OFFICIAL NBA GUIDE

2004-2005 EDITION

Editors/Official NBA Guide
CORRIE ANDERSON
ROB REHEUSER

Contributing Editors/Official NBA Guide
JEFF DENGATE
JOHN GARDELLA

ON THE COVER: Kevin Garnett by Robert Seale / TSN; Tony Parker by Chris Covatta / NBAE / Getty Images; Michael Redd by Gary Dineen / NBAE / Getty Images; Richard Jefferson by Nathaniel S. Butler / NBAE / Getty Images. ON THE SPINE: Kevin Garnett by Bob Leverone / TSN. ON THE BACK COVER: Carmelo Anthony by Robert Seale / TSN.

COVER DESIGN AND BOOK LAYOUT BY: Chad Painter / TSN.

Certain statistical data have been selected, compiled and exclusively supplied by NBA Properties, Inc.
Elias Sports Bureau, New York, is the official statistician of the NBA.

ISBN: 0-89204-742-9

10 9 8 7 6 5 4 3 2 1

CONTENTS

GV
885
.n26

2004-05 SEASON

- NBA directories
- Team by team
- NBA schedule
- Games on television and radio
- National Basketball Development League
- Women's National Basketball Association

NBA DIRECTORIES

LEAGUE OFFICE

NATIONAL BASKETBALL ASSOCIATION
NBA ENTERTAINMENT
WOMEN'S NATIONAL BASKETBALL ASSOCIATION
NATIONAL BASKETBALL DEVELOPMENT LEAGUE

New York
Olympic Tower
645 Fifth Avenue
New York, NY 10022
Telephone: 212-407-8000
Fax: 212-832-3861

New Jersey
450 Harmon Meadow Boulevard
Secaucus, NJ 07094
Telephone: 201-865-1500
Fax: 201-865-2626

100 Plaza Drive
Secaucus, NJ 07094
Telephone: 201-865-1500
Fax: 201-974-5973

Toronto
40 Bay Street, Suite 400
Toronto, Ontario, Canada
M5J 2X2
Telephone: (416) 364-2030
Fax: (416) 364-0205

Los Angeles
900 Wilshire Boulevard
Suite 310
Santa Monica, CA 90401
Telephone: 310-899-0483
Fax: 310-899-0596

NBDL
24 Vardry Street, Suite 201
Greenville, SC 29601
www.NBDL.com
(864) 248-1100, Fax: (864) 248-1102

INTERNATIONAL OFFICES

EUROPEAN HEADQUARTERS
40 Rue La Boetie
75008, Paris, France
Telephone: 011-33-1-53-53-6200
Fax: 011-33-1-53-53-6297

Spain
Mallorca 272 4-7
08037, Barcelona, Spain
Telephone: 011-34-93-272-1244
Fax: 011-34-93-215-6407

France
40 Rue La Boetie
75008, Paris, France
Telephone: 011-33-1-53-53-6200
Fax: 011-33-1-53-53-6297

ASIA/PACIFIC HEADQUARTERS
Man Yee Building
68 Des Voeux Road
Central Hong Kong
Telephone: 011-852-2843-9600
Fax: 011-852-2536-4808

Japan
Aioi Insurance Shinjuku Bldg.
3-25-03 Yoyogi, Shibuya-ku
Tokyo, Japan 151-0053
Telephone: 011-813-5351-2411
Fax: 011-813-3251-2470

Taiwan
Suite 1303, No. 88, Section 2
Chung Hsiao East Road
Taipei, Taiwan ROC
Telephone: 011-886-2-2358-1900
Fax: 011-886-2-2358-1098

China — Bejing
14/F, IBM Tower
Pacific Century Place
2A Workers Stadium Road North
Chaoyang District
Beijing 100027 China PRC
Telephone: 011-86-10-6539-1235
Fax: 011-86-10-6539-1277

China — Shanghai
35/F Citic Square
1168 Nanjing Road West
Shanghai 200041 China PRC
Telephone: 011-86-21-5111-9088
Fax: 011-86-21-5111-9090

LATIN AMERICAN HEADQUARTERS
5201 Blue Lagoon Drive
Suite 620
Miami, FL 33126
Telephone: 305-264-0607
Fax: 305-264-0760

Mexico
Jose Maria Castorena 324
Suite #206-207
Cuajimalpa, Mexico, D.F. C.P. 05000
Telephone: 011-5255-813-6699/7000
Fax: 011-5255-812-7464

NBA STORE
666 Fifth Avenue
New York, NY 10103
Telephone: 212-515-6221
Fax: 212-515-6249

NBA CITY
6068 Universal Boulevard
Orlando, FL 32819
Telephone: 407-363-5919
Fax: 407-370-3178

ATLANTA HAWKS
SOUTHEAST DIVISION

Hawks Schedule
Home games shaded; *—All-Star Game at Denver.

November

SUN	MON	TUE	WED	THU	FRI	SAT
	1	2	3 PHO	4	5 SEA	6
7 LAL	8	9 CLE	10	11	12 NO	13 SA
14	15	16 HOU	17 IND	18	19	20 UTH
21	22	23 NYK	24 MIA	25	26 ORL	27 CHA
28	29	30 NYK				

December

SUN	MON	TUE	WED	THU	FRI	SAT
			1	2	3 WAS	4 NJN
5	6 PHI	7	8 MEM	9	10 DET	11 NJN
12	13	14 IND	15 HOU	16	17 POR	18 DAL
19	20	21	22 DAL	23	24	25
26	27 MIA	28 CLE	29	30 SEA	31	

January

SUN	MON	TUE	WED	THU	FRI	SAT
						1
2 WAS	3	4	5 CLE	6	7 SAC	8
9	10	11 MIL	12	13	14 BOS	15 CHA
16	17 NJN	18	19 MIA	20	21 CHI	22 BOS
23	24 CHI	25	26 MIN	27	28 MIA	29 MEM
30	31 ORL					

February

SUN	MON	TUE	WED	THU	FRI	SAT
		1	2 DET	3	4 PHI	5 IND
6	7 LAL	8	9	10 ORL	11	12 MIL
13	14	15 DEN	16 CLE	17	18	19
20 *All-Star	21	22 SAC	23 GS	24	25 POR	26
27 LAC	28					

March

SUN	MON	TUE	WED	THU	FRI	SAT
		1 DEN	2 UTH	3	4	5 PHI
6	7	8 MIL	9 BOS	10	11 TOR	12 GS
13	14 DET	15	16 WAS	17	18 NYK	19
20	21 CHI	22 PHO	23	24	25 SA	26 TOR
27 ORL	28	29	30 WAS	31		

April

SUN	MON	TUE	WED	THU	FRI	SAT
					1 BOS	2
3 LAC	4	5 NO	6	7	8 TOR	9 MIN
10	11 CHA	12	13 CHA	14	15	16 CHI
17 NY	18	19 DET	20 PHI	21	22	23

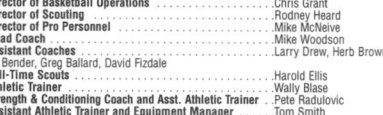

2004-05 SEASON
TEAM DIRECTORY

ATLANTA SPIRIT, LLC
Board of Managers . . . . Steven Belkin (Governor), Todd Foreman, Michael Gearon, Jr. (Alternate Governor), Bruce Levenson, Ed Peskowitz, Felix Riccio, Rutherford Seydel

EXECUTIVE MANAGEMENT – ATLANTA SPIRIT, LLC
President and CEO/Alternate Governor . . . . Bernie Mullin
Executive Vice President and General Manager . . . . Billy Knight
President of Philips Arena . . . . Bob Williams
Executive Vice President and Chief Financial Officer . . . . Bill Duffy
Executive Vice President of Business Development . . . . . . Lee Douglas
Senior Vice President of Broadcast and Corporate Partnerships . . Tracy White
Senior Vice President of Communications . . . . Tom Hughes
Senior Vice President of Ticket Sales and Service . . . . . Jeff Morander
Vice President and General Counsel . . . . T. Scott Wilkinson
Vice President of Basketball . . . . Dominique Wilkins
Vice President of Community Development . . . . Tiffany Stone
Vice President of Marketing, Advertising and Branding . . . Jim Pfeifer
Vice President of Strategic Planning/
Special Assistant to President . . . . Ailey Penningroth

BASKETBALL OPERATIONS
Director of Basketball Operations . . . . Chris Grant
Director of Scouting . . . . Rodney Heard
Director of Pro Personnel . . . . Mike McNeive
Head Coach . . . . Mike Woodson
Assistant Coaches . . . . Larry Drew, Herb Brown, Bob Bender, Greg Ballard, David Fizdale
Full-Time Scouts . . . . Harold Ellis
Athletic Trainer . . . . Wally Blase
Strength & Conditioning Coach and Asst. Athletic Trainer . . Pete Radulovic
Assistant Athletic Trainer and Equipment Manager . . . . . Tom Smith
Team Physicians . . . . Dr. Michael Bernot, Dr. Milton Frank III, Dr. Robert Marmer
Team Dentist . . . . Dr. Louis Freedman
Executive Assistant to the General Manager . . . . Carole Harding
Basketball Operations Coordinator . . . . Julie Hogg
Scouting Coordinator . . . . Lalita Haynes
Team Services Coordinator . . . . Cynthia Ellison
Video Coordinator . . . . Luke Steele
Assistant Video Coordinator . . . . John Beckett

BUSINESS OPERATIONS
Vice President of Public Relations . . . . Arthur Triche
Vice President of Suite Sales and Service . . . . Mike Harrison
Senior Director of Customer Service . . . . Michael Boswell
Senior Director of E Marketing and Interactive Services . . David Lee
Senior Director of Game Operations . . . . Peter Sorckoff
Senior Director of Suite Sales and Service . . . . Tim Stolz
Senior Director of Ticket Operations . . . . Wendell Byrne
Director of Accounting/Controller . . . . Michelle Walker
Director of Broadcast and Corporate Sales . . . . Bill Abercrombie
Director of Broadcast and Corporate Sales . . . . Terri Scalcucci-Cameron
Director of Corporate Partner Services . . . . Chris Carter
Director of CRM and Database Marketing . . . . Kyle Brunson
Director of Finance/Controller . . . . David Kane
Director of Group Ticket Sales and Service . . . . Tiffany Walker
Director of Human Resources . . . . Ginni Siler
Director of Media Relations . . . . Jon Steinberg
Director of Premium Seating/Season Ticket Special Services . Debbie Cagle
Director of Publications, Creative Services & Internet Marketing . Matt Musgrove
Senior Manager of Broadcast and Corporate Sales . . . . . . Stewart Tanner
Senior Manager of Finance . . . . Susie Hollis
Senior Manager of Promotions and Advertising . . . . Kimberly Hartley
Senior Manager of Ticket Operations . . . . Gilda Carlysle
Senior Financial Analyst . . . . Krista Halford
Assistant Controller . . . . Darius Nixon
Manager of Broadcast Services . . . . Diana Corbin
Manager of Club Seat Sales . . . . Matt Waller
Managers of Corporate Partnerships . . . . Chris Beaudin, Tamara Gehris, Maggie Hanes, Arden Robbins
Managers of Community Development . . . . Andrea Carter, Warren Grayson
Manager of Database Marketing . . . . David Elgin
Manager of Game Operations . . . . Ralph Humphlett
Managers of Group Ticket Sales and Service . . . . Evan Kellner, Jennifer Smith
Manager of Human Resources . . . . Jennifer Petit
Manager of Interactive Services . . . . Wes Taft
Manager of Media Relations . . . . Jason Roose
Manager of Payroll . . . . Sha Hinton
Manager of Promotions and Advertising . . . . Terese Smallwood
Manager of Rental Suites . . . . Alexandra Siciliano
Manager of Season Ticket Holder Retention . . . . Shayna Hoppe
Managers of Season Ticket Customer Service . . . . Scott Fillmore, Jonathan Tillman
Managers of Season Ticket Sales . . . . Jeff Tanzer, Keith Brennan
Manager of Shared Services . . . . Brian Hanley
Manager of Special Events . . . . Connie Zaleski
Manager of Suite Services . . . . Lauren Fisher
Managers of Telemarketing Sales . . . . Keith Bradshaw, JD Villasenor
Manager of Websites . . . . Kevin McCormack

Bernie Mullin

Billy Knight

Mike Woodson

ROSTER
Coach—Mike Woodson

Assistant coaches—Larry Drew, Herb Brown, Bob Bender, Greg Ballard, David Fizdale

No.	Name	Pos.	Ht./Wt.	Metric (m/kg)	Born	College/country
1	Josh Childress	G	6-8/210	2.03/95.3	6-20-83	Stanford
40	Jason Collier	F	7-0/260	2.13/117.9	9-8-77	Georgia Tech
4	Chris Crawford	F	6-9/235	2.05/106.6	5-13-75	Marquette
00	Tony Delk	G	6-2/189	1.88/85.7	1-28-74	Kentucky
13	Boris Diaw	G/F	6-8/215	2.03/97.5	4-16-82	France
14	Predrag Drobnjak	C	6-11/270	2.11/122.5	10-27-75	Yugoslavia
3	Al Harrington	F	6-9/250	2.05/113.4	2-17-80	St. Patrick HS
36	Royal Ivey	G	6-3/200	1.90/90.7	12-20-81	Texas
15	Donta Smith	G	6-7/215	2.00/97.5	11-27-83	SE Illinois College
42	Josh Smith	F	6-9/210	2.05/95.3	12-5-85	Oak Hill Academy
8	Antoine Walker	F	6-9/245	2.06/111.1	8-12-76	Kentucky

BROADCAST INFORMATION

Radio: WSB (750 AM). Broadcaster: Steve Holman.
TV: TBA
Cable TV: Turner South. Broadcasters: Bob Neal and TBA. FSN South. Broadcasters: Bob Rathbun, Mike Glenn.

TEAM INFORMATION

Team address .... Centennial Tower
101 Marietta St. NW, Suite 1900
Atlanta, GA 30303
Business phone 404-827-3800
Ticket information 404-827-DUNK; 800-4NBA-TIX
Website .... www.hawks.com
Arena (capacity) .... Philips Arena (19,445)
Game times .... 7:30 weeknights, 7 p.m. Saturdays
First Hawks game in arena .... November 4, 1999

2003-04 REVIEW

RESULTS

OCTOBER
29— at New Orleans	*83 -88	†0 -1	
31— at Chicago	*94 -100	0 -2	

NOVEMBER
1 — Indiana	*99 -103	†0 -3	
3 — New Orleans	90 -80	1 -3	
5 — at Golden State	*72 -99	1 -4	
8 — at Portland	*83 -90	1 -5	
9 — at Seattle	91 -81	2 -5	
11 — at L.A. Clippers	*103 -115	2 -6	
12— at Phoenix	99 -94	3 -6	
15— New Jersey	*85 -100	3 -7	
17— Washington	*97 -106	3 -8	
18— at Milwaukee	101 -93	4 -8	
21— at San Antonio	*75 -114	4 -9	
22— Cleveland	92 -83	5 -9	
24— Detroit	*89 -94	5 -10	
26— Toronto	*97 -99	†5 -11	
28— Miami	95 -83	6 -11	
29— at Philadelphia	*86 -98	6 -12	

DECEMBER
2 — Milwaukee	*94 -106	6 -13	
5 — at Toronto	*87 -92	6 -14	
6 — at Cleveland	*85 -95	6 -15	
9 — Denver	98 -112	7 -15	
10— at Memphis	*90 -103	7 -16	
12— at Indiana	*92 -103	7 -17	
13— Orlando	*102 -105	7 -18	
16— at Miami	*79 -97	7 -19	
17— Golden State	*85 -98	7 -20	

19— Sacramento	*86 -98	7 -21	
20— at New York	*92 -103	7 -22	
23— Boston	93 -88	8 -22	
26— at New Orleans	*79 -109	8 -23	
27— Detroit	*84 -87	8 -24	
30— at Washington	83 -73	9 -24	

JANUARY
2 — at Minnesota	*75 -93	9 -25	
3 — at Denver	84 -76	10 -25	
6 — at Sacramento	*89 -105	10 -26	
9 — at L.A. Lakers	*67 -113	10 -27	
10— at Utah	*71 -92	10 -28	
13— San Antonio	86 -77	11 -28	
14— at Indiana	*78 -85	11 -29	
17— Toronto	75 -70	12 -29	
19— Indiana	*97 -100	12 -30	
21— Chicago	97 -87	13 -30	
23— New York	*94 -96	13 -31	
25— at Detroit	91 -82	14 -31	
27— Phoenix	*85 -89	14 -32	
29— Portland	*85 -93	14 -33	
31— Milwaukee	93 -83	15 -33	

FEBRUARY
2 — L.A. Clippers	*95 -101	15 -34	
4 — Minnesota	97 -89	16 -34	
6 — at Boston	100 -96	17 -34	
7 — Houston	*77 -86	17 -35	
9 — Dallas	102 -96	18 -35	
18— at New Jersey	*92 -98	18 -36	
20— at Miami	*92 -125	18 -37	

22— at Houston	*121 -123	§18 -38	
24— Philadelphia	86 -75	19 -38	
27— at Detroit	*83 -105	19 -39	
28— Orlando	*99 -104	19 -40	

MARCH
2 — L.A. Lakers	94 -93	20 -40	
3 — at Cleveland	*80 -112	20 -41	
5 — at Orlando	*96 -101	20 -42	
8 — Cleveland	*102 -108	20 -43	
10— at Milwaukee	*80 -94	20 -44	
12— Washington	138 -124	21 -44	
14— at Toronto	*84 -101	21 -45	
16— Seattle	*110 -118	21 -46	
17— at Dallas	111 -110	22 -46	
19— at Washington	*84 -94	22 -47	
20— Utah	*81 -87	22 -48	
22— at New York	*84 -96	22 -49	
25— New Orleans	84 -76	23 -49	
27— Chicago	97 -88	24 -49	
29— Memphis	*133 -136	‡24 -50	
31— Miami	*97 -100	24 -51	

APRIL
2 — at Orlando	95 -87	25 -51	
4 — at New Jersey	*89 -106	25 -52	
6 — Philadelphia	*100 -103	†25 -53	
9 — at Chicago	116 -101	26 -53	
10— Boston	110 -99	27 -53	
12— New Jersey	129 -107	28 -53	
14— at Boston	*132 -137	28 -54	

*Loss. †Single overtime. ‡Double overtime. §Triple overtime.

TEAM LEADERS

Points: Stephen Jackson (1,450).
Field goals made: Jackson (536).
Free throws made: Shareef Abdur-Rahim (294).
3-pointers made: Jason Terry (146).
Rebounds: Abdur-Rahim (495).
Assists: Terry (437).
Steals: Jackson (142).
Blocks: Theo Ratliff (166).

RECORDS

Regular season: 28-54 (7th in Central); 10-18 in division; 20-35 in conference; 8-19 vs. Western Conference; 19-23 at home; 10-31 on road; 0-6 in overtime; 2-9 in games decided by three points or fewer; 12-26 in games decided by 10 points or more; held opponents under 100 points 48 times; held under 100 points 65 times.
Playoffs: None.
All-time franchise record: 2,170-2,168 in 55 seasons. Won one NBA title (1958), while franchise was located in St. Louis.
Team record past five years: 149-261 (.363, ranks 23rd in NBA in that span).

HIGHLIGHTS

Top players: Stephen Jackson led the Hawks in total points (1,450) and ranked 25th in the NBA with 18.1 ppg. He led Atlanta in steals (1.78 spg) and was second in 3-pointers made (145, T14th) and minutes (36.8 mpg, 36th). ... Jason Terry led the team in assists (5.4 apg, 19th in the NBA), 3-point field-goal percentage (.347), 3-pointers made (146, 13th) and minutes (37.3 mpg, 29th) and was second in scoring (16.8 ppg) and steals (1.5 spg). ... Bob Sura appeared in 27 games after a trade and more than doubled his scoring, rebounding and assist totals with the Hawks (14.7 ppg, 8.3 rpg, 5.3 apg). ... Jason Collier, another late-season acquisition, averaged career highs in scoring (11.3 ppg) and rebounding (5.6 rpg).
Key injuries: The Hawks lost a total of 318 player games because of injury or illness. Fourteen players missed games. Free-agent center Obinna Ekezie was expected to challenge for a backup spot before suffering a knee injury in the preseason and missing the entire season. Alan Henderson, bothered by back trouble for much of the year, missed 71 games. Terrell Brandon was released after missing 54 games, and midseason acquisitions Zeljko Rebraca (24 games), Wesley Person (20) and Joel Przybilla (17) all missed significant time.
Notable: Atlanta (28-54) ended the season in seventh place in the Central Division and failed to reach the playoffs for the fifth straight year. Coach Terry Stotts was released at the end of the season and replaced with former Detroit assistant coach Mike Woodson. ... The Hawks had 27 different players on the regular-season roster during the year. Bob Sura became the first Atlanta player —and the third in the NBA in 2003-04— to post consecutive triple-doubles. ... On March 12 vs. Washington, the Hawks had five players score 20 or more points in the game, a feat that had not been achieved in the NBA since January 26, 1993 when Orlando did the same against Atlanta. ... The Hawks also played a triple-overtime game on February 22 at Houston (a 123-121 loss), the NBA's first triple-overtime game since 2001. ... There were seven sellout crowds of 19,445 or better, an arena record.

– 9 –

BOSTON CELTICS
ATLANTIC DIVISION

Celtics Schedule
Home games shaded; *—All-Star Game at Denver.

November
SUN	MON	TUE	WED	THU	FRI	SAT
	1	2	3 PHI	4	5 IND	6 NYK
7	8	9	10 POR	11	12 CHA	13
14	15	16	17 WAS	18	19 SA	20
21 SEA	22	23 IND	24 PHI	25	26 CLE	27
28 MIA	29 ORL	30				

December
SUN	MON	TUE	WED	THU	FRI	SAT
			1 MIL	2	3 TOR	4
5 SAC	6 GS	7	8	9 POR	10	11 SEA
12 LAC	13	14	15 DEN	16	17 UTH	18 CLE
19	20	21 MIA	22 NYK	23	24	25
26 SA	27	28 DAL	29 MEM	30	31 WAS	

January
SUN	MON	TUE	WED	THU	FRI	SAT
						1
2 DET	3 NO	4	5 GS	6	7 DET	8 CHI
9	10 ORL	11	12 TOR	13	14 ATL	15
16	17	18	19 CHI	20	21 NJN	22 ATL
23	24	25 CHA	26 IND	27	28 PHO	29 CHI
30	31 HOU					

February
SUN	MON	TUE	WED	THU	FRI	SAT
		1	2 NJN	3	4 ORL	5
6 MIN	7	8 MIL	9 LAC	10	11 NYK	12
13 SAC	14	15	16 MEM	17	18	19
20 *All-Star	21	22 LAL	23 DEN	24	25 UTH	26
27 PHO	28					

March
SUN	MON	TUE	WED	THU	FRI	SAT
		1	2 LAL	3	4 CHA	5
6 MIN	7	8	9 ATL	10	11 DET	12
13 WAS	14 CHA	15	16 TOR	17	18 HOU	19 NO
20	21	22	23 NYK	24	25 CHI	26 DET
27	28	29	30 DAL	31		

April
SUN	MON	TUE	WED	THU	FRI	SAT
					1 ATL	2
3 PHI	4	5 WAS	6 MIL	7	8	9 NJN
10	11	12 PHI	13 MIL	14	15 MIA	16
17 TOR	18	19 CLE	20 NJN	21	22	23

2004-05 SEASON
TEAM DIRECTORY

CEO and Managing Partner ....Wyc Grousbeck
Executive Assistant ....Wendy Merritt
Basketball Operations
Executive Director, Basketball Operations ....Danny Ainge
President ....Arnold "Red" Auerbach
Head Coach ....Glenn "Doc" Rivers
Assistant Coaches ....Tony Brown, Jim Brewer, Kevin
   Eastman, Armond Hill, Paul Pressey, Dave Wohl
Strength and Conditioning Coaches ....Bryan Doo, Walter Norton, Jr.
Scout ....Paul Cormier
Special Assistant to Basketball Operations ....Ryan McDonough
Director, Player Personnel ....Leo Papile
Assistant to the Head Coach ....Sean Davis
Basketball Operations Assistants ....Frank Burke, Mike Procopio
Consultant ....Bill Russell
General Manager ....Chris Wallace
Video Coordinator ....Jamie Young
Sales and Marketing
Executive Assistant ....Susan Barabino
Sr. Director, Corp. Sales and Business Development .....Sean Barror
Game Operations and Entertainment Director ....Joe Bivona
Team Mascot ....Damon Blust
Account Executive ....Ashley Bryan
Director, Ticket Operations ....Paul Cacciatore
Market Services Coordinator ....Tessa Courtemanche
Marketing Consultant ....Bob Cousy
Account Executive ....Jon Crafts
Account Executive ....Jim Davis
Marketing Coordinator ....Nicole Federico
Executive VP, Sales and Corporate Development ....Rich Gotham
Vice President of Marketing ....Jon Hickey
Manager, Telemarketing ....Maureen Keyo
Marketing Services Manager ....Josh Kleinman
Director, Client Services/Charitable Foundation ....Duane Johnson
Account Executive ....Scott MacDonald
Director, Corporate Sales and Business Development .....Adam Marcus
Senior Account Executive ....Steve Markos
Account Executive ....Owen Morin
Director, Marketing ....Brian Robertson
Director, Ticket Sales ....Mackenzie Silverio
Creative Services Manager ....Keith Sliney
Manager, Game Operations ....Sean Sullivan
Vice President, Ticket Sales & Service ....Shawn Sullivan
Senior Account Executive ....Bobby Vines
Community Relations
Community Relations Coordinator ....Marcellus Heath
Director, Community Relations ....Wayne Levy
Director, Special Projects ....JoJo White
Media Relations
Vice President, Communications ....Bill Bonsiewicz
Communications Manager ....Farra D'Orazio
Media Relations Coordinator ....Brian Gleason
Vice President, Media Services/Alumni Affairs ....Jeff Twiss
Finance Administration
Reception/Office Assistant ....Kathleen Landers
Director Accounting ....Tim Rath
Director, HR & Investor Services ....Barbara Reed
Chief Financial Officer ....Bill Reissfelder
Team Services
Home Equipment Personnel ....Pete Chrisafideis
Team Travel & Equipment Manager ....John Conner
Security & Waltham Facility Manager ....Grant Gray
Director, Team Security ....Phil Lynch
Operation Liaison ....Francis O'Bryant
Locker Room Attendant ....Frank Randall
Medical Staff
Athletic Trainer ....Ed Lacerte, R.P.T., L/A.T.C.
Chief Medical Officer/Team Physician ....Arnold Scheller, M.D.
Massage Therapist ....Vladimir Shulman
Operations
Risk Management ....Rob Billings
Technical Analyst ....Elaine Burke
Sales Analyst ....Matt Griffin
Operations Manager/Staff Accountant ....Patrick Lynch
VP, Operations & Information ....Daryl Morey
Senior Director, Technology ....Jay Wessel

Red Auerbach

Danny Ainge

Doc Rivers

ROSTER
Coach—Glenn "Doc" Rivers
Assistant coaches—Jim Brewer, Tony Brown, Kevin Eastman, Armond Hill, Paul Pressey, Dave Wohl

No.	Name	Pos.	Ht./Wt.	Metric (m/kg)	Born	College/country
42	Tony Allen	G	6-4/213	1.93/96.6	1-11-82	Oklahoma State
	Marcus Banks	G	6-1/200	1.85/90.7	11-19-81	UNLV
30	Mark Blount	C	7-0/250	2.13/113.4	11-30-75	Pittsburgh
52	Ernest Brown	C	7-0/244	2.13/110.7	5-17-79	Indian Hills CC
12	Ricky Davis	G	6-7/195	2.00/88.5	9-23-79	Iowa
	Rick Fox	F	6-7/235	2.00/106.6	7-24-69	North Carolina
	Tom Gugliotta	F	6-10/240	2.08/108.9	12-19-69	N.C. State
8	Al Jefferson	F	6-10/265	2.08/120.2	1-4-85	Prentiss HS
45	Raef LaFrentz	F/C	6-11/240	2.10/108.4	5-29-76	Kansas
0	Walter McCarty	F	6-10/230	2.08/104.3	2-1-74	Kentucky
	Gary Payton	G	6-4/180	1.93/81.6	7-23-68	Oregon State
43	Kendrick Perkins	C	6-10/280	2.08/127.0	11-10-84	Ozen HS
34	Paul Pierce	G	6-6/230	1.98/104.3	10-13-77	Kansas
5	Michael Stewart	C	6-10/230	2.08/104.3	4-25-75	California
44	Jiri Welsch	G/F	6-7/208	2.00/94.3	1-27-80	Czech Republic
13	Delonte West	G	6-4/180	1.93/81.6	7-26-83	St. Joseph's

BROADCAST INFORMATION

Radio: WWZN (1510 AM) "The Zone".
Broadcasters: Sean Grande, Cedric Maxwell
Cable TV: FOX Sports Net New England.
Broadcasters: Mike Gorman, Tom Heinsohn.

TEAM INFORMATION

Team address . . . . .151 Merrimac Street
Boston, MA 02114
Business phone 617-854-8000
Ticket information 617-523-3030
Website . . . . .www.celtics.com
Arena (capacity) . . . . .FleetCenter (18,624)
Game times . . . . .7 & 7:30 p.m., Monday-Thursday; 7:30 & 8 p.m.,
Friday; 1 p.m., Saturday; Sunday as listed
First Celtics game in arena . . . . .November 3, 1995

2003-04 REVIEW

RESULTS

OCTOBER
29— Miami	98 -75	1 -0
31— at Memphis	93 -91	2 -0

NOVEMBER
1 — at New Orleans	*90 -97	2 -1
5 — Detroit	96 -88	2 -2
7 — New Jersey	*87 -94	2 -3
9 — Sacramento	91 -82	3 -3
11— Indiana	78 -76	4 -3
12— Chicago	*82 -89	4 -4
14— Cleveland	91 -82	5 -4
17— at New York	*86 -89	5 -5
19— New Orleans	*73 -81	5 -6
21— at Philadelphia	*85 -87	5 -7
24— New York	*88 -94	5 -8
26— at Orlando	94 -92	6 -8
28— Milwaukee	106 -96	7 -8
29— at Milwaukee	*94 -100	7 -9

DECEMBER
1 — Memphis	*89 -96	7 -10
3 — at Toronto	*95 -105	7 -11
5 — Phoenix	*106 -110	7 -12
7 — at Denver	116 -111	8 -12
8 — at Utah	102 -80	9 -12
10— Seattle	126 -112	10 -12
12— Toronto	114 -111	11 -12
13— at Cleveland	105 -98	12 -12
15— Minnesota	*95 -116	12 -13
17— Dallas	105 -103	13 -13
19— Utah	*96 -99	13 -14

21— Philadelphia	87 -84	14 -14
23— at Atlanta	*88 -93	14 -15
26— at Phoenix	104 -102	15 -15
28— at L.A. Lakers	*82 -105	15 -16
29— at Golden State	100 -91	16 -16
31— New Orleans	*94 -96	16 -17

JANUARY
2 — Indiana	*90 -103	16 -18
3 — at Chicago	88 -77	17 -18
5 — Detroit	*68 -78	17 -19
7 — Orlando	101 -93	18 -19
9 — Cleveland	107 -82	19 -19
11— at Houston	97 -93	20 -19
13— at Milwaukee	*103 -111	20 -20
14— Houston	*80- 95	20 -21
16— at Orlando	*118 -124	†20 -22
18— San Antonio	*92 -109	20 -23
20— at Miami	86 -84	21 -23
23— Washington	100 -89	22 -23
25— at New Jersey	*91 -110	22 -24
28— Detroit	*103 -106	22 -25
30— New York	*74 -92	22 -26
31— at Indiana	*98 -99	22 -27

FEBRUARY
4 — L.A. Clippers	*86 -95	22 -28
6 — Atlanta	*96 -100	22 -29
7 — at Philadelphia	110 -80	23 -29
9 — at Cleveland	*89 -97	23 -30
12— at Chicago	*87 -107	23 -31
17— at Sacramento	*111 -127	23 -32

19— at L.A. Clippers	*100 -102	23 -33
21— at Portland	*84 -105	23 -34
22— at Seattle	*87 -108	23 -35
25— Milwaukee	*104 -106	23 -36
27— Toronto	88 -75	24 -36
29— at Toronto	91 -82	25 -36

MARCH
1 — Orlando	117 -96	26 -36
5 — Washington	94 -90	27 -36
7 — at Minnesota	80 -77	28 -36
9 — at New York	87 -84	29 -36
10— L.A. Lakers	*109 -117	29 -37
12— Indiana	*81 -99	29 -38
13— at Washington	111 -102	30 -38
17— Denver	104 -100	31 -38
19— at Dallas	*104 -120	31 -39
20— at San Antonio	*87 -103	31 -40
26— New Jersey	102 -93	32 -40
28— Philadelphia	89 -65	33 -40
29— at New Jersey	84 -80	34 -40
31— Portland	*105 -98	34 -41

APRIL
2 — Golden State	111 -106	35 -41
4— at Washington	*102 -112	35 -42
7 — at Miami	*101 -104	35 -43
9 — at New Orleans	* 80 -89	35 -44
10— at Atlanta	*99 -110	35 -45
12— Miami	*77 -84	35 -46
14— Atlanta	137 -132	36 -46

*Loss. †Single overtime.

TEAM LEADERS

Points: Paul Pierce (1,836).
Field goals made: Pierce (602).
Free throws made: Pierce (517).
3-pointers made: Walter McCarty (137).
Rebounds: Mark Blount (589).
Assists: Pierce (410).
Steals: Pierce (131).
Blocks: Blount (109).

RECORDS

Regular season: 36-46 (4th in Atlantic); 14-10 in division; 24-30 in conference; 12-16 vs. Western Conference; 19-22 at home; 17-24 on road; 0-1 in overtime; 10-9 in games decided by three points or fewer; 11-18 in games decided by 10 points or more; held opponents under 100 points 48 times; held under 100 points 52 times.
Playoffs: 0-4, lost to Pacers, 4-0, in Eastern Conference first round.
All-time franchise record: 2,692-1,819 in 58 seasons. Won 16 NBA titles (1957, '59, '60, '61, '62, '63, '64, '65, '66, '68, '69, '74, '76, '81, '84, '86).
Team record past five years: 200-210 (.488, ranks 18th in NBA in that span).

HIGHLIGHTS

Top players: Paul Pierce led the Celtics in scoring (23.0 ppg, 5th in the NBA) and steals (1.64 spg). He scored his 10,000th career point March 12 vs. Indiana and accomplished the feat faster than any Celtic in history. Pierce also tied for the team lead with a career-high 19 double-doubles. ... Mark Blount led the Celtics in field-goal percentage (.566, 2nd in NBA), rebounding (7.2 rpg) and blocks (1.29 bpg). He recorded the Celtics' first 20-point, 20-rebound game in more than a decade with 28 points and a career-high 21 rebounds vs. Orlando on March 1. He tied with Pierce for the team lead with a career-high 19 double-doubles. ... Ricky Davis averaged 14.1 ppg on 48.8 percent shooting in 57 games with the Celtics.
Key injuries: The Celtics lost a total of 201 player games because of injury or illness. Raef LaFrentz missed 65 games, 59 with right knee tendinopothy. Kendrick Perkins missed 30 games, most with right knee tendinitis. Chucky Atkins missed three games with a lymph node

excision, and Jumaine Jones missed six games. Mark Blount was the only Celtic to appear in all 82 games.
Notable: The Celtics finished 36-46 and made the playoffs for the third consecutive season. The team was swept by the Indiana Pacers in the first round. ... The Celtics finished second in the NBA in steals per game, averaging 9.39 a contest, and rookie Marcus Banks led the NBA in steals per 48 minutes, averaging 3.05 in that frame. Paul Pierce made his third consecutive All-Star Game appearance. The Celtics increased their scoring average from 92.7 ppg in 2002-03 to 95.3 ppg in 2003-04.

CHARLOTTE BOBCATS
SOUTHEAST DIVISION

Bobcats Schedule
Home games shaded; *—All-Star Game at Denver.

November
SUN	MON	TUE	WED	THU	FRI	SAT
	1	2	3	4 WAS	5	6 ORL
7	8	9	10 MIL	11	12 BOS	13 GS
14	15	16 UTH	17	18 CLE	19	20 CLE
21 DET	22	23 DET	24	25	26 IND	27 ATL
28	29	30 NJN				

December
SUN	MON	TUE	WED	THU	FRI	SAT
			1	2	3	4 NYK
5 LAC	6	7 SAC	8	9	10 PHO	11
12 GS	13	14 NO	15	16	17	18 HOU
19	20	21 NJN	22 HOU	23	24	25
26 NYK	27 WAS	28	29 IND	30	31 SEA	

January
SUN	MON	TUE	WED	THU	FRI	SAT
						1 MIA
2	3 CLE	4	5 MIN	6	7 ORL	8
9	10	11 CLE	12	13	14 MEM	15 ATL
16	17 MIL	18	19 PHI	20	21 DAL	22
23 TOR	24	25 BOS	26	27 CHI	28 TOR	29
30 LAL	31					

February
SUN	MON	TUE	WED	THU	FRI	SAT
		1 UTH	2	3	4 POR	5 SEA
6	7	8 SA	9 IND	10	11 MIA	12
13 NYK	14 POR	15	16 DEN	17	18	19
20 *All-Star	21	22 MIL	23	24	25 NJN	26 CHI
27	28					

March
SUN	MON	TUE	WED	THU	FRI	SAT
		1 SAC	2 NO	3	4 BOS	5 WAS
6	7	8 MIN	9	10	11 PHI	12 LAL
13 BOS	14	15	16 DEN	17	18 SA	19 DAL
20 ORL	21	22	23 PHO	24 ORL	25	26 MIA
27	28 NJN	29	30 CHI	31		

April
SUN	MON	TUE	WED	THU	FRI	SAT
					1 TOR	2 CHI
3	4	5 LAC	6 PHI	7	8 MIL	9
10 MEM	11 ATL	12	13 ATL	14	15	16 NYK
17 WAS	18	19 MIA	20 DET	21	22	23

2004-05 SEASON

TEAM DIRECTORY

Owner/Governor	Robert L. Johnson
Alternate Governor	H. Van Sinclair
President/Alternate Governor	Ed Tapscott

ADMINISTRATION
Executive VP of Administration	Colleen Millsap
Vice President, Information Technology	Jamie Pope
Director of Human Resources	Kay Lowery

ARENA
Executive VP of Arena Development Operations & Entertainment	Barry Silberman
Senior Vice President of Event Booking and Marketing	Marty Bechtold

BASKETBALL OPERATIONS
General Manager/Head Coach	Bernie Bickerstaff
Assistant General Manager	Karl Hicks
Assistant Coaches	Gary Brokaw, John-Blair Bickerstaff, Jeff Capel, Gary Kloppenburg, John Outlaw
Director of Scouting	Kenny Williamson
Director of International Scouting	Tim Shea
Scout	Frank Ross
Head Athletic Trainer	Joe Sharpe
Assistant Athletic Trainer/Equipment Manager	Mark Coffelt
Strength & Conditioning Coach	Chris Munford
Team Physician	Dr. Glenn Perry
Video Coordinator	Drew Perry
Manager of Basketball Operations	Leslie Purcell

BROADCAST RIGHTS & ENTERTAINMENT
Executive Vice President of Media Rights & Entertainment	Naomi Travers
Vice President of Programming and Production	Jacque Coleman
VP of Professional Properties & Game Entertainment	John Guagliano

BUSINESS OPERATIONS
Executive Vice President/Chief Marketing Officer	Tom Ward
Vice President of Marketing	Andy Feffer
Vice President of Corporate Partnerships	Tod Rosensweig
Vice President of Ticket Sales and Service	Steve Swetoha
Director of Ticket Sales	Chris Gargani
Director of Ticket Operations	Jamie Hall
Director of Special Events	Polly Pearce
Director of Database Marketing, Research and Services	Dr. Pam Young

CORPORATE AFFAIRS
Executive Vice President/Chief of Staff	Chris Weiller
Vice President of Community Relations	LaRita Barber
Director of Player Programs	Dell Curry
Director of Public Relations	Scott Leightman
Manager of Public Relations	BJ Evans
Manager of Publications/New Media	Bo Hussey

FINANCE & BUSINESS AFFAIRS
Executive Vice President/Chief Financial Officer	Peter Smul
Senior Vice President of Legal and Business Affairs	Jonathan Fine
Controller	Sheryl Willie
Director of Financial Planning and Analysis	Greg Buonaccorsi
Director of Team Finance	Alvin Huggins

OFFICE OF THE PRESIDENT
VP of Government Relations and Business Diversity	Ed Lewis
Executive Assistant to the President	Cheryl Brown

Robert L. Johnson

Ed Tapscott

Bernie Bickerstaff

ROSTER
Coach—Bernie Bickerstaff
Asst. coaches—Gary Brokaw, John-Blair Bickerstaff, Jeff Capel, Gary Kloppenburg, John Outlaw

No.	Name	Pos.	Ht./Wt.	Metric (m/kg)	Born	College/country
25	Corey Benjamin	G	6-6/200	1.98/90.7	2-24-78	Oregon State
7	Primoz Brezec	C	7-1/252	2.16/114.3	10-2-79	Slovenia
10	Omar Cook	G	6-1/190	1.85/86.2	1-28-82	St. John's
2	Melvin Ely	F	6-10/261	2.08/118.4	5-2-78	Fresno State
1	Jason Hart	G	6-3/185	1.90/83.9	4-29-78	Syracuse
5	Eddie House	G	6-1/175	1.85/79.4	5-14-78	Arizona State
56	Brandon Hunter	F	6-7/260	2.00/117.9	11-24-80	Ohio University
24	Jason Kapono	F	6-8/213	2.03/96.6	2-2-81	UCLA
50	Emeka Okafor	F/C	6-10/252	2.08/114.3	9-28-82	Connecticut
21	Bernard Robinson	G/F	6-6/210	1.98/95.3	12-26-80	Michigan
31	Jamal Sampson	F	6-11/235	2.10/106.6	5-15-83	California
32	Tamar Slay	F	6-8/215	2.03/97.5	4-2-80	Marshall
0	Theron Smith	F	6-8/225	2.03/102.1	10-3-80	Ball State
3	Gerald Wallace	G	6-7/215	2.00/97.5	7-23-82	Alabama
55	Jahidi White	F/C	6-9/290	2.05/131.5	2-19-76	Georgetown

– 12 –

BROADCAST INFORMATION

Radio: WNMX (106.1 FM). Broadcaster: Steve Martin.
TV: WJZY (channel 46). Broadcasters: Matt Devlin, Adrian Branch.
Cable TV: C-SET (Carolinas Sports Entertainment Television). Broadcasters: Matt Devlin, Adrian Branch.

TEAM INFORMATION

Team address . . . . .129 West Trade Street, Suite 700
Charlotte, N.C. 28202
Business phone 704-424-4120
Ticket information 704-BOBCATS
Website .www.BobcatsBasketball.com
Arena (capacity) . . . . .Charlotte Coliseum (23,319)
Game times . . . . .7 p.m., Monday-Saturday
First Bobcats game in arena . . . .Scheduled for November 4, 2004

NBA Commissioner David Stern (left) passes the basketball to Bobcats majority owner Robert L. Johnson (center) and Charlotte mayor Pat McCrory during a street festival celebrating the team's name and logo unveiling on June 11, 2003, in Charlotte.

HIGHLIGHTS

The Charlotte Bobcats will tip off their inaugural 2004-05 campaign this fall after Robert L. Johnson was unanimously awarded ownership of the expansion franchise by the NBA Board of Governors on December 18, 2002. The team will play its inaugural season at Charlotte Coliseum before moving to a new Uptown Arena in 2005.

The franchise announced Bobcats as the team nickname on June 11, 2003, with its new logo and color scheme of orange as the primary color accompanied by blue, silver and black. An overflow crowd of 7,000 fans assembled in the Uptown Square of Trade and Tryon streets to witness the event, featuring Johnson, Charlotte Mayor Pat McCrory and NBA Commissioner David Stern.

On January 7, 2003, Johnson hired Ed Tapscott as the organization's chief operating officer to oversee the business and basketball operations for both the Charlotte Bobcats and WNBA Charlotte Sting. Tapscott then named NBA veteran Bernie Bickerstaff on October 16, 2003, to the dual role of Bobcats' general manager and head coach. With nearly 30 years of NBA experience, Bickerstaff served 10 seasons as an NBA head coach for three different teams (Seattle, Denver, Washington) in addition to roles as president and general manger for seven seasons and 12 years as an assistant coach.

The Bobcats began the process of building their inaugural team on June 21 by completing a trade with the Los Angeles Clippers for the second pick, swapping their fourth and 33rd selection in the 2004 NBA Draft for the second overall pick and center Predrag Drobnjak. On June 22, the team picked 19 players in the Charlotte Expansion Selection that included 10 players under contract and nine restricted free agents. By the rules of the Expansion Agreement, the restricted free agents became unrestricted free agents on July 1.

Those players under contract selected by the Bobcats included Primoz Brezec (Indiana), Brandon Hunter (Boston), Jason Kapono (Cleveland), Zaza Pachulia (Orlando), Aleksandar Pavlovic (Utah), Jamal Sampson (L.A. Lakers), Theron Smith (Memphis), Gerald Wallace (Sacramento) and Jahidi White (Phoenix). The team also chose restricted free agents Lonny Baxter (Washington), J.R. Bremer (Golden State), Maurice Carter (New Orleans), Desmond Ferguson (Portland), Marcus Fizer (Chicago), Richie Frahm (Seattle), Tamar Slay (New Jersey), Jeff Trepagnier (Denver) and Loren Woods (Miami). The following day, the Bobcats acquired the 45th overall pick in the 2004 NBA Draft from Milwaukee in exchange for Pachulia, and also acquired a future first-round pick from Cleveland in exchange for Pavlovic.

On June 24, the Bobcats chose center Emeka Okafor, the 2004 Co-College Basketball Player of the Year from the University of Connecticut, as the franchise's historical first rookie draft pick. In the second round, the team selected University of Michigan forward Bernard Robinson with the 45th overall selection.

When the NBA free agency period opened on July 14, the Bobcats signed free-agent guard Jason Hart and forward Tamar Slay. Charlotte also acquired forward Melvin Ely and guard Eddie House in a trade with the Los Angeles Clippers on the same day. In return, the Clippers received the Bobcats' second round draft picks in the 2005 and 2006 NBA Drafts.

The Bobcats unveiled their new uniforms on August 21, becoming the only NBA team to use orange as its primary road uniform color.

CHICAGO BULLS
CENTRAL DIVISION

Bulls Schedule
Home games shaded; *—All-Star Game at Denver.

November
SUN	MON	TUE	WED	THU	FRI	SAT
	1	2	3	4	5 NJN	6 IND
7	8	9 PHO	10	11	12	13 LAC
14	15	16 SAC	17 GS	18	19 DEN	20
21 LAL	22 PHO	23	24 UTH	25	26	27 CLE
28	29	30				

December
SUN	MON	TUE	WED	THU	FRI	SAT
			1 LAL	2	3 MIA	4 WAS
5 SA	6	7	8 CLE	9	10 PHI	11 MIN
12 DAL	13	14	15 MEM	16 MIL	17	18 IND
19	20 POR	21	22 DET	23	24	25
26 MIL	27	28 NJN	29	30	31	

January
SUN	MON	TUE	WED	THU	FRI	SAT
						1 ORL
2	3 DET	4	5 NO	6	7 UTH	8 BOS
9 GS	10	11	12 PHI	13	14	15 NYK
16 NYK	17	18	19 BOS	20	21 ATL	22 DET
23 ATL	24	25 DEN	26	27 CHA	28	29 BOS
30	31					

February
SUN	MON	TUE	WED	THU	FRI	SAT
		1 NJN	2	3	4	5 MIA
6	7	8 DAL	9 HOU	10	11	12
13 MIN	14	15 SAC	16 TOR	17	18	19
20 *All-Star	21	22 MIA	23 CLE	24	25 WAS	26 CHA
27	28					

March
SUN	MON	TUE	WED	THU	FRI	SAT
		1 HOU	2	3	4 SA	5 MIL
6	7 MIL	8	9 POR	10	11 SEA	12
13 LAC	14	15 SEA	16 NJN	17	18 NO	19 PHI
20	21 ATL	22	23 TOR	24	25 BOS	26 IND
27	28 MEM	29	30 CHA	31 CLE		

April
SUN	MON	TUE	WED	THU	FRI	SAT
					1	2 CHA
3	4	5 MIA	6 ORL	7	8 NYK	9 TOR
10	11 DET	12	13 WAS	14	15 ORL	16 ATL
17	18	19 NYK	20 IND	21	22	23

2004-05 SEASON
TEAM DIRECTORY

Chairman . . . . Jerry Reinsdorf
Assistant to Chairman . . . . Anita Fasano
Alternate NBA Governors . . . . Robert A. Judelson, Sanford Takiff
Executive Vice President, Business Operations . . . . Steve Schanwald
Executive Vice President, Basketball Operations . . . . John Paxson
Senior Vice President , Financial and Legal . . . . Irwin Mandel
Head Coach . . . . Scott Skiles
Assistant Coaches . . . . Ron Adams, Jim Boylan, Pete
Myers, Johnny Bach
Assistant Coach/Advance Scout . . . . Mike Wilhelm
Director of Player Personnel . . . . Gar Forman
Director of Pro Personnel . . . . Jay Hillock
Supervisor of European Scouting . . . . Ivica Dukan
Special Assistant to Executive VP of Basketball Operations . B.J. Armstrong
Assistant to Executive VP of Basketball Operations/
Manager, Berto Center . . . . Karen Stack-Umlauf
Senior Manager, Basketball Operations . . . . Matt Lloyd
Head Athletic Trainer . . . . Fred Tedeschi
Assistant Athletic Trainer . . . . TBA
Strength and Conditioning Consultant . . . . Al Vermeil
Strength and Conditioning Coach . . . . Erik Helland
Assistant Strength and Conditioning Coach . . . . Jeff Macy
Equipment Manager . . . . John Ligmanowski
Basketball Operations Assistants . . . . Wendy Knoll, Kristine Watson
Video Coordinator . . . . Greg Sabourin
Assistant Video Coordinator . . . . Wojciech Dron
Senior Director of Public and Media Relations . . . . Tim Hallam
Senior Director of Ticket Sales . . . . Keith Brown
Senior Director of Ticket Operations . . . . Joe O'Neil
Senior Director of Community Relations . . . . David Kurland
Director of Community Affairs . . . . Bob Love
Director of Premium Seating . . . . Greg Hanrahan
Director of Game Operations . . . . Jeff Wohlschlaeger
Director of Corporate Partnerships . . . . Scott Sonnenberg
Senior Manager, Public and Media Relations . . . . Sebrina Brewster
Senior Manager, Client Services . . . . Shannon Jordan
Senior Manager, Community Relations . . . . Tony Rokita
Senior Manager, Ticket Sales . . . . David Dowd
Senior Manager, Creative Services . . . . Jon Shoemaker
Manager, Corporate Communications . . . . Marianne Caponi
Manager, Rental Suites . . . . Curtis Baddeley
Manager, Publications . . . . Tony Hyde
Manager, Ticket Operations . . . . Pam Sher
Coordinator, Corporate Partnerships . . . . Liz Panich
Coordinator, Internet Services . . . . Adam Fluck
Coordinator, E-Marketing . . . . Jason Siok
Coordinator, Guest Services . . . . Jill Gayton
Coordinator, Public and Media Relations . . . . Brandon Faber
Corporate Partnerships Executive . . . . Whitney Garrott
Group Ticket Representatives . . . . Shannon Burney, Robby
Joseph, John Will
Ticket Executives . . . . Alan Bowman, Brandon
Caputo, Lauren Erickson, Brandon Wright
Graphic Designer . . . . Jeff Pitcock
Database Administrator . . . . Kristine Simantirakis
Assistant to the Executive VP, Business Operations . . . . . . Val Graham-Maxwell
Assistant, Public and Media Relations . . . . Matt Yob
Community Relations Assistants . . . . Jeff Schultz, Mike Ward
Corporate Partnerships Assistants . . . . Vanessa Weaver, DeBorah Wells
Group Ticket Assistant . . . . Jessica Sloan
Premium Seating Assistant . . . . Valerie Toth
Staff Assistant . . . . Gerard Longo
Ticket Operations Assistants . . . . Nancy DeFauw, Erin Hickok, Matt Shipley
Receptionist . . . . Alicia Santana
Team Photographer . . . . Bill Smith
Controller . . . . Stu Bookman
Assistant Controller . . . . Michele Chambers
Accountant . . . . Claudia Stevenson
Purchasing Agent . . . . Ben Adair
Assistant to Senior VP Financial and Legal . . . . Denise Aleman

Jerry Reinsdorf

John Paxson

Scott Skiles

ROSTER
Coach—Scott Skiles
Assistant coaches—Ron Adams, Johnny Bach, Jim Boylan, Pete Myers, Mike Wilhelm

No.	Name	Pos.	Ht./Wt.	Metric (m/kg)	Born	College/country
3	Tyson Chandler	F/C	7-1/235	2.16/106.6	10-2-82	Dominguez HS
2	Eddy Curry	C	6-11/285	2.10/129.3	12-5-82	Thornwood HS
34	Antonio Davis	F/C	6-9/245	2.05/111.1	10-31-68	Texas-El Paso
9	Luol Deng	F	6-8/220	2.03/99.8	4-16-85	Duke
21	Chris Duhon	G	6-1/185	1.85/83.9	8-31-82	Duke
7	Ben Gordon	G	6-3/200	1.90/90.7	4-4-83	Connecticut
24	Othella Harrington	F	6-9/235	2.06/106.6	1-31-74	Georgetown
12	Kirk Hinrich	G	6-3/190	1.90/86.2	1-2-81	Kansas
6	Chris Jefferies	F	6-8/230	2.03/104.3	2-13-80	Fresno State
55	Dikembe Mutombo	C	7-2/261	2.18/118.4	6-25-66	Georgetown
15	Jannero Pargo	G	6-1/175	1.85/79.4	9-22-79	Arkansas
33	Scottie Pippen	G/F	6-8/228	2.03/103.4	9-25-65	Central Arkansas
32	Eddie Robinson	G/F	6-9/210	2.05/95.3	4-19-76	Central Oklahoma
1	Tommy Smith	F	6-10/215	2.08/97.5	12-4-80	Arizona State
14	Cezary Trybanksi	C	7-2/240	2.18/108.9	9-22-79	Poland
30	Frank Williams	G	6-3/205	1.91/93.0	2-25-80	Illinois

BROADCAST INFORMATION

Radio: ESPN Radio (AM 1000). Broadcasters: Neil Funk, Bill Wennington.
TV: WGN-TV (Channel 9), WCIU-TV (Channel 26). Broadcasters: Wayne Larrivee, Johnny "Red" Kerr.
Cable TV: Comcast SportsNet Chicago. Broadcasters: Tom Dore, Johnny "Red" Kerr.

TEAM INFORMATION

Team address	.1901 W. Madison Street
	Chicago, IL 60612
Business phone	.312-455-4000
Ticket information	.312-559-1212
Website	.www.bulls.com
Arena (capacity)	.United Center (21,711)
Game times	.7:30 p.m., Monday-Saturday
First Bulls game in arena	.November 4, 1994

2003-04 REVIEW

RESULTS

OCTOBER
29— Washington	*74 -99	0 -1	
31— Atlanta	100 -94	1 -1	

NOVEMBER
1 — at Milwaukee	*68 -98	1 -2	
3— Houston	*66 -98	1 -3	
5— at Orlando	106 -100	2 -3	
7— Philadelphia	*85 -106	2 -4	
8 — at New Orleans	109 -106	3 -4	
10— Denver	*97 -105	3 -5	
12— at Boston	89 -82	4 -5	
13— Minnesota	*89 -92	†4 -6	
15— Seattle	*90 -98	4 -7	
18— at Phoenix	*82 -95	4 -8	
21— at L.A. Lakers	*94 -101	4 -9	
23— at Sacramento	*99 -110	4 -10	
25— at Dallas	*98 -124	4 -11	
26— at San Antonio	*98 -109	4 -12	

DECEMBER
1 — Milwaukee	97 -87	5 -12	
4 — at Philadelphia	*82 -83	5 -13	
6 — New Orleans	*91 -97	5 -14	
8 — San Antonio	*82 -96	5 -15	
12 — at Milwaukee	*95 -109	5 -16	
13— Indiana	86 -75	6 -16	
16— Orlando	102 -88	7 -16	
17— at Detroit	*73 -77	7 -17	
20— Cleveland	*87 -95	7 -18	
22— Utah	*80 -92	7 -19	
23— at New Jersey	*78 -95	7 -20	

26— at Cleveland	87 -80	8 -20
27— Washington	100 -86	9 -20
29— Miami	*83 -90	9 -21
30— at Minnesota	*93 -98	9 -22

JANUARY
2 — at New York	104 -99	10 -22
3 — Boston	*77 -88	10 -23
5 — Phoenix	87 -82	11 -23
7 — at Miami	*95 -102	11 -24
9 — Portland	*78 -87	11 -25
10 — New Orleans	89 -84	12 -25
13— Detroit	*89 -105	12 -26
15— at Memphis	*93 -108	12 -27
17— New York	*96 -101	12 -28
19— at Washington	*83 -93	12 -29
21— at Atlanta	*87 -97	12 -30
23— Dallas	*93 -106	12 -31
25— Toronto	96 -89	13 -31
27— at L.A. Clippers	*92 -102	13 -32
28— at Denver	*99 -115	13 -33
30— at Golden State	*81 -101	13 -34
31— at Portland	*95 -102	|13 -35

FEBRUARY
2 — at Seattle	*97 -109	13 -36
4 — at Utah	95 -79	14 -36
6 — at Houston	*80 -82	14 -37
10— Indiana	*84 -103	14 -38
12— Boston	107 -87	15 -38
17— Toronto	75 -73	16 -38
20— Sacramento	*83 -91	16 -39

21— Memphis	*98 -105	16 -40
25— Detroit	*88 -107	16 -41
26— at Washington	*87 -95	16 -42
28— Golden State	87 -81	†17 -42

MARCH
1 — Cleveland	92 -81	18 -42
3 — at New Orleans	*97 -100	†18 -43
6 — at Philadelphia	*88 -97	18 -44
9 — Philadelphia	*81 -89	18 -45
10— at Detroit	*65 -98	18 -46
12— at New Jersey	*76 -88	18 -47
13— L.A. Lakers	*81 -88	18 -48
16— at Cleveland	*87 -111	18 -49
19— at Toronto	96 -91	19 -49
20— New York	87 -81	20 -49
22— at Indiana	*77 -101	20 -50
23— New Jersey	*81 -84	20 -51
26— Milwaukee	*105 -115	20 -52
27— at Atlanta	*88 -97	20 -53
29— at Miami	*96 -105	20 -54
31— at Orlando	109 -91	21 -54

APRIL
2 — L.A. Clippers	114 -110	†22 -54
3 — Miami	*83 -97	22 -55
7 — at New York	*82 -96	22 -56
9 — Atlanta	*101 -116	22 -57
11— at Toronto	114 -108	†23 -57
12— Orlando	*84 -93	23 -58
14— at Indiana	*96 -101	23 -59

*Loss. †Single overtime.

TEAM LEADERS

Points: Jamal Crawford (1,383).
Field goals made: Crawford (509).
Free throws made: Eddy Curry (235).
3-pointers made: Crawford (165).
Rebounds: Antonio Davis (528).
Assists: Kirk Hinrich (517).
Steals: Crawford (111).
Blocks: Curry (83).

RECORDS

Regular season: 23-59 (8th in Central); 11-17 in division; 19-35 in conference; 4-24 vs. Western Conference; 14-27 at home; 9-32 on road; 3-3 in overtime; 2-5 in games decided by three points or fewer; 8-32 in games decided by 10 points or more; held opponents under 100 points 51 times; held under 100 points 70 times.
Playoffs: None.
All-time franchise record: 1,566-1,517 in 37 seasons. Won six NBA titles (1991, '92, '93, '96, '97, '98).
Team record past five years: 106-304 (.259, ranks 29th in NBA in that span).

HIGHLIGHTS

Top players: Jamal Crawford led the team in scoring (17.3 ppg) and steals (1.39 spg) and was second in assists (5.1 apg). He set career highs in minutes played (2,811), field goals (509), field-goal attempts (1,318), 3-point field goals (165), 3-point field-goal attempts (521), free throws (200), free throw attempts (240), assists (405), rebounds (283), steals (111), blocks (29) and points (1,383). He scored 30-plus points eight times, including one 50-point game. Crawford's 165 3-point field goals broke a franchise record. ... Eddy Curry tallied career highs of 14.7 ppg, 6.2 rpg, 1.14 bpg and 29.5 mpg. He led the team in scoring 20 times and in rebounding 12 times. ... Kirk Hinrich averaged 12.0 ppg, a team-high 6.8 apg (8th in the NBA), 1.33 spg and a team-high 35.6 mpg. He led all rookies with 14 double-doubles and was the only rookie to record a triple-double. He participated in the Rookie Challenge during All-Star Weekend and was named to the All-Rookie First Team. ... Antonio Davis was acquired via trade and posted averages of 8.9 ppg and a team-high 8.1 rpg.

Key injuries: The Bulls missed a total of 315 player games because of injury or illness, third most in the NBA. No Bulls player appeared in all 82 games. Scottie Pippen missed 58 games, most with a sore left knee. Tyson Chandler missed 44 games with injury and 43 with back problems. Jay Williams sat out the first 53 games of the season with injuries to his pelvis and left knee. Chris Jefferies missed 35 games with injury. Kendall Gill missed 26 games.
Notable: The Bulls ranked third in the NBA in attendance in 2003-04, averaging 19,736 fans per contest, and also hosted the seven largest NBA crowds of the season. ... The Bulls started a franchise record 18 different players in 2003-04. ... Scottie Pippen ended the season with 2,307 career steals and ranks fourth in NBA history. He needs just three more steals to tie Portland Trail Blazers coach Maurice Cheeks for third place on the all-time steals list.

CLEVELAND CAVALIERS
CENTRAL DIVISION

Cavaliers Schedule
Home games shaded; *—All-Star Game at Denver.

November

SUN	MON	TUE	WED	THU	FRI	SAT
	1	2	3 IND	4 MIA	5	6 MIL
7	8	9 ATL	10 PHO	11	12	13 WAS
14	15 GS	16	17	18 CHA	19	20 CHA
21 NYK	22	23	24 DET	25	26 BOS	27 CHI
28	29 LAC	30				

December

SUN	MON	TUE	WED	THU	FRI	SAT
			1 PHO	2 DEN	3	4 TOR
5	6	7 NJN	8 CHI	9	10	11 SA
12 MEM	13	14	15 POR	16 DET	17	18 BOS
19	20	21 MIN	22 NJN	23	24	25
26 NO	27	28 ATL	29 HOU	30	31	

January

SUN	MON	TUE	WED	THU	FRI	SAT
						1
2	3 CHA	4	5 ATL	6	7	8 NYK
9	10	11 CHA	12	13 LAL	14	15 UTH
16 SEA	17	18	19 POR	20 SAC	21	22 GS
23	24 WAS	25	26 MEM	27	28 NYK	29
30 MIL	31					

February

SUN	MON	TUE	WED	THU	FRI	SAT
		1 ORL	2	3 MIA	4	5 ORL
6	7	8 TOR	9	10	11 DEN	12
13 LAL	14	15	16 ATL	17 MIN	18	19
20 *All-Star	21	22	23 CHI	24	25 IND	26
27 NJN	28 SA					

March

SUN	MON	TUE	WED	THU	FRI	SAT
		1	2 SEA	3	4 PHI	5
6 MIA	7	8 ORL	9	10	11	12
13 IND	14	15 UTH	16 MIL	17	18 PHI	19
20 TOR	21	22 DET	23	24 HOU	25	26 DAL
27	28 NO	29 LAC	30	31 CHI		

April

SUN	MON	TUE	WED	THU	FRI	SAT
					1 SAC	2
3 DAL	4	5 NJN	6 IND	7	8 PHI	9 MIL
10	11 ORL	12	13	14 NYK	15 WAS	16
17 DET	18	19 BOS	20 TOR	21	22	23

2004-05 SEASON
TEAM DIRECTORY

Chairman . . . . .Gordon Gund
Vice Chairman . . . . .George Gund III
Vice Chairman . . . . .James C. Boland
Member, Board of Directors . . . . .John W. Graham
Secretary and Legal Counsel . . . . .Richard T. Watson
Chief Executive Officer . . . . .Mark R. Stornes
President . . . . .Len Komoroski
President/General Manager of Basketball Operations . .Jim Paxson
Head Coach . . . . .Paul Silas
Assistant Coaches . . . . .Kenny Natt, Stephen Silas
Assistant Coach/Strength & Conditioning . . . . .Stan Kellers
Dir. of Basketball Administration/Player Development . .Earl Patton
Director of Player Personnel . . . . .Mike Bratz
Athletic Trainer . . . . .Max Benton
Equipment Manager/Travel Coordinator . . . . .Mark Cashman
Special Projects Coordinator . . . . .Larry Nance
Director of Team Security .Marvin Cross
Head Scout . . . . .Darrell Hedric
Scouts . . . . .Rudy D'Amico, Don
Donoher,Wes Wilcox
Director of Public Relations . . . . .Amanda Mercado
Public Relations Coordinators . . . . .John Manuszak, Garin
Narain
Executive Assistant . . . . .Maura Naylon
Video Coordinator . . . . .Betsy McAllister
Basketball Operations Coordinator . . . . .Matt Yatsko
Team Physicians . . . . .John Bergfeld, M.D.,
Richard Parker, M.D., Alfred Cianflocco, M.D.
Team Dentist . . . . .Herb Litton, D.D.S.
Executive Vice President . . . . .Roy Jones
Vice President, Broadcasting . . . . .Joe Tait
Vice President, Communications . . . . .Tad Carper
Vice President, Corporate Sales . . . . .Kerry Bubolz
Vice President, Finance and Administration . . . . .John Wolf
Vice President, Marketing .Tracy Marek
Vice President, Operations .Pat Fitzgerald
Vice President, Sales and Business Development . . . . .Chad Estis
Vice President, Special Projects . . . . .Gayle Bibby-Creme
Senior Director, Broadcast Services . . . . .Dave Dombrowski
Senior Director, Guest Services . . . . .Mike Adams
Senior Director, Ticket Sales and Service . . . . .Maryann Kellermann
Controller . . . . .Noreen Byrne
Director, Advertising/Event Marketing . . . . .Chris Lesko
Director, Arena Public Relations . . . . .Phyllis Salem
Director, Booking/Assistant Building Manager . . . . . . .Peter Patton
Director, Community and Business Development . . . . . .Austin Carr
Director, Community Relations . . . . .Colleen Garrity
Director, Corporate Partner Services . . . . .Lisa Hudak
Director, Database Marketing . . . . .Damion Chatmon
Director, Game Presentation . . . . .Jay Moore
Director, Group Sales . . . . .John Fisher
Director, Housekeeping . . . . .Bob Pollard
Director, Human Resources . . . . .Farrell Finnin
Director, Information Technology . . . . .Ed Kordel
Director, Inside Sales . . . . .Mike Ondrejko
Director, Marketing . . . . .Brian Thornton
Director, Sales . . . . .Mike Ostrowski
Director, Suite Sales . . . . .Paul Mocho
Director, Suite Services . . . . .Dana Turk
Director, Ticketing Operations . . . . .Leisa Caton

Gordon Gund

Jim Paxson

Paul Silas

ROSTER
Coach—Paul Silas
Assistant coaches—Kenny Natt, Stephen Silas

No.	Name	Pos.	Ht./Wt.	Metric (m/kg)	Born	College/country
52	DeSagana Diop	C	7-0/280	2.13/127.0	1-30-82	Oak Hill Academy
	Drew Gooden	F	6-10/242	2.08/109.8	9-24-81	Kansas
11	Zydrunas Ilgauskas	C	7-3/260	2.21/117.9	6-5-75	Lithuania
33	Luke Jackson	G/F	6-7/215	2.00/97.5	11-6-81	Oregon
23	LeBron James	G/F	6-8/240	2.03/108.4	12-30-84	St. Vincent-St. Mary HS
0	Jeff McInnis	G	6-4/179	1.93/81.2	10-22-74	North Carolina
14	Ira Newble	F	6-7/220	2.00/99.8	1-20-75	Michigan (Ohio)
3	Aleksandar Pavlovic	G/F	6-7/210	2.00/95.3	11-15-83	Serbia-Montenegro
20	Eric Snow	G	6-3/205	1.90/93.0	4-24-73	Michigan State
32	Robert Traylor	F	6-8/284	2.03/128.8	2-1-77	Michigan
17	Anderson Varejao	F	6-10/230	2.08/104.3	9-28-82	Brazil
2	Dajuan Wagner	G	6-2/200	1.88/90.7	2-4-83	Memphis

BROADCAST INFORMATION
Radio: WTAM (1100 AM). Broadcaster: Joe Tait.
TV: WUAB (Channel 43). Broadcasters: Michael Reghi, Austin Carr.
Cable TV: FOX Sports Net (Ohio). Broadcasters: Michael Reghi.

TEAM INFORMATION
Team address	One Center Court
	Cleveland, OH 44115-4001
Business phone	216-420-2000
Ticket information	216-420-2100
Websites	www.clevelandcavaliers.com
Arena (capacity)	Gund Arena (20,562)
Game time	7 p.m., Sunday-Thursday
	7:30 p.m., Friday-Saturday
First Cavaliers game in arena	November 8, 1994

2003-04 REVIEW

RESULTS

OCTOBER
29 — at Sacramento	*92 -106	0 -1
30 — at Phoenix	*86 -95	0 -2

NOVEMBER
1 — at Portland	*85 -104	0 -3
5 — Denver	*89 -93	0 -4
7 — at Indiana	*90 -91	0 -5
8 — Washington	111 -98	1 -5
10 — New York	94 -80	2 -5
12 — at Miami	*83 -88	2 -6
14 — at Boston	*82 -91	2 -7
15 — Philadelphia	91 -88	†3 -7
18 — L.A. Clippers	103 -95	4 -7
19 — at Washington	*95 -106	4 -8
21 — Minnesota	*83 -97	4 -9
22 — at Atlanta	*83 -92	4 -10
26 — at New Orleans	*72 -82	4 -11
28 — at Detroit	*88 -92	4 -12
29 — Memphis	*125 -122	‡4 -13

DECEMBER
2 — at Denver	*103 -115	4 -14
3 — at L.A. Clippers	*80 -90	4 -15
6 — Atlanta	95 -85	5 -15
9 — Toronto	*93 -100	5 -16
11 — Detroit	95 -86	6 -16
13 — Boston	*98 -105	6 -17
15 — at Indiana	*85 -95	6 -18
17 — Houston	*85 -89	6 -19
19 — at Philadelphia	88 -81	7 -19
20 — at Chicago	95 -87	8 -19

23 — New Orleans	97 -86	9 -19
25 — at Orlando	*101 -113	†9 -20
26 — Chicago	*80 -87	9 -21
28 — Portland	86 -74	10 -21
30 — Indiana	*89 -92	10 -22

JANUARY
2 — at New Jersey	*82 -97	10 -23
6 — New York	107 -96	11 -23
7 — at Toronto	*69 -75	11 -24
9 — at Boston	*82 -107	11 -25
12 — at L.A. Lakers	*79 -89	11 -26
13 — at Seattle	104 -96	12 -26
15 — at Golden State	*102 -119	12 -27
17 — at Utah	102 -96	†13 -27
20 — Seattle	99 -94	14 -27
22 — Sacramento	*89 -95	14 -28
24 — Philadelphia	95 -87	15 -28
26 — Orlando	99 -98	16 -28
28 — Miami	94 -93	17 -28
30 — at Milwaukee	*95 -101	17 -29

FEBRUARY
1 — at Washington	104 -100	18 -29
3 — at Detroit	85 -82	19 -29
4 — L.A. Lakers	*106 -111	†19 -30
6 — at Minnesota	*92 -103	19 -31
7 — at Washington	*88 -106	19 -32
9 — Boston	97 -89	20 -32
11 — New Jersey	*85 -105	20 -33
18 — Dallas	*98 -114	20 -34
20 — San Antonio	89 -87	21 -34

22 — at New York	92 -86	22 -34
23 — New Orleans	104 -100	23 -34
25 — at Houston	*84 -90	23 -35
27 — at Orlando	112 -107	†24 -35

MARCH
1 — at Chicago	*81 -92	24 -36
3 — Atlanta	112 -80	25 -36
5 — at New Orleans	88 -85	26 -36
6 — Milwaukee	106 -97	27 -36
8 — at Atlanta	108 -102	28 -36
10 — at Toronto	106 -92	29 -36
14 — Indiana	107 -104	30 -36
16 — Chicago	111 -87	31 -36
19 — Utah	*88 -97	31 -37
21 — Detroit	*76 -96	31 -38
23 — Phoenix	*86 -103	31 -39
26 — at Philadelphia	*71 -86	31 -40
27 — New Jersey	107 -104	32 -40
29 — at San Antonio	*93 -101	32 -41
30 — at Dallas	*109 -126	32 -42

APRIL
2 — at Milwaukee	*09 -107	32 -43
3 — Golden State	*100 -103	32 -44
6 — Toronto	*86 -87	32 -45
7 — at Memphis	*74 -92	32 -46
9 — at Miami	*91 -106	32 -47
10 — Miami	91 -80	33 -47
12 — Milwaukee	93 -89	34 -47
14 — at New York	100 -90	35 -47

*Loss. †Single overtime. ‡Double overtime.

TEAM LEADERS
Points: LeBron James (1,654).
Field goals made: James (622).
Free throws made: James (347).
3-pointers made: James (63).
Rebounds: Carlos Boozer (627).
Assists: James (465).
Steals: James (130).
Blocks: Zydrunas Ilgauskas (201).

RECORDS
Regular season: 35-47 (5th in Central); 14-14 in division; 29-25 in conference; 6-22 vs. Western Conference; 23-18 at home; 12-29 on road; 3-3 in overtime; 8-4 in games decided by three points or fewer; 11-25 in games decided by 10 points or more; held opponents under 100 points 54 times; held under 100 points 59 times.
Playoffs: None.
All-time franchise record: 1,207-1,549 in 34 seasons.
Team record past five years: 143-267 (.349, ranks 26th in NBA in that span).

HIGHLIGHTS
Top players: LeBron James became the first Cavalier in franchise history and youngest player ever to be named the NBA Rookie of the Year. James became just the third rookie in NBA history to average 20-plus points (20.9), 5-plus rebounds (5.5) and 5-plus assists (5.9), joining Oscar Robertson and Michael Jordan. James was the Eastern Conference Rookie of the Month each month during the season. ... In the last 42 games of the season, Carlos Boozer averaged 17.8 ppg and 12.4 rpg and became the first Cavalier to average a double-double since Andre Miller in 2001-02. ... Boozer and Zydrunas Ilgauskas were Eastern Conference Players of the Week during the season. ... Boozer and James participated in the Rookie Challenge during All-Star Weekend.
Key injuries: The Cavaliers missed a total of 200 player games because of injury or illness. Dajuan Wagner missed the first 33 games of the season after undergoing right knee surgery. DeSagana Diop missed 16 games with a torn right meniscus. Jeff McInnis missed eight games with a bruised right shoulder, and Carlos Boozer missed six games with a right ankle sprain. LeBron James missed three games with a right ankle sprain.
Notable: Cleveland more than doubled its win total from last season (17 in 2002-03 to 35 in 2003-04) and won more games than any Cavaliers team since 1997-98 (47). ... The Cavaliers put together a seven-game win streak from March 3 to March 16, its longest of the season and longest since 1997. ... The Cavaliers were 20-11 with Jeff McInnis in the starting lineup. ... Cleveland increased its home attendance from 11,497 during the 2002-03 season to 18,288 during the 2003-04 season and sold out Gund Arena on 16 occasions. ... The Cavaliers selected Luke Jackson with the 10th overall pick in the 2004 Draft and acquired Eric Snow and Drew Gooden via trades during the offseason.

DALLAS MAVERICKS
SOUTHWEST DIVISION

Mavericks Schedule
Home games shaded; *—All-Star Game at Denver.

November
SUN	MON	TUE	WED	THU	FRI	SAT
	1	2 SAC	3 NO	4	5	6 MEM
7	8 GS	9 ORL	10	11 MIA	12	13 NJN
14 WAS	15	16 PHO	17	18	19 NYK	20
21 DEN	22 MIN	23	24 SA	25	26 POR	27 MEM
28	29	30 SA				

December
SUN	MON	TUE	WED	THU	FRI	SAT
			1	2 HOU	3	4 UTH
5	6 DET	7 MIN	8	9 SEA	10	11 HOU
12 CHI	13 GS	14	15	16	17	18 ATL
19	20	21 NYK	22 ATL	23	24	25
26 DEN	27	28 BOS	29	30	31	

January
SUN	MON	TUE	WED	THU	FRI	SAT
						1
2 MIL	3	4	5 LAL	6	7	8 IND
9	10	11	12 HOU	13	14 SA	15 NJN
16	17	18 WAS	19	20 LAC	21 CHA	22
23 DEN	24 LAC	25	26 POR	27	28	29 PHI
30	31					

February
SUN	MON	TUE	WED	THU	FRI	SAT
		1 MIA	2 NO	3 IND	4	5
6 TOR	7	8 CHI	9	10	11 SAC	12
13 SEA	14	15 GS	16	17 PHO	18	19
20 *All-Star	21	22	23 UTH	24 SAC	25	26 PHO
27	28 NO					

March
SUN	MON	TUE	WED	THU	FRI	SAT
		1	2 LAC	3	4 LAL	5
6 HOU	7 TOR	8	9	10 LAL	11 MIL	12
13 MIN	14	15 MIN	16	17 POR	18	19 CHA
20	21 NO	22	23 GS	24 SAC	25	26 CLE
27	28 DET	29	30 BOS	31		

April
SUN	MON	TUE	WED	THU	FRI	SAT
					1 PHI	2
3 CLE	4	5 ORL	6	7 SA	8	9 UTH
10	11 MEM	12	13 SEA	14 POR	15	16
17 LAL	18	19 SEA	20 MEM	21	22	23

2004-05 SEASON
TEAM DIRECTORY

Owner .... Mark Cuban
President and Chief Executive Officer .... Terdema Ussery
Senior Executive Assistant .... Cheryl Karalla
Senior Vice President of Human Resources .... Buddy Pittman
Receptionists .... Sandy Abel, Theta Hall
General Manager/Head Coach .... Don Nelson
President of Basketball Operations/Assistant Coach ... Donn Nelson
Assistant General Manager .... Keith Grant
Assistant Coaches .... Del Harris, Charlie Parker,
  Larry Riley
Basketball Executive Assistant .... Pat Russell
Basketball Travel Manager .... Leslie Tracy
Basketball Operations Coordinator .... Jason White
Coaches Assistant .... Kristy Cotten
Player Development Staff .... Rolando Blackman, Brad
  Davis, Paul Mokeski, Greg Dreiling
Free Throw Coach .... Gary Boren
Head Athletic Trainer .... Casey Smith
Assistant Athletic Trainer/Director of Rehabilitation ... Dionne Calhoun
Team Physician .... Dr. Tarek O. Souryal
Team Internist .... Dr. J. R. Zamorano
Strength and Conditioning Coach .... Robert Hackett
Equipment Manager .... Al Whitley
Performance Enhancement .... Don Kalkstein
Director of Business Development .... Brian Dameris
Scouts .... Dick Baker, Ray Dieringer,
  Alvydas Pazdrazdis, Kevin Stacom
Video Coordinator/Advance Scout .... Reginald Johnson
Assistant Video Coordinator .... Bill Reis
Director of Scouting .... Amadou Gallo Fall
Massage Therapist .... Gary Fineske
Chief Financial Officer .... Floyd Jahner
Controller .... Ronnie Fauss
Senior Accountant & Payroll Manager .... Lisa Tyner
Director of Technology & Information Systems .... Ken Bonzon
Systems Analyst .... Scott Powers
Ticket Manager .... Mary Jean Gaines
Financial Analyst/Ticket Systems Manager .... Mike Childers
Sr. Vice President of Marketing & Communications ... Matt Fitzgerald
Administrative Assistant .... Sandra Martinez
Director of Basketball Communications .... Sarah Melton
Basketball Communications Coordinator .... Sean McCloskey
Basketball Communications Coordinator .... Scott Tomlin
Director of Corporate and Community Relations ... Dawn Holgate
Project Manager, Communications & Events .... Danny Bollinger
Corporate Communications Coordinator .... Gina Calvert
Corp. Communications/Comm. Relations Coordinator ... Suzi LeBeau
Marketing Manager .... Kelly Weller
Player Relations Manager .... Tiffany Farha
Marketing Operations Manager .... Jeremy Armstrong
Marketing Coordinator .... Lesley Wright
Community Basketball Manager .... Jim Guy
Community Relations Coordinator .... Amy Cobb
Vice President of Merchandising .... Steve Shilts
Merchandise Assistant .... Alyssa Moog
Merchandising Staff .... Skip Titsworth, Matt Stewart,
  Ben Best
Director of Broadcasting .... Dave Evans
Executive Creative Producer .... Jill Lewis
Director of Production .... Tom Ward
Game Presentation Producer/Video Logging Coord. ... Anita Green
Vice President of Ticket Sales and Services .... George Prokos
Telemarketing Sales Manager .... Billy Widner
Vice President of Corporate Sponsorship .... George Killebrew
Sponsor Services Coordinator/Administrative Asst. ... Deadrah Smith
Senior Director of Corporate Sponsorship .... Billy Phillips
Directors of Corporate Sponsorship ..... Clay Christopher, Ryan Mackey
Vice President of Operations & Arena Development ... Steve Letson
Operations Manager .... Kirsten Seiter
Event Services Manager .... Melanie Lusk
Directory of Security .... Jim Colleran

Mark Cuban

Terdema Ussery

Don Nelson

ROSTER
Coach—Don Nelson
Assistant coaches—Del Harris, Donn Nelson, Charlie Parker, Larry Riley

No.	Name	Pos.	Ht./Wt.	Metric (m/kg)	Born	College/Country
9	Tariq Abdul-Wahad	G/F	6-6/235	1.98/106.6	11-3-74	San Jose State
52	Calvin Booth	C	6-11/231	2.10/104.8	5-7-76	Penn State
44	Shawn Bradley	C	7-6/275	2.28/124.7	3-22-72	Brigham Young
	Erick Dampier	C	6-11/265	2.11/120.2	7-14-75	Mississippi State
6	Marquis Daniels	G	6-6/200	1.98/90.7	1-7-81	Auburn
21	Dan Dickau	G	6-0/190	1.83/86.2	9-16-78	Gonzaga
4	Michael Finley	G/F	6-7/225	2.00/102.1	3-6-73	Wisconsin
34	Devin Harris	G	6-3/185	1.90/83.9	2-27-83	Wisconsin
	Alan Henderson	F	6-9/240	2.06/108.9	12-2-72	Indiana
5	Josh Howard	F	6-7/210	2.00/95.3	4-28-80	Wake Forest
	DJ Mbenga	C	7-0/220	2.13/99.8	12-30-80	Congo
41	Dirk Nowitzki	F/C	7-0/245	2.13/111.1	6-19-78	Germany
	Pavel Podkolzin	C	7-5/260	2.22/117.9	1-15-85	Russia
42	Jerry Stackhouse	G/F	6-6/218	1.98/98.9	11-5-74	North Carolina
10	Jon Stefansson	G	6-5/200	1.96/90.7	9-21-82	Iceland
31	Jason Terry	G	6-2/180	1.88/81.6	9-15-77	Arizona

BROADCAST INFORMATION

Radio: ESPN Radio (103.3 FM). Broadcasters: Mark Followill, Brad Davis. Spanish radio: KFLC (1270 AM). Broadcaster: TBA.
TV: UPN (Channel 21); CBS 11. Broadcasters: Matt Pinto, Bob Ortegel.
Cable TV: FSN Southwest. Broadcasters: Matt Pinto, Bob Ortegel.

TEAM INFORMATION

Team address . . . . .2500 Victory Avenue
Dallas, TX 75219
Team phone 214-665-4660
Business phone 214-747-6287
Ticket information 214-747-6287
Website . . . . .www.mavs.com
Arena (capacity) . . . . .American Airlines Center (19,200)
Game times . . . . .7:30 p.m.
First Mavericks game in arena . . . . .October 30, 2001

2003-04 REVIEW

RESULTS

OCTOBER
28— at L.A. Lakers	*93 -109	0 -1
29— at Golden State	95 -87	1 -1

NOVEMBER
1 — Utah	127 -102	2 -1
3 — Miami	103 -93	3 -1
5 — at Washington	*90 -100	3 -2
6 — at Toronto	*71 -77	3 -3
8 — at San Antonio	81 -78	4 -3
11— New Orleans	125 -97	5 -3
13— Houston	97 -86	6 -3
15— at Memphis	*101 -108	†6 -3
17— Portland	105 -98	7 -4
20— San Antonio	95 -92	8 -4
22— Denver	115 -101	9 -4
25— Chicago	124 -98	10 -4
26— at Phoenix	*90 -121	10 -5
28— at Denver	*103 -113	10 -6
29— at Minnesota	92 -88	11 -6

DECEMBER
2 — Washington	97 -72	12 -6
4 — L.A. Lakers	*103 -114	12 -7
6 — Orlando	110 -97	13 -7
10— at L.A. Clippers	*99 -109	13 -8
12— at L.A. Lakers	110 -93	14 -8
15— Toronto	111 -94	15 -8
17— at Boston	*103 -105	15 -9
18— at Minnesota	*109 -114	15 -10
20— L.A. Clippers	*105 -115	15 -11
23— at Portland	*88 -97	15 -12

25— at Sacramento	111 -103	16 -12
27— Memphis	104 -98	17 -12
30— Milwaukee	101 -92	18 -12

JANUARY
2 — at Milwaukee	*101 -109	18 -13
3 — Minnesota	119 -112	19 -13
5 — at Utah	*94 -108	19 -14
7 — Golden State	105 -99	20 -14
9 — Indiana	*80 -92	20 -15
11— at Detroit	*102 -115	20 -16
12— at New York	127 -121	†21 -16
14— Philadelphia	125 -122	‡22 -16
16— at Denver	91 -88	23 -16
17— at Portland	108 -104	24 -16
20— New Jersey	106 -93	25 -16
22— L.A. Lakers	106 -87	26 -16
23— at Chicago	106 -93	27 -16
25 — Sacramento	108 -99	28 -16
27— at Seattle	118 -116	29 -16
28— at Utah	*88 -91	29 -17
31— Denver	*102 -107	29 -18

FEBRUARY
3 — Golden State	107 -93	30 -18
4 — at New Orleans	113 -104	31 -18
7 — Detroit	111 -108	32 -18
9 — at Atlanta	*96 -102	32 -19
10— New York	105 -90	33 -19
17— at Memphis	*92 -109	33 -20
18— at Cleveland	114 -98	34 -20
21— Houston	97 -88	35 -20
24— L.A. Clippers	116 -91	36 -20

26— San Antonio	115 -91	37 -20
28— Portland	111 -91	38 -20

MARCH
2 — Seattle	107 -96	39 -20
3 — at Minnesota	*97 -121	39 -21
5 — at San Antonio	*100 -113	39 -22
7 — at Houston	*98 -101	39 -23
8—Phoenix	103 -90	40 -23
11— at Sacramento	*102 -120	40 -24
13— at Phoenix	113 -90	41 -24
14— at L.A. Clippers	101 -88	42 -24
17— Atlanta	*110 -111	42 -25
19— Boston	120 -104	43 -25
21— at New Jersey	101 -98	44 -25
22— at Philadelphia	*98 -107	44 -26
24— at Indiana	*99 -103	44 -27
26— at Miami	*118 -119	†44 -28
28— at Orlando	110 -00	45 -20
30— Cleveland	126 -109	46 -28

APRIL
1 — Sacramento	127 -117	47 -28
3 — Phoenix	124 -103	48 -28
6 — Seattle	118 -108	49 -28
8 — Utah	117 -94	50 -28
10— at Seattle	*99 -119	50 -29
11— at Golden State	*107 -108	50 -30
13— Memphis	110 -103	51 -30
14— at Houston	92 -89	52 -30

*Loss. †Single overtime. ‡Double overtime.

TEAM LEADERS

Points: Dirk Nowitzki (1,680).
Field goals made: Nowitzki (605).
Free throws made: Nowitzki (371).
3-pointers made: Michael Finley (150).
Rebounds: Antoine Walker (684).
Assists: Steve Nash (687).
Steals: Nowitzki (92).
Blocks: Nowitzki (104).

RECORDS

Regular season: 52-30 (3rd in Midwest Division); 14-10 in division, 33-19 in conference; 19-11 vs. Eastern Conference; 36-5 at home; 16-25 on road; 2-2 in overtime; 8-7 in games decided by three points or fewer; 30-14 in games decided by 10 points or more; held opponents under 100 points 40 times; held under 100 points 25 times.
Playoffs: 1-4, lost to Kings, 4-1, in Western Conference first round.
All-time franchise record: 866-1,070 in 24 seasons.
Team record past five years: 262-148 (.639, ranks 4th in NBA in that span).

HIGHLIGHTS

Top players: Dirk Nowitzki led the team in scoring (21.8 ppg, 9th in the NBA), rebounding (8.7, 16th), steals (1.19), blocks (1.35) and minutes (2,915). He was named to the Western Conference All-Star team. ... Michael Finley was the team's second-leading scorer (18.6 ppg) and led the team in 3-pointers (150) while shooting a career-high 40.5 percent from behind the arc (11th in the NBA). ... Steve Nash averaged a career-high 8.8 apg (3rd in the NBA). He also ranked second in the league with a career-high free throw percentage of 91.6 percent. ... Antawn Jamison earned the NBA's Sixth Man of the Year Award while playing in all 82 games and shooting a career-high 53.5 percent from the floor (4th in the league).
Key injuries: The Mavericks lost a total of 288 player games because of injury or illness. The most notable losses were Eduardo Najera, who missed 24 games with a left knee injury, Michael Finley, who missed 10 games with back spasms, a strained right calf and a sprained right great toe, and Dirk Nowitzki, who missed five games with a sprained right ankle.
Notable: The Mavericks had their most successful home record in franchise histo-ry with an NBA-best 36-5 mark. ... Dallas posted a Western Conference record of 33-19, just one win shy of tying the franchise record set a season earlier. ... The Mavericks were the highest scoring team in the league (105.2 ppg), led the NBA in free throw percentage (.796) and offensive rebounds (14.3) and had the fewest turnovers (11.8). ... Dallas is just one of four teams to post 50-win seasons the past four years (San Antonio, Sacramento and L.A. Lakers). ... Dirk Nowitzki earned All-NBA Third Team honors. ... Antawn Jamison earned the Sixth Man of the Year Award. ... Rookies Josh Howard and Marquis Daniels were named to the All-Rookie Second Team. Dallas sold out all 41 regular season games for the second straight season and has a streak of 112 consecutive sellouts.

DENVER NUGGETS
NORTHWEST DIVISION

Nuggets Schedule
Home games shaded; *---All-Star Game at Denver.

November
SUN	MON	TUE	WED	THU	FRI	SAT
	1	2 LAL	3	4 MIN	5	6 UTH
7	8 UTH	9 SEA	10	11 DET	12	13
14 SAC	15	16	17 TOR	18	19 CHI	20
21 DAL	22	23 NJN	24	25	26 SA	27 HOU
28	29 NO	30				

December
SUN	MON	TUE	WED	THU	FRI	SAT
			1	2 CLE	3	4 MIA
5	6 ORL	7	8 WAS	9	10 TOR	11
12 NYK	13	14 PHI	15 BOS	16	17 MIA	18 ORL
19	20 PHO	21	22 SEA	23	24	25
26 DAL	27 GS	28	29	30	31 PHI	

January
SUN	MON	TUE	WED	THU	FRI	SAT
						1
2 LAL	3 LAC	4	5	6	7	8 SA
9 HOU	10	11 SAC	12 LAL	13	14 MIN	15
16	17 GS	18 SEA	19	20	21 MEM	22
23 DAL	24	25 CHI	26 DET	27	28 MIL	29 IND
30	31					

February
SUN	MON	TUE	WED	THU	FRI	SAT
		1 NYK	2 POR	3	4	5 GS
6	7	8 UTH	9 MIN	10	11 CLE	12
13 NJN	14	15 ATL	16 CHA	17	18	19
20 *All-Star	21	22	23 BOS	24	25 MEM	26
27 NO	28					

March
SUN	MON	TUE	WED	THU	FRI	SAT
		1 ATL	2	3 IND	4	5 LAC
6	7 POR	8	9	10	11	12 SA
13 PHO	14	15	16 CHA	17	18 LAC	19
20 MIL	21	22 WAS	23	24 LAL	25	26 SAC
27	28 PHO	29	30 UT	31		

April
SUN	MON	TUE	WED	THU	FRI	SAT
					1 SA	2 POR
3	4	5 MEM	6 NO	7	8 MIN	9 SEA
10	11 GS	12	13 NO	14	15 MEM	16 HOU
17	18 PHO	19 POR	20	21	22	23

2004-05 SEASON

TEAM DIRECTORY

Owner . . . . .E. Stanley Kroenke
General Manager . . . . .Kiki Vandeweghe
Assistant General Manager . . . . .David Fredman
Assistant General Manager . . . . .Jeff Weltman
Head Coach . . . . .Jeff Bzdelik
Assistant Coaches .Scott Brooks, Michael
Cooper, Adrian Dantley
Assistant Coaches/Player Development . . . .Jarinn Akana, Chip
Engelland, Rex Kalamian
Assistant Coach/Director of Scouting . . . . . .Bill Branch
Assistant Coach/Coaching Consultant . . . . .Doug Moe
Head Athletic Trainer/Traveling Secretary . . .Jim Gillen
Assistant Athletic Trainer . . . . .Derrick Fitts
Assistant Coach/Strength and Conditioning . . . .Steve Hess
Assistant Strength and Conditioning Coach . . . .Rich Williams
Equipment Manager . . . . .Sparky Gonzales
Massage Therapist .Leonti Vinskevich
Scouts . . . . .Greg Bittner, John
Carideo, Mike Wilson, Masai Ujiri
Director of Media Relations . . . . .Eric Sebastian
Media Relations Assistant . . . . .Tim Gelt
Video Coordinator .Chad Iske
Scouting Coordinator . . . . .Stu Lash
Executive Assistant to the General Manager . . . .Carol Williams
Director of Basketball Administration . . . . . .Lisa Johnson
Manager, Basketball Operations . . . . .Greg Knight
Team Services Director . . . . .Tim Dixon
Team Physicians . . . . .Dr. Jim Benoist, Dr.
Steven Traina, Dr. Adam Liberman, Dr. Richard Beatty

E. Stanley Kroenke

Kiki Vandeweghe

Jeff Bzdelik

ROSTER
Coach—Jeff Bzdelik
Assistant coaches—Scott Brooks, Michael Cooper

No.	Name	Pos.	Ht./Wt.	Metric (m/kg)	Born	College/country
15	Carmelo Anthony	F	6-8/230	2.03/104.3	5-29-84	Syracuse
20	Jon Barry	G	6-5/205	1.96/93.0	7-25-69	Georgia Tech
32	Ryan Bowen	F	6-9/220	2.05/99.8	11-20-75	Iowa
11	Earl Boykins	G	5-5/133	1.65/60.3	6-2-76	Eastern Michigan
23	Marcus Camby	F/C	6-11/235	2.10/106.6	3-22-74	Massachusetts
56	Francisco Elson	F/C	7-0/235	2.13/106.6	2-28-76	California
1	Voshon Lenard	G	6-4/205	1.93/93.0	5-14-73	Minnesota
6	Kenyon Martin	F	6-9/240	2.05/108.9	12-30-77	Cincinnati
24	Andre Miller	G	6-2/200	1.88/90.7	3-19-76	Utah
31	Nene	F	6-11/260	2.10/117.9	9-13-82	Brazil
41	Mark Pope	F	6-10/235	2.08/106.6	9-11-72	Kentucky
22	Nikoloz Tskitishvili	F	7-0/245	2.13/111.1	4-14-83	Republic of Georgia
5	Rodney White	F	6-9/230	2.05/104.3	5-28-80	Charlotte

BROADCAST INFORMATION

Radio: KKFN (AM 950). Broadcaster: Jerry Schemmel.
Cable: Altitude. Broadcaster: TBA.

TEAM INFORMATION

Team address	.1000 Chopper Circle
	Denver, CO 80204
Business phone/Tickets	.303-405-1100
Ticket information	.303-405-1315
Internet address	.www.nuggets.com
Arena (capacity)	.Pepsi Center (19,099)
Game time	.7 p.m.
First Nuggets NBA game in arena	.November 2, 1999

2003-04 REVIEW

RESULTS

OCTOBER
29— San Antonio	80 -72	1 -0
30— at Houston	*85 -102	1 -1

NOVEMBER
1 — Sacramento	109 -88	2 -1
4 — at Indiana	*60 -71	2 -2
5 — at Cleveland	93 -89	3 -2
7 — L.A. Clippers	*102 -104	†3 -3
9 — at Toronto	*76 -89	3 -4
10—at Chicago	105 -97	4 -4
14—Orlando	106 -101	5 -4
18—at Minnesota	*76 -89	5 -5
19—Milwaukee	94 -86	6 -5
21—Washington	108 -87	7 -5
22—at Dallas	*101 -115	7 -6
25—Phoenix	110 -80	8 -6
28—Dallas	113 -103	9 -6
29—at L.A. Clippers	98 -86	10 -6

DECEMBER
2 — Cleveland	115 -103	11 -6
3 — at Golden State	117 -109	12 -6
5 — Golden State	98 -91	13 -6
7 — Boston	*111 -116	13 -7
9 — at Atlanta	*98 -112	13 -8
12—at Philadelphia	86 -77	14 -8
13—at New York	*88 -95	14 -9
16— New Orleans	116 -94	15 -9
17— at Seattle	99 -98	16 -9
19— at L.A. Lakers	*99 -101	16 -10
20— Seattle	*106 -115	16 -11

JANUARY (continued listing)
22— Memphis	106 -99	17 -11
26— Houston	95 -94	18 -11
28— Golden State	103 -79	19 -11
30— Toronto	*74 -81	19 -12
31— at L.A. Clippers	*104 -120	19 -13

JANUARY
2 — at Portland	106 -96	20 -13
3 — Atlanta	*76 -84	20 -14
5 — San Antonio	*74 -98	20 -15
7 — L.A. Lakers	113 -91	21 -15
9 — Utah	106 -96	22 -15
11— at Sacramento	*106 -117	22 -16
13— at Phoenix	105 -92	23 -16
14— at L.A. Lakers	*71 -97	23 -17
16— Dallas	*88 -91	23 -18
18— Miami	88 -80	24 -18
20— at Utah	96 -75	25 -18
21— Phoenix	97 -92	26 -18
23— at New Orleans	*91 -97	26 -19
25— at Memphis	*88 -106	26 -20
26— Minnesota	*95 -97	26 -21
28— Chicago	115 -99	27 -21
31— at Dallas	107 -102	28 -21

FEBRUARY
2 — Portland	116 -97	29 -21
6 — at Golden State	*87 -96	29 -22
8 — at Sacramento	*92 -115	29 -23
9 — Memphis	86 -83	30 -23
12— at Portland	107 -98	31 -23
17— Philadelphia	106 -85	32 -23

(continued)
20 — at Orlando	*98 -102	32 -24
21— at Miami	*81 -97	32 -25
23— at Memphis	*106 -109	32 -26
25— L.A. Lakers	*111 -112	32 -27
28— at San Antonio	*92 -117	32 -28
29— New York	107 -96	33 -28

MARCH
2 — New Jersey	*91 -95	33 -29
6 — Detroit	*66 -97	33 -30
7 — Indiana	*94 -103	33 -31
9 — at Washington	117 -87	34 -31
10— at New Jersey	*97 -98	34 -32
12— at Milwaukee	117 -111	35 -32
14— Utah	102 -75	36 -32
17— at Boston	*100 -104	36 -33
19— at Detroit	*75 -94	36 -34
21— at Minnesota	*77 -98	36 -35
22— L.A. Clippers	102 -80	37 -35
24— Minnesota	101 -92	38 -35
26— at Seattle	*86 -102	38 -36
27— at Utah	*83 -85	38 -37
30— Seattle	124 -119	39 -37

APRIL
2 — Houston	110 -100	40 -37
7 — at Phoenix	111 -96	41 -37
9 — at Houston	*103 -106	41 -38
10— Portland	110 -100	†42 -38
12— Sacramento	97 -89	43 -38
14— at San Antonio	*67 -93	43 -39

*Loss. †Single overtime.

TEAM LEADERS

Points: Carmelo Anthony (1,725).
Field goals made: Anthony (624).
Free throws made: Anthony (408).
3-pointers made: Voshon Lenard (106).
Rebounds: Marcus Camby (727).
Assists: Andre Miller (501).
Steals: Miller (142).
Blocks: Camby (187).

RECORDS

Regular season: 43-39 (6th in Midwest Division); 11-13 in division; 29-23 in conference; 14-16 vs. Eastern Conference; 29-12 at home; 14-27 on road; 1-1 in overtime; 3-9 in games decided by three points or fewer; 23-19 in games decided by 10 points or more; held opponents under 100 points 54 times; held under 100 points 42 times.
Playoffs: 1-4, lost to Minnesota, 4-1, in Western Conference first round.
All-time franchise record: 1,024-1,240 in 28 seasons in NBA; 413-331 in nine seasons in ABA.
Team record past five years: 162-248 (.395, ranks 22nd in NBA in that span).

HIGHLIGHTS

Top players: Carmelo Anthony earned All-Rookie First Team honors after leading the Nuggets in scoring (21.0 ppg, 12th in the NBA). He became the first rookie since David Robinson in 1989-90 to lead a playoff team in scoring. ... Marcus Camby played in a career-high 72 games and led the team in rebounding (10.1 rpg, 10th) and blocked shots (2.60 bpg, 5th). ... Andre Miller averaged 14.8 ppg and ranked 11th in the NBA with a team-high 6.1 apg. ... Voshon Lenard averaged 14.2 points a game—just short of a career high—and won the Footlocker 3-Point Shootout at All-Star Weekend. ... Earl Boykins averaged a career-high 10.2 ppg. ... Second-year forward Nene averaged 11.8 points and 6.5 rebounds a game.
Key injuries: The Nuggets lost a total of 218 player games because of injury or illness. Marcus Camby missed 10 games with various injuries, and Voshon Lenard missed nine.
Notable: The Nuggets made the playoffs for the first time since 1994-95, finishing with their most wins (43) since 1989-90. ... The Nuggets became the first team since the NBA went to an 82-game sched-ule in 1976 to make the playoffs after winning fewer than 20 games the year before. Their 26-game improvement was also the best in NBA history for a team that won fewer than 20 games the year before and tied for the sixth-best on the NBA's all-time list. ... The Nuggets led the league in fast-break points, averaging 19.9 per game. ... The Nuggets exceeded their previous year's win total (17) in just 29 games (18-11).

DETROIT PISTONS
CENTRAL DIVISION

Pistons Schedule
Home games shaded; *—All-Star Game at Denver.

November
SUN	MON	TUE	WED	THU	FRI	SAT
	1	2 HOU	3	4	5 TOR	6 PHI
7	8 LAC	9	10	11 DEN	12	13 UTH
14	15	16	17 MIN	18	19 IND	20
21 CHA	22	23 CHA	24 CLE	25	26 MIA	27 MIL
28	29	30 HOU				

December
SUN	MON	TUE	WED	THU	FRI	SAT
			1	2	3 SA	4 NO
5	6 DAL	7	8 TOR	9	10 ATL	11 MEM
12	13	14	15 NYK	16 CLE	17	18 POR
19	20	21	22 CHI	23	24	25 IND
26	27 NJN	28	29 WAS	30 MIA	31	

January
SUN	MON	TUE	WED	THU	FRI	SAT
						1
2 BOS	3 CHI	4	5	6 MEM	7 BOS	8
9	10	11 NJN	12 NO	13	14 ORL	15 PHI
16	17 PHO	18 ORL	19	20	21 MIL	22 CHI
23	24 MIN	25	26 DEN	27 IND	28	29 NYK
30	31					

February
SUN	MON	TUE	WED	THU	FRI	SAT
		1 WAS	2 ATL	3	4	5 NJN
6	7	8	9	10 LAL	11	12 WAS
13 MIL	14	15	16 PHI	17	18	19
20 *All-Star	21	22 NYK	23	24	25 LAL	26
27 GS	28					

March
SUN	MON	TUE	WED	THU	FRI	SAT
		1 POR	2	3 PHO	4 SEA	5
6 SAC	7	8	9 GS	10	11 BOS	12
13 UTH	14 ATL	15	16 SEA	17	18 TOR	19
20 SA	21	22 CLE	23 PHI	24	25 IND	26 BOS
27	28 DAL	29	30 SAC	31		

April
SUN	MON	TUE	WED	THU	FRI	SAT
					1 LAC	2
3 TOR	4	5	6 WAS	7	8 ORL	9
10 MIA	11 CHI	12	13 ORL	14	15 MIL	16
17 CLE	18	19 ATL	20 CHA	21	22	23

2004-05 SEASON

TEAM DIRECTORY

Managing Partner	William Davidson
Legal Counsel	Oscar H. Feldman
Advisory Board	Warren J. Coville, Milt Dresner, Bud Gerson, Dorothy Gerson, Eugene Mondry, Miriam Mondry, Ann Newman, Herbert Tyner, William M.Wetsman
President	Thomas S. Wilson
President of Basketball Operations	Joe Dumars
COO/Assistant General Manager	Alan Ostfield
VP of Basketball Operations	John Hammond
Head Coach	Larry Brown
Assistant Coaches	Phil Ford, Dave Hanners, Gar Heard, Igor Stefan Kokoskov, Pat Sullivan
Director of Player Personnel	Scott Perry
Director of Scouting	George David
Scouts	Brendan O'Connor, Tony Ronzone, Faruk Akagun
Head Athletic Trainer	Mike Abdenour
Strength and Conditioning Coach	Arnie Kander
Executive Vice President	John Ciszewski
Executive Vice President	Dan Hauser
Vice President of Public Relations	Matt Dobek
Senior Vice President	Marilyn Hauser
Senior Vice President	Lou Korpas
Senior Vice President	Stu Mayer
Senior Vice President/CFO	John O'Reilly
Senior Vice President	Pete Skorich
Vice President	Craig Turnbull
Director of Media Relations	Kevin Grigg
Media Relations Assistants	Bryant Fillmore, Cletus Lewis Jr.
Director of Box Office Operations	Bruce Trout
Basketball Operations Manager	Nancy Bontumasi
Team Physician	Dr. Ben Paolucci
Team Photographer	Allen Einstein

William Davidson

Joe Dumars

Larry Brown

ROSTER
Coach—Larry Brown
Assistant coaches—Phil Ford, Dave Hanners, Gar Heard, Igor Stefan Kokoskov, Pat Sullivan

No.	Name	Pos.	Ht./Wt.	Metric (m/kg)	Born	College/country
1	Chauncey Billups	G	6-3/202	1.90/91.6	9-25-76	Colorado
41	Elden Campbell	C	7-0/279	2.13/126.6	7-23-68	Clemson
44	Derrick Coleman	F	6-10/270	2,08/122,5	6-21-67	Syracuse
20	Carlos Delfino	G	6-6/230	1.98/104.3	8-29-82	Argentina
12	Ron Dupree	F	6-7/209	2.01/94.8	1-26-81	Louisiana State
8	Darvin Ham	F	6-7/240	2.01/108.9	7-23-73	Texas Tech
32	Richard Hamilton	G	6-7/193	1.98/83.9	2-14-78	Connecticut
	Lindsey Hunter	G	6-2/195	1.88/88.5	12-3-70	Jackson State
5	Horace Jenkins	G	6-1/180	1.85/81.8	10-14-74	William Paterson
24	Antonio McDyess	F	6-9/245	2.06/111.1	9-7-74	Alabama
31	Darko Milicic	C/F	7-0/245	2.13/111.1	6-20-85	Yugoslavia
22	Tayshaun Prince	G/F	6-9/215	2.05/97.5	2-28-80	Kentucky
3	Ben Wallace	C/F	6-9/240	2.05/108.9	9-10-74	Virginia Union
36	Rasheed Wallace	F	6-11/230	2.11/104.3	9-17-74	North Carolina

BROADCAST INFORMATION

Radio: Pistons Network WDFN (1130 AM). Broadcasters: George Blaha, Mark Champion, Rick Mahorn.
TV: WDWB (WB 20). Broadcasters: George Blaha, Bill Laimbeer.
Cable TV: FSN Detroit. Broadcasters: Fred McLeod, Greg Kelser.

TEAM INFORMATION

Team address	Four Championship Drive Auburn Hills, MI 48326
Business phone	248-377-0100
Ticket information	248-377-0100
Website	www.pistons.com
Arena (capacity)	The Palace of Auburn Hills (22,076)
Game times	7:30 p.m., Monday-Thursday; 8 p.m., Friday; 7:30 p.m., Saturday; 6 p.m., Sunday
First Pistons game in arena	November 5, 1988

2003-04 REVIEW

RESULTS

OCTOBER
29—	Indiana	*87 -89	0 -1
31—	at Miami	93 -81	1 -1

NOVEMBER
1—	at Orlando	96 -85	2 -1
5—	Boston	96 -88	3 -1
7—	Milwaukee	105 -99	4 -1
9—	New Jersey	98 -84	5 -1
11—	at Sacramento	*91 -97	5 -2
12—	at Golden State	*85 -87	†5 -3
14—	at L.A. Lakers	*89 -94	5 -4
15—	at Phoenix	100 -91	6 -4
18—	L.A. Lakers	106 -96	7 -4
19—	at Memphis	99 -92	8 -4
21—	New York	94 -85	9 -4
23—	New Orleans	*80 -81	9 -5
24—	at Atlanta	94 -89	10 -5
26—	at Philadelphia	*86 -90	10 -6
28—	Cleveland	92 -88	11 -6
29—	at Washington	80 -69	12 -6

DECEMBER
1—	at New York	79 -78	†13 -6
3—	Miami	87 -73	14 -6
6—	at Houston	*80 -86	14 -7
9—	Philadelphia	*76 -78	14 -8
11—	at Cleveland	*86 -95	14 -9
12—	Seattle	*72 -93	14 -10
17—	Chicago	77 -73	15 -10
19—	at Indiana	*75 -80	15 -11
21—	Utah	96 -75	16 -11

23—	at Milwaukee	*78 -83	16 -12
26—	New Jersey	*79 -82	16 -13
27—	at Atlanta	87 -84	17 -13
29—	New Orleans	108 -99	18 -13
31—	Portland	78 -71	19 -13

JANUARY
2—	Phoenix	93 -81	20 -13
3—	Golden State	99 -93	21 -13
5—	at Boston	78 -68	22 -13
7—	Houston	85 -66	23 -13
11—	Dallas	115 -102	24 -13
13—	at Chicago	105 -89	25 -13
14—	Toronto	95 -91	26 -13
16—	Washington	98 -77	27 -13
17—	at Milwaukee	99 -94	28 -13
19—	San Antonio	85 -77	29 -13
20—	at Indiana	*69 -81	29 -14
23—	at Minnesota	*79 -80	29 -15
25—	Atlanta	*82 -91	29 -16
28—	at Boston	106 -103	30 -16
30—	at Toronto	90 -89	†31 -16
31—	Memphis	80 -78	32 -16

FEBRUARY
2—	at Miami	102 -100	†33 -16
3—	Cleveland	*82 -85	33 -17
6—	at New Orleans	*81 -92	33 -18
7—	at Dallas	*108 -111	33 -19
10—	at New Jersey	*78 -89	33 -20
11—	Sacramento	*94 -96	33 -21
17—	at New York	*88 -92	33 -22

18—	Milwaukee	102 -98	34 -22
20—	Minnesota	*87 -88	34 -23
22—	Orlando	*86 -87	34 -24
23—	at Philadelphia	76 -66	35 -24
25—	at Chicago	107 -88	36 -24
27—	Atlanta	105 -83	37 -24
29—	at L.A. Clippers	100 -88	38 -24

MARCH
1 —	at Utah	*86 -94	38 -25
4 —	at Portland	83 -68	39 -25
6 —	at Denver	97 -66	40 -25
7 —	at Seattle	86 -65	41 -25
10—	Chicago	98 -65	42 -25
14—	Philadelphia	85 -69	43 -25
18—	at New Jersey	89 -71	44 -25
19—	Denver	94 -75	45 -25
21—	at Cleveland	96 -76	46 -25
23—	at New Orleans	*81 -82	46 -26
25—	at San Antonio	*75 -84	46 -27
27—	New York	100 -85	47 -27
31—	L.A. Clippers	108 -99	48 -27

APRIL
2 —	Miami	92 -84	49 -27
4 —	Indiana	79 -61	50 -27
6 —	Orlando	102 -86	51 -27
9 —	Toronto	74 -66	52 -27
10—	at Orlando	101 -89	53 -27
12—	Washington	101 -79	54 -27
13—	at Toronto	*78 -87	54 -28

*Loss. †Single overtime.

TEAM LEADERS

Points: Richard Hamilton (1,375).
Field goals made: Hamilton (530).
Free throws made: Chauncey Billups (404).
3-pointers made: Billups (130).
Rebounds: Ben Wallace (1,006).
Assists: Billups (446).
Steals: Wallace (143).
Blocks: Wallace (246).

RECORDS

Regular season: 54-28 (2nd in Central Division); 17-11 in division; 37-17 in conference; 17-11 vs. Western Conference; 31-10 at home; 23-18 on road; 3-1 in overtime; 6-12 in games decided by three points or fewer; 30-4 in games decided by 10 points or more; held opponents under 100 points 78 times; held under 100 points 64 times.
Playoffs: 16-7, defeated Bucks, 4-1, in Eastern Conference first round; defeated Nets, 4-3, in Eastern Conference semifinals; defeated Pacers, 4-2, in Eastern Conference finals; defeated Lakers, 4-1 in NBA Finals.
All-time franchise record: 2,131-2,269 in 56 seasons. Won three NBA titles (1989, '90, 2004).
Team record past five years: 228-182 (.556, ranks 10th in NBA in that span).

HIGHLIGHTS

Top players: Chauncey Billups was the NBA Finals MVP after averaging 21.0 ppg, 3.2 rpg, 5.2 apg and 1.20 spg in 38.4 mpg as Detroit won its third NBA title. He averaged a career-high 16.9 ppg and 5.7 apg during the regular season and was the first guard since Michael Jordan in 1998 to be named Finals MVP. ... Ben Wallace was named All-NBA Second Team, All-Defensive First Team and the Eastern Conference starting center at the All-Star game for the second consecutive season. He finished second in the NBA in rebounding (12.4 rpg), eighth in steals (1.77 spg) and second in blocks (3.04 bpg). He became the first player in NBA history since the league began recording steals and blocks (1973-74) to tally at least 1,000 rebounds, 100 steals and 100 blocks in four consecutive seasons. ... Richard Hamilton led Detroit with 17.6 ppg, dished out a career-best 4.0 apg in the regular season and averaged a team-leading 21.4 ppg in the playoffs. ... Rasheed Wallace averaged 13.7 ppg, 7.0 rpg, 2.3 apg and 2.05 bpg in 22 games. **Key injuries:** The Pistons lost a total of

197 player games because of injury or illness. Richard Hamilton broke his nose in the preseason and again in February. He missed three games after surgery. Lindsey Hunter missed 44 games, five with a sprained right hamstring and 39 with a strained left MCL. Chauncey Billups sprained his left ankle and missed the last four regular-season games.
Notable: The Pistons won the NBA Championship and finished 54-28, tying the third-best record in franchise history. ... Detroit ranked first in the NBA in attendance average for the second consecutive season with an average of 21,290 and 29 sellouts. ... Detroit tied for fewest points allowed with San Antonio at 84.3 points per game, the third-lowest in NBA history. ... Detroit set NBA records for holding opponents to fewer than 70 points in five consecutive games and 11 times overall. It set a franchise record for holding opponents to fewer than 100 points 78 times. ... Larry Brown became the seventh coach in NBA history to win 900 games.

GOLDEN STATE WARRIORS
PACIFIC DIVISION

Warriors Schedule
Home games shaded; *—All-Star Game at Denver.

November

SUN	MON	TUE	WED	THU	FRI	SAT
	1	2	3 POR	4	5 UTH	6 LAC
7	8 DAL	9	10 SA	11	12 MEM	13 CHA
14	15 CLE	16	17 CHI	18	19	20 MEM
21	22	23 NO	24	25	26 LAC	27
28 LAC	29	30				

December

SUN	MON	TUE	WED	THU	FRI	SAT
			1 MIN	2	3 LAL	4 IND
5	6 BOS	7 PHO	8	9	10 ORL	11
12 CHA	13	14 DAL	15 NO	16	17 HOU	18 SA
19	20 WAS	21	22 MEM	23	24	25
26 SAC	27 DEN	28	29 TOR	30	31	

January

SUN	MON	TUE	WED	THU	FRI	SAT
						1 POR
2	3 PHI	4	5 BOS	6	7 NJN	8
9 TOR	10 CHI	11	12 MIA	13	14 SEA	15 LAL
16	17 DEN	18	19	20	21 LAL	22 CLE
23	24	25	26 NJN	27	28 SEA	29 LAC
30	31					

February

SUN	MON	TUE	WED	THU	FRI	SAT
		1	2 SAC	3	4 NO	5 DEN
6	7 MIA	8 ORL	9	10	11 NO	12
13 PHO	14	15 DAL	16 SEA	17	18	19
20 *All-Star	21	22	23 ATL	24	25	26
27 DET	28					

March

SUN	MON	TUE	WED	THU	FRI	SAT
		1 MEM	2 MIN	3	4 WAS	5
6 NYK	7	8 PHI	9 DET	10	11 IND	12 ATL
13 HOU	14	15	16	17 SAC	18 PHO	19
20 SAC	21	22	23 DAL	24	25 MIL	26
27	28 NYK	29	30 MIL	31		

April

SUN	MON	TUE	WED	THU	FRI	SAT
					1 UTH	2
3 SEA	4	5 HOU	6 POR	7	8 PHO	9
10 SA	11 DEN	12	13 MIN	14	15 POR	16
17	18 LAL	19	20 UTH	21	22	23

TEAM DIRECTORY

Owner & Managing Member . . . . Christopher Cohan
Co-Owners . . . . Michael Marks, Jim Davidson, John Thompson, Fred Harman
President . . . . Robert Rowell

BASKETBALL OPERATIONS
Executive VP of Basketball Operations . . . . Chris Mullin
General Manager . . . . Rod Higgins
VP and Assistant General Manager . . . . Alvin Attles
Head Coach . . . . Mike Montgomery
Assistant Coaches . . . . Terry Stotts, Mario Elie, Keith Smart, Russell Turner
Athletic Trainer . . . . Tom Abdenour
Director of Athletic Development . . . . Mark Grabow
Strength and Conditioning Coach . . . . John Murray
Equipment Manager . . . . Eric Housen
Director of Basketball Operations . . . . Pete D'Alessandro
Director of Scouting . . . . Ron Meikle
Manager of Scouting . . . . Greg Stratton
Scouts . . . . Scott Pruneau, Bob Reinhart
Basketball Counseling Specialist . . . . Tom Mitchell
Video Coordinator . . . . Chuck Meyers

BUSINESS OPERATIONS
Executive VP, Team Marketing . . . . Travis Stanley

ARENA OPERATIONS
Executive Director, Arena Operations . . . . Terry Robinson

BROADCASTING
Executive Director of Broadcasting . . . . Dan Becker

BUSINESS DEVELOPMENT AND COMMUNITY RELATIONS
Vice President, Business Development . . . . Neda Kia
Community Relations Ambassador . . . . Nate Thurmond
Community Program Coordinator . . . . Rebecca Ward

CORPORATE SALES
VP, Corporate Sales & Services . . . . Victor Pelt

CREATIVE SERVICES
Director, Creative Services . . . . Julie Eriksen

EVENTS AND PROMOTIONS
Senior Executive Director, Entertainment . . . . . Joe Azzolina

FINANCE
VP, Finance . . . . Dwayne Redmon

HUMAN RESOURCES
Executive Director, Human Resources . . . . Erika Brown

INFORMATION TECHNOLOGY
VP, Business Systems & Technology . . . . Sandy Tacas
Director, Internet Communications . . . . Kyle Spencer

MERCHANDISE SALES
Manager, Merchandise Services . . . . Bill Del Colletti

PUBLIC RELATIONS
Executive Director, Public Relations . . . . Raymond Ridder
Director, Public Relations . . . . Dan Martinez
Manager, Public Relations . . . . Eric Govan

TICKET SALES AND SERVICES
Executive Director Ticket Sales & Operations . . . . Darryl Washington
Executive Director of Suite Services . . . . Tom Kaucic
Executive Director of Luxury Suite Sales . . . . . . Ben Shapiro
Director, Ticket Services . . . . Craig Lazarchik

Christopher Cohan

Chris Mullin

Mike Montgomery

ROSTER
Coach—Mike Montgomery
Assistant coaches—Terry Stotts, Mario Elie, Keith Smart, Russell Turner

No.	Name	Pos.	Ht./Wt.	Metric (m/kg)	Born	College/country
15	Andris Biedrins	F	6-11/240	2.10/108.4	4-2-86	Latvia
40	Calbert Cheaney	G/F	6-7/217	2.00/98.4	7-17-71	Indiana
10	Speedy Claxton	G	5-11/170	1.81/77.1	5-8-78	Hofstra
32	Dale Davis	F/C	6-11/252	2.10/114.3	3-25-69	Clemson
34	Mike Dunleavy	F	6-9/230	2.05/104.3	9-15-80	Duke
4	Derek Fisher	G	6-1/200	1.83/99.8	8-9-74	Arkansas-Little Rock
31	Adonal Foyle	C	6-10/270	2.08/122.5	3-19-75	Colgate
6	Avery Johnson	G	5-11/180	1.81/81.6	3-25-65	Southern
54	Popeye Jones	F	6-8/265	2.03/120.2	6-17-70	Murray State
	Christian Laettner	F/C	6-11/245	2.10/111.1	8-17-69	Duke
1	Troy Murphy	F	6-11/245	2.10/111.1	5-2-80	Notre Dame
	Eduardo Najera	F	6-8/235	2.03/106.6	7-11-76	Oklahoma
2	Mickael Pietrus	G/F	6-6/215	1.98/97.5	2-7-82	France
23	Jason Richardson	G	6-6/225	1.98/102.1	1-20-81	Michigan State
3	Clifford Robinson	F/C	6-10/240	2.08/108.4	12-16-66	Connecticut

BROADCAST INFORMATION

Radio: KNBR (680 AM) and KNBR (1050 AM).
Broadcaster: Tim Roye.
Cable TV: FOX Sports Net Bay Area.
Broadcasters: Bob Fitzgerald, Jim Barnett.

TEAM INFORMATION

Team address . . . . 1011 Broadway
Oakland, CA 94607
Business phone 510-986-2200
Ticket information 888-GSW-HOOP
Website . . . . www.warriors.com
Arena (capacity) . . . . The Arena in Oakland (19,596)
Game times . . . . 7:30 p.m. Monday-Saturday;
6 p.m. Sunday
First Warriors game in arena . . . . . . November 8, 1997

2003-04 REVIEW

RESULTS

OCTOBER
29— Dallas	*87 -95	0 -1

NOVEMBER
1—Philadelphia	104 -90	1 -1
2— at L.A. Lakers	*72 -87	1 -2
5— Atlanta	99 -72	2 -2
7— Utah	95 -89	3 -2
10— Phoenix	*96 -99	3 -3
12— Detroit	87 -85	†4 -3
14— L.A. Clippers	*98 -104	4 -4
16— at Sacramento	*104 -106	4 -5
18— at San Antonio	*81 -94	4 -6
19— at Houston	*83 -85	4 -7
21— Miami	101 -91	5 -7
23— Portland	78 -72	6 -7
28— at Phoenix	92 -83	7 -7
29— San Antonio	91 -89	8 -7

DECEMBER
3— Denver	*109 -117	8 -8
5— at Denver	*91 -98	8 -9
6— New York	104 -92	9 -9
9— at Minnesota	98 -95	10 -9
10— at Milwaukee	*89 -94	†10 -10
12— New Orleans	*85 -96	10 -11
16— at New York	104 -86	11 -11
17— at Atlanta	98 -85	12 -11
19— at Orlando	*93 -119	12 -12
21— at Miami	*93 -104	12 -13
23— L.A. Lakers	107 -98	13 -13
26— Sacramento	98 -91	14 -13

28— at Denver	*79 -103	14 -14
29— Boston	*91 -100	14 -15
31— at New Jersey	*70 -88	14 -16

JANUARY
2 — at Washington	*79 -97	14 -17
3 — at Detroit	*93 -99	14 -18
5 — at Houston	*65 -83	14 -19
7 — at Dallas	*99 -105	14 -20
10— Seattle	113 -110	†15 -20
12— Memphis	*113 -115	‡15 -21
13— at Utah	*80 -97	15 -22
15— Cleveland	119 -102	16 -22
16— at Phoenix	*93 -104	16 -23
19— Utah	101 -85	17 -23
21— at L.A. Clippers	*102 -106	17 -24
22— at Seattle	*87 -103	17 -25
24— at Portland	105 -87	18 -25
28— Minnesota	97 -90	19 -25
30—Chicago	101 -81	20 -25

FEBRUARY
2 — at Memphis	*101 -106	20 -26
3 — at Dallas	*93 -107	20 -27
6 — Denver	96 -87	21 -27
8 — Toronto	*81 -84	†21 -28
10— at Seattle	106 -97	22 -28
11— Phoenix	110 -99	23 -28
18— L.A. Lakers	*99 -100	23 -29
20— Portland	*93 -94	23 -30
21— Seattle	94 -92	24 -30
24— at Indiana	*96 -107	24 -31

25— at Memphis	99 -92	25 -31
27— at Minnesota	*81 -91	25 -32
28— at Chicago	*81 -87	†25 -33

MARCH
2 — Indiana	*88 -96	25 -34
5 — New Jersey	*74 -78	25 -35
7 — Memphis	*85 -95	25 -36
9 — at Sacramento	*92 -96	25 -37
10— at Utah	*77 -91	25 -38
12— at San Antonio	*74 -99	25 -39
13— at New Orleans	*84 -102	25 -40
15— San Antonio	97 -80	26 -40
17— Orlando	110 -85	27 -40
19— Houston	90 -84	28 -40
21— at L.A. Clippers	96 -85	29 -40
24— Milwaukee	98 -89	30 -40
26— Washington	99 -78	31 -40
28— L.A. Clippers	105 -77	32 -40
30— at Philadelphia	*71 -95	32 -41
31— at Toronto	85 -78	33 -41

APRIL
2 — at Boston	^106 -111	33 -42
3 — at Cleveland	103 -100	34 -42
6 — Houston	97 -90	35 -42
7 — at Portland	*81 -87	35 -43
9 — Minnesota	*74 -92	35 -44
11— Dallas	108 -107	36 -44
13— at L.A. Lakers	*104 -109	36 -45
14— Sacramento	97 -91	37 -45

*Loss. †Single overtime. ‡Double overtime.

TEAM LEADERS

Points: Jason Richardson (1,461).
Field goals made: Richardson (563).
Free throws made: Richardson (258).
3-pointers made: Clifford Robinson (112).
Rebounds: Erick Dampier (887).
Assists: Robinson (271).
Steals: Speedy Claxton (97).
Blocks: Dampier (137).

RECORDS

Regular season: 37-45 (tied, 4th in Pacific Division); 12-12 in division; 23-29 in conference; 14-16 vs. Eastern Conference; 27-14 at home; 10-31 on road; 2-4 in overtime; 7-7 in games decided by three points or fewer; 16-21 in games decided by 10 points or more; held opponents under 100 points 59 times; held under 100 points 59 times.
Playoff record: None.
All-time franchise record: 2,080-2,426 in 58 seasons. Won three NBA titles (1947, '56, '75), with first two championships while franchise located in Philadelphia.
Team record past five years: 132-278 (.322, ranks 28th in NBA in that span).

HIGHLIGHTS

Top players: Jason Richardson led the Warriors in scoring (18.7 ppg, 20th in NBA, 1st among NBA guards) and was second in rebounding (6.7 rpg). ... Erick Dampier led the Warriors in rebounding (12.0 rpg, 4th in NBA). ... Clifford Robinson was the only Warrior to appear in all 82 games and led the team in assists (271) and 3-pointers made (112). He also surpassed the 1,000 mark for 3-pointers made in his career, becoming just the 25th player and first player 6-10 or taller to do so. ... Mike Dunleavy improved his scoring average by 6 points per game and his rebounding by 3.3 rebounds per game from his rookie season, the eighth-largest improvement in the NBA. He averaged 16.3 ppg, 7.5 rpg, 3.7 apg and 1.1 spg in 30 games when playing 35 or more minutes. ... Speedy Claxton led the Warriors in steals (97), and his 1.62 steals per game would have ranked 15th in the NBA if he had met the statistical minimums.
Key injuries: The Warriors lost a total of 299 player games because of injury or illness, and 15 players missed games. Troy Murphy missed 54, Nick Van Exel 41, Adonal Foyle 34, Speedy Claxton 22, Erick Dampier eight and Mike Dunleavy seven. The projected starters (Van Exel, Richardson, Dampier, Dunleavy, Murphy) played together in only 11 games.
Notable: Golden State established a single-season attendance record for the second-straight season, drawing an average crowd of 16,235. ... Despite injury problems, the Warriors finished 37-45, one game behind the club's mark from 2002-03, when six players appeared in every game. ... The Warriors finished 27-14 at home, the team's best home record since 1993-94. ... During a seven-game win streak from March 15-28, Golden State held seven consecutive opponents under 90 points, the franchise's longest such streak during the shot clock era. ... The Warriors allowed 94.0 points per game (14th in NBA) in 2003-04 after allowing a league-high 103.6 in 2002-03, marking the best defensive improvement in the NBA (-9.6 ppg).

HOUSTON ROCKETS
SOUTHWEST DIVISION

HOUSTON ROCKETS

Rockets Schedule
Home games shaded; *—All-Star Game at Denver.

November

SUN	MON	TUE	WED	THU	FRI	SAT
	1	2 DET	3 TOR	4	5 MEM	6 SAC
7	8	9 MEM	10	11 MIN	12	13 LAL
14	15 NJN	16 ATL	17	18 NYK	19	20 LAC
21 POR	22	23 SAC	24	25	26 UTH	27 DEN
28	29	30 DET				

December

SUN	MON	TUE	WED	THU	FRI	SAT
		1	2 DAL	3	4 PHI
5	6	7 NO	8	9 SA	10	11 DAL
12	13	14	15 ATL	16	17 GS	18 CHA
19	20 TOR	21	22 CHA	23	24	25
26 LAC	27	28 MIL	29 CLE	30	31 MIL	

January

SUN	MON	TUE	WED	THU	FRI	SAT
						1
2 UTH	3	4	5 PHO	6	7 LAL	8
9 DEN	10	11	12 DAL	13 NJN	14	15 SA
16 MEM	17	18 IND	19	20 ORL	21 NYK	22
23	24 ORL	25	26 NO	27	28 SAC	29
30 MIA	31 BOS					

February

SUN	MON	TUE	WED	THU	FRI	SAT
		1	2 PHI	3	4 MIN	5
6 LAL	7	8	9 CHI	10	11 IND	12
13 POR	14	15 WAS	16	17	18	19
20 *All-Star	21	22 SEA	23 SA	24	25	26
27 UTH	28					

March

SUN	MON	TUE	WED	THU	FRI	SAT
		1 CHI	2 WAS	3	4	5
6 DAL	7	8 SEA	9	10	11 PHO	12
13 SAC	14 GS	15	16 POR	17	18 BOS	19
20 MIN	21	22 MIA	23	24 CLE	25 NO	26
27 SA	28 UTH	29	30 POR	31		

April

SUN	MON	TUE	WED	THU	FRI	SAT
					1 NO	2
3 PHO	4	5 GS	6	7 LAL	8	9 PHO
10	11 SEA	12	13 MEM	14	15	16 DEN
17	18 LAC	19	20 SEA	21	22	23

2004-05 SEASON
TEAM DIRECTORY

Owner . . . . .Leslie Alexander
President & Chief Executive Officer . .George Postolos
General Manager . . . . .Carroll Dawson
Head Coach . . . . .Jeff Van Gundy
Assistant Head Coach . . . . .Tom Thibodeau
Assistant Coaches . . . . .Steve Clifford, Patrick
  Ewing, Andy Greer
VP of Basketball Operations/
Player Personnel . . . . .Dennis Lindsey
VP of Basketball Operations/
Head Athletic Trainer . . . . .Keith Jones
Strength & Conditioning Coach . . . . .Anthony Falsone
Equipment Manager . . . . .Jay Namoc
Assistant Equipment Manager . . . . . .Anthony Nila
Coordinator of Sports Medicine . . . . .Michelle Leget
Rehabilitation Coordinator/Assistant
Strength & Conditioning Coach . . . . .David Macha
Personnel Scouts . . . . .Brent Johnson, Dean
  Cooper
Video Coordinators . . . . .Mike Longabardi, TBA
International Basketball Consultant . .Gianluca Pascucci
Chief Financial Officer . . . . .Marcus Jolibois
Senior VP, Marketing & Sales . . . . . .Thaddeus Brown
VP, Business Development . . . . .David Carlock
VP, Corporate Development . . . . .Todd Burnette
Vice President, Marketing . . . . .Tim McDougall
Vice President, Sales & Services . . . .Mark Norelli
Vice President & General Counsel . .Mark S. Biskamp
Director, Media Relations . . . . .Nelson Luis
Manager, Media Relations . . . . .Dan McKenna
Assistant Manager, Media Relations .Tracey Hughes
Coordinator, Media Relations . . . . . .Matt Rochinski

Leslie Alexander

Jeff Van Gundy

Carroll Dawson

ROSTER
Coach—Jeff Van Gundy
Assistant head coach—Tom Thibodeau
Assistant coaches—Steve Clifford, Patrick Ewing, Andy Greer

No.	Name	Pos.	Ht./Wt.	Metric (m/kg)	Born	College/country
4	Reece Gaines	G	6-6/205	1.98/93.0	1-7-81	Louisville
7	Adrian Griffin	G/F	6-5/230	1.96/104.3	7-4-74	Seton Hall
5	Juwan Howard	F	6-9/230	2.05/104.3	2-7-73	Michigan
21	Jim Jackson	G/F	6-6/220	1.98/99.8	10-14-70	Ohio State
10	Tyronn Lue	G	6-0/178	1.83/80.7	5-3-77	Nebraska
1	Tracy McGrady	G	6-8/210	2.03/95.3	5-24-79	Mt. Zion Christ. Acad.
9	Bostjan Nachbar	F	6-9/221	2.05/100.2	7-3-80	Slovenia
52	Eric Piatkowski	G/F	6-7/215	2.00/97.5	9-30-70	Nebraska
3	Bob Sura	G	6-5/200	1.96/90.7	3-25-73	Florida State
2	Maurice Taylor	F	6-9/255	2.05/115.7	10-30-76	Michigan
17	Charlie Ward	G	6-2/185	1.88/83.9	10-12-70	Florida State
30	Clarence Weatherspoon	F	6-7/270	2.00/122.5	9-8-70	Southern Miss.
11	Yao Ming	C	7 6/310	2.28/140.6	9-12-00	China

BROADCAST INFORMATION

Radio: KILT SportsRadio (610 AM).
Broadcasters: Gene Peterson, Jim Foley,
Craig Ackerman. Spanish radio: TBA.
Broadcasters: Adrian Chavarria, Alex Parra.
TV: KNWS Ch. 51. Broadcasters: Bill Worrell,
TBA.

TEAM INFORMATION

Team address . . . . .1510 Polk Street, Houston, TX 77002
Business phone 713-758-7200
Ticket information 713-627-DUNK
Arena (capacity) . . . . .Toyota Center (17,974)
Website .www.rockets.com
Game times . . . . .7:30 p.m., Monday-Sunday
First Rockets game in arena . . . . . .October 30, 2003

2003-04 REVIEW

RESULTS

OCTOBER
30— Denver	102 -85	1 -0

NOVEMBER
1 — Memphis	*71 -79	1 -1
3 — at Chicago	98 -66	2 -1
4 — at New Jersey	86 -75	3 -1
8 — Orlando	96 -86	4 -1
11— Miami	90 -70	5 -1
13— at Dallas	*86 -97	5 -2
14— Phoenix	90 -85	6 -2
16— at Toronto	*97 -101	‡6 -3
17— at Philadelphia	74 -66	7 -3
19— Golden State	85 -83	8 -3
21— at Portland	*78 -85	8 -4
24— at L.A. Clippers	105 -90	9 -4
26— at Utah	*76 -83	9 -5
28— at Sacramento	*74 -103	9 -6
29— at Seattle	*88 -95	9 -7

DECEMBER
3 — Utah	107 -101	†10 -7
5 at New Orleans	83 -74	11 -7
6 — Detroit	86 -80	12 -7
9 — Portland	93 -91	13 -7
11— San Antonio	*67 -71	13 -8
13— at San Antonio	*73 -86	13 -9
16— at Minnesota	*75 -92	13 -10
17— at Cleveland	89 -85	14 -10
19— L.A. Clippers	99 -85	15 -10
20— at Phoenix	*87 -102	15 -11
23— Indiana	*71 -79	15 -12

25— at L.A. Lakers	99 -87	16 -12
26— at Denver	*94 -95	16 -13
29— Seattle	*86 -87	16 -14
31— Philadelphia	80 -72	17 -14

JANUARY
3 — Utah	84 -63	18 -14
5 — Golden State	83 -65	19 -14
7 — at Detroit	*66 -85	19 -15
8 — at New York	111 -79	20 -15
11— Boston	*93 -97	20 -16
13— at Washington	93 -80	21 -16
14— at Boston	95 -80	22 -16
17— Minnesota	95 -76	23 -16
19— at Memphis	*83 -88	23 -17
21— New York	86 -71	24 -17
23— at Indiana	78 -74	25 -17
25— at Orlando	99 -87	26 -17
26— at Miami	*81 -95	26 -18
28— Sacramento	*94 -99	26 -19
31— New Jersey	*77 -88	26 -20

FEBRUARY
2 — at Phoenix	*79 -99	26 -21
4 — Milwaukee	103 -89	27 -21
6 — Chicago	82 -80	28 -21
7 — at Atlanta	86 -77	29 -21
9 — San Antonio	*82 -85	29 -22
11— L.A. Lakers	102 -87	30 -22
17— Washington	107 -81	31 -22
21— at Dallas	*88 -97	31 -23
22— Atlanta	123 -121	§32 -23

24— at San Antonio	*77 -86	32 -24
25— Cleveland	90 -84	33 -24
27— Portland	89 -85	34 -24
29— Seattle	*80 -97	34 -25

MARCH
3 — L.A. Lakers	*93 -96	34 -26
5 — at Minnesota	112 -109	35 -26
7 — Dallas	101 -98	36 -26
9 — L.A. Clippers	90 -85	37 -26
11— New Orleans	97 -86	38 -26
13— Memphis	88 -80	39 -26
15— Phoenix	*97 -99	†39 -27
19— at Golden State	*84 -90	39 -28
21— at Sacramento	*95 -100	39 -29
22— at Portland	93 -85	†40 -29
24— Toronto	90 -89	†41 -29
26— at Memphis	*86 -109	41 -30
28— at Milwaukee	111 -107	†42 -30
29— Minnesota	*88 -94	42 -31

APRIL
1 — at L A. Lakers	*85 -93	42 -32
2 — at Denver	*100 -110	42 -33
4 — Sacramento	*94 -99	42 -34
6 — at Golden State	*90 -97	42 -35
7 — at L.A. Clippers	102 -79	43 -35
9 — Denver	106 -103	44 -35
10— at Utah	*69 -82	44 -36
12— at Seattle	111 -107	45 -36
14— Dallas	*89 -92	45 -37

*Loss. †Single overtime. ‡Double over-
time. §Triple overtime.

TEAM LEADERS

Points: Yao Ming (1,431).
Field goals made: Yao (535).
Free throws made: Yao (361).
3-pointers made: Cuttino Mobley (164).
Rebounds: Yao (735).
Assists: Steve Francis (493).
Steals: Francis (139).
Blocks: Yao (156).

RECORDS

Regular season: 45-37 (5th in Midwest
Division); 8-16 in division; 21-31 in conference; 24-6 vs. Eastern Conference;
27-14 at home; 18-23 on road; 5-2 in
overtime; 8-6 in games decided by three
points or fewer; 21-13 in games decided
by 10 points or more; held opponents
under 100 points 70 times; held under
100 points 67 times.
Playoffs: 1-4, lost to Lakers, 4-1, in
Western Conference first round.
All-time franchise record: 1,492-1,510
in 37 seasons. Won two NBA titles
(1994, '95).
Team record past five years: 195-215
(.476, ranks 19th in NBA in that span).

HIGHLIGHTS

Top players: Yao Ming led the Rockets
with career highs of 17.5 ppg, 9.0 rpg and
1.90 bpg in 82 starts. He was one of six
NBA players to lead his team in points,
rebounds and blocks. In the NBA, Yao
ranked seventh in field-goal percentage
(.522), 13th in blocks per game and 15th
in rebounds per game. ... Jim Jackson
finished sixth in the NBA with a career-
high 162 3-pointers made. ... Tracy
McGrady will join the Rockets in 2004-05
after becoming just the ninth player in
NBA history to win consecutive scoring
titles. He led the NBA with a career-high
32.1 ppg in 2002-03 and 28.0 ppg last
season with Orlando. In NBA history, only
Wilt Chamberlain and Bob McAdoo won
multiple scoring titles at a younger age
than McGrady.
Key injuries: The Rockets lost a total of
152 player games because of injury or illness. Adrian Griffin missed 59 games with
medial surgery and chondomalacia in his
right knee. Mike Wilks was sidelined for
37 games with a shoulder contusion and
plantar fasciitis. Ben Davis missed 20
games with knee surgery. Eric Piatkowski

missed 12 games with ankle and index
finger sprains, and Kelvin Cato missed 11
games with left foot and shoulder sprains.
Notable: On June 29, 2004 the Houston
Rockets acquired Tracy McGrady, Juwan
Howard, Tyronn Lue and Reece Gaines
from Orlando for Steve Francis, Cuttino
Mobley and Kelvin Cato. ... In his first
season with Houston, Jeff Van Gundy
guided the Rockets to their first playoff
berth in five seasons. He has a career
coaching record of 293-209 and has had
a winning record in each of his eight NBA
seasons. ... Houston set franchise single-
season records in scoring defense (88.0
ppg, 5th in NBA) and field-goal percentage
defense (.412, 2nd). Only four teams in
NBA history have a better field-goal percentage defense, including Van Gundy's
1998-99 Knicks. ... For the second-
straight season, the Rockets increased
their home attendance, averaging 15,629
fans in their first season at Toyota Center.
The last time the Rockets had an attendance average this high was in 1998-99.
Toyota Center reached its sellout capacity
of 17,974 17 times in 2003-04.

– 27 –

INDIANA PACERS
CENTRAL DIVISION

Pacers Schedule
Home games shaded; *—All-Star Game at Denver.

November
SUN	MON	TUE	WED	THU	FRI	SAT
	1	2	3 CLE	4	5 BOS	6 CHI
7	8	9 MIN	10 LAC	11	12 PHI	13 NYK
14	15	16	17 ATL	18	19 DET	20 ORL
21	22	23 BOS	24	25 MIN	26 CHA	27
28 SEA	29	30				

December
SUN	MON	TUE	WED	THU	FRI	SAT
			1 LAC	2	3 SAC	4 GS
5	6	7 MIL	8	9	10 MIL	11 SAC
12	13	14 ATL	15	16	17 TOR	18 CHI
19	20	21	22 PHI	23	24	25 DET
26	27 NO	28	29 CHA	30 NJN	31	

January
SUN	MON	TUE	WED	THU	FRI	SAT
						1
2	3	4 MIL	5	6 SA	7	8 DAL
9 PHO	10	11 MEM	12	13	14 PHO	15 ORL
16	17	18 HOU	19 NO	20	21 MIA	22 WAS
23	24	25	26 BOS	27 DET	28	29 DEN
30	31 PHI					

February
SUN	MON	TUE	WED	THU	FRI	SAT
		1	2 TOR	3	4 DAL	5 ATL
6	7 WAS	8	9 CHA	10	11 HOU	12
13 MEM	14	15	16 POR	17	18	19
20 *All-Star	21	22 ORL	23 MIA	24	25 CLE	26 NYK
27	28					

March
SUN	MON	TUE	WED	THU	FRI	SAT
		1 SEA	2	3 DEN	4 POR	5
6 LAL	7	8 UTH	9	10	11 GS	12
13 CLE	14	15	16 UTH	17	18 LAL	19
20 NJN	21	22 NJN	23 SA	24	25 DET	26 CHI
27	28 MIL	29	30	31 MIA		

April
SUN	MON	TUE	WED	THU	FRI	SAT
					1	2
3 WAS	4	5 NYK	6 CLE	7	8 WAS	9
10 NYK	11 TOR	12	13 NJN	14	15 PHI	16
17 MIA	18 ORL	19	20 CHI	21	22	23

2004-05 SEASON

TEAM DIRECTORY

Owners	Melvin Simon, Herbert Simon
Chief Executive Officer and President	Donnie Walsh
President of Basketball Operations	Larry Bird
Executive Senior Vice President/ Executive Director of Conseco Fieldhouse	Rick Fuson
Senior VP/Basketball Administration	David Morway
Senior VP/Finance and Chief Financial Officer	Kevin Bower
Senior Vice President/Marketing	Larry Mago
Vice President/Budgeting	Jane Wardle
Vice President/Communications	Quinn Buckner
Vice President/Controller	Doug McKee
Vice President/Corporate Partnerships	TBA
Vice President/Entertainment	Jamie Berns
Vice President/Event Services and Merchandising	Rich Kapp
Vice President/Facilities Administration	Harry James
Vice President/Human Resources	Donna Wilkinson
Vice President/Management Information Systems	Larry Taylor
Vice President/Operations	Tom Rutledge
Vice President/Premium Sales and Services/ Corporate Relations	Jack Woodside
Vice President/Scheduling Production Services	Jeff Bowen
Vice President/Ticket Sales	Doug Dawson
Vice President/Team Development	Kathryn Jordan
Head Coach	Rick Carlisle
Manager/Basketball Administration	Sonya Clutinger
Director of Player Personnel/Assistant Coach	Mel Daniels
Director of Scouting/ Assistant to President of Basketball Operations	Joe Ash
Associate Head Coach	Mike Brown
Assistant Coaches	Dan Burke, Chad Forcier, Kevin O'Neill, Jimmy Powell
Scout/Assistant Coach	Nediljko "Misho" Ostarcevic
Scouts	Ryan Carr, George Felton, Kevin Mackey, Joe Touomou
Video Coordinator/Advance Scout	TBA
Head Athletic Trainer/Team Administrator	David Craig
Assistant Athletic Trainer	TBA
Equipment Manager	Joe Qatato
Strength & Conditioning Coach	Bill Dean
Physical Therapist	Julie Bender
Advance Scout	Derek Pierce
Director/Public Information	David Benner
Associate Director/Public Information	Jeff McCoy
Public Information Assistants	Tim Edwards, Krissy Myers
Executive Director/Pacers Foundation	Dale Ratermann
Director/Accounting	Ann Scott
Director/Box Office	Paul Congress
Director/Broadcast Engineering	Greg Smith
Director/Camps & Clinics/Alumni Relations	Darnell Hillman
Director/Community Relations	Vonda Brooks
Director/Creative Services	Wendy Sommers
Director/Game Operations and Promotions	Jeff Scalf
Director/Group Events	Rob Robinson
Director/Housekeeping	Ed Bland
Director/Human Resources	Angela Heady
Director/Internet Marketing	Conrad Brunner
Director/Management Information Systems	Kevin Naylor
Director/Merchandising	Gary Nelson
Director/Operations	Chuck Devers
Director/Premium Services	Heather Denton
Director/Production	Eric Nelson
Director/Safety/Crowd Management	Bob Shorter
Director/Sales Development	Mike Henn
Director/Sponsorship Sales	Mike McClure
Ticket Manager	Brenda Smith
Assistant Ticket Manager	Jill McQueeney

Melvin Simon

Herb Simon

Rick Carlisle

ROSTER
Coach—Rick Carlisle
Associate head coach—Mike Brown
Assistant coaches—Dan Burke, Chad Forcier, Kevin O'Neill

No.	Name	Pos.	Ht./Wt.	Metric (m/kg)	Born	College/country
23	Ron Artest	F	6-7/246	2.00/111.6	11-13-79	St. John's
24	Jonathan Bender	G/F	7-0/219	2.13/99.3	1-30-81	Picayune Memorial HS
44	Austin Croshere	F	6-10/242	2.08/109.8	5-1-75	Providence
10	Jeff Foster	F	6-11/242	2.10/109.8	1-16-77	Southwest Texas State
13	David Harrison	C	7-0/250	2.13/113.4	8-15-82	Colorado
1	Stephen Jackson	G/F	6-8/218	2.03/98.9	4-5-78	Oak Hill Academy
8	Anthony Johnson	G	6-3/190	1.90/86.2	10-10-74	College of Charleston
20	Fred Jones	G	6-2/218	1.88/98.9	3-11-79	Oregon
33	James Jones	G	6-8/215	2.03/97.5	10-4-80	Miami (Fla.)
31	Reggie Miller	G	6-7/195	2.00/88.4	8-24-65	UCLA
7	Jermaine O'Neal	F	6-11/242	2.10/109.8	10-13-78	Eau Claire H.S.
62	Scot Pollard	C	6-11/265	2.10/120.2	2-12-75	Kansas
11	Jamaal Tinsley	G	6-3/195	1.90/88.4	2-28-78	Iowa State
4	Eddie Gill	G	6-0/190	1.83/86.2	8-16-78	Weber State

BROADCAST INFORMATION

Radio: WIBC (1070 AM). Broadcasters: Mark Boyle, Bob Leonard.
TV: WB4 (Channel 4). Broadcasters: Al Albert, Clark Kellogg.
Cable TV: FOX Sports Net. Broadcasters: Al Albert, Quinn Buckner.

TEAM INFORMATION

Team address	125 S. Pennsylvania Street Indianapolis, IN 46204
Business phone	317-917-2500
Ticket information	317-239-5151
Websites	www.pacers.com; www.ConsecoFieldhouse.com
Arena (capacity)	Conseco Fieldhouse (18,345)
Game times	Mon.-Fri., 7 p.m.; Sat., 8 p.m.
First Pacers game in arena	November 6, 1999

2003-04 REVIEW

RESULTS

OCTOBER
29— at Detroit	89 -87	1 -0
31— Milwaukee	*79 -93	1 -1

NOVEMBER
1 — at Atlanta	103 -99	†2 -1
4 — Denver	71 -60	3 -1
6 — at New Jersey	87 -81	4 -1
7 — Cleveland	91 -90	5 -1
9 — at Philadelphia	85 -74	6 -1
11— Boston	*76 -78	6 -2
14— Seattle	101 -78	7 -2
15— at New York	95 -94	8 -2
19— L.A. Clippers	91 -78	9 -2
21— at New Orleans	76 -75	10 -2
24— at Orlando	89 -78	11 -2
25— Minnesota	98 -75	12 -2
27— New York	93 -70	13 -2
28— Philadelphia	90 -77	14 -2
30— at L.A. Lakers	*77 -99	14 -3

DECEMBER
1 — at Phoenix	89 -82	15 -3
3 — at Portland	*95 -97	†15 -4
5 — at Seattle	101 -94	16 -4
7 — at Sacramento	*88 -91	16 -5
9 — Washington	93 -79	17 -5
12— Atlanta	103 -92	18 -5
13— at Chicago	*75 -86	18 -6
15— Cleveland	95 -85	19 -6
17— Orlando	*90 -94	19 -7
19— Detroit	80 -75	20 -7

20— at Minnesota	*80 -102	20 -8
23— at Houston	79 -71	21 -8
26— at Milwaukee	*96 -101	21 -9
27— New Jersey	*75 -82	21 -10
29— Memphis	94 -86	22 -10
30— at Cleveland	92 -89	23 -10

JANUARY
2 — at Boston	103 -90	24 -10
3 — New Orleans	91 -84	25 -10
5 — at Miami	87 -65	26 -10
6 — Orlando	114 -107	27 -10
9 — at Dallas	92 -80	28 -10
10— at San Antonio	*88 -89	†28 -11
14— Atlanta	85 -78	29 -11
16— San Antonio	89 -79	30 -11
17— at New Jersey	90 -84	31 -11
19— at Atlanta	100 -97	32 -11
20— Detroit	81 -69	33 -11
23— Houston	*74 -78	33 -12
24— at Washington	*96 -107	33 -13
28— Phoenix	101 -79	34 -13
31— Boston	99 -98	35 -13

FEBRUARY
2 — L.A. Lakers	85 -72	36 -13
3 — at New York	*90 -97	36 -14
6 — at Toronto	83 -77	37 -14
8 — Miami	97 -91	38 -14
10— at Chicago	103 -84	39 -14
17— New Orleans	*75 -89	39 -15
20— at Washington	96 -87	40 -15

22— Utah	94 -80	41 -15
24— Golden State	107 -96	42 -15
27— at New Orleans	*77 -89	42 -16
28— Philadelphia	81 -74	43 -16

MARCH
2 — at Golden State	96 -88	44 -16
3 — at L.A. Clippers	101 -94	†45 -16
5 — at Utah	96 -88	46 -16
7 — at Denver	103 -94	47 -16
9 — Toronto	94 -84	†48 -16
12— at Boston	99 -81	49 -16
14— at Cleveland	*104 -107	49 -17
17— Portland	80 -71	50 -17
19— Sacramento	*92 -94	50 -18
20— at Memphis	*95 -99	50 -19
22— Chicago	101 -77	51 -19
24— Dallas	103 -99	52 -19
26— at Orlando	107 -92	53 -19
28— Miami	87 -80	54 -19
30— at Milwaukee	*86 -95	54 -20
31— Milwaukee	111 -78	55 -20

APRIL
2 — Toronto	84 -64	56 -20
4 — at Detroit	*61 -79	56 -21
6 — New York	107 -86	57 -21
7 — at Toronto	94 -90	58 -21
9 — New Jersey	90 -80	59 -21
12— at Philadelphia	107 -93	60 -21
14— Chicago	101 -96	61 -21

*Loss. †Single overtime.

TEAM LEADERS

Points: Jermaine O'Neal (1566).
Field goals made: O'Neal (608).
Free throws made: O'Neal (348).
3-pointers made: Reggie Miller (134).
Rebounds: O'Neal (778).
Assists: Jamaal Tinsley (303).
Steals: Ron Artest (152).
Blocks: O'Neal (199).

RECORDS

Regular season: 61-21 (1st in Central Division); 20-8 in division; 41-13 in conference; 20-8 vs. Western Conference; 34-7 at home; 27-14 on road; 3-2 in overtime; 7-6 in games decided by three points or fewer; 30-8 in games decided by 10 points or more; held opponents under 100 points 77 times; held under 100 points 62 times.
Playoffs: 10-6, defeated Celtics, 4-0, in Eastern Conference first round; defeated Heat, 4-2, in Eastern Conference semifinals; lost to Pistons, 4-2, in Eastern Conference Finals.
All-time franchise record: 1115-1149 in 28 seasons in NBA; 427-317 in nine seasons in ABA.
Team record past five years: 248-162 (.605, ranks 7th in NBA in that span).

HIGHLIGHTS

Top players: Jermaine O'Neal led the Pacers in scoring (20.1 ppg, 16th in the NBA), rebounds (10.0 rpg, 11th) and blocks (2.55 bpg, 6th) for the third consecutive season. He was selected to the All-NBA Second Team and was a starter in the All-Star Game, his third consecutive appearance. ... Ron Artest, the Defensive Player of the Year, earned a spot on the All-NBA Third Team as the Pacers' second-leading scorer (18.3 ppg, 24th in NBA) and ranked third in the NBA in steals (2.08 spg). Artest made his first All-Star appearance. ... Al Harrington averaged 13.3 ppg and 6.4 rpg and was second in the NBA Sixth Man Award balloting.
Key injuries: The Pacers lost a total of 281 player games because of injury or illness. Jamaal Tinsley missed 20 games, the majority with a sore lower back. Jonathan Bender missed 59 games, 48 with a sore left knee. Jeff Foster was the only player to play in all 82 games.
Notable: The Pacers finished with a franchise-best record (61-21) and

advanced to the Eastern Conference finals for the sixth time in the past 11 years. Their 61-21 record was the best in the NBA last season. Indiana began the season 14-2, the best start in the team's NBA history. With a record of 39-14 at the All-Star break, the Pacers earned their coaching staff All-Star honors for the second consecutive season. ... O'Neal was the only player in the Eastern Conference and one of five in the NBA to average 20-plus points and 10-plus rebounds per game. O'Neal finished third in the Most Valuable Player Award voting. ... Artest was named to the All-Defensive First Team. ... Fred Jones won the Sprite Rising Stars Slam Dunk contest at All-Star Saturday Night. ... Reggie Miller became just the 14th player in NBA history to score 24,000 points and finished the season 14th on the league's all-time scoring list (24,305). Miller made 100-plus 3-point field goals (134) for the 15th consecutive season, an NBA record.

LOS ANGELES CLIPPERS
PACIFIC DIVISION

Clippers Schedule
Home games shaded; *—All-Star Game at Denver.

November

SUN	MON	TUE	WED	THU	FRI	SAT
	1	2	3 SEA	4	5 POR	6 GS
7	8 DET	9	10 IND	11	12 NYK	13 CHI
14	15	16 TOR	17 LAL	18	19	20 HOU
21 PHO	22	23	24	25 NJN	26 GS	27
28 GS	29 CLE	30				

December

SUN	MON	TUE	WED	THU	FRI	SAT
		1 IND	2	3	4 MIN	
5	6 CHA	7	8	9	10	11 LAL
12	13 BOS	14 UTH	15	16	17 MIN	18
19 MEM	20	21 NO	22	23	24	25
26 HOU	27 MEM	28	29 UTH	30	31 SA	

January

SUN	MON	TUE	WED	THU	FRI	SAT
						1
2 PHI	3 DEN	4	5 POR	6	7	8 PHO
9	10	11 SEA	12 SEA	13	14 MIA	15 SAC
16 SAC	17	18	19 SA	20 DAL	21	22 NO
23 DAL	24 LAL	25	26 POR	27	28 POR	29 GS
30	31 NYK					

February

SUN	MON	TUE	WED	THU	FRI	SAT
		1	2	3 MEM	4 MIL	5
6 PHI	7	8	9 BOS	10	11 WAS	12
13 TOR	14	15 ORL	16 MIA	17	18	19
20 *All-Star	21	22	23 PHO	24 MIN	25	26
27 ATL	28 UTH					

March

SUN	MON	TUE	WED	THU	FRI	SAT
		1	2 DAL	3	4	5 DEN
6	7 MEM	8 LAL	9	10	11 SAC	12
13 CHI	14	15	16 ORL	17	18 DEN	19 SAC
20	21 POR	22	23 MIL	24	25 WAS	26
27 MIN	28	29 CLE	30 NJN	31		

April

SUN	MON	TUE	WED	THU	FRI	SAT
					1 DET	2
3 ATL	4	5 CHA	6 SA	7	8	9 SA
10	11	12 UTH	13	14	15 PHO	16 NO
17	18 HOU	19	20 NO	21	22	23

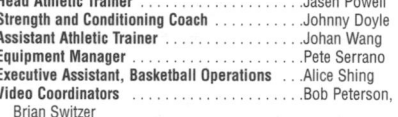

2004-05 SEASON
TEAM DIRECTORY

Chairman of the Board,
Owner & NBA Governor . . . . .Donald T. Sterling
Executive VP & NBA Alternate Governor . . . . . .Andy Roeser
BASKETBALL OPERATIONS
Vice President of Basketball Operations . . . . .Elgin Baylor
Head Coach . . . . .Mike Dunleavy
Assistant Coaches .Jim Eyen, Kim
  Hughes, Rory White, Neal Meyer
Director of Player Personnel . . . . .Barry Hecker
Assistant Director of Player Personnel . . . . . .Gary Sacks
Head Athletic Trainer . . . . .Jasen Powell
Strength and Conditioning Coach . . . . .Johnny Doyle
Assistant Athletic Trainer . . . . .Johan Wang
Equipment Manager . . . . .Pete Serrano
Executive Assistant, Basketball Operations . .Alice Shing
Video Coordinators .Bob Peterson,
  Brian Switzer
Team Physicians . . . . .Dr. Tony Daly, M.D.,
  Dr. Steven Krems, M.D., Dr. Mark Laska, D.D.S.
Scouts . . . . .Evan Pickman, Jim
  Mitchell, Jerry Holloway, Fabrizio Besnati
COMMUNICATIONS
Vice President of Communications . . . . .Joe Safety
Director of Communications . . . . .Rob Raichlen
Assistant Director of Communications . . . . . . .Nick Brown
Assistant Director of Media Services . . . . . . .Ta'Nisha Cooper
Media Services Assistant . . . . .Steven Esparza
MARKETING AND SALES
Senior Vice President of Marketing & Sales . .Carl Lahr
Group Sales Manager . . . . .Jana Suko
Group Sales Representative . . . . .Christie Freid
Account Executives .Sterling Dortch, Don
  Gore, Joni Maybury, Alan Mowrey, Rob Strikwerda, Cedric Wilson
Inside Sales Manager . . . . .Mat Warner
Ticket Manager . . . . .Rob Knepper
Dir. of Community Relations/Player Programs .Denise Booth
Community Relations Coordinator . . . . .David Brennan
Database and Ticket Operations Coordinator . .Trina Schwimmer
Game Entertainment Manager . . . . .Leslie Murata
Website Manager . . . . .David Callanan
MARKETING AND BROADCASTING
Vice President of Marketing & Broadcasting . .Christian Howard
Director of Sponsorship Sales . . . . .Chris Beyer
Director of Corporate Sales . . . . .Greg Flaherty
Marketing and Broadcasting Coordinator . . . .Jessica Bojorquez
Sponsor Services Coordinator . . . . .Annie Cornforth
Creative Services Coordinator . . . . .Kevin Cheung
FINANCE
Vice President of Finance . . . . .Donna Johnson
Sr. Accountant/Human Resources Administrator .Lori Balsamo
Staff Accountant . . . . .Jobel Rentino
Administrative Assistant . . . . .Nicole Williams

Donald T. Sterling

Elgin Baylor

Mike Dunleavy

ROSTER
Coach—Mike Dunleavy
Assistant coaches—Jim Eyen, Kim Hughes, Rory White, Neal Meyer

No.	Name	Pos.	Ht./Wt.	Metric (m/kg)	Born	College/country
42	Elton Brand	F	6-8/265	2.03/120.2	3-11-79	Duke
0	Lionel Chalmers	G	6-0/180	1.83/81.6	11-10-80	Xavier
20	Marko Jaric	G	6-7/217	2.00/98.4	10-12-78	Serbia & Montenegro
35	Chris Kaman	C	7-0/268	2.13/121.6	4-28-82	Central Michigan
14	Shaun Livingston	G	6-7/175	2.00/79.4	9-11-85	Peoria Central HS
50	Corey Maggette	F	6-6/228	1.98/103.4	11-12-79	Duke
34	Josh Moore	C	7-0/328	2.13/148.8	11-16-80	Michigan
	Mamadou N'diaye	C	7-0/255	2.13/115.7	6-16-75	Auburn
11	Zeljko Rebraca	C	7-0/257	2.13/116.6	4-9-72	Serbia & Montenegro
	Quinton Ross	G	6-6/195	1.98/88.5	4-30-81	SMU
21	Bobby Simmons	G	6-6/235	1.98/106.6	6-2-80	DePaul
54	Chris Wilcox	F	6-10/229	2.08/103.9	9-3-82	Maryland

BROADCAST INFORMATION

Radio: XTRA Sports (690/1150 AM).
Broadcaster: Mel Proctor.
TV: KTLA (Channel 5). Broadcasters: Ralph Lawler, Michael Smith.
Cable TV: FOX Sports Net West 2.
Broadcasters: Ralph Lawler, Michael Smith.

TEAM INFORMATION

Team address . . . . .1111 S. Figueroa Street, Suite 1100
                                          Los Angeles, CA 90015
Business phone 213-742-7500
Ticket information 213-742-7555
Website . . . . .www.clippers.com
Arena (capacity) . . . . .STAPLES Center (19,060)
Game times . . . . .7:30 p.m., Monday-Saturday;
                                          12:30 and 6:30 p.m., Sunday
First Clippers game in arena . . . . .November 2, 1999

2003-04 REVIEW

RESULTS

OCTOBER
30— at Seattle	*100 -109	0 -1	
31— Seattle	*105 -124	0 -2	

NOVEMBER
7— at Denver	104 -102	†1 -2	
11— Atlanta	115 -103	2 -2	
14— at Golden State	104 -98	3 -2	
15— Orlando	95 -92	4 -2	
18— at Cleveland	*95 -103	4 -3	
19— at Indiana	*78 -91	4 -4	
22— at Minnesota	*91 -103	4 -5	
24— Houston	*90 -105	4 -6	
27— New Jersey	*96 -102	4 -7	
29— Denver	*86 -98	4 -8	

DECEMBER
1— San Antonio	91 -83	5 -8	
3— Cleveland	90 -80	6 -8	
5— at Utah	*67 -86	6 -9	
7— Minnesota	*94 -96	6 -10	
9— at Sacramento	*95 -105	6 -11	
10— Dallas	100 -99	7 -11	
13— Phoenix	106 -91	8 -11	
15— New Orleans	109 -80	9 -11	
17— Milwaukee	93 -83	10 -11	
19— at Houston	*85 -99	10 -12	
20— at Dallas	115 -105	11 -12	
23— at San Antonio	*90 -111	11 -13	
26— Philadelphia	101 -98	12 -13	
28— Toronto	*88 -94	12 -14	
29— Phoenix	*105 -113	12 -15	

JANUARY
3 — Sacramento	*109 -116	13 -16	
4 — L.A. Lakers	101 -98	14 -16	
6 — at New Jersey	*75 -92	14 -17	
7 — at Philadelphia	*80 -100	14 -18	
9 — at Toronto	78 -68	15 -18	
11— Memphis	*107 -108	†15 -19	
13— Portland	103 -96	†16 -19	
16— Miami	*85 -87	16 -20	
17— at L.A. Lakers	*89 -91	16 -21	
19— Sacramento	*100 -125	16 -22	
21— Golden State	106 -102	17 -22	
23— Utah	93 -82	18 -22	
24— at Seattle	*97 -102	18 -23	
26— at Utah	*93 -98	18 -24	
27— Chicago	102 -92	19 -24	
30— at Miami	*88 -97	19 -25	
31— at Orlando	115 -106	20 -25	

FEBRUARY
2 — at Atlanta	101 -95	21 -25	
4 — at Boston	95 -86	22 -25	
6 — at Washington	*100 -112	22 -26	
8 — at New York	*104 -110	22 -27	
10— at Minnesota	*84 -96	22 -28	
11— at Memphis	*102 -110	22 -29	
18— at Portland	*86 -101	22 -30	
19— Boston	102 -100	23 -30	
21— at Milwaukee	105 -103	24 -30	
24— at Dallas	*91 -116	24 -31	

(continued)
31— Denver	120 -104	13 -15	
25— at New Orleans	*93 -99	24 -32	
27— New York	96 -94	25 -32	
29— Detroit	*88 -100	25 -33	

MARCH
2 — at Sacramento	*106 -113	25 -34	
3 — Indiana	*94 -101	†25 -35	
6 — Memphis	*92 -98	25 -36	
7 — Portland	91 -71	26 -36	
9 — at Houston	*85 -90	26 -37	
10— at San Antonio	*90 -108	26 -38	
12— at Memphis	*89 -98	26 -39	
14— Dallas	*88 -101	26 -40	
16— at Phoenix	110 -98	27 -40	
17— L.A. Lakers	*103 -106	27 -41	
19— at L.A. Lakers	*100 -106	27 -42	
21— Golden State	*85 -96	27 -43	
22— at Denver	*90 -102	27 -44	
24— at Portland	*85 -91	27 -45	
25— Washington	*94 -103	27 -46	
27— Minnesota	*82 -98	27 -47	
28— at Golden State	*77 -105	27 -48	
31— at Detroit	*99 -108	27 -49	

APRIL
2 — at Chicago	*110 -114	†27 -50	
4 — Utah	*92 -97	27 -51	
7 — Houston	*79 -102	27 -52	
11— San Antonio	*79 -88	27 -53	
13— at Phoenix	98 -96	28 -53	
14— Seattle	*87 -118	28 -54	

*Loss. †Single overtime.

TEAM LEADERS

Points: Corey Maggette (1,508).
Field goals made: Elton Brand (484).
Free throws made: Maggette (526).
3-pointers made: Quentin Richardson (120).
Rebounds: Brand (714).
Assists: Marko Jaric (281).
Steals: Jaric (93).
Blocks: Brand (154).

RECORDS

Regular season: 28-54 (7th in Pacific Division); 8-16 in division; 14-38 in conference; 14-16 vs. Eastern Conference; 18-23 at home; 10-31 on road; 2-3 in overtime; 9-5 in games decided by three points or fewer; 12-25 in games decided by 10 points or more; held opponents under 100 points 41 times; held under 100 points 51 times.
Playoffs: None.
All-time franchise record: 980-1776 in 34 seasons.
Team record past five years: 140-270 (.341, ranks 27th in the NBA in that span.)

HIGHLIGHTS

Top players: Corey Maggette averaged career highs of 20.7 ppg, 5.9 rpg and 3.1 apg. He led the NBA in free throws made (526) and was third in free throws attempted (620). He led the team and ranked 14th in the NBA in points per game. He led the Clippers in scoring 30 times. ... Elton Brand averaged 20.0 ppg, 10.3 rpg and 2.23 bpg. He recorded 40 points-rebounds double-doubles, was 10th in the NBA in blocks per game and 14th in field-goal percentage (.493). He led the team in scoring 27 times, rebounding 47 times and blocks 47 times. ... Chris Kaman was the only Clipper to play in all 82 games during his rookie season. ... Quentin Richardson averaged career highs of 17.2 ppg and 6.4 rpg.
Key injuries: The Clippers lost a total of 283 player games because of injury or illness (6th in the NBA) and were at full strength for just 36 of 82 regular-season games. Brand missed 13 of the first 14 games of the season with a hairline stress fracture in his right foot. Richardson missed 17 games with injury. Marko Jaric missed 24 games, including the final 20 of the season with a stress fracture in his left foot. Bobby

Simmons missed 25 games, 22 with a sprained left hip. Chris Wilcox missed 16 games with left groin and Achilles injuries. The Clippers' top seven played only 36 games together; the team was 15-21 in those games.
Notable: Coach Mike Dunleavy recorded his 400th NBA victory with a 115-103 win against Atlanta on November 11. Dunleavy joined Don Nelson, Larry Brown, Jerry Sloan, Rick Adelman and Hubie Brown as the only active coaches with 400 or more NBA victories. ... Richardson scored a career-high 44 points against Denver on December 31 to become the first Clipper to score 40 or more points since Dominique Wilkins scored 42 against the Lakers on April 16, 1994. Richardson's 44 points ranks as the second-highest point total by a Clipper since the franchise moved to Los Angeles, trailing only the 52 points scored by Charles Smith on December 1, 1990. ... Richardson connected on a franchise-record eight 3-point field goals in the Clippers 95-86 victory at Boston on February 4.

– 31 –

LOS ANGELES LAKERS
PACIFIC DIVISION

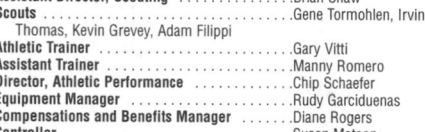

2003-04 SEASON

Lakers Schedule
Home games shaded; *—All-Star Game at Denver.

November

SUN	MON	TUE	WED	THU	FRI	SAT
	1	2 DEN	3 UTH	4	5 SA	6
7 ATL	8	9 NO	10 MEM	11	12 ORL	13 HOU
14	15	16	17 LAC	18	19 PHO	20
21 CHI	22	23 MIL	24	25	26 SAC	27
28 NO	29	30 MIL				

December

SUN	MON	TUE	WED	THU	FRI	SAT
			1 CHI	2	3 GS	4
5	6	7	8 PHO	9	10	11 LAC
12 ORL	13	14 SEA	15	16 SAC	17 WAS	18
19	20 MEM	21	22 NO	23	24	25 MIA
26	27	28 TOR	29	30	31	

January

SUN	MON	TUE	WED	THU	FRI	SAT
						1
2 DEN	3	4 SA	5 DAL	6	7 HOU	8
9	10 MIN	11	12 DEN	13 CLE	14	15 GS
16	17 UTH	18	19 MIN	20	21 GS	22
23	24	25 SEA	26 LAC	27	28 NJN	29
30 CHA	31					

February

SUN	MON	TUE	WED	THU	FRI	SAT
		1 POR	2	3 SA	4	5
6 HOU	7 ATL	8	9 NJN	10 DET	11	12
13 CLE	14	15 UTH	16	17	18	19
20 *All-Star	21	22 BOS	23 POR	24	25 DET	26
27 TOR	28 NYK					

March

SUN	MON	TUE	WED	THU	FRI	SAT
		1	2 BOS	3	4 DAL	5
6 IND	7	8 LAC	9	10 DAL	11	12 CHA
13	14 WAS	15 PHI	16	17 MIA	18 IND	19
20 SEA	21	22 UTH	23	24 DEN	25	26
27 PHI	28	29 NYK	30	31 MIN		

April

SUN	MON	TUE	WED	THU	FRI	SAT
					1	2 SA
3 MEM	4	5 PHO	6	7 HOU	8 SEA	9
10 SAC	11 PHO	12	13	14	15 SAC	16
17 DAL	18 GS	19	20 POR	21	22	23

TEAM DIRECTORY

Owner/Governor ....Dr. Jerry Buss
Co-Owner ....Phillip F. Anschutz
Co-Owner ....Edward P. Roski,Jr.
Co-Owner/Vice President ....Earvin Johnson
Executive Vice President, Marketing ....Frank Mariani
Executive Vice President, Business Operations .Jeanie Buss
General Counsel and Secretary ....Jim Perzik
Senior Vice President, Finance ....Joe McCormack
Senior Vice President, Business Operations . . .Tim Harris
General Manager ....Mitch Kupchak
Assistant General Manager ....Ronnie Lester
Assistant General Manager ....Jim Buss
Special Consultant ....Bill Sharman
Special Consultant ....Walt Hazzard
Head Coach ....Rudy Tomjanovich
Assistant Coaches ....Larry Smith, Frank
Hamblen, Mike Wells, Melvin Hunt, Chris Bodaken
Director, Scouting/Basketball Consultant .....Bill Bertka
Assistant Director, Scouting ....Brian Shaw
Scouts ....Gene Tormohlen, Irving
Thomas, Kevin Grevey, Adam Filippi
Athletic Trainer ....Gary Vitti
Assistant Trainer ....Manny Romero
Director, Athletic Performance ....Chip Schaefer
Equipment Manager ....Rudy Garciduenas
Compensations and Benefits Manager ......Diane Rogers
Controller ....Susan Matson
Executive Director, Multimedia Marketing .....Keith Harris
Director, Public Relations ....John Black
Assistant Director, Public Relations ....Alison Bogli
Director, Community Relations ....Eugenia Chow
Director, Charitable Services ....Janie Drexel
Director, Ticket Operations ....Veronica Lawlor
Director, Laker Girls ....Lisa Estrada
Basketball Operations Assistant ....Tania Jolly
Basketball Operations Assistant ....Kristen Luken
Executive Director Corporate Sponsorships
and Client Management ....Ron Rockoff
Executive Director, Corporate Sponsorships . . .Eva Campbell
Executive Director, Corporate Sponsorships . . .Blain Skinner
Team Physicians:
   Orthopedist ....Dr. Steve Lombardo
   Primary Internist ....Dr. John Moe
   Consultant ....Dr. Michael Mellman
   Dentist ....Jeffrey P. Hoy, D.D.S.
TV Announcers ....Paul Sunderland, Stu Lantz
Radio Announcers ....Joel Meyers, Mychal
   Thompson
Information Systems Manager ....Tommy Yamada
Director, Event Production ....Ian Levitt
Public Address Announcer ....Lawrence Tanter
Director of Camps/Assistant to G.M. ....Glen Carraro
Team Photographer ....Andrew Bernstein

Jerry Buss

Mitch Kupchak

Rudy Tomjanovich

ROSTER
Coach—Rudy Tomjanovich
Assistant coach—Larry Smith, Frank Hamblen, Mike Wells, Melvin Hunt, Chris Bodaken

No.	Name	Pos.	Ht./Wt.	Metric (m/kg)	Born	College/country
9	Chucky Atkins	G	5-11/160	1.80/72.6	8-14-74	South Florida
15	Tony Bobbitt	G	6-4/190	1.93/86.2	10-22-79	Cincinnati
8	Kobe Bryant	G	6-6/220	1.98/99.8	8-23-78	Lower Merion HS
1	Caron Butler	F	6-7/217	2.01/98.4	3-13-80	Connecticut
43	Brian Cook	F	6-9/234	2.05/106.1	12-4-80	Illinois
12	Vlade Divac	C	7-1/260	2.16/117.9	2-3-68	Serbia-Montenegro
3	Devean George	F	6-8/240	2.03/108.4	8-29-77	Augsburg
55	Brian Grant	F	6-9/254	2.06/115.2	3-5-72	Xavier
20	Jumaine Jones	F	6-8/218	2.03/98.9	2-10-79	Georgia
14	Stanislav Medvedenko	F/C	6-10/250	2.08/113.4	4-4-79	Ukraine
31	Chris Mihm	C	7-0/265	2.13/120.2	7-16-79	Texas
7	Lamar Odom	F	6-10/225	2.08/102.1	11-6-79	Rhode Island
21	Kareem Rush	G	6-6/215	1.98/97.5	10-30-80	Missouri
18	Sasha Vujacic	G	6-7/193	2.01/87.5	3-8-84	Slovenia
4	Luke Walton	F	6-8/235	2.03/106.6	3-28-80	Arizona

BROADCAST INFORMATION

Radio: KLAC (570 AM). Broadcasters: Joel Meyers, Mychal Thompson. Spanish Radio: KWKW (1330 AM). Broadcasters: Fernando Gonzalez, Jose "Pepe" Mantilla.
TV: KCAL (Channel 9). Broadcasters: Paul Sunderland, Stu Lantz.
Cable TV: FOX Sports Net. Broadcasters: Paul Sunderland, Stu Lantz.

TEAM INFORMATION

Team address	.555 N. Nash Street El Segundo, CA 90245
Business phone	.310-426-6000
Ticket information	.213-480-3232
Website	.www.lakers.com
Arena (capacity)	.STAPLES Center (18,997)
Game times	.5:30, 7 and 7:30 p.m., Monday-Saturday; 7:30 p.m. Friday; 12:30 and 6:30 p.m., Sunday
First Lakers game in arena	.November 3, 1999

2003-04 REVIEW

RESULTS

OCTOBER
28— Dallas	109 -93	1 -0

NOVEMBER
1 — at Phoenix	103 -99	2 -0
2 — Golden State	87 -72	3 -0
4 — at Milwaukee	113 -107	4 -0
6 — at San Antonio	120 -117	‡5 -0
7 — at New Orleans	*95 -114	5 -1
10— at Memphis	*95 -105	5 -2
12— Toronto	94 -79	6 -2
14— Detroit	94 -89	7 -2
16— Miami	99 -77	8 -2
18— at Detroit	*96 -106	8 -3
19— at New York	104 -83	9 -3
21— Chicago	101 -94	10 -3
23— Memphis	121 -89	11 -3
26— Washington	120 -99	12 -3
28— San Antonio	103 -87	13 -3
30— Indiana	99 -77	14 -3

DECEMBER
3 — at San Antonio	90 -86	15 -3
4 — at Dallas	114 -103	16 -3
7 — Utah	94 -92	17 -3
9 — New York	98 -90	18 -3
12— Dallas	*93 -110	18 -4
13— at Portland	*108 -112	18 -5
19— Denver	101 -99	19 -5
21— Phoenix	107 -101	20 -5
23— at Golden State	*98 -107	20 -6
25— Houston	*87 -99	20 -7

JANUARY
28— Boston	105 -82	21 -7
2 — at Seattle	*109 -111	21 -8
4 — at L.A. Clippers	*98 -101	21 -9
6 — at Minnesota	*90 -106	21 -10
7 — at Denver	*91 -113	21 -11
9 — Atlanta	113 -67	22 -11
12— Cleveland	89 -79	23 -11
14— Denver	97 -71	24 -11
16— at Sacramento	*83 -103	24 -12
17— L.A. Clippers	91 -89	25 -12
19— Phoenix	*85 -88	25 -13
21— at Memphis	*82 -88	25 -14
22— at Dallas	*87 -106	25 -15
24— at Utah	93 -86	26 -15
28— Seattle	96 -82	27 -15
30— Minnesota	*84 -97	27 -16

FEBRUARY
1 — at Toronto	84 -83	28 -16
2 — at Indiana	*72 -85	28 -17
4 — at Cleveland	111 -106	†29 -17
5 — at Philadelphia	*73 -96	29 -18
8 — at Orlando	98 -96	30 -18
10— at Miami	98 -83	31 -18
11— at Houston	*87 -102	31 -19
17— Portland	89 -86	32 -19
18— at Golden State	100 -99	33 -19
20— Philadelphia	116 -88	34 -19
22— at Phoenix	104 -92	35 -19
25— at Denver	112 -111	36 -19

26— Sacramento	*101 -103	36 -20
28— at Washington	122 -110	37 -20
29— at New Jersey	100 -83	38 -20

MARCH
2 — at Atlanta	*93 -94	38 -21
3 — at Houston	96 -93	39 -21
5 — Seattle	99 -91	40 -21
7 — New Jersey	94 -88	41 -21
8 — at Utah	*83 -88	41 -22
10— at Boston	117 -109	42 -22
12— at Minnesota	*86 -96	42 -23
13— at Chicago	88 -81	43 -23
15— Orlando	113 -110	†44 -23
17— at L.A. Clippers	106 -103	45 -23
19— L.A. Clippers	106 -100	46 -23
21— Milwaukee	104 -103	†47 -23
24— Sacramento	115 -91	48 -23
26— Minnesota	90 -73	49 -23
28— Utah	91 -84	50 -23
30— New Orleans	107 -88	51 -23

APRIL
1 — Houston	93 -85	52 -23
2 — at Seattle	97 -86	53 -23
4 — San Antonio	*89 -95	53 -24
6 — Portland	*80 -91	53 -25
9 — Memphis	103 -95	54 -25
11— at Sacramento	*85 -102	54 -26
13— Golden State	109 -104	55 -26
14— at Portland	105 -104	‡56 -26

*Loss. †Single overtime. ‡Double overtime.

TEAM LEADERS

Points: Kobe Bryant (1,557).
Field goals made: Shaquille O'Neal (554).
Free throws made: Bryant (454).
3-pointers made: Bryant (71).
Rebounds: O'Neal (769).
Assists: Gary Payton (449).
Steals: Bryant (112).
Blocks: O'Neal (166).

RECORDS

Regular season: 56-26 (1st in Pacific Division); 15-9 in division; 31-21 in conference; 25-5 vs. Eastern Conference; 34-7 at home; 22-19 on road; 5-0 in overtime; 14-5 in games decided by three points or fewer; 24-16 in games decided by 10 points or more; held opponents under 100 points 53 times; held under 100 points 48 times.
Playoffs: 13-9, defeated Rockets, 4-1, in Western Conference first round; defeated Spurs, 4-2, in Western Conference semifinals; defeated Timberwolves, 4-2, in Western Conference finals; lost to Pistons, 4-1, in NBA Finals.
All-time franchise record: 2,727-1,674 in 56 seasons. Won 14 NBA titles (1949, '50, '52, '53, '54, '72, '80, '82, '85, '87, '88, 2000, '01, '02).
Team record past five years: 287-123 (.700, ranks 1st in NBA in that span).

HIGHLIGHTS

Top players: Kobe Bryant led the Lakers in scoring (24.0, 4th in the NBA), free throw percentage (.852, 20th) and minutes per game (37.6, 25th). He made his sixth All-Star appearance and recorded his ninth career triple-double (25 points, 14 rebounds, 10 assists) February 28 at Washington. He was Western Conference Player of the Month for March. ... Shaquille O'Neal was the Lakers second-leading scorer (21.5, 11th in the NBA) and led the team in field-goal percentage (.584, 1st) and blocks per game (2.48, 8th). He tied for 5th in the NBA in double-doubles (43). He made his 11th All-Star appearance and was the All-Star MVP. ... Karl Malone ranked among league leaders in double-doubles (15, T40th in the NBA). On April 1, Malone moved past Mookie Blaylock and into ninth on the NBA's all-time career steals list. On November 28, he became the oldest player in NBA history to record a triple-double. ... Gary Payton ranked among league leaders in assists (5.5, 17th in the NBA) and field-goal percentage (.471, 30th). He had one triple-double and surpassed Clyde Drexler for fifth on the NBA's all-time steals list.
Key injuries: The Lakers lost a total of 258 player games because of injury or illness. Rick Fox missed 40 games after offseason surgery to repair a tendon in his left foot. Malone missed 39 games with a sprained medial collateral ligament in his right knee. Bryant missed 16 games with injury, including eight with a sprained ac joint in his right shoulder. O'Neal missed 14 games with a strained right calf. Derek Fisher, Devean George and Payton were the only players to compete in all 82 games.
Notables: The Lakers (56-26) recorded their 27th 50-win season in Los Angeles (28th overall for the Lakers franchise). They clinched their 18th Pacific Division championship and made the playoffs for the 10th straight year. ... On January 14 vs. Denver, Phil Jackson became the fastest coach to 800 career victories in NBA history (800-301). ... With their loss to Dallas on December 12 at STAPLES Center, the Lakers' Los Angeles-era franchise record for most consecutive regular-season home wins ended at 27.

MEMPHIS GRIZZLIES
SOUTHWEST DIVISION

Grizzlies Schedule
Home games shaded; *—All-Star Game at Denver.

November

SUN	MON	TUE	WED	THU	FRI	SAT
	1	2	3 WAS	4	5 HOU	6 DAL
7	8	9 HOU	10 LAL	11	12 GS	13
14 SEA	15	16	17 POR	18	19 SAC	20 GS
21 SA	22 SA	23	24 SEA	25	26 MIN	27 DAL
28	29	30 SAC				

December

SUN	MON	TUE	WED	THU	FRI	SAT
		1 NYK	2	3 PHI	4 ORL
5	6	7 NYK	8 ATL	9	10 MIA	11 DET
12	13 CLE	14	15 CHI	16	17 NJN	18
19 LAC	20 LAL	21	22 GS	23 PHO	24	25
26	27 LAC	28	29 BOS	30	31	

January

SUN	MON	TUE	WED	THU	FRI	SAT
						1 MIN
2	3 UTH	4	5	6 DET	7 NO	8
9	10	11 IND	12	13	14 CHA	15 MIL
16	17 HOU	18	19 PHO	20	21 DEN	22 UTH
23	24	25 ORL	26 CLE	27	28	29 ATL
30	31 NO					

February

SUN	MON	TUE	WED	THU	FRI	SAT
		1 PHO	2	3 LAC	4	5
6	7	8 MIN	9 PHI	10	11 POR	12
13 IND	14	15	16 BOS	17	18	19
20 *All-Star	21	22	23 WAS	24	25 DEN	26 SA
27	28					

March

SUN	MON	TUE	WED	THU	FRI	SAT
		1 GS	2	3	4 TOR	5
6	7 LAC	8 SAC	9	10	11 UTH	12 POR
13	14 POR	15	16 NO	17	18 MIN	19
20 PHO	21	22	23	24 NJN	25	26 NO
27	28 CHI	29 SEA	30	31		

April

SUN	MON	TUE	WED	THU	FRI	SAT
					1 MIL	2
3 LAL	4	5 DEN	6 TOR	7	8 MIA	9
10 CHA	11 DAL	12	13 HOU	14	15 DEN	16 SA
17	18 SA	19	20 DAL	21	22	23

2004-05 SEASON
TEAM DIRECTORY

OWNERSHIP
Majority Owner . . . . .Michael Heisley
Limited Partners . . . . .Pitt Hyde, Barbara Rosser
  Hyde, Andy Cates, Staley Cates, Charles Ewing, Fred Jones

BASKETBALL OPERATIONS
President, Basketball Operations . . . . .Jerry West
General Manager . . . . .Dick Versace
Assistant to the President, Basketball Operations . . . . .Gary Colson
Assistant General Manager/Legal Counsel . . . . .Tom Penn
Director, Team Operations . . . . .Steve Daniel
Director, Player Personnel . . . . .Tony Barone, Sr.
Director, Scouting . . . . .Tony Barone, Jr.
Special Advisor . . . . .Gene Bartow
Head Coach . . . . .Hubie Brown
Assistant Coaches .Tony Barone, Sr., Brendan
  Brown, Lionel Hollins, Hal Wissel
Assistant Coach/Workout Coach . . . . .John Welch
Strength & Conditioning Coach . . . . .Mike Curtis
Head Athletic Trainer . . . . .Scott McCullough
Assistant Trainer/Equipment Manager . . . . .Yusuf Boyd
Director, Team Travel . . . . .Dana Davis
Video Coordinator . . . . .T.J. Zanin

BUSINESS OPERATIONS
President, Business Operations . . . . .Andy Dolich
Senior Vice President, Business Operations . . . . .Mike Golub

BROADCAST
Vice President, Broadcast . . . . .Randy Stephens

COMMUNITY INVESTMENT
Director, Community Investment . . . . .Staci Franklin

EVENT MARKETING
Vice President, Event Marketing . . . . .Charlotte Allison

FINANCE
Senior Director, Finance . . . . .Arnetria Knowles

HUMAN RESOURCES
Director, Human Resources . . . . .Christy Haynes

INFORMATION TECHNOLOGY
Director, Information Technology . . . . .Mike Garrison

MARKETING COMMUNICATIONS
Vice President, Marketing Communications . . . . .Marla Taner
Director, Creative Services . . . . .Anna Lea Dahl

MEDIA RELATIONS
Director, Basketball Media Relations . . . . .Stacey Mitch

OPERATIONS
Vice President, Arena Operations . . . . .Don Hardman
Director, Event Operations . . . . .Todd Mastry
Director, Guest Relations . . . . .Nicole Spata
Director, Special Projects . . . . .Chris Stairs

PROMOTIONS & EVENT PRESENTATION
Senior Director, Promotions & Event Presentation . . . .Stephanie Willox

TICKET SALES & SERVICE
Vice President, Sales & Service . . . . .Mike Levy
Director, Sales & Service . . . . .Dennis O'Connor
Director, Ticket Operations . . . . .Garth Webster
Directors, Premium Sales . . . . .Paige Perkins, Gary Sommer

SPONSORSHIP SALES & SERVICE
Vice President, Sponsorship Sales & Service . . . . .Mike Redlick
Senior Director, Sponsorship Sales . . . . .Chad Bolen
Directors, Sponsorship Sales .Rob Reynolds, Rey Jordan

Michael Heisley

Jerry West

Hubie Brown

ROSTER
Coach—Hubie Brown
Assistant coaches—Tony Barone, Brendan Brown, Lionel Hollins, Hal Wissel

No.	Name	Pos.	Ht./Wt.	Metric (m/kg)	Born	College/country
31	Shane Battier	G/F	6-8/220	2.03/99.8	9-9-78	Duke
3	Troy Bell	G	6-1/180	1.85/81.6	11-10-80	Boston College
1	Antonio Burks	G	6-0/195	1.83/88.5	2-25-80	Memphis
35	Brian Cardinal	F	6-8/245	2.03/111.1	5-2-77	Purdue
14	Andre Emmett	G	6-5/230	1.96/104.3	8-27-82	Texas Tech
16	Pau Gasol	F	7-0/240	2.13/108.4	7-6-80	Spain
40	Ryan Humphrey	F	6-8/235	2.03/106.6	7-24-79	Notre Dame
30	Dahntay Jones	G/F	6-6/210	1.98/95.3	12-27-80	Duke
	Sergei Lishouk	F	6-11/232	2.10/105.2	3-31-82	Ukraine
33	Mike Miller	F	6-8/218	2.03/98.9	2-19-80	Florida
45	Bo Outlaw	F	6-8/220	2.03/99.8	4-13-71	Houston
41	James Posey	G/F	6-8/215	2.03/97.5	1-13-77	Xavier
4	Stromile Swift	F/C	6-9/230	2.05/104.3	11-21-79	Louisiana State
12	Jake Tsakalidis	C	7-2/290	2.18/131.5	6-10-79	Greece
25	Earl Watson	G	6-1/190	1.85/86.2	6-12-79	UCLA
6	Bonzi Wells	G/F	6-5/210	1.96/95.3	9-20-76	Ball State
2	Jason Williams	G	6-1/190	1.85/86.2	11-18-75	Florida
42	Lorenzen Wright	C	6-11/240	2.10/108.4	11-4-75	Memphis

BROADCAST INFORMATION
Radio: WRBO (103.5 FM).
TV: TBA.
Cable: TBA.

TEAM INFORMATION
Team address . . . . .191 Beale Street
                Memphis, TN 38103
Business phone 901-205-1234
Ticket information 901-888-HOOP
Website . . . . .www.grizzlies.com
Arena (capacity) . . . . .FedExForum (18,400)
Game times . . . . .7 p.m. Monday-Saturday; 3 p.m., Sunday
First Grizzlies game in arena . . . . . .Scheduled for Nov. 3, 2004

2003-04 REVIEW
RESULTS

OCTOBER
31— Boston	*91 -93	0 -1	

NOVEMBER
1 — at Houston	79 -71	1 -1
3 — San Antonio	88 -80	2 -1
5 — at Portland	*87 -93	2 -2
7 — at Phoenix	*88 -96	2 -3
8 — at Utah	*89 -96	2 -4
10— L.A. Lakers	105 -95	3 -4
12— at Orlando	107 -97	4 -4
15— Dallas	108 -101	†5 -4
19— Detroit	*92 -99	5 -5
21— at Seattle	98 -97	6 -5
23— at L.A. Lakers	*89 -121	6 -6
25—at Sacramento	*89 -109	6 -7
28— Minnesota	*98 -102	6 -8
29— at Cleveland	122 -115	‡7 -8

DECEMBER
1 — at Boston	96 -89	8 -8
3 — at New Jersey	96 -93	9 -8
5 — Washington	92 -77	10 -8
7 — Portland	93 -79	11 -8
10— Atlanta	103 -90	12 -8
12— at Miami	*88 -91	12 -9
13— New Jersey	110 -63	13 -9
15— at San Antonio	*67 -78	13 -10
16— Sacramento	105 -100	14 -10
19— Miami	97 -83	15 -10
20— at New Orleans	*89 -94	15 -11
22— at Denver	*99 -106	15 -12

23— at Sacramento	*97 -114	15 -13
26— New York	*94 -98	15 -14
27— at Dallas	*98 -104	15 -15
29— at Indiana	*86 -94	15 -16
30— Seattle	*99 -105	15 -17

JANUARY
2 — Utah	100 -88	16 -17
3 — Orlando	112 -103	17 -17
9 — at Seattle	*116 -122	17 -18
11— at L.A. Clippers	108 -107	†18 -18
12— at Golden State	115 -113	‡19 -18
15— Chicago	108 -93	20 -18
17— at Philadelphia	91 -87	21 -18
19— Houston	88 -83	22 -18
21— L.A. Lakers	88 -82	23 -18
23— Sacramento	109 -95	24 -18
25— Denver	106 -88	25 -18
28— Portland	*76 -88	25 -19
30— Utah	*79 -85	25 -20
31— at Detroit	*78 -80	25 -21

FEBRUARY
2 — Golden State	106 -101	26 -21
4 — at Washington	103 -101	27 -21
6 — Milwaukee	105 -85	28 -21
8 — at Minnesota	99 -98	29 -21
9 — at Denver	*83 -86	29 -22
11— L.A. Clippers	110 -102	30 -22
17— Dallas	109 -92	31 -22
20— Phoenix	97 -92	32 -22
21— at Chicago	105 -98	33 -22

23— Denver	109 -106	34 -22
25— Golden State	*92 -99	34 -23
27— at Milwaukee	*104 -106	34 -24
28— New Orleans	97 -92	35 -24

MARCH
1 — at San Antonio	81 -80	36 -24
3 — at Portland	97 -88	37 -24
6 — at L.A. Clippers	98 -92	38 -24
7 — at Golden State	95 -85	39 -24
9 — San Antonio	94 -88	40 -24
12— L.A. Clippers	98 -89	41 -24
13— at Houston	*80 -88	41 -25
16— Philadelphia	82 -79	42 -25
18— Seattle	*94 -97	42 -26
20— Indiana	99 -95	43 -26
23— Toronto	95 -86	44 -26
24— at New York	111 -97	45 -26
26— Houston	109 -86	46 -26
28— at Toronto	94 -88	47 -26
29— at Atlanta	136 -133	‡48 -26

APRIL
2 — Phoenix	109 -99	49 -26
4 — at Minnesota	*82 -90	49 -27
5 — at Utah	*81 -92	49 -28
7 — Cleveland	92 -74	50 -28
9 — at L.A. Lakers	*95 -103	50 -29
11— at Phoenix	*83 -89	50 -30
13— at Dallas	*103 -110	50 -31
14— Minnesota	*90 -107	50 -32

*Loss. †Single overtime. ‡Double overtime.

TEAM LEADERS
Points: Pau Gasol (1,381).
Field goals made: Gasol (506).
Free throws made: Gasol (365).
3-pointers made: Jason Williams (120).
Rebounds: Gasol (600).
Assists: Williams (492).
Steals: James Posey (137).
Blocks: Gasol (132).

RECORDS
Regular season: 50-32 (4th in Midwest Division); 12-12 in division; 28-24 in conference; 22-8 vs. Eastern Conference; 31-10 at home; 19-22 on road; 5-0 in overtime; 10-6 in games decided by three points or fewer; 18-7 in games decided by 10 points or more; held opponents under 100 points 59 times; held under 100 points 54 times.
Playoffs: 0-4, lost to Spurs, 4-0, in Western Conference first round.
All-time franchise record: 202-504 in nine seasons.
Team record past five years: 146-264 (.356, ranks 25th in NBA in that span.)

HIGHLIGHTS
Top players: Pau Gasol led the team in scoring (17.7 ppg), rebounding (7.7 rpg), blocks (1.69 bpg, 18th in NBA), minutes (31.5 mpg) and double-doubles (24). ... James Posey was a candidate for the NBA's Most Improved Player Award after averaging 13.7 ppg and 4.9 rpg. He led the team in steals (1.67 spg) and was second in 3-point field-goal percentage (38.6). He finished fifth in the NBA in steals-per-turnover ratio (1.22-to-1). ... Jason Williams led the team in assists (6.8 apg, 7th in the NBA) and finished fourth in the NBA in assists-to-turnover ratio (3.66-to-1). ... Shane Battier led the NBA in steals-per-turnover ratio (1.80-to-1).
Key injuries: The Grizzlies lost a total of 278 player games because of injury or illness. Gasol missed four games with a strained arch, the first time in his career he missed a game. It snapped a string of 240 consecutive games. Posey and Bo Outlaw were the only Grizzlies to play all 82 games.
Notable: The 2003-04 season was the best in team history. The Grizzlies went to the playoffs for the first time after compiling a team-record 50 wins but lost to San Antonio in the first round. ... President of basketball operations Jerry West was named the NBA's Executive of the Year, and head coach Hubie Brown won the Coach of the Year Award. ... The 50 wins marked the first time in team history the Grizzlies had a winning record, and they improved their win total by 22 from 2002-03, the 11th-best turnaround in NBA history. ... Brown won his 400th career game as an NBA coach, his 500th game as a professional coach (including the ABA) and is the Grizzlies' all-time winningest coach. ... The Grizzlies broke franchise records for wins (50), home wins (31), road wins (19) and consecutive wins (8). ... Gasol set a career high with 37 points on November 29 at Cleveland. ... Posey set a career high and a team high for the season with 38 points on March 29 at Atlanta. ... The Grizzlies set team records for margin of victory (+47), biggest lead in a game (+48), field-goal percentage (.620), fewest points allowed (63) and fewest points allowed in a first half (28) in a 110-63 win against New Jersey on December 13.

– 35 –

MIAMI HEAT
SOUTHEAST DIVISION

Heat Schedule
Home games shaded; *—All-Star Game at Denver.

November
SUN	MON	TUE	WED	THU	FRI	SAT
	1	2	3 NJN	4 CLE	5	6 WAS
7	8	9 WAS	10	11 DAL	12 SA	13
14 MIL	15	16 MIN	17 MIL	18	19 UTH	20
21 PHI	22	23 POR	24 ATL	25	26 DET	27
28 BOS	29	30 TOR				

December
SUN	MON	TUE	WED	THU	FRI	SAT
			1	2	3 CHI	4 DEN
5 UTH	6	7	8 MIL	9	10 MEM	11
12 TOR	13 WAS	14	15 WAS	16	17 DEN	18
19 ORL	20	21 BOS	22	23 SAC	24	25 LAL
26	27 ATL	28	29	30 DET	31	

January
SUN	MON	TUE	WED	THU	FRI	SAT
						1 CHA
2	3 SEA	4	5 NYK	6	7 POR	8
9 SEA	10	11 PHO	12 GS	13	14 LAC	15
16	17	18	19 ATL	20	21 IND	22
23 PHI	24 NO	25	26 TOR	27	28 ATL	29
30 HOU	31					

February
SUN	MON	TUE	WED	THU	FRI	SAT
		1 DAL	2	3 CLE	4	5 CHI
6	7 GS	8	9 NYK	10	11 CHA	12
13 SA	14	15	16 LAC	17	18	19
20 *All-Star	21	22 CHI	23 IND	24	25	26 ORL
27 ORL	28					

March
SUN	MON	TUE	WED	THU	FRI	SAT
		1	2	3 NJN	4 SAC	5
6 CLE	7 PHI	8	9	10 MIN	11	12 NJN
13	14 MIL	15 NYK	16	17 LAL	18	19 NYK
20	21	22 HOU	23	24	25 PHO	26 CHA
27	28	29 TOR	30	31 IND		

April
SUN	MON	TUE	WED	THU	FRI	SAT
					1	2 NO
3	4	5 CHI	6	7	8 MEM	9
10 DET	11	12	13	14 PHI	15 BOS	16
17 IND	18	19 CHA	20 ORL	21	22	23

2004-05 SEASON

TEAM DIRECTORY

Managing General Partner . . . . .Micky Arison
President . . . . .Pat Riley
General Manager . . . . .Randy Pfund
President, Business Operations . . . . .Eric Woolworth
Head Coach . . . . .Stan Van Gundy
Executive Vice President/CMO . . . . .Michael McCullough
Executive VP, HEAT Group Enterprises . . . . . . .Mike Walker
General Counsel . . . . .Raquel Libman
Limited Partners . . . . .Julio Iglesias, Raanan
    Katz, Sidney Kimmel, Robert Sturges
Senior Vice President/CFO . . . . .Sammy Schulman
Senior Vice President, Sales and Service . . . . .Stephen Weber
Senior VP, Basketball Operations . . . . .Andy Elisburg
Vice President, Sports Media Relations . . . . . .Tim Donovan
Vice President, Chief Information Officer . . . . . .Tony Coba
Vice President, Premium &
Season Ticket Services & Retention . . . . .Lorraine Mondich
VP, Arena Marketing and Bookings . . . . .Eric Bresler
VP, Facilities & General Manager . . . . .Alexander M. Diaz
Chief of Staff & VP Business Development . . . .Kim Stone
Vice President, Marketing Division . . . . .Jeff Craney
Executive Assistant to the President . . . . .Karen Merrill
Executive Assistant, Basketball Operations . . . .Yvette Morrell
Assistant Coaches . . . . .Bob McAdoo, Keith
    Askins, Erik Spoelstra
Trainer/Travel Coordinator . . . . .Ron Culp
Assistant Coach/Strength & Conditioning . . . . .Bill Foran
Assistant Trainer/Assistant Strength &
Conditioning Coach/Equipment Manager . . . . . .Jay Sabol
Senior Director, Team Services . . . . .Marjie Kates
Director of Player Personnel . . . . .Chet Kammerer
Director of Sports Media Relations . . . . .Rob Wilson
Director of Team Security . . . . .David Holcombe
Scout/Director of College Scouting . . . . .Adam Simon
Team Physicians . . . . .Dr. Harlan Selesnick,
    Dr. Allan Herskowitz, Dr. Edward Neff, Dr. Steve Tarkan, Dr. Jim
    Losito, Dr. Stuart Leeds, Dr. Richard Mariani, Dr. Larry Brown, Dr.
    Angelo Thrower, Dr. Henry Trattler
Neuromuscular Therapist . . . . .Vinny Aquilino
Scout . . . . .Randy Embry
Scouting Information Coordinator . . . . .Brian Hecker
Video Coordinator . . . . .Pat Delany
Assistant Director of Sports Media Relations . . .Michael Lissack
Sports Media Relations Assistant . . . . .Nick Maiorana
Assistant to the Coaches . . . . .Dave Beyer
Administrative Assistant . . . . .Kenny McCraney
Team Assistant . . . . .Carlos Estrada

Micky Arison

Pat Riley

Stan Van Gundy

ROSTER
Head Coach—Stan Van Gundy
Assistant Coaches—Bob McAdoo, Keith Askins, Erik Spoelstra, Bill Foran

No.	Name	Pos.	Ht./Wt.	Metric (m/kg)	Born	College/country
35	Malik Allen	F	6-10/255	2.08/115.7	6-27-78	Villanova
24	Jerome Beasley	F	6-10/241	2.08/109.3	5-17-80	North Dakota
45	Rasual Butler	F	6-7/205	2.00/93.0	5-23-79	La Salle
12	Bimbo Coles	G	6-2/182	1.88/82.6	4-22-68	Virginia Tech
51	Michael Doleac	C	6-11/262	2.11/118.8	6-15-77	Utah
5	Keyon Dooling	G	6-3/196	1.91/88.9	5-8-80	Missouri
50	Matt Freije	F	6-10/249	2.08/112.9	10-2-81	Vanderbilt
40	Udonis Haslem	F/C	6-8/230	2.03/104.3	6-9-80	Florida
19	Damon Jones	G	6-3/185	1.91/83.9	8-25-76	Houston
6	Eddie Jones	G	6-6/200	1.98/90.7	10-20-71	Temple
32	Shaquille O'Neal	C	7-1/315	2.16/142.9	3-6-72	Louisiana State
7	Wesley Person	G/F	6-6/200	1.98/90.7	3-28-71	Auburn
3	Dwyane Wade	G	6-4/210	1.93/95.3	1-17-82	Marquette
15	Wang Zhi-Zhi	C	7-0/255	2.13/115.7	7-8-77	China
1	Dorell Wright	F	6-7/190	2.01/07.6	12-2-85	South Kent Prep

BROADCAST INFORMATION

Radio: WIOD (610 AM). Broadcaster: Mike Inglis. Spanish Radio: WQBA (1140 AM). Broadcaster: Jose Paneda.
Cable TV: Sunshine Network. Broadcasters: Eric Reid, Mike Fratello, Tony Fiorentino.

TEAM INFORMATION

Team address ....601 Biscayne Blvd.
Miami, FL 33132
Business phone 786-777-HEAT
Ticket information 786-777-HEAT
Website ....www.heat.com
Arena (capacity) ....AmericanAirlines Arena (19,600)
Game times ....1, 6, 7:30 and 8 p.m.
First Heat game in arena ....January 2, 2000

2003-04 REVIEW

RESULTS

OCTOBER

28— at Philadelphia	*74 -89	0 -1
29— at Boston	*75 -98	0 -2
31— Detroit	*81 -93	0 -3

NOVEMBER

3 — at Dallas	*93 -103	0 -4
4 — at San Antonio	*73 -80	0 -5
8 — Minnesota	*79 -88	0 -6
11 — at Houston	*70 -90	0 -7
12— Cleveland	88 -83	1 -7
14— Washington	105 -101	†2 -7
16— at L.A. Lakers	*77 -99	2 -8
18— at Seattle	105 -98	3 -8
19— at Portland	*93 -94	3 -9
21— at Golden State	*91 -101	3 -10
22— at Phoenix	*98 -100	3 -11
25— New Orleans	91 -87	4 -11
28— at Atlanta	*83 95	4 -12
29— Toronto	78 -66	5 -12

DECEMBER

3 — at Detroit	*73 -87	5 -13
5 — Philadelphia	*90 -93	5 -14
6 — San Antonio	*70 -86	5 -15
9 — Phoenix	92 -72	6 -15
12— Memphis	91 -88	7 -15
14— at Toronto	90 -89	8 -15
16— Atlanta	97 -79	9 -15
17— at Philadelphia	*76 -87	9 -16
19— at Memphis	*83 -97	9 -17
21— Golden State	104 -93	10 -17

23— Washington	79 -72	11 -17
26— at Washington	92 -84	12 -17
27— New York	*80 -100	12 -18
29— at Chicago	90 -83	13 -18
30— at New York	*73 -102	13 -19

JANUARY

2 — Orlando	112 -101	14 -19
5 — Indiana	* 65 -87	14 -20
7 — Chicago	102 -95	15 -20
9 — at Milwaukee	*94 -103	15 -21
10— at Minnesota	*77 -83	15 -22
13— at Sacramento	*86 -90	15 -23
15— at Utah	*85 -97	15 -24
16— at L.A. Clippers	87 -85	16 -24
18— at Denver	*80 -88	16 -25
20— Boston	*84 -86	16 -26
23— New Jersey	85 -64	17 -26
24— at New York	86 -77	18 -26
26— Houston	95 -81	19 -26
28— at Cleveland	*93 -94	19 -27
30— L.A. Clippers	97 -88	20 -27
31— at New Orleans	94 -70	21 -27

FEBRUARY

2 — Detroit	*100 -102	†21 -28
4 — at New Jersey	*88 -99	21 -29
7 — New York	*64 -76	21 -30
8 — at Indiana	*91 -97	21 -31
10— L.A. Lakers	*83 -98	21 -32
11— at Orlando	111 -98	22 -32
17— Utah	97 -85	23 -32

20— Atlanta	125 -92	24 -32
21— Denver	97 -81	25 -32
23— Portland	*81 -89	25 -33
28— at New Jersey	*86 -92	25 -34
29— at Milwaukee	*104 -108	25 -35

MARCH

2 — Toronto	*86 -89	25 -36
4 — Milwaukee	104 -98	26 -36
6 — Sacramento	102 -96	27 -36
9 — Orlando	100 -89	28 -36
10— at New Orleans	*84 -95	28 -37
12— Seattle	82 -74	29 -37
14— New Jersey	104 -95	30 -37
16— New Orleans	96 -83	31 -37
20— Philadelphia	101 -69	32 -37
21— at Washington	101 -81	33 -37
24— at Orlando	105 -90	34 -37
2C— Dallas	119 -110	‖35 -37
28— at Indiana	*80 -87	35 -38
29— Chicago	105 -96	36 -38
31— at Atlanta	100 -97	37 -38

APRIL

2—at Detroit	*84 -92	37 -39
3—at Chicago	97 -83	38 -39
7 — Boston	104 -101	39 -39
9 — Cleveland	106 -91	40 -39
10— at Cleveland	*80 -91	40 -40
12— at Boston	84 -77	41 -40
14— New Jersey	96 -84	42 -40

*Loss. †Single overtime.

TEAM LEADERS

Points: Eddie Jones (1,401).
Field goals made: Lamar Odom (485).
Free throws made: Odom (340).
3-pointers made: Jones (177).
Rebounds: Odom (776).
Assists: Rafer Alston (372).
Steals: Alston (114).
Blocks: Odom (71).

RECORDS

Regular season: 42-40 (2nd in Atlantic); 15-10 in division; 30-24 in conference; 12-16 vs. Western Conference; 29-12 at home; 13-28 on road; 2-1 in overtime; 6-7 in games decided by three points or less; 20-21 in games decided by 10 points or more; held opponents under 100 points 70 times; held under 100 points 61 times.
Playoffs: 6-7, defeated Hornets, 4-3, in Eastern Conference first round; lost to Pacers, 4-2, in Eastern Conference semifinals.
All-time franchise record: 601-679 in 16 seasons.
Team record past five years: 205-205 (.500, tied for 15th in NBA in that span).

HIGHLIGHTS

Top players: Dwyane Wade ranked in the top five among rookies in points, rebounds, assists, field-goal percentage, steals and minutes. He was a unanimous selection to the All-Rookie First Team and a member of the U.S. Olympic team. ... Eddie Jones led the team and ranked third in the NBA in 3-point field goals made (177) and fifth in 3-point field-goal attempts. He was second in field goals made (473) for the Heat. ... Udonis Haslem ranked in the top 10 among rookies in points, rebounds, field-goal percentage, free throw percentage and minutes. He was named to the All-Rookie Second Team.
Key injuries: The Heat missed a total of 279 player games because of injury or illness. Jerome Beasley missed 69 games with a lower back strain, the most on the team. Wade missed a total 21 games (16 with bone contusions). Jones missed one game with a right calf strain. Caron Butler missed 14 games (six with left quad deficiency, five because of arthroscopic surgery on his left knee, one game with a right elbow bone contusion and one game

with lower back spasms).
Notable: The Heat began 0-7 and then 5-15 but mounted a turnaround and earned its ninth postseason berth in franchise history. The team finished 42-40. Miami went from last place in the Atlantic Division during the 2002-03 season to second place in the division and fourth in the Eastern Conference in 2003-04. The club's 17-game improvement from the previous season was the second-best improvement in franchise history and the fourth best in the NBA last year. ... Stan Van Gundy became the third coach in Heat history to lead the team to the playoffs in his first year of coaching. ... The team won 17 of its final 21 regular-season games, including 12 consecutive regular-season home games and 18 consecutive home games including the playoffs. ... The Heat broke the 100-point barrier 21 times.

MILWAUKEE BUCKS
CENTRAL DIVISION

Milwaukee Bucks

2004-05 SEASON

Bucks Schedule
Home games shaded; *—All-Star Game at Denver.

November

SUN	MON	TUE	WED	THU	FRI	SAT
	1	2	3 ORL	4	5	6 CLE
7	8	9	10 CHA	11	12	13 NO
14 MIA	15	16	17 MIA	18	19 POR	20
21 SAC	22	23 LAL	24 PHO	25	26	27 DET
28	29	30 LAL				

December

SUN	MON	TUE	WED	THU	FRI	SAT
			1 BOS	2	3	4 SA
5	6	7 IND	8 MIA	9	10 IND	11
12 PHI	13	14 SAC	15	16 CHI	17	18 PHI
19	20	21	22 POR	23	24	25
26 CHI	27	28 HOU	29 ORL	30	31 HOU	

January

SUN	MON	TUE	WED	THU	FRI	SAT
2 DAL	3	4 IND	5 NJN	6	7 TOR	8 UTH
9	10	11 ATL	12 SA	13	14 WAS	15 MEM
16	17 CHA	18	19 NJN	20	21 DET	22
23 NYK	24	25	26 PHO	27	28 DEN	29
30 CLE	31					

February

SUN	MON	TUE	WED	THU	FRI	SAT
		1 MIN	2	3	4 LAC	5 WAS
6	7	8 BOS	9 TOR	10	11	12 ATL
13	14 DET	15	16 NYK	17	18	19
20 *All-Star	21	22 CHA	23 NJN	24	25 TOR	26
27 SEA	28					

March

SUN	MON	TUE	WED	THU	FRI	SAT
		1 PHI	2	3	4 MIN	5 CHI
6	7 CHI	8 ATL	9	10	11 DAL	12 NO
13 MIA	14	15	16 CLE	17	18 WAS	19
20 DEN	21	22 SEA	23 LAC	24	25 GS	26 UTH
27	28 IND	29	30 GS	31		

April

SUN	MON	TUE	WED	THU	FRI	SAT
					1 MEM	2
3 NYK	4	5	6 BOS	7	8 CHA	9 CLE
10	11 WAS	12	13 BOS	14	15 DET	16 ORL
17	18 PHI	19 TOR	20	21	22	23

2004-05 SEASON

TEAM DIRECTORY

EXECUTIVE STAFF
President .... Herb Kohl
General Manager .... Larry Harris
Vice President, Business Operations .... John Steinmiller
Vice President, Alternate Governor .... Ron Walter
Chief Financial Officer .... Mike Burr

BASKETBALL OPERATIONS
Head Coach .... Terry Porter
Assistant Coaches .... Mike Schuler,
  Bob Ociepka, Jim Boylen, Jerome Kersey
Assistant General Manager .... Dan Kohl
Assistant to Head Coach .... Liz DuPlanty
Director of Scouting .... Dave Babcock
Director of European Scouting .... Jacinto Castillo
Scouts .... Chris Gilmartin, Scott Roth
Athletic Trainer/Traveling Secretary .... Andre Daniel
Strength and Conditioning Coach .... Tim Wilson
Assistant Trainer/Asst. Strength & Conditioning Coach .. John Anderson
Equipment and Team Facilities Manager .... Harold Lewis
Video Coordinator .... Anthony Houston
Assistant Video Coordinator .... Mike Sergo
Assistant to the General Manager .... Sharon Walls
Player Personnel/Scouting Assistant .... Dave Dean
Medical Advisors .... John Heinrich, M.D.,
  Samuel Idarraga, M.D., Dr. Tom Tongas, D.D.S., Dr. Robert Wallock, D.D.S.
Physicians Emeritus .... David Haskell, M.D.,
  Conrad Heinzelmann, M.D.

FINANCE
Director of Finance .... Jim Woloszyk
Accounting Manager .... Michelle Bondar
Accountant .... Tanya French

PUBLIC RELATIONS
Director of Public Relations .... Cheri Hanson
Manager of Public Relations .... Dan Smyczek
Public Relations Assistant .... Matt Wessel

TICKET SALES
Director of Sales .... Jim Grayson
Assistant Director of Sales .... David Trattner
Senior Account Representatives .... Patty Cox, Michael Grahl
Account Representative .... Mike Dammen
Customer Service Coordinator .... Brad Hamacher
Sales Associates .... Pat Bowdish, Ryan
  Morgan, Ryan Neils, Lori Warczak
Group Tickets Sales Manager .... Steve Tarachow
Group Tickets Service Manager .... Rick Wermager
Group Sales Representative .... Tricia Rasberry

TICKET OPERATIONS
Ticket Manager .... Sue Thompson
Assistant to the Ticket Manager .... Ben Conrad
Ticket Office Associates .... Sandy Short, Kim
  Klefstad, Sabrina Talavera, Matt Kern

CORPORATE AND BROADCAST SALES
Account Executives .... Deb Logan, David Snyder
Corporate Sales Coordinator/Account Executive .. Kareeda Chones
Sales Associate/Legal Associate .... Mike Sneathern

BROADCAST
Television Coordinator-Development .... Jim Paschke
Broadcast Sales-Traffic Administrator .... Deborah Kulaf

COMMUNITY RELATIONS
Director of Community Relations .... Skip Robinson
Community Relations Assistant .... Jessie Vavera

GAME OPERATIONS
Director of Game Operations .... Bryan Larive
Game Operations Assistant .... Kris Brunelli
Mascot Coordinator .... Kevin Vanderkolk

INFORMATION TECHNOLOGY
Information Technology Coordinator .... Ron Kiepert

ADMINISTRATION
Director of Team Services .... Clark Hillery
Executive Secretary to VP, Business Operations .. Rita Huber
Team Services Assistant .... Claudia Sylvester
Administrative Assistant .... Wade Waugus
Administrative Assistant/Sales .... Shakura Luckett
Receptionist .... Vanessa Murphy

Herb Kohl

Larry Harris

Terry Porter

ROSTER
Coach—Terry Porter
Assistant coaches—Mike Schuler, Bob Ociepka, Jim Boylen, Jerome Kersey

No.	Name	Pos.	Ht./Wt.	Metric (m/kg)	Born	College/country
11	T.J. Ford	G	6-0/165	1.83/74.8	3-24-83	Texas
50	Dan Gadzuric	C	6-11/240	2.10/108.4	2-2-78	UCLA
12	Marcus Haislip	F	6-10/230	1.08/104/3	12-22-80	Tennessee
31	Zendon Hamilton	C	6-11/240	2.11/108.9	4-29-75	St. John's
13	Mike James	G	6-2/188	1.88/85.3	6-23-75	Duquesne
45	Lonnie Jones	C	7-0/235	2.13/106.6	11-8-79	Ball State
6	Brevin Knight	G	5-10/170	1.78/77.1	11-8-75	Stanford
7	Toni Kukoc	F	6-11/235	2.10/106.6	9-18-68	Croatia
24	Desmond Mason	G/F	6-5/222	1.96/100.7	10-11-77	Oklahoma State
27	Zaza Pachulia	F/C	6-11/240	2.10/108.4	2-10-84	Turkey
22	Michael Redd	G	6-6/215	1.98/97.5	8-24-79	Ohio State
15	Daniel Santiago	C	7-1/260	2.16/117.9	6-24-76	St. Vincent (Pa.)
8	Joe Smith	F	6-10/225	1.08/102.1	7-26-75	Maryland
20	Erick Strickland	G	6-3/210	1.90/94.3	11-25-73	Nebraska
44	Keith Van Horn	F	6-10/240	1.08/108.4	10-23-75	Utah
	Maurice Williams	G	6-1/105	1.05/03.9	12/19/28	Alabama

– 38 –

BROADCAST INFORMATION

Radio: WTMJ (620 AM). Broadcasters: Ted Davis calls play-by-play (all games).
TV: UPN-24. Broadcasters: Jim Paschke and Jon McGlocklin.
Cable TV: FOX Sports Net. Broadcasters: Jim Paschke and Jon McGlocklin.

TEAM INFORMATION

Team address	1001 N. Fourth St. Milwaukee, WI 53203
Business phone	414-227-0500
Website	www.bucks.com
Ticket information	414-227-0500, 800-4-NBA-Tix
Arena (capacity)	Bradley Center (18,717)
Game times	7, 8 and 8:30 p.m., Monday-Thursday; 7:30 p.m., Friday; 7:30 and 8 p.m., Saturday; noon, 2 and 6 p.m. Sunday
First Bucks game in arena	November 5, 1988

2003-04 REVIEW

RESULTS

OCTOBER
29— at Minnesota	*89 -95	0 -1
31— at Indiana	93 -79	1 -1

NOVEMBER
1 — Chicago	98 -68	2 -1
4 — L.A. Lakers	*107 -113	2 -2
5 — at New York	106 -90	3 -2
7 — at Detroit	*99 -105	3 -3
8 — New York	90 -87	4 -3
12— Seattle	*99 -104	4 -4
15— Utah	100 -95	5 -4
18— Atlanta	*93 -101	5 -5
19— at Denver	*86 -94	5 -6
21— at Utah	*90 -99	5 -7
23— at Toronto	82 -62	6 -7
25— Philadelphia	95 -91	7 -7
28— at Boston	*96 -106	7 -8
29— Boston	100 -94	8 -8

DECEMBER
1 — at Chicago	*87 -97	8 -9
2 — at Atlanta	106 -94	9 -9
5 — at New Jersey	*86 -93	9 -10
6 — Washington	*109 -114	†9 -11
8 — at New Orleans	*85 -91	9 -12
10— Golden State	94 -89	†10 -12
12— Chicago	109 -95	11 -12
14— at Seattle	*102 -108	11 -13
16— at Portland	106 -99	12 -13
17— at L.A. Clippers	*83 -93	12 -14
20— New Jersey	92 -87	13 -14

23— Detroit	83 -78	14 -14
26— Indiana	101 -96	15 -14
28— at San Antonio	*74 -89	15 -15
30— at Dallas	*92 -101	15 -16

JANUARY
2 — Dallas	109 -101	16 -16
4 — at Washington	100 -94	17 -16
5 — at Philadelphia	88 -76	18 -16
7 — Phoenix	95 -87	19 -16
9 — Miami	103 -94	20 -16
10— at New York	*88 -94	20 -17
13— Boston	111 -103	21 -17
15— New Jersey	86 -83	22 -17
17— Detroit	*94 -99	22 -18
19— at Orlando	*99 -106	22 -19
21— Orlando	113 -102	23 -19
23— Toronto	98 -86	24 -19
26— San Antonio	93 -92	25 -19
28— at New Orleans	*100 -101	25 -20
30— Cleveland	101 -95	26 -20
31— at Atlanta	*83 -93	26 -21

FEBRUARY
4 — at Houston	*89 -103	26 -22
6 — at Memphis	*85 -105	26 -23
7 — New Orleans	107 -97	27 -23
10— Sacramento	*117 -124	27 -24
17— Orlando	127 -104	28 -24
18— at Detroit	*98 -102	28 -25
21— L.A. Clippers	*103 -105	28 -26
22— at Washington	113 -85	29 -26

24— Minnesota	*102 -108	29 -27
25— at Boston	106 -104	30 -27
27— Memphis	106 -104	31 -27
29— Miami	108 -104	32 -27

MARCH
3 — at Orlando	105 -97	33 -27
4 — at Miami	*98 -104	33 -28
6 — at Cleveland	*97 -106	33 -29
8 — at Philadelphia	*92 -97	33 -30
10— Atlanta	94 -80	34 -30
12— Denver	*111 -117	34 -31
14— New York	*100 -103	34 -32
16— Portland	*99 -100	34 -33
20— at Phoenix	*111 -123	34 -34
21— at L.A. Lakers	*103 -104	†34 -35
23— at Sacramento	112 -101	35 -35
24— at Golden State	*89 -98	35 -36
26— at Chicago	115 -105	36 -36
28— Houston	*107 -111	†36 -37
30— Indiana	95 -86	37 -37
31— at Indiana	*78 -111	37 -38

APRIL
2 — Cleveland	107 -89	38 -38
4 — at Toronto	90 -83	39 -38
6 — at New Jersey	103 -98	40 -38
7 — Washington	116 -107	41 -38
10— New Orleans	*87 -92	41 -39
12— at Cleveland	*89 -93	41 -40
14— Toronto	*87 -89	41 -41

*Loss. †Single overtime.

TEAM LEADERS

Points: Michael Redd (1,776).
Field goals made: Redd (633).
Free throws made: Redd (383).
3-pointers made: Redd (127).
Rebounds: Joe Smith (643).
Assists: Damon Jones (478).
Steals: Redd (81).
Blocks: Dan Gadzuric (105).

RECORDS

Regular season: 41-41 (tied, 3rd in Central); 15-13 in division; 33-21 in conference; 8-20 vs. Western Conference; 27-14 at home; 14-27 on road; 1-3 in overtime; 5-6 in games decided by three points or less; 16-9 in games decided by 10 points or more; held opponents under 100 points 47 times; held under 100 points 45 times.
Playoffs: 1-4, lost to Pistons, 4-1, in Eastern Conference first round.
All-time franchise record: 1,586-1,334 in 36 seasons. Won one NBA title (1971).
Team record past five years: 218-192 (.532, ranks 12th in NBA in that span).

HIGHLIGHTS

Top players: Michael Redd led the Bucks in scoring (21.7 ppg, 10th in the NBA) as he earned his first All-Star selection. He also was named to the All-NBA Third Team, and he finished 5th in the NBA in points (1,776), 10th in free throws made (383) and 12th in free throw percentage (86.8). ... Desmond Mason was one of the top sixth men in the league by averaging a career-high 14.4 ppg on 47.2 percent shooting. ... Keith Van Horn, acquired from New York on February 15, finished second on the team in scoring (15.7 ppg) in 25 games. He ranked 16th in the league in 3-point percentage (.400) and 17th in free throw percentage (.859). ... Joe Smith led the team in rebounds (8.5 rpg, 18th in NBA) and double-doubles (20). ... T.J. Ford finished second among all rookies and would have finished ninth in the NBA in assists (6.5 apg) if he had met the statistical minimums. He was named to the All-Rookie Second Team. ... Dan Gadzuric led the Bucks in blocks (1.4 bpg, 25th in NBA). ... Damon Jones started at point guard after the injury to Ford and was 14th in assists (5.8 apg) and second in assists-to-turnover ratio (4.64-to-1) in the NBA.

Key injuries: The Bucks lost a total of 127 player games because of injury or illness. Ford missed 26 games with a back injury. Brian Skinner missed 25 games with a left knee injury, and Toni Kukoc missed nine games with back spasms. Redd, Mason and Jones were the only players to appear in all 82 games.
Notable: Under first-year coach Terry Porter, the Bucks finished tied for third in the Central Division at 41-41, earning a playoff berth for the fifth time in six seasons and the 24th time in the team's 36-year history. Porter was the first coach since Rick Carlisle (Detroit) and Maurice Cheeks (Portland) in 2001-02 to guide his team to a playoff berth in his first season. ... The Bucks led the Eastern Conference in scoring (98.0 ppg) and ranked fourth in the league. ... Milwaukee ranked first in the Eastern Conference and third overall in fewest turnovers per game (13.0). ... The Bucks won their 100th playoff game in franchise history by defeating Detroit 92-88 at the Palace in Game 2. ... Milwaukee was the first road team to win a game in the 2004 playoffs.

– 39 –

MINNESOTA TIMBERWOLVES
NORTHWEST DIVISION

Timberwolves Schedule
Home games shaded; *—All-Star Game at Denver.

November
SUN	MON	TUE	WED	THU	FRI	SAT
	1	2	3 NYK	4 DEN	5	6 NO
7	8	9 IND	10	11 HOU	12	13
14	15	16 MIA	17 DET	18	19	20 NO
21	22 DAL	23 SEA	24	25 IND	26 MEM	27
28 SAC	29	30				

December
SUN	MON	TUE	WED	THU	FRI	SAT
		1 GS	2	3 PHO	4 LAC	
5	6	7 DAL	8 PHI	9	10 SAC	11 CHI
12	13	14 POR	15 TOR	16	17 LAC	18
19	20	21 CLE	22	23 SA	24	25
26 WAS	27	28	29 NYK	30	31	

January
SUN	MON	TUE	WED	THU	FRI	SAT
						1 MEM
2	3	4 PHO	5 CHA	6	7 PHI	8 WAS
9	10 LAL	11	12 ORL	13	14 DEN	15 POR
16	17 TOR	18	19 LAL	20	21 SEA	22 POR
23	24 DET	25	26 ATL	27	28 UTH	29
30 SAC	31					

February
SUN	MON	TUE	WED	THU	FRI	SAT
		1 MIL	2 PHO	3	4 HOU	5
6 BOS	7	8 MEM	9 DEN	10	11 UTH	12
13 CHI	14	15 NJN	16	17 CLE	18	19
20 *All-Star	21	22	23	24 LAC	25 SEA	26
27 POR	28					

March
SUN	MON	TUE	WED	THU	FRI	SAT
		1	2 GS	3	4 MIL	5
6 BOS	7	8 CHA	9	10 MIA	11 ORL	12
13 DAL	14	15 DAL	16 SA	17	18 MEM	19
20 HOU	21	22	23 NO	24	25	26 NJN
27 LAC	28	29	30	31 LAL		

April
SUN	MON	TUE	WED	THU	FRI	SAT
					1 PHO	2
3 SAC	4	5	6 UTH	7	8 DEN	9 ATL
10	11	12	13 GS	14	15 UTH	16
17 SEA	18 NO	19	20 SA	21	22	23

2004-05 SEASON

TEAM DIRECTORY

Owner . . . . .Glen Taylor
President . . . . .Rob Moor
Executive VP/Chief Financial Officer . .Roger Griffith
VP of Basketball Operations . . . . . . .Kevin McHale
General Manager . . . . .Jim Stack
Head Coach . . . . .Flip Saunders
Director of Scouting and
Player Personnel/Assistant Coach . . . .Jerry Sichting
Assistant Coaches . . . . .Randy Wittman,
Sid Lowe, Don Zierden
Trainer . . . . .Gregg Farnam
Strength and Conditioning Coach . . . .Thomas McKinney
Senior VP & Chief Marketing Officer . .Chris Wright
Vice President of Corporate Sales . . . .Conrad Smith
Controller . . . . .Jean Stankoski
Director of Communications . . . . .Ted Johnson
Director of Corporate Sales . . . . .Ethan Casson
Director of Fan Relations . . . . .Jeff Munneke
Director of Marketing . . . . .Jason LaFrenz
Director of Ticket Sales . . . . .Bryant Pfeiffer
Director of Broadcasting . . . . .Skip Krueger
Director of Security . . . . .Bob Goedderz
Manager of Public Relations . . . . . . .Mike Cristaldi
Assistant Manager of Public Relations .Paul Thompson
Manager of Corporate Services . . . . .Scott Coleman
Manager of Game Operations . . . . . . .Greg Vanderwilt
Production Manager . . . . .John Schissel
Suite Sales Manager . . . . .Kristen Rose
Box Office Manager . . . . .Molly Tomczak
Community Foundation Manager . . . . .Terrell Battle
Advertising Manager . . . . .Liz Hogenson
Information Systems Manager . . . . . . .Jeff Creamer
Publications Manager . . . . .Dan Bell
Human Resources Manager . . . . .Chris Johnson
Internet Managing Editor . . . . .Crystal Colby
Medical Director . . . . .Sheldon Burns, M.D.
Orthopedic Surgeon . . . . .David Fischer, M.D

Glen Taylor

Kevin McHale

Flip Saunders

ROSTER
Coach—Phil "Flip" Saunders
Assistant coaches—Randy Wittman, Sid Lowe, Jerry Sichting, Don Zierden

No.	Name	Pos.	Ht./Wt.	Metric (m/kg)	Born	College/country
19	Sam Cassell	G	6-3/185	1.90/83.9	11-18-69	Florida State
44	Ndudi Ebi	F	6-9/200	2.05/90.7	6-21-78	Westbury Christian HS
21	Kevin Garnett	F	6-11/240	2.10/108.4	5-19-76	Farragut Academy HS
23	Trenton Hassell	G	6-5/200	1.96/90.7	3-4-79	Austin Peay
32	Fred Hoiberg	G	6-5/210	1.96/95.3	10-15-72	Iowa State
16	Troy Hudson	G	6-1/175	1.85/79.4	3-13-76	Southern Illinois
40	Ervin Johnson	C	6-11/255	2.10/115.7	12-21-67	New Orleans
35	Mark Madsen	F	6-9/245	2.05/111.1	1-28-76	Stanford
34	Michael Olowokandi	C	7-0/270	2.13/122.5	4-3-75	Pacific
8	Latrell Sprewell	G/F	6-5/195	1.96/88.4	9-8-70	Alabama
10	Wally Szczerbiak	F	6-7/235	2.00/106.6	3-5-77	Miami (Ohio)

BROADCAST INFORMATION

Radio: KFAN (1130 AM). Broadcasters: Chad Hartman, TBA.
TV: KSTC-TV. Broadcasters: Tom Hanneman, Jim Petersen.
Cable TV: Fox Sports Net. Broadcasters: Tom Hanneman, Jim Petersen.

TEAM INFORMATION

Team address . . . . .600 First Ave. North
                                            Minneapolis, MN 55403
Business phone 612-673-1600
Ticket information . . . . .612-673-1645, ext. 1
Website .www.timberwolves.com
Arena (capacity) . . . . .Target Center (19,356)
Game times . . . . .7 p.m., Monday-Saturday;
                                            2, 2:30 and 7 p.m., Sunday
First Timberwolves game in arena . .November 2, 1990

Minnesota Timberwolves

2004-05 SEASON

2003-04 REVIEW

RESULTS

OCTOBER
29— Milwaukee	95 -89	1 -0	
31— at New Jersey	*61 -84	1 -1	

NOVEMBER
1 — Toronto	73 -56	2 -1	
3 — at Utah	*88 -93	2 -2	
5 — Sacramento	*121 -125	†2 -3	
7 — at Orlando	100 -71	3 -3	
8 — at Miami	88 -79	4 -3	
11— Seattle	*87 -89	4 -4	
13— at Chicago	92 -89	†5 -4	
14— Utah	*77 -85	5 -5	
18— Denver	89 -76	6 -5	
21— at Cleveland	97 -83	7 -5	
22— L.A. Clippers	103 -91	8 -5	
25— at Indiana	*75 -98	8 -6	
26— New York	*92 -97	8 -7	
28— at Memphis	102 -98	9 -7	
29— at Dallas	*88 -92	9 -8	

DECEMBER
3 — at Phoenix	92 -79	10-8	
5 — at Sacramento	112 -109	†11-8	
7 — at L.A. Clippers	96 -94	12-8	
9 — Golden State	*95 -98	12-9	
12— at Washington	110 -91	13-9	
15— at Boston	116 -95	14-9	
16— Houston	92 -75	15-9	
18— Dallas	114 -109	16-9	
20— Indiana	102 -80	17-9	
23— at New York	98 -92	18-9	

JANUARY
26— at Portland	*92 -101	18 -10	
27— at Seattle	104 -86	19 -10	
30— Chicago	98 - 93	20 -10	
2 — Atlanta	93 -75	21 -10	
3 — at Dallas	*112 -119	21 -11	
6 — L.A. Lakers	106 -90	22 -11	
8 — Portland	96 -75	23 -11	
10— Miami	83 -77	24 -11	
13— at New Orleans	94 -89	25 -11	
14— at San Antonio	100 -93	26 -11	
17— at Houston	*76 -95	26 -12	
19— New Orleans	97 -90	27 -12	
21— at Toronto	108 -97	28 -12	
23— Detroit	80 -79	29 -12	
25— Phoenix	99 -95	30 -12	
26— at Denver	97 -95	31 -12	
28— at Golden State	*90 -97	31 -13	
30— at L.A. Lakers	97 -84	32 -13	

FEBRUARY
1 — Philadelphia	106 -101	33 -13	
3 — Orlando	113 -100	34 -13	
4 — at Atlanta	*89 -97	34 -14	
6 — Cleveland	103 -92	35 -14	
8 — Memphis	*98 -99	35 -15	
10— L.A. Clippers	96 -84	36 -15	
11— at Utah	77 -66	37 -15	
17— Phoenix	110 -95	38 -15	
19— Sacramento	92 -75	39 -15	
20— at Detroit	88 -87	40 -15	

(continued)
22— San Antonio	*92 -94	40 -16	
24— at Milwaukee	108 -102	41 -16	
25— New Jersey	81 -68	42 -16	
27— Golden State	91 -81	43 -16	
29— at Philadelphia	*74 -81	43 -17	

MARCH
3 — Dallas	121 -97	44 -17	
5 — Houston	*109 -112	44 -18	
7 — Boston	*77 -80	44 -19	
9 — at Seattle	105 -92	45 -19	
10— at Portland	*79 -92	45 -20	
12— L.A. Lakers	96 -86	46 -20	
14— Portland	*83 -92	46 -21	
18— at San Antonio	*86 -106	46 -22	
19— at Phoenix	93 -80	47 -22	
21— Denver	98 -77	48 -22	
23— San Antonio	86 -81	49 -22	
24— at Denver	*92 -101	49 -23	
26— at L.A. Lakers	*73 -90	49 -24	
27— at L.A. Clippers	98 -82	50 -24	
29— at Houston	94 -88	51 -24	
31— Seattle	90 -83	52 -24	

APRIL
2 — Washington	91 -73	53 -24	
4 — Memphis	90 -82	54 -24	
8 — at Sacramento	94 -86	55 -24	
9 — at Golden State	92 -74	56 -24	
12— Utah	104 -90	57 -24	
14— at Memphis	107 -90	58 -24	

*Loss. †Single overtime.

TEAM LEADERS

Points: Kevin Garnett (1,987).
Field goals made: Garnett (804).
Free throws made: Garnett (368).
3-pointers made: Latrell Sprewell (99).
Rebounds: Garnett (1,139).
Assists: Sam Cassell (592).
Steals: Garnett (120).
Blocks: Garnett (178).

RECORDS

Regular season: 58-24 (1st in Midwest Division); 14-10 in division; 34-18 in conference; 24-6 vs. Eastern Conference; 31-10 at home; 27-14 on road; 2-1 in overtime; 6-6 in games decided by three points or fewer; 34-6 in games decided by 10 points or more; held opponents under 100 points 71 times; held under 100 points 58 times.
Playoffs: 10-8, defeated Nuggets, 4-1, in Western Conference first round; defeated Kings, 4-3, in Western Conference semifinals; lost to Lakers, 4-2, in Western Conference finals.
All-time franchise record: 518-680 in 15 seasons.
Team record past five years: 256-154 (.624, ranks 5th in NBA in that span).

HIGHLIGHTS

Top players: Kevin Garnett posted career highs in scoring (24.2 ppg, 3rd in the NBA) and rebounds (13.9 rpg, 1st). He averaged 5.0 apg (24th) for his fifth consecutive 20/10/5 season; he and Larry Bird are the only players to do so. Garnett finished with 1,987 points and 1,139 rebounds, becoming the fifth player in NBA history to lead the league in both categories. He set 11 franchise records, including those for points, rebounds, point-rebound double-doubles (71), 20-point games (67) and blocked shots (178). He was named Western Conference Player of the Month four times, the first player in the award's 25-year history to do so. ... Sam Cassell had career bests in points per game (19.8, 18th in the NBA), field-goal (48.8, 15th) and 3-point percentage (39.8, 17th). He made his All-Star debut and ranked fifth in the NBA in assists (7.3 apg) and 11th in free throw accuracy (87.3).
Key injuries: The Timberwolves lost a total of 189 player games because of injury or illness. Wally Szczerbiak missed the first 53 games with a strained plantar fascia in his left foot, and Michael Olowokandi was sidelined for 36 games and underwent arthroscopic surgery on his right knee December 12. Troy Hudson missed 45 games with a sprained right ankle and the final seven with a sprained left ankle. Garnett and Latrell Sprewell were the only players to appear in every game.
Notable: Minnesota finished with its best record ever (58-24) and made the playoffs for the eighth consecutive year. ... The Timberwolves captured their first Midwest Division title and posted playoff series wins against Denver and Sacramento before losing in the Western Conference Finals to the Lakers. ... Minnesota was 21-3 when scoring 100-plus points and 53-18 when allowing fewer than 100 points. ... The Timberwolves ranked second in the NBA in field-goal accuracy (.462) and finished fourth by holding opponents to 41.4 percent from the floor. ... Minnesota had a 14-game home winning streak, the best in the NBA. ... Garnett was the NBA's MVP and was All-NBA First Team and All-Defensive First Team. ... Cassell was All-NBA Second Team.

– 41 –

NEW JERSEY NETS
ATLANTIC DIVISION

Nets Schedule
Home games shaded; *—All-Star Game at Denver.

November

SUN	MON	TUE	WED	THU	FRI	SAT
	1	2	3 MIA	4	5 CHI	6 PHO
7	8	9 POR	10 PHI	11	12	13 DAL
14 HOU	15	16	17 SEA	18	19	20 WAS
21	22	23 DEN	24	25 LAC	26 SEA	27
28 POR	29	30 CHA				

December

SUN	MON	TUE	WED	THU	FRI	SAT
			1 WAS	2	3	4 ATL
5	6 TOR	7 CLE	8	9	10 NO	11 ATL
12	13	14 NYK	15	16	17 MEM	18
19 TOR	20	21 CHA	22 CLE	23	24	25
26	27 DET	28 CHI	29	30 IND	31	

January

SUN	MON	TUE	WED	THU	FRI	SAT
						1 NYK
2	3	4 WAS	5 MIL	6	7 GS	8 ORL
9	10	11 DET	12	13 HOU	14	15 DAL
16 ATL	17	18	19 MIL	20	21 BOS	22
23 PHO	24	25 SAC	26 GS	27	28 LAL	29 UTH
30	31					

February

SUN	MON	TUE	WED	THU	FRI	SAT
		1 CHI	2 BOS	3	4	5 DET
6	7 PHI	8	9 LAL	10	11 SA	12
13 DEN	14	15 MIN	16 SAC	17	18	19
20 *All-Star	21	22 TOR	23 MIL	24	25 CHA	26
27 CLE	28					

March

SUN	MON	TUE	WED	THU	FRI	SAT
		1	2 PHI	3 MIA	4	5 ORL
6	7	8 SA	9 NO	10	11	12 MIA
13 ORL	14	15	16 CHI	17	18 UTH	19
20 IND	21	22 IND	23	24 MEM	25	26 MIN
27 CHA	28	29	30 LAC	31		

April

SUN	MON	TUE	WED	THU	FRI	SAT
					1 NYK	2 ORL
3	4	5 CLE	6	7 NYK	8	9 BOS
10	11	12	13 IND	14	15 TOR	16
17 PHI	18	19 WAS	20 BOS	21	22	23

2004-05 SEASON

TEAM DIRECTORY

EXECUTIVE MANAGEMENT
Chief Executive Officer ....Rod Thorn
Chief Financial Officer ....Gordon Lavalette
Vice President of Sales and Marketing ....Leo Ehrline
Vice President of Operations ....Mark Gheduzzi
Vice President of Public Relations ....Gary Sussman

BASKETBALL OPERATIONS
General Manager ....Ed Stefanski
Head Coach ....Lawrence Frank
Assistant Coach ....Brian Hill
Assistant Coach ....John Kuester
Assistant Coach ....Tom Barrise
Advance Scout ....Travis Hyland
Athletic Trainer ....Tim Walsh
Assistant Trainer/Equipment Manager ....Drew Graham
Strength Coach ....Rich Dalatri
Assistant Strength Coach ....Phil Keplar
Director of Basketball Administration ....Bobby Marks
Basketball Administrative Assistant ....Ian Rubel
Director of Video Operations ....Mitch Kaufman
Video Coordinator ....Travis Hyland

ADMINISTRATION
Director of Facility Operations ....Jun Yasunaga
Operations Assistants ....Lewis Gibbons, Victor Liu
Executive Assistant ....Natalie Canto
Receptionist ....Crystal Anderson

COMMUNITY RELATIONS
Director of Community Relations ....Michele Alongi
Community Relations Assistant ....Joan Twine

CORPORATE SALES
Executive Director of Corporate Sales ....Joe Hockenjos
Senior Director of Corporate Sales ....Lou Terminello
Director of Corporate Sales ....Mitch Hall
Sponsorship Coordinators ....John Alfano, Eric Perugini

ENTERTAINMENT DEVELOPMENT
Director of Game Presentation ....Jennifer MacLure
Manager, Game Presentation ....Paul Kamras
Coordinator, Game Presentation ....Rich Mallon

FINANCE
Controller ....Paul Koehler
Staff Accountants ....Kimberly Blanco, Janet
   Dally, Michael Lysak
Finance Assistant ....Rachel Jones

MARKETING/COMMUNICATIONS
Director of Marketing ....Matt Pazaras
Marketing Manager ....Shauna Sikorski
Manager of Broadcast Operations ....Chris Carrino
Manager of Publications/Website ....Jennifer Epstein
Marketing Assistant ....Nikia Bynum

MIS
Director of Information Technology ....Mimi Viau
IT Assistant ....Jay Knutsen

PUBLIC RELATIONS
Assistant Director of Public Relations ....Aaron Harris
Public Relations Assistant ....Jeff Slavinsky

TICKET OPERATIONS
Director, Ticket Operations ....Daniel Harris
Ticketing Coordinators ....Gail Bryant, Debbie
   Ramos, Millie Roman

TICKET SALES
Director of Ticket Sales ....Fred Mangione
Account Managers ....Joe Cominski, Nick
   DeSimone, Scott Elkisch, Brett Fischer, Catherine Getty, Mark Higuera, Peter
   Juncaj, Cedric King, Rick Lottermann, Joe Mantia, Patrick Quinn, Brent Rogol,
   Tony Wollerman, Jasmine Zamanian
Director of Group Sales ....Frank Sullivan
Group Sales Managers ....Rich Davis, Rich Larcara,
   Ashwin Puri
Telemarketing Supervisors ....Stan Dombrowski, Drew Green
Ticket Sales Receptionist ....Nicole Jones

TICKET SERVICES
Director, Ticket Services ....Michael West
Manager of Premier Services ....Jack Lensky
Ticket Services Coordinator ....Christine Gillespie,
   Kristen Keane, Mark Laqui, Michael Verna

Rod Thorn

Lawrence Frank

ROSTER
Coach—Lawrence Frank
Assistant coach—Brian Hill, John Kuester, Tom Barrise

No.	Name	Pos.	Ht./Wt.	Metric (m/kg)	Born	College/country
	Rodney Buford	G/F	6-5/195	1.96/85.7	11-2-77	Creighton
35	Jason Collins	C	7-0/255	2.13/115.7	12-2-78	Stanford
7	Kyle Davis	C	6-10//235	2.08/106.6	6-3-82	Auburn
12	Lucious Harris	G	6-5/205	1.96/93.0	12-18-70	Long Beach State
24	Richard Jefferson	F	6-7/222	2.00/100.7	6-21-80	Arizona
5	Jason Kidd	G	6-4/210	1.93/95.3	3-23-73	California
	Nenad Krstic	F/C	6-11/210	2.10/95.3	7-25-83	Serbia-Montenegro
1	Ron Mercer	G/F	6-7/210	2.00/95.3	5-18-76	Kentucky
33	Alonzo Mourning	C	6-10/261	2.08/118.4	2-8-70	Georgetown
10	Zoran Planinic	G	6-7/195	2.00/88.4	9-12-82	Croatia
21	Brian Scalabrine	F	6-9/235	2.05/106.6	3-18-78	Southern California
11	Jacque Vaughn	G	6-1/190	1.85/86.2	2-11-75	Kansas
34	Aaron Williams	F/C	6-9/240	2.05/108.4	10-2-71	Xavier
55	Eric Williams	F	6-8/220	2.03/99.8	7-17-72	Providence

BROADCAST INFORMATION
Radio: WFAN (660 AM). Broadcasters: Chris Carrino, Tim Capstraw.
Cable TV: YES Network. Broadcasters: Ian Eagle, Kelly Tripucka.

TEAM INFORMATION

Team address	.390 Murray Hill Parkway
	East Rutherford, NJ 07073
Business phone	.201-935-8888
Fax	.201-935-1088
Website	.www.njnets.com
Arena (capacity)	.Continental Airlines Arena (20,174)
Game time	.7:30 p.m.
First Nets game in arena	.October 30, 1981

2003-04 REVIEW
RESULTS

OCTOBER
29— at Toronto	*87 -90	0 -1
31— Minnesota	84 -61	1 -1

NOVEMBER
1 — at Washington	98 -85	2 -1
4 — Houston	*75 -86	2 -2
6 — Indiana	*81 -87	2 -3
7 — at Boston	94 -87	3 -3
9 — at Detroit	*84 -98	3 -4
12— San Antonio	*71 -85	3 -5
14— New York	85 -80	4 -5
15— at Atlanta	100 -85	5 -5
18— New Orleans	*85 -88	5 -6
22— Toronto	*80 -81	5 -7
25— at Seattle	93 -70	6 -7
27— at L.A. Clippers	102 -96	7 -7
28— at Portland	*93 -97	7 -8
30— at Sacramento	*92 -105	7 -9

DECEMBER
1 — at Utah	*84 -91	7 -10
3 — Memphis	*93 -96	7 -11
5 — Milwaukee	93 -86	8 -11
6 — Phoenix	99 -88	9 -11
9 — Seattle	101 -88	10 -11
12— at Orlando	99 -95	11 -11
13— at Memphis	*63 -110	11 -12
17— Utah	87 -74	12 -12
19— Washington	97 -87	13 -12
20— at Milwaukee	*87 -92	13 -13
23— Chicago	95 -78	14 -13

26— at Detroit	82 -79	15 -13
27— at Indiana	82 -75	16 -13
29— Portland	*87 -91	16 -14
31— Golden State	88 -70	17 -14

JANUARY
2 — Cleveland	97 -82	18 -14
4 — at New York	95 -85	19 -14
6 — L.A. Clippers	92 -75	20 -14
9 — at Philadelphia	*81 -97	20 -15
14— Washington	115 -103	21 -15
15— at Milwaukee	*83 -86	21 -16
17— Indiana	*84 -90	21 -17
20— at Dallas	*93 -106	21 -18
21— at San Antonio	*76 -99	21 -19
23— at Miami	*64 -85	21 -20
25— Boston	110 -91	22 -20
27— at Philadelphia	94 -76	23 -20
29— at Orlando	80 79	24 -20
31— at Houston	88 -77	25 -20

FEBRUARY
2 — at New Orleans	91 -70	26 -20
4 — Miami	99 -88	27 -20
6 — Orlando	120 -99	28 -20
8 — Philadelphia	99 -87	29 -20
10— Detroit	89 -78	30 -20
11— at Cleveland	105 -85	31 -20
18— Atlanta	98 -92	32 -20
20— at Toronto	91 -72	33 -20
21— New Orleans	97 -84	34 -20
24— Toronto	86 -74	35 -20

25— at Minnesota	*68 -81	35 -21
28— Miami	92 -86	36 -21
29— L.A. Lakers	*83 -100	36 -22

MARCH
2 — at Denver	95 -91	37 -22
3 — at Phoenix	*74 -87	37 -23
5 — at Golden State	78 -74	38 -23
7 — at L.A. Lakers	*88 -94	38 -24
10— Denver	98 -97	39 -24
12— Chicago	88 -76	40 -24
14— at Miami	*95 -104	40 -25
16— Sacramento	94 -77	41 -25
18— Detroit	*71 -89	41 -26
19— at New York	*65 -79	41 -27
21— Dallas	*98 -101	41 -28
23— at Chicago	84 -81	42 -28
26— at Boston	*93 -102	42 -29
27— at Cleveland	*104 -107	42 -30
29— Boston	*80 -84	42 -31
31— at Washington	103 -99	†43 -31

APRIL
2 — New York	108 -83	44 -31
4 — Atlanta	106 -89	45 -31
6 — Milwaukee	*98 -103	45 -32
8 — Orlando	101 -81	46 -32
9 — at Indiana	*80 -90	46 -33
11— Philadelphia	89 -75	47 -33
12— at Atlanta	*107 -129	47 -34
14— at Miami	*84 -96	47 -35

*Loss. †Single overtime.

TEAM LEADERS
Points: Richard Jefferson (1,515).
Field goals made: Jefferson (555).
Free throws made: Jefferson (357).
3-pointers made: Kerry Kittles (97).
Rebounds: Kenyon Martin (617).
Assists: Jason Kidd (618).
Steals: Kittles (125).
Blocks: Martin (82).

RECORDS
Regular season: 47-35 (1st in Atlantic Division); 18-7 in division; 34-20 in conference; 13-15 vs. Western Conference; 28-13 at home; 19-22 on road; 1-0 in overtime; 3-7 in games decided by three points or fewer; 33-17 in games decided by 10 points or more; held opponents under 100 points 71 times; held under 100 points 69 times.
Playoffs: 7-4, defeated Knicks, 4-0, in Eastern Conference first round; lost to Pistons, 4-3, in Eastern Conference semifinals.
All-time franchise record: 950-1314 in 28 NBA seasons; 374-370 in nine ABA seasons.
Team record past five years: 205-205 (.500, tied for 15th in NBA in that span).

HIGHLIGHTS
Top players: Jason Kidd led the Nets in assists (9.2 apg, 1st in NBA) and steals (1.82 spg) and finished second in minutes per game (36.6), rebounds per game (6.4) and 3-pointers made (94) and third in points per game (15.5) and total minutes (2,450). He ranked first in the NBA in triple-doubles (9), 12th in assists-per-turnover ratio (2.89-to-1) and tied for 13th in double-doubles (34). He led the league in assists for the fifth time and became the first Nets player to lead the NBA in assists in back-to-back years. He scored his 10,000th point against the Washington Wizards in the third quarter on December 19 and became one of 23 players (five active) in NBA history with 10,000 points and 6,000 assists. ... Richard Jefferson ranked first on the team in points (a career-high 18.5 ppg) and minutes (38.2) and third in rebounds (5.7) on 49.8 percent shooting (12th in NBA). He ranked 17th in the NBA in minutes per game.
Key injuries: The Nets lost a total of 270 player games because of injury or illness. Alonzo Mourning missed 70 games with focal glomerulosclerosis. Kidd missed 15 games with injury—nine with a sore left knee and four with a bone bruise in his left knee. Lucious Harris missed 13 games with injury—12 games with lower back spasms and one with a sprained left ankle.
Notable: The Nets finished the regular season 47-35 and won the Atlantic Division for the third time in franchise history. They lost in the second round to the NBA Champion Detroit Pistons but made the playoffs in three consecutive years for the first time since 1991-94. ... The Nets tied their best road record in franchise history at 19-22 and recorded the best winning percentage in a month in franchise history in February, when they went 11-2 (.846). Their 10 straight victories by 10 or more points from January 25th to February 11th tied an NBA record held by the 1946-47 Washington Capitals. ... In his first full month on the job, Lawrence Frank was named February's Eastern Conference Coach of the Month. ... Kidd became the first Nets player to be selected to three consecutive All-Star games. He also earned spots on the All-NBA First Team and All-Defensive Second Team.

NEW ORLEANS HORNETS
SOUTHWEST DIVISION

Hornets Schedule
Home games shaded; *—All-Star Game at Denver.

November

SUN	MON	TUE	WED	THU	FRI	SAT
	1	2	3 DAL	4	5 ORL	6 MIN
7	8	9 LAL	10	11	12 ATL	13 MIL
14	15	16	17 PHO	18	19	20 MIN
21	22 UTH	23 GS	24	25	26 PHO	27
28 LAL	29 DEN	30				

December

SUN	MON	TUE	WED	THU	FRI	SAT
			1	2	3	4 DET
5	6	7 HOU	8 NYK	9	10 NJN	11
12 WAS	13	14 CHA	15 GS	16	17 SA	18
19 SAC	20	21 LAC	22 LAL	23	24	25
26 CLE	27 IND	28	29 PHO	30	31	

January

SUN	MON	TUE	WED	THU	FRI	SAT
						1
2	3 BOS	4	5 CHI	6	7 MEM	8 SAC
9	10	11 NYK	12 DET	13	14 POR	15
16 TOR	17 PHI	18	19 IND	20	21	22 LAC
23 MIA	24	25	26 HOU	27	28 PHI	29 SA
30	31 MEM					

February

SUN	MON	TUE	WED	THU	FRI	SAT
		1	2 DAL	3	4 GS	5 UTH
6	7	8 SEA	9 POR	10	11 GS	12
13 ORL	14 WAS	15	16 SA	17	18	19
20 *All-Star	21	22	23 SEA	24	25	26
27 DEN	28 DAL					

March

SUN	MON	TUE	WED	THU	FRI	SAT
		1	2 CHA	3	4 UTH	5
6 TOR	7	8	9 NJN	10	11	12 MIL
13	14 SA	15	16 MEM	17	18 CHI	19 BOS
20	21 DAL	22	23 MIN	24	25 HOU	26 MEM
27	28 CLE	29	30	31		

April

SUN	MON	TUE	WED	THU	FRI	SAT
					1 HOU	2 MIA
3	4	5 ATL	6 DEN	7	8 UTH	9
10 POR	11	12 PHO	13 DEN	14	15 SEA	16 LAC
17	18 MIN	19	20 LAC	21	22 SA	23

2004-05 SEASON
TEAM DIRECTORY

Majority Owner	George Shinn
Minority Owner	Ray Wooldridge
Executive VP/Chief Operating Officer	Jack Capella
Executive VP of Business	Sam Russo
Sr. VP of Marketing & Business Development	John Lee
Sr. VP of Communications & Public Affairs	Steve Martin
VP of Community Relations	Suzanne Werdann
VP of Corp. Affairs & Strategic Planning	Kristy McKearn
VP of Finance	Barbara Booth
VP of Public Relations	Harold Kaufman
VP of Sponsorship Sales	Todd Santino
General Manager	Allan Bristow
Vice President of Basketball Operations	Willis Reed
Director of Player Personnel	Jeff Bower
Head Coach	Byron Scott
Assistant Coaches	Darrell Walker, Jim Cleamons, Kenny Gattison
Trainer/Director of Team Travel	Terry Kofler
College/Pro Scouting	Kip Bass
College Scouting	Kelly Bass
Scout	Robert Werdann
Video Coordinator	Brian Hagen
Strength and Conditioning Coach	Marc Boff
Strength and Core Trainer	Jack Manson
Equipment Manager	David Jovanovic
Sports PR Manager	Scott Hall
Corporate PR Manager	Michael Thompson
Director of Broadcasting	Lew Shuman
Director of Creative Services	Brian Deese
Director of Game Operations	Josh Richardson
Director of Payroll/Personnel	Penny Middleton
Director of Promotions & Special Events	Jessica Dippel
Director of Security	Jimmy Keen
Director of Technology	Tim Spero
Director of Ticket Operations	Dave Felsen
Director of Ticket Sales	Brendan Donohue
Assistant to George Shinn	Meredith Silmon
Assistants to Ray Wooldridge	Winnie Beaucaire and Phyllis Shubert
Executive Assistant, Basketball Ops	JoAnn LaCaze
Director of Basketball Administration	Andrew Loomis
Executive Assistant	Kristy Fitzpatrick

George Shinn

Allan Bristow

Byron Scott

ROSTER
Coach—Byron Scott
Assistant coaches—Darrell Walker, Jim Cleamons, Kenny Gattison

No.	Name	Pos.	Ht./Wt.	Metric (m/kg)	Born	College/country
12	Chris Andersen	F/C	6-10/220	2.08/99.8	7-7-78	Blinn J.C.
10	Darrell Armstrong	G	6-1/180	1.85/81.6	6-22-68	Fayetteville State
42	P.J. Brown	F	6-11/239	2.10/108.0	10-14-69	Louisiana Tech
1	Baron Davis	G	6-3/223	1.90/101.2	4-13-79	UCLA
20	Alex Garcia	G/F	6-3/195	1.90/88.4	3-4-80	Brazil
9	George Lynch	F	6-8/235	2.03/106.6	9-3-70	North Carolina
21	Jamaal Magloire	C	6-11/259	2.10/117.5	5-21-78	Kentucky
24	Jamal Mashburn	F	6-8/247	2.03/112.0	11-29-72	Kentucky
22	Tim Pickett	G	6-4/207	1.93/88.5	4-18-81	Florida State
54	Rodney Rogers	F	6-7/255	2.00/115.7	6-20-71	Wake Forest
23	J.R. Smith	G	6-6/220	1.98/99.8	9-9-85	St. Benedict's HS
4	David Wesley	G	6-1/203	1.85/92.1	11-14-70	Baylor
30	David West	F	6-9/240	2.05/108.0	8-20-80	Xavier

BROADCAST INFORMATION

Radio: WODT (1280 AM), WRNO (99.5 FM).
Broadcasters: Bob Licht, Gerry Vaillancourt.
TV: Cox Sports Television (Channel 37).
Broadcasters: Gil McGregor, Jordy Hultberg.

TEAM INFORMATION

Team address . . . . .1501 Girod St.
New Orleans, LA 70113
Business phone 504-301-4000
Ticket information 504-525-HOOP
Website . . . . .www.hornets.com
Arena (capacity) . . . . .New Orleans Arena (17,200)
Game times . . . . .7:00 p.m.
First Hornets game in arena . . . . . . .October 30, 2002

2003-04 REVIEW

RESULTS

OCTOBER
29— Atlanta	88 -83	†1 -0
30— at Orlando	100 -98	2 -0

NOVEMBER
1 — Boston	97 -90	3 -0
3 — at Atlanta	*80 -90	3 -1
5 — at Philadelphia	106 -99	†4 -1
7 — L.A. Lakers	114 -95	5 -1
8 — Chicago	*106 -109	5 -2
11 — at Dallas	*97 -125	5 -3
12— Utah	96 -89	6 -3
15— Portland	101 -79	7 -3
18— at New Jersey	88 -85	8 -3
19— at Boston	81 -73	9 -3
21— Indiana	*75 -76	9 -4
23— at Detroit	81 -80	10 -4
25— at Miami	*87 -91	10 -5
26— Cleveland	82 -72	11 -5
29— at New York	*74 -79	11 -6

DECEMBER
2 — at Orlando	100 -91	12 -6
3 — Orlando	106 -91	13 -6
5 — Houston	*74 -83	13 -7
6 — at Chicago	97 -91	14 -7
8 — Milwaukee	91 -85	15 -7
11 — at Phoenix	111 -101	16 -7
12— at Golden State	96 -85	17 -7
15— at L.A. Clippers	*80 -109	17 -8
16— at Denver	*94 -116	17 -9
18— Sacramento	*90 -101	17 -10

20— Memphis	94 -89	18 -10
23— at Cleveland	*86 -97	18 -11
26— Atlanta	109 -79	19 -11
29— at Detroit	*99 -108	19 -12
31— at Boston	96 -94	20 -12

JANUARY
2 — at Toronto	86 -74	21 -12
3 — at Indiana	*84 -91	21 -13
7 — Washington	97 -87	22 -13
9 — San Antonio	*84 -94	22 -14
10— at Chicago	*84 -89	22 -15
13— Minnesota	*89 -94	22 -16
15— Toronto	*74 -78	†22 -17
17— Orlando	91 -90	23 -17
19— at Minnesota	*90 -97	23 -18
21— Philadelphia	*86 -92	23 -19
23— Denver	97 -91	24 -19
24— at San Antonio	98 -96	25 -19
28— Milwaukee	101 -100	26 -19
30— at Philadelphia	*82 -85	26 -20
31— Miami	*70 -94	26 -21

FEBRUARY
2 — New Jersey	*70 -91	26 -22
4 — Dallas	*104 -113	26 -23
6 — Detroit	92 -81	27 -23
7 — at Milwaukee	*97 -107	27 -24
11 — New York	106 -98	28 -24
17— at Indiana	89 -75	29 -24
18— Washington	120 -98	30 -24
21— at New Jersey	*84 -97	30 -25

23— at Cleveland	*100 -104	30 -26
25— L.A. Clippers	99 -93	31 -26
27— Indiana	89 -77	32 -26
28— at Memphis	*92 -97	32 -27

MARCH
1 — at Washington	*106 -111	†32 -28
3 — Chicago	100 -97	†33 -28
5 — Cleveland	*85 -88	33 -29
7 — at Toronto	*76 -84	33 -30
10— Miami	95 -84	34 -30
11 — at Houston	*86 -97	34 -31
13— Golden State	102 -84	35 -31
16— at Miami	*83 -96	35 -32
17— Philadelphia	104 -80	36 -32
19— Seattle	*80 -91	36 -33
21— Toronto	*120 -121	†36 -34
23— Detroit	82 -81	37 -34
25— at Atlanta	*76 -84	37 -35
26— Phoenix	*94 -99	37 -36
30— at L.A. Lakers	*88 -107	37 -37
31— at Utah	*76 -89	37 -38

APRIL
3 — at Portland	94 -81	38 -38
4 — at Seattle	*88 -96	38 -39
6 — at Sacramento	*91 -105	38 -40
9 — Boston	89 -80	39 -40
10— at Milwaukee	92 -87	40 -40
12— New York	*97 -101	40 -41
14— at Washington	94 -78	41 -41

*Loss. †Single overtime.

TEAM LEADERS

Points: Baron Davis (1,532).
Field goals made: Davis (554).
Free throws made: Davis (237).
3-pointers made: Davis (187).
Rebounds: Jamaal Magloire (847).
Assists: Davis (501).
Steals: Davis (158).
Blocks: Magloire (101).

RECORDS

Regular season: 41-41 (tied, 3rd in Central Division); 14-14 in division; 30-24 in conference; 11-17 vs. Western Conference; 25-16 at home; 16-25 on road; 3-3 in overtime; 9-5 in games decided by three points or fewer; 18-17 in games decided by 10 points or more; held opponents under 100 points 66 times; held under 100 points 63 times
Playoffs: 3-4, lost to Heat, 4-3, in Eastern Conference first round.
All-time franchise record: 630-650 in 16 seasons.
Team record past five years: 227-183 (.554, ranks 11th in NBA in that span).

HIGHLIGHTS

Top players: Baron Davis finished sixth in the NBA in scoring (22.9 ppg), fourth in assists (7.5 apg) and first in steals (2.36 spg) to become the third player since 1976-77 to finish in the top 10 in those categories (joining Gary Payton and Michael Adams) and the third Hornet to lead the league in any statistical category. ... Jamal Mashburn averaged 20.8 ppg in 19 games for the Hornets. ... David Wesley was the third-leading scorer (14.0 ppg). ... Jamaal Magloire ranked third in the NBA with 45 double-doubles and averaged career highs in points (13.6) and rebounds (10.3). ... Darrell Armstrong led the bench with 10.6 ppg and finished 11th in the league in steals (1.69 spg).
Key injuries: The Hornets lost a total of 194 player games because of injury or illness. Mashburn missed 63 games, including the first 44 of the season, because of arthroscopic surgery on his right knee. He missed the final 19 games of the season with a patella femoral irritation of his right knee. Davis missed 15 games with a sprained left ankle, and

Wesley sat out 21 contests with a sprained left big toe. Courtney Alexander missed the entire season after he ruptured his right Achilles' tendon in a preseason game.
Notable: The Hornets advanced to the playoffs for the seventh time in eight seasons and clinched their 12th straight season with a .500 or better record with their win in the season finale at Washington. ... Davis made the All-Star team and the All-NBA Third Team, was Eastern Conference Player of the Month for November and set a franchise record for 3-pointers attempted. ... Magloire made his first All-Star appearance and was Eastern Conference Player of the Month for April. He was one of 11 players in the NBA to average a double-double and one of four Hornets all-time to average a point-rebound double-double. ... P.J. Brown won the NBA Sportsmanship Award. ... Wesley scored his 10,000th point on March 25 at Atlanta, becoming one of three players to score 10,000 points after going undrafted (joining John Starks and Moses Malone).

NEW YORK KNICKS
ATLANTIC DIVISION

Knicks Schedule
Home games shaded; *—All-Star Game at Denver.

November

SUN	MON	TUE	WED	THU	FRI	SAT
	1	2	3 MIN	4	5	6 BOS
7	8	9 PHI	10	11	12 LAC	13 IND
14	15	16 SA	17	18 HOU	19 DAL	20
21 CLE	22	23 ATL	24 TOR	25	26	27 TOR
28	29	30 ATL				

December

SUN	MON	TUE	WED	THU	FRI	SAT
			1 MEM	2	3 ORL	4 CHA
5	6	7 MEM	8 NO	9	10 WAS	11
12 DEN	13	14 NJN	15 DET	16	17 PHI	18
19 UTH	20	21 DAL	22 BOS	23	24	25
26 CHA	27 ORL	28	29 MIN	30	31	

January

SUN	MON	TUE	WED	THU	FRI	SAT
						1 NJN
2	3	4 SAC	5 MIA	6	7	8 CLE
9 POR	10	11 NO	12	13	14	15 CHI
16	17 CHI	18	19 TOR	20	21 HOU	22
23 MIL	24	25 PHO	26	27	28 CLE	29 DET
30	31 LAC					

February

SUN	MON	TUE	WED	THU	FRI	SAT
		1 DEN	2	3	4 SAC	5 PHO
6	7 UTH	8	9 MIA	10	11 BOS	12
13 CHA	14 PHI	15	16 MIL	17	18	19
20 *All-Star	21	22 DET	23	24 PHI	25	26 IND
27	28 LAL					

March

SUN	MON	TUE	WED	THU	FRI	SAT
		1	2	3	4 ORL	5
6 GS	7	8 WAS	9	10	11	12
13 SEA	14	15 MIA	16	17	18 ATL	19 MIA
20	21 SA	22	23 BOS	24	25 SEA	26 POR
27 GS	28	29 LAL	30	31		

April

SUN	MON	TUE	WED	THU	FRI	SAT
					1 NJN	2
3 MIL	4	5 IND	6	7 NJN	8 CHI	9
10 IND	11	12 TOR	13	14 CLE	15	16 CHA
17 ATL	18	19 CHI	20 WAS	21	22	23

2004-05 SEASON

TEAM DIRECTORY

OFFICE OF THE CHAIRMAN, MADISON SQUARE GARDEN
President & CEO, Cablevision Systems Corporation
Chairman, MSG ....James L. Dolan
Vice Chairman, Cablevision Systems Corporation
Vice Chairman, MSG ....Hank J. Ratner
President & Chief Operating Officer, MSG Sports ....Steve Mills
President, Basketball Operations, New York Knicks ....Isiah Thomas
President & General Manager, New York Rangers ....Glen Sather

TEAM EXECUTIVE MANAGEMENT
Governor ....James L. Dolan
President & COO, MSG Sports, Alternate Governor .....Steve Mills
President, Alternate Governor ....Isiah Thomas
Senior Vice President, Marketing & Business Operations .....Anucha Browne Sanders
Senior Vice President, Basketball Affairs ....Frank Murphy
Senior Vice President, Legal Affairs, MSG ....Marc Schoenfeld
Senior Vice President, Finance & Controller, MSG ....John Cudmore
Vice President, Public Relations ....Joe Favorito
Vice President, Marketing ....Jordan Schlachter
Vice President, Community Relations & Fan Development ....Karin Buchholz
Vice President, Sports Team Publicity, MSG ....Dan Schoenberg

MADISON SQUARE GARDEN EXECUTIVE MANAGEMENT
President, MSG Networks ....Mike McCarthy
Executive Vice President, Finance ....Robert Pollichino
Executive Vice President, Ad Sales ....Neil Davis
Executive Vice President, Facilities ....Tim Hassett
Senior Vice President, Sports & Facility Event Sales .....Joel Fisher
Senior Vice President, Communications ....Barry Watkins
Senior Vice President, Team Sales, Tickets/Suites ......Brian Lafemina

BASKETBALL STAFF
Assistant Coach, Player Development ....Greg Brittenham
Head Athletic Trainer ....Mike Saunders
Assistant Athletic Trainer ....Said Hamdan
Video Coordinator ....Matt Harding
Assistant Video Coordinator ....Mike Smith
Team Assistant ....Chris Bernard
Equipment Manager ....Mike Martinez

BASKETBALL OPERATIONS
Assistant General Manager ....Jeff Nix
Director, Pro Player Personnel ....Brendan Suhr
Senior Basketball Consultant ....Dick McGuire
Director, Security ....John Donohue
Director, Team Travel ....Darren Blake
Director, Basketball Administration ....Jamie Mathews
Executive Administrative Assistant ....Catherine O'Gorman
Senior Secretary ....Raquel Burnette
Scouts ....Dell Demps, Gerald Madkins,
Scott McGuire, Walker D. Russell, James Thomas, Steve Yoder
International Scout ....Kevin Wilson
Advance Scout ....Jack Nolan

PUBLIC RELATIONS
Director, Media Relations ....Jonathan Supranowitz
Manager, Public Relations ....Sammy Steinlight
Manager, Public Relations ....Vince Jackson

FINANCE
Senior Staff, Accounting ....Dean Cannizzo, Pat
McDonough, Jeanine McGrory,
Administrative Assistant ....Carrie Delorme

MARKETING
Director, Event Presentation & Broadcasting ....Gary Winkler
Director, Marketing ....Hunter Lochmann
Director, New Media & Technology ....Steven Mau
Director, Entertainment Marketing, MSG ....Petra Pope
Manager, Event Presentation ....Michael Chant
Coordinator, Marketing & Promotions ....Brett Hurwitz
Assistant, Ticket Sales & Events ....Susan Williamson
Administrative Assistant ....Faye Brown

COMMUNITY RELATIONS & FAN DEVELOPMENT
Director, Special Projects & CR Representative ....Cal Ramsey
Director, Field Marketing ....Dan Gladstone
Assistant, Community Relations & Fan Development ......Alexia Katsaounis
Field Marketing Coordinator ....Troy Bowers
Field Marketing Assistant ....Vernon Manuel

MEDICAL STAFF
Team Physician ....Dr. Norman Scott
Team Physician ....Dr. Fred Cushner
Team Dentist ....Dr. George Bergofin

Steve Mills

Isiah Thomas

Lenny Wilkens

ROSTER

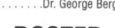

Coach—Lenny Wilkens
Assistant coaches—Mark Aguirre, Greg Brittenham, George Glymph, Dick Helm, Michael Malone, Herb Williams

No.	Name	Pos.	Ht./Wt.	Metric (m/kg)	Born	College/country
49	Shandon Anderson	F	6-6/210	1.98/95.3	12-31-73	Georgia
21	Trevor Ariza	F	6-8/200	2.03/90.7	6-30-85	UCLA
42	Vin Baker	F	6-11/250	2.10/113.4	11-23-71	Hartford
11	Jamal Crawford	G	6-5/190	1.96/86.2	3-20-80	Michigan
1	Anfernee Hardaway	G/F	6-7/215	2.00/97.5	7-18-71	Memphis
20	Allan Houston	G	6-6/205	1.98/93.0	4-20-71	Tennessee
4	DerMarr Johnson	G	6-9/201	2.05/91.2	5-5-80	Cincinnati
3	Stephon Marbury	G	6-2/205	1.88/93.0	2-20-77	Georgia Tech
13	Nazr Mohammed	C	6-10/250	2.08/113.4	9-5-77	Kentucky
25	Moochie Norris	G	6-1/175	1.85/79.4	7-23-73	West Florida
50	Michael Sweetney	F	6-8/275	2.03/124.7	10-25-82	Georgetown
40	Kurt Thomas	F/C	6-9/235	2.05/106.6	10-4-72	Texas Christian
5	Tim Thomas	F	6-10/230	2.08/104.3	2-26-77	Villanova
31	Jerome Williams	F	6-9/206	2.05/93.4	5-10-73	Georgetown

BROADCAST INFORMATION

Radio: ESPN Radio (1050 AM). Broadcasters: TBA. Spanish Radio: WADO (1280 AM). Broadcasters: Alfredo Bejar, Juan Antonio Cains, Clemson Smith-Muniz
Cable TV: MSG Network. Broadcasters: TBA.

TEAM INFORMATION

Team address	Two Pennsylvania Plaza
	New York, NY 10121-0091
Business phone	212-465-6471
Ticket information	877-NYK-DUNK
Website	www.nyknicks.com
Arena (capacity)	Madison Square Garden (19,763)
Game time	7:30 p.m.
First Knicks game in arena	February 14, 1968

2003-04 REVIEW

RESULTS

OCTOBER
29— Orlando	*83 -85	†0 -1	

NOVEMBER
1 — at San Antonio	*74 -86	0 -2
3 — at Orlando	75 -68	1 -2
5 — Milwaukee	*90 -106	1 -3
7 — Sacramento	114 -111	2 -3
8 — at Milwaukee	*87 -90	2 -4
10— at Cleveland	*80 -94	2 -5
14— at New Jersey	*80 -85	2 -6
15— Indiana	*94 -95	2 -7
17— Boston	89 -86	3 -7
19— L.A. Lakers	*83 -104	3 -8
21—at Detroit	*85 -94	3 -9
22— Philadelphia	99 -88	4 -9
24— at Boston	94 -88	5 -9
26— at Minnesota	97 -92	6 -9
27— at Indiana	*70 -93	6 -10
29— New Orleans	79 -74	7 -10

DECEMBER
1 — Detroit	*78 -79	†7 -11
3 — at Seattle	*87 -95	7 -12
5 — at Portland	*81 -88	7 -13
6 — at Golden State	*92 -104	7 -14
9 — at L.A. Lakers	*90 -98	7 -15
10— at Utah	*73 -95	7 -16
13— Denver	95 -88	8 -16
14— Washington	89 -87	9 -16
16— Golden State	*86 -104	9 -17
19— at Toronto	*99 -105	†9 -18

20— Atlanta	103 -92	10 -18
23— Minnesota	*92 -98	10 -19
26— at Memphis	98 -94	11 -19
27— at Miami	100 -80	12 -19
29— at Orlando	114 -86	13 -19
30— Miami	102 -73	14 -19

JANUARY
2 — Chicago	*99 -104	14 -20
4 — New Jersey	*85 - 95	14 -21
6 — at Cleveland	*96 -107	14 -22
8 — Houston	*79 -111	14 -23
10— Milwaukee	94 - 88	15 -23
12— Dallas	*121 -127	†15 -24
14— Orlando	120 -110	16 -24
16— Seattle	108 - 88	17 -24
17— at Chicago	101 - 96	18 -24
19— Toronto	90 - 79	19 -24
21— at Houston	*71 - 86	19 -25
23— at Atlanta	96 - 94	20 -25
24— Miami	*77 - 85	20 -26
27— San Antonio	*67 - 77	20 -27
30— at Boston	92 - 74	21 -27
31— Phoenix	110 -105	22 -27

FEBRUARY
3 — Indiana	97 -90	23 -27
7 — at Miami	76 -64	24 -27
8 — L.A. Clippers	110 -104	25 -27
10— at Dallas	*90 -105	25 -28
11— at New Orleans	*98 -106	25 -29
17— Detroit	92 -88	26 -29

20— Utah	*78 -92	26 -30
22— Cleveland	*86 -92	26 -31
24— at Sacramento	*99 -107	26 -32
25— at Phoenix	*95 -113	26 -33
27— at L.A. Clippers	*94 -96	26 -34
29— at Denver	*96 -107	26 -35

MARCH
3 — Philadelphia	88 -77	27 -35
5 — at Toronto	109 -103	28 -35
7 — at Washington	99 -86	29 -35
9 — Boston	*84 -87	29 -36
12— at Philadelphia	*94 -99	‡29 -37
14— at Milwaukee	103 -100	30 -37
16— Washington	114 -110	†31 -37
19— New Jersey	79 -65	32 -37
20— at Chicago	*81 -87	32 -38
22— Atlanta	96 -84	33 -38
24— Memphis	*97 -111	33 -39
26— Toronto	108 -101	34 -39
27— at Detroit	*85 -100	34 -40
29— Portland	92 - 91	35 -40

APRIL
2 — at New Jersey	*83 -108	35 -41
3 — at Philadelphia	86 -75	36 -41
6 — at Indiana	*86 -107	36 -42
7 — Chicago	96 -82	37 -42
10—at Washington	102 - 98	†38 -42
12—at New Orleans	101 -97	39 -42
14— Cleveland	*90 -100	39 -43

*Loss. †Single overtime. ‡Double overtime.

TEAM LEADERS

Points: Stephon Marbury (931).
Field goals made: Kurt Thomas (392).
Free throws made: Marbury (209).
3-pointers made: Allan Houston (87).
Rebounds: Kurt Thomas (662).
Assists: Marbury (438).
Steals: Shandon Anderson (68).
Blocks: Dikembe Mutombo (123).

RECORDS

Regular season: 39-43 (3rd in Atlantic Division); 17-7 in division; 31-23 in conference; 8-20 vs. Western Conference; 23-18 at home; 16-25 on road; 2-5 in overtime; 6-6 in games decided by three points or fewer; 16-22 in games decided by 10 points or more; held opponents under 100 points 55 times; held under 100 points 65 times.
Playoffs: 0-4, lost to Nets, 4-0, in Eastern Conference first round.
All-time franchise record: 2,310-2,197 in 58 seasons. Won two NBA titles (1970, '73).
Team record past five years: 204-206 (.498, ranks 17th in NBA in that span).

HIGHLIGHTS

Top players: Acquired midseason from Phoenix, Stephon Marbury was the only player to rank among NBA top 20 in scoring (20.2 ppg, 15th), assists (8.9 apg, 2nd), steals (1.59 spg, 15th) and assists-to-turnover ratio (2.89, 13th). He led the NBA in total assists (719). ... Dikembe Mutombo was 14th in the NBA in blocks per game (1.89). ... Allan Houston ranked third in the NBA in free throw pct. (.913). ... Mutombo (November 30) and Marbury (January 18) were honored as Eastern Conference Players of the Week, giving the Knicks two winners for the first time since 1991-92.
Key injuries: The Knicks lost a total of 234 player games because of injury or illness, the 15th highest in the NBA. Houston (back, knee, quad) missed 30 games, as well as the playoffs. Michael Sweetney (patella, 22 games), Mutombo (abdomen, 15 games) and Frank Williams (groin, 13 games) also missed considerable time. Before being traded, Antonio McDyess missed 17 games (knee). Seventeen different Knicks missed at least one game with injury or illness.

Notable: The midseason hirings of president of basketball operations Isiah Thomas and coach Lenny Wilkens and the January 5 deal that landed two-time All-Star Marbury led to the Knicks' first playoff berth since 2001. They finished 39-43 in the regular season. ... The Knicks were swept by New Jersey in the first round of the playoffs. ... With a two-game improvement from 2002-03, the Knicks and Indiana are the only Eastern Conference teams to increase their win totals in each of the past two seasons. ... In addition to Marbury, the midseason roster renovation resulted in acquisitions of Anfernee Hardaway, Vin Baker, Nazr Mohammed, Moochie Norris, DerMarr Johnson and Tim Thomas. ... The Knicks used a franchise-record 22 players during the regular season, and at season's end, seven players remained from the 15-man opening night roster. ... The Knicks were third in the NBA in free throw percentage (.793) and fourth in 3-point percentage (.364). ... The Knicks dedicated the season to the memory of Hall of Famer Dave DeBusschere.

– 47 –

ORLANDO MAGIC
SOUTHEAST DIVISION

Magic Schedule
Home games shaded; *—All-Star Game at Denver.

November

SUN	MON	TUE	WED	THU	FRI	SAT
	1	2	3 MIL	4	5 NO	6 CHA
7	8	9 DAL	10 WAS	11	12 LAL	13
14 PHI	15	16	17 UTH	18	19	20 IND
21	22	23	24 POR	25	26 ATL	27 PHI
28	29 BOS	30				

December

SUN	MON	TUE	WED	THU	FRI	SAT
		1 TOR	2	3 NYK		4 MEM
5 DEN	6	7 UTH	8	9	10 GS	11
12 LAL	13 PHO	14	15 SA	16	17	18 DEN
19 MIA	20	21	22 SA	23	24	25
26	27 NYK	28	29 MIL	30	31	

January

SUN	MON	TUE	WED	THU	FRI	SAT
						1 CHI
2	3 TOR	4	5 SEA	6	7 CHA	8 NJN
9	10 BOS	11	12 MIN	13	14 DET	15 IND
16	17	18 DET	19	20 HOU	21	22 PHI
23	24 HOU	25 MEM	26	27	28 WAS	29 WAS
30	31 ATL					

February

SUN	MON	TUE	WED	THU	FRI	SAT
		1 CLE	2	3	4 BOS	5 CLE
6	7	8 GS	9	10 ATL	11	12 PHI
13 NO	14	15 LAC	16	17	18	19
20 *All-Star	21	22 IND	23	24	25	26 MIA
27 MIA	28					

March

SUN	MON	TUE	WED	THU	FRI	SAT
		1	2 SAC	3	4 NYK	5 NJN
6	7	8 CLE	9 TOR	10	11 MIN	12
13 NJN	14	15 SAC	16 LAC	17	18 SEA	19 POR
20 CHA	21	22	23 CHA	24	25	26 PHO
27 ATL	28	29	30 TOR	31		

April

SUN	MON	TUE	WED	THU	FRI	SAT
					1 WAS	2 NJN
3	4	5 DAL	6 CHI	7	8 DET	9
10	11 CLE	12	13 DET	14 CHI	15	16 MIL
17	18 IND	19	20 MIA	21	22	23

2004-05 SEASON

TEAM DIRECTORY

RDV SPORTS/BASKETBALL OPERATIONS
Chairman . . . . Rich DeVos
Executive Vice Chairman . . . . Cheri Vander Weide
Vice Chairmen . . . . Dan DeVos, Dick DeVos, Doug DeVos
President/Chief Executive Officer . . . . Bob Vander Weide
COO/General Manager . . . . John Weisbrod
Head Coach . . . . Johnny Davis
Assistant Coaches . . . . Paul Westhead, Ron Ekker, Chris Jent, Clifford Ray, Morlon Wiley
Assistant Coach, Strength & Conditioning . . . Mick Smith
Athletic Trainer . . . . Ted Arzonico
Equipment Manager/Travel Coordinator . . . . . . Rodney Powell
Physical Therapist . . . . Vinnie Hudson
Director of Basketball Administration . . . . Scott Herring
Director of Player Personnel . . . . David Twardzik
Director of Player Development . . . . Otis Smith
Assistant Equipment Manager . . . . Jason Rivera
Assistant Athletic Trainer . . . . Keon Weise
Staff . . . . Patricia Barnard, Carolyn Cote, Ellis Dawson, Sam Foggin, Tom Jorgensen, Charles Klask

BROADCASTING
Director of Broadcasting . . . . Kevin Cosgrove
Staff . . . . Kati Ennis, Rick Price, Jack McCabe, Tye Eastham, Joe Canali, Dante Marchitelli, Derek Fuchs, Jil Gossard-Cook, Jason Dewberry, Paul Connolly, Kevin Holden

COMMUNICATIONS
Director of Communications . . . . Joel Glass
Staff . . . . George Galante, Michelle Andres, Trish Wingerson, Jason Wallace

FAN & COMMUNITY RELATIONS
Vice President of Franchise Relations . . . . . . Scott Bowman
Staff . . . . Kari Conley, Cindy Anderson, Deborah Rios-Barnes, Laurel Lamb, Paul Molettiere, Bill Mauger, Sarah Bagwell, John Febres, John Larson, David Turner

CORPORATE OFFICE
Senior Vice President . . . . Pat Williams
Director of Business Strategy . . . . Charles Freeman
Staff . . . . Melanie Held, Diana Basch

CORPORATE SALES
VP of Corporate Sales & Broadcasting . . . . . . Jack Swope
Director of Corporate Sales . . . . Cameron Scholvin
Staff . . . . Derek Houston, Brian Crews, Brian Gartz, Ritch Shamey, Ruben Navas, Carlos Velez, Carmen Smallwood, Janet Beckish, Natalie Brokaw, Krista Darting, John Shumate, Sabrina Riggs

FINANCE
Executive VP of Finance & Business Operations . . Jim Fritz
Controller . . . . Jeff Bissey
Staff . . . . Peg Michalski, Jane Mackey, Leslie Monahan, Alicia Mauger, Nina Kovach, Nancy Cook

HUMAN RESOURCES/ADMINISTRATION
VP of Human Resources/Administration . . . . . Lorisse Garcia
Staff . . . . Audra Hollifield, Rebecca Totten, Monica Peery, Page Willner, Cynthia Ohlhues, Robin Tate, Vince Pileggi

INFORMATION TECHNOLOGY
Staff . . . . David Chase, Joel Massey, Cheryl Alli, Chris Sayre, Maggie Ambra-Perez

MARKETING
Vice President of Marketing . . . . Chris D'Orso
Staff . . . . Matt Biggers, Joe Casalese, Rick Crawford, Phillip Hastings, Shawn Bennett, Rusty Morris, Stephanie Kuhn, Lauren Sanderson, Brian Saxon, Jeanine Thomas, Scott Hesington, Tonya Armento

TICKET SALES
Director of Ticket Sales . . . . Evangeline "Van" Leventhal
Staff . . . . Bobby Bridges, Matt Blayney, Steve Chamberland, Leonard Edwards, Jessica Goodwin, Juan Londono, Salman Lewis, Buzz Wilkie, Mike Centanni, Dan Karlsberg, Jeanine Jones-Nelson

MAGIC CARPET AVIATION
Director of Aviation . . . . Harry Mitchel
Staff . . . . Betty Serapin, Jim Hinchman, Danny Hamby, Larry Bennett, Sebastien Syssau, Missy Conroy, Pattie Stacy, Todd Hyatt

Rich DeVos

John Weisbrod

Johnny Davis

ROSTER
Coach—Johnny Davis
Assistant coaches—Ron Ekker, Chris Jent, Clifford Ray, Paul Westhead, Morlon Wiley

No.	Name	Pos.	Ht./Wt.	Metric (m/kg)	Born	College/country
2	Stacey Augmon	F	6-8/213	2.03/96.6	8-1-68	UNLV
4	Tony Battie	F/C	6-11/240	2.10/108.4	2-11-76	Texas Tech
10	Keith Bogans	G	6-5/215	1.96/97.5	5-12-80	Kentucky
7	Michael Bradley	F	6-10/245	2.08/111.1	4-18-79	Villanova
13	Kelvin Cato	C	6-11/275	2.10/124.7	8-26-74	Iowa State
55	Andrew DeClercq	C	6-10/255	2.08/115.7	2-1-73	Florida
3	Steve Francis	G	6-3/200	1.90/90.7	2-21-77	Maryland
8	Pat Garrity	F	6-9/238	2.05/108.0	8-23-76	Notre Dame
33	Grant Hill	F	6-8/225	2.03/102.1	10-5-72	Duke
12	Dwight Howard	F/C	6-11/240	2.10/108.4	12-8-85	SW Atl. Chris. Acad.
	Mario Kasun	C	7-1/260	2.13/117.9	4-5-80	Croatia
5	Cuttino Mobley	G	6-4/215	1.93/97.5	9-1-75	Rhode Island
14	Jameer Nelson	G	6-0/190	1.83/86.2	2-9-82	St. Joseph's
	DeShawn Stevenson	G	6-5/210	1.96/95.3	4-3-81	Washington Union HS
15	Hedo Turkoglu	F	6-10/220	2.08/99.8	3-19-79	Turkey

BROADCAST INFORMATION

Radio: WDBO (580 AM). Broadcasters: Dennis Neumann, Jeff Turner. Spanish radio: WPRD (1440 AM), WSDO (1400 AM); WOTS (1220 AM). Broadcaster: Joey Colon.
TV: WRBW UPN-65. Broadcasters: David Steele, TBA.
Cable TV: Sunshine Network. Broadcasters: David Steele, TBA.

TEAM INFORMATION

Team address .... .8701 Maitland Summit Blvd.
Orlando, FL 32810
Business phone 407-916-2400
Ticket information 1-800-338-0005; 407-89-MAGIC
Website .... .www.orlandomagic.com
Arena (capacity) .... .TD Waterhouse Centre (17,283)
Game times .... .7 p.m.
First Magic game in arena .... .November 4, 1989

2003-04 REVIEW

RESULTS

OCTOBER
29—	at New York	85 -83	†1 -0
30—	New Orleans	*98 -100	1 -1

NOVEMBER
1 —	Detroit	*85 -96	1 -2
3 —	New York	*68 -75	1 -3
5 —	Chicago	*100 -106	1 -4
7 —	Minnesota	*71 -100	1 -5
8 —	at Houston	*86 -96	1 -6
12—	Memphis	*97 -107	1 -7
14—	at Denver	*101 -106	1 -8
15—	at L.A. Clippers	*92 -95	1 -9
17—	at Utah	*88 -90	1 -10
20—	at Phoenix	*89 -96	1 -11
21—	at Sacramento	*92 -122	1 -12
24—	Indiana	*78 -89	1 -13
26—	Boston	*92 -94	1 -14
28—	Toronto	*86 -87	1 -15

DECEMBER
2 —	New Orleans	*91 -100	1 -16
3 —	at New Orleans	*91 -106	1 -17
5	San Antonio	*94 -105	1 -18
6 —	at Dallas	*97 -110	1 -19
8 —	Phoenix	105 -98	2 -19
10—	at Washington	95 -91	3 -19
12—	New Jersey	*95 -99	3 -20
13—	at Atlanta	105 -102	4 -20
16—	at Chicago	*88 -102	4 -21
17—	at Indiana	94 -90	5 -21
19—	Golden State	119 -93	6 -21

21—	at Toronto	104 -93	7 -21
22—	at Philadelphia	*73 -95	7 -22
25—	Cleveland	113 -101	†8 -22
26—	at San Antonio	*83 -98	8 -23
29—	New York	*86 -114	8 -24

JANUARY
2 —	at Miami	*101 -112	8 -25
3 —	at Memphis	*103 -112	8 -26
6 —	at Indiana	*107 -114	8 -27
7 —	at Boston	*93 -101	8 -28
9 —	Washington	103 -92	9 -28
12—	Philadelphia	*82 -87	9 -29
14—	at New York	*110 -120	9 -30
16—	Boston	124 -118	†10 -30
17—	at New Orleans	*90 -91	10 -31
19—	Milwaukee	106 -99	11 -31
21—	at Milwaukee	*102 -113	11 -32
23—	at Philadelphia	98 -93	12 -32
25—	Houston	*87 -99	12 -33
26—	at Cleveland	*98 -99	12 -34
28—	at Washington	104 -100	13 -34
29—	New Jersey	*79 -89	13 -35
31—	L.A. Clippers	*106 -115	13 -36

FEBRUARY
3 —	at Minnesota	*100 -113	13 -37
4 —	at Toronto	*90 -110	13 -38
6 —	at New Jersey	*99 -120	13 -39
8 —	L.A. Lakers	*96 -98	13 -40
11—	Miami	*98 -111	13 -41
17—	at Milwaukee	*104 -127	13 -42

18—	Utah	90 -77	14 -42
20—	Denver	102 -98	15 -42
22—	at Detroit	87 -86	16 -42
24—	Portland	*91 -94	†16 -43
27—	Cleveland	*107 -112	†16 -44
28—	at Atlanta	104 -99	17 -44

MARCH
1 —	at Boston	*96 -117	17 -45
3 —	Milwaukee	*97 -105	17 -46
5 —	Atlanta	101 -96	18 -46
7 —	Sacramento	*90 -107	18 -47
9 —	at Miami	*89 -100	18 -48
10—	Washington	108 -99	19 -48
13—	Seattle	*101 -115	19 -49
15—	at L.A. Lakers	*110 -113	†19 -50
17—	at Golden State	*85 -110	19 -51
20—	at Portland	*73 -92	19 -52
21—	at Seattle	*67 -84	19 -53
24—	Miami	*90 -105	19 -54
26—	Indiana	*92 -107	19 -55
28—	Dallas	*88 -118	19 -56
31—	Chicago	*91 -109	19 -57

APRIL
2 —	Atlanta	*87 -95	19 -58
6 —	at Detroit	*86 -102	19 -59
8 —	at New Jersey	*81 -101	19 -60
10—	Detroit	*89 -101	19 -61
12—	at Chicago	93 -84	20 -61
14—	at Philadelphia	95 -89	21 -61

*Loss. †Single overtime.

TEAM LEADERS

Points: Tracy McGrady (1,878).
Field goals made: McGrady (653).
Free throws made: McGrady (398).
3-pointers made: McGrady (174).
Rebounds: Juwan Howard (570).
Assists: McGrady (370).
Steals: McGrady (93).
Blocks: Steven Hunter (73).

RECORDS

Regular season: 21-61 (8th in Atlantic Division); 8-16 in division; 17-37 in conference; 4-24 vs. Western Conference; 11-30 at home; 10-31 on road; 3-3 in overtime; 3-10 in games decided by three points or fewer; 5-37 in games decided by 10 points or more; held opponents under 100 points 39 times; held under 100 points 56 times.
Playoffs: None.
All-time franchise record: 588-610 in 15 seasons.
Team record past five years: 191-219 (.466, tied for 20th in NBA in that span).

HIGHLIGHTS

Top players: Tracy McGrady led the NBA in scoring for the second straight season, averaging 28.0 ppg. McGrady, an All-NBA Second Team selection, also led the Magic in assists (5.5 apg), steals (1.39 spg) and minutes played (39.9 mpg). ... Juwan Howard led the team in rebounding with 7.0 rpg. He also finished second on the club in scoring with 17.0 ppg.
Key injuries: The Magic lost a total of 254 player games because of injury or illness. Grant Hill missed the entire season because of left ankle rehabilitation. Pat Garrity missed 80 games with a right knee injury. McGrady missed 15 games because of left patella tendinitis, upper back spasms, a lower back contusion, a sprained left ankle and personal reasons.
Notable: The Magic acquired the high school player of the year (Dwight Howard) and college player of the year (Jameer Nelson) on draft day. ... In a blockbuster deal, Orlando traded two-time NBA scoring champion McGrady to Houston for three starters—three-time All-Star Steve Francis, his backcourt mate Cuttino Mobley and big man Kelvin Cato.

... Francis, Oscar Robertson, Magic Johnson and Grant Hill are the only players in NBA history to average at least 15 points, five rebounds and five assists in each of their first five seasons. Mobley ranks fifth in total points scored among players from the 1998 draft class (trailing only Paul Pierce, Vince Carter, Dirk Nowitzki, Antawn Jamison). ... The Magic has advanced to postseason play eight times in the past 11 years.

PHILADELPHIA 76ERS
ATLANTIC DIVISION

76ers Schedule
Home games shaded; *—All-Star Game at Denver.

November

SUN	MON	TUE	WED	THU	FRI	SAT
	1	2	3 BOS	4	5 PHO	6 DET
7	8	9 NYK	10 NJN	11	12 IND	13
14 ORL	15	16 SEA	17	18 SA	19	20
21 MIA	22	23	24 BOS	25	26 WAS	27 ORL
28	29	30				

December

SUN	MON	TUE	WED	THU	FRI	SAT
			1 SA	2	3 MEM	4 HOU
5	6 ATL	7	8 MIN	9	10 CHI	11
12 MIL	13	14 DEN	15	16	17 NYK	18 MIL
19	20 UTH	21	22 IND	23	24	25
26	27 POR	28 SEA	29	30	31 DEN	

January

SUN	MON	TUE	WED	THU	FRI	SAT
						1
2 LAC	3 GS	4	5 UTH	6	7 MIN	8
9	10 POR	11	12 CHI	13	14 TOR	15 DET
16	17 NO	18	19 CHA	20	21	22 ORL
23 MIA	24	25	26 WAS	27	28 NO	29 DAL
30	31 IND					

February

SUN	MON	TUE	WED	THU	FRI	SAT
		1	2 HOU	3	4 ATL	5
6 LAC	7 NJN	8	9 MEM	10	11 TOR	12 ORL
13	14 NYK	15	16 DET	17	18	19
20 *All-Star	21	22	23	24 NYK	25	26 SAC
27	28					

March

SUN	MON	TUE	WED	THU	FRI	SAT
		1 MIL	2 NJN	3	4 CLE	5 ATL
6 MIA	7	8 GS	9	10	11 CHA	12
13 TOR	14	15 LAL	16	17	18 CLE	19 CHI
20	21	22	23 DET	24	25 TOR	26
27 LAL	28 SAC	29 PHO	30	31		

April

SUN	MON	TUE	WED	THU	FRI	SAT
					1 DAL	2
3 BOS	4	5	6 CHA	7	8 CLE	9 WAS
10	11	12 BOS	13	14 MIA	15 IND	16
17 NJN	18 MIL	19	20 ATL	21	22	23

2004-05 SEASON

TEAM DIRECTORY

Chairman . . . . Ed Snider
President and General Manager . . . . Billy King
Head Coach . . . . Jim O'Brien
Executive Assistant to the President . . . . . Marlene Barnes
Associate Head Coach . . . . Lester Conner
European Scouting Coordinator . . . . Danko Cvjeticanin
Scout . . . . Frank DiLeo
Senior VP and Assistant General Manager Tony DiLeo
Team Orthopaedic Consultant . . . . Dr. Nick DiNubile
Team Physician . . . . Dr. Brad Fenton
Pro Personnel Scout . . . . Chris Ford
Assistant Coach . . . . Joe Gallagher
Assistant Coach . . . . Dick Harter
Scout . . . . Bobby Hurley
Head Trainer . . . . Kevin Johnson
Video Coordinator . . . . Brad Leinbach
Team Chiropractor . . . . Dr. Neil Liebman
Director of Travel and Team Services . . . . Allen Lumpkin
Director of Sports Medicine . . . . Jim McNulty
Team Physician . . . . Dr. Jack McPhilemy
Assistant Equipment Manager . . . . Jeff Millman
Scouting Coordinator . . . . Jake Neff
Locker Room Attendant . . . . Lenny Oakes
Scouting Department Manager . . . . Mary Purcell-Davis
Equipment Manager . . . . Scott Rego
Scout . . . . Mike VandeGarde
Director of Player Personnel . . . . Courtney Witte
Assistant Coach . . . . Frank Vogel
Assistant Coach/Advance Scout . . . . Frank Zanin

76ERS STAFF
President, Comcast-Spectacor Team
Marketing & Communications Group . . . . Dave Coskey
Sr. Vice President of Business Operations Lara Price
Senior Vice President of Finance . . . . Andy Speiser
Executive Advisor . . . . Sonny Hill
Vice President of Communications . . . . . Karen Frascona
Vice President of Sales . . . . Jim Van Stone

76ERS BROADCASTING
Senior Director of Broadcasting . . . . Shawn Oleksiak
Staff . . . . J.R. Aguila, Tom McGinnis, Steve Mix, Max Negin, Marc Zumoff

76ERS COMMUNICATIONS
Staff . . . . Kevin Fischer, Donna Katzman, Brian Kirschner, Harvey Pollack, Chris Wallace
76ers Community Relations . . . . World B. Free, Bree Jones

76ERS CUSTOMER SERVICE
Senior Director of Ticket Operations . . . . . Larry Meli
Staff . . . . John Fierko, Steve Suppa, Suhaiba Cannon, Kristen DiAngelo, Michele Huntington, Scott Rendeiro, Michelle Stallings

76ERS FINANCE
Staff . . . . Jackie Kurzenski, Nicole Posillico, Tisa Wilkins-Sproul

76ERS GAME OPERATIONS
Staff . . . . Kathy Drysdale, Matt Cord, Jerry McElhenney

76ERS MARKETING/PROMOTIONS
Staff . . . . Debbie Apalucci, Shana Booker, Patty Butler, Jaime Cheng, Joe Masters, Bill Roth, Beth Schwartz

76ERS SALES
Staff . . . . Mara Harris, Craig Broderdorp, Derek Goldfarb, Al Guido, Lindsay Heck, Melissa Latorra, Brad McCleary, Jacqueline Halligan, Bryan Anton, Bob Capewell, Scott Conti, Amy Cordes, Mike DiMuzio, Jacqueline Halligan, Jen Kozlowski, Travis Kraus, Brian McAfee, Lindsey McNamara, Courtney Parker

Jim O'Brien

Billy King

Dave Coskey

ROSTER
Coach—Jim O'Brien
Associate head coach—Lester Conner
Assistant coaches—Joe Gallagher, Dick Harter, Frank Vogel

No.	Name	Pos.	Ht./Wt.	Metric (m/kg)	Born	College
5	Kedrick Brown	G/F	6-7/222	2.00/100.7	3-18-81	Okaloosa-Walton CC
21	Greg Buckner	G/F	6-4/210	1.93/95.3	9-16-76	Clemson
1	Samuel Dalembert	C	6-11/250	2.10/113.4	5-10-81	Seton Hall
33	Willie Green	G	6-4/200	1.93/90.7	7-28-81	Detroit Mercy
4	Andre Iguodala	F	6-6/207	1.98/93.9	1-28-84	Arizona
3	Allen Iverson	G	6-0/165	1.83/74.8	6-07-75	Georgetown
25	Marc Jackson	F/C	6-10/253	2.08/114.8	1-16-75	Temple
26	Kyle Korver	F	6-7/210	2.00/95.3	3-17-81	Creighton
11	Todd MacCulloch	C	7-0/280	2.13/127.0	1-27-76	Washington
8	Aaron McKie	G	6-5/209	1.96/94.8	10-02-72	Temple
12	Kevin Ollie	G	6-2/195	1.88/88.5	12-27-72	Connecticut
31	Glenn Robinson	F	6-7/240	2.00/108.9	1-10-73	Purdue
7	John Salmons	G	6-7/210	2.00/95.3	12-12-79	Miami (Fla.)
54	Brian Skinner	F/C	6-9/265	2.05/120.2	5-19-76	Baylor
9	Kenny Thomas	F	6-7/245	2.00/111.1	7-25-77	New Mexico
30	Corliss Williamson	F	6-7/245	2.00/111.1	12-4-73	Arkansas

BROADCAST INFORMATION

Radio: WIP (610 AM). Broadcaster: Tom McGinnis.
TV: WPSG (Channel 57). Broadcasters: Marc Zumoff, Steve Mix.
Cable TV: Comcast SportsNet. Broadcasters: Marc Zumoff, Steve Mix.
Network TV: WPVI (Channel 6).

TEAM INFORMATION

Team address	3601 South Broad Street
	Philadelphia, PA 19148
Business phone	215-339-7600
Ticket information	215-339-7676
Website	www.sixers.com
Arena (capacity)	Wachovia Center (20,294)
Game times	1, 2, 6, 7, 7:30, 8, 8:30, 10 and 10:30 p.m.
First 76ers game in arena	November 1, 1996

2003-04 REVIEW

RESULTS

OCTOBER
28— Miami	89 -74	1 -0	
31— at Sacramento	*89 -100	1 -1	

NOVEMBER
1 — at Golden State	*90 -104	1 -2	
3 — at Portland	94 -83	2 -2	
5 — New Orleans	*99 -106	†2 -3	
7 — at Chicago	106 -85	3 -3	
9 — Indiana	*74 -85	3 -4	
11— at Washington	112 -105	4 -4	
14— San Antonio	100 -96	5 -4	
15— at Cleveland	*88 -91	†5 -5	
17— Houston	*66 -74	5 -6	
19— at Toronto	81 -75	6 -6	
21— Boston	87 -85	7 -6	
22— at New York	*88 -99	7 -7	
25— at Milwaukee	*91 -95	7 -8	
26— Detroit	90 -86	8 -8	
28— at Indiana	*77 -90	8 -9	
29— Atlanta	98 -86	9 -9	

DECEMBER
2 — Toronto	*88 -95	9 -10	
4 — Chicago	83 -82	10 -10	
5 — at Miami	93 -90	11 -10	
9 — at Detroit	78 -76	12 -10	
12— Denver	*77 -86	12 -11	
14— Utah	*86 -94	12 -12	
17— Miami	87 -76	13 -12	
19— Cleveland	*81 -88	13 -13	
21— at Boston	*84 -87	13 -14	

22— Orlando	95 -73	14 -14
26— at L.A. Clippers	*98 -101	14 -15
28— at Phoenix	*92 -100	14 -16
29— at Utah	*97 -106	14 -17
31— at Houston	*72 -80	14 -18

JANUARY
3 — at San Antonio	83 -77	15 -18
5 — Milwaukee	*76 -88	15 -19
7 — L.A. Clippers	100 -80	16 -19
9 — New Jersey	97 -81	17 -19
10— at Washington	*87 -94	17 -20
12— Orlando	87 -82	18 -20
14— at Dallas	*122 -125	‡18 -21
17— Memphis	*87 -91	18 -22
19— Seattle	*81 -90	18 -23
21— at New Orleans	92 -86	19 -23
23— Orlando	*93 -98	19 -24
24— at Cleveland	*87 -95	19 -25
27— New Jersey	*76 -94	19 -26
28— at Toronto	*84 -94	19 -27
30— New Orleans	85 -82	20 -27

FEBRUARY
1 — at Minnesota	*101 -106	20 -28
3 — Toronto	*80 - 93	20 -29
5 — L.A. Lakers	96 - 73	21 -29
7 — Boston	*80 -110	21 -30
8 — at New Jersey	*87 - 99	21 -31
11— Washington	113 - 88	22 -31
17— at Denver	*85 -106	22 -32
19— at Seattle	112 -101	23 -32

20 — at L.A. Lakers	*88 -116	23 -33
23— Detroit	*66 -76	23 -34
24— at Atlanta	*75 -86	23 -35
28— at Indiana	*74 -81	23 -36
29— Minnesota	81 -74	24 -36

MARCH
3 — at New York	*77 -88	24 -37
4 — Sacramento	*105 -114	24 -38
6 — Chicago	97 -88	25 -38
8 — Milwaukee	97 -92	26 -38
9 — at Chicago	89 -81	27 -38
12— New York	99 -94	‡28 -38
14— at Detroit	*69 -85	28 -39
16— at Memphis	*79 -82	28 -40
17— at New Orleans	*80 -104	28 -41
20— at Miami	*69 -101	28 -42
22— Dallas	107 -98	29 -42
24— Phoenix	99 -94	30 -42
26— Cleveland	86 -71	31 -42
28— at Boston	*65 -89	31 -43
30— Golden State	95 -71	32 -43

APRIL
1 — Portland	*82 -88	32 -44
3 — New York	*75 -86	32 -45
6 — at Atlanta	103 -100	†33 -45
9 — Washington	*80 -83	33 -46
11— at New Jersey	*75 -89	33 -47
12— Indiana	*93 -107	33 -48
14— at Orlando	*89- 95	33- 49

*Loss. †Single overtime. ‡Double overtime.

TEAM LEADERS

Points: Allen Iverson (1,266).
Field goals made: Iverson (435).
Free throws made: Iverson (339).
3-pointers made: Kyle Korver (81).
Rebounds: Kenny Thomas (750).
Assists: Eric Snow (563).
Steals: Iverson (115).
Blocks: Samuel Dalembert (189).

RECORDS

Regular season: 33-49 (5th in Atlantic Division); 10-14 in division; 23-31 in conference; 10-18 vs. Western Conference; 21-20 at home; 12-29 on road; 2-3 in overtime; 6-6 in games decided by three points or fewer; 13-23 in games decided by 10 points or more; held opponents under 100 points 64 times; held under 100 points 71 times.
Playoffs: None.
All-time franchise record: 2,345-1,991 in 55 seasons. Won three NBA titles (1955, '67, '83), with the first title coming while the franchise was located in Syracuse, N.Y.
Team record past five years: 229-181 (.559, ranks 9th in NBA in that span).

HIGHLIGHTS

Top players: Allen Iverson led the team in scoring (26.4 ppg). ... Samuel Dalembert ranked ninth in the NBA in blocks per game (2.30) and finished with 189 blocks (6th in the NBA), the seventh-best Sixers single-season record. ... Kenny Thomas ranked ninth in the NBA in rebounds per game (10.1) and was one of just 11 NBA players to average a double-double this season. At 6-7, Thomas was one of only two players shorter than 6-9 who ranked in the top 30 in rebounds per game. Phoenix's Shawn Marion was the other. ...Rookie Willie Green finished the season ranked 13th among NBA rookies in scoring (6.9 ppg) and averaged 13.6 points in the team's final 12 games.
Key injuries: The Sixers lost a total of 350 player games because of injury or illness. Thirteen different players missed at least one game with injury. On March 30, it was announced that Iverson would miss the remainder of the regular season with persistent pain and inflammation in his right knee. The cause of the inflammation was a small articular cartilage lesion in the trochlear groove of the femur under the patella. Iverson missed a career-high 34 games during the 2003-04 season.

Notable: Chris Ford was named interim head coach of the Philadelphia 76ers on February 10, replacing Randy Ayers (21-31), who was hired on June 20, 2003. Ford led the team to a 12-18 record. ... Twelve different players scored 20 points or more in a game at least once during the 2003-04 season, the most since the 1995-96 season, when 14 different players eclipsed the 20-point plateau. ... Rookie Kyle Korver ranked second among all rookies and 23rd overall in 3-point field-goal percentage (.391). ... The Sixers used 25 different starting lineup combinations in 2003-04, with 11 players making at least one start.

PHOENIX SUNS
PACIFIC DIVISION

Suns Schedule
Home games shaded; *—All-Star Game at Denver.

November

SUN	MON	TUE	WED	THU	FRI	SAT
	1	2	3 ATL	4	5 PHI	6 NJN
7	8	9 CHI	10 CLE	11	12	13 SAC
14	15	16 DAL	17 NO	18	19 LAL	20
21 LAC	22 CHI	23	24 MIL	25	26 NO	27
28	29	30 UTH				

December

SUN	MON	TUE	WED	THU	FRI	SAT
		1 CLE	2	3 MIN	4	
5 POR	6	7 GS	8 LAL	9	10 CHA	11
12	13 ORL	14	15 UTH	16	17 SEA	18 WAS
19	20 DEN	21	22	23 MEM	24	25
26 TOR	27	28 SA	29 NO	30	31	

January

SUN	MON	TUE	WED	THU	FRI	SAT
						1
2 POR	3	4 MIN	5 HOU	6	7	8 LAC
9 IND	10	11 MIA	12 UTH	13	14 IND	15 WAS
16	17 DET	18	19 MEM	20	21 SA	22
23 NJN	24	25 NYK	26 MIL	27	28 BOS	29
30 TOR	31					

February

SUN	MON	TUE	WED	THU	FRI	SAT
		1 MEM	2 MIN	3	4	5 NYK
6	7	8 SAC	9	10	11 SEA	12
13 GS	14 UTH	15	16	17 DAL	18	19
20 *All-Star	21	22	23 LAC	24	25	26 DAL
27 BOS	28					

March

SUN	MON	TUE	WED	THU	FRI	SAT
		1	2	3 DET	4	5 POR
6 SEA	7	8	9 SA	10	11 HOU	12
13 DEN	14	15	16	17	18 GS	19
20 MEM	21	22 ATL	23 CHA	24	25 MIA	26 ORL
27	28 DEN	29	30 PHI	31		

April

SUN	MON	TUE	WED	THU	FRI	SAT
					1 MIN	2
3 HOU	4	5 LAL	6	7	8 GS	9 HOU
10	11 LAL	12 NO	13	14	15 LAC	16 SAC
17	18 DEN	19	20 SAC	21	22	23

2004-05 SEASON

TEAM DIRECTORY

Chairman & Chief Executive Officer	Jerry Colangelo
Vice Chairman & Managing Partner	Robert Sarver
President & General Manager	Bryan Colangelo
President & Chief Operating Officer	Rick Welts
Executive Vice President, Finance/Administration	Jim Pitman
Sr. Executive Vice President	Dick Van Arsdale
Sr. Vice President, Community Affairs	Tom Ambrose
Sr. Vice President, Marketing Communications	Ray Artigue
Sr. Vice President, Broadcasting	Al McCoy
Sr. Vice President and General Counsel	Tom O'Malley
Sr. Vice President, Corporate Sales	Harvey Shank
Assistant General Manager	Mark West
Head Coach	Mike D'Antoni
Assistant Coaches	Marc Iavaroni, Alvin Gentry, Phil Weber, Todd Quinter
Head Athletic Trainer	Aaron Nelson
Strength & Conditioning/Assistant Athletic Trainer	Erik Phillips
Assistant Trainer	Mike Elliott
Team Physicians	Dr. Tom Carter, Dr. Craig Phelps
Equipment Managers	Richard Howell, Jay Gaspar
Director of Player Personnel	David Griffin
Director of Basketball Operations	Rex Chapman
Director of International Scouting	Marco Crespi
Assistant to the Chairman	Ruth Dryjanski
Assistant to the President/G.M.	Jacque Alonzo
Executive Assistants	Sharon Chinn, Glenna Martinez, Bonnie Meadows, Sherry Reed, Debbie Villa, Connie Wallen
Vice President, Basketball Communications	Julie Fie
Basketball Communications Managers	DC Headley, Dustin Krugel
Vice President & Associate General Counsel	Nona Lee
Paralegal	Melissa Santello
Vice President, Public Relations	Rob Harris
Public Relations Staff	Jamie Morris, Mark Gretter
Community Affairs Staff	Stephanie Clarke, Connie Hawkins, Cassidy Kersten
Vice President, Corporate Sales	Lynn Agnello
Corporate Sales Staff	Megan Montgomery, Rachel Reinsmoen, Kristen Snell-Anzalone, Leah Staten, Matt Wright, Angela Yock
Game Operations Staff	Maggie Garcia, Kip Helt, Bob Woolf
Receptionist	Ceola Coaston
Staff Assistants	Travis Agenter, Mark Sanchez
Vice President, Business Development	John Walker
SES Sr. Director, Ticket Operations and Sales	Brett Wojtulewicz
Vice President, Retail Operations	Bob Nanberg
Merchandising Staff	Matt Altman, Kim Magnussen, Terri Tucker
Producer/Director Suns TV	Dan Siekmann, Bob Adlhoch
Suns Productions	Tommy Arguelles, Dave Grapentine, Marc Goldberg, Hap Hopper, David Hughes, Tom Leander, Jason Lewis, Richard Mendez
Vice President, Marketing and Fan Development	Jim Brewer
Sr. Director of Publishing	Jeramie McPeek

Jerry Colangelo

Bryan Colangelo

Mike D'Antoni

ROSTER
Coach—Mike D'Antoni
Assistant coaches—Marc Iavaroni, Alvin Gentry, Phil Weber, Todd Quinter

No.	Name	Pos.	Ht./Wt.	Metric (m/kg)	Born	College/country
10	Leandro Barbosa	G	6-3/188	1.90/85.3	11-28-82	Brazil
11	Zarko Cabarkapa	F	6-11/225	2.10/102.1	5-21-81	Serbia
12	Howard Eisley	G	6-2/185	1.88/83.9	12-4-72	Boston College
45	Steven Hunter	C	7-0/240	2.13/108.9	10-31-81	DePaul
23	Casey Jacobsen	G/F	6-6/215	1.98/97.5	3-19-81	Stanford
2	Joe Johnson	G	6-7/230	2.00/104.3	6-29-81	Arkansas
30	Maciej Lampe	F/C	6-11/275	2.10/124.7	2-5-85	Spain
31	Shawn Marion	F	6-7/228	2.00/103.4	5-7-78	UNLV
13	Steve Nash	G	6-3/195	1.90/88.5	2-7-74	Santa Clara
3	Quentin Richardson	G	6-6/236	1.98/107.0	4-13-80	DePaul
32	Amaré Stoudemire	F	6-10/245	2.08/111.1	11-16-82	Cypress Creek HS
43	Jake Voskuhl	C	6-11/250	2.10/113.4	11-1-77	Connecticut
4	Jackson Vroman	F/C	6-10/220	2.08/99.8	1-6-81	Iowa State

BROADCAST INFORMATION

Radio: KTAR (620 AM). Broadcasters: Al McCoy, TBA. Spanish radio: TBA.
TV: UPN 45. Broadcasters: Tom Leander, Eddie Johnson, Dan Majerle.
Cable TV: FSN Arizona. Broadcasters: Gary Bender, Eddie Johnson, Dan Majerle.

TEAM INFORMATION

Team address . . . . .201 E. Jefferson St.
  Phoenix, AZ 85004
Business phone 602-379-7900
Ticket information 602-379-7867
Website .www.suns.com
Arena (capacity) . . . . .America West Arena (18,422)
Game times . . . . .7:00 p.m.; 6 p.m., Sunday
First Suns game in arena . . . . .November 7, 1992

2003-04 REVIEW

RESULTS

OCTOBER
28— at San Antonio	*82 -83	0 -1	
30— Cleveland	95 -86	1 -1	

NOVEMBER
1 — L.A. Lakers	*99 -103	1 -2	
5 — at Utah	*80 -91	1 -3	
7 — Memphis	96 -88	2 -3	
10 —at Golden State	99 -96	3 -3	
12— Atlanta	*94 -99	3 -4	
14— at Houston	*85 -90	3 -5	
15— Detroit	*91 -100	3 -6	
18— Chicago	95 -82	4 -6	
20— Orlando	96 -89	5 -6	
22— Miami	100 -98	6 -6	
25— at Denver	*80 -110	6 -7	
26— Dallas	121 -90	7 -7	
28— Golden State	*83 -92	7 -8	

DECEMBER
1 — Indiana	*82 -89	7 -9	
3 — Minnesota	*79 -92	7 -10	
5 — at Boston	110 -106	8 -10	
6 — at New Jersey	*88 -99	8 -11	
8 — at Orlando	*98 -105	8 -12	
9 — at Miami	*72 -92	8 -13	
11— New Orleans	*101 -111	8 -14	
13— at L.A. Clippers	*91 -106	8 -15	
14— at Sacramento	*102 -107	8 -16	
16— Seattle	92 -91	†9 -16	
18— at Portland	*94 -101	9 -17	
20— Houston	102 -87	10 -17	

(continued)
21— at L.A. Lakers	*101 -107	10 -18	
23— at Seattle	*90 -116	10 -19	
26— Boston	*102 -104	10 -20	
28— Philadelphia	100 -92	11 -20	
29— at L.A. Clippers	113 -105	12 -20	

JANUARY
2 — at Detroit	*81 -93	12 -21	
4 — at Toronto	*73 -83	12 -22	
5 — at Chicago	*82 -87	12 -23	
7 — at Milwaukee	*87 -95	12 -24	
9 — Sacramento	*93 -113	12 -25	
13— Denver	*92 -105	12 -26	
15— at Portland	105 -96	13 -26	
16— Golden State	104 -93	14 -26	
18— Portland	96 -92	15 -26	
19— at L.A. Lakers	88 -85	16 -26	
21— at Denver	*92 -97	16 -27	
23— San Antonio	*84 -86	16 -28	
25— at Minnesota	*95 -99	16 -29	
27— at Atlanta	89 -85	17 -29	
28— at Indiana	*79 -101	17 -30	
30— at Washington	*100 -105	17 -31	
31— at New York	*105 -110	17 -32	

FEBRUARY
2 — Houston	99 -79	18 -32	
4 — Portland	*97 -101	18 -33	
6 — Seattle	*105 -107	18 -34	
7 — Utah	*92 -96	18 -35	
10— Toronto	*94 -101	18 -36	
11— at Golden State	*99 -110	18 -37	

(continued)
17— at Minnesota	*95 -110	18 -38	
20— at Memphis	*92 -97	18 -39	
22— L.A. Lakers	*92 -104	18 -40	
25— New York	113 -95	19 -40	
27— at Seattle	104 -99	20 -40	
29— at Sacramento	*94 -108	20 -41	

MARCH
3 — New Jersey	87 -74	21 -41	
6 — San Antonio	*86 -107	21 -42	
8 — at Dallas	*90 -103	21 -43	
12— Utah	*90 -99	21 -44	
13— Dallas	*90 -113	21 -45	
15— at Houston	99 -97	†22 -45	
16— L.A. Clippers	*98 -110	22 -46	
19— Minnesota	*80 -93	22 -47	
20— Milwaukee	123 -111	23 -47	
23— at Cleveland	103 -86	24 -47	
24— at Philadelphia	*94 -99	24 -48	
26— at New Orleans	99 -94	25 -48	
27— at San Antonio	*76 -105	25 -49	
29— Washington	101 -95	26 -49	

APRIL
2 — at Memphis	*99 -109	26 -50	
3 — at Dallas	*103 -124	26 -51	
7 — Denver	*96 -111	26 -52	
9 — Sacramento	101 -96	27 -52	
11— Memphis	89 -83	28 -52	
13— L.A. Clippers	*96 -98	28 -53	
14— at Utah	89 -84	29 -53	

*Loss. †Single overtime.

TEAM LEADERS

Points: Shawn Marion (1,498).
Field goals made: Marion (590).
Free throws made: Amaré Stoudemire (310).
3-pointers made: Marion (90).
Rebounds: Marion (737).
Assists: Joe Johnson (362).
Steals: Marion (167).
Blocks: Marion (104).

RECORDS

Regular season: 29-53 (6th in Pacific Division); 9-15 in division; 16-36 in conference; 13-17 vs. Eastern Conference; 18-23 at home; 11-30 on road; 2-0 in overtime; 5-5 in games decided by three points or fewer; 9-26 in games decided by 10 points or more; held opponents under 100 points 48 times; held under 100 points 60 times.
Playoffs: None.
All-time franchise record: 1,582-1,338 in 36 seasons.
Team record past five years: 213-197 (.520, ranks 13th in NBA in that span).

HIGHLIGHTS

Top players: Amaré Stoudemire led the team in scoring (20.6 ppg) and would have ranked 14th in the NBA in scoring but did not play in the minimum number of games required. In the final 32 games, he averaged 23.9 ppg and 9.6 rpg in 39.3 mpg. ... Shawn Marion was one of two NBA players (Kevin Garnett) to rank in top 30 in points (19.0, 19th), rebounds (9.3, 14th), steals (2.1, 2nd), blocks (1.3, 27th) and minutes (40.7, 2nd). He led the NBA with 167 steals. ... Joe Johnson was one of 11 NBA players to average more than 16 points, four rebounds and four assists (16.7 ppg, 4.7 rpg, 4.4 apg). After the Suns completed an eight-player trade on January 5, Johnson averaged 19.6 ppg, 5.1 rpg and 5.1 apg in the final 48 games. He led the NBA with 3,331 minutes, the third-highest single-season total in franchise history.
Key injuries: The Suns lost a total of 191 player games because of injury or illness. Zarko Cabarkapa (28), Stoudemire (27), Scott Williams (21), Jake Voskuhl (15), Antonio McDyess (15), Robert Archibald (15), Maciej Lampe (10) and Howard Eisley (10) missed double-figure games.

Johnson was the only Suns player to play in all 82 games.
Notable: Phoenix's 29-53 record was its worst since 1987-88, when it finished 28-54. ... Phoenix opened the season as the sixth-youngest team in the NBA but finished as the youngest. ... Phoenix rallied from a 29-point deficit to defeat the Celtics on December 5, the biggest comeback in club history. ... Mike D'Antoni was named the franchise's 12th head coach after Frank Johnson was let go after an 8-13 start. ... Stoudemire led the Suns in scoring in 11 consecutive games, tying the second-longest streak in franchise history. ... Johnson ended the season having logged at least 40 minutes in 35 consecutive games, the longest streak in the NBA since 1968-69 (37). ... Stoudemire set the Rookie Challenge scoring record with 36 points. ... Stoudemire tied a franchise record and set an AWA record with 10 blocks vs. Utah on February 7. ... In his first NBA start, Barbosa scored 27 points, the most points by a Suns rookie in his first start.

PORTLAND TRAIL BLAZERS
NORTHWEST DIVISION

Trail Blazers Schedule
Home games shaded; *—All-Star Game at Denver.

November
SUN	MON	TUE	WED	THU	FRI	SAT
	1	2	3 GS	4	5 LAC	6
7 TOR	8	9 NJN	10 BOS	11	12	13 TOR
14	15	16	17 MEM	18	19 MIL	20
21 HOU	22	23 MIA	24 ORL	25	26 DAL	27
28 NJN	29	30 SEA				

December
SUN	MON	TUE	WED	THU	FRI	SAT
			1	2	3	4 SEA
5 PHO	6	7	8	9 BOS	10 UTH	11
12 UTH	13	14 MIN	15 CLE	16	17 ATL	18 DET
19	20 CHI	21	22 MIL	23	24	25
26	27 PHI	28	29	30 SA	31	

January
SUN	MON	TUE	WED	THU	FRI	SAT
						1 GS
2 PHO	3	4	5 LAC	6	7 MIA	8
9 NYK	10 PHI	11	12 WAS	13	14 NO	15 MIN
16	17	18 SAC	19 CLE	20	21	22 MIN
23	24 SA	25	26 DAL	27	28 LAC	29
30	31					

February
SUN	MON	TUE	WED	THU	FRI	SAT
		1 LAL	2 DEN	3	4 CHA	5 SAC
6	7	8	9 NO	10	11 MEM	12
13 HOU	14 CHA	15	16 IND	17	18	19
20 *All-Star	21	22	23 LAL	24	25 ATL	26
27 MIN	28					

March
SUN	MON	TUE	WED	THU	FRI	SAT
		1 DET	2	3	4 IND	5 PHO
6	7 DEN	8	9 CHI	10	11	12 MEM
13	14 MEM	15	16 HOU	17 DAL	18	19 ORL
20	21 LAC	22 SAC	23	24 SEA	25	26 NYK
27	28 WAS	29	30 HOU	31		

April
SUN	MON	TUE	WED	THU	FRI	SAT
					1 SEA	2 DEN
3	4	5 UTH	6 GS	7	8 SAC	9
10 NO	11	12 SA	13	14 DAL	15 GS	16
17 UTH	18	19 DEN	20 LAL	21	22	23

2004-05 SEASON

TEAM DIRECTORY

Chairman . . . . Paul Allen
President . . . . Steve Patterson
General Manager . . . . John Nash
Chief Marketing Officer . . . . Declan Bolger
Sr. Vice President of Business Affairs . . . . . J.E. Isaac
Chief Financial Officer . . . . Gregg Olson
Vice President, General Counsel . . . . Mike Fennell
VP, Marketing & Communications . . . . Marta Monetti
VP, Corporate Sales & Service . . . . Sarah Mensah
VP, Broadcasting & Production . . . . Dick Vardanega
VP, Ticket Sales & Service . . . . Todd Taylor
VP, Chief Information Officer . . . . Chris Dill
Head Coach . . . . Maurice Cheeks
Assistant Coaches . . . . Tim Grgurich,
John Loyer, Jim Lynam, Dan Panaggio, Bernard Smith
Director of Player Personnel . . . . TBD
Trainer . . . . Jay Jensen
Assistant Trainer & Equipment Manager . . . Geoff Clark
Strength & Conditioning Coach . . . . Bob Medina
Scouts . . . . Chico Averbuck,
Tates Locke
Advance Scouts . . . . Dennis Johnson,
Jim Sleeper
Executive Director of Communications . . . . Mike Hanson
Director of Community Relations . . . . Traci Rose
Manager, Sports Communications . . . . Rich Austin
Manager, Corporate Communications . . . . . TBD
Director of Community Outreach . . . . Jerry Moss
Director of Events Presentations . . . . TBD
Director of Services . . . . Traci Richardson
Director of Human Resources . . . . Traci Reandeau
Director of Ticket Operations . . . . Lori Spencer
Dir. of Engineering & Technical Operations Mike Janes
Director of Blazers Broadcasting . . . . Chris McMurtry
Producer of Blazers Broadcasting . . . . Scott Zachry
Radio Broadcasters . . . . Brian Wheeler,
Mike Rice
TV Broadcasters . . . . Steve Jones, Mike
Barrett
Special Assistant to the G.M. . . . . Tates Locke

Paul Allen

John Nash

Maurice Cheeks

ROSTER
Coach—Maurice Cheeks
Assistant coaches— Tim Grgurich, John Loyer, Jim Lynam, Dan Panaggio, Bernard Smith

No.	Name	Pos.	Ht./Wt.	Metric (m/kg)	Born	College/country
33	Shareef Abdur-Rahim	F	6-9/245	2.06/111.1	12-11-76	California
1	Derek Anderson	G	6-5/206	1.96/93.4	7-18-74	Kentucky
14	Richie Frahm	G	6-5/210	1.96/95.3	8-14-77	Gonzaga
38	Viktor Khryapa	F	6-9/210	2.05/95.3	8-3-82	Russia
23	Darius Miles	F	6-9/210	2.06/95.3	10-9-81	East St. Louis HS
25	Travis Outlaw	F	6-9/205	2.06/93.0	9-18-84	Starkville HS
21	Ruben Patterson	F	6-6/223	1.98/101.2	7-31-75	Cincinnati
50	Zach Randolph	F	6-9/256	2.06/116.1	7-16-81	Michigan State
42	Theo Ratliff	C	6-10/235	2.08/106.6	4-17-73	Wyoming
11	Vladimir Stepania	C	7-1/244	2.16/110.7	5-8-76	Republic of Georgia
3	Damon Stoudamire	G	5-10/174	1.73/78.9	9-3-73	Arizona
23	Sebastian Telfair	G	6-0/165	1.78/74.8	6-9-85	Abraham Lincoln HS
19	Nick Van Exel	G	6-1/195	1.85/88.4	11-27-71	Trinity Valley CC
24	Qyntel Woods	F	6-8/221	2.03/100.2	2/16/81	NE Mississippi CC

BROADCAST INFORMATION

Radio: KXL (750 AM). Broadcasters: Brian Wheeler, Mike Rice.
TV: KGW (Channel 8). Broadcasters: Steve Jones, Mike Barrett.
Cable: Fox Sports Net. Broadcasters: Steve Jones, Mike Barrett.

TEAM INFORMATION

Team address . . . . .One Center Court, Suite 200
Portland, OR 97227
Business phone 503-234-9291
Ticket information 503-797-9600
Website . . . . .www.blazers.com
Arena (capacity) . . . . .The Rose Garden (19,980)
Game times . . . . .7 p.m., Monday-Saturday; 6 p.m. Sunday
First Trail Blazers game in arena . . . .November 3, 1995

2003-04 REVIEW

RESULTS

OCTOBER
29— at Utah	*92 -99	0 -1	

NOVEMBER
1 — Cleveland	104 -85	1 -1
3 — Philadelphia	*83 -94	1 -2
5 — Memphis	93 -87	2 -2
7 — at Seattle	*82 -100	2 -3
8 — Atlanta	90 -83	3 -3
11— Toronto	83 -80	4 -3
13— Sacramento	112 -110	†5 -3
15— at New Orleans	*79 -101	5 -4
17— at Dallas	*98 -105	5 -5
19— Miami	94 -93	6 -5
21— Houston	85 -78	7 -5
23— at Golden State	*72 -78	7 -6
25— Washington	*80 -81	7 -7
28— New Jersey	97 -93	8 -7

DECEMBER
3 — Indiana	97 -95	†9 -7
5 — New York	88 -81	10 -7
7 — at Memphis	*79 -93	10 -8
9 — at Houston	*91 -93	10 -9
10— at San Antonio	*77 -102	10 -10
13— L.A. Lakers	112 -108	11 -10
16— Milwaukee	*99 -106	11 -11
18— Phoenix	101 -94	12 -11
20— San Antonio	*91 -101	12 -12
21— at Sacramento	*98 -117	12 -13
23— Dallas	97 -88	13 -13
26— Minnesota	101 -92	14 -13

28— at Cleveland	*74 -86	14 -14
29— at New Jersey	91 -87	15 -14
31— at Detroit	*71 -78	15 -15

JANUARY
2 — Denver	*96 -106	15 -16
5 — at Seattle	*108 -119	†15 -17
8 — at Minnesota	*75 -96	15 -18
9 — at Chicago	87 -78	16 -18
11— at Toronto	*72 -83	16 -19
13— at L.A. Clippers	*96 -103	†16 -20
15— Phoenix	*96 -105	16 -21
17— Dallas	*104 -108	16 -22
18— at Phoenix	*92 -96	16 -23
20— at Sacramento	109 -104	†17 -23
24— Golden State	*87 -105	17 -24
26— at Washington	94 -83	18 -24
28— at Memphis	88 -76	19 -24
29— at Atlanta	93 -85	20 -24
31— Chicago	102 -95	†21 -24

FEBRUARY
2 — at Denver	*97 -116	21 -25
4 — at Phoenix	101 -97	22 -25
6 — at Utah	87 -73	23 -25
8 — Seattle	95 -85	24 -25
10— Utah	*81 -86	24 -26
12— Denver	*98 -107	24 -27
17— at L.A. Lakers	*86 -89	24 -28
18— L.A. Clippers	101 -86	25 -28
20— at Golden State	94 -93	26 -28
21— Boston	105 -84	27 -28

23— at Miami	89 -81	28 -28
24— at Orlando	94 -91	†29 -28
27— at Houston	*85 -89	29 -29
28— at Dallas	*91 -111	29 -30

MARCH
3 — Memphis	*88 -97	29 -31
4 — Detroit	*68 -83	29 -32
6 — Utah	91 -70	30 -32
7 — at L.A. Clippers	*71 -91	30 -33
10— Minnesota	92 -79	31 -33
12— Sacramento	83 -81	32 -33
14— at Minnesota	92 -83	33 -33
16— at Milwaukee	100 -99	34 -33
17— at Indiana	*71 -80	34 -34
20— Orlando	92 -73	35 -34
22— Houston	*85 -93	†35 -35
24— L.A. Clippers	91 -85	36 -35
27— Seattle	115 -108	†37 -35
29— at New York	*91 -92	37 -36
31— at Boston	105 -98	38 -36

APRIL
1 — at Philadelphia	88 -82	39 -36
3 — New Orleans	*01 -94	39 -37
6 — at L.A. Lakers	91 -80	40 -37
7 — Golden State	87 -81	41 -37
9 — at San Antonio	*74 -84	41 -38
10— at Denver	*100 -110	†41 -39
12— San Antonio	*66 -78	41 -40
14— L.A. Lakers	*104 -105	†41 -41

*Loss. †Single overtime. ‡Double overtime.

TEAM LEADERS

Points: Zach Randolph (1,626).
Field goals made: Randolph (663).
Free throws made: Randolph (229).
3-pointers made: Damon Stoudamire (156).
Rebounds: Randolph (851).
Assists: Stoudamire (500).
Steals: Stoudamire (99).
Blocks: Theo Ratliff (141).

RECORDS

Regular season: 41-41 (3rd in Pacific Division); 13-11 in division; 22-30 in conference; 19-11 vs. Eastern Conference; 25-16 at home; 16-25 on road; 6-5 in overtime games; 8-5 in games decided by three points or fewer; 11-21 in games decided by 10 points or more; held opponents under 100 points 60 times; held under 100 points 65 times.
Playoffs: None.
All-time franchise record: 1,467-1,207 in 33 seasons. Won one NBA title (1977).
Team record past five years: 249-161 (.607, ranks 6th in NBA in that span).

HIGHLIGHTS

Top players: NBA Most Improved Player Zach Randolph led the Trail Blazers in scoring (20.1 ppg, 17th in the NBA) and rebounding (10.5 rpg, 6th) and ranked in the top 20 in the league in 19 categories. He had 43 double-doubles, fifth best in the NBA and the most for a Blazer since 1981-82. ... Theo Ratliff, the NBA leader in blocked shots and a All-Defensive Second Team selection, played 32 games for the Blazers after coming to Portland in a February 9 trade, but his 141 blocks in that span were the fifth-highest for a full season in club history. His 4.41 bpg as a Blazer was the best in franchise history. ... Guards Derek Anderson (13.6 ppg) and Damon Stoudamire (13.4 ppg) were the team's second- and third-leading scorers. Stoudamire led the Blazers in assists (6.1, 12th in the NBA) and steals (1.21 spg) His 87.6 free throw percentage ranked 10th in the NBA. ... Shareef Abdur-Rahim was 12th in the NBA in free throw percentage (.869).
Key injuries: The Trail Blazers lost a total of 171 player games because of injury or illness. Anderson missed three games early in the season because of back spasms, then went on the injured list for 28 games with a herniated disc. He returned on January 8 and started the final 46 games. Portland was 25-21 with him as a starter. Ruben Patterson sat out seven early games with tendonitis in his left Achillies' tendon.
Notable: The Trail Blazers missed the playoffs, which snapped the club's NBA-best run of 21 straight postseason appearances and denied them an opportunity to tie the Syracuse/Philadelphia franchise's record of 22. ... The Trail Blazers finished 41-41, the 15th year in a row and the 25th time in the past 28 seasons they have finished at .500 or better. ... Portland was seven games under .500 with the third-worst road record in the league at the halfway point of the season but was 24-17 in the second half. ... Portland was 6-5 in a club-record 11 overtime games. ... A franchise-record 24 players played in Blazers' games, and Maurice Cheeks used 15 different starting combinations; the most games started by a single group was 28.

SACRAMENTO KINGS
PACIFIC DIVISION

Sacramento Kings

2004-05 SEASON

Kings Schedule
Home games shaded; *—All-Star Game at Denver.

November

SUN	MON	TUE	WED	THU	FRI	SAT
	1	2 DAL	3 SA	4	5	6 HOU
7	8	9 TOR	10 SEA	11	12	13 PHO
14 DEN	15	16 CHI	17	18	19 MEM	20
21 MIL	22	23 HOU	24	25	26 LAL	27
28 MIN	29	30 MEM				

December

SUN	MON	TUE	WED	THU	FRI	SAT
			1 NO	2	3 IND	4
5 BOS	6	7 CHA	8	9	10 MIN	11 IND
12	13	14 MIL	15	16 LAL	17	18
19 NO	20	21 WAS	22	23 MIA	24	25
26 GS	27	28	29	30	31 UTH	

January

SUN	MON	TUE	WED	THU	FRI	SAT
						1
2 SA	3	4 NYK	5 TOR	6	7 ATL	8 NO
9	10	11 DEN	12	13 UTH	14	15 LAC
16 LAC	17 POR	18	19	20 CLE	21	22
23 SA	24	25 NJN	26	27 SA	28 HOU	29
30 MIN	31					

February

SUN	MON	TUE	WED	THU	FRI	SAT
		1 SEA	2 GS	3	4 NYK	5 POR
6	7	8 PHO	9	10 SEA	11 DAL	12
13 BOS	14	15 CHI	16 NJN	17	18	19
20 *All-Star	21	22 ATL	23	24 DAL	25	26 PHI
27 WAS	28					

March

SUN	MON	TUE	WED	THU	FRI	SAT
		1 CHA	2 ORL	3	4 MIA	5
6 DET	7	8 MEM	9	10	11 LAC	12
13 HOU	14	15 ORL	16	17 GS	18	19 LAC
20 GS	21	22 POR	23	24 DAL	25	26 DEN
27	28 PHI	29	30 DET	31		

April

SUN	MON	TUE	WED	THU	FRI	SAT
					1 CLE	2
3 MIN	4	5 SEA	6	7	8 POR	9
10 LAL	11	12	13	14	15 LAL	16 PHO
17 UTH	18	19	20 PHO	21	22	23

2004-05 SEASON

TEAM DIRECTORY

Ownership . . . . .Maloof Sports and Entertainment
President, Basketball Operations . . . . . .Geoff Petrie
President . . . . .John Thomas
Vice President, Ticket Sales and Services . . .Orin Anderson
Vice President, Arena Programming . . . .Mike Duncan
Vice President, Strategic Alliances . . . . .Blake Edwards
Vice President, Service Development . . .Tom Peterson
Vice President, Finance . . . . .John Rinehart
Vice President, Human Resources . . . . .Donna Ruiz
Vice President, Arena Services . . . . .Mark Stone
Sr. Dir., Communications/Public Relations .Sonja Brown
Senior Director, Marketing and
Monarchs Business Operations . . . . .Danette Leighton

BASKETBALL OPERATIONS

Head Coach . . . . .Rick Adelman
VP, Basketball Operations . . . . .Wayne Cooper
Director, Player Personnel/TV Color Analyst .Jerry Reynolds
Director, Scouting . . . . .Scotty Stirling
Assistant Coaches . . . . .Elston Turner, Pete Carril, T.R. Dunn
Assistant Coach/Advance NBA Scout . . . .Bubba Burrage
Athletic Trainer . . . . .Pete Youngman
Regional Scout .Keith Drum
International Scout . . . . .Jack Mai
Video Coordinator . . . . .Steve Shuman
Video Scout . . . . .Mike Petrie
Assistant Video Coordinator . . . . .R.J. Adelman
Strength and Conditioning Coach . . . . . . .Al Biancani
Assistant Athletic Trainer/
Equipment Manager . . . . .Robert Pimental
Director, Basketball Operations . . . . .Sheli Everman
Director, Facility Operations/
Team Security .Joe Nolan
Director, Systems Development
Maintenance & Research . . . . .Steve Schmidt
Basketball Operations Coordinator . . . . . .Tiffany Tudsbury
Guest Information Specialist . . . . .Dayna Simondi
VP of Media Relations/
Basketball Operations . . . . .Troy Hanson
Executive Director of Media Relations/
Basketball Operations . . . . .Darrin May
Manager, Basketball Information . . . . .Darryl Arata
Kings Web Content Coordinator . . . . .Devin Blankenship
Media Relations Intern . . . . .Chris Clark
Team Physicians . . . . .Dr. Richard Marder
(orthopaedic), Dr. Jeff Tanji (general), Dr. Eric Heiden (orthopaedic),
Dr. Dave Cosca (general), Dr. Matthew Campbell (dental)
Team Counsel .David Price

Joe Maloof

Gavin Maloof

Rick Adelman

ROSTER
Coach—Rick Adelman
Assistant coaches—Bubba Burrage, Pete Carril, T.R. Dunn, Elston Turner

No.	Name	Pos.	Ht./Wt.	Metric (m/kg)	Born	College/country
10	Mike Bibby	G	6-1/190	1.85/86.2	5-13-78	Arizona
3	David Bluthenthal	F	6-7/220	2.00/99.8	7-18-80	USC
13	Doug Christie	G/F	6-6/205	1.98/93.0	5-9-70	Pepperdine
24	Bobby Jackson	G	6-1/185	1.85/83.9	12-9-68	Minnesota
23	Kevin Martin	G	6-7/185	2.00/83.9	2-1-83	Western Carolina
52	Brad Miller	F/C	7-0/260	2.13/117.9	4-12-76	Purdue
22	Ricky Minard	G	6-4/200	1.93/90.7	9-11-82	Morehead State
00	Greg Ostertag	C	7-2/280	2.18/127.0	3-6-73	Kansas
25	Darius Songaila	F	6-9/248	2.05/112.5	2-14-78	Wake Forest
16	Peja Stojakovic	G/F	6-10/229	2.08/103.9	9-6-77	Sebria and Montenegro
4	Chris Webber	F	6-10/245	2.08/111.1	3-1-73	Michigan

BROADCAST INFORMATION

Radio: KHTK (1140 AM). Broadcasters: Gary Gerould, Jim Kozimor.
TV: News10 (ABC, Channel 10). Broadcasters: Grant Napear, Jerry Reynolds.
Cable TV: TBA.

TEAM INFORMATION

Team address .... One Sports Parkway
Sacramento, CA 95834
Business phone 916-928-0000
Ticket information 916-928-3650
Website .... www.kings.com
Arena (capacity) .... ARCO Arena (17,317)
Game times .... 7 p.m.; 6 p.m. Sundays
First Kings game in arena .... November 8, 1988

2003-04 REVIEW

RESULTS

OCTOBER
29— Cleveland	106 -92	1 -0	
31— Philadelphia	100 -89	2 -0	

NOVEMBER
1 — at Denver	*88 -109	2 -1	
5 — at Minnesota	125 -121	†3 -1	
7 — at New York	*111 -114	3 -2	
9 — at Boston	*82 -91	3 -3	
11— Detroit	97 -91	4 -3	
13— at Portland	*110 -112	†4 -4	
14— Toronto	94 -64	5 -4	
16— Golden State	106 -104	6 -4	
19— at Utah	118 -110	7 -4	
21— Orlando	122 -92	8 -4	
23— Chicago	110 -99	9 -4	
25— Memphis	109 -89	10 -4	
28— Houston	103 -74	11 -4	
30— New Jersey	105 -92	12 -4	

DECEMBER
5 — Minnesota	*109 -112	†12 -5	
7 — Indiana	91 -88	13 -5	
9 — L.A. Clippers	105 -95	14 -5	
12— at Utah	100 -93	15 -5	
14— Phoenix	107 -102	16 -5	
16— at Memphis	*100 -105	16 -6	
18— at New Orleans	101 -90	17 -6	
19— at Atlanta	98 -86	18 -6	
21— Portland	117 -98	19 -6	
23— Memphis	114 -97	20 -6	
25— Dallas	*103 -111	20 -7	

JANUARY
3 — at L.A. Clippers	116 -109	22 -8	
4 — Seattle	130 -99	23 -8	
6 — Atlanta	105 -89	24 -8	
7 — at Seattle	*93 -104	24 -9	
9 — at Phoenix	113 -93	25 -9	
11— Denver	117 -106	26 -9	
13— Miami	90 -86	27 -9	
16— L.A. Lakers	103 -83	28 -9	
19— at L.A. Clippers	125 -100	29 -9	
20— Portland	*104 -109	†29 -10	
22— at Cleveland	95 -89	30 -10	
23— at Memphis	*95 -109	30 -11	
25— at Dallas	*99 -108	30 -12	
28— at Houston	99 -94	31 -12	
29— at San Antonio	96 -91	32 -12	
31— at Seattle	110 -103	33 -12	

FEBRUARY
3 — Seattle	117 -101	34 -12	
6 — San Antonio	*94 -102	34 -13	
8 — Denver	115 -92	35 -13	
10— at Milwaukee	124 -117	36 -13	
11— at Detroit	96 -94	37 -13	
17— Boston	127 -111	38 -13	
19— at Minnesota	*75 -92	38 -14	
20— at Chicago	91 -83	39 -14	
22— at Toronto	96 -81	40 -14	
24— New York	107 -99	41 -14	

MARCH
26— at L.A. Lakers	103 -101	42 -14	
27— Utah	*97 -102	42 -15	
29— Phoenix	108 -94	43 -15	
2 — L.A. Clippers	113 -106	44 -15	
4 — at Philadelphia	114 -105	45 -15	
6 — at Miami	*96 -102	45 -16	
7 — at Orlando	107 -90	46 -16	
9 — Golden State	96 -92	47 -16	
11— Dallas	120 -102	48 -16	
12— at Portland	*81 -83	48 -17	
14— San Antonio	101 -87	49 -17	
16— at New Jersey	*77 -94	49 -18	
17— at Washington	*108 -114	49 -19	
19— at Indiana	94 -92	50 -19	
21— Houston	100 -95	51 -19	
23— Milwaukee	*101 -112	51 -20	
24— at L.A. Lakers	*91 -115	51 -21	
28— Washington	100 -92	52 -21	
31— at San Antonio	*89 -107	52 -22	

APRIL
1 — at Dallas	*117 -127	52 -23	
4 — at Houston	99 -94	53 -23	
6 — New Orleans	105 -91	54 -23	
8 — Minnesota	*86 -94	54 -24	
9 — at Phoenix	*96 -101	54 -25	
11— L.A. Lakers	102 -85	55 -25	
12— at Denver	*89 -97	55 -26	
14— at Golden State	*91 -97	55 -27	

*Loss. †Single overtime.

TEAM LEADERS

Points: Peja Stojakovic (1,964).
Field goals made: Stojakovic (665).
Free throws made: Stojakovic (394).
3-pointers made: Stojakovic (240).
Rebounds: Brad Miller (743).
Assists: Mike Bibby (444).
Steals: Doug Christie (151).
Blocks: Brad Miller (86).

RECORDS

Regular season: 55-27 (2nd in Pacific Division); 16-8 in division; 31-21 in conference; 24-6 vs. Eastern Conference; 34-7 at home; 21-20 on road; 1-3 in overtime; 5-4 in games decided by three points or fewer; 29-9 in games decided by 10 points or more; held opponents under 100 points 48 times; held under 100 points 33 times.
Playoffs: 7-5, defeated Mavericks, 4-1, in Western Conference first round; lost to Timberwolves, 4-3, in Western Conference semifinals.
All-time franchise record: 2,093-2,308 in 56 seasons. Won one NBA title (1951) while franchise was located in Rochester.
Team record past five years: 274-136 (.668, ranks 3rd in NBA in that span).

HIGHLIGHTS

Top players: Peja Stojakovic led the Kings in scoring (24.2 ppg, 2nd in the NBA) and free throw shooting (.927, 1st in the NBA). He became the first King since Spud Webb in 1994-95 to lead the NBA in free throw percentage. ... Chris Webber, despite playing in 23 games, was second in scoring (18.7 ppg). ... Mike Bibby had a team-high 5.4 apg (18th in the NBA) while averaging 18.4 ppg (third-best on the team). ... Anthony Peeler shot an NBA-best 48.2 percent (68-of-141) from beyond the arc, becoming the first King to lead the league in 3-point accuracy since Jim Les in 1990-91. ... In his first season with the Kings, Brad Miller averaged 14.1 ppg and led the team in field-goal percentage (.510, 8th in the NBA) and blocks (1.19 bpg).
Key injuries: The Kings lost a total of 190 player games because of injury or illness. The regular starting lineup of Webber, Stojakovic, Vlade Divac, Doug Christie and Bibby played together in only 22 games. Webber suffered an injury to his left knee in the 2003 playoffs and didn't play until March 2. Bibby and Christie

were the only Kings to play in all 82 games; Stojakovic and Divac each missed one game. Bobby Jackson suffered an abdominal strain and missed 28 of the last 29 regular-season contests and all of the playoffs.
Notable: The Kings won 55 games, marking the fourth straight year they have won 55 or more. ... Sacramento led the NBA in field-goal percentage (.462), 3-point field-goal percentage (.401), assists (26.2 apg) and steals (8.66 spg) and was second in scoring (102.8 ppg) and free throw percentage (.795). ... In the playoffs, the Kings beat Dallas in five games but fell to Minnesota in seven. ... Sacramento has sold out 226 consecutive home contests, the longest active sellout streak in the NBA. ... For the fifth straight season, the Kings won 20 or more road games. ... On March 19 at Indiana, Rick Adelman became the franchise leader in coaching victories. ... Miller and Stojakovic were All-Stars. ... Stojakovic was named to the All-NBA Second Team, and Christie made the All-Defensive Second Team.

– 57 –

SAN ANTONIO SPURS
SOUTHWEST DIVISION

Spurs Schedule
Home games shaded; *—All-Star Game at Denver.

November

SUN	MON	TUE	WED	THU	FRI	SAT
	1	2	3 SAC	4	5 LAL	6
7 SEA	8	9	10 GS	11	12 MIA	13 ATL
14	15	16 NYK	17	18 PHI	19 BOS	20
21 TOR	22 MEM	23	24 DAL	25	26 DEN	27 UTH
28	29	30 DAL				

December

SUN	MON	TUE	WED	THU	FRI	SAT
			1 PHI	2	3 DET	4 MIL
5	6 CHI	7	8 SEA	9 HOU	10	11 CLE
12	13	14	15 ORL	16	17 NO	18 GS
19	20	21	22 ORL	23 MIN	24	25
26 BOS	27	28 PHO	29	30 POR	31 LAC	

January

SUN	MON	TUE	WED	THU	FRI	SAT
						1
2 SAC	3	4 LAL	5	6 IND	7	8 DEN
9	10 UTH	11	12 MIL	13	14 DAL	15 HOU
16	17 WAS	18	19 LAC	20	21 PHO	22
23 SAC	24 POR	25	26	27 SAC	28	29 NO
30	31 SEA					

February

SUN	MON	TUE	WED	THU	FRI	SAT
		1	2	3 LAL	4	5
6	7	8 CHA	9 WAS	10	11 NJN	12
13 MIA	14	15	16 NO	17	18	19
20 *All-Star	21	22	23 HOU	24	25	26 MEM
27	28 CLE					

March

SUN	MON	TUE	WED	THU	FRI	SAT
		1	2 TOR	3	4 CHI	5
6 UTH	7	8 NJN	9 PHO	10	11	12 DEN
13	14 NO	15	16 MIN	17	18 CHA	19
20 DET	21 NYK	22	23 IND	24	25 ATL	26
27 HOU	28	29	30 SEA	31		

April

SUN	MON	TUE	WED	THU	FRI	SAT
					1 DEN	2 LAL
3	4	5	6 LAC	7 DAL	8	9 LAC
10 GS	11	12 POR	13 UTH	14	15	16 MEM
17 MEM	18	19	20 MIN	21	22	23

TEAM DIRECTORY

Chairman and CEO . . . . Peter M. Holt

BASKETBALL OPERATIONS

Head Coach . . . . Gregg Popovich
General Manager . . . . R.C. Buford
Assistant Coaches . . . . P.J. Carlesimo, Mike Budenholzer, Don Newman
Director of Basketball Operations . . . . Danny Ferry
Assistant Coach/Dir. of Player Development . . Brett Brown
Assistant Coach/Scout . . . . Joe Prunty
Head Athletic Trainer . . . . Will Sevening
Assistant Athletic Trainer . . . . Joe Gutzwiller
Director of Scouting . . . . Lance Blanks
Director of Player Personnel . . . . Sam Presti
Video Coordinator . . . . James Borrego
Strength and Conditioning Coach . . . . Mike Brungardt
Team Physicians . . . . Dr. David Schmidt, Dr. Paul Saenz

BUSINESS OPERATIONS

Executive VP/Business Operations . . . . Russ Bookbinder
Executive VP/Corporate Development . . . . . . Rick Pych
Senior Vice President/Broadcasting . . . . Lawrence Payne
Vice President/Marketing . . . . Bruce Guthrie
Vice President/Sales . . . . Joe Clark
Vice President/Finance . . . . Lori Warren
Vice President/Community Relations . . . . Alison Fox
Vice President/Public Affairs . . . . Robert Peche
Vice President/Human Resources . . . . Paula Winslow
Director of Game Operations & Promotions . . Don Costante
Director of Ticket Operations . . . . Patricia Quinn
Director of Broadcasting . . . . Mike Kickirillo
Director of Internet and New Media . . . . Jeff Brody
Director of Guest Services . . . . Rebecca Caven
Director of Sponsorship Sales . . . . Judy Grier
Controller . . . . Craig Howard
Director of Media Services . . . . Tom James
Media Services Manager . . . . Brian Facchini
Media Services Coordinator . . . . Cliff Puchalski
SBC Center General Manager . . . . Steve Zito
SBC Center Assistant General Manager . . . . . John Sparks
Silver Stars Chief Operating Officer . . . . Clarissa Davis-Wrightsil
Silver Stars Media Services Manager . . . . Kris Davis
Director of Hockey Business Operations . . . . . Rick Carden
Rampage Media Services Manager . . . . Tobin Ernst

Peter M. Holt

Gregg Popovich

R.C. Buford

ROSTER
Coach—Gregg Popovich
Assistant coaches—Brett Brown, Mike Budenholzer, P.J. Carlesimo, Don Newman

No.	Name	Pos.	Ht./Wt.	Metric (m/kg)	Born	College/country
17	Brent Barry	G	6-6/203	1.98/92.1	12-31-71	Oregon State
12	Bruce Bowen	G	6-7/200	2.00/90.7	6-14-71	Cal State Fullerton
23	Devin Brown	G	6-5/235	1.96/106.6	12-30-78	Texas-San Antonio
21	Tim Duncan	F/C	7-0/260	2.13/117.9	4-25-76	Wake Forest
20	Manu Ginobili	G	6-6/210	1.98/95.3	7-28-77	Argentina
8	Rasho Nesterovic	C	7-0/248	2.13/112.5	5-30-76	Slovenia
9	Tony Parker	G	6-2/180	1.88/81.6	5-17-82	France
31	Malik Rose	F	6-7/255	2.00/115.6	11-23-74	Drexel
10	Romain Sato	G	6-5/205	1.96/93.0	3-2-81	Xavier
14	Beno Udrih	G	6-3/203	1.90/92.1	7-5-82	Slovenia
5	Robert Horry	F	6-10/240	2.08/108.9	8-25-70	Alabama
4	Sean Marks	F	6-10/250	2.08/113.4	8-23-75	California
34	Tony Massenburg	F	6-9/250	2.05/113.4	7-31-67	Maryland

BROADCAST INFORMATION

Radio: WOAI (1200 AM). Broadcaster: Bill Schoening; KCOR (1350 AM-Spanish). Broadcaster: Paul Castro.
TV: KENS (Channel 5), KRRT (Channel 35), FOX Sports Net. Broadcasters: Bill Land, Sean Elliot, Lance Banks.

TEAM INFORMATION

Team address	SBC Center, One SBC Center San Antonio, TX 78219
Business phone	210-444-5000
Ticket information	210-225-TEAM
Website	www.spurs.com
Arena (capacity)	SBC Center (18,797)
Game times	7:30 p.m.
First Spurs game in arena	November 1, 2002

2003-04 REVIEW

RESULTS

OCTOBER

28— Phoenix	83 -82	1 -0
29— at Denver	*72 -80	1 -1

NOVEMBER

1 — New York	86 -74	2 -1
3 — at Memphis	*80 -88	2 -2
4 — Miami	80 -73	3 -2
6 — L.A. Lakers	*117 -120	‡3 -3
8 — Dallas	*78 -81	3 -4
10— Utah	87 -78	4 -4
12— at New Jersey	85 -71	5 -4
14— at Philadelphia	*96 -100	5 -5
15— at Washington	95 -71	6 -5
18— Golden State	94 -81	7 -5
20— at Dallas	*92 -95	7 -6
21— Atlanta	114 -75	8 -6
26— Chicago	109 -98	9 -6
28— at L.A. Lakers	*87 -103	9 -7
29— at Golden State	*89 -91	9 -8

DECEMBER

1 — at L.A. Clippers	*83 -91	9 -9
3 — L.A. Lakers	*86 -90	9 -10
5 — at Orlando	105 -94	10 -10
6 — at Miami	86 -70	11 -10
8 — at Chicago	96 -82	12 -10
10— Portland	102 -77	13 -10
11— at Houston	71 -67	14 -10
13— Houston	86 -73	15 -10
15— Memphis	78 -67	16 -10
17— Toronto	73 -70	17 -10

19— at Seattle	87 -73	18 -10
20— at Portland	101 -91	19 -10
23— L.A. Clippers	111 -90	20 -10
26— Orlando	98 -83	21 -10
28— Milwaukee	89 -74	22 -10

JANUARY

3 — Philadelphia	*77 -83	22 -11
5 — at Denver	98 -74	23 -11
6 — Washington	94 -72	24 -11
9 — at New Orleans	94 -84	25 -11
10— Indiana	89 -88	†26 -11
13— at Atlanta	*77 -86	26 -12
14— Minnesota	*93 -100	26 -13
16— at Indiana	*79 -89	26 -14
18— at Boston	109 -92	27 -14
19— at Detroit	*77 -85	27 -15
21— New Jersey	99 -76	28 -15
23— at Phoenix	86 -84	29 -15
24— New Orleans	*96 -98	29 -16
26— at Milwaukee	*92 -93	29 -17
27— at New York	77 -67	30 -17
29— Sacramento	*91 -96	30 -18
31— Utah	85 -81	31 -18

FEBRUARY

2 — at Utah	83 -65	32 -18
5 — at Seattle	96 -90	33 -18
6 — at Sacramento	102 -94	34 -18
9 — at Houston	85 -82	35 -18
18— at Toronto	86 -82	36 -18
20— at Cleveland	*87 -89	36 -19

22— at Minnesota	94 -92	37 -19
24— Houston	86 -77	38 -19
26— at Dallas	*91 -115	38 -20
28— Denver	117 -92	39 -20

MARCH

1 — Memphis	*80 -81	39 -21
3 — Seattle	88 -84	40 -21
5 — Dallas	113 -100	41 -21
6 — at Phoenix	107 -86	42 -21
9 — at Memphis	*88 -94	42 -22
10— L.A. Clippers	108 -90	43 -22
12— Golden State	99 -74	44 -22
14— at Sacramento	*87 -101	44 -23
15— at Golden State	*80 -97	44 -24
18— Minnesota	106 -86	45 -24
20— Boston	103 -87	46 -24
23— at Minnesota	*81 -86	46 -25
25— Detroit	84 -75	47 -25
27— Phoenix	105 -76	48 -25
29— Cleveland	101 -93	49 -25
31— Sacramento	107 -89	50 -25

APRIL

2 — at Utah	94 -81	51 -25
4 — at L.A. Lakers	95 -89	52 -25
7 — Seattle	96 -75	53 -25
9 — Portland	84 -74	54 -25
11— at L.A. Clippers	88 -79	55 -25
12— at Portland	78 -66	56 -25
14— Denver	93 -67	57 -25

*Loss. †Single overtime. ‡Double overtime.

TEAM LEADERS

Points: Tim Duncan (1,538).
Field goals made: Duncan (592).
Free throws made: Duncan (352).
3-pointers made: Hedo Turkoglu (101).
Rebounds: Duncan (859).
Assists: Tony Parker (411).
Steals: Manu Ginobili (136).
Blocks: Duncan (185).

RECORDS

Regular season: 57-25 (2nd in Midwest Division); 15-9 in division; 35-17 in conference; 22-8 vs. Eastern Conference; 33-8 at home; 24-17 on road; 1-1 in overtime; 6-8 in games decided by three points or fewer; 38-5 in games decided by 10 points or more; held opponents under 100 points 75 times; held under 100 points 64 times.
Playoffs: 6-4, defeated Grizzlies, 4-0, in Western Conference first round; lost to Lakers, 4-2, in Western Conference semifinals.
All-time franchise record: 1,313-951 in 28 NBA seasons; 378-366 in nine ABA seasons. Won two NBA titles (1999, 2003).
Team record past five years: 286-124 (.698, ranks 2nd in NBA in that span).

HIGHLIGHTS

Top players: Tim Duncan led San Antonio in scoring (22.3 ppg, 8th in the NBA), rebounding (12.4 rpg, 2nd), blocks (2.68 bpg, 4th) and minutes (36.6 mpg). He had 56 double-doubles and was an All-Star and All-NBA First Team. ... Tony Parker led the Spurs in assists (5.5 apg, 16th in the NBA). ... Bruce Bowen was named to the NBA's All-Defensive First Team. He also shot 36.3 percent (77-212) from 3-point range. ... Off the bench, Manu Ginobili averaged 12.8 ppg, 4.5 rpg, 3.8 apg and 1.77 spg (7th in the NBA). He was selected to the sophomore squad in the Rookie Challenge and finished third in the Sixth Man of the Year voting. ... Rasho Nesterovic averaged 8.7 ppg, 7.7 rpg and 2.01 bpg (12th in the NBA).
Key injuries: Injuries cost San Antonio a total of 249 player games in 2003-04. Parker suffered a sprained left ankle in the preseason and sat out seven regular-season games. Duncan sat out 12 games with a left knee injury. Bowen and Nesterovic were the only Spurs to appear in all 82 games. San Antonio used eight different starting lineup combinations during the season.

Notable: The Spurs welcomed nine new faces into a lineup that had won an NBA Championship five months earlier. They wrapped up the 2003-04 season with a 57-25 record. ... Coach Gregg Popovich, who entered the season as one of just three active coaches to have won an NBA title (including Pat Riley and Phil Jackson), finished the year four wins shy of his 400th career coaching victory. He was the NBA's Coach of the Month in December. ... San Antonio's 2003-04 roster featured seven players born outside the United States. ... The Spurs first-round playoff sweep of the Memphis Grizzlies was the franchise's first playoff sweep since the 1999 season. ... Malik Rose became one of seven Spurs in franchise history to record a 20/20 game with his 20-point, 22-rebound performance vs. Dallas on November 8. ... Kevin Willis scored his 17,000th career point on November 4 vs. Miami. ... In the past six seasons, the Spurs own the NBA's best record with a 323-137 (.702) mark. ... On February 4, *ESPN the Magazine* named the Spurs the top franchise among all major professional sports.

SEATTLE SUPERSONICS
NORTHWEST DIVISION

SuperSonics Schedule
Home games shaded; *—All-Star Game at Denver.

November
SUN	MON	TUE	WED	THU	FRI	SAT
	1	2	3 LAC	4	5 ATL	6
7 SA	8	9 DEN	10 SAC	11	12 TOR	13
14 MEM	15	16 PHI	17 NJN	18	19 TOR	20
21 BOS	22	23 MIN	24 MEM	25	26 NJN	27
28 IND	29	30 POR				

December
SUN	MON	TUE	WED	THU	FRI	SAT
			1 UTH	2	3	4 POR
5	6	7	8 SA	9 DAL	10	11 BOS
12	13	14 LAL	15	16	17 PHO	18
19	20	21	22 DEN	23	24	25
26	27 UTH	28 PHI	29	30 ATL	31 CHA	

January
SUN	MON	TUE	WED	THU	FRI	SAT
						1
2	3 MIA	4	5 ORL	6 WAS	7	8
9 MIA	10	11 LAC	12 LAC	13	14 GS	15
16 CLE	17	18 DEN	19	20	21 MIN	22
23 UTH	24	25 LAL	26 UTH	27	28 GS	29
30	31 SA					

February
SUN	MON	TUE	WED	THU	FRI	SAT
		1 SAC	2	3	4	5 CHA
6	7	8 NO	9	10 SAC	11 PHO	12
13 DAL	14	15	16 GS	17	18	19
20 *All-Star	21	22 HOU	23 NO	24	25 MIN	26
27 MIL	28					

March
SUN	MON	TUE	WED	THU	FRI	SAT
		1 IND	2 CLE	3	4 DET	5
6 PHO	7	8 HOU	9	10	11 CHI	12
13 NYK	14	15 CHI	16 DET	17	18 ORL	19
20 LAL	21	22 MIL	23	24 POR	25 NYK	26
27 WAS	28	29 MEM	30 SA	31		

April
SUN	MON	TUE	WED	THU	FRI	SAT
					1 POR	2
3 GS	4	5 SAC	6	7	8 LAL	9 DEN
10	11 HOU	12	13 DAL	14	15 NO	16
17 MIN	18	19 DAL	20 HOU	21	22	23

2004-05 SEASON
TEAM DIRECTORY

Chairman . . . . .Howard Schultz
President/Chief Executive Officer . . . . .Wally Walker

BASKETBALL OPERATIONS
General Manager . . . . .Rick Sund
Head Coach . . . . .Nate McMillan
Associate Head Coach .Dwane Casey
Assistant Coaches . . . . .Dean Demopoulos, Bob Weiss
Special Assignments Coach . . . . .Jack Sikma
Special Assignments Coach/Video Coordinator . . . . .Walt Rock
Director of Player Personnel . . . . .David Pendergraft
Assistant G.M./Associate Legal Counsel . . . . .Rich Cho
Head Scout . . . . .Steve Rosenberry
Regional Scouts . . . . .Yvan Kelly, Bill Langloh
European Scout . . . . .Lojze Milosavljevic
Athletic Trainer . . . . .Mike Shimensky
Assistant Coach/Player Development . . . . .Dwight Daub
Equipment Manager/Furtado Center Manager . . . . . .Marc St. Yves
Executive Assistant to the General Manager . . . . . . .Denice Vezetinski
Basketball Operations Assistant . . . . .Linda Figurelli
Furtado Center Security .Al Lima, Jack Chaves
Team Physicians . . . . .Dr. Jeffrey Cary, Dr. Richard Zorn

SEATTLE SONICS
Executive Vice President/CFO . . . . .Danny Barth
Executive Vice President of Administration . . . . .Terry McLaughlin
Executive Vice President of Sales & Marketing . . . . .Mike Humes
VP of Business Development & Broadcasting . . . . . .John Croley
Vice President of Marketing . . . . .Rob Martin
Vice President of Ticket Sales . . . . .Kevin Terry
Vice President of Service Development . . . . .Pete Winemiller
Sr. Director of Public Relations & Community Relations .Valerie O'Neil
Art Director . . . . .Lisa Gardner
Controller . . . . .Stephanie Grube
Director of Broadcasting . . . . .Bridget Billig Backschies
Director of Business Development . . . . .Chip Bowers
Director of Information Technology . . . . .Rick Shrum
Director of Merchandising . . . . .Jeremy Owen
Director of Operations . . . . .Mark Henry
Director of Public Relations . . . . .Marc Moquin
Director of Sales Administration . . . . .Martin Walker
Accounting Staff . . . . .Ellis Bannister, Aesha Evans, Denae Johnson, Linda Krueger, Teresa Wong
Administration Staff . . . . .Allan Hoffman, Lorna Kennedy, Corin Mochnick, Katy Semtner, George Waterstraat
Business Development & Broadcast Staff . . . . .Noelle Anderson, Jack Breeden, Garrick Dorn, Arlene Escobar, Janna Ford, Steve Hood, Kevin Kepler, Natalie Larsen, Steve Ransom, Sharon Wortman
Facilities Staff . . . . .Keith Boyd, Philip Guerrier, Michael Johnson, Glinda Mathews
Guest Relations Staff . . . . .Gabriella Buono, Debby Dunn, Jason Hanson, Crissy Hathaway, Ali Hummels, Susie Kandzor
Marketing Staff . . . . .Mike Bellerive, RK Cobban, Michelle Odo, Marshall Sele, Ben Wilson
Merchandising Staff . . . . .Krista Armas, Joel Bowyer, David Cromar, James Kyle, Mark Pillo
Operations Staff . . . . .Mickey Ahrens, Marc Taylor, Pat Walker, Rebecca Wilson
Public Relations & Community Relations Staff . . . . . .Jennifer Carroll, Pat Coussens, Robyn Jamilosa, Ronee Meredith, Liam O'Mahony, Kevin Parker
Ticket Sales Staff . . . . .Nick Affolter, Chris Butler, Megan Cifala, Zack Daniels, Matt Difebo, Scott Earle, Chris Fryar, Jenny Guile, Keegan Hall, Travis Herman, Chad Langdon, Tanya Longoria, Kelly Nigh, John Paik, Nate Silverman, Brian Simpson, Stacy Slade, Jennifer Tucker
Ticket Operations Staff .Derrick Casey, Val Kato, Jason Krull, Darrin Miller

Howard Schultz

Wally Walker

Nate McMillan

ROSTER
Coach—Nate McMillan
Associate head coach—Dwane Casey
Assistant coaches—Dean Demopoulos, Bob Weiss

No.	Name	Pos.	Ht./Wt.	Metric (m/kg)	Born	College/country
34	Ray Allen	G	6-5/205	1.96/93.0	7-20-75	Connecticut
4	Nick Collison	F	6-9/255	2.05/115.7	10-26-80	Kansas
33	Antonio Daniels	G	6-4/205	1.93/93.0	3-19-75	Bowling Green
30	Reggie Evans	F	6-8/245	2.03/111.1	5-18-80	Iowa
21	Danny Fortson	F	6-8/260	2.03/117.9	3-27-76	Cincinnati
13	Jerome James	C	7-1/272	2.16/123.4	11-17-75	Florida A&M
7	Rashard Lewis	F	6-10/215	2.08/97.5	8-8-79	Alief Elsik HS
22	Ronald Murray	G	6-4/190	1.93/86.2	7-29-79	Shaw
9	Vitaly Potapenko	F/C	6-10/285	2.08/129.3	3-21-75	Wright State
77	Vladimir Radmanovic	F	6-10/234	2.08/106.1	11-19-80	Serbia-Montenegro
8	Luke Ridnour	G	6-2/175	1.88/79.4	2-13-81	Oregon
35	Leon Smith	F	6-10/235	2.08/106.6	11-2-80	Martin Luther King HS
31	Robert Swift	C	7-0/245	2.13/111.1	12-3-85	Bakersfield HS
24	David Young	G	6-5/205	1.06/93.0	8-18-81	North Carolina Central

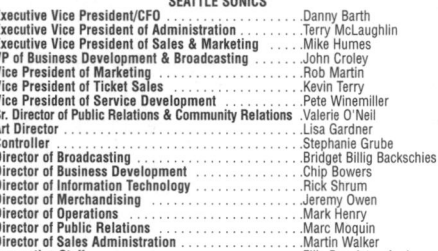

BROADCAST INFORMATION
Radio: SportsRadio 950 KJR-AM.
Broadcasters: Kevin Calabro, Craig Ehlo.
TV: FOX Sports Northwest. Broadcaster: Kevin Calabro, Craig Ehlo.
.

TEAM INFORMATION
Team address ....351 Elliott Avenue West, Suite 500
Seattle, WA 98119
Business phone 206-281-5800
Ticket information 206-283-3865
Website ....www.supersonics.com
Arena (capacity) ....KeyArena (17,072)
Game times ....7 p.m.
First SuperSonics game in arena ....November 4, 1995

2003-04 REVIEW

RESULTS

OCTOBER
30— L.A. Clippers	109 -100	1 -0
31— at L.A. Clippers	124 -105	2 -0

NOVEMBER
7 — Portland	100 -82	3 -0
9 — Atlanta	*81 -91	3 -1
11— at Minnesota	89 -87	4 -1
12— at Milwaukee	104 -99	5 -1
14— at Indiana	*78 -101	5 -2
15— at Chicago	98 -90	6 -2
18— Miami	*98 -105	6 -3
21— Memphis	*97 -98	6 -4
23— Washington	88 -85	7 -4
25— New Jersey	*70 -93	7 -5
28— at Utah	98 -81	7 -6
29— Houston	95 -88	8 -6

DECEMBER
3 — New York	95 -87	9 -6
5 — Indiana	*94 -101	9 -7
7 — at Toronto	*98 -108	9 -8
9 — at New Jersey	*88 -101	9 -9
10— at Boston	*112 -126	9 -10
12— at Detroit	93 -72	10 -10
14— Milwaukee	108 -102	11 -10
16— at Phoenix	*91 -92	†11 -11
17— Denver	*98 -99	11 -12
19— San Antonio	*73 -87	11 -13
20— at Denver	115 -106	12 -13
23— Phoenix	116 -90	13 -13
27— Minnesota	*86 -104	13 -14

JANUARY
29— at Houston	87 -86	14 -14
30— at Memphis	105 -99	15 -14
2 — L.A. Lakers	111 -109	16 -14
4 — at Sacramento	*99 -130	16 -15
5 — Portland	119 -108	†17 -15
7 — Sacramento	104 -93	18 -15
9 — Memphis	122 -116	19 -15
10— at Golden State	*110 -113	†19 -16
13— Cleveland	*96 -104	19 -17
16— at New York	*88 -108	19 -18
17— at Washington	*84 -99	19 -19
19— at Philadelphia	90 -81	20 -19
20— at Cleveland	*94 -99	20 -20
22— Golden State	103 -87	21 -20
24— L.A. Clippers	102 -97	22 -20
27— Dallas	*116 -118	22 -21
28— at L.A. Lakers	*82 -96	22 -22
31— Sacramento	*103 -110	22 -23

FEBRUARY
2 — Chicago	109 -97	23 -23
3 — at Sacramento	*101 -117	23 -24
5 — San Antonio	*90 -96	23 -25
6 — at Phoenix	107 -105	24 -25
8 — at Portland	*85 -95	24 -26
10— Golden State	*97 -106	24 -27
12— Toronto	94 -74	25 -27
19— Philadelphia	*101 -112	25 -28
21— at Golden State	*92 -94	25 -29
22— Boston	108 -87	26 -29

MARCH
24— at Utah	*86 -99	26 -30
25— Utah	*92 -93	†26 -31
27— Phoenix	*99 -104	26 -32
29— at Houston	97 -80	27 -32
2 — at Dallas	*96 -107	27 -33
3 — at San Antonio	*84 -88	27 -34
5 — at L.A. Lakers	*91 -99	27 -35
7 — Detroit	*65 -86	27 -36
9 — Minnesota	*92 -105	27 -37
12— at Miami	*74 -82	27 -38
13— at Orlando	115 -101	28 -38
16— at Atlanta	118 -110	29 -38
18— at Memphis	97 -94	30 -38
19— at New Orleans	91 -80	31 -38
21— Orlando	84 -67	32 -38
24— Utah	84 -77	33 -38
26— Denver	102 -86	34 -38
27— at Portland	*108 -115	†34 -39
30— at Denver	*119 -124	34 -40
31— at Minnesota	*83 -90	34 -41

APRIL
2 — L.A. Lakers	*86 -97	34 -42
4 — New Orleans	96 -88	35 -42
6 — at Dallas	*108 -118	35 -43
7 — at San Antonio	*75 -96	35 -44
10— Dallas	119 -99	36 -44
12— Houston	*107 -111	36 -45
14— at L.A. Clippers	118 -87	37 -45

*Loss. †Single overtime.

TEAM LEADERS
Points: Rashard Lewis (1,421).
Field goals made: Lewis (535).
Free throws made: Ray Allen (245).
3-pointers made: Allen (148).
Rebounds: Lewis (518).
Assists: Brent Barry (342).
Steals: Lewis (99).
Blocks: Calvin Booth (101).

RECORDS
Regular season: 37-45 (tied, fourth in Pacific Division); 11-13 in division; 22-30 in conference; 15-15 vs. Eastern Conference; 21-20 at home; 16-25 on road; 1-4 in overtime; 6-7 in games decided by three points or fewer; 17-23 in games decided by 10 points or more; held opponents under 100 points 49 times; held under 100 points 50 times.
Playoffs: None.
All-time franchise record: 1,607-1,395 in 37 seasons. Won one NBA title (1979).
Team record past five years: 211-199 (.515, ranks 14th in NBA in that span).

HIGHLIGHTS

Top players: Ray Allen averaged 23.0 ppg, 5.1 rpg, 4.8 apg and shot 90.4 percent from the foul line. ... Rashard Lewis led the team in rebounding (6.5 rpg) and was second on the team in scoring (17.8 ppg). ... Brent Barry averaged 10.8 ppg and finished second in the league in 3-point shooting percentage (.452). ... Ronald Murray finished third on the team in scoring, averaging 12.4 ppg. ... Vladimir Radmanovic averaged 12.0 ppg and 5.3 rpg.
Key injuries: The Sonics lost a total of 185 player games because of injury or illness. Allen missed 26 games, 25 because of surgery on his right ankle. Barry missed 23 games, 20 with a fractured right hand. First-round draft pick Nick Collison missed the entire season because of surgery on both shoulders. Murray was the only Sonic player to appear in all 82 games.
Notable: Seattle traveled to Japan to open the season and recorded two victories against the L.A. Clippers. ... Lewis scored a career-high 50 points in the second game against the Clippers. He also was named Western Conference

Player of the Week after averaging 37.5 points, 6.0 rebounds and 3.5 assists. ... Allen was named Western Conference Player of the Week for January 12 after scoring a season-high 42 points vs. Portland on January 5. He also was named a reserve for the Western Conference All-Star team. ... Barry and Lewis were chosen for the 3-point shootout during All-Star weekend, and Ronald Murray was selected for the Rookie Challenge. ... The Sonics won a season-high seven straight games from March 13-26. ... Seattle finished sixth in the NBA in scoring, averaging 97.1 ppg. ... The Sonics led the league in 3-point field goals made (723) and attempted (1936) and finished second in 3-point percentage (.373). ... Coach Nate McMillan recorded his 150th career victory February 29 vs. Houston.

TORONTO RAPTORS
ATLANTIC DIVISION

Raptors Schedule
Home games shaded; *—All-Star Game at Denver.

November
SUN	MON	TUE	WED	THU	FRI	SAT
	1	2	3 HOU	4	5 DET	6
7 POR	8	9 SAC	10 UTH	11	12 SEA	13 POR
14	15	16 LAC	17 DEN	18	19 SEA	20
21 SA	22	23 WAS	24 NYK	25	26	27 NYK
28 WAS	29	30 MIA				

December
SUN	MON	TUE	WED	THU	FRI	SAT
			1 ORL	2	3 BOS	4 CLE
5	6 NJN	7	8 DET	9	10 DEN	11
12 MIA	13	14	15 MIN	16	17 IND	18
19 NJN	20 HOU	21	22 UTH	23	24	25
26 PHO	27	28 LAL	29 GS	30	31	

January
SUN	MON	TUE	WED	THU	FRI	SAT
						1
2	3 ORL	4	5 SAC	6	7 MIL	8
9 GS	10	11	12 BOS	13	14 PHI	15
16 NO	17 MIN	18	19 NYK	20	21 WAS	22
23 CHA	24	25	26 MIA	27	28 CHA	29
30 PHO	31					

February
SUN	MON	TUE	WED	THU	FRI	SAT
		1	2 IND	3	4 WAS	5
6 DAL	7	8 CLE	9 MIL	10	11 PHI	12
13 LAC	14	15	16 CHI	17	18	19
20 *All-Star	21	22 NJN	23	24	25 MIL	26
27 LAL	28					

March
SUN	MON	TUE	WED	THU	FRI	SAT
		1	2 SA	3	4 MEM	5
6 NO	7 DAL	8	9 ORL	10	11 ATL	12
13 PHI	14	15	16 BOS	17	18 DET	19
20 CLE	21	22	23 CHI	24	25 PHI	26 ATL
27	28	29 MIA	30 ORL	31		

April
SUN	MON	TUE	WED	THU	FRI	SAT
					1 CHA	2
3 DET	4	5	6 MEM	7	8 ATL	9 CHI
10	11 IND	12 NYK	13	14	15 NJN	16
17 BOS	18	19 MIL	20 CLE	21	22	23

2004-05 SEASON
TEAM DIRECTORY

Board of Directors . . . . Larry M. Tanenbaum
(Chairman of the Board), Robert G. Bertram, Ken Dryden, Ivan Fecan, Dale H. Lastman, James W. Leech, John MacIntyre, Dean Metcalf, Richard Peddie
Chairman of the Board/NBA Governor . . . . Larry M. Tanenbaum
President/CEO/Alternate NBA Governor . . . . Richard Peddie
Executive VP and General Manager, Air Canada Centre . Bob Hunter
Executive VP and COO . . . . Tom Anselmi
Executive VP, CFO and Business Development . . . . Ian Clarke
Senior VP/General Counsel/Corporate Secretary . . . . . . Robin Brudner
VP, Communications and Community Development . . . . John Lashway
Vice President, People . . . . Mardi Walker
VP and Executive Producer, Leafs TV and Raptors NBA TV . . John Shannon
VP, Corporate Sales and Service . . . . Dave Hopkinson
Vice President, Finance . . . . Kevin Nonomura
Vice President, Marketing . . . . Beth Robertson
Vice President, Operations . . . . Diego Roccasalva
General Manager . . . . Rob Babcock
Senior Advisor to the General Manager . . . . Wayne Embry
Head Coach . . . . Sam Mitchell
Director of Player Development/Assistant Coach . . . . . Alex English
Assistant Coaches . . . . Jim Todd, Jay Triano
Assistant Coach/Strength and Conditioning Coordinator . . Shaun Brown
Massage Therapist . . . . Ray Chow
Director, NBA Player Personnel . . . . Pete Babcock
Director, International Player Personnel . . . . Scott Howard
Director, Player Personnel . . . . Jim Kelly
Director, Basketball Operations . . . . Steve Fruitman
Assistant Director, Player Personnel/
Director, Video Scouting . . . . Mike McCollow
Head Scout . . . . Bob Zuffelato
Scouts . . . . Mike Evans, Norm Goodman, Steve Young
Advance Scout . . . . Micah Nori
Equipment Manager/Travel Coordinator . . . . Kevin DiPietro
Executive Assistant to the General Manager . . . . Jacquie Allinson
Financial Assistant Basketball Operations . . . . Doreen Doyle
Assistant, Basketball Operations . . . . Graeme McIntosh
Assistant Equipment Manager . . . . Paul Elliott
Administrative Assistant, Basketball Operations . . . . . . Casey Whalen
Director, Media Relations . . . . Jim LaBumbard
Coordinators, Media Relations . . . . Michael Cvitkovic, James Lamont
Executive Director, Raptors Foundation/Director, Community Relations . . Beverley Deeth
Manager, Community Relations . . . . David De Freitas
Manager, Corporate Communications . . . . Rajani Kamath
Manager, Raptors Foundation . . . . Andrea Smith
Coordinator, Raptors Foundation Fund Develop. . . . . . . Tanya Phillips
Executive Assistant, Communications and
Community Development . . . . Rose Politi
Director, Consumer Products . . . . Marc Petitpas
Director, Food and Beverage Finance . . . . Aldrick Britto
Director, Event Operations and Production . . . . Jim Roe
Director, Executive Suite Services . . . . Kristy Fletcher
Director, Finance . . . . Suzanne Scott
Director, Food and Beverage . . . . Michael Doyle
Director, Guest Services . . . . Chris Gibbs
Director, Information Technology . . . . Sasha Puric
Director, People Relations . . . . Craig Richardson
Director, Programming and Event Marketing . . . . Patti-Anne Tarlton
Director, Restaurant Operations/Executive Chef . . . . . . Brad Long
Director, Sales . . . . Jim Edmands
Director, Service and Ticketing . . . . Paul Bierne
Director, Ticket Operations . . . . Donna Henderson
Legal Counsel . . . . Peter Miller
Manager, Broadcasting . . . . Liana Ward
Associate Producer, Broadcasting . . . . Forbes Robertson

Rob Babcock

Sam Mitchell

ROSTER
Coach—Sam Mitchell
Assistant coaches—Alex English, Jim Todd, Jay Triano

No.	Name	Pos.	Ht./Wt.	Metric (m/kg)	Born	College/country
11	Rafer Alston	G	6-2/175	1.88/79.4	7-24-76	Fresno State
55	Rafael Araujo	C	6-11/290	2.10/131.5	8-12-80	Brigham Young
4	Chris Bosh	F/C	6-10/228	2.08/103.4	3-24-84	Georgia Tech
15	Vince Carter	G/F	6-6/220	1.98/99.8	1-26-77	North Carolina
42	Donyell Marshall	F	6-9/230	2.05/104.3	5-18-73	Connecticut
31	Roger Mason Jr.	G	6-5/200	1.96/90.7	9-10-80	Virginia
6	Jerome Moiso	F	6-10/240	2.08/108.9	6-15-78	UCLA
21	Lamond Murray	F	6-7/235	2.00/106.6	4-20-73	California
10	Milt Palacio	G	6-3/215	1.90/97.5	2-07-78	Colorado State
24	Morris Peterson	G/F	6-7/220	2.00/99.8	8-26-77	Michigan State
5	Jalen Rose	G/F	6-8/215	2.03/97.5	1-30-73	Michigan
20	Alvin Williams	G	6-5/195	1.96/88.4	8-06-74	Villanova

BROADCAST INFORMATION

Radio: The Fan (590 AM). Broadcasters: TBA.
TV: SportsNet. Broadcasters: Chuck Swirsky, Leo Rautins and Norma Wick.

TEAM INFORMATION

Team address ....40 Bay Street, Suite 400
Toronto, Ontario, M5J 2X2
Business phone 416-815-5600
Ticket information 416-366-DUNK
Website ....www.raptors.com
Arena (capacity) ....Air Canada Centre (19,800)
Game times ....7 p.m., Monday-Saturday;
1, 3, 3:30 and 6 p.m., Sunday
First Raptors game in arena ......February 21, 1999

2003-04 REVIEW

RESULTS

OCTOBER
29— New Jersey	90 -87	1 -0
31— Washington	82 -79	2 -0

NOVEMBER
1 — at Minnesota	*56 -73	2 -1
6 — Dallas	77 -71	3 -1
7 — at Washington	*60 -86	3 -2
9 — Denver	89 -76	4 -2
11— at Portland	*80 -83	4 -3
12— at L.A. Lakers	*79 -94	4 -4
14— at Sacramento	*64 -94	4 -5
16— Houston	101 -97	‡5 -5
19— Philadelphia	*75 -81	5 -6
22— at New Jersey	81 -80	6 -6
23— Milwaukee	*62 -82	6 -7
26— at Atlanta	99 -97	†7 -7
28— at Orlando	87 -86	8 -7
29— at Miami	*66 -78	8 -8

DECEMBER
2 — at Philadelphia	95 -88	9 -8
3 — Boston	105 -95	10 -8
5 — Atlanta	92 -87	11 -8
7 — Seattle	108 -98	12 -8
9 — at Cleveland	100 -93	13 -8
12— at Boston	*111 -114	13 -9
14— Miami	*89 -90	13 -10
15— at Dallas	*94 -111	13 -11
17— at San Antonio	*70 -73	13 -12
19— New York	105 -99	†14 -12
21— Orlando	*93 -104	14 -13

26— at Utah	*94 -97	†14 -14
28— at L.A. Clippers	94 -88	15 -14
30— at Denver	81 -74	16 -14

JANUARY
2 — New Orleans	*74 -86	16 -15
4 — Phoenix	83 -73	17 -15
7 — Cleveland	75 -69	18 -15
9 — L.A. Clippers	*68 -78	18 -16
11— Portland	83 -72	19 -16
14— at Detroit	*91 -95	19 -17
15— at New Orleans	78 -74	†20 -17
17— at Atlanta	*70 -75	20 -18
19— at New York	*79 -90	20 -19
21— Minnesota	*97 -108	20 -20
23— at Milwaukee	*86 -98	20 -21
25— at Chicago	*89 -96	20 -22
28— Philadelphia	94 -84	21 -22
30— Detroit	*89 -90	†21 -23

FEBRUARY
1 — L.A. Lakers	*83 -84	21 -24
3 — at Philadelphia	93 -80	22 -24
4 — Orlando	110 -90	23 -24
6 — Indiana	*77 -83	23 -25
8 — at Golden State	84 -81	†24 -25
10— at Phoenix	101 -94	25 -25
12— at Seattle	*74 -94	25 -26
17— at Chicago	*73 -75	25 -27
18— San Antonio	*82 -86	25 -28
20— New Jersey	*72 -91	25 -29
22— Sacramento	*81 -96	25 -30

24— at New Jersey	*74 -86	25 -31
25— Washington	*74 -76	25 -32
27— at Boston	*75 -88	25 -33
29— Boston	*82 -91	25 -34

MARCH
2 — at Miami	89 -86	26 -34
3 — at Washington	*70 -84	26 -35
5 — New York	*103 -109	26 -36
7 — New Orleans	84 -76	27 -36
9 — at Indiana	*84 -94	†27 -37
10— Cleveland	*92 -106	27 -38
14— Atlanta	101 -84	28 -38
17— Utah	85 -81	29 -38
19— Chicago	*91 -96	29 -39
21— at New Orleans	121 -120	†30 -39
23— at Memphis	*86 -95	30 -40
24— at Houston	*89 -90	†30 -41
26— at New York	*101 -108	30 -42
28— Memphis	*88 -94	30 -43
31— Golden State	*78 -85	30 -44

APRIL
2 — at Indiana	*04 -04	30 45
4 — Milwaukee	*83 -90	30 -46
6 — at Cleveland	87 -86	31 -46
7 — Indiana	*90 -94	31 -47
9 — at Detroit	*66 -74	31 -48
11— Chicago	*108 -114	†31 -49
13— Detroit	87 -78	32 -49
14— at Milwaukee	89 -87	33 -49

*Loss. †Single overtime. ‡Double overtime.

TEAM LEADERS

Points: Vince Carter (1,645).
Field goals made: Carter (608).
Free throws made: Carter (336).
3-pointers made: Morris Peterson (126).
Rebounds: Marshall (709).
Assists: Carter (348).
Steals: Carter and Peterson (88).
Blocks: Chris Bosh (106).

RECORDS

Records: 33-49 (6th in Central Division); 11-17 in division; 22-32 in conference; 11-17 vs. Western Conference; 18-23 at home; 15-26 on road; 6-5 in overtime; 10-10 in games decided by three points or fewer; 9-22 in games decided by 10 points or more; held opponents under 100 points 73 times; held under 100 points 69 times.
Playoffs: None.
All-time franchise record: 281-425 in nine seasons.
Team record past five years: 191-219 (.466, tied for 20th in NBA in that span).

HIGHLIGHTS

Top players: Vince Carter led the Raptors in scoring (22.5 ppg, 7th in the NBA) for the sixth consecutive season. ... Chris Bosh was selected to the All-Rookie First Team, led all rookies in rebounds and blocks (106) and set a franchise record for rebounds in a rookie season with 557. ... Donyell Marshall was the only player in the league to finish in the top 25 in rebounds (9.9 rpg, 12th), 3-point field-goal percentage (.403, 13th) and blocks (1.51, 22nd). ... Jalen Rose scored his 10,000th career point December 14 vs. Miami. ... Morris Peterson ranked fourth in the NBA with a 1.28-to-1 steals-to-turnover ratio.
Key injuries: The Raptors lost a total of 270 player games because of injury or illness. Alvin Williams missed 26 games and had two stints on the injured list, primarily because of arthroscopic surgery on his right knee. Rose missed 16 games with a fracture of the fourth metacarpal on his left hand. Before the injury, Rose had played in 286 consecutive contests, which was the second-longest streak among active players (Antawn Jamison). Carter spent six games on the injured list with a moderate left ankle sprain. Peterson was the lone Raptor to appear in all 82 games. He has played in a franchise-best 196 consecutive contests.
Notable: The Raptors finished 33-49, nine wins better than the 2002-03 campaign. They did not advance to the playoffs for a second consecutive season. ... Toronto was 25-25 with one game left before the All-Star break and then lost its next nine contests. ... Toronto ranked in the top 10 in opponent points, field-goal percentage, 3-point field-goal percentage, assists, steals and blocks. ... Toronto ranked last in points, free throw attempts and offensive rebounds. ... Toronto set NBA season lows and franchise lows with 56 points and 19 field goals November 1 at Minnesota. ... The Raptors had 23 players suit up during the season, second-most in franchise history. ... Toronto played in 20 games decided by three points or fewer, the most by any team in the NBA.

– 63 –

UTAH JAZZ
NORTHWEST DIVISION

Jazz Schedule
Home games shaded; *—All-Star Game at Denver.

November

SUN	MON	TUE	WED	THU	FRI	SAT
	1	2	3 LAL	4	5 GS	6 DEN
7	8 DEN	9	10 TOR	11	12	13 DET
14	15	16 CHA	17 ORL	18	19 MIA	20 ATL
21	22 NO	23	24 CHI	25	26 HOU	27 SA
28	29	30 PHO				

December

SUN	MON	TUE	WED	THU	FRI	SAT
			1 SEA	2	3	4 DAL
5	6 MIA	7	8 ORL	9	10 POR	11
12 POR	13	14 LAC	15 PHO	16	17 BOS	18
19 NYK	20 PHI	21	22 TOR	23	24	25
26	27 SEA	28	29 LAC	30	31 SAC	

January

SUN	MON	TUE	WED	THU	FRI	SAT
						1
2 HOU	3 MEM	4	5 PHI	6	7 CHI	8 MIL
9	10 SA	11	12 PHO	13 SAC	14	15 CLE
16	17 LAL	18	19	20	21	22 MEM
23 SEA	24	25	26 SEA	27	28 MIN	29 NJN
30	31					

February

SUN	MON	TUE	WED	THU	FRI	SAT
		1 CHA	2	3	4	5 NO
6	7 NYK	8 DEN	9	10	11 MIN	12
13	14 PHO	15 LAL	16	17	18	19
20 *All-Star	21	22	23 DAL	24	25 BOS	26
27 HOU	28 LAC					

March

SUN	MON	TUE	WED	THU	FRI	SAT
		1	2 ATL	3	4 NO	5
6 SA	7	8 IND	9	10	11 MEM	12
13 DET	14	15 CLE	16 IND	17	18 NJN	19 WAS
20	21	22 LAL	23	24 WAS	25	26 MIL
27	28 HOU	29	30 DEN	31		

April

SUN	MON	TUE	WED	THU	FRI	SAT
					1 GS	2
3	4	5 POR	6 MIN	7	8 NO	9 DAL
10	11	12 LAC	13 SA	14	15 MIN	16
17 POR	18 SAC	19	20 GS	21	22	23

2004-05 SEASON

TEAM DIRECTORY

Owner . . . . .Larry H. Miller
President . . . . .Dennis Haslam
Senior VP, Basketball Operations . . . . .Kevin O'Connor
Head Coach .Jerry Sloan
Assistant Coaches . . . . .Phil Johnson,
   Gordon Chiesa, Tyrone Corbin
Player Development Assistant Coach . .Mark McKown
Athletic Trainer . . . . .Gary Briggs
Asst. Athletic Trainer/Equipment Manager . .Brian Zettler
Senior VP, Sales & Marketing . . . . .Jay Francis
Senior VP, Business Administration . . .Bob Hyde
Senior Vice President, Broadcasting . . .Randy Rigby
VP, Promotions/ Game Operations . . . .Grant Harrison
Vice President, Communications . . . . .Caroline Shaw
Vice President, Sales . . . . .Mike Snarr
Vice President, Ticket Sales . . . . .Jim Olson
Director, Broadcasting . . . . .Rob Howell
Director, Media Relations . . . . .Kim Turner
Director, Public Relations . . . . .Cindy Edman
Team Counsel . . . . .Robert Tingey
Team Orthropedic Surgeon . . . . .Lyle Mason
Team Internist . . . . .Russell Shields

Larry H. Miller

Kevin O'Connor

Jerry Sloan

ROSTER
Coach—Jerry Sloan
Assistant coaches—Gordon Chiesa, Tyrone Corbin, Phil Johnson

No.	Name	Pos.	Ht./Wt.	Metric (m/kg)	Born	College/country
30	Carlos Arroyo	G	6-2/202	1.88/91.6	7-30-79	Florida International
19	Raja Bell	G	6-5/210	1.96/95.3	9-19-76	Florida International
5	Carlos Boozer	F	6-9/258	2.05/117.0	11-20-81	Duke
22	Curtis Borchardt	C	7-0/240	2.13/108.9	9-13-80	Stanford
31	Jarron Collins	F/C	6-11/255	2.10/115.7	12-02-78	Stanford
10	Gordan Giricek	G	6-5/210	1.96/95.3	6-20-77	Croatia
15	Matt Harpring	F	6-7/231	2.00/104.8	5-31-76	Georgia Tech
43	Kris Humphries	F	6-9/235	2.05/106.6	2-5-85	Minnesota
47	Andrei Kirilenko	F	6-9/225	2.05/102.1	2-18-81	Russia
24	Raul Lopez	G	6-0/160	1.83/72.6	4-15-80	Spain
13	Mehmet Okur	F	6-11/249	2.10/112.9	5-26-79	Turkey
3	Kirk Snyder	G/F	6 6/225	1.98/102.1	0-5-03	Nevada

BROADCAST INFORMATION

Radio: KFNZ (1320 AM). Broadcasters: Rod Hundley, Ron Boone.
TV: KJZZ. Broadcasters: Rod Hundley, Ron Boone.
Cable TV: FOX Sports Rocky Mountain. Broadcasters: Rod Hundley, Ron Boone.

TEAM INFORMATION

Team address	.301 West South Temple
	Salt Lake City, UT 84101
Business phone	.801-325-2500
Ticket information	.801-325-7328
Arena (capacity)	.Delta Center (19,911)
Game times	.7 p.m.
First Jazz game in arena	.November 7, 1991

2003-04 REVIEW

RESULTS

OCTOBER
29— Portland	99 -92	1 -0	

NOVEMBER
1 — at Dallas	*102 -127	1 -1	
3 — Minnesota	93 -88	2 -1	
5 — Phoenix	91 -80	3 -1	
7 — at Golden State	*89 -95	3 -2	
8 — Memphis	96 -89	4 -2	
10— at San Antonio	*78 -87	4 -3	
12— at New Orleans	*89 -96	4 -4	
14— at Minnesota	85 -77	5 -4	
15— at Milwaukee	*95 -100	5 -5	
17— Orlando	90 -88	6 -5	
19— Sacramento	*110 -118	6 -6	
21— Milwaukee	99 -90	7 -6	
26— Houston	83 -76	8 -6	
28— Seattle	98 -81	9 -6	

DECEMBER
1 — New Jersey	91 -84	10 -6	
3 — at Houston	*101 -107	†10 -7	
5 — L.A. Clippers	86 -67	11 -7	
7 — at L.A. Lakers	*92 -94	11 -8	
8 — Boston	*80 -102	11 -9	
10— New York	95 -73	12 -9	
12— Sacramento	*93 -100	12 -10	
14— at Philadelphia	94 -86	13 -10	
16— at Washington	*87 -91	13 -11	
17— at New Jersey	*74 -87	13 -12	
19— at Boston	99 -96	14 -12	
21— at Detroit	*75 -96	14 -13	

22— at Chicago	92 -80	15 -13	
26— Toronto	97 -94	†16 -13	
28— at Sacramento	*89 -98	16 -14	
29— Philadelphia	106 -97	17 -14	

JANUARY
2 — at Memphis	*88 -100	17 -15	
3 — at Houston	*63 -84	17 -16	
5 — Dallas	108 -94	18 -16	
9 — at Denver	*96 -106	18 -17	
10— Atlanta	92 -71	19 -17	
13— Golden State	97 -80	20 -17	
15— Miami	97 -85	21 -17	
17— Cleveland	*96 -102	†21 -18	
19— at Golden State	*85 -101	21 -19	
20— Denver	*75 -96	21 -20	
23— at L.A. Clippers	*82 -93	21 -21	
24— L.A. Lakers	*86 -93	21 -22	
26— L.A. Clippers	98 -93	22 -22	
28— Dallas	91 -88	23 -22	
30— at Memphis	85 -79	24 -22	
31— at San Antonio	*81 -85	24 -23	

FEBRUARY
2 — San Antonio	*65 -83	24 -24	
4 — Chicago	*79 -95	24 -25	
6 — Portland	*73 -87	24 -26	
7 — at Phoenix	96 -92	25 -26	
10— at Portland	86 -81	26 -26	
11— Minnesota	*66 -77	26 -27	
17— at Miami	*85 -97	26 -28	
18— at Orlando	*77 -90	26 -29	

20— at New York	92 -78	27 -29	
22— at Indiana	*94 -80	27 -30	
24— Seattle	99 -86	28 -30	
25— at Seattle	93 -92	†29 -30	
27— at Sacramento	102 -97	30 -30	

MARCH
1 — Detroit	94 -86	31 -30	
5 — Indiana	*88 -96	31 -31	
6 — at Portland	*70 -91	31 -32	
8 — L.A. Lakers	88 -83	32 -32	
10— Golden State	91 -77	33 -32	
12— at Phoenix	99 -90	34 -32	
14— at Denver	*75 -102	34 -33	
17— at Toronto	*81 -85	34 -34	
19— at Cleveland	97 -88	35 -34	
20— at Atlanta	87 -81	36 -34	
23— Washington	85 -77	37 -34	
24— at Seattle	*77 -84	37 -35	
27— Denver	85 -83	38 -35	
28— at L.A. Lakers	*84 -91	38 -36	
31— New Orleans	89 -76	39 -36	

APRIL
2 — San Antonio	*81 -94	39 -37	
4 — at L.A. Clippers	97 -92	40 -37	
5 — Memphis	92 -81	41 -37	
8 — at Dallas	*94 -117	41 -38	
10— Houston	82 -69	42 -38	
12— at Minnesota	*90 -104	42 -39	
14— Phoenix	*84 -89	42 -40	

*Loss. †Single overtime.

TEAM LEADERS

Points: Andrei Kirilenko (1,284).
Field goals made: Kirilenko (412).
Free throws made: Kirilenko (392).
3-pointers made: Kirilenko (68).
Rebounds: Kirilenko (629).
Assists: Carlos Arroyo (355).
Steals: Kirilenko (150).
Blocks: Kirilenko (215).

RECORDS

Regular season: 42-40 (7th in Midwest Division); 10-14 in division; 25-27 in conference; 17-13 vs. Eastern Conference; 28-13 at home; 14-27 on road; 2-2 in overtime; 6-1 in games decided by three points or fewer; 15-22 in games decided by 10 points or more; held opponents under 100 points 69 times; held under 100 points 76 times.
Playoffs: None.
All-time franchise record: 1,321-1,107 in 30 seasons.
Team record past five years: 241-169 (.588, ranks 8th in NBA in that span).

HIGHLIGHTS

Top players: Andrei Kirilenko led the team in scoring (16.5 ppg), rebounding (8.1 rpg), steals (1.92 spg, 4th in the NBA), blocked shots (2.76 bpg, 3rd) and minutes per game (37.1). He was fifth in balloting for the NBA's Defensive Player of the Year. He became the first player in history to record two 5x5s in the same season. He had 10 points, 12 rebounds, 6 assists, 6 steals and 5 blocks vs. New York on December 10 and 19 points, 5 rebounds, 7 assists, 8 steals and 5 blocks at Houston on December 3. ... Matt Harpring was the team's second-leading scorer with 16.2 ppg. ... Carlos Arroyo led the team in assists (5.0 apg) and was second in steals (0.9 spg).
Key injuries: The Jazz lost a total of 257 player games because of injury. Harpring missed 51 games with a strained right knee that required surgery. Curtis Borchardt missed 65 games, including five with a nondisplaced fracture of his left index finger and 60 with a broken right wrist.

Michael Ruffin missed 34 games with an abdominal strain, and Arroyo missed 11 games with a sprained right ankle.
Notable: The Jazz had its streak of 19 consecutive years in the playoffs broken when it failed to advance to the 2004 playoffs and earned a spot in the draft lottery for the first time in franchise history. ... On opening night, the Jazz was the second-youngest team in the league after being the second-oldest team during the 2002-03 season. ... The Jazz opened the season for the first time since the 1985-86 season without future Hall of Famers John Stockton and Karl Malone. ... The team recorded its 19th consecutive season with a winning record. ... Jerry Sloan recorded his 900th NBA win at Phoenix on February 7 and posted his 800th win as Jazz coach on January 10 against Hawks. Sloan finished second in voting for the NBA's Coach of the Year to the Grizzlies' Hubie Brown.

WASHINGTON WIZARDS
SOUTHEAST DIVISION

WIZARDS

Wizards Schedule
Home games shaded; *—All-Star Game at Denver.

November
SUN	MON	TUE	WED	THU	FRI	SAT
	1	2	3 MEM	4 CHA	5	6 MIA
7	8	9 MIA	10 ORL	11	12	13 CLE
14 DAL	15	16	17 BOS	18	19	20 NJN
21	22	23 TOR	24	25	26 PHI	27
28 TOR	29	30				

December
SUN	MON	TUE	WED	THU	FRI	SAT
			1 NJN	2	3 ATL	4 CHI
5	6	7	8 DEN	9	10 NYK	11
12 NO	13 MIA	14	15 MIA	16	17 LAL	18 PHO
19	20 GS	21 SAC	22	23	24	25
26 MIN	27 CHA	28	29 DET	30	31 BOS	

January
SUN	MON	TUE	WED	THU	FRI	SAT
						1
2 ATL	3	4 NJN	5	6 SEA	7	8 MIN
9	10	11	12 POR	13	14 MIL	15 PHO
16 SA	17 DAL	18	19	20	21 TOR	22 IND
23	24 CLE	25	26 PHI	27	28 ORL	29 ORL
30	31					

February
SUN	MON	TUE	WED	THU	FRI	SAT
		1 DET	2	3	4 TOR	5 MIL
6	7 IND	8	9 SA	10	11 LAC	12 DET
13	14 NO	15 HOU	16	17	18	19
20 *All-Star	21	22	23 MEM	24	25 CHI	26
27 SAC	28					

March
SUN	MON	TUE	WED	THU	FRI	SAT
		1	2 HOU	3	4 GS	5 CHA
6	7	8 NYK	9	10	11	12
13 BOS	14 LAL	15	16 ATL	17	18 MIL	19 UTH
20	21	22 DEN	23	24 UTH	25 LAC	26
27 SEA	28 POR	29	30 ATL	31		

April
SUN	MON	TUE	WED	THU	FRI	SAT
					1 ORL	2
3 IND	4	5 BOS	6 DET	7	8 IND	9 PHI
10	11 MIL	12	13 CHI	14	15 CLE	16
17 CHA	18 NJN	19 NYK	20	21	22	23

2004-05 SEASON

TEAM DIRECTORY

Chairman . . . . .Abe Pollin
President . . . . .Susan O'Malley
President, Basketball Operations . . . . .Ernie Grunfeld
Director, Player Personnel . . . . .Milt Newton
Director, Basketball Administration . . . . .Tommy Sheppard
Assistant Director, Player Personnel . . . . .Tim Connelly
Head Coach . . . . .Eddie Jordan
Assistant Coaches . . . . .Mike O'Koren, Phil
Hubbard, Tom Young
Head Athletic Trainer . . . . .TBD
Assistant Athletic Trainer . . . . .Ernest Eugene
Strength and Conditioning Coach . . . . .Andrew Cleary
Director of Scouting . . . . .Chuck Douglas
Professional Scouts . . . . .Wes Unseld
Video Coordinator . . . . .Jim Lynam, Jr.
Equipment Managers . . . . .Jerry Walter, Rob Suller
Director, Player Services . . . . .Jennifer Thomas
Team Physicians . . . . .Dr. Stephen Haas, Dr
Barry Talesnick, Dr. Paul Taylor
Team Dentist . . . . .Dr. Howard Salob
Sr. VP, Community Relations and Mystics . . . . . .Judy Holland-Burton
Sr. VP, Corporate Marketing/Executive Seating . . .Rick Moreland
Sr. VP, Communications . . . . .Matt Williams
Sr. VP, Customer Service and Ticket Operations . .Rhonda Ballute
Vice President, Marketing . . . . .Ann Nicolaides
Vice President, Sales .Mark Schiponi
Controller . . . . .Paula Paul
Senior Director, Corporate Marketing . . . . .Lew Strudler
Director, Community Relations . . . . .Sashia Jones
Director, Customer Service . . . . .Kim Jackson
Director, Game Operations . . . . .Ken Bradford
Director, Marketing . . . . .Ira Frankel
Director, Public Relations . . . . .TBD
Executive Assistants . . . . .Pam Medlock, Cathy Smith
Coaches' Assistant . . . . .Dwayne Shannon
Communications . . . . .Josh Sekine
Website .Will Fan, Eric Hernandez,
Brian Sereno
Community Relations .Jen Hudnell, Ingrid
Harrell-Lee, Agnes Berrena
Customer Service . . . . .Sally Reilly, Laura Bryer,
Heidi Kibirsky, Greg Hall, Micketta Slade, Bo Nielsen
Finance .Rose Miller, Jill Davis,
Velma Allen, Catrina Williams, Rodney Coleman
Game Operations . . . . .Damian Bass, Bobby Zaal,
Alexis Miller
Marketing . . . . .Amy Flax, Kelly Youngs,
Susan Tarrant, Cathy Jerome
Corporate Marketing .Vincent Vanni, Roger
Moskowitz, Tracy Kelly, Brian Cawley, Ron Schnieder, Richard Garrard,
Kevin May, Amy Costello, Christy Ford, Chariss Gillom
Group Sales . . . . .Gene Kearney, Jill
Buxbaum, Stacy Donnelly
Ticket Sales . . . . .Bill Anderson, Jim
Anderson, Steve Bowen, Sam Burnette, Adam Cooley, Tamara Edgerton,
Oronde Garrett, Michael Glasser, Zari Gomez, Harris Handwerker, Bill Holt,
Pete Leibman, Ariel Levis, Paul Niermann, Rachelle Powell, Ralph Rosello,
Jessica Savitz, Marc Stern, Kelvin Stevens, Kira Stoutamire, David
Strousberg, Brandi Wiggins, Shavannia Willaims, Steve Zarick

Susan O'Malley

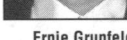

Ernie Grunfeld

Eddie Jordan

ROSTER
Coach—Eddie Jordan
Assistant coaches—Phil Hubbard, Mike O'Koren, Tom Young

No.	Name	Pos.	Ht./Wt.	Metric (m/kg)	Born	College/country
0	Gilbert Arenas	G	6-3/191	1.90/86.6	1-6-82	Arizona
2	Steve Blake	G	6-3/172	1.90/78.0	2-26-80	Maryland
5	Kwame Brown	F/C	6-11/248	2.10/112.5	3-10-82	Glynn Academy
3	Juan Dixon	G	6-3/164	1.90/74.4	10-9-78	Maryland
24	Jarvis Hayes	G/F	6-7/220	2.00/99.8	8-9-81	Georgia
33	Brendan Haywood	C	7-0/268	2.13/121.6	11-27-79	North Carolina
20	Larry Hughes	G	6-5/184	1.96/83.5	1-23-79	St. Louis
4	Antawn Jamison	F	6-9/225	2.05/102.1	6-12-76	North Carolina
1	Jared Jeffries	F	6-11/230	2.10/104.3	11-25-81	Indiana
8	Anthony Peeler	G	6-4/208	1.93/94.3	11-25-69	Missouri
34	Peter John Ramos	C	7-3/275	2.21/124.7	5-13-85	Puerto Rico
51	Michael Ruffin	F/C	6-8/246	2.03/111.6	1-21-77	Tulsa
36	Etan Thomas	C	6-10/260	2.08/117.9	4-1-78	Syracuse
52	Samaki Walker	F	6-9/260	2.05/117.9	2-25-76	Louisville

BROADCAST INFORMATION

Radio: WTEM (980 AM). Broadcaster: Dave Johnson.
TV: WBDC (Channel 50). Broadcasters: Steve Buckhantz, Phil Chenier.
Cable TV: Comcast SportsNet. Broadcasters: Steve Buckhantz, Phil Chenier.

TEAM INFORMATION

Team address ....601 F Street, NW
Washington, DC 20004
Business phone 202-661-5000
Ticket information 202-661-5050
Arena (capacity) ....MCI Center (20,173)
Game times ....noon, 1, 6, 7 and 8 p.m.
First Wizards game in arena ....December 2, 1997

2003-04 REVIEW

RESULTS

OCTOBER
29— at Chicago	99 -74	1 -0
31— at Toronto	*79 -82	1 -1

NOVEMBER
1 — New Jersey	*85 -98	1 -2
5 — Dallas	100 -90	2 -2
7 — Toronto	86 -60	3 -2
8 — at Cleveland	*98 -111	3 -3
11— Philadelphia	*105 -112	3 -4
14— at Miami	*101 -105	†3 -5
15— San Antonio	*71 -95	3 -6
17— at Atlanta	106 -97	4 -6
19— Cleveland	106 -95	5 -6
21— at Denver	*87 -108	5 -7
23— at Seattle	*85 -88	5 -8
25— at Portland	81 -80	6 -8
26— at L.A. Lakers	*99 -120	6 -9
29— Detroit	*69 -80	6 -10

DECEMBER
2 — at Dallas	*72 -97	6 -11
5 — at Memphis	*77 -92	6 -12
6 — at Milwaukee	114 -109	†7 -12
9 — at Indiana	*79 -93	7 -13
10— Orlando	*91 -95	7 -14
12— Minnesota	*91 -110	7 -15
14— at New York	*87 -89	7 -16
16— Utah	91 -87	8 -16
19— at New Jersey	*87 -97	8 -17
23— at Miami	*72 -79	8 -18
26— Miami	*84 -92	8 -19

27— at Chicago	*86 -100	8 -20
30— Atlanta	*73 -83	8 -21

JANUARY
2 — Golden State	97 -79	9 -21
4 — Milwaukee	*94 -100	9 -22
6 — at San Antonio	*72 -94	9 -23
7 — at New Orleans	*87 -97	9 -24
9 — at Orlando	*92 -103	9 -25
10— Philadelphia	94 -87	10 -25
13— Houston	*80 -93	10 -26
14— at New Jersey	*103 -115	10 -27
16— at Detroit	*77 -98	10 -28
17— Seattle	99 -84	11 -28
19— Chicago	93 -83	12 -28
23— at Boston	*89 -100	12 -29
24— Indiana	107 -96	13 -29
26— Portland	*83 -94	13 -30
28— Orlando	*100 -104	13 -31
30— Phoenix	105 -100	14 -31

FEBRUARY
1 — Cleveland	*100 -104	14 -32
4 — Memphis	*101 -103	14 -33
6 — L.A. Clippers	112 -100	15 -33
7 — at Cleveland	106 -88	16 -33
11— at Philadelphia	*88 -113	16 -34
17— at Houston	*81 -107	16 -35
18— at New Orleans	*98 -120	16 -36
20— Indiana	*87 -96	16 -37
22— Milwaukee	*85 -113	16 -38
25— at Toronto	76 -74	17 -38

26— Chicago	95 -87	18 -38
28— L.A. Lakers	*110 -122	18 -39

MARCH
1 — New Orleans	111 -106	†19 -39
3 — Toronto	84 -70	20 -39
5 — at Boston	*90 -94	20 -40
7 — New York	*86 -99	20 -41
9 — Denver	*87 -117	20 -42
10— at Orlando	*99 -108	20 -43
12— at Atlanta	*124 -138	20 -44
13— Boston	*102 -111	20 -45
16— at New York	*110 -114	†20 -46
17— Sacramento	114 -108	21 -46
19— Atlanta	94 -84	22 -46
21— Miami	*81 -101	22 -47
23— at Utah	*77 -85	22 -48
25— at L.A. Clippers	103 -94	23 -48
26— at Golden State	*78 -99	23 -49
28— at Sacramento	*92 -100	23 -50
29— at Phoenix	*95 -101	23 -51
31— New Jersey	*99 -103	†23 -52

APRIL
2 — at Minnesota	*73 -91	23 -53
4 — Boston	112 -102	24 -53
7 — at Milwaukee	*107 -116	24 -54
9 — at Philadelphia	83 -80	25 -54
10— New York	*98 -102	†25 -55
12— at Detroit	*79 -101	25 -56
14— New Orleans	*78 -94	25 -57

*Loss. †Single overtime.

TEAM LEADERS

Points: Larry Hughes (1,148).
Field goals made: Hughes (401).
Free throws made: Hughes (267).
3-pointers made: Gilbert Arenas (125).
Rebounds: Kwame Brown (550).
Assists: Arenas (275).
Steals: Arenas (103).
Blocks: Etan Thomas (123).

RECORDS

Regular season: 25-57 (6th in Atlantic Division); 3-21 in division; 16-38 in conference; 9-19 vs. Western Conference; 17-24 at home; 8-33 on road; 2-4 in overtime; 3-4 in games decided by three points or fewer; 13-34 in games decided by 10 points or more; held opponents under 100 points 45 times; held under 100 points 59 times.

Playoffs: None.

All-time franchise record: 1,585-1,898 in 43 seasons. Won one NBA title (1978).

Team record past five years: 147-263 (.359, ranks 24th in NBA in that span).

HIGHLIGHTS

Top players: Gilbert Arenas led the team with 19.6 ppg. He scored 40 points at Orlando on March 10 and 35 against the Lakers on February 28, when he set a career mark and tied a franchise record with eight 3-point field goals. ... Larry Hughes led the Wizards with 1,148 total points and averaged a career-best 18.8 ppg. Hughes started 61 games, the highest total of any Wizards player and the most in his six-year career. ... Jerry Stackhouse averaged 13.9 ppg and shot 80.6 percent from the free throw line. ... Kwame Brown was the fourth Wizards player to average double digits in scoring (10.9 ppg). He led the team in rebounds per game (7.4), total rebounds (550) and minutes played (2,239) and was third in total blocks (52).

Key injuries: The Wizards lost a total of 224 player games because of injury or illness, 102 by their three top scorers. Arenas missed 27 games between an abdominal injury and a sprained right ankle, Hughes missed 21 games (one with right knee tendinitis, one with a sore Achilles and 19 with a fractured left wrist), and Stackhouse missed 54 games,

the majority with arthroscopic surgery on his right knee that delayed his season debut until February 1. Chris Whitney missed 48 games with a left ankle sprain. Jared Jeffries was the only Wizards player to appear in all 82 games.

Notable: On November 7, Washington held the Raptors to a franchise-low four points in the second quarter, which ties the all-time NBA mark for the second fewest points allowed in the second quarter. The Wizards also set team records with 23 points allowed in the first half and 60 points allowed in the game. ... Jarvis Hayes was selected to play in the 2004 Rookie Challenge as part of All-Star Weekend. He also was named to the All-Rookie Second Team. ... Brown set new career bests in points and rebounds with a 30-point, 19-rebound effort against Sacramento on March 17. ... Arenas finished the season with three triple-doubles (2nd in the NBA), the first triple-doubles of his career.

NBA SCHEDULE

(All game times listed are local.)

TUESDAY, NOVEMBER 2
Houston at Detroit . . . . 8:00 PM
Sacramento at Dallas . . . . 7:30 PM
Denver at L.A. Lakers . . . . 7:30 PM

WEDNESDAY, NOVEMBER 3
Houston at Toronto . . . . 7:00 PM
Milwaukee at Orlando . . . . 7:00 PM
Indiana at Cleveland . . . . 7:00 PM
Philadelphia at Boston . . . . . . 7:30 PM
Miami at New Jersey . . . . 8:00 PM
Washington at Memphis . . . . . 7:00 PM
Dallas at New Orleans . . . . 7:00 PM
New York at Minnesota . . . . . . 7:00 PM
Sacramento at San Antonio . . 7:30 PM
Atlanta at Phoenix . . . . 7:00 PM
L.A. Lakers at Utah . . . . 8:30 PM
Seattle at L.A. Clippers . . . . . . 7:30 PM
Portland at Golden State . . . . . 7:30 PM

THURSDAY, NOVEMBER 4
Washington at Charlotte . . . . . 7:00 PM
Cleveland at Miami . . . . 8:00 PM
Minnesota at Denver . . . . 8:30 PM

FRIDAY, NOVEMBER 5
Detroit at Toronto . . . . 7:00 PM
Phoenix at Philadelphia . . . . . . 7:00 PM
Indiana at Boston . . . . 7:30 PM
Houston at Memphis . . . . 7:00 PM
Orlando at New Orleans . . . . . 7:00 PM
New Jersey at Chicago . . . . . . 7:30 PM
L.A. Clippers at Portland . . . . . 7:30 PM
San Antonio at L.A. Lakers . . . 7:30 PM
Utah at Golden State . . . . 7:30 PM
Atlanta at Seattle . . . . 7:30 PM

SATURDAY, NOVEMBER 6
Miami at Washington . . . . 7:00 PM
Orlando at Charlotte . . . . 7:00 PM
Boston at New York . . . . 7:30 PM
Philadelphia at Detroit . . . . . . 7:30 PM
Phoenix at New Jersey . . . . . . 8:00 PM
Chicago at Indiana . . . . 8:00 PM
New Orleans at Minnesota . . . 7:00 PM
Cleveland at Milwaukee . . . . . . 7:30 PM
Sacramento at Houston . . . . . . 7:30 PM
Memphis at Dallas . . . . 7:30 PM
Utah at Denver . . . . 7:00 PM
L.A. Clippers at Golden State . 7:30 PM

SUNDAY, NOVEMBER 7
Portland at Toronto . . . . 1:00 PM
San Antonio at Seattle . . . . . . 5:00 PM
Atlanta at L.A. Lakers . . . . 6:30 PM

MONDAY, NOVEMBER 8
Golden State at Dallas . . . . . . 7:30 PM
Denver at Utah . . . . 7:00 PM
Detroit at L.A. Clippers . . . . . . 7:30 PM

TUESDAY, NOVEMBER 9
Dallas at Orlando . . . . 7:00 PM
Portland at New Jersey . . . . . . 7:30 PM
Philadelphia at New York . . . . 7:30 PM
Cleveland at Atlanta . . . . 7:30 PM
Washington at Miami . . . . 7:30 PM
L.A. Lakers at New Orleans . . . 7:00 PM
Indiana at Minnesota . . . . 7:00 PM
Phoenix at Chicago . . . . 7:30 PM
Memphis at Houston . . . . 7:30 PM

Seattle at Denver . . . . 7:00 PM
Toronto at Sacramento . . . . . . 7:00 PM

WEDNESDAY, NOVEMBER 10
Portland at Boston . . . . 7:00 PM
New Jersey at Philadelphia . . . 7:00 PM
Orlando at Washington . . . . . . 7:00 PM
L.A. Clippers at Indiana . . . . . . 7:00 PM
Phoenix at Cleveland . . . . 8:00 PM
Charlotte at Milwaukee . . . . . . 7:00 PM
L.A. Lakers at Memphis . . . . . . 7:00 PM
Golden State at San Antonio . . 7:30 PM
Toronto at Utah . . . . 7:00 PM
Sacramento at Seattle . . . . 7:30 PM

THURSDAY, NOVEMBER 11
Dallas at Miami . . . . 8:00 PM
Minnesota at Houston . . . . . . 7:30 PM
Detroit at Denver . . . . 8:30 PM

FRIDAY, NOVEMBER 12
Indiana at Philadelphia . . . . . . 7:00 PM
L.A. Lakers at Orlando . . . . . . 7:00 PM
Charlotte at Boston . . . . 7:30 PM
L.A. Clippers at New York . . . . 7:30 PM
Golden State at Memphis . . . . 7:00 PM
Atlanta at New Orleans . . . . . . 7:00 PM
Miami at San Antonio . . . . 7:00 PM
Toronto at Seattle . . . . 7:30 PM

SATURDAY, NOVEMBER 13
Dallas at New Jersey . . . . 1:00 PM
Washington at Cleveland . . . . . 1:00 PM
Golden State at Charlotte . . . . 7:00 PM
San Antonio at Atlanta . . . . . . 7:00 PM
New York at Indiana . . . . 8:00 PM
L.A. Clippers at Chicago . . . . . 7:30 PM
New Orleans at Milwaukee . . 7:30 PM
L.A. Lakers at Houston . . . . . . 7:30 PM
Detroit at Utah . . . . 7:00 PM
Sacramento at Phoenix . . . . . . 7:00 PM
Toronto at Portland . . . . 7:00 PM

SUNDAY, NOVEMBER 14
Dallas at Washington . . . . 1:00 PM
Orlando at Philadelphia . . . . . . 2:00 PM
Milwaukee at Miami . . . . 6:00 PM
Memphis at Seattle . . . . 5:00 PM
Denver at Sacramento . . . . . . 6:00 PM

MONDAY, NOVEMBER 15
Golden State at Cleveland . . . . 7:00 PM
Houston at New Jersey . . . . . . 7:30 PM

TUESDAY, NOVEMBER 16
Seattle at Philadelphia . . . . . . 7:00 PM
Utah at Charlotte . . . . 7:00 PM
Houston at Atlanta . . . . 7:30 PM
Miami at Minnesota . . . . 7:00 PM
Phoenix at Dallas . . . . 7:30 PM
New York at San Antonio . . . . 7:30 PM
Chicago at Sacramento . . . . . . 7:00 PM
Toronto at L.A. Clippers . . . . . 7:30 PM

WEDNESDAY, NOVEMBER 17
Boston at Washington . . . . . . 7:00 PM
Utah at Orlando . . . . 7:00 PM
Atlanta at Indiana . . . . 7:00 PM
Seattle at New Jersey . . . . 7:30 PM
Minnesota at Detroit . . . . 7:30 PM
Phoenix at New Orleans . . . . . 7:00 PM

Miami at Milwaukee . . . . 8:00 PM
Toronto at Denver . . . . 7:00 PM
Memphis at Portland . . . . 7:00 PM
L.A. Clippers at L.A. Lakers . . . 7:30 PM
Chicago at Golden State . . . . . 7:30 PM

THURSDAY, NOVEMBER 18
San Antonio at Philadelphia . . 7:00 PM
Cleveland at Charlotte . . . . 7:00 PM
New York at Houston . . . . 8:30 PM

FRIDAY, NOVEMBER 19
Seattle at Toronto . . . . 7:00 PM
San Antonio at Boston . . . . . . 7:30 PM
Utah at Miami . . . . 7:30 PM
Indiana at Detroit . . . . 8:00 PM
New York at Dallas . . . . 7:30 PM
Chicago at Denver . . . . 7:00 PM
L.A. Lakers at Phoenix . . . . . . 7:00 PM
Milwaukee at Portland . . . . . . 7:00 PM
Memphis at Sacramento . . . . . 7:30 PM

SATURDAY, NOVEMBER 20
Houston at L.A. Clippers . . . . 12:30 PM
Utah at Atlanta . . . . 7:00 PM
Charlotte at Cleveland . . . . 7:30 PM
Washington at New Jersey . . . 8:00 PM
Orlando at Indiana . . . . 8:00 PM
Minnesota at New Orleans . . . 7:00 PM
Memphis at Golden State . . . . 7:30 PM

SUNDAY, NOVEMBER 21
San Antonio at Toronto . . . . . . 1:00 PM
Phoenix at L.A. Clippers . . . . 12:30 PM
Seattle at Boston . . . . 6:00 PM
Philadelphia at Miami . . . . 6:00 PM
Charlotte at Detroit . . . . 6:00 PM
Cleveland at New York . . . . . . 7:30 PM
Houston at Portland . . . . 5:00 PM
Dallas at Denver . . . . 7:00 PM
Milwaukee at Sacramento . . . . 6:00 PM
Chicago at L.A. Lakers . . . . . . 6:30 PM

MONDAY, NOVEMBER 22
San Antonio at Memphis . . . . 7:00 PM
Minnesota at Dallas . . . . 7:30 PM
New Orleans at Utah . . . . 7:00 PM
Chicago at Phoenix . . . . 7:00 PM

TUESDAY, NOVEMBER 23
Toronto at Washington . . . . . . 7:00 PM
Detroit at Charlotte . . . . 7:00 PM
Boston at Indiana . . . . 7:00 PM
Atlanta at New York . . . . 7:30 PM
Portland at Miami . . . . 7:30 PM
Seattle at Minnesota . . . . 7:00 PM
New Jersey at Denver . . . . 7:00 PM
Houston at Sacramento . . . . . 7:00 PM
Milwaukee at L.A. Lakers . . . . 7:30 PM
New Orleans at Golden State . . 7:30 PM

WEDNESDAY, NOVEMBER 24
New York at Toronto . . . . 7:00 PM
Boston at Philadelphia . . . . . . 7:00 PM
Portland at Orlando . . . . 7:00 PM
Detroit at Cleveland . . . . 7:00 PM
Miami at Atlanta . . . . 7:30 PM
Seattle at Memphis . . . . 7:00 PM
Dallas at San Antonio . . . . 7:30 PM
Chicago at Utah . . . . 7:00 PM
Milwaukee at Phoenix . . . . 7:00 PM

THURSDAY, NOVEMBER 25
Minnesota at Indiana . . . . 8:00 PM
New Jersey at L.A. Clippers . . 7:30 PM

FRIDAY, NOVEMBER 26
Portland at Dallas . . . . noon
Cleveland at Boston . . . . 7:30 PM
Washington at Philadelphia . . 7:30 PM
Orlando at Atlanta . . . . 7:30 PM
Miami at Detroit . . . . 8:00 PM
Charlotte at Indiana . . . . 8:00 PM
Memphis at Minnesota . . . . . . 7:00 PM
San Antonio at Denver . . . . . . 7:00 PM
Houston at Utah . . . . 7:00 PM
New Orleans at Phoenix . . . . . 7:00 PM
Sacramento at L.A. Lakers . . 7:30 PM
L.A. Clippers at Golden State . 7:30 PM
New Jersey at Seattle . . . . 7:30 PM

SATURDAY, NOVEMBER 27
Toronto at New York . . . . 1:00 PM
Atlanta at Charlotte . . . . 7:00 PM
Philadelphia at Orlando . . . . . . 7:00 PM
Chicago at Cleveland . . . . 7:30 PM
Dallas at Memphis . . . . 7:00 PM
Denver at Houston . . . . 7:30 PM
Utah at San Antonio . . . . 7:30 PM
Detroit at Milwaukee . . . . 8:00 PM

SUNDAY, NOVEMBER 28
Washington at Toronto . . . . . . 3:00 PM
Golden State at L.A. Clippers . 12:30 PM
Boston at Miami . . . . 6:00 PM
New Jersey at Portland . . . . . . 3:00 PM
Minnesota at Sacramento . . . . 6:00 PM
Indiana at Seattle . . . . 6:00 PM
New Orleans at L.A. Lakers . . 6:30 PM

MONDAY, NOVEMBER 29
Boston at Orlando . . . . 7:00 PM
New Orleans at Denver . . . . . . 7:00 PM
Cleveland at L.A. Clippers . . . 7:30 PM

TUESDAY, NOVEMBER 30
Charlotte at New Jersey . . . . . 7:30 PM
New York at Atlanta . . . . 7:30 PM
Toronto at Miami . . . . 7:30 PM
L.A. Lakers at Milwaukee . . . . 7:00 PM
Sacramento at Memphis . . . . . 7:00 PM
Detroit at Houston . . . . 7:30 PM
San Antonio at Dallas . . . . . . 7:30 PM
Phoenix at Utah . . . . 7:00 PM
Seattle at Portland . . . . 7:00 PM

WEDNESDAY, DECEMBER 1
Milwaukee at Boston . . . . 7:00 PM
New Jersey at Washington . . . 7:00 PM
Toronto at Orlando . . . . 7:00 PM
Memphis at New York . . . . . . 7:30 PM
Sacramento at New Orleans . . 7:00 PM
L.A. Lakers at Chicago . . . . . . 7:30 PM
Philadelphia at San Antonio . . 7:30 PM
Cleveland at Phoenix . . . . 7:00 PM
Utah at Seattle . . . . 7:00 PM
Indiana at L.A. Clippers . . . . . . 7:30 PM
Minnesota at Golden State . . . 7:30 PM

THURSDAY, DECEMBER 2
Houston at Dallas . . . . 7:00 PM
Cleveland at Denver . . . . 8:30 PM

FRIDAY, DECEMBER 3
Toronto at Boston . . . . 7:30 PM
Orlando at New York . . . . 7:30 PM
Washington at Atlanta . . . . . . 7:30 PM
Philadelphia at Memphis . . . . . 7:00 PM

Detroit at San Antonio . . . . . . 7:00 PM
Miami at Chicago . . . . 7:30 PM
Minnesota at Phoenix . . . . 7:00 PM
Golden State at L.A. Lakers . . 7:30 PM
Indiana at Sacramento . . . . . . 7:30 PM

SATURDAY, DECEMBER 4
New York at Charlotte . . . . 7:00 PM
Memphis at Orlando . . . . 7:00 PM
Atlanta at New Jersey . . . . 7:30 PM
Toronto at Cleveland . . . . 7:30 PM
Chicago at Washington . . . . . . 8:00 PM
Detroit at New Orleans . . . . . . 7:00 PM
San Antonio at Milwaukee . . . . 7:30 PM
Philadelphia at Houston . . . . . 7:30 PM
Utah at Dallas . . . . 7:30 PM
Miami at Denver . . . . 7:00 PM
Minnesota at L.A. Clippers . . . 7:30 PM
Indiana at Golden State . . . . . . 7:30 PM
Portland at Seattle . . . . 7:30 PM

SUNDAY, DECEMBER 5
Boston at Sacramento . . . . . . 6:00 PM
Phoenix at Portland . . . . 6:00 PM

MONDAY, DECEMBER 6
Toronto at New Jersey . . . . . . 7:30 PM
Philadelphia at Atlanta . . . . . . 7:30 PM
San Antonio at Chicago . . . . . 7:30 PM
Detroit at Dallas . . . . 7:30 PM
Orlando at Denver . . . . 7:00 PM
Miami at Utah . . . . 7:00 PM
Charlotte at L.A. Clippers . . . . 7:30 PM
Boston at Golden State . . . . . . 7:30 PM

TUESDAY, DECEMBER 7
New Jersey at Cleveland . . . . . 7:00 PM
Milwaukee at Indiana . . . . 7:00 PM
New York at Memphis . . . . 7:00 PM
Dallas at Minnesota . . . . 7:00 PM
New Orleans at Houston . . . . . 7:30 PM
Golden State at Phoenix . . . . . 7:00 PM
Charlotte at Sacramento . . . . . 7:00 PM

WEDNESDAY, DECEMBER 8
Minnesota at Philadelphia . . . . 7:00 PM
Denver at Washington . . . . 7:00 PM
Memphis at Atlanta . . . . 7:30 PM
Toronto at Detroit . . . . 7:30 PM
Miami at Milwaukee . . . . 7:00 PM
New York at New Orleans . . . . 7:00 PM
Cleveland at Chicago . . . . 7:30 PM
Seattle at San Antonio . . . . . . 7:30 PM
Orlando at Utah . . . . 7:00 PM
Phoenix at L.A. Lakers . . . . . . 7:30 PM

THURSDAY, DECEMBER 9
San Antonio at Houston . . . . . 7:00 PM
Seattle at Dallas . . . . 7:30 PM
Boston at Portland . . . . 7:30 PM

FRIDAY, DECEMBER 10
Denver at Toronto . . . . 7:00 PM
New York at Washington . . . . 7:00 PM
New Orleans at New Jersey . . 7:30 PM
Memphis at Miami . . . . 7:30 PM
Atlanta at Detroit . . . . 8:00 PM
Philadelphia at Chicago . . . . . 7:00 PM
Sacramento at Minnesota . . . . 7:00 PM
Indiana at Milwaukee . . . . 7:30 PM
Charlotte at Phoenix . . . . 7:00 PM
Portland at Utah . . . . 8:30 PM
Orlando at Golden State . . . . . 7:30 PM

SATURDAY, DECEMBER 11
New Jersey at Atlanta . . . . 7:00 PM
Sacramento at Indiana . . . . . . 8:00 PM
Detroit at Memphis . . . . 7:00 PM
Minnesota at Chicago . . . . 7:30 PM
Dallas at Houston . . . . 7:30 PM
Cleveland at San Antonio . . . . 7:30 PM
Boston at Seattle . . . . 7:00 PM
L.A. Lakers at L.A. Clippers . . . 7:30 PM

SUNDAY, DECEMBER 12
Denver at New York . . . . noon
Miami at Toronto . . . . 1:00 PM
New Orleans at Washington . . 1:00 PM
Milwaukee at Philadelphia . . . . 2:00 PM
Utah at Portland . . . . 5:00 PM
Charlotte at Golden State . . . . 6:00 PM
Orlando at L.A. Lakers . . . . . . 6:30 PM

MONDAY, DECEMBER 13
Washington at Miami . . . . 7:30 PM
Cleveland at Memphis . . . . . . 7:00 PM
Dallas at Chicago . . . . 7:30 PM
Orlando at Phoenix . . . . 7:00 PM
Boston at L.A. Clippers . . . . . . 7:30 PM

TUESDAY, DECEMBER 14
Denver at Philadelphia . . . . . . 7:00 PM
New Orleans at Charlotte . . . . 7:00 PM
New York at New Jersey . . . . . 7:30 PM
Indiana at Atlanta . . . . 7:30 PM
Sacramento at Milwaukee . . . . 7:00 PM
Portland at Minnesota . . . . . . 7:00 PM
Golden State at Dallas . . . . . . 7:30 PM
L.A. Clippers at Utah . . . . 7:00 PM
L.A. Lakers at Seattle . . . . 7:00 PM

WEDNESDAY, DECEMBER 15
Denver at Boston . . . . 7:00 PM
Minnesota at Toronto . . . . 7:00 PM

Miami at Washington . . . . 7:00 PM
Portland at Cleveland . . . . 7:00 PM
Detroit at New York . . . . 8:00 PM
Chicago at Memphis . . . . 7:00 PM
Golden State at New Orleans . . 7:00 PM
Atlanta at Houston . . . . 7:30 PM
Orlando at San Antonio . . . . . . 7:30 PM
Utah at Phoenix . . . . 8:30 PM

THURSDAY, DECEMBER 16
Cleveland at Detroit . . . . 8:00 PM
Milwaukee at Chicago . . . . 7:30 PM
L.A. Lakers at Sacramento . . . 7:30 PM

FRIDAY, DECEMBER 17
New York at Philadelphia . . . . 7:00 PM
Toronto at Indiana . . . . 7:00 PM
Utah at Boston . . . . 7:30 PM
Portland at Atlanta . . . . 7:30 PM
Denver at Miami . . . . 8:00 PM
New Jersey at Memphis . . . . . 7:00 PM
San Antonio at New Orleans . . 7:00 PM
L.A. Clippers at Minnesota . . . 7:00 PM
Golden State at Houston . . . . . 7:30 PM
Washington at L.A. Lakers . . . 7:30 PM
Phoenix at Seattle . . . . 7:30 PM

SATURDAY, DECEMBER 18
Houston at Charlotte . . . . 7:00 PM
Denver at Orlando . . . . 7:00 PM
Portland at Detroit . . . . 7:30 PM
Boston at Cleveland . . . . 7:30 PM
Indiana at Chicago . . . . 7:30 PM
Philadelphia at Milwaukee . . . . 7:30 PM
Atlanta at Dallas . . . . 7:30 PM

– 69 –

Golden State at San Antonio . . 7:30 PM
Washington at Phoenix. . . . . . 7:00 PM

SUNDAY, DECEMBER 19
New Jersey at Toronto . . . . . . 1:00 PM
Utah at New York . . . . 3:00 PM
Orlando at Miami . . . . 6:00 PM
New Orleans at Sacramento . . 6:00 PM
Memphis at L.A. Clippers . . . . 6:30 PM

MONDAY, DECEMBER 20
Utah at Philadelphia . . . . 7:00 PM
Portland at Chicago . . . . 7:30 PM
Toronto at Houston . . . . 7:30 PM
Phoenix at Denver . . . . 7:00 PM
Memphis at L.A. Lakers . . . . . 7:30 PM
Washington at Golden State . . 7:30 PM

TUESDAY, DECEMBER 21
New Jersey at Charlotte . . . . . 7:00 PM
Minnesota at Cleveland. . . . . . 7:00 PM
Dallas at New York . . . . 7:30 PM
Boston at Miami . . . . 7:30 PM
Washington at Sacramento. . . 7:00 PM
New Orleans at L.A. Clippers. . 7:30 PM

WEDNESDAY, DECEMBER 22
New York at Boston . . . . 7:00 PM
Utah at Toronto . . . . 7:00 PM
San Antonio at Orlando. . . . . . 7:00 PM
Philadelphia at Indiana . . . . . . 7:00 PM
Cleveland at New Jersey . . . . 7:30 PM
Dallas at Atlanta . . . . 7:30 PM
Chicago at Detroit . . . . 7:30 PM
Portland at Milwaukee . . . . . . 7:00 PM
Charlotte at Houston. . . . . . . 7:30 PM
Memphis at Golden State . . . . 7:00 PM
Denver at Seattle . . . . 7:00 PM
New Orleans at L.A. Lakers. . . 7:30 PM

THURSDAY, DECEMBER 23
Minnesota at San Antonio. . . . 7:00 PM
Memphis at Phoenix. . . . . . . 7:00 PM
Miami at Sacramento . . . . . . 7:30 PM

SATURDAY, DECEMBER 25
Detroit at Indiana . . . . . . 12:30 PM
Miami at L.A. Lakers . . . . noon

SUNDAY, DECEMBER 26
Charlotte at New York. . . . . . 1:00 PM
New Orleans at Cleveland. . . . 7:00 PM
Chicago at Milwaukee. . . . . . 6:00 PM
Boston at San Antonio . . . . . 6:00 PM
Washington at Minnesota . . . . 7:00 PM
Toronto at Phoenix . . . . . . 6:00 PM
L.A. Clippers at Houston. . . . . 7:30 PM
Dallas at Denver . . . . 7:00 PM
Golden State at Sacramento . . 6:00 PM

MONDAY, DECEMBER 27
Charlotte at Washington . . . . . 7:00 PM
New York at Orlando. . . . . . . 7:00 PM
New Orleans at Indiana . . . . . 7:00 PM
Atlanta at Miami . . . . 7:30 PM
New Jersey at Detroit . . . . . . 7:30 PM
L.A. Clippers at Memphis . . . . 7:00 PM
Seattle at Utah . . . . 7:00 PM
Philadelphia at Portland . . . . . 7:00 PM
Denver at Golden State . . . . . 7:30 PM

TUESDAY, DECEMBER 28
Cleveland at Atlanta . . . . 7:30 PM
Houston at Milwaukee . . . . . . 7:00 PM
New Jersey at Chicago . . . . . 7:30 PM
Boston at Dallas . . . . 7:30 PM

Phoenix at San Antonio . . . . . 7:30 PM
Philadelphia at Seattle. . . . . . 7:00 PM
Toronto at L.A. Lakers . . . . . . 7:30 PM

WEDNESDAY, DECEMBER 29
Detroit at Washington. . . . . . . 7:00 PM
Indiana at Charlotte . . . . 7:00 PM
Milwaukee at Orlando. . . . . . . 7:00 PM
Houston at Cleveland . . . . . . 7:00 PM
Minnesota at New York. . . . . . 7:30 PM
Boston at Memphis . . . . 7:00 PM
Phoenix at New Orleans . . . . . 7:00 PM
Utah at L.A. Clippers. . . . . . . 7:30 PM
Toronto at Golden State . . . . . 7:30 PM

THURSDAY, DECEMBER 30
Seattle at Atlanta . . . . 2:00 PM
Indiana at New Jersey . . . . . . 7:30 PM
Miami at Detroit . . . . 8:00 PM
San Antonio at Portland . . . . . 7:30 PM

FRIDAY, DECEMBER 31
Washington at Boston . . . . . . 3:00 PM
Seattle at Charlotte . . . . 7:00 PM
Philadelphia at Denver. . . . . . 6:00 PM
Sacramento at Utah . . . . 6:00 PM
San Antonio at L.A. Clippers . . 6:30 PM
Milwaukee at Houston . . . . . . 9:00 PM

SATURDAY, JANUARY 1
New Jersey at New York. . . . . 7:30 PM
Charlotte at Miami . . . . 7:30 PM
Memphis at Minnesota . . . . . . 7:00 PM
Orlando at Chicago . . . . 7:30 PM
Golden State at Portland. . . . . 7:00 PM

SUNDAY, JANUARY 2
Atlanta at Washington . . . . noon
Philadelphia at L.A. Clippers . 12:30 PM
Boston at Detroit . . . . 6:00 PM
Portland at Phoenix . . . . 6:00 PM
Utah at Houston . . . . 7:30 PM
Milwaukee at Dallas . . . . 7:30 PM
San Antonio at Sacramento . . 6:00 PM
Denver at L.A. Lakers . . . . . . 6:30 PM

MONDAY, JANUARY 3
New Orleans at Boston. . . . . . 7:00 PM
Orlando at Toronto . . . . 7:00 PM
Cleveland at Charlotte. . . . . . 7:00 PM
Seattle at Miami . . . . 7:30 PM
Utah at Memphis . . . . 7:00 PM
Detroit at Chicago . . . . 7:30 PM
L.A. Clippers at Denver. . . . . . 7:00 PM
Philadelphia at Golden State . . 7:30 PM

TUESDAY, JANUARY 4
New Jersey at Washington . . . 7:00 PM
Milwaukee at Indiana . . . . . . 7:00 PM
Sacramento at New York . . . . 7:30 PM
Phoenix at Minnesota . . . . . . 7:00 PM
L.A. Lakers at San Antonio . . . 7:30 PM

WEDNESDAY, JANUARY 5
Golden State at Boston. . . . . . 7:00 PM
Sacramento at Toronto . . . . . . 7:00 PM
Minnesota at Charlotte . . . . . . 7:00 PM
Seattle at Orlando . . . . 7:00 PM
Atlanta at Cleveland . . . . 7:00 PM
New York at Miami . . . . 7:30 PM
New Jersey at Milwaukee . . . . 7:00 PM
Chicago at New Orleans . . . . . 7:00 PM
L.A. Lakers at Dallas . . . . 7:30 PM
Phoenix at Houston . . . . 8:00 PM
Philadelphia at Utah . . . . 7:00 PM
Portland at L.A. Clippers. . . . . 7:30 PM

THURSDAY, JANUARY 6
Seattle at Washington. . . . . . . 7:00 PM
Memphis at Detroit . . . . 7:00 PM
Indiana at San Antonio . . . . . . 8:30 PM

FRIDAY, JANUARY 7
Milwaukee at Toronto . . . . . . 7:00 PM
Charlotte at Orlando . . . . 7:00 PM
Detroit at Boston . . . . 7:30 PM
Golden State at New Jersey . . 7:30 PM
Sacramento at Atlanta . . . . . . 7:30 PM
New Orleans at Memphis . . . . 7:00 PM
Philadelphia at Minnesota. . . . 7:00 PM
Utah at Chicago . . . . 7:30 PM
Miami at Portland . . . . 7:00 PM
Houston at L.A. Lakers . . . . . . 7:30 PM

SATURDAY, JANUARY 8
New York at Cleveland . . . . . . 1:30 PM
Denver at San Antonio . . . . . 12:30 PM
Phoenix at L.A. Clippers . . . . . 1:00 PM
Minnesota at Washington . . . . 7:00 PM
New Jersey at Orlando . . . . . . 7:00 PM
Sacramento at New Orleans . . 7:00 PM
Boston at Chicago . . . . 7:30 PM
Utah at Milwaukee . . . . 7:30 PM
Indiana at Dallas . . . . 7:30 PM

SUNDAY, JANUARY 9
Golden State at Toronto . . . . . 1:00 PM
Portland at New York . . . . . . 7:30 PM
Indiana at Phoenix . . . . 6:00 PM
Miami at Seattle . . . . 5:00 PM
Houston at Denver . . . . 7:00 PM

MONDAY, JANUARY 10
Orlando at Boston . . . . 7:00 PM
Portland at Philadelphia . . . . . 7:00 PM
L.A. Lakers at Minnesota . . . . 7:00 PM
Golden State at Chicago . . . . . 7:30 PM
San Antonio at Utah . . . . 7:00 PM

TUESDAY, JANUARY 11
Charlotte at Cleveland. . . . . . . 7:00 PM
Detroit at New Jersey . . . . . . 7:30 PM
New Orleans at New York . . . . 7:30 PM
Milwaukee at Atlanta. . . . . . . 7:30 PM
Indiana at Memphis . . . . 7:00 PM
Miami at Phoenix . . . . 7:00 PM
Denver at Sacramento . . . . . . 7:00 PM
L.A. Clippers at Seattle . . . . . . 7:00 PM

WEDNEDSAY, JANUARY 12
Boston at Toronto . . . . 7:00 PM
Portland at Washington . . . . . 7:00 PM
New Orleans at Detroit . . . . . . 7:30 PM
Orlando at Minnesota . . . . 7:00 PM
Philadelphia at Chicago. . . . . . 7:30 PM
Milwaukee at San Antonio. . . . 7:30 PM
Houston at Dallas . . . . 8:00 PM
L.A. Lakers at Denver . . . . 7:00 PM
Phoenix at Utah . . . . 7:00 PM
Seattle at L.A. Clippers . . . . . . 7:30 PM
Miami at Golden State . . . . . . 7:30 PM

THURSDAY, JANUARY 13
New Jersey at Houston. . . . . . 7:00 PM
Utah at Sacramento . . . . 7:00 PM
Cleveland at L.A. Lakers . . . . . 7:30 PM

FRIDAY, JANUARY 14
Toronto at Philadelphia. . . . . . 7:00 PM
Memphis at Charlotte . . . . . . 7:00 PM
Phoenix at Indiana . . . . 7:00 PM
Atlanta at Boston . . . . 7:30 PM
Orlando at Detroit . . . . 8:00 PM

– 70 –

Portland at New Orleans..... 7:00 PM
Dallas at San Antonio....... 7:00 PM
Washington at Milwaukee.... 7:30 PM
Minnesota at Denver........ 8:30 PM
Miami at L.A. Clippers...... 7:30 PM
Golden State at Seattle...... 7:30 PM

SATURDAY, JANUARY 15
New York at Chicago....... 2:30 PM
Phoenix at Washington...... 7:00 PM
Charlotte at Atlanta......... 7:00 PM
Philadelphia at Detroit...... 7:30 PM
Orlando at Indiana......... 8:00 PM
Milwaukee at Memphis...... 7:00 PM
Portland at Minnesota...... 7:00 PM
San Antonio at Houston...... 7:30 PM
New Jersey at Dallas....... 7:30 PM
Cleveland at Utah......... 7:00 PM
L.A. Clippers at Sacramento . 7:00 PM
L.A. Lakers at Golden State... 7:30 PM

SUNDAY, JANUARY 16
New Orleans at Toronto...... 1:00 PM
Cleveland at Seattle........ 6:00 PM

MONDAY, JANUARY 17
Chicago at New York....... 1:00 PM
Milwaukee at Charlotte...... 1:00 PM
New Orleans at Philadelphia .. 2:00 PM
New Jersey at Atlanta...... 2:00 PM
Phoenix at Detroit......... 3:30 PM
Sacramento at L.A. Clippers . 12:30 PM
Washington at San Antonio .. 4:00 PM
Toronto at Minnesota....... 5:00 PM
Houston at Memphis....... 7:00 PM
Utah at L.A. Lakers........ 7:30 PM
Denver at Golden State...... 7:30 PM

TUESDAY, JANUARY 18
Detroit at Orlando......... 7:00 PM
Indiana at Houston......... 7:30 PM
Washington at Dallas....... 7:30 PM
Portland at Sacramento..... 7:00 PM
Denver at Seattle......... 7:00 PM

WEDNESDAY, JANUARY 19
Chicago at Boston......... 7:00 PM
New York at Toronto........ 7:00 PM
Philadelphia at Charlotte..... 7:00 PM
Milwaukee at New Jersey.... 7:30 PM
Atlanta at Miami......... 7:30 PM
Indiana at New Orleans...... 7:00 PM
L.A. Clippers at San Antonio.. 7:30 PM
Memphis at Phoenix........ 7:00 PM
Cleveland at Portland....... 7:00 PM
Minnesota at L.A. Lakers.... 7:30 PM

THURSDAY, JANUARY 20
L.A. Clippers at Dallas...... 6:00 PM
Houston at Orlando........ 8:00 PM
Cleveland at Sacramento.... 7:30 PM

FRIDAY, JANUARY 21
Toronto at Washington...... 7:00 PM
Dallas at Charlotte......... 7:00 PM
Boston at New Jersey....... 7:30 PM
Houston at New York....... 7:30 PM
Indiana at Miami......... 8:00 PM
Atlanta at Chicago........ 7:30 PM
Detroit at Milwaukee........ 7:30 PM
San Antonio at Phoenix..... 7:00 PM
Memphis at Denver........ 8:30 PM
Golden State at L.A. Lakers... 7:30 PM
Minnesota at Seattle........ 7:30 PM

SATURDAY, JANUARY 22
Boston at Atlanta......... 7:00 PM
Philadelphia at Orlando...... 7:00 PM
Chicago at Detroit......... 7:30 PM
Washington at Indiana...... 8:00 PM
L.A. Clippers at New Orleans.. 7:00 PM
Memphis at Utah......... 7:00 PM
Minnesota at Portland...... 7:00 PM
Cleveland at Golden State.... 7:30 PM

SUNDAY, JANUARY 23
Charlotte at Toronto........ 1:00 PM
Denver at Dallas........... noon
Milwaukee at New York...... 3:00 PM
Miami at Philadelphia....... 6:00 PM
New Jersey at Phoenix...... 6:00 PM
San Antonio at Sacramento .. 6:00 PM
Utah at Seattle......... 6:00 PM

MONDAY, JANUARY 24
Washington at Cleveland.... 7:00 PM
Chicago at Atlanta........ 7:30 PM
New Orleans at Miami...... 7:30 PM
Detroit at Minnesota........ 7:00 PM
Orlando at Houston........ 7:30 PM
San Antonio at Portland..... 7:00 PM
Dallas at L.A. Clippers...... 7:30 PM

TUESDAY, JANUARY 25
Boston at Charlotte........ 7:00 PM
Phoenix at New York....... 7:30 PM
Orlando at Memphis........ 7:00 PM
Denver at Chicago........ 7:30 PM
New Jersey at Sacramento .. 7:00 PM
Seattle at L.A. Lakers....... 7:30 PM

WEDNESDAY, JANUARY 26
Indiana at Boston......... 7:00 PM
Miami at Toronto......... 7:00 PM
Philadelphia at Washington... 7:00 PM
Memphis at Cleveland...... 7:00 PM
Denver at Detroit......... 7:30 PM
Phoenix at Milwaukee....... 7:00 PM
Houston at New Orleans..... 7:00 PM
Atlanta at Minnesota....... 7:00 PM
Seattle at Utah......... 7:00 PM
Dallas at Portland......... 7:00 PM
L.A. Lakers at L.A. Clippers... 7:30 PM
New Jersey at Golden State .. 7:30 PM

THURSDAY, JANUARY 27
Detroit at Indiana......... 7:00 PM
Charlotte at Chicago........ 7:30 PM
Sacramento at San Antonio .. 8:30 PM

FRIDAY, JANUARY 28
Cleveland at New York...... 7:00 PM
Toronto at Charlotte........ 7:00 PM
Washington at Orlando...... 7:00 PM
Phoenix at Boston......... 7:30 PM
Miami at Atlanta......... 7:30 PM
Philadelphia at New Orleans .. 7:00 PM
Utah at Minnesota......... 7:00 PM
Denver at Milwaukee....... 7:30 PM
Sacramento at Houston..... 8:30 PM
L.A. Clippers at Portland..... 7:00 PM
New Jersey at L.A. Lakers.... 7:30 PM
Seattle at Golden State...... 7:30 PM

SATURDAY, JANUARY 29
Orlando at Washington...... 7:00 PM
New York at Detroit........ 7:30 PM
Denver at Indiana......... 8:00 PM
Atlanta at Memphis........ 7:00 PM
Boston at Chicago......... 7:30 PM
Philadelphia at Dallas....... 7:30 PM

New Orleans at San Antonio .. 7:30 PM
New Jersey at Utah........ 7:00 PM
Golden State at L.A. Clippers.. 7:30 PM

SUNDAY, JANUARY 30
Houston at Miami......... 1:00 PM
Phoenix at Toronto........ 3:30 PM
Sacramento at Minnesota.... 2:30 PM
Milwaukee at Cleveland..... 6:30 PM
Charlotte at L.A. Lakers..... 6:30 PM

MONDAY, JANUARY 31
Houston at Boston......... 7:00 PM
Indiana at Philadelphia...... 7:00 PM
Orlando at Atlanta......... 7:30 PM
Memphis at New Orleans..... 7:00 PM
San Antonio at Seattle...... 7:00 PM
New York at L.A. Clippers.... 7:30 PM

TUESDAY, FEBRUARY 1
Detroit at Washington....... 7:00 PM
Cleveland at Orlando....... 7:00 PM
Chicago at New Jersey...... 7:30 PM
Minnesota at Milwaukee..... 7:00 PM
Phoenix at Memphis........ 7:00 PM
Miami at Dallas......... 7:30 PM
New York at Denver........ 7:00 PM
Charlotte at Utah......... 7:00 PM
Seattle at Sacramento....... 7:00 PM
Portland at L.A. Lakers...... 7:30 PM

WEDNESDAY, FEBRUARY 2
New Jersey at Boston........ 7:00 PM
Houston at Philadelphia..... 7:00 PM
Toronto at Indiana......... 7:00 PM
Atlanta at Detroit......... 7:30 PM
Dallas at New Orleans....... 7:00 PM
Phoenix at Minnesota....... 7:00 PM
Denver at Portland........ 7:00 PM
Sacramento at Golden State .. 7:30 PM

THURSDAY, FEBRUARY 3
Cleveland at Miami........ 8:00 PM
L.A. Clippers at Memphis.... 7:00 PM
San Antonio at L.A. Lakers... 7:30 PM

FRIDAY, FEBRUARY 4
Washington at Toronto...... 7:00 PM
Atlanta at Philadelphia...... 7:00 PM
Dallas at Indiana......... 7:00 PM
Orlando at Boston......... 7:30 PM
L.A. Clippers at Milwaukee... 7:30 PM
Houston at Minnesota...... 8:30 PM
New York at Sacramento..... 7:00 PM
Charlotte at Portland........ 7:00 PM
New Orleans at Golden State.. 7:30 PM

SATURDAY, FEBRUARY 5
Detroit at New Jersey....... 1:00 PM
Milwaukee at Washington.... 7:00 PM
Indiana at Atlanta......... 7:00 PM
Chicago at Miami......... 7:30 PM
Orlando at Cleveland........ 7:30 PM
Golden State at Denver...... 7:00 PM
New Orleans at Utah....... 7:00 PM
New York at Phoenix....... 7:00 PM
Sacramento at Portland..... 7:00 PM
Charlotte at Seattle........ 7:00 PM

SUNDAY, FEBRUARY 6
Dallas at Toronto......... 1:00 PM
L.A. Clippers at Philadelphia .. 1:00 PM
Boston at Minnesota.......... noon
L.A. Lakers at Houston...... 2:30 PM

MONDAY, FEBRUARY 7
Indiana at Washington . . . . . . 7:00 PM
Philadelphia at New Jersey . . . 7:30 PM
L.A. Lakers at Atlanta . . . . 7:30 PM
Golden State at Miami . . . . . . 7:30 PM
New York at Utah . . . . 7:00 PM

TUESDAY, FEBRUARY 8
San Antonio at Charlotte . . . . . 7:00 PM
Golden State at Orlando . . . . . 7:00 PM
Toronto at Cleveland . . . . 7:00 PM
Boston at Milwaukee . . . . 7:00 PM
Minnesota at Memphis . . . . . . 7:00 PM
Chicago at Dallas . . . . 7:30 PM
Utah at Denver . . . . 7:00 PM
Phoenix at Sacramento . . . . . . 7:00 PM
New Orleans at Seattle . . . . . . 7:00 PM

WEDNESDAY, FEBRUARY 9
L.A. Clippers at Boston . . . . . . 7:00 PM
Milwaukee at Toronto . . . . 7:00 PM
Memphis at Philadelphia . . . . . 7:00 PM
San Antonio at Washington . . 7:00 PM
Charlotte at Indiana . . . . 7:00 PM
L.A. Lakers at New Jersey . . . . 7:30 PM
Miami at New York . . . . 7:30 PM
Denver at Minnesota . . . . 7:00 PM
Chicago at Houston . . . . 7:30 PM
New Orleans at Portland . . . . . 7:00 PM

THURSDAY, FEBRUARY 10
Atlanta at Orlando . . . . 7:00 PM
L.A. Lakers at Detroit . . . . 8:00 PM
Sacramento at Seattle . . . . . . 7:30 PM

FRIDAY, FEBRUARY 11
Philadelphia at Toronto . . . . . . 7:00 PM
L.A. Clippers at Washington . . 7:00 PM
Miami at Charlotte . . . . 7:00 PM
Houston at Indiana . . . . 7:00 PM
New York at Boston . . . . 7:30 PM
San Antonio at New Jersey . . . 7:30 PM
Denver at Cleveland . . . . 8:00 PM
Portland at Memphis . . . . 7:00 PM
Golden State at New Orleans . . 7:00 PM
Minnesota at Utah . . . . 7:00 PM
Seattle at Phoenix . . . . 7:00 PM
Dallas at Sacramento . . . . . . 7:30 PM

SATURDAY, FEBRUARY 12
Orlando at Philadelphia . . . . . . 7:00 PM
Washington at Detroit . . . . 7:30 PM
Atlanta at Milwaukee . . . . 7:30 PM

SUNDAY, FEBRUARY 13
San Antonio at Miami . . . . 1:00 PM
L.A. Lakers at Cleveland . . . . . 3:30 PM
Chicago at Minnesota . . . . 2:30 PM
Sacramento at Boston . . . . . . 6:00 PM
L.A. Clippers at Toronto . . . . . 6:00 PM
Denver at New Jersey . . . . 6:00 PM
Charlotte at New York . . . . 6:00 PM
New Orleans at Orlando . . . . . 6:00 PM
Memphis at Indiana . . . . 6:00 PM
Dallas at Seattle . . . . 5:00 PM
Portland at Houston . . . . 7:30 PM
Phoenix at Golden State . . . . . 6:00 PM

MONDAY, FEBRUARY 14
New York at Philadelphia . . . . 7:00 PM
Portland at Charlotte . . . . 7:00 PM
Milwaukee at Detroit . . . . 7:30 PM
Washington at New Orleans . . 7:00 PM
Utah at Phoenix . . . . 7:00 PM

TUESDAY, FEBRUARY 15
L.A. Clippers at Orlando . . . . . 7:00 PM
Denver at Atlanta . . . . 7:30 PM
New Jersey at Minnesota . . . . 7:00 PM
Sacramento at Chicago . . . . . . 7:30 PM
Washington at Houston . . . . . . 7:30 PM
Utah at L.A. Lakers . . . . 7:30 PM
Dallas at Golden State . . . . . . 7:30 PM

WEDNESDAY, FEBRUARY 16
Memphis at Boston . . . . 7:00 PM
Chicago at Toronto . . . . 7:00 PM
Detroit at Philadelphia . . . . . . 7:00 PM
Denver at Charlotte . . . . 7:00 PM
Atlanta at Cleveland . . . . 7:00 PM
Portland at Indiana . . . . 7:00 PM
Sacramento at New Jersey . . . 7:30 PM
Milwaukee at New York . . . . . . 7:30 PM
L.A. Clippers at Miami . . . . . . 7:30 PM
San Antonio at New Orleans . . 8:00 PM
Golden State at Seattle . . . . . . 7:00 PM

THURSDAY, FEBRUARY 17
Cleveland at Minnesota . . . . . . 7:00 PM
Dallas at Phoenix . . . . 8:30 PM

TUESDAY, FEBRUARY 22
Milwaukee at Charlotte . . . . . . 7:00 PM
Indiana at Orlando . . . . 7:00 PM
Toronto at New Jersey . . . . . . 7:30 PM
New York at Detroit . . . . 7:30 PM
Miami at Chicago . . . . 7:30 PM
Seattle at Houston . . . . 7:30 PM
Atlanta at Sacramento . . . . . . 7:00 PM
Boston at L.A. Lakers . . . . 7:30 PM

WEDNESDAY, FEBRUARY 23
Memphis at Washington . . . . . 7:00 PM
Chicago at Cleveland . . . . 7:00 PM
Miami at Indiana . . . . 7:00 PM
New Jersey at Milwaukee . . . . 7:00 PM
Seattle at New Orleans . . . . . . 7:00 PM
Houston at San Antonio . . . . . 8:00 PM
Boston at Denver . . . . 7:00 PM
Dallas at Utah . . . . 7:00 PM
L.A. Clippers at Phoenix . . . . . 7:00 PM
L.A. Lakers at Portland . . . . . . 7:00 PM
Atlanta at Golden State . . . . . . 7:30 PM

THURSDAY, FEBRUARY 24
Philadelphia at New York . . . . 7:00 PM
Sacramento at Dallas . . . . 8:30 PM
Minnesota at L.A. Clippers . . . 7:30 PM

FRIDAY, FEBRUARY 25
Charlotte at New Jersey . . . . . 7:30 PM
Cleveland at Indiana . . . . 8:00 PM
Denver at Memphis . . . . 7:00 PM
Washington at Chicago . . . . . . 7:30 PM
Toronto at Milwaukee . . . . 7:30 PM
Boston at Utah . . . . 7:00 PM
Atlanta at Portland . . . . 7:00 PM
Detroit at L.A. Lakers . . . . 7:30 PM
Minnesota at Seattle . . . . 7:30 PM

SATURDAY, FEBRUARY 26
Orlando at Miami . . . . 1:00 PM
Chicago at Charlotte . . . . 7:00 PM
Indiana at New York . . . . 7:30 PM
Sacramento at Philadelphia . . . 7:30 PM
Phoenix at Dallas . . . . 7:30 PM
Memphis at San Antonio . . . . 7:30 PM

SUNDAY, FEBRUARY 27
L.A. Lakers at Toronto . . . . . . 1:00 PM

Cleveland at New Jersey . . . . . 1:00 PM
Seattle at Milwaukee . . . . 2:00 PM
Utah at Houston . . . . 3:00 PM
Sacramento at Washington . . . 6:00 PM
Denver at New Orleans . . . . . . 6:00 PM
Miami at Orlando . . . . 7:30 PM
Boston at Phoenix . . . . 6:00 PM
Minnesota at Portland . . . . . . 5:00 PM
Detroit at Golden State . . . . . . 6:00 PM
Atlanta at L.A. Clippers . . . . . . 6:30 PM

MONDAY, FEBRUARY 28
San Antonio at Cleveland . . . . 7:00 PM
L.A. Lakers at New York . . . . . 7:30 PM
New Orleans at Dallas . . . . . . 7:30 PM
L.A. Clippers at Utah . . . . 7:00 PM

TUESDAY, MARCH 1
Golden State at Memphis . . . . 1:00 PM
Sacramento at Charlotte . . . . . 7:00 PM
Seattle at Indiana . . . . 7:00 PM
Philadelphia at Milwaukee . . . 7:00 PM
Houston at Chicago . . . . 7:30 PM
Atlanta at Denver . . . . 7:00 PM
Detroit at Portland . . . . 7:00 PM

WEDNESDAY, MARCH 2
New Jersey at Philadelphia . . 7:00 PM
Houston at Washington . . . . . 7:00 PM
Sacramento at Orlando . . . . . . 7:00 PM
Seattle at Cleveland . . . . 7:00 PM
L.A. Lakers at Boston . . . . 7:30 PM
Golden State at Minnesota . . . 7:00 PM
Toronto at San Antonio . . . . . . 7:30 PM
Charlotte at New Orleans . . . . 8:00 PM
Atlanta at Utah . . . . 7:00 PM
Dallas at L.A. Clippers . . . . . . 7:30 PM

THURSDAY, MARCH 3
Miami at New Jersey . . . . 7:30 PM
Indiana at Denver . . . . 6:00 PM
Detroit at Phoenix . . . . 8:30 PM

FRIDAY, MARCH 4
Cleveland at Philadelphia . . . . 7:00 PM
Golden State at Washington . . 7:00 PM
New York at Orlando . . . . 7:00 PM
Charlotte at Boston . . . . 7:30 PM
Sacramento at Miami . . . . 8:00 PM
Toronto at Memphis . . . . 7:00 PM
Utah at New Orleans . . . . 7:00 PM
Milwaukee at Minnesota . . . . . 7:00 PM
Chicago at San Antonio . . . . . 7:30 PM
Indiana at Portland . . . . 7:00 PM
Dallas at L.A. Lakers . . . . 7:30 PM
Detroit at Seattle . . . . 7:30 PM

SATURDAY, MARCH 5
Denver at L.A. Clippers . . . . noon
Washington at Charlotte . . . . . 7:00 PM

Philadelphia at Atlanta . . . . . . 7:00 PM
Orlando at New Jersey . . . . . . 7:30 PM
Chicago at Milwaukee . . . . 7:30 PM
Portland at Phoenix . . . . 7:00 PM

SUNDAY, MARCH 6
Dallas at Houston . . . . noon
Detroit at Sacramento . . . . . . 12:30 PM
Minnesota at Boston . . . . 6:00 PM
Toronto at New Orleans . . . . . 6:00 PM
Utah at San Antonio . . . . 6:00 PM
Golden State at New York . . . . 7:30 PM
Miami at Cleveland . . . . 7:30 PM
Phoenix at Seattle . . . . 6:00 PM
Indiana at L.A. Lakers . . . . 6:30 PM

MONDAY, MARCH 7
Philadelphia at Miami . . . . 7:30 PM
Milwaukee at Chicago . . . . 7:30 PM
Toronto at Dallas . . . . 7:30 PM
Portland at Denver . . . . 7:00 PM
Memphis at L.A. Clippers . . . . 7:30 PM

TUESDAY, MARCH 8
Golden State at Philadelphia . . 7:00 PM
Orlando at Cleveland. . . . . 7:00 PM
Washington at New York . . . . 7:30 PM
Atlanta at Milwaukee. . . . . 7:00 PM
Charlotte at Minnesota . . . . . . 7:00 PM
New Jersey at San Antonio. . . 7:30 PM
Indiana at Utah . . . . 7:00 PM
Memphis at Sacramento. . . . . . 7:00 PM
Houston at Seattle . . . . 7:00 PM
L.A. Clippers at L.A. Lakers. . . 7:30 PM

WEDNESDAY, MARCH 9
Atlanta at Boston . . . . 7:00 PM
Orlando at Toronto . . . . 7:00 PM
Golden State at Detroit. . . . . . 7:30 PM
New Jersey at New Orleans . . 7:00 PM
San Antonio at Phoenix . . . . . 7:00 PM
Chicago at Portland . . . . 7:00 PM

THURSDAY, MARCH 10
Minnesota at Miami . . . . 7:00 PM
L.A. Lakers at Dallas. . . . . 8:30 PM

FRIDAY, MARCH 11
Atlanta at Toronto . . . . 7:00 PM
Charlotte at Philadelphia. . . . . 7:00 PM
Minnesota at Orlando . . . . 7:00 PM
Golden State at Indiana . . . . . 7:00 PM
Detroit at Boston . . . . 7:30 PM
Dallas at Milwaukee . . . . 7:30 PM
Memphis at Utah . . . . 7:00 PM
Houston at Phoenix . . . . 7:00 PM
L.A. Clippers at Sacramento . . 7:00 PM
Chicago at Seattle . . . . 7:30 PM

SATURDAY, MARCH 12
New Jersey at Miami . . . . 1:00 PM
L.A. Lakers at Charlotte . . . . . 7:00 PM
Golden State at Atlanta. . . . . . 7:00 PM
Milwaukee at New Orleans . . . 7:00 PM
Denver at San Antonio . . . . . . 7:30 PM
Memphis at Portland . . . . 7:00 PM

SUNDAY, MARCH 13
Dallas at Minnesota . . . . noon
Chicago at L.A. Clippers . . . . 12:30 PM

Houston at Sacramento . . . . 12:30 PM
Washington at Boston . . . . . . 6:00 PM
Philadelphia at Toronto. . . . . . 6:00 PM
Seattle at New York . . . . 6:00 PM
New Jersey at Orlando . . . . . . 6:00 PM
Utah at Detroit . . . . 6:00 PM
Indiana at Cleveland . . . . 7:00 PM
Phoenix at Denver . . . . 7:00 PM

MONDAY, MARCH 14
L.A. Lakers at Washington . . . 7:00 PM
Boston at Charlotte . . . . 7:00 PM
Detroit at Atlanta . . . . 7:30 PM
Milwaukee at Miami . . . . 7:30 PM
Portland at Memphis . . . . 7:00 PM
New Orleans at San Antonio . . 7:30 PM
Houston at Golden State. . . . . 7:30 PM

TUESDAY, MARCH 15
L.A. Lakers at Philadelphia . . . 7:00 PM
Utah at Cleveland . . . . 7:00 PM

Miami at New York . . . . 7:30 PM
Seattle at Chicago . . . . 7:30 PM
Minnesota at Dallas . . . . 7:30 PM
Orlando at Sacramento. . . . . . 7:00 PM

WEDNESDAY, MARCH 16
Toronto at Boston . . . . 7:00 PM
Utah at Indiana . . . . 7:00 PM
Chicago at New Jersey . . . . . . 7:30 PM
Washington at Atlanta . . . . . . 7:30 PM
Seattle at Detroit . . . . 7:30 PM
Cleveland at Milwaukee. . . . . . 7:00 PM
Memphis at New Orleans . . . . 7:00 PM
Portland at Houston . . . . 7:30 PM
Minnesota at San Antonio. . . . 8:00 PM
Charlotte at Denver . . . . 7:00 PM
Orlando at L.A. Clippers . . . . . 7:30 PM

THURSDAY, MARCH 17
L.A. Lakers at Miami. . . . . 8:00 PM
Portland at Dallas . . . . 7:30 PM
Sacramento at Golden State . . 7:30 PM

FRIDAY, MARCH 18
Utah at New Jersey . . . . 7:30 PM
New York at Atlanta . . . . 7:30 PM
Philadelphia at Cleveland . . . . 7:30 PM
L.A. Lakers at Indiana. . . . . . . 7:30 PM
Toronto at Detroit . . . . 8:00 PM
Minnesota at Memphis. . . . . . 7:00 PM
New Orleans at Chicago . . . . . 7:30 PM
Washington at Milwaukee. . . . 7:30 PM
Boston at Houston . . . . 7:30 PM
Charlotte at San Antonio. . . . . 7:30 PM
L.A. Clippers at Denver. . . . . . 7:00 PM
Golden State at Phoenix . . . . . 7:00 PM
Orlando at Seattle . . . . 7:30 PM

SATURDAY, MARCH 19
Chicago at Philadelphia. . . . . . 7:00 PM
Utah at Washington . . . . 7:00 PM
New York at Miami . . . . 7:30 PM
Boston at New Orleans . . . . . . 7:00 PM
Charlotte at Dallas . . . . 7:30 PM
Orlando at Portland . . . . 7:00 PM
Sacramento at L.A. Clippers . . 7:30 PM

SUNDAY, MARCH 20
Cleveland at Toronto. . . . . 1:00 PM
San Antonio at Detroit . . . . . . 3:30 PM
New Jersey at Indiana . . . . . . 3:30 PM
Phoenix at Memphis. . . . . 3:00 PM
Houston at Minnesota . . . . . . 6:30 PM
Milwaukee at Denver . . . . 7:00 PM
Golden State at Sacramento . . 6:00 PM
Seattle at L.A. Lakers . . . . 6:30 PM

MONDAY, MARCH 21
Orlando at Charlotte . . . . 7:00 PM
San Antonio at New York . . . . 7:30 PM
Atlanta at Chicago . . . . 7:30 PM
New Orleans at Dallas. . . . . . . 7:30 PM
Portland at L.A. Clippers. . . . . 7:30 PM

TUESDAY, MARCH 22
Detroit at Cleveland . . . . 7:00 PM
Indiana at New Jersey . . . . . . 7:30 PM
Phoenix at Atlanta . . . . 7:30 PM
Washington at Denver . . . . . . 7:00 PM
L.A. Lakers at Utah . . . . 7:00 PM
Miami at Houston . . . . 8:30 PM
Portland at Sacramento . . . . . 7:00 PM
Milwaukee at Seattle. . . . . 7:00 PM

WEDNESDAY, MARCH 23
Chicago at Toronto . . . . 7:00 PM

Phoenix at Charlotte . . . . 7:00 PM
San Antonio at Indiana . . . . . . 7:00 PM
Boston at New York . . . . 7:30 PM
Detroit at Philadelphia . . . . . . 8:00 PM
New Orleans at Minnesota . . . 7:00 PM
Milwaukee at L.A. Clippers . . . 7:30 PM
Dallas at Golden State . . . . . . 7:30 PM

THURSDAY, MARCH 24
Charlotte at Orlando . . . . 7:00 PM
Memphis at New Jersey . . . . . 7:30 PM
Cleveland at Houston . . . . 7:30 PM
L.A. Lakers at Denver . . . . 7:00 PM
Washington at Utah . . . . 7:00 PM
Dallas at Sacramento . . . . 7:00 PM
Seattle at Portland . . . . 7:00 PM

FRIDAY, MARCH 25
Toronto at Philadelphia. . . . . . 7:00 PM
Chicago at Boston . . . . 7:30 PM
Phoenix at Miami . . . . 8:00 PM
Indiana at Detroit . . . . 8:00 PM
Houston at New Orleans. . . . . 7:00 PM
Atlanta at San Antonio . . . . . . 7:30 PM
Washington at L.A. Clippers . . 7:30 PM
Milwaukee at Golden State . . . 7:30 PM
New York at Seattle . . . . 7:30 PM

SATURDAY, MARCH 26
Minnesota at New Jersey . . . . 1:00 PM
Miami at Charlotte . . . . 7:00 PM
Toronto at Atlanta . . . . 7:00 PM
Phoenix at Orlando . . . . 7:00 PM
Boston at Detroit . . . . 7:30 PM
New Orleans at Memphis . . . . 7:00 PM
Indiana at Chicago . . . . 7:30 PM
Cleveland at Dallas . . . . 7:30 PM
Sacramento at Denver . . . . . . 7:00 PM
Milwaukee at Utah . . . . 7:00 PM
New York at Portland . . . . 7:00 PM

SUNDAY, MARCH 27
Houston at San Antonio. . . . . noon
L.A. Clippers at Minnesota . . . 2:30 PM
Philadelphia at L.A. Lakers. . . . 4:30 PM
Washington at Seattle. . . . . . . 5:00 PM

MONDAY, MARCH 28
New Jersey at Charlotte . . . . . 7:00 PM
Atlanta at Orlando . . . . 7:00 PM
Dallas at Detroit . . . . 7:30 PM
Indiana at Milwaukee. . . . . 7:00 PM
Cleveland at New Orleans . . . . 7:00 PM
Memphis at Chicago. . . . . 7:30 PM
Houston at Utah . . . . 7:00 PM
Denver at Phoenix . . . . 7:00 PM
Philadelphia at Sacramento. . . 7:00 PM
Washington at Portland . . . . . 7:00 PM
New York at Golden State. . . . 7:30 PM

TUESDAY, MARCH 29
L.A. Clippers at Cleveland . . . . 7:00 PM
Toronto at Miami . . . . 7:30 PM
Seattle at Memphis . . . . 7:00 PM
New York at L.A. Lakers . . . . . 7:30 PM

WEDNESDAY, MARCH 30
Dallas at Boston . . . . 7:00 PM
Atlanta at Washington . . . . . . 7:00 PM
Chicago at Charlotte. . . . . 7:00 PM
Toronto at Orlando . . . . 7:00 PM
L.A. Clippers at New Jersey . . 7:30 PM
Sacramento at Detroit. . . . . . . 7:30 PM
Golden State at Milwaukee . . . 7:00 PM
Seattle at San Antonio . . . . . . 7:30 PM
Denver at Utah . . . . 7:00 PM

Philadelphia at Phoenix. . . . . . 7:00 PM
Houston at Portland . . . . 7:00 PM

THURSDAY, MARCH 31
Miami at Indiana . . . . 8:00 PM
Cleveland at Chicago . . . . . . 7:30 PM
Minnesota at L.A. Lakers . . . . 7:30 PM

FRIDAY, APRIL 1
Dallas at Philadelphia . . . . 7:00 PM
Toronto at Charlotte . . . . 7:00 PM
Washington at Orlando. . . . . . 7:00 PM
Boston at Atlanta . . . . 7:30 PM
New Jersey at New York. . . . . 8:00 PM
L.A. Clippers at Detroit. . . . . 8:00 PM
Sacramento at Cleveland . . . . 8:00 PM
Memphis at Milwaukee. . . . . . 7:30 PM
New Orleans at Houston . . . . . 7:30 PM
Golden State at Utah. . . . . . . 7:00 PM
Minnesota at Phoenix. . . . . . . 7:00 PM
San Antonio at Denver . . . . . 8:30 PM
Portland at Seattle . . . . 7:30 PM

SATURDAY, APRIL 2
Orlando at New Jersey . . . . . . 7:30 PM
Miami at New Orleans . . . . . . 7:00 PM
Charlotte at Chicago . . . . 7:30 PM
L.A. Lakers at San Antonio . . 7:30 PM
Denver at Portland . . . . 7:00 PM

SUNDAY, APRIL 3
Indiana at Washington . . . . . . 1:00 PM
Dallas at Cleveland . . . . 1:00 PM
New York at Milwaukee. . . . . 12:00 PM
Minnesota at Sacramento . . . 12:30 PM
Philadelphia at Boston . . . . . . 6:00 PM
Detroit at Toronto . . . . 6:00 PM
L.A. Clippers at Atlanta. . . . . . 6:00 PM
Seattle at Golden State . . . . . . 3:00 PM
L.A. Lakers at Memphis . . . . . 7:00 PM
Phoenix at Houston . . . . 7:30 PM

TUESDAY, APRIL 5
Boston at Washington . . . . . . 7:00 PM
L.A. Clippers at Charlotte . . . . 7:00 PM
New Jersey at Cleveland . . . . . 7:00 PM
Indiana at New York . . . . 7:30 PM
New Orleans at Atlanta . . . . . . 7:30 PM
Chicago at Miami . . . . 7:30 PM
Denver at Memphis . . . . 7:00 PM
Orlando at Dallas . . . . 7:30 PM
Portland at Utah . . . . 7:00 PM
L.A. Lakers at Phoenix . . . . . . 7:00 PM
Seattle at Sacramento. . . . . . . 7:00 PM
Houston at Golden State. . . . . 7:30 PM

WEDNESDAY, APRIL 6,
Milwaukee at Boston . . . . 7:00 PM
Memphis at Toronto . . . . 7:00 PM
Charlotte at Philadelphia . . . . . 7:00 PM
Chicago at Orlando . . . . 7:00 PM
Cleveland at Indiana . . . . 6:00 PM
Washington at Detroit. . . . . . . 7:30 PM
Denver at New Orleans . . . . . . 7:00 PM
L.A. Clippers at San Antonio . . 7:30 PM
Utah at Minnesota . . . . 8:30 PM
Golden State at Portland. . . . . 7:00 PM

THURSDAY, APRIL 7
New York at New Jersey. . . . . 7:30 PM
San Antonio at Dallas . . . . 7:00 PM
Houston at L.A. Lakers . . . . . . 7:30 PM

FRIDAY, APRIL 8
Atlanta at Toronto . . . . 7:00 PM
Cleveland at Philadelphia . . . . 7:00 PM

Detroit at Orlando . . . . 7:00 PM
Chicago at New York . . . . 8:00 PM
Washington at Indiana . . . . . . 7:00 PM
Miami at Memphis . . . . 7:00 PM
Utah at New Orleans. . . . . . . 7:00 PM
Charlotte at Milwaukee . . . . . . 7:30 PM
Denver at Minnesota . . . . 8:30 PM
Sacramento at Portland . . . . 7:00 PM
Phoenix at Golden State . . . . 7:30 PM
L.A. Lakers at Seattle . . . . 7:30 PM

SATURDAY, APRIL 9
Boston at New Jersey. . . . . . . 1:00 PM
Philadelphia at Washington. . . 7:00 PM
Minnesota at Atlanta. . . . . . . 7:00 PM
Milwaukee at Cleveland. . . . . 7:30 PM
Toronto at Chicago . . . . 7:30 PM
Utah at Dallas . . . . 7:30 PM
Seattle at Denver . . . . 7:00 PM
Houston at Phoenix . . . . 7:00 PM
San Antonio at L.A. Clippers . . 7:30 PM

SUNDAY, APRIL 10
Detroit at Miami . . . . 1:00 PM
New York at Indiana. . . . . noon
L.A. Lakers at Sacramento . . 12:30 PM
Portland at New Orleans . . . . . 6:00 PM
Charlotte at Memphis . . . . . . 7:00 PM
San Antonio at Golden State . . 6:00 PM

MONDAY, APRIL 11
Indiana at Toronto . . . . 7:00 PM
Milwaukee at Washington. . . . 7:00 PM
Cleveland at Orlando. . . . . 7:00 PM
Charlotte at Atlanta . . . . 7:30 PM
Detroit at Chicago . . . . 7:30 PM
Memphis at Dallas . . . . 7:30 PM
Golden State at Denver. . . . . . 7:00 PM
Houston at Seattle . . . . 7:00 PM
Phoenix at L.A. Lakers . . . . . . 7:30 PM

TUESDAY, APRIL 12
Boston at Philadelphia . . . . . . 7:00 PM
Toronto at New York. . . . . 7:30 PM
Portland at San Antonio . . . . . 7:30 PM
New Orleans at Phoenix . . . . . 7:00 PM
Utah at L.A. Clippers. . . . . 7:30 PM

WEDNESDAY, APRIL 13
Chicago at Washington. . . . . . 7:00 PM
Atlanta at Charlotte . . . . 7:00 PM
Orlando at Detroit . . . . 7:30 PM
New Jersey at Indiana . . . . . . 7:00 PM
Boston at Milwaukee . . . . 7:00 PM
Golden State at Minnesota . . 7:00 PM
Memphis at Houston . . . . 7:30 PM
New Orleans at Denver . . . . . . 7:00 PM
Dallas at Seattle . . . . 7:00 PM
San Antonio at Utah . . . . 8:30 PM

THURSDAY, APRIL 14
Miami at Philadelphia . . . . 7:00 PM
New York at Cleveland . . . . . . 8:00 PM
Dallas at Portland . . . . 7:30 PM

FRIDAY, APRIL 15
New Jersey at Toronto . . . . . . 7:00 PM
Cleveland at Washington . . . . 7:00 PM
Miami at Boston . . . . 7:30 PM
Milwaukee at Detroit. . . . . . . 8:00 PM
Philadelphia at Indiana . . . . . . 7:00 PM
Orlando at Chicago . . . . 7:30 PM
Memphis at Denver . . . . 7:00 PM
Minnesota at Utah . . . . 7:00 PM
L.A. Clippers at Phoenix . . . . . 7:00 PM
Sacramento at L.A. Lakers . . . 7:30 PM

Portland at Golden State. . . . . 7:30 PM
New Orleans at Seattle . . . . . 7:30 PM

SATURDAY, APRIL 16
New York at Charlotte. . . . . . . 1:00 PM
Chicago at Atlanta . . . . 7:00 PM
Denver at Houston . . . . 6:30 PM
Orlando at Milwaukee. . . . . . . 7:30 PM
Memphis at San Antonio . . . . 7:30 PM
Sacramento at Phoenix . . . . . 7:00 PM
New Orleans at L.A. Clippers. . 7:30 PM

SUNDAY, APRIL 17
Charlotte at Washington . . . . . 1:00 PM
Indiana at Miami . . . . 1:00 PM
Cleveland at Detroit . . . . 1:00 PM
Seattle at Minnesota. . . . . . . 2:30 PM
Dallas at L.A. Lakers. . . . . . . 12:30 PM
Boston at Toronto . . . . 6:00 PM
Philadelphia at New Jersey . . . 6:00 PM
Atlanta at New York . . . . 7:30 PM
Utah at Portland . . . . 5:00 PM

MONDAY, APRIL 18
Milwaukee at Philadelphia. . . . 7:00 PM
Indiana at Orlando . . . . 7:00 PM
San Antonio at Memphis . . . . 7:00 PM
Minnesota at New Orleans . . . 7:00 PM
L.A. Clippers at Houston. . . . . 7:30 PM
Sacramento at Utah . . . . 7:00 PM
Denver at Phoenix . . . . 7:00 PM
L.A. Lakers at Golden State. . . 7:30 PM

TUESDAY, APRIL 19
Boston at Cleveland . . . . 7:00 PM
Washington at New Jersey . . . 7:30 PM
Detroit at Atlanta . . . . 7:30 PM
Charlotte at Miami . . . . 7:30 PM
Toronto at Milwaukee . . . . 7:00 PM
New York at Chicago . . . . 7:30 PM
Seattle at Dallas . . . . 7:30 PM
Portland at Denver . . . . 7:00 PM

WEDNESDAY, APRIL 20
New Jersey at Boston. . . . . . . 7:00 PM
Cleveland at Toronto. . . . . 7:00 PM
Atlanta at Philadelphia . . . . . . 7:00 PM
Detroit at Charlotte . . . . 7:00 PM
Miami at Orlando . . . . 7:00 PM
Washington at New York . . . . 7:30 PM
Chicago at Indiana . . . . 7:00 PM
Dallas at Memphis . . . . 7:00 PM
L.A. Clippers at New Orleans. . 7:00 PM
San Antonio at Minnesota. . . . 7:00 PM
Seattle at Houston . . . . 7:30 PM
L.A. Lakers at Portland . . . . . . 7:00 PM
Utah at Golden State. . . . . . . 7:30 PM
Phoenix at Sacramento. . . . . . 7:30 PM

GAMES ON TELEVISION & RADIO

(All times Eastern)

ABC SCHEDULE

Dec. 25—Miami at L.A. Lakers . . . . 3:00 PM	Mar. 20—New Jersey at Indiana . . . . 3:30 PM
Jan. 8—New York at Cleveland . . . . 1:30 PM	Mar. 27—Houston at San Antonio . . . . 1:00 PM
Jan. 8—Denver at San Antonio . . . . 1:30 PM	Apr. 3—Dallas at Cleveland . . . . 1:00 PM
Jan. 30—Houston at Miami . . . . 1:00 PM	Apr. 3—New York at Milwaukee. . . . . 1:00 PM
Feb. 6—L.A. Lakers at Houston . . . . 3:30 PM	Apr. 3—Minnesota at Sacramento . . . . 3:30 PM
Feb. 13—San Antonio at Miami . . . . 1:00 PM	Apr. 10—Detroit at Miami. . . . . 1:00 PM
Feb. 13—L.A. Lakers at Cleveland . . . . 3:30 PM	Apr. 10—New York at Indiana. . . . . 1:00 PM
Mar. 6—Dallas at Houston . . . . 1:00 PM	Apr. 10—L.A. Lakers at Sacramento . . . . 3:30 PM
Mar. 6—Detroit at Sacramento . . . . 3:30 PM	Apr. 17—Indiana at Miami . . . . 1:00 PM
Mar. 13—Dallas at Minnesota. . . . . 1:00 PM	Apr. 17—Cleveland at Detroit . . . . 1:00 PM
Mar. 13—Houston at Sacramento. . . . . 3:30 PM	Apr. 17—Dallas at L.A. Lakers . . . . 3:30 PM
Mar. 20—San Antonio at Detroit. . . . . 3:30 PM	

NBA TV SCHEDULE

Nov. 6—Sacramento at Houston . . . . 8:30 PM	Jan. 24—Orlando at Houston . . . . 8:30 PM
Nov. 7—San Antonio at Seattle . . . . 8:00 PM	Jan. 25—Phoenix at New York . . . . 7:30 PM
Nov. 8—Detroit at L.A. Clippers. . . . . 10:30 PM	Jan. 26—Denver at Detroit. . . . . 7:30 PM
Nov. 9—Portland at New Jersey . . . . 7:30 PM	Jan. 26—Dallas at Portland . . . . 10:00 PM
Nov. 13—L.A. Lakers at Houston . . . . 8:30 PM	Jan. 29—Orlando at Washington . . . . 7:00 PM
Nov. 14—Denver at Sacramento. . . . . 9:00 PM	Jan. 31—Indiana at Philadelphia. . . . . 7:00 PM
Nov. 15—Golden State at Cleveland . . . . 7:00 PM	Feb. 1—Miami at Dallas . . . . 8:30 PM
Nov. 16—Miami at Minnesota . . . . 8:00 PM	Feb. 5—New Orleans at Utah. . . . . 9:00 PM
Nov. 20—Orlando at Indiana . . . . 8:00 PM	Feb. 7—Indiana at Washington . . . . 7:30 PM
Nov. 21—Cleveland at New York. . . . . 7:30 PM	Feb. 8—Phoenix at Sacramento. . . . . 10:00 PM
Nov. 22—Minnesota at Dallas. . . . . 8:30 PM	Feb. 9—Miami at New York. . . . . 7:30 PM
Nov. 23—Toronto at Washington . . . . 7:00 PM	Feb. 13—Denver at New Jersey . . . . 6:00 PM
Nov. 27—Denver at Houston . . . . 8:30 PM	Feb. 14—Utah at Phoenix. . . . . 9:00 PM
Nov. 28—Minnesota at Sacramento . . . . 9:00 PM	Feb. 15—New Jersey at Minnesota. . . . . 8:00 PM
Nov. 29—Cleveland at L.A. Clippers . . . . 10:30 PM	Feb. 22—Boston at L.A. Lakers . . . . 10:30 PM
Nov. 30—San Antonio at Dallas . . . . 8:30 PM	Feb. 26—Indiana at New York . . . . 7:30 PM
Dec. 1—Milwaukee at Boston . . . . 7:00 PM	Feb. 27—Utah at Houston . . . . 4:00 PM
Dec. 4—Miami at Denver . . . . 9:00 PM	Feb. 28—L.A. Lakers at New York . . . . 7:30 PM
Dec. 5—Phoenix at Portland . . . . 9:00 PM	Mar. 1—Sacramento at Charlotte. . . . . 7:00 PM
Dec. 6—Detroit at Dallas. . . . . 8:30 PM	Mar. 5—Chicago at Milwaukee . . . . 8:30 PM
Dec. 7—New Orleans at Houston . . . . 8:30 PM	Mar. 7—Philadelphia at Miami. . . . . 7:30 PM
Dec. 8—Minnesota at Philadelphia . . . . 7:00 PM	Mar. 8—Memphis at Sacramento . . . . 10:00 PM
Dec. 11—Sacramento at Indiana . . . . 8:00 PM	Mar. 9—New Jersey at New Orleans . . . . 8:00 PM
Dec. 11—L.A. Lakers at L.A. Clippers . . . . 10:30 PM	Mar. 11—Dallas at Milwaukee . . . . 8:30 PM
Dec. 12—Utah at Portland . . . . 8:00 PM	Mar. 12—Denver at San Antonio . . . . 8:30 PM
Dec. 13—Cleveland at Memphis. . . . . 8:00 PM	Mar. 13—Indiana at Cleveland . . . . 7:00 PM
Dec. 14—New Orleans at Charlotte. . . . . 7:00 PM	Mar. 14—Milwaukee at Miami . . . . 7:30 PM
Dec. 18—Portland at Detroit . . . . 7:30 PM	Mar. 14—Houston at Golden State . . . . 10:30 PM
Dec. 19—Orlando at Miami . . . . 6:00 PM	Mar. 15—Minnesota at Dallas. . . . . 8:30 PM
Dec. 20—Utah at Philadelphia . . . . 7:00 PM	Mar. 19—Utah at Washington. . . . . 7:00 PM
Dec. 21—Minnesota at Cleveland . . . . 7:00 PM	Mar. 21—San Antonio at New York. . . . . 7:30 PM
Dec. 26—L.A. Clippers at Houston . . . . 8:30 PM	Mar. 24—L.A. Lakers at Denver . . . . 9:00 PM
Dec. 27—New Jersey at Detroit . . . . 7:30 PM	Mar. 26—Cleveland at Dallas . . . . 8:30 PM
Dec. 28—Philadelphia at Seattle. . . . . 10:00 PM	Mar. 28—Indiana at Milwaukee. . . . . 8:00 PM
Dec. 29—Minnesota at New York . . . . 7:30 PM	Mar. 29—Seattle at Memphis . . . . 8:00 PM
Jan. 1—Orlando at Chicago. . . . . 8:30 PM	Apr. 2—L.A. Lakers at San Antonio . . . . 8:30 PM
Jan. 2—Boston at Detroit . . . . 6:00 PM	Apr. 3—Philadelphia at Boston . . . . 6:00 PM
Jan. 3—Utah at Memphis . . . . 8:00 PM	Apr. 5—Denver at Memphis . . . . 8:00 PM
Jan. 4—L.A. Lakers at San Antonio . . . . 8:30 PM	Apr. 9—Milwaukee at Cleveland. . . . . 7:30 PM
Jan. 8—Indiana at Dallas. . . . . 8:30 PM	Apr. 10—San Antonio at Golden State . . . . 9:00 PM
Jan. 9—Miami at Seattle. . . . . 8:00 PM	Apr. 11—Phoenix at L.A. Lakers . . . . 10:30 PM
Jan. 10—L.A. Lakers at Minnesota . . . . 8:00 PM	Apr. 12—Toronto at New York . . . . 7:30 PM
Jan. 11—New Orleans at New York . . . . 7:30 PM	Apr. 16—Sacramento at Phoenix . . . . 10:00 PM
Jan. 15—San Antonio at Houston. . . . . 8:30 PM	Apr. 17—Philadelphia at New Jersey. . . . . 6:00 PM
Jan. 16—Cleveland at Seattle . . . . 9:00 PM	Apr. 18—San Antonio at Memphis . . . . 8:00 PM
Jan. 17—Phoenix at Detroit . . . . 3:30 PM	Apr. 19—Portland at Denver. . . . . 9:00 PM
Jan. 18—Portland at Sacramento . . . . 10:00 PM	
Jan. 22—Boston at Atlanta. . . . . 7:00 PM	
Jan. 23—Miami at Philadelphia . . . . 6:00 PM	

ESPN SCHEDULE

Nov. 3—Miami at New Jersey	8:00 PM
Nov. 3—L.A. Lakers at Utah	10:30 PM
Nov. 5—Houston at Memphis	8:00 PM
Nov. 5—San Antonio at L.A. Lakers	10:30 PM
Nov. 10—Phoenix at Cleveland	8:00 PM
Nov. 10—Sacramento at Seattle	10:30 PM
Nov. 17—Miami at Milwaukee	9:00 PM
Nov. 19—Indiana at Detroit	8:00 PM
Nov. 19—Memphis at Sacramento	10:30 PM
Nov. 24—Detroit at Cleveland	7:00 PM
Nov. 26—Miami at Detroit	8:00 PM
Nov. 26—Sacramento at L.A. Lakers	10:30 PM
Dec. 3—Detroit at San Antonio	8:00 PM
Dec. 3—Indiana at Sacramento	10:30 PM
Dec. 10—Philadelphia at Chicago	8:00 PM
Dec. 10—Portland at Utah	10:30 PM
Dec. 15—Detroit at New York	8:00 PM
Dec. 15—Utah at Phoenix	10:30 PM
Dec. 17—Denver at Miami	8:00 PM
Dec. 17—Phoenix at Seattle	10:30 PM
Dec. 22—Memphis at Golden State	*10:00 PM
Dec. 25—Detroit at Indiana	12:30 PM
Dec. 31—Philadelphia at Denver	*8:00 PM
Jan. 5—Phoenix at Houston	9:00 PM
Jan. 7—Philadelphia at Minnesota	*8:00 PM
Jan. 7—Houston at L.A. Lakers	10:30 PM
Jan. 12—Houston at Dallas	9:00 PM
Jan. 14—Dallas at San Antonio	*8:00 PM
Jan. 14—Minnesota at Denver	10:30 PM
Jan. 19—Minnesota at L.A. Lakers	10:30 PM
Jan. 21—Indiana at Miami	8:00 PM
Jan. 21—Memphis at Denver	10:30 PM
Jan. 28—Cleveland at New York	7:00 PM
Jan. 28—Sacramento at Houston	*9:30 PM
Jan. 30—Milwaukee at Cleveland	6:30 PM
Feb. 2—Denver at Portland	10:00 PM
Feb. 4—Dallas at Indiana	7:00 PM
Feb. 4—Houston at Minnesota	9:30 PM
Feb. 11—Denver at Cleveland	8:00 PM
Feb. 11—Dallas at Sacramento	10:30 PM
Feb. 16—San Antonio at New Orleans	9:00 PM
Feb. 23—Houston at San Antonio	9:00 PM
Feb. 25—Cleveland at Indiana	8:00 PM
Feb. 25—Detroit at L.A. Lakers	10:30 PM
Feb. 27—Miami at Orlando	7:30 PM
Mar. 2—Charlotte at New Orleans	9:00 PM
Mar. 4—Sacramento at Miami	8:00 PM
Mar. 4—Dallas at L.A. Lakers	10:30 PM
Mar. 6—Miami at Cleveland	7:30 PM
Mar. 16—Minnesota at San Antonio	9:00 PM
Mar. 18—L.A. Lakers at Indiana	7:30 PM
Mar. 20—Houston at Minnesota	7:30 PM
Mar. 23—Detroit at Philadelphia	8:00 PM
Mar. 23—Dallas at Golden State	10:30 PM
Mar. 25—Phoenix at Miami	8:00 PM
Mar. 25—New York at Seattle	10:30 PM
Mar. 27—Philadelphia at L.A. Lakers	7:30 PM
Mar. 30—Houston at Portland	10:00 PM
Apr. 1—Sacramento at Cleveland	8:00 PM
Apr. 1—San Antonio at Denver	10:30 PM
Apr. 6—Cleveland at Indiana	7:00 PM
Apr. 6—Utah at Minnesota	9:30 PM
Apr. 8—Detroit at Orlando	7:00 PM
Apr. 8—Denver at Minnesota	9:30 PM
Apr. 13—New Jersey at Indiana	8:00 PM
Apr. 13—San Antonio at Utah	10:30 PM
Apr. 15—Milwaukee at Detroit	8:00 PM
Apr. 15—Sacramento at L.A. Lakers	10:30 PM
Apr. 16—Denver at Houston	7:30 PM
Apr. 20—San Antonio at Minnesota	8:00 PM
Apr. 20—Phoenix at Sacramento	10:30 PM
*Game on ESPN2	

TNT SCHEDULE

Nov. 2—Houston at Detroit	8:00 PM
Nov. 2—Denver at L.A. Lakers	10:30 PM
Nov. 4—Cleveland at Miami	8:00 PM
Nov. 4—Minnesota at Denver	10:30 PM
Nov. 11—Dallas at Miami	8:00 PM
Nov. 11—Detroit at Denver	10:30 PM
Nov. 18—San Antonio at Philadelphia	7:00 PM
Nov. 18—New York at Houston	9:30 PM
Nov. 25—Minnesota at Indiana	8:00 PM
Nov. 25—New Jersey at L.A. Clippers	10:30 PM
Dec. 2—Houston at Dallas	8:00 PM
Dec. 2—Cleveland at Denver	10:30 PM
Dec. 9—San Antonio at Houston	8:00 PM
Dec. 9—Boston at Portland	10:30 PM
Dec. 16—Cleveland at Detroit	8:00 PM
Dec. 16—L.A. Lakers at Sacramento	10:30 PM
Dec. 23—Minnesota at San Antonio	8:00 PM
Dec. 23—Miami at Sacramento	10:30 PM
Dec. 30—Miami at Detroit	8:00 PM
Dec. 30—San Antonio at Portland	10:30 PM
Jan. 6—Memphis at Detroit	7:00 PM
Dec. 6—Indiana at San Antonio	9:30 PM
Jan. 13—New Jersey at Houston	8:00 PM
Jan. 13—Cleveland at L.A. Lakers	10:30 PM
Jan. 17—Houston at Memphis	8:00 PM
Jan. 17—Denver at Golden State	10:30 PM
Jan. 20—Houston at Orlando	8:00 PM
Jan. 20—Cleveland at Sacramento	10:30 PM
Jan. 27—Detroit at Indiana	7:00 PM
Jan. 27—Sacramento at San Antonio	9:30 PM
Feb. 3—Cleveland at Miami	8:00 PM
Feb. 3—San Antonio at L.A. Lakers	10:30 PM
Feb. 10—L.A. Lakers at Detroit	8:00 PM
Feb. 10—Sacramento at Seattle	10:30 PM
Feb. 17—Cleveland at Minnesota	8:00 PM
Feb. 17—Dallas at Phoenix	10:30 PM
Feb. 24—Philadelphia at New York	7:00 PM
Feb. 24—Sacramento at Dallas	9:30 PM
Mar. 3—Indiana at Denver	8:00 PM
Mar. 3—Detroit at Phoenix	10:30 PM
Mar. 10—Minnesota at Miami	7:00 PM
Mar. 10—L.A. Lakers at Dallas	9:30 PM
Mar. 17—L.A. Lakers at Miami	8:00 PM
Mar. 17—Sacramento at Golden State	10:30 PM
Mar. 22—Detroit at Cleveland	7:00 PM
Mar. 22—Miami at Houston	9:30 PM
Mar. 31—Miami at Indiana	8:00 PM
Mar. 31—Minnesota at L.A. Lakers	10:30 PM
Apr. 7—San Antonio at Dallas	8:00 PM
Apr. 7—Houston at L.A. Lakers	10:30 PM
Apr. 14—New York at Cleveland	8:00 PM
Apr. 14—Dallas at Portland	10:30 PM

ESPN RADIO SCHEDULE

Nov. 2—Houston at Detroit . . . . 7:40 PM
Nov. 4—Cleveland at Miami . . . . 7:40 PM
Nov. 11—Dallas at Miami. . . . . 7:40 PM
Nov. 18—New York at Houston . . . . 9:05 PM
Nov. 25—Minnesota at Indiana. . . . . 7:40 PM
Dec. 2—Cleveland at Denver . . . . 10:05 PM
Dec. 9—San Antonio at Houston . . . . 7:40 PM
Dec. 16—Cleveland at Detroit. . . . . 7:40 PM
Dec. 25—Miami at L.A. Lakers . . . . 2:40 PM
Dec. 30—Miami at Detroit . . . . 7:40 PM
Jan. 8—Denver at San Antonio . . . . 1:05 PM
Jan. 13—Cleveland at L.A. Lakers. . . . . 10:05 PM
Jan. 20—Houston at Orlando . . . . 7:40 PM
Jan. 30—Houston at Miami . . . . 12:40 PM
Feb. 6—L.A. Lakers at Houston . . . . 3:05 PM

Feb. 13—San Antonio at Miami . . . . 12:40 PM
Feb. 13—L.A. Lakers at Cleveland . . . . Following
Feb. 27—Miami at Orlando. . . . . 7:05 PM
Mar. 6—Dallas at Houston. . . . . 12:40 PM
Mar. 6—Detroit at Sacramento. . . . . Following
Mar. 13—Dallas at Minnesota. . . . . 12:40 PM
Mar. 13—Houston at Sacramento . . . . Following
Mar. 20—San Antonio at Detroit. . . . . 3:05 PM
Mar. 27—Houston at San Antonio . . . . 12:40 PM
Apr. 3—Dallas at Cleveland . . . . 12:40 PM
Apr. 3—Minnesota at Sacramento . . . . Following
Apr. 10—Detroit at Miami. . . . . 12:40 PM
Apr. 10—L.A. Lakers at Sacramento . . . . Following
Apr. 17—Indiana at Miami . . . . 12:40 PM
Apr. 17—Dallas at L.A. Lakers . . . . Following

NATIONAL BASKETBALL DEVELOPMENT LEAGUE

National Basketball Development League
24 Vardry Street, Suite 201
Greenville, SC 29601
NBDL.com
Tel: (864) 248-1100
Fax: (864) 248-1102
Sr. Director of Communications: Kent Partridge

ASHEVILLE ALTITUDE
87 Haywood Street
Asheville, NC 28801
Tel: (828) 782-1000
Fax: (828) 782-1002
Arena: Asheville Civic Center
Media and Community Relations Manager: Patricia Harvey

FLORIDA FLAME
13130 Westlinks Terrace, Suite 7
Ft. Myers, FL 33913
Tel: (239) 561-8130
Fax: (239) 561-9782
Arena: Germaine Arena
Media Relations Contact: TBA

COLUMBUS RIVERDRAGONS
18 E 11th Street
Columbus, GA 31902
Tel: (706) 225-1100
Fax: (706) 225-1102
Arena: Columbus Civic Center
Media Relations Coordinator/Acct. Executive: Tim Becwar

HUNTSVILLE FLIGHT
700 Monroe Street
Huntsville, AL 35801
Tel: (256) 429-1000
Fax: (256) 429-1002
Arena: Von Braun Center
Manager of Sales and Communications: Matt O'Halloran

FAYETTEVILLE PATRIOTS
400 Westwood Shopping Center, Suite 220
Fayetteville, NC 28314
Tel: (910) 213-1000
Fax: (910) 213-1002
Arena: Crown Coliseum
Manager of Sales, Marketing and Media Relations: Chrissie Macko

ROANOKE DAZZLE
710 Williamson Road
Roanoke, VA 24022
Tel: (540) 266-1000
Fax: (540) 266-1002
Arena: Roanoke Civic Center
Coordinator of Sales, Marketing, CR and Media Relations: Melissa May

2003-04 SEASON
FINAL STANDINGS

	W-L	HOME W-L	AWAY W-L	Pct	Gb	Last 5
Asheville Altitude	28-18	15-8	13-10	.608	—	5-0
Charleston Lowgators	27-19	17-6	10-13	.586	1.0	4-1
Huntsville Flight	24-22	10-13	14-9	.521	4.0	2-3
Fayetteville Patriots	21-25	10-13	11-12	.456	7.0	3-2
Roanoke Dazzle	20-26	10-13	10-13	.434	8.0	0-5
Columbus Riverdragons	18-28	9-14	9-14	.391	10.0	2-3

PLAYOFF RESULTS

SINGLE-ELIMINATION SEMIFINALS
Saturday, April 17

Asheville 116, Fayetteville 111
Huntsville 108, Charleston 100

CHAMPIONSHIP GAME
Saturday, April 24

Asheville 108, Huntsville 106 OT

AWARD WINNERS

Most Valuable Player: Tierre Brown, Charleston Lowgators
Defensive Player of the Year: Karim Shabazz, Charleston Lowgators
Rookie of the Year: Desmond Penigar, Asheville Altitude
Regular Season Champion: Asheville Altitude
Postseason Champion: Asheville Altitude

INDIVIDUAL LEADERS

SCORING

	G	Pts.	Avg.
Desmond Penigar, Asheville	38	746	19.6
Tierre Brown, Charleston	41	763	18.6
Ime Udoke, Charleston	41	694	16.9
Junie Sanders, Fayetteville	44	743	16.9
Marque Perry, Roanoke	44	678	15.4
Jason Collier, Fayetteville	30	462	15.4
Alpha Bangura, Charleston	45	676	15.0
Britton Johnsen, Fayetteville	34	495	14.6
Josh Asselin, Roanoke	46	664	14.4
Philip Ricci, Huntsville	45	632	14.0
Rod Grizzard, Huntsville	44	615	14.0
Mateen Cleaves, Huntsville	42	576	13.7
Terrence Shannon, Roanoke	34	465	13.7
Brandon Kurtz, Asheville	33	446	13.5
Bryan Lucas, Fayetteville	45	606	13.5
Damone Brown, Huntsville	26	342	13.2

FIELD-GOAL PERCENTAGE

	FGM	FGA	Pct.
Kris Lang, Asheville	206	336	.613
Greg Stevenson, Asheville	189	332	.569
Karim Shabazz, Charleston	113	206	.549
Rodney Bias, Huntsville	81	153	.529
Josh Asselin, Roanoke	238	452	.527
Darrell Johns, Roanoke	145	275	.527
Philip Ricci, Huntsville	247	470	.526
Rolan Roberts, Charleston	177	337	.525

FREE THROW PERCENTAGE

	FTM	FTA	Pct.
Jeff Myers, Columbus	131	154	.851
Rick Apodaca, Huntsville	62	73	.849
Curtis Staples, Roanoke	78	92	.848
Rusty LaRue, Asheville	41	49	.837
Jason Capel, Fayetteville	107	129	.829
Lavor Postell, Asheville	149	182	.819
Damone Brown, Huntsville	82	101	.812
Jason Collier, Fayetteville	142	175	.811

3-POINT FIELD-GOAL PERCENTAGE

	3PM	3PA	Pct.
Rusty LaRue, Asheville	43	87	.494
Kent Williams, Fayetteville	45	100	.450
Jeff Myers, Columbus	28	68	.412
Rick Apodaca, Huntsville	23	59	.390
Damone Brown, Huntsville	24	62	.387

	3PM	3PA	Pct.
Chuck Eidson, Charleston	12	32	.375
Desmond Penigar, Asheville	32	86	.372
Britton Johnsen, Fayetteville	18	49	.367

REBOUNDS PER GAME

	G	Reb.	Avg.
Rodney Bias, Huntsville	36	364	10.1
Courtney James, Columbus	46	377	8.2
Bryan Lucas, Fayetteville	45	367	8.2
Karim Shabazz, Charleston	46	348	7.6
Terence Morris, Columbus	46	340	7.4
Jason Collier, Fayetteville	30	216	7.2
Ime Udoke, Charleston	41	295	7.2
Brandon Kurtz, Asheville	33	232	7.0

ASSISTS PER GAME

	G	Ast.	Avg.
Omar Cook, Fayetteville	24	215	9.0
Kareem Reid, Asheville	43	290	6.7
Marque Perry, Roanoke	44	295	6.7
Tierre Brown, Charleston	41	265	6.5
Mateen Cleaves, Huntsville	42	248	5.9
Derrick Zimmerman, Columbus	45	238	5.3
Brandin Knight, Asheville	38	186	4.9
Jeff Myers, Columbus	36	156	4.3

BLOCKED SHOTS PER GAME

	G	Blk.	Avg.
Ken Johnson, Huntsville	40	97	2.4
Karim Shabazz, Charleston	46	96	2.1
Hiram Fuller, Charleston	40	76	1.9
Kevin Lyde, Columbus	46	75	1.6
Terence Morris, Columbus	46	72	1.6
Kris Lang, Asheville	44	63	1.4
Rodney Bias, Huntsville	36	45	1.3
Rolan Roberts, Charleston	46	55	1.2

STEALS PER GAME

	G	Stl.	Avg.
Omar Cook, Fayetteville	24	63	2.6
Tierre Brown, Charleston	41	74	1.8
Brandin Knight, Asheville	38	68	1.8
Ime Udoke, Charleston	41	64	1.6
Erick Barkley, Huntsville	42	64	1.5
Marque Perry, Roanoke	44	67	1.5
Chuck Eidson, Charleston	32	47	1.5
Jeff Myers, Columbus	36	52	1.4

2003-04 NBDL TO NBA CALL-UPS

Player	NBDL team	NBA team
Rusty LaRue	Asheville Altitude	Golden State Warriors
Omar Cook	Fayetteville Patriots	Portland Trail Blazers
Mikki Moore	Roanoke Dazzle	Utah Jazz
Tierre Brown	North Charleston Lowgators	New Orleans Hornets
Ronald Dupree	Huntsville Flight	Chicago Bulls
Ime Udoka	Charleston Lowgators	LA Lakers
Mamadou N'Diaye	Asheville Altitude	Atlanta Hawks
Desmond Penigar	Asheville Altitude	Orlando Magic
Hiram Fuller	Charleston Lowgators	Atlanta Hawks
Matt Carroll	Roanoke Dazzle	San Antonio Spurs
Jason Collier	Fayetteville Patriots	Atlanta Hawks
Britton Johnsen	Fayetteville Patriots	Orlando Magic
Mateen Cleaves	Huntsville Flight	Cleveland Cavaliers
Ernest Brown	Fayetteville Patriots	Boston Celtics

Coach	NBDL team	NBA team
Stephanie Ready	Greenville Groove asst. coach	Washington Mystics asst. coach
Ty Corbin	Charleston player mentor	Utah Jazz assistant coach
Jeff Capel	Fayetteville head coach	Charlotte Bobcats asst coach

WOMEN'S NATIONAL BASKETBALL ASSOCIATION

Women's National Basketball Association
Olympic Tower, 645 Fifth Avenue
New York, NY 10022
Main Number: 212-688-WNBA (9622)

CHARLOTTE STING
129 W. Trade St., Suite 700
Charlotte, NC 28202
704-420-4120
704-333-2340 (fax)
www.charlottesting.com

CONNECTICUT SUN
1 Mohegan Sun Boulevard
Uncasville, CT 06382
860-862-4000
860-862-4006 (fax)
www.connecticutsun.com

DETROIT SHOCK
The Palace of Auburn Hills
Three Championship Drive
Auburn Hills, MI 48326
248-377-0100
248-377-3260 (fax)
www.wnba.com/shock

HOUSTON COMETS
Toyota Center
1510 Polk Street
Houston, Texas 77002
713-758-7200
713-758-7339 (fax)
www.houstoncomets.com

INDIANA FEVER
One Conseco Court
125 S. Pennsylvania St.
Indianapolis, IN 46204
317-917-2500
317-917-2599 (fax)
www.wnba.com/fever

LOS ANGELES SPARKS
2151 E. Grand Ave.
El Segundo, CA 90245
310-341-1000
310-341-1029 (fax)
www.wnba.com/sparks

MINNESOTA LYNX
Target Center
600 First Avenue North
Minneapolis, MN 55403
612-673-1600
612-673-8367 (fax)
www.wnba.com/lynx

NEW YORK LIBERTY
Two Pennsylvania Plaza—14th Floor
New York, NY 10121
212-465-6256
212-465-6250 (fax)
www.nyliberty.com

PHOENIX MERCURY
America West Arena
201 E. Jefferson
Phoenix, AZ 85004
602-514-8333
602-514-8303 (fax)
www.phoenixmercury.com

SACRAMENTO MONARCHS
ARCO Arena
One Sports Parkway
Sacramento, CA 95834
916-928-0000
916-928-0727 (fax)
www.sacramentomonarchs.com

SAN ANTONIO SILVER STARS
One SBC Center
San Antonio, TX 78219
210-444-5000
210-444-5003 (fax)
www.sasilverstars.com

SEATTLE STORM
351 Elliot Ave. W. Suite 500
Seattle, WA 98119
206-281-5800
206-281-5839 (fax)
www.storm.wnba.com

WASHINGTON MYSTICS
MCI Center
601 F Street, NW
Washington, DC 20001
202-661-5000
202-661-5108 (fax)
www.washingtonmystics.com

2003-04 REVIEW

- Year in review
- Regular-season statistics
- Playoffs
- NBA Finals
- NBA Draft
- Award winners

YEAR IN REVIEW

HIGHLIGHTS

By ROB REHEUSER

2003-04 REVIEW *Year in review*

ATLANTIC DIVISION

New Jersey Nets (47-35): Jason Kidd's decision to re-sign with New Jersey during the summer of 2003 meant most, if not all, of the key pieces would be in place for the Nets to make a run at a third consecutive trip to the NBA Finals. Unfortunately, Alonzo Mourning's kidney condition resurfaced, robbing New Jersey of a much-needed interior presence, while nagging injuries saddled much of team's remaining core. The results were a third-consecutive Atlantic Division crown, followed by a second-round exit from the playoffs at the hands of eventual NBA champ Detroit. Kenyon Martin elevated his play, earning his first trip to the All-Star game, while Richard Jefferson (18.5 ppg) continued to blossom into one of the NBA's top young players.

Miami Heat (42-40): Things got off to a rocky start, with Pat Riley stepping down as head coach prior to the start of the season and the Heat losing its first seven games. Caron Butler, the team's top returning player, had not fully recovered from off-season surgery. Toss in a rookie point guard (Dwyane Wade) and a talented, yet underachieving, forward (Lamar Odom) playing out of position, and it appeared that first-time coach Stan Van Gundy had his hands full. As it turned out, Odom emerged as one of the top forwards in the Eastern Conference, and Wade showed flashes of brilliance, especially in the playoffs, where Miami advanced to the second round before falling to Indiana in six hard-fought games.

New York Knicks (39-43): Looking back, it felt as if the Knicks managed to cram eight seasons into one in 2003-04. There was the Scott Layden/Don Chaney era, followed by the arrival of Isiah Thomas as president, followed by the trade for Stephon Marbury, followed by the hiring of Lenny Wilkens, followed by the trade for Tim Thomas. Additional subplots included Allan Houston's injury problems, Dikembe Mutombo's bruised ego, players moving in and out of the rotation and so on. When the smoke cleared, New York earned its first trip to the playoffs since 2001, losing to New Jersey in four games.

Boston Celtics (36-46): It began with Antoine Walker being handed his walking papers before the season. It continued with a swap that brought Ricky Davis to Boston and sent Eric Williams and Tony Battie to Cleveland, which led to Jim O'Brien tendering his resignation. You get the picture. Danny Ainge arrived in Boston with a clear vision of what he wanted the Celtics to resemble on the court and spent much of the season trying to bring the vision to life by tinkering with his roster. Boston managed to sneak into the playoffs but was swept in the first round by Indiana. Paul Pierce made his third straight trip to the All-Star Game.

Philadelphia 76ers (33-49): The Sixers pretty much begin and end with Allen Iverson. So, when the former MVP and three-time scoring champ pulled up lame with a bad knee, that spelled the end for Philadelphia. After missing a large chunk of December, Iverson tried to play through the pain before going on the shelf for good in March. The Sixers missed the playoffs for the first time since 1998. Some bright spots included the emergence of third-year center Samuel Dalembert, who averaged 8.0 points, 7.6 rebounds and 2.3 blocks, as well as solid contributions from 2003 second-round picks Willie Greene and Kyle Korver. Kenny Thomas was one of only nine players in the league to average a double-double (13.6 ppg, 10.1 rpg).

Washington Wizards (25-57): The Wizards made a big splash in the free-agent market, convincing Gilbert Arenas to head east to run the show in Washington, D.C. Unfortunately, Jerry Stackhouse could barely get his feet in the water, appearing in only 26 games, while Arenas and Larry Hughes also battled the injury bug. And although it opened up playing time for promising rookies like Jarvis Hayes (9.6 ppg) and Steve Blake, it meant another trip to the lottery for the Wizards. Kwame Brown had his usual ups and down but seemed to make overall progress, averaging 10.9 points and 7.4 rebounds.

Orlando Magic (21-61): On opening night in 2003, Tracy McGrady scored 26 points as the Magic stole an overtime victory at Madison Square Garden against the Knicks. Orlando then proceeded to lose its next 19 games, costing Doc Rivers his job and the team any chance of making the playoffs. The absence of Darrell Armstrong (signed with Hornets) and Pat Garrity (knee) had a much larger impact than originally anticipated, and the team never was able to establish any lasting chemistry. McGrady did win his second consecutive scoring title but was traded to Houston in the offseason.

CENTRAL DIVISION

Indiana Pacers (61-21): A pair of familiar faces returned to Conseco Fieldhouse in 2003-04— Larry Bird took over basketball operations, and Rick Carlisle assumed head coaching duties—and after several seasons in which many felt the Pacers underachieved, Indiana went wire-to-wire in the Eastern Conference, led the NBA in victories and advanced to the Eastern Conference Finals, losing to the Pistons in six games. Jermaine O'Neal turned in another spectacular season, making his third consecutive trip to the All-Star Game, earning All-NBA Second Team honors and finishing fourth in the league MVP voting, while Ron Artest came into his own, earning his first trip to the All-Star Game, capturing All-NBA Third Team honors and being named the NBA's Defensive Player of the Year.

– 82 –

Detroit Pistons (54-28): All year long, Pistons coach Larry Brown talked about playing the game the right way. When it was all said and done, the Pistons were NBA Champions, easily defeating the heavily favored Lakers in The Finals. To single out one player would be to go against what Detroit stood for in 2003-04. Richard Hamilton was brilliant in the playoffs, Chauncey Billups raised his game in the Finals, Rasheed Wallace joined the team in February and became that missing piece along a frontline that already had Ben Wallace rebounding and blocking everything in sight. There were solid contributions from Tayshaun Prince, who became a full-time starter in his second year, and Mehmet Okur, who started 33 games but graciously stepped aside when Wallace joined the fold.

New Orleans Hornets (41-41): The song pretty much remained the same down in New Orleans: enough good players to do some damage in the Eastern Conference, just not enough healthy ones. Jamal Mashburn appeared in only 19 games. The normally indestructible David Wesley missed 21 games. Baron Davis did his best to keep things afloat, earning his second trip to the All-Star Game with a monster first half. He started to break down in the second half and wound up missing 15 games. Jamaal Magloire turned in his best season as a pro, averaging 13.6 points and 10.3 rebounds and joining Davis at the All-Star Game. Darrell Armstrong proved to be a solid acquisition, as he appeared in 79 games, averaging 10.6 points and 3.9 assists.

Michael Redd played in his first All-Star Game and was named to the All-NBA Third Team.

Milwaukee Bucks (41-41): You were not alone if you thought the Bucks would finish at the bottom of the Eastern Conference after losing Ray Allen and Sam Cassell and not adding a legitimate post presence. In one of the major surprises of the 2003-04 season, the team led by rookie head coach Terry Porter didn't sink to the bottom of the standings, finishing sixth in the East before losing in the first round of the playoffs to Detroit. Michael Redd proved to be a more than adequate replacement for Allen, making the All-Star team and earning All-NBA Third Team honors after averaging 21.7 points. As for the lack of a post player, Joe Smith (10.9 ppg, 8.5 rpg) and Brian Skinner (10.5 ppg, 7.3 rpg) were more than solid.

Cleveland Cavaliers (35-47): It began with a 25-point, nine-rebound, six-assist performance in Sacramento and ended with the Cavaliers winning 18 more games than they did the previous season and missing the playoffs by two games. Not a bad debut for LeBron James, arguably the most heralded rookie ever to enter the NBA. James exceeded expectations—becoming only the third rookie in NBA history to average at least 20 points, five rebounds and five assists (including Michael Jordan and Oscar Robertson)—and raised the level of play of teammates like Carlos Boozer (15.5 ppg, 11.4 rpg) and Zydrunas Ilgauskas (15.3 ppg, 8.1 rpg).

Toronto Raptors (33-49): The good news is Vince Carter was able to stay reasonably healthy

and showed flashes of his old form. Unfortunately, Alvin Williams wasn't able to stay healthy, and a severe lack of depth across the board kept Toronto from staying in the playoff picture. The arrival of Donyell Marshall and Jalen Rose via trade with Chicago helped in terms of scoring, but the loss of Antonio Davis and Jerome Williams created a huge void up front, leaving rookie Chris Bosh to learn the hard way. Bosh turned in a solid rookie season, earning All-Rookie First Team honors and averaging 11.5 points and 7.4 rebounds.

Atlanta Hawks (28-54): If basketball were simply a two-man sport consisting of two guards on each team, the Hawks would have been in pretty good shape in 2003-04 with Stephen Jackson (18.1 ppg) and Jason Terry (16.8 ppg, 5.4 apg) leading the way. It's the other three spots Atlanta had trouble filling—after trading Shareef Abdur-Rahim, Theo Ratliff and Nazr Mohammed—which resulted in the Hawks missing the playoffs for the fifth straight season. The trades did allow the Hawks to clear significant cap space, which they planned to use on big-name free agents.

Chicago Bulls (23-59): Many felt 2003-04 was the year Chicago would sneak back into the playoffs on the way to becoming a relevant NBA franchise once again. Things didn't go according to plan, with Bill Cartwright being replaced by Scott Skiles, Tyson Chandler and Scottie Pippen missing most of the season with injuries and Jalen Rose and Donyell Marshall being traded to

Sam Cassell turned in the finest season of his 11-year career, earning All-NBA Second Team honors and playing in his first All-Star Game.

Toronto. There were some bright spots. Kirk Hinrich overcame some early health issues to become of the league's top rookies, averaging 12.0 points and a team-high 6.8 assists, and Jamal Crawford (17.3 ppg) became the team's primary scoring option.

MIDWEST DIVISION

Minnesota Timberwolves (58-24): After seven consecutive first-round playoff exits, the Timberwolves broke through in a big way, finishing with the best record in the West and advancing to the Conference Finals before being eliminated by the Lakers in six games. Kevin Garnett was named the league's MVP, and new sidekicks Sam Cassell and Latrell Sprewell flourished playing alongside Garnett. Cassell earned his first trip to the All-Star Game and was named to the All-NBA Second Team. Sprewell's energy and willingness to fit in uplifted the entire team. Role players like Trenton Hassell, Fred Hoiberg and Ervin Johnson made up for injuries to Wally Szczerbiak, Troy Hudson and Michael Olowokandi.

San Antonio Spurs (57-25): The Spurs reshuffled the deck around Tim Duncan, bringing in Rasho Nesterovic to replace David Robinson and Hedo Turkoglu and Ron Mercer to fill the void left by Stephen Jackson. It worked for the most part, with the Spurs having the second-best record in the West and a great chance to win a second consecutive championship. After breezing past Memphis in Round 1, the Spurs took a 2-0 lead on the Lakers in the second round, then dropped four straight to Shaq & Co. Duncan had another brilliant season, the only blemish his poor free throw shooting. Manu Ginobili took on increased role as Tony Parker continued to develop into a top-flight point guard.

Dallas Mavericks (52-30): After coming up a tad short of a Finals berth in 2002-03, Dallas tinkered with its lineup, adding Antawn Jamison and Antoine Walker to the mix in place of playoff hero Nick Van Exel and Raef LaFentz. In the end, the Mavericks still suffered from the lack of a true interior presence and spotty defense and lost in the first round of the playoffs to Sacramento. Dirk Nowitzki averaged a team-high 21.8 ppg and earned his third straight trip to the All-Star Game. After a slow start, Michael Finley (18.6 ppg) had another good season, while Jamison (14.8 ppg) was named the NBA's Sixth Man of the Year. Rookies Josh Howard and Marquis Daniels were named to the All-Rookie Second Team.

Memphis Grizzlies (50-32): What a difference a West makes. And a Hubie. Two years ago, the Grizzlies began the season 0-8 and finished with 28 wins. Last year, Memphis finished with the sixth-best record in a deep Western Conference and made the playoffs for the first time in franchise history. The philosophy was pretty straightforward: Bring in as many good players as possible, regardless of position, and allow Brown to coach them and come up with winning combinations. The result was a versatile roster that went close to 12 deep and gave teams fits with its pressure defense and attack mentality. Eight players averaged at least eight points, led by Pau Gasol (17.7 ppg) and James Posey (13.7 ppg).

Houston Rockets (45-37): As expected, Houston transformed into one of the NBA's top defensive teams under Jeff Van Gundy, which resulted in the Rockets making the playoffs for the first time since 1999. Yao Ming showed significant improvement, leading the team in scoring (17.5 ppg), rebounding (9.0 rpg) and blocks (1.9 bpg). As a result of Van Gundy preaching inside/out basketball, which featured Yao, Steve Francis (16.6 ppg) and Cuttino Mobley (15.8 ppg) saw their numbers decline. Jim Jackson turned out to be a solid free-agent pickup, as he averaged 12.3 points and made 40 percent of his 3-point attempts. Maurice Taylor (11.5 ppg) provided a nice offensive lift off the bench.

Denver Nuggets (43-39): After winning 17 games in 2002-03, then losing to Cleveland in the LeBron James sweepstakes, G.M. Kiki Vandeweghe put his plan into full motion. It started with the drafting of Carmelo Anthony, who led all rookies in scoring (21.0 ppg). It continued with the free-agent signing of Andre Miller, who looked much more like the Miller of his Cleveland days than the one who made a forgettable cameo with the Clippers in 2002-03. Marcus Camby bucked his history of injury, appearing in a career-high 72 games, averaging 8.6 points and 10.1 rebounds. Voshon Lenard (14.2 ppg) provided nice scoring punch from the backcourt, while Earl Boykins (10.2 ppg) continued to show he belongs in the NBA.

Utah Jazz (42-40): Without John Stockton (retirement) and Karl Malone (Lakers) in the lineup for the first time since 1983, Jerry Sloan figured to have his work cut out for him to keep Utah at the mediocre level in a stacked Western Conference. When all was said and done, the team many picked to finish at the bottom of the standings missed the playoffs by one game. Much of Utah's success had to do with the excellent all-around play from third-year forward Andrei Kirilenko, who was named to the All-Star team. Carlos Arroyo also did an excellent job running the show (12.6 ppg, 5.0 apg). An injury to Matt Harpring opened up minutes for Gordan Giricek (13.5 ppg) and Raja Bell (11.2).

PACIFIC DIVISION

Los Angeles Lakers (56-26): The Lakers pretty much covered all bases in the soap opera department and nearly came away with a fourth title in five years before being upended by the Pistons in The Finals. Kobe Bryant's legal troubles made for interesting fodder, as did his persistent problems with Shaquille O'Neal and Phil Jackson. Karl Malone and Gary Payton signing for less money over the summer made great headlines before Malone's stint on the injured list and Payton's difficulties with Jackson's system soiled both gestures. Still, Bryant had moments of brilliance, and O'Neal, though not as big an offensive factor, still could dominate when motivated. The result was a huge second-round win against San Antonio and a record 28th trip to the Finals.

Sacramento Kings (55-27): Even without Chris Webber in the lineup for much of the regular season, the Kings, at times, looked like the odds-on favorites to finally emerge from the Western Conference. Peja Stojakovic had an MVP-type regular season, finishing second in the league in scoring. Brad Miller turned out to be an excellent free-agent acquisition and was named to the All-Star team for the second straight year. Mike Bibby upped his scoring (18.4 ppg), while Vlade Divac (5.3 apg) and Doug Christie (1.8 spg) continued to do all the little things needed to win championships. Webber returned late in the season, and the Kings never quite gelled, losing to Minnesota in the second round of the playoffs.

Portland Trail Blazers (41-41): Two eras in Blazers history came to an abrupt end in 2003-04, as the team missed the playoffs for the first time since 1982 and also traded Rasheed Wallace after a tumultuous eight-year reign. It was also the start of

a new era—the Zach Randolph era. The third-year forward ran away with the NBA's Most Improved Player Award, averaging 20.1 points and 10.5 rebounds, one of only five players in the NBA to average at least 20 points and 10 rebounds. In-season trades netted Darius Miles, Shareef Abdur-Rahim and Theo Ratliff. Miles flourished, and Ratliff was a much-needed defensive presence, but Abdur-Rahim struggled to find a role.

Golden State Warriors (37-45): Although the record didn't quite show it, the Warriors took a step back last season, which was to be expected given the departure of Gilbert Arenas and Antawn Jamison. Speedy Claxton and Nick Van Exel both battled injuries, as did Troy Murphy, who after averaging a double-double in 2002-03 appeared in only 28 games. Jason Richardson (18.7 ppg) and Erick Dampier (12.3 ppg, 12.0 rpg) had career seasons, and there was a surprising contribution from Brian Cardinal, but in the end the Warriors missed the playoffs for the 10th straight season.

Seattle SuperSonics (37-45): Not having Ray Allen for the first few months of the season was a mixed bag for the Sonics. The team was robbed of its best player, go-to scorer and leader. In his absence, though, Ronald Murray emerged as a player to be reckoned with, as the second-year guard from Shaw University averaged close to 20 points for the first chunk of the season. His minutes diminished when Allen returned and Brent Barry got healthy, but Murray was a nice surprise for Seattle. An unwelcome surprise was the loss of first-round pick Nick Collison for the season (shoulder surgery). Seattle was hoping he would provide much needed interior defense and rebounding.

Phoenix Suns (29-53): The Suns had great expectations in 2003-04 after making the playoffs in 2002-03 and taking the Spurs to six games in the opening round. The season began with an unfortunate injury to last year's top rookie Amare Stoudemire, and things were never able to get on track. As a result, Stephon Marbury and Penny Hardaway were traded to New York, which resulted in an intriguing collection of young prospects and cap space. The trade also opened up minutes for Joe Johnson (16.7 ppg) and rookie Leandro Barbosa (7.9 ppg). When healthy, Stoudemire (20.6 ppg) showed significant improvement, and Shawn Marion had another solid campaign.

Los Angeles Clippers (28-54): In his first game after signing a big contact extension over the summer, Elton Brand had 21 points, 15 rebounds and eight blocks. He also added one broken foot, which immediately set the Clippers back. Corey Maggette (20.7 ppg) and Quentin Richardson (17.2 ppg) did their best to try to keep the Clippers above water, but the lack of a solid point guard coupled with a fairly inexperienced roster led to another season of missing the playoffs. When healthy, Brand (20.0 ppg, 10.3 rpg, 2.2 bpg) was one of the more effective power forwards in the league, and second-year forward Chris Wilcox (8.6 ppg) showed improvement.

2003-04 NBA Playoffs

Western Conference

Minnesota
Denver
— Minnesota, 4-1

Sacramento
Dallas
— Sacramento, 4-1

— Minnesota, 4-3

L.A. Lakers
Houston
— L.A. Lakers, 4-1

San Antonio
Memphis
— San Antonio, 4-0

— L.A. Lakers, 4-2

L.A. Lakers, 4-2

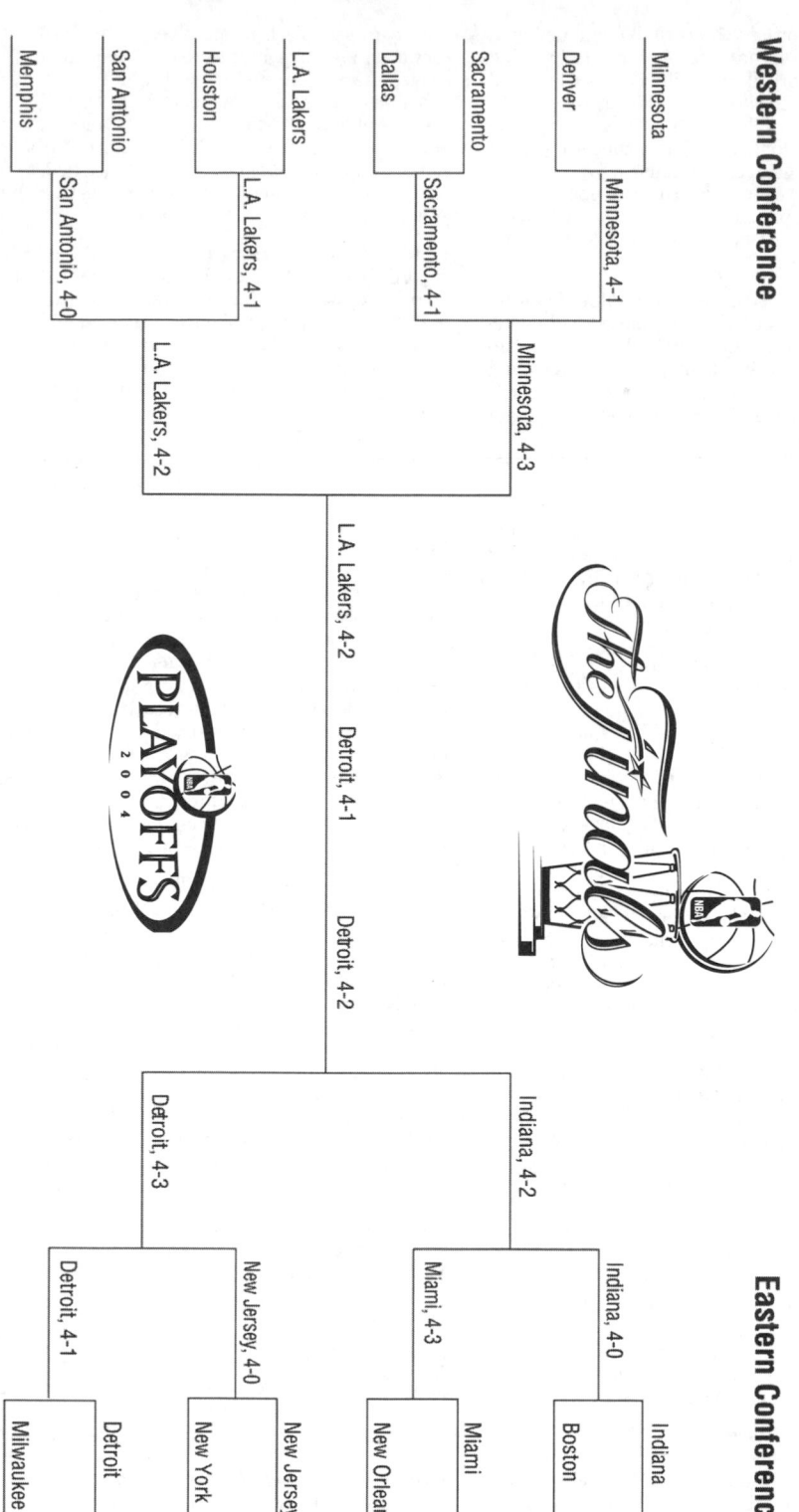

Detroit, 4-1

Detroit, 4-2

Indiana, 4-2

Eastern Conference

Indiana
Boston
— Indiana, 4-0

Miami
New Orleans
— Miami, 4-3

New Jersey
New York
— New Jersey, 4-0

Detroit
Milwaukee
— Detroit, 4-1

— Detroit, 4-3

2003-04 NBA CHAMPION DETROIT PISTONS

Front row (from left): assistant coach Herb Brown, assistant coach John Kuester, head coach Larry Brown, president of basketball operations Joe Dumars, managing partner William Davidson, vice president of basketball operations John Hammond, assistant coach Mike Woodson, assistant coach Dave Hanners. Second row (from left): Tremaine Fowlkes, Lindsey Hunter, athletic trainer Mike Abdenour, assistant coach Igor Kokoskov, assistant coach Pat Sullivan, strength and conditioning coach Arnie Kander, Mike James, Richard Hamilton, Chauncey Billups. Back row (from left): Ben Wallace, Mehmet Okur, Darko Milicic, Rasheed Wallace, Elden Campbell, Tayshaun Prince, Corliss Williamson, Darvin Ham.

FINAL STANDINGS

ATLANTIC DIVISION

TM	Atl	Bos	Chi	Cle	Dal	Den	Det	GS	Hou	Ind	LAC	LAL	Mem	Mia	Mil	Min	NJ	NO	NY	Orl	Phi	Pho	Por	SAC	SA	Sea	Tor	Uta	Was	W	L	Pct	GB	Last-10	Streak
NJ	3	2	3	2	0	2	2	2	1	1	2	0	0	2	1	—	2	3	4	3	1	0	1	0	2	2	1	4		47	35	.573	-	5-5	Lost 2
MIA	3	2	4	2	1	1	0	1	1	0	2	0	1	—	1	0	3	3	1	4	1	1	0	1	0	2	2	1	4	42	40	.512	5	7-3	Won 2
NY	3	3	2	0	0	1	1	0	0	1	1	0	1	3	2	1	1	2	—	3	3	1	1	1	0	1	3	0	4	39	43	.476	8	6-4	Lost 1
BOS	1	—	1	3	1	2	0	1	1	0	0	1	2	1	1	2	0	1	3	3	1	0	1	0	1	3	1	3		36	46	.439	11	4-6	Won 1
PHI	2	1	4	1	1	0	2	1	0	0	1	1	0	3	1	1	1	2	1	2	—	1	1	0	2	1	1	0	2	33	49	.402	14	3-7	Lost 4
WAS	2	1	3	2	1	0	0	1	0	1	2	0	0	0	1	0	0	0	1	0	0	0	2	1	1	0	1	3	1	25	57	.305	22	2-8	Lost 3
ORL	3	1	1	1	0	1	1	1	0	1	0	0	0	0	1	0	0	0	1	—	2	1	0	0	0	1	1	4		21	61	.256	26	2-8	Won 2

CENTRAL DIVISION

TM	Atl	Bos	Chi	Cle	Dal	Den	Det	GS	Hou	Ind	LAC	LAL	Mem	Mia	Mil	Min	NJ	NO	NY	Orl	Phi	Pho	Por	SAC	SA	Sea	Tor	Uta	Was	W	L	Pct	GB	Last-10	Streak
IND	4	3	3	3	2	2	3	2	1	—	2	1	1	3	1	1	3	2	3	3	4	2	1	0	1	2	4	2	2	61	21	.744	-	8-2	Won 5
DET	3	3	4	2	1	2	—	1	1	1	2	4	3	0	2	1	3	3	2	2	2	0	1	1	3	1	3	1	3	54	28	.659	7	8-2	Lost 1
NO	2	4	2	1	0	1	3	2	0	2	1	1	1	3	0	1	—	1	4	2	1	2	0	1	0	1	1	4	1	41	41	.500	20	4-6	Won 1
MIL	2	3	3	2	1	0	1	1	0	3	0	0	1	2	—	0	3	1	2	3	2	1	1	1	0	3	1	3		41	41	.500	20	5-5	Lost 3
CLE	3	1	2	—	0	0	2	0	0	1	1	0	0	2	2	0	1	3	4	2	3	0	1	0	1	2	1	1	2	35	47	.427	26	3-7	Won 3
TOR	3	1	0	3	1	2	1	1	1	0	1	0	0	1	1	0	2	3	1	2	3	2	1	0	0	1	—	1	1	33	49	.402	28	3-7	Won 2
ATL	—	3	3	1	2	2	1	0	0	0	0	1	0	1	2	1	1	2	0	1	1	1	0	0	1	1	1	0	2	28	54	.341	33	5-5	Lost 1
CHI	1	2	—	2	0	0	0	1	0	1	1	0	0	0	1	0	0	1	2	2	2	3	0	1	0	0	0	4	1	1	23	59	.280	38	3-7	Lost 2

MIDWEST DIVISION

TM	Atl	Bos	Chi	Cle	Dal	Den	Det	GS	Hou	Ind	LAC	LAL	Mem	Mia	Mil	Min	NJ	NO	NY	Orl	Phi	Pho	Por	SAC	SA	Sea	Tor	Uta	Was	W	L	Pct	GB	Last-10	Streak
MIN	1	1	2	2	2	3	2	2	2	1	4	3	3	2	2	—	1	2	1	2	1	4	1	3	2	3	2	2		58	24	.707	-	9-1	Won 9
SA	1	2	2	1	1	3	1	2	4	1	3	1	1	2	1	2	2	1	2	2	0	4	4	2	—	4	2	4	2	57	25	.695	1	10-0	Won 11
DAL	0	1	2	2	—	2	1	3	3	0	2	2	2	1	1	2	2	2	2	2	1	3	3	3	3	3	1	2	1	52	30	.634	6	8-2	Won 2
MEM	2	1	2	2	0	3	3	1	4	2	—	1	1	1	2	1	2	1	2	2	2	2	3	1	2	1	2	2	2	50	32	.610	8	4-6	Lost 4
HOU	2	1	2	2	1	2	1	2	—	1	4	2	1	1	2	2	1	2	2	2	2	1	3	0	0	1	1	2	2	45	37	.549	13	3-7	Lost 1
DEN	0	0	2	2	2	—	0	3	2	0	2	1	2	1	2	1	1	0	1	1	1	2	4	4	2	1	2	0	3	43	39	.524	15	6-4	Lost 1
UTA	2	1	1	1	2	1	1	2	2	0	3	1	3	1	1	2	1	1	2	1	2	1	2	3	2	1	0	3	1	—	42	40	.512	16	5-5	Lost 2

PACIFIC DIVISION

TM	Atl	Bos	Chi	Cle	Dal	Den	Det	GS	Hou	Ind	LAC	LAL	Mem	Mia	Mil	Min	NJ	NO	NY	Orl	Phi	Pho	Por	SAC	SA	Sea	Tor	Uta	Was	W	L	Pct	GB	Last-10	Streak
LAL	1	2	2	2	2	3	1	3	2	1	3	—	2	2	2	1	2	1	2	2	1	3	2	1	3	3	2	3	2	56	26	.683	-	7-3	Won 2
SAC	2	1	2	2	1	2	2	2	4	2	4	3	2	1	1	1	1	1	2	1	2	2	3	—	2	3	2	3	1	55	27	.671	1	4-6	Lost 2
POR	2	2	1	1	0	0	2	1	1	2	2	2	2	1	3	2	0	1	1	2	1	1	—	3	0	2	1	2	1	41	41	.500	15	4-6	Lost 4
GS	2	0	1	2	1	1	—	2	0	2	1	1	1	1	2	0	0	2	1	1	2	2	2	2	3	1	2	1		37	45	.451	19	5-5	Won 1
SEA	1	1	2	0	1	2	1	1	3	0	4	1	3	0	2	1	0	2	1	2	1	2	2	1	0	—	1	1	3	37	45	.451	19	3-7	Won 1
PHO	1	1	1	2	1	0	0	2	3	0	1	1	1	0	1	1	0	1	1	—	2	1	0	2	0	1	1	0		29	53	.354	27	5-5	Won 1
LAC	2	2	1	1	2	2	0	2	0	0	—	1	0	0	2	0	0	1	1	2	1	3	2	0	1	0	1	1	1	0	28	54	.341	28	1-9	Lost 1

REGULAR-SEASON STATISTICS

TEAM

OFFENSIVE

Team	G	Field Goals Made	Att.	Pct.	3-Pointers Made	Att.	Pct.	Free Throws Made	Att.	Pct.	Rebounds Off.	Def.	Tot.	Misc. Ast	PF	Dq	Stl	TO	Blk	Scoring Pts	Avg.
Dall.	82	3322	7230	.459	507	1456	.348	1475	1854	.796	1174	2538	3712	1963	1609	16	656	1000	437	8626	105.2
Sac.	82	3103	6711	.462	601	1498	.401	1626	2044	.795	888	2492	3380	2152	1586	12	710	1137	325	8433	102.8
LA-L.	82	3028	6676	.454	365	1115	.327	1631	2352	.693	1001	2535	3536	1948	1732	13	682	1132	379	8052	98.2
Milw.	82	2970	6650	.447	401	1145	.350	1698	2192	.775	960	2502	3462	1872	1668	12	554	1110	383	8039	98.0
Den.	82	2993	6763	.443	331	985	.336	1655	2159	.767	1083	2387	3470	1794	1804	13	745	1278	520	7972	97.2
Sea.	82	2939	6590	.446	723	1936	.373	1363	1782	.765	907	2318	3225	1782	1784	11	661	1188	387	7964	97.1
Mem.	82	2963	6657	.445	447	1314	.340	1557	2143	.727	1047	2381	3428	1915	1903	24	795	1226	565	7930	96.7
Bos.	82	2843	6415	.443	553	1599	.346	1572	2095	.750	851	2440	3291	1683	1837	15	770	1332	331	7811	95.3
LA-C.	82	2817	6579	.428	329	1024	.321	1808	2302	.785	1149	2416	3565	1653	1816	16	594	1344	376	7771	94.8
Minn.	82	3033	6571	.462	326	897	.363	1361	1743	.781	875	2645	3520	1890	1731	12	561	1043	462	7753	94.5
Phoe.	82	2958	6671	.443	415	1202	.345	1392	1865	.746	924	2406	3330	1586	1862	31	734	1249	383	7723	94.2
Orl.	82	2904	6768	.429	429	1248	.344	1474	2000	.737	1003	2350	3353	1584	1744	13	547	1123	308	7711	94.0
G.S.	82	2875	6511	.442	429	1283	.334	1470	2028	.725	1002	2533	3535	1681	1691	14	576	1211	389	7649	93.3
Clev.	82	2922	6753	.433	247	786	.314	1528	2030	.753	1118	2619	3737	1808	1743	8	585	1216	537	7619	92.9
Atl.	82	2829	6529	.433	419	1249	.335	1534	1976	.776	996	2507	3503	1648	1826	20	627	1350	408	7611	92.8
N.Y.	82	2881	6513	.442	406	1115	.364	1374	1732	.793	950	2543	3493	1695	1897	21	608	1289	391	7542	92.0
N.O.	82	2772	6605	.420	531	1666	.319	1454	1937	.751	1091	2418	3509	1716	1715	18	708	1228	346	7529	91.8
Wash.	82	2758	6556	.421	433	1269	.341	1579	2211	.714	1115	2392	3507	1537	1712	11	733	1439	406	7528	91.8
S.A.	82	2842	6434	.442	408	1140	.358	1409	2069	.681	1029	2669	3698	1676	1667	8	661	1203	537	7501	91.5
Ind.	82	2753	6322	.435	449	1281	.351	1538	2014	.764	965	2452	3417	1774	1709	8	726	1182	411	7493	91.4
Port.	82	2898	6467	.448	381	1102	.346	1263	1728	.731	1040	2376	3416	1768	1554	8	613	1213	443	7440	90.7
Miami.	82	2729	6417	.425	485	1357	.357	1459	1915	.762	940	2459	3399	1565	1812	14	590	1137	313	7402	90.3
N.J.	82	2813	6372	.441	377	1123	.336	1398	1856	.753	862	2473	3335	2009	1722	11	709	1209	322	7401	90.3
Det.	82	2747	6314	.435	333	968	.344	1561	2074	.753	1014	2492	3506	1702	1664	7	659	1241	570	7388	90.1
Hou.	82	2738	6195	.442	515	1406	.366	1371	1774	.773	847	2647	3494	1579	1762	14	560	1373	443	7362	89.8
Chi.	82	2798	6753	.414	429	1256	.342	1330	1834	.725	1048	2519	3567	1793	1911	35	659	1321	396	7355	89.7
Utah.	82	2690	6172	.436	252	786	.321	1639	2196	.746	1103	2272	3375	1671	2096	18	583	1365	494	7271	88.7
Phil.	82	2682	6260	.428	339	992	.342	1512	2009	.753	941	2408	3349	1640	1701	11	654	1307	358	7215	88.0
Tor.	82	2654	6348	.418	461	1294	.356	1237	1650	.750	830	2419	3249	1574	1748	9	604	1164	402	7006	85.4

DEFENSIVE

Team	Field Goals Made	Att.	Pct.	3-Pointers Made	Att.	Pct.	Free Throws Made	Att.	Pct.	Rebounds Off.	Def.	Tot.	Misc. Ast	PF	Dq	Stl	TO	Blk	Scoring Pts	Avg.	Dif.
S.A.	2613	6388	.409	311	951	.327	1372	1844	.744	909	2459	3368	1419	1837	18	635	1254	380	6909	84.3	+7.2
Det.	2633	6378	.413	356	1180	.302	1287	1730	.744	980	2353	3333	1561	1877	21	649	1310	410	6909	84.3	+5.8
Ind.	2671	6180	.432	329	1014	.324	1350	1800	.750	867	2423	3290	1649	1794	18	582	1301	512	7021	85.6	+5.8
N.J.	2693	6302	.427	418	1193	.350	1392	1830	.761	873	2471	3344	1627	1739	15	656	1321	374	7196	87.8	+2.5
Hou.	2636	6405	.412	457	1227	.372	1491	2024	.737	907	2351	3258	1689	1695	16	710	1103	359	7220	88.0	+1.7
Tor.	2722	6365	.428	273	889	.307	1536	2055	.747	1034	2662	3696	1518	1619	10	590	1196	332	7253	88.5	-3.0
Minn.	2741	6625	.414	395	1181	.334	1426	1893	.753	1001	2400	3401	1701	1656	12	547	1106	296	7303	89.1	+5.5
Miami.	2658	6205	.428	431	1256	.343	1612	2100	.768	892	2486	3378	1526	1729	14	578	1207	439	7359	89.7	+0.5
Utah.	2541	5879	.432	415	1209	.343	1474	2431	.771	868	2131	2999	1528	1999	26	666	1262	530	7371	89.9	-1.2
Phil.	2751	6369	.432	443	1329	.333	1474	1982	.744	996	2398	3394	1747	1757	21	678	1245	463	7419	90.5	-2.5
N.O.	2843	6443	.441	444	1301	.341	1407	1877	.750	972	2477	3449	1790	1734	14	613	1282	429	7537	91.9	-0.1
Port.	2954	6567	.450	417	1222	.341	1219	1618	.753	1016	2292	3308	1912	1534	13	657	1120	390	7544	92.0	-1.3
N.Y.	2785	6491	.429	415	1228	.338	1678	2198	.763	950	2444	3394	1676	1600	7	675	1132	383	7663	93.5	-1.5
G.S.	2948	6630	.445	414	1107	.374	1399	1875	.746	981	2532	3513	1762	1801	16	666	1145	418	7709	94.0	-0.7
Mem.	2859	6550	.436	369	1091	.338	1643	2150	.764	1099	2508	3607	1674	1891	26	673	1395	461	7730	94.3	+2.4
LA-L.	2920	6640	.440	420	1247	.337	1472	1964	.749	922	2558	3480	1708	2024	25	616	1254	308	7732	94.3	+3.9
Clev.	2956	6759	.437	431	1162	.371	1491	1990	.749	971	2475	3446	1783	1656	8	635	1071	434	7834	95.5	-2.6
Chi.	2882	6611	.436	439	1235	.355	1673	2238	.748	1011	2682	3693	1890	1684	13	694	1250	446	7876	96.0	-6.4
Den.	3019	6662	.453	376	1056	.356	1470	2020	.728	1056	2465	3521	1931	1895	16	664	1399	479	7884	96.1	+1.1
Bos.	2894	6626	.437	515	1534	.362	1587	2156	.736	1069	2524	3593	1882	1819	7	719	1406	408	7930	96.7	-1.5
Milw.	3034	6719	.452	456	1296	.352	1428	1932	.739	983	2521	3504	1870	1878	14	615	1164	406	7952	97.0	+1.1
Wash.	3061	6740	.454	424	1208	.342	1444	1874	.771	1048	2520	3568	1966	1783	17	786	1321	448	7990	97.4	-5.6
Atl.	2968	6740	.440	482	1345	.358	1574	2072	.760	1048	2485	3533	1803	1699	15	731	1151	416	7992	97.5	-4.6
Sea.	2980	6622	.450	486	1394	.349	1570	2028	.774	1068	2430	3498	1728	1658	7	629	1211	387	8016	97.8	-0.6
Sac.	3140	6920	.454	409	1205	.339	1333	1780	.749	1080	2521	3601	1743	1817	20	651	1225	413	8022	97.8	+5.0
Phoe.	2975	6671	.446	479	1374	.349	1601	2093	.765	1038	2550	3588	1760	1589	3	649	1304	431	8030	97.9	-3.7
LA-C.	3075	6687	.460	452	1256	.360	1545	2086	.741	1033	2358	3391	1874	1861	11	693	1122	437	8147	99.4	-4.6
Dall.	3133	6824	.459	534	1471	.363	1462	1960	.746	1009	2562	3571	1937	1690	11	582	1242	382	8262	100.8	+4.4
Orl.	3169	6804	.466	491	1301	.377	1458	1964	.742	1072	2570	3642	2004	1691	9	625	1111	450	8287	101.1	-7.0
AVG.	2871	6545	.439	425	1224	.347	1492	1985	.752	991	2469	3461	1747	1759	15	650	1228	415	7659	93.4	—

HOME/ROAD

	Total	Home	Road		Total	Home	Road
Atlanta	28-54	19-23	10-31	Minnesota	58-24	31-10	27-14
Boston	36-46	19-22	17-24	New Jersey	47-35	28-13	19-23
Chicago	23-59	14-27	9-32	New Orleans	41-41	25-16	16-25
Cleveland	35-47	23-18	12-29	New York	39-43	23-18	16-25
Dallas	52-30	36-5	16-25	Orlando	21-61	11-30	10-31
Denver	43-39	29-12	14-27	Philadelphia	33-49	21-20	12-29
Detroit	54-28	31-10	23-18	Phoenix	29-53	18-23	11-30
Golden State	37-45	27-14	10-31	Portland	41-41	25-16	16-25
Houston	45-37	27-14	18-23	Sacramento	55-27	34-7	21-20
Indiana	61-21	34-7	27-14	San Antonio	57-25	33-8	27-14
L.A. Clippers	28-54	18-23	10-31	Seattle	37-45	21-20	16-25
L.A. Lakers	56-26	34-7	22-19	Toronto	33-49	18-23	15-26
Memphis	50-32	31-10	19-22	Utah	42-40	28-13	14-27
Miami	42-40	29-12	13-28	Washington	25-57	17-24	8-33
Milwaukee	41-41	27-14	14-27				

INDIVIDUAL LEADERS

SCORING
(minimum 70 games or 1,400 points)

	G	FGM	FTM	Pts.	Avg.
McGrady, Orl.	67	653	398	1878	28.0
Stojakovic, Sac.	81	665	394	1964	24.2
Garnett, Min.	82	804	368	1987	24.2
Bryant, LA-L.	65	516	454	1557	24.0
Pierce, Bos.	80	602	517	1836	23.0
Davis, N.O.	67	554	237	1532	22.9
Carter, Tor.	73	608	336	1645	22.5
Duncan, S.A.	69	592	352	1538	22.3
Nowitzki, Dal.	77	605	371	1680	21.8
Redd, Mil.	82	633	383	1776	21.7
O'Neal, LA-L.	67	554	331	1439	21.5
Anthony, Den.	82	624	408	1725	21.0
James, Cle.	79	622	347	1654	20.9
Maggette, LA-C.	73	453	526	1508	20.7
Marbury, Pho.-N.Y.	81	598	356	1639	20.2
O'Neal, Ind.	78	608	348	1566	20.1
Randolph, Por.	81	663	299	1626	20.1
Cassell, Min.	81	620	289	1603	19.8
Marion, Pho.	79	590	228	1498	19.0

FIELD-GOAL PERCENTAGE
(minimum 300 made)

	FGM	FGA	Pct.
O'Neal, LA-L.	554	948	.584
Blount, Bos.	342	604	.566
Dampier, G.S.	348	650	.535
Jamison, Dal.	488	913	.535
Nene, Den.	334	630	.530
Boozer, Cle.	471	900	.523
Yao, Hou.	535	1025	.522
Miller, Sac.	373	731	.510
Williamson, Det.	304	602	.505
Duncan, S.A.	592	1181	.501

FREE THROW PERCENTAGE
(minimum 125 made)

	FTM	FTA	Pct.
Stojakovic, Sac.	394	425	.927
Nash, Dal.	230	251	.916
Houston, N.Y.	157	172	.913
Allen, Sea.	245	271	.904
Miller, Ind.	146	165	.885
Billups, Det.	404	460	.878
Cardinal, G.S.	238	271	.878
Nowitzki, Dal.	371	423	.877
Boykins, Den.	142	162	.877
Stoudamire, Por.	127	145	.876

ASSISTS
(minimum 70 games or 400 assists)

	G	No.	Avg.
Kidd, N.J.	67	618	9.2
Marbury, Pho.-N.Y.	81	719	8.9
Nash, Dal.	78	687	8.8
Davis, N.O.	67	501	7.5
Cassell, Min.	81	592	7.3
Snow, Phi.	82	563	6.9
Williams, Mem.	72	492	6.8
Hinrich, Chi.	76	517	6.8
Francis, Hou.	79	493	6.2
McInnis, Por.-Cle.	70	430	6.1
Miller, Den.	82	501	6.1
Stoudamire, Por.	82	500	6.1
James, Cle.	79	465	5.9
Jones, Mil.	82	478	5.8
Billups, Det.	78	446	5.7
Parker, S.A.	75	411	5.5
Payton, LA-L.	82	449	5.5
Bibby, Sac.	82	444	5.4
Terry, Atl.	81	437	5.4
Divac, Sac.	81	432	5.3

REBOUNDS
(minimum 70 games or 800 rebounds)

	G	Off.	Def.	Tot.	Avg.
Garnett, Min.	82	245	894	1139	13.9
Duncan, S.A.	69	227	632	859	12.4
B. Wallace, Det.	81	324	682	1006	12.4
Dampier, G.S.	74	344	543	887	12.0
Boozer, Cle.	75	230	627	857	11.4
Randolph, Por.	81	242	609	851	10.5
Magloire, N.O.	82	268	579	847	10.3
Miller, Sac.	72	191	552	743	10.3
Thomas, Phi.	74	261	489	750	10.1
Camby, Den.	72	211	516	727	10.1
O'Neal, Ind.	78	193	585	778	10.0
Marshall, Chi.-Tor.	82	210	598	808	9.9
Odom, Mia.	80	160	616	776	9.7
Marion, Pho.	79	212	525	737	9.3
Yao, Hou.	82	197	538	735	9.0
Nowitzki, Dal.	77	90	580	670	8.7
P. Brown, N.O.	80	237	453	690	8.6
Smith, Mil.	76	230	413	643	8.5
Davis, Tor.-Chi.	80	207	464	671	8.4
Walker, Dal.	82	198	486	684	8.3

STEALS
(minimum 70 games or 125 steals)

	G	No.	Avg.
Davis, N.O.	67	158	2.36
Marion, Pho.	79	167	2.11
Artest, Ind.	73	152	2.08
Kirilenko, Utah	78	150	1.92
Christie, Sac.	82	151	1.84
Jackson, Atl.	80	142	1.78
Ginobili, S.A.	77	136	1.77
B. Wallace, Det.	81	143	1.77
Francis, Hou.	79	139	1.76
Miller, Den.	82	142	1.73

2003-04 REVIEW Regular-season statistics

BLOCKED SHOTS
(minimum 70 games or 100 blocked shots)

	G	No.	Avg.
Ratliff, Atl.-Por.	85	307	3.61
B. Wallace, Det.	81	246	3.04
Kirilenko, Utah	78	215	2.76
Duncan, S.A.	69	185	2.68
Camby, Den.	72	187	2.60
O'Neal, Ind.	78	199	2.55
Ilgauskas, Cle.	81	201	2.48
O'Neal, LA-L	67	166	2.48
Dalembert, Phi.	82	189	2.30
Brand, LA-C	69	154	2.23

3-POINT FIELD GOALS
(minimum 55 made)

	FGM	FGA	Pct.
Peeler, Sac.	68	141	.482
Barry, Sea.	114	252	.452
Cardinal, G.S.	55	124	.444
Hoiberg, Min.	76	172	.442
McKie, Phi.	75	172	.436
Stojakovic, Sac.	240	554	.433
Houston, N.Y.	87	202	.431
Turkoglu, S.A.	101	241	.419
Jacobsen, Pho.	75	180	.417
Ward, N.Y.-Pho.-S.A.	84	206	.408

INDIVIDUAL STATISTICS, TEAM BY TEAM

ATLANTA HAWKS

	G	Min.	FGM	FGA	Pct.	FTM	FTA	Pct.	Off.	Def.	Tot.	Ast.	PF	Dq.	Stl.	TO	Blk.	Pts.	Avg.	Hi.
Shareef Abdur-Rahim(>)	53	1956	383	790	.485	294	334	.880	141	354	495	127	147	1	44	131	19	1065	20.1	43
Rasheed Wallace(>)	1	42	8	24	.333	3	3	1.000	1	5	6	2	0	0	1	3	5	20	20.0	20
Stephen Jackson	80	2940	536	1261	.425	233	297	.785	97	273	370	244	216	3	142	223	20	1450	18.1	42
Jason Terry	81	3018	499	1196	.417	215	260	.827	49	287	336	437	192	2	124	229	16	1359	16.8	30
Jason Collier	20	545	79	165	.479	67	85	.788	36	75	111	17	71	3	11	31	11	226	11.3	22
Chris Crawford	56	1207	211	471	.448	103	119	.866	58	117	175	45	131	4	37	55	20	569	10.2	27
Dion Glover(>)	55	1465	205	524	.391	110	142	.775	54	183	237	115	106	0	40	83	17	556	10.1	23
Theo Ratliff(>)	53	1648	171	373	.458	96	147	.653	105	276	381	51	189	2	30	86	166	438	8.3	16
Bob Sura(*)	27	956	131	312	.420	123	157	.783	70	153	223	144	72	0	25	66	5	397	14.7	32
Bob Sura(!)	80	1663	202	485	.416	171	226	.757	100	226	326	233	158	0	62	105	14	596	7.5	32
Nazr Mohammed(>)	53	938	138	280	.493	69	110	.627	101	166	267	20	113	0	22	55	27	345	6.5	13
Wesley Person(*)	9	132	13	39	.333	6	6	1.000	2	23	25	5	5	0	3	4	1	40	4.4	15
Wesley Person(!)	58	1037	126	314	.401	31	39	.795	16	101	117	66	38	0	19	38	9	338	5.8	20
Lee Nailon(>)	27	300	63	138	.457	16	19	.842	26	37	63	17	48	0	10	24	7	142	5.3	15
Boris Diaw	76	1919	140	313	.447	56	93	.602	111	231	342	182	191	2	59	126	37	342	4.5	15
Alan Henderson	6	68	10	21	.476	4	6	.667	11	10	21	2	1	0	1	3	2	24	4.0	9
Jacque Vaughn	71	1271	107	277	.386	53	68	.779	12	104	116	195	126	0	44	84	2	270	3.8	23
Zeljko Rebraca(*)	3	51	12	23	.522	1	2	.500	4	5	9	2	7	1	0	4	2	25	8.3	18
Zeljko Rebraca(!)	24	273	34	77	.442	23	30	.767	23	35	58	6	52	1	5	17	11	91	3.8	18
Mamadou N'diaye(*)	25	359	27	68	.397	44	59	.746	43	68	111	0	58	1	8	17	24	98	3.9	15
Mamadou N'diaye(!)	28	366	27	69	.391	44	59	.746	43	69	112	0	59	1	8	18	25	98	3.5	15
Travis Hansen	41	507	46	130	.354	22	27	.815	30	40	70	19	67	0	10	15	9	123	3.0	14
Joel Przybilla(*)	12	314	18	50	.360	12	29	.414	31	70	101	4	48	1	5	16	17	48	4.0	9
Joel Przybilla(!)	17	347	18	50	.360	13	31	.419	32	79	111	7	53	1	5	18	17	49	2.9	9
Dan Dickau(>)	23	143	21	49	.429	4	6	.667	4	12	16	18	22	0	9	13	0	49	2.1	7
Hiram Fuller	4	43	3	8	.375	2	6	.333	4	7	11	2	5	0	0	4	1	8	2.0	4
Josh Davis	4	23	2	5	.400	1	1	1.000	1	4	5	0	3	0	0	2	0	5	1.3	5
Michael Bradley(*)	11	60	6	12	.500	0	0	—	5	7	12	0	8	0	2	4	0	12	1.1	10
Michael Bradley(!)	16	98	7	15	.467	1	2	.500	6	17	23	1	14	0	3	7	0	15	0.9	10
Atlanta	82	19905	2829	6529	.433	1534	1976	.776	996	2507	3503	1648	1826	20	627	1350	408	7611	92.8	138
Opponents	82	19905	2968	6740	.440	1574	2072	.760	1048	2485	3533	1803	1699	15	731	1151	416	7992	97.5	137

3-pt. FG: Atlanta 419-1249 (.335)

Abdur-Rahim(>) 5-23 (.217); Wallace(>) 1-6 (.167); Jackson 145-427 (.340); Terry 146-421 (.347); Collier 1-4 (.250)
Crawford 44-113 (.389); Glover(>) 36-105 (.343); Sura(*) 12-43 (.279); Sura(!) 21-79 (.266); Person(!) 8-19 (.421)
Person(!) 55-138 (.399); Diaw 6-26 (.231); Vaughn 3-20 (.150); Hansen 9-30 (.300); Dickau(>) 3-10 (.300); Davis 0-2 (.000)
Opponents 482-1345 (.358)

BOSTON CELTICS

	G	Min.	FGM	FGA	Pct.	FTM	FTA	Pct.	Off.	Def.	Tot.	Ast.	PF	Dq.	Stl.	TO	Blk.	Pts.	Avg.	Hi.
Paul Pierce	80	3099	602	1497	.402	517	631	.819	69	453	522	410	234	3	131	303	52	1836	23.0	41
Ricky Davis(*)	57	1678	312	639	.488	145	198	.732	59	178	237	148	120	0	71	121	14	804	14.1	33
Ricky Davis(!)	79	2474	446	950	.469	196	273	.718	77	281	358	259	171	1	96	189	22	1140	14.4	33
Eric Williams(>)	21	513	77	177	.435	78	109	.716	21	74	95	25	52	0	22	31	1	243	11.6	21
Vin Baker(>)	37	1000	168	333	.505	82	112	.732	76	134	210	54	98	1	22	52	23	418	11.3	24
Mike James(>)	55	1684	213	510	.418	76	95	.800	20	156	176	244	113	0	70	83	2	588	10.7	24
Mark Blount	82	2402	342	604	.566	159	221	.719	207	382	589	75	253	4	80	150	106	843	10.3	29
Jiri Welsch	81	2179	262	612	.428	153	206	.743	60	236	296	183	176	0	101	129	7	746	9.2	22
Chucky Atkins(*)	24	793	104	249	.418	42	54	.778	3	42	45	128	42	0	26	44	1	289	12.0	21
Chucky Atkins(!)	64	1544	192	484	.397	73	97	.753	9	84	93	223	102	0	45	92	2	538	8.4	21
Walter McCarty	77	1900	203	523	.388	62	82	.756	28	211	239	124	179	1	72	91	22	605	7.9	21
Raef LaFrentz	17	328	57	124	.460	10	13	.769	30	49	79	24	47	1	8	11	13	132	7.8	17
Chris Mihm(*)	54	939	127	254	.500	76	118	.644	109	164	273	11	150	2	28	65	41	330	6.1	16
Chris Mihm(!)	76	1330	186	381	.488	110	166	.663	156	257	413	21	208	3	37	90	63	482	6.3	21
Dana Barros	1	11	2	3	.667	2	2	1.000	0	0	0	2	0	0	0	0	0	6	6.0	6
Marcus Banks	81	1385	177	442	.400	99	131	.756	30	103	133	175	171	2	88	125	13	480	5.9	21
Tony Battie(>)	23	501	56	117	.479	23	33	.697	39	79	118	21	55	0	8	24	20	136	5.9	15
Kedrick Brown(>)	21	408	45	99	.455	8	13	.615	18	50	68	25	38	1	17	12	2	110	5.2	18

	G	Min.	FGM	FGA	Pct.	FTM	FTA	Pct.	REBOUNDS Off.	Def.	Tot.	Ast.	PF	Dq.	Stl.	TO	Blk.	SCORING Pts.	Avg.	Hi.
Brandon Hunter	36	406	53	116	.457	19	43	.442	50	68	118	19	40	0	13	22	1	125	3.5	17
Jumaine Jones	42	373	33	96	.344	14	23	.609	24	44	68	14	48	0	12	19	9	93	2.2	10
Kendrick Perkins	10	35	8	15	.533	6	9	.667	5	9	14	3	6	0	0	5	2	22	2.2	7
Michael Stewart(*)	17	71	2	5	.400	1	2	.500	3	8	11	0	13	0	1	2	2	5	0.3	2
Michael Stewart(!)	25	147	5	12	.417	3	4	.750	8	21	29	0	34	0	2	3	10	13	0.5	6
Boston	82	19705	2843	6415	.443	1572	2095	.750	851	2440	3291	1683	1837	15	770	1332	331	7811	95.3	137
Opponents	82	19705	2894	6626	.437	1587	2156	.736	1069	2524	3593	1882	1819	7	719	1406	408	7930	96.7	132

3-pt. FG: Boston 553-1599 (.346)
Pierce 115-384 (.299); Davis(*) 35-92 (.380); Davis(!) 52-140 (.371); Williams(>) 11-32 (.344); Baker(>) 0-1 (.000); James(>) 86-226 (.381); Welsch 69-181 (.381); Atkins(*) 39-111 (.351); Atkins(!) 81-241 (.336); McCarty 137-366 (.374); LaFrentz 8-40 (.200); Banks 27-86 (.314); Battie(>) 1-1 (1.000); K. Brown(>) 12-32 (.375); B. Hunter 0-3 (.000); Jones 13-44 (.295); Opponents 555-1534 (.362)

CHICAGO BULLS

	G	Min.	FGM	FGA	Pct.	FTM	FTA	Pct.	REBOUNDS Off.	Def.	Tot.	Ast.	PF	Dq.	Stl.	TO	Blk.	SCORING Pts.	Avg.	Hi.
Jamal Crawford	80	2811	509	1318	.386	200	240	.833	46	237	283	405	161	0	111	193	29	1383	17.3	50
Eddy Curry	73	2154	417	840	.496	235	350	.671	143	308	451	68	258	11	24	177	83	1070	14.7	28
Jalen Rose(>)	16	529	75	200	.375	39	51	.765	7	57	64	56	45	0	12	37	4	212	13.3	34
Kirk Hinrich	76	2706	318	823	.386	135	168	.804	42	217	259	517	276	9	101	204	21	915	12.0	29
Kendall Gill	56	1411	215	548	.392	100	136	.735	61	129	190	89	107	0	65	83	16	539	9.6	29
Antonio Davis(*)	65	2032	220	540	.407	139	181	.768	158	370	528	123	161	1	29	93	57	579	8.9	18
Antonio Davis(!)	80	2570	266	660	.403	176	230	.765	207	464	671	137	206	1	37	114	65	708	8.9	18
Donyell Marshall(>)	16	408	57	136	.419	14	20	.700	28	71	99	28	47	1	13	22	20	139	8.7	25
Marcus Fizer	46	738	134	350	.383	90	120	.750	61	141	202	43	97	0	16	51	8	360	7.8	30
Eddie Robinson	51	1024	157	326	.482	28	43	.651	27	77	104	58	57	1	33	45	10	343	6.7	17
Jannero Pargo(*)	13	345	66	154	.429	23	27	.852	8	19	27	47	38	2	7	30	5	175	13.5	34
Jannero Pargo(!)	31	479	81	199	.407	23	27	.852	8	29	37	70	50	2	13	47	6	207	6.7	34
Ronald Dupree	47	893	111	282	.394	66	105	.629	55	112	167	55	134	4	32	51	18	292	6.2	18
Jerome Williams(*)	53	1230	130	279	.466	85	126	.675	142	205	347	61	104	0	71	51	5	345	6.5	15
Jerome Williams(!)	68	1637	158	336	.470	106	155	.684	177	298	475	72	134	0	90	74	8	422	6.2	17
Tyson Chandler	35	782	67	158	.424	79	118	.669	82	188	270	23	87	2	17	38	43	213	6.1	22
Scottie Pippen	23	412	53	140	.379	17	27	.630	20	48	68	50	38	0	21	29	9	136	5.9	17
Corie Blount(>)	46	756	97	206	.471	13	24	.542	76	130	206	45	86	0	38	35	19	207	4.5	13
Lonny Baxter(>)	14	147	27	49	.551	5	8	.625	11	24	35	5	31	2	1	11	6	60	4.3	19
Linton Johnson	41	734	72	203	.355	22	37	.595	59	124	183	27	90	2	37	37	32	173	4.2	12
Chris Jefferies(*)	19	187	24	66	.364	12	19	.632	5	23	28	6	36	0	4	18	7	76	4.0	15
Chris Jefferies(!)	21	195	27	72	.375	13	20	.650	5	24	29	7	36	0	4	19	7	84	4.0	15
Paul Shirley	7	86	10	23	.435	1	3	.333	8	8	16	4	9	0	1	9	1	21	3.0	6
Rick Brunson(*)	37	402	38	101	.376	27	31	.871	9	28	37	80	44	0	25	33	3	114	3.1	12
Rick Brunson(!)	40	412	40	105	.381	27	31	.871	9	28	37	82	44	0	25	33	3	118	3.0	12
Roger Mason(>)	3	43	1	11	.091	0	0	—	0	3	3	3	5	0	1	2	0	3	1.0	3
Chicago	82	19830	2798	6753	.414	1330	1834	.725	1048	2519	3567	1793	1911	35	659	1321	396	7355	89.7	114
Opponents	82	19830	2882	6611	.436	1673	2238	.748	1011	2682	3693	1890	1684	13	694	1250	446	7876	96.0	124

3-pt. FG: Chicago 429-1256 (.342)
Crawford 165-521 (.317); Curry 1-1 (1.000); Rose(>) 23-54 (.426); Hinrich 144-369 (.390); Gill 9-38 (.237); Fizer 2-17 (.118); Marshall(>) 11-27 (.407); Robinson 1-5 (.200); Pargo(*) 20-53 (.377); Pargo(!) 22-62 (.355); Dupree 4-9 (.444); Shirley 0-1 (.000); Williams(*) 0-7 (.000); Williams(!) 0-8 (.000); Chandler 0-1 (.000); Pippen 13-48 (.271); Blount(>) 0-3 (.000); Baxter(>) 1-1 (1.000); Johnson 7-33 (.212); Jefferies(*) 16-39 (.410); Jefferies(!) 17-42 (.405); Brunson(*) 11-23 (.478); Brunson(!) 11-23 (.478); Mason(>) 1-6 (.167); Opponents 439-1235 (.355)

CLEVELAND CAVALIERS

	G	Min.	FGM	FGA	Pct.	FTM	FTA	Pct.	REBOUNDS Off.	Def.	Tot.	Ast.	PF	Dq.	Stl.	TO	Blk.	SCORING Pts.	Avg.	Hi.
LeBron James	79	3122	622	1492	.417	347	460	.754	99	333	432	465	149	0	130	273	58	1654	20.9	41
Carlos Boozer	75	2592	471	900	.523	219	285	.768	230	627	857	148	199	0	74	134	55	1162	15.5	32
Ricky Davis(>)	22	796	134	311	.431	51	75	.680	18	103	121	111	51	1	25	68	8	336	15.3	27
Zydrunas Ilgauskas	81	2539	466	965	.483	303	406	.746	279	374	653	109	277	2	39	163	201	1237	15.3	31
Jeff McInnis(*)	31	1096	138	331	.417	56	67	.836	17	65	82	234	69	2	36	59	4	363	11.7	21
Jeff McInnis(!)	70	2365	334	747	.447	114	143	.797	33	143	176	430	163	4	72	120	6	828	11.8	21
Eric Williams(*)	50	1373	154	421	.366	137	174	.787	44	147	191	95	128	0	48	57	8	469	9.4	22
Eric Williams(!)	71	1886	231	598	.386	215	283	.760	65	221	286	120	180	0	70	88	9	712	10.0	22
Darius Miles(>)	37	888	143	331	.432	39	72	.542	48	119	167	80	84	0	25	56	27	330	8.9	26
Chris Mihm(>)	22	391	59	127	.465	34	48	.708	47	93	140	10	58	1	9	25	22	152	6.9	21
Dajuan Wagner	44	708	112	306	.366	32	47	.681	9	49	58	51	89	0	26	41	7	287	6.5	21
Lee Nailon(*)	22	397	73	162	.451	24	30	.800	30	36	66	17	36	0	4	21	1	170	7.7	23
Lee Nailon(!)	57	780	147	327	.450	47	58	.810	64	79	143	38	93	0	15	45	8	341	6.0	23
Tony Battie(*)	50	977	114	267	.427	43	56	.768	79	162	241	37	104	0	18	39	47	272	5.4	17
Tony Battie(!)	73	1478	170	384	.443	66	89	.742	118	241	359	58	159	0	26	63	67	408	5.6	17
Kedrick Brown(*)	34	561	72	155	.465	9	14	.643	23	55	78	39	42	0	13	17	5	179	5.3	13
Kedrick Brown(!)	55	969	117	254	.461	17	27	.630	41	105	146	64	80	1	30	29	7	289	5.3	18
Kevin Ollie	82	1401	95	257	.370	147	176	.835	23	147	170	234	119	0	51	81	8	341	4.2	12
Ira Newble	64	1245	108	276	.391	36	46	.783	65	90	155	72	109	1	25	54	19	254	4.0	16
Mateen Cleaves	4	92	7	23	.304	1	2	.500	1	6	7	19	13	0	4	5	2	15	3.8	8
J.R. Bremer(>)	31	403	39	137	.285	13	20	.650	7	26	33	39	27	0	18	19	4	110	3.5	20
Jason Kapono	41	427	52	129	.403	20	24	.833	19	36	55	14	41	0	13	21	2	145	3.5	19
DeSagana Diop	56	730	57	147	.388	12	20	.600	72	127	199	34	116	1	26	29	51	126	2.3	8

	G	Min.	FGM	FGA	Pct.	FTM	FTA	Pct.	Off.	Def.	Tot.	Ast.	PF	Dq.	Stl.	TO	Blk.	Pts.	Avg.	Hi.
Bruno Sundov(>)	4	29	3	9	.333	3	6	.500	2	8	10	0	7	0	0	3	0	9	2.3	4
Michael Stewart(>)	8	76	3	7	.429	2	2	1.000	5	13	18	0	21	0	1	1	8	8	1.0	6
Ruben Boumtje Boumtj(*)	0	0	0	0	—	0	0	—	0	0	0	0	0	0	0	0	0	0	—	0
Ruben Boumtje Boumtj(!)	9	26	1	5	.200	2	2	1.000	0	1	1	1	2	0	0	0	1	4	0.4	2
Jelani McCoy	2	12	0	0	—	0	0	—	1	3	4	0	4	0	0	1	0	0	0.0	0
Cleveland	82	19855	2922	6753	.433	1528	2030	.753	1118	2619	3737	1808	1743	8	585	1216	537	7619	92.9	115
Opponents	82	19855	2956	6759	.437	1491	1990	.749	971	2475	3446	1783	1656	8	635	1071	434	7834	95.5	126

3-pt. FG: Cleveland 247-786 (.314)
James 63-217 (.290); Boozer 1-6 (.167); Davis(>) 17-48 (.354); Ilgauskas 2-7 (.286); McInnis(*) 31-80 (.388); Miles(>) 5-30 (.167)
McInnis(!) 46-127 (.362); Williams(*) 24-95 (.253); Williams(!) 35-127 (.276); Wagner 31-86 (.360); Nailon(*) 0-3 (.000)
Nailon(!) 0-3 (.000); Battie(*) 1-8 (.125); Battie(!) 2-9 (.222); Brown(*) 26-67 (.388); Brown(!) 38-99 (.384); Ollie 4-9 (.444)
Newble 2-19 (.105); Cleaves 0-1 (.000); Bremer(>) 19-66 (.288); Kapono 21-44 (.477); Opponents 431-1162 (.371)

DALLAS MAVERICKS

	G	Min.	FGM	FGA	Pct.	FTM	FTA	Pct.	Off.	Def.	Tot.	Ast.	PF	Dq.	Stl.	TO	Blk.	Pts.	Avg.	Hi.
Dirk Nowitzki	77	2915	605	1310	.462	371	423	.877	90	580	670	207	216	3	92	135	104	1680	21.8	43
Michael Finley	72	2778	514	1159	.443	164	193	.850	78	247	325	212	118	0	84	83	39	1342	18.6	38
Antawn Jamison	82	2376	488	913	.535	220	294	.748	233	287	520	70	174	2	83	81	30	1212	14.8	26
Steve Nash	78	2612	397	845	.470	230	251	.916	59	173	232	687	139	0	67	209	8	1128	14.5	31
Antoine Walker	82	2840	483	1129	.428	103	186	.554	198	486	684	369	212	3	65	202	65	1151	14.0	30
Josh Howard	67	1589	229	532	.430	97	138	.703	149	219	368	97	168	6	69	67	54	575	8.6	19
Marquis Daniels	56	1039	203	411	.494	60	78	.769	66	80	146	116	51	0	53	44	12	477	8.5	33
Tony Delk	33	509	70	184	.380	37	44	.841	16	43	59	28	46	0	27	17	7	197	6.0	22
Scott Williams(*)	27	260	37	85	.435	7	14	.500	15	45	60	11	50	0	5	10	9	81	3.0	16
Scott Williams(!)	43	527	90	186	.484	16	27	.593	38	94	132	17	95	0	20	16	16	198	4.6	16
Danny Fortson	56	625	71	139	.511	75	92	.815	114	136	250	9	148	0	12	37	11	217	3.9	11
Shawn Bradley	66	773	89	188	.473	41	49	.837	72	101	173	20	130	1	33	17	74	219	3.3	13
Eduardo Najera	58	720	72	162	.444	30	46	.652	67	89	156	25	90	1	35	29	19	176	3.0	11
Travis Best	61	762	64	172	.372	40	46	.870	17	51	68	112	66	0	31	33	4	171	2.8	13
Mamadou N'diaye(>)	3	7	0	1	.000	0	0	—	0	1	1	0	1	0	0	1	1	0	0.0	0
Dallas	82	19805	3322	7230	.459	1475	1854	.796	1174	2538	3712	1963	1609	16	656	1000	437	8626	105.2	127
Opponents	82	19805	3133	6824	.459	1462	1960	.746	1009	2562	3571	1937	1690	11	582	1242	382	8262	100.8	122

3-pt. FG: Dallas 507-1456 (.348)
Nowitzki 99-290 (.341); Finley 150-370 (.405); Jamison 16-40 (.400); Nash 104-257 (.405); Walker 82-305 (.269); Delk 20-66 (.303)
Howard 20-66 (.303); Daniels 11-36 (.306); Williams(*) 0-1 (.000); Williams(!) 2-3 (.667); Bradley 0-1 (.000); Najera 2-4 (.500)
Best 3-20 (.150); Opponents 534-1471 (.363)

DENVER NUGGETS

	G	Min.	FGM	FGA	Pct.	FTM	FTA	Pct.	Off.	Def.	Tot.	Ast.	PF	Dq.	Stl.	TO	Blk.	Pts.	Avg.	Hi.
Carmelo Anthony	82	2995	624	1465	.426	408	525	.777	183	315	498	227	225	1	97	247	41	1725	21.0	41
Andre Miller	82	2838	430	941	.457	342	411	.832	127	239	366	501	194	2	142	215	25	1214	14.8	30
Voshon Lenard	73	2233	394	933	.422	144	182	.791	46	154	200	151	177	1	61	101	12	1038	14.2	38
Nene Hilario	77	2504	334	630	.530	240	352	.682	154	349	503	168	280	3	116	183	41	908	11.8	25
Earl Boykins	82	1849	321	766	.419	142	162	.877	42	101	143	295	84	0	51	100	3	839	10.2	27
Marcus Camby	72	2162	262	549	.477	98	136	.721	211	516	727	132	239	4	86	98	187	622	8.6	23
Rodney White	72	985	215	468	.459	78	104	.750	44	121	165	60	105	0	32	78	20	541	7.5	24
Jon Barry	57	1101	120	297	.404	60	71	.845	25	98	123	147	66	0	57	53	8	351	6.2	20
Michael Doleac(*)	26	344	40	97	.412	14	16	.875	28	48	76	14	58	0	6	11	6	94	3.6	10
Michael Doleac(!)	72	1029	140	322	.435	45	52	.865	88	177	265	44	142	1	23	48	36	325	4.5	18
Francisco Elson	62	875	94	199	.472	30	45	.667	65	138	203	32	145	2	35	35	39	218	3.5	16
Chris Andersen	71	1029	90	203	.443	63	107	.589	89	209	298	35	119	0	34	48	114	243	3.4	15
Nikoloz Tskitishvili	39	307	40	122	.328	23	29	.793	24	39	63	10	50	0	6	17	8	106	2.7	14
Jeff Trepagnier	11	96	10	38	.263	3	6	.500	6	9	15	4	7	0	3	6	0	25	2.3	11
Ryan Bowen	52	392	18	53	.340	10	12	.833	39	48	87	18	47	0	18	6	16	46	0.9	6
Mark Pope	4	20	1	2	.500	0	1	.000	0	3	3	0	8	0	1	3	0	2	0.5	2
Denver	82	19730	2993	6763	.443	1655	2159	.767	1083	2387	3470	1794	1804	13	745	1278	520	7972	97.2	124
Opponents	82	19730	3019	6662	.453	1470	2020	.728	1056	2465	3521	1931	1895	16	664	1399	479	7884	96.1	120

3-pt. FG: Denver 331-985 (.336)
Anthony 69-214 (.322); Miller 12-65 (.185); Lenard 106-289 (.367); Hilario 0-2 (.000); Boykins 55-171 (.322); Camby 0-2 (.000)
White 33-87 (.379); Barry 51-138 (.370); Elson 0-1 (.000); Andersen 0-1 (.000); Tskitishvili 3-11 (.273); Trepagnier 2-4 (.500)
Opponents 376-1056 (.356)

DETROIT PISTONS

	G	Min.	FGM	FGA	Pct.	FTM	FTA	Pct.	Off.	Def.	Tot.	Ast.	PF	Dq.	Stl.	TO	Blk.	Pts.	Avg.	Hi.
Richard Hamilton	78	2772	530	1166	.455	297	342	.868	78	201	279	310	222	3	103	210	17	1375	17.6	44
Chauncey Billups	78	2758	392	996	.394	404	460	.878	35	241	276	446	177	2	84	189	8	1318	16.9	33
Rasheed Wallace(*)	22	673	121	281	.431	38	54	.704	32	123	155	40	59	0	24	29	45	302	13.7	27
Rasheed Wallace(!)	68	2390	425	974	.436	156	212	.736	102	357	459	156	190	1	61	119	122	1088	16.0	31
Tayshaun Prince	82	2701	338	723	.467	108	141	.766	93	297	390	191	149	0	63	119	69	841	10.3	25
Mehmet Okur	71	1580	251	542	.463	162	209	.775	160	261	421	69	138	0	36	101	63	682	9.6	27
Ben Wallace	81	3050	315	748	.421	142	290	.490	324	682	1006	138	162	0	143	123	246	773	9.5	30
Corliss Williamson	79	1574	304	602	.505	144	197	.731	88	168	256	57	204	2	30	113	20	752	9.5	22
Mike James(*)	26	512	59	147	.401	27	32	.844	8	50	58	95	43	0	26	41	1	165	6.3	21

	G	Min.	FGM	FGA	Pct.	FTM	FTA	Pct.	Off.	Def.	Tot.	Ast.	PF	Dq.	Stl.	TO	Blk.	Pts.	Avg.	Hi.
									REBOUNDS									**SCORING**		
Mike James(!)	81	2196	272	657	.414	103	127	.811	28	206	234	339	156	0	96	124	3	753	9.3	24
Chucky Atkins(>)	40	751	88	235	.374	31	43	.721	6	42	48	95	60	0	19	48	1	249	6.2	19
Elden Campbell	65	892	138	314	.439	85	124	.685	52	157	209	45	137	0	21	63	50	361	5.6	13
Bob Sura(>)	53	707	71	173	.410	48	69	.696	30	73	103	89	86	0	37	39	9	199	3.8	13
Lindsey Hunter	33	661	49	143	.343	5	8	.625	13	54	67	85	45	0	39	34	6	117	3.5	13
Zeljko Rebraca(>)	21	222	22	54	.407	22	28	.786	19	30	49	4	45	0	5	13	9	66	3.1	10
Darvin Ham	54	484	37	75	.493	21	35	.600	47	46	93	16	63	0	13	31	8	96	1.8	11
Darko Milicic	34	159	17	65	.262	14	24	.583	11	32	43	7	33	0	7	13	15	48	1.4	6
Tremaine Fowlkes	36	261	15	48	.313	13	18	.722	18	35	53	14	37	0	9	12	3	44	1.2	8
Hubert Davis(>)	3	23	0	2	.000	0	0	—	0	0	0	1	4	0	1	0	0	0	0.0	0
Detroit	82	19780	2747	6314	.435	1561	2074	.753	1014	2492	3506	1702	1664	7	659	1241	570	7388	90.1	115
Opponents	82	19780	2633	6378	.413	1287	1730	.744	980	2353	3333	1561	1877	21	649	1310	410	6909	84.3	111

3-pt. FG: Detroit 333-968 (.344)
Hamilton 18-68 (.265); Billups 130-335 (.388); R. Wallace(*) 22-69 (.319); R. Wallace(!) 82-248 (.331); Prince 57-157 (.363)
Okur 18-48 (.375); B. Wallace 1-8 (.125); James(*) 20-55 (.364); James(!) 106-281 (.377); Atkins(>) 42-130 (.323); Ham 1-2 (.500)
Sura(>) 9-36 (.250); Hunter 14-50 (.280); Milicic 0-1 (.000); Fowlkes 1-8 (.125); Davis(>) 0-1 (.000); Opponents 356-1180 (.302)

GOLDEN STATE WARRIORS

	G	Min.	FGM	FGA	Pct.	FTM	FTA	Pct.	Off.	Def.	Tot.	Ast.	PF	Dq.	Stl.	TO	Blk.	Pts.	Avg.	Hi.
									REBOUNDS									**SCORING**		
Jason Richardson	78	2936	563	1284	.438	258	377	.684	124	400	524	226	182	1	86	196	41	1461	18.7	35
Nick Van Exel	39	1255	187	479	.390	70	99	.707	16	88	104	206	57	0	20	78	2	490	12.6	29
Erick Dampier	74	2403	348	650	.535	217	332	.654	344	543	887	60	227	3	33	131	137	913	12.3	26
Clifford Robinson	82	2846	366	945	.387	123	173	.711	54	268	322	271	237	2	68	173	73	967	11.8	35
Mike Dunleavy	75	2336	323	720	.449	137	185	.741	87	355	442	220	169	2	68	143	13	877	11.7	32
Speedy Claxton	60	1595	224	524	.427	182	224	.813	38	118	156	267	146	2	97	102	9	634	10.6	28
Troy Murphy	28	610	107	243	.440	60	80	.750	48	125	173	20	58	1	12	34	17	279	10.0	32
Brian Cardinal	76	1634	220	466	.472	238	271	.878	100	217	317	103	206	4	66	84	20	733	9.6	32
Calbert Cheaney	79	2067	278	578	.481	47	77	.610	77	183	260	136	184	1	60	85	12	603	7.6	24
Mickael Pietrus	53	748	96	231	.416	52	75	.693	48	71	119	27	100	1	32	40	12	279	5.3	20
Avery Johnson	46	637	80	199	.402	52	78	.667	3	30	33	111	34	0	26	51	3	212	4.6	16
Sean Lampley	10	63	13	20	.650	8	12	.667	2	9	11	2	2	0	0	3	1	34	3.4	14
J.R. Bremer(*)	5	40	4	21	.190	0	0	—	2	1	3	12	5	0	0	5	0	8	1.6	4
J.R. Bremer(!)	36	443	43	158	.272	13	20	.650	9	27	36	51	32	0	18	24	4	118	3.3	20
Adonal Foyle	44	572	59	130	.454	19	35	.543	54	113	167	17	68	1	6	21	46	137	3.1	20
Dan Langhi(>)	4	17	2	6	.333	2	2	1.000	0	3	3	0	5	0	0	2	0	6	1.5	4
Rusty LaRue	4	22	1	3	.333	1	2	.500	0	3	3	2	2	0	2	4	0	4	1.0	3
Cherokee Parks	12	64	4	10	.400	4	6	.667	4	6	10	1	7	0	0	2	3	12	1.0	4
Popeye Jones	5	10	0	2	.000	0	0	—	1	0	1	0	2	0	0	0	0	0	0.0	0
Golden State	82	19855	2875	6511	.442	1470	2028	.725	1002	2533	3535	1681	1691	14	576	1211	389	7649	93.3	119
Opponents	82	19855	2948	6630	.445	1399	1875	.746	981	2532	3513	1762	1801	16	666	1145	418	7709	94.0	119

3-pt. FG: Golden State 429-1283 (.334)
Richardson 77-273 (.282); Van Exel 46-150 (.307); Dampier 0-2 (.000); Robinson 112-314 (.357); Dunleavy 94-254 (.370)
Claxton 4-22 (.182); Murphy 5-17 (.294); Cardinal 55-124 (.444); Cheaney 0-10 (.000); Pietrus 35-105 (.333); Johnson 0-3 (.000)
Bremer(*) 0-8 (.000); Bremer(!) 19-74 (.257); LaRue 1-1 (1.000); Opponents 414-1107 (.374)

HOUSTON ROCKETS

	G	Min.	FGM	FGA	Pct.	FTM	FTA	Pct.	Off.	Def.	Tot.	Ast.	PF	Dq.	Stl.	TO	Blk.	Pts.	Avg.	Hi.
									REBOUNDS									**SCORING**		
Yao Ming	82	2692	535	1025	.522	361	446	.809	197	538	735	122	273	4	22	204	156	1431	17.5	41
Steve Francis	79	3194	450	1117	.403	337	435	.775	116	317	433	493	257	3	139	294	35	1310	16.6	33
Cuttino Mobley	80	3229	460	1081	.426	176	217	.811	40	322	362	258	179	0	107	180	33	1260	15.8	32
Jim Jackson	80	3119	382	900	.424	107	127	.843	52	435	487	226	227	1	86	175	23	1033	12.9	28
Maurice Taylor	75	2081	367	765	.480	128	174	.736	131	253	384	107	253	5	43	149	47	862	11.5	25
Kelvin Cato	69	1743	161	360	.447	96	142	.676	153	319	472	72	203	0	52	84	96	418	6.1	16
Clarence Weatherspoo(*)	37	652	86	171	.503	35	53	.660	60	94	154	17	56	0	22	26	13	207	5.6	16
Clarence Weatherspoo(!)	52	868	104	211	.493	53	72	.736	74	130	204	30	75	0	30	35	15	261	5.0	16
Eric Piatkowski	49	703	72	191	.377	14	16	.875	10	63	73	26	42	0	16	29	5	201	4.1	14
Scott Padgett	58	547	74	167	.443	24	32	.750	46	93	139	23	73	0	12	22	13	200	3.4	18
Torraye Braggs(>)	11	132	13	28	.464	8	12	.667	15	19	34	6	21	0	4	12	2	34	3.1	6
Bostjan Nachbar	45	516	47	132	.356	21	29	.724	8	62	70	30	72	1	14	23	14	138	3.1	12
Moochie Norris(>)	30	401	27	87	.310	18	24	.750	2	28	30	48	16	0	16	30	2	80	2.7	8
Mark Jackson	42	577	34	100	.340	28	39	.718	10	60	70	119	41	0	17	53	1	103	2.5	25
Mike Wilks	26	145	17	36	.472	10	12	.833	3	13	16	17	15	0	3	7	0	50	1.9	13
Alton Ford	9	41	6	11	.545	3	6	.500	3	8	11	3	9	0	0	3	1	15	1.7	7
Charles Oakley	7	25	2	6	.333	5	6	.833	0	5	5	2	8	0	0	1	0	9	1.3	4
Adrian Griffin	19	133	5	18	.278	0	4	.000	1	18	19	10	17	0	7	3	2	11	0.6	3
Houston	82	19930	2738	6195	.442	1371	1774	.773	847	2647	3494	1579	1762	14	560	1373	443	7362	89.8	123
Opponents	82	19930	2636	6405	.412	1491	2024	.737	907	2351	3258	1689	1695	16	710	1103	359	7220	88.0	121

3-pt. FG: Houston 515-1406 (.366)
Yao 0-2 (.000); Francis 73-250 (.292); Mobley 164-420 (.390); J. Jackson 162-405 (.400); Taylor 0-2 (.000); Padgett 28-65 (.431)
Weatherspoon(*) 0-1 (.000); Weatherspoon(!) 0-1 (.000); Piatkowski 43-122 (.352); Nachbar 23-63 (.365); Norris(>) 8-23 (.348)
M. Jackson 7-41 (.171); Wilks 6-10 (.600); Griffin 1-2 (.500); Opponents 457-1227 (.372)

INDIANA PACERS

	G	Min.	FGM	FGA	Pct.	FTM	FTA	Pct.	Off.	Def.	Tot.	Ast.	PF	Dq.	Stl.	TO	Blk.	Pts.	Avg.	Hi.
Jermaine O'Neal	78	2788	608	1400	.434	348	460	.757	193	585	778	164	248	2	59	181	199	1566	20.1	34
Ron Artest	73	2714	468	1112	.421	322	439	.733	100	285	385	272	194	2	152	202	50	1333	18.3	35
Al Harrington	79	2441	421	909	.463	185	252	.734	163	345	508	131	250	1	80	163	22	1048	13.3	27
Reggie Miller	80	2254	260	594	.438	146	165	.885	18	170	188	249	96	0	65	68	11	800	10.0	31
Jamaal Tinsley	52	1378	153	370	.414	49	67	.731	28	108	136	303	132	2	84	110	17	432	8.3	19
Jonathan Bender	21	271	50	106	.472	39	47	.830	9	31	40	9	23	0	5	33	11	148	7.0	16
Anthony Johnson	73	1598	167	411	.406	75	94	.798	28	102	130	202	138	0	64	75	8	450	6.2	21
Jeff Foster	82	1961	197	362	.544	103	154	.669	248	362	610	64	189	1	71	60	27	497	6.1	19
Kenny Anderson	44	905	113	256	.441	35	48	.729	19	62	81	125	73	0	26	50	5	262	6.0	14
Austin Croshere	77	1051	119	307	.388	93	104	.894	60	183	243	52	101	0	24	55	14	387	5.0	16
Fred Jones	81	1508	123	311	.395	124	149	.832	25	101	126	173	132	0	65	73	18	397	4.9	18
Jamison Brewer	13	160	13	35	.371	1	6	.167	2	9	11	17	9	0	7	10	0	32	2.5	12
Scot Pollard	61	678	47	114	.412	12	21	.571	67	97	164	10	110	0	23	22	26	106	1.7	8
Primoz Brezec	18	72	12	26	.462	4	6	.667	5	10	15	3	13	0	0	6	3	28	1.6	5
James Jones	6	26	2	9	.222	2	2	1.000	0	2	2	0	1	0	1	0	0	7	1.2	3
Indiana	82	19805	2753	6322	.435	1538	2014	.764	965	2452	3417	1774	1709	8	726	1182	411	7493	91.4	114
Opponents	82	19805	2671	6180	.432	1350	1800	.750	867	2423	3290	1649	1794	18	582	1301	512	7021	85.6	107

3-pt. FG: Indiana 449-1281 (.351)
O'Neal 2-18 (.111); Artest 75-242 (.310); Harrington 21-77 (.273); Miller 134-334 (.401); Tinsley 77-207 (.372); Foster 0-4 (.000)
Bender 9-22 (.409); Johnson 41-122 (.336); Anderson 1-4 (.250); Croshere 56-144 (.389); F. Jones 27-89 (.303); Brewer 5-14 (.357)
J. Jones 1-4 (.250); Opponents 329-1014 (.324)

LOS ANGELES CLIPPERS

	G	Min.	FGM	FGA	Pct.	FTM	FTA	Pct.	Off.	Def.	Tot.	Ast.	PF	Dq.	Stl.	TO	Blk.	Pts.	Avg.	Hi.
Corey Maggette	73	2628	453	1013	.447	526	620	.848	96	334	430	224	217	2	65	207	16	1508	20.7	34
Elton Brand	69	2670	484	982	.493	411	532	.773	269	445	714	227	229	1	64	193	154	1379	20.0	39
Quentin Richardson	65	2338	425	1068	.398	204	740	.146	146	268	414	139	130	0	67	141	19	1121	17.2	44
Chris Wilcox	65	1340	227	436	.521	105	150	.700	125	180	305	51	183	4	29	80	20	559	8.6	24
Marko Jaric	58	1760	185	477	.388	74	101	.733	44	131	175	281	132	1	93	115	20	495	8.5	23
Bobby Simmons	56	1376	147	373	.394	141	169	.834	115	147	262	96	169	2	51	73	17	437	7.8	24
Eddie House	60	1188	161	449	.359	36	45	.800	28	110	138	148	92	1	65	63	4	409	6.8	22
Predrag Drobnjak	61	949	149	379	.393	73	86	.849	54	142	196	39	85	1	22	48	24	382	6.3	24
Keyon Dooling	58	1137	137	352	.389	78	94	.830	17	62	79	130	108	2	45	65	6	360	6.2	20
Chris Kaman	82	1843	200	435	.460	99	142	.697	126	335	461	85	211	1	23	155	73	499	6.1	19
Matt Barnes	38	724	63	138	.457	43	61	.705	53	98	151	48	76	0	27	44	3	171	4.5	14
Melvin Ely	42	510	66	153	.431	25	42	.595	48	53	101	22	68	0	9	20	17	157	3.7	15
Doug Overton(*)	55	1011	96	237	.405	21	29	.724	16	69	85	134	85	1	25	56	2	216	3.9	16
Doug Overton(!)	61	1033	99	245	.404	23	31	.742	16	70	86	138	89	1	26	58	2	224	3.7	16
Glen Rice	18	262	22	76	.289	17	17	1.000	9	32	41	24	22	0	6	13	0	66	3.7	11
Randy Livingston	4	48	2	10	.200	4	6	.667	2	5	7	4	7	0	2	4	0	8	2.0	6
Zhizhi Wang(>)	2	9	0	1	.000	4	4	1.000	0	4	4	0	0	0	0	0	1	4	2.0	2
Olden Polynice	2	12	0	0	—	0	0	—	1	1	2	1	2	0	1	4	0	0	0.0	0
L.A. Clippers	82	19805	2817	6579	.428	1808	2302	.785	1149	2416	3565	1653	1816	16	594	1344	376	7771	94.8	120
Opponents	82	19805	3075	6687	.460	1545	2086	.741	1033	2358	3391	1874	1861	11	693	1122	437	8147	99.4	125

3-pt. FG: L.A. Clippers 329-1024 (.321)
Maggette 76-231 (.329); Brand 0-1 (.000); Richardson 120-341 (.352); Wilcox 0-1 (.000); Jaric 51-150 (.340); Simmons 2-12 (.167)
House 51-136 (.375); Drobnjak 11-36 (.306); Dooling 8-46 (.174); Kaman 0-2 (.000); Barnes 2-13 (.154); Ely 0-1 (.000)
Overton(*) 3-23 (.130); Overton(!) 3-23 (.130); Rice 5-28 (.179); Livingston 0-3 (.000); Opponents 452-1256 (.360)

LOS ANGELES LAKERS

	G	Min.	FGM	FGA	Pct.	FTM	FTA	Pct.	Off.	Def.	Tot.	Ast.	PF	Dq.	Stl.	TO	Blk.	Pts.	Avg.	Hi.
Kobe Bryant	65	2447	516	1178	.438	454	533	.852	103	256	359	330	176	0	112	171	28	1557	24.0	45
Shaquille O'Neal	67	2464	554	948	.584	331	676	.490	246	523	769	196	225	3	34	195	166	1439	21.5	37
Gary Payton	82	2825	482	1024	.471	180	252	.714	72	270	342	449	169	0	96	151	19	1199	14.6	30
Karl Malone	42	1373	193	400	.483	168	225	.747	61	306	367	163	116	1	50	103	20	554	13.2	20
Slava Medvedenko	68	1442	237	537	.441	89	116	.767	148	195	343	57	191	1	38	59	18	563	8.3	26
Devean George	71	1951	233	571	.408	73	96	.760	87	245	332	112	189	4	81	88	38	604	7.4	24
Derek Fisher	82	1769	203	576	.352	122	153	.797	30	122	152	187	115	0	103	79	4	580	7.1	18
Kareem Rush	72	1244	190	432	.440	31	52	.596	20	77	97	59	109	0	33	48	20	459	6.4	30
Maurice Carter(>)	4	50	5	14	.357	11	12	.917	0	3	3	2	5	0	0	6	0	22	5.5	9
Rick Fox	38	846	73	186	.392	22	30	.733	29	73	102	98	99	2	29	48	4	183	4.8	11
Brian Cook	35	442	67	141	.475	21	28	.750	31	70	101	20	64	0	16	17	16	155	4.4	16
Horace Grant	55	1106	92	224	.411	39	54	.722	79	154	233	71	70	1	24	29	21	223	4.1	14
Bryon Russell	72	945	98	244	.402	50	65	.769	32	114	146	71	110	0	32	37	12	289	4.0	17
Jamal Sampson	10	130	11	23	.478	7	12	.583	23	29	52	7	16	0	2	6	4	29	2.9	9
Luke Walton	72	730	65	153	.425	31	44	.705	39	88	127	113	70	1	28	44	8	174	2.4	9
Ime Udoka	4	28	3	9	.333	2	4	.500	1	4	5	2	3	0	2	3	1	8	2.0	4
Jannero Pargo(>)	13	63	6	16	.375	0	0	—	0	6	6	11	5	0	2	12	0	14	1.1	5
L.A. Lakers	82	19855	3028	6676	.454	1631	2352	.693	1001	2535	3536	1948	1732	13	682	1132	379	8052	98.2	122
Opponents	82	19855	2920	6640	.440	1472	1964	.749	922	2558	3480	1708	2024	25	616	1254	308	7732	94.3	117

3-pt. FG: L.A. Lakers 365-1115 (.327)
Bryant 71-217 (.327); Payton 55-165 (.333); Malone 0-1 (.000); Medvedenko 0-3 (.000); George 65-186 (.349); Fisher 52-179 (.291)
Rush 48-138 (.348); Carter(>) 1-3 (.333); Fox 15-61 (.246); Cook 0-5 (.000); Grant 0-1 (.000); Russell 43-112 (.384)
Walton 13-39 (.333); Udoka 0-1 (.000); Pargo(>) 2-4 (.500); Opponents 420-1247 (.337)

MEMPHIS GRIZZLIES

	G	Min.	FGM	FGA	Pct.	FTM	FTA	Pct.	Off.	Def.	Tot.	Ast.	PF	Dq.	Stl.	TO	Blk.	Pts.	Avg.	Hi.
									REBOUNDS									SCORING		
Pau Gasol 78	78	2458	506	1049	.482	365	511	.714	206	394	600	198	185	1	44	187	132	1381	17.7	37
James Posey 82	82	2451	368	770	.478	278	335	.830	92	311	403	122	248	5	137	112	40	1126	13.7	38
Bonzi Wells(*) 59	59	1468	295	675	.437	117	156	.750	57	142	199	104	159	2	71	129	16	728	12.3	30
Bonzi Wells(!) 72	72	1872	363	850	.427	138	183	.754	78	182	260	139	197	2	91	161	19	886	12.3	30
Mike Miller 65	65	1770	270	616	.438	102	141	.723	42	174	216	232	162	3	59	107	14	722	11.1	27
Jason Williams 72	72	2115	290	713	.407	82	98	.837	25	122	147	492	97	0	92	136	5	782	10.9	28
Stromile Swift 77	77	1528	268	571	.469	190	262	.725	141	237	378	38	188	4	56	88	118	727	9.4	24
Lorenzen Wright 65	65	1674	257	586	.439	96	131	.733	144	301	445	71	192	4	45	77	58	610	9.4	21
Shane Battier 79	79	1947	242	543	.446	120	164	.732	102	201	303	101	187	1	101	56	58	669	8.5	22
Earl Watson 81	81	1669	172	464	.371	90	138	.652	49	129	178	402	175	3	91	146	19	460	5.7	20
Wesley Person(>) . . 16	16	284	33	107	.308	6	8	.750	2	16	18	23	11	0	5	16	2	83	5.2	12
Bo Outlaw 82	82	1606	159	312	.510	61	116	.526	125	217	342	90	170	0	73	69	70	379	4.6	15
Jake Tsakalidis 40	40	533	67	133	.504	36	61	.590	37	91	128	18	79	1	9	23	22	170	4.3	15
Theron Smith 20	20	178	16	43	.372	6	8	.750	13	28	41	7	18	0	5	14	5	44	2.2	7
Troy Bell 6	6	34	4	18	.222	3	3	1.000	3	1	4	4	6	0	1	6	0	11	1.8	5
Dahntay Jones 20	20	154	15	53	.283	5	11	.455	7	16	23	12	23	0	5	12	6	36	1.8	7
Ryan Humphrey 2	2	11	1	4	.250	0	0	—	2	1	3	1	3	0	1	2	0	2	1.0	2
Memphis 82	82	19880	2963	6657	.445	1557	2143	.727	1047	2381	3428	1915	1903	24	795	1226	565	7930	96.7	136
Opponents 82	82	19880	2859	6550	.436	1643	2150	.764	1099	2508	3607	1674	1891	26	673	1395	461	7730	94.3	133

3-pt. FG: Memphis 447-1314 (.340)
Gasol 4-15 (.267); Posey 112-290 (.386); Wells(*) 21-61 (.344); Wells(!) 22-69 (.319); Miller 80-215 (.372); Swift 1-4 (.250)
Williams 120-364 (.330); Wright 0-5 (.000); Battier 65-186 (.349); Watson 26-106 (.245); Person(>) 11-43 (.256); Outlaw 0-4 (.000)
Smith 6-12 (.500); Bell 0-4 (.000); Jones 1-4 (.250); Humphrey 0-1 (.000); Opponents 369-1091 (.338)

MIAMI HEAT

	G	Min.	FGM	FGA	Pct.	FTM	FTA	Pct.	Off.	Def.	Tot.	Ast.	PF	Dq.	Stl.	TO	Blk.	Pts.	Avg.	Hi.
									REBOUNDS									SCORING		
Eddie Jones 81	81	2998	473	1156	.409	278	333	.835	38	270	308	258	226	2	92	129	34	1401	17.3	33
Lamar Odom 80	80	3003	485	1127	.430	340	458	.742	160	616	776	327	273	5	85	236	71	1371	17.1	30
Dwyane Wade 61	61	2126	371	798	.465	233	312	.747	85	162	247	275	140	0	86	196	34	991	16.2	33
Rafer Alston 82	82	2581	287	764	.376	103	134	.769	26	200	226	372	212	1	114	128	18	838	10.2	23
Caron Butler 68	68	2030	240	631	.380	133	176	.756	92	234	326	126	162	0	75	91	13	623	9.2	30
Brian Grant 76	76	2303	289	613	.471	86	110	.782	174	350	524	69	254	4	51	82	35	664	8.7	19
Udonis Haslem 75	75	1795	205	447	.459	140	183	.765	189	284	473	51	197	2	33	74	24	550	7.3	20
Rasual Butler 45	45	675	119	250	.476	16	21	.762	4	57	61	23	72	0	10	28	13	304	6.8	20
John Wallace 37	37	368	61	145	.421	31	40	.775	12	47	59	14	38	0	5	24	8	158	4.3	19
Malik Allen 45	45	616	83	198	.419	25	33	.758	42	77	119	16	81	0	12	27	28	191	4.2	14
Loren Woods 38	38	506	44	96	.458	33	55	.600	65	69	134	10	52	0	11	26	19	121	3.2	12
Samaki Walker 33	33	418	38	99	.384	29	44	.659	42	70	112	6	54	0	9	15	11	105	3.2	9
Zhizhi Wang(*) 14	14	105	17	45	.378	5	6	.833	4	10	14	2	13	0	3	6	4	43	3.1	11
Zhizhi Wang(!) 16	16	114	17	46	.370	9	10	.900	4	14	18	2	13	0	3	6	5	47	2.9	11
Tyrone Hill 5	5	38	3	5	.600	3	4	.750	5	3	8	0	10	0	0	2	1	9	1.8	9
Kirk Penney 2	2	18	1	6	.167	0	0	—	0	1	1	1	1	0	1	3	0	3	1.5	3
Bimbo Coles 22	22	170	12	34	.353	4	6	.667	2	8	10	15	27	0	3	9	0	28	1.3	4
Jerome Beasley 2	2	5	1	3	.333	0	0	—	0	1	1	0	0	0	0	0	0	2	1.0	2
Miami 82	82	19755	2729	6417	.425	1459	1915	.762	940	2459	3399	1565	1812	14	590	1137	313	7402	90.3	125
Opponents 82	82	19755	2658	6205	.428	1612	2100	.768	892	2486	3378	1526	1729	14	578	1207	439	7359	89.7	118

3-pt. FG: Miami 485-1357 (.357)
Jones 177-479 (.370); Odom 61-205 (.298); Wade 16-53 (.302); Alston 161-434 (.371); C. Butler 10-42 (.238); Grant 0-1 (.000)
Haslem 0-3 (.000); R. Butler 50-108 (.463); Wallace 5-13 (.385); Walker 0-2 (.000); Wang(*) 4-14 (.286); Wang(!) 4-14 (.286)
Penney 1-3 (.333); Opponents 431-1256 (.343)

MILWAUKEE BUCKS

	G	Min.	FGM	FGA	Pct.	FTM	FTA	Pct.	Off.	Def.	Tot.	Ast.	PF	Dq.	Stl.	TO	Blk.	Pts.	Avg.	Hi.
									REBOUNDS									SCORING		
Michael Redd 82	82	3021	633	1439	.440	383	441	.868	118	289	407	185	152	0	81	116	6	1776	21.7	40
Keith Van Horn(*) 25	25	766	137	290	.472	86	91	.945	51	107	158	37	64	2	16	50	15	393	15.7	32
Keith Van Horn(!) . . . 72	72	2340	410	903	.454	249	290	.859	149	352	501	120	215	6	68	169	33	1162	16.1	32
Desmond Mason 82	82	2534	409	867	.472	356	463	.769	93	266	359	152	191	2	60	148	24	1183	14.4	27
Tim Thomas(>) 42	42	1343	226	510	.443	93	122	.762	38	167	205	90	127	3	40	73	15	592	14.1	25
Joe Smith 76	76	2254	311	708	.439	207	241	.859	230	413	643	78	209	1	47	82	94	830	10.9	25
Brian Skinner 56	56	1577	255	513	.497	79	138	.572	119	292	411	49	165	3	30	78	61	589	10.5	21
Toni Kukoc 73	73	1522	211	506	.417	145	199	.729	60	211	271	200	110	0	59	110	21	616	8.4	24
T.J. Ford 55	55	1472	153	398	.384	80	98	.816	37	140	177	356	123	0	60	139	3	391	7.1	17
Damon Jones 82	82	2016	210	524	.401	55	72	.764	15	155	170	478	92	0	30	103	4	573	7.0	23
Dan Gadzuric 75	75	1260	183	349	.524	58	118	.492	126	220	346	28	186	0	51	45	105	424	5.7	19
Erick Strickland 43	43	571	79	196	.403	44	51	.863	13	58	71	90	63	0	26	54	2	231	5.4	16
Brevin Knight(*) 21	21	420	46	105	.438	30	38	.789	3	45	48	98	56	1	29	25	0	123	5.9	12
Brevin Knight(!) 56	56	1037	105	246	.427	49	65	.754	14	98	112	204	107	1	84	72	1	261	4.7	13
Daniel Santiago 54	54	708	78	163	.479	61	90	.678	35	97	132	24	98	0	19	32	21	217	4.0	13
Marcus Haislip 31	31	263	36	74	.486	20	28	.714	21	32	53	4	25	0	6	9	12	93	3.0	13
Dan Langhi(*) 2	2	20	3	8	.375	0	0	—	0	1	1	0	2	0	0	0	0	7	3.5	5
Dan Langhi(!) 6	6	37	5	14	.357	2	2	1.000	0	4	4	0	7	0	0	2	0	13	2.2	5
Joel Przybilla(>) 5	5	33	0	0	—	1	2	.500	1	9	10	3	5	0	0	2	0	1	0.2	1

	G	Min.	FGM	FGA	Pct.	FTM	FTA	Pct.	REBOUNDS Off.	Def.	Tot.	Ast.	PF	Dq.	Stl.	TO	Blk.	SCORING Pts.	Avg.	Hi.
Milwaukee	82	19780	2970	6650	.447	1698	2192	.775	960	2502	3462	1872	1668	12	554	1110	383	8039	98.0	127
Opponents	82	19780	3034	6719	.452	1428	1932	.739	983	2521	3504	1870	1878	14	615	1164	406	7952	97.0	124

3-pt. FG: Milwaukee 401-1145 (.350).
Redd 127-363 (.350); Van Horn(*) 33-72 (.458); Van Horn(!) 93-233 (.399); Mason 9-39 (.231); Thomas(>) 47-130 (.362)
Smith 1-5 (.200); Kukoc 49-168 (.292); Ford 5-21 (.238); Jones 98-273 (.359); Gadzuric 0-1 (.000); Strickland 29-66 (.439)
Knight(*) 1-3 (.333); Knight(!) 2-8 (.250); Haislip 1-2 (.500); Langhi(*) 1-2 (.500); Langhi(!) 1-2 (.500)
Opponents 456-1296 (.352)

MINNESOTA TIMBERWOLVES

	G	Min.	FGM	FGA	Pct.	FTM	FTA	Pct.	REBOUNDS Off.	Def.	Tot.	Ast.	PF	Dq.	Stl.	TO	Blk.	SCORING Pts.	Avg.	Hi.
Kevin Garnett	82	3231	804	1611	.499	368	465	.791	245	894	1139	409	202	1	120	212	178	1987	24.2	35
Sam Cassell	81	2838	620	1270	.488	289	331	.873	44	227	271	592	247	2	102	220	18	1603	19.8	36
Latrell Sprewell	82	3100	518	1266	.409	240	295	.814	56	254	310	286	101	0	88	158	21	1375	16.8	37
Wally Szczerbiak	28	622	106	236	.449	53	64	.828	24	64	88	33	42	0	12	28	1	285	10.2	24
Troy Hudson	29	503	80	207	.386	27	33	.818	4	31	35	70	32	0	7	34	0	218	7.5	29
Fred Hoiberg	79	1804	178	383	.465	98	116	.845	21	247	268	109	136	0	66	44	10	530	6.7	21
Michael Olowokandi	43	925	121	285	.425	36	61	.590	78	167	245	24	137	3	16	54	68	278	6.5	14
Gary Trent	68	1025	155	328	.473	69	91	.758	83	133	216	49	129	2	12	54	17	379	5.6	22
Trenton Hassell	81	2264	177	381	.465	48	61	.787	68	189	257	133	200	1	36	46	54	406	5.0	15
Mark Madsen	72	1246	101	204	.495	57	118	.483	134	138	272	28	175	2	33	47	18	259	3.6	11
Darrick Martin	16	172	20	67	.299	9	9	1.000	2	5	7	23	23	0	2	7	1	55	3.4	11
Keith McLeod	33	391	27	82	.329	33	43	.767	5	29	34	59	39	0	16	29	1	88	2.7	7
Anthony Goldwire(>)	5	66	5	14	.357	1	1	1.000	1	5	6	10	5	0	3	2	0	13	2.6	5
Oliver Miller	48	506	53	100	.530	15	23	.652	46	84	130	36	91	0	19	33	26	121	2.5	9
Ervin Johnson	66	965	55	103	.534	17	28	.607	61	171	232	24	156	1	27	30	43	127	1.9	10
Quincy Lewis	14	65	7	20	.350	0	0	—	1	6	7	2	10	0	2	3	2	16	1.1	5
Ndudi Ebi	17	32	6	14	.429	1	4	.250	2	1	3	3	6	0	0	4	3	13	0.8	4
Minnesota	82	19755	3033	6571	.462	1361	1743	.781	875	2645	3520	1890	1731	12	561	1043	462	7753	94.5	121
Opponents	82	19755	2741	6625	.414	1426	1893	.753	1001	2400	3401	1701	1656	12	547	1106	296	7303	89.1	125

3-pt. FG: Minnesota 326-897 (.363)
Garnett 11-43 (.256); Cassell 74-186 (.398); Sprewell 99-299 (.331); Szczerbiak 20-46 (.435); Hudson 31-77 (.403)
Hoiberg 76-172 (.442); Trent 0-6 (.000); Hassell 4-13 (.308); Madsen 0-6 (.000); Martin 6-26 (.231); McLeod 1-10 (.100)
Goldwire(>) 2-6 (.333); Miller 0-1 (.000); Johnson 0-1 (.000); Lewis 2-5 (.400); Opponents 395-1181 (.334)

NEW JERSEY NETS

	G	Min.	FGM	FGA	Pct.	FTM	FTA	Pct.	REBOUNDS Off.	Def.	Tot.	Ast.	PF	Dq.	Stl.	TO	Blk.	SCORING Pts.	Avg.	Hi.
Richard Jefferson	82	3133	555	1115	.498	357	468	.763	109	355	464	315	224	1	92	198	28	1515	18.5	35
Kenyon Martin	65	2252	439	900	.488	201	294	.684	133	484	617	160	230	5	95	168	82	1086	16.7	29
Jason Kidd	67	2450	368	959	.384	206	249	.827	85	343	428	618	110	0	122	214	14	1036	15.5	35
Kerry Kittles	82	2842	434	959	.453	107	136	.787	56	271	327	206	144	0	125	95	40	1072	13.1	34
Alonzo Mourning	12	215	33	71	.465	30	34	.882	8	19	27	8	32	0	2	10	6	96	8.0	15
Rodney Rogers	69	1409	207	505	.410	75	98	.765	100	207	307	137	183	2	59	98	27	539	7.8	15
Lucious Harris	69	1504	187	463	.404	66	78	.846	39	101	140	135	74	0	41	53	2	478	6.9	24
Aaron Williams	72	1337	172	342	.503	105	155	.677	101	193	294	81	187	0	34	89	46	450	6.3	17
Jason Collins	78	2220	163	384	.424	136	184	.739	143	257	400	153	251	2	67	97	56	462	5.9	19
Brian Scalabrine	69	928	86	218	.394	58	70	.829	42	131	173	65	113	0	21	42	14	240	3.5	15
Zoran Planinic	49	473	53	129	.411	38	60	.633	14	41	55	68	70	1	13	36	3	153	3.1	14
Brandon Armstrong	56	434	65	175	.371	2	4	.500	12	31	43	14	49	0	12	24	2	151	2.7	14
Tamar Slay	22	165	21	60	.350	7	14	.500	10	15	25	14	20	0	7	11	1	53	2.4	9
Robert Pack	26	220	22	52	.423	5	6	.833	4	14	18	27	20	0	12	16	1	49	1.9	10
Anthony Goldwire(*)	6	19	2	8	.250	0	0	—	0	1	1	1	0	0	2	1	0	4	0.7	4
Anthony Goldwire(!)	11	85	7	22	.318	1	1	1.000	1	6	7	11	5	0	5	3	0	17	1.5	5
Doug Overton(>)	6	22	3	8	.375	2	2	1.000	0	1	1	4	4	0	1	2	0	8	1.3	2
Damone Brown	3	17	1	10	.100	1	2	.500	3	2	5	0	2	0	2	1	0	3	1.0	2
Mikki Moore(>)	4	10	1	5	.200	0	0	—	1	1	2	0	1	0	0	0	0	2	0.5	2
Hubert Davis(*)	14	55	1	9	.111	2	2	1.000	2	6	8	3	8	0	2	2	0	4	0.3	2
Hubert Davis(!)	17	78	1	11	.091	2	2	1.000	2	6	8	4	12	0	2	3	0	4	0.2	2
New Jersey	82	19705	2813	6372	.441	1398	1856	.753	862	2473	3335	2009	1722	11	709	1209	322	7401	90.3	120
Opponents	82	19705	2693	6302	.427	1392	1830	.761	873	2471	3344	1627	1739	15	656	1321	374	7196	87.8	129

3-pt. FG: New Jersey 377-1123 (.336)
Jefferson 48-132 (.364); Martin 7-25 (.280); Kidd 94-293 (.321); Kittles 97-276 (.351); Rogers 50-152 (.329); Harris 38-101 (.376)
Williams 1-3 (.333); Collins 0-2 (.000); Scalabrine 10-41 (.244); Planinic 9-32 (.281); Armstrong 19-52 (.365); Slay 4-12 (.333)
Goldwire(*) 0-2 (.000); Goldwire(!) 2-8 (.250); Davis(!) 0-1 (.000); Opponents 418-1193 (.350)

NEW ORLEANS HORNETS

	G	Min.	FGM	FGA	Pct.	FTM	FTA	Pct.	REBOUNDS Off.	Def.	Tot.	Ast.	PF	Dq.	Stl.	TO	Blk.	SCORING Pts.	Avg.	Hi.
Baron Davis	67	2686	554	1402	.395	237	352	.673	66	221	287	501	178	2	158	215	27	1532	22.9	37
Jamal Mashburn	19	730	156	398	.392	65	80	.813	19	98	117	47	42	0	14	37	5	396	20.8	28
David Wesley	61	2001	311	800	.389	137	182	.753	28	106	134	175	147	1	71	100	14	851	14.0	32
Jamaal Magloire	82	2777	383	809	.473	353	470	.751	268	579	847	86	278	6	43	201	101	1119	13.6	27
Darrell Armstrong	79	2247	291	736	.395	123	144	.854	63	163	226	311	148	1	133	155	16	840	10.6	35
P.J. Brown	80	2753	339	712	.476	158	185	.854	237	453	690	155	203	2	78	101	73	836	10.5	24
Stacey Augmon	60	1416	143	347	.412	110	139	.701	52	122	174	85	114	2	55	76	16	397	6.6	21

	G	Min.	FGM	FGA	Pct.	FTM	FTA	Pct.	Off.	Def.	Tot.	Ast.	PF	Dq.	Stl.	TO	Blk.	Pts.	Avg.	Hi.
Robert Traylor	71	942	145	287	.505	70	128	.547	106	156	262	43	161	3	39	62	37	362	5.1	20
Steve Smith	71	929	119	293	.406	77	83	.928	27	54	81	56	91	0	15	42	6	358	5.0	18
Shammond Williams(*)	16	238	28	81	.346	11	13	.846	0	17	17	52	22	0	14	21	1	72	4.5	14
Shammond Williams(!)	53	763	87	232	.375	51	58	.879	5	51	60	116	62	0	37	47	2	255	4.8	17
George Lynch	78	1701	149	375	.397	34	51	.667	96	216	312	117	159	1	48	64	18	375	4.8	15
Maurice Carter(*)	6	60	6	21	.286	5	8	.625	2	6	8	2	5	0	0	3	0	20	3.3	7
Maurice Carter(!)	10	110	11	35	.314	16	20	.800	2	9	11	4	10	0	0	9	0	42	4.2	9
David West	71	930	108	228	.474	57	80	.713	117	180	297	60	117	0	27	48	28	273	3.8	15
Sean Rooks(>)	35	325	34	94	.362	12	15	.800	10	40	50	11	48	0	9	15	5	80	2.3	7
Tierre Brown	3	17	2	4	.500	2	4	.500	0	1	1	2	1	0	0	7	0	6	2.0	3
Bryce Drew	15	78	4	18	.222	3	3	1.000	0	6	6	13	1	0	4	8	0	12	0.8	5
New Orleans	82	19830	2772	6605	.420	1454	1937	.751	1091	2418	3509	1716	1715	18	708	1228	346	7529	91.8	120
Opponents	82	19830	2843	6443	.441	1407	1877	.750	972	2477	3449	1790	1734	14	613	1282	429	7537	91.9	125

3-pt. FG: New Orleans 531-1666 (.319)
Davis 187-582 (.321); Mashburn 19-67 (.284); Wesley 92-285 (.323); Magloire 0-1 (.000); Armstrong 135-429 (.315); West 0-2 (.000)
P. Brown 0-1 (.000); Augmon 1-7 (.143); Traylor 2-5 (.400); Smith 43-107 (.402); Williams(*) 5-26 (.192); Lynch 43-139 (.309)
Williams(!) 30-100 (.300); Carter(*) 3-8 (.375); Carter(!) 4-11 (.364); Drew 1-7 (.143); Opponents 444-1301 (.341)

NEW YORK KNICKERBOCKERS

	G	Min.	FGM	FGA	Pct.	FTM	FTA	Pct.	Off.	Def.	Tot.	Ast.	PF	Dq.	Stl.	TO	Blk.	Pts.	Avg.	Hi.
Stephon Marbury(*)	47	1839	336	780	.431	209	251	.833	39	107	146	438	98	0	65	152	4	931	19.8	42
Stephon Marbury(!)	81	3254	598	1386	.431	356	436	.817	58	205	263	719	172	0	129	249	9	1639	20.2	42
Allan Houston	50	1799	340	781	.435	157	172	.913	20	101	121	99	105	1	38	102	2	924	18.5	39
Keith Van Horn(>)	47	1574	273	613	.445	163	199	.819	98	245	343	83	151	4	52	119	18	769	16.4	30
Tim Thomas(*)	24	746	137	303	.452	78	96	.813	26	89	115	34	69	1	24	43	5	378	15.8	33
Tim Thomas(!)	66	2089	363	813	.446	171	218	.784	64	256	320	124	196	4	64	116	20	970	14.7	33
Kurt Thomas	80	2548	392	829	.473	106	127	.835	145	517	662	149	298	4	56	132	80	890	11.1	28
Vin Baker(*)	17	313	40	99	.404	32	45	.711	36	34	70	12	62	2	7	25	9	113	6.6	16
Vin Baker(!)	54	1313	208	432	.481	114	157	.726	112	168	280	66	160	3	29	77	32	531	9.8	24
Anfernee Hardaway(*)	42	1219	159	408	.390	69	89	.775	42	147	189	79	81	0	42	65	12	403	9.6	21
Anfernee Hardaway(!)	76	2095	279	679	.411	111	138	.804	69	218	287	176	146	1	70	107	20	699	9.2	22
Charlie Ward(>)	35	827	115	260	.442	16	21	.762	10	86	96	170	74	2	47	69	8	305	8.7	18
Antonio McDyess(>)	18	421	65	142	.458	22	38	.579	31	88	119	20	46	0	12	27	11	152	8.4	19
Shandon Anderson	80	1974	238	564	.422	123	161	.764	53	169	222	122	182	1	68	118	17	635	7.9	28
Nazr Mohammed(*)	27	673	108	192	.563	31	59	.525	77	130	207	16	82	1	33	41	25	247	9.1	20
Nazr Mohammed(!)	80	1611	246	472	.521	100	169	.592	178	296	474	36	195	1	55	96	52	592	7.4	20
Howard Eisley(>)	33	730	80	202	.396	32	36	.889	7	59	66	156	85	1	30	50	3	220	6.7	26
Dikembe Mutombo	65	1494	141	295	.478	81	119	.681	145	292	437	25	141	0	17	54	123	363	5.6	18
DerMarr Johnson	21	287	36	97	.371	28	31	.903	5	34	39	11	32	0	8	16	7	113	5.4	22
Michael Doleac(>)	46	685	100	225	.444	31	36	.861	60	129	189	30	84	1	17	37	30	231	5.0	18
Othella Harrington	56	872	100	202	.495	58	78	.744	58	119	177	29	134	3	12	65	14	258	4.6	14
Michael Sweetney	42	494	69	140	.493	42	58	.724	68	89	157	14	57	0	18	32	12	180	4.3	16
Frank Williams	56	714	80	208	.385	41	48	.854	8	45	53	121	58	0	25	63	6	219	3.9	18
Clarence Weatherspoo(>)	15	216	18	40	.450	18	19	.947	14	36	50	13	19	0	8	9	2	54	3.6	12
Moochie Norris(*)	36	446	53	130	.408	36	47	.766	8	27	35	73	35	0	28	34	3	154	4.3	21
Moochie Norris(!)	66	847	80	217	.369	54	71	.761	10	55	65	121	51	0	44	64	5	234	3.5	21
Bruno Sundov(*)	1	4	1	1	1.000	0	0	—	0	0	0	1	2	0	0	0	0	2	2.0	2
Bruno Sundov(!)	5	33	4	10	.400	3	6	.500	2	8	10	1	9	0	0	3	0	11	2.2	4
Cezary Trybanski(*)	3	5	0	2	.000	1	2	.500	0	0	0	2	0	1	0	0	0	1	0.3	1
Cezary Trybanski(!)	7	15	0	4	.000	2	2	.500	0	1	1	0	3	0	1	2	1	1	0.1	1
New York	82	19880	2881	6513	.442	1374	1732	.793	950	2543	3493	1695	1897	21	608	1289	391	7542	92.0	121
Opponents	82	19880	2785	6491	.429	1678	2198	.763	950	2444	3394	1676	1600	7	675	1132	383	7663	93.5	127

3-pt. FG: New York 406-1115 (.364)
Marbury(*) 50-156 (.321); Marbury(!) 87-274 (.318); Houston 87-202 (.431); Van Horn(>) 60-161 (.373); T. Thomas(*) 26-64 (.406)
T. Thomas(!) 73-194 (.376); K. Thomas 0-3 (.000); Baker(*) 1-2 (.500); Baker(!) 1-3 (.333); Hardaway(*) 16-44 (.364)
Hardaway(!) 30-79 (.380); Ward(>) 59-138 (.428); Anderson 36-128 (.281); Eisley(>) 28-85 (.329); Johnson 13-36 (.361)
Sweetney 0-1 (.000); Williams 18-60 (.300); Norris(*) 12-35 (.343); Norris(!) 20-58 (.345); Opponents 415-1228 (.338)

ORLANDO MAGIC

	G	Min.	FGM	FGA	Pct.	FTM	FTA	Pct.	Off.	Def.	Tot.	Ast.	PF	Dq.	Stl.	TO	Blk.	Pts.	Avg.	Hi.
Tracy McGrady	67	2675	653	1566	.417	398	500	.796	95	307	402	370	129	1	93	179	42	1878	28.0	62
Juwan Howard	81	2877	529	1169	.453	318	393	.809	171	399	570	158	284	1	54	178	22	1376	17.0	38
Drew Gooden	79	2134	369	829	.445	167	262	.637	160	356	516	89	196	2	62	126	72	914	11.6	32
DeShawn Stevenson(*)	26	933	115	285	.404	49	71	.690	36	84	120	66	54	0	24	40	1	291	11.2	21
DeShawn Stevenson(!)	80	2444	376	871	.432	138	204	.676	79	219	298	158	140	0	52	120	17	909	11.4	24
Tyronn Lue	76	2332	309	714	.433	101	131	.771	26	161	187	317	185	0	61	124	5	799	10.5	32
Gordan Giricek(>)	48	1435	188	427	.440	67	81	.827	37	127	164	80	98	0	41	63	10	489	10.2	25
Keith Bogans	73	1787	183	454	.403	65	103	.631	106	211	317	98	128	2	46	75	10	498	6.8	21
Rod Strickland(>)	46	915	122	269	.454	57	76	.750	24	94	118	185	59	0	27	67	7	311	6.8	15
Shammond Williams(>)	37	525	59	151	.391	40	45	.889	9	34	43	64	40	0	23	26	1	183	4.9	17
Donnell Harvey(>)	24	345	36	89	.404	26	39	.667	29	43	72	8	44	0	10	22	11	98	4.1	16
Lee Nailon(>)	8	83	11	27	.407	7	9	.778	8	6	14	4	9	0	1	0	0	29	3.6	12
Zaza Pachulia	59	664	68	175	.389	58	90	.644	69	105	174	13	87	0	21	34	12	194	3.3	14
Andrew DeClercq	71	1211	93	195	.477	44	54	.815	131	186	317	44	217	7	47	54	32	230	3.2	14
Desmond Penigar	10	89	14	28	.500	4	4	1.000	6	18	24	3	14	0	2	6	2	32	3.2	6

	G	Min.	FGM	FGA	Pct.	FTM	FTA	Pct.	Off.	Def.	Tot.	Ast.	PF	Dq.	Stl.	TO	Blk.	Pts.	Avg.	Hi.
Steven Hunter	59	789	82	155	.529	23	69	.333	54	116	170	12	101	0	5	29	73	187	3.2	15
Derrick Dial.........	9	86	9	28	.321	6	8	.750	5	8	13	2	6	0	6	1	0	26	2.9	5
Sean Rooks(*)	20	270	20	57	.351	21	22	.955	14	33	47	18	41	0	5	7	5	61	3.1	7
Sean Rooks(!).......	55	595	54	151	.358	33	37	.892	24	73	97	29	89	0	14	22	10	141	2.6	7
Britton Johnsen	20	290	17	59	.288	7	16	.438	15	30	45	12	28	0	7	14	1	42	2.1	8
Robert Archibald(>) ...	1	4	1	2	.500	0	2	.000	0	1	1	0	0	0	1	0	0	2	2.0	2
Reece Gaines	38	364	25	86	.291	16	25	.640	8	31	39	40	22	0	11	18	2	69	1.8	14
Mengke Bateer(*)....	0	0	0	0	—	0	0	—	0	0	0	0	0	0	0	0	0	0	—	0
Mengke Bateer(!) ...	7	40	4	7	.571	0	0	—	5	3	8	1	10	0	1	2	0	8	1.1	2
Pat Garrity	2	22	1	3	.333	0	0	—	0	0	0	1	2	0	0	0	0	2	1.0	2
Orlando	82	19830	2904	6768	.429	1474	2000	.737	1003	2350	3353	1584	1744	13	547	1123	308	7711	94.0	124
Opponents	82	19830	3169	6804	.466	1458	1964	.742	1072	2570	3642	2004	1691	9	625	1111	450	8287	101.1	127

3-pt. FG: Orlando 429-1248 (.344)
McGrady 174-513 (.339); Howard 0-1 (.000); Gooden 9-42 (.214); Stevenson(*) 12-41 (.293); Stevenson(!) 19-71 (.268)
Lue 80-209 (.383); Giricek(>) 46-113 (.407); Bogans 67-187 (.358); Strickland(>) 10-33 (.303); S. Williams(>) 25-74 (.338)
Harvey(>) 0-3 (.000); Dial 2-9 (.222); Rooks(*) 0-1 (.000); Rooks(!) 0-1 (.000); Johnsen 1-12 (.083); Gaines 3-10 (.300)
Opponents 491-1301 (.377)

PHILADELPHIA 76ERS

	G	Min.	FGM	FGA	Pct.	FTM	FTA	Pct.	Off.	Def.	Tot.	Ast.	PF	Dq.	Stl.	TO	Blk.	Pts.	Avg.	Hi.
Allen Iverson........	48	2040	435	1125	.387	339	455	.745	34	144	178	324	87	0	115	209	5	1266	26.4	50
Glenn Robinson	42	1336	275	614	.448	114	137	.832	46	143	189	57	96	1	42	106	9	698	16.6	34
Kenny Thomas	74	2699	381	813	.469	243	323	.752	261	489	750	111	219	2	82	172	33	1006	13.6	27
Eric Snow..........	82	2966	295	715	.413	252	316	.797	62	219	281	563	213	1	97	187	6	844	10.3	22
Marc Jackson	22	598	71	171	.415	64	81	.790	45	81	126	18	45	0	12	24	6	206	9.4	23
Aaron McKie	75	2112	265	577	.459	84	111	.757	45	208	253	195	142	1	85	103	23	689	9.2	24
Derrick Coleman	34	843	107	259	.413	49	65	.754	45	147	192	46	79	0	23	57	26	271	8.0	20
Samuel Dalembert...	82	2198	270	490	.541	112	174	.644	194	432	626	21	273	4	44	86	189	652	8.0	24
Willie Green	53	767	143	357	.401	59	81	.728	16	49	65	53	83	0	26	59	5	364	6.9	26
John Salmons.......	77	1603	161	416	.387	71	92	.772	38	158	196	134	122	0	62	77	16	443	5.8	22
Kyle Korver........	74	882	115	327	.352	19	24	.792	30	81	111	40	102	2	25	41	8	330	4.5	18
Zendon Hamilton.....	45	472	51	95	.537	67	96	.698	49	97	146	13	74	0	8	27	8	169	3.8	21
Greg Buckner	53	703	66	175	.377	20	27	.741	28	75	103	45	77	0	21	34	4	164	3.1	20
Amal McCaskill......	59	636	47	117	.402	19	27	.704	48	85	133	20	89	0	12	25	20	113	1.9	9
Philadelphia	82	19855	2682	6260	.428	1512	2009	.753	941	2408	3349	1640	1701	11	654	1307	358	7215	88.0	122
Opponents	82	19855	2751	6369	.432	1474	1982	.744	996	2398	3394	1747	1757	21	678	1245	463	7419	90.5	125

3-pt. FG: Philadelphia 339-992 (.342)
Iverson 57-199 (.286); Robinson 34-100 (.340); Thomas 1-5 (.200); Snow 2-18 (.111); Jackson 0-1 (.000); McKie 75-172 (.436)
Coleman 8-36 (.222); Dalembert 0-1 (.000); Green 19-61 (.311); Salmons 50-147 (.340); Korver 81-207 (.391); Buckner 12-44 (.273)
McCaskill 0-1 (.000); Opponents 443-1329 (.333)

PHOENIX SUNS

	G	Min.	FGM	FGA	Pct.	FTM	FTA	Pct.	Off.	Def.	Tot.	Ast.	PF	Dq.	Stl.	TO	Blk.	Pts.	Avg.	Hi.
Stephon Marbury(>) ..	34	1415	262	606	.432	147	185	.795	19	98	117	281	74	0	64	97	5	708	20.8	40
Amare Stoudemire ...	55	2025	411	865	.475	310	435	.713	157	339	496	78	188	5	64	177	89	1133	20.6	33
Shawn Marion	79	3217	590	1341	.440	228	268	.851	212	525	737	214	203	1	167	156	104	1498	19.0	32
Joe Johnson........	82	3331	555	1291	.430	174	232	.750	80	305	385	362	177	1	93	199	26	1367	16.7	31
Anfernee Hardaway(>).	34	876	120	271	.443	42	49	.857	27	71	98	97	65	1	28	42	8	296	8.7	22
Leandro Barbosa ...	70	1500	210	470	.447	47	61	.770	23	100	123	165	184	6	93	120	7	550	7.9	27
Scott Williams(>)	16	267	53	101	.525	9	13	.692	23	49	72	6	45	0	15	6	7	117	7.3	14
Antonio McDyess(*) ..	24	506	61	126	.484	16	31	.516	39	99	138	16	71	5	25	30	13	138	5.8	16
Antonio McDyess(!) ..	42	927	126	268	.470	38	69	.551	70	187	257	36	117	5	37	57	24	290	6.9	19
Howard Eisley(*)....	34	727	86	249	.345	44	53	.830	13	50	63	117	52	0	26	48	2	240	7.1	16
Howard Eisley(!).....	67	1457	166	451	.368	76	89	.854	20	109	129	273	137	1	56	98	5	460	6.9	26
Jake Voskuhl.......	66	1606	152	300	.507	134	181	.740	123	220	343	57	258	8	42	77	25	438	6.6	18
Casey Jacobsen	78	1828	150	360	.417	91	111	.820	42	159	201	98	144	0	48	68	9	466	6.0	18
Maciej Lampe	21	224	43	88	.489	10	13	.769	9	35	44	9	28	0	3	15	3	96	4.6	17
Jahidi White(*).......	61	861	99	189	.524	63	126	.500	97	164	261	7	176	4	25	65	50	261	4.3	15
Jahidi White(!)......	62	865	99	190	.521	63	126	.500	97	164	261	7	176	4	25	66	51	261	4.2	15
Zarko Cabarkapa.....	49	570	81	197	.411	35	53	.660	26	73	99	40	75	0	10	54	13	203	4.1	17
Donnell Harvey(*)...	36	438	53	112	.473	35	44	.795	19	73	92	13	85	0	14	23	16	141	3.9	10
Donnell Harvey(!)....	60	783	89	201	.443	61	83	.735	48	116	164	21	129	0	24	45	27	239	4.0	16
Tom Gugliotta(>)....	30	304	31	99	.313	6	8	.750	15	41	56	21	34	0	14	20	4	68	2.3	8
Keon Clark(*)	0	0	0	0	—	0	0	—	0	0	0	0	0	0	0	0	0	0	—	0
Keon Clark(!)	2	27	2	6	.333	0	0	—	1	6	7	1	1	0	1	0	0	4	2.0	4
Robert Archibald(>) ...	1	6	0	1	.000	1	2	.500	0	1	1	1	1	0	0	1	0	1	1.0	1
Brevin Knight(>)......	3	19	1	3	.333	0	0	—	0	3	3	4	1	0	3	3	1	2	0.7	2
Cezary Trybanski(>) ..	4	10	0	2	.000	0	0	—	0	1	1	0	1	0	0	2	1	0	0.0	0
Phoenix	82	19730	2958	6671	.443	1392	1865	.746	924	2406	3330	1586	1862	31	734	1249	383	7723	94.2	123
Opponents	82	19730	2975	6671	.446	1601	2093	.765	1038	2550	3588	1760	1589	3	649	1304	431	8030	97.9	124

3-pt. FG: Phoenix 415-1202 (.345)
Marbury(>) 37-118 (.314); Stoudemire 1-5 (.200); Marion 90-265 (.340); Johnson 83-272 (.305); Hardaway(>) 14-35 (.400)
Barbosa 83-210 (.395); Williams(>) 2-2 (1.000); Eisley(*) 24-78 (.308); Eisley(!) 52-163 (.319); Jacobsen 75-180 (.417)
Lampe 0-4 (.000); Cabarkapa 6-32 (.188); Harvey(!) 0-3 (.000); Gugliotta(>) 0-1 (.000); Opponents 479-1374 (.349)

PORTLAND TRAIL BLAZERS

	G	Min.	FGM	FGA	Pct.	FTM	FTA	Pct.	Off.	Def.	Tot.	Ast.	PF	Dq.	Stl.	TO	Blk.	Pts.	Avg.	Hi.
									REBOUNDS									SCORING		
Zach Randolph	81	3067	663	1368	.485	299	393	.761	242	609	851	163	227	0	68	247	41	1626	20.1	34
Rasheed Wallace(>)	45	1675	296	669	.442	115	155	.742	69	229	298	114	131	1	36	87	72	766	17.0	31
Shareef Abdur-Rahim(*)	32	728	118	264	.447	79	95	.832	48	96	144	47	75	0	24	53	18	319	10.0	20
Shareef Abdur-Rahim(!)	85	2684	501	1054	.475	373	429	.869	189	450	639	174	222	1	68	184	37	1384	16.3	43
Derek Anderson	51	1810	230	612	.376	155	188	.824	26	156	182	228	79	0	66	90	3	694	13.6	29
Damon Stoudamire	82	3118	408	1018	.401	127	145	.876	52	256	308	500	173	2	99	180	9	1099	13.4	32
Bonzi Wells(>)	13	404	68	175	.389	21	27	.778	21	40	61	35	38	0	20	32	3	158	12.2	27
Jeff McInnis(>)	39	1269	196	416	.471	58	76	.763	16	78	94	196	94	2	36	61	2	465	11.9	21
Darius Miles(*)	42	1191	222	422	.526	85	121	.702	64	128	192	82	84	0	42	74	34	531	12.6	31
Darius Miles(!)	79	2079	365	753	.485	124	193	.642	112	247	359	162	168	0	67	130	61	861	10.9	31
Theo Ratliff(*)	32	1016	95	176	.540	44	70	.629	90	143	233	20	111	1	24	34	141	234	7.3	18
Theo Ratliff(!)	85	2664	266	549	.485	140	217	.645	195	419	614	71	300	3	54	120	307	672	7.9	18
Ruben Patterson	73	1651	200	395	.506	105	190	.553	129	139	268	139	152	0	84	105	21	507	6.9	24
Wesley Person(>)	33	621	80	168	.476	19	25	.760	12	62	74	38	22	0	11	18	6	215	6.5	20
Dale Davis	76	1682	133	281	.473	65	106	.613	158	240	398	72	154	1	43	40	62	331	4.4	15
Qyntel Woods	62	673	88	237	.371	38	60	.633	46	90	136	46	88	1	20	52	14	224	3.6	16
Vladimir Stepania	42	453	43	103	.417	22	36	.611	50	75	125	23	61	0	11	19	15	108	2.6	10
Kaniel Dickens	3	12	3	3	1.000	1	2	.500	2	0	2	0	3	0	0	1	0	7	2.3	4
Eddie Gill	22	157	15	36	.417	17	20	.850	4	13	17	16	16	0	9	12	1	50	2.3	11
Dan Dickau(*)	20	151	16	49	.327	7	8	.875	3	7	10	20	22	0	8	13	0	46	2.3	9
Dan Dickau(!)	43	294	37	98	.378	11	14	.786	7	19	26	38	44	0	17	26	0	95	2.2	9
Desmond Ferguson	7	32	5	12	.417	0	2	.000	0	4	4	1	0	0	0	1	0	13	1.9	5
Tracy Murray	7	35	3	12	.250	0	1	.000	3	2	5	1	3	0	1	2	0	8	1.1	5
Matt Carroll(>)	13	48	5	11	.455	2	2	1.000	0	3	3	1	3	0	0	2	0	13	1.0	7
Travis Outlaw	8	19	3	7	.429	2	4	.500	2	2	4	1	1	0	1	1	0	8	1.0	4
Omar Cook	17	139	7	27	.259	0	0	—	3	3	6	24	14	0	10	10	0	14	0.8	2
Ruben Boumtje Boumtj(>)	9	26	1	5	.200	2	2	1.000	0	1	1	1	2	0	0	0	1	4	0.4	2
Slavko Vranes	1	3	0	1	.000	0	0	—	0	0	0	0	1	0	0	0	0	0	0.0	0
Portland	82	19980	2898	6467	.448	1263	1728	.731	1040	2376	3416	1768	1554	8	613	1213	443	7440	90.7	115
Opponents	82	19980	2954	6567	.450	1219	1618	.753	1016	2292	3308	1912	1534	13	657	1120	390	7544	92.0	119

3-pt. FG: Portland 381-1102 (.346)
Randolph 1-5 (.200); Wallace(>) 59-173 (.341); Abdur-Rahim(*) 4-11 (.364); Abdur-Rahim(!) 9-34 (.265); Anderson 79-259 (.305)
Stoudamire 156-427 (.365); Wells(>) 1-8 (.125); McInnis(>) 15-47 (.319); Miles(*) 2-10 (.200); Miles(!) 7-40 (.175)
Patterson 2-12 (.167); Person(>) 36-76 (.474); Woods 10-29 (.345); Gill 3-8 (.375); Dickau(*) 7-20 (.350); Dickau(!) 10-30 (.333)
Ferguson 3-8 (.375); Murray 2-5 (.400); Carroll(>) 1-3 (.333); Cook 0-1 (.000); Opponents 417-1222 (.341)

SACRAMENTO KINGS

	G	Min.	FGM	FGA	Pct.	FTM	FTA	Pct.	Off.	Def.	Tot.	Ast.	PF	Dq.	Stl.	TO	Blk.	Pts.	Avg.	Hi.
									REBOUNDS									SCORING		
Peja Stojakovic	81	3264	665	1386	.480	394	425	.927	91	417	508	173	159	0	108	153	14	1964	24.2	41
Chris Webber	23	831	174	421	.413	81	114	.711	48	152	200	105	76	1	31	60	20	430	18.7	26
Mike Bibby	82	2980	527	1170	.450	304	373	.815	67	210	277	444	146	0	112	175	18	1506	18.4	31
Brad Miller	82	2621	373	731	.510	256	329	.778	191	552	743	312	247	7	68	144	86	1014	14.1	35
Bobby Jackson	50	1185	263	592	.444	82	109	.752	55	119	174	105	106	1	49	63	8	689	13.8	29
Doug Christie	82	2780	317	688	.461	148	172	.860	69	260	329	347	186	0	151	155	41	831	10.1	28
Vlade Divac	81	2317	314	668	.470	170	260	.654	136	327	463	432	222	2	57	173	77	800	9.9	26
Anthony Peeler	75	1391	156	348	.448	51	61	.836	31	122	153	120	103	0	56	77	10	431	5.7	18
Darius Songaila	73	976	133	273	.487	71	88	.807	91	134	225	48	126	1	42	43	12	337	4.6	17
Tony Massenburg	59	789	104	219	.475	43	63	.683	57	131	188	29	144	0	14	45	18	251	4.3	14
Jabari Smith	31	168	26	70	.371	12	20	.600	11	20	31	11	25	0	2	7	6	64	2.1	6
Gerald Wallace	37	337	32	89	.360	11	24	.458	35	39	74	19	37	0	14	8	14	75	2.0	6
Rodney Buford	22	141	19	56	.339	3	6	.500	6	9	15	7	9	0	6	4	1	41	1.9	6
Sacramento	82	19780	3103	6711	.462	1626	2044	.795	888	2492	3380	2152	1586	12	710	1137	325	8433	102.8	130
Opponents	82	19780	3140	6920	.454	1333	1780	.749	1080	2521	3601	1743	1817	20	651	1225	413	8022	97.8	127

3-pt. FG: Sacramento 601-1498 (.401)
Stojakovic 240-554 (.433); Webber 1-5 (.200); Bibby 148-378 (.392); Miller 12-38 (.316); Jackson 81-219 (.370); Divac 2-13 (.154)
Christie 49-142 (.345); Peeler 68-141 (.482); Massenburg 0-1 (.000); Smith 0-3 (.000); Wallace 0-2 (.000); Buford 0-2 (.000)
Opponents 409-1205 (.339)

SAN ANTONIO SPURS

	G	Min.	FGM	FGA	Pct.	FTM	FTA	Pct.	Off.	Def.	Tot.	Ast.	PF	Dq.	Stl.	TO	Blk.	Pts.	Avg.	Hi.
									REBOUNDS									SCORING		
Tim Duncan	69	2527	592	1181	.501	352	588	.599	227	632	859	213	164	1	62	183	185	1538	22.3	47
Tony Parker	75	2577	423	946	.447	191	272	.702	43	194	237	411	148	0	61	179	7	1099	14.7	29
Manu Ginobili	77	2260	330	789	.418	239	298	.802	86	258	344	291	181	0	136	161	16	987	12.8	33
Hedo Turkoglu	80	2073	262	645	.406	114	161	.708	52	306	358	154	165	0	80	94	32	739	9.2	21
Rasho Nesterovic	82	2353	328	700	.469	54	114	.474	257	376	633	114	247	5	51	107	165	710	8.7	23
Malik Rose	67	1256	173	404	.428	183	225	.813	110	210	320	69	164	1	36	112	24	529	7.9	26
Bruce Bowen	82	2624	211	502	.420	66	114	.579	45	208	253	113	166	1	84	90	33	565	6.9	16
Charlie Ward(*)	36	425	45	130	.346	4	6	.667	2	46	48	45	33	0	17	27	3	119	3.3	13
Charlie Ward(!)	71	1252	160	390	.410	20	27	.741	12	132	144	215	107	2	64	96	11	424	6.0	18
Ron Mercer	39	516	90	211	.427	13	17	.765	10	39	49	22	37	0	14	26	5	195	5.0	14
Robert Horry	81	1290	141	348	.405	69	107	.645	108	164	272	101	165	0	48	55	49	392	4.8	14
Anthony Carter	5	87	11	37	.297	0	0	—	2	9	11	12	9	0	4	2	0	22	4.4	10
Devin Brown	58	627	85	196	.434	60	74	.811	38	92	130	33	61	0	15	36	4	234	4.0	19

	G	Min.	FGM	FGA	Pct.	FTM	FTA	Pct.	Off.	Def.	Tot.	Ast.	PF	Dq.	Stl.	TO	Blk.	Pts.	Avg.	Hi.
Shane Heal	6	72	7	24	.292	4	5	.800	1	3	4	5	2	0	1	5	0	22	3.7	11
Kevin Willis	48	373	70	150	.467	24	39	.615	37	61	98	11	61	0	21	32	9	164	3.4	17
Jason Hart	53	660	71	159	.447	33	43	.767	10	69	79	81	59	0	28	29	5	177	3.3	14
Alex Garcia	2	13	1	7	.143	1	2	.500	0	0	0	0	0	0	2	1	0	3	1.5	3
Matt Carroll(*)	3	22	2	5	.400	2	4	.500	1	2	3	1	5	0	1	4	0	6	2.0	4
Matt Carroll(!)	16	70	7	16	.438	4	6	.667	1	5	6	2	8	0	1	6	0	19	1.2	7
San Antonio	82	19755	2842	6434	.442	1409	2069	.681	1029	2669	3698	1676	1667	8	661	1203	537	7501	91.5	117
Opponents	82	19755	2613	6388	.409	1372	1844	.744	909	2459	3368	1419	1837	18	635	1254	380	6909	84.3	120

3-pt. FG: San Antonio 408-1140 (.358)
Duncan 2-12 (.167); Parker 62-199 (.312); Ginobili 88-245 (.359); Turkoglu 101-241 (.419); Rose 0-3 (.000); Bowen 77-212 (.363)
Ward(*) 25-68 (.368); Ward(!) 84-206 (.408); Mercer 2-7 (.286); Horry 41-108 (.380); Carter 0-3 (.000); Brown 4-14 (.286)
Heal 4-18 (.222); Willis 0-1 (.000); Hart 2-9 (.222); Carroll(!) 1-3 (.333); Opponents 311-951 (.327)

SEATTLE SUPERSONICS

	G	Min.	FGM	FGA	Pct.	FTM	FTA	Pct.	Off.	Def.	Tot.	Ast.	PF	Dq.	Stl.	TO	Blk.	Pts.	Avg.	Hi.
Ray Allen	56	2152	447	1017	.440	245	271	.904	69	217	286	268	132	2	71	156	11	1287	23.0	42
Rashard Lewis	80	2931	535	1229	.435	206	270	.763	133	385	518	175	233	3	99	135	54	1421	17.8	50
Ronald Murray	82	2021	389	915	.425	168	235	.715	45	159	204	205	158	0	81	149	28	1013	12.4	31
Vladimir Radmanovic	77	2321	345	812	.425	95	127	.748	104	302	406	142	187	1	80	109	42	925	12.0	25
Brent Barry	59	1803	215	427	.504	91	110	.827	21	183	204	342	121	0	85	139	16	635	10.8	28
Antonio Daniels	71	1512	187	398	.470	155	184	.842	23	119	142	298	64	0	45	61	6	571	8.0	30
Vitaly Potapenko	65	1419	200	409	.489	59	92	.641	101	188	289	53	161	2	22	77	28	459	7.1	21
Luke Ridnour	69	1114	145	350	.414	65	79	.823	35	73	108	163	105	0	52	80	7	382	5.5	17
Jerome James	65	990	129	259	.498	66	100	.660	78	152	230	32	180	1	20	82	60	324	5.0	16
Calvin Booth	71	1206	135	290	.466	75	94	.798	86	194	280	28	150	2	17	45	101	345	4.9	12
Ansu Sesay	57	583	81	178	.455	32	46	.696	43	49	92	19	66	0	19	23	20	200	3.5	19
Richie Frahm	54	469	63	139	.453	23	26	.885	12	44	56	24	50	0	16	7	4	183	3.4	31
Reggie Evans	75	1280	67	165	.406	83	148	.561	156	252	408	33	176	0	54	65	10	217	2.9	16
Leon Smith	1	4	1	2	.500	0	0	—	1	1	2	0	1	0	0	0	0	2	2.0	2
Seattle	82	19805	2939	6590	.446	1363	1782	.765	907	2318	3225	1782	1784	11	661	1188	387	7964	97.1	124
Opponents	82	19805	2980	6622	.450	1570	2028	.774	1068	2430	3498	1728	1658	7	629	1211	387	8016	97.8	130

3-pt. FG: Seattle 723-1936 (.373)
Allen 148-378 (.392); Lewis 145-386 (.376); Murray 67-229 (.293); Radmanovic 140-377 (.371); Barry 114-252 (.452)
Daniels 42-116 (.362); Ridnour 27-80 (.338); Booth 0-2 (.000); Sesay 6-21 (.286); Frahm 34-92 (.370); Evans 0-3 (.000)
Opponents 486-1394 (.349)

TORONTO RAPTORS

	G	Min.	FGM	FGA	Pct.	FTM	FTA	Pct.	Off.	Def.	Tot.	Ast.	PF	Dq.	Stl.	TO	Blk.	Pts.	Avg.	Hi.
Vince Carter	73	2785	608	1457	.417	336	417	.806	95	254	349	348	212	1	88	223	65	1645	22.5	43
Jalen Rose(*)	50	1968	308	752	.410	148	180	.822	27	175	202	273	139	2	39	171	18	810	16.2	32
Jalen Rose(!)	66	2497	383	952	.402	187	231	.810	34	232	266	329	184	2	51	208	22	1022	15.5	34
Donyell Marshall(*)	66	2580	413	884	.467	120	162	.741	182	527	709	94	200	0	80	95	104	1066	16.2	32
Donyell Marshall(!)	82	2988	470	1020	.461	134	182	.736	210	598	808	122	247	1	93	117	124	1205	14.7	32
Chris Bosh	75	2510	327	712	.459	202	288	.701	191	366	557	78	215	2	59	107	106	861	11.5	25
Dion Glover(*)	14	178	25	65	.385	10	14	.714	4	25	29	15	17	0	10	19	2	64	4.6	13
Dion Glover(!)	69	1643	230	589	.390	120	156	.769	58	208	266	130	123	0	50	102	19	620	9.0	23
Alvin Williams	56	1730	201	496	.405	66	85	.776	18	132	150	224	114	1	55	78	10	494	8.8	20
Antonio Davis(>)	15	538	46	120	.383	37	49	.755	49	94	143	14	45	0	8	21	8	129	8.6	15
Morris Peterson	82	2148	238	587	.405	76	94	.809	35	226	261	113	206	0	88	69	14	678	8.3	27
Rod Strickland(*)	15	282	28	84	.333	15	22	.682	10	27	37	59	17	0	8	14	4	71	4.7	14
Rod Strickland(!)	61	1197	150	353	.425	72	98	.735	34	121	155	244	76	0	35	85	11	382	6.3	15
Lamond Murray	33	518	76	215	.353	24	35	.686	14	76	90	28	47	0	15	38	7	197	6.0	15
Jerome Williams(>)	15	407	28	57	.491	21	29	.724	35	93	128	11	30	0	19	23	3	77	5.1	17
Milt Palacio	59	1211	104	298	.349	45	68	.662	15	87	102	184	90	0	41	87	11	257	4.4	19
Lonny Baxter(>)	36	487	60	128	.469	30	56	.536	42	79	121	10	69	1	14	22	18	150	4.2	13
Chris Jefferies(>)	2	8	3	6	.500	1	1	1.000	0	1	1	1	0	0	0	1	0	8	4.0	5
Corie Blount(*)	16	294	18	47	.383	2	3	.667	22	47	69	10	49	0	11	8	5	38	2.4	6
Corie Blount(!)	62	1050	115	253	.455	15	27	.556	98	177	275	55	135	0	49	43	24	245	4.0	13
Roger Mason(*)	23	285	31	87	.356	19	22	.864	1	27	28	23	31	1	10	18	6	93	4.0	18
Roger Mason(!)	26	328	32	98	.327	19	22	.864	1	30	31	26	36	1	11	20	6	96	3.7	18
Jannero Pargo(>)	5	71	9	29	.310	0	0	—	0	4	4	12	7	0	4	5	1	18	3.6	8
Michael Curry	70	1229	76	196	.388	49	58	.845	22	65	87	53	153	1	23	48	5	204	2.9	10
Jerome Moiso	35	417	40	84	.476	22	38	.579	41	72	113	8	42	0	17	25	12	102	2.9	11
Rick Brunson(>)	3	10	2	4	.500	0	0	—	0	0	0	2	0	0	0	0	0	4	1.3	2
Mengke Bateer(>)	7	40	4	7	.571	0	0	—	5	3	8	1	10	0	1	2	0	8	1.1	2
Robert Archibald(*)	30	246	8	30	.267	13	27	.481	21	29	50	12	49	0	13	9	3	29	1.0	6
Robert Archibald(!)	32	256	9	33	.273	14	31	.452	21	31	52	13	50	0	14	10	3	32	1.0	6
Michael Bradley(>)	5	38	1	3	.333	1	2	.500	1	10	11	1	6	0	1	3	0	3	0.6	3
Toronto	82	19980	2654	6348	.418	1237	1650	.750	830	2419	3249	1574	1748	9	604	1164	402	7006	85.4	121
Opponents	82	19980	2722	6365	.428	1536	2055	.747	1034	2662	3696	1518	1619	10	590	1196	333	7253	88.5	120

3-pt. FG: Toronto 461-1294 (.356)
Carter 93-243 (.383); Rose(*) 46-148 (.311); Rose(!) 69-202 (.342); Marshall(*) 120-298 (.403); Marshall(!) 131-325 (.403)
Bosh 5-14 (.357); Glover(*) 4-14 (.286); Glover(!) 40-119 (.336); A. Williams 26-89 (.292); Peterson 126-340 (.371)
Strickland(*) 0-3 (.000); Strickland(!) 10-36 (.278); Murray 21-60 (.350); J. Williams(>) 0-1 (.000); Palacio 4-26 (.154)
Baxter(>) 0-1 (.000); Jefferies(>) 1-3 (.333); Blount(!) 0-3 (.000); Mason(*) 12-33 (.364); Mason(!) 13-39 (.333)
Pargo(>) 0-5 (.000); Curry 3-15 (.200); Moiso 0-1 (.000); Opponents 273-889 (.307)

UTAH JAZZ

	G	Min.	FGM	FGA	Pct.	FTM	FTA	Pct.	Off.	Def.	Tot.	Ast.	PF	Dq.	Stl.	TO	Blk.	Pts.	Avg.	Hi.
Andrei Kirilenko	78	2895	412	931	.443	392	496	.790	226	403	629	244	174	0	150	215	215	1284	16.5	31
Matt Harpring	31	1134	193	410	.471	108	157	.688	91	156	247	63	102	1	22	65	2	502	16.2	32
Carlos Arroyo	71	2008	339	768	.441	181	225	.804	41	144	185	355	165	0	63	156	5	897	12.6	30

	G				Pct.			Pct.													
DeShawn Stevenson(>)	54	1511	261	586	.445	89	133	.669	43	135	178	92	86	0	28	80	16	618	11.4	24
Gordan Giricek(*)	25	606	128	297	.431	68	77	.883	14	48	62	42	46	0	15	40	5	338	13.5	33
Gordan Giricek(!)	73	2041	316	724	.436	135	158	.854	51	175	226	122	144	0	56	103	15	827	11.3	33
Raja Bell	82	2020	329	805	.409	195	248	.786	60	181	241	107	262	6	63	111	13	915	11.2	26
Raul Lopez	82	1617	223	517	.431	101	117	.863	24	131	155	305	200	2	62	174	2	572	7.0	25
Greg Ostertag	78	2153	208	437	.476	113	195	.579	221	357	578	123	228	1	30	99	139	529	6.8	18
Jarron Collins	81	1732	147	295	.498	188	262	.718	117	199	316	77	255	3	26	79	18	482	6.0	14
Maurice Williams	57	772	115	303	.380	44	56	.786	23	49	72	76	87	0	28	51	2	284	5.0	20
Aleksandar Pavlovic	79	1144	149	376	.396	65	84	.774	44	115	159	60	187	3	41	67	16	382	4.8	18
Mikki Moore(*)	28	385	49	94	.521	30	35	.857	28	54	82	19	64	1	7	22	13	128	4.6	15
Mikki Moore(!)	32	395	50	99	.505	30	35	.857	29	55	84	19	65	1	7	22	13	130	4.1	15
Ben Handlogten	17	172	25	47	.532	18	27	.667	22	33	55	6	32	0	3	10	4	68	4.0	13
Curtis Borchardt	16	258	22	56	.393	14	18	.778	13	41	54	15	40	0	4	18	14	58	3.6	11
Tom Gugliotta(*)	25	515	39	104	.375	14	20	.700	50	81	131	42	47	0	17	19	8	93	3.7	8
Tom Gugliotta(!)	55	819	70	203	.345	20	28	.714	65	122	187	63	81	0	31	39	12	161	2.9	8
Paul Grant	10	98	11	23	.478	3	8	.375	7	10	17	3	17	0	1	7	1	25	2.5	6
Michael Ruffin	41	733	38	117	.325	16	38	.421	78	129	207	41	103	1	22	42	21	92	2.2	6
Keon Clark(>)	2	27	2	6	.333	0	0	—	1	6	7	1	1	0	1	0	0	4	2.0	4
Utah	82	19780	2690	6172	.436	1639	2196	.746	1103	2272	3375	1671	2096	18	583	1365	494	7271	88.7	110
Opponents	82	19780	2541	5879	.432	1874	2431	.771	868	2131	2999	1528	1999	26	666	1262	530	7371	89.9	127

3-pt. FG: Utah 252-786 (.321).
Kirilenko 68-201 (.338); Harpring 8-33 (.242); Arroyo 38-117 (.325); Stevenson(>) 7-30 (.233); Giricek(*) 14-39 (.359)
Giricek(!) 60-152 (.395); Bell 62-166 (.373); Lopez 25-85 (.294); Ostertag 0-1 (.000); Collins 0-1 (.000); Williams 10-39 (.256)
Pavlovic 19-70 (.271); Borchardt 0-1 (.000); Gugliotta(*) 1-3 (.333); Gugliotta(!) 1-4 (.250); Opponents 415-1209 (.343)

WASHINGTON WIZARDS

	G	Min.	FGM	FGA	Pct.	FTM	FTA	Pct.	REBOUNDS			Ast.	PF	Dq.	Stl.	TO	Blk.	SCORING		
									Off.	Def.	Tot.							Pts.	Avg.	Hi.
Gilbert Arenas	55	2066	358	914	.392	237	317	.748	55	199	254	275	176	2	103	226	12	1078	19.6	40
Larry Hughes	61	2061	401	1009	.397	267	335	.797	96	230	326	148	147	2	95	152	26	1148	18.8	43
Jerry Stackhouse	26	774	128	321	.399	83	103	.806	16	78	94	103	49	0	24	88	3	362	13.9	29
Kwame Brown	74	2239	288	589	.489	228	334	.683	178	372	550	112	144	0	66	140	52	805	10.9	30
Jarvis Hayes	70	2044	278	695	.400	77	98	.786	71	193	264	106	157	1	71	110	11	673	9.6	23
Juan Dixon	71	1478	247	637	.388	111	139	.799	30	118	148	137	111	1	82	104	4	664	9.4	30
Etan Thomas	79	1901	257	526	.489	191	295	.647	183	345	528	68	219	1	36	113	123	705	8.9	21
Brendan Haywood	77	1484	200	388	.515	137	234	.585	186	201	387	43	154	0	32	80	100	537	7.0	23
Steve Blake	75	1392	157	407	.386	55	67	.821	18	99	117	209	100	0	57	128	7	444	5.9	21
Christian Laettner	48	984	119	256	.465	40	50	.800	50	182	232	89	102	1	37	42	28	284	5.9	17
Jared Jeffries	82	1913	177	469	.377	105	171	.614	180	244	424	93	212	3	48	107	28	464	5.7	14
Brevin Knight(>)	32	598	58	138	.420	19	27	.704	11	50	61	102	50	0	52	44	0	136	4.3	13
Lonny Baxter(*)	12	132	16	32	.500	9	12	.750	11	20	31	5	23	0	2	5	5	41	3.4	12
Lonny Baxter(!)	62	766	103	209	.493	44	76	.579	64	123	187	20	123	3	17	38	29	251	4.0	19
Mitchell Butler	41	552	54	124	.435	15	24	.625	24	47	71	32	54	0	22	24	4	134	3.3	13
Chris Whitney	16	186	17	45	.378	5	5	1.000	3	12	15	14	6	0	6	6	2	47	2.9	11
Torraye Braggs(*)	4	22	3	5	.600	0	0	—	3	2	5	1	8	0	0	1	0	6	1.5	2
Torraye Braggs(!)	15	154	16	33	.485	8	12	.667	18	21	39	7	29	0	4	13	2	40	2.7	6
Jahidi White(>)	1	4	0	1	.000	0	0	—	0	0	0	0	0	0	1	1	0	0	0.0	0
Washington	82	19830	2758	6556	.421	1579	2211	.714	1115	2392	3507	1537	1712	11	733	1439	406	7528	91.8	124
Opponents	82	19830	3061	6740	.454	1444	1874	.771	1048	2520	3568	1966	1783	17	786	1321	448	7990	97.4	138

3-pt. FG: Washington 433-1269 (.341)
Arenas 125-333 (.375); Hughes 79-232 (.341); Stackhouse 23-65 (.354); Brown 1-2 (.500); Hayes 40-131 (.305); Dixon 59-198 (.298)
Haywood 0-1 (.000); Blake 75-202 (.371); Laettner 6-21 (.286); Jeffries 5-30 (.167); Knight(>) 1-5 (.200); Baxter(*) 0-1 (.000)
Baxter 1-3 (.333); Butler 11-30 (.367); Whitney 8-18 (.444); Opponents 424-1238 (.342)

(*) Statistics with this team only
(!) Totals with all teams
(>) Continued season with another team

ACTIVE CAREER LEADERS

(Players who were on active rosters or on injured list during 2003-04 season)

SCORING
(minimum 400 games or 10,000 points)

	G	FGM	FTM	Pts.	Avg.
Shaquille O'Neal	809	8,670	4,573	21,914	27.1
Allen Iverson	535	5,104	3,539	14,436	27.0
Karl Malone	1476	13,528	9,787	36,928	25.0
Paul Pierce	444	3,429	2,689	10,317	23.2
Tim Duncan	520	4,524	2,796	11,862	22.8
Chris Webber	619	5,716	1,983	13,639	22.0
Kobe Bryant	561	4,317	3,093	12,215	21.8
Tracy McGrady	487	3,791	2,289	10,420	21.4
Grant Hill	482	3,645	2,756	10,104	21.0
Jerry Stackhouse	608	4,126	3,779	12,737	20.9

FIELD-GOAL PERCENTAGE
(minimum 2,000 made)

	FGM	FGA	Pct.
Shaquille O'Neal	8,670	15,020	.577
Dale Davis	3,438	6,447	.533
Alonzo Mourning	4,538	8,654	.524
Dikembe Mutombo	3,878	7,487	.518
Karl Malone	13,528	26,210	.516
Horace Grant	5,439	10,695	.509
Tim Duncan	4,524	8,896	.509
Olden Polynice	3,557	7,037	.505
Tyrone Hill	2,834	5,643	.502
Vlade Divac	5,192	10,479	.495

FREE THROW PERCENTAGE
(minimum 1,200 made)

	FTM	FTA	Pct.
Steve Nash	1,258	1,409	.893
Reggie Miller	5,987	6,758	.886
Peja Stojakovic	1,373	1,551	.885
Ray Allen	2,199	2,486	.885
Darrell Armstrong	1,279	1,446	.885
Chauncey Billups	1,493	1,709	.874
Terrell Brandon	1,784	2,043	.873
Allan Houston	2,536	2,936	.864
Sam Cassell	2,857	3,328	.858
Dana Barros	1,249	1,456	.8583

3-POINT FIELD-GOAL PERCENTAGE
(minimum 250 made)

	FGM	FGA	Pct.
Hubert Davis	728	1,651	.441
Wesley Person	1,109	2,665	.416
Steve Nash	673	1,618	.416
Pat Garrity	513	1,242	.413
Dana Barros	1,090	2,652	.411
Brent Barry	990	2,430	.407
Michael Redd	397	980	.405
Allan Houston	1,274	3,167	.402
Ray Allen	1,277	3,187	.401
Glen Rice	1,559	3,896	.400

GAMES
Karl Malone	1,476
Kevin Willis	1,390
Reggie Miller	1,323
Mark Jackson	1,296
Charles Oakley	1,282
Clifford Robinson	1,179
Scottie Pippen	1,178
Horace Grant	1,165
Vlade Divac	1,119
Gary Payton	1,109

MINUTES
Karl Malone	54,852
Reggie Miller	45,514
Scottie Pippen	41,069
Gary Payton	40,768
Charles Oakley	40,280
Mark Jackson	39,121
Horace Grant	38,621
Clifford Robinson	38,054
Kevin Willis	37,975
Glen Rice	34,985

POINTS
Karl Malone	36,928
Reggie Miller	24,305
Shaquille O'Neal	21,914
Gary Payton	19,956
Scottie Pippen	18,940
Glen Rice	18,336
Clifford Robinson	18,305
Kevin Willis	17,154
Latrell Sprewell	15,691
Allen Iverson	14,436

FIELD GOALS MADE
Karl Malone	13,528
Shaquille O'Neal	8,670
Gary Payton	7,995
Reggie Miller	7,927
Scottie Pippen	7,420
Kevin Willis	7,055
Clifford Robinson	6,887
Glen Rice	6,776
Chris Webber	5,716
Latrell Sprewell	5,678

FIELD GOALS ATTEMPTED
Karl Malone	26,210
Gary Payton	17,060
Reggie Miller	16,780
Scottie Pippen	15,700
Clifford Robinson	15,621
Shaquille O'Neal	15,020
Glen Rice	14,867
Kevin Willis	14,469
Latrell Sprewell	13,333
Allen Iverson	12,247

FREE THROWS MADE
Karl Malone	9,787
Reggie Miller	5,987
Shaquille O'Neal	4,573
Jerry Stackhouse	3,779
Alonzo Mourning	3,612
Allen Iverson	3,539
Clifford Robinson	3,430
Rod Strickland	3,423
Shareef Abdur-Rahim	3,394
Derrick Coleman	3,323

FREE THROWS ATTEMPTED
Karl Malone	13,188
Shaquille O'Neal	8,508
Reggie Miller	6,758
Alonzo Mourning	5,113
Clifford Robinson	4,953
Rod Strickland	4,749
Allen Iverson	4,668
Jerry Stackhouse	4,648
Dikembe Mutombo	4,585
Scottie Pippen	4,437

3-POINT FIELD GOALS MADE
Reggie Miller	2,464
Glen Rice	1,559
Nick Van Exel	1,373
Ray Allen	1,277
Allan Houston	1,274
Eddie Jones	1,159
Wesley Person	1,109
Steve Smith	1,107
Clifford Robinson	1,101
Dana Barros	1,090

3-POINT FIELD GOALS ATTEMPTED
Reggie Miller	6,188
Glen Rice	3,896
Nick Van Exel	3,867
Ray Allen	3,187
Allan Houston	3,167
Steve Smith	3,103
Gary Payton	3,088
Clifford Robinson	3,081
Latrell Sprewell	3,061
Eddie Jones	3,053

REBOUNDS
Karl Malone	14,968
Charles Oakley	12,205
Kevin Willis	11,817
Dikembe Mutombo	10,907
Shaquille O'Neal	9,781
Horace Grant	9,443
Vlade Divac	9,294
Dale Davis	8,040
Scottie Pippen	7,494
Kevin Garnett	7,493

ASSISTS
Mark Jackson	10,334
Gary Payton	8,039
Rod Strickland	7,948
Jason Kidd	6,738
Scottie Pippen	6,135
Avery Johnson	5,846
Nick Van Exel	5,427
Karl Malone	5,248
Kenny Anderson	5,093
Stephon Marbury	4,830

PERSONAL FOULS
Karl Malone	4,578
Charles Oakley	4,421
Kevin Willis	4,108
Clifford Robinson	3,690
Vlade Divac	3,584
Scottie Pippen	3,329
Elden Campbell	2,949
Dikembe Mutombo	2,898
Tyrone Hill	2,893
Olden Polynice	2,835

STEALS
Scottie Pippen	2,307
Gary Payton	2,243
Karl Malone	2,085
Rod Strickland	1,613
Mark Jackson	1,608
Kendall Gill	1,505
Jason Kidd	1,502
Doug Christie	1,463
Reggie Miller	1,455
Charles Oakley	1,351

BLOCKED SHOTS
Dikembe Mutombo	2,996
Shaquille O'Neal	2,102
Shawn Bradley	2,056
Alonzo Mourning	1,889
Vlade Divac	1,630
Elden Campbell	1,595
Theo Ratliff	1,569
Tim Duncan	1,314
Clifford Robinson	1,274
Ben Wallace	1,243

DISQUALIFICATIONS
Shawn Bradley	66
Clifford Robinson	64
Tyrone Hill	63
Charles Oakley	63
Vlade Divac	55
Kurt Thomas	50
P.J. Brown	48
Christian Laettner	48
Alonzo Mourning	48
Vin Baker	44

Denotes number of overtime periods.

POINTS

	FG	FT	Pts.
Tracy McGrady, Orlando vs. Washington, March 10, 2004	20	17	62
Tracy McGrady, Orlando at Denver, November 14, 2003	20	3	51
Rashard Lewis, Seattle at L.A. Clippers, October 31, 2003	18	10	50
Allen Iverson, Philadelphia vs. Atlanta, November 29, 2003	20	6	50
Jamal Crawford, Chicago at Toronto, April 11, 2004	*18	8	50
Tim Duncan, San Antonio at Orlando, December 5, 2003	19	9	47
Kobe Bryant, L.A. Lakers vs. Golden State, April 13, 2004	14	17	45
Richard Hamilton, Detroit vs. Cleveland, November 28, 2003	15	13	44
Quentin Richardson, L.A. Clippers vs. Denver, December 31, 2003	17	5	44
Kobe Bryant, L.A. Lakers at L.A. Clippers, January 4, 2004	14	12	44
Tracy McGrady, Orlando vs. Boston, January 16, 2004	*16	7	44
Vince Carter, Toronto at Atlanta, November 26, 2003	*18	5	43
Shareef Abdur-Rahim, Atlanta at Cleveland, December 6, 2003	17	9	43
Tracy McGrady, Orlando at Indiana, January 6, 2004	14	7	43
Larry Hughes, Washington vs. Philadelphia, January 10, 2004	17	7	43
Dirk Nowitzki, Dallas at Seattle, January 27, 2004	16	3	43
Tracy McGrady, Orlando vs. Utah, February 18, 2004	13	14	43
Jamal Crawford, Chicago vs. Washington, December 27, 2003	16	5	42
Ray Allen, Seattle vs. Portland, January 5, 2004	*16	5	42
Stephon Marbury, New York vs. L.A. Clippers, February 8, 2004	15	8	42
Stephen Jackson, Atlanta vs. Washington, March 12, 2004	14	10	42
Vince Carter, Toronto at New Orleans, March 21, 2004	*13	12	42
Paul Pierce, Boston at Cleveland, December 13, 2003	12	16	41
Peja Stojakovic, Sacramento vs. Memphis, December 23, 2003	11	14	41
Tracy McGrady, Orlando vs. Cleveland, December 25, 2003	*15	6	41
Ray Allen, Seattle vs. L.A. Clippers, January 24, 2004	14	7	41
Tracy McGrady, Orlando at Milwaukee, February 17, 2004	15	8	41
Yao Ming, Houston vs. Atlanta, February 22, 2004	***15	11	41
LeBron James, Cleveland vs. New Jersey, March 27, 2004	15	10	41
Carmelo Anthony, Denver vs. Seattle, March 30, 2004	19	1	41
Allen Iverson, Philadelphia at Washington, November 11, 2003	12	14	40
Stephon Marbury, Phoenix at L.A. Clippers, December 29, 2003	15	7	40
Michael Redd, Milwaukee vs. Orlando, January 21, 2004	16	6	40
Michael Redd, Milwaukee at New Orleans, January 28, 2004	16	4	40
Dirk Nowitzki, Dallas vs. Detroit, February 7, 2004	15	7	40
Allen Iverson, Philadelphia at Seattle, February 19, 2004	10	17	40
Kobe Bryant, L.A. Lakers at Phoenix, February 22, 2004	15	8	40
Ray Allen, Seattle vs. Utah, February 25, 2004	*13	8	40
Gilbert Arenas, Washington at Orlando, March 10, 2004	15	8	40
Tracy McGrady, Orlando vs. Seattle, March 13, 2004	12	13	40
Vince Carter, Toronto at New York, March 26, 2004	13	9	40

FIELD GOALS MADE

	FTA	FTM
Tracy McGrady, Orlando at Denver, November 14, 2003	30	20
Allen Iverson, Philadelphia vs. Atlanta, November 29, 2003	34	20
Tracy McGrady, Orlando vs. Washington, March 10, 2004	37	20
Tim Duncan, San Antonio at Orlando, December 5, 2003	34	19
Carmelo Anthony, Denver vs. Seattle, March 30, 2004	29	19
Rashard Lewis, Seattle at L.A. Clippers, October 31, 2003	25	18
Vince Carter, Toronto at Atlanta, November 26, 2003	* 28	18
Jamal Crawford, Chicago at Toronto, April 11, 2004	* 34	18
Shareef Abdur-Rahim, Atlanta at Cleveland, December 6, 2003	27	17
Michael Finley, Dallas at L.A. Clippers, December 10, 2003	26	17
Quentin Richardson, L.A. Clippers vs. Denver, December 31, 2003	30	17
Larry Hughes, Washington vs. Philadelphia, January 10, 2004	29	17
Tim Duncan, San Antonio vs. Sacramento, January 29, 2004	27	17
Kobe Bryant, L.A. Lakers at San Antonio, November 6, 2003	** 29	16
Jamal Crawford, Chicago vs. Washington, December 27, 2003	27	16
Ray Allen, Seattle vs. Portland, January 5, 2004	* 27	16
Tracy McGrady, Orlando vs. Boston, January 16, 2004	* 31	16
Michael Redd, Milwaukee vs. Orlando, January 21, 2004	25	16
Dirk Nowitzki, Dallas at Seattle, January 27, 2004	22	16
Michael Redd, Milwaukee at New Orleans, January 28, 2004	33	16
Michael Finley, Dallas vs. Denver, January 31, 2004	25	16
Kevin Garnett, Minnesota vs. Cleveland, February 6, 2004	29	16

Regular-season statistics

2003-04 REVIEW

FREE THROWS MADE

	FTA	FTM
Corey Maggette, L.A. Clippers vs. Houston, November 24, 2003	20	18
Allen Iverson, Philadelphia vs. Toronto, December 2, 2003	23	18
Allen Iverson, Philadelphia at Seattle, February 19, 2004	21	17
Tracy McGrady, Orlando vs. Washington, March 10, 2004	26	17
Corey Maggette, L.A. Clippers at L.A. Lakers, March 19, 2004	20	17
Kobe Bryant, L.A. Lakers vs. Utah, March 28, 2004	21	17
Kobe Bryant, L.A. Lakers vs. Golden State, April 13, 2004	18	17
Allen Iverson, Philadelphia at Miami, December 5, 2003	17	16
LeBron James, Cleveland vs. Boston, December 13, 2003	18	16
Paul Pierce, Boston at Cleveland, December 13, 2003	18	16
Paul Pierce, Boston vs. Philadelphia, December 21, 2003	18	16
Shareef Abdur-Rahim, Atlanta vs. Indiana, January 19, 2004	17	16
Speedy Claxton, Golden State at Memphis, February 25, 2004	18	16
Paul Pierce, Boston vs. Golden State, April 2, 2004	23	16

REBOUNDS

	Off.	Def.	Total
Shaquille O'Neal, L.A. Lakers vs. Milwaukee, March 21, 2004	*1	25	26
Kevin Garnett, Minnesota at Sacramento, December 5, 2003	*2	23	25
Erick Dampier, Golden State vs. L.A. Clippers, March 28, 2004	13	12	25
Erick Dampier, Golden State vs. Utah, January 19, 2004	10	14	24
Marcus Camby, Denver vs. Chicago, January 28, 2004	5	19	24
Donyell Marshall, Toronto at Chicago, February 17, 2004	7	17	24
Kevin Garnett, Minnesota vs. Sacramento, February 19, 2004	2	22	24
Erick Dampier, Golden State at L.A. Lakers, November 2, 2003	8	15	23
Shaquille O'Neal, L.A. Lakers vs. Orlando, March 15, 2004	*12	11	23
Tyson Chandler, Chicago vs. Atlanta, October 31, 2003	9	13	22
Malik Rose, San Antonio vs. Dallas, November 8, 2003	9	13	22
Ben Wallace, Detroit vs. Phoenix, January 2, 2004	7	15	22
Kevin Garnett, Minnesota at Dallas, January 3, 2004	9	13	22
Erick Dampier, Golden State vs. Memphis, January 12, 2004	**10	12	22
Kevin Garnett, Minnesota vs. Memphis, April 4, 2004	7	15	22

ASSISTS

	No.
Steve Nash, Dallas vs. Sacramento, April 1, 2004	19

STEALS

	No.
Dirk Nowitzki, Dallas at Houston, March 7, 2004	9
Allen Iverson, Philadelphia at Chicago, November 7, 2003	8
Andrei Kirilenko, Utah at Houston, December 3, 2003	*8
Juan Dixon, Washington vs. Indiana, February 20, 2004	8
Gilbert Arenas, Washington vs. Sacramento, March 17, 2004	8
Ron Artest, Indiana vs. Dallas, March 24, 2004	8
Walter McCarty, Boston at Philadelphia, February 7, 2004	7
Speedy Claxton, Golden State vs. Phoenix, February 11, 2004	7
Marcus Banks, Boston vs. Golden State, April 2, 2004	7

BLOCKED SHOTS

	No.
Dikembe Mutombo, New York vs. New Jersey, January 4, 2004	10
Calvin Booth, Seattle vs. Cleveland, January 13, 2004	10
Amare Stoudemire, Phoenix vs. Utah, February 7, 2004	10
Ben Wallace, Detroit vs. New York, November 21, 2003	9
Shaquille O'Neal, L.A. Lakers at San Antonio, December 3, 2003	9
Theo Ratliff, Portland at Orlando, February 24, 2004	*9
Samuel Dalembert, Philadelphia vs. New York, April 3, 2004	9
Tim Duncan, San Antonio at Denver, October 29, 2003	8
Elton Brand, L.A. Clippers at Seattle, October 30, 2003	8
Jermaine O'Neal, Indiana at Phoenix, December 1, 2003	8
Ben Wallace, Detroit vs. Chicago, December 17, 2003	8
Marcus Camby, Denver vs. Utah, January 9, 2004	8
Ben Wallace, Detroit vs. Milwaukee, February 18, 2004	8
Pau Gasol, Memphis vs. Phoenix, February 20, 2004	8
Theo Ratliff, Portland vs. Sacramento, March 12, 2004	8
Greg Ostertag, Utah vs. Denver, March 27, 2004	8
Theo Ratliff, Portland vs. Golden State, April 7, 2004	8

PLAYOFFS
RESULTS

EASTERN CONFERENCE
FIRST ROUND

INDIANA vs. BOSTON
(Pacers win series 4-0)
Apr. 17—Boston 88 at Indiana 104
Apr. 20—Boston 90 at Indiana 103
Apr. 23—Indiana 108 at Boston 85
Apr. 25—Indiana 90 at Boston 75

NEW JERSEY vs. NEW YORK
(Nets win series 4-0)
Apr. 17—New York 83 at New Jersey 107
Apr. 20—New York 81 at New Jersey 99
Apr. 22—New Jersey 81 at New York 78
Apr. 25—New Jersey 100 at New York 94

DETROIT vs. MILWAUKEE
(Pistons win series 4-1)
Apr. 18—Milwaukee 82 at Detroit 108
Apr. 21—Milwaukee 92 at Detroit 88
Apr. 24—Detroit 95 at Milwaukee 85
Apr. 26—Detroit 109 at Milwaukee 92
Apr. 29—Milwaukee 77 at Detroit 91

MIAMI vs. NEW ORLEANS
(Heat wins series 4-3)
Apr. 18—New Orleans 79 at Miami 81
Apr. 21—New Orleans 63 at Miami 93
Apr. 24—Miami 71 at New Orleans 77
Apr. 27—Miami 85 at New Orleans 96
Apr. 30—New Orleans 83 at Miami 87
May 2—Miami 83 at New Orleans 89
May 4—New Orleans 77 at Miami 85

SEMIFINALS

INDIANA vs. MIAMI
(Pacers win series 4-2)
May 6—Miami 81 at Indiana 94
May 8—Miami 80 at Indiana 91
May 10—Indiana 87 at Miami 94
May 12—Indiana 88 at Miami 100
May 15—Miami 83 at Indiana 94
May 18—Indiana 73 at Miami 70

NEW JERSEY vs. DETROIT
(Pistons win series 4-3)
May 3—New Jersey 56 at Detroit 78
May 7—New Jersey 80 at Detroit 95
May 9—Detroit 64 at New Jersey 82
May 11—Detroit 79 at New Jersey 94
May 14—New Jersey 127 at Detroit 120 (3OT)
May 16—Detroit 81 at New Jersey 75
May 20—New Jersey 69 at Detroit 90

FINALS

DETROIT vs. INDIANA
(Pistons win series 4-2)
May 22—Detroit 74 at Indiana 78
May 24—Detroit 72 at Indiana 67
May 26—Indiana 78 at Detroit 85
May 28—Indiana 83, Detroit 68
May 30—Detroit 83 at Indiana 65
Jun. 1—Indiana 65 at Detroit 69

WESTERN CONFERENCE
FIRST ROUND

MINNESOTA vs. DENVER
(Timberwolves win series 4-1)
Apr. 18—Denver 92 at Minnesota 106
Apr. 21—Denver 81 at Minnesota 95
Apr. 24—Minnesota 86 at Denver 107
Apr. 27—Minnesota 84 at Denver 82
Apr. 30—Denver 91 at Minnesota 102

L.A. LAKERS vs. HOUSTON
(Lakers win series 4-1)
Apr. 17—Houston 71 at L.A. Lakers 72
Apr. 19—Houston 84 at L.A. Lakers 98
Apr. 23—L.A. Lakers 91 at Houston 102
Apr. 25—L.A. Lakers 92 at Houston 88 (OT)
Apr. 28—Houston 78 at L.A. Lakers 97

SAN ANTONIO vs. MEMPHIS
(Spurs win series 4-0)
Apr. 17—Memphis 74 at San Antonio 98
Apr. 19—Memphis 70 at San Antonio 87
Apr. 22—San Antonio 95 at Memphis 93
Apr. 26—San Antonio 110 at Memphis 97

SACRAMENTO vs. DALLAS
(Kings win series 4-1)
Apr. 18—Dallas 105 at Sacramento 116
Apr. 20—Dallas 79 at Sacramento 83
Apr. 24—Sacramento 79 at Dallas 104
Apr. 26—Sacramento 94 at Dallas 92
Apr. 29—Dallas 118 at Sacramento 119

SEMIFINALS

MINNESOTA vs. SACRAMENTO
(Timberwolves win series 4-3)
May 4—Sacramento 104 at Minnesota 98
May 8—Sacramento 89 at Minnesota 94
May 10—Minnesota 114 at Sacramento 113 (OT)
May 12—Minnesota 81 at Sacramento 87
May 14—Sacramento 74 at Minnesota 86
May 16—Minnesota 87 at Sacramento 104
May 19—Sacramento 80 at Minnesota 83

L.A. LAKERS vs. SAN ANTONIO
(Lakers win series 4-2)
May 2—L.A. Lakers 78 at San Antonio 88
May 5—L.A. Lakers 85 at San Antonio 95
May 9—San Antonio 81 at L.A. Lakers 105
May 11—San Antonio 90 at L.A. Lakers 98
May 13—L.A. Lakers 74 at San Antonio 73
May 15—San Antonio 76 at L.A. Lakers 88

FINALS

L.A. LAKERS vs. MINNESOTA
(Lakers win series 4-2)
May 21—L.A. Lakers 97 at Minnesota 88
May 23—L.A. Lakers 71 at Minnesota 89
May 25—Minnesota 89 at L.A. Lakers 100
May 27—Minnesota 85 at L.A. Lakers 92
May 29—L.A. Lakers 96 at Minnesota 98
May 31—Minnesota 90 at L.A. Lakers 96

NBA FINALS

DETROIT vs. L.A. LAKERS
(Pistons win series 4-1)
Jun. 6—Detroit 87 at L.A. Lakers 75
Jun. 8—Detroit 91 at L.A. Lakers 99 (OT)
Jun. 10—L.A. Lakers 68 at Detroit 88
Jun. 13—L.A. Lakers 80 at Detroit 88
Jun. 15—L.A. Lakers 87 at Detroit 100

TEAM STATISTICS

OFFENSIVE

Team	G	Field Goals			3-pointers			Free Throws			Rebounds			Miscellaneous						Scoring	
		Made	Att.	Pct.	Made	Att.	Pct.	Made	Att.	Pct.	Off.	Def.	Tot.	Ast	PF	Dq	Stl	TO	Blk	Pts	Avg.
Dall....	5	191	482	.396	25	87	.287	91	118	.771	102	159	261	103	108	0	46	68	33	498	99.6
Sac....	12	423	995	.425	70	201	.348	226	298	.758	131	397	528	274	253	2	113	172	44	1142	95.2
Minn...	18	611	1387	.441	106	274	.387	327	419	.780	174	582	756	347	437	4	119	270	93	1655	91.9
Den....	5	186	436	.427	22	65	.338	59	84	.702	72	144	216	102	121	2	39	71	14	453	90.6
S.A...	10	335	762	.440	69	189	.365	154	239	.644	126	297	423	194	228	1	77	155	42	893	89.3
N.J...	11	339	801	.423	49	180	.272	243	333	.730	117	353	470	225	286	8	95	204	59	970	88.2
LA-L..	22	727	1639	.444	109	340	.321	376	614	.612	224	661	885	498	503	2	161	278	93	1939	88.1
Det...	23	722	1754	.412	97	319	.304	462	629	.734	296	735	1031	447	518	6	184	342	164	2003	87.1
Milw...	5	162	389	.416	24	72	.333	80	108	.741	56	140	196	103	112	1	41	82	21	428	85.6
Ind....	16	491	1202	.408	95	285	.333	291	397	.733	173	501	674	286	376	6	139	217	100	1368	85.5
Hou...	5	159	372	.427	23	76	.303	82	114	.719	48	174	222	86	114	4	26	84	18	423	84.6
Bos....	4	115	282	.408	21	63	.333	87	108	.806	37	127	164	70	81	1	26	79	20	338	84.5
Miami.	13	397	972	.408	48	174	.276	251	333	.754	148	396	544	212	317	3	98	184	53	1093	84.1
N.Y...	4	123	320	.384	17	58	.293	73	101	.723	49	105	154	78	112	2	37	65	16	336	84.0
Mem...	4	123	290	.424	15	51	.294	73	94	.777	38	100	138	58	100	0	38	57	20	334	83.5
N.O....	7	205	534	.384	41	130	.315	113	145	.779	86	210	296	135	146	1	43	120	32	564	80.6

DEFENSIVE

Team	Field Goals			3-pointers			Free Throws			Rebounds			Miscellaneous						Scoring		
	Made	Att.	Pct.	Made	Att.	Pct.	Made	Att.	Pct.	Off.	Def.	Tot.	Ast	PF	Dq	Stl	TO	Blk	Pts	Avg	Dif.
Det...	678	1729	.392	108	390	.277	392	544	.721	250	683	933	427	597	12	183	358	117	1856	80.7	+6.4
Ind...	462	1164	.397	59	192	.307	314	405	.775	172	506	678	271	367	3	104	249	101	1297	81.1	+4.4
N.O...	213	527	.404	28	110	.255	131	178	.736	84	216	300	114	164	1	57	106	28	585	83.6	-3.0
Miami.	385	951	.405	77	229	.336	244	330	.739	148	397	545	244	284	3	82	206	65	1091	83.9	+0.2
N.J...	341	871	.392	48	162	.296	213	291	.732	137	324	461	213	291	6	97	176	64	943	85.7	+2.5
S.A...	320	707	.453	41	127	.323	181	271	.668	88	293	381	179	227	0	80	149	52	862	86.2	+3.1
LA-L..	705	1669	.422	113	363	.311	396	550	.720	254	693	947	394	529	7	145	320	75	1919	87.2	+0.9
Hou...	169	394	.429	23	67	.343	89	140	.636	50	152	202	122	108	0	50	52	20	450	90.0	-5.4
Minn..	626	1458	.429	97	284	.342	307	447	.687	212	545	757	417	391	4	135	227	62	1656	92.0	-0.1
Den...	173	376	.460	32	65	.492	95	131	.725	46	155	201	100	108	0	34	82	30	473	94.6	+0.0
Sac...	429	1036	.414	68	199	.342	215	279	.771	176	398	574	238	272	2	98	179	76	1141	95.1	+0.1
N.Y...	137	288	.476	17	63	.270	96	129	.744	37	137	174	89	90	2	38	76	20	387	96.8	-12.8
Mem...	146	288	.507	31	65	.477	67	101	.663	46	122	168	87	81	0	30	65	25	390	97.5	-14.0
Dall..	186	421	.442	33	90	.367	86	121	.711	63	176	239	111	109	1	50	82	23	491	98.2	+1.4
Milw..	184	400	.460	27	84	.321	96	126	.762	65	161	226	120	103	2	48	70	40	491	98.2	-12.6
Bos...	155	338	.459	29	74	.392	66	91	.725	49	123	172	92	91	0	51	51	24	405	101.3	-16.8
AVG...	332	789	.421	52	160	.324	187	258	.723	117	318	435	201	238	3	80	153	51	902	88.0	---

INDIVIDUAL STATISTICS, TEAM BY TEAM

BOSTON CELTICS

	G	Min.	FGM	FGA	Pct.	FTM	FTA	Pct.	REBOUNDS			Ast.	PF	Dq.	Stl.	TO	Blk.	SCORING		
									Off.	Def.	Tot.							Pts.	Avg.	Hi.
Paul Pierce	4	162	26	76	.342	26	31	.839	6	29	35	10	12	0	5	25	4	83	20.8	27
Chucky Atkins	4	133	17	39	.436	17	19	.895	3	11	14	15	2	0	3	10	0	54	13.5	21
Mark Blount	4	145	17	35	.486	14	19	.737	10	27	37	4	17	0	6	9	8	48	12.0	21
Ricky Davis	4	123	16	40	.400	11	16	.688	3	9	12	14	7	0	2	12	0	47	11.8	19
Jiri Welsch	4	104	11	23	.478	9	9	1.000	0	12	12	9	7	0	2	8	0	32	8.0	11
Walter McCarty	4	127	11	23	.478	0	0	---	3	18	21	8	7	0	2	4	2	28	7.0	12
Marcus Banks	4	60	7	16	.438	4	4	1.000	1	6	7	7	9	0	2	3	1	20	5.0	9
Chris Mihm	4	65	7	22	.318	6	10	.600	8	10	18	0	12	1	4	3	4	20	5.0	9
Jumaine Jones	2	28	2	6	.333	0	0	---	1	4	5	2	4	0	0	0	0	4	2.0	4
Brandon Hunter	3	10	1	1	1.000	0	0	---	2	1	3	1	2	0	0	1	1	2	0.7	2
Dana Barros	1	1	0	1	.000	0	0	---	0	0	0	0	0	0	0	0	0	0	0.0	0
Michael Stewart	1	2	0	0	---	0	0	---	0	0	0	0	2	0	0	0	0	0	0.0	0
Boston	4	960	115	282	.408	87	108	.806	37	127	164	70	81	1	26	79	20	338	84.5	90
Opponents	4	960	155	338	.459	66	91	.725	49	123	172	92	91	0	51	51	24	405	101.3	108

3-pt FG: Boston 21-63 (.333)
Pierce 5-17 (.294); Atkins 3-10 (.300); Davis 4-10 (.400); Welsch 1-4 (.250); McCarty 6-15 (.400); Banks 2-5 (.400)
Jones 0-2 (.000); Opponents 29-74 (.392)

DALLAS MAVERICKS

	G	Min.	FGM	FGA	Pct.	FTM	FTA	Pct.	REBOUNDS			Ast.	PF	Dq.	Stl.	TO	Blk.	SCORING		
									Off.	Def.	Tot.							Pts.	Avg.	Hi.
Dirk Nowitzki	5	212	45	100	.450	36	42	.857	13	46	59	7	16	0	7	6	13	133	26.6	32
Marquis Daniels	5	184	32	75	.427	14	22	.636	10	21	31	15	14	0	10	15	3	79	15.8	22
Steve Nash	5	197	27	70	.386	8	9	.889	6	20	26	45	14	0	4	12	0	68	13.6	24
Michael Finley	5	196	26	68	.382	6	10	.600	6	10	16	13	8	0	4	9	3	65	13.0	18
Antawn Jamison	5	109	26	57	.456	11	15	.733	10	15	25	2	15	0	5	5	2	65	13.0	20
Antoine Walker	5	140	22	61	.361	4	7	.571	23	27	50	12	13	0	6	9	3	49	9.8	15
Josh Howard	5	86	8	36	.222	10	11	.909	17	15	32	4	12	0	6	7	6	27	5.4	11
Eduardo Najera	5	57	5	11	.455	2	2	1.000	10	7	17	3	12	0	3	2	2	12	2.4	6
Shawn Bradley	2	3	0	0	---	0	0	---	0	0	0	0	1	0	0	0	0	0	0.0	0
Tony Delk	1	5	0	0	---	0	0	---	0	1	1	2	0	0	1	0	0	0	0.0	0
Scott Williams	3	11	0	1	.000	0	0	---	2	2	4	0	0	0	0	0	1	0	0.0	0

	G	Min.	FGM	FGA	Pct.	FTM	FTA	Pct.	Off.	Def.	Tot.	Ast.	PF	Dq.	Stl.	TO	Blk.	Pts.	Avg.	Hi.
Dallas	5	1200	191	482	.396	91	118	.771	102	159	261	103	108	0	46	68	33	498	99.6	118
Opponents	5	1200	186	421	.442	86	121	.711	63	176	239	111	109	1	50	82	23	491	98.2	119

3-pt. FG: Dallas 25-87 (.287)

Nowitzki 7-15 (.467); Daniels 1-7 (.143); Nash 6-16 (.375); Finley 7-26 (.269); Jamison 2-8 (.250); Walker 1-10 (.100)
Howard 1-5 (.200); Opponents 33-90 (.367)

DENVER NUGGETS

	G	Min.	FGM	FGA	Pct.	FTM	FTA	Pct.	Off.	Def.	Tot.	Ast.	PF	Dq.	Stl.	TO	Blk.	Pts.	Avg.	Hi.
Voshon Lenard	5	161	32	75	.427	10	14	.714	4	9	13	12	13	0	4	9	0	85	17.0	28
Andre Miller	5	174	34	72	.472	9	11	.818	15	8	23	16	16	1	8	10	0	77	15.4	21
Carmelo Anthony	4	143	21	64	.328	16	20	.800	7	26	33	11	11	1	5	17	0	60	15.0	24
Earl Boykins	5	121	28	63	.444	6	7	.857	6	6	12	19	6	0	5	6	1	67	13.4	19
Marcus Camby	5	194	27	55	.491	8	14	.571	14	43	57	12	21	0	4	6	7	63	12.6	21
Nene Hilario	5	132	16	36	.444	7	13	.538	12	13	25	15	22	0	5	9	3	39	7.8	14
Jon Barry	5	100	8	24	.333	2	3	.667	4	14	18	10	4	0	3	4	0	21	4.2	9
Francisco Elson......	4	60	7	12	.583	1	2	.500	1	8	9	2	14	0	2	3	1	15	3.8	7
Michael Doleac	5	49	5	10	.500	0	0	—	2	5	7	3	8	0	0	1	0	10	2.0	4
Rodney White........	4	26	4	15	.267	0	0	—	1	4	5	0	3	0	2	2	0	8	2.0	6
Chris Andersen	5	34	3	9	.333	0	0	—	6	8	14	2	3	0	1	2	2	6	1.2	4
Ryan Bowen	4	6	1	1	1.000	0	0	—	0	0	0	0	0	0	0	0	0	2	0.5	2
Denver	5	1200	186	436	.427	59	84	.702	72	144	216	102	121	2	39	71	14	453	90.6	107
Opponents	5	1200	173	376	.460	95	131	.725	46	155	201	100	108	0	34	82	30	473	94.6	106

3-pt. FG: Denver 22-65 (.338)

Lenard 11-24 (.458); Miller 0-2 (.000); Anthony 2-11 (.182); Boykins 5-14 (.357); Camby 1-2 (.500); Barry 3-9 (.333)
White 0-3 (.000); Opponents 32-65 (.492)

DETROIT PISTONS

	G	Min.	FGM	FGA	Pct.	FTM	FTA	Pct.	Off.	Def.	Tot.	Ast.	PF	Dq.	Stl.	TO	Blk.	Pts.	Avg.	Hi.
Richard Hamilton	23	924	181	405	.447	117	138	.848	32	74	106	97	72	2	27	72	1	494	21.5	33
Chauncey Billups....	23	881	110	286	.385	121	136	.890	14	56	70	136	57	1	31	60	2	378	16.4	31
Rasheed Wallace.....	23	803	118	286	.413	46	60	.767	47	132	179	37	78	1	13	43	45	299	13.0	26
Ben Wallace	23	924	93	205	.454	50	117	.427	95	233	328	44	58	1	44	37	56	236	10.3	18
Tayshaun Prince	23	795	87	212	.410	41	55	.745	41	96	137	53	61	1	25	19	31	228	9.9	24
Corliss Williamson ...	22	327	44	121	.364	38	47	.809	20	29	49	15	59	0	6	24	3	126	5.7	14
Mehmet Okur	22	252	31	66	.470	18	26	.692	16	45	61	8	20	0	5	15	9	82	3.7	9
Mike James	22	195	21	53	.396	9	16	.563	7	19	26	24	23	0	5	15	0	57	2.6	10
Lindsey Hunter	23	273	19	65	.292	11	12	.917	5	28	33	21	42	0	18	13	4	56	2.4	8
Elden Campbell......	14	124	10	35	.286	10	18	.556	10	15	25	10	28	0	6	9	9	30	2.1	6
Darvin Ham	22	108	8	16	.500	0	0	—	8	6	14	1	19	0	3	8	4	16	0.8	4
Darko Milicic........	8	14	0	4	.000	1	4	.250	1	2	3	1	1	0	1	3	0	1	0.1	1
Detroit	23	5620	722	1754	.412	462	629	.734	296	735	1031	447	518	6	184	342	164	2003	87.1	120
Opponents	23	5620	678	1729	.392	392	544	.721	250	683	933	427	597	12	183	358	117	1856	80.7	127

3-pt. FG: Detroit 97-319 (.304)

Hamilton 15-39 (.385); Billups 37-107 (.346); R. Wallace 17-70 (.243); B. Wallace 0-3 (.000); Prince 13-49 (.265); Okur 2-5 (.400)
Williamson 0-1 (.000); James 6-14 (.429); Hunter 7-30 (.233); Ham 0-1 (.000); Opponents 108-390 (.277)

HOUSTON ROCKETS

	G	Min.	FGM	FGA	Pct.	FTM	FTA	Pct.	Off.	Def.	Tot.	Ast.	PF	Dq.	Stl.	TO	Blk.	Pts.	Avg.	Hi.
Steve Francis	5	222	30	70	.429	29	40	.725	6	36	42	38	18	1	7	21	1	96	19.2	27
Yao Ming	5	185	31	68	.456	13	17	.765	11	26	37	9	20	2	2	13	7	75	15.0	21
Jim Jackson	5	221	29	73	.397	8	12	.667	3	49	52	10	9	0	5	9	1	74	14.8	19
Cuttino Mobley	5	210	29	75	.387	8	10	.800	5	19	24	14	14	0	3	18	3	72	14.4	21
Maurice Taylor	5	115	18	38	.474	13	17	.765	5	11	16	5	20	0	0	7	1	49	9.8	16
Kelvin Cato	5	148	13	22	.591	3	7	.429	14	20	34	2	18	1	5	5	4	29	5.8	12
Clarence Weatherspoo .	2	22	2	5	.400	3	6	.500	2	2	4	0	3	0	0	0	0	7	3.5	4
Bostjan Nachbar	5	41	4	9	.444	5	5	1.000	1	5	6	2	9	0	1	2	0	14	2.8	5
Scott Padgett	4	14	2	5	.400	0	0	—	1	2	3	0	1	0	1	1	1	5	1.3	3
Mark Jackson	5	38	1	6	.167	0	0	—	0	3	3	5	1	0	2	2	0	2	0.4	2
Eric Piatkowski.......	1	4	0	1	.000	0	0	—	0	1	1	0	1	0	0	0	0	0	0.0	0
Mike Wilks	2	5	0	0	—	0	0	—	0	0	0	1	0	0	0	1	0	0	0.0	0
Houston	5	1225	159	372	.427	82	114	.719	48	174	222	86	114	4	26	84	18	423	84.6	102
Opponents	5	1225	169	394	.429	89	140	.636	50	152	202	122	108	0	50	52	20	450	90.0	98

3-pt. FG: Houston 23-76 (.303)

Francis 7-17 (.412); J. Jackson 8-29 (.276); Mobley 6-21 (.286); Nachbar 1-3 (.333); Padgett 1-3 (.333); M. Jackson 0-3 (.000)
Opponents 23-67 (.343)

INDIANA PACERS

	G	Min.	FGM	FGA	Pct.	FTM	FTA	Pct.	Off.	Def.	Tot.	Ast.	PF	Dq.	Stl.	TO	Blk.	Pts.	Avg.	Hi.
Jermaine O'Neal	16	604	115	272	.423	77	110	.700	29	117	146	19	53	0	8	29	36	307	19.2	37
Ron Artest	15	584	98	259	.378	61	85	.718	24	74	98	48	45	2	21	37	16	276	18.4	28
Reggie Miller	16	455	45	112	.402	47	51	.922	3	34	37	45	23	0	18	28	3	161	10.1	21
Al Harrington	16	427	60	140	.429	30	55	.545	33	69	102	12	56	1	23	28	9	152	9.5	19

	G	Min.	FGM	FGA	Pct.	FTM	FTA	Pct.	Off.	Def.	Tot.	Ast.	PF	Dq.	Stl.	TO	Blk.	Pts.	Avg.	Hi.
Jamaal Tinsley	16	422	49	123	.398	15	16	.938	6	40	46	80	56	2	28	31	3	129	8.1	17
Austin Croshere	13	214	19	55	.345	17	21	.810	13	27	40	12	17	1	4	6	3	63	4.8	14
Jonathan Bender	16	200	28	69	.406	12	16	.750	10	18	28	7	19	0	2	12	14	77	4.8	19
Fred Jones	14	263	25	51	.490	5	7	.714	3	30	33	16	31	0	7	9	7	66	4.7	17
Anthony Johnson	16	332	25	69	.362	17	22	.773	7	27	34	34	34	0	13	11	4	73	4.6	9
Jeff Foster	16	307	25	43	.581	8	10	.800	44	61	105	12	37	0	13	13	5	58	3.6	20
Kenny Anderson	4	19	2	7	.286	0	0	—	0	1	1	1	3	0	1	5	0	4	1.0	4
Scot Pollard	3	13	0	2	.000	2	4	.500	1	3	4	0	2	0	1	0	0	2	0.7	1
Indiana	16	3840	491	1202	.408	291	397	.733	173	501	674	286	376	6	139	217	100	1368	85.5	108
Opponents	16	3840	462	1164	.397	314	405	.775	172	506	678	271	367	3	104	249	101	1297	81.1	100

3-pt. FG: Indiana 95-285 (.333)
O'Neal 0-4 (.000); Artest 19-66 (.288); Miller 24-64 (.375); Harrington 2-5 (.400); Tinsley 16-54 (.296); Croshere 8-24 (.333)
Bender 9-25 (.360); F. Jones 11-22 (.500); Johnson 6-20 (.300); Foster 0-1 (.000); Opponents 59-192 (.307)

LOS ANGELES LAKERS

	G	Min.	FGM	FGA	Pct.	FTM	FTA	Pct.	Off.	Def.	Tot.	Ast.	PF	Dq.	Stl.	TO	Blk.	Pts.	Avg.	Hi.
Kobe Bryant	22	973	190	460	.413	135	166	.813	18	86	104	121	59	0	42	61	7	539	24.5	42
Shaquille O'Neal	22	917	182	307	.593	109	254	.429	91	200	291	55	90	1	7	55	61	473	21.5	36
Karl Malone	21	798	98	218	.450	46	73	.630	37	148	185	72	65	0	24	47	2	242	11.5	30
Gary Payton	22	772	68	186	.366	21	28	.750	19	53	72	116	60	0	23	28	4	171	7.8	18
Derek Fisher	22	507	60	148	.405	23	35	.657	10	46	56	49	47	0	18	19	0	166	7.5	17
Devean George	22	470	43	100	.430	13	20	.650	11	39	50	11	45	0	21	11	8	121	5.5	16
Slava Medvedenko	21	237	33	75	.440	17	21	.810	23	30	53	10	50	0	4	5	4	83	4.0	12
Kareem Rush	22	315	30	78	.385	2	3	.667	0	16	16	17	33	0	10	14	3	82	3.7	18
Luke Walton	17	134	10	29	.345	7	10	.700	5	17	22	26	24	1	7	14	2	32	1.9	7
Rick Fox	16	145	8	20	.400	1	2	.500	6	17	23	18	21	0	3	9	2	18	1.1	6
Brian Cook	13	46	5	15	.333	2	2	1.000	3	9	12	1	7	0	1	3	0	12	0.9	4
Bryon Russell	6	16	0	3	.000	0	0	—	1	0	1	2	2	0	1	0	0	0	0.0	0
L.A. Lakers	22	5330	727	1639	.444	376	614	.612	224	661	885	498	503	2	161	278	93	1939	88.1	105
Opponents	22	5330	705	1669	.422	396	550	.720	254	693	947	394	529	7	145	320	75	1919	87.2	100

3-pt. FG: L.A. Lakers 109-340 (.321).
Bryant 24-97 (.247); Malone 0-1 (.000); Payton 14-56 (.250); Fisher 23-55 (.418); George 22-59 (.373); Rush 20-50 (.400)
Walton 5-13 (.385); Fox 1-7 (.143); Russell 0-2 (.000); Opponents 113-363 (.311)

MEMPHIS GRIZZLIES

	G	Min.	FGM	FGA	Pct.	FTM	FTA	Pct.	Off.	Def.	Tot.	Ast.	PF	Dq.	Stl.	TO	Blk.	Pts.	Avg.	Hi.
Pau Gasol	4	134	28	49	.571	18	20	.900	4	16	20	10	10	0	4	5	6	74	18.5	22
James Posey	4	130	15	37	.405	19	21	.905	8	14	22	4	13	0	9	6	2	50	12.5	20
Bonzi Wells	4	94	19	37	.514	9	14	.643	2	10	12	4	8	0	4	9	1	47	11.8	16
Jason Williams	4	130	15	46	.326	7	7	1.000	1	8	9	18	10	0	2	7	0	43	10.8	16
Mike Miller	4	98	12	34	.353	1	3	.333	0	12	12	3	4	0	5	5	0	30	7.5	12
Stromile Swift	4	74	9	26	.346	6	8	.750	6	13	19	3	6	0	3	3	6	24	6.0	9
Lorenzen Wright	4	100	10	23	.435	2	6	.333	5	12	17	2	15	0	4	5	2	22	5.5	8
Shane Battier	4	69	6	15	.400	4	6	.667	6	6	12	1	17	0	0	4	1	19	4.8	6
Earl Watson	4	62	8	15	.533	3	3	1.000	4	5	9	7	8	0	5	6	0	19	4.8	13
Jake Tsakalidis	1	3	0	0	—	2	2	1.000	0	0	0	0	0	0	0	3	0	2	2.0	2
Ryan Humphrey	3	5	1	1	1.000	0	0	—	1	1	2	0	2	0	0	0	0	2	0.7	2
Bo Outlaw	4	61	0	7	.000	2	4	.500	1	3	4	6	9	0	2	3	2	2	0.5	1
Memphis	4	960	123	290	.424	73	94	.777	38	100	138	58	100	0	38	57	20	334	83.5	97
Opponents	4	960	146	288	.507	67	101	.663	46	122	168	78	87	81	0	30	65	25	390	97.5	110

3-pt. FG: Memphis 15-51 (.294).
Posey 1-6 (.167); Wells 0-1 (.000); Williams 6-21 (.286); Miller 5-13 (.385); Battier 3-7 (.429); Watson 0-3 (.000)
Opponents 31-65 (.477)

MIAMI HEAT

	G	Min.	FGM	FGA	Pct.	FTM	FTA	Pct.	Off.	Def.	Tot.	Ast.	PF	Dq.	Stl.	TO	Blk.	Pts.	Avg.	Hi.
Dwyane Wade	13	510	86	189	.455	59	75	.787	16	36	52	73	45	0	17	54	4	234	18.0	27
Lamar Odom	13	512	81	182	.445	49	72	.681	32	76	108	37	58	2	15	42	10	219	16.8	25
Eddie Jones	13	478	56	153	.366	40	50	.800	3	44	47	29	37	0	18	19	11	172	13.2	25
Caron Butler	13	511	59	153	.386	47	57	.825	18	92	110	31	45	0	28	23	7	167	12.8	24
Brian Grant	13	399	42	98	.429	8	14	.571	45	67	112	10	52	1	7	18	8	92	7.1	15
Rafer Alston	13	295	29	91	.319	21	25	.840	4	25	29	22	22	0	5	10	1	91	7.0	17
Malik Allen	10	138	22	49	.449	6	9	.667	12	18	30	4	21	0	2	4	9	50	5.0	13
Udonis Haslem	13	199	13	33	.394	21	31	.677	18	26	44	3	22	0	5	3	3	47	3.6	8
Rasual Butler	10	58	9	22	.409	0	0	—	0	11	11	2	12	0	1	1	0	21	2.1	5
Samaki Walker	4	11	0	2	.000	0	0	—	0	1	1	0	2	0	0	0	0	0	0.0	0
Zhizhi Wang	3	7	0	0	—	0	0	—	0	0	0	1	1	0	0	1	0	0	0.0	0
Loren Woods	1	2	0	0	—	0	0	—	0	0	0	0	0	0	0	0	0	0	0.0	0
Miami	13	3120	397	972	.408	251	333	.754	148	396	544	212	317	3	98	184	53	1093	84.1	100
Opponents	13	3120	385	951	.405	244	330	.739	148	397	545	244	284	3	82	206	65	1091	83.9	96

3-pt. FG: Miami 48-174 (.276)
Wade 3-8 (.375); Odom 8-26 (.308); Jones 20-67 (.299); C. Butler 2-11 (.182); Grant 0-1 (.000); Alston 12-52 (.231)
R. Butler 3-9 (.333); Opponents 77-229 (.336)

MILWAUKEE BUCKS

	G	Min.	FGM	FGA	Pct.	FTM	FTA	Pct.	REBOUNDS			Ast.	PF	Dq.	Stl.	TO	Blk.	SCORING		
									Off.	Def.	Tot.							Pts.	Avg.	Hi.
Michael Redd	5	192	34	83	.410	16	21	.762	6	19	25	13	16	0	0	19	0	90	18.0	26
Desmond Mason	5	198	25	74	.338	22	26	.846	4	20	24	12	16	0	4	12	2	72	14.4	19
Joe Smith	5	175	27	55	.491	12	13	.923	23	27	50	2	15	0	4	6	10	66	13.2	17
Damon Jones	5	144	18	34	.529	4	6	.667	2	18	20	37	14	0	5	9	0	50	10.0	17
Toni Kukoc	5	105	17	34	.500	4	8	.500	4	10	14	4	11	0	3	6	2	42	8.4	15
Keith Van Horn	5	137	16	48	.333	4	6	.667	5	18	23	7	15	0	7	10	3	40	8.0	11
Brian Skinner	5	94	11	21	.524	5	12	.417	8	14	22	0	8	0	1	7	3	27	5.4	8
Erick Strickland	3	41	5	12	.417	4	4	1.000	0	5	5	9	3	0	2	3	0	14	4.7	10
Brevin Knight	5	101	6	23	.261	9	11	.818	3	8	11	17	12	1	14	7	1	21	4.2	11
Dan Gadzuric	1	9	2	4	.500	0	1	.000	0	1	1	2	1	0	1	0	0	4	4.0	4
Marcus Haislip	1	3	1	1	1.000	0	0	—	1	0	1	0	0	0	0	0	0	2	2.0	2
Daniel Santiago	1	1	0	0	—	0	0	—	0	0	0	0	1	0	0	0	0	0	0.0	0
Milwaukee	5	1200	162	389	.416	80	108	.741	56	140	196	103	112	1	41	82	21	428	85.6	92
Opponents	5	1200	184	400	.460	96	126	.762	65	161	226	120	103	2	48	70	40	491	98.2	109

3-pt. FG: Milwaukee 24-72 (.333).
Redd 6-20 (.300); Mason 0-2 (.000); Smith 0-1 (.000); Jones 10-21 (.476); Kukoc 4-12 (.333); Van Horn 4-11 (.364)
Strickland 0-5 (.000); Opponents 27-84 (.321).

MINNESOTA TIMBERWOLVES

	G	Min.	FGM	FGA	Pct.	FTM	FTA	Pct.	REBOUNDS			Ast.	PF	Dq.	Stl.	TO	Blk.	SCORING		
									Off.	Def.	Tot.							Pts.	Avg.	Hi.
Kevin Garnett	18	783	168	372	.452	97	125	.776	39	224	263	92	57	2	24	75	41	438	24.3	32
Latrell Sprewell	18	771	130	309	.421	60	77	.779	11	68	79	72	35	0	29	47	12	357	19.8	34
Sam Cassell	16	497	94	202	.465	52	61	.852	3	37	40	70	53	2	12	43	3	265	16.6	40
Wally Szczerbiak	12	298	47	112	.420	38	41	.927	9	30	39	20	31	0	6	24	2	142	11.8	21
Trenton Hassell	18	472	62	119	.521	13	16	.813	21	23	44	27	42	0	10	16	7	138	7.7	17
Fred Hoiberg	18	438	39	86	.453	15	16	.938	9	57	66	23	29	0	16	8	0	115	6.4	14
Darrick Martin	16	182	14	51	.275	16	20	.800	5	9	14	23	17	0	4	8	0	50	3.1	15
Mark Madsen	17	221	17	32	.531	13	29	.448	28	30	58	2	43	0	5	7	4	47	2.8	8
Ervin Johnson	18	356	19	38	.500	10	16	.625	27	57	84	13	56	0	11	6	10	48	2.7	9
Michael Olowokandi	15	224	12	37	.324	7	8	.875	16	36	52	2	50	0	2	17	11	31	2.1	10
Gary Trent	13	71	8	25	.320	5	8	.625	6	6	12	2	11	0	0	3	0	21	1.6	10
Oliver Miller	8	31	1	4	.250	1	2	.500	0	5	5	1	13	0	0	3	3	3	0.4	2
Minnesota	18	4345	611	1387	.441	327	419	.780	174	582	756	347	437	4	119	270	93	1655	91.9	114
Opponents	18	4345	626	1458	.429	307	447	.687	212	545	757	417	391	4	135	227	62	1656	92.0	113

3-pt. FG: Minnesota 106-274 (.387).
Garnett 5-16 (.313); Sprewell 37-96 (.385); Cassell 25-60 (.417); Szczerbiak 10-29 (.345); Hassell 1-2 (.500); Martin 6-20 (.300)
Hoiberg 22-48 (.458); Olowokandi 0-1 (.000); Trent 0-2 (.000); Opponents 97-284 (.342).

NEW JERSEY NETS

	G	Min.	FGM	FGA	Pct.	FTM	FTA	Pct.	REBOUNDS			Ast.	PF	Dq.	Stl.	TO	Blk.	SCORING		
									Off.	Def.	Tot.							Pts.	Avg.	Hi.
Richard Jefferson	11	460	66	158	.418	77	108	.713	14	55	69	42	35	0	14	43	8	218	19.8	31
Kenyon Martin	11	409	81	152	.533	48	64	.750	25	96	121	12	50	3	13	32	14	210	19.1	36
Kerry Kittles	11	415	60	134	.448	21	34	.618	10	37	47	23	28	0	22	11	10	158	14.4	20
Jason Kidd	11	474	43	129	.333	43	53	.811	16	57	73	99	15	0	25	43	6	139	12.6	22
Rodney Rogers	11	228	23	72	.319	16	20	.800	9	46	55	12	31	1	6	17	3	67	6.1	13
Lucious Harris	11	182	19	49	.388	14	18	.778	10	12	22	10	16	0	7	5	1	55	5.0	12
Aaron Williams	11	149	18	33	.545	6	10	.600	7	15	22	4	41	2	0	15	7	42	3.8	12
Jason Collins	11	266	14	38	.368	12	16	.750	18	26	44	17	49	2	3	15	10	40	3.6	8
Brian Scalabrine	9	73	11	17	.647	3	6	.500	7	5	12	1	15	0	3	4	0	30	3.3	17
Brandon Armstrong	8	32	3	12	.250	0	0	—	1	1	2	3	4	0	1	0	0	6	0.8	2
Tamar Slay	6	12	1	5	.200	2	2	1.000	0	2	2	0	0	0	1	0	0	4	0.7	2
Zoran Planinic	6	15	0	2	.000	1	2	.500	0	1	1	2	2	0	0	2	0	1	0.2	1
New Jersey	11	2715	339	801	.423	243	333	.730	117	353	470	225	286	8	95	204	59	970	88.2	127
Opponents	11	2715	341	871	.392	213	291	.732	137	324	461	213	291	6	97	176	64	943	85.7	120

3-pt. FG: New Jersey 49-180 (.272).
Jefferson 9-33 (.273); Martin 0-4 (.000); Kittles 17-52 (.327); Kidd 10-48 (.208); Rogers 5-22 (.227); Harris 3-12 (.250)
Scalabrine 5-6 (.833); Armstrong 0-1 (.000); Slay 0-1 (.000); Planinic 0-1 (.000); Opponents 48-162 (.296).

NEW ORLEANS HORNETS

	G	Min.	FGM	FGA	Pct.	FTM	FTA	Pct.	REBOUNDS			Ast.	PF	Dq.	Stl.	TO	Blk.	SCORING		
									Off.	Def.	Tot.							Pts.	Avg.	Hi.
Baron Davis	7	260	43	114	.377	25	33	.758	6	23	29	49	21	0	11	19	5	127	18.1	33
Jamaal Magloire	7	239	28	67	.418	21	28	.750	16	48	64	5	22	1	3	11	7	77	11.0	14
David Wesley	7	243	24	74	.324	15	21	.714	1	15	16	17	21	0	5	16	0	74	10.6	18
P.J. Brown	7	256	26	71	.366	10	11	.909	29	39	68	15	16	0	3	13	11	62	8.9	16
George Lynch	7	147	25	57	.439	5	8	.625	13	24	37	12	15	0	3	7	3	58	8.3	16
Stacey Augmon	7	168	18	48	.375	16	18	.889	4	15	19	7	13	0	6	13	1	52	7.4	17
Steve Smith	5	46	12	26	.462	2	3	.667	2	6	8	1	5	0	0	3	0	32	6.4	25
David West	7	111	15	28	.536	11	13	.846	8	22	30	8	10	0	2	7	4	41	5.9	16
Darrell Armstrong	7	150	8	34	.235	3	3	1.000	6	9	15	16	10	0	6	13	0	24	3.4	8
Robert Traylor	4	40	4	9	.444	2	3	.667	1	9	10	1	8	0	3	2	1	10	2.5	4
Shammond Williams	3	18	2	5	.400	3	4	.750	0	4	5	0	4	0	1	4	0	7	2.3	7
Maurice Carter	1	2	0	1	.000	0	0	—	0	0	0	0	0	0	0	0	0	0	0.0	0
New Orleans	7	1680	205	534	.384	113	145	.779	86	210	296	135	146	1	43	120	32	564	80.6	96
Opponents	7	1680	213	527	.404	131	178	.736	84	216	300	114	164	1	57	106	28	585	83.6	93

3-pt. FG: New Orleans 41-130 (.315).
Davis 16-49 (.327); Magloire 0-1 (.000); Wesley 11-30 (.367); Lynch 3-12 (.250); Augmon 0-1 (.000); Smith 6-11 (.545)
Armstrong 5-25 (.200); Williams 0-1 (.000); Opponents 28-110 (.255).

NEW YORK KNICKERBOCKERS

	G	Min.	FGM	FGA	Pct.	FTM	FTA	Pct.	Off.	Def.	Tot.	Ast.	PF	Dq.	Stl.	TO	Blk.	Pts.	Avg.	Hi.
Stephon Marbury	4	174	31	83	.373	17	25	.680	5	12	17	26	9	0	7	14	0	85	21.3	31
Anfernee Hardaway	4	168	23	63	.365	15	18	.833	4	14	18	23	8	0	6	10	1	66	16.5	18
Kurt Thomas	4	139	21	49	.429	9	12	.750	9	37	46	6	17	0	7	10	3	51	12.8	18
Tim Thomas	1	22	4	10	.400	4	5	.800	1	4	5	3	5	0	0	2	0	12	12.0	12
Nazr Mohammed	4	97	15	30	.500	11	16	.688	10	13	23	1	18	1	6	7	3	41	10.3	18
Vin Baker	4	57	8	14	.571	6	9	.667	6	6	12	1	8	1	3	2	2	22	5.5	12
Frank Williams	4	74	6	22	.273	3	5	.600	1	1	2	5	13	0	3	4	0	19	4.8	11
Shandon Anderson	4	117	7	27	.259	1	2	.500	5	4	9	11	19	0	4	8	1	17	4.3	9
Michael Sweetney	4	57	6	11	.545	4	6	.667	4	6	10	0	7	0	0	0	1	16	4.0	12
Dikembe Mutombo	3	38	2	6	.333	3	3	1.000	4	6	10	0	6	0	1	3	4	7	2.3	5
DerMarr Johnson	3	17	0	5	.000	0	0	—	0	2	2	2	2	0	0	0	1	0	0.0	0
New York	4	960	123	320	.384	73	101	.723	49	105	154	78	112	2	37	65	16	336	84.0	94
Opponents	4	960	137	288	.476	96	129	.744	37	137	174	89	90	2	38	76	20	387	96.8	107

3-pt. FG: New York 17-58 (.293).
Marbury 6-20 (.300); Hardaway 5-14 (.357); T. Thomas 0-1 (.000); Williams 4-13 (.308); Anderson 2-7 (.286); Johnson 0-3 (.000)
Opponents 17-63 (.270).

SACRAMENTO KINGS

	G	Min.	FGM	FGA	Pct.	FTM	FTA	Pct.	Off.	Def.	Tot.	Ast.	PF	Dq.	Stl.	TO	Blk.	Pts.	Avg.	Hi.
Mike Bibby	12	497	84	196	.429	48	55	.873	9	41	50	84	40	1	23	35	5	240	20.0	36
Chris Webber	12	446	90	199	.452	40	65	.615	24	75	99	44	34	0	16	38	10	221	18.4	28
Peja Stojakovic	12	517	76	198	.384	35	39	.897	15	69	84	18	26	0	22	14	3	210	17.5	29
Doug Christie	12	461	56	141	.397	41	48	.854	17	57	74	47	35	0	22	22	5	166	13.8	24
Brad Miller	12	366	48	91	.527	29	48	.604	30	74	104	38	46	0	9	20	11	126	10.5	21
Vlade Divac	12	235	31	71	.437	17	23	.739	22	37	59	22	31	0	4	14	5	79	6.6	14
Anthony Peeler	11	236	19	63	.302	5	6	.833	7	28	35	15	19	0	14	14	2	50	4.5	11
Darius Songaila	7	85	10	16	.625	6	6	1.000	6	7	13	2	14	1	0	5	1	26	3.7	8
Rodney Buford	5	32	5	12	.417	1	2	.500	0	5	5	3	2	0	2	0	0	12	2.4	7
Gerald Wallace	3	20	3	6	.500	1	2	.500	0	2	2	1	4	0	1	3	1	7	2.3	5
Jabari Smith	4	10	1	2	.500	3	4	.750	1	2	3	0	2	0	0	0	1	5	1.3	3
Sacramento	12	2905	423	995	.425	226	298	.758	131	397	528	274	253	2	113	172	44	1142	95.2	119
Opponents	12	2905	429	1036	.414	215	279	.771	176	398	574	238	272	2	98	179	76	1141	95.1	118

3-pt. FG: Sacramento 70-201 (.348).
Bibby 24-55 (.436); Webber 1-4 (.250); Stojakovic 23-73 (.315); Christie 13-33 (.394); Miller 1-7 (.143); Peeler 7-26 (.269)
Buford 1-3 (.333); Opponents 68-199 (.342)

SAN ANTONIO SPURS

	G	Min.	FGM	FGA	Pct.	FTM	FTA	Pct.	Off.	Def.	Tot.	Ast.	PF	Dq.	Stl.	TO	Blk.	Pts.	Avg.	Hi.
Tim Duncan	10	405	83	159	.522	55	87	.632	33	80	113	32	34	0	8	42	20	221	22.1	30
Tony Parker	10	386	72	168	.429	23	35	.657	5	16	21	70	15	0	13	31	1	184	18.4	30
Manu Ginobili	10	280	42	94	.447	36	44	.818	15	38	53	31	30	0	17	21	1	130	13.0	21
Hedo Turkoglu	10	271	26	81	.321	11	18	.611	5	40	45	15	20	0	9	16	1	77	7.7	18
Robert Horry	10	211	20	43	.465	13	14	.929	25	38	63	9	31	0	8	10	2	61	6.1	14
Bruce Bowen	10	298	23	63	.365	3	13	.231	6	23	29	10	24	0	4	4	3	60	6.0	10
Rasho Nesterovic	10	261	29	67	.433	1	6	.167	21	34	55	10	38	0	3	8	11	59	5.9	12
Devin Brown	9	130	18	37	.486	10	17	.588	4	14	18	9	18	1	3	7	1	52	5.8	16
Jason Hart	7	62	11	20	.550	0	0	—	0	3	3	1	5	0	5	1	0	22	3.1	6
Charlie Ward	5	13	4	6	.667	0	0	—	0	0	0	1	2	0	2	2	0	11	2.2	6
Malik Rose	7	58	4	16	.250	2	4	.500	12	5	17	6	6	0	4	8	2	10	1.4	4
Kevin Willis	7	25	3	8	.375	0	1	1.000	0	6	6	0	5	0	1	0	0	6	0.9	4
San Antonio	10	2400	335	762	.440	154	239	.644	126	297	423	194	228	1	77	155	42	893	89.3	90
Opponents	10	2400	320	707	.453	181	271	.668	88	293	381	179	227	0	80	149	52	862	86.2	105

3-pt. FG: San Antonio 69-189 (.365).
Duncan 0-1 (.000); Parker 17-43 (.395); Ginobili 10-35 (.286); Turkoglu 14-42 (.333); Horry 8-22 (.364); Bowen 11-29 (.379)
Nesterovic 0-1 (.000); Brown 6-10 (.600); Ward 3-3 (1.000); Rose 0-2 (.000); Willis 0-1 (.000); Opponents 41-127 (.323)

(*) Statistics with this team only
(!) Totals with all teams
(>) Continued season with another team

SINGLE-GAME BESTS

*Denotes number of overtime periods.

SCORING

Player, Team	Points	Opponent	Date
Bryant, LA-L	42	vs. S.A.	05/11
Cassell, Min.	40	vs. Den.	04/18
Cassell, Min.	40	vs. Sac.	05/04
O'Neal, Ind.	37	at Miami	05/12
Bryant, LA-L	36	vs. Hou.	04/19
Martin, N.J.	36	at N.Y.	04/25
Bibby, Sac	36	vs. Dall.	04/29
O'Neal, LA-L	36	at Det.	06/13

REBOUNDS

Player, Team	Rebounds	Opponent	Date
B. Wallace, Det.	24	at N.J.	05/09
Garnett, Min.	22	vs. Den.	04/21
D. Wallace, Det.	22	at Ind.	05/22
B. Wallace, Det.	22	vs. LA-L	06/15
B. Wallace, Det.	21	at Milw.	04/24
Garnett, Min.	21	at Sac.	05/12
Duncan, S.A.	21	vs. LA-L	05/13
Garnett, Min.	21	vs. Sac.	05/19

ASSISTS

Player, Team	Assists	Opponent	Date
Nash, Dal.	14	at Sac.	04/29
Kidd, N.J.	13	vs. N.Y.	04/17
Parker, S.A.	13	at Mem.	04/25
Billups, Det.	13	vs. N.J.	05/07
Francis, Hou.	12	at LA-L	04/19
Webber, Sac.	12	vs. Dall.	04/20
Davis, N.O.	12	vs. Miami	05/02
Kidd, N.J.	12	vs. Det.	05/09
Bibby, Sac.	12	vs. Minn.	05/12

Minutes ....57, Kidd, NJ at DET, 5/14 (3 OT)
48, Marbury, NY vs. NJ, 4/22
48, Nowitzki, DAL at SAC, 4/29
Field Goals ....16, Cassell, MIN vs. DEN, 4/18
16, O'Neal, LAL at DET, 6/13
FG Attempts ....30, Garnett, MIN vs. DEN, 4/18
3-Pt. Field Goals ....7, Sprewell, MIN vs. DEN, 4/21
7, Cassell, MIN vs. SAC, 5/4
3-Pt. FG Attempts ....13, Stojakovic, SAC vs. MIN, 5/10 (OT)
12, Davis, NO vs. MIA, 4/27
Free Throws ....16, Bryant, LAL vs. HOU, 4/19
FT Attempts ....22, O'Neal, LAL vs. MIN, 5/25
Off. Rebounds ....11, B. Wallace, DET at NJ, 5/9
Def. Rebounds ....20, Garnett, MIN vs. DEN, 4/21
20, Garnett, MIN vs. SAC, 5/19
Rebounds ....24, B. Wallace, DET at NJ, 5/9
Assists ....14, Nash, DAL at SAC, 4/29
Steals ....5, (9 times, most recently) Billups, DET at IND, 5/24
Turnovers ....8, (3 times, most recently) Garnett, MIN at LAL, 5/31
Blocks ....8, O'Neal, LAL at SA, 5/9
Points ....42, Bryant, LAL vs. SA, 5/11

TEAM HIGHS AND LOWS

Field Goals ....48, Sacramento, vs. DAL, 4/29
Fewest Field Goals ....19, New Jersey, at DET, 5/3
FG Attempts ....111, Detroit, vs. NJ, 5/14 (3 OT)
100, Dallas, vs. SAC, 4/24
100, Dallas, at SAC, 4/29
Fewest FG Attempts ....63, San Antonio, at MEM, 4/25
63, Detroit, vs. NJ, 5/3
Field Goal Pct. ....587, San Antonio, at MEM, 4/25
Lowest Field Goal Pct. ....244, New Orleans, at MIA, 4/21
3-Pt. Field Goals ....11, New Jersey, at DET, 5/14 (3 OT)
11, (4 times, most recently) San Antonio, at LAL, 5/9
27, San Antonio, at LAL, 5/9
27, L.A. Lakers, at DET, 6/10
3-Pt. FG Pct. ....647, San Antonio, at MEM, 4/25
Free Throws ....42, New Jersey, at DET, 5/14 (3 OT)
31, Boston, at IND, 4/20
31, New Jersey, at NY, 4/25
Fewest Free Throws ....6, Denver, at MIN, 4/30
6, L.A. Lakers, at SA, 5/13
FT Attempts ....55, New Jersey, at DET, 5/14 (3 OT)
43, L.A. Lakers, vs. MIN, 5/25
Fewest FT Attempts ....10, Denver, at MIN, 4/30
Free Throw Pct. ....1.000, Dallas, at SAC, 4/29
Lowest Free Throw Pct. ....389, L.A. Lakers, at SA, 5/5
Off. Rebounds ....24, Sacramento, at DAL, 4/26
Fewest Off. Rebounds ....3, Minnesota, vs. LAL, 5/21
Def. Rebounds ....44, New Jersey, at DET, 5/14 (3 OT)
44, Sacramento, at DAL, 4/26
Fewest Def. Rebounds ....21, Memphis, vs. SA, 4/22
Rebounds ....68, Sacramento, at DAL, 4/26
Fewest Rebounds ....29, New Jersey, at DET, 5/3
Assists ....31, (3 times, most recently) L.A. Lakers, vs. MIN, 5/31
Fewest Assists ....7, Miami, vs. IND, 5/18
Personal Fouls ....42, New Jersey, at DET, 5/14 (3 OT)
36, Minnesota, at LAL, 5/25
Fewest Personal Fouls ....14, Milwaukee, vs. DET, 4/26
Steals ....19, Dallas, vs. SAC, 4/24
19, Indiana, at BOS, 4/25
Turnovers ....28, New Jersey, at DET, 5/14 (3 OT)
26, Sacramento, at DAL, 4/24
26, Boston, vs. IND, 4/25
Fewest Turnovers ....5, L.A. Lakers, at HOU, 4/23
Blocks ....19, Detroit at IND, 5/24
Points ....127, New Jersey, at DET, 5/14 (3 OT)
119, Sacramento, vs. DAL, 4/29
Fewest Points ....56, New Jersey, at DET, 5/3

ACTIVE CAREER LEADERS

(Players who were on active rosters or on injured list during 2003-04 season)

SCORING AVERAGE
(25 games or 625 points)

	G	FGM	FTM	Pts.	Avg.
Allen Iverson	57	618	404	1,743	30.6
Shaquille O'Neal	158	1,658	978	4,294	27.2
Dirk Nowitzki	40	337	287	1,024	25.6
Paul Pierce	30	225	247	748	24.9
Karl Malone	193	1,743	1,269	4,761	24.7
Ray Allen	26	223	107	629	24.2
Tim Duncan	82	720	518	1,960	23.9
Kobe Bryant	119	969	635	2,694	22.6
Kevin Garnett	47	415	207	1,049	22.3
Richard Hamilton	40	315	223	877	21.9

FIELD-GOAL PERCENTAGE
(minimum 150 made)

	FGM	FGA	Pct.
Shaquille O'Neal	1,658	2,951	.562
Dale Davis	337	615	.548
Horace Grant	786	1,483	.530
Dikembe Mutombo	286	559	.512
Tim Duncan	720	1,420	.507
Alonzo Mourning	374	769	.486
Avery Johnson	398	819	.486
Kevin Willis	398	823	.484
Antonio Davis	291	604	.482
Scott Williams	201	419	.480

FREE THROW PERCENTAGE
(minimum 100 made)

	FTM	FTA	Pct.
Peja Stojakovic	190	212	.896
Chauncey Billups	220	247	.891
Reggie Miller	722	811	.890
Dirk Nowitzki	287	323	.889
Steve Nash	132	149	.886
Allan Houston	268	303	.884
Ray Allen	107	121	.884
Wally Szczerbiak	100	114	.877
Richard Hamilton	223	255	.875
Steve Smith	314	366	.858

3-POINT FIELD-GOAL PERCENTAGE
(minimum 35 made)

	FGM	FGA	Pct.
Ray Allen	76	164	.463
Steve Nash	81	185	.438
Tim Thomas	39	90	.433
Derek Fisher	144	334	.431
Tony Delk	47	110	.427
Keith Van Horn	55	129	.426
Dirk Nowitzki	63	150	.420
Allan Houston	76	181	.420
Voshon Lenard	65	155	.419
David Wesley	68	170	.400

GAMES

Scottie Pippen	208
Karl Malone	193
Robert Horry	175
Horace Grant	170
Shaquille O'Neal	158
Charles Oakley	144
Mark Jackson	131
Reggie Miller	131
Clifford Robinson	125
Gary Payton	122

MINUTES

Scottie Pippen	8,105
Karl Malone	7,907
Shaquille O'Neal	6,382
Horace Grant	6,172
Robert Horry	5,466
Charles Oakley	5,108
Reggie Miller	4,878
Gary Payton	4,650
Kobe Bryant	4,556
Mark Jackson	3,776

POINTS

Karl Malone	4,761
Shaquille O'Neal	4,294
Scottie Pippen	3,642
Reggie Miller	2,779
Kobe Bryant	2,694
Tim Duncan	1,960
Gary Payton	1,950
Horace Grant	1,907
Allen Iverson	1,743
Robert Horry	1,570

FIELD GOALS MADE

Karl Malone	1,743
Shaquille O'Neal	1,658
Scottie Pippen	1,335
Kobe Bryant	969
Reggie Miller	879
Horace Grant	786
Gary Payton	773
Tim Duncan	720
Allen Iverson	618
Charles Oakley	584

FIELD GOALS ATTEMPTED

Karl Malone	3,768
Scottie Pippen	3,009
Shaquille O'Neal	2,951
Kobe Bryant	2,233
Reggie Miller	1,952
Gary Payton	1,745
Allen Iverson	1,559
Horace Grant	1,483
Tim Duncan	1,420
Clifford Robinson	1,300

FREE THROWS MADE

Karl Malone	1,269
Shaquille O'Neal	978
Scottie Pippen	772
Reggie Miller	722
Kobe Bryant	635
Tim Duncan	518
Allen Iverson	404
Vlade Divac	373
Charles Oakley	367
Sam Cassell	340
Alonzo Mourning	340

FREE THROWS ATTEMPTED

Shaquille O'Neal	1,889
Karl Malone	1,725
Scottie Pippen	1,067
Reggie Miller	811
Kobe Bryant	802
Tim Duncan	742
Allen Iverson	533
Alonzo Mourning	512
Vlade Divac	510
Charles Oakley	486

3-POINT FIELD GOALS MADE

Reggie Miller	299
Scottie Pippen	200
Robert Horry	199
Derek Fisher	144
Steve Smith	136
Bryon Russell	126
Kobe Bryant	121
Gary Payton	119
Nick Van Exel	111
Allen Iverson	103
Toni Kukoc	103

3-POINT FIELD GOALS ATTEMPTED

Reggie Miller	754
Scottie Pippen	660
Robert Horry	567
Kobe Bryant	375
Gary Payton	362
Steve Smith	345
Bryon Russell	344
Nick Van Exel	342
Derek Fisher	334
Jason Kidd	326

REBOUNDS

Karl Malone	2,062
Shaquille O'Neal	2,040
Scottie Pippen	1,583
Horace Grant	1,457
Charles Oakley	1,445
Robert Horry	1,086
Tim Duncan	1,076
Dale Davis	989
Vlade Divac	913
Dikembe Mutombo	868

ASSISTS

Scottie Pippen	1,048
Mark Jackson	905
Gary Payton	740
Jason Kidd	661
Karl Malone	610
Avery Johnson	562
Kobe Bryant	528
Sam Cassell	498
Shaquille O'Neal	492
Robert Horry	480

PERSONAL FOULS

Scottie Pippen	686
Karl Malone	662
Robert Horry	569
Shaquille O'Neal	552
Horace Grant	515
Charles Oakley	503
Clifford Robinson	447
Vlade Divac	439
Kobe Bryant	376
Gary Payton	366

STEALS

Scottie Pippen	395
Karl Malone	258
Robert Horry	234
Gary Payton	187
Charles Oakley	178
Horace Grant	171
Kobe Bryant	161
Jason Kidd	146
Reggie Miller	136
Mark Jackson	131

BLOCKED SHOTS

Shaquille O'Neal	374
Tim Duncan	241
Dikembe Mutombo	228
Scottie Pippen	185
Horace Grant	173
Robert Horry	167
Vlade Divac	165
Greg Ostertag	163
Alonzo Mourning	155
Elden Campbell	137

DISQUALIFICATIONS

Vlade Divac	14
Scottie Pippen	11
Robert Horry	9
Shaquille O'Neal	9
Clifford Robinson	9
P.J. Brown	9
Sam Cassell	8
Horace Grant	8
Kenyon Martin	8
Chris Webber	8

NBA FINALS

Frank Sinatra did it his way. Kobe Bryant and Shaquille O'Neal tried to do it their own way. The Detroit Pistons did it the right way.

In one for the ages, the Pistons completed one of the biggest upsets in NBA Finals history, toppling the mighty Los Angeles Lakers with a 100-87 Game 5 victory that was entirely emblematic of a team triumphing over individuals.

In front of a raucous and unrelenting sellout crowd at The Palace of Auburn Hills, Detroit closed out the series in five games for its first title in 14 years, harkening back to the days of the "Bad Boys."

"It's about players," said Pistons coach Larry Brown, emotionally drained from winning his first title. "This sport is about players playing the right way and showing kids that you can be a team and be successful, and it's great for our league."

Leading the way was Brown, the nomadic coach who fronted for a group of cast-offs and convinced them that they could overcome tremendous odds by playing "the right way." In his seventh NBA stop, Brown finally broke through, becoming the first coach to win championships on the pro and college levels.

"We did it, man," said Finals MVP Chauncey Billups, who has found a home with his seventh team. "We came into this series, nobody gave us a chance, but we felt we had a great chance. We knew as a team we just felt we were a better team."

"Chauncey's career is a lot like mine," Brown said. "I think I might have been a couple more places than him, but he's still been through a lot."

As time wound down in Game 5, Brown emptied his bench, sending in rookie Darko Milicic, the "Human Victory Cigar." Brown put his face in his hands and took a moment to himself, contemplating the victory that completes his Hall of Fame career.

Brown's way began with defense. The Pistons limited the Lakers to an average of 81.8 points in the series, turning counterpart Phil Jackson's vaunted triangle offense into a disfigured new shape.

"They do play the right way, and I'm very proud of them," Brown said.

And while the Lakers leaned too hard on superstars Shaquille O'Neal and Kobe Bryant, the Pistons shared the ball and the spotlight. In fact, Billups was named MVP despite having little impact in the clincher.

"It's unbelievable," Billups said. "Really, I'm just speechless."

Fittingly, Detroit's leading man was center Ben Wallace, who baited O'Neal into early foul trouble from which Los Angeles never recovered. A

In The Finals, Richard Hamilton led Detroit's balanced attack, averaging a team-high 21.4 points.

throw-in in the deal that sent Grant Hill out of town four years ago, Wallace had 18 points and 22 rebounds in Game 5 and displayed the hunger, determination and backbone that are the trademarks of his team. For the series, Wallace averaged 10.8 points and 13.6 rebounds.

Detroit flashed a little offense in Game 5, as all five starters were in double figures. Richard Hamilton, who averaged a team-high 21.4 points in The Finals, scored 21 points. Tayshaun Prince, who harassed Bryant the whole series, added 17. Billups contributed 14 and outscored Gary Payton, 105-21, over five games. And Rasheed Wallace again overcame foul trouble to offer 11.

"I never thought of this Piston ballclub as my team," said Wallace, who was acquired in a trade in February and instantly became Detroit's best all-around player. "It's a band of guys. It's veteran guys. I think when you have veterans who are hungry and are willing to sacrifice things to win, you don't necessarily need to be a leader because everyone knew what they have to do."

Bryant scored 24 points but was just 7-of-21 from the floor and shot 38 percent for the series. By firing away at will, he helped the Pistons neutralize the effectiveness of O'Neal, who scored 20 points but made just 6-of-16 free throws.

When the series began, the Lakers were odds-on favorites to win their fourth title in five years.

The Pistons show off the 2004 NBA championship trophy after bringing Detroit its third NBA title.

But their dreams of a dynasty died amid defense, dysfunction and dissension.

It also did not help that Karl Malone was hobbled by a sprained MCL for the entire series and sat out Game 5. His pursuit of an elusive championship continues, as does Payton's.

"We missed (Malone) tonight, a lot, and we missed him through this series," said Lakers coach Phil Jackson, who lost in The Finals for the first time in 10 tries and remains tied with the legendary Red Auerbach with nine titles.

The Pistons ended the five-year stranglehold the Lakers and San Antonio Spurs had held on the league and became the first champ from the East since Michael Jordan's Chicago Bulls in 1998.

The victory was especially sweet for Detroit's President of Basketball Operations Joe Dumars, who wore a uniform the last time the Pistons captured the title. After 100 wins in two seasons, Dumars made the difficult decision to fire Rick Carlisle in favor of Brown. Some 12 months later, the Pistons parade through Detroit's streets as champs thanks in large part to Dumars' ability to evaluate talent and make excellent personnel decisions.

At age 62, Brown is the oldest coach to win an NBA title. Brown also took longer than any coach in NBA history, 22 years, to capture a crown, easily outpacing Bill Fitch (12) and Red Auerbach.

GAME 1
AT LOS ANGELES, JUNE 6, 2004

Detroit	Pos	Min	FG	FGA	3P	3PA	FT	FTA	Off	Def	Tot	Ast	PF	Stl	TO	Tec	Pts
Richard Hamilton	G	43	5	16	0	0	2	4	3	4	7	5	0	1	6	0	12
Chauncey Billups	G	39	8	14	2	4	4	4	1	2	3	4	1	3	2	0	22
Tayshaun Prince	F	35	5	10	1	4	0	0	1	5	6	4	3	2	0	0	11
Rasheed Wallace	F	29	3	4	2	2	6	6	1	7	8	1	3	0	1	0	14
Ben Wallace	C	41	4	8	0	0	1	2	1	7	8	0	1	1	2	0	9
Elden Campbell		18	2	5	0	0	2	6	1	0	1	4	1	2	1	0	6
Lindsey Hunter		13	1	5	1	2	2	2	0	1	1	0	2	0	1	0	5
Corliss Williamson		11	2	3	0	0	3	4	1	1	2	1	3	0	0	0	7
Mehmet Okur		6	0	0	0	0	1	2	0	0	0	0	1	0	1	0	1
Darvin Ham		4	0	0	0	0	0	0	0	0	0	0	2	0	0	0	0
Mike James		1	0	0	0	0	0	0	0	0	0	0	0	0	0	0	0
Darko Milicic							DNP										
TOTALS		240	30	65	6	12	21	30	9	27	36	19	17	9	14	0	87

PERCENTAGES: 46.2 50.0 70.0   TM REB: 11 TOT TO: 14

Los Angeles	Pos	Min	FG	FGA	3P	3PA	FT	FTA	Off	Def	Tot	Ast	PF	Stl	Tec	BS	Pts
Kobe Bryant	G	47	10	27	1	6	4	4	1	3	4	4	2	4	0	2	25
Gary Payton	G	31	1	4	1	1	0	0	1	1	2	3	5	2	0	0	3
Karl Malone	F	44	2	9	0	0	0	0	3	8	11	3	1	0	0	1	4
Devean George	F	27	2	5	1	2	0	0	0	3	3	0	2	1	0	0	5
Shaquille O'Neal	C	45	13	16	0	0	8	12	5	6	11	1	4	0	0	1	34
Derek Fisher		20	1	9	0	2	0	0	3	0	3	3	2	1	0	0	2
Kareem Rush		16	0	3	0	2	0	0	0	2	2	0	4	0	0	0	0
Stanislav Medvedenko		6	0	0	0	0	2	2	0	1	1	0	3	0	0	0	2
Rick Fox		4	0	0	0	0	0	0	0	0	0	1	2	0	0	0	0
Brian Cook							DNP										
Luke Walton							DNP										
Bryon Russell							DNP										
TOTALS		240	29	73	3	13	14	18	13	24	37	15	25	8	15	4	75

PERCENTAGES: 39.7 23.1 77.8   TM REB: 8 TOT TO: 16

Score by periods	1st	2nd	3rd	4th	Totals
Pistons	22	18	24	23	87
Lakers	19	22	17	17	75

BLOCKED SHOTS
Pistons 4   Lakers.......4
Campbell 2   Bryant.......2
B. Wallace 1   Malone 1
R. Wallace 1   O'Neal.......1

TECHNICAL FOULS
Pistons 0   Lakers 0

FLAGRANT FOUL
Pistons 0   Lakers.......0

OFFICIALS: Joe Crawford Bob Delaney Bernie Fryer TIME OF GAME: 2:30
ATTENDANCE: 18,997

GAME 2
AT LOS ANGELES, JUNE 8, 2004

Detroit	Pos	Min	FG	FGA	3P	3PA	FT	FTA	Off	Def	Tot	Ast	PF	Stl	TO	Tec	Pts
Richard Hamilton	G	47	10	25	2	2	4	5	5	3	8	2	2	0	5	1	26
Chauncey Billups	G	47	6	15	2	2	13	14	2	2	4	9	1	0	3	0	27
Tayshaun Prince	F	47	2	6	1	2	0	0	4	1	5	0	2	3	0	0	5
Rasheed Wallace	F	34	5	14	0	3	1	2	1	6	7	3	4	0	0	0	11
Ben Wallace	C	43	5	11	0	0	2	8	4	10	14	1	5	2	0	0	12
Mehmet Okur		18	0	2	0	0	1	2	0	2	2	1	2	0	3	0	1
Lindsey Hunter		12	2	4	1	3	0	0	0	0	0	0	2	1	0	0	5
Elden Campbell		9	1	2	0	0	0	0	2	2	4	1	4	0	1	0	2
Corliss Williamson		7	1	2	0	0	0	0	1	1	2	0	2	0	2	0	2
Mike James		1	0	0	0	0	0	0	0	0	0	0	0	0	0	0	0
Darvin Ham							DNP										
Darko Milicic							DNP										
TOTALS		265	32	81	6	12	21	31	19	27	46	19	23	6	14	1	91

PERCENTAGES: 39.5 50.0 67.7 TM REB: 12 TOT TO: 17

NBA Finals

2003-04 REVIEW

Los Angeles	Pos	Min	FG	FGA	3P	3PA	FT	FTA	Rebounds Off	Def	Tot	Ast	PF	Stl	TO	Tec	Pts
Kobe Bryant	G	49	14	27	1	5	4	5	0	4	4	7	5	2	5	0	33
Gary Payton	G	28	1	3	0	1	0	0	1	2	3	3	4	1	3	0	2
Karl Malone	F	39	3	9	0	1	3	4	3	6	9	2	3	1	1	0	9
Devean George	F	21	3	7	1	3	0	0	0	2	2	1	2	1	0	0	7
Shaquille O'Neal	C	48	10	20	0	0	9	14	3	4	7	3	5	0	3	0	29
Luke Walton		27	3	3	1	1	0	0	1	4	5	8	3	0	0	0	7
Derek Fisher		25	2	6	2	4	1	2	0	3	3	2	4	2	0	0	7
Kareem Rush		18	2	4	1	2	0	0	0	2	2	2	0	0	1	0	5
Stanislav Medvedenko		9	0	1	0	0	0	0	1	2	3	0	1	0	0	0	0
Brian Cook		1	0	0	0	0	0	0	0	0	0	0	0	0	1	0	0
Rick Fox							DNP										
Bryon Russell							DNP										
TOTALS		265	38	80	6	17	17	25	9	29	38	28	27	7	14	0	99

PERCENTAGES: 47.5 35.3 68.0 TM REB: 13 TOT TO: 14

Score by periods	1st	2nd	3rd	4th	OT	Totals
Pistons	16	20	30	23	2	91
Lakers	18	26	24	21	10	99

BLOCKED SHOTS

Pistons 6	Lakers.......3		
Prince ..2	Walton 2		
B. Wallace 2	O'Neal.......1		
R. Wallace 2			

TECHNICAL FOULS

Pistons 1   Lakers 0
Hamilton ... 1

FLAGRANT FOUL

Pistons 0   Lakers.......0

OFFICIALS: Joe DeRosa Steve Javie Bennett Salvatore TIME OF GAME: 3:04
ATTENDANCE: 18,997

GAME 3

AT AUBURN HILLS, MICH., JUNE 10, 2004

Los Angeles	Pos	Min	FG	FGA	3P	3PA	FT	FTA	Rebounds Off	Def	Tot	Ast	PF	Stl	TO	Tec	Pts
Kobe Bryant	G	45	4	13	0	4	3	3	0	3	3	5	3	1	4	0	11
Gary Payton	G	35	2	7	1	5	1	2	1	3	4	7	2	1	0	0	6
Devean George	F	21	3	8	2	6	0	0	0	3	3	0	3	2	1	0	8
Karl Malone	F	18	2	4	0	0	1	2	0	4	4	2	2	0	1	0	5
Shaquille O'Neal	C	38	7	14	0	0	0	2	2	6	8	1	5	1	2	0	14
Stanislav Medvedenko		21	1	3	0	0	1	2	2	6	8	1	4	0	1	0	3
Luke Walton		19	1	5	0	2	2	2	1	2	3	2	4	1	2	0	4
Kareem Rush		18	3	8	2	7	0	0	0	1	1	0	2	1	2	0	8
Derek Fisher		16	4	9	1	3	0	0	1	1	2	1	1	0	3	0	9
Brian Cook		8	0	3	0	0	0	0	0	3	3	0	2	0	0	0	0
Bryon Russell		1	0	0	0	0	0	0	0	0	0	0	0	0	0	0	0
Rick Fox							DNP										
TOTALS		240	27	74	6	27	8	13	7	32	39	19	28	7	16	0	68

PERCENTAGES: 36.5 22.2 61.5 TM REB: 8 TOT TO: 16

Detroit	Pos	Min	FG	FGA	3P	3PA	FT	FTA	Rebounds Off	Def	Tot	Ast	PF	Stl	TO	Tec	Pts
Richard Hamilton	G	43	11	22	2	4	7	7	3	3	6	3	1	2	3	0	31
Chauncey Billups	G	36	5	11	2	5	7	7	0	2	2	3	1	1	2	0	19
Tayshaun Prince	F	36	5	13	1	5	0	2	3	3	6	2	1	3	1	0	11
Rasheed Wallace	F	26	1	4	0	0	1	4	2	8	10	1	3	0	1	0	3
Ben Wallace	C	38	3	9	0	1	1	4	2	9	11	3	3	2	3	0	7
Lindsey Hunter		16	1	3	0	0	0	0	1	4	5	2	4	0	0	0	2
Corliss Williamson		15	2	4	0	0	2	2	0	3	3	0	0	0	1	0	6
Elden Campbell		13	1	4	0	0	3	4	2	0	2	1	3	3	0	0	5
Mehmet Okur		8	1	4	0	0	0	0	1	3	4	1	0	0	0	0	2
Mike James		4	0	0	0	0	0	0	1	0	1	1	0	0	0	0	0
Darvin Ham		3	1	1	0	0	0	0	0	0	0	0	0	0	0	0	2
Darko Milicic		2	0	1	0	0	0	0	0	1	1	0	0	0	0	0	0
TOTALS		240	31	76	5	15	21	30	15	36	51	17	16	11	11	0	88

PERCENTAGES: 40.8 .33.3 70.0 TM REB: 8 TOT TO: 12

Score by periods	1st	2nd	3rd	4th	Totals
Lakers	16	16	19	17	68
Pistons	24	15	24	25	88

GAME 4

AT AUBURN HILLS, MICH., JUNE 13, 2004

Los Angeles	Pos	Min	FG	FGA	3P	3PA	FT	FTA	Off	Def	Tot	Ast	PF	Stl	TO	Tec	Pts
Kobe Bryant	G	45	8	25	2	6	2	2	0	0	0	2	3	1	3	1	20
Gary Payton	G	43	4	11	0	2	0	0	1	1	2	5	4	0	1	0	8
Karl Malone	F	21	1	2	0	0	0	0	2	3	5	2	2	0	2	0	2
Devean George	F	15	1	2	1	2	2	4	1	2	3	0	5	1	0	0	5
Shaquille O'Neal	C	47	16	21	0	0	4	11	3	17	20	2	4	0	2	0	36
Derek Fisher		21	1	6	0	3	2	3	1	4	5	2	4	0	0	0	4
Rick Fox		16	1	4	0	1	0	0	0	1	1	6	3	0	0	0	2
Stanislav Medvedenko		13	1	5	0	1	1	2	1	0	1	1	3	0	0	1	3
Luke Walton		12	0	1	0	1	0	0	0	1	1	3	6	2	2	0	0
Kareem Rush		6	0	1	0	1	0	0	0	0	0	0	1	0	0	0	0
Bryon Russell		1	0	0	0	0	0	0	0	0	0	0	0	0	0	0	0
Brian Cook		DNP															
TOTALS		240	33	78	3	16	11	22	9	29	38	23	35	4	10	2	80

PERCENTAGES: 42.3 18.8 50.0 TM REB: 10 TOT TO: 10

Detroit	Pos	Min	FG	FGA	3P	3PA	FT	FTA	Off	Def	Tot	Ast	PF	Stl	TO	Tec	Pts
Richard Hamilton	G	44	5	11	0	0	7	7	1	1	2	6	5	0	5	0	17
Chauncey Billups	G	37	7	12	2	5	7	9	0	4	4	4	3	2	3	0	23
Rasheed Wallace	F	41	10	23	0	5	6	6	2	11	13	2	4	2	2	1	26
Tayshaun Prince	F	40	3	10	0	3	0	1	4	3	7	2	1	0	0	0	6
Ben Wallace	C	39	2	5	0	0	4	14	2	11	13	2	3	1	1	1	8
Elden Campbell		14	0	3	0	0	0	0	0	2	2	0	2	0	0	1	0
Lindsey Hunter		11	0	1	0	0	4	4	0	0	0	0	1	0	0	0	4
Mike James		6	2	2	0	0	0	0	0	2	2	0	0	0	1	0	4
Corliss Williamson		5	0	1	0	0	0	0	0	2	2	0	0	0	0	0	0
Darvin Ham		2	0	0	0	0	0	0	0	0	0	0	1	0	0	0	0
Darko Milicic		1	0	0	0	0	0	0	0	0	0	0	0	0	0	0	0
Mehmet Okur		DNP															
TOTALS		240	29	68	2	13	28	41	9	36	45	16	20	5	12	1	88

PERCENTAGES: 42.6 15.4 68.3 TM REB: 15 TOT TO: 13

Score by periods	1st	2nd	3rd	4th	Totals
Lakers	22	17	17	24	80
Pistons	21	20	15	32	88

GAME 5

AT AUBURN HILLS, MICH., JUNE 15, 2004

Los Angeles	Pos	Min	FG	FGA	3P	3PA	FT	FTA	Off	Def	Tot	Ast	PF	Stl	TO	Tec	Pts
Kobe Bryant	G	45	7	21	0	2	10	11	1	2	3	4	2	1	3	0	24
Gary Payton	G	31	1	3	0	1	0	0	2	2	4	4	2	2	1	1	2
Stanislav Medvedenko	F	23	4	8	0	0	2	2	2	3	5	1	1	0	1	0	10
Devean George	F	20	2	6	0	2	0	0	2	1	3	2	4	0	0	1	4

	Pos	Min	FG	FGA	3P	3PA	FT	FTA	Off	Def	Tot	Ast	PF	Stl	TO	Tec	Pts
										Rebounds							
Shaquille O'Neal C	C	35	7	13	0	0	6	16	2	6	8	1	4	1	1	0	20
Kareem Rush		20	2	6	1	4	0	0	0	0	0	0	3	0	0	0	5
Luke Walton		19	1	4	0	2	0	0	1	2	3	5	2	3	3	0	2
Derek Fisher		19	3	6	3	4	1	2	2	2	2	1	5	2	0	0	10
Brian Cook		12	1	3	0	0	2	2	3	2	5	0	2	1	1	0	4
Rick Fox		10	3	3	0	0	0	0	0	2	2	0	1	0	1	0	6
Bryon Russell		6	0	2	0	1	0	0	1	0	1	0	1	0	0	0	0
Karl Malone								DNP									
TOTAL		240	31	75	4	16	21	33	14	22	36	18	27	10	11	2	873

PERCENTAGES: 41.3 .25.0 63.6   TM REB: 12 TOT TO: 12

Detroit	Pos	Min	FG	FGA	3P	3PA	FT	FTA	Off	Def	Tot	Ast	PF	Stl	TO	Tec	Pts
										Rebounds							
Richard Hamilton ......G	G	45	6	18	0	4	9	11	0	3	3	4	1	1	4	1	21
Chauncey Billups ....G	G	33	3	5	0	1	8	8	0	3	3	6	2	0	3	0	14
Tayshaun Prince ....F	F	38	6	15	0	2	5	8	3	7	10	2	2	1	1	0	17
Rasheed Wallace ....F	F	21	5	8	1	2	0	0	1	0	1	0	5	0	0	0	11
Ben Wallace C	C	42	8	13	0	1	2	6	10	12	22	1	3	3	0	0	18
Elden Campbell		14	2	2	0	0	0	0	1	3	4	2	3	0	1	0	4
Corliss Williamson		14	1	5	0	0	4	4	2	1	3	0	2	0	1	0	6
Lindsey Hunter		13	1	4	0	3	0	0	0	1	1	0	3	2	0	0	2
Mike James		10	0	2	0	0	0	0	1	0	1	3	2	0	0	0	0
Mehmet Okur		7	3	3	1	1	0	0	0	0	0	0	4	0	0	0	7
Darko Milicic		2	0	1	0	0	0	2	1	0	1	0	0	1	1	0	0
Darvin Ham		1	0	0	0	0	0	0	1	0	1	0	0	1	0	0	0
TOTAL		240	35	76	2	14	28	39	20	30	50	18	27	8	12	1	100

PERCENTAGES: 46.1 14.3 71.8   TM REB: 10 TOT TO: 13

Score by periods	1st	2nd	3rd	4th	Totals
Lakers 24	24	21	14	28	87
Pistons 25	25	30	27	18	100

BLOCKED SHOTS
Lakers 2   Pistons 2
Payton 1   R. Wallace.... 1
George 1   B. Wallace.... 1

TECHNICAL FOULS
Lakers 2   Pistons.... 1
Payton 1   Jefferson .. 1
George..... 1

FLAGRANT FOUL
Lakers 0   Pistons 0

OFFICIALS: Joe Crawford   Bernie Fryer   Bennett Salvatore   TIME OF GAME: 2:32
ATTENDANCE: 22,076

DETROIT PISTONS

	G	Min.	FGM	FGA	Pct.	FTM	FTA	Pct.	REBOUNDS Off.	REBOUNDS Def.	REBOUNDS Tot.	Ast.	PF	Dq.	Stl.	TO	Blk.	SCORING Pts.	SCORING Avg.	SCORING Hi.
Richard Hamilton	5	222	37	92	.402	29	34	.853	12	14	26	20	9	0	4	23	0	107	21.4	31
Chauncey Billups	5	192	29	57	.509	39	42	.929	3	13	16	26	8	0	6	13	0	105	21.0	27
Rasheed Wallace.	5	151	24	53	.453	14	18	.778	7	32	39	7	19	0	2	4	8	65	13.0	26
Ben Wallace	5	203	22	46	.478	10	34	.294	19	49	68	7	15	0	9	6	5	54	10.8	18
Tayshaun Prince	5	196	21	54	.389	5	11	.455	15	19	34	10	9	0	9	2	2	50	10.0	17
Corliss Williamson	5	52	6	15	.400	9	10	.900	4	8	12	1	7	0	0	4	0	21	4.2	7
Lindsey Hunter	5	65	5	17	.294	6	6	1.000	1	6	7	4	11	0	3	1	2	18	3.6	5
Elden Campbell	5	68	6	16	.375	5	10	.500	6	7	13	8	13	0	5	3	3	17	3.4	6
Mehmet Okur	4	39	4	9	.444	2	4	.500	1	5	6	2	7	0	0	4	0	11	2.8	7
Mike James	5	22	2	4	.500	0	0	—	2	2	4	4	2	0	0	1	0	4	0.8	4
Darvin Ham	4	10	1	1	1.000	0	0	—	1	0	1	0	3	0	0	1	0	2	0.5	2
Darko Milicic.	3	5	0	2	.000	0	2	.000	1	1	2	0	0	0	1	1	0	0	0.0	0
Detroit	5	1225	157	366	.429	119	171	.696	72	156	228	89	103	0	39	69	20	454	90.8	100
Opponents	5	1225	158	380	.416	71	111	.640	52	136	188	103	142	1	36	68	14	409	81.8	99

3-pt. FG: Detroit 21-66 (.318).
Hamilton 4-10 (.400); Billups 8-17 (.471); R. Wallace 3-12 (.250); B. Wallace 0-2 (.000); Prince 3-16 (.188); Hunter 2-8 (.250)
Okur 1-1 (1.000); Opponents 22-89 (.247).

LOS ANGELES LAKERS

	G	Min.	FGM	FGA	Pct.	FTM	FTA	Pct.	REBOUNDS Off.	REBOUNDS Def.	REBOUNDS Tot.	Ast.	PF	Dq.	Stl.	TO	Blk.	SCORING Pts.	SCORING Avg.	SCORING Hi.
Shaquille O'Neal	5	213	53	84	.631	27	55	.491	15	39	54	8	22	0	2	14	3	133	26.6	36
Kobe Bryant	5	231	43	113	.381	23	25	.920	2	12	14	22	15	0	9	18	3	113	22.6	33
Derek Fisher	5	101	11	36	.306	4	7	.571	5	10	15	9	16	0	5	4	0	32	6.4	10
Devean George	5	104	11	28	.393	2	4	.500	3	11	14	3	16	0	5	2	2	29	5.8	8
Karl Malone	4	122	8	24	.333	4	6	.667	8	21	29	9	8	0	1	4	1	20	5.0	9
Gary Payton	5	168	9	28	.321	1	2	.500	6	9	15	22	17	0	6	7	2	21	4.2	8
Slava Medvedenko	5	72	6	17	.353	6	8	.750	6	12	18	3	12	0	0	2	1	18	3.6	10
Kareem Rush	5	78	7	22	.318	0	0	—	0	5	5	2	10	0	1	5	0	18	3.6	8
Luke Walton	4	77	5	13	.385	2	2	1.000	4	3	7	6	16	0	7	2	0	13	3.3	7
Rick Fox	3	30	4	7	.571	0	0	—	0	3	3	7	6	0	0	1	0	8	2.7	6
Brian Cook	3	21	1	6	.167	2	2	1.000	3	5	8	0	4	0	1	2	0	4	1.3	4
Bryon Russell	3	8	0	2	.000	0	0	—	1	0	1	0	1	0	0	0	0	0	0.0	0
L.A. Lakers	5	1225	158	380	.416	71	111	.640	52	136	188	103	142	1	36	68	14	409	81.8	99
Opponents	5	1225	157	366	.429	119	171	.696	72	156	228	89	103	0	39	69	20	454	90.8	100

3-pt. FG: L.A. Lakers 22-89 (.247).
Bryant 4-23 (.174); Fisher 6-16 (.375); George 5-15 (.333); Malone 0-1 (.000); Payton 2-10 (.200); Rush 4-16 (.250)
Walton 1-6 (.167); Fox 0-1 (.000); Russell 0-1 (.000); Opponents 21-66 (.318).

2003-04 REVIEW NBA Finals

ALL-STAR GAME

West	Pos	Min	FG	FGA	3P	3PA	FT	FTA	Off	Def	Tot	Ast	PF	Stl	TO	BS	Pts
Kobe Bryant	G	36	9	12	2	3	0	1	1	3	4	4	3	5	6	1	20
Steve Francis	G	23	6	9	1	2	0	0	1	3	4	4	1	0	1	0	13
Kevin Garnett	F	29	6	14	0	1	0	0	3	4	7	6	0	2	1	1	12
Tim Duncan	F	26	6	11	0	0	2	4	2	11	13	5	2	1	2	0	14
Yao Ming	C	18	8	14	0	2	0	0	2	2	4	1	2	0	0	0	16
Shaquille O'Neal		24	12	19	0	0	0	1	5	6	11	1	3	2	4	2	24
Ray Allen		23	6	13	1	4	3	4	2	1	3	4	2	1	3	0	16
Sam Cassell		13	2	3	0	0	0	0	0	1	1	7	0	1	1	0	4
Dirk Nowitzki		13	1	3	0	1	0	0	0	0	0	1	0	2	2	0	2
Peja Stojakovic		13	2	5	1	4	0	0	0	1	1	1	0	0	2	0	5
Andrei Kirilenko		12	1	3	0	1	0	0	0	1	1	0	0	0	0	1	2
Brad Miller		10	4	5	0	0	0	0	1	2	3	0	0	0	2	0	8
TOTAL		240	63	111	5	18	5	10	17	35	52	34	13	14	24	5	136
PERCENTAGES			56.8	27.8		50.0	TM REB: 4			TOT TO: 24							

East	Pos	Min	FG	FGA	3P	3PA	FT	FTA	Off	Def	Tot	Ast	PF	Stl	TO	BS	Pts
Allen Iverson	G	23	1	6	0	0	1	4	0	1	1	11	3	0	4	0	3
Tracy McGrady	G	23	5	11	1	6	2	4	1	3	4	3	0	0	1	0	13
Jermaine O'Neal	F	28	7	13	0	0	2	4	2	7	9	2	0	1	2	0	16
Vince Carter	F	16	5	7	1	3	0	0	1	1	2	0	1	2	2	0	11
Ben Wallace	C	23	2	5	0	1	0	0	2	5	7	0	0	3	0	1	4
Kenyon Martin		23	8	10	0	0	1	2	4	3	7	3	1	0	3	0	17
Jason Kidd		22	4	6	3	4	3	4	0	3	3	10	1	2	3	0	14
Jamaal Magloire		21	9	16	0	1	1	2	3	5	8	0	2	1	1	1	19
Ron Artest		17	3	5	0	1	1	2	1	2	3	3	2	1	1	0	7
Baron Davis		16	3	9	1	6	0	0	0	0	0	7	0	1	1	0	7
Michael Redd		15	5	12	3	6	0	0	2	1	3	2	0	3	1	0	13
Paul Pierce		13	4	8	0	1	0	0	0	1	1	2	2	1	1	0	8
TOTALS		240	56	108	9	28	11	22	16	32	48	43	12	15	20	2	132
PERCENTAGES			51.9	32.1		50.0	TM REB: 12			TOTI TO: 20							

Score by periods	1st	2nd	3rd	4th	Totals
West	31	27	45	33	136
East	33	31	37	31	132

TECHNICAL FOULS
West 0   East 0

FLAGRANT FOUL
West 0   East 0

OFFICIALS: Steve Javie, Blane Reichelt, Tom Washington TIME OF GAME: 2:59
ATTENDANCE: 19, 662

NBA DRAFT

When the Orlando Magic selected Dwight Howard with the top pick in the 2004 NBA Draft, it touched off high school hyperactivity never seen before in the history of the draft.

Howard was one of a record eight high school players chosen, all in the first round. An astounding six were taken in an eight-pick stretch in the middle of the first round, including three in a row.

The Magic opted for Howard over Connecticut junior Emeka Okafor, who went second to the expansion Charlotte Bobcats.

Orlando took high schooler Dwight Howard and passed on NCAA champ Emeka Okafor.

"I was surprised," said Howard, an 18-year-old from Atlanta Southwest Christian Academy. "The whole day, I couldn't sleep. I couldn't do anything. I was thinking about this moment right here. And it's here. I'm very happy with the way things have fallen for me, and I'm ready to go to work."

Howard is the third high school player taken with the top pick, all in the last four years. Washington took Kwame Brown first in 2001, and Cleveland selected LeBron James with the top choice last year.

The Bobcats were delighted to land the 6-9 Okafor, who left college after leading the Huskies to a national title in 2004.

"I think he is ready right now to step in and impact a basketball team," said Bobcats coach and general manager Bernie Bickerstaff. "He is a tremendous young man, and I know the fans in Charlotte will really enjoy him on and off the court."

An Academic All-American, Okafor brings more of a defensive presence at this stage of his career, but he's a quick learner with an excellent work ethic. Okafor's college teammate, guard Ben Gordon, went next to the Chicago Bulls, who also added Duke's Luol Deng via a trade with Phoenix.

Okafor and Gordon joined Duke's Jay Williams (2) and Mike Dunleavy (3) in 2002 as the second-highest-drafted college teammates in NBA history. Kareem Abdul-Jabbar (1) and Lucius Allen (3) of UCLA were the highest drafted college teammates ever in 1969.

With the fourth pick, the Los Angeles Clippers selected Shaun Livingston, a 6-7 point guard from Peoria Central High School in Illinois. The Wizards chose Wisconsin junior guard Devin Harris fifth and made one of five trades in the first round, sending his rights to Dallas with guard Jerry Stackhouse and forward Christian Laettner for Sixth Man Award winner Antawn Jamison and cash.

There were eight international players selected in the first round, one shy of the record nine set in 2003. This year's selections were No. 7 Deng (born in The Sudan, raised in England), No. 8 Rafael Araujo (Brazil), No. 11 Andris Biedrins (Latvia), No. 21 Pavel Podkolzine (Russia), No. 22 Viktor Khryapa (Russia), No. 23 Sergei Monia (Russia), No. 27 Sasha Vujacic (Slovenia) and No. 28 Beno Udrih (Slovenia).

In 2003, there were nine college seniors chosen in the first round. This year, there were four—Araujo (8), Luke Jackson (10), Jameer Nelson (20) and Tony Allen (25).

Picking 12th, the Seattle SuperSonics continued the high school trend, taking 7-foot center Robert Swift from Bakersfield High School. The Portland Trail Blazers followed by selecting 6-foot guard Sebastian Telfair from Lincoln High in New York. With the 15th pick, Boston picked Al Jefferson from Prentiss High School in Mississippi. With the 17th pick and their second first-rounder, the Hawks tabbed high school forward Josh Smith, a Georgia native who played at basketball factory Oak Hill Academy in Virginia.

Guard J.R. Smith of St. Benedict's Prep in Newark, New Jersey went next to the New Orleans Hornets, and the Miami Heat chose forward Dorell Wright of South Kent Prep in Connecticut, ending the high school frenzy.

That was followed by a flurry of trades. The Denver Nuggets selected college player of the year Nelson at No. 20 and dealt him to Orlando for a future first-round pick.

There were a total of 20 international players selected in the 2004 NBA Draft, one shy of the record 21 set in 2003. The breakdown was eight in the first round and 12 in the second round.

2003-04 REVIEW NBA Draft

FIRST ROUND

	Team	Name	College/country	Ht.
1.	Orlando	Dwight Howard	SW Atlanta Christian Acad. (Ga.)	6-11
2.	Charlotte (from L.A. Clippers)	Emeka Okafor	Connecticut	6-10
3.	Chicago	Ben Gordon	Connecticut	6-3
4.	L.A. Clippers (from Charlotte)	Shaun Livingston	Peoria Central HS (Ill.)	6-7
5.	Washington	Devin Harris*	Wisconsin	6-3
6.	Atlanta	Josh Childress	Stanford	6-8
7.	Phoenix	Luol Deng**	Duke	6-8
8.	Toronto	Rafael Araujo	Brigham Young	6-11
9.	Philadelphia	Andre Iguodala	Arizona	6-6
10.	Cleveland	Luke Jackson	Oregon	6-7
11.	Golden State	Andris Biedrins	BK Skonto Riga (Latvia)	6-11
12.	Seattle	Robert Swift	Bakersfield HS (Calif.)	7-0
13.	Portland	Sebastian Telfair	Abraham Lincoln HS (N.Y.)	6-0
14.	Utah	Kris Humphries	Minnesota	6-9
15.	Boston	Al Jefferson	Prentiss HS (Miss.)	6-10
16.	Utah (from N.Y. through Phoenix)	Kirk Snyder	Nevada	6-6
17.	Atlanta (from Mil. through Denver and Detroit)	Josh Smith	Oak Hill Academy (Va.)	6-9
18.	New Orleans	J.R. Smith	St. Benedict's Prep (N.J.)	6-6
19.	Miami	Dorell Wright	South Kent Prep (Conn.)	6-7
20.	Denver	Jameer Nelson†	St. Joseph's	6-0
21.	Utah (from Houston)	Pavel Podkolzine‡	Varese (Italy)	7-5
22.	New Jersey	Viktor Khryapa§	CSKA Moscow (Russia)	6-9
23.	Portland (from Memphis)	Sergei Monia	CSKA Moscow (Russia)	6-8
24.	Boston (from Dallas)	Delonte West	St. Joseph's	6-4
25.	Boston (from Detroit)	Tony Allen	Oklahoma State	6-4
26.	Sacramento	Kevin Martin	Western Carolina	6-7
27.	L.A. Lakers	Sasha Vujacic	Snaidero Udine (Italy)	6-7
28.	San Antonio	Beno Udrih	Breil Milano (Italy)	6-3
29.	Indiana	David Harrison	Colorado	7-0

SECOND ROUND

	Team	Name	College/country	Ht.
30.	Orlando	Anderson Varejao	F.C. Barcelona (Spain)	6-10
31.	Chicago	Jackson Vroman∞	Iowa State	6-10
32.	Washington	Peter John Ramos	Criollos de Caguas (Puerto Rico)	7-3
33.	L.A. Clippers (from Charlotte)	Lionel Chalmers	Xavier	6-0
34.	Atlanta	Donta Smith	Southeastern Illinois College	6-7
35.	Seattle (from L.A. Clippers)	Andre Emmett▲	Texas Tech	6-5
36.	Orlando (from Phoenix)	Antonio Burks@	Memphis	6-0
37.	Atlanta (from Philadelphia)	Royal Ivey	Texas	6-3
38.	Chicago (from Toronto)	Chris Duhon	Duke	6-1
39.	Toronto (from Cleveland)	Albert Miralles	Roseto (Italy)	6-10
40.	Boston	Justin Reed	Mississippi	6-8
41.	Seattle	David Young	North Carolina Central	6-5
42.	Atlanta (from Orlando through Phil. and Golden St.	Viktor Sanikidze	SAOS JDA Dijon (France)	6-8
43.	New York	Trevor Ariza	UCLA	6-7
44.	New Orleans	Tim Pickett	Florida State	6-4
45.	Charlotte (from Milwaukee)	Bernard Robinson	Michigan	6-6
46.	Portland	Ha Seung-Jin	Yonsei University (South Korea)	7-3
47.	Miami	Pape Sow	Cal State Fullerton	6-10
48.	Sacramento (from Utah)	Ricky Minard	Morehead State	6-4
49.	Memphis (from Denver through Orlando)	Sergei Lishouk	Khimik Yuzhniy (Ukraine)	6-11
50.	Dallas (from Houston through Denver)	Vassillis Spanoulis	Maroussi (Greece)	6-4
51.	New Jersey	Christian Drejer	FC Barcelona (Spain)	6-9
52.	San Antonio (from Memphis)	Romain Sato	Xavier	6-5
53.	Miami (from Dallas)	Matt Freije	Vanderbilt	6-10
54.	Detroit	Rickey Paulding	Missouri	6-5
55.	Houston (from Sacramento through Utah)	Luis Flores	Manhattan	6-2
56.	L.A. Lakers	Marcus Douthit	Providence	6-11
57.	San Antonio	Sergei Karaulov	Yakutsk (Russia)	7-1
58.	Minnesota	Blake Stepp	Gonzaga	6-4
59.	Indiana	Rashad Wright	Georgia	6-2

NOTE: Minnesota forfeited its first-round pick
*Washington traded the draft rights to Devin Harris, plus the rights to Christian Laettner and Jerry Stackhouse, to Dallas for cash considerations and Antawn Jamison.
**Phoenix traded the draft rights to Luol Deng to Chicago for a future first-round selection, the draft rights to Jackson Vroman and cash considerations.
† Denver traded the draft rights to Jameer Nelson to Orlando for a future first-round selection.
‡ Utah traded the draft rights traded to Pavel Podkolzine to Dallas for a future first-round selection.
§ New Jersey traded the draft rights to Viktor Khryapa to Portland for cash considerations and the rights to Eddie Gill.
∞ Chicago traded the draft rights to Jackson Vroman, a future first-round selection and cash considerations to Phoenix for the draft rights to Luol Deng.
▲ Seattle traded the draft rights to Andre Emmett to Memphis for a future second-round selection.
@ Orlando traded the draft rights to Antonio Burks to Memphis for cash considerations.

AWARD WINNERS

MAJOR AWARDS

NBA Most Valuable Player:
Kevin Garnett, Minnesota

IBM NBA Red Auerbach Coach of the Year:
Hubie Brown, Memphis

Got Milk? NBA Rookie of the Year:
LeBron James, Cleveland

NBA Most Improved Player:
Zach Randolph, Portland

NBA Executive of the Year:
Jerry West, Memphis

J. Walter Kennedy Citizenship Award:
Reggie Miller, Indiana

NBA Sportsmanship Award:
P.J. Brown, New Orleans

NBA Defensive Player of the Year:
Ron Artest, Indiana

NBA Sixth Man Award:
Antawn Jamison, Dallas

NBA Finals Most Valuable Player:
Chauncey Billups, Detroit

All-Star Game Most Valuable Player:
Shaquille O'Neal, L.A. Lakers

ALL-NBA TEAMS

FIRST
Kevin Garnett, Minnesota
Tim Duncan, San Antonio
Shaquille O'Neal, L.A. Lakers
Kobe Bryant, L.A. Lakers
Jason Kidd, New Jersey

SECOND
Jermaine O'Neal, Indiana
Peja Stojakovic, Sacramento
Ben Wallace, Detroit
Sam Cassell, Minnesota
Tracy McGrady, Orlando

THIRD
Dirk Nowitzki, Dallas
Ron Artest, Indiana
Yao Ming, Houston
Michael Redd, Milwaukee
Baron Davis, New Orleans

GOT MILK? ALL-ROOKIE TEAMS

FIRST
Carmelo Anthony, Denver
LeBron James, Cleveland
Dwyane Wade, Miami
Chris Bosh, Toronto
Kirk Hinrich, Chicago

SECOND
Josh Howard, Dallas
T.J. Ford, Milwaukee
Udonis Haslem, Miami
Jarvis Hayes, Washington
Marquis Daniels, Dallas

ALL-DEFENSIVE TEAMS

FIRST
Ron Artest, Indiana
Kevin Garnett, Minnesota
Ben Wallace, Detroit
Bruce Bowen, San Antonio
Kobe Bryant, L.A. Lakers

SECOND
Andre Kirilenko, Utah
Tim Duncan, San Antonio
Theo Ratliff, Portland
Doug Christie, Sacramento
Jason Kidd, New Jersey

NBA PLAYERS OF THE WEEK

Oct. 28	Baron Davis, New Orleans(E)
	Rashard Lewis, Seattle (W)
Nov. 9	Ron Artest, Indiana (E)
	Andrei Kirilenko, Utah (W)
Nov. 10	Allen Iverson, Phil. (E)
	Q. Richardson, L.A. C. (W)
Nov. 17	Chauncey Billups, Detroit (E)
	Kevin Garnett, Minnesota (W)
Nov. 24	Dikembe Mutombo, N.Y. (E)
	Voshon Lenard, Denver (W)
Dec. 1	Vince Carter, Toronto (E)
	Shaquille O'Neal, L.A. L. (W)
Dec. 8	Paul Pierce, Boston (E)
	Peja Stojakovic, Sac. (W)
Dec. 15	Tracy McGrady, Orlando (E)
	Kevin Garnett, Minnesota (W)
Dec. 22	Jason Kidd, New Jersey (E)
	Sam Cassell, Minnesota (W)
Dec. 29	Ben Wallace, Detroit (E)
	Elton Brand, L.A. C. (W)
Jan. 5	Paul Pierce, Boston (E)
	Ray Allen, Seattle (W)
Jan. 12	Stephon Marbury, N.Y. (E)
	Michael Finley, Dallas (W)
Jan. 19	Carlos Boozer, Cleveland (E)
	Kevin Garnett, Minnesota (W)
Jan. 26	Jason Kidd, New Jersey (E)
	Kevin Garnett, Minnesota (W)
Feb. 2	Kenyon Martin, N.J. (E)
	Tim Duncan, S.A. (W)
Feb. 9	All-Star Week (no award)
Feb. 17	Dwyane Wade, Miami (E)
	Kobe Bryant, L.A. Lakers (W)
Feb. 23	Ben Wallace, Detroit (E)
	Andrei Kirilenko, Utah (W)
Mar. 1	Lamar Odom, Miami (E)
	Yao Ming, Houston (W)
Mar. 8	Zydrunas Ilgauskas, Clev. (E)
	Carmelo Anthony, Den. (W)
Mar. 15	Vince Carter, Toronto (E)
	Shaquille O'Neal, L.A. L. (W)
Mar. 22	Ron Artest, Indiana (E)
	Kobe Bryant, L.A. Lakers (W)
Mar. 29	Richard Jefferson, N.J. (E)
	Dirk Nowitzki, Dallas (W)
Apr. 5	Jamaal Magloire, N. Orl. (E)
	Carmelo Anthony, Den. (W)

NBA PLAYERS OF THE MONTH

Nov.—Baron Davis, New Orleans (E)
      Peja Stojakovic, Sacramento (W)
Dec.—Jermaine O'Neal, Indiana (E)
      Kevin Garnett, Minnesota (W)
Jan..—Michael Redd, Bucks (E)
      Kevin Garnett, Minnesota (W)
Feb.—Kenyon Martin, New Jersey (E)
      Kevin Garnett, Minnesota (W)
Mar.—Lamar Odom, Miami (E)
      Kobe Bryant, L.A. Lakers (W)
Apr.—Jamaal Magloire, New Orleans (E)
      Kevin Garnett, Minnesota (W)

GOT MILK? ROOKIES OF THE MONTH

Nov.—LeBron James, Cleveland (E)
      Carmelo Anthony, Denver (W)
Dec.—LeBron James, Cleveland (E)
      Carmelo Anthony, Denver (W)
Jan.—LeBron James, Cleveland (E)
      Carmelo Anthony, Denver (W)
Feb.—LeBron James, Cleveland (E)
      Carmelo Anthony, Denver (W)
Mar.—LeBron James, Cleveland (E)
      Carmelo Anthony, Denver (W)
Apr.—LeBron James, Cleveland (E)
      Carmelo Anthony, Denver (W)

NBA COACHES OF THE MONTH

Nov.—Rick Carlisle, Indiana (E)
      Phil Jackson, L.A. Lakers (W)
Dec.—Byron Scott, New Jersey (E)
      Gregg Popovich, San Ant. (W)
Jan. Larry Brown, Detroit (E)
      Rick Adelman, Sacramento. (W)
Feb.—Lawrence Frank, New Jersey (E)
      Hubie Brown, Memphis (W)
Mar.—Stan Van Gundy, Miami (E)
      Hubie Brown, Memphis (W)
Apr.—Larry Brown, Detroit (E)
      Flip Saunders, Minnesota (W)

COMMUNITY ASSIST AWARD

Oct.—Rashard Lewis, Seattle
Nov.—Marc Jackson, Aaron McKie, Phi.
Dec.—Jermaine O'Neal, Indiana
Jan.—Karl Malone, L.A. Lakers
Feb.—Dirk Nowitski, Dallas
Mar.—Carlos Boozer, Cleveland
Apr.—Derek Fisher, L.A. Lakers
May—Lamar Odom, Miami

(Ranked according to overall total)

REGULAR SEASON

	HOME				ROAD		
	G.	Total	Avg.		G.	Total	Avg.
Atlanta Hawks	41	565,728	13,798		41	667,598	16,283
Boston Celtics	41	664,248	16,201		41	695,160	16,955
Chicago Bulls	41	809,177	19,736		41	677,203	16,517
Cleveland Cavaliers	41	749,790	18,288		41	768,973	18,755
Dallas Mavericks	41	825,594	20,136		41	715,560	17,453
Denver Nuggets	41	721,476	17,597		41	704,573	17,185
Detroit Pistons	41	872,902	21,290		41	702,245	17,128
Golden State Warriors	41	665,648	16,235		41	651,304	15,885
Houston Rockets	41	640,794	15,629		41	728,522	17,769
Indiana Pacers	41	678,326	16,545		41	726,142	17,711
Los Angeles Clippers	41	665,396	16,229		41	666,582	16,258
Los Angeles Lakers	41	777,757	18,970		41	794,595	19,380
Memphis Grizzlies	41	622,723	15,188		41	684,513	16,695
Miami Heat	41	624,809	15,239		41	677,500	16,524
Milwaukee Bucks	41	690,200	16,834		41	664,773	16,214
Minnesota Timberwolves	41	723,071	17,636		41	732,361	17,862
New Jersey Nets	41	613,051	14,952		41	711,678	17,358
New Orleans Hornets	41	587,613	14,332		41	683,875	16,680
New York Knickerbockers	41	785,739	19,164		41	721,154	17,589
Orlando Magic	41	589,144	14,369		41	688,551	16,794
Philadelphia 76ers	41	788,128	19,223		41	724,580	17,673
Phoenix Suns	41	670,385	16,351		41	674,937	16,462
Portland Trail Blazers	41	684,038	16,684		41	667,592	16,283
Sacramento Kings	41	709,997	17,317		41	730,342	17,813
San Antonio Spurs	41	739,706	18,042		41	711,250	17,348
Seattle SuperSonics	41	625,474	15,255		41	690,548	16,843
Toronto Raptors	41	750,608	18,308		41	675,737	16,481
Utah Jazz	41	785,330	19,154		41	678,034	16,537
Washington Wizards	41	645,363	15,741		41	656,333	16,008
TOTALS	1189	20,272,215	17,050		1189	20,272,215	17,050

PLAYOFFS

	HOME				ROAD		
	G.	Total	Avg.		G.	Total	Avg.
Boston Celtics	2	34,069	17,035		2	33,952	16,976
Dallas Mavericks	2	41,257	20,629		3	51,951	17,317
Denver Nuggets	2	39,407	19,704		3	56,494	18,831
Detroit Pistons	13	286,988	22,076		10	187,890	18,789
Houston Rockets	2	36,445	18,223		3	56,991	18,997
Indiana Pacers	8	144,022	18,003		8	160,676	20,085
Los Angeles Lakers	11	208,967	18,997		11	218,432	19,857
Memphis Grizzlies	2	38,702	19,351		2 3	7,594	18,797
Miami Heat	7	141,103	20,158		6	102,592	17,099
Milwaukee Bucks	2	36,033	18,017		3	66,228	22,076
Minnesota Timberwolves	10	194,015	19,402		8	148,349	18,544
New Jersey Nets	5	96,952	19,390		6	127,830	21,305
New Orleans Hornets	3	47,557	15,852		4	80,724	20,181
New York Knickerbockers	2	39,526	19,763		2	38,124	19,062
Sacramento Kings	6	103,902	17,317		6	119,410	19,902
San Antonio Spurs	5	93,985	18,797		5	95,693	19,139
TOTALS	82	1,582,930	19,304		82	1,582,930	19,304

2003-04 REVIEW *Attendance*

HISTORY

- Team by team
- Award winners
- Regular season
- Playoffs
- NBA Finals
- All-Star Game
- Hall of Fame
- Memorable games
- American Basketball Association

TEAM BY TEAM

ANDERSON PACKERS

YEAR-BY-YEAR RECORDS

Season	Coach	Finish	REGULAR SEASON W	L	PLAYOFFS W	L
1949-50	Howard Schultz, 21-14					
	Ike Duffey, 1-2					
	Doxie Moore, 15-11	2nd/Western Div.	37	27	4	4

ATLANTA HAWKS

YEAR-BY-YEAR RECORDS

Season	Coach	Finish	REGULAR SEASON W	L	PLAYOFFS W	L
1949-50*	Roger Potter, 1-6					
	Red Auerbach, 28-29	3rd/Western Div.	29	35	1	2
1950-51*	Dave McMillan, 9-14					
	John Logan, 2-1					
	M. Todorovich, 14-28	5th/Western Div.	25	43	—	—
1951-52†	Doxie Moore	5th/Western Div.	17	49	—	—
1952-53†	Andrew Levane	5th/Western Div.	27	44	—	—
1953-54†	Andrew Levane, 11-35					
	Red Holzman, 10-16	4th/Western Div.	21	51	—	—
1954-55†	Red Holzman	4th/Western Div.	26	46	—	—
1955-56‡	Red Holzman	T2nd/Western Div.	33	39	4	5
1956-57‡	Red Holzman, 14-19					
	Slater Martin, 5-3					
	Alex Hannum, 15-16	T1st/Western Div.	34	38	8	4
1957-58‡	Alex Hannum	1st/Western Div.	41	31	8	3
1958-59‡	Andy Phillip, 6-4					
	Ed Macauley, 43-19	1st/Western Div.	49	23	2	4
1959-60‡	Ed Macauley	1st/Western Div.	46	29	7	7
1960-61‡	Paul Seymour	1st/Western Div.	51	28	5	7
1961-62‡	Paul Seymour, 5-9					
	Andrew Levane, 20-40					
	Bob Pettit, 4-2	4th/Western Div.	29	51	—	—
1962-63‡	Harry Gallatin	2nd/Western Div.	48	32	6	5
1963-64‡	Harry Gallatin	2nd/Western Div.	46	34	6	6
1964-65‡	Harry Gallatin, 17-16					
	Richie Guerin, 28-19	2nd/Western Div.	45	35	1	3
1965-66‡	Richie Guerin	3rd/Western Div.	36	44	6	4
1966-67‡	Richie Guerin	2nd/Western Div.	39	42	5	4
1967-68‡	Richie Guerin	1st/Western Div.	56	26	2	4
1968-69	Richie Guerin	2nd/Western Div.	48	34	5	6
1969-70	Richie Guerin	1st/Western Div.	48	34	4	5
1970-71	Richie Guerin	2nd/Central Div.	36	46	1	4
1971-72	Richie Guerin	2nd/Central Div.	36	46	2	4
1972-73	Cotton Fitzsimmons	2nd/Central Div.	46	36	2	4
1973-74	Cotton Fitzsimmons	2nd/Central Div.	35	47	—	—
1974-75	Cotton Fitzsimmons	4th/Central Div.	31	51	—	—
1975-76	C. Fitzsimmons, 28-46					
	Gene Tormohlen, 1-7	5th/Central Div.	29	53	—	—
1976-77	Hubie Brown	6th/Central Div.	31	51	—	—
1977-78	Hubie Brown	4th/Central Div.	41	41	0	2
1978-79	Hubie Brown	3rd/Central Div.	46	36	5	4
1979-80	Hubie Brown	1st/Central Div.	50	32	1	4
1980-81	Hubie Brown, 31-48					
	Mike Fratello, 0-3	4th/Central Div.	31	51	—	—
1981-82	Kevin Loughery	2nd/Central Div.	42	40	0	2
1982-83	Kevin Loughery	2nd/Central Div.	43	39	1	2
1983-84	Mike Fratello	3rd/Central Div.	40	42	2	3
1984-85	Mike Fratello	5th/Central Div.	34	48	—	—
1985-86	Mike Fratello	2nd/Central Div.	50	32	4	5
1986-87	Mike Fratello	1st/Central Div.	57	25	4	5
1987-88	Mike Fratello	T2nd/Central Div.	50	32	6	6
1988-89	Mike Fratello	3rd/Central Div.	52	30	2	3
1989-90	Mike Fratello	6th/Central Div.	41	41	—	—

FIRST-ROUND DRAFT PICKS

- 1950—Bob Cousy, Holy Cross
- 1951—Mel Hutchins, Brigham Young
- 1952—Mark Workman, West Virginia
- 1953—Bob Houbregs, Washington
- 1954—Bob Pettit, Louisiana State
- 1955—Dick Ricketts, Duquesne
- 1956—Bill Russell, San Francisco
- 1957—Win Wilfong, Memphis State
- 1958—Dave Gambee, Oregon State
- 1959—Bob Ferry, St. Louis
- 1960—Lenny Wilkens, Providence
- 1961—Cleo Hill, Winston-Salem
- 1962—Zelmo Beaty, Prairie View
- 1963—Jerry Ward, Boston College
- 1964—Jeff Mullins, Duke
- 1965—Jim Washington, Villanova
- 1966—Lou Hudson, Minnesota
- 1967—Tim Workman, Seattle
- 1968—Skip Harlicka, South Carolina
- 1969—Butch Beard, Louisville
- 1970—Pete Maravich, Louisiana State
- John Vallely, UCLA
- 1971—Tom Payne, Kentucky†
- George Trapp, Long Beach State
- 1972—None
- 1973—Dwight Jones, Houston
- John Brown, Missouri
- 1974—Tom Henderson, Hawaii
- Mike Sojourner, Utah
- 1975—David Thompson, N.C. State*
- Marvin Webster, Morgan State
- 1976—Armond Hill, Princeton
- 1977—Tree Rollins, Clemson
- 1978—Butch Lee, Marquette
- Jack Givens, Kentucky
- 1979—None
- 1980—Don Collins, Washington State
- 1981—Al Wood, North Carolina
- 1982—Keith Edmonson, Purdue
- 1983—None
- 1984—Kevin Willis, Michigan State
- 1985—Jon Koncak, Southern Methodist
- 1986—Billy Thompson, Louisville
- 1987—Dallas Comegys, DePaul
- 1988—None
- 1989—Roy Marble, Iowa
- 1990—Rumeal Robinson, Michigan
- 1991—Stacey Augmon, UNLV
- Anthony Avent, Seton Hall
- 1992—None
- 1993—Douglas Edwards, Florida State
- 1994—None
- 1995—Alan Henderson, Indiana
- 1996—Priest Lauderdale, Central State (O.)
- 1997—Ed Gray, California

HISTORY Team by team

Season	Coach	Finish	REGULAR SEASON W	L	PLAYOFFS W	L
1990-91	Bob Weiss	4th/Central Div.	43	39	2	3
1991-92	Bob Weiss	5th/Central Div.	38	44	—	—
1992-93	Bob Weiss	4th/Central Div.	43	39	0	3
1993-94	Lenny Wilkens	1st/Central Div.	57	25	5	6
1994-95	Lenny Wilkens	5th/Central Div.	42	40	0	3
1995-96	Lenny WIlkens	T4th/Central Div.	46	36	4	6
1996-97	Lenny Wilkens	2nd/Central Div.	56	26	4	6
1997-98	Lenny Wilkens	4th/Central Div.	50	32	1	3
1998-99	Lenny Wilkens	2nd/Central Div.	31	19	3	6
1999-00	Lenny Wilkens	7th/Central Div.	28	54	—	—
2000-01	Lon Kruger	7th/Central Div.	25	57	—	—
2001-02	Lon Kruger	6th/Central Div.	33	49	—	—
2002-03	Lon Kruger, 11-16					
	Terry Stotts, 24-31	5th/Central Div.	35	47	—	—
2003-04	Terry Stotts	7th/Central Div.	28	54	—	—
Totals.			2170	2168	119	153

*Tri-Cities Blackhawks.
†Milwaukee Hawks.
‡St. Louis Hawks.

1998— Roshown McLeod, Duke
1999— Jason Terry, Arizona
       Cal Bowdler, Old Dominion
       Dion Glover, Georgia Tech
2000— DerMarr Johnson, Cincinnati
2001— Pau Gasol, Spain
2002— None
2003— Boris Diaw, France
2004— Josh Childress, Stanford
       Josh Smith, Oak Hill Acad. (Va.)
*First overall pick of draft.
†Payne was selected in the 1971 supplementary draft of hardship cases. The
Hawks had to forfeit their 1972 first-
round choice.

RETIRED NUMBERS
9 Bob Pettit
21 Dominique Wilkins
23 Lou Hudson

BALTIMORE BULLETS

YEAR-BY-YEAR RECORDS

Season	Coach	Finish	REGULAR SEASON W	L	PLAYOFFS W	L
1947-48	Buddy Jeannette	2nd/Western Div.	28	20	9	3
1948-49	Buddy Jeannette	3rd/Eastern Div.	29	31	1	2
1949-50	Buddy Jeannette	5th/Eastern Div.	25	43	—	—
1950-51	Buddy Jeannette, 14-23					
	Walter Budko, 10-19	5th/Eastern Div.	24	42	—	—
1951-52	Fred Scolari, 12-27					
	Chick Reiser, 8-19	5th/Eastern DIv.	20	46	—	—
1952-53	Chick Reiser, 0-3					
	Clair Bee, 16-51	4th/Eastern Div.	16	54	0	2
1953-54	Clair Bee	5th/Eastern Div.	16	56	—	—
1954-55*	Clair Bee, 2-9					
	Al Barthelme, 1-2		3	11	—	—
Totals.			161	303	10	7

*Team disbanded November 27.

FIRST-ROUND DRAFT PICKS
1947— Larry Killick, Vermont
1948— Walter Budko, Columbia
1949— Ron Livingstone, Wyoming
1950— Don Rehfeldt, Wisconsin
1951— Gene Melchiorre, Bradley*
1952— Jim Baechtold, Eastern Kentucky
1953— Ray Felix, Long Island U.
1954— Frank Selvy, Furman*
*First overall pick of draft.

BOSTON CELTICS

YEAR-BY-YEAR RECORDS

Season	Coach	Finish	REGULAR SEASON W	L	PLAYOFFS W	L
1946-47	John Russell	T5th/Eastern Div.	22	38	—	—
1947-48	John Russell	3rd/Eastern Div.	20	28	1	2
1948-49	Alvin Julian	5th/Eastern Div.	25	35	—	—
1949-50	Alvin Julian	6th/Eastern Div.	22	46	—	—
1950-51	Red Auerbach	2nd/Eastern Div.	39	30	0	2
1951-52	Red Auerbach	2nd/Eastern Div.	39	27	1	2
1952-53	Red Auerbach	3rd/Eastern Div.	46	25	3	3
1953-54	Red Auerbach	T2nd/Eastern Div.	42	30	2	4
1954-55	Red Auerbach	3rd/Eastern Div.	36	36	3	4
1955-56	Red Auerbach	2nd/Eastern Div.	39	33	1	2
1956-57	Red Auerbach	1st/Eastern Div.	44	28	7	3
1957-58	Red Auerbach	1st/Eastern Div.	49	23	6	5
1958-59	Red Auerbach	1st/Eastern Div.	52	20	8	3
1959-60	Red Auerbach	1st/Eastern Div.	59	16	8	5
1960-61	Red Auerbach	1st/Eastern Div.	57	22	8	2
1961-62	Red Auerbach	1st/Eastern Div.	60	20	8	6
1962-63	Red Auerbach	1st/Eastern Div.	58	22	8	5
1963-64	Red Auerbach	1st/Eastern Div.	59	21	8	2
1964-65	Red Auerbach	1st/Eastern Div.	62	18	8	4
1965-66	Red Auerbach	2nd/Eastern Div.	54	26	11	6
1966-67	Bill Russell	2nd/Eastern Div.	60	21	4	5

FIRST-ROUND DRAFT PICKS
1947— Eddie Ehlers, Purdue
1948— George Hauptfuehrer, Harvard
1949— Tony Lavelli, Yale
1950— Charlie Share, Bowling Green*
1951— Ernie Barrett, Kansas State
1952— Bill Stauffer, Missouri
1953— Frank Ramsey, Kentucky
1954— Togo Palazzi, Holy Cross
1955— Jim Loscutoff, Oregon
1956— Tom Heinsohn, Holy Cross
1957— Sam Jones, North Carolina College
1958— Ben Swain, Texas Southern
1959— John Richter, North Carolina State
1960— Tom Sanders, New York University
1961— Gary Phillips, Houston
1962— John Havlicek, Ohio State
1963— Bill Green, Colorado State
1964— Mel Counts, Oregon State
1965— Ollie Johnson, San Francisco
1966— Jim Barnett, Oregon
1967— Mal Graham, New York University
1968— Don Chaney, Houston
1969— Jo Jo White, Kansas
1970— Dave Cowens, Florida State
1971— Clarence Glover, Western Kentucky
1972— Paul Westphal, Southern California

Season	Coach	Finish	REGULAR SEASON W	L	PLAYOFFS W	L
1967-68	Bill Russell	2nd/Eastern Div.	54	28	12	7
1968-69	Bill Russell	4th/Eastern Div.	48	34	12	6
1969-70	Tom Heinsohn	6th/Eastern Div.	34	48	—	—
1970-71	Tom Heinsohn	3rd/Atlantic Div.	44	38	—	—
1971-72	Tom Heinsohn	1st/Atlantic Div.	56	26	5	6
1972-73	Tom Heinsohn	1st/Atlantic Div.	68	14	7	6
1973-74	Tom Heinsohn	1st/Atlantic Div.	56	26	12	6
1974-75	Tom Heinsohn	1st/Atlantic Div.	60	22	6	5
1975-76	Tom Heinsohn	1st/Atlantic Div.	54	28	12	6
1976-77	Tom Heinsohn	2nd/Atlantic Div.	44	38	5	4
1977-78	Tom Heinsohn, 11-23					
	Tom Sanders, 21-27	3rd/Atlantic Div.	32	50	—	—
1978-79	Tom Sanders, 2-12					
	Dave Cowens, 27-41	5th/Atlantic Div.	29	53	—	—
1979-80	Bill Fitch	1st/Atlantic Div.	61	21	5	4
1980-81	Bill Fitch	T1st/Atlantic Div.	62	20	12	5
1981-82	Bill Fitch	1st/Atlantic Div.	63	19	7	5
1982-83	Bill Fitch	2nd/Atlantic Div.	56	26	2	5
1983-84	K.C. Jones	1st/Atlantic Div.	62	20	15	8
1984-85	K.C. Jones	1st/Atlantic Div.	63	19	13	8
1985-86	K.C. Jones	1st/Atlantic Div.	67	15	15	3
1986-87	K.C. Jones	1st/Atlantic Div.	59	23	13	10
1987-88	K.C. Jones	1st/Atlantic Div.	57	25	9	8
1988-89	Jimmy Rodgers	3rd/Atlantic Div.	42	40	0	3
1989-90	Jimmy Rodgers	2nd/Atlantic Div.	52	30	2	3
1990-91	Chris Ford	1st/Atlantic Div.	56	26	5	6
1991-92	Chris Ford	T1st/Atlantic Div.	51	31	6	4
1992-93	Chris Ford	2nd/Atlantic Div.	48	34	1	3
1993-94	Chris Ford	5th/Atlantic Div.	32	50	—	—
1994-95	Chris Ford	3rd/Atlantic Div.	35	47	1	3
1995-96	M.L. Carr	5th/Atlantic Div.	33	49	—	—
1996-97	M.L. Carr	7th/Atlantic Div.	15	67	—	—
1997-98	Rick Pitino	6th/Atlantic Div.	36	46	—	—
1998-99	Rick Pitino	5th/Atlantic Div.	19	31	—	—
1999-00	Rick Pitino	5th/Atlantic Div.	35	47	—	—
2000-01	Rick Pitino, 12-22					
	Jim O'Brien, 24-24	5th/Atlantic Div.	36	46	—	—
2001-02	Jim O'Brien	2nd/Atlantic Div.	49	33	9	7
2002-03	Jim O'Brien	3rd/Atlantic Div.	44	38	4	6
2003-04	Jim O'Brien, 22-24	4th/Atlantic Div.	36	46	0	4
	John Carroll, 14-22					
Totals			2692	1819	285	206

1973— Steve Downing, Indiana
1974— Glenn McDonald, Long Beach State
1975— Tom Boswell, South Carolina
1976— Norm Cook, Kansas
1977— Cedric Maxwell, UNC Charlotte
1978— Larry Bird, Indiana State
Freeman Williams, Portland State
1979— None
1980— Kevin McHale, Minnesota
1981— Charles Bradley, Wyoming
1982— Darren Tillis, Cleveland State
1983— Greg Kite, Brigham Young
1984— Michael Young, Houston
1985— Sam Vincent, Michigan State
1986— Len Bias, Maryland
1987— Reggie Lewis, Northeastern
1988— Brian Shaw, Cal.-Santa Barbara
1989— Michael Smith, Brigham Young
1990— Dee Brown, Jacksonville
1991— Rick Fox, North Carolina
1992— Jon Barry, Georgia Tech
1993— Acie Earl, Iowa
1994— Eric Montross, North Carolina
1995— Eric Williams, Providence
1996— Antoine Walker, Kentucky
1997— Chauncey Billups, Colorado
Ron Mercer, Kentucky
1998— Paul Pierce, Kansas
1999— None
2000— Jerome Moiso, UCLA
2001— Joe Johnson, Arkansas
Kedrick Brown, Okaloosa-Walton C.C. (Fla.)
Joseph Forte, North Carolina
2002— None
2003— Troy Bell, Boston College
Dahntay Jones, Duke
2004— Al Jefferson, Prentiss HS (Miss.)
Delonte West, St. Joseph's
Tony Allen, Oklahoma State

RETIRED NUMBERS

00 Robert Parish	* Jim Loscutoff
1 Walter Brown	19 Don Nelson
2 Red Auerbach	21 Bill Sharman
3 Dennis Johnson	22 Ed Macauley
6 Bill Russell	23 Frank Ramsey
10 Jo Jo White	24 Sam Jones
14 Bob Cousy	25 K.C. Jones
15 Tom Heinsohn	31 Cedric Maxwell
16 Tom Sanders	32 Kevin McHale
17 John Havlicek	33 Larry Bird
18 Dave Cowens	35 Reggie Lewis

*Loscutoff's jersey was retired, but number 18 was kept active for Dave Cowens. So, "Loscy" was suspended from the rafters.

Note: Microphone retired in honor of broadcaster Johnny Most.

CHICAGO BULLS

YEAR-BY-YEAR RECORDS

Season	Coach	Finish	REGULAR SEASON W	L	PLAYOFFS W	L
1966-67	Red Kerr	4th/Western Div.	33	48	0	3
1967-68	Red Kerr	4th/Western Div.	29	53	1	4
1968-69	Dick Motta	5th/Western Div.	33	49	—	—
1969-70	Dick Motta	T3rd/Western Div.	39	43	1	4
1970-71	Dick Motta	2nd/Midwest Div.	51	31	3	4
1971-72	Dick Motta	2nd/Midwest Div.	57	25	0	4
1972-73	Dick Motta	2nd/Midwest Div.	51	31	3	4
1973-74	Dick Motta	2nd/Midwest Div.	54	28	4	7
1974-75	Dick Motta	1st/Midwest Div.	47	35	7	6
1975-76	Dick Motta	4th/Midwest Div.	24	58	—	—
1976-77	Ed Badger	T2nd/Midwest Div.	44	38	1	2
1977-78	Ed Badger	3rd/Midwest Div.	40	42	—	—

FIRST-ROUND DRAFT PICKS

1966— Dave Schellhase, Purdue
1967— Clem Haskins, Western Kentucky
1968— Tom Boerwinkle, Tennessee
1969— Larry Cannon, La Salle
1970— Jimmy Collins, New Mexico State
1971— Kennedy McIntosh, E. Michigan
1972— Ralph Simpson, Michigan State
1973— Kevin Kunnert, Iowa
1974— Maurice Lucas, Marquette
Cliff Pondexter, Long Beach State
1975— None
1976— Scott May, Indiana
1977— Tate Armstrong, Duke
1978— Reggie Theus, UNLV

Season	Coach	Finish	REGULAR SEASON W	L	PLAYOFFS W	L
1978-79	Larry Costello, 20-36					
	S. Robertson, 11-15	5th/Midwest Div.	31	51	—	—
1979-80	Jerry Sloan	T3rd/Midwest Div.	30	52	—	—
1980-81	Jerry Sloan	2nd/Central Div.	45	37	2	4
1981-82	Jerry Sloan, 19-32					
	Phil Johnson, 0-1					
	Rod Thorn, 15-15	5th/Central Div.	34	48	—	—
1982-83	Paul Westhead	4th/Central Div.	28	54	—	—
1983-84	Kevin Loughery	5th/Central Div.	27	55	—	—
1984-85	Kevin Loughery	3rd/Central Div.	38	44	1	3
1985-86	Stan Albeck	4th/Central Div.	30	52	0	3
1986-87	Doug Collins	5th/Central Div.	40	42	0	3
1987-88	Doug Collins	T2nd/Central Div.	50	32	4	6
1988-89	Doug Collins	5th/Central Div.	47	35	9	8
1989-90	Phil Jackson	2nd/Central Div.	55	27	10	6
1990-91	Phil Jackson	1st/Central Div.	61	21	15	2
1991-92	Phil Jackson	1st/Central Div.	67	15	15	7
1992-93	Phil Jackson	1st/Central Div.	57	25	15	4
1993-94	Phil Jackson	2nd/Central Div.	55	27	6	4
1994-95	Phil Jackson	3rd/Central Div.	47	35	5	5
1995-96	Phil Jackson	1st/Central Div.	72	10	15	3
1996-97	Phil Jackson	1st/Central Div.	69	13	15	4
1997-98	Phil Jackson	1st/Central Div.	62	20	15	6
1998-99	Tim Floyd	8th/Central Div.	13	37	—	—
1999-00	Tim Floyd	8th/Central Div.	17	65	—	—
2000-01	Tim Floyd	8th/Central Div.	15	67	—	—
2001-02	Tim Floyd, 4-21					
	Bill Berry, 0-2					
	Bill Cartwright, 17-38	8th/Central Div.	21	61	—	—
2002-03	Bill Cartwright	6th/Central Div.	30	52	—	—
2003-04	Bill Cartwright, 4-10					
	Pete Myers, 0-2					
	Scott Skiles, 19-47	8th/Central Div.	23	59	—	—
	Totals............................		1566	1517	147	106

1979— David Greenwood, UCLA
1980— Kelvin Ransey, Ohio State
1981— Orlando Woolridge, Notre Dame
1982— Quintin Dailey, San Francisco
1983— Sidney Green, UNLV
1984— Michael Jordan, North Carolina
1985— Keith Lee, Memphis State
1986— Brad Sellers, Ohio State
1987— Olden Polynice, Virginia
         Horace Grant, Clemson
1988— Will Perdue, Vanderbilt
1989— Stacey King, Oklahoma
         B.J. Armstrong, Iowa
         Jeff Sanders, Georgia Southern
1990— None
1991— Mark Randall, Kansas
1992— Byron Houston, Oklahoma State
1993— Corie Blount, Cincinnati
1994— Dickey Simpkins, Providence
1995— Jason Caffey, Alabama
1996— Travis Knight, Connecticut
1997— Keith Booth, Maryland
1998— Corey Benjamin, Oregon State
1999— Elton Brand, Duke*
         Ron Artest, St. John's
2000— Marcus Fizer, Iowa State
         Chris Mihm, Texas
         Dalibor Bagaric, Croatia
2001— Eddy Curry, Thornwood HS (Ill.)
2002— Jay Williams, Duke
2003— Kirk Hinrich, Kansas
2004— Ben Gordon, Connecticut
*First overall pick of draft.

RETIRED NUMBERS

4 Jerry Sloan   23 Michael Jordan
10 Bob Love

CHICAGO STAGS

YEAR-BY-YEAR RECORDS

Season	Coach	Finish	REGULAR SEASON W	L	PLAYOFFS W	L
1946-47	Harold Olsen	1st/Western Div.	39	22	5	6
1947-48	Harold Olsen	T2nd/Western Div.	28	20	3	4
1948-49	Harold Olsen, 28-21	3rd/Western Div.	38	22	0	2
	*P. Brownstein, 10-1					
1949-50	Philip Brownstein	T3rd/Central Div.	40	28	0	3
	Totals............................		145	92	8	15

*Substituted during Olsen's illness.

FIRST-ROUND DRAFT PICKS

1947— Paul Huston, Ohio State
1948— Ed Mikan, DePaul
1949— Ralph Beard, Kentucky
         Jack Kerric, Loyola (Ill.)
1950— Larry Foust, La Salle

CLEVELAND CAVALIERS

YEAR-BY-YEAR RECORDS

Season	Coach	Finish	REGULAR SEASON W	L	PLAYOFFS W	L
1970-71	Bill Fitch	4th/Central Div.	15	67	—	—
1971-72	Bill Fitch	4th/Central Div.	23	59	—	—
1972-73	Bill Fitch	4th/Central Div.	32	50	—	—
1973-74	Bill Fitch	4th/Central Div.	29	53	—	—
1974-75	Bill Fitch	3rd/Central Div.	40	42	—	—
1975-76	Bill Fitch	1st/Central Div.	49	33	6	7
1976-77	Bill Fitch	4th/Central Div.	43	39	1	2
1977-78	Bill Fitch	3rd/Central Div.	43	39	0	2
1978-79	Bill Fitch	T4th/Central Div.	30	52	—	—
1979-80	Stan Albeck	T4th/Central Div.	37	45	—	—
1980-81	Bill Musselman, 25-46					
	Don Delaney, 3-8	5th/Central Div.	28	54	—	—
1981-82	Don Delaney, 4-11					

FIRST-ROUND DRAFT PICKS

1970— John Johnson, Iowa
1971— Austin Carr, Notre Dame*
1972— Dwight Davis, Houston
1973— Jim Brewer, Minnesota
1974— Campy Russell, Michigan
1975— John Lambert, Southern California
1976— Chuckie Williams, Kansas State
1977— None
1978— Mike Mitchell, Auburn
1979— None
1980— Chad Kinch, UNC Charlotte
1981— None
1982— John Bagley, Boston College

Season	Coach	Finish	W	L	W	L
	Bob Kloppenburg, 0-3					
1981-82	Chuck Daly, 9-32					
	Bill Musselman, 2-21	6th/Central Div.	15	67	—	—
1982-83	Tom Nissalke	5th/Central Div.	23	59	—	—
1983-84	Tom Nissalke	4th/Central Div.	28	54	—	—
1984-85	George Karl	4th/Central Div.	36	46	1	3
1985-86	George Karl, 25-42					
	Gene Littles, 4-11	5th/Central Div.	29	53	—	—
1986-87	Lenny Wilkens	6th/Central Div.	31	51	—	—
1987-88	Lenny Wilkens	T4th/Central Div.	42	40	2	3
1988-89	Lenny Wilkens	2nd/Central Div.	57	25	2	3
1989-90	Lenny Wilkens	T4th/Central Div.	42	40	2	3
1990-91	Lenny Wilkens	6th/Central Div.	33	49	—	—
1991-92	Lenny Wilkens	2nd/Central Div.	57	25	9	8
1992-93	Lenny Wilkens	2nd/Central Div.	54	28	3	6
1993-94	Mike Fratello	T3rd/Central Div.	47	35	0	3
1994-95	Mike Fratello	4th/Central Div.	43	39	1	3
1995-96	Mike Fratello	3rd/Central Div.	47	35	0	3
1996-97	Mike Fratello	5th/Central Div.	42	40	—	—
1997-98	Mike Fratello	5th/Central Div.	47	35	1	3
1998-99	Mike Fratello	7th/Central Div.	22	28	—	—
1999-00	Randy Wittman	6th/Central Div.	32	50	—	—
2000-01	Randy Wittman	6th/Central Div.	30	52	—	—
2001-02	John Lucas	7th/Central Div.	29	53	—	—
2002-03	John Lucas, 8-34					
	Keith Smart, 9-31	8th/Central Div.	17	65	—	—
2003-04	Paul Silas	5th/Central Div.	35	47	—	—
Totals			1207	1549	28	49

1983— Roy Hinson, Rutgers
Stewart Granger, Villanova
1984— Tim McCormick, Michigan
1985— Charles Oakley, Virginia Union
1986— Brad Daugherty, North Carolina*
Ron Harper, Miami (O.)
1987— Kevin Johnson, California
1988— Randolph Keys, Southern Miss.
1989— John Morton, Seton Hall
1990— None
1991— Terrell Brandon, Oregon
1992— None
1993— Chris Mills, Arizona
1994— None
1995— Bob Sura, Florida State
1996— Vitaly Potapenko, Wright State
Zydrunas Ilgauskas, Lithuania
1997— Derek Anderson, Kentucky
Brevin Knight, Stanford
1998— None
1999— Andre Miller, Utah
Trajan Langdon, Duke
2000— Jamal Crawford, Michigan
2001— DeSagana Diop, Oak Hill Ac. (Va.)
Brendan Haywood, North Carolina
2002— Dajuan Wagner, Memphis
2003— LeBron James, St. Vincent-St.
Mary HS (Ohio)*
2004— Luke Jackson, Oregon
*First overall pick of draft.

RETIRED NUMBERS

7 Bingo Smith	34 Austin Carr
22 Larry Nance	42 Nate Thurmond
25 Mark Price	43 Brad Daugherty

CLEVELAND REBELS

YEAR-BY-YEAR RECORDS

Season	Coach	Finish	W	L	W	L
1946-47	Dutch Dehnert, 17-20					
	Roy Clifford, 13-10	3rd/Western Div.	30	30	1	2

DALLAS MAVERICKS

YEAR-BY-YEAR RECORDS

Season	Coach	Finish	W	L	W	L
1980-81	Dick Motta	6th/Midwest Div.	15	67	—	—
1981-82	Dick Motta	5th/Midwest Div.	28	54	—	—
1982-83	Dick Motta	4th/Midwest Div.	38	44	—	—
1983-84	Dick Motta	2nd/Midwest Div.	43	39	4	6
1984-85	Dick Motta	3rd/Midwest Div.	44	38	1	3
1985-86	Dick Motta	3rd/Midwest Div.	44	38	5	5
1986-87	Dick Motta	1st/Midwest Div.	55	27	1	3
1987-88	John MacLeod	2nd/Midwest Div.	53	29	10	7
1988-89	John MacLeod	4th/Midwest Div.	38	44	—	—
1989-90	John MacLeod, 5-6					
	Richie Adubato, 42-29	3rd/Midwest Div.	47	35	0	3
1990-91	Richie Adubato	6th/Midwest Div.	28	54	—	—
1991-92	Richie Adubato	5th/Midwest Div.	22	60	—	—
1992-93	Richie Adubato, 2-27					
	Gar Heard, 9-44	6th/Midwest Div.	11	71	—	—
1993-94	Quinn Buckner	6th/Midwest Div.	13	69	—	—
1994-95	Dick Motta	5th/Midwest Div.	36	46	—	—
1995-96	Dick Motta	T5th/Midwest Div.	26	56	—	—
1996-97	Jim Cleamons	4th/Midwest Div.	24	58	—	—
1997-98	Jim Cleamons, 4-12					
	Don Nelson, 16-50	5th/Midwest Div.	20	62	—	—
1998-99	Don Nelson	5th/Midwest Div.	19	31	—	—
1999-00	Don Nelson	4th/Midwest Div.	40	42	—	—
2000-01	Don Nelson	T2nd/Midwest Div.	53	29	4	6
2001— None						

FIRST-ROUND DRAFT PICKS

1980— Kiki Vandeweghe, UCLA
1981— Mark Aguirre, DePaul*
Rolando Blackman, Kansas State
1982— Bill Garnett, Wyoming
1983— Dale Ellis, Tennessee
Derek Harper, Illinois
1984— Sam Perkins, North Carolina
Terence Stansbury, Temple
1985— Detlef Schrempf, Washington
Bill Wennington, St. John's
Uwe Blab, Indiana
1986— Roy Tarpley, Michigan
1987— Jim Farmer, Alabama
1988— None
1989— Randy White, Louisiana Tech
1990— None
1991— Doug Smith, Missouri
1992— Jim Jackson, Ohio State
1993— Jamal Mashburn, Kentucky
1994— Jason Kidd, California
Tony Dumas, Missouri-Kan. City
1995— Cherokee Parks, Duke
Loren Meyer, Iowa State
1996— Samaki Walker, Louisville
1997— Kelvin Cato, Iowa State
1998— Robert Traylor, Michigan
1999— None
2000— Etan Thomas, Syracuse
2001— None

Season	Coach	REGULAR SEASON Finish	W	L	PLAYOFFS W	L
2001-02	Don Nelson	2nd/Midwest Div.	57	25	4	4
2002-03	Don Nelson	2nd/Midwest Div.	60	22	10	10
2003-04	Don Nelson	3rd/Midwest Div.	52	30	1	4
Totals			866	1070	40	51

2002— None
2003— Josh Howard, Wake Forest
2004— None
*First overall pick of draft.

RETIRED NUMBERS
15 Brad Davis
22 Rolando Blackman

DENVER NUGGETS

YEAR-BY-YEAR RECORDS

Season	Coach	REGULAR SEASON Finish	W	L	PLAYOFFS W	L
1949-50	James Darden	6th/Western Div.	11	51	—	—

DENVER NUGGETS

YEAR-BY-YEAR RECORDS

Season	Coach	REGULAR SEASON Finish	W	L	PLAYOFFS W	L
1967-68*	Bob Bass	3rd/Western Div.	45	33	2	3
1968-69*	Bob Bass	3rd/Western Div.	44	34	3	4
1969-70*	John McLendon, 9-19					
	Joe Belmont, 42-14	1st/Western Div.	51	33	5	7
1970-71*	Joe Belmont, 3-10					
	Stan Albeck, 27-44	5th/Western Div.	30	54	—	—
1971-72*	Alex Hannum	4th/Western Div.	34	50	3	4
1972-73*	Alex Hannum	3rd/Western Div.	47	37	1	4
1973-74*	Alex Hannum	4th/Western Div.	37	47	—	—
1974-75†	Larry Brown	1st/Western Div.	65	19	7	6
1975-76†	Larry Brown	1st	60	24	6	7
1976-77	Larry Brown	1st/Midwest Div.	50	32	2	4
1977 78	Larry Brown	1st/Midwest Div.	48	34	6	7
1978-79	Larry Brown, 28-25					
	Donnie Walsh, 19-10	2nd/Midwest Div.	47	35	1	2
1979-80	Donnie Walsh	T3rd/Midwest Div.	30	52	—	—
1980-81	Donnie Walsh, 11-20					
	Doug Moe, 26-25	4th/Midwest Div.	37	45	—	—
1981-82	Doug Moe	T2nd/Midwest Div.	46	36	1	2
1982-83	Doug Moe	T2nd/Midwest Div.	45	37	3	5
1983-84	Doug Moe	T3rd/Midwest Div.	38	44	2	3
1984-85	Doug Moe	1st/Midwest Div.	52	30	8	7
1985-86	Doug Moe	2nd/Midwest Div.	47	35	5	5
1986-87	Doug Moe	4th/Midwest Div.	37	45	0	3
1987-88	Doug Moe	1st/Midwest Div.	54	28	5	6
1988-89	Doug Moe	3rd/Midwest Div.	44	38	0	3
1909-90	Doug Moe	4th/Midwest Div.	43	39	0	3
1990-91	Paul Westhead	7th/Midwest Div.	20	62		
1991-92	Paul Westhead	4th/Midwest Div.	24	58	—	—
1992-93	Dan Issel	4th/Midwest Div.	36	46	—	—
1993-94	Dan Issel	4th/Midwest Div.	42	40	6	6
1994-95	Dan Issel, 18-16					
	Gene Littles, 3-13					
	B. Bickerstaff, 20-12	4th/Midwest Div.	41	41	0	3
1995-96	Bernie Bickerstaff	4th/Midwest Div.	35	47	—	—
1996-97	Bernie Bickerstaff, 4-9					
	Dick Motta, 17-52	5th/Midwest Div.	21	61	—	—
1997-98	Bill Hanzlik	7th/Midwest Div.	11	71	—	—
1998-99	Mike D'Antoni	6th/Midwest Div.	14	36	—	—
1999-00	Dan Issel	5th/Midwest Div.	35	47	—	—
2000-01	Dan Issel	6th/Midwest Div.	40	42	—	—
2001-02	Dan Issel, 9-17					
	Mike Evans, 18-38	6th/Midwest Div.	27	55	—	—
2002-03	Jeff Bzdelik	7th/Midwest Div.	17	65	—	—
2003-04	Jeff Bzdelik	6th/Pacific Div.	43	39	1	4

		W	L	W	L
ABA totals		413	331	27	35
NBA totals		1024	1240	40	63

*Denver Rockets; club in ABA.
†Denver Nuggets; club in ABA.

FIRST-ROUND DRAFT PICKS
1967— Walt Frazier, Southern Illinois
1968— Tom Boerwinkle, Tennessee
1969— Bob Presley, California
1970— Spencer Haywood, Detroit
1971— Cliff Meely, Colorado
1972— Bud Stallworth, Kansas
1973— Mike Bantom, St. Joseph's
       Ed Ratleff, Long Beach State
1974— James Williams, Austin Peay
1975— Marvin Webster, Morgan State
1976— None
1977— Tom LaGarde, North Carolina
       Anthony Roberts, Oral Roberts
1978— Rod Griffin, Wake Forest
       Mike Evans, Kansas State
1979— None
1980— James Ray, Jacksonville
       Carl Nicks, Indiana State
1981— None
1982— Rob Williams, Houston
1983— Howard Carter, Louisiana State
1984— None
1985— Blair Rasmussen, Oregon
1986— Maurice Martin, St. Joseph's
       Mark Alarie, Duke
1987— None
1988— Jerome Lane, Pittsburgh
1989— Todd Lichti, Stanford
1990— Mahmoud Abdul-Rauf, LSU
1991— Dikembe Mutombo, Georgetown
       Mark Macon, Temple
1992— LaPhonso Ellis, Notre Dame
       Bryant Stith, Virginia
1993— Rodney Rogers, Wake Forest
1994— Jalen Rose, Michigan
1995— Brent Barry, Oregon State
1996— Efthimis Rentzias, Greece
1997— Tony Battie, Texas Tech
1998— Raef LaFrentz, Kansas
       Tyronn Lue, Nebraska
1999— James Posey, Xavier
2000— Mamadou N'diaye, Auburn
2001— None
2002— Nikoloz Tskitishvili, Italy
       Frank Williams, Illinois
2003— Carmelo Anthony, Syracuse
2004— Jameer Nelson, St. Joseph's
NOTE: Denver's first-round selections from 1967-75 were made while a member of the ABA.

RETIRED NUMBERS
2 Alex English
33 David Thompson
40 Byron Beck
44 Dan Issel
432 Doug Moe

DETROIT FALCONS
YEAR-BY-YEAR RECORDS

Season	Coach	Finish	REGULAR SEASON W	L	PLAYOFFS W	L
1946-47	Glenn Curtis, 12-22					
	Philip Sachs, 8-18	4th/Western Div.	20	40	—	—

DETROIT PISTONS
YEAR-BY-YEAR RECORDS

Season	Coach	Finish	REGULAR SEASON W	L	PLAYOFFS W	L
1948-49*	Carl Bennett, 0-6					
	Paul Armstrong, 22-32	5th/Western Div.	22	38	—	—
1949-50*	Murray Mendenhall	T3rd/Central Div.	40	28	3	2
1950-51*	Murray Mendenhall	3rd/Western Div.	32	36	1	2
1951-52*	Paul Birch	4th/Western Div.	29	37	0	2
1952-53*	Paul Birch	3rd/Western Div.	36	33	4	4
1953-54*	Paul Birch	3rd/Western Div.	40	32	0	4
1954-55*	Charles Eckman	1st/Western Div.	43	29	6	5
1955-56*	Charles Eckman	1st/Western Div.	37	35	4	6
1956-57*	Charles Eckman	T1st/Western Div.	34	38	0	3
1957-58	Charles Eckman, 9-16					
	Red Rocha, 24-23	T2nd/Western Div.	33	39	3	4
1958-59	Red Rocha	3rd/Western Div.	28	44	1	2
1959-60	Red Rocha, 13-21					
	Dick McGuire, 17-24	2nd/Western Div.	30	45	0	2
1960-61	Dick McGuire	3rd/Western Div.	34	45	2	3
1961-62	Dick McGuire	3rd/Western Div.	37	43	5	5
1962-63	Dick McGuire	3rd/Western Div.	34	46	1	3
1963-64	Charles Wolf	5th/Western Div.	23	57	—	—
1964-65	Charles Wolf, 2-9					
	D. DeBusschere, 29-40	4th/Western Div.	31	49	—	—
1965-66	Dave DeBusschere	5th/Western Div.	22	58	—	—
1966-67	D. DeBusschere, 28-45					
	Donnis Butcher, 2-6	5th/Western Div.	30	51	—	—
1967-68	Donnis Butcher	4th/Eastern Div.	40	42	2	4
1968-69	Donnis Butcher, 10-12					
	Paul Seymour, 22-38	6th/Eastern Div.	32	50	—	—
1969-70	Bill van Breda Kolff	7th/Eastern Div.	31	51	—	—
1970-71	Bill van Breda Kolff	4th/Midwest Div.	45	37	—	—
1971-72	B. van Breda Kolff, 6-4					
	Terry Dischinger, 0-2					
	Earl Lloyd, 20-50	4th/Midwest Div.	26	56	—	—
1972-73	Earl Lloyd, 2-5					
	Ray Scott, 38-37	3rd/Midwest Div.	40	42	—	—
1973-74	Ray Scott	3rd/Midwest Div.	52	30	3	4
1974-75	Ray Scott	3rd/Midwest Div.	40	42	1	2
1975-76	Ray Scott, 17-25					
	Herb Brown, 19-21	2nd/Midwest Div.	36	46	4	5
1976-77	Herb Brown	T2nd/Midwest Div.	44	38	1	2
1977-78	Herb Brown, 9-15					
	Bob Kauffman, 29-29	4th/Midwest Div.	38	44	—	—
1978-79	Dick Vitale	T4th/Central Div.	30	52	—	—
1979-80	Dick Vitale, 4-8					
	Richie Adubato, 12-58	6th/Central Div.	16	66	—	—
1980-81	Scotty Robertson	6th/Central Div.	21	61	—	—
1981-82	Scotty Robertson	3rd/Central Div.	39	43	—	—
1982-83	Scotty Robertson	3rd/Central Div.	37	45	—	—
1983-84	Chuck Daly	2nd/Central Div.	49	33	2	3
1984-85	Chuck Daly	2nd/Central Div.	46	36	5	4
1985-86	Chuck Daly	3rd/Central Div.	46	36	1	3
1986-87	Chuck Daly	2nd/Central Div.	52	30	10	5
1987-88	Chuck Daly	1st/Central Div.	54	28	14	9
1988-89	Chuck Daly	1st/Central Div.	63	19	15	2
1989-90	Chuck Daly	1st/Central Div.	59	23	15	5
1990-91	Chuck Daly	2nd/Central Div.	50	32	7	8
1991-92	Chuck Daly	3rd/Central Div.	48	34	2	3
1992-93	Ron Rothstein	6th/Central Div.	40	42	—	—
1993-94	Don Chaney	T6th/Central Div.	20	62	—	—

FIRST-ROUND DRAFT PICKS

1949— Bob Harris, Oklahoma A&M
1950— George Yardley, Stanford
1951— Zeke Sinicola, Niagara
1952— Dick Groat, Duke
1953— Jack Molinas, Columbia
1954— Dick Rosenthal, Notre Dame
1955— John Horan, Dayton
1956— Ron Sobieszczk, DePaul
1957— Charles Tyra, Louisville
1958— None
1959— Bailey Howell, Mississippi State
1960— Jackie Moreland, Louisiana Tech
1961— Ray Scott, Portland
1962— Dave DeBusschere, Detroit
1963— Eddie Miles, Seattle
1964— Joe Caldwell, Arizona State
1965— Bill Buntin, Michigan
1966— Dave Bing, Syracuse
1967— Jimmy Walker, Providence*
      Sonny Dove, St. John's
1968— Otto Moore, Pan American
1969— Terry Driscoll, Boston College
1970— Bob Lanier, St. Bonaventure*
1971— Curtis Rowe, UCLA
1972— Bob Nash, Hawaii
1973— None
1974— Al Eberhard, Missouri
1975— None
1976— Leon Douglas, Alabama
1977— None
1978— None
1979— Greg Kelser, Michigan State
      Roy Hamilton, UCLA
      Phil Hubbard, Michigan
1980— Larry Drew, Missouri
1981— Isiah Thomas, Indiana
      Kelly Tripucka, Notre Dame
1982— Cliff Levingston, Wichita State
      Ricky Pierce, Rice
1983— Antoine Carr, Wichita State
1984— Tony Campbell, Ohio State
1985— Joe Dumars, McNeese State
1986— John Salley, Georgia Tech
1987— None
1988— None
1989— Kenny Battle, Illinois
1990— Lance Blanks, Texas
1991— None
1992— Don MacLean, UCLA
1993— Lindsey Hunter, Jackson State
      Allan Houston, Tennessee
1994— Grant Hill, Duke
1995— Theo Ratliff, Wyoming
      Randolph Childress, Wake Forest
1996— Jerome Williams, Georgetown
1997— Scot Pollard, Kansas
1998— Bonzi Wells, Ball State
1999— None
2000— Mateen Cleaves, Michigan State
2001— Rodney White, Charlotte

Season	Coach	Finish	W	L	W	L
			REGULAR SEASON		**PLAYOFFS**	
1994-95	Don Chaney	7th/Central Div.	28	54	—	—
1995-96	Doug Collins	T4th/Central Div.	46	36	0	3
1996-97	Doug Collins	T3rd/Central Div.	54	28	2	3
1997-98	Doug Collins, 21-24					
	Alvin Gentry, 16-21	6th/Central Div.	37	45	—	—
1998-99	Alvin Gentry	3rd/Central Div.	29	21	2	3
1999-00	Alvin Gentry, 28-30					
	George Irvine, 14-10	T4th/Central Div.	42	40	0	3
2000-01	George Irvine	5th/Central Div.	32	50	—	—
2001-02	Rick Carlisle	1st/Central Div.	50	32	4	6
2002-03	Rick Carlisle	1st/Central Div.	50	32	8	9
2003-04	Larry Brown	2nd/Central Div.	54	28	16	7
Totals................................			2131	2269	142	140

*Fort Wayne Pistons.

2002—Tayshaun Prince, Kentucky
2003—Darko Milicic, Serbia & Monten.
 Carlos Delfino, Argentina
2004—None
*First overall pick of draft.

RETIRED NUMBERS

2 Chuck Daly	16 Bob Lanier
4 Joe Dumars	21 Dave Bing
11 Isiah Thomas	40 Bill Laimbeer
15 Vinnie Johnson	

GOLDEN STATE WARRIORS

YEAR-BY-YEAR RECORDS

Season	Coach	Finish	W	L	W	L
			REGULAR SEASON		**PLAYOFFS**	
1946-47*	Edward Gottlieb	2nd/Eastern Div.	35	25	8	2
1947-48*	Edward Gottlieb	1st/Eastern Div.	27	21	6	7
1948-49*	Edward Gottlieb	4th/Eastern Div.	28	32	0	2
1949-50*	Edward Gottlieb	4th/Eastern Div.	26	42	0	2
1950-51*	Edward Gottlieb	1st/Eastern Div.	40	26	0	2
1951-52*	Edward Gottlieb	4th/Eastern Div.	33	33	1	2
1952-53*	Edward Gottlieb	5th/Eastern Div.	12	57	—	—
1953-54*	Edward Gottlieb	4th/Eastern Div.	29	43	—	—
1954-55*	Edward Gottlieb	4th/Eastern Div.	33	39	—	—
1955-56	George Senesky	1st/Eastern Div.	45	27	7	3
1956-57*	George Senesky	3rd/Eastern Div.	37	35	0	2
1957-58*	George Senesky	3rd/Easterm Div.	37	35	3	5
1958-59*	Al Cervi	4th/Eastern Div.	32	40	—	—
1959-60*	Neil Johnston	2nd/Eastern Div.	49	26	4	5
1960-61*	Neil Johnston	2nd/Eastern Div.	46	33	0	3
1961-62*	Frank McGuire	2nd/Eastern Div.	49	31	6	6
1962-63†	Bob Feerick	4th/Western Div.	31	49	—	—
1963-64†	Alex Hannum	1st/Western Div.	48	32	5	7
1964-65†	Alex Hannum	5th/Western Div.	17	63	—	—
1965-66†	Alex Hannum	4th/Western Div.	35	45	—	—
1966-67†	Bill Sharman	1st/Western Div.	44	37	9	6
1967-68†	Bill Sharman	3rd/Western Div.	43	39	4	6
1968-69†	George Lee	3rd/Western Div.	41	41	2	4
1969-70†	George Lee, 22-30					
	Al Attles, 8-22	6th/Western Div.	30	52	—	—
1970-71†	Al Attles	2nd/Pacific Div.	41	41	1	4
1971-72	Al Attles	2nd/Pacific Div.	51	31	1	4
1972-73	Al Attles	2nd/Pacific Div.	47	35	5	6
1973-74	Al Attles	2nd/Pacific Div.	44	38	—	—
1974-75	Al Attles	1st/Pacific Div.	48	34	12	5
1975-76	Al Attles	1st/Pacific Div.	59	23	7	6
1976-77	Al Attles	3rd/Pacific Div.	46	36	5	5
1977-78	Al Attles	5th/Pacific Div.	43	39	—	—
1978-79	Al Attles	6th/Pacific Div.	38	44	—	—
1979-80	Al Attles, 18-43					
	John Bach, 6-15	6th/Pacific Div.	24	58	—	—
1980-81	Al Attles	4th/Pacific Div.	39	43	—	—
1981-82	Al Attles	4th/Pacific Div.	45	37	—	—
1982-83	Al Attles	5th/Pacific Div.	30	52	—	—
1983-84	John Bach	5th/Pacific Div.	37	45	—	—
1984-85	John Bach	6th/Pacific Div.	22	60	—	—
1985-86	John Bach	6th/Pacific Div.	30	52	—	—
1986-87	George Karl	3rd/Pacific Div.	42	40	4	6
1987-88	George Karl, 16-48					
	Ed Gregory, 4-14	5th/Pacific Div.	20	62	—	—
1988-89	Don Nelson	4th/Pacific Div.	43	39	4	4
1989-90	Don Nelson	5th/Pacific Div.	37	45	—	—
1990-91	Don Nelson	4th/Pacific Div.	44	38	4	5

FIRST-ROUND DRAFT PICKS

1947—Francis Crossin, Pennsylvania
1948—Phil Farbman, CCNY
1949—Vern Gardner, Utah
1950—Paul Arizin, Villanova
1951—Don Sunderlage, Illinois
1952—Bill Mlkvy, Temple
1953—Ernie Beck, Pennsylvania*
1954—Gene Shue, Maryland
1955—Tom Gola, La Salle
1956—Hal Lear, Temple
1957—Len Rosenbluth, North Carolina
1958—Guy Rodgers, Temple
1959—Wilt Chamberlain, Kansas
1960—Al Bunge, Maryland
1961—Tom Meschery, St. Mary's (Cal.)
1962—Wayne Hightower, Kansas
1963—Nate Thurmond, Bowling Green
1964—Barry Kramer, New York University
1965—Fred Hetzel, Davidson*
 Rick Barry, Miami (Fla.)
1966—Clyde Lee, Vanderbilt
1967—Dave Lattin, Texas Western
1968—Ron Williams, West Virginia
1969—Bob Portman, Creighton
1970—None
1971—Cyril Baptiste, Creighton†
 Darnell Hillman, San Jose State
1972—None
1973—Kevin Joyce, South Carolina
1974—Jamaal Wilkes, UCLA
1975—Joe Bryant, La Salle
1976—Robert Parish, Centenary
 Sonny Parker, Texas A&M
1977—Rickey Green, Michigan
 Wesley Cox, Louisville
1978—Purvis Short, Jackson State
 Raymond Townsend, UCLA
1979—None
1980—Joe Barry Carroll, Purdue*
 Rickey Brown, Mississippi State
1981—None
1982—Lester Conner, Oregon State
1983—Russell Cross, Purdue
1984—None
1985—Chris Mullin, St. John's
1986—Chris Washburn, N. Carolina St.
1987—Tellis Frank, Western Kentucky
1988—Mitch Richmond, Kansas State
1989—Tim Hardaway, Texas-El Paso
1990—Tyrone Hill, Xavier
1991—Chris Gatling, Old Dominion
 Victor Alexander, Iowa State
 Shaun Vandiver, Colorado

HISTORY *Team by team*

Season	Coach	REGULAR SEASON Finish	W	L	PLAYOFFS W	L
1991-92	Don Nelson	2nd/Pacific Div.	55	27	1	3
1992-93	Don Nelson	6th/Pacific Div.	34	48	—	—
1993-94	Don Nelson	3rd/Pacific Div.	50	32	0	3
1994-95	Don Nelson, 14-31					
	Bob Lanier, 12-25	6th/Pacific Div.	26	56	—	—
1995-96	Rick Adelman	6th/Pacific Div.	36	46	—	—
1996-97	Rick Adelman	7th/Pacific Div.	30	52	—	—
1997-98	P.J. Carlesimo	6th/Pacific Div.	19	63	—	—
1998-99	P.J. Carlesimo	6th/Pacific Div.	21	29	—	—
1999-00	P.J. Carlesimo, 6-21					
	Garry St. Jean, 13-42	6th/Pacific Div.	19	63	—	—
2000-01	Dave Cowens	7th/Pacific Div.	17	65	—	—
2001-02	Dave Cowens, 8-15					
	Brian Winters, 13-46	7th/Pacific Div.	21	61	—	—
2002-03	Eric Musselman	6th/Pacific Div.	38	44	—	—
2003-04	Eric Musselman	T4th/Pacific Div.	37	45	—	—
Totals.			2080	2426	99	115

*Philadelphia Warriors.
†San Francisco Warriors.

1992—Latrell Sprewell, Alabama
1993—Anfernee Hardaway, Memphis St.
1994—Clifford Rozier, Louisville
1995—Joe Smith, Maryland*
1996—Todd Fuller, North Carolina State
1997—Adonal Foyle, Colgate
1998—Vince Carter, North Carolina
1999—Jeff Foster, Southwest Texas St.
2000—None
2001—Jason Richardson, Michigan State
        Troy Murphy, Notre Dame
2002—Mike Dunleavy, Duke
2003—Mickael Pietrus, France
2004—Andris Biedrins, Latvia
*First overall pick of draft.
†Baptiste was selected in the 1971 supplementary draft of hardship cases. The Warriors had to forfeit their 1972 first-round choice.

RETIRED NUMBERS

13 Wilt Chamberlain	24 Rick Barry
14 Tom Meschery	42 Nate Thurmond
16 Al Attles	

HOUSTON ROCKETS

YEAR-BY-YEAR RECORDS

Season	Coach	REGULAR SEASON Finish	W	L	PLAYOFFS W	L
1967-68*	Jack McMahon	6th/Western Div.	15	67	—	—
1968-69*	Jack McMahon	4th/Western Div.	37	45	2	4
1969-70*	Jack McMahon, 9-17					
	Alex Hannum, 18-38	7th/Western Div.	27	55	—	—
1970-71*	Alex Hannum	3rd/Pacific Div.	40	42	—	—
1971-72	Tex Winter	4th/Pacific Div.	34	48	—	—
1972-73	Tex Winter, 17-30					
	John Egan, 16-19	3rd/Central Div.	33	49	—	—
1973-74	John Egan	3rd/Central Div.	32	50	—	—
1974-75	John Egan	2nd/Central Div.	41	41	3	5
1975-76	John Egan	3rd/Central Div.	40	42	—	—
1976-77	Tom Nissalke	1st/Central Div.	49	33	6	6
1977-78	Tom Nissalke	6th/Central Div.	28	54	—	—
1978-79	Tom Nissalke	2nd/Central Div.	47	35	0	2
1979-80	Del Harris	T2nd/Central Div.	41	41	2	5
1980-81	Del Harris	T2nd/Midwest Div.	40	42	12	9
1981-82	Del Harris	T2nd/Midwest Div.	46	36	1	2
1982-83	Del Harris	6th/Midwest Div.	14	68	—	—
1983-84	Bill Fitch	6th/Midwest Div.	29	53	—	—
1984-85	Bill Fitch	2nd/Midwest Div.	48	34	2	3
1985-86	Bill Fitch	1st/Midwest Div.	51	31	13	7
1986-87	Bill Fitch	3rd/Midwest Div.	42	40	5	5
1987-88	Bill Fitch	4th/Midwest Div.	46	36	1	3
1988-89	Don Chaney	2nd/Midwest Div.	45	37	1	3
1989-90	Don Chaney	5th/Midwest Div.	41	41	1	3
1990-91	Don Chaney	3rd/Midwest Div.	52	30	0	3
1991-92	Don Chaney, 26-26					
	R. Tomjanovich, 16-14	3rd/Midwest Div.	42	40	—	—
1992-93	Rudy Tomjanovich	1st/Midwest Div.	55	27	6	6
1993-94	Rudy Tomjanovich	1st/Midwest Div.	58	24	15	8
1994-95	Rudy Tomjanovich	3rd/Midwest Div.	47	35	15	7
1995-96	Rudy Tomjanovich	3rd/Midwest Div.	48	34	3	5
1996-97	Rudy Tomjanovich	2nd/Midwest Div.	57	25	9	7
1997-98	Rudy Tomjanovich	4th/Midwest Div.	41	41	2	3
1998-99	Rudy Tomjanovich	3rd/Midwest Div.	31	19	1	3
1999-00	Rudy Tomjanovich	6th/Midwest Div.	34	48	—	—
2000-01	Rudy Tomjanovich	5th/Midwest Div.	45	37	—	—
2001-02	Rudy Tomjanovich	5th/Midwest Div.	28	54	—	—
2002-03	Rudy Tomjanovich	5th/Midwest Div.	43	39	—	—
2003-04	Jeff Van Gundy	5th/Midwest Div.	45	37	1	4
Totals.			1492	1510	101	103

*San Diego Rockets.

FIRST-ROUND DRAFT PICKS

1967—Pat Riley, Kentucky
1968—Elvin Hayes, Houston*
1969—Bobby Smith, Tulsa
1970—Rudy Tomjanovich, Michigan
1971—Cliff Meely, Colorado
1972—None
1973—Ed Ratleff, Long Beach State
1974—Bobby Jones, North Carolina
1975—Joe Meriweather, Southern Illinois
1976—John Lucas, Maryland*
1977—None
1978—None
1979—Lee Johnson, East Texas State
1980—None
1981—None
1982—Terry Teagle, Baylor
1983—Ralph Sampson, Virginia*
        Rodney McCray, Louisville
1984—Hakeem Olajuwon, Houston*
1985—Steve Harris, Tulsa
1986—Buck Johnson, Alabama
1987—None
1988—Derrick Chievous, Missouri
1989—None
1990—Alec Kessler, Georgia
1991—John Turner, Phillips
1992—Robert Horry, Alabama
1993—Sam Cassell, Florida State
1994—None
1995—None
1996—None
1997—Rodrick Rhodes, Southern California
1998—Michael Dickerson, Arizona
        Bryce Drew, Valparaiso
        Mirsad Turkcan, Turkey
1999—Kenny Thomas, New Mexico
2000—Joel Przybilla, Minnesota
2001—Richard Jefferson, Arizona
        Jason Collins, Stanford
        Brandon Armstrong, Pepperdine
2002—Yao Ming, China*
        Bostjan Nachbar, Slovenia
2003—None
2004—None
*First overall pick of draft.

RETIRED NUMBERS

22 Clyde Drexler	34 Hakeem
23 Calvin Murphy	Olajuwon
24 Moses Malone	45 Rudy
	Tomjanovich

INDIANA PACERS

YEAR-BY-YEAR RECORDS

Season	Coach	Finish	REGULAR SEASON W	L	PLAYOFFS W	L
1967-68*	Larry Staverman	3rd/Eastern Div.	38	40	0	3
1968-69*	Larry Staverman, 2-7					
	Bob Leonard, 42-27	1st/Eastern Div.	44	34	9	8
1969-70*	Bob Leonard	1st/Eastern Div.	59	25	12	3
1970-71*	Bob Leonard	1st/Western Div.	58	26	7	4
1971-72*	Bob Leonard	2nd/Western Div.	47	37	12	8
1972-73*	Bob Leonard	2nd/Western Div.	51	33	12	6
1973-74*	Bob Leonard	2nd/Western Div.	46	38	7	7
1974-75*	Bob Leonard	3rd/Western Div.	45	39	9	9
1975-76*	Bob Leonard	5th	39	45	1	2
1976-77	Bob Leonard	5th/Midwest Div.	36	46	—	—
1977-78	Bob Leonard	T5th/Midwest Div.	31	51	—	—
1978-79	Bob Leonard	T3rd/Midwest Div.	38	44	—	—
1979-80	Bob Leonard	T4th/Central Div.	37	45	—	—
1980-81	Jack McKinney	3rd/Central Div.	44	38	0	2
1981-82	Jack McKinney	4th/Central Div.	35	47	—	—
1982-83	Jack McKinney	6th/Central Div.	20	62	—	—
1983-84	Jack McKinney	6th/Central Div.	26	56	—	—
1984-85	George Irvine	6th/Central Div.	22	60	—	—
1985-86	George Irvine	6th/Central Div.	26	56	—	—
1986-87	Jack Ramsay	4th/Central Div.	41	41	1	3
1987-88	Jack Ramsay	6th/Central Div.	38	44	—	—
1988-89	Jack Ramsay, 0-7					
	Mel Daniels, 0-2					
	George Irvine, 6-14					
	Dick Versace, 22-31	6th/Central Div.	28	54	—	—
1989-90	Dick Versace	T4th/Central Div.	42	40	0	3
1990-91	Dick Versace, 9-16					
	Bob Hill, 32-25	5th/Central Div.	41	41	2	3
1991-92	Bob Hill	4th/Central Div.	40	42	0	3
1992-93	Bob Hill	5th/Central Div.	41	41	1	3
1993-94	Larry Brown	T3rd/Central Div.	47	35	10	6
1994-95	Larry Brown	1st/Central Div.	52	30	10	7
1995-96	Larry Brown	2nd/Central Div.	52	30	2	3
1996-97	Larry Brown	6th/Central Div.	39	43	—	—
1997-98	Larry Bird	2nd/Central Div.	58	24	10	6
1998-99	Larry Bird	1st/Central Div.	33	17	9	4
1999-00	Larry Bird	1st/Central Div.	56	26	13	10
2000-01	Isiah Thomas	4th/Central Div.	41	41	1	3
2001-02	Isiah Thomas	T3rd/Central Div.	42	40	2	3
2002-03	Isiah Thomas	2nd/Central Div.	48	34	2	4
2003-04	Rick Carlisle	1st/Central Div.	61	21	10	6
ABA totals	. . . .		427	317	69	50
NBA totals	. . . .		1115	1149	73	69

*Club in ABA.

FIRST-ROUND DRAFT PICKS

1967—Jimmy Walker, Providence
1968—Don May, Dayton
1969—None
1970—Rick Mount, Purdue
1971—None
1972—None
1973—Steve Downing, Indiana
      Mike Green, Louisiana Tech
1974—Billy Knight, Pittsburgh
1975—Dan Roundfield, Central Michigan
1976—None
1977—None
1978—Rick Robey, Kentucky
1979—Dudley Bradley, North Carolina
1980—None
1981—Herb Williams, Ohio State
1982—Clark Kellogg, Ohio State
1983—Steve Stipanovich, Missouri
      Mitchell Wiggins, Florida State
1984—Vern Fleming, Georgia
1985—Wayman Tisdale, Oklahoma
1986—Chuck Person, Auburn
1987—Reggie Miller, UCLA
1988—Rik Smits, Marist (N.Y.)
1989—George McCloud, Florida State
1990—None
1991—Dale Davis, Clemson
1992—Malik Sealy, St. John's
1993—Scott Haskin, Oregon State
1994—Eric Piatkowski, Nebraska
1995—Travis Best, Georgia Tech
1996—Erick Dampier, Mississippi State
1997—Austin Croshere, Providence
1998 Al Harrington, St. Patrick's HS (N.J.)
1999—Vonteego Cummings, Pittsburgh
2000—Primoz Brezec, Slovenia
2001—None
2002—Fred Jones, Oregon
2003—None
2004—David Harrison, Colorado
NOTE: Indiana's first-round selections from 1967-75 were made while a member of the ABA.

RETIRED NUMBERS

30 George McGinnis   529 Bob "Slick"
34 Mel Daniels   Leonard
35 Roger Brown

INDIANAPOLIS JETS

YEAR-BY-YEAR RECORDS

Season	Coach	Finish	REGULAR SEASON W	L	PLAYOFFS W	L
1948-49	Bruce Hale, 4-13					
	Burl Friddle, 14-29	6th/Western Div.	18	42	—	—

FIRST-ROUND DRAFT PICKS

1948—George Kok, Indianapolis

INDIANAPOLIS OLYMPIANS

YEAR-BY-YEAR RECORDS

Season	Coach	Finish	REGULAR SEASON W	L	PLAYOFFS W	L
1949-50	Clifford Barker	1st/Western Div.	39	25	3	3
1950-51	Clifford Barker, 24-32					
	Wallace Jones, 7-5	4th/Western Div.	31	37	1	2
1951-52	Herman Schaefer	3rd/Western Div.	34	32	0	2
1952-53	Herman Schaefer	4th/Western Div.	28	43	0	2
Totals	. . . .		132	137	4	9

FIRST-ROUND DRAFT PICKS

1949—Alex Groza, Kentucky
1950—Bob Lavoy, Western Kentucky
1951—Marcus Freiberger, Oklahoma
1952—Joe Dean, Louisiana State

YEAR-BY-YEAR RECORDS

Season	Coach	Finish	W	L	W	L
		REGULAR SEASON			**PLAYOFFS**	
1970-71*	Dolph Schayes	4th/Atlantic Div.	22	60	—	—
1971-72*	Dolph Schayes, 0-1					
	John McCarthy, 22-59	4th/Atlantic Div.	22	60	—	—
1972-73*	Jack Ramsay	3rd/Atlantic Div.	21	61	—	—
1973-74*	Jack Ramsay	3rd/Atlantic Div.	42	40	2	4
1974-75*	Jack Ramsay	2nd/Atlantic Div.	49	33	3	4
1975-76*	Jack Ramsay	T2nd/Atlantic Div.	46	36	4	5
1976-77*	Tates Locke, 16-30					
	Bob MacKinnon, 3-4					
	Joe Mullaney, 11-18	4th/Atlantic Div.	30	52	—	—
1977-78*	Cotton Fitzsimmons	4th/Atlantic Div.	27	55	—	—
1978-79†	Gene Shue	5th/Pacific Div.	43	39	—	—
1979-80†	Gene Shue	5th/Pacific Div.	35	47	—	—
1980-81†	Paul Silas	5th/Pacific Div.	36	46	—	—
1981-82†	Paul Silas	6th/Pacific Div.	17	65	—	—
1982-83†	Paul Silas	6th/Pacific Div.	25	57	—	—
1983-84†	Jim Lynam	6th/Pacific Div.	30	52	—	—
1984-85	Jim Lynam, 22-39					
	Don Chaney, 9-12	T4th/Pacific Div.	31	51	—	—
1985-86	Don Chaney	T3rd/Pacific Div.	32	50	—	—
1986-87	Don Chaney	6th/Pacific Div.	12	70	—	—
1987-88	Gene Shue	6th/Pacific Div.	17	65	—	—
1988-89	Gene Shue, 10-28					
	Don Casey, 11-33	7th/Pacific Div.	21	61	—	—
1989-90	Don Casey	6th/Pacific Div.	30	52	—	—
1990-91	Mike Schuler	6th/Pacific Div.	31	51	—	—
1991-92	Mike Schuler, 21-24					
	Mack Calvin, 1-1					
	Larry Brown, 23-12	5th/Pacific Div.	45	37	2	3
1992-93	Larry Brown	4th/Pacific Div.	41	41	2	3
1993-94	Bob Weiss	7th/Pacific Div.	27	55	—	—
1994-95	Bill Fitch	7th/Pacific Div.	17	65	—	—
1995-96	Bill Fitch	7th/Pacific Div.	29	53	—	—
1996-97	Bill Fitch	5th/Pacific Div.	36	46	0	3
1997-98	Bill Fitch	7th/Pacific Div.	17	65	—	—
1998-99	Chris Ford	7th/Pacific Div.	9	41	—	—
1999-00	Chris Ford, 11-34					
	Jim Todd, 4-33	7th/Pacific Div.	15	67	—	—
2000-01	Alvin Gentry	6th/Pacific Div.	31	51	—	—
2001-02	Alvin Gentry	5th/Pacific Div.	39	43	—	—
2002-03	Alvin Gentry, 19-39					
	Dennis Johnson, 8-16	7th/Pacific Div.	27	55	—	—
2003-04	Mike Dunleavy Sr.	7th/Pacific Div.	28	54	—	—
Totals			980	1776	13	22

*Buffalo Braves.
†San Diego Clippers.

FIRST-ROUND DRAFT PICKS

1970— John Hummer, Princeton
1971— Elmore Smith, Kentucky State
1972— Bob McAdoo, North Carolina
1973— Ernie DiGregorio, Providence
1974— Tom McMillen, Maryland
1975— None
1976— Adrian Dantley, Notre Dame
1977— None
1978— None
1979— None
1980— Michael Brooks, La Salle
1981— Tom Chambers, Utah
1982— Terry Cummings, DePaul
1983— Byron Scott, Arizona State
1984— Lancaster Gordon, Louisville
      Michael Cage, San Diego State
1985— Benoit Benjamin, Creighton
1986— None
1987— Reggie Williams, Georgetown
      Joe Wolf, North Carolina
      Ken Norman, Illinois
1988— Danny Manning, Kansas*
      Hersey Hawkins, Bradley
1989— Danny Ferry, Duke
1990— Bo Kimble, Loyola Marymount
      Loy Vaught, Michigan
1991— LeRon Ellis, Syracuse
1992— Randy Woods, La Salle
      Elmore Spencer, UNLV
1993— Terry Dehere, Seton Hall
1994— Lamond Murray, California
      Greg Minor, Louisville
1995— Antonio McDyess, Alabama
1996— Lorenzen Wright, Memphis
1997— Maurice Taylor, Michigan
1998— Michael Olowokandi, Pacific (Cal.)*
      Brian Skinner, Baylor
1999— Lamar Odom, Rhode Island
2000— Darius Miles, E. St. Louis HS (Ill.)
      Quentin Richardson, DePaul
2001— Tyson Chandler, Dominguez HS (Calif.)
2002— Chris Wilcox, Maryland
      Melvin Ely, Fresno State
2003— Chris Kaman, Central Michigan
2004— Shaun Livingston, Peoria Central HS (Ill.)

*First overall pick of draft.

RETIRED NUMBERS

None

YEAR-BY-YEAR RECORDS

Season	Coach	Finish	W	L	W	L
		REGULAR SEASON			**PLAYOFFS**	
1948-49*	John Kundla	2nd/Western Div.	44	16	8	2
1949-50*	John Kundla	T1st/Central Div.	51	17	10	2
1950-51*	John Kundla	1st/Western Div.	44	24	3	4
1951-52*	John Kundla	2nd/Western Div.	40	26	9	4
1952-53*	John Kundla	1st/Western Div.	48	22	9	3
1953-54*	John Kundla	1st/Western Div.	46	26	9	4
1954-55*	John Kundla	2nd/Western Div.	40	32	3	4
1955-56*	John Kundla	T2nd/Western Div.	33	39	1	2
1956-57*	John Kundla	T1st/Western Div.	34	38	2	3
1957-58*	George Mikan, 9-30					
	John Kundla, 10-23	4th/Western Div.	19	53	—	—
1958-59*	John Kundla	2nd/Western Div.	33	39	6	7
1959-60*	John Castellani, 11-25					
	Jim Pollard, 14-25	3rd/Western Div.	25	50	5	4
1960-61	Fred Schaus	2nd/Western Div.	36	43	6	6

FIRST-ROUND DRAFT PICKS

1948— Arnie Ferrin, Utah
1949— Vern Mikkelsen, Hamline
1950— Kevin O'Shea, Notre Dame
1951— Whitey Skoog, Minnesota
1952— Not available
1953— Jim Fritsche, Hamline
1954— Ed Kalafat, Minnesota
1955— Not available
1956— Jim Paxson, Dayton
1957— Jim Krebs, Southern Methodist
1958— Elgin Baylor, Seattle*
1959— Tom Hawkins, Notre Dame
1960— Jerry West, West Virginia
1961— Wayne Yates, Memphis State
1962— LeRoy Ellis, St. John's
1963— Roger Strickland, Jacksonville
1964— Walt Hazzard, UCLA
1965— Gail Goodrich, UCLA

Season	Coach	Finish	REGULAR SEASON W	L	PLAYOFFS W	L
1961-62	Fred Schaus	1st/Western Div.	54	26	7	6
1962-63	Fred Schaus	1st/Western Div.	53	27	6	7
1963-64	Fred Schaus	3rd/Western Div.	42	38	2	3
1964-65	Fred Schaus	1st/Western Div.	49	31	5	6
1965-66	Fred Schaus	1st/Western Div.	45	35	7	7
1966-67	Fred Schaus	3rd/Western Div.	36	45	0	3
1967-68	Bill van Breda Kolff	2nd/Western Div.	52	30	10	5
1968-69	Bill van Breda Kolff	1st/Western Div.	55	27	11	7
1969-70	Joe Mullaney	2nd/Western Div.	46	36	11	7
1970-71	Joe Mullaney	1st/Pacific Div.	48	34	5	7
1971-72	Bill Sharman	1st/Pacific Div.	69	13	12	3
1972-73	Bill Sharman	1st/Pacific Div.	60	22	9	8
1973-74	Bill Sharman	1st/Pacific Div.	47	35	1	4
1974-75	Bill Sharman	5th/Pacific Div.	30	52	—	—
1975-76	Bill Sharman	4th/Pacific Div.	40	42	—	—
1976-77	Jerry West	1st/Pacific Div.	53	29	4	7
1977-78	Jerry West	4th/Pacific Div.	45	37	1	2
1978-79	Jerry West	3rd/Pacific Div.	47	35	3	5
1979-80	Jack McKinney, 10-4					
	Paul Westhead, 50-18	1st/Pacific Div.	60	22	12	4
1980-81	Paul Westhead	2nd/Pacific Div.	54	28	1	2
1981-82	Paul Westhead, 7-4					
	Pat Riley, 50-21	1st/Pacific Div.	57	25	12	2
1982-83	Pat Riley	1st/Pacific Div.	58	24	8	7
1983-84	Pat Riley	1st/Pacific Div.	54	28	14	7
1984-85	Pat Riley	1st/Pacific Div.	62	20	15	4
1985-86	Pat Riley	1st/Pacific Div.	62	20	8	6
1986-87	Pat Riley	1st/Pacific Div.	65	17	15	3
1987-88	Pat Riley	1st/Pacific Div.	62	20	15	9
1988-89	Pat Riley	1st/Pacific Div.	57	25	11	4
1989-90	Pat Riley	1st/Pacific Div.	63	19	4	5
1990-91	Mike Dunleavy	2nd/Pacific Div.	58	24	12	7
1991-92	Mike Dunleavy	6th/Pacific Div.	43	39	1	3
1992-93	Randy Pfund	5th/Pacific Div.	39	43	2	3
1993-94	Randy Pfund, 27-37					
	Bill Bertka, 1-1					
	Magic Johnson, 5-11	5th/Pacific Div.	33	49	—	—
1994-95	Del Harris	3rd/Pacific Div.	48	34	5	5
1995-96	Del Harris	2nd/Pacific Div.	53	29	1	3
1996-97	Del Harris	2nd/Pacific Div.	56	26	4	5
1997-98	Del Harris	T1st/Pacific Div.	61	21	7	6
1998-99	Del Harris, 6-6					
	Bill Bertka, 1-0					
	Kurt Rambis, 24-13	2nd/Pacific Div.	31	19	3	5
1999-00	Phil Jackson	1st/Pacific Div.	67	15	15	8
2000-01	Phil Jackson	1st/Pacific Div.	56	26	15	1
2001-02	Phil Jackson	2nd/Pacific Div.	58	24	15	4
2002-03	Phil Jackson	T2nd/Pacific Div.	50	32	6	6
2003-04	Phil Jackson	1st/Pacific Div.	56	26	13	9
Totals..................................			2727	1674	379	250

*Minneapolis Lakers

1966—Jerry Chambers, Utah
1967—None
1968—Bill Hewitt, Southern California
1969—Willie McCarter, Drake
      Rick Roberson, Cincinnati
1970—Jim McMillian, Columbia
1971—Jim Cleamons, Ohio State
1972—Travis Grant, Kentucky State
1973—Kermit Washington, American
1974—Brian Winters, South Carolina
1975—David Meyers, UCLA
      Junior Bridgeman, Louisville
1976—None
1977—Kenny Carr, North Carolina State
      Brad Davis, Maryland
      Norm Nixon, Duquesne
1978—None
1979—Magic Johnson, Michigan State*
      Brad Holland, UCLA
1980—None
1981—Mike McGee, Michigan
1982—James Worthy, North Carolina*
1983—None
1984—Earl Jones, District of Columbia
1985—A.C. Green, Oregon State
1986—Ken Barlow, Notre Dame
1987—None
1988—David Rivers, Notre Dame
1989—Vlade Divac, Yugoslavia
1990—Elden Campbell, Clemson
1991—None
1992—Anthony Peeler, Missouri
1993—George Lynch, North Carolina
1994—Eddie Jones, Temple
1995—None
1996—Derek Fisher, Arkansas-Little Rock
1997—None
1998—Sam Jacobson, Minnesota
1999—Devean George, Augsburg (Minn.)
2000—Mark Madsen, Stanford
2001—None
2002—Chris Jefferies, Fresno State
2003—Brian Cook, Illinois
2004—Sasha Vujacic, Slovenia
*First overall pick of draft.

RETIRED NUMBERS

13 Wilt Chamberlain	42 James Worthy
22 Elgin Baylor	44 Jerry West
25 Gail Goodrich	Note: Microphone
32 Magic Johnson	retired in honor of
33 Kareem Abdul-	broadcaster Chick
Jabbar	Hearn.

MEMPHIS GRIZZLIES

YEAR-BY-YEAR RECORDS

Season	Coach	Finish	REGULAR SEASON W	L	PLAYOFFS W	L
1995-96*	Brian Winters	7th/Midwest Div.	15	67	—	—
1996-97*	Brian Winters, 8-35					
	Stu Jackson, 6-33	7th/Midwest Div.	14	68	—	—
1997-98*	Brian Hill	6th/Midwest Div.	19	63	—	—
1998-99*	Brian Hill	7th/Midwest Div.	8	42	—	—
1999-00*	Brian Hill, 4-18					
	Lionel Hollins, 18-42	7th/Midwest Div.	22	60	—	—
2000-01*	Sidney Lowe	7th/Midwest Div.	23	59	—	—
2001-02	Sidney Lowe	7th/Midwest Div.	23	59	—	—
2002-03	Sidney Lowe, 0-8					
	Hubie Brown, 28-46	6th/Midwest Div.	28	54	—	—
2003-04	Hubie Brown	4th/Midwest Div.	50	32	0	4
Totals............................			202	504	0	4

*Vancouver Grizzlies.

FIRST-ROUND DRAFT PICKS

1995—Bryant Reeves, Oklahoma State
1996—Shareef Abdur-Rahim, California
      Roy Rogers, Alabama
1997—Antonio Daniels, Bowling Green
1998—Mike Bibby, Arizona
1999—Steve Francis, Maryland
2000—Stromile Swift, Louisiana State
2001—Shane Battier, Duke
      Jamaal Tinsley, Iowa State
2002—Drew Gooden, Kansas
2003—Marcus Banks, UNLV
      Kendrick Perkins, Clifton J. Ozen
      HS (Texas)
2004—None

RETIRED NUMBERS

None

MIAMI HEAT

YEAR-BY-YEAR RECORDS

Season	Coach	Finish	REGULAR SEASON W	L	PLAYOFFS W	L
1988-89	Ron Rothstein	6th/Midwest Div.	15	67	—	—
1989-90	Ron Rothstein	5th/Atlantic Div.	18	64	—	—
1990-91	Ron Rothstein	6th/Atlantic Div.	24	58	—	—
1991-92	Kevin Loughery	4th/Atlantic Div.	38	44	0	3
1992-93	Kevin Loughery	5th/Atlantic Div.	36	46	—	—
1993-94	Kevin Loughery	4th/Atlantic Div.	42	40	2	3
1994-95	Kevin Loughery, 17-29					
	Alvin Gentry, 15-21	4th/Atlantic Div.	32	50	—	—
1995-96	Pat Riley	3rd/Atlantic Div.	42	40	0	3
1996-97	Pat Riley	1st/Atlantic Div.	61	21	8	9
1997-98	Pat Riley	1st/Atlantic Div.	55	27	2	3
1998-99	Pat Riley	T1st/Atlantic Div.	33	17	2	3
1999-00	Pat Riley	1st/Atlantic Div.	52	30	6	4
2000-01	Pat Riley	2nd/Atlantic Div.	50	32	0	3
2001-02	Pat Riley	6th/Atlantic Div.	36	46	—	—
2002-03	Pat Riley	7th/Atlantic Div.	25	57	—	—
2003-04	Stan Van Gundy	4th/Midwest Div.	42	40	6	7
Totals			601	679	28	42

FIRST-ROUND DRAFT PICKS

1988— Rony Seikaly, Syracuse
       Kevin Edwards, DePaul
1989— Glen Rice, Michigan
1990— Willie Burton, Minnesota
       Dave Jamerson, Ohio
1991— Steve Smith, Michigan State
1992— Harold Miner, Southern California
1993— None
1994— Khalid Reeves, Arizona
1995— Kurt Thomas, Texas Christian
1996— None
1997— Charles Smith, New Mexico
1998— None
1999— Tim James, Miami (Fla.)
2000— None
2001— None
2002— Caron Butler, Connecticut
2003— Dwyane Wade, Marquette
2004— Dorell Wright, Leuzinger HS (Calif.)

RETIRED NUMBERS

None

MILWAUKEE BUCKS

YEAR-BY-YEAR RECORDS

Season	Coach	Finish	REGULAR SEASON W	L	PLAYOFFS W	L
1968-69	Larry Costello	7th/Eastern Div.	27	55	—	—
1969-70	Larry Costello	2nd/Eastern Div.	56	26	5	5
1970-71	Larry Costello	1st/Midwest Div.	66	16	12	2
1971-72	Larry Costello	1st/Midwest Div.	63	19	6	5
1972-73	Larry Costello	1st/Midwest Div.	60	22	2	4
1973-74	Larry Costello	1st/Midwest Div.	59	23	11	5
1974-75	Larry Costello	4th/Midwest Div.	38	44	—	—
1975-76	Larry Costello	1st/Midwest Div.	38	44	1	2
1976-77	Larry Costello, 3-15					
	Don Nelson, 27-37	6th/Midwest Div.	30	52	—	—
1977-78	Don Nelson	2nd/Midwest Div.	44	38	5	4
1978-79	Don Nelson	T3rd/Midwest Div.	38	44	—	—
1979-80	Don Nelson	1st/Midwest Div.	49	33	3	4
1980-81	Don Nelson	1st/Central Div.	60	22	3	4
1981-82	Don Nelson	1st/Central Div.	55	27	2	4
1982-83	Don Nelson	1st/Central Div.	51	31	5	4
1983-84	Don Nelson	1st/Central Div.	50	32	8	8
1984-85	Don Nelson	1st/Central Div.	59	23	3	5
1985-86	Don Nelson	1st/Central Div.	57	25	7	7
1986-87	Don Nelson	3rd/Central Div.	50	32	6	6
1987-88	Del Harris	T4th/Central Div.	42	40	2	3
1988-89	Del Harris	4th/Central Div.	49	33	3	6
1989-90	Del Harris	3rd/Central Div.	44	38	1	3
1990-91	Del Harris	3rd/Central Div.	48	34	0	3
1991-92	Del Harris, 8-9					
	Frank Hamblen, 23-42	T6th/Central Div.	31	51	—	—
1992-93	Mike Dunleavy	7th/Central Div.	28	54	—	—
1993-94	Mike Dunleavy	T6th/Central Div.	20	62	—	—
1994-95	Mike Dunleavy	6th/Central Div.	34	48	—	—
1995-96	Mike Dunleavy	7th/Central Div.	25	57	—	—
1996-97	Chris Ford	7th/Central Div.	33	49	—	—
1997-98	Chris Ford	7th/Central Div.	36	46	—	—
1998-99	George Karl	4th/Central Div.	28	22	0	3
1999-00	George Karl	T4th/Central Div.	42	40	2	3
2000-01	George Karl	1st/Central Div.	52	30	10	8
2001-02	George Karl	5th/Central Div.	41	41	—	—
2002-03	George Karl	4th/Central Div.	42	40	2	4
2003-04	Terry Porter	T3rd/Central Div.	41	41	1	4
Totals			1586	1334	100	106

FIRST-ROUND DRAFT PICKS

1968— Charlie Paulk, NE Oklahoma
1969— Kareem Abdul-Jabbar, UCLA*
1970— Gary Freeman, Oregon State
1971— Collis Jones, Notre Dame
1972— Russell Lee, Marshall
       Julius Erving, Massachusetts
1973— Swen Nater, UCLA
1974— Gary Brokaw, Notre Dame
1975— None
1976— Quinn Buckner, Indiana
1977— Kent Benson, Indiana*
       Marques Johnson, UCLA
       Ernie Grunfeld, Tennessee
1978— George Johnson, St. John's
1979— Sidney Moncrief, Arkansas
1980— None
1981— Alton Lister, Arizona State
1982— Paul Pressey, Tulsa
1983— Randy Breuer, Minnesota
1984— Kenny Fields, UCLA
1985— Jerry Reynolds, Louisiana State
1986— Scott Skiles, Michigan State
1987— None
1988— Jeff Grayer, Iowa State
1989— None
1990— Terry Mills, Michigan
1991— Kevin Brooks, SW Louisiana
1992— Todd Day, Arkansas
       Lee Mayberry, Arkansas
1993— Vin Baker, Hartford
1994— Glenn Robinson, Purdue*
       Eric Mobley, Pittsburgh
1995— Gary Trent, Ohio University
1996— Stephon Marbury, Georgia Tech
1997— Danny Fortson, Cincinnati
1998— Dirk Nowitzki, Germany
       Pat Garrity, Notre Dame
1999— None
2000— Jason Collier, Georgia Tech
2001— None
2002— Marcus Haislip, Tennessee
2003— T.J. Ford, Texas
2004— None
*First overall pick of draft.

RETIRED NUMBERS

1 Oscar Robertson   16 Bob Lanier
2 Junior Bridgeman 32 Brian Winters
4 Sidney Moncrief   33 Kareem Abdul-
14 Jon McGlocklin   Jabbar

MINNESOTA TIMBERWOLVES

YEAR-BY-YEAR RECORDS

		REGULAR SEASON			PLAYOFFS	
Season	Coach	Finish	W	L	W	L
1989-90	Bill Musselman	6th/Midwest Div.	22	60	—	—
1990-91	Bill Musselman	5th/Midwest Div.	29	53	—	—
1991-92	Jimmy Rodgers	6th/Midwest Div.	15	67	—	—
1992-93	Jimmy Rodgers, 6-23					
	Sidney Lowe, 13-40	5th/Midwest Div.	19	63	—	—
1993-94	Sidney Lowe	5th/Midwest Div.	20	62	—	—
1994-95	Bill Blair	6th/Midwest Div.	21	61	—	—
1995-96	Bill Blair, 6-14					
	Flip Saunders, 20-42	T5th/Midwest Div.	26	56	—	—
1996-97	Flip Saunders	3rd/Midwest Div.	40	42	0	3
1997-98	Flip Saunders	3rd/Midwest Div.	45	37	2	3
1998-99	Flip Saunders	4th/Midwest Div.	25	25	1	3
1999-00	Flip Saunders	3rd/Midwest Div.	50	32	1	3
2000-01	Flip Saunders	4th/Midwest Div.	47	35	1	3
2001-02	Flip Saunders	3rd/Midwest Div.	50	32	0	3
2002-03	Flip Saunders	3rd/Midwest Div.	51	31	2	4
2003-04	Flip Saunders	1st/Midwest Div.	58	24	10	8
Totals			518	680	17	30

FIRST-ROUND DRAFT PICKS

1989— Pooh Richardson, UCLA
1990— Felton Spencer, Louisville
Gerald Glass, Mississippi
1991— Luc Longley, New Mexico
1992— Christian Laettner, Duke
1993— J.R. Rider, UNLV
1994— Donyell Marshall, Connecticut
1995— Kevin Garnett, Farragut Acad. (IL)
1996— Ray Allen, Connecticut
1997— Paul Grant, Wisconsin
1998— Radoslav Nesterovic, Italy
1999— Wally Szczerbiak, Miami (Ohio)
William Avery, Duke
2000— None*
2001— None*
2002— None*
2003— Ndudi Ebi, Westbury Christian HS (Texas)
2004— None*
*Minnesota forfeited its first-round picks in 2000-2002 and 2004 because of salary cap violations.

RETIRED NUMBERS

2 Malik Sealy

NEW JERSEY NETS

YEAR-BY-YEAR RECORDS

		REGULAR SEASON			PLAYOFFS	
Season	Coach	Finish	W	L	W	L
1967-68*	Max Zaslofsky	5th/Eastern Div.	36	42	—	—
1968-69†	Max Zaslofsky	5th/Eastern Div.	17	61	—	—
1969-70†	York Larese	4th/Eastern Div.	39	45	3	4
1970-71†	Lou Carnesecca	3rd/Eastern Div.	40	44	2	4
1971-72†	Lou Carnesecca	3rd/Eastern Div.	44	40	10	9
1972-73†	Lou Carnesecca	4th/Eastern Div.	30	54	1	4
1973-74†	Kevin Loughery	1st/Eastern Div.	55	29	12	2
1974-75†	Kevin Loughery	T1st/Eastern Div.	58	26	1	4
1975-76†	Kevin Loughery	2nd	55	29	8	5
1976-77‡	Kevin Loughery	5th/Atlantic Div.	22	60	—	—
1977-78	Kevin Loughery	5th/Atlantic Div.	24	58	—	—
1978-79	Kevin Loughery	3rd/Atlantic Div.	37	45	0	2
1979-80	Kevin Loughery	5th/Atlantic Div.	34	48	—	—
1980-81	Kevin Loughery, 12-23					
	Bob MacKinnon, 12-35	5th/Atlantic Div.	24	58	—	—
1981-82	Larry Brown	3rd/Atlantic Div.	44	38	0	2
1982-83	Larry Brown, 47-29					
	Bill Blair, 2-4	3rd/Atlantic Div.	49	33	0	2
1983-84	Stan Albeck	4th/Atlantic Div.	45	37	5	6
1984-85	Stan Albeck	3rd/Atlantic Div.	42	40	0	3
1985-86	Dave Wohl	T3rd/Atlantic Div.	39	43	0	3
1986-87	Dave Wohl	T4th/Atlantic Div.	24	58	—	—
1987-88	Dave Wohl, 2-13					
	Bob MacKinnon, 10-29					
	Willis Reed, 7-21	5th/Atlantic Div.	19	63	—	—
1988-89	Willis Reed	5th/Atlantic Div.	26	56	—	—
1989-90	Bill Fitch	6th/Atlantic Div.	17	65	—	—
1990-91	Bill Fitch	5th/Atlantic Div.	26	56	—	—
1991-92	Bill Fitch	3rd/Atlantic Div.	40	42	1	3
1992-93	Chuck Daly	3rd/Atlantic Div.	43	39	2	3
1993-94	Chuck Daly	3rd/Atlantic Div.	45	37	1	3
1994-95	Butch Beard	5th/Atlantic Div.	30	52	—	—
1995-96	Butch Beard	6th/Atlantic Div.	30	52	—	—
1996-97	John Calipari	5th/Atlantic Div.	26	56	—	—
1997-98	John Calipari	T2nd/Atlantic Div.	43	39	0	3
1998-99	John Calipari, 3-17					
	Don Casey, 13-17	7th/Atlantic Div.	16	34	—	—
1999-00	Don Casey	6th/Atlantic Div.	31	51	—	—

FIRST-ROUND DRAFT PICKS

1967—Sonny Dove, St. John's
1968—Joe Allen, Bradley
1969—Kareem Abdul-Jabbar, UCLA
1970—Bob Lanier, St. Bonaventure
1971—Charles Davis, Wake Forest
1972—Jim Chones, Marquette
1973—Doug Collins, Illinois State
Jim Brewer, Minnesota
1974—Brian Winters, South Carolina
1975—John Lucas, Maryland
1976—None
1977—Bernard King, Tennessee
1978—Winford Boynes, San Francisco
1979—Calvin Natt, Northeast Louisiana
Cliff Robinson, Southern California
1980—Mike O'Koren, North Carolina
Mike Gminski, Duke
1981—Buck Williams, Maryland
Albert King, Maryland
Ray Tolbert, Indiana
1982—Sleepy Floyd, Georgetown
Eddie Phillips, Alabama
1983—None
1984—Jeff Turner, Vanderbilt
1985—None
1986—Dwayne Washington, Syracuse
1987—Dennis Hopson, Ohio State
1988—Chris Morris, Auburn
1989—Mookie Blaylock, Oklahoma
1990—Derrick Coleman, Syracuse*
Tate George, Connecticut
1991—Kenny Anderson, Georgia Tech
1992—None
1993—Rex Walters, Kansas
1994—Yinka Dare, George Washington
1995—Ed O'Bannon, UCLA
1996—Kerry Kittles, Villanova
1997—Tim Thomas, Villanova
Anthony Parker, Bradley
1998—None
1999—None
2000—Kenyon Martin, Cincinnati*
2001—Eddie Griffin, Seton Hall
2002—Nenad Krstic, Yugoslavia

HISTORY Team by team

Season	Coach	Finish	REGULAR SEASON W	L	PLAYOFFS W	L
2000-01	Byron Scott	6th/Atlantic Div.	26	56	—	—
2001-02	Byron Scott	1st/Atlantic Div.	52	30	11	9
2002-03	Byron Scott	1st/Atlantic Div.	49	33	14	6
2003-04	Byron Scott, 22-20					
	Lawrence Frank, 25-15	1st/Atlantic Div.	47	35	7	4
ABA totals			374	370	37	32
NBA totals			950	1314	41	49

*New Jersey Americans; club in ABA.
†New York Nets; club in ABA.
‡New York Nets; club in NBA.

2003— Zoran Planinic, Croatia
2004— Viktor Khryapa, Russia
*First overall pick of draft.
NOTE: New Jersey's first-round selections from 1967-75 were made while a member of the ABA.

RETIRED NUMBERS

3 Drazen Petrovic 32 Julius Erving
4 Wendell Ladner 52 Buck Williams
23 John Williamson
25 Bill Melchionni

NEW ORLEANS HORNETS

YEAR-BY-YEAR RECORDS

Season	Coach	Finish	REGULAR SEASON W	L	PLAYOFFS W	L
1988-89*	Dick Harter	6th/Atlantic Div.	20	62	—	—
1989-90*	Dick Harter, 8-32					
	Gene Littles, 11-31	7th/Midwest Div.	19	63	—	—
1990-91*	Gene Littles	7th/Central Div.	26	56	—	—
1991-92*	Allan Bristow	6th/Central Div.	31	51	—	—
1992-93*	Allan Bristow	3rd/Central Div.	44	38	4	5
1993-94*	Allan Bristow	5th/Central Div.	41	41	—	—
1994-95*	Allan Bristow	2nd/Central Div.	50	32	1	3
1995-96*	Allan Bristow	6th/Central Div.	41	41	—	—
1996-97*	Dave Cowens	T3rd/Central Div.	54	28	0	3
1997-98*	Dave Cowens	3rd/Central Div.	51	31	4	5
1998-99*	Dave Cowens, 4-11					
	Paul Silas, 22-13	5th/Central Div.	26	24	—	—
1999-00*	Paul Silas	2nd/Central Div.	49	33	1	3
2000-01	Paul Silas	3rd/Central Div.	46	36	6	4
2001-02	Paul Silas	2nd/Central Div.	44	38	4	5
2002-03	Paul Silas	3rd/Central Div.	47	35	2	4
2003-04	Tim Floyd	T3rd/Central Div.	41	41	3	4
Totals			630	650	25	36

*Charlotte Hornets

FIRST-ROUND DRAFT PICKS

1988— Rex Chapman, Kentucky
1989— J.R. Reid, North Carolina
1990— Kendall Gill, Illinois
1991— Larry Johnson, UNLV*
1992— Alonzo Mourning, Georgetown
1993— Greg Graham, Indiana
         Scott Burrell, Connecticut
1994— None
1995— George Zidek, UCLA
1996— Kobe Bryant, Low. Merion HS (Pa.)
         Tony Delk, Kentucky
1997— None
1998— Ricky Davis, Iowa
1999— Baron Davis, UCLA
2000— Jamaal Magloire, Kentucky
2001— Kirk Haston, Indiana
2002— None†
2003— David West, Xavier
2004— J.R. Smith, St. Benedict's Prep
         (N.J.)
*First overall pick of draft.
†Moved to New Orleans prior to draft.

RETIRED NUMBERS

7 "Pistol" Pete Maravich
13 Bobby Phills

NEW YORK KNICKERBOCKERS

YEAR-BY-YEAR RECORDS

Season	Coach	Finish	REGULAR SEASON W	L	PLAYOFFS W	L
1946-47	Neil Cohalan	3rd/Eastern Div.	33	27	2	3
1947-48	Joe Lapchick	2nd/Eastern Div.	26	22	1	2
1948-49	Joe Lapchick	2nd/Eastern Div.	32	28	3	3
1949-50	Joe Lapchick	2nd/Eastern Div.	40	28	3	2
1950-51	Joe Lapchick	3rd/Eastern Div.	36	30	8	6
1951-52	Joe Lapchick	3rd/Eastern Div.	37	29	8	6
1952-53	Joe Lapchick	1st/Eastern Div.	47	23	6	5
1953-54	Joe Lapchick	1st/Eastern Div.	44	28	0	4
1954-55	Joe Lapchick	2nd/Eastern Div.	38	34	1	2
1955-56	Joe Lapchick, 26-25					
	Vince Boryla, 9-12	T3rd/Eastern Div.	35	37	—	—
1956-57	Vince Boryla	4th/Eastern Div.	36	36	—	—
1957-58	Vince Boryla	4th/Eastern Div.	35	37	—	—
1958-59	Andrew Levane	2nd/Eastern Div.	40	32	0	2
1959-60	Andrew Levane, 8-19					
	Carl Braun, 19-29	4th/Eastern Div.	27	48	—	—
1960-61	Carl Braun	4th/Eastern Div.	21	58	—	—
1961-62	Eddie Donovan	4th/Eastern Div.	29	51	—	—
1962-63	Eddie Donovan	4th/Eastern Div.	21	59	—	—
1963-64	Eddie Donovan	4th/Eastern Div.	22	58	—	—
1964-65	Eddie Donovan, 12-26					
	Harry Gallatin, 19-23	4th/Eastern Div.	31	49	—	—
1965-66	Harry Gallatin, 6-15					
	Dick McGuire, 24-35	4th/Eastern Div.	30	50	—	—
1966-67	Dick McGuire	4th/Eastern Div.	36	45	1	3
1967-68	Dick McGuire, 15-23					
	Red Holzman, 28-16	3rd/Eastern Div.	43	39	2	4

FIRST-ROUND DRAFT PICKS

1947— Wat Misaka, Utah
1948— Harry Gallatin, NE Missouri State
1949— Dick McGuire, St. John's
1950— Not available
1951— Not available
1952— Ralph Polson, Whitworth
1953— Walter Dukes, Seton Hall
1954— Jack Turner, Western Kentucky
1955— Ken Sears, Santa Clara
1956— Ronnie Shavlik, N.C. State
1957— Brendan McCann, St. Bonaventure
1958— Pete Brannan, North Carolina
1959— Johnny Green, Michigan State
1960— Darrall Imhoff, California
1961— Tom Stith, St. Bonaventure
1962— Paul Hogue, Cincinnati
1963— Art Heyman, Duke
1964— Jim Barnes, Texas Western
1965— Bill Bradley, Princeton
         Dave Stallworth, Wichita State
1966— Cazzie Russell, Michigan*
1967— Walt Frazier, Southern Illinois
1968— Bill Hosket, Ohio State
1969— John Warren, St. John's
1970— Mike Price, Illinois
1971— Dean Meminger, Marquette
1972— Tom Riker, South Carolina
1973— Mel Davis, St. John's
1974— None
1975— Eugene Short, Jackson State
1976— None

NEW YORK KNICKS

			REGULAR SEASON		PLAYOFFS	
Season	Coach	Finish	W	L	W	L
1968-69	Red Holzman	3rd/Eastern Div.	54	28	6	4
1969-70	Red Holzman	1st/Eastern Div.	60	22	12	7
1970-71	Red Holzman	1st/Atlantic Div.	52	30	7	5
1971-72	Red Holzman	2nd/Atlantic Div.	48	34	9	7
1972-73	Red Holzman	2nd/Atlantic Div.	57	25	12	5
1973-74	Red Holzman	2nd/Atlantic Div.	49	33	5	7
1974-75	Red Holzman	3rd/Atlantic Div.	40	42	1	2
1975-76	Red Holzman	4th/Atlantic Div.	38	44	—	—
1976-77	Red Holzman	3rd/Atlantic Div.	40	42	—	—
1977-78	Willis Reed	2nd/Atlantic Div.	43	39	2	4
1978-79	Willis Reed, 6-8					
	Red Holzman, 25-43	4th/Atlantic Div.	31	51	—	—
1979-80	Red Holzman	T3rd/Atlantic Div.	39	43	—	—
1980-81	Red Holzman	3rd/Atlantic Div.	50	32	0	2
1981-82	Red Holzman	5th/Atlantic Div.	33	49	—	—
1982-83	Hubie Brown	4th/Atlantic Div.	44	38	2	4
1983-84	Hubie Brown	3rd/Atlantic Div.	47	35	6	6
1984-85	Hubie Brown	5th/Atlantic Div.	24	58	—	—
1985-86	Hubie Brown	5th/Atlantic Div.	23	59	—	—
1986-87	Hubie Brown, 4-12					
	Bob Hill, 20-46	T4th/Atlantic Div.	24	58	—	—
1987-88	Rick Pitino	T2nd/Atlantic Div.	38	44	1	3
1988-89	Rick Pitino	1st/Atlantic Div.	52	30	5	4
1989-90	Stu Jackson	3rd/Atlantic Div.	45	37	4	6
1990-91	Stu Jackson, 7-8					
	John MacLeod, 32-35	3rd/Atlantic Div.	39	43	0	3
1991-92	Pat Riley	T1st/Atlantic Div.	51	31	6	6
1992-93	Pat Riley	1st/Atlantic Div.	60	22	9	6
1993-94	Pat Riley	1st/Atlantic Div.	57	25	14	11
1994-95	Pat Riley	2nd/Atlantic Div.	55	27	6	5
1995-96	Don Nelson, 34-25					
	Jeff Van Gundy, 13-10	2nd/Atlantic Div.	47	35	4	4
1996-97	Jeff Van Gundy	2nd/Atlantic Div.	57	25	6	4
1997-98	Jeff Van Gundy	T2nd/Atlantic Div.	43	39	4	6
1998-99	Jeff Van Gundy	4th/Atlantic Div.	27	23	12	8
1999-00	Jeff Van Gundy	2nd/Atlantic Div.	50	32	9	7
2000-01	Jeff Van Gundy	3rd/Atlantic Div.	48	34	2	3
2001-02	Jeff Van Gundy, 10-9					
	Don Chaney, 20-43	7th/Atlantic Div.	30	52	—	—
2002-03	Don Chaney	T5th/Atlantic Div.	37	45	—	—
2003-04	Don Chaney, 15-24					
	Lenny Wilkens, 23-19	3rd/Atlantic Div.	39	43	0	4
Totals.			2310	2197	179	175

1977—Ray Williams, Minnesota
1978—Micheal Ray Richardson, Montana
1979—Bill Cartwright, San Francisco
  Larry Demic, Arizona
  Sly Williams, Rhode Island
1980—Mike Woodson, Indiana
1981—None
1982—Trent Tucker, Minnesota
1983—Darrell Walker, Arkansas
1984—None
1985—Patrick Ewing, Georgetown*
1986—Kenny Walker, Kentucky
1987—Mark Jackson, St. John's
1988—Rod Strickland, DePaul
1989—None
1990—Jerrod Mustaf, Maryland
1991—Greg Anthony, UNLV
1992—Hubert Davis, North Carolina
1993—None
1994—Monty Williams, Notre Dame
  Charlie Ward, Florida State
1995—None
1996—John Wallace, Syracuse
  Walter McCarty, Kentucky
  Dontae' Jones, Mississippi State
1997—John Thomas, Minnesota
1998—None
1999—Frederic Weis, France
2000—Donnell Harvey, Florida
2001—None
2002—Nene Hilario, Brazil
2003—Mike Sweetney, Georgetown
2004—None
*First overall pick of draft.

RETIRED NUMBERS

10	Walt Frazier	22	Dave
12	Dick Barnett		DeBusschere
15	Earl Monroe	24	Bill Bradley
15	Dick McGuire	33	Patrick Ewing
19	Willis Reed	613	Red Holzman

ORLANDO MAGIC

YEAR-BY-YEAR RECORDS

			REGULAR SEASON		PLAYOFFS	
Season	Coach	Finish	W	L	W	L
1989-90	Matt Guokas	7th/Central Div.	18	64	—	—
1990-91	Matt Guokas	4th/Midwest Div.	31	51	—	—
1991-92	Matt Guokas	7th/Atlantic Div.	21	61	—	—
1992-93	Matt Guokas	4th/Atlantic Div.	41	41	—	—
1993-94	Brian Hill	2nd/Atlantic Div.	50	32	0	3
1994-95	Brian Hill	1st/Atlantic Div.	57	25	11	10
1995-96	Brian Hill	1st/Atlantic Div.	60	22	7	5
1996-97	Brian Hill, 24-25					
	Richie Adubato, 21-12	3rd/Atlantic Div.	45	37	2	3
1997-98	Chuck Daly	5th/Atlantic Div.	41	41	—	—
1998-99	Chuck Daly	T1st/Atlantic Div.	33	17	1	3
1999-00	Doc Rivers	4th/Atlantic Div.	41	41	—	—
2000-01	Doc Rivers	4th/Atlantic Div.	43	39	1	3
2001-02	Doc Rivers	3rd/Atlantic Div.	44	38	1	3
2002-03	Doc Rivers	4th/Atlantic Div.	42	40	3	4
2003-04	Doc Rivers, 1-10					
	Johnny Davis, 20-51	7th/Atlantic Div.	21	61	—	—
Totals.			588	610	26	34

FIRST-ROUND DRAFT PICKS

1989—Nick Anderson, Illinois
1990—Dennis Scott, Georgia Tech
1991—Brian Williams, Arizona
  Stanley Roberts, Louisiana State
1992—Shaquille O'Neal, Louisiana State*
1993—Chris Webber, Michigan*
  Geert Hammink, Louisiana State
1994—Brooks Thompson, Oklahoma State
1995—David Vaughn, Memphis
1996—Brian Evans, Indiana
1997—Johnny Taylor, UT-Chattanooga
1998—Michael Doleac, Utah
  Keon Clark, UNLV
  Matt Harpring, Georgia Tech
1999—None
2000—Mike Miller, Florida
  Keyon Dooling, Missouri
  Courtney Alexander, Fresno State
2001—Steven Hunter, DePaul
  Jeryl Sasser, Southern Methodist
2002—Curtis Borchardt, Stanford
2003—Reece Gaines, Louisville
2004—Dwight Howard, SW Atlanta
  Christian (Ga.)*
*First overall pick of draft.

RETIRED NUMBERS

6 Fans

HISTORY Team by team

YEAR-BY-YEAR RECORDS

Season	Coach	Finish	REGULAR SEASON W	L	PLAYOFFS W	L
1949-50*	Al Cervi	1st/Eastern Div.	51	13	6	5
1950-51*	Al Cervi	4th/Eastern Div.	32	34	4	3
1951-52*	Al Cervi	1st/Eastern Div.	40	26	3	4
1952-53*	Al Cervi	2nd/Eastern Div.	47	24	0	2
1953-54*	Al Cervi	T2nd/Eastern Div.	42	30	9	4
1954-55*	Al Cervi	1st/Eastern Div.	43	29	7	4
1955-56*	Al Cervi	3rd/Eastern Div.	35	37	5	4
1956-57*	Al Cervi, 4-8					
	Paul Seymour, 34-26	2nd/Eastern Div.	38	34	2	3
1957-58*	Paul Seymour	2nd/Eastern Div.	41	31	1	2
1958-59*	Paul Seymour	3rd/Eastern Div.	35	37	5	4
1959-60*	Paul Seymour	3rd/Eastern Div.	45	30	1	2
1960-61*	Alex Hannum	3rd/Eastern Div.	38	41	4	4
1961-62*	Alex Hannum	3rd/Eastern Div.	41	39	2	3
1962-63*	Alex Hannum	2nd/Eastern Div.	48	32	2	3
1963-64	Dolph Schayes	3rd/Eastern Div.	34	46	2	3
1964-65	Dolph Schayes	3rd/Eastern Div.	40	40	6	5
1965-66	Dolph Schayes	1st/Eastern Div.	55	25	1	4
1966-67	Alex Hannum	1st/Eastern Div.	68	13	11	4
1967-68	Alex Hannum	1st/Eastern Div.	62	20	7	6
1968-69	Jack Ramsay	2nd/Eastern Div.	55	27	1	4
1969-70	Jack Ramsay	4th/Eastern Div.	42	40	1	4
1970-71	Jack Ramsay	2nd/Atlantic Div.	47	35	3	4
1971-72	Jack Ramsay	3rd/Atlantic Div.	30	52	—	—
1972-73	Roy Rubin, 4-47					
	Kevin Loughery, 5-26	4th/Atlantic Div.	9	73	—	—
1973-74	Gene Shue	4th/Atlantic Div.	25	57	—	—
1974-75	Gene Shue	4th/Atlantic Div.	34	48	—	—
1975-76	Gene Shue	T2nd/Atlantic Div.	46	36	1	2
1976-77	Gene Shue	1st/Atlantic Div.	50	32	10	9
1977-78	Gene Shue, 2-4					
	B. Cunningham, 53-23	1st/Atlantic Div.	55	27	6	4
1978-79	Billy Cunningham	2nd/Atlantic Div.	47	35	5	4
1979-80	Billy Cunningham	2nd/Atlantic Div.	59	23	12	6
1980-81	Billy Cunningham	T1st/Atlantic Div.	62	20	9	7
1981-82	Billy Cunningham	2nd/Atlantic Div.	58	24	12	9
1982-83	Billy Cunningham	1st/Atlantic Div.	65	17	12	1
1983-84	Billy Cunningham	2nd/Atlantic Div.	52	30	2	3
1984-85	Billy Cunningham	2nd/Atlantic Div.	58	24	8	5
1985-86	Matt Guokas	2nd/Atlantic Div.	54	28	6	6
1986-87	Matt Guokas	2nd/Atlantic Div.	45	37	2	3
1987-88	Matt Guokas, 20-23					
	Jim Lynam, 16-23	4th/Atlantic Div.	36	46	—	—
1988-89	Jim Lynam	2nd/Atlantic Div.	46	36	0	3
1989-90	Jim Lynam	1st/Atlantic Div.	53	29	4	6
1990-91	Jim Lynam	2nd/Atlantic Div.	44	38	4	4
1991-92	Jim Lynam	5th/Atlantic Div.	35	47	—	—
1992-93	Doug Moe, 19-37					
	Fred Carter, 7-19	6th/Atlantic Div.	26	56	—	—
1993-94	Fred Carter	6th/Atlantic Div.	25	57	—	—
1994-95	John Lucas	6th/Atlantic Div.	24	58	—	—
1995-96	John Lucas	7th/Atlantic Div.	18	64	—	—
1996-97	Johnny Davis	6th/Atlantic Div.	22	60	—	—
1997-98	Larry Brown	7th/Atlantic Div.	31	51	—	—
1998-99	Larry Brown	3rd/Atlantic Div.	28	22	3	5
1999-00	Larry Brown	3rd/Atlantic Div.	49	33	5	5
2000-01	Larry Brown	1st/Atlantic Div.	56	26	12	11
2001-02	Larry Brown	4th/Atlantic Div.	43	39	2	3
2002-03	Larry Brown	2nd/Atlantic Div.	48	34	6	6
2003-04	Randy Ayers, 21-31					
	Chris Ford, 12-18	5th/Atlantic Div.	33	49	—	—
Totals.			2345	1991	204	183

*Syracuse Nationals.

FIRST-ROUND DRAFT PICKS

1964—Luke Jackson, Pan American
1965—Billy Cunningham, North Carolina
1966—Matt Guokas, St. Joseph's
1967—Craig Raymond, Brigham Young
1968—Shaler Halimon, Utah State
1969—Bud Ogden, Santa Clara
1970—Al Henry, Wisconsin
1971—Dana Lewis, Tulsa
1972—Fred Boyd, Oregon State
1973—Doug Collins, Illinois State*
    Raymond Lewis, Los Angeles State
1974—Marvin Barnes, Providence
1975—Darryl Dawkins, Maynard Evans HS (Fla.)
1976—Terry Furlow, Michigan State
1977—Glenn Mosley, Seton Hall
1978—None
1979—Jim Spanarkel, Duke
1980—Andrew Toney, SW Louisiana
    Monti Davis, Tennessee State
1981—Franklin Edwards, Cleveland State
1982—Mark McNamara, California
1983—Leo Rautins, Syracuse
1984—Charles Barkley, Auburn
    Leon Wood, Fullerton State
    Tom Sewell, Lamar
1985—Terry Catledge, South Alabama
1986—None
1987—Chris Welp, Washington
1988—Charles Smith, Pittsburgh
1989—Kenny Payne, Louisville
1990—None
1991—None
1992—Clarence Weatherspoon, Sou. Miss.
1993—Shawn Bradley, Brigham Young
1994—Sharone Wright, Clemson
    B.J. Tyler, Texas
1995—Jerry Stackhouse, North Carolina
1996—Allen Iverson, Georgetown*
1997—Keith Van Horn, Utah
1998—Larry Hughes, St. Louis
1999—None
2000—Speedy Claxton, Hofstra
2001—Samuel Dalembert, Seton Hall
2002—Jiri Welsch, Slovenia
2003—None
2004—Andre Iguodala, Arizona
*First overall pick of draft.

RETIRED NUMBERS

6 Julius Erving
10 Maurice Cheeks
13 Wilt Chamberlain
15 Hal Greer
24 Bobby Jones
32 Billy Cunningham
34 Charles Barkley

Note: Microphone retired in honor of broadcaster Dave Zinkoff.

HISTORY *Team by team*

YEAR-BY-YEAR RECORDS

Season	Coach	Finish	W	L	W	L
		REGULAR SEASON			PLAYOFFS	
1968-69	Johnny Kerr	7th/Western Div.	16	66	—	—
1969-70	Johnny Kerr, 15-23					
	Jerry Colangelo, 24-20	T3rd/Western Div.	39	43	3	4
1970-71	Cotton Fitzsimmons	3rd/Midwest Div.	48	34	—	—
1971-72	Cotton Fitzsimmons	3rd/Midwest Div.	49	33	—	—
1972-73	B. van Breda Kolff, 3-4					
	Jerry Colangelo, 35-40	3rd/Pacific Div.	38	44	—	—
1973-74	John MacLeod	4th/Pacific Div.	30	52	—	—
1974-75	John MacLeod	4th/Pacific Div.	32	50	—	—
1975-76	John MacLeod	3rd/Pacific Div.	42	40	10	9
1976-77	John MacLeod	5th/Pacific Div.	34	48	—	—
1977-78	John MacLeod	2nd/Pacific Div.	49	33	0	2
1978-79	John MacLeod	2nd/Pacific Div.	50	32	9	6
1979-80	John MacLeod	3rd/Pacific Div.	55	27	3	5
1980-81	John MacLeod	1st/Pacific Div.	57	25	3	4
1981-82	John MacLeod	3rd/Pacific Div.	46	36	2	5
1982-83	John MacLeod	2nd/Pacific Div.	53	29	1	2
1983-84	John MacLeod	4th/Pacific Div.	41	41	9	8
1984-85	John MacLeod	3rd/Pacific Div.	36	46	0	3
1985-86	John MacLeod	T3rd/Pacific Div.	32	50	—	—
1986-87	John MacLeod, 22-34					
	D. Van Arsdale, 14-12	5th/Pacific Div.	36	46	—	—
1987-88	John Wetzel	4th/Pacific Div.	28	54	—	—
1988-89	Cotton Fitzsimmons	2nd/Pacific Div.	55	27	7	5
1989-90	Cotton Fitzsimmons	3rd/Pacific Div.	54	28	9	7
1990-91	Cotton Fitzsimmons	3rd/Pacific Div.	55	27	1	3
1991-92	Cotton Fitzsimmons	3rd/Pacific Div.	53	29	4	4
1992-93	Paul Westphal	1st/Pacific Div.	62	20	13	11
1993-94	Paul Westphal	2nd/Pacific Div.	56	26	6	4
1994-95	Paul Westphal	1st/Pacific Div.	59	23	6	4
1995-96	Paul Westphal, 14-19					
	C. Fitzsimmons, 27-22	4th/Pacific Div.	41	41	1	3
1996-97	Cotton Fitzsimmons, 0-8					
	Danny Ainge, 40-34	4th/Pacific Div.	40	42	2	3
1997-98	Danny Ainge	3rd/Pacific Div.	56	26	1	3
1998-99	Danny Ainge	T3rd/Pacific Div.	27	23	0	3
1999-00	Danny Ainge, 13-7					
	Scott Skiles, 40-22	3rd/Pacific Div.	53	29	4	5
2000-01	Scott Skiles	3rd/Pacific Div.	51	31	1	3
2001-02	Scott Skiles, 25-26					
	Frank Johnson, 11-20	6th/Pacific Div.	36	46	—	—
2002-03	Frank Johnson	4th/Pacific Div.	44	38	2	4
2003-04	Frank Johnson, 8-13					
	Mike D'Antoni, 21-40	6th/Pacific Div.	29	53	—	—
Totals			1582	1338	97	110

FIRST-ROUND DRAFT PICKS

1968— Gary Gregor, South Carolina
1969— Neal Walk, Florida
1970— Greg Howard, New Mexico
1971— John Roche, South Carolina
1972— Corky Calhoun, Pennsylvania
1973— Mike Bantom, St. Joseph's
1974— John Shumate, Notre Dame
1975— Alvan Adams, Oklahoma
    Ricky Sobers, UNLV
1976— Ron Lee, Oregon
1977— Walter Davis, North Carolina
1978— Marty Byrnes, Syracuse
1979— Kyle Macy, Kentucky
1980— None
1981— Larry Nance, Clemson
1982— David Thirdkill, Bradley
1983— None
1984— Jay Humphries, Colorado
1985— Ed Pinckney, Villanova
1986— William Bedford, Memphis State
1987— Armon Gilliam, UNLV
1988— Tim Perry, Temple
    Dan Majerle, Central Michigan
1989— Anthony Cook, Arizona
1990— Jayson Williams, St. John's
1991— None
1992— Oliver Miller, Arkansas
1993— Malcolm Mackey, Georgia Tech
1994— Wesley Person, Auburn
1995— Michael Finley, Wisconsin
    Mario Bennett, Arizona State
1996— Steve Nash, Santa Clara
1997— None
1998— None
1999— Shawn Marion, UNLV
2000— Iakovos Tsakalidis, Rep. of Georgia
2001— None
2002— Amare Stoudemire, Cypress Creek
    HS (Fla.)
    Casey Jacobsen, Stanford
2003— Zarko Cabarkapa, Serbia & Mont.
2004— Luol Deng, Duke

RETIRED NUMBERS

5 Dick Van Arsdale	33 Alvan Adams
6 Walter Davis	34 Charles Barkley
7 Kevin Johnson	42 Connie Hawkins
9 Dan Majerle	44 Paul Westphal
24 Tom Chambers	

YEAR-BY-YEAR RECORDS

Season	Coach	Finish	W	L	W	L
		REGULAR SEASON			PLAYOFFS	
1946-47	Paul Birch	5th/Western Div.	15	45	—	—

FIRST-ROUND DRAFT PICKS

1947—Clifton McNeeley, Texas Western

YEAR-BY-YEAR RECORDS

Season	Coach	Finish	W	L	W	L
		REGULAR SEASON			PLAYOFFS	
1970-71	Rolland Todd	5th/Pacific Div.	29	53	—	—
1971-72	Rolland Todd, 12-44					
	Stu Inman, 6-20	5th/Pacific Div.	18	64	—	—
1972-73	Jack McCloskey	5th/Pacific Div.	21	61	—	—
1973-74	Jack McCloskey	5th/Pacific Div.	27	55	—	—
1974-75	Lenny Wilkens	3rd/Pacific Div.	38	44	—	—
1975-76	Lenny Wilkens	5th/Pacific Div.	37	45	—	—

FIRST-ROUND DRAFT PICKS

1970— Geoff Petrie, Princeton
1971— Sidney Wicks, UCLA
1972— LaRue Martin, Loyola*
1973— Barry Parkhill, Virginia
1974— Bill Walton, UCLA*
1975— Lionel Hollins, Arizona State
1976— Wally Walker, Virginia
1977— Rich Laurel, Hofstra
1978— Mychal Thompson, Minnesota*
    Ron Brewer, Arkansas
1979— Jim Paxson, Dayton
1980— Ronnie Lester, Iowa

Season	Coach	REGULAR SEASON Finish	W	L	PLAYOFFS W	L
1976-77	Jack Ramsay	2nd/Pacific Div.	49	33	14	5
1977-78	Jack Ramsay	1st/Pacific Div.	58	24	2	4
1978-79	Jack Ramsay	4th/Pacific Div.	45	37	1	2
1979-80	Jack Ramsay	4th/Pacific Div.	38	44	1	2
1980-81	Jack Ramsay	3rd/Pacific Div.	45	37	1	2
1981-82	Jack Ramsay	5th/Pacific Div.	42	40	—	—
1982-83	Jack Ramsay	4th/Pacific Div.	46	36	3	4
1983-84	Jack Ramsay	2nd/Pacific Div.	48	34	2	3
1984-85	Jack Ramsay	2nd/Pacific Div.	42	40	4	5
1985-86	Jack Ramsay	2nd/Pacific Div.	40	42	1	3
1986-87	Mike Schuler	2nd/Pacific Div.	49	33	1	3
1987-88	Mike Schuler	2nd/Pacific Div.	53	29	1	3
1988-89	Mike Schuler, 25-22 Rick Adelman, 14-21	5th/Pacific Div.	39	43	0	3
1989-90	Rick Adelman	2nd/Pacific Div.	59	23	12	9
1990-91	Rick Adelman	1st/Pacific Div.	63	19	9	7
1991-92	Rick Adelman	1st/Pacific Div.	57	25	13	8
1992-93	Rick Adelman	3rd/Pacific Div.	51	31	1	3
1993-94	Rick Adelman	4th/Pacific Div.	47	35	1	3
1994-95	P.J. Carlesimo	4th/Pacific Div.	44	38	0	3
1995-96	P.J. Carlesimo	3rd/Pacific Div.	44	38	2	3
1996-97	P.J. Carlesimo	3rd/Pacific Div.	49	33	1	3
1997-98	Mike Dunleavy	4th/Pacific Div.	46	36	1	3
1998-99	Mike Dunleavy	1st/Pacific Div.	35	15	7	6
1999-00	Mike Dunleavy	2nd/Pacific Div.	59	23	10	6
2000-01	Mike Dunleavy	4th/Pacific Div.	50	32	0	3
2001-02	Maurice Cheeks	3rd/Pacific Div.	49	33	0	3
2002-03	Maurice Cheeks	T2nd/Pacific Div.	50	32	3	4
2003-04	Maurice Cheeks	3rd/Pacific Div.	41	41	—	—
Totals			1508	1248	91	103

1981— Jeff Lamp, Virginia
      Darnell Valentine, Kansas
1982— Lafayette Lever, Arizona State
1983— Clyde Drexler, Houston
1984— Sam Bowie, Kentucky
      Bernard Thompson, Fresno State
1985— Terry Porter, Wis.-Stevens Point
1986— Walter Berry, St. John's
      Arvydas Sabonis, Soviet Union
1987— Ronnie Murphy, Jacksonville
1988— Mark Bryant, Seton Hall
1989— Byron Irvin, Missouri
1990— Alaa Abdelnaby, Duke
1991— None
1992— Dave Johnson, Syracuse
1993— James Robinson, Alabama
1994— Aaron McKie, Temple
1995— Shawn Respert, Michigan State
1996— Jermaine O'Neal, Eau Claire HS (S.C.)
1997— Chris Anstey, Australia
1998— None
1999— None
2000— Erick Barkley, St. John's
2001— Zach Randolph, Michigan State
2002— Qyntel Woods, NE Mississippi C.C.
2003— Travis Outlaw, Starkville HS (Miss.)
2004— Sebastian Telfair, Abraham Lincoln HS (N.Y.)
      Sergei Monia, Russia
*First overall pick of draft.

RETIRED NUMBERS

1 Larry Weinberg   32 Bill Walton
13 Dave Twardzik   36 Lloyd Neal
15 Larry Steele   45 Geoff Petrie
20 Maurice Lucas   77 Jack Ramsay
22 Clyde Drexler

PROVIDENCE STEAMROLLERS

YEAR-BY-YEAR RECORDS

Season	Coach	REGULAR SEASON Finish	W	L	PLAYOFFS W	L
1946-47	Robert Morris	4th/Eastern Div.	28	32	—	—
1947-48	Albert Soar, 2-17 Nat Hickey, 4-25	4th/Eastern Div.	6	42	—	—
1948-49	Ken Loeffler	6th/Eastern Div.	12	48	—	—
Totals			46	122	—	—

FIRST-ROUND DRAFT PICKS

1947—Walt Dropo, Connecticut
1948—Howie Shannon, Kansas State
1949—Paul Courty, Oklahoma

SACRAMENTO KINGS

YEAR-BY-YEAR RECORDS

Season	Coach	REGULAR SEASON Finish	W	L	PLAYOFFS W	L
1948-49*	Les Harrison	1st/Western Div.	45	15	2	2
1949-50*	Les Harrison	T1st/Central Div.	51	17	0	2
1950-51*	Les Harrison	2nd/Western Div.	41	27	9	5
1951-52*	Les Harrison	1st/Western Div.	41	25	3	3
1952-53*	Les Harrison	2nd/Western Div.	44	26	1	2
1953-54*	Les Harrison	2nd/Western Div.	44	28	3	3
1954-55*	Les Harrison	3rd/Western Div.	29	43	1	2
1955-56*	Bob Wanzer	4th/Western Div.	31	41	—	—
1956-57*	Bob Wanzer	4th/Western Div.	31	41	—	—
1957-58†	Bob Wanzer	T2nd/Western Div.	33	39	0	2
1958-59†	Bob Wanzer, 3-15 Tom Marshall, 16-38	4th/Western Div.	19	53	—	—
1959-60†	Tom Marshall	4th/Western Div.	19	56	—	—
1960-61†	Charles Wolf	4th/Western Div.	33	46	—	—
1961-62†	Charles Wolf	2nd/Western Div.	43	37	1	3
1962-63†	Charles Wolf	3rd/Eastern Div.	42	38	6	6
1963-64†	Jack McMahon	2nd/Eastern Div.	55	25	4	6
1964-65†	Jack McMahon	2nd/Eastern Div.	48	32	1	3
1965-66†	Jack McMahon	3rd/Eastern Div.	45	35	2	3

FIRST-ROUND DRAFT PICKS

1949—Frank Saul, Seton Hall
1950—Joe McNamee, San Francisco
1951—Sam Ranzino, North Carolina State
1952—Not available
1953—Richie Regan, Seton Hall
1954—Tom Marshall, Western Kentucky
1955—Not available
1956—Si Green, Duquesne*
1957—Rod Hundley, West Virginia*
1958—Archie Dees, Indiana
1959—Bob Boozer, Kansas State*
1960—Oscar Robertson, Cincinnati*
1961—Larry Siegfried, Ohio State
1962—Jerry Lucas, Ohio State
1963—Tom Thacker, Cincinnati
1964—George Wilson, Cincinnati
1965—Nate Bowman, Wichita State
1966—Walt Wesley, Kansas
1967—Mel Daniels, New Mexico
1968—Don Smith (Abdul Aziz), Iowa State

Season	Coach	Finish	REGULAR SEASON		PLAYOFFS	
			W	L	W	L
1966-67†	Jack McMahon	3rd/Eastern Div.	39	42	1	3
1967-68†	Ed Jucker	5th/Eastern Div.	39	43	—	—
1968-69†	Ed Jucker	5th/Eastern Div.	41	41	—	—
1969-70†	Bob Cousy	5th/Eastern Div.	36	46	—	—
1970-71†	Bob Cousy	3rd/Central Div.	33	49	—	—
1971-72†	Bob Cousy	3rd/Central Div.	30	52	—	—
1972-73‡	Bob Cousy	4th/Midwest Div.	36	46	—	—
1973-74‡	Bob Cousy, 6-16					
	Draff Young, 0-3					
	Phil Johnson, 27-30	4th/Midwest Div.	33	49	—	—
1974-75‡	Phil Johnson	2nd/Midwest Div.	44	38	2	4
1975-76§	Phil Johnson	3rd/Midwest Div.	31	51	—	—
1976-77§	Phil Johnson	4th/Midwest Div.	40	42	—	—
1977-78§	Phil Johnson, 13-24					
	L. Staverman, 18-27	T5th/Midwest Div.	31	51	—	—
1978-79§	Cotton Fitzsimmons	1st/Midwest Div.	48	34	1	4
1979-80§	Cotton Fitzsimmons	2nd/Midwest Div.	47	35	1	2
1980-81§	Cotton Fitzsimmons	T2nd/Midwest Div.	40	42	7	8
1981-82§	Cotton Fitzsimmons	4th/Midwest Div.	30	52	—	—
1982-83§	Cotton Fitzsimmons	T2nd/Midwest Div.	45	37	—	—
1983-84§	Cotton Fitzsimmons	T3rd/Midwest Div.	38	44	0	3
1984-85§	Jack McKinney, 1-8					
	Phil Johnson, 30-43	6th/Midwest Div.	31	51	—	—
1985-86	Phil Johnson	5th/Midwest Div.	37	45	0	3
1986-87	Phil Johnson, 14-32					
	Jerry Reynolds, 15-21	5th/Midwest Div.	29	53	—	—
1987-88	Bill Russell, 17-41					
	Jerry Reynolds, 7-17	6th/Midwest Div.	24	58	—	—
1988-89	Jerry Reynolds	6th/Pacific Div.	27	55	—	—
1989-90	Jerry Reynolds, 7-21					
	Dick Motta, 16-38	7th/Pacific Div.	23	59	—	—
1990-91	Dick Motta	7th/Pacific Div.	25	57	—	—
1991-92	Dick Motta, 7-18					
	Rex Hughes, 22-35	7th/Pacific Div.	29	53	—	—
1992-93	Garry St. Jean	7th/Pacific Div.	25	57	—	—
1993-94	Garry St. Jean	6th/Pacific Div.	28	54	—	—
1994-95	Garry St. Jean	5th/Pacific Div.	39	43	—	—
1995-96	Garry St. Jean	5th/Pacific Div.	39	43	1	3
1996-97	Garry St. Jean, 28-39					
	Eddie Jordan, 6-9	6th/Pacific Div.	34	48	—	—
1997-98	Eddie Jordan	5th/Pacific Div.	27	55	—	—
1998-99	Rick Adelman	T3rd/Pacific Div.	27	23	2	3
1999-00	Rick Adelman	5th/Pacific Div.	44	38	2	3
2000-01	Rick Adelman	2nd/Pacific Div.	55	27	3	5
2001-02	Rick Adelman	1st/Pacific Div.	61	21	10	6
2002-03	Rick Adelman	1st/Pacific Div.	59	23	7	5
2003-04	Rick Adelman	2nd/Pacific Div.	55	27	7	5
Totals.			2093	2308	77	99

*Rochester Royals.
†Cincinnati Royals.
‡Kansas City/Omaha Kings.
§Kansas City Kings.

1969—Herm Gilliam, Purdue
1970—Sam Lacey, New Mexico State
1971—Ken Durrett, La Salle
    Nate Williams, Utah State†
1972—None
1973—Ron Behagen, Minnesota
1974—Scott Wedman, Colorado
1975—Bill Robinzine, DePaul
    Bob Bigelow, Pennsylvania
1976—Richard Washington, UCLA
1977—Otis Birdsong, Houston
1978—Phil Ford, North Carolina
1979—Reggie King, Alabama
1980—Hawkeye Whitney, N.C. State
1981—Steve Johnson, Oregon State
    Kevin Loder, Alabama State
1982—LaSalle Thompson, Texas
    Brook Steppe, Georgia Tech
1983—Ennis Whatley, Alabama
1984—Otis Thorpe, Providence
1985—Joe Kleine, Arkansas
1986—Harold Pressley, Villanova
1987—Kenny Smith, North Carolina
1988—Ricky Berry, San Jose State
1989—Pervis Ellison, Louisville*
1990—Lionel Simmons, La Salle
    Travis Mays, Texas
    Duane Causwell, Temple
    Anthony Bonner, St. Louis
1991—Billy Owens, Syracuse
    Pete Chilcutt, North Carolina
1992—Walt Williams, Maryland
1993—Bobby Hurley, Duke
1994—Brian Grant, Xavier
1995—Corliss Williamson, Arkansas
1996—Predrag Stojakovic, Greece
1997—Olivier Saint-Jean, San Jose State
1998—Jason Williams, Florida
1999—None
2000—Hidayet Turkoglu, Turkey
2001—Gerald Wallace, Alabama
2002—Dan Dickau, Gonzaga
2003—None
2004—Kevin Martin, Western Carolina
*First overall pick of draft.
†Williams was selected in the 1971 supplementary draft of hardship cases. The Royals had to forfeit their 1972 first-round choice.

RETIRED NUMBERS

1	Nate Archibald	12	Maurice Stokes
2	Mitch Richmond	14	Oscar Robertson
6	Sixth man (fan)	27	Jack Twyman
11	Bob Davies	44	Sam Lacey

ST. LOUIS BOMBERS

YEAR-BY-YEAR RECORDS

Season	Coach	Finish	REGULAR SEASON		PLAYOFFS	
			W	L	W	L
1946-47	Ken Loeffler	2nd/Western Div.	38	23	1	2
1947-48	Ken Loeffler	1st/Western Div.	29	19	3	4
1948-49	Grady Lewis	4th/Western Div.	29	31	0	2
1949-50	Grady Lewis	5th/Central Div.	26	42	—	—
Totals.			122	115	4	8

FIRST-ROUND DRAFT PICKS

1947—Jack Underman, Ohio State
1948—Not available
1949—Ed Macauley, St. Louis

SAN ANTONIO SPURS

YEAR-BY-YEAR RECORDS

Season	Coach	Finish	REGULAR SEASON W	L	PLAYOFFS W	L
1967-68*	Cliff Hagan	2nd/Western Div.	46	32	4	4
1968-69*	Cliff Hagan	4th/Western Div.	41	37	3	4
1969-70*	Cliff Hagan, 22-21					
	Max Williams, 23-18	2nd/Western Div.	45	39	2	4
1970-71†	Max Williams, 5-14					
	Bill Blakely, 25-40	4th/Western Div.	30	54	0	4
1971-72*	Tom Nissalke	3rd/Western Div.	42	42	0	4
1972-73*	Babe McCarthy, 24-48					
	Dave Brown, 4-8	5th/Western Div.	28	56	—	—
1973-74‡	Tom Nissalke	3rd/Western Div.	45	39	3	4
1974-75‡	Tom Nissalke, 17-10					
	Bob Bass, 34-23	2nd/Western Div.	51	33	2	4
1975-76‡	Bob Bass	3rd in ABA	50	34	3	4
1976-77	Doug Moe	3rd/Central Div.	44	38	0	2
1977-78	Doug Moe	1st/Central Div.	52	30	2	4
1978-79	Doug Moe	1st/Central Div.	48	34	7	7
1979-80	Doug Moe, 33-33					
	Bob Bass, 8-8	2nd/Central Div.	41	41	1	2
1980-81	Stan Albeck	1st/Midwest Div.	52	30	3	4
1981-82	Stan Albeck	1st/Midwest Div.	48	34	4	5
1982-83	Stan Albeck	1st/Midwest Div.	53	29	6	5
1983-84	Morris McHone, 11-20					
	Bob Bass, 26-25	5th/Midwest Div.	37	45	—	—
1984-85	Cotton Fitzsimmons	T4th/Midwest Div.	41	41	2	3
1985-86	Cotton Fitzsimmons	6th/Midwest Div.	35	47	0	3
1986-87	Bob Weiss	6th/Midwest Div.	28	54	—	—
1987-88	Bob Weiss	5th/Midwest Div.	31	51	0	3
1988-89	Larry Brown	5th/Midwest Div.	21	61	—	—
1989-90	Larry Brown	1st/Midwest Div.	56	26	6	4
1990-91	Larry Brown	1st/Midwest Div.	55	27	1	3
1991-92	Larry Brown, 21-17					
	Bob Bass, 26-18	2nd/Midwest Div.	47	35	0	3
1992-93	Jerry Tarkanian, 9-11					
	Rex Hughes, 1-0					
	John Lucas, 39-22	2nd/Midwest Div.	49	33	5	5
1993-94	John Lucas	2nd/Midwest Div.	55	27	1	3
1994-95	Bob Hill	1st/Midwest Div.	62	20	9	6
1995-96	Bob Hill	1st/Midwest Div.	59	23	5	5
1996-97	Bob Hill, 3-15					
	Gregg Popovich, 17-47	6th/Midwest Div.	20	62	—	—
1997-98	Gregg Popovich	2nd/Midwest Div.	56	26	4	5
1998-99	Gregg Popovich	T1st/Midwest Div.	37	13	15	2
1999-00	Gregg Popovich	2nd/Midwest Div.	53	29	1	3
2000-01	Gregg Popovich	1st/Midwest Div.	58	24	7	6
2001-02	Gregg Popovich	1st/Midwest Div.	58	24	4	6
2002-03	Gregg Popovich	1st/Midwest Div.	60	22	16	8
2003-04	Gregg Popovich	2nd/Midwest Div.	57	25	6	4
	ABA totals		378	366	17	32
	NBA totals		1313	951	105	101

*Dallas Chaparrals; club in ABA.
†Texas Chaparrals; club in ABA.
‡San Antonio Spurs; club in ABA.

FIRST-ROUND DRAFT PICKS

1967—Matt Aitch, Michigan State
1968—Shaler Halimon, Utah State
1969—Willie Brown, Middle Tennessee
1970—Nate Archibald, Texas-El Paso
1971—Stan Love, Oregon
1972—LaRue Martin, Loyola
1973—Kevin Kunnert, Iowa
      Mike D'Antoni, Marshall
1974—Leonard Robinson, Tennessee
1975—Mark Olberding, Minnesota
1976—None
1977—None
1978—Frankie Sanders, Southern
1979—Wiley Peck, Mississippi State
1980—Reggie Johnson, Tennessee
1981—None
1982—None
1983—John Paxson, Notre Dame
1984—Alvin Robertson, Arkansas
1985—Alfredrick Hughes, Loyola (Ill.)
1986—Johnny Dawkins, Duke
1987—David Robinson, Navy*
      Greg Anderson, Houston
1988—Willie Anderson, Georgia
1989—Sean Elliott, Arizona
1990—Dwayne Schintzius, Florida
1991—None
1992—Tracy Murray, UCLA
1993—None
1994—Bill Curley, Boston College
1995—Cory Alexander, Virginia
1996—None
1997—Tim Duncan, Wake Forest*
1998—Felipe Lopez, St. John's
1999—Leon Smith, Martin Luther King
      HS (Ill.)
2000—None
2001—Tony Parker, France
2002—John Salmons, Miami (Fla.)
2003—Leandrinho Barbosa, Brazil
2004—Beno Udrih, Slovenia
*First overall pick of draft.
NOTE: San Antonio's first-round selections from 1967-75 were made while a member of the ABA.

RETIRED NUMBERS

00 Johnny Moore
13 James Silas
44 George Gervin
50 David Robinson

SEATTLE SUPERSONICS

YEAR-BY-YEAR RECORDS

Season	Coach	Finish	REGULAR SEASON W	L	PLAYOFFS W	L
1967-68	Al Bianchi	5th/Western Div.	23	59	—	—
1968-69	Al Bianchi	6th/Western Div.	30	52	—	—
1969-70	Lenny Wilkens	5th/Western Div.	36	46	—	—
1970-71	Lenny Wilkens	4th/Pacific Div.	38	44	—	—
1971-72	Lenny Wilkens	3rd/Pacific Div.	47	35	—	—
1972-73	Tom Nissalke, 13-32					
	B. Buckwalter, 13-24	4th/Pacific Div.	26	56	—	—
1973-74	Bill Russell	3rd/Pacific Div.	36	46	—	—

FIRST-ROUND DRAFT PICKS

1967—Al Tucker, Oklahoma Baptist
1968—Bob Kauffman, Guilford
1969—Lucius Allen, UCLA
1970—Jim Ard, Cincinnati
1971—Fred Brown, Iowa
1972—Bud Stallworth, Kansas
1973—Mike Green, Louisiana Tech
1974—Tom Burleson, North Carolina St.
1975—Frank Oleynick, Seattle University
1976—Bob Wilkerson, Indiana

Season	Coach	Finish	REGULAR SEASON W	L	PLAYOFFS W	L
1974-75	Bill Russell	2nd/Pacific Div.	43	39	4	5
1975-76	Bill Russell	2nd/Pacific Div.	43	39	2	4
1976-77	Bill Russell	4th/Pacific Div.	40	42	—	—
1977-78	Bob Hopkins, 5-17					
	Lenny Wilkens, 42-18	3rd/Pacific Div.	47	35	13	9
1978-79	Lenny Wilkens	1st/Pacific Div.	52	30	12	5
1979-80	Lenny Wilkens	2nd/Pacific Div.	56	26	7	8
1980-81	Lenny Wilkens	6th/Pacific Div.	34	48		
1981-82	Lenny Wilkens	2nd/Pacific Div.	52	30	3	5
1982-83	Lenny Wilkens	3rd/Pacific Div.	48	34	0	2
1983-84	Lenny Wilkens	3rd/Pacific Div.	42	40	2	3
1984-85	Lenny Wilkens	T4th/Pacific Div.	31	51	—	—
1985-86	Bernie Bickerstaff	5th/Pacific Div.	31	51	—	—
1986-87	Bernie Bickerstaff	4th/Pacific Div.	39	43	7	7
1987-88	Bernie Bickerstaff	3rd/Pacific Div.	44	38	2	3
1988-89	B. Bickerstaff, 46-30	3rd/Pacific Div.	47	35	3	5
	*Tom Newell, 0-1					
	*Bob Kloppenburg, 1-4					
1989-90	Bernie Bickerstaff	4th/Pacific Div.	41	41	—	—
1990-91	K.C. Jones	5th/Pacific Div.	41	41	2	3
1991-92	K.C. Jones, 18-18					
	Bob Kloppenburg, 2-2					
	George Karl, 27-15	4th/Pacific Div.	47	35	4	5
1992-93	George Karl	2nd/Pacific Div.	55	27	10	9
1993-94	George Karl	1st/Pacific Div.	63	19	2	3
1994-95	George Karl	2nd/Pacific Div.	57	25	1	3
1995-96	George Karl	1st/Pacific Div.	64	18	13	8
1996-97	George Karl	1st/Pacific Div.	57	25	6	6
1997-98	George Karl	T1st/Pacific Div.	61	21	4	6
1998-99	Paul Westphal	5th/Pacific Div.	25	25	—	—
1999-00	Paul Westphal	4th/Pacific Div.	45	37	2	3
2000-01	Paul Westphal, 6-9					
	Nate McMillan, 38-29	5th/Pacific Div.	44	38	—	—
2001-02	Nate McMillan	4th/Pacific Div.	45	37	2	3
2002-03	Nate McMillan	5th/Pacific Div.	40	42	—	—
2003-04	Nate McMillan	T4th/Pacific Div.	37	45	—	—

Totals. 1607 1395 101 105

*Substituted during Bickerstaff's illness

FIRST-ROUND DRAFT PICKS (right column)

1977—Jack Sikma, Illinois Wesleyan
1978—None
1979—James Bailey, Rutgers
      Vinnie Johnson, Baylor
1980—Bill Hanzlik, Notre Dame
1981—Danny Vranes, Utah
1982—None
1983—Jon Sundvold, Missouri
1984—None
1985—Xavier McDaniel, Wichita State
1986—None
1987—Scottie Pippen, Central Arkansas
      Derrick McKey, Alabama
1988—Gary Grant, Michigan
1989—Dana Barros, Boston College
      Shawn Kemp, Concord HS (Ind.)
1990—Gary Payton, Oregon State
1991—Rich King, Nebraska
1992—Doug Christie, Pepperdine
1993—Ervin Johnson, New Orleans
1994—Carlos Rogers, Tennessee State
1995—Sherell Ford, Illinois-Chicago
1996—None
1997—Bobby Jackson, Minnesota
1998—Vladimir Stepania, Slovenia
1999—Corey Maggette, Duke
2000—Desmond Mason, Oklahoma State
2001—Vladimir Radmanovic, Yugoslavia
2002—None
2003—Nick Collison, Kansas
      Luke Ridnour, Oregon
2004—Robert Swift, Bakersfield HS
      (Calif.)

RETIRED NUMBERS

1 Gus Williams
10 Nate McMillan
19 Lenny Wilkens
32 Fred Brown
43 Jack Sikma

Note: Microphone retired in honor of broadcaster Bob Blackburn.

SHEBOYGAN REDSKINS

YEAR-BY-YEAR RECORDS

Season	Coach	Finish	REGULAR SEASON W	L	PLAYOFFS W	L
1949-50	Ken Suesens	4th/Western Div.	22	40	1	2

TORONTO HUSKIES

YEAR-BY-YEAR RECORDS

Season	Coach	Finish	REGULAR SEASON W	L	PLAYOFFS W	L
1946-47	Ed Sadowski, 3-9					
	Lew Hayman, 0-1					
	Dick Fitzgerald, 2-1					
	Robert Rolfe, 17-27	T5th/Eastern Div.	22	38	—	—

FIRST-ROUND DRAFT PICKS

1947—Glen Selbo, Wisconsin

TORONTO RAPTORS

YEAR-BY-YEAR RECORDS

Season	Coach	Finish	REGULAR SEASON W	L	PLAYOFFS W	L
1995-96	Brendan Malone	8th/Central Div.	21	61	—	—
1996-97	Darrell Walker	8th/Central Div.	30	52	—	—
1997-98	Darrell Walker, 11-38					
	Butch Carter, 5-28	8th/Central Div.	16	66	—	—
1998-99	Butch Carter	6th/Central Div.	23	27	—	—
1999-00	Butch Carter	3rd/Central Div.	45	37	0	3
2000-01	Lenny Wilkens	2nd/Central Div.	47	35	6	6
2001-02	Lenny Wilkens	T3rd/Central Div.	42	40	2	3
2002-03	Lenny Wilkens	7th/Central Div.	24	58	—	—
2003-04	Kevin O'Neill	6th/Central Div.	33	49	—	—

Totals. 281 425 8 12

FIRST-ROUND DRAFT PICKS

1995— Damon Stoudamire, Arizona
1996— Marcus Camby, Massachusetts
1997— Tracy McGrady, Mt. Zion Christian Academy (N.C.)
1998— Antawn Jamison, North Carolina
1999— Jonathan Bender, Picayune HS
     (Miss.)
     Aleksandar Radojevic, Barton County
     C.C. (Kan.)
2000— Morris Peterson, Michigan State
2001— Michael Bradley, Villanova
2002— Kareem Rush, Missouri
2003— Chris Bosh, Georgia Tech
2004— Rafael Araujo, Brigham Young

RETIRED NUMBERS

None

UTAH JAZZ

YEAR-BY-YEAR RECORDS

Season	Coach	Finish	REGULAR SEASON W	L	PLAYOFFS W	L
1974-75*	Scotty Robertson, 1-14					
	Elgin Baylor, 0-1					
	B. van Breda Kolff, 22-44	5th/Central Div.	23	59	—	—
1975-76*	Butch van Breda Kolff	4th/Central Div.	38	44	—	—
1976-77*	B. van Breda Kolff, 14-12					
	Elgin Baylor, 21-35	5th/Central Div.	35	47	—	—
1977-78*	Elgin Baylor	5th/Central Div.	39	43	—	—
1978-79*	Elgin Baylor	6th/Central Div.	26	56	—	—
1979-80	Tom Nissalke	5th/Midwest Div.	24	58	—	—
1980-81	Tom Nissalke	5th/Midwest Div.	28	54	—	—
1981-82	Tom Nissalke, 8-12					
	Frank Layden, 17-45	6th/Midwest Div.	25	57	—	—
1982-83	Frank Layden	5th/Midwest Div.	30	52	—	—
1983-84	Frank Layden	1st/Midwest Div.	45	37	5	6
1984-85	Frank Layden	T4th/Midwest Div.	41	41	4	6
1985-86	Frank Layden	4th/Midwest Div.	42	40	1	3
1986-87	Frank Layden	2nd/Midwest Div.	44	38	2	3
1987-88	Frank Layden	3rd/Midwest Div.	47	35	6	5
1988-89	Frank Layden, 11-6					
	Jerry Sloan, 40-25	1st/Midwest Div.	51	31	0	3
1989-90	Jerry Sloan	2nd/Midwest Div.	55	27	2	3
1990-91	Jerry Sloan	2nd/Midwest Div.	54	28	4	5
1991-92	Jerry Sloan	1st/Midwest Div.	55	27	9	7
1992-93	Jerry Sloan	3rd/Midwest Div.	47	35	2	3
1993-94	Jerry Sloan	3rd/Midwest Div.	53	29	8	8
1994-95	Jerry Sloan	2nd/Midwest Div.	60	22	2	3
1995-96	Jerry Sloan	2nd/Midwest Div.	55	27	10	8
1996-97	Jerry Sloan	1st/Midwest Div.	64	18	13	7
1997-98	Jerry Sloan	1st/Midwest Div.	62	20	13	7
1998-99	Jerry Sloan	T1st/Midwest Div.	37	13	5	6
1999-00	Jerry Sloan	1st/Midwest Div.	55	27	4	6
2000-01	Jerry Sloan	T2nd/Midwest Div.	53	29	2	3
2001-02	Jerry Sloan	4th/Midwest Div.	44	38	1	3
2002-03	Jerry Sloan	4th/Midwest Div.	47	35	1	4
2003-04	Jerry Sloan	7th/Midwest Div.	42	40	—	—
Totals.			1321	1107	94	99

*New Orleans Jazz.

FIRST-ROUND DRAFT PICKS

1974— None
1975— Rich Kelley, Stanford
1976— None
1977— None
1978— James Hardy, San Francisco
1979— Larry Knight, Loyola
1980— Darrell Griffith, Louisville
        John Duren, Georgetown
1981— Danny Schayes, Syracuse
1982— Dominique Wilkins, Georgia
1983— Thurl Bailey, North Carolina State
1984— John Stockton, Gonzaga
1985— Karl Malone, Louisiana Tech
1986— Dell Curry, Virginia Tech
1987— Jose Ortiz, Oregon State
1988— Eric Leckner, Wyoming
1989— Blue Edwards, East Carolina
1990— None
1991— Eric Murdock, Providence
1992— None
1993— Luther Wright, Seton Hall
1994— None
1995— Greg Ostertag, Kansas
1996— Martin Muursepp, Estonia
1997— Jacque Vaughn, Kansas
1998— Nazr Mohammed, Kentucky
1999— Quincy Lewis, Minnesota
        Andrei Kirilenko, Russia
        Scott Padgett, Kentucky
2000— DeShawn Stevenson, Washington
        Union HS (Calif.)
2001— Raul Lopez, Spain
2002— Ryan Humphrey, Notre Dame
2003— Aleksandar Pavlovic, Serbia &
        Montenegro
2004— Kris Humphries, Minnesota
        Kirk Snyder, Nevada
        Pavel Podkolzin, Russia

RETIRED NUMBERS

1 Frank Layden	35 Darrell Griffith
7 Pete Maravich	53 Mark Eaton
14 Jeff Hornacek	

WASHINGTON CAPITOLS

YEAR-BY-YEAR RECORDS

Season	Coach	Finish	REGULAR SEASON W	L	PLAYOFFS W	L
1946-47	Red Auerbach	1st/Eastern Div.	49	11	2	4
1947-48	Red Auerbach	T2nd/Western Div.	28	20	—	—
1948-49	Red Auerbach	1st/Eastern Div.	38	22	6	5
1949-50	Robert Feerick	3rd/Eastern Div.	32	36	0	2
1950-51*	Horace McKinney		10	25	—	—
Totals.			157	114	8	11

*Team disbanded January 9.

FIRST-ROUND DRAFT PICKS

1947— Dick O'Keefe, Santa Clara
1948— Not available
1949— Wallace Jones, Kentucky
1950— Dick Schnittker, Ohio State

WASHINGTON WIZARDS

YEAR-BY-YEAR RECORDS

Season	Coach	Finish	REGULAR SEASON W	L	PLAYOFFS W	L
1961-62*	Jim Pollard	5th/Western Div.	18	62	—	—
1962-63†	Jack McMahon, 12-26					
	Bob Leonard, 13-29	5th/Western Div.	25	55	—	—
1963-64‡	Bob Leonard	4th/Western Div.	31	49	—	—
1964-65‡	Buddy Jeannette	3rd/Western Div.	37	43	5	5
1965-66‡	Paul Seymour	2nd/Western Div.	38	42	0	3
1966-67‡	Mike Farmer, 1-8					
	Buddy Jeannette, 3-13					
	Gene Shue, 16-40	5th/Eastern Div.	20	61	—	—

FIRST-ROUND DRAFT PICKS

1961— Walt Bellamy, Indiana*
1962— Billy McGill, Utah
1963— Rod Thorn, West Virginia
1964— Gary Bradds, Ohio State
1965— None
1966— Jack Marin, Duke
1967— Earl Monroe, Winston-Salem
1968— Wes Unseld, Louisville
1969— Mike Davis, Virginia Union
1970— George Johnson, Stephen F. Austin

		REGULAR SEASON			PLAYOFFS	
Season	Coach	Finish	W	L	W	L
1967-68‡	Gene Shue	6th/Eastern Div.	36	46	—	—
1968-69‡	Gene Shue	1st/Eastern Div.	57	25	0	4
1969-70‡	Gene Shue	3rd/Eastern Div.	50	32	3	4
1970-71‡	Gene Shue	1st/Central Div.	42	40	8	10
1971-72‡	Gene Shue	1st/Central Div.	38	44	2	4
1972-73‡	Gene Shue	1st/Central Div.	52	30	1	4
1973-74§	K. C. Jones	1st/Central Div.	47	35	3	4
1974-75∞	K. C. Jones	1st/Central Div.	60	22	8	9
1975-76∞	K. C. Jones	2nd/Central Div.	48	34	3	4
1976-77∞	Dick Motta	2nd/Central Div.	48	34	4	5
1977-78∞	Dick Motta	2nd/Central Div.	44	38	14	7
1978-79∞	Dick Motta	1st/Atlantic Div.	54	28	9	10
1979-80∞	Dick Motta	T3rd/Atlantic Div.	39	43	0	2
1980-81∞	Gene Shue	4th/Atlantic Div.	39	43	—	—
1981-82∞	Gene Shue	4th/Atlantic Div.	43	39	3	4
1982-83∞	Gene Shue	5th/Atlantic Div.	42	40	—	—
1983-84∞	Gene Shue	5th/Atlantic Div.	35	47	1	3
1984-85∞	Gene Shue	4th/Atlantic Div.	40	42	1	3
1985-86∞	Gene Shue, 32-37					
	Kevin Loughery, 7-6	T3rd/Atlantic Div.	39	43	2	3
1986-87∞	Kevin Loughery	3rd/Atlantic Div.	42	40	0	3
1987-88∞	Kevin Loughery, 8-19					
	Wes Unseld, 30-25	T2nd/Atlantic Div.	38	44	2	3
1988-89∞	Wes Unseld	4th/Atlantic Div.	40	42	—	—
1989-90∞	Wes Unseld	4th/Atlantic Div.	31	51	—	—
1990-91∞	Wes Unseld	4th/Atlantic Div.	30	52	—	—
1991-92∞	Wes Unseld	6th/Atlantic Div.	25	57	—	—
1992-93∞	Wes Unseld	7th/Atlantic Div.	22	60	—	—
1993-94∞	Wes Unseld	7th/Atlantic Div.	24	58	—	—
1994-95∞	Jim Lynam	7th/Atlantic Div.	21	61	—	—
1995-96∞	Jim Lynam	4th/Atlantic Div.	39	43	—	—
1996-97∞	Jim Lynam, 22-24					
	Bob Staak, 0-1					
	Bernie Bickerstaff, 22-13	4th/Atlantic Div.	44	38	0	3
1997-98	Bernie Bickerstaff	4th/Atlantic Div.	42	40	—	—
1998-99	Bernie Bickerstaff, 13-19					
	Jim Brovelli, 5-13	6th/Atlantic Div.	18	32	—	—
1999-00	Gar Heard, 14-30					
	Darrell Walker, 15-23	7th/Atlantic Div.	29	53	—	—
2000-01	Leonard Hamilton	7th/Atlantic Div.	19	63	—	—
2001-02	Doug Collins	5th/Atlantic Div.	37	45	—	—
2002-03	Doug Collins	T5th/Atlantic Div.	37	45	—	—
2003-04	Eddie Jordan	6th?Atlantic Div.	25	57	—	—
Totals..............................			1585	1898	69	97

*Chicago Packers.
†Chicago Zephyrs.
‡Baltimore Bullets.
§Capital Bullets.
∞Washington Bullets.

1971—Phil Chenier, California†
    Stan Love, Oregon
1972—None
1973—Nick Weatherspoon, Illinois
1974—Len Elmore, Maryland
1975—Kevin Grevey, Kentucky
1976—Mitch Kupchak, North Carolina
    Larry Wright, Grambling
1977—Greg Ballard, Oregon
    Bo Ellis, Marquette
1978—Roger Phegley, Bradley
    Dave Corzine, DePaul
1979—None
1980—Wes Matthews, Wisconsin
1981—Frank Johnson, Wake Forest
1982—None
1983—Jeff Malone, Mississippi State
    Randy Wittman, Indiana
1984—Melvin Turpin, Kentucky
1985—Kenny Green, Wake Forest
1986—John Williams, Louisiana State
    Anthony Jones, UNLV
1987—Tyrone Bogues, Wake Forest
1988—Harvey Grant, Oklahoma
1989—Tom Hammonds, Georgia Tech
1990—None
1991—LaBradford Smith, Louisville
1992—Tom Gugliotta, N.C. State
1993—Calbert Cheaney, Indiana
1994—Juwan Howard, Michigan
1995—Rasheed Wallace, N. Carolina
1996—None
1997—None‡
1998—None
1999—Richard Hamilton, Connecticut
2000—None
2001—Kwame Brown, Glynn Acad. (Ga.)*
2002—Jared Jeffries, Indiana
    Juan Dixon, Maryland
2003—Jarvis Hayes, Georgia
2004—Devin Harris, Wisconsin
*First overall pick of draft.
†Chenier was selected in the 1971 supplementary draft of hardship cases. The Bullets had to forfeit their 1972 first-round choice.
‡The Wizards forfeited their 1997 first-round draft pick as compensation for re-signing free agent Juwan Howard in 1996.

RETIRED NUMBERS

11 Elvin Hayes
25 Gus Johnson
41 Wes Unseld

WATERLOO HAWKS

YEAR-BY-YEAR RECORDS

		REGULAR SEASON			PLAYOFFS	
Season	Coach	Finish	W	L	W	L
1949-50	Charles Shipp, 8-27					
	Jack Smiley, 11-16	5th/Western Div.	19	43	—	—

AWARD WINNERS

NBA MOST VALUABLE PLAYER
(Maurice Podoloff Trophy)
Selected by vote of NBA players until 1979-80; by writers and broadcasters since 1980-81.

1955-56— Bob Pettit, St. Louis	1971-72— Kareem Abdul-Jabbar, Milw.	1987-88— Michael Jordan, Chicago
1956-57— Bob Cousy, Boston	1972-73— Dave Cowens, Boston	1988-89— Magic Johnson, L.A. Lakers
1957-58— Bill Russell, Boston	1973-74— Kareem Abdul-Jabbar, Milw.	1989-90— Magic Johnson, L.A. Lakers
1958-59— Bob Pettit, St. Louis	1974-75— Bob McAdoo, Buffalo	1990-91— Michael Jordan, Chicago
1959-60— Wilt Chamberlain, Phil.	1975-76— Kareem Abdul-Jabbar, L.A.	1991-92— Michael Jordan, Chicago
1960-61— Bill Russell, Boston	1976-77— Kareem Abdul-Jabbar, L.A.	1992-93— Charles Barkley, Phoenix
1961-62— Bill Russell, Boston	1977-78— Bill Walton, Portland	1993-94— Hakeem Olajuwon, Houston
1962-63— Bill Russell, Boston	1978-79— Moses Malone, Houston	1994-95— David Robinson, San Antonio
1963-64— Oscar Robertson, Cincinnati	1979-80— Kareem Abdul-Jabbar, L.A.	1995-96— Michael Jordan, Chicago
1964-65— Bill Russell, Boston	1980-81— Julius Erving, Philadelphia	1996-97— Karl Malone, Utah
1965-66— Wilt Chamberlain, Phil.	1981-82— Moses Malone, Houston	1997-98— Michael Jordan, Chicago
1966-67— Wilt Chamberlain, Phil.	1982-83— Moses Malone, Philadelphia	1998-99— Karl Malone, Utah
1967-68— Wilt Chamberlain, Phil.	1983-84— Larry Bird, Boston	1999-00— Shaquille O'Neal, L.A. Lakers
1968-69— Wes Unseld, Baltimore	1984-85— Larry Bird, Boston	2000-01— Allen Iverson, Philadelphia
1969-70— Willis Reed, New York	1985-86— Larry Bird, Boston	2001-02— Tim Duncan, San Antonio
1970-71— Kareem Abdul-Jabbar, Milw.	1986-87— Magic Johnson, L.A. Lakers	2002-03—Tim Duncan, San Antonio
		2003-04—Kevin Garnett, Minnesota

NBA COACH OF THE YEAR
(Red Auerbach Trophy)
Selected by writers and broadcasters.

1962-63— Harry Gallatin, St. Louis	1976-77— Tom Nissalke, Houston	1990-91— Don Chaney, Houston
1963-64— Alex Hannum, San Francisco	1977-78— Hubie Brown, Atlanta	1991-92— Don Nelson, Golden State
1964-65— Red Auerbach, Boston	1978-79— Cotton Fitzsimmons, K.C.	1992-93— Pat Riley, New York
1965-66— Dolph Schayes, Philadelphia	1979-80— Bill Fitch, Boston	1993-94— Lenny Wilkens, Atlanta
1966-67— Johnny Kerr, Chicago	1980-81— Jack McKinney, Indiana	1994-95— Del Harris, L.A. Lakers
1967-68— Richie Guerin, St. Louis	1981-82— Gene Shue, Washington	1995-96— Phil Jackson, Chicago
1968-69— Gene Shue, Baltimore	1982-83— Don Nelson, Milwaukee	1996-97— Pat Riley, Miami
1969-70— Red Holzman, New York	1983-84— Frank Layden, Utah	1997-98— Larry Bird, Indiana
1970-71— Dick Motta, Chicago	1984-85— Don Nelson, Milwaukee	1998-99— Mike Dunleavy, Portland
1971-72— Bill Sharman, Los Angeles	1985-86— Mike Fratello, Atlanta	1999-00— Glenn "Doc" Rivers, Orlando
1972-73— Tom Heinsohn, Boston	1986-87— Mike Schuler, Portland	2000-01— Larry Brown, Philadelphia
1973-74— Ray Scott, Detroit	1987-88— Doug Moe, Denver	2001-02— Rick Carlisle, Detroit
1974-75— Phil Johnson, K.C./Omaha	1988-89— Cotton Fitzsimmons, Pho.	2002-03—Gregg Popovich, S. Antonio
1975-76— Bill Fitch, Cleveland	1989-90— Pat Riley, L.A. Lakers	2003-04—Hubie Brown, Memphis

GOT MILK? NBA ROOKIE OF THE YEAR
(Eddie Gottlieb Trophy)
Selected by writers and broadcasters.

1952-53— Don Meineke, Fort Wayne	1970-71— Dave Cowens, Boston	1987-88— Mark Jackson, New York
1953-54— Ray Felix, Baltimore	Geoff Petrie, Portland	1988-89— Mitch Richmond, Golden St.
1954-55— Bob Pettit, Milwaukee	1971-72— Sidney Wicks, Portland	1989-90— David Robinson, San Antonio
1955-56— Maurice Stokes, Rochester	1972-73— Bob McAdoo, Buffalo	1990-91— Derrick Coleman, New Jersey
1956-57— Tom Heinsohn, Boston	1973-74— Ernie DiGregorio, Buffalo	1991-92— Larry Johnson, Charlotte
1957-58— Woody Sauldsberry, Phil.	1974-75— Keith Wilkes, Golden State	1992-93— Shaquille O'Neal, Orlando
1958-59— Elgin Baylor, Minneapolis	1975-76— Alvan Adams, Phoenix	1993-94— Chris Webber, Golden State
1959-60— Wilt Chamberlain, Phil.	1976-77— Adrian Dantley, Buffalo	1994-95— Grant Hill, Detroit
1960-61— Oscar Robertson, Cincinnati	1977-78— Walter Davis, Phoenix	Jason Kidd, Dallas
1961-62— Walt Bellamy, Chicago	1978-79— Phil Ford, Kansas City	1995-96— Damon Stoudamire, Toronto
1962-63— Terry Dischinger, Chicago	1979-80— Larry Bird, Boston	1996-97— Allen Iverson, Philadelphia
1963-64— Jerry Lucas, Cincinnati	1980-81— Darrell Griffith, Utah	1997-98— Tim Duncan, San Antonio
1964-65— Willis Reed, New York	1981-82— Buck Williams, New Jersey	1998-99— Vince Carter, Toronto
1965-66— Rick Barry, San Francisco	1982-83— Terry Cummings, San Diego	1999-00— Elton Brand, Chicago
1966-67— Dave Bing, Detroit	1983-84— Ralph Sampson, Houston	Steve Francis, Houston
1967-68— Earl Monroe, Baltimore	1984-85— Michael Jordan, Chicago	2000-01— Mike Miller, Orlando
1968-69— Wes Unseld, Baltimore	1985-86— Patrick Ewing, New York	2001-02— Pau Gasol, Memphis
1969-70— Kareem Abdul-Jabbar, Milw.	1986-87— Chuck Person, Indiana	2002-03—Amare Stoudemire, Phoenix
		2003-04—LeBron James, Cleveland

HISTORY *Award winners*

NBA MOST IMPROVED PLAYER

Selected by writers and broadcasters.

1985-86— Alvin Robertson, San Ant.
1986-87— Dale Ellis, Seattle
1987-88— Kevin Duckworth, Portland
1988-89— Kevin Johnson, Phoenix
1989-90— Rony Seikaly, Miami
1990-91— Scott Skiles, Orlando
1991-92— Pervis Ellison, Washington

1992-93— Mahmoud Abdul-Rauf, Den.
1993-94— Don MacLean, Washington
1994-95— Dana Barros, Philadelphia
1995-96— Gheorghe Muresan, Was.
1996-97— Isaac Austin, Miami
1997-98— Alan Henderson, Atlanta
1998-99— Darrell Armstrong, Orlando

1999-00— Jalen Rose, Indiana
2000-01— Tracy McGrady, Orlando
2001-02— Jermaine O'Neal, Indiana
2002-03—Gilbert Arenas, Golden State
2003-04—Zach Randolph, Portland

NBA EXECUTIVE OF THE YEAR

Selected by NBA executives for The Sporting News.

1972-73— Joe Axelson, K.C./Omaha
1973-74— Eddie Donovan, Buffalo
1974-75— Dick Vertlieb, Golden State
1975-76— Jerry Colangelo, Phoenix
1976-77— Ray Patterson, Houston
1977-78— Angelo Drossos, San Ant.
1978-79— Bob Ferry, Washington
1979-80— Red Auerbach, Boston
1980-81— Jerry Colangelo, Phoenix
1981-82— Bob Ferry, Washington
1982-83— Zollie Volchok, Seattle

1983-84— Frank Layden, Utah
1984-85— Vince Boryla, Denver
1985-86— Stan Kasten, Atlanta
1986-87— Stan Kasten, Atlanta
1987-88— Jerry Krause, Chicago
1988-89— Jerry Colangelo, Phoenix
1989-90— Bob Bass, San Antonio
1990-91— Bucky Buckwalter, Portland
1991-92— Wayne Embry, Cleveland
1992-93— Jerry Colangelo, Phoenix
1993-94— Bob Whitsitt, Seattle

1994-95— Jerry West, L.A. Lakers
1995-96— Jerry Krause, Chicago
1996-97— Bob Bass, Charlotte
1997-98— Wayne Embry, Cleveland
1998-99— Geoff Petrie, Sacramento
1999-00— John Gabriel, Orlando
2000-01— Geoff Petrie, Sacramento
2001-02— Rod Thorn, New Jersey
2002-03—Joe Dumars, Detroit
2003-04—Jerry West, Memphis

J. WALTER KENNEDY CITIZENSHIP AWARD

Selected by the Pro Basketball Writers Association.

1974-75— Wes Unseld, Washington
1975-76— Slick Watts, Seattle
1976-77— Dave Bing, Washington
1977-78— Bob Lanier, Detroit
1978-79— Calvin Murphy, Houston
1979-80— Austin Carr, Cleveland
1980-81— Mike Glenn, New York
1981-82— Kent Benson, Detroit
1982-83— Julius Erving, Philadelphia
1983-84— Frank Layden, Utah
1984-85— Dan Issel, Denver

1985-86— Michael Cooper, L.A. Lakers
            Rory Sparrow, New York
1986-87— Isiah Thomas, Detroit
1987-88— Alex English, Denver
1988-89— Thurl Bailey, Utah
1989-90— Doc Rivers, Atlanta
1990-91— Kevin Johnson, Phoenix
1991-92— Magic Johnson, L.A. Lakers
1992-93— Terry Porter, Portland
1993-94— Joe Dumars, Detroit
1994-95— Joe O'Toole, Atlanta

1995-96— Chris Dudley, Portland
1996-97— P.J. Brown, Miami
1997-98— Steve Smith, Atlanta
1998-99— Brian Grant, Portland
1999-00— Vlade Divac, Sacramento
2000-01— Dikembe Mutombo, Phil.
2001-02— Alonzo Mourning, Miami
2002-03—David Robinson, S. Antonio
2003-04—Reggie Miller, Indiana

NBA DEFENSIVE PLAYER OF THE YEAR

Selected by writers and broadcasters.

1982-83— Sidney Moncrief, Milwaukee
1983-84— Sidney Moncrief, Milwaukee
1984-85— Mark Eaton, Utah
1985-86— Alvin Robertson, San Ant.
1986-87— Michael Cooper, L.A. Lakers
1987-88— Michael Jordan, Chicago
1988-89— Mark Eaton, Utah

1989-90— Dennis Rodman, Detroit
1990-91— Dennis Rodman, Detroit
1991-92— David Robinson, San Ant.
1992-93— Hakeem Olajuwon, Houston
1993-94— Hakeem Olajuwon, Houston
1994-95— Dikembe Mutombo, Denver
1995-96— Gary Payton, Seattle

1996-97— Dikembe Mutombo, Atlanta
1997-98— Dikembe Mutombo, Atlanta
1998-99— Alonzo Mourning, Miami
1999-00— Alonzo Mourning, Miami
2000-01— Dikembe Mutombo, Phil.
2001-02— Ben Wallace, Detroit
2002-03—Ben Wallace, Detroit
2003-04—Ron Artest, Indiana

NBA SIXTH MAN AWARD

Selected by writers and broadcasters.

1982-83— Bobby Jones, Philadelphia
1983-84— Kevin McHale, Boston
1984-85— Kevin McHale, Boston
1985-86— Bill Walton, Boston
1986-87— Ricky Pierce, Milwaukee
1987-88— Roy Tarpley, Dallas
1988-89— Eddie Johnson, Phoenix
1989-90— Ricky Pierce, Milwaukee

1990-91— Detlef Schrempf, Indiana
1991-92— Detlef Schrempf, Indiana
1992-93— Clifford Robinson, Portland
1993-94— Dell Curry, Charlotte
1994-95— Anthony Mason, New York
1995-96— Toni Kukoc, Chicago
1996-97— John Starks, New York
1997-98— Danny Manning, Phoenix

1998-99— Darrell Armstrong, Orlando
1999-00— Rodney Rogers, Phoenix
2000-01— Aaron McKie, Philadelphia
2001-02— Corliss Williamson, Detroit
2002-03—Bobby Jackson, Sacramento
2003-04—Antawn Jamison, Dallas

NBA SPORTSMANSHIP AWARD

Selected by writers and broadcasters.

Inaugural—Joe Dumars, Detroit
1996-97—Terrell Brandon, Cleveland
1996-97 Divisional winners:
Atlantic—Buck Williams, New York
Central—Terrell Brandon, Clev.
Midwest—Jeff Hornacek, Utah
Pacific—Mitch Richmond, Sac.
1997-98—Avery Johnson, San Antonio
1997-98 Divisional winners:
Atlantic—Allan Houston, New York
Central—Bobby Phills, Charlotte
Midwest—Avery Johnson, San Ant.
Pacific—Hersey Hawkins, Seattle
1998-99—Hersey Hawkins, Seattle
1998-99 Divisional winners:
Atlantic—Eric Snow, Philadelphia
Central—Vince Carter, Toronto

Midwest—Kevin Garnett, Minnesota
Pacific—Hersey Hawkins, Seattle
1999-00—Eric Snow, Philadelphia
1999-00 Divisional winners:
Atlantic—Eric Snow, Philadelphia
Central—LaPhonso Ellis, Atlanta
Midwest—Hakeem Olajuwon, Hou.
Pacific—Jason Kidd, Phoenix
2000-01—David Robinson, San Ant.
2000-01 Divisional winners:
Atlantic—Chris Whitney, Wash.
Central—Sam Perkins, Indiana
Midwest—David Robinson, San Ant.
Pacific—Antawn Jamison, G.S.
2001-02—Steve Smith, San Antonio
2001-02 Divisional winners:
Atlantic—LaPhonso Ellis, Miami

Central—P.J. Brown, Charlotte
Midwest—Steve Smith, San Antonio
Pacific—Shawn Marion, Phoenix
2002-03—Ray Allen, Seattle
2002-03 Divisional winners
Atlantic—Allan Houston, New York
Central—P.J. Brown, New Orleans
Midwest—Michael Finley, Dallas
Pacific—Ray Allen, Seattle
2003-04—P.J. Brown, New Orleans
2003-04 Divisional winners
Atlantic—Kerry Kittles, New Jersey
Central—P.J. Brown, New Orleans
Midwest—Shane Battier, Memphis
Pacific—Elton Brand, L.A. Clippers

IBM AWARD

Determined by computer formula.

1983-84— Magic Johnson, Los Ang.
1984-85— Michael Jordan, Chicago
1985-86— Charles Barkley, Philadelphia
1986-87— Charles Barkley, Philadelphia
1987-88— Charles Barkley, Philadelphia
1988-89— Michael Jordan, Chicago
1989-90— David Robinson, San Ant.

1990-91— David Robinson, San Ant.
1991-92— Dennis Rodman, Detroit
1992-93— Hakeem Olajuwon, Houston
1993-94— David Robinson, San Ant.
1994-95— David Robinson, San Ant.
1995-96— David Robinson, San Ant.
1996-97— Grant Hill, Detroit

1997-98— Karl Malone, Utah
1998-99— Dikembe Mutombo, Atlanta
1999-00— Shaquille O'Neal, L.A. Lakers
2000-01— Shaquille O'Neal, L.A. Lakers
2001-02— Tim Duncan, San Antonio

NBA FINALS MOST VALUABLE PLAYER

Selected by writers and broadcasters.

1969— Jerry West, Los Angeles
1970— Willis Reed, New York
1971— Kareem Abdul-Jabbar, Milw.
1972— Wilt Chamberlain, Los Angeles
1973— Willis Reed, New York
1974— John Havlicek, Boston
1975— Rick Barry, Golden State
1976— Jo Jo White, Boston
1977— Bill Walton, Portland
1978— Wes Unseld, Washington
1979— Dennis Johnson, Seattle
1980— Magic Johnson, Los Angeles

1981— Cedric Maxwell, Boston
1982— Magic Johnson, Los Angeles
1983— Moses Malone, Philadelphia
1984— Larry Bird, Boston
1985— K. Abdul-Jabbar, L.A. Lakers
1986— Larry Bird, Boston
1987— Magic Johnson, L.A. Lakers
1988— James Worthy, L.A. Lakers
1989— Joe Dumars, Detroit
1990— Isiah Thomas, Detroit
1991— Michael Jordan, Chicago
1992— Michael Jordan, Chicago

1993— Michael Jordan, Chicago
1994— Hakeem Olajuwon, Houston
1995— Hakeem Olajuwon, Houston
1996— Michael Jordan, Chicago
1997— Michael Jordan, Chicago
1998— Michael Jordan, Chicago
1999— Tim Duncan, San Antonio
2000— Shaquille O'Neal, L.A. Lakers
2001— Shaquille O'Neal, L.A. Lakers
2002— Shaquille O'Neal, L.A. Lakers
2003— Tim Duncan, San Antonio
2004— Chauncey Billups, Detroit

ALL-NBA TEAMS

Selected by writers and broadcasters.

1946-47
FIRST
Joe Fulks, Philadelphia
Bob Feerick, Washington
Stan Miasek, Detroit
Bones McKinney, Washington
Max Zaslofsky, Chicago
SECOND
Ernie Calverley, Providence
Frank Baumholtz, Cleveland
John Logan, St. Louis
Chuck Halbert, Chicago
Fred Scolari, Washington

1947-48
FIRST
Joe Fulks, Philadelphia
Max Zaslofsky, Chicago
Ed Sadowski, Boston
Howie Dallmar, Philadelphia
Bob Feerick, Washington

SECOND
John Logan, St. Louis
Carl Braun, New York
Stan Miasek, Chicago
Fred Scolari, Washington
Buddy Jeannette, Baltimore

1948-49
FIRST
George Mikan, Minneapolis
Joe Fulks, Philadelphia
Bob Davies, Rochester
Max Zaslofsky, Chicago
Jim Pollard, Minneapolis
SECOND
Arnie Risen, Rochester
Bob Feerick, Washington
Bones McKinney, Washington
Ken Sailors, Providence
John Logan, St. Louis

1949-50
FIRST
George Mikan, Minneapolis
Jim Pollard, Minneapolis
Alex Groza, Indianapolis
Bob Davies, Rochester
Max Zaslofsky, Chicago
SECOND
Frank Brian, Anderson
Fred Schaus, Fort Wayne
Dolph Schayes, Syracuse
Al Cervi, Syracuse
Ralph Beard, Indianapolis

1950-51
FIRST
George Mikan, Minneapolis
Alex Groza, Indianapolis
Ed Macauley, Boston
Bob Davies, Rochester
Ralph Beard, Indianapolis

SECOND
Dolph Schayes, Syracuse
Frank Brian, Tri-Cities
Vern Mikkelsen, Minneapolis
Joe Fulks, Philadelphia
Dick McGuire, New York

1951-52
FIRST
George Mikan, Minneapolis
Ed Macauley, Boston
Paul Arizin, Philadelphia
Bob Cousy, Boston
Bob Davies, Rochester
Dolph Schayes, Syracuse
SECOND
Larry Foust, Fort Wayne
Vern Mikkelsen, Minneapolis
Jim Pollard, Minneapolis
Bob Wanzer, Rochester
Andy Phillip, Philadelphia

1952-53
FIRST
George Mikan, Minneapolis
Bob Cousy, Boston
Neil Johnston, Philadelphia
Ed Macauley, Boston
Dolph Schayes, Syracuse
SECOND
Bill Sharman, Boston
Vern Mikkelsen, Minneapolis
Bob Wanzer, Rochester
Bob Davies, Rochester
Andy Phillip, Philadelphia

1953-54
FIRST
Bob Cousy, Boston
Neil Johnston, Philadelphia
George Mikan, Minneapolis
Dolph Schayes, Syracuse
Harry Gallatin, New York
SECOND
Ed Macauley, Boston
Jim Pollard, Minneapolis
Carl Braun, New York
Bob Wanzer, Rochester
Paul Seymour, Syracuse

1954-55
FIRST
Neil Johnston, Philadelphia
Bob Cousy, Boston
Dolph Schayes, Syracuse
Bob Pettit, Milwaukee
Larry Foust, Fort Wayne
SECOND
Vern Mikkelsen, Minneapolis
Harry Gallatin, New York
Paul Seymour, Syracuse
Slater Martin, Minneapolis
Bill Sharman, Boston

1955-56
FIRST
Bob Pettit, St. Louis
Paul Arizin, Philadelphia
Neil Johnston, Philadelphia
Bob Cousy, Boston
Bill Sharman, Boston

SECOND
Dolph Schayes, Syracuse
Maurice Stokes, Rochester
Clyde Lovellette, Minneapolis
Slater Martin, Minneapolis
Jack George, Philadelphia

1956-57
FIRST
Paul Arizin, Philadelphia
Dolph Schayes, Syracuse
Bob Pettit, St. Louis
Bob Cousy, Boston
Bill Sharman, Boston
SECOND
George Yardley, Fort Wayne
Maurice Stokes, Rochester
Neil Johnston, Philadelphia
Dick Garmaker, Minneapolis
Slater Martin, St. Louis

1957-58
FIRST
Dolph Schayes, Syracuse
George Yardley, Detroit
Bob Pettit, St. Louis
Bob Cousy, Boston
Bill Sharman, Boston
SECOND
Cliff Hagan, St. Louis
Maurice Stokes, Cincinnati
Bill Russell, Boston
Tom Gola, Philadelphia
Slater Martin, St. Louis

1958-59
FIRST
Bob Pettit, St. Louis
Elgin Baylor, Minneapolis
Bill Russell, Boston
Bob Cousy, Boston
Bill Sharman, Boston
SECOND
Paul Arizin, Philadelphia
Cliff Hagan, St. Louis
Dolph Schayes, Syracuse
Slater Martin, St. Louis
Richie Guerin, New York

1959-60
FIRST
Bob Pettit, St. Louis
Elgin Baylor, Minneapolis
Wilt Chamberlain, Philadelphia
Bob Cousy, Boston
Gene Shue, Detroit
SECOND
Jack Twyman, Cincinnati
Dolph Schayes, Syracuse
Bill Russell, Boston
Richie Guerin, New York
Bill Sharman, Boston

1960-61
FIRST
Elgin Baylor, Los Angeles
Bob Pettit, St. Louis
Wilt Chamberlain, Philadelphia
Bob Cousy, Boston
Oscar Robertson, Cincinnati

SECOND
Dolph Schayes, Syracuse
Tom Heinsohn, Boston
Bill Russell, Boston
Larry Costello, Syracuse
Gene Shue, Detroit

1961-62
FIRST
Bob Pettit, St. Louis
Elgin Baylor, Los Angeles
Wilt Chamberlain, Philadelphia
Jerry West, Los Angeles
Oscar Robertson, Cincinnati
SECOND
Tom Heinsohn, Boston
Jack Twyman, Cincinnati
Bill Russell, Boston
Richie Guerin, New York
Bob Cousy, Boston

1962-63
FIRST
Elgin Baylor, Los Angeles
Bob Pettit, St. Louis
Bill Russell, Boston
Oscar Robertson, Cincinnati
Jerry West, Los Angeles
SECOND
Tom Heinsohn, Boston
Bailey Howell, Detroit
Wilt Chamberlain, San Francisco
Bob Cousy, Boston
Hal Greer, Syracuse

1963-64
FIRST
Bob Pettit, St. Louis
Elgin Baylor, Los Angeles
Wilt Chamberlain, San Francisco
Oscar Robertson, Cincinnati
Jerry West, Los Angeles
SECOND
Tom Heinsohn, Boston
Jerry Lucas, Cincinnati
Bill Russell, Boston
John Havlicek, Boston
Hal Greer, Philadelphia

1964-65
FIRST
Elgin Baylor, Los Angeles
Jerry Lucas, Cincinnati
Bill Russell, Boston
Oscar Robertson, Cincinnati
Jerry West, Los Angeles
SECOND
Bob Pettit, St. Louis
Gus Johnson, Baltimore
Wilt Chamberlain, S.F.-Phila.
Sam Jones, Boston
Hal Greer, Philadelphia

1965-66
FIRST
Rick Barry, San Francisco
Jerry Lucas, Cincinnati
Wilt Chamberlain, Philadelphia
Oscar Robertson, Cincinnati
Jerry West, Los Angeles

SECOND
John Havlicek, Boston
Gus Johnson, Baltimore
Bill Russell, Boston
Sam Jones, Boston
Hal Greer, Philadelphia

1966-67
FIRST
Rick Barry, San Francisco
Elgin Baylor, Los Angeles
Wilt Chamberlain, Philadelphia
Jerry West, Los Angeles
Oscar Robertson, Cincinnati
SECOND
Willis Reed, New York
Jerry Lucas, Cincinnati
Bill Russell, Boston
Hal Greer, Philadelphia
Sam Jones, Boston

1967-68
FIRST
Elgin Baylor, Los Angeles
Jerry Lucas, Cincinnati
Wilt Chamberlain, Philadelphia
Dave Bing, Detroit
Oscar Robertson, Cincinnati
SECOND
Willis Reed, New York
John Havlicek, Boston
Bill Russell, Boston
Hal Greer, Philadelphia
Jerry West, Los Angeles

1968-69
FIRST
Billy Cunningham, Philadelphia
Elgin Baylor, Los Angeles
Wes Unseld, Baltimore
Earl Monroe, Baltimore
Oscar Robertson, Cincinnati
SECOND
John Havlicek, Boston
Dave DeBusschere, Detroit-New York
Willis Reed, New York
Hal Greer, Philadelphia
Jerry West, Los Angeles

1969-70
FIRST
Billy Cunningham, Philadelphia
Connie Hawkins, Phoenix
Willis Reed, New York
Jerry West, Los Angeles
Walt Frazier, New York
SECOND
John Havlicek, Boston
Gus Johnson, Baltimore
Kareem Abdul-Jabbar, Milwaukee
Lou Hudson, Atlanta
Oscar Robertson, Cincinnati

1970-71
FIRST
John Havlicek, Boston
Billy Cunningham, Philadelphia
Kareem Abdul-Jabbar, Milwaukee
Jerry West, Los Angeles
Dave Bing, Detroit

SECOND
Gus Johnson, Baltimore
Bob Love, Chicago
Willis Reed, New York
Walt Frazier, New York
Oscar Robertson, Milwaukee

1971-72
FIRST
John Havlicek, Boston
Spencer Haywood, Seattle
Kareem Abdul-Jabbar, Milwaukee
Jerry West, Los Angeles
Walt Frazier, New York
SECOND
Bob Love, Chicago
Billy Cunningham, Philadelphia
Wilt Chamberlain, Los Angeles
Nate Archibald, Cincinnati
Archie Clark, Phila.-Balt.

1972-73
FIRST
John Havlicek, Boston
Spencer Haywood, Seattle
Kareem Abdul-Jabbar, Milwaukee
Nate Archibald, Kansas City/Omaha
Jerry West, Los Angeles
SECOND
Elvin Hayes, Baltimore
Rick Barry, Golden State
Dave Cowens, Boston
Walt Frazier, New York
Pete Maravich, Atlanta

1973-74
FIRST
John Havlicek, Boston
Rick Barry, Golden State
Kareem Abdul-Jabbar, Milwaukee
Walt Frazier, New York
Gail Goodrich, Los Angeles
SECOND
Elvin Hayes, Capital
Spencer Haywood, Seattle
Bob McAdoo, Buffalo
Dave Bing, Detroit
Norm Van Lier, Chicago

1974-75
FIRST
Rick Barry, Golden State
Elvin Hayes, Washington
Bob McAdoo, Buffalo
Nate Archibald, Kansas City/Omaha
Walt Frazier, New York
SECOND
John Havlicek, Boston
Spencer Haywood, Seattle
Dave Cowens, Boston
Phil Chenier, Washington
Jo Jo White, Boston

1975-76
FIRST
Rick Barry, Golden State
George McGinnis, Philadelphia
Kareem Abdul-Jabbar, Los Angeles
Nate Archibald, Kansas City
Pete Maravich, New Orleans

SECOND
Elvin Hayes, Washington
John Havlicek, Boston
Dave Cowens, Boston
Randy Smith, Buffalo
Phil Smith, Golden State

1976-77
FIRST
Elvin Hayes, Washington
David Thompson, Denver
Kareem Abdul-Jabbar, Los Angeles
Pete Maravich, New Orleans
Paul Westphal, Phoenix
SECOND
Julius Erving, Philadelphia
George McGinnis, Philadelphia
Bill Walton, Portland
George Gervin, San Antonio
Jo Jo White, Boston

1977-78
FIRST
Leonard Robinson, New Orleans
Julius Erving, Philadelphia
Bill Walton, Portland
George Gervin, San Antonio
David Thompson, Denver
SECOND
Walter Davis, Phoenix
Maurice Lucas, Portland
Kareem Abdul-Jabbar, Los Angeles
Paul Westphal, Phoenix
Pete Maravich, New Orleans

1978-79
FIRST
Marques Johnson, Milwaukee
Elvin Hayes, Washington
Moses Malone, Houston
George Gervin, San Antonio
Paul Westphal, Phoenix
SECOND
Walter Davis, Phoenix
Bobby Dandridge, Washington
Kareem Abdul-Jabbar, Los Angeles
World B. Free, San Diego
Phil Ford, Kansas City

1979-80
FIRST
Julius Erving, Philadelphia
Larry Bird, Boston
Kareem Abdul-Jabbar, Los Angeles
George Gervin, San Antonio
Paul Westphal, Phoenix
SECOND
Dan Roundfield, Atlanta
Marques Johnson, Milwaukee
Moses Malone, Houston
Dennis Johnson, Seattle
Gus Williams, Seattle

1980-81
FIRST
Julius Erving, Philadelphia
Larry Bird, Boston
Kareem Abdul-Jabbar, Los Angeles
George Gervin, San Antonio
Dennis Johnson, Phoenix

SECOND
Marques Johnson, Milwaukee
Adrian Dantley, Utah
Moses Malone, Houston
Otis Birdsong, Kansas City
Nate Archibald, Boston

1981-82
FIRST
Larry Bird, Boston
Julius Erving, Philadelphia
Moses Malone, Houston
George Gervin, San Antonio
Gus Williams, Seattle
SECOND
Alex English, Denver
Bernard King, Golden State
Robert Parish, Boston
Magic Johnson, Los Angeles
Sidney Moncrief, Milwaukee

1982-83
FIRST
Larry Bird, Boston
Julius Erving, Philadelphia
Moses Malone, Philadelphia
Magic Johnson, Los Angeles
Sidney Moncrief, Milwaukee
SECOND
Alex English, Denver
Buck Williams, New Jersey
Kareem Abdul-Jabbar, Los Angeles
George Gervin, San Antonio
Isiah Thomas, Detroit

1983-84
FIRST
Larry Bird, Boston
Bernard King, New York
Kareem Abdul-Jabbar, Los Angeles
Magic Johnson, Los Angeles
Isiah Thomas, Detroit
SECOND
Julius Erving, Philadelphia
Adrian Dantley, Utah
Moses Malone, Philadelphia
Sidney Moncrief, Milwaukee
Jim Paxson, Portland

1984-85
FIRST
Larry Bird, Boston
Bernard King, New York
Moses Malone, Philadelphia
Magic Johnson, L.A. Lakers
Isiah Thomas, Detroit
SECOND
Terry Cummings, Milwaukee
Ralph Sampson, Houston
Kareem Abdul-Jabbar, L.A. Lakers
Michael Jordan, Chicago
Sidney Moncrief, Milwaukee

1985-86
FIRST
Larry Bird, Boston
Dominique Wilkins, Atlanta
Kareem Abdul-Jabbar, L.A. Lakers
Magic Johnson, L.A. Lakers
Isiah Thomas, Detroit

SECOND
Charles Barkley, Philadelphia
Alex English, Denver
Hakeem Olajuwon, Houston
Sidney Moncrief, Milwaukee
Alvin Robertson, San Antonio

1986-87
FIRST
Larry Bird, Boston
Kevin McHale, Boston
Hakeem Olajuwon, Houston
Magic Johnson, L.A. Lakers
Michael Jordan, Chicago
SECOND
Dominique Wilkins, Atlanta
Charles Barkley, Philadelphia
Moses Malone, Washington
Isiah Thomas, Detroit
Fat Lever, Denver

1987-88
FIRST
Larry Bird, Boston
Charles Barkley, Philadelphia
Hakeem Olajuwon, Houston
Michael Jordan, Chicago
Magic Johnson, L.A. Lakers
SECOND
Karl Malone, Utah
Dominique Wilkins, Atlanta
Patrick Ewing, New York
Clyde Drexler, Portland
John Stockton, Utah

1988-89
FIRST
Karl Malone, Utah
Charles Barkley, Philadelphia
Hakeem Olajuwon, Houston
Magic Johnson, L.A. Lakers
Michael Jordan, Chicago
SECOND
Tom Chambers, Phoenix
Chris Mullin, Golden State
Patrick Ewing, New York
John Stockton, Utah
Kevin Johnson, Phoenix
THIRD
Dominique Wilkins, Atlanta
Terry Cummings, Milwaukee
Robert Parish, Boston
Dale Ellis, Seattle
Mark Price, Cleveland

1989-90
FIRST
Karl Malone, Utah
Charles Barkley, Philadelphia
Patrick Ewing, New York
Magic Johnson, L.A. Lakers
Michael Jordan, Chicago
SECOND
Larry Bird, Boston
Tom Chambers, Phoenix
Hakeem Olajuwon, Houston
John Stockton, Utah
Kevin Johnson, Phoenix
THIRD
James Worthy, L.A. Lakers
Chris Mullin, Golden State
David Robinson, San Antonio
Clyde Drexler, Portland
Joe Dumars, Detroit

1990-91
FIRST
Karl Malone, Utah
Charles Barkley, Philadelphia
David Robinson, San Antonio
Michael Jordan, Chicago
Magic Johnson, L.A. Lakers
SECOND
Dominique Wilkins, Atlanta
Chris Mullin, Golden State
Patrick Ewing, New York
Kevin Johnson, Phoenix
Clyde Drexler, Portland
THIRD
James Worthy, L.A. Lakers
Bernard King, Washington
Hakeem Olajuwon, Houston
John Stockton, Utah
Joe Dumars, Detroit

1991-92
FIRST
Karl Malone, Utah
Chris Mullin, Golden State
David Robinson, San Antonio
Michael Jordan, Chicago
Clyde Drexler, Portland
SECOND
Scottie Pippen, Chicago
Charles Barkley, Philadelphia
Patrick Ewing, New York
Tim Hardaway, Golden State
John Stockton, Utah
THIRD
Dennis Rodman, Detroit
Kevin Willis, Atlanta
Brad Daugherty, Cleveland
Mark Price, Cleveland
Kevin Johnson, Phoenix

1992-93
FIRST
Charles Barkley, Phoenix
Karl Malone, Utah
Hakeem Olajuwon, Houston
Michael Jordan, Chicago
Mark Price, Cleveland
SECOND
Dominique Wilkins, Atlanta
Larry Johnson, Charlotte
Patrick Ewing, New York
John Stockton, Utah
Joe Dumars, Detroit
THIRD
Scottie Pippen, Chicago
Derrick Coleman, New Jersey
David Robinson, San Antonio
Tim Hardaway, Golden State
Drazen Petrovic, New Jersey

1993-94
FIRST
Scottie Pippen, Chicago
Karl Malone, Utah
Hakeem Olajuwon, Houston
John Stockton, Utah
Latrell Sprewell, Golden State
SECOND
Shawn Kemp, Seattle
Charles Barkley, Phoenix
David Robinson, San Antonio
Mitch Richmond, Sacramento
Kevin Johnson, Phoenix

THIRD
Derrick Coleman, New Jersey
Dominique Wilkins, Atl.-LAC
Shaquille O'Neal, Orlando
Mark Price, Cleveland
Gary Payton, Seattle

1994-95

FIRST
Scottie Pippen, Chicago
Karl Malone, Utah
David Robinson, San Antonio
John Stockton, Utah
Anfernee Hardaway, Orlando
SECOND
Shawn Kemp, Seattle
Charles Barkley, Phoenix
Shaquille O'Neal, Orlando
Mitch Richmond, Sacramento
Gary Payton, Seattle
THIRD
Detlef Schrempf, Seattle
Dennis Rodman, San Antonio
Hakeem Olajuwon, Houston
Reggie Miller, Indiana
Clyde Drexler, Portland-Houston

1995-96

FIRST
Scottie Pippen, Chicago
Karl Malone, Utah
David Robinson, San Antonio
Michael Jordan, Chicago
Anfernee Hardaway, Orlando
SECOND
Shawn Kemp, Seattle
Grant Hill, Detroit
Hakeem Olajuwon, Houston
Gary Payton, Seattle
John Stockton, Utah
THIRD
Charles Barkley, Phoenix
Juwan Howard, Washington
Shaquille O'Neal, Orlando
Mitch Richmond, Sacramento
Reggie Miller, Indiana

1996-97

FIRST
Grant Hill, Detroit
Karl Malone, Utah
Hakeem Olajuwon, Houston
Michael Jordan, Chicago
Tim Hardaway, Miami
SECOND
Scottie Pippen, Chicago
Glen Rice, Charlotte
Patrick Ewing, New York
Gary Payton, Seattle
Mitch Richmond, Sacramento
THIRD
Anthony Mason, Charlotte
Vin Baker, Milwaukee
Shaquille O'Neal, L.A. Lakers
John Stockton, Utah
Anfernee Hardaway, Orlando

1997-98

FIRST
Karl Malone, Utah
Tim Duncan, San Antonio
Shaquille O'Neal, L.A. Lakers

Michael Jordan, Chicago
Gary Payton, Seattle
SECOND
Grant Hill, Detroit
Vin Baker, Seattle
David Robinson, San Antonio
Tim Hardaway, Miami
Rod Strickland, Washington
THIRD
Scottie Pippen, Chicago
Glen Rice, Charlotte
Dikembe Mutombo, Atlanta
Mitch Richmond, Sacramento
Reggie Miller, Indiana

1998-99

FIRST
Karl Malone, Utah
Tim Duncan, San Antonio
Alonzo Mourning, Miami
Allen Iverson, Philadelphia
Jason Kidd, Phoenix
SECOND
Chris Webber, Sacramento
Grant Hill, Detroit
Shaquille O'Neal, L.A. Lakers
Gary Payton, Seattle
Tim Hardaway, Miami
THIRD
Kevin Garnett, Minnesota
Antonio McDyess, Denver
Hakeem Olajuwon, Houston
Kobe Bryant, L.A. Lakers
John Stockton, Utah

1999-2000

FIRST
Kevin Garnett, Minnesota
Tim Duncan, San Antonio
Shaquille O'Neal, L.A. Lakers
Gary Payton, Seattle
Jason Kidd, Phoenix
SECOND
Karl Malone, Utah
Grant Hill, Detroit
Alonzo Mourning, Miami
Allen Iverson, Philadelphia
Kobe Bryant, L.A. Lakers
THIRD
Chris Webber, Sacramento
Vince Carter, Toronto
David Robinson, San Antonio
Eddie Jones, Charlotte
Stephon Marbury, New Jersey

2000-01

FIRST
Tim Duncan, San Antonio
Chris Webber, Sacramento
Shaquille O'Neal, L.A. Lakers
Allen Iverson, Philadelphia
Jason Kidd, Phoenix
SECOND
Kevin Garnett, Minnesota
Vince Carter, Toronto
Dikembe Mutombo, Atl.-Phil.
Kobe Bryant, L.A. Lakers
Tracy McGrady, Orlando
THIRD
Karl Malone, Utah
Dirk Nowitzki, Dallas

David Robinson, San Antonio
Gary Payton, Seattle
Ray Allen, Milwaukee

2001-02

FIRST
Tim Duncan, San Antonio
Tracy McGrady, Orlando
Shaquille O'Neal, L.A. Lakers
Jason Kidd, New Jersey
Kobe Bryant, L.A. Lakers
SECOND
Kevin Garnett, Minnesota
Chris Webber, Sacramento
Dirk Nowitzki, Dallas
Gary Payton, Seattle
Allen Iverson, Philadelphia
THIRD
Ben Wallace, Detroit
Jermaine O'Neal, Indiana
Dikembe Mutombo, Philadelphia
Paul Pierce, Boston
Steve Nash, Dallas

2002-03

FIRST
Tim Duncan, San Antonio
Kevin Garnett, Minnesota
Shaquille O'Neal, L.A. Lakers
Kobe Bryant, L.A. Lakers
Tracy McGrady, Orlando
SECOND
Dirk Nowitzki, Dallas
Chris Webber, Sacramento
Ben Wallace, Detroit
Jason Kidd, New Jersey
Allen Iverson, Philadelphia
THIRD
Paul Pierce, Boston
Jamal Mashburn, New Orleans
Jermaine O'Neal, Indiana
Stephon Marbury, Phoenix
Steve Nash, Dallas

2003-04

FIRST
Kevin Garnett, Minnesota
Tim Duncan, San Antonio
Shaquille O'Neal, L.A. Lakers
Kobe Bryant, L.A. Lakers
Jason Kidd, New Jersey
SECOND
Jermaine O'Neal, Indiana
Peja Stojakovic, Sacramento
Ben Wallace, Detroit
Sam Cassell, Minnesota
Tracy McGrady, Orlando
THIRD
Dirk Nowitzki, Dallas
Ron Artest, Indiana
Yao Ming, Houston
Michael Redd, Milwaukee
Baron Davis, New Orleans

PLAYERS WHO HAVE MADE ALL-NBA TEAMS

(Official All-NBA teams at end of season; active 2003-04 players in CAPS.)

Player	1st Team	2nd	3rd
KARL MALONE	11	2	1
Kareem Abdul-Jabbar	10	5	0
Bob Cousy	10	2	0
Jerry West	10	2	0
Michael Jordan	10	1	0
Bob Pettit	10	1	0
Elgin Baylor	10	0	0
Oscar Robertson	9	2	0
Larry Bird	9	1	0
Magic Johnson	9	1	0
Wilt Chamberlain	7	3	0
TIM DUNCAN	7	0	0
Dolph Schayes	6	6	0
Hakeem Olajuwon	6	3	3
SHAQUILLE O'NEAL	6	2	3
George Mikan	6	0	0
Charles Barkley	5	5	1
Julius Erving	5	2	0
George Gervin	5	2	0
Rick Barry	5	1	0
JASON KIDD	5	1	0
John Havlicek	4	7	0
Moses Malone	4	4	0
Bill Sharman	4	3	0
David Robinson	4	2	4
Walt Frazier	4	2	0
Bob Davies	4	1	0
Neil Johnston	4	1	0
Max Zaslofsky	4	0	0
Bill Russell	3	8	0
Elvin Hayes	3	3	0
SCOTTIE PIPPEN	3	2	2
KOBE BRYANT	3	2	1
KEVIN GARNETT	3	2	1
Nate Archibald	3	2	0
Jerry Lucas	3	2	0
Isiah Thomas	3	2	0
Paul Arizin	3	1	0
Billy Cunningham	3	1	0
Joe Fulks	3	1	0
Ed Macauley	3	1	0
Paul Westphal	3	1	0
John Stockton	2	6	3
GARY PAYTON	2	5	2
ALLEN IVERSON	2	3	0
Spencer Haywood	2	2	0
Pete Maravich	2	2	0
TRACY McGRADY	2	2	0
Jim Pollard	2	2	0
Bernard King	2	1	1
Dave Bing	2	1	0
Bob Feerick	2	1	0
ANFERNEE HARDAWAY	2	0	1
Alex Groza	2	0	0
David Thompson	2	0	0
Patrick Ewing	1	6	0
Dominique Wilkins	1	4	2
GRANT HILL	1	4	0
Sidney Moncrief	1	4	0
Willis Reed	1	4	0
Clyde Drexler	1	2	2
Tim Hardaway	1	3	1
CHRIS WEBBER	1	3	1
Chris Mullin	1	2	1
Marques Johnson	1	2	0
Shawn Kemp	1	2	0
Ralph Beard	1	1	0
Larry Foust	1	1	0
Harry Gallatin	1	1	0
Dennis Johnson	1	1	0
Bob McAdoo	1	1	0
George McGinnis	1	1	0
Bones McKinney	1	1	0
Stan Miasek	1	1	0
Alonzo Mourning	1	1	0
Gene Shue	1	1	0
Bill Walton	1	1	0
Gus Williams	1	1	0
George Yardley	1	1	0
Mark Price	1	0	3
Howie Dallmar	1	0	0
Gail Goodrich	1	0	0
Connie Hawkins	1	0	0
Kevin McHale	1	0	0
Earl Monroe	1	0	0
Truck Robinson	1	0	0
LATRELL SPREWELL	1	0	0
Wes Unseld	1	0	0
Hal Greer	0	7	0
Slater Martin	0	5	0
Kevin Johnson	0	4	1
Tom Heinsohn	0	4	0
Gus Johnson	0	4	0
Vern Mikkelsen	0	4	0
MITCH RICHMOND	0	3	2
Dave Cowens	0	3	0
Alex English	0	3	0
Richie Guerin	0	3	0
Sam Jones	0	3	0
John Logan	0	3	0
Maurice Stokes	0	3	0
Bob Wanzer	0	3	0
DIRK NOWITZKI	0	2	2
Carl Braun	0	2	0
Frank Brian	0	2	0
Tom Chambers	0	2	0
Adrian Dantley	0	2	0
Walter Davis	0	2	0
Cliff Hagan	0	2	0
Bob Love	0	2	0
Andy Phillip	0	2	0
Fred Scolari	0	2	0
Paul Seymour	0	2	0
Jack Twyman	0	2	0
Jo Jo White	0	2	0
Joe Dumars	0	1	2
DIKEMBE MUTOMBO	0	1	2
JERMAINE O'NEAL	0	1	2
VIN BAKER	0	1	1
VINCE CARTER	0	1	1
Terry Cummings	0	1	1
Robert Parish	0	1	1
GLEN RICE	0	1	1
BEN WALLACE	0	1	1
Frank Baumholtz	0	1	0
Otis Birdsong	0	1	0
Ernie Calverley	0	1	0
SAM CASSELL	0	1	0
Al Cervi	0	1	0
Phil Chenier	0	1	0
Archie Clark	0	1	0
Larry Costello	0	1	0
Bobby Dandridge	0	1	0
Dave DeBusschere	0	1	0
Phil Ford	0	1	0
World B. Free	0	1	0
Dick Garmaker	0	1	0
Jack George	0	1	0
Tom Gola	0	1	0
Chuck Halbert	0	1	0
Bailey Howell	0	1	0
Lou Hudson	0	1	0
Buddy Jeannette	0	1	0
Larry Johnson	0	1	0
Fat Lever	0	1	0
Clyde Lovellette	0	1	0
Maurice Lucas	0	1	0
Dick McGuire	0	1	0
Jim Paxson	0	1	0
Arnie Risen	0	1	0
Alvin Robertson	0	1	0
Dan Roundfield	0	1	0
Ken Sailors	0	1	0
Ralph Sampson	0	1	0
Fred Schaus	0	1	0
Phil Smith	0	1	0
Randy Smith	0	1	0
PEJA STOJAKOVIC	0	1	0
ROD STRICKLAND	0	1	0
Norm Van Lier	0	1	0
Buck Williams	0	1	0
REGGIE MILLER	0	0	3
DERRICK COLEMAN	0	0	2
STEPHON MARBURY	0	0	2
STEVE NASH	0	0	2
PAUL PIERCE	0	0	2
Dennis Rodman	0	0	2
James Worthy	0	0	2
RAY ALLEN	0	0	1
RON ARTEST	0	0	1
Brad Daugherty	0	0	1
BARON DAVIS	0	0	1
Dale Ellis	0	0	1
JUWAN HOWARD	0	0	1
EDDIE JONES	0	0	1
JAMAL MASHBURN	0	0	1
Anthony Mason	0	0	1
ANTONIO McDYESS	0	0	1
YAO MING	0	0	1
Drazen Petrovic	0	0	1
MICHAEL REDD	0	0	1
Detlef Schrempf	0	0	1
KEVIN WILLIS	0	0	1

HISTORY *Award winners*

Selected by NBA coaches.

1962-63
Terry Dischinger, Chicago
Chet Walker, Syracuse
Zelmo Beaty, St. Louis
John Havlicek, Boston
Dave DeBusschere, Detroit

1963-64
Jerry Lucas, Cincinnati
Gus Johnson, Baltimore
Nate Thurmond, San Francisco
Art Heyman, New York
Rod Thorn, Baltimore

1964-65
Willis Reed, New York
Jim Barnes, New York
Howard Komives, New York
Lucious Jackson, Philadelphia
Wally Jones, Baltimore
Joe Caldwell, Detroit

1965-66
Rick Barry, San Francisco
Billy Cunningham, Philadelphia
Tom Van Arsdale, Detroit
Dick Van Arsdale, New York
Fred Hetzel, San Francisco

1966-67
Lou Hudson, St. Louis
Jack Marin, Baltimore
Erwin Mueller, Chicago
Cazzie Russell, New York
Dave Bing, Detroit

1967-68
Earl Monroe, Baltimore
Bob Rule, Seattle
Walt Frazier, New York
Al Tucker, Seattle
Phil Jackson, New York

1968-69
Wes Unseld, Baltimore
Elvin Hayes, San Diego
Bill Hewitt, Los Angeles
Art Harris, Seattle
Gary Gregor, Phoenix

1969-70
Kareem Abdul-Jabbar, Milwaukee
Bob Dandridge, Milwaukee
Jo Jo White, Boston
Mike Davis, Baltimore
Dick Garrett, Los Angeles

1970-71
Geoff Petrie, Portland
Dave Cowens, Boston
Pete Maravich, Atlanta
Calvin Murphy, San Diego
Bob Lanier, Detroit

1971-72
Elmore Smith, Buffalo
Sidney Wicks, Portland
Austin Carr, Cleveland
Phil Chenier, Baltimore
Clifford Ray, Chicago

1972-73
Bob McAdoo, Buffalo
Lloyd Neal, Portland
Fred Boyd, Philadelphia
Dwight Davis, Cleveland
Jim Price, Los Angeles

1973-74
Ernie DiGregorio, Buffalo
Ron Behagen, Kansas City/Omaha
Mike Bantom, Phoenix
John Brown, Atlanta
Nick Weatherspoon, Capital

1974-75
Keith Wilkes, Golden State
John Drew, Atlanta
Scott Wedman, Kansas City/Omaha
Tom Burleson, Seattle
Brian Winters, Los Angeles

1975-76
Alvan Adams, Phoenix
Gus Williams, Golden State
Joe Meriweather, Houston
John Shumate, Phoenix-Buffalo
Lionel Hollins, Portland

1976-77
Adrian Dantley, Buffalo
Scott May, Chicago
Mitch Kupchak, Washington
John Lucas, Houston
Ron Lee, Phoenix

1977-78
Walter Davis, Phoenix
Marques Johnson, Milwaukee
Bernard King, New Jersey
Jack Sikma, Seattle
Norm Nixon, Los Angeles

1978-79
Phil Ford, Kansas City
Mychal Thompson, Portland
Ron Brewer, Portland
Reggie Theus, Chicago
Terry Tyler, Detroit

1979-80
Larry Bird, Boston
Magic Johnson, Los Angeles
Bill Cartwright, New York
Calvin Natt, New Jersey-Portland
David Greenwood, Chicago

1980-81
Joe Barry Carroll, Golden State
Darrell Griffith, Utah
Larry Smith, Golden State
Kevin McHale, Boston
Kelvin Ransey, Portland

1981-82
Kelly Tripucka, Detroit
Jay Vincent, Dallas
Isiah Thomas, Detroit
Buck Williams, New Jersey
Jeff Ruland, Washington

1982-83
Terry Cummings, San Diego
Clark Kellogg, Indiana
Dominique Wilkins, Atlanta
James Worthy, Los Angeles
Quintin Dailey, Chicago

1983-84
Ralph Sampson, Houston
Steve Stipanovich, Indiana
Byron Scott, Los Angeles
Jeff Malone, Washington
Thurl Bailey, Utah
Darrell Walker, New York

1984-85
Michael Jordan, Chicago
Hakeem Olajuwon, Houston
Sam Bowie, Portland
Charles Barkley, Philadelphia
Sam Perkins, Dallas

1985-86
Xavier McDaniel, Seattle
Patrick Ewing, New York
Karl Malone, Utah
Joe Dumars, Detroit
Charles Oakley, Chicago

1986-87
Brad Daugherty, Cleveland
Ron Harper, Cleveland
Chuck Person, Indiana
Roy Tarpley, Dallas
John Williams, Cleveland

1987-88
Mark Jackson, New York
Armon Gilliam, Phoenix
Kenny Smith, Sacramento
Greg Anderson, San Antonio
Derrick McKey, Seattle

1988-89
FIRST
Mitch Richmond, Golden State
Willie Anderson, San Antonio
Hersey Hawkins, Philadelphia
Rik Smits, Indiana
Charles Smith, L.A. Clippers
SECOND
Brian Shaw, Boston
Rex Chapman, Charlotte
Chris Morris, New Jersey
Rod Strickland, New York
Kevin Edwards, Miami

1989-90
FIRST
David Robinson, San Antonio
Tim Hardaway, Golden State
Vlade Divac, L.A. Lakers
Sherman Douglas, Miami
Pooh Richardson, Minnesota
SECOND
J.R. Reid, Charlotte
Sean Elliott, San Antonio
Stacey King, Chicago
Blue Edwards, Utah
Glen Rice, Miami

1990-91
FIRST
Kendall Gill, Charlotte
Dennis Scott, Orlando
Dee Brown, Boston
Lionel Simmons, Sacramento
Derrick Coleman, New Jersey
SECOND
Chris Jackson, Denver
Gary Payton, Seattle
Felton Spencer, Minnesota
Travis Mays, Sacramento
Willie Burton, Miami

1991-92
FIRST
Larry Johnson, Charlotte
Dikembe Mutombo, Denver
Billy Owens, Golden State
Steve Smith, Miami
Stacey Augmon, Atlanta
SECOND
Rick Fox, Boston
Terrell Brandon, Cleveland
Larry Stewart, Washington
Stanley Roberts, Orlando
Mark Macon, Denver

1992-93
FIRST
Shaquille O'Neal, Orlando
Alonzo Mourning, Charlotte
Christian Laettner, Minnesota
Tom Gugliotta, Washington
LaPhonso Ellis, Denver
SECOND
Walt Williams, Sacramento
Robert Horry, Houston
Latrell Sprewell, Golden State
Clarence Weatherspoon, Philadelphia
Richard Dumas, Phoenix

1993-94
FIRST
Chris Webber, Golden State
Anfernee Hardaway, Orlando
Vin Baker, Milwaukee
Jamal Mashburn, Dallas
Isaiah Rider, Minnesota
SECOND
Dino Radja, Boston
Nick Van Exel, L.A. Lakers
Shawn Bradley, Philadelphia
Toni Kukoc, Chicago
Lindsey Hunter, Detroit

1994-95
FIRST
Jason Kidd, Dallas
Grant Hill, Detroit
Glenn Robinson, Milwaukee
Eddie Jones, L.A. Lakers
Brian Grant, Sacramento
SECOND
Juwan Howard, Washington
Eric Montross, Boston

Wesley Person, Phoenix
Jalen Rose, Denver
Donyell Marshall, Minnesota-Golden St.
Sharone Wright, Philadelphia

1995-96
FIRST
Damon Stoudamire, Toronto
Joe Smith, Golden State
Jerry Stackhouse, Philadelphia
Antonio McDyess, Denver
Arvydas Sabonis, Portland
Michael Finley, Phoenix
SECOND
Kevin Garnett, Minnesota
Bryant Reeves, Vancouver
Brent Barry, L.A. Clippers
Rasheed Wallace, Washington
Tyus Edney, Sacramento

1996-97
FIRST
Shareef Abdur-Rahim, Vancouver
Allen Iverson, Philadelphia
Stephon Marbury, Minnesota
Marcus Camby, Toronto
Antoine Walker, Boston
SECOND
Kerry Kittles, New Jersey
Ray Allen, Milwaukee
Travis Knight, L.A. Lakers
Kobe Bryant, L.A. Lakers
Matt Maloney, Houston

1997-98
FIRST
Tim Duncan, San Antonio
Keith Van Horn, New Jersey
Brevin Knight, Cleveland
Zydrunas Ilgauskas, Cleveland
Ron Mercer, Boston
SECOND
Tim Thomas, Philadelphia
Cedric Henderson, Cleveland
Derek Anderson, Cleveland
Maurice Taylor, L.A. Clippers
Bobby Jackson, Denver

1998-99
FIRST
Vince Carter, Toronto
Paul Pierce, Boston
Jason Williams, Sacramento
Mike Bibby, Vancouver
Matt Harpring, Orlando
SECOND
Michael Dickerson, Houston
Michael Doleac, Orlando
Cuttino Mobley, Houston
Michael Olowokandi, L.A. Clippers
Antawn Jamison, Golden State

1999-2000
FIRST
Elton Brand, Chicago
Steve Francis, Houston
Lamar Odom, L.A. Clippers

Wally Szczerbiak, Minnesota
Andre Miller, Cleveland
SECOND
Shawn Marion, Phoenix
Ron Artest, Chicago
James Posey, Denver
Jason Terry, Atlanta
Chucky Atkins, Orlando

2000-01
FIRST
Mike Miller, Orlando
Kenyon Martin, New Jersey
Marc Jackson, Golden State
Morris Peterson, Toronto
Darius Miles, L.A. Clippers
SECOND
Hidayet Turkoglu, Sacramento
Desmond Mason, Seattle
Courtney Alexander, Washington
Marcus Fizer, Chicago
Chris Mihm, Cleveland

2001-02
FIRST
Pau Gasol, Memphis
Shane Battier, Memphis
Jason Richardson, Golden State
Tony Parker, San Antonio
Andrei Kirilenko, Utah
SECOND
Jamaal Tinsley, Indiana
Richard Jefferson, New Jersey
Eddie Griffin, Houston
Zeljko Rebraca, Detroit
Vladimir Radmanovic, Seattle
Joe Johnson, Phoenix

2002-03
FIRST
Yao Ming, Houston
Amare Staudemire, Phoenix
Caron Butler, Miami
Drew Gooden, Orlando
Nene Hilario, Denver
SECOND
Emanuel Ginobili, San Antonio
Gordan Giricek, Orlando
Carlos Boozer, Cleveland
Jay Williams, Chicago
J.R. Bremer, Boston

2003-04
FIRST
Carmelo Anthony, Denver
LeBron James, Cleveland
Dwyane Wade, Miami
Chris Bosh, Toronto
Kirk Hinrich, Chicago
SECOND
Josh Howard, Dallas
T.J. Ford, Milwaukee
Udonis Haslem, Miami
Jarvis Hayes, Washington
Marquis Daniels, Dallas

Selected by NBA coaches.

1968-69
FIRST
Dave DeBusschere, Detroit-New York
Nate Thurmond, San Francisco
Bill Russell, Boston
Walt Frazier, New York
Jerry Sloan, Chicago
SECOND
Rudy LaRusso, San Francisco
Tom Sanders, Boston
John Havlicek, Boston
Jerry West, Los Angeles
Bill Bridges, Atlanta

1969-70
FIRST
Dave DeBusschere, New York
Gus Johnson, Baltimore
Willis Reed, New York
Walt Frazier, New York
Jerry West, Los Angeles
SECOND
John Havlicek, Boston
Bill Bridges, Atlanta
Kareem Abdul-Jabbar, Milwaukee
Joe Caldwell, Atlanta
Jerry Sloan, Chicago

1970-71
FIRST
Dave DeBusschere, New York
Gus Johnson, Baltimore
Nate Thurmond, San Francisco
Walt Frazier, New York
Jerry West, Los Angeles
SECOND
John Havlicek, Boston
Paul Silas, Phoenix
Kareem Abdul-Jabbar, Milwaukee
Jerry Sloan, Chicago
Norm Van Lier, Cincinnati

1971-72
FIRST
Dave DeBusschere, New York
John Havlicek, Boston
Wilt Chamberlain, Los Angeles
Jerry West, Los Angeles
Walt Frazier, New York
Jerry Sloan, Chicago
SECOND
Paul Silas, Phoenix
Bob Love, Chicago
Nate Thurmond, Golden State
Norm Van Lier, Chicago
Don Chaney, Boston

1972-73
FIRST
Dave DeBusschere, New York
John Havlicek, Boston
Wilt Chamberlain, Los Angeles
Jerry West, Los Angeles
Walt Frazier, New York

SECOND
Paul Silas, Boston
Mike Riordan, Baltimore
Nate Thurmond, Golden State
Norm Van Lier, Chicago
Don Chaney, Boston

1973-74
FIRST
Dave DeBusschere, New York
John Havlicek, Boston
Kareem Abdul-Jabbar, Milwaukee
Norm Van Lier, Chicago
Walt Frazier, New York
Jerry Sloan, Chicago
SECOND
Elvin Hayes, Capital
Bob Love, Chicago
Nate Thurmond, Golden State
Don Chaney, Boston
Dick Van Arsdale, Phoenix
Jim Price, Los Angeles

1974-75
FIRST
John Havlicek, Boston
Paul Silas, Boston
Kareem Abdul-Jabbar, Milwaukee
Jerry Sloan, Chicago
Walt Frazier, New York
SECOND
Elvin Hayes, Washington
Bob Love, Chicago
Dave Cowens, Boston
Norm Van Lier, Chicago
Don Chaney, Boston

1975-76
FIRST
Paul Silas, Boston
John Havlicek, Boston
Dave Cowens, Boston
Norm Van Lier, Chicago
Don Watts, Seattle
SECOND
Jim Brewer, Cleveland
Jamaal Wilkes, Golden State
Kareem Abdul-Jabbar, Los Angeles
Jim Cleamons, Cleveland
Phil Smith, Golden State

1976-77
FIRST
Bobby Jones, Denver
E.C. Coleman, New Orleans
Bill Walton, Portland
Don Buse, Indiana
Norm Van Lier, Chicago
SECOND
Jim Brewer, Cleveland
Jamaal Wilkes, Golden State
Kareem Abdul-Jabbar, Los Angeles
Brian Taylor, Kansas City
Don Chaney, Los Angeles

1977-78
FIRST
Bobby Jones, Denver
Maurice Lucas, Portland
Bill Walton, Portland
Lionel Hollins, Portland
Don Buse, Phoenix
SECOND
E.C. Coleman, Golden State
Bob Gross, Portland
Kareem Abdul-Jabbar, Los Angeles
Artis Gilmore, Chicago
Norm Van Lier, Chicago
Quinn Buckner, Milwaukee

1978-79
FIRST
Bobby Jones, Philadelphia
Bobby Dandridge, Washington
Kareem Abdul-Jabbar, Los Angeles
Dennis Johnson, Seattle
Don Buse, Phoenix
SECOND
Maurice Lucas, Portland
M.L. Carr, Detroit
Moses Malone, Houston
Lionel Hollins, Portland
Eddie Johnson, Atlanta

1979-80
FIRST
Bobby Jones, Philadelphia
Dan Roundfield, Atlanta
Kareem Abdul-Jabbar, Los Angeles
Dennis Johnson, Seattle
Don Buse, Phoenix
Micheal Ray Richardson, New York
SECOND
Scott Wedman, Kansas City
Kermit Washington, Portland
Dave Cowens, Boston
Quinn Buckner, Milwaukee
Eddie Johnson, Atlanta

1980-81
FIRST
Bobby Jones, Philadelphia
Caldwell Jones, Philadelphia
Kareem Abdul-Jabbar, Los Angeles
Dennis Johnson, Phoenix
Micheal Ray Richardson, New York
SECOND
Dan Roundfield, Atlanta
Kermit Washington, Portland
George Johnson, San Antonio
Quinn Buckner, Milwaukee
Dudley Bradley, Indiana
Michael Cooper, Los Angeles

1981-82
FIRST
Bobby Jones, Philadelphia
Dan Roundfield, Atlanta
Caldwell Jones, Philadelphia
Michael Cooper, Los Angeles
Dennis Johnson, Phoenix

SECOND
Larry Bird, Boston
Lonnie Shelton, Seattle
Jack Sikma, Seattle
Quinn Buckner, Milwaukee
Sidney Moncrief, Milwaukee

1982-83
FIRST
Bobby Jones, Philadelphia
Dan Roundfield, Atlanta
Moses Malone, Philadelphia
Sidney Moncrief, Milwaukee
Dennis Johnson, Phoenix
Maurice Cheeks, Philadelphia
SECOND
Larry Bird, Boston
Kevin McHale, Boston
Tree Rollins, Atlanta
Michael Cooper, Los Angeles
T.R. Dunn, Denver

1983-84
FIRST
Bobby Jones, Philadelphia
Michael Cooper, Los Angeles
Tree Rollins, Atlanta
Maurice Cheeks, Philadelphia
Sidney Moncrief, Milwaukee
SECOND
Larry Bird, Boston
Dan Roundfield, Atlanta
Kareem Abdul-Jabbar, Los Angeles
Dennis Johnson, Boston
T.R. Dunn, Denver

1984-85
FIRST
Sidney Moncrief, Milwaukee
Paul Pressey, Milwaukee
Mark Eaton, Utah
Michael Cooper, L.A. Lakers
Maurice Cheeks, Philadelphia
SECOND
Bobby Jones, Philadelphia
Danny Vranes, Seattle
Hakeem Olajuwon, Houston
Dennis Johnson, Boston
T.R. Dunn, Denver

1985-86
FIRST
Paul Pressey, Milwaukee
Kevin McHale, Boston
Mark Eaton, Utah
Sidney Moncrief, Milwaukee
Maurice Cheeks, Philadelphia
SECOND
Michael Cooper, L.A. Lakers
Bill Hanzlik, Denver
Manute Bol, Washington
Alvin Robertson, San Antonio
Dennis Johnson, Boston

1986-87
FIRST
Kevin McHale, Boston
Michael Cooper, L.A. Lakers
Hakeem Olajuwon, Houston
Alvin Robertson, San Antonio
Dennis Johnson, Boston

SECOND
Paul Pressey, Milwaukee
Rodney McCray, Houston
Mark Eaton, Utah
Maurice Cheeks, Philadelphia
Derek Harper, Dallas

1987-88
FIRST
Kevin McHale, Boston
Rodney McCray, Houston
Hakeem Olajuwon, Houston
Michael Cooper, L.A. Lakers
Michael Jordan, Chicago
SECOND
Buck Williams, New Jersey
Karl Malone, Utah
Mark Eaton, Utah
Patrick Ewing, New York
Alvin Robertson, San Antonio
Fat Lever, Denver

1988-89
FIRST
Dennis Rodman, Detroit
Larry Nance, Cleveland
Mark Eaton, Utah
Michael Jordan, Chicago
Joe Dumars, Detroit
SECOND
Kevin McHale, Boston
A.C. Green, L.A. Lakers
Patrick Ewing, New York
John Stockton, Utah
Alvin Robertson, San Antonio

1989-90
FIRST
Dennis Rodman, Detroit
Buck Williams, Portland
Hakeem Olajuwon, Houston
Michael Jordan, Chicago
Joe Dumars, Detroit
SECOND
Kevin McHale, Boston
Rick Mahorn, Philadelphia
David Robinson, San Antonio
Derek Harper, Dallas
Alvin Robertson, Milwaukee

1990-91
FIRST
Michael Jordan, Chicago
Alvin Robertson, Milwaukee
David Robinson, San Antonio
Dennis Rodman, Detroit
Buck Williams, Portland
SECOND
Joe Dumars, Detroit
John Stockton, Utah
Hakeem Olajuwon, Houston
Scottie Pippen, Chicago
Dan Majerle, Phoenix

1991-92
FIRST
Dennis Rodman, Detroit
Scottie Pippen, Chicago
David Robinson, San Antonio
Michael Jordan, Chicago
Joe Dumars, Detroit

SECOND
Larry Nance, Cleveland
Buck Williams, Portland
Patrick Ewing, New York
John Stockton, Utah
Micheal Williams, Indiana

1992-93
FIRST
Scottie Pippen, Chicago
Dennis Rodman, Detroit
Hakeem Olajuwon, Houston
Michael Jordan, Chicago
Joe Dumars, Detroit
SECOND
Horace Grant, Chicago
Larry Nance, Cleveland
David Robinson, San Antonio
Dan Majerle, Phoenix
John Starks, New York

1993-94
FIRST
Scottie Pippen, Chicago
Charles Oakley, New York
Hakeem Olajuwon, Houston
Gary Payton, Seattle
Mookie Blaylock, Atlanta
SECOND
Dennis Rodman, San Antonio
Horace Grant, Chicago
David Robinson, San Antonio
Nate McMillan, Seattle
Latrell Sprewell, Golden State

1994-95
FIRST
Scottie Pippen, Chicago
Dennis Rodman, San Antonio
David Robinson, San Antonio
Gary Payton, Seattle
Mookie Blaylock, Atlanta
SECOND
Horace Grant, Chicago
Derrick McKey, Indiana
Dikembe Mutombo, Denver
John Stockton, Utah
Nate McMillan, Seattle

1995-96
FIRST
Scottie Pippen, Chicago
Dennis Rodman, Chicago
David Robinson, San Antonio
Gary Payton, Seattle
Michael Jordan, Chicago
SECOND
Horace Grant, Orlando
Derrick McKey, Indiana
Hakeem Olajuwon, Houston
Mookie Blaylock, Atlanta
Bobby Phills, Cleveland

1996-97
FIRST
Scottie Pippen, Chicago
Karl Malone, Utah
Dikembe Mutombo, Atlanta
Michael Jordan, Chicago
Gary Payton, Seattle

SECOND
Anthony Mason, Charlotte
P.J. Brown, Miami
Hakeem Olajuwon, Houston
Mookie Blaylock, Atlanta
John Stockton, Utah

1997-98
FIRST
Scottie Pippen, Chicago
Karl Malone, Utah
Dikembe Mutombo, Atlanta
Michael Jordan, Chicago
Gary Payton, Seattle
SECOND
Tim Duncan, San Antonio
Charles Oakley, New York
David Robinson, San Antonio
Mookie Blaylock, Atlanta
Eddie Jones, L.A. Lakers

1998-99
FIRST
Tim Duncan, San Antonio
Karl Malone, Utah
Scottie Pippen, Houston
Alonzo Mourning, Miami
Gary Payton, Seattle
Jason Kidd, Phoenix
SECOND
P.J. Brown, Miami
Theo Ratliff, Philadelphia
Dikembe Mutombo, Atlanta
Mookie Blaylock, Atlanta
Eddie Jones, L.A.Lakers-Charlotte

1999-2000
FIRST
Tim Duncan, San Antonio
Kevin Garnett, Minnesota

Alonzo Mourning, Miami
Gary Payton, Seattle
Kobe Bryant, L.A. Lakers
SECOND
Scottie Pippen, Portland
Clifford Robinson, Phoenix
Shaquille O'Neal, L.A. Lakers
Eddie Jones, Charlotte
Jason Kidd, Phoenix

2000-01
FIRST
Tim Duncan, San Antonio
Kevin Garnett, Minnesota
Dikembe Mutombo, Atl.-Phi.
Gary Payton, Seattle
Jason Kidd, Phoenix
SECOND
Bruce Bowen, Miami
P.J. Brown, Charlotte
Shaquille O'Neal, L.A. Lakers
Kobe Bryant, L.A. Lakers
Doug Christie, Sacramento

2001-02
FIRST
Tim Duncan, San Antonio
Kevin Garnett, Minnesota
Ben Wallace, Detroit
Gary Payton, Seattle
Jason Kidd, New Jersey
SECOND
Bruce Bowen, San Antonio
Clifford Robinson, Detroit
Dikembe Mutombo, Philadelphia
Kobe Bryant, L.A. Lakers
Doug Christie, Sacramento

2002-03
FIRST
Kevin Garnett, Minnesota
Tim Duncan, San Antonio
Ben Wallace, Detroit
Doug Christie, Sacramento
Kobe Bryant, L.A. Lakers
SECOND
Ron Artest, Indiana
Bruce Bowen, San Antonio
Shaquille O'Neal, L.A. Lakers
Jason Kidd, New Jersey
Eric Snow, Philadelphia

2003-04
FIRST
Ron Artest, Indiana
Kevin Garnett, Minnesota
Ben Wallace, Detroit
Bruce Bowen, San Antonio
Kobe Bryant, L.A. Lakers
SECOND
Andrei Kirilenko, Utah
Tim Duncan, San Antonio
Theo Ratliff, Portland
Doug Christie, Sacramento
Jason Kidd, New Jersey

REGULAR SEASON

YEARLY

SCORING

Season	Pts.	
1946-47	1,389	Joe Fulks, Philadelphia
1947-48	1,007	Max Zaslofsky, Chicago
1948-49	1,698	George Mikan, Minneapolis
1949-50	1,865	George Mikan, Minneapolis
1950-51	1,932	George Mikan, Minneapolis
1951-52	1,674	Paul Arizin, Philadelphia
1952-53	1,564	Neil Johnston, Philadelphia
1953-54	1,759	Neil Johnston, Philadelphia
1954-55	1,631	Neil Johnston, Philadelphia
1955-56	1,849	Bob Pettit, St. Louis
1956-57	1,817	Paul Arizin, Philadelphia
1957-58	2,001	George Yardley, Detroit
1958-59	2,105	Bob Pettit, St. Louis
1959-60	2,707	Wilt Chamberlain, Philadelphia
1960-61	3,033	Wilt Chamberlain, Philadelphia
1961-62	4,029	Wilt Chamberlain, Philadelphia
1962-63	3,586	Wilt Chamberlain, San Francisco
1963-64	2,948	Wilt Chamberlain, San Francisco
1964-65	2,534	Wilt Chamberlain, S.F.-Phil.
1965-66	2,649	Wilt Chamberlain, Philadelphia
1966-67	2,775	Rick Barry, San Francisco
1967-68	2,142	Dave Bing, Detroit
1968-69	2,327	Elvin Hayes, San Diego
1969-70	31.2*	Jerry West, Los Angeles
1970-71	31.7*	Kareem Abdul-Jabbar, Milwaukee
1971-72	34.8*	Kareem Abdul-Jabbar, Milwaukee
1972-73	34.0*	Nate Archibald, K.C./Omaha
1973-74	30.6*	Bob McAdoo, Buffalo
1974-75	34.5*	Bob McAdoo, Buffalo
1975-76	31.1*	Bob McAdoo, Buffalo
1976-77	31.1*	Pete Maravich, New Orleans
1977-78	27.2*	George Gervin, San Antonio
1978-79	29.6*	George Gervin, San Antonio
1979-80	33.1*	George Gervin, San Antonio
1980-81	30.7*	Adrian Dantley, Utah
1981-82	32.3*	George Gervin, San Antonio
1982-83	28.4*	Alex English, Denver
1983-84	30.6*	Adrian Dantley, Utah
1984-85	32.9*	Bernard King, New York
1985-86	30.3*	Dominique Wilkins, Atlanta
1986-87	37.1*	Michael Jordan, Chicago
1987-88	35.0*	Michael Jordan, Chicago
1988-09	32.5*	Michael Jordan, Chicago
1989-90	33.6*	Michael Jordan, Chicago
1990-91	31.5*	Michael Jordan, Chicago
1991-92	30.1*	Michael Jordan, Chicago
1992-93	32.6*	Michael Jordan, Chicago
1993-94	29.8*	David Robinson, San Antonio
1994-95	29.3*	Shaquille O'Neal, Orlando
1995-96	30.4*	Michael Jordan, Chicago
1996-97	29.6*	Michael Jordan, Chicago
1997-98	28.7*	Michael Jordan, Chicago
1998-99	26.8*	Allen Iverson, Philadelphia
1999-00	29.7*	Shaquille O'Neal, L.A. Lakers
2000-01	31.1*	Allen Iverson, Philadelphia
2001-02	31.4*	Allen Iverson, Philadelphia
2002-03	32.1*	Tracy McGrady, Orlando
2003-04	28.0*	Tracy McGrady, Orlando

*Based on average per game.

FIELD-GOAL PERCENTAGE

Season	Pct.	
1946-47	.401	Bob Feerick, Washington
1947-48	.340	Bob Feerick, Washington
1948-49	.423	Arnie Risen, Rochester
1949-50	.478	Alex Groza, Indianapolis
1950-51	.470	Alex Groza, Indianapolis
1951-52	.448	Paul Arizin, Philadelphia
1952-53	.452	Neil Johnston, Philadelphia
1953-54	.486	Ed Macauley, Boston
1954-55	.487	Larry Foust, Fort Wayne
1955-56	.457	Neil Johnston, Philadelphia
1956-57	.447	Neil Johnston, Philadelphia
1957-58	.452	Jack Twyman, Cincinnati
1958-59	.490	Ken Sears, New York
1959-60	.477	Ken Sears, New York
1960-61	.509	Wilt Chamberlain, Philadelphia
1961-62	.519	Walt Bellamy, Chicago
1962-63	.528	Wilt Chamberlain, San Francisco
1963-64	.527	Jerry Lucas, Cincinnati
1964-65	.510	Wilt Chamberlain, S.F.-Phil.
1965-66	.540	Wilt Chamberlain, Philadelphia
1966-67	.683	Wilt Chamberlain, Philadelphia
1967-68	.595	Wilt Chamberlain, Philadelphia
1968-69	.583	Wilt Chamberlain, Los Angeles
1969-70	.559	Johnny Green, Cincinnati
1970-71	.587	Johnny Green, Cincinnati
1971-72	.649	Wilt Chamberlain, Los Angeles
1972-73	.727	Wilt Chamberlain, Los Angeles
1973-74	.547	Bob McAdoo, Buffalo
1974-75	.539	Don Nelson, Boston
1975-76	.561	Wes Unseld, Washington
1976-77	.579	Kareem Abdul-Jabbar, Los Angeles
1977-78	.578	Bobby Jones, Denver
1978-79	.584	Cedric Maxwell, Boston
1979-80	.609	Cedric Maxwell, Boston
1980-81	.670	Artis Gilmore, Chicago
1981-82	.652	Artis Gilmore, Chicago
1982-83	.626	Artis Gilmore, San Antonio
1983-84	.631	Artis Gilmore, San Antonio
1984-85	.637	James Donaldson, L.A. Clippers
1985-86	.632	Steve Johnson, San Antonio
1986-87	.604	Kevin McHale, Boston
1987-88	.604	Kevin McHale, Boston
1988-89	.595	Dennis Rodman, Detroit
1989-90	.625	Mark West, Phoenix
1990-91	.602	Buck Williams, Portland
1991-92	.604	Buck Williams, Portland
1992-93	.576	Cedric Ceballos, Phoenix
1993-94	.599	Shaquille O'Neal, Orlando
1994-95	.633	Chris Gatling, Golden State
1995-96	.504	Gheorghe Muresan, Washington
1996-97	.604	Gheorghe Muresan, Washington
1997-98	.584	Shaquille O'Neal, L.A. Lakers
1998-99	.576	Shaquille O'Neal, L.A. Lakers
1999-00	.574	Shaquille O'Neal, L.A. Lakers
2000-01	.572	Shaquille O'Neal, L.A. Lakers
2001-02	.579	Shaquille O'Neal, L.A. Lakers
2002-03	.585	Eddy Curry, Chicago
2003-04	.584	Shaquille O'Neal, L.A. Lakers

FREE THROW PERCENTAGE

Season	Pct.	
1946-47	.811	Fred Scolari, Washington
1947-48	.788	Bob Feerick, Washington
1948-49	.859	Bob Feerick, Washington
1949-50	.843	Max Zaslofsky, Chicago
1950-51	.855	Joe Fulks, Philadelphia
1951-52	.904	Bob Wanzer, Rochester
1952-53	.850	Bill Sharman, Boston
1953-54	.844	Bill Sharman, Boston
1954-55	.897	Bill Sharman, Boston
1955-56	.867	Bill Sharman, Boston
1956-57	.905	Bill Sharman, Boston
1957-58	.904	Dolph Schayes, Syracuse
1958-59	.932	Bill Sharman, Boston

Season	Pct.	
1959-60—.892	Dolph Schayes, Syracuse	
1960-61—.921	Bill Sharman, Boston	
1961-62—.896	Dolph Schayes, Syracuse	
1962-63—.881	Larry Costello, Syracuse	
1963-64—.853	Oscar Robertson, Cincinnati	
1964-65—.877	Larry Costello, Philadelphia	
1965-66—.881	Larry Siegfried, Boston	
1966-67—.903	Adrian Smith, Cincinnati	
1967-68—.873	Oscar Robertson, Cincinnati	
1968-69—.864	Larry Siegfried, Boston	
1969-70—.898	Flynn Robinson, Milwaukee	
1970-71—.859	Chet Walker, Chicago	
1971-72—.894	Jack Marin, Baltimore	
1972-73—.902	Rick Barry, Golden State	
1973-74—.902	Ernie DiGregorio, Buffalo	
1974-75—.904	Rick Barry, Golden State	
1975-76—.923	Rick Barry, Golden State	
1976-77—.945	Ernie DiGregorio, Buffalo	
1977-78—.924	Rick Barry, Golden State	
1978-79—.947	Rick Barry, Houston	
1979-80—.935	Rick Barry, Houston	
1980-81—.958	Calvin Murphy, Houston	
1981-82—.899	Kyle Macy, Phoenix	
1982-83—.920	Calvin Murphy, Houston	
1983-84—.888	Larry Bird, Boston	
1984-85—.907	Kyle Macy, Phoenix	
1985-86—.896	Larry Bird, Boston	
1986-87—.910	Larry Bird, Boston	
1987-88—.922	Jack Sikma, Milwaukee	
1988-89—.911	Magic Johnson, L.A. Lakers	
1989-90—.930	Larry Bird, Boston	
1990-91—.918	Reggie Miller, Indiana	
1991-92—.947	Mark Price, Cleveland	
1992-93—.948	Mark Price, Cleveland	
1993-94—.956	Mahmoud Abdul-Rauf, Denver	
1994-95—.934	Spud Webb, Sacramento	
1995-96—.930	Mahmoud Abdul-Rauf, Denver	
1996-97—.906	Mark Price, Golden State	
1997-98—.939	Chris Mullin, Indiana	
1998-99—.915	Reggie Miller, Indiana	
1999-00—.950	Jeff Hornacek, Utah	
2000-01—.928	Reggie Miller, Indiana	
2001-02—.911	Reggie Miller, Indiana	
2002-03—.919	Allan Houston, New York	
2003-04—.927	Peja Stojakovic, Sacramento	

3-POINT FIELD-GOAL PERCENTAGE

Season	Pct.	
1979-80—.443	Fred Brown, Seattle	
1980-81—.383	Brian Taylor, San Diego	
1981-82—.439	Campy Russell, New York	
1982-83—.345	Mike Dunleavy, San Antonio	
1983-84—.361	Darrell Griffith, Utah	
1984-85—.433	Byron Scott, L.A. Lakers	
1985-86—.451	Craig Hodges, Milwaukee	
1986-87—.481	Kiki Vandeweghe, Portland	
1987-88—.491	Craig Hodges, Mil.-Pho.	
1988-89—.522	Jon Sundvold, Miami	
1989-90—.507	Steve Kerr, Cleveland	
1990-91—.461	Jim Les, Sacramento	
1991-92—.446	Dana Barros, Seattle	
1992-93—.453	B.J. Armstrong, Chicago	
1993-94—.459	Tracy Murray, Portland	
1994-95—.524	Steve Kerr, Chicago	
1995-96—.522	Tim Legler, Washington	
1996-97—.470	Glen Rice, Charlotte	
1997-98—.464	Dale Ellis, Seattle	
1998-99—.476	Dell Curry, Milwaukee	
1999-00—.491	Hubert Davis, Dallas	
2000-01—.476	Brent Barry, Seattle	
2001-02—.472	Steve Smith, San Antonio	
2002-03—.441	Bruce Bowen, San Antonio	
2003-04—.482	Anthony Peeler, Sacramento	

MINUTES

Season	No.	
1951-52—2,939	Paul Arizin, Philadelphia	
1952-53—3,166	Neil Johnston, Philadelphia	
1953-54—3,296	Neil Johnston, Philadelphia	
1954-55—2,953	Paul Arizin, Philadelphia	
1955-56—2,838	Slater Martin, Minneapolis	
1956-57—2,851	Dolph Schayes, Syracuse	
1957-58—2,918	Dolph Schayes, Syracuse	
1958-59—2,979	Bill Russell, Boston	
1959-60—3,338	Wilt Chamberlain, Philadelphia	
	Gene Shue, Detroit	
1960-61—3,773	Wilt Chamberlain, Philadelphia	
1961-62—3,882	Wilt Chamberlain, Philadelphia	
1962-63—3,806	Wilt Chamberlain, San Francisco	
1963-64—3,689	Wilt Chamberlain, San Francisco	
1964-65—3,466	Bill Russell, Boston	
1965-66—3,737	Wilt Chamberlain, Philadelphia	
1966-67—3,682	Wilt Chamberlain, Philadelphia	
1967-68—3,836	Wilt Chamberlain, Philadelphia	
1968-69—3,695	Elvin Hayes, San Diego	
1969-70—3,665	Elvin Hayes, San Diego	
1970-71—3,678	John Havlicek, Boston	
1971-72—3,698	John Havlicek, Boston	
1972-73—3,681	Nate Archibald, K.C./Omaha	
1973-74—3,602	Elvin Hayes, Capital	
1974-75—3,539	Bob McAdoo, Buffalo	
1975-76—3,379	Kareem Abdul-Jabbar, Los Angeles	
1976-77—3,364	Elvin Hayes, Washington	
1977-78—3,638	Len Robinson, New Orleans	
1978-79—3,390	Moses Malone, Houston	
1979-80—3,226	Norm Nixon, Los Angeles	
1980-81—3,417	Adrian Dantley, Utah	
1981-82—3,398	Moses Malone, Houston	
1982-83—3,093	Isiah Thomas, Detroit	
1983-84—3,082	Jeff Ruland, Washington	
1984-85—3,182	Buck Williams, New Jersey	
1985-86—3,270	Maurice Cheeks, Philadelphia	
1986-87—3,281	Michael Jordan, Chicago	
1987-88—3,311	Michael Jordan, Chicago	
1988-89—3,255	Michael Jordan, Chicago	
1989-90—3,238	Rodney McCray, Sacramento	
1990-91—3,315	Chris Mullin, Golden State	
1991-92—3,346	Chris Mullin, Golden State	
1992-93—3,323	Larry Johnson, Charlotte	
1993-94—3,533	Latrell Sprewell, Golden State	
1994-95—3,361	Vin Baker, Milwaukee	
1995-96—3,457	Anthony Mason, New York	
1996-97—3,362	Glen Rice, Charlotte	
1997-98—3,394	Michael Finley, Dallas	
1998-99—2,060	Jason Kidd, Phoenix	
1999-00—3,464	Michael Finley, Dallas	
2000-01—3,443	Michael Finley, Dallas	
2001-02—3,406	Antoine Walker, Boston	
2002-03—3,485	Allen Iverson, Philadelphia	
2003-04—3,331	Joe Johnson, Phoenix	

REBOUNDING

Season	No.	
1950-51—1,080	Dolph Schayes, Syracuse	
1951-52—880	Larry Foust, Fort Wayne	
	Mel Hutchins, Milwaukee	
1952-53—1,007	George Mikan, Minneapolis	
1953-54—1,098	Harry Gallatin, New York	
1954-55—1,085	Neil Johnston, Philadelphia	
1955-56—1,164	Bob Pettit, St. Louis	
1956-57—1,256	Maurice Stokes, Rochester	
1957-58—1,564	Bill Russell, Boston	
1958-59—1,612	Bill Russell, Boston	
1959-60—1,941	Wilt Chamberlain, Philadelphia	
1960-61—2,149	Wilt Chamberlain, Philadelphia	
1961-62—2,052	Wilt Chamberlain, Philadelphia	
1962-63—1,946	Wilt Chamberlain, San Francisco	
1963-64—1,930	Bill Russell, Boston	
1964-65—1,878	Bill Russell, Boston	
1965-66—1,943	Wilt Chamberlain, Philadelphia	
1966-67—1,957	Wilt Chamberlain, Philadelphia	
1967-68—1,952	Wilt Chamberlain, Philadelphia	

1968-69—1,712	Wilt Chamberlain, Los Angeles
1969-70—16.9*	Elvin Hayes, San Diego
1970-71—18.2*	Wilt Chamberlain, Los Angeles
1971-72—19.2*	Wilt Chamberlain, Los Angeles
1972-73—18.6*	Wilt Chamberlain, Los Angeles
1973-74—18.1*	Elvin Hayes, Capital
1974-75—14.8*	Wes Unseld, Washington
1975-76—16.9*	Kareem Abdul-Jabbar, Los Angeles
1976-77—14.4*	Bill Walton, Portland
1977-78—15.7*	Len Robinson, New Orleans
1978-79—17.6*	Moses Malone, Houston
1979-80—15.0*	Swen Nater, San Diego
1980-81—14.8*	Moses Malone, Houston
1981-82—14.7*	Moses Malone, Houston
1982-83—15.3*	Moses Malone, Philadelphia
1983-84—13.4*	Moses Malone, Philadelphia
1984-85—13.1*	Moses Malone, Philadelphia
1985-86—13.1*	Bill Laimbeer, Detroit
1986-87—14.6*	Charles Barkley, Philadelphia
1987-88—13.03*	Michael Cage, L.A. Clippers
1988-89—13.5*	Hakeem Olajuwon, Houston
1989-90—14.0*	Hakeem Olajuwon, Houston
1990-91—13.0*	David Robinson, San Antonio
1991-92—18.7*	Dennis Rodman, Detroit
1992-93—18.3*	Dennis Rodman, Detroit
1993-94—17.3*	Dennis Rodman, San Antonio
1994-95—16.8*	Dennis Rodman, San Antonio
1995-96—14.9*	Dennis Rodman, Chicago
1996-97—16.1*	Dennis Rodman, Chicago
1997-98—15.0*	Dennis Rodman, Chicago
1998-99—13.0*	Chris Webber, Sacramento
1999-00—14.1*	Dikembe Mutombo, Atlanta
2000-01—13.5*	Dikembe Mutombo, Atl.-Phil.
2001-02—13.0*	Ben Wallace, Detroit
2002-03—15.4*	Ben Wallace, Detroit
2003-04—13.9*	Kevin Garnett, Minnesota

*Based on average per game.

ASSISTS

Season	No.	
1946-47—202		Ernie Calverly, Providence
1947-48—120		Howie Dallmar, Philadelphia
1948-49—321		Bob Davies, Rochester
1949-50—396		Dick McGuire, New York
1950-51—414		Andy Phillip, Philadelphia
1951-52—539		Andy Phillip, Philadelphia
1952-53—547		Bob Cousy, Boston
1953-54—518		Bob Cousy, Boston
1954-55—557		Bob Cousy, Boston
1955-56—642		Bob Cousy, Boston
1956-57—478		Bob Cousy, Boston
1957-58—463		Bob Cousy, Boston
1958-59—557		Bob Cousy, Boston
1959-60—715		Bob Cousy, Boston
1960-61—690		Oscar Robertson, Cincinnati
1961-62—899		Oscar Robertson, Cincinnati
1962-63—825		Guy Rodgers, San Francisco
1963-64—868		Oscar Robertson, Cincinnati
1964-65—861		Oscar Robertson, Cincinnati
1965-66—847		Oscar Robertson, Cincinnati
1966-67—908		Guy Rodgers, Chicago
1967-68—702		Wilt Chamberlain, Philadelphia
1968-69—772		Oscar Robertson, Cincinnati
1969-70—9.1*		Lenny Wilkens, Seattle
1970-71—10.1*		Norm Van Lier, Cincinnati
1971-72—9.7*		Jerry West, Los Angeles
1972-73—11.4*		Nate Archibald, K.C./Omaha
1973-74—8.2*		Ernie DiGregorio, Buffalo
1974-75—8.0*		Kevin Porter, Washington
1975-76—8.1*		Don Watts, Seattle
1976-77—8.5*		Don Buse, Indiana
1977-78—10.2*		Kevin Porter, Detroit-New Jersey
1978-79—13.4*		Kevin Porter, Detroit
1979-80—10.1*		Micheal Ray Richardson, New York
1980-81—9.1*		Kevin Porter, Washington
1981-82—9.6*		Johnny Moore, San Antonio
1982-83—10.5*		Magic Johnson, Los Angeles
1983-84—13.1*		Magic Johnson, Los Angeles

Season	No.	
1984-85—13.98*		Isiah Thomas, Detroit
1985-86—12.6*		Magic Johnson, L.A. Lakers
1986-87—12.2*		Magic Johnson, L.A. Lakers
1987-88—13.8*		John Stockton, Utah
1988-89—13.6*		John Stockton, Utah
1989-90—14.5*		John Stockton, Utah
1990-91—14.2*		John Stockton, Utah
1991-92—13.7*		John Stockton, Utah
1992-93—12.0*		John Stockton, Utah
1993-94—12.6*		John Stockton, Utah
1994-95—12.3*		John Stockton, Utah
1995-96—11.2*		John Stockton, Utah
1996-97—11.4*		Mark Jackson, Denver-Indiana
1997-98—10.5*		Rod Strickland, Washington
1998-99—10.8*		Jason Kidd, Phoenix
1999-00—10.1*		Jason Kidd, Phoenix
2000-01—9.8*		Jason Kidd, Phoenix
2001-02—10.9*		Andre Miller, Cleveland
2002-03—8.9*		Jason Kidd, New Jersey
2003-04—9.2*		Jason Kidd, New Jersey

*Based on average per game.

PERSONAL FOULS

Season	No.	
1946-47—208		Stan Miasek, Detroit
1947-48—231		Charles Gilmur, Chicago
1948-49—273		Ed Sadowski, Philadelphia
1949-50—297		George Mikan, Minneapolis
1950-51—308		George Mikan, Minneapolis
1951-52—286		George Mikan, Minneapolis
1952-53—334		Don Meineke, Fort Wayne
1953-54—303		Earl Lloyd, Syracuse
1954-55—319		Vern Mikkelsen, Minneapolis
1955-56—319		Vern Mikkelsen, Minneapolis
1956-57—312		Vern Mikkelsen, Minneapolis
1957-58—311		Walter Dukes, Detroit
1958-59—332		Walter Dukes, Detroit
1959-60—311		Tom Gola, Philadelphia
1960-61—335		Paul Arizin, Philadelphia
1961-62—330		Tom Meschery, Philadelphia
1962-63—312		Zelmo Beaty, St. Louis
1963-64—325		Wayne Embry, Cincinnati
1964-65—345		Bailey Howell, Baltimore
1965-66—344		Zelmo Beaty, St. Louis
1966-67—344		Joe Strawder, Detroit
1967-68—366		Bill Bridges, St. Louis
1968-69—329		Billy Cunningham, Philadelphia
1969-70—335		Jim Davis, Atlanta
1970-71—350		Dave Cowens, Boston
1971-72—314		Dave Cowens, Boston
1972-73—323		Neal Walk, Phoenix
1973-74—319		Kevin Porter, Capital
1974-75—330		Bob Dandridge, Milwaukee
		Phil Jackson, New York
1975-76—356		Charlie Scott, Boston
1976-77—363		Lonnie Shelton, N.Y. Knicks
1977-78—350		Lonnie Shelton, New York
1978-79—367		Bill Robinzine, Kansas City
1979-80—328		Darryl Dawkins, Philadelphia
1980-81—342		Ben Poquette, Utah
1981-82—372		Steve Johnson, Kansas City
1982-83—379		Darryl Dawkins, New Jersey
1983-84—386		Darryl Dawkins, New Jersey
1984-85—344		Hakeem Olajuwon, Houston
1985-86—333		Charles Barkley, Philadelphia
1986-87—340		Steve Johnson, Portland
1987-88—332		Patrick Ewing, New York
1988-89—337		Grant Long, Miami
1989-90—328		Rik Smits, Indiana
1990-91—338		Sam Mitchell, Minnesota
1991-92—315		Tyrone Hill, Golden State
1992-93—332		Stanley Roberts, L.A. Clippers
1993-94—312		Shawn Kemp, Seattle
1994-95—338		Shawn Bradley, Philadelphia
1995-96—300		Elden Campbell, L.A. Lakers
		Otis Thorpe, Detroit
1996-97—320		Shawn Kemp, Seattle

Season	No.	
1997-98—321	Ervin Johnson, Milwaukee	
1998-99—212	Danny Fortson, Denver	
1999-00—371	Shawn Kemp, Cleveland	
2000-01—319	Aaron Williams, New Jersey	
2001-02—341	Kurt Thomas, New York	
2002-03—344	Kurt Thomas, New York	
2003-04—300	Theo Ratliff, Atlanta-Portland	

STEALS PER GAME

Season Avg.	
1973-74—2.68*	Larry Steele, Portland
1974-75—2.85*	Rick Barry, Golden State
1975-76—3.18*	Don Watts, Seattle
1976-77—3.47*	Don Buse, Indiana
1977-78—2.74*	Ron Lee, Phoenix
1978-79—2.46*	M.L. Carr, Detroit
1979-80—3.23*	Micheal Ray Richardson, New York
1980-81—3.43*	Magic Johnson, L.A. Lakers
1981-82—2.67*	Magic Johnson, L.A. Lakers
1982-83—2.84*	Micheal Ray Richardson, G.S.-N.J.
1983-84—2.65*	Rickey Green, Utah
1984-85—2.96*	Micheal Ray Richardson, New Jersey
1985-86—3.67*	Alvin Robertson, San Antonio
1986-87—3.21*	Alvin Robertson, San Antonio
1987-88—3.16*	Michael Jordan, Chicago
1988-89—3.21*	John Stockton, Utah
1989-90—2.77*	Michael Jordan, Chicago
1990-91—3.04*	Alvin Robertson, Milwaukee
1991-92—2.98*	John Stockton, Utah
1992-93—2.83*	Michael Jordan, Chicago
1993-94—2.96*	Nate McMillan, Seattle
1994-95—2.94*	Scottie Pippen, Chicago
1995-96—2.85*	Gary Payton, Seattle
1996-97—2.72*	Mookie Blaylock, Atlanta
1997-98—2.61*	Mookie Blaylock, Atlanta
1998-99—2.68*	Kendall Gill, New Jersey
1999-00—2.67*	Eddie Jones, Charlotte
2000-01—2.51*	Allen Iverson, Philadelphia
2001-02—2.80*	Allen Iverson, Philadelphia
2002-03—2.74*	Allen Iverson, Philadelphia
2003-04—2.36*	Baron Davis, New Orleans

*Based on average per game.

BLOCKED SHOTS PER GAME

Season Avg.	
1973-74—4.85*	Elmore Smith, Los Angeles
1974-75—3.26*	Kareem Abdul-Jabbar, Milwaukee
1975-76—4.12*	Kareem Abdul-Jabbar, Los Angeles
1976-77—3.25*	Bill Walton, Portland
1977-78—3.38*	George Johnson, New Jersey
1978-79—3.95*	Kareem Abdul-Jabbar, Los Angeles
1979-80—3.41*	Kareem Abdul-Jabbar, Los Angeles
1980-81—3.39*	George Johnson, San Antonio
1981-82—3.12*	George Johnson, San Antonio
1982-83—4.29*	Tree Rollins, Atlanta
1983-84—4.28*	Mark Eaton, Utah
1984-85—5.56*	Mark Eaton, Utah
1985-86—4.96*	Manute Bol, Washington
1986-87—4.06*	Mark Eaton, Utah
1987-88—3.71*	Mark Eaton, Utah
1988-89—4.31*	Manute Bol, Golden State
1989-90—4.59*	Hakeem Olajuwon, Houston
1990-91—3.95*	Hakeem Olajuwon, Houston
1991-92—4.49*	David Robinson, San Antonio
1992-93—4.17*	Hakeem Olajuwon, Houston
1993-94—4.10*	Dikembe Mutombo, Denver
1994-95—3.91*	Dikembe Mutombo, Denver
1995-96—4.49*	Dikembe Mutombo, Denver
1996-97—3.40*	Shawn Bradley, New Jersey-Dallas
1997-98—3.65*	Marcus Camby, Toronto
1998-99—3.91*	Alonzo Mourning, Miami
1999-00—3.72*	Alonzo Mourning, Miami
2000-01—3.74*	Theo Ratliff, Phil.-Atl.
2001-02—3.48*	Ben Wallace, Detroit
2002-03—3.23*	Theo Ratliff, Atlanta
2003-04—3.61*	Theo Ratliff, Atlanta-Portland

*Based on average per game.

DISQUALIFICATIONS

Season	No.	
1950-51—19	Cal Christensen, Tri-Cities
1951-52—18	Don Boven, Milwaukee
1952-53—26	Don Meineke, Fort Wayne
1953-54—12	Earl Lloyd, Syracuse
1954-55—17	Charley Share, Milwaukee
1955-56—17	Vern Mikkelsen, Minneapolis
	Arnie Risen, Boston
1956-57—18	Vern Mikkelsen, Minneapolis
1957-58—20	Vern Mikkelsen, Minneapolis
1958-59—22	Walter Dukes, Detroit
1959-60—20	Walter Dukes, Detroit
1960-61—16	Walter Dukes, Detroit
1961-62—20	Walter Dukes, Detroit
1962-63—13	Frank Ramsey, Boston
1963-64—11	Zelmo Beaty, St. Louis
	Gus Johnson, Baltimore
1964-65—15	Tom Sanders, Boston
1965-66—19	Tom Sanders, Boston
1966-67—19	Joe Strawder, Detroit
1967-68—18	John Tresvant, Det.-Cin.
	Joe Strawder, Detroit
1968-69—14	Art Harris, Seattle
1969-70—18	Norm Van Lier, Cincinnati
1970-71—16	John Trapp, San Diego
1971-72—14	Curtis Perry, Hou.-Mil.
1972-73—16	Elmore Smith, Buffalo
1973-74—15	Mike Bantom, Phoenix
1974-75—12	Kevin Porter, Washington
1975-76—19	Bill Robinzine, Kansas City
1976-77—21	Joe Meriweather, Atlanta
1977-78—20	George Johnson, New Jersey
1978-79—19	John Drew, Atlanta
	Tree Rollins, Atlanta
1979-80—12	Tree Rollins, Atlanta
	James Edwards, Indiana
	George McGinnis, Den.-Ind.
1980-81—18	Ben Poquette, Utah
1981-82—25	Steve Johnson, Kansas City
1982-83—23	Darryl Dawkins, New Jersey
1983-84—22	Darryl Dawkins, New Jersey
1984-85—16	Ken Bannister, New York
1985-86—13	Joe Barry Carroll, Golden State
	Steve Johnson, San Antonio
1986-87—16	Steve Johnson, Portland
1987-88—11	Jack Sikma, Milwaukee
	Frank Brickowski, San Antonio
1988-89—14	Rik Smits, Indiana
1989-90—11	Grant Long, Miami
	Rik Smits, Indiana
	LaSalle Thompson, Indiana
1990-91—15	Blair Rasmussen, Denver
1991-92—13	Shawn Kemp, Seattle
1992-93—15	Stanley Roberts, L.A. Clippers
1993-94—11	Shawn Kemp, Seattle
	Rik Smits, Indiana
1994-95—18	Shawn Bradley, Philadelphia
1995-96—11	Matt Geiger, Charlotte
1996-97—11	Shawn Kemp, Seattle
	Walt Williams, Toronto
1997-98—15	Shawn Kemp, Cleveland
1998-99—9	Danny Fortson, Denver
	Otis Thorpe, Washington
1999-00—13	Shawn Kemp, Cleveland
	Lamar Odom, L.A. Clippers
2000-01—10	Travis Best, Indiana
	Michael Doleac, Orlando
	Kenyon Martin, New Jersey
2001-02—11	Raef LaFrentz, Den.-Dal.
2002-03—12	Kurt Thomas, New York
2003-04—11	Eddy Curry, Chicago

HISTORY *Regular season*

*Denotes number of overtime periods.

POINTS

	FG	FT	Pts.
Wilt Chamberlain, Philadelphia vs. New York at Hershey, Pa., March 2, 1962	.36	28	100
Wilt Chamberlain, Philadelphia vs. Los Angeles at Philadelphia, December 8, 1961***	.31	16	78
Wilt Chamberlain, Philadelphia vs. Chicago at Philadelphia, January 13, 1962	.29	15	73
Wilt Chamberlain, San Francisco at New York, November 16, 1962	.29	15	73
David Thompson, Denver at Detroit, April 9, 1978	.28	17	73
Wilt Chamberlain, San Francisco at Los Angeles, November 3, 1962	.29	14	72
Elgin Baylor, Los Angeles at New York, November 15, 1960	.28	15	71
David Robinson, San Antonio at L.A. Clippers, April 24, 1994	.26	18	71
Wilt Chamberlain, San Francisco at Syracuse, March 10, 1963	.27	16	70
Michael Jordan, Chicago at Cleveland, March 28, 1990*	.23	21	69
Wilt Chamberlain, Philadelphia at Chicago, December 16, 1967	.30	8	68
Pete Maravich, New Orleans vs. N.Y. Knicks, February 25, 1977	.26	16	68
Wilt Chamberlain, Philadelphia vs. New York at Philadelphia, March 9, 1961	.27	13	67
Wilt Chamberlain, Philadelphia at St. Louis, February 17, 1962	.26	15	67
Wilt Chamberlain, Philadelphia vs. New York at Philadelphia, February 25, 1962	.25	17	67
Wilt Chamberlain, San Francisco vs. Los Angeles at San Francisco, January 11, 1963	.28	11	67
Wilt Chamberlain, Los Angeles vs. Phoenix, February 9, 1969	.29	8	66
Wilt Chamberlain, Philadelphia at Cincinnati, February 13, 1962	.24	17	65
Wilt Chamberlain, Philadelphia at St. Louis, February 27, 1962	.25	15	65
Wilt Chamberlain, Philadelphia vs. Los Angeles at Philadelphia, February 7, 1966	.28	9	65
Elgin Baylor, Minneapolis vs. Boston at Minneapolis, November 8, 1959	.25	14	64
Rick Barry, Golden State vs. Portland at Oakland, March 26, 1974	.30	4	64
Michael Jordan, Chicago vs. Orlando at Chicago, January 16, 1993*	.27	9	64
Joe Fulks, Philadelphia vs. Indianapolis at Philadelphia, February 10, 1949	.27	9	63
Elgin Baylor, Los Angeles at Philadelphia, December 8, 1961***	.23	17	63
Jerry West, Los Angeles vs. New York at Los Angeles, January 17, 1962	.22	19	63
Wilt Chamberlain, San Francisco vs. Los Angeles at San Francisco, December 14, 1962	.24	15	63
Wilt Chamberlain, San Francisco at Philadelphia, November 26, 1964	.27	9	63
George Gervin, San Antonio at New Orleans, April 9, 1978	.23	17	63
Wilt Chamberlain, Philadelphia at Boston, January 14, 1962	.27	8	62
Wilt Chamberlain, Philadelphia vs. St. Louis at Detroit, January 17, 1962*	.24	14	62
Wilt Chamberlain, Philadelphia vs. Syracuse at Utica, N. Y., January 21, 1962*	.25	12	62
Wilt Chamberlain, San Francisco at New York, January 29, 1963	.27	8	62
Wilt Chamberlain, San Francisco at Cincinnati, November 15, 1964	.26	10	62
Wilt Chamberlain, Philadelphia vs. San Francisco at Philadelphia, March 3, 1966	.26	10	62
Tracy McGrady, Orlando vs. Washington, March 10, 2004	.20	17	62
George Mikan, Minneapolis vs. Rochester at Minneapolis, January 20, 1952**	.22	17	61
Wilt Chamberlain, Philadelphia vs. Chicago at Philadelphia, December 9, 1961	.28	5	61
Wilt Chamberlain, Philadelphia vs. St. Louis at Philadelphia, February 22, 1962	.21	19	61
Wilt Chamberlain, Philadelphia at Chicago, February 28, 1962	.24	13	61
Wilt Chamberlain, San Francisco vs. Cincinnati at San Francisco, November 21, 1962	.27	7	61
Wilt Chamberlain, San Francisco vs. Syracuse at San Francisco, December 11, 1962	.27	7	61
Wilt Chamberlain, San Francisco vs. St. Louis at San Francisco, December 18, 1962	.26	9	61
Michael Jordan, Chicago at Detroit, March 4, 1987*	.22	17	61
Michael Jordan, Chicago vs. Atlanta, April 16, 1987	.22	17	61
Karl Malone, Utah vs. Milwaukee, January 27, 1990	.21	19	61
Shaquille O'Neal, L.A. Lakers at L.A. Clippers, March 6, 2000	.24	13	61
Wilt Chamberlain, Philadelphia at Los Angeles, December 1, 1961	.22	16	60
Wilt Chamberlain, Philadelphia vs. Los Angeles at Hershey, Pa., December 29, 1961	.24	12	60
Wilt Chamberlain, Los Angeles vs. Cincinnati at Cleveland, January 26, 1969	.22	16	60
Bernard King, New York vs. New Jersey, December 25, 1984	.19	22	60
Larry Bird, Boston vs. Atlanta at New Orleans, March 12, 1985	.22	15	60
Tom Chambers, Phoenix vs. Seattle, March 24, 1990	.22	16	60
Jack Twyman, Cincinnati vs. Minneapolis at Cincinnati, January 15, 1960	.21	17	59
Wilt Chamberlain, Philadelphia at New York, December 25, 1961**	.23	13	59
Wilt Chamberlain, Philadelphia vs. New York at Syracuse, February 8, 1962	.23	13	59
Wilt Chamberlain, San Francisco vs. New York at San Francisco, October 30, 1962	.24	11	59
Wilt Chamberlain, San Francisco at Cincinnati, November 18, 1962	.24	11	59
Wilt Chamberlain, San Francisco vs. St. Louis at San Francisco, December 2, 1962	.25	9	59
Wilt Chamberlain, San Francisco vs. Los Angeles at San Francisco, December 6, 1963	.22	15	59
Wilt Chamberlain, San Francisco at Philadelphia, January 28, 1964	.24	11	59
Wilt Chamberlain, San Francisco at Detroit, February 11, 1964*	.25	9	59
Purvis Short, Golden State vs. New Jersey, November 17, 1984	.20	15	59
Michael Jordan, Chicago at Detroit, April 3, 1988	.21	17	59
Wilt Chamberlain, Philadelphia vs. Detroit at Bethlehem, Pa., January 25, 1960	.24	10	58
Wilt Chamberlain, Philadelphia at New York, February 21, 1960	.26	6	58
Wilt Chamberlain, Philadelphia at Cincinnati, February 25, 1961	.25	8	58
Wilt Chamberlain, Philadelphia vs. Detroit at Philadelphia, November 4, 1961	.24	10	58
Wilt Chamberlain, Philadelphia at Detroit, November 8, 1961	.23	12	58
Wilt Chamberlain, Philadelphia at New York, March 4, 1962	.24	10	58
Wilt Chamberlain, San Francisco vs. Detroit at Bakersfield, Calif., January 24, 1963	.25	8	58
Wilt Chamberlain, San Francisco at New York, December 15, 1964*	.25	8	58
Wilt Chamberlain, Philadelphia vs. Cincinnati at Philadelphia, February 13, 1967	.26	6	58

	FG	FT	Pts.
Fred Brown, Seattle at Golden State, March 23, 1974	.24	10	58
Michael Jordan, Chicago vs. New Jersey, February 26, 1987	.16	26	58
Allen Iverson, Philadelphia vs. Houston, January 15, 2002*	.21	14	58
Richie Guerin, New York vs. Syracuse at New York, December 11, 1959	.18	21	57
Elgin Baylor, Los Angeles at Detroit, February 16, 1961	.23	11	57
Bob Pettit, St. Louis at Detroit, February 18, 1961	.25	7	57
Wilt Chamberlain, Philadelphia vs. Los Angeles at Philadelphia, October 20, 1961	.24	9	57
Wilt Chamberlain, Philadelphia at Cincinnati, December 19, 1961	.24	9	57
Wilt Chamberlain, San Francisco vs. Chicago at San Francisco, November 10, 1962	.24	9	57
Rick Barry, San Francisco at New York, December 14, 1965	.18	21	57
Rick Barry, San Francisco at Cincinnati, October 29, 1966	.21	15	57
Lou Hudson, Atlanta vs. Chicago at Auburn, Ala., November 10, 1969	.25	7	57
Calvin Murphy, Houston vs. New Jersey at Houston, March 18, 1978	.24	9	57
Adrian Dantley, Utah vs. Chicago, December 4, 1982	.20	17	57
Purvis Short, Golden State vs. San Antonio, January 7, 1984	.24	7	57
Dominique Wilkins, Atlanta vs. New Jersey, April 10, 1986	.21	15	57
Dominique Wilkins, Atlanta vs. Chicago, December 10, 1986	.19	19	57
Reggie Miller, Indiana at Charlotte, November 28, 1992	.16	21	57
Michael Jordan, Chicago vs. Washington at Chicago, December 23, 1992	.22	7	57
Jerry Stackhouse, Detroit at Chicago, April 3, 2001	.21	11	57
Wilt Chamberlain, Philadelphia vs. New York at Philadelphia, January 2, 1961	.23	10	56
Wilt Chamberlain, Philadelphia vs. Syracuse at Philadelphia, January 5, 1961	.20	16	56
Wilt Chamberlain, Philadelphia vs. Los Angeles at Philadelphia, January 21, 1961	.25	6	56
Elgin Baylor, Los Angeles vs. Syracuse at Los Angeles, January 24, 1961	.19	18	56
Wilt Chamberlain, Philadelphia at Syracuse, March 1, 1961	.22	12	56
Wilt Chamberlain, Philadelphia vs. Los Angeles at Philadelphia, November 17, 1961	.24	8	56
Wilt Chamberlain, San Francisco vs. Detroit at San Francisco, October 23, 1962	.23	10	56
Wilt Chamberlain, San Francisco at Cincinnati, February 7, 1963	.23	10	56
Wilt Chamberlain, San Francisco at Los Angeles, February 16, 1963**	.26	4	56
Wilt Chamberlain, San Francisco vs. Baltimore at San Francisco, December 1, 1964**	.22	12	56
Oscar Robertson, Cincinnati vs. Los Angeles at Cincinnati, December 18, 1964	.17	22	56
Earl Monroe, Baltimore vs. Los Angeles, February 13, 1968*	.20	16	56
Chet Walker, Chicago vs. Cincinnati at Chicago, February 6, 1972	.22	12	56
Kelly Tripucka, Detroit vs. Chicago, January 29, 1983	.18	20	56
Kevin McHale, Boston vs. Detroit, March 3, 1985	.22	12	56
Michael Jordan, Chicago vs. Philadelphia, March 24, 1987	.22	12	56
Tom Chambers, Phoenix at Golden State, February 18, 1990	.19	16	56
Glen Rice, Miami vs. Orlando, April 15, 1995	.20	9	56
Karl Malone, Utah at Golden State, April 7, 1998	.18	19	56
Kobe Bryant, L.A. Lakers vs. Memphis, January 14, 2002	.21	11	56

FIELD GOALS

	FGM	FGA
Wilt Chamberlain, Philadelphia vs. New York at Hershey, Pa., March 2, 1962	36	63
Wilt Chamberlain, Philadelphia vs. Los Angeles at Philadelphia, December 8, 1961***	31	62
Wilt Chamberlain, Philadelphia at Chicago, December 16, 1967	30	40
Rick Barry, Golden State vs. Portland at Oakland, March 26, 1974	30	45
Wilt Chamberlain, Philadelphia vs. Chicago at Philadelphia, January 13, 1962	29	48
Wilt Chamberlain, San Francisco at Los Angeles, November 3, 1962	29	48
Wilt Chamberlain, San Francisco at New York, November 16, 1962	29	43
Wilt Chamberlain, Los Angeles vs. Phoenix, February 9, 1969	29	35
Elgin Baylor, Los Angeles at New York, November 15, 1960	28	48
Wilt Chamberlain, Philadelphia vs. Chicago at Philadelphia, December 9, 1961	28	48
Wilt Chamberlain, San Francisco vs. Los Angeles at San Francisco, January 11, 1963	28	47
Wilt Chamberlain, Philadelphia vs. Los Angeles at Philadelphia, February 7, 1966	28	43
David Thompson, Denver at Detroit, April 9, 1978	28	38
Joe Fulks, Philadelphia vs. Indianapolis at Philadelphia, February 10, 1949	27	56
Wilt Chamberlain, Philadelphia vs. New York at Philadelphia, March 9, 1961	27	37
Wilt Chamberlain, Philadelphia at Boston, January 14, 1962	27	45
Wilt Chamberlain, San Francisco vs. Cincinnati at San Francisco, November 21, 1962	27	52
Wilt Chamberlain, San Francisco vs. Syracuse at San Francisco, December 11, 1962	27	57
Wilt Chamberlain, San Francisco at New York, January 29, 1963	27	44
Wilt Chamberlain, San Francisco at Syracuse, March 10, 1963	27	38
Wilt Chamberlain, San Francisco at Philadelphia, November 26, 1964	27	58
Michael Jordan, Chicago vs. Orlando at Chicago, January 16, 1993*	27	49
Wilt Chamberlain, Philadelphia at New York, February 21, 1960	26	47
Wilt Chamberlain, Philadelphia at St. Louis, February 17, 1962	26	44
Wilt Chamberlain, San Francisco vs. St. Louis at San Francisco, December 18, 1962	26	53
Wilt Chamberlain, San Francisco at Los Angeles, February 16, 1963**	26	47
Wilt Chamberlain, San Francisco at Cincinnati, November 15, 1964	26	44
Wilt Chamberlain, Philadelphia vs. San Francisco at Philadelphia, March 3, 1966	26	39
Wilt Chamberlain, Philadelphia vs. Cincinnati at Philadelphia, February 13, 1967	26	34
Pete Maravich, New Orleans vs. N.Y. Knicks at New Orleans, February 25, 1977	26	43
David Robinson, San Antonio at L.A. Clippers, April 24, 1994	26	41
Elgin Baylor, Minneapolis vs. Boston at Minneapolis, November 8, 1959	25	47
Wilt Chamberlain, Philadelphia vs. Boston at New York, February 23, 1960	25	44
Wilt Chamberlain, Philadelphia vs. Los Angeles at Philadelphia, January 21, 1961	25	46

	FGM	FGA
Bob Pettit, St. Louis at Detroit, February 18, 1961.	25	42
Wilt Chamberlain, Philadelphia at Cincinnati, February 25, 1961	25	38
Wilt Chamberlain, Philadelphia vs. Syracuse at Utica, N.Y., January 21, 1962*	25	42
Wilt Chamberlain, Philadelphia vs. New York at Philadelphia, February 25, 1962	25	38
Wilt Chamberlain, Philadelphia at St. Louis, February 27, 1962	25	43
Wilt Chamberlain, San Francisco vs. St. Louis at San Francisco, December 2, 1962.	25	36
Wilt Chamberlain, San Francisco vs. Detroit at Bakersfield, Calif., January 24, 1963.	25	36
Wilt Chamberlain, San Francisco at Detroit, February 11, 1964*	25	50
Wilt Chamberlain, San Francisco at New York, December 15, 1964*	25	45
Lou Hudson, Atlanta vs. Chicago at Auburn, Ala., November 10, 1969	25	34

FREE THROWS

	FTM	FTA
Wilt Chamberlain, Philadelphia vs. New York at Hershey, Pa., March 2, 1962	28	32
Adrian Dantley, Utah vs. Houston, at Las Vegas, January 4, 1984	28	29
Adrian Dantley, Utah vs. Denver, November 25, 1983	27	31
Adrian Dantley, Utah vs. Dallas at Utah, October 31, 1980	26	29
Michael Jordan, Chicago vs. New Jersey, February 26, 1987	26	27
Frank Selvy, Milwaukee vs. Minneapolis at Ft. Wayne, December 2, 1954.	24	26
Willie Burton, Philadelphia vs. Miami, December 13, 1994.	24	28
Dolph Schayes, Syracuse vs. Minneapolis at Syracuse, January 17, 1952***	23	27
Nate Archibald, Cincinnati vs. Detroit at Cincinnati, February 5, 1972*	23	24
Nate Archibald, K.C./Omaha vs. Portland at Kansas City, January 21, 1975	23	25
Pete Maravich, New Orleans vs. New York, October 26, 1975**	23	26
Kevin Johnson, Phoenix vs. Utah, April 9, 1990*.	23	24
Dominique Wilkins, Atlanta vs. Chicago at Atlanta, December 8, 1992	23	23
Kobe Bryant, L.A. Lakers at Cleveland, January 30, 2001.	23	26
Larry Foust, Minneapolis vs. St. Louis at Minneapolis, November 30, 1957	22	26
Richie Guerin, New York at Boston, February 11, 1961	22	23
Oscar Robertson, Cincinnati vs. Los Angeles at Cincinnati, December 18, 1964	22	23
Oscar Robertson, Cincinnati at Baltimore, December 27, 1964.	22	26
Oscar Robertson, Cincinnati vs. Baltimore at Cincinnati, November 20, 1966.	22	23
John Williamson, New Jersey vs. San Diego at New Jersey, December 9, 1978	22	24
World B. Free, San Diego at Atlanta, January 13, 1979	22	29
Bernard King, New York vs. New Jersey, December 25, 1984	22	26
Rolando Blackman, Dallas at New Jersey, February 17, 1986.	22	23
Eric Floyd, Houston vs. Golden State, February 3, 1991**	22	27
Detlef Schrempt, Indiana at Golden State, December 8, 1992.	22	23
Charles Barkley, Phoenix vs. Washington, December 20, 1995*.	22	27
Latrell Sprewell, Golden State at L.A. Clippers, March 10, 1997.	22	25
Michael Jordan, Chicago vs. New York, April 18, 1998	22	24
Vince Carter, Toronto at Phoenix, December 30, 2000	22	27
Dolph Schayes, Syracuse vs. New York at Syracuse, February 15, 1953.	21	25
Richie Guerin, New York vs. Syracuse at New York, December 11, 1959	21	26
Rick Barry, San Francisco at New York, December 14, 1965	21	22
Rick Barry, San Francisco vs. Baltimore at San Francisco, November 6, 1966	21	25
Flynn Robinson, Milwaukee vs. Atlanta at Baltimore, February 17, 1969.	21	22
Lenny Wilkens, Seattle at Philadelphia, November 8, 1969.	21	25
Connie Hawkins, Phoenix vs. Seattle, January 17, 1970.	21	25
Spencer Haywood, Seattle vs. K.C./Omaha at Seattle, January 3, 1973.	21	27
John Drew, Atlanta at Phoenix, April 5, 1977.	21	28
Rich Kelley, New Orleans vs. New Jersey at New Orleans, March 21, 1978.	21	25
Moses Malone, Houston vs. Washington, February 27, 1980.	21	23
Jack Sikma, Seattle vs. Kansas City at Seattle, November 14, 1980	21	23
Moses Malone, Philadelphia vs. New York, February 13, 1985.	21	23
Moses Malone, Washington vs. Golden State, December 29, 1986	21	22
Charles Barkley, Philadelphia at Atlanta, February 9, 1988	21	26
Michael Jordan, Chicago at Cleveland, March 28, 1990*	21	23
Reggie Miller, Indiana at Charlotte, November 28, 1992.	21	23
Michael Jordan, Chicago at Miami, December 30, 1992.	21	24
George Mikan, Minneapolis at Anderson, November 19, 1949	20	23
George Mikan, Minneapolis at Chicago, December 3, 1949	20	23
Dolph Schayes, Syracuse at Cincinnati, October 26, 1957	20	22
George Yardley, Detroit at St. Louis, December 26, 1957.	20	24
Walter Dukes, Detroit at Los Angeles, November 19, 1960	20	24
Elgin Baylor, Los Angeles at St. Louis, December 21, 1962	20	21
Jerry West, Los Angeles vs. San Francisco at Los Angeles, October 30, 1965	20	21
Oscar Robertson, Cincinnati at Los Angeles, December 3, 1965.	20	24
Jerry West, Los Angeles at New York, January 8, 1966	20	24
Jerry West, Los Angeles vs. San Francisco at Los Angeles, January 21, 1966	20	23
Zelmo Beaty, St. Louis at Seattle, December 3, 1967.	20	23
Kareem Abdul-Jabbar, Milwaukee at Boston, March 8, 1970	20	25
Lenny Wilkens, Seattle vs. Baltimore at U. of Washington, January 14, 1971.	20	21
Artis Gilmore, Chicago vs. Kansas City at Chicago, March 18, 1977.	20	25
David Thompson, Denver at New Orleans, April 10, 1977	20	22
Nate Archibald, Boston vs. Chicago, January 16, 1980	20	22
Rolando Blackman, Dallas vs. San Antonio, January 5, 1983	20	21

	FTM	FTA
Kelly Tripucka, Detroit vs. Chicago, January 29, 1983	20	22
Moses Malone, Philadelphia vs. Golden State, February 20, 1985	20	22
Michael Jordan, Chicago at New York, November 1, 1986	20	22
Moses Malone, Washington vs. Houston, November 21, 1986	20	23
Dominique Wilkins, Atlanta at Seattle, February 10, 1987	20	22
Moses Malone, Washington at Atlanta, November 6, 1987	20	23
Moses Malone, Washington at San Antonio, March 14, 1988	20	22
Charles Barkley, Philadelphia vs. New York, March 16, 1988	20	24
Karl Malone, Utah at Minnesota, December 17, 1989	20	24
Karl Malone, Utah vs. Golden State, April 13, 1992	20	24
Dominique Wilkins, Atlanta at New York, March 2, 1993	20	22
Kenny Anderson, New Jersey vs. Detroit, April 15, 1994*	20	23
Shawn Kemp, Seattle at L.A. Clippers, December 10, 1994**	20	22
Paul Pierce, Boston at New York, November 2, 2002	20	21

REBOUNDS

	No.
Wilt Chamberlain, Philadelphia vs. Boston at Philadelphia, November 24, 1960	55
Bill Russell, Boston vs. Syracuse at Boston, February 5, 1960	51
Bill Russell, Boston vs. Philadelphia at Boston, November 16, 1957	49
Bill Russell, Boston vs. Detroit at Providence, March 11, 1965	49
Wilt Chamberlain, Philadelphia vs. Syracuse at Philadelphia, February 6, 1960	45
Wilt Chamberlain, Philadelphia vs. Los Angeles at Philadelphia, January 21, 1961	45
Wilt Chamberlain, Philadelphia vs. New York at Philadelphia, November 10, 1959	43
Wilt Chamberlain, Philadelphia vs. Los Angeles at Philadelphia, December 8, 1961***	43
Bill Russell, Boston vs. Los Angeles at Boston, January 20, 1963	43
Wilt Chamberlain, Philadelphia vs. Boston at Philadelphia, March 6, 1965	43
Wilt Chamberlain, Philadelphia vs. Boston at Philadelphia, January 15, 1960	42
Wilt Chamberlain, Philadelphia vs. Detroit at Bethlehem, Pa., January 25, 1960	42
Nate Thurmond, San Francisco vs. Detroit at San Francisco, November 9, 1965	42
Wilt Chamberlain, Philadelphia vs. Boston at Philadelphia, January 14, 1966	42
Wilt Chamberlain, Los Angeles vs. Boston, March 7, 1969*	42
Bill Russell, Boston vs. Syracuse at Boston, February 12, 1958	41
Wilt Chamberlain, San Francisco vs. Detroit at San Francisco, October 26, 1962*	41
Bill Russell, Boston vs. San Francisco at Boston, March 14, 1965	41
Bill Russell, Boston vs. Cincinnati at Boston, December 12, 1958*	40
Wilt Chamberlain, Philadelphia vs. Syracuse at Philadelphia, November 4, 1959	40
Bill Russell, Boston vs. Philadelphia at Boston, February 12, 1961	40
Jerry Lucas, Cincinnati at Philadelphia, February 29, 1964	40
Wilt Chamberlain, San Francisco vs. Detroit at San Francisco, November 22, 1964	40
Wilt Chamberlain, Philadelphia vs. Boston at Philadelphia, December 28, 1965	40
Neil Johnston, Philadelphia vs. Syracuse at Philadelphia, December 4, 1954	39
Bill Russell, Boston vs. Detroit at Boston, January 25, 1959	39
Bill Russell, Boston vs. New York at Boston, December 19, 1959	39
Wilt Chamberlain, Philadelphia vs. Cincinnati at St. Louis, December 28, 1959	39
Wilt Chamberlain, Philadelphia vs. Syracuse at Boston, January 13, 1960*	39
Wilt Chamberlain, Philadelphia vs. Boston at Philadelphia, January 29, 1960	39
Wilt Chamberlain, Philadelphia vs. Detroit at Philadelphia, November 4, 1960	39
Bill Russell, Boston vs. New York at Providence, R.I., December 21, 1961	39
Maurice Stokes, Rochester vs. Syracuse at Rochester, January 14, 1956	38
Bill Russell, Boston vs. Philadelphia at Providence, February 23, 1958	38
Bill Russell, Boston vs. New York at Boston, December 4, 1959	38
Wilt Chamberlain, Philadelphia vs. Los Angeles at New York, November 29, 1960	38
Wilt Chamberlain, Philadelphia at Cincinnati, December 18, 1960	38
Wilt Chamberlain, Philadelphia vs. Chicago at Philadelphia, November 25, 1961	38
Bill Russell, Boston at San Francisco, February 21, 1963	38
Wilt Chamberlain, San Francisco vs. Boston at San Francisco, February 21, 1963	38
Wilt Chamberlain, San Francisco vs. Boston at San Francisco, April 24, 1964	38
Bill Russell, Boston at New York, January 30, 1965	38
Bill Russell, Boston vs. Los Angeles at Boston, March 3, 1965	38
Wilt Chamberlain, Philadelphia vs. San Francisco at Philadelphia, March 2, 1967	38
Wilt Chamberlain, Philadelphia at Seattle, December 20, 1967	38
Wilt Chamberlain, Los Angeles vs. Baltimore at Los Angeles, March 9, 1969	38

ASSISTS

	No.
Scott Skiles, Orlando vs. Denver at Orlando, December 30, 1990	30
Kevin Porter, New Jersey vs. Houston at New Jersey, February 24, 1978	29
Bob Cousy, Boston vs. Minneapolis at Boston, February 27, 1959	28
Guy Rodgers, San Francisco vs. St. Louis at San Francisco, March 14, 1963	28
John Stockton, Utah vs. San Antonio, January 15, 1991	28
Geoff Huston, Cleveland vs. Golden State at Cleveland, January 27, 1982	27
John Stockton, Utah at New York, December 19, 1989	27
John Stockton, Utah vs. Portland, April 14, 1988	26
Ernie DiGregorio, Buffalo at Portland, January 1, 1974	25
Kevin Porter, Detroit vs. Boston at Detroit, March 9, 1979	25
Kevin Porter, Detroit at Phoenix, April 1, 1979	25
Isiah Thomas, Detroit vs. Dallas, February 13, 1985	25

No.

Nate McMillan, Seattle vs. L.A. Clippers, February 23, 1987 .... .25
Kevin Johnson, Phoenix vs. San Antonio, April 6, 1994 .... .25
Jason Kidd, Dallas vs. Utah, February 8, 1996** .... .25
Guy Rodgers, Chicago vs. New York at Chicago, December 21, 1966 .... .24
Kevin Porter, Washington vs. Detroit, March 23, 1980 .... .24
John Lucas, San Antonio vs. Denver, April 15, 1984 .... .24
Isiah Thomas, Detroit at Washington, February 7, 1985** .... .24
John Stockton, Utah at Houston, January 3, 1989 .... .24
Magic Johnson, L.A. Lakers vs. Denver, November 17, 1989 .... .24
Magic Johnson, L.A. Lakers at Phoenix, January 9, 1990* .... .24
Jerry West, Los Angeles vs. Philadelphia at Los Angeles, February 1, 1967 ... .23
Kevin Porter, Detroit vs. Houston at Detroit, December 27, 1978 .... .23
Kevin Porter, Detroit at Los Angeles, March 30, 1979 .... .23
Nate Archibald, Boston vs. Denver at Boston, February 5, 1982 .... .23
Magic Johnson, Los Angeles vs. Seattle, February 21, 1984 .... .23
Magic Johnson, L.A. Lakers at Dallas, April 20, 1988 .... .23
Fat Lever, Denver at Golden State, April 21, 1989 .... .23
John Stockton, Utah vs. L.A. Lakers, April 12, 1990 .... .23
John Stockton, Utah at L.A. Clippers, December 8, 1990 .... .23
John Stockton, Utah vs. Golden State, November 29, 1991 .... .23
John Stockton, Utah vs. Minnesota, April 17, 1992 .... .23
Mookie Blaylock, Atlanta vs. Utah at Atlanta, March 6, 1993 .... .23
Nick Van Exel, L.A. Lakers at Vancouver, January 5, 1997 .... .23
Jamaal Tinsley, Indiana vs. Washington, November 22, 2001 .... .23
Oscar Robertson, Cincinnati vs. Syracuse at Cincinnati, October 29, 1961 .. .22
Oscar Robertson, Cincinnati vs. New York at Cincinnati, March 5, 1966* .... .22
Art Williams, San Diego at Phoenix, December 28, 1968 .... .22
Art Williams, San Diego vs. San Francisco, February 14, 1970 .... .22
Kevin Porter, Washington vs. Atlanta at Washington, March 5, 1975 .... .22
Kevin Porter, Detroit vs. San Antonio at Detroit, December 23, 1978 ...... .22
Phil Ford, Kansas City vs. Milwaukee at Kansas City, February 21, 1979 ... .22
Kevin Porter, Detroit at Chicago, February 27, 1979 .... .22
John Lucas, Golden State at Denver, February 27, 1981 .... .22
Allan Leavell, Houston vs. New Jersey, January 25, 1983 .... .22
Magic Johnson, Los Angeles vs. Cleveland, November 17, 1983 .... .22
Ennis Whatley, Chicago vs. New York, January 14, 1984 .... .22
Ennis Whatley, Chicago vs. Atlanta, March 3, 1984 .... .22
John Stockton, Utah vs. L.A. Lakers, January 8, 1987 .... .22
John Stockton, Utah vs. Cleveland, December 11, 1989* .... .22
Magic Johnson, L.A. Lakers vs. Portland, November 6, 1990* .... .22
John Stockton, Utah at Philadelphia, December 18, 1992 .... .22
Sherman Douglas, Boston at Philadelphia, April 3, 1994 .... .22
Tim Hardaway, Golden State vs. Orlando, December 16, 1994* .... .22
Robert Pack, New Jersey vs. Dallas, November 23, 1996 .... .22
Mark Jackson, Denver vs. New Jersey, January 20, 1997 .... .22
George McCloud, Denver at Chicago, March 26, 2001* .... .22
Andre Miller, Cleveland vs. Philadelphia, December 15, 2001 .... .22
Richie Guerin, New York vs. St. Louis at New York, December 12, 1958 . .21
Bob Cousy, Boston vs. St. Louis at Boston, December 21, 1960 .... .21
Oscar Robertson, Cincinnati vs. New York at Cincinnati, February 14, 1964 .21
Guy Rodgers, Chicago vs. San Francisco at Chicago, October 18, 1966 . .21
Wilt Chamberlain, Philadelphia vs. Detroit, February 2, 1968 .... .21
Guy Rodgers, Milwaukee vs. Detroit, October 31, 1968 .... .21
Clem Haskins, Chicago vs. Boston, December 6, 1969* .... .21
Larry Siegfried, San Diego at Portland, November 16, 1970 .... .21
Nate Archibald, K.C./Omaha vs. Detroit at Omaha, December 15, 1972* .21
Kevin Porter, Washington vs. Los Angeles at Washington, March 2, 1975 .21
Kevin Porter, Detroit at Houston, February 6, 1979 .... .21
Phil Ford, Kansas City vs. Phoenix at Kansas City, February 23, 1979 .21
Maurice Cheeks, Philadelphia vs. New Jersey, October 30, 1982 .... .21
Magic Johnson, Los Angeles at Atlanta, January 15, 1983 .... .21
Isiah Thomas, Detroit at Kansas City, December 22, 1984 .... .21
Ennis Whatley, Chicago vs. Golden State, February 23, 1985 ..... .21
Norm Nixon, L.A. Clippers vs. Detroit, March 18, 1985 .... .21
Isiah Thomas, Detroit vs. Washington, April 12, 1985 .... .21
Doc Rivers, Atlanta vs. Philadelphia, March 4, 1986 .... .21
Nate McMillan, Seattle vs. Sacramento, March 31, 1987 .... .21
John Stockton, Utah at L.A. Clippers, February 19, 1988 ..... .21
John Stockton, Utah vs. L.A. Clippers, February 20, 1988 ... .21
John Stockton, Utah vs. Phoenix, March 22, 1988 .... .21
John Stockton, Utah at L.A. Clippers, April 20, 1988 ...... .21
John Stockton, Utah vs. Phoenix, November 19, 1988 ...... .21
Magic Johnson, L.A. Lakers at L.A. Clippers, December 6, 1988 .21
John Stockton, Utah vs. Denver, February 14, 1989 ...... .21
Kevin Johnson, Phoenix at L.A. Lakers, February 26, 1989 .21
Magic Johnson, L.A. Lakers vs. Seattle, April 23, 1989 . .21
Gary Grant, L.A. Clippers vs. Milwaukee, November 29, 1989 .21

– 171 –

HISTORY Regular season

Magic Johnson, L.A. Lakers at Boston, December 15, 1989 21
Gary Grant, L.A. Clippers vs. Seattle, January 18, 1990 21
John Stockton, Utah vs. Portland, March 1, 1990 21
John Stockton, Utah vs. Phoenix, March 13, 1990 21
John Stockton, Utah vs. Golden State, December 11, 1990 21
Magic Johnson, L.A. Lakers vs. Indiana, December 16, 1990 21
John Stockton, Utah at San Antonio, April 19, 1992 21
Scott Skiles, Orlando at Cleveland, April 16, 1993 21
Sherman Douglas, Boston vs. Sacramento, December 8, 1993 21

STEALS

No.

Larry Kenon, San Antonio at Kansas City, December 26, 1976 11
Kendall Gill, New Jersey vs. Miami, April 3, 1999 11
Jerry West, Los Angeles vs. Seattle at Los Angeles, December 7, 1973 10
Larry Steele, Portland vs. Los Angeles at Portland, November 16, 1974 10
Fred Brown, Seattle at Philadelphia, December 3, 1976 10
Gus Williams, Seattle at New Jersey, February 22, 1978 10
Eddie Jordan, New Jersey at Philadelphia, March 23, 1979 10
Johnny Moore, San Antonio vs. Indiana, March 6, 1985 10
Fat Lever, Denver vs. Indiana, March 9, 1985 10
Clyde Drexler, Portland at Milwaukee, January 10, 1986 10
Alvin Robertson, San Antonio vs. Phoenix, February 18, 1986 10
Alvin Robertson, San Antonio at L.A. Clippers, November 22, 1986 10
Ron Harper, Cleveland vs. Philadelphia, March 10, 1987 10
Michael Jordan, Chicago vs. New Jersey, January 29, 1988 10
Alvin Robertson, San Antonio vs. Houston, January 11, 1989* 10
Alvin Robertson, Milwaukee vs. Utah, November 19, 1990 10
Kevin Johnson, Phoenix vs. Washington, December 9, 1993 10
Clyde Drexler, Houston vs. Sacramento, November 1, 1996 10
Mookie Blaylock, Atlanta vs. Philadelphia, April 14, 1998 10
Michael Finley, Dallas vs. Philadelphia, January 23, 2001 10
Calvin Murphy, Houston vs. Boston at Houston, December 14, 1973 9
Larry Steele, Portland vs. Los Angeles at Portland, March 5, 1974 9
Rick Barry, Golden State vs. Buffalo at Oakland, October 29, 1974 9
Don Watts, Seattle vs. Philadelphia at Seattle, February 23, 1975 9
Larry Steele, Portland vs. Phoenix at Portland, March 7, 1975 9
Larry Steele, Portland vs. Detroit at Portland, March 14, 1976 9
Quinn Buckner, Milwaukee vs. Indiana at Milwaukee, January 2, 1977 9
Don Watts, Seattle vs. Phoenix at Seattle, March 27, 1977 9
Earl Tatum, Detroit at Los Angeles, November 28, 1978 9
Gus Williams, Seattle at Washington, January 23, 1979 9
Ron Lee, Detroit vs. Houston, March 16, 1980 9
Dudley Bradley, Indiana at Utah, November 10, 1980 9
Dudley Bradley, Indiana vs. Cleveland at Indiana, November 29, 1980 9
Micheal Ray Richardson, New York at Chicago, December 23, 1980 9
Johnny High, Phoenix at Washington, January 28, 1981 9
Magic Johnson, Los Angeles vs. Phoenix at Los Angeles, November 6, 1981 9
Jack Sikma, Seattle vs. Kansas City at Kansas City, January 27, 1982 9
Rickey Green, Utah vs. Denver, November 10, 1982 9
Rickey Green, Utah at Philadelphia, November 27, 1982 9
Micheal Ray Richardson, Golden State vs. San Antonio, February 5, 1983 9
Darwin Cook, New Jersey vs. Portland, December 3, 1983* 9
Gus Williams, Washington vs. Atlanta, October 30, 1984 9
Johnny Moore, San Antonio vs. Golden State, January 8, 1985 9
Larry Bird, Boston at Utah, February 18, 1985 9
Micheal Ray Richardson, New Jersey vs. Indiana, October 30, 1985*** 9
Maurice Cheeks, Philadelphia vs. L.A. Clippers, January 5, 1987 9
T.R. Dunn, Denver at New Jersey, January 6, 1988 9
Michael Jordan, Chicago at Boston, November 9, 1988 9
Hersey Hawkins, Philadelphia vs. Boston, January 25, 1991 9
John Stockton, Utah vs. Houston, February 12, 1991 9
Michael Adams, Washington at Indiana, November 1, 1991 9
Doc Rivers, L.A. Clippers vs. Phoenix, November 6, 1991 9
Michael Jordan, Chicago vs. New Jersey at Chicago, April 2, 1993 9
Fat Lever, Dallas vs. Washington, February 10, 1994 9
Scottie Pippen, Chicago vs. Atlanta, March 8, 1994 9
Eric Murdock, Milwaukee at Washington, April 2, 1994 9
Mookie Blaylock, Atlanta at Houston, February 17, 1997 9
Doug Christie, Toronto at Denver, February 25, 1997* 9
Eddie Jones, Charlotte vs. Indiana, November 4, 1999 9
Paul Pierce, Boston vs. Miami, December 3, 1999 9
Allen Iverson, Philadelphia vs. Orlando, March 19, 2000 9
Andre Miller, Cleveland vs. Philadelphia, December 15, 2001 9

HISTORY *Regular season*

Allen Iverson, Philadelphia vs. L.A. Lakers, December 20,, 2002* 9
Dirk Nowitzki, Dallas at Houston, March 7, 2004. 9

BLOCKED SHOTS

No.

Elmore Smith, Los Angeles vs. Portland at Los Angeles, October 28, 1973 17
Manute Bol, Washington vs. Atlanta, January 25, 1986 15
Manute Bol, Washington vs. Indiana, February 26, 1987 15
Shaquille O'Neal, Orlando at New Jersey, November 20, 1993 15
Elmore Smith, Los Angeles vs. Detroit at Los Angeles, October 26, 1973 14
Elmore Smith, Los Angeles vs. Houston at Los Angeles, November 4, 1973 14
Mark Eaton, Utah vs. Portland, January 18, 1985 14
Mark Eaton, Utah vs. San Antonio, February 18, 1989 14
George Johnson, San Antonio vs. Golden State at San Antonio, February 24, 1981 13
Mark Eaton, Utah vs. Portland, February 18, 1983 13
Darryl Dawkins, New Jersey vs. Philadelphia, November 5, 1983 13
Ralph Sampson, Houston at Chicago, December 9, 1983* 13
Manute Bol, Golden State vs. New Jersey, February 2, 1990 13
Shawn Bradley, Dallas vs. Portland, April 7, 1998 13
Nate Thurmond, Chicago vs. Atlanta at Chicago, October 18, 1974 12
George Johnson, New Jersey at New Orleans, March 21, 1978 12
Tree Rollins, Atlanta vs. Portland at Atlanta, February 21, 1979 12
Mark Eaton, Utah at Denver, February 5, 1983 12
Mark Eaton, Utah vs. Dallas, March 17, 1984 12
Mark Eaton, Utah at Dallas, February 26, 1985 12
Manute Bol, Washington vs. Milwaukee, December 12, 1985* 12
Mark Eaton, Utah vs. Portland, November 1, 1986 12
Manute Bol, Washington vs. Cleveland, February 5, 1987 12
Hakeem Olajuwon, Houston vs. Seattle, March 10, 1987** 12
Manute Bol, Washington vs. Boston, March 26, 1987 12
Manute Bol, Golden State at San Antonio, February 22, 1989 12
Hakeem Olajuwon, Houston vs. Utah, November 11, 1989 12
David Robinson, San Antonio vs. Minnesota, February 23, 1990 12
Dikembe Mutombo, Denver vs. L.A. Clippers at Denver, April 18, 1993 12
Shawn Bradley, New Jersey vs. Toronto, April 17, 1996 12
Vlade Divac, Charlotte vs. New Jersey, February 12, 1997 12
Keon Clark, Toronto vs. Atlanta, March 23, 2001 12

CAREER SCORING

TOP NBA CAREER SCORERS (10,000 OR MORE POINTS)
Active players are shown in capital letters.

CAREER shows the calendar year in which the player's earliest and latest seasons ended. For example, if the earliest season was 1969-1970 and the latest season was 1988-1989, the display will show "70-89".

Player	Yrs.	G	Min.	FGM	FGA	Pct.	FTM	FTA	Pct.	Reb.	Ast.	PF	Pts.	Avg.	Career
Kareem Abdul-Jabbar	20	1560	57446	15837	28307	.559	6712	9304	.721	17440	5660	4657	38387	24.6	70-89
KARL MALONE	19	1476	54852	13528	26210	.516	9787	13188	.742	14968	5248	4578	36928	25.0	86-04
Michael Jordan	15	1072	41011	12192	24537	.497	7327	8772	.835	6672	5633	2783	32292	30.1	85-03
Wilt Chamberlain	14	1045	47859	12681	23497	.540	6057	11862	.511	23924	4643	2075	31419	30.1	60-73
Moses Malone	19	1329	45071	9435	19225	.491	8531	11090	.769	16212	1796	3076	27409	20.6	77-95
Elvin Hayes	16	1303	50000	10976	24272	.452	5356	7999	.670	16279	2398	4193	27313	21.0	69-84
Hakeem Olajuwon	18	1238	44222	10749	20991	.512	5423	7621	.712	13748	3058	4383	26946	21.8	85-02
Oscar Robertson	14	1040	43886	9508	19620	.485	7694	9185	.838	7804	9887	2931	26710	25.7	61-74
Dominique Wilkins	15	1074	38113	9963	21589	.461	6031	7438	.811	7169	2677	2061	26668	24.8	83-99
John Havlicek	16	1270	46471	10513	23930	.439	5369	6589	.815	8007	6114	3281	26395	20.8	63-78
Alex English	15	1193	38063	10659	21036	.507	4277	5141	.832	6538	4351	3027	25613	21.5	77-91
Jerry West	14	932	36571	9016	19032	.474	7160	8801	.814	5376	6238	2435	25192	27.0	61-74
Patrick Ewing	17	1183	40594	9702	19241	.504	5392	7289	.740	11607	2215	4034	24815	21.0	85-02
REGGIE MILLER	17	1323	45514	7927	16780	.472	5987	6758	.886	4026	3995	2621	24305	18.4	88-04
Charles Barkley	16	1073	39330	8435	15605	.541	6349	8643	.735	12546	4215	3287	23757	22.1	85-00
Robert Parish	21	1611	45704	9614	17914	.537	4106	5694	.721	14715	2180	4443	23334	14.5	77-97
Adrian Dantley	15	955	34151	8169	15121	.540	6832	8351	.818	5455	2830	2550	23177	24.3	77-91
Elgin Baylor	14	846	33863	8693	20171	.431	5763	7391	.780	11463	3650	2596	23149	27.4	59-72
Clyde Drexler	15	1086	37537	8335	17673	.472	4698	5962	.788	6677	6125	3285	22195	20.4	84-98
SHAQUILLE O'NEAL	12	809	30493	8670	15020	.577	4573	8508	.537	9781	2309	2745	21914	27.1	93-04
Larry Bird	13	897	34443	8591	17334	.496	3960	4471	.886	8974	5695	2279	21791	24.3	80-92
Hal Greer	15	1122	39788	8504	18811	.452	4578	5717	.801	5665	4540	3855	21586	19.2	59-73
Walt Bellamy	14	1043	38940	7914	15340	.516	5113	8088	.632	14241	2544	3536	20941	20.1	62-75
Bob Pettit	11	792	30690	7349	16872	.436	6182	8119	.761	12849	2369	2529	20880	26.4	55-65
David Robinson	14	987	34271	7365	14221	.518	6035	8201	.736	10497	2441	2835	20790	21.1	90-03
George Gervin	10	791	26536	8045	15747	.511	4541	5383	.844	3607	2214	2331	20708	26.2	77-86
Mitch Richmond	14	976	34309	7305	16038	.455	4561	5365	.850	3801	3398	2503	20497	21.0	89-02
Tom Chambers	16	1107	33922	7378	15749	.468	5066	6274	.807	6703	2283	3742	20049	18.1	82-98
GARY PAYTON	14	1109	40768	7995	17060	.469	2974	4096	.726	4668	8039	2810	19956	18.0	91-04
John Stockton	19	1504	47764	7039	13658	.515	4788	5796	.826	4051	15806	3942	19711	13.1	85-03
Bernard King	14	874	29417	7830	15109	.518	3972	5444	.730	5060	2863	2885	19655	22.5	78-93
Walter Davis	15	1033	28859	8118	15871	.511	3128	3676	.851	3053	3878	2454	19521	18.9	78-92

HISTORY *Regular season*

Player	Yrs.	G	Min.	FGM	FGA	Pct.	FTM	FTA	Pct.	Reb.	Ast.	PF	Pts.	Avg.	Career
Terry Cummings	18	1183	33898	8045	16628	.484	3326	4711	.706	8630	2190	3836	19460	16.4	83-00
Bob Lanier	14	959	32103	7761	15092	.514	3724	4858	.767	9698	3007	3048	19248	20.1	71-84
Dolph Schayes	16	1059	29800	6134	15427	.380	6979	8274	.843	11256	3072	3664	19247	18.2	49-64
Eddie A. Johnson	17	1199	32604	7727	16361	.472	3186	3792	.840	4832	2550	2962	19202	16.0	82-99
Gail Goodrich	14	1031	33527	7431	16300	.456	4319	5354	.807	3279	4805	2775	19181	18.6	66-79
Reggie Theus	13	1026	34603	7057	14973	.471	4663	5644	.826	3349	6453	3008	19015	18.5	79-91
Dale Ellis	17	1209	34778	7323	15275	.479	2639	3365	.784	4201	1746	2480	19004	15.7	84-00
SCOTTIE PIPPEN	17	1178	41069	7420	15700	.473	3122	4437	.704	7494	6135	3329	18940	16.1	88-04
Chet Walker	13	1032	33433	6876	14628	.470	5079	6384	.796	7314	2126	2727	18831	18.2	63-75
Isiah Thomas	13	979	35516	7194	15904	.452	4036	5316	.759	3478	9061	2971	18822	19.2	82-94
Bob McAdoo	14	852	28327	7420	14751	.503	3944	5229	.754	8048	1951	2726	18787	22.1	73-86
Mark Aguirre	13	923	27730	7201	14865	.484	3664	4944	.741	4578	2871	2599	18458	20.0	82-94
Rick Barry	10	794	28825	7252	16163	.449	3818	4243	.900	5168	4017	2264	18395	23.2	66-80
Julius Erving	11	836	28677	7237	14276	.507	3844	4950	.777	5601	3224	2286	18364	22.0	77-87
GLEN RICE	15	1000	34985	6776	14867	.456	3225	3813	.846	4387	2097	2361	18336	18.3	90-04
Dave Bing	12	901	32769	6962	15769	.441	4403	5683	.775	3420	5397	2615	18327	20.3	67-78
CLIFFORD ROBINSON	15	1179	38054	6887	15621	.441	3430	4953	.693	5708	2850	3690	18305	15.5	90-04
World B. Free	13	886	26893	6512	14294	.456	4718	6264	.753	2430	3319	2270	17955	20.3	76-88
Calvin Murphy	13	1002	30607	7247	15030	.482	3445	3864	.892	2103	4402	3250	17949	17.9	71-83
Lou Hudson	13	890	29794	7392	15129	.489	3156	3960	.797	3926	2432	2439	17940	20.2	67-79
Chris Mullin	16	986	32163	6740	13243	.509	3616	4178	.865	4034	3450	2050	179111	8.2	86-01
Lenny Wilkens	15	1077	38064	6189	14327	.432	5394	6973	.774	5030	7211	3285	17772	16.5	61-75
Bailey Howell	12	950	30627	6515	13585	.480	4740	6224	.762	9383	1853	3498	17770	18.7	60-71
Magic Johnson	13	906	33245	6211	11951	.520	4960	5850	.848	6559	10141	2050	17707	19.5	80-96
Rolando Blackman	13	980	32087	6887	13969	.493	3620	4309	.840	3278	2981	1634	17623	18.0	82-94
Otis Thorpe	17	1257	39822	6872	12593	.546	3853	5612	.687	10370	2730	4146	17600	14.0	85-01
Earl Monroe	13	926	29636	6906	14898	.464	3642	4513	.807	2796	3594	2416	17454	18.8	68-80
Kevin McHale	13	971	30118	6830	12334	.554	3634	4554	.798	7122	1670	2758	17335	17.9	81-93
Jack Sikma	14	1107	36943	6396	13792	.464	4292	5053	.849	10816	3488	3879	17287	15.6	78-91
Jeff Malone	13	905	29660	7099	14674	.484	2947	3383	.871	2364	2154	1695	17231	19.0	84-96
KEVIN WILLIS	19	1390	37975	7055	14469	.488	3004	4213	.713	11817	1318	4108	17154	12.3	85-04
Bob Cousy	14	924	30165	6168	16648	.375	4624	5756	.803	4786	6955	2242	16960	18.4	51-70
Buck Williams	17	1307	42464	6404	11661	.549	3971	5979	.664	13017	1646	4267	16784	12.8	82-98
Nate Archibald	13	876	31159	5899	12628	.467	4664	5760	.810	2046	6476	2002	16481	18.8	71-84
Joe Dumars	14	1018	35139	5994	13026	.460	3423	4059	.843	2203	4612	1826	16401	16.1	86-99
James Worthy	12	926	30001	6878	13204	.521	2447	3184	.769	4708	2791	1975	16320	17.6	83-94
Paul Arizin	10	713	24897	5628	13356	.421	5010	6189	.810	6129	1665	2764	16266	22.8	51-62
Randy Smith	12	976	31444	6676	14218	.470	2893	3705	.781	3597	4487	2556	16262	16.7	72-83
Derek Harper	16	1199	37786	6191	13384	.463	2554	3426	.745	2884	6577	2755	16006	13.3	84-99
Kiki Vandeweghe	13	810	24521	6139	11699	.525	3484	3997	.872	2785	1668	1560	15980	19.7	81-93
Pete Maravich	10	658	24316	6187	14025	.441	3564	4344	.820	2747	3563	1865	15948	24.2	71-80
Jack Twyman	11	823	26147	6237	13873	.450	3366	4325	.778	5424	1861	2782	15840	19.2	56-66
Detlef Schrempf	16	1136	33597	5400	10995	.491	4486	5584	.803	7023	3833	3360	15761	13.9	86-01
LATRELL SPREWELL	12	833	32820	5678	13333	.426	3300	4110	.803	3470	3485	1565	15691	18.8	93-04
Larry Nance	13	920	30697	6370	11664	.546	2939	3892	.755	7352	2393	2703	15687	17.1	82-94
Jeff Hornacek	14	1077	33964	5929	11957	.496	2973	3390	.877	3646	5281	2364	15659	14.5	87-00
Terry Porter	17	1274	35354	5428	11734	.463	3433	4107	.836	3872	7160	2203	15586	12.2	86-02
Walt Frazier	13	825	30965	6130	12516	.490	3321	4226	.786	4830	5040	2180	15581	18.9	68-80
Artis Gilmore	12	909	29685	5732	9570	.599	4114	5768	.713	9161	1777	2986	15579	17.1	77-88
Dennis Johnson	14	1100	35954	5832	13100	.445	3791	4754	.797	4249	5499	3087	15535	14.1	77-90
Bob Dandridge	13	839	29502	6445	13317	.484	2638	3382	.780	5715	2846	2940	15530	18.5	70-82
Sam Jones	12	871	24285	6271	13745	.456	2869	3572	.803	4305	2209	1735	15411	17.7	58-69
Tim Hardaway	13	867	30626	5640	13076	.431	2551	3263	.782	2855	7095	2027	15373	17.7	90-03
Dick Barnett	14	971	28937	6034	13227	.456	3290	4324	.761	2812	2729	2514	15358	15.8	60-74
Shawn Kemp	14	1051	29293	5505	11278	.488	4304	5805	.742	8834	1704	3826	15347	14.6	90-03
Sam Perkins	17	1286	36598	5498	11984	.459	3479	4292	.811	7666	1975	3177	15324	11.9	85-01
John Drew	11	739	21828	5481	11658	.470	4319	5774	.748	5088	1224	2641	15291	20.7	75-85
Byron Scott	14	1073	30152	5918	12268	.482	2486	2985	.833	2987	2729	2051	15097	14.1	84-97
Dick Van Arsdale	12	921	31771	5413	11661	.464	4253	5385	.790	3807	3060	2575	15079	16.4	66-77
Mike Mitchell	10	759	24537	6371	12912	.493	2255	2894	.779	4246	1010	2012	15016	19.8	79-88
James Edwards	19	1168	28356	5802	11724	.495	3257	4666	.698	6004	1499	4042	14862	12.7	78-96
Richie Guerin	13	848	27449	5174	12451	.416	4328	5549	.780	4278	4211	2769	14676	17.3	57-70
Dan Issel	9	718	22342	5424	10711	.506	3792	4756	.797	5707	1804	2022	14659	20.4	77-85
Jamaal Wilkes	12	828	27275	6226	12471	.499	2185	2878	.759	5117	2050	2296	14644	17.7	75-86
Purvis Short	12	842	24549	5934	12507	.474	2614	3174	.824	3625	2123	2479	14607	17.3	79-90
Spencer Haywood	12	760	25600	5790	12447	.465	3011	3766	.800	7038	1351	2167	14592	19.2	71-83
Bill Russell	13	963	40726	5687	12930	.440	3148	5614	.561	21620	4100	2592	14522	15.1	57-69
Hersey Hawkins	13	983	32034	4889	10612	.461	3466	3985	.870	3554	2860	2043	14470	14.7	89-01
Ricky Pierce	16	969	23665	5391	10925	.493	3389	3871	.875	2296	1826	2213	14467	14.9	83-98
Nate Thurmond	14	964	35875	5521	13105	.421	3395	5089	.667	14464	2575	2624	14437	15.0	64-77
ALLEN IVERSON	8	535	22164	5104	12247	.417	3539	4668	.758	2175	3046	1178	14436	27.0	97-04
ROD STRICKLAND	16	1078	33438	5409	11885	.455	3423	4749	.721	4057	7948	2033	14435	13.4	89-04
Jo Jo White	12	837	29941	6169	13884	.444	2060	2471	.834	3345	4095	2056	14399	17.2	70-81
ALLAN HOUSTON	11	819	27779	5252	11812	.445	2536	2936	.864	2411	1948	2022	14314	17.5	94-04
Tom Van Arsdale	12	929	28682	5505	12763	.431	3222	4226	.762	3942	2085	2922	14232	15.3	66-77
GLENN ROBINSON	10	679	25189	5537	12052	.459	2452	2993	.819	4165	1871	1828	14144	20.8	95-04
Gus Williams	11	825	25645	5793	12570	.461	2399	3173	.756	2222	4597	1637	14093	17.1	76-87

Player	Yrs.	G	Min.	FGM	FGA	Pct.	FTM	FTA	Pct.	Reb.	Ast.	PF	Pts.	Avg.	Career
Dave DeBusschere	12	875	31202	5722	13249	.432	2609	3730	.699	9618	2497	2801	14053	16.1	63-74
Jerry Lucas	11	829	32131	5709	11441	.499	2635	3365	.783	12942	2730	2389	14053	17.0	64-74
Fred Brown	13	963	24422	6006	12568	.478	1896	2211	.858	2637	3160	1937	14018	14.6	72-84
Alvan Adams	13	988	27203	5709	11464	.498	2490	3160	.788	6937	4012	3214	13910	14.1	76-88
Ron Harper	15	1009	31199	5326	11946	.446	2735	3799	.720	4309	3916	2324	13910	13.8	87-01
Bob Love	11	789	25120	5447	12688	.429	3001	3728	.805	4653	1123	2130	13895	17.6	67-77
Marques Johnson	11	691	23694	5733	11065	.518	2412	3265	.739	4817	2502	1766	13892	20.1	78-90
KEVIN GARNETT	9	693	26462	5628	11522	.488	2470	3245	.761	7493	3059	1758	13864	20.0	96-04
Chuck Person	13	943	28941	5576	12176	.458	1486	2056	.723	4763	2645	2565	13858	14.7	87-00
Bill Laimbeer	14	1068	33956	5574	11198	.498	2440	2916	.837	10400	2184	3633	13790	12.9	81-94
CHRIS WEBBER	11	619	23637	5716	11649	.491	1983	3158	.628	6302	2746	2107	13639	22.0	94-04
Billy Cunningham	9	654	22406	5116	11467	.446	3394	4717	.720	6638	2625	2431	13626	20.8	66-76
Orlando Woolridge	13	851	24041	5150	10037	.513	3315	4501	.737	3696	1609	2166	13623	16.0	82-94
Xavier McDaniel	12	870	25201	5673	11685	.485	2186	3046	.718	5313	1775	2557	13606	15.6	86-98
Dave Cowens	11	766	29565	5744	12499	.460	2027	2590	.783	10444	2910	2920	13516	17.6	71-83
Cliff Hagan	10	745	21731	5239	11630	.450	2969	3722	.798	5116	2242	2388	13447	18.0	57-66
Rudy Tomjanovich	11	768	25714	5630	11240	.501	2089	2666	.784	6198	1573	1937	13383	17.4	71-81
VLADE DIVAC	15	1119	33708	5192	10479	.495	2880	4164	.692	9294	3522	3584	13364	11.9	90-04
Kevin Johnson	12	735	25061	4512	9160	493	3943	4691	.841	2404	6711	1541	13127	17.9	88-00
STEVE SMITH	13	892	28105	4507	10237	.440	2995	3545	.845	2995	2851	2196	13116	14.7	92-04
Jeff Mullins	12	802	24574	5383	11631	.463	2251	2764	.814	3427	3023	2165	13017	16.2	65-76
HORACE GRANT	17	1165	38621	5439	10695	.509	2114	3053	.692	9443	2575	2832	12996	11.2	88-04
JUWAN HOWARD	10	730	27080	5225	11100	.471	2534	3356	.755	5408	2183	2498	12990	17.8	95-04
MICHAEL FINLEY	9	671	26528	5053	11196	.451	2036	2526	.806	3477	2581	1308	12971	19.3	96-04
Bob Boozer	11	874	25449	4961	10738	.462	3042	3998	.761	7119	1237	2519	12964	14.8	61-71
Wayman Tisdale	12	840	23868	5338	10575	.505	2202	2897	.760	5117	1077	2801	12878	15.3	86-97
DERRICK COLEMAN	14	776	25853	4613	10321	.447	3323	4323	.769	7217	1985	2056	12875	16.6	91-04
Rik Smits	11	867	23100	5301	10461	.507	2266	2932	.773	5277	1215	3011	12871	14.8	89-00
KENDALL GILL	14	952	29197	5036	11592	.434	2445	3247	.753	3965	2918	2478	12829	13.5	91-04
Mychal Thompson	12	935	27764	5191	10306	.504	2427	3707	655	6951	2141	2692	12810	13.7	79-91
Paul Westphal	12	823	20947	5079	10084	.504	2596	3166	.820	1580	3591	1705	12809	15.6	73-84
Sidney Wicks	10	760	25762	5046	11002	.459	2711	3955	.685	6620	2437	2524	12803	16.8	72-81
Mickey Johnson	12	904	25005	4733	10544	.449	3253	4066	.800	6465	2677	3101	12748	14.1	75-86
Johnny Newman	16	1159	28435	4456	9671	.461	3228	3984	.810	2536	1688	3199	12740	11.0	87-02
JERRY STACKHOUSE	9	608	22169	4128	10077	.409	3770	4648	.813	2273	2487	1342	12737	20.9	96-04
Bill Cartwright	15	963	27491	4656	8868	.525	3401	4412	.771	6106	1390	2833	12713	13.2	80-95
ALONZO MOURNING	11	634	22010	4538	8654	.524	3612	5113	.706	6137	892	2276	12710	20.0	93-04
Armen Gilliam	13	929	26421	4838	9895	.489	3024	3896	.776	6401	1088	2009	12700	13.7	88-00
Dell Curry	16	1083	23549	5090	11146	.457	1245	1476	.843	2617	1909	1795	12670	11.7	87-02
Bill Sharman	11	711	21793	4761	11168	.426	3143	3559	.883	2779	2101	1925	12665	17.8	51-61
Otis Birdsong	12	696	21627	5347	10562	.506	1801	2748	.655	2072	2260	1783	12544	18.0	78-89
Jack Marin	11	849	24590	5068	10890	.465	2405	2852	.843	4405	1813	2416	12541	14.8	67-77
Mike Newlin	11	837	24574	4720	10133	.466	3005	3456	.870	2494	3364	2542	12507	14.9	72-82
MARK JACKSON	17	1296	39121	4793	10731	.447	2169	2818	.770	4963	10334	2230	12489	9.6	88-04
Johnny Kerr	12	905	27784	4909	11751	.418	2662	3682	.723	10092	2004	2287	12480	13.8	55-66
Joe Barry Carroll	10	705	22838	5021	10583	.474	2413	3232	.747	5404	1264	2212	12455	17.7	81-91
SHAREEF ABDUR-RAHIM	8	618	22988	4452	9545	.466	3394	4173	.813	5082	1736	1695	12429	20.1	97-04
CHARLES OAKLEY	19	1282	40280	4835	10263	.471	2679	3522	.761	12205	3217	4421	12417	9.7	86-04
Darrell Griffith	10	765	21403	5237	11305	.403	1307	1061	.707	2519	1627	1689	12391	16.2	81-91
Cazzzie Russell	12	817	22213	5172	11154	.464	2033	2459	.827	3068	1838	1693	12377	15.1	67-78
Danny Manning	15	883	24202	5026	9835	.511	2274	3120	.729	4615	2063	2895	12367	14.0	89-03
Maurice Lucas	12	855	24787	4870	10297	.473	2595	3399	.763	7520	1987	2865	12339	14.4	77-88
A.C. Green	16	1278	36552	4544	9202	.494	3119	4250	.734	9473	1400	2436	12331	9.6	86-01
Johnny Green	14	1057	24624	4973	10091	.493	2335	4226	.553	9083	1449	2856	12281	11.6	60-73
Sleepy Floyd	13	957	26383	4448	10015	.444	2846	3493	.815	2494	5175	1972	12260	12.8	83-95
KOBE BRYANT	8	561	19273	4317	9506	.454	3093	3710	.834	2817	2390	1499	12215	21.8	97-04
Maurice Cheeks	15	1101	34845	4906	9374	.523	2331	2938	.793	3088	7392	2258	12195	11.1	79-93
Tom Heinsohn	9	654	19254	4773	11787	.405	2648	3353	.790	5749	1318	2454	12194	18.6	57-65
Willis Reed	10	650	23073	4859	10202	.476	2465	3298	.747	8414	1186	2411	12183	18.7	64-74
SAM CASSELL	11	743	22956	4392	9602	.457	2857	3328	.858	2474	4663	2135	12161	16.4	94-04
ANTOINE WALKER	9	610	23667	4712	11392	.414	1728	2630	.657	5268	2564	1859	12146	19.9	97-04
Kelly Tripucka	10	707	20959	4434	9380	.473	3106	3660	.849	2703	2090	1634	12142	17.2	82-91
John Long	15	893	22680	5108	10929	.467	1814	2104	.862	2492	1738	1868	12131	13.6	79-98
Norm Nixon	10	768	27250	5219	10805	.483	1527	1978	.772	1991	6386	1983	12065	15.7	78-89
Truck Robinson	11	772	25141	4816	9971	.483	2355	3556	.662	7267	1348	2253	11988	15.5	75-85
Danny Ainge	14	1042	27755	4643	9905	.469	1676	1980	.846	2768	4199	2549	11964	11.5	82-95
Mookie Blaylock	13	889	31026	4705	11499	.409	1269	1724	.736	3659	5972	1687	11962	13.5	90-02
Clyde Lovellette	11	704	19075	4784	10795	.443	2379	3141	.757	6663	1097	2289	11947	17.0	54-64
Herb Williams	18	1102	28484	5037	10781	.467	1862	2675	.696	6509	1856	2876	11944	10.8	82-99
Sidney Moncrief	11	767	23150	4117	8198	.502	3587	4319	.831	3575	2793	1635	11931	15.6	80-91
Scott Wedman	13	906	25927	5153	10713	.481	1526	1923	.794	4355	1771	2549	11916	13.2	75-87
STEPHON MARBURY	8	583	22450	4272	9914	.431	2678	3414	.784	1793	4830	1409	11908	20.4	97-04

Player	Yrs.	G	Min.	FGM	FGA	Pct.	FTM	FTA	Pct.	Reb.	Ast.	PF	Pts.	Avg.	Career
JIM JACKSON	12	781	26568	4516	10505	.430	2124	2580	.823	3807	2633	1768	11897	15.2	93-04
TIM DUNCAN	7	520	20253	4524	8896	.509	2796	4028	.694	6407	1660	1470	11862	22.8	98-04
Thurl Bailey	12	928	24873	4753	10056	.473	2324	2863	.812	4718	1298	1843	11834	12.8	84-99
Vinnie Johnson	13	984	24308	4882	10515	.464	1978	2673	.740	3109	3212	2063	11825	12.0	80-92
Jerome Kersey	17	1153	28115	4723	10166	.465	2321	3364	.690	6339	2134	3455	11825	10.3	85-01
Archie Clark	10	725	23581	4693	9784	.480	2433	3163	.769	2427	3498	1806	11819	16.3	67-76
Paul Silas	16	1254	34989	4293	9949	.432	3196	4748	.673	12357	2572	3105	11782	9.4	65-80
VIN BAKER	11	756	25448	4672	9618	.486	2394	3752	.638	5809	1495	2509	11777	15.6	94-04
George Mikan	9	520	8350	4097	8783	.404	3570	4588	.777	4167	1245	2162	11764	22.6	47-56
Dick Snyder	13	964	25676	4890	10019	.488	1975	2398	.824	2732	2767	2453	11755	12.2	67-79
Gerald Wilkins	13	900	26084	4754	10564	.450	1810	2429	.745	2646	2697	1853	11736	13.0	86-99
NICK VAN EXEL	11	762	26364	4286	10554	.406	1772	2226	.796	2293	5427	1250	11717	15.4	94-04
RAY ALLEN	8	579	21294	4101	9144	.448	2199	2486	.885	2709	2299	1467	11678	20.2	97-04
Jimmy Walker	9	698	23590	4624	10039	.461	2407	2903	.829	1860	2429	1735	11655	16.7	68-76
JAMAL MASHBURN	11	611	22762	4277	10222	.418	2323	3032	.766	3271	2414	1533	11644	19.1	94-04
EDDIE JONES	10	688	24986	4045	9142	.442	2334	2874	.812	2851	2245	1835	11583	16.8	95-04
Kevin Loughery	11	755	22208	4477	10829	.413	2621	3262	.803	2254	2803	2543	11575	15.3	63-73
Don Ohl	10	727	22413	4685	10806	.434	2179	2975	.732	2163	2243	2014	11549	15.9	61-70
Nick Anderson	13	800	24922	4416	9891	.446	1642	2461	.667	4064	2087	1502	11529	14.4	90-02
Junior Bridgeman	12	849	21257	4801	10099	.475	1875	2216	.846	2995	2066	1969	11517	13.6	76-87
Rudy LaRusso	10	736	24487	4102	9521	.431	3303	4308	.767	6936	1556	2553	11507	15.6	60-69
Happy Hairston	11	776	24330	4240	8872	.478	3025	4080	.741	8019	1268	2334	11505	14.8	65-75
Larry Johnson	10	707	25685	4401	9086	.484	2281	2978	.766	5300	2298	1893	11450	16.2	92-01
Dan Roundfield	11	746	23443	4289	8852	.485	2733	3702	.738	7243	1620	2561	11318	15.2	77-87
Willie Naulls	10	716	20620	4526	11145	.406	2253	2774	.812	6508	1114	2216	11305	15.8	57-66
David Thompson	8	509	16305	4213	8365	.504	2815	3616	.778	1921	1631	1287	11264	22.1	77-84
Ed Macauley	10	641	18071	3742	8589	.436	3750	4929	.761	4325	2079	1667	11234	17.5	50-59
John Johnson	12	869	25681	4575	10254	.446	2050	2633	.779	4778	3285	2505	11200	12.9	71-82
Jim J. Paxson	11	784	21357	4545	9134	.498	2011	2493	.807	1593	2300	1442	11199	14.3	80-90
Larry Foust	12	817	21890	3814	9414	.405	3570	4816	.741	8041	1368	2909	11198	13.7	51-62
Bill Bridges	13	926	30878	4181	9463	.442	2650	3824	.693	11054	2553	3375	11012	11.9	63-75
Mark Price	12	722	21560	3939	8345	.472	2135	2362	.904	1848	4863	964	10989	15.2	87-98
Mike Woodson	11	786	20021	4368	9364	.466	2125	2615	.813	1838	1822	1847	10981	14.0	81-91
Mike Gminski	14	938	24058	4208	9047	.465	2531	3002	.843	6480	1203	1574	10953	11.7	81-94
Dan Majerle	14	955	30206	3950	9171	.431	1665	2246	.741	4265	2755	1927	10925	11.4	89-02
Vernon Maxwell	13	855	24309	3932	9878	.398	1792	2446	.733	2200	2912	1766	10912	12.8	89-01
Ricky Sobers	11	821	22992	4250	9262	.459	2272	2695	.843	2132	3525	2622	10902	13.3	76-86
Don Nelson	14	1053	21685	4017	8373	.480	2864	3744	.765	5192	1526	2451	10898	10.3	63-76
Alvin Robertson	10	779	24669	4412	9245	.477	1822	2451	.743	4066	3929	2638	10882	14.0	85-96
Bingo Smith	11	865	22407	4776	10642	.449	1307	1637	.798	3630	1734	2059	10882	12.6	70-80
DIKEMBE MUTOMBO	13	929	32620	3878	7487	.518	3118	4585	.680	10907	1208	2898	10874	11.7	92-04
CHRISTIAN LAETTNER	12	819	25021	3929	8221	.478	2912	3545	.821	5675	2183	2690	10861	13.3	93-04
John Starks	13	866	23514	3953	9590	.412	1701	2211	.769	2129	3085	2293	10829	12.5	89-02
Cliff T. Robinson	11	629	19284	4493	9596	.468	1830	2533	.722	5237	1249	1870	10823	17.2	80-92
JALEN ROSE	10	741	22986	3997	9015	.443	2178	2737	.796	2683	3121	2040	10730	14.5	95-04
ELDEN CAMPBELL	13	1004	25386	4023	8712	.462	2637	3777	.698	6023	1180	2949	10685	10.6	91-04
JASON KIDD	10	720	27020	3832	9529	.402	2158	2766	.780	4585	6738	1357	10666	14.8	95-04
Carl Braun	13	788	18409	3912	10211	.383	2801	3484	.804	2122	2892	2164	10625	13.5	48-62
Wes Unseld	13	984	35832	4369	8586	.509	1883	2976	.633	13769	3822	2762	10624	10.8	69-81
KENNY ANDERSON	13	815	25125	3917	9311	.421	2211	2796	.791	2553	5093	1887	10586	13.0	92-04
Jerry Sloan	11	755	25750	4116	9646	.427	2339	3239	.722	5615	1925	2700	10571	14.0	66-76
Billy Knight	9	671	18412	4064	8026	.506	2399	2892	.830	3037	1435	1204	10561	15.7	77-85
Sean Elliott	12	742	24502	3852	8290	.465	2251	2816	.799	3204	1897	1626	10544	14.2	90-01
Brian Winters	9	650	19938	4490	9457	.475	1443	1713	.842	1688	2674	1830	10537	16.2	75-83
Austin Carr	10	682	19660	4359	9714	.449	1753	2181	.804	1990	1878	1394	10473	15.4	72-81
Cedric Maxwell	11	835	23769	3433	6293	.546	3598	4592	.784	5261	1862	2273	10465	12.5	78-88
Robert Reid	13	919	25109	4443	9706	.458	1459	1992	.732	4168	2500	2893	10448	11.4	78-91
Fat Lever	11	752	23814	4244	9504	.447	1783	2312	.771	4523	4696	1803	10433	13.9	83-94
TRACY MCGRADY	7	487	16375	3791	8490	.447	2289	3028	.756	3115	2007	965	10420	21.4	98-04
Guy Rodgers	12	892	28663	4125	10908	.378	2165	3003	.721	3791	6917	2630	10415	11.7	59-70
Brad Daugherty	8	548	20029	3823	7189	.532	2741	3670	.747	5227	2028	1466	10389	19.0	87-94
Wayne Embry	11	831	21763	3993	9067	.440	2394	3741	.640	7544	1194	2838	10380	12.5	59-69
CLARENCE WEATHERSPOON	12	875	27211	3978	8423	.472	2394	3226	.742	6724	1329	1954	10360	11.8	93-04
ANFERNEE HARDAWAY	11	647	22420	3859	8397	.460	2147	2774	.774	3012	3408	1452	10345	16.0	94-04
PAUL PIERCE	6	444	16832	3429	7946	.432	2689	3410	.789	2893	1609	1325	10317	23.2	99-04
Sam Lacey	13	1002	31873	4276	9693	.441	1748	2369	.738	9687	3754	3473	10303	10.3	71-83
Calvin Natt	11	599	18818	4003	7580	.528	2269	2954	.768	4070	1306	1386	10291	17.2	80-90
Derrick McKey	15	937	27229	3908	8048	.486	2247	2885	.779	4387	2254	2700	10266	11.0	88-02
Ray Scott	9	684	21339	3906	9641	.405	2372	3293	.720	7154	1618	2035	10184	14.9	62-70
Leroy Ellis	14	1048	27520	4143	9378	.442	1890	2595	.728	8709	1405	2661	10176	9.7	63-76
Eddie Johnson	10	675	19975	4015	8436	.476	2029	2564	.791	1522	3436	1706	10163	15.1	78-87
Ray Williams	10	655	18462	3962	8794	.451	2143	2673	.802	2370	3779	2165	10158	15.5	78-87
Vern Fleming	12	893	24721	3964	7954	.498	2159	2826	.764	3012	4293	2003	10125	11.3	85-96
DAVID WESLEY	11	763	24774	3666	8547	.429	1890	2423	.780	1964	3653	1851	10119	13.3	94-04
GRANT HILL	9	482	18495	3645	7674	.475	2756	3670	.751	3773	2931	1226	10104	21.0	95-04
RASHEED WALLACE	9	632	21812	4038	8175	.494	1597	2251	.709	4261	1229	1894	10096	16.0	96-04
Gene Shue	10	699	23338	3715	9378	.396	2638	3273	.806	2855	2608	1405	10068	14.4	55-64
Vern Mikkelsen	10	699	18443	3547	8812	.403	2969	3874	.766	5940	1515	2812	10063	14.4	50-59
Charlie Scott	9	560	19278	4113	9266	.444	1809	2344	.772	2034	2696	2059	10037	17.9	72-80
Neil Johnston	8	516	10290	3303	7435	.444	3417	4447	.768	5856	1269	1681	10023	19.4	52-59

(active players in 2003-04 in CAPS)

SCORING AVERAGE

(minimum 400 games or 10,000 points)

	G	FGM	FTM	Pts.	Avg.
MICHAEL JORDAN	1072	7,327	12,192	32,292	30.12
Wilt Chamberlain	1045	6,057	12,681	31,419	30.07
Elgin Baylor	846	5,763	8,693	23,149	27.4
SHAQUILLE O'NEAL	809	4,573	8,670	21,914	27.1
Jerry West	932	7,160	9,016	25,192	27.0
ALLEN IVERSON	535	3,539	5,104	14,436	27.0
Bob Pettit	792	6,182	7,349	20,880	26.4
George Gervin	791	4,541	8,045	20,708	26.2
Oscar Robertson	1040	7,694	9,508	26,710	25.7
KARL MALONE	1476	9,787	13,528	36,928	5.0

FREE THROW PERCENTAGE

(minimum 1,200 made)

	FTM	FTA	Pct.
Mark Price	2,135	2,362	.904
Rick Barry	3,818	4,243	.900
STEVE NASH	1,258	1,409	.893
Calvin Murphy	3,445	3,864	.892
Scott Skiles	1,548	1,741	.889
REGGIE MILLER	5,987	6,758	.886
Larry Bird	3,960	4,471	.886
PEJA STOJAKOVIC	1,373	1,551	.885
RAY ALLEN	2,199	2,486	.885
Bill Sharman	3,143	3,559	.883

FIELD-GOAL PERCENTAGE

(minimum 2,000 made)

	FGM	FGA	Pct.
Artis Gilmore	5,732	9,570	.599
Mark West	2,528	4,356	.580
SHAQUILLE O'NEAL	8,670	15,020	.577
Steve Johnson	2,841	4,965	.572
Darryl Dawkins	3,477	6,079	572
James Donaldson	3,105	5,442	.571
Jeff Ruland	2,105	3,734	.564
Kareem Abdul-Jabbar	15,837	28,307	.559
Kevin McHale	6,830	12,334	.554
Bobby Jones	3,412	6,199	.550

3-POINT FIELD-GOAL PERCENTAGE

(minimum 250 made)

	FGM	FGA	Pct.
Steve Kerr	726	1,599	.454
HUBERT DAVIS	728	1,651	.441
Drazen Petrovic	255	583	.437
Tim Legler	260	603	.431
B.J. Armstrong	436	1,026	.425
WESLEY PERSON	1,109	2,665	.416
STEVE NASH	673	1,618	.416
PAT GARRITY	513	1,242	.413
DANA BARROS	1,090	2,652	.411
Trent Tucker	575	1,410	.408

GAMES

Robert Parish	1,611
Kareem Abdul-Jabbar	1,560
John Stockton	1,504
KARL MALONE	1,476
KEVIN WILLIS	1,390
Moses Malone	1,329
REGGIE MILLER	1,323
Buck Williams	1,307
Elvin Hayes	1,303
MARK JACKSON	1,296

FIELD GOALS ATTEMPTED

Kareem Abdul-Jabbar	28,307
KARL MALONE	26,210
Michael Jordan	24,537
Elvin Hayes	24,272
John Havlicek	23,930
Wilt Chamberlain	23,497
Dominique Wilkins	21,589
Alex English	21,036
Hakeem Olajuwon	20,991
Elgin Baylor	20,171

3-POINT FIELD GOALS MADE

REGGIE MILLER	2,464
Dale Ellis	1,719
GLEN RICE	1,559
Tim Hardaway	1,542
NICK VAN EXEL	1,373
Dan Majerle	1,360
Mitch Richmond	1,326
Terry Porter	1,297
Mookie Blaylock	1,283
RAY ALLEN	1,277

MINUTES

Kareem Abdul-Jabbar	57,446
KARL MALONE	54,852
Elvin Hayes	50,000
Wilt Chamberlain	47,859
John Stockton	47,764
John Havlicek	46,471
Robert Parish	45,704
REGGIE MILLER	45,514
Moses Malone	45,071
Hakeem Olajuwon	44,222

FREE THROWS MADE

KARL MALONE	9,787
Moses Malone	8,531
Oscar Robertson	7,694
Michael Jordan	7,327
Jerry West	7,160
Dolph Schayes	6,979
Adrian Dantley	6,832
Kareem Abdul-Jabbar	6,712
Charles Barkley	6,349
Bob Pettit	6,182

3-POINT FIELD GOALS ATTEMPTED

REGGIE MILLER	6,188
Tim Hardaway	4,345
Dale Ellis	4,266
Vernon Maxwell	3,931
GLEN RICE	3,896
NICK VAN EXEL	3,867
Mookie Blaylock	3,816
Dan Majerle	3,798
John Starks	3,591
Mitch Richmond	3,417

FIELD GOALS MADE

Kareem Abdul-Jabbar	15,837
KARL MALONE	13,528
Wilt Chamberlain	12,681
Michael Jordan	12,192
Elvin Hayes	10,976
Hakeem Olajuwon	10,749
Alex English	10,659
John Havlicek	10,513
Dominique Wilkins	9,963
Patrick Ewing	9,702

FREE THROWS ATTEMPTED

KARL MALONE	13,188
Wilt Chamberlain	11,862
Moses Malone	11,090
Kareem Abdul-Jabbar	9,304
Oscar Robertson	9,185
Jerry West	8,801
Michael Jordan	8,772
Charles Barkley	8,643
SHAQUILLE O'NEAL	8,508
Adrian Dantley	8,351

REBOUNDS

Wilt Chamberlain	23,924
Bill Russell	21,620
Kareem Abdul-Jabbar	17,440
Elvin Hayes	16,279
Moses Malone	16,212
KARL MALONE	14,968
Robert Parish	14,715
Nate Thurmond	14,464
Walt Bellamy	14,241
Wes Unseld	13,769

HISTORY Regular season

ASSISTS

John Stockton	15,806
MARK JACKSON	10,334
Magic Johnson	10,141
Oscar Robertson	9,887
Isiah Thomas	9,061
GARY PAYTON	8,039
ROD STRICKLAND	7,948
Maurice Cheeks	7,392
Lenny Wilkens	7,211
Terry Porter	7,160

STEALS

John Stockton	3,265
Michael Jordan	2,514
Maurice Cheeks	2,310
SCOTTIE PIPPEN	2,307
GARY PAYTON	2,243
Clyde Drexler	2,207
Hakeem Olajuwon	2,162
Alvin Robertson	2,112
KARL MALONE	2,085
Mookie Blaylock	2,075

DISQUALIFICATIONS

Vern Mikkelsen	127
Walter Dukes	121
Shawn Kemp	115
Charlie Share	105
Paul Arizin	101
Darryl Dawkins	100
James Edwards	96
Tom Gola	94
Tom Sanders	94
Steve Johnson	93

PERSONAL FOULS

Kareem Abdul-Jabbar	4,657
KARL MALONE	4,578
Robert Parish	4,443
CHARLES OAKLEY	4,421
Hakeem Olajuwon	4,383
Buck Williams	4,267
Elvin Hayes	4,193
Otis Thorpe	4,146
KEVIN WILLIS	4,108
James Edwards	4,042

BLOCKED SHOTS

Hakeem Olajuwon	3,830
Kareem Abdul-Jabbar	3,189
Mark Eaton	3,064
DIKEMBE MUTOMBO	2,996
David Robinson	2,954
Patrick Ewing	2,894
Tree Rollins	2,542
Robert Parish	2,361
SHAQUILLE O'NEAL	2,102
Manute Bol	2,086

POINTS

Kareem Abdul-Jabbar	38,387
KARL MALONE	36,928
Michael Jordan	32,292
Wilt Chamberlain	31,419
Moses Malone	27,409
Elvin Hayes	27,313
Hakeem Olajuwon	26,946
Oscar Robertson	26,710
Dominique Wilkins	26,668
John Havlicek	26,395

COMBINED NBA/ABA, CAREER SCORING

(active players in 2003-04 in CAPS)

Player	Yrs.	G	Pts.	Avg.	Player	Yrs.	G	Pts.	Avg.
Kareem Abdul-Jabbar	20	1560	38,387	24.6	Mark Aguirre	13	923	18,458	20.0
KARL MALONE	19	1476	36,928	25.0	GLEN RICE	15	1000	18,336	18.3
Michael Jordan	15	1072	32,292	30.1	Dave Bing	12	901	18,327	20.3
Wilt Chamberlain	14	1045	31,419	30.1	CLIFFORD ROBINSON	15	1179	18,305	15.5
Julius Erving	16	1243	30,026	24.2	World B. Free	13	886	17,955	20.3
Moses Malone	21	1455	29,580	20.3	Calvin Murphy	13	1002	17,949	17.9
Dan Issel	15	1218	27,482	22.6	Lou Hudson	13	890	17,940	20.2
Elvin Hayes	16	1303	27,313	21.0	Chris Mullin	16	986	17,911	18.2
Hakeem Olajuwon	18	1238	26,946	21.8	Len Wilkens	15	1077	17,772	16.5
Oscar Robertson	14	1040	26,710	25.7	Bailey Howell	12	950	17,770	18.7
Dominique Wilkins	15	1074	26,668	24.8	Magic Johnson	13	906	17,707	19.5
George Gervin	14	1060	26,595	25.1	Rolando Blackman	13	980	17,623	18.0
John Havlicek	16	1270	26,395	20.8	Otis Thorpe	17	1257	17,600	14.0
Alex English	15	1193	25,613	21.5	Earl Monroe	13	926	17,454	18.8
Rick Barry	14	1020	25,279	24.8	Ron Boone	13	1041	17,437	16.8
Jerry West	14	932	25,192	27.0	Kevin McHale	13	971	17,335	17.9
Artis Gilmore	17	1329	24,941	18.8	Jack Sikma	14	1107	17,287	15.6
Patrick Ewing	17	1183	24,815	21.0	Jeff Malone	13	905	17,231	19.0
REGGIE MILLER	17	1323	24,305	18.4	KEVIN WILLIS	19	1390	17,154	12.3
Charles Barkley	16	1073	23,757	22.1	Spencer Haywood	13	844	17,111	20.3
Robert Parish	21	1611	23,334	14.5	George McGinnis	11	842	17,009	20.2
Adrian Dantley	15	955	23,177	24.3	Bob Cousy	14	924	16,960	18.4
Elgin Baylor	14	846	23,149	27.4	Buck Williams	17	1307	16,784	12.8
Clyde Drexler	15	1086	22,195	20.4	Nate Archibald	13	876	16,481	18.8
SHAQUILLE O'NEAL	12	809	21,914	27.1	Joe Dumars	14	1018	16,401	16.1
Larry Bird	13	897	21,791	24.3	James Worthy	12	926	16,320	17.6
Hal Greer	15	1122	21,586	19.2	Billy Cunningham	11	770	16,310	21.2
Walt Bellamy	14	1043	20,941	20.1	Paul Arizin	10	713	16,266	22.8
Bob Pettit	11	792	20,880	26.4	Randy Smith	12	976	16,262	16.7
David Robinson	14	987	20,790	21.1	Derek Harper	16	1199	16,006	13.3
Mitch Richmond	14	976	20,497	21.0	Kiki Vandeweghe	13	810	15,980	19.7
Tom Chambers	16	1107	20,049	18.1	Pete Maravich	10	658	15,948	24.2
GARY PAYTON	14	1109	19,956	18.0	Jack Twyman	11	823	15,840	19.2
John Stockton	19	1504	19,711	13.1	Detlef Schrempf	16	1136	15,761	13.9
Bernard King	14	874	19,655	22.5	LATRELL SPREWELL	12	833	15,691	18.8
Walter Davis	15	1033	19,521	18.9	Larry Nance	13	920	15,687	17.1
Terry Cummings	18	1183	19,460	16.4	Jeff Hornacek	14	1077	15,659	14.5
Dolph Schayes	16	1059	19,249	18.2	Terry Porter	17	1274	15,586	12.2
Bob Lanier	14	959	19,248	20.1	Walt Frazier	13	825	15,581	18.9
Eddie A. Johnson	17	1199	19,202	16.0	Dennis Johnson	14	1100	15,535	14.1
Gail Goodrich	14	1031	19,181	18.6	Bob Dandridge	13	839	15,530	18.5
Reggie Theus	13	1026	19,015	18.5	Sam Jones	12	871	15,411	17.7
Dale Ellis	17	1209	19,004	15.7	Tim Hardaway	13	867	15,373	17.7
SCOTTIE PIPPEN	17	1178	18,940	16.1	Dick Barnett	14	971	15,358	15.8
Chet Walker	13	1032	18,831	18.2	Shawn Kemp	14	1051	15,347	14.6
Isiah Thomas	13	979	18,822	19.2	Sam Perkins	17	1286	15,324	11.9
Bob McAdoo	14	852	18,787	22.1	John Drew	11	739	15,291	20.7
					Louie Dampier	12	900	15,279	15.9

(active players in 2003-04 in CAPS)

SCORING AVERAGE
(minimum 400 games or 10,000 points)

	G	FGM	FTM	Pts.	Avg.
Michael Jordan	1072	12,192	7,327	32,292	30.12
Wilt Chamberlain	1045	12,681	6,057	31,419	30.07
Elgin Baylor	846	8,693	5,763	23,149	27.4
SHAQUILLE O'NEAL	809	8,670	4,573	21,914	27.1
Jerry West	932	9,016	7,160	25,192	27.0
ALLEN IVERSON	535	5,104	3,539	14,436	27.0
Bob Pettit	792	7,349	6,182	20,880	26.4
Oscar Robertson	1040	9,508	7,694	26,710	25.7
George Gervin	1060	10,368	5,737	26,595	25.1
KARL MALONE	1476	13,528	9,787	36,928	25.0

FREE THROW PERCENTAGE
(minimum 1,200 made)

	FTM	FTA	Pct.
Mark Price	2,135	2,362	.904
Rick Barry	5,713	6,397	.893
STEVE NASH	1,258	1,409	.893
Calvin Murphy	3,445	3,864	.892
Scott Skiles	1,548	1,741	.889
REGGIE MILLER	5,987	6,758	.886
Larry Bird	3,960	4,471	.886
PEJA STOJAKOVIC	1,373	1,551	.885
RAY ALLEN	2,199	2,486	.885
DARRELL ARMSTRONG	1,279	1,446	.885

FIELD-GOAL PERCENTAGE
(minimum 2,000 made)

	FGM	FGA	Pct.
Artis Gilmore	9,403	16,158	.582
Mark West	2,528	4,356	.580
SHAQUILLE O'NEAL	8,670	15,020	.577
Steve Johnson	2,841	4,965	.572
Darryl Dawkins	3,477	6,079	.572
James Donaldson	3,105	5,442	.571
Jeff Ruland	2,105	3,734	.564
Bobby Jones	4,451	7,953	.560
Kareem Abdul-Jabbar	15,837	28,307	.559
Kevin McHale	6,830	12,334	.554

3-POINT FIELD-GOAL PERCENTAGE
(minimum 250 made)

	FGM	FGA	Pct.
Steve Kerr	726	1,599	.454
HUBERT DAVIS	728	1,651	.441
Drazen Petrovic	255	583	.437
Tim Legler	260	603	.431
B.J. Armstrong	436	1,026	.425
WESLEY PERSON	1,109	2,665	.416
STEVE NASH	673	1,618	.416
PAT GARRITY	513	1,242	.413
DANA BARROS	1,090	2,652	.411
Trent Tucker	575	1,410	.408

GAMES

Robert Parish	1,611
Kareem Abdul-Jabbar	1,560
John Stockton	1,504
KARL MALONE	1,476
Moses Malone	1,455
KEVIN WILLIS	1,390
Artis Gilmore	1,329
REGGIE MILLER	1,323
Buck Williams	1,307
Elvin Hayes	1,303

MINUTES

Kareem Abdul-Jabbar	57,446
KARL MALONE	54,852
Elvin Hayes	50,000
Moses Malone	49,444
Wilt Chamberlain	47,859
John Stockton	47,764
Artis Gilmore	47,134
John Havlicek	46,471
Robert Parish	45,704
REGGIE MILLER	45,514

FIELD GOALS MADE

Kareem Abdul-Jabbar	15,837
KARL MALONE	13,528
Wilt Chamberlain	12,681
Michael Jordan	12,192
Julius Erving	11,818
Elvin Hayes	10,976
Hakeem Olajuwon	10,749
Alex English	10,659
John Havlicek	10,513
Dan Issel	10,431

FIELD GOALS ATTEMPTED

Kareem Abdul-Jabbar	28,307
KARL MALONE	26,210
Michael Jordan	24,537
Elvin Hayes	24,272
John Havlicek	23,930
Wilt Chamberlain	23,497
Julius Erving	23,370
Dominique Wilkins	21,589
Rick Barry	21,283
Alex English	21,036

FREE THROWS MADE

KARL MALONE	9,787
Moses Malone	9,018
Oscar Robertson	7,694
Michael Jordan	7,327
Jerry West	7,160
Dolph Schayes	6,979
Adrian Dantley	6,832
Kareem Abdul-Jabbar	6,712
Dan Issel	6,591
Charles Barkley	6,349

FREE THROWS ATTEMPTED

KARL MALONE	12,963
Moses Malone	11,864
Wilt Chamberlain	11,862
Kareem Abdul-Jabbar	9,304
Oscar Robertson	9,185
Jerry West	8,801
Artis Gilmore	8,790
Michael Jordan	8,772
Charles Barkley	8,643
SHAQUILLE O'NEAL	8,508

3-POINT FIELD GOALS MADE

REGGIE MILLER	2,464
Dale Ellis	1,719
GLEN RICE	1,559
Tim Hardaway	1,542
NICK VAN EXEL	1,373
Dan Majerle	1,360
Mitch Richmond	1,326
Terry Porter	1,297
Mookie Blaylock	1,283
RAY ALLEN	1,277

3-POINT FIELD GOALS ATTEMPTED

REGGIE MILLER	6,188
Tim Hardaway	4,345
Dale Ellis	4,266
Vernon Maxwell	3,931
GLEN RICE	3,896
NICK VAN EXEL	3,867
Mookie Blaylock	3,816
Dan Majerle	3,798
John Starks	3,591
Mitch Richmond	3,417

REBOUNDS

Wilt Chamberlain	23,924
Bill Russell	21,620
Moses Malone	17,834
Kareem Abdul-Jabbar	17,440
Artis Gilmore	16,330
Elvin Hayes	16,279
KARL MALONE	14,968
Robert Parish	14,715
Nate Thurmond	14,464
Walt Bellamy	14,241

ASSISTS

John Stockton	15,806
MARK JACKSON	10,334
Magic Johnson	10,141
Oscar Robertson	9,887
Isiah Thomas	9,061
GARY PAYTON	8,039
ROD STRICKLAND	7,948
Maurice Cheeks	7,392
Lenny Wilkens	7,211
Terry Porter	7,160

HISTORY Regular season

PERSONAL FOULS

Kareem Abdul-Jabbar	4,657
KARL MALONE	4,578
Artis Gilmore	4,529
Robert Parish	4,443
Caldwell Jones	4,436
CHARLES OAKLEY	4,421
Hakeem Olajuwon	4,383
Buck Williams	4,267
Elvin Hayes	4,193
Otis Thorpe	4,146

STEALS

John Stockton	3,265
Michael Jordan	2,514
Maurice Cheeks	2,310
SCOTTIE PIPPEN	2,307
Julius Erving	2,272
GARY PAYTON	2,243
Clyde Drexler	2,207
Hakeem Olajuwon	2,162
Alvin Robertson	2,112
KARL MALONE	2,085

BLOCKED SHOTS

Hakeem Olajuwon	3,830
Kareem Abdul-Jabbar	3,189
Artis Gilmore	3,178
Mark Eaton	3,064
DIKEMBE MUTOMBO	2,996
David Robinson	2,954
Patrick Ewing	2,894
Tree Rollins	2,542
Robert Parish	2,361
Caldwell Jones	2,297

DISQUALIFICATIONS

Vern Mikkelsen	127
Walter Dukes	121
Shawn Kemp	115
Charlie Share	105
Paul Arizin	101
Darryl Dawkins	100
James Edwards	96
Tom Gola	94
Tom Sanders	94
Steve Johnson	93

ALL-TIME TEAM STANDINGS

OVERALL

Team	W	L	Pct.
Los Angeles Lakers	2727	1674	.620
Chicago Stags*	145	92	.612
Boston Celtics	2692	1819	.597
San Antonio Spurs	1313	951	.580
Washington Capitols*	157	114	.579
Anderson Packers*	37	27	.578
Portland Trail Blazers	1508	1248	.547
Utah Jazz	1321	1107	.544
Milwaukee Bucks	1586	1334	.543
Phoenix Suns	1582	1338	.542
Philadelphia 76ers	2345	1991	.541
Seattle SuperSonics	1607	1395	.535
St. Louis Bombers*	122	115	.515
New York Knickerbockers	2310	2197	.513
Chicago Bulls	1566	1517	.508
Atlanta Hawks	2170	2168	.500
Cleveland Rebels*	30	30	.500
Houston Rockets	1492	1510	.497
Indiana Pacers	1115	1149	.493
New Orleans Hornets	630	650	.492
Orlando Magic	588	610	.491
Indianapolis Olympians*	132	137	.491
Detroit Pistons	2131	2269	.484
Sacramento Kings	2093	2308	.476
Miami Heat	601	679	.470
Golden State Warriors	2080	2426	.462
Washington Wizards	1585	1898	.455
Denver Nuggets	1024	1240	.452
Dallas Mavericks	866	1070	.447
Cleveland Cavaliers	1207	1549	.438
Minnesota Timberwolves	518	680	.432
New Jersey Nets	950	1314	.420
Toronto Raptors	281	425	.398
Toronto Huskies*	22	38	.367
Los Angeles Clippers	980	1776	.356
Sheboygan Redskins*	22	40	.355
Baltimore Bullets*	158	292	.351
Detroit Falcons*	20	40	.333
Waterloo Hawks*	19	43	.306
Indianapolis Jets*	18	42	.300
Memphis Grizzlies	202	504	.286
Providence Steamrollers*	46	122	.274
Pittsburgh Ironmen*	15	45	.250
Denver Nuggets*	11	51	.177
Totals	42024	42024	.500

*Defunct

HOME

Team	W	L	Pct.
Los Angeles Lakers	1547	521	.748
Washington Capitols*	98	37	.726
Anderson Packers*	23	9	.719
San Antonio Spurs	807	325	.713
Boston Celtics	1471	596	.712
Utah Jazz	849	365	.699
Indianapolis Olympians*	86	37	.699
Portland Trail Blazers	957	418	.696
Phoenix Suns	1007	445	.694
Chicago Stags*	70	33	.680
Seattle SuperSonics	996	480	.675
Philadelphia 76ers	1343	667	.668
Milwaukee Bucks	953	481	.665
Atlanta Hawks	1319	720	.647
St. Louis Bombers*	73	41	.640
Indiana Pacers	719	413	.635
New York Knickerbockers	1333	784	.630
Houston Rockets	928	549	.628
Sacramento Kings	1284	761	.628
Denver Nuggets	710	422	.627
Chicago Bulls	952	568	.626
Orlando Magic	370	229	.618
Detroit Pistons	1269	791	.616
New Orleans Hornets	379	261	.592
Golden State Warriors	1218	862	.586
Washington Wizards	975	702	.581
Miami Heat	367	273	.573
Cleveland Cavaliers	789	589	.573
Cleveland Rebels*	17	13	.567
New Jersey Nets	621	511	.549
Sheboygan Redskins*	17	14	.548
Dallas Mavericks	527	441	.544
Minnesota Timberwolves	319	280	.533
Waterloo Hawks*	17	15	.531
Baltimore Bullets*	111	100	.526
Toronto Huskies*	15	15	.500
Indianapolis Jets*	14	15	.483
Los Angeles Clippers	649	715	.476
Toronto Raptors	166	187	.470
Detroit Falcons*	12	18	.400
Denver Nuggets*	9	15	.375
Memphis Grizzlies	132	221	.374
Pittsburgh Ironmen*	11	19	.367
Providence Steamrollers*	29	55	.345
Totals	25558	15013	.630

*Defunct

HISTORY *Regular season*

ROAD

Team	W	L	Pct.
Chicago Stags*	63	58	.521
Los Angeles Lakers	1040	1031	.502
Boston Celtics	1019	1135	.473
San Antonio Spurs	506	626	.447
Washington Capitols*	57	72	.442
Cleveland Rebels*	13	17	.433
Milwaukee Bucks	609	838	.421
Philadelphia 76ers	841	1191	.414
Portland Trail Blazers	549	818	.402
Seattle SuperSonics	593	884	.402
New York Knickerbockers	844	1278	.398
Phoenix Suns	566	875	.393
New Orleans Hornets	251	389	.392
Chicago Bulls	583	916	.389
Utah Jazz	472	742	.389
St. Louis Bombers*	45	71	.388
Anderson Packers*	11	18	.379
Houston Rockets	539	929	.367
Miami Heat	234	406	.366
Orlando Magic	218	381	.364
Atlanta Hawks	724	1284	.361
Detroit Pistons	717	1296	.356
Dallas Mavericks	339	629	.350
Indiana Pacers	396	736	.350
Washington Wizards	553	1102	.334
Minnesota Timberwolves	199	400	.332
Golden State Warriors	697	1434	.327
Toronto Raptors	115	238	.326
Sacramento Kings	660	1404	.320
Cleveland Cavaliers	412	955	.301
New Jersey Nets	329	803	.291
Denver Nuggets	314	818	.277
Detroit Falcons*	8	22	.267
Indianapolis Olympians*	31	89	.258
Los Angeles Clippers	321	1043	.235
Toronto Huskies*	7	23	.233
Providence Steamrollers*	17	65	.207
Baltimore Bullets*	36	141	.203
Memphis Grizzlies	70	283	.198
Sheboygan Redskins*	5	22	.185
Indianapolis Jets*	4	22	.154
Pittsburgh Ironmen*	4	26	.133
Waterloo Hawks*	1	22	.043
Denver Nuggets*	1	26	.037
Totals	15013	25558	.370

*Defunct

NEUTRAL COURT

(Neutral-court records kept prior to the 1973-74 season)

Team	W	L	Pct.
Anderson Duffey Packers*	3	0	1.000
Chicago Stags*	12	1	.923
Boston Celtics	202	88	.697
Milwaukee Bucks	24	15	.615
Indianapolis Olympians*	15	11	.577
St. Louis Bombers*	4	3	.571
Golden State Warriors	165	130	.559
Philadelphia 76ers	161	133	.548
Cleveland Cavaliers	6	5	.545
Los Angeles Lakers	140	122	.534
Sacramento Kings	149	143	.510
New York Knickerbockers	133	135	.496
Chicago Bulls	31	33	.484
Detroit Pistons	145	182	.443
Houston Rockets	25	32	.439
Altanta Hawks	127	164	.436
Washington Wizards	57	94	.377
Seattle SuperSonics	18	31	.367
Los Angeles Clippers	10	18	.357
Phoenix Suns	9	18	.333
Washington Capitols*	2	5	.286
Baltimore Bullets*	11	51	.177
Portland Trail Blazers	2	12	.143
Waterloo Hawks*	1	6	.143
Denver Nuggets*	1	10	.091
Providence Steamrollers*	0	2	.000
Sheboygan Redskins*	0	4	.000
Indianapolis Jets*	0	5	.000
Totals	1453	1453	.500

*Defunct

TOP SINGLE-SEASON WINNING PERCENTAGES

OVERALL

1.	.878	1995-96—Chicago	(72-10)
2.	.841	1971-72—Los Angeles	(69-13)
		1996-97—Chicago	(69-13)
4.	.840	1966-67—Philadelphia	(68-13)
5.	.829	1972-73—Boston	(68-14)
6.	.8171	1985-86—Boston	(67-15)
		1991-92—Chicago	(67-15)
		1999-00—L.A. Lakers	(67-15)
9.	.8167	1946-47—Washington	(49-11)
10.	.805	1970-71—Milwaukee	(66-16)

HOME

1.	.976	1985-86—Boston	(40-1)
2.	.971	1949-50 Rochester	(33-1)
3.	.969	1949-50—Syracuse	(31-1)
4.	.968	1949-50—Minneapolis	(30-1)
5.	.967	1946-47—Washington	(29-1)
6.	.951	1986-87—Boston	(39-2)
		1994-95—Orlando	(39-2)
		1995-96—Chicago	(39-2)
		1996-97—Chicago	(39-2)
10.	.944	1970-71—Milwaukee	(34-2)

ROAD

1.	.816	1971-72—Los Angeles	(31-7)
2.	.805	1995-96—Chicago	(33-8)
3.	.800	1972-73—Boston	(32-8)
4.	.780	1974-75—Boston	(32-9)
		1996-97—Miami	(32-9)
6.	.765	1966-67—Philadelphia	(26-8)
7.	.756	1991-92—Chicago	(31-10)
		1999-00—L.A. Lakers	(31-10)
9.	.732	1982-83—Philadelphia	(30-11)
		1996-97—Chicago	(30-11)

Team	WINNING STREAK Games	WINNING STREAK Dates		LOSING STREAK Games	LOSING STREAK Dates	
Atlanta	14	11-16-93 to	12-14-93	16	3-11-76 to	4-9-76
Boston	18	2-24-82 to	3-26-82	13	2-1-94 to	3-2-94
					2-5-97 to	3-1-97
Chicago	18	12-29-95 to	2-2-96	16	1-8-01 to	2-6-01
Cleveland	11	12-15-88 to	1-7-89	19	3-19-82 to	4-18-82
		12-20-91 to	1-11-92			
		2-18-94 to	3-8-94			
		12-9-94 to	12-30-94			
Dallas	14	10-30-02 to	11-27-02	20	11-13-93 to	12-22-93
Denver	12	3-10-82 to	4-2-82	23	12-9-97 to	1-23-98
Detroit	13	1-23-90 to	2-21-90	14	3-7-80 to	3-30-80
		12-27-03 to	1-19-04		12-20-93 to	1-18-94
Golden State	11	12-29-71 to	1-22-72	17	*12-20-64 to	1-26-65
				16	12-29-84 to	1-31-85
Houston	15	2-13-93 to	3-18-93	17	†1-18-68 to	2-16-68
		11-5-93 to	12-2-93	15	11-23-01 to	12-20-01
Indiana	9	11-2-02 to	11-22-02	12	2-16-83 to	3-11-83
					3-14-85 to	4-3-85
					1-26-89 to	2-23-89
Los Angeles Clippers	11	‡11-3-74 to	11-23-74	19	†3-11-82 to	4-13-82
	8	11-30-91 to	12-15-91		12-30-88 to	2-6-89
Los Angeles Lakers	33	11-5-71 to	1-7-72	10	4-8-94 to	4-24-94
Memphis	8	1-11-04 to	1-25-04	23	■2-16-96 to	4-2-96
				13	10-30-02 to	11-22-02
Miami	11	1-27-97 to	2-20-97	17	11-5-88 to	12-12-88
Milwaukee	20	2-6-71 to	3-8-71	15	3-4-96 to	3-30-96
Minnesota	11	1-17-01 to	2-7-01	16	2-29-92 to	3-29-92
New Jersey	14	1-25-04 to	2-24-04	16	1-5-78 to	2-3-78
New Orleans	10	@2-21-98 to	3-13-98	12	1-19-90 to	2-14-90
New York	18	10-24-69 to	11-28-69	12	3-23-85 to	4-13-85
Orlando	9	11-12-94 to	12-2-94	19	10-30-03 to	12-6-03
		1-30-01 to	2-18-01			
Philadelphia	14	12-21-82 to	1-21-83	20	1-9-73 to	2-11-73
Phoenix	14	12-1-92 to	12-30-92	13	11-1-96 to	11-26-96
Portland	16	3-20-91 to	4-19-91	13	2-12-72 to	3-4-72
Sacramento	15	§2-17-50 to	3-19-50	14	▲1-16-60 to	2-10-60
	12	12-23-01 to	1-21-02		▲12-12-71 to	1-9-72
				12	3-9-98 to	4-3-98
San Antonio	17	2-29-96 to	3-31-96	13	2-4-89 to	3-2-89
Seattle	14	2-3-96 to	3-5-96	10	12-12-68 to	12-29-68
					1-16-76 to	2-8-76
Toronto	9	3-22-02 to	4-9-02	17	11-6-97 to	12-9-97
Utah	15	11-13-96 to	12-10-96	18	2-24-82 to	3-29-82
		3-12-97 to	4-11-97			
Washington	9	◆12-4-68 to	12-25-68	13	◆12-17-66 to	1-8-67
		◆11-9-69 to	11-27-69		3-21-95 to	4-13-95
		11-14-78 to	12-1-78			
		12-6-01 to	12-22-01			

*Club located in San Francisco. †Club located in San Diego. ‡Club located in Buffalo. §Club located in Rochester. ▲Club located in Cincinnati. ◆Club located in Baltimore. ■Club located in Vancouver. @Club located in Charlotte.

HISTORY *Regular season*

(2003-04 head coaches in CAPS)

BY VICTORIES

(minimum 200 victories)

Coach	W	L	Pct.
LENNY WILKENS	1,315	1,133	.537
DON NELSON	1,148	858	.572
Pat Riley	1,110	569	.661
Bill Fitch	944	1,106	.460
Red Auerbach	938	479	.662
Dick Motta	935	1,017	.479
LARRY BROWN	933	713	.567
JERRY SLOAN	917	561	.620
Jack Ramsay	864	783	.525
Cotton Fitzsimmons	832	775	.518
PHIL JACKSON	832	316	.725
Gene Shue	784	861	.477
George Karl	708	499	.587
John MacLeod	707	657	.518
Red Holzman	696	604	.535
RICK ADELMAN	658	411	.616
Chuck Daly	638	437	.593
Doug Moe	628	529	.543
Mike Fratello	572	465	.552
Alvin Attles	557	518	.518
Del Harris	556	457	.549
K.C. Jones	522	252	.674
Rudy Tomjanovich	503	397	.559
Kevin Loughery	474	662	.417
Alex Hannum	471	412	.533
Billy Cunningham	454	196	.698
Larry Costello	430	300	.589
Tom Heinsohn	427	263	.619
MIKE DUNLEAVY	426	444	.490
John Kundla	423	302	.583
HUBIE BROWN	419	488	.462
GREGG POPOVICH	396	210	.653
FLIP SAUNDERS	386	300	.563
Bill Russell	341	290	.540
Bernie Bickerstaff	338	348	.493
DON CHANEY	337	494	.406
Bill Sharman	333	240	.581
Doug Collins	332	287	.536
Jim Lynam	328	392	.456
Richie Guerin	327	291	.529
Al Cervi	326	241	.575
Joe Lapchick	326	247	.569
CHRIS FORD	323	376	.462
PAUL SILAS	321	370	.465
Fred Schaus	315	245	.563
Stan Albeck	307	267	.535
Lester Harrison	295	181	.620
JEFF VAN GUNDY	293	209	.584
Frank Layden	277	294	.485
Paul Seymour	271	241	.529
Paul Westphal	267	159	.627
Butch Van Breda Kolff	266	253	.513
Eddie Gottlieb	263	318	.453
Jack McMahon	260	289	.474
Bob Hill	257	212	.548
Tom Nissalke	248	391	.388
Phil Johnson	236	306	.435
Matt Guokas	230	305	.430
Brian Hill	222	227	.494
Bob Weiss	210	282	.427
Allan Bristow	207	203	.505
Wes Unseld	202	345	.369

BY WINNING PERCENTAGE

(minimum 400 games)

Coach	Pct.	W	L
PHIL JACKSON	.725	832	316
Billy Cunningham	.698	454	196
K.C. Jones	.674	522	252
Red Auerbach	.662	938	479
Pat Riley	.661	1,110	569
GREGG POPOVICH	.653	396	210
Paul Westphal	.627	267	159
JERRY SLOAN	.620	917	561
Lester Harrison	.620	295	181
Tom Heinsohn	.619	427	263
RICK ADELMAN	.616	658	411
Chuck Daly	.593	638	437
Larry Costello	.589	430	300
George Karl	.587	708	499
Jeff Van Gundy	.584	293	209
John Kundla	.583	423	302
Bill Sharman	.581	333	240
Al Cervi	.575	326	241
DON NELSON	.572	1,148	858
Joe Lapchick	.569	326	247

BY GAMES

Coach	G
LENNY WILKENS	2,448
Bill Fitch	2,050
DON NELSON	2,006
Dick Motta	1,952
Pat Riley	1,679
Jack Ramsay	1,647
LARRY BROWN	1,646
Gene Shue	1,645
Cotton Fitzsimmons	1,607
JERRY SLOAN	1,478
Red Auerbach	1,417
John MacLeod	1,364
Red Holzman	1,300
George Karl	1,207
Doug Moe	1,157
PHIL JACKSON	1,148
Kevin Loughery	1,136
Alvin Attles	1,075
Chuck Daly	1,075
RICK ADELMAN	1,069

HISTORY *Regular season*

BY VICTORIES, COMBINED NBA/ABA

Coach	W-L	Pct.	Coach	W-L	Pct.
LENNY WILKENS	1,315-1,133	.537	PHIL JACKSON	832-316	.725
LARRY BROWN	1,162- 820	.586	Gene Shue	784-861	.477
DON NELSON	1,148- 858	.572	George Karl	708-499	.587
Pat Riley	1,110- 569	.661	John MacLeod	707-657	.518
Bill Fitch	944-1,106	.460	Red Holzman	696-604	.535
Red Auerbach	938- 479	.662	RICK ADELMAN	658-411	.616
Dick Motta	935-1,017	.479	Alex Hannum	649-564	.535
JERRY SLOAN	917-561	.620	Kevin Loughery	642-746	.463
Jack Ramsay	864-783	.525	Chuck Daly	638-437	.593
Cotton Fitzsimmons	832-775	.518	Doug Moe	628-529	.543

BY WINNING PERCENTAGE, COMBINED NBA/ABA

(minimum 400 games)

Coach	Pct.	W	L
PHIL JACKSON	.725	832	316
Billy Cunningham	.698	454	196
Red Auerbach	.662	938	479
Pat Riley	.661	1,110	569
GREGG POPOVICH	.653	396	210
K.C. Jones	.643	552	306
Paul Westphal	.627	267	159
JERRY SLOAN	.620	917	561
Tom Heinsohn	.619	427	263
Les Harrison	.618	299	185
RICK ADELMAN	.616	658	411
Johnny Kundla	.594	466	319
Chuck Daly	.593	638	437
Larry Costello	.589	430	300
George Karl	.587	708	499
LARRY BROWN	.586	1,162	820
JEFF VAN GUNDY	.584	293	209
Al Cervi	.581	366	264
DON NELSON	.572	1,148	858
Bill Sharman	.569	466	353

BY GAMES, COMBINED NBA/ABA

Coach	G
LENNY WILKENS	2,448
Bill Fitch	2,050
DON NELSON	2,006
LARRY BROWN	1,982
Dick Motta	1,952
Pat Riley	1,679
Jack Ramsay	1,647
Gene Shue	1,645
Cotton Fitzsimmons	1,607
JERRY SLOAN	1,478
Red Auerbach	1,417
Kevin Loughery	1,388
John MacLeod	1,364
Red Holzman	1,300
Alex Hannum	1,213
George Karl	1,207
Doug Moe	1,157
PHIL JACKSON	1,148
Bob Leonard	1,107
Alvin Attles	1,075
HUBIE BROWN	1,075
Chuck Daly	1,075

ATTENDANCE
TOP SINGLE-GAME CROWDS

REGULAR SEASON

62,046— March 27, 1998
Chicago at Atlanta (Georgia Dome)
61,983— January 29, 1988
Boston at Detroit (Silverdome)
52,745— February 14, 1987
Philadelphia at Detroit (Silverdome)
49,551— April 17, 1990
Denver at Minnesota (Metrodome)
47,692— March 30, 1988
Atlanta at Detroit (Silverdome)

45,790— November 7, 1997
Chicago at Atlanta (Georgia Dome)
45,458— April 13, 1990
Orlando at Minnesota (Metrodome)
44,970— February 21, 1987
Atlanta at Detroit (Silverdome)
44,180— February 15, 1986
Philadelphia at Detroit (Silverdome)
43,816— February 16, 1985
Philadelphia at Detroit (Silverdome)

PLAYOFFS

41,732— June 16, 1988
L.A. Lakers at Detroit (Silverdome)
1988 NBA Finals, Game 5
40,172— April 15, 1980
Milwaukee at Seattle (Kingdome)
1980 Western Conference
Semifinals, Game 5

39,554— June 18, 1999
New York at San Antonio (Alamodome)
1999 NBA Finals, Game 2
39,514— June 16, 1999
New York at San Antonio (Alamodome)
1999 NBA Finals, Game 1
39,457— May 30, 1978
Washington at Seattle (Kingdome)
1978 NBA Finals, Game 4

ALL-STAR GAMES

44,735— February 12, 1989
Houston, Tex. (Astrodome)
43,146— February 10, 1985
Indianapolis, Ind. (Hoosier Dome)
36,037— February 11, 1996
San Antonio, Tex. (Alamodome)

34,275— February 8, 1987
Seattle, Wash. (Kingdome)
31,745— February 4, 1979
Pontiac, Mich. (Silverdome)

PLAYOFFS

STATISTICAL LEADERS
SINGLE-GAME BESTS

*Denotes number of overtime periods.

POINTS

	FG	FT	Pts.
Michael Jordan, Chicago at Boston, April 20, 1986**	.22	19	63
Elgin Baylor, Los Angeles at Boston, April 14, 1962	.22	17	61
Wilt Chamberlain, Philadelphia vs. Syracuse at Philadelphia, March 22, 1962	.22	12	56
Michael Jordan, Chicago at Miami, April 29, 1992	.20	16	56
Charles Barkley, Phoenix at Golden State, May 4, 1994	.23	7	56
Rick Barry, San Francisco vs. Philadelphia at San Francisco, April 18, 1967	.22	11	55
Michael Jordan, Chicago vs. Cleveland, May 1, 1988	.24	7	55
Michael Jordan, Chicago vs. Phoenix, June 16, 1993	.21	13	55
Michael Jordan, Chicago vs. Washington, April 27, 1997	.22	10	55
Allen Iverson, Philadelphia vs. New Orleans, April 20, 2003	.21	10	55
John Havlicek, Boston vs. Atlanta at Boston, April 1, 1973	.24	6	54
Michael Jordan, Chicago vs. New York, May 31, 1993	.18	12	54
Allen Iverson, Philadelphia vs. Toronto, May 9, 2001	.21	9	54
Wilt Chamberlain, Philadelphia vs. Syracuse at Philadelphia, March 14, 1960	.24	5	53
Jerry West, Los Angeles vs. Boston, April 23, 1969	.21	11	53
Jerry West, Los Angeles vs. Baltimore at Los Angeles, April 5, 1965	.16	20	52
Allen Iverson, Philadelphia vs. Toronto, May 16, 2001	.21	2	52
Sam Jones, Boston at New York, March 28, 1967	.19	13	51
Eric Floyd, Golden State vs. L.A. Lakers, May 10, 1987	.18	13	51
Bob Cousy, Boston vs. Syracuse at Boston, March 21, 1953****	.10	30	50
Bob Pettit, St. Louis vs. Boston at St. Louis, April 12, 1958	.19	12	50
Wilt Chamberlain, Philadelphia at Boston, March 22, 1960	.22	6	50
Wilt Chamberlain, San Francisco vs. St. Louis at San Francisco, April 10, 1964	.22	6	50
Billy Cunningham, Philadelphia vs. Milwaukee at Philadelphia, April 1, 1970	.22	8	50
Bob McAdoo, Buffalo vs. Washington at Buffalo, April 18, 1975	.20	10	50
Dominique Wilkins, Atlanta vs. Detroit, April 19, 1986	.19	12	50
Michael Jordan, Chicago vs. Cleveland, April 28, 1988	.19	12	50
Michael Jordan, Chicago vs. Cleveland, May 5, 1989*	.14	22	50
Karl Malone, Utah vs. Seattle, April 22, 2000	.18	13	50
Vince Carter, Toronto vs. Philadelphia, May 11, 2001	.19	3	50
Elgin Baylor, Los Angeles vs. Detroit at Los Angeles, March 15, 1961	.17	15	49
Jerry West, Los Angeles vs. Baltimore at Los Angeles, April 3, 1965	.15	19	49
Michael Jordan, Chicago at Boston, April 17, 1986	.18	13	49
Hakeem Olajuwon, Houston at Seattle, May 14, 1987**	.19	11	49
Michael Jordan, Chicago at Philadelphia, May 11, 1990	.19	7	49
Jerry West, Los Angeles at Baltimore, April 9, 1965	.20	8	48
Michael Jordan, Chicago at Milwaukee, May 1, 1990	.20	7	48
Michael Jordan, Chicago at Charlotte, April 28, 1995*	.18	11	48
Kobe Bryant, L.A. Lakers at Sacramento, May 13, 2001	.15	17	48
Allen Iverson, Philadelphia at L.A. Lakers, June 6, 2001*	.18	9	48
George Mikan, Minneapolis at Rochester, March 29, 1952	.15	17	47
Elgin Baylor, Los Angeles at Detroit, March 18, 1961	.17	13	47
Elgin Baylor, Los Angeles at St. Louis, March 27, 1961	.17	13	47
Sam Jones, Boston vs. Cincinnati at Boston, April 10, 1963	.18	11	47
Rick Barry, San Francisco vs. St. Louis at San Francisco, April 1, 1967	.17	13	47
Dominique Wilkins, Atlanta at Boston, May 22, 1988	.19	8	47
Michael Jordan, Chicago vs. New York, May 14, 1989	.12	23	47
Michael Jordan, Chicago vs. Detroit, May 26, 1990	.17	11	47
Charles Barkley, Phoenix at Portland, May 2, 1995	.16	11	47

FIELD GOALS

	FGM	FGA
Wilt Chamberlain, Philadelphia vs. Syracuse at Philadelphia, March 14, 1960	24	42
John Havlicek, Boston vs. Atlanta at Boston, April 1, 1973	24	36
Michael Jordan, Chicago vs. Cleveland, May 1, 1988	24	45
Charles Barkley, Phoenix at Golden State, May 4, 1994	23	31
Wilt Chamberlain, Philadelphia at Boston, March 22, 1960	22	42
Wilt Chamberlain, Philadelphia vs. Syracuse at Philadelphia, March 22, 1962	22	48
Elgin Baylor, Los Angeles at Boston, April 14, 1962	22	46
Wilt Chamberlain, San Francisco vs. St. Louis at San Francisco, April 10, 1964	22	32
Rick Barry, San Francisco vs. Philadelphia at San Francisco, April 18, 1967	22	48
Billy Cunningham, Philadelphia vs. Milwaukee at Philadelphia, April 1, 1970	22	39
Michael Jordan, Chicago at Boston, April 20, 1986**	22	41
Michael Jordan, Chicago vs. Washington, April 27, 1997	22	35
Jerry West, Los Angeles vs. Boston, April 23, 1969	21	41

	FGM	FGA
Bob McAdoo, Buffalo vs. Boston at Buffalo, April 6, 1974	21	40
Michael Jordan, Chicago vs. Miami, April 24, 1992	21	34
Michael Jordan, Chicago vs. Phoenix, June 16, 1993	21	37
Shaquille O'Neal, L.A. Lakers vs. Sacramento, April 23, 2000	21	33
Shaquille O'Neal, L.A. Lakers vs. Indiana, June 7, 2000	21	31
Allen Iverson, Philadelphia vs. Toronto, May 9, 2001	21	39
Allen Iverson, Philadelphia vs. Toronto, May 16, 2001	21	32
Allen Iverson, Philadelphia vs. New Orleans, April 20, 2003	21	32
Jerry West, Los Angeles at Baltimore, April 9, 1965	20	43
Wilt Chamberlain, Los Angeles vs. New York at Los Angeles, May 6, 1970.	20	27
Kareem Abdul-Jabbar, Milwaukee at Chicago, April 18, 1974	20	29
Bob McAdoo, Buffalo vs. Washington at Buffalo, April 18, 1975	20	32
Xavier McDaniel, Seattle vs. L.A. Lakers, May 23, 1987	20	29
Michael Jordan, Chicago at Milwaukee, May 1, 1990	20	35
Michael Jordan, Chicago at Philadelphia, May 10, 1991	20	34
Michael Jordan, Chicago at Miami, April 29, 1992	20	30
Hakeem Olajuwon, Houston at Utah, April 27, 1995.	20	30
Bob Pettit, St. Louis vs. Boston at St. Louis, April 12, 1958.	19	34
Wilt Chamberlain, Philadelphia vs. Syracuse at Philadelphia, March 14, 1961.	19	36
Wilt Chamberlain, San Francisco at St. Louis, April 5, 1964.	19	36
Wilt Chamberlain, San Francisco vs. St. Louis at San Francisco, April 16, 1964	19	29
Wilt Chamberlain, Philadelphia vs. Boston at Philadelphia, April 12, 1966	19	34
Jerry West, Los Angeles vs. Boston at Los Angeles, April 22, 1966	19	31
Wilt Chamberlain, Philadelphia vs. Cincinnati at Philadelphia, March 21, 1967	19	30
Sam Jones, Boston at New York, March 28, 1967	19	30
Dave Bing, Detroit vs. Boston, April 1, 1968	19	38
Gail Goodrich, Los Angeles vs. Golden State at Los Angeles, April 25, 1973	19	26
Elvin Hayes, Capital at New York, March 29, 1974	19	29
Elvin Hayes, Washington vs. Buffalo at Washington, April 20, 1975	19	26
Fred Brown, Seattle vs. Phoenix at Seattle, April 15, 1976	19	35
George Gervin, San Antonio vs. Washington at San Antonio, May 11, 1979	19	31
George Gervin, San Antonio vs. Houston, April 4, 1980	19	29
Kareem Abdul-Jabbar, Los Angeles vs. Philadelphia, May 7, 1980	19	31
Calvin Murphy, Houston at San Antonio, April 17, 1981.	19	28
Bernard King, New York vs. Detroit, April 22, 1984	19	27
Rolando Blackman, Dallas vs. Portland, April 18, 1985**	19	33
Dominique Wilkins, Atlanta vs. Detroit, April 19, 1986.	19	28
Mark Aguirre, Dallas vs. L.A. Lakers, May 4, 1986.	19	30
Hakeem Olajuwon, Houston at Seattle, May 14, 1987**	19	33
Michael Jordan, Chicago vs. Cleveland, April 28, 1988	19	35
Dominique Wilkins, Atlanta at Boston, May 22, 1988.	19	33
Michael Jordan, Chicago at Philadelphia, May 11, 1990.	19	34
Michael Jordan, Chicago vs. Phoenix, June 13, 1993***	19	43
Hakeem Olajuwon, Houston vs. San Antonio, May 26, 1995	19	32
Hakeem Olajuwon, Houston at San Antonio, May 30, 1995	19	30
Shaquille O'Neal, L.A. Lakers vs. Indiana, June 19, 2000	19	32
Vince Carter, Toronto vs. Philadelphia, May 11, 2001.	19	29
Kobe Bryant, L.A. Lakers at San Antonio, May 19, 2001	19	35

FREE THROWS

	FTM	FTA
Bob Cousy, Boston vs. Syracuse at Boston, March 21, 1953****	30	32
Michael Jordan, Chicago vs. New York, May 14, 1989.	23	28
Michael Jordan, Chicago vs. Cleveland, May 5, 1989*	22	27
Karl Malone, Utah vs. L.A. Clippers at Anaheim, May 3, 1992	22	24
Oscar Robertson, Cincinnati at Boston, April 10, 1963.	21	22
Derrick Coleman, New Jersey vs. New York, May 6, 1994	21	25
Kevin Johnson, Phoenix vs. Houston, May 20, 1995	21	22
Paul Pierce, Boston vs. Indiana, April 19, 2003	21	21
Bob Cousy, Boston vs. Syracuse at Boston, March 17, 1954*	20	25
Jerry West, Los Angeles at Detroit, April 3, 1962.	20	23
Jerry West, Los Angeles vs. Baltimore at Los Angeles, April 5, 1965	20	21
Magic Johnson, L.A. Lakers vs. Golden State, May 8, 1991	20	22
Karl Malone, Utah at Portland, May 9, 1991	20	22
Bob Pettit, St. Louis at Boston, April 9, 1958.	19	24
Jerry West, Los Angeles vs. Baltimore at Los Angeles, April 3, 1965	19	21
Michael Jordan, Chicago at Boston, April 20, 1986**	19	21
Charles Barkley, Phoenix vs. Seattle, June 5, 1993	19	22
Tim Duncan, San Antonio at L.A. Lakers, May 22, 1999.	19	23
Allen Iverson, Philadelphia vs. Boston, April 28, 2002	19	20

REBOUNDS

	No.
Wilt Chamberlain, Philadelphia vs. Boston at Philadelphia, April 5, 1967	41
Bill Russell, Boston vs. Philadelphia at Boston, March 23, 1958	40
Bill Russell, Boston vs. St. Louis at Boston, March 29, 1960	40

Bill Russell, Boston vs. Los Angeles at Boston, April 18, 1962* 40
Bill Russell, Boston vs. Philadelphia at Boston, March 19, 1960 39
Bill Russell, Boston vs. Syracuse at Boston, March 23, 1961 39
Wilt Chamberlain, Philadelphia vs. Boston at Philadelphia, April 6, 1965 39
Bill Russell, Boston vs. St. Louis at Boston, April 11, 1961 38
Bill Russell, Boston vs. Los Angeles at Boston, April 16, 1963 38
Wilt Chamberlain, San Francisco vs. Boston at San Francisco, April 24, 1964 38
Wilt Chamberlain, Philadelphia vs. San Francisco at Philadelphia, April 16, 1967 38

ASSISTS

No.
Magic Johnson, Los Angeles vs. Phoenix, May 15, 1984 24
John Stockton, Utah at L.A. Lakers, May 17, 1988 24
Magic Johnson, L.A. Lakers at Portland, May 3, 1985 23
John Stockton, Utah vs. Portland, April 25, 1996 23
Doc Rivers, Atlanta vs. Boston, May 16, 1988 22
Magic Johnson, Los Angeles vs. Boston, June 3, 1984 21
Magic Johnson, L.A. Lakers vs. Houston, April 27, 1991 21
Magic Johnson, L.A. Lakers at Portland, May 18, 1991 21
John Stockton, Utah vs. L.A. Clippers, April 24, 1992 21
Johnny Moore, San Antonio vs. Denver, April 27, 1983 20
Magic Johnson, L.A. Lakers at Houston, May 16, 1986 20
Magic Johnson, L.A. Lakers vs. Boston, June 4, 1987 20
John Stockton, Utah at L.A. Lakers, May 21, 1988 20
Magic Johnson, L.A. Lakers at Dallas, May 31, 1988 20
Magic Johnson, L.A. Lakers at Phoenix, May 28, 1989 20
Tim Hardaway, Golden State at L.A. Lakers, May 14, 1991* 20
Magic Johnson, L.A. Lakers vs. Chicago, June 12, 1991 20
Bob Cousy, Boston vs. St. Louis at Boston, April 9, 1957 19
Bob Cousy, Boston at Minneapolis, April 7, 1959 19
Wilt Chamberlain, Philadelphia vs. Cincinnati at Philadelphia, March 24, 1967 19
Walt Frazier, New York vs. Los Angeles at New York, May 8, 1970 19
Jerry West, Los Angeles vs. Chicago at Los Angeles, April 1, 1973 19
Norm Nixon, Los Angeles vs. Seattle at Los Angeles, April 22, 1979 19
Magic Johnson, Los Angeles vs. San Antonio, May 18, 1983 19
Magic Johnson, L.A. Lakers vs. Phoenix, April 18, 1985 19
Magic Johnson, L.A. Lakers vs. Portland, May 7, 1985 19
Magic Johnson, L.A. Lakers vs. Denver, May 22, 1985 19
Magic Johnson, L.A. Lakers vs. Houston, May 13, 1986 19
Magic Johnson, L.A. Lakers vs. Boston, June 14, 1987 19
Magic Johnson, L.A. Lakers vs. Dallas, May 25, 1988 19
Magic Johnson, L.A. Lakers vs. Detroit, June 19, 1988 19
John Stockton, Utah at Phoenix, May 2, 1990 19
Magic Johnson, L.A. Lakers vs. Portland, May 24, 1991 19
Kevin Johnson, Phoenix vs. San Antonio, April 26, 1992 19
John Stockton, Utah vs. L.A. Clippers, April 26, 1992 19
John Stockton, Utah at San Antonio, May 7, 1996 19

STEALS

No.
Allen Iverson, Philadelphia vs. Orlando, May 13, 1999 10
Rick Barry, Golden State vs. Seattle, April 14, 1975 8
Lionel Hollins, Portland at Los Angeles, May 8, 1977 8
Maurice Cheeks, Philadelphia vs. New Jersey, April 11, 1979 8
Craig Hodges, Milwaukee at Philadelphia, May 9, 1986 8
Tim Hardaway, Golden State at L.A. Lakers, May 8, 1991 8
Tim Hardaway, Golden State at Seattle, April 30, 1992 8
Mookie Blaylock, Atlanta vs. Indiana, April 29, 1996 8
Rick Barry, Golden State at Chicago, May 11, 1975 7
Rick Barry, Golden State vs. Detroit, April 28, 1976 7
Bobby Jones, Denver at Portland, April 24, 1977 7
Magic Johnson, Los Angeles vs. Portland, April 24, 1983 7
Darrell Walker, New York at Detroit, April 17, 1984 7
T.R. Dunn, Denver vs. Portland, April 20, 1986 7
Dennis Johnson, Boston vs. Atlanta, April 29, 1986 7
Derek Harper, Dallas at L.A. Lakers, April 30, 1986 7
Patrick Ewing, New York vs. Boston, May 4, 1990 7
Byron Scott, L.A. Lakers at Golden State, May 10, 1991 7
Charles Barkley, Phoenix vs. San Antonio, May 13, 1993 7
Haywoode Workman, Indiana at Orlando, April 28, 1994 7
Robert Horry, Houston at Orlando, June 9, 1995 7
Allen Iverson, Philadelphia vs. Toronto, May 6, 2001 7
Baron Davis, Charlotte at New Jersey, May 5, 2002 7
Baron Davis, Charlotte vs. New Jersey, May 9, 2002 7
Ben Wallace, Detroit vs. Orlando, April 27, 2003 7

HISTORY Playoffs

	No.
Mark Eaton, Utah vs. Houston, April 26, 1985	10
Hakeem Olajuwon, Houston at L.A. Lakers, April 29, 1990	10
Kareem Abdul-Jabbar, Los Angeles vs. Golden State, April 22, 1977	9
Manute Bol, Washington at Philadelphia, April 18, 1986	9
Hakeem Olajuwon, Houston vs. L.A. Clippers, April 29, 1993	9
Derrick Coleman, New Jersey vs. Cleveland, May 7, 1993	9
Greg Ostertag, Utah vs. L.A. Lakers, May 12, 1997*	9
Alonzo Mourning, Miami vs. Detroit, April 22, 2000	9
George T. Johnson, Golden State at Seattle, April 24, 1975	8
Elvin Hayes, Washington vs. Cleveland, April 26, 1976*	8
Kareem Abdul-Jabbar, Los Angeles at Portland, May 10, 1977	8
Bill Walton, Portland vs. Philadelphia, June 5, 1977	8
Caldwell Jones, Philadelphia vs. Washington, May 3, 1978	8
Darryl Dawkins, Philadelphia vs. Atlanta, April 21, 1982	8
Kareem Abdul-Jabbar, Los Angeles at Portland, May 1, 1983	8
Mark Eaton, Utah at Houston, April 19, 1985	8
Manute Bol, Washington at Philadelphia, April 20, 1986	8
Manute Bol, Washington vs. Philadelphia, April 22, 1986	8
Hakeem Olajuwon, Houston vs. Boston, June 5, 1986	8
Hakeem Olajuwon, Houston vs. Portland, April 28, 1987	8
Alton Lister, Seattle vs. Houston, April 28, 1989	8
David Robinson, San Antonio vs. Portland, May 10, 1990	8
David Robinson, San Antonio vs. Golden State, April 25, 1991	8
Hakeem Olajuwon, Houston vs. Seattle, May 16, 1993	8
Dikembe Mutombo, Denver vs. Seattle, May 5, 1994*	8
Dikembe Mutombo, Denver at Seattle, May 7, 1994*	8
Dikembe Mutombo, Denver at Utah, May 12, 1994	8
Patrick Ewing, New York vs. Houston, June 17, 1994	8
Shaquille O'Neal, L.A. Lakers at Seattle, May 12, 1998	8
Samaki Walker, San Antonio vs. Phoenix, April 25, 2000	8
Shaquille O'Neal, L.A. Lakers vs. Philadelphia, June 8, 2001	8
Tim Duncan, San Antonio vs. New Jersey, June 15, 2003	8
Shaquille O'Neal, L.A. Lakers vs. San Antonio, May 9, 2004	8

CAREER SCORING

(Active players in 2003-04 in CAPS)

Figures from National Basketball League are included below; NBL did not record field-goal attempts, however, so all field-goal percentages listed here are based only on field goals and attempts in NBA competition. Minutes played not compiled prior to 1952; rebounds not compiled prior to 1951.

Player	Yrs.	G	Min.	FGM	FGA	Pct.	FTM	FTA	Pct.	Reb.	Ast.	PF	Pts.	Avg.
Michael Jordan	13	179	7474	2188	4497	.487	1463	1766	.828	1152	1022	541	5987	33.4
Kareem Abdul-Jabbar	18	237	8851	2356	4422	.533	1050	1419	.740	2481	767	797	5762	24.3
KARL MALONE	19	193	7907	1743	3768	.463	1269	1725	.736	2062	610	662	4761	24.7
Jerry West	13	153	6321	1622	3460	.469	1213	1506	.805	855	970	451	4457	29.1
SHAQUILLE O'NEAL	11	158	6382	1658	2951	.562	978	1889	.518	2040	492	552	4294	27.2
Larry Bird	12	164	6886	1458	3090	.472	901	1012	.890	1683	1062	466	3897	23.8
John Havlicek	13	172	6860	1451	3329	.436	874	1046	.836	1186	825	527	3776	22.0
Hakeem Olajuwon	15	145	5749	1504	2847	.528	743	1034	.719	1621	458	562	3755	25.9
Magic Johnson	13	190	7538	1291	2552	.506	1068	1274	.838	1465	2346	524	3701	19.5
SCOTTIE PIPPEN	16	208	8105	1335	3009	.444	772	1067	.724	1583	1048	686	3642	17.5
Elgin Baylor	12	134	5510	1388	3161	.439	847	1098	.771	1724	541	435	3623	27.0
Wilt Chamberlain	13	160	7559	1425	2728	.522	757	1627	.465	3913	673	412	3607	22.5
Kevin McHale	13	169	5716	1204	2145	.561	766	972	.788	1253	274	571	3182	18.8
Dennis Johnson	13	180	6994	1167	2661	.439	756	943	.802	781	1006	575	3116	17.3
Julius Erving	11	141	5288	1187	2441	.486	707	908	.779	994	594	403	3088	21.9
James Worthy	9	143	5297	1267	2329	.544	474	652	.727	747	463	352	3022	21.1
Clyde Drexler	15	145	5572	1076	2408	.447	670	851	.787	1002	891	486	2963	20.4
Sam Jones	12	154	4654	1149	2571	.447	611	753	.811	718	358	391	2909	18.9
Charles Barkley	13	123	4849	1009	1965	.513	751	1048	.717	1582	482	408	2833	23.0
Robert Parish	16	184	6177	1132	2239	.506	556	770	.722	1765	234	617	2820	15.3
Patrick Ewing	14	139	5207	1104	2353	.469	597	831	.718	1435	275	522	2813	20.2
REGGIE MILLER	14	131	4878	879	1952	.450	722	811	.890	376	337	247	2779	21.2
KOBE BRYANT	8	119	4556	969	2233	.434	635	802	.792	577	528	376	2694	22.6
Bill Russell	13	165	7497	1003	2335	.430	667	1106	.603	4104	770	546	2673	16.2
Byron Scott	13	183	5365	934	1937	.482	449	548	.819	536	390	445	2451	13.4
John Stockton	19	182	6398	855	1809	.473	615	759	.810	608	1839	539	2436	13.4
Isiah Thomas	9	111	4216	825	1869	.441	530	689	.769	524	987	363	2261	20.4
Bob Pettit	9	88	3545	766	1834	.418	708	915	.774	1304	241	277	2240	25.5
David Robinson	12	123	4221	768	1604	.479	684	966	.708	1301	280	423	2221	18.1
Elvin Hayes	10	96	4160	883	1901	.464	428	656	.652	1244	185	378	2194	22.9

HISTORY *Playoffs*

Player	Yrs.	G	Min.	FGM	FGA	Pct.	FTM	FTA	Pct.	Reb.	Ast.	PF	Pts.	Avg.
George Mikan......... 9	9	91	1500	723	1394	.404	695	901	.771	665	155	390	2141	23.5
Jeff Hornacek.......... 11	11	140	4766	741	1578	.470	488	551	.886	527	525	384	2092	14.9
Moses Malone 12	12	94	3796	750	1566	.479	576	756	.762	1295	136	244	2077	22.1
Tom Heinsohn 9	9	104	3223	818	2035	.402	422	568	.743	954	215	417	2058	19.8
Kevin Johnson 11	11	105	3879	705	1504	.469	594	713	.833	349	935	233	2026	19.3
Bob Cousy 13	13	109	4120	689	2016	.342	640	799	.801	546	937	314	2018	18.5
Dolph Schayes 15	15	103	2687	609	1491	.390	755	918	.822	1051	257	397	1973	19.2
Bob Dandridge 8	8	98	3882	823	1716	.480	321	422	.761	754	365	377	1967	20.1
TIM DUNCAN 6	6	82	3439	720	1420	.507	518	742	.698	1076	318	251	1960	23.9
GARY PAYTON 12	12	122	4650	773	1745	.443	285	405	.704	502	740	366	1950	16.0
Gus Williams 10	10	99	3215	782	1644	.476	356	483	.737	308	469	243	1929	19.5
Walt Frazier 8	8	93	3953	767	1500	.511	393	523	.751	666	599	285	1927	20.7
Chet Walker 13	13	105	3688	687	1531	.449	542	689	.787	737	212	286	1916	18.2
Maurice Cheeks 13	13	133	4848	772	1509	.512	362	466	.777	453	922	324	1910	14.4
Oscar Robertson...... 10	10	86	3673	675	1466	.460	560	655	.855	578	769	267	1910	22.2
HORACE GRANT....... 13	13	170	6172	786	1483	.530	334	468	.714	1457	360	515	1907	11.2
Danny Ainge.......... 12	12	193	5038	717	1571	.456	296	357	.829	443	656	533	1902	9.9
Hal Greer 13	13	92	3642	705	1657	.425	466	574	.812	505	393	357	1876	20.4
Sam Perkins 15	15	167	4785	656	1479	.444	397	506	.785	936	246	441	1861	11.1
Cliff Hagan........... 9	9	90	2965	701	1544	.454	432	540	.800	744	305	320	1834	20.4
Rick Barry 7	7	74	2723	719	1688	.426	392	448	.875	418	340	232	1833	24.8
Terry Porter 16	16	124	3939	620	1320	.470	437	529	.826	371	624	245	1828	14.7
Jamaal Wilkes 10	10	113	3799	785	1689	.465	250	344	.727	718	246	326	1820	16.1
Joe Dumars 10	10	112	4097	646	1398	.462	407	476	.855	257	512	227	1752	15.6
Mark Aguirre 9	9	102	2958	696	1435	.485	310	417	.743	537	262	281	1747	17.1
ALLEN IVERSON 5	5	57	2584	618	1559	.396	404	533	.758	247	328	131	1743	30.6
Jo Jo White 6	6	80	3428	732	1629	.449	256	309	.828	358	452	241	1720	21.5
Bob McAdoo 9	9	94	2714	698	1423	.491	320	442	.724	711	127	318	1718	18.3
Dave Cowens 7	7	89	3768	733	1627	.451	218	293	.744	1285	333	398	1684	18.9
Terry Cummings 13	13	110	2959	678	1351	.502	307	435	.706	742	173	353	1664	15.1
Tom Chambers........ 10	10	108	3061	607	1380	.440	421	509	.827	569	183	359	1662	15.4
Alex English 10	10	68	2427	668	1328	.503	325	377	.862	371	293	188	1661	24.4
George Gervin 9	9	59	2202	622	1225	.508	348	424	.821	341	186	207	1592	27.0
Michael Cooper....... 11	11	168	4744	582	1244	.468	293	355	.825	574	703	474	1581	9.4
Don Nelson 11	11	150	3209	585	1175	.498	407	498	.817	719	210	399	1577	10.5
ROBERT HORRY 12	12	175	5466	545	1266	.430	281	392	.717	1086	480	569	1570	9.0
Adrian Dantley 7	7	73	2515	531	1012	.525	496	623	.796	395	169	188	1558	21.3
Jerome Kersey 15	15	126	3394	599	1277	.469	357	491	.727	717	233	427	1557	12.4
CHARLES OAKLEY 15	15	144	5108	584	1272	.459	367	486	.755	1445	283	503	1550	10.8
Dick Barnett 11	11	102	3027	603	1317	.458	333	445	.748	273	247	282	1539	15.1
Rik Smits 10	10	104	2747	623	1230	.507	290	350	.829	540	135	419	1537	14.8
Dave DeBusschere 8	8	96	3682	634	1523	.416	268	384	.698	1155	253	327	1536	16.0
Shawn Kemp 10	10	88	2937	514	1032	.498	491	616	.797	853	161	346	1522	17.3
Sidney Moncrief 11	11	93	3226	491	1033	.475	488	602	.811	469	317	285	1487	16.0
Earl Monroe 8	8	82	2715	567	1292	.439	337	426	.791	266	264	216	1471	17.9
VLADE DIVAC......... 14	14	121	3728	541	1128	.480	373	510	.731	913	286	439	1468	12.1
Jack Sikma........... 11	11	102	3558	556	1249	.445	338	407	.830	945	244	432	1461	14.3
Bobby Jones 10	10	125	3431	553	1034	.535	347	429	.809	614	284	400	1453	11.6
Walter Davis.......... 10	10	78	2184	591	1192	.496	263	317	.830	240	312	186	1450	18.6
Gail Goodrich 8	8	80	2622	542	1227	.442	366	447	.819	250	333	219	1450	18.1
Ricky Pierce 12	12	97	2050	532	1142	.466	350	404	.866	229	187	266	1447	14.9
Bill Sharman.......... 10	10	78	2573	538	1262	.426	370	406	.911	285	201	220	1446	18.5
Dan Majerle 13	13	123	4239	508	1222	.416	244	324	.753	609	304	285	1441	11.7
Detlef Schrempf 14	14	114	3338	488	1049	.465	399	506	.789	565	296	309	1432	12.6
Dominique Wilkins 10	10	56	2172	515	1201	.429	366	444	.824	375	143	123	1423	25.4
Bailey Howell 10	10	86	2712	542	1165	.465	317	433	.732	697	130	376	1401	16.3
Vinnie Johnson 10	10	116	2671	578	1275	.453	214	284	.754	364	306	234	1387	12.0
CLIFFORD ROBINSON ... 14	14	125	3598	514	1300	.395	282	451	.625	518	240	447	1386	11.1
Darryl Dawkins....... 10	10	109	2734	542	992	.546	291	414	.703	665	119	438	1375	12.6
John Starks 9	9	96	3035	450	1069	.421	287	378	.759	271	393	323	1363	14.2
Willis Reed 7	7	78	2641	570	1203	.474	218	285	.765	801	149	275	1358	17.4
Bill Laimbeer 9	9	113	3735	549	1174	.468	212	259	.819	1097	195	408	1354	12.0
SAM CASSELL 9	9	103	2871	455	1086	.419	340	398	.854	286	498	337	1346	13.1
Rudy LaRusso 9	9	93	3188	467	1152	.405	410	546	.751	779	194	366	1344	14.5
STEVE SMITH......... 12	12	98	2894	444	1040	.427	314	366	.858	268	195	221	1338	15.4
Paul Westphal 9	9	107	2449	553	1149	.481	225	285	.789	153	353	241	1337	12.5
Frank Ramsey......... 9	9	98	2396	469	1105	.424	393	476	.826	494	151	362	1331	13.6
A.C. Green 13	13	153	4119	455	958	.475	393	532	.739	1084	130	340	1315	8.6
ANFERNEE HARDAWAY ... 8	8	64	2640	456	1018	.448	291	390	.746	303	394	197	1304	20.4
Lou Hudson 9	9	61	2199	519	1164	.446	262	326	.804	318	164	196	1300	21.3
Wes Unseld 12	12	119	4889	513	1040	.493	234	385	.608	1777	453	371	1260	10.6
Andrew Toney 6	6	72	2146	485	1015	.478	272	346	.786	168	323	265	1254	17.4
Bob Lanier............ 9	9	67	2361	508	955	.532	228	297	.768	645	235	233	1244	18.6
CHRIS WEBBER 8	8	59	2310	512	1109	.462	209	339	.617	567	253	215	1242	21.1

Player	Yrs.	G	Min.	FGM	FGA	Pct.	FTM	FTA	Pct.	Reb.	Ast.	PF	Pts.	Avg.
LATRELL SPREWELL	5	62	2548	446	1067	.418	269	335	.803	269	211	135	1223	19.7
Bill Bradley	8	95	3161	510	1165	.438	202	251	.805	333	263	313	1222	12.9
ALLAN HOUSTON	6	63	2525	435	970	.448	268	303	.884	184	139	151	1214	19.3
Buck Williams	14	108	3710	436	839	.520	338	503	.672	941	113	386	1211	11.2
JASON KIDD	8	73	3028	432	1102	.392	261	329	.793	515	661	164	1210	16.6
Fred Brown	8	83	1900	499	1082	.461	186	227	.819	196	193	144	1197	14.4
Jim McMillian	7	72	2722	497	1101	.451	200	253	.791	377	137	169	1194	16.6
Paul Arizin	8	49	1815	411	1001	.411	364	439	.829	404	128	177	1186	24.2
Bill Bridges	12	113	3521	475	1135	.419	235	349	.673	1305	219	408	1185	10.5
MARK JACKSON	14	131	3776	438	1013	.432	212	273	.777	477	905	225	1185	9.0
Derrick McKey	13	142	3786	436	939	.464	265	356	.744	626	319	436	1176	8.3
Eddie A. Johnson	10	89	2114	452	1054	.429	197	228	.864	312	102	199	1168	13.1
Marques Johnson	6	54	2112	471	964	.489	218	311	.701	427	198	156	1163	21.5
RASHEED WALLACE	7	73	2695	450	977	.461	206	287	.718	485	132	260	1163	15.9
Maurice Lucas	9	82	2426	472	975	.484	215	289	.744	690	225	310	1159	14.1
Satch Sanders	11	130	3039	465	1066	.436	212	296	.716	760	127	508	1142	8.8
Vern Mikkelsen	9	85	2103	396	999	.396	349	446	.783	585	152	397	1141	13.5
Mychal Thompson	11	104	2708	449	897	.501	234	361	.648	627	126	309	1132	10.9
Archie Clark	10	71	2387	444	977	.454	237	307	.772	229	297	197	1125	15.8
Paul Silas	14	163	4619	396	998	.397	332	480	.692	1527	335	469	1124	6.9
Sean Elliott	9	85	2836	384	862	.445	277	346	.801	341	207	220	1118	13.2
Cedric Maxwell	8	102	2731	375	688	.545	366	471	.777	553	194	260	1116	10.9
Rolando Blackman	8	69	2137	434	897	.484	233	268	.869	200	217	119	1110	16.1
Bill Cartwright	10	124	3496	417	866	.482	266	367	.725	668	162	412	1100	8.9
Jim Pollard	8	82	1724	397	1029	.339	306	413	.741	407	259	234	1100	13.4
ALONZO MOURNING	8	55	2062	374	769	.486	340	512	.664	524	72	226	1095	19.9
Derek Harper	10	97	3094	415	925	.449	168	236	.712	233	513	237	1094	11.3
Kiki Vandeweghe	12	68	1890	419	822	.510	235	259	.907	188	134	132	1093	16.1
Phil Chenier	7	60	2088	438	974	.450	212	251	.845	230	131	152	1088	18.1
Jeff Mullins	10	83	2255	462	1030	.449	160	213	.751	304	259	217	1084	13.1
Dennis Rodman	11	169	4789	442	902	.490	190	352	.540	1676	205	630	1081	6.4
Alvan Adams	9	78	2288	440	930	.473	196	256	.766	588	320	251	1076	13.8
Bob Love	6	47	2061	441	1023	.431	194	250	.776	352	87	144	1076	22.9
Zelmo Beaty	7	63	2345	399	857	.466	273	370	.738	696	98	267	1071	17.0
Larry Nance	8	68	2428	440	813	.541	190	256	.742	535	160	220	1070	15.7
KEVIN GARNETT	8	47	2003	415	907	.458	207	272	.761	628	236	149	1049	22.3
Hersey Hawkins	8	74	2529	326	716	.455	292	322	.907	286	195	188	1043	14.1
TONI KUKOC	8	96	2611	378	864	.438	183	262	.698	382	308	207	1042	10.9
BRYON RUSSELL	10	102	3072	355	805	.441	199	263	.757	444	135	249	1035	10.1
Lenny Wilkens	7	64	2403	359	899	.399	313	407	.769	373	372	258	1031	16.1
James Edwards	11	111	2212	399	853	.468	232	340	.682	354	84	325	1030	9.3
Dan Issel	7	53	1599	402	810	.496	223	269	.829	393	145	157	1029	19.4
Norm Nixon	6	58	2287	440	921	.478	142	186	.763	195	465	201	1027	17.7
DIRK NOWITZKI	4	40	1690	337	740	.455	287	323	.889	441	76	132	1024	25.6
Robert Reid	9	79	2740	430	983	.437	157	217	.724	391	335	277	1025	13.0
Ron Harper	10	112	3000	397	883	.450	162	232	.698	417	305	245	1013	9.0
Dale Ellis	10	73	1981	403	909	.443	134	171	.784	273	92	163	1011	13.8
NICK VAN EXEL	6	64	2257	365	913	.400	165	222	.743	209	325	165	1006	15.7

CAREER, OTHER CATEGORIES

(Active players in 2003-04 in CAPS)

SCORING AVERAGE
(minimum 25 games or 625 points)

	G	FGM	FTM	Pts.	Avg.
Michael Jordan	179	2,188	1,463	5,987	33.4
ALLEN IVERSON	57	618	404	1,743	30.6
Jerry West	153	1,622	1,213	4,457	29.1
SHAQUILLE O'NEAL	158	1,658	978	4,294	27.2
Elgin Baylor	134	1,388	847	3,623	27.0
George Gervin	59	622	348	1,592	27.0
Hakeem Olajuwon	145	1,504	743	3,755	25.9
DIRK NOWITZKI	40	337	287	1,024	25.6
Bob Pettit	88	766	708	2,240	25.5
Dominique Wilkins	56	515	366	1,423	25.4

FIELD-GOAL PERCENTAGE
(minimum 150 made)

	FGM	FGA	Pct.
James Donaldson	153	244	.627
Kurt Rambis	284	495	.574
Otis Thorpe	321	564	.569
Artis Gilmore	179	315	.568
Mark West	201	355	.566
SHAQUILLE O'NEAL	1,658	2,951	.562
Kevin McHale	1,204	2,145	.561
Bernard King	269	481	.559
DALE DAVIS	337	615	.548
Darryl Dawkins	542	992	.546

FREE THROW PERCENTAGE
(minimum 100 made)

	FTM	FTA	Pct.
Mark Price	202	214	.944
Calvin Murphy	165	177	.932
Bill Sharman	370	406	.911
Kiki Vandeweghe	235	259	.907
Hersey Hawkins	292	322	.907
PEJA STOJAKOVIC	190	212	.896
CHAUNCEY BILLUPS	220	247	.891
Larry Bird	901	1,012	.890
REGGIE MILLER	722	811	.890
Vince Boryla	120	135	.889

3-POINT FIELD-GOAL PERCENTAGE
(minimum 35 made)

	FGM	FGA	Pct.
Bob Hansen	38	76	.500
RAY ALLEN	76	164	.463
B.J. Armstrong	51	113	.451
Kenny Smith	117	261	.448
STEVE NASH	81	185	.438
TIM THOMAS	39	90	.433
Jeff Hornacek	122	282	.433
DEREK FISHER	144	334	.431
TONY DELK	47	110	.427
KEITH VAN HORN	55	129	.426

YEARS

KARL MALONE 19
John Stockton 19
Kareem Abdul-Jabbar 18
Robert Parish 16
SCOTTIE PIPPEN 16
Terry Porter. 16
Many tied 15

GAMES

Kareem Abdul-Jabbar 237
SCOTTIE PIPPEN 208
Danny Ainge 193
KARL MALONE 193
Magic Johnson 190
Robert Parish 184
Byron Scott 183
John Stockton 182
Dennis Johnson 180
Michael Jordan 179

MINUTES

Kareem Abdul-Jabbar 8,851
SCOTTIE PIPPEN 8,105
KARL MALONE 7,907
Wilt Chamberlain 7,559
Magic Johnson 7,538
Bill Russell 7,497
Michael Jordan 7,474
Dennis Johnson 6,994
Larry Bird 6,886
John Havlicek 6,860

FIELD GOALS MADE

Kareem Abdul-Jabbar 2,356
Michael Jordan 2,188
KARL MALONE 1,743
SHAQUILLE O'NEAL 1,658
Jerry West 1,622
Hakeem Olajuwon 1,504
Larry Bird 1,458
John Havlicek 1,451
Wilt Chamberlain 1,425
Elgin Baylor 1,388

FIELD GOALS ATTEMPTED

Michael Jordan 4,497
Kareem Abdul-Jabbar 4,422
KARL MALONE 3,768
Jerry West 3,460
John Havlicek 3,329
Elgin Baylor 3,161
Larry Bird 3,090
SCOTTIE PIPPEN 3,009
SHAQUILLE O'NEAL 2,951
Hakeem Olajuwon 2,847

FREE THROWS MADE

Michael Jordan 1,463
KARL MALONE 1,269
Jerry West 1,213
Magic Johnson 1,068
Kareem Abdul-Jabbar 1,050
SHAQUILLE O'NEAL 978
Larry Bird 901
John Havlicek 874
Elgin Baylor 847
SCOTTIE PIPPEN 772

FREE THROWS ATTEMPTED

SHAQUILLE O'NEAL 1,889
Michael Jordan 1,766
KARL MALONE 1,725
Wilt Chamberlain 1,627
Jerry West 1,506
Kareem Abdul-Jabbar 1,419
Magic Johnson 1,274
Bill Russell 1,106
Elgin Baylor 1,098
SCOTTIE PIPPEN 1,067

3-POINT FIELD GOALS MADE

REGGIE MILLER 299
SCOTTIE PIPPEN 200
ROBERT HORRY 199
Dan Majerle 181
John Starks 176
Danny Ainge 172
Sam Perkins 152
Terry Porter 151
Michael Jordan 148
DEREK FISHER 144

3-POINT FIELD GOALS ATTEMPTED

REGGIE MILLER 754
SCOTTIE PIPPEN 660
ROBERT HORRY 567
Dan Majerle 513
Clyde Drexler 489
John Starks 475
Michael Jordan 446
Danny Ainge 433
Sam Perkins 419
Terry Porter 406

REBOUNDS

Bill Russell 4,104
Wilt Chamberlain 3,913
Kareem Abdul-Jabbar 2,481
KARL MALONE 2,062
SHAQUILLE O'NEAL 2,040
Wes Unseld 1,777
Robert Parish 1,765
Elgin Baylor 1,724

Larry Bird 1,683
Dennis Rodman 1,676

ASSISTS

Magic Johnson 2,346
John Stockton 1,839
Larry Bird 1,062
SCOTTIE PIPPEN 1,048
Michael Jordan 1,022
Dennis Johnson 1,006
Isiah Thomas 987
Jerry West 970
Bob Cousy 937
Kevin Johnson 935

PERSONAL FOULS

Kareem Abdul-Jabbar 797
SCOTTIE PIPPEN 686
KARL MALONE 662
Dennis Rodman 630
Robert Parish 617
Dennis Johnson 575
Kevin McHale 571
ROBERT HORRY 569
Hakeem Olajuwon 562
SHAQUILLE O'NEAL 552

STEALS

SCOTTIE PIPPEN 395
Michael Jordan 376
Magic Johnson 358
John Stockton 338
Larry Bird 296
Maurice Cheeks 295
Clyde Drexler 278
KARL MALONE 258
Dennis Johnson 247
Hakeem Olajuwon 245

BLOCKED SHOTS

Kareem Abdul-Jabbar 476
Hakeem Olajuwon 472
SHAQUILLE O'NEAL 374
David Robinson 312
Robert Parish 309
Patrick Ewing 303
Kevin McHale 281
TIM DUNCAN 241
Julius Erving 239
DIKEMBE MUTOMBO 228

DISQUALIFICATIONS

Tom Sanders 26
Vern Mikkelsen 24
Bailey Howell 21
Charlie Share 17
Jack Sikma 17
Darryl Dawkins 16
Robert Parish 16
Dave Cowens 15
Five tied 14

HISTORY Playoffs

OVERALL

Team	W	L	Pct.
Los Angeles Lakers	379	250	.603
Chicago Bulls	147	106	.581
Boston Celtics	285	206	.580
Baltimore Bullets*	9	7	.563
Philadelphia 76ers	203	183	.526
Indiana Pacers	73	69	.514
San Antonio Spurs	105	101	.510
Detroit Pistons	143	139	.507
New York Knickerbockers	179	175	.506
Anderson Packers*	4	4	.500
Houston Rockets	101	103	.495
Seattle SuperSonics	101	105	.490
Utah Jazz	94	99	.487
Milwaukee Bucks	100	106	.485
Portland Trail Blazers	91	103	.469
Phoenix Suns	97	110	.469
Golden State Warriors	99	115	.463
New Jersey Nets	41	49	.456
Dallas Mavericks	40	51	.440
Sacramento Kings	77	99	.438
Atlanta Hawks	117	152	.435
Orlando Magic	26	34	.433
Washington Capitols*	8	11	.421
Washington Wizards	69	97	.416
New Orleans Hornets	25	36	.410
Miami Heat	26	38	.406
Toronto Raptors	8	12	.400
Denver Nuggets	40	63	.388
Los Angeles Clippers	13	22	.371
Cleveland Cavaliers	28	49	.364
Minnesota Timberwolves	17	30	.362
Chicago Stags*	7	13	.350
Cleveland Rebels*	1	2	.333
Sheboygan Redskins*	1	2	.333
St. Louis Bombers*	4	8	.333
Indianapolis Olympians*	4	9	.308
Memphis Grizzlies	0	4	.000
Totals	2762	2762	.500

*Defunct

SERIES WON-LOST

Team	W	L	Pct.
Los Angeles Lakers	93	38	.710
Boston Celtics	66	28	.702
Anderson Packers*	2	1	.667
Chicago Bulls	34	18	.654
Baltimore Bullets*	3	2	.600
New York Knickerbockers	40	35	.533
Houston Rockets	22	20	.524
Philadelphia 76ers	42	39	.519
Seattle SuperSonics	21	20	.512
Detroit Pistons	30	31	.492
San Antonio Spurs	21	22	.488
Golden State Warriors	22	24	.478
Utah Jazz	18	20	.474
Indiana Pacers	13	16	.448
Dallas Mavericks	8	10	.444
Phoenix Suns	19	24	.442
Milwaukee Bucks	18	23	.439
Portland Trail Blazers	18	25	.419
Washington Capitols*	2	3	.400
Washington Wizards	13	20	.394
Orlando Magic	5	8	.385
New Jersey Nets	8	13	.381
Atlanta Hawks	20	35	.364
Sacramento Kings	14	26	.350
Chicago Stags*	2	4	.333

Team	W	L	Pct.
Denver Nuggets	7	15	.318
Miami Heat	4	9	.308
New Orleans Hornets	4	9	.308
Toronto Raptors	1	3	.250
Cleveland Cavaliers	4	13	.235
Indianapolis Olympians*	1	4	.200
Minnesota Timberwolves	2	8	.200
Los Angeles Clippers	1	6	.143
Cleveland Rebels*	0	1	.000
Memphis Grizzlies	0	1	.000
Sheboygan Redskins*	0	1	.000
St. Louis Bombers*	0	3	.000
Totals	578	578	.500

*Defunct

HOME

Team	W	L	Pct.
Cleveland Rebels*	1	0	1.000
Sheboygan Redskins*	1	0	1.000
Baltimore Bullets*	7	1	.875
Chicago Bulls	98	30	.766
Anderson Packers*	3	1	.750
Los Angeles Lakers	246	83	.748
Boston Celtics	190	72	.725
Utah Jazz	70	30	.700
Indiana Pacers	48	21	.696
Portland Trail Blazers	67	30	.691
New York Knickerbockers	119	56	.680
Philadelphia 76ers	129	61	.679
Detroit Pistons	94	45	.676
Seattle SuperSonics	71	35	.670
San Antonio Spurs	64	37	.634
Atlanta Hawks	81	48	.628
Golden State Warriors	65	39	.625
Toronto Raptors	5	3	.625
Houston Rockets	62	39	.614
Dallas Mavericks	27	17	.614
Milwaukee Bucks	62	41	.602
Phoenix Suns	62	41	.602
Los Angeles Clippers	9	6	.600
Washington Capitols*	6	4	.600
New Orleans Hornets	16	11	.593
Washington Wizards	48	33	.593
Miami Heat	20	14	.588
Orlando Magic	18	13	.581
Denver Nuggets	28	21	.571
Indianapolis Olympians*	4	3	.571
Sacramento Kings	47	37	.560
Cleveland Cavaliers	21	18	.538
Minnesota Timberwolves	12	11	.522
New Jersey Nets	22	21	.512
St. Louis Bombers*	3	4	.429
Chicago Stags*	3	5	.375
Memphis Grizzlies	0	2	.000
Totals	1829	933	.662

*Defunct

ROAD

Team	W	L	Pct.
Los Angeles Lakers	133	167	.443
Boston Celtics	95	134	.415
New Jersey Nets	19	28	.404
Chicago Bulls	49	76	.392
San Antonio Spurs	41	64	.390
Houston Rockets	39	64	.379
Philadelphia 76ers	74	122	.378
Milwaukee Bucks	38	65	.369
Detroit Pistons	49	94	.343
Indiana Pacers	25	48	.342

Team	W	L	Pct.
Phoenix Suns	35	69	.337
New York Knickerbockers	60	119	.335
Chicago Stags*	4	8	.333
Sacramento Kings	30	62	.326
Golden State Warriors	34	76	.309
Seattle SuperSonics	30	70	.300
Dallas Mavericks	13	34	.277
Orlando Magic	8	21	.276
New Orleans Hornets	9	25	.265
Utah Jazz	24	69	.258
Atlanta Hawks	36	104	.257
Anderson Packers*	1	3	.250
Baltimore Bullets*	2	6	.250
Toronto Raptors	3	9	.250
Portland Trail Blazers	24	73	.247

Team	W	L	Pct.
Washington Wizards	21	64	.247
Denver Nuggets	12	42	.222
Washington Capitols*	2	7	.222
Minnesota Timberwolves	5	19	.208
Los Angeles Clippers	4	16	.200
Miami Heat	6	24	.200
St. Louis Bombers*	1	4	.200
Cleveland Cavaliers	7	31	.184
Cleveland Rebels*	0	2	.000
Memphis Grizzlies	0	2	.000
Sheboygan Redskins*	0	2	.000
Indianapolis Olympians*	0	6	.000
Totals	933	1829	.338

*Defunct

COACHES RANKINGS

(2003-04 head coaches in CAPS)

BY VICTORIES

Coach	W	L	Pct.
PHIL JACKSON	175	69	.717
Pat Riley	155	100	.608
Red Auerbach	99	69	.589
LARRY BROWN	85	79	.518
K.C. Jones	81	57	.587
LENNY WILKENS	80	98	.449
JERRY SLOAN	78	80	.494
Chuck Daly	75	51	.595
DON NELSON	70	85	.452
RICK ADELMAN	67	60	.528
Billy Cunningham	66	39	.629
John Kundla	60	35	.632
George Karl	59	67	.468
Red Holzman	58	47	.552
Dick Motta	56	70	.444
Bill Fitch	55	54	.505

Coach	W	L	Pct.
GREGG POPOVICH	53	34	.609
Rudy Tomjanovich	51	39	.567
Tom Heinsohn	47	33	.588
John MacLeod	47	54	.465
Alex Hannum	45	34	.570
Jack Ramsay	44	58	.431
Del Harris	38	50	.432
JEFF VAN GUNDY	38	36	.514
Larry Costello	37	23	.617
Cotton Fitzsimmons	35	49	.417
Bill Sharman	35	27	.565
Bill Russell	34	27	.557
Al Cervi	33	26	.559
Doug Moe	33	50	.398
Fred Schaus	33	38	.465

BY WINNING PERCENTAGE

(minimum 25 games)

Coach	Pct.	W	L
PHIL JACKSON	.717	175	69
Butch van Breda Kolff	.636	21	12
John Kundla	.632	60	35
Billy Cunningham	.629	66	39
BYRON SCOTT	.625	25	15
Larry Costello	.617	37	23
Larry Bird	.615	32	20
GREGG POPOVICH	.609	53	34
Pat Riley	.608	155	100
Chuck Daly	.595	75	51
Red Auerbach	.589	99	69
Tom Heinsohn	.588	47	33
K.C. Jones	.587	81	57
Alex Hannum	.570	45	34
Rudy Tomjanovich	.567	51	39

BY GAMES

Coach	G
PAT RILEY	255
PHIL JACKSON	244
LENNY WILKENS	178
Red Auerbach	168
LARRY BROWN	164
JERRY SLOAN	158
DON NELSON	155
K.C. Jones	138
RICK ADELMAN	127
Chuck Daly	126
George Karl	126
Dick Motta	126
Bill Fitch	109
Billy Cunningham	105
Red Holzman	105

NBA FINALS

Year	Dates	Winner (coach)	Loser (coach)	Games
1947	Apr. 16- Apr. 22	Philadelphia (Ed Gottlieb)	Chicago (Harold Olsen)	4-1
1948	Apr. 10- Apr. 21	Baltimore (Buddy Jeannette)	Philadelphia (Ed Gottlieb)	4-2
1949	Apr. 4- Apr. 13	Minneapolis (John Kundla)	Washington (Red Auerbach)	4-2
1950	Apr. 8- Apr. 23	Minneapolis (John Kundla)	*Syracuse (Al Cervi)	4-2
1951	Apr. 7- Apr. 21	Rochester (Les Harrison)	New York (Joe Lapchick)	4-3
1952	Apr. 12- Apr. 25	Minneapolis (John Kundla)	New York (Joe Lapchick)	4-3
1953	Apr. 4- Apr. 10	*Minneapolis (John Kundla)	New York (Joe Lapchick)	4-1
1954	Mar. 31- Apr. 12	*Minneapolis (John Kundla)	Syracuse (Al Cervi)	4-3
1955	Mar. 31- Apr. 10	*Syracuse (Al Cervi)	*Fort Wayne (Charles Eckman)	4-3
1956	Mar. 31- Apr. 7	*Philadelphia (George Senesky)	Fort Wayne (Charles Eckman)	4-1
1957	Mar. 30- Apr. 13	*Boston (Red Auerbach)	St. Louis (Alex Hannum)	4-3
1958	Mar. 29- Apr. 12	St. Louis (Alex Hannum)	*Boston (Red Auerbach)	4-2
1959	Apr. 4- Apr. 9	*Boston (Red Auerbach)	Minneapolis (John Kundla)	4-0
1960	Mar. 27- Apr. 9	*Boston (Red Auerbach)	St. Louis (Ed Macauley)	4-3
1961	Apr. 2- Apr. 11	*Boston (Red Auerbach)	St. Louis (Paul Seymour)	4-1
1962	Apr. 7- Apr. 18	*Boston (Red Auerbach)	Los Angeles (Fred Schaus)	4-3
1963	Apr. 14- Apr. 24	*Boston (Red Auerbach)	Los Angeles (Fred Schaus)	4-2
1964	Apr. 18- Apr. 26	*Boston (Red Auerbach)	San Francisco (Alex Hannum)	4-1
1965	Apr. 18- Apr. 25	*Boston (Red Auerbach)	Los Angeles (Fred Schaus)	4-1
1966	Apr. 17- Apr. 28	Boston (Red Auerbach)	Los Angeles (Fred Schaus)	4-3
1967	Apr. 14- Apr. 24	*Philadelphia (Alex Hannum)	San Francisco (Bill Sharman)	4-2
1968	Apr. 21- May 2	Boston (Bill Russell)	Los Angeles (Butch van Breda Kolff)	4-2
1969	Apr. 23- May 5	Boston (Bill Russell)	Los Angeles (Butch van Breda Kolff)	4-3
1970	Apr. 24- May 8	*New York (Red Holzman)	Los Angeles (Joe Mullaney)	4-3
1971	Apr. 21- Apr. 30	*Milwaukee (Larry Costello)	Baltimore (Gene Shue)	4-0
1972	Apr. 26- May 7	*Los Angeles (Bill Sharman)	New York (Red Holzman)	4-1
1973	May 1- May 10	New York (Red Holzman)	Los Angeles (Bill Sharman)	4-1
1974	Apr. 28- May 12	Boston (Tom Heinsohn)	*Milwaukee (Larry Costello)	4-3
1975	May 18- May 25	Golden State (Al Attles)	*Washington (K.C. Jones)	4-0
1976	May 23- June 6	Boston (Tom Heinsohn)	Phoenix (John MacLeod)	4-2
1977	May 22- June 5	Portland (Jack Ramsay)	Philadelphia (Gene Shue)	4-2
1978	May 21- June 7	Washington (Dick Motta)	Seattle (Lenny Wilkens)	4-3
1979	May 20- June 1	Seattle (Lenny Wilkens)	*Washington (Dick Motta)	4-1
1980	May 4- May 16	Los Angeles (Paul Westhead)	Philadelphia (Billy Cunningham)	4-2
1981	May 5- May 14	*Boston (Bill Fitch)	Houston (Del Harris)	4-2
1982	May 27- June 8	Los Angeles (Pat Riley)	Philadelphia (Billy Cunningham)	4-2
1983	May 22- May 31	*Philadelphia (Billy Cunningham)	Los Angeles (Pat Riley)	4-0
1984	May 27- June 12	*Boston (K.C. Jones)	Los Angeles (Pat Riley)	4-3
1985	May 27- June 9	Los Angeles Lakers (Pat Riley)	*Boston (K.C. Jones)	4-2
1986	May 26- June 8	*Boston (K.C. Jones)	Houston (Bill Fitch)	4-2
1987	June 2- June 14	*Los Angeles Lakers (Pat Riley)	Boston (K.C. Jones)	4-2
1988	June 7- June 21	*Los Angeles Lakers (Pat Riley)	Detroit (Chuck Daly)	4-3
1989	June 6- June 13	*Detroit (Chuck Daly)	Los Angeles Lakers (Pat Riley)	4-0
1990	June 5- June 14	Detroit (Chuck Daly)	Portland (Rick Adelman)	4-1
1991	June 2- June 12	Chicago (Phil Jackson)	Los Angeles Lakers (Mike Dunleavy)	4-1
1992	June 3- June 14	*Chicago (Phil Jackson)	Portland (Rick Adelman)	4-2
1993	June 9- June 20	Chicago (Phil Jackson)	*Phoenix (Paul Westphal)	4-2
1994	June 8- June 22	Houston (Rudy Tomjanovich)	New York (Pat Riley)	4-3
1995	June 7- June 14	Houston (Rudy Tomjanovich)	Orlando (Brian Hill)	4-0
1996	June 5- June 16	*Chicago (Phil Jackson)	Seattle (George Karl)	4-2
1997	June 1- June 13	*Chicago (Phil Jackson)	Utah (Jerry Sloan)	4-2
1998	June 3- June 14	*Chicago (Phil Jackson)	*Utah (Jerry Sloan)	4-2
1999	June 16-June 25	*San Antonio (Gregg Popovich)	New York (Jeff Van Gundy)	4-1
2000	June 7-June 19	*L.A. Lakers (Phil Jackson)	Indiana (Larry Bird)	4-2
2001	June 6-June 15	L.A. Lakers (Phil Jackson)	Philadelphia (Larry Brown)	4-1
2002	June 5-June 12	L.A. Lakers (Phil Jackson)	New Jersey (Byron Scott)	4-0
2003	June 4-June 15	San Antonio (Gregg Popovich)	New Jersey (Byron Scott)	4-2
2004	June 6-June 15	Detroit (Larry Brown)	L.A. Lakers (Phil Jackson)	4-1

*Had best record (or tied for best record) during regular season.

STATISTICAL LEADERS
SINGLE-GAME BESTS

*Denotes number of overtime periods.

POINTS

	FG	FT	Pts.
Elgin Baylor, Los Angeles at Boston, April 14, 1962	.22	17	61
Rick Barry, San Francisco vs. Philadelphia, April 18, 1967	.22	11	55

	FG	FT	Pts.
Michael Jordan, Chicago vs. Phoenix, June 16, 1993	21	13	55
Jerry West, Los Angeles vs. Boston, April 23, 1969	21	11	53
Bob Pettit, St. Louis vs. Boston, April 12, 1958	19	12	50
Allen Iverson, Philadelphia at L.A. Lakers, June 6, 2001*	18	9	48
Michael Jordan, Chicago at Portland, June 12, 1992	14	16	46
Jerry West, Los Angeles at Boston, April 19, 1965	17	11	45
Jerry West, Los Angeles vs. Boston, April 22, 1966	19	7	45
Wilt Chamberlain, Los Angeles vs. New York, May 6, 1970	20	5	45
Michael Jordan, Chicago at Utah, June 14, 1998	15	12	45
Rick Barry, San Francisco vs. Philadelphia, April 24, 1967	16	12	44
Michael Jordan, Chicago vs. Phoenix, June 13, 1993***	19	3	44
Shaquille O'Neal, L.A. Lakers vs. Philadelphia, June 6, 2001*	17	10	44
Elgin Baylor, Los Angeles at Boston, April 21, 1963	15	13	43
Jerry West, Los Angeles vs. Boston, April 21, 1965	13	17	43
Rick Barry, San Francisco vs. Philadelphia, April 20, 1967	17	9	43
John Havlicek, Boston at Los Angeles, April 25, 1969	15	13	43
Isiah Thomas, Detroit at L.A. Lakers, June 19, 1988	18	5	43
Shaquille O'Neal, L.A. Lakers vs. Indiana, June 7, 2000	21	1	43
George Mikan, Minneapolis vs. Washington, April 4, 1949	14	14	42
Jerry West, Los Angeles vs. Boston, April 17, 1963	14	14	42
Jerry West, Los Angeles vs. Boston, May 5, 1969	14	14	42
Magic Johnson, Los Angeles at Philadelphia, May 16, 1980	14	14	42
Charles Barkley, Phoenix vs. Chicago, June 11, 1993	16	10	42
Michael Jordan, Chicago at Phoenix, June 11, 1993	18	4	42
Elgin Baylor, Los Angeles at Boston, April 18, 1962*	13	15	41
Jerry West, Los Angeles at Boston, April 17, 1966*	15	11	41
Elgin Baylor, Los Angeles at Boston, April 24, 1966	13	15	41
Jerry West, Los Angeles vs. Boston, April 25, 1969	12	17	41
Michael Jordan, Chicago vs. Phoenix, June 18, 1993	16	7	41
Shaquille O'Neal, L.A. Lakers vs. Indiana, June 19, 2000	19	3	41
George Mikan, Minneapolis vs. Syracuse, April 23, 1950	13	14	40
Cliff Hagan, St. Louis at Boston, April 5, 1961	16	8	40
Bob Pettit, St. Louis vs. Boston, April 9, 1961	14	12	40
Jerry West, Los Angeles at Boston, April 8, 1962	13	14	40
John Havlicek, Boston at Los Angeles, May 2, 1968	14	12	40
Jerry West, Los Angeles at Boston, April 29, 1969	15	10	40
Julius Erving, Philadelphia at Portland, June 5, 1977	17	6	40
Kareem Abdul-Jabbar, Los Angeles vs. Philadelphia, May 14, 1980	16	8	40
James Worthy, L.A. Lakers vs. Detroit, June 13, 1989	17	4	40
Shaquille O'Neal, L.A. Lakers vs. Indiana, June 9, 2000	11	18	40
Shaquille O'Neal, L.A. Lakers vs. New Jersey, June 7, 2002	14	12	40

FIELD GOALS

	FGM	FGA
Elgin Baylor, Los Angeles at Boston, April 14, 1962	22	46
Rick Barry, San Francisco vs. Philadelphia, April 18, 1967	22	48
Jerry West, Los Angeles vs. Boston, April 23, 1969	21	41
Michael Jordan, Chicago vs. Phoenix, June 16, 1993	21	37
Shaquille O'Neal, L.A. Lakers vs. Indiana, June 7, 2000	21	31
Wilt Chamberlain, Los Angeles vs. New York, May 6, 1970	20	27
Bob Pettit, St. Louis vs. Boston, April 12, 1958	19	34
Jerry West, Los Angeles vs. Boston, April 22, 1966	19	31
Kareem Abdul-Jabbar, Los Angeles vs. Philadelphia, May 7, 1980	19	31
Michael Jordan, Chicago vs. Phoenix, June 13, 1993***	19	43
Shaquille O'Neal, L.A. Lakers vs. Indiana, June 19, 2000	19	32
Isiah Thomas, Detroit at L.A. Lakers, June 19, 1988	18	32
Michael Jordan, Chicago at Phoenix, June 11, 1993	18	36
Allen Iverson, Philadelphia at L.A. Lakers, June 6, 2001*	18	41
Tom Heinsohn, Boston vs. St. Louis, April 13, 1957**	17	33
Sam Jones, Boston at Los Angeles, April 16, 1962	17	27
Jerry West, Los Angeles vs. Boston, April 17, 1963	17	30
Jerry West, Los Angeles at Boston, April 19, 1965	17	38
Rick Barry, San Francisco vs. Philadelphia, April 20, 1967	17	41
Willis Reed, New York at Los Angeles, April 29, 1970*	17	30
Julius Erving, Philadelphia at Portland, June 5, 1977	17	29
James Worthy, L.A. Lakers vs. Detroit, June 13, 1989	17	26
Karl Malone, Utah at Chicago, June 12, 1998	17	27
Shaquille O'Neal, L.A. Lakers vs. Indiana, June 16, 2000	17	27
Shaquille O'Neal, L.A. Lakers vs. Philadelphia, June 6, 2001*	17	28
Cliff Hagan, St. Louis at Boston, April 5, 1961	16	28
Sam Jones, Boston at Los Angeles, April 23, 1965	16	27
Rick Barry, San Francisco vs. Philadelphia, April 24, 1967	16	38
Jerry West, Los Angeles vs. Boston, May 1, 1969	16	31
Willis Reed, New York vs. Los Angeles, April 24, 1970	16	30
Kareem Abdul-Jabbar, Milwaukee vs. Boston, May 7, 1974	16	31
Kareem Abdul-Jabbar, Milwaukee at Boston, May 10, 1974**	16	26
Kareem Abdul-Jabbar, Los Angeles vs. Philadelphia, May 14, 1980	16	24
Jamaal Wilkes, Los Angeles at Philadlephia, May 16, 1980	16	30
Kareem Abdul-Jabbar, L.A. Lakers vs. Boston, June 7, 1985	16	28

	FGM	FGA
James Worthy, L.A. Lakers vs. Boston, June 2, 1987	16	23
Michael Jordan, Chicago vs. Portland, June 3, 1992	16	27
Michael Jordan, Chicago vs. Portland, June 5, 1992*	16	32
Charles Barkley, Phoenix vs. Chicago, June 11, 1993	16	26
Michael Jordan, Chicago vs. Phoenix, June 18, 1993	16	29
Shaquille O'Neal, L.A. Lakers at Detroit, June 13, 2004	16	21

FREE THROWS

	FTM	FTA
Bob Pettit, St. Louis at Boston, April 9, 1958	19	24
Shaquille O'Neal, L.A. Lakers vs. Indiana, June 9, 2000	18	39
Cliff Hagan, St. Louis at Boston, March 30, 1958	17	18
Elgin Baylor, Los Angeles at Boston, April 14, 1962	17	19
Jerry West, Los Angeles vs. Boston, April 21, 1965	17	20
Jerry West, Los Angeles vs. Boston, April 25, 1969	17	20
Bob Pettit, St. Louis vs. Boston, April 11, 1957	16	22
Michael Jordan, Chicago at Portland, June 12, 1992	16	19
Bob Pettit, St. Louis at Boston, March 30, 1957**	15	20
Frank Ramsey, Boston vs. Los Angeles, April 18, 1962*	15	16
Elgin Baylor, Los Angeles at Boston, April 18, 1962*	15	21
Elgin Baylor, Los Angeles at Boston, April 24, 1966	15	17
Jerry West, Los Angeles at New York, April 24, 1970	15	17
Terry Porter, Portland at Detroit, June 7, 1990*	15	15
Michael Jordan, Chicago vs. Utah, June 4, 1997	15	21
Joe Fulks, Philadelphia vs. Chicago, April 22, 1947	14	17
George Mikan, Minneapolis vs. Washington, April 4, 1949	14	16
George Mikan, Minneapolis vs. Syracuse, April 23, 1950	14	17
Dolph Schayes, Syracuse vs. Fort Wayne, April 9, 1955	14	17
Jerry West, Los Angeles at Boston, April 8, 1962	14	15
Jerry West, Los Angeles at Boston, April 10, 1962	14	16
Bill Russell, Boston vs. Los Angeles, April 18, 1962*	14	17
Jerry West, Los Angeles vs. Boston, May 5, 1969	14	18
Rick Barry, Golden State vs. Washington, May 23, 1975	14	16
Magic Johnson, Los Angeles at Philadelphia, May 16, 1980	14	14
Cedric Maxwell, Boston vs. Los Angeles, June 12, 1984	14	17
Shawn Kemp, Seattle at Chicago, June 5, 1996	14	16

REBOUNDS

	No.
Bill Russell, Boston vs. St. Louis, March 29, 1960	40
Bill Russell, Boston vs. Los Angeles, April 18, 1962*	40
Bill Russell, Boston vs. St. Louis, April 11, 1961	38
Bill Russell, Boston vs. Los Angeles, April 16, 1963	38
Wilt Chamberlain, San Francisco vs. Boston, April 24, 1964	38
Wilt Chamberlain, Philadelphia vs. San Francisco, April 16, 1967	38
Bill Russell, Boston vs. St. Louis, April 9, 1960	35
Wilt Chamberlain, Philadelphia vs. San Francisco, April 14, 1967*	33
Bill Russell, Boston vs. St. Louis, April 13, 1957**	32
Bill Russell, Boston at San Francisco, April 22, 1964	32
Bill Russell, Boston vs. Los Angeles, April 28, 1966	32
Bill Russell, Boston vs. St. Louis, April 2, 1961	31
Nate Thurmond, San Francisco at Philadelphia, April 14, 1967*	31
Wilt Chamberlain, Los Angeles at Boston, April 29, 1969	31
Wilt Chamberlain, Los Angeles vs. Boston, May 1, 1969	31
Bill Russell, Boston vs. Minneapolis, April 5, 1959	30
Bill Russell, Boston at Minneapolis, April 7, 1959	30
Bill Russell, Boston at Minneapolis, April 9, 1959	30
Bill Russell, Boston vs. Los Angeles, April 25, 1965	30

ASSISTS

	No.
Magic Johnson, Los Angeles vs. Boston, June 3, 1984	21
Magic Johnson, L.A. Lakers vs. Boston, June 4, 1987	20
Magic Johnson, L.A. Lakers vs. Chicago, June 12, 1991	20
Bob Cousy, Boston vs. St. Louis, April 9, 1957	19
Bob Cousy, Boston at Minneapolis, April 7, 1959	19
Walt Frazier, New York vs. Los Angeles, May 8, 1970	19
Magic Johnson, L.A. Lakers vs. Boston, June 14, 1987	19
Magic Johnson, L.A. Lakers vs. Detroit, June 19, 1988	19
Jerry West, Los Angeles vs. New York, May 1, 1970*	18
Magic Johnson, Los Angeles vs. Boston, June 6, 1984*	17
Dennis Johnson, Boston at L.A. Lakers, June 7, 1985	17
Magic Johnson, L.A. Lakers vs. Boston, June 7, 1985	17
Robert Reid, Houston vs. Boston, June 5, 1986	17
Magic Johnson, L.A. Lakers at Detroit, June 16, 1988	17
Magic Johnson, L.A. Lakers vs. Boston, June 2, 1985	16
Bob Cousy, Boston vs. Minneapolis, April 5, 1959	15
Magic Johnson, Los Angeles at Boston, June 12, 1984	15

STEALS

BLOCKED SHOTS

CAREER

(active players in 2003-04 in CAPS)

SCORING AVERAGE

(minimum 10 games)

	G	FGM	FTM	Pts.	Avg.
Rick Barry	10	138	87	363	36.3
Michael Jordan	35	438	258	1,176	33.6
SHAQUILLE O'NEAL	24	306	171	783	32.6
Jerry West	55	612	455	1,679	30.5
Bob Pettit	25	241	227	709	28.4
Hakeem Olajuwon	17	187	91	467	27.5
Elgin Baylor	44	442	277	1,161	26.4
TIM DUNCAN	11	105	72	282	25.6
Julius Erving	22	216	128	561	25.5
Joe Fulks	11	84	104	272	24.7

FIELD-GOAL PERCENTAGE

(minimum 50 made)

	FGM	FGA	Pct.
SHAQUILLE O'NEAL	306	509	.601
John Paxson	71	120	.592
Bill Walton	74	130	.569
Wilt Chamberlain	264	472	.559
Luc Longley	59	107	.551
Kevin McHale	210	386	.544
Bobby Jones	77	143	.538
Walt Frazier	129	240	.538
James Worthy	314	589	.533
Kurt Rambis	78	147	.531

HISTORY *NBA Finals*

FREE THROW PERCENTAGE
(minimum 40 made)

	FTM	FTA	Pct.
REGGIE MILLER	45	46	.978
Bill Sharman	126	136	.926
Joe Dumars	79	89	.888
SAM CASSELL	45	51	.882
Magic Johnson	284	325	.874
Larry Bird	177	203	.872
Paul Seymour	79	91	.868
Terry Porter	68	79	.861
Adrian Dantley	55	64	.859
Shawn Kemp	42	49	.857

3-POINT FIELD-GOAL PERCENTAGE
(minimum 10 made)

	FGM	FGA	Pct.
GLEN RICE	12	19	.632
Scott Wedman	10	17	.588
DEREK FISHER	31	59	.525
RICK FOX	17	35	.486
John Paxson	17	36	.472
Isiah Thomas	18	39	.462
B.J. Armstrong	11	24	.458
ANFERNEE HARDAWAY	11	24	.458
SAM CASSELL	14	31	.452
Mario Elie	14	32	.438

GAMES

Bill Russell	70
Sam Jones	64
Kareem Abdul-Jabbar	56
Jerry West	55
Tom Heinsohn	52
Magic Johnson	50
John Havlicek	47
Frank Ramsey	47
Michael Cooper	46
Elgin Baylor	44
K.C. Jones	44

MINUTES

Bill Russell	3,185
Jerry West	2,375
Kareem Abdul-Jabbar	2,082
Magic Johnson	2,044
John Havlicek	1,872
Sam Jones	1,871
Elgin Baylor	1,850
Wilt Chamberlain	1,657
Bob Cousy	1,639
Tom Heinsohn	1,602

POINTS

Jerry West	1,679
Kareem Abdul-Jabbar	1,317
Michael Jordan	1,176
Elgin Baylor	1,161
Bill Russell	1,151
Sam Jones	1,143
Tom Heinsohn	1,035
John Havlicek	1,020
Magic Johnson	971
SHAQUILLE O'NEAL	783

FIELD GOALS MADE

Jerry West	612
Kareem Abdul-Jabbar	544
Sam Jones	458
Elgin Baylor	442
Michael Jordan	438
Bill Russell	415
Tom Heinsohn	407
John Havlicek	390
Magic Johnson	339
James Worthy	314

FIELD GOALS ATTEMPTED

Jerry West	1,333
Kareem Abdul-Jabbar	1,040
Elgin Baylor	1,034
Tom Heinsohn	1,016
Sam Jones	994
John Havlicek	926
Michael Jordan	911
Bill Russell	910
Bob Cousy	766
Magic Johnson	657

FREE THROWS MADE

Jerry West	455
Bill Russell	321
Magic Johnson	284
Elgin Baylor	277
George Mikan	259
Michael Jordan	258
John Havlicek	240
Kareem Abdul-Jabbar	229
Sam Jones	227
Bob Pettit	227

FREE THROWS ATTEMPTED

Jerry West	551
Bill Russell	524
Elgin Baylor	367
SHAQUILLE O'NEAL	334
Wilt Chamberlain	329
Kareem Abdul-Jabbar	327
George Mikan	326
Magic Johnson	325
Michael Jordan	320
Bob Pettit	301

3-POINT FIELD GOALS MADE

Michael Jordan	42
ROBERT HORRY	38
Michael Cooper	35
DEREK FISHER	31
SCOTTIE PIPPEN	30
Danny Ainge	27
TONI KUKOC	27
BRYON RUSSELL	21
Sam Perkins	20
Larry Bird	19

3-POINT FIELD GOALS ATTEMPTED

SCOTTIE PIPPEN	117
Michael Jordan	114
ROBERT HORRY	104
Michael Cooper	92
TONI KUKOC	73
Danny Ainge	65
DEREK FISHER	59
JASON KIDD	57
BRIAN SHAW	57
BRYON RUSSELL	56

REBOUNDS

Bill Russell	1,718
Wilt Chamberlain	862
Elgin Baylor	593
Kareem Abdul-Jabbar	507
Tom Heinsohn	473
Bob Pettit	416
Magic Johnson	397
Larry Bird	361
John Havlicek	350
SHAQUILLE O'NEAL	332

ASSISTS

Magic Johnson	584
Bob Cousy	400
Bill Russell	315
Jerry West	306
Dennis Johnson	228
Michael Jordan	209
SCOTTIE PIPPEN	207
John Havlicek	195
Larry Bird	187
Kareem Abdul-Jabbar	181

PERSONAL FOULS

Bill Russell	225
Tom Heinsohn	209
Kareem Abdul-Jabbar	196
Satch Sanders	179
Frank Ramsey	178
Michael Cooper	159
Jerry West	159
John Havlicek	154
Sam Jones	151
Slater Martin	148

STEALS

Magic Johnson	102
SCOTTIE PIPPEN	67
Larry Bird	63
Michael Jordan	62
Michael Cooper	59
Dennis Johnson	48
Danny Ainge	46
Kareem Abdul-Jabbar	45
Julius Erving	44
ROBERT HORRY	41

BLOCKED SHOTS

Kareem Abdul-Jabbar	116
SHAQUILLE O'NEAL	57
Hakeem Olajuwon	54
Robert Parish	54
Kevin McHale	44
TIM DUNCAN	43
Caldwell Jones	42
Julius Erving	40
Dennis Johnson	39
SCOTTIE PIPPEN	39

DISQUALIFICATIONS

Satch Sanders	12
Tom Heinsohn	9
George Mikan	7
Frank Ramsey	7
Arnie Risen	7
Vern Mikkelsen	6
Cliff Hagan	5
Art Hillhouse	5
Slater Martin	5
Charlie Scott	5

OVERALL

Team	W	L	Pct.
San Antonio Spurs	8	3	.727
Chicago Bulls	24	11	.686
Baltimore Bullets*	4	2	.667
Milwaukee Bucks	7	4	.636
Boston Celtics	70	46	.603
Detroit Pistons	19	14	.576
Sacramento Kings	4	3	.571
Golden State Warriors	17	14	.548
Houston Rockets	12	11	.522
Seattle SuperSonics	9	9	.500
Los Angeles Lakers	79	82	.491
Philadelphia 76ers	24	29	.453
Atlanta Hawks	11	14	.440
New York Knickerbockers	20	28	.417
Portland Trail Blazers	7	10	.412
Indiana Pacers	2	4	.333
Phoenix Suns	4	8	.333
Utah Jazz	4	8	.333
Washington Capitols*	2	4	.333
Washington Bullets	5	15	.250
Chicago Stags*	1	4	.200
New Jersey Nets	2	8	.200
Orlando Magic	0	4	.000
Totals	335	335	.500

*Defunct

SERIES WON-LOST

Team	W	L	Pct.
Chicago Bulls	6	0	1.000
San Antonio Spurs	2	0	1.000
Baltimore Bullets*	1	0	1.000
Sacramento Kings	1	0	1.000
Boston Celtics	16	3	.842
Los Angeles Lakers	14	14	.500
Detroit Pistons	3	3	.500
Golden State Warriors	3	3	.500
Houston Rockets	2	2	.500
Milwaukee Bucks	1	1	.500
Philadelphia 76ers	3	6	.333
Portland Trail Blazers	1	2	.333
Seattle SuperSonics	1	2	.333
Atlanta Hawks	1	3	.250
New York Knickerbockers	2	6	.250
Washington Bullets	1	3	.250
Chicago Stags*	0	1	.000
Indiana Pacers	0	1	.000
Orlando Magic	0	1	.000
Washington Capitols*	0	1	.000
New Jersey Nets	0	2	.000
Phoenix Suns	0	2	.000
Utah Jazz	0	2	.000
Totals	58	58	.500

*Defunct

HOME

Team	W	L	Pct.
Baltimore Bullets*	3	0	1.000
Detroit Pistons	12	3	.800
San Antonio Spurs	4	1	.800
Golden State Warriors	12	4	.750
Sacramento Kings	3	1	.750
Boston Celtics	44	17	.721
Chicago Bulls	12	5	.706
Houston Rockets	8	4	.667
Indiana Pacers	2	1	.667
Seattle SuperSonics	6	3	.667
Washington Capitols*	2	1	.667
Atlanta Hawks	7	4	.636
Philadelphia 76ers	16	11	.593
Los Angeles Lakers	47	33	.588
New York Knickerbockers	12	11	.522
Chicago Stags*	1	1	.500
Milwaukee Bucks	3	3	.500
Utah Jazz	3	3	.500
Portland Trail Blazers	4	5	.444
Phoenix Suns	2	4	.333
Washington Bullets	3	7	.300
New Jersey Nets	1	4	.200
Orlando Magic	0	2	.000
Totals	207	128	.618

*Defunct

ROAD

Team	W	L	Pct.
Milwaukee Bucks	4	1	.800
Chicago Bulls	12	6	.667
San Antonio Spurs	4	2	.667
Boston Celtics	26	29	.473
Los Angeles Lakers	32	49	.395
Detroit Pistons	7	11	.389
Portland Trail Blazers	3	5	.375
Houston Rockets	4	7	.364
Baltimore Bullets*	1	2	.333
Golden State Warriors	5	10	.333
Phoenix Suns	2	4	.333
Sacramento Kings	1	2	.333
Seattle SuperSonics	3	6	.333
New York Knickerbockers	8	17	.320
Philadelphia 76ers	8	18	.308
Atlanta Hawks	4	10	.286
New Jersey Nets	1	4	.200
Washington Bullets	2	8	.200
Utah Jazz	1	5	.167
Orlando Magic	0	2	.000
Chicago Stags*	0	3	.000
Indiana Pacers	0	3	.000
Washington Capitols*	0	3	.000
Totals	128	207	.382

*Defunct

HISTORY *NBA Finals*

ALL-STAR GAME

RESULTS

Year	Result, Location	Winning coach	Losing coach	Most Valuable Player
1951	East 111, West 94 at Boston	Joe Lapchick	John Kundla	Ed Macauley, Boston
1952	East 108, West 91 at Boston	Al Cervi	John Kundla	Paul Arizin, Philadelphia
1953	West 79, East 75 at Fort Wayne	John Kundla	Joe Lapchick	George Mikan, Minneapolis
1954	East 98, West 93 (OT) at New York	Joe Lapchick	John Kundla	Bob Cousy, Boston
1955	East 100, West 91 at New York	Al Cervi	Charley Eckman	Bill Sharman, Boston
1956	West 108, East 94 at Rochester	Charley Eckman	George Senesky	Bob Pettit, St. Louis
1957	East 109, West 97 at Boston	Red Auerbach	Bobby Wanzer	Bob Cousy, Boston
1958	East 130, West 118 at St. Louis	Red Auerbach	Alex Hannum	Bob Pettit, St. Louis
1959	West 124, East 108 at Detroit	Ed Macauley	Red Auerbach	Elgin Baylor, Minneapolis Bob Pettit, St. Louis
1960	East 125, West 115 at Philadelphia	Red Auerbach	Ed Macauley	Wilt Chamberlain, Phil.
1961	West 153, East 131 at Syracuse	Paul Seymour	Red Auerbach	Oscar Robertson, Cincinnati
1962	West 150, East 130 at St. Louis	Fred Schaus	Red Auerbach	Bob Pettit, St. Louis
1963	East 115, West 108 at Los Angeles	Red Auerbach	Fred Schaus	Bill Russell, Boston
1964	East 111, West 107 at Boston	Red Auerbach	Fred Schaus	Oscar Robertson, Cincinnati
1965	East 124, West 123 at St. Louis	Red Auerbach	Alex Hannum	Jerry Lucas, Cincinnati
1966	East 137, West 94 at Cincinnati	Red Auerbach	Fred Schaus	Adrian Smith, Cincinnati
1967	West 135, East 120 at San Francisco	Fred Schaus	Red Auerbach	Rick Barry, San Francisco
1968	East 144, West 124 at New York	Alex Hannum	Bill Sharman	Hal Greer, Philadelphia
1969	East 123, West 112 at Baltimore	Gene Shue	Richie Guerin	Oscar Robertson, Cincinnati
1970	East 142, West 135 at Philadelphia	Red Holzman	Richie Guerin	Willis Reed, New York
1971	West 108, East 107 at San Diego	Larry Costello	Red Holzman	Lenny Wilkens, Seattle
1972	West 112, East 110 at Los Angeles	Bill Sharman	Tom Heinsohn	Jerry West, Los Angeles
1973	East 104, West 84 at Chicago	Tom Heinsohn	Bill Sharman	Dave Cowens, Boston
1974	West 134, East 123 at Seattle	Larry Costello	Tom Heinsohn	Bob Lanier, Detroit
1975	East 108, West 102 at Phoenix	K.C. Jones	Al Attles	Walt Frazier, New York
1976	East 123, West 109 at Philadelphia	Tom Heinsohn	Al Attles	Dave Bing, Washington
1977	West 125, East 124 at Milwaukee	Larry Brown	Gene Shue	Julius Erving, Philadelphia
1978	East 133, West 125 at Atlanta	Billy Cunningham	Jack Ramsay	Randy Smith, Buffalo
1979	West 134, East 129 at Detroit	Lenny Wilkens	Dick Motta	David Thompson, Denver
1980	East 144, West 136 (OT) at Landover	Billy Cunningham	Lenny Wilkens	George Gervin, San Antonio
1981	East 123, West 120 at Cleveland	Billy Cunningham	John MacLeod	Nate Archibald, Boston
1982	East 120, West 118 at E. Rutherford	Bill Fitch	Pat Riley	Larry Bird, Boston
1983	East 132, West 123 at Los Angeles	Billy Cunningham	Pat Riley	Julius Erving, Philadelphia
1984	East 154, West 145 (OT) at Denver	K.C. Jones	Frank Layden	Isiah Thomas, Detroit
1985	West 140, East 129 at Indianapolis	Pat Riley	K.C. Jones	Ralph Sampson, Houston
1986	East 139, West 132 at Dallas	K.C. Jones	Pat Riley	Isiah Thomas, Detroit
1987	West 154, East 149 (OT) at Seattle	Pat Riley	K.C. Jones	Tom Chambers, Seattle
1988	East 138, West 133 at Chicago	Mike Fratello	Pat Riley	Michael Jordan, Chicago
1989	West 143, East 134 at Houston	Pat Riley	Lenny Wilkens	Karl Malone, Utah
1990	East 130, West 113 at Miami	Chuck Daly	Pat Riley	Magic Johnson, L.A. Lakers
1991	East 116, West 114 at Charlotte	Chris Ford	Rick Adelman	Charles Barkley, Philadelphia
1992	West 153, East 113 at Orlando	Don Nelson	Phil Jackson	Magic Johnson, L.A. Lakers
1993	West 135, East 132 (OT) at Salt Lake City	Paul Westphal	Pat Riley	Karl Malone, Utah John Stockton, Utah
1994	East 127, West 118 at Minneapolis	Lenny Wilkens	George Karl	Scottie Pippen, Chicago
1995	West 139, East 112 at Phoenix	Paul Westphal	Brian Hill	Mitch Richmond, Sacramento
1996	East 129, West 118 at San Antonio	Phil Jackson	George Karl	Michael Jordan, Chicago
1997	East 132, West 120 at Cleveland	Doug Collins	Rudy Tomjanovich	Glen Rice, Charlotte
1998	East 135, West 114 at New York	Larry Bird	George Karl	Michael Jordan, Chicago
1999	No game played.			
2000	West 137, East 126 at Oakland	Phil Jackson	Jeff Van Gundy	Tim Duncan, San Antonio Shaquille O'Neal, L.A. Lakers
2001	East 111, West 110 at Washington	Larry Brown	Rick Adelman	Allen Iverson, Philadelphia
2002	West 135, East 120 at Philadelphia	Don Nelson	Byron Scott	Kobe Bryant, L.A. Lakers
2003	West 155, East 145 (2 OT) at Atlanta	Rick Adelman	Isiah Thomas	Kevin Garnett, Minnesota
2004	West 136, East 132 at Los Angeles	Flip Saunders	Rick Carlisle	Shaquille O'Neal, L.A. Lakers

STATISTICAL LEADERS

CAREER SCORING

(Active players in 2003-04 in CAPS)

Player	G	Min.	FGM	FGA	Pct.	FTM	FTA	Pct.	Reb.	Ast.	PF	Dq.	Pts.	Avg.
Michael Jordan*	13	382	110	233	.472	39	52	.750	61	54	31	0	262	20.2
Kareem Abdul-Jabbar*	18	449	105	213	.493	41	50	.820	149	51	57	1	251	13.9
Oscar Robertson	12	380	88	172	.512	70	98	.714	69	81	41	0	246	20.5
Bob Pettit	11	360	81	193	.420	62	80	.775	178	23	25	0	224	20.4
Julius Erving	11	316	85	178	.478	50	63	.794	70	35	31	0	221	20.1
Elgin Baylor	11	321	70	164	.427	78	98	.796	99	38	31	0	218	19.8
Wilt Chamberlain	13	388	72	122	.590	47	94	.500	197	36	23	0	191	14.7
Isiah Thomas*	11	318	76	133	.571	27	35	.771	27	97	17	0	186	16.8

John Havlicek	13	303	74	154	.481	31	41	.756	46	31	20	0	179	13.8
Magic Johnson*	11	331	64	131	.489	38	42	.905	57	127	25	0	176	16.0
Jerry West	12	341	62	137	.453	36	50	.720	47	55	28	0	160	13.3
Bob Cousy	3	368	52	158	.329	43	51	.843	78	86	27	2	147	11.3
SHAQUILLE O'NEAL***	8	198	61	116	.526	24	50	.480	71	8	20	0	146	18.3
KARL MALONE**	2	244	58	107	.542	29	40	.725	74	19	16	0	145	12.1
David Robinson	0	184	50	85	.588	41	59	.695	62	8	26	0	141	14.1
Dolph Schayes*	11	248	48	109	.440	42	50	.840	105	17	32	1	138	12.5
Paul Arizin	9	206	54	116	.466	29	36	.806	47	6	29	1	137	15.2
George Gervin	9	215	54	108	.500	28	36	.778	33	12	25	0	137	15.2
Larry Bird**	10	287	52	123	.423	27	32	.844	79	41	28	0	134	13.4
Rick Barry*	7	195	54	111	.486	20	24	.833	29	31	30	2	128	18.3
Moses Malone*	11	271	44	98	.449	40	67	.597	108	15	26	0	128	11.6
Elvin Hayes	12	264	52	129	.403	22	34	.647	92	17	37	0	126	10.5
KOBE BRYANT	6	182	52	103	.505	12	16	.750	27	26	17	0	125	20.8
Hal Greer	10	207	47	102	.461	26	37	.703	45	28	29	0	120	12.0
Bill Russell	12	343	51	111	.459	18	34	.529	139	39	37	1	120	10.0
KEVIN GARNETT	7	195	54	102	.529	11	11	1.000	55	23	7	0	119	17.0
Hakeem Olajuwon	12	270	45	110	.409	26	50	.520	94	17	31	1	117	9.8
Charles Barkley**	9	209	45	91	.495	20	32	.625	60	16	18	0	113	12.6
Patrick Ewing**	9	190	44	82	.537	18	26	.692	60	7	27	0	106	11.8
Dominique Wilkins	8	159	38	95	.400	28	38	.737	27	15	13	0	106	13.3
Bill Sharman	8	194	40	104	.385	22	27	.815	31	16	16	0	102	12.8
Paul Westphal	5	128	43	68	.632	11	16	.688	7	24	14	0	97	19.4
Clyde Drexler*	9	166	40	79	.506	12	12	1.000	44	23	19	0	96	10.7
ALLEN IVERSON	5	144	35	77	.455	20	26	.769	14	35	5	0	94	18.8
Jerry Lucas	7	183	35	64	.547	19	21	.905	64	12	20	0	89	12.7
Jack Twyman	6	117	38	68	.559	13	20	.650	21	8	14	0	89	14.8
Walt Frazier	7	183	35	78	.449	18	21	.857	27	26	10	0	88	12.6
Willis Reed	7	161	38	84	.452	12	16	.750	58	7	20	1	88	12.6
TIM DUNCAN	6	170	39	69	.565	9	11	.818	81	17	9	0	87	14.5
Robert Parish	9	142	36	68	.529	14	21	.667	53	8	15	0	86	9.6
GARY PAYTON	9	195	34	78	.436	11	11	1.000	30	73	13	0	85	9.4
SCOTTIE PIPPEN	7	173	34	77	.442	10	16	.625	39	17	8	0	85	12.1
Lenny Wilkens	9	182	30	75	.400	25	32	.781	22	26	15	0	85	9.4
Ed Macauley	7	154	24	62	.387	35	41	.854	32	18	13	0	83	11.9
John Stockton	10	197	35	66	.530	4	6	.667	17	71	20	0	81	8.1
George Mikan	4	100	28	80	.350	22	27	.815	51	7	14	0	78	19.5
Tom Chambers	4	84	29	56	.518	17	22	.773	16	5	11	0	77	19.3
Dave DeBusschere	8	167	37	81	.457	3	4	.750	51	11	12	0	77	9.6
Dave Cowens*	6	154	33	66	.500	10	14	.714	81	12	21	0	76	12.7
David Thompson	4	115	33	49	.673	9	17	.529	16	10	13	0	75	18.8
Nate Archibald	6	162	27	60	.450	20	24	.833	18	40	10	0	74	12.3
Bob Lanier	8	121	32	55	.582	10	12	.833	45	12	15	0	74	9.3
James Worthy	7	142	34	77	.442	6	9	.667	26	9	10	0	74	10.6
Alex English	8	148	36	72	.500	1	2	.500	18	15	8	0	73	9.1
Rolando Blackman	6	88	29	49	.592	13	16	.813	13	13	5	0	71	17.8
Neil Johnston	6	132	27	63	.429	16	23	.696	52	6	13	0	70	11.7
TRACY McGRADY	4	103	25	47	.532	11	14	.786	15	9	4	0	68	17.0
Gus Johnson	5	99	24	56	.429	19	25	.760	35	6	12	0	67	13.4
Vern Mikkelsen	6	110	27	70	.386	13	20	.650	52	8	20	0	67	11.2
Lou Hudson	6	99	26	61	.426	14	15	.933	13	6	11	0	66	11.0
Gene Shue	5	130	29	51	.569	8	12	.667	20	19	11	0	66	13.2
Jo Jo White	7	124	29	60	.483	6	11	.545	27	21	6	0	64	9.1
George Yardley	6	131	26	60	.433	12	17	.706	35	4	13	0	64	10.7
Adrian Dantley	6	130	23	54	.426	17	19	.895	23	7	13	0	63	10.5
Richie Guerin	6	122	23	56	.411	17	26	.654	19	18	17	1	63	10.5
Kevin McHale	7	25	24	48	.500	12	14	.857	37	8	21	0	61	8.7
RAY ALLEN	4	84	23	58	.397	8	10	.800	10	13	7	0	60	15.0

*Denotes number of additional games in which player was selected but did not play.

CAREER, OTHER CATEGORIES

(Active players in 2003-04 in CAPS)

SCORING AVERAGE
(minimum three games or 60 points)

	G	FGM	FTM	Pts.	Avg.
KOBE BRYANT	6	52	12	125	20.8
Oscar Robertson	12	88	70	246	20.5
Bob Pettit	11	81	62	224	20.4
Michael Jordan	13	110	39	262	20.2
Julius Erving	11	85	50	221	20.1
Elgin Baylor	11	70	78	218	19.8
George Mikan	4	28	22	78	19.5
Paul Westphal	5	43	11	97	19.4
Tom Chambers	4	29	17	77	19.3
ALLEN IVERSON	5	35	20	94	18.8

FIELD-GOAL PERCENTAGE
(minimum 15 made)

	FGM	FGA	Pct.
Larry Nance	15	21	.714
Randy Smith	15	21	.714
David Thompson	33	49	.673
Eddie Johnson	18	28	.643
Ralph Sampson	21	33	.636
Paul Westphal	43	68	.632
ANFERNEE HARDAWAY	20	32	.625
Artis Gilmore	18	29	.621
DIKEMBE MUTOMBO	22	37	.595
Rolando Blackman	29	49	.592

FREE THROW PERCENTAGE
(minimum 10 made)

	FTM	FTA	Pct.
Clyde Drexler	12	12	1.000
Archie Clark	11	11	1.000
KEVIN GARNETT	11	11	1.000
GARY PAYTON	11	11	1.000
Larry Foust	15	16	.938
Lou Hudson	14	15	.933
Don Ohl	14	15	.933
Magic Johnson	38	42	.905
Jerry Lucas	19	21	.905
Adrian Dantley	17	19	.895

GAMES PLAYED
Kareem Abdul-Jabbar 18
Wilt Chamberlain 13
Bob Cousy 13
John Havlicek 13
Michael Jordan 13
Elvin Hayes 12
KARL MALONE 12
Hakeem Olajuwon 12
Oscar Robertson 12
Bill Russell 12
Jerry West 12

MINUTES
Kareem Abdul-Jabbar 449
Wilt Chamberlain 388
Michael Jordan 382
Oscar Robertson 380
Bob Cousy 368
Bob Pettit 360
Bill Russell 343
Jerry West 341
Magic Johnson 331
Elgin Baylor 321

POINTS
Michael Jordan 262
Kareem Abdul-Jabbar 251
Oscar Robertson 246
Bob Pettit 224
Julius Erving 221
Elgin Baylor 218
Wilt Chamberlain 191
Isiah Thomas 185
John Havlicek 179
Magic Johnson 176

FIELD GOALS MADE
Michael Jordan 110
Kareem Abdul-Jabbar 105
Oscar Robertson 88
Julius Erving 85
Bob Pettit 81
Isiah Thomas 76
John Havlicek 74
Wilt Chamberlain 72
Elgin Baylor 70
Magic Johnson 64

FIELD GOALS ATTEMPTED
Michael Jordan 233
Kareem Abdul-Jabbar 213
Bob Pettit 193
Julius Erving 178
Oscar Robertson 172
Elgin Baylor 164
Bob Cousy 158
John Havlicek 154
Jerry West 137
Isiah Thomas 133

FREE THROWS MADE
Elgin Baylor 78
Oscar Robertson 70
Bob Pettit 62
Julius Erving 50
Wilt Chamberlain 47
Bob Cousy 43
Dolph Schayes 42
Kareem Abdul-Jabbar 41
David Robinson 41
Moses Malone 40

FREE THROWS ATTEMPTED
Elgin Baylor 98
Oscar Robertson 98
Wilt Chamberlain 94
Bob Pettit 80
Moses Malone 67
Julius Erving 63
David Robinson 59
Michael Jordan 52
Bob Cousy 51
Five tied 50

3-POINT FIELD GOALS MADE
JASON KIDD 11
Magic Johnson 10
KOBE BRYANT 9
Mark Price 9
GLEN RICE 9
Tim Hardaway 8
TRACY MCGRADY 7
SCOTTIE PIPPEN 7
John Stockton 7
Four tied 6

3-POINT FIELD GOALS ATTEMPTED
RAY ALLEN 27
GARY PAYTON 23
SCOTTIE PIPPEN 22
KOBE BRYANT 21
Tim Hardaway 21
Magic Johnson 21
JASON KIDD 21
John Stockton 21
REGGIE MILLER 19
Mark Price 9

REBOUNDS
Wilt Chamberlain 197
Bob Pettit 178
Kareem Abdul-Jabbar 149
Bill Russell 139
Moses Malone 108
Dolph Schayes 105
Elgin Baylor 99
Hakeem Olajuwon 94
Elvin Hayes 92
Dave Cowens 81
TIM DUNCAN 81

ASSISTS
Magic Johnson 127
Isiah Thomas 97
Bob Cousy 86
Oscar Robertson 81
GARY PAYTON 73
John Stockton 71
JASON KIDD 58
Jerry West 55
Michael Jordan 54

Kareem Abdul-Jabbar 51

PERSONAL FOULS
Kareem Abdul-Jabbar 57
Oscar Robertson 41
Elvin Hayes 37
Bill Russell 37
Dolph Schayes 32
Elgin Baylor 31
Julius Erving 31
Michael Jordan 31
Hakeem Olajuwon 31
Rick Barry 30

STEALS
Michael Jordan 37
Isiah Thomas 31
Larry Bird 23
Magic Johnson 21
JASON KIDD 19
GARY PAYTON 19
Julius Erving 18
SCOTTIE PIPPEN 17
Rick Barry 16
George Gervin 16
John Stockton 16

BLOCKED SHOTS
Kareem Abdul-Jabbar 31
Hakeem Olajuwon 23
Patrick Ewing 16
SHAQUILLE O'NEAL 14
David Robinson 13
Kevin McHale 12
Julius Erving 11
DIKEMBE MUTOMBO 10
George Gervin 9
KEVIN GARNETT 8
ALONZO MOURNING 8
Robert Parish 8

DISQUALIFICATIONS
Rick Barry 2
Bob Cousy 2
Kareem Abdul-Jabbar 1
Paul Arizin 1
Walt Bellamy 1
John Green 1
Richie Guerin 1
Hakeem Olajuwon 1
Willis Reed 1
Bill Russell 1
Dolph Schayes 1
Bobby Wanzer 1

HISTORY *All-Star Game*

PLAYERS WHO HAVE MADE ALL-STAR TEAMS

(midseason All-Star Games; active 2003-04 players in CAPS)

	No.		No.		No.
Kareem Abdul-Jabbar*	19	Jack Twyman	6	Dan Majerle	3
Michael Jordan*	14	George Yardley	6	George McGinnis	3
KARL MALONE**	14	Carl Braun*	5	Jeff Mullins	3
Jerry West**	14	VINCE CARTER*	5	Larry Nance	3
Wilt Chamberlain	13	Brad Daugherty	5	DIRK NOWITZKI	3
Bob Cousy	13	Wayne Embry*	5	JERMAINE O'NEAL	3
John Havlicek	13	Tom Gola*	5	PAUL PIERCE	3
Larry Bird**	12	Gail Goodrich	5	GLEN RICE	3
Elvin Hayes	12	Cliff Hagan*	5	Dan Roundfield**	3
Magic Johnson*	12	Tim Hardaway	5	Detlef Schrempf	3
Moses Malone*	12	ALLEN IVERSON	5	Charlie Scott	3
Hakeem Olajuwon	12	Dennis Johnson	5	Paul Seymour	3
Oscar Robertson	12	Gus Johnson	5	Maurice Stokes	3
Bill Russell	12	Marques Johnson	5	PEJA STOJAKOVIC	3
Dolph Schayes*	12	Sam Jones	5	Dick Van Arsdale	3
Isiah Thomas*	12	Rudy LaRusso*	5	Tom Van Arsdale	3
Charles Barkley**	11	Pete Maravich*	5	Norm Van Lier	3
Elgin Baylor	11	Bob McAdoo	5	ANTOINE WALKER	3
Julius Erving	11	REGGIE MILLER	5	Jamaal Wilkes	3
Patrick Ewing**	11	Sidney Moncrief	5	Buck Williams	3
SHAQUILLE O'NEAL***	11	Chris Mullin*	5	Leo Barnhorst	2
Bob Pettit	11	Don Ohl	5	Zelmo Beaty	2
Paul Arizin*	10	Andy Phillip	5	Terrell Brandon	2
Clyde Drexler*	10	Gene Shue	5	Frank Brian	2
Hal Greer	10	Rudy Tomjanovich	5	Joe Caldwell	2
David Robinson	10	Wes Unseld	5	Archie Clark	2
John Stockton	10	Bobby Wanzer	5	Terry Cummings	2
George Gervin	9	CHRIS WEBBER*	5	BARON DAVIS	2
Robert Parish	9	Paul Westphal	5	John Drew	2
GARY PAYTON	9	RAY ALLEN	4	Kevin Duckworth	2
Lenny Wilkens	9	VIN BAKER	4	Walter Dukes	2
Dominique Wilkins*	9	Walt Bellamy	4	Dike Eddleman	2
Rick Barry*	8	Otis Birdsong	4	Sean Elliot	2
Dave DeBusschere	8	Rolando Blackman	4	MICHAEL FINLEY	2
Alex English	8	Tom Chambers	4	Joe Fulks	2
Larry Foust*	8	Maurice Cheeks	4	Jack George	2
Bob Lanier	8	Doug Collins*	4	ALLAN HOUSTON	2
DIKEMBE MUTOMBO	8	Billy Cunningham	4	Rod Hundley	2
Bill Sharman	8	Bob Dandridge	4	Eddie Johnson	2
Dave Bing	7	Bob Davies	4	John Johnson	2
Dave Cowens*	7	Dick Garmaker	4	Larry Johnson	2
Walt Frazier	7	Johnny Green	4	Larry Kenon	2
Harry Gallatin	7	ANFERNEE HARDAWAY	4	Don Kojis	2
KEVIN GARNETT	7	Connie Hawkins	4	Fat Lever	2
JASON KIDD	7	Spencer Haywood	4	Jeff Malone	2
Jerry Lucas	7	Mel Hutchins	4	Danny Manning	2
Ed Macauley	7	Bobby Jones	4	STEPHON MARBURY	2
Slater Martin	7	Bernard King	4	Jack Marin	2
Dick McGuire	7	Bill Laimbeer	4	BRAD MILLER	2
Kevin McHale	7	Maurice Lucas	4	YAO MING	2
Alonzo Mourning***	7	George Mikan	4	STEVE NASH	2
SCOTTIE PIPPEN	7	TRACY McGRADY	4	Norm Nixon	2
Willis Reed	7	Earl Monroe	4	Jim Paxson	2
Jack Sikma	7	Willie Naulls	4	Geoff Petrie	2
Nate Thurmond**	7	Jim Pollard	4	Terry Porter	2
Chet Walker	7	Mark Price	4	GLENN ROBINSON	2
Jo Jo White	7	Micheal Ray Richardson	4	Truck Robinson	2
James Worthy	7	Arnie Risen*	4	Red Rocha	2
Nate Archibald	6	Alvin Robertson	4	Dennis Rodman	2
KOBE BRYANT	6	Guy Rodgers	4	Fred Scolari*	2
Larry Costello*	6	Ralph Sampson*	4	Ken Sears	2
Adrian Dantley	6	LATRELL SPREWELL	4	Frank Selvy	2
Walter Davis	6	David Thompson	4	Paul Silas	2
Joe Dumars	6	Sidney Wicks	4	Jerry Sloan	2
TIM DUNCAN	6	Mark Aguirre	3	Phil Smith	2
Artis Gilmore	6	Bill Bridges	3	Randy Smith	2
Richie Guerin	6	Phil Chenier	3	JERRY STACKHOUSE	2
Tom Heinsohn*	6	Terry Dischinger	3	Reggie Theus	2
GRANT HILL*	6	STEVE FRANCIS	3	Andrew Toney	2
Bailey Howell	6	Kevin Johnson	3	Kelly Tripucka	2
Lou Hudson	6	EDDIE JONES	3	Kiki Vandeweghe	2
Neil Johnston	6	Bob Kauffman	3	Jimmy Walker	2
Shawn Kemp	6	Red Kerr	3	BEN WALLACE	2
Vern Mikkelsen	6	Bob Love	3	RASHEED WALLACE	2
Mitch Richmond*	6	Clyde Lovellette	3	Bill Walton*	2

	No.
Gus Williams	2
Brian Winters	2
SHAREEF ABDUR-RAHIM	1
Alvan Adams	1
Michael Adams	1
Danny Ainge	1
KENNY ANDERSON	1
B.J. Armstrong	1
RON ARTEST	1
Don Barksdale	1
Dick Barnett	1
DANA BARROS	1
Butch Beard	1
Ralph Beard	1
Mookie Blaylock	1
John Block	1
Bob Boozer	1
Vince Boryla	1
Bill Bradley	1
ELTON BRAND	1
Fred Brown	1
Don Buse	1
Austin Carr	1
Joe Barry Carroll	1
Bill Cartwright	1
SAM CASSELL	1
Cedric Ceballos*	1
Len Chappell	1
Nat Clifton	1
DERRICK COLEMAN	1
Jack Coleman	1
ANTONIO DAVIS	1
DALE DAVIS	1
VLADE DIVAC	1
James Donaldson	1
Mark Eaton	1
Dale Ellis	1
Ray Felix	1
Sleepy Floyd	1

	No.
World B. Free	1
Billy Gabor	1
Chris Gatling	1
HORACE GRANT	1
A.C. Green	1
Rickey Green	1
Alex Groza	1
TOM GUGLIOTTA	1
Bob Harrison	1
Hersey Hawkins	1
Walt Hazzard	1
TYRONE HILL	1
Lionel Hollins	1
Jeff Hornacek	1
JUWAN HOWARD	1
ZYDRUNAS ILGAUSKAS	1
Darrall Imhoff	1
Dan Issel	1
Luke Jackson	1
MARK JACKSON	1
Steve Johnson*	1
Jim King	1
ANDREI KIRILENKO	1
Billy Knight	1
Sam Lacey	1
CHRISTIAN LAETTNER	1
Clyde Lee	1
Reggie Lewis	1
JAMAAL MAGLOIRE	1
SHAWN MARION	1
KENYON MARTIN	1
JAMAL MASHBURN	1
Anthony Mason	1
Xavier McDaniel	1
ANTONIO McDYESS	1
Jon McGlocklin	1
Tom Meschery	1
Eddie Miles	1
Mike Mitchell	1

	No.
Steve Mix	1
Calvin Murphy	1
Calvin Natt	1
Chuck Noble	1
CHARLES OAKLEY	1
Ricky Pierce	1
Jim Price	1
THEO RATLIFF*	1
MICHAEL REDD	1
Richie Regan	1
Doc Rivers	1
CLIFFORD ROBINSON	1
Flynn Robinson	1
Curtis Rowe	1
Jeff Ruland	1
Bob Rule	1
Campy Russell	1
Cazzie Russell	1
Woody Sauldsberry	1
Fred Schaus	1
Lee Shaffer	1
Lonnie Shelton	1
Adrian Smith	1
STEVE SMITH	1
Rik Smits	1
John Starks	1
Don Sunderlage	1
WALLY SZCZERBIAK	1
Otis Thorpe	1
NICK VAN EXEL	1
Paul Walther	1
Kermit Washington	1
Scott Wedman	1
Jayson Williams	1
KEVIN WILLIS	1
Max Zaslofsky	1

*Denotes number of games in which player was selected but did not play.

ALL-STAR SATURDAY RESULTS

SPRITE RISING STARS SLAM DUNK

1984— Larry Nance, Phoenix
1985— Dominique Wilkins, Atlanta
1986— Spud Webb, Atlanta
1987— Michael Jordan, Chicago
1988— Michael Jordan, Chicago
1989— Kenny Walker, New York
1990— Dominique Wilkins, Atlanta
1991— Dee Brown, Boston
1992— Cedric Ceballos, Phoenix
1993— Harold Miner, Miami
1994— Isaiah Rider, Minnesota
1995— Harold Miner, Miami
1996— Brent Barry, L.A. Clippers
1997— Kobe Bryant, L.A. Lakers
1998— No competition held.
1999— No competition held.
2000— Vince Carter, Toronto
2001— Desmond Mason, Seattle
2002— Jason Richardson, Golden State
2003— Jason Richardson, Golden State
2004— Fred Jones, Indiana

FOOT LOCKER 3-POINT SHOOTOUT

1986— Larry Bird, Boston
1987— Larry Bird, Boston
1988— Larry Bird, Boston
1989— Dale Ellis, Seattle
1990— Craig Hodges, Chicago
1991— Craig Hodges, Chicago
1992— Craig Hodges, Chicago
1993— Mark Price, Cleveland
1994— Mark Price, Cleveland
1995— Glen Rice, Miami

1996— Tim Legler, Washington
1997— Steve Kerr, Chicago
1998— Jeff Hornacek, Utah
1999— No competition held.
2000— Jeff Hornacek, Utah
2001— Ray Allen, Milwaukee
2002— Peja Stojakovic, Sacramento
2003— Peja Stojakovic, Sacramento
2004— Voshon Lenard, Denver

GOT MILK? ROOKIE CHALLENGE

1994— Phenoms 74, Sensations 68
1995— White 83, Green 79 (OT)
1996— East 94, West 92
1997— East 96, West 91
1998— East 85, West 80
1999— No game played.
2000— 2000 Rookies 92,
       1999 Rookies 81 (OT)
2001— 2000 Rookies 121,
       2001 Rookies 113
2002— Rookies 103, Sophomores 97
2003— Sophomores 132, Rookies 112
2004— Sophomores 142, Rookies 118

SONY ALL-STAR 2BALL

1998— Clyde Drexler, Houston Rockets
       Cynthia Cooper, Houston
       Comets (WNBA)
1999— No competition held.
2000— Jeff Hornacek, Utah Jazz
       Natalie Williams, Utah Starzz
       (WNBA)
2001— Predrag Stojakovic, Sac. Kings
       Ruthie Bolton-Holifield,
       Sac. Monarchs (WNBA)

JEEP ALL-STAR HOOP-IT-UP

2002— Hedo Turkoglu, Sacramento
       Kings; Ticha Penicheiro,
       Sacramento Monarchs
       (WNBA); Sarunas
       Marciulionis (former NBA
       player); Tom Cavanaugh
       (actor)
2003— Marko Jaric, L.A. Clippers; Lisa
       Leslie, L.A. Sparks
       (WNBA); Magic Johnson
       (former NBA Player);
       Ashton Kutcher (actor)

RADIOSHACK SHOOTING STARS

2004— Magic Johnson, Derek Fisher,
       L.A. Lakers; Lisa Leslie,
       L.A. Sparks (WNBA)

989 SPORTS SKILLS CHALLENGE

2003— Jason Kidd, New Jersey
2004— Baron Davis, New Orleans

SCHICK LEGENDS CLASSIC

1984— West 64, East 63
1985— East 63, West 53
1986— West 53, East 44
1987— West 54, East 43
1988— East 47, West 45 (OT)
1989— West 54, East 53
1990— East 37, West 36
1991— East 41, West 34
1992— West 46, East 38
1993— East 58, West 45

HISTORY *All-Star Game*

HALL OF FAME
LIST OF ENSHRINEES

CONTRIBUTORS

Name	Year enshrined
Abbott, Senda	1984
Bee, Clair F.	**1967**
Biasone, Danny	**2000**
Brown, Walter A.	**1965**
Bunn, John W.	1964
Colangelo, Jerry	**2004**
Douglas, Robert L. (Bob)	1971
Duer, Al	1981
Embry, Wayne	**1999**
Fagan, Clifford	1983
Fisher, Harry A.	1973
Fleisher, Larry	**1991**
Gottlieb, Edward	**1971**
Gulick, Dr. Luther H.	1959
Harrison, Les	**1979**
Hearn, Francis D. (Chick)	2003
Hepp, Ferenc	1980
Hickox, Edward J.	1959
Hinkle, Paul D. (Tony)	1965
Irish, Ned	**1964**
Jones, R. William	1964
Kennedy, J. Walter	**1980**
Liston, Emil S.	1974
McLendon, John B.	1978
Mokray, William G. (Bill)	**1965**
Morgan, Ralph	1959
Morgenweck, Frank	1962
Naismith, Dr. James	1959
Newell, Peter F.	**1978**
Newton, C.M.	2000
O'Brien, John J.	1961
O'Brien, Larry	**1991**
Olsen, Harold G.	**1959**
Podoloff, Maurice	**1973**
Porter, H.V.	1960
Reid, William A.	1963
Ripley, Elmer	1972
St. John, Lynn W.	1962
Saperstein, Abe	1970
Schabinger, Arthur A.	1961
Stagg, Amos Alonzo	1959
Stankovic, Boris	1991
Steitz, Edward	1983
Taylor, Charles H. (Chuck)	1968
Teague, Bertha	1984
Tower, Oswald	1959
Trester, Arthur L.	1961
Wells, Clifford	1971
Wilke, Lou	1982
Zollner, Fred	**1999**

PLAYERS

Name	Year enshrined
Abdul-Jabbar, Kareem	**1995**
Archibald, Nathaniel (Nate)	**1991**
Arizin, Paul J.	**1977**
Barlow, Thomas B.	1980
Barry, Richard F.D. (Rick)	**1987**
Baylor, Elgin	**1977**
Beckman, John	1972
Bellamy, Walt	**1993**
Belov, Sergei	1992
Bing, Dave	**1990**
Bird, Larry	**1998**
Blazejowski, Carol	1994
Borgmann, Bennie	1961

Name	Year enshrined
Bradley, Bill	**1982**
Brennan, Joseph	1974
Cervi, Al	**1985**
Chamberlain, Wilt	**1978**
Cooper, Charles (Tarzan)	1976
Cosic, Kresimir	1996
Cousy, Robert J. (Bob)	**1970**
Cowens, David (Dave)	**1991**
Crawford, Joan	1997
Cunningham, William J. (Billy)	**1986**
Curry, Denise	1997
Dalipagic, Drazen	2004
Davies, Robert E. (Bob)	**1970**
DeBernardi, Forrest S.	1961
DeBusschere, Dave	**1982**
Dehnert, H.G. (Dutch)	1968
Drexler, Clyde	**2004**
Donovan, Anne	1995
Endacott, Paul	1971
English, Alex	**1997**
Erving, Julius	**1993**
Foster, Harold (Bud)	1964
Frazier, Walter	**1987**
Friedman, Max (Marty)	1971
Fulks, Joseph F. (Joe)	**1978**
Gale, Lauren (Laddie)	1976
Gallatin, Harry J.	**1991**
Gates, William	1989
Gervin, George	**1996**
Gola, Tom	**1975**
Goodrich, Gail	**1996**
Greer, Hal	**1982**
Gruenig, Robert (Ace)	1963
Hagan, Clifford O.	**1978**
Hanson, Victor	1960
Harris, Lusia	1992
Havlicek, John	**1984**
Hawkins, Connie	**1992**
Hayes, Elvin	**1990**
Haynes, Marques	1998
Heinsohn, Thomas W. (Tom)	**1986**
Holman, Nat	1964
Houbregs, Robert J.	**1987**
Howell, Bailey	**1997**
Hyatt, Charles (Chuck)	1959
Issel, Dan	**1993**
Jeannette, Harry Edward (Buddy)	**1994**
Johnson, Earvin Jr. (Magic)	**2002**
Johnson, William C.	1976
Johnston, D. Neil	**1990**
Jones, K.C.	**1989**
Jones, Sam	**1984**
Krause, Edward (Moose)	1975
Kurland, Robert (Bob)	1961
Lanier, Bob	**1992**
Lapchick, Joe	1966
Lemon, Meadowlark	2003
Lieberman, Nancy	1996
Lloyd, Earl	**2003**
Lovellette, Clyde	**1988**
Lucas, Jerry	**1980**
Luisetti, Angelo (Hank)	1959
Macauley, C. Edward (Ed)	**1960**
Malone, Moses	**2001**
Maravich, Peter P. (Pete)	**1987**
Martin, Slater	**1982**
McAdoo, Bob	**2000**
McCracken, Branch	1960

Name	Year enshrined
McCracken, Jack	1962
McDermott, Bobby	1988
McGuire, Dick	**1993**
McHale, Kevin	**1999**
Meneghin, Dino	2003
Meyers, Ann	1993
Mikan, George L.	**1959**
Mikkelsen, Vern	**1995**
Miller, Cheryl	1995
Monroe, Earl	**1990**
Murphy, Calvin	**1993**
Murphy, Charles (Stretch)	1960
Page, H.O. (Pat)	1962
Parish, Robert	**2003**
Petrovic, Drazen	**2002**
Pettit, Robert L. (Bob)	**1970**
Phillip, Andy	**1961**
Pollard, James C. (Jim)	**1978**
Ramsey, Frank	**1981**
Reed, Willis	**1982**
Risen, Arnie	**1998**
Robertson, Oscar	**1980**
Roosma, Col. John S.	1961
Russell, John (Honey)	1964
Russell, William (Bill)	**1975**
Schayes, Adolph (Dolph)	**1973**
Schmidt, Ernest J.	1973
Schommer, John J.	1959
Sedran, Barney	1962
Semenova, Juliana	1993
Sharman, Bill	**1976**
Steinmetz, Christian	1961
Stokes, Maurice	**2004**
Thomas, Isiah	**2000**
Thompson, David	**1996**
Thompson, John A. (Cat)	1962
Thurmond, Nate	**1985**
Twyman, Jack	**1983**
Unseld, Wes	**1988**
Vandivier, Robert (Fuzzy)	1974
Wachter, Edward A.	1961
Walton, Bill	**1993**
Wanzer, Robert F.	**1987**
West, Jerry	**1980**
White, Nera	1992
Wilkens, Lenny	**1989**
Woodard, Lynette	2004
Wooden, John R.	1960
Worthy, James	**2003**
Yardley, George	**1996**

COACHES

Name	Year enshrined
Allen, Dr. Forrest C. (Phog)	1959
Anderson, Harold	1984
Auerbach, A.J. (Red)	**1968**
Barmore, Leon	2003
Barry, Sam	1978
Blood, Ernest A.	1960
Brown, Larry	**2002**
Cann, Howard G.	1967
Carlson, Dr. H. Clifford	1959
Carnesecca, Lou	1992
Carnevale, Ben	1969
Carril, Pete	1997
Case, Everett	1981
Chaney, John	2001
Conradt, Jody	1998
Crum, Denny	1994
Daly, Chuck	**1994**
Dean, Everett S.	1966
Diaz-Miguel, Antonio	1997
Diddle, Edgar A.	1971
Drake, Bruce	1972
Gaines, Clarence	1981

Name	Year enshrined
Gardner, Jack	1983
Gill, Amory T. (Slats)	1967
Gomelsky, Aleksandr	1995
Hannum, Alex	**1998**
Harshman, Marv	1984
Haskins, Don	1997
Hickey, Edgar S.	1978
Hobson, Howard A.	1965
Holzman, William (Red)	**1986**
Iba, Henry P. (Hank)	1968
Julian, Alvin F. (Doggie)	**1967**
Keaney, Frank W.	1960
Keogan, George E.	1961
Knight, Bob	1991
Krzyzewski, Mike	2001
Kundla, John	**1995**
Lambert, Ward L.	1960
Litwack, Harry	1975
Loeffler, Kenneth D.	**1964**
Lonborg, A.C. (Dutch)	1972
McCutchan, Arad A.	1980
McGuire, Al	1992
McGuire, Frank	**1976**
Meanwell, Dr. Walter E.	1959
Meyer, Raymond J.	1978
Miller, Ralph	1988
Moore, Billie	1999
Nikolic, Aleksandar	1998
Olson, Lute	2002
Ramsay, Jack	**1992**
Rubini, Cesare	1994
Rupp, Adolph F.	1968
Sachs, Leonard D.	1961
Sharman, Bill	**2004**
Shelton, Everett F.	1979
Smith, Dean	1982
Summitt, Pat	2000
Taylor, Fred R.	1985
Thompson, John	1999
Wade, Margaret	1984
Watts, Stanley H.	1985
Wilkens, Lenny	**1998**
Wooden, John R.	1972
Woolpert, Phil	1992
Wootten, Morgan	2000
Yow, Kay	2002

REFEREES

Name	Year enshrined
Enright, James E.	**1978**
Hepbron, George T.	1960
Hoyt, George	1961
Kennedy, Matthew P.	**1959**
Leith, Lloyd	1982
Mihalik, Zigmund J.	1986
Nucatola, John P.	**1977**
Quigley, Ernest C.	1961
Shirley, J. Dallas	**1979**
Strom, Earl	**1995**
Tobey, David	1961
Walsh, David H.	1961

TEAMS

Name	Year enshrined
First Team	1959
Original Celtics	1959
Buffalo Germans	1961
New York Renaissance	1963
Harlem Globetrotters	2002

Individuals associated with the NBA in boldface.
Individuals elected—253.
Teams elected—5.

MEMORABLE GAMES

WILT CHAMBERLAIN'S 100-POINT GAME

MARCH 2, 1962, AT HERSHEY, PA.

Philadelphia Warriors (169)

	Pos.	FGM	FGA	FTM	FTA	Pts.
Paul Arizin	F	7	18	2	2	16
Tom Meschery	F	7	12	2	2	16
Wilt Chamberlain	C	36	63	28	32	100
Guy Rodgers	G	1	4	9	12	11
Al Attles	G	8	8	1	1	17
York Larese		4	5	1	1	9
Ed Conlin		0	4	0	0	0
Joe Ruklick		0	1	0	2	0
Ted Luckenbill		0	0	0	0	0
Totals		63	115	43	52	169

FG pct.: .548. FT pct.: .827. Team rebounds: 3.

New York Knickerbockers (147)

	Pos.	FGM	FGA	FTM	FTA	Pts.
Willie Naulls	F	9	22	13	15	31
Johnny Green	F	3	7	0	0	6
Darrall Imhoff	C	3	7	1	1	7
Richie Guerin	G	13	29	13	17	39
Al Butler	G	4	13	0	0	8
Cleveland Buckner		16	26	1	1	33
Dave Budd		6	8	1	1	13
Donnie Butcher		3	6	4	6	10
Totals		57	118	33	41	147

FG pct.: .483. FT pct.: .805. Team rebounds: 4.

Score by periods:	1st	2nd	3rd	4th	Totals
Philadelphia	42	37	46	44	169
New York	26	42	38	41	147

Officials: Willie Smith, Pete D'Ambrosio.
Attendance: 4,124.

CHAMBERLAIN'S SCORING BY PERIODS

	Min.	FGM	FGA	FTM	FTA	Reb.	Ast.	Pts.
1st	12	7	14	9	9	10	0	23
2nd	12	7	12	4	5	4	1	18
3rd	12	10	16	8	8	6	1	28
4th	12	12	21	7	10	5	0	31
Totals	48	63	36	32	28	25	2	100

LOWEST-SCORING GAME IN NBA HISTORY

NOVEMBER 22, 1950, AT MINNEAPOLIS

Fort Wayne Pistons (19)

	Pos.	FGM	FGA	FTM	FTA	Pts.
Fred Schaus	F	0	1	3	3	3
Jack Kerris	F	0	1	2	4	2
Larry Foust	C	1	2	1	1	3
John Hargis	G	1	1	0	0	2
John Oldham	G	1	5	3	4	5
Paul Armstrong		1	2	2	2	4
Bob Harris		0	0	0	1	0
Ralph Johnson		0	1	0	0	0
Totals		4	13	11	15	19

FG pct.: .308. FT pct.: .733. Rebounds—Oldham 4, Kerris 2, Foust 1, Harris 1. Assists—Hargis 1, Johnson 1, Schaus 1. Personal fouls—Kerris 5, Foust 3, Oldham 2, Armstrong 1, Harris 1, Johnson 1.

Minneapolis Lakers (18)

	Pos.	FGM	FGA	FTM	FTA	Pts.
Jim Pollard	F	0	1	1	1	1
Vern Mikkelsen	F	0	2	0	0	0
George Mikan	C	4	11	7	11	15
Slater Martin	G	0	2	0	3	0
Bob Harrison	G	0	2	2	2	2
Bud Grant		0	0	0	0	0
Joe Hutton		0	0	0	0	0
Arnie Ferrin		0	0	0	0	0
Totals		4	18	10	17	18

FG pct.: .222. FT pct.: .588. Rebounds—Mikan 4, Mikkelsen 3, Martin 1, Pollard 1. Assists—Martin 2, Grant 1, Pollard 1. Personal fouls—Harrison 3, Martin 2, Mikkelsen 2, Pollard 2, Grant 1, Mikan 1.

Score by periods:	1st	2nd	3rd	4th	Totals
Fort Wayne	8	3	5	3	19
Minneapolis	7	6	4	1	18

Referees: Jocko Collins, Stan Stutz.
Attendance: 7,021.

HIGHEST-SCORING GAME IN NBA HISTORY

DECEMBER 13, 1983, AT DENVER

Detroit Pistons (186)

	Pos.	FGM	FGA	FTM	FTA	Pts.
Kelly Tripucka	F	14	25	7	9	35
Cliff Levingston	F	1	2	0	0	2
Bill Laimbeer	C	6	10	5	9	17
Isiah Thomas	G	18	34	10	19	47
John Long	G	18	25	5	6	41
Terry Tyler		8	15	2	3	18
Vinnie Johnson		4	12	4	5	12
Earl Cureton		3	6	3	5	9
Ray Tolbert		1	4	1	4	3
Walker Russell		1	2	0	0	2
Kent Benson		0	1	0	0	0
David Thirdkill		0	0	0	0	0
Totals		74	136	37	60	186

FG pct.: .544. FT pct.: .617. Team rebounds: 16. Minutes played—Thomas 52, Laimbeer 47, Long 46, Tripucka 39, Cureton 34, Tyler 28, Johnson 21, Tolbert 15, Benson 13, Levingston 13, Russell 6, Thirdkill 1. Total rebounds—Laimbeer 12, Tyler 8, Cureton 7, Long 6, Tolbert 6, Johnson 5, Thomas 5, Tripucka 4, Levingston 2, Benson 1. Assists—Thomas 17, Johnson 8, Long 8, Laimbeer 6, Cureton 2, Tolbert 2, Tripucka 2, Russell 1, Tyler 1.

Denver Nuggets (184)

	Pos.	FGM	FGA	FTM	FTA	Pts.
Alex English	F	18	30	11	13	47
Kiki Vandeweghe	F	21	29	9	11	51
Dan Issel	C	11	19	6	8	28
Rob Williams	G	3	8	3	4	9
T.R. Dunn	G	3	3	1	2	7
Mike Evans		7	13	2	2	16
Richard Anderson		5	6	2	3	13
Danny Schayes		0	1	11	12	11
Bill Hanzlik		0	4	2	2	2
Howard Carter		0	1	0	0	0
Ken Dennard		0	1	0	0	0
Totals		68	115	47	57	184

FG pct.: .591. FT pct.: .825. Team rebounds: 13. Minutes played—English 50, Vandeweghe 50, Evans 40, Hanzlik 38, Dunn 36, Issel 35, Schayes 24, Williams 21, Anderson 14, Carter 4, Dennard 3. Total rebounds—English 12, Vandeweghe 9, Issel 8, Hanzlik 7, Schayes 7, Anderson 5, Dunn 4, Williams 3, Evans 2. Assists—Vandeweghe 8, English 7, Evans 7, Hanzlik 7, Issel 5, Williams 5, Dunn 2, Schayes 2, Anderson 1, Carter 1, Dennard 1.

Score by periods:	1st	2nd	3rd	4th	OT	OT	OT	Totals
Detroit	38	36	34	37	14	12	15	186
Denver	34	40	39	32	14	12	13	184

3-pt. field goals: Thomas 1-2, Anderson 1-1, Issel 0-1.
Officials: Joe Borgia, Jesse Hall.
Attendance: 9,655.
Time of game: 3:11.

AMERICAN BASKETBALL ASSOCIATION

CHAMPIONSHIP SERIES RESULTS

1968—Pittsburgh defeated New Orleans, four games to three
1969—Oakland defeated Indiana, four games to one
1970—Indiana defeated Los Angeles, four games to two
1971—Utah defeated Kentucky, four games to three
1972—Indiana defeated New York, four games to two

1973—Indiana defeated Kentucky, four games to three
1974—New York defeated Utah, four games to one
1975—Kentucky defeated Indiana, four games to one
1976—New York defeated Denver, four games to two

ALL-TIME RECORDS OF TEAMS

	Years	REGULAR SEASON			PLAYOFFS		
		W	L	Pct.	W	L	Pct.
Anaheim Amigos	1	25	53	.321	0	0	.000
Carolina Cougars	5	215	205	.512	7	13	.350
Dallas Chaparrals	5	202	206	.408	9	16	.360
Denver Nuggets	2	125	43	.744	13	13	.500
Denver Rockets	7	288	288	.500	14	22	.389
Floridians	2	73	95	.435	2	8	.250
Houston Mavericks	2	52	104	.333	0	3	.000
Indiana Pacers	9	427	317	.574	69	50	.580
Kentucky Colonels	9	448	296	.602	55	46	.545
Los Angeles Stars	2	76	86	.469	10	7	.588
Memphis Sounds	5	139	281	.331	1	8	.111
Miami Floridians	2	66	96	.407	5	7	.417
Minnesota Muskies	1	50	28	.641	4	6	.400
Minnesota Pipers	1	36	42	.462	3	4	.429
New Jersey Americans	1	36	42	.462	0	0	.000
New Orleans Buccaneers	3	136	104	.567	14	14	.500
New York Nets	8	338	328	.508	37	32	.536
Oakland Oaks	2	82	74	.526	12	4	.750
Pittsburgh Condors	2	61	107	.363	0	0	.000
Pittsburgh Pipers	2	83	79	.512	11	4	.733
San Antonio Spurs	3	146	106	.579	8	12	.400
San Diego Conquistadors	4	98	154	.389	2	8	.250
San Diego Sails	1	3	8	.273	0	0	.000
Spirits of St. Louis	2	67	101	.399	5	5	.500
Texas Chaparrals	1	30	54	.357	0	4	.000
Utah Stars	6	265	171	.608	36	27	.571
Virginia Squires	6	200	303	.398	15	18	.455
Washington Capitols	1	44	40	.524	3	4	.429

Anaheim moved to Los Angeles after the 1967-68 season and then to Utah after the 1969-70 season. Houston moved to Carolina after the 1968-69 season. Minnesota Muskies moved to Miami after the 1967-68 season. New Jersey moved to New York after the 1967-68 season. Oakland moved to Washington after the 1968-69 season and then to Virginia after the 1969-70 season. Pittsburgh moved to Minnesota and retained nickname after the 1967-68 season and returned to Pittsburgh after the 1968-69 season and changed nickname to Condors in 1970-71. New Orleans moved to Memphis after the 1969-70 season. Dallas moved to San Antonio after the 1972-73 season. San Diego was an expansion team in 1972-73 and changed nickname to Sails in 1975-76 before folding after 11 games. Carolina moved to St. Louis after the 1973-74 season. Baltimore (not shown) folded before the 1975-76 season even started and Utah folded after 16 games of the 1975-76 season.

YEARLY STATISTICAL LEADERS

Year	Scoring	Rebounding	Assists
1968	Connie Hawkins, 26.8	Mel Daniels, 15.6	Larry Brown, 6.5
1969	Rick Barry, 34.0	Mel Daniels, 16.5	Larry Brown, 7.1
1970	Spencer Haywood, 30.0	Spencer Haywood, 19.5	Larry Brown, 7.1
1971	Dan Issel, 29.9	Mel Daniels, 18.0	Bill Melchionni, 8.3
1972	Charlie Scott, 34.6	Artis Gilmore, 17.8	Bill Melchionni, 8.4
1973	Julius Erving, 31.9	Artis Gilmore, 17.5	Bill Melchionni, 7.5
1974	Julius Erving, 27.4	Artis Gilmore, 18.3	Al Smith, 8.2
1975	George McGinnis, 29.8	Swen Nater, 16.4	Mack Calvin, 7.7
1976	Julius Erving, 29.3	Artis Gilmore, 15.5	Don Buse, 8.2

David Thompson, who was the ABA's last Rookie of the Year in 1976, went on to have a Hall of Fame career in the NBA. He scored 73 points (the most of any NBA player in one game except Wilt Chamberlain) on April 9, 1978, for Denver at Detroit in the final game of the 1977-78 regular season. Later that day, George Gervin of the San Antonio Spurs (needing to score at least 58 points) had 63 points against the New Orleans Jazz to nip Thompson for the scoring title by 0.07 points per game.

AWARD WINNERS

MOST VALUABLE PLAYER

1968—Connie Hawkins, Pittsburgh	1972—Artis Gilmore, Kentucky	1975—Julius Erving, New York
1969—Mel Daniels, Indiana	1973—Billy Cunningham, Carolina	George McGinnis, Indiana
1970—Spencer Haywood, Denver	1974—Julius Erving, New York	1976—Julius Erving, New York
1971—Mel Daniels, Indiana		

ROOKIE OF THE YEAR

1968—Mel Daniels, Minnesota	1971—Charlie Scott, Virginia	1974—Swen Nater, San Antonio
1969—Warren Armstrong, Oakland	Dan Issel, Kentucky	1975—Marvin Barnes, St. Louis
1970—Spencer Haywood, Denver	1972—Artis Gilmore, Kentucky	1976—David Thompson, Denver
	1973—Brian Taylor, New York	

COACH OF THE YEAR

1968—Vince Cazzetta, Pittsburgh	1971—Al Bianchi, Virginia	1974—Babe McCarthy, Kentucky
1969—Alex Hannum, Oakland	1972—Tom Nissalke, Dallas	Joe Mullaney, Utah
1970—Bill Sharman, Los Angeles	1973—Larry Brown, Carolina	1975—Larry Brown, Denver
Joe Belmont, Denver		1976—Larry Brown, Denver

HISTORY American Basketball Association

PLAYERS WHO MADE ALL-ABA TEAMS

	1st Team	2nd		1st Team	2nd
Marvin Barnes	0	1	Dan Issel	1	4
Rick Barry	4	0	Warren Jabali	1	0
John Beasley	0	2	Bobby Jones	0	1
Zelmo Beaty	0	2	James Jones	3	0
Ron Boone	1	1	Larry Jones	3	0
John Brisker	0	1	Billy Knight	1	0
Larry Brown	0	1	George McGinnis	2	1
Roger Brown	1	2	Bill Melchionni	1	0
Don Buse	0	1	Doug Moe	1	1
Joe Caldwell	0	1	Swen Nater	0	2
Mack Calvin	3	1	Bob Netolicky	0	1
Larry Cannon	0	1	Cincy Powell	0	1
Billy Cunningham	1	0	Red Robbins	0	2
Louie Dampier	0	4	Charlie Scott	1	1
Mel Daniels	4	1	James Silas	1	1
Julius Erving	4	1	Ralph Simpson	1	2
Don Freeman	1	3	Brian Taylor	0	1
George Gervin	0	2	David Thompson	0	1
Artis Gilmore	5	0	Bob Verga	1	0
Connie Hawkins	2	0	Charlie Williams	1	0
Spencer Haywood	1	0	Willie Wise	0	2

ALL-STAR GAME RESULTS

EAST 5, WEST 3

Date	Site	Att.	East coach	Score	West coach	MVP
Jan. 9,1968—Indianapolis		10,872	Pollard	East, 126-120	McCarthy	L. Brown
Jan. 28,1969—Louisville		5,407	Rhodes	West, 133-127	Hannum	J. Beasley
Jan. 24,1970—Indianapolis		11,932	Leonard	West, 128-98	McCarthy	S. Haywood
Jan. 23,1971—Greensboro		14,407	Bianchi	East, 126-122	Sharman	M. Daniels
Jan. 29,1972—Louisville		15,738	Mullaney	East, 142-115	Andersen	Dan Issel
Feb. 6,1973—Salt Lake City		12,556	Brown	West, 123-111	Andersen	W. Jabali
Jan. 30,1974—Norfolk		10,624	McCarthy	East, 128-112	Mullaney	A. Gilmore
Jan. 28,1975—San Antonio		10,449	Loughery	East, 151-124	L. Brown	F. Lewis
Jan. 27,1976—Denver		17,798	*Loughery	*Denver, 144-138	*L. Brown	D. Thompson

*The final ABA All-Star Game in 1976 was a contest between the Denver Nuggets, coached by Larry Brown, and a team of ABA All-Stars, coached by Kevin Loughery.

COACHES RANKINGS

BY VICTORIES

Coach	W-L	Pct.
Bob Leonard	387-270	.589
Babe McCarthy	280-284	.496
Bob Bass	252-249	.503
Al Bianchi	230-280	.451
Larry Brown	229-107	.682
Joe Mullaney	217-156	.582
Alex Hannum	178-152	.539
Kevin Loughery	168-84	.667
Bill Sharman	133-113	.541
Gene Rhodes	128-110	.538

BY WINNING PERCENTAGE

(minimum 100 games)

Coach	Pct.	W	L
LaDell Andersen	.685	115	53
Larry Brown	.682	229	107
Kevin Loughery	.667	168	84
Hubie Brown	.619	104	64
Bob Leonard	.589	387	270
Joe Mullaney	.582	217	156
Joe Pollard	.557	98	78
Cliff Hagan	.548	109	90
Bill Sharman	.541	133	113
Alex Hannum	.539	178	152

BY GAMES

Coach	G
Bob Leonard	657
Babe McCarthy	564
Al Bianchi	510
Bob Bass	501
Joe Mullaney	373
Larry Brown	336
Alex Hannum	330
Lou Carnesecca	252
Kevin Loughery	252
Bill Sharman	246

RECORDS

- Regular season
- Playoffs
- NBA Finals
- All-Star Game

REGULAR SEASON

Compiled by Elias Sports Bureau

Throughout this all-time NBA record section, records for "fewest" and "lowest" exclude games and seasons before 1954-55, when the 24-second clock was introduced.

INDIVIDUAL

SEASONS

Most seasons
21—Robert Parish, Golden State, 1976-77—1979-80; Boston, 1980-81—1993-94; Charlotte, 1994-95—1995-96; Chicago, 1996-97
20—Kareem Abdul-Jabbar, Milwaukee, 1969-70—1974-75; L.A. Lakers, 1975-76—1988-89
19—James Edwards, Los Angeles, 1977-78; Indiana, 1977-78—1980-81; Cleveland, 1981-82—1982-83; Phoenix, 1982-83—1987-88; Detroit, 1987-88—1990-91; L.A. Clippers, 1991-92; L.A. Lakers, 1992-93—1993-94; Portland, 1994-95; Chicago, 1995-96
Moses Malone, Buffalo, 1976-77; Houston, 1976-77—1981-82; Philadelphia, 1982-83—1985-86; Washington,1986-87—1987-88; Atlanta, 1988-89—1990-91; Milwaukee, 1991-92—1992-93; Philadelphia, 1993-94; San Antonio, 1994-95
John Stockton, Utah, 1984-85—2002-03
Karl Malone, Utah, 1985-86—2002-03; L.A. Lakers, 2003-04
Charles Oakley, Chicago, 1985-86—1987-88; New York, 1988-89—1997-98; Toronto, 1998-99—2000-01; Chicago, 2001-02; Washington, 2002-03; Houston, 2003-04
Kevin Willis, Atlanta, 1984-85—1994-95; Miami, 1994-95—1995-96; Golden State, 1995-96; Houston, 1996-97—1997-98; Toronto, 1998-99—2000-01; Denver, 2000-01; Houston, 2001-02; San Antonio, 2002-03—2003-04

GAMES

Most games, career
1,611—Robert Parish, Golden State, 1976-77—1979-80; Boston, 1980-81—1993-94; Charlotte, 1994-95—1995-96; Chicago, 1996-97
1,560—Kareem Abdul-Jabbar, Milwaukee, 1969-70—1974-75; L.A. Lakers, 1975-76—1988-89
1,504—John Stockton, Utah, 1984-85—2002-03
1,476—Karl Malone, Utah, 1985-86—2002-03; L.A. Lakers, 2003-04
1,390—Kevin Willis, Atlanta, 1984-85—1994-95; Miami, 1994-95—1995-96; Golden State, 1995-96; Houston, 1996-97—1997-98; Toronto, 1998-99—2000-01; Denver, 2000-01; Houston, 2001-02; San Antonio, 2002-03—2003-04

Most consecutive games, career
1,192—A.C. Green, L.A. Lakers, Phoenix, Dallas, Miami, November 19, 1986—April 18, 2001
906—Randy Smith, Buffalo, San Diego, Cleveland, New York, San Diego, February 18, 1972—March 13, 1983
844—John Kerr, Syracuse, Philadelphia, Baltimore, October 31, 1954—November 4, 1965

Most games, season
88—Walt Bellamy, New York, Detroit, 1968-69
87—Tom Henderson, Atlanta, Washington, 1976-77
86—McCoy McLemore, Cleveland, Milwaukee, 1970-71
Garfield Heard, Buffalo, Phoenix, 1975-76

MINUTES

Minutes have been compiled since 1951-52

Most seasons leading league, minutes
8—Wilt Chamberlain, Philadelphia, 1959-60—1961-62; San Francisco, 1962-63—1963-64; Philadelphia,1965-66—1967-68

4—Elvin Hayes, San Diego, 1968-69—1969-70; Capital, 1973-74; Washington, 1976-77
3—Michael Jordan, Chicago, 1986-87—1988-89
Michael Finley, Dallas, 1997-98, 1999-00—2000-01

Most consecutive seasons leading league, minutes
5—Wilt Chamberlain, Philadelphia, 1959-60—1961-62; San Francisco, 1962-63—1963-64
3—Wilt Chamberlain, Philadelphia, 1965-66—1967-68
Michael Jordan, Chicago, 1986-87—1988-89

Most minutes, career
57,446—Kareem Abdul-Jabbar, Milwaukee, 1969-70—1974-75; L.A. Lakers, 1975-76—1988-89
54,852—Karl Malone, Utah, 1985-86—2002-03; L.A. Lakers, 2003-04
50,000—Elvin Hayes, San Diego, 1968-69—1970-71; Houston, 1971-72; Baltimore, 1972-73; Capital, 1973-74; Washington, 1974-75—1980-81; Houston, 1981-82—1983-84
47,859—Wilt Chamberlain, Philadelphia, 1959-60—1961-62; San Francisco, 1962-63—1964-65; Philadelphia,1964-65—1967-68; Los Angeles, 1968-69—1972-73
47,764—John Stockton, Utah, 1984-85—2002-03

Highest average, minutes per game, career
(minimum: 400 games)
45.8—Wilt Chamberlain, Philadelphia, 1959-60—1961-62; San Francisco, 1962-63—1964-65; Philadelphia, 1964-65—1967-68; Los Angeles, 1968-69—1972-73 (47,859/1,045)
42.3—Bill Russell, Boston, 1956-57—1968-69 (40,726/963)
42.2—Oscar Robertson, Cincinnati, 1960-61—1969-70; Milwaukee, 1970-71—1973-74 (43,866/1,040)

Most minutes, season
3,882—Wilt Chamberlain, Philadelphia, 1961-62
3,836—Wilt Chamberlain, Philadelphia, 1967-68
3,806—Wilt Chamberlain, San Francisco, 1962-63
3,773—Wilt Chamberlain, Philadelphia, 1960-61
3,737—Wilt Chamberlain, Philadelphia, 1965-66

Highest average, minutes per game, season
48.5—Wilt Chamberlain, Philadelphia, 1961-62 (3,882/80)
47.8—Wilt Chamberlain, Philadelphia, 1960-61 (3,773/79)
47.6—Wilt Chamberlain, San Francisco, 1962-63 (3,806/80)
47.3—Wilt Chamberlain, Philadelphia, 1965-66 (3,737/79)
46.8—Wilt Chamberlain, Philadelphia, 1967-68 (3,836/82)

Most minutes, rookie, season
3,695—Elvin Hayes, San Diego, 1968-69
3,534—Kareem Abdul-Jabbar, Milwaukee, 1969-70
3,344—Walt Bellamy, Chicago, 1961-62

Most minutes, game
69—Dale Ellis, Seattle at Milwaukee, November 9, 1989 (5 ot)
68—Xavier McDaniel, Seattle at Milwaukee, November 9, 1989 (5 ot)
64—Norm Nixon, Los Angeles at Cleveland, January 29, 1980 (4 ot)
Eric Floyd, Golden State vs. New Jersey, February 1, 1987 (4 ot)

COMPLETE GAMES

Most complete games, season
79—Wilt Chamberlain, Philadelphia, 1961-62

Most consecutive complete games, season
47—Wilt Chamberlain, Philadelphia, January 5—March 14, 1962

SCORING

Most seasons leading league
10—Michael Jordan, Chicago, 1986-87—1992-93, 1995-96—1997-98
7—Wilt Chamberlain, Philadelphia, 1959-60—1961-62; San Francisco, 1962-63—1963-64; San Francisco, Philadelphia, 1964-65; Philadelphia, 1965-66
4—George Gervin, San Antonio, 1977-78—1979-80, 1981-82

Most consecutive seasons leading league
7—Wilt Chamberlain, Philadelphia, 1959-60—1961-62; San Francisco, 1962-63—1963-64; San Francisco, Philadelphia, 1964-65; Philadelphia, 1965-66
Michael Jordan, Chicago, 1986-87—1992-93
3—George Mikan, Minneapolis, 1948-49—1950-51
Neil Johnston, Philadelphia, 1952-53—1954-55
Bob McAdoo, Buffalo, 1973-74—1975-76
George Gervin, San Antonio, 1977-78—1979-80
Michael Jordan, Chicago, 1995-96—1997-98

Most points, lifetime
38,387—Kareem Abdul-Jabbar, Milwaukee, 1969-70—1974-75; L.A. Lakers, 1975-76—1988-89
36,928—Karl Malone, Utah, 1985-86—2002-03; L.A. Lakers, 2003-04
32,292—Michael Jordan, Chicago, 1984-85—1992-93, 1994-95—1997-98; Washington, 2001-02—2002-03
31,419—Wilt Chamberlain, Philadelphia, 1959-60—1961-62; San Francisco, 1962-63—1964-65; Philadelphia, 1964-65—1967-68; Los Angeles, 1968-69—1972-73
27,409—Moses Malone, Buffalo, 1976-77; Houston, 1976-77—1981-82; Philadelphia, 1982-83—1985-86; Washington, 1986-87—1987-88; Atlanta, 1988-89—1990-91; Milwaukee, 1991-92—1992-93; Philadelphia, 1993-94; San Antonio, 1994-95

Highest average, points per game, career
(minimum: 400 games)
30.12—Michael Jordan, Chicago, 1984-85—1992-93, 1994-95—1997-98; Washington, 2001-02—2002-03 (32,292/1,072)
30.07—Wilt Chamberlain, Philadelphia, 1959-60—1961-62; San Francisco, 1962-63—1964-65; Philadelphia, 1964-65—1967-68; Los Angeles, 1968-69—1972-73 (31,419/1,045)
27.4—Elgin Baylor, Minneapolis, 1958-59—1959-60; Los Angeles, 1960-61—1971-72 (23,149/846)
27.1—Shaquille O'Neal, Orlando, 1992-93—1995-96; L.A. Lakers, 1996-97—2003-04 (21,914/809)
27.0—Jerry West, Los Angeles, 1960-61—1973-74 (25,192/932)

Most points, season
4,029—Wilt Chamberlain, Philadelphia, 1961-62
3,586—Wilt Chamberlain, San Francisco, 1962-63
3,041—Michael Jordan, Chicago, 1986-87
3,033—Wilt Chamberlain, Philadelphia, 1960-61
2,948—Wilt Chamberlain, San Francisco, 1963-64

Highest average, points per game, season
(minimum: 70 games)
50.4—Wilt Chamberlain, Philadelphia, 1961-62 (4,029/80)
44.8—Wilt Chamberlain, San Francisco, 1962-63 (3,586/80)
38.4—Wilt Chamberlain, Philadelphia, 1960-61 (3,033/79)
37.6—Wilt Chamberlain, Philadelphia, 1959-60 (2,707/72)
37.1—Michael Jordan, Chicago, 1986-87 (3,041/82)

Most points, rookie, season
2,707—Wilt Chamberlain, Philadelphia, 1959-60
2,495—Walt Bellamy, Chicago, 1961-62

2,361—Kareem Abdul-Jabbar, Milwaukee, 1969-70

Highest average, points per game, rookie, season
37.6—Wilt Chamberlain, Philadelphia, 1959-60 (2,707/72)
31.6—Walt Bellamy, Chicago, 1961-62 (2,495/79)
30.5—Oscar Robertson, Cincinnati, 1960-61 (2,165/71)

Most seasons, 2,000 or more points
12—Karl Malone, Utah, 1987-88—1997-98, 1999-00
11—Michael Jordan, Chicago, 1984-85, 1986-87—1992-93, 1995-96—1997-98
9—Kareem Abdul-Jabbar, Milwaukee, 1969-70—1973-74; Los Angeles, 1975-76—1976-77, 1979-80—1980-81

Most consecutive seasons, 2,000 or more points
11—Karl Malone, Utah, 1987-88—1997-98
8—Alex English, Denver, 1981-82—1988-89
7—Wilt Chamberlain, Philadelphia, 1959-60—1961-62; San Francisco, 1962-63—1963-64; San Francisco, Philadelphia, 1964-65; Philadelphia, 1965-66
Oscar Robertson, Cincinnati, 1960-61—1966-67
Dominique Wilkins, Atlanta, 1984-85—1990-91
Michael Jordan, Chicago, 1986-87—1992-93

Most seasons, 1,000 or more points
19—Kareem Abdul-Jabbar, Milwaukee, 1969-70—1974-75; L.A. Lakers, 1975-76—1987-88
18—Karl Malone, Utah, 1985-86—2002-03
16—John Havlicek, Boston, 1962-63—1977-78

Most consecutive seasons, 1,000 or more points
19—Kareem Abdul-Jabbar, Milwaukee, 1969-70—1974-75; L.A. Lakers, 1975-76—1987-88
18—Karl Malone, Utah, 1985-86—2002-03 (current)
16—John Havlicek, Boston, 1962-63—1977-78

Most points, game
100—Wilt Chamberlain, Philadelphia vs. New York, at Hershey, Pa., March 2, 1962
78—Wilt Chamberlain, Philadelphia vs. Los Angeles, December 8, 1961 (3 ot)
73—Wilt Chamberlain, Philadelphia vs. Chicago, January 13, 1962
Wilt Chamberlain, San Francisco at New York, November 16, 1962
David Thompson, Denver at Detroit, April 9, 1978
72—Wilt Chamberlain, San Francisco at Los Angeles, November 3, 1962
71—Elgin Baylor, Los Angeles at New York, November 15, 1960
David Robinson, San Antonio at L.A. Clippers, April 24, 1994

Most points, rookie, game
58—Wilt Chamberlain, Philadelphia vs. Detroit, at Bethlehem, Pa., January 25, 1960
Wilt Chamberlain, Philadelphia at New York, February 21, 1960
57—Rick Barry, San Francisco at New York, December 14, 1965
56—Earl Monroe, Baltimore vs. Los Angeles, February 13, 1968 (ot)

Most games, 50 or more points, career
118—Wilt Chamberlain, Philadelphia, 1959-60—1961-62; San Francisco, 1962-63—1964-65; Philadelphia, 1964-65—1967-68; Los Angeles, 1968-69—1972-73
31—Michael Jordan, Chicago, 1984-85—1992-93, 1994-95—1997-98; Washington, 2001-02—2002-03
17—Elgin Baylor, Minneapolis, 1958-59—1959-60; Los Angeles, 1960-61—1971-72
14—Rick Barry, San Francisco, 1965-66—1966-67; Golden State, 1972-73—1977-78; Houston, 1978-79—1979-80

Most games, 50 or more points, season
45—Wilt Chamberlain, Philadelphia, 1961-62
30—Wilt Chamberlain, San Francisco, 1962-63
9—Wilt Chamberlain, San Francisco, 1963-64
Wilt Chamberlain, San Francisco, Philadelphia, 1964-65

Most consecutive games, 50 or more points
7—Wilt Chamberlain, Philadelphia, December 16—December 29, 1961

6—Wilt Chamberlain, Philadelphia, January 11—January 19, 1962
5—Wilt Chamberlain, Philadelphia, December 8—December 13, 1961
Wilt Chamberlain, Philadelphia, February 25—March 4, 1962

Most games, 40 or more points, career
271—Wilt Chamberlain, Philadelphia, 1959-60—1961-62; San Francisco, 1962-63—1964-65; Philadelphia, 1964-65—1967-68; Los Angeles, 1968-69—1972-73
173—Michael Jordan, Chicago, 1984-85—1992-93, 1994-95—1997-98; Washington, 2001-02—2002-03
88—Elgin Baylor, Minneapolis, 1958-59—1959-60; Los Angeles, 1960-61—1971-72

Most games, 40 or more points, season
63—Wilt Chamberlain, Philadelphia, 1961-62
52—Wilt Chamberlain, San Francisco, 1962-63
37—Michael Jordan, Chicago, 1986-87

Most consecutive games, 40 or more points
14—Wilt Chamberlain, Philadelphia, December 8—December 30, 1961
Wilt Chamberlain, Philadelphia, January 11—February 1, 1962
10—Wilt Chamberlain, San Francisco, November 9—November 25, 1962
9—Michael Jordan, Chicago, November 28—December 12, 1986
Kobe Bryant, L.A. Lakers, February 2-23, 2003

Most consecutive games, 30 or more points
65—Wilt Chamberlain, Philadelphia, November 4, 1961—February 22, 1962
31—Wilt Chamberlain, Philadelphia, San Francisco, February 25—December 8, 1962
25—Wilt Chamberlain, Philadelphia, November 11—December 27, 1960

Most consecutive games, 20 or more points
126—Wilt Chamberlain, Philadelphia, San Francisco, October 19, 1961—January 19, 1963
92—Wilt Chamberlain, San Francisco, February 26, 1963—March 18, 1964
79—Oscar Robertson, Cincinnati, October 22, 1963—October 20, 1964

Most consecutive games, 10 or more points
866—Michael Jordan, Chicago, Washington, March 25, 1986—December 26, 2001
787—Kareem Abdul-Jabbar, L.A. Lakers, December 4, 1977—December 2, 1987
575—Karl Malone, Utah, December 18, 1991—March 26, 1999

Most points, one half
59—Wilt Chamberlain, Philadelphia vs. New York, at Hershey, Pa., March 2, 1962 (2nd Half)
53—David Thompson, Denver at Detroit, April 9, 1978 (1st Half)
George Gervin, San Antonio at New Orleans, April 9, 1978 (1st Half)
47—David Robinson, San Antonio at L.A. Clippers, April 24, 1994 (2nd Half)

Most points, one quarter
33—George Gervin, San Antonio at New Orleans, April 9, 1978 (2nd Qtr.)
32—David Thompson, Denver at Detroit, April 9, 1978 (1st Qtr.)
31—Wilt Chamberlain, Philadelphia vs. New York, at Hershey, Pa., March 2, 1962 (4th Qtr.)

Most points, overtime period
14—Butch Carter, Indiana vs. Boston, March 20, 1984
13—Earl Monroe, Baltimore vs. Detroit, February 6, 1970
Joe Caldwell, Atlanta vs. Cincinnati, at Memphis, February 18, 1970
Steve Smith, Atlanta vs. Washington, January 24, 1997
Darrell Armstrong, Orlando at Philadelphia, February 2, 2001
Paul Pierce, Boston at New Jersey, December 1, 2001

FIELD-GOAL PERCENTAGE

Most seasons, leading league
9—Wilt Chamberlain, Philadelphia, 1960-61; San Francisco, 1962-63; San Francisco, Philadelphia, 1964-65; Philadelphia, 1965-66—1967-68; Los Angeles, 1968-69, 1971-72—1972-73

7—Shaquille O'Neal, Orlando, 1993-94; L.A. Lakers, 1997-98—2001-02, 2003-04
4—Artis Gilmore, Chicago, 1980-81—1981-82; San Antonio, 1982-83—1983-84

Most consecutive seasons leading league
5—Wilt Chamberlain, San Francisco, Philadelphia, 1964-65; Philadelphia, 1965-66—1967-68; Los Angeles, 1968-69
Shaquille O'Neal, L.A. Lakers, 1997-98—2001-02
4—Artis Gilmore, Chicago, 1980-81—1981-82; San Antonio, 1982-83—1983-84
2—By many

Highest field-goal percentage, career
(minimum: 2,000 field goals)
.599—Artis Gilmore, Chicago, 1976-77—1981-82; San Antonio, 1982-83—1986-87; Chicago, 1987-88; Boston, 1987-88 (5,732/9,570)
.580—Mark West, Dallas, 1983-84; Milwaukee, 1984-85; Cleveland, 1984-85—1987-88; Phoenix, 1987-88—1993-94; Detroit, 1994-95—1995-96; Cleveland, 1996-97; Indiana, 1997-98; Atlanta, 1998-99; Phoenix, 1999-00 (2,528/4,356)
.577—Shaquille O'Neal, Orlando, 1992-93—1995-96; L.A. Lakers, 1996-97—2003-04 (8,670/15,020)
.5722—Steve Johnson, Kansas City, 1981-82—1983-84; Chicago, 1983-84—1984-85; San Antonio, 1985-86; Portland, 1986-87—1988-89; Minnesota, 1989-90; Seattle, 1989-90; Golden State, 1990-91 (2,841/4,965)
.5720—Darryl Dawkins, Philadelphia, 1975-76—1981-82; New Jersey, 1982-83—1986-87; Utah, 1987-88; Detroit, 1987-88—1988-89 (3,477/6,079)

Highest field-goal percentage, season (qualifiers)
.727—Wilt Chamberlain, Los Angeles, 1972-73 (426/586)
.683—Wilt Chamberlain, Philadelphia, 1966-67 (785/1,150)
.670—Artis Gilmore, Chicago, 1980-81 (547/816)
.652—Artis Gilmore, Chicago, 1981-82 (546/837)
.649—Wilt Chamberlain, Los Angeles, 1971-72 (496/764)

Highest field-goal percentage, rookie, season (qualifiers)
.613—Steve Johnson, Kansas City, 1981-82 (395/644)
.600—Otis Thorpe, Kansas City, 1984-85 (411/685)
.582—Buck Williams, New Jersey, 1981-82 (513/881)

Highest field-goal percentage, game
(minimum: 15 field goals)
1.000—Wilt Chamberlain, Philadelphia vs. Los Angeles, January 20, 1967 (15/15)
Wilt Chamberlain, Philadelphia vs. Baltimore, at Pittsburgh, February 24, 1967 (18/18)
Wilt Chamberlain, Philadelphia at Baltimore, March 19, 1967 (16/16)
.947—Wilt Chamberlain, San Francisco vs. New York, at Boston, November 27, 1963 (18/19)
.944—George Gervin, San Antonio vs. Chicago, February 18, 1978 (17/18)

Most field goals, no misses, game
18—Wilt Chamberlain, Philadelphia vs. Baltimore, at Pittsburgh, February 24, 1967
16—Wilt Chamberlain, Philadelphia at Baltimore, March 19, 1967
15—Wilt Chamberlain, Philadelphia vs. Los Angeles, January 20, 1967
14—Bailey Howell, Baltimore vs. San Francisco, January 3, 1965
Wilt Chamberlain, Los Angeles vs. Detroit, March 11, 1969
Billy McKinney, Kansas City vs. Boston, at St. Louis, December 27, 1978
Gary Payton, Seattle at Cleveland, January 4, 1995

Most field-goal attempts, none made, game
17—Tim Hardaway, Golden State at Minnesota, December 27, 1991 (ot)
15—Howie Dallmar, Philadelphia vs. New York, November 27, 1947
Howie Dallmar, Philadelphia vs. Washington, November 25, 1948
Dick Ricketts, Rochester vs. St. Louis, March 7, 1956

Corky Devlin, Ft. Wayne vs. Minneapolis, at Rochester, December 25, 1956
Charlie Tyra, New York at Philadelphia, November 7, 1957
Frank Ramsey, Boston vs. Cincinnati, at Philadelphia, December 8, 1960
Bob Love, Chicago vs. Kansas City, March 12, 1976
Ray Williams, New Jersey vs. Indiana, December 28, 1981
Rodney McCray, Sacramento at Utah, November 9,1988
14—Ed Leede, Boston at Washington, December 13, 1950
Jack George, Philadelphia at Syracuse, November 1, 1953
Sihugo Green, St. Louis vs. Boston, at Philadelphia, December 14, 1961
Bailey Howell, Detroit vs. St. Louis, January 4, 1963
Bill Russell, Boston vs. Philadelphia, at Syracuse, January 23, 1965
Adrian Smith, Cincinnati at New York, December 18, 1965
Connie Dierking, Cincinnati at San Francisco, November 1, 1969
Junior Bridgeman, Milwaukee at Washington, January 24, 1984 (2 OT)
Dino Radja, Boston at San Antonio, December 26, 1993

FIELD GOALS

Most seasons leading league
10—Michael Jordan, Chicago, 1986-87—1992-93, 1995-96—1997-98
7—Wilt Chamberlain, Philadelphia, 1959-60—1961-62; San Francisco, 1962-63—1963-64; San Francisco, Philadelphia, 1964-65; Philadelphia, 1965-66
5—Kareem Abdul-Jabbar, Milwaukee, 1969-70—1971-72, 1973-74; Los Angeles, 1976-77
Shaquille O'Neal, Orlando, 1993-94—1994-95; L.A. Lakers, 1998-99—2000-01

Most consecutive seasons leading league
7—Wilt Chamberlain, Philadelphia, 1959-60—1961-62; San Francisco, 1962-63—1963-64; San Francisco, Philadelphia, 1964-65; Philadelphia, 1965-66
Michael Jordan, Chicago, 1986-87—1992-93
3—George Mikan, Minneapolis, 1948-49—1950-51
Kareem Abdul-Jabbar, Milwaukee, 1969-70—1971-72
George Gervin, San Antonio, 1977-78—1979-80
Michael Jordan, Chicago, 1995-96—1997-98
Shaquille O'Neal, L.A. Lakers, 1998-99—2000-01

Most field goals, career
15,837—Kareem Abdul-Jabbar, Milwaukee, 1969-70—1974-75; L.A. Lakers, 1975-76—1988-89
13,528—Karl Malone, Utah, 1985-86—2002-03; L.A. Lakers, 2003-04
12,681—Wilt Chamberlain, Philadelphia, 1959-60—1961-62; San Francisco, 1962-63—1964-65; Philadelphia, 1964-65—1967-68; Los Angeles, 1968-69—1972-73

Most field goals, season
1,597—Wilt Chamberlain, Philadelphia, 1961-62
1,463—Wilt Chamberlain, San Francisco, 1962-63
1,251—Wilt Chamberlain, Philadelphia, 1960-61

Most consecutive field goals, no misses, season
35—Wilt Chamberlain, Philadelphia, February 17—February 28, 1967

Most field goals, game
36—Wilt Chamberlain, Philadelphia vs. New York, at Hershey, Pa., March 2, 1962
31—Wilt Chamberlain, Philadelphia vs. Los Angeles, December 8, 1961 (3 ot)
30—Wilt Chamberlain, Philadelphia at Chicago, December 16, 1967
Rick Barry, Golden State vs. Portland, March 26, 1974

Most field goals, one half
22—Wilt Chamberlain, Philadelphia vs. New York, at Hershey, Pa., March 2, 1962 (2nd Half)
21—Rick Barry, Golden State vs. Portland, March 26, 1974 (2nd Half)

20—David Thompson, Denver at Detroit, April 9, 1978 (1st Half)
Most field goals, one quarter
13—David Thompson, Denver at Detroit, April 9, 1978 (1st Qtr.)
12—Cliff Hagan, St. Louis at New York, February 4, 1958 (4th Qtr.)
Wilt Chamberlain, Philadelphia vs. New York, at Hershey, Pa., March 2, 1962 (4th Qtr.)
George Gervin, San Antonio at New Orleans, April 9, 1978 (2nd Qtr.)
Jeff Malone, Washington at Phoenix, February 27, 1988 (3rd Qtr.)

FIELD-GOAL ATTEMPTS

Most seasons leading league
9—Michael Jordan, Chicago, 1986-87—1987-88, 1989-90—1992-93, 1995-96—1997-98
7—Wilt Chamberlain, Philadelphia, 1959-60—1961-62; San Francisco, 1962-63—1963-64; San Francisco, Philadelphia, 1964-65; Philadelphia, 1965-66
3—Joe Fulks, Philadelphia, 1946-47—1948-49
George Mikan, Minneapolis, 1949-50—1951-52
Elvin Hayes, San Diego, 1968-69—1970-71
George Gervin, San Antonio, 1978-79—1979-80, 1981-82
Allen Iverson, Philadelphia, 1998-99—1999-00, 2002-03

Most consecutive seasons leading league
7—Wilt Chamberlain, Philadelphia, 1959-60—1961-62; San Francisco, 1962-63—1963-64; San Francisco, Philadelphia, 1964-65; Philadelphia, 1965-66
4—Michael Jordan, Chicago, 1989-90—1992-93
3—Joe Fulks, Philadelphia, 1946-47—1948-49
George Mikan, Minneapolis, 1949-50—1951-52
Elvin Hayes, San Diego, 1968-69—1970-71
Michael Jordan, Chicago, 1995-96—1997-98

Most field-goal attempts, career
28,307—Kareem Abdul-Jabbar, Milwaukee, 1969-70—1974-75; L.A. Lakers, 1975-76—1988-09
26,210—Karl Malone, Utah, 1985-86—2002-03; L.A. Lakers, 2003-04
24,537—Michael Jordan, Chicago, 1984-85—1997-98; Washington, 2001-02—2002-03

Most field-goal attempts, season
3,159—Wilt Chamberlain, Philadelphia, 1961-62
2,770—Wilt Chamberlain, San Francisco, 1962-63
2,457—Wilt Chamberlain, Philadelphia, 1960-61

Most field-goal attempts, game
63—Wilt Chamberlain, Philadelphia vs. New York, at Hershey, Pa., March 2, 1962
62—Wilt Chamberlain, Philadelphia vs. Los Angeles, December 8, 1961 (3 ot)
60—Wilt Chamberlain, San Francisco at Cincinnati, October 28, 1962 (ot)

Most field-goal attempts, one half
37—Wilt Chamberlain, Philadelphia vs. New York, at Hershey, Pa., March 2, 1962 (2nd Half)
34—George Gervin, San Antonio at New Orleans, April 9, 1978 (1st Half)
32—Wilt Chamberlain, Philadelphia vs. Chicago, at Boston, January 24, 1962

Most field-goal attempts, one quarter
21—Wilt Chamberlain, Philadelphia vs. New York, at Hershey, Pa., March 2, 1962 (4th Qtr.)
20—Wilt Chamberlain, Philadelphia vs. Chicago, at Boston, January 24, 1962
George Gervin, San Antonio at New Orleans, April 9, 1978 (2nd Qtr.)
19—Bob Pettit, St. Louis at Philadelphia, December 6, 1961

3-POINT FIELD-GOAL PERCENTAGE

Most seasons leading league
2—Craig Hodges, Milwaukee, 1985-86; Milwaukee, Phoenix, 1987-88

– 215 –

Steve Kerr, Cleveland, 1989-90; Chicago, 1994-95
1—by many

Highest 3-point field-goal percentage, career
(minimum: 250 3-point FGs)
.454—Steve Kerr, Phoenix, 1988-89; Cleveland, 1989-90—
      1992-93, Orlando, 1992-93; Chicago, 1993-94—
      1997-98; San Antonio, 1998-99—2002-03
      (726/1,599)
.441—Hubert Davis, New York, 1992-93—1995-96; Toronto,
      1996-97; Dallas, 1997-98—2000-01; Washington,
      2001-02; Detroit, 2002-03—2003-04; New Jersey,
      2003-04 (728/1,651)
.437—Drazen Petrovic, Portland, 1989-90—1990-91; New
      Jersey, 1990-91—1992-93 (255/583)

Highest 3-point field-goal percentage, season (qualifiers)
.524—Steve Kerr, Chicago, 1994-95 (89/170)
.5224—Tim Legler, Washington, 1995-96 (128/245)
.5217—Jon Sundvold, Miami, 1988-89 (48/92)

Most 3-point field goals, no misses, game
9—Latrell Sprewell, New York vs. L.A. Clippers, February 4, 2003
8—Jeff Hornacek, Utah vs. Seattle, November 23, 1994
   Sam Perkins, Seattle vs. Toronto, January 15, 1997
   Steve Smith, San Antonio at Portland, November 3, 2001
7—Terry Porter, Portland at Golden State, November 14, 1992
   Sam Perkins, Seattle vs. Denver, November 9, 1993
   Sasha Danilovic, Miami at New York, December 3, 1996
   Mitch Richmond, Sacramento at Boston, February 26, 1997

Most three-point field-goal attempts, none made, game
11—Antoine Walker, Boston at Philadelphia, December 17, 2001
10—George McCloud, Dallas at Toronto, March 10, 1996
    Antoine Walker, Boston at Cleveland, December 21, 2002
    Baron Davis, New Orleans vs. Milwaukee, December 8, 2003
9—By many

3-POINT FIELD GOALS

Most seasons leading league
2—Darrell Griffith, Utah, 1983-84—1984-85
   Larry Bird, Boston, 1985-86—1986-87
   Michael Adams, Denver, 1988-89—1989-90
   Vernon Maxwell, Houston, 1990-91—1991-92
   Dan Majerle, Phoenix, 1992-93—1993-94
   Reggie Miller, Indiana, 1992-93, 1996-97
   Ray Allen, Milwaukee, 2001-02; Milwaukee-Seattle, 2002-03
1—by many

Most 3-point field goals, career
2,464—Reggie Miller, Indiana, 1987-88—2003-04
1,719—Dale Ellis, Dallas, 1983-84—1985-86; Seattle, 1986-
      87—1990-91; Milwaukee, 1990-91—1991-92; San
      Antonio, 1992-93—1993-94; Denver, 1994-95—
      1996-97; Seattle, 1997-98—1998-99; Milwaukee,
      1999-00; Charlotte, 1999-00
1,559—Glen Rice, Miami, 1989-90—1994-95; Charlotte,
      1995-96—1997-98; L.A. Lakers, 1998-99—1999-
      00; New York, 2000-01; Houston, 2001-02—2002-
      03; L.A. Clippers, 2003-04

Most 3-point field goals, season
267—Dennis Scott, Orlando, 1995-96
257—George McCloud, Dallas, 1995-96
240—Peja Stojakovic, Sacramento, 2003-04

Most consecutive 3-point field goals, no misses, season
13—Brent Price, Washington, January 15—January 19, 1996
    Terry Mills, Detroit, December 4—December 7, 1996
11—Scott Wedman, Boston, December 21, 1984—March 31, 1985
    Jeff Hornacek, Utah, December 30, 1994—January 11, 1995

Most 3-point field goals, game
12—Kobe Bryant, L.A. Lakers vs. Seattle, January 7, 2003
11—Dennis Scott, Orlando vs. Atlanta, April 18, 1996
10—Brian Shaw, Miami at Milwaukee, April 8, 1993
    Joe Dumars, Detroit vs. Minnesota, November 8, 1994
    George McCloud, Dallas vs. Phoenix, December 16, 1995 (ot)

Ray Allen, Milwaukee vs. Charlotte, April 14, 2002

Most consecutive games, 3-point field goals made
89—Dana Barros, Philadelphia, Boston, December 23,
    1994—January 10, 1996 (58 games in 1994-95; 31
    games in 1995-96)
79—Michael Adams, Denver, January 28, 1988—January 23,
    1989 (43 games in 1987-88; 36 games in 1988-89)
78—Dennis Scott, Orlando, April 17, 1995—April 4, 1996 (4
    games in 1994-95; 74 games in 1995-96)

Most 3-point field goals, rookie, season
158—Kerry Kittles, New Jersey, 1996-97
155—Allen Iverson, Philadelphia, 1996-97
154—Matt Maloney, Houston, 1996-97

Most 3-point field goals made, one half
8—Tim Thomas, Milwaukee at Portland, January 5, 2001
   Michael Redd, Milwaukee vs. Houston, February 20, 2002
   Ray Allen, Milwaukee vs. Charlotte, April 14, 2002
   Kobe Bryant, L.A. Lakers vs. Washington, March 28, 2003
   Tracy McGrady, Orlando at Cleveland, January 26, 2004
7—John Roche, Denver vs. Seattle, January 9, 1982
   Michael Adams, Denver vs. Milwaukee, January 21, 1989
   John Starks, New York vs. Miami, November 22, 1993
   Allan Houston, Detroit at Chicago, February 17, 1995
   Joe Dumars, Detroit at Orlando, April 5, 1995
   George McCloud, Dallas vs. Phoenix, December 16, 1995
   George McCloud, Dallas vs. Philadelphia, February 27, 1996
   Dennis Scott, Orlando vs. Atlanta, April 18, 1996
   Steve Smith, Atlanta vs. Seattle, March 14, 1997
   Henry James, Atlanta vs. New Jersey, April 15, 1997
   Lindsey Hunter, Detroit at Chicago, February 15, 1998
   Glen Rice, L.A. Lakers vs. Portland, May 5, 1999

Most 3-point field goals made, one quarter
8—Michael Redd, Milwaukee vs. Houston, February 20, 2002
7—John Roche, Denver vs. Seattle, January 9, 1982
   Steve Smith, Atlanta vs. Seattle, March 14, 1997
   Henry James, Atlanta vs. New Jersey, April 15, 1997

3-POINT FIELD-GOAL ATTEMPTS

Most seasons leading league
4—Michael Adams, Denver, 1987-88—1990-91
3—Antoine Walker, Boston, 2000-01—2002-03
2—Darrell Griffith, Utah, 1983-84—1984-85
   Dan Majerle, Phoenix, 1992-93—1993-94

Most 3-point field-goal attempts, career
6,188—Reggie Miller, Indiana, 1987-88—2003-04
4,345—Tim Hardaway, Golden State, 1989-90—1995-96;
      Miami, 1995-96—2000-01; Dallas, 2001-02; Denver,
      2001-02; Indiana, 2002-03
4,266—Dale Ellis, Dallas, 1983-84—1985-86; Seattle, 1986-
      87—1990-91; Milwaukee, 1990-91—1991-92; San
      Antonio,
      1992-93—1993-94; Denver, 1994-95—1996-97;
      Seattle, 1997-98—1998-99; Milwaukee, 1999-00;
      Charlotte, 1999-00

Most 3-point field-goal attempts, season
678—George McCloud, Dallas, 1995-96
645—Antoine Walker, Boston, 2001-02
628—Dennis Scott, Orlando, 1995-96

Most 3-point field-goal attempts, game
20—Michael Adams, Denver at L.A. Clippers, April 12, 1991
    George McCloud, Dallas vs. New Jersey, March 5, 1996
19—Dennis Scott, Orlando vs. Milwaukee, April 13, 1993
18—Joe Dumars, Detroit vs. Minnesota, November 8, 1994
    Dee Brown, Toronto at Milwaukee, April 28, 1999
    Kobe Bryant, L.A. Lakers vs. Seattle, January 7, 2003

Most 3-point field-goal attempts, one half
13—Michael Adams, Denver at L.A. Clippers, April 12, 1991
12—Manute Bol, Philadelphia at Phoenix, March 3, 1993
    Dennis Scott, Orlando vs. Milwaukee, April 13, 1993
    Allan Houston, Detroit at Denver, March 10, 1995
    Vernon Maxwell, Philadelphia vs. New Jersey, April 8, 1996

Jason Williams, Sacramento vs. Minnesota, April 23, 1999
Michael Redd, Milwaukee vs. Houston, February 20, 2002
Tracy McGrady, Orlando at Atlanta, February 2, 2003

FREE THROW PERCENTAGE

Most seasons leading league
7—Bill Sharman, Boston, 1952-53—1956-57, 1958-59, 1960-61
6—Rick Barry, Golden State, 1972-73, 1974-75—1975-76,
    1977-78; Houston, 1978-79—1979-80
4—Larry Bird, Boston, 1983-84, 1985-86—1986-87, 1989-90
    Reggie Miller, Indiana, 1990-91, 1998-99, 2000-01—2001-02

Most consecutive seasons leading league
5—Bill Sharman, Boston, 1952-53—1956-57
3—Rick Barry, Golden State, 1977-78; Houston, 1978-79—
    1979-80
2—Bob Feerick, Washington, 1947-48—1948-49
    Rick Barry, Golden State, 1974-75—1975-76
    Larry Bird, Boston, 1985-86—1986-87
    Mark Price, Cleveland, 1991-92—1992-93
    Reggie Miller, Indiana, 2000-01—2001-02

Highest free throw percentage, career
(minimum: 1,200 free throws made)
.904—Mark Price, Cleveland, 1986-87—1994-95;
    Washington, 1995-96; Golden State, 1996-97;
    Orlando, 1997-98 (2,135/2,362)
.900—Rick Barry, San Francisco, 1965-66—1966-67; Golden
    State, 1972-73—1977-78; Houston,
    1978-79—1979-80 (3,818/4,243)
.893—Steve Nash, Phoenix, 1996-97—1997-98; Dallas,
    1998-99—2003-04 (1,258/1,409)

Highest free throw percentage, season (qualifiers)
.958—Calvin Murphy, Houston, 1980-81 (206/215)
.956—Mahmoud Abdul-Rauf, Denver, 1993-94 (219/229)
.950—Jeff Hornacek, Utah, 1999-00 (171/180)
.948—Mark Price, Cleveland, 1992-93 (289/305)
.947—Mark Price, Cleveland, 1991-92 (270/285)

Highest free throw percentage, rookie, season (qualifiers)
.902—Ernie DiGregorio, Buffalo, 1973-74 (174/193)
.896—Chris Mullin, Golden State, 1985-86 (189/211)
.879—Winston Garland, Golden State, 1987-88 (138/157)

Most free throws made, no misses, game
23—Dominique Wilkins, Atlanta vs. Chicago, December 8, 1992
19—Bob Pettit, St. Louis at Boston, November 22, 1961
    Bill Cartwright, New York vs. Kansas City, November 17, 1981
    Adrian Dantley, Detroit vs. Chicago, December 15, 1987 (ot)
18—By many

Most free throw attempts, none made, game
11—Shaquille O'Neal, L.A. Lakers vs. Seattle, December 8, 2000
10—Wilt Chamberlain, Philadelphia vs. Detroit, November 4, 1960
 9—Wilt Chamberlain, Philadelphia at St. Louis, February 19, 1967
    Truck Robinson, Phoenix vs. Chicago, November 28, 1980

FREE THROWS MADE

Most seasons leading league
8—Karl Malone, Utah, 1988-89—1992-93, 1996-97—1998-99
5—Adrian Dantley, Indiana, Los Angeles, 1977-78; Utah,
    1980-81—1981-82; 1983-84, 1985-86
4—Oscar Robertson, Cincinnati, 1963-64—1964-65. 1967-
    68—1968-69

Most consecutive seasons leading league
5—Karl Malone, Utah, 1988-89—1992-93
3—George Mikan, Minneapolis, 1948-49—1950-51
    Neil Johnston, Philadelphia, 1952-53—1954-55
    David Robinson, San Antonio, 1993-94—1995-96
    Karl Malone, Utah, 1996-97—1998-99

Most free throws made, career
9,787—Karl Malone, Utah, 1985-86—2002-03; L.A. Lakers,
    2003-04
8,531—Moses Malone, Buffalo, 1976-77; Houston, 1976-

77—1981-82; Philadelphia, 1982-83—1985-86;
    Washington, 1986-87—1987-88; Atlanta, 1988-
    89—1990-91; Milwaukee, 1991-92—1992-93;
    Philadelphia, 1993-94; San Antonio, 1994-95
7,694—Oscar Robertson, Cincinnati, 1960-61—1969-70;
    Milwaukee, 1970-71—1973-74

Most free throws made, season
840—Jerry West, Los Angeles, 1965-66
835—Wilt Chamberlain, Philadelphia, 1961-62
833—Michael Jordan, Chicago, 1986-87

Most consecutive free throws made
97—Micheal Williams, Minnesota, March 24, 1993—
    November 9, 1993
81—Mahmoud Abdul-Rauf, Denver, March 15, 1993—
    November 16, 1993
78—Calvin Murphy, Houston, December 27, 1980—February
    28, 1981

Most free throws made, game
28—Wilt Chamberlain, Philadelphia vs. New York, at Hershey,
    Pa., March 2, 1962 Adrian Dantley, Utah vs.
    Houston, at Las Vegas, January 4, 1984
27—Adrian Dantley, Utah vs. Denver, November 25, 1983
26—Adrian Dantley, Utah vs. Dallas, October 31, 1980
    Michael Jordan, Chicago vs. New Jersey, February 26, 1987

Most free throws made, one half
20—Michael Jordan, Chicago at Miami, December 30, 1992
    (2nd Half)
19—Oscar Robertson, Cincinnati at Baltimore, December 27, 1964
18—Michael Jordan, Chicago vs. New York, January 21, 1990
    (2nd Half)
    Detlef Schrempf, Indiana at Golden State, December 8, 1992
    (2nd Half)
    Willie Burton, Philadelphia vs. Miami, December 13,
    1994 (2nd Half)

Most free throws made, one quarter
14—Rick Barry, San Francisco at New York, December 6,
    1966 (3rd Qtr.)
    Pete Maravich, Atlanta vs. Buffalo, November 28, 1973 (3rd Qtr.)
    Adrian Dantley, Detroit vs. Sacramento, December 10, 1986
    (4th Qtr.)
    Michael Jordan, Chicago at Utah, November 15, 1989 (4th Qtr.)
    Michael Jordan, Chicago at Miami, December 30, 1992 (4th Qtr.)
    Johnny Newman, Denver vs. Boston, February 10, 1998 (4th Qtr.)
13—Ken Sears, New York at Boston, November 3, 1956
    Oscar Robertson, Cincinnati at Baltimore, December 27, 1964
    John Drew, Atlanta vs. New Orleans, January 20, 1979 (3rd Qtr.)
    Willie Burton, Philadelphia vs. Miami, December 13,
    1994 (4th Qtr.)
    Mitch Richmond, Sacramento vs. Detroit, January 22, 1997
    (4th Qtr.)
    Michael Jordan, Chicago vs. New York, April 18, 1998 (2nd Qtr.)
    Shawn Kemp, Cleveland vs. New York, November 6,
    1999 (1st Qtr.)
    Speedy Claxton, Golden State vs. Denver, February 6, 2004

FREE THROW ATTEMPTS

Most seasons leading league
9—Wilt Chamberlain, Philadelphia, 1959-60—1961-62; San
    Francisco, 1962-63—1963-64; San Francisco,
    Philadelphia, 1964-65; Philadelphia, 1966-67—
    1967-68; Los Angeles, 1968-69
7—Karl Malone, Utah, 1988-89—1992-93, 1996-97—1997-98
6—Shaquille O'Neal, Orlando, 1994-95; L.A. Lakers, 1998-
    99—2001-02, 2003-04

Most consecutive seasons leading league
6—Wilt Chamberlain, Philadelphia, 1959-60—1961-62; San
    Francisco, 1962-63—1963-64; San Francisco,
    Philadelphia, 1964-65
5—Karl Malone, Utah, 1988-89—1992-93
4—Moses Malone, Houston, 1979-80—1981-82;
    Philadelphia, 1982-83
    Shaquille O'Neal, L.A. Lakers, 1998-99—2001-02

RECORDS   Regular season

Most free throw attempts, career
13,188—Karl Malone, Utah, 1985-86—2002-03; L.A. Lakers, 2003-04
11,862—Wilt Chamberlain, Philadelphia, 1959-60—1961-62; San Francisco, 1962-63—1964-65; Philadelphia, 1964-65—1967-68; Los Angeles, 1968-69—1972-73
11,090—Moses Malone, Buffalo, 1976-77; Houston, 1976-77—1981-82; Philadelphia, 1982-83—1985-86; Washington, 1986-87—1987-88; Atlanta, 1988-89—1990-91; Milwaukee, 1991-92—1992-93; Philadelphia, 1993-94; San Antonio, 1994-95

Most free throw attempts, season
1,363—Wilt Chamberlain, Philadelphia, 1961-62
1,113—Wilt Chamberlain, San Francisco, 1962-63
1,054—Wilt Chamberlain, Philadelphia, 1960-61

Most free throw attempts, game
34—Wilt Chamberlain, Philadelphia vs. St. Louis, February 22, 1962
32—Wilt Chamberlain, Philadelphia vs. New York, at Hershey, Pa., March 2, 1962
31—Wilt Chamberlain, Philadelphia vs. Los Angeles, December 8, 1961 (3 OT)
    Adrian Dantley, Utah vs. Denver, November 25, 1983
    Shaquille O'Neal, L.A. Lakers vs. Chicago, November 19, 1999

Most free throw attempts, one half
23—Michael Jordan, Chicago at Miami, December 30, 1992
22—Oscar Robertson, Cincinnati at Baltimore, December 27, 1964
    Tony Campbell, Minnesota vs. L.A. Clippers, March 8, 1990
    Willie Burton, Philadelphia vs. Miami, December 13, 1994
    Karl Malone, Utah at Dallas, November 4, 2000
21—Adrian Dantley, Utah vs. New Jersey, February 25, 1981

Most free throw attempts, one quarter
16—Oscar Robertson, Cincinnati at Baltimore, December 27, 1964
    Stan McKenzie, Phoenix at Philadelphia, February 15, 1970
    Pete Maravich, Atlanta at Chicago, January 2, 1973 (2nd Qtr.)
    Michael Jordan, Chicago at Miami, December 30, 1992
    Willie Burton, Philadelphia vs. Miami, December 13, 1994
    Johnny Newman, Denver vs. Boston, February 10, 1998
15—by many

REBOUNDS

Rebounds have been compiled since 1950-51

Most seasons leading league
11—Wilt Chamberlain, Philadelphia, 1959-60—1961-62; San Francisco, 1962-63; Philadelphia, 1965-66—1967-68; Los Angeles, 1968-69, 1970-71—1972-73
7—Dennis Rodman, Detroit, 1991-92—1992-93; San Antonio, 1993-94—1994-95; Chicago, 1995-96—1997-98
6—Moses Malone, Houston, 1978-79, 1980-81—1981-82; Philadelphia, 1982-83—1984-85

Most consecutive seasons leading league
7—Dennis Rodman, Detroit, 1991-92—1992-93; San Antonio, 1993-94—1994-95; Chicago, 1995-96—1997-98
5—Moses Malone, Houston, 1980-81—1981-82; Philadelphia, 1982-83—1984-85
4—Wilt Chamberlain, Philadelphia, 1959-60—1961-62; San Francisco, 1962-63
    Wilt Chamberlain, Philadelphia, 1965-66—1967-68; Los Angeles, 1968-69

Most rebounds, career
23,924—Wilt Chamberlain, Philadelphia, 1959-60—1961-62; San Francisco, 1962-63—1964-65; Philadelphia, 1964-65—1967-68; Los Angeles, 1968-69—1972-73
21,620—Bill Russell, Boston 1956-57—1968-69
17,440—Kareem Abdul-Jabbar, Milwaukee, 1969-70—1974-75; L.A. Lakers, 1975-76—1988-89
16,279—Elvin Hayes, San Diego, 1968-69—1970-71; Houston, 1971-72; Baltimore, 1972-73; Capital, 1973-74; Washington, 1974-75—1980-81; Houston, 1981-82—1983-84
16,212—Moses Malone, Buffalo, 1976-77; Houston, 1976-77—1981-82; Philadelphia, 1982-83—1985-86; Washington, 1986-87—1987-88; Atlanta, 1988-89—1990-91; Milwaukee, 1991-92—1992-93; Philadelphia, 1993-94; San Antonio, 1994-95

Highest average, rebounds per game, career
(minimum: 400 games)
22.9—Wilt Chamberlain, Philadelphia, 1959-60—1961-62; San Francisco, 1962-63—1964-65; Philadelphia, 1964-65—1967-68; Los Angeles, 1968-69—1972-73 (23,924/1,045)

22.5—Bill Russell, Boston 1956-57—1968-69 (21,620/963)
16.2—Bob Pettit, Milwaukee, 1954-55; St. Louis, 1955-56—1964-65 (12,849/792)
15.6—Jerry Lucas, Cincinnati, 1963-64—1969-70; San Francisco, 1969-70—1970-71; New York, 1971-72—1973-74 (12,942/829)
15.0—Nate Thurmond, San Francisco, 1963-64—1970-71; Golden State, 1971-72—1973-74; Chicago, 1974-75—1975-76; Cleveland, 1975-76—1976-77 (14,464/964)

Most rebounds, season
2,149—Wilt Chamberlain, Philadelphia, 1960-61
2,052—Wilt Chamberlain, Philadelphia, 1961-62
1,957—Wilt Chamberlain, Philadelphia, 1966-67
1,952—Wilt Chamberlain, Philadelphia, 1967-68
1,946—Wilt Chamberlain, San Francisco, 1962-63

Most rebounds, rookie, season
1,941—Wilt Chamberlain, Philadelphia, 1959-60
1,500—Walt Bellamy, Chicago, 1961-62
1,491—Wes Unseld, Baltimore, 1968-69

Most seasons, 1,000-or-more rebounds
13—Wilt Chamberlain, Philadelphia, 1959-60—1961-62; San Francisco, 1962-63—1963-64; San Francisco, Philadelphia, 1964-65; Philadelphia 1965-66—1967-68; Los Angeles, 1968-69, 1970-71—1972-73
12—Bill Russell, Boston, 1957-58—1968-69
9—Bob Pettit, St. Louis, 1955-56—1963-64
    Walt Bellamy, Chicago, 1961-62—1962-63; Baltimre, 1963-64—1964-65; Baltimore, New York, 1965-66; New York, 1966-67; New York, Detroit, 1968-69; Atlanta, 1970-71—1971-72
    Elvin Hayes, San Diego, 1968-69—1970-71; Houston, 1971-72; Baltimore, 1972-73; Capital, 1973-74; Washington, 1974-75, 1976-77—1977-78

Most consecutive seasons, 1,000-or-more rebounds
12—Bill Russell, Boston, 1957-58—1968-69
10—Wilt Chamberlain, Philadelphia, 1959-60—1961-62; San Francisco, 1962-63—1963-64; San Francisco, Philadelphia,1964-65; Philadelphia 1965-66—1967-68; Los Angeles, 1968-69
9—Bob Pettit, St. Louis, 1955-56—1963-64

Highest average, rebounds per game, season
27.2—Wilt Chamberlain, Philadelphia, 1960-61 (2,149/79)
27.0—Wilt Chamberlain, Philadelphia, 1959-60 (1,941/72)
25.7—Wilt Chamberlain, Philadelphia, 1961-62 (2,052/80)
24.7—Bill Russell, Boston, 1963-64 (1,930/78)
24.6—Wilt Chamberlain, Philadelphia, 1965-66 (1,943/79)

Most rebounds, game
55—Wilt Chamberlain, Philadelphia vs. Boston, November 24, 1960
51—Bill Russell, Boston vs. Syracuse, February 5, 1960
49—Bill Russell, Boston vs. Philadelphia, November 16, 1957
    Bill Russell, Boston vs. Detroit, at Providence, March 11, 1965
45—Wilt Chamberlain, Philadelphia vs. Syracuse, February 6, 1960
    Wilt Chamberlain, Philadelphia vs. Los Angeles, January 21, 1961

Most rebounds, rookie, game
45—Wilt Chamberlain, Philadelphia vs. Syracuse, February 6, 1960
43—Wilt Chamberlain, Philadelphia vs. New York, November 10, 1959
42—Wilt Chamberlain, Philadelphia vs. Boston, January 15, 1960
    Wilt Chamberlain, Philadelphia vs. Detroit, at Bethlehem, Pa., January 25, 1960

Most rebounds, one half
32—Bill Russell, Boston vs. Philadelphia, November 16, 1957
31—Wilt Chamberlain, Philadelphia vs. Boston, November 24, 1960
28—Wilt Chamberlain, Philadelphia vs. Syracuse, February 6, 1960

Most rebounds, one quarter
18—Nate Thurmond, San Francisco at Baltimore, February 28, 1965
17—Bill Russell, Boston vs. Philadelphia, November 16, 1957
    Bill Russell, Boston vs. Cincinnati, December 12, 1958
    Bill Russell, Boston vs. Syracuse, February 5, 1960
    Wilt Chamberlain, Philadelphia vs. Syracuse, February 6, 1960

OFFENSIVE REBOUNDS

Offensive Rebounds have been compiled since 1973-74

Most seasons leading league
8—Moses Malone, Buffalo, Houston, 1976-77; Houston, 1977-78—1981-82; Philadelphia, 1982-83; Atlanta 1989-90
6—Dennis Rodman, Detroit, 1990-91—1992-93; San Antonio, 1993-94; Chicago, 1995-96—1996-97
3—Charles Barkley, Philadelphia, 1986-87—1988-89

Most consecutive seasons leading league
7—Moses Malone, Buffalo, Houston, 1976-77; Houston, 1977-78—1981-82; Philadelphia, 1982-83
4—Dennis Rodman, Detroit, 1990-91—1992-93; San Antonio, 1993-94
3—Charles Barkley, Philadelphia, 1986-87—1988-89

Most offensive rebounds, career
6,731—Moses Malone, Buffalo, Houston, 1976-77; Houston, 1976-77—1981-82; Philadelphia, 1982-83—1985-86; Washington, 1986-87—1987-88; Atlanta, 1988-89—1990-91; Milwaukee, 1991-92—1992-93; Philadelphia, 1993-94; San Antonio, 1994-95
4,598—Robert Parish, Golden State, 1976-77—1979-80; Boston, 1980-81—1993-94; Charlotte, 1994-95—1995-96; Chicago, 1996-97
4,526—Buck Williams, New Jersey, 1981-82—1988-89; Portland, 1989-90—1995-96; New York, 1996-97—1997-98

Highest average, offensive rebounds per game, career
(minimum: 400 games)
5.1—Moses Malone, Buffalo, Houston, 1976-77; Houston, 1976-77—1981-82; Philadelphia, 1982-83—1985-86; Washington, 1986-87—1987-88; Atlanta, 1988-89—1990-91; Milwaukee, 1991-92—1992-93; Philadelphia, 1993-94; San Antonio, 1994-95 (6,731/1,329)
4.8—Dennis Rodman, Detroit, 1986-87—1992-93; San Antonio, 1993-94—1994-95; Chicago, 1995-96—1997-98; L.A. Lakers, 1998-99; Dallas, 1999-00 (4,329/911)
4.0—Charles Barkley, Philadelphia, 1984-85—1991-92; Phoenix, 1992-93—1995-96; Houston, 1996-97—1999-2000 (4,260/1,073)

Most offensive rebounds, season
587—Moses Malone, Houston, 1978-79
573—Moses Malone, Houston, 1979-80
558—Moses Malone, Houston, 1981-82

Most offensive rebounds, game
21—Moses Malone, Houston vs. Seattle, February 11, 1982
19—Moses Malone, Houston at New Orleans, February 9, 1979
18—Charles Oakley, Chicago vs. Milwaukee, March 15, 1986 (ot)
Dennis Rodman, Detroit vs. Indiana, March 4, 1992 (ot)

Most offensive rebounds, one half
13—Charles Barkley, Philadelphia vs. New York, March 4, 1987
12—Moses Malone, Houston vs. San Antonio, February 10, 1978
Larry Smith, Golden State vs. Denver, March 23, 1986
Larry Smith, Houston vs. Phoenix, February 16, 1991

Most offensive rebounds, one quarter
11—Charles Barkley, Philadelphia vs. New York, March 4, 1987
Larry Smith, Golden State vs. Denver, March 23, 1986
10—Moses Malone, Milwaukee vs. Sacramento, January 11, 1992

DEFENSIVE REBOUNDS

Defensive Rebounds have been compiled since 1973-74

Most seasons leading league
3—Dennis Rodman, Detroit, 1991-92; San Antonio, 1993-94; Chicago, 1997-98
2—Kareem Abdul-Jabbar, Los Angeles, 1975-76—1976-77
Swen Nater, San Diego, 1979-80—1980-81
Moses Malone, Houston, 1978-79; Philadelphia, 1982-83
Jack Sikma, Seattle, 1981-82, 1983-84
Charles Oakley, Chicago, 1986-87—1987-88
Hakeem Olajuwon, Houston, 1988-89—1989-90
Karl Malone, Utah, 1990-91, 1994-95
Dikembe Mutombo, Atlanta, 1998-99—1999-00
Kevin Garnett, Minnesota, 2002-03—2003-04

Most consecutive seasons leading league
2—Kareem Abdul-Jabbar, Los Angeles, 1975-76—1976-77
Swen Nater, San Diego, 1979-80—1980-81
Charles Oakley, Chicago, 1986-87—1987-88
Hakeem Olajuwon, Houston, 1988-89—1989-90
Dikembe Mutombo, Atlanta, 1998-99—1999-00
Kevin Garnett, Minnesota, 2002-03—2003-04

Most defensive rebounds, career
11,406—Karl Malone, Utah, 1985-86—2002-03; L.A. Lakers, 2003-04
10,117—Robert Parish, Golden State, 1976-77—1979-80; Boston, 1980-81—1993-94; Charlotte, 1994-95—1995-96; Chicago, 1996-97
9,714—Hakeem Olajuwon, Houston, 1984-85—2000-01; Toronto, 2001-02

Highest average, defensive rebounds per game, career
(minimum: 400 games)
9.8—Dave Cowens, Boston, 1973-74—1979-80; Milwaukee, 1982-83 (5,122/524)
9.0—Tim Duncan, San Antonio, 1997-98—2003-04 (4,699/520)
8.4—Wes Unseld, Baltimore, 1968-69—1972-73; Capital, 1973-74; Washington, 1974-75—1980-81

Most defensive rebounds, season
1,111—Kareem Abdul-Jabbar, Los Angeles, 1975-76
1,109—Elvin Hayes, Capital, 1973-74
1,007—Dennis Rodman, Detroit, 1991-92

Most defensive rebounds, game
29—Kareem Abdul-Jabbar, Los Angeles vs. Detroit, December 14, 1975
28—Elvin Hayes, Capital at Atlanta, November 17, 1973
26—Rony Seikaly, Miami vs. Washington, March 3, 1993

Most defensive rebounds, one half
18—Swen Nater, San Diego vs. Denver, December 14, 1979
17—Marvin Webster, Seattle at Atlanta, November 1, 1977

Most defensive rebounds, one quarter
13—Happy Hairston, Los Angeles vs. Philadelphia, November 15, 1974
12—John Lambert, Cleveland vs. New Jersey, February 6, 1979
Kevin Willis, Atlanta vs. Seattle, February 3, 1992
Charles Barkley, Houston at Philadelphia, January 10, 1997

ASSISTS

Most seasons leading league
9—John Stockton, Utah, 1987-88—1995-96
8—Bob Cousy, Boston, 1952-53—1959-60
6—Oscar Robertson, Cincinnati, 1960-61—1961-62, 1963-64—1965-66, 1968-69

Most consecutive seasons leading league
9—John Stockton, Utah, 1987-88—1995-96
8—Bob Cousy, Boston, 1952-53—1959-60
3—Oscar Robertson, Cincinnati, 1963-64—1965-66
Jason Kidd, Phoenix, 1998-99—2000-01

Most assists, career
15,806—John Stockton, Utah, 1984-85—2002-03
10,334—Mark Jackson, New York, 1987-88—1991-92; L.A. Clippers, 1992-93—1993-94; Indiana, 1994-95—1995-96; Denver, 1996-97; Indiana, 1996-97—1999-00; Toronto, 2000-01; New York, 2000-01—2001-02; Utah, 2002-03; Houston, 2003-04
10,141—Magic Johnson, L.A. Lakers, 1979-80—1990-91, 1995-96
9,887—Oscar Robertson, Cincinnati, 1960-61—1969-70; Milwaukee, 1970-71—1973-74
9,061—Isiah Thomas, Detroit, 1981-82—1993-94

Highest average, assists per game, career
(minimum:400 games)
11.2—Magic Johnson, L.A. Lakers, 1979-80—1990-91, 1995-96 (10,141/906)
10.5—John Stockton, Utah, 1984-85—2002-03 (15,806/1,504)
9.5—Oscar Robertson, Cincinnati, 1960-61—1969-70; Milwaukee, 1970-71—1973-74 (9,887/1,040)
9.4—Jason Kidd, Dallas, 1994-95—1996-97; Phoenix, 1996-97—2000-01; New Jersey, 2001-02—2003-04 (6,738/720)
9.3—Isiah Thomas, Detroit, 1981-82—1993-94 (9,061/979)

Most assists, season
1,164—John Stockton, Utah, 1990-91
1,134—John Stockton, Utah, 1989-90
1,128—John Stockton, Utah, 1987-88

Most assists, rookie, season
868—Mark Jackson, New York, 1987-88
690—Oscar Robertson, Cincinnati, 1960-61
689—Tim Hardaway, Golden State, 1989-90

Highest average, assists per game, season
(minimum: 70 games)
14.5—John Stockton, Utah, 1989-90 (1,134/78)
14.2—John Stockton, Utah, 1990-91 (1,164/82)
13.9—Isiah Thomas, Detroit, 1984-85 (1,123/81)

Most assists, game
30—Scott Skiles, Orlando vs. Denver, December 30, 1990
29—Kevin Porter, New Jersey vs. Houston, February 24, 1978
28—Bob Cousy, Boston vs. Minneapolis, February 27, 1959
    Guy Rodgers, San Francisco vs. St. Louis, March 14, 1963
    John Stockton, Utah vs. San Antonio, January 15, 1991

Most assists, rookie, game
25—Ernie DiGregorio, Buffalo at Portland, January 1, 1974
    Nate McMillan, Seattle vs. L.A. Clippers, February 23, 1987
23—Jamaal Tinsley, Indiana vs. Washington, November 22, 2001
22—Phil Ford, Kansas City vs. Milwaukee, February 21, 1979
    Ennis Whatley, Chicago vs. New York, January 14, 1984
    Ennis Whatley, Chicago vs. Atlanta, March 3, 1984

Most assists, one half
19—Bob Cousy, Boston vs. Minneapolis, February 27, 1959
18—Magic Johnson, Los Angeles vs. Seattle, February 21, 1984 (1st Half)
17—Nate McMillan, Seattle vs. L.A. Clippers, February 23, 1987 (2nd Half)

Most assists, one quarter
14—John Lucas, San Antonio vs. Denver, April 15, 1984 (2nd Qtr.)
12—Bob Cousy, Boston vs. Minneapolis, February 27, 1959
    John Lucas, Houston vs. Milwaukee, October 27, 1977 (3rd Qtr.)
    John Lucas, Golden State vs. Chicago, November 17, 1978 (1st Qtr.)
    Magic Johnson, Los Angeles vs. Seattle, February 21, 1984 (1st Qtr.)
    Mark Jackson, Denver vs. New Jersey, January 20, 1997
    Avery Johnson, San Antonio vs. L.A. Clippers, December 10, 1997
11—by many

PERSONAL FOULS

Most seasons leading league
3—George Mikan, Minneapolis, 1949-50—1951-52
    Vern Mikkelsen, Minneapolis, 1954-55—1956-57
    Darryl Dawkins, Philadelphia, 1979-80; New Jersey, 1982-83—1983-84
    Shawn Kemp, Seattle, 1993-94, 1996-97; Cleveland, 1999-00
2—Walter Dukes, Detroit, 1957-58—1958-59
    Zelmo Beaty, St. Louis, 1962-63—1965-66
    Dave Cowens, Boston, 1970-71—1971-72
    Lonnie Shelton, N.Y. Knicks, 1976-77—1977-78
    Steve Johnson, Kansas City, 1981-82; Portland, 1986-87
    Kurt Thomas, New York, 2001-02—2002-03

Most consecutive seasons leading league
3—George Mikan, Minneapolis, 1949-50—1951-52
    Vern Mikkelsen, Minneapolis, 1954-55—1956-57
2—Walter Dukes, Detroit, 1957-58—1958-59
    Dave Cowens, Boston, 1970-71—1971-72
    Lonnie Shelton, N.Y. Knicks, 1976-77—1977-78
    Darryl Dawkins, New Jersey, 1982-83—1983-84
    Kurt Thomas, New York, 2001-02—2002-03

Most personal fouls, career
4,657—Kareem Abdul-Jabbar, Milwaukee, 1969-70—1974-75; L.A. Lakers, 1975-76—1988-89
4,578—Karl Malone, Utah, 1985-86—2002-03; L.A. Lakers, 2003-04
4,443—Robert Parish, Golden State, 1976-77—1979-80; Boston, 1980-81—1993-94; Charlotte, 1994-95—1995-96; Chicago, 1996-97

Most personal fouls, season
386—Darryl Dawkins, New Jersey, 1983-84
379—Darryl Dawkins, New Jersey, 1982-83
372—Steve Johnson, Kansas City, 1981-82

Most personal fouls, game
8—Don Otten, Tri-Cities at Sheboygan, November 24, 1949

7—Alex Hannum, Syracuse at Boston, December 26, 1950
    Cal Bowdler, Atlanta at Portland, November 13, 1999
6—by many

Most personal fouls, one half
6—by many

Most personal fouls, one quarter
6—by many

DISQUALIFICATIONS
Disqualifications have been compiled since 1950-51

Most seasons leading league
5—Shawn Kemp, Seattle, 1991-92, 1993-94, 1996-97; Cleveland, 1997-98, 1999-00
4—Walter Dukes, Detroit, 1958-59—1961-62
3—Vern Mikkelsen, Minneapolis, 1955-56—1957-58
    Steve Johnson, Kansas City, 1981-82; San Antonio, 1985-86; Portland, 1986-87
    Rik Smits, Indiana, 1988-89—1989-90, 1993-94

Most consecutive seasons leading league
4—Walter Dukes, Detroit, 1958-59—1961-62
3—Vern Mikkelsen, Minneapolis, 1955-56—1957-58
2—By many

Most disqualifications, career
127—Vern Mikkelsen, Minneapolis, 1950-51—1958-59
 21—Walter Dukes, New York, 1955-56; Minneapolis, 1956-57; Detroit, 1957-58—1962-63
115—Shawn Kemp, Seattle, 1989-90—1996-97; Cleveland, 1997-98—1999-00; Portland, 2000-01—2001-02; Orlando, 2002-03

Highest percentage, games disqualified, career
(minimum: 400 games)
21.88—Walter Dukes, New York, 1955-56; Minneapolis, 1956-57; Detroit, 1957-58—1962-63 (121/553)
20.13—Vern Mikkelsen, Minneapolis, 1950-51—1958-59 (127/631)
18.14—Alex Hannum, Syracuse, 1950-51—Baltimore, 1951-52; Rochester, 1951-52—1953-54; Milwaukee, 1954-55; St. Louis, 1955-56; Ft. Wayne, 1956-57; St. Louis, 1956-57 (82/452)

Lowest percentage, games disqualified, career
(minimum: 400 games)
0.00—Wilt Chamberlain, Philadelphia, 1959-60—1961-62; San Francisco, 1962-63—1964-65; Philadelphia, 1964-65—1967-68; Los Angeles, 1968-69—1972-73 (0/1,045)
    Steve Kerr, Phoenix, 1988-89; Cleveland, 1989-90—1992-93; Orlando, 1992-93; Chicago, 1993-94—1997-98; San Antonio, 1998-99—2002-03 (0/910)
    Don Buse, Indiana, 1976-77; Phoenix, 1977-78—1979-80; Indiana, 1980-81—1981-82; Portland, 1982-83; Kansas City, 1983-84—1984-85 (0/648)
    John Battle, Atlanta, 1985-86—1990-91; Cleveland 1991-92—1994-95 (0/612)
    Jerry Sichting, Indiana, 1980-81—1984-85; Boston 1985-86—1987-88; Portland, 1987-88—1988-89; Charlotte, 1989-90; Milwaukee, 1989-90 (0/598)
    Danny Young, Seattle, 1984-85—1987-88; Portland, 1988-89—1991-92; L.A. Clippers, 1991-92; Detroit, 1992-93; Milwaukee, 1994-95; L.A. Lakers, 1994-95 (0/574)
    Randy Wittman, Atlanta, 1983-84—1987-88; Sacramento, 1988-89; Indiana, 1988-89—1991-92 (0/543)
    Steve Colter, Portland, 1984-85—1985-86; Chicago, 1986-87; Philadelphia, 1986-87—1987-88; Washington, 1987-88—1989-90; Sacramento, 1990-91; Cleveland, 1994-95 (0/526)
    Antonio Daniels, Vancouver, 1997-98; San Antonio, 1998-99—2001-02; Portland, 2002-03; Seattle, 2003-04 (0/488)

Jason Williams, Sacramento, 1998-99—2000-01; Memphis,
   2001-02—2003-04 (0/421)
Charlie Criss, Atlanta, 1977-78—1981-82; San Diego,
   1981-82; Milwaukee, 1982-83—1983-84; Atlanta,
   1983-84—1984-85 (0/418)
0.102—Rolando Blackman, Dallas, 1981-82—1991-92; New
   York, 1992-93—1993-94 (1/980)
0.107—Mike Gminski, New Jersey, 1980-81—1987-88;
   Philadelphia, 1987-88—1990-91; Charlotte, 1990-
   91—1993-94; Milwaukee, 1993-94 (1/938)

Most consecutive games without disqualification, career
1,213—Mark Jackson, New York, L.A. Clippers, Indiana,
   Denver, Indiana, Toronto, New York, Utah, Houston,
   November 5, 1988—April 14, 2004 (current)
1,212—Moses Malone, Houston, Philadelphia, Washington,
   Atlanta, Milwaukee, Philadelphia, San Antonio,
   January 7, 1978—December 27, 1994
1,045—Wilt Chamberlain, Philadelphia, San Francisco,
   Philadelphia, Los Angeles, October 24, 1959—
   March 28, 1973

Most disqualifications, season
26—Don Meineke, Ft. Wayne, 1952-53
25—Steve Johnson, Kansas City, 1981-82
23—Darryl Dawkins, New Jersey, 1982-83

Fewest minutes, disqualified, game
3—Bubba Wells, Dallas at Chicago, December 29, 1997
5—Dick Farley, Syracuse at St. Louis, March 12, 1956
   Mark Bryant, Dallas vs. L.A. Lakers, December 22, 2000
6—by many

STEALS

Steals have been compiled since 1973-74

Most seasons leading league
3—Micheal Ray Richardson, New York, 1979-80; Golden
      State, New Jersey, 1982-83; New Jersey, 1984-85
   Alvin Robertson, San Antonio, 1985-86—1986-87;
      Milwaukee, 1990-91
   Michael Jordan, Chicago, 1987-88, 1989-90, 1992-93
   Allen Iverson, Philadelphia, 2000-01—2002-03
2—Magic Johnson, Los Angeles, 1980-81—1981-82
   John Stockton, Utah, 1988-89, 1991-92
   Mookie Blaylock, Atlanta, 1996-97—1997-98

Most consecutive seasons leading league
3—Allen Iverson, Philadelphia, 2000-01—2002-03
2—Magic Johnson, Los Angeles, 1980-81—1981-82
   Alvin Robertson, San Antonio, 1985-86—1986-87
   Mookie Blaylock, Atlanta, 1996-97—1997-90

Most steals, career
3,265—John Stockton, Utah, 1984-85—2002-03
2,514—Michael Jordan, Chicago, 1984-85—1992-93, 1994-
   95—1997-98; Washington, 2001-02—2002-03
2,310—Maurice Cheeks, Philadelphia, 1978-79—1988-89;
   San Antonio, 1989-90; New York, 1989-90—1990-
   91;
   Atlanta, 1991-92; New Jersey, 1992-93

Highest average, steals per game, career
(minimum: 400 games)
2.71—Alvin Robertson, San Antonio, 1984-85—1988-89;
   Milwaukee, 1989-90—1992-93; Detroit, 1992-93;
   Toronto, 1995-96 (2,112/779)
2.63—Micheal Ray Richardson, New York, 1978-79—1981-
   82; Golden State, New Jersey, 1982-83; New Jersey,
   1983-84—1985-86 (1,463/556)
2.38—Allen Iverson, Philadelphia, 1996-97—2003-04
   (1,273/535)

Most steals, season
301—Alvin Robertson, San Antonio, 1985-86

281—Don Buse, Indiana, 1976-77
265—Micheal Ray Richardson, New York, 1979-80

Highest average, steals per game, season (qualifiers)
3.67—Alvin Robertson, San Antonio, 1985-86 (301/82)
3.47—Don Buse, Indiana, 1976-77 (281/81)
3.43—Magic Johnson, Los Angeles, 1980-81 (127/37)

Most steals, rookie, season
211—Dudley Bradley, Indiana, 1979-80
209—Ron Harper, Cleveland, 1986-87
205—Mark Jackson, New York, 1987-88

Highest average, steals per game, rookie, season (qualifiers)
2.57—Dudley Bradley, Indiana, 1979-80 (211/82)
2.55—Ron Harper, Cleveland, 1986-87 (209/82)
2.50—Mark Jackson, New York, 1987-88 (205/82)

Most steals, game
11—Larry Kenon, San Antonio at Kansas City, December 26, 1976
   Kendall Gill, New Jersey vs. Miami, April 3, 1999
10—Jerry West, Los Angeles vs. Seattle, December 7, 1973
   Larry Steele, Portland vs. Los Angeles, November 16, 1974
   Fred Brown, Seattle at Philadelphia, December 3, 1976
   Gus Williams, Seattle at New Jersey, February 22, 1978
   Eddie Jordan, New Jersey at Philadelphia, March 23, 1979
   Johnny Moore, San Antonio vs. Indiana, March 6, 1985
   Lafayette Lever, Denver vs. Indiana, March 9, 1985
   Clyde Drexler, Portland at Milwaukee, January 10, 1986
   Alvin Robertson, San Antonio vs. Phoenix, February 18, 1986
   Alvin Robertson, San Antonio at L.A. Clippers, November
      22, 1986
   Ron Harper, Cleveland vs. Philadelphia, March 10, 1987
   Michael Jordan, Chicago vs. New Jersey, January 29, 1988
   Alvin Robertson, San Antonio vs. Houston, January 11,
      1989 (ot)
   Alvin Robertson, Milwaukee vs. Utah, November 19, 1990
   Kevin Johnson, Phoenix vs. Washington, December 9, 1993
   Clyde Drexler, Houston vs. Sacramento, November 1, 1996
   Mookie Blaylock, Atlanta vs. Philadelphia, April 14, 1998
   Michael Finley, Dallas vs. Philadelphia, January 23, 2001

Most steals, one half
8—Quinn Buckner, Milwaukee vs. N.Y. Nets, November 27,
      1976
   Fred Brown, Seattle at Philadelphia, December 3, 1976
   Gus Williams, Seattle at Washington, January 23, 1979
   Eddie Jordan, New Jersey at Chicago, October 23, 1979
   Dudley Bradley, Indiana at Utah, November 10, 1980
   Rob Williams, Denver at New Jersey, February 17, 1983
   Lafayette Lever, Denver vs. Indiana, March 9, 1985
   Michael Jordan, Chicago at Boston, November 9, 1988
   Clyde Drexler, Houston vs. Sacramento, November 1, 1996
   Doug Christie, Toronto at Philadelphia, April 2, 1997
   Michael Finley, Dallas vs. Philadelphia, January 23, 2001

Most steals, one quarter
8—Lafayette Lever, Denver vs. Indiana, March 9, 1985
7—Quinn Buckner, Milwaukee vs. N.Y. Nets, November 27, 1976
   Alvin Robertson, San Antonio vs. Detroit, March 25, 1988
   Michael Adams, Washington at Atlanta, November 26, 1993
   Tom Gugliotta, Minnesota at Portland, February 21, 1995

BLOCKED SHOTS

Blocked Shots have been compiled since 1973-74

Most seasons leading league
4—Kareem Abdul-Jabbar, Milwaukee, 1974-75; Los Angeles,
      1975-76, 1978-79—1979-80
   Mark Eaton, Utah, 1983-84—1984-85; 1986-87—1987-88

3—George T. Johnson, New Jersey, 1977-78; San Antonio, 1980-81—1981-82
Hakeem Olajuwon, Houston, 1989-90—1990-91, 1992-93
Dikembe Mutombo, Denver, 1993-94—1995-96
Theo Ratliff, Philadelphia-Atlanta, 2000-01; Atlanta, 2002-03; Atlanta-Portland, 2003-04

Most consecutive seasons leading league
3—Dikembe Mutombo, Denver, 1993-94—1995-96
2—Kareem Abdul-Jabbar, Milwaukee, 1974-75; Los Angeles, 1975-76
Kareem Abdul-Jabbar, Los Angeles, 1978-79—1979-80
George T. Johnson, San Antonio, 1980-81—1981-82
Mark Eaton, Utah, 1983-84—1984-85;
Mark Eaton, Utah, 1986-87—1987-88
Hakeem Olajuwon, Houston, 1989-90—1990-91
Alonzo Mourning, Miami, 1998-99—1999-00
Theo Ratliff, Atlanta, 2002-03; Atlanta-Portland, 2003-04

Most blocked shots, career
3,830—Hakeem Olajuwon, Houston, 1984-85—2000-01; Toronto, 2001-02
3,189—Kareem Abdul-Jabbar, Milwaukee, 1973-74—1974-75; L.A. Lakers, 1975-76—1988-89
3,064—Mark Eaton, Utah, 1982-83—1992-93

Highest average, blocked shots per game, career
(minimum: 400 games)
3.50—Mark Eaton, Utah, 1982-83—1992-93 (3,064/875)
3.34—Manute Bol, Washington, 1985-86—1987-88; Golden State, 1988-89—1989-90; Philadelphia, 1990-91—1992-93; Miami, 1993-94; Washington, 1993-94; Philadelphia, 1993-94; Golden State, 1994-95 (2,086/624)
3.22—Dikembe Mutombo, Denver, 1991-92—1995-96; Atlanta, 1996-97—2000-01; Philadelphia, 2000-01—2001-02; New Jersey, 2002-03; New York, 2003-04 (2,996/929)

Most blocked shots, season
456—Mark Eaton, Utah, 1984-85
397—Manute Bol, Washington, 1985-86
393—Elmore Smith, Los Angeles, 1973-74

Highest average, blocked shots per game, season (qualifiers)
5.56—Mark Eaton, Utah, 1984-85 (456/82)
4.97—Manute Bol, Washington, 1985-86 (397/80)
4.85—Elmore Smith, Los Angeles, 1973-74 (393/81)

Most blocked shots, rookie, season
397—Manute Bol, Washington, 1985-86
319—David Robinson, San Antonio, 1989-90
286—Shaquille O'Neal, Orlando, 1992-93

Highest average, blocked shots per game, rookie, season (qualifiers)
4.97—Manute Bol, Washington, 1985-86 (397/80)
3.89—David Robinson, San Antonio, 1989-90 (319/82)
3.53—Shaquille O'Neal, Orlando, 1992-93 (286/81)

Most blocked shots, game
17—Elmore Smith, Los Angeles vs. Portland, October 28, 1973

15—Manute Bol, Washington vs. Atlanta, January 25, 1986
Manute Bol, Washington vs. Indiana, February 26, 1987
Shaquille O'Neal, Orlando at New Jersey, November 20, 1993
14—Elmore Smith, Los Angeles vs. Detroit, October 26, 1973
Elmore Smith, Los Angeles vs. Houston, November 4, 1973
Mark Eaton, Utah vs. Portland, January 18, 1985
Mark Eaton, Utah vs. San Antonio, February 18, 1989

Most blocked shots, one half
11—Elmore Smith, Los Angeles vs. Portland, October 28, 1973
George Johnson, San Antonio vs. Golden State, February 24, 1981
Manute Bol, Washington vs. Milwaukee, December 12, 1985
10—Harvey Catchings, Philadelphia vs. Atlanta, March 21, 1975
Manute Bol, Washington vs. Indiana, February 26, 1987
Keon Clark, Toronto vs. Atlanta, March 23, 2001

Most blocked shots, one quarter
8—Manute Bol, Washington vs. Milwaukee, December 12, 1985
Manute Bol, Washington vs. Indiana, February 26, 1987
Dikembe Mutombo, Philadelphia at Chicago, December 1, 2001
Erick Dampier, Golden State vs. L.A. Clippers, April 17, 2002

TURNOVERS

Turnovers have been compiled since 1977-78

Most turnovers, career
4,524—Karl Malone, Utah, 1985-86—2002-03; L.A. Lakers, 2003-04
4,244—John Stockton, Utah, 1984-85—2002-03
3,804—Moses Malone, Houston, 1977-78—1981-82; Philadelphia, 1982-83—1985-86; Washington, 1986-87—1987-88; Atlanta, 1988-89—1990-91; Milwaukee, 1991-92—1992-93; Philadelphia, 1993-94; San Antonio, 1994-95

Most turnovers, season
366—Artis Gilmore, Chicago, 1977-78
360—Kevin Porter, Detroit, New Jersey, 1977-78
359—Micheal Ray Richardson, New York, 1979-80

Most turnovers, game
14—John Drew, Atlanta at New Jersey, March 1, 1978
Jason Kidd, Phoenix vs. New York, November 17, 2000
13—Chris Mullin, Golden State at Utah, March 31, 1988
12—Kevin Porter, New Jersey at Philadelphia, November 9, 1977
Artis Gilmore, Chicago vs. Atlanta, January 31, 1978 (ot)
Kevin Porter, Detroit at Philadelphia, February 7, 1979
Maurice Lucas, Portland vs. Phoenix, November 25, 1979
Moses Malone, Houston at Phoenix, February 6, 1981
Eric Floyd, Golden State vs. Denver, October 25, 1985
Scottie Pippen, Chicago at New Jersey, February 25, 1990 (ot)
Scottie Pippen, Chicago at Houston, January 30, 1996
Damon Stoudamire, Toronto at Chicago, January 25, 1997
Jason Kidd, New Jersey at Atlanta, January 6, 2003
Jason Kidd, New Jersey vs. Philadelphia, March 16, 2003

TEAM OFFENSE

SCORING

Highest average, points per game, season
126.5—Denver, 1981-82 (10,371/82)
125.4—Philadelphia, 1961-62 (10,035/80)
125.2—Philadelphia, 1966-67 (10,143/81)

Lowest average, points per game, season
81.9—Chicago, 1998-99 (4,095/50)
84.2—Denver, 2002-03 (6,901/82)

84.8—Chicago, 1999-00 (6,952/82)

Most consecutive games, 100 or more points
136—Denver, January 21, 1981—December 8, 1982
129—San Antonio, December 12, 1978—March 14, 1980
81—Cincinnati, November 18, 1960—November 21, 1961

Most consecutive games, 100 or more points, season
82—Denver, October 30, 1981—April 17, 1982 (entire season)
77—New York, October 23, 1966—March 19, 1967

73—Syracuse, November 4, 1961—March 14, 1962
   Philadelphia, November 8, 1966—March 19, 1967
Most consecutive games, fewer than 100 points, season
35—Miami, October 31, 2001—January 14, 2002
29—Orlando, December 13, 1997—February 16, 1998
   Chicago, November 3, 1999—January 5, 2000
27—Golden State, December 18, 1997—February 13, 1998

Most points, game
186—Detroit at Denver, December 13, 1983 (3 ot)
184—Denver vs. Detroit, December 13, 1983 (3 ot)
173—Boston vs. Minneapolis, February 27, 1959
   Phoenix vs. Denver, November 10, 1990
171—San Antonio vs. Milwaukee, March 6, 1982 (3 ot)
169—Philadelphia vs. New York, at Hershey, Pa., March 2, 1962

Fewest points, game
49—Chicago vs. Miami, April 10, 1999
53—Denver at Detroit, November 16, 2002
55—Indiana vs. San Antonio, March 29, 1998

Most points, both teams, game
370—Detroit (186) at Denver (184), December 13, 1983 (3 ot)
337—San Antonio (171) vs. Milwaukee (166), March 6, 1982 (3 ot)
320—Golden State (162) at Denver (158), November 2, 1990
318—Denver (163) vs. San Antonio (155), January 11, 1984
316—Philadelphia (169) vs. New York (147), at Hershey, Pa.,
   March 2, 1962
   Cincinnati (165) vs. San Diego (151), March 12, 1970
   Phoenix (173) vs. Denver (143), November 10, 1990

Fewest points, both teams, game
119—Milwaukee (57) vs. Boston (62), at Providence, February 27, 1955
121—Miami (56) at Charlotte (65), December 20, 2000
123—Philadelphia (57) vs. Miami (66), February 21, 1996
   Cleveland (59) at San Antonio (64), March 25, 1997

Largest margin of victory, game
68—Cleveland vs. Miami, December 17, 1991 (148-80)
65—Indiana vs. Portland, February 27, 1998 (124-59)
63—Los Angeles vs. Golden State, March 19, 1972 (162-99)
62—Syracuse vs. New York, December 25, 1960 (162-100)
   Golden State vs. Sacramento, November 2, 1991 (153-91)
59—Golden State vs. Indiana, March 19, 1977 (150-91)
   Milwaukee vs. Detroit, December 26, 1978 (143-84)

BY HALF

Most points, first half
107—Phoenix vs. Denver, November 10, 1990
 90—Denver at San Antonio, November 7, 1990
 89—Cincinnati vs. San Diego, March 12, 1970
   L.A. Lakers vs. Phoenix, January 2, 1987

Fewest points, first half
19—L.A. Clippers at L.A. Lakers, December 14, 1999
20—New Orleans at Seattle, January 4, 1975
21—Utah at L.A. Lakers, February 4, 2000

Most points, both teams, first half
174—Phoenix (107) vs. Denver (67), November 10, 1990
173—Denver (90) at San Antonio (83), November 7, 1990
170—Golden State (87) at Denver (83), November 2, 1990

Fewest points, both teams, first half
55—Houston (25) vs. San Antonio (30), December 11, 2003
57—Detroit (28) vs. Denver (29), November 16, 2002
   New York (27) vs. Miami (30), January 20, 2003
58—Syracuse (27) vs. Ft. Wayne (31), at Buffalo, January 25,
   1955 Dallas (24) at Indiana (34), February 13, 1998

Most points, second half
97—Atlanta at San Diego, February 11, 1970
95—Philadelphia at Seattle, December 20, 1967
94—Houston at Denver, January 10, 1991

Fewest points, second half
19—Miami at Orlando, March 26, 2000
   Charlotte at New York, November 11, 2000

21—Miami at Atlanta, November 15, 1996
   Indiana vs. San Antonio, March 29, 1998
   Minnesota vs. Golden State, December 11, 1999
   Orlando vs. Miami, January 27, 2001
22—Milwaukee at Seattle, February 21, 2003

Most points, both teams, second half
172—San Antonio (91) at Denver (81), January 11, 1984
170—Philadelphia (90) vs. Cincinnati (80), March 19, 1971
169—Philadelphia (90) vs. New York (79), at Hershey, Pa.,
   March 2, 1962

Fewest points, both teams, second half
51—Boston (25) vs. Milwaukee (26), at Providence, February 27, 1955
   Charlotte (19) at New York (32), November 11, 2000
52—Cleveland (24) at San Antonio (28), March 25, 1997
53—Indiana (21) vs. San Antonio (32), March 29, 1998

BY QUARTER

Most points, first quarter
50—Syracuse at San Francisco, December 16, 1962
   Boston vs. Denver, February 5, 1982
   Utah vs. Denver, April 10, 1982
   Milwaukee vs. Orlando, November 16, 1989
   Phoenix vs. Denver, November 10, 1990
49—Atlanta vs. New Jersey, January 5, 1985
   Portland vs. San Antonio, November 25, 1990

Fewest points, first quarter
3—Denver at San Antonio, November 27, 2002
4—Sacramento at L.A. Lakers, February 4, 1987
5—Syracuse at Milwaukee, November 13, 1954
   New York vs. Ft. Wayne, at Boston, November 21, 1956
   Cleveland at Chicago, December 15, 1990

Most points, both teams, first quarter
91—Utah (50) vs. Denver (41), April 10, 1982
87—Denver (47) vs. San Antonio (40), January 11, 1984
   Phoenix (50) vs. Denver (37), November 10, 1990
86—Denver (47) vs. San Antonio (39), November 20, 1987
   Houston (44) vs. Denver (42), November 6, 1990

Fewest points, both teams, first quarter
18—Ft. Wayne (9) at Syracuse (9), November 29, 1956
22—Utah (9) at New Jersey (13), December 17, 2003
24—San Antonio (11) at Vancouver (13), March 20, 1999
   Miami (8) at Orlando (16), April 22, 1999
   Denver (3) at San Antonio (21), November 27, 2002
   Toronto (8) at Atlanta (16), January 17, 2004

Most points, second quarter
57—Phoenix vs. Denver, November 10, 1990
52—Baltimore vs. Detroit, December 18, 1965
50—San Diego vs. Utah, April 14, 1984
   San Antonio at Houston, November 17, 1984

Fewest points, second quarter
3—L.A. Clippers at L.A. Lakers, December 14, 1999
4—Cleveland vs. Boston, November 28, 2000
   Toronto at Washington, November 7, 2003
5—Utah at Los Angeles, December 1, 1981
   New York at Chicago, March 12, 1999

Most points, both teams, second quarter
91—Seattle (46) at Golden State (45), March 23, 1974
90—New York (47) at Philadelphia (43), November 18, 1988
89—Denver (45) at Dallas (44), January 14, 1983
   San Antonio (47) vs. Denver (42), November 7, 1990

Fewest points, both teams, second quarter
19—Philadelphia (8) at Charlotte (11), April 5, 1995
20—L.A. Clippers (3) at L.A. Lakers (17), December 14, 1999
   Houston (8) vs. San Antonio (12), December 11, 2003
22—San Francisco (11) at Detroit (11), January 15, 1964
   Phoenix (8) at Vancouver (14), November 14, 1996
   Indiana (10) vs. Dallas (12), February 13, 1998

Most points, third quarter

57—Golden State vs. Sacramento, March 4, 1989
54—Atlanta at San Diego, February 11, 1970
51—Syracuse vs. Detroit, March 2, 1963
    Cincinnati at Philadelphia, February 28, 1964
    Seattle vs. Baltimore, February 13, 1970
    Denver vs. San Diego, January 6, 1982

Fewest points, third quarter

2—Dallas at L.A. Lakers, April 6, 1997
4—Buffalo vs. Milwaukee, October 21, 1972
5—New York at Portland, February 26, 1997

Most points, both teams, third quarter

90—Cincinnati (51) at Philadelphia (39), February 28, 1964
89—Atlanta (49) vs. Philadelphia (40), March 4, 1973
88—Los Angeles (44) vs. San Diego (44), March 23, 1979

Fewest points, both teams, third quarter

18—Boston (9) vs. Toronto (9), January 12, 2001
19—New York (8) at Atlanta (11), April 28, 1999
21—New York (9) vs. Detroit (12), December 1, 2003

Most points, fourth quarter

58—Buffalo at Boston, October 20, 1972
54—Boston vs. San Diego, February 25, 1970
53—by many

Fewest points, fourth quarter

2—Golden State vs. Toronto, February 8, 2004
6—Detroit at Orlando, December 7, 1993
    Golden State at Phoenix, February 28, 1999
    Memphis vs. Phoenix, February 21, 2002
    Toronto at San Antonio, November 1, 2002
7—Many times

Most points, both teams, fourth quarter

99—San Antonio (53) at Denver (46), January 11, 1984
96—Boston (52) vs. Minneapolis (44), February 27, 1959
    Detroit (53) vs. Cincinnati (43), January 7, 1972
93—San Antonio (48) at Denver (45), November 20, 1987
    Houston (50) at Denver (43), January 10, 1991

Fewest points, both teams, fourth quarter

19—Miami (8) vs. Toronto (11), March 2, 2004
20—Golden State (2) vs. Toronto (18), February 8, 2004
21—Cleveland (10) at San Antonio (11), March 25, 1997
    New York (9) at Boston (12), February 26, 1999
    Toronto (9) vs. Boston (12), December 2, 2001

OVERTIME

Most points, overtime period

25—New Jersey at L.A. Clippers, November 30, 1996
24—Sacramento vs. Utah, March 17, 1990
23—L.A. Clippers vs. Phoenix, November 12, 1988
    Dallas at L.A. Lakers, December 12, 1990
    Indiana vs. Golden State, March 31, 1991
    Dallas at Houston, April 11, 1995
    Houston vs. Dallas, April 11, 1995
    Denver at Phoenix, December 23, 1996

Fewest points, overtime period

0—Houston vs. Portland, January 22, 1983
    L.A. Lakers vs. Detroit, December 1, 1989
    Seattle at Philadelphia, February 16, 1990
    Indiana at Portland, March 10, 1996
    Denver vs. Charlotte, January 13, 1997
    Washington at Atlanta, November 18, 1997
    L.A. Clippers vs. Chicago, November 21, 1997
    Vancouver vs. Indiana, December 1, 2000
1—Washington at Atlanta, March 16, 1983
2—by many

Most points, both teams, overtime period

46—Dallas (23) at Houston (23), April 11, 1995
43—Denver (23) at Phoenix (20), December 23, 1996
39—Indiana (23) vs. Golden State (16), March 31, 1991
    New Jersey (25) at L.A. Clippers (14), November 30, 1996

Fewest points, both teams, overtime period

2—Denver (0) vs. Charlotte (2), January 13, 1997
4—San Diego (2) vs. St. Louis (2), January 3, 1968
    Seattle (0) at Philadelphia (4), February 16, 1990
    San Antonio (2) at New York (2), December 10, 1995
5—Indiana (0) at Portland (5), March 10, 1996
    Seattle (2) at Phoenix (3), December 16, 2003

Largest margin of victory, overtime game

17—Portland at Houston, January 22, 1983 (113-96 game, 17-0 overtime)
16—Milwaukee vs. New Jersey, December 4, 1977 (134-118 game, 18-2 overtime)
15—Boston at San Francisco, January 2, 1963 (135-120 game, 21-6 overtime)
    Dallas at L.A. Lakers, December 12, 1990 (112-97 game, 23-8 overtime)

PLAYERS SCORING

Most players, 2,000 or more points, season

2—Los Angeles, 1964-65 (West 2,292; Baylor 2,009)
    Atlanta, 1972-73 (Maravich 2,063; Hudson 2,029)
    Denver, 1982-83 (English 2,326; Vandeweghe 2,186)
    Denver, 1983-84 (Vandeweghe 2,295; English 2,167)
    Boston, 1986-87 (Bird 2,076; McHale 2,008)

Most players, 1,000 or more points, season

6—Syracuse, 1960-61 (Schayes 1,868; Greer 1,551; Barnett 1,320; Gambee 1,085; Costello 1,084; Kerr 1,056)
    Denver, 1987-88 (English 2,000; Lever 1,546; Adams 1,137; Schayes 1,129; Vincent 1,124; Rasmussen 1,002)
    Boston, 1990-91 (Lewis 1,478; Gamble 1,281; McHale 1,251; Parish 1,207; Bird 1,164; Shaw 1,091)

Most players, 40 or more points, game

2—Baltimore vs. Los Angeles, November 14, 1964 (Johnson 41, Bellamy 40)
    Los Angeles at San Francisco, February 11, 1970 (Baylor 43, West 43)
    New Orleans vs. Denver, April 10, 1977 (Maravich 45, Williams 41)
    Phoenix at Boston, January 5, 1978 (Westphal 43, Davis 40)
    San Antonio vs. Milwaukee, March 6, 1982 (3 ot) (Gervin 50, Mitchell 45)
    Detroit at Denver, December 13, 1983 (3 ot) (Thomas 47, Long 41)
    Denver vs. Detroit, December 13, 1983 (3 ot) (Vandeweghe 51, English 47)
    Utah vs. Detroit, March 19, 1984 (Dantley 43, Drew 42)
    Chicago at Indiana, February 18, 1996 (Jordan 44, Pippen 40)

Most players, 40 or more points, both teams, game

4—Denver vs. Detroit, December 13, 1983 (3 ot) (Detroit: Thomas 47, Long 41; Denver: Vandeweghe 51, English 47)
3—New Orleans (2) vs. Denver (1), April 10, 1977 (New Orleans: Maravich 45, Williams 41; Denver: Thompson 40)
    San Antonio (2) vs. Milwaukee (1), March 6, 1982 (3 ot) (San Antonio: Gervin 50, Mitchell 45; Milwaukee: Winters 42)

FIELD-GOAL PERCENTAGE

Highest field-goal percentage, season

.545—L.A. Lakers, 1984-85 (3,952/7,254)
.532—Los Angeles, 1983-84 (3,854/7,250)
.529—Los Angeles, 1979-80 (3,898/7,368)

Lowest field-goal percentage, season

.362—Milwaukee, 1954-55 (2,187/6,041)
.3688—Syracuse, 1956-57 (2,550/6,915)
.3695—Rochester, 1956-57 (2,515/6,807)

Highest field-goal percentage, game

.707—San Antonio at Dallas, April 16, 1983 (53/75)

.705—Chicago at Golden State, December 2, 1981 (43/61)
.699—Chicago vs. Detroit, January 22, 1980 (58/83)
.697—Portland vs. L.A. Clippers, February 1, 1986 (62/89)
.696—Phoenix at Golden State, March 12, 1980 (48/69)

Lowest field-goal percentage, game
.229—Milwaukee vs. Minneapolis, at Buffalo, November 6,
　　　1954 (22/96)
.234—Chicago vs. Miami, April 10, 1999 (18/77)
.235—New York vs. Milwaukee, at Providence, December 31,
　　　1954 (24/102)

Highest field-goal percentage, both teams, game
.632—Boston (.650) vs. New Jersey (.615) at Hartford,
　　　December 11, 1984 (108/171)
.630—Portland (.697) vs. L.A. Clippers (.560), February 1,
　　　1986 (109/173)
.628—New York (.642) vs. Denver (.612), December 8, 1981
　　　(113/180)
.625—Chicago (.699) vs. Detroit (.559), January 22, 1980
　　　(110/176)
　　　Phoenix (.696) at Golden State (.566), March 12, 1980
　　　(95/152)

Lowest field-goal percentage, both teams, game
.246—Milwaukee (.229) vs. Minneapolis (.263), at Buffalo,
　　　November 6, 1954 (48/195)
.260—Rochester (.250) at St. Louis (.270), November 23,
　　　1955 (61/235)
.273—St. Louis (.239) vs. Syracuse (.315), November 12,
　　　1955 (56/205)

FIELD GOALS

Most field goals per game, season
49.9—Boston, 1959-60 (3,744/75)
49.0—Philadelphia, 1961-62 (3,917/80)
48.5—Denver, 1981-82 (3,900/02)

Fewest field goals per game, season
30.4—Milwaukee, 1954-55 (2,187/72)
30.8—Chicago, 1998-99 (1,539/50)
　　　Atlanta, 1998-99 (1,539/50)
31.2—Cleveland, 1998-99 (1,562/50)

Most field goals, game
74—Detroit at Denver, December 13, 1983 (3 ot)
72—Boston vs. Minneapolis, February 27, 1959
69—Syracuse vs. San Francisco, March 10, 1963
　　Los Angeles vs. Golden State, March 19, 1972
　　Detroit vs. Boston, March 9, 1979
　　Milwaukee vs. New Orleans, March 14, 1979
　　Los Angeles vs. Denver, April 9, 1982

Fewest field goals, game
18—Chicago vs. Miami, April 10, 1999
19—Indiana at New York, December 10, 1985
　　Utah at San Antonio, November 8, 1997
　　New York at Chicago, March 12, 1999
　　Miami at Charlotte, December 20, 2000
　　Toronto at Minnesota, November 1, 2003
20—by many

Most field goals, both teams, game
142—Detroit (74) at Denver (68), December 13, 1983 (3 ot)
136—Milwaukee (68) at San Antonio (68), March 6, 1982 (3 ot)
134—Cincinnati (67) vs. San Diego (67), March 12, 1970

Fewest field goals, both teams, game
45—Minnesota (22) vs. Atlanta (23), April 12, 1997
　　New York (19) at Chicago (26), March 12, 1999
　　Miami (19) at Charlotte (26), December 20, 2000
46—Boston (23) vs. Milwaukee (23), at Providence, February 27, 1955
　　Dallas (20) at Utah (26), February 26, 1999
　　Chicago (22) vs. Washington (24), January 19, 2002
47—many times

Most field goals, one half
43—Phoenix vs. Denver, November 10, 1990 (1st Half)

Most field goals, both teams, one half
71—Denver (37) at San Antonio (34), November 7, 1990 (1st Half)

Most field goals, one quarter
24—Phoenix vs. Denver, November 10, 1990 (2nd Qtr.)

Most field goals, both teams, one quarter
40—Boston (23) vs. Minneapolis (17), February 27, 1959 (4th Qtr.)

FIELD-GOAL ATTEMPTS

Most field-goal attempts per game, season
119.6—Boston, 1959-60 (8,971/75)
117.7—Boston, 1960-61 (9,295/79)
115.7—Philadelphia, 1959-60 (8,678/75)

Fewest field-goal attempts per game, season
71.22—Cleveland, 1998-99 (3,561/50)
71.30—Miami, 1998-99 (3,565/50)
72.40—Utah, 1998-99 (3,620/50)

Most field-goal attempts, game
153—Philadelphia vs. Los Angeles, December 8, 1961 (3 ot)
150—Boston vs. Philadelphia, March 2, 1960
149—Boston vs. Detroit, January 27, 1961

Fewest field-goal attempts, game
53—Cleveland vs. Boston, November 29, 1997
　　Utah vs. Dallas, December 12, 1997
54—Houston vs. Utah, February 4, 2002
55—Ft. Wayne at Milwaukee, February 20, 1955
　　Philadelphia vs. Atlanta, April 1, 1988
　　Milwaukee at Detroit, December 27, 1994
　　Detroit at Cleveland, March 4, 1999
　　Utah vs. Miami, January 28, 2002

Most field-goal attempts, both teams, game
291—Philadelphia (153) vs. Los Angeles (138), December 8,
　　　1961 (3 ot)
274—Boston (149) vs. Detroit (125), January 27, 1961
　　　Philadelphia (141) at Boston (133), March 5, 1961
272—Boston (150) vs. Philadelphia (122), March 2, 1960
　　　New York (138) at Boston (134), March 9, 1960

Fewest field-goal attempts, both teams, game
116—Utah (53) vs. Dallas (63), December 12, 1997
118—Detroit (55) at Cleveland (63), March 4, 1999
121—Seattle (60) at Cleveland (61), February 25, 1997
　　　Detroit (60) at Cleveland (61), March 17, 1997

Most field-goal attempts, one half
83—Philadelphia vs. Syracuse, November 4, 1959
　　Boston at Philadelphia, December 27, 1960

Most field-goal attempts, both teams, one half
153—Boston (80) vs. Minneapolis (73), February 27, 1959
　　　(2nd Half)

Most field-goal attempts, one quarter
47—Boston vs. Minneapolis, February 27, 1959 (4th Qtr.)

Most field-goal attempts, both teams, one quarter
86—Boston (47) vs. Minneapolis (39), February 27, 1959 (4th Qtr.)

3-POINT FIELD-GOAL PERCENTAGE

Highest 3-point field-goal percentage, season
.428 —Charlotte, 1996-97 (591/1,382)
.40677—Washington, 1995-96 (493/1,212)
.40676—San Antonio, 2000-01 (445/1,094)

Lowest 3-point field-goal percentage, season
.104—Los Angeles, 1982-83 (10/96)
.122—Atlanta, 1980-81 (10/82)
.138—Los Angeles, 1981-82 (13/94)

Most 3-point field goals, no misses, game
7—Indiana vs. Atlanta, January 20, 1995
6—Cleveland at Utah, January 24, 1985
　　L.A. Lakers at Portland, January 1, 1987
　　Houston vs. Denver, February 17, 1989

San Antonio vs. Milwaukee, December 22, 1990
Utah at Minnesota, March 15, 1999

Most 3-point field goals, no misses, both teams, game
5—San Antonio (4) at Philadelphia (1), December 19, 1984
4—Washington (4) at Kansas City (0), January 8, 1981
Washington (3) vs. Atlanta (1), December 3, 1987

Most 3-point field goal attempts, none made, game
15—Houston at Orlando, March 30, 1991
Golden State vs. Indiana, December 6, 1996
Milwaukee vs. Phoenix, January 22, 2002
14—Philadelphia at Houston, February 22, 1988
Cleveland at Golden State, November 12, 1992 (2 ot)
Golden State vs. Minnesota, April 9, 2004
13—Portland at Philadelphia, March 1, 1991
New York vs. Utah, November 20, 1993
Phoenix at San Antonio, March 31, 1996
Philadelphia vs. Golden State, January 15, 1997
Vancouver at Miami, March 14, 1997
Cleveland at Houston, October 31, 1997
Detroit vs. Orlando, April 3, 1999
Sacramento at San Antonio, November 29, 2000
Golden State vs. Miami, December 16, 2000

3-POINT FIELD GOALS

Most 3-point field goals per game, season
8.96—Dallas, 1995-96 (735/82)
8.82—Seattle, 2003-04 (723/82)
8.77—Boston, 2002-03 (719/82)

Fewest 3-point field goals per game, season
0.12—Atlanta, 1980-81 (10/82)
Los Angeles, 1982-83 (10/82)
0.16—Atlanta, 1979-80 (13/82)
Detroit, 1980-81 (13/82)
Los Angeles, 1981-82 (13/82)

Most 3-point field goals, game
19—Atlanta at Dallas, December 17, 1996
18—Dallas at Denver, February 29, 1996
Dallas vs. New Jersey, March 5, 1996
Dallas at Atlanta, January 15, 2002
Seattle vs. Boston, February 22, 2004
17—Many times

Most 3-point field goals, both teams, game
29—Denver (16) at Seattle (13), March 20, 1997
28—Dallas (15) at Houston (13), April 11, 1995 (2 ot)
Dallas (15) vs. Philadelphia (13), February 27, 1996
Houston (16) vs. Philadelphia (12), December 7, 1996
Seattle (17) at Vancouver (11), April 3, 1998
27—Denver (14) at Utah (13), December 7, 1995

Most 3-point field goals, one half
12—Dallas at Denver, February 29, 1996
Milwaukee at Portland, January 5, 2001
Houston vs. Milwaukee, December 22, 2001
Sacramento vs. Chicago, November 23, 2003
Seattle vs. Boston, February 22, 2004

Most 3-point field goals, one quarter
10—Boston at Atlanta, November 17, 2001

3-POINT FIELD-GOAL ATTEMPTS

Most 3-point field-goal attempts per game, season
26.28—Boston, 2002-03 (2,155/82)
24.87—Dallas, 1995-96 (2,039/82)
23.73—Boston, 2001-02 (1,946/82)

Fewest 3-point field-goal attempts per game, season
0.91—Atlanta, 1979-80 (75/82)
1.00—Atlanta, 1980-81 (82/82)
1.02—Detroit, 1980-81 (84/82)
Philadelphia, 1980-81 (84/82)

Most 3-point field-goal attempts, game
49—Dallas vs. New Jersey, March 5, 1996

44—Dallas at Vancouver, March 1, 1996
42—Dallas vs. Phoenix, March 3, 1996

Most 3-point field-goal attempts, both teams, game
64—Houston (33) vs. Dallas (31), April 11, 1995 (2 ot)
Cleveland (40) vs. Portland (24), December 30, 1995 (2 ot)
Houston (37) vs. L.A. Lakers (27), November 12, 1996 (2 ot)
63—Dallas (40) at L.A. Lakers (23), March 17, 2002
Boston (35) vs. Houston (28), February 24, 2003 (ot)
62—Dallas (40) vs. Philadelphia (22), February 27, 1996
Seattle (33) vs. Atlanta (29), November 5, 1996
Seattle (35) at Golden State (27), January 10, 2004 (ot)

Most 3-point field-goal attempts, one half
28—Phoenix at New York, January 29, 1995

FREE THROW PERCENTAGE

Highest free throw percentage, season
.832—Boston, 1989-90 (1,791/2,153)
.829—Dallas, 2002-03 (1,486/1,793)
.824—Boston, 1990-91 (1,646/1,997)

Lowest free throw percentage, season
.635—Philadelphia, 1967-68 (2,121/3,338)
.638—San Francisco, 1963-64 (1,800/2,821)
.640—San Francisco, 1964-65 (1,819/2,844)

Most free throws made, no misses, game
39—Utah at Portland, December 7, 1982
35—Boston vs. Miami, April 12, 1990
33—Boston vs. New Jersey, March 18, 1990
Golden State vs. Houston, April 11, 1991
30—Buffalo vs. Los Angeles, November 18, 1975
Utah vs. Boston, December 28, 1985
Portland at Indiana, November 30, 1986
Miami at Boston, March 24, 1993
29—Syracuse at Boston, November 2, 1957
Utah at Boston, December 14, 1984

Lowest free throw percentage, game
.000—Toronto vs. Charlotte, January 9, 1996 (0/3)
.200—New Orleans at Houston, November 19, 1977 (1/5)
New Jersey at Minnesota, February 25, 2004 (1/5)
.214—Houston vs. Portland, February 22, 1983 (3/14)
.231—Miami at L.A. Lakers, April 5, 1991 (3/13)
.261—Orlando at New Jersey, December 12, 1994 (6/23)

Highest free throw percentage, both teams, game
1.000—Atlanta (1.000) vs. Toronto (1.000), December 22, 2000 (16/16)
.977—Minnesota (1.000) at Phoenix (.950), April 5, 2003 (43/44)
.973—Denver (1.000) vs. Phoenix (.938), April 4, 1997 (36/37)

Lowest free throw percentage, both teams, game
.410—Los Angeles (.386) at Chicago (.471), December 7, 1968 (25/61)
.442—Cleveland (.316) at Detroit (.542), November 22, 1986 (19/43)
.450—Milwaukee (.375) at Cleveland (.500), November 3, 1977 (9/20)

FREE THROWS MADE

Most free throws made per game, season
31.9—New York, 1957-58 (2,300/72)
31.2—Minneapolis, 1957-58 (2,246/72)
30.9—Syracuse, 1952-53 (2,197/71)

Fewest free throws made per game, season
14.9—Boston, 1998-99 (745/50)
15.0—Vancouver, 1996-97 (1,230/82)
15.1—Miami, 2001-02 (1,236/82)

Most free throws made, game
61—Phoenix vs. Utah, April 9, 1990 (ot)
60—Washington vs. New York, November 13, 1987
59—Syracuse vs. Anderson, November 24, 1949 (5 ot)

Fewest free throws made, game
0—Toronto vs. Charlotte, January 9, 1996

1—New Orleans at Houston, November 19, 1977
  New Jersey at Minnesota, February 25, 2004
2—by many

Most free throws made, both teams, game
116—Syracuse (59) vs. Anderson (57), November 24, 1949 (5 ot)
103—Boston (56) at Minneapolis (47), November 28, 1954
 96—Philadelphia (48) vs. Minneapolis (48), November 2, 1957

Fewest free throws made, both teams, game
 7—Milwaukee (3) vs. Baltimore (4), January 1, 1973
 9—Milwaukee (3) at Cleveland (6), November 3, 1977
  Los Angeles (2) vs. San Diego (7), March 28, 1980
10—New Orleans (1) at Houston (9), November 19, 1977

Most free throws made, one half
36—Chicago vs. Phoenix, January 8, 1970
  Golden State vs. Utah, March 29, 1990
  Seattle at Denver, April 7, 1991

Most free throws made, both teams, one half
62—Golden State (33) vs. Sacramento (29), January 26, 1996
Most free throws made, one quarter
26—Atlanta at Milwaukee, March 3, 1991
Most free throws made, both teams, one quarter
41—Milwaukee (32) vs. L.A. Lakers (19), March 21, 2001

FREE THROW ATTEMPTS

Most free throw attempts per game, season
42.4—New York, 1957-58 (3,056/72)
42.3—St. Louis, 1957-58 (3,047/72)
42.1—Philadelphia, 1966-67 (3,411/81)

Fewest free throw attempts per game, season
19.8—New York, 2002-03 (1,620/82)
19.9—Phoenix, 2001-02 (1,630/02)
20.1—Toronto, 2003-04 (1,650/82)

Most free throw attempts, game
86—Syracuse vs. Anderson, November 24, 1949 (5 ot)
80—Phoenix vs. Utah, April 9, 1990 (ot)
74—Anderson at Syracuse, November 24, 1949 (5 ot)
  San Francisco vs. New York, November 6, 1964 (2 ot)
71—Chicago vs. Phoenix, January 8, 1970

Fewest free throw attempts, game
2—Cleveland vs. Golden State, November 26, 1994
3—Los Angeles vs. San Diego, March 28, 1980
  Toronto vs. Charlotte, January 9, 1996
  Milwaukee vs. Houston, February 20, 2002
4—Many times

Most free throw attempts, both teams, game
160—Syracuse (86) vs. Anderson (74), November 24, 1949 (5 ot)
136—Baltimore (70) vs. Syracuse (66), November 15, 1952 (ot)
127—Ft. Wayne (67) vs. Minneapolis (60), December 31, 1954

Fewest free throw attempts, both teams, game
12—Los Angeles (3) vs. San Diego (9), March 28, 1980
14—Milwaukee (6) vs. Baltimore (8), January 1, 1973
15—New Orleans (5) at Houston (10), November 19, 1977

Most free throw attempts, one half
48—Chicago vs. Phoenix, January 8, 1970
Most free throw attempts, both teams, one half
79—Golden State (43) vs. Sacramento (36), January 26, 1996

Most free throw attempts, one quarter
32—Vancouver vs. L.A. Clippers, November 11, 1997

Most free throw attempts, both teams, one quarter
50—New York (26) at St. Louis (24), December 14, 1957
  Cincinnati (29) at Baltimore (21), December 27, 1964

REBOUNDS

Rebounds have been compiled since 1950-51
Team rebounds not included

Most rebounds per game, season
71.5—Boston, 1959-60 (5,365/75)
70.7—Boston, 1960-61 (5,582/79)
70.2—Boston, 1958-59 (5,055/72)

Fewest rebounds per game, season
35.6—Cleveland, 1995-96 (2,922/82)

35.8—Cleveland, 1998-99 (1,788/50)
36.3—Minnesota, 1994-95 (2,973/82)

Most rebounds, game
109—Boston vs. Detroit, December 24, 1960
105—Boston vs. Minneapolis, February 26, 1960
104—Philadelphia vs. Syracuse, November 4, 1959
  Philadelphia vs. Cincinnati, November 8, 1959

Fewest rebounds, game
18—Detroit vs. Charlotte, November 28, 2001
19—Seattle vs. Phoenix, April 14, 1999
20—New York vs. Ft. Wayne, at Miami, February 14, 1955
  Buffalo at Houston, February 17, 1974
  Seattle at Charlotte, March 6, 1998

Most rebounds, both teams, game
188—Philadelphia (98) vs. Los Angeles (90), December 8, 1961 (3 ot)
177—Philadelphia (104) vs. Syracuse (73), November 4, 1959
  Boston (89) at Philadelphia (88), December 27, 1960

Fewest rebounds, both teams, game
48—New York (20) vs. Ft. Wayne (28), at Miami, February 14, 1955
50—New York (23) vs. Indiana (27), January 10, 1995
51—Cleveland (22) at Indiana (29), March 29, 1995
  Seattle (19) vs. Phoenix (32), April 14, 1999

Most rebounds, one half
65—Boston vs. Cincinnati, January 12, 1962

Most rebounds, one quarter
40—Philadelphia vs. Syracuse, November 9, 1961

Highest rebound percentage, season
.553—Portland, 1994-95
.548—Boston, 1972-73
.543—Dallas, 1994-95

Lowest rebound percentage, season
.438—Golden State, 1989-90
.458—Dallas, 1999-2000
.459—Minnesota, 1994-95

Highest rebound percentage, game
.727—Portland vs. Houston, December 19, 1989
.714—Atlanta at Phoenix, April 5, 1977
.713—Chicago vs. Portland, January 16, 1981

OFFENSIVE REBOUNDS

Offensive rebounds have been compiled since 1973-74

Most offensive rebounds per game, season
18.54—Denver, 1990-91 (1,520/82)
18.46—Dallas, 1994-95 (1,514/82)
 18.4—New Jersey, 1991-92 (1,512/82)

Fewest offensive rebounds per game, season
9.43—New York, 2000-01 (773/82)
9.44—Cleveland, 1998-99 (472/50)
 9.6—Charlotte, 1998-99 (480/50)

Most offensive rebounds, game
39—Boston at Capital, October 20, 1973
37—Kansas City at Denver, January 4, 1983
  San Antonio at Golden State, February 28, 1990 (ot)
  New Jersey vs. Golden State, April 6, 1990
  Dallas vs. Vancouver, December 28, 1995 (2 ot)
36—Detroit at Los Angeles, December 14, 1975

Fewest offensive rebounds, game
0—San Antonio at Utah, January 23, 2002
1—Cleveland vs. Houston, March 23, 1975
  New York vs. Boston, March 4, 1978
  Denver vs. Portland, December 5, 1996
  Cleveland vs. Toronto, March 30, 1999
  Cleveland at Washington, April 29, 1999
  Miami at Portland, January 18, 2001
  Indiana vs. Detroit, January 18, 2002
  L.A. Lakers vs. Indiana, March 1, 2002
  Houston at Chicago, November 3, 2003
2—by many

Most offensive rebounds, both teams, game
60—Golden State (33) vs. Vancouver (27), April 18, 2001

57—Los Angeles (29) vs. Cleveland (28), January 22, 1974 (ot)
    Detroit (29) vs. Indiana (28), January 30, 1977
56—Los Angeles (30) vs. Utah (26), November 13, 1983

Fewest offensive rebounds, both teams, game
6—Indiana (1) vs. Detroit (5), January 18, 2002
7—Houston (3) vs. New Jersey (4), March 15, 2001
    New York (3) vs. Houston (4), February 25, 2003
8—Detroit (4) at Boston (4), November 11, 1988
    Cleveland (3) vs. Utah (5), March 16, 1995
    Portland (3) vs. Houston (5), November 11, 2000
    Milwaukee (2) vs. Indiana (6), December 26, 2003

Most offensive rebounds, one half
25—San Antonio vs. Denver, April 8, 1997

Highest offensive rebound percentage, season
.391—New Jersey, 1991-92
.389—Dallas, 1994-95
.388—Golden State, 1980-81

Lowest offensive rebound percentage, season
.236—Boston, 2002-03
.238—Toronto, 2003-04
.241—Dallas, 2000-01

Highest offensive rebound percentage, game
.659—New York vs. Washington, December 1, 1983 (29-44)
.647—Houston vs. Seattle, February 11, 1982 (33-51)
.642—Indiana vs. Milwaukee, March 17, 1993 (34-53)

DEFENSIVE REBOUNDS

Defensive rebounds have been compiled since 1973-74

Most defensive rebounds per game, season
37.5—Boston, 1973-74, (3,074/82)
37.0—Golden State, 1973-74 (3,035/82)
36.2—Boston, 1975-76 (2,972/82)

Fewest defensive rebounds per game, season
24.9—Boston, 1997-98 (2,044/82)
25.0—Minnesota, 1989-90 (2,053/82)
25.1—Cleveland, 1995-96 (2,055/82)

Most defensive rebounds, game
61—Boston vs. Capital, March 17, 1974
58—Los Angeles vs. Seattle, October 19, 1973
56—Portland vs. Cleveland, October 18, 1974 (4 ot)

Fewest defensive rebounds, game
10—Utah at L.A. Lakers, April 1, 1990
11—Charlotte vs. Indiana, February 2, 1994
    Golden State vs. New York, November 7, 1996
12—Indiana at New Jersey, February 27, 1987
    Philadelphia at Boston, January 20, 1989

Most defensive rebounds, both teams, game
106—Portland (56) vs. Cleveland (50), October 18, 1974 (4 ot)
103—Philadelphia (54) vs. Washington (49), November 15, 1975 (3 ot)
101—Indiana (53) vs. Denver (48), January 23, 1989

Fewest defensive rebounds, both teams, game
31—Utah (10) at L.A. Lakers (21), April 1, 1990
32—Golden State (14) vs. Toronto (18), February 2, 1996
33—Philadelphia (16) at Milwaukee (17), December 14, 1984
    Cleveland (15) at New York (18), April 11, 1996

Most defensive rebounds, one half
36—Los Angeles vs. Seattle, October 19, 1973

Highest defensive rebound percentage, season
.7459—San Antonio, 2003-04
.7456—Chicago, 1975-76
.745—Charlotte, 2000-01

Lowest defensive rebound percentage, season
.615—Golden State, 1989-90
.619—New York, 1986-87
.623—Minnesota, 1991-92

Highest defensive rebound percentage, game
1.000—Utah vs. San Antonio, January 23, 2002 (25-25)
.974—Portland vs. Miami, January 18, 2001 (38-39)
    Indiana at L.A. Lakers, March 1, 2002 (38-39)
.973—Boston at New York, March 4, 1978 (36-37)

ASSISTS

Most assists per game, season
31.4—L.A. Lakers, 1984-85 (2,575/82)
31.2—Milwaukee, 1978-79 (2,562/82)

30.7—Los Angeles, 1982-83 (2,519/82)

Fewest assists per game, season
15.6—Atlanta, 1998-99 (782/50)
16.4—L.A. Clippers, 1998-99 (820/50)
16.6—Minneapolis, 1956-57 (1,195/72)

Most assists, game
53—Milwaukee vs. Detroit, December 26, 1978
52—Chicago vs. Atlanta, March 20, 1971
    Seattle vs. Denver, March 18, 1983
    Denver at Golden State, April 21, 1989
51—Sheboygan vs. Denver, March 10, 1950
    Phoenix vs. San Antonio, February 2, 1979
    Los Angeles vs. Denver, February 23, 1982

Fewest assists, game
3—Boston vs. Minneapolis, at Louisville, November 28, 1956
    Baltimore vs. Boston, October 16, 1963
    Cincinnati vs. Chicago, at Evansville, December 5, 1967
    New York at Boston, March 28, 1976
4—By many

Most assists, both teams, game
93—Detroit (47) at Denver (46), December 13, 1983 (3 ot)
90—Rochester (48) vs. Minnesota (42), at Kentucky, January 23, 1957
89—Detroit (48) at Cleveland (41), March 28, 1973 (ot)

Fewest assists, both teams, game
10—Boston (3) vs. Minneapolis (7), at Louisville, November 28, 1956
11—Baltimore (3) vs. Boston (8), October 16, 1963
12—Ft. Wayne (6) vs. New York (6), at Miami, February 17, 1955
    Chicago (6) vs. St. Louis (6), October 27, 1961

Most assists, one half
33—Phoenix vs. Denver, November 10, 1990

Most assists, both teams, one half
51—Denver (27) at San Antonio (24), November 7, 1990

Most assists, one quarter
19—Milwaukee vs. Detroit, December 26, 1978
    San Antonio vs. Denver, April 15, 1984 (2nd Qtr.)

Most assists, both teams, one quarter
28—Minnesota (15) vs. Charlotte (13), April 19, 1992

PERSONAL FOULS

Most personal fouls per game, season
32.1—Tri-Cities, 1949-50 (2,057/64)
31.6—Rochester, 1952-53 (2,210/70)
30.8—Tri-Cities, 1950-51 (2,092/68)

Since 1954-55 season
30.1—Atlanta, 1977-78 (2,470/82)

Fewest personal fouls per game, season
18.0—Houston, 2001-02 (1,476/82)
18.1—Philadelphia, 1993-94 (1,488/82)
18.6—L.A. Lakers, 1990-91 (1,524/82)

Most personal fouls, game
66—Anderson at Syracuse, November 24, 1949 (5 ot)
60—Syracuse at Baltimore, November 15, 1952 (ot)
56—Syracuse vs. Anderson, November 24, 1949 (5 ot)
55—Milwaukee at Baltimore, November 12, 1952

Since 1954-55 season
52—Utah at Phoenix, April 9, 1990 (ot)

Since 1954-55 season (regulation game)
46—New York at Phoenix, December 3, 1987

Fewest personal fouls, game
5—Dallas at San Antonio, November 20, 1999
7—San Antonio at Houston, April 13, 1984 (ot)
    Phoenix at San Antonio, April 18, 1997
    Houston at Milwaukee, February 20, 2004
    Houston at Sacramento, December 1, 2002
8—Detroit at Phoenix, March 27, 1975
    Indiana at New Jersey, November 3, 1984
    Dallas at Seattle, January 7, 1985
    Utah vs. Washington, December 4, 1991

Houston at Minnesota, February 4, 2000

Most personal fouls, both teams, game
122—Anderson (66) at Syracuse (56), November 24, 1949 (5 ot)
114—Syracuse (60) at Baltimore (54), November 15, 1952 (ot)
 97—Syracuse (50) vs. New York (47), February 15. 1953

Since 1954-55 season
87—Portland (44) vs. Chicago (43), March 16, 1984 (4 ot)
 Detroit (44) at Denver (43), December 13, 1983 (3 ot)

Since 1954-55 season (regulation game)
84—Indiana (44) vs. Kansas City (40), October 22, 1977

Fewest personal fouls, both teams, game
21—Phoenix (9) at Portland (12), December 1, 2001
 Portland (10) vs. Atlanta (11), November 8, 2003
 Dallas (10) vs. Seattle (11), April 6, 2004
22—New Jersey (10) at Philadelphia (12), December 22, 1984
 Dallas (10) at New York (12), December 22, 1997
 Houston (7) at Sacramento (15), December 1, 2002
23—Detroit (8) at Phoenix (15), March 27, 1975
 Cleveland (10) at Washington (13), March 16, 1992
 Houston (10) at Sacramento (13), November 21, 1999
 Portland (9) at Vancouver (14), April 12, 2001
 New Orleans (10) vs. Sacramento (13), February 5, 2003
 Dallas (10) at Seattle (13), April 10, 2004

Most personal fouls, one half
30—Rochester at Syracuse, January 15, 1953

Most personal fouls, both teams, one half
51—Syracuse (28) at Boston (23), December 26, 1950

Most personal fouls, one quarter
19—Dallas at Denver, January 15, 1982

Most personal fouls, both teams, one quarter
32—Dallas (19) at Denver (13), January 15, 1902

DISQUALIFICATIONS

Disqualifications have been compiled since 1950-51

Most disqualifications per game, season
1.53—Rochester, 1952-53 (107/70)
1.41—Ft. Wayne, 1952-53 (97/69)
1.31—Baltimore, 1952-53 (93/71)
 Milwaukee, 1952-53 (93/71)

Since 1954-55 season
0.98—Atlanta, 1977-78 (80/82)

Fewest disqualifications per game, season
0.02—L.A. Lakers, 1988-89 (2/82)
0.04—Detroit, 1991-92 (3/82)
0.05—Chicago, 1991-92 (4/82)
 San Antonio, 1993-94 (4/82)
 Houston, 2002-03 (4/82)

Most disqualifications, game
8—Syracuse at Baltimore, November 15, 1952 (ot)
6—Syracuse at Boston, December 26, 1950
5—Pittsburgh at Philadelphia, November 7, 1946
 Boston vs. Syracuse, December 26, 1950
 Baltimore vs. Syracuse, November 15, 1952 (ot)
 Rochester at Philadelphia, December 11, 1952
 Minneapolis vs. St. Louis, February 17, 1957 (ot)
 Indiana at New Jersey, February 8, 1978 (ot)
 Kansas City at Denver, November 11, 1978
 Chicago at Portland, March 16, 1984 (4 ot)
 Atlanta at Utah, February 19, 1986 (ot)

Most disqualifications, both teams, game
13—Syracuse (8) at Baltimore (5), November 15, 1952 (ot)
11—Syracuse (6) at Boston (5), December 26, 1950
 9—Minneapolis (5) vs. St. Louis (4), February 17, 1957 (ot)

Since 1954-55 season (regulation game)
8—Kansas City (5) at Denver (3), November 11, 1978

STEALS

Steals have been compiled since 1973-74

Most steals per game, season
12.9—Phoenix, 1977-78 (1,059/82)
12.8—Seattle, 1993-94 (1,053/82)

12.0—Boston, 1997-98 (987/82)

Fewest steals per game, season
5.94—Detroit, 1990-91 (487/82)
5.98—L.A. Clippers, 2000-01 (490/82)
6.10—Atlanta, 1999-00 (500/82)

Most steals, game
27—Seattle vs. Toronto, January 15, 1997
25—Golden State vs. Los Angeles, March 25, 1975
 Golden State vs. San Antonio, February 15, 1989
24—by many

Fewest steals, game
0—Accomplished 21 times. Most recent:
 Minnesota at San Antonio, March 18, 2004

Most steals, both teams, game
40—Golden State (24) vs. Los Angeles (16), January 21, 1975
 Philadelphia (24) vs. Detroit (16), November 11, 1978
 Golden State (25) vs. San Antonio (15), February 15, 1989
39—Golden State (25) vs. Los Angeles (14), March 25, 1975
 Atlanta (22) vs. Detroit (17), January 3, 1978
 Phoenix (20) at New York (19), February 25, 1978
 Seattle (27) vs. Toronto (12), January 15, 1997

Fewest steals, both teams, game
2—Detroit (1) at New York (1), October 9, 1973
 San Antonio (1) at Charlotte (1), February 6, 1996
3—New York (1) vs. Chicago (2), October 20, 1973
 Golden State (0) at New York (3), November 24, 1973
 Cleveland (1) at Boston (2), January 30, 1974
 Phoenix (1) at Utah (2), March 5, 1981
 Cleveland (1) vs. Philadelphia (2), December 3, 1994
 Denver (1) at L.A. Clippers (2), April 18, 1999

Most steals, one half
17—Golden State vs. San Antonio, February 15, 1989

Most steals, one quarter
11—Los Angeles vs. Chicago, March 12, 1982
 New Jersey vs. L.A. Clippers, March 1, 1988
 Miami at L.A. Clippers, February 28, 1992
 Milwaukee vs. Orlando, March 6, 1992
 L.A. Lakers at Dallas, December 13, 1994
 Seattle vs. Toronto, January 15, 1997
 Boston at Chicago, April 1, 1997
 Boston vs. Houston, December 10, 1999

BLOCKED SHOTS

Blocked shots have been compiled since 1973-74

Most blocked shots per game, season
8.7—Washington, 1985-86 (716/82)
8.5—Utah, 1984-85 (697/82)
8.4—Denver, 1993-94 (686/82)

Fewest blocked shots per game, season
2.6 Dallas, 1980 81 (214/82)
2.7—Philadelphia, 1973-74 (220/82)
2.8—Atlanta, 1974-75 (227/82)

Most blocked shots, game
23—Toronto vs. Atlanta, March 23, 2001
22—New Jersey vs. Denver, December 12, 1991
21—Detroit vs. Atlanta, October 18, 1980 (2 ot)
 Los Angeles vs. Denver, April 9, 1982
 Cleveland vs. New York, January 7, 1989

Fewest blocked shots, game
0—by many

Most blocked shots, both teams, game
34—Detroit (19) vs. Washington (15), November 19, 1981
32—New Jersey (19) at New Orleans (13), March 21, 1978
 New Orleans (19) vs. Indiana (13), March 27, 1979
 Philadelphia (20) vs. Seattle (12), March 9, 1984
31—Houston (20) at Denver (11), November 16, 1984
 Washington (20) vs. Indiana (11), February 26, 1987
 Toronto (16) vs. Portland (15), January 28, 1997
 Toronto (23) vs. Atlanta (8), March 23, 2001

Fewest blocked shots, both teams, game
0—Seattle at Portland, November 22, 1973
 Atlanta at Phoenix, December 3, 1974
 Kansas City at New York, October 30, 1975

Detroit at New York, November 29, 1975
Houston at Los Angeles, January 22, 1978
Buffalo at Atlanta, January 29, 1978
Phoenix at Portland, November 25, 1979
Washington at Dallas, February 10, 1982
Miami at Detroit, January 2, 1994
San Antonio at Milwaukee, November 14, 1995

Most blocked shots, one half
16—Toronto vs. Atlanta, March 23, 2001
15—San Antonio vs. Golden State, February 24, 1981
    Detroit vs. Washington, November 19, 1981
    New Jersey vs. Seattle, February 1, 1994

TURNOVERS

Turnovers have been compiled since 1970-71

Most turnovers per game, season
24.5—Denver, 1976-77 (2,011/82)
24.4—Buffalo, 1972-73 (2,001/82)
23.4—Philadelphia, 1976-77 (1,915/82)

Fewest turnovers per game, season
11.6—Dallas, 2002-03 (949/82)
12.1—Dallas, 2001-02 (992/82)
12.2—Dallas, 2003-04 (1,000/82)

Most turnovers, game
45—San Francisco vs. Boston, March 9, 1971
43—Los Angeles vs. Seattle, February 15, 1974

41—New Jersey vs. Detroit, November 16, 1980

Fewest turnovers, game
3—Portland vs. Phoenix, February 22, 1991
    Orlando vs. New York, March 31, 1996
    Toronto at Houston, January 16, 2001
    L.A. Lakers vs. Houston, December 30, 2001
    Sacramento at San Antonio, December 8, 2002
    Washington at Indiana, February 25, 2003
4—by many

Most turnovers, both teams, game
73—Philadelphia (38) vs. San Antonio (35), October 22, 1976
    Denver (38) vs. Phoenix (35), October 24, 1980
71—New Jersey (41) vs. Detroit (30), November 16, 1980
70—San Francisco (45) vs. Boston (25), March 9, 1971
    Portland (36) vs. New Orleans (34), November 30, 1974
    Denver (35) at Detroit (35), March 1, 1977

Fewest turnovers, both teams, game
11—Dallas (4) vs. New Jersey (7), January 20, 2004
12—Cleveland (6) at Boston (6), March 7, 1993
13—Detroit (6) vs. Philadelphia (7), April 21, 1989
    Washington (6) at Detroit (7), December 30, 1992
    Phoenix (5) at San Antonio (8), February 14, 1998
    Atlanta (6) vs. New York (7), April 7, 1998
    Minnesota (4) vs. Denver (9), March 23, 2001
    Portland (5) at L.A. Lakers (8), April 15, 2001
    Washington (6) vs. Toronto (7), February 5, 2002

TEAM DEFENSE

POINTS

Fewest points allowed per game, season
83.4—Atlanta, 1998-99 (4,170/50)
84.0—Miami, 1998-99 (4,201/50)
84.3—Detroit, 2003-04 (6,909/82)
    San Antonio, 2003-04 (6,909/82)

Most points allowed per game, season
130.8—Denver, 1990-91 (10,723/82)
126.5—Denver, 1981-82 (10,371/82)
125.1—Seattle, 1967-68 (10,261/82)

Most consecutive games, fewer than 100 points allowed, season
36—Detroit, October 29, 2003—January 7, 2004
33—New York, November 11, 2000—January 21, 2001
30—Detroit, February 10—April 13, 2004

Most consecutive games, 100-or-more points allowed, season
82—Denver, October 30, 1981—April 17, 1982 (entire season)
    Denver, November 2, 1990—April 21, 1991 (entire season)
80—Seattle, October 13, 1967—March 16, 1968
79—New York, October 20, 1960—March 12, 1961

FIELD-GOAL PERCENTAGE

Opponents' field-goal percentage has been compiled since 1970-71

Lowest opponents' field-goal percentage, season
.402—San Antonio, 1998-99 (1,631/4,061)
.403—New York, 1998-99 (1,528/3,790)
.409—San Antonio, 2003-04 (2,613/6,388)

Highest opponents' field-goal percentage, season
.536—Golden State, 1984-85 (3,839/7,165)
.529—San Diego, 1982-83 (3,652/6,910)
.526—San Diego, 1981-82 (3,739/7,105)

TURNOVERS

Opponents' turnovers have been compiled since 1970-71

Most opponents' turnovers per game, season
24.1—Atlanta, 1977-78 (1,980/82)
24.0—Phoenix, 1977-78 (1,969/82)
23.7—Denver, 1976-77 (1,944/82)

Fewest opponents' turnovers per game, season
12.0—Houston, 2001-02 (988/82)
12.21—Atlanta, 1999-00 (1,001/82)
12.23—Boston, 1989-90 (1,003/82)

TEAM MISCELLANEOUS

GAMES WON & LOST

Highest winning percentage, season
.878—Chicago, 1995-96 (72-10)
.841—Los Angeles, 1971-72 (69-13)
    Chicago, 1996-97 (69-13)
.840—Philadelphia, 1966-67 (68-13)
.829—Boston, 1972-73 (68-14)

Lowest winning percentage, season
.110—Philadelphia, 1972-73 (9-73)
.125—Providence, 1947-48 (6-42)
.134—Dallas, 1992-93 (11-71)
    Denver, 1997-98 (11-71)

Most consecutive games won
33—Los Angeles, November 5, 1971—January 7, 1972
20—Washington, March 13—December 4, 1948 (5 games in
    1947-48; 15 games in 1948-49)
    Milwaukee, February 6—March 8, 1971
19—L.A. Lakers, February 4—March 13, 2000

Most consecutive games won, one season
33—Los Angeles, November 5, 1971—January 7, 1972
20—Milwaukee, February 6—March 8, 1971
9—L.A. Lakers, February 4—March 13, 2000

Most consecutive games won, start of season
15—Washington, November 3—December 4, 1948
    Houston, November 5—December 2, 1993

14—Boston, October 22—November 27, 1957
   Dallas, October 30—November 27, 2002
12—Seattle, October 29—November 19, 1982
   Chicago, November 1—November 21, 1996

Most consecutive games won, end of season
15—Rochester, February 17—March 19, 1950
14—Milwaukee, February 28—March 27, 1973
11—Philadelphia, March 3—March 20, 1966
   San Antonio, March 25—April 14, 2004

Most consecutive games lost
24—Cleveland, March 19—November 5, 1982 (19 games in
   1981-82; 5 games in 1982-83)
23—Vancouver, February 16—April 2, 1996
   Denver, December 9, 1997—January 23, 1998
21—Detroit, March 7—October 22, 1980 (14 games in 1979-
   80; 7 games in 1980-81)
20—Philadelphia, January 9—February 11, 1973
   New York, March 23—November 9, 1985 (12 games in
   1984-85; 8 games in 1985-86)
   Dallas, November 13—December 22, 1993
   L.A. Clippers, April 18—December 5, 1994 (4 games in
   1993-94; 16 games in 1994-95)

Most consecutive games lost, one season
23—Vancouver, February 16—April 2, 1996
   Denver, December 9, 1997—January 23, 1998
20—Philadelphia, January 9—February 11, 1973
   Dallas, November 13—December 22, 1993
19—Cleveland, March 19—April 18, 1982
   San Diego, March 11—April 13, 1982
   L.A. Clippers, December 30, 1988—February 6, 1989
   Dallas, February 6—March 15, 1993
   Vancouver, November 7—December 13, 1995
   Orlando, October 30—December 6, 2003

Most consecutive games lost, start of season
17—Miami, November 5—December 12, 1988
   L.A. Clippers, February 5—March 10, 1999
16—L.A. Clippers, November 4—December 5, 1994
15—Denver, October 29—November 25, 1949
   Cleveland, October 14—November 10, 1970
   Philadelphia, October 10—November 10, 1972

Most consecutive games lost, end of season
19—Cleveland, March 19—April 18, 1982
15—San Diego, February 23—March 20, 1968
14—Detroit, March 7—March 30, 1980
   L.A. Clippers, March 27—April 19, 1987

Highest winning percentage, home games, season
.976—Boston, 1985-86 (40-1)
.971—Rochester, 1949-50 (33-1)
.969—Syracuse, 1949-50 (31-1)
.968—Minneapolis, 1949-50 (30-1)
.967—Washington, 1946-47 (29-1)

Lowest winning percentage, home games, season
.125—Providence, 1947-48 (3-21)
.146—Dallas, 1993-94 (6-35)
.161—Philadelphia, 1972-73 (5-26)

Most consecutive home games won
44—Chicago, March 30, 1995—April 4, 1996 (7 games in
   1994-95; 37 games in 1995-96)
40—Orlando, March 21, 1995—March 19, 1996 (7 games in
   1994-95; 33 games in 1995-96)
38—Boston, December 10, 1985—November 28, 1986 (31
   games in 1985-86; 7 games in 1986-87)

Most consecutive home games won, start of season
37—Chicago, November 3, 1995—April 4, 1996
33—Orlando, November 3, 1995—March 19, 1996
27—Washington, November 20, 1946—March 19, 1947

Most consecutive home games won, end of season
31—Boston, December 10, 1985—April 13, 1986
29—Boston, December 17, 1986—April 19, 1987
27—Minneapolis, November 30, 1949—March 15, 1950

Most consecutive home games lost
19—Dallas, November 6, 1993—January 21, 1994
16—Providence, November 13, 1948—January 6, 1949
   Orlando, March 1—November 6, 1990 (14 games in
   1989-90; 2 games in 1990-91)
15—Cleveland, March 20—November 26, 1982 (9 games in
   1981-82; 6 games in 1982-83)

Most consecutive home games lost, start of season
19—Dallas, November 6, 1993—January 21, 1994
11—Cleveland, October 28—December 4, 1970
   Miami, November 5—December 21, 1988
   Orlando, October 30—December 15, 2003
10—San Diego, October 14—November 8, 1967
   Philadelphia, October 11—December 1, 1972
   Minnesota, November 5—December 14, 1994

Most consecutive home games lost, end of season
14—Orlando, March 1—April 20, 1990
13—Charlotte, February 28—April 21, 1989
11—San Francisco, February 13—March 12, 1965
   Houston, March 1—April 16, 1983

Highest winning percentage, road games, season
.816—Los Angeles, 1971-72 (31-7)
.805—Chicago, 1995-96 (33-8)
.800—Boston, 1972-73 (32-8)
.780—Boston, 1974-75 (32-9)
   Miami, 1996-97 (32-9)

Lowest winning percentage, road games, season
.000—Baltimore, 1953-54 (0-20)
.024—Sacramento, 1990-91 (1-40)
.034—Philadelphia, 1952-53 (1-28)

Most consecutive road games won
16—Los Angeles, November 6, 1971—January 7, 1972
15—Utah, November 27, 1994—January 26, 1995
14—Boston, February 25—December 17, 1961 (4 in 1960-
   61; 10 in 1961-62)
   Miami, November 19—December 29, 1996

Most consecutive road games won, start of season
12—New York, October 15—December 10, 1969
10—Boston, October 28—December 5, 1960
   Boston, November 3—December 17, 1961
 9—Houston, November 7—December 2, 1993

Most consecutive road games won, end of season
8—Milwaukee, March 4—March 27, 1973
7—Chicago, April 2—April 21, 1996
   L.A. Lakers, March 31—April 14, 1998
   Phoenix, March 31—April 19, 1998
6—Washington, February 20—March 13, 1947
   Phoenix, April 6—April 22, 1989

Most consecutive road games lost
43—Sacramento, November 21, 1990—November 22, 1991
   (37 games in 1990-91; 6 games in 1991-92)
34—New Jersey, December 23, 1989—November 21, 1990
   (28 games in 1989-90; 6 games in 1990-91)
   Cleveland, January 13—December 15, 2003 (21 games
   in 2002-03; 13 games in 2003-04)
32—Baltimore, January 2, 1953—March 14, 1954 (12 games
   in 1952-53; 20 games in 1953-54)

Most consecutive road games lost, start of season
29—Dallas, November 10, 1992—March 13, 1993
28—New Orleans, October 17, 1974—February 7, 1975
22—Waterloo, November 10, 1949—February 18, 1950
   Denver, November 1, 1997—Janaury 23, 1998

Most consecutive road games lost, end of season
37—Sacramento, November 21, 1990—April 19, 1991

28—New Jersey, December 23, 1989—April 21, 1990
23—Vancouver, February 19—May 5, 1999

OVERTIME GAMES

Most overtime games, season
14—Philadelphia, 1990-91
13—New York, 1950-51
   L.A. Clippers, 2000-01
   Sacramento, 2000-01
12—Baltimore, 1952-53
   Milwaukee, 1952-53
   Rochester, 1952-53

Most consecutive overtime games, season
3—Ft. Wayne, November 14-17-18, 1951
   Rochester, November 18-20-22, 1951
   San Francisco, October 26-27-28, 1962
   Houston, November 17-20-24, 1976
   Milwaukee, February 24-26-28, 1978
   Kansas City, March 2-4-7, 1979
   Phoenix, April 4-6-7, 1987
   L.A. Lakers, November 1-2-5, 1991
   Boston, March 24-27-29, 1994
   Atlanta, January 7-9-11, 1997
   Denver, February 25-28, March 2, 1997
   Milwaukee, December 26-30, 1997
   Houston, November 26—December 1, 1999
   Sacramento, December 30, 2000—January 5, 2001
   Orlando, January 18-23, 2001

Most overtime games won, season
9—Sacramento, 2000-01
8—Milwaukee, 1977-78
   Philadelphia, 1990-91
   Detroit, 2002-03
7—New York, 1949-50
   New York, 1955-56
   Boston, 1958-59
   Los Angeles, 1961-62
   Chicago, 1969-70
   New York, 1990-91
   Orlando, 1994-95
   Minnesota, 1999-00
   Miami, 2001-02

Most overtime games won, no losses, season
8—Detroit, 2002-03
7—Los Angeles, 1961-62
5—New York, 1946-47
   San Antonio, 1980-81
   Philadelphia, 1982-83
   Portland, 1986-87
   Orlando, 1995-96
   Atlanta, 1996-97
   Charlotte, 1996-97
   Philadelphia, 1999-00
   Memphis, 2003-04

Most consecutive overtime games won
11—San Antonio, November 13, 1979—February 8, 1983 (2
   games in 1979-80; 5 games in 1980-81; 1 game in
   1981-82; 3 games in 1982-83) Atlanta, April 11,
   1995—November 26, 1997 (1 game in 1994-95; 2
   games in 1995-96; 5 games in 1996-97; 3 games in
   1997-98)
10—Milwaukee, February 26, 1972—November 30, 1974 (3
   games in 1971-72; 3 games in 1972-73; 3 games in
   1973-74; 1 game in 1974-75)
 9—Boston, March 24, 1974—October 23, 1976 (1 game in
   1973-74; 3 games in 1974-75; 3 games in 1975-76;
   2 games in 1976-77) Houston, November 3, 1976—
   January 19, 1979 (4 games in 1976-77; 2 games in
   1977-78; 3 games in 1978-79)
   New York, November 11, 1988—February 17, 1990
   (4 games in 1988-89; 5 games in 1989-90)

Most overtime games lost, season
10—Baltimore, 1952-53
   L.A. Clippers, 2000-01
8—Milwaukee, 1952-53
   Golden State, 1979-80
   Chicago, 2002-03
7—by many

Most overtime games lost, no wins, season
8—Golden State, 1979-80
6—Ft. Wayne, 1951-52
   Seattle, 1990-91
   Minnesota, 1992-93
   Atlanta, 2003-04

Most consecutive overtime games lost
10—Golden State, October 13, 1979—March 15, 1981 (8
   games in 1979-80; 2 games in 1980-81)
   Minnesota, November 7, 1992—January 3, 1995 (6
   games in 1992-93; 2 games in 1993-94; 2 games in
   1994-95)
 9—Baltimore, January 14, 1953—February 22, 1954 (6
   games in 1952-53; 3 games in 1953-54)
   Syracuse, January 13, 1960—January 21, 1962 (2
   games in 1959-60; 4 games in 1960-61; 3 games in
   1961-62)
   New Jersey, March 18, 1986—April 19, 1988 (1 game in
   1985-86; 4 games in 1986-87; 4 games in 1987-88)
   Miami, January 2, 1992—February 14, 1993 (3 games in
   1991-92; 6 games in 1992-93)
   Portland, November 26, 1996—February 14, 1999 (5
   games in 1996-97; 3 games in 1997-98; 1 game in
   1998-99)
   L.A. Clippers, April 15, 2000—February 18, 2001 (1
   game in 1999-00; 8 games in 2000-01)

Most overtime periods, game
6—Indianapolis (75) at Rochester (73), January 6, 1951
5—Anderson (123) at Syracuse (125), November 24, 1949
   Seattle (154) at Milwaukee (155), November 9, 1989
4—New York (92) at Rochester (102), January 23, 1951
   Indianapolis (96) at Rochester (99), November 8, 1952
   Cleveland (129) at Portland (131), October 18, 1974
   Los Angeles (153) at Cleveland (154), January 29, 1980
   Atlanta (127) at Seattle (122), February 19, 1982
   Chicago (156) at Portland (155), March 16, 1984
   New Jersey (147) at Golden State (150), February 1, 1987
   Phoenix (140) at Portland (139), November 14, 1997

PLAYOFFS

INDIVIDUAL, SERIES

MOST POINTS

2-game series
68—Bob McAdoo, New York vs. Cleveland, 1978
65—Elgin Baylor, Minneapolis vs. Detroit, 1960
   Gus Williams, Seattle vs. Portland, 1983

3-game series
135—Michael Jordan, Chicago vs. Miami, 1992
131—Michael Jordan, Chicago vs. Boston, 1986

4-game series
150—Hakeem Olajuwon, Houston vs. Dallas, 1988
147—Michael Jordan, Chicago vs. Milwaukee, 1990

5-game series
226—Michael Jordan, Chicago vs. Cleveland, 1988
215—Michael Jordan, Chicago vs. Philadelphia, 1990

6-game series
278—Jerry West, Los Angeles vs. Baltimore, 1965
246—Michael Jordan, Chicago vs. Phoenix, 1993

7-game series
284—Elgin Baylor, Los Angeles vs. Boston, 1962
270—Wilt Chamberlain, San Francisco vs. St. Louis, 1964

MOST MINUTES PLAYED

2-game series
95—John Kerr, Syracuse vs. New York, 1959
92—John Williamson, New Jersey vs. Philadelphia, 1979
   Elvin Hayes, Washington vs. Philadelphia, 1980

3-game series
144—Wilt Chamberlain, Philadelphia vs. Syracuse, 1961
142—Wilt Chamberlain, Philadelphia vs. Syracuse, 1960
   Bill Bridges, St. Louis vs. Baltimore, 1966
   Bob McAdoo, Buffalo vs. Philadelphia, 1976
   Moses Malone, Houston vs. Los Angeles, 1981

4-game series
195—Wilt Chamberlain, Philadelphia vs. Cincinnati, 1965
   Jerry Lucas, Cincinnati vs. Philadelphia, 1965
   Oscar Robertson, Cincinnati vs. Philadelphia, 1965
   Wilt Chamberlain, Los Angeles vs. Atlanta, 1970
192—Wilt Chamberlain, Philadelphia vs. Cincinnati, 1967
   Wilt Chamberlain, Los Angeles vs. Chicago, 1972

5-game series
243—Oscar Robertson, Cincinnati vs. Syracuse, 1963
242—Kareem Abdul-Jabbar, Los Angeles vs. Seattle, 1979

6-game series
296—Wilt Chamberlain, Philadelphia vs. New York, 1968
292—Bill Russell, Boston vs. Los Angeles, 1968

7-game series
345—Kareem Abdul-Jabbar, Milwaukee vs. Boston, 1974
341—Wilt Chamberlain, Philadelphia vs. Boston, 1965

HIGHEST FIELD-GOAL PERCENTAGE

(minimum: 4 FG per game)

2-game series
.773—Darryl Dawkins, New Jersey vs. New York, 1983
.750—Mike Bantom, Indiana vs. Philadelphia, 1981

3-game series
.778—Rick Mahorn, Philadelphia vs. Milwaukee, 1991
.750—Alton Lister, Milwaukee vs. New Jersey, 1986

4-game series
.783—Dale Davis, Indiana vs. Cleveland, 1998
.739—Derrek Dickey, Golden State vs. Washington, 1975

5-game series
.721—James Worthy, L.A. Lakers vs. Denver, 1985
.714—Bobby Jones, Philadelphia vs. Boston, 1985
   Robert Parish, Boston vs. Indiana, 1991

6-game series
.781—James Donaldson, Dallas vs. L.A. Lakers, 1986
.675—Clifford Ray, Golden State vs. Detroit, 1976

7-game series
.744—James Donaldson, Dallas vs. L.A. Lakers, 1988
.690—Shawn Kemp, Seattle vs. Utah, 1996
   Dale Davis, Indiana vs. Chicago, 1998

MOST FIELD GOALS

2-game series
28—Bob McAdoo, New York vs. Cleveland, 1978
27—Jo Jo White, Boston vs. San Antonio, 1977

3-game series
53—Michael Jordan, Chicago vs. Miami, 1992
51—Wilt Chamberlain, Philadelphia vs. Syracuse, 1960

4-game series
65—Kareem Abdul-Jabbar, Milwaukee vs. Chicago, 1974
56—Hakeem Olajuwon, Houston vs. Dallas, 1988
   Hakeem Olajuwon, Houston vs. Orlando, 1995

5-game series
86—Michael Jordan, Chicago vs. Philadelphia, 1990
85—Michael Jordan, Chicago vs. Cleveland, 1988

6-game series
101—Michael Jordan, Chicago vs. Phoenix, 1993
 96—Jerry West, Los Angeles vs. Baltimore, 1965
   Shaquille O'Neal, L.A. Lakers vs. Indiana, 2000

7-game series
113—Wilt Chamberlain, San Francisco vs. St. Louis, 1964
104—Bob McAdoo, Buffalo vs. Washington, 1975

MOST FIELD-GOAL ATTEMPTS

2-game series
62—John Williamson, New Jersey vs. Philadelphia, 1979
53—Neil Johnston, Philadelphia vs. Syracuse, 1957
   George Yardley, Ft. Wayne vs. Minneapolis, 1957
   Elgin Baylor, Minneapolis vs. Detroit, 1960

3-game series
104—Wilt Chamberlain, Philadelphia vs. Syracuse, 1960
 96—Wilt Chamberlain, Philadelphia vs. Syracuse, 1961

4-game series
123—Tracy McGrady, Orlando vs. Milwaukee, 2001
116—Hakeem Olajuwon, Houston vs. Orlando, 1995

5-game series
162—Allen Iverson, Philadelphia vs. L.A. Lakers, 2001
159—Wilt Chamberlain, Philadelphia vs. Syracuse, 1962

6-game series
235—Rick Barry, San Francisco vs. Philadelphia, 1967
212—Jerry West, Los Angeles vs. Baltimore, 1965

7-game series
235—Elgin Baylor, Los Angeles vs. Boston, 1962
216—Elgin Baylor, Los Angeles vs. St. Louis, 1961
   Bob McAdoo, Buffalo vs. Washington, 1975

HIGHEST 3-POINT FIELD-GOAL PERCENTAGE

(minimum: 1 F3 per game)
2-game series
1.000—Kevin Grevey, Washington vs. New Jersey, 1982
 .500—Kevin Grevey, Washington vs. Philadelphia, 1980

3-game series
1.000—Pat Garrity, Phoenix vs. Portland, 1999
 .857—Muggsy Bogues, Charlotte vs. New York, 1997

4-game series
1.000—Dana Barros, Seattle vs. Golden State, 1992
 .818—Bob Hansen, Utah vs. Portland, 1988

5-game series
 .857—John Stockton, Utah vs. Seattle, 2000
 .800—Byron Scott, L.A. Lakers vs. Golden State, 1991

6-game series
 .667—Danny Ainge, Phoenix vs. Chicago, 1993
    Travis Best, Indiana vs. New York, 2000
    Devin Brown, San Antonio vs. L.A. Lakers, 2004
 .654—Bruce Bowen, San Antonio vs. L.A. Lakers, 2003

7-game series
 .636—Craig Hodges, Chicago vs. New York, 1992
    Rasheed Wallace, Portland vs. L.A. Lakers, 2000
 .611—Brian Shaw, L.A. Lakers vs. Portland, 2000

MOST 3-POINT FIELD GOALS MADE

2-game series
5—Kevin Grevey, Washington vs. Philadelphia, 1980
4—Kevin Grevey, Washington vs. New Jersey, 1982

3-game series
14—John Starks, New York vs. Cleveland, 1996
13—Reggie Miller, Indiana vs. Atlanta, 1995

4-game series
15—Reggie Miller, Indiana vs. Philadelphia, 2001
    Derek Fisher, L.A. Lakers vs. San Antonio, 2001
14—Nick Van Exel, L.A. Lakers vs. Seattle, 1995
    Robert Horry, Houston vs. Seattle, 1996

5-game series
22—Rex Chapman, Phoenix vs. Seattle, 1997
20—Paul Pierce, Boston vs. Philadelphia, 2002
    Antoine Walker, Boston vs. Philadelphia, 2002

6-game series
21—Derek Fisher, L.A. Lakers vs. Minnesota, 2003
18—Terry Porter, Portland vs. Utah, 1992

7-game series
28—Dennis Scott, Orlando vs. Indiana, 1995
    Ray Allen, Milwaukee vs. Philadelphia, 2001
25—Reggie Miller, Indiana vs. Orlando, 1995

MOST 3-POINT FIELD-GOAL ATTEMPTS

2-game series
10—Kevin Grevey, Washington vs. Philadelphia, 1980
 6—John Williamson, Washington vs. Philadelphia, 1980

3-game series
35—Reggie Miller, Indiana vs. Milwaukee, 1999
31—Reggie Miller, Indiana vs. Atlanta, 1995

4-game series
42—Nick Anderson, Orlando vs. Philadelphia, 1999
35—Reggie Miller, Indiana vs. Philadelphia, 2001

5-game series
48—Rex Chapman, Phoenix vs. Seattle, 1997
46—Mookie Blaylock, Atlanta vs. Chicago, 1997

6-game series
43—Dennis Scott, Orlando vs. Chicago, 1995
42—Antoine Walker, Boston vs. New Jersey, 2002

7-game series
65—Dennis Scott, Orlando vs. Indiana, 1995
55—Reggie Miller, Indiana vs. Orlando, 1995
    Ray Allen, Milwaukee vs. Philadelphia, 2001

MOST FREE THROWS MADE, NONE MISSED

2-game series
8—Jo Jo White, Boston vs. Seattle, 1977
    Rick Barry, Houston vs. Atlanta, 1979
    Caldwell Jones, Philadelphia vs. New Jersey, 1979
    Mike Newlin, Houston vs. Atlanta, 1979
    Bobby Jones, Philadelphia vs. Washington, 1980

3-game series
25—Jamal Mashburn, Charlotte vs. Miami, 2001
18—Kiki Vandeweghe, Denver vs. Phoenix, 1982

4-game series
32—Kiki Vandeweghe, Portland vs. Denver, 1986
27—Kevin Johnson, Phoenix vs. L.A. Lakers, 1989

5-game series
30—Mark Price, Cleveland vs. Philadelphia, 1990
25—Jeff Malone, Utah vs. Portland, 1991

6-game series
32—Michael Finley, Dallas vs. San Antonio, 2003
24—Caron Butler, Miami vs. Indiana, 2004

7-game series
35—Jack Sikma, Milwaukee vs. Boston, 1987
23—Calvin Murphy, Houston vs. San Antonio, 1981

MOST FREE THROWS MADE

2-game series
21—George Yardley, Detroit vs. Cincinnati, 1958
19—Larry Foust, Ft. Wayne vs. Minneapolis, 1957
    John Kerr, Syracuse vs. New York, 1959
    Reggie Theus, Chicago vs. New York, 1981

3-game series
43—Kevin Johnson, Phoenix vs. Denver, 1989
42—Dolph Schayes, Syracuse vs. Boston, 1957

4-game series
51—Kobe Bryant, L.A. Lakers vs. Sacramento, 2001
49—Jerry West, Los Angeles vs. Atlanta, 1970

5-game series
62—Oscar Robertson, Cincinnati vs. Philadelphia, 1964
61—Oscar Robertson, Cincinnati vs. Boston, 1966
    Karl Malone, Utah vs. L.A. Clippers, 1992

6-game series
86—Jerry West, Los Angeles vs. Baltimore, 1965
68—Michael Jordan, Chicago vs. New York, 1989

7-game series
83—Dolph Schayes, Syracuse vs. Boston, 1959
82—Elgin Baylor, Los Angeles vs. Boston, 1962

MOST FREE THROW ATTEMPTS

2-game series
24—George Yardley, Detroit vs. Cincinnati, 1958
    Bernard King, New Jersey vs. Philadelphia, 1979
    Calvin Natt, Portland vs. Seattle, 1983
23—Larry Foust, Ft. Wayne vs. Minneapolis, 1957

3-game series
47—Dolph Schayes, Syracuse vs. Boston, 1957
46—Kevin Johnson, Phoenix vs. Denver, 1989

4-game series
68—Shaquille O'Neal, L.A. Lakers vs. New Jersey, 2002
61—Shaquille O'Neal, L.A. Lakers vs. San Antonio, 1999

5-game series
79—Karl Malone, Utah vs. L.A. Clippers, 1992
78—Karl Malone, Utah vs. Houston, 1995

6-game series
95—Jerry West, Los Angeles vs. Baltimore, 1965
93—Shaquille O'Neal, L.A. Lakers vs. Indiana, 2000
    Shaquille O'Neal, L.A. Lakers vs. Minnesota, 2004

7-game series
100—Charles Barkley, Philadelphia vs. Milwaukee, 1986
99—Elgin Baylor, Los Angeles vs. Boston, 1962
    Shaquille O'Neal, L.A. Lakers vs. Portland, 2000

MOST REBOUNDS

2-game series
41—Moses Malone, Houston vs. Atlanta, 1979
39—John Kerr, Syracuse vs. Philadelphia, 1957

3-game series
84—Bill Russell, Boston vs. Syracuse, 1957
69—Wilt Chamberlain, Philadelphia vs. Syracuse, 1961

4-game series
118—Bill Russell, Boston vs. Minneapolis, 1959
106—Wilt Chamberlain, Philadelphia vs. Cincinnati, 1967

5-game series
160—Wilt Chamberlain, Philadelphia vs. Boston, 1967
155—Bill Russell, Boston vs. Syracuse, 1961

6-game series
171—Wilt Chamberlain, Philadelphia vs. San Francisco, 1967
165—Wilt Chamberlain, Philadelphia vs. Boston, 1960

7-game series
220—Wilt Chamberlain, Philadelphia vs. Boston, 1965
189—Bill Russell, Boston vs. Los Angeles, 1962

MOST OFFENSIVE REBOUNDS

2-game series
25—Moses Malone, Houston vs. Atlanta, 1979
13—Dan Roundfield, Atlanta vc. Houston, 1979
    Lonnie Shelton, Seattle vs. Portland, 1983

3-game series
28—Moses Malone, Houston vs. Seattle, 1982
23—Dennis Rodman, Chicago vs. New Jersey, 1998

4-game series
27—Moses Malone, Philadelphia vs. Los Angeles, 1983
26—Dennis Rodman, Chicago vs. Orlando, 1996
    Shaquille O'Neal, L.A. Lakers vs. San Antonio, 1999
    Shaquille O'Neal, L.A. Lakers vs. Sacramento, 2001

5-game series
36—Larry Smith, Golden State vs. L.A. Lakers, 1987
35—Charles Barkley, Philadelphia vs. Chicago, 1990

6-game series
46—Moses Malone, Houston vs. Boston, 1981
45—Moses Malone, Houston vs. Philadelphia, 1977

7-game series
45—Wes Unseld, Washington vs. San Antonio, 1979
    Dikembe Mutombo, Philadelphia vs. Milwaukee, 2001
44—Roy Tarpley, Dallas vs. L.A. Lakers, 1988

MOST DEFENSIVE REBOUNDS

2-game series
23—Wes Unseld, Washington vs. Atlanta, 1978
21—Wes Unseld, Washington vs. Philadelphia, 1980

3-game series
43—Bob McAdoo, Buffalo vs. Philadelphia, 1976
42—Dirk Nowitzki, Dallas vs. Minnesota, 2002

4-game series
62—Kareem Abdul-Jabbar, Milwaukee vs. Chicago, 1974
53—Wes Unseld, Washington vs. Golden State, 1975
    Ben Wallace, Detroit vs. New Jersey, 2003

5-game series
66—Kevin Garnett, Minnesota vs. Denver, 2004
64—Tim Duncan, San Antonio vs. L.A. Lakers, 2002

6-game series
91—Bill Walton, Portland vs. Philadelphia, 1977

83—Kevin Garnett, Minnesota vs. L.A. Lakers, 2003
7-game series
95—Kareem Abdul-Jabbar, Los Angeles vs. Golden State, 1977
91—Dirk Nowitzki, Dallas vs. Sacramento, 2003

MOST ASSISTS

2-game series
20—Frank Johnson, Washington vs. New Jersey, 1982
19—Paul Westphal, Phoenix vs. Milwaukee, 1978

3-game series
48—Magic Johnson, Los Angeles vs. San Antonio, 1986
47—Kevin Johnson, Phoenix vs. San Antonio, 1992

4-game series
57—Magic Johnson, L.A. Lakers vs. Phoenix, 1989
54—Magic Johnson, L.A. Lakers vs. Houston, 1990

5-game series
85—Magic Johnson, L.A. Lakers vs. Portland, 1985
81—Magic Johnson, L.A. Lakers vs. Houston, 1986

6-game series
90—Johnny Moore, San Antonio vs. Los Angeles, 1983
87—Magic Johnson, Los Angeles vs. Phoenix, 1984

7-game series
115—John Stockton, Utah vs. L.A. Lakers, 1988
96—Magic Johnson, L.A. Lakers vs. Dallas, 1988

MOST PERSONAL FOULS

2-game series
12—Bob Lochmueller, Syracuse vs. Boston, 1953
    Walter Dukes, Detroit vs. Cincinnati, 1958
    Ray Felix, New York vs. Syracuse, 1959
    Dave Cowens, Boston vs. San Antonio, 1977
    Dan Roundfield, Atlanta vc. Houston, 1979
    Albert King, New Jersey vs. New York, 1983
    Buck Williams, New Jersey vs. New York, 1983

3-game series
18—Charlie Share, St. Louis vs. Minneapolis, 1956
    Vern Mikkelsen, Minneapolis vs. St. Louis, 1957
    Chris Webber, Washington vs. Chicago, 1997
17—Walter Dukes, Minneapolis vs. St. Louis, 1957
    Paul Arizin, Philadelphia vs. Syracuse, 1961
    Larry Costello, Syracuse vs. Philadelphia, 1961
    Dave Twardzik, Portland vs. Chicago, 1977
    Kevin Duckworth, Portland vs. L.A. Lakers, 1989
    Sam Perkins, Dallas vs. Portland, 1990
    Jay Humphries, Milwaukee vs. Philadelphia, 1991

4-game series
22—Al Attles, San Francisco vs. Los Angeles, 1968
    Doc Rivers, Atlanta vs. Detroit, 1986
    Zydrunas Ilgauskas, Cleveland vs. Indiana, 1998
21—Hakeem Olajuwon, Houston vs. Portland, 1987
    Mark Eaton, Utah vs. Portland, 1988
    Roy Tarpley, Dallas vs. Houston, 1988
    Rik Smits, Indiana vs. Cleveland, 1998

5-game series
27—George Mikan, Minneapolis vs. New York, 1953
    Red Rocha, Syracuse vs. Philadelphia, 1956
    Larry Costello, Syracuse vs. Cincinnati, 1963
    Luc Longley, Chicago vs. New York, 1996
26—Tom Gola, Philadelphia vs. Syracuse, 1962
    Bailey Howell, Boston vs. Philadelphia, 1969
    Antoine Carr, Utah vs. Houston, 1995
    Kurt Thomas, New York vs. Toronto, 2001

6-game series
35—Charlie Scott, Boston vs. Phoenix, 1976
33—Tom Heinsohn, Boston vs. St. Louis, 1958
    Tom Meschery, San Francisco vs. Philadelphia, 1967

7-game series
37—Arnie Risen, Boston vs. St. Louis, 1957
    Tom Sanders, Boston vs. Philadelphia, 1965
36—Vern Mikkelsen, Minneapolis vs. New York, 1952
    Jack McMahon, St. Louis vs. Boston, 1957
    Alonzo Mourning, Miami vs. New York, 1997
    Vlade Divac, Sacramento vs. L.A. Lakers, 2002

MOST DISQUALIFICATIONS

2-game series
2—Bob Lochmueller, Syracuse vs. Boston, 1953
    Walter Dukes, Detroit vs. Cincinnati, 1958
    Ray Felix, New York vs. Syracuse, 1959
    Dave Cowens, Boston vs. San Antonio, 1977
    Dan Roundfield, Atlanta vs. Houston, 1979
    Albert King, New Jersey vs. New York, 1983
    Buck Williams, New Jersey vs. New York, 1983

3-game series
3—Charlie Share, St. Louis vs. Minneapolis, 1956
    Vern Mikkelsen, Minneapolis vs. St. Louis, 1957
    Chris Webber, Washington vs. Chicago, 1997

4-game series
2—Walter Dukes, Detroit vs. Cincinnati, 1962
    Zelmo Beaty, St. Louis vs. Detroit, 1963
    Al Attles, San Francisco vs. Los Angeles, 1968
    Bill Turner, San Francisco vs. Los Angeles, 1968
    Lou Hudson, Atlanta vs. Los Angeles, 1970
    Earl Tatum, Los Angeles vs. Portland, 1977
    Dennis Johnson, Phoenix vs. Los Angeles, 1982
    Lonnie Shelton, Cleveland vs. Boston, 1985
    Ben Poquette, Cleveland vs. Boston, 1985
    Sam Bowie, Portland vs. Dallas, 1985
    Doc Rivers, Atlanta vs. Detroit, 1986
    Alton Lister, Seattle vs. L.A. Lakers, 1987
    Mark Eaton, Utah vs. Portland, 1988
    Greg Anderson, Milwaukee vs. Chicago, 1990
    Tyrone Hill, Golden State vs. San Antonio, 1991
    Zydrunas Ilgauskas, Cleveland vs. Indiana, 1998
    Rik Smits, Indiana vs. Cleveland, 1998
    Walt Williams, Portland vs. L.A. Lakers, 1998
    Chris Crawford, Atlanta vs. New York, 1999
    Vlade Divac, Sacramento vs. Utah, 2002
    Antoine Walker, Boston vs. New Jersey, 2003

5-game series
5—Art Hillhouse, Philadelphia vs. Chicago, 1947
4—Chuck Gilmur, Chicago vs. Philadelphia, 1947

6-game series
5—Charlie Scott, Boston vs. Phoenix, 1976
7-game series
5—Arnie Risen, Boston vs. St. Louis, 1957
4—Frank Ramsey, Boston vs. Syracuse, 1959
    Alvin Attles, Philadelphia vs. Boston, 1962
    Hal Greer, Philadelphia vs. Baltimore, 1971

MOST STEALS

2-game series
10—Maurice Cheeks, Philadelphia vs. New Jersey, 1979
 9—Maurice Cheeks, Philadelphia vs. Indiana, 1981

3-game series
13—Clyde Drexler, Portland vs. Dallas, 1990
    Hersey Hawkins, Philadelphia vs. Milwaukee, 1991
12—Alvin Robertson, San Antonio vs. L.A. Lakers, 1988

4-game series
17—Lionel Hollins, Portland vs. Los Angeles, 1977
16—Jason Kidd, Phoenix vs. San Antonio, 1998
    Allen Iverson, Philadelphia vs. Orlando, 1999

5-game series
21—Micheal Ray Richardson, New Jersey vs. Philadelphia, 1984
    Baron Davis, Charlotte vs. New Jersey, 2002
20—Isiah Thomas, Detroit vs. Washington, 1988
    Michael Jordan, Chicago vs. Philadelphia, 1990

6-game series
19—Rick Barry, Golden State vs. Seattle, 1975
18—Slick Watts, Seattle vs. Golden State, 1975
    Gus Williams, Seattle vs. Portland, 1978

7-game series
28—John Stockton, Utah vs. L.A. Lakers, 1988
27—Maurice Cheeks, Philadelphia vs. San Antonio, 1979

MOST BLOCKED SHOTS

2-game series
10—Darryl Dawkins, Philadelphia vs. Atlanta, 1982
 9—Artis Gilmore, Chicago vs. New York, 1981

3-game series
18—Manute Bol, Golden State vs. Utah, 1989
15—Kareem Abdul-Jabbar, Los Angeles vs. Denver, 1979

4-game series
23—Hakeem Olajuwon, Houston vs. L.A. Lakers, 1990
20—Hakeem Olajuwon, Houston vs. Portland, 1987

5-game series
31—Dikembe Mutombo, Denver vs. Seattle, 1994
29—Mark Eaton, Utah vs. Houston, 1985
    Manute Bol, Washington vs. Philadelphia, 1986
    Hakeem Olajuwon, Houston vs. L.A. Clippers, 1993

6-game series
32—Tim Duncan, San Antonio vs. New Jersey, 2003
27—Marvin Webster, Seattle vs. Denver, 1978

7-game series
38—Dikembe Mutombo, Denver vs. Utah, 1994
30—Hakeem Olajuwon, Houston vs. Seattle, 1993
    Patrick Ewing, New York vs. Houston, 1994

MOST TURNOVERS

2-game series
14—John Williamson, New Jersey vs. Philadelphia, 1979
12—Wes Unseld, Washington vs. Atlanta, 1978
    Frank Johnson, Washington vs. New Jersey, 1982

3-game series
20—Anfernee Hardaway, Orlando vs. Indiana, 1994
17—Walter Davis, Phoenix vs. Portland, 1979

4-game series
25—Darrell Armstrong, Orlando vs. Philadelphia, 1999
    Paul Pierce, Boston vs. New Jersey, 2003
    Paul Pierce, Boston vs. Indiana, 2004
24—Magic Johnson, Los Angeles vs. Philadelphia, 1983

5-game series
29—Larry Bird, Boston vs. Milwaukee, 1984
28—Charles Barkley, Philadelphia vs. Washington, 1986
6-game series
30—Magic Johnson, Los Angeles vs. Philadelphia, 1980
    Sidney Moncrief, Milwaukee vs. New Jersey, 1984
29—George McGinnis, Philadelphia vs. Washington, 1978

7-game series
37—Charles Barkley, Philadelphia vs. Milwaukee, 1986
34—John Johnson, Seattle vs. Phoenix, 1979

MOST POINTS

2-game series
260—Syracuse vs. New York, 1959
241—Minneapolis vs. Ft. Wayne, 1957
   New York vs. Cleveland, 1978

3-game series
408—L.A. Lakers vs. Phoenix, 1985
407—L.A. Lakers vs. Denver, 1987

4-game series
498—Philadelphia vs. New York, 1978
492—Portland vs. Dallas, 1985

5-game series
664—San Antonio vs. Denver, 1983
662—L.A. Lakers vs. Denver, 1985

6-game series
747—Philadelphia vs. San Francisco, 1967
735—Los Angeles vs. Detroit, 1962

7-game series
869—Boston vs. Syracuse, 1959
867—Boston vs. Cincinnati, 1963

FEWEST POINTS

2-game series
171—Atlanta vs. Philadelphia, 1982
175—New Jersey vs. Washington, 1982

3-game series
235—Miami vs. Charlotte, 2001
239—Cleveland vs. New York, 1996
   Detroit vs. Miami, 2000

4-game series
304—Portland vs. San Antonio, 1999
306—Atlanta vs. New York, 1999

5-game series
393—Miami vs. Chicago, 1997
395—Miami vs. New York, 1999

6-game series
436—Indiana vs. Detroit, 2004
451—Detroit vs. Indiana, 2004

7-game series
562—Miami vs. New York, 2000
564—New Orleans vs. Miami, 2004

HIGHEST FIELD-GOAL PERCENTAGE

2-game series
.555—New York vs. Cleveland, 1978
.541—Philadelphia vs. Atlanta, 1982

3-game series
.600—L.A. Lakers vs. Phoenix, 1985
.596—L.A. Lakers vs. San Antonio, 1986

4-game series
.561—Milwaukee vs. Chicago, 1974
.554—Boston vs. Chicago, 1981

5-game series
.565—L.A. Lakers vs. Denver, 1985
.560—Los Angeles vs. Dallas, 1984

6-game series
.536—Los Angeles vs. Phoenix, 1984
.534—L.A. Lakers vs. Dallas, 1986

7-game series
.534—L.A. Lakers vs. Dallas, 1988
.526—Detroit vs. Boston, 1987

LOWEST FIELD-GOAL PERCENTAGE

2-game series
.321—Cincinnati vs. Detroit, 1958
.355—Philadelphia vs. Syracuse, 1957

3-game series
.308—Syracuse vs. Boston, 1957
.324—Syracuse vs. Philadelphia, 1958

4-game series
.316—Atlanta vs. New York, 1999
.323—Minneapolis vs. Ft. Wayne, 1955

5-game series
.348—Syracuse vs. Boston, 1961
.352—Cincinnati vs. Boston, 1964

6-game series
.349—Indiana vs. Detroit, 2004
.355—Boston vs. St. Louis, 1958

7-game series
.339—Syracuse vs. Ft. Wayne, 1955
.369—Boston vs. St. Louis, 1957

MOST FIELD GOALS

2-game series
101—New York vs. Cleveland, 1978
 93—Minneapolis vs. Ft. Wayne, 1957

3-game series
165—L.A. Lakers vs. Phoenix, 1985
156—San Antonio vs. Denver, 1990

4-game series
206—Portland vs. Dallas, 1985
198—Milwaukee vs. Chicago, 1974

5-game series
274—San Antonio vs. Denver, 1983
   L.A. Lakers vs. Denver, 1985
252—Los Angeles vs. Dallas, 1984

6-game series
293—Boston vs. Atlanta, 1972
292—Houston vs. Denver, 1986

7-game series
333—Boston vs. Cincinnati, 1963
332—New York vs. Los Angeles, 1970
   Milwaukee vs. Denver, 1978

FEWEST FIELD GOALS

2-game series
63—Atlanta vs. Philadelphia, 1982
69—Cincinnati vs. Detroit, 1958

3-game series
83—Toronto vs. New York, 2000
84—Detroit vs. Miami, 2000

4-game series
101—Atlanta vs. New York, 1999
107—New Jersey vs. New York, 1994
   Cleveland vs. Indiana, 1998

5-game series
131—Miami vs. Chicago, 1997
136—Miami vs. New York, 1999

6-game series
156—Indiana vs. Detroit, 2004
163—Detroit vs. Indiana, 2004

7-game series
202—New Jersey vs. Detroit, 2004
204—Miami vs. New York, 1997
   New York vs. Miami, 2000

MOST FIELD-GOAL ATTEMPTS

2-game series
248—New York vs. Syracuse, 1959
215—Cincinnati vs. Detroit, 1958
    Detroit vs. Minneapolis, 1960

3-game series
349—Philadelphia vs. Syracuse, 1960
344—Minneapolis vs. St. Louis, 1957

4-game series
464—Minneapolis vs. Boston, 1959
463—Boston vs. Minneapolis, 1959
5-game series
568—Boston vs. Los Angeles, 1965
565—Boston vs. Philadelphia, 1967

6-game series
743—San Francisco vs. Philadelphia, 1967
712—Boston vs. Philadelphia, 1960

7-game series
835—Boston vs. Syracuse, 1959
799—Boston vs. St. Louis, 1957

FEWEST FIELD-GOAL ATTEMPTS

2-game series
150—Atlanta vs. Philadelphia, 1982
157—Milwaukee vs. Phoenix, 1978
    Philadelphia vs. Atlanta, 1982

3-game series
199—Portland vs. Phoenix, 1999
201—New York vs. Cleveland, 1996
    New York vs. Toronto, 2000

4-game series
246—Cleveland vs. Indiana, 1998
262—New York vs. Cleveland, 1995

5-game series
337—San Antonio vs. New York, 1999
340—Miami vs. New York, 1999

6-game series
408—San Antonio vs. Utah, 1996
415—Portland vs. Utah, 1999
7-game series
454—Seattle vs. Utah, 1996
476—Indiana vs. Chicago, 1998

MOST 3-POINT FIELD GOALS MADE

2-game series
7—Washington vs. Philadelphia, 1980
4—Washington vs. New Jersey, 1982

3-game series
35—Houston vs. Minnesota, 1997
33—Indiana vs. Milwaukee, 1999

4-game series
43—Houston vs. Seattle, 1996
41—Orlando vs. Houston, 1995
    Seattle vs. Houston, 1996

5-game series
58—Boston vs. Philadelphia, 2002
54—Seattle vs. Phoenix, 1997

6-game series
57—Boston vs. Indiana, 2003
52—Dallas vs. San Antonio, 2003

7-game series
77—Orlando vs. Indiana, 1995
75—Dallas vs. Sacramento, 2003

MOST 3-POINT FIELD-GOAL ATTEMPTS

2-game series
19—Washington vs. Philadelphia, 1980
10—New York vs. Chicago, 1981

3-game series
85—Indiana vs. Milwaukee, 1999
81—Houston vs. Minnesota, 1997

4-game series
118—Orlando vs. Houston, 1995
     Houston vs. Seattle, 1996
 94—Boston vs. New Jersey, 2003

5-game series
145—Phoenix vs. Seattle, 1997
132—Seattle vs. Phoenix, 1997
     Detroit vs. Boston, 2002

6-game series
150—Boston vs. New Jersey, 2002
149—Boston vs. Indiana, 2003

7-game series
187—Dallas vs. Sacramento, 2003
180—Houston vs. Seattle, 1997

HIGHEST FREE THROW PERCENTAGE

2-game series
.865—Syracuse vs. New York, 1959
.839—Chicago vs. New York, 1981

3-game series
.877—Dallas vs. Minnesota, 2002
.872—Denver vs. San Antonio, 1990

4-game series
.882—Houston vs. Boston, 1980
.869—Cincinnati vs. Philadelphia, 1965

5-game series
.894—Dallas vs. Seattle, 1984
.881—Utah vs. Portland, 1991

6-game series
.896—Dallas vs. San Antonio, 2003
.852—Indiana vs. L.A. Lakers, 2000

7-game series
.849—Dallas vs. Portland, 2003
.842—Milwaukee vs. Philadelphia, 2001

LOWEST FREE THROW PERCENTAGE

2-game series
.610—New Jersey vs. Washington, 1982
.629—San Antonio vs. Boston, 1977

3-game series
.611—Baltimore vs. St. Louis, 1966
.618—Kansas City vs. Phoenix, 1980

4-game series
.543—Orlando vs. Chicago, 1996
.607—Charlotte vs. Atlanta, 1998

5-game series
.567—Houston vs. Utah, 1985
.587—Orlando vs. Atlanta, 1996

6-game series
.570—L.A. Lakers vs. Indiana, 2000
.581—L.A. Lakers vs. Minnesota, 2004

7-game series
.582—San Francisco vs. St. Louis, 1964
.606—Philadelphia vs. Boston, 1968

MOST FREE THROWS MADE

2-game series
90—Syracuse vs. New York, 1959
62—Detroit vs. Cincinnati, 1958

3-game series
131—Minneapolis vs. St. Louis, 1956
121—St. Louis vs. Minneapolis, 1956

4-game series
144—L.A. Lakers vs. Seattle, 1987
135—Syracuse vs. Boston, 1955
    Minneapolis vs. Ft. Wayne, 1955

5-game series
183—Philadelphia vs. Syracuse, 1956
176—Boston vs. Syracuse, 1961

6-game series
232—Boston vs. St. Louis, 1958
215—St. Louis vs. Boston, 1958

7-game series
244—St. Louis vs. Boston, 1957
239—Los Angeles vs. Boston, 1962

FEWEST FREE THROWS MADE

2-game series
25—New Jersey vs. Washington, 1982
31—Phoenix vs. Milwaukee, 1978
    Washington vs. Philadelphia, 1980

3-game series
35—Cleveland vs. New York, 1996
    New York vs. Charlotte, 1997
37—Kansas City vs. Portland, 1981

4-game series
46—Milwaukee vs. Chicago, 1974
50—Phoenix vs. San Antonio, 2000

5-game series
57—Detroit vs. Atlanta, 1999
59—Denver vs. Minnesota, 2004

6-game series
82—Chicago vs. Phoenix, 1993
    New York vs. Indiana, 2000
84—Cleveland vs. Boston, 1976
    Utah vs. San Antonio, 1996

7-game series
 97—Toronto vs. Philadelphia, 2001
100—Milwaukee vs. Boston, 1974

MOST FREE THROW ATTEMPTS

2-game series
104—Syracuse vs. New York, 1959
 82—Detroit vs. Cincinnati, 1958

3-game series
174—St. Louis vs. Minneapolis, 1956
173—Minnneapolis vs. St. Louis, 1956

4-game series
186—Syracuse vs. Boston, 1955

5-game series
238—Philadelphia vs. Syracuse, 1956
232—Boston vs. Syracuse, 1961

6-game series
 298—Boston vs. St. Louis, 1958
 292—St. Louis vs. Boston, 1958

7-game series
341—St. Louis vs. Boston, 1957
303—Cincinnati vs. Boston, 1963

FEWEST FREE THROW ATTEMPTS

2-game series
38—Phoenix vs. Milwaukee, 1978
41—New Jersey vs. Washington, 1982

3-game series
45—Cleveland vs. New York, 1996
49—Houston vs. L.A. Lakers, 1991

4-game series
57—Milwaukee vs. Chicago, 1974
69—Boston vs. Charlotte, 1993

5-game series
72—Detroit vs. Atlanta, 1999
82—Charlotte vs. Chicago, 1998

6-game series
105—Boston vs. Buffalo, 1974
109—Utah vs. San Antonio, 1996

7-game series
120—Milwaukee vs. Philadelphia, 2001
124—Toronto vs. Philadelphia, 2001

HIGHEST REBOUND PERCENTAGE

2-game series
.585—Boston vs. San Antonio, 1977
.559—Washington vs. Atlanta, 1978

3-game series
.652—L.A. Lakers vs. San Antonio, 1986
.590—Boston vs. Indiana, 1992

4-game series
.595—Chicago vs. Orlando, 1996
.580—New Jersey vs. Detroit, 2003

5-game series
.595—Seattle vs. Los Angeles, 1979
.575—New York vs. Detroit, 1992

6-game series
.583—Los Angeles vs. Philadelphia, 1980
.568—New Jersey vs. Milwaukee, 2003

7-game series
.560—Chicago vs. Indiana, 1998
.556—Seattle vs. Phoenix, 1979

MOST REBOUNDS

2-game series
137—New York vs. Syracuse, 1959
127—Cincinnati vs. Detroit, 1958
    Detroit vs. Cincinnati, 1958

3-game series
225—Philadelphia vs. Syracuse, 1960
212—San Francisco vs. Los Angeles, 1967

4-game series
295—Boston vs. Minneapolis, 1959
268—Minneapolis vs. Boston, 1959

5-game series
396—Boston vs. Syracuse, 1961
371—Boston vs. Philadelphia, 1958

6-game series
457—Boston vs. Philadelphia, 1960
435—San Francisco vs. Philadelphia, 1967

7-game series
525—Boston vs. Syracuse, 1959
517—Boston vs. Philadelphia, 1962

FEWEST REBOUNDS

2-game series
71—Atlanta vs. Philadelphia, 1982
76—San Antonio vs. Boston, 1977

3-game series
79—San Antonio vs. L.A. Lakers, 1986
99—Miami vs. Chicago, 1992
  Phoenix vs. Portland, 1999
4-game series
115—Cleveland vs. New York, 1995
123—Orlando vs. Chicago, 1996
5-game series
159—Detroit vs. Atlanta, 1997
171—Houston vs. Utah, 1995
  Atlanta vs. Orlando, 1996
6-game series
201—Chicago vs. New York, 1993
212—Milwaukee vs. New Jersey, 2003
 7-game series
240—Orlando vs. Indiana, 1995
248—Chicago vs. New York, 1992
  New York vs. Indiana, 1995
  Utah vs. Seattle, 1996

MOST OFFENSIVE REBOUNDS

2-game series
51—Houston vs. Atlanta, 1979
43—Philadelphia vs. New Jersey, 1979

3-game series
72—Golden State vs. Detroit, 1977
65—Sacramento vs. Houston, 1986

4-game series
77—Seattle vs. L.A. Lakers, 1989
76—San Antonio vs. Los Angeles, 1982
  Seattle vs. L.A. Lakers, 1987
  Portland vs. Utah, 1988

5-game series
111—Phoenix vs. Golden State, 1989
110—Houston vs. Utah, 1985

6-game series
124—Golden State vs. Detroit, 1976
117—Washington vs. Philadelphia, 1978

7-game series
142—Washington vs. San Antonio, 1979
141—Boston vs. Philadelphia, 1982

FEWEST OFFENSIVE REBOUNDS

2-game series
19—Milwaukee vs. Phoenix, 1978
22—Portland vs. Seattle, 1983

3-game series
18—Detroit vs. Miami, 2000
20—Milwaukee vs. Detroit, 1976

4-game series
27—Houston vs. L.A. Lakers, 1996
29—Cleveland vs. New York, 1995

5-game series
33—Houston vs. Utah, 1995
39—New York vs. Toronto, 2001

6-game series
46—New York vs. Indiana, 2000
50—Milwaukee vs. New Jersey, 2003
  L.A. Lakers vs. San Antonio, 2004

7-game series
52—Seattle vs. Utah, 1996
60—New York vs. Miami, 2000

MOST DEFENSIVE REBOUNDS

2-game series
79—Boston vs. San Antonio, 1977
77—Milwaukee vs. Phoenix, 1978

3-game series
119—L.A. Lakers vs. Denver, 1987
118—Phoenix vs. Denver, 1989
  San Antonio vs. Denver, 1990
4-game series
161—Philadelphia vs. New York, 1978
158—Milwaukee vs. Chicago, 1974
5-game series
208—San Antonio vs. Denver, 1983
197—Boston vs. New York, 1974
6-game series
240—Boston vs. Phoenix, 1976
228—Portland vs. Philadelphia, 1977
7-game series
250—Sacramento vs. Dallas, 2003
246—Houston vs. Phoenix, 1994

FEWEST DEFENSIVE REBOUNDS

2-game series
45—Atlanta vs. Philadelphia, 1982
49—Cleveland vs. New York, 1978
3-game series
58—San Antonio vs. L.A. Lakers, 1986
66—Miami vs. Chicago, 1992
4-game series
84—Detroit vs. Chicago, 1991
  Orlando vs. Chicago, 1996
86—Cleveland vs. New York, 1995
5-game series
108—Golden State vs. L.A. Lakers, 1987
112—Seattle vs. Utah, 1992
6-game series
134—Milwaukee vs. Philadelphia, 1982
138—Chicago vs. New York, 1993
7-game series
162—Dallas vs. L.A. Lakers, 1988
165—Chicago vs. New York, 1992

MOST ASSISTS

2-game series
62—New York vs. Cleveland, 1978
  Philadelphia vs. New Jersey, 1979
59—Boston vs. San Antonio, 1977
3-game series
107—L.A. Lakers vs. Denver, 1987
104—L.A. Lakers vs. Phoenix, 1985
4-game series
129—Los Angeles vs. San Antonio, 1982
123—Portland vs. Dallas, 1985
5-game series
181—San Antonio vs. Denver, 1983
179—L.A. Lakers vs. Denver, 1985
6-game series
197—Los Angeles vs. Phoenix, 1984
196—Los Angeles vs. San Antonio, 1983
7-game series
233—Milwaukee vs. Denver, 1978
218—Los Angeles vs. Phoenix, 1970

FEWEST ASSISTS

2-game series
24—Cincinnati vs. Detroit, 1958
30—Detroit vs. Cincinnati, 1958
3-game series
36—Syracuse vs. Philadelphia, 1958
  New York vs. Toronto, 2000
39—Syracuse vs. Boston, 1957

4-game series
44—Atlanta vs. New York, 1999
58—Minneapolis vs. Ft. Wayne, 1955
  Memphis vs. San Antonio, 2004

5-game series
64—New York vs. Miami, 1999
66—Orlando vs. Miami, 1997

6-game series
85—Indiana vs. Detroit, 2004
91—Portland vs. Utah, 1999

7-game series
 95—New York vs. Miami, 2000
105—Washington vs. Cleveland, 1976

MOST PERSONAL FOULS

2-game series
70—New York vs. Syracuse, 1959
61—Atlanta vs. Washington, 1978
  Atlanta vs. Philadelphia, 1982

3-game series
105—Denver vs. San Antonio, 1995
 99—Minneapolis vs. St. Louis, 1957

4-game series
126—Detroit vs. Chicago, 1991
124—New York vs. Philadelphia, 1978
  Portland vs. Denver, 1986
  Utah vs. L.A. Lakers, 1998

5-game series
165—Syracuse vs. Boston, 1961
157—Los Angeles vs. Detroit, 1961

6-game series
197—Milwaukee vs. New Jersey, 1984
194—Boston vs. St. Louis, 1958
  St. Louis vs. Boston, 1958

7-game series
221—Boston vs. St. Louis, 1957
216—Boston vs. Cincinnati, 1963

FEWEST PERSONAL FOULS

2-game series
40—Milwaukee vs. Phoenix, 1978
41—Philadelphia vs. Washington, 1980

3-game series
51—New York vs. Cleveland, 1996
55—Chicago vs. New York, 1991
  L.A. Lakers vs. Houston, 1991

4-game series
69—Chicago vs. Milwaukee, 1974
71—San Antonio vs. Minnesota, 1999

5-game series
86—Atlanta vs. Detroit, 1999
89—Philadelphia vs. Boston, 1958

6-game series
108—Los Angeles vs. Milwaukee, 1972
116—L.A. Lakers vs. Portland, 1991

7-game series
122—Philadelphia vs. Milwaukee, 2001
124—Cleveland vs. Boston, 1992

MOST DISQUALIFICATIONS

2-game series
4—New York vs. Syracuse, 1959
  New Jersey vs. New York, 1983
3—San Antonio vs. Boston, 1977
  Atlanta vs. Philadelphia, 1982

3-game series
8—Minneapolis vs. St. Louis, 1957
7—St. Louis vs. Minneapolis, 1956

4-game series
7—San Francisco vs. Los Angeles, 1968
5—Minneapolis vs. Ft. Wayne, 1955
  Cleveland vs. Boston, 1985
  Atlanta vs. Detroit, 1986
  L.A. Lakers vs. San Antonio, 1999

5-game series
9—Chicago vs. Philadelphia, 1947
8—Philadelphia vs. Chicago, 1947

6-game series
11—Boston vs. St. Louis, 1958
10—Detroit vs. Los Angeles, 1962

7-game series
10—Boston vs. St. Louis, 1957
 9—Minneapolis vs. New York, 1952
  St. Louis vs. Boston, 1957
  Boston vs. Los Angeles, 1962

MOST STEALS

2-game series
23—Philadelphia vs. Washington, 1980
22—Indiana vs. Philadelphia, 1981
  Philadelphia vs. Indiana, 1981

3-game series
38—Indiana vs. Orlando, 1994
37—Chicago vs. New York, 1991
  Charlotte vs. Miami, 2001

4-game series
57—Portland vs. Los Angeles, 1977
55—Golden State vs. Washington, 1975

5-game series
66—Kansas City vs. Phoenix, 1979
59—Golden State vs. L.A. Lakers, 1987

6-game series
81—Golden State vs. Seattle, 1975
73—Golden State vs. Detroit, 1976

7-game series
94—Golden State vs. Phoenix, 1976
78—Los Angeles vs. Golden State, 1977

FEWEST STEALS

2-game series
10—New York vs. Cleveland, 1978
  Atlanta vs. Philadelphia, 1982
11—Portland vs. Seattle, 1983
  Seattle vs. Portland, 1983

3-game series
 8—Detroit vs. Orlando, 1996
11—Indiana vs. Detroit, 1990

4-game series
10—Detroit vs. Milwaukee, 1989
16—Detroit vs. L.A. Lakers, 1989

5-game series
17—Dallas vs. Seattle, 1984
19—Boston vs. New York, 1974
  Dallas vs. Utah, 2001

6-game series
24—Detroit vs. Boston, 1991
26—Boston vs. Detroit, 1991

7-game series
21—Milwaukee vs. Boston, 1974
25—Detroit vs. Chicago, 1974

MOST BLOCKED SHOTS

2-game series
22—Philadelphia vs. Atlanta, 1982
20—Houston vs. Atlanta, 1979

3-game series
34—L.A. Lakers vs. Denver, 1987
   Golden State vs. Utah, 1989
32—Los Angeles vs. Kansas City, 1984

4-game series
39—Phoenix vs. San Antonio, 2000
35—Seattle vs. Houston, 1989

5-game series
53—Boston vs. Washington, 1982
48—Denver vs. Seattle, 1994

6-game series
60—Philadelphia vs. Los Angeles, 1980
59—San Antonio vs. New Jersey, 2003

7-game series
71—Denver vs. Utah, 1994
62—Philadelphia vs. Milwaukee, 1981

FEWEST BLOCKED SHOTS

2-game series
4—New York vs. Chicago, 1981
5—Boston vs. San Antonio, 1977
   Indiana vs. Philadelphia, 1981

3-game series
3—Cleveland vs. Chicago, 1994
4—Seattle vs. Los Angeles, 1978

4-game series
6—Indiana vs. Atlanta, 1987
8—Boston vs. Milwaukee, 1983
   Milwaukee vs. Detroit, 1989
   New Jersey vs. Boston, 2003

5-game series
7—New York vs. Miami, 1998
9—Detroit vs. Atlanta, 1999

6-game series
10—Boston vs. Phoenix, 1976
11—Boston vs. Washington, 1975

7-game series
7—Boston vs. Milwaukee, 1974
19—Indiana vs. Orlando, 1995

MOST TURNOVERS

2-game series
47—Boston vs. San Antonio, 1977
46—Philadelphia vs. New Jersey, 1979

3-game series
82—Chicago vs. Portland, 1977
67—New York vs. Chicago, 1991

4-game series
94—Golden State vs. Washington, 1975
92—Milwaukee vs. Baltimore, 1971

5-game series
128—Phoenix vs. Kansas City, 1979
113—San Antonio vs. Denver, 1985

6-game series
149—Portland vs. Philadelphia, 1977
144—Boston vs. Phoenix, 1976

7-game series
147—Phoenix vs. Golden State, 1976
146—Seattle vs. Phoenix, 1979

FEWEST TURNOVERS

2-game series
23—Seattle vs. Portland, 1983
24—Portland vs. Seattle, 1983

3-game series
28—Houston vs. Seattle, 1982
   Minnesota vs. Houston, 1997
31—Boston vs. Chicago, 1987

4-game series
36—Milwaukee vs. Detroit, 1989
41—Houston vs. Orlando, 1995
   Philadelphia vs. Indiana, 1999

5-game series
48—Detroit vs. Atlanta, 1997
49—San Antonio vs. Seattle, 2002

6-game series
46—Detroit vs. Boston, 1991
60—Boston vs. Detroit, 1991

7-game series
76—Atlanta vs. Boston, 1988
77—Utah vs. Denver, 1994
   New York vs. Miami, 2000

INDIVIDUAL

MINUTES

Most minutes, game
67—Red Rocha, Syracuse at Boston, March 21, 1953 (4 ot)
   Paul Seymour, Syracuse at Boston, March 21, 1953 (4 ot)
66—Bob Cousy, Boston vs. Syracuse, March 21, 1953 (4 ot)

Highest average, minutes per game, one playoff series
49.33—Wilt Chamberlain, Philadelphia vs. New York, 1968 (296/6)
49.29—Kareem Abdul-Jabbar, Milwaukee vs. Boston, 1974 (345/7)
48.75—Wilt Chamberlain, Philadelphia vs. Cincinnati, 1965 (195/4)
   Jerry Lucas, Cincinnati vs. Philadelphia, 1965 (195/4)
   Oscar Robertson, Cincinnati vs. Philadelphia, 1965 (195/4)
   Wilt Chamberlain, Los Angeles vs. Atlanta, 1970 (195/4)

SCORING

Highest scoring average, one playoff series
46.3—Jerry West, Los Angeles vs. Baltimore, 1965 (278/6)
45.2—Michael Jordan, Chicago vs. Cleveland, 1988 (226/5)
45.0—Michael Jordan, Chicago vs. Miami, 1992 (135/3)

Most points, game
63—Michael Jordan, Chicago at Boston, April 20, 1986 (2 ot)
61—Elgin Baylor, Los Angeles at Boston, April 14, 1962
56—Wilt Chamberlain, Philadelphia vs. Syracuse, March 22, 1962

No player has scored more points in a playoff game than Michael Jordan, who scorched the Celtics for 63 in a two-overtime game on April 20, 1986. Boston, however, won the game, 135-131, and eventually the series 3-0.

Michael Jordan, Chicago at Miami, April 29, 1992
Charles Barkley, Phoenix at Golden State, May 4, 1994

Most points, rookie, game
53—Wilt Chamberlain, Philadelphia vs. Syracuse, March 14, 1960
50—Wilt Chamberlain, Philadelphia at Boston, March 22, 1960
46—Kareem Abdul-Jabbar, Milwaukee vs. Philadelphia, at Madison, Wis., April 3, 1970

Most consecutive games, 10 or more points
179—Michael Jordan, Chicago, April 19, 1985—June 14, 1998
147—Karl Malone, Utah, April 18, 1986—May 25, 1999
137—Shaquille O'Neal, Orlando-L.A. Lakers, April 28, 1994—April 17, 2004

Most consecutive games, 20 or more points
60—Michael Jordan, Chicago, June 2, 1989—May 11, 1993
57—Kareem Abdul-Jabbar, Milwaukee, Los Angeles, April 13, 1973—April 5, 1981
49—Elgin Baylor, Minneapolis, Los Angeles, March 17, 1960—March 30, 1964

Most consecutive games, 30 or more points
11—Elgin Baylor, Los Angeles, March 27, 1962—April 18, 1962
9—Kareem Abdul-Jabbar, Milwaukee, March 25, 1970—April 19, 1970
   Bob McAdoo, Buffalo, April 12, 1974—April 15, 1976
8—Elgin Baylor, Los Angeles, April 7—April 21, 1963
   Michael Jordan, Chicago, April 23, 1987—May 8, 1988
   Michael Jordan, Chicago, June 9, 1993—April 30, 1995

Most consecutive games, 40 or more points
6—Jerry West, Los Angeles, April 3—April 13, 1965
4—Bernard King, New York, April 19—April 27, 1984
   Michael Jordan, Chicago, June 11, 1993—June 18, 1993
3—Kareem Abdul-Jabbar, Los Angeles, April 26—May 1, 1977
   Michael Jordan, Chicago, May 3—May 7, 1989
   Michael Jordan, Chicago, May 9—May 13, 1990
   Allen Iverson, Philadelphia, June 1—June 6, 2001

Most points, one half
39—Eric Floyd, Golden State vs. L.A. Lakers, May 10, 1987
38—Charles Barkley, Phoenix at Golden State, May 4, 1994

Most points, one quarter
29—Eric Floyd, Golden State vs. L.A. Lakers, May 10, 1987
27—Mark Aguirre, Dallas at Houston, May 5, 1988
   Charles Barkley, Phoenix at Golden State, May 4, 1994

Most points, overtime period
13—Clyde Drexler, Portland at L.A. Lakers, April 29, 1992

FIELD GOALS

Highest field-goal percentage, game
(minimum: 8 field goals)
1.000—Wilt Chamberlain, Los Angeles at Atlanta, April 17, 1969 (9/9)
   Don Nelson, Boston at Buffalo, April 6, 1974 (10/10)
   Tom Kozelko, Capital at New York, April 12, 1974 (8/8)
   Larry McNeill, K.C.-Omaha vs. Chicago, April 13, 1975 (12/12)
   Clifford Ray, Golden State at Detroit, April 14, 1977 (8/8)
   Scott Wedman, Boston vs. L.A. Lakers, May 27, 1985 (11/11)
   Brad Davis, Dallas at Utah, April 25, 1986 (8/8)
   Bob Hansen, Utah vs. Dallas, April 25, 1986 (9/9)
   Robert Parish, Boston at Atlanta, May 16, 1988 (8/8)
   John Paxson, Chicago vs. L.A. Lakers, June 5, 1991 (8/8)
   Horace Grant, Chicago vs. Cleveland, May 13, 1993 (8/8)
   David Robinson, San Antonio vs. Phoenix, April 19, 2003 (OT) (8/8)

.929—Dikembe Mutombo, Atlanta vs. Detroit, May 10, 1999 (13/14)
.923—Wes Unseld, Washington vs. San Antonio, May 6, 1979 (12/13)

Most field goals, none missed, game
12—Larry McNeill, K.C.-Omaha vs. Chicago, April 13, 1975
11—Scott Wedman, Boston vs. L.A. Lakers, May 27, 1985
10—Don Nelson, Boston at Buffalo, April 6, 1974

Most field goals, game
24—Wilt Chamberlain, Philadelphia vs. Syracuse, March 14, 1960
   John Havlicek, Boston vs. Atlanta, April 1, 1973
   Michael Jordan, Chicago vs. Cleveland, May 1, 1988
23—Charles Barkley, Phoenix at Golden State, May 4, 1994

Most field goals, one half
16—Dave Bing, Detroit vs. Boston, April 1, 1968
15—Eric Floyd, Golden State vs. L.A. Lakers, May 10, 1987
   Charles Barkley, Phoenix at Golden State, May 4, 1994

Most field goals, one quarter
12—Eric Floyd, Golden State vs. L.A. Lakers, May 10, 1987
11—Gus Williams, Seattle at Dallas, April 17, 1984
   Isiah Thomas, Detroit at L.A. Lakers, June 19, 1988
   Charles Barkley, Phoenix at Golden State, May 4, 1994

Most field-goal attempts, game
48—Wilt Chamberlain, Philadelphia vs. Syracuse, March 22, 1962
   Rick Barry, San Francisco vs. Philadelphia, April 18, 1967
46—Joe Fulks, Philadelphia vs. St. Louis, March 30, 1948
   Elgin Baylor, Los Angeles at Boston, April 14, 1962
45—Elgin Baylor, Los Angeles at St. Louis, March 27, 1961
   Michael Jordan, Chicago vs. Cleveland, May 1, 1988

Most field-goal attempts, none made, game
14—Chick Reiser, Baltimore at Philadelphia, April 10, 1948
   Dennis Johnson, Seattle vs. Washington, June 7, 1978
12—Tom Gola, Philadelphia at Boston, March 23, 1958
   Guy Rodgers, San Francisco at Boston, April 18, 1964
   Paul Pressey, Milwaukee at Boston, May 5, 1987

Most field-goal attempts, one half
25—Wilt Chamberlain, Philadelphia vs. Syracuse, March 22, 1962
   Elgin Baylor, Los Angeles at Boston, April 14, 1962
   Michael Jordan, Chicago vs. Cleveland, May 1, 1988

Most field-goal attempts, one quarter
17—Rick Barry, San Francisco at Philadelphia, April 14, 1967

3-POINT FIELD GOALS

Most 3-point field goals, none missed, game
7—Robert Horry, L.A. Lakers at Utah, May 6, 1997
5—Brad Davis, Dallas at Utah, April 25, 1986
   Byron Scott, L.A. Lakers vs. Golden State, May 5, 1991
   Nate McMillan, Seattle vs. Houston, May 6, 1996
   Mario Elie, Houston vs. Seattle, May 5, 1997
   Larry Johnson, New York vs. Indiana, May 29, 2000
   Baron Davis, Charlotte at Milwaukee, May 15, 2001
   Mike Bibby, Sacramento at Dallas, May 9, 2002

Most 3-point field goals, game
9—Rex Chapman, Phoenix at Seattle, April 25, 1997
   Vince Carter, Toronto vs. Philadelphia, May 11, 2001
   Ray Allen, Milwaukee vs. Philadelphia, June 1, 2001
8—Dan Majerle, Phoenix vs. Seattle, June 1, 1993
   Gary Payton, Seattle at Phoenix, April 29, 1997
   Mookie Blaylock, Atlanta at Chicago, May 8, 1997
   Matt Maloney, Houston at Seattle, May 11, 1997 (ot)
   Allen Iverson, Philadelphia vs. Toronto, May 16, 2001
   Paul Pierce, Boston vs. Philadelphia, May 3, 2002

Most 3-point field goals, one half
8—Vince Carter, Toronto vs. Philadelphia, May 11, 2001
7—Antoine Walker, Boston at Philadelphia, April 28, 2002
   Sam Cassell, Minnesota vs. Sacramento, May 4, 2004

Most 3-point field goals, one quarter
6—Antoine Walker, Boston at Philadelphia, April 28, 2002
5—Reggie Miller, Indiana at New York, June 1, 1994
   Kenny Smith, Houston at Orlando, June 7, 1995

Robert Horry, Houston vs. Seattle, May 12, 1996
Gary Payton, Seattle at Phoenix, April 29, 1997
Ray Allen, Milwaukee at Indiana, May 11, 1999
Vince Carter, Toronto vs. Philadelphia, May 11, 2001
Tim Thomas, Milwaukee at New Jersey, April 19, 2003
Chauncey Billups, Detroit at Orlando, May 2, 2003

Most 3-point field-goal attempts, game
17—Rex Chapman, Phoenix at Seattle, April 25, 1997
16—Reggie Miller, Indiana vs. Milwaukee, May 11, 1999 (ot)

Most 3-point field-goal attempts, one half
11—Gary Payton, Seattle vs. Houston, May 4, 1996
    Kobe Bryant, L.A. Lakers at San Antonio, May 13, 2003

FREE THROWS

Most free throws made, none missed, game
21—Paul Pierce, Boston at Indiana, April 19, 2003
18—Karl Malone, Utah at L.A. Lakers, May 10, 1997

Most free throws made, game
30—Bob Cousy, Boston vs. Syracuse, March 21, 1953 (4 ot)
23—Michael Jordan, Chicago vs. New York, May 14, 1989
22—Michael Jordan, Chicago vs. Cleveland, May 5, 1989 (ot)
    Karl Malone, Utah at L.A. Clippers, May 3, 1992

Most free throws made, one half
19—Magic Johnson, L.A. Lakers vs. Golden State, May 8, 1991
    Karl Malone, Utah at Portland, May 9, 1991
    Charles Barkley, Phoenix vs. Seattle, June 5, 1993

Most free throws made, one quarter
13—Michael Jordan, Chicago vs. Detroit, May 21, 1991
12—Reggie Miller, Indiana at New York, April 30, 1993
    Shaquille O'Neal, L.A. Lakers vs. Portland, May 20, 2000

Most free throw attempts, game
39—Shaquille O'Neal, L.A. Lakers vs. Indiana, June 9, 2000
32—Bob Cousy, Boston vs. Syracuse, March 21, 1953 (4 ot)

Most free throw attempts, one half
27—Shaquille O'Neal, L.A. Lakers vs. Portland, May 20, 2000
22—Shaquille O'Neal, L.A. Lakers vs. Indiana, June 9, 2000

Most free throw attempts, one quarter
25—Shaquille O'Neal, L.A. Lakers vs. Portland, May 20, 2000
16—Shaquille O'Neal, L.A. Lakers vs. Indiana, June 9, 2000
    Shaquille O'Neal, L.A. Lakers vs. New Jersey, June 5, 2002
    Ben Wallace, Detroit at Orlando, May 2, 2003

REBOUNDS

Highest average, rebounds per game, one playoff series
32.0—Wilt Chamberlain, Philadelphia vs. Boston, 1967 (160/5)
31.4—Wilt Chamberlain, Philadelphia vs. Boston, 1965 (200/7)
31.0—Bill Russell, Boston vs. Syracuse, 1961 (155/5)

Most rebounds, game
41—Wilt Chamberlain, Philadelphia vs. Boston, April 5, 1967
40—Bill Russell, Boston vs. Philadelphia, March 23, 1958
 Bill Russell, Boston vs. St. Louis, March 29, 1960
 Bill Russell, Boston vs. Los Angeles, April 18, 1962 (ot)

Most rebounds, rookie, game
35—Wilt Chamberlain, Philadelphia at Boston, March 22, 1960

Most rebounds, one half
26—Wilt Chamberlain, Philadelphia vs. San Francisco, April 16, 1967

Most rebounds, one quarter
19—Bill Russell, Boston vs. Los Angeles, April 18, 1962

Most offensive rebounds, game
15—Moses Malone, Houston vs. Washington, April 21, 1977 (ot)
14—Shaquille O'Neal, Orlando vs. Chicago, May 16, 1995
13—Moses Malone, Houston at Atlanta, April 13, 1979

Most defensive rebounds, game
20— Dave Cowens, Boston at Houston, April 22, 1975
     Dave Cowens, Boston at Philadelphia, May 1, 1977

Bill Walton, Portland at Philadelphia, June 3, 1977
Bill Walton, Portland vs. Philadelphia, June 5, 1977
Tim Duncan, San Antonio at L.A. Lakers, May 14, 2002
Tim Duncan, San Antonio at Phoenix, April 25, 2003
Kevin Garnett, Minnesota vs. Denver, April 21, 2004
Kevin Garnett, Minnesota vs. Sacramento, May 19, 2004
19— Sam Lacey, K.C.-Omaha vs. Chicago, April 13, 1975
     Dave Cowens, Boston at Buffalo, April 28, 1976
     Elvin Hayes, Washington at Cleveland, April 15, 1977
     Larry Bird, Boston at Philadelphia, April 23, 1980
     Hakeem Olajuwon, Houston at Dallas, April 30, 1988
     Shaquille O'Neal, L.A. Lakers vs. Indiana, June 9, 2000
     Kevin Garnett, Minnesota vs. L.A. Lakers, April 22, 2003
     Jermaine O'Neal, Indiana vs. Boston, April 29, 2003 (ot)
     Jim Jackson, Houston vs. L.A. Lakers, April 25, 2004 (ot)
     Ben Wallace, Detroit at Indiana, May 22, 2004

ASSISTS

Highest average, assists per game, one playoff series
17.0—Magic Johnson, L.A. Lakers vs. Portland, 1985 (85/5)
16.4—John Stockton, Utah vs. L.A. Lakers, 1988 (115/7)
16.2—Magic Johnson, L.A. Lakers vs. Houston, 1986 (81/5)

Most assists, game
24—Magic Johnson, Los Angeles vs. Phoenix, May 15, 1984
    John Stockton, Utah at L.A. Lakers, May 17, 1988
23—Magic Johnson, L.A. Lakers at Portland, May 3, 1985
    John Stockton, Utah vs. Portland, April 25, 1996
22—Doc Rivers, Atlanta vs. Boston, May 16, 1988

Most assists, rookie, game
18—Spud Webb, Atlanta vs. Detroit, April 19, 1986

Most assists, one half
15—Magic Johnson, L.A. Lakers at Portland, May 3, 1985
    Doc Rivers, Atlanta vs. Boston, May 16, 1988

Most assists, one quarter
11—John Stockton, Utah vs. San Antonio, May 5, 1994

PERSONAL FOULS

Most personal fouls, game
8—Jack Toomay, Baltimore at New York, March 26, 1949 (ot)
7—Al Cervi, Syracuse at Boston, March 21, 1953 (4 ot)
6—by many

Most personal fouls, one half
6—by many

Most personal fouls, one quarter
6—Paul Mokeski, Milwaukee vs. Philadelphia, May 7, 1986
5—by many

Most minutes played, no personal fouls, game
59—Dan Majerle, Phoenix at Chicago, June 13, 1993 (3 ot)
54—Randy Wittman, Atlanta at Detroit, April 25, 1986 (2 ot)
52—Allen Iverson, Philadelphia at L.A. Lakers, June 6, 2001 (ot)

DISQUALIFICATIONS

Fewest minutes played, diqualified player, game
6—Travis Knight, L.A. Lakers vs. San Antonio, May 23, 1999
7—Bob Lochmueller, Syracuse vs. Boston, March 19, 1953
    Will Perdue, Chicago at New York, May 14, 1992
    Scot Pollard, Sacramento vs. L.A. Lakers, April 30, 2000
    Brian Shaw, L.A. Lakers vs. Portland, May 30, 2000
    Aaron Williams, New Jersey vs. L.A. Lakers, June 9, 2002

STEALS

Most steals, game
10—Allen Iverson, Philadelphia vs. Orlando, May 13, 1999

8—Rick Barry, Golden State vs. Seattle, April 14, 1975
  Lionel Hollins, Portland at Los Angeles, May 8, 1977
  Maurice Cheeks, Philadelphia vs. New Jersey, April 11, 1979
  Craig Hodges, Milwaukee at Philadelphia, May 9, 1986
  Tim Hardaway, Golden State at L.A. Lakers, May 8, 1991
  Tim Hardaway, Golden State at Seattle, April 30, 1992
  Mookie Blaylock, Atlanta vs. Indiana, April 29, 1996
7—by many

BLOCKED SHOTS

Most blocked shots, game
10—Mark Eaton, Utah vs. Houston, April 26, 1985
  Hakeem Olajuwon, Houston at L.A. Lakers, April 29, 1990
9—Kareem Abdul-Jabbar, Los Angeles vs. Golden State, April 22, 1977
  Manute Bol, Washington at Philadelphia, April 18, 1986
  Hakeem Olajuwon, Houston vs. L.A. Clippers, April 29, 1993
  Derrick Coleman, New Jersey vs. Cleveland, May 7, 1993
  Greg Ostertag, Utah vs. L.A. Lakers, May 12, 1997 (ot)
  Alonzo Mourning, Miami vs. Detroit, April 22, 2000

8—by many

TURNOVERS

Most turnovers, game
11—John Williamson, New Jersey at Philadelphia, April 11, 1979
10—Quinn Buckner, Milwaukee vs. Phoenix, April 14, 1978
  Magic Johnson, Los Angeles vs. Philadelphia, May 14, 1980
  Larry Bird, Boston vs. Chicago, April 7, 1981
  Moses Malone, Philadelphia at New Jersey, April 24, 1984
  Kevin Johnson, Phoenix at L.A. Lakers, May 23, 1989
  Anfernee Hardaway, Orlando at Indiana, May 2, 1994
  Kevin Garnett, Minnesota at Seattle, May 2, 1998
  Tim Duncan, San Antonio at L.A. Lakers, May 7, 2002

Most minutes played, no turnovers, game
59—Dan Majerle, Phoenix at Chicago, June 13, 1993 (3 ot)
56—Peja Stojakovic, Sacramento vs. Dallas, May 10, 2003 (2 ot)
52—Baron Davis, Charlotte at Orlando, April 27, 2002 (ot)
  Kobe Bryant, L.A. Lakers at Sacramento, June 2, 2002 (ot)
  Ben Wallace, Detroit at Philadelphia, May 16, 2003 (ot)

TEAM

WON-LOST

Most consecutive games won, all playoff series
13—L.A. Lakers, 1988-89
12—Detroit, 1989-90
  San Antonio, 1999
  L.A. Lakers, 2000-01

Most consecutive games won, one year
12—San Antonio, 1999
11—L.A. Lakers, 1989
  L.A. Lakers, 2001

Most consecutive games won at home, all playoff series
15—Chicago, 1990-91
14—Minneapolis, 1949-51
  Boston, 1986-87
  Detroit, 1989-90

Most consecutive games won at home, one year
10—Portland, 1977
  Boston, 1986
  L.A. Lakers, 1987
  Detroit, 1990
  Chicago, 1996
  Utah, 1997
9—Boston, 1976
  Seattle, 1978
  Boston, 1984
  Boston, 1985
  Portland, 1990
  L.A. Lakers, 2004

Most consecutive games won on road, all playoff series
12—L.A. Lakers, 2001-02
8—Chicago, 1991-92
  Houston, 1995-96

Most consecutive games won on road, one year
8—L.A. Lakers, 2001
7—Houston, 1995

Most consecutive games lost, all playoff series
11—Baltimore, 1965-66, 1969-70
  Denver, 1988-90, 1994
10—New Jersey, 1984-86, 1992
  Kansas City, Sacramento, 1981, 1984, 1986, 1996
  Portland, 2000-03

Most consecutive games lost at home, all playoff series
9—Philadelphia, 1968-71
7—Cleveland, 1993-96

Most consecutive games lost at home, one year
4—Los Angeles, 1983
  San Antonio, 1995
3—New York, 1953
  Philadelphia, 1969
  San Francisco, 1969
  San Antonio, 1983
  New Jersey, 1984
  Philadelphia, 1984
  Milwaukee, 1989
  Portland, 1990
  L.A. Lakers, 1991
  Phoenix, 1993
  Philadelphia, 2001
  Dallas, 2003

Most consecutive games lost on road, all playoff series
18—Chicago, 1967-68, 1970-73
14—Los Angeles, 1973-74, 1977-79
  Cleveland, 1976-78, 1985, 1988-89
  Portland, 1992-98

Most consecutive games lost on road, one year
7—Boston, 1987
6—Los Angeles, 1971
  Miami, 2004

Most games, one year
25—New York, 1994
24—L.A. Lakers, 1988
  Phoenix, 1993
  San Antonio, 2003
23—Boston, 1984
  Boston, 1987
  Detroit, 1988
  Houston, 1994
  Indiana, 2000
  L.A. Lakers, 2000
  Philadelphia, 2001
  Detroit, 2004

Most home games, one year
14—L.A. Lakers, 1988
13—Boston, 1984
  Boston, 1987
  Phoenix, 1993
  Houston, 1994
  New York, 1994
  L.A. Lakers, 2000
  Philadelphia, 2001
  Detroit, 2004

Most road games, one year
12—Houston, 1981
New York, 1994
Houston, 1995
San Antonio, 2003
11—Washington, 1978
Philadelphia, 1982
Detroit, 1988
Phoenix, 1993
Indiana, 2000
L.A. Lakers, 2004

Most wins at home, one year
12—Boston, 1984
L.A. Lakers, 1988
11—Boston, 1987
New York, 1994
L.A. Lakers, 2000

Most wins on road, one year
9—Houston, 1995
8—Houston, 1981
San Antonio, 1999
L.A. Lakers, 2001
San Antonio, 2003

Most games lost, one year
11—Phoenix, 1993
New York, 1994
Philadelphia, 2001
10—Baltimore, 1971
Washington, 1979
Boston, 1987
Orlando, 1995
Indiana, 2000
Dallas, 2003

Most games lost at home, one year
6—Phoenix, 1993
Philadelphia, 2001
5—Washington, 1979
Houston, 1981
Dallas, 2003

Most games lost on road, one year
9—New York, 1994
8—Boston, 1987
L.A. Lakers, 2004

Most games won at home without a loss, one year
10—Portland, 1977
Boston, 1986
L.A. Lakers, 1987
Chicago, 1996
9—Boston, 1976

Most games lost on road without a win, one year
6—Los Angeles, 1971
Miami, 2004
5—Cincinnati, 1964
Los Angeles, 1977
Philadelphia, 1990
Utah, 2000

Highest won-lost percentage, one year
.938—L.A. Lakers, 2001 (15-1)
.923—Philadelphia, 1983 (12-1)

SCORING

Most points, game
157—Boston vs. New York, April 28, 1990
156—Milwaukee at Philadelphia, March 30, 1970
153—L.A. Lakers vs. Denver, May 22, 1985
Portland at Phoenix, May 11, 1992 (2 ot)

Fewest points, game
54—Utah at Chicago, June 7, 1998
56—New Jersey at Detroit, May 3, 2004

63—Atlanta at Detroit, May 12, 1999
Portland vs. San Antonio, June 4, 1999
Toronto at Detroit, April 21, 2002
New Orleans at Miami, April 21, 2004

Most points, both teams, game
304—Portland (153) at Phoenix (151), May 11, 1992 (2 ot)
285—San Antonio (152) vs. Denver (133), April 26, 1983
Boston (157) vs. New York (128), April 28, 1990
280—Dallas (151) vs. Seattle (129), April 23, 1987

Fewest points, both teams, game
130—Detroit (64) at Boston (66), May 10, 2002
134—New Jersey (56) at Detroit (78), May 3, 2004
Indiana (65) at Detroit (69), June 1, 2004
139—Indiana (67) vs. Detroit (72), May 24, 2004

Largest margin of victory, game
58—Minneapolis vs. St. Louis, March 19, 1956 (133-75)
56—Los Angeles at Golden State, April 21, 1973 (126-70)
50—Milwaukee vs. San Francisco, April 4, 1971 (136-86)

BY HALF

Most points, first half
83—Dallas vs. Sacramento, May 8, 2003
82—San Antonio vs. Denver, April 26, 1983
L.A. Lakers vs. Denver, April 23, 1987

Fewest points, first half
23—Phoenix at L.A. Lakers, May 16, 2000
24—Portland at Utah, May 5, 1996

Most points, both teams, first half
150—San Antonio (82) vs. Denver (68), April 26, 1983
147—L.A. Lakers (79) at Denver (68), May 17, 1985
Phoenix (74) at Golden State (73), May 4, 1994

Fewest points, both teams, first half
60—Detroit (27) vs. Indiana (33), June 1, 2004
62—New Jersey (25) at Detroit (37), May 3, 2004

Largest lead at halftime
40—Detroit vs. Washington, April 26, 1987 (led 76-36; won 128-85)
36—Milwaukee at Philadelphia, March 30, 1970 (led 77-41; won 156-120)

Largest deficit at halftime overcome to win a game
21—Baltimore at Philadelphia, April 13, 1948 (trailed 20-41; won 66-63)
20—Boston vs. New Jersey, May 25, 2002 (trailed 34-54; won 94-90)

Most points, second half
87—Milwaukee vs. Denver, April 23, 1978
83—Houston vs. San Antonio, April 6, 1980
Detroit vs. Boston, May 24, 1987
Boston vs. New York, April 28, 1990

Fewest points, second half
23—Utah at Chicago, June 7, 1998
24—Miami vs. Charlotte, April 23, 2001
Indiana vs. Detroit, May 24, 2004

Most points, both teams, second half
158—Milwaukee (79) at Philadelphia (79), March 30, 1970
152—Boston (83) vs. New York (69), April 28, 1990

Fewest points, both teams, second half
59—Indiana (24) vs. Detroit (35), May 24, 2004
60—Atlanta (29) at New York (31), May 24, 1999
Boston (29) vs. Detroit (31), May 10, 2002

BY QUARTER, OVERTIME PERIOD

Most points, first quarter
45—L.A. Lakers vs. Phoenix, April 18, 1985
Dallas vs. L.A. Lakers, May 4, 1986
44—Atlanta vs. Orlando, May 13, 1996
Dallas vs. Sacramento, May 8, 2003

Fewest points, first quarter
8—Utah at L.A. Lakers, May 8, 1988
9—Atlanta at Boston, May 13, 1988
Utah at San Antonio, May 9, 1996
Toronto at Detroit, April 21, 2002

Most points, both teams, first quarter
84—Philadelphia (43) at San Francisco (41), April 24, 1967
   Phoenix (42) at Golden State (42), May 4, 1994
   Dallas (44) vs. Sacramento (40), May 8, 2003
79—Boston (41) vs. New York (38), April 28, 1990

Fewest points, both teams, first quarter
25—Utah (11) vs. Portland (14), May 20, 1999
   Toronto (9) at Detroit (16), April 21, 2002
26—Detroit (10) vs. Boston (16), May 30, 1988

Largest lead, end of first quarter
26—Milwaukee at Philadelphia, March 30, 1970 (led 40-14;
   won 156-120)
25—Miami vs. Orlando, April 24, 1997 (led 35-10; won 99-64)

Largest deficit end of first quarter overcome to win
20—L.A. Lakers at Seattle, May 14, 1989 (trailed 12-32; won 97-95)
   L.A. Lakers vs. Sacramento, May 26, 2002 (trailed 20-40;
   won 100-99)
18—San Francisco at St. Louis, April 12, 1967 (trailed 21-39;
   won 112-107)
   Indiana vs. New York, May 5, 1998 (trailed 13-31; won 93-83)

Most points, second quarter
46—Boston vs. St. Louis, March 27, 1960
   Boston vs. Detroit, March 24, 1968
45—New York vs. Boston, March 19, 1955
   St. Louis vs. Ft. Wayne, March 14, 1957

Fewest points, second quarter
7—Utah at Seattle, May 3, 2000
8—New York at Indiana, May 31, 2000
   Utah at Sacramento, April 19, 2003

Most points, both teams, second quarter
80—Boston (42) vs. Syracuse (38), March 18, 1959
77—Cincinnati (42) at Boston (35), March 31, 1963

Fewest points, both teams, second quarter
23—Utah (10) vs. Houston (13), May 29, 1994
25—Golden State (11) at Los Angeles (14), April 22, 1977
   Milwaukee (10) at Detroit (15), April 29, 2004
   Detroit (9) vs. Indiana (16), May 26, 2004

Most points, third quarter
49—L.A. Lakers vs. Golden State, May 5, 1987
47—Milwaukee at Philadelphia, March 30, 1970
   Los Angeles vs. Boston, June 3, 1984

Fewest points, third quarter
6—Atlanta at Boston, May 6, 1986
7—Miami vs. Charlotte, April 23, 2001

Most points, both teams, third quarter
82—San Francisco (44) vs. St. Louis (38), April 1, 1967
0—Los Angeles (47) vs. Boston (33), June 3, 1984

Fewest points, both teams, third quarter
23—San Antonio (9) vs. Phoenix (14), April 25, 2000
25—Atlanta (11) at New York (14), May 23, 1999

Largest lead end of third quarter
52—Milwaukee at Philadelphia, March 30, 1970 (led 124-72;
   won 156-120)
48—Milwaukee vs. San Francisco, April 4, 1971 (led 105-57;
   won 136-86)

Largest deficit end of third quarter overcome to win
21—Boston vs. New Jersey, May 25, 2002 (trailed 53-74;
   won 94-90)
18—Phoenix at Houston, May 11, 1994 (trailed 100-82; won
   124-117 in ot)

Most points, fourth quarter
51—Los Angeles vs. Detroit, March 31, 1962
49—Golden State at San Antonio, April 25, 1991

Fewest points, fourth quarter
5—Portland at Utah, May 18, 1999
8—New Jersey vs. Cleveland, May 7, 1993
   Houston vs. Phoenix, May 11, 1994
   San Antonio at L.A. Lakers, May 25, 2001

Most points, both teams, fourth quarter
86—Golden State (49) at San Antonio (37), April 25, 1991
83—Milwaukee (47) vs. Denver (36), April 23, 1978

Fewest points, both teams, fourth quarter
24—Portland (5) at Utah (19), May 18, 1999
25—New York (12) vs. Miami (13), May 12, 2000
   Milwaukee (11) vs. Philadelphia (14), May 26, 2001

Most points, overtime period
22—Los Angeles vs. New York, May 1, 1970
20—Portland vs. Utah, May 26, 1992

Fewest points, overtime period
0—Minneapolis at Ft. Wayne, March 22, 1955
   Boston at Indiana, April 29, 2003
1—Ft. Wayne vs. Minneapolis, March 22, 1955
   Boston vs. Charlotte, May 1, 1993

Most points, both teams, overtime period
38—Los Angeles (22) vs. New York (16), May 1, 1970
36—L.A. Lakers (19) vs. Portland (17), April 29, 1992

Fewest points, both teams, overtime period
1—Minneapolis (0) at Ft. Wayne (1), March 22, 1955
3—Boston (1) vs. Charlotte (2), May 1, 1993

PLAYERS SCORING

Most players, 40-or-more points, game
2—Los Angeles at Detroit, March 29, 1962
   Houston at Dallas, April 30, 1988
   Houston vs. Utah, May 5, 1995
   Indiana vs. Philadelphia, May 6, 2000

Most players, 30-or-more points, game
3—Denver at Utah, April 19, 1984
   San Antonio vs. Golden State, April 25, 1991
2—by many

Most players, 30-or-more points, both teams, game
4—Houston (2) at Orlando (2), June 9, 1995
3—by many

Most players, 20-or-more points, game
5—Boston vs. Los Angeles, April 19, 1965
   Philadelphia vs. Boston, April 11, 1967
   Phoenix at Los Angeles, May 23, 1984
   Boston vs. Milwaukee, May 15, 1986
   L.A. Lakers vs. Boston, June 4, 1987
   Boston vs. L.A. Lakers, June 11, 1987

Most players, 20-or-more points, both teams, game
8—Cincinnati (4) at Detroit (4), March 16, 1962
   Boston (4) at Los Angeles (4), April 26, 1966
   Phoenix (5) at Los Angeles (3), May 23, 1984
   Boston (5) vs. Milwaukee (3), May 15, 1986
   L.A. Lakers (5) vs. Boston (3), June 4, 1987
   Portland (4) at Phoenix (4), May 11, 1992 (2 ot)

Most players, 10-or-more points, game
10—Minneapolis vs. St. Louis, March 19, 1956
9—Cincinnati at Boston, March 31, 1963
   Dallas vs. Seattle, April 23, 1987
   Cleveland vs. New Jersey, April 29, 1993

Most players, 10-or-more points, both teams, game
15—Philadelphia (8) vs. Milwaukee (7), March 30, 1970
   L.A. Lakers (8) vs. Phoenix (7), April 18, 1985
   Dallas (9) vs. Seattle (6), April 23, 1987
   Dallas (8) vs. Houston (7), April 28, 1988
14—Ft. Wayne (7) at Minneapolis (7), March 17, 1957
   St. Louis (7) at Boston (7), March 27, 1960
   Detroit (7) at Cincinnati (7), March 17, 1962
   Boston (7) at Detroit (7), March 25, 1968
   Philadelphia (7) at Washington (7), May 5, 1978
   Phoenix (7) at L.A. Lakers (7), April 20, 1985
   Denver (7) at L.A. Lakers (7), April 25, 1987
   Boston (8) vs. New York (6), April 28, 1990

Fewest players, 10 or more points, game
1—Golden State vs. Los Angeles, April 21, 1973
   Phoenix vs. Kansas City, April 8, 1981
   Utah at San Antonio, April 28, 1994
   Utah at San Antonio, May 9, 1998
   Utah at Chicago, June 7, 1998
   Detroit at Atlanta, May 8, 1999
   Sacramento at L.A. Lakers, May 5, 2000
   Phoenix at L.A. Lakers, May 16, 2000
   Orlando at Detroit, April 23, 2003
   New Orleans at Miami, April 21, 2004
   Detroit at New Jersey, May 11, 2004
2—by many

Fewest players, 10 or more points, both teams, game
4—Chicago (2) at Miami (2), May 24, 1997
   Utah (2) at Chicago (2), June 10, 1998
   Utah (2) at Chicago (2), June 12, 1998
   Phoenix (1) at L.A. Lakers (3), May 16, 2000
5—many times

FIELD-GOAL PERCENTAGE

Highest field-goal percentage, game
.670—Boston vs. New York, April 28, 1990 (63-94)
.663—L.A. Lakers vs. San Antonio, April 17, 1986 (57-86)

Lowest field-goal percentage, game
.233—Golden State vs. Los Angeles, April 21, 1973 (27-116)
.242—St. Louis at Minneapolis, March 19, 1956 (22-91)

Highest field-goal percentage, both teams, game
.591—L.A. Lakers (.640) vs. Denver (.543), May 11, 1985
.588—Boston (.608) vs. Atlanta (.571), May 22, 1988
   Boston (.670) vs. New York (.510), April 20, 1990

Lowest field-goal percentage, both teams, game
.277—Syracuse (.275) vs. Ft. Wayne (.280), at Indianapolis, April 7, 1955
.288—Minneapolis (.283) vs. Rochester (.293), March 16, 1955

FIELD GOALS

Most field goals, game
67—Milwaukee at Philadelphia, March 30, 1970
   San Antonio vs. Denver, May 4, 1983
   L.A. Lakers vs. Denver, May 22, 1985
64—Milwaukee vs. Denver, April 23, 1978

Fewest field goals, game
19—Portland vs. San Antonio, June 4, 1999
   New Jersey at Detroit, May 3, 2004
20—New Orleans at Miami, April 21, 2004

Most field goals, both teams, game
119—Milwaukee (67) at Philadelphia (52), March 30, 1970
114—San Antonio (62) vs. Denver (52), April 26, 1983
   Boston (63) vs. New York (51), April 28, 1990

Fewest field goals, both teams, game
45—Indiana (22) vs. Detroit (23), May 24, 2004
47—Indiana (22) at Miami (25), May 18, 2004

FIELD-GOAL ATTEMPTS

Most field-goal attempts, game
140—Boston vs. Syracuse, March 18, 1959
   San Francisco at Philadelphia, April 14, 1967 (ot)
135—Boston vs. Syracuse, April 1, 1959
   Boston vs. Philadelphia, March 22, 1960

Fewest field-goal attempts, game
53—Cleveland at New York, April 29, 1995
   Seattle at Utah, May 26, 1996
54—Houston at Utah, May 7, 1995

Most field-goal attempts, both teams, game
257—Boston (135) vs. Philadelphia (122), March 22, 1960
256—San Francisco (140) at Philadelphia (116), April 14, 1967 (ot)

Fewest field-goal attempts, both teams, game
113—Cleveland (53) at New York (60), April 29, 1995
118—Cleveland (56) vs. Indiana (62), April 30, 1998

3-POINT FIELD GOALS

Most 3-point field goals, game
20—Seattle vs. Houston, May 6, 1996
19—Houston at Utah, April 29, 1995
   Boston vs. Philadelphia, May 3, 2002
   Dallas at Sacramento, May 10, 2003 (2 ot)

Most 3-point field goals, both teams, game
33—Seattle (20) vs. Houston (13), May 6, 1996
28—Houston (19) at Utah (9), April 29, 1995
   Dallas (19) at Sacramento (9), May 10, 2003 (2 ot)

Most 3-point field goals, none missed, game
5—Dallas at Utah, April 25, 1986
   Dallas vs. L.A. Lakers, May 4, 1986
4—Washington vs. New Jersey, April 23, 1982
   L.A. Lakers vs. Denver, May 11, 1985

Most 3-point field goals, one half
11—Houston at Utah, April 29, 1995
   New York at Cleveland, April 25, 1996
   Boston vs. Philadelphia, May 3, 2002
   Dallas vs. Sacramento, May 8, 2003

Most 3-point field goals, one quarter
9—Boston vs. Philadelphia, May 3, 2002

3-POINT FIELD-GOAL ATTEMPTS

Most 3-point field-goal attempts, game
42—Dallas at Sacramento, May 10, 2003 (2 ot)
34—Houston vs. Seattle, May 12, 1996 (ot)
33—Seattle at Phoenix, May 1, 1997 (ot)
   Indiana at Milwaukee, May 13, 1999

Most 3-point field-goal attempts, both teams, game
68—Dallas (42) at Sacramento (26), May 10, 2003 (2 ot)
63—Seattle (33) at Phoenix (30), May 1, 1997 (ot)
62—Houston (32) at Orlando (30), June 7, 1995 (ot)
59—Seattle (30) at Phoenix (29), April 29, 1997

Most 3-point field-goal attempts, one half
26—L.A. Lakers vs. Sacramento, May 24, 2002

FREE THROW PERCENTAGE

Highest free throw percentage, game
1.000—Detroit at Milwaukee, April 18, 1976 (15-15)
   Dallas vs. Seattle, April 19, 1984 (24-24)
   Detroit vs. Chicago, May 18, 1988 (23-23)
   Phoenix vs. Golden State, May 9, 1989 (28-28)
   Chicago vs. Cleveland, May 19, 1992 (19-19)
   Portland at Chicago, June 14, 1992 (21-21)
   New Jersey vs. Cleveland, May 7, 1993 (3-3)
   Indiana at New York, June 11, 1999 (9-9)
   Indiana vs. New York, May 23, 2000 (12-12)
   Philadelphia vs. Toronto, May 16, 2001 (16-16)
   Dallas at San Antonio, May 27, 2003 (23-23)
   Dallas at Sacramento, April 29, 2004 (18-18)
.980—Dallas at San Antonio, May 19, 2003 (49-50)

Lowest free throw percentage, game
.261—Philadelphia at Boston, March 19, 1960 (6-23)
.333—Orlando at Chicago, May 19, 1996 (8-24)
   Milwaukee at Philadelphia, May 24, 2001 (2-6)

Highest free throw percentage, both teams, game
.957—Chicago (.964) at Boston (.947), April 23, 1987
.946—Phoenix (1.000) vs. Golden State (.893), May 9, 1989

Lowest free throw percentage, both teams, game
.444—Orlando (.333) at Chicago (.667), May 19, 1996
.500—Philadelphia (.261) at Boston (.762), March 19, 1960

L.A. Lakers (.435) at Phoenix (.571), May 2, 1993
L.A. Lakers (.462) at San Antonio (.529), May 13, 2004

FREE THROWS MADE

Most free throws made, game
57—Boston vs. Syracuse, March 21, 1953 (4 ot)
   Phoenix vs. Seattle, June 5, 1993
54—St. Louis vs. Minneapolis, March 17, 1956

Fewest free throws made, game
2—Milwaukee at Philadelphia, May 24, 2001
3—Houston vs. Washington, April 19, 1977
   Los Angeles at Philadelphia, May 26, 1983
   New Jersey vs. Cleveland, May 7, 1993

Most free throws made, both teams, game
108—Boston (57) vs. Syracuse (51), March 21, 1953 (4 ot)
 98—New York (51) vs. Baltimore (47), March 26, 1949 (ot)
 91—St. Louis (54) vs. Minneapolis (37), March 17, 1956

Fewest free throws made, both teams, game
12—Boston (6) at Buffalo (6), April 6, 1974
14—Houston (4) vs. Phoenix (10), May 8, 1994

FREE THROW ATTEMPTS

Most free throw attempts, game
70—St. Louis vs. Minneapolis, March 17, 1956
68—Minneapolis vs. St. Louis, March 21, 1956

Fewest free throw attempts, game
3—New Jersey vs. Cleveland, May 7, 1993
5—Los Angeles at Philadelphia, May 26, 1983
   Boston at Cleveland, May 2, 1992
   Utah at San Antonio, May 9, 1996

Most free throw attempts, both teams, game
128—Boston (64) vs. Syracuse (64), March 21, 1953 (4 ot)
122—St. Louis (70) vs. Minneapolis (52), March 17, 1956
   Minneapolis (68) vs. St. Louis (54), March 21, 1956

Fewest free throw attempts, both teams, game
16—New Jersey (3) vs. Cleveland (13), May 7, 1993
18—Boston (7) at Buffalo (11), April 6, 1974

TOTAL REBOUNDS

Highest rebound percentage, game
.694—Chicago vs. Atlanta, April 30, 1993
   Chicago vs. Atlanta, May 13, 1997
.688—Boston vs. Milwaukee, May 17, 1987

Most rebounds, game
97—Boston vs. Philadelphia, March 19, 1960
95—Boston vs. Syracuse, March 18, 1959

Fewest rebounds, game
18—San Antonio at L.A. Lakers, April 17, 1986
21—Detroit vs. Atlanta, April 29, 1997
   New Jersey vs. Chicago, April 29, 1998

Most rebounds, both teams, game
169—Boston (89) vs. Philadelphia (80), March 22, 1960
   Philadelphia (93) vs. San Francisco (76), April 16, 1967
163—Boston (95) vs. Syracuse (68), March 18, 1959

Fewest rebounds, both teams, game
51—Milwaukee (25) vs. Philadelphia (26), May 1, 1982
55—Cleveland (24) at New York (31), April 29, 1995
   Orlando (24) vs. Chicago (31), May 27, 1996
   Chicago (22) at Utah (33), June 14, 1998

OFFENSIVE REBOUNDS

Highest offensive rebound percentage, game
.609—New York vs. Indiana, June 5, 1994 (28-46)
.583—Houston vs. Philadelphia, May 11, 1977 (28-48)

Most offensive rebounds, game
30—Seattle vs. Portland, April 23, 1978
29—Washington at Atlanta, April 26, 1979

Kansas City at Phoenix, April 27, 1979

Fewest offensive rebounds, game
2—New York at Boston, April 19, 1974
   Golden State at Chicago, April 30, 1975
   Houston vs. L.A. Clippers, April 29, 1993
   Cleveland at New York, April 29, 1995
   Seattle vs. Utah, May 20, 1996
3—Many times

Most offensive rebounds, both teams, game
51—Houston (27) vs. Atlanta (24), April 11, 1979
   Utah (27) at Houston (24), April 28, 1985
50—Washington (28) at San Antonio (22), May 11, 1979

Fewest offensive rebounds, both teams, game
 9—New York (4) at Indiana (5), May 7, 1998
   Indiana (4) at New York (5), May 27, 2000
10—Minnesota (3) vs. L.A. Lakers (7), May 21, 2004

DEFENSIVE REBOUNDS

Highest defensive rebound percentage, game
.952—Chicago vs. Golden State, April 30, 1975 (40-42)
.947—Boston vs. New York, April 19, 1974 (36-38)

Most defensive rebounds, game
56—San Antonio vs. Denver, May 4, 1983
49—Philadelphia vs. New York, April 16, 1978
   Denver vs. Portland, May 1, 1977 (ot)

Fewest defensive rebounds, game
12—Golden State at Seattle, April 28, 1992
13—San Antonio at L.A. Lakers, April 17, 1986

Most defensive rebounds, both teams, game
92—Denver (49) vs. Portland (43), May 1, 1977 (ot)
86—San Antonio (56) vs. Denver (30), May 4, 1983

Fewest defensive rebounds, both teams, game
30—New Jersey (14) vs. Chicago (16), April 29, 1998
34—Milwaukee (15) vs. Philadelphia (19), May 1, 1982

ASSISTS

Most assists, game
51—San Antonio vs. Denver, May 4, 1983
46—Milwaukee at Philadelphia, March 30, 1970
   Milwaukee vs. Denver, April 23, 1978
   Boston vs. New York, April 28, 1990

Fewest assists, game
5—Boston at St. Louis, April 3, 1960
   Detroit at Chicago, April 5, 1974
6—Chicago vs. Los Angeles, March 29, 1968

Most assists, both teams, game
79—L.A. Lakers (44) vs. Boston (35), June 4, 1987
78—Denver (40) at San Antonio (38), April 26, 1983

Fewest assists, both teams, game
16—Chicago (6) vs. Los Angeles (10), March 29, 1968
17—Cincinnati (7) at Detroit (10), March 15, 1958
   Miami (7) vs. Indiana (10), May 18, 2004

PERSONAL FOULS

Most personal fouls, game
55—Syracuse at Boston, March 21, 1953 (4 ot)
53—Baltimore at New York, March 26, 1949 (ot)
51—Boston vs. Syracuse, March 21, 1953 (4 ot)
47—New York vs. Baltimore, March 26, 1949 (ot)
45—Syracuse at New York, April 8, 1952

Fewest personal fouls, game
 9—Cleveland vs. Boston, May 2, 1992
10—Cleveland at New Jersey, May 7, 1993

Most personal fouls, both teams, game
106—Syracuse (55) at Boston (51), March 21, 1953 (4 ot)
100—Baltimore (53) at New York (47), March 26, 1949 (ot)

83—New Jersey (42) at Detroit (41), May 14, 2004 (3 ot)
82—Syracuse (45) at New York (37), April 8, 1952

Fewest personal fouls, both teams, game
25—Cleveland (10) at New Jersey (15), May 7, 1993
27—Philadelphia (12) at Boston (15), March 23, 1958
    Houston (13) vs. Utah (14), May 23, 1994

DISQUALIFICATIONS

Most disqualifications, game
7—Syracuse at Boston, March 21, 1953 (4 ot)
6—Baltimore at New York, March 26, 1949 (ot)
5—New York vs. Baltimore, March 26, 1949 (ot)
    Boston vs. Syracuse, March 21, 1953 (4 ot)
4—by many

Most disqualifications, both teams, game
12—Syracuse (7) at Boston (5), March 21, 1953 (4 ot)
11—Baltimore (6) at New York (5), March 26, 1949 (ot)
 8—Detroit (4) vs. New Jersey (4), May 14, 2004 (3 ot)
 7—Los Angeles (4) at Detroit (3), April 3, 1962
    Boston (4) vs. Los Angeles (3), April 18, 1962 (ot)

STEALS

Most steals, game
22—Golden State vs. Seattle, April 14, 1975
20—Golden State vs. Phoenix, May 2, 1976
 Philadelphia vs. Orlando, May 13, 1999

Fewest steals, game
0—Buffalo at Boston, March 30, 1974
    Phoenix at Seattle, April 15, 1976
    Indiana vs. Orlando, May 27, 1995
    Indiana vs. Philadelphia, May 2, 2001
1—by many

Most steals, both teams, game
35—Golden State (22) vs. Seattle (13), April 14, 1975
32—Seattle (18) at Golden State (14), April 16, 1975
    Los Angeles (19) vs. Golden State (13), May 4, 1977
    Milwaukee (19) at Philadelphia (13), May 9, 1986

Fewest steals, both teams, game
2—Phoenix (0) at Seattle (2), April 15, 1976
3—New York (1) at Boston (2), April 14, 1974

BLOCKED SHOTS

Most blocked shots, game
20—Philadelphia vs. Milwaukee, April 5, 1981
19—Detroit at Indiana, May 24, 2004

Fewest blocked shots, game
0—Accomplished 52 times. Most recent:
    Philadelphia vs. Detroit, May 10, 2003

Most blocked shots, both teams, game
29—Philadelphia (20) vs. Milwaukee (9), April 5, 1981
26—Detroit (19) at Indiana (7), May 24, 2004

Fewest blocked shots, both teams, game
1—Dallas (1) at Portland (0), April 25, 1985
    Houston (0) vs. Seattle (1), May 17, 1997
    New York (0) vs. Miami (1), April 30, 1998
2—New York (0) at Boston (2), April 19, 1974
    Philadelphia (1) at Milwaukee (1), April 12, 1981
    Boston (0) at Houston (2), May 14, 1981
    Boston (1) at Milwaukee (1), May 18, 1986
    Chicago (0) vs. New York (2), April 25, 1991
    Portland (0) vs. Phoenix (2), May 2, 1995
    Charlotte (1) at New York (1), April 24, 1997
    Milwaukee (0) at Indiana (2), May 4, 2000
    Minnesota (0) vs. Dallas (2), April 28, 2002
    Dallas (0) vs. Portland (2), April 23, 2003
    Portland (0) at Dallas (2), April 25, 2003

TURNOVERS

Most turnovers, game
36—Chicago at Portland, April 17, 1977
35—Indiana at New York, May 9, 1995
34—Portland at Philadelphia, May 22, 1977

Fewest turnovers, game
4—Detroit at Boston, May 9, 1991
5—Chicago vs. Los Angeles, March 30, 1971
    Boston vs. Chicago, April 26, 1987
    Detroit vs. Milwaukee, May 12, 1989
    Boston at Detroit, May 13, 1991
    Chicago at L.A. Lakers, June 9, 1991
    New York at Cleveland, April 25, 1996
    Houston vs. L.A. Lakers, April 30, 1996
    Minnesota at Houston, April 24, 1997
    L.A. Lakers vs. Indiana, June 19, 2000
    Boston vs. Philadelphia, May 3, 2002
    L.A. Lakers at Houston, April 23, 2004

Most turnovers, both teams, game
60—Golden State (31) at Washington (29), May 25, 1975
56—Phoenix (30) vs. Kansas City (26), April 22, 1979

Fewest turnovers, both teams, game
13—Detroit (4) at Boston (9), May 9, 1991
    Portland (6) at Minnesota (7), April 30, 2000
    Seattle (6) at San Antonio (7), May 3, 2002
14—Boston (5) at Detroit (9), May 13, 1991
    Houston (5) vs. L.A. Lakers (9), April 30, 1996
    New York (6) at Miami (8), May 21, 2000
    L.A. Lakers (5) vs. Indiana (9), June 19, 2000

NBA FINALS

POINTS

4-game series
145—Shaquille O'Neal, L.A. Lakers, 2002
131—Hakeem Olajuwon, Houston, 1995

5-game series
178—Allen Iverson, Philadelphia, 2001
169—Jerry West, Los Angeles, 1965

6-game series
246—Michael Jordan, Chicago, 1993
245—Rick Barry, San Francisco, 1967

7-game series
284—Elgin Baylor, Los Angeles, 1962
265—Jerry West, Los Angeles, 1969

MINUTES PLAYED

4-game series
187—Robert Horry, Houston, 1995
186—Bob Cousy, Boston, 1959
     Bill Russell, Boston, 1959

5-game series
240—Wilt Chamberlain, Los Angeles, 1973
237—Allen Iverson, Philadelphia, 2001

6-game series
292—Bill Russell, Boston, 1968
291—John Havlicek, Boston, 1968

7-game series
345—Kareem Abdul-Jabbar, Milwaukee, 1974
338—Bill Russell, Boston, 1962

FIELD-GOAL PERCENTAGE

(minimum: 4 FG per game)

4-game series
.739—Derrek Dickey, Golden State, 1975
.649—Mario Elie, Houston, 1995

5-game series
.702—Bill Russell, Boston, 1965
.653—John Paxson, Chicago, 1991

6-game series
.667—Bob Gross, Portland, 1977
.611—Shaquille O'Neal, L.A. Lakers, 2000

7-game series
.638—James Worthy, Los Angeles, 1984
.625—Wilt Chamberlain, Los Angeles, 1970

MOST FIELD GOALS

4-game series
56—Hakeem Olajuwon, Houston, 1995
50—Shaquille O'Neal, L.A. Lakers, 2002

5-game series
66—Allen Iverson, Philadelphia, 2001
63—Michael Jordan, Chicago, 1991
     Shaquille O'Neal, L.A. Lakers, 2001

6-game series
101—Michael Jordan, Chicago, 1993
 96—Shaquille O'Neal, L.A. Lakers, 2000

7-game series
101—Elgin Baylor, Los Angeles, 1962
 97—Kareem Abdul-Jabbar, Milwaukee, 1974

MOST FIELD-GOAL ATTEMPTS

4-game series
116—Hakeem Olajuwon, Houston, 1995
102—Elgin Baylor, Minneapolis, 1959

5-game series
162—Allen Iverson, Philadelphia, 2001
139—Jerry West, Los Angeles, 1965

6-game series
235—Rick Barry, San Francisco, 1967
199—Michael Jordan, Chicago, 1993

7-game series
235—Elgin Baylor, Los Angeles, 1962
196—Jerry West, Los Angeles, 1969

3-POINT FIELD-GOAL PERCENTAGE

4-game series
.667—Derek Fisher, L.A. Lakers, 2002
.571—Mario Elie, Houston, 1995

5-game series
.688—Isiah Thomas, Detroit, 1990
.615—Robert Horry, L.A. Lakers, 2001

6-game series
.667—Danny Ainge, Phoenix, 1993
.643—John Paxson, Chicago, 1993

7-game series
.438—Sam Cassell, Houston, 1994
.436—Derek Harper, New York, 1994

3-POINT FIELD GOALS MADE

4-game series
11—Anfernee Hardaway, Orlando, 1995
     Robert Horry, Houston, 1995
10—Nick Anderson, Orlando, 1995
     Brian Shaw, Orlando, 1995

5-game series
11—Isiah Thomas, Detroit, 1990
     Allen Iverson, Philadelphia, 2001
10—Derek Fisher, L.A. Lakers, 2001

6-game series
17—Dan Majerle, Phoenix, 1993
15—Bryon Russell, Utah, 1997
     Reggie Miller, Indiana, 2000

7-game series
17—Derek Harper, New York, 1994
16—John Starks, New York, 1994

3-POINT FIELD-GOAL ATTEMPTS

4-game series
31—Nick Anderson, Orlando, 1995
29—Robert Horry, Houston, 1995
     Dennis Scott, Orlando, 1995

5-game series
39—Allen Iverson, Philadelphia, 2001
25—Terry Porter, Portland, 1990

6-game series
40—Reggie Miller,Indiana, 2000
39—Dan Majerle, Phoenix, 1993
     Scottie Pippen, Chicago, 1996

7-game series
50—John Starks, New York, 1994
40—Vernon Maxwell, Houston, 1994

FREE THROW PERCENTAGE

(minimum: 2 FTM per game)

4-game series
1.000—Dennis Scott, Orlando, 1995
.944—Phil Chenier, Washington, 1975

5-game series
1.000—Bill Laimbeer, Detroit, 1990
        Vlade Divac, L.A. Lakers, 1991
  .957—Jim McMillian, Los Angeles, 1972

6-game series
.978—Reggie Miller, Indiana, 2000
.968—Bill Sharman, Boston, 1958

7-game series
.959—Bill Sharman, Boston, 1957
.947—Don Meineke, Ft. Wayne, 1955

FREE THROWS MADE

4-game series
45—Shaquille O'Neal, L.A. Lakers, 2002
34—Phil Chenier, Washington, 1975

5-game series
51—Jerry West, Los Angeles, 1965
48—Bob Pettit, St. Louis, 1961

6-game series
67—George Mikan, Minneapolis, 1950
61—Joe Fulks, Philadelphia, 1948

7-game series
82—Elgin Baylor, Los Angeles, 1962
75—Jerry West, Los Angeles, 1970

FREE THROW ATTEMPTS

4-game series
68—Shaquille O'Neal, L.A. Lakers, 2002
47—Moses Malone, Philadelphia, 1983

5-game series
76—Shaquille O'Neal, L.A. Lakers, 2001
60—Bob Pettit, St. Louis, 1961

6-game series
93—Shaquille O'Neal, L.A. Lakers, 2000
86—George Mikan, Minneapolis, 1950

7-game series
99—Elgin Baylor, Los Angeles, 1962
97—Bob Pettit, St. Louis, 1957

REBOUNDS

4-game series
118—Bill Russell, Boston, 1959
  76—Wes Unseld, Baltimore, 1971

5-game series
144—Bill Russell, Boston, 1961
138—Wilt Chamberlain, San Francisco, 1964

6-game series
171—Wilt Chamberlain, Philadelphia, 1967
160—Nate Thurmond, San Francisco, 1967

7-game series
189—Bill Russell, Boston, 1962
175—Wilt Chamberlain, Los Angeles, 1969

OFFENSIVE REBOUNDS

4-game series
27—Moses Malone, Philadelphia, 1983
19—Horace Grant, Orlando, 1995

5-game series
31—Shaquille O'Neal, L.A. Lakers, 2001
21—Elvin Hayes, Washington, 1979

6-game series
46—Moses Malone, Houston, 1981
41—Dennis Rodman, Chicago, 1996

7-game series
33—Elvin Hayes, Washington, 1978
     Marvin Webster, Seattle, 1978
32—Patrick Ewing, New York, 1994

DEFENSIVE REBOUNDS

4-game series
53—Wes Unseld, Washington, 1975
45—Moses Malone, Philadelphia, 1983

5-game series
62—Jack Sikma, Seattle, 1979
56—Tim Duncan, San Antonio, 1999

6-game series
91—Bill Walton, Portland, 1977
79—Tim Duncan, San Antonio, 2003

7-game series
72—Larry Bird, Boston, 1984
64—Marvin Webster, Seattle, 1978

ASSISTS

4-game series
51—Bob Cousy, Boston, 1959
50—Magic Johnson, Los Angeles, 1983

5-game series
62—Magic Johnson, L.A. Lakers, 1991
57—Michael Jordan, Chicago, 1991

6-game series
84—Magic Johnson, L.A. Lakers, 1985
78—Magic Johnson, L.A. Lakers, 1987

7-game series
95—Magic Johnson, Los Angeles, 1984
91—Magic Johnson, L.A. Lakers, 1988

PERSONAL FOULS

4-game series
20—Michael Cooper, Los Angeles, 1983
19—Kevin Porter, Washington, 1975
     Tony Campbell, L.A. Lakers, 1989
     Jason Collins, New Jersey, 2002

5-game series
27—George Mikan, Minneapolis, 1953
25—Art Hillhouse, Philadelphia, 1947
     Lonnie Shelton, Seattle, 1979
     Bill Laimbeer, Detroit, 1990
     Marcus Camby, New York, 1999

6-game series
35—Charlie Scott, Boston, 1976
33—Tom Heinsohn, Boston, 1958
     Tom Meschery, San Francisco, 1967

7-game series
37—Arnie Risen, Boston, 1957
36—Vern Mikkelsen, Minneapolis, 1952
     Jack McMahon, St. Louis, 1957

DISQUALIFICATIONS

4-game series
1—John Tresvant, Baltimore, 1971
    Elvin Hayes, Washington, 1975
    George Johnson, Golden State, 1975
    Kevin Porter, Washington, 1975
    Marc Iavaroni, Philadelphia, 1983
    Michael Cooper, Los Angeles, 1983

Tony Campbell, L.A. Lakers, 1989
A.C. Green, L.A. Lakers, 1989
Rick Mahorn, Detroit, 1989
Jason Collins, New Jersey, 2002
Keith Van Horn, New Jersey, 2002
Aaron Williams, New Jersey, 2002

5-game series
5—Art Hillhouse, Philadelphia, 1947
4—Chuck Gilmur, Chicago, 1947

6-game series
5—Charlie Scott, Boston, 1976

7-game series
5—Arnie Risen, Boston, 1957
3—Mel Hutchins, Ft. Wayne, 1955
   Jack McMahon, St. Louis, 1957
   Jack Sikma, Seattle, 1978

STEALS

4-game series
14—Rick Barry, Golden State, 1975
12—Robert Horry, Houston, 1995

5-game series
14—Michael Jordan, Chicago, 1991
13—Charlie Ward, New York, 1999

6-game series
16—Julius Erving, Philadelphia, 1977
   Magic Johnson, Los Angeles, 1980
   Larry Bird, Boston, 1986
15—Maurice Cheeks, Philadelphia, 1980
   Magic Johnson, Los Angeles, 1982
   Byron Scott, L.A. Lakers, 1985
   Danny Ainge, Boston, 1986

7-game series
20—Isiah Thomas, Detroit, 1988
17—Derek Harper, New York, 1994

BLOCKED SHOTS

4-game series
11—Elvin Hayes, Washington, 1975
   George Johnson, Golden State, 1975
   Julius Erving, Philadelphia, 1983
   John Salley, Detroit, 1989
   Shaquille O'Neal, L.A. Lakers, 2002
10—Shaquille O'Neal, Orlando, 1995

5-game series
17—Shaquille O'Neal, L.A. Lakers, 2001
16—Jack Sikma, Seattle, 1979

6-game series
32—Tim Duncan, San Antonio, 2003
23—Kareem Abdul-Jabbar, Los Angeles, 1980

7-game series
30—Patrick Ewing, New York, 1994
27—Hakeem Olajuwon, Houston, 1994

TURNOVERS

4-game series
24—Magic Johnson, Los Angeles, 1983
21—Shaquille O'Neal, Orlando, 1995

5-game series
25—Isiah Thomas, Detroit, 1990
23—Richard Hamilton, Detroit, 2004

6-game series
30—Magic Johnson, Los Angeles, 1980
26—Magic Johnson, Los Angeles, 1982
   Kevin Johnson, Phoenix, 1993
   Scottie Pippen, Chicago, 1993
   Stephen Jackson, San Antonio, 2003

7-game series
31—Magic Johnson, Los Angeles, 1984
26—Gus Williams, Seattle, 1978
   Isiah Thomas, Detroit, 1988

TEAM, SERIES

MOST POINTS

4-game series
487—Boston vs. Minneapolis, 1959
456—Houston vs. Orlando, 1995

5-game series
617—Boston vs. Los Angeles, 1965
605—Boston vs. St. Louis, 1961

6-game series
747—Philadelphia vs. San Francisco, 1967
707—San Francisco vs. Philadelphia, 1967

7-game series
827—Boston vs. Los Angeles, 1966
824—Boston vs. Los Angeles, 1962

FEWEST POINTS

4-game series
376—Baltimore vs. Milwaukee, 1971
382—Washington vs. Golden State, 1975

5-game series
399—New York vs. San Antonio, 1999
409—L.A. Lakers vs. Detroit, 2004

6-game series
481—Utah vs. Chicago, 1998
492—New Jersey vs. San Antonio, 2003

7-game series
603—Houston vs. New York, 1994
608—New York vs. Houston, 1994

HIGHEST FIELD-GOAL PERCENTAGE

4-game series
.527—Detroit vs. L.A. Lakers, 1989
.505—L.A. Lakers vs. New Jersey, 2002

5-game series
.527—Chicago vs. L.A. Lakers, 1991
.470—New York vs. Los Angeles, 1972

6-game series
.515—L.A. Lakers vs. Boston, 1987
.512—L.A. Lakers vs. Boston, 1985

7-game series
.515—Los Angeles vs. Boston, 1984
.494—Los Angeles vs. New York, 1970

LOWEST FIELD-GOAL PERCENTAGE

4-game series
.384—Baltimore vs. Milwaukee, 1971
.388—Minneapolis vs. Boston, 1959

5-game series
.365—Ft. Wayne vs. Philadelphia, 1956
.372—St. Louis vs. Boston, 1961

6-game series
.355—Boston vs. St. Louis, 1958
.370—New Jersey vs. San Antonio, 2003

7-game series
.339—Syracuse vs. Ft. Wayne, 1955
.369—Boston vs. St. Louis, 1957

MOST FIELD GOALS

4-game series
188—Boston vs. Minneapolis, 1959
180—Minneapolis vs. Boston, 1959

5-game series
243—Boston vs. Los Angeles, 1965
238—Boston vs. St. Louis, 1961

6-game series
287—Philadelphia vs. San Francisco, 1967
    San Francisco vs. Philadelphia, 1967
280—L.A. Lakers vs. Boston, 1987

7-game series
332—New York vs. Los Angeles, 1970
327—Los Angeles vs. Boston, 1984

FEWEST FIELD GOALS

4-game series
144—L.A. Lakers vs. Detroit, 1989
146—L.A. Lakers vs. New Jersey, 2002

5-game series
150—San Antonio vs. New York, 1999
154—New York vs. San Antonio, 1999

6-game series
182—New Jersey vs. San Antonio, 2003
185—Utah vs. Chicago, 1997

7-game series
207—Syracuse vs. Ft. Wayne, 1955
217—Ft. Wayne vs. Syracuse, 1955

MOST FIELD-GOAL ATTEMPTS

4-game series
464—Minneapolis vs. Boston, 1959
463—Boston vs. Minneapolis, 1959

5-game series
568—Boston vs. Los Angeles, 1965
555—Boston vs. St. Louis, 1961

6-game series
743—San Francisco vs. Philadelphia, 1967
640—Boston vs. L.A. Lakers, 1963

7-game series
799—Boston vs. St. Louis, 1957
769—Boston vs. St. Louis, 1960

FEWEST FIELD-GOAL ATTEMPTS

4-game series
289—L.A. Lakers vs. New Jersey, 2002
310—L.A. Lakers vs. Detroit, 1989

5-game series
337—San Antonio vs. New York, 1999
366—Detroit vs. L.A. Lakers, 2004

6-game series
418—Seattle vs. Chicago, 1996
430—Utah vs. Chicago, 1997

7-game series
523—Houston vs. New York, 1994
531—L.A. Lakers vs. Detroit, 1988

HIGHEST 3-POINT FIELD-GOAL PERCENTAGE

4-game series
.475—L.A. Lakers vs. New Jersey, 2002
.402—Houston vs. Orlando, 1995

5-game series
.480—L.A. Lakers vs. Philadelphia, 2001
.446—Detroit vs. Portland, 1990

6-game series
.464—Chicago vs. Phoenix, 1993
.435—Phoenix vs. Chicago, 1993

7-game series
.375—Boston vs. Los Angeles, 1984
.343—New York vs. Houston, 1994

MOST 3-POINT FIELD GOALS MADE

4-game series
41—Orlando vs. Houston, 1995
37—Houston vs. Orlando, 1995

5-game series
36—L.A. Lakers vs. Philadelphia, 2001
25—Detroit vs. Portland, 1990

6-game series
49—Indiana vs. L.A. Lakers, 2000
39—Chicago vs. Utah, 1997

7-game series
37—Houston vs. New York, 1994
36—New York vs. Houston, 1994

MOST 3-POINT FIELD-GOAL ATTEMPTS

4-game series
118—Orlando vs. Houston, 1995
 92—Houston vs. Orlando, 1995

5-game series
89—L.A. Lakers vs. Detroit, 2004
75—L.A. Lakers vs. Philadelphia, 2001

6-game series
137—Chicago vs. Seattle, 1996
116—Indiana vs. L.A. Lakers, 2000

7-game series
121—Houston vs. New York, 1994
105—New York vs. Houston, 1994

HIGHEST FREE THROW PERCENTAGE

4-game series
.785—Los Angeles vs. Philadelphia, 1983
.776—Detroit vs. L.A. Lakers, 1989

5-game series
.826—Chicago vs. L.A. Lakers, 1991
.810—L.A. Lakers vs. Chicago, 1991

6-game series
.852—Indiana vs. L.A. Lakers, 2000
.851—Seattle vs. Chicago, 1996

7-game series
.827—Boston vs. Los Angeles, 1966
.805—Los Angeles vs. Boston, 1962

LOWEST FREE THROW PERCENTAGE

4-game series
.670—New Jersey vs. L.A. Lakers, 2002
.675—Baltimore vs. Milwaukee, 1971

5-game series
.616—San Francisco vs. Boston, 1964
.640—L.A. Lakers vs. Detroit, 2004

6-game series
.570—L.A. Lakers vs. Indiana, 2000
.613—Philadelphia vs. San Francisco, 1967

7-game series
.641—Los Angeles vs. Boston, 1969
.688—Los Angeles vs. New York, 1970

MOST FREE THROWS MADE

4-game series
111—Boston vs. Minneapolis, 1959
108—L.A. Lakers vs. Detroit, 1989

5-game series
146—Los Angeles vs. Boston, 1965
145—New York vs. Minneapolis, 1953

6-game series
232—Boston vs. St. Louis, 1958
215—St. Louis vs. Boston, 1958

7-game series
244—St. Louis vs. Boston, 1957
239—Los Angeles vs. Boston, 1962

FEWEST FREE THROWS MADE

4-game series
52—Baltimore vs. Milwuakee, 1971
59—New Jersey vs. L.A. Lakers, 2002

5-game series
71—L.A. Lakers vs. Detroit, 2004
73—New York vs. Los Angeles, 1973

6-game series
82—Chicago vs. Phoenix, 1993
86—Utah vs. Chicago, 1998

7-game series
100—Milwaukee vs. Boston, 1974
108—New York vs. Houston, 1994

MOST FREE THROW ATTEMPTS

4-game series
159—Boston vs. Minneapolis, 1959
144—L.A. Lakers vs. Detroit, 1989

5-game series
211—San Francisco vs. Boston, 1964
199—New York vs. Minneapolis, 1953
     Los Angeles vs. Boston, 1965

6-game series
298—Boston vs. St. Louis, 1958
292—St. Louis vs. Boston, 1958

7-game series
341—St. Louis vs. Boston, 1957
299—Boston vs. St. Louis, 1957

FEWEST FREE THROW ATTEMPTS

4-game series
77—Baltimore vs. Milwaukee, 1971
88—New Jersey vs. L.A. Lakers, 2002

5-game series
92—Chicago vs. L.A. Lakers, 1991
96—New York vs. Los Angeles, 1973

6-game series
112—Utah vs. Chicago, 1998
129—Boston vs. Houston, 1981

7-game series
137—Milwaukee vs. Boston, 1974
148—New York vs. Houston, 1994

HIGHEST REBOUND PERCENTAGE

4-game series
.556—Golden State vs. Washington, 1975
.533—Milwaukee vs. Baltimore, 1971

5-game series
.5483—Boston vs. St. Louis, 1961
.5481—Detroit vs. L.A. Lakers, 2004

6-game series
.583—Los Angeles vs. Philadelphia, 1980
.558—Boston vs. Phoenix, 1976

7-game series
.541—Rochester vs. New York, 1951
.538—Detroit vs. L.A. Lakers, 1988

MOST REBOUNDS

4-game series
295—Boston vs. Minneapolis, 1959
268—Minneapolis vs. Boston, 1959

5-game series
369—Boston vs. St. Louis, 1961
316—Boston vs. Los Angeles, 1965

6-game series
435—San Francisco vs. Philadelphia, 1967
425—Philadelphia vs. San Francisco, 1967

7-game series
487—Boston vs. St. Louis, 1957
448—Boston vs. St. Louis, 1960

FEWEST REBOUNDS

4-game series
145—L.A. Lakers vs. Detroit, 1989
156—New Jersey vs. L.A. Lakers, 2002

5-game series
178—L.A. Lakers vs. Chicago, 1991
188—L.A. Lakers vs. Detroit, 2004

6-game series
223—Philadelphia vs. Los Angeles, 1980
     Seattle vs. Chicago, 1996
225—Chicago vs. Portland, 1992

7-game series
263—L.A. Lakers vs. Detroit, 1988
280—Houston vs. New York, 1994

HIGHEST OFFENSIVE REBOUND PERCENTAGE

4-game series
.396—Philadelphia vs. Los Angeles, 1983
.375—Golden State vs. Washington, 1975

5-game series
.346—Detroit vs. L.A. Lakers, 2004
.336—Washington vs. Seattle, 1979

6-game series
.410—Boston vs. Houston, 1981
.407—Los Angeles vs. Philadelphia, 1982

7-game series
.384—Boston vs. Los Angeles, 1984
.366—Seattle vs. Washington, 1978

MOST OFFENSIVE REBOUNDS

4-game series
72—Golden State vs. Washington, 1975
     Philadelphia vs. Los Angeles, 1983

5-game series
82—Washington vs. Seattle, 1979
72—Detroit vs. Portland, 1990
     Detroit vs. L.A. Lakers, 2004

6-game series
112—Houston vs. Boston, 1981
111—Houston vs. Boston, 1986

7-game series
131—Boston vs. Los Angeles, 1984
127—Seattle vs. Washington, 1978

FEWEST OFFENSIVE REBOUNDS

4-game series
43—L.A. Lakers vs. New Jersey, 2002
44—Houston vs. Orlando, 1995

5-game series
42—San Antonio vs. New York, 1999
49—New York vs. San Antonio, 1999

6-game series
52—Indiana vs. L.A. Lakers, 2000
57—Philadelphia vs. Los Angeles, 1980

7-game series
72—L.A. Lakers vs. Detroit, 1988
74—Houston vs. New York, 1994

HIGHEST DEFENSIVE REBOUND PERCENTAGE

4-game series
.756—Orlando vs. Houston, 1995
.737—Golden State vs. Washington, 1975

5-game series
.772—New York vs. San Antonio, 1999
.767—San Antonio vs. New York, 1999

6-game series
.782—Los Angeles vs. Philadelphia, 1980
.771—L.A. Lakers vs. Indiana, 2000

7-game series
.745—Detroit vs. L.A. Lakers, 1988
.726—New York vs. Houston, 1994

MOST DEFENSIVE REBOUNDS

4-game series
143—Golden State vs. Washington, 1975
136—Orlando vs. Houston, 1995

5-game series
162—Seattle vs. Washington, 1979
161—San Antonio vs. New York, 1999

6-game series
240—Boston vs. Phoenix, 1976
228—Portland vs. Philadelphia, 1977

7-game series
223—Seattle vs. Washington, 1978
220—Milwaukee vs. Boston, 1974
     Washington vs. Seattle, 1978

FEWEST DEFENSIVE REBOUNDS

4-game series
96—New Jersey vs. L.A. Lakers, 2002
98—L.A. Lakers vs. Detroit, 1989

5-game series
119—L.A. Lakers vs. Chicago, 1991
136—L.A. Lakers vs. Detroit, 2004

6-game series
144—Houston vs. Boston, 1981
     Chicago vs. Seattle, 1996
153—Chicago vs. Utah, 1998

7-game series
191—L.A. Lakers vs. Detroit, 1988
196—New York vs. Houston, 1994

MOST ASSISTS

4-game series
114—Boston vs. Minneapolis, 1959

110—Orlando vs. Houston, 1995

5-game series
139—Chicago vs. L.A. Lakers, 1991
130—Boston vs. St. Louis, 1961

6-game series
192—L.A. Lakers vs. Boston, 1985
188—Los Angeles vs. Philadelphia, 1982

7-game series
198—Los Angeles vs. Boston, 1984
192—New York vs. Los Angeles, 1970

FEWEST ASSISTS

4-game series
78—Baltimore vs. Milwaukee, 1971
82—Golden State vs. Washington, 1975

5-game series
70—New York vs. San Antonio, 1999
88—San Francisco vs. Boston, 1964
     Los Angeles vs. New York, 1973

6-game series
100—New Jersey vs. San Antonio, 2003
101—Seattle vs. Chicago, 1996

7-game series
121—Seattle vs. Washington, 1978
135—Los Angeles vs. Boston, 1962
     Boston vs. Los Angeles, 1969

MOST PERSONAL FOULS

4-game series
120—Los Angeles vs. Philadelphia, 1983
116—Golden State vs. Washington, 1975

5-game series
149—Portland vs. Detroit, 1990
140—Boston vs. San Francisco, 1964

6-game series
194—Boston vs. St. Louis, 1958
     St. Louis vs. Boston, 1958
182—San Francisco vs. Philadelphia, 1967
     Portland vs. Philadelphia, 1977

7-game series
221—Boston vs. St. Louis, 1957
210—Boston vs. Los Angeles, 1962

FEWEST PERSONAL FOULS

4-game series
78—L.A. Lakers vs. New Jersey, 2002
83—Houston vs. Orlando, 1995

5-game series
96—L.A. Lakers vs. Chicago, 1991
100—San Antonio vs. New York, 1999

6-game series
121—Houston vs. Boston, 1981
123—San Antonio vs. New Jersey, 2003

7-game series
149—Houston vs. New York, 1994
150—Los Angeles vs. New York, 1970

MOST DISQUALIFICATIONS

4-game series
3—New Jersey vs. L.A. Lakers, 2002
2—Washington vs. Golden State, 1975
    L.A. Lakers vs. Detroit, 1989

5-game series
9—Chicago vs. Philadelphia, 1947
8—Philadelphia vs. Chicago, 1947

6-game series
11—Boston vs. St. Louis, 1958
 9—Minneapolis vs. Syracuse, 1950

7-game series
10—Boston vs. St. Louis, 1957
 9—Minneapolis vs. New York, 1952
    St. Louis vs. Boston, 1957
    Boston vs. Los Angeles, 1962

FEWEST DISQUALIFICATIONS

4-game series
0—Boston vs. Minneapolis, 1959
    Minneapolis vs. Boston, 1959
    Milwaukee vs. Baltimore, 1971
    Houston vs. Orlando, 1995
    Orlando vs. Houston, 1995
    L.A. Lakers vs. New Jersey, 2002

5-game series
0—Los Angeles vs. New York, 1972
    San Antonio vs. New York, 1999
    Detroit vs. L.A. Lakers, 2004
1—New York vs. Los Angeles, 1972
    Chicago vs. L.A. Lakers, 1991
    L.A. Lakers vs. Detroit, 2004

6-game series
0—Los Angeles vs. Philadelphia, 1980
    Boston vs. Houston, 1986
    Houston vs. Boston, 1986
    Chicago vs. Seattle, 1996
1—by nine teams

7-game series
0—St. Louis vs. Boston, 1960
    L.A. Lakers vs. Detroit, 1988
1—Los Angeles vs. Boston, 1969
    Los Angeles vs. New York, 1970
    Houston vs. New York, 1994

MOST STEALS

4-game series
55—Golden State vs. Washington, 1975
45—Washington vs. Golden State, 1975

5-game series
49—Chicago vs. L.A. Lakers, 1991
41—L.A. Lakers vs. Philadelphia, 2001

6-game series
71—Philadelphia vs. Portland, 1977
64—Portland vs. Philadelphia, 1977
    Los Angeles vs. Philadelphia, 1982

7-game series
65—Boston vs. Los Angeles, 1984
59—Los Angeles vs. Boston, 1984

FEWEST STEALS

4-game series
16—Detroit vs. L.A. Lakers, 1989
21—Orlando vs. Houston, 1995

5-game series
28—Detroit vs. Portland, 1990
29—Washington vs. Seattle, 1979

6-game series
30—Boston vs. L.A. Lakers, 1987
33—Indiana vs. L.A. Lakers, 2000

7-game series
21—Milwaukee vs. Boston, 1974
40—Seattle vs. Washington, 1978

MOST BLOCKED SHOTS

4-game series
32—Golden State vs. Washington, 1975
    Philadelphia vs. Los Angeles, 1983
29—Los Angeles vs. Philadelphia, 1983

5-game series
44—L.A. Lakers vs. Philadelphia, 2001
39—Seattle vs. Washington, 1979

6-game series
60—Philadelphia vs. Los Angeles, 1980
59—San Antonio vs. New Jersey, 2003

7-game series
49—Seattle vs. Washington, 1978
43—New York vs. Houston, 1994

FEWEST BLOCKED SHOTS

4-game series
16—L.A. Lakers vs. Detroit, 1989
18—New Jersey vs. L.A. Lakers, 2002

5-game series
14—L.A. Lakers vs. Detroit, 2004
17—Portland vs. Detroit, 1990
    New York vs. San Antonio, 1999

6-game series
10—Boston vs. Phoenix, 1976
15—Utah vs. Chicago, 1998

7-game series
 7—Boston vs. Milwaukee, 1974
21—L.A. Lakers vs. Detroit, 1988

MOST TURNOVERS

4-game series
94—Golden State vs. Washington, 1975
92—Milwaukee vs. Baltimore, 1971

5-game series
104—Los Angeles vs. New York, 1973
 88—New York vs. Los Angeles, 1972

6-game series
149—Portland vs. Philadelphia, 1977
144—Boston vs. Phoenix, 1976

7-game series
142—Milwaukee vs. Boston, 1974
126—Seattle vs. Washington, 1978

FEWEST TURNOVERS

4-game series
41—Houston vs. Orlando, 1995
45—New Jersey vs. L.A. Lakers, 2002

5-game series
64—New York vs. San Antonio, 1999
65—Philadelphia vs. L.A. Lakers, 2001

6-game series
68—L.A. Lakers vs. Boston, 1987
    L.A. Lakers vs. Indiana, 2000
69—Chicago vs. Utah, 1997

7-game series
87—Detroit vs. L.A. Lakers, 1988
92—New York vs. Houston, 1994

INDIVIDUAL

MINUTES

Most minutes, game

62—Kevin Johnson, Phoenix at Chicago, June 13, 1993 (3 ot)
61—Garfield Heard, Phoenix at Boston, June 4, 1976 (3 ot)

60—Jo Jo White, Boston vs. Phoenix, June 4, 1976 (3 ot)

Most minutes per game, one championship series
49.3—Kareem Abdul-Jabbar, Milwaukee vs. Boston, 1974 (345/7)
48.7—Bill Russell, Boston vs. Los Angeles, 1968 (292/6)
48.5—John Havlicek, Boston vs. Los Angeles, 1968 (291/6)

SCORING

Most points, game
61—Elgin Baylor, Los Angeles at Boston, April 14, 1962
55—Rick Barry, San Francisco vs. Philadelphia, April 18, 1967
   Michael Jordan, Chicago vs. Phoenix, June 16, 1993
53—Jerry West, Los Angeles vs. Boston, April 23, 1969

Most points, rookie, game
42—Magic Johnson, Los Angeles at Philadelphia, May 16, 1980
37—Joe Fulks, Philadelphia vs. Chicago, April 16, 1947
   Tom Heinsohn, Boston vs. St. Louis, April 13, 1957 (2 ot)
34—Joe Fulks, Philadelphia vs. Chicago, April 22, 1947
   Elgin Baylor, Minneapolis at Boston, April 4, 1959

Highest scoring average, one championship series
41.0—Michael Jordan, Chicago vs. Phoenix, 1993 (246/6)
40.8—Rick Barry, San Francisco vs. Philadelphia, 1967 (245/6)
40.6—Elgin Baylor, Los Angeles vs. Boston, 1962 (284/7)

Highest scoring average, rookie, one championship series
26.2—Joe Fulks, Philadelphia vs. Chicago, 1947 (131/5)
24.0—Tom Heinsohn, Boston vs. St. Louis, 1957 (168/7)
23.0—Alvan Adams, Phoenix vs. Boston, 1976 (138/6)

Most consecutive games, 20-or-more points
35—Michael Jordan, Chicago, June 2, 1991—June 14, 1998
25—Jerry West, Los Angeles, April 20, 1966—May 8, 1970
21—Shaquille O'Neal, Orlando-L.A. Lakers, June 7, 1995—
   June 8, 2004

Most consecutive games, 30-or-more points
13—Elgin Baylor, Minneapolis-Los Angeles, April 9, 1959—
   April 21, 1963
9—Michael Jordan, Chicago, June 10, 1992—June 20, 1993
7—Shaquille O'Neal, L.A. Lakers, June 7, 2000—June 6, 2001

Most consecutive games, 40-or-more points
4—Michael Jordan, June 11, 1993—June 18, 1993
2—Jerry West, Los Angeles, April 19, 1965—April 21, 1965
   Rick Barry, San Francisco, April 18, 1967—April 20, 1967
   Jerry West, Los Angeles, April 23, 1969—April 25, 1969
   Shaquille O'Neal, L.A. Lakers, June 7, 2000—June 9, 2000
   Shaquille O'Neal, L.A. Lakers, June 19, 2000—June 6, 2001

Scoring 30-or-more points in all games in championship series
Elgin Baylor, Los Angeles vs. Boston, 1962 (7-game series)
Rick Barry, San Francisco vs. Philadelphia, 1967 (6-game series)
Michael Jordan, Chicago vs. Phoenix, 1993 (6-game series)
Hakeem Olajuwon, Houston vs. Orlando, 1995 (4-game series)
Shaquille O'Neal, L.A. Lakers vs. Indiana, 2000 (6-game series)
Shaquille O'Neal, L.A. Lakers vs. New Jersey, 2002 (4-game series)

Scoring 20-or-more points in all games of 7-game championship series
Bob Pettit, St. Louis vs. Boston, 1960
Elgin Baylor, Los Angeles vs. Boston, 1962
Jerry West, Los Angeles vs. Boston, 1962
Jerry West, Los Angeles vs. Boston, 1969
Jerry West, Los Angeles vs. New York, 1970
Kareem Abdul-Jabbar, Milwaukee vs. Boston, 1974
Larry Bird, Boston vs. Los Angeles, 1984
Hakeem Olajuwon, Houston vs. New York, 1994

Most points, one half
35—Michael Jordan, Chicago vs. Portland, June 3, 1992

Most points, one quarter
25—Isiah Thomas, Detroit at L.A. Lakers, June 19, 1988

Most points, overtime period
9—John Havlicek, Boston vs. Milwaukee, May 10, 1974
   Bill Laimbeer, Detroit vs. Portland, June 7, 1990
   Danny Ainge, Portland at Chicago, June 5, 1992

FIELD GOALS

Highest field-goal percentage, game
(minimum: 8 field goals)
1.000—Scott Wedman, Boston vs. L.A. Lakers, May 27, 1985 (11/11)
   John Paxson, Chicago vs. L.A. Lakers, June 5, 1991 (8/8)
.917—Bill Bradley, New York at Los Angeles, April 26, 1972
   (11/12)
   James Worthy, Los Angeles at Boston, May 31, 1984
   (11/12) (ot)

Most field goals, game
22—Elgin Baylor, Los Angeles at Boston, April 14, 1962
   Rick Barry, San Francisco vs. Philadelphia, April 18, 1967
21—Jerry West, Los Angeles vs. Boston, April 23, 1969
   Michael Jordan, Chicago vs. Phoenix, June 16, 1993
   Shaquille O'Neal, L.A. Lakers vs. Indiana, June 7, 2000

Most field goals, one half
14—Isiah Thomas, Detroit at L.A. Lakers, June 19, 1988
   Michael Jordan, Chicago vs. Portland, June 3, 1992
   Michael Jordan, Chicago vs. Phoenix, June 16, 1993

Most field goals, one quarter
11—Isiah Thomas, Detroit at L.A. Lakers, June 19, 1988

Most field-goal attempts, game
48—Rick Barry, San Francisco vs. Philadelphia, April 18, 1967
46—Elgin Baylor, Los Angeles at Boston, April 14, 1962
43—Rick Barry, San Francisco at Philadelphia, April 14, 1967 (ot)
   Michael Jordan, Chicago vs. Phoenix, June 13, 1993 (3 ot)

Most field-goal attempts, one half
25—Elgin Baylor, Los Angeles at Boston, April 14, 1962

Most field-goal attempts, one quarter
17—Rick Barry, San Francisco at Philadelphia, April 14, 1967

3-POINT FIELD GOALS

Most 3-point field goals, none missed, game
4—Scott Wedman, Boston vs. L.A. Lakers, May 27, 1985
3—Danny Ainge, Boston at L.A. Lakers, June 2, 1987
   Isiah Thomas, Detroit at Portland, June 14, 1990
   Sam Cassell, Houston at New York, June 12, 1994
   Glen Rice, L.A. Lakers vs. Indiana, June 19, 2000
   Robert Horry, L.A. Lakers at Philadelphia, June 10, 2001
   Robert Horry, L.A. Lakers at Philadelphia, June 13, 2001
   Rick Fox, L.A. Lakers at Philadelphia, June 15, 2001
   Kobe Bryant, L.A. Lakers vs. New Jersey, June 7, 2002
   Derek Fisher, L.A. Lakers at New Jersey, June 9, 2002

Most 3-point field goals, game
7—Kenny Smith, Houston at Orlando, June 7, 1995 (ot)
   Scottie Pippen, Chicago at Utah, June 6, 1997
6—Michael Cooper, L.A. Lakers vs. Boston, June 4, 1987
   Bill Laimbeer, Detroit vs. Portland, June 7, 1990 (ot)
   Michael Jordan, Chicago vs. Portland, June 3, 1992
   Dan Majerle, Phoenix at Chicago, June 13, 1993 (3 ot)
   Reggie Miller, Indiana vs. L.A. Lakers, June 14, 2000 (ot)
   Derek Fisher, L.A. Lakers at Philadelphia, June 15, 2001

Most 3-point field goals, one half
6—Michael Jordan, Chicago vs. Portland, June 3, 1992
   Kenny Smith, Houston at Orlando, June 7, 1995

Most 3-point field goals, one quarter
5—Kenny Smith, Houston at Orlando, June 7, 1995

Most 3-point field-goal attempts, game
12—Nick Anderson, Orlando at Houston, June 11, 1995
11—John Starks, New York at Houston, June 22, 1994
   Kenny Smith, Houston at Orlando, June 7, 1995 (ot)
   Brian Shaw, Orlando at Houston, June 14, 1995
   Scottie Pippen, Chicago at Utah, June 6, 1997
   Allen Iverson, Philadelphia vs. L.A. Lakers, June 15, 2001

Most 3-point field-goal attempts, one half
10—John Starks, New York at Houston, June 22, 1994

FREE THROWS

Most free throws made, none missed, game
15—Terry Porter, Portland at Detroit, June 7, 1990 (ot)
14—Magic Johnson, Los Angeles at Philadelphia, May 16, 1980

Most free throws made, game
19—Bob Pettit, St. Louis at Boston, April 9, 1958
18—Shaquille O'Neal, L.A. Lakers vs. Indiana, June 9, 2000

Most free throws made, one half
13—Shaquille O'Neal, L.A. Lakers vs. Indiana, June 9, 2000

Most free throws made, one quarter
9—Frank Ramsey, Boston vs. Minneapolis, April 4, 1959
   Michael Jordan, Chicago at Utah, June 11, 1997
   Shaquille O'Neal, L.A. Lakers vs. Indiana, June 9, 2000
   Austin Croshere, Indiana vs. L.A. Lakers, June 16, 2000
   Allen Iverson, Philadelphia vs. L.A. Lakers, June 10, 2001

Most free throw attempts, game
39—Shaquille O'Neal, L.A. Lakers vs. Indiana, June 9, 2000
24—Bob Pettit, St. Louis at Boston, April 9, 1958

Most free throw attempts, one half
22—Shaquille O'Neal, L.A. Lakers vs. Indiana, June 9, 2000

Most free throw attempts, one quarter
16—Shaquille O'Neal, L.A. Lakers vs. Indiana, June 9, 2000
   Shaquille O'Neal, L.A. Lakers vs. New Jersey, June 5, 2002

REBOUNDS

Most rebounds, game
40—Bill Russell, Boston vs. St. Louis, March 29, 1960
   Bill Russell, Boston vs. Los Angeles, April 18, 1962 (ot)
38—Bill Russell, Boston vs. St. Louis, April 11, 1961
   Bill Russell, Boston vs. Los Angeles, April 16, 1963
   Wilt Chamberlain, San Francisco vs. Boston, April 24, 1964
   Wilt Chamberlain, Philadelphia vs. San Francisco, April 16, 1967

Most rebounds, rookie, game
32—Bill Russell, Boston vs. St. Louis, April 13, 1957 (2 ot)
25—Bill Russell, Boston vs. St. Louis, March 31, 1957
23—Bill Russell, Boston vs. St. Louis, April 9, 1957
   Bill Russell, Boston at St. Louis, April 11, 1957
   Tom Heinsohn, Boston vs. St. Louis, April 13, 1957 (2 ot)

Highest average, rebounds per game, one championship series
29.5—Bill Russell, Boston vs. Minneapolis, 1959 (118/4)
28.8—Bill Russell, Boston vs. St. Louis, 1961 (144/5)
28.5—Wilt Chamberlain, Philadelphia vs. San Francisco, 1967
   (171/6)

Highest average, rebounds per game, rookie, one
championship series
22.9—Bill Russell, Boston vs. St. Louis, 1957 (160/7)
13.0—Nate Thurmond, San Francisco vs. Boston, 1964 (65/5)
12.6—Tom Heinsohn, Boston vs. St. Louis, 1957 (88/7)

Most consecutive games, 20-or-more rebounds
15—Bill Russell, Boston, April 9, 1960—April 16, 1963
12—Wilt Chamberlain, San Francisco-Philadelphia-Los
   Angeles, April 18, 1964—April 23, 1969

Most consecutive games, 30-or-more rebounds
3—Bill Russell, Boston, April 5, 1959—April 9, 1959
2—Bill Russell, Boston, April 9, 1960—April 2, 1961
   Wilt Chamberlain, Philadelphia, April 14, 1967—April 16, 1967
   Wilt Chamberlain, Los Angeles, April 29, 1969—May 1, 1969

20-or-more rebounds in all championship series games
Bill Russell, Boston vs. Minneapolis, 1959 (4-game series)
Bill Russell, Boston vs. St. Louis, 1961 (5-game series)
Bill Russell, Boston vs. Los Angeles, 1962 (7-game series)
Wilt Chamberlain, San Francisco vs. Boston, 1964 (5-game series)
Wilt Chamberlain, Philadelphia vs. San Francisco, 1967
   (6-game series)
Nate Thurmond, San Francisco vs. Philadelphia, 1967 (6-game series)

Most rebounds, one half
26—Wilt Chamberlain, Philadelphia vs. San Francisco, April 16, 1967

Most rebounds, one quarter
19—Bill Russell, Boston vs. Los Angeles, April 18, 1962

Most offensive rebounds, game
11—Elvin Hayes, Washington at Seattle, May 27, 1979
   Dennis Rodman, Chicago vs. Seattle, June 7, 1996
   Dennis Rodman, Chicago vs. Seattle, June 16, 1996
10—Marvin Webster, Seattle vs. Washington, June 7, 1978
   Robert Reid, Houston vs. Boston, May 10, 1981
   Moses Malone, Houston vs. Boston, May 14, 1981
   Ben Wallace, Detroit vs. L.A. Lakers, June 15, 2004

Most defensive rebounds, game
20—Bill Walton, Portland at Philadelphia, June 3, 1977
   Bill Walton, Portland vs. Philadelphia, June 5, 1977
19—Shaquille O'Neal, L.A. Lakers vs. Indiana, June 9, 2000

ASSISTS

Most assists, game
21—Magic Johnson, Los Angeles vs. Boston, June 3, 1984
20—Magic Johnson, L.A. Lakers vs. Boston, June 4, 1987
   Magic Johnson, L.A. Lakers vs. Chicago, June 12, 1991

Highest average, assists per game, one championship series
14.0—Magic Johnson, L.A. Lakers vs. Boston, 1985 (84/6)
13.6—Magic Johnson, Los Angeles vs. Boston, 1984 (95/7)
13.0—Magic Johnson, L.A. Lakers vs. Boston, 1987 (78/6)
   Magic Johnson, L.A. Lakers vs. Detroit, 1988 (91/7)

Most assists, rookie, game
11—Magic Johnson, Los Angeles vs. Philadelphia, May 7, 1980
10—Tom Gola, Philadelphia vs. Ft. Wayne, March 31, 1956
   Walt Hazzard, Los Angeles at Boston, April 25, 1965
   Magic Johnson, Los Angeles vs. Philadelphia, May 4, 1980
   Magic Johnson, Los Angeles vs. Philadelphia, May 14, 1980

Highest average, assists per game, rookie, one
championship series
8.7—Magic Johnson, Los Angeles vs. Philadelphia, 1980 (52/6)
6.0—Tom Gola, Philadelphia vs. Ft. Wayne, 1956 (30/5)
5.2—Walt Hazzard, Los Angeles vs. Boston, 1965 (26/5)

Most consecutive games 10-or-more assists
13—Magic Johnson, L.A. Lakers, June 3, 1984—June 4, 1987
6—Magic Johnson, Los Angeles, June 8, 1982—May 27, 1984

Most assists, one half
14—Magic Johnson, L.A. Lakers vs. Detroit, June 19, 1988
13—Robert Reid, Houston vs. Boston, June 5, 1986
   Magic Johnson, L.A. Lakers vs. Boston, June 4, 1987

Most assists, one quarter
8—Bob Cousy, Boston vs. St. Louis, April 9, 1957
   Magic Johnson, Los Angeles vs. Boston, June 3, 1984
   Robert Reid, Houston vs. Boston, June 5, 1986
   Michael Cooper, L.A. Lakers vs. Boston, June 4, 1987
   Magic Johnson, L.A. Lakers vs. Boston, June 4, 1987
   Magic Johnson, L.A. Lakers at Detroit, June 16, 1988
   Magic Johnson, L.A. Lakers vs. Detroit, June 19, 1988
   John Stockton, Utah at Chicago, June 10, 1998

PERSONAL FOULS

Most minutes played, no personal fouls, game
59—Dan Majerle, Phoenix at Chicago, June 13, 1993 (3 ot)
52—Allen Iverson, Philadelphia at L.A. Lakers, June 6, 2001 (ot)

DISQUALIFICATIONS

Most consecutive games, disqualified
5—Art Hillhouse, Philadelphia, 1947
   Charlie Scott, Boston, 1976
4—Arnie Risen, Boston, 1957

Fewest minutes played, disqualified player, game
7—Aaron Williams, New Jersey vs. L.A. Lakers, June 9, 2002

9—Bob Harrison, Minneapolis vs. New York, April 13, 1952

STEALS

Most steals, game
7—Robert Horry, Houston at Orlando, June 9, 1995
6—John Havlicek, Boston vs. Milwaukee, May 3, 1974
Steve Mix, Philadelphia vs. Portland, May 22, 1977
Maurice Cheeks, Philadelphia at Los Angeles, May 7, 1980
Isiah Thomas, Detroit at L.A. Lakers, June 19, 1988

BLOCKED SHOTS

Most blocked shots, game
8—Bill Walton, Portland vs. Philadelphia, June 5, 1977
Hakeem Olajuwon, Houston vs. Boston, June 5, 1986
Patrick Ewing, New York vs. Houston, June 17, 1994
Shaquille O'Neal, L.A. Lakers vs. Philadelphia, June 8, 2001
Tim Duncan, San Antonio vs. New Jersey, June 15, 2003

7—Dennis Johnson, Seattle at Washington, May 28, 1978
Patrick Ewing, New York vs. Houston, June 12, 1994
Hakeem Olajuwon, Houston at New York, June 12, 1994
Tim Duncan, San Antonio vs. New Jersey, June 4, 2003
Tim Duncan, San Antonio at New Jersey, June 11, 2003

TURNOVERS

Most turnovers, game
10—Magic Johnson, Los Angeles vs. Philadelphia,
May 14, 1980
9—Magic Johnson, Los Angeles vs. Philadelphia, May 31, 1983

Most minutes played, no turnovers, game
59—Dan Majerle, Phoenix at Chicago, June 13, 1993 (3 ot)
50—Wes Unseld, Washington at Seattle, May 29, 1979 (ot)
48—Rodney McCray, Houston vs. Boston, June 5, 1986

TEAM

WON-LOST

Most consecutive games won, all championship series
8—L.A. Lakers, 2001-02
6—Houston, 1994-95 (current)

Most consecutive games won, one championship series
4—Minneapolis vs. New York, 1953 (5-game series)
Boston vs. Minneapolis, 1959 (4-game series)
Milwaukee vs. Baltimore, 1971 (4-game series)
Los Angeles vs. New York, 1972 (5-game series)
New York vs. Los Angeles, 1973 (5-game series)
Golden State vs. Washington, 1975 (4-game series)
Portland vs. Philadelphia, 1977 (6-game series)
Seattle vs. Washington, 1979 (5-game series)
Philadelphia vs. Los Angeles, 1983 (4-game series)
Detroit vs. L.A. Lakers, 1989 (4-game series)
Chicago vs. L.A. Lakers, 1991 (5-game series)
Houston vs. Orlando, 1995 (4-game series)
L.A. Lakers vs. Philadelphia, 2001 (5-game series)
L.A. Lakers vs. New Jersey, 2002 (4-game series)

Most consecutive games won at home, all championship series
8—Chicago, 1996-98
7—Minneapolis, 1949-52

Most consecutive games won at home, one championship series
4—Syracuse vs. Ft. Wayne, 1955 (7-game series)

Most consecutive games won on road, all championship series
6—Detroit, 1989-90, 2004
5—Chicago, 1992-93, 1996
L.A. Lakers, 2001-02

Most consecutive games won on road, one championship series
3—Minneapolis vs. New York, 1953 (5-game series)
Detroit vs. Portland, 1990 (5-game series)
Chicago vs. L.A. Lakers, 1991 (5-game series)
Chicago vs. Phoenix, 1993 (6-game series)
L.A. Lakers vs. Philadelphia, 2001 (5-game series)

Most consecutive games lost, all championship series
9—Baltimore/Washington, 1971-78
5—Minneapolis/Los Angeles, 1959-62
New York, 1972-73
Philadelphia, 1977-80
New Jersey, 2002-03

Most consecutive games lost at home, all championship series
5—L.A. Lakers, 1989-91
4—Baltimore/Washington, 1971-75
Portland, 1990-92
Phoenix, 1976-93 (current)

Most consecutive games lost on road, all championship series
7—Ft. Wayne, 1955-56
5—Philadelphia, 1947-56
St. Louis, 1960-61
Syracuse/Philadelphia, 1954-67
San Francisco, 1964-67
Los Angeles, 1968-70
Baltimore/Washington, 1971-78
Utah, 1997-98

SCORING

Most points, game
148—Boston vs. L.A. Lakers (114), May 27, 1985
142—Boston vs. Los Angeles (110), April 18, 1965
141—Philadelphia vs. San Francisco (135), April 14, 1967 (ot)
L.A. Lakers vs. Boston (122), June 4, 1987

Fewest points, game
54—Utah at Chicago, June 7, 1998
67—New York at San Antonio, June 18, 1999
68—L.A. Lakers at Detroit, June 10, 2004

Most points, both teams, game
276—Philadelphia (141) vs. San Francisco (135), April 14, 1967 (ot)
263—L.A. Lakers (141) vs. Boston (122), June 4, 1987

Fewest points, both teams, game
145—Syracuse (71) vs. Ft. Wayne (74), at Indianapolis, April 7, 1955
147—New York (67) at San Antonio (80), June 18, 1999

Largest margin of victory, game
42—Chicago vs. Utah, June 7, 1998 (96-54)
35—Washington vs. Seattle, June 4, 1978 (117-82)
34—Boston vs. St. Louis, April 2, 1961 (129-95)
Boston vs. L.A. Lakers, May 27, 1985 (148-114)

BY HALF

Most points, first half
79—Boston vs. L.A. Lakers, May 27, 1985
76—Boston vs. St. Louis, March 27, 1960

Fewest points, first half
30—Houston vs. Boston, May 9, 1981
Utah at Chicago, June 12, 1998
New Jersey vs. San Antonio, June 8, 2003
31—Syracuse vs. Ft. Wayne, at Indianapolis, April 7, 1955
Utah at Chicago, June 4, 1997
Utah at Chicago, June 7, 1998

Most points, both teams, first half
140—San Francisco (72) vs. Philadelphia (68), April 24, 1967
138—Philadelphia (73) vs. San Francisco (65), April 14, 1967

Fewest points, both teams, first half
63—New Jersey (30) vs. San Antonio (33), June 8, 2003
66—Utah (30) at Chicago (36), June 12, 1998

Largest lead at halftime
30—Boston vs. L.A. Lakers, May 27, 1985 (led 79-49; won 148-114)
27—New York vs. Los Angeles, May 8, 1970 (led 69-42; won 113-99)

Largest deficit at halftime, overcome to win
21—Baltimore at Philadelphia, April 13, 1948 (trailed 20-41; won 66-63)
14—New York at Los Angeles, April 29, 1970 (trailed 42-56; won 111-108 in ot)
    Golden State at Washington, May 18, 1975 (trailed 40-54; won 101-95)
    Philadelphia at Los Angeles, May 31, 1983 (trailed 51-65; won 115-108)

Most points, second half
81—Philadelphia vs. Los Angeles, June 6, 1982
80—Los Angeles vs. Boston, June 3, 1984

Fewest points, second half
23—Utah at Chicago, June 7, 1998
30—Washington vs. Seattle, May 24, 1979

Most points, both teams, second half
139—Boston (78) vs. Los Angeles (61), April 18, 1965
138—Los Angeles (71) at Boston (67), April 21, 1963
    Los Angeles (80) vs. Boston (58), June 3, 1984

Fewest points, both teams, second half
63—Houston (31) vs. New York (32), June 8, 1994
70—Utah (23) at Chicago (47), June 7, 1998

BY QUARTER, OVERTIME PERIOD

Most points, first quarter
43—Philadelphia vs. San Francisco, April 14, 1967
    Philadelphia at San Francisco, April 24, 1967
41—San Francisco vs. Philadelphia, April 24, 1967

Fewest points, first quarter
13—Ft. Wayne at Syracuse, April 2, 1955
    Milwaukee at Boston, May 3, 1974
14—Houston at New York, June 15, 1994
    Philadelphia vs. L.A. Lakers, June 13, 2001
    New Jersey at L.A. Lakers, June 5, 2002

Most points, both teams, first quarter
84—Philadelphia (43) at San Francisco (41), April 24, 1967
73—Philadelphia (43) vs. San Francisco (30), April 14, 1967

Fewest points, both teams, first quarter
31—Los Angeles (15) at Boston (16), April 29, 1969
33—Ft. Wayne (13) at Syracuse (20), April 2, 1955
    Houston (14) at New York (19), June 15, 1994

Largest lead at end of first quarter
20—Los Angeles vs. New York, May 6, 1970 (led 36-16; won 135-113)
19—San Francisco vs. Boston, April 22, 1964 (led 40-21; won 115-91)
    Boston vs. Milwaukee, May 3, 1974 (led 32-13; won 95-83)

Largest deficit at end of first quarter, overcome to win
15—Boston at St. Louis, April 7, 1957 (trailed 21-36; won 123-118)
14—Los Angeles at Boston, April 17, 1966 (trailed 20-34; won 133-129 in ot)

Most points, second quarter
46—Boston vs. St. Louis, March 27, 1960
43—Los Angeles at Boston, April 8, 1962

Fewest points, second quarter
9—New Jersey vs. San Antonio, June 8, 2003
10—New York at San Antonio, June 16, 1999

Most points, both teams, second quarter
73—St. Louis (38) vs. Boston (35), April 8, 1961
    Boston (38) vs. Los Angeles (35), April 14, 1962
72—St. Louis (42) at Boston (30), March 29, 1958
    Boston (46) vs. St. Louis (26), March 27, 1960

Fewest points, both teams, second quarter
27—New Jersey (9) vs. San Antonio (18), June 8, 2003
29—Syracuse (13) vs. Ft. Wayne (16), at Indianapolis, April 7, 1955

Most points, third quarter
47—Los Angeles vs. Boston, June 3, 1984
41—Portland vs. Philadelphia, May 31, 1977
    Los Angeles at Philadelphia, May 27, 1982

Fewest points, third quarter
11—New York at Los Angeles, April 30, 1972
    New Jersey vs. San Antonio, June 11, 2003
12—Boston at St. Louis, April 7, 1960
    Boston at L.A. Lakers, June 14, 1987

Most points, both teams, third quarter
80—Los Angeles (47) vs. Boston (33), June 3, 1984
75—Boston (40) vs. Los Angeles (35), April 21, 1963

Fewest points, both teams, third quarter
31—Portland (15) vs. Chicago (16), June 7, 1992
    Chicago (15) at Utah (16), June 6, 1997
32—New York (15) at San Antonio (17), June 18, 1999
    New York (16) vs. San Antonio (16), June 21, 1999
    Detroit (15) vs. L.A. Lakers (17), June 13, 2004

Largest lead at end of third quarter
36—Chicago vs. Portland, June 3, 1992 (led 104-68; won 122-89)
31—Portland vs. Philadelphia, May 31, 1977 (led 98-67; won 130-98)

Largest deficit at end of third quarter, overcome to win
15—Chicago vs. Portland, June 14, 1992 (trailed 64-79; won 97-93)
12—San Francisco at Philadelphia, April 23, 1967 (trailed 84-96; won 117-109)

Most points, fourth quarter
44—Philadelphia vs. Los Angeles, June 6, 1982
42—Boston vs. Los Angeles, April 25, 1965
    Portland vs. Philadelphia, May 29, 1977

Fewest points, fourth quarter
9—Utah at Chicago, June 7, 1998
12—Chicago at Phoenix, June 20, 1993
    Utah vs. Chicago, June 3, 1998

Most points, both teams, fourth quarter
76—Philadelphia (38) at Los Angeles (38), June 1, 1982
75—Boston (40) vs. L.A. Lakers (35), May 27, 1985

Fewest points, both teams, fourth quarter
28—Houston (13) vs. New York (15), June 8, 1994
31—Chicago (12) at Phoenix (19), June 20, 1993

Most points, overtime period
22—Los Angeles vs. New York, May 1, 1970
18—Portland at Chicago, June 5, 1992

Fewest points, overtime period
2—Detroit at L.A. Lakers, June 8, 2004
4—Boston vs. Milwaukee, May 10, 1974
    Milwaukee at Boston, May 10, 1974
    L.A. Lakers vs. Chicago, June 7, 1991
    Chicago vs. Phoenix, June 13, 1993
    Phoenix at Chicago, June 13, 1993

Most points, both teams, overtime period
38—Los Angeles (22) vs. New York (16), May 1, 1970
30—Boston (16) vs. Phoenix (14), June 4, 1976
    L.A. Lakers (16) at Indiana (14), June 14, 2000

Fewest points, both teams, overtime period
8—Boston (4) vs. Milwaukee (4), May 10, 1974
    Chicago (4) vs. Phoenix (4), June 13, 1993
12—Boston (6) vs. Phoenix (6), June 4, 1976
    Detroit (2) at L.A. Lakers (10), June 8, 2004

100-POINT GAMES

Most consecutive games, 100-or-more points,
all championship series
20—Minneapolis/Los Angeles, 1959-65
    L.A. Lakers, 1983-87
19—Boston, 1981-86
    Philadelphia, 1977-2001
17—Boston, 1960-63

Most consecutive games scoring fewer than 100 points, all
championship series
15—Chicago, 1996-98 (current)
12—New York, 1994-99 (current)
 9—Utah, 1997-98 (current)

PLAYERS SCORING

Most players, 30-or-more points, game
2—Accomplished 29 times. Most recent:
    L.A. Lakers at New Jersey, June 9, 2002

Most players, 30-or-more points, both teams, game
4—Houston (2) at Orlando (2), June 9, 1995
3—by many

Most players, 20-or-more points, game
5—Boston vs. Los Angeles, April 19, 1965
    L.A. Lakers vs. Boston, June 4, 1987
    Boston vs. L.A. Lakers, June 11, 1987
4—by many

Most players, 20-or-more points, both teams, game
8—Boston (4) at Los Angeles (4), April 26, 1966
    L.A. Lakers (5) vs. Boston (3), June 4, 1987
7—Boston (5) vs. Los Angeles (2), April 19, 1965
    Philadelphia (4) vs. San Francisco (3), April 14, 1967 (ot)
    Boston (4) vs. Los Angeles (3), April 30, 1968 (ot)
    Phoenix (4) at Boston (3), June 4, 1976 (3 ot)
    Philadelphia (4) at Los Angeles (3), May 31, 1983
    Los Angeles (4) vs. Boston (3), June 10, 1984
    Boston (4) at L.A. Lakers (3), June 7, 1985

Most players, 10-or-more points, game
8—Boston vs. Los Angeles, May 31, 1984 (ot)
7—Accomplished 17 times. Most recent:
    Phoenix at Chicago, June 13, 1993 (3 ot)

Most players, 10-or-more points, both teams, game
14—Boston (7) vs. St. Louis (7), March 27, 1960
13—Los Angeles (7) at Boston (6), April 19, 1966
    Boston (8) vs. Los Angeles (5), May 31, 1984 (ot)

Fewest players, 10-or-more points, game
1—Utah at Chicago, June 7, 1998
2—by many

Fewest players, 10-or-more points, both teams, game
4—Utah (2) at Chicago (2), June 10, 1998
    Utah (2) at Chicago (2), June 12, 1998
5—Ft. Wayne (2) vs. Philadelphia (3), April 1, 1956
    Chicago (2) vs. Utah (3), June 1, 1997
    Utah (1) at Chicago (4), June 7, 1998
    Chicago (2) at Utah (3), June 14, 1998
    San Antonio (2) vs. New Jersey (3), June 8, 2003
    L.A. Lakers (2) at Detroit (3), June 10, 2004
    L.A. Lakers (2) at Detroit (3), June 13, 2004

FIELD-GOAL PERCENTAGE

Highest field-goal percentage, game
.617—Chicago vs. L.A. Lakers, June 5, 1991 (50/81)

.615—L.A. Lakers vs. Boston, June 4, 1987 (56/91)
.608—Boston vs. L.A. Lakers, May 27, 1985 (62/102)

Lowest field-goal percentage, game
.275—Syracuse vs. Ft. Wayne, at Indianapolis, April 7, 1955 (25/91)
.280—Ft. Wayne vs. Syracuse, at Indianapolis, April 7, 1955 (23/82)
.289—San Antonio at New Jersey, June 11, 2003 (26/90)
.293—Boston at St. Louis, April 6, 1957 (29/99)
.295—San Francisco at Philadelphia, April 16, 1967 (38/129)

Highest field-goal percentage, both teams, game
.582—L.A. Lakers (.615) vs. Boston (.548), June 4, 1987
      (107/184)
.553—L.A. Lakers (.556) vs. Boston (.549), June 2, 1987
      (100/181)

Lowest field-goal percentage, both teams, game
.277—Syracuse (.275) vs. Ft. Wayne (.280), at Indianapolis,
      April 7, 1955 (48/173)
.312—Boston (.304) at St. Louis (.320), April 11, 1957
      (68/218)

Highest field-goal percentage, one half
.706—Philadelphia vs. Los Angeles, June 6, 1982 (36/51)
.667—Philadelphia at Los Angeles, May 7, 1980 (26/39)
      Philadelphia at Los Angeles, June 8, 1982 (30/45)
      Los Angeles vs. Boston, June 6, 1984 (28/42)
.659—Chicago vs. L.A. Lakers, June 5, 1991 (27/41)

Highest field-goal percentage, one quarter
.850—Chicago vs. L.A. Lakers, June 5, 1991 (17/20)
.824—Detroit vs. L.A. Lakers, June 6, 1989 (14/17)
.813—Los Angeles vs. Boston, June 6, 1984 (13/16)
      Boston at Houston, June 3, 1986 (13/16)

FIELD GOALS

Most field goals, game
62—Boston vs. L.A. Lakers, May 27, 1985
61—Boston vs. St. Louis, March 27, 1960

Fewest field goals, game
21—Utah at Chicago, June 7, 1998
23—Ft. Wayne vs. Syracuse, at Indianapolis, April 7, 1955

Most field goals, both teams, game
112—Philadelphia (57) vs. San Francisco (55), April 14, 1967 (ot)
111—Boston (62) vs. L.A. Lakers (49), May 27, 1985

Fewest field goals, both teams, game
48—Ft. Wayne (23) vs. Syracuse (25), at Indianapolis, April 7, 1955
54—San Antonio (27) vs. New York (27), June 18, 1999
    San Antonio (26) at New Jersey (28), June 11, 2003

FIELD-GOAL ATTEMPTS

Most field-goal attempts, game
140—San Francisco at Philadelphia, April 14, 1967 (ot)
133—Boston vs. St. Louis, March 27, 1960

Fewest field-goal attempts, game
60—Seattle vs. Chicago, June 9, 1996
63—San Antonio vs. New York, June 18, 1999

Most field-goal attempts, both teams, game
256—San Francisco (140) at Philadelphia (116), April 14, 1967 (ot)
250—Boston (130) vs. Minneapolis (120), April 4, 1959

Fewest field-goal attempts, both teams, game
131—Utah (64) vs. Chicago (67), June 14, 1998
136—Seattle (60) vs. Chicago (76), June 9, 1996
      Utah (67) at Chicago (69), June 4, 1997

3-POINT FIELD GOALS MADE

Most 3-point field goals made, game
14—Houston at Orlando, June 7, 1995 (ot)

Orlando at Houston, June 14, 1995
12—Chicago at Utah, June 6, 1997
  Indiana at L.A. Lakers, June 19, 2000
  L.A. Lakers at Philadelphia, June 15, 2001

Most 3-point field goals made, both teams, game
25—Orlando (14) at Houston (11), June 14, 1995
23—Houston (14) at Orlando (9), June 7, 1995 (ot)

Most 3-point field goals made, one half
9—Houston at Orlando, June 7, 1995
  Orlando at Houston, June 14, 1995

Most 3-point field goals made, one quarter
7—Houston at Orlando, June 7, 1995
  Orlando at Houston, June 14, 1995

3-POINT FIELD-GOAL ATTEMPTS

Most 3-point field-goal attempts, game
32—Houston at Orlando, June 7, 1995 (ot)
  Chicago at Utah, June 6, 1997
31—Orlando at Houston, June 11, 1995
  Orlando at Houston, June 14, 1995

Most 3-point field-goal attempts, both teams, game
62—Houston (32) at Orlando (30), June 7, 1995 (ot)
58—Orlando (31) at Houston (27), June 14, 1995

Most 3-point field-goal attempts, one half
19—Chicago vs. Seattle, June 16, 1996

FREE THROW PERCENTAGE

Highest free throw percentage, game
1.000—Portland at Chicago, June 14, 1992 (21/21)
 .958—Boston vs. Houston, May 29, 1986 (23/24)

Lowest free throw percentage, game
.417—Chicago at Utah, June 8, 1997 (5/12)
.421—L.A. Lakers at Indiana, June 11, 2000 (8/19)

Highest free throw percentage, both teams, game
.933—L.A. Lakers (.955) at Chicago (.875), June 5, 1991 (28/30)
.903—Boston (.926) vs. Los Angeles (.889), April 14, 1962 (65/72)

Lowest free throw percentage, both teams, game
.538—Philadelphia (.444) vs. San Francisco (.655), April 16, 1967 (35/65)
.541—San Francisco (.478) at Boston (.615), April 18, 1964 (46/85)

FREE THROWS MADE

Most free throws made, game
45—St. Louis at Boston, April 13, 1957 (2 ot)
44—St. Louis at Boston, April 9, 1958

Fewest free throws made, game
3—Los Angeles at Philadelphia, May 26, 1983
5—Chicago at Utah, June 8, 1997

Most free throws made, both teams, game
80—St. Louis (44) at Boston (36), April 9, 1958
77—Syracuse (39) vs. Ft. Wayne (38), April 9, 1955
  Boston (43) at St. Louis (34), April 12, 1958

Fewest free throws made, both teams, game
17—Utah (7) at Chicago (10), June 1, 1997
20—Chicago (5) at Utah (15), June 8, 1997

FREE THROW ATTEMPTS

Most free throw attempts, game
64—Philadelphia at San Francisco, April 24, 1967

62—St. Louis at Boston, April 13, 1957 (2 ot)

Fewest free throw attempts, game
5—Los Angeles at Philadelphia, May 26, 1983
8—Chicago vs. L.A. Lakers, June 5, 1991

Most free throw attempts, both teams, game
116—St. Louis (62) at Boston (54), April 13, 1957 (2 ot)
107—Boston (60) at St. Louis (47), April 2, 1958
  St. Louis (57) at Boston (50), April 9, 1958

Fewest free throw attempts, both teams, game
26—Utah (11) at Chicago (15), June 1, 1997
30—Chicago (8) vs. L.A. Lakers (22), June 5, 1991
  Seattle (10) at Chicago (20), June 16, 1996

TOTAL REBOUNDS

Highest rebound percentage, game
.667—Boston vs. St. Louis, April 9, 1960 (78/117)
.632—Los Angeles vs. New York, May 7, 1972 (67/106)

Most rebounds, game
93—Philadelphia vs. San Francisco, April 16, 1967
86—Boston vs. Minneapolis, April 4, 1959

Fewest rebounds, game
22—Chicago at Utah, June 14, 1998
27—New Jersey vs. L.A. Lakers, June 9, 2002

Most rebounds, both teams, game
169—Philadelphia (93) vs. San Francisco (76), April 16, 1967
159—San Francisco (80) at Philadelphia (79), April 14, 1967 (ot)

Fewest rebounds, both teams, game
55—Chicago (22) at Utah (33), June 14, 1998
65—Seattle (32) vs. Chicago (33), June 9, 1996

OFFENSIVE REBOUNDS

Highest offensive rebound percentage, game
.556—Detroit vs. L.A. Lakers, June 16, 1988 (20/36)
.529—Seattle vs. Washington, June 7, 1978 (27/51)

Most offensive rebounds, game
28—Houston vs. Boston, May 10, 1981
27—Seattle vs. Washington, June 7, 1978
  Boston at Los Angeles, June 6, 1984 (ot)
  Chicago vs. Phoenix, June 13, 1993 (3 ot)

Fewest offensive rebounds, game
3—Boston vs. L.A. Lakers, May 30, 1985
  Houston vs. New York, June 22, 1994
4—San Antonio vs. New York, June 16, 1999
  New York vs. San Antonio, June 25, 1999

Most offensive rebounds, both teams, game
45—Houston (28) vs. Boston (17), May 10, 1981
44—Seattle (27) vs. Washington (17), June 7, 1978
  Boston (25) vs. Houston (19), May 5, 1981

Fewest offensive rebounds, both teams, game
12—New Jersey (5) vs. L.A. Lakers (7), June 9, 2002
13—New York (4) vs. San Antonio (9), June 25, 1999

DEFENSIVE REBOUNDS

Highest defensive rebound percentage, game
.921—L.A. Lakers at Boston, May 30, 1985 (35/38)
.897—New York at Houston, June 22, 1994 (26/29)

Most defensive rebounds, game
48—Portland at Philadelphia, June 3, 1977
46—Philadelphia vs. Portland, May 26, 1977

Fewest defensive rebounds, game
16—L.A. Lakers at Detroit, June 16, 1988
17—Chicago at Utah, June 14, 1998

Most defensive rebounds, both teams, game
84—Portland (48) at Philadelphia (36), June 3, 1977

82—Philadelphia (46) vs. Portland (36), May 26, 1977

Fewest defensive rebounds, both teams, game
40—Chicago (17) at Utah (23), June 14, 1998
43—L.A. Lakers (21) at Detroit (22), June 8, 1989

ASSISTS

Most assists, game
44—Los Angeles vs. New York, May 6, 1970
    L.A. Lakers vs. Boston, June 4, 1987
43—Boston vs. L.A. Lakers, May 27, 1985

Fewest assists, game
5—Boston at St. Louis, April 3, 1960
8—New York at San Antonio, June 18, 1999

Most assists, both teams, game
79—L.A. Lakers (44) vs. Boston (35), June 4, 1987
76—L.A. Lakers (40) vs. Boston (36), June 7, 1985

Fewest assists, both teams, game
21—Los Angeles (10) at Boston (11), April 29, 1969
22—Los Angeles (9) at Boston (13), April 28, 1966

PERSONAL FOULS

Most personal fouls, game
42—Minneapolis vs. Syracuse, April 23, 1950
40—Portland vs. Philadelphia, May 31, 1977

Fewest personal fouls, game
13—L.A. Lakers at Detroit, June 12, 1988
    San Antonio vs. New York, June 18, 1999
14—San Antonio vs. New Jersey, June 15, 2003

Most personal fouls, both teams, game
77—Minneapolis (42) vs. Syracuse (35), April 23, 1950
76—Minneapolis (39) at New York (37), April 18, 1952 (ot)

Fewest personal fouls, both teams, game
35—Boston (17) at Milwaukee (18), April 28, 1974
    Boston (17) at Houston (18), June 3, 1986
    L.A. Lakers (15) at Chicago (20), June 5, 1991
    Chicago (15) vs. Seattle (20), June 16, 1996
36—Baltimore (17) vs. Milwaukee (19), April 25, 1971
    Boston (17) vs. Houston (19), May 26, 1986
    L.A. Lakers (13) at Detroit (23), June 12, 1988
    Chicago (17) at Phoenix (19), June 9, 1993

DISQUALIFICATIONS

Most disqualifications, game
4—Minneapolis vs. Syracuse, April 23, 1950
    Minneapolis vs. New York, April 4, 1953
    New York vs. Minneapolis, April 10, 1953
    St. Louis at Boston, April 13, 1957 (2 ot)
    Boston vs. Los Angeles, April 18, 1962 (ot)

Most disqualifications, both teams, game
7—Boston (4) vs. Los Angeles (3), April 18, 1962 (ot)
6—St. Louis (4) at Boston (2), April 13, 1957 (2 ot)

STEALS

Most steals, game
17—Golden State vs. Washington, May 23, 1975
16—Philadelphia vs. Portland, May 22, 1977

Fewest steals, game
1—Milwaukee at Boston, May 10, 1974 (2 ot)
    Boston vs. Phoenix, May 23, 1976
2—Milwaukee at Boston, May 3, 1974
    Milwaukee at Boston, May 5, 1974
    Milwaukee vs. Boston, May 12, 1974
    Detroit vs. L.A. Lakers, June 6, 1989
    Detroit vs. Portland, June 7, 1990 (ot)
    Indiana at L.A. Lakers, June 19, 2000

Most steals, both teams, game
31—Golden State (17) vs. Washington (14), May 23, 1975
28—Golden State (15) at Washington (13), May 25, 1975

Fewest steals, both teams, game
6—Detroit (3) vs. L.A. Lakers (3), June 8, 1989

L.A. Lakers (3) vs. Detroit (3), June 13, 1989
7—Chicago (3) at Seattle (4), June 14, 1996
    Indiana (2) at L.A. Lakers (5), June 19, 2000

BLOCKED SHOTS

Most blocked shots, game
13—Seattle at Washington, May 28, 1978
    Philadelphia at Los Angeles, May 4, 1980
    Philadelphia vs. Los Angeles, June 6, 1982
    Philadelphia vs. Los Angeles, May 22, 1983
    Houston vs. Boston, June 5, 1986
    L.A. Lakers vs. Philadelphia, June 8, 2001
    New Jersey vs. San Antonio, June 11, 2003
    San Antonio vs. New Jersey, June 15, 2003
12—Golden State vs. Washington, May 20, 1975
    Phoenix vs. Chicago, June 11, 1993
    San Antonio vs. New Jersey, June 4, 2003

Fewest blocked shots, game
0—Boston vs. Milwaukee, May 5, 1974
    Boston vs. Milwaukee, May 10, 1974 (2 ot)
    Boston vs. Phoenix, June 4, 1976 (3 ot)
    Philadelphia vs. Portland, May 22, 1977
    Washington at Seattle, May 21, 1978
    Boston at Houston, May 14, 1981
    L.A. Lakers vs. Boston, June 5, 1985
    L.A. Lakers vs. Detroit, June 7, 1988
    Utah at Chicago, June 1, 1997
    Utah at Chicago, June 4, 1997
    Utah vs. Chicago, June 14, 1998

Most blocked shots, both teams, game
23—New Jersey (13) vs. San Antonio (10), June 11, 2003
22—Philadelphia (13) at Los Angeles (9), May 4, 1980
    Philadelphia (13) vs. Los Angeles (9), June 6, 1982

Fewest blocked shots, both teams, game
2—Boston (0) at Houston (2), May 14, 1981
3—Boston (0) vs. Milwaukee (3), May 5, 1974
    Boston (0) vs. Milwaukee (3), May 10, 1974 (2 ot)
    Boston (1) vs. Phoenix (2), May 23, 1976
    L.A. Lakers (1) vs. Detroit (2), June 21, 1988
    Chicago (1) vs. L.A. Lakers (2), June 5, 1991
    Utah (1) at Chicago (2), June 10, 1998
    New York (1) vs. San Antonio (2), June 25, 1999

TURNOVERS

Most turnovers, game
34—Portland at Philadelphia, May 22, 1977
31—Golden State at Washington, May 25, 1975

Fewest turnovers, game
5—Chicago at L.A. Lakers, June 9, 1991
    L.A. Lakers vs. Indiana, June 19, 2000
6—Indiana at L.A. Lakers, June 9, 2000

Most turnovers, both teams, game
60—Golden State (31) at Washington (29), May 25, 1975
54—Phoenix (29) at Boston (25), June 4, 1976 (3 ot)
    Portland (34) at Philadelphia (20), May 22, 1977

Fewest turnovers, both teams, game
14—L.A. Lakers (5) vs. Indiana (9), June 19, 2000
15—Chicago (5) at L.A. Lakers (10), June 9, 1991

ALL-STAR GAME

INDIVIDUAL

CAREER

Most games played
18—Kareem Abdul-Jabbar
13—Wilt Chamberlain
   Bob Cousy
   John Havlicek
   Michael Jordan
12—Elvin Hayes
   Karl Malone
   Hakeem Olajuwon
   Oscar Robertson
   Bill Russell
   Jerry West

Most minutes played
449—Kareem Abdul-Jabbar
388—Wilt Chamberlain
382—Michael Jordan

Highest scoring average
(minimum: 60 points)
20.8—Kobe Bryant (125/6)
20.5—Oscar Robertson (246/12)
20.4—Bob Pettit (224/11)

Most field goals made
110—Michael Jordan
105—Kareem Abdul-Jabbar
 88—Oscar Robertson

Most field-goal attempts
233—Michael Jordan
213—Kareem Abdul-Jabbar
193—Bob Pettit

Highest field-goal percentage
(minimum: 15 field goals made)
.714—Larry Nance (15/21)
   Randy Smith (15/21)
.673—David Thompson (33/49)

Most free throws made
78—Elgin Baylor
70—Oscar Robertson
62—Bob Pettit

Most free throw attempts
98—Elgin Baylor
   Oscar Robertson
94—Wilt Chamberlain

Highest free throw percentage
(minimum: 10 free throws made)
1.000—Archie Clark (11/11)
   Clyde Drexler (12/12)
   Kevin Garnett (11/11)
   Gary Payton (11/11)
 .938—Larry Foust (15/16)

Most 3-point field goals made
11—Jason Kidd
10—Magic Johnson
 9—Kobe Bryant
   Mark Price
   Glen Rice

Most 3-point field-goal attempts
27—Ray Allen
23—Gary Payton
22—Scottie Pippen

Most rebounds
197—Wilt Chamberlain
178—Bob Pettit
149—Kareem Abdul-Jabbar

Most assists
127—Magic Johnson
 97—Isiah Thomas
 86—Bob Cousy

Most steals
37—Michael Jordan
31—Isiah Thomas
23—Larry Bird

Most blocked shots
31—Kareem Abdul-Jabbar
23—Hakeem Olajuwon
16—Patrick Ewing

Most personal fouls
57—Kareem Abdul-Jabbar
41—Oscar Robertson
37—Elvin Hayes
   Bill Russell

SINGLE GAME

Most minutes played
42—Oscar Robertson, 1964
   Bill Russell, 1964
   Jerry West, 1964
   Nate Thurmond, 1967

Most points scored
42—Wilt Chamberlain, 1962

Most field goals made
17—Wilt Chamberlain, 1962
   Michael Jordan, 1988
   Kevin Garnett, 2003 (2 ot)

Most field-goal attempts
27—Rick Barry, 1967
   Michael Jordan, 2003 (2 ot)

Most free throws made
12—Elgin Baylor, 1962
   Oscar Robertson, 1965

Most free throw attempts
16—Wilt Chamberlain, 1962

Most 3-point field goals made
6—Mark Price, 1993 (ot)
5—Scottie Pippen, 1994

Most 3-point field-goal attempts
10—Ray Allen, 2002

Most rebounds
27—Bob Pettit, 1962

Most offensive rebounds
9—Dan Roundfield, 1980 (ot)
   Hakeem Olajuwon, 1990

Most defensive rebounds
19—Dikembe Mutombo, 2001

Most assists
22—Magic Johnson, 1984 (ot)
19—Magic Johnson, 1988

Most steals
8—Rick Barry, 1975

Most blocked shots
6—Kareem Abdul-Jabbar, 1980 (ot)
5—Patrick Ewing, 1990
   Hakeem Olajuwon, 1994

Most personal fouls
6—Bob Wanzer, 1954
   Paul Arizin, 1956
   Bob Cousy, 1956 and 1961
   Dolph Schayes, 1959
   Walt Bellamy, 1962
   Richie Guerin, 1962
   Bill Russell, 1965
   John Green, 1965
   Rick Barry, 1966 and 1978
   Kareem Abdul-Jabbar, 1970
   Willis Reed, 1970
   Hakeem Olajuwon, 1987

ONE HALF

Most points
24—Glen Rice, 1997

Most field goals made
10—Wilt Chamberlain, 1962

Most field-goal attempts
17—Glen Rice, 1997

Most free throws made
10—Zelmo Beaty, 1966

Most free throw attempts
12—Zelmo Beaty, 1966

Most 3-point field goals made
6—Mark Price, 1993

Most 3-point field-goal attempts
7—Scottie Pippen, 1994

Most rebounds
16—Wilt Chamberlain, 1960
   Bob Pettit, 1962

Most assists
13—Magic Johnson, 1984

Most personal fouls
5—Randy Smith, 1978

Most steals
5—Larry Bird, 1986

Most blocked shots
4—Kareem Abdul-Jabbar, 1980
   Kareem Abdul-Jabbar, 1981
   Michael Jordan, 1988
   Hakeem Olajuwon, 1994

ONE QUARTER

Most points
20—Glen Rice, 1997

Most field goals made
8—Dave DeBusschere, 1967
　　Glen Rice, 1997

Most field-goal attempts
12—Bill Sharman, 1960

Most free throws made
9—Zelmo Beaty, 1966
　　Julius Erving, 1978

Most free throw attempts
11—Julius Erving, 1978

Most 3-point field goals made
4—Glen Rice, 1997

Most rebounds
10—Bob Pettit, 1962

Most assists
9—John Stockton, 1989

Most personal fouls
4—Vern Mikkelsen, 1955
　　Cliff Hagan, 1959
　　Bob McAdoo, 1976
　　Randy Smith, 1976
　　David Robinson, 1991

Most steals
4—Fred Brown, 1976
　　Larry Bird, 1986
　　Isiah Thomas, 1989

Most blocked shots
4—Kareem Abdul-Jabbar, 1981

ONE CLUB, FULL GAME

Most points
155—West, 2003 (2 ot)
154—East, 1984 (ot)
　　　West, 1987 (ot)
153—West, 1961
　　　West, 1992

Most field goals made
67—West, 2003 (2 ot)
64—West, 1992

Most field-goal attempts
135—East, 1960

Most free throws made
40—East, 1959

Most free throw attempts
57—West, 1970

Most 3-point field goals made
13—West, 2002

Most 3-point field-goal attempts
30—West, 2002

Most rebounds
83—East, 1966
79—West, 1956
　　　West, 1960
　　　West, 1962

Highest rebound percentage
.632—East, 1997

Most offensive rebounds
33—East, 1985

Highest offensive rebound percentage
.500—East, 1980

Most defensive rebounds
46—West, 2003 (2 ot)
44—East, 1982
　　　West, 1993 (ot)

Highest defensive rebound percentage
.840—East, 1997

Most assists
46—West, 1984 (ot)
45—West, 1986

Most steals
24—East, 1989

Most blocked shots
16—West, 1980 (ot)
12—West, 1994

Most personal fouls
36—East, 1965

Most disqualifications
2—East, 1956
　　East, 1965
　　East, 1970

ONE CLUB, ONE HALF

Most points
87—West, 1989

Most field goals made
36—West, 1989

Most field-goal attempts
73—East, 1960

Most free throws made
26—East, 1959

Most free throw attempts
31—East, 1959

Most rebounds
51—East, 1966

Most assists
28—West, 1984

Most personal fouls
18—West, 1954
　　　East, 1962
　　　East, 1970
　　　West, 1986
　　　East, 1987

Most disqualifications
2—East, 1956
　　East, 1970

ONE CLUB, ONE QUARTER

Most points
50—West, 1970

Most field goals made
21—West, 2004

Most field-goal attempts
38—East, 1960

Most free throws made
19—East, 1986

Most free throw attempts
25—West, 1970

Most rebounds
29—West, 1962
　　　East, 1962

Most assists
15—West, 1977
　　　West, 1984

Most personal fouls
13—East, 1970

Most disqualifications
2—East, 1956
　　East, 1970

BOTH CLUBS, FULL GAME

Most points
303—(West 154, East 149), 1987 (ot)
300—(West 155, East 145), 2003 (2 ot)
299—(East 154, West 145), 1984 (ot)
284—(West 153, East 131), 1961

Most field goals made
126—(East 63, West 63), 1984 (ot)
123—(West 67, East 56), 2003 (2 ot)
119—(West 63, East 56), 2004

Most field-goal attempts
256—(East 135, West 121), 1960

Most free throws made
71—(West 39, East 32), 1987 (ot)
70—(West 37, East 33), 1961

Most free throw attempts
95—(East 53, West 42), 1956

Most 3-point field goals made
22—(West 13, East 9), 2002

Most 3-point field-goal attempts
59—(West 30, East 29), 2002

Most rebounds
175—(West 95, East 80), 1962

Most offensive rebounds
55—(East 31, West 24), 1980 (ot)
51—(West 28, East 23), 1987 (ot)
45—(West 24, East 21), 1994

Most defensive rebounds
81—(East 44, West 37), 1982

Most assists
85—(West 46, East 39), 1984 (ot)
77—(West 45, East 32), 1986
　　　(West 44, East 33), 1995
　　　(East 43, West 34), 2004

Most steals
40—(East 24, West 16), 1989

Most blocked shots
25—(West 16, East 9), 1980 (ot)
21—(West 12, East 9), 1994

Most personal fouls
64—(East 36, West 28), 1965

Most disqualifications
2—(East 2, West 0), 1956
　(East 1, West 1), 1962
　(East 2, West 0), 1965
　(East 2, West 0), 1970

BOTH CLUBS, ONE HALF

Most points
157—(West 79, East 78), 1988

Most field goals made
65—(West 35, East 30), 1962

Most field-goal attempts
135—(East 73, West 62), 1960

Most free throws made
36—(West 20, East 16), 1961

Most free throw attempts
57—(West 29, East 28), 1962

Most rebounds
98—(East 50, West 48), 1962
　(East 51, West 47), 1966

Most assists
45—(West 28, East 17), 1984

Most personal fouls
37—(West 22, East 15), 1980

Most disqualifications
2—(East 2, West 0), 1956
　(East 1, West 1), 1962
　(East 2, West 0), 1970

BOTH CLUBS, ONE QUARTER

Most points
86—(West 50, East 36), 1970

Most field goals made
37—(West 21, East 16), 2004

Most field-goal attempts
71—(East 37, West 34), 1962

Most free throws made
27—(East 19, West 8), 1986

Most free throw attempts
33—(East 20, West 13), 1962
　(West 21, East 12), 1993

Most rebounds
58—(West 30, East 28), 1966

Most assists
26—(East 14, West 12), 2004

Most personal fouls
20—(East 11, West 9), 1985
　(East 12, West 8), 1987

Most disqualifications
2—(East 2, West 0), 1956
　(East 1, West 1), 1962
　(East 2, West 0), 1970

YEAR-BY-YEAR REVIEWS

- Final standings
- Team statistics
- Individual leaders
- Individual statistics, team by team
- Playoff results

2002-03 NBA CHAMPION SAN ANTONIO SPURS

Front row (from left): strength and conditioning coach Mike Brungardt, head athletic trainer Will Sevening, director of player development Brett Brown, NBA scout Joe Prunty, Speedy Claxton, Manu Ginobili, Stephen Jackson, Tony Parker, Steve Kerr, assistant coach P.J. Carlesimo, assistant coach Mike Brown, assistant coach Mike Budenholzer, general manager R.C. Buford. Second row (from left): senior VP/broadcasting Lawrence Payne, executive VP/business operations Russ Bookbinder, team physician Dr. Paul Saenz, executive VP/corporate development Rick Pych, team physician Dr. David Schmidt, chairman Peter Holt, Malik Rose, Danny Ferry, Kevin Willis, Tim Duncan, David Robinson, Mengke Bateer, Steve Smith, Bruce Bowen, head coach Gregg Popovich, equipment manager Clarence Rinehart, assistant trainer Joe Gutzwiller, assistant strength coach Chris White, assistant video coordinator Scott Peterson, interpreter Jimmy Chang, video coordinator Kyle Cummins.

FINAL STANDINGS

ATLANTIC DIVISION

TM	Atl	Bos	Chi	Cle	Dal	Den	Det	GS	Hou	Ind	LAC	LAL	Mem	Mia	Mil	Min	NJ	NO	NY	Orl	Phi	Pho	Por	SAC	SA	Sea	Tor	Uta	Was	W	L	Pct	GB	Last-10	Streak
NJ	3	3	2	2	0	2	1	1	1	2	1	2	1	4	2	2	—	2	3	2	1	1	2	0	1	1	4	0	3	49	33	.598	-	5-5	Lost 2
PHI	1	2	3	4	0	2	2	0	0	2	2	1	2	4	2	2	1	3	1	2	—	0	2	0	1	1	3	1	4	48	34	.585	1	5-5	Won 1
BOS	3	—	2	4	0	1	2	1	0	2	2	1	2	2	1	2	1	2	1	3	4	3	2	0	1	0	0	2	1	44	38	.537	5	6-4	Won 2
ORL	1	2	3	4	1	2	1	1	0	1	1	1	0	4	2	1	2	3	2	—	2	0	0	1	0	2	1	2		42	40	.512	7	4-6	Won 1
NY	3	0	1	2	0	2	2	0	2	1	1	1	1	2	1	0	1	1	—	2	2	2	2	0	1	2	1	3	1	37	45	.451	12	5-5	Lost 1
WAS	2	3	3	4	0	1	1	0	1	2	2	1	3	1	0	1	1	2	2	0	1	1	0	1	1	1	1		—	37	45	.451	12	3-7	Lost 3
MIA	3	2	2	2	0	0	1	1	1	0	0	1	0	—	1	1	0	0	2	0	0	2	0	1	0	0	4	0	1	25	57	.305	24	3-7	Won 1

CENTRAL DIVISION

TM	Atl	Bos	Chi	Cle	Dal	Den	Det	GS	Hou	Ind	LAC	LAL	Mem	Mia	Mil	Min	NJ	NO	NY	Orl	Phi	Pho	Por	SAC	SA	Sea	Tor	Uta	Was	W	L	Pct	GB	Last-10	Streak
DET	3	2	4	4	0	2	—	1	2	2	1	2	3	1	1	2	2	2	2	2	1	0	1	0	1	3	2	3		50	32	.610	-	4-6	Lost 1
IND	2	2	4	1	1	2	1	—	2	0	1	4	3	2	1	3	3	2	1	1	0	0	0	2	3	1	2			48	34	.585	2	6-4	Won 2
NO	2	1	3	3	0	2	2	1	1	1	1	1	4	2	1	2	—	3	1	2	2	1	0	1	0	2	4	2	2	47	35	.573	3	7-3	Won 3
MIL	2	2	2	4	2	1	3	2	1	1	1	0	0	3	—	0	2	2	3	2	2	0	2	0	0	1	0	2		42	40	.512	8	8-2	Won 4
ATL	—	0	2	4	0	2	1	0	1	2	2	1	1	1	2	0	1	2	1	2	3	0	0	1	1	1	1	1	2	35	47	.427	15	6-4	Lost 1
CHI	2	2	—	3	0	1	0	1	0	1	1	1	2	0	2	1	2	1	2	1	1	1	1	0	0	0	2	1	1	30	52	.366	20	4-6	Won 1
TOR	3	2	2	1	0	1	1	0	0	1	1	0	1	2	1	0	0	1	2	0	1	2	0	—	0	3	2	4		24	58	.293	26	1-9	Lost 8
CLE	0	0	1	—	0	1	0	1	1	0	2	1	0	1	0	0	2	1	1	0	0	0	0	0	1	3	1	0		17	65	.207	33	3-7	Won 1

MIDWEST DIVISION

TM	Atl	Bos	Chi	Cle	Dal	Den	Det	GS	Hou	Ind	LAC	LAL	Mem	Mia	Mil	Min	NJ	NO	NY	Orl	Phi	Pho	Por	SAC	SA	Sea	Tor	Uta	Was	W	L	Pct	GB	Last-10	Streak
SA	1	2	2	2	2	3	2	3	3	2	3	4	3	2	2	2	1	2	0	2	1	1	2	3	—	3	2	4	1	60	22	.732	-	8-2	Lost 1
DAL	2	2	2	2	—	4	2	4	4	1	4	1	4	2	0	2	2	2	2	1	2	1	2	2	1	2	2	2	2	60	22	.732	-	6-4	Won 3
MIN	2	0	2	2	4	1	3	2	0	3	2	4	1	2	—	0	1	2	1	1	3	3	2	2	1	1	2			51	31	.622	9	5-5	Won 3
UTA	1	1	1	2	4	0	2	3	1	3	1	3	2	2	3	2	0	1	1	1	3	3	1	0	2	2	—	1		47	35	.573	13	4-6	Lost 2
HOU	2	1	0	4	0	3	—	1	2	2	3	1	1	2	1	1	0	2	2	3	1	2	1	2	1	1	1	1		43	39	.524	17	6-4	Won 3
MEM	1	0	1	2	0	2	0	2	1	1	2	0	—	2	2	0	1	1	1	2	0	1	1	0	1	1	1	1	1	28	54	.341	32	2-8	Lost 3
DEN	0	1	1	1	0	—	0	0	0	1	1	0	2	2	1	0	0	0	0	0	0	0	1	2	0	1	1	1	0	17	65	.207	43	1-9	Lost 8

PACIFIC DIVISION

TM	Atl	Bos	Chi	Cle	Dal	Den	Det	GS	Hou	Ind	LAC	LAL	Mem	Mia	Mil	Min	NJ	NO	NY	Orl	Phi	Pho	Por	SAC	SA	Sea	Tor	Uta	Was	W	L	Pct	GB	Last-10	Streak
SAC	1	2	2	2	3	4	1	4	2	2	3	2	4	1	2	2	2	1	1	1	1	2	3	—	1	3	1	3	2	59	23	.720	-	8-2	Won 2
LAL	1	1	1	3	4	1	2	2	2	4	—	4	1	2	2	0	1	1	1	1	3	2	2	0	2	2	3	1		50	32	.610	9	8-2	Won 2
POR	1	1	2	2	2	4	2	4	3	2	3	2	0	1	0	2	2	2	0	1	—	1	2	4	2	1	1			50	32	.610	9	5-5	Lost 1
PHO	2	2	1	2	2	3	2	1	1	3	1	3	0	2	1	1	0	0	2	2	—	3	2	3	1	1	1	1		44	38	.537	15	6-4	Lost 2
SEA	1	0	2	1	2	3	1	2	2	0	3	2	3	2	1	2	1	0	1	0	1	3	0	1	1	—	2	2	1	40	42	.488	19	5-5	Won 1
GS	2	1	1	1	0	4	1	—	1	1	2	2	2	1	0	1	1	1	1	1	2	2	0	0	1	2	2	2		38	44	.463	21	3-7	Lost 4
LAC	0	0	2	0	0	3	1	2	2	0	—	0	2	2	1	1	1	1	1	1	0	1	1	1	1	1	1	1	0	27	55	.329	32	5-5	Won 3

TEAM STATISTICS

OFFENSIVE

Team	G	FG Made	Att.	Pct.	3P Made	Att.	Pct.	FT Made	Att.	Pct.	Off.	Def.	Tot.	Ast	PF	Dq	Stl	TO	Blk	Pts	Avg.
Dall.	82	3161	6982	.453	636	1668	.381	1486	1793	.829	912	2544	3456	1837	1730	19	665	949	449	8444	103.0
G.S.	82	3061	6941	.441	425	1235	.344	1853	2382	.778	1284	2546	3830	1712	1786	13	594	1295	506	8400	102.4
Sac.	82	3242	6990	.464	491	1288	.381	1367	1832	.746	900	2751	3651	2034	1666	8	736	1192	457	8342	101.7
LA-L.	82	3091	6856	.451	486	1367	.356	1562	2129	.734	1078	2554	3632	1909	1874	20	639	1192	470	8230	100.4
Milw.	82	3045	6670	.457	585	1526	.383	1483	1911	.776	876	2367	3243	1823	1820	19	622	1044	344	8158	99.5
Orl.	82	2947	6763	.436	568	1590	.357	1616	2079	.777	958	2392	3350	1676	1888	14	696	1177	300	8078	98.5
Minn.	82	3172	6809	.466	296	804	.368	1406	1826	.770	959	2614	3573	2070	1704	14	553	1124	433	8046	98.1
Mem.	82	3049	6743	.452	467	1279	.365	1430	1936	.739	943	2466	3409	1892	1678	16	651	1262	500	7995	97.5
Phil.	82	2975	6640	.448	245	787	.311	1746	2253	.775	1042	2415	3457	1771	1804	19	844	1212	284	7941	96.8
Ind.	82	2911	6608	.441	379	1119	.339	1739	2271	.766	1004	2622	3626	1910	1811	18	696	1210	443	7940	96.8
N.Y.	82	2967	6725	.441	606	1582	.383	1320	1620	.815	842	2376	3218	1800	1888	22	579	1149	255	7860	95.9
S.A.	82	2908	6297	.462	449	1270	.354	1591	2194	.725	939	2556	3495	1636	1672	12	629	1295	529	7856	95.8
Phoe.	82	3005	6776	.443	394	1149	.343	1430	1928	.742	1049	2440	3489	1719	1801	9	665	1208	404	7834	95.5
N.J.	82	2906	6585	.441	346	1041	.332	1662	2195	.757	991	2528	3519	1887	1772	20	717	1212	374	7820	95.4
Port.	82	2987	6491	.460	379	1150	.330	1450	1947	.745	992	2378	3370	1860	1634	8	725	1248	316	7803	95.2
Chi.	82	2991	6714	.445	349	997	.350	1455	2014	.722	985	2541	3526	1782	2028	18	605	1388	461	7786	95.0
Utah.	82	2894	6189	.468	224	641	.349	1750	2349	.745	1021	2381	3402	2103	1837	15	708	1374	467	7762	94.7
Atl.	82	2859	6434	.444	402	1141	.352	1594	2011	.793	937	2558	3495	1679	1783	9	611	1367	473	7714	94.1
N.O.	82	2914	6695	.435	404	1075	.376	1467	1910	.768	1097	2475	3572	1807	1769	15	636	1212	394	7699	93.9
LA-C	82	2835	6490	.437	390	1178	.331	1633	2177	.750	1008	2462	3470	1605	1784	28	574	1291	461	7693	93.8
Hou.	82	2840	6411	.440	439	1267	.346	1469	2044	.768	1024	2564	3588	1506	1602	4	594	1276	493	7688	93.8
Bos.	82	2700	6509	.415	719	2155	.334	1480	1994	.742	849	2471	3320	1575	1758	12	720	1147	303	7599	92.7
Sea.	82	2887	6599	.437	456	1291	.353	1325	1780	.744	963	2385	3348	1775	1712	11	679	1085	295	7555	92.1
Wash.	82	2816	6394	.440	253	811	.312	1617	2077	.779	917	2395	3312	1612	1644	9	621	1095	390	7502	91.5
Clev.	82	2850	6746	.422	293	896	.327	1502	2012	.747	1118	2542	3660	1712	1864	23	636	1501	521	7495	91.4
Det.	82	2700	6277	.430	533	1488	.358	1559	2021	.771	883	2445	3328	1620	1748	9	556	1104	468	7492	91.4
Tor.	82	2847	6664	.427	409	1193	.343	1350	1879	.718	1023	2355	3378	1583	1761	10	609	1181	392	7453	90.9
Miami.	82	2688	6517	.412	348	1100	.316	1292	1689	.765	948	2464	3412	1501	1856	21	592	1167	324	7016	85.6
Den.	82	2689	6544	.411	229	824	.278	1294	1850	.699	1112	2363	3475	1737	2056	23	712	1514	422	6901	84.2

DEFENSIVE

Team	FG Made	Att.	Pct.	3P Made	Att.	Pct.	FT Made	Att.	Pct.	Off.	Def.	Tot.	Ast	PF	Dq	Stl	TO	Blk	Pts	Avg.	Dif.
Det.	2744	6269	.438	289	839	.344	1413	1895	.746	859	2528	3387	1501	1904	20	568	1149	355	7190	87.7	+3.7
N.J.	2757	6461	.427	425	1185	.359	1453	1941	.749	932	2461	3393	1607	1880	15	693	1358	423	7392	90.1	+5.2
S.A.	2862	6703	.427	354	1043	.339	1334	1737	.768	1029	2322	3351	1559	1915	24	665	1231	422	7412	90.4	+5.4
Miami.	2713	6208	.437	406	1149	.353	1598	2129	.751	872	2587	3459	1482	1671	9	626	1173	436	7430	90.6	-5.0
N.O.	2857	6518	.438	338	1001	.338	1474	1925	.766	909	2368	3277	1630	1754	12	647	1196	427	7526	91.8	+2.1
Sea.	2871	6424	.447	472	1371	.344	1351	1821	.742	938	2462	3400	1703	1671	13	500	1209	409	7565	92.3	-0.1
Utah.	2751	6346	.434	437	1252	.349	1627	2143	.759	1011	2120	3131	1601	1950	20	723	1305	427	7566	92.3	+2.4
Hou.	2891	6681	.433	386	1113	.347	1399	1805	.775	979	2353	3332	1683	1794	14	663	1082	381	7567	92.3	+1.5
Den.	2696	6087	.443	420	1134	.370	1768	2337	.757	861	2443	3304	1764	1789	16	742	1405	538	7580	92.4	-8.3
Wash.	2877	6507	.442	449	1242	.362	1382	1792	.771	949	2447	3396	1776	1804	16	612	1171	358	7585	92.5	-1.0
Port.	2942	6540	.450	438	1285	.341	1267	1659	.764	912	2292	3204	1863	1670	11	683	1270	391	7589	92.5	+2.6
Bos.	2804	6450	.435	463	1400	.331	1560	2084	.749	937	2750	3687	1824	1798	13	617	1315	367	7631	93.1	-0.4
Ind.	2860	6690	.428	407	1197	.340	1527	1992	.767	1006	2458	3464	1696	1923	21	620	1258	513	7654	93.3	+3.5
Phoe.	2913	6658	.438	436	1361	.320	1479	1932	.766	1031	2487	3518	1824	1763	20	639	1309	453	7741	94.4	+1.1
Phil.	2876	6363	.452	453	1278	.354	1547	2035	.760	908	2400	3308	1809	1885	20	639	1405	521	7741	94.5	+2.3
Dall.	2926	6687	.438	477	1401	.340	1477	2032	.727	1045	2682	3727	1781	1746	18	547	1316	322	7806	95.2	+7.8
Sac.	2991	7125	.420	373	1166	.320	1454	1962	.741	1145	2614	3759	1759	1635	9	684	1262	356	7809	95.2	+6.5
Minn.	3005	6873	.437	472	1362	.347	1394	1853	.752	974	2444	3418	1871	1686	11	571	1116	405	7876	96.0	+2.1
Tor.	3037	6592	.461	370	986	.375	1490	1964	.759	976	2601	3577	1729	1702	7	604	1125	406	7934	96.8	-5.9
N.Y.	2961	6478	.457	358	1053	.340	1691	2193	.771	935	2613	3548	1732	1631	11	627	1179	308	7971	97.2	-1.4
Atl.	3015	6908	.436	446	1243	.359	1530	2013	.760	1073	2420	3493	1771	1668	9	738	1068	409	8006	97.6	-3.6
LA-C.	3035	6787	.447	454	1244	.365	1507	1946	.774	1046	2460	3506	1840	1844	15	652	1152	418	8031	97.9	-4.1
LA-L.	2976	6725	.443	465	1223	.380	1622	2133	.760	957	2495	3452	1753	1916	28	644	1190	311	8039	98.0	+2.3
Orl.	3007	6602	.455	405	1211	.334	1648	2150	.767	970	2596	3566	1837	1823	15	643	1341	411	8067	98.4	+0.1
Milw.	3043	6641	.458	479	1278	.375	1574	2114	.745	1021	2541	3562	1892	1685	8	543	1182	333	8139	99.3	+0.2
Chi.	2991	6817	.439	431	1333	.323	1794	2394	.749	1117	2572	3689	1949	1796	10	768	1208	413	8207	100.1	-5.1
Mem.	3224	7008	.460	431	1188	.363	1381	1819	.759	1126	2555	3681	1991	1782	21	714	1213	430	8260	100.7	-3.2
Clev.	3072	6786	.453	428	1197	.358	1712	2219	.772	932	2491	3423	1972	1709	7	802	1162	494	8284	101.0	-9.6
G.S.	3240	7175	.452	438	1177	.372	1575	2084	.756	1204	2388	3592	1934	1936	25	710	1121	491	8493	103.6	-1.1
Avgs.	2929	6624	.442	421	1204	.349	1518	2004	.758	988	2481	3469	1763	1784	15	651	1223	411	7797	95.1	—

2002-03

	Home	Road	Total		Home	Road	Total
Atlanta	9-32	26-15	35-47	Minnesota	33-8	18-23	51-31
Boston	25-16	19-22	44-38	New Jersey	33-8	16-25	49-33
Chicago	3-38	27-14	30-52	New Orleans	18-23	29-12	47-35
Cleveland	14-27	3-38	17-65	New York	24-17	13-28	37-45
Dallas	33-8	27-14	60-22	Orlando	26-15	16-25	42-40
Denver	13-28	4-37	17-65	Philadelphia	25-16	23-18	48-34
Detroit	30-11	20-21	50-32	Phoenix	30-11	14-27	44-38
Golden State	24-17	14-27	38-44	Portland	27-14	23-18	50-32
Houston	28-13	15-26	43-39	Sacramento	35-6	24-17	59-23
Indiana	16-25	32-9	48-34	San Antonio	33-8	27-14	60-22
L.A. Clippers	16-25	11-30	27-55	Seattle	25-16	15-26	40-42
L.A. Lakers	31-10	19-22	50-32	Toronto	15-26	9-32	24-58
Memphis	20-21	8-33	28-54	Utah	29-12	18-23	47-35
Miami	16-25	9-32	25-57	Washington	23-18	14-27	37-45
Milwaukee	17-24	25-16	42-40	Total	671-518	518-671	1,189-1,189

INDIVIDUAL LEADERS

POINTS

(minimum 70 games or 1,400 points)

	G	FGM	FTM	Pts.	Avg.
McGrady, Orl.	.75	829	576	2407	32.1
Bryant, LA-L	.82	868	601	2461	30.0
Iverson, Phi.	.82	804	570	2262	27.6
O'Neal, LA-L	.67	695	451	1841	27.5
Pierce, Bos.	.79	663	604	2048	25.9
Nowitzki, Dal.	.80	690	483	2011	25.1
Duncan, S.A.	.81	714	450	1884	23.3
Webber, Sac.	.67	661	215	1542	23.0
Garnett, Min.	.82	743	377	1883	23.0
Allen, Mil.-Sea.	.76	598	316	1713	22.5

FIELD GOALS

(minimum 300 made)

	FGM	FGA	Pct.
Curry, Chi.	.335	573	.585
O'Neal, LA-L	.695	1211	.574
Boozer, Cle.	.331	618	.536
Brown, N.O.	.319	601	.531
Nesterovic, Min.	.400	762	.525
Hilario, Den.	.321	619	.519
Duncan, S.A.	.714	1392	.513
Harpring, Utah	.521	1020	.511
Gasol, Mem.	.569	1116	.510
Grant, Mia.	.344	676	.509

FREE THROWS

(minimum 125 made)

	FTM	FTA	Pct.
Houston, N.Y.	.363	395	.919
Allen, Mil.-Sea.	.316	345	.916
Nash, Dal.	.308	339	.909
Hudson, Min.	.208	231	.900
R. Miller, Ind.	.207	230	.900
Terry, Atl.	.259	292	.887
Nowitzki, Dal.	.483	548	.881
Billups, Det.	.318	362	.878
Stackhouse, Was.	.455	518	.878
Armstrong, Orl.	.165	188	.878

ASSISTS

(minimum 70 games or 400 assists)

	G	No.	Avg.
Kidd, N.J.	.80	711	8.9
Williams, Mem.	.76	631	8.3
Payton, Sea.-Mil.	.80	663	8.3
Marbury, Pho.	.81	654	8.1
Stockton, Utah	.82	629	7.7
Tinsley, Ind.	.73	548	7.5
Terry, Atl.	.81	600	7.4
Nash, Dal.	.82	598	7.3
Miller, LA-C	.80	537	6.7
Snow, Phi.	.82	544	6.6

REBOUNDS

(minimum 70 games or 800 rebounds)

	G	Off.	Def.	Tot.	Avg.
Wallace, Det.	.73	293	833	1126	15.4
Garnett, Min.	.82	244	858	1102	13.4
Duncan, S.A.	.81	259	784	1043	12.9
O'Neal, Ind.	.77	202	594	796	10.3
Grant, Mia.	.82	241	596	837	10.2
Murphy, G.S.	.79	228	578	806	10.2
Nowitzki, Dal.	.80	81	710	791	9.9
Marion, Pho.	.81	199	574	773	9.5
J. Williams, Tor.	.71	231	419	650	9.2
Brown, N.O.	.78	243	458	701	9.0

STEALS

(minimum 70 games or 125 steals)

	G	No.	Avg.
Iverson, Phi.	.82	225	2.74
Artest, Ind.	.69	159	2.30
Marion, Pho.	.81	185	2.28
Christie, Sac.	.80	180	2.25
Kidd, N.J.	.80	179	2.24
Bryant, LA-L	.82	181	2.21
Pierce, Bos.	.79	139	1.76
C. Butler, Mia.	.78	137	1.76
Francis, Hou.	.81	141	1.74
Tinsley, Ind.	.73	125	1.71

BLOCKED SHOTS

(minimum 70 games or 100 blocked shots)

	G	No.	Avg.
Ratliff, Atl.	.81	262	3.23
Wallace, Det.	.73	230	3.15
Duncan, S.A.	.81	237	2.93
Brand, LA-C	.62	158	2.55
Foyle, G.S.	.82	205	2.50
O'Neal, LA-L	.67	159	2.37
O'Neal, Ind.	.77	178	2.31
Kirilenko, Utah	.80	175	2.19
Bradley, Dal.	.81	170	2.10
Dampier, G.S.	.82	154	1.88

3-POINT FIELD GOALS

(minimum 55 made)

	FGM	FGA	Pct.
Bowen, S.A.	.101	229	.441
Redd, Mil.	.182	416	.437
Person, Mem.	.100	231	.433
Wesley, N.O.	.134	316	.424
Szczerbiak, Min.	.61	145	.421
Nash, Dal.	.111	269	.413
Harpring, Utah	.66	160	.412
Peeler, Min.	.87	212	.410
Bibby, Sac.	.56	137	.409
Jones, Mia.	.98	241	.407

2002-03

ATLANTA HAWKS

	G	Min.	FGM	FGA	Pct.	FTM	FTA	Pct.	REBOUNDS Off.	Def.	Tot.	Ast.	PF	Dq.	Stl.	TO	Blk.	SCORING Pts.	Avg.	Hi.
Glenn Robinson 69	69	2591	539	1248	.432	268	306	.876	86	371	457	205	183	0	91	248	26	1436	20.8	37
Shareef Abdur-Rahim . 81	81	3087	566	1183	.478	455	541	.841	175	502	677	242	240	2	87	212	38	1608	19.9	33
Jason Terry. 81	81	3081	488	1141	.428	259	292	.887	37	242	279	600	175	2	126	249	14	1395	17.2	33
Dion Glover. 76	76	1890	277	648	.427	127	162	.784	62	220	282	141	146	0	71	108	15	737	9.7	28
Theo Ratliff. 81	81	2518	276	595	.464	154	214	.720	154	453	607	73	271	3	56	137	262	706	8.7	20
Ira Newble 73	73	1931	231	467	.495	70	90	.778	86	185	271	99	174	1	50	69	26	564	7.7	23
Mike Wilks(>) 15	15	364	29	81	.358	21	29	.724	9	32	41	42	38	0	16	16	1	85	5.7	19
Alan Henderson 82	82	1494	153	327	.468	88	138	.638	156	242	398	41	168	1	33	61	32	394	4.8	17
Chris Crawford 5	5	38	8	13	.615	7	8	.875	3	4	7	1	7	0	2	2	3	24	4.8	14
Nazr Mohammed 35	35	445	67	159	.421	26	41	.634	47	82	129	6	79	0	16	25	21	160	4.6	16
Corey Benjamin. 9	9	152	13	43	.302	12	16	.750	10	21	31	10	20	0	1	6	2	40	4.4	14
Emanual Davis 24	24	340	32	88	.364	17	22	.773	5	38	43	36	28	0	12	25	2	88	3.7	14
Dan Dickau 50	50	515	70	170	.412	21	26	.808	9	34	43	85	66	0	14	53	2	183	3.7	16
Darvin Ham 75	75	926	71	159	.447	38	79	.481	73	80	153	38	127	0	16	65	19	180	2.4	12
Jermaine Jackson(*). . 29	29	273	19	42	.452	17	28	.607	9	23	32	35	27	0	10	15	3	55	1.9	10
Jermaine Jackson(!) . . 53	53	559	40	110	.364	40	55	.727	19	38	57	74	51	0	19	34	6	121	2.3	10
Mikki Moore(*). 5	5	31	5	12	.417	8	10	.800	5	2	7	3	1	0	0	2	2	18	3.6	8
Mikki Moore(!) 8	8	43	5	13	.385	8	10	.800	6	2	8	3	7	0	0	2	4	18	2.3	8
Matt Maloney 14	14	103	8	25	.320	3	5	.600	1	6	7	17	9	0	4	5	0	24	1.7	5
Antonio Harvey 4	4	32	2	5	.400	0	0	—	1	5	6	0	7	0	1	3	4	4	1.0	2
Amal McCaskill 11	11	70	4	17	.235	3	4	.750	7	15	22	5	13	0	3	2	1	11	1.0	7
Brandon Williams 6	6	19	1	7	.143	0	0	—	2	0	2	0	4	0	2	3	0	2	0.3	2
Paul Shirley 3	3	5	0	4	.000	0	0	—	0	1	1	0	0	0	0	0	0	0	0.0	0

3-pt. FG: Atlanta 402-1141 (.352)
Robinson 90-263 (.342); Abdur-Rahim 21-60 (.350); Terry 160-431 (.371); Glover 56-158 (.354); Newble 32-84 (.381); Ham 0-3 (.000)
Wilks(>) 6-17 (.353); Henderson 0-2 (.000); Crawford 1-3 (.333); Benjamin 2-13 (.154); Davis 7-29 (.241); Dickau 22-61 (.361)
Jackson(*) 0-1 (.000); Jackson(!) 1-10 (.100); Maloney 5-15 (.333); Williams 0-1 (.000); Opponents 446-1243 (.359)

BOSTON CELTICS

	G	Min.	FGM	FGA	Pct.	FTM	FTA	Pct.	REBOUNDS Off.	Def.	Tot.	Ast.	PF	Dq.	Stl.	TO	Blk.	SCORING Pts.	Avg.	Hi.
Paul Pierce 79	79	3096	663	1592	.416	604	753	.802	106	472	578	349	227	2	139	288	62	2048	25.9	46
Antoine Walker 78	78	3235	603	1554	.388	176	286	.615	99	464	563	373	221	4	116	260	31	1570	20.1	38
Tony Delk 67	67	1873	233	560	.416	68	87	.782	41	191	232	146	124	0	72	69	10	654	9.8	26
Eric Williams. 82	82	2350	254	575	.442	201	268	.750	143	239	382	140	234	0	86	97	19	746	9.1	21
J.R. Bremer 64	64	1503	171	464	.369	85	111	.766	18	127	145	164	80	1	38	59	3	528	8.3	25
Shammond Williams(>)51	51	1169	134	338	.396	48	57	.842	12	98	110	128	84	0	61	61	3	372	7.3	21
Tony Battie 67	67	1683	199	369	.539	88	118	.746	148	285	433	49	197	2	33	48	81	487	7.3	24
Walter McCarty 82	82	1949	173	418	.414	61	98	.622	64	224	288	106	188	1	78	67	28	498	6.1	24
Vin Baker 52	52	942	99	207	.478	72	107	.673	90	108	198	29	146	1	22	61	30	270	5.2	16
Mark Blount(*) 27	27	518	45	80	.563	30	40	.750	49	76	125	21	75	1	20	33	17	120	4.4	13
Mark Blount(!) 81	81	1403	150	347	.432	101	139	.727	111	197	308	56	187	2	42	103	68	401	5.0	15
Bimbo Coles(*). 14	14	175	22	49	.449	8	8	1.000	1	10	11	16	17	0	6	10	0	52	3.7	12
Bimbo Coles(!) 35	35	691	56	168	.333	35	42	.833	11	48	59	72	60	0	17	28	4	154	4.4	12
Kedrick Brown 51	51	666	61	171	.357	20	32	.625	45	95	140	20	68	0	34	23	13	145	2.8	14
Grant Long 41	41	488	27	70	.386	18	23	.783	24	59	83	25	62	0	9	19	1	72	1.8	8
Bruno Sundov. 26	26	138	14	56	.250	0	2	.000	8	20	28	7	24	0	6	9	3	32	1.2	5
Mark Bryant(*) 2	2	9	0	1	.000	0	0	—	0	2	2	1	2	0	0	0	0	0	0.0	0
Mark Bryant(!) 16	16	100	5	19	.263	3	4	.750	8	12	20	4	18	0	1	7	1	13	0.8	6
Ruben Wolkowyski . . . 7	7	24	2	4	.500	1	4	.250	0	1	1	1	3	0	0	1	0	5	0.7	2
Mikki Moore 3	3	12	0	1	.000	0	0	—	1	0	1	0	6	0	0	0	2	0	0.0	0

3-pt. FG: Boston 719-2155 (.334)
Pierce 118-391 (.302); Walker 188-582 (.323); Delk 120-304 (.395); E. Williams 37-110 (.336); Bremer 101-286 (.353)
S. Williams(>) 56-159 (.352); Battie 1-5 (.200); McCarty 91-248 (.367); Baker 0-4 (.000); Coles(*) 0-7 (.000); Brown 3-39 (.077)
Coles(!) 7-32 (.219); Long 0-3 (.000); Sundov 4-16 (.250); Wolkowyski 0-1 (.000); Opponents 463-1400 (.331)

CHICAGO BULLS

	G	Min.	FGM	FGA	Pct.	FTM	FTA	Pct.	REBOUNDS Off.	Def.	Tot.	Ast.	PF	Dq.	Stl.	TO	Blk.	SCORING Pts.	Avg.	Hi.
Jalen Rose 82	82	3351	642	1583	.406	399	467	.854	68	283	351	395	271	2	72	285	23	1816	22.1	38
Donyell Marshall. . . . 78	78	2378	421	918	.459	167	221	.756	234	465	699	137	234	3	95	135	85	1042	13.4	32
Marcus Fizer 38	38	809	178	383	.465	88	134	.657	80	136	216	48	89	0	14	57	17	445	11.7	28
Jamal Crawford. 80	80	1992	334	808	.413	104	129	.806	21	164	185	334	126	0	77	134	25	858	10.7	33
Eddy Curry. 81	81	1571	335	573	.585	179	287	.624	116	237	353	37	226	3	18	137	62	849	10.5	31
Jay Williams 75	75	1961	273	685	.399	103	161	.640	27	168	195	350	179	1	86	171	17	714	9.5	26
Tyson Chandler 75	75	1827	257	484	.531	177	291	.608	169	345	514	76	220	3	37	135	106	691	9.2	27
Eddie Robinson 64	64	1355	165	315	.492	51	63	.810	76	124	200	66	122	0	62	52	13	364	5.7	15
Lonny Baxter 55	55	682	96	206	.466	70	103	.680	65	100	165	16	135	1	9	46	22	262	4.8	17
Trenton Hassell 82	82	1999	144	392	.367	41	55	.745	37	218	255	151	197	2	45	83	61	342	4.2	15
Rick Brunson 17	17	196	23	50	.460	10	12	.833	4	15	19	36	20	0	10	17	3	60	3.5	17

2002-03

	G	Min.	FGM	FGA	Pct.	FTM	FTA	Pct.	Off.	Def.	Tot.	Ast.	PF	Dq.	Stl.	TO	Blk.	Pts.	Avg.	Hi.
Corie Blount 50	50	836	65	134	.485	20	35	.571	68	137	205	50	121	1	33	43	19	150	3.0	10
Fred Hoiberg 63	63	784	49	126	.389	41	50	.820	11	126	137	70	59	0	40	25	5	144	2.3	11
Dalibor Bagaric 10	10	76	8	26	.308	3	4	.750	7	13	20	4	11	0	3	5	3	19	1.9	4
Roger Mason 17	17	113	11	31	.355	2	2	1.000	2	10	12	12	20	0	4	5	0	30	1.8	6

3-pt. FG: Chicago 349-997 (.350)
Rose 133-359 (.370); Marshall 33-87 (.379); Fizer 1-6 (.167); Crawford 86-242 (.355); Williams 65-202 (.322); Robinson 3-14 (.214)
Baxter 0-2 (.000); Hassell 13-40 (.325); Brunson 4-6 (.667); Hoiberg 5-21 (.238); Mason 6-18 (.333); Opponents 431-1333 (.323)

CLEVELAND CAVALIERS

									REBOUNDS									SCORING		
	G	Min.	FGM	FGA	Pct.	FTM	FTA	Pct.	Off.	Def.	Tot.	Ast.	PF	Dq.	Stl.	TO	Blk.	Pts.	Avg.	Hi.
Ricky Davis 79	79	3131	602	1470	.410	348	465	.748	97	293	390	436	180	0	125	277	36	1626	20.6	45
Zydrunas Ilgauskas . . . 81	81	2432	495	1122	.441	400	512	.781	240	371	611	127	274	4	56	210	152	1390	17.2	35
Dajuan Wagner 47	47	1385	223	605	.369	128	160	.800	20	62	82	130	107	2	38	85	7	629	13.4	33
Carlos Boozer 81	81	2049	331	618	.536	148	192	.771	202	407	609	106	224	2	59	103	50	810	10.0	27
Jumaine Jones 80	80	2204	308	710	.434	57	83	.687	106	299	405	112	176	1	67	107	22	784	9.8	25
Darius Miles 67	67	2008	263	642	.410	92	155	.594	113	250	363	176	159	3	67	178	69	618	9.2	19
Tyrone Hill(>) 32	32	855	85	197	.431	33	45	.733	70	197	267	32	104	4	31	52	19	203	6.3	17
Smush Parker 66	66	1103	136	338	.402	98	118	.831	29	90	119	162	106	1	48	133	12	408	6.2	21
Chris Mihm 52	52	809	116	287	.404	76	105	.724	93	138	231	28	124	0	18	48	38	308	5.9	19
Milt Palacio 80	80	1976	162	388	.418	65	87	.747	48	187	235	259	168	2	68	131	16	397	5.0	20
Bimbo Coles(>) 21	21	516	34	119	.286	27	34	.794	10	38	48	56	43	0	11	18	4	102	4.9	12
Tierre Brown 15	15	168	27	59	.458	11	14	.786	8	22	30	39	9	0	13	22	0	65	4.3	16
DeSagana Diop 80	80	943	54	154	.351	11	30	.367	63	152	215	43	148	4	33	56	81	119	1.5	10
Michael Stewart 47	47	251	14	37	.378	8	12	.667	19	36	55	6	42	0	2	10	15	36	0.8	5
Cleveland 82	82	19830	2850	6746	.422	1502	2012	.747	1118	2542	3660	1712	1864	23	636	1501	521	7495	91.4	133
Opponents 82	82	19830	3072	6786	.453	1712	2219	.772	932	2491	3423	1972	1709	7	802	1162	494	8284	101.0	140

3-pt. FG: Cleveland 293-896 (.327)
Davis 74-204 (.363); Ilgauskas 0-5 (.000); Wagner 55-174 (.316); Boozer 0-1 (.000); Jones 111-314 (.354); Miles 0-14 (.000)
Parker 38-118 (.322); Mihm 0-3 (.000); Palacio 8-37 (.216); Coles(>) 7-25 (.280); Brown 0-1 (.000); Opponents 428-1197 (.358)

DALLAS MAVERICKS

									REBOUNDS									SCORING		
	G	Min.	FGM	FGA	Pct.	FTM	FTA	Pct.	Off.	Def.	Tot.	Ast.	PF	Dq.	Stl.	TO	Blk.	Pts.	Avg.	Hi.
Dirk Nowitzki 80	80	3117	690	1489	.463	483	548	.881	81	710	791	239	206	2	111	152	82	2011	25.1	44
Michael Finley 69	69	2642	507	1193	.425	198	230	.861	107	295	402	205	105	0	76	114	21	1331	19.3	42
Steve Nash 82	82	2711	518	1114	.465	308	339	.909	63	171	234	598	134	0	85	192	6	1455	17.7	32
Nick Van Exel 73	73	2026	342	831	.412	110	144	.764	35	173	208	312	86	1	42	123	4	912	12.5	35
Raef LaFrentz 69	69	1611	266	514	.518	60	88	.682	125	205	330	54	264	8	35	46	91	639	9.3	26
Shawn Bradley 81	81	1731	201	375	.536	141	175	.806	151	325	476	54	242	5	65	67	170	543	6.7	16
Eduardo Najera 48	48	1103	129	231	.558	62	91	.681	90	133	223	47	129	1	40	23	22	320	6.7	16
Walt Williams 66	66	1161	134	341	.393	31	50	.620	53	154	207	59	141	0	42	35	26	363	5.5	18
Adrian Griffin 74	74	1373	146	337	.433	27	32	.844	88	176	264	105	157	0	77	47	6	325	4.4	17
Tariq Abdul-Wahad . . . 14	14	204	27	58	.466	3	6	.500	14	26	40	21	26	0	6	7	3	57	4.1	12
Avery Johnson 48	48	430	63	150	.420	30	39	.769	10	21	31	64	26	0	15	29	1	156	3.3	12
Raja Bell 75	75	1173	93	211	.441	23	34	.676	47	98	145	57	134	1	52	43	8	230	3.1	13
Popeye Jones 26	26	222	24	62	.387	5	11	.455	29	30	59	8	31	0	5	15	1	53	2.0	11
Antoine Rigaudeau . . . 11	11	91	8	35	.229	0	0		4	4	8	6	11	0	3	6	0	17	1.5	6
Evan Eschmeyer 17	17	135	7	19	.368	3	4	.750	10	19	29	6	35	1	10	6	7	17	1.0	5
Mark Strickland 4	4	13	2	5	.400	0	0		5	2	7	0	1	0	1	0	1	4	1.0	2
Adam Harrington(>) . . 13	13	37	4	17	.235	2	2	1.000	0	2	2	2	2	0	1	2	1	11	0.8	5

3-pt. FG: Dallas 636-1668 (.381)
Nowitzki 148-390 (.379); Finley 119-322 (.370); Nash 111-269 (.413); Van Exel 118-312 (.378); LaFrentz 47-116 (.405)
Bradley 0-1 (.000); Najera 0-1 (.000); Williams 64-171 (.374); Griffin 6-24 (.250); Abdul-Wahad 0-1 (.000); Johnson 0-2 (.000)
Bell 21-51 (.412); Rigaudeau 1-5 (.200); Harrington(>) 1-3 (.333); Opponents 477-1401 (.340)

DENVER NUGGETS

									REBOUNDS									SCORING		
	G	Min.	FGM	FGA	Pct.	FTM	FTA	Pct.	Off.	Def.	Tot.	Ast.	PF	Dq.	Stl.	TO	Blk.	Pts.	Avg.	Hi.
Juwan Howard 77	77	2730	567	1261	.450	282	351	.803	181	404	585	234	239	2	77	189	27	1418	18.4	30
James Posey(>) 25	25	872	121	324	.373	86	102	.843	38	107	145	78	63	1	29	66	6	352	14.1	24
Nene Hilario 80	80	2258	321	619	.519	197	341	.578	208	283	491	149	295	4	127	181	65	839	10.5	24
Chris Whitney(>) 29	29	762	94	261	.360	46	57	.807	1	45	46	124	77	1	17	55	1	277	9.6	23
Rodney White 72	72	1563	260	638	.408	98	125	.784	43	170	213	121	134	1	45	156	32	650	9.0	23
Shammond Williams(*) 27	27	712	94	241	.390	30	45	.667	12	49	61	138	56	0	16	53	3	255	9.4	22
Shammond Williams(!) 78	78	1881	228	579	.394	78	102	.765	24	147	171	266	140	0	77	114	6	627	8.0	22
Donnell Harvey 77	77	1613	246	551	.446	118	176	.670	125	284	409	100	203	2	48	123	27	611	7.9	23
Marcus Camby 29	29	616	93	227	.410	33	50	.660	75	133	208	47	69	1	20	27	40	221	7.6	18
Vincent Yarbrough . . . 59	59	1381	168	428	.393	49	62	.790	36	126	162	130	145	2	57	81	33	406	6.9	18
Jeff Trepagnier 8	8	97	17	40	.425	7	7	1.000	8	8	16	6	5	0	8	8	0	45	5.6	15
Kenny Satterfield(>) . . 22	22	420	51	165	.309	16	23	.696	12	23	35	53	30	0	18	36	2	123	5.6	15
Mark Blount(>) 54	54	885	105	267	.393	71	99	.717	62	121	183	35	112	1	22	70	51	281	5.2	15
Chris Andersen 59	59	907	114	285	.400	77	140	.550	109	165	274	32	90	1	30	60	60	305	5.2	16
Junior Harrington 82	82	2003	169	467	.362	73	112	.652	44	206	250	277	250	6	80	157	15	418	5.1	17
Nikoloz Tskitishvili 81	81	1320	115	393	.293	48	65	.738	64	117	181	91	136	1	31	84	29	315	3.9	17

	G	Min.	FGM	FGA	Pct.	FTM	FTA	Pct.	Off.	Def.	Tot.	Ast.	PF	Dq.	Stl.	TO	Blk.	Pts.	Avg.	Hi.
									REBOUNDS									SCORING		
Ryan Bowen	62	996	97	197	.492	27	41	.659	78	79	157	54	82	0	65	43	29	223	3.6	14
John Crotty	12	180	14	41	.341	9	15	.600	1	14	15	29	16	0	3	9	0	41	3.4	8
Predrag Savovic	27	256	29	93	.312	21	29	.724	9	16	25	22	33	0	14	21	1	83	3.1	11
Devin Brown(*)	3	71	7	25	.280	4	6	.667	4	7	11	5	11	0	4	4	1	18	6.0	8
Devin Brown(!)	10	93	12	35	.343	6	8	.750	8	10	18	7	14	0	4	9	1	30	3.0	8
Adam Harrington(*)	6	74	7	20	.350	1	2	.500	1	5	6	10	6	0	1	0	0	19	3.2	9
Adam Harrington(!)	19	111	11	37	.297	3	4	.750	1	7	8	12	8	0	2	2	1	30	1.6	9
Mark Bryant(>)	3	14	0	1	.000	1	2	.500	1	1	2	2	4	0	0	2	0	1	0.3	1

3-pt. FG: Denver 229-824 (.278)
Howard 2-4 (.500); Posey(>) 24-88 (.273); Hilario 0-3 (.000); Whitney(>) 43-128 (.336); White 32-134 (.239); Harvey 1-7 (.143)
Williams(*) 37-102 (.363); Williams(!) 93-261 (.356); Camby 2-5 (.400); Yarbrough 21-78 (.269); Trepagnier 4-8 (.500)
Satterfield(>) 5-28 (.179); Andersen 0-1 (.000); J. Harrington 7-28 (.250); Tskitishvili 37-152 (.243); Bowen 2-7 (.286)
Crotty 4-13 (.308); Savovic 4-26 (.154); Brown(*) 0-1 (.000); Brown(!) 0-1 (.000); A. Harrington(*) 4-11 (.364)
A. Harrington(!) 5-14 (.357); Opponents 420-1134 (.370)

DETROIT PISTONS

	G	Min.	FGM	FGA	Pct.	FTM	FTA	Pct.	Off.	Def.	Tot.	Ast.	PF	Dq.	Stl.	TO	Blk.	Pts.	Avg.	Hi.
									REBOUNDS									SCORING		
Richard Hamilton	82	2640	570	1286	.443	440	528	.833	88	230	318	208	249	2	64	200	13	1612	19.7	34
Chauncey Billups	74	2327	366	870	.421	318	362	.878	38	235	273	287	136	0	63	134	15	1199	16.2	33
Clifford Robinson	81	2825	372	935	.398	161	238	.676	81	237	318	268	259	5	87	158	88	992	12.2	25
Corliss Williamson	82	2061	374	826	.453	237	300	.790	147	211	358	104	238	1	44	126	27	987	12.0	22
Chucky Atkins	65	1398	168	465	.361	40	49	.816	21	75	96	175	108	0	27	77	4	462	7.1	21
Jon Barry	80	1473	191	424	.450	86	100	.860	33	147	180	206	104	0	63	81	14	555	6.9	19
Ben Wallace	73	2873	210	437	.481	85	189	.450	293	833	1126	120	179	0	104	88	230	506	6.9	17
Mehmet Okur	72	1366	180	423	.426	96	131	.733	117	218	335	71	167	0	25	66	39	494	6.9	22
Zeljko Rebraca	30	488	80	145	.552	38	48	.792	27	65	92	9	79	1	6	29	17	198	6.6	21
Tayshaun Prince	42	435	53	118	.449	11	17	.647	5	40	45	24	25	0	10	21	14	137	3.3	13
Michael Curry	78	1555	92	229	.402	36	45	.800	16	111	127	104	163	0	44	43	4	236	3.0	11
Danny Manning	13	89	13	32	.406	5	6	.833	7	11	18	7	11	0	9	7	3	34	2.6	18
Hubert Davis	43	328	31	70	.302	5	6	.833	6	30	36	29	23	0	5	11	0	79	1.8	11
Don Reid	1	10	0	3	.000	1	2	.500	0	0	0	0	4	0	0	0	0	1	1.0	1
Pepe Sanchez	9	37	0	5	.000	0	0	—	4	2	6	8	3	0	5	2	0	0	0.0	0

3-pt. FG: Detroit 533-1488 (.358)
Hamilton 32-119 (.209); Billups 140-380 (.392); Robinson 87-259 (.336); Williamson 2-11 (.182); Atkins 86-242 (.355)
Barry 87-214 (.407); Wallace 1-6 (.167); Okur 38-112 (.339); Prince 20-47 (.426); Curry 16-54 (.296); Manning 3-8 (.375)
Davis 12-36 (.333); Opponents 289-839 (.344)

GOLDEN STATE WARRIORS

	G	Min.	FGM	FGA	Pct.	FTM	FTA	Pct.	Off.	Def.	Tot.	Ast.	PF	Dq.	Stl.	TO	Blk.	Pts.	Avg.	Hi.
									REBOUNDS									SCORING		
Antawn Jamison	82	3226	691	1471	.470	375	475	.789	195	383	578	156	197	1	76	177	45	1822	22.2	41
Gilbert Arenas	82	2866	509	1180	.431	370	468	.791	97	289	386	514	260	3	124	290	17	1497	18.3	41
Jason Richardson	82	2698	476	1161	.410	207	271	.764	111	267	378	247	201	1	90	179	23	1282	15.6	39
Troy Murphy	79	2510	338	749	.451	244	290	.841	228	578	806	106	246	1	65	111	30	923	11.7	24
Earl Boykins	68	1321	199	464	.429	173	200	.865	35	53	88	221	75	0	38	73	4	600	8.8	28
Erick Dampier	82	1978	259	522	.496	155	222	.698	248	295	543	58	242	3	27	112	154	673	8.2	31
Bob Sura	55	1130	135	328	.412	103	148	.696	58	109	167	177	108	0	45	82	2	401	7.3	16
Mike Dunleavy	82	1305	168	417	.403	78	100	.780	66	148	214	106	120	0	53	86	19	466	5.7	21
Adonal Foyle	82	1787	185	345	.536	70	104	.673	176	314	490	37	214	3	40	73	205	440	5.4	10
Chris Mills	21	262	39	106	.368	16	18	.889	19	31	50	22	29	0	7	10	3	101	4.8	14
Danny Fortson	17	223	20	54	.370	19	29	.655	28	45	73	12	43	0	9	15	0	59	3.5	11
Oscar Torres	17	109	16	36	.444	14	20	.700	3	9	12	3	9	0	4	8	2	53	3.1	16
Jiri Welsch	37	234	19	75	.253	22	29	.759	12	16	28	27	32	1	8	19	2	61	1.6	8
Dean Oliver	15	93	7	29	.241	7	8	.875	8	8	16	23	9	0	7	10	0	22	1.5	5
A.J. Guyton	2	9	0	4	.000	0	0	—	0	0	0	2	0	0	1	1	0	0	0.0	0
Guy Rucker	3	4	0	0	—	0	0	—	0	1	1	1	0	0	0	0	0	0	0.0	0

3-pt. FG: Golden State 425-1235 (.344)
Jamison 65-209 (.311); Arenas 109-313 (.348); Richardson 123-334 (.368); Murphy 3-14 (.214); Boykins 29-77 (.377)
Dampier 0-2 (.000); Sura 28-85 (.329); Dunleavy 52-150 (.347); Foyle 0-1 (.000); Mills 7-25 (.280); Fortson 0-1 (.000)
Torres 7-13 (.538); Welsch 1-4 (.250); Oliver 1-6 (.167); Guyton 0-1 (.000); Opponents 438-1177 (.372)

HOUSTON ROCKETS

	G	Min.	FGM	FGA	Pct.	FTM	FTA	Pct.	Off.	Def.	Tot.	Ast.	PF	Dq.	Stl.	TO	Blk.	Pts.	Avg.	Hi.
									REBOUNDS									SCORING		
Steve Francis	81	3318	571	1312	.435	476	595	.800	159	340	499	502	251	2	141	299	41	1703	21.0	44
Cuttino Mobley	73	3044	463	1067	.434	242	282	.858	70	233	303	208	185	0	95	166	36	1280	17.5	31
Ming Yao	82	2382	401	805	.498	301	371	.811	196	479	675	137	230	1	31	173	147	1104	13.5	30
James Posey(*)	58	1646	188	428	.439	119	144	.826	52	229	281	106	134	0	77	78	9	541	9.3	26
James Posey(!)	83	2518	309	752	.411	205	246	.833	90	336	426	184	197	1	106	144	15	893	10.8	26
Kenny Thomas(>)	20	586	82	190	.432	33	45	.733	45	92	137	39	49	0	16	40	6	197	9.9	29
Glen Rice	62	1532	196	457	.429	63	83	.759	28	126	154	65	99	0	23	55	5	556	9.0	25
Eddie Griffin	77	1890	271	678	.400	58	94	.617	138	323	461	86	136	1	52	76	111	664	8.6	23
Maurice Taylor	67	1377	231	535	.432	100	138	.725	95	143	238	66	151	0	22	100	22	562	8.4	30

	G	Min.	FGM	FGA	Pct.	FTM	FTA	Pct.	Off.	Def.	Tot.	Ast.	PF	Dq.	Stl.	TO	Blk.	Pts.	Avg.	Hi.
Kelvin Cato	73	1247	133	256	.520	66	124	.532	132	296	428	20	176	0	38	56	85	332	4.5	22
Moochie Norris	82	1375	134	330	.406	78	114	.684	37	122	159	196	72	0	55	86	4	357	4.4	16
Terence Morris	49	632	82	176	.466	11	14	.786	40	88	128	25	35	0	8	29	17	182	3.7	17
Jason Collier	13	104	17	36	.472	2	2	1.000	12	17	29	1	10	0	2	2	1	36	2.8	11
Juaquin Hawkins	58	685	57	148	.385	10	20	.500	16	62	78	47	57	0	29	29	6	134	2.3	14
Bostjan Nachbar	14	77	11	31	.355	5	10	.500	3	8	11	3	13	0	2	6	2	29	2.1	5
Tito Maddox	9	35	3	12	.250	5	8	.625	1	6	7	5	4	0	3	3	1	11	1.2	5

3-pt. FG: Houston 439-1267 (.346)
Francis 85-240 (.354); Mobley 112-318 (.352); Yao 1-2 (.500); Posey(*) 46-141 (.326); Posey(!) 70-229 (.306); Rice 101-254 (.398) Griffin 64-192 (.333); Taylor 0-2 (.000); Cato 0-4 (.000); Norris 11-45 (.244); Morris 7-32 (.219); Hawkins 10-24 (.417) Nachbar 2-10 (.200); Maddox 0-3 (.000); Opponents 386-1113 (.347)

INDIANA PACERS

	G	Min.	FGM	FGA	Pct.	FTM	FTA	Pct.	Off.	Def.	Tot.	Ast.	PF	Dq.	Stl.	TO	Blk.	Pts.	Avg.	Hi.
Jermaine O'Neal	77	2864	610	1260	.484	373	510	.731	202	594	796	155	277	5	66	180	178	1600	20.8	38
Ron Artest	69	2317	362	846	.428	273	371	.736	101	261	362	198	242	7	159	145	50	1068	15.5	32
Brad Miller	73	2270	329	667	.493	292	357	.818	185	418	603	193	203	0	65	118	43	955	13.1	29
Reggie Miller	70	2117	281	637	.441	207	230	.900	21	151	172	170	89	0	62	66	4	882	12.6	28
Al Harrington	82	2467	389	896	.434	211	274	.770	159	352	511	125	280	3	71	163	33	1002	12.2	40
Jamaal Tinsley	73	2237	220	556	.396	80	112	.714	58	202	260	548	201	2	125	192	18	566	7.8	21
Ron Mercer	72	1671	244	597	.409	65	81	.802	32	122	154	112	123	1	49	54	14	556	7.7	22
Jonathan Bender	46	819	112	254	.441	60	84	.714	42	91	133	42	86	0	8	42	56	303	6.6	22
Erick Strickland	71	1275	163	380	.429	70	87	.805	23	122	145	209	111	0	38	98	7	458	6.5	22
Austin Croshere	49	633	86	209	.411	53	65	.815	40	115	155	56	48	0	6	28	13	252	5.1	17
Tim Hardaway	10	127	18	49	.367	2	4	.500	1	14	15	24	8	0	9	11	0	49	4.9	14
Jamison Brewer	10	80	9	17	.529	4	9	.444	5	4	9	18	11	0	2	6	1	22	2.2	8
Jeff Foster	77	802	64	178	.360	34	63	.540	118	161	279	51	103	0	28	34	21	162	2.1	12
Primoz Brezec	22	111	15	38	.395	12	20	.600	13	10	23	4	16	0	2	7	4	42	1.9	6
Fred Jones	19	115	9	24	.375	3	4	.750	4	5	9	5	13	0	6	6	1	23	1.2	6

3-pt. FG: Indiana 379-1119 (.339)
O'Neal 7-21 (.333); Artest 71-211 (.336); B. Miller 5-16 (.313); R. Miller 113-318 (.355); Harrington 13-46 (.283) Tinsley 46-166 (.277); Mercer 3-16 (.188); Bender 19-53 (.358); Strickland 62-160 (.388); Croshere 27-69 (.391); Brewer 0-2 (.000) Hardaway 11-31 (.355); J. Foster 0-2 (.000); Brezec 0-1 (.000); Jones 2-7 (.286); Opponents 407-1197 (.340)

LOS ANGELES CLIPPERS

	G	Min.	FGM	FGA	Pct.	FTM	FTA	Pct.	Off.	Def.	Tot.	Ast.	PF	Dq.	Stl.	TO	Blk.	Pts.	Avg.	Hi.
Elton Brand	62	2454	451	899	.502	244	356	.685	283	420	703	157	204	3	71	161	158	1146	18.5	34
Corey Maggette	64	2006	343	773	.444	325	405	.802	77	245	322	123	194	6	55	147	16	1073	16.8	34
Lamar Odom	49	1679	268	611	.439	136	175	.777	59	267	326	178	181	6	42	140	41	714	14.6	30
Andre Miller	80	2913	377	928	.406	311	391	.795	84	232	316	537	203	3	99	206	11	1088	13.6	37
Michael Olowokandi	36	1369	186	436	.427	69	105	.657	57	271	328	47	110	5	18	98	79	441	12.3	24
Eric Piatkowski	62	1360	210	446	.471	101	122	.828	44	112	156	70	92	0	33	56	9	601	9.7	27
Quentin Richardson	59	1368	203	546	.372	85	124	.685	98	183	281	52	92	0	35	64	10	552	9.4	24
Marko Jaric	66	1379	179	446	.401	79	105	.752	35	125	160	193	125	0	97	103	11	490	7.4	25
Keyon Dooling	55	969	128	329	.389	44	57	.772	9	63	72	89	93	0	24	60	6	350	6.4	18
Cherokee Parks	30	648	82	163	.503	23	38	.605	46	86	132	21	52	0	16	18	20	188	6.3	18
Melvin Ely	52	802	92	186	.495	52	74	.703	64	110	174	15	95	0	10	50	32	236	4.5	14
Zhizhi Wang	41	412	62	162	.383	42	58	.724	26	51	77	10	41	0	8	31	10	182	4.4	21
Tremaine Fowlkes	37	573	56	128	.438	50	59	.847	41	62	103	23	63	0	25	20	2	164	4.4	16
Sean Rooks	70	1344	125	297	.421	47	58	.810	53	163	216	69	174	3	34	66	44	297	4.2	16
Chris Wilcox	46	479	73	140	.521	25	50	.500	32	72	104	21	65	2	7	26	12	171	3.7	16

3-pt. FG: L.A. Clippers 390-1178 (.331)
Brand 0-1 (.000); Maggette 62-177 (.350); Odom 42-129 (.326); Miller 23-108 (.213); Piatkowski 80-201 (.398); Jaric 53-166 (.319) Richardson 61-198 (.308); Dooling 50-139 (.360); Parks 1-2 (.500); Wang 16-47 (.340); Fowlkes 2-9 (.222); Rooks 0-1 (.000) Opponents 454-1244 (.365)

LOS ANGELES LAKERS

	G	Min.	FGM	FGA	Pct.	FTM	FTA	Pct.	Off.	Def.	Tot.	Ast.	PF	Dq.	Stl.	TO	Blk.	Pts.	Avg.	Hi.
Kobe Bryant	82	3401	868	1924	.451	601	713	.843	106	458	564	481	218	0	181	288	67	2461	30.0	55
Shaquille O'Neal	67	2535	695	1211	.574	451	725	.622	259	483	742	206	229	4	38	196	159	1841	27.5	48
Derek Fisher	82	2829	339	775	.437	100	125	.800	40	199	239	298	195	4	93	94	15	863	10.5	24
Rick Fox	76	2181	262	621	.422	52	69	.754	64	259	323	253	215	4	69	121	14	681	9.0	23
Devean George	71	1613	180	461	.390	83	105	.790	91	195	286	92	180	2	56	65	38	492	6.9	25
Robert Horry	80	2343	184	476	.387	103	134	.769	181	333	514	233	247	2	96	112	61	522	6.5	17
Samaki Walker	67	1243	115	274	.420	66	101	.653	115	253	368	64	143	4	20	56	55	296	4.4	14
Slava Medvedenko	58	620	112	258	.434	31	43	.721	66	75	141	18	118	0	11	37	8	255	4.4	15
Brian Shaw	72	900	101	261	.387	10	15	.667	20	99	119	103	62	0	32	54	13	250	3.5	20
Mark Madsen	54	781	69	163	.423	36	61	.590	86	73	159	38	116	0	15	27	19	174	3.2	12
Kareem Rush	76	872	96	244	.393	16	23	.696	26	68	94	68	71	0	10	63	11	227	3.0	11
Jannero Pargo	34	342	37	93	.398	4	4	1.000	9	28	37	39	45	0	13	23	2	85	2.5	18
Tracy Murray	31	193	23	71	.324	7	9	.778	5	18	23	12	22	0	5	14	3	61	2.0	11
Soumaila Samake	13	77	10	24	.417	2	2	1.000	10	13	23	4	13	0	0	2	5	22	1.7	10

3-pt. FG: L.A. Lakers 486-1367 (.356)
Bryant 124-324 (.383); Fisher 85-212 (.401); Fox 105-280 (.375); George 49-132 (.371); Horry 51-177 (.288); Walker 0-1 (.000) Medvedenko 0-2 (.000); Shaw 38-109 (.340); Rush 19-68 (.279); Pargo 7-24 (.292); Murray 8-38 (.211); Opponents 465-1223 (.380)

MEMPHIS GRIZZLIES

	G	Min.	FGM	FGA	Pct.	FTM	FTA	Pct.	Off.	Def.	Tot.	Ast.	PF	Dq.	Stl.	TO	Blk.	Pts.	Avg.	Hi.
Pau Gasol	82	2948	569	1116	.510	416	565	.736	192	528	720	229	220	3	34	213	148	1555	19.0	32
Mike Miller(*)	16	360	77	151	.510	29	36	.806	6	49	55	31	34	1	6	26	5	205	12.8	29
Mike Miller(!)	65	2186	373	859	.434	156	186	.839	46	295	341	170	173	2	42	125	21	1011	15.6	33
Jason Williams	76	2407	333	859	.388	110	131	.840	25	187	212	631	130	0	91	168	10	919	12.1	28
Drew Gooden(>)	51	1329	255	576	.443	92	132	.697	105	190	295	63	121	1	38	105	22	616	12.1	25
Lorenzen Wright	70	1982	325	716	.454	147	223	.659	170	358	528	80	209	7	51	110	54	797	11.4	24
Gordan Giricek(>)	49	1187	207	478	.433	88	107	.822	18	90	108	70	104	0	22	94	6	548	11.2	31
Wesley Person	66	1941	274	601	.456	79	97	.814	24	168	192	112	64	0	42	56	19	727	11.0	27
Shane Battier	78	2383	275	569	.483	120	145	.828	128	217	345	105	207	0	102	68	88	756	9.7	22
Stromile Swift	67	1478	235	489	.481	177	245	.722	114	270	384	45	152	3	55	99	104	647	9.7	24
Mike Batiste	75	1248	197	467	.422	69	88	.784	82	175	257	52	120	1	42	69	16	481	6.4	18
Earl Watson	79	1366	170	391	.436	62	86	.721	46	118	164	225	138	0	89	88	14	433	5.5	21
Michael Dickerson	6	87	10	24	.417	5	5	1.000	1	5	6	8	16	0	5	6	1	29	4.8	7
Chris Owens	1	6	2	3	.667	0	0	—	1	0	1	0	0	0	0	1	0	4	4.0	4
Brevin Knight	55	928	97	228	.425	20	37	.541	15	66	81	233	123	0	69	94	2	216	3.9	11
Ryan Humphrey(*)	13	122	12	35	.343	5	11	.455	4	26	30	4	18	0	5	2	2	29	2.2	5
Ryan Humphrey(!)	48	444	35	120	.292	23	39	.590	34	65	99	11	75	1	9	23	18	93	1.9	8
Robert Archibald	12	72	6	20	.300	7	18	.389	6	11	17	3	9	0	0	7	3	19	1.6	4
Cezary Trybanski	15	86	5	20	.250	4	10	.400	6	8	14	1	13	0	0	8	6	14	0.9	5

3-pt. FG: Memphis 467-1279 (.365).
Gasol 1-10 (.100); Miller(*) 22-44 (.500); Miller(!) 109-300 (.363); Williams 143-404 (.354); Gooden(>) 14-46 (.304)
Wright 0-5 (.000); Giricek(>) 46-130 (.354); Person 100-231 (.433); Battier 86-216 (.398); Swift 0-2 (.000); Batiste 18-81 (.222)
Watson 31-91 (.341); Dickerson 4-11 (.364); Knight 2-8 (.250); Opponents 431-1188 (.363)

MIAMI HEAT

	G	Min.	FGM	FGA	Pct.	FTM	FTA	Pct.	Off.	Def.	Tot.	Ast.	PF	Dq.	Stl.	TO	Blk.	Pts.	Avg.	Hi.
Eddie Jones	47	1789	291	688	.423	189	230	.822	35	191	226	173	137	1	64	85	31	869	18.5	38
Caron Butler	78	2858	429	1032	.416	309	375	.824	135	262	397	213	230	3	137	192	31	1201	15.4	35
Brian Grant	82	2641	344	676	.509	158	205	.771	241	596	837	104	300	8	63	129	47	846	10.3	24
Malik Allen	80	2318	335	790	.424	97	121	.802	134	291	425	54	234	1	37	128	78	767	9.6	23
Travis Best	72	1807	231	583	.396	105	123	.854	20	121	147	265	174	6	44	106	7	603	8.4	22
Mike James	78	1722	218	585	.373	104	142	.732	26	123	149	246	176	1	64	108	5	607	7.8	20
Rasual Butler	72	1514	207	572	.362	76	104	.731	29	157	186	93	105	0	21	77	43	540	7.5	22
Eddie House	55	1025	172	444	.387	31	36	.861	17	84	101	87	73	0	44	46	1	411	7.5	21
Vladimir Stepania	79	1594	105	427	.133	71	134	.530	211	343	554	24	169	0	45	69	40	441	5.6	17
LaPhonso Ellis	55	784	100	262	.382	50	66	.758	44	113	157	15	88	0	15	31	15	277	5.0	16
Sean Lampley	35	487	56	129	.434	57	82	.695	26	57	83	31	43	0	7	25	3	169	4.8	18
Anthony Carter	49	912	83	233	.356	33	50	.660	12	71	83	203	70	0	45	81	5	199	4.1	12
Sean Marks	23	223	22	59	.373	10	15	.667	8	27	35	3	37	1	5	14	6	54	2.3	6
Ken Johnson	16	156	15	37	.405	2	6	.333	4	28	32	0	20	0	1	6	12	32	2.0	8

3-pt. FG: Miami 348-1100 (.316)
Jones 98-241 (.407); C. Butler 34-107 (.318); Allen 0-4 (.000); Best 36-109 (.330); James 67-228 (.294); R. Butler 50-171 (.292)
House 36-120 (.300); Ellis 27-107 (.252); Lampley 0-4 (.000); Carter 0-8 (.000); Marks 0-1 (.000); Opponents 406-1149 (.353)

MILWAUKEE BUCKS

	G	Min.	FGM	FGA	Pct.	FTM	FTA	Pct.	Off.	Def.	Tot.	Ast.	PF	Dq.	Stl.	TO	Blk.	Pts.	Avg.	Hi.
Ray Allen(>)	47	1683	351	803	.437	178	195	.913	45	173	218	164	149	2	57	117	11	1003	21.3	37
Gary Payton(*)	28	1085	221	474	.466	88	118	.746	23	63	86	206	64	0	40	56	8	550	19.6	28
Gary Payton(!)	80	3208	665	1466	.454	250	352	.710	79	255	334	663	181	0	133	187	20	1634	20.4	40
Sam Cassell	78	2700	546	1162	.470	385	447	.861	57	285	342	450	216	1	88	177	14	1536	19.7	39
Michael Redd	82	2316	455	971	.469	149	185	.805	98	273	371	117	143	0	100	74	13	1241	15.1	35
Desmond Mason(*)	28	952	166	350	.474	78	102	.765	66	122	188	68	74	0	20	41	11	415	14.8	24
Desmond Mason(!)	80	2763	457	1017	.449	212	283	.749	154	369	523	163	210	1	67	115	32	1147	14.3	30
Tim Thomas	80	2358	412	930	.443	145	186	.780	97	292	389	102	257	5	70	133	49	1066	13.3	27
Toni Kukoc	63	1704	249	577	.432	137	194	.706	67	199	266	230	134	0	81	122	29	730	11.6	26
Anthony Mason	65	2199	191	393	.486	84	117	.718	90	326	416	209	147	0	32	79	12	466	7.2	21
Jason Caffey	51	894	113	248	.456	69	106	.651	68	108	176	38	122	3	19	56	15	295	5.8	16
Kevin Ollie(>)	53	1127	117	255	.459	68	91	.747	12	87	99	181	71	0	37	36	4	303	5.7	14
Marcus Haislip	39	441	66	153	.431	26	38	.684	21	32	53	9	55	1	7	21	18	161	4.1	12
Dan Gadzuric	49	760	70	145	.483	29	56	.518	66	131	197	9	125	3	22	27	52	169	3.4	12
Ervin Johnson	69	1170	61	135	.452	30	44	.682	117	177	294	24	178	3	34	34	63	152	2.2	12
Ronald Murray(>)	12	42	9	26	.346	5	8	.625	0	1	1	3	0	0	4	4	0	23	1.9	6
Joel Przybilla	32	546	18	46	.391	12	24	.500	48	97	145	12	85	1	10	19	45	48	1.5	5
Jamal Sampson	5	8	0	2	.000	0	0	—	1	1	2	1	0	0	1	0	0	0	0.0	0

3-pt. FG: Milwaukee 585-1526 (.383)
Allen(>) 123-311 (.395); Payton(*) 20-68 (.294); Payton(!) 54-182 (.297); Cassell 59-163 (.362); Redd 182-416 (.438)
D. Mason(*) 5-17 (.294); D. Mason(!) 21-72 (.292); Thomas 97-265 (.366); Kukoc 95-263 (.361); A. Mason 0-1 (.000)
Ollie(>) 1-5 (.200); Haislip 3-12 (.250); Gadzuric 0-1 (.000); Murray(>) 0-4 (.000); Opponents 479-1278 (.375)

MINNESOTA TIMBERWOLVES

	G	Min.	FGM	FGA	Pct.	FTM	FTA	Pct.	Off.	Def.	Tot.	Ast.	PF	Dq.	Stl.	TO	Blk.	Pts.	Avg.	Hi.
Kevin Garnett	82	3321	743	1481	.502	377	502	.751	244	858	1102	495	199	0	113	229	129	1883	23.0	37
Wally Szczerbiak	52	1886	351	729	.482	150	173	.867	53	188	241	136	123	0	44	87	22	913	17.6	44
Troy Hudson	79	2600	409	956	.428	208	231	.900	42	141	183	452	160	1	60	182	7	1123	14.2	31
Rasho Nesterovic	77	2337	400	762	.525	61	95	.642	146	358	504	114	256	9	39	99	116	861	11.2	23

2002-03

	G	Min.	FGM	FGA	Pct.	FTM	FTA	Pct.	REBOUNDS			Ast.	PF	Dq.	Stl.	TO	Blk.	SCORING		
									Off.	Def.	Tot.							Pts.	Avg.	Hi.
Kendall Gill	82	2068	286	677	.422	123	161	.764	51	197	248	156	176	2	78	108	15	714	8.7	22
Anthony Peeler	82	2245	252	609	.414	39	50	.780	40	201	241	244	161	0	72	82	13	630	7.7	23
Joe Smith	54	1117	151	328	.460	102	131	.779	111	159	270	38	171	2	14	43	55	404	7.5	25
Rod Strickland	47	956	120	278	.432	79	107	.738	20	75	95	215	55	0	46	76	6	320	6.8	16
Gary Trent	80	1222	208	389	.535	60	101	.594	106	185	291	77	142	0	32	59	23	476	6.0	19
Marc Jackson	77	1041	153	349	.438	114	149	.765	86	139	225	37	137	0	24	59	30	421	5.5	18
Mike Wilks(*)	31	324	21	67	.313	16	18	.889	11	19	30	50	31	0	11	12	3	62	2.0	8
Mike Wilks(!)	46	688	50	148	.338	37	47	.787	20	51	71	92	69	0	27	28	4	147	3.2	19
Reggie Slater	26	141	27	50	.540	27	45	.600	18	13	31	4	31	0	6	9	1	81	3.1	10
Loren Woods	38	353	29	76	.382	21	27	.778	27	68	95	19	37	0	10	23	13	80	2.1	18
Igor Rakocevic	42	244	22	58	.379	29	36	.806	4	13	17	33	25	0	4	23	0	78	1.9	9

3-pt. FG: Minnesota 296-804 (.368)
Garnett 20-71 (.282); Szczerbiak 61-145 (.421); Hudson 97-266 (.365); Nesterovic 0-2 (.000); Gill 19-59 (.322); Smith 0-2 (.000)
Peeler 87-212 (.410); Strickland 1-11 (.091); Trent 0-2 (.000); Jackson 1-1 (1.000); Wilks(*) 4-18 (.222); Wilks(!) 10-35 (.286)
Woods 1-3 (.333); Rakocevic 5-12 (.417); Opponents 472-1362 (.347)

NEW JERSEY NETS

	G	Min.	FGM	FGA	Pct.	FTM	FTA	Pct.	REBOUNDS			Ast.	PF	Dq.	Stl.	TO	Blk.	SCORING		
									Off.	Def.	Tot.							Pts.	Avg.	Hi.
Jason Kidd	80	2989	515	1244	.414	339	403	.841	110	394	504	711	127	0	179	296	25	1495	18.7	41
Kenyon Martin	77	2628	509	1082	.470	256	392	.653	164	476	640	185	294	6	98	192	70	1283	16.7	35
Richard Jefferson	80	2879	456	911	.501	324	436	.743	150	364	514	201	216	1	80	156	44	1242	15.5	39
Kerry Kittles	65	1951	332	711	.467	106	135	.785	52	200	252	170	110	1	101	55	30	848	13.0	35
Lucious Harris	77	1973	298	721	.413	152	189	.804	63	169	232	155	95	0	53	71	8	795	10.3	26
Rodney Rogers	68	1303	183	455	.402	68	90	.756	61	202	263	107	192	2	50	91	31	478	7.0	18
Aaron Williams	81	1597	199	439	.453	102	130	.785	137	194	331	88	206	5	27	85	57	500	6.2	15
Dikembe Mutombo	24	514	49	131	.374	40	55	.727	54	99	153	19	54	0	4	34	37	138	5.8	16
Jason Collins	81	1900	140	338	.414	180	236	.763	136	232	368	87	252	4	47	85	44	460	5.7	15
Anthony Johnson	66	842	103	231	.446	51	74	.689	13	65	78	86	93	1	37	41	5	270	4.1	16
Brian Scalabrine	59	724	68	169	.402	30	36	.833	40	101	141	46	77	0	16	46	18	180	3.1	16
Tamar Slay	36	274	39	103	.379	7	10	.700	8	23	31	14	31	0	14	20	3	92	2.6	14
Brandon Armstrong	17	69	9	27	.333	5	6	.833	0	4	4	2	8	0	3	5	1	24	1.4	5
Chris Childs	12	106	6	20	.300	2	3	.667	3	2	5	16	17	0	8	6	1	15	1.3	5
Donny Marshall	3	6	0	3	.000	0	0	—	0	3	3	0	0	0	0	1	0	0	0.0	0

3-pt. FG: New Jersey 346-1041 (.332)
Kidd 126-370 (.341); Martin 9-43 (.209); Jefferson 6-24 (.250); Kittles 78-219 (.356); Harris 47-136 (.346); Rogers 44-132 (.333)
Williams 0-1 (.000); Collins 0-4 (.000); Johnson 13-35 (.371); Scalabrine 14-39 (.359); Slay 7-25 (.280); Armstrong 1-6 (.167)
Childs 1-6 (.167); Marshall 0-1 (.000); Opponents 425-1185 (.359)

NEW ORLEANS HORNETS

	G	Min.	FGM	FGA	Pct.	FTM	FTA	Pct.	REBOUNDS			Ast.	PF	Dq.	Stl.	TO	Blk.	SCORING		
									Off.	Def.	Tot.							Pts.	Avg.	Hi.
Jamal Mashburn	82	3321	670	1586	.422	313	369	.848	66	432	498	462	196	0	83	230	17	1772	21.6	50
Baron Davis	50	1889	332	798	.416	93	131	.710	56	130	186	320	148	3	91	140	22	856	17.1	33
David Wesley	73	2710	449	1037	.433	185	237	.781	38	137	175	251	173	0	109	132	9	1217	16.7	35
P.J. Brown	78	2609	319	601	.531	194	232	.836	243	458	701	147	203	3	67	98	80	832	10.7	20
Jamaal Magloire	82	2443	305	635	.480	231	322	.717	260	464	724	88	276	4	49	158	111	841	10.3	22
Courtney Alexander	66	1360	193	505	.382	118	146	.808	39	79	118	79	125	0	31	68	6	523	7.9	23
Elden Campbell(>)	41	685	101	247	.409	93	115	.809	34	108	142	42	102	2	24	42	31	295	7.2	24
Kenny Anderson(*)	23	446	61	150	.407	16	22	.727	14	31	45	77	43	0	18	42	4	139	6.0	12
Kenny Anderson(!)	61	1135	163	382	.427	45	57	.789	31	101	132	198	106	0	58	75	5	372	6.1	17
Robert Pack	28	440	52	129	.403	41	55	.745	11	40	51	81	35	0	25	40	0	145	5.2	18
George Lynch	81	1497	147	359	.409	41	74	.554	139	214	353	104	136	1	66	52	19	363	4.5	19
Jerome Moiso	51	644	89	171	.520	27	41	.659	59	119	178	22	87	1	19	46	44	205	4.0	13
Robert Traylor	69	851	105	237	.443	57	88	.648	108	154	262	50	153	1	45	53	37	268	3.9	15
Stacey Augmon	70	862	79	192	.411	54	72	.750	26	93	119	69	80	0	27	40	9	212	3.0	12
Randy Livingston	2	12	2	4	.500	2	2	1.000	0	0	0	1	0	0	0	0	0	6	3.0	4
Bryce Drew	13	79	8	27	.296	0	0	---	4	9	13	11	2	0	2	3	0	19	1.5	7
Kirk Haston	12	57	2	17	.118	2	4	.500	0	7	7	3	10	0	0	7	5	6	0.5	2
New Orleans	82	19905	2914	6695	.435	1467	1910	.768	1097	2475	3572	1807	1769	15	656	1212	394	7699	93.9	125
Opponents	82	19905	2857	6518	.438	1474	1925	.766	909	2368	3277	1630	1754	12	647	1196	427	7526	91.8	123

3-pt. FG: New Orleans 404-1075 (.376)
Mashburn 119-306 (.389); Davis 99-283 (.350); Wesley 134-316 (.424); Brown 0-3 (.000); Magloire 0-3 (.000); Alexander 19-57 (.333)
Campbell(>) 0-1 (.000); Anderson(*) 1-2 (.500); Anderson(!) 1-7 (.143); Pack 0-5 (.000); Lynch 28-79 (.354); Traylor 1-3 (.333)
Augmon 0-7 (.000); Drew 3-7 (.429); Haston 0-3 (.000); Opponents 338-1001 (.338)

NEW YORK KNICKERBOCKERS

	G	Min.	FGM	FGA	Pct.	FTM	FTA	Pct.	REBOUNDS			Ast.	PF	Dq.	Stl.	TO	Blk.	SCORING		
									Off.	Def.	Tot.							Pts.	Avg.	Hi.
Allan Houston	82	3108	652	1465	.445	363	395	.919	26	205	231	220	191	2	54	178	7	1845	22.5	53
Latrell Sprewell	74	2859	454	1127	.403	173	218	.794	45	240	285	332	134	2	102	172	22	1215	16.4	38
Kurt Thomas	81	2577	497	1028	.483	138	184	.750	160	477	637	162	344	12	81	138	97	1134	14.0	33
Howard Eisley	82	2243	262	628	.417	89	105	.848	24	162	186	444	222	1	71	149	9	744	9.1	30
Shandon Anderson	82	1731	248	537	.462	139	190	.732	64	190	254	87	177	1	73	114	20	687	8.4	21
Othella Harrington	74	1850	225	443	.508	123	150	.820	165	311	476	62	231	2	12	90	23	573	7.7	21
Charlie Ward	66	1465	165	414	.399	41	53	.774	25	152	177	306	146	1	78	95	11	472	7.2	17
Clarence Weatherspoon	79	2024	186	414	.449	149	194	.768	214	385	599	68	174	0	69	63	36	521	6.6	18
Lee Nailon	38	405	84	190	.442	42	51	.824	32	38	70	26	46	0	6	32	3	210	5.5	20
Michael Doleac	75	1041	146	343	.426	36	46	.783	65	154	219	42	150	1	16	49	16	328	4.4	16

2002-03

	G	Min.	FGM	FGA	Pct.	FTM	FTA	Pct.	Off.	Def.	Tot.	Ast.	PF	Dq.	Stl.	TO	Blk.	Pts.	Avg.	Hi.
									REBOUNDS									**SCORING**		
Lavor Postell	12	98	14	38	.368	13	15	.867	1	3	4	3	9	0	2	7	0	43	3.6	9
Travis Knight........	32	287	25	65	.385	10	13	.769	18	44	62	14	44	0	8	10	9	60	1.9	10
Frank Williams	21	167	9	33	.273	4	6	.667	3	15	18	34	20	0	7	17	2	28	1.3	11

3-pt. FG: New York 606-1582 (.383)
Houston 178-450 (.396); Sprewell 134-360 (.372); Thomas 2-3 (.667); Eisley 131-337 (.389); Anderson 52-140 (.371)
Ward 101-267 (.378); Nailon 0-1 (.000); Postell 2-7 (.286); Knight 0-1 (.000); Williams 6-16 (.375); Opponents 358-1053 (.340)

ORLANDO MAGIC

	G	Min.	FGM	FGA	Pct.	FTM	FTA	Pct.	Off.	Def.	Tot.	Ast.	PF	Dq.	Stl.	TO	Blk.	Pts.	Avg.	Hi.
									REBOUNDS									**SCORING**		
Tracy McGrady	75	2954	829	1813	.457	576	726	.793	121	367	488	411	156	0	124	195	59	2407	32.1	52
Mike Miller(>).......	49	1826	296	708	.418	127	150	.847	40	246	286	139	139	1	36	99	16	806	16.4	33
Grant Hill	29	843	151	307	.492	118	144	.819	40	166	206	122	46	0	28	84	13	421	14.5	29
Drew Gooden(*).....	19	544	100	201	.498	59	80	.738	58	102	160	20	51	1	15	45	13	259	13.6	26
Drew Gooden(!)	70	1873	355	777	.457	151	212	.712	163	292	455	83	172	2	53	150	35	875	12.5	26
Gordan Giricek(*) ...	27	961	143	325	.440	62	76	.816	18	112	130	67	55	0	30	51	2	387	14.3	21
Gordan Giricek(!)	76	2148	350	803	.436	150	183	.820	36	202	238	137	159	0	52	145	8	935	12.3	31
Pat Garrity	81	2584	312	744	.419	83	100	.830	72	234	306	121	255	1	62	77	20	868	10.7	24
Darrell Armstrong....	82	2350	263	643	.409	165	188	.878	91	204	295	323	167	1	135	160	13	769	9.4	21
Chris Whitney(*).....	22	290	30	88	.341	11	12	.917	2	19	21	21	15	0	12	16	1	78	3.5	11
Chris Whitney(!)	51	1052	124	349	.355	57	69	.826	3	64	67	145	92	1	29	71	2	355	7.0	23
Shawn Kemp	79	1633	211	505	.418	115	155	.742	147	304	451	55	239	2	66	102	33	537	6.8	22
Jacque Vaughn	80	1686	184	411	.448	97	125	.776	26	92	118	232	169	1	64	97	2	473	5.9	16
Horace Grant	5	85	13	25	.520	0	0	—	2	6	8	7	5	0	3	1	0	26	5.2	14
Andrew DeClercq	77	1327	149	279	.534	67	104	.644	142	197	339	52	258	5	39	84	36	365	4.7	14
Pat Burke	62	783	113	296	.382	40	58	.690	57	89	146	23	99	1	19	47	25	267	4.3	14
Steven Hunter.......	33	447	56	103	.544	18	44	.409	38	55	93	6	56	0	9	15	36	130	3.9	15
Jeryl Sasser	75	1025	64	207	.309	53	78	.679	64	120	184	65	91	0	45	39	12	194	2.6	26
Ryan Humphrey(>) ..	35	322	23	85	.271	18	28	.643	30	39	69	7	57	1	4	21	16	64	1.8	8
Olumide Oyedeji	45	145	10	23	.435	7	11	.636	10	40	50	5	30	0	5	5	3	27	1.0	6

3-pt. FG: Orlando 568-1590 (.357)
McGrady 173-448 (.386); Miller(>) 87-256 (.340); Hill 1-4 (.250); Gooden(*) 0-2 (.000); Gooden(!) 14-48 (.292); Kemp 0-1 (.000)
Giricek(*) 39-119 (.328); Giricek(!) 85-249 (.341); Garrity 161-407 (.396); Armstrong 78-232 (.336); Whitney(*) 7-36 (.194)
Whitney(!) 50-164 (.305); Vaughn 8-34 (.235); Burke 1-7 (.143); Sasser 13-44 (.295); Opponents 405-1211 (.334)

PHILADELPHIA 76ERS

	G	Min.	FGM	FGA	Pct.	FTM	FTA	Pct.	Off.	Def.	Tot.	Ast.	PF	Dq.	Stl.	TO	Blk.	Pts.	Avg.	Hi.
									REBOUNDS									**SCORING**		
Allen Iverson........	82	3485	804	1940	.414	570	736	.774	68	276	344	454	149	2	225	286	13	2262	27.6	42
Keith Van Horn	74	2337	459	952	.482	193	240	.804	159	365	524	93	251	7	63	150	30	1176	15.9	33
Eric Snow	82	3108	361	799	.452	325	379	.858	71	230	301	544	235	2	133	194	11	1054	12.9	25
Kenny Thomas(*)....	46	1392	178	369	.482	114	152	.750	140	252	392	73	120	2	46	76	22	470	10.2	24
Kenny Thomas(!)	66	1978	260	559	.465	147	197	.746	185	344	529	112	169	2	62	116	28	667	10.1	29
Derrick Coleman	64	1742	223	498	.448	134	171	.784	151	299	450	87	171	2	53	96	69	602	9.4	22
Aaron McKie........	80	2374	286	666	.429	112	134	.836	61	289	350	278	177	2	131	109	9	721	9.0	22
Todd MacCulloch ..	42	812	123	238	.517	53	79	.671	66	130	196	20	107	0	19	35	32	299	7.1	17
Greg Buckner	75	1514	185	398	.465	65	81	.802	72	144	216	96	203	0	72	62	16	450	6.0	16
Brian Skinner	77	1381	182	331	.550	97	161	.602	136	230	366	19	176	1	47	62	53	461	6.0	20
Tyrone Hill(*)	24	496	44	109	.404	21	35	.600	56	68	124	9	68	0	15	16	7	109	4.5	14
Tyrone Hill(!)	56	1351	129	306	.422	54	80	.675	126	265	391	41	172	4	46	68	26	312	5.6	17
Monty Williams......	21	276	34	80	.425	24	32	.750	12	33	45	26	33	0	12	17	5	92	4.4	10
Kenny Satterfield(*) ..	17	82	4	18	.222	1	2	.500	4	4	8	15	6	0	2	7	0	9	0.5	2
Kenny Satterfield(!)..	39	502	55	183	.301	17	25	.680	16	27	43	68	36	0	20	43	2	132	3.4	15
Art Long(>)..........	19	131	19	50	.380	1	5	.200	13	27	40	2	22	0	2	9	8	40	2.1	5
John Salmons.......	64	504	48	116	.414	26	35	.743	16	43	59	47	53	1	17	29	6	132	2.1	9
Efthimios Rentzias ...	35	144	20	59	.339	8	9	.889	10	16	26	7	21	0	6	4	2	52	1.5	9
Mark Bryant(>).......	11	77	5	17	.294	2	2	1.000	7	9	16	1	12	0	1	5	1	12	1.1	6

3-pt. FG: Philadelphia 245-787 (.311)
Iverson 84-303 (.277); Van Horn 65-176 (.369); Snow 7-32 (.219); Coleman 22-67 (.328); McKie 37-112 (.330); Buckner 15-55 (.273)
Williams 0-2 (.000); Satterfield(!) 5-28 (.179); Long(>) 1-1 (1.000); Salmons 10-31 (.323); Rentzias 4-8 (.500)
Opponents 453-1278 (.354)

PHOENIX SUNS

	G	Min.	FGM	FGA	Pct.	FTM	FTA	Pct.	Off.	Def.	Tot.	Ast.	PF	Dq.	Stl.	TO	Blk.	Pts.	Avg.	Hi.
									REBOUNDS									**SCORING**		
Stephon Marbury	81	3240	671	1530	.439	375	467	.803	53	210	263	654	200	1	108	263	20	1806	22.3	43
Shawn Marion.......	81	3373	662	1466	.452	251	295	.851	199	574	773	198	208	0	185	157	95	1716	21.2	36
Amare Stoudemire ...	82	2570	392	830	.472	320	484	.661	250	471	721	78	269	3	62	189	87	1106	13.5	38
Anfernee Hardaway ..	58	1777	256	573	.447	77	97	.794	66	192	258	235	150	1	66	145	26	615	10.6	24
Joe Johnson	82	2255	316	796	.397	96	124	.774	57	207	264	210	143	0	62	108	19	803	9.8	27
Casey Jacobsen	72	1147	122	327	.373	72	105	.686	29	54	83	73	90	0	35	55	6	368	5.1	19
Jake Tsakalidis	33	543	61	135	.452	39	58	.672	45	77	122	13	80	1	6	26	17	161	4.9	13

	G	Min.	FGM	FGA	Pct.	FTM	FTA	Pct.	Off.	Def.	Tot.	Ast.	PF	Dq.	Stl.	TO	Blk.	Pts.	Avg.	Hi.
Tom Gugliotta	27	447	60	132	.455	9	9	1.000	25	75	100	31	35	0	14	31	5	129	4.8	14
Bo Outlaw	80	1800	153	278	.550	72	116	.621	134	234	368	112	194	1	50	76	71	378	4.7	19
Scott Williams	69	872	120	292	.411	33	42	.786	72	121	193	22	159	2	27	32	21	273	4.0	16
Jake Voskuhl	65	947	92	163	.564	64	96	.667	97	128	225	36	172	0	18	48	29	248	3.8	14
Dan Langhi	60	541	81	202	.401	12	20	.600	19	68	87	21	58	0	15	16	6	183	3.1	11
Randy Brown	32	262	16	43	.372	9	12	.750	3	23	26	35	36	0	17	17	2	41	1.3	4
Alton Ford	11	31	3	9	.333	1	3	.333	0	6	6	1	7	0	0	2	0	7	0.6	4

3-pt. FG: Phoenix 394-1149 (.343):
Marbury 89-296 (.301); Marion 141-364 (.387); Stoudemire 2-10 (.200); Hardaway 26-73 (.356); Johnson 75-205 (.366)
Jacobsen 52-165 (.315); Gugliotta 0-1 (.000); Outlaw 0-2 (.000); Williams 0-2 (.000); Langhi 9-31 (.290)
Opponents 436-1361 (.320)

PORTLAND TRAIL BLAZERS

	G	Min.	FGM	FGA	Pct.	FTM	FTA	Pct.	Off.	Def.	Tot.	Ast.	PF	Dq.	Stl.	TO	Blk.	Pts.	Avg.	Hi.
Rasheed Wallace	74	2684	515	1094	.471	200	272	.735	113	435	548	153	223	2	70	140	77	1340	18.1	38
Bonzi Wells	75	2396	437	990	.441	226	313	.722	98	296	394	246	220	2	123	215	18	1138	15.2	37
Derek Anderson	76	2556	355	832	.427	231	269	.859	53	211	264	325	141	1	90	128	16	1057	13.9	31
Scottie Pippen	64	1911	265	597	.444	121	148	.818	57	221	278	285	149	0	105	164	25	689	10.8	26
Zach Randolph	77	1301	264	515	.513	122	161	.758	139	204	343	41	141	0	42	62	14	650	8.4	31
Ruben Patterson	78	1655	254	516	.492	138	220	.627	120	144	264	101	161	0	73	117	29	649	8.3	26
Dale Davis	78	2282	237	438	.541	105	166	.633	233	331	564	94	189	1	51	71	70	579	7.4	17
Damon Stoudamire	59	1315	156	415	.376	53	67	.791	40	115	155	204	67	0	39	82	6	409	6.9	21
Arvydas Sabonis	78	1209	172	361	.476	129	164	.787	88	247	335	142	141	0	61	75	49	476	6.1	16
Jeff McInnis	75	1311	188	423	.444	50	67	.746	22	75	97	170	117	1	21	75	2	432	5.8	17
Antonio Daniels	67	872	84	186	.452	65	76	.855	11	61	72	85	43	0	33	32	9	251	3.7	16
Qyntel Woods	53	334	59	118	.500	7	20	.350	15	38	53	12	36	1	15	23	1	128	2.4	14
Charles Smith	3	13	1	4	.250	3	4	.750	0	0	0	1	3	0	1	1	0	5	1.7	4
Ruben Boumtje-Boumtj.	2	5	0	1	.000	0	0	—	1	0	1	1	0	0	0	0	0	0	0.0	0
Chris Dudley	3	11	0	1	.000	0	0	—	2	0	2	0	3	0	0	0	0	0	0.0	0

3-pt. FG: Portland 379-1150 (.330)
Wallace 110-307 (.358); Wells 38-130 (.292); Anderson 116-331 (.350); Pippen 38-133 (.286); Randolph 0-5 (.000); Woods 3-9 (.333)
Patterson 3-20 (.150); Stoudamire 44-114 (.386); Sabonis 3-6 (.500); McInnis 6-35 (.171); Daniels 18-59 (.305); Smith 0-1 (.000)
Opponents 438-1285 (.341)

SACRAMENTO KINGS

	G	Min.	FGM	FGA	Pct.	FTM	FTA	Pct.	Off.	Def.	Tot.	Ast.	PF	Dq.	Stl.	TO	Blk.	Pts.	Avg.	Hi.
Chris Webber	67	2622	661	1433	.461	215	354	.607	160	544	704	364	204	1	106	215	88	1542	23.0	36
Peja Stojakovic	72	2450	497	1034	.481	231	264	.875	61	336	397	141	143	1	72	101	5	1380	19.2	37
Mike Bibby	55	1835	329	700	.470	161	187	.861	34	113	147	285	93	0	72	127	8	875	15.9	30
Bobby Jackson	59	1676	340	732	.464	126	149	.846	57	162	219	182	126	0	71	106	3	895	15.2	31
Vlade Divac	80	2384	305	655	.466	179	251	.713	157	417	574	274	239	3	83	152	105	795	9.9	24
Doug Christie	80	2710	267	557	.479	141	174	.810	61	281	342	376	186	1	180	144	37	748	9.4	25
Jim Jackson	63	1309	204	462	.442	47	55	.855	84	178	262	118	132	0	31	80	4	487	7.7	23
Keon Clark	80	1780	226	451	.501	84	128	.656	138	313	451	80	227	2	38	94	150	536	6.7	19
Hedo Turkoglu	67	1175	165	391	.422	88	110	.800	35	153	188	87	125	0	25	50	12	447	6.7	22
Gerald Wallace	47	571	90	183	.492	39	74	.527	38	90	128	23	68	0	24	44	15	220	4.7	21
Damon Jones	49	709	80	210	.381	20	27	.741	11	59	70	80	42	0	18	23	4	224	4.6	18
Scot Pollard	23	325	40	87	.460	23	38	.605	46	60	106	6	50	0	13	15	15	103	4.5	15
Lawrence Funderburke	27	229	32	72	.444	10	17	.588	17	38	55	8	25	0	1	6	11	74	2.7	10
Mateen Cleaves	12	55	6	23	.261	3	4	.750	1	7	8	10	6	0	2	14	0	16	1.3	7

3-pt. FG: Sacramento 491-1288 (.381).
Webber 5-21 (.238); Stojakovic 155-406 (.382); Bibby 56-137 (.409); B. Jackson 89-235 (.379); Divac 6-25 (.240); Clark 0-4 (.000)
Christie 73-185 (.395); J. Jackson 32-71 (.451); Turkoglu 29-78 (.372); Wallace 1-4 (.250); Jones 44-121 (.364)
Cleaves 1-1 (1.000); Opponents 373-1166 (.320)

SAN ANTONIO SPURS

	G	Min.	FGM	FGA	Pct.	FTM	FTA	Pct.	Off.	Def.	Tot.	Ast.	PF	Dq.	Stl.	TO	Blk.	Pts.	Avg.	Hi.
Tim Duncan	81	3181	714	1392	.513	450	634	.710	259	784	1043	316	231	2	55	248	237	1884	23.3	38
Tony Parker	82	2774	484	1043	.464	219	290	.755	33	183	216	432	174	2	71	198	4	1269	15.5	32
Stephen Jackson	80	2254	356	818	.435	139	183	.760	66	220	286	183	202	1	125	176	30	946	11.8	28
Malik Rose	79	1933	289	630	.459	242	306	.791	148	358	506	124	206	2	57	170	40	822	10.4	34
David Robinson	64	1676	197	420	.469	152	214	.710	163	345	508	61	126	1	52	83	111	546	8.5	20
Manu Ginobili	69	1431	174	397	.438	126	171	.737	47	114	161	138	170	3	96	100	17	525	7.6	20
Bruce Bowen	82	2566	223	479	.466	36	89	.404	59	180	239	113	195	0	66	72	42	583	7.1	21
Steve Smith	53	1032	113	291	.388	95	114	.833	21	78	99	70	79	0	28	43	9	360	6.8	15
Speedy Claxton	30	471	67	145	.462	39	57	.684	22	34	56	75	43	0	22	35	7	173	5.8	16
Kevin Willis	71	840	123	257	.479	51	83	.614	83	143	226	24	120	1	20	60	20	297	4.2	15
Steve Kerr	75	952	110	256	.430	30	34	.882	12	48	60	70	49	0	27	35	3	299	4.0	17
Danny Ferry	64	601	44	124	.355	10	13	.769	20	55	75	21	55	0	7	27	9	119	1.9	10
Devin Brown(>)	7	22	5	10	.500	2	2	1.000	4	3	7	2	3	0	0	5	0	12	1.7	4
Anthony Goldwire(>)	10	51	5	18	.278	0	2	.000	0	3	3	3	5	0	3	2	0	12	1.2	7

	G	Min.	FGM	FGA	Pct.	FTM	FTA	Pct.	Off.	Def.	Tot.	Ast.	PF	Dq.	Stl.	TO	Blk.	Pts.	Avg.	Hi.
									REBOUNDS									**SCORING**		
Mengke Bateer	12	46	4	17	.235	0	2	.000	2	8	10	4	14	0	0	6	0	9	0.8	5

3-pt. FG: San Antonio 449-1270 (.354).
Duncan 6-22 (.273); Parker 82-243 (.337); Jackson 95-297 (.320); Rose 2-5 (.400); Ginobili 51-148 (.345); Bowen 101-229 (.441)
Smith 39-118 (.331); Claxton 0-11 (.000); Willis 0-2 (.000); Kerr 49-124 (.395); Ferry 21-60 (.350); Goldwire(>) 2-8 (.250)
Bateer 1-3 (.333); Opponents 354-1043 (.339)

SEATTLE SUPERSONICS

	G	Min.	FGM	FGA	Pct.	FTM	FTA	Pct.	Off.	Def.	Tot.	Ast.	PF	Dq.	Stl.	TO	Blk.	Pts.	Avg.	Hi.
									REBOUNDS									**SCORING**		
Ray Allen(*)	29	1197	247	560	.441	138	150	.920	49	114	163	170	71	2	46	81	3	710	24.5	40
Ray Allen(!)	76	2880	598	1363	.439	316	345	.916	94	287	381	334	220	4	103	198	14	1713	22.5	40
Gary Payton(>)	52	2123	444	992	.448	162	234	.692	56	192	248	457	117	0	93	131	12	1084	20.8	40
Rashard Lewis	77	3044	519	1149	.452	283	345	.820	152	351	503	133	205	1	99	143	35	1396	18.1	37
Desmond Mason(>)	52	1811	291	667	.436	134	181	.740	88	247	335	95	136	1	47	74	21	732	14.1	30
Brent Barry	75	2480	264	577	.458	128	161	.795	48	253	301	384	199	1	113	142	15	774	10.3	25
Vladimir Radmanovic	72	1910	274	668	.410	72	102	.706	76	247	323	97	136	0	64	100	22	724	10.1	29
Predrag Drobnjak	82	1984	325	789	.412	91	115	.791	111	209	320	86	180	0	48	65	38	771	9.4	26
Kevin Ollie(*)	29	770	82	186	.441	66	87	.759	13	70	83	110	51	0	32	36	1	231	8.0	15
Kevin Ollie(!)	82	1897	199	441	.451	134	178	.753	25	157	182	291	122	0	69	72	5	534	6.5	15
Kenny Anderson(>)	38	689	102	232	.440	29	35	.829	17	70	87	121	63	0	40	33	1	233	6.1	17
Elden Campbell(*)	15	184	16	48	.333	16	21	.762	13	26	39	9	27	0	9	8	8	48	3.2	10
Elden Campbell(!)	56	869	117	295	.397	109	136	.801	47	134	181	51	129	2	33	50	39	343	6.1	24
Jerome James	51	766	111	232	.478	54	92	.587	78	138	216	27	166	3	12	75	82	276	5.4	13
Vitaly Potapenko	26	403	41	93	.441	22	29	.759	25	64	89	4	46	0	9	25	8	104	4.0	13
Reggie Evans	67	1365	66	140	.471	80	154	.519	167	278	445	34	173	2	38	52	11	212	3.2	13
Calvin Booth	47	575	52	119	.437	34	47	.723	32	77	109	12	74	0	11	22	33	138	2.9	10
Ansu Sesay	45	448	41	107	.383	12	21	.571	34	39	73	23	62	1	14	25	5	94	2.1	8
Ronald Murray(*)	2	20	2	5	.400	0	0	—	0	3	3	2	0	0	0	4	0	4	2.0	4
Ronald Murray(!)	14	62	11	31	.355	5	8	.625	0	4	4	5	0	0	4	8	0	27	1.9	6
Joseph Forte	17	86	10	35	.286	4	6	.667	4	7	11	11	6	0	4	10	1	24	1.4	7

3-pt. FG: Seattle 456-1291 (.353).
Allen(*) 78-222 (.351); Allen(!) 201-533 (.377); Payton(>) 34-114 (.298); Lewis 75-217 (.346); Mason(>) 16-55 (.291)
Barry 118-293 (.403); Radmanovic 104-293 (.355); Drobnjak 30-85 (.353); Ollie(*) 1-1 (1.000); Ollie(!) 2-6 (.333)
Anderson(>) 0-5 (.000); Campbell(!) 0-1 (.000); Booth 0-2 (.000); Murray(*) 0-1 (.000); Murray(!) 0-5 (.000); Forte 0-3 (.000)
Opponents 472-1371 (.344)

TORONTO RAPTORS

	G	Min.	FGM	FGA	Pct.	FTM	FTA	Pct.	Off.	Def.	Tot.	Ast.	PF	Dq.	Stl.	TO	Blk.	Pts.	Avg.	Hi.
									REBOUNDS									**SCORING**		
Vince Carter	43	1471	355	760	.467	129	160	.806	59	129	188	143	121	2	48	74	41	884	20.6	43
Voshon Lenard	63	1929	325	809	.402	156	194	.804	48	164	212	144	156	1	59	103	21	898	14.3	30
Morris Peterson	82	2949	421	1073	.392	195	247	.789	97	266	363	188	232	1	88	128	32	1153	14.1	33
Antonio Davis	53	1894	261	641	.407	216	280	.771	130	307	437	131	150	0	23	118	62	738	13.9	27
Alvin Williams	78	2638	396	905	.438	187	239	.782	55	190	245	416	170	0	111	128	21	1027	13.2	32
Jerome Williams	71	2346	267	535	.499	156	281	.555	231	419	650	95	197	2	116	98	26	691	9.7	30
Lindsey Hunter	29	673	106	302	.351	34	47	.723	15	44	59	71	50	1	35	57	5	280	9.7	23
Rafer Alston	47	980	139	335	.415	37	54	.685	21	86	107	192	120	0	38	86	15	366	7.8	23
Jelani McCoy	67	1367	194	395	.491	69	126	.548	95	260	355	43	162	2	28	96	60	457	6.8	16
Damone Brown	5	115	11	35	.314	6	8	.750	3	12	15	3	14	0	1	6	0	28	5.6	13
Mamadou N'diaye	22	364	43	96	.448	34	47	.723	29	53	82	7	58	0	8	21	32	120	5.5	13
Michael Bradley	67	1314	151	314	.481	35	67	.522	162	247	409	67	125	0	16	76	32	338	5.0	16
Greg Foster	29	539	47	122	.385	26	32	.813	30	72	102	13	82	1	1	30	9	121	4.2	11
Chris Jefferies	51	666	75	194	.387	29	43	.674	16	43	59	22	56	0	19	45	16	197	3.9	15
Nate Huffman	7	76	9	25	.360	5	8	.625	9	14	23	5	13	0	1	3	3	23	3.3	10
Jermaine Jackson(>)	24	286	21	68	.309	23	27	.852	10	15	25	39	24	0	9	19	3	66	2.8	10
Maceo Baston	16	106	15	25	.600	10	12	.833	4	19	23	0	16	0	4	6	11	40	2.5	8
Art Long(*)	7	80	9	25	.360	1	5	.200	8	12	20	4	13	0	3	11	3	20	2.9	10
Art Long(!)	26	211	28	75	.373	2	10	.200	21	39	60	6	35	0	5	20	11	60	2.3	10
Zendon Hamilton	3	12	2	5	.400	2	2	1.000	1	3	4	0	2	0	1	1	0	6	2.0	4

3-pt. FG: Toronto 409-1193 (.343).
Carter 45-131 (.344); Lenard 92-252 (.365); Peterson 116-344 (.337); A. Williams 48-146 (.329); J. Williams 1-6 (.167)
Hunter 34-107 (.318); Alston 51-130 (.392); Brown 0-2 (.000); Bradley 1-6 (.167); Foster 1-4 (.250); Jefferies 18-54 (.333)
Jackson(>) 1-9 (.111); Long(*) 1-2 (.500); Long(!) 2-3 (.667); Opponents 370-986 (.375)

UTAH JAZZ

	G	Min.	FGM	FGA	Pct.	FTM	FTA	Pct.	Off.	Def.	Tot.	Ast.	PF	Dq.	Stl.	TO	Blk.	Pts.	Avg.	Hi.
									REBOUNDS									**SCORING**		
Karl Malone	81	2936	595	1289	.462	474	621	.763	113	515	628	379	204	0	136	210	31	1667	20.6	40
Matt Harpring	78	2557	521	1020	.511	262	331	.792	190	324	514	133	217	4	73	160	17	1370	17.6	33
Andrei Kirilenko	80	2213	315	642	.491	296	370	.800	147	273	420	138	185	0	118	136	175	963	12.0	30
John Stockton	82	2275	309	640	.483	237	287	.826	51	150	201	629	184	1	137	182	16	884	10.8	25
Calbert Cheaney	81	2351	325	651	.499	40	69	.580	73	211	284	163	225	1	65	108	13	700	8.6	18

- 281 -

	G	Min.	FGM	FGA	Pct.	FTM	FTA	Pct.	REBOUNDS			Ast.	PF	Dq.	Stl.	TO	Blk.	SCORING		
									Off.	Def.	Tot.							Pts.	Avg.	Hi.
Scott Padgett	82	1321	170	423	.402	81	107	.757	83	189	272	86	148	1	41	70	24	466	5.7	15
Jarron Collins	22	421	38	86	.442	44	62	.710	32	28	60	14	70	2	5	19	6	120	5.5	18
Greg Ostertag	81	1926	169	326	.518	100	196	.510	180	323	503	55	235	4	20	104	147	438	5.4	16
Tony Massenburg	58	792	104	232	.448	65	84	.774	59	97	156	17	144	1	17	50	19	273	4.7	20
Mark Jackson	82	1467	147	369	.398	61	80	.763	34	142	176	375	90	0	48	152	3	382	4.7	10
DeShawn Stevenson	61	760	114	284	.401	47	68	.691	22	63	85	40	57	0	22	49	8	279	4.6	18
Carlos Arroyo	44	287	50	109	.459	18	22	.818	11	15	26	53	28	0	12	30	1	121	2.8	16
John Amaechi	50	474	37	118	.314	25	52	.481	26	51	77	21	50	1	14	34	7	99	2.0	12

3-pt. FG: Utah 224-641 (.349)

Malone 3-14 (.214); Harpring 66-160 (.413); Kirilenko 37-114 (.325); Stockton 29-80 (.363); Cheaney 10-25 (.400) Padgett 45-133 (.338); Collins 0-1 (.000); Jackson 27-95 (.284); Stevenson 4-12 (.333); Arroyo 3-7 (.429) Opponents 437-1252 (.349)

WASHINGTON WIZARDS

	G	Min.	FGM	FGA	Pct.	FTM	FTA	Pct.	REBOUNDS			Ast.	PF	Dq.	Stl.	TO	Blk.	SCORING		
									Off.	Def.	Tot.							Pts.	Avg.	Hi.
Jerry Stackhouse	70	2747	491	1201	.409	455	518	.878	61	197	258	316	130	1	65	193	28	1508	21.5	38
Michael Jordan	82	3031	679	1527	.445	266	324	.821	71	426	497	311	171	1	123	173	39	1640	20.0	45
Larry Hughes	67	2137	346	741	.467	136	186	.731	67	241	308	205	149	1	86	136	24	857	12.8	24
Tyronn Lue	75	1986	248	573	.433	91	104	.875	22	127	149	263	151	0	47	77	1	647	8.6	21
Christian Laettner	76	2215	255	516	.494	120	144	.833	114	388	502	235	206	0	82	87	40	632	8.3	21
Kwame Brown	80	1773	224	502	.446	145	217	.668	128	298	426	58	159	1	50	110	80	593	7.4	20
Juan Dixon	42	647	104	271	.384	37	46	.804	13	59	72	40	54	0	26	42	3	270	6.4	27
Brendan Haywood	81	1930	173	339	.510	155	245	.633	192	212	404	29	225	3	32	65	119	501	6.2	16
Etan Thomas	38	513	61	124	.492	60	94	.638	70	95	165	3	66	0	8	33	23	182	4.8	14
Bryon Russell	70	1388	108	306	.353	53	69	.768	43	165	208	72	130	1	70	55	7	315	4.5	16
Jahidi White	16	230	25	53	.472	17	25	.680	37	36	73	2	33	1	1	9	12	67	4.2	10
Jared Jeffries	20	292	30	63	.476	16	29	.552	26	32	58	16	28	0	8	21	5	79	4.0	14
Bobby Simmons	36	378	44	112	.393	32	35	.914	33	44	77	20	51	0	10	8	3	120	3.3	15
Charles Oakley	42	514	23	55	.418	28	34	.824	37	70	107	40	90	0	13	21	6	74	1.8	6
Anthony Goldwire(*)	5	34	4	7	.571	4	5	.800	0	3	3	1	1	0	0	4	0	13	2.6	10
Anthony Goldwire(!)	15	85	9	25	.360	4	7	.571	0	6	6	4	6	0	3	6	0	25	1.7	10
Brian Cardinal	5	15	1	4	.250	2	2	1.000	3	2	5	1	0	0	0	1	0	4	0.8	2

3-pt. FG: Washington 253-811 (.312)

Stackhouse 71-245 (.290); Jordan 16-55 (.291); Hughes 29-79 (.367); Lue 60-176 (.341); Laettner 2-16 (.125); Brown 0-3 (.000) Dixon 25-84 (.298); Russell 46-140 (.329); Jeffries 3-6 (.500); Simmons 0-5 (.000); Goldwire(*) 1-1 (1.000); Cardinal 0-1 (.000) Goldwire(!) 3-9 (.333); Opponents 449-1242 (.362)

(*) Statistics with this team only
(!) Totals with all teams
(>) Continued season with another team

2002-03

PLAYOFFS
RESULTS

EASTERN CONFERENCE
FIRST ROUND

DETROIT vs. ORLANDO
(Pistons win series 4-3)
Apr. 20—Orl. 99 at Det. 94
Apr. 23—Orl. 77 at Det. 89
Apr. 25—Det. 80 at Orl. 89
Apr. 27—Det. 92 at Orl. 100
Apr. 30—Orl. 67 at Det. 98
May 2—Det. 103 at Orl. 88
May 4—Orl. 93 at Det. 108

NEW JERSEY vs. MILWAUKEE
(Nets win series 4-2)
Apr. 19—Mil. 96 at N.J. 109
Apr. 22—Mil. 88 at at N.J. 85
Apr. 24—N.J. 103 at Mil. 101
Apr. 26—N.J. 114 at Mil. 119 (OT)
Apr. 29—Mil. 82 at N.J. 89
May 1 —N.J. 113 at Mil. 101

INDIANA vs. BOSTON
(Celtics win series 4-2)
Apr. 19—Bos. 103 at Ind. 100
Apr. 21—Bos. 77 at Ind. 89
Apr. 24—Ind. 83 at Bos. 101
Apr. 27—Ind. 92 at Bos. 102
Apr. 29—Bos. 88 at Ind. 93 (OT)
May 1 —Ind. 90 at Bos. 110

PHILADELPHIA vs. NEW ORLEANS
(76ers wins series 4-2)
Apr. 20—N.O. 90 at Phil. 98
Apr. 23—N.O. 85 at Phil. 90
Apr. 26—Phil. 85 at N.O. 99
Apr. 28—Phil. 96 at N.O. 87
Apr. 30—N.O. 93 at Phil. 91
May 2 —Phil. 107 at N.O. 103

SEMIFINALS

DETROIT vs. PHILADELPHIA
(Pistons win series 4-2)
May 6 —Phil. 87 at Det. 98
May 8 —Phil. 97 at Det. 104 (OT)
May 10—Det. 83 at Phil. 93
May 11—Det. 82 at Phil. 95
May 14—Phil. 77 at Det. 78
May 16—Det. 93 at Phil. 89 (OT)

NEW JERSEY vs. BOSTON
(Nets win series 4-0)
May 5 —Bos. 93 at N.J. 97
May 7 —Bos. 95 at N.J. 104
May 9 —N.J. 94 at Bos. 76
May 12—N.J. 110 at Bos. 101 (2OT)

FINALS

DETROIT vs. NEW JERSEY
(Nets win series 4-0)
May 18—N.J. 76 at Det. 74
May 20—N.J. 88 at Det. 86
May 22—Det. 85 at N.J. 97
May 24—Det. 82 at N.J. 102

WESTERN CONFERENCE
FIRST ROUND

SAN ANTONIO vs. PHOENIX
(Spurs win series 4-2)
Apr. 19—Pho. 96 at S.A. 95 (OT)
Apr. 21—Pho. 76 at S.A. 84
Apr. 25—S.A. 99 at Pho. 86
Apr. 27—S.A. 84 at Pho. 86
Apr. 29—Pho. 82 at S.A. 94
May 1 —S.A. 87 at Pho. 85

SACRAMENTO vs. UTAH
(Kings win series 4-1)
Apr. 19—Utah 90 at Sac. 96
Apr. 21—Utah 95 at Sac. 108
Apr. 26—Sac. 104 at Utah 107
Apr. 28—Sac. 99 at Utah 82
Apr. 30—Utah 91 at Sac. 111

DALLAS vs. PORTLAND
(Mavericks win series 4-3)
Apr. 19—Port. 86 at Dal. 96
Apr. 23—Port. 99 at Dal. 103
Apr. 25—Dal. 115 at Port. 103
Apr. 27—Dal. 79 at Port. 98
Apr. 30—Port. 103 at Dal. 99
May 2 —Dal. 103 at Port. 125
May 4 —Port. 95 at Dal. 107

MINNESOTA vs. L.A. LAKERS
(Lakers win series 4-2)
Apr. 20   LAL 117 at Minn. 98
Apr. 22—LAL 91 at Minn. 119
Apr. 24—Minn. 114 at LAL 110 (OT)
Apr. 27—Minn. 97 at LAL 102
Apr. 29—LAL 120 at Minn. 90
May 1 —Minn. 85 at LAL 101

SEMIFINALS

SAN ANTONIO vs. L.A. LAKERS
(Spurs win series 4-2)
May 5 —LAL 82 at S.A. 87
May 7 —LAL 95 at S.A. 114
May 9 —S.A. 95 at LAL 110
May 11—S.A. 95 at LAL 99
May 13—LAL 94 at S.A. 96
May 15—S.A. 110 at LAL 82

DALLAS vs. SACRAMENTO
(Mavericks win series 4-3)
May 6 —Sac. 124 at Dal. 113
May 8 —Sac. 110 at Dal. 132
May 10—Dal. 141 at Sac. 137 (2OT)
May 11—Dal. 83 at Sac. 99
May 13—Sac. 93 at Dal. 112
May 15—Dal. 109 at Sac. 115
May 17—Sac. 99 at Dal. 112

FINALS

SAN ANTONIO vs. DALLAS
(Spurs win series 4-2)
May 19—Dal. 113 at S.A. 110
May 21—Dal. 106 at S.A. 119
May 23—S.A. 96 at Dal. 83
May 25—S.A. 102 at Dal. 95
May 27—Dal. 103 at S.A. 91
May 29— S.A. 90 at Dal. 78

NBA FINALS

SAN ANTONIO vs. NEW JERSEY
(Spurs win series 4-2)
Jun. 4 —N.J. 89 at S.A. 101
Jun. 6 —N.J. 87 at S.A. 85
Jun. 8 —S.A. 84 at N.J. 79
Jun. 11—S.A. 76 at N.J. 77
Jun. 13—S.A. 93 at N.J. 83
Jun. 15—N.J. 77 at S.A. 88

2001-02

2001-02 NBA CHAMPION LOS ANGELES LAKERS

Front row (from left) Devean George, Jelani McCoy, Stanislav Medvedenko, Shaquille O'Neal, owner Jerry Buss, Samaki Walker, Robert Horry, Mark Madsen. Center row (from left) massage therapist Dan Garcia, Lindsey Hunter, Brian Shaw, Rick Fox, Kobe Bryant, Mitch Richmond, Derek Fisher, equipment manager Rudy Garciduenas. Back row (from left) athletic trainer Gary Vitti, athletic performance coordinator Chip Schaeffer, assistant coach Jim Cleamons, head coach Phil Jackson, assistant coach Kurt Rambis, assistant coach Tex Winter, assistant coach Frank Hamblen, strength and conditioning coach Jim Cotta.

FINAL STANDINGS

ATLANTIC DIVISION

	Atl.	Bos.	Cha.	Chi.	Cle.	Dal.	Den.	Det.	G.S.	Hou.	Ind.	LA-C	LA-L	Mia.	Mem.	Mil.	Min.	N.J.	N.Y.	Orl.	Phi.	Pho.	Por.	Sac.	S.A.	Sea.	Tor.	Uta.	Was.	W	L	Pct.	GB
N.J. 1	1	3	4	3	0	1	1	1	2	3	2	1	2	3	2	1	..	4	3	2	1	1	1	2	1	2	1		3	52	30	.634	..
Bos. ..2	..	2	2	4	0	2	2	1	0	3	2	2	2	1	1	3	4	3	1	1	1	0	0	1	2	1			3	49	33	.598	3
Orl. ...3	1	1	3	3	1	2	2	2	2	1	0	2	1	1	1	1	4	..	3	2	0	1	0	0	3	1			2	44	38	.537	8
Phi. ...3	3	3	2	3	1	1	1	1	1	1	2	1	0	3	3	1	2	3	1	..	2	0	0	1	1	1	0		2	43	39	.524	9
Was. ..3	1	1	3	2	1	2	0	1	1	1	1	0	2	2	1	0	1	3	2	3	2	0	1	0	1	2	0		..	37	45	.451	15
Mia. ..1	1	0	3	1	1	2	1	2	2	2	0	1	1	..	3	0	1	2	3	1	1	1	0	1	2	1	0		2	36	46	.439	16
N.Y. ..3	0	2	1	2	1	0	1	1	1	1	0	0	1	2	3	0	0	..	0	1	1	1	1	1	0	2	3	1	1	30	52	.366	22

CENTRAL DIVISION

	Atl.	Bos.	Cha.	Chi.	Cle.	Dal.	Den.	Det.	G.S.	Hou.	Ind.	LA-C	LA-L	Mia.	Mem.	Mil.	Min.	N.J.	N.Y.	Orl.	Phi.	Pho.	Por.	Sac.	S.A.	Sea.	Tor.	Uta.	Was.	W	L	Pct.	GB
Det. 3	2	3	3	3	1	2	..	1	1	3	1	0	2	2	2	1	3	3	2	2	1	0	0	0	1	3	1		4	50	32	.610	..
Cha. ..2	1	..	4	3	0	2	1	2	1	3	1	0	1	3	2	0	1	2	3	1	2	1	0	1	1	2	1		3	44	38	.537	6
Ind. ...3	0	1	4	3	0	2	1	2	2	..	1	0	1	2	1	1	2	3	3	1	1	2	1	0	1	1			3	42	40	.512	8
Tor. 4	2	2	4	3	1	1	1	2	1	3	1	1	1	3	0	1	2	0	1	3	1	1	0	1	0	..	1		1	42	40	.512	8
Mil. 3	3	2	2	1	0	2	2	2	1	3	1	0	2	1	..	0	1	1	2	1	0	0	0	2	0	4	2		3	41	41	.500	9
Atl.	2	2	3	3	0	2	1	2	1	1	1	1	2	3	1	0	2	1	1	1	1	0	0	0	1	0			4	33	49	.402	17
Cle. 1	0	1	3	..	0	1	1	1	2	2	0	0	1	3	3	2	1	2	1	0	1	0	0	1	0	1	0		1	29	53	.354	21
Chi. 1	2	0	..	1	0	0	1	1	2	0	0	2	1	1	2	0	0	3	0	1	1	0	0	0	1	0	0		1	21	61	.256	29

MIDWEST DIVISION

	Atl.	Bos.	Cha.	Chi.	Cle.	Dal.	Den.	Det.	G.S.	Hou.	Ind.	LA-C	LA-L	Mia.	Mem.	Mil.	Min.	N.J.	N.Y.	Orl.	Phi.	Pho.	Por.	Sac.	S.A.	Sea.	Tor.	Uta.	Was.	W	L	Pct.	GB
S.A. 2	2	1	2	1	3	4	2	4	4	1	3	1	4	1	0	2	0	2	2	1	3	3	1	..	2	1	4		2	58	24	.707	..
Dal. 2	2	2	2	2	..	4	1	4	2	2	1	4	1	2	2	2	1	1	1	3	2	3	1	3	1	3	1		1	57	25	.695	1
Min. ..2	1	2	2	0	2	2	1	3	2	1	2	2	4	2	2	..	1	2	1	2	2	1	2	2	1	3	2			50	32	.610	8
Utah 1	2	1	1	2	2	1	3	1	4	2	1	4	1	1	2	0	1	1	1	2	2	3	0	0	3	1	..		2	44	38	.537	14
Hou. ..1	2	1	0	0	2	2	1	3	..	0	1	0	1	0	1	2	0	1	0	1	2	1	0	0	2	1	2		1	28	54	.341	30
Den. ..0	0	0	2	1	0	..	0	1	2	0	1	1	3	0	0	2	1	0	1	3	2	0	0	3	1	1	0		27	55	.329	31
Mem. 0	0	1	1	1	0	1	0	1	3	1	1	1	..	1	0	0	1	0	2	1	2	1	0	0	1	3	0		23	59	.280	35

PACIFIC DIVISION

	Atl.	Bos.	Cha.	Chi.	Cle.	Dal.	Den.	Det.	G.S.	Hou.	Ind.	LA-C	LA-L	Mia.	Mem.	Mil.	Min.	N.J.	N.Y.	Orl.	Phi.	Pho.	Por.	Sac.	S.A.	Sea.	Tor.	Uta.	Was.	W	L	Pct.	GB
Sac. ..2	2	2	2	2	1	4	2	4	4	0	3	3	2	3	1	1	2	3	2	..	3	2	2	4	1			1		61	21	.744	..
L.A.L. 1	0	2	0	2	3	3	2	3	4	2	3	..	3	1	2	2	1	2	2	3	3	3	1	3	2			2		58	24	.707	3
Por. 1	1	1	2	2	2	2	2	2	3	1	3	2	2	1	2	2	1	1	2	2	2	..	2	1	3	1	1		2	49	33	.598	12
Sea. ..2	1	1	1	2	1	1	1	4	2	3	1	4	0	2	2	1	0	2	1	2	1	2	..	2	1	1			45	37	.549	16
L.A.C. 1	0	1	2	2	3	1	2	3	1	..	1	3	2	1	2	0	2	1	0	3	1	1	1	1	1	0		1	39	43	.476	22
Pho. ..1	1	0	1	1	1	1	1	4	2	1	1	2	3	1	2	2	1	1	0	0	..	2	1	1	2	1	2		0	36	46	.439	25
G.S. ..0	1	0	1	1	0	3	1		1	0	2	1	3	0	0	1	1	1	0	1	0	2	0	0	0	0	0		I	21	61	.256	40

OFFENSIVE

	G	FGM	FGA	Pct.	FTM	FTA	Pct.	REBOUNDS Off.	Def.	Tot.	Ast.	PF	Dq.	Stl.	TO	Blk.	SCORING Pts.	Avg.
Dallas.........	82	3200	6930	.462	1608	1994	.806	918	2568	3486	1811	1842	21	581	992	392	8629	105.2
Sacramento ...	82	3267	7003	.467	1618	2154	.751	1013	2702	3715	1958	1560	7	741	1128	375	8578	104.6
L.A. Lakers....	82	3150	6840	.461	1494	2138	.699	1022	2607	3629	1882	1823	10	625	1040	478	8304	101.3
Orlando	82	3087	6893	.448	1446	1917	.754	942	2440	3382	1804	1700	9	665	1119	384	8240	100.5
Minnesota	82	3175	6887	.461	1399	1754	.798	1059	2562	3621	1993	1739	8	524	1097	427	8145	99.3
Seattle	82	3131	6681	.469	1263	1672	.755	968	2333	3301	1926	1732	15	698	1124	364	8014	97.7
Golden State .	82	2998	6989	.429	1693	2344	.722	1334	2493	3827	1706	1884	20	650	1378	523	8009	97.7
Milwaukee	82	3041	6577	.462	1321	1767	.748	841	2557	3398	1847	1788	14	596	1157	388	7996	97.5
Indiana.......	82	2935	6580	.446	1663	2155	.772	930	2568	3498	1884	1876	31	658	1249	436	7938	96.8
San Antonio...	82	2913	6363	.458	1668	2249	.742	907	2566	3473	1643	1575	10	625	1180	537	7932	96.7
Portland......	82	3004	6671	.450	1451	1901	.763	1085	2444	3529	1926	1613	7	702	1172	368	7925	96.6
Boston........	82	2852	6731	.424	1498	1960	.764	891	2570	3461	1722	1776	13	793	1114	292	7901	96.4
New Jersey ...	82	3042	6816	.446	1402	1907	.735	1039	2515	3554	1990	1734	22	716	1189	490	7889	96.2
Utah.........	82	2869	6374	.450	1853	2430	.763	1109	2349	3458	1999	1971	17	749	1353	523	7871	96.0
L.A. Clippers .	82	2970	6668	.445	1498	2026	.739	1083	2474	3557	1714	1624	14	510	1214	540	7846	95.7
Cleveland	82	2948	6582	.448	1529	1980	.772	968	2483	3451	1891	1752	24	572	1196	470	7812	95.3
Phoenix	82	3097	6934	.447	1250	1630	.767	1072	2430	3502	1838	1785	9	668	1205	401	7802	95.1
Detroit	82	2845	6300	.452	1478	1954	.756	810	2366	3176	1765	1695	9	648	1193	565	7735	94.3
Atlanta.......	82	2901	6610	.439	1486	1942	.765	955	2445	3400	1656	1702	15	667	1275	350	7711	94.0
Charlotte	82	2893	6580	.440	1568	2105	.745	1059	2505	3564	1759	1747	8	653	1150	456	7700	93.9
Washington ..	82	2938	6664	.441	1428	1866	.765	1055	2393	3448	1715	1763	13	570	1068	354	7609	92.8
Houston.......	82	2837	6629	.428	1402	1893	.741	1025	2411	3436	1482	1476	17	537	1156	445	7572	92.3
Denver.......	82	2915	6870	.424	1306	1756	.744	1117	2310	3427	1817	1873	22	613	1205	462	7559	92.2
New York.....	82	2817	6520	.432	1406	1786	.787	876	2458	3334	1720	1800	17	558	1192	288	7514	91.6
Toronto	82	2919	6727	.434	1269	1717	.739	1114	2336	3450	1779	1771	18	688	1174	454	7494	91.4
Philadelphia ..	82	2804	6436	.436	1639	2104	.779	1092	2534	3626	1638	1645	7	705	1256	363	7461	91.0
Memphis	82	2851	6535	.436	1334	1883	.708	984	2413	3397	1785	1571	11	646	1344	488	7372	89.9
Chicago	82	2811	6491	.433	1413	1958	.722	924	2359	3283	1817	1834	23	633	1252	361	7335	89.5
Miami	82	2801	6382	.439	1236	1708	.724	902	2544	3446	1664	1846	24	547	1217	448	7150	87.2

DEFENSIVE

	FGM	FGA	Pct.	FTM	FTA	Pct.	REBOUNDS Off.	Def.	Tot.	Ast.	PF	Dq.	Stl.	TO	Blk.	SCORING Pts.	Avg.	Dif.
Miami	2666	6279	.425	1565	2127	.736	894	2484	3378	1461	1709	21	620	1134	353	7276	88.7	-1.5
Philadelphia....	2771	6500	.426	1350	1798	.751	981	2348	3329	1768	1827	19	654	1208	458	7330	89.4	+1.6
San Antonio....	2883	6775	.426	1283	1651	.777	1003	2429	3432	1543	1896	22	635	1192	428	7423	90.5	+6.2
Toronto	2820	6390	.441	1513	2011	.752	995	2436	3431	1629	1612	10	628	1250	393	7530	91.8	-0.4
New Jersey	2858	6668	.429	1423	1890	.753	999	2517	3516	1563	1667	9	669	1317	439	7548	92.0	+4.2
Detroit........	2926	6546	.447	1349	1787	.755	991	2511	3502	1638	1874	14	651	1273	335	7560	92.2	+2.1
Charlotte	2850	6594	.432	1488	1938	.768	963	2399	3362	1639	1703	13	625	1140	422	7621	92.9	+1.0
Portland	2951	6508	.453	1312	1771	.741	890	2328	3218	1945	1651	12	612	1208	410	7680	93.7	+3.0
L.A. Lakers....	2872	6777	.424	1577	2072	.761	1016	2526	3542	1643	1890	30	587	1148	354	7720	94.1	+7.1
Boston........	2797	6579	.425	1612	2091	.771	954	2807	3761	1802	1734	12	623	1335	476	7720	94.1	+2.2
Washington	2953	6534	.452	1396	1849	.755	960	2376	3336	1818	1713	8	573	1095	414	7724	94.2	-1.4
Seattle	2966	6605	.449	1362	1844	.739	1091	2326	3417	1832	1627	9	568	1254	400	7766	94.7	+3.0
Utah	2777	6218	.447	1779	2308	.771	927	2204	3131	1585	2069	32	748	1371	548	7798	95.1	+0.9
New York......	2924	6570	.445	1550	2047	.757	959	2540	3499	1762	1670	8	686	1103	385	7841	95.6	-4.0
Phoenix	2957	6663	.444	1511	2013	.751	1030	2493	3523	1821	1521	9	685	1265	475	7858	95.8	-0.7
Minnesota	2962	6654	.445	1452	1958	.742	912	2326	3238	1855	1676	16	542	1097	407	7868	96.0	+3.4
L.A. Clippers ..	3074	6866	.448	1329	1783	.745	1064	2379	3443	1859	1775	15	612	1055	439	7884	96.1	-0.5
Indiana........	2977	6800	.438	1544	2062	.749	1048	2514	3562	1771	1855	15	618	1173	466	7916	96.5	+0.3
Sacramento....	3128	7108	.440	1312	1764	.744	1065	2617	3682	1839	1827	18	633	1246	387	7954	97.0	+7.6
Houston	3191	6875	.464	1221	1623	.752	1045	2507	3552	1838	1647	7	576	988	415	7973	97.2	-4.9
Memphis	3119	6829	.457	1346	1788	.753	1135	2560	3695	1961	1784	12	781	1207	457	7982	97.3	-7.4
Milwaukee	3016	6846	.441	1489	1967	.757	1050	2438	3488	1883	1642	18	599	1054	361	8014	97.7	-0.2
Chicago.......	3027	6514	.465	1560	2090	.746	944	2553	3497	2066	1720	15	681	1178	399	8035	98.0	-8.5
Denver........	3005	6540	.459	1602	2144	.747	995	2529	3524	1968	1646	11	671	1173	560	8036	98.0	-5.8
Atlanta.......	3065	6675	.459	1456	1957	.744	1004	2523	3527	1856	1647	8	705	1239	509	8058	98.3	-4.2
Cleveland......	3053	6678	.457	1506	2014	.748	928	2382	3310	1989	1638	13	602	1063	459	8085	98.6	-3.3
Orlando	3116	6828	.456	1470	1994	.737	1086	2633	3719	1930	1740	17	659	1292	384	8111	98.9	+1.6
Dallas........	3094	6851	.452	1640	2184	.751	1065	2600	3665	1865	1788	16	589	1155	377	8280	101.0	+4.3
Golden State ..	3213	6993	.459	1622	2125	.763	1100	2450	3550	2002	1949	26	706	1176	512	8452	103.1	-5.4
Avgs........	2966	6664	.445	1470	1953	.752	1003	2474	3477	1798	1741	15	639	1186	428	7829	95.5	...

2001-02

HOME/ROAD

	Home	Road	Total		Home	Road	Total
Atlanta	23-18	10-31	33-49	Milwaukee	25-16	16-25	41-41
Boston	27-14	22-19	49-33	Minnesota	29-12	21-20	50-32
Charlotte	21-20	23-18	44-38	New Jersey	33-8	19-22	52-30
Chicago	14-27	7-34	21-61	New York	19-22	11-30	30-52
Cleveland	20-21	9-32	29-53	Orlando	27-14	17-24	44-38
Dallas	30-11	27-14	57-25	Philadelphia	22-19	21-20	43-39
Denver	20-21	7-34	27-55	Phoenix	23-18	13-28	36-46
Detroit	26-15	24-17	50-32	Portland	30-11	19-22	49-33
Golden State	14-27	7-34	21-61	Sacramento	36-5	25-16	61-21
Houston	18-23	10-31	28-54	San Antonio	32-9	26-15	58-24
Indiana	25-16	17-24	42-40	Seattle	26-15	19-22	45-37
L.A. Clippers	25-16	14-27	39-43	Toronto	24-17	18-23	42-40
L.A. Lakers	34-7	24-17	58-24	Utah	25-16	19-22	44-38
Memphis	15-26	8-33	23-59	Washington	22-19	15-26	37-45
Miami	18-23	18-23	36-46	Totals	703-486	486-703	1,189-1,189

INDIVIDUAL LEADERS

POINTS

(minimum 70 games or 1,400 points)

	G	FGM	FTM	Pts.	Avg.
Allen Iverson, Philadelphia	60	665	475	1883	31.4
Shaquille O'Neal, L.A. Lakers	67	712	398	1822	27.2
Paul Pierce, Boston	82	707	520	2144	26.1
Tracy McGrady, Orlando	76	715	415	1948	25.6
Tim Duncan, San Antonio	82	764	560	2089	25.5
Kobe Bryant, L.A. Lakers	80	749	488	2019	25.2
Vince Carter, Toronto	60	559	245	1484	24.7
Dirk Nowitzki, Dallas	76	600	440	1779	23.4
Karl Malone, Utah	80	635	509	1788	22.4
Antoine Walker, Boston	81	666	240	1794	22.1
Gary Payton, Seattle	82	737	267	1815	22.1

REBOUNDS

(minimum 70 games or 800 rebounds)

	G	Off.	Def.	Tot.	Avg.
Ben Wallace, Detroit	80	318	721	1039	13.0
Tim Duncan, San Antonio	82	268	774	1042	12.7
Kevin Garnett, Minnesota	81	243	738	981	12.1
Danny Fortson, Golden State	77	290	609	899	11.7
Elton Brand, L.A. Clippers	80	396	529	925	11.6
Dikembe Mutombo, Philadelphia	80	254	609	863	10.8
Jermaine O'Neal, Indiana	72	188	569	757	10.5
Dirk Nowitzki, Dallas	76	120	635	755	9.9
Shawn Marion, Phoenix	81	211	592	803	9.9
P.J. Brown, Charlotte	80	273	513	786	9.8

FIELD GOALS

(minimum 300 made)

	FGM	FGA	Pct.
Shaquille O'Neal, L.A. Lakers	712	1229	.579
Elton Brand, L.A. Clippers	532	1010	.527
Donyell Marshall, Utah	343	661	.519
Pau Gasol, Memphis	551	1064	.518
John Stockton, Utah	401	775	.517
Alonzo Mourning, Miami	447	866	.516
Ruben Patterson, Portland	319	619	.515
Corliss Williamson, Detroit	411	806	.510
Tim Duncan, San Antonio	764	1504	.508
Brent Barry, Seattle	401	790	.508

STEALS

(minimum 70 games or 125 steals)

	G	No.	Avg.
Allen Iverson, Philadelphia	60	168	2.80
Ron Artest, Chi.-Ind.	55	141	2.56
Jason Kidd, New Jersey	82	175	2.13
Baron Davis, Charlotte	82	172	2.10
Doug Christie, Sacramento	81	160	1.98
Darrell Armstrong, Orlando	82	157	1.91
Karl Malone, Utah	80	152	1.90
Paul Pierce, Boston	82	154	1.88
Kenny Anderson, Boston	76	141	1.86
John Stockton, Utah	82	152	1.85

FREE THROWS

(minimum 125 made)

	FTM	FTA	Pct.
Reggie Miller, Indiana	296	325	.911
Richard Hamilton, Washington	300	337	.890
Darrell Armstrong, Orlando	182	205	.888
Damon Stoudamire, Portland	174	196	.888
Steve Nash, Dallas	260	293	.887
Chauncey Billups, Minnesota	207	234	.885
Chris Whitney, Washington	154	175	.880
Steve Smith, San Antonio	159	181	.878
Predrag Stojakovic, Sacramento	283	323	.876
Troy Hudson, Orlando	176	201	.876

BLOCKED SHOTS

(minimum 70 games or 100 blocked shots)

	G	No.	Avg.
Ben Wallace, Detroit	80	278	3.48
Raef LaFrentz, Den.-Dal.	78	213	2.73
Alonzo Mourning, Miami	75	186	2.48
Tim Duncan, San Antonio	82	203	2.48
Dikembe Mutombo, Philadelphia	80	190	2.38
Jermaine O'Neal, Indiana	72	166	2.31
Erick Dampier, Golden State	73	167	2.29
Adonal Foyle, Golden State	79	168	2.13
Pau Gasol, Memphis	82	169	2.06
Shaquille O'Neal, L.A. Lakers	67	137	2.04

ASSISTS

(minimum 70 games or 400 assists)

	G	No.	Avg.
Andre Miller, Cleveland	81	882	10.9
Jason Kidd, New Jersey	82	808	9.9
Gary Payton, Seattle	82	737	9.0
Baron Davis, Charlotte	82	698	8.5
John Stockton, Utah	82	674	8.2
Stephon Marbury, Phoenix	82	666	8.1
Jamaal Tinsley, Indiana	80	647	8.1
Jason Williams, Memphis	65	519	8.0
Steve Nash, Dallas	82	634	7.7
Mark Jackson, New York	82	605	7.4

3-POINT FIELD GOALS

(minimum 55 made)

	FGM	FGA	Pct.
Steve Smith, San Antonio	116	246	.472
Jon Barry, Detroit	121	258	.469
Eric Piatkowski, L.A. Clippers	111	238	.466
Wally Szczerbiak, Minnesota	87	191	.455
Steve Nash, Dallas	156	343	.455
Hubert Davis, Washington	57	126	.452
Tyronn Lue, Washington	63	141	.447
Michael Redd, Milwaukee	88	198	.444
Wesley Person, Cleveland	143	322	.444
Ray Allen, Milwaukee	229	528	.434

2001-02

INDIVIDUAL STATISTICS, TEAM BY TEAM

ATLANTA HAWKS

	G	Min.	FGM	FGA	Pct.	FTM	FTA	Pct.	Off.	Def.	Tot.	Ast.	PF	Dq.	Stl.	TO	Blk.	Pts.	Avg.	Hi.
									REBOUNDS									SCORING		
Shareef Abdur-Rahim . 77	77	2980	598	1297	.461	419	523	.801	198	498	696	239	214	2	98	250	81	1636	21.2	50
Jason Terry......... 78	78	2967	524	1219	.430	284	340	.835	40	230	270	444	156	0	144	181	13	1504	19.3	46
Toni Kukoc 59	59	1494	211	504	.419	109	153	.712	43	175	218	210	91	0	48	113	17	584	9.9	24
Nazr Mohammed..... 82	82	2168	329	713	.461	137	222	.617	242	409	651	33	252	2	63	118	61	795	9.7	30
Dion Glover......... 55	55	1156	192	456	.421	78	103	.757	36	133	169	84	89	1	45	76	14	492	8.9	25
Theo Ratliff......... 3	3	82	10	20	.500	6	11	.545	5	11	16	1	8	0	1	7	8	26	8.7	12
DerMarr Johnson 72	72	1727	214	540	.396	85	105	.810	59	188	247	81	163	1	62	102	56	602	8.4	28
Ira Newble 42	42	1273	131	263	.498	75	88	.852	80	142	222	45	117	2	38	49	20	338	8.0	17
Chris Crawford 7	7	131	21	45	.467	11	15	.733	9	16	25	5	21	1	2	10	5	53	7.6	14
Emanual Davis 28	28	774	70	198	.354	16	18	.889	19	55	74	68	68	0	27	52	5	185	6.6	16
Jacque Vaughn..... 82	82	1856	206	438	.470	104	126	.825	18	150	168	349	183	0	65	112	2	540	6.6	20
Alan Henderson 26	26	422	59	116	.509	24	45	.533	31	66	97	11	40	0	11	21	15	143	5.5	16
Hanno Mottola 82	82	1371	169	384	.440	57	76	.750	81	187	268	50	174	5	20	70	19	396	4.8	14
Mark Strickland...... 46	46	654	91	204	.446	25	44	.568	41	90	131	20	48	0	19	28	17	208	4.5	17
Cal Bowdler 52	52	585	61	174	.351	39	47	.830	38	72	110	11	64	1	18	11	15	162	3.1	14
Reggie Slater† 4	4	37	5	13	.385	6	9	.667	5	2	7	1	2	0	1	0	1	16	4.0	8
Reggie Slater‡ 8	8	47	7	15	.467	7	10	.700	5	4	9	1	3	0	1	1	1	21	2.6	8
Leon Smith......... 14	14	100	10	26	.385	11	17	.647	10	21	31	3	12	0	5	3	1	31	2.2	6
Dickey Simpkins... 1	1	3	0	0	...	0	0	...	0	0	0	1	0	0	0	0	0	0.0	0

3-pt. FG: Atlanta 423-1194 (.354)—Abdur-Rahim 21-70 (.300); Terry 172-444 (.387); Kukoc 53-171 (.310); Mohammed 0-1 (.000); Glover 30-91 (.330); Newble 1-7 (.143); Johnson 89-247 (.360); Crawford 0-1 (.000); Davis 29-85 (.341); Vaughn 24-54 (.444); Henderson 1-1 (1.000); Mottola 1-13 (.077); Strickland 1-4 (.250); Bowdler 1-5 (.200). Opponents 472-1329 (.355).

BOSTON CELTICS

	G	Min.	FGM	FGA	Pct.	FTM	FTA	Pct.	Off.	Def.	Tot.	Ast.	PF	Dq.	Stl.	TO	Blk.	Pts.	Avg.	Hi.
									REBOUNDS									SCORING		
Paul Pierce 82	82	3302	707	1598	.442	520	643	.809	81	485	566	261	237	1	154	241	86	2144	26.1	48
Antoine Walker 81	81	3406	666	1689	.394	240	324	.741	150	564	714	407	237	2	122	251	38	1794	22.1	42
Rodney Rogers† 27	27	626	107	222	.482	35	50	.700	34	73	107	40	78	1	16	42	12	288	10.7	25
Rodnoy Rogers‡ 77	77	1880	356	756	.471	117	149	.785	129	219	348	112	226	3	66	108	29	917	11.9	29
Kenny Anderson 76	76	2430	312	716	.436	98	132	.742	57	218	275	403	210	4	141	119	10	731	9.6	19
Tony Delk† 22	22	570	60	172	.349	22	30	.733	20	59	79	51	38	0	22	19	6	162	7.4	19
Tony Delk‡ 63	63	1447	226	588	.384	78	97	.804	58	145	203	132	98	0	53	59	10	597	9.5	27
Erick Strickland..... 79	79	1643	190	488	.389	131	155	.845	22	191	213	184	145	1	56	94	1	606	7.7	23
Tony Battie 74	74	1819	211	390	.541	88	130	.677	184	297	481	35	219	3	60	51	67	510	6.9	20
Eric Williams........ 74	74	1747	144	385	.374	160	219	.731	58	163	221	109	179	1	77	95	8	472	6.4	19
Joe Johnson*....... 48	48	1003	130	296	.439	20	26	.769	40	99	139	74	59	0	33	28	9	304	6.3	23
Vitaly Potapenko 79	79	1343	137	301	.455	89	120	.742	167	180	347	30	174	0	37	63	18	363	4.6	14
Walter McCarty 56	56	718	80	180	.444	13	19	.684	32	96	128	41	83	0	18	22	7	212	3.8	18
Milt Palacio*........ 41	41	518	52	135	.385	36	51	.706	8	42	50	54	38	0	21	24	3	152	3.7	19
Kedrick Brown 29	29	245	23	70	.329	12	20	.600	11	39	50	15	18	0	18	7	7	63	2.2	12
Mark Blount 44	44	415	32	76	.421	30	37	.811	26	59	85	10	59	0	16	23	19	94	2.1	11
Joseph Forte........ 8	8	39	1	12	.083	4	4	1.000	1	5	6	6	1	0	2	3	0	6	0.8	2
Randy Brown 1	1	6	0	1	.000	0	0	...	0	0	0	0	2	1	0	0	0	0	0.0	0

3-pt. FG: Boston 699-1946 (.359)—Pierce 210-520 (.404); Walker 222-645 (.344); Rogers† 39-95 (.411); Rogers‡ 88-235 (.374); Anderson 9-33 (.273); Delk† 20-67 (.299); Delk‡ 67-214 (.313); Strickland 95-247 (.385); Battie 0-2 (.000); Williams 24-86 (.279); Forte 0-3 (.000); Johnson* 24-88 (.273); McCarty 39-99 (.394); Palacio* 12-34 (.353); K. Brown 5-27 (.185). Opponents 514-1511 (.340).

CHARLOTTE HORNETS

	G	Min.	FGM	FGA	Pct.	FTM	FTA	Pct.	Off.	Def.	Tot.	Ast.	PF	Dq.	Stl.	TO	Blk.	Pts.	Avg.	Hi.
									REBOUNDS									SCORING		
Jamal Mashburn..... 40	40	1601	303	744	.407	211	241	.876	31	211	242	171	80	0	45	110	6	858	21.5	36
Baron Davis 82	82	3318	559	1341	.417	196	338	.580	93	256	349	698	241	0	172	246	47	1484	18.1	38
David Wesley 67	67	2487	364	910	.400	138	188	.734	44	99	143	236	147	0	74	119	15	951	14.2	30
Elden Campbell...... 77	77	2156	384	794	.484	306	384	.797	133	397	530	102	264	4	60	138	137	1074	13.9	26
Lee Nailon 79	79	1912	369	764	.483	112	150	.747	103	188	291	94	175	1	59	96	17	851	10.8	27
Jamaal Magloire 82	82	1549	228	414	.551	243	333	.730	153	308	461	31	201	0	27	118	86	699	8.5	22
P.J. Brown 80	80	2563	250	527	.474	169	197	.858	273	513	786	107	222	1	59	85	78	669	8.4	18
Stacey Augmon...... 77	77	1319	140	328	.427	77	101	.762	59	166	225	103	115	0	56	54	12	357	4.6	16
George Lynch 45	45	893	73	198	.369	25	40	.625	70	116	186	54	75	1	40	41	14	172	3.8	12
Robert Traylor..... 61	61	678	87	204	.426	53	84	.631	67	120	187	37	127	1	24	45	37	228	3.7	15
Bryce Drew......... 61	61	774	78	182	.429	23	29	.793	14	58	72	101	49	0	32	33	2	210	3.4	15
Matt Bullard 31	31	350	39	115	.339	11	12	.917	10	37	47	16	29	0	2	12	2	105	3.4	19
Kirk Haston........ 15	15	77	11	39	.282	4	8	.500	5	15	20	5	9	0	0	3	1	26	1.7	4
Jerome Moiso....... 15	15	76	8	20	.400	0	0	...	4	21	25	4	12	0	3	8	2	16	1.1	4
Eldridge Recasner*.... 1	1	2	0	0	...	0	0	...	0	0	0	0	1	0	0	0	0	0	0.0	0

3-pt. FG: Charlotte 346-994 (.348)—Mashburn 41-112 (.366); Davis 170-478 (.356); Wesley 85-256 (.332); Campbell 0-2 (.000); Nailon 1-2 (.500); Magloire 0-1 (.000); Augmon 0-3 (.000); Lynch 1-6 (.167); Traylor 1-1 (1.000); Drew 31-73 (.425); Bullard 16-57 (.281); Haston 0-3 (.000). Opponents 433-1156 (.375).

– 287 –

CHICAGO BULLS

	G	Min.	FGM	FGA	Pct.	FTM	FTA	Pct.	Off.	Def.	Tot.	Ast.	PF	Dq.	Stl.	TO	Blk.	Pts.	Avg.	Hi.
Jalen Rose†	30	1216	276	587	.470	125	149	.839	14	110	124	158	103	1	33	96	16	714	23.8	44
Jalen Rose‡	83	3153	663	1458	.455	281	335	.839	43	330	373	355	251	2	78	201	45	1696	20.4	44
Ron Mercer*	40	1503	286	717	.399	84	108	.778	44	111	155	118	86	1	30	79	10	673	16.8	31
Ron Artest*	27	823	152	351	.433	81	129	.628	40	91	131	77	108	6	75	69	23	421	15.6	29
Brad Miller*	48	1391	208	452	.460	190	253	.751	176	225	401	101	156	2	52	74	29	608	12.7	32
Marcus Fizer	76	1963	371	848	.438	189	283	.668	128	299	427	120	186	1	49	131	24	938	12.3	30
Jamal Crawford	23	481	89	187	.476	10	13	.769	5	29	34	55	18	0	18	32	5	214	9.3	18
Eddie Robinson	29	653	112	247	.453	36	48	.750	24	54	78	37	35	0	23	36	11	262	9.0	18
Trenton Hassell	78	2237	267	628	.425	87	114	.763	65	190	255	172	184	2	55	101	44	681	8.7	22
Greg Anthony*	36	961	113	287	.394	47	70	.671	16	72	88	203	72	1	49	58	4	302	8.4	19
Travis Best†	30	793	112	254	.441	47	51	.922	10	71	81	149	72	3	32	40	1	279	9.3	21
Travis Best‡	74	1747	228	518	.440	104	116	.897	20	131	151	324	173	6	89	99	7	581	7.9	21
Eddy Curry	72	1150	189	377	.501	105	160	.656	111	161	272	25	173	0	16	69	53	483	6.7	19
Tyson Chandler	71	1389	151	304	.497	134	222	.604	114	229	343	54	179	1	28	99	93	436	6.1	21
Kevin Ollie*	52	1146	97	253	.383	109	130	.838	18	110	128	193	64	1	36	80	1	304	5.8	15
A.J. Guyton	45	607	88	244	.361	22	27	.815	12	32	44	81	23	0	10	37	7	244	5.4	19
Fred Hoiberg	79	1408	121	291	.416	79	94	.840	18	192	210	136	87	2	61	32	5	345	4.4	18
Charles Oakley	57	1383	97	263	.369	21	28	.750	72	271	343	114	175	2	49	87	11	216	3.8	12
Dalibor Bagaric	50	638	72	178	.404	41	70	.586	55	107	162	23	108	0	17	46	24	185	3.7	16
Norm Richardson†	8	63	10	23	.435	6	9	.667	2	5	7	1	5	0	0	3	0	30	3.8	10
Norm Richardson‡	11	67	10	26	.385	6	9	.667	3	5	8	2	5	0	0	3	0	30	2.7	10

3-pt. FG: Chicago 300-868 (.346)—Rose† 37-100 (.370); Rose‡ 89-246 (.362); Mercer* 17-57 (.298); Artest* 36-91 (.396); Miller* 2-4 (.500); Fizer 7-41 (.171); Crawford 26-58 (.448); Robinson 2-5 (.400); Hassell 60-165 (.364); Anthony* 29-90 (.322); Best† 8-25 (.320); Best‡ 21-59 (.356); Ollie* 1-2 (.500); Guyton 46-123 (.374); Hoiberg 24-92 (.261); Oakley 1-6 (.167); Bagaric 0-1 (.000); Richardson† 4-8 (.500); Richardson‡ 4-8 (.500). Opponents 421-1177 (.358).

CLEVELAND CAVALIERS

	G	Min.	FGM	FGA	Pct.	FTM	FTA	Pct.	Off.	Def.	Tot.	Ast.	PF	Dq.	Stl.	TO	Blk.	Pts.	Avg.	Hi.
Lamond Murray	71	2312	430	986	.436	215	263	.817	81	291	372	157	148	1	70	141	43	1176	16.6	40
Andre Miller	81	3023	474	1045	.454	365	447	.817	108	271	379	882	228	1	126	245	34	1335	16.5	37
Wesley Person	78	2793	467	944	.495	99	124	.798	50	244	294	173	93	0	77	74	37	1176	15.1	33
Ricky Davis	82	1954	376	781	.481	196	248	.790	63	180	243	178	145	0	69	148	23	959	11.7	35
Zydrunas Ilgauskas	62	1329	241	567	.425	208	276	.754	136	198	334	70	187	4	17	94	84	690	11.1	26
Jumaine Jones	81	2142	287	640	.448	45	68	.662	125	365	490	116	184	3	75	79	46	671	8.3	28
Tyrone Hill	26	810	71	182	.390	67	103	.650	79	195	274	23	102	3	17	48	13	209	8.0	16
Chris Mihm	74	1659	221	526	.420	124	179	.693	133	259	392	24	260	7	18	97	89	569	7.7	20
Trajan Langdon	44	477	70	176	.398	42	46	.913	13	42	55	60	49	0	13	40	5	209	4.8	24
Michael Doleac	42	705	78	187	.417	38	46	.826	47	121	168	25	98	4	15	37	11	194	4.6	17
Bryant Stith	50	665	70	188	.372	44	52	.846	20	65	85	42	42	0	29	30	6	208	4.2	20
Brian Skinner	65	1107	88	162	.543	48	79	.608	93	188	281	17	130	1	24	42	61	224	3.4	11
Bimbo Coles	47	693	56	146	.384	33	37	.892	12	43	55	107	59	0	13	31	4	149	3.2	13
Jeff Trepagnier	12	77	7	23	.304	4	7	.571	3	9	12	12	8	0	8	11	4	18	1.5	8
DeSagana Diop	18	109	12	29	.414	1	5	.200	5	12	17	5	19	0	1	12	10	25	1.4	6

3-pt. FG: Cleveland 387-1026 (.377)—Murray 101-238 (.424); Miller 22-87 (.253); Person 143-322 (.444); Davis 11-35 (.314); Ilgauskas 0-5 (.000); Jones 52-168 (.310); Hill 0-1 (.000); Mihm 3-7 (.429); Langdon 27-74 (.365); Stith 24-68 (.353); Coles 4-20 (.200); Trepagnier 0-1 (.000). Opponents 473-1200 (.394).

DALLAS MAVERICKS

	G	Min.	FGM	FGA	Pct.	FTM	FTA	Pct.	Off.	Def.	Tot.	Ast.	PF	Dq.	Stl.	TO	Blk.	Pts.	Avg.	Hi.
Dirk Nowitzki	76	2891	600	1258	.477	440	516	.853	120	635	755	186	222	2	83	145	77	1779	23.4	40
Michael Finley	69	2754	569	1228	.463	210	251	.837	90	270	360	230	144	1	65	117	25	1424	20.6	39
Nick Van Exel†	27	757	129	314	.411	65	77	.844	9	76	85	113	35	0	14	40	4	357	13.2	27
Nick Van Exel‡	72	2496	501	1226	.409	201	251	.801	28	226	254	478	104	0	44	156	11	1322	18.4	44
Steve Nash	82	2837	525	1088	.483	260	293	.887	50	204	254	634	164	0	53	229	4	1466	17.9	39
Raef LaFrentz†	27	787	114	261	.437	35	46	.761	59	141	200	29	108	6	24	34	60	292	10.8	30
Raef LaFrentz‡	78	2455	421	920	.458	105	151	.695	176	403	579	89	281	11	55	94	213	1051	13.5	30
Juwan Howard*	53	1659	270	585	.462	144	191	.754	138	252	390	93	170	1	28	78	30	684	12.9	36
Tim Hardaway*	54	1276	199	494	.362	65	78	.833	13	84	97	201	84	0	40	73	8	518	9.6	21
Avery Johnson†	17	152	21	49	.429	12	17	.706	0	5	5	28	17	0	5	9	1	54	3.2	15
Avery Johnson‡	68	1352	207	432	.479	121	163	.742	14	55	69	286	86	0	40	76	9	535	7.9	23
Adrian Griffin	58	1383	179	359	.499	41	49	.837	68	161	229	106	142	2	75	42	12	415	7.2	23
Eduardo Najera	62	1357	150	300	.500	100	148	.676	149	193	342	38	156	2	56	40	30	400	6.5	19
Greg Buckner	44	885	104	198	.525	40	58	.690	67	106	173	48	124	1	31	27	19	253	5.8	18
Tariq Abdul-Wahad†	4	24	0	2	.000	0	1	.000	2	4	6	2	5	0	2	3	1	0	0.0	0
Tariq Abdul-Wahad‡	24	441	55	147	.374	21	33	.727	41	43	84	24	50	1	20	27	10	135	5.6	14

	G	Min.	FGM	FGA	Pct.	FTM	FTA	Pct.	Off.	Def.	Tot.	Ast.	PF	Dq.	Stl.	TO	Blk.	Pts.	Avg.	Hi.
									REBOUNDS									SCORING		
Zhizhi Wang	55	600	109	248	.440	42	57	.737	19	92	111	22	84	0	11	25	18	308	5.6	18
Johnny Newman	47	724	67	148	.453	42	58	.724	9	40	49	14	88	2	29	21	4	198	4.2	17
Shawn Bradley	53	757	78	163	.479	59	64	.922	53	123	176	20	128	3	28	25	64	215	4.1	15
Danny Manning	41	552	71	149	.477	22	33	.667	25	83	108	30	80	0	21	25	21	165	4.0	13
Donnell Harvey*	18	162	14	26	.538	10	22	.455	12	34	46	5	27	0	4	8	5	38	2.1	12
Evan Eschmeyer	31	299	21	50	.420	20	33	.606	35	63	98	9	60	1	10	16	9	62	2.0	6
Charlie Bell†	2	2	0	0	...	0	0	...	0	1	1	0	0	0	0	0	0	0	0.0	0
Charlie Bell‡	7	44	3	11	.273	2	2	1.000	2	3	5	2	3	0	0	5	0	8	1.1	4
Darrick Martin	3	22	0	10	.000	1	2	.500	0	1	1	3	4	0	2	1	0	1	0.3	1

3-pt. FG: Dallas 621-1645 (.378)—Nowitzki 139-350 (.397); Finley 76-224 (.339); Van Exel† 34-98 (.347); Van Exel‡ 119-350 (.340); Nash 156-343 (.455); LaFrentz† 29-95 (.305); LaFrentz‡ 104-268 (.388); Howard* 0-1 (.000); Hardaway* 95-279 (.341); Johnson‡ 0-5 (.000); Griffin 16-54 (.296); Najera 0-2 (.000); Buckner 5-16 (.313); Abdul-Wahad‡ 1-2 (.500); Wang 48-116 (.414); Newman 22-57 (.386); Bradley 0-1 (.000); Manning 1-7 (.143); Bell‡ 0-6 (.000); Martin 0-2 (.000). Opponents 452-1293 (.350).

DENVER NUGGETS

	G	Min.	FGM	FGA	Pct.	FTM	FTA	Pct.	Off.	Def.	Tot.	Ast.	PF	Dq.	Stl.	TO	Blk.	Pts.	Avg.	Hi.
									REBOUNDS									SCORING		
Nick Van Exel*	45	1739	372	912	.408	136	174	.782	19	150	169	365	69	0	30	116	7	965	21.4	44
Raef LaFrentz*	51	1668	307	659	.466	70	105	.667	117	262	379	60	173	5	31	60	153	759	14.9	30
Juwan Howard†	28	979	192	420	.457	117	152	.770	85	137	222	76	95	3	18	74	17	501	17.9	30
Juwan Howard‡	81	2635	462	1005	.460	261	343	.761	223	389	612	169	265	4	46	152	47	1185	14.6	36
Voshon Lenard	71	1665	315	769	.410	94	120	.783	38	145	183	130	105	0	59	91	25	813	11.5	29
Antonio McDyess	10	236	43	75	.573	27	33	.818	18	37	55	18	20	0	10	20	8	113	11.3	19
James Posey	73	2238	277	736	.376	161	203	.793	109	320	429	180	224	3	114	127	39	782	10.7	33
Tim Hardaway†	14	325	47	126	.373	12	19	.632	1	26	27	77	25	0	17	38	2	134	9.6	22
Tim Hardaway‡	68	1601	226	620	.365	77	97	.794	14	110	124	278	109	0	57	111	10	652	9.6	22
Avery Johnson*	51	1200	186	383	.486	109	146	.747	14	50	64	258	69	0	35	67	8	481	9.4	23
Isaiah Rider	10	173	37	81	.457	13	17	.765	10	23	33	12	11	0	3	14	2	93	9.3	28
George McCloud	69	1830	206	576	.358	132	163	.810	67	184	251	204	175	3	58	144	19	604	8.8	26
Calbert Cheaney	68	1631	224	466	.481	46	67	.687	57	183	240	110	156	1	34	70	21	494	7.3	22
Tariq Abdul-Wahad*	20	417	55	145	.379	24	32	.750	39	39	78	22	51	1	18	24	9	135	6.8	14
Zendon Hamilton	54	848	103	245	.420	118	181	.652	110	143	253	14	104	0	21	60	18	324	6.0	20
Donnell Harvey†	29	679	94	191	.492	44	68	.647	68	113	181	32	88	1	17	25	19	232	8.0	18
Donnell Harvey‡	47	841	108	217	.498	54	90	.600	80	147	227	37	115	1	21	33	24	270	5.7	18
Kenny Satterfield	36	560	73	199	.367	36	46	.783	17	35	52	108	43	0	31	53	1	189	5.3	21
Mengke Bateer	27	408	53	132	.402	29	37	.784	32	64	96	22	94	3	10	32	5	139	5.1	12
Scott Williams	41	737	86	217	.396	30	41	.732	82	127	209	13	98	1	17	35	33	202	4.9	16
Ryan Bowen	75	1686	147	307	.479	69	92	.750	134	165	299	52	171	1	75	41	41	364	4.9	18
Shawnelle Scott	21	252	37	75	.493	8	20	.400	53	50	103	8	49	0	3	15	6	82	3.9	9
Chris Andersen	24	262	25	74	.338	22	28	.786	38	38	76	7	35	0	7	13	28	72	3.0	17
Carlos Arroyo†	20	275	36	82	.439	9	12	.750	9	19	28	49	18	0	5	11	1	81	4.1	12
Carlos Arroyo‡	37	371	49	111	.441	13	18	.722	12	28	40	70	30	0	11	23	1	111	3.0	12

3-pt. FG: Denver 423-1285 (.329)—Van Exel* 85-252 (.337); LaFrentz* 75-173 (.434); Howard† 0-1 (.000); Howard‡ 0-2 (.000); Lenard 89-240 (.371); Posey 67-237 (.283); Hardaway† 28-75 (.373); Hardaway‡ 123-354 (.347); Johnson* 0-5 (.000); Rider 6-15 (.400); McCloud 60-222 (.270); Cheaney 0-4 (.000); Abdul-Wahad* 1-2 (.500); Satterfield 7-27 (.259); Bateer 4-12 (.333); Williams 0-2 (.000); Bowen 1-12 (.083); Andersen 0-4 (.000); Arroyo† 0-2 (.000); Arroyo‡ 0-2 (.000). Opponents 424 1173 (.361).

DETROIT PISTONS

	G	Min.	FGM	FGA	Pct.	FTM	FTA	Pct.	Off.	Def.	Tot.	Ast.	PF	Dq.	Stl.	TO	Blk.	Pts.	Avg.	Hi.
									REBOUNDS									SCORING		
Jerry Stackhouse	76	2685	524	1319	.397	495	577	.858	77	238	315	403	163	0	77	266	37	1629	21.4	40
Clifford Robinson	80	2855	454	1069	.425	143	206	.694	79	307	386	202	243	4	89	151	95	1166	14.6	35
Corliss Williamson	78	1701	411	806	.510	240	298	.805	117	202	319	94	226	1	49	137	26	1063	13.6	25
Chucky Atkins	79	2285	368	790	.466	83	120	.692	31	127	158	263	177	1	72	128	11	957	12.1	26
Jon Barry	82	1985	255	522	.489	116	124	.931	42	192	234	274	134	0	94	111	20	739	9.0	25
Ben Wallace	80	2921	255	480	.531	99	234	.423	318	721	1039	115	178	2	138	70	278	609	7.6	19
Zeljko Rebraca	74	1179	189	374	.505	135	175	.771	84	206	290	38	192	0	28	84	73	513	6.9	24
Dana Barros	29	582	74	192	.385	21	27	.778	1	56	57	78	37	0	14	33	2	193	6.7	17
Damon Jones	67	1083	114	284	.401	43	59	.729	13	90	103	140	83	0	23	61	1	340	5.1	17
Ratko Varda	1	6	2	3	.667	1	1	1.000	0	1	1	0	3	0	0	1	0	5	5.0	5
Michael Curry	82	1912	125	276	.453	72	91	.791	15	153	168	127	207	1	47	60	10	329	4.0	14
Rodney White	16	129	21	60	.350	12	14	.857	2	16	18	12	6	0	9	14	2	56	3.5	7
Victor Alexander	15	97	18	51	.353	4	8	.500	7	22	29	6	6	0	0	5	1	40	2.7	12
Mikki Moore	30	271	29	61	.475	20	26	.769	22	31	53	11	35	0	7	14	9	79	2.6	8
Brian Cardinal	8	43	6	13	.462	2	2	1.000	2	4	6	2	5	0	1	0	0	17	2.1	6

3-pt. FG: Detroit 567-1509 (.376)—Stackhouse 86-300 (.287); Robinson 115-304 (.378); Williamson 1-5 (.200); Atkins 138-336 (.411); Barry 121-258 (.469); Wallace 0-3 (.000); Barros 24-71 (.338); Jones 69-186 (.371); Curry 7-26 (.269); White 2-9 (.222); Alexander 0-2 (.000); Moore 1-2 (.500); Cardinal 3-7 (.429). Opponents 359-993 (.362).

2001-02

GOLDEN STATE WARRIORS

	G	Min.	FGM	FGA	Pct.	FTM	FTA	Pct.	Off.	Def.	Tot.	Ast.	PF	Dq.	Stl.	TO	Blk.	Pts.	Avg.	Hi.
Antawn Jamison	82	3033	614	1375	.447	323	440	.734	211	345	556	161	187	0	70	161	45	1619	19.7	35
Jason Richardson . . .	80	2629	464	1090	.426	141	210	.671	124	216	340	236	195	2	106	160	31	1151	14.4	40
Larry Hughes	73	2049	343	810	.423	191	259	.737	83	162	245	316	150	0	113	171	23	895	12.3	31
Danny Fortson	77	2216	309	722	.428	245	308	.795	290	609	899	127	255	5	44	160	17	864	11.2	25
Gilbert Arenas	47	1155	174	384	.453	124	160	.775	41	91	132	174	115	3	69	97	11	511	10.9	32
Bob Sura	78	1780	250	590	.424	236	328	.720	89	167	256	275	160	1	88	133	17	778	10.0	23
Erick Dampier	73	1740	209	480	.435	136	211	.645	167	220	387	87	235	4	17	156	167	554	7.6	22
Chris Mills	66	1237	178	427	.417	85	107	.794	51	139	190	72	120	0	31	56	13	489	7.4	20
Troy Murphy	82	1448	178	423	.421	121	156	.776	99	223	322	70	217	2	36	84	21	480	5.9	17
Marc Jackson*	17	169	22	65	.338	40	48	.833	17	26	43	7	25	0	5	12	3	84	4.9	13
Adonal Foyle	79	1485	171	385	.444	37	93	.398	150	234	384	41	179	2	36	76	168	379	4.8	14
Mookie Blaylock	35	599	50	146	.342	4	8	.500	8	44	52	114	20	0	24	37	4	119	3.4	13
Cedric Henderson . .	12	70	15	31	.484	4	7	.571	1	2	3	4	4	0	6	8	2	36	3.0	11
Dean Oliver	20	139	17	46	.370	6	9	.667	0	8	8	21	16	1	3	11	0	42	2.1	15
Dean Garrett†	5	31	4	15	.267	0	0	. . .	3	7	10	1	6	0	2	3	1	8	1.6	2
Dean Garrett‡	34	183	18	55	.327	0	3	.000	16	41	57	5	32	0	7	10	10	36	1.1	6

3-pt. FG: Golden State 320-994 (.322)—Jamison 68-210 (.324); Richardson 82-246 (.333); Hughes 18-93 (.194); Fortson 1-4 (.250); Arenas 39-113 (.345); Sura 42-133 (.316); Mills 48-127 (.378); Murphy 3-9 (.333); Blaylock 15-42 (.357); Henderson 2-4 (.500); Oliver 2-13 (.154). Opponents 404-1162 (.348).

HOUSTON ROCKETS

	G	Min.	FGM	FGA	Pct.	FTM	FTA	Pct.	Off.	Def.	Tot.	Ast.	PF	Dq.	Stl.	TO	Blk.	Pts.	Avg.	Hi.
Cuttino Mobley	74	3116	595	1358	.438	267	314	.850	63	237	300	187	189	3	109	180	37	1606	21.7	41
Steve Francis	57	2343	420	1007	.417	326	422	.773	102	299	401	362	172	2	71	221	25	1234	21.6	36
Kenny Thomas	72	2484	396	829	.478	223	336	.664	158	358	516	137	195	5	85	143	66	1015	14.1	31
Walt Williams	48	1117	166	396	.419	40	51	.784	37	125	162	69	106	0	18	53	10	450	9.4	31
Eddie Griffin	73	1896	244	666	.366	64	86	.744	117	299	416	53	117	1	17	47	134	642	8.8	25
Glen Rice	20	606	65	167	.389	24	30	.800	5	42	47	31	34	0	12	24	3	172	8.6	20
Moochie Norris	82	2249	251	631	.398	127	169	.751	73	173	246	403	130	0	81	156	4	665	8.1	28
Kelvin Cato	75	1917	190	326	.583	113	194	.582	176	349	525	29	208	5	40	53	95	493	6.6	18
Kevin Willis	52	865	125	284	.440	65	87	.747	105	194	299	14	98	0	25	41	23	315	6.1	18
Oscar Torres	65	1075	135	341	.396	82	105	.781	47	75	122	40	64	0	25	49	9	389	6.0	28
Jason Collier	25	365	41	95	.432	24	32	.750	31	51	82	9	40	0	6	13	4	106	4.2	12
Terence Morris	68	1110	111	289	.384	18	28	.643	77	134	211	64	72	1	21	45	27	255	3.8	13
Dan Langhi	34	434	49	125	.392	8	11	.727	22	45	67	14	25	0	8	9	5	107	3.1	17
Tierre Brown	40	403	49	115	.426	21	28	.750	12	30	42	70	26	0	19	40	3	123	3.1	16

3-pt. FG: Houston 496-1480 (.335)—Mobley 149-377 (.395); Francis 68-210 (.324); Thomas 0-16 (.000); Williams 78-183 (.426); Griffin 90-273 (.330); Rice 18-64 (.281); Norris 36-134 (.269); Cato 0-1 (.000); Willis 0-1 (.000); Torres 37-126 (.294); Collier 0-1 (.000); Morris 15-78 (.192); Langhi 1-4 (.250); Brown 4-12 (.333). Opponents 370-1028 (.360).

INDIANA PACERS

	G	Min.	FGM	FGA	Pct.	FTM	FTA	Pct.	Off.	Def.	Tot.	Ast.	PF	Dq.	Stl.	TO	Blk.	Pts.	Avg.	Hi.
Jermaine O'Neal	72	2707	543	1133	.479	284	413	.688	188	569	757	118	269	4	45	174	166	1371	19.0	38
Jalen Rose*	53	1937	387	871	.444	156	186	.839	29	220	249	197	148	1	45	105	29	982	18.5	43
Reggie Miller	79	2889	414	913	.453	296	325	.911	23	196	219	253	143	0	88	120	10	1304	16.5	30
Ron Mercer†	13	213	25	67	.373	11	11	1.000	6	17	23	10	22	0	2	9	3	62	4.8	17
Ron Mercer‡	53	1716	311	784	.397	95	119	.798	50	128	178	128	108	1	32	88	13	735	13.9	31
Brad Miller†	28	872	158	281	.562	107	130	.823	76	144	220	51	88	1	24	41	12	424	15.1	25
Brad Miller‡	76	2263	366	733	.499	297	383	.775	252	369	621	152	244	3	76	115	41	1032	13.6	32
Ron Artest†	28	819	117	285	.411	55	75	.733	33	107	140	50	109	4	66	49	16	306	10.9	24
Ron Artest‡	55	1642	269	636	.423	136	204	.667	73	198	271	127	217	10	141	118	39	727	13.2	29
Al Harrington	44	1313	230	484	.475	115	144	.799	96	180	276	54	166	4	41	78	21	576	13.1	26
Jamaal Tinsley	80	2442	289	760	.380	131	186	.704	78	220	298	647	248	9	138	270	40	751	9.4	30
Jonathan Bender	78	1647	198	460	.430	140	181	.773	64	180	244	62	147	1	19	96	49	581	7.4	20
Travis Best*	44	954	116	264	.439	57	65	.877	10	60	70	175	101	3	57	59	6	302	6.9	18
Austin Croshere	76	1286	185	448	.413	97	114	.851	74	220	294	77	106	0	26	67	29	516	6.8	32
Kevin Ollie†	29	577	40	100	.400	78	97	.804	7	49	56	98	33	0	26	26	1	158	5.4	16
Kevin Ollie‡	81	1723	137	353	.388	187	227	.824	25	159	184	291	97	1	62	106	2	462	5.7	16
Jeff Foster	82	1786	177	394	.449	111	182	.610	206	350	556	70	232	4	71	79	38	467	5.7	17
Carlos Rogers	22	168	24	43	.558	10	19	.526	14	24	38	3	17	0	5	5	6	59	2.7	15
Primoz Brezec	22	160	14	29	.483	15	25	.600	16	12	28	6	28	0	0	6	7	43	2.0	8
Bruno Sundov	22	88	16	40	.400	0	2	.000	7	14	21	3	16	0	3	4	3	32	1.5	6
Jamison Brewer	13	43	2	5	.400	0	0	. . .	2	6	8	9	3	0	2	3	0	4	0.3	2
Norm Richardson*	3	4	0	3	.000	0	0	. . .	1	0	1	1	0	0	0	0	0	0	0.0	0

3-pt. FG: Indiana 405-1195 (.339)—O'Neal 1-14 (.071); Rose* 52-146 (.356); R. Miller 180-443 (.406); Mercer† 1-5 (.200); Mercer‡ 18-62 (.290); B. Miller† 1-3 (.333); B. Miller‡ 3-7 (.429); Artest† 17-79 (.215); Artest‡ 53-170 (.312); Harrington 1-3 (.333); Tinsley 42-175 (.240); Bender 45-125 (.360); Best* 13-34 (.382); Croshere 49-145 (.338); Ollie‡ 1-2 (.500); Foster 2-15 (.133) Rogers 1-6 (.167); Sundov 0-1 (.000); Brewer 0-1 (.000). Opponents 418-1200 (.348).

LOS ANGELES CLIPPERS

								REBOUNDS									SCORING		
	G	Min.	FGM	FGA	Pct.	FTM	FTA	Pct.	Off.	Def.	Tot.	Ast.	PF	Dq.	Stl.	TO	Blk.	Pts.	Avg.	Hi.
Elton Brand........	80	3020	532	1010	.527	389	524	.742	396	529	925	191	254	3	80	173	163	1453	18.2	31
Jeff McInnis........	81	3030	463	1121	.413	183	219	.836	45	168	213	500	202	2	63	147	6	1184	14.6	31
Quentin Richardson...	81	2152	400	926	.432	143	187	.765	113	221	334	128	142	2	78	102	21	1076	13.3	31
Lamar Odom........	29	999	151	360	.419	61	93	.656	31	145	176	171	91	3	23	97	36	379	13.1	27
Corey Maggette......	63	1615	235	530	.443	201	251	.801	54	177	231	112	155	0	41	116	19	717	11.4	28
Michael Olowokandi ..	80	2568	384	886	.433	117	188	.622	164	547	711	90	217	1	55	175	145	885	11.1	30
Darius Miles........	82	2227	309	642	.481	158	255	.620	109	344	453	184	184	2	71	160	103	779	9.5	20
Eric Piatkowski	71	1718	207	471	.439	101	113	.894	43	141	184	112	110	0	41	64	12	626	8.8	36
Keyon Dooling	14	155	22	57	.386	10	12	.833	0	3	3	12	20	0	4	10	3	58	4.1	17
Earl Boykins........	68	761	110	275	.400	47	61	.770	27	27	54	145	44	0	20	44	2	280	4.1	12
Tremaine Fowlkes	22	343	25	64	.391	24	31	.774	32	32	64	17	39	0	11	13	1	74	3.4	11
Sean Rooks	61	728	81	194	.418	21	29	.724	32	92	124	25	114	1	12	20	21	183	3.0	16
Doug Overton	18	130	14	44	.318	4	7	.571	1	11	12	13	10	0	3	12	1	39	2.2	8
Harold Jamison	25	176	22	43	.512	10	15	.667	24	15	39	6	23	0	5	6	1	54	2.2	14
Obinna Ekezie	29	152	13	39	.333	28	40	.700	12	22	34	3	16	0	2	10	6	54	1.9	11
Eldridge Recasner†....	5	31	2	6	.333	1	1	1.000	0	0	0	5	3	0	1	1	0	5	1.0	3
Eldridge Recasner‡....	6	33	2	6	.333	1	1	1.000	0	0	0	5	4	0	1	1	0	5	0.8	3

3-pt. FG: L.A. Clippers 408-1147 (.356)—McInnis 75-234 (.321); Richardson 133-349 (.381); Odom 16-84 (.190); Maggette 46-139 (.331); Miles 3-19 (.158); Piatkowski 111-238 (.466); Dooling 4-14 (.286); Boykins 13-42 (.310); Overton 7-27 (.259); Recasner† 0-1 (.000); Recasner‡ 0-1 (.000). Opponents 407-1145 (.355).

LOS ANGELES LAKERS

								REBOUNDS									SCORING		
	G	Min.	FGM	FGA	Pct.	FTM	FTA	Pct.	Off.	Def.	Tot.	Ast.	PF	Dq.	Stl.	TO	Blk.	Pts.	Avg.	Hi.
Shaquille O'Neal	67	2422	712	1229	.579	398	717	.555	235	480	715	200	199	2	41	171	137	1822	27.2	46
Kobe Bryant	80	3063	749	1597	.469	488	589	.829	112	329	441	438	228	1	118	223	35	2019	25.2	56
Derek Fisher	70	1974	274	666	.411	94	111	.847	15	131	146	181	121	0	66	62	9	786	11.2	28
Rick Fox	82	2289	255	605	.421	70	85	.824	90	299	389	283	244	2	67	132	21	645	7.9	18
Devean George	82	1759	215	523	.411	85	126	.675	78	225	303	111	190	3	71	66	42	581	7.1	17
Robert Horry........	81	2140	183	460	.398	108	138	.783	130	349	479	232	208	1	77	88	89	550	6.8	23
Samaki Walker	69	1655	187	365	.512	86	129	.667	129	352	481	64	170	1	20	53	88	460	6.7	18
Lindsey Hunter	82	1616	187	490	.382	20	40	.500	18	103	121	129	120	0	66	55	19	473	5.8	18
Stanislav Medvedenko.	71	729	145	304	.477	41	62	.661	85	73	158	43	119	0	29	42	11	331	4.7	18
Mitch Richmond	64	709	100	247	.405	42	44	.955	14	80	94	57	61	0	18	40	6	260	4.1	13
Brian Shaw	58	631	61	173	.353	18	26	.692	19	93	112	89	43	0	25	32	3	169	2.9	16
Mark Madsen	59	650	66	146	.452	35	54	.648	89	73	162	44	104	0	16	22	13	167	2.8	10
Joseph Crispin*	6	27	3	12	.250	4	5	.800	0	1	1	2	2	0	1	1	0	10	1.7	5
Mike Penberthy.......	3	12	1	2	.500	3	4	.750	0	2	2	2	0	0	2	0	0	5	1.7	2
Jelani McCoy	21	104	12	21	.571	2	8	.250	8	17	25	7	14	0	0	8	5	26	1.2	6

3-pt. FG: L.A. Lakers 510-1439 (.354)—O'Neal 0-1 (.000); Bryant 33-132 (.250); Fisher 144-349 (.413); Fox 65-208 (.313); George 66-178 (.371); Horry 76-203 (.374); Hunter 79-208 (.380); Medvedenko 0-4 (.000); Richmond 18-62 (.290); Shaw 29-88 (.330); Madsen 0-2 (.000); Crispin* 0-4 (.000). Opponents 399-1259 (.317).

MEMPHIS GRIZZLIES

								REBOUNDS									SCORING		
	G	Min.	FGM	FGA	Pct.	FTM	FTA	Pct.	Off.	Def.	Tot.	Ast.	PF	Dq.	Stl.	TO	Blk.	Pts.	Avg.	Hi.
Pau Gasol..........	82	3007	551	1064	.518	338	477	.709	238	492	730	223	195	2	41	224	169	1441	17.6	32
Jason Williams	65	2236	376	985	.382	80	101	.792	22	173	195	519	102	0	111	214	7	959	14.8	38
Shane Battier	78	3097	412	961	.429	198	283	.700	180	238	418	216	215	2	121	155	81	1125	14.4	30
Lorenzen Wright.....	43	1251	223	486	.459	70	123	.569	130	275	405	44	126	0	30	72	23	516	12.0	33
Stromile Swift.......	68	1805	293	611	.480	217	305	.711	161	269	430	50	178	3	53	122	113	803	11.8	31
Michael Dickerson.....	4	124	15	48	.313	5	6	.833	3	9	12	9	12	0	3	8	1	43	10.8	15
Rodney Buford	63	1769	258	593	.435	58	80	.725	52	220	272	71	110	1	42	63	12	591	9.4	21
Brevin Knight	53	1151	141	334	.422	87	115	.757	11	98	109	302	135	1	79	111	7	371	7.0	24
Grant Long..........	66	1868	164	385	.426	86	123	.699	31	200	231	136	123	0	63	103	12	417	6.3	19
Tony Massenburg ...	73	1247	159	349	.456	84	117	.718	100	224	324	26	174	2	30	65	31	403	5.5	23
Elliot Perry	2	48	5	10	.500	1	2	.500	0	4	4	7	6	0	3	7	0	11	5.5	7
Willie Solomon	62	872	113	331	.341	49	73	.671	12	56	68	92	76	0	35	62	7	321	5.2	23
Eddie Gill	23	384	39	92	.424	31	39	.795	7	21	28	49	38	0	11	34	1	116	5.0	20
Nick Anderson	15	219	21	76	.276	5	9	.556	1	32	33	14	17	0	6	14	6	60	4.0	17
Antonis Fotsis.......	28	320	42	104	.404	17	20	.850	25	37	62	10	22	0	9	21	11	108	3.9	21
Isaac Austin	21	307	36	92	.391	4	4	1.000	11	60	71	13	36	0	9	11	5	76	3.6	10
Ike Fontaine	6	75	3	14	.214	4	6	.667	0	5	5	4	6	0	0	4	0	11	1.8	8

3-pt. FG: Memphis 336-1096 (.307)—Gasol 1-5 (.200); Williams 127-430 (.295); Battier 103-276 (.373); Wright 0-2 (.000); Swift 0-3 (.000); Dickerson 8-21 (.381); Buford 17-70 (.243); Knight 2-8 (.250); Long 3-17 (.176); Massenburg 1-1 (1.000); Solomon 46-162 (.284); Gill 7-22 (.318); Anderson 13-48 (.271); Fotsis 7-23 (.304); Austin 0-3 (.000); Fontaine 1-5 (.200). Opponents 398-1112 (.358).

MIAMI HEAT

	G	Min.	FGM	FGA	Pct.	FTM	FTA	Pct.	Off.	Def.	Tot.	Ast.	PF	Dq.	Stl.	TO	Blk.	Pts.	Avg.	Hi.
									REBOUNDS									SCORING		
Eddie Jones	81	3156	517	1198	.432	297	355	.837	61	317	378	262	258	2	117	148	77	1480	18.3	37
Alonzo Mourning	75	2455	447	866	.516	283	431	.657	182	450	632	87	258	7	27	182	186	1178	15.7	28
Jim Jackson	55	1825	238	538	.442	75	87	.862	54	236	290	140	145	0	42	106	14	589	10.7	24
Rod Strickland	76	2294	316	714	.443	154	201	.766	49	183	232	463	114	0	82	159	11	794	10.4	24
Brian Grant	72	2256	286	610	.469	101	119	.849	168	407	575	137	236	6	48	122	31	673	9.3	22
Eddie House	64	1230	209	524	.399	42	49	.857	17	93	110	123	98	1	43	80	5	514	8.0	28
LaPhonso Ellis	66	1684	189	452	.418	53	84	.631	107	180	287	56	196	4	30	73	37	469	7.1	24
Chris Gatling	54	809	131	293	.447	82	117	.701	71	135	206	25	109	1	17	58	11	345	6.4	19
Kendall Gill	65	1410	162	422	.384	42	62	.677	29	155	184	100	140	0	44	55	8	372	5.7	13
Sean Marks	21	319	38	88	.432	20	34	.588	19	56	75	8	40	0	5	19	10	96	4.6	15
Malik Allen	12	161	22	51	.431	8	10	.800	15	23	38	5	16	0	3	2	8	52	4.3	16
Anthony Carter	46	1050	89	260	.342	19	36	.528	19	98	117	214	85	2	50	72	3	198	4.3	12
Vladimir Stepania	67	884	117	249	.470	50	104	.481	100	170	270	16	103	1	24	52	44	285	4.3	19
Sam Mack	12	159	14	49	.286	5	7	.714	2	12	14	4	17	0	5	7	1	40	3.3	11
Mike James	15	119	15	43	.349	4	7	.571	2	12	14	19	17	0	6	13	1	42	2.8	12
Tang Hamilton	9	98	10	19	.526	0	1	.000	6	12	18	5	10	0	4	2	0	20	2.2	8
Ernest Brown	3	21	1	6	.167	1	4	.250	1	5	6	0	4	0	0	3	1	3	1.0	3

3-pt. FG: Miami 312-899 (.347)—Jones 149-382 (.390); Mourning 1-3 (.333); Jackson 38-81 (.469); Strickland 8-26 (.308); Grant 0-2 (.000); House 54-157 (.344); Ellis 38-124 (.306); Gatling 1-8 (.125); Gill 6-44 (.136); Allen 0-1 (.000); Carter 1-19 (.053); Stepania 1-2 (.500); Mack 7-28 (.250); James 8-21 (.381); Hamilton 0-1 (.000). Opponents 379-1109 (.342).

MILWAUKEE BUCKS

	G	Min.	FGM	FGA	Pct.	FTM	FTA	Pct.	Off.	Def.	Tot.	Ast.	PF	Dq.	Stl.	TO	Blk.	Pts.	Avg.	Hi.
									REBOUNDS									SCORING		
Ray Allen	69	2525	530	1148	.462	214	245	.873	81	231	312	271	157	0	88	159	18	1503	21.8	47
Glenn Robinson	66	2346	536	1147	.467	236	282	.837	70	336	406	168	173	1	97	174	41	1366	20.7	38
Sam Cassell	74	2605	554	1197	.463	282	328	.860	54	258	312	493	208	3	90	177	12	1461	19.7	33
Tim Thomas	74	1987	316	753	.420	142	179	.793	64	236	300	105	200	3	65	127	32	869	11.7	25
Michael Redd	67	1417	294	609	.483	91	115	.791	77	147	224	91	96	0	42	57	7	767	11.4	27
Anthony Mason	82	3143	316	626	.505	154	221	.697	124	522	646	346	187	0	57	130	22	787	9.6	23
Greg Anthony†	24	553	70	188	.372	13	21	.619	6	38	44	79	42	0	28	36	1	172	7.2	20
Greg Anthony‡	60	1514	183	475	.385	60	91	.659	22	110	132	282	114	1	77	94	5	474	7.9	20
Darvin Ham	70	1208	120	211	.569	62	123	.504	91	111	202	73	175	0	25	83	37	303	4.3	14
Jason Caffey	23	283	36	72	.500	27	43	.628	24	26	50	12	39	0	4	19	5	99	4.3	17
Rafer Alston	50	600	66	191	.346	18	29	.621	10	62	72	143	42	0	32	40	2	177	3.5	14
Joel Przybilla	71	1128	76	142	.535	38	90	.422	78	205	283	21	199	3	20	43	118	190	2.7	12
Ervin Johnson	81	1660	89	193	.461	30	66	.455	142	324	466	27	219	4	37	52	82	208	2.6	10
Mark Pope	45	426	36	91	.396	11	21	.524	20	53	73	17	47	0	11	15	11	87	1.9	10
Greg Foster	6	24	2	9	.222	3	4	.750	0	8	8	1	4	0	0	0	0	7	1.2	3

3-pt. FG: Milwaukee 593-1583 (.375)—Allen 229-528 (.434); Robinson 58-178 (.326); Cassell 71-204 (.348); Thomas 95-291 (.326); Redd 88-198 (.444); Mason 1-1 (1.000); Anthony† 19-73 (.260); Anthony‡ 48-163 (.294); Ham 1-7 (.143); Caffey 0-1 (.000); Alston 27-71 (.380); Przybilla 0-1 (.000); Johnson 0-1 (.000); Pope 4-25 (.160); Foster 0-4 (.000). Opponents 493-1377 (.358).

MINNESOTA TIMBERWOLVES

	G	Min.	FGM	FGA	Pct.	FTM	FTA	Pct.	Off.	Def.	Tot.	Ast.	PF	Dq.	Stl.	TO	Blk.	Pts.	Avg.	Hi.
									REBOUNDS									SCORING		
Kevin Garnett	81	3175	659	1401	.470	359	448	.801	243	738	981	422	184	0	96	229	126	1714	21.2	37
Wally Szczerbiak	82	3117	609	1200	.508	226	272	.831	120	271	391	257	188	1	66	181	21	1531	18.7	37
Chauncey Billups	82	2355	348	823	.423	207	234	.885	35	191	226	450	169	1	66	138	17	1027	12.5	36
Terrell Brandon	32	962	155	365	.425	83	84	.988	17	76	93	264	49	1	52	43	6	397	12.4	22
Joe Smith	72	1922	297	581	.511	171	206	.830	152	301	453	82	250	2	39	86	59	767	10.7	26
Anthony Peeler	82	2060	288	684	.421	50	58	.862	37	169	206	177	137	0	61	76	11	737	9.0	26
Rasho Nesterovic	82	2218	324	657	.493	39	71	.549	200	334	534	75	262	3	45	94	109	687	8.4	24
Gary Trent	64	1140	193	381	.507	92	144	.639	104	166	270	60	160	0	21	58	27	478	7.5	20
Marc Jackson†	22	326	38	99	.384	26	32	.813	31	54	85	7	44	0	6	18	3	102	4.6	12
Marc Jackson‡	39	495	60	164	.366	66	80	.825	48	80	128	14	69	0	11	30	6	186	4.8	13
Robert Pack	16	252	25	68	.368	11	15	.733	7	16	23	49	32	0	13	20	0	62	3.9	12
Sam Mitchell	74	726	98	227	.432	38	49	.776	18	64	82	45	79	0	12	26	4	244	3.3	11
Will Avery	28	258	26	90	.289	13	19	.684	4	20	24	36	17	0	7	19	0	71	2.5	14
Felipe Lopez	67	581	59	156	.378	37	55	.673	29	51	80	39	73	0	18	36	1	169	2.5	13
Maurice Evans	10	45	9	19	.474	3	4	.750	3	1	4	4	9	0	0	2	0	21	2.1	11
Loren Woods	60	516	33	96	.344	44	60	.733	46	76	122	22	60	0	17	36	34	110	1.8	11
Dean Garrett*	29	152	14	40	.350	0	3	.000	13	34	47	4	26	0	5	7	9	28	1.0	6

3-pt. FG: Minnesota 396-1047 (.378)—Garnett 37-116 (.319); Szczerbiak 87-191 (.455); Billups 124-315 (.394); Brandon 4-23 (.174); Smith 2-3 (.667); Trent 0-2 (.000); Peeler 111-283 (.392); Nesterovic 0-1 (.000); Jackson† 0-1 (.000); Jackson‡ 0-1 (.000); Pack 1-4 (.250); Mitchell 10-35 (.286); Avery 6-35 (.171); Lopez 14-33 (.424); Evans 0-3 (.000); Woods 0-2 (.000). Opponents 492-1321 (.372).

NEW JERSEY NETS

	G	Min.	FGM	FGA	Pct.	FTM	FTA	Pct.	Off.	Def.	Tot.	Ast.	PF	Dq.	Stl.	TO	Blk.	Pts.	Avg.	Hi.
									REBOUNDS									SCORING		
Kenyon Martin	73	2504	445	962	.463	181	267	.678	113	275	388	192	261	8	90	172	121	1086	14.9	31
Keith Van Horn	81	2465	471	1089	.433	156	195	.800	137	472	609	164	221	1	63	146	42	1199	14.8	34
Jason Kidd	82	3056	445	1138	.391	201	247	.814	130	465	595	808	136	0	175	286	20	1208	14.7	33
Kerry Kittles	82	2601	438	940	.466	128	172	.744	68	207	275	216	108	0	130	109	31	1102	13.4	30
Todd MacCulloch	62	1502	247	465	.531	110	164	.671	157	221	378	78	181	1	24	66	89	604	9.7	29
Richard Jefferson	79	1917	270	591	.457	189	265	.713	85	208	293	140	211	5	64	107	48	742	9.4	22
Lucious Harris	74	1553	249	537	.464	133	158	.842	49	158	207	116	99	1	53	61	6	675	9.1	23
Aaron Williams	82	1546	231	439	.526	130	186	.699	115	224	339	77	212	5	29	79	76	592	7.2	23
Jason Collins	77	1407	117	278	.421	115	164	.701	132	169	301	81	173	1	29	72	47	350	4.5	18
Derrick Dial*	25	249	30	94	.319	13	18	.722	12	33	45	31	12	0	8	13	4	73	2.9	13
Anthony Johnson	34	366	37	90	.411	16	25	.640	10	19	29	48	30	0	31	20	1	94	2.8	13
Brian Scalabrine	28	290	23	67	.343	11	15	.733	12	39	51	21	39	0	9	24	2	60	2.1	16
Brandon Armstrong	35	196	27	85	.318	5	10	.500	10	6	16	8	26	0	7	8	1	64	1.8	13
Donny Marshall	20	118	8	29	.276	12	18	.667	8	13	21	5	14	0	3	2	0	30	1.5	6
Reggie Slater*	4	10	2	2	1.000	1	1	1.000	0	2	2	0	1	0	0	1	0	5	1.3	3
Steve Goodrich	9	50	2	10	.200	1	2	.500	1	4	5	5	10	0	1	3	2	5	0.6	2

3-pt. FG: New Jersey 403-1194 (.338)—Martin 15-67 (.224); Van Horn 101-293 (.345); Kidd 117-364 (.321); Kittles 98-242 (.405); Jefferson 13-56 (.232); Harris 44-118 (.373); Williams 0-2 (.000); Collins 1-2 (.500); Dial* 0-7 (.000); Johnson 4-12 (.333); Scalabrine 3-10 (.300); Armstrong 5-17 (.294); Marshall 2-4 (.500). Opponents 409-1175 (.348).

NEW YORK KNICKERBOCKERS

	G	Min.	FGM	FGA	Pct.	FTM	FTA	Pct.	Off.	Def.	Tot.	Ast.	PF	Dq.	Stl.	TO	Blk.	Pts.	Avg.	Hi.
									REBOUNDS									SCORING		
Allan Houston	77	2914	568	1301	.437	295	339	.870	37	215	252	190	182	0	54	170	10	1567	20.4	44
Latrell Sprewell	81	3326	573	1419	.404	284	346	.821	59	239	298	313	161	0	94	223	14	1575	19.4	49
Kurt Thomas	82	2771	463	938	.494	216	265	.815	214	533	747	87	341	8	71	153	79	1143	13.9	33
Marcus Camby	29	1007	130	290	.448	62	99	.626	89	233	322	33	107	3	34	42	50	322	11.1	26
Clarence Weatherspoon	56	1728	189	452	.418	116	146	.795	149	311	460	60	132	0	37	47	48	494	8.8	20
Mark Jackson	82	2367	260	592	.439	87	110	.791	56	253	309	605	162	0	74	150	1	686	8.4	22
Othella Harrington	77	1503	237	450	.527	122	172	.709	125	224	349	37	250	5	30	95	36	596	7.7	18
Charlie Ward	63	1058	113	303	.373	47	58	.810	15	112	127	203	100	0	68	75	14	326	5.2	14
Shandon Anderson	82	1596	149	373	.399	74	107	.692	57	192	249	76	134	1	48	97	15	411	5.0	22
Howard Eisley	39	609	59	175	.337	39	49	.796	9	40	49	100	55	0	24	53	3	171	4.4	14
Lavor Postell	23	179	28	84	.333	31	41	.756	2	14	16	5	7	0	6	11	0	93	4.0	20
Travis Knight	49	429	41	113	.363	16	21	.762	48	56	104	8	95	0	11	27	10	98	2.0	8
Larry Robinson	2	10	1	4	.250	0	0	...	0	2	2	0	1	0	0	0	0	3	1.5	3
Felton Spencer	32	248	6	26	.231	17	33	.515	16	34	50	3	73	0	7	12	8	29	0.9	4

3-pt. FG: New York 474-1344 (.353)—Houston 136-346 (.393); Sprewell 145-403 (.360); Thomas 1-6 (.167); Camby 0-1 (.000); Jackson 79-195 (.405); Harrington 0-2 (.000); Ward 53-164 (.323); Anderson 39-141 (.277); Eisley 14-58 (.241); Postell 6-26 (.231); Robinson 1-2 (.500). Opponents 443-1256 (.353).

ORLANDO MAGIC

	G	Min.	FGM	FGA	Pct.	FTM	FTA	Pct.	Off.	Def.	Tot.	Ast.	PF	Dq.	Stl.	TO	Blk.	Pts.	Avg.	Hi.
									REBOUNDS									SCORING		
Tracy McGrady	76	2912	715	1586	.451	415	555	.748	150	447	597	400	139	1	119	189	73	1948	25.6	50
Grant Hill	14	512	83	195	.426	69	80	.863	29	96	125	64	40	2	8	37	4	235	16.8	28
Mike Miller	63	2123	351	802	.438	138	181	.762	49	224	273	198	145	0	47	108	23	956	15.2	32
Darrell Armstrong	82	2730	347	828	.419	182	205	.888	83	236	319	453	166	2	157	175	10	1015	12.4	29
Troy Hudson	81	1854	354	815	.434	176	201	.876	30	115	145	255	119	0	57	163	6	950	11.7	34
Pat Garrity	80	2406	327	767	.426	61	73	.836	77	261	338	99	230	1	61	68	28	884	11.1	29
Horace Grant	76	2210	264	515	.513	80	111	.721	159	322	481	104	118	0	57	51	49	608	8.0	22
Monty Williams	68	1284	198	362	.547	88	134	.657	80	155	235	96	134	1	49	86	17	484	7.1	23
Patrick Ewing	65	901	148	333	.444	94	134	.701	60	203	263	35	129	0	22	65	45	390	6.0	22
Jaren Jackson	9	144	15	37	.405	2	4	.500	1	16	17	8	13	0	5	8	0	39	4.3	11
Steven Hunter	53	516	67	147	.456	55	94	.585	40	57	97	5	81	0	5	16	43	189	3.6	17
Charles Outlaw*	10	160	13	21	.619	8	18	.444	15	14	29	5	23	0	9	11	9	34	3.4	11
Don Reid	68	714	90	190	.474	44	68	.647	65	111	176	27	180	2	20	54	44	224	3.3	15
Andrew DeClercq	61	633	67	149	.450	28	50	.560	74	89	163	22	130	0	23	34	24	162	2.7	12
Jud Buechler†	60	630	42	112	.375	2	4	.500	27	81	108	29	46	0	20	14	8	105	1.8	9
Jud Buechler‡	66	684	44	118	.373	2	4	.500	29	87	116	32	53	0	21	15	8	111	1.7	9
Jeryl Sasser	7	36	3	14	.214	4	5	.800	3	4	7	2	3	0	3	2	0	10	1.4	5
Dee Brown	7	65	3	20	.150	0	0	...	0	9	9	2	4	0	3	4	1	7	1.0	5

3-pt. FG: Orlando 620-1660 (.373)—McGrady 103-283 (.364); Hill 0-2 (.000); Miller 116-303 (.383); Armstrong 139-398 (.349); Hudson 66-187 (.353); Ewing 0-1 (.000); Garrity 169-396 (.427); Williams 0-4 (.000); Jackson 7-20 (.350); Buechler† 19-54 (.352); Buechler‡ 21-60 (.350); Brown 1-12 (.083). Opponents 409-1161 (.352).

PHILADELPHIA 76ERS

	G	Min.	FGM	FGA	Pct.	FTM	FTA	Pct.	Off.	Def.	Tot.	Ast.	PF	Dq.	Stl.	TO	Blk.	Pts.	Avg.	Hi.
									REBOUNDS									SCORING		
Allen Iverson	60	2622	665	1669	.398	475	585	.812	44	225	269	331	102	0	168	237	13	1883	31.4	58
Derrick Coleman	58	2080	331	735	.450	185	227	.815	167	342	509	98	158	0	42	119	51	875	15.1	25
Aaron McKie	48	1471	220	490	.449	96	122	.787	26	166	192	179	74	0	56	93	14	587	12.2	24
Eric Snow	61	2225	276	624	.442	183	227	.806	33	182	215	400	167	1	95	138	9	738	12.1	26
Matt Harpring	81	2541	386	838	.461	165	222	.743	203	370	573	107	201	1	70	127	5	958	11.8	25
Dikembe Mutombo	80	2907	321	641	.501	278	364	.764	254	609	863	83	242	2	29	156	190	920	11.5	24
Speedy Claxton	67	1528	181	452	.400	114	136	.838	46	114	160	198	145	1	95	95	6	480	7.2	23
Corie Blount	72	1426	115	251	.458	29	45	.644	149	219	368	44	176	1	49	52	26	259	3.6	15
Raja Bell	74	890	103	240	.429	36	48	.750	31	80	111	71	109	0	21	48	4	254	3.4	16
Ira Bowman	3	29	5	7	.714	0	0	...	0	1	1	1	3	0	2	0	0	10	3.3	8
Vonteego Cummings	58	501	78	187	.417	24	32	.750	14	38	52	60	53	0	18	36	5	192	3.3	28
Jabari Smith†	11	110	20	42	.476	15	20	.750	6	8	14	5	19	1	4	3	2	55	5.0	14
Jabari Smith‡	23	181	26	63	.413	21	32	.656	8	20	28	11	31	1	6	5	6	73	3.2	14
Derrick McKey	41	784	52	122	.426	10	14	.714	48	79	127	45	90	0	41	22	4	119	2.9	10
Samuel Dalembert	34	177	22	50	.440	7	18	.389	25	43	68	5	30	0	6	14	13	51	1.5	6
Damone Brown	17	67	8	21	.381	7	8	.875	2	2	4	2	11	0	1	9	1	23	1.4	8
Tim James	9	41	5	13	.385	2	6	.333	5	2	7	1	5	0	0	3	1	12	1.3	7
Alvin Jones	23	126	8	20	.400	10	20	.500	13	23	36	3	35	0	3	11	9	26	1.1	8
Michael Ruffin	15	169	7	26	.269	2	8	.250	23	28	51	5	23	0	5	11	8	16	1.1	5
Matt Geiger	4	36	1	8	.125	1	2	.500	3	3	6	0	2	0	0	2	2	3	0.8	3

3-pt. FG: Philadelphia 214-715 (.299)—Iverson 78-268 (.291); Coleman 28-83 (.337); McKie 51-128 (.398); Snow 3-27 (.111); Harpring 21-69 (.304); Claxton 4-33 (.121); Blount 0-1 (.000); Bell 12-44 (.273); Bowman 0-1 (.000); Cummings 12-46 (.261); Smith† 0-2 (.000); Smith‡ 0-3 (.000); McKey 5-12 (.417); Brown 0-1 (.000). Opponents 438-1322 (.331).

PHOENIX SUNS

	G	Min.	FGM	FGA	Pct.	FTM	FTA	Pct.	Off.	Def.	Tot.	Ast.	PF	Dq.	Stl.	TO	Blk.	Pts.	Avg.	Hi.
									REBOUNDS									SCORING		
Stephon Marbury	82	3187	625	1413	.442	353	452	.781	75	191	266	666	186	0	77	284	13	1674	20.4	36
Shawn Marion	81	3109	654	1395	.469	191	226	.845	211	592	803	162	214	0	149	144	86	1547	19.1	32
Rodney Rogers*	50	1254	249	534	.466	82	99	.828	95	146	241	72	148	2	50	66	17	629	12.6	29
Anfernee Hardaway	80	2462	389	931	.418	158	195	.810	98	252	350	324	184	0	122	189	32	959	12.0	31
Tony Delk*	41	877	166	416	.399	56	67	.836	38	86	124	81	60	0	31	40	4	435	10.6	27
Joe Johnson†	29	913	121	288	.420	21	27	.778	35	83	118	105	55	0	26	43	11	277	9.6	23
Joe Johnson‡	77	1916	251	584	.430	41	53	.774	75	182	257	179	114	0	59	71	20	581	7.5	23
Jake Tsakalidis	67	1582	190	400	.475	111	159	.698	130	244	374	23	193	4	23	78	69	491	7.3	23
Tom Gugliotta	44	1129	127	301	.422	28	37	.757	59	162	221	77	116	1	39	61	30	285	6.5	18
John Wallace	46	490	93	214	.435	40	46	.870	27	58	85	29	60	0	11	29	9	231	5.0	23
Jake Voskuhl	59	900	107	193	.554	82	109	.752	103	147	250	18	139	1	11	48	23	296	5.0	20
Dan Majerle	65	1180	99	289	.343	23	39	.590	28	148	176	90	104	0	48	35	15	300	4.6	14
Charles Outlaw†	73	1768	153	278	.550	35	84	.417	132	203	335	122	182	1	61	85	83	342	4.7	16
Charles Outlaw‡	83	1928	166	299	.555	43	102	.422	147	217	364	127	205	1	70	96	92	376	4.5	16
Joseph Crispin†	15	129	23	56	.411	8	8	1.000	2	8	10	24	8	0	4	9	0	69	4.6	13
Joseph Crispin‡	21	156	26	68	.382	12	13	.923	2	9	11	26	10	0	5	10	0	79	3.8	13
Milt Palacio†	28	272	30	79	.380	18	23	.783	3	20	23	29	23	0	9	16	1	79	2.8	15
Milt Palacio‡	69	790	82	214	.383	54	74	.730	11	62	73	83	61	0	30	40	4	231	3.3	19
Alton Ford	53	452	61	118	.517	42	57	.737	32	75	107	7	99	0	6	32	7	164	3.1	14
Daniel Santiago	3	24	4	8	.500	0	0	...	0	7	7	2	4	0	0	2	1	8	2.7	4
Charlie Bell*	5	42	3	11	.273	2	2	1.000	2	2	4	2	3	0	0	5	0	8	1.6	4
Jud Buechler*	6	54	2	6	.333	0	0	...	2	6	8	3	7	0	1	1	0	6	1.0	3
Vinny Del Negro	2	6	1	4	.250	0	0	...	0	0	0	2	0	0	0	0	0	2	1.0	2

3-pt. FG: Phoenix 358-1096 (.327)—Marbury 71-248 (.286); Marion 48-122 (.393); Rogers* 49-140 (.350); Hardaway 23-83 (.277); Delk* 47-147 (.320); Johnson† 14-42 (.333); Johnson‡ 38-130 (.292); Tsakalidis 0-1 (.000); Gugliotta 3-9 (.333); Wallace 5-13 (.385); Majerle 79-235 (.336); Outlaw† 1-2 (.500); Outlaw‡ 1-2 (.500); Crispin† 15-35 (.429); Crispin‡ 15-39 (.385); Palacio† 1-7 (.143); Palacio‡ 13-41 (.317); Bell* 0-6 (.000); Buechler* 2-6 (.333). Opponents 433-1208 (.358).

PORTLAND TRAIL BLAZERS

	G	Min.	FGM	FGA	Pct.	FTM	FTA	Pct.	Off.	Def.	Tot.	Ast.	PF	Dq.	Stl.	TO	Blk.	Pts.	Avg.	Hi.
									REBOUNDS									SCORING		
Rasheed Wallace	79	2963	603	1287	.469	201	274	.734	136	509	645	152	212	0	101	131	101	1521	19.3	37
Bonzi Wells	74	2348	487	1039	.469	215	290	.741	121	323	444	204	208	0	113	191	25	1255	17.0	35
Damon Stoudamire	75	2796	369	918	.402	174	196	.888	78	214	292	490	153	0	67	149	7	1016	13.5	29
Ruben Patterson	75	1765	319	619	.515	192	274	.701	155	143	298	107	140	1	79	114	37	839	11.2	31
Derek Anderson	70	1860	247	612	.404	178	208	.856	47	142	189	216	113	1	68	87	8	757	10.8	26
Scottie Pippen	62	1996	246	599	.411	113	146	.774	77	244	321	363	162	3	101	171	35	659	10.6	28
Dale Davis	78	2447	296	580	.510	150	212	.708	262	426	688	96	193	1	62	62	83	742	9.5	25

2001-02

	G	Min.	FGM	FGA	Pct.	FTM	FTA	Pct.	REBOUNDS Off.	Def.	Tot.	Ast.	PF	Dq.	Stl.	TO	Blk.	SCORING Pts.	Avg.	Hi.
Shawn Kemp	75	1232	175	407	.430	104	131	.794	90	198	288	52	184	1	43	81	33	454	6.1	21
Steve Kerr	65	775	102	217	.470	39	40	.975	6	54	60	63	49	0	13	24	1	269	4.1	16
Erick Barkley	19	228	24	68	.353	9	10	.900	5	13	18	34	29	0	17	12	1	58	3.1	12
Zach Randolph	41	238	48	107	.449	18	27	.667	31	38	69	13	29	0	7	15	4	114	2.8	14
Mitchell Butler	11	90	10	23	.458	8	12	.667	6	8	14	5	10	0	0	5	1	29	2.6	8
Rick Brunson	59	520	45	113	.398	29	41	.707	23	45	68	114	51	0	25	47	2	125	2.1	10
Ruben Boumtje-Boumtje	33	245	13	32	.406	13	25	.520	21	34	55	4	38	0	3	14	16	39	1.2	5
Chris Dudley	43	327	20	50	.400	8	15	.533	27	53	80	13	42	0	3	14	14	48	1.1	10

3-pt. FG: Portland 466-1318 (.354)—Wallace 114-317 (.360); Wells 66-172 (.384); Stoudamire 104-295 (.353); Patterson 9-36 (.250); Anderson 85-228 (.373); Pippen 54-177 (.305); Kemp 0-4 (.000); Kerr 26-66 (.394); Barkley 1-7 (.143); Butler 1-3 (.333); Brunson 6-11 (.545); Dudley 0-2 (.000). Opponents 466-1285 (.363).

SACRAMENTO KINGS

	G	Min.	FGM	FGA	Pct.	FTM	FTA	Pct.	REBOUNDS Off.	Def.	Tot.	Ast.	PF	Dq.	Stl.	TO	Blk.	SCORING Pts.	Avg.	Hi.
Chris Webber	54	2071	532	1075	.495	253	338	.749	150	396	546	258	181	1	90	158	76	1322	24.5	39
Predrag Stojakovic	71	2649	547	1130	.484	283	323	.876	72	301	373	175	120	0	81	140	14	1506	21.2	36
Mike Bibby	80	2659	446	985	.453	155	193	.803	37	185	222	403	133	0	87	134	15	1098	13.7	27
Doug Christie	81	2798	338	735	.460	206	242	.851	74	300	374	340	209	3	160	164	25	972	12.0	23
Vlade Divac	80	2420	338	716	.472	209	340	.615	205	466	671	297	229	1	79	158	94	888	11.1	27
Bobby Jackson	81	1750	334	754	.443	149	184	.810	82	169	251	164	145	1	73	93	11	896	11.1	22
Hidayet Turkoglu	80	1970	290	687	.422	167	230	.726	63	300	363	163	184	0	57	81	31	810	10.1	31
Scot Pollard	80	1881	197	358	.550	115	166	.693	188	377	565	53	202	1	70	68	76	509	6.4	23
Lawrence Funderburke	56	722	115	245	.469	34	56	.607	76	122	198	32	65	0	11	33	18	264	4.7	29
Gerald Wallace	54	430	75	175	.429	23	46	.500	49	40	89	27	46	0	19	22	6	173	3.2	20
Mateen Cleaves	32	153	30	68	.441	8	9	.889	1	7	8	25	9	0	7	27	0	70	2.2	13
Brent Price	20	89	9	27	.333	9	13	.692	4	4	8	9	13	0	3	10	1	31	1.6	6
Jabari Smith*	12	71	6	21	.286	6	12	.500	2	12	14	6	12	0	2	2	4	18	1.5	4
Chucky Brown	18	92	10	27	.370	1	2	.500	10	23	33	6	12	0	2	5	4	21	1.2	6

3-pt. FG: Sacramento 426-1160 (.367)—Webber 5-19 (.263); Stojakovic 129-310 (.416); Bibby 51-138 (.370); Christie 90-256 (.352); Divac 3-13 (.231); Wallace 0-7 (.000); Jackson 79-219 (.361); Turkoglu 63-171 (.368); Funderburke 0-3 (.000); Cleaves 2-8 (.250); Price 4-15 (.267); Smith* 0-1 (.000). Opponents 386-1145 (.337).

SAN ANTONIO SPURS

	G	Min.	FGM	FGA	Pct.	FTM	FTA	Pct.	REBOUNDS Off.	Def.	Tot.	Ast.	PF	Dq.	Stl.	TO	Blk.	SCORING Pts.	Avg.	Hi.
Tim Duncan	82	3329	764	1504	.508	560	701	.799	268	774	1042	307	217	2	61	263	203	2089	25.5	53
David Robinson	78	2303	341	672	.507	269	395	.681	191	456	647	94	193	3	86	104	140	951	12.2	27
Steve Smith	77	2211	310	682	.455	159	181	.878	45	148	193	151	158	0	54	108	15	895	11.6	36
Malik Rose	82	1725	293	633	.463	185	257	.720	172	320	492	61	208	2	70	140	42	772	9.4	26
Antonio Daniels	82	2175	269	612	.440	158	210	.752	23	153	176	228	104	0	48	70	12	753	9.2	21
Tony Parker	77	2267	268	639	.419	108	160	.675	33	164	197	334	166	1	89	151	7	705	9.2	22
Charles Smith	60	1141	182	428	.425	42	65	.646	34	99	133	80	114	1	52	59	44	441	7.4	32
Bruce Bowen	59	1699	155	398	.389	46	96	.479	42	120	162	88	116	0	62	66	25	412	7.0	21
Terry Porter	72	1294	136	321	.424	68	83	.819	12	152	164	205	89	0	45	85	16	399	5.5	22
Danny Ferry	50	799	76	177	.429	34	36	.944	15	75	90	48	70	0	16	22	9	229	4.6	18
Stephen Jackson	23	227	34	91	.374	12	17	.706	3	23	26	11	29	0	15	23	3	89	3.9	16
Jason Hart	10	92	10	19	.526	6	6	1.000	4	9	13	12	16	0	7	8	1	26	2.6	6
Amal McCaskill	27	153	20	49	.408	12	26	.462	16	20	36	4	23	0	6	14	10	52	1.9	8
Mark Bryant	30	206	25	55	.455	6	8	.750	25	19	44	10	38	1	7	6	2	56	1.9	12
Cherokee Parks	42	234	30	83	.361	3	8	.375	24	34	58	10	34	0	7	14	8	63	1.5	7

3-pt. FG: San Antonio 438-1211 (.362)—Duncan 1-10 (.100); S. Smith 116-246 (.472); Rose 1-12 (.083); Daniels 57-196 (.291); Parker 61-189 (.323); C. Smith 35-131 (.267); Bowen 56-148 (.378); Porter 59-142 (.415); Ferry 43-99 (.434); Jackson 9-36 (.250); Hart 0-2 (.000). Opponents 374-1108 (.338).

SEATTLE SUPERSONICS

	G	Min.	FGM	FGA	Pct.	FTM	FTA	Pct.	REBOUNDS Off.	Def.	Tot.	Ast.	PF	Dq.	Stl.	TO	Blk.	SCORING Pts.	Avg.	Hi.
Gary Payton	82	3301	737	1578	.467	267	335	.797	80	316	396	737	179	0	131	209	26	1815	22.1	43
Rashard Lewis	71	2585	455	972	.468	162	200	.810	139	359	498	123	174	3	104	97	40	1195	16.8	36
Brent Barry	81	3040	401	790	.508	198	234	.846	58	383	441	426	182	3	147	165	37	1164	14.4	31
Vin Baker	55	1710	315	649	.485	143	226	.633	168	182	350	72	197	4	22	127	36	774	14.1	32
Desmond Mason	75	2420	357	769	.464	201	237	.848	92	259	351	104	170	0	67	104	27	931	12.4	36
Predrag Drobnjak	64	1174	191	414	.461	55	73	.753	75	144	219	51	109	0	20	51	31	437	6.8	19
Vladimir Radmanovic	61	1230	146	354	.412	49	72	.681	45	185	230	81	119	0	56	72	24	407	6.7	21
Ansu Sesay	9	142	22	44	.500	14	20	.700	7	13	20	8	18	0	3	2	2	58	6.4	12
Calvin Booth	15	279	35	82	.427	23	24	.958	20	34	54	16	47	1	6	16	13	93	6.2	24
Jerome James	56	949	134	273	.491	30	60	.500	89	143	232	24	174	0	25	74	86	298	5.3	18
Art Long	63	989	120	244	.492	45	85	.529	107	144	251	41	180	4	22	63	28	285	4.5	13
Shammond Williams	50	603	81	193	.420	31	39	.795	16	47	63	83	35	0	21	35	2	221	4.4	16
Earl Watson	64	964	96	212	.453	23	36	.639	31	52	83	125	93	0	60	51	5	231	3.6	14

	G	Min.	FGM	FGA	Pct.	FTM	FTA	Pct.	Off.	Def.	Tot.	Ast.	PF	Dq.	Stl.	TO	Blk.	Pts.	Avg.	Hi.
Randy Livingston	13	176	15	54	.278	10	11	.909	9	16	25	26	11	0	9	2	2	41	3.2	6
Antonio Harvey	5	47	4	12	.333	1	2	.500	5	4	9	5	8	0	1	3	3	9	1.8	2
Olumide Oyedeji	36	221	22	41	.537	11	18	.611	27	52	79	4	36	0	4	14	2	55	1.5	6

3-pt. FG: Seattle 489-1292 (.378)—Payton 74-236 (.314); Lewis 123-316 (.389); Barry 164-387 (.424); Baker 1-8 (.125); Mason 16-59 (.271); Drobnjak 0-2 (.000); Radmanovic 66-157 (.420); Williams 28-75 (.373); Watson 16-44 (.364); Livingston 1-8 (.125). Opponents 472-1374 (.344).

TORONTO RAPTORS

									REBOUNDS									SCORING		
	G	Min.	FGM	FGA	Pct.	FTM	FTA	Pct.	Off.	Def.	Tot.	Ast.	PF	Dq.	Stl.	TO	Blk.	Pts.	Avg.	Hi.
Vince Carter	60	2385	559	1307	.428	245	307	.798	138	175	313	239	191	4	94	154	43	1484	24.7	43
Antonio Davis	77	2978	410	963	.426	293	358	.818	254	486	740	155	225	3	54	159	83	1113	14.5	29
Morris Peterson	63	1988	336	768	.438	127	169	.751	91	132	223	153	174	2	73	86	11	883	14.0	29
Alvin Williams	82	2927	403	971	.415	103	140	.736	58	223	281	468	191	1	135	150	26	971	11.8	28
Keon Clark	81	2185	380	775	.490	155	230	.674	182	421	603	88	258	4	58	140	122	915	11.3	26
Jerome Williams	68	1641	190	388	.490	138	204	.676	165	221	386	75	153	0	78	68	25	518	7.6	22
Hakeem Olajuwon . . .	61	1378	194	418	.464	47	84	.560	98	268	366	66	147	0	74	98	90	435	7.1	16
Dell Curry	56	886	141	347	.406	33	37	.892	23	58	81	61	50	0	22	41	6	360	6.4	18
Tracy Murray	40	473	85	207	.411	17	21	.810	18	35	53	19	38	0	11	25	8	227	5.7	16
Chris Childs	69	1576	97	296	.328	58	71	.817	18	136	154	351	177	3	56	123	5	285	4.1	14
Mamadou N'diaye . . .	5	46	6	10	.600	8	10	.800	6	5	11	0	6	0	0	1	2	20	4.0	8
Derrick Dial†	7	50	11	26	.423	5	6	.833	2	9	11	4	1	0	2	3	0	28	4.0	9
Derrick Dial‡	32	299	41	120	.342	18	24	.750	14	42	56	35	13	0	10	16	4	101	3.2	13
Jermaine Jackson . . .	24	280	20	42	.476	16	24	.667	3	24	27	57	24	0	9	14	1	57	2.4	10
Eric Montross	49	655	53	132	.402	10	31	.323	36	104	140	16	92	1	12	25	23	116	2.4	10
Michael Stewart	11	93	8	23	.348	6	11	.545	12	13	25	3	22	0	4	4	3	22	2.0	7
Carlos Arroyo*	17	96	13	29	.448	4	6	.667	3	9	12	21	12	0	6	12	0	30	1.8	6
Michael Bradley	26	118	13	25	.520	4	8	.500	7	17	24	3	10	0	0	6	6	30	1.2	6

3-pt. FG: Toronto 387-1109 (.349)—Carter 121-313 (.387); Davis 0-1 (.000); Peterson 84-231 (.364); A. Williams 62-193 (.321); Clark 0-5 (.000); Olajuwon 0-2 (.000); Curry 45-131 (.344); Murray 40-104 (.385); Childs 33-120 (.275); Dial† 1-4 (.250); Dial‡ 1-11 (.091); Jackson 1-2 (.500); Montross 0-1 (.000); Bradley 0-2 (.000). Opponents 377-1089 (.346).

UTAH JAZZ

									REBOUNDS									SCORING		
	G	Min.	FGM	FGA	Pct.	FTM	FTA	Pct.	Off.	Def.	Tot.	Ast.	PF	Dq.	Stl.	TO	Blk.	Pts.	Avg.	Hi.
Karl Malone	80	3040	635	1399	.454	509	639	.797	142	544	686	341	229	1	152	263	59	1788	22.4	39
Donyell Marshall	58	1750	343	661	.519	160	226	.708	158	285	443	101	150	1	50	124	67	859	14.8	32
John Stockton	82	2566	401	775	.517	275	321	.857	59	204	263	674	209	1	152	208	24	1102	13.4	26
Andrei Kirilenko	82	2151	285	633	.450	285	371	.768	149	253	402	94	156	2	116	108	159	880	10.7	27
Bryon Russell	66	1998	222	584	.380	115	140	.821	79	216	295	136	205	1	64	110	19	636	9.6	25
John Crotty	41	802	98	208	.471	57	66	.864	16	59	75	141	77	1	19	51	1	284	6.9	17
Scott Padgett	75	1295	188	395	.476	75	102	.735	111	174	285	82	140	0	43	69	13	500	6.7	21
Jarron Collins	70	1440	158	343	.461	134	181	.740	138	158	296	58	234	4	29	56	22	450	6.4	22
Rusty LaRue	33	542	73	185	.395	30	35	.857	11	38	49	71	58	0	17	43	7	193	5.8	14
DeShawn Stevenson . .	67	1134	143	371	.385	37	53	.698	44	87	131	116	82	0	29	68	24	325	4.9	16
John Starks	66	929	114	310	.368	33	41	.805	15	53	68	70	126	1	33	52	0	290	4.4	20
Quincy Lewis	36	490	64	143	.448	13	20	.650	10	33	43	36	89	4	23	32	9	144	4.0	18
Greg Ostertag	74	1107	91	201	.453	63	130	.485	125	188	313	50	152	1	15	51	109	245	3.3	14
John Amaechi	54	586	54	166	.325	67	105	.638	52	57	109	29	64	0	7	55	10	175	3.2	18

3-pt. FG: Utah 280-842 (.333)—Malone 9-25 (.360); Marshall 13-42 (.310); Stockton 25-78 (.321); Kirilenko 25-100 (.250); Russell 77-226 (.341); Crotty 31-69 (.449); Padgett 49-113 (.434); Collins 0-1 (.000); LaRue 17-50 (.340); Stevenson 2-25 (.080); Starks 29-95 (.305); Lewis 3-18 (.167). Opponents 465-1215 (.383).

WASHINGTON WIZARDS

									REBOUNDS									SCORING		
	G	Min.	FGM	FGA	Pct.	FTM	FTA	Pct.	Off.	Def.	Tot.	Ast.	PF	Dq.	Stl.	TO	Blk.	Pts.	Avg.	Hi.
Michael Jordan	60	2093	551	1324	.416	263	333	.790	50	289	339	310	119	0	85	162	26	1375	22.9	51
Richard Hamilton	63	2203	472	1084	.435	300	337	.890	73	143	216	171	136	0	38	132	14	1260	20.0	34
Chris Whitney	82	2171	274	656	.418	154	175	.880	11	141	152	314	182	1	72	85	6	833	10.2	22
Courtney Alexander . .	56	1325	223	474	.470	98	121	.810	43	105	148	86	113	0	35	60	7	549	9.8	32
Tyronn Lue	71	1458	222	520	.427	48	63	.762	14	108	122	246	120	2	49	96	0	555	7.8	26
Hubert Davis	51	1231	146	326	.448	16	21	.762	7	70	77	107	58	0	28	44	3	365	7.2	22
Christian Laettner	57	1441	168	362	.464	66	76	.868	74	227	301	151	129	1	60	85	25	404	7.1	29
Popeye Jones	79	1920	222	508	.437	106	130	.815	233	345	578	127	209	4	50	88	19	554	7.0	18
Tyrone Nesby	70	1498	183	421	.435	64	93	.688	105	213	318	91	164	1	61	49	22	443	6.3	18
Jahidi White	71	1346	150	279	.538	83	154	.539	159	285	444	17	163	0	25	65	75	383	5.4	22
Brendan Haywood . . .	62	1266	109	221	.493	97	160	.606	143	179	322	29	158	1	21	50	91	315	5.1	19
Kwame Brown	57	817	94	243	.387	70	99	.707	63	135	198	43	105	2	16	43	26	258	4.5	14
Etan Thomas	47	618	81	151	.536	41	74	.554	55	126	181	6	76	0	17	26	35	203	4.3	14
Bobby Simmons	30	343	43	95	.453	22	30	.733	25	27	52	17	31	1	13	14	5	112	3.7	15

3-pt. FG: Washington 305-786 (.388)—Jordan 10-53 (.189); Hamilton 16-42 (.381); Whitney 131-323 (.406); Alexander 5-18 (.278); Lue 63-141 (.447); Davis 57-126 (.452); Laettner 2-10 (.200); Jones 4-11 (.364); Nesby 13-47 (.277); Brown 0-1 (.000); Simmons 4-14 (.286). Opponents 422-1191 (.354).

* Finished season with another team. † Totals with this team only. ‡ Totals with all teams.

PLAYOFFS
RESULTS

EASTERN CONFERENCE
FIRST ROUND

New Jersey 3, Indiana 2

Apr. 20—Sat.	Indiana 89 at New Jersey	.83
Apr. 22—Mon.	Indiana 79 at New Jersey	.95
Apr. 26—Fri.	New Jersey 85 at Indiana	.84
Apr. 30—Tue.	New Jersey 74 at Indiana	.97
May 2—Thur.	Indiana 109 at New Jersey	**120

Detroit 3, Toronto 2

Apr. 21—Sun.	Toronto 63 at Detroit	.85
Apr. 24—Wed.	Toronto 91 at Detroit	.96
Apr. 27—Sat.	Detroit 84 at Toronto	.94
Apr. 29—Mon.	Detroit 83 at Toronto	.89
May 2—Thur.	Toronto 82 at Detroit	.85

Boston 3, Philadelphia 2

Apr. 21—Sun.	Philadelphia 82 at Boston	.92
Apr. 25—Thur.	Philadelphia 85 at Boston	.93
Apr. 28—Sun.	Boston 103 at Philadelphia	.108
May 1—Wed.	Boston 81 at Philadelphia	.83
May 3—Fri.	Philadelphia 87 at Boston	.120

Charlotte 3, Orlando 1

Apr. 20—Sat.	Orlando 79 at Charlotte	.80
Apr. 23—Tue.	Orlando 111 at Charlotte	*103
Apr. 27—Sat.	Charlotte 110 at Orlando	*100
Apr. 30—Tue.	Charlotte 102 at Orlando	.85

SEMIFINALS

New Jersey 4, Charlotte 1

May 5—Sun.	Charlotte 93 at New Jersey	.99
May 7—Tue.	Charlotte 88 at New Jersey	.102
May 9—Thur.	New Jersey 97 at Charlotte	.115
May 12—Sun.	New Jersey 89 at Charlotte	.79
May 15—Wed.	Charlotte 95 at New Jersey	.103

Boston 4, Detroit 1

May 5—Sun.	Boston 84 at Detroit	.96
May 8—Wed.	Boston 85 at Detroit	.77
May 10—Fri.	Detroit 64 at Boston	.66
May 12—Sun.	Detroit 79 at Boston	.90
May 14—Tue.	Boston 90 at Detroit	.81

FINALS

New Jersey 4, Boston 2

May 19—Sun.	Boston 97 at New Jersey	.104
May 21—Tue.	Boston 93 at New Jersey	.86
May 25—Sat.	New Jersey 90 at Boston	.94
May 27—Mon.	New Jersey 94 at Boston	.92
May 29—Wed.	Boston 92 at New Jersey	.103
May 31—Fri.	New Jersey 96 at Boston	.88

WESTERN CONFERENCE
FIRST ROUND

Sacramento 3, Utah 1

Apr. 20—Sat.	Utah 86 at Sacramento	.89
Apr. 23—Tue.	Utah 93 at Sacramento	.86
Apr. 27—Sat.	Sacramento 90 at Utah	.87
Apr. 29—Mon.	Sacramento 91 at Utah	.86

San Antonio 3, Seattle 2

Apr. 20—Sat.	Seattle 89 at San Antonio	.110
Apr. 22—Mon.	Seattle 98 at San Antonio	.90
Apr. 27—Sat.	San Antonio 102 at Seattle	.75
May 1—Wed.	San Antonio 79 at Seattle	.91
May 3—Fri.	Seattle 78 at San Antonio	.101

L.A. Lakers 3, Portland 0

Apr. 21—Sun.	Portland 87 at L.A. Lakers	.95
Apr. 25—Thur.	Portland 96 at L.A. Lakers	.103
Apr. 28—Sun.	L.A. Lakers 92 at Portland	.91

Dallas 3, Minnesota 0

Apr. 21—Sun.	Minnesota 94 at Dallas	.101
Apr. 24—Wed.	Minnesota 110 at Dallas	.122
Apr. 28—Sun.	Dallas 115 at Minnesota	.102

SEMIFINALS

Sacramento 4, Dallas 1

May 4—Sat.	Dallas 91 at Sacramento	.108
May 6—Mon.	Dallas 110 at Sacramento	.102
May 9—Thur.	Sacramento 125 at Dallas	.119
May 11—Sat.	Sacramento 115 at Dallas	*113
May 13—Mon.	Dallas 101 at Sacramento	.114

L.A. Lakers 4, San Antonio 1

May 5—Sun.	San Antonio 80 at L.A. Lakers	.86
May 7—Tue.	San Antonio 88 at L.A. Lakers	.85
May 10—Fri.	L.A. Lakers 99 at San Antonio	.89
May 12—Sun.	L.A. Lakers 87 at San Antonio	.85
May 14—Tue.	San Antonio 87 at L.A. Lakers	.93

FINALS

L.A. Lakers 4, Sacramento 3

May 18—Sat.	L.A. Lakers 106 at Sacramento	.99
May 20—Mon.	L.A. Lakers 90 at Sacramento	.96
May 24—Fri.	Sacramento 103 at L.A. Lakers	.90
May 26—Sun.	Sacramento 99 at L.A. Lakers	.100
May 28—Tue.	L.A. Lakers 91 at Sacramento	.92
May 31—Fri.	Sacramento 102 at L.A. Lakers	.106
June 2—Sun.	L.A. Lakers 112 at Sacramento	*106

2001-02

NBA FINALS

L.A. Lakers 4, New Jersey 0

June 5—Wed.	New Jersey 94 at L.A. Lakers	.99
June 7—Fri.	New Jersey 83 at L.A. Lakers	.106
June 9—Sun.	L.A. Lakers 106 at New Jersey	.103
June 12—Wed.	L.A. Lakers 113 at New Jersey	.107

*Denotes number of overtime periods.

2000-01 NBA CHAMPION LOS ANGELES LAKERS

Front row (from left): Devean George, Stanislav Medvedenko, Greg Foster, Shaquille O'Neal, owner Jerry Buss, Horace Grant, Robert Horry, Mark Madsen. Center row (from left): Tyronn Lue, Mike Penberthy, Ron Harper, Rick Fox, Kobe Bryant, Brian Shaw, Isaiah Rider, Derek Fisher, massage therapist Dan Garcia. Back row (from left): athletic trainer Gary Vitti, athletic performance coordinator Chip Schaefer, assistant coach Bill Bertka, assistant coach Frank Hamblen, head coach Phil Jackson, assistant coach Tex Winter, assistant coach Jim Cleamons, strength and conditioning coach Jim Cotta, equipment manager Rudy Garciduenas.

FINAL STANDINGS

ATLANTIC DIVISION

	Atl.	Bos.	Cha.	Chi.	Cle.	Dal.	Den.	Det.	G.S.	Hou.	Ind.	LA-C	LA-L	Mia.	Mil.	Min.	N.J.	N.Y.	Orl.	Phi.	Pho.	Por.	Sac.	S.A.	Sea.	Tor.	Uta.	Van.	Was.	W	L	Pct.	GB
Phi.	3	4	2	3	4	1	1	4	2	1	3	1	1	3	2	1	3	3	1	..	1	1	1	1	1	1	1	2	4	56	26	.683	..
Mia.	3	2	2	3	2	0	2	4	2	1	2	2	1	..	1	1	3	2	3	1	0	1	1	1	2	1	2	4		50	32	.610	6
N.Y.	2	3	2	3	2	1	1	2	2	0	2	1	2	3	2	2	2	..	3	1	1	1	2	1	1	0	1	4		43	39	.524	13
Orl.	3	3	1	3	3	1	2	2	2	1	2	1	0	1	0	1	3	1	..	3	1	0	0	1	1	2	0	2	3	43	39	.524	13
Bos.	3	..	0	2	2	0	2	3	0	1	1	2	0	2	1	1	4	1	1	0	2	1	0	2	1	1	0	3		36	46	.439	20
N.J.	3	0	0	2	0	0	1	0	1	1	2	2	0	1	0	1	..	2	1	1	1	0	0	1	1	1	0	3		26	56	.317	30
Was.	2	1	2	1	2	0	1	2	2	0	0	1	0	0	1	1	1	0	1	0	1	1	0	0	0	0	0	0	..	19	63	.232	37

CENTRAL DIVISION

	Atl.	Bos.	Cha.	Chi.	Cle.	Dal.	Den.	Det.	G.S.	Hou.	Ind.	LA-C	LA-L	Mia.	Mil.	Min.	N.J.	N.Y.	Orl.	Phi.	Pho.	Por.	Sac.	S.A.	Sea.	Tor.	Uta.	Van.	Was.	W	L	Pct.	GB
Mil.	3	3	1	4	3	1	1	3	2	0	2	1	2	2	..	0	4	1	4	2	0	0	2	2	0	3	2	1	3	52	30	.634	..
Tor.	2	3	1	4	4	0	2	2	2	0	4	1	0	2	1	0	2	3	1	3	0	0	0	1	2	..	1	2	4	47	35	.573	5
Cha.	4	4	..	3	2	0	2	2	0	3	2	0	2	3	1	4	1	2	2	0	0	1	1	0	3	1	1	2	4	46	36	.561	6
Ind.	2	3	1	4	3	1	1	3	0	0	..	2	1	1	2	1	2	2	2	0	1	0	2	0	1	0	0	2	4	41	41	.500	11
Det.	1	2	4	2	1	1	..	1	0	1	0	0	0	1	0	4	1	2	0	1	0	0	0	2	2	0	1	1	1	32	50	.390	20
Cle.	2	2	3	..	1	1	2	2	0	1	1	0	0	2	1	0	3	2	1	0	0	1	1	0	0	0	1	1	2	30	52	.366	22
Atl.	..	1	0	2	2	0	1	0	2	0	2	1	1	0	1	0	1	2	1	0	0	1	1	0	0	1	2	0	1	25	57	.305	27
Chi.	2	1	1	..	1	0	0	0	0	0	0	0	0	1	0	0	2	1	1	1	1	0	0	0	1	0	0	0	1	15	67	.183	37

MIDWEST DIVISION

	Atl.	Bos.	Cha.	Chi.	Cle.	Dal.	Den.	Det.	G.S.	Hou.	Ind.	LA-C	LA-L	Mia.	Mil.	Min.	N.J.	N.Y.	Orl.	Phi.	Pho.	Por.	Sac.	S.A.	Sea.	Tor.	Uta.	Van.	Was.	W	L	Pct.	GB
S.A.	2	2	1	1	2	3	2	2	4	3	2	4	2	1	0	3	1	0	1	1	2	3	2	..	3	1	4	4	2	58	24	.707	..
Dal.	2	2	2	1	..	3	1	4	2	1	4	0	2	1	3	2	1	1	1	1	2	1	3	2	2	3	1	4	2	53	29	.646	5
Utah	2	1	1	2	1	2	3	2	3	3	2	4	1	0	2	2	2	2	1	2	1	1	0	4	1	..	4	2		53	29	.646	5
Min.	2	1	1	2	2	1	2	2	2	1	2	1	1	2	..	1	0	1	1	3	3	2	1	3	2	2	3	1		47	35	.573	11
Hou.	2	2	2	2	1	2	3	..	2	1	1	1	2	1	2	1	2	1	1	1	1	0	1	2	2	1	4	2	1	45	37	.549	13
Den.	1	0	2	2	1	1	..	1	4	3	1	2	2	0	1	2	1	1	0	1	0	2	2	2	2	0	1	4	1	40	42	.488	18
Van.	1	2	1	1	1	1	0	1	3	0	0	2	0	0	1	1	1	1	0	0	1	2	0	0	1	0	0	..	2	23	59	.280	35

PACIFIC DIVISION

	Atl.	Bos.	Cha.	Chi.	Cle.	Dal.	Den.	Det.	G.S.	Hou.	Ind.	LA-C	LA-L	Mia.	Mil.	Min.	N.J.	N.Y.	Orl.	Phi.	Pho.	Por.	Sac.	S.A.	Sea.	Tor.	Uta.	Van.	Was.	W	L	Pct.	GB
L.A.L.	1	2	2	2	2	4	2	2	3	3	1	3	..	1	0	3	2	0	2	1	3	2	3	2	0	2	2	4	2	56	26	.683	..
Sac.	1	2	1	2	1	2	2	2	4	4	0	3	1	1	0	2	2	1	2	1	3	3	..	2	2	3	4	2		55	27	.671	1
Pho.	2	0	2	2	2	3	4	1	2	3	1	2	1	2	1	1	1	1	1	3	..	1	3	2	3	2	2	3	1	51	31	.622	5
Por.	1	1	2	2	1	2	2	4	3	2	2	2	1	1	0	1	2	1	2	1	1	..	1	1	2	2	3	2		50	32	.610	6
Sea.	1	0	2	2	1	2	0	4	2	1	4	4	1	1	1	1	1	1	1	1	1	2	1	..	0	0	3	2		44	38	.537	12
L.A.C.	1	0	0	2	2	0	2	3	3	0	..	1	0	1	2	0	1	1	1	2	1	0	0	1	0	2	1	51	.378	25				
G.S.	0	2	0	2	0	0	0	1	..	1	2	1	1	0	0	2	1	0	0	0	2	0	0	0	0	0	1	1	0	17	65	.207	39

TEAM STATISTICS

OFFENSIVE

	G	FGM	FGA	Pct.	FTM	FTA	Pct.	REBOUNDS Off.	Def.	Tot.	Ast.	PF	Dq.	Stl.	TO	Blk.	SCORING Pts.	Avg.
Sacramento	82	3132	6969	.449	1600	2075	.771	987	2705	3692	1852	1596	13	793	1221	432	8343	101.7
Milwaukee	82	3112	6798	.458	1474	1874	.787	975	2500	3475	1844	1928	31	672	1123	386	8260	100.7
L.A. Lakers	82	3109	6685	.465	1594	2333	.683	1085	2583	3668	1888	1872	20	564	1184	490	8251	100.6
Dallas	82	3085	6716	.459	1552	1954	.794	831	2571	3402	1740	1907	18	618	1141	492	8239	100.5
Toronto	82	3048	6972	.437	1482	1984	.747	1118	2529	3647	2004	1745	10	599	1080	519	8007	97.6
Orlando	82	3013	6873	.438	1476	2068	.714	1069	2450	3519	1803	2071	29	674	1245	481	7992	97.5
Minnesota	82	3148	6871	.458	1364	1737	.785	1002	2470	3472	2083	1900	20	682	1136	456	7982	97.3
Seattle	82	3029	6649	.456	1454	1986	.732	999	2422	3421	1792	1733	7	657	1252	409	7978	97.3
Houston	82	2943	6494	.453	1582	2086	.758	919	2524	3443	1613	1657	19	587	1204	358	7972	97.2
Utah	82	2960	6289	.471	1714	2280	.752	943	2383	3326	2110	2107	10	661	1296	463	7959	97.1
Denver	82	2979	6877	.433	1448	1964	.737	1044	2583	3627	1970	1820	20	552	1136	538	7918	96.6
San Antonio	82	2884	6262	.461	1673	2340	.715	902	2712	3614	1778	1551	5	568	1145	576	7886	96.2
Detroit	82	2919	6880	.424	1610	2233	.721	1108	2626	3734	1629	1955	12	613	1304	447	7837	95.6
Portland	82	3004	6417	.468	1447	1899	.762	960	2481	3441	1963	1745	11	672	1257	419	7824	95.4
Philadelphia	82	2902	6487	.447	1697	2277	.745	1075	2600	3675	1692	1673	11	690	1292	408	7763	94.7
Boston	82	2773	6485	.428	1621	2190	.740	897	2367	3264	1708	1952	13	769	1285	336	7759	94.6
Phoenix	82	2944	6757	.436	1490	1973	.755	970	2529	3499	1905	1863	20	775	1250	429	7710	94.0
Washington	82	2833	6453	.439	1704	2245	.759	1016	2370	3386	1647	1913	15	630	1391	383	7645	93.2
Indiana	82	2828	6431	.440	1539	2009	.766	921	2595	3516	1763	1926	26	563	1244	487	7591	92.6
Golden State	82	2937	7175	.409	1428	2024	.706	1345	2385	3730	1788	1727	17	742	1301	410	7584	92.5
L.A. Clippers	82	2896	6467	.448	1429	2061	.693	962	2559	3521	1585	1775	14	490	1293	513	7581	92.5
Cleveland	82	2890	6532	.442	1561	2040	.765	1015	2440	3455	1708	1904	6	642	1350	436	7561	92.2
New Jersey	82	2781	6550	.425	1629	2146	.759	909	2337	3246	1603	1982	35	649	1208	407	7552	92.1
Charlotte	82	2800	6501	.431	1599	2146	.745	1033	2608	3641	1900	1753	12	665	1183	455	7539	91.9
Vancouver	82	2870	6539	.439	1457	1892	.770	894	2431	3325	1899	1733	12	586	1291	359	7522	91.7
Atlanta	82	2876	6668	.431	1374	1811	.759	1028	2490	3518	1559	1863	18	634	1368	387	7459	91.0
Miami	82	2694	6258	.430	1423	1874	.759	813	2435	3248	1630	1726	25	633	1122	304	7289	88.9
New York	82	2755	6108	.444	1374	1727	.796	773	2524	3297	1520	1863	22	545	1189	346	7275	88.7
Chicago	82	2721	6411	.424	1410	1909	.739	926	2260	3186	1810	1902	26	675	1292	379	7181	87.6

DEFENSIVE

	FGM	FGA	Pct.	FTM	FTA	Pct.	REBOUNDS Off.	Def.	Tot.	Ast.	PF	Dq.	Stl.	TO	Blk.	SCORING Pts.	Avg.	Dif.
New York	2568	6159	.417	1478	2015	.733	872	2418	3290	1573	1754	16	596	1216	338	7059	86.1	+2.6
Miami	2701	6261	.431	1339	1818	.737	914	2528	3442	1421	1824	23	598	1275	424	7101	86.6	+2.3
San Antonio	2837	6770	.419	1233	1664	.741	967	2432	3399	1617	1946	27	600	1107	426	7250	88.4	+7.8
Charlotte	2767	6501	.426	1444	1910	.756	892	2436	3328	1748	1768	13	616	1204	375	7367	89.8	+2.1
Philadelphia	2871	6699	.429	1243	1660	.749	985	2366	3351	1771	1938	20	672	1261	458	7412	90.4	+4.3
Portland	2819	6436	.438	1436	1930	.744	946	2238	3184	1745	1738	11	646	1216	324	7480	91.2	+4.2
Phoenix	2792	6422	.435	1618	2127	.761	902	2588	3490	1652	1819	14	682	1433	416	7529	91.8	+2.2
Utah	2667	6076	.439	1830	2391	.765	874	2183	3057	1564	2006	33	649	1320	453	7574	92.4	+4.7
Indiana	2829	6683	.423	1572	2074	.758	1042	2495	3537	1695	1882	13	589	1115	387	7607	92.8	-0.2
Houston	3020	6733	.449	1385	1862	.744	988	2420	3408	1735	1771	17	605	1092	400	7784	94.9	+2.3
L.A. Clippers	2995	6800	.440	1474	1983	.743	1042	2439	3481	1791	1795	16	638	1045	412	7818	95.3	-2.9
Toronto	3009	6725	.447	1425	1890	.754	926	2511	3437	1696	1792	20	561	1156	439	7822	95.4	+2.3
Sacramento	3087	7139	.432	1291	1724	.749	1121	2643	3764	1816	1766	14	666	1334	476	7866	95.9	+5.8
Minnesota	2977	6588	.452	1567	2164	.724	967	2505	3472	1834	1655	5	583	1246	357	7871	96.0	+1.4
Atlanta	2922	6609	.442	1646	2153	.765	1029	2534	3563	1737	1890	11	098	1212	513	7886	96.2	-5.2
Dallas	2938	6693	.439	1631	2231	.731	1068	2623	3691	1778	1848	21	622	1273	379	7888	96.2	+4.3
Cleveland	2927	6582	.445	1633	2125	.768	990	2400	3390	1880	1810	12	694	1229	542	7909	96.5	-4.2
Orlando	2830	6499	.435	1885	2566	.735	1061	2609	3670	1793	1946	15	695	1408	440	7911	96.5	+1.0
Chicago	2987	6330	.472	1607	2202	.730	957	2551	3508	1932	1754	11	635	1217	426	7927	96.7	-9.1
Boston	2935	6392	.459	1634	2178	.750	888	2650	3538	1885	1903	17	650	1402	440	7934	96.8	-2.1
Milwaukee	2912	6626	.439	1679	2186	.768	1014	2490	3504	1883	1778	13	592	1273	350	7942	96.9	+3.9
New Jersey	2937	6452	.455	1664	2231	.746	1001	2622	3623	1840	1808	21	619	1304	522	7966	97.1	-5.0
L.A. Lakers	2983	6815	.438	1595	2114	.754	981	2407	3388	1659	2002	24	619	1073	324	7974	97.2	+3.4
Seattle	3076	6783	.453	1353	1824	.742	1046	2431	3477	1957	1816	12	648	1228	510	7976	97.3	+0.0
Detroit	2976	6850	.434	1596	2169	.736	1012	2671	3683	1860	2062	23	669	1274	397	7976	97.3	-1.7
Vancouver	3143	6791	.463	1317	1798	.732	1052	2534	3586	1935	1768	16	710	1217	476	7992	97.5	-5.7
Denver	3081	6914	.446	1542	2049	.753	1012	2642	3654	2042	1758	23	588	1075	497	8120	99.0	-2.5
Washington	3100	6596	.470	1509	2088	.747	931	2410	3341	1902	1974	18	688	1230	511	8192	99.9	-6.7
Golden State	3179	6740	.472	1529	2011	.760	1039	2693	3732	2045	1765	18	722	1348	493	8326	101.5	-9.0
Avgs.	2926	6609	.443	1524	2039	.748	983	2499	3482	1786	1832	17	641	1234	431	7774	94.8	...

2000-01

– 299 –

HOME/ROAD

	Home	Road	Total		Home	Road	Total
Atlanta	18-23	7-34	25-57	Minnesota	30-11	17-24	47-35
Boston	20-21	16-25	36-46	New Jersey	18-23	8-33	26-56
Charlotte	28-13	18-23	46-36	New York	30-11	18-23	48-34
Chicago	10-31	5-36	15-67	Orlando	26-15	17-24	43-39
Cleveland	20-21	10-31	30-52	Philadelphia	29-12	27-14	56-26
Dallas	28-13	25-16	53-29	Phoenix	31-10	20-21	51-31
Denver	29-12	11-30	40-42	Portland	28-13	22-19	50-32
Detroit	18-23	14-27	32-50	Sacramento	33-8	22-19	55-27
Golden State	11-30	6-35	17-65	San Antonio	33-8	25-16	58-24
Houston	24-17	21-20	45-37	Seattle	26-15	18-23	44-38
Indiana	26-15	15-26	41-41	Toronto	27-14	20-21	47-35
L.A. Clippers	22-19	9-32	31-51	Utah	28-13	25-16	53-29
L.A. Lakers	31-10	25-16	56-26	Vancouver	15-26	8-33	23-59
Miami	29-12	21-20	50-32	Washington	12-29	7-34	19-63
Milwaukee	31-10	21-20	52-30	Totals	711-478	478-711	1,189-1,189

INDIVIDUAL LEADERS

POINTS

(minimum 70 games or 1,400 points)

	G	FGM	FTM	Pts.	Avg.
Allen Iverson, Philadelphia	71	762	585	2207	31.1
Jerry Stackhouse, Detroit	80	774	666	2380	29.8
Shaquille O'Neal, L.A. Lakers	74	813	499	2125	28.7
Kobe Bryant, L.A. Lakers	68	701	475	1938	28.5
Vince Carter, Toronto	75	762	384	2070	27.6
Chris Webber, Sacramento	70	786	324	1898	27.1
Tracy McGrady, Orlando	77	788	430	2065	26.8
Paul Pierce, Boston	82	687	550	2071	25.3
Antawn Jamison, Golden State	82	800	382	2044	24.9
Stephon Marbury, New Jersey	67	563	362	1598	23.9

REBOUNDS

(minimum 70 games or 800 rebounds)

	G	Off.	Def.	Tot.	Avg.
Dikembe Mutombo, Atl.-Phi.	75	307	708	1015	13.5
Ben Wallace, Detroit	80	303	749	1052	13.2
Shaquille O'Neal, L.A. Lakers	74	291	649	940	12.7
Tim Duncan, San Antonio	82	259	738	997	12.2
Antonio McDyess, Denver	70	240	605	845	12.1
Kevin Garnett, Minnesota	81	219	702	921	11.4
Chris Webber, Sacramento	70	179	598	777	11.1
Shawn Marion, Phoenix	79	220	628	848	10.7
Antonio Davis, Toronto	78	274	513	787	10.1
Elton Brand, Chicago	74	285	461	746	10.1

FIELD GOALS

(minimum 300 made)

	FGM	FGA	Pct.
Shaquille O'Neal, L.A. Lakers	813	1422	.572
Bonzi Wells, Portland	387	726	.533
Marcus Camby, New York	304	580	.524
Kurt Thomas, New York	314	614	.511
Wally Szczerbiak, Minnesota	469	920	.510
Darius Miles, L.A. Clippers	318	630	.505
John Stockton, Utah	328	651	.504
Donyell Marshall, Utah	427	849	.503
Corliss Williamson, Tor.-Det.	325	647	.502
Clarence Weatherspoon, Cleveland	347	692	.501
Rasheed Wallace, Portland	590	1178	.501

STEALS

(minimum 70 games or 125 steals)

	G	No.	Avg.
Allen Iverson, Philadelphia	71	178	2.51
Mookie Blaylock, Golden State	69	163	2.36
Doug Christie, Sacramento	81	183	2.26
Jason Kidd, Phoenix	77	166	2.16
Baron Davis, Charlotte	82	170	2.07
Terrell Brandon, Minnesota	78	161	2.06
Ron Artest, Chicago	76	152	2.00
Darrell Armstrong, Orlando	75	135	1.80
Steve Francis, Houston	80	141	1.76
Antoine Walker, Boston	81	138	1.70

FREE THROWS

(minimum 125 made)

	FTM	FTA	Pct.
Reggie Miller, Indiana	323	348	.928
Allan Houston, New York	279	307	.909
Doug Christie, Sacramento	280	312	.897
Steve Nash, Dallas	231	258	.895
Mitch Richmond, Washington	143	160	.894
Steve Smith, Portland	309	347	.890
Ray Allen, Milwaukee	348	392	.888
Darrell Armstrong, Orlando	220	249	.884
Eric Piatkowski, L.A. Clippers	158	181	.873
Terrell Brandon, Minnesota	195	224	.871

BLOCKED SHOTS

(minimum 70 games or 100 blocked shots)

	G	No.	Avg.
Theo Ratliff, Philadelphia	50	187	3.74
Jermaine O'Neal, Indiana	81	228	2.81
Shawn Bradley, Dallas	82	228	2.78
Shaquille O'Neal, L.A. Lakers	74	204	2.76
Dikembe Mutombo, Atl.-Phi.	75	203	2.71
Adonal Foyle, Golden State	58	156	2.69
Raef LaFrentz, Denver	78	206	2.64
David Robinson, San Antonio	80	197	2.46
Tim Duncan, San Antonio	82	192	2.34
Ben Wallace, Detroit	80	186	2.33

ASSISTS

(minimum 70 games or 400 assists)

	G	No.	Avg.
Jason Kidd, Phoenix	77	753	9.8
John Stockton, Utah	82	713	8.7
Nick Van Exel, Denver	71	600	8.5
Mike Bibby, Vancouver	82	685	8.4
Gary Payton, Seattle	79	642	8.1
Andre Miller, Cleveland	82	657	8.0
Mark Jackson, Tor.-N.Y.	83	661	8.0
Sam Cassell, Milwaukee	76	580	7.6
Stephon Marbury, New Jersey	67	506	7.6
Terrell Brandon, Minnesota	78	583	7.5

3-POINT FIELD GOALS

(minimum 55 made)

	FGM	FGA	Pct.
Brent Barry, Seattle	109	229	.476
John Stockton, Utah	61	132	.462
Shammond Williams, Seattle	61	133	.459
Hubert Davis, Dal.-Was.	78	171	.456
Danny Ferry, San Antonio	70	156	.449
Toni Kukoc, Phi.-Atl.	70	157	.446
Pat Garrity, Orlando	97	224	.433
Ray Allen, Milwaukee	202	467	.433
Rashard Lewis, Seattle	123	285	.432
Dell Curry, Toronto	62	146	.420

ATLANTA HAWKS

	G	Min.	FGM	FGA	Pct.	FTM	FTA	Pct.	Off.	Def.	Tot.	Ast.	PF	Dq.	Stl.	TO	Blk.	Pts.	Avg.	Hi.
Jason Terry	82	3089	596	1367	.436	303	358	.846	42	227	269	403	204	2	104	239	12	1619	19.7	38
Jim Jackson*	17	550	77	217	.355	73	85	.859	17	62	79	50	42	0	19	48	4	243	14.3	34
Lorenzen Wright	71	1988	363	811	.448	155	216	.718	180	355	535	87	232	2	42	125	63	881	12.4	31
Toni Kukoc†	17	618	124	252	.492	49	72	.681	19	78	97	106	36	0	13	51	5	335	19.7	31
Toni Kukoc‡	65	1597	275	582	.473	101	160	.631	66	193	259	199	98	0	48	111	11	721	11.1	31
Alan Henderson	73	1810	298	671	.444	173	271	.638	180	226	406	50	164	2	51	126	29	769	10.5	23
Roshown McLeod*	34	907	144	330	.436	45	51	.882	37	81	118	58	88	0	23	57	8	335	9.9	24
Dikembe Mutombo*	49	1716	169	354	.477	107	154	.695	188	505	693	54	139	2	20	92	137	445	9.1	22
Nazr Mohammed†	28	716	135	281	.480	75	98	.765	97	155	252	17	73	0	23	55	28	345	12.3	24
Nazr Mohammed‡	58	912	176	369	.477	89	126	.706	115	192	307	19	113	0	29	64	35	441	7.6	24
Chris Crawford	47	901	122	270	.452	68	83	.819	28	82	110	37	117	3	21	62	16	318	6.8	27
Matt Maloney	55	1403	146	348	.420	26	34	.765	14	103	117	154	94	1	56	70	5	369	6.7	18
Brevin Knight†	47	1364	137	356	.385	49	60	.817	22	139	161	286	138	2	95	84	3	324	6.9	31
Brevin Knight‡	53	1457	139	371	.375	54	66	.818	23	145	168	311	155	2	101	91	4	333	6.3	31
Dion Glover	57	929	141	336	.420	47	69	.681	39	92	131	69	92	1	49	54	10	338	5.9	28
Larry Robinson†	33	631	67	184	.364	21	24	.875	23	64	87	36	46	0	28	24	2	199	6.0	21
Larry Robinson‡	34	632	67	184	.364	21	24	.875	23	64	87	36	46	0	28	25	2	199	5.9	21
DerMarr Johnson	78	1313	146	390	.374	64	87	.736	56	122	178	64	134	0	43	93	30	397	5.1	19
Hanno Mottola	73	989	123	277	.444	73	90	.811	49	125	174	25	163	3	11	67	9	319	4.4	11
Cal Bowdler	44	375	53	114	.465	33	40	.825	30	47	77	4	45	0	10	11	21	140	3.2	15
Tony Smith	6	78	8	23	.348	1	2	.500	2	1	3	10	12	0	7	9	0	17	2.8	9
Anthony Johnson*	25	279	26	71	.366	12	17	.706	3	20	23	34	41	0	17	20	5	64	2.6	7
Anthony Miller*	2	6	1	2	.500	0	0	...	0	2	2	0	0	0	0	1	0	2	1.0	2
Ira Bowman	3	19	0	2	.000	0	0	...	1	1	2	7	0	0	0	1	0	0	0.0	0
Sean Colson*	3	14	0	5	.000	0	0	...	0	3	3	3	0	0	0	2	0	0	0.0	0
Andy Panko	1	1	0	0	...	0	0	...	0	0	0	0	0	0	0	0	0	0	0.0	0
Pepe Sanchez	5	34	0	7	.000	0	0	...	1	0	1	5	3	0	2	3	0	0	0.0	0

3-pt. FG: Atlanta 333-933 (.357)—Terry 124-314 (.395); Jackson* 16-38 (.421); Wright 0-2 (.000); Kukoc† 38-79 (.481); Kukoc‡ 70-157 (.446); Smith 0-2 (.000); Henderson 0-1 (.000); McLeod* 2-21 (.095); Mohammed† 0-1 (.000); Mohammed‡ 0-1 (.000); Crawford 6-22 (.273); Maloney 51-142 (.359); Knight† 1-10 (.100); Knight‡ 1-10 (.100); Glover 9-46 (.196); Robinson† 44-116 (.379); Robinson‡ 44-116 (.379); D. Johnson 41-127 (.323); Mottola 0-3 (.000); Bowdler 1-5 (.200); A. Johnson* 0-3 (.000); Colson* 0-1 (.000). Opponents 396-1080 (.367).

BOSTON CELTICS

	G	Min.	FGM	FGA	Pct.	FTM	FTA	Pct.	Off.	Def.	Tot.	Ast.	PF	Dq.	Stl.	TO	Blk.	Pts.	Avg.	Hi.
Paul Pierce	82	3120	687	1513	.454	550	738	.745	94	428	522	253	251	3	138	262	69	2071	25.3	44
Antoine Walker	81	3396	711	1720	.413	249	348	.716	151	568	719	445	251	2	138	301	49	1892	23.4	47
Bryant Stith	78	2504	245	611	.401	175	207	.845	65	219	284	168	182	0	93	90	14	756	9.7	29
Kenny Anderson	33	849	88	227	.388	59	71	.831	16	57	73	134	62	0	44	52	2	246	7.5	20
Vitaly Potapenko	82	1901	248	521	.476	115	158	.728	206	289	495	64	228	2	52	105	23	611	7.5	16
Eric Williams	81	1745	162	448	.362	165	231	.714	64	143	207	112	179	1	64	76	13	535	6.6	22
Tony Battie	40	845	108	201	.537	44	69	.638	73	160	233	16	126	3	27	37	60	260	6.5	19
Milt Palacio	58	1141	126	267	.472	78	92	.848	25	77	102	151	83	0	48	80	0	342	5.9	19
Doug Overton*	7	144	15	44	.341	7	11	.636	3	12	15	19	15	0	4	13	0	38	5.4	10
Chris Carr	35	309	53	112	.473	46	60	.767	11	33	44	11	45	1	4	19	0	169	4.8	15
Randy Brown	54	1238	100	237	.422	23	40	.575	23	76	99	154	132	1	62	56	10	223	4.1	16
Mark Blount	64	1098	101	200	.505	46	66	.697	97	134	231	32	183	0	39	62	76	248	3.9	12
Rick Brunson*	7	142	10	35	.286	4	9	.444	2	7	9	24	16	0	7	9	1	26	3.7	7
Chris Herren	25	408	29	96	.302	9	12	.750	4	17	21	56	43	0	14	20	0	83	3.3	13
Walter McCarty	60	478	45	126	.357	22	28	.786	24	57	81	39	82	0	14	20	7	131	2.2	27
Adrian Griffin	44	377	33	97	.340	18	24	.750	27	60	87	27	45	0	18	18	5	93	2.1	10
Jerome Moiso	24	135	12	30	.400	11	26	.423	12	30	42	3	29	0	3	18	4	35	1.5	5

3-pt. FG: Boston 592-1633 (.363)—Pierce 147-384 (.383); Walker 221-603 (.367); Stith 91-242 (.376); Anderson 11-33 (.333); Williams 46-139 (.331); Brown 0-3 (.000); Battie 0-3 (.000); Palacio 12-36 (.333); Overton* 1-4 (.250); Carr 17-37 (.459); Brunson* 2-11 (.182); Herren 16-55 (.291); McCarty 19-56 (.339); Griffin 9-26 (.346); Moiso 0-1 (.000). Opponents 430-1170 (.368).

CHARLOTTE HORNETS

	G	Min.	FGM	FGA	Pct.	FTM	FTA	Pct.	Off.	Def.	Tot.	Ast.	PF	Dq.	Stl.	TO	Blk.	Pts.	Avg.	Hi.
Jamal Mashburn	76	2989	573	1388	.413	279	364	.766	92	484	576	411	185	1	85	211	13	1528	20.1	33
David Wesley	82	3106	523	1239	.422	271	339	.799	64	160	224	361	220	2	128	171	16	1414	17.2	32
Baron Davis	82	3192	409	957	.427	228	337	.677	129	279	408	598	267	1	170	226	36	1131	13.8	28
Elden Campbell	78	2337	367	834	.440	288	406	.709	157	451	608	104	280	1	60	144	140	1022	13.1	26
P.J. Brown	80	2811	249	561	.444	178	209	.852	257	485	742	127	260	6	78	108	92	676	8.5	22
Derrick Coleman	34	683	97	255	.380	63	92	.685	46	138	184	39	53	1	10	42	21	277	8.1	18
Eddie Robinson	67	1201	216	407	.531	64	88	.727	60	138	198	59	66	0	50	43	32	498	7.4	21
Jamaal Magloire	74	1095	122	271	.450	95	145	.655	103	192	295	27	139	0	18	61	78	339	4.6	16
Scott Burrell	4	41	7	15	.467	1	4	.250	1	2	3	1	8	0	3	0	0	17	4.3	5
Lee Nailon	42	469	66	136	.485	32	43	.744	29	63	92	24	60	0	9	27	5	164	3.9	15
Hersey Hawkins	59	681	56	137	.409	54	63	.857	17	63	80	72	45	0	33	19	9	183	3.1	15

2000-01

	G	Min.	FGM	FGA	Pct.	FTM	FTA	Pct.	REBOUNDS Off.	Def.	Tot.	Ast.	PF	Dq.	Stl.	TO	Blk.	SCORING Pts.	Avg.	Hi.
Otis Thorpe	49	647	59	131	.450	20	24	.833	50	95	145	29	108	0	12	32	7	138	2.8	10
Eldridge Recasner	43	403	38	114	.333	14	18	.778	13	37	50	39	30	0	6	27	1	103	2.4	11
Doug Overton*	2	15	2	2	1.000	0	0	...	0	0	0	0	2	0	1	3	0	4	2.0	4
Tim James	30	197	16	52	.308	12	14	.857	15	20	35	8	27	0	2	8	5	45	1.5	6
Terrance Roberson	3	13	0	2	.000	0	0	...	0	1	1	1	3	0	0	2	0	0	0.0	0

3-pt. FG: Charlotte 340-984 (.346)—Mashburn 103-289 (.356); Wesley 97-258 (.376); Davis 85-274 (.310); Campbell 0-6 (.000); Brown 0-4 (.000); Coleman 20-51 (.392); Robinson 2-4 (.500); Magloire 0-2 (.000); Burrell 2-6 (.333); Nailon 0-1 (.000); Hawkins 17-46 (.370); Recasner 13-39 (.333); James 1-3 (.333); Roberson 0-1 (.000). Opponents 389-1081 (.360).

CHICAGO BULLS

	G	Min.	FGM	FGA	Pct.	FTM	FTA	Pct.	REBOUNDS Off.	Def.	Tot.	Ast.	PF	Dq.	Stl.	TO	Blk.	SCORING Pts.	Avg.	Hi.
Elton Brand	74	2906	578	1215	.476	334	472	.708	285	461	746	240	243	4	71	219	118	1490	20.1	31
Ron Mercer	61	2535	500	1121	.446	188	228	.825	72	164	236	201	148	3	78	129	27	1202	19.7	39
Ron Artest	76	2363	327	815	.401	210	280	.750	59	235	294	228	254	7	152	159	45	907	11.9	29
Marcus Fizer	72	1580	278	646	.430	117	161	.727	76	237	313	76	175	0	30	124	19	683	9.5	26
Fred Hoiberg	74	2247	217	495	.438	136	157	.866	21	287	308	263	155	0	98	74	12	673	9.1	28
Brad Miller	57	1434	168	386	.435	168	226	.743	144	275	419	107	176	5	33	73	38	505	8.9	22
Bryce Drew	48	1305	124	327	.379	14	19	.737	12	57	69	185	99	1	32	68	3	302	6.3	24
Khalid El-Amin	50	936	115	311	.370	56	72	.778	21	60	81	145	99	0	48	54	2	314	6.3	21
A.J. Guyton	33	630	78	192	.406	15	18	.833	10	26	36	64	35	0	9	24	5	198	6.0	24
Corey Benjamin	65	857	115	302	.381	56	83	.675	38	62	100	69	128	2	28	63	16	307	4.7	17
Jamal Crawford	61	1050	107	304	.352	27	34	.794	9	80	89	141	68	0	43	85	14	282	4.6	17
Michael Ruffin	45	879	40	90	.444	39	77	.506	101	161	262	39	131	2	30	46	38	119	2.6	10
Dragan Tarlac	43	598	39	99	.394	25	33	.758	37	85	122	31	95	2	7	38	19	103	2.4	10
Jake Voskuhl	16	143	11	25	.440	8	14	.571	12	22	34	5	38	0	5	12	6	30	1.9	6
Steve Goodrich	12	133	7	18	.389	4	7	.571	7	14	21	6	14	0	2	8	1	19	1.6	4
Dalibor Bagaric	35	259	17	65	.262	13	28	.464	22	34	56	10	44	0	9	21	16	47	1.3	5

3-pt. FG: Chicago 329-950 (.346)—Brand 0-2 (.000); Mercer 14-46 (.304); Artest 43-148 (.291); Fizer 10-39 (.256); Hoiberg 103-250 (.412); Miller 1-5 (.200); Drew 40-105 (.381); El-Amin 28-84 (.333); Guyton 27-69 (.391); Benjamin 21-81 (.259); Crawford 41-117 (.350); Goodrich 1-3 (.333); Bagaric 0-1 (.000). Opponents 346-973 (.356).

CLEVELAND CAVALIERS

	G	Min.	FGM	FGA	Pct.	FTM	FTA	Pct.	REBOUNDS Off.	Def.	Tot.	Ast.	PF	Dq.	Stl.	TO	Blk.	SCORING Pts.	Avg.	Hi.
Andre Miller	82	2848	452	999	.452	375	450	.833	94	266	360	657	229	0	119	265	28	1296	15.8	30
Lamond Murray	78	2225	391	925	.423	155	211	.735	104	236	340	124	173	0	83	141	27	998	12.8	30
Zydrunas Ilgauskas	24	616	114	234	.487	53	78	.679	65	95	160	18	78	0	15	60	37	281	11.7	24
Jim Jackson†	39	1140	162	415	.390	66	84	.786	36	109	145	113	97	0	34	82	6	400	10.3	23
Jim Jackson‡	56	1690	239	632	.378	139	169	.822	53	171	224	163	139	0	53	130	10	643	11.5	34
Chris Gatling	74	1670	329	733	.449	156	228	.684	99	292	391	61	185	0	52	119	27	842	11.4	38
Clarence Weatherspoon	82	2774	347	692	.501	230	291	.790	223	573	796	103	171	0	85	112	105	924	11.3	24
Matt Harpring	56	1615	238	524	.454	134	165	.812	90	152	242	102	161	1	42	90	17	623	11.1	34
Chris Mihm	59	1166	173	391	.442	100	126	.794	106	174	280	16	156	2	20	80	53	446	7.6	18
Wesley Person	44	958	128	292	.438	24	30	.800	11	119	130	64	62	0	27	40	11	314	7.1	24
Trajan Langdon	65	1116	135	313	.431	68	76	.895	12	77	89	81	114	0	38	52	9	389	6.0	31
Robert Traylor	70	1212	161	324	.497	80	141	.567	124	176	300	63	204	3	49	98	76	402	5.7	17
Bimbo Coles	47	804	91	239	.381	48	56	.857	9	39	48	138	87	0	27	59	6	232	4.9	17
Cedric Henderson	55	961	102	262	.389	30	46	.652	19	71	90	79	101	0	29	63	23	235	4.3	15
Chucky Brown†	20	265	31	75	.413	16	24	.667	5	31	36	6	27	0	6	6	6	78	3.9	12
Chucky Brown‡	26	339	40	95	.421	22	34	.647	8	46	54	11	37	0	9	8	7	102	3.9	12
Anthony Johnson†	28	232	27	81	.333	11	16	.688	7	14	21	44	21	0	6	14	1	66	2.4	16
Anthony Johnson‡	53	511	53	152	.349	23	33	.697	10	34	44	78	62	0	23	34	6	130	2.5	16
J.R. Reid	6	39	2	5	.400	6	8	.750	5	3	8	1	4	0	2	1	1	10	1.7	5
Brevin Knight*	6	93	2	15	.133	5	6	.833	1	6	7	25	17	0	6	7	1	9	1.5	4
Etdrick Bohannon	6	19	2	4	.500	4	4	1.000	3	4	7	0	4	0	0	1	2	8	1.3	4
Michael Hawkins	10	76	3	9	.333	0	0	...	2	3	5	13	13	0	2	6	0	8	0.8	3
Larry Robinson*	1	1	0	0	...	0	0	...	0	0	0	0	0	0	0	1	0	0	0.0	0

3-pt. FG: Cleveland 220-659 (.334)—Miller 17-64 (.266); Murray 61-165 (.370); Ilgauskas 0-2 (.000); Jackson† 10-42 (.238); Jackson‡ 26-80 (.325); Mihm 0-1 (.000); Gatling 28-92 (.304); Harpring 13-52 (.250); Person 34-84 (.405); Langdon 51-124 (.411); Traylor 0-2 (.000); Coles 2-16 (.125); Henderson 1-8 (.125); Brown† 0-1 (.000); Brown‡ 0-3 (.000); Johnson† 1-2 (.500); Johnson‡ 1-5 (.200); Hawkins 2-4 (.500). Opponents 422-1155 (.365).

DALLAS MAVERICKS

	G	Min.	FGM	FGA	Pct.	FTM	FTA	Pct.	REBOUNDS Off.	Def.	Tot.	Ast.	PF	Dq.	Stl.	TO	Blk.	SCORING Pts.	Avg.	Hi.
Dirk Nowitzki	82	3125	591	1247	.474	451	538	.838	119	635	754	173	245	1	78	198	101	1784	21.8	38
Michael Finley	82	3443	711	1552	.458	252	325	.775	109	316	425	360	174	2	118	190	32	1765	21.5	38
Juwan Howard†	27	993	191	391	.488	99	127	.780	50	143	193	70	102	1	29	73	16	481	17.8	32
Juwan Howard‡	81	2974	583	1218	.479	296	383	.773	171	401	572	224	292	2	75	242	37	1462	18.0	35
Steve Nash	70	2387	386	792	.487	231	258	.895	46	177	223	509	158	0	72	205	5	1092	15.6	31
Howard Eisley	82	2426	265	675	.393	104	126	.825	23	174	197	295	218	3	99	102	12	741	9.0	27
Christian Laettner*	53	930	165	323	.511	67	82	.817	75	137	212	67	159	1	40	70	27	398	7.5	17

	G	Min.	FGM	FGA	Pct.	FTM	FTA	Pct.	REBOUNDS Off.	Def.	Tot.	Ast.	PF	Dq.	Stl.	TO	Blk.	SCORING Pts.	Avg.	Hi.
Hubert Davis*	51	1261	139	314	.443	35	41	.854	18	91	109	61	92	0	29	56	1	371	7.3	32
Shawn Bradley	82	2001	219	447	.490	140	178	.787	160	448	608	38	256	6	36	88	228	579	7.1	22
Greg Buckner	37	820	84	192	.438	59	81	.728	60	97	157	49	118	2	33	27	9	229	6.2	15
Calvin Booth†	15	293	46	84	.548	20	33	.606	24	48	72	19	55	0	12	17	30	112	7.5	12
Calvin Booth‡	55	933	120	252	.476	53	78	.679	77	169	246	42	146	1	29	53	111	293	5.3	18
Wang Zhizhi	5	38	8	19	.421	8	10	.800	1	6	7	0	8	0	0	1	0	24	4.8	13
Vernon Maxwell†	19	285	31	98	.316	6	10	.600	1	28	29	20	31	0	9	17	3	81	4.3	11
Vernon Maxwell‡	43	660	73	223	.327	21	32	.656	4	62	66	49	64	0	21	35	3	201	4.7	15
Courtney Alexander*	38	472	62	178	.348	33	45	.733	20	43	63	21	76	1	16	21	3	160	4.2	20
Gary Trent	33	319	57	130	.438	19	36	.528	39	53	92	10	52	0	13	22	8	133	4.0	10
Eduardo Najera	40	431	58	111	.523	14	33	.424	41	54	95	27	48	0	13	17	8	114	3.1	10
Loy Vaught*	37	392	55	121	.455	4	6	.667	35	88	123	16	61	0	15	18	5	114	3.1	10
Obinna Ekezie†	8	8	0	4	.000	0	0	...	0	2	2	0	2	0	0	0	0	0	0.0	0
Obinna Ekezie‡	33	281	32	81	.395	37	53	.698	31	47	78	9	48	0	5	14	5	101	3.1	13
Donnell Harvey	18	65	8	14	.571	6	16	.375	6	14	20	2	15	0	3	7	1	22	1.2	5
Mark Bryant	18	101	8	20	.400	3	5	.600	4	17	21	3	29	1	1	5	2	19	1.1	6
Bill Curley*	5	15	1	4	.250	1	4	.250	0	0	0	0	4	0	1	2	1	3	0.6	2

3-pt. FG: Dallas 517-1357 (.381)—Nowitzki 151-390 (.387); Finley 91-263 (.346); Howard† 0-3 (.000); Howard‡ 0-3 (.000); Nash 89-219 (.406); Bradley 1-6 (.167); Eisley 107-269 (.398); Laettner* 1-3 (.333); Davis* 58-133 (.436); Buckner 2-7 (.286); Wang 0-2 (.000); Trent 0-1 (.000); Maxwell† 13-47 (.277); Maxwell‡ 34-111 (.306); Alexander* 3-10 (.300); Najera 1-3 (.333); Curley* 0-1 (.000). Opponents 381-1140 (.334).

DENVER NUGGETS

	G	Min.	FGM	FGA	Pct.	FTM	FTA	Pct.	REBOUNDS Off.	Def.	Tot.	Ast.	PF	Dq.	Stl.	TO	Blk.	SCORING Pts.	Avg.	Hi.
Antonio McDyess	70	2555	577	1165	.495	304	434	.700	240	605	845	146	220	2	43	162	102	1458	20.8	40
Nick Van Exel	71	2688	460	1112	.414	204	249	.819	44	197	241	600	109	1	61	165	18	1259	17.7	41
Raef LaFrentz	78	2457	387	812	.477	183	262	.698	173	434	607	107	290	9	37	97	206	1008	12.9	32
Voshon Lenard	80	2331	336	846	.397	153	192	.797	47	184	231	190	170	1	65	102	18	972	12.2	30
George McCloud	76	2007	250	655	.382	152	181	.840	55	169	224	279	165	1	53	117	27	729	9.6	24
Kevin Willis†	43	1059	180	421	.428	52	66	.788	109	200	309	29	138	0	38	47	31	413	9.6	25
Kevin Willis‡	78	1830	304	690	.441	113	147	.769	177	355	502	50	216	0	57	87	52	722	9.3	25
James Posey	82	2255	243	590	.412	115	141	.816	125	306	431	163	226	2	93	102	40	666	8.1	23
Keon Clark*	35	752	82	199	.412	63	105	.600	58	128	186	34	101	3	16	48	44	227	6.5	16
Robert Pack	74	1260	181	426	.425	105	137	.766	30	107	137	293	114	0	65	135	1	479	6.5	26
Mark Strickland*	46	517	82	185	.443	37	59	.627	43	77	120	17	58	0	12	24	19	201	4.4	16
Anthony Goldwire	20	201	30	80	.375	13	17	.765	1	11	12	34	13	0	9	15	0	82	4.1	10
Tracy Murray*	13	135	17	55	.309	9	10	.900	4	18	22	9	8	0	4	6	1	50	3.8	17
Tariq Abdul-Wahad	29	420	43	111	.387	21	36	.583	14	45	59	22	54	0	14	34	13	111	3.8	15
Ryan Bowen	57	696	80	144	.556	27	44	.614	62	51	113	30	95	0	37	24	12	191	3.4	12
Dan McClintock	6	58	9	18	.500	0	5	.000	10	7	17	1	11	1	0	3	2	18	3.0	8
Calbert Cheaney	9	153	10	30	.333	1	2	.500	5	15	20	9	14	0	4	5	2	21	2.3	6
Terry Davis	19	228	12	25	.480	9	22	.409	24	29	53	7	34	0	1	5	1	33	1.7	6
Garth Joseph†	2	8	0	3	.000	0	2	.000	0	0	0	1	1	0	0	2	1	0	0.0	0
Garth Joseph‡	4	16	1	5	.200	0	2	.000	2	0	2	1	1	0	0	2	1	2	0.5	2

3-pt. FG: Denver 512-1444 (.355)—Van Exel 135-358 (.377); LaFrentz 51-139 (.367); Lenard 147-382 (.385); McCloud 77-234 (.329); Willis† 1-4 (.250); Willis‡ 1-6 (.167); Posey 65-217 (.300); Pack 12-31 (.387); Strickland* 0-1 (.000); Goldwire 9-34 (.265); Bowen 4-11 (.364); Murray* 7-23 (.304); Abdul-Wahad 4-10 (.400). Opponents 416-1168 (.356).

DETROIT PISTONS

	G	Min.	FGM	FGA	Pct.	FTM	FTA	Pct.	REBOUNDS Off.	Def.	Tot.	Ast.	PF	Dq.	Stl.	TO	Blk.	SCORING Pts.	Avg.	Hi.
Jerry Stackhouse	80	3215	774	1927	.402	666	810	.822	99	216	315	410	160	1	97	326	54	2380	29.8	57
Joe Smith	69	1941	308	765	.403	231	287	.805	160	331	491	79	258	5	47	88	50	847	12.3	28
Chucky Atkins	81	2363	380	952	.399	90	130	.692	28	145	173	330	184	2	67	149	5	971	12.0	36
Corliss Williamson†	27	800	172	322	.534	67	107	.626	53	115	168	28	87	0	35	45	8	411	15.2	26
Corliss Williamson‡	69	1686	325	647	.502	151	237	.637	110	211	321	61	185	0	50	110	21	801	11.6	26
Dana Barros	60	1079	183	412	.444	68	80	.850	6	88	94	110	63	0	30	60	2	478	8.0	22
Jerome Williams*	33	804	88	201	.438	65	90	.722	98	180	278	32	81	0	39	47	10	241	7.3	15
Ben Wallace	80	2760	215	439	.490	80	238	.336	303	749	1052	123	192	0	107	117	186	511	6.4	18
John Wallace	40	527	100	236	.424	35	45	.778	25	58	83	23	72	1	13	36	16	237	5.9	21
Cedric Ceballos*	13	166	28	71	.394	8	10	.800	7	19	26	7	19	0	6	9	3	75	5.8	19
Mateen Cleaves	78	1268	160	400	.400	97	137	.708	26	106	132	207	153	1	49	139	1	422	5.4	19
Michael Curry	68	1485	145	319	.455	62	73	.849	21	100	121	132	173	0	27	61	3	356	5.2	17
Mikki Moore	81	1154	132	268	.493	95	130	.731	121	195	316	33	202	2	24	74	61	359	4.4	16
Billy Owens	45	793	88	230	.383	19	40	.475	84	121	205	55	93	0	32	39	12	198	4.4	14
Jud Buechler	57	737	76	164	.463	9	12	.750	20	74	94	39	83	0	21	25	10	193	3.4	13
Eric Montross*	42	568	50	121	.413	7	26	.269	43	101	144	15	100	0	8	37	23	107	2.5	13
Kornel David†	10	69	10	22	.455	0	0	...	6	13	19	3	8	0	4	4	1	20	2.0	6
Kornel David‡	27	209	25	51	.490	12	13	.923	15	37	52	7	28	0	6	11	0	62	2.3	10
Brian Cardinal	15	126	10	31	.323	11	18	.611	8	15	23	3	27	0	7	9	2	31	2.1	9

3-pt. FG: Detroit 389-1112 (.350)—Stackhouse 166-473 (.351); Smith 0-5 (.000); Atkins 121-339 (.357); Williamson† 0-2 (.000); Barros 44-105 (.419); Williams* 0-2 (.000); B. Wallace 1-4 (.250); J. Wallace 2-15 (.133); Ceballos* 11-40 (.275); Cleaves 5-17 (.294); Curry 4-9 (.444); Moore 0-1 (.000); Owens 3-20 (.150); Buechler 32-77 (.416); Cardinal 0-5 (.000). Opponents 428-1229 (.348).

GOLDEN STATE WARRIORS

	G	Min.	FGM	FGA	Pct.	FTM	FTA	Pct.	REBOUNDS Off.	Def.	Tot.	Ast.	PF	Dq.	Stl.	TO	Blk.	SCORING Pts.	Avg.	Hi.
Antawn Jamison	82	3394	800	1812	.442	382	534	.715	280	435	715	164	225	2	114	199	28	2044	24.9	51
Danny Fortson	6	203	29	50	.580	42	54	.778	29	69	98	5	22	1	2	10	0	100	16.7	21
Larry Hughes	50	1846	308	805	.383	193	252	.766	76	200	276	223	147	2	96	152	29	823	16.5	29
Marc Jackson	48	1410	237	508	.467	154	192	.802	119	242	361	59	138	1	34	93	27	633	13.2	31
Chris Mills	15	493	71	191	.372	31	36	.861	24	69	93	18	43	1	9	20	5	180	12.0	19
Bob Sura	53	1684	202	518	.390	135	189	.714	54	173	227	242	127	0	54	160	8	586	11.1	31
Mookie Blaylock	69	2352	317	801	.396	53	76	.697	71	201	272	462	134	1	163	128	20	760	11.0	25
Chris Porter	51	1147	173	445	.389	94	141	.667	89	100	189	61	111	2	45	59	6	440	8.6	24
Erick Dampier	43	1038	126	314	.401	67	126	.532	97	153	250	59	123	3	17	82	58	319	7.4	20
Vonteego Cummings	66	1495	178	517	.344	79	116	.681	47	90	137	227	160	2	67	91	14	483	7.3	22
Adonal Foyle	58	1457	156	375	.416	30	68	.441	156	249	405	48	136	0	31	79	156	342	5.9	16
Chris Mullin	20	374	36	106	.340	24	28	.857	10	31	41	19	28	0	16	19	10	115	5.8	16
Paul McPherson†	22	287	62	120	.517	24	34	.706	20	11	31	22	32	0	13	24	1	150	6.8	26
Paul McPherson‡	55	595	109	216	.505	42	58	.724	40	39	79	38	80	0	25	47	4	262	4.8	26
Corie Blount†	38	918	107	247	.433	43	68	.632	146	169	315	51	90	1	29	55	17	259	6.8	15
Corie Blount‡	68	1305	130	294	.442	51	83	.614	181	219	400	59	165	3	42	73	22	313	4.6	15
Chucky Brown*	6	74	9	20	.450	6	10	.600	3	15	18	5	10	0	3	2	1	24	4.0	9
Bill Curley†	15	177	24	43	.558	11	15	.733	21	16	37	3	41	1	6	14	8	60	4.0	11
Bill Curley‡	20	192	25	47	.532	12	19	.632	21	16	37	3	45	1	7	16	9	63	3.2	11
Vinny Del Negro*	29	396	30	90	.333	16	16	1.000	4	27	31	62	36	0	6	15	0	77	2.7	9
Adam Keefe	67	836	64	159	.403	39	63	.619	90	119	209	36	102	0	28	40	20	168	2.5	12
Chris Garner	8	149	7	37	.189	5	6	.833	2	10	12	18	18	0	7	9	1	19	2.4	13
Ruben Garces†	3	11	0	7	.000	0	0	...	4	3	7	1	0	0	1	0	1	0	0.0	0
Ruben Garces‡	13	73	7	22	.318	2	8	.250	16	13	29	5	14	0	3	5	2	16	1.2	6
John Coker	6	32	1	8	.125	0	0	...	3	2	5	2	4	0	1	2	0	2	0.3	2
Randy Livingston	2	7	0	2	.000	0	0	...	0	1	1	1	0	0	0	0	0	0	0.0	0

3-pt. FG: Golden State 282-964 (.293)—Jamison 62-205 (.302); Hughes 14-75 (.187); Jackson 5-23 (.217); Mills 7-25 (.280); Sura 47-172 (.273); Blaylock 73-225 (.324); Porter 0-5 (.000); Dampier 0-2 (.000); Cummings 48-143 (.336); Mullin 19-52 (.365); McPherson† 2-6 (.333); Blount† 2-8 (.250); McPherson‡ 2-12 (.167); Blount‡ 2-8 (.250); Brown* 0-2 (.000); Curley† 1-1 (1.000); Curley‡ 1-2 (.500); Keefe 1-3 (.333); Del Negro* 1-9 (.111); Garner 0-7 (.000); Livingston 0-1 (.000). Opponents 439-1159 (.379).

HOUSTON ROCKETS

	G	Min.	FGM	FGA	Pct.	FTM	FTA	Pct.	REBOUNDS Off.	Def.	Tot.	Ast.	PF	Dq.	Stl.	TO	Blk.	SCORING Pts.	Avg.	Hi.
Steve Francis	80	3194	550	1219	.451	358	438	.817	190	363	553	517	274	7	141	265	31	1591	19.9	36
Cuttino Mobley	79	3002	527	1214	.434	394	474	.831	83	314	397	195	169	1	84	165	26	1538	19.5	41
Maurice Taylor	69	1972	390	797	.489	119	162	.735	109	269	378	104	208	3	28	125	38	899	13.0	34
Hakeem Olajuwon	58	1545	283	568	.498	123	198	.621	124	307	431	72	141	0	70	81	88	689	11.9	27
Shandon Anderson	82	2396	263	590	.446	138	188	.734	72	261	333	189	202	0	82	131	40	710	8.7	26
Walt Williams	72	1583	202	513	.394	97	126	.770	31	214	245	97	153	2	30	73	28	599	8.3	18
Kenny Thomas	74	1820	206	465	.443	91	126	.722	122	295	417	77	178	4	40	116	43	528	7.1	18
Moochie Norris	82	1654	184	413	.446	151	194	.778	44	154	198	283	84	0	69	107	2	544	6.6	18
Matt Bullard	61	1000	129	305	.423	10	14	.714	22	108	130	42	76	0	10	12	9	354	5.8	18
Kelvin Cato	35	624	64	111	.577	37	57	.649	47	94	141	11	89	1	13	25	31	165	4.7	15
Carlos Rogers	39	544	75	110	.682	29	52	.558	48	91	139	9	33	0	10	17	18	179	4.6	22
Jason Collier	23	222	27	71	.380	17	24	.708	12	25	37	6	27	1	2	11	3	71	3.1	12
Dan Langhi	33	241	37	99	.374	16	29	.552	13	28	41	4	16	0	7	8	1	90	2.7	13
Sean Colson†	10	30	6	19	.316	2	4	.500	2	1	3	7	6	0	1	0	0	15	1.5	6
Sean Colson‡	13	44	6	24	.250	2	4	.500	2	4	6	10	6	0	1	2	0	15	1.2	6
Anthony Miller*	1	3	0	0	...	0	0	...	0	0	0	0	1	0	0	0	0	0	0.0	0

3-pt. FG: Houston 504-1412 (.357)—Francis 133-336 (.396); Mobley 90-252 (.357); Taylor 0-4 (.000); Olajuwon 0-1 (.000); Anderson 46-170 (.271); Thomas 25-92 (.272); Williams 98-248 (.395); Norris 25-89 (.281); Bullard 86-213 (.404); Rogers 0-1 (.000); Collier 0-1 (.000); Langhi 0-1 (.000); Colson† 1-4 (.250); Colson‡ 1-5 (.200). Opponents 359-1015 (.354).

INDIANA PACERS

	G	Min.	FGM	FGA	Pct.	FTM	FTA	Pct.	REBOUNDS Off.	Def.	Tot.	Ast.	PF	Dq.	Stl.	TO	Blk.	SCORING Pts.	Avg.	Hi.
Jalen Rose	72	2943	567	1242	.457	285	344	.828	37	322	359	435	230	2	65	211	43	1478	20.5	42
Reggie Miller	81	3181	517	1176	.440	323	348	.928	38	247	285	260	162	0	81	133	15	1527	18.9	41
Jermaine O'Neal	81	2641	404	868	.465	233	388	.601	249	545	794	98	280	5	49	161	228	1041	12.9	30
Travis Best	77	2457	347	788	.440	187	226	.827	38	184	222	473	246	10	110	127	11	918	11.9	30
Austin Croshere	81	1874	276	701	.394	200	231	.866	123	264	387	92	180	1	36	136	50	822	10.1	32
Al Harrington	78	1892	241	543	.444	103	157	.656	119	262	381	130	223	2	63	148	18	586	7.5	22
Tyus Edney	24	263	35	91	.385	35	39	.897	5	19	24	54	17	0	17	25	0	106	4.4	16
Zan Tabak	55	777	98	186	.527	20	47	.426	65	148	213	33	125	0	10	57	30	216	3.9	16
Bruno Sundov	11	120	20	41	.488	3	5	.600	4	19	23	2	21	1	2	3	4	43	3.9	17
Sam Perkins	64	999	86	226	.381	32	38	.842	32	136	168	41	61	0	33	19	18	242	3.8	16
Jeff Foster	71	1152	100	213	.469	47	91	.516	144	245	389	33	152	3	39	52	28	249	3.5	15
Jonathan Bender	59	574	66	186	.355	50	68	.735	14	60	74	32	73	0	7	42	28	193	3.3	20
Derrick McKey	66	987	60	136	.441	21	27	.778	49	127	176	74	136	1	48	47	13	145	2.2	9
Terry Mills	14	113	11	34	.324	0	0	...	4	17	21	5	20	1	3	10	1	25	1.8	8
Lari Ketner	3	7	0	0	...	0	0	...	0	0	0	1	0	0	0	2	0	0	0.0	0

3-pt. FG: Indiana 396-1159 (.342)—Rose 59-174 (.339); Miller 170-464 (.366); O'Neal 0-5 (.000); Best 37-97 (.381); Croshere 70-207 (.338); Harrington 1-7 (.143); Edney 1-6 (.167); Sundov 0-4 (.000); Perkins 38-110 (.345); Foster 2-7 (.286); Bender 11-41 (.268); McKey 4-20 (.200); Mills 3-17 (.176). Opponents 377-1121 (.336).

LOS ANGELES CLIPPERS

	G	Min.	FGM	FGA	Pct.	FTM	FTA	Pct.	Off.	Def.	Tot.	Ast.	PF	Dq.	Stl.	TO	Blk.	Pts.	Avg.	Hi.
Lamar Odom	76	2836	481	1046	.460	262	386	.679	110	482	592	392	236	4	74	264	122	1304	17.2	34
Jeff McInnis	81	2831	432	933	.463	130	161	.807	41	179	220	447	199	2	75	113	7	1046	12.9	33
Eric Piatkowski	81	2144	291	672	.433	158	181	.873	54	187	241	96	123	0	46	76	19	860	10.6	30
Corey Maggette	69	1359	225	487	.462	223	288	.774	88	203	291	82	140	1	35	106	9	690	10.0	23
Darius Miles	81	2133	318	630	.505	124	238	.521	127	350	477	99	191	1	51	147	125	761	9.4	26
Michael Olowokandi	82	2127	308	708	.435	85	156	.545	168	357	525	46	250	4	30	169	108	701	8.5	24
Quentin Richardson	76	1358	232	525	.442	99	158	.627	105	152	257	62	98	0	42	64	7	613	8.1	21
Tyrone Nesby*	14	333	40	123	.325	18	23	.783	16	26	42	11	28	0	10	10	4	108	7.7	19
Earl Boykins	10	149	25	63	.397	14	17	.824	4	7	11	32	9	0	5	9	0	65	6.5	15
Keyon Dooling	76	1237	148	362	.409	125	179	.698	8	81	89	177	107	0	41	94	11	449	5.9	14
Sean Rooks	82	1553	169	395	.428	107	143	.748	91	212	303	77	197	2	34	73	64	446	5.4	15
Cherokee Parks†	52	876	116	236	.492	19	27	.704	58	131	189	39	102	0	19	31	25	251	4.8	16
Cherokee Parks‡	65	1054	134	274	.489	31	44	.705	71	158	229	46	122	0	25	41	36	299	4.6	16
Derek Strong	28	491	45	117	.385	28	37	.757	34	74	108	7	30	0	14	22	1	118	4.2	17
Brian Skinner	39	584	64	161	.398	32	59	.542	55	113	168	18	61	0	14	32	11	160	4.1	23
Zendon Hamilton	3	19	2	9	.222	5	8	.625	3	5	8	0	4	0	0	2	0	9	3.0	5

3-pt. FG: L.A. Clippers 360-1063 (.339)—Odom 80-253 (.316); McInnis 52-144 (.361); Piatkowski 120-297 (.404); Maggette 17-56 (.304); Miles 1-19 (.053); Boykins 1-8 (.125); Richardson 50-151 (.331); Nesby* 10-46 (.217); Dooling 28-80 (.350); Rooks 1-2 (.500); Parks† 0-6 (.000); Parks‡ 0-6 (.000); Strong 0-1 (.000). Opponents 354-1075 (.329).

LOS ANGELES LAKERS

	G	Min.	FGM	FGA	Pct.	FTM	FTA	Pct.	Off.	Def.	Tot.	Ast.	PF	Dq.	Stl.	TO	Blk.	Pts.	Avg.	Hi.
Shaquille O'Neal	74	2924	813	1422	.572	499	972	.513	291	649	940	277	256	6	47	218	204	2125	28.7	41
Kobe Bryant	68	2783	701	1510	.464	475	557	.853	104	295	399	338	222	3	114	220	43	1938	28.5	51
Derek Fisher	20	709	77	187	.412	50	62	.806	5	54	59	87	50	0	39	29	2	229	11.5	26
Rick Fox	82	2291	287	646	.444	95	122	.779	80	245	325	262	225	1	70	136	29	787	9.6	22
Horace Grant	77	2390	263	569	.462	131	169	.775	220	325	545	121	181	2	51	48	61	657	8.5	19
Isaiah Rider	67	1206	201	472	.426	71	83	.855	44	112	156	111	105	0	27	98	7	507	7.6	24
Ron Harper	47	1109	127	271	.460	34	48	.708	46	120	166	113	70	0	39	62	25	307	6.5	21
Brian Shaw	80	1833	164	411	.399	51	64	.797	48	256	304	258	159	1	49	97	27	421	5.3	22
Robert Horry	79	1587	147	380	.387	59	83	.711	93	203	296	128	210	3	54	79	54	407	5.2	20
Mike Penberthy	53	851	92	222	.414	28	31	.903	10	53	63	71	57	0	22	34	2	267	5.0	16
Stanislav Medvedenko	7	39	12	25	.480	7	12	.583	1	8	9	2	9	0	1	3	1	32	4.6	10
Tyronn Lue	38	468	50	117	.427	19	24	.792	5	27	32	45	54	1	10	27	0	130	3.4	10
Devean George	59	593	64	207	.309	39	55	.709	35	75	110	19	87	1	15	34	15	182	3.1	10
Greg Foster	62	451	56	133	.421	10	14	.714	29	83	112	32	76	0	9	25	12	125	2.0	13
Mark Madsen	70	641	55	113	.487	26	37	.703	74	78	152	24	111	2	8	27	8	137	2.0	15

3-pt. FG: L.A. Lakers 439-1275 (.344)—O'Neal 0-2 (.000); Bryant 61-200 (.305); Fisher 25-63 (.397); Fox 118-300 (.393); Grant 0-3 (.000); Rider 34-92 (.370); Harper 19-72 (.264); Shaw 42-135 (.311); Horry 54-156 (.346); Penberthy 55-139 (.396); Medvedenko 1-1 (1.000); Lue 11-34 (.324); George 15-68 (.221); Foster 3-9 (.333); Madsen 1-1 (1.000). Opponents 413-1168 (.354).

MIAMI HEAT

	G	Min.	FGM	FGA	Pct.	FTM	FTA	Pct.	Off.	Def.	Tot.	Ast.	PF	Dq.	Stl.	TO	Blk.	Pts.	Avg.	Hi.
Eddie Jones	63	2282	388	871	.445	228	270	.844	75	217	292	171	183	5	110	135	58	1094	17.4	31
Anthony Mason	80	3254	460	954	.482	370	474	.781	169	601	770	248	231	5	80	179	25	1290	16.1	29
Brian Grant	82	2771	484	1010	.479	282	354	.797	217	501	718	101	293	5	60	170	71	1250	15.2	33
Tim Hardaway	77	2613	408	1042	.392	145	181	.801	28	178	204	403	155	1	90	189	6	1150	14.9	26
Alonzo Mourning	13	306	73	141	.518	31	55	.564	35	66	101	12	24	0	4	28	31	177	13.6	25
Bruce Bowen	82	2685	211	581	.363	98	161	.609	45	200	245	132	269	8	83	74	53	623	7.6	20
Cedric Ceballos†	27	393	73	158	.462	29	33	.879	27	53	80	13	42	0	10	23	4	186	6.9	21
Cedric Ceballos‡	40	559	101	229	.441	37	43	.860	34	72	106	20	61	0	16	32	7	261	6.5	21
Anthony Carter	72	1630	195	480	.406	65	103	.631	46	134	180	268	154	1	73	119	10	461	6.4	19
Dan Majerle	53	1306	87	259	.336	36	44	.818	20	146	166	88	98	0	53	35	15	267	5.0	13
Eddie House	50	550	104	247	.421	24	35	.686	5	37	42	52	58	0	13	35	0	251	5.0	23
Ricky Davis	7	70	12	29	.414	7	8	.875	1	6	7	11	7	0	5	5	2	32	4.6	11
A.C. Green	82	1411	144	324	.444	79	111	.712	107	206	313	39	119	0	30	45	8	367	4.5	19
Don MacLean	8	76	10	20	.500	9	12	.750	7	11	18	4	9	0	5	10	1	31	3.9	16
Todd Fuller	10	77	10	35	.286	8	8	1.000	7	11	18	1	10	0	3	3	2	28	2.8	12
Duane Causwell	31	384	32	85	.376	12	25	.480	23	60	83	5	67	0	8	23	18	76	2.5	9
Jamal Robinson	6	72	3	22	.136	0	0	...	3	8	11	2	7	0	6	3	0	6	1.0	2

3-pt. FG: Miami 478-1384 (.345)—Jones 90-238 (.378); Grant 0-1 (.000); Hardaway 189-517 (.366); Mourning 0-1 (.000); Bowen 103-307 (.336); Carter 6-40 (.150); Ceballos† 11-33 (.333); Ceballos‡ 22-73 (.301); Majerle 57-181 (.315); House 19-55 (.345); Davis 1-1 (1.000); Green 0-6 (.000); MacLean 2-2 (1.000); Robinson 0-2 (.000). Opponents 360-1087 (.331).

MILWAUKEE BUCKS

	G	Min.	FGM	FGA	Pct.	FTM	FTA	Pct.	Off.	Def.	Tot.	Ast.	PF	Dq.	Stl.	TO	Blk.	Pts.	Avg.	Hi.
Glenn Robinson	76	2813	684	1460	.468	251	306	.820	124	402	526	252	191	2	86	219	62	1674	22.0	45
Ray Allen	82	3129	628	1309	.480	348	392	.888	101	327	428	374	192	2	124	204	20	1806	22.0	43
Sam Cassell	76	2709	537	1132	.474	277	323	.858	46	244	290	580	214	5	88	220	8	1381	18.2	40

	G	Min.	FGM	FGA	Pct.	FTM	FTA	Pct.	Off.	Def.	Tot.	Ast.	PF	Dq.	Stl.	TO	Blk.	Pts.	Avg.	Hi.
Tim Thomas	76	2086	326	758	.430	195	253	.771	79	234	313	138	194	5	78	114	45	954	12.6	39
Lindsey Hunter	82	2002	298	783	.381	77	96	.802	32	137	169	222	172	1	102	68	12	825	10.1	24
Jason Caffey	70	1460	179	367	.488	142	211	.673	135	218	353	53	184	8	38	77	25	500	7.1	17
Scott Williams	66	1272	171	361	.474	60	70	.857	97	267	364	35	178	1	48	41	32	403	6.1	24
Darvin Ham	29	540	39	80	.488	29	49	.592	56	65	121	25	85	0	17	33	21	109	3.8	10
Jerome Kersey	22	243	32	69	.464	8	16	.500	8	37	45	15	36	1	14	6	8	72	3.3	12
Ervin Johnson	82	1981	108	198	.545	50	93	.538	205	408	613	40	257	4	44	47	97	266	3.2	13
Mark Pope	63	942	62	142	.437	22	35	.629	56	91	147	38	140	2	16	17	26	151	2.4	10
Michael Redd	6	35	5	19	.263	3	6	.500	3	1	4	1	2	0	1	1	0	13	2.2	8
Rafer Alston	37	288	30	84	.357	9	13	.692	4	27	31	68	27	0	13	20	0	77	2.1	12
Jason Hart	1	10	1	1	1.000	0	0	...	0	0	0	1	0	0	0	2	0	2	2.0	2
Joel Przybilla	33	270	12	35	.343	3	11	.273	29	42	71	2	56	0	3	13	30	27	0.8	3

3-pt. FG: Milwaukee 562-1481 (.379)—Robinson 55-184 (.299); Allen 202-467 (.433); Cassell 30-98 (.306); Thomas 107-260 (.412); Hunter 152-407 (.373); Ham 2-3 (.667); Williams 1-4 (.250); Kersey 0-1 (.000); Pope 5-24 (.208); Redd 0-3 (.000); Alston 8-30 (.267). Opponents 439-1246 (.352).

MINNESOTA TIMBERWOLVES

	G	Min.	FGM	FGA	Pct.	FTM	FTA	Pct.	Off.	Def.	Tot.	Ast.	PF	Dq.	Stl.	TO	Blk.	Pts.	Avg.	Hi.
Kevin Garnett	81	3202	704	1475	.477	357	467	.764	219	702	921	401	204	0	111	230	145	1784	22.0	40
Terrell Brandon	78	2821	511	1134	.451	195	224	.871	60	238	298	583	138	1	161	155	21	1250	16.0	34
Wally Szczerbiak	82	2856	469	920	.510	181	208	.870	133	314	447	260	226	4	59	138	33	1145	14.0	28
Anthony Peeler	75	2126	308	732	.421	75	87	.862	44	148	192	192	166	1	91	105	18	791	10.5	28
LaPhonso Ellis	82	1948	298	642	.464	169	214	.790	199	295	494	93	290	7	67	108	74	772	9.4	24
Chauncey Billups	77	1790	248	587	.422	144	171	.842	32	126	158	260	178	2	51	111	11	713	9.3	31
Felipe Lopez†	23	457	69	152	.454	19	33	.576	25	49	74	34	46	0	21	27	12	170	7.4	18
Felipe Lopez‡	70	1565	211	478	.441	109	156	.699	55	179	234	107	156	0	62	83	30	550	7.9	26
Reggie Slater	55	686	90	175	.514	74	110	.673	78	108	186	26	126	1	18	43	9	254	4.6	14
Rasho Nesterovic	73	1233	147	319	.461	34	65	.523	99	187	286	45	189	3	25	55	63	328	4.5	16
Todd Day	31	345	44	118	.373	18	23	.783	10	27	37	28	52	0	10	24	7	132	4.3	11
Sam Mitchell	82	983	118	289	.408	40	55	.727	28	95	123	57	117	0	26	36	10	285	3.5	20
Will Avery	55	463	55	144	.382	28	36	.778	5	24	29	75	48	0	13	45	4	154	2.8	16
Dean Garrett	70	831	75	156	.481	27	39	.692	65	152	217	24	93	0	26	25	49	177	2.5	10
Sam Jacobson	14	59	9	18	.500	2	3	.667	3	3	6	4	19	0	3	0	0	20	1.4	12
Tom Hammonds	7	30	3	10	.300	1	2	.500	2	2	4	1	8	1	0	3	0	7	1.0	4

3-pt. FG: Minnesota 322-901 (.357)—Garnett 19-66 (.288); Brandon 33-91 (.363); Szczerbiak 26-77 (.338); Peeler 100-256 (.391); Ellis 7-22 (.318); Day 26-69 (.377); Billups 73-194 (.376); Lopez† 13-23 (.565); Lopez‡ 19-52 (.365); Nesterovic 0-1 (.000); Mitchell 9-43 (.209); Avery 16-59 (.271). Opponents 350-996 (.351).

NEW JERSEY NETS

	G	Min.	FGM	FGA	Pct.	FTM	FTA	Pct.	Off.	Def.	Tot.	Ast.	PF	Dq.	Stl.	TO	Blk.	Pts.	Avg.	Hi.
Stephon Marbury	67	2557	563	1277	.441	362	458	.790	53	152	205	506	150	1	79	197	5	1598	23.9	50
Keith Van Horn	49	1733	308	708	.435	150	186	.806	78	269	347	82	150	4	40	103	20	831	17.0	31
Kenyon Martin	68	2272	346	777	.445	121	192	.630	137	365	502	131	281	10	78	138	113	814	12.0	26
Johnny Newman	82	2049	291	695	.419	254	297	.855	34	142	176	115	229	3	63	106	10	895	10.9	27
Aaron Williams	82	2336	297	650	.457	244	310	.787	211	379	590	88	319	9	59	132	113	838	10.2	23
Lucious Harris	73	2071	265	624	.425	107	139	.770	71	217	288	135	127	1	74	64	16	683	9.4	27
Kendall Gill	31	892	107	323	.331	65	90	.722	32	99	131	87	64	0	47	48	7	283	9.1	22
Stephen Jackson	77	1660	243	572	.425	97	135	.719	41	167	208	140	166	2	86	130	14	635	8.2	25
Doug Overton†	12	316	35	93	.376	3	5	.600	1	23	24	53	20	0	3	15	0	83	6.9	17
Doug Overton‡	21	475	52	139	.374	10	16	.625	4	35	39	72	37	0	8	31	0	125	6.0	17
Sherman Douglas	59	1094	122	303	.403	86	115	.748	21	53	74	144	93	0	36	79	4	338	5.7	22
Eddie Gill	8	152	16	41	.390	4	5	.800	0	9	9	24	9	0	4	10	1	39	4.9	9
Mark Strickland†	9	202	21	54	.389	8	11	.727	11	30	41	7	14	0	4	10	3	51	5.7	9
Mark Strickland‡	55	719	103	239	.431	45	70	.643	54	107	161	24	72	0	16	34	22	252	4.6	16
Jamie Feick	6	149	8	23	.348	6	12	.500	12	44	56	5	15	0	8	7	3	22	3.7	9
Evan Eschmeyer	74	1331	92	200	.460	67	102	.657	135	231	366	40	220	5	41	53	58	251	3.4	12
Vladimir Stepania	29	280	28	88	.318	25	34	.735	35	74	109	16	47	0	10	19	11	82	2.8	8
Jamel Thomas	5	56	6	19	.316	0	0	...	4	5	9	0	6	0	3	6	0	13	2.6	9
Jim McIlvaine	18	193	10	28	.357	8	12	.667	8	27	35	4	35	0	7	9	15	28	1.6	8
Soumaila Samake	34	226	18	48	.375	10	24	.417	22	31	53	1	23	0	2	4	14	46	1.4	5
Kevin Ollie*	19	161	5	27	.185	12	19	.632	3	20	23	25	14	0	5	9	0	22	1.2	5

3-pt. FG: New Jersey 361-1084 (.333)—Marbury 110-335 (.328); Van Horn 65-170 (.382); Martin 1-11 (.091); Newman 59-176 (.335); Williams 0-2 (.000); K. Gill 4-14 (.286); Harris 46-132 (.348); Jackson 52-155 (.335); Overton† 10-32 (.313); Overton‡ 11-36 (.306); Douglas 8-40 (.200); E. Gill 3-9 (.333); Strickland† 1-1 (1.000); Strickland‡ 1-2 (.500); Stepania 1-4 (.250); Thomas 1-3 (.333). Opponents 428-1189 (.360).

NEW YORK KNICKERBOCKERS

	G	Min.	FGM	FGA	Pct.	FTM	FTA	Pct.	Off.	Def.	Tot.	Ast.	PF	Dq.	Stl.	TO	Blk.	Pts.	Avg.	Hi.
Allan Houston	78	2858	542	1208	.449	279	307	.909	20	263	283	173	190	5	52	161	10	1459	18.7	39
Latrell Sprewell	77	3017	524	1219	.430	275	351	.783	49	298	347	269	159	1	106	218	28	1364	17.7	32
Marcus Camby	63	2127	304	580	.524	150	225	.667	196	527	723	52	205	4	66	63	136	759	12.0	27

	G	Min.	FGM	FGA	Pct.	FTM	FTA	Pct.	Off.	Def.	Tot.	Ast.	PF	Dq.	Stl.	TO	Blk.	Pts.	Avg.	Hi.
Glen Rice	75	2212	331	752	.440	155	182	.852	61	246	307	89	179	1	41	96	13	899	12.0	32
Kurt Thomas	77	2125	314	614	.511	171	210	.814	172	343	515	63	287	6	61	99	69	800	10.4	23
Larry Johnson	65	2105	246	598	.411	102	128	.797	90	273	363	127	209	2	39	97	29	645	9.9	25
Othella Harrington†	30	548	67	121	.554	51	70	.729	37	62	99	20	101	1	15	41	19	185	6.2	18
Othella Harrington‡	74	1815	247	507	.487	171	224	.763	139	249	388	56	237	4	34	145	45	665	9.0	24
Mark Jackson†	29	786	74	180	.411	9	17	.529	21	99	120	163	56	0	21	58	0	170	5.9	15
Mark Jackson‡	83	2588	244	583	.419	73	93	.785	63	242	305	661	139	0	84	175	7	631	7.6	23
Charlie Ward	61	1492	155	373	.416	56	70	.800	32	127	159	273	132	0	70	112	10	433	7.1	19
Chris Childs*	51	1309	93	222	.419	39	46	.848	14	124	138	236	160	2	37	98	7	245	4.8	17
Erick Strickland*	28	421	40	131	.305	24	28	.857	9	43	52	29	46	0	22	21	1	120	4.3	11
Lavor Postell	26	169	17	54	.315	22	27	.815	8	17	25	5	12	0	4	17	2	59	2.3	10
Felton Spencer	18	113	12	20	.600	15	25	.600	16	19	35	2	24	0	2	11	2	39	2.2	15
Rick Brunson†	15	66	8	19	.421	4	6	.667	3	9	12	7	5	0	1	8	0	20	1.3	6
Rick Brunson‡	22	208	18	54	.333	8	15	.533	5	16	21	31	21	0	8	17	1	46	2.1	7
Luc Longley	25	301	18	54	.333	13	17	.765	26	40	66	7	51	0	3	22	9	49	2.0	7
Travis Knight	45	256	10	53	.189	9	18	.500	19	34	53	5	47	0	5	10	11	29	0.6	6

3-pt. FG: New York 391-1115 (.351)—Houston 96-252 (.381); Sprewell 41-135 (.304); Camby 1-8 (.125); Rice 82-211 (.389); Thomas 1-3 (.333); Johnson 51-163 (.313); Harrington‡ 0-3 (.000); Jackson† 13-42 (.310); Jackson‡ 70-207 (.338); Ward 67-175 (.383); Childs* 20-64 (.313); Strickland* 16-47 (.340); Postell 3-11 (.273); Brunson† 0-3 (.000); Brunson‡ 2-14 (.143); Knight 0-1 (.000). Opponents 445-1266 (.352).

ORLANDO MAGIC

	G	Min.	FGM	FGA	Pct.	FTM	FTA	Pct.	Off.	Def.	Tot.	Ast.	PF	Dq.	Stl.	TO	Blk.	Pts.	Avg.	Hi.
Tracy McGrady	77	3087	788	1724	.457	430	587	.733	192	388	580	352	160	0	116	198	118	2065	26.8	49
Darrell Armstrong	75	2767	413	1002	.412	220	249	.884	94	249	343	524	155	2	135	200	13	1189	15.9	34
Grant Hill	4	133	19	43	.442	16	26	.615	8	17	25	25	9	0	5	11	2	55	13.8	19
Mike Miller	82	2390	368	845	.436	91	128	.711	66	261	327	140	200	2	51	97	19	975	11.9	28
Pat Garrity	76	1579	223	576	.387	85	98	.867	51	159	210	51	241	3	40	68	15	628	8.3	21
John Amaechi	82	1710	237	592	.400	176	279	.631	77	191	268	74	175	1	28	124	29	650	7.9	27
Charles Outlaw	80	2534	226	368	.614	129	225	.573	211	408	619	225	241	4	105	141	137	582	7.3	21
Dee Brown	7	155	16	44	.364	4	5	.800	0	11	11	12	10	0	4	7	0	48	6.9	17
Michael Doleac	77	1398	220	527	.417	50	59	.847	70	203	273	65	239	10	37	59	41	490	6.4	17
Monty Williams	82	1211	162	364	.445	85	133	.639	86	157	243	79	136	1	29	85	16	410	5.0	22
Troy Hudson	75	1008	125	372	.336	85	104	.817	38	67	105	162	82	0	37	92	3	357	4.8	30
Andrew DeClercq	67	903	107	193	.554	47	82	.573	91	145	236	32	198	2	41	51	33	261	3.9	15
Don Reid	65	764	82	145	.566	46	75	.613	84	158	242	21	190	4	23	48	54	210	3.2	13
Cory Alexander	26	227	18	56	.321	12	18	.667	0	25	25	36	29	0	16	25	0	52	2.0	9
Elliot Perry*	6	39	5	11	.455	0	0	...	1	3	4	5	1	0	3	6	0	10	1.7	4
James Robinson	6	50	4	11	.364	0	0	...	0	8	8	5	0	0	4	4	1	10	1.7	8

3-pt. FG: Orlando 490-1346 (.364)—McGrady 59-166 (.355); Armstrong 143-403 (.355); Hill 1-1 (1.000); Miller 148-364 (.407); Garrity 97-224 (.433); Outlaw 1-2 (.500); Amaechi 0-7 (.000); Brown 12-32 (.375); Doleac 0-3 (.000); Williams 1-13 (.077); Hudson 22-109 (.202); Alexander 4-16 (.250); Perry* 0-1 (.000); Robinson 2-5 (.400). Opponents 366-1059 (.346).

PHILADELPHIA 76ERS

	G	Min.	FGM	FGA	Pct.	FTM	FTA	Pct.	Off.	Def.	Tot.	Ast.	PF	Dq.	Stl.	TO	Blk.	Pts.	Avg.	Hi.
Allen Iverson	71	2979	762	1813	.420	585	719	.814	50	223	273	325	147	0	178	237	20	2207	31.1	54
Theo Ratliff	50	1800	228	457	.499	165	217	.760	125	288	413	58	165	3	30	126	187	621	12.4	22
Aaron McKie	76	2394	338	714	.473	149	194	.768	33	278	311	377	178	3	106	203	8	878	11.6	24
Dikembe Mutombo†	26	875	100	202	.495	104	137	.759	119	203	322	22	65	0	9	52	66	304	11.7	27
Dikembe Mutombo‡	75	2591	269	556	.484	211	291	.725	307	708	1015	76	204	2	29	144	203	749	10.0	27
Eric Snow	50	1740	182	435	.418	122	154	.792	27	139	166	369	123	1	77	124	7	491	9.8	25
Roshown McLeod†	1	15	1	2	.500	0	0	...	1	1	2	0	2	0	0	1	0	2	2.0	2
Roshown McLeod‡	35	922	145	332	.437	45	51	.882	38	82	120	58	90	0	23	58	8	337	9.6	24
Tyrone Hill	76	2363	278	587	.474	172	273	.630	239	448	687	48	242	2	37	127	27	728	9.6	21
George Lynch	82	2649	274	616	.445	123	171	.719	200	390	590	139	222	2	99	109	30	686	8.4	23
Toni Kukoc*	48	979	151	330	.458	52	88	.591	47	115	162	93	62	0	35	60	6	386	8.0	25
Matt Geiger	35	542	88	224	.393	37	54	.685	50	89	139	14	73	0	12	25	8	213	6.1	15
Rodney Buford	47	573	104	241	.432	24	29	.828	16	58	74	17	68	0	17	29	6	248	5.3	16
Vernon Maxwell*	24	375	42	125	.336	15	22	.682	3	34	37	29	33	0	12	18	0	120	5.0	15
Jumaine Jones	65	866	122	275	.444	40	53	.755	63	126	189	32	68	0	30	39	15	304	4.7	26
Todd MacCulloch	63	597	109	185	.589	42	66	.636	69	99	168	10	96	0	7	27	19	260	4.1	21
Nazr Mohammed*	30	196	41	88	.466	14	28	.500	18	37	55	2	40	0	6	9	7	96	3.2	12
Kevin Ollie†	51	764	71	165	.430	51	70	.729	13	59	72	121	70	0	25	40	1	194	3.8	13
Kevin Ollie‡	70	925	76	192	.396	63	89	.708	16	79	95	146	84	0	30	49	1	216	3.1	13
Raja Bell	5	30	2	7	.286	0	0	...	0	1	1	0	1	0	1	2	0	5	1.0	3
Pepe Sanchez†	24	116	9	21	.429	2	2	1.000	2	12	14	36	18	0	9	3	1	20	0.8	4
Pepe Sanchez‡	29	150	9	28	.321	2	2	1.000	3	12	15	41	21	0	11	6	1	20	0.7	4
Anthony Miller†	1	2	0	0	...	0	0	...	0	0	0	0	0	0	0	0	0	0	0.0	0
Anthony Miller‡	4	11	1	2	.500	0	0	...	0	2	2	0	1	0	0	1	0	2	0.5	2

3-pt. FG: Philadelphia 262-803 (.326)—Iverson 98-306 (.320); McKie 53-170 (.312); Snow 5-19 (.263); McLeod† 0-1 (.000); McLeod‡ 2-22 (.091); Hill 0-1 (.000); Lynch 15-57 (.263); Kukoc* 32-78 (.410); Geiger 0-2 (.000); Buford 16-38 (.421); Maxwell* 21-64 (.328); Jones 20-60 (.333); Ollie† 1-3 (.333); Ollie‡ 1-3 (.333); Bell 1-3 (.333); Sanchez† 0-1 (.000); Sanchez‡ 0-1 (.000). Opponents 427-1248 (.342).

2000-01

PHOENIX SUNS

	G	Min.	FGM	FGA	Pct.	FTM	FTA	Pct.	Off.	Def.	Tot.	Ast.	PF	Dq.	Stl.	TO	Blk.	Pts.	Avg.	Hi.
Shawn Marion	79	2857	557	1160	.480	234	289	.810	220	628	848	160	211	2	132	129	108	1369	17.3	38
Jason Kidd	77	3065	451	1097	.411	328	403	.814	91	403	494	753	171	1	166	286	23	1299	16.9	43
Clifford Robinson	82	2751	501	1186	.422	253	357	.709	105	229	334	237	258	6	87	186	82	1345	16.4	42
Tony Delk	82	2288	383	923	.415	185	235	.787	76	185	261	160	171	1	75	101	17	1005	12.3	53
Rodney Rogers	82	2183	377	876	.430	188	247	.761	94	265	359	180	269	5	97	157	47	998	12.2	27
Anfernee Hardaway	4	112	15	36	.417	7	11	.636	5	13	18	15	6	0	6	3	1	39	9.8	16
Tom Gugliotta	57	1159	149	380	.392	61	77	.792	76	179	255	55	110	0	47	51	21	362	6.4	25
Iakovos Tsakalidis	57	947	101	215	.470	54	91	.593	83	159	242	19	137	1	10	66	55	256	4.5	17
Mario Elie	68	1506	104	246	.423	55	69	.797	38	117	155	131	112	0	58	60	12	299	4.4	17
Vinny Del Negro†	36	526	76	144	.528	25	28	.893	8	43	51	64	42	0	20	19	3	177	4.9	14
Vinny Del Negro‡	65	922	106	234	.453	41	44	.932	12	70	82	126	78	0	26	34	3	254	3.9	14
Paul McPherson*	33	308	47	96	.490	18	24	.750	20	28	48	16	48	0	12	23	3	112	3.4	20
Daniel Santiago	54	581	64	134	.478	42	61	.689	35	67	102	11	101	1	17	47	21	170	3.1	15
Elliot Perry†	43	460	60	129	.465	16	22	.727	8	34	42	74	28	0	19	32	1	137	3.2	18
Elliot Perry‡	49	499	65	140	.464	16	22	.727	9	37	46	79	29	0	22	38	1	147	3.0	18
Corie Blount*	30	387	23	47	.489	8	15	.533	35	50	85	8	75	2	13	18	5	54	1.8	8
Ruben Garces*	10	62	7	15	.467	2	8	.250	12	10	22	4	14	0	2	5	1	16	1.6	6
Chris Dudley	53	613	29	73	.397	14	36	.389	64	119	183	18	111	1	14	26	29	72	1.4	8

3-pt. FG: Phoenix 332-1054 (.315)—Marion 21-82 (.256); Kidd 69-232 (.297); Robinson 90-249 (.361); Delk 54-168 (.321); Rogers 56-189 (.296); Hardaway 2-8 (.250); Gugliotta 3-12 (.250); Elie 36-100 (.360); Del Negro† 0-4 (.000); Del Negro‡ 1-13 (.077); McPherson* 0-6 (.000); Perry† 1-4 (.250); Perry‡ 1-5 (.200). Opponents 327-937 (.349).

PORTLAND TRAIL BLAZERS

	G	Min.	FGM	FGA	Pct.	FTM	FTA	Pct.	Off.	Def.	Tot.	Ast.	PF	Dq.	Stl.	TO	Blk.	Pts.	Avg.	Hi.
Rasheed Wallace	77	2940	590	1178	.501	245	320	.766	147	455	602	212	206	2	90	158	135	1477	19.2	42
Steve Smith	81	2542	359	788	.456	309	347	.890	87	185	272	213	203	0	48	137	24	1105	13.6	26
Damon Stoudamire	82	2655	406	935	.434	172	207	.831	69	234	303	468	202	1	106	191	8	1066	13.0	32
Bonzi Wells	75	1995	387	726	.533	159	240	.663	120	247	367	208	203	1	94	169	20	950	12.7	28
Scottie Pippen	64	2133	269	596	.451	119	161	.739	70	263	333	294	158	2	94	154	35	721	11.3	28
Arvydas Sabonis	61	1299	247	516	.479	121	156	.776	51	280	331	91	137	2	40	85	62	616	10.1	32
Rod Strickland†	21	351	41	98	.418	15	26	.577	11	24	35	72	21	0	10	24	1	97	4.6	11
Rod Strickland‡	54	1371	182	429	.424	130	173	.751	36	104	140	303	76	0	53	107	5	498	9.2	26
Dale Davis	81	2162	242	487	.497	96	152	.632	233	373	606	103	199	0	44	67	76	580	7.2	18
Shawn Kemp	68	1083	168	413	.407	101	131	.771	63	196	259	65	184	3	45	99	23	441	6.5	21
Greg Anthony	58	856	97	253	.383	23	35	.657	21	40	61	82	63	0	40	43	3	282	4.9	20
Stacey Augmon	66	1182	127	266	.477	57	87	.655	60	99	159	98	105	0	48	48	21	311	4.7	13
Detlef Schrempf	26	397	39	95	.411	23	27	.852	17	61	78	44	43	0	7	28	3	104	4.0	13
Antonio Harvey	12	72	13	28	.464	5	6	.833	5	9	14	4	10	0	1	3	6	31	2.6	15
Gary Grant	4	17	5	7	.714	0	0	...	0	0	0	1	1	0	0	0	0	10	2.5	4
Erick Barkley	8	38	8	22	.364	0	0	...	0	3	3	6	2	0	2	5	0	19	2.4	9
Will Perdue	13	58	6	9	.667	2	4	.500	6	12	18	2	8	0	3	0	2	14	1.1	6

3-pt. FG: Portland 369-1057 (.349)—Wallace 52-162 (.321); Smith 78-230 (.339); Stoudamire 82-219 (.374); Wells 17-50 (.340); Pippen 64-186 (.344); Davis 0-4 (.000); Sabonis 1-15 (.067); Strickland† 0-1 (.000); Strickland‡ 4-17 (.235); Kemp 4-11 (.364); Anthony 65-159 (.409); Augmon 0-4 (.000); Schrempf 3-8 (.375); Barkley 3-8 (.375). Opponents 406-1103 (.368).

SACRAMENTO KINGS

	G	Min.	FGM	FGA	Pct.	FTM	FTA	Pct.	Off.	Def.	Tot.	Ast.	PF	Dq.	Stl.	TO	Blk.	Pts.	Avg.	Hi.
Chris Webber	70	2836	786	1635	.481	324	461	.703	179	598	777	294	226	1	93	195	118	1898	27.1	51
Predrag Stojakovic	75	2905	559	1189	.470	267	312	.856	93	341	434	164	144	0	91	146	13	1529	20.4	39
Doug Christie	81	2939	311	788	.395	280	312	.897	95	260	355	289	224	2	183	154	45	996	12.3	32
Vlade Divac	81	2420	364	755	.482	242	350	.691	207	466	673	231	242	5	87	192	93	974	12.0	34
Jason Williams	77	2290	281	690	.407	60	76	.789	19	166	185	416	114	0	94	160	9	720	9.4	24
Bobby Jackson	79	1648	231	526	.439	65	88	.739	74	172	246	161	139	0	87	103	7	566	7.2	18
Scot Pollard	77	1658	185	395	.468	128	171	.749	173	292	465	47	206	4	48	66	97	498	6.5	22
Hidayet Turkoglu	74	1245	138	335	.412	87	112	.777	49	161	210	69	139	1	52	55	24	391	5.3	18
Jon Barry	62	1010	103	255	.404	64	73	.877	16	78	94	130	66	0	28	53	6	316	5.1	15
Lawrence Funderburke	59	698	120	242	.496	48	77	.623	74	122	196	17	44	0	9	32	13	288	4.9	18
Darrick Martin	31	176	29	76	.382	31	35	.886	2	14	16	14	27	0	7	10	0	103	3.3	15
Jabari Smith	9	66	11	22	.500	4	6	.667	1	7	8	6	7	0	4	3	0	26	2.9	9
Nick Anderson	21	169	14	57	.246	0	0	...	3	22	25	13	13	0	10	7	4	38	1.8	5
Art Long	9	20	0	4	.000	0	2	.000	2	6	8	1	5	0	0	2	3	0	0.0	0

3-pt. FG: Sacramento 479-1353 (.354)—Webber 2-28 (.071); Stojakovic 144-360 (.400); Christie 94-250 (.376); Divac 4-14 (.286); Williams 98-311 (.315); Jackson 39-104 (.375); Pollard 0-2 (.000); Turkoglu 28-86 (.326); Barry 46-132 (.348); Martin 14-27 (.519); Anderson 10-39 (.256). Opponents 401-1131 (.355).

SAN ANTONIO SPURS

	G	Min.	FGM	FGA	Pct.	FTM	FTA	Pct.	Off.	Def.	Tot.	Ast.	PF	Dq.	Stl.	TO	Blk.	Pts.	Avg.	Hi.
Tim Duncan	82	3174	702	1406	.499	409	662	.618	259	738	997	245	247	0	70	242	192	1820	22.2	42
Derek Anderson	82	2859	413	993	.416	342	402	.851	75	288	363	301	188	1	120	165	14	1269	15.5	30
David Robinson	80	2371	400	823	.486	351	470	.747	208	483	691	116	212	1	80	122	197	1151	14.4	34

	G	Min.	FGM	FGA	Pct.	FTM	FTA	Pct.	Off.	Def.	Tot.	Ast.	PF	Dq.	Stl.	TO	Blk.	Pts.	Avg.	Hi.
Antonio Daniels	79	2060	275	588	.468	121	156	.776	26	137	163	304	120	0	61	109	14	745	9.4	26
Sean Elliott	52	1229	147	339	.434	60	84	.714	17	153	170	81	80	0	23	51	25	409	7.9	19
Malik Rose	57	1219	160	368	.435	114	160	.713	95	213	308	48	148	1	59	74	40	437	7.7	26
Terry Porter	80	1678	197	440	.448	92	116	.793	24	177	201	251	88	1	52	104	11	573	7.2	18
Avery Johnson	55	1290	134	300	.447	41	60	.683	21	64	85	237	90	0	33	60	4	310	5.6	14
Danny Ferry	80	1688	178	375	.475	22	30	.733	55	168	223	71	169	1	28	50	21	448	5.6	16
Samaki Walker	61	963	121	252	.480	78	124	.629	67	176	243	29	103	0	10	68	41	321	5.3	16
Steve Kerr	55	650	67	159	.421	14	15	.933	6	29	35	57	30	0	16	21	1	181	3.3	12
Derrick Dial	33	207	36	83	.434	12	21	.571	12	26	38	21	22	0	4	12	6	86	2.6	15
Jaren Jackson	16	114	16	40	.400	0	2	.000	1	11	12	7	13	0	5	3	0	39	2.4	14
Ira Newble	27	184	21	55	.382	8	16	.500	13	22	35	6	18	0	2	7	4	54	2.0	14
Shawnelle Scott	27	144	17	41	.415	9	22	.409	23	27	50	4	23	0	5	11	6	43	1.6	14

3-pt. FG: San Antonio 445-1094 (.407)—Duncan 7-27 (.259); Anderson 101-253 (.399); Robinson 0-1 (.000); Daniels 74-183 (.404); Elliott 55-129 (.426); Rose 3-17 (.176); Porter 87-205 (.424); Johnson 1-6 (.167); Ferry 70-156 (.449); Walker 1-3 (.333); Kerr 33-77 (.429); Dial 2-10 (.200); Jackson 7-18 (.389); Newble 4-9 (.444). Opponents 343-1043 (.329).

SEATTLE SUPERSONICS

	G	Min.	FGM	FGA	Pct.	FTM	FTA	Pct.	Off.	Def.	Tot.	Ast.	PF	Dq.	Stl.	TO	Blk.	Pts.	Avg.	Hi.
Gary Payton	79	3244	725	1591	.456	271	354	.766	73	288	361	642	184	0	127	209	26	1823	23.1	44
Rashard Lewis	78	2720	426	887	.480	176	213	.826	143	398	541	125	191	2	91	129	45	1151	14.8	28
Ruben Patterson	76	2059	370	749	.494	246	361	.681	183	199	382	161	176	1	103	155	45	988	13.0	26
Vin Baker	76	2129	347	822	.422	232	321	.723	179	251	430	90	264	2	38	158	73	927	12.2	24
Patrick Ewing	79	2107	294	684	.430	172	251	.685	124	461	585	92	229	1	53	151	91	760	9.6	21
Brent Barry	67	1778	198	401	.494	84	103	.816	33	178	211	225	126	1	80	86	14	589	8.8	22
Shammond Williams	69	1238	161	368	.438	84	96	.875	34	98	132	190	83	0	31	82	4	467	6.8	21
David Wingate	1	9	3	3	1.000	0	0	...	0	0	0	2	1	0	0	0	0	6	6.0	6
Desmond Mason	78	1522	189	439	.431	67	91	.736	72	177	249	63	146	0	39	53	20	463	5.9	25
Emanual Davis	62	1290	133	318	.418	45	55	.818	28	126	154	137	101	0	64	77	12	361	5.8	19
Jelani McCoy	70	1143	138	264	.523	41	93	.441	92	159	251	57	141	0	18	75	49	317	4.5	13
Ruben Wolkowyski	34	305	25	79	.316	25	34	.735	12	34	46	3	38	0	6	12	18	75	2.2	7
Olumide Oyedeji	30	221	18	37	.486	9	12	.750	24	43	67	2	40	0	7	11	10	45	1.5	10
Pervis Ellison	9	40	2	7	.286	2	2	1.000	2	10	12	3	13	0	0	3	2	6	0.7	2

3-pt. FG: Seattle 466-1169 (.399)—Payton 102-272 (.375); Lewis 123-285 (.432); Patterson 2-36 (.056); Baker 1-16 (.063); Ewing 0-2 (.000); Barry 109-229 (.476); Williams 61-133 (.459); Mason 18-67 (.269); Davis 50-127 (.394); Wolkowyski 0-2 (.000). Opponents 471-1351 (.349).

TORONTO RAPTORS

	G	Min.	FGM	FGA	Pct.	FTM	FTA	Pct.	Off.	Def.	Tot.	Ast.	PF	Dq.	Stl.	TO	Blk.	Pts.	Avg.	Hi.
Vince Carter	75	2979	762	1656	.460	384	502	.765	176	240	416	291	205	1	114	167	82	2070	27.6	48
Antonio Davis	78	2729	375	866	.433	319	423	.754	274	513	787	106	230	4	22	135	151	1069	13.7	31
Alvin Williams	82	2394	330	767	.430	109	145	.752	50	162	212	407	171	1	123	103	26	802	9.8	23
Charles Oakley	78	2767	305	786	.388	127	152	.836	142	599	741	264	258	0	76	139	48	748	9.6	23
Morris Peterson	80	1809	290	673	.431	104	145	.717	112	147	259	105	164	0	63	78	20	747	9.3	29
Corliss Williamson*	42	886	153	325	.471	84	130	.646	57	96	153	33	98	0	15	65	13	390	9.3	22
Kevin Willis*	35	771	124	269	.461	61	81	.753	68	155	223	21	78	0	19	40	21	309	8.8	23
Mark Jackson*	54	1802	170	403	.422	64	76	.842	42	143	185	498	83	0	63	117	7	461	8.5	23
Keon Clark†	46	968	167	320	.522	79	135	.585	78	170	248	38	143	3	16	42	110	413	9.0	23
Keon Clark‡	81	1720	249	519	.480	142	240	.592	136	298	434	72	244	6	32	90	154	640	7.9	23
Jerome Williams†	26	378	48	93	.516	35	45	.778	35	69	104	13	43	0	18	16	10	131	5.0	13
Jerome Williams‡	79	1182	136	294	.463	100	135	.741	133	249	382	45	124	0	57	63	20	372	6.3	15
Dell Curry	71	956	162	382	.424	43	51	.843	16	69	85	75	66	0	27	39	8	429	6.0	23
Tracy Murray†	38	453	77	193	.399	24	32	.750	18	41	59	14	45	0	8	20	6	207	5.4	20
Tracy Murray‡	51	588	94	248	.379	33	42	.786	22	59	81	23	53	0	12	26	7	257	5.0	20
Chris Childs†	26	550	42	113	.372	21	25	.840	10	54	64	119	82	1	22	58	8	117	4.5	12
Chris Childs‡	77	1859	135	335	.403	60	71	.845	24	178	202	355	242	3	59	156	15	362	4.7	17
Kornel David*	17	140	15	29	.517	12	13	.923	9	24	33	4	20	0	2	7	3	42	2.5	10
Eric Montross†	12	81	6	17	.353	1	5	.200	9	20	29	4	15	0	3	4	3	13	1.1	6
Eric Montross‡	54	649	56	138	.406	8	31	.258	52	121	173	19	115	0	11	41	26	120	2.2	13
Tyrone Corbin	15	117	9	38	.237	2	4	.500	3	10	13	4	18	0	2	3	0	20	1.3	6
Mamadou N'diaye	3	10	1	4	.250	2	2	1.000	1	1	2	0	3	0	0	0	0	4	1.3	2
Michael Stewart	26	123	11	34	.324	11	18	.611	16	13	29	2	19	0	4	5	3	33	1.3	6
Garth Joseph*	2	8	1	2	.500	0	0	...	2	0	2	1	1	0	0	1	0	2	1.0	2
Muggsy Bogues*	3	34	0	2	.000	0	0	...	3	3	3	2	4	0	0	0	0	0	0.0	0

3-pt. FG: Toronto 429-1164 (.369)—Carter 162-397 (.408); Davis 0-1 (.000); A. Williams 33-108 (.306); Oakley 11-49 (.224); Peterson 63-165 (.382); Corbin 0-5 (.000); Williamson* 0-2 (.000); Willis* 0-2 (.000); Jackson* 57-165 (.345); Clark† 0-1 (.000); Clark‡ 0-1 (.000); J. Williams† 0-1 (.000); J. Williams‡ 0-3 (.000); Curry 62-145 (.428); Murray† 29-80 (.363); Murray‡ 36-103 (.350); Childs† 12-42 (.286); Childs‡ 32-106 (.302); Bogues* 0-1 (.000). Opponents 379-1045 (.363).

UTAH JAZZ

	G	Min.	FGM	FGA	Pct.	FTM	FTA	Pct.	Off.	Def.	Tot.	Ast.	PF	Dq.	Stl.	TO	Blk.	Pts.	Avg.	Hi.
Karl Malone	81	2895	670	1345	.498	536	676	.793	114	555	669	361	216	0	93	244	62	1878	23.2	41
Donyell Marshall	81	2326	427	849	.503	205	273	.751	172	394	566	133	196	0	85	128	78	1100	13.6	31
Bryon Russell	78	2473	308	700	.440	222	285	.779	94	236	330	160	229	1	96	113	20	933	12.0	24
John Stockton	82	2397	328	651	.504	227	278	.817	54	173	227	713	194	1	132	203	21	944	11.5	22

2000-01

	G	Min.	FGM	FGA	Pct.	FTM	FTA	Pct.	REBOUNDS			Ast.	PF	Dq.	Stl.	TO	Blk.	SCORING		
									Off.	Def.	Tot.							Pts.	Avg.	Hi.
John Starks	75	2122	273	686	.398	89	111	.802	29	125	154	178	217	2	73	94	10	699	9.3	21
Danny Manning	82	1305	247	500	.494	102	140	.729	66	148	214	92	219	0	47	96	29	603	7.4	25
Jacque Vaughn	82	1620	170	393	.433	128	164	.780	18	132	150	323	145	0	48	129	3	498	6.1	18
Olden Polynice	81	1619	206	415	.496	17	65	.262	157	221	378	31	241	2	27	78	77	429	5.3	15
Greg Ostertag	81	1491	139	281	.495	84	151	.556	164	251	415	22	215	3	22	63	142	363	4.5	25
David Benoit	49	446	71	147	.483	31	39	.795	20	61	81	22	75	0	6	28	6	178	3.6	18
Quincy Lewis	35	402	50	123	.407	15	21	.714	14	33	47	18	78	1	10	17	10	124	3.5	14
DeShawn Stevenson	40	293	36	91	.341	26	38	.684	9	19	28	18	29	0	10	28	2	89	2.2	11
John Crotty	31	264	22	65	.338	17	19	.895	13	15	28	34	32	0	6	19	0	65	2.1	8
Scott Padgett	27	127	18	43	.419	15	20	.750	19	20	39	5	21	0	6	10	3	56	2.1	13

3-pt. FG: Utah 325-852 (.381)—Malone 2-5 (.400); Marshall 41-128 (.320); Russell 95-230 (.413); Stockton 61-132 (.462); Starks 64-182 (.352); Benoit 5-13 (.385); Manning 7-28 (.250); Vaughn 30-78 (.385); Polynice 0-1 (.000); Ostertag 1-2 (.500); Lewis 9-25 (.360); Stevenson 1-12 (.083); Crotty 4-7 (.571); Padgett 5-9 (.556). Opponents 410-1194 (.343).

VANCOUVER GRIZZLIES

	G	Min.	FGM	FGA	Pct.	FTM	FTA	Pct.	REBOUNDS			Ast.	PF	Dq.	Stl.	TO	Blk.	SCORING		
									Off.	Def.	Tot.							Pts.	Avg.	Hi.
Shareef Abdur-Rahim	81	3241	604	1280	.472	443	531	.834	175	560	735	250	238	1	90	231	77	1663	20.5	38
Michael Dickerson	70	2618	425	1020	.417	206	270	.763	70	159	229	233	207	0	62	162	27	1142	16.3	32
Mike Bibby	82	3190	525	1157	.454	143	188	.761	47	257	304	685	148	1	107	248	12	1301	15.9	37
Othella Harrington*	44	1267	180	386	.466	120	154	.779	102	187	289	36	136	3	19	104	26	480	10.9	24
Bryant Reeves	75	1832	254	552	.460	113	142	.796	132	320	452	80	243	5	43	90	54	622	8.3	31
Damon Jones	71	1415	170	416	.409	37	52	.712	16	108	124	224	58	0	36	76	1	461	6.5	25
Mahmoud Abdul-Rauf	41	486	120	246	.488	22	29	.759	5	20	25	76	50	0	9	26	1	266	6.5	25
Grant Long	66	1507	140	319	.439	112	157	.713	76	198	274	83	160	2	72	62	15	396	6.0	16
Erick Strickland†	22	409	41	136	.301	44	51	.863	9	67	76	66	42	0	22	27	1	140	6.4	15
Erick Strickland‡	50	830	81	267	.303	68	79	.861	18	110	128	95	88	0	44	48	2	260	5.2	15
Stromile Swift	80	1312	153	339	.451	85	141	.603	109	175	284	28	160	0	62	64	82	391	4.9	17
Tony Massenburg	52	823	92	199	.462	49	70	.700	75	135	210	9	122	0	10	48	28	233	4.5	14
Isaac Austin	52	845	96	270	.356	28	40	.700	50	172	222	58	94	0	20	54	23	226	4.3	15
Kevin Edwards	46	634	56	170	.329	43	53	.811	23	59	82	52	46	0	29	37	8	160	3.5	13
Brent Price	6	30	3	11	.273	6	7	.857	1	3	4	5	8	0	2	4	0	13	2.2	5
Doug West	15	171	11	38	.289	6	7	.857	4	11	15	14	21	0	3	4	4	28	1.9	6

3-pt. FG: Vancouver 325-947 (.343)—Abdur-Rahim 12-64 (.188); Dickerson 86-230 (.374); Bibby 108-285 (.379); Harrington* 0-3 (.000); Reeves 1-4 (.250); Jones 84-231 (.364); Abdul-Rauf 4-14 (.286); Long 4-15 (.267); Strickland† 14-48 (.292); Strickland‡ 30-95 (.316); Swift 0-4 (.000); Austin 6-24 (.250); Edwards 5-19 (.263); Price 1-4 (.250); West 0-2 (.000). Opponents 389-1075 (.362).

WASHINGTON WIZARDS

	G	Min.	FGM	FGA	Pct.	FTM	FTA	Pct.	REBOUNDS			Ast.	PF	Dq.	Stl.	TO	Blk.	SCORING		
									Off.	Def.	Tot.							Pts.	Avg.	Hi.
Juwan Howard*	54	1981	392	827	.474	197	256	.770	121	258	379	154	186	1	46	169	21	981	18.2	35
Richard Hamilton	78	2519	547	1249	.438	277	319	.868	75	163	238	224	203	2	75	201	10	1411	18.1	41
Mitch Richmond	37	1216	205	504	.407	143	160	.894	15	94	109	111	86	0	43	84	7	598	16.2	29
Rod Strickland*	33	1020	141	331	.426	115	147	.782	25	80	105	231	55	0	43	83	4	401	12.2	26
Courtney Alexander†	27	910	177	395	.448	90	105	.857	22	58	80	41	63	0	29	54	2	458	17.0	33
Courtney Alexander‡	65	1382	239	573	.417	123	150	.820	42	101	143	62	139	1	45	75	5	618	9.5	33
Chris Whitney	59	1532	182	470	.387	101	113	.894	12	94	106	248	150	5	55	103	3	558	9.5	27
Christian Laettner†	25	733	112	228	.491	103	122	.844	43	110	153	57	83	0	31	67	19	330	13.2	26
Christian Laettner‡	78	1663	277	551	.503	170	204	.833	118	247	365	124	242	1	71	137	46	728	9.3	26
Jahidi White	68	1609	203	408	.498	177	312	.567	178	343	521	20	211	3	32	136	111	583	8.6	22
Tyrone Nesby†	48	1223	149	407	.366	67	83	.807	35	96	131	65	127	1	41	55	16	404	8.4	22
Tyrone Nesby‡	62	1556	189	530	.357	85	106	.802	51	122	173	76	155	1	51	65	20	512	8.3	22
Felipe Lopez*	47	1108	142	326	.436	90	123	.732	30	130	160	73	110	0	41	56	18	380	8.1	26
Hubert Davis†	15	431	57	119	.479	19	21	.905	10	20	30	49	29	0	6	25	0	153	10.2	21
Hubert Davis‡	66	1692	196	433	.453	54	62	.871	28	111	139	110	121	0	35	81	1	524	7.9	25
David Vanterpool	22	411	46	110	.418	30	50	.600	15	22	37	66	44	0	23	37	3	122	5.5	21
Gerard King	45	706	90	176	.511	36	45	.800	39	90	129	31	94	2	14	47	11	216	4.8	17
Calvin Booth*	40	640	74	168	.440	33	45	.733	53	121	174	23	91	1	17	36	81	181	4.5	18
Laron Profit	35	605	56	142	.394	33	45	.733	18	46	64	89	43	0	36	46	11	152	4.3	18
Michael Smith	79	1610	106	218	.486	89	154	.578	172	390	562	101	156	0	57	62	37	301	3.8	18
Cherokee Parks*	13	178	18	38	.474	12	17	.706	13	27	40	7	20	0	6	10	11	48	3.7	13
Popeye Jones	45	638	60	153	.392	41	55	.745	83	137	220	31	95	0	19	21	8	162	3.6	14
Obinna Ekezie	29	273	32	77	.416	37	53	.684	31	45	76	9	46	0	5	14	5	101	3.5	13
Loy Vaught†	14	157	25	48	.521	4	4	1.000	16	34	50	7	13	0	6	8	2	54	3.9	10
Loy Vaught‡	51	549	80	169	.473	8	10	.800	51	122	173	23	74	0	21	26	7	168	3.3	10
Mike Smith	17	180	19	59	.322	10	16	.625	10	12	22	10	8	0	5	7	3	51	3.0	11

3-pt. FG: Washington 275-848 (.324)—Hamilton 40-146 (.274); Richmond 45-133 (.338); Strickland* 4-16 (.250); Alexander† 14-36 (.389); Alexander‡ 17-46 (.370); Whitney 93-248 (.375); Laettner† 3-10 (.300); Laettner‡ 4-13 (.308); White 0-1 (.000); Nesby† 39-134 (.291); Nesby‡ 49-180 (.272); Lopez* 6-29 (.207); Davis† 20-38 (.526); Davis‡ 78-171 (.456); Vanterpool 0-6 (.000); Profit 7-26 (.269); Mic. Smith 0-1 (.000); Jones 1-6 (.167); Mik. Smith 3-18 (.167). Opponents 433-1093 (.396).

* Finished season with another team   † Totals with this team only   ‡ Totals with all teams

PLAYOFFS

RESULTS

EASTERN CONFERENCE

FIRST ROUND

Philadelphia 3, Indiana 1

Apr. 21—Sat.	Indiana 79 at Philadelphia	.78
Apr. 24—Tue.	Indiana 98 at Philadelphia	.116
Apr. 28—Sat.	Philadelphia 92 at Indiana	.87
May 2—Wed.	Philadelphia 88 at Indiana	.85

Toronto 3, New York 2

Apr. 22—Sun.	Toronto 85 at New York	.92
Apr. 26—Thur.	Toronto 94 at New York	.74
Apr. 29—Sun.	New York 97 at Toronto	.89
May 2—Wed.	New York 93 at Toronto	.100
May 4—Fri.	Toronto 93 at New York	.89

Charlotte 3, Miami 0

Apr. 21—Sat.	Charlotte 106 at Miami	.80
Apr. 23—Mon.	Charlotte 102 at Miami	.76
Apr. 27—Fri.	Miami 79 at Charlotte	.94

Milwaukee 3, Orlando 1

Apr. 22—Sun.	Orlando 90 at Milwaukee	.103
Apr. 25—Wed.	Orlando 96 at Milwaukee	.103
Apr. 28—Sat.	Milwaukee 116 at Orlando	*121
May 1—Tue.	Milwaukee 112 at Orlando	.104

SEMIFINALS

Philadelphia 4, Toronto 3

May 6—Sun.	Toronto 96 at Philadelphia	.93
May 9—Wed.	Toronto 92 at Philadelphia	.97
May 11—Fri.	Philadelphia 78 at Toronto	.102
May 13—Sun.	Philadelphia 84 at Toronto	.79
May 16—Wed.	Toronto 88 at Philadelphia	.121
May 18—Fri.	Philadelphia 89 at Toronto	.101
May 20—Sun.	Toronto 87 at Philadelphia	.88

Milwaukee 4, Charlotte 3

May 6—Sun.	Charlotte 92 at Milwaukee	.104
May 8—Tue.	Charlotte 90 at Milwaukee	.91
May 10—Thur.	Milwaukee 92 at Charlotte	.102
May 13—Sun.	Milwaukee 78 at Charlotte	.85
May 15—Tue.	Charlotte 94 at Milwaukee	.86
May 17—Thur.	Milwaukee 104 at Charlotte	.97
May 20—Sun.	Charlotte 95 at Milwaukee	.104

FINALS

Philadelphia 4, Milwaukee 3

May 22—Tue.	Milwaukee 85 at Philadelphia	.93
May 24—Thur.	Milwaukee 92 at Philadelphia	.78
May 26—Sat.	Philadelphia 74 at Milwaukee	.80
May 28—Mon.	Philadelphia 89 at Milwaukee	.83
May 30—Wed.	Milwaukee 88 at Philadelphia	.89
June 1—Fri.	Philadelphia 100 at Milwaukee	.110
June 3—Sun.	Milwaukee 91 at Philadelphia	.108

WESTERN CONFERENCE

FIRST ROUND

San Antonio 3, Minnesota 1

Apr. 21—Sat.	Minnesota 82 at San Antonio	.87
Apr. 23—Mon.	Minnesota 69 at San Antonio	.86
Apr. 28—Sat.	San Antonio 84 at Minnesota	.93
Apr. 30—Mon.	San Antonio 97 at Minnesota	.84

Dallas 3, Utah 2

Apr. 21—Sat.	Dallas 86 at Utah	.88
Apr. 24—Tue.	Dallas 98 at Utah	.109
Apr. 28—Sat.	Utah 91 at Dallas	.94
May 1—Tue.	Utah 77 at Dallas	.107
May 3—Thur.	Dallas 84 at Utah	.83

Sacramento 3, Phoenix 1

Apr. 22—Sun.	Phoenix 86 at Sacramento	.83
Apr. 25—Wed.	Phoenix 90 at Sacramento	.116
Apr. 29—Sun.	Sacramento 104 at Phoenix	.96
May 2—Wed.	Sacramento 80 at Phoenix	.78

L.A. Lakers 3, Portland 0

Apr. 22—Sun.	Portland 93 at L.A. Lakers	.106
Apr. 26—Thur.	Portland 88 at L.A. Lakers	.106
Apr. 29—Sun.	L.A. Lakers 99 at Portland	.86

SEMIFINALS

San Antonio 4, Dallas 1

May 5—Sat.	Dallas 78 at San Antonio	.94
May 7—Mon.	Dallas 86 at San Antonio	.100
May 9—Wed.	San Antonio 104 at Dallas	.90
May 12—Sat.	San Antonio 108 at Dallas	.112
May 14—Mon.	Dallas 87 at San Antonio	.105

L.A. Lakers 4, Sacramento 0

May 6—Sun.	Sacramento 105 at L.A. Lakers	.108
May 8—Tue.	Sacramento 90 at L.A. Lakers	.96
May 11—Fri.	L.A. Lakers 103 at Sacramento	.81
May 13—Sun.	L.A. Lakers 119 at Sacramento	.113

FINALS

L.A. Lakers 4, San Antonio 0

May 19—Sat.	L.A. Lakers 104 at San Antonio	.90
May 21—Mon.	L.A. Lakers 88 at San Antonio	.81
May 25—Fri.	San Antonio 72 at L.A. Lakers	.111
May 27—Sun.	San Antonio 82 at L.A. Lakers	.111

NBA FINALS

L.A. Lakers 4, Philadelphia 1

June 6—Wed.	Philadelphia 107 at L.A. Lakers	*101
June 8—Fri.	Philadelphia 89 at L.A. Lakers	.98
June 10—Sun.	L.A. Lakers 96 at Philadelphia	.91
June 13—Wed.	L.A. Lakers 100 at Philadelphia	.86
June 15—Fri.	L.A. Lakers 108 at Philadelphia	.96

*Denotes number of overtime periods.

2000-01

1999-2000

1999-2000 NBA CHAMPION LOS ANGELES LAKERS

Front row (from left): Glen Rice, Robert Horry, Shaquille O'Neal, owner Dr. Jerry Buss, Travis Knight, John Salley, A.C. Green. Center row (from left): Tyronn Lue, Devean George, Ron Harper, Rick Fox, Kobe Bryant, Brian Shaw, John Celestand, Derek Fisher. Back row (from left): athletic trainer Gary Vitti, athletic performance coordinator Chip Schaefer, assistant coach Bill Bertka, assistant coach Frank Hamblen, head coach Phil Jackson, assistant coach Tex Winter, assistant coach Jim Cleamons, strength and conditioning coach Jim Cotta, equipment manager Rudy Garciduenas.

FINAL STANDINGS

ATLANTIC DIVISION

	Atl.	Bos.	Cha.	Chi.	Cle.	Dal.	Den.	Det.	G.S.	Hou.	Ind.	LA-C	LA-L	Mia.	Mil.	Min.	N.J.	N.Y.	Orl.	Phi.	Pho.	Por.	Sac.	S.A.	Sea.	Tor.	Uta.	Van.	Was.	W	L	Pct.	GB
Mia.	2	3	2	2	3	2	2	2	1	1	2	2	0	..	2	2	2	3	3	3	1	1	2	1	1	1	1	1	4	52	30	.634	..
N.Y.	1	2	3	3	1	2	1	3	2	2	2	1	0	1	4	1	3	..	3	3	1	2	1	1	2	1	0	2	2	50	32	.610	2
Phi.	4	3	1	4	4	2	0	2	2	1	2	1	0	1	3	1	3	1	2	..	0	0	1	0	2	3	1	2	3	49	33	.598	3
Orl.	3	2	2	4	1	1	2	2	1	2	1	2	0	1	0	1	2	1	..	2	0	0	0	1	1	2	1	2	4	41	41	.500	11
Bos.	3	..	1	2	2	1	2	0	1	1	1	1	0	1	1	0	3	2	2	1	1	0	1	0	1	2	1	1	3	35	47	.427	17
N.J.	1	1	1	1	2	2	1	1	2	1	1	1	0	2	3	1	..	1	3	1	0	1	1	0	0	2	0	0	1	31	51	.378	21
Was.	3	1	0	2	1	1	1	1	2	1	1	1	1	1	0	1	2	3	2	0	1	0	0	0	1	0	2	0	..	29	53	.354	23

CENTRAL DIVISION

	Atl.	Bos.	Cha.	Chi.	Cle.	Dal.	Den.	Det.	G.S.	Hou.	Ind.	LA-C	LA-L	Mia.	Mil.	Min.	N.J.	N.Y.	Orl.	Phi.	Pho.	Por.	Sac.	S.A.	Sea.	Tor.	Uta.	Van.	Was.	W	L	Pct.	GB
Ind.	3	3	2	3	4	1	2	3	2	2	..	1	1	2	2	1	3	2	2	2	1	2	1	1	1	3	2	2	2	56	26	.683	..
Cha.	3	3	..	4	3	1	1	2	2	1	2	2	0	2	3	2	2	1	2	3	1	0	0	0	1	3	0	2	3	49	33	.598	7
Tor.	2	2	1	4	4	1	0	2	2	2	1	2	1	2	2	0	2	3	2	0	1	1	1	1	2	..	1	1	2	45	37	.549	11
Det.	3	3	2	3	2	0	1	..	2	1	1	2	0	2	3	0	2	1	2	2	0	1	0	1	2	2	0	2	2	42	40	.512	14
Mil.	4	2	1	3	3	2	0	1	1	2	2	2	0	2	..	0	1	0	4	0	1	0	1	2	1	2	1	1	3	42	40	.512	14
Cle.	1	2	1	3	..	2	2	2	1	1	0	2	0	0	1	0	2	3	2	0	0	1	0	1	0	0	0	2	3	32	50	.390	24
Atl.	..	1	1	3	3	0	1	1	0	1	1	1	0	2	0	1	3	2	0	0	0	2	0	1	2	0	1	1	1	28	54	.341	28
Chi.	1	2	0	..	1	0	1	1	0	0	1	2	0	2	1	0	2	0	0	0	0	0	0	1	0	0	0	0	2	17	65	.207	39

MIDWEST DIVISION

	Atl.	Bos.	Cha.	Chi.	Cle.	Dal.	Den.	Det.	G.S.	Hou.	Ind.	LA-C	LA-L	Mia.	Mil.	Min.	N.J.	N.Y.	Orl.	Phi.	Pho.	Por.	Sac.	S.A.	Sea.	Tor.	Uta.	Van.	Was.	W	L	Pct.	GB
Utah	2	1	2	2	2	3	2	2	4	3	0	4	1	1	1	1	2	2	1	1	4	1	3	2	2	1	..	3	2	55	27	.671	..
S.A.	2	2	2	2	1	2	3	1	4	4	1	4	3	1	0	1	2	1	1	2	2	1	..	2	1	2	4	1		53	29	.646	2
Min.	1	2	0	2	2	2	2	2	3	4	1	3	0	0	2	..	1	1	1	1	2	3	3	2	2	3	4	0		50	32	.610	5
Dal.	2	1	1	2	0	..	3	2	4	1	1	4	1	0	0	2	0	0	1	0	3	2	1	2	1	1	3	1		40	42	.488	15
Den.	1	0	1	1	0	1	..	1	2	2	0	3	1	0	2	2	1	1	0	2	1	2	2	1	1	2	2	2	1	35	47	.427	20
Hou.	1	1	1	2	1	3	2	1	3	..	0	4	2	1	0	0	0	0	0	1	2	2	1	0	1	0	1	1		34	48	.415	21
Van.	1	1	0	2	0	1	2	0	1	2	0	3	0	1	1	0	2	0	0	0	0	1	1	0	0	1	1	..	1	22	60	.268	30

PACIFIC DIVISION

	Atl.	Bos.	Cha.	Chi.	Cle.	Dal.	Den.	Det.	G.S.	Hou.	Ind.	LA-C	LA-L	Mia.	Mil.	Min.	N.J.	N.Y.	Orl.	Phi.	Pho.	Por.	Sac.	S.A.	Sea.	Tor.	Uta.	Van.	Was.	W	L	Pct.	GB
L.A.L.	2	2	2	2	2	3	3	2	4	2	1	4	..	2	2	4	2	2	2	2	4	2	3	1	3	1	3	4	1	67	15	.817	..
Por.	2	2	2	2	1	2	2	1	4	2	0	4	2	1	2	2	1	0	2	2	3	..	4	3	4	1	3	3	2	59	23	.720	8
Pho.	2	1	1	2	2	1	3	2	4	2	1	4	0	1	1	3	2	1	2	2	..	1	4	2	2	1	0	4	2	53	29	.646	14
Sea.	1	1	1	1	2	3	3	0	4	3	1	3	1	1	2	2	0	1	0	2	2	..	0	2	4	2				45	37	.549	22
Sac.	0	1	2	2	2	3	2	2	3	3	1	3	1	1	1	1	1	2	1	0	0	..	3	2	1	1	3	2		44	38	.537	23
G.S.	2	1	0	2	1	0	2	0	..	1	0	1	0	0	0	1	1	1	0	0	0	1	0	0	0	0	3	1		19	63	.232	48
L.A.C.	1	1	0	0	0	0	1	0	3	0	1	..	0	0	0	1	1	1	0	1	0	0	1	0	0	1	1			15	67	.183	52

TEAM STATISTICS

OFFENSIVE

	G	FGM	FGA	Pct.	FTM	FTA	Pct.	REBOUNDS Off.	Def.	Tot.	Ast.	PF	Dq.	Stl.	TO	Blk.	SCORING Pts.	Avg.
Sacramento ...	82	3276	7288	.450	1521	2016	.754	1056	2635	3691	1953	1729	15	787	1325	381	8607	105.0
Detroit	82	3044	6635	.459	1956	2506	.781	917	2458	3375	1707	2011	27	665	1288	273	8483	103.5
Dallas........	82	3195	7047	.453	1407	1751	.804	931	2444	3375	1810	1770	22	592	1124	416	8316	101.4
Indiana.......	82	3047	6640	.459	1629	2008	.811	842	2612	3454	1857	1786	6	559	1159	422	8306	101.3
Milwaukee	82	3174	6827	.465	1558	1982	.786	1016	2373	3389	1852	2020	26	671	1230	381	8300	101.2
L.A. Lakers....	82	3137	6836	.459	1649	2368	.696	1117	2738	3855	1921	1841	10	613	1143	534	8267	100.8
Orlando	82	3169	7014	.452	1574	2142	.735	1145	2540	3685	1709	1967	11	743	1443	467	8206	100.1
Houston......	82	3001	6664	.450	1573	2145	.733	1008	2586	3594	1774	1663	7	613	1425	438	8156	99.5
Boston.......	82	3054	6880	.444	1621	2175	.745	1108	2420	3528	1741	2223	36	795	1259	286	8146	99.3
Seattle.......	82	3108	6946	.447	1363	1960	.695	1042	2483	3525	1878	1776	11	657	1152	345	8125	99.1
Denver.......	82	3057	6911	.442	1531	2116	.724	1073	2590	3663	1911	1962	25	554	1281	618	8115	99.0
Phoenix	82	3093	6771	.457	1467	1934	.759	1022	2558	3580	2098	1973	17	744	1368	433	8111	98.9
Minnesota ...	82	3226	6910	.467	1379	1769	.780	1016	2471	3487	2205	1913	25	622	1139	444	8079	98.5
Charlotte	82	2935	6533	.449	1863	2458	.758	884	2635	3519	2023	1670	16	732	1206	480	8072	98.4
New Jersey ...	82	2979	6881	.433	1601	2041	.784	1040	2315	3355	1688	1913	19	720	1119	393	8036	98.0
Portland......	82	3021	6430	.470	1542	2029	.760	966	2560	3526	1925	1865	11	633	1243	396	7991	97.5
Toronto	82	2980	6882	.433	1583	2068	.765	1098	2449	3547	1947	1989	22	666	1137	544	7968	97.2
Cleveland.....	82	2977	6734	.442	1653	2205	.750	1010	2499	3509	1941	2219	34	715	1427	363	7950	97.0
Washington ...	82	3010	6681	.451	1566	2107	.743	1064	2438	3502	1771	2149	20	593	1320	383	7921	96.6
Utah.........	82	2962	6380	.464	1661	2150	.773	936	2426	3362	2041	2013	11	629	1220	446	7914	96.5
San Antonio ...	82	2952	6393	.462	1652	2214	.746	927	2666	3593	1819	1716	6	614	1233	551	7886	96.2
Golden State ..	82	2996	7140	.420	1497	2147	.697	1300	2438	3738	1851	2043	27	731	1302	356	7834	95.5
Philadelphia...	82	2993	6776	.442	1577	2226	.708	1147	2468	3615	1817	1939	17	791	1284	386	7771	94.8
Miami	82	2974	6462	.460	1345	1827	.736	921	2619	3540	1931	1947	23	582	1231	524	7739	94.4
Atlanta.......	82	3000	6807	.441	1477	1987	.743	1146	2570	3716	1548	1718	16	500	1266	461	7735	94.3
Vancouver	82	2892	6441	.449	1594	2060	.774	1005	2324	3329	1700	1881	19	608	1381	346	7702	93.9
New York	82	2897	6374	.455	1410	1805	.781	802	2521	3323	1588	1983	23	515	1201	349	7555	92.1
L.A. Clippers ..	82	2877	6757	.426	1363	1826	.746	955	2377	3332	1479	1821	37	578	1325	494	7546	92.0
Chicago	82	2565	6180	.415	1482	2089	.709	1032	2323	3355	1645	1908	18	646	1557	383	6952	84.8

DEFENSIVE

	FGM	FGA	Pct.	FTM	FTA	Pct.	REBOUNDS Off.	Def.	Tot.	Ast.	PF	Dq.	Stl.	TO	Blk.	SCORING Pts.	Avg.	Dif.
San Antonio....	2884	6781	.425	1276	1726	.739	986	2410	3396	1667	1893	25	645	1181	429	7399	90.2	+5.9
New York......	2711	6398	.424	1609	2153	.747	927	2441	3368	1609	1799	17	603	1161	354	7435	90.7	+1.5
Portland.......	2825	6557	.431	1422	1985	.716	978	2220	3198	1705	1872	22	652	1186	350	7466	91.0	+6.4
Miami	2782	6595	.422	1512	2022	.748	974	2341	3315	1582	1795	12	621	1150	364	7484	91.3	+3.1
Utah	2781	6240	.446	1598	2141	.746	887	2236	3123	1620	2023	16	588	1270	411	7548	92.0	+4.5
L.A. Lakers....	2838	6824	.416	1518	2045	.742	1007	2531	3538	1597	2099	42	627	1196	345	7566	92.3	+8.5
Philadelphia....	2867	6595	.435	1510	2001	.755	1065	2501	3566	1828	1977	29	631	1444	531	7661	93.4	+1.3
Phoenix.......	2825	6665	.424	1630	2205	.739	1071	2465	3536	1700	1794	11	733	1422	427	7683	93.7	+5.2
Chicago.......	2916	6396	.456	1533	2070	.741	1000	2416	3416	1902	1966	18	853	1244	461	7723	94.2	-9.4
Charlotte	3048	6811	.448	1347	1807	.745	966	2550	3516	1903	2076	21	604	1297	421	7853	95.8	+2.7
Minnesota	2924	6576	.445	1644	2185	.752	916	2440	3356	1737	1685	19	591	1232	344	7872	96.0	+2.5
Indiana	3113	6982	.446	1374	1821	.755	1040	2545	3585	1735	1910	18	610	1126	333	7929	96.7	+4.6
Toronto	3002	6615	.454	1631	2136	.764	961	2552	3513	1790	1874	15	557	1250	434	7981	97.3	-0.2
Seattle........	3132	6941	.451	1343	1795	.748	1084	2611	3695	1939	1839	13	590	1258	433	8047	98.1	+1.0
New Jersey	3125	6741	.464	1503	2012	.747	1129	2657	3786	1866	1869	14	568	1368	350	8121	99.0	-1.0
Orlando	3076	6919	.445	1567	2104	.745	1094	2473	3567	1991	2008	17	724	1488	475	8150	99.4	+0.7
Vancouver	3136	6613	.474	1530	1989	.769	970	2336	3306	1932	1912	28	725	1234	519	8163	99.5	-5.6
Atlanta........	3211	7060	.455	1381	1796	.769	1052	2474	3526	1886	1830	13	655	1001	404	8176	99.7	-5.4
Washington	3005	6547	.459	1790	2405	.744	962	2418	3380	1793	1967	17	686	1225	503	8190	99.9	-3.3
Boston........	2960	6304	.470	1929	2563	.753	857	2534	3391	1798	1928	21	638	1395	473	8208	100.1	-0.8
Houston	3226	7074	.456	1425	1829	.779	1027	2451	3478	1863	1833	17	735	1126	433	8227	100.3	-0.9
Cleveland.....	2983	6736	.443	1851	2385	.776	1013	2586	3599	1942	2058	26	659	1389	500	8237	100.5	-3.5
Milwaukee	3033	6644	.457	1685	2241	.752	1037	2368	3405	1987	1870	14	637	1303	340	8282	101.0	+0.2
Denver........	3129	6953	.450	1632	2174	.751	1027	2606	3633	2003	1937	22	616	1179	462	8289	101.1	-2.1
Dallas	3225	7053	.457	1484	2005	.740	1251	2719	3970	1901	1814	12	604	1318	416	8363	102.0	-0.6
Detroit........	3119	6706	.465	1669	2237	.746	973	2504	3477	1893	2219	33	652	1400	396	8365	102.0	+1.4
Sacramento....	3269	7239	.452	1434	1910	.751	1143	2761	3904	1950	1943	19	753	1437	404	8368	102.0	+2.9
L.A. Clippers ...	3281	6879	.477	1512	2041	.741	1038	2699	3737	1975	1731	8	621	1172	377	8491	103.5	-11.5
Golden State ...	3165	6776	.467	1755	2328	.754	1091	2691	3782	2036	1887	18	690	1338	495	8512	103.8	-8.3
Avgs.........	3020	6732	.449	1555	2073	.750	1018	2501	3519	1832	1911	19	651	1269	424	7993	97.5	...

HOME/ROAD

	Home	Road	Total		Home	Road	Total
Atlanta	21-20	7-34	28-54	Minnesota	26-15	24-17	50-32
Boston	26-15	9-32	35-47	New Jersey	22-19	9-32	31-51
Charlotte	30-11	19-22	49-33	New York	33-8	17-24	50-32
Chicago	12-29	5-36	17-65	Orlando	26-15	15-26	41-41
Cleveland	22-19	10-31	32-50	Philadelphia	29-12	20-21	49-33
Dallas	22-19	18-23	40-42	Phoenix	32-9	21-20	53-29
Denver	25-16	10-31	35-47	Portland	30-11	29-12	59-23
Detroit	27-14	15-26	42-40	Sacramento	30-11	14-27	44-38
Golden State	12-29	7-34	19-63	San Antonio	31-10	22-19	53-29
Houston	22-19	12-29	34-48	Seattle	24-17	21-20	45-37
Indiana	36-5	20-21	56-26	Toronto	26-15	19-22	45-37
L.A. Clippers	10-31	5-36	15-67	Utah	31-10	24-17	55-27
L.A. Lakers	36-5	31-10	67-15	Vancouver	12-29	10-31	22-60
Miami	33-8	19-22	52-30	Washington	17-24	12-29	29-53
Milwaukee	23-18	19-22	42-40	Totals	726-463	463-726	1,189-1,189

INDIVIDUAL LEADERS

POINTS

(minimum 70 games or 1,400 points)

	G	FGM	FTM	Pts.	Avg.
Shaquille O'Neal, L.A. Lakers	79	956	432	2344	29.7
Allen Iverson, Philadelphia	70	729	442	1989	28.4
Grant Hill, Detroit	74	696	480	1906	25.8
Vince Carter, Toronto	82	788	436	2107	25.7
Karl Malone, Utah	82	752	589	2095	25.5
Chris Webber, Sacramento	75	748	311	1834	24.5
Gary Payton, Seattle	82	747	311	1982	24.2
Jerry Stackhouse, Detroit	82	619	618	1939	23.6
Tim Duncan, San Antonio	74	628	459	1716	23.2
Kevin Garnett, Minnesota	81	759	309	1857	22.9

REBOUNDS

(minimum 70 games or 800 rebounds)

	G	Off.	Def.	Tot.	Avg.
Dikembe Mutombo, Atlanta	82	304	853	1157	14.1
Shaquille O'Neal, L.A. Lakers	79	336	742	1078	13.6
Tim Duncan, San Antonio	74	262	656	918	12.4
Kevin Garnett, Minnesota	81	223	733	956	11.8
Chris Webber, Sacramento	75	189	598	787	10.5
Shareef Abdur-Rahim, Vancouver	82	218	607	825	10.1
Elton Brand, Chicago	81	348	462	810	10.0
Dale Davis, Indiana	74	256	473	729	9.9
David Robinson, San Antonio	80	193	577	770	9.6
Jerome Williams, Detroit	82	277	512	789	9.6

FIELD GOALS

(minimum 300 made)

	FGM	FGA	Pct.
Shaquille O'Neal, L.A. Lakers	956	1665	.574
Dikembe Mutombo, Atlanta	322	573	.562
Alonzo Mourning, Miami	652	1184	.551
Ruben Patterson, Seattle	354	661	.536
Rasheed Wallace, Portland	542	1045	.519
David Robinson, San Antonio	528	1031	.512
Wally Szczerbiak, Minnesota	342	669	.511
Karl Malone, Utah	752	1476	.509
Antonio McDyess, Denver	614	1211	.507
Othella Harrington, Vancouver	420	830	.506

STEALS

(minimum 70 games or 125 steals)

	G	No.	Avg.
Eddie Jones, Charlotte	72	192	2.67
Paul Pierce, Boston	73	152	2.08
Darrell Armstrong, Orlando	82	169	2.06
Allen Iverson, Philadelphia	70	144	2.06
Mookie Blaylock, Golden State	73	146	2.00
Jason Kidd, Phoenix	67	134	2.00
Terrell Brandon, Minnesota	71	134	1.89
Gary Payton, Seattle	82	153	1.87
Kendall Gill, New Jersey	76	139	1.83
John Stockton, Utah	82	143	1.74

FREE THROWS

(minimum 125 made)

	FTM	FTA	Pct.
Jeff Hornacek, Utah	171	180	.950
Reggie Miller, Indiana	373	406	.919
Darrell Armstrong, Orlando	225	247	.911
Terrell Brandon, Minnesota	187	208	.899
Ray Allen, Milwaukee	353	398	.887
Predrag Stojakovic, Sacramento	135	153	.882
Jim Jackson, Atlanta	186	212	.877
Derek Anderson, L.A. Clippers	271	309	.877
Mitch Richmond, Washington	298	340	.876
Sam Cassell, Milwaukee	390	445	.876

BLOCKED SHOTS

(minimum 70 games or 100 blocked shots)

	G	No.	Avg.
Alonzo Mourning, Miami	79	294	3.72
Dikembe Mutombo, Atlanta	82	269	3.28
Shaquille O'Neal, L.A. Lakers	79	239	3.03
Theo Ratliff, Philadelphia	57	171	3.00
Shawn Bradley, Dallas	77	190	2.47
David Robinson, San Antonio	80	183	2.29
Tim Duncan, San Antonio	74	165	2.23
Raef LaFrentz, Denver	81	180	2.22
Greg Ostertag, Utah	81	172	2.12
Marcus Camby, New York	59	116	1.97

ASSISTS

(minimum 70 games or 400 assists)

	G	No.	Avg.
Jason Kidd, Phoenix	67	678	10.1
Nick Van Exel, Denver	79	714	9.0
Sam Cassell, Milwaukee	81	729	9.0
Gary Payton, Seattle	82	732	8.9
Terrell Brandon, Minnesota	71	629	8.9
John Stockton, Utah	82	703	8.6
Stephon Marbury, New Jersey	74	622	8.4
Mike Bibby, Vancouver	82	665	8.1
Mark Jackson, Indiana	81	650	8.0
Eric Snow, Philadelphia	82	624	7.6

3-POINT FIELD GOALS

(minimum 55 made)

	FGM	FGA	Pct.
Hubert Davis, Dallas	82	167	.491
Jeff Hornacek, Utah	66	138	.478
Matt Bullard, Houston	79	177	.446
Rodney Rogers, Phoenix	115	262	.439
Allan Houston, New York	106	243	.436
Terry Porter, San Antonio	90	207	.435
Lindsey Hunter, Detroit	168	389	.432
Tracy Murray, Washington	113	263	.430
Jon Barry, Sacramento	66	154	.429
Wesley Person, Cleveland	106	250	.424

INDIVIDUAL STATISTICS, TEAM BY TEAM

ATLANTA HAWKS

	G	Min.	FGM	FGA	Pct.	FTM	FTA	Pct.	Off.	Def.	Tot.	Ast.	PF	Dq.	Stl.	TO	Blk.	Pts.	Avg.	Hi.
									REBOUNDS									SCORING		
Isaiah Rider 60	60	2084	449	1072	.419	204	260	.785	63	195	258	219	132	3	41	168	6	1158	19.3	38
Jim Jackson 79	79	2767	507	1235	.411	186	212	.877	101	293	394	230	167	0	57	185	10	1317	16.7	33
Alan Henderson 82	82	2775	429	930	.461	224	334	.671	265	306	571	77	233	3	81	139	54	1083	13.2	24
Dikembe Mutombo .. 82	82	2984	322	573	.562	298	421	.708	304	853	1157	105	248	3	27	174	269	942	11.5	27
LaPhonso Ellis 58	58	1309	209	464	.450	66	95	.695	98	192	290	59	133	1	32	52	25	487	8.4	17
Jason Terry 81	81	1888	249	600	.415	113	140	.807	24	142	166	346	133	0	90	156	10	657	8.1	22
Bimbo Coles 80	80	1924	276	607	.455	85	104	.817	30	142	172	290	178	1	58	103	11	645	8.1	25
Roshown McLeod 44	44	860	131	332	.395	54	70	.771	41	97	138	52	84	0	16	59	5	318	7.2	22
Dion Glover 30	30	446	66	171	.386	51	70	.729	15	23	38	27	28	0	15	28	4	195	6.5	18
Lorenzen Wright 75	75	1205	180	361	.499	87	135	.644	117	188	305	21	203	3	29	66	40	448	6.0	23
Chris Crawford 55	55	668	91	229	.397	63	81	.778	51	48	99	33	83	1	17	37	16	252	4.6	18
Cal Bowdler 46	46	423	49	115	.426	24	38	.632	22	63	85	14	46	1	14	21	9	122	2.7	13
Drew Barry† 8	8	74	6	15	.400	3	3	1.000	0	4	4	16	9	0	0	7	0	19	2.4	8
Drew Barry‡ 16	16	159	15	33	.455	4	5	.800	0	12	12	33	23	0	2	13	0	41	2.6	8
Anthony Johnson* ... 38	38	423	36	103	.350	19	24	.792	15	24	39	59	41	0	23	24	2	92	2.4	8

3-pt. FG: Atlanta 258-814 (.317)—Rider 56-180 (.311); Jackson 117-303 (.386); Henderson 1-10 (.100); Ellis 3-21 (.143); Terry 46-157 (.293); Coles 8-39 (.205); McLeod 2-13 (.154); Glover 12-45 (.267); Wright 1-3 (.333); Crawford 7-27 (.259); Bowdler 0-1 (.000); Barry† 4-9 (.444); Barry‡ 7-18 (.389); Johnson* 1-6 (.167). Opponents 373-1015 (.367).

BOSTON CELTICS

	G	Min.	FGM	FGA	Pct.	FTM	FTA	Pct.	Off.	Def.	Tot.	Ast.	PF	Dq.	Stl.	TO	Blk.	Pts.	Avg.	Hi.
									REBOUNDS									SCORING		
Antoine Walker 82	82	3003	648	1506	.430	311	445	.699	199	453	652	305	263	4	117	259	32	1680	20.5	39
Paul Pierce 73	73	2583	486	1099	.442	359	450	.798	83	313	396	221	237	5	152	178	62	1427	19.5	38
Kenny Anderson 82	82	2593	434	986	.440	196	253	.775	55	170	225	420	230	4	139	130	8	1149	14.0	33
Vitaly Potapenko 79	79	1797	307	615	.499	109	160	.681	182	317	499	77	239	4	41	145	29	723	9.2	22
Danny Fortson 55	55	856	140	265	.528	139	189	.735	141	225	366	29	180	4	20	67	5	419	7.6	23
Eric Williams........ 68	68	1378	165	386	.427	134	169	.793	55	101	156	93	165	3	44	66	16	489	7.2	23
Dana Barros 72	72	1139	196	435	.451	66	76	.868	13	86	99	133	80	0	31	66	4	517	7.2	19
Adrian Griffin 72	72	1927	175	413	.424	119	158	.753	128	244	372	177	222	3	116	93	15	485	6.7	23
Tony Battie 82	82	1505	219	459	.477	102	151	.675	152	258	410	63	249	4	47	67	70	541	6.6	18
Calbert Cheaney 67	67	1309	120	273	.440	9	21	.429	23	115	138	80	158	3	44	46	14	267	4.0	12
Walter McCarty 61	61	879	78	230	.339	39	54	.722	33	77	110	70	83	1	24	67	23	229	3.8	20
Jamel Thomas 3	3	19	5	10	.500	1	1	1.000	0	2	2	2	0	0	0	1	0	11	3.7	5
Doug Overton 48	48	432	61	154	.396	20	21	.952	14	19	33	53	46	0	10	20	0	152	3.2	11
Pervis Ellison 30	30	269	19	43	.442	15	21	.714	29	38	67	13	67	1	10	13	8	53	1.8	5
Wayne Turner 3	3	41	1	6	.167	2	6	.333	1	2	3	5	4	0	0	3	0	4	1.3	3

3-pt. FG: Boston 417-1260 (.331)—Walker 73-285 (.256); Pierce 96-280 (.343); Anderson 85-220 (.386); Potapenko 0-1 (.000); Williams 25-72 (.347); Battie 1-8 (.125); Barros 59-144 (.410); Griffin 16-57 (.281); Cheaney 18-54 (.333); McCarty 34-110 (.309); Thomas 0-1 (.000); Overton 10-28 (.357). Opponents 359-995 (.361).

CHARLOTTE HORNETS

	G	Min.	FGM	FGA	Pct.	FTM	FTA	Pct.	Off.	Def.	Tot.	Ast.	PF	Dq.	Stl.	TO	Blk.	Pts.	Avg.	Hi.
									REBOUNDS									SCORING		
Eddie Jones 72	72	2807	478	1119	.427	362	419	.864	81	262	343	305	176	1	192	160	49	1446	20.1	34
Derrick Coleman 74	74	2347	446	979	.456	296	377	.785	124	508	632	175	195	2	34	173	130	1239	16.7	34
David Wesley 82	82	2760	407	955	.426	214	275	.778	39	186	225	463	186	2	109	159	11	1116	13.6	30
Bobby Phills 28	28	825	152	335	.454	47	65	.723	17	54	71	79	72	2	41	48	8	381	13.6	27
Elden Campbell...... 78	78	2538	370	829	.446	247	358	.690	168	422	590	129	269	6	56	127	150	987	12.7	27
Anthony Mason...... 82	82	3133	317	661	.480	314	421	.746	145	554	699	367	220	0	74	160	29	948	11.6	31
Brad Miller 55	55	961	135	293	.461	153	195	.785	113	180	293	45	111	1	23	48	35	423	7.7	20
Eddie Robinson...... 67	67	1112	212	386	.549	47	64	.734	54	130	184	32	67	0	48	39	25	471	7.0	19
Baron Davis 82	82	1523	182	433	.420	97	153	.634	48	117	165	309	201	1	97	140	19	486	5.9	19
Chucky Brown† 33	33	494	66	152	.434	11	21	.524	24	66	90	25	61	1	12	17	8	144	4.4	12
Chucky Brown‡...... 63	63	1096	148	328	.451	36	52	.692	35	132	167	66	114	1	20	45	18	334	5.3	16
Ricky Davis........ 48	48	570	94	187	.503	39	51	.765	29	54	83	62	39	0	30	46	8	227	4.7	16
Dale Ellis† 24	24	240	19	58	.328	3	4	.750	6	16	22	8	22	0	7	13	0	55	2.3	9
Dale Ellis‡.......... 42	42	564	66	159	.415	9	13	.692	13	43	56	14	45	0	13	20	0	178	4.2	17
Todd Fuller 41	41	399	51	122	.418	32	53	.604	36	74	110	5	46	0	9	27	8	134	3.3	11
Eldridge Recasner..... 7	7	28	3	7	.429	0	0	...	0	4	4	5	1	0	0	0	0	7	1.0	4
Michael Hawkins 12	12	36	3	13	.231	1	2	.500	0	7	7	13	2	0	0	3	0	8	0.7	5
Derek Hood 2	2	4	0	3	.000	0	0	...	0	1	1	0	0	0	0	0	0	0	0.0	0
Jason Miskiri 1	1	3	0	1	.000	0	0	...	0	0	0	1	2	0	0	0	0	0	0.0	0

3-pt. FG: Charlotte 339-1001 (.339)—Jones 128-341 (.375); Coleman 51-141 (.362); Wesley 88-248 (.355); Phills 30-91 (.330); Campbell 0-6 (.000); Mason 0-1 (.000); Miller 0-2 (.000); Robinson 0-4 (.000); B. Davis 25-111 (.225); Brown† 1-7 (.143); Brown‡ 2-10 (.200); R. Davis 0-4 (.000); Ellis† 14-35 (.400); Ellis‡ 37-100 (.370); Recasner 1-4 (.250); Hawkins 1-5 (.200); Miskiri 0-1 (.000). Opponents 410-1086 (.378).

1999-2000

CHICAGO BULLS

	G	Min.	FGM	FGA	Pct.	FTM	FTA	Pct.	REBOUNDS Off.	Def.	Tot.	Ast.	PF	Dq.	Stl.	TO	Blk.	SCORING Pts.	Avg.	Hi.
Elton Brand	81	2999	630	1306	.482	367	536	.685	348	462	810	155	259	3	66	228	132	1627	20.1	44
Toni Kukoc*	24	868	148	388	.381	118	155	.761	37	93	130	124	51	0	44	75	19	432	18.0	33
John Starks†	4	82	11	34	.324	5	5	1.000	0	10	10	11	9	0	5	3	1	30	7.5	17
John Starks‡	37	1190	203	542	.375	50	59	.847	10	91	101	181	102	1	42	67	4	515	13.9	28
Ron Artest	72	2238	309	759	.407	188	279	.674	62	246	308	202	159	0	119	166	39	866	12.0	24
Chris Carr†	50	1092	185	463	.400	91	106	.858	36	124	160	81	101	0	30	112	14	492	9.8	19
Chris Carr‡	57	1166	196	496	.395	107	125	.856	41	132	173	84	113	0	30	117	15	531	9.3	19
Rusty LaRue	4	129	15	43	.349	5	7	.714	1	9	10	11	9	0	7	7	0	37	9.3	13
Fred Hoiberg	31	845	89	230	.387	69	76	.908	7	103	110	85	66	0	40	43	2	279	9.0	20
Hersey Hawkins	61	1622	159	375	.424	107	119	.899	31	144	175	134	146	1	74	100	15	480	7.9	30
Corey Benjamin	48	862	145	350	.414	49	82	.598	21	67	88	54	122	2	31	74	22	370	7.7	21
Dedric Willoughby	25	508	61	179	.341	39	51	.765	11	40	51	66	32	0	23	37	2	190	7.6	21
B.J. Armstrong	27	583	83	186	.446	22	25	.880	2	45	47	78	34	0	7	40	1	201	7.4	22
Kornel David*	26	443	63	148	.426	42	52	.808	22	51	73	16	49	0	13	31	2	168	6.5	17
Randy Brown	59	1625	157	435	.361	62	84	.738	23	121	144	202	120	1	61	105	15	379	6.4	18
Matt Maloney	51	1175	114	318	.358	37	45	.822	10	54	64	138	42	0	32	63	3	327	6.4	19
Chris Anstey	73	1007	161	364	.442	116	147	.789	90	190	280	65	180	4	29	80	25	439	6.0	19
Dickey Simpkins	69	1651	111	274	.405	65	120	.542	124	248	372	100	217	4	22	128	22	287	4.2	17
Khalid Reeves	3	48	3	12	.250	5	5	1.000	2	2	4	13	8	0	2	6	0	11	3.7	4
Will Perdue	67	1012	59	168	.351	50	105	.476	88	174	262	65	126	1	14	78	42	168	2.5	13
Michael Ruffin	71	975	58	138	.420	43	88	.489	117	133	250	44	170	1	26	59	26	159	2.2	14
Lari Ketner*	6	41	4	10	.400	2	2	1.000	0	7	7	4	8	1	1	3	1	10	1.7	6

3-pt. FG: Chicago 340-1032 (.329)—Brand 0-2 (.000); Kukoc* 18-78 (.231); Starks† 3-10 (.300); Starks‡ 59-171 (.345); Artest 60-191 (.314); LaRue 2-14 (.143); Carr† 31-93 (.333); Carr‡ 32-101 (.317); Hoiberg 32-94 (.340); Hawkins 55-141 (.390); Benjamin 31-89 (.348); Brown 3-6 (.500); Willoughby 29-98 (.296); Armstrong 13-29 (.448); David* 0-3 (.000); Maloney 62-174 (.356); Anstey 1-6 (.167); Reeves 0-3 (.000); Simpkins 0-1 (.000). Opponents 358-1049 (.341).

CLEVELAND CAVALIERS

	G	Min.	FGM	FGA	Pct.	FTM	FTA	Pct.	REBOUNDS Off.	Def.	Tot.	Ast.	PF	Dq.	Stl.	TO	Blk.	SCORING Pts.	Avg.	Hi.
Shawn Kemp	82	2492	484	1160	.417	493	635	.776	231	494	725	138	371	13	100	291	96	1463	17.8	36
Lamond Murray	74	2365	460	1019	.451	204	268	.761	127	296	423	132	208	2	105	184	36	1175	15.9	38
Bob Sura	73	2216	356	815	.437	175	251	.697	50	238	288	284	201	0	91	148	19	1009	13.8	31
Andre Miller	82	2093	339	755	.449	226	292	.774	85	195	280	476	194	1	84	166	17	914	11.1	28
Brevin Knight	65	1754	230	558	.412	140	184	.761	38	155	193	458	185	2	107	157	21	602	9.3	20
Wesley Person	79	2056	280	654	.428	61	77	.792	44	223	267	146	119	1	40	60	19	727	9.2	24
Danny Ferry	63	1326	189	380	.497	52	57	.912	55	183	238	67	181	1	22	55	24	463	7.3	19
Andrew DeClercq	82	1831	225	443	.508	94	160	.588	156	283	439	58	275	6	63	108	66	544	6.6	19
Mark Bryant	75	1712	174	346	.503	76	94	.809	126	226	352	61	250	5	31	87	31	424	5.7	18
Kornel David†	6	31	4	9	.444	3	4	.750	4	4	8	1	7	0	4	2	1	11	1.8	5
Kornel David‡	32	474	67	157	.427	45	56	.804	26	55	81	17	56	0	17	33	3	179	5.6	17
Cedric Henderson	61	1107	129	326	.396	69	104	.663	34	106	140	55	99	0	39	68	17	328	5.4	20
Earl Boykins†	25	253	53	112	.473	18	23	.783	11	14	25	45	23	0	12	17	1	132	5.3	22
Earl Boykins‡	26	261	56	116	.483	18	23	.783	12	14	26	48	23	0	12	17	1	138	5.3	22
Trajan Langdon	10	145	15	40	.375	11	11	1.000	4	11	15	11	16	0	5	6	0	49	4.9	12
Ryan Stack	25	198	17	51	.333	18	27	.667	15	30	45	5	47	3	4	17	11	52	2.1	8
Donny Marshall	6	39	3	11	.273	5	6	.833	0	1	1	0	7	0	2	3	0	11	1.8	7
Lari Ketner†	16	91	9	22	.409	6	10	.600	12	15	27	0	12	0	3	7	2	24	1.5	4
Lari Ketner‡	22	132	13	32	.406	8	12	.667	12	22	34	1	20	1	4	10	3	34	1.5	6
Mark Hendrickson*	10	47	5	7	.714	2	2	1.000	2	9	11	3	7	0	2	3	1	12	1.2	4
A.J. Bramlett	8	61	4	21	.190	0	0	...	12	10	22	0	13	0	1	3	0	8	1.0	2
Benoit Benjamin	3	8	1	3	.333	0	0	...	0	1	1	0	1	0	0	0	1	2	0.7	2
Pete Chilcutt*	6	30	0	2	.000	0	0	...	4	5	9	1	3	0	0	0	0	0	0.0	0

3-pt. FG: Cleveland 343-919 (.373)—Kemp 2-6 (.333); Murray 51-139 (.367); Sura 122-332 (.367); Miller 10-49 (.204); Knight 2-10 (.200); Person 106-250 (.424); Ferry 33-75 (.440); David‡ 0-3 (.000); Henderson 1-15 (.067); Boykins† 8-20 (.400); Boykins‡ 8-20 (.400); Stack 0-1 (.000); Langdon 8-19 (.421); Marshall 0-3 (.000). Opponents 420-1229 (.342).

DALLAS MAVERICKS

	G	Min.	FGM	FGA	Pct.	FTM	FTA	Pct.	REBOUNDS Off.	Def.	Tot.	Ast.	PF	Dq.	Stl.	TO	Blk.	SCORING Pts.	Avg.	Hi.
Michael Finley	82	3464	748	1636	.457	260	317	.820	122	396	518	438	171	1	109	196	32	1855	22.6	38
Dirk Nowitzki	82	2938	515	1118	.461	289	348	.830	102	430	532	203	256	4	63	141	68	1435	17.5	32
Cedric Ceballos	69	2064	447	1002	.446	209	248	.843	172	290	462	90	165	3	56	125	24	1147	16.6	39
Gary Trent	11	301	70	142	.493	11	21	.524	20	32	52	22	28	0	8	25	3	151	13.7	22
Erick Strickland	68	2025	316	730	.433	162	195	.831	69	254	323	211	190	3	105	102	13	867	12.8	36
Robert Pack	29	665	96	230	.417	63	78	.808	7	35	42	168	44	0	31	76	3	259	8.9	27
Steve Nash	56	1532	173	363	.477	75	85	.882	34	87	121	272	122	1	37	102	3	481	8.6	24
Shawn Bradley	77	1901	266	555	.479	114	149	.765	160	337	497	60	260	7	71	74	190	647	8.4	26
Hubert Davis	79	1817	217	464	.468	67	77	.870	17	117	134	141	109	0	24	70	3	583	7.4	27

	G	Min.	FGM	FGA	Pct.	FTM	FTA	Pct.	Off.	Def.	Tot.	Ast.	PF	Dq.	Stl.	TO	Blk.	Pts.	Avg.	Hi.
Greg Buckner	48	923	111	233	.476	43	63	.683	56	118	174	55	148	1	38	36	20	275	5.7	25
Sean Rooks	71	1001	122	283	.431	65	89	.730	82	166	248	68	169	0	29	70	52	309	4.4	13
Damon Jones†	42	416	55	154	.357	25	39	.641	12	27	39	57	21	0	12	25	1	165	3.9	18
Damon Jones‡	55	612	80	208	.385	32	48	.667	12	43	55	96	34	0	18	40	1	233	4.2	18
Rick Hughes	21	224	35	72	.486	12	26	.462	24	25	49	9	30	0	3	14	1	82	3.9	13
Dennis Rodman	12	389	12	31	.387	10	14	.714	48	123	171	14	41	2	2	19	1	34	2.8	6
Bruno Sundov.......	14	61	12	31	.387	2	2	1.000	5	7	12	2	16	0	2	4	2	26	1.9	4
Randell Jackson	1	1	0	0	...	0	0	...	0	0	0	0	0	0	0	0	0	0	0.0	0
Rodrick Rhodes	1	8	0	3	.000	0	0	...	1	0	1	0	0	0	2	2	0	0	0.0	0

3-pt. FG: Dallas 519-1326 (.391)—Finley 99-247 (.401); Nowitzki 116-306 (.379); Ceballos 44-134 (.328); Trent 0-2 (.000); Strickland 73-186 (.392); Pack 4-11 (.364); Nash 60-149 (.403); Bradley 1-5 (.200); Davis 82-167 (.491); Buckner 10-26 (.385); Jones† 30-91 (.330); Jones‡ 41-114 (.360); Hughes 0-1 (.000); Rodman 0-1 (.000). Opponents 429-1244 (.345).

DENVER NUGGETS

									REBOUNDS									SCORING		
	G	Min.	FGM	FGA	Pct.	FTM	FTA	Pct.	Off.	Def.	Tot.	Ast.	PF	Dq.	Stl.	TO	Blk.	Pts.	Avg.	Hi.
Antonio McDyess	81	2698	614	1211	.507	323	516	.626	234	451	685	159	316	12	69	230	139	1551	19.1	40
Ron Mercer*........	37	1408	272	612	.444	119	151	.788	29	123	152	104	75	0	33	87	15	678	18.3	31
Nick Van Exel	79	2950	473	1213	.390	196	240	.817	34	277	311	714	148	0	68	221	11	1275	16.1	44
Raef LaFrentz	81	2435	392	879	.446	162	236	.686	170	471	641	97	292	6	42	96	180	1006	12.4	32
Chris Gatling†	40	770	155	340	.456	95	128	.742	63	142	205	31	104	2	34	64	13	416	10.4	25
Chris Gatling‡......	85	1811	365	802	.455	266	373	.713	154	348	502	71	246	2	82	169	23	1014	11.9	31
Tariq Abdul-Wahad† ..	15	373	51	131	.389	31	42	.738	24	28	52	26	31	0	6	19	12	134	8.9	17
Tariq Abdul-Wahad‡ ..	61	1578	274	646	.424	146	193	.756	101	190	291	98	147	1	59	106	28	697	11.4	23
George McCloud	78	2118	266	638	.417	148	181	.818	72	213	285	246	180	2	48	134	26	787	10.1	28
Chauncey Billups.....	13	305	34	101	.337	37	44	.841	8	26	34	39	27	0	10	24	2	112	8.6	20
Keon Clark	81	1850	286	528	.542	121	176	.688	162	343	505	71	231	1	45	125	114	694	8.6	29
James Posey	81	2052	230	536	.429	120	150	.800	85	232	317	146	207	1	98	95	33	662	8.2	25
Bryant Stith	45	691	86	189	.455	64	77	.831	23	61	84	61	56	0	18	33	12	253	5.6	27
Chris Herren	45	597	45	124	.363	27	40	.675	12	40	52	111	74	0	15	42	2	141	3.1	18
Cory Alexander	29	329	28	98	.286	17	22	.773	8	34	42	58	39	0	24	28	2	82	2.8	11
Popeye Jones	40	330	44	104	.423	14	19	.737	41	62	103	19	50	1	3	13	6	104	2.6	12
Ryan Bowen	52	589	46	117	.393	38	53	.717	75	39	114	20	95	0	39	14	13	131	2.5	12
Roy Rogers.........	40	355	35	88	.398	19	41	.463	33	47	80	9	36	0	2	10	38	89	2.2	18
Johnny Taylor*.......	1	5	0	2	.000	0	0	...	0	1	1	0	1	0	0	0	0	0	0.0	0

3-pt. FG: Denver 470-1397 (.336)—McDyess 0-2 (.000); Mercer* 15-39 (.385); Van Exel 133-401 (.332); LaFrentz 60-183 (.328); Gatling† 11-47 (.234); Gatling‡ 18-70 (.257); Abdul-Wahad† 1-2 (.500); Abdul-Wahad‡ 3-23 (.130); McCloud 107-283 (.378); Billups 7-41 (.171); Clark 1-8 (.125); Posey 82-220 (.373); Stith 17-56 (.304); Herren 24-67 (.358); Alexander 9-35 (.257); Jones 2-3 (.667); Bowen 1-9 (.111); Rogers 0-1 (.000). Opponents 399-1126 (.354).

DETROIT PISTONS

									REBOUNDS									SCORING		
	G	Min.	FGM	FGA	Pct.	FTM	FTA	Pct.	Off.	Def.	Tot.	Ast.	PF	Dq.	Stl.	TO	Blk.	Pts.	Avg.	Hi.
Grant Hill	74	2776	696	1422	.489	480	604	.795	97	393	490	385	190	0	103	240	43	1906	25.8	42
Jerry Stackhouse	82	3148	619	1447	.428	618	758	.815	118	197	315	365	188	1	103	311	36	1939	23.6	40
Lindsey Hunter	82	2919	379	892	.425	117	154	.760	35	215	250	327	216	2	129	145	22	1043	12.7	29
Christian Laettner ...	82	2443	379	801	.473	237	292	.812	175	378	553	186	326	10	83	186	45	1002	12.2	28
Jerome Williams.....	82	2102	257	456	.564	175	284	.616	277	512	789	68	196	0	95	105	21	689	8.4	26
Mikki Moore	29	488	87	140	.621	54	68	.794	44	68	112	17	104	5	9	23	31	228	7.9	15
Terry Mills	82	1842	214	488	.439	25	34	.735	50	340	390	85	242	4	38	46	24	548	6.7	24
Michael Curry	82	1611	182	379	.480	141	168	.839	21	83	104	87	209	3	33	73	5	506	6.2	23
John Crotty.........	69	937	106	251	.422	80	93	.860	17	58	75	128	104	0	27	54	5	325	4.7	14
Jud Buechler.......	58	657	55	156	.353	2	7	.286	30	61	91	33	50	1	25	13	16	130	2.2	14
Loy Vaught.........	43	292	32	89	.360	11	16	.688	26	65	91	11	45	0	6	11	4	75	1.7	10
Marcus Brown	6	45	4	14	.286	2	2	1.000	3	4	7	3	8	0	0	3	0	10	1.7	6
Don Reid*	21	165	16	34	.471	3	6	.500	5	20	25	1	45	1	5	11	12	35	1.7	9
Jermaine Jackson ...	7	73	1	11	.091	5	8	.625	1	10	11	4	7	0	3	7	0	7	1.0	4
Eric Montross.......	51	332	17	55	.309	6	12	.500	18	54	72	7	81	0	6	22	9	40	0.8	4

3-pt. FG: Detroit 439-1223 (.359)—Hill 34-98 (.347); Stackhouse 83-288 (.288); Hunter 168-389 (.432); Laettner 7-24 (.292); Williams 0-3 (.000); Mills 95-242 (.393); Curry 1-5 (.200); Crotty 33-80 (.413); Buechler 18-83 (.217); Vaught 0-3 (.000); Brown 0-7 (.000); Jackson 0-1 (.000). Opponents 458-1234 (.371).

GOLDEN STATE WARRIORS

									REBOUNDS									SCORING		
	G	Min.	FGM	FGA	Pct.	FTM	FTA	Pct.	Off.	Def.	Tot.	Ast.	PF	Dq.	Stl.	TO	Blk.	Pts.	Avg.	Hi.
Antawn Jamison	43	1556	356	756	.471	127	208	.611	172	187	359	90	115	0	30	113	15	841	19.6	37
Chris Mills	20	649	123	292	.421	68	84	.810	46	77	123	47	60	0	18	25	4	322	16.1	24
Larry Hughes†	32	1306	267	686	.389	173	235	.736	61	129	190	130	97	2	61	100	16	725	22.7	44
Larry Hughes‡	82	2324	459	1147	.400	279	377	.740	113	236	349	205	191	2	115	195	28	1226	15.0	44
John Starks*	33	1108	192	508	.378	45	54	.833	10	81	91	170	93	1	37	64	3	485	14.7	28

	G	Min.	FGM	FGA	Pct.	FTM	FTA	Pct.	Off.	Def.	Tot.	Ast.	PF	Dq.	Stl.	TO	Blk.	Pts.	Avg.	Hi.
Donyell Marshall	64	2071	331	840	.394	199	255	.780	189	448	637	167	180	1	68	123	68	910	14.2	37
Jason Caffey	71	2159	323	675	.479	206	345	.597	189	293	482	119	269	11	62	170	20	852	12.0	26
Mookie Blaylock	73	2459	327	837	.391	67	95	.705	55	215	270	489	122	0	146	143	22	822	11.3	25
Vonteego Cummings	75	1793	265	655	.405	127	169	.751	57	127	184	247	174	4	91	132	13	706	9.4	23
Terry Cummings	22	398	76	177	.429	32	39	.821	45	62	107	21	74	0	13	27	8	184	8.4	18
Erick Dampier	21	495	70	173	.405	27	51	.529	48	86	134	19	75	1	8	29	15	167	8.0	16
Tony Farmer	74	1199	127	312	.407	203	265	.766	118	177	295	74	167	1	66	82	16	465	6.3	19
Mark Davis	23	464	56	137	.409	31	47	.660	31	53	84	38	52	0	25	40	4	143	6.2	25
Billy Owens†	16	386	38	100	.380	25	42	.595	36	73	109	38	47	0	7	24	5	103	6.4	18
Billy Owens‡	62	1305	150	358	.419	63	106	.594	99	202	301	97	166	1	33	85	21	374	6.0	18
Chris Carr*	7	74	11	33	.333	16	19	.842	5	8	13	3	12	0	0	5	1	39	5.6	14
Adonal Foyle	76	1654	193	380	.508	34	90	.378	174	250	424	42	218	2	26	71	136	420	5.5	18
Damon Jones*	13	196	25	54	.463	7	9	.778	0	16	16	39	13	0	6	15	0	68	5.2	17
Sam Mack	23	333	37	122	.303	19	20	.950	7	32	39	24	45	0	18	19	1	114	5.0	16
Sam Jacobson†	49	663	103	203	.507	30	39	.769	25	45	70	30	112	3	29	31	3	245	5.0	19
Sam Jacobson‡	52	681	108	212	.509	30	41	.732	25	46	71	32	113	3	30	33	3	255	4.9	19
Tim Legler	23	284	28	78	.359	14	18	.778	4	19	23	24	33	0	4	6	1	77	3.3	14
Drew Barry*	8	85	9	18	.500	1	2	.500	0	8	8	17	14	0	2	6	0	22	2.8	7
Bill Curley†	24	259	23	57	.404	18	25	.720	14	28	42	14	51	1	11	17	4	64	2.7	10
Bill Curley‡	28	309	29	68	.426	18	25	.720	18	32	50	14	61	2	13	21	4	76	2.7	10
Tim Young	25	137	13	39	.333	28	36	.778	13	22	35	5	18	0	2	9	1	54	2.2	6
Jamel Thomas†	4	27	3	8	.375	0	0	...	1	2	3	4	2	0	1	4	0	6	1.5	4
Jamel Thomas‡	7	46	8	18	.444	1	1	1.000	1	4	5	6	2	0	1	5	0	17	2.4	5

3-pt. FG: Golden State 345-1069 (.323)—Jamison 2-7 (.286); Mills 8-30 (.267); Hughes† 18-74 (.243); Hughes‡ 29-125 (.232); Starks* 56-161 (.348); Caffey 0-2 (.000); Marshall 49-138 (.355); Blaylock 101-301 (.336); V. Cummings 49-151 (.325); Farmer 8-44 (.182); Davis 0-2 (.000); Owens† 2-7 (.286); Owens‡ 11-34 (.324); Carr* 1-8 (.125); Jones* 11-23 (.478); Mack 21-64 (.328); Jacobson† 9-24 (.375); Jacobson‡ 9-24 (.375); Legler 7-21 (.333); Barry* 3-9 (.333); Curley† 0-1 (.000); Curley‡ 0-1 (.000); Thomas† 0-2 (.000); Thomas‡ 0-3 (.000). Opponents 427-1163 (.367).

HOUSTON ROCKETS

	G	Min.	FGM	FGA	Pct.	FTM	FTA	Pct.	Off.	Def.	Tot.	Ast.	PF	Dq.	Stl.	TO	Blk.	Pts.	Avg.	Hi.
Steve Francis	77	2776	497	1117	.445	287	365	.786	152	257	409	507	231	2	118	306	29	1388	18.0	34
Cuttino Mobley	81	2496	437	1016	.430	299	353	.847	59	229	288	208	171	0	87	186	32	1277	15.8	35
Charles Barkley	20	620	106	222	.477	71	110	.645	71	138	209	63	48	0	14	44	4	289	14.5	26
Shandon Anderson	82	2700	368	778	.473	194	253	.767	91	293	384	239	182	0	96	194	32	1009	12.3	35
Walt Williams	76	1859	312	681	.458	101	123	.821	69	237	306	157	190	2	49	113	44	827	10.9	24
Hakeem Olajuwon	44	1049	193	421	.458	69	112	.616	65	209	274	61	88	0	41	73	70	455	10.3	31
Kelvin Cato	65	1581	216	402	.537	135	208	.649	102	287	389	26	175	1	33	71	124	567	8.7	27
Kenny Thomas	72	1797	212	531	.399	138	209	.660	147	290	437	113	167	0	54	112	22	594	8.3	22
Carlos Rogers	53	1101	170	324	.525	81	137	.591	98	177	275	42	77	0	14	63	34	422	8.0	28
Moochie Norris	30	502	69	159	.434	57	73	.781	16	52	68	94	32	0	23	30	1	207	6.9	19
Matt Bullard	56	1024	139	340	.409	25	30	.833	13	125	138	63	85	0	19	36	13	382	6.8	24
Bryce Drew	72	1293	158	413	.383	45	53	.849	23	80	103	162	79	0	41	66	1	420	5.8	20
Tony Massenburg	10	109	16	36	.444	14	16	.875	7	20	27	3	13	0	2	9	5	46	4.6	8
Thomas Hamilton	22	273	35	79	.443	12	23	.522	31	59	90	15	25	0	4	28	14	82	3.7	12
Anthony Miller	35	476	52	97	.536	26	51	.510	49	115	164	16	68	1	11	19	10	130	3.7	19
Bill Curley*	4	50	6	11	.545	0	0	...	4	4	8	0	10	1	2	4	0	12	3.0	8
Devin Gray	21	124	15	37	.405	19	29	.655	11	14	25	5	22	0	5	4	3	49	2.3	6

3-pt. FG: Houston 581-1625 (.358)—Francis 107-310 (.345); Mobley 104-292 (.356); Barkley 6-26 (.231); Anderson 79-225 (.351); Williams 102-261 (.391); Olajuwon 0-2 (.000); Cato 0-4 (.000); Thomas 32-122 (.262); Rogers 1-14 (.071); Norris 12-29 (.414); Bullard 79-177 (.446); Drew 59-163 (.362). Opponents 350-990 (.354).

INDIANA PACERS

	G	Min.	FGM	FGA	Pct.	FTM	FTA	Pct.	Off.	Def.	Tot.	Ast.	PF	Dq.	Stl.	TO	Blk.	Pts.	Avg.	Hi.
Jalen Rose	80	2978	563	1196	.471	254	307	.827	42	345	387	320	234	1	84	188	49	1457	18.2	35
Reggie Miller	81	2987	466	1041	.448	373	406	.919	50	189	239	187	126	0	85	129	25	1470	18.1	32
Rik Smits	79	1852	431	890	.484	156	211	.739	94	307	401	85	249	1	20	108	100	1018	12.9	29
Austin Croshere	81	1885	288	653	.441	196	231	.848	135	381	516	89	203	2	44	121	60	835	10.3	22
Dale Davis	74	2127	302	602	.502	139	203	.685	256	473	729	64	203	1	52	91	94	743	10.0	23
Travis Best	82	1691	271	561	.483	156	190	.821	16	126	142	272	204	1	76	107	5	733	8.9	27
Mark Jackson	81	2190	246	570	.432	79	98	.806	63	233	296	650	111	0	76	174	10	660	8.1	23
Sam Perkins	81	1620	184	441	.417	80	97	.825	64	225	289	68	136	0	31	63	33	537	6.6	22
Al Harrington	50	854	121	264	.458	78	111	.703	47	112	159	38	130	0	25	65	9	328	6.6	19
Chris Mullin	47	582	80	187	.428	37	41	.902	14	62	76	37	60	0	28	28	9	242	5.1	21
Derrick McKey	32	634	43	108	.398	43	56	.768	29	106	135	35	81	0	29	19	13	139	4.3	14
Jonathan Bender	24	130	23	70	.329	16	24	.667	4	17	21	3	18	0	1	7	5	64	2.7	11
Jeff Foster	19	86	13	23	.565	17	25	.680	12	20	32	5	18	0	5	2	1	43	2.3	11
Zan Tabak	18	114	16	34	.471	5	8	.625	16	16	32	4	13	0	3	11	9	37	2.1	10

3-pt. FG: Indiana 583-1487 (.392)—Rose 77-196 (.393); Miller 165-404 (.408); Smits 0-1 (.000); Croshere 63-174 (.362); Best 35-93 (.376); Jackson 89-221 (.403); Perkins 89-218 (.408); Harrington 8-34 (.235); Mullin 45-110 (.409); McKey 10-23 (.435); Bender 2-12 (.167); Foster 0-1 (.000). Opponents 329-1006 (.327).

LOS ANGELES CLIPPERS

	G	Min.	FGM	FGA	Pct.	FTM	FTA	Pct.	REBOUNDS Off.	Def.	Tot.	Ast.	PF	Dq.	Stl.	TO	Blk.	SCORING Pts.	Avg.	Hi.
Maurice Taylor	62	2227	458	988	.464	143	201	.711	96	304	400	101	217	4	51	169	48	1060	17.1	31
Derek Anderson	64	2201	377	860	.438	271	309	.877	80	178	258	220	149	2	90	167	11	1080	16.9	35
Lamar Odom	76	2767	449	1024	.438	302	420	.719	159	436	595	317	291	13	91	258	95	1259	16.6	33
Tyrone Nesby	73	2317	364	915	.398	151	191	.791	82	193	275	121	205	5	75	102	31	973	13.3	29
Michael Olowokandi ..	80	2493	330	756	.437	123	189	.651	194	462	656	38	304	10	35	177	140	783	9.8	27
Troy Hudson........	62	1592	204	541	.377	77	95	.811	28	120	148	242	65	0	43	108	0	545	8.8	22
Eric Piatkowski	75	1712	238	573	.415	85	100	.850	74	148	222	81	140	0	44	57	13	654	8.7	35
Jeff McInnis	25	597	80	186	.430	13	17	.765	18	54	72	89	55	0	15	27	2	180	7.2	20
Eric Murdock	40	693	79	205	.385	51	80	.638	15	62	77	108	67	0	47	58	5	225	5.6	16
Brian Skinner	33	775	68	134	.507	43	65	.662	63	138	201	11	75	0	16	37	44	179	5.4	18
Keith Closs	57	820	96	197	.487	46	78	.590	65	114	179	25	80	0	13	34	73	238	4.2	14
Charles Jones	56	662	66	201	.328	17	23	.739	17	45	62	94	46	0	30	28	5	188	3.4	13
Etdrick Bohannon† ..	11	113	7	13	.538	12	20	.600	12	18	30	5	24	0	2	8	6	26	2.4	7
Etdrick Bohannon‡ ..	13	118	7	13	.538	15	24	.625	13	18	31	5	25	0	2	10	6	29	2.2	7
Pete Chilcutt†	24	347	31	63	.492	6	6	1.000	27	52	79	16	39	2	10	11	6	73	3.0	13
Pete Chilcutt‡	56	601	53	127	.417	8	8	1.000	46	85	131	27	73	2	15	20	10	120	2.1	13
Anthony Avent	49	377	29	96	.302	23	32	.719	23	51	74	11	62	1	16	24	15	81	1.7	11
Marty Conlon	3	9	1	2	.500	0	0	...	1	1	2	0	1	0	0	0	0	2	0.7	2
Mario Bennett.......	1	3	0	3	.000	0	0	...	1	1	2	0	1	0	0	0	0	0	0.0	0

3-pt. FG: L.A. Clippers 429-1267 (.339)—Taylor 1-8 (.125); Anderson 55-178 (.309); Odom 59-164 (.360); Nesby 94-281 (.335); Hudson 60-193 (.311); Piatkowski 93-243 (.383); McInnis 7-21 (.333); Murdock 16-42 (.381); Closs 0-3 (.000); Jones 39-118 (.331); Chilcutt† 5-16 (.313); Chilcutt‡ 6-26 (.231). Opponents 417-1077 (.387).

LOS ANGELES LAKERS

	G	Min.	FGM	FGA	Pct.	FTM	FTA	Pct.	REBOUNDS Off.	Def.	Tot.	Ast.	PF	Dq.	Stl.	TO	Blk.	SCORING Pts.	Avg.	Hi.
Shaquille O'Neal	79	3163	956	1665	.574	432	824	.524	336	742	1078	299	255	2	36	223	239	2344	29.7	61
Kobe Bryant	66	2524	554	1183	.468	331	403	.821	108	308	416	323	220	4	106	182	62	1485	22.5	40
Glen Rice	80	2530	421	980	.430	346	396	.874	56	271	327	176	179	0	47	114	12	1272	15.9	29
Ron Harper.........	80	2042	212	531	.399	100	147	.680	96	241	337	270	164	0	85	132	39	557	7.0	18
Rick Fox	82	1473	206	498	.414	63	78	.808	63	135	198	138	203	1	52	87	26	534	6.5	20
Derek Fisher	78	1803	167	483	.346	105	145	.724	22	121	143	216	150	1	80	75	3	491	6.3	20
Tyronn Lue	8	146	19	39	.487	6	8	.750	2	10	12	17	17	0	3	9	0	48	6.0	13
Robert Horry........	76	1685	159	363	.438	89	113	.788	133	228	361	118	189	0	84	73	80	436	5.7	20
A.C. Green	82	1929	173	387	.447	66	95	.695	160	326	486	80	127	0	53	53	18	413	5.0	14
Brian Shaw	74	1249	123	322	.382	41	54	.759	45	171	216	201	105	0	35	75	14	305	4.1	14
Sam Jacobson*	3	18	5	9	.556	0	2	.000	0	1	1	2	1	0	1	2	0	10	3.3	6
Devean George	49	345	56	144	.389	27	41	.659	29	46	75	12	54	0	10	21	4	155	3.2	14
John Celestand	16	185	15	45	.333	5	6	.833	1	10	11	20	22	0	7	16	0	37	2.3	8
Travis Knight........	63	410	46	118	.390	17	28	.607	46	83	129	23	88	1	6	26	23	109	1.7	9
John Salley.........	45	303	25	69	.362	21	28	.750	20	45	65	26	67	1	8	18	14	71	1.6	8

3-pt. FG: L.A. Lakers 344-1047 (.329)—O'Neal 0-1 (.000); Bryant 46-144 (.319); Rice 84-229 (.367); Harper 33-106 (.311); Fox 59-181 (.326); Fisher 52-166 (.313); Lue 4-8 (.500); Horry 29-94 (.309); Green 1-4 (.250); Shaw 18-58 (.310); George 16-47 (.340); Celestand 2-9 (.222). Opponents 372-1142 (.326).

MIAMI HEAT

	G	Min.	FGM	FGA	Pct.	FTM	FTA	Pct.	REBOUNDS Off.	Def.	Tot.	Ast.	PF	Dq.	Stl.	TO	Blk.	SCORING Pts.	Avg.	Hi.
Alonzo Mourning.....	79	2748	652	1184	.551	414	582	.711	215	538	753	123	308	8	40	217	294	1718	21.7	43
Jamal Mashburn.....	76	2828	515	1158	.445	186	239	.778	64	317	381	298	215	3	79	180	14	1328	17.5	34
Tim Hardaway.......	52	1672	246	638	.386	110	133	.827	25	125	150	385	112	0	49	119	4	696	13.4	32
Voshon Lenard	53	1434	228	560	.407	84	106	.792	37	116	153	136	127	2	41	80	15	629	11.9	29
P.J. Brown.........	80	2302	322	671	.480	120	159	.755	216	384	600	145	264	4	65	100	61	764	9.6	25
Dan Majerle	69	2308	170	422	.403	56	69	.812	27	306	333	206	156	1	89	62	17	506	7.3	33
Clarence Weatherspoon	78	1615	215	419	.513	135	183	.738	128	321	449	93	165	1	51	100	49	565	7.2	15
Anthony Carter	79	1859	201	509	.395	93	124	.750	48	151	199	378	167	0	93	173	5	498	6.3	21
Otis Thorpe.........	51	777	125	243	.514	29	48	.604	56	110	166	33	136	4	26	59	9	279	5.5	17
Mark Strickland......	58	663	122	224	.545	40	56	.714	44	96	140	22	68	0	15	24	18	284	4.9	13
Rodney Buford	34	386	62	151	.411	16	22	.727	10	38	48	21	44	0	10	9	8	147	4.3	17
Bruce Bowen†.......	27	567	46	121	.380	19	31	.613	13	47	60	18	81	0	14	14	10	137	5.1	16
Bruce Bowen‡.......	69	878	72	194	.371	25	43	.581	27	69	96	34	118	0	23	19	15	196	2.8	16
Rex Walters	33	389	38	91	.418	12	16	.750	8	28	36	65	44	0	6	29	0	93	2.8	10
Tim James	4	23	5	14	.357	1	3	.333	3	1	4	2	1	0	0	2	3	11	2.8	4
Duane Causwell	25	185	20	37	.541	26	38	.684	11	36	47	2	42	0	2	10	16	66	2.6	13
Harold Jamison.....	12	74	7	20	.350	4	18	.222	16	5	21	4	17	0	2	4	1	18	1.5	6

3-pt. FG: Miami 446-1202 (.371)—Mourning 0-4 (.000); Mashburn 112-278 (.403); Hardaway 94-256 (.367); Lenard 89-228 (.390); Brown 0-1 (.000); Carter 3-23 (.130); Majerle 110-304 (.362); Thorpe 0-3 (.000); Buford 7-29 (.241); Bowen† 26-56 (.464); Bowen‡ 27-58 (.466); Walters 5-20 (.250). Opponents 408-1130 (.361).

MILWAUKEE BUCKS

	G	Min.	FGM	FGA	Pct.	FTM	FTA	Pct.	Off.	Def.	Tot.	Ast.	PF	Dq.	Stl.	TO	Blk.	Pts.	Avg.	Hi.
Ray Allen	82	3070	642	1411	.455	353	398	.887	83	276	359	308	187	1	110	183	19	1809	22.1	36
Glenn Robinson	81	2909	690	1461	.472	227	283	.802	107	378	485	193	212	3	78	223	41	1693	20.9	38
Sam Cassell	81	2899	545	1170	.466	390	445	.876	69	232	301	729	255	5	102	267	8	1506	18.6	35
Tim Thomas	80	2093	347	753	.461	188	243	.774	100	232	332	113	227	3	59	129	31	945	11.8	26
Scott Williams	68	1488	213	426	.500	94	129	.729	177	271	448	28	230	3	40	65	66	520	7.6	19
Dale Ellis*	18	324	47	101	.465	6	9	.667	7	27	34	6	23	0	6	7	0	123	6.8	17
Vinny Del Negro	67	1211	153	325	.471	35	39	.897	9	98	107	160	81	0	36	48	0	349	5.2	16
Darvin Ham	35	792	71	128	.555	35	78	.449	85	87	172	42	102	1	29	29	29	177	5.1	13
Ervin Johnson	80	2129	144	279	.516	95	157	.605	233	415	648	44	298	6	81	80	127	383	4.8	15
Danny Manning	72	1217	149	339	.440	34	52	.654	50	158	208	73	183	2	62	55	29	333	4.6	19
J.R. Reid	34	602	53	127	.417	43	56	.768	29	88	117	18	81	2	19	20	5	150	4.4	15
Robert Traylor	44	447	58	122	.475	41	68	.603	50	65	115	20	79	0	25	27	25	157	3.6	8
Haywoode Workman*	23	248	23	62	.371	9	13	.692	1	16	17	44	23	0	11	14	0	66	2.9	14
Rafer Alston	27	361	27	95	.284	3	4	.750	5	18	23	70	29	0	12	29	0	60	2.2	10
Mirsad Turkcan†	10	65	12	28	.429	5	8	.625	11	12	23	4	10	0	1	7	1	29	2.9	6
Mirsad Turkcan‡	17	90	14	38	.368	5	8	.625	13	20	33	5	14	0	3	8	1	33	1.9	6

3-pt. FG: Milwaukee 394-1069 (.369)—Allen 172-407 (.423); Robinson 86-237 (.363); Cassell 26-90 (.289); Thomas 63-182 (.346); Ellis* 23-65 (.354); Ham 0-1 (.000); Del Negro 8-24 (.333); Johnson 0-1 (.000); Manning 1-4 (.250); Reid 1-7 (.143); Traylor 0-4 (.000); Workman* 11-29 (.379); Alston 3-14 (.214); Turkcan† 0-4 (.000); Turkcan‡ 0-6 (.000). Opponents 531-1357 (.391).

MINNESOTA TIMBERWOLVES

	G	Min.	FGM	FGA	Pct.	FTM	FTA	Pct.	Off.	Def.	Tot.	Ast.	PF	Dq.	Stl.	TO	Blk.	Pts.	Avg.	Hi.
Kevin Garnett	81	3243	759	1526	.497	309	404	.765	223	733	956	401	205	1	120	268	126	1857	22.9	40
Terrell Brandon	71	2587	486	1042	.466	187	208	.899	44	194	238	629	158	1	134	184	30	1212	17.1	30
Wally Szczerbiak	73	2171	342	669	.511	133	161	.826	89	183	272	201	175	3	58	83	23	845	11.6	27
Malik Sealy	82	2392	371	780	.476	177	218	.812	119	233	352	197	197	1	76	110	19	929	11.3	27
Joe Smith	78	1975	289	623	.464	195	258	.756	186	298	484	88	302	8	45	119	85	774	9.9	26
Anthony Peeler	82	2073	316	725	.436	87	109	.798	58	174	232	195	171	1	62	85	10	804	9.8	22
Sam Mitchell	66	1227	168	376	.447	81	92	.880	28	110	138	111	116	0	27	44	14	427	6.5	20
Radoslav Nesterovic	82	1723	206	433	.476	59	103	.573	135	244	379	93	262	9	21	71	85	471	5.7	23
Bobby Jackson	73	1034	140	346	.405	76	98	.776	50	103	153	172	114	0	48	58	7	369	5.1	21
William Avery	59	484	56	181	.309	24	36	.667	8	32	40	88	60	0	14	42	2	154	2.6	13
Tom Hammonds	56	372	42	97	.433	33	56	.589	34	67	101	10	55	0	8	21	3	117	2.1	12
Dean Garrett	56	604	48	108	.444	18	26	.692	41	99	140	19	94	1	8	21	40	114	2.0	8
Andrae Patterson	5	20	3	4	.750	0	0	...	1	1	2	1	4	0	1	1	0	6	1.2	2

3-pt. FG: Minnesota 248-716 (.346)—Garnett 30-81 (.370); Brandon 53-132 (.402); Szczerbiak 28-78 (.359); Sealy 10-35 (.286); Smith 1-1 (1.000); Peeler 85-255 (.333); Mitchell 10-23 (.435); Nesterovic 0-2 (.000); Jackson 13-46 (.283); Avery 18-63 (.286). Opponents 380-1066 (.356).

NEW JERSEY NETS

	G	Min.	FGM	FGA	Pct.	FTM	FTA	Pct.	Off.	Def.	Tot.	Ast.	PF	Dq.	Stl.	TO	Blk.	Pts.	Avg.	Hi.
Stephon Marbury	74	2881	569	1317	.432	436	536	.813	61	179	240	622	195	4	112	270	15	1640	22.2	42
Keith Van Horn	80	2782	559	1257	.445	333	393	.847	200	476	676	158	258	5	64	245	60	1535	19.2	32
Kendall Gill	76	2355	396	956	.414	181	255	.710	82	201	283	210	211	3	139	89	41	993	13.1	25
Kerry Kittles	62	1896	305	698	.437	101	127	.795	46	179	225	142	120	0	79	56	19	807	13.0	33
Johnny Newman	82	1763	278	623	.446	192	229	.838	39	115	154	65	207	0	53	89	11	820	10.0	29
Lucious Harris	77	1510	198	463	.428	79	99	.798	53	134	187	100	98	0	65	42	6	513	6.7	22
Scott Burrell	74	1336	165	419	.394	39	50	.780	65	191	256	72	173	1	67	38	44	451	6.1	19
Sherman Douglas	20	309	45	90	.500	25	28	.893	13	16	29	34	26	0	17	24	0	120	6.0	15
Jamie Feick	81	2241	181	423	.428	94	133	.707	264	491	755	68	206	2	43	59	38	459	5.7	16
Elliot Perry	60	803	128	294	.435	50	62	.806	13	48	61	139	47	0	39	60	1	317	5.3	20
Gheorghe Muresan	30	267	41	90	.456	23	38	.605	24	44	68	9	52	0	0	16	12	105	3.5	12
Evan Eschmeyer	31	373	38	72	.528	15	30	.500	40	68	108	21	84	2	8	21	21	91	2.9	9
Jim McIlvaine	66	1048	64	154	.416	29	56	.518	106	124	230	36	205	2	26	38	117	157	2.4	8
Michael Cage	20	242	12	24	.500	3	3	1.000	33	48	81	9	30	0	8	4	8	27	1.4	6
Mark Hendrickson†	5	24	0	1	.000	1	2	.500	1	1	2	3	1	0	0	0	0	1	0.2	1
Mark Hendrickson‡	15	71	5	8	.625	3	4	.750	3	10	13	6	8	0	2	3	1	13	0.9	4

3-pt. FG: New Jersey 477-1374 (.347)—Marbury 66-233 (.283); Van Horn 84-228 (.368); Gill 20-78 (.256); Kittles 96-240 (.400); Newman 72-190 (.379); Douglas 5-16 (.313); Harris 38-115 (.330); Burrell 82-232 (.353); Feick 3-3 (1.000); Perry 11-39 (.282). Opponents 368-1013 (.363).

NEW YORK KNICKERBOCKERS

	G	Min.	FGM	FGA	Pct.	FTM	FTA	Pct.	Off.	Def.	Tot.	Ast.	PF	Dq.	Stl.	TO	Blk.	Pts.	Avg.	Hi.
Allan Houston	82	3169	614	1271	.483	280	334	.838	38	233	271	224	219	1	65	186	14	1614	19.7	37
Latrell Sprewell	82	3276	568	1305	.435	344	397	.866	49	300	349	332	184	0	109	226	22	1524	18.6	33
Patrick Ewing	62	2035	361	775	.466	207	283	.731	140	464	604	58	196	1	36	142	84	929	15.0	30
Larry Johnson	70	2281	282	652	.433	128	167	.766	87	293	380	175	205	1	42	94	7	750	10.7	24

	G	Min.	FGM	FGA	Pct.	FTM	FTA	Pct.	REBOUNDS Off.	Def.	Tot.	Ast.	PF	Dq.	Stl.	TO	Blk.	SCORING Pts.	Avg.	Hi.
Marcus Camby	59	1548	226	471	.480	148	221	.670	174	287	461	49	204	5	43	72	116	601	10.2	23
Kurt Thomas	80	1971	270	535	.505	100	128	.781	144	361	505	82	278	6	51	105	42	641	8.0	20
Charlie Ward	72	1986	189	447	.423	48	58	.828	22	206	228	300	176	3	95	102	16	528	7.3	25
John Wallace	60	798	155	332	.467	82	102	.804	42	93	135	22	103	0	10	63	14	392	6.5	20
Chris Childs	71	1675	146	357	.409	47	59	.797	17	130	147	285	240	4	36	105	4	376	5.3	16
Andrew Lang	19	244	28	64	.438	3	7	.429	16	44	60	3	31	0	8	5	6	59	3.1	10
Rick Brunson	37	289	29	70	.414	11	18	.611	3	24	27	49	35	0	9	31	1	71	1.9	9
Etdrick Bohannon*	2	5	0	0	...	3	4	.750	1	0	1	0	1	0	0	2	0	3	1.5	3
DeMarco Johnson	5	37	3	9	.333	0	0	...	3	4	7	0	5	0	1	3	0	6	1.2	4
Chris Dudley	47	459	23	67	.343	9	27	.333	63	73	136	5	95	2	7	18	21	55	1.2	7
Mirsad Turkcan*	7	25	2	10	.200	0	0	...	2	8	10	1	4	0	2	1	0	4	0.6	2
David Wingate	7	32	1	9	.111	0	0	...	1	1	2	3	7	0	1	2	2	2	0.3	2

3-pt. FG: New York 351-937 (.375)—Houston 106-243 (.436); Sprewell 44-127 (.346); Ewing 0-2 (.000); L. Johnson 58-174 (.333); Camby 1-2 (.500); Thomas 1-3 (.333); Ward 102-264 (.386); Wallace 0-3 (.000); Childs 37-104 (.356); Brunson 2-13 (.154); Turkcan* 0-2 (.000). Opponents 404-1197 (.338).

ORLANDO MAGIC

	G	Min.	FGM	FGA	Pct.	FTM	FTA	Pct.	REBOUNDS Off.	Def.	Tot.	Ast.	PF	Dq.	Stl.	TO	Blk.	SCORING Pts.	Avg.	Hi.
Ron Mercer†	31	969	188	468	.402	94	119	.790	35	63	98	54	76	2	42	64	8	470	15.2	27
Ron Mercer‡	68	2377	460	1080	.426	213	270	.789	64	186	250	158	151	2	75	151	23	1148	16.9	31
Darrell Armstrong	82	2590	484	1119	.433	225	247	.911	65	205	270	501	137	0	169	248	9	1330	16.2	33
Chris Gatling*	45	1041	210	462	.455	171	245	.698	91	206	297	40	142	0	48	105	10	598	13.3	31
Tariq Abdul-Wahad*	46	1205	223	515	.433	115	151	.762	77	162	239	72	116	1	53	87	16	563	12.2	23
John Amaechi	80	1684	306	700	.437	223	291	.766	62	204	266	95	161	1	35	139	37	836	10.5	31
Chucky Atkins	82	1626	314	741	.424	97	133	.729	20	106	126	306	137	1	52	142	3	782	9.5	22
Monty Williams	75	1501	263	538	.489	123	166	.741	96	154	250	106	187	1	46	109	17	651	8.7	19
Corey Maggette	77	1370	224	469	.478	196	261	.751	123	180	303	61	169	1	24	138	26	646	8.4	20
Pat Garrity	82	1479	258	585	.441	80	111	.721	44	166	210	58	197	1	31	85	19	675	8.2	32
Michael Doleac	81	1335	242	535	.452	80	95	.842	89	245	334	63	224	3	29	65	34	565	7.0	23
Earl Boykins*	1	8	3	4	.750	0	0	...	1	0	1	3	0	0	0	0	0	6	6.0	6
Charles Outlaw	82	2326	204	339	.602	82	162	.506	202	323	525	245	203	0	113	133	148	490	6.0	16
Ben Wallace	81	1959	168	334	.503	54	114	.474	211	454	665	67	162	0	72	67	130	390	4.8	14
Matt Harpring	4	63	4	17	.235	6	7	.857	5	7	12	8	7	0	5	1	1	16	4.0	16
Anthony Parker	16	185	24	57	.421	8	11	.727	5	22	27	10	13	0	8	11	4	57	3.6	8
Anthony Johnson†	18	214	26	61	.426	9	15	.600	6	6	12	13	17	0	10	8	2	62	3.4	12
Anthony Johnson‡	56	637	62	164	.378	28	39	.718	21	30	51	72	58	0	33	32	4	154	2.8	12
Derek Strong	20	148	21	48	.438	11	14	.786	11	33	44	4	15	0	5	12	2	54	2.7	13
Johnny Taylor†	5	29	5	12	.417	0	0	...	2	3	5	1	4	0	1	2	1	11	2.2	4
Johnny Taylor‡	6	34	5	14	.357	0	0	...	2	4	6	1	5	0	1	2	1	11	1.8	4
Kiwane Garris*	3	23	2	10	.200	0	0	...	1	0	1	1	2	0	0	1	0	4	1.3	4

3-pt. FG: Orlando 294-870 (.338)—Mercer† 0-9 (.000); Mercer‡ 15-48 (.313); Armstrong 137-403 (.340); Gatling* 7-23 (.304); Abdul-Wahad* 2-21 (.095); Amaechi 1-6 (.167); Atkins 57-163 (.350); Williams 2-5 (.400); Maggette 2-11 (.182); Garrity 79-197 (.401); Doleac 1-2 (.500); Outlaw 0-3 (.000); Harpring 2-2 (1.000); Parker 1-14 (.071); Johnson† 1-5 (.200); Johnson‡ 2-11 (.182); Strong 1-4 (.250); Taylor† 1-1 (1.000); Taylor‡ 1-1 (1.000); Garris 0-1 (.000). Opponents 431-1277 (.338).

PHILADELPHIA 76ERS

	G	Min.	FGM	FGA	Pct.	FTM	FTA	Pct.	REBOUNDS Off.	Def.	Tot.	Ast.	PF	Dq.	Stl.	TO	Blk.	SCORING Pts.	Avg.	Hi.
Allen Iverson	70	2853	729	1733	.421	442	620	.713	71	196	267	328	162	1	144	230	5	1989	28.4	50
Toni Kukoc†	32	916	149	340	.438	74	110	.673	38	105	143	141	61	0	33	71	9	398	12.4	23
Toni Kukoc‡	56	1784	297	728	.408	192	265	.725	75	198	273	265	112	0	77	146	28	830	14.8	33
Tyrone Hill	68	2155	318	656	.485	179	259	.691	220	405	625	52	243	3	64	124	27	815	12.0	22
Theo Ratliff	57	1795	247	491	.503	182	236	.771	140	295	435	36	185	4	32	108	171	676	11.9	25
Larry Hughes*	50	1018	192	461	.416	106	142	.746	52	107	159	75	94	0	54	95	12	501	10.0	27
Matt Geiger	65	1406	260	589	.441	109	140	.779	154	233	387	39	194	1	29	91	22	629	9.7	26
George Lynch	75	2416	297	644	.461	113	183	.617	216	366	582	136	231	2	119	120	38	722	9.6	26
Aaron McKie	82	1952	244	593	.411	121	146	.829	47	199	246	240	194	3	108	113	18	653	8.0	25
Eric Snow	82	2866	257	597	.430	126	177	.712	42	219	261	624	243	2	140	162	8	651	7.9	21
Billy Owens*	46	919	112	258	.434	38	64	.594	63	129	192	59	119	1	26	61	16	271	5.9	18
Todd MacCulloch	56	528	89	161	.553	28	54	.519	48	98	146	13	94	0	11	26	37	206	3.7	16
Stanley Roberts	5	51	5	16	.313	0	3	.000	6	9	15	3	15	0	1	2	1	10	2.0	4
Nazr Mohammed	28	190	21	54	.389	12	22	.545	16	34	50	2	29	0	4	18	12	54	1.9	7
Kevin Ollie	40	290	22	49	.449	28	37	.757	4	27	31	46	27	0	10	10	0	72	1.8	7
Jumaine Jones	33	138	22	58	.379	11	18	.611	16	22	38	5	10	0	6	14	5	57	1.7	6
Bruce Bowen*	42	311	26	73	.356	6	12	.500	14	22	36	16	37	0	9	5	5	59	1.4	10
Antonio Lang†	3	6	1	1	1.000	1	1	1.000	0	0	0	1	1	0	0	0	0	3	1.0	3
Antonio Lang‡	10	38	1	6	.167	4	5	.800	0	5	5	2	8	0	4	2	1	6	0.6	3
Ira Bowman	11	20	2	2	1.000	1	2	.500	0	2	2	1	0	0	1	0	0	5	0.5	2

3-pt. FG: Philadelphia 208-643 (.323)—Iverson 89-261 (.341); Kukoc† 26-90 (.289); Kukoc‡ 44-168 (.262); Hill 0-1 (.000); Hughes* 11-51 (.216); Geiger 0-4 (.000); Lynch 15-36 (.417); McKie 44-121 (.364); Snow 11-45 (.244); Owens* 9-27 (.333); Roberts 0-1 (.000); Jones 2-4 (.500); Bowen* 1-2 (.500). Opponents 417-1172 (.356).

1999-2000

PHOENIX SUNS

	G	Min.	FGM	FGA	Pct.	FTM	FTA	Pct.	Off.	Def.	Tot.	Ast.	PF	Dq.	Stl.	TO	Blk.	Pts.	Avg.	Hi.
									REBOUNDS									SCORING		
Clifford Robinson	80	2839	530	1142	.464	298	381	.782	105	254	359	224	239	3	90	166	61	1478	18.5	50
Anfernee Hardaway ...	60	2253	378	798	.474	226	286	.790	91	256	347	315	164	1	94	153	38	1015	16.9	33
Jason Kidd	67	2616	350	855	.409	203	245	.829	96	387	483	678	148	2	134	226	28	959	14.3	32
Rodney Rogers	82	2286	428	881	.486	159	249	.639	138	309	447	170	290	5	94	163	47	1130	13.8	36
Tom Gugliotta	54	1767	310	645	.481	117	151	.775	141	284	425	124	152	2	80	106	31	738	13.7	27
Shawn Marion.......	51	1260	222	471	.471	72	85	.847	105	227	332	69	113	0	38	51	53	520	10.2	27
Todd Day	58	941	130	330	.394	72	108	.667	31	98	129	65	127	1	44	50	22	396	6.8	20
Kevin Johnson	6	113	16	28	.571	7	7	1.000	0	16	16	24	6	0	2	7	0	40	6.7	14
Rex Chapman	53	957	124	320	.388	59	78	.756	10	70	80	62	70	0	22	38	1	348	6.6	29
Oliver Miller	51	1088	137	233	.588	49	73	.671	87	174	261	68	132	1	42	74	80	323	6.3	17
Luc Longley	72	1417	186	399	.466	80	97	.825	100	223	323	77	221	1	22	136	42	452	6.3	20
Randy Livingston	79	1081	155	373	.416	52	62	.839	25	105	130	170	129	1	49	92	13	381	4.8	23
Toby Bailey	46	449	58	140	.414	45	65	.692	26	46	72	30	55	0	13	24	4	163	3.5	12
Corie Blount	38	446	44	89	.494	19	33	.576	52	61	113	10	78	0	15	28	7	107	2.8	11
Don MacLean	16	143	18	49	.367	4	6	.667	6	17	23	8	24	0	2	8	1	42	2.6	13
Ben Davis	5	22	2	6	.333	0	0	...	3	6	9	2	2	0	1	3	1	4	0.8	4
Mark West	22	127	5	12	.417	5	8	.625	6	25	31	2	23	0	2	6	4	15	0.7	4

3-pt. FG: Phoenix 458-1246 (.368)—Robinson 120-324 (.370); Hardaway 33-102 (.324); Kidd 56-166 (.337); Rogers 115-262 (.439); Gugliotta 1-8 (.125); Marion 4-22 (.182); Day 64-165 (.388); Johnson 1-1 (1.000); Chapman 41-123 (.333); Livingston 19-55 (.345); Bailey 2-10 (.200); Blount 0-2 (.000); MacLean 2-6 (.333). Opponents 403-1146 (.352).

PORTLAND TRAIL BLAZERS

	G	Min.	FGM	FGA	Pct.	FTM	FTA	Pct.	Off.	Def.	Tot.	Ast.	PF	Dq.	Stl.	TO	Blk.	Pts.	Avg.	Hi.
									REBOUNDS									SCORING		
Rasheed Wallace.....	81	2845	542	1045	.519	233	331	.704	129	437	566	142	216	2	87	157	107	1325	16.4	34
Steve Smith	82	2689	420	900	.467	289	340	.850	123	190	313	209	214	0	71	117	31	1225	14.9	27
Damon Stoudamire ...	78	2372	386	894	.432	122	145	.841	61	182	243	405	173	0	77	149	1	974	12.5	31
Scottie Pippen.......	82	2749	388	860	.451	160	223	.717	114	399	513	406	208	0	117	208	41	1022	12.5	25
Arvydas Sabonis.....	66	1688	302	598	.505	167	198	.843	97	416	513	118	184	3	43	97	78	778	11.8	23
Bonzi Wells	66	1162	236	480	.492	88	129	.682	78	104	182	97	153	3	69	97	12	580	8.8	29
Detlef Schrempf	77	1662	187	433	.432	179	215	.833	79	253	332	197	182	0	37	100	17	574	7.5	22
Brian Grant	63	1322	173	352	.491	112	166	.675	121	223	344	64	166	2	32	84	28	459	7.3	21
Greg Anthony	82	1548	169	416	.406	88	114	.772	17	116	133	208	143	0	59	85	9	514	6.3	24
Gary Grant	3	24	6	14	.429	0	0	...	0	3	3	3	1	3	0	1	2	0	12	4.0	6
Jermaine O'Neal	70	859	108	222	.486	57	98	.582	97	132	229	18	127	1	11	47	55	273	3.9	17
Stacey Augmon......	59	692	83	175	.474	37	55	.673	42	74	116	53	69	0	27	38	11	203	3.4	12
Antonio Harvey......	19	137	17	30	.567	7	12	.583	8	25	33	5	20	0	1	12	6	41	2.2	9
Joe Kleine	7	31	4	11	.364	3	3	1.000	0	6	6	2	7	0	1	2	0	11	1.6	4

3-pt. FG: Portland 407-1128 (.361)—Wallace 8-50 (.160); Smith 96-241 (.398); Stoudamire 80-212 (.377); Pippen 86-263 (.327); Sabonis 7-19 (.368); Wells 20-53 (.377); Schrempf 21-52 (.404); B. Grant 1-2 (.500); Anthony 88-233 (.378); O'Neal 0-1 (.000); Augmon 0-2 (.000); Opponents 394-1195 (.330).

SACRAMENTO KINGS

	G	Min.	FGM	FGA	Pct.	FTM	FTA	Pct.	Off.	Def.	Tot.	Ast.	PF	Dq.	Stl.	TO	Blk.	Pts.	Avg.	Hi.
									REBOUNDS									SCORING		
Chris Webber	75	2880	748	1548	.483	311	414	.751	189	598	787	345	264	7	120	218	128	1834	24.5	39
Jason Williams	81	2760	363	973	.373	128	170	.753	22	208	230	589	140	0	117	296	8	999	12.3	28
Vlade Divac........	82	2374	384	764	.503	230	333	.691	174	482	656	244	251	2	103	190	103	1005	12.3	27
Predrag Stojakovic ...	74	1749	321	717	.448	135	153	.882	74	202	276	106	97	0	52	88	7	877	11.9	30
Nick Anderson	72	2094	306	782	.391	37	76	.487	83	256	339	123	118	0	94	95	16	781	10.8	29
Corliss Williamson ...	76	1707	311	622	.500	163	212	.769	122	168	290	82	192	0	38	110	19	785	10.3	28
Jon Barry	62	1281	161	346	.465	107	116	.922	38	121	159	150	104	1	75	85	7	495	8.0	19
Lawrence Funderburke	75	1026	184	352	.523	115	163	.706	98	136	234	33	91	0	32	40	20	483	6.4	18
Tony Delk	46	682	120	279	.430	47	59	.797	36	52	88	55	58	0	35	32	5	296	6.4	14
Darrick Martin.......	71	893	133	350	.380	98	119	.824	7	37	44	122	89	0	28	62	2	402	5.7	21
Scot Pollard	76	1336	149	283	.527	114	159	.717	168	236	404	43	213	3	55	50	59	412	5.4	17
Ryan Robertson	1	25	2	6	.333	1	1	1.000	0	0	0	0	0	0	0	0	0	5	5.0	5
Tyrone Corbin	54	941	88	247	.356	33	39	.846	40	125	165	60	99	2	36	29	5	219	4.1	14
Bill Wennington	7	57	6	19	.316	2	2	1.000	5	14	19	1	13	0	2	1	2	14	2.0	6

3-pt. FG: Sacramento 534-1656 (.322)—Webber 27-95 (.284); Williams 145-505 (.287); Divac 7-26 (.269); Stojakovic 100-267 (.375); Anderson 132-397 (.332); Barry 66-154 (.429); Funderburke 0-2 (.000); Delk 9-40 (.225); Martin 38-124 (.306); Robertson 0-2 (.000); Corbin 10-44 (.227). Opponents 396-1123 (.353).

SAN ANTONIO SPURS

	G	Min.	FGM	FGA	Pct.	FTM	FTA	Pct.	Off.	Def.	Tot.	Ast.	PF	Dq.	Stl.	TO	Blk.	Pts.	Avg.	Hi.
									REBOUNDS									SCORING		
Tim Duncan 74	74	2875	628	1281	.490	459	603	.761	262	656	918	234	210	1	66	242	165	1716	23.2	46
David Robinson 80	80	2557	528	1031	.512	371	511	.726	193	577	770	142	247	1	97	164	183	1427	17.8	38
Avery Johnson 82	82	2571	402	850	.473	114	155	.735	33	125	158	491	150	0	76	140	18	919	11.2	24
Terry Porter 68	68	1613	207	463	.447	137	170	.806	24	167	191	221	79	0	50	100	9	641	9.4	22
Mario Elie 79	79	2217	195	457	.427	126	149	.846	48	201	249	193	156	0	73	130	9	590	7.5	25
Malik Rose 74	74	1341	176	385	.457	143	198	.722	133	202	335	47	232	2	35	99	52	496	6.7	21
Chucky Brown* 30	30	602	82	176	.466	25	31	.806	11	66	77	41	53	0	8	28	10	190	6.3	16
Jaren Jackson 81	81	1691	186	488	.381	33	51	.647	34	147	181	118	157	1	54	66	7	513	6.3	23
Antonio Daniels. 68	68	1195	163	344	.474	72	101	.713	16	70	86	177	73	0	55	58	5	420	6.2	18
Sean Elliott 19	19	391	38	106	.358	25	32	.781	6	41	47	28	34	0	12	19	2	114	6.0	15
Samaki Walker 71	71	980	137	305	.449	86	126	.683	77	195	272	38	108	1	10	64	35	360	5.1	18
Derrick Dial. 8	8	95	17	46	.370	3	5	.600	14	12	26	5	10	0	1	6	1	40	5.0	9
Jerome Kersey 72	72	1310	146	354	.412	29	41	.707	58	167	225	69	161	0	67	51	47	321	4.5	14
Steve Kerr. 32	32	268	32	74	.432	9	11	.818	3	16	19	12	14	0	4	7	0	89	2.8	9
Felton Spencer 26	26	149	15	33	.455	20	30	.667	15	24	39	3	32	0	6	9	8	50	1.9	5

3-pt. FG: San Antonio 330-882 (.374)—Duncan 1-11 (.091); Robinson 0-2 (.000); Johnson 1-9 (.111); Porter 90-207 (.435); Elie 74-186 (.398); Rose 1-3 (.333); Brown* 1-3 (.333); Jackson 108-306 (.353); Daniels 22-66 (.333); Elliott 13-37 (.351); Dial 3-12 (.250); Kersey 0-9 (.000); Kerr 16-31 (.516). Opponents 355-1036 (.343).

SEATTLE SUPERSONICS

	G	Min.	FGM	FGA	Pct.	FTM	FTA	Pct.	Off.	Def.	Tot.	Ast.	PF	Dq.	Stl.	TO	Blk.	Pts.	Avg.	Hi.
									REBOUNDS									SCORING		
Gary Payton 82	82	3425	747	1666	.448	311	423	.735	100	429	529	732	178	0	153	224	18	1982	24.2	43
Vin Baker 79	79	2849	514	1129	.455	281	412	.682	227	378	605	148	288	6	47	213	66	1311	16.6	33
Brent Barry 80	80	2726	327	707	.463	127	157	.809	50	322	372	291	228	4	103	142	31	945	11.8	24
Ruben Patterson 81	81	2097	354	661	.536	222	321	.692	218	216	434	126	190	0	94	144	40	942	11.6	32
Vernon Maxwell 47	47	989	169	490	.345	108	148	.730	15	64	79	75	83	0	38	53	9	513	10.9	29
Rashard Lewis 82	82	1575	275	566	.486	84	123	.683	127	209	336	70	163	0	62	78	36	674	8.2	30
Horace Grant 76	76	2688	266	599	.444	80	111	.721	167	424	591	188	192	0	55	61	60	612	8.1	26
Shammond Williams . . 43	43	517	84	225	.373	33	51	.647	12	40	52	78	39	0	10	40	0	225	5.2	28
Jelani McCoy 58	58	746	102	177	.576	45	91	.495	54	125	179	24	127	0	15	45	46	249	4.3	15
Emanual Davis 54	54	701	80	220	.364	26	38	.684	15	85	100	70	72	0	38	44	5	217	4.0	18
Lazaro Borrell 17	17	167	28	63	.444	6	11	.545	14	26	40	10	9	0	6	6	3	62	3.6	15
Greg Foster 60	60	718	91	224	.406	18	28	.643	16	91	107	41	105	0	10	28	18	203	3.4	17
Chuck Person 37	37	340	37	123	.301	4	8	.500	6	47	53	22	56	1	5	12	2	102	2.8	9
Vladimir Stepania 30	30	202	29	79	.367	17	36	.472	21	26	47	3	44	0	10	22	11	75	2.5	11
Fred Vinson 8	8	40	5	17	.294	1	2	.500	0	1	1	2	0	3	4	0	0	13	1.6	7

3-pt. FG: Seattle 546-1611 (.339)—Payton 177-520 (.340); Baker 2-8 (.250); Barry 164-399 (.411); Patterson 12-27 (.444); Maxwell 67-223 (.300); Lewis 40-120 (.333); Grant 0-4 (.000); Williams 24-81 (.296); Davis 31-103 (.301); Borrell 0-3 (.000); Foster 3-15 (.200); Person 24-95 (.253); Stepania 0-6 (.000); Vinson 2-7 (.286). Opponents 440-1293 (.340).

TORONTO RAPTORS

	G	Min.	FGM	FGA	Pct.	FTM	FTA	Pct.	Off.	Def.	Tot.	Ast.	PF	Dq.	Stl.	TO	Blk.	Pts.	Avg.	Hi.
									REBOUNDS									SCORING		
Vince Carter 82	82	3126	788	1696	.465	436	551	.791	150	326	476	322	263	2	110	178	92	2107	25.7	51
Tracy McGrady 79	79	2462	459	1018	.451	277	392	.707	188	313	501	263	201	2	90	160	151	1213	15.4	28
Doug Christie 73	73	2264	311	764	.407	182	216	.843	63	222	285	321	167	1	102	144	43	903	12.4	31
Antonio Davis 79	79	2479	313	712	.440	284	371	.765	235	461	696	105	267	2	38	121	100	910	11.5	28
Kevin Willis. 79	79	1679	236	569	.415	131	164	.799	201	281	482	49	256	3	36	98	48	604	7.6	21
Dell Curry 67	67	1095	194	454	.427	24	32	.750	11	89	100	89	66	0	32	40	9	507	7.6	17
Dee Brown 38	38	673	93	258	.360	11	16	.688	9	45	54	86	62	1	24	39	5	264	6.9	19
Charles Oakley 80	80	2431	234	560	.418	66	85	.776	117	423	540	253	294	6	102	154	45	548	6.9	20
Alvin Williams 55	55	779	114	287	.397	48	65	.738	27	58	85	126	78	0	34	47	11	292	5.3	17
Muggsy Bogues 80	80	1731	157	358	.439	79	87	.908	25	110	135	299	119	0	65	59	4	410	5.1	24
Haywoode Workman† . 13	13	102	8	28	.286	1	2	.500	0	9	9	17	14	1	9	4	0	20	1.5	10
Haywoode Workman‡ . 36	36	350	31	90	.344	10	15	.667	1	25	26	61	37	1	20	18	0	86	2.4	14
Aleksandar Radojevic . . 3	3	24	2	7	.286	3	6	.500	2	6	8	1	5	0	2	5	1	7	2.3	6
John Thomas 55	55	477	49	107	.458	16	41	.390	37	38	75	9	106	1	12	14	14	114	2.1	11
Sean Marks 5	5	12	2	6	.333	4	4	1.000	0	2	2	0	3	0	1	3	1	8	1.6	4
Michael Stewart 42	42	389	20	53	.377	18	32	.563	33	61	94	6	81	3	5	17	19	58	1.4	11
Antonio Lang* 7	7	32	0	5	.000	3	4	.750	0	5	5	1	7	0	4	2	1	3	0.4	2

3-pt. FG: Toronto 425-1171 (.363)—Carter 95-236 (.403); McGrady 18-65 (.277); Christie 99-275 (.360); Willis 1-3 (.333); Curry 95-242 (.393); Brown 67-187 (.358); Oakley 14-41 (.341); Williams 16-55 (.291); Bogues 17-51 (.333); Workman† 3-14 (.214); Workman‡ 14-43 (.326); Marks 0-1 (.000); Thomas 0-1 (.000). Opponents 346-1021 (.339).

1999-2000

UTAH JAZZ

	G	Min.	FGM	FGA	Pct.	FTM	FTA	Pct.	Off.	Def.	Tot.	Ast.	PF	Dq.	Stl.	TO	Blk.	Pts.	Avg.	Hi.
									REBOUNDS									SCORING		
Karl Malone	82	2947	752	1476	.509	589	739	.797	169	610	779	304	229	1	79	231	71	2095	25.5	40
Bryon Russell	82	2900	408	914	.446	237	316	.750	99	328	427	158	255	3	128	101	23	1159	14.1	25
Jeff Hornacek	77	2133	358	728	.492	171	180	.950	49	133	182	202	149	1	66	113	16	953	12.4	27
John Stockton	82	2432	363	725	.501	221	257	.860	45	170	215	703	192	0	143	179	15	990	12.1	23
Howard Eisley	82	2096	282	675	.418	84	102	.824	23	147	170	347	223	2	59	132	9	708	8.6	23
Armen Gilliam	50	782	133	305	.436	67	86	.779	72	137	209	42	83	0	12	55	16	333	6.7	19
Olden Polynice	82	1819	203	398	.510	28	90	.311	166	287	453	37	260	1	30	70	84	435	5.3	13
Greg Ostertag	81	1606	124	267	.464	119	187	.636	172	310	482	18	196	2	20	79	172	367	4.5	11
Quincy Lewis	74	896	111	298	.372	38	52	.731	46	67	113	40	158	0	24	46	15	283	3.8	14
Jacque Vaughn	78	884	109	262	.416	57	76	.750	11	54	65	121	92	0	32	77	0	289	3.7	12
Scott Padgett	47	432	44	140	.314	19	27	.704	24	64	88	25	55	1	14	22	8	120	2.6	16
Adam Keefe	62	604	53	130	.408	29	36	.806	45	91	136	34	90	0	17	46	13	135	2.2	9
Pete Chilcutt*	26	224	22	62	.355	2	2	1.000	15	28	43	10	31	0	5	9	4	47	1.8	7

3-pt. FG: Utah 329-854 (.385)—Malone 2-8 (.250); Russell 106-268 (.396); Hornacek 66-138 (.478); Stockton 43-121 (.355); Eisley 60-163 (.368); Keefe 0-1 (.000); Gilliam 0-1 (.000); Polynice 1-2 (.500); Ostertag 0-1 (.000); Lewis 23-63 (.365); Vaughn 14-34 (.412); Padgett 13-44 (.295); Chilcutt* 1-10 (.100). Opponents 388-1097 (.354).

VANCOUVER GRIZZLIES

	G	Min.	FGM	FGA	Pct.	FTM	FTA	Pct.	Off.	Def.	Tot.	Ast.	PF	Dq.	Stl.	TO	Blk.	Pts.	Avg.	Hi.
									REBOUNDS									SCORING		
Shareef Abdur-Rahim	82	3223	594	1277	.465	446	551	.809	218	607	825	271	244	3	89	249	87	1663	20.3	36
Michael Dickerson	82	3103	554	1270	.436	269	324	.830	78	201	279	208	226	0	116	165	45	1496	18.2	40
Mike Bibby	82	3155	459	1031	.445	195	250	.780	73	233	306	665	171	1	132	247	15	1190	14.5	33
Othella Harrington	82	2677	420	830	.506	236	298	.792	196	367	563	97	287	3	36	217	58	1076	13.1	27
Bryant Reeves	69	1773	252	562	.448	107	165	.648	126	264	390	82	245	8	33	119	38	611	8.9	31
Dennis Scott	66	1263	125	333	.375	48	57	.842	16	90	106	69	104	0	28	30	9	369	5.6	16
Grant Long	42	920	74	167	.443	55	71	.775	86	148	234	43	108	1	45	49	10	203	4.8	13
Felipe Lopez	65	781	111	261	.425	67	109	.615	59	65	124	44	94	0	32	53	17	292	4.5	14
Doug West	38	581	59	145	.407	34	40	.850	18	53	71	43	80	1	12	19	8	152	4.0	12
Brent Price	41	424	41	119	.345	34	39	.872	8	29	37	69	63	0	17	47	1	141	3.4	13
Obinna Ekezie	39	351	41	88	.466	43	64	.672	34	58	92	8	61	0	9	26	4	125	3.2	11
Antoine Carr	21	221	28	64	.438	11	14	.786	8	24	32	7	42	0	3	9	6	67	3.2	12
Joe Stephens	13	181	19	51	.373	3	4	.750	13	23	36	11	9	0	7	6	3	41	3.2	10
Cherokee Parks	56	808	72	145	.497	24	37	.649	55	128	183	35	115	2	29	28	45	168	3.0	12
Milt Palacio	53	394	43	98	.439	22	37	.595	17	34	51	48	32	0	20	44	0	108	2.0	11

3-pt. FG: Vancouver 324-898 (.361)—Abdur-Rahim 29-96 (.302); Dickerson 119-291 (.409); Bibby 77-212 (.363); Harrington 0-2 (.000); Reeves 0-4 (.000); Long 0-4 (.000); Scott 71-189 (.376); Lopez 3-18 (.167); West 0-3 (.000); Price 25-68 (.368); Stephens 0-8 (.000); Parks 0-1 (.000); Palacio 0-2 (.000). Opponents 361-1083 (.333).

WASHINGTON WIZARDS

	G	Min.	FGM	FGA	Pct.	FTM	FTA	Pct.	Off.	Def.	Tot.	Ast.	PF	Dq.	Stl.	TO	Blk.	Pts.	Avg.	Hi.
									REBOUNDS									SCORING		
Mitch Richmond	74	2397	447	1049	.426	298	340	.876	37	176	213	185	191	2	110	154	13	1285	17.4	33
Juwan Howard	82	2909	509	1108	.459	202	275	.735	132	338	470	247	299	2	67	225	21	1220	14.9	36
Rod Strickland	69	2188	327	762	.429	214	305	.702	73	186	259	519	147	1	94	187	18	869	12.6	27
Tracy Murray	80	1831	290	670	.433	120	141	.851	63	208	271	72	185	2	45	84	24	813	10.2	27
Richard Hamilton	71	1373	254	605	.420	103	133	.774	38	91	129	108	142	2	28	84	6	639	9.0	26
Chris Whitney	82	1627	217	521	.417	112	132	.848	20	114	134	313	166	1	55	107	5	642	7.8	29
Aaron Williams	81	1545	235	450	.522	146	201	.726	159	250	409	58	234	3	41	80	92	616	7.6	27
Jahidi White	80	1537	228	450	.507	113	211	.536	202	351	553	15	234	2	31	94	83	569	7.1	23
Isaac Austin	59	1173	151	352	.429	94	137	.686	64	218	282	74	128	0	17	107	38	397	6.7	20
Michael Smith	46	1145	108	192	.563	73	101	.723	121	210	331	56	127	0	27	45	23	289	6.3	20
Gerard King	62	1060	139	277	.502	49	66	.742	84	166	250	49	132	1	34	41	15	327	5.3	20
Calvin Booth	11	143	16	46	.348	10	14	.714	15	17	32	7	23	0	3	6	14	42	3.8	10
Don Reid†	17	333	44	78	.564	21	28	.750	26	51	77	10	73	4	19	12	19	109	6.4	15
Don Reid‡	38	498	60	112	.536	24	34	.706	31	71	102	11	118	5	24	23	31	144	3.8	15
Lorenzo Williams	8	76	7	9	.778	0	0	...	12	13	25	1	13	0	3	3	6	14	1.8	4
Laron Profit	33	225	21	59	.356	4	10	.400	2	24	26	25	26	0	7	19	4	49	1.5	10
Reggie Jordan	36	243	17	53	.321	7	13	.538	16	25	41	32	29	0	12	19	2	41	1.1	7

3-pt. FG: Washington 335-890 (.376)—Richmond 93-241 (.386); Howard 0-7 (.000); Strickland 1-21 (.048); Murray 113-263 (.430); Hamilton 28-77 (.364); Austin 1-4 (.250); Whitney 96-255 (.376); A. Williams 0-3 (.000); Smith 0-1 (.000); Profit 3-17 (.176); Jordan 0-1 (.000). Opponents 390-1052 (.371).

* Finished season with another team. † Totals with this team only. ‡ Totals with all teams.

PLAYOFFS
RESULTS

EASTERN CONFERENCE
FIRST ROUND

Indiana 3, Milwaukee 2

Apr. 23—Sun.	Milwaukee 85 at Indiana	.88
Apr. 27—Thur.	Milwaukee 104 at Indiana	.91
Apr. 29—Sat.	Indiana 109 at Milwaukee	.96
May 1—Mon.	Indiana 87 at Milwaukee	.100
May 4—Thur.	Milwaukee 95 at Indiana	.96

Philadelphia 3, Charlotte 1

Apr. 22—Sat.	Philadelphia 92 at Charlotte	.82
Apr. 24—Mon.	Philadelphia 98 at Charlotte	*108
Apr. 28—Fri.	Charlotte 76 at Philadelphia	.81
May 1—Mon.	Charlotte 99 at Philadelphia	.105

New York 3, Toronto 0

Apr. 23—Sun.	Toronto 88 at New York	.92
Apr. 26—Wed.	Toronto 83 at New York	.84
Apr. 30—Sun.	New York 87 at Toronto	.80

Miami 3, Detroit 0

Apr. 22—Sat.	Detroit 85 at Miami	.95
Apr. 25—Tue.	Detroit 82 at Miami	.84
Apr. 29—Sat.	Miami 91 at Detroit	.72

SEMIFINALS

Indiana 4, Philadelphia 2

May 6—Sat.	Philadelphia 91 at Indiana	.108
May 8—Mon.	Philadelphia 97 at Indiana	.103
May 10—Wed.	Indiana 97 at Philadelphia	.89
May 13—Sat.	Indiana 90 at Philadelphia	.92
May 15—Mon.	Philadelphia 107 at Indiana	.86
May 19—Fri.	Indiana 106 at Philadelphia	.90

New York 4, Miami 3

May 7—Sun.	New York 83 at Miami	.87
May 9—Tue.	New York 82 at Miami	.76
May 12—Fri.	Miami 77 at New York	*76
May 14—Sun.	Miami 83 at New York	.91
May 17—Wed.	New York 81 at Miami	.87
May 19—Fri.	Miami 70 at New York	.72
May 21—Sun.	New York 83 at Miami	.82

FINALS

Indiana 4, New York 2

May 23—Tue.	New York 88 at Indiana	.102
May 25—Thur.	New York 84 at Indiana	.88
May 27—Sat.	Indiana 95 at New York	.98
May 29—Mon.	Indiana 89 at New York	.91
May 31—Wed.	New York 79 at Indiana	.88
June 2—Fri.	Indiana 93 at New York	.80

WESTERN CONFERENCE
FIRST ROUND

L.A. Lakers 3, Sacramento 2

Apr. 23—Sun.	Sacramento 107 at L.A. Lakers	.117
Apr. 27—Thur.	Sacramento 89 at L.A. Lakers	.113
Apr. 30—Sun.	L.A. Lakers 91 at Sacramento	.99
May 2—Tue.	L.A. Lakers 88 at Sacramento	.101
May 5—Fri.	Sacramento 86 at L.A. Lakers	.113

Phoenix 3, San Antonio 1

Apr. 22—Sat.	Phoenix 72 at San Antonio	.70
Apr. 25—Tue.	Phoenix 70 at San Antonio	.85
Apr. 29—Sat.	San Antonio 94 at Phoenix	.101
May 2—Tue.	San Antonio 78 at Phoenix	.89

Portland 3, Minnesota 1

Apr. 23—Sun.	Minnesota 88 at Portland	.91
Apr. 26—Wed.	Minnesota 82 at Portland	.86
Apr. 30—Sun.	Portland 87 at Minnesota	.94
May 2—Tue.	Portland 85 at Minnesota	.77

Utah 3, Seattle 2

Apr. 22—Sat.	Seattle 93 at Utah	.104
Apr. 24—Mon.	Seattle 87 at Utah	.101
Apr. 29—Sat.	Utah 78 at Seattle	.89
May 3—Wed.	Utah 93 at Seattle	.104
May 5—Fri.	Seattle 93 at Utah	.96

SEMIFINALS

L.A. Lakers 4, Phoenix 1

May 7—Sun.	Phoenix 77 at L.A. Lakers	.105
May 10—Wed.	Phoenix 96 at L.A. Lakers	.97
May 12—Fri.	L.A. Lakers 105 at Phoenix	.99
May 14—Sun.	L.A. Lakers 98 at Phoenix	.117
May 16—Tue.	Phoenix 65 at L.A. Lakers	.87

Portland 4, Utah 1

May 7—Sun.	Utah 75 at Portland	.94
May 9—Tue.	Utah 85 at Portland	.103
May 11—Thur.	Portland 103 at Utah	.84
May 14—Sun.	Portland 85 at Utah	.88
May 16—Tue.	Utah 79 at Portland	.81

FINALS

L.A. Lakers 4, Portland 3

May 20—Sat.	Portland 94 at L.A. Lakers	.109
May 22—Mon.	Portland 106 at L.A. Lakers	.77
May 26—Fri.	L.A. Lakers 93 at Portland	.91
May 28—Sun.	L.A. Lakers 103 at Portland	.91
May 30—Tue.	Portland 96 at L.A. Lakers	.88
June 2—Fri.	L.A. Lakers 93 at Portland	.103
June 4—Sun.	Portland 84 at L.A. Lakers	.89

NBA FINALS

L.A. Lakers 4, Indiana 2

June 7—Wed.	Indiana 87 at L.A. Lakers	.104
June 9—Fri.	Indiana 104 at L.A. Lakers	.111
June 11—Sun.	L.A. Lakers 91 at Indiana	.100
June 14—Wed.	L.A. Lakers 120 at Indiana	*118
June 16—Fri.	L.A. Lakers 87 at Indiana	.120
June 19—Mon.	Indiana 111 at L.A. Lakers	.116

*Denotes number of overtime periods.

1999-2000

1998-99

1998-99 NBA CHAMPION SAN ANTONIO SPURS

Front row (from left): chairman Peter M. Holt, Andrew Gaze, Antonio Daniels, Steve Kerr, Avery Johnson, Jaren Jackson, Mario Elie, Brandon Williams, executive VP/business operations Russ Bookbinder, Sr. VP/Broadcasting Lawrence Payne. Center row (from left): assistant video coordinator Marty Verdugo, strength & conditioning coach Mike Brungardt, equipment manager Clarence Rinehart. Back row (from left): video coordinator Joe Prunty, assistant coach Mike Budenholzer, head coach & general manager Gregg Popovich, Jerome Kersey, Gerard King, Will Perdue, David Robinson, Tim Duncan, Sean Elliott, Malik Rose, assistant coach Paul Pressey, assistant coach Hank Egan, head athletic trainer Will Sevening.

FINAL STANDINGS

ATLANTIC DIVISION

	Atl.	Bos.	Cha.	Chi.	Cle.	Dal.	Den.	Det.	G.S.	Hou.	Ind.	LA-C	LA-L	Mia.	Mil.	Min.	N.J.	N.Y.	Orl.	Phi.	Pho.	Por.	Sac.	S.A.	Sea.	Tor.	Uta.	Van.	Was.	W	L	Pct.	GB
Mia.	..3	0	2	2	3	1	1	1	0	1	2	0	0	..	2	0	3	2	2	2	0	0	0	0	0	3	0	0	3	33	17	.660	-
Orl.	2	2	2	3	2	0	0	4	1	1	2	0	0	1	2	0	3	3	..	1	0	0	1	0	0	1	0	0	2	33	17	.660	-
Phi.	1	2	2	2	2	0	0	3	0	0	2	0	1	1	2	0	2	1	2	.	0	0	1	0	0	2	0	1	1	28	22	.560	5
N.Y.	1	2	3	2	2	0	0	1	0	0	1	1	0	2	1	1	3	..	0	3	1	0	0	0	0	1	0	0	2	27	23	.540	6
Bos.	..0	..	1	2	2	0	1	0	0	0	0	1	0	3	0	0	1	1	1	1	0	0	0	0	0	1	0	1	3	19	31	.380	14
Was.	..1	1	1	2	2	0	1	1	0	0	0	0	0	1	1	1	2	0	0	0	0	1	2	0	0	..				18	32	.360	15
N.J.	2	2	0	1	0	1	0	1	0	0	1	0	0	1	1	0	..	0	0	1	0	0	0	0	1	2	0	0	2	16	34	.320	17

CENTRAL DIVISION

	Atl.	Bos.	Cha.	Chi.	Cle.	Dal.	Den.	Det.	G.S.	Hou.	Ind.	LA-C	LA-L	Mia.	Mil.	Min.	N.J.	N.Y.	Orl.	Phi.	Pho.	Por.	Sac.	S.A.	Sea.	Tor.	Uta.	Van.	Was.	W	L	Pct.	GB
Ind.	1	3	2	3	3	0	1	1	0	0	..	0	1	2	3	0	3	2	1	1	0	0	0	0	2	0	1	3		33	17	.660	-
Atl.	......	3	3	3	2	0	0	1	0	1	3	1	0	0	1	0	1	2	2	2	1	0	0	0	2	0	1	2	31	19	.620	2
Det.	...2	3	0	3	2	1	0	..	0	0	2	0	0	2	2	0	2	2	0	1	1	0	0	0	1	2	1	0	2	29	21	.580	4
Mil.	...2	3	2	3	2	0	0	1	1	0	0	0	0	1	..	1	2	2	1	1	0	0	0	0	1	3	0	0	2	28	22	.560	5
Cha.	..0	2	..	2	2	0	0	3	0	0	1	0	0	1	2	0	3	1	1	1	1	0	0	0	2	1	0	2	2	26	24	.520	7
Tor.	...1	2	1	2	2	0	0	1	1	0	0	1	1	1	2	2	1	0	0	0	0	1	0	..	0	1	2			23	27	.460	10
Cle.	...1	2	1	3	..	0	0	1	1	0	0	1	0	1	0	3	1	1	1	1	0	0	1	0	2	0	0	1	1	22	28	.440	11
Chi.	...1	1	1	..	0	0	0	0	0	0	1	0	1	1	0	2	1	1	0	0	0	0	0	0	1	0	1	1	1	13	37	.260	20

MIDWEST DIVISION

	Atl.	Bos.	Cha.	Chi.	Cle.	Dal.	Den.	Det.	G.S.	Hou.	Ind.	LA-C	LA-L	Mia.	Mil.	Min.	N.J.	N.Y.	Orl.	Phi.	Pho.	Por.	Sac.	S.A.	Sea.	Tor.	Uta.	Van.	Was.	W	L	Pct.	GB
S.A.	0	0	0	1	0	3	4	1	3	3	0	3	1	0	0	2	0	0	1	1	2	3	2	..	2	0	2	3	0	37	13	.740	-
Utah	...0	0	0	1	1	3	2	0	4	3	0	3	3	1	0	3	0	0	0	0	2	2	2	1	2	0	..	3	1	37	13	.740	-
Hou.	..0	0	0	0	1	2	4	0	3	..	0	3	1	0	0	2	1	0	0	0	2	2	3	0	2	1	0	4	0	31	19	.620	6
Min.	..0	1	0	0	0	2	3	1	2	1	0	2	1	1	1	..	0	0	0	0	1	0	3	2	2	0	0	3	0	25	25	.500	12
Dal.	1	0	0	1	0	..	2	0	2	2	0	3	0	0	0	1	0	0	1	0	1	0	2	1	0	0	0	2	0	19	31	.380	18
Den.	..0	0	0	0	0	1	..	0	1	0	0	3	1	0	1	0	1	0	0	0	0	0	2	0	1	3	0			14	36	.280	23
Van.	..0	0	0	0	0	1	1	0	0	0	0	3	1	0	0	1	0	0	0	0	0	0	0	0	1	0	0	..	0	8	42	.160	29

PACIFIC DIVISION

	Atl.	Bos.	Cha.	Chi.	Cle.	Dal.	Den.	Det.	G.S.	Hou.	Ind.	LA-C	LA-L	Mia.	Mil.	Min.	N.J.	N.Y.	Orl.	Phi.	Pho.	Por.	Sac.	S.A.	Sea.	Tor.	Uta.	Van.	Was.	W	L	Pct.	GB
Por.	0	1	0	0	0	3	3	0	2	1	1	2	0	0	0	3	1	0	0	1	3	..	4	1	2	0	1	3	1	35	15	.700	-
L.A.L.	0	0	1	0	0	3	2	0	2	2	0	4	..	0	0	2	0	1	1	0	3	2	1	2	2	0	1	2	0	31	19	.620	4
Pho.	..0	0	0	0	0	3	3	0	2	2	0	3	1	0	1	2	0	0	0	0	..	0	0	2	3	0	2	3	0	27	23	.540	8
Sac.	..0	1	1	0	0	2	3	0	2	0	0	2	0	0	1	0	1	0	0	3	0	..	1	2	0	1	4	1		27	23	.540	8
Sea.	..0	0	0	1	0	3	2	0	2	1	0	3	2	0	0	1	0	0	0	1	0	2	2	1	..	0	2	2	0	25	25	.500	10
G.S.	..0	0	1	0	0	2	3	0	..	0	1	2	1	0	0	2	0	0	0	1	2	1	0	1	0	0	3	1		21	29	.420	14
L.A.C.	0	0	0	0	0	0	0	0	1	1	0	..	0	0	0	2	1	0	0	0	1	1	0	0	0	1	1	0		9	41	.180	26

OFFENSIVE

	G	FGM	FGA	Pct.	FTM	FTA	Pct.	REBOUNDS Off.	Def.	Tot.	Ast.	PF	Dq.	Stl.	TO	Blk.	SCORING Pts.	Avg.
Sacramento ...	50	1918	4307	.445	883	1293	.683	706	1573	2279	1129	1016	6	444	842	232	5009	100.2
L.A. Lakers....	50	1841	3935	.468	1027	1503	.683	619	1482	2101	1095	1231	16	389	754	287	4950	99.0
Phoenix	50	1797	4004	.449	924	1215	.760	598	1418	2016	1249	1022	4	444	681	200	4779	95.6
Seattle	50	1756	3976	.442	922	1354	.681	676	1422	2098	1087	1047	5	393	765	201	4743	94.9
Portland......	50	1747	3956	.442	1002	1349	.743	646	1570	2216	1073	1126	14	411	771	290	4742	94.8
Indiana......	50	1731	3866	.448	977	1228	.796	574	1452	2026	1005	1082	7	316	649	223	4733	94.7
Houston......	50	1755	3798	.462	865	1187	.729	536	1539	2075	1058	960	5	386	812	260	4711	94.2
Denver.......	50	1681	3989	.421	1010	1325	.762	647	1392	2039	969	1144	19	376	739	275	4674	93.5
Utah........	50	1684	3620	.465	1158	1510	.767	555	1508	2063	1204	1133	6	398	814	276	4666	93.3
Boston.......	50	1816	4164	.436	745	1077	.692	680	1458	2138	1073	1193	15	453	807	255	4650	93.0
Minnesota	50	1838	4327	.425	849	1143	.743	754	1392	2146	1218	1185	13	426	641	272	4647	92.9
Charlotte	50	1671	3718	.449	1034	1384	.747	480	1493	1973	1110	1101	9	443	796	247	4644	92.9
San Antonio ...	50	1740	3812	.456	988	1415	.698	614	1584	2198	1101	1010	4	421	759	351	4640	92.8
Milwaukee	50	1753	3818	.459	847	1155	.733	570	1369	1939	1030	1142	8	442	719	202	4584	91.7
Dallas.......	50	1749	4033	.434	881	1210	.728	645	1478	2123	921	1065	16	352	692	292	4581	91.6
New Jersey ...	50	1691	4160	.406	962	1251	.769	715	1437	2152	923	1134	15	491	750	273	4569	91.4
Washington ...	50	1768	3969	.445	845	1198	.705	595	1403	1998	1064	1151	12	393	736	193	4560	91.2
Toronto	50	1660	3940	.421	1011	1330	.760	712	1447	2159	1036	1139	10	439	799	321	4557	91.1
L.A. Clippers ..	50	1711	4007	.427	883	1225	.721	665	1293	1958	820	1223	17	424	796	236	4519	90.4
Detroit.......	50	1660	3716	.447	950	1283	.740	605	1412	2017	1009	1139	8	444	790	208	4518	90.4
Philadelphia ...	50	1656	3883	.426	1073	1486	.722	729	1428	2157	934	1152	18	542	822	271	4483	89.7
Orlando	50	1687	3943	.428	876	1252	.700	688	1445	2133	1067	935	3	496	819	213	4473	89.5
Miami	50	1616	3565	.453	928	1262	.735	503	1512	2015	1019	1035	6	327	744	304	4449	89.0
Vancouver	50	1643	3838	.428	1009	1408	.717	650	1359	2009	964	1123	7	420	848	199	4443	88.9
Golden State ..	50	1730	4173	.415	794	1175	.676	816	1559	2375	1037	1270	15	414	768	221	4416	88.3
Cleveland.....	50	1562	3561	.439	1016	1356	.749	472	1316	1788	1093	1208	13	452	785	203	4322	86.4
New York.....	50	1610	3704	.435	892	1218	.732	551	1510	2061	963	1140	9	395	804	262	4320	86.4
Atlanta.......	50	1539	3760	.409	1040	1422	.731	676	1499	2175	782	987	7	346	745	260	4315	86.3
Chicago......	50	1539	3837	.401	840	1185	.709	573	1394	1967	1017	1112	7	436	774	169	4095	81.9

DEFENSIVE

	FGM	FGA	Pct.	FTM	FTA	Pct.	REBOUNDS Off.	Def.	Tot.	Ast.	PF	Dq.	Stl.	TO	Blk.	SCORING Pts.	Avg.	Dif.
Atlanta........	1598	3873	.413	784	1076	.729	581	1369	1950	895	1202	10	379	675	243	4170	83.4	+2.9
Miami	1565	3805	.411	860	1167	.737	619	1342	1961	853	1102	9	387	677	188	4201	84.0	+5.0
San Antonio ...	1631	4061	.402	805	1148	.701	696	1406	2102	941	1148	19	437	730	243	4237	84.7	+8.1
New York......	1528	3790	.403	979	1335	.733	616	1426	2042	923	1035	1	425	766	215	4269	85.4	+1.0
Utah	1595	3863	.413	936	1299	.721	635	1294	1929	904	1309	29	431	744	264	4340	86.8	+6.5
Orlando	1708	3856	.443	697	986	.707	595	1424	2019	1039	1111	5	468	863	239	4343	86.9	+2.6
Detroit........	1585	3639	.436	941	1317	.715	548	1377	1925	1043	1113	14	424	770	225	4347	86.9	+3.4
Philadelphia....	1599	3784	.423	941	1288	.731	619	1402	2021	999	1185	13	435	896	263	4380	87.6	+2.1
Cleveland.....	1597	3664	.436	978	1316	.743	591	1405	1996	1056	1198	14	392	821	282	4408	88.2	-1.7
Portland	1644	3939	.417	916	1263	.725	616	1388	2004	962	1142	10	411	785	244	4424	88.5	+6.4
Milwaukee.....	1600	3746	.427	1029	1369	.752	657	1398	2055	1018	1020	4	399	830	194	4501	90.0	+1.7
Golden State ..	1617	3848	.420	1114	1531	.728	656	1503	2159	1023	1027	8	400	735	304	4541	90.8	-2.5
Indiana	1706	3935	.434	928	1227	.756	626	1426	2052	955	1127	8	357	652	238	4546	90.9	+3.7
Chicago.......	1723	3786	.455	914	1247	.733	551	1568	2119	1099	1074	7	444	782	285	4568	91.4	-9.5
Houston.......	1793	4136	.434	779	1062	.734	664	1391	2055	1034	1030	2	441	663	245	4595	91.9	+2.3
Minnesota	1680	3823	.439	1055	1470	.718	591	1563	2154	1114	1017	9	363	836	262	4628	92.6	+0.4
Toronto	1694	3855	.439	996	1368	.728	614	1393	2007	1095	1088	10	446	773	258	4639	92.8	-1.6
Charlotte	1739	4003	.434	959	1306	.734	655	1491	2146	1092	1151	13	443	762	232	4649	93.0	-0.1
Phoenix.......	1772	3936	.450	850	1224	.694	614	1506	2120	1064	1065	8	410	812	205	4666	93.3	+2.3
Washington	1705	3826	.446	1044	1418	.736	617	1517	2134	1079	1087	8	402	792	212	4672	93.4	-2.2
Dallas	1815	4037	.450	855	1193	.717	660	1519	2179	1073	1042	4	361	699	244	4701	94.0	-2.4
Boston........	1725	3896	.443	1118	1506	.742	642	1544	2186	1018	1001	9	461	841	253	4743	94.9	-1.9
New Jersey	1796	3968	.453	943	1298	.727	624	1581	2205	968	1084	7	395	813	326	4758	95.2	-3.8
Seattle........	1838	4026	.457	857	1187	.722	652	1446	2098	1111	1165	12	399	746	224	4797	95.9	-1.1
L.A. Lakers	1759	3992	.441	1064	1501	.709	628	1403	2031	1062	1271	21	408	716	196	4799	96.0	+3.0
Vancouver	1813	3917	.463	1021	1400	.729	673	1456	2129	1189	1164	15	490	779	328	4876	97.5	-8.7
L.A. Clippers ...	1830	3858	.474	1078	1445	.746	640	1506	2146	1101	1042	10	419	782	289	4960	99.2	-8.8
Denver........	1885	4017	.469	997	1339	.745	620	1502	2122	1175	1103	7	396	701	274	5004	100.1	-6.6
Sacramento	2009	4500	.446	793	1113	.712	750	1598	2348	1165	1102	8	490	790	221	5030	100.6	-0.4
Avgs........	1709	3910	.437	939	1290	.728	629	1453	2083	1036	1111	10	418	766	248	4579	91.6	...

HOME/ROAD

	Home	Road	Total		Home	Road	Total
Atlanta	16-9	15-10	31-19	Minnesota	18-7	7-18	25-25
Boston	10-15	9-16	19-31	New Jersey	12-13	4-21	16-34
Charlotte	16-9	10-15	26-24	New York	19-6	8-17	27-23
Chicago	8-17	5-20	13-37	Orlando	21-4	12-13	33-17
Cleveland	15-10	7-18	22-28	Philadelphia	17-8	11-14	28-22
Dallas	15-10	4-21	19-31	Phoenix	15-10	12-13	27-23
Denver	12-13	2-23	14-36	Portland	22-3	13-12	35-15
Detroit	17-8	12-13	29-21	Sacramento	16-9	11-14	27-23
Golden State	13-12	8-17	21-29	San Antonio	21-4	16-9	37-13
Houston	19-6	12-13	31-19	Seattle	17-8	8-17	25-25
Indiana	18-7	15-10	33-17	Toronto	14-11	9-16	23-27
L.A. Clippers	6-19	3-22	9-41	Utah	22-3	15-10	37-13
L.A. Lakers	18-7	13-12	31-19	Vancouver	7-18	1-24	8-42
Miami	18-7	15-10	33-17	Washington	13-12	5-20	18-32
Milwaukee	17-8	11-14	28-22	Totals	452-273	273-452	725-725

INDIVIDUAL LEADERS

POINTS

(minimum 43 games or 854 points)

	G	FGM	FTM	Pts.	Avg.
Allen Iverson, Philadelphia	48	435	356	1284	26.8
Shaquille O'Neal, L.A. Lakers	49	510	269	1289	26.3
Karl Malone, Utah	49	393	378	1164	23.8
Shareef Abdur-Rahim, Vancouver	50	386	369	1152	23.0
Keith Van Horn, New Jersey	42	322	256	916	21.8
Tim Duncan, San Antonio	50	418	247	1084	21.7
Gary Payton, Seattle	50	401	199	1084	21.7
Stephon Marbury, Min.-N.J.	49	378	222	1044	21.3
Antonio McDyess, Denver	50	415	230	1061	21.2
Grant Hill, Detroit	50	384	285	1053	21.1

REBOUNDS

(minimum 43 games or 488 rebounds)

	G	Off.	Def.	Tot.	Avg.
Chris Webber, Sacramento	42	149	396	545	13.0
Charles Barkley, Houston	42	167	349	516	12.3
Dikembe Mutombo, Atlanta	50	192	418	610	12.2
Danny Fortson, Denver	50	210	371	581	11.6
Tim Duncan, San Antonio	50	159	412	571	11.4
Alonzo Mourning, Miami	46	166	341	507	11.0
Antonio McDyess, Denver	50	168	369	537	10.7
Shaquille O'Neal, L.A. Lakers	49	187	338	525	10.7
Kevin Garnett, Minnesota	47	166	323	489	10.4
David Robinson, San Antonio	49	148	344	492	10.0

FIELD GOALS

(minimum 183 made)

	FGM	FGA	Pct.
Shaquille O'Neal, L.A. Lakers	510	885	.576
Otis Thorpe, Washington	240	440	.545
Hakeem Olajuwon, Houston	373	725	.514
Alonzo Mourning, Miami	324	634	.511
David Robinson, San Antonio	268	527	.509
Rasheed Wallace, Portland	242	476	.508
Bison Dele, Detroit	216	431	.501
Vitaly Potapenko, Cleveland-Boston	204	412	.495
Danny Fortson, Denver	191	386	.495
Tim Duncan, San Antonio	418	845	.495

STEALS

(minimum 43 games or 76 steals)

	G	No.	Avg.
Kendall Gill, New Jersey	50	134	2.68
Eddie Jones, L.A. Lakers-Charlotte	50	125	2.50
Allen Iverson, Philadelphia	48	110	2.29
Jason Kidd, Phoenix	50	114	2.28
Doug Christie, Toronto	50	113	2.26
Anfernee Hardaway, Orlando	50	111	2.22
Gary Payton, Seattle	50	109	2.18
Darrell Armstrong, Orlando	50	108	2.16
Eric Snow, Philadelphia	48	100	2.08
Mookie Blaylock, Atlanta	48	99	2.06

FREE THROWS

(minimum 76 made)

	FTM	FTA	Pct.
Reggie Miller, Indiana	226	247	.915
Chauncey Billups, Denver	157	172	.913
Darrell Armstrong, Orlando	161	178	.904
Ray Allen, Milwaukee	176	195	.903
Hersey Hawkins, Seattle	119	132	.902
Jeff Hornacek, Utah	125	140	.893
Chris Mullin, Indiana	80	92	.870
Glenn Robinson, Milwaukee	140	161	.870
Mario Elie, San Antonio	103	119	.866
Eric Piatkowski, L.A. Clippers	88	102	.863

BLOCKED SHOTS

(minimum 43 games or 61 blocked shots)

	G	No.	Avg.
Alonzo Mourning, Miami	46	180	3.91
Shawn Bradley, Dallas	49	159	3.24
Theo Ratliff, Philadelphia	50	149	2.98
Dikembe Mutombo, Atlanta	50	147	2.94
Greg Ostertag, Utah	48	131	2.73
Patrick Ewing, New York	38	100	2.63
Tim Duncan, San Antonio	50	126	2.52
Hakeem Olajuwon, Houston	50	123	2.46
David Robinson, San Antonio	49	119	2.43
Antonio McDyess, Denver	50	115	2.30

ASSISTS

(minimum 43 games or 244 assists)

	G	No.	Avg.
Jason Kidd, Phoenix	50	539	10.8
Rod Strickland, Washington	44	434	9.9
Stephon Marbury, Minnesota-New Jersey	49	437	8.9
Gary Payton, Seattle	50	436	8.7
Terrell Brandon, Milwaukee-Minnesota	36	309	8.6
Mark Jackson, Indiana	49	386	7.9
Brevin Knight, Cleveland	39	302	7.7
John Stockton, Utah	50	374	7.5
Avery Johnson, San Antonio	50	369	7.4
Nick Van Exel, Denver	50	368	7.4

3-POINT FIELD GOALS

(minimum 34 made)

	FGM	FGA	Pct.
Dell Curry, Milwaukee	69	145	.476
Chris Mullin, Indiana	73	157	.465
Hubert Davis, Dallas	65	144	.451
Walt Williams, Portland	63	144	.438
Dale Ellis, Seattle	94	217	.433
Michael Dickerson, Houston	71	164	.433
Jeff Hornacek, Utah	34	81	.420
Clifford Robinson, Phoenix	58	139	.417
George McCloud, Phoenix	69	166	.416
Jud Buechler, Detroit	61	140	.412

ATLANTA HAWKS

	G	Min.	FGM	FGA	Pct.	FTM	FTA	Pct.	Off.	Def.	Tot.	Ast.	PF	Dq.	Stl.	TO	Blk.	Pts.	Avg.	Hi.
									REBOUNDS									SCORING		
Steve Smith	36	1314	217	540	.402	191	225	.849	50	101	151	118	100	2	36	99	11	672	18.7	30
Mookie Blaylock	48	1763	247	651	.379	69	91	.758	45	179	224	278	61	0	99	115	9	640	13.3	30
Alan Henderson	38	1142	187	423	.442	100	149	.671	100	150	250	28	96	1	33	58	19	474	12.5	24
Dikembe Mutombo	50	1829	173	338	.512	195	285	.684	192	418	610	57	145	2	16	94	147	541	10.8	24
LaPhonso Ellis	20	539	80	190	.421	43	61	.705	25	84	109	18	48	1	8	34	7	204	10.2	21
Grant Long	50	1380	151	359	.421	184	235	.783	100	196	296	53	143	0	57	74	16	489	9.8	22
Tyrone Corbin	47	1066	131	335	.391	52	80	.650	37	108	145	43	74	0	31	43	7	352	7.5	18
Chris Crawford	42	784	110	255	.431	57	70	.814	37	53	90	24	106	1	10	48	13	288	6.9	18
Anthony Johnson	49	885	91	225	.404	57	82	.695	16	59	75	107	67	0	35	65	7	244	5.0	17
Ed Gray	30	337	53	182	.291	28	37	.757	7	21	28	12	30	0	12	29	1	146	4.9	12
Roshown McLeod	34	348	62	163	.380	37	45	.822	12	38	50	14	24	0	2	23	1	162	4.8	16
Jeff Sheppard	18	185	15	39	.385	8	13	.615	6	16	22	16	12	0	3	7	0	40	2.2	8
Shammond Williams	2	4	0	1	.000	3	4	.750	0	0	0	1	0	0	0	0	0	3	1.5	3
Mark West	49	499	22	59	.373	16	45	.356	49	76	125	13	81	0	4	17	22	60	1.2	6

3-pt. FG: Atlanta 197-644 (.306)—Smith 47-139 (.338); Blaylock 77-251 (.307); Henderson 0-1 (.000); Ellis 1-5 (.200); Long 3-18 (.167); Corbin 38-119 (.319); Crawford 11-33 (.333); Johnson 5-19 (.263); Gray 12-42 (.286); McLeod 1-10 (.100); Sheppard 2-7 (.286). Opponents 190-634 (.300).

BOSTON CELTICS

	G	Min.	FGM	FGA	Pct.	FTM	FTA	Pct.	Off.	Def.	Tot.	Ast.	PF	Dq.	Stl.	TO	Blk.	Pts.	Avg.	Hi.
									REBOUNDS									SCORING		
Antoine Walker	42	1549	303	735	.412	113	202	.559	106	253	359	130	142	2	63	119	28	784	18.7	32
Ron Mercer	41	1551	305	707	.431	83	105	.790	37	118	155	104	81	1	67	89	12	698	17.0	35
Paul Pierce	48	1632	284	647	.439	139	195	.713	117	192	309	115	139	1	82	113	50	791	16.5	31
Kenny Anderson	34	1010	161	357	.451	84	101	.832	24	79	103	193	78	1	33	71	2	412	12.1	23
Vitaly Potapenko†	33	927	149	286	.521	58	106	.547	91	147	238	59	116	2	24	72	20	356	10.8	26
Vitaly Potapenko‡	50	1394	204	412	.495	91	155	.587	114	218	332	75	169	4	35	100	36	499	10.0	26
Dana Barros	50	1156	168	371	.453	64	73	.877	16	89	105	208	64	1	52	88	5	464	9.3	27
Tony Battie	50	1121	147	283	.519	41	61	.672	96	204	300	53	159	1	29	45	71	335	6.7	16
Walter McCarty	32	659	64	177	.362	40	57	.702	36	79	115	40	88	0	24	40	13	181	5.7	17
Andrew DeClercq*	14	258	28	57	.491	19	29	.655	33	30	63	10	51	1	13	22	9	75	5.4	14
Damon Jones†	13	213	29	75	.387	3	4	.750	4	27	31	29	16	0	6	12	0	76	5.8	15
Damon Jones‡	24	344	43	119	.361	14	17	.824	6	38	44	42	23	0	13	17	0	125	5.2	15
Greg Minor	44	765	85	204	.417	36	48	.750	31	86	117	50	69	1	20	38	6	214	4.9	14
Popeye Jones	18	206	20	51	.392	14	17	.824	28	24	52	15	31	0	5	7	0	54	3.0	13
Bruce Bowen	30	494	26	93	.280	11	24	.458	15	37	52	28	51	2	21	13	9	70	2.3	10
Eric Riley	35	337	28	54	.519	22	31	.710	36	63	99	13	73	2	9	26	26	78	2.2	9
Marlon Garnett	24	205	15	51	.294	15	20	.750	3	18	21	18	18	0	5	12	1	51	2.1	10
Dwayne Schintzius	16	67	4	16	.250	3	4	.750	7	12	19	8	17	0	0	10	3	11	0.7	5

3-pt. FG: Boston 273-758 (.360)—Walker 65-176 (.369); Mercer 5-30 (.167); Pierce 84-204 (.412); Anderson 6-24 (.250); Potapenko‡ 0-1 (.000); Battie 0-3 (.000); Barros 64-160 (.400); McCarty 13-50 (.260); D. Jones† 15-33 (.455); D. Jones‡ 25-62 (.403); Minor 8-28 (.286); P. Jones 0-1 (.000); Bowen 7-26 (.269); Garnett 6-23 (.261). Opponents 175-561 (.312).

CHARLOTTE HORNETS

	G	Min.	FGM	FGA	Pct.	FTM	FTA	Pct.	Off.	Def.	Tot.	Ast.	PF	Dq.	Stl.	TO	Blk.	Pts.	Avg.	Hi.
									REBOUNDS									SCORING		
Eddie Jones†	30	1157	164	368	.446	153	191	.801	30	88	118	125	86	1	90	72	34	509	17.0	29
Eddie Jones‡	50	1881	260	595	.437	212	271	.782	50	144	194	186	128	1	125	93	58	780	15.6	29
J.R. Reid*	16	556	88	169	.521	67	84	.798	21	92	113	25	63	2	22	28	10	243	15.2	29
Bobby Phills	43	1574	215	497	.433	115	168	.685	39	135	174	149	124	1	60	92	25	613	14.3	24
David Wesley	50	1848	243	545	.446	159	191	.832	23	138	161	322	130	2	100	142	10	706	14.1	24
Derrick Coleman	37	1178	168	406	.414	143	190	.753	76	252	328	78	96	1	24	90	42	486	13.1	28
Elden Campbell†	32	1134	178	364	.489	134	207	.647	88	213	301	61	108	1	38	58	57	490	15.3	32
Elden Campbell‡	49	1459	222	465	.477	172	269	.639	126	271	397	69	159	3	39	80	73	616	12.6	32
Chucky Brown	48	1192	176	373	.472	40	59	.678	36	138	174	57	106	0	16	38	19	407	8.5	19
Brad Miller	38	649	78	138	.565	81	102	.794	35	82	117	22	65	0	9	32	18	238	6.3	32
Chuck Person	50	990	112	289	.388	24	32	.750	17	115	132	60	90	0	20	41	8	303	6.1	21
B.J. Armstrong*	10	178	21	43	.488	9	10	.900	1	15	16	27	16	0	3	10	0	57	5.7	17
Eldridge Recasner	44	708	82	184	.446	34	39	.872	20	57	77	91	66	0	17	58	1	222	5.0	26
Ricky Davis	46	557	81	200	.405	45	59	.763	40	44	84	58	46	0	30	54	7	209	4.5	32
Charles Shackleford	32	367	44	90	.489	19	29	.655	41	88	129	13	66	1	5	27	13	107	3.3	13
Corey Beck†	16	150	14	31	.452	6	13	.462	3	20	23	20	21	0	7	11	2	35	2.2	11
Corey Beck‡	24	180	18	39	.462	8	15	.533	6	22	28	20	26	0	9	13	2	45	1.9	11
Travis Williams	8	62	6	13	.462	3	4	.750	6	13	19	2	10	0	2	6	1	15	1.9	5
Willie Burton	3	18	1	7	.143	2	4	.500	4	2	6	0	2	0	0	1	0	4	1.3	4
Joe Wolf	3	12	0	1	.000	0	2	.000	1	0	1	0	6	0	0	0	0	0	0.0	0

3-pt. FG: Charlotte 268-735 (.365)—Jones† 28-78 (.359); Jones‡ 48-142 (.338); Phills 68-172 (.395); Wesley 61-170 (.359); Coleman 7-33 (.212); Brown 15-40 (.375); Campbell† 0-1 (.000); Campbell‡ 0-1 (.000); Miller 1-2 (.500); Person 55-157 (.350); Armstrong* 6-8 (.750); Recasner 24-60 (.400); Davis 2-12 (.167); Beck† 1-1 (1.000); Beck‡ 1-1 (1.000); Burton 0-1 (.000). Opponents 212-637 (.333).

1998-99

CHICAGO BULLS

	G	Min.	FGM	FGA	Pct.	FTM	FTA	Pct.	Off.	Def.	Tot.	Ast.	PF	Dq.	Stl.	TO	Blk.	Pts.	Avg.	Hi.
Toni Kukoc	44	1654	315	750	.420	159	215	.740	65	245	310	235	82	0	49	121	11	828	18.8	32
Ron Harper	35	1107	147	390	.377	71	101	.703	49	131	180	115	80	0	60	65	35	392	11.2	25
Brent Barry	37	1181	141	356	.396	78	101	.772	39	105	144	116	98	2	42	72	11	412	11.1	22
Dickey Simpkins	50	1448	150	324	.463	156	242	.645	110	229	339	65	128	1	36	72	13	456	9.1	21
Mark Bryant	45	1204	168	348	.483	71	110	.645	92	140	232	48	149	2	34	68	16	407	9.0	25
Randy Brown	39	1139	132	319	.414	78	103	.757	27	105	132	149	93	1	68	80	8	342	8.8	20
Kornel David	50	902	109	243	.449	90	111	.811	70	103	173	40	88	0	23	48	17	308	6.2	20
Rusty LaRue	43	732	78	217	.359	17	17	1.000	9	47	56	63	66	0	33	34	3	203	4.7	15
Cory Carr	42	624	71	216	.329	24	32	.750	8	41	49	66	66	0	21	46	7	171	4.1	18
Andrew Lang	21	386	32	99	.323	16	23	.696	33	60	93	13	43	0	5	17	12	80	3.8	14
Corey Benjamin	31	320	44	117	.376	27	40	.675	15	25	40	10	46	0	11	21	8	118	3.8	15
Bill Wennington	38	451	62	178	.348	18	22	.818	20	59	79	18	79	1	13	17	12	143	3.8	12
Charles Jones	29	476	39	123	.317	11	22	.500	9	33	42	41	30	0	18	29	5	108	3.7	15
Keith Booth	39	432	49	151	.325	21	42	.500	25	68	93	38	60	0	22	39	11	120	3.1	16
Mario Bennett	3	19	2	6	.333	3	4	.750	2	3	5	0	4	0	1	1	0	7	2.3	4

3-pt. FG: Chicago 177-612 (.289)—Kukoc 39-137 (.285); Harper 27-85 (.318); Barry 52-172 (.302); Simpkins 0-1 (.000); Bryant 0-1 (.000); Brown 0-10 (.000); David 0-1 (.000); LaRue 30-89 (.337); Carr 5-30 (.167); Benjamin 3-14 (.214); Wennington 1-1 (1.000); Jones 19-61 (.311); Booth 1-10 (.100). Opponents 208-612 (.340).

CLEVELAND CAVALIERS

	G	Min.	FGM	FGA	Pct.	FTM	FTA	Pct.	Off.	Def.	Tot.	Ast.	PF	Dq.	Stl.	TO	Blk.	Pts.	Avg.	Hi.
Shawn Kemp	42	1475	277	575	.482	307	389	.789	131	257	388	101	159	2	48	127	45	862	20.5	32
Zydrunas Ilgauskas	5	171	29	57	.509	18	30	.600	17	27	44	4	24	1	4	9	7	76	15.2	22
Wesley Person	45	1342	198	437	.453	32	53	.604	19	123	142	80	52	0	37	41	16	503	11.2	24
Derek Anderson	38	978	125	314	.398	138	165	.836	20	89	109	145	73	0	48	82	4	409	10.8	28
Brevin Knight	39	1186	134	315	.425	105	141	.745	16	115	131	302	115	1	70	105	7	373	9.6	20
Cedric Henderson	50	1517	189	453	.417	74	91	.813	45	152	197	113	136	2	58	97	24	454	9.1	22
Vitaly Potapenko*	17	467	55	126	.437	33	49	.673	23	71	94	16	53	2	11	28	16	143	8.4	17
Andrew DeClercq†	33	844	110	219	.502	76	112	.679	71	121	192	21	110	2	37	32	20	296	9.0	17
Andrew DeClercq‡	47	1102	138	276	.500	95	141	.674	104	151	255	31	161	3	50	54	29	371	7.9	17
Danny Ferry	50	1058	141	296	.476	29	33	.879	16	86	102	53	113	0	23	39	10	349	7.0	22
Johnny Newman	50	949	106	251	.422	68	84	.810	15	60	75	41	126	2	28	41	12	303	6.1	18
Mitchell Butler	31	418	67	139	.482	23	32	.719	13	31	44	22	41	0	15	29	4	168	5.4	21
Bob Sura	50	841	70	210	.333	65	103	.631	21	81	102	152	98	1	46	67	14	214	4.3	19
Earl Boykins†	17	170	20	58	.345	2	3	.667	6	7	13	27	17	0	5	13	0	44	2.6	9
Earl Boykins‡	22	221	30	79	.380	2	3	.667	7	10	17	33	20	0	6	20	0	65	3.0	9
Corie Blount†	20	368	23	67	.343	22	42	.524	34	71	105	10	47	0	18	15	12	68	3.4	11
Corie Blount‡	34	530	36	100	.360	28	54	.519	58	93	151	12	74	0	19	21	16	100	2.9	11
Ryan Stack	18	199	14	37	.378	19	20	.950	19	15	34	5	31	0	2	9	11	47	2.6	11
Antonio Lang	10	65	4	6	.667	5	9	.556	6	10	16	1	13	0	2	4	1	13	1.3	4
Litterial Green	1	2	0	1	.000	0	0	...	0	0	0	0	0	0	0	0	0	0	0.0	0

3-pt. FG: Cleveland 182-534 (.341)—Kemp 1-2 (.500); Person 75-200 (.375); Anderson 21-69 (.304); Knight 0-5 (.000); Henderson 2-12 (.167); Potapenko* 0-1 (.000); Ferry 38-97 (.392); Newman 23-61 (.377); Butler 11-29 (.379); Sura 9-45 (.200); Boykins† 2-13 (.154); Boykins‡ 3-18 (.167); Blount‡ 0-1 (.000). Opponents 236-675 (.350).

DALLAS MAVERICKS

	G	Min.	FGM	FGA	Pct.	FTM	FTA	Pct.	Off.	Def.	Tot.	Ast.	PF	Dq.	Stl.	TO	Blk.	Pts.	Avg.	Hi.
Michael Finley	50	2051	389	876	.444	186	226	.823	69	194	263	218	96	1	66	107	15	1009	20.2	36
Gary Trent	45	1362	287	602	.477	145	235	.617	127	224	351	77	122	1	29	66	23	719	16.0	33
Cedric Ceballos	13	352	59	140	.421	34	49	.694	23	62	85	12	23	1	7	28	5	163	12.5	26
Hubert Davis	50	1378	174	397	.438	44	50	.880	3	83	86	89	76	0	21	57	3	457	9.1	21
Robert Pack	25	468	75	174	.431	72	88	.818	9	27	36	81	41	0	20	49	1	222	8.9	31
Shawn Bradley	49	1294	167	348	.480	86	115	.748	130	262	392	40	153	2	35	56	159	420	8.6	20
Dirk Nowitzki	47	958	136	336	.405	99	128	.773	41	121	162	47	105	5	29	73	27	385	8.2	29
Steve Nash	40	1269	114	314	.363	38	46	.826	32	82	114	219	98	2	37	83	2	315	7.9	24
Erick Strickland	33	567	89	221	.403	53	65	.815	12	71	83	64	44	0	40	36	2	249	7.5	20
Samaki Walker	39	568	88	190	.463	53	98	.541	46	97	143	6	87	3	9	37	16	229	5.9	16
A.C. Green	50	924	108	256	.422	30	52	.577	82	146	228	25	69	0	28	19	8	246	4.9	19
Chris Anstey	41	470	50	139	.360	34	48	.708	35	62	97	27	98	1	18	26	13	134	3.3	12
Bruno Sundov	3	11	2	7	.286	0	0	...	0	0	0	1	4	0	0	1	0	4	1.3	4
John Williams	25	403	11	33	.333	7	10	.700	36	47	83	15	49	0	13	13	18	29	1.2	6

3-pt. FG: Dallas 202-595 (.339)—Finley 45-136 (.331); Trent 0-5 (.000); Ceballos 11-28 (.393); Davis 65-144 (.451); Pack 0-4 (.000); Bradley 0-4 (.000); Nowitzki 14-68 (.206); Nash 49-131 (.374); Strickland 18-59 (.305); Walker 0-1 (.000); Green 0-8 (.000); Anstey 0-7 (.000). Opponents 216-686 (.315).

1998-99

DENVER NUGGETS

	G	Min.	FGM	FGA	Pct.	FTM	FTA	Pct.	Off.	Def.	Tot.	Ast.	PF	Dq.	Stl.	TO	Blk.	Pts.	Avg.	Hi.
									REBOUNDS									SCORING		
Antonio McDyess	50	1937	415	882	.471	230	338	.680	168	369	537	82	175	5	73	138	115	1061	21.2	46
Nick Van Exel	50	1802	306	769	.398	142	175	.811	14	99	113	368	90	0	40	121	3	826	16.5	41
Chauncey Billups. . . .	45	1488	191	495	.386	157	172	.913	24	72	96	173	115	0	58	98	14	624	13.9	32
Raef LaFrentz	12	387	59	129	.457	36	48	.750	33	58	91	8	38	2	9	9	17	166	13.8	24
Danny Fortson	50	1417	191	386	.495	168	231	.727	210	371	581	32	212	9	31	77	22	550	11.0	22
Eric Williams.	38	780	80	219	.365	111	139	.799	34	47	81	37	76	0	27	49	8	277	7.3	21
Cory Alexander	36	778	97	260	.373	37	44	.841	7	67	74	119	77	0	35	69	5	261	7.3	28
Bryant Stith	46	1194	114	290	.393	61	71	.859	30	77	107	82	65	0	28	45	15	320	7.0	23
Johnny Taylor	36	724	82	198	.414	17	23	.739	30	71	101	24	97	1	28	34	17	207	5.8	21
Eric Washington	38	761	73	184	.397	22	32	.688	35	54	89	30	87	2	25	34	18	205	5.4	19
Tyson Wheeler	1	3	1	1	1.000	1	2	.500	0	0	0	2	1	0	0	0	0	4	4.0	4
Keon Clark	28	409	36	80	.450	21	37	.568	36	60	96	10	52	0	10	21	31	93	3.3	13
Carl Herrera†	24	265	27	63	.429	5	9	.556	20	34	54	1	38	0	12	12	7	59	2.5	8
Carl Herrera‡	28	307	30	76	.395	5	11	.455	25	37	62	4	41	0	12	16	7	65	2.3	8
Kelly McCarty	2	4	2	3	.667	0	0	. . .	2	1	3	0	0	0	0	2	0	4	2.0	4
Loren Meyer	14	70	7	28	.250	1	2	.500	4	12	16	1	22	0	4	3	3	16	1.1	5
Monty Williams.	1	6	0	2	.000	1	2	.500	0	0	0	0	0	0	0	0	0	1	1.0	1

3-pt. FG: Denver 302-922 (.328)—McDyess 1-9 (.111); Van Exel 72-234 (.308); Billups 85-235 (.362); LaFrentz 12-31 (.387); Fortson 0-3 (.000); Stith 31-106 (.292); E. Williams 6-26 (.231); Alexander 30-105 (.286); Taylor 26-68 (.382); Washington 37-97 (.381); Wheeler 1-1 (1.000); Clark 0-1 (.000); Herrera† 0-1 (.000); Herrera‡ 0-1 (.000); Meyer 1-5 (.200). Opponents 237-640 (.370).

DETROIT PISTONS

	G	Min.	FGM	FGA	Pct.	FTM	FTA	Pct.	Off.	Def.	Tot.	Ast.	PF	Dq.	Stl.	TO	Blk.	Pts.	Avg.	Hi.
									REBOUNDS									SCORING		
Grant Hill	50	1852	384	802	.479	285	379	.752	65	290	355	300	114	0	80	184	27	1053	21.1	46
Jerry Stackhouse . . .	42	1188	181	488	.371	210	247	.850	26	81	107	118	79	0	34	121	19	607	14.5	34
Lindsey Hunter	49	1755	228	524	.435	67	89	.753	26	142	168	193	126	2	86	92	8	582	11.9	25
Joe Dumars	38	1116	144	350	.411	51	61	.836	12	56	68	134	51	0	23	53	2	428	11.3	26
Bison Dele	49	1177	216	431	.501	81	118	.686	92	180	272	71	181	3	38	111	40	513	10.5	23
Christian Laettner . .	16	337	38	106	.358	44	57	.772	21	33	54	24	30	0	15	19	12	121	7.6	17
Jerome Williams	50	1154	124	248	.500	107	159	.673	158	191	349	23	108	0	63	41	7	355	7.1	22
Jud Buechler	50	1056	100	240	.417	13	18	.722	29	104	133	57	83	0	37	21	13	274	5.5	16
Don Reid	47	935	97	174	.557	48	79	.608	66	104	170	33	150	2	27	36	43	242	5.1	25
Korleone Young	3	15	5	10	.500	2	2	1.000	2	2	4	1	3	0	0	1	0	13	4.3	5
Loy Vaught	37	481	59	155	.381	9	14	.643	36	110	146	11	54	0	15	17	6	127	3.4	18
Charles O'Bannon . .	18	165	24	56	.429	8	8	1.000	18	16	34	12	22	0	2	8	3	56	3.1	14
Khalid Reeves	11	112	8	21	.381	8	14	.571	3	4	7	11	13	0	4	7	0	25	2.3	5
Eric Montross	46	577	42	80	.525	11	32	.344	45	94	139	14	107	1	12	16	27	95	2.1	9
Mikki Moore	2	6	1	1	1.000	2	2	1.000	0	1	1	0	0	0	0	0	0	4	2.0	2
Mark Macon	7	69	4	20	.200	0	0	. . .	3	2	5	4	6	0	5	6	1	9	1.3	7
Corey Beck*	8	30	4	8	.500	2	2	1.000	3	2	5	5	2	0	2	2	0	10	1.3	6
Steve Henson	4	25	1	2	.500	2	2	1.000	0	0	0	3	1	0	1	3	0	4	1.0	2

3-pt. FG: Detroit 248-679 (.365)—Hill 0-14 (.000); Stackhouse 35-126 (.278); Hunter 59-153 (.386); Dumars 89-221 (.403); Dele 0-1 (.000); Laettner 1-3 (.333); Buechler 61-148 (.412); Young 1-4 (.250); Vaught 0-1 (.000); O'Bannon 0-1 (.000); Reeves 1-3 (.333); Montross 0-1 (.000); Macon 1-3 (.333). Opponents 236-682 (.346).

GOLDEN STATE WARRIORS

	G	Min.	FGM	FGA	Pct.	FTM	FTA	Pct.	Off.	Def.	Tot.	Ast.	PF	Dq.	Stl.	TO	Blk.	Pts.	Avg.	Hi.
									REBOUNDS									SCORING		
John Starks	50	1686	269	728	.370	74	100	.740	33	130	163	235	135	3	69	83	5	690	13.8	27
Donyell Marshall	48	1250	208	494	.421	88	121	.727	115	227	342	66	123	1	47	80	37	530	11.0	36
Chris Mills	47	1395	186	453	.411	79	96	.823	49	188	237	103	125	1	39	58	14	483	10.3	23
Antawn Jamison	47	1058	178	394	.452	90	153	.588	131	170	301	34	102	1	38	68	16	449	9.6	24
Bimbo Coles	48	1272	183	414	.442	83	101	.822	21	96	117	222	113	2	45	82	11	455	9.5	24
Terry Cummings	50	1011	186	424	.439	81	114	.711	95	160	255	58	168	4	46	58	10	454	9.1	24
Erick Dampier	50	1414	161	414	.389	120	204	.588	164	218	382	54	165	2	26	92	58	442	8.8	22
Jason Caffey	35	876	123	277	.444	62	98	.633	79	126	205	18	113	1	24	75	9	308	8.8	20
Tony Delk	36	630	92	253	.364	46	71	.648	11	43	54	45	47	0	16	45	6	246	6.8	18
Muggsy Bogues	36	714	76	154	.494	31	36	.861	16	57	73	134	44	0	43	47	1	183	5.1	9
Adonal Foyle	44	614	52	121	.430	25	51	.490	79	115	194	18	90	0	15	31	43	129	2.9	11
Felton Spencer	26	159	15	33	.455	12	26	.462	18	28	46	0	41	0	5	9	10	42	1.6	11
Duane Ferrell	8	46	1	14	.071	3	4	.750	5	1	6	0	4	0	1	1	1	5	0.6	2

3-pt. FG: Golden State 162-565 (.287)—Starks 78-269 (.290); Marshall 26-72 (.361); Mills 32-115 (.278); Jamison 3-10 (.300); Coles 6-25 (.240); Cummings 1-1 (1.000); Caffey 0-1 (.000); Delk 16-66 (.242); Bogues 0-6 (.000). Opponents 193-575 (.336).

HOUSTON ROCKETS

	G	Min.	FGM	FGA	Pct.	FTM	FTA	Pct.	Off.	Def.	Tot.	Ast.	PF	Dq.	Stl.	TO	Blk.	Pts.	Avg.	Hi.
									REBOUNDS									SCORING		
Hakeem Olajuwon . .	50	1784	373	725	.514	195	272	.717	106	372	478	88	160	3	82	139	123	945	18.9	32
Charles Barkley	42	1526	240	502	.478	192	267	.719	167	349	516	192	89	0	43	100	13	676	16.1	35

	G	Min.	FGM	FGA	Pct.	FTM	FTA	Pct.	Off.	Def.	Tot.	Ast.	PF	Dq.	Stl.	TO	Blk.	Pts.	Avg.	Hi.
Scottie Pippen	50	2011	261	604	.432	132	183	.721	63	260	323	293	118	0	98	159	37	726	14.5	31
Michael Dickerson	50	1558	215	462	.465	46	72	.639	26	57	83	95	90	0	27	66	11	547	10.9	31
Sam Mack†	25	506	81	172	.471	23	28	.821	7	35	42	32	41	0	15	13	3	230	9.2	21
Sam Mack‡	44	1083	167	384	.435	51	58	.879	14	81	95	55	94	1	35	33	4	472	10.7	26
Cuttino Mobley	49	1456	172	405	.425	90	110	.818	22	89	111	121	98	0	44	79	23	487	9.9	26
Othella Harrington	41	903	156	304	.513	88	122	.721	72	174	246	15	103	0	6	61	25	400	9.8	23
Brent Price	40	806	100	207	.483	46	61	.754	18	60	78	113	90	0	33	65	1	292	7.3	19
Eddie Johnson	3	18	6	13	.462	0	0	...	0	2	2	1	3	0	0	2	0	12	4.0	6
Bryce Drew	34	441	47	129	.364	8	8	1.000	3	29	32	52	61	2	12	31	4	118	3.5	18
Rodrick Rhodes*	3	33	2	8	.250	5	6	.833	2	2	4	1	5	0	1	5	0	9	3.0	7
Matt Bullard	44	413	43	114	.377	7	10	.700	9	33	42	18	28	0	13	14	4	117	2.9	14
Antoine Carr	18	152	21	52	.404	5	7	.714	9	22	31	9	31	0	1	9	10	47	2.6	7
Anthony Miller	29	249	28	60	.467	14	22	.636	26	41	67	7	34	0	7	9	5	70	2.4	9
Stanley Roberts	6	33	5	13	.385	4	8	.500	4	7	11	0	2	0	0	4	1	14	2.3	10
Matt Maloney	15	186	5	28	.179	10	11	.909	2	8	10	21	7	0	4	14	0	21	1.4	6

3-pt. FG: Houston 336-914 (.368)—Olajuwon 4-13 (.308); Barkley 4-25 (.160); Pippen 72-212 (.340); Dickerson 71-164 (.433); Mack† 45-111 (.405); Drew 16-49 (.327); Mack‡ 87-219 (.397); Mobley 53-148 (.358); Price 46-112 (.411); Johnson 0-1 (.000); Bullard 24-62 (.387); Carr 0-1 (.000); Miller 0-1 (.000); Maloney 1-15 (.067). Opponents 230-645 (.357).

INDIANA PACERS

	G	Min.	FGM	FGA	Pct.	FTM	FTA	Pct.	Off.	Def.	Tot.	Ast.	PF	Dq.	Stl.	TO	Blk.	Pts.	Avg.	Hi.
Reggie Miller	50	1787	294	671	.438	226	247	.915	25	110	135	112	101	1	37	76	9	920	18.4	34
Rik Smits	49	1271	310	633	.490	108	132	.818	73	202	275	52	159	1	18	75	52	728	14.9	35
Jalen Rose	49	1238	200	496	.403	125	158	.791	34	120	154	93	128	0	50	72	15	542	11.1	28
Chris Mullin	50	1179	177	371	.477	80	92	.870	25	135	160	81	101	0	47	60	13	507	10.1	22
Antonio Davis	49	1271	164	348	.471	135	192	.703	116	228	344	33	136	3	22	50	42	463	9.4	22
Dale Davis	50	1374	161	302	.533	76	123	.618	155	261	416	22	115	0	20	43	57	398	8.0	21
Mark Jackson	49	1382	138	329	.419	65	79	.823	33	151	184	386	58	0	42	99	3	373	7.6	16
Travis Best	49	1043	127	305	.416	70	83	.843	19	61	80	169	111	2	42	62	4	347	7.1	20
Sam Perkins	48	789	80	200	.400	43	60	.717	36	102	138	25	74	0	15	22	14	238	5.0	15
Derrick McKey	13	244	23	52	.442	14	17	.824	18	23	41	13	24	0	12	12	4	60	4.6	15
Austin Croshere	27	249	32	75	.427	20	23	.870	16	29	45	10	32	0	7	23	8	92	3.4	9
Al Harrington	21	160	18	56	.321	9	15	.600	20	19	39	5	26	0	4	11	2	45	2.1	8
Fred Hoiberg	12	87	6	21	.286	6	6	1.000	2	9	11	4	11	0	0	3	0	19	1.6	5
Mark Pope	4	26	1	7	.143	0	1	.000	2	2	4	0	6	0	0	1	0	2	0.5	2

3-pt. FG: Indiana 294-799 (.368)—Miller 106-275 (.385); Smits 0-2 (.000); Rose 17-65 (.262); Mullin 73-157 (.465); Jackson 32-103 (.311); Best 22-59 (.373); Perkins 35-90 (.389); McKey 0-1 (.000); Croshere 8-29 (.276); Harrington 0-5 (.000); Hoiberg 1-9 (.111); Pope 0-4 (.000). Opponents 206-634 (.325).

LOS ANGELES CLIPPERS

	G	Min.	FGM	FGA	Pct.	FTM	FTA	Pct.	Off.	Def.	Tot.	Ast.	PF	Dq.	Stl.	TO	Blk.	Pts.	Avg.	Hi.
Maurice Taylor	46	1505	311	675	.461	150	206	.728	100	142	242	67	179	5	16	120	29	773	16.8	29
Lamond Murray	50	1317	226	578	.391	126	157	.803	59	136	195	61	107	1	58	99	20	612	12.2	30
Eric Piatkowski	49	1242	180	417	.432	88	102	.863	39	101	140	53	86	0	44	53	6	513	10.5	29
Tyrone Nesby	50	1288	182	405	.449	104	133	.782	57	118	175	82	143	2	77	53	20	503	10.1	30
Michael Olowokandi	45	1279	172	399	.431	57	118	.483	120	237	357	25	137	2	27	85	55	401	8.9	17
Sherman Douglas	30	842	96	219	.438	55	87	.632	16	42	58	124	54	0	27	61	3	247	8.2	19
Darrick Martin	37	941	102	278	.367	61	76	.803	5	43	48	144	82	1	43	67	4	296	8.0	22
James Robinson*	14	280	39	98	.398	20	27	.741	10	17	27	18	29	0	14	16	3	106	7.6	17
Rodney Rogers	47	968	131	297	.441	68	101	.673	65	114	179	77	140	2	47	66	22	348	7.4	19
Troy Hudson	25	524	60	150	.400	34	38	.895	15	40	55	92	28	1	11	38	2	169	6.8	20
Lorenzen Wright	48	1135	119	260	.458	81	117	.692	142	219	361	33	162	2	26	48	36	319	6.6	18
Brian Skinner	21	258	33	71	.465	20	33	.606	20	33	53	1	20	0	10	19	13	86	4.1	14
Charles Smith	23	317	35	97	.361	7	16	.438	7	17	24	13	35	0	17	20	14	84	3.7	16
Pooh Richardson	11	130	12	36	.333	4	4	1.000	1	12	13	30	5	0	4	9	0	28	2.5	10
Keith Closs	15	87	12	23	.522	8	10	.800	5	20	25	0	14	1	3	6	9	32	2.1	9
Stojko Vrankovic	2	12	1	4	.250	0	0	...	4	2	6	0	2	0	0	0	2	2	1.0	2

3-pt. FG: L.A. Clippers 214-668 (.320)—Taylor 1-6 (.167); Murray 34-103 (.330); Piatkowski 65-165 (.394); Nesby 35-96 (.365); Douglas 0-11 (.000); Martin 31-106 (.292); Robinson* 8-30 (.267); Rogers 18-63 (.286); Hudson 15-47 (.319); Wright 0-1 (.000); Smith 7-33 (.212); Richardson 0-6 (.000); Closs 0-1 (.000). Opponents 222-627 (.354).

LOS ANGELES LAKERS

	G	Min.	FGM	FGA	Pct.	FTM	FTA	Pct.	Off.	Def.	Tot.	Ast.	PF	Dq.	Stl.	TO	Blk.	Pts.	Avg.	Hi.
Shaquille O'Neal	49	1705	510	885	.576	269	498	.540	187	338	525	114	155	4	36	122	82	1289	26.3	38
Kobe Bryant	50	1896	362	779	.465	245	292	.839	53	211	264	190	153	3	72	157	50	996	19.9	38
Glen Rice	27	985	171	396	.432	77	90	.856	0	00	00	71	07	1	17	45	6	472	17.5	40

	G	Min.	FGM	FGA	Pct.	FTM	FTA	Pct.	Off.	Def.	Tot.	Ast.	PF	Dq.	Stl.	TO	Blk.	Pts.	Avg.	Hi.
									REBOUNDS									SCORING		
Eddie Jones*	20	724	96	227	.423	59	80	.738	20	56	76	61	42	0	35	21	24	271	13.6	21
J.R. Reid†	25	473	44	108	.407	38	53	.717	24	75	99	23	72	1	15	23	0	126	5.0	15
J.R. Reid‡	41	1029	132	277	.477	105	137	.766	45	167	212	48	135	3	37	51	10	369	9.0	29
Rick Fox	44	944	148	330	.448	66	89	.742	26	63	89	89	114	1	28	56	10	394	9.0	24
Elden Campbell*	17	325	44	101	.436	38	62	.613	38	58	96	8	51	2	1	22	16	126	7.4	24
Derek Harper	45	1120	120	291	.412	26	32	.813	13	54	67	187	66	0	44	52	4	309	6.9	20
Derek Fisher	50	1131	99	263	.376	60	79	.759	21	70	91	197	95	0	61	77	1	296	5.9	20
Tyronn Lue	15	188	28	65	.431	12	21	.571	2	4	6	25	28	0	5	11	0	75	5.0	15
Robert Horry	38	744	67	146	.459	34	46	.739	56	96	152	56	103	2	36	49	39	188	4.9	22
Travis Knight	37	525	67	130	.515	22	29	.759	34	94	128	31	108	2	21	35	27	156	4.2	15
Sam Jacobson	2	12	3	5	.600	2	2	1.000	0	3	3	0	2	0	0	1	0	8	4.0	6
Sean Rooks	36	315	32	79	.405	34	48	.708	33	39	72	9	61	0	2	21	9	98	2.7	11
Ruben Patterson	24	144	21	51	.412	22	31	.710	17	13	30	2	16	0	5	12	3	65	2.7	11
Corie Blount*	14	162	13	33	.394	6	12	.500	24	22	46	2	27	0	1	6	4	32	2.3	7
Dennis Rodman	23	657	16	46	.348	17	39	.436	62	196	258	30	71	0	10	31	12	49	2.1	7

3-pt. FG: L.A. Lakers 241-685 (.352)—O'Neal 0-1 (.000); Bryant 27-101 (.267); Rice 53-135 (.393); Jones* 20-64 (.313); Reid† 0-1 (.000); Reid‡ 0-1 (.000); Fox 32-95 (.337); Harper 43-117 (.368); Fisher 38-97 (.392); Lue 7-16 (.438); Horry 20-45 (.444); Knight 0-1 (.000); Jacobson 0-1 (.000); Rooks 0-2 (.000); Patterson 1-6 (.167); Blount* 0-1 (.000); Rodman 0-2 (.000). Opponents 217-653 (.332).

MIAMI HEAT

	G	Min.	FGM	FGA	Pct.	FTM	FTA	Pct.	Off.	Def.	Tot.	Ast.	PF	Dq.	Stl.	TO	Blk.	Pts.	Avg.	Hi.
									REBOUNDS									SCORING		
Alonzo Mourning	46	1753	324	634	.511	276	423	.652	166	341	507	74	161	1	34	139	180	924	20.1	34
Tim Hardaway	48	1772	301	752	.400	121	149	.812	15	137	152	352	102	1	57	131	6	835	17.4	32
Jamal Mashburn	24	855	134	297	.451	75	104	.721	24	122	146	75	58	0	20	60	3	356	14.8	25
P.J. Brown	50	1611	229	477	.480	113	146	.774	115	231	346	66	166	2	46	69	48	571	11.4	24
Terry Porter	50	1365	172	370	.465	123	148	.831	13	127	140	146	97	0	48	74	11	525	10.5	21
Terry Mills	1	29	3	8	.375	1	2	.500	3	1	4	0	3	0	1	3	0	9	9.0	9
Clarence Weatherspoon	49	1040	141	264	.534	115	143	.804	72	171	243	34	107	0	28	61	17	397	8.1	22
Dan Majerle	48	1624	118	298	.396	33	46	.717	21	187	208	150	100	0	38	55	7	337	7.0	22
Voshon Lenard	12	190	31	79	.392	8	11	.727	4	12	16	10	18	0	3	7	1	82	6.8	14
Mark Strickland	32	357	50	101	.495	19	26	.731	26	52	78	9	28	0	7	13	8	119	3.7	13
Blue Edwards	24	283	32	72	.444	9	13	.692	7	26	33	30	23	0	17	21	5	77	3.2	12
Rex Walters	33	506	35	95	.368	19	23	.826	10	40	50	58	63	0	10	32	3	101	3.1	9
Duane Causwell	19	137	20	35	.571	4	12	.333	14	21	35	2	32	1	0	18	11	44	2.3	10
Mark Davis	4	35	2	6	.333	5	6	.833	2	5	7	1	12	1	1	7	0	9	2.3	6
Keith Askins	33	415	20	62	.323	5	8	.625	10	34	44	10	58	0	17	13	3	53	1.6	6
Marty Conlon	7	35	3	13	.231	2	2	1.000	1	4	5	1	6	0	0	3	1	8	1.1	4
Jamie Watson	3	18	1	2	.500	0	0	...	0	1	1	1	1	0	0	1	0	2	0.7	2

3-pt. FG: Miami 289-804 (.359)—Mourning 0-2 (.000); Hardaway 112-311 (.360); Mashburn 13-30 (.433); Porter 58-141 (.411); Mills 2-4 (.500); Majerle 68-203 (.335); Lenard 12-35 (.343); Strickland 0-1 (.000); Edwards 4-10 (.400); Walters 12-38 (.316); Askins 8-29 (.276). Opponents 211-606 (.348).

MILWAUKEE BUCKS

	G	Min.	FGM	FGA	Pct.	FTM	FTA	Pct.	Off.	Def.	Tot.	Ast.	PF	Dq.	Stl.	TO	Blk.	Pts.	Avg.	Hi.
									REBOUNDS									SCORING		
Glenn Robinson	47	1579	347	756	.459	140	161	.870	73	203	276	100	114	1	46	106	41	865	18.4	33
Ray Allen	50	1719	303	673	.450	176	195	.903	57	155	212	178	117	0	53	122	7	856	17.1	31
Sam Cassell†	4	99	18	44	.409	18	19	.947	4	5	9	17	9	0	6	8	0	55	13.8	16
Sam Cassell‡	8	199	39	93	.419	47	50	.940	5	10	15	36	22	1	9	20	0	127	15.9	36
Terrell Brandon*	15	505	85	208	.409	26	31	.839	11	42	53	104	25	0	24	36	3	203	13.5	20
Dell Curry	42	864	163	336	.485	28	34	.824	18	67	85	48	42	0	36	45	3	423	10.1	20
Tyrone Hill*	17	517	50	118	.424	46	81	.568	51	83	134	17	68	0	18	24	8	146	8.6	20
Armen Gilliam	34	668	101	223	.453	79	101	.782	33	93	126	19	48	0	22	36	12	281	8.3	17
Tim Thomas†	33	624	105	212	.495	54	88	.614	42	51	93	31	86	2	23	31	9	280	8.5	21
Tim Thomas‡	50	812	132	279	.473	73	112	.652	49	77	126	46	107	2	26	46	12	358	7.2	21
Haywoode Workman	29	815	73	170	.429	37	47	.787	14	88	102	172	53	0	32	63	1	200	6.9	19
Vinny Del Negro	48	1093	114	270	.422	40	50	.800	14	88	102	174	62	0	33	55	3	281	5.9	16
Chris Gatling†	30	494	81	168	.482	25	69	.362	31	83	114	20	78	0	24	33	6	188	6.3	16
Chris Gatling‡	48	775	117	265	.442	37	93	.398	52	127	179	32	118	0	32	62	10	272	5.7	16
Robert Traylor	49	786	108	201	.537	43	80	.538	80	102	182	38	140	4	44	42	44	259	5.3	15
Ervin Johnson	50	1027	96	189	.508	64	105	.610	120	200	320	19	151	1	29	47	57	256	5.1	12
Michael Curry	50	1146	90	206	.437	63	79	.797	19	89	108	78	135	0	42	37	7	244	4.9	14
Elliot Perry*	5	47	9	17	.529	1	2	.500	1	7	8	12	3	0	4	2	0	20	4.0	10
Scott Williams†	5	29	5	15	.333	4	7	.571	2	10	12	0	5	0	1	2	1	14	2.8	8
Scott Williams‡	7	46	5	17	.294	4	7	.571	3	11	14	1	9	0	3	4	2	14	2.0	8
Jerald Honeycutt*	3	12	2	5	.400	1	2	.500	0	1	1	0	6	0	1	1	0	5	1.7	3
Adonis Jordan	4	18	2	4	.500	2	4	.500	0	0	0	3	0	0	3	2	0	6	1.5	3

	G	Min.	FGM	FGA	Pct.	FTM	FTA	Pct.	Off.	Def.	Tot.	Ast.	PF	Dq.	Stl.	TO	Blk.	Pts.	Avg.	Hi.
									REBOUNDS									SCORING		
Paul Grant†	2	5	1	2	.500	0	0	...	0	0	0	0	0	0	1	1	0	2	1.0	2
Paul Grant‡	6	13	2	6	.333	0	0	...	1	0	1	0	4	0	1	2	0	4	0.7	2
Jamie Feick*	2	3	0	1	.000	0	0	...	0	2	2	0	0	0	0	0	0	0	0.0	0

3-pt. FG: Milwaukee 231-619 (.373)—Robinson 31-79 (.392); R. Allen 74-208 (.356); Cassell† 1-3 (.333); Cassell‡ 2-10 (.200); Brandon* 7-28 (.250); D. Curry 69-145 (.476); Gilliam 0-1 (.000); Thomas† 16-49 (.327); Thomas‡ 21-68 (.309); Workman 17-47 (.362); Del Negro 13-30 (.433); Gatling† 1-7 (.143); Gatling‡ 1-8 (.125); Traylor 0-1 (.000); M. Curry 1-15 (.067); Jordan 0-2 (.000); Perry* 1-1 (1.000); Honeycutt* 0-3 (.000). Opponents 272-814 (.334).

MINNESOTA TIMBERWOLVES

	G	Min.	FGM	FGA	Pct.	FTM	FTA	Pct.	Off.	Def.	Tot.	Ast.	PF	Dq.	Stl.	TO	Blk.	Pts.	Avg.	Hi.
									REBOUNDS									SCORING		
Kevin Garnett	47	1780	414	900	.460	145	206	.704	166	323	489	202	152	5	78	135	83	977	20.8	30
Stephon Marbury*	18	661	124	304	.408	63	87	.724	17	45	62	167	44	0	29	55	5	319	17.7	40
Terrell Brandon†	21	712	127	299	.425	39	47	.830	16	65	81	205	57	0	39	38	7	298	14.2	22
Terrell Brandon‡	36	1217	212	507	.418	65	78	.833	27	107	134	309	82	0	63	74	10	501	13.9	22
Joe Smith	43	1418	223	522	.427	142	188	.755	154	200	354	68	147	3	32	66	66	588	13.7	30
Sam Mitchell	50	1344	213	522	.408	126	165	.764	55	127	182	98	111	1	35	34	16	561	11.2	25
Anthony Peeler	28	810	103	272	.379	30	41	.732	30	54	84	78	60	0	35	38	6	270	9.6	20
Malik Sealy	31	731	95	231	.411	55	61	.902	23	69	92	36	68	0	30	33	5	251	8.1	18
Bobby Jackson	50	941	141	348	.405	61	79	.772	43	92	135	167	75	1	39	75	3	353	7.1	17
Dennis Scott†	21	532	70	157	.446	22	27	.815	5	33	38	32	32	0	12	14	2	191	9.1	22
Dennis Scott‡	36	738	87	213	.408	23	31	.742	8	50	58	40	49	0	15	19	3	234	6.5	22
James Robinson†	17	226	28	87	.322	8	14	.571	8	27	35	38	31	0	8	28	5	77	4.5	15
James Robinson‡	31	506	67	185	.362	28	41	.683	18	44	62	56	60	0	22	44	8	183	5.9	17
Dean Garrett	49	1054	116	231	.502	38	51	.745	99	158	257	28	113	0	30	29	45	270	5.5	22
Tom Hammonds	49	716	82	179	.458	48	75	.640	54	82	136	20	88	1	8	32	7	212	4.3	23
Radoslav Nesterovic	2	30	3	12	.250	2	2	1.000	3	5	8	1	5	0	0	1	0	8	4.0	4
Andrae Patterson	35	284	43	97	.443	28	36	.778	30	35	65	15	62	1	19	22	7	114	3.3	12
Bill Curley	35	372	29	72	.403	19	22	.864	20	31	51	14	83	1	17	10	9	78	2.2	8
Brian Evans†	5	24	2	10	.200	0	0	...	2	0	2	1	1	0	2	0	0	4	0.8	2
Brian Evans‡	16	145	13	44	.295	4	4	1.000	6	13	19	15	8	0	5	2	3	34	2.1	12
Chris Carr*	11	81	9	26	.346	2	4	.500	0	12	12	7	9	0	1	4	1	23	2.1	4
Reggie Jordan	27	296	15	54	.278	21	38	.553	27	32	59	41	38	0	12	14	5	51	1.9	9
Paul Grant*	4	8	1	4	.250	0	0	...	1	0	1	0	4	0	0	1	0	2	0.5	2
Trevor Winter	1	5	0	0	...	0	0	...	1	2	3	0	5	0	0	0	0	0	0.0	0

3-pt. FG: Minnesota 122-410 (.298)—Garnett 4-14 (.286); Marbury* 8-39 (.205); Brandon† 5-19 (.263); Brandon‡ 12-47 (.255); Smith 0-3 (.000); Sealy 6-23 (.261); Mitchell 9-38 (.237); Peeler 34-114 (.298); Jackson 10-27 (.370); Scott† 29-68 (.426); Scott‡ 37-97 (.381); Curley 1-5 (.200); Robinson† 13-44 (.295); Robinson‡ 21-74 (.284); Patterson 0-5 (.000); Evans† 0-2 (.000); Evans‡ 4-13 (.308); Carr* 3-9 (.333). Opponents 213-654 (.326).

NEW JERSEY NETS

	G	Min.	FGM	FGA	Pct.	FTM	FTA	Pct.	Off.	Def.	Tot.	Ast.	PF	Dq.	Stl.	TO	Blk.	Pts.	Avg.	Hi.
									REBOUNDS									SCORING		
Keith Van Horn	42	1576	322	752	.428	256	298	.859	114	244	358	65	134	2	43	133	53	916	21.8	35
Stephon Marbury†	31	1234	254	579	.439	159	191	.832	20	60	80	270	81	0	30	109	3	725	23.4	41
Stephon Marbury‡	49	1895	378	883	.428	222	278	.799	37	105	142	437	125	0	59	164	8	1044	21.3	41
Sam Cassell*	4	100	21	49	.429	29	31	.935	1	5	6	19	13	1	3	12	0	72	18.0	36
Kerry Kittles	46	1570	227	613	.370	88	114	.772	52	139	191	116	82	0	79	66	26	592	12.9	31
Kendall Gill	50	1606	236	593	.398	114	167	.683	61	183	244	123	162	4	134	71	26	588	11.8	25
Jayson Williams	30	1020	97	218	.445	48	85	.565	147	213	360	33	126	3	24	46	60	242	8.1	23
Doug Overton*	8	174	25	57	.439	12	14	.857	6	11	17	16	14	0	3	15	1	64	8.0	18
Eric Murdock	15	401	45	114	.395	21	26	.808	3	32	35	66	35	1	22	29	2	119	7.9	23
Scott Burrell	32	706	75	208	.361	34	42	.810	32	87	119	45	82	2	40	23	11	212	6.6	18
Jamie Feick†	26	849	67	133	.504	43	60	.717	112	174	286	24	73	0	25	34	18	177	6.8	17
Jamie Feick‡	28	852	67	134	.500	43	60	.717	112	176	288	24	73	0	25	34	18	177	6.3	17
Mark Hendrickson	22	399	39	88	.443	42	50	.840	27	41	68	13	39	0	12	15	1	120	5.5	19
Lucious Harris	36	602	73	181	.403	36	48	.750	21	46	67	31	52	1	18	18	7	193	5.4	17
Chris Carr†	28	364	67	179	.374	25	36	.694	23	36	59	16	36	0	7	24	1	184	6.6	24
Chris Carr‡	39	445	76	205	.371	27	40	.675	23	48	71	23	45	0	8	28	2	207	5.3	24
Chris Gatling*	18	281	36	97	.371	12	24	.500	21	44	65	12	40	0	8	29	4	84	4.7	14
Damon Jones*	11	131	14	44	.318	11	13	.846	2	11	13	13	7	0	7	5	0	49	4.5	17
Earl Boykins*	5	51	10	21	.476	0	0	...	1	3	4	6	3	0	1	7	0	21	4.2	6
David Vaughn	10	103	13	24	.542	8	10	.800	13	21	34	1	22	0	2	11	8	34	3.4	8
Elliot Perry†	30	243	30	86	.349	9	12	.750	6	20	26	35	22	0	16	32	0	78	2.6	10
Elliot Perry‡	35	290	39	103	.379	10	14	.714	7	27	34	47	25	0	20	34	0	98	2.8	10
Brian Evans*	11	121	11	34	.324	4	4	1.000	4	13	17	14	7	0	3	2	3	30	2.7	12
Jim McIlvaine	22	269	22	51	.431	4	6	.667	31	23	54	2	59	1	9	13	32	48	2.2	6
Rony Seikaly	9	88	4	20	.200	7	18	.389	5	16	21	2	15	0	4	10	6	15	1.7	7
William Cunningham†	15	161	3	18	.167	0	2	.000	13	15	28	1	30	0	1	5	11	6	0.4	2
William Cunningham‡	16	162	3	18	.167	0	2	.000	13	15	28	1	30	0	1	5	11	6	0.4	2
Gheorghe Muresan	1	1	0	1	.000	0	0	...	0	0	0	0	0	0	0	0	0	0	0.0	0

3-pt. FG: New Jersey 225-679 (.331)—Van Horn 16-53 (.302); Marbury† 58-158 (.367); Marbury‡ 66-197 (.335); Cassell* 1-7 (.143); Kittles 50-158 (.316); Gill 2-17 (.118); Williams 0-2 (.000); Overton* 2-4 (.500); Murdock 8-22 (.364); Burrell 28-72 (.389); Hendrickson 0-1 (.000); Harris 11-50 (.220); Carr† 25-66 (.379); Carr‡ 28-75 (.373); Gatling* 0-1 (.000); Jones* 10-29 (.345); Boykins* 1-5 (.200); Perry† 9-23 (.391); Perry‡ 10-24 (.417); Evans* 4-11 (.364). Opponents 223-654 (.341),

NEW YORK KNICKERBOCKERS

	G	Min.	FGM	FGA	Pct.	FTM	FTA	Pct.	Off.	Def.	Tot.	Ast.	PF	Dq.	Stl.	TO	Blk.	Pts.	Avg.	Hi.
Patrick Ewing	38	1300	247	568	.435	163	231	.706	74	303	377	43	105	1	30	99	100	657	17.3	37
Latrell Sprewell	37	1233	215	518	.415	155	191	.812	41	115	156	91	65	0	46	79	2	606	16.4	31
Allan Houston	50	1815	294	703	.418	168	195	.862	20	132	152	137	115	1	35	130	9	813	16.3	30
Larry Johnson	49	1639	210	458	.459	134	164	.817	91	193	284	119	147	1	34	89	10	587	12.0	23
Kurt Thomas	50	1182	170	368	.462	66	108	.611	82	204	286	55	159	3	45	73	17	406	8.1	20
Charlie Ward	50	1556	135	334	.404	55	78	.705	23	149	172	271	105	0	103	131	8	378	7.6	18
Marcus Camby	46	945	136	261	.521	57	103	.553	102	151	253	12	131	2	29	39	74	329	7.2	22
Chris Childs	48	1297	114	267	.427	64	78	.821	18	115	133	193	156	0	44	85	1	328	6.8	15
Dennis Scott*	15	206	17	56	.304	1	4	.250	3	17	20	8	17	0	3	5	1	43	2.9	9
Chris Dudley	46	685	48	109	.440	19	40	.475	79	114	193	7	116	1	13	24	38	115	2.5	10
Ben Davis	8	21	7	17	.412	3	6	.500	9	2	11	3	4	0	0	1	0	17	2.1	7
Herb Williams	6	34	4	8	.500	2	2	1.000	3	3	6	0	2	0	0	2	2	10	1.7	4
Rick Brunson	17	95	6	21	.286	5	18	.278	3	7	10	19	8	0	9	12	0	17	1.0	4
David Wingate	20	92	7	16	.438	0	0	...	3	5	8	5	10	0	4	6	0	14	0.7	4

3-pt. FG: New York 208-589 (.353)—Ewing 0-2 (.000); Sprewell 21-77 (.273); Houston 57-140 (.407); Johnson 33-92 (.359); Thomas 0-1 (.000); Ward 53-149 (.356); Childs 36-94 (.383); Scott* 8-29 (.276); Brunson 0-5 (.000). Opponents 234-662 (.353).

ORLANDO MAGIC

	G	Min.	FGM	FGA	Pct.	FTM	FTA	Pct.	Off.	Def.	Tot.	Ast.	PF	Dq.	Stl.	TO	Blk.	Pts.	Avg.	Hi.
Anfernee Hardaway	50	1944	301	717	.420	149	211	.706	74	210	284	266	111	0	111	150	23	791	15.8	30
Nick Anderson	47	1581	253	640	.395	99	162	.611	51	226	277	91	72	0	64	83	15	701	14.9	40
Darrell Armstrong	50	1502	230	522	.441	161	178	.904	53	127	180	335	90	0	108	158	4	690	13.8	28
Isaac Austin	49	1259	185	453	.408	105	157	.669	83	154	237	89	125	1	47	114	35	477	9.7	23
Horace Grant	50	1660	198	456	.434	47	70	.671	117	234	351	90	99	0	46	44	60	443	8.9	20
Matt Harpring	50	1114	148	320	.463	102	143	.713	88	126	214	45	112	0	30	73	6	408	8.2	18
Charles Outlaw	31	851	84	154	.545	35	81	.432	54	113	167	56	79	1	40	58	43	203	6.5	16
Michael Doleac	49	780	125	267	.468	54	80	.675	66	82	148	20	117	1	19	26	17	304	6.2	25
Derek Strong	44	695	76	180	.422	71	99	.717	66	95	161	17	64	0	15	37	7	223	5.1	14
Dominique Wilkins	27	252	50	132	.379	29	42	.690	30	41	71	16	19	0	4	23	1	134	5.0	19
B.J. Armstrong†	22	180	19	45	.422	9	11	.818	1	22	23	34	15	0	9	15	0	48	2.2	9
B.J. Armstrong‡	32	358	40	88	.455	18	21	.857	2	37	39	61	31	0	12	25	0	105	3.3	17
Doug Overton*	6	33	6	12	.500	6	6	1.000	1	1	2	3	2	0	1	3	0	18	3.0	0
Kevin Ollie†	1	4	0	1	.000	1	2	.500	0	1	1	0	1	0	0	0	0	1	1.0	1
Kevin Ollie‡	8	72	4	14	.286	5	7	.714	0	7	7	3	9	0	3	3	1	13	1.6	6
Danny Schayes	19	143	11	29	.379	6	8	.750	3	11	14	4	23	0	1	8	2	28	1.5	6
Gerald Wilkins	3	28	0	9	.000	2	2	1.000	0	1	1	1	3	0	0	3	0	2	0.7	2
Miles Simon	5	19	1	5	.200	0	0	...	1	1	2	0	1	0	1	3	0	2	0.4	2
Jonathan Kerner	1	5	0	1	.000	0	0	...	0	0	0	0	0	0	0	0	0	0	0.0	0

3-pt. FG: Orlando 223-675 (.330)—Hardaway 40-140 (.286); Anderson 96-277 (.347); D. Armstrong 69-189 (.365); Austin 2-7 (.286); Grant 0-2 (.000); Outlaw 0-3 (.000); Harpring 10-25 (.400); Strong 0-2 (.000); D. Wilkins 5-19 (.263); B. Armstrong† 1-7 (.143); B. Armstrong‡ 7-15 (.467); Overton* 0-2 (.000); Simon 0-2 (.000). Opponents 230-667 (.345).

PHILADELPHIA 76ERS

	G	Min.	FGM	FGA	Pct.	FTM	FTA	Pct.	Off.	Def.	Tot.	Ast.	PF	Dq.	Stl.	TO	Blk.	Pts.	Avg.	Hi.
Allen Iverson	48	1990	435	1056	.412	356	474	.751	66	170	236	223	98	0	110	167	7	1284	26.8	46
Matt Geiger	50	1540	266	555	.479	141	177	.797	137	225	362	58	157	2	39	101	40	674	13.5	26
Theo Ratliff	50	1627	197	419	.470	166	229	.725	139	268	407	30	180	8	45	92	149	560	11.2	23
Larry Hughes	50	988	170	414	.411	107	151	.709	83	106	189	77	97	0	44	68	14	455	9.1	22
Eric Snow	48	1716	149	348	.428	110	150	.733	25	137	162	301	149	2	100	111	1	413	8.6	20
Tyrone Hill†	21	587	72	150	.480	35	69	.507	64	89	153	18	77	2	16	35	8	179	8.5	23
Tyrone Hill‡	38	1104	122	268	.455	81	150	.540	115	172	287	35	145	2	34	59	16	325	8.6	23
George Lynch	43	1315	147	349	.421	53	84	.631	110	169	279	76	142	2	85	79	22	356	8.3	21
Aaron McKie	50	959	95	237	.401	44	62	.710	27	113	140	100	90	1	63	57	3	240	4.8	15
Tim Thomas*	17	188	27	67	.403	19	24	.792	7	26	33	15	21	0	3	15	3	78	4.6	13
Doug Overton†	10	37	5	15	.333	0	0	...	0	2	2	4	2	0	1	2	0	10	1.0	4
Doug Overton‡	24	244	36	84	.429	18	20	.900	7	14	21	23	18	0	5	20	1	92	3.8	18
Harvey Grant	47	798	62	168	.369	21	29	.724	36	74	110	23	73	1	20	21	16	146	3.1	12
Jerald Honeycutt†	13	90	7	27	.259	6	8	.750	3	8	11	3	10	0	4	8	2	25	1.9	6
Jerald Honeycutt‡	16	102	9	32	.281	7	10	.700	3	9	12	3	16	0	5	9	2	30	1.9	6
Nazr Mohammed	26	121	15	42	.357	12	21	.571	18	19	37	2	22	0	5	12	4	42	1.6	8
Anthony Parker	2	3	1	1	1.000	0	0	...	0	0	0	0	0	0	0	0	0	2	1.0	2
Rick Mahorn	13	127	5	18	.278	3	8	.375	7	16	23	2	22	0	5	6	1	13	0.8	4
Benoit Benjamin	6	33	2	7	.286	0	0	...	3	5	8	1	6	0	0	3	0	4	0.7	2
Casey Shaw	9	14	1	8	.125	0	0	...	1	1	2	3	2	0	0	2	0	2	0.2	2
Scott Williams*	2	17	0	2	.000	0	0	...	1	1	2	1	4	0	2	2	1	0	0.0	0

3-pt. FG: Philadelphia 98-371 (.264)—Iverson 58-199 (.291); Geiger 1-5 (.200); Hughes 8-52 (.154); Snow 5-21 (.238); Lynch 9-23 (.391); McKie 6-31 (.194); Thomas* 5-19 (.263); Overton† 0-1 (.000); Overton‡ 2-7 (.286); Grant 1-6 (.167); Honeycutt† 5-14 (.357); Honeycutt‡ 5-17 (.294). Opponents 241-716 (.337).

PHOENIX SUNS

	G	Min.	FGM	FGA	Pct.	FTM	FTA	Pct.	Off.	Def.	Tot.	Ast.	PF	Dq.	Stl.	TO	Blk.	Pts.	Avg.	Hi.
									REBOUNDS									**SCORING**		
Tom Gugliotta	43	1563	277	573	.483	173	218	.794	131	250	381	121	110	0	59	88	21	729	17.0	33
Jason Kidd	50	2060	310	698	.444	181	239	.757	87	252	339	539	108	1	114	150	19	846	16.9	30
Clifford Robinson	50	1740	299	629	.475	163	234	.697	69	158	227	128	153	2	75	88	59	819	16.4	30
Rex Chapman	38	1183	165	459	.359	76	91	.835	12	92	104	109	46	0	34	54	9	459	12.1	25
Randy Livingston	1	22	5	8	.625	2	2	1.000	0	2	2	3	1	0	2	1	0	12	12.0	12
Danny Manning	50	1184	187	386	.484	78	112	.696	62	157	219	113	129	1	36	69	38	453	9.1	19
George McCloud	48	1245	142	324	.438	75	87	.862	34	128	162	79	128	0	45	49	14	428	8.9	24
Luc Longley	39	933	140	290	.483	59	76	.776	59	162	221	45	119	0	23	53	21	339	8.7	21
Pat Garrity	39	538	85	170	.500	40	56	.714	26	49	75	18	62	0	8	20	3	217	5.6	25
Chris Morris	44	535	64	149	.430	40	46	.870	54	67	121	23	54	0	16	21	11	184	4.2	17
Shawn Respert	12	99	13	36	.361	7	10	.700	2	11	13	8	10	0	5	5	0	37	3.1	12
Toby Bailey	27	249	34	86	.395	9	13	.692	24	30	54	13	24	0	9	11	2	78	2.9	12
Alvin Sims	4	25	4	10	.400	2	5	.400	3	1	4	5	2	0	2	6	0	11	2.8	6
Gerald Brown	33	236	33	89	.371	11	14	.786	5	17	22	31	21	0	5	22	1	80	2.4	10
Joe Kleine	31	374	30	74	.405	8	12	.667	27	40	67	12	46	0	8	10	1	68	2.2	10
Jimmy Oliver	2	11	1	3	.333	0	0	...	0	0	0	0	2	0	0	0	0	3	1.5	3
Marko Milic	11	53	8	20	.400	0	0	...	3	2	5	2	7	0	3	6	1	16	1.5	4

3-pt. FG: Phoenix 261-702 (.372)—Gugliotta 2-7 (.286); Kidd 45-123 (.366); Robinson 58-139 (.417); Chapman 53-151 (.351); Manning 1-9 (.111); McCloud 69-166 (.416); Garrity 7-18 (.389); Morris 16-56 (.286); Respert 4-13 (.308); Bailey 1-5 (.200); Sims 1-1 (1.000); Brown 3-10 (.300); Kleine 0-2 (.000); Oliver 1-1 (1.000); Milic 0-1 (.000). Opponents 272-755 (.360).

PORTLAND TRAIL BLAZERS

	G	Min.	FGM	FGA	Pct.	FTM	FTA	Pct.	Off.	Def.	Tot.	Ast.	PF	Dq.	Stl.	TO	Blk.	Pts.	Avg.	Hi.
									REBOUNDS									**SCORING**		
Isaiah Rider	47	1385	249	605	.412	111	147	.755	59	137	196	104	100	0	25	95	9	651	13.9	30
Rasheed Wallace	49	1414	242	476	.508	131	179	.732	57	184	241	60	175	6	48	80	54	628	12.8	26
Damon Stoudamire	50	1673	249	629	.396	89	122	.730	41	126	167	312	81	0	49	110	4	631	12.6	31
Arvydas Sabonis	50	1349	232	478	.485	135	175	.771	88	305	393	119	147	2	34	85	63	606	12.1	28
Brian Grant	48	1525	183	382	.479	184	226	.814	173	297	470	67	136	1	21	96	34	550	11.5	25
Walt Williams	48	1044	147	347	.424	89	107	.832	36	107	143	80	101	2	37	63	28	446	9.3	28
Jim Jackson	49	1175	152	370	.411	85	101	.842	36	123	159	128	80	0	43	82	6	414	8.4	21
Greg Anthony	50	806	104	251	.414	62	89	.697	14	49	63	100	75	0	66	55	3	319	6.4	23
Bonzi Wells	7	35	11	20	.550	8	18	.444	4	5	9	3	5	0	1	6	1	31	4.4	12
Stacey Augmon	48	874	78	174	.448	52	76	.684	47	78	125	58	81	0	57	30	18	208	4.3	12
John Crotty*	3	19	4	8	.500	3	3	1.000	0	1	1	5	1	0	2	0	0	12	4.0	8
Kelvin Cato	43	545	58	129	.450	34	67	.507	49	101	150	19	100	3	23	27	56	151	3.5	14
Jermaine O'Neal	36	311	36	83	.434	18	35	.514	42	55	97	13	41	0	4	14	14	90	2.5	9
Carlos Rogers	2	8	2	2	1.000	1	4	.250	0	1	1	1	2	0	0	0	0	5	2.5	3
Gary Grant	2	7	0	1	.000	0	0	...	0	0	0	3	0	0	1	0	0	0	0.0	0
Brian Shaw	1	5	0	1	.000	0	0	...	0	1	1	1	1	0	0	1	0	0	0.0	0

3-pt. FG: Portland 246-675 (.364)—Rider 42-111 (.378); Wallace 13-31 (.419); Stoudamire 44-142 (.310); Sabonis 7-24 (.292); Williams 63-144 (.438); Wells 1-3 (.333); Jackson 25-90 (.278); Anthony 49-125 (.392); Augmon 0-2 (.000); Crotty* 1-1 (1.000); Cato 1-1 (1.000); O'Neal 0-1 (.000). Opponents 220-691 (.318).

SACRAMENTO KINGS

	G	Min.	FGM	FGA	Pct.	FTM	FTA	Pct.	Off.	Def.	Tot.	Ast.	PF	Dq.	Stl.	TO	Blk.	Pts.	Avg.	Hi.
									REBOUNDS									**SCORING**		
Chris Webber	42	1719	378	778	.486	79	174	.454	149	396	545	173	145	1	60	148	89	839	20.0	36
Vlade Divac	50	1761	262	557	.470	179	255	.702	140	361	501	215	166	2	44	131	51	714	14.3	29
Corliss Williamson	50	1374	269	555	.485	120	188	.638	85	121	206	66	118	1	30	75	8	659	13.2	29
Jason Williams	50	1805	231	617	.374	79	105	.752	14	139	153	299	91	0	95	143	1	641	12.8	27
Vernon Maxwell	46	1007	164	421	.390	84	114	.737	13	72	85	76	111	1	30	67	3	492	10.7	33
Tariq Abdul-Wahad	49	1205	177	407	.435	94	136	.691	72	114	186	50	121	0	50	70	16	454	9.3	19
Lawrence Funderburke	47	936	167	299	.559	85	120	.708	101	121	222	30	77	0	22	52	23	420	8.9	18
Predrag Stojakovic	48	1025	141	373	.378	63	74	.851	43	100	143	72	43	0	41	53	7	402	8.4	26
Scot Pollard	16	259	33	61	.541	16	23	.696	38	44	82	4	41	0	8	5	18	82	5.1	16
Jon Barry	43	736	59	138	.428	71	84	.845	25	71	96	112	61	1	53	47	5	213	5.0	20
Oliver Miller	4	35	5	11	.455	0	0	...	7	1	8	0	3	0	0	4	2	10	2.5	6
Terry Dehere*	4	20	4	11	.364	0	0	...	2	0	2	1	2	0	2	2	0	9	2.3	5
Kevin Ollie*	7	68	4	13	.308	4	5	.800	0	6	6	3	8	0	3	3	1	12	1.7	6
Michael Hawkins	24	203	14	40	.350	3	3	1.000	10	15	25	27	14	0	3	13	1	36	1.5	11
Jerome James	16	42	9	24	.375	6	12	.500	6	11	17	1	11	0	2	9	6	24	1.5	5
Peter Aluma	2	5	1	2	.500	0	0	...	1	1	2	0	4	0	1	2	1	2	1.0	2

3-pt. FG: Sacramento 290-943 (.308)—Webber 4-34 (.118); Divac 11-43 (.256); Williamson 1-5 (.200); Williams 100-323 (.310); Maxwell 80-231 (.346); Barry 24-79 (.304); Abdul-Wahad 6-21 (.286); Funderburke 1-5 (.200); Stojakovic 57-178 (.320); Dehere* 1-5 (.200); Hawkins 5-19 (.263). Opponents 219-652 (.336).

1998-99

SAN ANTONIO SPURS

	G	Min.	FGM	FGA	Pct.	FTM	FTA	Pct.	Off.	Def.	Tot.	Ast.	PF	Dq.	Stl.	TO	Blk.	Pts.	Avg.	Hi.
Tim Duncan	50	1963	418	845	.495	247	358	.690	159	412	571	121	147	2	45	146	126	1084	21.7	39
David Robinson	49	1554	268	527	.509	239	363	.658	148	344	492	103	143	0	69	108	119	775	15.8	29
Sean Elliott	50	1509	208	507	.410	106	140	.757	35	178	213	117	104	1	26	71	17	561	11.2	22
Avery Johnson	50	1672	218	461	.473	50	88	.568	22	96	118	369	101	0	51	112	11	487	9.7	24
Mario Elie	47	1291	156	331	.471	103	119	.866	36	101	137	89	91	0	46	61	12	455	9.7	23
Jaren Jackson.......	47	861	108	284	.380	32	39	.821	21	78	99	49	63	0	41	37	9	301	6.4	21
Malik Rose	47	608	93	201	.463	98	146	.671	90	92	182	29	120	0	40	56	22	284	6.0	22
Antonio Daniels.....	47	614	83	183	.454	49	65	.754	13	41	54	106	39	0	30	44	6	220	4.7	13
Steve Kerr..........	44	734	68	174	.391	31	35	.886	6	38	44	49	28	0	23	22	3	192	4.4	14
Jerome Kersey	45	699	68	200	.340	6	14	.429	42	88	130	41	92	1	37	30	14	145	3.2	10
Will Perdue.........	37	445	38	60	.633	14	26	.538	33	105	138	18	63	0	9	22	10	90	2.4	8
Gerard King	19	63	6	14	.429	11	18	.611	6	8	14	4	12	0	2	4	1	23	1.2	5
Andrew Gaze.......	19	58	8	25	.320	0	0	...	2	3	5	6	7	0	2	4	1	21	1.1	6
Brandon Williams	3	4	0	0	...	2	4	.500	1	0	1	0	0	0	0	0	0	2	0.7	1

3-pt. FG: San Antonio 172-521 (.330)—Duncan 1-7 (.143); Robinson 0-1 (.000); Elliott 39-119 (.328); Johnson 1-12 (.083); Elie 40-107 (.374); Jackson 53-147 (.361); Rose 0-1 (.000); Daniels 5-17 (.294); Kerr 25-80 (.313); Kersey 3-14 (.214); Gaze 5-16 (.313). Opponents 170-559 (.304).

SEATTLE SUPERSONICS

	G	Min.	FGM	FGA	Pct.	FTM	FTA	Pct.	Off.	Def.	Tot.	Ast.	PF	Dq.	Stl.	TO	Blk.	Pts.	Avg.	Hi.
Gary Payton	50	2008	401	923	.434	199	276	.721	62	182	244	436	115	0	109	154	12	1084	21.7	34
Detlef Schrempf	50	1765	259	549	.472	200	243	.823	77	293	370	184	152	0	41	103	26	752	15.0	28
Vin Baker	34	1162	198	437	.453	72	160	.450	86	125	211	56	121	2	32	76	34	468	13.8	31
Don MacLean	17	365	63	159	.396	50	80	.625	18	47	65	16	34	0	5	25	5	185	10.9	24
Hersey Hawkins	50	1644	171	408	.419	119	132	.902	51	150	201	123	90	1	80	80	18	516	10.3	24
Dale Ellis..........	48	1232	174	395	.441	53	70	.757	25	90	115	38	77	1	25	45	3	495	10.3	22
Billy Owens.........	21	451	65	165	.394	28	35	.800	35	45	80	38	37	0	12	33	4	163	7.8	19
Olden Polynice	48	1481	160	368	.472	29	94	.309	184	241	425	43	150	0	20	49	30	368	7.7	18
John Crotty†	24	363	47	116	.405	40	47	.851	8	22	30	58	30	0	9	33	0	147	6.1	19
John Crotty‡.........	27	382	51	124	.411	43	50	.860	8	23	31	63	31	0	11	33	0	159	5.9	19
Vladimir Stepania	23	313	53	125	.424	21	40	.525	27	48	75	12	58	0	10	32	23	127	5.5	17
Jelani McCoy	26	331	56	76	.737	21	42	.500	27	52	79	4	42	0	11	10	20	133	5.1	14
Aaron Williams	40	458	52	123	.423	54	74	.730	54	74	128	22	75	1	14	30	24	158	4.0	14
Moochie Norris......	12	140	13	40	.325	6	16	.375	4	16	20	24	17	0	7	16	0	38	3.2	12
James Cotton	10	59	6	18	.333	13	18	.722	2	8	10	0	6	0	3	3	0	25	2.5	10
Rashard Lewis	20	145	19	52	.365	8	14	.571	13	12	25	4	19	0	8	20	1	47	2.4	8
Drew Barry	17	183	10	32	.313	9	13	.692	3	17	20	29	24	0	7	12	1	37	2.2	8

3-pt. FG: Seattle 309-899 (.344)—Payton 83-281 (.295); Schrempf 34-86 (.395); Baker 0-3 (.000); MacLean 9-33 (.273); Hawkins 55-180 (.306); Ellis 94-217 (.433); Owens 5-11 (.455); Polynice 1-1 (1.000); Crotty† 13-35 (.371); Crotty‡ 14-36 (.389); Stepania 0-3 (.000); Williams 0-1 (.000); Norris 6-15 (.400); Cotton 0-3 (.000); Lewis 1-6 (.167); Barry 8-24 (.333). Opponents 264-765 (.345).

TORONTO RAPTORS

	G	Min.	FGM	FGA	Pct.	FTM	FTA	Pct.	Off.	Def.	Tot.	Ast.	PF	Dq.	Stl.	TO	Blk.	Pts.	Avg.	Hi.
Vince Carter	50	1760	345	766	.450	204	268	.761	94	189	283	149	140	2	55	110	77	913	18.3	32
Doug Christie	50	1768	252	650	.388	207	246	.841	59	148	207	187	111	1	113	119	26	700	15.2	20
Kevin Willis.........	42	1216	187	447	.418	130	155	.839	109	241	350	67	134	1	28	86	28	504	12.0	28
Dee Brown	49	1377	187	495	.378	40	55	.727	15	88	103	143	75	0	56	80	8	549	11.2	29
Tracy McGrady	49	1106	168	385	.436	114	157	.726	120	158	278	113	94	1	52	80	66	458	9.3	27
John Wallace	48	812	153	354	.432	105	150	.700	54	117	171	46	92	0	12	70	43	411	8.6	21
Charles Oakley	50	1633	140	327	.428	67	83	.807	96	278	374	168	182	4	46	96	21	348	7.0	18
Alvin Williams......	50	1051	95	237	.401	44	52	.846	19	63	82	130	94	1	51	56	12	248	5.0	11
John Thomas	39	593	71	123	.577	27	48	.563	65	69	134	15	82	0	17	21	9	169	4.3	13
Reggie Slater	30	263	31	81	.383	53	85	.624	36	34	70	5	50	0	3	25	3	115	3.8	12
Michael Stewart	42	394	22	53	.415	17	25	.680	43	56	99	5	76	0	4	12	28	61	1.5	9
Sean Marks	8	28	5	8	.625	1	2	.500	0	1	1	0	3	0	1	3	0	11	1.4	4
Negele Knight........	6	56	3	8	.375	2	4	.500	1	5	6	8	5	0	1	7	0	8	1.3	2
Micheal Williams.....	2	15	1	5	.200	0	0	...	1	0	1	0	1	0	0	1	0	2	1.0	2
Mark Baker..........	1	2	0	1	.000	0	0	...	0	0	0	0	0	0	0	1	0	0	0.0	0
William Cunningham*..	1	1	0	0	...	0	0	...	0	0	0	0	0	0	0	0	0	0	0.0	0

3-pt. FG: Toronto 226-662 (.341)—Carter 19-66 (.288); Christie 49-161 (.304); Willis 0-2 (.000); Brown 135-349 (.387); McGrady 8-35 (.229); Oakley 1-5 (.200); A. Williams 14-42 (.333); Thomas 0-1 (.000); Knight 0-1 (.000). Opponents 255-686 (.372).

UTAH JAZZ

	G	Min.	FGM	FGA	Pct.	FTM	FTA	Pct.	Off.	Def.	Tot.	Ast.	PF	Dq.	Stl.	TO	Blk.	Pts.	Avg.	Hi.
Karl Malone	49	1832	393	797	.493	378	480	.788	107	356	463	201	134	0	62	162	28	1164	23.8	38
Bryon Russell.......	50	1770	217	468	.464	136	171	.795	65	201	266	74	154	3	76	76	15	622	12.4	25

	G	Min.	FGM	FGA	Pct.	FTM	FTA	Pct.	REBOUNDS			Ast.	PF	Dq.	Stl.	TO	Blk.	SCORING		
									Off.	Def.	Tot.							Pts.	Avg.	Hi.
Jeff Hornacek	48	1435	214	449	.477	125	140	.893	33	127	160	192	95	0	52	82	14	587	12.2	23
John Stockton	50	1410	200	410	.488	137	169	.811	31	115	146	374	107	0	81	110	13	553	11.1	26
Shandon Anderson	50	1072	162	363	.446	89	125	.712	49	83	132	56	89	0	39	66	10	427	8.5	18
Howard Eisley	50	1038	140	314	.446	67	80	.838	12	82	94	185	122	0	30	109	2	368	7.4	17
Greg Ostertag	48	1340	99	208	.476	75	121	.620	105	243	348	23	140	2	12	45	131	273	5.7	16
Thurl Bailey	43	543	78	175	.446	25	34	.735	36	58	94	26	78	0	9	27	28	181	4.2	11
Adam Keefe	44	642	56	124	.452	62	89	.697	51	91	142	28	63	0	16	33	12	174	4.0	15
Todd Fuller	42	462	56	124	.452	30	50	.600	28	73	101	6	60	0	6	27	14	142	3.4	12
Greg Foster	42	458	52	138	.377	13	21	.619	28	55	83	25	63	1	6	24	8	118	2.8	12
Jacque Vaughn	19	87	11	30	.367	20	24	.833	1	10	11	12	14	0	5	14	0	44	2.3	10
Anthony Avent	5	44	4	13	.308	1	2	.500	8	4	12	1	6	0	2	7	0	9	1.8	5
Chris King	8	42	2	7	.286	0	4	.000	1	10	11	1	8	0	2	4	1	4	0.5	2

3-pt. FG: Utah 140-388 (.361)—Malone 0-1 (.000); Russell 52-147 (.354); Hornacek 34-81 (.420); Stockton 16-50 (.320); Anderson 14-41 (.341); Eisley 21-50 (.420); Bailey 0-2 (.000); Keefe 0-4 (.000); Foster 1-4 (.250); Vaughn 2-8 (.250). Opponents 214-666 (.321).

VANCOUVER GRIZZLIES

	G	Min.	FGM	FGA	Pct.	FTM	FTA	Pct.	REBOUNDS			Ast.	PF	Dq.	Stl.	TO	Blk.	SCORING		
									Off.	Def.	Tot.							Pts.	Avg.	Hi.
Shareef Abdur-Rahim	50	2021	386	893	.432	369	439	.841	114	260	374	172	137	1	69	186	55	1152	23.0	39
Mike Bibby	50	1758	260	605	.430	127	169	.751	30	106	136	325	122	0	78	146	5	662	13.2	26
Sam Mack*	19	577	86	212	.406	28	30	.933	7	46	53	23	53	1	20	20	1	242	12.7	26
Tony Massenburg	43	1143	189	388	.487	103	155	.665	83	174	257	23	108	0	26	64	39	481	11.2	28
Bryant Reeves	25	702	102	251	.406	67	116	.578	50	88	138	37	103	3	13	47	8	271	10.8	28
Felipe Lopez	47	1218	169	379	.446	87	135	.644	69	97	166	62	128	0	49	82	14	437	9.3	23
Doug West	14	294	31	65	.477	19	25	.760	5	20	25	19	38	1	16	12	7	81	5.8	16
Cherokee Parks	48	1118	118	275	.429	30	55	.545	75	168	243	36	114	0	28	49	28	266	5.5	14
Michael Smith	48	1098	77	144	.535	76	128	.594	135	215	350	48	107	0	46	60	18	230	4.8	12
DeJuan Wheat	46	590	73	193	.378	40	55	.727	11	34	45	102	59	0	26	48	2	208	4.5	11
Pete Chilcutt	46	697	63	172	.366	14	17	.824	29	88	117	30	52	0	22	28	12	166	3.6	16
Rodrick Rhodes†	10	123	11	44	.250	11	19	.579	7	6	13	10	16	0	4	15	2	34	3.4	10
Rodrick Rhodes‡	13	156	13	52	.250	16	25	.640	9	8	17	11	21	0	5	20	2	43	3.3	10
J.R. Henderson	30	331	35	96	.365	25	45	.556	20	27	47	22	29	1	9	18	4	97	3.2	10
Terry Dehere†	22	271	27	74	.365	5	7	.714	5	17	22	26	28	0	5	14	3	74	3.4	9
Terry Dehere‡	26	291	31	85	.365	5	7	.714	7	17	24	27	30	0	7	16	3	83	3.2	9
Lee Mayberry	9	126	7	19	.368	4	5	.800	0	3	3	23	13	0	7	11	0	20	2.2	5
Jason Sasser	6	39	5	11	.455	1	2	.500	2	5	7	2	4	0	2	2	0	11	1.8	5
Carl Herrera*	4	42	3	13	.231	0	2	.000	5	3	8	3	3	0	0	4	0	6	1.5	4
Makhtar Ndiaye	4	27	1	4	.250	3	4	.750	3	2	5	1	9	0	0	1	1	5	1.3	4

3-pt. FG: Vancouver 148-453 (.327)—Abdur-Rahim 11-36 (.306); Bibby 15-74 (.203); Mack* 42-108 (.389); Massenburg 0-2 (.000); Reeves 0-1 (.000); Lopez 12-44 (.273); West 0-2 (.000); Parks 0-1 (.000); Smith 0-1 (.000); Wheat 22-60 (.367); Chilcutt 26-68 (.382); Rhodes† 1-7 (.143); Rhodes‡ 1-7 (.143); Henderson 2-5 (.400); Dehere† 15-34 (.441); Dehere‡ 16-39 (.410); Mayberry 2-10 (.200). Opponents 229-653 (.351).

WASHINGTON WIZARDS

	G	Min.	FGM	FGA	Pct.	FTM	FTA	Pct.	REBOUNDS			Ast.	PF	Dq.	Stl.	TO	Blk.	SCORING		
									Off.	Def.	Tot.							Pts.	Avg.	Hi.
Mitch Richmond	50	1912	331	803	.412	251	293	.857	30	142	172	122	121	1	64	136	10	983	19.7	35
Juwan Howard	36	1430	286	604	.474	110	146	.753	90	203	293	107	130	1	42	95	14	682	18.9	29
Rod Strickland	44	1632	251	603	.416	176	236	.746	56	156	212	434	91	0	76	142	5	690	15.7	31
Otis Thorpe	49	1539	240	440	.545	74	106	.698	96	238	334	101	196	9	42	88	19	554	11.3	22
Calbert Cheaney	50	1266	172	415	.414	33	67	.493	33	108	141	73	146	0	39	42	16	385	7.7	22
Tracy Murray	36	653	83	237	.350	34	42	.810	18	63	81	27	65	0	21	29	6	233	6.5	20
Ben Wallace	46	1231	115	199	.578	47	132	.356	137	247	384	18	111	0	50	36	90	277	6.0	20
Chris Whitney	39	441	64	156	.410	27	31	.871	8	39	47	69	49	0	18	36	2	187	4.8	13
Randell Jackson	27	271	46	108	.426	21	32	.656	30	24	54	8	29	0	3	26	11	114	4.2	17
Tim Legler	30	377	51	115	.443	3	6	.500	8	32	40	21	42	0	4	14	3	119	4.0	13
Jeff McInnis	35	427	50	134	.373	21	28	.750	9	12	21	73	36	0	19	30	1	130	3.7	19
Terry Davis	37	578	49	92	.533	28	38	.737	50	89	139	10	79	0	11	16	3	126	3.4	12
Jahidi White	20	191	17	32	.531	15	35	.429	23	35	58	1	39	1	3	16	11	49	2.5	9
John Coker	14	98	13	31	.419	5	6	.833	7	15	22	0	17	0	1	2	2	31	2.2	8
Etdrick Bohannon	2	4	0	0	...	0	0	...	0	0	0	0	0	0	0	0	0	0	0.0	0

3-pt. FG: Washington 179-580 (.309)—Richmond 70-221 (.317); Howard 0-3 (.000); Strickland 12-42 (.286); Thorpe 0-2 (.000); Cheaney 8-37 (.216); Murray 33-103 (.320); Whitney 32-95 (.337); Jackson 1-7 (.143); Legler 14-35 (.400); McInnis 9-35 (.257). Opponents 218-619 (.352).

* Finished season with another team. † Totals with this team only. ‡ Totals with all teams.

EASTERN CONFERENCE
FIRST ROUND

New York 3, Miami 2

May 8—Sat.	New York 95 at Miami	.75
May 10—Mon.	New York 73 at Miami	.83
May 12—Wed.	Miami 73 at New York	.97
May 14—Fri.	Miami 87 at New York	.72
May 16—Sun.	New York 78 at Miami	.77

Atlanta 3, Detroit 2

May 8—Sat.	Detroit 70 at Atlanta	.90
May 10—Mon.	Detroit 69 at Atlanta	.89
May 12—Wed.	Atlanta 63 at Detroit	.79
May 14—Fri.	Atlanta 82 at Detroit	.103
May 16—Sun.	Detroit 75 at Atlanta	.87

Indiana 3, Milwaukee 0

May 9—Sun.	Milwaukee 88 at Indiana	.110
May 11—Tue.	Milwaukee 107 at Indiana	.*108
May 13—Thur.	Indiana 99 at Milwaukee	.91

Philadelphia 3, Orlando 1

May 9—Sun.	Philadelphia 104 at Orlando	.90
May 11—Tue.	Philadelphia 68 at Orlando	.79
May 13—Thur.	Orlando 85 at Philadelphia	.97
May 15—Sat.	Orlando 91 at Philadelphia	.101

SEMIFINALS

Indiana 4, Philadelphia 0

May 17—Mon.	Philadelphia 90 at Indiana	.94
May 19—Wed.	Philadelphia 82 at Indiana	.85
May 21—Fri.	Indiana 97 at Philadelphia	.86
May 23—Sun.	Indiana 89 at Philadelphia	.86

New York 4, Atlanta 0

May 18—Tue.	New York 100 at Atlanta	.92
May 20—Thur.	New York 77 at Atlanta	.70
May 23—Sun.	Atlanta 78 at New York	.90
May 24—Mon.	Atlanta 66 at New York	.79

FINALS

New York 4, Indiana 2

May 30—Sun.	New York 93 at Indiana	.90
June 1—Tue.	New York 86 at Indiana	.88
June 5—Sat.	Indiana 91 at New York	.92
June 7—Mon.	Indiana 90 at New York	.78
June 9—Wed.	New York 101 at Indiana	.94
June 11—Fri.	Indiana 82 at New York	.90

WESTERN CONFERENCE
FIRST ROUND

San Antonio 3, Minnesota 1

May 9—Sun.	Minnesota 86 at San Antonio	.99
May 11—Tue.	Minnesota 80 at San Antonio	.71
May 13—Thur.	San Antonio 85 at Minnesota	.71
May 15—Sat.	San Antonio 92 at Minnesota	.85

L.A. Lakers 3, Houston 1

May 9—Sun.	Houston 100 at L.A. Lakers	.101
May 11—Tue.	Houston 98 at L.A. Lakers	.110
May 13—Thur.	L.A. Lakers 88 at Houston	.102
May 15—Sat.	L.A. Lakers 98 at Houston	.88

Portland 3, Phoenix 0

May 8—Sat.	Phoenix 85 at Portland	.95
May 10—Mon.	Phoenix 99 at Portland	.110
May 12—Wed.	Portland 103 at Phoenix	.93

Utah 3, Sacramento 2

May 8—Sat.	Sacramento 87 at Utah	.117
May 10—Mon.	Sacramento 101 at Utah	.90
May 12—Wed.	Utah 81 at Sacramento	.*84
May 14—Fri.	Utah 90 at Sacramento	.89
May 16—Sun.	Sacramento 92 at Utah	.*99

SEMIFINALS

San Antonio 4, L.A. Lakers 0

May 17—Mon.	L.A. Lakers 81 at San Antonio	.87
May 19—Wed.	L.A. Lakers 76 at San Antonio	.79
May 22—Sat.	San Antonio 103 at L.A. Lakers	.91
May 23—Sun.	San Antonio 118 at L.A. Lakers	.107

Portland 4, Utah 2

May 18—Tue.	Portland 83 at Utah	.93
May 20—Thur.	Portland 84 at Utah	.81
May 22—Sat.	Utah 87 at Portland	.97
May 23—Sun.	Utah 75 at Portland	.81
May 25—Tue.	Portland 71 at Utah	.88
May 27—Thur.	Utah 80 at Portland	.92

FINALS

San Antonio 4, Portland 0

May 29—Sat.	Portland 76 at San Antonio	.80
May 31—Mon.	Portland 85 at San Antonio	.86
June 4—Fri.	San Antonio 85 at Portland	.63
June 6—Sun.	San Antonio 94 at Portland	.80

1998-99

NBA FINALS

San Antonio 4, New York 1

June 16—Wed.	New York 77 at San Antonio	.89
June 18—Fri.	New York 67 at San Antonio	.80
June 21—Mon.	San Antonio 81 at New York	.89
June 23—Wed.	San Antonio 96 at New York	.89
June 25—Fri.	San Antonio 78 at New York	.77

*Denotes number of overtime periods.

1997-98

1997-98 NBA CHAMPION CHICAGO BULLS

Front row (from left): Randy Brown, Ron Harper, Scottie Pippen, Michael Jordan, Dennis Rodman, Jud Buechler, Steve Kerr. Center row (from left): Rusty LaRue, Dickey Simpkins, Toni Kukoc, Joe Kleine, Luc Longley, Bill Wennington, Scott Burrell, Keith Booth. Back row (from left): trainer Robert "Chip" Schaefer, assistant coach Frank Hamblen, assistant coach Bill Cartwright, head coach Phil Jackson, assistant coach Jimmy Rodgers, assistant coach Tex Winter, equipment manager John Ligmanowski.

FINAL STANDINGS

ATLANTIC DIVISION

	Atl.	Bos.	Cha.	Chi.	Cle.	Dal.	Den.	Det.	G.S.	Hou.	Ind.	LA-C	LA-L	Mia.	Mil.	Min.	N.J.	N.Y.	Orl.	Phi.	Pho.	Por.	Sac.	S.A.	Sea.	Tor.	Uta.	Van.	Was.	W	L	Pct.	GB
Mia.	3	4	1	1	3	2	2	2	2	2	1	2	1	..	3	1	3	2	3	4	0	2	2	0	0	4	1	2	2	55	27	.671	-
N.J.	2	2	2	0	1	2	2	2	1	1	1	1	1	4	0	1	..	2	3	3	1	1	2	1	0	3	0	2	1	43	39	.524	12
N.Y.	2	2	3	0	2	1	2	2	1	1	1	2	1	2	1	1	2	..	4	2	2	1	1	0	1	3	0	2	1	43	39	.524	12
Was.	0	2	2	1	2	1	1	2	2	1	0	2	1	2	2	2	3	3	1	1	1	1	1	1	1	3	2	1	..	42	40	.512	13
Orl.	2	2	1	1	2	2	2	2	1	2	1	2	1	1	1	2	1	0	..	4	0	2	0	0	1	3	0	2	3	41	41	.500	14
Bos.	1	..	1	1	1	1	1	2	1	1	0	2	1	0	2	1	2	2	2	3	0	1	1	0	1	3	0	2	3	36	46	.439	19
Phi.	1	1	1	1	1	2	2	1	2	1	0	1	2	0	2	0	1	2	0	..	1	1	1	0	0	2	0	2	3	31	51	.378	24

CENTRAL DIVISION

	Atl.	Bos.	Cha.	Chi.	Cle.	Dal.	Den.	Det.	G.S.	Hou.	Ind.	LA-C	LA-L	Mia.	Mil.	Min.	N.J.	N.Y.	Orl.	Phi.	Pho.	Por.	Sac.	S.A.	Sea.	Tor.	Uta.	Van.	Was.	W	L	Pct.	GB
Chi.	3	3	3	..	2	1	2	3	2	2	2	2	1	2	4	1	4	4	3	2	1	1	2	2	1	4	0	2	3	62	20	.756	..
Ind.	3	4	1	2	2	1	2	3	2	1	..	2	0	3	4	2	2	3	4	1	1	2	0	0	4	1	2	4	4	58	24	.707	4
Cha.	0	2	..	1	2	2	2	3	1	2	3	2	1	3	3	1	2	1	3	2	1	2	1	1	4	1	2	2	2	51	31	.622	11
Atl.	..	2	4	1	4	2	2	2	1	1	2	0	1	3	0	1	2	2	3	1	2	1	1	4	0	2	4	0	2	50	32	.610	12
Cle.	0	3	2	2	..	1	2	3	2	1	2	2	3	1	2	3	2	1	3	2	1	0	0	3	1	2	1	1	1	47	35	.573	15
Det.	2	2	1	1	1	2	2	..	2	1	1	2	0	1	2	0	2	2	1	3	1	0	1	1	0	4	0	0	2	37	45	.451	25
Mil.	1	2	1	0	2	2	2	2	2	1	0	2	0	1	..	1	3	2	2	2	0	2	2	0	1	3	0	1	1	36	46	.439	26
Tor.	0	0	0	0	1	1	2	0	2	0	0	1	0	0	0	1	1	1	1	2	0	1	0	0	0	..	0	1	0	16	66	.195	46

MIDWEST DIVISION

	Atl.	Bos.	Cha.	Chi.	Cle.	Dal.	Den.	Det.	G.S.	Hou.	Ind.	LA-C	LA-L	Mia.	Mil.	Min.	N.J.	N.Y.	Orl.	Phi.	Pho.	Por.	Sac.	S.A.	Sea.	Tor.	Uta.	Van.	Was.	W	L	Pct.	GB
Utah	2	2	1	2	1	4	4	2	4	4	1	3	1	1	2	3	2	2	2	3	1	2	3	2	2	2	..	4	0	62	20	.756	..
S.A.	1	2	1	0	2	4	4	1	3	2	2	3	0	2	2	3	1	2	2	2	1	2	4	..	2	2	1	4	1	56	26	.683	6
Min.	2	1	1	1	0	2	3	2	4	3	0	4	0	1	1	..	2	1	1	2	0	3	1	3	1	1	1	4	0	45	37	.549	17
Hou.	1	1	0	0	1	4	4	1	3	..	1	4	1	0	1	1	1	1	0	1	1	1	4	2	1	2	0	3	1	41	41	.500	21
Dal.	2	1	0	1	1	..	3	0	1	0	1	1	0	0	0	2	0	1	0	0	0	0	0	2	1	0	4	1	1	20	62	.244	42
Van.	0	0	0	0	0	3	2	3	1	0	3	0	0	0	1	0	0	0	0	0	2	2	0	1	0	1	0	..	1	19	63	.232	43
Den.	0	1	0	0	0	1	..	0	1	0	0	2	0	0	0	1	0	0	0	0	2	1	0	0	0	0	1	1	1	11	71	.134	51

PACIFIC DIVISION

	Atl.	Bos.	Cha.	Chi.	Cle.	Dal.	Den.	Det.	G.S.	Hou.	Ind.	LA-C	LA-L	Mia.	Mil.	Min.	N.J.	N.Y.	Orl.	Phi.	Pho.	Por.	Sac.	S.A.	Sea.	Tor.	Uta.	Van.	Was.	W	L	Pct.	GB
L.A.L.	2	1	1	1	1	4	4	2	3	3	2	4	..	1	2	4	1	1	1	0	2	2	4	4	1	2	3	4	1	61	21	.744	..
Sea.	1	1	1	2	2	4	2	3	3	2	4	3	2	1	3	2	1	1	2	2	4	3	2	2	..	2	2	4	1	61	21	.744	..
Pho.	2	2	1	1	0	4	4	1	4	3	1	4	2	2	2	1	1	0	2	1	..	2	3	3	2	2	1	4	1	56	26	.683	5
Por.	1	0	1	1	4	2	2	3	1	4	2	3	2	2	3	1	1	0	1	2	2	..	3	2	2	3	2	2	1	46	36	.561	15
Sac.	0	1	1	0	0	4	3	1	2	0	0	2	0	1	2	1	1	0	1	2	1	1	..	0	1	1	2	2	1	27	55	.329	34
G.S.	0	1	1	0	0	3	3	0	..	1	0	1	1	0	0	0	1	1	0	1	2	1	1	0	0	1	1	0	0	19	63	.232	42
L.A.C.	0	0	0	0	3	2	0	3	0	0	..	0	0	0	0	1	0	1	0	1	0	3	1	0	1	1	1	1	0	17	65	.207	44

OFFENSIVE

	G	FGM	FGA	Pct.	FTM	FTA	Pct.	REBOUNDS Off.	Def.	Tot.	Ast.	PF	Dq.	Stl.	TO	Blk.	SCORING Pts.	Avg.
L.A. Lakers....	82	3146	6536	.481	1863	2743	.679	1079	2471	3550	2009	1859	15	734	1256	556	8652	105.5
Minnesota...	82	3157	6844	.461	1673	2253	.743	1063	2429	3492	2068	1882	14	639	1138	427	8290	101.1
Utah.........	82	2993	6113	.490	2044	2644	.773	962	2405	3367	2070	1961	13	648	1260	412	8279	101.0
Seattle.......	82	3052	6458	.473	1521	2109	.721	931	2225	3156	1986	1812	11	804	1145	376	8246	100.6
New Jersey ...	82	3055	6928	.441	1750	2351	.744	1344	2137	3481	1685	1917	21	777	1180	314	8170	99.6
Phoenix......	82	3138	6710	.468	1459	1948	.749	991	2452	3443	2124	1765	20	756	1236	429	8166	99.6
Houston......	82	2946	6513	.452	1634	2120	.771	987	2350	3337	1799	1653	7	686	1298	294	8099	98.8
Washington ...	82	3080	6811	.452	1489	2156	.691	1121	2341	3462	1900	1839	20	689	1156	379	7969	97.2
Chicago......	82	3064	6801	.451	1492	2009	.743	1243	2438	3681	1952	1691	12	696	1178	353	7931	96.7
Charlotte	82	2968	6344	.468	1641	2186	.751	985	2341	3326	1941	1757	12	691	1247	312	7923	96.6
Vancouver	82	3006	6567	.458	1586	2145	.739	1081	2313	3394	1960	1809	10	614	1405	349	7923	96.6
Indiana.......	82	2921	6223	.469	1631	2136	.764	874	2348	3222	1889	1859	23	645	1168	368	7874	96.0
Atlanta.......	82	2887	6352	.455	1749	2314	.756	1105	2418	3523	1569	1671	13	653	1214	491	7860	95.9
Boston.......	82	3012	6934	.434	1425	1964	.726	1196	2044	3240	1816	2203	21	987	1330	366	7864	95.9
L.A. Clippers ..	82	2930	6690	.438	1480	2047	.723	1040	2276	3316	1533	1827	22	625	1323	456	7865	95.9
Miami	82	2850	6327	.450	1539	2082	.739	1028	2419	3447	1758	1982	28	665	1226	429	7787	95.0
Toronto	82	2965	6813	.435	1479	2060	.718	1187	2149	3336	1746	1851	21	769	1371	663	7781	94.9
Milwaukee ...	82	2918	6399	.456	1663	2167	.767	1035	2236	3271	1649	1915	23	733	1383	357	7748	94.5
Portland......	82	2885	6397	.451	1640	2226	.737	1086	2522	3608	1766	1859	23	585	1383	464	7734	94.3
Detroit.......	82	2862	6373	.449	1704	2288	.745	1044	2338	3382	1597	1805	19	678	1198	344	7721	94.2
Philadelphia ...	82	2837	6409	.443	1734	2352	.737	1125	2294	3419	1729	1878	16	729	1354	490	7651	93.3
Sacramento ...	82	2957	6684	.442	1440	2096	.687	1094	2304	3398	1836	1810	17	596	1271	420	7637	93.1
Cleveland.....	82	2817	6207	.454	1653	2187	.756	955	2331	3286	1894	1939	29	814	1418	419	7585	92.5
San Antonio ...	82	2898	6187	.468	1489	2164	.688	984	2638	3622	1839	1731	13	516	1318	568	7587	92.5
New York	82	2864	6413	.447	1399	1812	.772	978	2434	3412	1787	1947	24	634	1247	278	7509	91.6
Dallas.......	82	2882	6754	.427	1308	1738	.753	1007	2281	3288	1535	1643	20	646	1182	466	7494	91.4
Orlando	82	2771	6455	.429	1552	2138	.726	1178	2203	3381	1694	1617	6	649	1258	441	7387	90.1
Denver.......	82	2677	6412	.417	1658	2147	.772	1040	2157	3197	1547	1937	17	664	1311	393	7300	89.0
Golden State ..	82	2845	6884	.413	1358	1912	.710	1288	2473	3761	1708	1859	22	621	1369	448	7237	88.3

DEFENSIVE

	FGM	FGA	Pct.	FTM	FTA	Pct.	REBOUNDS Off.	Def.	Tot.	Ast.	PF	Dq.	Stl.	TO	Blk.	SCORING Pts.	Avg.	Dif.
San Antonio....	2737	6656	.411	1448	1956	.740	1017	2236	3253	1556	1845	20	730	1045	378	7260	88.5	+4.0
New York......	2624	6131	.428	1728	2304	.750	854	2341	3195	1585	1705	14	653	1138	313	7307	89.1	+2.5
Chicago.......	2797	6483	.431	1425	1956	.729	1016	2239	3255	1595	1774	24	657	1268	356	7348	89.6	+7.1
Cleveland......	2689	6214	.433	1642	2175	.755	948	2229	3177	1790	1904	21	707	1444	455	7361	89.8	+2.7
Indiana.......	2788	6451	.432	1525	2096	.728	1114	2254	3368	1591	1847	19	644	1237	366	7375	89.9	+6.1
Miami	2723	6355	.428	1632	2195	.744	1058	2232	3290	1630	1851	18	637	1214	370	7383	90.0	+5.0
Orlando	2930	6460	.454	1302	1769	.736	1089	2268	3357	1740	1866	16	747	1259	388	7475	91.2	-1.1
Atlanta........	2961	6698	.442	1302	1772	.735	1081	2152	3233	1753	1892	26	617	1184	372	7572	92.3	+3.6
Detroit........	2840	6377	.445	1549	2077	.746	991	2334	3325	1753	1874	18	648	1263	382	7592	92.6	+1.6
Portland	2810	6520	.431	1626	2253	.722	1011	2201	3212	1764	1823	13	770	1160	445	7619	92.9	+1.4
Seattle........	2896	6491	.446	1449	2001	.724	1141	2314	3455	1825	1824	14	640	1394	403	7658	93.4	+7.2
Phoenix.......	2923	6618	.442	1501	2051	.732	1051	2343	3394	1803	1769	17	720	1363	323	7741	94.4	+5.2
Utah	2806	6390	.439	1730	2284	.757	984	2012	2996	1690	2133	41	645	1157	423	7743	94.4	+6.6
Charlotte	2977	6417	.464	1436	1964	.731	965	2259	3224	1806	1902	18	582	1240	372	7759	94.6	+2.0
Philadelphia ...	2906	6440	.451	1651	2262	.730	1115	2341	3450	1927	1904	21	766	1318	508	7847	95.7	-2.4
Milwaukee.....	2911	6319	.461	1779	2393	.743	1001	2260	3261	1746	1808	15	765	1348	398	7905	96.4	-1.9
Washington....	2975	6540	.455	1623	2172	.747	1029	2468	3497	1725	1924	16	632	1328	372	7921	96.6	+0.6
Golden State ...	2992	6742	.444	1667	2266	.729	1134	2535	3669	2011	1638	6	757	1154	478	7985	97.4	-9.1
Dallas	3138	6819	.460	1333	1868	.714	1223	2644	3867	1882	1608	6	658	1240	374	7995	97.5	-6.1
L.A. Lakers	2984	6800	.439	1669	2281	.732	1123	2339	3462	1841	2151	32	660	1281	423	8017	97.8	+7.7
New Jersey	3016	6406	.471	1653	2211	.748	1079	2316	3395	1771	2023	23	616	1482	515	8041	98.1	+1.5
Boston........	2864	5981	.479	2052	2756	.745	1015	2446	3461	1826	1719	16	696	1688	406	8079	98.5	-2.6
Sacramento	3095	6776	.457	1560	2102	.742	1157	2533	3690	1824	1775	12	694	1256	466	8095	98.7	-5.6
Houston	3173	6769	.469	1406	1891	.744	1041	2326	3367	1914	1747	11	732	1170	365	8161	99.5	-0.7
Minnesota.....	3076	6860	.448	1648	2220	.742	1116	2411	3527	1909	1863	24	609	1228	412	8232	100.4	+0.7
Denver........	3015	6370	.473	1817	2410	.754	1095	2401	3496	1983	1782	13	662	1243	535	8266	100.8	-11.8
L.A. Clippers ...	3236	6832	.474	1663	2267	.734	1169	2469	3638	1826	1747	14	726	1158	412	8469	103.3	-7.4
Vancouver	3230	6797	.475	1634	2233	.732	1144	2358	3502	2101	1832	12	836	1163	538	8522	103.9	-7.3
Toronto	3271	6826	.479	1603	2289	.700	1270	2506	3776	2219	1748	12	737	1370	514	8541	104.2	-9.3
Avgs..........	2944	6536	.450	1588	2155	.737	1070	2337	3407	1806	1837	18	688	1270	416	7837	95.6	...

1997-98

HOME/ROAD

	Home	Road	Total		Home	Road	Total
Atlanta	29-12	21-20	50-32	Minnesota	26-15	19-22	45-37
Boston	24-17	12-29	36-46	New Jersey	26-15	17-24	43-39
Charlotte	32-9	19-22	51-31	New York	28-13	15-26	43-39
Chicago	37-4	25-16	62-20	Orlando	24-17	17-24	41-41
Cleveland	27-14	20-21	47-35	Philadelphia	19-22	12-29	31-51
Dallas	13-28	7-34	20-62	Phoenix	30-11	26-15	56-26
Denver	9-32	2-39	11-71	Portland	26-15	20-21	46-36
Detroit	25-16	12-29	37-45	Sacramento	21-20	6-35	27-55
Golden State	12-29	7-34	19-63	San Antonio	31-10	25-16	56-26
Houston	24-17	17-24	41-41	Seattle	35-6	26-15	61-21
Indiana	32-9	26-15	58-24	Toronto	9-32	7-34	16-66
L.A. Clippers	11-30	6-35	17-65	Utah	36-5	26-15	62-20
L.A. Lakers	33-8	28-13	61-21	Vancouver	14-27	5-36	19-63
Miami	30-11	25-16	55-27	Washington	24-17	18-23	42-40
Milwaukee	21-20	15-26	36-46	Totals	708-481	481-708	1189-1189

INDIVIDUAL LEADERS

POINTS

(minimum 70 games or 1,400 points)

	G	FGM	FTM	Pts.	Avg.
Michael Jordan, Chicago	82	881	565	2357	28.7
Shaquille O'Neal, L.A. Lakers	60	670	359	1699	28.3
Karl Malone, Utah	81	780	628	2190	27.0
Mitch Richmond, Sacramento	70	543	407	1623	23.2
Antoine Walker, Boston	82	722	305	1840	22.4
Shareef Abdur-Rahim, Vancouver	82	653	502	1829	22.3
Glen Rice, Charlotte	82	634	428	1826	22.3
Allen Iverson, Philadelphia	80	649	390	1758	22.0
Chris Webber, Washington	71	647	196	1555	21.9
David Robinson, San Antonio	73	544	485	1574	21.6

REBOUNDS

(minimum 70 games or 800 rebounds)

	G	Off.	Def.	Tot.	Avg.
Dennis Rodman, Chicago	80	421	780	1201	15.0
Jayson Williams, New Jersey	65	443	440	883	13.6
Tim Duncan, San Antonio	82	274	703	977	11.9
Dikembe Mutombo, Atlanta	82	276	656	932	11.4
David Robinson, San Antonio	73	239	536	775	10.6
Karl Malone, Utah	81	189	645	834	10.3
Anthony Mason, Charlotte	81	177	649	826	10.2
Antoine Walker, Boston	82	270	566	836	10.2
Arvydas Sabonis, Portland	73	149	580	729	10.0
Kevin Garnett, Minnesota	82	222	564	786	9.6

FIELD GOALS

(minimum 300 made)

	FGM	FGA	Pct.
Shaquille O'Neal, L.A. Lakers	670	1147	.584
Charles Outlaw, Orlando	301	543	.554
Alonzo Mourning, Miami	403	732	.551
Tim Duncan, San Antonio	706	1287	.549
Vin Baker, Seattle	631	1164	.542
Dikembe Mutombo, Atlanta	399	743	.537
Antonio McDyess, Phoenix	497	927	.536
Rasheed Wallace, Portland	466	875	.533
Karl Malone, Utah	780	1472	.530
Bryant Reeves, Vancouver	492	941	.523

STEALS

(minimum 70 games or 125 steals)

	G	No.	Avg.
Mookie Blaylock, Atlanta	70	183	2.61
Brevin Knight, Cleveland	80	196	2.45
Doug Christie, Toronto	78	190	2.44
Gary Payton, Seattle	82	185	2.26
Allen Iverson, Philadelphia	80	176	2.20
Eddie Jones, L.A. Lakers	80	160	2.00
Jason Kidd, Phoenix	82	162	1.98
Kendall Gill, New Jersey	81	156	1.93
Hersey Hawkins, Seattle	82	148	1.80
Clyde Drexler, Houston	70	126	1.80

FREE THROWS

(minimum 125 made)

	FTM	FTA	Pct.
Chris Mullin, Indiana	154	164	.939
Jeff Hornacek, Utah	285	322	.885
Ray Allen, Milwaukee	342	391	.875
Derek Anderson, Cleveland	275	315	.873
Kevin Johnson, Phoenix	162	186	.871
Tracy Murray, Washington	182	209	.871
Reggie Miller, Indiana	382	440	.868
Hersey Hawkins, Seattle	177	204	.868
Christian Laettner, Atlanta	306	354	.864
Mitch Richmond, Sacramento	407	471	.864

BLOCKED SHOTS

(minimum 70 games or 100 blocked shots)

	G	No.	Avg.
Marcus Camby, Toronto	63	230	3.65
Dikembe Mutombo, Atlanta	82	277	3.38
Shawn Bradley, Dallas	64	214	3.34
Theo Ratliff, Detroit-Philadelphia	82	258	3.15
David Robinson, San Antonio	73	192	2.63
Tim Duncan, San Antonio	82	206	2.51
Michael Stewart, Sacramento	81	195	2.41
Shaquille O'Neal, L.A. Lakers	60	144	2.40
Alonzo Mourning, Miami	58	130	2.24
Charles Outlaw, Orlando	82	181	2.21

ASSISTS

(minimum 70 games or 400 assists)

	G	No.	Avg.
Rod Strickland, Washington	76	801	10.5
Jason Kidd, Phoenix	82	745	9.1
Mark Jackson, Indiana	82	713	8.7
Stephon Marbury, Minnesota	82	704	8.6
John Stockton, Utah	64	543	8.5
Tim Hardaway, Miami	81	672	8.3
Gary Payton, Seattle	82	679	8.3
Brevin Knight, Cleveland	80	656	8.2
Damon Stoudamire, Toronto-Portland	71	580	8.2
Sam Cassell, New Jersey	75	603	8.0

3-POINT FIELD GOALS

(minimum 55 made)

	FGM	FGA	Pct.
Dale Ellis, Seattle	127	274	.464
Jeff Hornacek, Utah	56	127	.441
Chris Mullin, Indiana	107	243	.440
Hubert Davis, Dallas	101	230	.439
Steve Kerr, Chicago	57	130	.438
Glen Rice, Charlotte	130	300	.433
Wesley Person, Cleveland	192	447	.430
Reggie Miller, Indiana	164	382	.429
Dell Curry, Charlotte	61	145	.421
Eldridge Recasner, Atlanta	62	148	.419

1997-98

ATLANTA HAWKS

	G	Min.	FGM	FGA	Pct.	FTM	FTA	Pct.	REBOUNDS Off.	Def.	Tot.	Ast.	PF	Dq.	Stl.	TO	Blk.	SCORING Pts.	Avg.	Hi.
Steve Smith	73	2857	489	1101	.444	389	455	.855	133	176	309	292	219	4	75	176	29	1464	20.1	35
Alan Henderson	69	2000	365	753	.485	253	388	.652	199	243	442	73	175	1	42	110	36	986	14.3	39
Christian Laettner	74	2282	354	730	.485	306	354	.864	142	345	487	190	246	6	71	183	73	1020	13.8	25
Dikembe Mutombo	82	2917	399	743	.537	303	452	.670	276	656	932	82	254	1	34	168	277	1101	13.4	34
Mookie Blaylock	70	2700	368	938	.392	95	134	.709	81	260	341	469	122	0	183	176	21	921	13.2	26
Tyrone Corbin	79	2699	328	747	.439	101	128	.789	78	284	362	173	197	1	105	86	7	806	10.2	23
Eldridge Recasner	59	1454	206	452	.456	74	79	.937	32	110	142	117	94	0	41	91	1	548	9.3	23
Ed Gray	30	472	77	202	.381	55	65	.846	9	36	45	34	73	0	15	30	11	227	7.6	20
Chucky Brown	77	1202	161	372	.433	63	87	.724	57	126	183	55	100	0	23	51	13	387	5.0	14
Chris Crawford	40	256	46	110	.418	57	68	.838	20	21	41	9	27	0	12	18	7	150	3.8	9
Brian Oliver	5	61	7	19	.368	1	4	.250	3	6	9	2	4	0	1	1	0	15	3.0	7
Anthony Miller	37	228	29	52	.558	21	39	.538	30	40	70	3	41	0	15	14	3	79	2.1	12
Drew Barry	27	256	18	38	.474	11	13	.846	5	30	35	49	28	0	10	30	1	56	2.1	8
Greg Anderson	50	398	36	81	.444	16	41	.390	39	79	118	15	85	0	19	17	10	88	1.8	6
Randy Livingston	12	82	3	12	.250	4	5	.800	1	5	6	5	6	0	7	6	2	10	0.8	5
Donald Whiteside	3	16	1	2	.500	0	2	.000	0	1	1	1	0	0	0	1	0	2	0.7	2

3-pt. FG: Atlanta 337-1016 (.332)—Smith 97-276 (.351); Henderson 3-6 (.500); Laettner 6-27 (.222); Blaylock 90-334 (.269); Corbin 49-141 (.348); Recasner 62-148 (.419); Gray 18-46 (.391); Brown 2-8 (.250); Crawford 1-3 (.333); Barry 9-21 (.429); Anderson 0-5 (.000); Whiteside 0-1 (.000). Opponents 348-1017 (.342).

BOSTON CELTICS

	G	Min.	FGM	FGA	Pct.	FTM	FTA	Pct.	REBOUNDS Off.	Def.	Tot.	Ast.	PF	Dq.	Stl.	TO	Blk.	SCORING Pts.	Avg.	Hi.
Antoine Walker	82	3268	722	1705	.423	305	473	.645	270	566	836	273	262	2	142	292	60	1840	22.4	49
Ron Mercer	80	2662	515	1145	.450	188	224	.839	109	171	280	176	213	2	125	132	17	1221	15.3	31
Kenny Anderson†	16	386	64	147	.435	41	49	.837	3	36	39	100	36	0	26	29	0	179	11.2	21
Kenny Anderson‡	61	1858	268	674	.398	153	194	.789	39	134	173	345	135	1	87	143	1	746	12.2	31
Chauncey Billups*	51	1290	177	454	.390	147	100	.017	40	73	113	217	118	1	77	118	2	666	11.1	26
Dana Barros	80	1686	281	609	.461	122	144	.847	28	125	153	286	124	0	83	107	6	784	9.8	29
Walter McCarty	82	2340	295	730	.404	144	194	.742	141	223	364	177	274	6	110	141	44	788	9.6	20
Dee Brown*	41	811	109	255	.427	19	28	.679	10	52	62	53	76	1	44	32	6	280	6.8	32
Travis Knight	74	1503	193	438	.441	81	103	.786	146	219	365	104	253	3	54	87	82	482	6.5	21
Bruce Bowen	61	1305	122	298	.409	76	122	.623	79	95	174	81	174	0	87	52	29	340	5.6	16
Andrew DeClercq	81	1523	169	340	.497	101	168	.601	180	212	392	59	277	3	85	84	49	439	5.4	17
Zan Tabak†	18	232	26	55	.473	7	13	.538	25	33	58	12	46	1	5	17	11	59	3.3	11
Zan Tabak‡	57	984	142	304	.467	23	61	.377	84	128	212	48	163	2	20	61	38	307	5.4	23
Tyus Edney	52	623	93	216	.431	88	111	.793	20	35	55	139	69	0	51	66	1	277	5.3	17
Greg Minor	69	1126	140	321	.436	59	86	.686	55	95	150	88	100	0	53	43	11	345	5.0	17
John Thomas*	33	368	41	80	.513	26	33	.788	32	38	70	13	65	0	19	33	9	108	3.3	13
Pervis Ellison	33	447	40	70	.571	20	34	.588	52	57	109	31	90	2	20	28	31	100	3.0	8
Dontae Jones	15	91	19	57	.333	0	0	...	3	6	9	5	12	0	2	11	3	44	2.9	15
Roy Rogers*	9	37	3	8	.375	1	2	.500	0	5	5	1	6	0	2	1	4	7	0.8	3
Reggie Hanson	8	26	3	6	.500	0	0	...	3	3	6	1	6	0	2	3	1	6	0.8	4

3-pt. FG: Boston 415-1249 (.332)—Walker 91-292 (.312); Mercer 3-28 (.107); Anderson† 10-27 (.370); Anderson‡ 57-160 (.356); Billups* 64-189 (.339); Barros 100-246 (.407); McCarty 54-175 (.309); Brown* 43-113 (.381); Knight 15-55 (.273); Bowen 20-59 (.339); DeClercq 0-1 (.000); Tabak‡ 0-1 (.000); Edney 3-10 (.300); Minor 6-31 (.194); Jones 6-23 (.261). Opponents 299-940 (.318).

CHARLOTTE HORNETS

	G	Min.	FGM	FGA	Pct.	FTM	FTA	Pct.	REBOUNDS Off.	Def.	Tot.	Ast.	PF	Dq.	Stl.	TO	Blk.	SCORING Pts.	Avg.	Hi.
Glen Rice	82	3295	634	1386	.457	428	504	.849	89	264	353	182	200	0	77	182	22	1826	22.3	42
David Wesley	81	2845	383	864	.443	229	288	.795	49	164	213	529	229	3	140	226	30	1054	13.0	32
Anthony Mason	81	3148	389	764	.509	261	402	.649	177	649	826	342	182	1	68	146	18	1039	12.8	29
Matt Geiger	78	1839	358	709	.505	168	236	.712	196	325	521	78	191	1	68	111	87	885	11.3	29
Vlade Divac	64	1805	267	536	.498	130	188	.691	183	335	518	172	179	1	83	114	94	667	10.4	25
Bobby Phills	62	1887	246	552	.446	106	140	.757	59	157	216	187	181	2	81	108	18	642	10.4	22
Dell Curry	52	971	194	434	.447	41	52	.788	26	75	101	69	85	2	31	54	4	490	9.4	23
Vernon Maxwell†	31	467	77	180	.428	25	34	.735	9	35	44	40	51	1	14	28	3	210	6.8	22
Vernon Maxwell‡	42	636	103	258	.399	48	60	.800	14	43	57	52	71	1	16	40	4	291	6.9	22
J.R. Reid	79	1109	146	318	.459	89	122	.730	72	138	210	51	172	1	35	65	19	384	4.9	14
B.J. Armstrong†	62	772	99	194	.510	37	43	.860	12	57	69	144	68	0	25	35	0	244	3.9	15
B.J. Armstrong‡	66	831	105	213	.493	42	50	.840	16	60	76	150	74	0	29	42	0	261	4.0	15
Travis Williams	39	365	56	119	.471	24	46	.522	53	39	92	20	55	0	18	30	5	136	3.5	11
Corey Beck	59	738	73	159	.459	43	59	.729	27	63	90	98	100	0	33	70	7	191	3.2	16
Muggsy Bogues*	2	16	2	5	.400	2	2	1.000	0	1	1	4	2	0	2	1	0	6	3.0	6
Tony Delk*	3	34	3	4	.750	1	2	.500	0	2	2	3	8	0	0	4	0	8	2.7	5
Donald Royal†	29	305	24	63	.381	26	29	.897	16	21	37	16	30	0	6	7	1	74	2.6	9
Donald Royal‡	31	323	25	69	.362	29	33	.879	18	23	41	17	35	0	7	10	1	79	2.5	9
Tony Farmer	17	169	17	53	.321	31	39	.795	16	16	32	5	23	0	10	9	4	67	2.5	11
Jeff Grayer*	1	11	0	4	.000	0	0	...	0	0	0	1	0	0	0	2	0	0	0.0	0
Michael McDonald	1	4	0	0	...	0	0	...	0	0	0	1	0	0	0	2	0	0	0.0	0

3-pt. FG: Charlotte 346-904 (.383)—Rice 130-300 (.433); Wesley 59-170 (.347); Mason 0-4 (.000); Geiger 1-11 (.091); Divac 3-14 (.214); Phills 44-114 (.386); Curry 61-145 (.421); Maxwell† 31-86 (.360); Maxwell‡ 37-112 (.330); Reid 3-8 (.375); Armstrong† 9-34 (.265); Armstrong‡ 9-35 (.257); Williams 0-1 (.000); Beck 2-4 (.500); Delk* 1-1 (1.000); Farmer 2-9 (.222); Grayer* 0-3 (.000). Opponents 369-1063 (.347).

1997-98

CHICAGO BULLS

	G	Min.	FGM	FGA	Pct.	FTM	FTA	Pct.	REBOUNDS Off.	Def.	Tot.	Ast.	PF	Dq.	Stl.	TO	Blk.	SCORING Pts.	Avg.	Hi.
Michael Jordan	82	3181	881	1893	.465	565	721	.784	130	345	475	283	151	0	141	185	45	2357	28.7	49
Scottie Pippen	44	1652	315	704	.447	150	193	.777	53	174	227	254	116	0	79	109	43	841	19.1	33
Toni Kukoc	74	2235	383	841	.455	155	219	.708	121	206	327	314	149	0	76	154	37	984	13.3	30
Luc Longley	58	1703	277	609	.455	109	148	.736	113	228	341	161	206	7	34	130	62	663	11.4	24
Ron Harper	82	2284	293	665	.441	162	216	.750	107	183	290	241	181	0	108	91	48	764	9.3	21
Steve Kerr	50	1119	137	302	.454	45	49	.918	14	63	77	96	71	0	26	27	5	376	7.5	21
Jason Caffey*	51	710	100	199	.503	68	103	.660	76	97	173	36	92	1	13	48	17	268	5.3	18
Scott Burrell	80	1096	159	375	.424	47	64	.734	80	118	198	65	131	1	64	50	37	416	5.2	24
Dennis Rodman	80	2856	155	360	.431	61	111	.550	421	780	1201	230	238	2	47	147	18	375	4.7	13
Randy Brown	71	1147	116	302	.384	56	78	.718	34	60	94	151	118	0	71	63	12	288	4.1	14
Rusty LaRue	14	140	20	49	.408	5	8	.625	1	7	8	5	12	0	3	6	1	49	3.5	9
Bill Wennington	48	467	75	172	.436	17	21	.810	32	48	80	19	77	1	4	16	5	167	3.5	14
Dickey Simpkins†	21	237	26	41	.634	26	44	.591	8	23	31	17	35	0	4	13	3	78	3.7	17
Dickey Simpkins‡	40	433	48	89	.539	36	70	.514	27	50	77	33	54	0	9	32	5	132	3.3	17
Jud Buechler	74	608	85	176	.483	3	6	.500	24	53	77	49	47	0	22	21	15	198	2.7	11
Joe Kleine	46	397	39	106	.368	15	18	.833	27	50	77	30	63	0	4	28	5	93	2.0	6
Keith Booth	6	17	2	6	.333	6	6	1.000	2	2	4	1	3	0	0	3	0	10	1.7	4
David Vaughn*	3	6	1	1	1.000	2	4	.500	0	1	1	0	1	0	0	0	0	4	1.3	4

3-pt. FG: Chicago 311-962 (.323)—Jordan 30-126 (.238); Pippen 61-192 (.318); Kukoc 63-174 (.362); Harper 16-84 (.190); Kerr 57-130 (.438); Caffey* 0-1 (.000); Burrell 51-144 (.354); Rodman 4-23 (.174); Brown 0-5 (.000); LaRue 4-16 (.250); Simpkins† 0-1 (.000); Simpkins‡ 0-2 (.000); Buechler 25-65 (.385); Booth 0-1 (.000). Opponents 329-1022 (.322).

CLEVELAND CAVALIERS

	G	Min.	FGM	FGA	Pct.	FTM	FTA	Pct.	REBOUNDS Off.	Def.	Tot.	Ast.	PF	Dq.	Stl.	TO	Blk.	SCORING Pts.	Avg.	Hi.
Shawn Kemp	80	2769	518	1164	.445	404	556	.727	219	526	745	197	310	15	108	271	90	1442	18.0	31
Wesley Person	82	3198	440	957	.460	132	170	.776	65	298	363	188	108	0	129	110	49	1204	14.7	33
Zydrunas Ilgauskas	82	2379	454	876	.518	230	302	.762	279	444	723	71	288	4	52	146	135	1139	13.9	32
Derek Anderson	66	1839	239	586	.408	275	315	.873	55	132	187	227	136	0	86	128	13	770	11.7	30
Cedric Henderson	82	2527	348	725	.480	136	190	.716	71	254	325	168	238	3	96	165	45	832	10.1	30
Brevin Knight	80	2483	261	592	.441	201	251	.801	67	186	253	656	271	5	196	194	18	723	9.0	22
Vitaly Potapenko	80	1412	234	488	.480	102	144	.708	110	203	313	57	198	2	27	132	28	570	7.1	18
Bob Sura	46	942	87	231	.377	74	131	.565	25	69	94	171	113	0	44	93	7	267	5.8	30
Danny Ferry	69	1034	113	286	.395	32	40	.800	23	91	114	59	118	0	26	53	17	291	4.2	15
Carl Thomas†	29	272	27	70	.386	8	13	.615	6	31	37	9	27	0	16	12	5	77	2.7	13
Carl Thomas‡	43	426	56	140	.400	16	25	.640	10	37	47	19	39	0	21	18	7	148	3.4	14
Henry James	28	166	24	59	.407	21	22	.955	2	13	15	5	24	0	1	12	1	80	2.9	14
Greg Graham	6	56	7	12	.583	2	2	1.000	0	1	1	6	7	0	1	10	0	16	2.7	10
Mitchell Butler	18	206	15	47	.319	6	10	.600	6	16	22	18	26	0	8	8	0	37	2.1	11
Tony Dumas	7	47	6	12	.500	0	3	.000	1	4	5	5	5	0	0	5	0	14	2.0	5
Scott Brooks	43	312	28	66	.424	18	20	.900	6	24	30	49	25	0	18	12	3	79	1.8	10
Shawnelle Scott	41	188	16	36	.444	12	18	.667	20	39	59	8	45	0	6	10	8	44	1.1	5

3-pt. FG: Cleveland 298-801 (.372)—Kemp 2-8 (.250); Person 192-447 (.430); Ilgauskas 1-4 (.250); Anderson 17-84 (.202); Henderson 0-4 (.000); Knight 0-7 (.000); Potapenko 0-1 (.000); Sura 19-60 (.317); Ferry 33-99 (.333); Thomas† 15-38 (.395); Thomas‡ 20-59 (.339); James 11-25 (.440); Graham 0-3 (.000); Butler 1-6 (.167); Dumas 2-4 (.500); Brooks 5-11 (.455). Opponents 341-992 (.344).

DALLAS MAVERICKS

	G	Min.	FGM	FGA	Pct.	FTM	FTA	Pct.	REBOUNDS Off.	Def.	Tot.	Ast.	PF	Dq.	Stl.	TO	Blk.	SCORING Pts.	Avg.	Hi.
Michael Finley	82	3394	675	1505	.449	326	416	.784	149	289	438	405	163	0	132	219	30	1763	21.5	39
Dennis Scott*	52	1797	258	666	.387	97	118	.822	39	158	197	129	121	1	43	92	32	707	13.6	33
Shawn Bradley	64	1822	300	711	.422	130	180	.722	164	354	518	60	214	9	51	96	214	731	11.4	26
Cedric Ceballos†	12	364	75	157	.478	47	61	.770	24	48	72	25	29	0	11	33	8	203	16.9	25
Cedric Ceballos‡	47	990	204	415	.492	107	145	.738	75	146	221	60	88	0	33	72	16	536	11.4	25
Hubert Davis	81	2378	350	767	.456	97	116	.836	34	135	169	157	117	0	43	88	5	898	11.1	25
Samaki Walker	41	1027	156	321	.486	53	97	.546	96	206	302	24	127	2	30	61	40	365	8.9	26
Khalid Reeves	82	1950	248	593	.418	165	213	.775	54	131	185	230	195	3	80	130	10	717	8.7	28
Robert Pack	12	292	33	98	.337	25	36	.694	8	26	34	42	17	0	20	38	1	94	7.8	23
Erick Strickland	67	1505	199	558	.357	65	84	.774	35	126	161	167	140	1	56	106	8	511	7.6	30
Kurt Thomas	5	73	17	45	.378	3	3	1.000	8	16	24	3	19	1	1	10	0	37	7.4	13
A.C. Green	82	2649	242	534	.453	116	162	.716	219	449	668	123	157	0	78	68	27	600	7.3	25
Shawn Respert†	10	215	36	84	.429	4	7	.571	7	20	27	17	17	0	5	15	0	82	8.2	14
Shawn Respert‡	57	911	130	293	.444	48	61	.787	37	63	100	61	75	0	34	48	1	339	5.9	20
Chris Anstey	64	680	92	231	.398	53	74	.716	53	104	157	35	95	1	31	41	27	240	5.9	26
Martin Muursepp	41	603	83	191	.435	51	67	.761	46	68	114	30	96	1	29	29	14	233	5.7	24
Eric Riley	39	544	56	135	.415	27	36	.750	43	90	133	22	80	0	15	37	46	139	3.6	16
Bubba Wells	39	395	48	116	.414	31	43	.721	22	46	68	34	40	1	15	31	4	128	3.3	21
Kevin Ollie*	16	214	14	42	.333	18	25	.720	6	15	21	32	16	0	6	16	0	46	2.9	11
Adrian Caldwell	1	3	0	0	...	0	0	...	0	0	0	0	0	0	0	0	0	0	0.0	0

3-pt. FG: Dallas 422-1183 (.357)—Finley 87-244 (.357); Scott* 94-273 (.344); Bradley 1-3 (.333); Ceballos† 6-20 (.300); Ceballos‡ 21-70 (.300); Davis 101-230 (.439); Walker 0-1 (.000); Reeves 56-152 (.368); Pack 3-6 (.500); Strickland 48-163 (.294); Green 0-4 (.000); Respert† 6-26 (.231); Respert‡ 31-93 (.333); Anstey 3-16 (.188); Muursepp 16-38 (.421); Riley 0-1 (.000); Wells 1-6 (.167). Opponents 386-1130 (.342).

1997-98

DENVER NUGGETS

	G	Min.	FGM	FGA	Pct.	FTM	FTA	Pct.	Off.	Def.	Tot.	Ast.	PF	Dq.	Stl.	TO	Blk.	Pts.	Avg.	Hi.
									REBOUNDS									SCORING		
Eric Williams.........	4	145	24	61	.393	31	45	.689	10	11	21	12	9	0	4	9	0	79	19.8	26
Johnny Newman....	74	2176	344	799	.431	365	445	.820	50	91	141	138	208	2	77	147	24	1089	14.7	35
LaPhonso Ellis......	76	2575	410	1007	.407	206	256	.805	146	398	544	213	226	2	65	173	49	1083	14.3	26
Bobby Jackson.....	68	2042	310	791	.392	149	183	.814	78	224	302	317	160	0	105	184	11	790	11.6	28
Danny Fortson	80	1811	276	611	.452	263	339	.776	182	266	448	76	314	7	44	157	30	816	10.2	26
Anthony Goldwire ...	82	2212	269	636	.423	150	186	.806	40	107	147	277	149	0	86	85	7	751	9.2	22
Tony Battie	65	1506	234	525	.446	73	104	.702	138	213	351	60	199	6	54	98	69	544	8.4	19
Cory Alexander†	23	797	111	255	.435	55	65	.846	10	89	99	138	45	0	45	65	6	323	14.0	25
Cory Alexander‡	60	1298	171	400	.428	80	102	.784	17	129	146	209	98	2	70	112	11	488	8.1	25
Eric Washington	66	1539	201	498	.404	65	83	.783	47	80	127	78	143	0	53	72	25	511	7.7	22
Bryant Stith	31	718	75	225	.333	75	86	.872	15	50	65	50	52	0	21	35	8	235	7.6	22
Dean Garrett	82	2632	242	565	.428	114	176	.648	227	417	644	90	197	0	57	84	133	598	7.3	18
Harold Ellis........	27	344	62	111	.559	40	63	.635	27	23	50	18	53	0	19	19	4	164	6.1	22
Priest Lauderdale ...	39	345	53	127	.417	38	69	.551	27	73	100	21	63	0	7	46	17	144	3.7	16
George Zidek*	6	42	4	15	.267	10	12	.833	4	9	13	1	5	0	0	3	2	18	3.0	9
Kiwane Garris	28	225	22	65	.338	19	25	.760	3	16	19	28	22	0	7	15	1	68	2.4	7
Joe Wolf...........	57	621	40	121	.331	5	10	.500	36	90	126	30	92	0	20	22	7	87	1.5	8

3-pt. FG: Denver 288-893 (.323)—Newman 36-105 (.343); Ellis 57-201 (.284); Jackson 21-81 (.259); Fortson 1-3 (.333); Goldwire 63-164 (.384); Battie 3-14 (.214); Alexander† 46-112 (.411); Alexander‡ 66-176 (.375); Washington 44-137 (.321); Stith 10-48 (.208); Ellis 0-4 (.000); Garris 5-14 (.357); Wolf 2-10 (.200). Opponents 419-1105 (.379).

DETROIT PISTONS

	G	Min.	FGM	FGA	Pct.	FTM	FTA	Pct.	Off.	Def.	Tot.	Ast.	PF	Dq.	Stl.	TO	Blk.	Pts.	Avg.	Hi.
									REBOUNDS									SCORING		
Grant Hill	81	3294	615	1361	.452	479	647	.740	93	530	623	551	196	1	143	285	53	1712	21.1	37
Brian Williams......	78	2619	531	1040	.511	198	280	.707	223	472	695	94	252	4	67	181	55	1261	16.2	31
Jerry Stackhouse† ...	57	1797	296	692	.428	273	349	.782	77	113	190	174	119	1	58	150	38	896	15.7	35
Jerry Stackhouse‡ ...	79	2545	424	975	.435	354	450	.787	105	161	266	241	175	2	89	224	59	1249	15.8	35
Joe Dumars	72	2326	329	791	.416	127	154	.825	14	90	104	253	99	0	44	84	2	943	13.1	33
Lindsey Hunter	71	2505	316	826	.383	145	196	.740	61	186	247	224	174	3	123	110	10	862	12.1	35
Malik Sealy........	77	1641	216	505	.428	150	182	.824	48	171	219	100	156	2	65	79	20	591	7.7	22
Theo Ratliff*	24	586	57	111	.514	43	63	.683	46	75	121	15	83	2	12	34	55	157	6.5	15
Jerome Williams.....	77	1305	151	288	.524	108	166	.651	170	209	379	48	144	1	51	60	10	410	5.3	22
Aaron McKie*.......	24	472	43	104	.413	20	23	.070	24	44	68	38	47	0	23	24	1	109	4.5	12
Grant Long	40	739	50	117	.427	41	57	.719	57	93	150	25	91	2	29	22	12	141	3.5	13
Don Reid	68	994	94	176	.534	50	71	.704	77	98	175	26	183	2	25	28	55	238	3.5	16
Eric Montross†	28	354	31	68	.456	9	21	.429	41	66	107	4	66	1	6	14	15	71	2.5	6
Eric Montross‡	48	691	61	144	.424	16	40	.400	69	130	199	11	127	1	13	29	27	138	2.9	9
Scot Pollard	33	317	35	70	.500	19	23	.826	34	40	74	9	48	0	8	12	10	89	2.7	11
Rick Mahorn.......	59	707	59	129	.457	23	34	.676	65	130	195	15	123	0	14	37	7	141	2.4	10
Charles O'Bannon ...	30	234	26	69	.377	12	15	.800	14	19	33	17	15	0	9	9	1	64	2.1	8
Steve Henson	23	65	13	26	.500	7	7	1.000	0	2	2	4	9	0	1	6	0	36	1.6	9

3-pt. FG: Detroit 293-938 (.312)—Hill 3-21 (.143); B. Williams 1-3 (.333); Stackhouse† 31-149 (.208); Stackhouse‡ 47-195 (.241); Dumars 158-426 (.371); Hunter 85-265 (.321); Sealy 9-41 (.220); J. Williams 0-1 (.000); McKie* 3-17 (.176); Long 0-4 (.000); O'Bannon 0-3 (.000); Henson 3-8 (.375). Opponents 363-1100 (.330).

GOLDEN STATE WARRIORS

	G	Min.	FGM	FGA	Pct.	FTM	FTA	Pct.	Off.	Def.	Tot.	Ast.	PF	Dq.	Stl.	TO	Blk.	Pts.	Avg.	Hi.
									REBOUNDS									SCORING		
Latrell Sprewell......	14	547	110	277	.397	70	94	.745	7	44	51	68	26	0	19	44	5	299	21.4	45
Joe Smith*........	49	1645	343	800	.429	160	208	.769	141	197	338	67	169	2	44	106	38	846	17.3	36
Jim Jackson†	31	1258	230	572	.402	103	128	.805	61	112	173	158	74	0	38	118	2	585	18.9	33
Jim Jackson‡	79	3046	476	1107	.430	229	282	.812	130	270	400	381	186	0	79	263	8	1242	15.7	33
Donyell Marshall....	73	2611	451	1091	.413	158	216	.731	210	418	628	159	226	1	95	147	73	1123	15.4	30
Erick Dampier	82	2656	352	791	.445	267	399	.669	272	443	715	94	281	6	39	175	139	971	11.8	23
Tony Delk†	74	1647	311	794	.392	110	149	.738	38	132	170	169	88	0	73	105	12	773	10.4	26
Tony Delk‡	77	1681	314	798	.393	111	151	.735	38	134	172	172	96	0	73	109	12	781	10.1	26
Clarence Weatherspoon†	31	1035	127	277	.458	77	103	.748	89	169	258	49	86	1	42	50	22	331	10.7	20
Clarence Weatherspoon‡	79	2325	268	608	.441	200	277	.722	198	396	594	89	194	2	85	119	74	736	9.3	20
Bimbo Coles	53	1471	166	438	.379	78	88	.886	17	106	123	248	135	2	51	89	13	423	8.0	19
Jason Caffey†	29	713	126	267	.472	63	97	.649	84	87	171	31	89	3	12	57	3	315	10.9	28
Jason Caffey‡	80	1423	226	466	.485	131	200	.655	160	184	344	67	181	4	25	105	20	583	7.3	28
Brian Shaw*	39	1028	103	307	.336	24	33	.727	20	131	151	173	93	3	35	75	14	251	6.4	20
Carl Thomas*	10	139	25	65	.385	7	10	.700	4	6	10	9	12	0	5	6	1	62	6.2	14
Muggsy Bogues† ...	59	1554	139	318	.437	59	66	.894	30	101	131	327	56	0	65	104	3	341	5.8	12
Muggsy Bogues‡ ...	61	1570	141	323	.437	61	68	.897	30	102	132	331	58	0	67	105	3	347	5.7	12
David Vaughn*	22	322	46	114	.404	22	34	.647	34	68	102	18	48	1	10	31	6	114	5.2	12
B.J. Armstrong*......	4	59	6	19	.316	5	7	.714	4	3	7	6	6	0	4	7	0	17	4.3	6
Brandon Williams	9	140	16	50	.320	2	4	.500	4	11	15	3	18	0	6	9	3	37	4.1	11
Todd Fuller	57	613	86	205	.420	55	80	.688	61	135	196	10	89	0	6	37	16	227	4.0	17
Adonal Foyle........	55	656	69	170	.406	27	62	.435	73	111	184	14	94	0	13	50	52	165	3.0	16
Dickey Simpkins*	19	196	22	48	.458	10	26	.385	19	27	46	16	19	0	5	19	2	54	2.8	7
Felton Spencer	68	813	59	129	.457	44	79	.557	93	133	226	17	175	3	23	49	37	162	2.4	10

	G	Min.	FGM	FGA	Pct.	FTM	FTA	Pct.	Off.	Def.	Tot.	Ast.	PF	Dq.	Stl.	TO	Blk.	Pts.	Avg.	Hi.
Jeff Grayer†	4	23	4	7	.571	0	0	...	0	4	4	1	7	0	2	2	0	10	2.5	8
Jeff Grayer‡	5	34	4	11	.364	0	0	...	0	4	4	2	7	0	2	4	0	10	2.0	8
Gerald Madkins	19	243	13	34	.382	5	7	.714	2	13	15	45	18	0	13	13	1	37	1.9	10
Duane Ferrell	50	461	41	111	.369	12	22	.545	25	22	47	26	50	0	21	18	6	94	1.9	8

3-pt. FG: Golden State 189-696 (.272)—Sprewell 9-48 (.188); Smith* 0-7 (.000); Jackson† 22-79 (.278); Jackson‡ 61-191 (.319); Marshall 63-201 (.313); Dampier 0-2 (.000); Delk† 41-156 (.263); Delk‡ 42-157 (.268); Coles 13-57 (.228); Caffey† 0-1 (.000); Caffey‡ 0-2 (.000); Shaw* 21-67 (.313); Thomas* 5-21 (.238); Bogues† 4-16 (.250); Bogues‡ 4-16 (.250); Vaughn* 0-1 (.000); Armstrong* 0-1 (.000); Williams 3-9 (.333); Fuller 0-4 (.000); Foyle 0-1 (.000); Simpkins* 0-1 (.000); Grayer† 2-3 (.667); Grayer‡ 2-6 (.333); Madkins 6-15 (.400); Ferrell 0-6 (.000). Opponents 334-962 (.347).

HOUSTON ROCKETS

	G	Min.	FGM	FGA	Pct.	FTM	FTA	Pct.	Off.	Def.	Tot.	Ast.	PF	Dq.	Stl.	TO	Blk.	Pts.	Avg.	Hi.
Clyde Drexler	70	2473	452	1059	.427	277	346	.801	105	241	346	382	193	0	126	189	42	1287	18.4	43
Hakeem Olajuwon	47	1633	306	633	.483	160	212	.755	116	344	460	143	152	0	84	126	96	772	16.4	33
Kevin Willis	81	2528	531	1041	.510	242	305	.793	232	447	679	78	235	1	55	170	38	1305	16.1	33
Charles Barkley	68	2243	361	744	.485	296	397	.746	241	553	794	217	187	2	71	147	28	1036	15.2	43
Matt Maloney	78	2217	239	586	.408	65	78	.833	16	126	142	219	99	0	62	107	5	669	8.6	24
Eddie Johnson	75	1490	227	544	.417	113	136	.831	50	103	153	88	89	0	32	62	3	633	8.4	37
Mario Elie	73	1988	206	456	.452	145	174	.833	39	117	156	221	115	0	81	100	8	612	8.4	23
Matt Bullard	67	1190	175	389	.450	20	27	.741	25	121	146	60	104	0	31	39	24	466	7.0	20
Othella Harrington	58	903	129	266	.485	92	122	.754	73	134	207	24	112	1	10	47	27	350	6.0	18
Rodrick Rhodes	58	1070	112	305	.367	111	180	.617	28	42	70	110	125	0	62	97	10	337	5.8	16
Brent Price	72	1332	128	310	.413	77	98	.786	37	70	107	192	163	3	52	111	4	406	5.6	13
Emanual Davis	45	599	63	142	.444	31	37	.838	10	37	47	59	55	0	17	52	3	184	4.1	13
Joe Stephens	7	37	10	28	.357	4	6	.667	3	3	6	1	2	0	2	2	0	27	3.9	5
Charles Jones	24	127	7	10	.700	1	2	.500	12	12	24	5	22	0	1	4	6	15	0.6	3

3-pt. FG: Houston 573-1670 (.343)—Drexler 106-334 (.317); Olajuwon 0-3 (.000); Willis 1-7 (.143); Barkley 18-84 (.214); Maloney 126-346 (.364); Johnson 66-198 (.333); Elie 55-189 (.291); Bullard 96-231 (.416); Harrington 0-1 (.000); Rhodes 2-8 (.250); Price 73-187 (.390); Davis 27-72 (.375); Stephens 3-10 (.300). Opponents 409-1120 (.365).

INDIANA PACERS

	G	Min.	FGM	FGA	Pct.	FTM	FTA	Pct.	Off.	Def.	Tot.	Ast.	PF	Dq.	Stl.	TO	Blk.	Pts.	Avg.	Hi.
Reggie Miller	81	2795	516	1081	.477	382	440	.868	46	186	232	171	148	2	78	128	11	1578	19.5	35
Rik Smits	73	2085	514	1038	.495	188	240	.783	127	378	505	101	243	9	40	134	88	1216	16.7	29
Chris Mullin	82	2177	333	692	.481	154	164	.939	38	211	249	186	186	0	95	117	39	927	11.3	27
Antonio Davis	82	2191	254	528	.481	277	398	.696	192	368	560	61	234	6	45	103	72	785	9.6	28
Jalen Rose	82	1706	290	607	.478	166	228	.728	28	167	195	155	171	0	56	132	14	771	9.4	26
Mark Jackson	82	2413	249	598	.416	137	180	.761	67	255	322	713	132	0	84	174	2	678	8.3	28
Dale Davis	78	2174	273	498	.548	80	172	.465	233	378	611	70	209	1	51	73	87	626	8.0	22
Travis Best	82	1547	201	480	.419	112	131	.855	28	94	122	281	193	3	85	111	5	535	6.5	21
Derrick McKey	57	1316	150	327	.459	55	77	.714	74	137	211	88	156	1	57	79	30	359	6.3	16
Fred Hoiberg	65	874	85	222	.383	59	69	.855	14	109	123	45	101	0	40	22	3	261	4.0	20
Austin Croshere	26	243	32	86	.372	8	14	.571	10	35	45	8	32	1	9	13	5	76	2.9	17
Mark West	15	105	10	21	.476	3	6	.500	6	9	15	2	15	0	2	8	4	23	1.5	5
Mark Pope	28	193	14	41	.341	10	17	.588	9	17	26	7	36	0	3	10	6	39	1.4	7
Etdrick Bohannon	5	11	0	4	.000	0	0	...	2	4	6	1	3	0	0	3	2	0	0.0	0

3-pt. FG: Indiana 401-1029 (.390)—Miller 164-382 (.429); Smits 0-3 (.000); Mullin 107-243 (.440); A. Davis 0-3 (.000); Rose 25-73 (.342); Jackson 43-137 (.314); Best 21-70 (.300); McKey 4-17 (.235); Hoiberg 32-85 (.376); Croshere 4-13 (.308); Pope 1-3 (.333). Opponents 274-867 (.316).

LOS ANGELES CLIPPERS

	G	Min.	FGM	FGA	Pct.	FTM	FTA	Pct.	Off.	Def.	Tot.	Ast.	PF	Dq.	Stl.	TO	Blk.	Pts.	Avg.	Hi.
Lamond Murray	79	2579	473	984	.481	220	294	.748	172	312	484	142	193	3	118	171	54	1220	15.4	32
Rodney Rogers	76	2499	426	935	.456	225	328	.686	155	269	424	202	242	5	93	193	38	1149	15.1	34
Brent Barry*	41	1341	190	444	.428	103	122	.844	27	116	143	132	88	0	50	95	23	561	13.7	26
Isaac Austin†	26	895	154	339	.454	88	135	.652	80	147	227	88	69	0	18	89	22	396	15.2	24
Isaac Austin‡	78	2266	406	871	.466	243	363	.669	199	358	557	175	231	5	61	206	56	1055	13.5	33
Maurice Taylor	71	1513	321	675	.476	173	244	.709	118	178	296	53	222	7	34	107	40	815	11.5	26
Eric Piatkowski	67	1740	257	568	.452	140	170	.824	70	166	236	85	137	0	51	80	12	760	11.3	29
Darrick Martin	82	2299	275	730	.377	184	217	.848	19	145	164	331	198	2	82	154	10	841	10.3	21
Lorenzen Wright	69	2067	241	542	.445	141	214	.659	180	426	606	55	237	2	55	81	87	623	9.0	32
James Robinson	70	1231	195	501	.389	77	107	.720	37	74	111	135	101	0	37	97	10	541	7.7	26
Loy Vaught	10	265	36	84	.429	3	8	.375	16	49	65	7	33	0	4	13	2	75	7.5	14
Pooh Richardson	69	1252	124	333	.372	30	43	.698	17	79	96	226	71	0	44	54	3	289	4.2	14
Keith Closs	58	740	93	207	.449	46	77	.597	63	105	168	19	73	0	12	38	81	232	4.0	15
Charles Smith†	23	260	45	107	.421	5	9	.556	8	11	19	19	21	0	10	21	5	109	4.7	16
Charles Smith‡	34	292	49	125	.392	6	11	.545	13	14	27	21	24	0	12	27	6	119	3.5	15
Stojko Vrankovic	65	996	79	186	.425	37	65	.569	71	192	263	36	130	3	11	46	66	195	3.0	9
James Collins	23	103	21	55	.382	8	14	.571	7	7	14	3	12	0	6	8	3	59	2.6	15

3-pt. FG: L.A. Clippers 525-1468 (.358)—Murray 54-153 (.353); Rogers 72-212 (.340); Barry* 78-195 (.400); Austin† 0-5 (.000); Austin‡ 0-8 (.000); Taylor 0-1 (.000); Piatkowski 106-259 (.409); Martin 107-293 (.365); Wright 0-2 (.000); Robinson 74-225 (.329); Vaught 0-2 (.000); Richardson 11-57 (.193); Smith† 14-44 (.318); Smith‡ 15-47 (.310); Collins 9-20 (.450). Opponents 334-923 (.362).

LOS ANGELES LAKERS

	G	Min.	FGM	FGA	Pct.	FTM	FTA	Pct.	REBOUNDS Off.	Def.	Tot.	Ast.	PF	Dq.	Stl.	TO	Blk.	SCORING Pts.	Avg.	Hi.
Shaquille O'Neal	60	2175	670	1147	.584	359	681	.527	208	473	681	142	193	1	39	175	144	1699	28.3	50
Eddie Jones	80	2910	486	1005	.484	234	306	.765	85	217	302	246	164	0	160	146	55	1349	16.9	35
Kobe Bryant	79	2056	391	913	.428	363	457	.794	79	163	242	199	180	1	74	157	40	1220	15.4	33
Nick Van Exel	64	2053	311	743	.419	136	172	.791	31	163	194	442	120	0	64	104	6	881	13.8	35
Rick Fox	82	2709	363	771	.471	171	230	.743	78	280	358	276	309	4	100	201	48	983	12.0	31
Elden Campbell	81	1784	289	624	.463	237	342	.693	143	312	455	78	209	1	35	115	102	816	10.1	25
Robert Horry	72	2192	200	420	.476	117	169	.692	186	356	542	163	238	5	112	99	94	536	7.4	23
Derek Fisher	82	1760	164	378	.434	115	152	.757	38	155	193	333	126	1	75	119	5	474	5.8	21
Mario Bennett	45	354	80	135	.593	16	44	.364	60	66	126	18	61	0	19	21	11	177	3.9	21
Corie Blount	70	1029	107	187	.572	39	78	.500	114	184	298	37	157	2	29	51	25	253	3.6	12
Sean Rooks	41	425	46	101	.455	47	79	.595	46	72	118	24	68	0	2	19	23	139	3.4	15
Jon Barry	49	374	38	104	.365	27	29	.931	8	29	37	51	33	0	24	22	3	121	2.5	13
Shea Seals	4	9	1	8	.125	2	4	.500	3	1	4	0	1	0	1	0	0	4	1.0	2

3-pt. FG: L.A. Lakers 497-1415 (.351)—Jones 143-368 (.389); Bryant 75-220 (.341); Van Exel 123-316 (.389); Fox 86-265 (.325); Campbell 1-2 (.500); Horry 19-93 (.204); Fisher 31-81 (.383); Bennett 1-2 (.500); Blount 0-4 (.000); Barry 18-61 (.295); Seals 0-3 (.000). Opponents 380-1071 (.355).

MIAMI HEAT

	G	Min.	FGM	FGA	Pct.	FTM	FTA	Pct.	REBOUNDS Off.	Def.	Tot.	Ast.	PF	Dq.	Stl.	TO	Blk.	SCORING Pts.	Avg.	Hi.
Alonzo Mourning	58	1939	403	732	.551	309	465	.665	193	365	558	52	208	4	40	179	130	1115	19.2	39
Tim Hardaway	81	3031	558	1296	.431	257	329	.781	48	251	299	672	200	2	136	224	16	1528	18.9	33
Jamal Mashburn	48	1729	251	577	.435	184	231	.797	72	164	236	132	137	1	43	108	14	723	15.1	32
Isaac Austin*	52	1371	252	532	.474	155	228	.680	119	211	330	87	162	5	43	117	34	659	12.7	33
Voshon Lenard	81	2621	363	854	.425	141	179	.788	72	220	292	180	219	0	58	99	16	1020	12.6	28
Brent Barry†	17	259	23	62	.371	12	12	1.000	2	26	28	21	30	0	14	9	4	70	4.1	10
Brent Barry‡	58	1600	213	506	.421	115	134	.858	29	142	171	153	118	0	64	104	27	631	10.9	26
P.J. Brown	74	2362	278	590	.471	151	197	.766	235	400	635	103	264	9	66	97	98	707	9.6	21
Dan Majerle	72	1928	184	439	.419	40	51	.784	48	220	268	157	139	2	68	65	15	519	7.2	22
Mark Strickland	51	847	145	269	.539	59	82	.720	80	133	213	26	87	0	18	47	34	349	6.8	23
Eric Murdock	82	1395	177	419	.422	125	156	.801	39	117	156	219	173	1	103	104	13	507	6.2	17
Todd Day	5	69	11	31	.355	6	9	.667	4	2	6	7	10	0	7	3	0	30	6.0	13
Marty Conlon	18	209	28	62	.452	32	44	.727	16	30	46	12	27	0	9	11	5	88	4.9	11
Terry Mills	50	782	81	206	.393	25	33	.758	34	118	152	39	129	1	19	45	9	212	4.2	20
Keith Askins	46	681	39	122	.320	12	19	.632	28	73	101	29	107	3	27	26	12	111	2.4	15
Duane Causwell	37	363	37	89	.416	15	26	.577	29	70	99	5	73	0	7	18	27	89	2.4	15
Rex Walters†	19	108	13	24	.542	9	11	.818	2	13	15	14	11	0	3	10	1	38	2.0	9
Rex Walters‡	38	235	24	53	.453	26	28	.929	5	19	24	35	28	0	8	27	1	80	2.1	11
Antonio Lang	6	29	3	5	.600	6	8	.750	2	3	5	1	3	0	2	4	0	12	2.0	6
Charles Smith*	11	32	4	18	.222	1	2	.500	5	3	8	2	3	0	2	6	1	10	0.9	3

3-pt. FG: Miami 548-1544 (.355)—Hardaway 155-442 (.351); Mashburn 37-122 (.303); Austin* 0-3 (.000); Lenard 153-378 (.405); Barry† 12-34 (.353); Barry‡ 90-229 (.393); Majerle 111-295 (.376); Strickland 0-1 (.000); Murdock 28-91 (.308); Day 2-12 (.167); Mills 25-81 (.309); Askins 21-74 (.284); Walters† 3-8 (.375); Walters‡ 6-22 (.273); Smith* 1-3 (.333). Opponents 305-921 (.331).

MILWAUKEE BUCKS

	G	Min.	FGM	FGA	Pct.	FTM	FTA	Pct.	REBOUNDS Off.	Def.	Tot.	Ast.	PF	Dq.	Stl.	TO	Blk.	SCORING Pts.	Avg.	Hi.
Glenn Robinson	56	2294	534	1136	.470	215	266	.808	82	225	307	158	164	2	69	200	34	1308	23.4	42
Ray Allen	82	3287	563	1315	.428	342	391	.875	127	278	405	356	244	2	111	263	12	1602	19.5	40
Terrell Brandon	50	1784	339	731	.464	132	156	.846	23	153	176	387	120	1	111	145	17	841	16.8	29
Armon Gilliam	82	2114	327	676	.484	267	333	.802	146	293	439	104	177	1	65	148	37	921	11.2	29
Tyrone Hill	57	2064	208	418	.498	155	255	.608	212	396	608	88	230	8	67	106	30	571	10.0	18
Ervin Johnson	81	2261	253	471	.537	143	238	.601	242	443	685	59	321	7	79	117	158	649	8.0	24
Elliot Perry	81	1752	241	561	.430	92	109	.844	21	87	108	230	129	1	90	128	2	591	7.3	25
Michael Curry	82	1978	196	418	.469	147	176	.835	26	72	98	137	218	1	56	77	14	543	6.6	25
Jerald Honeycutt	38	530	90	221	.407	36	58	.621	27	66	93	33	83	0	20	49	6	245	6.4	20
Ricky Pierce	39	442	52	143	.364	43	52	.827	19	26	45	34	35	0	9	21	0	151	3.9	13
Tony Smith	7	80	8	24	.333	3	4	.750	4	3	7	10	7	0	5	9	2	19	2.7	10
Andrew Lang	57	692	54	143	.378	44	57	.772	56	97	153	16	101	0	18	33	27	152	2.7	13
Jamie Feick	45	450	39	90	.433	20	41	.488	45	79	124	16	67	0	25	21	17	102	2.3	12
Tim Breaux	6	30	4	11	.364	1	2	.500	0	2	2	2	1	0	2	1	1	10	1.7	5
Jeff Nordgaard	13	48	5	18	.278	8	9	.889	4	10	14	3	7	0	2	3	0	18	1.4	4
Litterial Green	21	124	5	23	.217	15	20	.750	1	6	7	16	11	0	4	8	0	25	1.2	5

3-pt. FG: Milwaukee 249-703 (.354)—Robinson 25-65 (.385); Allen 134-368 (.364); Brandon 31-93 (.333); Gilliam 0-4 (.000); Hill 0-1 (.000); Perry 17-50 (.340); Curry 4-9 (.444); Honeycutt 29-77 (.377); Pierce 4-13 (.308); Smith 0-4 (.000); Lang 0-1 (.000); Feick 4-13 (.308); Breaux 1-3 (.333); Green 0-2 (.000). Opponents 304-929 (.327).

MINNESOTA TIMBERWOLVES

	G	Min.	FGM	FGA	Pct.	FTM	FTA	Pct.	REBOUNDS Off.	Def.	Tot.	Ast.	PF	Dq.	Stl.	TO	Blk.	SCORING Pts.	Avg.	Hi.
Tom Gugliotta	41	1582	319	635	.502	183	223	.821	106	250	356	167	102	0	61	109	22	823	20.1	33
Kevin Garnett	82	3222	635	1293	.491	245	332	.738	222	564	786	348	224	1	139	192	150	1518	18.5	32
Stephon Marbury	82	3112	513	1237	.415	329	450	.731	58	172	230	704	222	0	104	256	7	1450	17.7	38

	G	Min.	FGM	FGA	Pct.	FTM	FTA	Pct.	Off.	Def.	Tot.	Ast.	PF	Dq.	Stl.	TO	Blk.	Pts.	Avg.	Hi.
Sam Mitchell	81	2239	371	800	.464	243	292	.832	118	267	385	107	200	0	64	66	22	1000	12.3	29
Anthony Peeler†	30	991	155	348	.445	32	41	.780	31	72	103	114	81	0	52	45	6	390	13.0	23
Anthony Peeler‡	38	1193	190	420	.452	36	47	.766	37	86	123	137	97	0	61	51	6	469	12.3	23
Chris Carr	51	1165	190	452	.420	84	99	.848	43	112	155	85	129	1	17	69	11	504	9.9	20
Terry Porter	82	1786	259	577	.449	167	195	.856	37	131	168	271	103	0	63	104	16	777	9.5	22
Cherokee Parks	79	1703	224	449	.499	110	169	.651	140	297	437	53	237	4	36	66	86	558	7.1	20
Stanley Roberts	74	1328	191	386	.495	75	156	.481	109	254	363	27	226	5	24	70	72	457	6.2	20
Tom Hammonds	57	1140	127	246	.516	92	132	.697	100	171	271	36	127	1	15	48	17	346	6.1	19
Doug West	38	688	64	171	.374	29	40	.725	23	59	82	45	97	1	11	21	5	157	4.1	13
Bill Curley	11	146	16	33	.485	2	3	.667	11	17	28	4	28	1	3	3	1	34	3.1	8
Reggie Jordan	57	487	54	113	.478	41	72	.569	57	40	97	50	63	0	35	30	9	149	2.6	18
Micheal Williams	25	161	16	48	.333	32	33	.970	2	12	14	32	24	0	9	16	2	64	2.6	6
DeJuan Wheat	34	150	20	50	.400	9	15	.600	3	8	11	25	12	0	6	9	1	57	1.7	19
Clifford Rozier	6	30	3	6	.500	0	1	.000	3	3	6	0	7	0	0	4	0	6	1.0	4

3-pt. FG: Minnesota 303-873 (.347)—Gugliotta 2-17 (.118); Garnett 3-16 (.188); Marbury 95-304 (.313); Mitchell 15-43 (.349); Peeler† 48-106 (.453); Peeler‡ 53-125 (.424); Carr 40-127 (.315); Porter 92-233 (.395); Parks 0-1 (.000); Hammonds 0-1 (.000); West 0-2 (.000); Curley 0-1 (.000); Jordan 0-1 (.000); Williams 0-4 (.000); Wheat 8-17 (.471). Opponents 432-1206 (.358).

NEW JERSEY NETS

	G	Min.	FGM	FGA	Pct.	FTM	FTA	Pct.	Off.	Def.	Tot.	Ast.	PF	Dq.	Stl.	TO	Blk.	Pts.	Avg.	Hi.
Keith Van Horn	62	2325	446	1047	.426	258	305	.846	142	266	408	106	216	0	64	164	25	1219	19.7	33
Sam Cassell	75	2606	510	1156	.441	436	507	.860	73	155	228	603	262	5	121	269	20	1471	19.6	35
Kerry Kittles	77	2814	508	1154	.440	202	250	.808	132	230	362	176	152	0	132	106	37	1328	17.2	31
Kendall Gill	81	2733	418	974	.429	225	327	.688	112	279	391	200	268	4	156	124	64	1087	13.4	27
Rony Seikaly†	9	152	13	41	.317	16	27	.593	16	20	36	8	27	0	3	12	4	42	4.7	10
Rony Seikaly‡	56	1636	250	579	.432	246	332	.741	146	247	393	77	164	2	28	146	43	746	13.3	37
Jayson Williams	65	2343	321	645	.498	195	293	.666	443	440	883	67	236	7	45	95	49	837	12.9	27
Chris Gatling	57	1359	248	545	.455	159	265	.600	118	216	334	53	152	2	52	99	29	656	11.5	25
Sherman Douglas	80	1699	255	515	.495	115	172	.669	52	83	135	319	156	2	55	110	7	639	8.0	25
David Benoit*	53	799	102	269	.379	37	44	.841	42	99	141	17	120	0	26	39	16	282	5.3	14
Brian Evans†	28	332	46	106	.434	6	9	.667	18	34	52	24	44	0	7	14	5	115	4.1	16
Brian Evans‡	72	893	123	312	.394	46	57	.807	49	88	137	55	101	0	29	38	13	321	4.5	16
David Vaughn†	15	161	19	33	.576	6	9	.667	19	30	49	2	34	0	5	9	4	44	2.9	6
David Vaughn‡	40	489	66	148	.446	30	47	.638	53	99	152	20	83	1	15	40	10	162	4.1	12
Lucious Harris	50	671	69	177	.390	41	55	.745	21	31	52	42	77	0	42	21	5	191	3.8	15
Kevin Edwards*	27	352	37	106	.349	13	15	.867	11	23	34	26	20	0	21	20	0	91	3.4	15
Jack Haley	16	51	5	18	.278	12	21	.571	5	10	15	0	9	0	0	4	1	22	1.4	10
Michael Cage	79	1201	43	84	.512	20	36	.556	115	193	308	32	105	1	45	23	44	106	1.3	8
Xavier McDaniel	20	180	10	30	.333	5	8	.625	12	19	31	9	23	0	3	8	2	25	1.3	7
Yinka Dare	10	60	4	18	.222	4	8	.500	10	7	17	1	9	0	0	2	2	12	1.2	4
Don MacLean	9	42	1	10	.100	0	0	...	3	2	5	0	7	0	0	2	0	3	0.3	3

3-pt. FG: New Jersey 310-937 (.331)—Van Horn 69-224 (.308); Cassell 15-80 (.188); Kittles 110-263 (.418); Gill 26-101 (.257); Seikaly‡ 0-2 (.000); Williams 0-4 (.000); Gatling 1-4 (.250); Douglas 14-46 (.304); Benoit* 41-119 (.345); Evans† 17-42 (.405); Evans‡ 29-87 (.333); Vaughn† 0-1 (.000); Harris 12-39 (.308); Edwards* 4-11 (.364); Haley 0-1 (.000); Cage 0-1 (.000); MacLean 1-2 (.500). Opponents 356-1030 (.346).

NEW YORK KNICKERBOCKERS

	G	Min.	FGM	FGA	Pct.	FTM	FTA	Pct.	Off.	Def.	Tot.	Ast.	PF	Dq.	Stl.	TO	Blk.	Pts.	Avg.	Hi.
Patrick Ewing	26	848	203	403	.504	134	186	.720	59	206	265	28	74	0	16	77	58	540	20.8	34
Allan Houston	82	2848	571	1277	.447	285	335	.851	43	231	274	212	207	2	63	200	24	1509	18.4	34
Larry Johnson	70	2412	429	884	.485	214	283	.756	175	226	401	150	193	2	40	127	13	1087	15.5	35
John Starks	82	2188	372	947	.393	185	235	.787	48	182	230	219	205	2	78	143	5	1059	12.9	34
Chris Mills	80	2183	292	675	.433	152	189	.804	120	288	408	133	218	3	45	107	30	776	9.7	23
Charles Oakley	79	2734	307	698	.440	97	114	.851	218	506	724	201	280	4	123	126	22	711	9.0	19
Charlie Ward	82	2317	235	516	.455	91	113	.805	32	242	274	466	195	3	144	175	37	642	7.8	19
Terry Cummings†	30	529	103	216	.477	28	40	.700	42	93	135	26	79	0	16	34	5	234	7.8	23
Terry Cummings‡	74	1185	200	428	.467	67	98	.684	97	186	283	47	181	1	38	51	10	467	6.3	23
Chris Childs	68	1599	149	354	.421	104	126	.825	29	133	162	268	179	2	56	103	6	429	6.3	17
Buck Williams	41	738	75	149	.503	52	71	.732	78	105	183	21	93	1	17	38	15	202	4.9	15
Chris Dudley	51	858	58	143	.406	41	92	.446	108	167	275	21	139	4	13	44	51	157	3.1	10
Anthony Bowie	27	224	32	59	.542	8	9	.889	9	17	26	11	25	1	6	7	2	75	2.8	16
Brooks Thompson†	17	121	13	29	.448	3	5	.600	0	10	10	24	16	0	6	11	1	33	1.9	11
Brooks Thompson‡	30	167	23	56	.411	4	8	.500	1	14	15	27	22	0	10	16	1	59	2.0	11
Pete Myers	9	40	5	10	.500	4	6	.667	5	5	10	3	7	0	4	4	0	14	1.6	7
Herb Williams	27	178	18	43	.419	1	8	.125	6	23	29	4	34	0	6	5	9	37	1.4	5
Ben Davis	7	13	2	10	.200	0	0	...	6	0	6	0	3	0	1	0	0	4	0.6	2

3-pt. FG: New York 382-1139 (.335)—Ewing 0-2 (.000); Houston 82-213 (.385); Johnson 15-63 (.238); Starks 130-398 (.327); Mills 40-137 (.292); Oakley 0-6 (.000); Ward 81-215 (.377); Cummings‡ 0-1 (.000); Childs 27-87 (.310); Bowie 3-4 (.750); Thompson† 4-14 (.286); Thompson‡ 9-30 (.300). Opponents 331-1045 (.317).

ORLANDO MAGIC

	G	Min.	FGM	FGA	Pct.	FTM	FTA	Pct.	Off.	Def.	Tot.	Ast.	PF	Dq.	Stl.	TO	Blk.	Pts.	Avg.	Hi.
Anfernee Hardaway	19	625	103	273	.377	90	118	.763	8	68	76	68	45	0	28	46	15	311	16.4	32
Nick Anderson	58	1701	343	754	.455	127	199	.638	98	199	297	119	98	1	72	85	23	890	15.3	38

								REBOUNDS									SCORING		
	G	Min.	FGM	FGA	Pct.	FTM	FTA	Pct.	Off.	Def.	Tot.	Ast.	PF	Dq.	Stl.	TO	Blk.	Pts.	Avg.	Hi.
Rony Seikaly*	47	1484	237	538	.441	230	305	.754	130	227	357	69	137	2	25	134	39	704	15.0	37
Derek Strong	58	1638	259	617	.420	218	279	.781	152	275	427	51	122	0	31	74	24	736	12.7	25
Horace Grant	76	2803	393	857	.459	135	199	.678	228	390	618	172	180	0	81	88	79	921	12.1	26
Charles Outlaw	82	2953	301	543	.554	180	313	.575	255	382	637	216	260	1	107	175	181	783	9.5	29
Mark Price	63	1430	229	531	.431	87	103	.845	24	105	129	297	92	0	53	162	5	597	9.5	23
Darrell Armstrong	48	1236	156	380	.411	105	123	.854	65	94	159	236	96	1	58	112	5	442	9.2	24
Derek Harper	66	1761	226	542	.417	55	79	.696	23	80	103	233	140	0	72	101	10	566	8.6	26
Vernon Maxwell*	11	169	26	78	.333	23	26	.885	5	8	13	12	20	0	2	12	1	81	7.4	18
Danny Schayes	74	1272	155	371	.418	96	119	.807	97	145	242	44	182	0	34	61	33	406	5.5	19
David Benoit†	24	324	50	139	.360	24	30	.800	18	44	62	8	37	0	9	13	4	138	5.8	19
David Benoit‡	77	1123	152	408	.373	61	74	.824	60	143	203	25	157	0	35	52	20	420	5.5	19
Gerald Wilkins	72	1252	141	434	.325	69	98	.704	16	74	90	78	78	0	34	79	6	380	5.3	23
Brian Evans*	44	561	77	206	.374	40	48	.833	31	54	85	31	57	0	22	24	8	206	4.7	16
Kevin Edwards†	12	135	20	59	.339	17	20	.850	9	11	20	13	8	0	5	10	1	59	4.9	12
Kevin Edwards‡	39	487	57	165	.345	30	35	.857	20	34	54	39	28	0	26	30	1	150	3.8	15
Kevin Ollie†	19	216	23	56	.411	31	45	.689	3	15	18	33	15	0	7	28	0	77	4.1	14
Kevin Ollie‡	35	430	37	98	.378	49	70	.700	9	30	39	65	31	0	13	44	0	123	3.5	14
Johnny Taylor	12	108	13	37	.351	11	16	.688	4	9	13	1	22	0	3	8	2	38	3.2	10
Spud Webb	4	34	5	12	.417	2	2	1.000	2	1	3	5	6	0	1	7	0	12	3.0	8
Donald Royal*	2	18	1	6	.167	3	4	.750	2	2	4	1	5	0	1	3	0	5	2.5	5
Carl Thomas*	4	15	4	5	.800	1	2	.500	0	0	0	1	0	0	0	0	1	9	2.3	4
Jason Lawson	17	80	9	15	.600	8	10	.800	8	19	27	5	14	1	4	2	4	26	1.5	6
Tim Kempton*	3	15	0	2	.000	0	0	...	0	1	1	1	3	0	0	0	0	0	0.0	0

3-pt. FG: Orlando 293-907 (.323)—Hardaway 15-50 (.300); Anderson 77-214 (.360); Seikaly* 0-2 (.000); Strong 0-4 (.000); Grant 0-7 (.000); Outlaw 1-4 (.250); Price 52-155 (.335); Armstrong 25-68 (.368); Harper 59-164 (.360); Maxwell* 6-26 (.231); Benoit† 14-51 (.275); Benoit‡ 55-170 (.324); Wilkins 29-109 (.266); Evans* 12-45 (.267); Edwards† 2-4 (.500); Edwards‡ 6-15 (.400); Ollie† 0-1 (.000); Ollie‡ 0-1 (.000); Taylor 1-2 (.500); Webb 0-1 (.000). Opponents 313-967 (.324).

PHILADELPHIA 76ERS

								REBOUNDS									SCORING		
	G	Min.	FGM	FGA	Pct.	FTM	FTA	Pct.	Off.	Def.	Tot.	Ast.	PF	Dq.	Stl.	TO	Blk.	Pts.	Avg.	Hi.
Allen Iverson	80	3150	649	1407	.461	390	535	.729	86	210	296	494	200	2	176	244	25	1758	22.0	43
Derrick Coleman	59	2135	356	867	.411	302	391	.772	149	438	587	145	144	1	46	157	68	1040	17.6	35
Jerry Stackhouse*	22	748	128	283	.452	81	101	.802	28	48	76	67	56	1	31	74	21	353	16.0	32
Joe Smith†	30	699	121	270	.448	67	85	.788	58	75	133	27	94	0	18	52	13	309	10.3	27
Joe Smith‡	79	2344	464	1070	.434	227	293	.775	199	272	471	94	263	2	62	158	51	1155	14.6	36
Jim Jackson*	48	1788	246	535	.460	126	154	.818	69	158	227	223	112	0	41	145	6	657	13.7	28
Tim Thomas	77	1779	306	684	.447	171	231	.740	107	181	288	90	185	2	54	118	17	845	11.0	27
Theo Ratliff†	58	1861	249	486	.512	154	218	.706	175	251	426	42	209	6	38	82	203	652	11.2	27
Theo Ratliff‡	82	2447	306	597	.513	197	281	.701	221	326	547	57	292	8	50	116	258	809	9.9	27
Clarence Weatherspoon*	48	1290	141	331	.426	123	174	.707	109	227	336	40	108	1	43	69	52	405	8.4	19
Brian Shaw†	20	502	51	139	.367	12	19	.632	17	47	64	88	55	1	14	24	3	121	6.1	24
Brian Shaw‡	59	1530	154	446	.345	36	52	.692	37	178	215	261	148	4	49	99	17	372	6.3	24
Tom Chambers	1	10	2	2	1.000	2	2	1.000	2	2	2	2	0	2	0	1	0	6	6.0	6
Terry Cummings*	44	656	97	212	.458	39	58	.672	55	93	148	21	102	1	22	17	5	233	5.3	16
Benoit Benjamin	14	197	22	41	.537	19	30	.633	18	35	53	3	26	0	4	12	4	63	4.5	10
Aaron McKie†	57	1341	96	277	.347	22	32	.688	34	129	163	137	117	0	78	52	12	223	3.9	15
Aaron McKie‡	81	1813	139	381	.365	42	55	.764	58	173	231	175	164	0	101	76	13	332	4.1	15
Scott Williams	58	801	93	213	.437	51	63	.810	87	124	211	29	132	0	17	30	21	237	4.1	14
Mark Davis	71	906	109	244	.447	64	101	.634	64	94	158	73	95	1	49	91	18	282	4.0	16
Eric Montross*	20	337	30	76	.395	7	19	.368	28	64	92	7	61	0	7	15	12	67	3.4	9
Eric Snow†	47	844	69	161	.429	44	61	.721	19	58	77	164	99	0	60	51	4	184	3.9	9
Eric Snow‡	64	918	79	184	.429	49	71	.690	19	62	81	177	114	0	60	63	5	209	3.3	9
Doug Overton	23	277	24	63	.381	14	16	.875	2	12	14	37	34	0	8	23	1	62	2.7	9
Kebu Stewart	15	110	12	26	.462	16	25	.640	9	22	31	2	13	0	5	8	2	40	2.7	11
Rex Walters*	19	127	11	29	.379	17	17	1.000	3	6	9	21	17	0	5	17	0	42	2.2	11
Anthony Parker	37	196	25	63	.397	13	20	.650	8	18	26	19	17	0	11	11	3	72	1.9	9
William Cunningham†	1	0	0	0	...	0	0	...	0	2	2	0	0	0	0	0	0	0	0.0	0
William Cunningham‡	7	39	4	9	.444	0	0	...	4	6	10	1	10	0	2	0	0	8	1.1	2

3-pt. FG: Philadelphia 243-810 (.300)—Iverson 70-235 (.298); Coleman 26-98 (.265); Stackhouse* 16-46 (.348); Smith† 0-1 (.000); Smith‡ 0-8 (.000); Jackson* 39-112 (.348); Thomas 62-171 (.363); Shaw† 7-28 (.250); Shaw‡ 28-95 (.295); Cummings* 0-1 (.000); McKie† 9-46 (.196); McKie‡ 12-63 (.190); Williams 0-5 (.000); Davis 0-6 (.000); Snow† 2-16 (.125); Snow‡ 2-17 (.118); Overton 0-3 (.000); Walters* 3-14 (.214); Parker 9-28 (.321). Opponents 384-1115 (.344).

PHOENIX SUNS

								REBOUNDS									SCORING		
	G	Min.	FGM	FGA	Pct.	FTM	FTA	Pct.	Off.	Def.	Tot.	Ast.	PF	Dq.	Stl.	TO	Blk.	Pts.	Avg.	Hi.
Rex Chapman	68	2263	408	956	.427	146	187	.781	30	143	173	203	102	0	71	116	14	1082	15.9	33
Antonio McDyess	81	2441	497	927	.536	231	329	.702	206	407	613	106	292	6	100	142	135	1225	15.1	37
Clifford Robinson	80	2359	429	895	.479	248	360	.689	152	258	410	170	249	5	92	140	90	1133	14.2	36
Danny Manning	70	1794	390	756	.516	167	226	.739	110	282	392	139	201	2	71	100	46	947	13.5	35
Jason Kidd	82	3118	357	859	.416	167	209	.799	108	402	510	745	142	0	162	261	26	954	11.6	29
Dennis Scott†	29	493	71	162	.438	8	12	.667	8	42	50	24	31	0	10	12	7	181	6.2	19
Dennis Scott‡	81	2290	329	828	.397	105	130	.808	47	200	247	153	152	1	53	104	39	888	11.0	33
Kevin Johnson	50	1290	155	347	.447	162	186	.871	35	129	164	245	57	0	27	101	8	476	9.5	30
Cedric Ceballos*	35	626	129	258	.500	60	84	.714	51	98	149	35	59	0	22	39	8	333	9.5	22

	G	Min.	FGM	FGA	Pct.	FTM	FTA	Pct.	REBOUNDS Off.	Def.	Tot.	Ast.	PF	Dq.	Stl.	TO	Blk.	SCORING Pts.	Avg.	Hi.
Steve Nash	76	1664	268	584	.459	74	86	.860	32	128	160	262	145	1	63	98	4	691	9.1	24
George McCloud	63	1213	173	427	.405	39	51	.765	45	173	218	84	132	1	54	63	13	456	7.2	25
Mark Bryant	70	1110	109	225	.484	73	95	.768	92	152	244	46	180	3	36	58	15	291	4.2	11
John Williams	71	1333	95	202	.470	65	93	.699	107	205	312	49	138	2	33	29	60	255	3.6	16
Horacio Llamas	8	42	8	21	.381	7	10	.700	4	14	18	1	14	0	1	9	3	24	3.0	7
Marko Milic	33	163	39	64	.609	11	17	.647	10	15	25	12	17	0	10	21	0	92	2.8	13
Brooks Thompson*	13	46	10	27	.370	1	3	.333	1	4	5	3	6	0	4	5	0	26	2.0	8

3-pt. FG: Phoenix 431-1211 (.356)—Chapman 120-311 (.386); McDyess 0-2 (.000); Robinson 27-84 (.321); Manning 0-7 (.000); Kidd 73-233 (.313); Scott† 31-69 (.449); Scott‡ 125-342 (.365); Johnson 4-26 (.154); Ceballos* 15-50 (.300); Nash 81-195 (.415); McCloud 71-208 (.341); Bryant 0-1 (.000); Llamas 1-3 (.333); Milic 3-6 (.500); Thompson* 5-16 (.313). Opponents 394-1091 (.361).

PORTLAND TRAIL BLAZERS

	G	Min.	FGM	FGA	Pct.	FTM	FTA	Pct.	REBOUNDS Off.	Def.	Tot.	Ast.	PF	Dq.	Stl.	TO	Blk.	SCORING Pts.	Avg.	Hi.
Isaiah Rider	74	2786	551	1302	.423	221	267	.828	99	247	346	231	188	1	55	187	19	1458	19.7	38
Damon Stoudamire†	22	806	94	258	.364	59	75	.787	24	57	81	181	38	0	33	64	2	273	12.4	24
Damon Stoudamire‡	71	2839	448	1091	.411	238	287	.829	87	211	298	580	150	0	113	223	7	1225	17.3	36
Arvydas Sabonis	73	2333	407	826	.493	323	405	.798	149	580	729	218	267	7	65	190	80	1167	16.0	32
Rasheed Wallace	77	2896	466	875	.533	184	278	.662	132	346	478	195	268	6	75	167	88	1124	14.6	28
Kenny Anderson*	45	1472	204	527	.387	112	145	.772	36	98	134	245	99	1	61	114	1	567	12.6	31
Brian Grant	61	1921	283	557	.508	171	228	.750	197	358	555	86	184	3	44	110	45	737	12.1	34
Gary Trent*	41	1005	177	359	.493	113	163	.693	80	154	234	58	115	2	27	72	19	471	11.5	27
Walt Williams†	31	594	85	225	.378	59	65	.908	23	59	82	53	61	0	19	40	12	260	8.4	20
Walt Williams‡	59	1470	210	544	.386	108	125	.864	50	150	200	122	161	2	59	92	35	608	10.3	39
Alvin Williams*	41	864	109	238	.458	58	79	.734	19	41	60	83	60	0	30	50	2	283	6.9	19
Stacey Augmon	71	1445	154	372	.414	94	156	.603	104	131	235	88	144	0	57	81	32	403	5.7	18
Carlos Rogers†	3	25	2	4	.500	0	0	...	1	1	2	2	1	0	1	1	0	4	1.3	2
Carlos Rogers‡	21	376	47	91	.516	18	32	.563	35	32	67	18	35	0	10	14	8	112	5.3	14
Gary Grant	22	359	43	93	.462	12	14	.857	8	40	48	84	30	0	17	24	2	105	4.8	12
Jermaine O'Neal	60	808	112	231	.485	45	89	.506	80	121	201	17	101	0	15	55	58	269	4.5	21
Rick Brunson	38	622	49	141	.348	42	62	.677	14	42	56	100	55	0	25	52	3	162	4.3	19
Kelvin Cato	74	1007	98	229	.428	86	125	.688	91	161	252	23	164	3	29	44	94	282	3.8	16
John Crotty	26	379	29	90	.322	32	34	.941	4	28	32	63	28	0	10	42	1	96	3.7	17
Vincent Askew	30	443	19	54	.352	28	39	.718	21	47	68	38	39	0	19	35	5	66	2.2	10
Alton Lister	7	44	3	8	.375	0	0	...	2	9	11	1	12	0	1	2	1	6	0.9	6
Dontonio Wingfield	3	9	0	3	.000	1	2	.500	2	2	4	0	2	0	1	1	0	1	0.3	1
Sean Higgins	2	12	0	5	.000	0	0	...	0	0	0	3	0	0	2	1	0	0	0.0	0

3-pt. FG: Portland 324-1047 (.309)—Rider 135-420 (.321); Stoudamire† 26-99 (.263); Stoudamire‡ 91-304 (.299); Sabonis 30-115 (.261); Wallace 8-39 (.205); Anderson* 47-133 (.353); B. Grant 0-1 (.000); Trent* 4-9 (.444); W. Williams† 31-90 (.344); W. Williams‡ 80-219 (.365); A. Williams* 7-24 (.292); Augmon 1-7 (.143); Rogers† 0-1 (.000); Rogers‡ 0-2 (.000); G. Grant 7-19 (.368); O'Neal 0-2 (.000); Brunson 22-61 (.361); Cato 0-3 (.000); Crotty 6-20 (.300); Askew 0-2 (.000); Higgins 0-2 (.000). Opponents 373-1087 (.343).

SACRAMENTO KINGS

	G	Min.	FGM	FGA	Pct.	FTM	FTA	Pct.	REBOUNDS Off.	Def.	Tot.	Ast.	PF	Dq.	Stl.	TO	Blk.	SCORING Pts.	Avg.	Hi.
Mitch Richmond	70	2569	543	1220	.445	407	471	.864	50	179	229	279	154	0	88	181	15	1623	23.2	35
Corliss Williamson	79	2819	561	1134	.495	279	443	.630	162	284	446	230	252	4	76	199	48	1401	17.7	40
Billy Owens	78	2348	338	728	.464	116	197	.589	170	412	582	219	231	5	93	153	38	818	10.5	27
Otis Thorpe†	27	623	89	194	.459	46	70	.657	51	115	166	61	80	1	18	37	7	224	8.3	22
Otis Thorpe‡	74	2197	294	624	.471	164	240	.683	151	386	537	222	238	4	48	152	30	752	10.2	22
Lawrence Funderburke	52	1094	191	390	.490	110	162	.679	80	154	234	63	56	0	19	62	15	493	9.5	18
Olden Polynice	70	1458	249	542	.459	52	115	.452	173	266	439	107	158	0	37	98	45	550	7.9	26
Anthony Johnson	77	2266	226	609	.371	80	110	.727	51	120	171	329	188	1	64	120	6	574	7.5	22
Mahmoud Abdul-Rauf	31	530	103	273	.377	16	16	1.000	6	31	37	58	31	0	16	19	1	227	7.3	20
Tariq Abdul-Wahad	59	959	144	357	.403	84	125	.672	44	72	116	51	81	0	35	65	13	376	6.4	31
Terry Dehere	77	1410	180	451	.399	79	99	.798	21	85	106	196	150	0	52	96	4	489	6.4	21
Michael Stewart	81	1761	155	323	.480	65	142	.458	197	339	536	61	251	6	29	85	195	375	4.6	14
Chris Robinson†	19	271	42	111	.378	7	14	.500	9	24	33	29	29	0	12	18	3	108	5.7	22
Chris Robinson‡	35	414	65	174	.374	8	16	.500	9	37	46	39	50	0	19	33	4	162	4.6	22
Michael Smith*	18	347	26	61	.426	17	30	.567	35	65	100	29	35	0	15	15	9	69	3.8	12
Bobby Hurley*	34	417	47	115	.409	30	37	.811	7	29	36	80	36	0	13	42	0	128	3.8	11
Mark Hendrickson	48	737	58	149	.389	47	57	.825	33	110	143	41	60	0	26	31	9	163	3.4	10
Derek Grimm	9	34	4	14	.286	2	2	1.000	0	4	4	0	6	0	3	3	1	14	1.6	6
Kevin Salvadori	16	87	1	13	.077	3	6	.500	5	15	20	3	12	0	0	5	11	5	0.3	2

3-pt. FG: Sacramento 283-806 (.351)—Richmond 130-334 (.389); Williamson 0-9 (.000); Owens 26-70 (.371); Thorpe† 0-1 (.000); Thorpe‡ 0-5 (.000); Funderburke 1-7 (.143); Polynice 0-1 (.000); Johnson 42-128 (.328); Abdul-Rauf 5-31 (.161); Abdul-Wahad 4-19 (.211); Dehere 50-132 (.379); Robinson† 17-42 (.405); Robinson‡ 24-66 (.364); Hurley* 4-15 (.267); Hendrickson 0-5 (.000); Grimm 4-12 (.333). Opponents 345-968 (.356).

SAN ANTONIO SPURS

	G	Min.	FGM	FGA	Pct.	FTM	FTA	Pct.	REBOUNDS Off.	Def.	Tot.	Ast.	PF	Dq.	Stl.	TO	Blk.	SCORING Pts.	Avg.	Hi.
David Robinson	73	2457	544	1065	.511	485	660	.735	239	536	775	199	204	2	64	202	192	1574	21.6	39
Tim Duncan	82	3204	706	1287	.549	319	482	.662	274	703	977	224	254	1	55	279	206	1731	21.1	35
Avery Johnson	75	2674	321	671	.478	122	168	.726	30	120	150	591	140	0	84	165	18	766	10.2	27

	G	Min.	FGM	FGA	Pct.	FTM	FTA	Pct.	Off.	Def.	Tot.	Ast.	PF	Dq.	Stl.	TO	Blk.	Pts.	Avg.	Hi.
Vinny Del Negro	54	1721	211	479	.441	74	93	.796	13	139	152	183	113	0	39	53	6	513	9.5	23
Sean Elliott	36	1012	122	303	.403	56	78	.718	16	108	124	62	92	1	24	57	14	334	9.3	23
Jaren Jackson	82	2226	258	654	.394	94	118	.797	55	155	210	156	222	3	60	104	8	722	8.8	31
Chuck Person	61	1455	143	398	.359	28	37	.757	17	187	204	86	121	1	29	67	10	409	6.7	32
Monty Williams	72	1314	165	368	.448	122	182	.670	67	112	179	89	133	1	34	82	24	453	6.3	16
Will Perdue	79	1491	162	295	.549	70	133	.526	177	358	535	57	137	0	22	81	50	394	5.0	21
Cory Alexander*	37	501	60	145	.414	25	37	.676	7	40	47	71	53	2	25	47	5	165	4.5	17
Malik Rose	53	429	59	136	.434	39	61	.639	40	50	90	19	79	1	21	44	7	158	3.0	12
Carl Herrera	58	516	76	175	.434	18	44	.409	24	67	91	22	71	1	19	38	12	170	2.9	12
Reggie Geary	62	685	56	169	.331	28	56	.500	19	48	67	74	95	0	37	42	12	152	2.5	13
Brad Lohaus	9	102	7	21	.333	1	3	.333	3	9	12	5	10	0	1	3	2	19	2.1	9
Willie Burton	13	43	8	21	.381	8	12	.667	3	6	9	1	7	0	2	1	2	27	2.1	7

3-pt. FG: San Antonio 302-863 (.350)—Robinson 1-4 (.250); Duncan 0-10 (.000); Johnson 2-13 (.154); Del Negro 17-39 (.436); Elliott 34-90 (.378); Jackson 112-297 (.377); Person 95-276 (.344); Williams 1-2 (.500); Perdue 0-1 (.000); Alexander* 20-64 (.313); Rose 1-3 (.333); Herrera 0-1 (.000); Geary 12-40 (.300); Lohaus 4-14 (.286); Burton 3-9 (.333). Opponents 338-1029 (.328).

SEATTLE SUPERSONICS

	G	Min.	FGM	FGA	Pct.	FTM	FTA	Pct.	Off.	Def.	Tot.	Ast.	PF	Dq.	Stl.	TO	Blk.	Pts.	Avg.	Hi.
Vin Baker	82	2944	631	1164	.542	311	526	.591	286	370	656	152	278	7	91	174	86	1574	19.2	41
Gary Payton	82	3145	579	1278	.453	279	375	.744	77	299	376	679	195	0	185	229	18	1571	19.2	31
Detlef Schrempf	78	2742	437	898	.487	297	352	.844	135	419	554	341	205	0	60	168	19	1232	15.8	26
Dale Ellis	79	1939	348	700	.497	111	142	.782	51	133	184	89	128	0	60	74	5	934	11.8	23
Hersey Hawkins	82	2597	280	636	.440	177	204	.868	71	263	334	221	153	0	148	102	17	862	10.5	29
Sam Perkins	81	1675	196	471	.416	101	128	.789	53	202	255	113	158	0	62	62	29	580	7.2	21
Jerome Kersey	37	717	97	233	.416	39	65	.600	56	79	135	44	104	1	52	36	14	234	6.3	18
Greg Anthony	80	1021	150	349	.430	53	80	.663	18	93	111	205	97	0	64	91	3	419	5.2	16
Aaron Williams	65	757	115	220	.523	66	85	.776	48	99	147	14	119	0	19	50	38	296	4.6	20
Nate McMillan	18	279	23	67	.343	1	1	1.000	13	27	40	55	41	0	14	12	4	62	3.4	9
Jim McIlvaine	78	1211	101	223	.453	45	81	.556	96	163	259	14	240	3	24	54	137	247	3.2	10
James Cotton	9	33	8	21	.381	8	9	.889	2	4	6	0	3	0	1	6	1	24	2.7	8
David Wingate	58	546	66	140	.471	15	29	.517	19	60	79	37	58	0	21	37	3	150	2.6	9
George Zidek†	6	22	3	14	.214	4	4	1.000	0	4	4	1	5	0	0	1	0	11	1.8	4
George Zidek‡	12	64	7	29	.241	14	16	.875	4	13	17	2	10	0	0	4	2	29	2.4	9
Stephen Howard	13	53	8	21	.381	9	18	.500	6	6	12	3	13	0	3	6	1	25	1.9	6
Eric Snow*	17	74	10	23	.435	5	10	.500	0	4	4	13	15	0		12	1	25	1.5	4

3-pt. FG: Seattle 621-1569 (.396)—Baker 1-7 (.143); Payton 134-397 (.338); Schrempf 61-147 (.415); Ellis 127-274 (.464); Hawkins 125-301 (.415); Perkins 87-222 (.392); Kersey 1-10 (.100); Anthony 66-159 (.415); Williams 0-1 (.000); McMillan 15-34 (.441); McIlvaine 0-3 (.000); Cotton 0-4 (.000); Wingate 3-7 (.429); Zidek† 1-2 (.500); Zidek‡ 0-1 (.000); Snow* 0-1 (.000). Opponents 417-1287 (.324).

TORONTO RAPTORS

	G	Min.	FGM	FGA	Pct.	FTM	FTA	Pct.	Off.	Def.	Tot.	Ast.	PF	Dq.	Stl.	TO	Blk.	Pts.	Avg.	Hi.
Damon Stoudamire*	49	2033	354	833	.425	179	212	.844	63	154	217	399	112	0	80	159	5	952	19.4	36
Doug Christie	78	2939	458	1071	.428	271	327	.829	94	310	404	282	198	3	190	228	57	1287	16.5	35
John Wallace	82	2361	468	979	.478	210	293	.717	117	256	373	110	239	7	62	172	101	1147	14.0	30
Walt Williams	28	876	125	319	.392	49	60	.817	27	91	118	69	100	2	40	52	23	348	12.4	39
Marcus Camby	63	2002	308	747	.412	149	244	.611	203	263	466	111	200	1	68	134	230	765	12.1	28
Gary Trent†	13	355	64	146	.438	31	49	.633	43	61	104	14	46	1	8	22	8	159	12.2	25
Gary Trent‡	54	1360	241	505	.477	144	212	.679	123	215	338	72	161	3	35	94	27	630	11.7	27
Chauncey Billups†	29	920	103	295	.349	79	86	.919	22	55	77	97	54	1	30	56	2	328	11.3	27
Chauncey Billups‡	80	2216	280	749	.374	226	266	.850	62	128	190	314	172	2	107	174	4	893	11.2	27
Dee Brown†	31	908	137	307	.446	39	43	.907	14	76	90	101	47	0	38	41	17	378	12.2	30
Dee Brown‡	72	1719	246	562	.438	58	71	.817	24	128	152	154	123	1	82	73	23	658	9.1	32
Popeye Jones	14	352	52	127	.409	14	19	.737	50	52	102	18	39	0	10	16	3	120	8.6	21
Reggie Slater	82	1662	211	459	.460	203	322	.630	134	171	305	74	201	4	45	102	30	625	8.0	20
Tracy McGrady	64	1179	179	398	.450	79	111	.712	105	164	269	98	86	0	49	66	61	451	7.0	22
Zan Tabak*	39	752	116	249	.466	16	48	.333	59	95	154	36	117	1	15	44	27	248	6.4	23
Oliver Miller	41	1628	170	369	.461	61	101	.604	146	254	400	196	184	1	58	131	72	401	6.3	22
Carlos Rogers*	18	351	45	87	.517	18	32	.563	34	31	65	16	34	0	9	13	8	108	6.0	14
Alvin Williams†	13	207	16	44	.364	7	11	.636	5	16	21	20	19	0	8	8	1	41	3.2	6
Alvin Williams‡	54	1071	125	282	.443	65	90	.722	24	57	81	103	79	0	38	58	3	324	6.0	19
Lloyd Daniels	6	82	12	29	.414	8	10	.800	4	3	7	4	4	0	3	4	2	34	5.7	21
Shawn Respert*	47	696	94	209	.450	44	54	.815	30	43	73	44	58	0	29	33	1	257	5.5	20
John Thomas†	21	167	14	33	.424	15	21	.714	16	20	36	4	32	0	3	13	3	43	2.0	7
John Thomas‡	54	335	55	113	.487	41	54	.759	48	58	106	17	97	0	22	46	12	151	2.8	13
Sharone Wright	7	44	7	14	.500	2	4	.500	1	8	9	4	7	0	0	2	0	16	2.3	4
Chris Garner	38	293	23	70	.329	3	7	.429	7	17	24	45	50	0	21	25	4	53	1.4	7
Roy Rogers†	6	69	6	17	.353	1	4	.250	8	4	12	1	12	0	1	4	4	13	2.2	4
Roy Rogers‡	15	106	9	25	.360	2	6	.333	8	9	17	2	18	0	3	5	8	20	1.3	4
Ed Stokes	4	17	1	3	.333	1	2	.500	1	3	4	1	4	0	1	2	2	3	0.8	2
Tim Kempton†	5	32	2	7	.286	0	0	...	4	1	5	2	7	0	1	4	2	4	0.8	2
Tim Kempton‡	8	47	2	9	.222	0	0	...	4	2	6	3	10	0	1	4	2	4	0.5	2
Bob McCann	1	5	0	1	.000	0	0	...	1	0	1	0	1	0	0	0	0	0	0.0	0

3-pt. FG: Toronto 372-1086 (.343)—Stoudamire* 65-205 (.317); Christie 100-307 (.326); Wallace 1-2 (.500); W. Williams* 49-129 (.380); Camby 0-2 (.000); Trent† 0-3 (.000); Trent‡ 4-12 (.333); Billups† 43-136 (.316); Billups‡ 107-325 (.329); Brown† 65-158 (.411); Brown‡ 108-271 (.399); Jones 2-3 (.667); McGrady 14-41 (.341); Tabak* 0-1 (.000); Miller 0-4 (.000); Rogers* 0-1 (.000); A. Williams† 2-4 (.500); A. Williams‡ 9-28 (.321); Daniels 2-9 (.222); Respert* 25-67 (.373); Garner 4-14 (.286). Opponents 396-1034 (.383).

1997-98

UTAH JAZZ

	G	Min.	FGM	FGA	Pct.	FTM	FTA	Pct.	Off.	Def.	Tot.	Ast.	PF	Dq.	Stl.	TO	Blk.	Pts.	Avg.	Hi.
Karl Malone	81	3030	780	1472	.530	628	825	.761	189	645	834	316	237	0	96	247	70	2190	27.0	56
Jeff Hornacek	80	2460	399	828	.482	285	322	.885	65	205	270	349	175	1	109	132	15	1139	14.2	31
John Stockton.	64	1858	270	511	.528	191	231	.827	35	131	166	543	138	0	89	161	10	770	12.0	24
Bryon Russell	82	2219	226	525	.430	213	278	.766	78	248	326	101	229	2	90	81	31	738	9.0	21
Shandon Anderson . . .	82	1602	269	500	.538	136	185	.735	86	141	227	89	145	0	66	92	18	681	8.3	26
Adam Keefe	80	2047	229	424	.540	162	200	.810	179	259	438	89	172	0	52	71	24	620	7.8	25
Howard Eisley	82	1726	229	519	.441	127	149	.852	25	141	166	346	182	3	54	160	13	633	7.7	22
Antoine Carr	66	1086	151	325	.465	76	98	.776	42	89	131	48	195	3	11	48	53	378	5.7	19
Greg Foster.	78	1446	186	418	.445	67	87	.770	85	188	273	51	187	2	15	68	28	441	5.7	18
Greg Ostertag	63	1288	115	239	.481	67	140	.479	134	240	374	25	166	1	28	74	132	297	4.7	21
Chris Morris	54	538	85	207	.411	44	61	.721	35	79	114	24	61	0	25	33	17	233	4.3	20
Jacque Vaughn	45	419	44	122	.361	48	68	.706	4	34	38	84	63	1	9	56	1	139	3.1	9
Troy Hudson.	8	23	6	14	.429	0	0	. . .	1	1	2	4	1	0	2	1	0	12	1.5	6
William Cunningham*. .	6	38	4	9	.444	0	0	. . .	4	4	8	1	10	0	2	0	0	8	1.3	2

3-pt. FG: Utah 249-670 (.372)—Malone 2-6 (.333); Hornacek 56-127 (.441); Stockton 39-91 (.429); Russell 73-214 (.341); Anderson 7-32 (.219); Eisley 48-118 (.407); Foster 2-9 (.222); Morris 19-62 (.306); Vaughn 3-8 (.375); Hudson 0-3 (.000). Opponents 401-1122 (.357).

VANCOUVER GRIZZLIES

	G	Min.	FGM	FGA	Pct.	FTM	FTA	Pct.	Off.	Def.	Tot.	Ast.	PF	Dq.	Stl.	TO	Blk.	Pts.	Avg.	Hi.
Shareef Abdur-Rahim .	82	2950	653	1347	.485	502	640	.784	227	354	581	213	201	0	89	257	76	1829	22.3	32
Bryant Reeves.	74	2527	492	941	.523	223	316	.706	196	389	585	155	278	6	39	156	80	1207	16.3	41
Otis Thorpe*.	47	1574	205	430	.477	118	170	.694	100	271	371	161	158	3	30	115	23	528	11.2	21
Sam Mack	57	1414	222	559	.397	62	77	.805	30	103	133	101	117	0	41	69	11	616	10.8	28
Blue Edwards	81	1968	326	742	.439	180	215	.837	61	156	217	201	183	0	86	134	27	872	10.8	27
Anthony Peeler*	8	202	35	72	.486	4	6	.667	6	14	20	23	16	0	9	6	0	79	9.9	19
Antonio Daniels	74	1956	228	548	.416	112	170	.659	22	121	143	334	88	0	55	164	10	579	7.8	23
George Lynch	82	1493	248	516	.481	111	158	.703	147	215	362	122	161	0	65	104	41	616	7.5	19
Tony Massenburg	61	894	148	309	.479	100	137	.730	80	152	232	21	123	0	25	60	24	396	6.5	34
Michael Smith†	30	706	67	133	.504	48	73	.658	85	121	206	59	60	0	26	36	6	182	6.1	14
Michael Smith‡	48	1053	93	194	.479	65	103	.631	120	186	306	88	95	0	41	51	15	251	5.2	14
Pete Chilcutt	82	1420	156	359	.435	39	59	.661	77	229	306	104	158	0	53	62	37	405	4.9	17
Lee Mayberry	79	1835	131	349	.375	38	51	.745	19	95	114	349	164	1	65	113	10	363	4.6	14
Bobby Hurley†	27	458	46	123	.374	29	39	.744	5	25	30	97	43	0	10	44	0	122	4.5	17
Bobby Hurley‡	61	875	93	238	.391	59	76	.776	12	54	66	177	79	0	23	86	0	250	4.1	17
Chris Robinson*	16	143	23	63	.365	1	2	.500	0	13	13	10	21	0	7	15	1	54	3.4	9
Larry Robinson	6	41	6	19	.316	2	2	1.000	2	10	12	1	0	0	4	2	0	17	2.8	12
Ivano Newbill	28	249	20	57	.351	17	30	.567	24	45	69	9	38	0	10	17	3	58	2.1	8

3-pt. FG: Vancouver 325-898 (.362)—Abdur-Rahim 21-51 (.412); Reeves 0-4 (.000); Thorpe* 0-4 (.000); Mack 110-269 (.409); Edwards 40-120 (.333); Peeler* 5-19 (.263); Daniels 11-52 (.212); Lynch 9-30 (.300); Smith† 0-1 (.000); Smith‡ 0-1 (.000); Chilcutt 54-130 (.415); Mayberry 63-180 (.350); Hurley† 1-7 (.143); Hurley‡ 5-22 (.227); C. Robinson* 7-24 (.292); L. Robinson 3-6 (.500); Newbill 1-1 (1.000). Opponents 428-1111 (.385).

WASHINGTON WIZARDS

	G	Min.	FGM	FGA	Pct.	FTM	FTA	Pct.	Off.	Def.	Tot.	Ast.	PF	Dq.	Stl.	TO	Blk.	Pts.	Avg.	Hi.
Chris Webber	71	2809	647	1341	.482	196	333	.589	176	498	674	273	269	4	111	185	124	1555	21.9	36
Juwan Howard	64	2559	463	991	.467	258	358	.721	161	288	449	208	225	3	82	185	23	1184	18.5	29
Rod Strickland	76	3020	490	1130	.434	357	492	.726	112	293	405	801	182	2	126	266	25	1349	17.8	37
Tracy Murray.	82	2227	449	1007	.446	182	209	.871	75	202	277	84	167	0	67	102	25	1238	15.1	50
Calbert Cheaney	82	2841	448	981	.457	139	215	.647	82	242	324	173	264	4	96	104	36	1050	12.8	30
Ledell Eackles	42	547	75	175	.429	52	59	.881	25	50	75	16	43	0	17	29	0	218	5.2	24
Chris Whitney	82	1073	126	355	.355	118	129	.915	16	99	115	196	106	0	34	65	6	422	5.1	21
Jimmy Oliver	1	10	2	4	.500	0	0	. . .	0	2	2	1	1	0	0	0	0	5	5.0	5
Terry Davis	74	1705	127	256	.496	69	119	.580	209	271	480	30	193	4	41	56	24	323	4.4	15
Ben Wallace	67	1124	85	164	.518	35	98	.357	112	212	324	18	116	1	61	28	72	205	3.1	11
God Shammgod	20	146	19	58	.328	23	30	.767	2	5	7	36	27	0	7	21	1	61	3.1	12
Harvey Grant	65	895	75	196	.383	19	30	.633	60	108	168	39	94	1	23	26	15	170	2.6	17
Darvin Ham	71	635	55	104	.529	35	74	.473	72	59	131	16	118	1	21	37	25	145	2.0	9
Lorenzo Williams	14	111	13	17	.765	0	2	.000	16	10	26	3	17	0	2	2	3	26	1.9	8
Tim Legler	8	76	3	19	.158	3	4	.750	2	2	4	3	11	0	1	4	0	9	1.1	5
Lawrence Moten	8	27	3	13	.231	3	4	.750	1	0	1	3	6	0	0	1	0	9	1.1	4

3-pt. FG: Washington 320-944 (.339)—Webber 65-205 (.317); Howard 0-2 (.000); Strickland 12-48 (.250); Murray 158-403 (.392); Cheaney 15-53 (.283); Eackles 16-46 (.348); Whitney 52-169 (.308); Oliver 1-2 (.500); Davis 0-1 (.000); Shammgod 0-2 (.000); Grant 1-6 (.167); Legler 0-6 (.000); Moten 0-1 (.000). Opponents 348-977 (.356).

* Finished season with another team. † Totals with this team only. ‡ Totals with all teams.

EASTERN CONFERENCE

FIRST ROUND

Chicago 3, New Jersey 0

Apr. 24—Fri.	New Jersey 93 at Chicago	*96
Apr. 26—Sun.	New Jersey 91 at Chicago	96
Apr. 29—Wed.	Chicago 116 at New Jersey	101

New York 3, Miami 2

Apr. 24—Fri.	New York 79 at Miami	94
Apr. 26—Sun.	New York 96 at Miami	86
Apr. 28—Tue.	Miami 91 at New York	85
Apr. 30—Thur.	Miami 85 at New York	90
May 3—Sun.	New York 98 at Miami	81

Indiana 3, Cleveland 1

Apr. 23—Thur.	Cleveland 77 at Indiana	106
Apr. 25—Sat.	Cleveland 86 at Indiana	92
Apr. 27—Mon.	Indiana 77 at Cleveland	86
Apr. 30—Thur.	Indiana 80 at Cleveland	74

Charlotte 3, Atlanta 1

Apr. 23—Thur.	Atlanta 87 at Charlotte	97
Apr. 25—Sat.	Atlanta 85 at Charlotte	92
Apr. 28—Tue.	Charlotte 64 at Atlanta	96
May 1—Fri.	Charlotte 91 at Atlanta	82

SEMIFINALS

Chicago 4, Charlotte 1

May 3—Sun.	Charlotte 70 at Chicago	83
May 6—Wed.	Charlotte 78 at Chicago	76
May 8—Fri.	Chicago 103 at Charlotte	89
May 10—Sun.	Chicago 94 at Charlotte	80
May 13—Wed.	Charlotte 84 at Chicago	93

Indiana 4, New York 1

May 5—Tue.	New York 83 at Indiana	93
May 7—Thur.	New York 77 at Indiana	85
May 9—Sat.	Indiana 76 at New York	83
May 10—Sun.	Indiana 118 at New York	*107
May 13—Wed.	New York 88 at Indiana	99

FINALS

Chicago 4, Indiana 3

May 17—Sun.	Indiana 79 at Chicago	85
May 19—Tue.	Indiana 98 at Chicago	104
May 23—Sat.	Chicago 105 at Indiana	107
May 25—Mon.	Chicago 94 at Indiana	96
May 27—Wed.	Indiana 87 at Chicago	106
May 29—Fri.	Chicago 89 at Indiana	92
May 31—Sun.	Indiana 83 at Chicago	88

WESTERN CONFERENCE

FIRST ROUND

Utah 3, Houston 2

Apr. 23—Thur.	Houston 103 at Utah	90
Apr. 25—Sat.	Houston 90 at Utah	105
Apr. 29—Wed.	Utah 85 at Houston	89
May 1—Fri.	Utah 93 at Houston	71
May 3—Sun.	Houston 70 at Utah	84

Seattle 3, Minnesota 2

Apr. 24—Fri.	Minnesota 83 at Seattle	108
Apr. 26—Sun.	Minnesota 98 at Seattle	93
Apr. 28—Tue.	Seattle 90 at Minnesota	98
Apr. 30—Thur.	Seattle 92 at Minnesota	88
May 2—Sat.	Minnesota 84 at Seattle	97

L.A. Lakers 3, Portland 1

Apr. 24—Fri.	Portland 102 at L.A. Lakers	104
Apr. 26—Sun.	Portland 99 at L.A. Lakers	108
Apr. 28—Tue.	L.A. Lakers 94 at Portland	99
Apr. 30—Thur.	L.A. Lakers 110 at Portland	99

San Antonio 3, Phoenix 1

Apr. 23—Thur.	San Antonio 102 at Phoenix	96
Apr. 25—Sat.	San Antonio 101 at Phoenix	108
Apr. 27—Mon.	Phoenix 88 at San Antonio	100
Apr. 29—Wed.	Phoenix 80 at San Antonio	99

SEMIFINALS

Utah 4, San Antonio 1

May 5—Tue.	San Antonio 82 at Utah	83
May 7—Thur.	San Antonio 106 at Utah	*109
May 9—Sat.	Utah 64 at San Antonio	86
May 10—Sun.	Utah 82 at San Antonio	73
May 12—Tue.	San Antonio 77 at Utah	87

L.A. Lakers 4, Seattle 1

May 4—Mon.	L.A. Lakers 92 at Seattle	106
May 6—Wed.	L.A. Lakers 92 at Seattle	68
May 8—Fri.	Seattle 103 at L.A. Lakers	119
May 10—Sun.	Seattle 100 at L.A. Lakers	112
May 12—Tue.	L.A. Lakers 110 at Seattle	95

FINALS

Utah 4, L.A. Lakers 0

May 16—Sat.	L.A. Lakers 77 at Utah	112
May 18—Mon.	L.A. Lakers 95 at Utah	99
May 22—Fri.	Utah 109 at L.A. Lakers	98
May 24—Sun.	Utah 96 at L.A. Lakers	92

NBA FINALS

Chicago 4, Utah 2

June 3—Wed.	Chicago 85 at Utah	*88
June 5—Fri.	Chicago 93 at Utah	88
June 7—Sun.	Utah 54 at Chicago	96
June 10—Wed.	Utah 82 at Chicago	86
June 12—Fri.	Utah 83 at Chicago	81
June 14—Sun.	Chicago 87 at Utah	86

*Denotes number of overtime periods.

1997-98

1996-97

1996-97 NBA CHAMPION CHICAGO BULLS

Front row (from left): Luc Longley, Dennis Rodman, Michael Jordan, Scottie Pippen, Ron Harper. Center row (from left): Jud Buechler, Jason Caffey, Toni Kukoc, Bill Wennington, Robert Parish, Dickey Simpkins, Steve Kerr, Randy Brown. Back row (from left): equipment manager John Ligmanowski, assistant coach Frank Hamblen, assistant coach Jimmy Rodgers, head coach Phil Jackson, assistant coach Tex Winter, trainer Robert "Chip" Schaefer.

FINAL STANDINGS

ATLANTIC DIVISION

	Atl.	Bos.	Cha.	Chi.	Cle.	Dal.	Den.	Det.	G.S.	Hou.	Ind.	LA-C	LA-L	Mia.	Mil.	Min.	N.J.	N.Y.	Orl.	Phi.	Pho.	Por.	Sac.	S.A.	Sea.	Tor.	Uta.	Van.	Was.	W	L	Pct.	GB
Mia.	2	4	2	2	4	2	2	4	2	2	3	2	1	..	4	1	3	1	2	3	2	1	2	2	0	3	0	2	3	61	21	.744	..
N.Y.	3	4	1	2	3	1	2	2	2	1	3	2	1	3	2	1	2	..	3	3	1	1	2	2	0	3	1	2	4	57	25	.695	4
Orl.	1	4	2	0	2	1	2	2	1	2	3	1	1	2	2	1	3	1	..	2	1	2	1	1	4	0	1	1		45	37	.549	16
Was.	1	4	1	1	3	2	1	0	2	0	3	2	0	1	3	1	3	0	3	3	1	2	2	2	0	2	0	1	..	44	38	.537	17
N.J.	1	4	0	1	0	1	1	0	0	0	2	1	0	1	1	0	..	2	1	2	1	0	1	2	1	0	0	2	1	26	56	.317	35
Phi.	0	3	0	0	0	0	1	1	0	0	0	1	0	1	1	1	2	2	2	..	1	1	0	1	0	1	0	2	1	22	60	.268	39
Bos.	1	..	0	0	1	1	1	0	1	0	1	0	1	0	1	0	0	0	0	0	1	1	0	1	0	3	0	0	0	15	67	.183	46

CENTRAL DIVISION

	Atl.	Bos.	Cha.	Chi.	Cle.	Dal.	Den.	Det.	G.S.	Hou.	Ind.	LA-C	LA-L	Mia.	Mil.	Min.	N.J.	N.Y.	Orl.	Phi.	Pho.	Por.	Sac.	S.A.	Sea.	Tor.	Uta.	Van.	Was.	W	L	Pct.	GB
Chi.	3	4	4	..	3	2	2	3	2	1	4	2	1	2	4	2	3	2	3	4	2	2	2	2	3	1	2	2	2	69	13	.841	..
Atl.	..	3	1	1	3	2	1	1	2	1	3	2	1	1	4	2	3	1	3	4	1	2	2	2	1	4	1	2	2	56	26	.683	13
Cha.	3	4	..	0	3	1	2	2	2	2	2	1	1	1	2	2	4	3	1	4	1	0	2	2	2	2	0	2	3	54	28	.659	15
Det.	3	4	2	1	2	2	2	..	2	1	3	2	1	0	3	2	4	1	2	2	0	1	1	2	1	3	1	2	4	54	28	.659	15
Cle.	1	2	1	1	..	2	1	2	1	0	3	2	1	0	0	2	2	4	1	2	3	1	2	0	0	3	1	2	1	42	40	.512	27
Ind.	1	2	2	0	1	1	2	1	1	1	..	2	1	1	2	2	2	1	1	3	1	1	1	1	4	0	2	1	1	39	43	.476	30
Mil.	0	3	2	0	2	2	1	1	1	1	2	0	..	0	0	2	2	1	3	1	0	0	3	1	2	1				33	49	.402	36
Tor.	0	1	2	1	1	2	1	1	0	1	0	0	1	1	1	1	3	0	0	3	2	2	1	1	0	..	1	1	2	30	52	.366	39

MIDWEST DIVISION

	Atl.	Bos.	Cha.	Chi.	Cle.	Dal.	Den.	Det.	G.S.	Hou.	Ind.	LA-C	LA-L	Mia.	Mil.	Min.	N.J.	N.Y.	Orl.	Phi.	Pho.	Por.	Sac.	S.A.	Sea.	Tor.	Uta.	Van.	Was.	W	L	Pct.	GB
Utah	1	2	2	1	1	3	4	1	4	2	2	3	3	2	1	3	2	1	2	2	3	2	4	3	3	1	..	4	2	64	18	.780	..
Hou.	1	2	0	1	2	4	3	1	4	..	1	3	3	0	1	4	2	1	0	2	2	2	4	3	3	1	2	3	2	57	25	.695	7
Min.	0	2	0	0	0	3	4	0	3	0	0	3	1	1	2	..	2	1	1	3	2	0	4	0	1	1	4	1		40	42	.488	24
Dal.	0	1	1	0	0	..	3	0	0	0	1	2	0	0	0	1	1	1	1	2	1	1	2	1	1	0	1	3	0	24	58	.293	40
Den.	1	1	0	0	1	1	..	0	1	1	0	1	0	0	1	0	1	0	0	1	1	0	2	0	2	0	1	0	3	21	61	.256	43
S.A.	0	1	0	0	2	3	2	0	1	1	1	0	2	0	1	0	0	0	1	1	1	0	1	..	0	1	1	1	0	20	62	.244	44
Van.	0	2	0	0	0	1	1	0	1	1	0	0	0	0	0	0	0	1	0	2	0	0	3	0	1	0	..		1	14	68	.171	50

PACIFIC DIVISION

	Atl.	Bos.	Cha.	Chi.	Cle.	Dal.	Den.	Det.	G.S.	Hou.	Ind.	LA-C	LA-L	Mia.	Mil.	Min.	N.J.	N.Y.	Orl.	Phi.	Pho.	Por.	Sac.	S.A.	Sea.	Tor.	Uta.	Van.	Was.	W	L	Pct.	GB
Sea.	1	2	0	0	2	3	4	1	4	1	1	3	2	1	2	1	2	1	2	3	3	4	..	2	1	4	2			57	25	.695	..
L.A.L.	1	1	1	1	1	4	4	1	4	1	1	2	..	1	2	3	2	1	2	4	1	4	2	3	1	1	4	2		56	26	.683	1
Por.	0	1	2	0	1	3	4	1	2	2	1	4	3	1	2	2	2	1	0	1	3	..	2	4	1	0	2	4	0	49	33	.598	8
Pho.	1	1	1	0	1	3	2	2	4	2	2	0	1	1	1	1	1	..	1	4	3	2	0	1	2	1	4	2		40	42	.488	17
L.A.C.	0	2	1	0	0	2	3	0	3	1	0	..	2	0	2	1	0	1	1	0	2	4	1	2	1	2	1	4	0	36	46	.439	21
Sac.	0	2	0	0	0	2	2	1	3	0	1	2	0	0	0	4	1	0	1	2	0	2	..	3	1	1	0	4	0	34	48	.415	23
G.S.	0	1	0	0	1	4	3	0	..	0	1	1	0	0	0	1	2	0	1	2	0	2	1	4	0	2	0	3	0	30	52	.366	27

OFFENSIVE

	G	FGM	FGA	Pct.	FTM	FTA	Pct.	REBOUNDS Off.	Def.	Tot.	Ast.	PF	Dq.	Stl.	TO	Blk.	SCORING Pts.	Avg.
Chicago	82	3277	6923	.473	1381	1848	.747	1235	2461	3696	2142	1617	10	716	1109	332	8458	103.1
Utah	82	3131	6217	.504	1858	2416	.769	889	2410	3299	2199	1981	12	748	1259	418	8454	103.1
Phoenix	82	3143	6705	.469	1618	2125	.761	916	2376	3292	2067	1727	21	664	1180	322	8431	102.8
Seattle	82	2995	6415	.467	1725	2295	.752	1010	2271	3281	1931	1803	17	904	1231	388	8274	100.9
Houston	82	3037	6484	.468	1503	1992	.755	927	2565	3492	2013	1610	10	685	1365	347	8248	100.6
Boston	82	3066	6967	.440	1649	2199	.750	1095	2188	3283	1792	1915	13	810	1342	315	8248	100.6
Philadelphia	82	3003	6850	.438	1776	2450	.725	1267	2355	3622	1695	1733	24	683	1437	394	8215	100.2
L.A. Lakers	82	3018	6642	.454	1613	2330	.692	1092	2414	3506	1845	1818	17	740	1222	575	8200	100.0
Golden State	82	2997	6567	.456	1696	2180	.778	1086	2259	3345	1822	1787	14	611	1410	359	8171	99.6
Washington	82	3208	6678	.480	1400	1979	.707	1010	2420	3430	1921	1815	20	712	1289	402	8147	99.4
Portland	82	3000	6465	.464	1613	2261	.713	1058	2494	3552	1710	1928	23	640	1357	435	8114	99.0
Charlotte	82	2988	6342	.471	1541	1984	.777	910	2298	3208	2021	1702	17	597	1203	349	8108	98.9
Denver	82	2934	6687	.439	1516	1992	.761	994	2452	3446	1889	1784	25	503	1359	487	8020	97.8
New Jersey	82	2994	7091	.422	1502	2031	.740	1410	2376	3786	1726	1865	23	677	1290	481	7974	97.2
L.A. Clippers	82	2989	6696	.446	1517	2074	.731	1092	2242	3334	1662	1964	27	733	1311	441	7969	97.2
Sacramento	82	3000	6611	.454	1494	2067	.723	1100	2307	3407	1799	1946	24	588	1332	362	7908	96.4
Minnesota	82	2937	6436	.456	1637	2180	.751	957	2302	3259	1874	1818	16	618	1243	557	7882	96.1
Toronto	82	2897	6632	.437	1446	2008	.720	1135	2254	3389	1714	1883	34	722	1347	517	7829	95.5
New York	82	2882	6227	.463	1585	2119	.748	973	2516	3489	1809	2033	28	629	1462	378	7819	95.4
Indiana	82	2851	6254	.456	1687	2336	.722	1029	2390	3419	1750	1977	22	585	1338	394	7819	95.4
Milwaukee	82	2967	6303	.471	1560	2104	.741	955	2263	3218	1610	1892	22	632	1285	348	7818	95.3
Miami	82	2822	6235	.453	1454	2022	.719	957	2402	3359	1735	1919	36	650	1306	439	7776	94.8
Atlanta	82	2812	6307	.446	1491	1955	.763	1021	2350	3371	1557	1591	17	701	1228	427	7774	94.8
Detroit	82	2827	6095	.464	1487	1995	.745	858	2292	3150	1554	1652	12	632	1041	283	7723	94.2
Orlando	82	2839	6497	.437	1474	1975	.746	1071	2221	3292	1689	1643	15	694	1250	363	7719	94.1
Dallas	82	2813	6452	.436	1375	1918	.717	1040	2262	3302	1663	1798	16	654	1324	351	7431	90.6
San Antonio	82	2827	6391	.442	1386	1929	.719	1101	2129	3230	1661	1764	11	646	1243	431	7418	90.5
Vancouver	82	2819	6453	.437	1230	1734	.709	1023	2155	3178	1862	1755	8	657	1301	464	7313	89.2
Cleveland	82	2704	5972	.453	1282	1773	.723	909	2159	3068	1714	1882	16	655	1188	315	7173	87.5

DEFENSIVE

	FGM	FGA	Pct.	FTM	FTA	Pct.	REBOUNDS Off.	Def.	Tot.	Ast.	PF	Dq.	Stl.	TO	Blk.	SCORING Pts.	Avg.	Dif.
Cleveland	2488	5638	.441	1587	2138	.742	845	2186	3031	1647	1748	16	549	1331	350	7022	85.6	+1.8
Detroit	2768	6231	.444	1229	1668	.737	964	2264	3228	1795	1784	18	488	1195	282	7293	88.9	+5.2
Miami	2687	6226	.432	1541	2108	.731	999	2321	3320	1512	1831	15	646	1324	392	7326	89.3	+5.5
Atlanta	2804	6451	.435	1235	1676	.737	1045	2225	3270	1665	1747	18	605	1267	332	7328	89.4	+5.4
New York	2665	6272	.425	1752	2389	.733	911	2220	3131	1589	1882	35	727	1333	295	7563	92.2	+3.1
Chicago	2898	6653	.436	1305	1770	.737	1088	2205	3293	1619	1732	18	624	1293	286	7572	92.3	+10.8
Seattle	2759	6259	.441	1513	2042	.741	1015	2256	3271	1751	1927	18	634	1535	423	7644	93.2	+7.7
Utah	2708	6188	.438	1796	2395	.750	957	2101	3058	1593	2045	28	639	1330	373	7733	94.3	+8.8
Indiana	2799	6357	.440	1642	2182	.753	1004	2261	3265	1737	1952	29	693	1289	418	7739	94.4	+1
Orlando	2966	6539	.454	1361	1860	.732	1080	2398	3478	1798	1769	16	704	1314	417	7748	94.5	-0.4
Portland	2798	6423	.436	1719	2327	.739	952	2197	3149	1703	1887	23	656	1242	428	7772	94.8	+4.2
L.A. Lakers	2922	6619	.441	1527	2126	.718	1110	2368	3478	1880	1934	30	620	1341	388	7850	95.7	+4.3
Houston	3030	6845	.443	1302	1785	.729	1029	2332	3361	1835	1735	17	731	1172	365	7881	96.1	+4.5
Dallas	2966	6469	.458	1482	1974	.751	1098	2428	3526	1794	1720	18	687	1284	433	7952	97.0	-6.4
Charlotte	3056	6650	.460	1356	1857	.730	1077	2256	3333	1783	1781	20	532	1143	335	7955	97.0	+1.9
Milwaukee	2999	6355	.472	1606	2197	.731	975	2257	3232	1820	1777	21	688	1201	392	7973	97.2	-1.9
Minnesota	2945	6539	.450	1646	2184	.754	1069	2364	3433	1885	1829	27	654	1283	445	8003	97.6	-1.5
Washington	3011	6637	.454	1500	2004	.749	1022	2336	3358	1671	1769	19	665	1356	334	8014	97.7	+1.6
San Antonio	3002	6379	.471	1508	2042	.738	1048	2302	3350	1955	1646	4	664	1180	448	8064	98.3	-7.9
Toronto	2971	6390	.465	1646	2274	.724	1033	2352	3385	1967	1799	9	675	1338	442	8085	98.6	-3.1
Vancouver	3092	6556	.472	1468	2018	.727	1206	2426	3632	1974	1593	15	725	1251	461	8152	99.4	-10.2
L.A. Clippers	2975	6445	.462	1732	2312	.749	1051	2450	3501	1654	1860	14	737	1369	419	8162	99.5	-2.4
Sacramento	3010	6521	.462	1723	2337	.737	1063	2341	3404	1777	1789	18	716	1257	429	8185	99.8	-3.4
New Jersey	3100	6684	.464	1628	2185	.745	1065	2464	3529	1925	1780	14	675	1257	516	8348	101.8	-4.6
Phoenix	3183	6818	.467	1466	1984	.739	1048	2461	3509	1996	1840	20	662	1298	372	8377	102.2	+0.7
Denver	3297	7063	.467	1457	1943	.750	1086	2459	3545	1846	1725	10	724	1057	453	8535	104.1	-6.3
Golden State	3199	6735	.475	1578	2103	.750	1089	2272	3361	2159	1886	22	824	1288	395	8557	104.4	-4.7
Philadelphia	3314	7045	.470	1565	2134	.733	1186	2453	3639	2066	2008	16	822	1278	494	8751	106.7	-6.5
Boston	3365	6696	.503	1626	2257	.720	1005	2628	3633	2130	1827	22	720	1446	557	8849	107.9	-7.3
Avgs.	2958	6503	.455	1534	2078	.738	1039	2330	3369	1808	1814	19	672	1285	403	7946	96.9	...

1996-97

HOME/ROAD

	Home	Road	Total		Home	Road	Total
Atlanta	36-5	20-21	56-26	Minnesota	25-16	15-26	40-42
Boston	11-30	4-37	15-67	New Jersey	16-25	10-31	26-56
Charlotte	30-11	24-17	54-28	New York	31-10	26-15	57-25
Chicago	39-2	30-11	69-13	Orlando	26-15	19-22	45-37
Cleveland	25-16	17-24	42-40	Philadelphia	11-30	11-30	22-60
Dallas	14-27	10-31	24-58	Phoenix	25-16	15-26	40-42
Denver	12-29	9-32	21-61	Portland	29-12	20-21	49-33
Detroit	30-11	24-17	54-28	Sacramento	22-19	12-29	34-48
Golden State	18-23	12-29	30-52	San Antonio	12-29	8-33	20-62
Houston	30-11	27-14	57-25	Seattle	31-10	26-15	57-25
Indiana	21-20	18-23	39-43	Toronto	18-23	12-29	30-52
L.A. Clippers	21-20	15-26	36-46	Utah	38-3	26-15	64-18
L.A. Lakers	31-10	25-16	56-26	Vancouver	8-33	6-35	14-68
Miami	29-12	32-9	61-21	Washington	25-16	19-22	44-38
Milwaukee	20-21	13-28	33-49	Totals	684-505	505-684	1189-1189

INDIVIDUAL LEADERS

POINTS

(minimum 70 games or 1,400 points)

	G	FGM	FTM	Pts.	Avg.
Michael Jordan, Chicago	82	920	480	2431	29.6
Karl Malone, Utah	82	864	521	2249	27.4
Glen Rice, Charlotte	79	722	464	2115	26.8
Mitch Richmond, Sacramento	81	717	457	2095	25.9
Latrell Sprewell, Golden State	80	649	493	1938	24.2
Allen Iverson, Philadelphia	76	625	382	1787	23.5
Hakeem Olajuwon, Houston	78	727	351	1810	23.2
Patrick Ewing, New York	78	655	439	1751	22.4
Kendall Gill, New Jersey	82	644	427	1789	21.8
Gary Payton, Seattle	82	706	254	1785	21.8

FIELD GOALS

(minimum 300 made)

	FGM	FGA	Pct.
Gheorghe Muresan, Washington	327	541	.604
Tyrone Hill, Cleveland	357	595	.600
Rasheed Wallace, Portland	380	681	.558
Shaquille O'Neal, L.A. Lakers	552	991	.557
Chris Mullin, Golden State	438	792	.553
Karl Malone, Utah	864	1571	.550
John Stockton, Utah	416	759	.548
Dale Davis, Indiana	370	688	.538
Danny Manning, Phoenix	426	795	.536
Gary Trent, Portland	361	674	.536

FREE THROWS

(minimum 125 made)

	FTM	FTA	Pct.
Mark Price, Golden State	155	171	.906
Terrell Brandon, Cleveland	268	297	.902
Jeff Hornacek, Utah	293	326	.899
Ricky Pierce, Denver-Charlotte	139	155	.897
Mario Elie, Houston	207	231	.896
Reggie Miller, Indiana	418	475	.880
Malik Sealy, L.A. Clippers	254	290	.876
Hersey Hawkins, Seattle	258	295	.875
Darrick Martin, L.A. Clippers	218	250	.872
Glen Rice, Charlotte	464	535	.867
Joe Dumars, Detroit	222	256	.867

ASSISTS

(minimum 70 games or 400 assists)

	G	No.	Avg.
Mark Jackson, Denver-Indiana	82	935	11.4
John Stockton, Utah	82	860	10.5
Kevin Johnson, Phoenix	70	653	9.3
Jason Kidd, Dallas-Phoenix	55	496	9.0
Rod Strickland, Washington	82	727	8.9
Damon Stoudamire, Toronto	81	709	8.8
Tim Hardaway, Miami	81	695	8.6
Nick Van Exel, L.A. Lakers	79	672	8.5
Robert Pack, New Jersey-Dallas	54	452	8.4
Stephon Marbury, Minnesota	67	522	7.8

REBOUNDS

(minimum 70 games or 800 rebounds)

	G	Off.	Def.	Tot.	Avg.
Dennis Rodman, Chicago	55	320	563	883	16.1
Dikembe Mutombo, Atlanta	80	268	661	929	11.6
Anthony Mason, Charlotte	73	186	643	829	11.4
Ervin Johnson, Denver	82	231	682	913	11.1
Patrick Ewing, New York	78	175	659	834	10.7
Chris Webber, Washington	72	238	505	743	10.3
Vin Baker, Milwaukee	78	267	537	804	10.3
Loy Vaught, L.A. Clippers	82	222	595	817	10.0
Shawn Kemp, Seattle	81	275	532	807	10.0
Tyrone Hill, Cleveland	74	259	477	736	9.9
Karl Malone, Utah	82	193	616	809	9.9

STEALS

(minimum 70 games or 125 steals)

	G	No.	Avg.
Mookie Blaylock, Atlanta	78	212	2.72
Doug Christie, Toronto	81	201	2.48
Gary Payton, Seattle	82	197	2.40
Eddie Jones, L.A. Lakers	80	189	2.36
Rick Fox, Boston	76	167	2.20
David Wesley, Boston	74	162	2.19
Allen Iverson, Philadelphia	76	157	2.07
John Stockton, Utah	82	166	2.02
Greg Anthony, Vancouver	65	129	1.98
Kenny Anderson, Portland	82	162	1.98

BLOCKED SHOTS

(minimum 70 games or 100 blocked shots)

	G	No.	Avg.
Shawn Bradley, New Jersey-Dallas	73	248	3.40
Dikembe Mutombo, Atlanta	80	264	3.30
Shaquille O'Neal, L.A. Lakers	51	147	2.88
Alonzo Mourning, Miami	66	189	2.86
Ervin Johnson, Denver	82	227	2.77
Patrick Ewing, New York	78	189	2.42
Vlade Divac, Charlotte	81	180	2.22
Hakeem Olajuwon, Houston	78	173	2.22
Kevin Garnett, Minnesota	77	163	2.12
Marcus Camby, Toronto	63	130	2.06

3-POINT FIELD GOALS

(minimum 82 made)

	FGM	FGA	Pct.
Glen Rice, Charlotte	207	440	.470
Steve Kerr, Chicago	110	237	.464
Kevin Johnson, Phoenix	89	202	.441
Joe Dumars, Detroit	166	384	.432
Mitch Richmond, Sacramento	204	477	.428
Reggie Miller, Indiana	229	536	.427
Dell Curry, Charlotte	126	296	.426
Terry Mills, Detroit	175	415	.422
Mario Elie, Houston	120	286	.420
Voshon Lenard, Miami	183	442	.414

INDIVIDUAL STATISTICS, TEAM BY TEAM

ATLANTA HAWKS

	G	Min.	FGM	FGA	Pct.	FTM	FTA	Pct.	REBOUNDS Off.	Def.	Tot.	Ast.	PF	Dq.	Stl.	TO	Blk.	SCORING Pts.	Avg.	Hi.
Steve Smith 72	72	2818	491	1145	.429	333	393	.847	90	148	238	305	173	2	62	176	23	1445	20.1	41
Christian Laettner 82	82	3140	548	1128	.486	359	440	.816	212	508	720	223	277	8	102	218	64	1486	18.1	37
Mookie Blaylock . . . 78	78	3056	501	1159	.432	131	174	.753	114	299	413	463	141	0	212	185	20	1354	17.4	39
Dikembe Mutombo . . 80	80	2973	380	721	.527	306	434	.705	268	661	929	110	249	3	49	186	264	1066	13.3	27
Tyrone Corbin 70	70	2305	253	600	.422	86	108	.796	76	218	294	124	176	1	90	85	7	666	9.5	22
Henry James. 53	53	945	125	306	.408	30	36	.833	27	54	81	21	98	1	11	29	1	356	6.7	26
Alan Henderson 30	30	501	77	162	.475	45	75	.600	47	69	116	23	73	1	21	29	6	199	6.6	19
Willie Burton. 24	24	380	39	116	.336	57	68	.838	11	30	41	11	55	0	8	26	3	148	6.2	20
Eldridge Recasner 71	71	1207	148	350	.423	51	58	.879	35	80	115	94	97	0	38	65	4	405	5.7	23
Jon Barry 58	58	965	100	246	.407	37	46	.804	26	73	99	115	56	0	55	59	3	285	4.9	17
Ken Norman 17	17	220	27	94	.287	4	12	.333	8	31	39	12	17	0	7	18	3	64	3.8	16
Priest Lauderdale . . 35	35	180	49	89	.551	13	23	.565	16	27	43	12	39	0	1	37	9	111	3.2	14
Donnie Boyce 22	22	154	21	63	.333	11	22	.500	7	8	15	13	17	0	10	16	4	55	2.5	8
Darrin Hancock† . . . 14	14	86	13	27	.481	8	12	.667	3	10	13	7	6	0	7	7	1	34	2.4	12
Darrin Hancock‡ 24	24	133	16	35	.457	10	14	.714	4	14	18	12	15	0	9	11	1	42	1.8	12
Ivano Newbill 72	72	850	40	91	.440	20	52	.385	76	128	204	24	115	1	28	42	15	100	1.4	7
Derrick Alston. 2	2	11	0	5	.000	0	2	.000	3	1	4	0	0	0	0	0	0	0	0.0	0
Anthony Miller 1	1	14	0	5	.000	0	0	. . .	2	5	7	0	2	0	0	0	0	0	0.0	0

3-pt. FG: Atlanta 659-1834 (.359)—Smith 130-388 (.335); Laettner 31-88 (.352); Blaylock 221-604 (.366); Corbin 74-208 (.356); James 76-181 (.420); Burton 13-46 (.283); Recasner 58-140 (.414); Barry 48-124 (.387); Norman 6-38 (.158); Lauderdale 0-1 (.000); Boyce 2-16 (.125). Opponents 485-1399 (.347).

BOSTON CELTICS

	G	Min.	FGM	FGA	Pct.	FTM	FTA	Pct.	REBOUNDS Off.	Def.	Tot.	Ast.	PF	Dq.	Stl.	TO	Blk.	SCORING Pts.	Avg.	Hi.
Antoine Walker 82	82	2970	576	1354	.425	231	366	.631	288	453	741	262	271	1	105	230	53	1435	17.5	37
David Wesley 74	74	2991	456	974	.468	225	288	.781	67	197	264	537	221	1	162	211	13	1240	16.8	34
Rick Fox 76	76	2050	400	860	.456	207	263	.787	114	280	394	286	279	4	167	178	40	1174	15.4	34
Eric Williams 72	72	2435	374	820	.456	328	436	.752	126	203	329	129	213	0	72	139	13	1070	15.0	20
Todd Day 81	81	2277	398	999	.398	256	331	.773	109	221	330	117	208	0	108	127	48	1178	14.5	33
Dino Radja 25	25	874	149	339	.440	51	71	.718	44	167	211	48	76	2	23	70	48	349	14.0	26
Dana Barros 24	24	708	110	253	.435	37	43	.860	5	43	48	81	34	0	26	39	6	300	12.5	24
Greg Minor 23	23	547	94	196	.480	31	38	.801	30	50	80	34	45	0	15	22	2	220	9.6	16
Marty Conlon 74	74	1614	214	454	.471	144	171	.842	128	195	323	104	154	2	46	109	18	574	7.8	22
Dee Brown 21	21	522	61	166	.367	18	22	.818	8	40	48	67	45	0	31	24	7	160	7.6	17
Frank Brickowski. . . . 17	17	255	32	73	.438	10	14	.714	6	28	34	15	42	1	5	19	4	81	4.8	12
Michael Hawkins. 29	29	326	29	68	.426	12	15	.800	9	22	31	64	40	0	16	28	1	80	2.8	14
Pervis Ellison 6	6	125	6	16	.375	3	5	.600	9	17	26	4	21	1	5	7	9	15	2.5	7
Nate Driggers 15	15	132	13	43	.302	10	14	.714	12	10	22	6	10	0	3	6	2	36	2.4	8
Stacey King* 5	5	33	5	7	.714	2	3	.667	1	8	9	1	3	0	0	1	1	12	2.4	6
Brett Szabo 70	70	662	54	121	.446	45	61	.738	56	109	165	17	119	0	16	41	32	153	2.2	15
Steve Hamer. 35	35	268	30	57	.526	16	29	.552	17	43	60	7	39	0	2	13	4	76	2.2	9
Alton Lister 53	53	516	32	77	.416	23	31	.742	66	102	168	13	95	1	8	30	14	87	1.6	10

3-pt. FG: Boston 467-1331 (.351)—Walker 52-159 (.327); Wesley 103-286 (.360); Fox 101-278 (.363); Williams 2-8 (.250); Day 126-348 (.362); Radja 0-1 (.000); Barros 43-105 (.410); Minor 1-8 (.125); Conlon 2-10 (.200); Brown 20-65 (.308); Brickowski 7-20 (.350); Hawkins 10-31 (.323); Driggers 0-9 (.000); Szabo 0-1 (.000); Hamer 0-2 (.000). Opponents 493-1351 (.365).

CHARLOTTE HORNETS

	G	Min.	FGM	FGA	Pct.	FTM	FTA	Pct.	REBOUNDS Off.	Def.	Tot.	Ast.	PF	Dq.	Stl.	TO	Blk.	SCORING Pts.	Avg.	Hi.
Glen Rice 79	79	3362	722	1513	.477	464	535	.867	67	251	318	160	190	0	72	177	26	2115	26.8	48
Anthony Mason. 73	73	3143	433	825	.525	319	428	.745	186	643	829	414	202	3	76	165	33	1186	16.2	28
Dell Curry 68	68	2078	384	836	.459	114	142	.803	40	171	211	118	147	0	60	93	14	1008	14.8	38
Vlade Divac. 81	81	2840	418	847	.494	177	259	.683	241	484	725	301	277	6	103	193	180	1024	12.6	29
Ricky Pierce† 27	27	650	119	237	.502	56	63	.889	19	49	68	49	48	0	14	30	4	324	12.0	24
Ricky Pierce‡ 60	60	1250	239	497	.481	139	155	.897	36	85	121	80	97	0	28	68	9	659	11.0	25
Matt Geiger. 49	49	1044	171	350	.489	89	127	.701	100	158	258	38	153	1	20	67	27	437	8.9	25
Muggsy Bogues 65	65	1880	204	443	.460	54	64	.844	25	116	141	469	114	0	82	108	2	522	8.0	24
Anthony Goldwire* . . . 33	33	576	62	154	.403	30	40	.750	3	35	38	94	58	1	19	41	1	190	5.8	18
Tony Delk 61	61	867	119	256	.465	42	51	.824	31	68	99	99	71	1	36	68	6	332	5.4	25
Scott Burrell* 28	28	482	45	131	.344	42	53	.792	24	55	79	39	60	0	14	25	11	151	5.4	12
Tony Smith 69	69	1291	138	337	.409	38	59	.644	38	56	94	150	110	2	48	73	19	346	5.0	20
Donald Royal† 25	25	320	21	40	.525	28	35	.800	18	40	58	10	42	0	12	22	2	70	2.8	10
Donald Royal‡ 62	62	858	62	146	.425	94	117	.803	52	102	154	25	100	0	23	47	11	218	3.5	12
Rafael Addison 41	41	355	49	122	.402	22	28	.786	19	26	45	34	52	0	8	17	3	128	3.1	18
Malik Rose 54	54	525	61	128	.477	38	62	.613	70	94	164	32	114	3	28	41	17	160	3.0	14
George Zidek* 36	36	288	33	85	.388	25	32	.781	25	38	63	9	44	0	4	23	3	91	2.5	12
Jamie Feick* 3	3	10	2	4	.500	0	2	.000	1	2	3	0	3	0	0	1	1	5	1.7	5
Tom Chambers 12	12	83	7	31	.226	3	4	.750	3	11	14	4	14	0	1	9	0	19	1.6	8
Eric Leckner* 1	1	11	0	3	.000	0	0	. . .	0	1	1	1	3	0	0	0	0	0	0.0	0

3-pt. FG: Charlotte 591-1382 (.428)—Rice 207-440 (.470); Mason 1-3 (.333); Curry 126-296 (.426); Divac 11-47 (.234); Pierce† 30-56 (.536); Pierce‡ 42-95 (.442); Geiger 6-20 (.300); Bogues 60-144 (.417); Goldwire* 36-82 (.439); Delk 52-112 (.464); Burrell* 19-55 (.345); Smith 32-99 (.323); Royal‡ 0-2 (.000); Addison 8-20 (.400); Rose 0-2 (.000); Zidek* 0-2 (.000); Feick* 1-1 (1.000); Chambers 2-3 (.667). Opponents 487-1364 (.357).

1996-97

CHICAGO BULLS

	G	Min.	FGM	FGA	Pct.	FTM	FTA	Pct.	Off.	Def.	Tot.	Ast.	PF	Dq.	Stl.	TO	Blk.	Pts.	Avg.	Hi.
									REBOUNDS									SCORING		
Michael Jordan	82	3106	920	1892	.486	480	576	.833	113	369	482	352	156	0	140	166	44	2431	29.6	51
Scottie Pippen	82	3095	648	1366	.474	204	291	.701	160	371	531	467	213	2	154	214	45	1656	20.2	47
Toni Kukoc	57	1610	285	605	.471	134	174	.770	94	167	261	256	97	1	60	91	29	754	13.2	31
Luc Longley	59	1472	221	485	.456	95	120	.792	121	211	332	141	191	5	23	111	66	537	9.1	17
Steve Kerr	82	1861	249	467	.533	54	67	.806	29	101	130	175	98	0	67	43	3	662	8.1	20
Jason Caffey	75	1405	205	385	.532	139	211	.659	135	166	301	89	149	0	25	97	9	549	7.3	23
Brian Williams	9	138	26	63	.413	11	15	.733	14	19	33	12	20	0	3	11	5	63	7.0	10
Ron Harper	76	1740	177	406	.436	58	82	.707	46	147	193	191	138	0	86	50	38	480	6.3	22
Dennis Rodman	55	1947	128	286	.448	50	88	.568	320	563	883	170	172	1	32	111	19	311	5.7	16
Randy Brown	72	1057	140	333	.420	57	84	.679	34	77	111	133	116	0	81	58	17	341	4.7	14
Bill Wennington	61	783	118	237	.498	44	53	.830	46	83	129	41	132	1	10	31	11	280	4.6	18
Robert Parish	43	406	70	143	.490	21	31	.677	42	47	89	22	40	0	6	28	19	161	3.7	12
Dickey Simpkins	48	395	31	93	.333	28	40	.700	36	56	92	31	44	0	5	35	5	91	1.9	11
Jud Buechler	76	703	58	158	.367	5	14	.357	45	81	126	60	50	0	23	27	21	139	1.8	12
Matt Steigenga	2	12	1	4	.250	1	2	.500	0	3	3	2	1	0	1	2	1	3	1.5	2

3-pt. FG: Chicago 523-1403 (.373)—Jordan 111-297 (.374); Pippen 156-424 (.368); Kukoc 50-151 (.331); Longley 0-2 (.000); Kerr 110-237 (.464); Caffey 0-1 (.000); Harper 68-188 (.362); Rodman 5-19 (.263); Brown 4-22 (.182); Wennington 0-2 (.000); Simpkins 1-4 (.250); Buechler 18-54 (.333); Steigenga 0-2 (.000). Opponents 471-1408 (.335).

CLEVELAND CAVALIERS

	G	Min.	FGM	FGA	Pct.	FTM	FTA	Pct.	Off.	Def.	Tot.	Ast.	PF	Dq.	Stl.	TO	Blk.	Pts.	Avg.	Hi.
									REBOUNDS									SCORING		
Terrell Brandon	78	2868	575	1313	.438	268	297	.902	48	253	301	490	177	1	138	178	30	1519	19.5	33
Chris Mills	80	3167	405	894	.453	176	209	.842	118	379	497	198	222	1	86	120	41	1072	13.4	25
Tyrone Hill	74	2582	357	595	.600	241	381	.633	259	477	736	92	268	6	63	147	30	955	12.9	26
Bobby Phills	69	2375	328	766	.428	125	174	.718	63	182	245	233	174	1	113	135	21	866	12.6	27
Danny Ferry	82	2633	341	794	.429	74	87	.851	82	255	337	151	245	1	56	94	32	870	10.6	23
Bob Sura	82	2269	253	587	.431	196	319	.614	76	232	308	390	218	3	90	181	33	755	9.2	23
Vitaly Potapenko	80	1238	186	423	.440	92	125	.736	105	112	217	40	216	3	26	109	34	465	5.8	22
Mark West	70	959	100	180	.556	27	56	.482	69	117	186	19	142	0	11	52	55	227	3.2	16
Donny Marshall	56	548	52	160	.325	38	54	.704	22	48	70	24	60	0	24	32	3	175	3.1	17
Antonio Lang	64	843	68	162	.420	35	48	.729	52	75	127	33	111	0	33	50	30	171	2.7	14
Reggie Geary	39	246	22	58	.379	5	11	.455	4	11	15	36	36	0	13	15	2	57	1.5	11
Shawnelle Scott	16	50	8	16	.500	4	11	.364	8	8	16	0	6	0	0	0	3	20	1.3	5
Carl Thomas	19	77	9	24	.375	1	1	1.000	3	10	13	8	7	0	2	6	1	21	1.1	5

3-pt. FG: Cleveland 483-1284 (.376)—Brandon 101-271 (.373); Mills 86-220 (.391); Hill 0-1 (.000); Phills 85-216 (.394); Ferry 114-284 (.401); Sura 53-164 (.323); Potapenko 1-2 (.500); Marshall 33-87 (.379); Lang 0-6 (.000); Geary 8-21 (.381); Thomas 2-12 (.167). Opponents 459-1230 (.373).

DALLAS MAVERICKS

	G	Min.	FGM	FGA	Pct.	FTM	FTA	Pct.	Off.	Def.	Tot.	Ast.	PF	Dq.	Stl.	TO	Blk.	Pts.	Avg.	Hi.
									REBOUNDS									SCORING		
Chris Gatling*	44	1191	309	580	.533	221	313	.706	126	222	348	25	125	1	35	114	31	840	19.1	35
Jim Jackson*	46	1676	260	588	.442	148	188	.787	81	146	227	156	113	0	57	107	15	714	15.5	28
Michael Finley†	56	1994	334	774	.432	142	176	.807	54	198	252	156	96	0	50	120	20	897	16.0	33
Michael Finley‡	83	2790	475	1071	.444	198	245	.808	88	284	372	224	138	0	68	164	24	1249	15.0	33
Robert Pack†	20	597	79	219	.361	62	73	.849	13	47	60	127	56	0	35	67	3	229	11.5	23
Robert Pack‡	54	1782	272	693	.392	196	243	.807	28	118	146	452	139	0	94	217	6	771	14.3	33
George McCloud*	41	1207	204	482	.423	77	92	.837	29	114	143	92	106	1	52	52	8	563	13.7	28
Shawn Bradley†	33	1060	207	449	.461	68	106	.642	103	183	286	32	115	3	17	70	88	482	14.6	32
Shawn Bradley‡	73	2288	406	905	.449	149	228	.654	221	390	611	52	237	7	40	134	248	961	13.2	32
Sasha Danilovic†	13	438	73	174	.420	48	57	.842	8	26	34	25	37	0	15	22	1	216	16.6	23
Sasha Danilovic‡	56	1789	248	570	.435	121	151	.801	29	107	136	102	160	2	54	116	9	702	12.5	23
Sam Cassell*	16	398	70	165	.424	42	50	.840	14	36	50	57	48	2	17	41	6	197	12.3	21
Jamal Mashburn*	37	975	140	376	.372	72	111	.649	28	87	115	93	69	0	35	57	5	394	10.6	27
Erick Strickland	28	759	102	256	.398	65	80	.813	21	69	90	68	75	3	27	66	5	297	10.6	25
Derek Harper	75	2210	299	674	.444	95	128	.742	30	107	137	321	144	0	92	132	12	753	10.0	29
Jason Kidd*	22	791	75	203	.369	46	69	.667	30	60	90	200	42	0	45	66	8	217	9.9	25
Khalid Reeves†	13	384	43	111	.387	9	12	.750	12	19	31	56	40	0	11	26	2	102	7.8	14
Khalid Reeves‡	63	1432	184	470	.391	65	87	.747	34	85	119	226	159	3	34	108	9	516	8.2	25
A.C. Green†	56	1944	173	356	.486	97	149	.651	189	329	518	52	111	0	52	54	15	444	7.9	21
A.C. Green‡	83	2492	234	484	.483	128	197	.650	222	434	656	69	145	0	70	74	16	597	7.2	21
Samaki Walker	43	602	83	187	.444	48	74	.649	47	100	147	17	71	0	15	39	22	214	5.0	13
Oliver Miller*	42	836	76	154	.494	28	53	.528	82	151	233	58	133	1	34	70	50	180	4.3	13
Loren Meyer*	19	259	34	78	.436	9	12	.750	14	35	49	7	52	1	6	27	3	78	4.1	11
Tony Dumas*	18	227	27	77	.351	15	23	.652	3	11	14	22	36	0	10	15	1	72	4.0	15
Eric Montross*	47	984	86	187	.460	10	34	.294	66	170	236	32	150	2	9	51	34	182	3.9	12
Martin Muursepp†	32	321	49	117	.419	38	56	.679	33	29	62	17	55	1	12	15	10	139	4.3	18
Martin Muursepp‡	42	348	54	131	.412	44	70	.629	35	32	67	20	58	1	12	18	11	156	3.7	18
Ed O'Bannon†	19	175	17	72	.236	11	12	.917	9	27	36	11	19	0	5	6	2	46	2.4	7
Ed O'Bannon‡	64	809	93	279	.333	31	35	.886	50	98	148	39	97	0	29	20	12	235	3.7	12
Jamie Watson†	10	211	20	47	.426	2	4	.500	14	15	29	23	18	0	11	15	2	45	4.5	10
Jamie Watson‡	23	340	31	72	.431	12	16	.750	18	29	47	33	34	0	22	24	4	78	3.4	10

								REBOUNDS									SCORING		
	G	Min.	FGM	FGA	Pct.	FTM	FTA	Pct.	Off.	Def.	Tot.	Ast.	PF	Dq.	Stl.	TO	Blk.	Pts.	Avg.	Hi.
Jason Sasser†	2	7	1	4	.250	0	0	...	1	0	1	1	0	0	1	0	0	2	1.0	2
Jason Sasser‡	8	69	9	23	.391	0	0	...	1	7	8	2	11	0	3	2	0	19	2.4	11
Stacey King†	6	70	6	15	.400	0	4	.000	10	8	18	0	11	0	2	5	0	12	2.0	6
Stacey King‡	11	103	11	22	.500	2	7	.286	11	16	27	1	14	0	2	6	1	24	2.2	6
Greg Dreiling	40	389	34	74	.459	11	27	.407	19	57	76	11	65	1	8	9	7	80	2.0	9
Fred Roberts	12	40	6	15	.400	10	14	.714	2	8	10	0	2	0	5	1	0	22	1.8	6
Stevin Smith	8	60	6	18	.333	1	1	1.000	2	8	10	4	9	0	1	4	0	14	1.8	6

3-pt. FG: Dallas 430-1316 (.327)—Gatling* 1-6 (.167); Jackson* 46-139 (.331); Finley† 87-225 (.387); Finley‡ 101-280 (.361); Pack† 9-38 (.237); Pack‡ 31-112 (.277); McCloud* 78-205 (.380); Bradley† 0-3 (.000); Bradley‡ 0-8 (.000); Danilovic† 22-60 (.367); Danilovic‡ 85-236 (.360); Cassell* 15-49 (.306); Mashburn* 42-131 (.321); Strickland 28-92 (.304); Harper 60-176 (.341); Kidd* 21-65 (.323); Reeves† 7-35 (.200); Reeves‡ 83-227 (.366); Green† 1-17 (.059); Green‡ 1-20 (.050); Walker 0-1 (.000); Miller* 0-1 (.000); Meyer* 1-2 (.500); Dumas* 3-24 (.125); Muursepp† 3-20 (.150); Muursepp‡ 4-24 (.167); O'Bannon† 1-10 (.100); O'Bannon‡ 18-70 (.257); Watson† 3-9 (.333); Watson‡ 4-12 (.333); Sasser† 0-1 (.000); Sasser‡ 1-3 (.333); Dreiling 1-1 (1.000); Smith 1-6 (.167). Opponents 538-1444 (.373).

DENVER NUGGETS

								REBOUNDS									SCORING		
	G	Min.	FGM	FGA	Pct.	FTM	FTA	Pct.	Off.	Def.	Tot.	Ast.	PF	Dq.	Stl.	TO	Blk.	Pts.	Avg.	Hi.
LaPhonso Ellis	55	2002	445	1014	.439	218	282	.773	107	279	386	131	181	7	44	117	41	1203	21.9	39
Antonio McDyess	74	2565	536	1157	.463	274	387	.708	155	382	537	106	276	9	62	199	126	1352	18.3	35
Dale Ellis	82	2940	477	1151	.414	215	263	.817	99	194	293	165	178	0	60	146	7	1361	16.6	37
Bryant Stith	52	1788	251	603	.416	202	234	.863	74	143	217	133	119	1	60	101	20	774	14.9	37
Mark Jackson*	52	2001	192	452	.425	109	136	.801	71	200	271	641	104	0	51	172	9	541	10.4	22
Ricky Pierce*	33	600	120	260	.462	83	92	.902	17	36	53	31	49	0	14	38	5	335	10.2	25
Ervin Johnson	82	2599	243	467	.520	96	156	.615	231	682	913	71	288	5	65	118	227	582	7.1	21
Sarunas Marciulionis	17	255	38	101	.376	29	36	.806	12	18	30	25	38	0	12	40	1	116	6.8	14
Brooks Thompson†	65	1047	162	405	.400	24	38	.632	18	78	96	179	125	0	55	86	2	445	6.8	26
Brooks Thompson‡	67	1055	162	406	.399	24	38	.632	18	78	96	180	126	0	55	87	2	445	6.6	26
Anthony Goldwire†	27	612	69	176	.392	31	38	.816	9	37	46	125	46	0	14	35	1	197	7.3	20
Anthony Goldwire‡	60	1188	131	330	.397	61	78	.782	12	72	84	219	104	1	33	76	2	387	6.5	20
Kenny Smith†	33	654	87	206	.422	35	41	.854	3	34	37	102	25	0	18	62	0	260	7.9	18
Kenny Smith‡	48	765	101	239	.423	39	45	.867	4	40	44	116	30	0	19	71	0	300	6.3	18
Tom Hammonds	81	1758	191	398	.480	124	172	.721	135	266	401	64	205	0	16	88	24	506	6.2	29
Aaron Williams*	1	10	3	5	.600	0	0	...	2	3	5	0	0	0	0	4	3	6	6.0	6
Vincent Askew†	1	9	2	3	.667	2	2	1.000	0	0	0	0	0	0	0	4	0	6	6.0	6
Vincent Askew‡	43	838	81	186	.435	70	88	.795	25	73	98	90	123	5	17	46	6	239	5.6	13
Jeff Molnnio	13	117	23	49	.469	7	10	.700	2	4	6	18	16	0	2	13	1	65	5.0	10
Eric Murdock	12	114	15	33	.455	11	12	.917	1	10	11	24	9	0	9	11	4	45	3.8	7
Jerome Allen†	25	251	21	74	.284	15	25	.600	12	21	33	43	17	0	4	33	2	64	2.6	7
Jerome Allen‡	76	943	78	221	.353	42	72	.583	25	73	98	152	84	0	31	69	4	228	3.0	12
Rich King	2	22	2	6	.333	2	4	.500	2	0	2	2	2	0	3	1	0	6	3.0	5
George Zidek†	16	88	16	33	.485	20	25	.800	10	13	23	5	17	0	1	4	0	52	3.3	10
George Zidek‡	52	376	49	118	.415	45	57	.789	35	51	86	14	61	0	5	27	3	143	2.8	12
Elmer Bennett†	5	59	4	13	.308	2	4	.500	0	3	3	7	6	0	2	10	0	12	2.4	6
Elmer Bennett‡	9	75	6	19	.316	7	10	.700	0	4	4	11	7	0	4	10	0	22	2.4	6
Darvin Ham*	35	313	32	61	.525	16	33	.485	29	27	56	14	57	3	8	21	8	80	2.3	13
Melvin Booker*	5	21	2	4	.500	0	0	...	0	1	1	3	0	0	0	7	0	5	1.0	3
LaSalle Thompson*	17	105	3	16	.188	1	2	.500	5	21	26	0	26	0	3	7	6	7	0.4	2

3-pt. FG: Denver 636-1711 (.372)—L. Ellis 95-259 (.367); McDyess 6-35 (.171); D. Ellis 192-528 (.364); Stith 70-182 (.385); Jackson* 48-121 (.397); Pierce* 12-39 (.308); Johnson 0-2 (.000); Marciulionis 11-30 (.367); B. Thompson† 97-244 (.398); B. Thompson‡ 97-244 (.398); Goldwire† 28-71 (.394); Goldwire‡ 64-153 (.418); Smith† 51-120 (.425); Smith‡ 59-135 (.437); Hammonds 0-2 (.000); Askew‡ 7-24 (.292); McInnis 12-26 (.462); Murdock 4-10 (.400); Allen† 7-34 (.206); Allen‡ 30-93 (.323); Zidek‡ 0-2 (.000); Bennett† 2-6 (.333); Bennett‡ 3-9 (.333); Booker* 1-2 (.500). Opponents 484-1232 (.393).

DETROIT PISTONS

								REBOUNDS									SCORING		
	G	Min.	FGM	FGA	Pct.	FTM	FTA	Pct.	Off.	Def.	Tot.	Ast.	PF	Dq.	Stl.	TO	Blk.	Pts.	Avg.	Hi.
Grant Hill	80	3147	625	1259	.496	450	633	.711	123	598	721	583	186	0	144	259	48	1710	21.4	38
Joe Dumars	79	2923	385	875	.440	222	256	.867	38	153	191	318	97	0	57	128	1	1158	14.7	29
Lindsey Hunter	82	3023	421	1042	.404	158	203	.778	59	174	233	154	206	1	129	96	24	1166	14.2	30
Otis Thorpe	82	2661	419	787	.532	198	303	.653	226	396	622	133	298	7	59	145	17	1036	13.1	27
Terry Mills	79	1997	312	702	.444	58	70	.829	68	309	377	99	161	1	35	85	27	857	10.8	29
Theo Ratliff	76	1292	179	337	.531	81	116	.698	109	147	256	13	181	2	29	56	111	439	5.8	25
Aaron McKie†	42	850	97	209	.464	51	61	.836	27	101	128	77	69	0	43	42	7	263	6.3	18
Aaron McKie‡	83	1625	150	365	.411	92	110	.836	40	181	221	161	130	1	77	90	22	433	5.2	18
Grant Long	65	1166	123	275	.447	63	84	.750	88	134	222	39	106	0	43	48	6	326	5.0	15
Stacey Augmon*	20	292	31	77	.403	28	41	.683	14	35	49	15	29	0	10	27	10	90	4.5	12
Michael Curry	81	1217	99	221	.448	97	108	.898	23	96	119	43	128	0	31	28	12	318	3.9	17
Don Reid	47	462	54	112	.482	24	32	.750	36	65	101	14	105	1	16	23	15	132	2.8	14
Kenny Smith*	9	64	8	20	.400	2	2	1.000	0	5	5	10	2	0	1	3	0	23	2.6	7
Rick Mahorn	22	218	20	54	.370	16	22	.727	19	34	53	6	34	0	4	10	3	56	2.5	13
Litterial Green	45	311	30	64	.469	30	47	.638	6	16	22	41	27	0	16	15	1	90	2.0	8
Randolph Childress†	3	30	4	10	.400	0	0	...	0	1	1	2	5	0	2	5	0	10	2.5	8
Randolph Childress‡	23	155	14	40	.350	6	8	.750	1	5	6	17	16	0	9	18	0	39	1.7	8
Jerome Williams	33	177	20	51	.392	9	17	.529	22	28	50	7	18	0	13	13	1	49	1.5	9

3-pt. FG: Detroit 582-1499 (.388)—Hill 10-33 (.303); Dumars 166-384 (.432); Hunter 166-468 (.355); Thorpe 0-2 (.000); Mills 175-415 (.422); McKie† 18-48 (.375); McKie‡ 41-103 (.398); Long 17-47 (.362); Curry 23-77 (.299); Reid 0-1 (.000); Smith* 5-10 (.500); Mahorn 0-1 (.000); Green 0-10 (.000); Childress† 2-3 (.667); Childress‡ 5-19 (.263). Opponents 528-1430 (.369).

GOLDEN STATE WARRIORS

	G	Min.	FGM	FGA	Pct.	FTM	FTA	Pct.	Off.	Def.	Tot.	Ast.	PF	Dq.	Stl.	TO	Blk.	Pts.	Avg.	Hi.
									REBOUNDS									SCORING		
Latrell Sprewell	80	3353	649	1444	.449	493	585	.843	58	308	366	507	153	0	132	322	45	1938	24.2	46
Joe Smith	80	3086	587	1293	.454	307	377	.814	261	418	679	125	244	3	74	192	86	1493	18.7	38
Chris Mullin	79	2733	438	792	.553	184	213	.864	75	242	317	322	155	0	130	192	33	1143	14.5	28
Mark Price	70	1876	263	589	.447	155	171	.906	36	143	179	342	100	0	67	161	3	793	11.3	32
B.J. Armstrong	49	1020	148	327	.453	68	79	.861	7	67	74	126	56	0	25	53	2	389	7.9	24
Donyell Marshall	61	1022	174	421	.413	61	98	.622	92	184	276	54	96	0	25	55	46	444	7.3	30
Bimbo Coles	51	1183	122	314	.389	37	49	.755	39	79	118	149	96	0	35	59	7	311	6.1	14
Melvin Booker†	16	409	44	101	.436	18	20	.900	7	21	28	50	28	0	3	20	2	117	7.3	16
Melvin Booker‡	21	430	46	105	.438	18	20	.900	7	22	29	53	28	0	3	27	2	122	5.8	16
Andrew DeClercq	71	1065	142	273	.520	91	151	.603	122	176	298	32	229	3	33	76	27	375	5.3	17
Scott Burrell†	29	457	53	140	.379	15	23	.652	25	54	79	35	60	0	14	28	8	143	4.9	21
Scott Burrell‡	57	939	98	271	.362	57	76	.750	49	109	158	74	120	0	28	53	19	294	5.2	21
Felton Spencer†	72	1539	137	282	.486	94	161	.584	152	258	410	21	273	7	34	87	50	368	5.1	14
Felton Spencer‡	73	1558	139	284	.489	94	161	.584	157	259	416	22	275	7	34	88	50	372	5.1	14
Todd Fuller	75	949	114	266	.429	76	110	.691	108	141	249	24	146	0	10	52	20	304	4.1	18
Donald Royal*	36	509	37	96	.385	62	78	.795	33	62	95	14	55	0	11	22	9	136	3.8	9
Ray Owes	57	592	75	180	.417	26	46	.565	64	99	163	15	86	1	15	23	20	177	3.1	18
Lou Roe	17	107	14	48	.292	9	19	.474	7	7	14	6	10	0	3	11	1	40	2.4	6
Clifford Rozier*	1	5	0	1	.000	0	0	...	0	0	0	0	0	0	0	0	0	0	0.0	0

3-pt. FG: Golden State 481-1363 (.353)—Sprewell 147-415 (.354); Smith 12-46 (.261); Mullin 83-202 (.411); Price 112-283 (.396); Armstrong 25-90 (.278); Marshall 35-111 (.315); Coles 30-102 (.294); Booker† 11-35 (.314); Booker‡ 12-37 (.324); Burrell† 22-61 (.361); Burrell‡ 41-116 (.353); Royal* 0-2 (.000); Owes 1-5 (.200); Roe 3-11 (.273). Opponents 581-1558 (.373).

HOUSTON ROCKETS

	G	Min.	FGM	FGA	Pct.	FTM	FTA	Pct.	Off.	Def.	Tot.	Ast.	PF	Dq.	Stl.	TO	Blk.	Pts.	Avg.	Hi.
									REBOUNDS									SCORING		
Hakeem Olajuwon	78	2852	727	1426	.510	351	446	.787	173	543	716	236	249	3	117	281	173	1810	23.2	48
Charles Barkley	53	2009	335	692	.484	288	415	.694	212	504	716	248	153	2	69	151	25	1016	19.2	35
Clyde Drexler	62	2271	397	899	.442	201	268	.750	118	255	373	354	151	0	119	156	36	1114	18.0	39
Mario Elie	78	2687	291	585	.497	207	231	.896	60	175	235	310	200	2	92	135	12	909	11.7	26
Kevin Willis	75	1964	350	728	.481	140	202	.693	146	415	561	71	216	1	42	119	32	842	11.2	31
Matt Maloney	82	2386	271	615	.441	71	93	.763	19	141	160	303	125	0	82	122	1	767	9.4	24
Eddie Johnson†	24	607	101	226	.447	35	41	.854	24	74	98	35	48	0	10	30	1	277	11.5	27
Eddie Johnson‡	52	913	160	362	.442	55	68	.809	27	111	138	52	81	0	15	47	2	424	8.2	27
Sam Mack	52	904	105	262	.401	35	42	.833	20	86	106	58	67	0	29	42	6	292	5.6	20
Brent Price	25	390	44	105	.419	21	21	1.000	10	19	29	65	34	0	17	32	0	126	5.0	20
Emanual Davis	13	230	24	54	.444	5	8	.625	2	20	22	26	20	0	9	17	2	65	5.0	19
Othella Harrington	57	860	112	204	.549	49	81	.605	75	123	198	18	112	2	12	57	22	273	4.8	13
Matt Bullard	71	1025	114	284	.401	25	34	.735	13	104	117	67	68	0	21	38	18	320	4.5	24
Randy Livingston	64	981	100	229	.437	42	65	.646	32	62	94	155	107	0	39	102	12	251	3.9	12
Tracy Moore	27	237	33	85	.388	22	31	.710	11	15	26	20	19	0	5	14	0	99	3.7	12
Sedale Threatt	21	334	28	74	.378	6	8	.750	5	19	24	40	29	0	15	13	3	70	3.3	15
Elmer Bennett*	4	16	2	6	.333	5	6	.833	0	1	1	4	1	0	2	0	0	10	2.5	4
Joe Stephens	2	9	1	5	.200	0	0	...	2	1	3	0	3	0	3	3	0	3	1.5	3
Charles Jones	12	93	2	5	.400	0	0	...	5	8	13	3	8	0	2	0	4	4	0.3	2

3-pt. FG: Houston 671-1839 (.365)—Olajuwon 5-16 (.313); Barkley 58-205 (.283); Drexler 119-335 (.355); Elie 120-286 (.420); Willis 2-14 (.143); Maloney 154-381 (.404); Johnson† 40-103 (.388); Johnson‡ 49-131 (.374); Mack 47-142 (.331); Price 17-53 (.321); Davis 12-27 (.444); Harrington 0-3 (.000); Bullard 67-183 (.366); Livingston 9-22 (.409); Moore 11-43 (.256); Threatt 8-20 (.400); Bennett* 1-3 (.333); Stephens 1-3 (.333). Opponents 519-1547 (.335).

INDIANA PACERS

	G	Min.	FGM	FGA	Pct.	FTM	FTA	Pct.	Off.	Def.	Tot.	Ast.	PF	Dq.	Stl.	TO	Blk.	Pts.	Avg.	Hi.
									REBOUNDS									SCORING		
Reggie Miller	81	2966	552	1244	.444	418	475	.880	53	233	286	273	172	1	75	166	25	1751	21.6	40
Rik Smits	52	1518	356	733	.486	173	217	.797	105	256	361	67	175	3	22	126	59	887	17.1	40
Antonio Davis	82	2335	308	641	.481	241	362	.666	190	408	598	65	260	4	42	141	84	858	10.5	30
Dale Davis	80	2589	370	688	.538	92	215	.428	301	471	772	59	233	3	60	108	77	832	10.4	23
Travis Best	76	2064	274	620	.442	149	197	.756	36	130	166	318	221	3	98	153	5	754	9.9	27
Mark Jackson†	30	1053	97	227	.427	59	77	.766	20	104	124	294	57	0	46	102	3	271	9.0	18
Mark Jackson‡	82	3054	289	679	.426	168	213	.789	91	304	395	935	161	0	97	274	12	812	9.9	22
Derrick McKey	50	1449	148	379	.391	89	123	.724	80	161	241	135	141	1	47	83	30	400	8.0	17
Jalen Rose	66	1188	172	377	.456	117	156	.750	27	94	121	155	136	1	57	107	18	482	7.3	21
Duane Ferrell	62	1115	159	337	.472	58	94	.617	57	84	141	66	120	0	38	55	6	394	6.4	17
Vincent Askew*	41	822	79	183	.432	68	86	.791	25	73	98	90	122	5	17	42	6	233	5.7	13
Haywoode Workman	4	81	11	20	.550	0	1	.000	4	3	7	11	10	0	3	5	0	22	5.5	8
Eddie Johnson*	28	306	59	136	.434	20	27	.741	3	37	40	17	33	0	5	17	1	147	5.3	14
Erick Dampier	72	1052	131	336	.390	107	168	.637	96	198	294	43	153	1	19	84	73	370	5.1	15
Fred Hoiberg	47	572	67	156	.429	61	77	.792	13	68	81	41	51	0	27	22	6	224	4.8	21
Jerome Allen*	51	692	57	147	.388	27	47	.574	13	52	65	109	67	0	27	56	0	164	3.2	12
Reggie Williams*	2	33	2	9	.222	1	2	.500	1	6	7	2	5	0	0	2	0	5	2.5	5
Darvin Ham‡	36	318	33	62	.532	17	35	.486	29	27	56	14	57	3	9	22	8	83	2.3	13
Darvin Ham†	1	5	1	1	1.000	1	2	.500	0	0	0	0	0	0	1	0	0	3	3.0	3
Brent Scott	16	55	8	17	.471	3	6	.500	3	6	9	3	14	0	1	4	1	19	1.2	6
LaSalle Thompson†	9	35	0	3	.000	3	4	.750	2	6	8	2	7	0	0	2	0	3	0.3	2
LaSalle Thompson‡	26	140	3	19	.158	4	6	.667	7	27	34	2	33	0	3	9	6	10	0.4	2

3-pt. FG: Indiana 430-1130 (.381)—Miller 229-536 (.427); Smits 2-8 (.250); A. Davis 1-14 (.071); Best 57-155 (.368); Jackson† 18-57 (.316); Jackson‡ 66-178 (.371); McKey 15-58 (.259); Rose 21-72 (.292); Ferrell 18-44 (.409); Askew* 7-24 (.292); Workman 0-3 (.000); Johnson* 9-28 (.321); Dampier 1-1 (1.000); Hoiberg 29-70 (.414); Allen* 23-59 (.390); Williams* 0-1 (.000). Opponents 499-1440 (.347).

LOS ANGELES CLIPPERS

	G	Min.	FGM	FGA	Pct.	FTM	FTA	Pct.	Off.	Def.	Tot.	Ast.	PF	Dq.	Stl.	TO	Blk.	Pts.	Avg.	Hi.
									REBOUNDS									SCORING		
Loy Vaught	82	2838	542	1084	.500	134	191	.702	222	595	817	110	241	3	85	137	25	1220	14.9	31
Malik Sealy	80	2456	373	942	.396	254	290	.876	59	179	238	165	185	4	124	154	45	1079	13.5	30
Rodney Rogers	81	2480	408	884	.462	191	288	.663	137	274	411	222	272	5	88	221	61	1072	13.2	34
Darrick Martin	82	1820	292	718	.407	218	250	.872	26	87	113	339	165	1	57	127	2	893	10.9	38
Stanley Roberts	18	378	63	148	.426	45	64	.703	24	67	91	9	57	2	8	23	23	171	9.5	21
Charles Outlaw	82	2195	254	417	.609	117	232	.504	174	280	454	157	227	5	94	107	142	625	7.6	19
Brent Barry	59	1094	155	379	.409	76	93	.817	30	80	110	154	88	1	51	76	15	442	7.5	18
Lamond Murray	74	1295	181	435	.416	156	211	.739	85	148	233	57	113	3	53	86	29	549	7.4	24
Lorenzen Wright	77	1936	236	491	.481	88	150	.587	206	265	471	49	211	2	48	79	60	561	7.3	24
Terry Dehere	73	1053	148	383	.386	122	148	.824	15	80	95	158	142	0	27	96	3	470	6.4	25
Eric Piatkowski	65	747	134	298	.450	69	84	.821	49	56	105	52	85	0	33	46	10	388	6.0	16
Pooh Richardson	59	1065	131	344	.381	26	43	.605	25	73	98	169	82	0	54	62	5	330	5.6	20
Kevin Duckworth	26	384	45	103	.437	11	16	.688	23	37	60	16	63	1	9	33	11	104	4.0	12
Rich Manning†	10	73	14	34	.412	3	6	.500	8	8	16	1	11	0	1	2	1	31	3.1	8
Rich Manning‡	26	201	32	82	.390	9	14	.643	16	23	39	3	29	0	4	7	2	75	2.9	10
Dwayne Schintzius	15	116	13	36	.361	7	8	.875	9	13	22	4	22	0	1	7	9	34	2.3	15

3-pt. FG: L.A. Clippers 474-1339 (.354)—Vaught 2-12 (.167); Sealy 79-222 (.356); Rogers 65-180 (.361); Martin 91-234 (.389); Outlaw 0-8 (.000); Barry 56-173 (.324); Murray 31-91 (.341); Wright 1-4 (.250); Dehere 52-160 (.325); Piatkowski 51-120 (.425); Richardson 42-128 (.328); Duckworth 3-4 (.750); Manning† 0-1 (.000); Manning‡ 2-4 (.500); Schintzius 1-2 (.500). Opponents 480-1345 (.357).

LOS ANGELES LAKERS

	G	Min.	FGM	FGA	Pct.	FTM	FTA	Pct.	Off.	Def.	Tot.	Ast.	PF	Dq.	Stl.	TO	Blk.	Pts.	Avg.	Hi.
									REBOUNDS									SCORING		
Shaquille O'Neal	51	1941	552	991	.557	232	479	.484	195	445	640	159	180	2	46	146	147	1336	26.2	42
Eddie Jones	80	2998	473	1081	.438	276	337	.819	90	236	326	270	226	3	189	169	49	1374	17.2	34
Nick Van Exel	79	2937	432	1075	.402	165	200	.825	44	182	226	672	110	0	75	212	10	1206	15.3	37
Elden Campbell	77	2516	442	942	.469	263	370	.711	207	400	615	126	276	6	46	130	117	1148	14.9	40
Cedric Ceballos*	8	279	34	83	.410	13	15	.867	11	42	53	15	19	0	5	17	6	86	10.8	22
George McCloud†	23	286	34	96	.354	6	9	.667	7	29	36	17	20	0	9	9	0	95	4.1	16
George McCloud‡	64	1493	238	578	.412	83	101	.822	36	143	179	109	126	1	61	61	8	658	10.3	28
Robert Horry†	22	676	75	165	.455	28	40	.700	28	90	118	56	72	1	38	26	29	203	9.2	15
Robert Horry‡	54	1395	157	360	.436	60	90	.667	68	169	237	110	153	2	66	72	55	423	7.0	19
Kobe Bryant	71	1103	176	422	.417	136	166	.819	47	85	132	91	102	0	49	112	23	539	7.6	24
Jerome Kersey	70	1766	194	449	.432	71	118	.602	112	251	363	89	219	0	119	74	49	476	6.8	16
Byron Scott	79	1440	163	379	.430	127	151	.841	21	97	118	99	72	0	46	53	16	526	6.7	19
Travis Knight	71	1156	140	275	.509	62	100	.620	130	189	319	39	170	2	31	49	58	342	4.8	19
Corie Blount	58	1009	92	179	.514	56	83	.675	113	163	276	35	121	2	22	50	26	241	4.2	17
Derek Fisher	80	921	104	262	.397	79	120	.658	25	72	97	119	87	0	41	71	5	309	3.9	21
Sean Rooks	69	735	87	185	.470	91	130	.700	56	107	163	42	123	1	17	51	38	265	3.8	20
Rumeal Robinson*	15	126	17	48	.354	5	8	.625	2	8	10	13	12	0	5	11	2	45	3.0	10
Larry Krystkowiak	3	11	1	2	.500	1	2	.500	2	3	5	3	3	0	2	1	0	3	1.0	3
Joe Kleine*	8	30	2	8	.250	2	2	1.000	2	7	9	0	6	0	0	0	0	6	0.8	2

3-pt. FG: L.A. Lakers 551-1500 (.367)—O'Neal 0-4 (.000); Jones 152-389 (.391); Van Exel 177-468 (.378); Campbell 1-4 (.250); Ceballos* 5-21 (.238); McCloud† 21-49 (.429); McCloud‡ 99-254 (.390); Horry† 25-76 (.329); Horry‡ 49-154 (.318); Bryant 51-136 (.375); Kersey 17-65 (.262); Scott 73-188 (.388); Blount 1-3 (.333); Fisher 22-73 (.301); Rooks 0-1 (.000); Robinson* 6-23 (.261). Opponents 479-1379 (.347).

MIAMI HEAT

	G	Min.	FGM	FGA	Pct.	FTM	FTA	Pct.	Off.	Def.	Tot.	Ast.	PF	Dq.	Stl.	TO	Blk.	Pts.	Avg.	Hi.
									REBOUNDS									SCORING		
Tim Hardaway	81	3136	575	1384	.415	291	364	.799	49	228	277	695	165	2	151	230	9	1644	20.3	45
Alonzo Mourning	66	2320	473	885	.534	363	565	.642	189	467	656	104	272	9	56	226	189	1310	19.8	35
Voshon Lenard	73	2111	314	684	.459	86	105	.819	38	179	217	161	168	1	50	109	18	897	12.3	38
Jamal Mashburn†	32	1189	146	367	.398	88	117	.752	41	138	179	111	117	4	43	57	7	428	13.4	29
Jamal Mashburn‡	69	2164	286	743	.385	160	228	.702	69	225	294	204	186	4	78	114	12	822	11.9	29
Sasha Danilovic*	43	1351	175	396	.442	73	94	.777	21	81	102	77	123	2	39	94	8	486	11.3	21
Dan Majerle	36	1264	141	347	.406	40	59	.678	45	117	162	116	75	0	54	50	14	390	10.8	26
Isaac Austin	82	1881	321	639	.502	150	226	.664	136	342	478	101	244	4	45	161	43	792	9.7	26
P.J. Brown	80	2592	300	656	.457	161	220	.732	239	431	670	92	283	7	85	113	98	761	9.5	21
Kurt Thomas	18	374	39	105	.371	35	46	.761	31	76	107	9	67	3	12	25	9	113	6.3	18
Keith Askins	78	1773	138	319	.433	39	58	.672	86	185	271	75	196	4	53	59	19	384	4.9	15
John Crotty	48	659	79	154	.513	54	64	.844	15	32	47	102	79	0	18	42	0	232	4.8	18
Gary Grant	28	365	39	110	.355	18	22	.818	8	30	38	45	39	0	16	27	0	110	3.9	12
Willie Anderson	28	303	29	64	.453	17	20	.850	15	27	42	34	36	0	14	19	4	83	3.0	11
Ed Pinckney	27	273	23	43	.535	20	25	.800	25	40	65	6	30	0	8	19	9	66	2.4	11
Mark Strickland	31	153	25	60	.417	12	21	.571	16	21	37	1	17	0	4	15	10	62	2.0	11
Martin Muursepp*	10	27	5	14	.357	6	14	.429	2	3	5	3	3	0	0	3	1	17	1.7	4
Matt Fish†	1	1	0	0	...	0	0	...	0	0	0	0	0	0	0	0	0	0	0.0	0
Matt Fish‡	6	8	1	3	.333	0	0	...	1	4	5	0	2	0	0	2	0	2	0.3	2
James Scott	8	32	0	8	.000	1	2	.500	1	5	6	3	5	0	2	2	0	1	0.1	1
Bruce Bowen	1	1	0	0	...	0	0	...	0	0	0	0	0	0	0	0	1	0	0.0	0

3-pt. FG: Miami 678-1865 (.364)—Hardaway 203-590 (.344); Mourning 1-9 (.111); Lenard 183-442 (.414); Mashburn† 48-146 (.329); Mashburn‡ 90-277 (.325); Danilovic* 63-176 (.358); Majerle 68-201 (.338); Austin 0-3 (.000); Brown 0-2 (.000); Thomas 0-1 (.000); Askins 69-172 (.401); Crotty 20-49 (.408); Grant 14-46 (.304); Anderson 8-19 (.421); Strickland 0-1 (.000); Muursepp* 1-4 (.250); Scott 0-4 (.000). Opponents 411-1134 (.362).

MILWAUKEE BUCKS

	G	Min.	FGM	FGA	Pct.	FTM	FTA	Pct.	Off.	Def.	Tot.	Ast.	PF	Dq.	Stl.	TO	Blk.	Pts.	Avg.	Hi.
									REBOUNDS									SCORING		
Glenn Robinson	80	3114	669	1438	.465	288	364	.791	130	372	502	248	225	5	103	269	68	1689	21.1	44
Vin Baker	78	3159	632	1251	.505	358	521	.687	267	537	804	211	275	8	81	245	112	1637	21.0	36
Ray Allen	82	2532	390	908	.430	205	249	.823	97	229	326	210	218	0	75	149	10	1102	13.4	32
Sherman Douglas	79	2316	306	610	.502	114	171	.667	57	136	193	427	191	0	78	153	10	764	9.7	26
Johnny Newman	82	2060	246	547	.450	189	247	.765	66	120	186	116	257	4	73	115	17	715	8.7	27
Armon Gilliam	80	2050	246	522	.471	199	259	.768	136	361	497	53	206	0	61	105	40	691	8.6	27
Elliot Perry	82	1595	217	458	.474	79	106	.745	24	100	124	247	117	0	98	111	3	562	6.9	19
Andrew Lang	52	1194	115	248	.464	44	61	.721	94	184	278	25	140	4	26	39	47	274	5.3	19
Acie Earl†	9	43	8	23	.348	10	14	.714	2	9	11	2	7	0	3	2	1	26	2.9	5
Acie Earl‡	47	500	67	180	.372	54	84	.643	35	61	96	20	61	0	15	35	28	188	4.0	23
Chucky Brown†	60	674	65	128	.508	39	59	.661	38	94	132	24	86	1	9	15	20	170	2.8	13
Chucky Brown‡	70	757	78	154	.506	47	70	.671	41	107	148	28	100	1	9	19	22	204	2.9	13
Joe Wolf	56	525	40	89	.449	14	19	.737	32	80	112	20	105	0	14	14	11	95	1.7	6
Shawn Respert*	14	83	6	19	.316	7	7	1.000	3	4	7	8	5	0	0	8	0	20	1.4	7
Keith Tower	5	72	3	8	.375	1	8	.125	2	7	9	1	12	0	2	2	1	7	1.4	3
Jimmy Carruth	4	21	2	3	.667	1	1	1.000	0	4	4	0	4	0	1	2	5	5	1.3	3
David Wood	46	240	20	38	.526	12	18	.667	5	22	27	13	36	0	7	6	6	57	1.2	8
Darrin Hancock*	9	39	2	6	.333	0	0	...	1	4	5	4	7	0	2	4	0	4	0.4	2
Cuonzo Martin	3	13	0	7	.000	0	0	...	1	0	1	1	0	0	1	0	0	0	0.0	0

3-pt. FG: Milwaukee 324-920 (.352)—Robinson 63-180 (.350); Baker 15-54 (.278); Allen 117-298 (.393); Douglas 38-114 (.333); Newman 34-98 (.347); Perry 49-137 (.358); Earl‡ 0-5 (.000); Brown† 1-6 (.167); Brown‡ 1-6 (.167); Wolf 1-7 (.143); Respert* 1-9 (.111); Wood 5-15 (.333); Martin 0-2 (.000). Opponents 369-1080 (.342).

MINNESOTA TIMBERWOLVES

	G	Min.	FGM	FGA	Pct.	FTM	FTA	Pct.	Off.	Def.	Tot.	Ast.	PF	Dq.	Stl.	TO	Blk.	Pts.	Avg.	Hi.
									REBOUNDS									SCORING		
Tom Gugliotta	81	3131	592	1339	.442	464	566	.820	187	515	702	335	237	3	130	293	89	1672	20.6	35
Kevin Garnett	77	2995	549	1100	.499	205	272	.754	190	428	618	236	199	2	105	175	163	1309	17.0	33
Stephon Marbury	67	2324	355	871	.408	245	337	.727	54	130	184	522	159	2	67	210	19	1057	15.8	33
Sam Mitchell	82	2044	269	603	.446	224	295	.759	112	214	326	79	232	1	51	93	20	766	9.3	28
James Robinson	69	1309	196	482	.407	78	114	.684	24	88	112	126	125	1	30	69	8	572	8.3	28
Dean Garrett	68	1665	223	389	.573	96	138	.696	149	346	495	38	158	1	40	34	95	542	8.0	25
Doug West	68	1920	226	484	.467	64	94	.681	37	111	148	113	218	3	61	66	24	531	7.8	19
Terry Porter	82	1568	187	449	.416	127	166	.765	31	145	176	295	104	0	54	128	11	568	6.9	20
Chris Carr	55	830	125	271	.461	56	73	.767	31	82	113	48	93	0	24	37	10	337	6.1	22
Stojko Vrankovic	53	766	78	139	.561	25	37	.676	57	111	168	14	121	1	10	52	67	181	3.4	11
Cherokee Parks	76	961	103	202	.510	46	76	.605	83	112	195	34	150	2	41	32	48	252	3.3	14
Reggie Jordan†	10	31	8	10	.800	4	7	.571	0	4	4	1	2	0	2	2	0	20	2.0	7
Reggie Jordan‡	19	130	16	26	.615	8	17	.471	11	16	27	12	15	0	7	8	3	40	2.1	8
Shane Heal	43	236	26	97	.268	3	5	.600	2	16	18	33	20	0	3	17	3	75	1.7	15

3-pt. FG: Minnesota 371-1093 (.339)—Gugliotta 24-93 (.258); Garnett 6-21 (.286); Marbury 102-288 (.354); Mitchell 4-25 (.160); Robinson 102-267 (.382); West 15-45 (.333); Porter 67-200 (.335); Carr 31-88 (.352); Parks 0-1 (.000); Heal 20-65 (.308). Opponents 467-1290 (.362).

NEW JERSEY NETS

	G	Min.	FGM	FGA	Pct.	FTM	FTA	Pct.	Off.	Def.	Tot.	Ast.	PF	Dq.	Stl.	TO	Blk.	Pts.	Avg.	Hi.
									REBOUNDS									SCORING		
Kendall Gill	82	3199	644	1453	.443	427	536	.797	183	316	499	326	225	2	154	218	46	1789	21.8	41
Chris Gatling†	3	92	18	43	.419	15	16	.938	8	14	22	3	13	0	4	6	0	51	17.0	21
Chris Gatling‡	47	1283	327	623	.525	236	329	.717	134	236	370	28	138	1	39	120	31	891	19.0	35
Kerry Kittles	82	3012	507	1189	.426	175	227	.771	106	213	319	249	165	1	157	127	35	1347	16.4	40
Robert Pack*	34	1185	193	474	.407	134	170	.788	15	71	86	325	83	0	59	150	3	542	15.9	33
Jim Jackson†	31	1155	184	441	.417	104	122	.852	51	133	184	160	81	0	29	101	17	512	16.5	33
Jim Jackson‡	77	2831	444	1029	.431	252	310	.813	132	279	411	316	194	0	86	208	32	1226	15.9	33
Sam Cassell†	23	777	167	377	.443	64	77	.831	21	61	82	149	86	3	37	67	7	445	19.3	30
Sam Cassell‡	61	1714	337	783	.430	212	251	.845	47	135	182	305	200	9	77	168	19	967	15.9	30
Jayson Williams	41	1432	221	540	.409	108	183	.590	242	311	553	51	158	5	24	82	36	550	13.4	28
Shawn Bradley*	40	1228	199	456	.436	81	122	.664	118	207	325	20	122	4	23	64	160	479	12.0	22
Khalid Reeves*	50	1048	141	359	.393	56	75	.747	22	66	88	170	119	3	23	82	7	414	8.3	25
Tony Massenburg	79	1954	219	452	.485	130	206	.631	222	295	517	23	217	2	38	91	50	568	7.2	26
Kevin Edwards	32	477	69	183	.377	37	43	.860	9	34	43	57	34	0	17	49	4	190	5.9	21
Reggie Williams†	11	167	27	67	.403	8	10	.800	4	20	24	8	28	0	8	10	4	71	6.5	14
Reggie Williams‡	13	200	29	76	.382	9	12	.750	5	26	31	10	33	0	8	12	4	76	5.8	14
Xavier McDaniel	62	1170	138	355	.389	65	89	.730	124	194	318	65	144	0	36	70	17	346	5.6	15
Lloyd Daniels†	17	282	34	103	.330	5	6	.833	18	21	39	25	29	0	9	11	3	92	5.4	11
Lloyd Daniels‡	22	310	36	119	.303	5	6	.833	19	24	43	26	33	0	10	14	3	98	4.5	11
Eric Montross†	31	844	73	162	.451	11	28	.393	115	167	282	29	118	3	11	26	39	157	5.1	14
Eric Montross‡	78	1828	159	349	.456	21	62	.339	181	337	518	61	268	5	20	77	73	339	4.3	14
Ed O'Bannon*	45	634	76	207	.367	20	23	.870	41	71	112	28	78	0	24	14	10	189	4.2	12
Joe Kleine†	28	453	35	82	.427	13	18	.722	39	75	114	23	57	0	8	21	12	84	3.0	8
Joe Kleine‡	59	848	69	170	.406	28	38	.737	62	141	203	35	110	0	17	41	18	168	2.8	11
Evric Gray	5	42	4	15	.267	4	4	1.000	1	2	3	2	5	0	1	3	0	13	2.6	7

								REBOUNDS									SCORING		
	G	Min.	FGM	FGA	Pct.	FTM	FTA	Pct.	Off.	Def.	Tot.	Ast.	PF	Dq.	Stl.	TO	Blk.	Pts.	Avg.	Hi.
Jack Haley 20	74	13	37	.351	14	19	.737	13	19	32	5	14	0	1	2	1	40	2.0	10
Adrian Caldwell*..... 18	204	10	35	.286	9	17	.529	20	36	56	5	27	0	8	12	1	29	1.6	7
Robert Werdann 6	31	3	7	.429	3	3	1.000	3	3	6	0	10	0	2	2	1	9	1.5	5
Yinka Dare 41	313	19	54	.352	19	37	.514	35	47	82	3	51	0	4	21	28	57	1.4	7
Vincent Askew* 1	7	0	0	...	0	0	...	0	0	0	0	1	0	0	0	0	0	0.0	0

3-pt. FG: New Jersey 484-1371 (.353)—Gill 74-220 (.336); Gatling‡ 1-6 (.167); Kittles 158-419 (.377); Pack* 22-74 (.297); Jackson† 40-108 (.370); Jackson‡ 86-247 (.348); Cassell† 47-120 (.392); Cassell‡ 81-231 (.351); J. Williams 0-4 (.000); Bradley* 0-5 (.000); Reeves* 76-192 (.396); Massenburg 0-1 (.000); Edwards 15-43 (.349); R. Williams† 9-33 (.273); R. Williams‡ 9-34 (.265); McDaniel 5-25 (.200); Daniels† 19-59 (.322); Daniels‡ 21-70 (.300); O'Bannon* 17-60 (.283); Kleine† 1-2 (.500); Kleine‡ 2-3 (.667); Gray 1-4 (.250); Caldwell* 0-2 (.000). Opponents 520-1398 (.372).

NEW YORK KNICKERBOCKERS

								REBOUNDS									SCORING		
	G	Min.	FGM	FGA	Pct.	FTM	FTA	Pct.	Off.	Def.	Tot.	Ast.	PF	Dq.	Stl.	TO	Blk.	Pts.	Avg.	Hi.
Patrick Ewing 78	2887	655	1342	.488	439	582	.754	175	659	834	156	250	2	69	269	189	1751	22.4	39
Allan Houston....... 81	2681	437	1032	.423	175	218	.803	43	197	240	179	233	6	41	167	18	1197	14.8	32
John Starks 77	2042	369	856	.431	173	225	.769	36	169	205	217	196	2	90	158	11	1061	13.8	31
Larry Johnson 76	2613	376	735	.512	190	274	.693	165	228	393	174	249	3	64	136	36	976	12.8	28
Charles Oakley 80	2873	339	694	.488	181	224	.808	246	535	781	221	305	4	111	171	21	864	10.8	21
Chris Childs 65	2076	211	510	.414	113	149	.758	22	169	191	398	213	6	78	180	11	605	9.3	24
Buck Williams 74	1496	175	326	.537	115	179	.642	166	231	397	53	204	2	40	79	38	465	6.3	17
Charlie Ward 79	1763	133	337	.395	95	125	.760	45	175	220	326	188	2	83	147	15	409	5.2	14
John Wallace 68	787	122	236	.517	79	110	.718	51	104	155	37	102	0	21	76	25	325	4.8	19
Chris Jent 3	10	2	6	.333	0	0	...	1	0	1	1	2	0	0	0	0	6	2.0	3
Herb Williams...... 21	184	18	46	.391	3	4	.750	9	22	31	5	18	0	4	5	5	39	1.9	10
Walter McCarty..... 35	192	26	68	.382	8	14	.571	8	15	23	13	38	0	7	17	9	64	1.8	8
Scott Brooks 38	251	19	39	.487	14	15	.933	6	12	18	29	35	1	21	17	0	57	1.5	7

3-pt. FG: New York 470-1294 (.363)—Ewing 2-9 (.222); Houston 148-384 (.385); Starks 150-407 (.369); Johnson 34-105 (.324); Oakley 5-19 (.263); Childs 70-181 (.387); B. Williams 0-1 (.000); Ward 48-154 (.312); Wallace 2-4 (.500); Jent 2-3 (.667); H. Williams 0-1 (.000); McCarty 4-14 (.286); Brooks 5-12 (.417). Opponents 481-1374 (.350).

ORLANDO MAGIC

								REBOUNDS									SCORING		
	G	Min.	FGM	FGA	Pct.	FTM	FTA	Pct.	Off.	Def.	Tot.	Ast.	PF	Dq.	Stl.	TO	Blk.	Pts.	Avg.	Hi.
Anfernee Hardaway... 59	2221	421	941	.447	283	345	.820	82	181	263	332	123	1	93	145	35	1210	20.5	35
Rony Seikaly 74	2615	460	907	.507	357	500	.714	274	427	701	92	275	4	49	218	107	1277	17.3	33
Horace Grant 67	2496	358	695	.515	128	179	.715	206	394	600	163	157	1	101	99	65	845	12.6	26
Dennis Scott....... 66	2166	298	749	.398	80	101	.792	40	163	203	139	138	2	74	81	19	823	12.5	27
Nick Anderson 63	2163	288	725	.397	38	94	.404	66	238	304	182	160	1	120	86	32	757	12.0	28
Donald Royal* 1	29	4	10	.400	4	4	1.000	1	0	1	1	3	0	0	3	0	12	12.0	12
Gerald Wilkins 80	2202	323	759	.426	136	190	.716	59	114	173	173	144	0	54	123	12	848	10.6	25
Derek Strong 82	2004	262	586	.447	175	218	.803	174	345	519	73	196	2	47	102	20	699	8.5	27
Brian Shaw........ 77	1867	189	516	.366	111	140	.793	47	147	194	319	197	3	67	170	26	552	7.2	17
Darrell Armstrong... 67	1010	132	345	.383	92	106	.868	35	41	76	175	114	1	61	99	9	411	6.1	19
Felton Spencer* 1	19	2	2	1.000	0	0	...	5	1	6	1	2	0	0	1	0	4	4.0	4
Danny Schayes...... 45	540	47	120	.392	39	52	.750	41	84	125	14	74	0	15	27	16	133	3.0	21
Kenny Smith*....... 6	47	6	13	.462	2	2	1.000	1	1	2	4	3	0	0	6	0	17	2.8	8
David Vaughn 35	298	31	72	.431	19	30	.633	35	60	95	7	43	0	8	29	15	81	2.3	12
Amal McCaskill...... 17	109	10	32	.313	8	12	.667	4	18	22	7	7	0	3	11	5	28	1.6	9
Brian Evans 14	59	8	22	.364	0	0	...	1	7	8	7	6	0	1	2	2	20	1.4	4
Dell Demps 2	10	0	3	.000	2	2	1.000	0	0	0	0	1	0	1	0	0	2	1.0	2

3-pt. FG: Orlando 567-1662 (.341)—Hardaway 85-267 (.318); Seikaly 0-3 (.000); Grant 1-6 (.167); Scott 147-373 (.394); Anderson 143-405 (.353); Wilkins 66-203 (.325); Strong 0-13 (.000); Shaw 63-194 (.325); Armstrong 55-181 (.304); Schayes 0-1 (.000); Smith* 3-5 (.600); McCaskill 0-2 (.000); Evans 4-8 (.500); Demps 0-1 (.000). Opponents 455-1327 (.343).

PHILADELPHIA 76ERS

								REBOUNDS									SCORING		
	G	Min.	FGM	FGA	Pct.	FTM	FTA	Pct.	Off.	Def.	Tot.	Ast.	PF	Dq.	Stl.	TO	Blk.	Pts.	Avg.	Hi.
Allen Iverson 76	3045	625	1504	.416	382	544	.702	115	197	312	567	233	5	157	337	24	1787	23.5	50
Jerry Stackhouse 81	3166	533	1308	.407	511	667	.766	156	182	338	253	219	2	93	316	63	1679	20.7	39
Derrick Coleman ... 57	2102	364	836	.435	272	365	.745	157	416	573	193	164	1	50	184	75	1032	18.1	35
Clarence Weatherspoon . 82	2949	398	811	.491	206	279	.738	219	460	679	140	187	0	74	137	86	1003	12.2	34
Don MacLean....... 37	733	163	365	.447	64	97	.660	41	99	140	37	71	0	12	47	10	402	10.9	29
Mark Davis......... 75	1700	251	535	.469	113	168	.673	138	185	323	135	230	7	85	118	31	639	8.5	27
Rex Walters 59	1041	148	325	.455	49	62	.790	21	86	107	113	75	1	28	61	3	402	6.8	27
Scott Williams 62	1317	162	318	.509	38	55	.691	155	242	397	41	206	5	44	50	41	362	5.8	20
Lucious Harris 54	813	112	294	.381	33	47	.702	27	44	71	50	45	0	41	34	3	293	5.4	19
Doug Overton 61	634	81	190	.426	45	48	.938	18	50	68	101	44	0	24	39	0	217	3.6	20
Joe Courtney* 4	52	6	14	.429	0	0	...	5	4	9	0	8	1	0	1	0	12	3.0	6
Mark Hendrickson .. 29	301	32	77	.416	18	26	.692	35	57	92	3	32	1	10	14	4	85	2.9	12
Frankie King 7	59	7	17	.412	5	5	1.000	4	10	14	5	7	0	4	3	0	20	2.9	6
Adrian Caldwell†..... 27	365	30	57	.526	12	33	.364	38	73	111	7	60	1	8	16	7	72	2.7	8
Adrian Caldwell‡..... 45	569	40	92	.435	21	50	.420	58	109	167	12	87	1	16	28	8	101	2.2	8
Michael Cage 82	1247	66	141	.468	19	41	.463	112	208	320	43	118	0	48	17	42	151	1.8	7
Mark Bradtke 36	251	25	58	.431	9	13	.692	26	42	68	7	34	0	5	9	5	59	1.6	8

3-pt. FG: Philadelphia 433-1356 (.319)—Iverson 155-455 (.341); Stackhouse 102-342 (.298); Coleman 32-119 (.269); Weatherspoon 1-6 (.167); MacLean 12-38 (.316); Davis 24-93 (.258); Walters 57-148 (.385); Williams 0-2 (.000); Harris 36-99 (.364); Overton 10-40 (.250); Hendrickson 3-12 (.250); King 1-2 (.500); Caldwell‡ 0-2 (.000). Opponents 558-1529 (.365).

1996-97

PHOENIX SUNS

	G	Min.	FGM	FGA	Pct.	FTM	FTA	Pct.	Off.	Def.	Tot.	Ast.	PF	Dq.	Stl.	TO	Blk.	Pts.	Avg.	Hi.
									REBOUNDS									SCORING		
Kevin Johnson	70	2658	441	890	.496	439	515	.852	54	199	253	653	141	0	102	217	12	1410	20.1	38
Sam Cassell*	22	539	100	241	.415	106	124	.855	12	38	50	99	66	4	23	60	6	325	14.8	30
Cedric Ceballos†	42	1147	248	534	.464	126	171	.737	91	186	277	49	94	0	28	68	17	643	15.3	32
Cedric Ceballos‡	50	1426	282	617	.457	139	186	.747	102	228	330	64	113	0	33	85	23	729	14.6	32
Rex Chapman	65	1833	332	749	.443	124	149	.832	25	156	181	182	108	1	52	96	7	898	13.8	32
Danny Manning	77	2134	426	795	.536	181	251	.721	137	332	469	173	268	7	81	161	74	1040	13.5	26
Wesley Person	80	2326	409	903	.453	91	114	.798	68	224	292	123	102	0	86	76	20	1080	13.5	33
Michael Finley*	27	796	141	297	.475	56	69	.812	34	86	120	68	42	0	18	44	4	352	13.0	25
Jason Kidd†	33	1173	138	326	.423	66	96	.688	34	125	159	296	72	0	79	76	12	382	11.6	33
Jason Kidd‡	55	1964	213	529	.403	112	165	.679	64	185	249	496	114	0	124	142	20	599	10.9	33
Mark Bryant	41	1018	152	275	.553	76	108	.704	67	145	212	47	136	4	22	46	5	380	9.3	24
John Williams	68	2137	204	416	.490	133	198	.672	178	384	562	100	176	1	67	66	88	541	8.0	22
Robert Horry*	32	719	82	195	.421	32	50	.640	40	79	119	54	81	1	28	46	26	220	6.9	19
Wayman Tisdale	53	778	158	371	.426	30	48	.625	35	85	120	20	111	0	8	36	21	346	6.5	20
A.C. Green*	27	548	61	128	.477	31	48	.646	33	105	138	17	34	0	18	20	1	153	5.7	21
Loren Meyer†	35	449	74	166	.446	37	52	.712	39	57	96	12	73	2	5	35	12	188	5.4	18
Loren Meyer‡	54	708	108	244	.443	46	64	.719	53	92	145	19	125	3	11	62	15	266	4.9	18
Tony Dumas†	6	51	6	19	.316	1	2	.500	0	2	2	3	9	0	0	1	1	14	2.3	7
Tony Dumas‡	24	278	33	96	.344	16	25	.640	3	13	16	25	45	0	10	16	2	86	3.6	15
Chucky Brown*	10	83	13	26	.500	8	11	.727	3	13	16	4	14	0	0	4	2	34	3.4	12
Joe Kleine*	23	365	32	80	.400	13	18	.722	21	59	80	12	47	0	9	20	6	78	3.4	11
Steve Nash	65	684	74	175	.423	42	51	.824	16	47	63	138	92	1	20	63	0	213	3.3	17
Rumeal Robinson*	12	87	16	34	.471	1	4	.250	1	6	7	8	8	0	1	5	0	36	3.0	9
Mike Brown	6	83	5	12	.417	6	10	.600	9	16	25	5	9	0	1	2	1	16	2.7	7
Dexter Boney	8	48	6	19	.316	6	8	.750	3	3	6	0	3	0	2	1	1	19	2.4	10
Horacio Llamas	20	101	15	28	.536	4	8	.500	4	14	18	4	25	0	10	11	5	34	1.7	6
Ben Davis	20	98	10	26	.385	9	20	.450	12	15	27	0	16	0	4	3	1	29	1.5	7

3-pt. FG: Phoenix 527-1428 (.369)—Johnson 89-202 (.441); Cassell* 19-62 (.306); Ceballos† 21-81 (.259); Ceballos‡ 26-102 (.255); Chapman 110-314 (.350); Manning 7-36 (.194); Person 171-414 (.413); Finley* 14-55 (.255); Kidd† 40-100 (.400); Kidd‡ 61-165 (.370); Williams 0-2 (.000); Horry* 24-78 (.308); Green* 0-3 (.000); Meyer† 3-5 (.600); Meyer‡ 4-7 (.571); Dumas† 1-4 (.250); Dumas‡ 4-28 (.143); Kleine* 1-1 (1.000); Nash 23-55 (.418); Robinson* 3-10 (.300); Boney 1-6 (.167). Opponents 545-1479 (.368).

PORTLAND TRAIL BLAZERS

	G	Min.	FGM	FGA	Pct.	FTM	FTA	Pct.	Off.	Def.	Tot.	Ast.	PF	Dq.	Stl.	TO	Blk.	Pts.	Avg.	Hi.
									REBOUNDS									SCORING		
Kenny Anderson	82	3081	485	1137	.427	334	435	.768	91	272	363	584	222	2	162	193	15	1436	17.5	35
Isaiah Rider	76	2563	456	983	.464	212	261	.812	94	210	304	198	199	2	45	212	19	1223	16.1	40
Rasheed Wallace	62	1892	380	681	.558	169	265	.638	122	297	419	74	198	1	48	114	59	938	15.1	38
Clifford Robinson	81	3077	444	1043	.426	215	309	.696	90	231	321	261	251	6	99	172	66	1224	15.1	33
Arvydas Sabonis	69	1762	328	658	.498	223	287	.777	114	433	547	146	203	4	63	151	84	928	13.4	33
Gary Trent	82	1918	361	674	.536	160	229	.699	156	272	428	87	186	2	48	129	35	882	10.8	24
Stacey Augmon†	40	650	74	143	.517	41	56	.732	33	56	89	41	58	0	32	37	7	189	4.7	13
Stacey Augmon‡	60	942	105	220	.477	69	97	.711	47	91	138	56	87	0	42	64	17	279	4.7	13
Dontonio Wingfield	47	569	79	193	.409	27	40	.675	63	74	137	45	101	1	14	49	6	211	4.5	16
Aaron McKie*	44	775	53	156	.340	41	49	.837	13	80	93	84	61	1	34	48	15	170	4.1	17
Jermaine O'Neal	45	458	69	153	.451	47	78	.603	39	85	124	8	46	0	2	27	26	185	4.1	20
Ruben Nembhard†	2	19	4	8	.500	0	0	...	0	0	0	5	3	0	3	5	0	8	4.0	6
Ruben Nembhard‡	10	113	16	37	.432	8	10	.800	3	5	8	17	12	0	9	8	0	40	4.0	12
Chris Dudley	81	1840	126	293	.430	65	137	.474	204	389	593	41	247	3	39	80	96	317	3.9	12
Marcus Brown	21	184	28	70	.400	13	19	.684	4	11	15	20	26	0	8	13	2	82	3.9	13
Rumeal Robinson†	27	295	33	82	.402	20	23	.870	3	27	30	52	40	0	18	27	0	95	3.5	14
Rumeal Robinson‡	54	508	66	164	.402	26	35	.743	6	41	47	73	60	0	24	43	2	176	3.3	14
Aleksandar Djordjevic	8	61	8	16	.500	4	5	.800	1	4	5	5	3	0	0	5	0	25	3.1	8
Mitchell Butler	49	465	52	125	.416	32	50	.64	19	34	53	30	55	1	13	27	2	148	3.0	17
Reggie Jordan*	9	99	8	16	.500	4	10	.400	11	12	23	11	13	0	5	6	3	20	2.2	8
Randolph Childress*	19	125	10	30	.333	6	8	.750	1	4	5	15	11	0	7	13	0	29	1.5	8
Ennis Whatley	3	22	2	4	.500	0	0	...	0	3	3	3	5	0	0	1	0	4	1.3	4

3-pt. FG: Portland 501-1401 (.358)—Anderson 132-366 (.361); Rider 99-257 (.385); Wallace 9-33 (.273); C. Robinson 121-350 (.346); Sabonis 49-132 (.371); Trent 0-11 (.000); Wingfield 26-77 (.338); McKie* 23-55 (.418); O'Neal 0-1 (.000); Nembhard† 0-2 (.000); Nembhard‡ 0-6 (.000); Brown 13-32 (.406); R. Robinson† 9-23 (.391); R. Robinson‡ 18-56 (.321); Djordjevic 5-7 (.714); Butler 12-39 (.308); Childress* 3-16 (.188). Opponents 457-1279 (.357).

SACRAMENTO KINGS

	G	Min.	FGM	FGA	Pct.	FTM	FTA	Pct.	Off.	Def.	Tot.	Ast.	PF	Dq.	Stl.	TO	Blk.	Pts.	Avg.	Hi.
									REBOUNDS									SCORING		
Mitch Richmond	81	3125	717	1578	.454	457	531	.861	59	260	319	338	211	1	118	237	24	2095	25.9	41
Mahmoud Abdul-Rauf	75	2131	411	924	.445	115	136	.846	16	106	122	189	174	3	56	119	6	1031	13.7	34
Olden Polynice	82	2893	442	967	.457	141	251	.562	272	500	772	178	298	4	46	166	80	1025	12.5	25
Corliss Williamson	79	1992	371	745	.498	173	251	.689	139	187	326	124	263	4	60	157	49	915	11.6	24
Billy Owens	66	1995	299	640	.467	101	145	.697	134	258	392	187	187	4	62	133	25	724	11.0	31
Brian Grant	24	607	91	207	.440	70	90	.778	49	93	142	28	75	0	19	44	25	252	10.5	20
Tyus Edney	70	1376	150	391	.384	177	215	.823	34	79	113	226	98	0	60	112	2	485	6.9	23
Michael Smith	81	2526	202	375	.539	128	258	.496	257	512	769	191	251	3	82	130	60	532	6.6	16
Kevin Gamble	62	953	123	286	.430	7	10	.700	13	94	107	77	76	0	21	27	17	307	5.0	23
Jeff Grayer	25	316	38	83	.458	11	20	.550	21	17	38	25	42	0	8	15	7	91	3.6	16
Lionel Simmons	41	521	45	136	.331	42	48	.875	30	74	104	57	63	0	8	34	13	139	3.4	11

	G	Min.	FGM	FGA	Pct.	FTM	FTA	Pct.	Off.	Def.	Tot.	Ast.	PF	Dq.	Stl.	TO	Blk.	Pts.	Avg.	Hi.
									REBOUNDS									**SCORING**		
Bobby Hurley	49	632	46	125	.368	37	53	.698	9	29	38	146	53	0	27	55	3	143	2.9	10
Devin Gray*	3	25	3	11	.273	2	4	.500	3	6	9	2	3	0	3	0	0	8	2.7	4
Duane Causwell	46	581	48	94	.511	20	37	.541	57	70	127	20	131	5	15	34	38	118	2.6	10
Kevin Salvadori	23	154	12	33	.364	13	18	.722	6	19	25	10	17	0	2	12	13	37	1.6	9
Lloyd Daniels*	5	28	2	16	.125	0	0	...	1	3	4	1	4	0	1	3	0	6	1.2	3

3-pt. FG: Sacramento 414-1058 (.391)—Richmond 204-477 (.428); Abdul-Rauf 94-246 (.382); Polynice 0-6 (.000); Williamson 0-3 (.000); Owens 25-72 (.347); Edney 8-42 (.190); Gamble 54-112 (.482); Grayer 4-11 (.364); Simmons 7-30 (.233); Hurley 14-45 (.311); Causwell 2-3 (.667); Daniels* 2-11 (.182). Opponents 442-1254 (.352).

SAN ANTONIO SPURS

	G	Min.	FGM	FGA	Pct.	FTM	FTA	Pct.	Off.	Def.	Tot.	Ast.	PF	Dq.	Stl.	TO	Blk.	Pts.	Avg.	Hi.
									REBOUNDS									**SCORING**		
Dominique Wilkins	63	1945	397	953	.417	281	350	.803	169	233	402	119	100	0	39	135	31	1145	18.2	33
David Robinson	6	147	36	72	.500	34	52	.654	19	32	51	8	9	0	6	8	6	106	17.7	27
Sean Elliott	39	1393	196	464	.422	148	196	.755	48	142	190	124	105	1	24	89	24	582	14.9	29
Vernon Maxwell	72	2068	340	906	.375	134	180	.744	27	132	159	153	168	1	87	121	19	929	12.9	34
Vinny Del Negro	72	2243	365	781	.467	112	129	.868	39	171	210	231	131	0	59	92	7	886	12.3	29
Avery Johnson	76	2472	327	685	.477	140	203	.690	32	115	147	513	158	1	96	146	15	800	10.5	26
Monty Williams	65	1345	234	460	.509	120	186	.645	98	108	206	91	161	1	55	116	52	588	9.0	30
Will Perdue	65	1918	233	410	.568	99	171	.579	251	387	638	38	184	2	32	87	102	565	8.7	19
Carl Herrera	75	1837	257	593	.433	81	118	.686	118	222	340	50	217	3	62	95	53	597	8.0	24
Cory Alexander	80	1454	194	490	.396	95	129	.736	29	94	123	254	148	0	82	146	16	577	7.2	26
Charles Smith	19	329	34	84	.405	20	26	.769	18	47	65	14	44	0	13	22	22	88	4.6	12
Gaylon Nickerson*	3	36	3	9	.333	7	7	1.000	1	3	4	1	1	0	0	0	1	13	4.3	6
Darrin Hancock*	1	8	1	2	.500	2	2	1.000	0	0	0	1	2	0	0	0	0	4	4.0	4
Greg Anderson	82	1659	130	262	.496	62	93	.667	157	291	448	34	225	2	63	73	67	322	3.9	14
Stephen Howard*	7	69	7	12	.583	12	14	.857	4	5	9	1	7	0	8	5	2	26	3.7	7
Jamie Feick†	38	614	54	153	.353	34	65	.523	81	130	211	26	75	0	16	31	13	146	3.8	15
Jamie Feick‡	41	624	56	157	.357	34	67	.507	82	132	214	26	78	0	16	31	14	151	3.7	15
Devin Gray†	3	24	5	15	.333	0	1	.000	3	2	5	0	8	0	1	5	0	10	3.3	8
Devin Gray‡	6	49	8	26	.308	2	5	.400	6	8	14	2	11	0	4	5	0	18	3.0	8
Jason Sasser*	6	62	8	19	.421	0	0	...	0	7	7	1	11	0	2	2	0	17	2.8	11
Joe Courtney†	5	48	5	16	.313	3	5	.600	4	3	7	0	6	0	0	2	0	13	2.6	7
Joe Courtney‡	9	100	11	30	.367	3	5	.600	9	7	16	0	14	1	0	3	0	25	2.8	7
Tim Kempton	10	59	1	5	.200	2	2	1.000	3	5	8	2	4	0	1	7	1	4	0.4	4

3-pt. FG: San Antonio 378-1180 (.320)—Wilkins 70-239 (.293); Elliott 42-126 (.333); Maxwell 115-372 (.309); Del Negro 44-140 (.314); Johnson 6-26 (.231); Williams 0-1 (.000); Herrera 2-6 (.333); Alexander 94-252 (.373); Smith 0-1 (.000); Nickerson* 0-1 (.000); Anderson 0-1 (.000); Feick† 4-13 (.308); Feick‡ 5-14 (.357); Sasser* 1-2 (.500). Opponents 552-1425 (.387).

SEATTLE SUPERSONICS

	G	Min.	FGM	FGA	Pct.	FTM	FTA	Pct.	Off.	Def.	Tot.	Ast.	PF	Dq.	Stl.	TO	Blk.	Pts.	Avg.	Hi.
									REBOUNDS									**SCORING**		
Gary Payton	82	3213	706	1482	.476	254	355	.715	106	272	378	583	208	1	197	215	13	1785	21.8	32
Shawn Kemp	81	2750	526	1032	.510	452	609	.742	275	532	807	156	320	11	125	280	81	1516	18.7	34
Detlef Schrempf	61	2192	356	724	.492	253	316	.801	87	307	394	266	151	0	63	150	16	1022	16.8	34
Hersey Hawkins	82	2755	369	795	.464	258	295	.875	92	228	320	250	146	1	159	130	12	1139	13.9	31
Sam Perkins	81	1976	290	661	.439	187	229	.817	74	226	300	103	134	0	69	77	49	889	11.0	26
Terry Cummings	45	828	155	319	.486	57	82	.695	70	113	183	39	113	0	33	45	7	370	8.2	18
Nate McMillan	37	798	61	149	.409	19	29	.655	15	103	118	140	78	0	58	32	6	169	4.6	13
Larry Stewart	70	982	112	252	.444	67	93	.720	75	96	171	52	108	0	31	63	23	300	4.3	19
Jim McIlvaine	82	1477	130	276	.471	53	107	.495	132	198	330	23	247	4	39	62	164	314	3.8	12
David Wingate	65	929	89	214	.416	33	40	.825	23	51	74	80	108	0	44	37	5	236	3.6	14
Craig Ehlo	62	848	87	248	.351	13	26	.500	39	71	110	68	71	0	36	45	4	214	3.5	14
Greg Graham	28	197	29	80	.363	26	40	.650	2	11	13	11	12	0	12	10	1	93	3.3	13
Eric Snow	67	775	74	164	.451	47	66	.712	17	53	70	159	94	0	37	48	3	199	3.0	11
Antonio Harvey	6	26	5	11	.455	5	6	.833	2	8	10	1	8	0	0	1	4	15	2.5	5
Steve Scheffler	7	29	6	7	.857	1	2	.500	1	2	3	0	5	0	0	5	0	13	1.9	5
Elmore Spencer	1	5	0	1	.000	0	0	...	0	0	0	0	0	0	1	1	0	0	0.0	0

3-pt. FG: Seattle 559-1583 (.353)—Payton 119-380 (.313); Kemp 12-33 (.364); Schrempf 57-161 (.354); Hawkins 143-355 (.403); Perkins 122-309 (.395); Cummings 3-5 (.600); McMillan 28-84 (.333); Stewart 9-37 (.243); McIlvaine 1-7 (.143); Wingate 25-71 (.352); Ehlo 27-95 (.284); Graham 9-31 (.290); Snow 4-15 (.267). Opponents 613-1644 (.373).

TORONTO RAPTORS

	G	Min.	FGM	FGA	Pct.	FTM	FTA	Pct.	Off.	Def.	Tot.	Ast.	PF	Dq.	Stl.	TO	Blk.	Pts.	Avg.	Hi.
									REBOUNDS									**SCORING**		
Damon Stoudamire	81	3311	564	1407	.401	330	401	.823	86	244	330	709	162	1	123	288	13	1634	20.2	35
Walt Williams	73	2647	419	982	.427	186	243	.765	103	264	367	197	282	11	97	174	62	1199	16.4	34
Marcus Camby	63	1897	375	778	.482	183	264	.693	131	263	394	97	214	7	66	134	130	935	14.8	37
Doug Christie	81	3127	396	949	.417	237	306	.775	85	347	432	315	245	6	201	200	45	1176	14.5	33
Carlos Rogers	56	1397	212	404	.525	102	170	.600	120	184	304	37	140	1	42	53	69	551	9.8	24
Reggie Slater	26	406	82	149	.550	39	75	.520	40	55	95	21	34	0	9	29	6	203	7.8	21
Popeye Jones	79	2421	258	537	.480	99	121	.818	270	410	680	84	269	3	58	116	39	616	7.8	22
Sharone Wright	60	1009	161	403	.400	68	133	.511	79	107	186	28	146	3	15	93	50	390	6.5	17
Zan Tabak	13	218	32	71	.451	20	29	.690	20	29	49	14	35	0	6	21	11	84	6.5	16
Hubert Davis	36	623	74	184	.402	17	23	.739	11	29	40	34	40	0	11	21	2	181	5.0	17
Oliver Miller†	19	316	47	84	.560	0	26	.769	23	50	73	29	48	0	13	20	13	114	6.0	13
Oliver Miller‡	61	1152	123	238	.517	48	79	.608	105	201	306	87	181	1	47	90	63	294	4.8	13

1996-97

	G	Min.	FGM	FGA	Pct.	FTM	FTA	Pct.	Off.	Def.	Tot.	Ast.	PF	Dq.	Stl.	TO	Blk.	Pts.	Avg.	Hi.
Clifford Rozier†	41	732	79	173	.457	31	61	.508	102	132	234	31	97	2	24	29	44	189	4.6	20
Clifford Rozier‡	42	737	79	174	.454	31	61	.508	102	132	234	31	97	2	24	29	44	189	4.5	20
Acie Earl*	38	457	59	157	.376	44	70	.629	33	52	85	18	54	0	12	33	27	162	4.3	23
Shawn Respert†	27	412	53	120	.442	27	32	.844	11	21	32	32	35	0	20	22	2	152	5.6	14
Shawn Respert‡	41	495	59	139	.424	34	39	.872	14	25	39	40	40	0	20	30	2	172	4.2	14
John Long	32	370	46	117	.393	25	28	.893	6	34	40	21	28	0	9	24	2	129	4.0	15
Benoit Benjamin	4	44	5	12	.417	3	4	.750	3	6	9	1	5	0	1	2	0	13	3.3	8
Jimmy Oliver	4	43	4	13	.308	2	2	1.000	1	4	5	1	2	0	2	3	0	11	2.8	5
Donald Whiteside	27	259	18	55	.327	11	15	.733	2	10	12	36	23	0	11	17	0	59	2.2	9
Brad Lohaus	6	45	4	15	.267	0	0	...	1	6	7	1	6	0	1	1	0	10	1.7	5
Martin Lewis	9	50	6	14	.429	1	2	.500	4	2	6	4	8	0	1	1	2	14	1.6	5
Earl Cureton	9	46	3	8	.375	1	3	.333	4	5	9	4	10	0	0	1	0	7	0.8	6

3-pt. FG: Toronto 589-1624 (.363)—Stoudamire 176-496 (.355); Williams 175-437 (.400); Camby 2-14 (.143); Christie 147-383 (.384); Rogers 25-66 (.379); Slater 0-2 (.000); Jones 1-13 (.077); Wright 0-1 (.000); Davis 16-70 (.229); Miller† 0-1 (.000); Miller‡ 0-2 (.000); Rozier† 0-2 (.000); Rozier‡ 0-2 (.000); Earl* 0-5 (.000); Respert† 19-48 (.396); Respert‡ 20-57 (.351); Long 12-34 (.353); Oliver 1-6 (.167); Whiteside 12-36 (.333); Lohaus 2-7 (.286); Lewis 1-3 (.333). Opponents 497-1427 (.348).

UTAH JAZZ

	G	Min.	FGM	FGA	Pct.	FTM	FTA	Pct.	Off.	Def.	Tot.	Ast.	PF	Dq.	Stl.	TO	Blk.	Pts.	Avg.	Hi.
Karl Malone	82	2998	864	1571	.550	521	690	.755	193	616	809	368	217	0	113	233	48	2249	27.4	41
Jeff Hornacek	82	2592	413	856	.482	293	326	.899	60	181	241	361	188	1	124	134	26	1191	14.5	30
John Stockton	82	2896	416	759	.548	275	325	.846	45	183	228	860	194	2	166	248	15	1183	14.4	31
Bryon Russell	81	2525	297	620	.479	171	244	.701	79	252	331	123	237	2	129	94	27	873	10.8	23
Antoine Carr	82	1460	252	522	.483	99	127	.780	60	135	195	74	214	2	24	75	63	603	7.4	17
Greg Ostertag	77	1818	210	408	.515	139	205	.678	180	385	565	27	233	2	24	74	152	559	7.3	21
Shandon Anderson	65	1066	147	318	.462	68	99	.687	52	127	179	49	113	0	27	73	8	386	5.9	20
Howard Eisley	82	1083	139	308	.451	70	89	.787	20	64	84	198	141	0	44	110	10	368	4.5	14
Chris Morris	73	977	122	299	.408	39	54	.722	37	125	162	43	121	3	29	45	24	314	4.3	15
Ruben Nembhard*	8	94	12	29	.414	8	10	.800	3	5	8	12	9	0	6	3	0	32	4.0	12
Adam Keefe	62	915	82	160	.513	71	103	.689	75	141	216	32	97	0	30	45	13	235	3.8	14
Stephen Howard†	42	349	55	96	.573	40	67	.597	25	51	76	10	55	0	11	20	10	150	3.6	16
Stephen Howard‡	49	418	62	108	.574	52	81	.642	29	56	85	11	62	0	19	25	12	176	3.6	16
Greg Foster	79	920	111	245	.453	54	65	.831	56	131	187	31	145	0	10	54	20	278	3.5	13
Jamie Watson*	13	129	11	25	.440	10	12	.833	4	14	18	10	16	0	11	9	2	33	2.5	5
Brooks Thompson*	2	8	0	1	.000	0	0	...	0	0	1	1	0	0	1	0	0	0	0.0	0

3-pt. FG: Utah 334-902 (.370)—Malone 0-13 (.000); Hornacek 72-195 (.369); Stockton 76-180 (.422); Russell 108-264 (.409); Carr 0-3 (.000); Ostertag 0-4 (.000); Anderson 24-47 (.511); Eisley 20-72 (.278); Morris 31-113 (.274); Nembhard* 0-4 (.000); Keefe 0-1 (.000); Foster 2-3 (.667); Watson* 1-3 (.333). Opponents 521-1480 (.352).

VANCOUVER GRIZZLIES

	G	Min.	FGM	FGA	Pct.	FTM	FTA	Pct.	Off.	Def.	Tot.	Ast.	PF	Dq.	Stl.	TO	Blk.	Pts.	Avg.	Hi.
Shareef Abdur-Rahim	80	2802	550	1214	.453	387	519	.746	216	339	555	175	199	0	79	225	79	1494	18.7	37
Bryant Reeves	75	2777	498	1025	.486	216	307	.704	174	436	610	160	270	3	29	175	67	1213	16.2	39
Anthony Peeler	72	2291	402	1011	.398	109	133	.820	54	193	247	256	168	0	105	157	17	1041	14.5	40
Greg Anthony	65	1863	199	507	.393	130	178	.730	25	159	184	407	122	0	129	129	4	616	9.5	24
George Lynch	41	1059	137	291	.471	60	97	.619	98	163	261	76	97	1	63	64	17	342	8.3	20
Blue Edwards	61	1439	182	458	.397	89	109	.817	49	140	189	114	135	0	38	81	20	478	7.8	34
Lawrence Moten	67	1214	171	441	.388	64	99	.646	43	76	119	129	83	0	48	81	24	447	6.7	21
Roy Rogers	82	1848	244	483	.505	54	94	.574	139	247	386	46	214	1	21	86	163	543	6.6	18
Aaron Williams†	32	553	82	143	.573	33	49	.673	60	78	138	15	72	1	16	28	26	197	6.2	16
Aaron Williams‡	33	563	85	148	.574	33	49	.673	62	81	143	15	72	1	16	32	29	203	6.2	16
Lee Mayberry	80	1952	149	370	.403	29	46	.630	29	105	134	329	159	0	60	90	8	410	5.1	17
Chris Robinson	41	681	69	182	.379	16	26	.615	23	48	71	65	85	2	28	34	9	188	4.6	15
Pete Chilcutt	54	662	72	165	.436	13	22	.591	67	89	156	47	52	0	26	28	17	182	3.4	13
Rich Manning*	16	128	18	48	.375	6	8	.750	8	15	23	2	18	0	3	5	1	44	2.8	10
Eric Mobley	28	307	28	63	.444	16	30	.533	30	28	58	14	44	0	5	29	10	72	2.6	11
Eric Leckner†	19	115	14	30	.467	6	12	.500	5	30	35	4	32	0	3	10	2	34	1.8	6
Eric Leckner‡	20	126	14	33	.424	6	12	.500	5	31	36	5	35	0	3	10	2	34	1.7	6
Moochie Norris	8	89	4	22	.182	2	5	.400	3	9	12	23	5	0	4	5	0	12	1.5	8

3-pt. FG: Vancouver 445-1274 (.349)—Abdur-Rahim 7-27 (.259); Reeves 1-11 (.091); Peeler 128-343 (.373); Anthony 88-238 (.370); Lynch 8-31 (.258); Edwards 25-89 (.281); Moten 41-141 (.291); Rogers 1-1 (1.000); Williams† 0-1 (.000); Williams‡ 0-1 (.000); Mayberry 83-221 (.376); Robinson 34-89 (.382); Chilcutt 25-69 (.362); Manning* 2-3 (.667); Norris 2-10 (.200). Opponents 500-1369 (.365).

WASHINGTON BULLETS

	G	Min.	FGM	FGA	Pct.	FTM	FTA	Pct.	Off.	Def.	Tot.	Ast.	PF	Dq.	Stl.	TO	Blk.	Pts.	Avg.	Hi.
Chris Webber	72	2806	604	1167	.518	177	313	.565	238	505	743	331	258	6	122	230	137	1445	20.1	34
Juwan Howard	82	3324	638	1313	.486	294	389	.756	202	450	652	311	259	3	93	246	23	1570	19.1	33
Rod Strickland	82	2997	515	1105	.466	367	497	.738	95	240	335	727	166	2	143	270	14	1410	17.2	34
Gheorghe Muresan	73	1849	327	541	.604	123	199	.618	141	340	481	29	230	3	43	117	96	777	10.6	24
Calbert Cheaney	79	2411	369	730	.505	95	137	.693	70	198	268	114	226	3	77	94	18	837	10.6	24
Tracy Murray	82	1814	288	678	.425	135	161	.839	84	169	253	78	150	1	69	86	19	817	10.0	24
Chris Whitney	82	1117	139	330	.421	94	113	.832	13	91	104	182	100	0	49	68	4	430	5.2	18
Jaren Jackson	75	1133	134	329	.407	53	69	.768	31	101	132	65	131	0	45	60	16	374	5.0	16
Harvey Grant	78	1604	129	314	.411	30	39	.769	63	193	256	68	167	2	46	30	48	316	4.1	14
Gaylon Nickerson†	1	6	1	3	.333	0	0	...	0	1	1	0	0	0	1	1	0	2	2.0	2
Gaylon Nickerson‡	4	42	4	12	.333	7	7	1.000	1	4	5	1	1	0	1	1	1	15	3.8	6

1996-97

	G	Min.	FGM	FGA	Pct.	FTM	FTA	Pct.	REBOUNDS			Ast.	PF	Dq.	Stl.	TO	Blk.	SCORING		
									Off.	Def.	Tot.							Pts.	Avg.	Hi.
Tim Legler	15	182	15	48	.313	6	7	.857	0	21	21	7	21	0	3	9	5	44	2.9	9
Lorenzo Williams	19	264	20	31	.645	5	7	.714	28	41	69	4	49	0	6	18	8	45	2.4	13
Ashraf Amaya	31	144	12	40	.300	15	28	.536	19	33	52	3	29	0	7	10	3	40	1.3	4
Ben Wallace	34	197	16	46	.348	6	20	.300	25	33	58	2	27	0	8	18	11	38	1.1	6
Matt Fish*	5	7	1	3	.333	0	0	...	1	4	5	0	2	0	0	2	0	2	0.4	2

3-pt. FG: Washington 331-1001 (.331)—Webber 60-151 (.397); Howard 0-2 (.000); Strickland 13-77 (.169); Cheaney 4-30 (.133); Murray 106-300 (.353); Whitney 58-163 (.356); Jackson 53-158 (.335); Grant 28-89 (.315); Nickerson† 0-1 (.000); Nickerson‡ 0-2 (.000); Legler 8-29 (.276); Amaya 1-1 (1.000). Opponents 492-1327 (.371).

* Finished season with another team. † Totals with this team only. ‡ Totals with all teams.

PLAYOFF RESULTS

EASTERN CONFERENCE

FIRST ROUND

Chicago 3, Washington 0
Apr. 25—Fri.	Washington 86 at Chicago	98
Apr. 27—Sun.	Washington 104 at Chicago	109
Apr. 30—Wed.	Chicago 96 at Washington	95

Miami 3, Orlando 2
Apr. 24—Thur.	Orlando 64 at Miami	99
Apr. 27—Sun.	Orlando 87 at Miami	104
Apr. 29—Tue.	Miami 75 at Orlando	88
May 1—Thur.	Miami 91 at Orlando	99
May 4—Sun.	Orlando 83 at Miami	91

New York 3, Charlotte 0
Apr. 24—Thur.	Charlotte 99 at New York	109
Apr. 26—Sat.	Charlotte 93 at New York	100
Apr. 28—Mon.	New York 104 at Charlotte	95

Atlanta 3, Detroit 2
Apr. 25—Fri.	Detroit 75 at Atlanta	89
Apr. 27—Sun.	Detroit 93 at Atlanta	80
Apr. 29—Tue.	Atlanta 91 at Detroit	99
May 2—Fri.	Atlanta 94 at Detroit	82
May 4—Sun.	Detroit 79 at Atlanta	84

SEMIFINALS

Chicago 4, Atlanta 1
May 6—Tue.	Atlanta 97 at Chicago	100
May 8—Thur.	Atlanta 103 at Chicago	95
May 10—Sat.	Chicago 100 at Atlanta	80
May 11—Sun.	Chicago 89 at Atlanta	80
May 13—Tue.	Atlanta 92 at Chicago	107

Miami 4, New York 3
May 7—Wed.	New York 88 at Miami	79
May 9—Fri.	New York 84 at Miami	88
May 11—Sun.	Miami 73 at New York	77
May 12—Mon.	Miami 76 at New York	89
May 14—Wed.	New York 81 at Miami	96
May 16—Fri.	Miami 95 at New York	90
May 18—Sun.	New York 90 at Miami	101

FINALS

Chicago 4, Miami 1
May 20—Tue.	Miami 77 at Chicago	84
May 22—Thur.	Miami 68 at Chicago	75
May 24—Sat.	Chicago 98 at Miami	74
May 26—Mon.	Chicago 80 at Miami	87
May 28—Wed.	Miami 87 at Chicago	100

WESTERN CONFERENCE

FIRST ROUND

Utah 3, L.A. Clippers 0
Apr. 24—Thur.	L.A. Clippers 86 at Utah	106
Apr. 26—Sat.	L.A. Clippers 99 at Utah	105
Apr. 28—Mon.	Utah 104 at L.A. Clippers	92

Seattle 3, Phoenix 2
Apr. 25—Fri.	Phoenix 106 at Seattle	101
Apr. 27—Sun.	Phoenix 78 at Seattle	122
Apr. 29—Tue.	Seattle 103 at Phoenix	110
May 1—Thur.	Seattle 122 at Phoenix	*115
May 3—Sat.	Phoenix 92 At Seattle	116

Houston 3, Minnesota 0
Apr. 24—Thur.	Minnesota 95 at Houston	112
Apr. 26—Sat.	Minnesota 84 at Houston	96
Apr. 29—Tue.	Houston 125 at Minnesota	120

L.A. Lakers 3, Portland 1
Apr. 25—Fri.	Portland 77 at L.A. Lakers	95
Apr. 27—Sun.	Portland 93 at L.A. Lakers	107
Apr. 30—Wed.	L.A. Lakers 90 at Portland	98
May 2—Fri.	L.A. Lakers 95 at Portland	91

SEMIFINALS

Utah 4, L.A. Lakers 1
May 4—Sun.	L.A. Lakers 77 at Utah	93
May 6—Tue.	L.A. Lakers 101 at Utah	103
May 8—Thur.	Utah 84 at L.A. Lakers	104
May 10—Sat.	Utah 110 at L.A. Lakers	95
May 12—Mon.	L.A. Lakers 93 at Utah	*98

Houston 4, Seattle 3
May 5—Mon.	Seattle 102 at Houston	112
May 7—Wed.	Seattle 106 at Houston	101
May 9—Fri.	Houston 97 at Seattle	93
May 11—Sun.	Houston 110 at Seattle	*106
May 13—Tue.	Seattle 100 at Houston	94
May 15—Thur.	Houston 96 at Seattle	99
May 17—Sat.	Seattle 91 at Houston	96

FINALS

Utah 4, Houston 2
May 19—Mon.	Houston 86 at Utah	101
May 21—Wed.	Houston 92 at Utah	104
May 23—Fri.	Utah 100 at Houston	118
May 25—Sun.	Utah 92 at Houston	95
May 27—Tue.	Houston 91 at Utah	96
May 29—Thur.	Utah 103 at Houston	100

NBA FINALS

Chicago 4, Utah 2
June 1—Sun.	Utah 82 at Chicago	84
June 4—Wed.	Utah 85 at Chicago	97
June 6—Fri.	Chicago 93 at Utah	104
June 8—Sun.	Chicago 73 at Utah	78
June 11—Wed.	Chicago 90 at Utah	88
June 13—Fri.	Utah 86 at Chicago	90

*Denotes number of overtime periods.

1996-97

1995-96

1995-96 NBA CHAMPION CHICAGO BULLS

Front row (from left): Toni Kukoc, Luc Longley, Dennis Rodman, Michael Jordan, Scottie Pippen, Ron Harper, Steve Kerr. Center row (from left): Jud Buechler, Jason Caffey, James Edwards, Bill Wennington, Dickey Simpkins, Jack Haley, Randy Brown. Back row (from left): assistant coach John Paxson, assistant coach Jimmy Rodgers, head coach Phil Jackson, assistant coach Jim Cleamons, assistant coach Tex Winter.

FINAL STANDINGS

ATLANTIC DIVISION

	Atl.	Bos.	Cha.	Chi.	Cle.	Dal.	Den.	Det.	G.S.	Hou.	Ind.	LA-C	LA-L	Mia.	Mil.	Min.	N.J.	N.Y.	Orl.	Phi.	Pho.	Por.	Sac.	S.A.	Sea.	Tor.	Uta.	Van.	Was.	W	L	Pct.	GB
Orl.	2	3	4	1	2	1	1	3	2	2	2	2	1	3	3	2	4	3	..	4	2	1	1	1	1	2	1	2	4	60	22	.732	..
N.Y.	1	4	0	1	1	2	1	4	2	2	3	1	1	3	2	2	2	..	1	3	0	0	0	1	4	1	1	3		47	35	.573	13
Mia.	2	1	2	1	3	2	2	3	1	2	0	1	0	..	3	1	5	1	1	3	1	0	1	1	0	2	0	1	2	42	40	.512	18
Was.	3	2	1	0	1	2	1	2	1	1	0	1	1	2	3	2	2	1	0	3	0	2	2	1	1	1	1	2	..	39	43	.476	21
Bos.	0	..	2	0	1	0	1	2	0	1	0	2	0	3	3	2	2	0	1	4	1	0	2	0	0	3	0	1	2	33	49	.402	27
N.J.	0	2	3	0	2	1	2	0	0	0	3	1	0	0	3	1	..	2	0	2	0	1	1	0	2	0	2	2		30	52	.366	30
Phi.	1	0	1	0	0	2	0	0	0	0	1	0	1	1	1	1	2	1	0	..	0	0	0	0	0	3	1	1	1	18	64	.220	42

CENTRAL DIVISION

	Atl.	Bos.	Cha.	Chi.	Cle.	Dal.	Den.	Det.	G.S.	Hou.	Ind.	LA-C	LA-L	Mia.	Mil.	Min.	N.J.	N.Y.	Orl.	Phi.	Pho.	Por.	Sac.	S.A.	Sea.	Tor.	Uta.	Van.	Was.	W	L	Pct.	GB
Chi.	4	3	3	..	4	2	1	4	2	2	2	2	2	3	4	2	3	3	3	4	1	2	2	2	1	3	2	2	4	72	10	.878	..
Ind.	3	4	3	2	2	2	2	2	1	0	..	2	1	3	3	1	1	1	2	3	1	1	0	1	2	4	0	2	3	52	30	.634	20
Cle.	1	3	1	0	..	2	1	2	2	1	2	2	1	4	2	1	3	1	4	2	1	1	0	0	3	0	2	3		47	35	.573	25
Atl.		4	3	0	3	1	1	2	1	–	1	1	2	0	2	2	1	4	2	2	2	0	2	2	0	0	4	1	2	1	46	36	.561	26
Det.	2	1	3	0	2	2	1	..	2	1	2	2	0	1	2	1	4	0	1	4	2	2	1	2	1	4	0	2	1	46	36	.561	26
Cha.	1	2	..	1	3	2	2	1	0	0	1	1	2	2	3	1	0	3	0	3	2	1	1	0	0	3	1	2	3	41	41	.500	31
Mil.	2	1	1	0	0	1	1	2	1	0	1	1	0	0	..	1	1	2	1	2	0	2	0	1	0	2	0	1	1	25	57	.305	47
Tor.	0	1	1	1	1	1	0	0	1	0	0	2	0	1	2	1	2	0	1	1	0	0	0	0	1	..	0	1	3	21	61	.256	51

MIDWEST DIVISION

	Atl.	Bos.	Cha.	Chi.	Cle.	Dal.	Den.	Det.	G.S.	Hou.	Ind.	LA-C	LA-L	Mia.	Mil.	Min.	N.J.	N.Y.	Orl.	Phi.	Pho.	Por.	Sac.	S.A.	Sea.	Tor.	Uta.	Van.	Was.	W	L	Pct.	GB
S.A.	2	2	2	0	2	2	4	0	3	3	1	3	3	1	1	3	2	1	1	2	3	3	3	..	2	2	3	4	1	59	23	.720	..
Utah	1	2	1	0	2	3	1	2	3	2	2	3	2	2	2	3	2	1	1	1	3	3	4	1	1	2	..	4	1	55	27	.671	4
Hou.	1	1	2	0	1	3	3	1	2	..	2	4	3	0	2	2	2	0	0	2	3	2	2	1	0	2	2	4	1	48	34	.585	11
Den.	1	0	1	1	2	..	1	2	1	0	1	2	0	1	4	0	1	1	2	3	0	0	0	1	2	3	3	1	0	35	47	.427	24
Dal.	1	2	0	0	0	..	2	0	2	1	0	2	0	0	1	0	1	0	1	0	1	0	2	2	2	1	1	4	0	26	56	.317	33
Min.	1	0	1	0	0	4	0	1	1	2	1	1	1	1	1	..	1	0	0	1	1	0	3	1	0	1	1	2	0	26	56	.317	33
Van.	0	1	0	0	0	0	1	0	0	0	0	1	0	1	1	2	0	1	0	1	0	2	2	0	1	1	0	..	0	15	67	.183	44

PACIFIC DIVISION

	Atl.	Bos.	Cha.	Chi.	Cle.	Dal.	Den.	Det.	G.S.	Hou.	Ind.	LA-C	LA-L	Mia.	Mil.	Min.	N.J.	N.Y.	Orl.	Phi.	Pho.	Por.	Sac.	S.A.	Sea.	Tor.	Uta.	Van.	Was.	W	L	Pct.	GB
Sea.	2	2	2	1	2	2	3	1	4	4	0	4	2	2	2	4	2	1	1	2	4	3	4	2	..	1	3	3	1	64	18	.780	..
L.A.L.	2	2	0	0	0	4	2	2	3	1	1	4	..	2	2	3	2	1	1	1	3	2	3	1	2	2	2	4	1	53	29	.646	11
Por.	2	1	0	1	4	4	0	3	2	1	2	2	2	0	4	1	2	1	2	2	..	1	1	1	2	1	2	0		44	38	.537	20
Pho.	2	1	0	1	0	3	1	0	3	1	1	1	1	1	2	3	2	2	0	2	..	2	2	1	0	2	1	4	2	41	41	.500	23
Sac.	0	0	1	0	1	2	4	1	3	2	2	2	1	1	2	1	1	2	1	2	2	3	..	1	0	2	0	2	0	39	43	.476	25
G.S.	1	2	2	0	0	2	2	0	..	2	1	3	1	1	1	3	2	0	0	2	1	1	1	1	0	1	1	4	1	36	46	.439	28
L.A.C.	0	0	1	0	0	2	3	0	1	0	0	..	0	1	1	3	1	1	0	2	3	2	2	1	0	0	1	3	1	29	53	.354	35

TEAM STATISTICS

OFFENSIVE

	G	FGM	FGA	Pct.	FTM	FTA	Pct.	REBOUNDS Off.	Def.	Tot.	Ast.	PF	Dq.	Stl.	TO	Blk.	SCORING Pts.	Avg.
Chicago	82	3293	6892	.478	1495	2004	.746	1247	2411	3658	2033	1807	10	745	1175	345	8625	105.2
Seattle	82	3074	6401	.480	1843	2424	.760	954	2449	3403	1999	1967	18	882	1441	393	8572	104.5
Orlando	82	3203	6640	.482	1543	2232	.691	966	2401	3367	2080	1709	19	663	1160	406	8571	104.5
Phoenix	82	3159	6673	.473	1907	2472	.771	1009	2501	3510	2001	1776	14	623	1207	331	8552	104.3
Boston	82	3163	6942	.456	1630	2284	.714	1050	2427	3477	1792	2041	14	653	1302	406	8495	103.6
San Antonio	82	3148	6602	.477	1663	2261	.736	937	2586	3523	2044	1820	6	645	1195	536	8477	103.4
L.A. Lakers	82	3216	6706	.480	1529	2049	.746	995	2303	3298	2080	1702	12	722	1163	516	8438	102.9
Charlotte	82	3108	6618	.470	1631	2119	.770	987	2256	3243	1907	1815	23	582	1241	277	8431	102.8
Dallas	82	3124	7431	.420	1426	1975	.722	1408	2379	3787	1913	1836	31	642	1270	342	8409	102.5
Washington	82	3202	6618	.484	1511	2076	.728	930	2327	3257	1815	1981	21	592	1327	506	8408	102.5
Utah	82	3129	6417	.488	1769	2302	.768	993	2373	3366	2139	2046	12	667	1215	418	8404	102.5
Houston	82	3078	6638	.464	1611	2106	.765	919	2455	3374	1982	1753	11	645	1245	476	8404	102.5
Golden State	82	3056	6700	.456	1775	2340	.759	1173	2285	3458	1889	1835	19	706	1343	470	8334	101.6
Sacramento	82	2971	6494	.457	1759	2407	.731	1114	2345	3459	1829	2131	29	643	1442	436	8163	99.5
L.A. Clippers	82	3126	6618	.472	1392	1984	.702	979	2190	3169	1672	2008	21	703	1355	411	8153	99.4
Portland	82	3064	6688	.458	1537	2321	.662	1160	2577	3737	1760	1859	20	594	1377	417	8145	99.3
Indiana	82	2979	6205	.480	1823	2416	.755	1010	2262	3272	1917	2031	17	579	1335	323	8144	99.3
Atlanta	82	2985	6665	.448	1523	2012	.757	1182	2148	3330	1609	1714	18	771	1228	319	8059	98.3
Minnesota	82	2974	6481	.459	1797	2314	.777	985	2271	3256	1867	1994	15	650	1426	481	8024	97.9
Denver	82	3001	6657	.451	1614	2173	.743	1057	2487	3544	1851	1882	21	521	1265	597	8013	97.7
Toronto	82	3084	6598	.467	1412	1953	.723	1071	2213	3284	1927	1987	27	745	1544	493	7994	97.5
New York	82	3003	6382	.471	1480	1954	.757	829	2449	3278	1822	1864	17	645	1272	377	7971	97.2
Miami	82	2902	6348	.457	1553	2187	.710	999	2495	3494	1752	2158	32	574	1394	439	7909	96.5
Milwaukee	82	3034	6490	.467	1412	1914	.738	973	2164	3137	1755	1943	16	582	1295	302	7837	95.6
Detroit	82	2810	6122	.459	1657	2206	.751	884	2440	3324	1610	1953	16	506	1215	352	7822	95.4
Philadelphia	82	2796	6418	.436	1662	2263	.734	1031	2161	3192	1629	1777	16	643	1414	420	7746	94.5
New Jersey	82	2881	6750	.427	1672	2244	.745	1350	2503	3853	1752	1880	23	627	1375	571	7684	93.7
Cleveland	82	2761	5998	.460	1355	1775	.763	867	2055	2922	1818	1685	14	674	1073	340	7473	91.1
Vancouver	82	2772	6483	.428	1446	1998	.724	957	2170	3127	1706	1852	14	728	1347	333	7362	89.8

DEFENSIVE

	FGM	FGA	Pct.	FTM	FTA	Pct.	REBOUNDS Off.	Def.	Tot.	Ast.	PF	Dq.	Stl.	TO	Blk.	SCORING Pts.	Avg.	Dif.
Cleveland	2674	5787	.462	1400	1844	.759	874	2167	3041	1818	1667	9	504	1282	336	7201	88.5	+2.6
Detroit	2827	6375	.443	1458	2039	.715	964	2268	3232	1729	1887	19	556	1153	385	7617	92.9	+2.5
Chicago	2880	6428	.448	1424	1985	.717	981	2136	3117	1592	1856	25	595	1405	312	7621	92.9	+12.2
New York	2859	6471	.442	1621	2191	.740	995	2425	3420	1671	1762	11	653	1293	281	7781	94.9	+2.3
Miami	2734	6303	.434	1878	2498	.752	982	2315	3297	1645	2031	30	662	1288	403	7792	95.0	+1.4
Utah	2747	6174	.445	1820	2422	.751	936	2149	3085	1640	1983	25	584	1284	409	7864	95.9	+6.6
Indiana	2841	6291	.452	1703	2302	.740	1004	2051	3055	1726	2041	27	663	1259	420	7878	96.1	+3.2
Seattle	2873	6553	.438	1654	2309	.716	1074	2255	3329	1776	2010	29	758	1517	391	7933	96.7	+7.8
Portland	2953	6677	.442	1574	2127	.740	932	2316	3248	1817	1996	18	708	1192	409	7952	97.0	+2.4
Atlanta	3044	6419	.474	1392	1865	.746	1054	2292	3346	1841	1807	15	580	1405	338	7959	97.1	+1.2
San Antonio	3017	6866	.439	1485	2034	.730	1109	2473	3582	1849	1972	19	604	1257	428	7960	97.1	+6.3
New Jersey	3006	6625	.454	1476	1994	.740	1028	2355	3383	1876	1925	14	665	1270	516	8031	97.9	-4.2
L.A. Lakers	3118	6806	.458	1395	1891	.738	1146	2316	3462	2006	1806	14	588	1334	483	8073	98.5	+4.5
Orlando	3060	6736	.454	1499	2037	.736	1087	2365	3452	1869	1827	19	644	1238	324	8115	99.0	+5.6
Vancouver	3080	6486	.475	1661	2129	.733	1102	2550	3652	1988	1785	9	698	1423	474	8180	99.8	-10.0
Denver	3091	6741	.459	1600	2105	.760	934	2385	3319	1875	1899	18	617	1130	418	8235	100.4	-2.7
Houston	3178	6910	.460	1423	2012	.707	1126	2499	3625	1945	1847	14	670	1224	400	8261	100.7	+1.7
Milwaukee	3084	6421	.480	1590	2193	.725	998	2305	3303	1940	1752	12	648	1212	373	8272	100.9	-5.3
Washington	3061	6650	.460	1822	2378	.766	1105	2370	3475	1690	1891	16	696	1362	390	8321	101.5	+1.1
Sacramento	2987	6461	.462	1950	2596	.751	1056	2312	3368	1805	2006	21	767	1356	505	8385	102.3	-2.7
L.A. Clippers	3090	6471	.478	1824	2444	.746	1034	2362	3396	1658	1860	16	689	1357	401	8448	103.0	-3.6
Golden State	3206	6753	.475	1564	2097	.746	1114	2292	3406	2098	1959	23	698	1375	385	8453	103.1	-1.5
Minnesota	3086	6586	.469	1761	2368	.744	1036	2317	3353	1966	1940	17	725	1343	498	8463	103.2	-5.4
Charlotte	3254	6651	.489	1440	1957	.736	953	2358	3311	2049	1829	14	536	1215	368	8478	103.4	-0.6
Phoenix	3217	6837	.471	1540	2083	.739	1003	2382	3385	2088	2011	28	586	1191	420	8525	104.0	+0.3
Philadelphia	3284	6796	.483	1472	1986	.741	1164	2478	3642	2109	1912	17	723	1288	469	8566	104.5	-10.0
Toronto	3146	6624	.475	1799	2416	.745	1098	2274	3372	1990	1739	10	766	1326	482	8610	105.0	-7.5
Boston	3296	6856	.481	1767	2366	.747	1040	2590	3630	1916	1965	22	667	1314	489	8774	107.0	-3.4
Dallas	3403	6921	.492	1535	2097	.732	1087	2726	3813	1978	1841	15	702	1348	531	8811	107.5	-4.9
Avgs.	3038	6575	.462	1601	2164	.740	1035	2348	3383	1860	1890	18	654	1298	415	8159	99.5	...

HOME/ROAD

	Home	Road	Total		Home	Road	Total
Atlanta	26-15	20-21	46-36	Minnesota	17-24	9-32	26-56
Boston	18-23	15-26	33-49	New Jersey	20-21	10-31	30-52
Charlotte	25-16	16-25	41-41	New York	26-15	21-20	47-35
Chicago	39-2	33-8	72-10	Orlando	37-4	23-18	60-22
Cleveland	26-15	21-20	47-35	Philadelphia	11-30	7-34	18-64
Dallas	16-25	10-31	26-56	Phoenix	25-16	16-25	41-41
Denver	24-17	11-30	35-47	Portland	26-15	18-23	44-38
Detroit	30-11	16-25	46-36	Sacramento	26-15	13-28	39-43
Golden State	23-18	13-28	36-46	San Antonio	33-8	26-15	59-23
Houston	27-14	21-20	48-34	Seattle	38-3	26-15	64-18
Indiana	32-9	20-21	52-30	Toronto	15-26	6-35	21-61
L.A. Clippers	19-22	10-31	29-53	Utah	34-7	21-20	55-27
L.A. Lakers	30-11	23-18	53-29	Vancouver	10-31	5-36	15-67
Miami	26-15	16-25	42-40	Washington	25-16	14-27	39-43
Milwaukee	14-27	11-30	25-57	Totals	718-471	471-718	1189-1189

INDIVIDUAL LEADERS

POINTS

(minimum 70 games or 1,400 points)

	G	FGM	FTM	Pts.	Avg.
Michael Jordan, Chicago	82	916	548	2491	30.4
Hakeem Olajuwon, Houston	72	768	397	1936	26.9
Shaquille O'Neal, Orlando	54	592	249	1434	26.6
Karl Malone, Utah	82	789	512	2106	25.7
David Robinson, San Antonio	82	711	626	2051	25.0
Charles Barkley, Phoenix	71	580	440	1649	23.2
Alonzo Mourning, Miami	70	563	488	1623	23.2
Mitch Richmond, Sacramento	81	611	425	1872	23.1
Patrick Ewing, New York	76	678	351	1711	22.5
Juwan Howard, Washington	81	733	319	1789	22.1

REBOUNDS

(minimum 70 games or 800 rebounds)

	G	Off.	Def.	Tot.	Avg.
Dennis Rodman, Chicago	64	356	596	952	14.9
David Robinson, San Antonio	82	319	681	1000	12.2
Dikembe Mutombo, Denver	74	249	622	871	11.8
Charles Barkley, Phoenix	71	243	578	821	11.6
Shawn Kemp, Seattle	79	276	628	904	11.4
Hakeem Olajuwon, Houston	72	176	608	784	10.9
Patrick Ewing, New York	76	157	649	806	10.6
Alonzo Mourning, Miami	70	218	509	727	10.4
Loy Vaught, L.A. Clippers	80	204	604	808	10.1
Jayson Williams, New Jersey	80	342	461	803	10.0

FIELD GOALS

(minimum 300 made)

	FGM	FGA	Pct.
Gheorge Muresan, Washington	466	798	.584
Chris Gatling, Golden State-Washington	326	567	.575
Shaquille O'Neal, Orlando	592	1033	.573
Anthony Mason, New York	449	798	.563
Shawn Kemp, Seattle	526	937	.561
Dale Davis, Indiana	334	599	.558
Arvydas Sabonis, Portland	394	723	.545
Brian Williams, L.A. Clippers	416	766	.543
Chucky Brown, Houston	300	555	.541
John Stockton, Utah	440	818	.538

STEALS

(minimum 70 games or 125 steals)

	G	No.	Avg.
Gary Payton, Seattle	81	231	2.85
Mookie Blaylock, Atlanta	81	212	2.62
Michael Jordan, Chicago	82	180	2.60
Jason Kidd, Dallas	81	175	2.16
Alvin Robertson, Toronto	77	166	2.16
Anfernee Hardaway, Orlando	82	166	2.02
Eric Murdock, Milwaukee-Vancouver	73	135	1.85
Eddie Jones, L.A. Lakers	70	129	1.84
Hersey Hawkins, Seattle	82	149	1.82
Tom Gugliotta, Minnesota	78	139	1.78

FREE THROWS

(minimum 125 made)

	FTM	FTA	Pct.
Mahmoud Abdul-Rauf, Denver	146	157	.930
Jeff Hornacek, Utah	259	290	.893
Terrell Brandon, Cleveland	338	381	.887
Dana Barros, Boston	130	147	.884
Brent Price, Washington	167	191	.874
Hersey Hawkins, Seattle	247	283	.873
Mitch Richmond, Sacramento	425	491	.866
Reggie Miller, Indiana	430	498	.863
Tim Legler, Washington	132	153	.863
Spud Webb, Atlanta-Minnesota	125	145	.862

BLOCKED SHOTS

(minimum 70 games or 100 blocked shots)

	G	No.	Avg.
Dikembe Mutombo, Denver	74	332	4.49
Shawn Bradley, Philadelphia-New Jersey	79	288	3.65
David Robinson, San Antonio	82	271	3.30
Hakeem Olajuwon, Houston	72	207	2.88
Alonzo Mourning, Miami	70	189	2.70
Elden Campbell, L.A. Lakers	82	212	2.59
Patrick Ewing, New York	76	184	2.42
Gheorge Muresan, Washington	76	172	2.26
Shaquille O'Neal, Orlando	54	115	2.13
Jim McIlvaine, Washington	80	166	2.08

ASSISTS

(minimum 70 games or 400 assists)

	G	No.	Avg.
John Stockton, Utah	82	916	11.2
Jason Kidd, Dallas	81	783	9.7
Avery Johnson, San Antonio	82	789	9.6
Rod Strickland, Portland	67	640	9.6
Damon Stoudamire, Toronto	70	653	9.3
Kevin Johnson, Phoenix	56	517	9.2
Kenny Anderson, New Jersey-Charlotte	69	575	8.3
Tim Hardaway, Golden State-Miami	80	640	8.0
Mark Jackson, Indiana	81	635	7.8
Gary Payton, Seattle	81	608	7.5

3-POINT FIELD GOALS

(minimum 82 made)

	FGM	FGA	Pct.
Tim Legler, Washington	128	245	.522
Steve Kerr, Chicago	122	237	.515
Hubert Davis, New York	127	267	.476
B.J. Armstrong, Golden State	98	207	.473
Jeff Hornacek, Utah	104	223	.466
Brent Price, Washington	139	301	.462
Bobby Phills, Cleveland	93	211	.441
Terry Dehere, L.A. Clippers	139	316	.440
Mitch Richmond, Sacramento	225	515	.437
Allan Houston, Detroit	191	447	.427

ATLANTA HAWKS

	G	Min.	FGM	FGA	Pct.	FTM	FTA	Pct.	Off.	Def.	Tot.	Ast.	PF	Dq.	Stl.	TO	Blk.	Pts.	Avg.	Hi.
Steve Smith 80	80	2856	494	1143	.432	318	385	.826	124	202	326	224	207	1	68	151	17	1446	18.1	32
Christian Laettner† . . . 30	30	977	159	325	.489	107	130	.823	86	150	236	68	119	3	31	75	28	425	14.2	28
Christian Laettner‡ . . . 74	74	2495	442	907	.487	324	396	.818	184	354	538	197	276	7	71	187	71	1217	16.4	29
Mookie Blaylock 81	81	2893	455	1123	.405	127	170	.747	110	222	332	478	151	1	212	188	17	1268	15.7	28
Grant Long 82	82	3008	395	838	.471	257	337	.763	248	540	788	183	233	3	108	157	34	1078	13.1	24
Andrew Lang* 51	51	1815	281	619	.454	95	118	.805	111	223	334	62	178	4	35	94	85	657	12.9	29
Stacey Augmon 77	77	2294	362	738	.491	251	317	.792	137	167	304	137	188	1	106	138	31	976	12.7	24
Ken Norman 34	34	770	127	273	.465	17	48	.354	40	92	132	63	68	0	15	46	16	304	8.9	26
Craig Ehlo 79	79	1758	253	591	.428	81	103	.786	65	191	256	138	138	0	85	104	9	669	8.5	28
Sean Rooks† 16	16	215	32	58	.552	29	43	.674	21	30	51	9	35	0	4	31	14	93	5.8	12
Sean Rooks‡ 65	65	1117	144	285	.505	135	202	.668	81	174	255	47	141	0	23	80	42	424	6.5	19
Alan Henderson 79	79	1416	192	434	.442	119	200	.595	164	192	356	51	217	5	44	87	43	503	6.4	16
Spud Webb* 51	51	817	104	222	.468	74	87	.851	19	41	60	140	68	0	27	51	2	300	5.9	16
Reggie Jordan 24	24	247	36	71	.507	22	38	.579	23	29	52	29	30	0	12	19	7	94	3.9	14
Matt Bullard 46	46	460	66	162	.407	16	20	.800	18	42	60	18	50	0	17	24	11	174	3.8	28
Donnie Boyce 8	8	41	9	23	.391	2	4	.500	5	5	10	3	2	0	3	6	1	24	3.0	8
Howard Nathan 5	5	15	5	9	.556	3	4	.750	0	0	0	2	2	0	3	8	0	13	2.6	6
Todd Mundt* 24	24	118	13	32	.406	5	8	.625	10	15	25	2	23	0	1	3	4	31	1.3	8
Ronnie Grandison* 4	4	19	2	4	.500	0	0	. . .	1	5	6	1	0	0	0	0	0	4	1.0	2
Tim Kempton 3	3	11	0	0	. . .	0	0	. . .	0	2	2	1	5	0	0	1	0	0	0.0	0

3-pt. FG: Atlanta 566-1595 (.355)—Smith 140-423 (.331); Laettner† 0-8 (.000); Laettner‡ 9-39 (.231); Blaylock 231-623 (.371); Long 31-86 (.360); Lang* 0-3 (.000); Augmon 1-4 (.250); Norman 33-84 (.393); Ehlo 82-221 (.371); Rooks† 0-1 (.000); Rooks‡ 1-7 (.143); Henderson 0-3 (.000); Webb* 18-57 (.316); Bullard 26-72 (.361); Boyce 4-8 (.500); Nathan 0-1 (.000); Grandison* 0-1 (.000). Opponents 479-1329 (.360).

BOSTON CELTICS

	G	Min.	FGM	FGA	Pct.	FTM	FTA	Pct.	Off.	Def.	Tot.	Ast.	PF	Dq.	Stl.	TO	Blk.	Pts.	Avg.	Hi.
Dino Radja 53	53	1984	426	852	.500	191	275	.695	113	409	522	83	161	2	48	117	81	1043	19.7	33
Rick Fox 81	81	2588	421	928	.454	196	254	.772	158	292	450	369	290	5	113	216	41	1137	14.0	33
Dana Barros 80	80	2328	379	806	.470	130	147	.884	21	171	192	306	116	1	58	120	3	1038	13.0	27
David Wesley 82	82	2104	338	736	.459	217	288	.753	68	196	264	390	207	0	100	159	11	1009	12.3	37
Todd Day† 71	71	1636	277	746	.371	200	261	.766	62	140	202	102	198	1	77	98	48	849	12.0	41
Todd Day‡ 79	79	1807	299	817	.366	224	287	.780	70	154	224	107	225	2	81	109	51	922	11.7	41
Eric Williams 64	64	1470	241	546	.441	200	298	.671	92	125	217	71	147	1	56	88	11	685	10.7	31
Dee Brown 65	65	1591	246	616	.399	135	158	.854	36	100	136	146	119	0	80	74	12	695	10.7	21
Sherman Douglas* . . . 10	10	234	36	84	.429	25	40	.625	6	17	23	39	16	0	2	29	0	98	9.8	19
Greg Minor 78	78	1761	320	640	.500	99	130	.762	93	164	257	146	161	0	36	78	11	746	9.6	24
Eric Montross 61	61	1432	196	346	.566	50	133	.376	119	233	352	43	181	1	19	83	29	442	7.2	19
Pervis Ellison 69	69	1431	145	295	.492	75	117	.641	151	300	451	62	207	2	39	84	99	365	5.3	23
Junior Burrough 61	61	495	64	170	.376	61	93	.656	45	64	109	15	74	0	15	40	10	189	3.1	13
Thomas Hamilton 11	11	70	9	31	.290	7	18	.389	10	12	22	1	12	0	0	9	9	25	2.3	13
Alton Lister† 57	57	647	47	96	.490	39	62	.629	60	191	251	15	121	1	6	44	39	133	2.3	10
Alton Lister‡ 64	64	735	51	105	.486	41	64	.641	67	213	280	19	136	1	6	48	42	143	2.2	10
Doug Smith 17	17	92	14	39	.359	5	8	.625	12	10	22	4	21	0	3	11	0	33	1.9	6
Todd Mundt† 9	9	33	3	9	.333	0	0	. . .	1	2	3	1	6	0	1	0	1	6	0.7	2
Todd Mundt‡ 33	33	151	16	41	.390	5	8	.625	11	17	28	3	29	0	2	3	5	37	1.1	8
Charles Claxton 3	3	7	1	2	.500	0	2	.000	2	0	2	0	4	0	0	1	1	2	0.7	2
Larry Sykes 1	1	2	0	0	. . .	0	0	. . .	1	1	2	0	0	0	1	0	0	0	0.0	0

3-pt. FG: Boston 539-1453 (.371)—Fox 99-272 (.364); Barros 150-368 (.408); Wesley 116-272 (.426); Day† 95-277 (.343); Day‡ 100-302 (.331); Williams 3-10 (.300); Brown 68-220 (.309); Douglas* 1-7 (.143); Minor 7-27 (.259). Opponents 415-1162 (.357).

CHARLOTTE HORNETS

	G	Min.	FGM	FGA	Pct.	FTM	FTA	Pct.	Off.	Def.	Tot.	Ast.	PF	Dq.	Stl.	TO	Blk.	Pts.	Avg.	Hi.
Glen Rice 79	79	3142	610	1296	.471	319	381	.837	86	292	378	232	217	1	91	163	19	1710	21.6	38
Larry Johnson 81	81	3274	583	1225	.476	427	564	.757	249	434	683	355	173	0	55	182	43	1660	20.5	44
Kenny Anderson† 38	38	1302	206	454	.454	109	150	.727	26	76	102	328	105	1	59	88	6	577	15.2	28
Kenny Anderson‡ 69	69	2344	349	834	.418	260	338	.769	63	140	203	575	178	1	111	146	14	1050	15.2	39
Dell Curry* 82	82	2371	441	974	.453	146	171	.854	68	196	264	176	173	2	108	130	25	1192	14.5	27
Scott Burrell 20	20	693	92	206	.447	42	56	.750	26	72	98	47	76	2	27	43	13	263	13.2	26
Kendall Gill* 36	36	1265	179	372	.481	89	117	.761	56	133	189	225	101	2	42	110	22	464	12.9	23
Matt Geiger 77	77	2399	357	666	.536	149	205	.727	201	448	649	60	290	11	46	137	63	866	11.2	28
Khalid Reeves* 20	20	418	54	118	.458	43	51	.843	11	29	40	72	46	0	16	30	1	162	8.1	19
Anthony Goldwire 42	42	621	76	189	.402	46	60	.767	8	35	43	112	79	0	16	63	0	231	5.5	20
Michael Adams 21	21	329	37	83	.446	26	35	.743	5	17	22	67	25	0	21	25	4	114	5.4	14
Darrin Hancock 63	63	838	112	214	.523	47	73	.644	40	58	98	47	94	2	28	56	5	272	4.3	16
George Zidek 71	71	888	105	248	.423	71	93	.763	69	114	183	16	170	2	9	38	7	281	4.0	21
Robert Parish 74	74	1086	120	241	.498	50	71	.704	89	214	303	29	80	0	21	50	54	290	3.9	16
Pete Myers* 32	32	453	29	87	.333	31	46	.674	14	53	67	48	57	0	20	25	6	92	2.9	9
Pete Myers‡ 71	71	1092	91	247	.368	80	122	.656	35	105	140	145	132	1	34	81	17	276	3.9	20
Greg Sutton* 18	18	190	20	50	.400	15	19	.789	4	11	15	39	36	0	8	17	0	62	3.4	12

	G	Min.	FGM	FGA	Pct.	FTM	FTA	Pct.	REBOUNDS Off.	Def.	Tot.	Ast.	PF	Dq.	Stl.	TO	Blk.	SCORING Pts.	Avg.	Hi.
Rafael Addison	53	516	77	165	.467	17	22	.773	25	65	90	30	74	0	9	27	9	171	3.2	16
Muggsy Bogues	6	77	6	16	.375	2	2	1.000	6	1	7	19	4	0	2	6	0	14	2.3	4
Gerald Glass†	5	15	2	5	.400	1	1	1.000	1	1	2	0	5	0	1	0	0	5	1.0	3
Gerald Glass‡	15	71	12	33	.364	1	1	1.000	6	2	8	4	10	0	3	0	1	26	1.7	5
Donald Hodge†	2	2	0	0	...	0	0	...	0	1	1	0	0	0	0	0	0	0	0.0	0
Donald Hodge‡	15	115	9	24	.375	0	0	...	9	14	23	4	26	0	1	2	8	18	1.2	8
Corey Beck	5	33	2	8	.250	1	2	.500	3	4	7	5	8	0	1	4	0	5	1.0	5
Joe Wolf*	1	18	0	1	.000	0	0	...	0	2	2	0	2	2	0	0	0	0	0.0	0

3-pt. FG: Charlotte 584-1520 (.384)—Rice 171-403 (.424); Johnson 67-183 (.366); Anderson† 56-157 (.357); Anderson‡ 92-256 (.359); Curry* 164-406 (.404); Burrell 37-98 (.378); Gill* 17-54 (.315); Geiger 3-8 (.375); Reeves* 11-36 (.306); Goldwire 33-83 (.398); Adams 14-41 (.341); Hancock 1-3 (.333); Myers† 3-16 (.188); Myers‡ 14-58 (.241); Sutton* 7-21 (.333); Addison 0-9 (.000); Bogues 0-1 (.000); Glass† 0-1 (.000); Glass‡ 1-6 (.167). Opponents 530-1340 (.396).

CHICAGO BULLS

	G	Min.	FGM	FGA	Pct.	FTM	FTA	Pct.	REBOUNDS Off.	Def.	Tot.	Ast.	PF	Dq.	Stl.	TO	Blk.	SCORING Pts.	Avg.	Hi.
Michael Jordan	82	3090	916	1850	.495	548	657	.834	148	395	543	352	195	0	180	197	42	2491	30.4	53
Scottie Pippen	77	2825	563	1216	.463	220	324	.679	152	344	496	452	198	0	133	207	57	1496	19.4	40
Toni Kukoc	81	2103	386	787	.490	206	267	.772	115	208	323	287	150	0	64	114	28	1065	13.1	34
Luc Longley	62	1641	242	502	.482	80	103	.777	104	214	318	119	223	4	22	114	84	564	9.1	21
Steve Kerr	82	1919	244	482	.506	78	84	.929	25	85	110	192	109	0	63	42	2	688	8.4	19
Ron Harper	80	1886	234	501	.467	98	139	.705	74	139	213	208	137	0	105	73	32	594	7.4	22
Dennis Rodman	64	2088	146	304	.480	56	106	.528	356	596	952	160	196	1	36	138	27	351	5.5	12
Bill Wennington	71	1065	169	343	.493	37	43	.860	58	116	174	46	171	1	21	37	16	376	5.3	18
Jack Haley	1	7	2	6	.333	1	2	.500	1	1	2	0	2	0	0	1	0	5	5.0	5
John Salley†	17	191	12	35	.343	12	20	.600	20	23	43	15	38	0	8	16	15	36	2.1	12
John Salley‡	42	673	63	140	.450	59	85	.694	46	94	140	54	110	3	19	55	27	185	4.4	15
Jud Buechler	74	740	112	242	.463	14	22	.636	45	66	111	56	70	0	34	39	7	278	3.8	14
Dickey Simpkins	60	685	77	160	.481	61	97	.629	66	90	156	38	78	0	9	56	8	216	3.6	12
James Edwards	28	274	41	110	.373	16	26	.615	15	25	40	11	61	1	1	21	8	98	3.5	12
Jason Caffey	57	545	71	162	.438	40	68	.588	51	60	111	24	91	3	12	48	7	182	3.2	13
Randy Brown	68	671	78	192	.406	28	46	.609	17	49	66	73	88	0	57	31	12	185	2.7	16

3-pt. FG: Chicago 544-1349 (.403)—Jordan 111-260 (.427); Pippen 150-401 (.374); Kukoc 87-216 (.403); Kerr 122-237 (.515); Harper 28-104 (.269); Rodman 3-27 (.111); Wennington 1-1 (1.000); Buechler 40-90 (.444); Simpkins 1-1 (1.000); Caffey 0-1 (.000); Brown 1-11 (.091). Opponents 437-1249 (.350).

CLEVELAND CAVALIERS

	G	Min.	FGM	FGA	Pct.	FTM	FTA	Pct.	REBOUNDS Off.	Def.	Tot.	Ast.	PF	Dq.	Stl.	TO	Blk.	SCORING Pts.	Avg.	Hi.
Terrell Brandon	75	2570	510	1096	.465	338	381	.887	47	201	248	487	146	1	132	142	33	1449	19.3	32
Chris Mills	80	3060	454	971	.468	218	263	.829	112	331	443	188	241	1	73	121	52	1205	15.1	30
Bobby Phills	72	2530	386	826	.467	186	240	.775	62	199	261	271	192	3	102	126	27	1051	14.6	43
Danny Ferry	82	2680	422	919	.459	103	134	.769	71	238	309	191	233	3	57	122	37	1090	13.3	32
Dan Majerle	82	2367	303	748	.405	120	169	.710	70	235	305	214	131	0	81	93	34	872	10.6	25
Tyrone Hill	44	929	130	254	.512	81	135	.600	94	150	244	33	144	3	31	64	20	341	7.8	19
Michael Cage	82	2631	220	396	.556	50	92	.543	288	441	729	53	215	0	87	54	79	490	6.0	20
Bob Sura	79	1150	148	360	.411	99	141	.702	34	101	135	233	126	1	56	115	21	422	5.3	19
Harold Miner	19	136	23	52	.442	13	13	1.000	4	8	12	8	23	1	0	14	0	61	3.2	13
John Crotty	58	617	51	114	.447	62	72	.861	20	34	54	102	60	0	22	51	6	172	3.0	19
Antonio Lang	41	367	41	77	.532	34	47	.723	17	36	53	12	61	0	14	24	12	116	2.8	14
John Amaechi	28	357	29	70	.414	19	33	.576	13	39	52	9	49	1	6	34	11	77	2.8	11
Donny Marshall	34	208	24	68	.353	22	35	.629	9	17	26	7	26	0	8	7	2	77	2.3	9
Joe Courtney	23	200	15	35	.429	8	18	.444	24	25	49	9	35	0	5	17	6	38	1.7	5
Darryl Johnson	11	28	5	12	.417	2	2	1.000	2	0	2	1	3	0	0	1	0	12	1.1	2

3-pt. FG: Cleveland 596-1582 (.377)—Brandon 91-235 (.387); Mills 79-210 (.376); Phills 93-211 (.441); Ferry 143-363 (.394); Majerle 146-414 (.353); Cage 0-1 (.000); Sura 27-78 (.346); Miner 2-10 (.200); Crotty 8-27 (.296); Lang 0-2 (.000); Marshall 7-30 (.233); Johnson 0-1 (.000). Opponents 513-1322 (.388).

DALLAS MAVERICKS

	G	Min.	FGM	FGA	Pct.	FTM	FTA	Pct.	REBOUNDS Off.	Def.	Tot.	Ast.	PF	Dq.	Stl.	TO	Blk.	SCORING Pts.	Avg.	Hi.
Jamal Mashburn	18	669	145	383	.379	97	133	.729	37	60	97	50	39	0	14	55	3	422	23.4	37
Jim Jackson	82	2820	569	1308	.435	345	418	.825	173	237	410	235	165	0	47	191	22	1604	19.6	38
George McCloud	79	2846	530	1281	.414	180	224	.804	116	263	379	212	212	1	113	166	38	1497	18.9	37
Jason Kidd	81	3034	493	1293	.381	229	331	.692	203	350	553	783	155	0	175	328	26	1348	16.6	37
Tony Dumas	67	1284	274	655	.418	154	257	.599	58	57	115	99	128	0	42	77	13	776	11.6	39
Popeye Jones	68	2322	327	733	.446	102	133	.767	260	477	737	132	262	8	54	109	27	770	11.3	24
Lucious Harris	61	1016	183	397	.461	68	87	.782	41	81	122	79	56	0	35	46	3	481	7.9	19
Scott Brooks	69	716	134	293	.457	59	69	.855	11	30	41	100	53	0	42	43	3	352	5.1	18
Loren Meyer	72	1266	145	330	.439	70	102	.686	114	205	319	57	224	6	20	67	32	363	5.0	14
Terry Davis	28	501	55	108	.509	27	47	.574	43	74	117	21	66	2	10	25	4	137	4.9	15
Cherokee Parks	64	869	101	247	.409	41	62	.661	66	150	216	29	100	0	25	31	32	250	3.9	25
David Wood†	37	642	67	154	.435	29	40	.725	42	91	133	27	118	5	16	19	9	182	4.9	19
David Wood‡	62	772	75	174	.431	38	50	.760	51	103	154	34	150	5	19	24	10	208	3.4	19
Lorenzo Williams	65	1806	87	214	.407	24	70	.343	234	287	521	85	226	9	48	78	122	198	3.0	10
Reggie Slater†	3	26	5	11	.455	1	2	.500	1	4	5	0	6	0	0	3	0	11	3.7	11
Reggie Slater‡	11	72	14	27	.519	3	7	.429	4	11	15	2	11	0	2	9	3	31	2.8	11
Donald Hodge*	13	113	9	24	.375	0	0	...	9	13	22	4	26	0	1	2	8	18	1.4	8

DENVER NUGGETS

	G	Min.	FGM	FGA	Pct.	FTM	FTA	Pct.	REBOUNDS Off.	Def.	Tot.	Ast.	PF	Dq.	Stl.	TO	Blk.	SCORING Pts.	Avg.	Hi.
Mahmoud Abdul-Rauf..	57	2029	414	955	.434	146	157	.930	26	112	138	389	117	0	64	115	3	1095	19.2	51
Dale Ellis..........	81	2626	459	959	.479	136	179	.760	88	227	315	139	191	1	57	98	7	1204	14.9	33
Bryant Stith	82	2810	379	911	.416	320	379	.844	125	275	400	241	187	3	114	157	16	1119	13.6	27
Antonio McDyess	76	2280	427	881	.485	166	243	.683	229	343	572	75	250	4	54	154	114	1020	13.4	32
Don MacLean	56	1107	233	547	.426	145	198	.732	62	143	205	89	105	1	21	68	5	625	11.2	38
Dikembe Mutombo ...	74	2713	284	569	.499	246	354	.695	249	622	871	108	258	4	38	150	332	814	11.0	22
LaPhonso Ellis	45	1269	189	432	.438	89	148	.601	93	229	322	74	163	3	36	83	33	471	10.5	22
Jalen Rose	80	2134	290	604	.480	191	277	.690	46	214	260	495	229	3	53	234	39	803	10.0	19
Tom Hammonds	71	1045	127	268	.474	88	115	.765	85	138	223	23	137	0	23	48	13	342	4.8	26
Reggie Williams	52	817	94	254	.370	33	39	.846	25	97	122	74	137	1	34	51	21	241	4.6	27
Reggie Slater*	4	26	6	11	.545	2	5	.400	3	4	7	2	4	0	1	3	1	14	3.5	6
Doug Overton	55	607	67	178	.376	40	55	.727	8	55	63	106	49	0	13	40	5	182	3.3	16
Matt Fish†	16	117	15	26	.577	10	18	.556	7	11	18	7	16	0	3	3	6	40	2.5	6
Matt Fish‡	18	134	21	36	.583	10	19	.526	10	11	21	8	19	0	3	3	7	52	2.9	10
Greg Grant†	10	109	6	23	.261	0	0	...	3	4	7	14	7	0	2	5	0	14	1.4	5
Greg Grant‡	31	527	35	99	.354	5	6	.833	7	27	34	97	43	0	22	30	2	83	2.7	14
Randy Woods........	8	72	6	22	.273	2	2	1.000	3	3	6	12	13	0	6	5	1	19	2.4	5
Rastko Cvetkovic.....	14	48	5	16	.313	0	4	.000	4	7	11	3	11	0	2	3	1	10	0.7	2
Elmore Spencer*	6	21	0	1	.000	0	0	...	1	3	4	0	8	1	0	3	0	0	0.0	0

DETROIT PISTONS

	G	Min.	FGM	FGA	Pct.	FTM	FTA	Pct.	REBOUNDS Off.	Def.	Tot.	Ast.	PF	Dq.	Stl.	TO	Blk.	SCORING Pts.	Avg.	Hi.
Grant Hill	80	3260	564	1221	.462	485	646	.751	127	656	783	548	242	1	100	263	48	1618	20.2	35
Allan Houston.......	82	3072	564	1244	.453	298	362	.823	54	246	300	250	233	1	61	233	16	1617	19.7	38
Otis Thorpe........	82	2841	452	853	.530	257	362	.710	211	477	688	158	300	7	53	195	39	1161	14.2	27
Joe Dumars	67	2193	255	598	.426	162	197	.822	28	110	138	265	106	0	43	97	3	793	11.8	41
Terry Mills	82	1656	283	675	.419	121	157	.771	108	244	352	98	197	0	42	98	20	769	9.4	24
Lindsey Hunter	80	2138	239	628	.381	84	120	.700	44	150	194	188	185	0	84	80	18	679	8.5	21
Michael Curry†	41	749	70	151	.464	41	58	.707	25	55	80	26	89	1	23	23	2	201	4.9	17
Michael Curry‡	46	783	73	161	.453	45	62	.726	27	58	85	27	92	1	24	24	2	211	4.6	17
Theo Ratliff........	75	1305	128	230	.557	85	120	.708	110	187	297	13	144	1	16	56	116	341	4.5	21
Don Reid	69	997	106	187	.567	51	77	.662	78	125	203	11	199	2	47	41	40	263	3.8	12
Mark Macon	23	287	29	67	.433	9	11	.818	10	12	22	16	34	0	15	9	0	74	3.2	12
Mark West	47	682	61	126	.484	28	45	.622	49	84	133	6	135	2	6	35	37	150	3.2	15
Steve Bardo	9	123	9	23	.391	4	6	.667	2	20	22	15	17	1	4	5	1	22	2.4	8
Eric Leckner	18	155	18	29	.621	8	13	.615	8	26	34	1	30	0	2	11	4	44	2.4	13
Lou Roe	49	372	32	90	.356	24	32	.750	30	48	78	15	42	0	10	17	8	90	1.8	14

GOLDEN STATE WARRIORS

	G	Min.	FGM	FGA	Pct.	FTM	FTA	Pct.	REBOUNDS Off.	Def.	Tot.	Ast.	PF	Dq.	Stl.	TO	Blk.	SCORING Pts.	Avg.	Hi.
Latrell Sprewell......	78	3064	515	1202	.428	352	446	.789	124	256	380	328	150	1	127	222	45	1473	18.9	32
Joe Smith..........	82	2821	469	1024	.458	303	392	.773	300	417	717	79	224	5	85	138	134	1251	15.3	30
Tim Hardaway*......	52	1487	255	606	.421	140	182	.769	22	109	131	360	131	3	74	125	11	735	14.1	31
Chris Mullin	55	1617	269	539	.499	137	160	.856	44	115	159	194	127	0	75	122	32	734	13.3	26
B.J. Armstrong	82	2262	340	727	.468	234	279	.839	22	162	184	401	147	0	68	128	6	1012	12.3	35
Rony Seikaly........	64	1813	285	568	.502	204	282	.723	166	333	499	71	219	5	40	180	69	776	12.1	31
Bimbo Coles†	29	733	87	218	.399	29	38	.763	11	48	59	126	78	2	31	48	5	228	7.9	18
Bimbo Coles‡	81	2615	318	777	.409	168	211	.796	49	211	260	422	253	5	94	171	17	892	11.0	26
Kevin Willis†	28	778	130	300	.433	54	77	.701	74	144	218	19	95	0	13	62	16	315	11.3	24
Kevin Willis‡	75	2135	325	712	.456	143	202	.708	208	430	638	53	253	4	32	161	41	794	10.6	25
Chris Gatling*	47	862	171	308	.555	84	132	.636	78	164	242	26	135	0	19	60	29	426	9.1	21
Jerome Kersey	76	1620	205	500	.410	97	147	.660	154	209	363	114	205	2	91	75	45	510	6.7	16
Donyell Marshall....	62	934	125	314	.398	64	83	.771	65	148	213	49	83	0	22	48	31	342	5.5	24
Jon Barry	68	712	91	185	.492	31	37	.838	17	46	63	85	51	1	33	42	11	257	3.8	19
Clifford Rozier.......	59	723	79	135	.585	26	55	.473	71	100	171	22	135	0	19	40	30	184	3.1	14
Andrew DeClercq	22	203	24	50	.480	11	19	.579	18	21	39	9	30	0	7	4	5	59	2.7	10
Robert Churchwell ...	4	20	3	8	.375	0	0	...	0	3	3	1	1	0	0	2	0	6	1.5	6
Geert Hammink†.....	3	10	1	2	.500	2	3	.667	1	1	0	1	0	0	0	0	0	4	1.3	4
Geert Hammink‡.....	6	17	2	4	.500	4	7	.571	2	2	4	0	2	0	0	2	0	8	1.3	4
David Wood*........	21	96	7	14	.500	7	8	.875	7	9	16	5	23	0	2	3	1	22	1.0	5

HOUSTON ROCKETS

	G	Min.	FGM	FGA	Pct.	FTM	FTA	Pct.	REBOUNDS Off.	Def.	Tot.	Ast.	PF	Dq.	Stl.	TO	Blk.	SCORING Pts.	Avg.	Hi.
Hakeem Olajuwon	72	2797	768	1494	.514	397	548	.724	176	608	784	257	242	0	113	247	207	1936	26.9	51
Clyde Drexler	52	1997	331	764	.433	265	338	.784	97	276	373	302	153	0	105	134	24	1005	19.3	41
Sam Cassell	61	1682	289	658	.439	235	285	.825	51	137	188	278	166	2	53	157	4	886	14.5	33
Robert Horry	71	2634	300	732	.410	111	143	.776	97	315	412	281	197	3	116	160	109	853	12.0	40
Tracy Moore	8	190	30	76	.395	18	19	.947	10	12	22	6	16	0	2	8	0	91	11.4	18
Mario Elie	45	1385	180	357	.504	98	115	.852	47	108	155	138	93	0	45	59	11	499	11.1	20
Sam Mack	31	868	121	287	.422	39	46	.848	18	80	98	79	75	0	22	28	9	335	10.8	38
Mark Bryant	71	1587	242	446	.543	127	177	.718	131	220	351	52	234	4	31	85	19	611	8.6	30
Chucky Brown.	82	2019	300	555	.541	104	150	.693	134	307	441	89	163	0	47	94	38	705	8.6	18
Kenny Smith	68	1617	201	464	.433	87	106	.821	21	75	96	245	116	1	47	100	3	580	8.5	22
Eldridge Recasner. . . .	63	1275	149	359	.415	57	66	.864	31	113	144	170	111	1	23	61	5	436	6.9	21
Henry James	7	58	10	24	.417	5	5	1.000	3	3	6	2	13	0	0	4	0	30	4.3	16
Melvin Booker.	11	131	16	50	.320	9	11	.818	1	8	9	21	18	0	5	12	1	44	4.0	9
Tim Breaux	54	570	59	161	.366	28	45	.622	22	38	60	24	42	0	11	30	8	161	3.0	17
Pete Chilcutt	74	651	73	179	.408	17	26	.654	51	105	156	26	65	0	19	22	14	200	2.7	15
Alvin Heggs	4	14	3	5	.600	2	3	.667	1	1	2	0	0	0	0	0	0	8	2.0	7
Jaren Jackson	4	33	0	8	.000	8	10	.800	0	3	3	0	5	0	1	0	0	8	2.0	7
Charles Jones	46	297	6	19	.316	4	13	.308	28	46	74	12	44	0	5	3	24	16	0.3	4

3-pt. FG: Houston 637-1761 (.362)—Olajuwon 3-14 (.214); Drexler 78-235 (.332); Cassell 73-210 (.348); Horry 142-388 (.366); Moore 13-30 (.433); Elie 41-127 (.323); Mack 54-135 (.400); Bryant 0-2 (.000); Brown 1-8 (.125); Smith 91-238 (.382); Recasner 81-191 (.424); James 5-15 (.333); Booker 3-19 (.158); Breaux 15-46 (.326); Chilcutt 37-98 (.378); Jackson 0-5 (.000). Opponents 482-1344 (.359).

INDIANA PACERS

	G	Min.	FGM	FGA	Pct.	FTM	FTA	Pct.	REBOUNDS Off.	Def.	Tot.	Ast.	PF	Dq.	Stl.	TO	Blk.	SCORING Pts.	Avg.	Hi.
Reggie Miller	76	2621	504	1066	.473	430	498	.863	38	176	214	253	175	0	77	189	13	1606	21.1	40
Rik Smits	63	1901	466	894	.521	231	293	.788	119	314	433	110	226	5	21	160	45	1164	18.5	44
Derrick McKey	75	2440	346	712	.486	170	221	.769	123	238	361	262	246	4	83	143	44	879	11.7	25
Dale Davis	78	2617	334	599	.558	135	289	.467	252	457	709	76	238	0	56	119	112	803	10.3	21
Mark Jackson	81	2643	296	626	.473	150	191	.785	66	241	307	635	153	0	100	201	5	806	10.0	21
Ricky Pierce	76	1404	264	590	.447	174	205	.849	40	96	136	101	188	1	57	93	6	737	9.7	26
Antonio Davis	82	2092	236	482	.490	246	345	.713	188	313	501	43	248	6	33	87	66	719	8.8	26
Eddie Johnson	62	1002	180	436	.413	70	79	.886	45	108	153	69	104	1	20	56	4	475	7.7	26
Travis Best	59	571	69	163	.423	75	90	.833	11	33	44	97	80	0	20	63	3	221	3.7	13
Duane Ferrell	54	591	80	166	.482	42	57	.737	32	61	93	30	83	0	23	34	3	202	3.7	14
Haywoode Workman . .	77	1164	101	259	.390	54	73	.740	27	97	124	213	152	0	65	93	4	279	3.6	14
Dwayne Schintzius . . .	33	297	49	110	.445	13	21	.619	23	55	78	14	53	0	9	19	12	111	3.4	17
Adrian Caldwell	51	327	46	83	.554	18	36	.500	42	68	110	6	73	0	9	35	5	110	2.2	11
Fred Hoiberg.	15	85	8	19	.421	15	18	.833	4	5	9	8	12	0	6	7	1	32	2.1	8

3-pt. FG: Indiana 363-973 (.373)—Miller 168-410 (.410); Smits 1-5 (.200); McKey 17-68 (.250); Jackson 64-149 (.430); Pierce 35-104 (.337); A. Davis 1-2 (.500); Johnson 45-128 (.352); Best 8-25 (.320); Ferrell 0-8 (.000); Workman 23-71 (.324); Hoiberg 1-3 (.333). Opponents 493-1368 (.360).

LOS ANGELES CLIPPERS

	G	Min.	FGM	FGA	Pct.	FTM	FTA	Pct.	REBOUNDS Off.	Def.	Tot.	Ast.	PF	Dq.	Stl.	TO	Blk.	SCORING Pts.	Avg.	Hi.
Loy Vaught	80	2966	571	1087	.525	149	205	.727	204	604	808	112	241	4	87	158	40	1298	16.2	28
Brian Williams.	65	2157	416	766	.543	196	267	.734	149	343	492	122	226	5	70	190	55	1029	15.8	35
Terry Dehere	82	2018	315	686	.459	247	327	.755	41	102	143	350	239	2	54	191	16	1016	12.4	31
Pooh Richardson	63	2013	281	664	.423	78	105	.743	35	123	158	340	134	0	77	95	13	734	11.7	31
Rodney Rogers.	67	1950	306	641	.477	113	180	.628	113	173	286	167	216	2	75	144	35	774	11.6	25
Malik Sealy.	62	1601	272	655	.415	147	184	.799	76	164	240	116	150	2	84	113	28	712	11.5	29
Brent Barry	79	1898	283	597	.474	111	137	.810	38	130	168	230	196	2	95	120	22	800	10.1	30
Lamond Murray	77	1816	257	575	.447	99	132	.750	89	157	246	84	151	0	61	108	25	650	8.4	22
Stanley Roberts	51	795	141	304	.464	74	133	.556	42	120	162	41	153	3	15	48	39	356	7.0	25
Eric Piatkowski	65	784	98	242	.405	67	82	.817	40	63	103	48	83	0	24	45	10	301	4.6	16
Antonio Harvey†	37	411	44	129	.341	18	40	.450	42	64	106	6	38	0	13	26	26	106	2.9	13
Antonio Harvey‡	55	821	83	224	.371	38	83	.458	69	131	200	15	76	0	27	44	47	204	3.7	13
Charles Outlaw	80	985	107	186	.575	72	162	.444	87	113	200	50	127	0	44	45	91	286	3.6	14
Keith Tower	34	305	32	72	.444	18	26	.692	22	29	51	5	50	1	4	16	11	82	2.4	19
Logan Vander Velden .	15	31	3	14	.214	3	4	.750	1	5	6	1	4	0	0	0	0	9	0.6	2

3-pt. FG: L.A. Clippers 509-1374 (.370)—Vaught 7-19 (.368); Williams 1-6 (.167); Dehere 139-316 (.440); Richardson 94-245 (.384); Rogers 49-153 (.320); Sealy 21-100 (.210); Barry 123-296 (.416); Murray 37-116 (.319); Piatkowski 38-114 (.333); Harvey‡ 0-2 (.000); Outlaw 0-3 (.000); Tower 0-1 (.000); Vander Velden 0-5 (.000). Opponents 444-1195 (.372).

LOS ANGELES LAKERS

	G	Min.	FGM	FGA	Pct.	FTM	FTA	Pct.	REBOUNDS Off.	Def.	Tot.	Ast.	PF	Dq.	Stl.	TO	Blk.	SCORING Pts.	Avg.	Hi.
Cedric Ceballos	78	2628	638	1203	.530	329	409	.804	215	321	536	119	144	0	94	167	22	1656	21.2	38
Nick Van Exel	74	2513	396	950	.417	163	204	.799	29	152	181	509	115	0	70	156	10	1099	14.9	30
Magic Johnson	32	958	137	294	.466	172	201	.856	40	143	183	220	48	0	26	103	13	468	14.6	30
Elden Campbell	82	2699	447	888	.503	249	349	.713	162	461	623	181	300	4	88	137	212	1143	13.9	29
Vlade Divac.	79	2470	414	807	.513	189	295	.641	198	481	679	261	274	5	76	199	131	1020	12.9	29
Eddie Jones	70	2184	337	685	.492	136	184	.739	45	188	233	246	162	0	129	99	45	893	12.8	27

	G	Min.	FGM	FGA	Pct.	FTM	FTA	Pct.	REBOUNDS Off.	Def.	Tot.	Ast.	PF	Dq.	Stl.	TO	Blk.	SCORING Pts.	Avg.	Hi.
Anthony Peeler	73	1608	272	602	.452	61	86	.709	45	92	137	118	139	0	59	56	10	710	9.7	25
Sedale Threatt	82	1687	241	526	.458	54	71	.761	20	75	95	269	178	0	68	74	11	596	7.3	27
George Lynch	76	1012	117	272	.430	53	80	.663	82	127	209	51	106	0	47	40	10	291	3.8	14
Fred Roberts	33	317	48	97	.495	22	28	.786	18	29	47	26	24	0	16	24	4	122	3.7	19
Derek Strong	63	746	72	169	.426	69	85	.812	60	118	178	32	80	1	18	20	12	214	3.4	16
Corie Blount	57	715	79	167	.473	25	44	.568	69	101	170	42	109	2	25	47	35	183	3.2	11
Anthony Miller	27	123	15	35	.429	6	10	.600	11	14	25	4	19	0	4	8	1	36	1.3	6
Frankie King	6	20	3	11	.273	1	3	.333	1	1	2	2	4	0	2	2	0	7	1.2	3

3-pt. FG: L.A. Lakers 477-1359 (.351)—Ceballos 51-184 (.277); Van Exel 144-403 (.357); Johnson 22-58 (.379); Campbell 0-5 (.000); Divac 3-18 (.167); Jones 83-227 (.366); Peeler 105-254 (.413); Threatt 60-169 (.355); Lynch 4-13 (.308); Roberts 4-14 (.286); Strong 1-9 (.111); Blount 0-2 (.000); Miller 0-2 (.000); King 0-1 (.000). Opponents 442-1203 (.367).

MIAMI HEAT

	G	Min.	FGM	FGA	Pct.	FTM	FTA	Pct.	REBOUNDS Off.	Def.	Tot.	Ast.	PF	Dq.	Stl.	TO	Blk.	SCORING Pts.	Avg.	Hi.
Alonzo Mourning	70	2671	563	1076	.523	488	712	.685	218	509	727	159	245	5	70	262	189	1623	23.2	50
Tim Hardaway†	28	1047	164	386	.425	101	123	.821	13	85	98	280	70	0	58	110	6	482	17.2	29
Tim Hardaway‡	28	2534	419	992	.422	241	305	.790	35	194	229	640	201	3	132	235	17	1217	15.2	31
Billy Owens*	40	1388	239	473	.505	112	177	.633	94	192	286	134	132	1	30	113	22	590	14.8	34
Rex Chapman	56	1865	289	679	.426	83	113	.735	22	123	145	166	117	0	45	79	10	786	14.0	39
Walt Williams†	28	788	124	268	.463	33	60	.550	37	75	112	65	87	0	32	48	16	337	12.0	27
Walt Williams‡	73	2169	359	808	.444	163	232	.703	99	220	319	230	238	0	85	151	58	995	13.6	29
Predrag Danilovic	19	542	83	184	.451	55	72	.764	12	34	46	47	49	0	15	37	3	255	13.4	30
Bimbo Coles*	52	1882	231	559	.413	139	173	.803	38	163	201	296	175	3	63	123	12	664	12.8	26
Chris Gatling†	24	565	155	259	.598	55	75	.733	51	124	175	17	82	0	17	35	11	365	15.2	24
Chris Gatling‡	71	1427	326	567	.575	139	207	.671	129	288	417	43	217	0	36	95	40	791	11.1	24
Kevin Willis*	47	1357	195	412	.473	89	125	.712	134	286	420	34	158	4	19	99	25	479	10.2	25
Kurt Thomas	74	1655	274	547	.501	118	178	.663	122	317	439	46	271	7	47	98	36	666	9.0	29
Kevin Gamble*	44	1033	117	297	.394	33	38	.868	14	72	86	82	119	2	31	32	5	305	6.9	37
Keith Askins	75	1897	157	391	.402	45	57	.789	113	211	324	121	271	6	48	82	61	458	6.1	21
Voshon Lenard	30	323	53	141	.376	34	43	.791	12	40	52	31	31	0	6	23	1	176	5.9	20
Tyrone Corbin†	22	354	38	92	.413	23	28	.821	26	39	65	23	51	0	16	17	3	101	4.6	13
Tyrone Corbin‡	71	1284	155	351	.442	100	120	.833	81	163	244	84	147	1	63	67	20	413	5.8	19
Jeff Malone†	7	103	13	33	.394	5	6	.833	0	8	8	7	6	0	3	3	0	31	4.4	10
Jeff Malone‡	32	510	76	193	.394	29	32	.906	8	32	40	26	25	0	16	22	0	186	5.8	21
Tony Smith†	25	410	46	101	.455	4	9	.444	6	33	39	60	46	1	16	26	5	109	4.4	16
Tony Smith‡	59	938	116	274	.423	28	46	.609	30	65	95	154	106	2	37	66	10	298	5.1	17
Pete Myers*	39	639	62	160	.388	49	76	.645	21	52	73	97	75	1	14	56	11	184	4.7	20
Danny Schayes	32	399	32	94	.340	37	46	.804	29	60	89	9	60	0	11	23	16	101	3.2	17
Terrence Rencher*	34	397	32	99	.323	30	43	.698	9	33	42	54	36	0	16	41	1	103	3.0	8
Stacey King	15	156	17	36	.472	4	8	.500	9	14	23	2	39	2	7	18	2	38	2.5	8
Ronnie Grandison*	18	235	13	39	.333	13	19	.684	14	22	36	10	27	0	8	11	1	43	2.4	8
LeRon Ellis	12	74	5	22	.227	3	6	.500	5	3	8	4	11	0	2	3	3	13	1.1	4

3-pt. FG: Miami 552-1458 (.379)—Mourning 9-30 (.300); Hardaway† 52-147 (.361); Hardaway‡ 138-379 (.364); Owens* 0-6 (.000); Chapman 125-337 (.371); Williams† 56-123 (.455); Williams‡ 114-293 (.389); Danilovic 34-78 (.436); Coles* 63-172 (.366); Gatling‡ 0-1 (.000); Willis* 0-5 (.000); Thomas 0-2 (.000); Gamble* 38-91 (.418); Askins 99-237 (.418); Lenard 36-101 (.356); Corbin† 2-6 (.333); Corbin‡ 3-18 (.167); Malone‡ 5-16 (.313); Smith† 13-39 (.333); Smith‡ 38-116 (.328); Myers* 11-42 (.262); Rencher* 9-29 (.310); Grandison* 4-13 (.308). Opponents 446-1237 (.361).

MILWAUKEE BUCKS

	G	Min.	FGM	FGA	Pct.	FTM	FTA	Pct.	REBOUNDS Off.	Def.	Tot.	Ast.	PF	Dq.	Stl.	TO	Blk.	SCORING Pts.	Avg.	Hi.
Vin Baker	82	3319	699	1429	.489	321	479	.670	263	545	808	212	272	3	68	216	91	1729	21.1	41
Glenn Robinson	82	3249	627	1382	.454	316	389	.812	136	368	504	293	236	2	95	282	42	1660	20.2	39
Sherman Douglas†	69	2101	309	601	.514	135	179	.754	49	108	157	397	147	0	61	165	5	792	11.5	26
Sherman Douglas‡	79	2335	345	685	.504	160	219	.731	55	125	180	436	163	0	63	194	5	890	11.3	26
Johnny Newman	82	2690	321	649	.495	186	232	.802	66	134	200	154	257	4	90	108	15	889	10.8	27
Todd Day*	8	171	22	71	.310	24	26	.923	8	14	22	5	27	1	4	11	3	73	9.1	22
Benoit Benjamin†	70	1492	223	429	.520	101	138	.732	110	326	436	48	184	0	35	110	70	547	7.8	21
Benoit Benjamin‡	83	1896	294	590	.498	140	194	.722	141	398	539	64	224	1	45	144	85	728	8.8	29
Terry Cummings	81	1777	270	584	.462	104	160	.650	162	283	445	89	263	2	56	69	30	645	8.0	24
Eric Murdock*	9	193	24	66	.364	8	12	.667	5	9	14	35	16	0	6	12	0	62	6.9	19
Marty Conlon	74	958	153	327	.468	84	110	.764	58	119	177	68	126	1	20	79	11	395	5.3	18
Lee Mayberry	82	1705	153	364	.420	41	68	.603	21	69	90	302	144	1	64	89	10	422	5.1	16
Shawn Respert	62	845	113	292	.387	35	42	.833	28	46	74	68	67	0	32	42	4	303	4.9	20
Randolph Keys	69	816	87	208	.418	36	43	.837	41	84	125	65	139	2	32	33	14	232	3.4	17
Jerry Reynolds	19	191	21	53	.396	13	21	.619	13	20	33	20	33	0	15	16	6	56	2.9	9
Alton Lister*	7	88	4	9	.444	2	2	1.000	7	22	29	4	15	0	0	4	3	10	1.4	8
Eric Mobley*	5	65	2	7	.286	2	4	.500	3	9	12	0	5	0	1	1	1	6	1.2	3
Kevin Duckworth	8	58	3	14	.214	3	6	.500	2	5	7	2	19	0	2	2	0	9	1.1	3
Mike Peplowski†	5	12	3	5	.600	1	3	.333	1	3	4	1	6	0	1	2	2	7	1.4	3
Mike Peplowski‡	7	17	3	5	.600	1	3	.333	1	4	4	1	10	0	1	2	2	7	1.0	3

3-pt. FG: Milwaukee 357-1056 (.338)—Baker 10-48 (.208); Robinson 90-263 (.342); Douglas† 39-103 (.379); Douglas‡ 40-110 (.364); Newman 61-162 (.377); Day* 5-25 (.200); Benjamin† 0-3 (.000); Benjamin‡ 0-3 (.000); Cummings 1-7 (.143); Murdock* 6-23 (.261); Conlon 5-30 (.167); Mayberry 75-189 (.397); Respert 42-122 (.344); Keys 22-71 (.310); Reynolds 1-10 (.100). Opponents 514-1296 (.397).

1995-96

MINNESOTA TIMBERWOLVES

	G	Min.	FGM	FGA	Pct.	FTM	FTA	Pct.	Off.	Def.	Tot.	Ast.	PF	Dq.	Stl.	TO	Blk.	Pts.	Avg.	Hi.
J.R. Rider	75	2594	560	1206	.464	248	296	.838	99	210	309	213	204	2	48	201	23	1470	19.6	33
Christian Laettner* . . .	44	1518	283	582	.486	217	266	.816	98	204	302	129	157	4	40	112	43	792	18.0	29
Tom Gugliotta	78	2835	473	1004	.471	289	374	.773	176	514	690	238	265	1	139	234	96	1261	16.2	36
Andrew Lang†	20	550	72	171	.421	30	38	.789	42	79	121	3	63	0	7	30	41	175	8.8	21
Andrew Lang‡	71	2365	353	790	.447	125	156	.801	153	302	455	65	241	4	42	124	126	832	11.7	29
Sam Mitchell	78	2145	303	618	.490	237	291	.814	107	232	339	74	220	3	49	87	26	844	10.8	23
Kevin Garnett	80	2293	361	735	.491	105	149	.705	175	326	501	145	189	2	86	110	131	835	10.4	33
Terry Porter	82	2072	269	608	.442	164	209	.785	36	176	212	452	154	0	89	173	15	773	9.4	23
Spud Webb†	26	645	82	208	.394	51	58	.879	7	33	40	154	41	0	25	59	5	244	9.4	21
Spud Webb‡	77	1462	186	430	.433	125	145	.862	26	74	100	294	109	0	52	110	7	544	7.1	21
Darrick Martin†	35	747	88	231	.381	63	74	.851	3	41	44	156	76	0	26	70	2	254	7.3	24
Darrick Martin‡	59	1149	147	362	.406	101	120	.842	16	66	82	217	123	0	53	107	3	415	7.0	24
Sean Rooks*	49	902	112	227	.493	106	159	.667	60	144	204	38	106	0	19	49	28	331	6.8	19
Doug West	73	1639	175	393	.445	114	144	.792	48	113	161	119	228	2	30	81	17	465	6.4	16
Micheal Williams	9	189	13	40	.325	28	33	.848	3	20	23	31	37	0	5	23	3	55	6.1	18
Eric Riley	25	310	35	74	.473	22	28	.786	32	44	76	5	42	0	8	17	16	92	3.7	9
Mark Davis	57	571	55	149	.369	74	116	.638	56	69	125	47	92	1	40	68	22	188	3.3	12
Jerome Allen	41	362	36	105	.343	26	36	.722	5	20	25	49	42	0	21	34	5	108	2.6	9
Marques Bragg	53	369	54	120	.450	23	41	.561	38	41	79	8	71	0	17	26	8	131	2.5	13
Chris Smith	8	39	3	10	.300	0	2	.000	0	5	5	6	7	0	1	5	0	6	0.8	4

3-pt. FG: Minnesota 279-857 (.326)—Rider 102-275 (.371); Laettner* 9-31 (.290); Gugliotta 26-86 (.302); Lang† 1-2 (.500); Lang‡ 1-5 (.200); Mitchell 1-18 (.056); Garnett 8-28 (.286); Porter 71-226 (.314); Webb† 29-72 (.403); Webb‡ 47-129 (.364); Martin† 15-47 (.319); Martin‡ 20-69 (.290); Rooks* 1-6 (.167); West 1-13 (.077); Williams 1-3 (.333); Riley 0-1 (.000); Davis 4-13 (.308); Allen 10-33 (.303); Smith 0-3 (.000). Opponents 530-1393 (.380).

NEW JERSEY NETS

	G	Min.	FGM	FGA	Pct.	FTM	FTA	Pct.	Off.	Def.	Tot.	Ast.	PF	Dq.	Stl.	TO	Blk.	Pts.	Avg.	Hi.
Armon Gilliam	78	2856	576	1216	.474	277	350	.791	241	472	713	140	180	1	73	177	53	1429	18.3	32
Kenny Anderson*	31	1042	143	380	.376	151	188	.803	37	64	101	247	73	0	52	58	8	473	15.3	39
Kendall Gill†	11	418	67	152	.441	49	59	.831	16	27	43	35	30	0	22	21	2	192	17.5	30
Kendall Gill‡	47	1683	246	524	.469	138	176	.784	72	160	232	260	131	2	64	131	24	656	14.0	30
Chris Childs	78	2408	324	778	.416	259	304	.852	51	194	245	548	246	3	111	230	8	1002	12.8	30
Shawn Bradley†	67	1995	344	776	.443	150	221	.679	187	345	532	55	244	5	41	148	250	839	12.5	32
Shawn Bradley‡	79	2329	387	873	.443	169	246	.687	221	417	638	63	286	5	49	179	288	944	11.9	32
Kevin Edwards	34	1007	142	390	.364	68	84	.810	14	61	75	71	67	0	54	68	7	394	11.6	26
P.J. Brown	81	2942	354	798	.444	204	265	.770	215	345	560	165	249	5	79	133	100	915	11.3	30
Jayson Williams	80	1858	279	660	.423	161	272	.592	342	461	803	47	238	4	35	106	57	721	9.0	35
Vern Fleming	77	1747	227	524	.433	133	177	.751	49	121	170	255	115	0	41	122	5	590	7.7	21
Ed O'Bannon	64	1253	156	400	.390	77	108	.713	65	103	168	63	95	0	44	62	11	399	6.2	19
Khalid Reeves†	31	415	41	109	.376	18	31	.581	7	32	39	46	69	2	21	33	2	117	3.8	14
Khalid Reeves‡	51	833	95	227	.419	61	82	.744	18	61	79	118	115	2	37	63	3	279	5.5	19
Greg Graham†	45	485	61	161	.379	37	51	.725	12	30	42	41	48	0	20	29	1	184	4.1	15
Greg Graham‡	53	613	78	193	.404	52	68	.765	17	40	57	52	64	0	25	46	1	240	4.5	15
Rex Walters*	11	87	12	33	.364	6	6	1.000	2	5	7	11	4	0	3	7	0	33	3.0	9
Robert Werdann	13	93	16	32	.500	7	13	.538	5	18	23	2	17	0	5	6	3	39	3.0	10
Yinka Dare	58	626	63	144	.438	38	62	.613	56	125	181	0	117	3	8	72	40	164	2.8	12
Rick Mahorn	50	450	43	122	.352	34	47	.723	31	79	110	16	72	0	14	30	13	120	2.4	11
Tim Perry†	22	167	23	47	.489	3	6	.500	15	20	35	6	11	0	2	7	10	52	2.4	14
Tim Perry‡	30	254	31	65	.477	5	9	.556	21	27	48	8	16	0	4	10	13	71	2.4	14
Gerald Glass*	10	56	10	28	.357	0	0	. . .	5	1	6	4	5	0	2	0	1	21	2.1	5

3-pt. FG: New Jersey 250-746 (.335)—Gilliam 0-1 (.000); Anderson* 36-99 (.364); Gill† 9-25 (.360); Gill‡ 26-79 (.329); Childs 95-259 (.367); Bradley† 1-4 (.250); Bradley‡ 1-4 (.250); Edwards 42-104 (.404); Brown 3-15 (.200); Williams 2-7 (.286); Fleming 3-28 (.107); O'Bannon 10-56 (.179); Reeves† 17-55 (.309); Reeves‡ 28-91 (.308); Graham† 25-68 (.368); Graham‡ 32-82 (.390); Walters* 3-12 (.250); Mahorn 0-1 (.000); Perry† 3-7 (.429); Perry‡ 4-8 (.500); Glass* 1-5 (.200). Opponents 543-1415 (.384).

NEW YORK KNICKERBOCKERS

	G	Min.	FGM	FGA	Pct.	FTM	FTA	Pct.	Off.	Def.	Tot.	Ast.	PF	Dq.	Stl.	TO	Blk.	Pts.	Avg.	Hi.
Patrick Ewing	76	2783	678	1456	.466	351	461	.761	157	649	806	160	247	2	68	221	184	1711	22.5	41
Anthony Mason	82	3457	449	798	.563	298	414	.720	220	544	764	363	246	3	69	211	34	1196	14.6	30
Derek Harper	82	2893	436	939	.464	156	206	.757	32	170	202	352	201	0	131	178	5	1149	14.0	25
John Starks	81	2491	375	846	.443	131	174	.753	31	206	237	315	226	2	103	156	11	1024	12.6	37
Charles Oakley	53	1775	211	448	.471	175	210	.833	162	298	460	137	195	6	58	104	14	604	11.4	20
Hubert Davis	74	1773	275	566	.486	112	129	.868	35	88	123	103	120	1	31	63	8	789	10.7	30
Willie Anderson†	27	496	56	133	.421	19	31	.613	13	47	60	48	59	0	17	24	8	136	5.0	15
Willie Anderson‡	76	2060	288	660	.436	132	163	.810	48	198	246	197	230	5	75	143	59	742	9.8	26
Charles Smith*	41	890	114	294	.388	73	103	.709	59	101	160	29	124	2	18	61	51	303	7.4	21
J.R. Reid†	33	670	88	160	.550	43	55	.782	38	94	132	28	89	0	18	30	7	219	6.6	22
J.R. Reid‡	65	1313	160	324	.494	107	142	.754	73	182	255	42	187	0	43	79	17	427	6.6	22
Matt Fish*	2	17	6	10	.600	0	1	.000	3	0	3	1	3	0	0	0	1	12	6.0	10
Gary Grant	47	596	88	181	.486	48	58	.828	12	40	52	69	91	0	39	45	3	232	4.9	15
Doug Christie*	23	218	35	73	.479	13	22	.591	8	26	34	25	41	1	12	19	3	93	4.0	16
Charlie Ward	62	787	87	218	.399	37	54	.685	29	73	102	132	98	0	54	79	6	244	3.9	15
Brad Lohaus†	23	325	32	79	.405	2	2	1.000	2	29	31	27	36	0	8	11	10	90	3.9	14

	G	Min.	FGM	FGA	Pct.	FTM	FTA	Pct.	Off.	Def.	Tot.	Ast.	PF	Dq.	Stl.	TO	Blk.	Pts.	Avg.	Hi.
									REBOUNDS									**SCORING**		
Brad Lohaus‡ 55	55	598	71	175	.406	4	5	.800	7	57	64	44	70	0	10	20	17	197	3.6	22
Herb Williams† 43	43	540	59	144	.410	13	20	.650	14	68	82	27	75	0	13	22	31	132	3.1	10
Herb Williams‡ 44	44	571	62	152	.408	13	20	.650	15	75	90	27	79	0	14	22	33	138	3.1	10
Ronnie Grandison† 6	6	57	7	15	.467	4	6	.667	5	8	13	2	4	0	4	1	1	18	3.0	7
Ronnie Grandison‡ . . . 28	28	311	22	58	.379	17	25	.680	20	35	55	13	31	0	12	12	2	65	2.3	8
Monty Williams* 14	14	62	7	22	.318	5	8	.625	9	8	17	4	9	0	2	5	0	19	1.4	4

3-pt. FG: New York 485-1285 (.377)—Ewing 4-28 (.143); Harper 121-325 (.372); Starks 143-396 (.361); Oakley 7-26 (.269); Davis 127-267 (.476); Anderson† 5-25 (.200); Anderson‡ 34-120 (.283); Smith* 2-15 (.133); Reid‡ 0-1 (.000); Grant 8-24 (.333); Christie* 10-19 (.526); Ward 33-99 (.333); Lohaus† 24-57 (.421); Lohaus‡ 51-122 (.418); H. Williams† 1-4 (.250); H. Williams‡ 1-4 (.250); Grandison‡ 4-14 (.286). Opponents 442-1311 (.337).

ORLANDO MAGIC

	G	Min.	FGM	FGA	Pct.	FTM	FTA	Pct.	Off.	Def.	Tot.	Ast.	PF	Dq.	Stl.	TO	Blk.	Pts.	Avg.	Hi.
									REBOUNDS									**SCORING**		
Shaquille O'Neal 54	54	1946	592	1033	.573	249	511	.487	182	414	596	155	193	1	34	155	115	1434	26.6	49
Anfernee Hardaway . . . 82	82	3015	623	1215	.513	445	580	.767	129	225	354	582	160	0	166	229	41	1780	21.7	42
Dennis Scott 82	82	3041	491	1117	.440	182	222	.820	63	246	309	243	169	1	90	122	29	1431	17.5	37
Nick Anderson 77	77	2717	400	904	.442	166	240	.692	92	323	415	279	135	0	121	141	46	1134	14.7	34
Horace Grant 63	63	2286	347	677	.513	152	207	.734	178	402	580	170	144	1	62	64	74	847	13.4	29
Brian Shaw 75	75	1679	182	486	.374	91	114	.798	58	166	224	336	160	1	58	173	11	496	6.6	19
Donald Royal 64	64	963	106	216	.491	125	164	.762	57	96	153	42	97	0	29	52	15	337	5.3	16
Joe Wolf† 63	63	1047	135	262	.515	21	29	.724	49	136	185	63	161	4	13	40	5	291	4.6	16
Joe Wolf‡ 64	64	1065	135	263	.513	21	29	.724	49	138	187	63	163	4	15	42	5	291	4.5	16
Brooks Thompson 33	33	246	48	103	.466	19	27	.704	4	20	24	31	35	0	12	24	0	140	4.2	21
Anthony Bowie 74	74	1078	128	272	.471	40	46	.870	40	83	123	105	112	0	34	55	10	308	4.2	20
Jeff Turner 13	13	192	18	51	.353	2	2	1.000	10	18	28	6	33	2	2	11	1	47	3.6	16
Anthony Bonner 4	4	43	5	15	.333	3	7	.429	6	13	19	4	11	0	3	3	0	13	3.3	11
Darrell Armstrong 13	13	41	16	32	.500	4	4	1.000	0	2	2	5	4	0	6	6	0	42	3.2	8
Jon Koncak 67	67	1288	84	175	.480	32	57	.561	63	209	272	51	226	7	27	41	44	203	3.0	11
David Vaughn 33	33	266	27	80	.338	10	18	.556	33	47	80	8	62	2	6	18	15	64	1.9	10
Geert Hammink* 3	3	7	1	2	.500	2	4	.500	2	1	3	0	1	0	0	2	0	4	1.3	4

3-pt. FG: Orlando 622-1645 (.378)—O'Neal 1-2 (.500); Hardaway 89-283 (.314); Scott 267-628 (.425); Anderson 168-430 (.391); Grant 1-6 (.167); Shaw 41-144 (.285); Royal 0-2 (.000); Wolf† 0-6 (.000); Wolf‡ 0-6 (.000); Thompson 25-64 (.391); Bowie 12-31 (.387); Turner 9-27 (.333); Armstrong 6-12 (.500); Koncak 3-9 (.333); Vaughn 0-1 (.000). Opponents 496-1357 (.366).

PHILADELPHIA 76ERS

	G	Min.	FGM	FGA	Pct.	FTM	FTA	Pct.	Off.	Def.	Tot.	Ast.	PF	Dq.	Stl.	TO	Blk.	Pts.	Avg.	Hi.
									REBOUNDS									**SCORING**		
Jerry Stackhouse 72	72	2701	452	1091	.414	387	518	.747	90	175	265	278	179	0	76	252	79	1384	19.2	34
Clarence Weatherspoon . 78	78	3096	491	1015	.484	318	426	.746	237	516	753	158	214	3	112	179	108	1300	16.7	35
Vernon Maxwell 75	75	2467	410	1052	.390	251	332	.756	39	190	229	330	182	1	96	215	12	1217	16.2	41
Trevor Ruffin 61	61	1551	263	648	.406	148	182	.813	21	111	132	269	132	0	43	149	2	778	12.8	32
Derrick Coleman 11	11	294	48	118	.407	20	32	.625	13	59	72	31	30	0	4	28	10	123	11.2	27
Sharone Wright* 46	46	1136	183	384	.477	117	186	.629	124	175	299	27	125	2	24	81	39	483	10.5	30
Tony Massenburg† 30	30	804	114	236	.483	68	92	.739	75	111	186	12	73	0	15	38	11	296	9.9	25
Tony Massenburg‡ 54	54	1463	214	432	.495	111	157	.707	127	225	352	30	140	0	28	73	20	539	10.0	25
Shawn Bradley* 12	12	334	43	97	.443	19	25	.760	34	72	106	8	42	0	8	31	38	105	8.8	23
Sean Higgins 44	44	916	134	323	.415	35	37	.946	20	72	92	55	90	1	24	49	11	351	8.0	27
Greg Graham* 8	8	128	17	32	.531	15	17	.882	5	10	15	11	16	0	5	17	0	56	7.0	13
Ed Pinckney† 27	27	679	54	102	.529	42	55	.764	74	102	176	22	55	1	33	23	11	150	5.6	14
Ed Pinckney‡ 74	74	1710	171	335	.510	136	179	.760	189	269	458	72	156	1	64	77	28	478	6.5	16
Scott Skiles 10	10	236	20	57	.351	8	10	.800	1	15	16	38	21	0	7	16	0	63	6.3	22
Jeff Malone* 25	25	407	63	160	.394	24	26	.923	8	24	32	19	19	0	13	19	0	155	6.2	21
Derrick Alston 73	73	1614	198	387	.512	55	112	.491	127	175	302	61	191	1	56	59	52	452	6.2	30
Richard Dumas 39	39	739	95	203	.468	49	70	.700	42	57	99	44	79	1	42	49	6	241	6.2	20
Greg Sutton† 30	30	465	65	167	.389	20	27	.741	4	31	35	63	56	0	17	45	2	190	6.3	15
Greg Sutton‡ 48	48	655	85	217	.392	35	46	.761	8	42	50	102	92	0	25	62	2	252	5.3	15
Rex Walters† 33	33	523	49	115	.426	36	46	.783	11	37	48	95	49	0	22	34	4	153	4.6	23
Rex Walters‡ 44	44	610	61	148	.412	42	52	.808	13	42	55	106	53	0	25	41	4	186	4.2	23
Greg Grant* 11	11	280	18	48	.375	5	6	.833	3	18	21	60	28	0	12	15	2	45	4.1	14
Trevor Wilson 6	6	79	10	20	.500	3	4	.750	7	7	14	4	9	0	3	1	0	23	3.8	12
Scott Williams‡ 13	13	193	15	29	.517	10	12	.833	13	33	46	5	27	0	6	8	7	40	3.1	10
Mike Brown 9	9	162	9	16	.563	8	17	.471	14	23	37	3	24	1	3	6	2	26	2.9	7
Tim Perry* 8	8	87	8	18	.444	2	3	.667	6	7	13	2	5	0	2	3	3	19	2.4	5
LaSalle Thompson . . . 44	44	773	33	83	.398	19	24	.792	62	137	199	26	125	5	19	37	20	85	1.9	10
Elmer Bennett 8	8	66	4	17	.235	3	4	.750	1	4	5	8	6	0	1	7	1	11	1.4	6

3-pt. FG: Philadelphia 492-1438 (.342)—Stackhouse 93-292 (.318); Weatherspoon 0-2 (.000); Maxwell 146-460 (.317); Ruffin 104-284 (.366); Coleman 7-21 (.333); Massenburg† 0-3 (.000); Massenburg‡ 0-3 (.000); Higgins 48-129 (.372); Graham* 7-14 (.500); Pinckney‡ 0-3 (.000); Skiles 15-34 (.441); Malone* 5-16 (.313); Alston 1-3 (.333); Dumas 2-9 (.222); Sutton† 40-96 (.417); Sutton‡ 47-117 (.402); Walters† 19-54 (.352); Walters‡ 22-66 (.333); Grant* 4-18 (.222); Williams 0-2 (.000); Perry* 1-1 (1.000). Opponents 526-1421 (.370).

PHOENIX SUNS

	G	Min.	FGM	FGA	Pct.	FTM	FTA	Pct.	Off.	Def.	Tot.	Ast.	PF	Dq.	Stl.	TO	Blk.	Pts.	Avg.	Hi.
									REBOUNDS									**SCORING**		
Charles Barkley 71	71	2632	580	1160	.500	440	566	.777	243	578	821	262	208	3	114	218	56	1649	23.2	45
Kevin Johnson 56	56	2007	342	674	.507	342	398	.859	42	179	221	517	144	0	82	170	13	1047	18.7	39

	G	Min.	FGM	FGA	Pct.	FTM	FTA	Pct.	Off.	Def.	Tot.	Ast.	PF	Dq.	Stl.	TO	Blk.	Pts.	Avg.	Hi.
Michael Finley	82	3212	465	976	.476	242	323	.749	139	235	374	289	199	1	85	133	31	1233	15.0	27
Danny Manning	33	816	178	388	.459	82	109	.752	30	113	143	65	121	2	38	77	24	441	13.4	32
Wesley Person	82	2609	390	877	.445	148	192	.771	56	265	321	138	148	0	55	89	22	1045	12.7	29
Wayman Tisdale	63	1152	279	564	.495	114	149	.765	55	159	214	58	188	2	15	63	36	672	10.7	30
Elliot Perry	81	1668	261	549	.475	151	194	.778	34	102	136	353	140	1	87	146	5	697	8.6	35
A.C. Green	82	2113	215	444	.484	168	237	.709	166	388	554	72	141	1	45	79	23	612	7.5	29
John Williams	62	1652	180	397	.453	95	130	.731	129	243	372	62	170	2	46	62	90	455	7.3	23
Tony Smith*	34	528	70	173	.405	24	37	.649	24	32	56	86	60	1	21	40	5	189	5.6	17
Mario Bennett	19	230	29	64	.453	27	42	.643	21	28	49	6	46	0	11	11	11	85	4.5	12
Chris Carr	60	590	90	217	.415	49	60	.817	27	75	102	43	77	1	10	40	5	240	4.0	15
Terrence Rencher†	2	8	1	1	1.000	1	3	.333	0	2	2	0	1	0	0	2	1	3	1.5	3
Terrence Rencher‡	36	405	33	100	.330	31	46	.674	9	35	44	54	37	0	16	43	2	106	2.9	8
Joe Kleine	56	663	71	169	.420	20	25	.800	36	96	132	44	113	0	13	37	6	164	2.9	15
John Coker	5	11	4	5	.800	0	0	...	2	0	2	1	1	0	0	0	1	8	1.6	4
Stefano Rusconi	7	30	3	9	.333	2	5	.400	3	3	6	3	10	0	0	3	2	8	1.1	7
David Wood*	4	34	1	6	.167	2	2	1.000	2	3	5	2	9	0	1	2	0	4	1.0	2

3-pt. FG: Phoenix 327-984 (.332)—Barkley 49-175 (.280); Johnson 21-57 (.368); Finley 61-186 (.328); Manning 3-14 (.214); Person 117-313 (.374); Perry 24-59 (.407); Green 14-52 (.269); Williams 0-1 (.000); Smith* 25-77 (.325); Bennett 0-1 (.000); Carr 11-42 (.262); Rencher‡ 9-29 (.310); Kleine 2-7 (.286). Opponents 551-1492 (.369).

PORTLAND TRAIL BLAZERS

	G	Min.	FGM	FGA	Pct.	FTM	FTA	Pct.	Off.	Def.	Tot.	Ast.	PF	Dq.	Stl.	TO	Blk.	Pts.	Avg.	Hi.
Clifford Robinson	78	2980	553	1306	.423	360	542	.664	123	320	443	190	248	3	86	194	68	1644	21.1	41
Rod Strickland	67	2526	471	1023	.460	276	423	.652	89	208	297	640	135	2	97	255	16	1256	18.7	32
Arvydas Sabonis	73	1735	394	723	.545	231	305	.757	147	441	588	130	211	2	64	154	78	1058	14.5	26
Aaron McKie	81	2259	337	722	.467	152	199	.764	86	218	304	205	205	5	92	135	21	864	10.7	24
Harvey Grant	76	2394	314	679	.462	60	110	.545	117	244	361	111	173	1	60	82	43	709	9.3	24
James Robinson	76	1627	229	574	.399	89	135	.659	44	113	157	150	146	0	34	111	16	649	8.5	22
Gary Trent	69	1219	220	429	.513	78	141	.553	84	154	238	50	116	0	25	92	11	518	7.5	21
Buck Williams	70	1672	192	384	.500	125	187	.668	159	245	404	42	187	1	40	90	47	511	7.3	21
Rumeal Robinson	43	715	92	221	.416	33	51	.647	19	59	78	142	79	1	26	72	5	247	5.7	20
Chris Dudley	80	1924	162	358	.453	80	157	.510	239	481	720	37	251	4	41	79	100	404	5.1	13
Dontonio Wingfield	44	487	60	157	.382	26	34	.765	45	59	104	28	73	1	20	31	6	165	3.8	17
Randolph Childress	28	250	25	79	.316	22	27	.815	1	18	19	32	22	0	8	28	1	85	3.0	18
Reggie Slater*	4	20	3	5	.600	0	0	...	0	3	3	0	1	0	1	3	2	6	1.5	4
Anthony Cook	11	60	7	16	.438	1	4	.250	5	7	12	2	8	0	0	1	1	15	1.4	4
Elmore Spencer†	11	37	5	12	.417	4	6	.667	2	7	9	1	4	0	0	3	2	14	1.3	5
Elmore Spencer‡	17	58	5	13	.385	4	6	.667	3	10	13	1	12	1	0	6	2	14	0.8	5

3-pt. FG: Portland 480-1358 (.353)—C. Robinson 178-471 (.378); Strickland 38-111 (.342); Sabonis 39-104 (.375); McKie 38-117 (.325); Grant 21-67 (.313); J. Robinson 102-284 (.359); Trent 0-9 (.000); Williams 2-3 (.667); R. Robinson 30-79 (.380); Dudley 0-1 (.000); Wingfield 19-63 (.302); Childress 13-47 (.277); Cook 0-2 (.000). Opponents 472-1355 (.348).

SACRAMENTO KINGS

	G	Min.	FGM	FGA	Pct.	FTM	FTA	Pct.	Off.	Def.	Tot.	Ast.	PF	Dq.	Stl.	TO	Blk.	Pts.	Avg.	Hi.
Mitch Richmond	81	2946	611	1368	.447	425	491	.866	54	215	269	255	233	6	125	220	19	1872	23.1	47
Walt Williams*	45	1381	235	540	.435	130	172	.756	62	145	207	165	151	0	53	103	42	658	14.6	29
Brian Grant	78	2398	427	842	.507	262	358	.732	175	370	545	127	269	9	40	185	103	1120	14.4	32
Billy Owens†	22	594	84	200	.420	45	70	.643	49	76	125	70	60	1	19	51	16	218	9.9	21
Billy Owens‡	62	1982	323	673	.480	157	247	.636	143	268	411	204	192	2	49	164	38	808	13.0	34
Olden Polynice	81	2441	431	818	.527	122	203	.601	257	507	764	58	250	3	52	127	66	985	12.2	27
Sarunas Marciulionis	53	1039	176	389	.452	155	200	.775	20	57	77	118	112	1	52	96	4	571	10.8	25
Tyus Edney	80	2481	305	740	.412	197	252	.782	63	138	201	491	203	2	89	192	3	860	10.8	20
Tyrone Corbin*	49	930	117	259	.452	77	92	.837	55	124	179	61	96	1	47	50	17	312	6.4	19
Kevin Gamble†	21	292	35	82	.427	5	10	.500	7	20	27	18	28	0	4	11	3	81	3.9	17
Kevin Gamble‡	65	1325	152	379	.401	38	48	.792	21	92	113	100	147	2	35	43	8	386	5.9	37
Corliss Williamson	53	609	125	268	.466	47	84	.560	56	58	114	23	115	2	11	76	9	297	5.6	26
Michael Smith	65	1384	144	238	.605	68	177	.384	143	246	389	110	166	0	47	72	46	357	5.5	15
Lionel Simmons	54	810	86	217	.396	55	75	.733	41	104	145	83	85	0	31	51	20	246	4.6	19
Byron Houston	25	276	32	64	.500	21	26	.808	31	53	84	7	59	2	13	17	7	86	3.4	8
Duane Causwell	73	1044	90	216	.417	70	96	.729	86	162	248	20	173	2	27	53	78	250	3.4	18
Bobby Hurley	72	1059	65	230	.283	68	85	.800	12	63	75	216	121	0	28	86	3	220	3.1	17
Clint McDaniel	12	71	8	23	.348	12	16	.750	3	7	10	7	10	0	5	2	0	30	2.5	8

3-pt. FG: Sacramento 462-1194 (.387)—Richmond 225-515 (.437); Williams* 58-170 (.341); Grant 4-17 (.235); Owens† 5-12 (.417); Owens‡ 5-18 (.278); Polynice 1-3 (.333); Marciulionis 64-157 (.408); Edney 53-144 (.368); Corbin* 1-12 (.083); Gamble† 6-23 (.261); Gamble‡ 44-114 (.386); Williamson 0-3 (.000); Smith 1-1 (1.000); Simmons 19-51 (.373); Houston 1-3 (.333); Causwell 0-1 (.000); Hurley 22-76 (.289); McDaniel 2-6 (.333). Opponents 461-1215 (.379).

SAN ANTONIO SPURS

	G	Min.	FGM	FGA	Pct.	FTM	FTA	Pct.	Off.	Def.	Tot.	Ast.	PF	Dq.	Stl.	TO	Blk.	Pts.	Avg.	Hi.
David Robinson	82	3019	711	1378	.516	626	823	.761	319	681	1000	247	262	1	111	190	271	2051	25.0	45
Sean Elliott	77	2901	525	1127	.466	326	423	.771	69	327	396	211	178	1	69	198	33	1537	20.0	36
Vinny Del Negro	82	2766	478	962	.497	178	214	.832	36	236	272	315	166	0	85	100	6	1191	14.5	31
Avery Johnson	82	3084	438	887	.494	189	262	.721	37	169	206	789	179	1	119	195	21	1071	13.1	26

	G	Min.	FGM	FGA	Pct.	FTM	FTA	Pct.	Off.	Def.	Tot.	Ast.	PF	Dq.	Stl.	TO	Blk.	Pts.	Avg.	Hi.
									REBOUNDS									**SCORING**		
Chuck Person	80	2131	308	705	.437	67	104	.644	76	337	413	100	197	2	49	91	26	873	10.9	25
Charles Smith†	32	826	130	284	.458	46	60	.767	74	128	202	36	100	1	32	45	29	306	9.6	18
Charles Smith‡	73	1716	244	578	.422	119	163	.730	133	229	362	65	224	3	50	106	80	609	8.3	21
J.R. Reid*	32	643	72	164	.439	64	87	.736	35	88	123	14	98	0	25	49	10	208	6.5	15
Will Perdue	80	1396	173	331	.523	67	125	.536	175	310	485	33	183	0	28	86	75	413	5.2	18
Doc Rivers	78	1235	108	290	.372	48	64	.750	30	108	138	123	175	0	73	57	21	311	4.0	11
Brad Lohaus*	32	273	39	96	.406	2	3	.667	5	28	33	17	34	0	2	9	7	107	3.3	22
Dell Demps	16	87	19	33	.576	14	17	.824	2	7	9	8	10	0	3	12	1	53	3.3	15
Cory Alexander	60	560	63	155	.406	16	25	.640	9	33	42	121	94	0	27	68	2	168	2.8	14
Monty Williams†	17	122	20	46	.435	9	12	.750	11	12	23	4	17	0	4	13	2	49	2.9	14
Monty Williams‡	31	184	27	68	.397	14	20	.700	20	20	40	8	26	0	6	18	2	68	2.2	14
Carl Herrera	44	393	40	97	.412	5	17	.294	30	51	81	16	61	0	9	29	8	85	1.9	6
Greg Anderson	46	344	24	47	.511	6	25	.240	29	71	100	10	66	0	9	22	24	54	1.2	6

3-pt. FG: San Antonio 518-1320 (.392)—Robinson 3-9 (.333); Elliott 161-392 (.411); Del Negro 57-150 (.380); Johnson 6-31 (.194); Person 190-463 (.410); Smith‡ 2-15 (.133); Reid* 0-1 (.000); Perdue 0-1 (.000); Rivers 47-137 (.343); Lohaus* 27-65 (.415); Demps 1-2 (.500); Alexander 26-66 (.394); Williams† 0-1 (.000); Williams‡ 0-1 (.000); Herrera 0-1 (.000); Anderson 0-1 (.000). Opponents 441-1337 (.330).

SEATTLE SUPERSONICS

	G	Min.	FGM	FGA	Pct.	FTM	FTA	Pct.	Off.	Def.	Tot.	Ast.	PF	Dq.	Stl.	TO	Blk.	Pts.	Avg.	Hi.
									REBOUNDS									**SCORING**		
Shawn Kemp	79	2631	526	937	.561	493	664	.742	276	628	904	173	299	6	93	315	127	1550	19.6	32
Gary Payton	81	3162	618	1276	.484	229	306	.748	104	235	339	608	221	1	231	260	19	1563	19.3	38
Detlef Schrempf	63	2200	360	740	.486	287	370	.776	73	255	328	276	179	0	56	146	8	1080	17.1	35
Hersey Hawkins	82	2823	443	936	.473	249	285	.874	86	211	297	218	172	0	149	164	14	1281	15.6	35
Sam Perkins	82	2169	325	797	.408	191	241	.793	101	266	367	120	174	1	83	82	48	970	11.8	26
Vincent Askew	69	1725	215	436	.493	123	161	.764	65	153	218	163	178	0	47	96	15	582	8.4	21
Ervin Johnson	81	1519	180	352	.511	85	127	.669	129	304	433	48	245	3	40	98	129	446	5.5	28
Frank Brickowski	63	986	123	252	.488	61	86	.709	26	125	151	58	185	4	26	78	8	339	5.4	21
Nate McMillan	55	1261	100	238	.420	29	41	.707	41	169	210	197	143	3	95	75	18	275	5.0	13
David Wingate	60	695	88	212	.415	32	41	.780	17	39	56	58	66	0	20	42	4	223	3.7	18
Sherell Ford	28	139	30	80	.375	26	34	.765	12	12	24	5	27	0	8	6	1	90	3.2	9
Eric Snow	43	389	42	100	.420	29	49	.592	9	34	43	73	53	0	28	38	0	115	2.7	9
Steve Scheffler	35	181	24	45	.533	9	19	.474	15	18	33	2	25	0	6	8	2	58	1.7	0

3-pt. FG: Seattle 581-1596 (.364)—Kemp 5-12 (.417); Payton 98-299 (.328); Schrempf 73-179 (.408); Hawkins 146-380 (.384); Perkins 129-363 (.355); Askew 29-86 (.337); Johnson 1-3 (.333); Brickowski 32-79 (.405); McMillan 46-121 (.380); Wingate 15-34 (.441); Ford 4-25 (.160); Snow 2-10 (.200); Scheffler 1-5 (.200). Opponents 533-1531 (.348).

TORONTO RAPTORS

	G	Min.	FGM	FGA	Pct.	FTM	FTA	Pct.	Off.	Def.	Tot.	Ast.	PF	Dq.	Stl.	TO	Blk.	Pts.	Avg.	Hi.
									REBOUNDS									**SCORING**		
Damon Stoudamire . . .	70	2865	481	1129	.426	236	296	.797	59	222	281	653	166	0	98	267	19	1331	19.0	30
Tracy Murray	82	2458	496	1092	.454	182	219	.831	114	238	352	131	208	2	87	132	40	1325	16.2	40
Oliver Miller	76	2516	418	795	.526	146	221	.661	177	385	562	219	277	4	108	202	143	982	12.9	35
Willie Anderson*	49	1564	232	527	.440	113	132	.856	35	151	186	149	171	5	58	119	51	606	12.4	26
Sharone Wright†	11	298	65	128	.508	50	73	.685	24	33	57	11	38	2	6	28	10	181	16.5	25
Sharone Wright‡	57	1434	248	512	.484	167	259	.645	148	208	356	38	163	4	30	109	49	664	11.6	30
Tony Massenburg*	24	659	100	196	.510	43	65	.662	52	114	166	18	67	0	13	35	9	243	10.1	24
Alvin Robertson	77	2478	285	607	.470	107	158	.677	110	232	342	323	268	5	166	183	36	718	9.3	30
Carlos Rogers	50	1043	178	344	.517	71	130	.546	80	90	170	35	87	0	25	61	48	430	7.7	28
Zan Tabak	67	1332	225	414	.543	64	114	.561	117	203	320	62	204	2	24	101	31	514	7.7	26
Doug Christie†	32	818	115	264	.436	56	71	.789	26	94	120	92	100	4	58	76	16	322	10.1	30
Doug Christie‡	55	1036	150	337	.445	69	93	.742	34	120	154	117	141	5	70	95	19	415	7.5	30
Acie Earl	42	655	117	276	.424	82	114	.719	51	78	129	27	73	0	18	49	37	316	7.5	40
Ed Pinckney*	47	1031	117	233	.502	94	124	.758	115	167	282	50	101	0	31	54	17	328	7.0	16
Dan O'Sullivan	5	139	13	35	.371	7	8	.875	13	19	32	2	13	0	2	5	4	33	6.6	15
Herb Williams*	1	31	3	8	.375	0	0	—	1	7	8	0	4	0	1	0	2	6	6.0	6
John Salley*	25	482	51	105	.486	47	65	.723	26	71	97	39	72	3	11	39	12	149	6.0	15
Dwayne Whitfield	8	122	13	30	.433	14	22	.636	9	16	25	2	14	0	3	8	2	40	5.0	16
Martin Lewis	16	189	29	60	.483	15	25	.600	15	14	29	3	21	0	8	14	3	75	4.7	17
Jimmy King	62	868	110	255	.431	54	77	.701	43	67	110	88	76	0	21	60	13	279	4.5	14
Vincenzo Esposito	30	282	36	100	.360	31	39	.795	4	12	16	23	27	0	7	39	0	116	3.9	18

3-pt. FG: Toronto 414-1168 (.354)—Stoudamire 133-337 (.395); Murray 151-358 (.422); Miller 0-11 (.000); Anderson* 29-95 (.305); Wright† 1-3 (.333); Wright‡ 1-3 (.333); Robertson 41-151 (.272); Rogers 3-21 (.143); Tabak 0-1 (.000); Christie† 36-87 (.414); Christie‡ 46-106 (.434); Earl 0-3 (.000); Pinckney* 0-3 (.000); O'Sullivan 0-1 (.000); Lewis 2-7 (.286); King 5-34 (.147); Esposito 13-56 (.232). Opponents 519-1416 (.367).

UTAH JAZZ

	G	Min.	FGM	FGA	Pct.	FTM	FTA	Pct.	Off.	Def.	Tot.	Ast.	PF	Dq.	Stl.	TO	Blk.	Pts.	Avg.	Hi.
									REBOUNDS									**SCORING**		
Karl Malone	82	3113	789	1520	.519	512	708	.723	175	629	804	345	245	1	138	199	56	2106	25.7	51
Jeff Hornacek	82	2588	442	880	.502	259	290	.893	62	147	209	340	171	1	106	127	20	1247	15.2	29
John Stockton	82	2915	440	818	.538	234	282	.830	54	172	226	916	207	1	140	246	15	1209	14.7	31
Chris Morris	66	1424	265	606	.437	98	127	.772	100	129	229	77	140	1	63	71	20	691	10.5	23
David Benoit	81	1961	255	581	.439	87	112	.777	90	293	383	82	166	2	43	71	49	661	8.2	24
Antoine Carr	80	1532	233	510	.457	114	144	.792	71	129	200	74	254	4	28	78	65	580	7.3	20
Adam Keefe	82	1708	180	346	.520	139	201	.692	176	279	455	64	174	0	51	88	41	499	6.1	16

1995-96

	G	Min.	FGM	FGA	Pct.	FTM	FTA	Pct.	REBOUNDS Off.	Def.	Tot.	Ast.	PF	Dq.	Stl.	TO	Blk.	SCORING Pts.	Avg.	Hi.
Felton Spencer	71	1267	146	281	.520	104	151	.689	100	206	306	11	240	1	20	77	54	396	5.6	16
Howard Eisley	65	961	104	242	.430	65	77	.844	22	56	78	146	130	0	29	77	3	287	4.4	14
Greg Foster	73	803	107	244	.439	61	72	.847	53	125	178	25	120	0	7	58	22	276	3.8	16
Greg Ostertag	57	661	86	182	.473	36	54	.667	57	118	175	5	91	1	5	25	63	208	3.6	14
Jamie Watson	16	217	18	43	.419	9	13	.692	5	22	27	24	30	0	8	17	2	48	3.0	7
Bryon Russell	59	577	56	142	.394	48	67	.716	28	62	90	29	66	0	29	36	8	174	2.9	19
Andy Toolson	13	53	8	22	.364	3	4	.750	0	6	6	1	12	0	0	2	0	22	1.7	5

3-pt. FG: Utah 377-1013 (.372)—Malone 16-40 (.400); Hornacek 104-223 (.466); Stockton 95-225 (.422); Morris 63-197 (.320); Benoit 64-192 (.333); Carr 0-3 (.000); Keefe 0-4 (.000); Eisley 14-62 (.226); Foster 1-8 (.125); Watson 3-7 (.429); Russell 14-40 (.350); Toolson 3-12 (.250). Opponents 550-1428 (.385).

VANCOUVER GRIZZLIES

	G	Min.	FGM	FGA	Pct.	FTM	FTA	Pct.	REBOUNDS Off.	Def.	Tot.	Ast.	PF	Dq.	Stl.	TO	Blk.	SCORING Pts.	Avg.	Hi.
Greg Anthony	69	2096	324	781	.415	229	297	.771	29	145	174	476	137	1	116	160	11	967	14.0	32
Benoit Benjamin*	13	404	71	161	.441	39	56	.696	31	72	103	16	40	1	10	34	15	181	13.9	29
Bryant Reeves	77	2460	401	877	.457	219	299	.732	178	392	570	109	226	2	43	157	55	1021	13.3	28
Blue Edwards	82	2773	401	956	.419	157	208	.755	98	248	346	212	243	1	118	170	46	1043	12.7	26
Byron Scott	80	1894	271	676	.401	203	243	.835	40	152	192	123	126	0	63	100	22	819	10.2	27
Kenny Gattison	25	570	91	190	.479	47	78	.603	35	79	114	14	75	0	10	40	11	229	9.2	20
Eric Murdock†	64	1480	220	521	.422	106	131	.809	21	134	155	292	124	0	129	120	9	585	9.1	20
Eric Murdock‡	73	1673	244	587	.416	114	143	.797	26	143	169	327	140	0	135	132	9	647	8.9	20
Chris King	80	1930	250	585	.427	90	136	.662	102	183	285	104	163	0	68	103	33	634	7.9	21
Gerald Wilkins	28	738	77	205	.376	20	23	.870	22	43	65	68	55	0	22	37	2	188	6.7	15
Darrick Martin*	24	402	59	131	.450	38	46	.826	13	25	38	61	47	0	27	37	1	161	6.7	15
Lawrence Moten	44	573	112	247	.453	49	75	.653	36	25	61	50	54	0	29	44	8	291	6.6	21
Ashraf Amaya	54	1104	121	252	.480	97	149	.651	114	189	303	33	151	3	22	57	10	339	6.3	18
Anthony Avent	71	1586	179	466	.384	57	77	.740	108	247	355	69	202	3	30	107	42	415	5.8	16
Antonio Harvey*	18	410	39	95	.411	20	43	.465	27	67	94	9	38	0	14	18	21	98	5.4	13
Eric Mobley†	34	611	72	131	.550	37	83	.446	51	77	128	22	82	1	13	49	23	182	5.4	12
Eric Mobley‡	39	676	74	138	.536	39	87	.448	54	86	140	22	87	1	14	50	24	188	4.8	12
Rich Manning	29	311	49	113	.434	9	14	.643	16	39	55	7	37	0	3	17	6	107	3.7	13
Doug Edwards	31	519	32	91	.352	29	38	.763	35	52	87	39	51	2	10	29	18	93	3.0	11
Cuonzo Martin	4	19	3	5	.600	0	2	.000	1	1	2	1	2	0	1	1	0	9	2.3	3

3-pt. FG: Vancouver 372-1129 (.329)—Anthony 90-271 (.332); Reeves 0-3 (.000); B. Edwards 84-245 (.343); Scott 74-221 (.335); Murdock† 39-122 (.320); Murdock‡ 45-145 (.310); King 44-113 (.389); Wilkins 14-64 (.219); D. Martin* 5-22 (.227); Moten 18-55 (.327); Amaya 0-1 (.000); Harvey* 0-2 (.000); Mobley† 1-2 (.500); Mobley‡ 1-2 (.500); Manning 0-1 (.000); D. Edwards 0-4 (.000); C. Martin 3-3 (1.000). Opponents 459-1226 (.374).

WASHINGTON BULLETS

	G	Min.	FGM	FGA	Pct.	FTM	FTA	Pct.	REBOUNDS Off.	Def.	Tot.	Ast.	PF	Dq.	Stl.	TO	Blk.	SCORING Pts.	Avg.	Hi.
Chris Webber	15	558	150	276	.543	41	69	.594	37	77	114	75	51	1	27	49	9	356	23.7	40
Juwan Howard	81	3294	733	1500	.489	319	426	.749	188	472	660	360	269	3	67	303	39	1789	22.1	42
Robert Pack	31	1084	190	444	.428	154	182	.846	29	103	132	242	68	0	62	114	1	560	18.1	35
Calbert Cheaney	70	2324	426	905	.471	151	214	.706	67	172	239	154	205	1	67	129	18	1055	15.1	29
Gheorghe Muresan	76	2242	466	798	.584	172	278	.619	248	480	728	56	297	8	52	143	172	1104	14.5	31
Rasheed Wallace	65	1788	275	565	.487	78	120	.650	93	210	303	85	206	4	42	103	54	655	10.1	22
Brent Price	81	2042	252	534	.472	167	191	.874	38	190	228	416	184	3	78	153	4	810	10.0	30
Tim Legler	77	1775	233	460	.507	132	153	.863	29	111	140	136	141	0	45	45	12	726	9.4	21
Ledell Eackles	55	1238	161	377	.427	98	118	.831	44	104	148	86	84	1	28	57	3	474	8.6	24
Mark Price	7	127	18	60	.300	10	10	1.000	1	6	7	18	7	0	6	10	0	56	8.0	13
Chris Whitney	21	335	45	99	.455	41	44	.932	2	31	33	51	46	0	18	23	1	150	7.1	19
Mitchell Butler	61	858	88	229	.384	48	83	.578	29	89	118	67	104	0	41	67	12	237	3.9	22
Kevin Pritchard	2	22	2	3	.667	2	3	.667	0	2	2	7	3	0	2	0	0	7	3.5	7
Bob McCann	62	653	76	153	.497	35	74	.473	46	97	143	24	116	0	21	42	15	188	3.0	13
Greg Grant*	10	138	11	28	.393	0	0	. . .	1	5	6	23	8	0	8	10	0	24	2.4	6
Jim McIlvaine	80	1195	62	145	.428	58	105	.552	66	164	230	11	171	0	21	36	166	182	2.3	12
Michael Curry*	5	34	3	10	.300	4	4	1.000	2	3	5	1	3	0	1	1	0	10	2.0	6
Jeff Webster	11	58	8	23	.348	0	0	. . .	2	5	7	3	7	0	4	3	0	18	1.6	12
Cedric Lewis	3	4	2	3	.667	0	0	. . .	2	0	2	0	0	0	1	0	0	4	1.3	2
Bob Thornton	7	31	1	6	.167	1	2	.500	6	6	12	0	7	0	1	1	0	3	0.4	2
Mike Peplowski*	2	5	0	0	. . .	0	0	. . .	0	0	0	4	0	0	0	0	0	0	0.0	0

3-pt. FG: Washington 493-1212 (.407)—Webber 15-34 (.441); Howard 4-13 (.308); Pack 26-98 (.265); Cheaney 52-154 (.338); Muresan 0-1 (.000); Wallace 27-82 (.329); B. Price 139-301 (.462); Legler 128-245 (.522); Eackles 54-128 (.422); M. Price 10-30 (.333); Whitney 19-44 (.432); Butler 13-60 (.217); Pritchard 1-1 (1.000); McCann 1-2 (.500); Grant* 2-10 (.200); Curry 0-3 (.000); Webster 2-6 (.333). Opponents 377-1103 (.342).

* Finished season with another team. † Totals with this team only. ‡ Totals with all teams.

PLAYOFF RESULTS

EASTERN CONFERENCE
FIRST ROUND

Chicago 3, Miami 0
Apr. 26—Fri.	Miami 85 at Chicago	102
Apr. 28—Sun.	Miami 75 at Chicago	106
May 1—Wed.	Chicago 112 at Miami	91

Orlando 3, Detroit 0
Apr. 26—Fri.	Detroit 92 at Orlando	112
Apr. 28—Sun.	Detroit 77 at Orlando	92
Apr. 30—Tue.	Orlando 101 at Detroit	98

Atlanta 3, Indiana 2
Apr. 25—Thur.	Atlanta 92 at Indiana	80
Apr. 27—Sat.	Atlanta 94 at Indiana	*102
Apr. 29—Mon.	Indiana 83 at Atlanta	90
May 2—Thur.	Indiana 83 at Atlanta	75
May 5—Sun.	Atlanta 89 at Indiana	87

New York 3, Cleveland 0
Apr. 25—Thur.	New York 106 at Cleveland	83
Apr. 27—Sat.	New York 84 at Cleveland	80
May 1—Wed.	Cleveland 76 at New York	81

SEMIFINALS

Chicago 4, New York 1
May 5—Sun.	New York 84 at Chicago	91
May 7—Tue.	New York 80 at Chicago	91
May 11—Sat.	Chicago 99 at New York	*102
May 12—Sun.	Chicago 91 at New York	91
May 14—Tue.	New York 81 at Chicago	94

Orlando 4, Atlanta 1
May 8—Wed.	Atlanta 105 at Orlando	117
May 10—Fri.	Atlanta 94 at Orlando	120
May 12—Sun.	Orlando 102 at Atlanta	96
May 13—Mon.	Orlando 99 at Atlanta	104
May 15—Wed.	Atlanta 88 at Orlando	96

FINALS

Chicago 4, Orlando 0
May 19—Sun.	Orlando 83 at Chicago	121
May 21—Tue.	Orlando 88 at Chicago	93
May 25—Sat.	Chicago 86 at Orlando	67
May 27—Mon.	Chicago 106 at Orlando	101

WESTERN CONFERENCE
FIRST ROUND

Seattle 3, Sacramento 1
Apr. 26—Fri.	Sacramento 85 at Seattle	97
Apr. 28—Sun.	Sacramento 90 at Seattle	81
Apr. 30—Tue.	Seattle 96 at Sacramento	89
May 2—Thur.	Seattle 101 at Sacramento	87

San Antonio 3, Phoenix 1
Apr. 26—Fri.	Phoenix 98 at San Antonio	120
Apr. 28—Sun.	Phoenix 105 at San Antonio	110
May 1—Wed.	San Antonio 93 at Phoenix	94
May 3—Fri.	San Antonio 116 at Phoenix	98

Utah 3, Portland 2
Apr. 25—Thur.	Portland 102 at Utah	110
Apr. 27—Sat.	Portland 90 at Utah	105
Apr. 29—Mon.	Utah 91 at Portland	*94
May 1—Wed.	Utah 90 at Portland	98
May 5—Sun.	Portland 64 at Utah	102

Houston 3, L.A. Lakers 1
Apr. 25—Thur.	Houston 87 at L.A. Lakers	83
Apr. 27—Sat.	Houston 94 at L.A. Lakers	104
Apr. 30—Tue.	L.A. Lakers 98 at Houston	104
May 2—Thur.	L.A. Lakers 94 at Houston	102

SEMIFINALS

Seattle 4, Houston 0
May 4—Sat.	Houston 75 at Seattle	108
May 6—Mon.	Houston 101 at Seattle	105
May 10—Fri.	Seattle 115 at Houston	112
May 12—Sun.	Seattle 114 at Houston	*107

Utah 4, San Antonio 2
May 7—Tue.	Utah 95 at San Antonio	75
May 9—Thur.	Utah 77 at San Antonio	88
May 11—Sat.	San Antonio 75 at Utah	105
May 12—Sun.	San Antonio 86 at Utah	101
May 14—Tue.	Utah 87 at San Antonio	98
May 16—Thur.	San Antonio 81 at Utah	108

FINALS

Seattle 4, Utah 3
May 18—Sat.	Utah 72 at Seattle	102
May 20—Mon.	Utah 87 at Seattle	91
May 24—Fri.	Seattle 76 at Utah	96
May 26—Sun.	Seattle 88 at Utah	86
May 28—Tue.	Utah 98 at Seattle	*95
May 30—Thur.	Seattle 83 at Utah	118
June 2—Sun.	Utah 86 at Seattle	90

NBA FINALS

Chicago 4, Seattle 2
June 5—Wed.	Seattle 90 at Chicago	107
June 7—Fri.	Seattle 88 at Chicago	92
June 9—Sun.	Chicago 108 at Seattle	86
June 12—Wed.	Chicago 86 at Seattle	107
June 14—Fri.	Chicago 78 at Seattle	89
June 16—Sun.	Seattle 75 at Chicago	87

*Denotes number of overtime periods.

1994-95

1994-95 NBA CHAMPION HOUSTON ROCKETS

Front row (from left): director of player development Robert Barr, assistant coach Carroll Dawson, Vernon Maxwell, Robert Horry, Hakeem Olajuwon, head coach Rudy Tomjanovich, Clyde Drexler, Carl Herrera, Kenny Smith, assistant coach Bill Berry, assistant coach Larry Smith. Back row (from left): equipment manager David Nordstrom, assistant trainer Dennis Terry, video coordinator Jim Boylen, Sam Cassell, Pete Chilcutt, Chucky Brown, Zan Tabak, Tracy Murray, Tim Breaux, Mario Elie, film coordinator Ed Bernholz, trainer Ray Melchiorre, scout Joe Ash. Not pictured: Charles Jones.

FINAL STANDINGS

ATLANTIC DIVISION

	Atl.	Bos.	Char.	Chi.	Cle.	Dal.	Den.	Det.	G.S.	Hou.	Ind.	L.A.C.	L.A.L.	Mia.	Mil.	Min.	N.J.	N.Y.	Orl.	Phi.	Pho.	Por.	Sac.	S.A.	Sea.	Uta.	Was.	W	L	Pct.	GB
Orlando 3	3	3	3	3	2	2	3	2	2	2	2	1	3	4	1	2	3	..	4	1	2	1	1	0	1	3	57	25	.695	..
New York 2	5	1	1	2	2	2	3	1	2	3	2	2	4	2	2	4	..	2	4	1	1	2	1	0	0	4	55	27	.671	2
Boston 1	..	1	0	2	1	1	3	2	1	2	0	1	4	1	2	2	0	2	3	1	0	1	0	1	0	3	35	47	.427	22
Miami 2	1	1	1	3	2	0	3	1	0	2	2	1	..	4	1	1	1	1	0	0	0	0	0	0	0	4	32	50	.390	25
New Jersey ..0	3	1	2	0	1	1	2	1	0	1	2	0	3	2	1	..	1	2	2	0	1	1	0	1	0	2	30	52	.366	27
Philadelphia ..1	1	1	0	1	0	1	0	1	0	0	1	1	4	1	1	3	0	1	..	0	2	1	0	0	0	3	24	58	.293	33
Washington ..0	1	1	2	1	1	0	1	0	0	1	2	0	1	1	1	3	0	2	2	0	0	1	0	0	0	..	21	61	.256	36

CENTRAL DIVISION

	Atl.	Bos.	Char.	Chi.	Cle.	Dal.	Den.	Det.	G.S.	Hou.	Ind.	L.A.C.	L.A.L.	Mia.	Mil.	Min.	N.J.	N.Y.	Orl.	Phi.	Pho.	Por.	Sac.	S.A.	Sea.	Uta.	Was.	W	L	Pct.	GB
Indiana 4	2	4	2	3	1	1	2	2	1	..	2	1	2	3	2	3	1	2	4	1	1	2	2	1	0	3	52	30	.634	..
Charlotte 2	3	..	2	3	0	1	5	2	0	1	2	0	3	4	1	3	3	1	3	0	2	1	1	2	2	3	50	32	.610	2
Chicago 4	4	2	..	2	1	1	5	2	1	2	1	1	3	2	3	1	4	1	1	0	1	0	0	0	2	3	47	35	.573	5
Cleveland 4	2	2	3	..	0	1	2	2	0	2	1	1	4	1	4	2	1	3	1	1	1	0	0	1	3	43	39	.524	9
Atlanta 3	2	1	1	2	2	3	2	0	1	2	0	2	1	2	4	2	1	3	1	1	1	1	0	0	4	42	40	.512	10
Milwaukee ...3	3	1	4	0	1	0	3	2	1	2	1	1	0	..	1	2	2	0	3	0	0	1	0	0	0	3	34	48	.415	18
Detroit 2	1	0	0	2	1	1	..	1	0	2	1	0	1	2	1	2	1	1	4	1	0	1	0	0	0	3	28	54	.341	24

MIDWEST DIVISION

	Atl.	Bos.	Char.	Chi.	Cle.	Dal.	Den.	Det.	G.S.	Hou.	Ind.	L.A.C.	L.A.L.	Mia.	Mil.	Min.	N.J.	N.Y.	Orl.	Phi.	Pho.	Por.	Sac.	S.A.	Sea.	Uta.	Was.	W	L	Pct.	GB
San Antonio ..1	2	1	1	2	3	4	2	3	5	0	4	3	2	2	5	2	1	1	2	2	3	4	..	2	3	2	62	20	.756	..
Utah 2	2	0	2	1	4	4	2	2	3	2	3	2	2	4	2	1	2	2	3	4	2	3	..	2	0	2	60	22	.732	2
Houston 2	1	2	1	2	3	4	2	4	..	1	3	0	2	1	3	2	0	0	2	3	1	3	1	0	2	2	47	35	.573	15
Denver 0	1	1	1	1	4	..	1	1	1	4	2	2	2	6	1	0	0	1	3	2	1	1	1	2	41	41	.500	21
Dallas 0	1	2	1	2	..	1	1	3	2	1	3	1	0	1	4	1	0	0	2	0	3	2	2	0	2	1	36	46	.439	26
Minnesota ...0	0	1	0	1	1	0	1	3	2	0	3	1	1	1	..	1	0	1	1	0	0	1	0	1	1	21	61	.256	41

PACIFIC DIVISION

	Atl.	Bos.	Char.	Chi.	Cle.	Dal.	Den.	Det.	G.S.	Hou.	Ind.	L.A.C.	L.A.L.	Mia.	Mil.	Min.	N.J.	N.Y.	Orl.	Phi.	Pho.	Por.	Sac.	S.A.	Sea.	Uta.	Was.	W	L	Pct.	GB
Phoenix 1	1	2	1	1	4	3	1	2	1	4	4	2	2	4	2	1	1	2	..	5	4	2	4	2	2	59	23	.720	..
Seattle 2	1	0	2	2	4	3	2	4	4	1	5	1	2	2	4	1	2	2	2	1	3	2	2	..	1	2	57	25	.695	2
L.A. Lakers ..2	1	2	1	1	3	2	2	2	4	1	3	..	1	1	3	2	0	1	1	1	2	3	1	4	2	2	48	34	.585	11
Portland 1	2	0	1	1	1	2	4	3	1	5	3	2	2	4	1	1	0	0	0	..	3	1	2	1	2	4	44	38	.537	15
Sacramento ..1	1	1	2	1	2	2	1	5	1	0	4	2	2	1	3	1	0	1	1	2	..	0	3	0	1	3	39	43	.476	20
Golden State .0	0	0	0	0	1	3	1	..	0	0	3	3	1	0	1	1	1	0	1	3	1	0	1	1	2	2	26	56	.317	33
L.A. Clippers .0	2	0	1	1	1	0	1	2	1	0	..	2	0	1	1	0	0	0	1	1	0	1	0	1	0	0	17	65	.207	42

TEAM STATISTICS

OFFENSIVE

	G	FGM	FGA	Pct.	FTM	FTA	Pct.	Off.	Def.	Tot.	Ast.	PF	Dq.	Stl.	TO	Blk.	Pts.	Avg.
Orlando	82	3460	6899	.502	1648	2465	.669	1149	2457	3606	2281	1726	11	672	1297	488	9091	110.9
Phoenix	82	3356	6967	.482	1777	2352	.756	1027	2403	3430	2198	1839	10	687	1167	312	9073	110.6
Seattle	82	3310	6741	.491	1944	2564	.758	1068	2337	3405	2115	2067	21	917	1295	392	9055	110.4
San Antonio	82	3236	6687	.484	1836	2487	.738	1029	2661	3690	1919	1871	11	656	1246	456	8742	106.6
Utah	82	3243	6339	.512	1939	2483	.781	874	2412	3286	2256	2045	16	758	1289	392	8726	106.4
Golden State	82	3217	6873	.468	1687	2395	.704	1101	2371	3472	2017	1804	20	649	1497	391	8667	105.7
L.A. Lakers	82	3284	7088	.463	1523	2072	.735	1126	2316	3442	2078	1933	22	750	1243	563	8616	105.1
Houston	82	3159	6579	.480	1527	2039	.749	880	2440	3320	2060	1714	10	721	1322	514	8491	103.5
Dallas	82	3227	7342	.440	1622	2210	.734	1514	2433	3947	1941	1811	17	579	1345	348	8462	103.2
Portland	82	3217	7134	.451	1555	2230	.697	1352	2443	3795	1846	2024	17	668	1212	467	8451	103.1
Boston	82	3179	6847	.464	1708	2268	.753	1156	2320	3476	1783	1975	21	612	1305	361	8428	102.8
Chicago	82	3191	6710	.476	1500	2065	.726	1106	2294	3400	1970	1962	20	797	1297	352	8325	101.5
Denver	82	3098	6461	.479	1700	2305	.738	1040	2402	3442	1836	2063	23	660	1381	585	8309	101.3
Miami	82	3144	6738	.467	1569	2133	.736	1092	2272	3364	1779	2000	25	662	1291	298	8293	101.1
Charlotte	82	3051	6438	.474	1587	2042	.777	832	2395	3227	2072	1685	11	620	1224	399	8249	100.6
Washington	82	3176	6899	.460	1457	2013	.724	1044	2219	3263	1749	1949	16	648	1301	404	8242	100.5
Milwaukee	82	3022	6586	.459	1608	2259	.712	1063	2187	3250	1737	1858	22	674	1393	359	8146	99.3
Indiana	82	2983	6248	.477	1796	2390	.751	1051	2290	3341	1877	1939	16	703	1340	363	8136	99.2
Sacramento	82	3025	6463	.468	1647	2317	.711	1073	2325	3398	1824	2040	15	650	1449	457	8056	98.2
Detroit	82	3060	6633	.461	1439	1941	.741	958	2204	3162	1872	2151	24	705	1318	420	8053	98.2
New York	82	2985	6394	.467	1552	2114	.734	929	2473	3402	2055	2102	22	591	1305	387	8054	98.2
New Jersey	82	2939	6738	.436	1750	2305	.759	1213	2569	3782	1884	1844	18	544	1300	548	8042	98.1
L.A. Clippers	82	3060	6888	.444	1476	2079	.710	1064	2076	3140	1805	2152	19	787	1334	435	7927	96.7
Atlanta	82	2986	6680	.447	1410	1948	.724	1104	2272	3376	1757	1804	13	738	1221	412	7921	96.6
Philadelphia	82	2949	6577	.448	1567	2125	.737	1105	2230	3335	1566	1835	34	643	1355	576	7820	95.4
Minnesota	82	2792	6219	.449	1824	2355	.775	883	2090	2973	1780	2074	14	609	1400	402	7726	94.2
Cleveland	82	2756	6255	.441	1507	1982	.760	1045	2237	3282	1672	1694	11	630	1176	349	7417	90.5

DEFENSIVE

	FGM	FGA	Pct.	FTM	FTA	Pct.	Off.	Def.	Tot.	Ast.	PF	Dq.	Stl.	TO	Blk.	Pts.	Avg.	Dif.
Cleveland	2803	6083	.461	1364	1801	.757	851	2246	3097	1812	1770	14	556	1213	433	7366	89.8	+0.7
New York	2800	6410	.437	1802	2449	.736	1021	2317	3338	1584	1907	21	639	1264	324	7799	95.1	+3.1
Atlanta	3001	6485	.463	1394	1919	.726	1051	2391	3442	1733	1815	12	608	1359	320	7816	95.3	+1.3
Indiana	2921	6408	.456	1516	2089	.726	1048	2156	3204	1804	2058	24	691	1370	416	7833	95.5	+3.7
Chicago	2923	6399	.457	1682	2280	.738	1068	2252	3320	1713	1892	14	687	1485	369	7929	96.7	+4.8
Charlotte	3088	6807	.454	1375	1859	.740	1102	2365	3467	1898	1859	20	535	1216	368	7980	97.3	+3.3
Utah	2845	6282	.453	1835	2477	.741	917	2125	3042	1713	2053	15	648	1353	429	8071	98.4	+8.0
Sacramento	2964	6549	.453	1833	2473	.741	1145	2268	3413	1820	2033	18	756	1348	515	8138	99.2	-1.0
Portland	2951	6465	.456	1794	2380	.754	883	2295	3178	1789	1938	21	638	1302	405	8138	99.2	+3.9
Philadelphia	3100	6663	.465	1569	2057	.763	1143	2317	3460	1992	1859	22	712	1299	422	8236	100.4	-5.0
Denver	3050	6695	.456	1721	2296	.750	1021	2207	3228	1784	1956	24	640	1167	460	8240	100.5	+0.8
San Antonio	3168	6974	.454	1491	2089	.714	1017	2303	3320	1878	2063	25	633	1182	408	8253	100.6	+6.0
New Jersey	3182	6904	.461	1495	2073	.721	1056	2435	3491	1826	1911	21	733	1104	440	8299	101.2	-3.1
Houston	3202	7061	.453	1407	1874	.751	1165	2386	3551	1940	1779	12	744	1274	365	8317	101.4	+2.1
Seattle	3008	6637	.453	1848	2514	.735	1064	2207	3271	1849	2024	17	652	1485	493	8384	102.2	+8.2
Miami	3092	6566	.471	1732	2340	.740	1036	2355	3391	1860	1896	21	656	1332	385	8427	102.8	-1.7
Minnesota	3088	6509	.474	1820	2491	.731	1169	2305	3474	2069	1982	15	703	1323	512	8464	103.2	-9.0
Milwaukee	3248	6589	.493	1517	2081	.729	1014	2337	3351	2103	1973	18	770	1359	407	8504	103.7	-4.4
Orlando	3242	7093	.457	1560	2106	.741	1136	2226	3362	1986	1954	21	700	1234	367	8512	103.8	+7.1
Boston	3303	6820	.484	1601	2225	.720	1064	2335	3399	1999	1922	17	653	1232	454	8582	104.7	-1.9
L.A. Lakers	3299	7050	.468	1580	2233	.708	1283	2474	3757	2203	1807	16	644	1390	489	8634	105.3	-0.2
Detroit	3120	6558	.476	1963	2720	.722	1147	2432	3579	2013	1746	9	693	1286	439	8651	105.5	-7.3
L.A. Clippers	3207	6470	.496	1876	2503	.750	1083	2536	3619	1917	1905	9	693	1506	459	8678	105.8	-9.1
Dallas	3407	6982	.488	1454	1981	.734	1053	2379	3432	1991	1925	17	722	1250	502	8700	106.1	-2.9
Washington	3246	6768	.480	1771	2315	.765	1107	2521	3628	1959	1775	13	701	1359	446	8701	106.1	-5.6
Phoenix	3320	6963	.477	1590	2138	.744	1038	2431	3469	2149	2026	22	658	1285	391	8755	106.8	+3.8
Golden State	3527	7233	.488	1565	2175	.720	1196	2527	3723	2345	2133	21	865	1326	412	9111	111.1	-5.4
Avgs.	3115	6682	.466	1635	2220	.736	1070	2338	3408	1916	1924	18	679	1308	423	8315	101.4	...

HOME/ROAD

	Home	Road	Total		Home	Road	Total
Atlanta	24-17	18-23	42-40	Milwaukee	22-19	12-29	34-48
Boston	20-21	15-26	35-47	Minnesota	13-28	8-33	21-61
Charlotte	29-12	21-20	50-32	New Jersey	20-21	10-31	30-52
Chicago	28-13	19-22	47-35	New York	29-12	26-15	55-27
Cleveland	26-15	17-24	43-39	Orlando	39-2	18-23	57-25
Dallas	19-22	17-24	36-46	Philadelphia	14-27	10-31	24-58
Denver	23-18	18-23	41-41	Phoenix	32-9	27-14	59-23
Detroit	22-19	6-35	28-54	Portland	26-15	18-23	44-38
Golden State	15-26	11-30	26-56	Sacramento	27-14	12-29	39-43
Houston	25-16	22-19	47-35	San Antonio	33-8	29-12	62-20
Indiana	33-8	19-22	52-30	Seattle	32-9	25-16	57-25
L.A. Clippers	13-28	4-37	17-65	Utah	33-8	27-14	60-22
L.A. Lakers	29-12	19-22	48-34	Washington	13-28	8-33	21-61
Miami	22-19	10-31	32-50	Totals	661-446	446-661	1107-1107

1994-95

POINTS

(minimum 70 games or 1,400 points)

	G	FGM	FTM	Pts.	Avg.
Shaquille O'Neal, Orlando	.79	930	455	2315	29.3
Hakeem Olajuwon, Houston	.72	798	406	2005	27.8
David Robinson, San Antonio	.81	788	656	2238	27.6
Karl Malone, Utah	.82	830	516	2187	26.7
Jamal Mashburn, Dallas	.80	683	447	1926	24.1
Patrick Ewing, New York	.79	730	420	1886	23.9
Charles Barkley, Phoenix	.68	554	379	1561	23.0
Mitch Richmond, Sacramento	.82	668	375	1867	22.8
Glen Rice, Miami	.82	667	312	1831	22.3
Glenn Robinson, Milwaukee	.80	636	397	1755	21.9

REBOUNDS

(minimum 70 games or 800 rebounds)

	G	Off.	Def.	Tot.	Avg.
Dennis Rodman, San Antonio	.49	274	549	823	16.8
Dikembe Mutombo, Denver	.82	319	710	1029	12.5
Shaquille O'Neal, Orlando	.79	328	573	901	11.4
Patrick Ewing, New York	.79	157	710	867	11.0
Shawn Kemp, Seattle	.82	318	575	893	10.9
Tyrone Hill, Cleveland	.70	269	496	765	10.9
David Robinson, San Antonio	.81	234	643	877	10.8
Hakeem Olajuwon, Houston	.72	172	603	775	10.8
Karl Malone, Utah	.82	156	715	871	10.6
Popeye Jones, Dallas	.80	329	515	844	10.6

FIELD GOALS

(minimum 300 made)

	FGM	FGA	Pct.
Chris Gatling, Golden State	.324	512	.633
Shaquille O'Neal, Orlando	.930	1594	.583
Horace Grant, Orlando	.401	707	.567
Otis Thorpe, Houston-Portland	.385	681	.565
Dale Davis, Indiana	.324	576	.563
Gheorghe Muresan, Washington	.303	541	.560
Dikembe Mutombo, Denver	.349	628	.556
Shawn Kemp, Seattle	.545	997	.547
Danny Manning, Phoenix	.340	622	.547
Olden Polynice, Sacramento	.376	691	.544

STEALS

(minimum 70 games or 125 steals)

	G	No.	Avg.
Scottie Pippen, Chicago	.79	232	2.94
Mookie Blaylock, Atlanta	.80	200	2.50
Gary Payton, Seattle	.82	204	2.49
John Stockton, Utah	.82	194	2.37
Nate McMillan, Seattle	.80	165	2.06
Eddie Jones, L.A. Lakers	.64	131	2.05
Jason Kidd, Dallas	.79	151	1.91
Elliot Perry, Phoenix	.82	156	1.90
Hakeem Olajuwon, Houston	.72	133	1.85
Dana Barros, Philadelphia	.82	149	1.82

FREE THROWS

(minimum 125 made)

	FTM	FTA	Pct.
Spud Webb, Sacramento	.226	242	.934
Mark Price, Cleveland	.148	162	.914
Dana Barros, Philadelphia	.347	386	.899
Reggie Miller, Indiana	.383	427	.897
Muggsy Bogues, Charlotte	.160	180	.889
Scott Skiles, Washington	.179	202	.886
Mahmoud Abdul-Rauf, Denver	.138	156	.885
B.J. Armstrong, Chicago	.206	233	.884
Jeff Hornacek, Utah	.284	322	.882
Keith Jennings, Golden State	.134	153	.876

BLOCKED SHOTS

(minimum 70 games or 100 blocked shots)

	G	No.	Avg.
Dikembe Mutombo, Denver	.82	321	3.91
Hakeem Olajuwon, Houston	.72	242	3.36
Shawn Bradley, Philadelphia	.82	274	3.34
David Robinson, San Antonio	.81	262	3.23
Alonzo Mourning, Charlotte	.77	225	2.92
Shaquille O'Neal, Orlando	.79	192	2.43
Vlade Divac, L.A. Lakers	.80	174	2.18
Patrick Ewing, New York	.79	159	2.01
Charles Outlaw, L.A. Clippers	.81	151	1.86
Elden Campbell, L.A. Lakers	.73	132	1.81
Oliver Miller, Detroit	.64	116	1.81

ASSISTS

(minimum 70 games or 400 assists)

	G	No.	Avg.
John Stockton, Utah	.82	1011	12.3
Kenny Anderson, New Jersey	.72	680	9.4
Tim Hardaway, Golden State	.62	578	9.3
Rod Strickland, Portland	.64	562	8.8
Muggsy Bogues, Charlotte	.78	675	8.7
Nick Van Exel, L.A. Lakers	.80	660	8.3
Avery Johnson, San Antonio	.82	670	8.2
Pooh Richardson, L.A. Clippers	.80	632	7.9
Mookie Blaylock, Atlanta	.80	616	7.7
Jason Kidd, Dallas	.79	607	7.7

3-POINT FIELD GOALS

(minimum 82 made)

	FGM	FGA	Pct.
Steve Kerr, Chicago	.89	170	.524
Detlef Schrempf, Seattle	.93	181	.514
Dana Barros, Philadelphia	.197	425	.464
Hubert Davis, New York	.131	288	.455
John Stockton, Utah	.102	227	.449
Hersey Hawkins, Charlotte	.131	298	.440
Wesley Person, Phoenix	.116	266	.436
Kenny Smith, Houston	.142	331	.429
Dell Curry, Charlotte	.154	361	.427
B.J. Armstrong, Chicago	.108	253	.427

INDIVIDUAL STATISTICS, TEAM BY TEAM

ATLANTA HAWKS

	G	Min.	FGM	FGA	Pct.	FTM	FTA	Pct.	REBOUNDS Off.	Def.	Tot.	Ast.	PF	Dq.	Stl.	TO	Blk.	SCORING Pts.	Avg.	Hi.
Kevin Willis*	2	89	16	41	.390	10	15	.667	10	26	36	3	7	0	1	7	3	42	21.0	24
Mookie Blaylock	80	3069	509	1198	.425	156	214	.729	117	276	393	616	164	3	200	242	26	1373	17.2	35
Steve Smith†	78	2603	417	976	.427	295	349	.845	100	170	270	267	216	2	60	151	32	1264	16.2	37
Steve Smith‡	80	2665	428	1005	.426	312	371	.841	104	172	276	274	225	2	62	155	33	1305	16.3	37
Stacey Augmon	76	2362	397	876	.453	252	346	.728	157	211	368	197	163	0	100	152	47	1053	13.9	34
Ken Norman	74	1879	388	856	.453	64	140	.457	103	259	362	94	154	0	34	96	20	938	12.7	34
Grant Long†	79	2579	337	704	.479	238	315	.756	190	405	595	127	232	2	107	151	34	923	11.7	33
Grant Long‡	81	2641	342	716	.478	244	325	.751	191	415	606	131	243	3	109	155	34	939	11.6	33
Andrew Lang	82	2340	320	677	.473	152	188	.809	154	302	456	72	271	4	45	108	144	794	9.7	21

	G	Min.	FGM	FGA	Pct.	FTM	FTA	Pct.	Off.	Def.	Tot.	Ast.	PF	Dq.	Stl.	TO	Blk.	Pts.	Avg.	Hi.
									REBOUNDS									**SCORING**		
Craig Ehlo.........	49	1166	191	422	.453	44	71	.620	55	92	147	113	86	0	46	73	6	477	9.7	22
Tyrone Corbin......	81	1389	205	464	.442	78	114	.684	98	164	262	67	161	1	55	74	16	502	6.2	21
Sergei Bazarevich..	10	74	11	22	.500	7	9	.778	1	6	7	14	10	0	1	7	1	30	3.0	9
Jon Koncak........	62	943	77	187	.412	13	24	.542	23	161	184	52	137	1	36	20	46	179	2.9	9
Greg Anderson.....	51	622	57	104	.548	34	71	.479	62	126	188	17	103	0	23	32	32	148	2.9	17
Ennis Whatley......	27	292	24	53	.453	20	32	.625	9	21	30	54	37	0	19	19	0	70	2.6	11
Jim Les	24	188	11	38	.289	23	27	.852	6	20	26	44	28	0	4	21	0	50	2.1	12
Doug Edwards	38	212	22	48	.458	23	32	.719	19	29	48	13	30	0	5	22	4	67	1.8	8
Morlon Wiley†	5	17	3	6	.500	0	0	...	0	4	4	6	0	0	1	4	1	7	1.4	7
Morlon Wiley‡	43	424	50	117	.427	7	10	.700	6	37	43	75	44	0	22	23	2	137	3.2	14
Fred Vinson	5	27	1	7	.143	1	1	1.000	0	0	0	1	4	0	0	2	0	4	0.8	3
Tom Hovasse	2	4	0	1	.000	0	0	...	0	0	0	0	1	0	1	0	0	0	0.0	0

3-pt. FG: Atlanta 539-1580 (.341)—Willis* 0-1 (.000); Blaylock 199-555 (.359); Smith† 135-404 (.334); Smith‡ 137-416 (.329); Augmon 7-26 (.269); Norman 98-285 (.344); Long† 11-31 (.355); Long‡ 11-31 (.355); Lang 2-3 (.667); Ehlo 51-134 (.381); Corbin 14-56 (.250); Bazarevich 1-6 (.167); Koncak 12-36 (.333); Whatley 2-8 (.250); Les 5-23 (.217); Edwards 0-1 (.000); Wiley† 1-4 (.250); Wiley‡ 30-79 (.380); Vinson 1-6 (.167); Hovasse 0-1 (.000). Opponents 420-1212 (.347).

BOSTON CELTICS

	G	Min.	FGM	FGA	Pct.	FTM	FTA	Pct.	Off.	Def.	Tot.	Ast.	PF	Dq.	Stl.	TO	Blk.	Pts.	Avg.	Hi.
									REBOUNDS									**SCORING**		
Dominique Wilkins ...	77	2423	496	1169	.424	266	340	.782	157	244	401	166	130	0	61	173	14	1370	17.8	43
Dino Radja	66	2147	450	919	.490	233	307	.759	149	424	573	111	232	5	60	159	86	1133	17.2	31
Dee Brown	79	2792	437	977	.447	236	277	.852	63	186	249	301	181	0	110	146	49	1236	15.6	41
Sherman Douglas ...	65	2048	365	769	.475	204	296	.689	48	122	170	446	152	0	80	162	2	954	14.7	33
Eric Montross.......	78	2315	307	575	.534	167	263	.635	196	370	566	36	299	10	29	112	61	781	10.0	28
Rick Fox	53	1309	169	351	.481	95	123	.772	61	94	155	139	154	1	52	78	19	464	8.8	21
Xavier McDaniel	68	1430	246	546	.451	89	125	.712	94	206	300	108	146	0	30	89	20	587	8.6	23
David Wesley	51	1380	128	313	.409	71	94	.755	31	86	117	266	144	0	82	87	9	378	7.4	23
Blue Edwards*	31	507	83	195	.426	43	48	.896	25	40	65	47	64	0	19	39	10	220	7.1	22
Pervis Ellison	55	1083	152	300	.507	71	99	.717	124	185	309	34	179	5	22	76	54	375	6.8	20
Derek Strong	70	1344	149	329	.453	141	172	.820	136	239	375	44	143	0	24	79	13	441	6.3	25
Greg Minor.........	63	946	166	301	.515	65	78	.833	49	88	137	66	89	0	32	44	16	377	6.0	31
Tony Harris.........	3	18	3	8	.375	8	9	.889	0	0	0	2	0	0	1	0	1	14	4.7	7
Tony Dawson	2	13	3	8	.375	1	1	1.000	0	3	3	1	4	0	0	2	0	8	4.0	8
Acie Earl..........	30	208	26	68	.382	14	29	.483	19	26	45	2	39	0	6	14	8	66	2.2	11
Jay Humphries†	6	52	4	9	.444	2	4	.500	2	1	3	10	10	0	2	5	0	10	1.7	4
Jay Humphries‡	18	201	8	34	.235	2	4	.500	4	9	13	19	35	0	9	17	0	20	1.1	4
James Blackwell†	9	61	6	10	.600	2	3	.667	2	6	8	6	7	0	3	3	0	14	1.6	6
James Blackwell‡	13	80	8	13	.615	2	3	.667	2	9	11	11	8	0	4	5	0	18	1.4	6

3-pt. FG: Boston 362-984 (.368)—Wilkins 112-289 (.388); Radja 0-1 (.000); Brown 126-327 (.385); Douglas 20-82 (.244); Montross 0-1 (.000); Fox 31-75 (.413); McDaniel 6-21 (.286); Wesley 51-119 (.429); Edwards* 11-43 (.256); Ellison 0-2 (.000); Strong 2-7 (.286); Minor 2-12 (.167); Harris 0-1 (.000); Dawson 1-3 (.333); Humphries† 0-1 (.000); Humphries‡ 2-4 (.500). Opponents 375-1047 (.358).

CHARLOTTE HORNETS

	G	Min.	FGM	FGA	Pct.	FTM	FTA	Pct.	Off.	Def.	Tot.	Ast.	PF	Dq.	Stl.	TO	Blk.	Pts.	Avg.	Hi.
									REBOUNDS									**SCORING**		
Alonzo Mourning.....	77	2941	571	1101	.519	490	644	.761	200	561	761	111	275	5	49	241	225	1643	21.3	36
Larry Johnson	81	3234	585	1219	.480	274	354	.774	190	395	585	369	174	2	78	207	28	1525	18.8	39
Hersey Hawkins	82	2731	390	809	.482	261	301	.867	60	254	314	262	178	1	122	150	18	1172	14.3	31
Dell Curry.........	69	1718	343	778	.441	95	111	.856	41	127	168	113	144	1	55	98	18	935	13.6	30
Scott Burrell	65	2014	277	593	.467	100	144	.694	96	272	368	161	187	1	75	85	40	750	11.5	25
Muggsy Bogues ...	78	2299	348	730	.477	160	180	.889	51	206	257	675	151	0	103	132	0	862	11.1	23
Michael Adams	29	443	67	148	.453	25	30	.833	6	23	29	95	41	0	23	26	1	188	6.5	15
Kenny Gattison	21	409	47	100	.470	31	51	.608	21	54	75	17	64	1	7	22	15	125	6.0	16
Greg Sutton	53	690	94	230	.409	32	45	.711	8	48	56	91	114	0	33	51	2	263	5.0	17
Robert Parish	81	1352	159	372	.427	71	101	.703	93	257	350	44	132	0	27	66	36	389	4.8	16
Tony Bennett........	3	46	6	13	.462	0	0	...	0	2	2	4	6	0	0	3	0	14	4.7	12
Darrin Hancock	46	424	68	121	.562	16	39	.410	14	39	53	30	48	0	19	30	4	153	3.3	15
David Wingate......	52	515	50	122	.410	18	24	.750	11	49	60	56	60	0	19	27	6	122	2.3	11
Joe Wolf...........	63	583	38	81	.469	12	16	.750	34	95	129	37	101	0	9	22	6	90	1.4	9
Tom Tolbert	10	57	6	18	.333	2	2	1.000	7	10	17	2	9	0	0	3	0	14	1.4	4
James Blackwell* ...	4	19	2	3	.667	0	0	...	0	3	3	5	1	0	1	2	0	4	1.0	4

3-pt. FG: Charlotte 560-1409 (.397)—Mourning 11-34 (.324); Johnson 81-210 (.386); Hawkins 131-298 (.440); Curry 154-361 (.427); Burrell 96-235 (.409); Bogues 6-30 (.200); Adams 29-81 (.358); Gattison 0-1 (.000); Sutton 43-115 (.374); Bennett 2-9 (.222); Hancock 1-3 (.333); Wingate 4-22 (.182); Wolf 2-6 (.333); Tolbert 0-4 (.000). Opponents 429-1289 (.333).

CHICAGO BULLS

	G	Min.	FGM	FGA	Pct.	FTM	FTA	Pct.	Off.	Def.	Tot.	Ast.	PF	Dq.	Stl.	TO	Blk.	Pts.	Avg.	Hi.
									REBOUNDS									**SCORING**		
Michael Jordan......	17	668	166	404	.411	109	136	.801	25	92	117	90	47	0	30	35	13	457	26.9	55
Scottie Pippen	79	3014	634	1320	.480	315	440	.716	175	464	639	409	238	4	232	271	89	1692	21.4	40
Toni Kukoc	81	2584	487	967	.504	235	314	.748	155	285	440	372	163	1	102	165	16	1271	15.7	43
B.J. Armstrong	82	2577	418	894	.468	206	233	.884	25	161	186	244	159	0	84	103	8	1150	14.0	27
Steve Kerr.........	82	1839	261	495	.527	63	81	.778	20	99	119	151	114	0	44	48	3	674	8.2	19

	G	Min.	FGM	FGA	Pct.	FTM	FTA	Pct.	Off.	Def.	Tot.	Ast.	PF	Dq.	Stl.	TO	Blk.	Pts.	Avg.	Hi.
									REBOUNDS									**SCORING**		
Will Perdue.........	78	1592	254	459	.553	113	194	.582	211	311	522	90	220	3	26	116	56	621	8.0	19
Ron Harper.........	77	1536	209	491	.426	81	131	.618	51	129	180	157	132	1	97	100	27	530	6.9	27
Luc Longley	55	1001	135	302	.447	88	107	.822	82	181	263	73	177	5	24	86	45	358	6.5	14
Greg Foster*........	17	299	41	86	.477	22	31	.710	18	36	54	16	54	0	2	17	8	104	6.1	16
Jo Jo English	8	127	15	39	.385	10	13	.769	1	2	3	7	19	0	7	6	1	43	5.4	11
Bill Wennington ...	73	956	156	317	.492	51	63	.810	64	126	190	40	198	5	22	39	17	363	5.0	16
Pete Myers	71	1270	119	287	.415	70	114	.614	57	82	139	148	125	1	58	88	15	318	4.5	14
Larry Krystkowiak....	19	287	28	72	.389	27	30	.900	19	40	59	26	34	0	9	25	2	83	4.4	14
Jud Buechler........	57	605	90	183	.492	22	39	.564	36	62	98	50	64	0	24	30	12	217	3.8	17
Corie Blount	68	889	100	210	.476	38	67	.567	107	133	240	60	146	0	26	59	33	238	3.5	16
Dickey Simpkins	59	586	78	184	.424	50	72	.694	60	91	151	37	72	0	10	45	7	206	3.5	16

3-pt. FG: Chicago 443-1187 (.373)—Jordan 16-32 (.500); Pippen 109-316 (.345); Kukoc 62-198 (.313); Armstrong 108-253 (.427); Kerr 89-170 (.524); Perdue 0-1 (.000); Harper 31-110 (.282); Longley 0-2 (.000); English 3-12 (.250); Wennington 0-4 (.000); Myers 10-39 (.256); Buechler 15-48 (.313); Blount 0-2 (.000). Opponents 401-1150 (.349).

CLEVELAND CAVALIERS

	G	Min.	FGM	FGA	Pct.	FTM	FTA	Pct.	Off.	Def.	Tot.	Ast.	PF	Dq.	Stl.	TO	Blk.	Pts.	Avg.	Hi.
									REBOUNDS									**SCORING**		
Mark Price	48	1375	253	612	.413	148	162	.914	25	87	112	335	50	0	35	142	4	757	15.8	36
Tyrone Hill	70	2397	350	694	.504	263	397	.662	269	496	765	55	245	4	55	151	41	963	13.8	29
Terrell Brandon	67	1961	341	762	.448	159	186	.855	35	151	186	363	118	0	107	144	14	889	13.3	31
John Williams.......	74	2641	366	810	.452	196	286	.685	173	334	507	192	211	2	83	149	101	929	12.6	24
Chris Mills	80	2814	359	855	.420	174	213	.817	99	267	366	154	242	2	59	120	35	986	12.3	26
Bobby Phills	80	2500	338	816	.414	183	235	.779	90	175	265	180	206	0	115	113	25	878	11.0	24
Danny Ferry	82	1290	223	500	.446	74	84	.881	30	113	143	96	131	0	27	59	22	614	7.5	24
Tony Campbell	78	1128	161	392	.411	132	159	.830	60	93	153	69	122	0	32	65	8	469	6.0	23
Michael Cage	82	2040	177	340	.521	53	88	.602	203	361	564	56	149	1	61	56	67	407	5.0	15
John Battle	28	280	43	114	.377	19	26	.731	3	8	11	37	28	0	8	17	1	116	4.1	17
Fred Roberts	21	223	28	72	.389	20	26	.769	13	21	34	8	26	1	6	7	3	80	3.8	14
Elmer Bennett........	4	18	6	11	.545	3	4	.750	0	1	1	3	3	0	4	3	0	15	3.8	6
Steve Colter	57	752	67	169	.396	54	71	.761	13	46	59	101	53	0	30	36	6	196	3.4	16
Greg Dreiling	58	483	42	102	.412	26	41	.634	32	84	116	22	108	1	6	25	22	110	1.9	11
Gerald Madkins.......	7	28	2	6	.333	3	4	.750	0	0	0	1	2	0	2	3	0	8	1.1	7

3-pt. FG: Cleveland 398-1033 (.385)—Price 103-253 (.407); Hill 0-1 (.000); Brandon 48-121 (.397); Williams 1-5 (.200); Mills 94-240 (.392); Phills 19-55 (.345); Ferry 94-233 (.403); Campbell 15-42 (.357); Cage 0-2 (.000); Battle 11-31 (.355); Roberts 4-11 (.364); Bennett 0-2 (.000); Colter 8-35 (.229); Madkins 1-2 (.500). Opponents 396-1108 (.357).

DALLAS MAVERICKS

	G	Min.	FGM	FGA	Pct.	FTM	FTA	Pct.	Off.	Def.	Tot.	Ast.	PF	Dq.	Stl.	TO	Blk.	Pts.	Avg.	Hi.
									REBOUNDS									**SCORING**		
Jim Jackson	51	1982	484	1026	.472	306	380	.805	120	140	260	191	92	0	28	160	12	1309	25.7	50
Jamal Mashburn.....	80	2980	683	1566	.436	447	605	.739	116	215	331	298	190	0	82	235	8	1926	24.1	50
Roy Tarpley.........	55	1354	292	610	.479	102	122	.836	142	307	449	58	155	2	45	109	55	691	12.6	26
Jason Kidd	79	2668	330	857	.385	192	275	.698	152	278	430	607	146	0	151	250	24	922	11.7	38
Popeye Jones	80	2385	372	839	.443	80	124	.645	329	515	844	163	267	5	35	124	27	825	10.3	25
George McCloud....	42	802	144	328	.439	80	96	.833	82	65	147	53	71	0	23	40	9	402	9.6	25
Lucious Harris	79	1695	280	610	.459	136	170	.800	85	135	220	132	105	0	58	77	14	751	9.5	31
Scott Brooks†.......	31	622	91	210	.433	46	58	.793	13	40	53	94	42	0	26	33	3	245	7.9	21
Scott Brooks‡.......	59	808	126	275	.458	64	79	.810	14	52	66	116	56	0	34	47	4	341	5.8	23
Doug Smith	63	826	131	314	.417	57	75	.760	43	101	144	40	132	1	29	37	26	320	5.1	18
Tony Dumas	58	613	96	250	.384	50	77	.649	32	30	62	57	78	0	13	50	4	264	4.6	24
Lorenzo Williams	82	2383	145	304	.477	38	101	.376	291	399	690	124	306	6	52	105	148	328	4.0	19
Donald Hodge	54	633	83	204	.407	39	51	.765	40	82	122	41	107	1	10	39	14	209	3.9	13
Morlon Wiley*	38	407	47	111	.423	7	10	.700	6	33	39	69	44	0	21	19	1	130	3.4	14
Terry Davis	46	580	49	113	.434	42	66	.636	63	93	156	10	76	2	6	30	3	140	3.0	11

3-pt. FG: Dallas 386-1200 (.322)—Jackson 35-110 (.318); Mashburn 113-344 (.328); Tarpley 5-18 (.278); Kidd 70-257 (.272); Jones 1-12 (.083); McCloud 34-89 (.382); Harris 55-142 (.387); Brooks† 17-52 (.327); Brooks‡ 25-69 (.362); Smith 1-12 (.083); Dumas 22-73 (.301); Hodge 4-14 (.286); Wiley* 29-75 (.387); Davis 0-2 (.000). Opponents 432-1181 (.366).

DENVER NUGGETS

	G	Min.	FGM	FGA	Pct.	FTM	FTA	Pct.	Off.	Def.	Tot.	Ast.	PF	Dq.	Stl.	TO	Blk.	Pts.	Avg.	Hi.
									REBOUNDS									**SCORING**		
Mahmoud Abdul-Rauf.	73	2082	472	1005	.470	138	156	.885	32	105	137	263	126	0	77	119	9	1165	16.0	36
Reggie Williams	74	2198	388	846	.459	132	174	.759	94	235	329	231	264	4	114	124	67	993	13.4	31
Rodney Rogers......	80	2142	375	769	.488	179	275	.651	132	253	385	161	281	7	95	173	46	979	12.2	31
Robert Pack	42	1144	170	395	.430	137	175	.783	19	94	113	290	101	1	61	134	6	507	12.1	30
Dikembe Mutombo ..	82	3100	349	628	.556	248	379	.654	319	710	1029	113	284	2	40	192	321	946	11.5	26
Dale Ellis...........	81	1996	351	774	.453	110	127	.866	56	166	222	57	142	0	37	81	9	918	11.3	24
Bryant Stith	81	2329	312	661	.472	267	324	.824	95	173	268	153	142	0	91	110	18	911	11.2	27
Jalen Rose	81	1798	227	500	.454	173	234	.739	57	160	217	389	206	0	65	160	22	663	8.2	21
Brian Williams.......	63	1261	196	333	.589	106	162	.654	98	200	298	53	210	7	38	114	43	498	7.9	29
Tom Hammonds	70	956	139	260	.535	132	177	.746	55	167	222	36	132	1	11	56	14	410	5.9	22
Reggie Slater	25	236	40	81	.494	40	55	.727	21	36	57	12	47	0	7	26	3	120	4.8	16

	G	Min.	FGM	FGA	Pct.	FTM	FTA	Pct.	REBOUNDS			Ast.	PF	Dq.	Stl.	TO	Blk.	SCORING		
									Off.	Def.	Tot.							Pts.	Avg.	Hi.
LaPhonso Ellis	6	58	9	25	.360	6	6	1.000	7	10	17	4	12	0	1	5	5	24	4.0	12
Cliff Levingston	57	469	55	130	.423	19	45	.422	49	75	124	27	91	0	13	21	20	129	2.3	9
Greg Grant	14	151	10	33	.303	9	12	.750	2	7	9	43	20	1	6	14	2	31	2.2	8
Eldridge Recasner	3	13	1	6	.167	4	4	1.000	0	2	2	1	0	0	3	2	0	6	2.0	4
Darnell Mee	2	8	1	5	.200	0	0	...	0	1	1	2	0	0	1	0	0	3	1.5	3
Mark Randall	8	39	3	10	.300	0		...	4	8	12	1	5	0	0	1	0	6	0.8	2

3-pt. FG: Denver 413-1160 (.356)—Abdul-Rauf 83-215 (.386); R. Williams 85-266 (.320); Rogers 50-148 (.338); Pack 30-72 (.417); D. Ellis 106-263 (.403); Stith 20-68 (.294); Rose 36-114 (.316); Hammonds 0-1 (.000); Levingston 0-1 (.000); Grant 2-7 (.286); Recasner 0-1 (.000); Mee 1-3 (.333); Randall 0-1 (.000). Opponents 419-1208 (.347).

DETROIT PISTONS

	G	Min.	FGM	FGA	Pct.	FTM	FTA	Pct.	REBOUNDS			Ast.	PF	Dq.	Stl.	TO	Blk.	SCORING		
									Off.	Def.	Tot.							Pts.	Avg.	Hi.
Grant Hill	70	2678	508	1064	.477	374	511	.732	125	320	445	353	203	1	124	202	62	1394	19.9	33
Joe Dumars	67	2544	417	970	.430	277	344	.805	47	111	158	368	153	0	72	219	7	1214	18.1	43
Terry Mills	72	2514	417	933	.447	175	219	.799	124	434	558	160	253	5	68	144	33	1118	15.5	37
Allan Houston	76	1996	398	859	.463	147	171	.860	29	138	167	164	182	0	61	113	14	1101	14.5	36
Oliver Miller	64	1558	232	418	.555	78	124	.629	162	313	475	93	217	1	60	115	116	545	8.5	21
Rafael Addison	79	1776	279	586	.476	74	99	.747	67	175	242	109	236	2	53	76	25	656	8.3	25
Mark West	67	1543	217	390	.556	66	138	.478	160	248	408	18	247	8	27	85	102	500	7.5	19
Lindsey Hunter	42	944	119	318	.374	40	55	.727	24	51	75	159	94	1	51	79	7	314	7.5	24
Johnny Dawkins	50	1170	125	270	.463	50	55	.909	28	85	113	205	74	1	52	86	1	325	6.5	17
Mark Macon	55	721	101	265	.381	54	68	.794	29	47	76	63	97	1	67	41	1	276	5.0	17
Negele Knight†	44	665	78	199	.392	14	21	.667	20	38	58	116	65	0	20	45	5	181	4.1	15
Negele Knight‡	47	708	85	214	.397	18	25	.720	21	40	61	127	70	0	21	49	5	199	4.2	15
Eric Leckner	57	623	87	165	.527	51	72	.708	47	127	174	14	122	1	15	39	15	225	3.9	16
Bill Curley	53	595	58	134	.433	27	36	.750	54	70	124	25	128	3	21	25	21	143	2.7	15
Walter Bond*	5	51	3	12	.250	3	4	.750	1	4	5	7	10	0	1	3	0	10	2.0	5
Mike Peplowski	6	21	5	5	1.000	1	2	.500	1	2	3	1	10	0	1	2	0	11	1.8	5
Ivano Newbill	34	331	16	45	.356	8	22	.364	40	41	81	17	60	0	12	12	11	40	1.2	6

3-pt. FG: Detroit 494-1396 (.354)—Hill 4-27 (.148); Dumars 103-338 (.305); Mills 109-285 (.382); Houston 158-373 (.424); Miller 3-13 (.231); Addison 24-83 (.289); Hunter 36-108 (.333); Dawkins 25-73 (.342); Macon 20-62 (.323); Knight† 11-28 (.393); Knight‡ 11-28 (.393); Leckner 0-2 (.000); Bond* 1-4 (.250). Opponents 448-1235 (.363).

GOLDEN STATE WARRIORS

	G	Min.	FGM	FGA	Pct.	FTM	FTA	Pct.	REBOUNDS			Ast.	PF	Dq.	Stl.	TO	Blk.	SCORING		
									Off.	Def.	Tot.							Pts.	Avg.	Hi.
Latrell Sprewell	69	2771	490	1171	.418	350	448	.781	58	198	256	279	108	0	112	230	46	1420	20.6	40
Tim Hardaway	62	2321	430	1007	.427	219	288	.760	46	144	190	578	155	1	88	214	12	1247	20.1	32
Chris Mullin	25	890	170	348	.489	94	107	.879	25	90	115	125	53	0	38	93	19	476	19.0	33
Donyell Marshall†	32	1050	187	453	.413	64	100	.640	73	136	209	48	94	1	20	57	38	475	14.8	29
Donyell Marshall‡	72	2086	345	876	.394	147	222	.662	137	268	405	105	157	1	45	115	88	906	12.6	30
Chris Gatling	58	1470	324	512	.633	148	250	.592	144	299	443	51	184	4	39	117	52	796	13.7	29
Ricky Pierce	27	673	111	254	.437	93	106	.877	12	52	64	40	38	0	22	24	2	338	12.5	27
Rony Seikaly	36	1035	162	314	.516	111	160	.694	77	189	266	45	122	1	20	104	37	435	12.1	38
Tom Gugliotta*	40	1324	176	397	.443	55	97	.567	100	197	297	122	98	2	50	93	23	435	10.9	27
Victor Alexander	50	1237	230	447	.515	36	60	.600	87	204	291	60	145	2	28	76	29	502	10.0	23
Carlos Rogers	49	1017	180	340	.529	76	146	.521	108	170	278	37	124	2	22	84	52	438	8.9	22
Keith Jennings	80	1722	190	425	.447	134	153	.876	26	122	148	373	133	0	95	120	2	589	7.4	23
Ryan Lorthridge	37	672	106	223	.475	57	88	.648	24	47	71	101	42	0	28	57	1	272	7.4	18
Tim Legler	24	371	60	115	.522	30	34	.882	12	28	40	27	33	0	12	20	1	176	7.3	24
Cliff Rozier	66	1494	189	390	.485	68	152	.447	200	286	486	45	196	2	35	89	39	448	6.8	26
David Wood	78	1336	153	326	.469	91	117	.778	83	158	241	65	217	4	28	53	13	428	5.5	20
Dwayne Morton	41	395	50	129	.388	58	85	.682	21	37	58	18	45	1	11	27	15	167	4.1	14
Manute Bol	5	81	6	10	.600	0	0	...	1	11	12	0	10	0	0	1	9	15	3.0	9
Rod Higgins	5	46	3	12	.250	3	4	.750	4	3	7	3	7	0	1	1	1	10	2.0	9

3-pt. FG: Golden State 546-1602 (.341)—Sprewell 90-326 (.276); Hardaway 168-444 (.378); Mullin 42-93 (.452); Marshall† 37-137 (.270); Marshall‡ 69-243 (.284); Gatling 0-1 (.000); Pierce 23-70 (.329); Gugliotta* 28-90 (.311); Alexander 6-25 (.240); Rogers 2-14 (.143); Jennings 75-204 (.368); Lorthridge 3-14 (.214); Legler 26-50 (.520); Rozier 2-7 (.286); Wood 31-91 (.341); Morton 9-25 (.360); Bol 3-5 (.600); Higgins 1-6 (.167). Opponents 492-1384 (.355).

HOUSTON ROCKETS

	G	Min.	FGM	FGA	Pct.	FTM	FTA	Pct.	REBOUNDS			Ast.	PF	Dq.	Stl.	TO	Blk.	SCORING		
									Off.	Def.	Tot.							Pts.	Avg.	Hi.
Hakeem Olajuwon	72	2853	798	1545	.517	406	537	.756	172	603	775	255	250	3	133	237	242	2005	27.8	47
Clyde Drexler†	35	1300	266	526	.506	157	194	.809	68	178	246	154	89	1	62	89	23	749	21.4	41
Clyde Drexler‡	76	2728	571	1238	.461	364	442	.824	152	328	480	362	206	1	136	186	45	1653	21.8	41
Vernon Maxwell	64	2038	306	777	.394	99	144	.688	18	146	164	274	157	1	75	137	13	854	13.3	27
Otis Thorpe*	36	1188	206	366	.563	67	127	.528	113	209	322	58	102	1	22	76	13	479	13.3	27
Kenny Smith	81	2030	287	593	.484	126	148	.851	27	128	155	323	109	1	71	123	10	842	10.4	29
Robert Horry	64	2074	240	537	.447	86	113	.761	81	243	324	216	161	0	94	122	76	652	10.2	21
Sam Cassell	82	1882	253	593	.427	214	254	.843	38	173	211	405	209	3	94	167	14	783	9.5	31
Mario Elie	81	1896	243	487	.499	144	171	.842	50	146	196	189	158	0	65	104	12	710	8.8	25

	G	Min.	FGM	FGA	Pct.	FTM	FTA	Pct.	Off.	Def.	Tot.	Ast.	PF	Dq.	Stl.	TO	Blk.	Pts.	Avg.	Hi.
Carl Herrera	61	1331	171	327	.523	73	117	.624	98	180	278	44	136	0	40	71	38	415	6.8	22
Chucky Brown	41	814	105	174	.603	38	62	.613	64	125	189	30	105	0	11	29	14	249	6.1	19
Pete Chilcutt	68	1347	146	328	.445	31	42	.738	106	211	317	66	117	0	25	61	43	358	5.3	25
Tracy Murray†	25	203	32	80	.400	5	8	.625	2	20	22	5	31	0	7	15	3	88	3.5	17
Tracy Murray‡	54	516	95	233	.408	33	42	.786	20	39	59	19	73	0	14	35	4	258	4.8	19
Scott Brooks*	28	186	35	65	.538	18	21	.857	1	12	13	22	14	0	8	14	1	96	3.4	23
Tim Breaux	42	340	45	121	.372	32	49	.653	16	18	34	15	25	0	11	16	4	128	3.0	12
Zan Tabak	37	182	24	53	.453	27	44	.614	23	34	57	4	37	0	2	18	7	75	2.0	10
Charles Jones	3	36	1	3	.333	1	2	.500	2	5	7	0	8	0	0	0	1	3	1.0	2
Adrian Caldwell	7	30	1	4	.250	3	6	.500	1	9	10	0	6	0	1	1	0	5	0.7	2

3-pt. FG: Houston 646-1757 (.368)—Olajuwon 3-16 (.188); Drexler† 60-168 (.357); Drexler‡ 147-408 (.360); Maxwell 143-441 (.324); Thorpe* 0-3 (.000); Smith 142-331 (.429); Horry 86-227 (.379); Cassell 63-191 (.330); Elie 80-201 (.398); Herrera 0-2 (.000); Brown 1-3 (.333); Chilcutt 35-86 (.407); Murray† 19-45 (.422); Murray‡ 35-86 (.407); Brooks* 8-17 (.471); Breaux 6-25 (.240); Tabak 0-1 (.000). Opponents 506-1345 (.376).

INDIANA PACERS

	G	Min.	FGM	FGA	Pct.	FTM	FTA	Pct.	Off.	Def.	Tot.	Ast.	PF	Dq.	Stl.	TO	Blk.	Pts.	Avg.	Hi.
Reggie Miller	81	2665	505	1092	.462	383	427	.897	30	180	210	242	157	0	98	151	16	1588	19.6	40
Rik Smits	78	2381	558	1060	.526	284	377	.753	192	409	601	111	278	6	40	189	79	1400	17.9	35
Derrick McKey	81	2805	411	833	.493	221	297	.744	125	269	394	276	260	5	125	168	49	1075	13.3	24
Dale Davis	74	2346	324	576	.563	138	259	.533	259	437	696	58	222	2	72	124	116	786	10.6	25
Byron Scott	80	1528	265	583	.455	193	227	.850	18	133	151	108	123	1	61	119	13	802	10.0	21
Mark Jackson	82	2402	239	566	.422	119	153	.778	73	233	306	616	148	0	105	210	16	624	7.6	22
Antonio Davis	44	1030	109	245	.445	117	174	.672	105	175	280	25	134	2	19	64	29	335	7.6	17
Sam Mitchell	81	1377	201	413	.487	126	174	.724	95	148	243	61	206	0	43	54	20	529	6.5	18
Vern Fleming	55	686	93	188	.495	65	90	.722	20	68	88	109	80	0	27	43	1	251	4.6	19
Haywoode Workman	69	1028	101	269	.375	55	74	.743	21	90	111	194	115	0	59	73	5	292	4.2	19
Duane Ferrell	56	607	83	173	.480	64	85	.753	50	38	88	31	79	0	26	43	6	231	4.1	11
LaSalle Thompson	38	453	49	118	.415	14	16	.875	28	61	89	18	76	0	18	33	10	112	2.9	13
Kenny Williams	34	402	41	115	.357	14	25	.560	23	39	62	27	48	0	10	35	2	100	2.9	10
Greg Kite†	9	61	3	14	.214	2	10	.200	10	8	18	1	13	0	0	5	0	8	0.9	6
Greg Kite‡	11	77	3	17	.176	2	10	.200	12	10	22	1	15	0	0	6	0	8	0.7	6
Mark Strickland	4	9	1	3	.333	1	2	.500	2	2	4	0	0	0	0	1	1	3	0.8	2

3-pt. FG: Indiana 374-985 (.380)—Miller 195-470 (.415); Smits 0-2 (.000); McKey 32-89 (.360); D. Davis 0-1 (.000); Scott 79-203 (.389); Jackson 27-87 (.310); Mitchell 1-10 (.100); Fleming 0-7 (.000); Workman 35-98 (.357); Ferrell 1-6 (.167); Williams 4-12 (.333). Opponents 475-1304 (.364).

LOS ANGELES CLIPPERS

	G	Min.	FGM	FGA	Pct.	FTM	FTA	Pct.	Off.	Def.	Tot.	Ast.	PF	Dq.	Stl.	TO	Blk.	Pts.	Avg.	Hi.
Loy Vaught	80	2966	609	1185	.514	176	248	.710	261	511	772	139	243	4	104	166	29	1401	17.5	33
Lamond Murray	81	2556	439	1093	.402	199	264	.754	132	222	354	133	180	3	72	163	55	1142	14.1	30
Malik Sealy	60	1604	291	669	.435	174	223	.780	77	137	214	107	173	2	72	83	25	778	13.0	34
Pooh Richardson	80	2864	353	897	.394	81	125	.648	38	223	261	632	218	1	129	171	12	874	10.9	32
Terry Dehere	80	1774	279	685	.407	229	292	.784	35	117	152	225	200	0	45	157	7	835	10.4	25
Tony Massenburg	80	2127	282	601	.469	177	235	.753	160	295	455	67	253	2	48	118	58	741	9.3	26
Eric Piatkowski	81	1208	201	456	.441	90	115	.783	63	70	133	77	150	1	37	63	15	566	7.0	23
Elmore Spencer	19	368	52	118	.441	28	50	.560	11	54	65	25	62	0	14	48	23	132	6.9	15
Gary Grant	33	470	78	166	.470	45	55	.818	8	27	35	93	66	0	29	44	3	205	6.2	19
Michael Smith	29	319	63	134	.470	26	30	.867	13	43	56	20	41	0	6	18	2	153	5.3	17
Charles Outlaw	81	1655	170	325	.523	82	186	.441	121	192	313	84	227	4	90	78	151	422	5.2	14
Matt Fish	26	370	49	103	.476	25	37	.676	32	52	84	17	70	1	16	28	7	123	4.7	10
Eric Riley	40	434	65	145	.448	47	64	.734	45	67	112	11	78	1	17	31	35	177	4.4	14
Harold Ellis	69	656	91	189	.481	69	117	.590	56	32	88	40	102	0	67	49	12	252	3.7	24
Randy Woods	62	495	83	117	.316	28	38	.737	10	34	44	134	87	0	41	55	0	124	2.0	9
Bob Martin	1	14	1	5	.200	0	0	...	2	0	2	1	2	0	0	0	1	2	2.0	2

3-pt. FG: L.A. Clippers 331-1051 (.315)—Vaught 7-33 (.212); Murray 65-218 (.298); Sealy 22-73 (.301); Richardson 87-244 (.357); Dehere 48-163 (.294); Massenburg 0-3 (.000); Piatkowski 74-198 (.374); Spencer 0-1 (.000); Grant 4-16 (.250); Smith 1-8 (.125); Outlaw 0-5 (.000); Fish 0-1 (.000); Riley 0-1 (.000); Ellis 1-13 (.077); Woods 22-74 (.297). Opponents 388-1049 (.370).

LOS ANGELES LAKERS

	G	Min.	FGM	FGA	Pct.	FTM	FTA	Pct.	Off.	Def.	Tot.	Ast.	PF	Dq.	Stl.	TO	Blk.	Pts.	Avg.	Hi.
Cedric Ceballos	58	2029	497	977	.509	209	292	.716	169	295	464	105	131	1	60	143	19	1261	21.7	50
Nick Van Exel	80	2944	465	1107	.420	235	300	.783	27	196	223	660	157	0	97	220	6	1348	16.9	40
Vlade Divac	80	2807	485	957	.507	297	382	.777	261	568	829	329	305	8	109	205	174	1277	16.0	30
Eddie Jones	64	1981	342	744	.460	122	169	.722	79	170	249	128	175	1	131	75	41	897	14.0	31
Elden Campbell	73	2076	360	785	.459	193	290	.666	168	277	445	92	246	4	69	98	132	913	12.5	32
Anthony Peeler	73	1559	285	659	.432	102	128	.797	62	106	168	122	143	1	52	82	13	756	10.4	27
Sedale Threatt	59	1384	217	437	.497	88	111	.793	21	103	124	248	139	1	54	70	12	558	9.5	38
Lloyd Daniels†	25	541	71	182	.390	20	25	.800	27	29	56	36	40	0	20	23	10	185	7.4	22
Lloyd Daniels‡	30	604	80	209	.383	22	27	.815	29	34	63	40	48	0	22	31	10	208	6.9	22
George Lynch	56	953	138	295	.468	62	86	.721	75	109	184	62	86	0	51	73	10	341	6.1	21
Tony Smith	61	1024	132	309	.427	44	63	.698	43	64	107	102	111	0	46	50	7	340	5.6	19

	G	Min.	FGM	FGA	Pct.	FTM	FTA	Pct.	Off.	Def.	Tot.	Ast.	PF	Dq.	Stl.	TO	Blk.	Pts.	Avg.	Hi.
									REBOUNDS									SCORING		
Sam Bowie	67	1225	118	267	.442	68	89	.764	72	216	288	118	182	4	21	91	80	306	4.6	19
Anthony Miller	46	527	70	132	.530	47	76	.618	67	85	152	35	77	2	20	38	7	189	4.1	18
Randolph Keys	6	83	9	26	.346	2	2	1.000	6	11	17	2	16	0	1	2	2	20	3.3	10
Antonio Harvey	59	572	77	176	.438	24	45	.533	39	63	102	23	87	0	15	25	41	179	3.0	18
Kurt Rambis	26	195	18	35	.514	8	12	.667	10	24	34	16	35	0	3	8	9	44	1.7	9
Lester Conner	2	5	0	0	...	2	2	1.000	0	0	0	3	0	1	0	0	0	2	1.0	2

3-pt. FG: L.A. Lakers 525-1492 (.352)—Ceballos 58-146 (.397); Van Exel 183-511 (.358); Divac 10-53 (.189); Jones 91-246 (.370); Campbell 0-1 (.000); Peeler 84-216 (.389); Threatt 36-95 (.379); Daniels† 23-86 (.267); Daniels‡ 26-100 (.260); Lynch 3-21 (.143); Smith 32-91 (.352); Bowie 2-11 (.182); Miller 2-5 (.400); Keys 0-9 (.000); Harvey 1-1 (1.000). Opponents 456-1294 (.352).

MIAMI HEAT

	G	Min.	FGM	FGA	Pct.	FTM	FTA	Pct.	Off.	Def.	Tot.	Ast.	PF	Dq.	Stl.	TO	Blk.	Pts.	Avg.	Hi.
									REBOUNDS									SCORING		
Glen Rice	82	3014	667	1403	.475	312	365	.855	99	279	378	192	203	1	112	153	14	1831	22.3	56
Steve Smith*	2	62	11	29	.379	17	22	.773	4	2	6	7	9	0	2	4	1	41	20.5	22
Kevin Willis†	65	2301	457	974	.469	195	282	.691	217	479	696	83	208	3	59	155	33	1112	17.1	31
Kevin Willis‡	67	2390	473	1015	.466	205	297	.690	227	505	732	86	215	3	60	162	36	1154	17.2	31
Billy Owens	70	2296	403	820	.491	194	313	.620	203	299	502	246	205	6	80	204	30	1002	14.3	30
Bimbo Coles	68	2207	261	607	.430	141	174	.810	46	145	191	416	185	1	99	156	13	679	10.0	25
Khalid Reeves	67	1462	206	465	.443	140	196	.714	52	134	186	288	139	1	77	132	10	619	9.2	32
Matt Geiger	74	1712	260	485	.536	93	143	.650	146	267	413	55	245	5	41	113	51	617	8.3	22
Grant Long*	2	62	5	12	.417	6	10	.600	1	10	11	4	11	1	2	4	0	16	8.0	11
Kevin Gamble	77	1223	220	450	.489	87	111	.784	29	93	122	119	130	0	52	49	10	566	7.4	23
John Salley	75	1955	197	395	.499	153	207	.739	110	226	336	123	279	5	47	97	85	547	7.3	21
Ledell Eackles	54	898	143	326	.439	91	126	.722	33	62	95	72	88	0	19	53	2	395	7.3	22
Harold Miner	45	871	123	305	.403	69	95	.726	38	79	117	69	85	0	15	77	6	329	7.3	23
Keith Askins	50	854	81	207	.391	46	57	.807	86	112	198	39	109	1	35	25	17	229	4.6	19
Brad Lohaus	61	730	97	231	.420	10	15	.667	28	74	102	43	85	2	20	29	25	267	4.4	18
Kevin Pritchard†	14	158	13	29	.448	15	17	.882	0	11	11	23	19	0	2	7	1	43	3.1	11
Kevin Pritchard‡	19	194	13	32	.406	16	21	.762	0	12	12	34	22	0	2	12	1	44	2.3	11

3-pt. FG: Miami 436-1182 (.369)—Rice 105-451 (.410); Smith* 2-12 (.167); Willis† 3-14 (.214); Willis‡ 3-15 (.200); Owens 2-22 (.091); Coles 16-76 (.211); Reeves 67-171 (.392); Geiger 4-10 (.400); Gamble 39-98 (.398); Eackles 18-41 (.439); Miner 14-49 (.286); Askins 21-78 (.269); Lohaus 63-155 (.406); Pritchard† 2-5 (.400); Pritchard‡ 2-8 (.250). Opponents 511-1417 (.361).

MILWAUKEE BUCKS

	G	Min.	FGM	FGA	Pct.	FTM	FTA	Pct.	Off.	Def.	Tot.	Ast.	PF	Dq.	Stl.	TO	Blk.	Pts.	Avg.	Hi.
									REBOUNDS									SCORING		
Glenn Robinson	80	2958	636	1410	.451	397	499	.796	169	344	513	197	234	2	115	313	22	1755	21.9	38
Vin Baker	82	3361	594	1229	.483	256	432	.593	289	557	846	296	277	5	86	221	116	1451	17.7	31
Todd Day	82	2717	445	1049	.424	257	341	.754	95	227	322	134	283	6	104	157	63	1310	16.0	34
Eric Murdock	75	2158	338	814	.415	211	267	.790	48	166	214	482	139	0	113	194	12	977	13.0	29
Marty Conlon	82	2064	344	647	.532	119	194	.613	160	266	426	110	218	3	42	123	18	815	9.9	22
Johnny Newman	82	1896	226	488	.463	137	171	.801	72	101	173	91	234	3	69	86	13	634	7.7	30
Lee Mayberry	82	1744	172	408	.422	58	83	.699	21	61	82	276	123	0	51	106	4	474	5.8	22
Eric Mobley	46	587	78	132	.591	22	45	.489	55	98	153	21	63	0	8	24	27	180	3.9	14
Jon Barry	52	602	57	134	.425	61	80	.763	15	34	49	85	54	0	30	41	4	191	3.7	13
Danny Young	7	77	9	17	.529	1	1	1.000	1	4	5	12	8	0	4	4	0	24	3.4	7
Alton Lister	60	776	66	134	.493	35	70	.500	67	169	236	12	146	3	16	38	57	167	2.8	10
Ed Pinckney	62	835	48	97	.495	44	62	.710	65	146	211	21	64	0	34	26	17	140	2.3	12
Aaron Williams	15	72	8	24	.333	8	12	.667	5	14	19	0	14	0	2	7	6	24	1.6	8
Tate George	3	8	1	3	.333	2	2	1.000	1	0	1	0	1	0	0	2	0	4	1.3	2

3-pt. FG: Milwaukee 489-1337 (.366)—Robinson 86-268 (.321); Baker 7-24 (.292); Day 163-410 (.390); Murdock 90-240 (.375); Conlon 8-29 (.276); Newman 45-128 (.352); Mayberry 72-177 (.407); Mobley 2-2 (1.000); Barry 16-48 (.333); Young 5-12 (.417); Lister 0-1 (.000); Williams 0-1 (1.000); George 0-1 (.000). Opponents 491-1242 (.395).

MINNESOTA TIMBERWOLVES

	G	Min.	FGM	FGA	Pct.	FTM	FTA	Pct.	Off.	Def.	Tot.	Ast.	PF	Dq.	Stl.	TO	Blk.	Pts.	Avg.	Hi.
									REBOUNDS									SCORING		
J.R. Rider	75	2645	558	1249	.447	277	339	.817	90	159	249	245	194	3	69	232	23	1532	20.4	42
Christian Laettner	81	2770	450	920	.489	409	500	.818	164	449	613	234	302	4	101	225	87	1322	16.3	26
Tom Gugliotta†	31	1018	162	357	.454	93	122	.762	49	173	222	139	86	0	61	81	28	445	14.4	30
Tom Gugliotta‡	77	2568	371	837	.443	174	252	.690	165	407	572	279	203	2	132	189	62	976	12.7	30
Doug West	71	2328	351	762	.461	206	246	.837	60	167	227	185	250	4	65	126	24	919	12.9	33
Sean Rooks	80	2405	289	615	.470	290	381	.761	165	321	486	97	208	1	29	142	71	868	10.9	28
Donyell Marshall*	40	1036	158	423	.374	83	122	.680	64	132	196	57	63	0	25	58	50	431	10.8	30
Darrick Martin	34	803	95	233	.408	57	65	.877	14	50	64	133	88	0	34	62	0	254	7.5	15
Winston Garland	73	1931	170	410	.415	89	112	.795	48	120	168	318	184	1	71	105	13	448	6.1	20
Micheal Williams	1	28	1	4	.250	4	5	.800	0	1	1	3	3	0	2	3	0	6	6.0	6
Stacey King	50	792	99	212	.467	68	102	.667	54	111	165	26	126	1	24	64	20	266	5.3	17
Pat Durham	59	852	117	237	.494	63	96	.656	37	57	94	53	114	0	36	45	32	302	5.1	16
Chris Smith	64	1073	116	264	.439	41	63	.651	14	59	73	146	119	0	32	50	22	320	5.0	24
Greg Foster†	61	845	109	232	.470	56	80	.700	67	138	205	23	129	0	13	54	20	281	4.6	15
Greg Foster‡	78	1144	150	318	.472	78	111	.703	85	174	259	39	183	0	15	71	28	385	4.9	16
Charles Shackleford	21	239	39	65	.600	16	20	.800	16	51	67	8	47	0	8	8	6	94	4.5	18

	G	Min.	FGM	FGA	Pct.	FTM	FTA	Pct.	Off.	Def.	Tot.	Ast.	PF	Dq.	Stl.	TO	Blk.	Pts.	Avg.	Hi.
									REBOUNDS									SCORING		
Askia Jones 11	11	139	15	44	.341	13	16	.813	6	5	11	16	19	0	6	9	0	45	4.1	8
Howard Eisley* 34	34	496	37	105	.352	31	40	.775	10	32	42	77	78	0	18	42	5	113	3.3	15
Andres Guibert 17	17	167	16	47	.340	13	19	.684	16	29	45	10	29	0	8	12	1	45	2.6	9
Mike Brown 27	27	213	10	40	.250	15	27	.556	9	36	45	10	35	0	7	16	0	35	1.3	9

3-pt. FG: Minnesota 318-1016 (.313)—Rider 139-396 (.351); Laettner 13-40 (.325); Gugliotta† 28-88 (.318); Gugliotta‡ 60-186 (.323); West 11-61 (.180); Rooks 0-5 (.000); Marshall* 32-106 (.302); Martin 7-38 (.184); Garland 19-75 (.253); King 0-1 (.000); Durham 5-26 (.192); Smith 47-108 (.435); Foster† 7-23 (.304); Foster‡ 7-23 (.304); Jones 2-12 (.167); Eisley* 8-32 (.250); Guibert 0-4 (.000); Brown 0-1 (.000). Opponents 468-1243 (.377).

NEW JERSEY NETS

	G	Min.	FGM	FGA	Pct.	FTM	FTA	Pct.	Off.	Def.	Tot.	Ast.	PF	Dq.	Stl.	TO	Blk.	Pts.	Avg.	Hi.
									REBOUNDS									SCORING		
Derrick Coleman 56	56	2103	371	875	.424	376	490	.767	167	424	591	187	162	2	35	172	94	1146	20.5	36
Kenny Anderson 72	72	2689	411	1031	.399	348	414	.841	73	177	250	680	184	1	103	225	14	1267	17.6	40
Armon Gilliam 82	82	2472	455	905	.503	302	392	.770	192	421	613	99	171	0	67	152	89	1212	14.8	33
Kevin Edwards 14	14	466	69	154	.448	40	42	.952	10	27	37	27	42	0	19	35	5	196	14.0	22
Chris Morris 71	71	2131	351	856	.410	142	195	.728	181	221	402	147	155	0	86	117	51	950	13.4	31
Benoit Benjamin 61	61	1598	271	531	.510	133	175	.760	94	346	440	38	151	3	23	125	64	675	11.1	30
P.J. Brown 80	80	2466	254	570	.446	139	207	.671	178	309	487	135	262	8	69	80	135	651	8.1	19
Rex Walters 80	80	1435	206	469	.439	40	52	.769	18	75	93	121	135	0	37	71	16	523	6.5	20
Chris Childs 53	53	1021	106	279	.380	55	73	.753	14	55	69	219	116	1	42	76	3	308	5.8	14
Jayson Williams 75	75	982	149	323	.461	65	122	.533	179	246	425	35	160	2	26	59	33	363	4.8	20
Sean Higgins 57	57	735	105	273	.385	35	40	.875	25	52	77	29	93	1	10	35	9	268	4.7	13
Sleepy Floyd 48	48	831	71	212	.335	30	43	.698	8	46	54	126	73	0	13	51	6	197	4.1	14
Rick Mahorn 58	58	630	79	151	.523	39	49	.796	45	117	162	26	93	0	11	34	12	198	3.4	17
Dwayne Schintzius ... 43	43	318	41	108	.380	6	11	.545	29	52	81	15	45	0	3	17	17	88	2.0	9
Yinka Dare 1	1	3	0	1	.000	0	0	...	0	1	1	0	2	0	1	0	0	0	0.0	0

3-pt. FG: New Jersey 414-1297 (.319)—Coleman 28-120 (.233); Anderson 97-294 (.330); Gilliam 0-2 (.000); Edwards 18-45 (.400); Morris 106-317 (.334); Brown 4-24 (.167); Walters 71-196 (.362); Childs 41-125 (.328); Williams 0-5 (.000); Higgins 23-78 (.295); Floyd 25-88 (.284); Mahorn 1-3 (.333). Opponents 440-1176 (.374).

NEW YORK KNICKERBOCKERS

	G	Min.	FGM	FGA	Pct.	FTM	FTA	Pct.	Off.	Def.	Tot.	Ast.	PF	Dq.	Stl.	TO	Blk.	Pts.	Avg.	Hi.
									REBOUNDS									SCORING		
Patrick Ewing 79	79	2920	730	1452	.503	420	560	.750	157	710	867	212	272	3	68	256	159	1886	23.9	46
John Starks 80	80	2725	419	1062	.395	168	228	.737	34	185	219	411	257	3	92	160	4	1223	15.3	35
Charles Smith 76	76	2150	352	747	.471	255	322	.792	144	180	324	120	286	6	49	147	95	966	12.7	29
Derek Harper 80	80	2716	337	756	.446	139	192	.724	31	163	194	458	219	0	79	151	10	919	11.5	26
Charles Oakley 50	50	1567	192	393	.489	119	150	.793	155	290	445	126	179	3	60	103	7	506	10.1	20
Hubert Davis 82	82	1697	296	617	.480	97	120	.808	30	80	110	150	146	1	35	87	11	820	10.0	27
Anthony Mason...... 77	77	2496	287	507	.566	191	298	.641	182	468	650	240	253	3	69	123	21	765	9.9	26
Doc Rivers* 3	3	47	4	13	.308	8	11	.727	2	7	9	8	8	1	4	4	0	19	6.3	9
Greg Anthony 61	61	943	128	293	.437	60	76	.789	7	57	64	160	99	1	50	57	7	372	6.1	19
Anthony Bonner 58	58	1126	88	193	.456	44	67	.657	113	149	262	80	159	0	48	79	23	221	3.8	15
Herb Williams 56	56	743	82	180	.456	23	37	.622	23	109	132	27	108	0	13	40	45	187	3.3	16
Monty Williams...... 41	41	503	60	133	.451	17	38	.447	42	56	98	49	87	0	20	41	4	137	3.3	9
Charlie Ward........ 10	10	44	4	19	.211	7	10	.700	1	5	6	4	7	0	2	8	0	16	1.6	4
Doug Christie 12	12	79	5	22	.227	4	5	.800	3	10	13	8	18	1	2	13	1	15	1.3	4
Ronnie Grandison 2	2	8	1	4	.250	0	0	...	3	2	5	2	2	0	0	0	0	2	1.0	2
Greg Kite* 2	2	16	0	3	.000	0	0	...	2	2	4	0	2	0	0	1	0	0	0.0	0

3-pt. FG: New York 532-1446 (.368)—Ewing 6-21 (.286); Starks 217-611 (.355); Smith 7-31 (.226); Harper 106-292 (.363); Oakley 3-12 (.250); Davis 131-288 (.455); Mason 0-1 (.000); Rivers* 3-5 (.600); Anthony 56-155 (.361); Bonner 1-5 (.200); M. Williams 0-8 (.000); Ward 1-10 (.100); Christie 1-7 (.143). Opponents 397-1165 (.341).

ORLANDO MAGIC

	G	Min.	FGM	FGA	Pct.	FTM	FTA	Pct.	Off.	Def.	Tot.	Ast.	PF	Dq.	Stl.	TO	Blk.	Pts.	Avg.	Hi.
									REBOUNDS									SCORING		
Shaquille O'Neal 79	79	2923	930	1594	.583	455	854	.533	328	573	901	214	258	1	73	204	192	2315	29.3	46
Anfernee Hardaway... 77	77	2901	585	1142	.512	356	463	.769	139	197	336	551	158	1	130	258	26	1613	20.9	39
Nick Anderson 76	76	2588	439	923	.476	143	203	.704	85	250	335	314	124	0	125	141	22	1200	15.8	35
Dennis Scott........ 62	62	1499	283	645	.439	86	114	.754	25	121	146	131	119	1	45	57	14	802	12.9	38
Horace Grant 74	74	2693	401	707	.567	146	211	.692	223	492	715	173	203	2	76	85	88	948	12.8	29
Donald Royal 70	70	1841	206	434	.475	223	299	.746	83	196	279	198	156	0	45	125	16	635	9.1	21
Brian Shaw 78	78	1836	192	494	.389	70	95	.737	52	189	241	406	184	1	73	184	18	502	6.4	17
Anthony Bowie 77	77	1261	177	369	.480	61	73	.836	54	85	139	159	138	1	47	86	21	427	5.5	22
Jeff Turner 49	49	576	73	178	.410	26	29	.897	23	74	97	38	102	2	12	22	3	199	4.1	16
Geert Hammink....... 1	1	7	1	3	.333	2	2	1.000	0	2	2	1	1	0	0	0	0	4	4.0	4
Anthony Avent 71	71	1066	105	244	.430	48	75	.640	97	196	293	41	170	1	28	53	50	258	3.6	11
Darrell Armstrong..... 3	3	8	3	8	.375	2	2	1.000	1	0	1	3	3	0	1	1	0	10	3.3	5
Brooks Thompson.... 38	38	246	45	114	.395	8	12	.667	7	16	23	43	46	1	10	27	2	116	3.1	20
Tree Rollins......... 51	51	478	20	42	.476	21	31	.677	31	64	95	9	63	0	7	23	36	61	1.2	8
Keith Tower.......... 3	3	7	0	2	.000	1	2	.500	1	2	3	0	1	0	0	1	0	1	0.3	1

3-pt. FG: Orlando 523-1412 (.370)—O'Neal 0-5 (.000); Hardaway 87-249 (.349); Anderson 179-431 (.415); Scott 150-352 (.426); Grant 0-8 (.000); Royal 0-4 (.000); Shaw 48-184 (.261); Bowie 12-40 (.300); Turner 27-75 (.360); Armstrong 2-6 (.333); Thompson 18-58 (.310). Opponents 468-1239 (.378).

PHILADELPHIA 76ERS

	G	Min.	FGM	FGA	Pct.	FTM	FTA	Pct.	Off.	Def.	Tot.	Ast.	PF	Dq.	Stl.	TO	Blk.	Pts.	Avg.	Hi.
									REBOUNDS									SCORING		
Dana Barros 82	82	3318	571	1165	.490	347	386	.899	27	247	274	619	159	1	149	242	4	1686	20.6	50
Jeff Malone 19	19	660	144	284	.507	51	59	.864	11	44	55	29	35	0	15	29	0	350	18.4	34
Clarence Weatherspoon . 76	76	2991	543	1238	.439	283	377	.751	144	382	526	215	195	1	115	191	67	1373	18.1	31
Willie Burton 53	53	1564	243	606	.401	220	267	.824	49	115	164	96	167	3	32	122	19	812	15.3	53
Sharone Wright 79	79	2044	361	776	.465	182	282	.645	191	281	472	48	246	5	37	151	104	904	11.4	23
Shawn Bradley 82	82	2365	315	693	.455	148	232	.638	243	416	659	53	338	18	54	142	274	778	9.5	28
Jeff Grayer 47	47	1098	163	381	.428	58	83	.699	58	91	149	74	80	1	27	56	4	389	8.3	22
Scott Williams. 77	77	1781	206	434	.475	79	107	.738	173	312	485	59	237	4	71	84	40	491	6.4	19
Greg Graham 50	50	775	95	223	.426	55	73	.753	19	43	62	66	76	0	29	48	6	251	5.0	20
Corey Gaines 11	11	280	24	51	.471	5	11	.455	1	17	18	33	23	0	8	14	1	55	5.0	11
Derrick Alston 64	64	1032	120	258	.465	59	120	.492	98	121	219	33	107	1	39	53	35	299	4.7	22
Jerome Harmon 10	10	158	21	53	.396	3	6	.500	9	14	23	12	12	0	9	7	0	46	4.6	14
Lloyd Daniels* 5	5	63	9	27	.333	2	2	1.000	2	5	7	4	8	0	2	8	0	23	4.6	9
Alphonso Ford 5	5	98	9	39	.231	1	2	.500	8	12	20	9	5	0	1	8	0	19	3.8	8
B.J. Tyler 55	55	809	72	189	.381	35	50	.700	13	49	62	174	58	0	36	97	2	195	3.5	16
Jaren Jackson 21	21	257	25	68	.368	16	24	.667	18	24	42	19	33	0	9	17	5	70	3.3	11
Tim Perry 42	42	446	27	78	.346	22	40	.550	38	51	89	12	51	0	10	21	15	76	1.8	5
Alaa Abdelnaby† 3	3	30	1	11	.091	0	0	. . .	3	5	8	0	2	0	0	5	0	2	0.7	2
Alaa Abdelnaby‡ 54	54	506	118	231	.511	20	35	.571	37	77	114	13	104	1	15	45	12	256	4.7	24
Kevin Pritchard* 5	5	36	0	3	.000	1	4	.250	0	1	1	11	3	0	0	5	0	1	0.2	1

3-pt. FG: Philadelphia 355-936 (.379)—Barros 197-425 (.464); Malone 11-28 (.393); Weatherspoon 4-21 (.190); Burton 106-275 (.385); Wright 0-8 (.000); Bradley 0-3 (.000); Grayer 5-15 (.333); Williams 0-7 (.000); Graham 6-28 (.214); Gaines 2-15 (.133); Alston 0-4 (.000); Abdelnaby‡ 0-2 (.000); Harmon 1-1 (1.000); Daniels* 3-14 (.214); Ford 0-9 (.000); Tyler 16-51 (.314); Jackson 4-15 (.267); Perry 0-14 (.000); Pritchard* 0-3 (.000). Opponents 467-1287 (.363).

PHOENIX SUNS

	G	Min.	FGM	FGA	Pct.	FTM	FTA	Pct.	Off.	Def.	Tot.	Ast	PF	Dq.	Stl.	TO	Blk.	Pts.	Avg.	Hi.
									REBOUNDS									SCORING		
Charles Barkley 68	68	2382	554	1141	.486	379	507	.748	203	553	756	276	201	3	110	150	45	1561	23.0	45
Danny Manning. 46	46	1510	340	622	.547	136	202	.673	97	179	276	154	176	1	41	121	57	822	17.9	33
Dan Majerle 82	82	3091	438	1031	.425	206	282	.730	104	271	375	340	155	0	96	105	38	1281	15.6	33
Kevin Johnson 47	47	1352	246	523	.470	234	289	.810	32	83	115	360	88	0	47	105	18	730	15.5	31
A.C. Green 82	82	2687	311	617	.504	251	343	.732	194	475	669	127	146	0	55	114	31	916	11.2	24
Wesley Person 78	78	1800	309	638	.484	80	101	.792	67	134	201	105	149	0	48	79	24	814	10.4	26
Wayman Tisdale 65	65	1276	278	574	.484	94	122	.770	83	164	247	45	190	3	29	64	27	650	10.0	24
Elliot Perry 82	82	1977	306	588	.520	158	195	.810	51	100	151	394	142	0	156	163	4	795	9.7	24
Danny Ainge 74	74	1374	194	422	.460	105	130	.808	25	84	109	210	155	1	46	79	7	571	7.7	23
Richard Dumas 15	15	167	37	73	.507	8	16	.500	18	11	29	7	22	0	10	9	2	82	5.5	20
Trevor Ruffin. 49	49	319	84	197	.426	27	38	.711	8	15	23	48	52	0	14	47	2	233	4.8	20
Dan Schayes 69	69	823	126	248	.508	50	69	.725	57	151	208	89	170	0	20	64	37	303	4.4	17
Joe Kleine 75	75	968	119	265	.449	42	49	.857	82	177	259	39	174	2	14	35	18	280	3.7	13
Aaron Swinson 9	9	51	10	18	.556	4	5	.800	3	5	8	3	8	0	1	5	0	24	2.7	12
Antonio Lang 12	12	53	4	10	.400	3	4	.750	3	1	4	1	11	0	0	5	2	11	0.9	6

3-pt. FG: Phoenix 584-1584 (.369)—Barkley 74-219 (.338); Manning 6-21 (.286); Majerle 199-548 (.363); Johnson 4-26 (.154); Green 43-127 (.339); Person 116-266 (.436); Perry 25-60 (.417); Ainge 78-214 (.364); Dumas 0-1 (.000); Ruffin 38-99 (.384); Schayes 1-1 (1.000); Kleine 0-2 (.000). Opponents 525-1544 (.340).

PORTLAND TRAIL BLAZERS

	G	Min.	FGM	FGA	Pct.	FTM	FTA	Pct.	Off.	Def.	Tot.	Ast.	PF	Dq.	Stl.	TO	Blk.	Pts.	Avg.	Hi.
									REBOUNDS									SCORING		
Clyde Drexler* 41	41	1428	305	712	.428	207	248	.835	84	150	234	208	117	0	74	97	22	904	22.0	41
Clifford Robinson 75	75	2725	597	1320	.452	265	382	.694	152	271	423	198	240	3	79	158	82	1601	21.3	33
Rod Strickland 64	64	2267	441	946	.466	283	380	.745	73	244	317	562	118	0	123	209	9	1211	18.9	36
Otis Thorpe† 34	34	908	179	315	.568	100	154	.649	89	147	236	54	122	2	19	56	15	458	13.5	27
Otis Thorpe‡ 70	70	2096	385	681	.565	167	281	.594	202	356	558	112	224	3	41	132	28	937	13.4	27
Buck Williams 82	82	2422	309	604	.512	138	205	.673	251	418	669	78	254	2	67	119	69	757	9.2	25
James Robinson 71	71	1539	255	624	.409	65	110	.591	42	90	132	180	142	0	48	127	13	651	9.2	30
Harvey Grant. 75	75	1771	286	621	.461	103	146	.705	103	181	284	82	163	0	56	62	53	683	9.1	24
Terry Porter 35	35	770	105	267	.393	58	82	.707	18	63	81	133	60	0	30	58	2	312	8.9	36
Jerome Kersey 63	63	1143	203	489	.415	95	124	.766	93	163	256	82	173	1	52	64	35	508	8.1	18
Aaron McKie 45	45	827	116	261	.444	50	73	.685	35	94	129	89	97	1	36	39	16	293	6.5	24
Negele Knight* 3	3	43	7	15	.467	4	4	1.000	1	2	3	11	5	0	1	4	0	18	6.0	13
Tracy Murray 29	29	313	63	153	.412	28	34	.824	18	19	37	14	42	0	7	20	1	170	5.9	19
Chris Dudley 82	82	2245	181	446	.406	85	183	.464	325	439	764	34	286	6	43	81	126	447	5.5	17
Mark Bryant 49	49	658	101	192	.526	41	63	.651	55	106	161	28	109	1	19	39	16	244	5.0	18
Steve Henson 37	37	380	37	86	.430	22	25	.880	3	23	26	85	52	1	9	30	0	119	3.2	13
James Edwards. 28	28	266	32	83	.386	11	17	.647	10	33	43	8	44	0	5	14	8	75	2.7	11

3-pt. FG: Portland 462-1266 (.365)—Drexler* 87-240 (.363); C. Robinson 142-383 (.371); Strickland 46-123 (.374); Thorpe† 0-4 (.000); Thorpe‡ 0-7 (.000); Williams 1-2 (.500); J. Robinson 76-223 (.341); Grant 8-26 (.308); Porter 44-114 (.386); Kersey 7-27 (.259); McKie 11-28 (.393); Murray* 16-41 (.390); Dudley 0-1 (.000); Bryant 1-2 (.500); Henson 23-52 (.442). Opponents 442-1189 (.372).

1994-95

SACRAMENTO KINGS

	G	Min.	FGM	FGA	Pct.	FTM	FTA	Pct.	Off.	Def.	Tot.	Ast.	PF	Dq.	Stl.	TO	Blk.	Pts.	Avg.	Hi.
Mitch Richmond	82	3172	668	1497	.446	375	445	.843	69	288	357	311	227	2	91	234	29	1867	22.8	44
Walt Williams	77	2739	445	998	.446	266	364	.731	100	245	345	316	265	3	123	243	63	1259	16.4	31
Brian Grant	80	2289	413	809	.511	231	363	.636	207	391	598	99	276	4	49	163	116	1058	13.2	29
Spud Webb	76	2458	302	689	.438	226	242	.934	29	145	174	468	148	0	75	185	8	878	11.6	24
Olden Polynice	81	2534	376	691	.544	124	194	.639	277	448	725	62	238	0	48	113	52	877	10.8	27
Michael Smith	82	1736	220	406	.542	127	262	.485	174	312	486	67	235	1	61	106	49	567	6.9	18
Lionel Simmons	58	1064	131	312	.420	59	84	.702	61	135	196	89	118	0	28	70	23	327	5.6	18
Alaa Abdelnaby*	51	476	117	220	.532	20	35	.571	34	72	106	13	102	1	15	40	12	254	5.0	24
Randy Brown	67	1086	124	287	.432	55	82	.671	24	84	108	133	153	0	99	78	19	317	4.7	18
Bobby Hurley	68	1105	103	284	.363	58	76	.763	14	56	70	226	79	0	29	110	0	285	4.2	14
Duane Causwell	58	820	76	147	.517	57	98	.582	57	117	174	15	146	4	14	33	80	209	3.6	14
Trevor Wilson	15	147	18	40	.450	11	14	.786	10	16	26	12	12	0	4	6	2	47	3.1	7
Henry Turner	30	149	23	57	.404	20	35	.571	17	11	28	7	20	0	8	12	1	68	2.3	10
Doug Lee	22	75	9	25	.360	18	21	.857	0	5	5	5	18	0	6	5	3	43	2.0	10
Derrick Phelps	3	5	0	1	.000	0	2	.000	0	0	0	1	3	0	0	0	0	0	0.0	0

3-pt. FG: Sacramento 359-1037 (.346)—Richmond 156-424 (.368); Williams 103-296 (.348); Grant 1-4 (.250); Webb 48-145 (.331); Polynice 1-1 (1.000); M. Smith 0-2 (.000); Simmons 6-16 (.375); Abdelnaby* 0-2 (.000); Brown 14-47 (.298); Hurley 21-76 (.276); Causwell 0-1 (.000); Turner 2-5 (.400); Lee 7-18 (.389). Opponents 377-1240 (.304).

SAN ANTONIO SPURS

	G	Min.	FGM	FGA	Pct.	FTM	FTA	Pct.	Off.	Def.	Tot.	Ast.	PF	Dq.	Stl.	TO	Blk.	Pts.	Avg.	Hi.
David Robinson	81	3074	788	1487	.530	656	847	.774	234	643	877	236	230	2	134	233	262	2238	27.6	43
Sean Elliott	81	2858	502	1072	.468	326	404	.807	63	224	287	206	216	2	78	151	38	1466	18.1	32
Avery Johnson	82	3011	448	863	.519	202	295	.685	49	159	208	670	154	0	114	207	13	1101	13.4	29
Vinny Del Negro	75	2360	372	766	.486	128	162	.790	28	164	192	226	179	0	61	56	14	938	12.5	31
Chuck Person	81	2033	317	750	.423	66	102	.647	49	209	258	106	198	0	45	102	12	872	10.8	27
Dennis Rodman	49	1568	137	240	.571	75	111	.676	274	549	823	97	159	1	31	98	23	349	7.1	17
J.R. Reid	81	1566	201	396	.508	160	233	.687	120	273	393	55	230	2	60	113	32	563	7.0	16
Terry Cummings	76	1273	224	464	.483	72	123	.585	138	240	378	59	188	1	36	95	19	520	6.8	19
Doc Rivers†	60	942	104	289	.360	52	71	.732	13	87	100	154	142	1	61	56	21	302	5.0	17
Doc Rivers‡	63	989	108	302	.358	60	82	.732	15	94	109	162	150	2	65	60	21	321	5.1	17
Willie Anderson	38	556	76	162	.469	30	41	.732	15	40	55	52	71	1	26	38	10	185	4.9	15
Moses Malone	17	149	13	35	.371	22	32	.688	20	26	46	6	15	0	2	11	3	49	2.9	12
Jack Haley	31	117	26	61	.426	21	32	.656	8	19	27	2	31	0	3	13	5	73	2.4	10
Chris Whitney	25	179	14	47	.298	11	11	1.000	4	9	13	28	34	1	4	18	0	42	1.7	10
Julius Nwosu	23	84	9	28	.321	13	17	.765	11	13	24	3	20	0	0	9	3	31	1.3	5
Corey Crowder	7	29	2	10	.200	2	6	.333	1	2	3	1	1	0	1	2	0	6	0.9	4
Howard Eisley†	15	56	3	17	.176	0	0	.	2	4	6	18	3	0	0	8	1	7	0.5	3
Howard Eisley‡	49	552	40	122	.328	31	40	.775	12	36	48	95	81	0	18	50	6	120	2.4	15

3-pt. FG: San Antonio 434-1158 (.375)—Robinson 6-20 (.300); Elliott 136-333 (.408); Johnson 3-22 (.136); Del Negro 66-162 (.407); Person 172-445 (.387); Rodman 0-2 (.000); Reid 1-2 (.500); Rivers† 42-122 (.344); Rivers‡ 45-127 (.354); Anderson 3-19 (.158); Malone 1-2 (.500); Haley 0-1 (.000); Whitney 3-19 (.158); Crowder 0-4 (.000); Eisley† 1-5 (.200); Eisley‡ 9-37 (.243). Opponents 426-1251 (.341).

SEATTLE SUPERSONICS

	G	Min.	FGM	FGA	Pct.	FTM	FTA	Pct.	Off.	Def.	Tot.	Ast.	PF	Dq.	Stl.	TO	Blk.	Pts.	Avg.	Hi.
Gary Payton	82	3015	685	1345	.509	249	348	.716	108	173	281	583	206	1	204	201	13	1689	20.6	33
Detlef Schrempf	82	2886	521	997	.523	437	521	.839	135	373	508	310	252	0	93	176	35	1572	19.2	33
Shawn Kemp	82	2679	545	997	.547	438	585	.749	318	575	893	149	337	9	102	259	122	1530	18.7	42
Kendall Gill	73	2125	392	858	.457	155	209	.742	99	191	290	192	186	0	117	138	28	1002	13.7	34
Sam Perkins	82	2356	346	742	.466	215	269	.799	96	302	398	135	186	0	72	77	45	1043	12.7	31
Vincent Askew	71	1721	248	504	.492	176	238	.739	65	116	181	176	191	1	49	85	13	703	9.9	20
Sarunas Marciulionis	66	1194	216	457	.473	145	198	.732	17	51	68	110	126	1	72	98	3	612	9.3	21
Nate McMillan	80	2070	166	397	.418	34	58	.586	65	237	302	421	275	8	165	126	53	419	5.2	15
Byron Houston	39	258	49	107	.458	28	38	.737	20	35	55	6	50	0	13	20	5	132	3.4	14
Ervin Johnson	64	907	85	192	.443	29	46	.630	101	188	289	16	163	1	17	54	67	199	3.1	15
Bill Cartwright	29	430	27	69	.391	15	24	.625	25	62	87	10	70	0	6	18	3	69	2.4	8
Dontonio Wingfield	20	81	18	51	.353	8	10	.800	11	19	30	3	15	0	5	8	3	46	2.3	6
Steve Scheffler	18	102	12	23	.522	15	18	.833	8	15	23	4	9	0	2	3	2	39	2.2	8
Rich King	2	6	0	2	.000	0	2	.000	0	0	0	0	1	0	0	0	0	0	0.0	0

3-pt. FG: Seattle 491-1305 (.376)—Payton 70-232 (.302); Schrempf 93-181 (.514); Kemp 2-7 (.286); Gill 63-171 (.368); Perkins 136-343 (.397); Askew 31-94 (.330); Marciulionis 35-87 (.402); McMillan 53-155 (.342); Houston 6-22 (.273); Johnson 0-1 (.000); Wingfield 2-12 (.167). Opponents 520-1514 (.343).

UTAH JAZZ

	G	Min.	FGM	FGA	Pct.	FTM	FTA	Pct.	Off.	Def.	Tot.	Ast.	PF	Dq.	Stl.	TO	Blk.	Pts.	Avg.	Hi.
Karl Malone	82	3126	830	1548	.536	516	695	.742	156	715	871	285	269	2	129	236	85	2187	26.7	45
Jeff Hornacek	81	2696	482	937	.514	284	322	.882	53	157	210	347	181	1	129	145	17	1337	16.5	40
John Stockton	82	2867	429	791	.542	246	306	.804	57	194	251	1011	215	3	194	267	22	1206	14.7	28
David Benoit	71	1841	285	587	.486	132	157	.841	96	272	368	58	183	1	45	75	47	740	10.4	24
Antoine Carr	78	1677	290	546	.531	165	201	.821	81	184	265	67	253	4	24	87	68	746	9.6	22

	G	Min.	FGM	FGA	Pct.	FTM	FTA	Pct.	Off.	Def.	Tot.	Ast.	PF	Dq.	Stl.	TO	Blk.	Pts.	Avg.	Hi.
Felton Spencer	34	905	105	215	.488	107	135	.793	90	170	260	17	131	3	12	68	32	317	9.3	19
Blue Edwards†	36	605	98	198	.495	32	42	.762	25	40	65	30	79	1	24	42	6	239	6.6	22
Blue Edwards‡	67	1112	181	393	.461	75	90	.833	50	80	130	77	143	1	43	81	16	459	6.9	22
Tom Chambers	81	1240	195	427	.457	109	135	.807	66	147	213	73	173	1	25	52	30	503	6.2	16
Adam Keefe	75	1270	172	298	.577	117	173	.676	135	192	327	30	141	0	36	62	25	461	6.1	18
Walter Bond†	18	239	36	72	.500	11	16	.688	7	20	27	17	37	0	5	14	4	97	5.4	14
Walter Bond‡	23	290	39	84	.464	14	20	.700	8	24	32	24	47	0	6	17	4	107	4.7	14
Bryon Russell	63	860	104	238	.437	62	93	.667	44	97	141	34	101	0	48	42	11	283	4.5	17
John Crotty	80	1019	93	231	.403	98	121	.810	27	70	97	205	105	0	39	70	6	295	3.7	14
Jamie Watson	60	673	76	152	.500	38	56	.679	16	58	74	59	86	0	35	51	11	195	3.3	14
James Donaldson	43	613	44	74	.595	22	31	.710	19	88	107	14	66	0	6	22	28	110	2.6	10
Jay Humphries*	12	149	4	25	.160	0	0	...	2	8	10	9	25	0	7	12	0	10	0.8	3

3-pt. FG: Utah 301-801 (.376)—Malone 11-41 (.268); Hornacek 89-219 (.406); Stockton 102-227 (.449); Benoit 38-115 (.330); Carr 1-4 (.250); Edwards† 11-32 (.344); Edwards‡ 22-75 (.293); Chambers 4-24 (.167); Bond† 14-37 (.378); Bond‡ 15-41 (.366); Russell 13-44 (.295); Crotty 11-36 (.306); Watson 5-19 (.263); Humphries* 2-3 (.667). Opponents 546-1431 (.382).

WASHINGTON BULLETS

	G	Min.	FGM	FGA	Pct.	FTM	FTA	Pct.	Off.	Def.	Tot.	Ast.	PF	Dq.	Stl.	TO	Blk.	Pts.	Avg.	Hi.
Chris Webber	54	2067	464	938	.495	117	233	.502	200	318	518	256	186	2	83	167	85	1085	20.1	31
Juwan Howard	65	2348	455	931	.489	194	292	.664	184	361	545	165	236	2	52	166	15	1104	17.0	31
Calbert Cheaney	78	2651	512	1129	.453	173	213	.812	105	216	321	177	215	0	80	151	21	1293	16.6	32
Rex Chapman	45	1468	254	639	.397	137	159	.862	23	90	113	128	85	0	67	62	15	731	16.2	35
Tom Gugliotta*	6	226	33	83	.398	26	33	.788	16	37	53	18	19	0	21	15	11	96	16.0	24
Scott Skiles	62	2077	265	583	.455	179	202	.886	26	133	159	452	135	2	70	172	6	805	13.0	28
Don MacLean	39	1052	158	361	.438	104	136	.765	46	119	165	51	97	0	15	44	3	430	11.0	23
Gheorghe Muresan	73	1720	303	541	.560	124	175	.709	179	309	488	38	259	6	48	115	127	730	10.0	30
Mitchell Butler	76	1554	214	508	.421	123	185	.665	43	127	170	91	155	0	61	106	10	597	7.9	26
Kevin Duckworth	40	818	118	267	.442	45	70	.643	65	130	195	20	110	3	21	59	24	283	7.1	20
Doug Overton	82	1704	207	498	.416	109	125	.872	26	117	143	246	126	1	53	104	2	576	7.0	30
Anthony Tucker	62	982	96	210	.457	51	83	.614	44	126	170	68	129	0	46	56	11	243	3.9	18
Larry Stewart	40	346	41	89	.461	20	30	.667	28	39	67	18	52	0	16	16	9	102	2.6	18
Kenny Walker	24	266	18	42	.429	21	28	.750	19	28	47	7	42	0	5	15	5	57	2.4	8
Brian Oliver	6	42	4	9	.444	6	8	.750	0	4	4	4	8	0	0	3	0	14	2.3	8
Jim McIlvaine	55	534	34	71	.479	28	41	.683	40	65	105	10	95	0	10	19	60	96	1.7	10

3-pt. FG: Washington 433-1264 (.343)—Webber 40-145 (.276); Howard 0-7 (.000); Cheaney 96-283 (.339); Chapman 86-274 (.314); Gugliotta* 4-8 (.500); Skiles 96-228 (.421); MacLean 10-40 (.250); Butler 46-141 (.326); Duckworth 2-10 (.200); Overton 53-125 (.424); Tucker 0-1 (.000); Stewart 0-2 (.000). Opponents 438-1145 (.383).

* Finished season with another team. † Totals with this team only. ‡ Totals with all teams.

1994-95

PLAYOFF RESULTS

EASTERN CONFERENCE

FIRST ROUND

Orlando 3, Boston 1
Apr. 28—Fri.	Boston 77 at Orlando	124
Apr. 30—Sun.	Boston 99 at Orlando	92
May 3—Wed.	Orlando 82 at Boston	77
May 5—Fri.	Orlando 95 at Boston	92

Indiana 3, Atlanta 0
Apr. 27—Thur.	Atlanta 82 at Indiana	90
Apr. 29—Sat.	Atlanta 97 at Indiana	105
May 2—Tue.	Indiana 105 at Atlanta	89

New York 3, Cleveland 1
Apr. 27—Thur.	Cleveland 79 at New York	103
Apr. 29—Sat.	Cleveland 90 at New York	84
May 1—Mon.	New York 83 at Cleveland	81
May 4—Thur.	New York 93 at Cleveland	80

Chicago 3, Charlotte 1
Apr. 28—Fri.	Chicago 108 at Charlotte	*100
Apr. 30—Sun.	Chicago 89 at Charlotte	106
May 2—Tue.	Charlotte 80 at Chicago	103
May 4—Thur.	Charlotte 84 at Chicago	85

SEMIFINALS

Indiana 4, New York 3
May 7—Sun.	Indiana 107 at New York	105
May 9—Tue.	Indiana 77 at New York	96
May 11—Thur.	New York 95 at Indiana	*97
May 13—Sat.	New York 84 at Indiana	98
May 17—Wed.	Indiana 95 at New York	96
May 19—Fri.	New York 92 at Indiana	82
May 21—Sun.	Indiana 97 at New York	95

Orlando 4, Chicago 2
May 7—Sun.	Chicago 91 at Orlando	94
May 10—Wed.	Chicago 104 at Orlando	94
May 12—Fri.	Orlando 110 at Chicago	101
May 14—Sun.	Orlando 95 at Chicago	106
May 16—Tue.	Chicago 95 at Orlando	103
May 18—Thur.	Orlando 108 at Chicago	102

FINALS

Orlando 4, Indiana 3
May 23—Tue.	Indiana 101 at Orlando	105
May 25—Thur.	Indiana 114 at Orlando	119
May 27—Sat.	Orlando 100 at Indiana	105
May 29—Mon.	Orlando 93 at Indiana	94
May 31—Wed.	Indiana 106 at Orlando	108
June 2—Fri.	Orlando 96 at Indiana	123
June 4—Sun.	Indiana 81 at Orlando	105

WESTERN CONFERENCE

FIRST ROUND

San Antonio 3, Denver 0
Apr. 28—Fri.	Denver 88 at San Antonio	104
Apr. 30—Sun.	Denver 96 at San Antonio	122
May 2—Tue.	San Antonio 99 at Denver	95

Phoenix 3, Portland 0
Apr. 28—Fri.	Portland 102 at Phoenix	129
Apr. 30—Sun.	Portland 94 at Phoenix	103
May 2—Tue.	Phoenix 117 at Portland	109

Houston 3, Utah 2
Apr. 27—Thur.	Houston 100 at Utah	102
Apr. 29—Sat.	Houston 140 at Utah	126
May 3—Wed.	Utah 95 at Houston	82
May 5—Fri.	Utah 106 at Houston	123
May 7—Sun.	Houston 95 at Utah	91

L.A. Lakers 3, Seattle 1
Apr. 27—Thur.	L.A. Lakers 71 at Seattle	96
Apr. 29—Sat.	L.A. Lakers 84 at Seattle	82
May 1—Mon.	Seattle 101 at L.A. Lakers	105
May 4—Thur.	Seattle 110 at L.A. Lakers	114

SEMIFINALS

San Antonio 4, L.A. Lakers 2
May 6—Sat.	L.A. Lakers 94 at San Antonio	110
May 8—Mon.	L.A. Lakers 90 at San Antonio	*97
May 12—Fri.	San Antonio 85 at L.A. Lakers	92
May 14—Sun.	San Antonio 80 at L.A. Lakers	71
May 16—Tue.	L.A. Lakers 98 at San Antonio	*96
May 18—Thur.	San Antonio 100 at L.A. Lakers	88

Houston 4, Phoenix 3
May 9—Tue.	Houston 108 at Phoenix	130
May 11—Thur.	Houston 94 at Phoenix	118
May 13—Sat.	Phoenix 85 at Houston	118
May 14—Sun.	Phoenix 114 at Houston	110
May 16—Tue.	Houston 103 at Phoenix	*97
May 18—Thur.	Phoenix 103 at Houston	116
May 20—Sat.	Houston 115 at Phoenix	114

FINALS

Houston 4, San Antonio 2
May 22—Mon.	Houston 94 at San Antonio	93
May 24—Wed.	Houston 106 at San Antonio	96
May 26—Fri.	San Antonio 107 at Houston	102
May 28—Sun.	San Antonio 103 at Houston	81
May 30—Tue.	Houston 111 at San Antonio	90
June 1—Thur.	San Antonio 95 at Houston	100

NBA FINALS

Houston 4, Orlando 0
June 7—Wed.	Houston 120 at Orlando	*118
June 9—Fri.	Houston 117 at Orlando	106
June 11—Sun.	Orlando 103 at Houston	106
June 14—Wed.	Orlando 101 at Houston	113

*Denotes number of overtime periods.

1994-95

1993-94

1993-94 NBA CHAMPION HOUSTON ROCKETS
Front row (from left): assistant coach Carroll Dawson, Robert Horry, Kenny Smith, Otis Thorpe, head coach Rudy Tomjanovich, Hakeem Olajuwon, Vernon Maxwell, assistant coach Larry Smith, assistant coach Bill Berry. Back row (from left): equipment manager David Nordstrom, scout Joe Ash, strength coach Robert Barr, Sam Cassell, Carl Herrera, Matt Bullard, Eric Riley, Richard Petruska, Larry Robinson, Mario Elie, Scott Brooks, video coordinator Jim Boylen, film coordinator Ed Bernholz, trainer Ray Melchiorre. Not pictured: Earl Cureton, Chris Jent.

FINAL STANDINGS

ATLANTIC DIVISION

	Atl.	Bos.	Char.	Chi.	Cle.	Dal.	Den.	Det.	G.S.	Hou.	Ind.	L.A.C.	L.A.L.	Mia.	Mil.	Min.	N.J.	N.Y.	Orl.	Phi.	Pho.	Por.	Sac.	S.A.	Sea.	Uta.	Was.	W	L	Pct.	GB
New York	2	4	1	3	4	2	1	4	1	0	4	2	2	2	4	2	1	..	3	3	1	2	2	1	1	0	5	57	25	.695	..
Orlando	1	2	2	2	2	2	1	3	1	1	2	1	0	3	3	1	5	2	..	4	1	2	2	0	1	2	4	50	32	.610	7
New Jersey	3	4	2	1	2	2	1	3	2	0	1	1	2	3	3	1	..	4	0	3	0	0	1	1	1	1	3	45	37	.549	12
Miami	1	3	3	2	3	2	1	2	0	0	1	1	1	..	4	2	2	2	4	0	0	1	0	2	1	1	3	42	40	.512	15
Boston	0	..	0	2	1	2	1	3	1	1	0	1	1	2	3	1	1	0	2	4	1	1	1	0	0	0	3	32	50	.390	25
Philadelphia	0	1	1	1	0	2	2	3	1	0	2	1	1	1	3	0	1	2	0	..	0	0	0	0	0	1	2	25	57	.305	32
Washington	0	2	2	0	1	1	1	2	0	1	1	1	1	3	2	1	0	1	3	0	0	0	0	0	0	1	..	24	58	.293	33

CENTRAL DIVISION

	Atl.	Bos.	Char.	Chi.	Cle.	Dal.	Den.	Det.	G.S.	Hou.	Ind.	L.A.C.	L.A.L.	Mia.	Mil.	Min.	N.J.	N.Y.	Orl.	Phi.	Pho.	Por.	Sac.	S.A.	Sea.	Uta.	Was.	W	L	Pct.	GB
Atlanta	..	4	4	2	3	2	1	4	0	1	3	1	1	3	5	2	1	2	3	4	1	1	2	1	1	1	4	57	25	.695	..
Chicago	3	2	4	..	1	2	1	5	2	1	4	2	1	2	4	2	3	1	2	3	1	0	1	1	1	2	4	55	27	.671	2
Cleveland	3	4	3	4	..	2	1	3	0	0	2	2	1	1	3	2	2	0	2	4	2	2	0	1	0	0	3	47	35	.573	10
Indiana	2	4	2	1	3	2	1	4	1	1	..	2	0	3	3	2	3	0	2	2	1	1	2	0	1	1	3	47	35	.573	10
Charlotte	1	4	..	1	1	1	1	4	0	1	2	1	2	1	3	2	2	3	2	3	2	0	1	0	0	1	2	41	41	.500	16
Milwaukee	0	1	2	0	2	2	0	4	0	1	1	0	0	1	..	0	1	0	1	1	0	1	1	0	0	0	1	20	62	.244	37
Detroit	0	1	0	0	2	1	0	..	0	0	1	1	0	2	1	2	1	0	1	1	1	0	1	1	1	0	2	20	62	.244	37

MIDWEST DIVISION

	Atl.	Bos.	Char.	Chi.	Cle.	Dal.	Den.	Det.	G.S.	Hou.	Ind.	L.A.C.	L.A.L.	Mia.	Mil.	Min.	N.J.	N.Y.	Orl.	Phi.	Pho.	Por.	Sac.	S.A.	Sea.	Uta.	Was.	W	L	Pct.	GB
Houston	1	1	1	1	2	4	2	2	4	..	1	4	3	2	1	4	2	2	1	2	2	4	4	2	2	3	1	58	24	.707	..
San Antonio	1	2	2	1	2	5	4	1	2	3	2	3	4	2	2	4	1	1	2	2	1	3	3	..	0	0	2	55	27	.671	3
Utah	2	1	0	1	5	4	2	1	3	1	3	2	1	2	4	1	2	0	1	2	3	3	5	1	1	..	2	53	29	.646	5
Denver	1	1	1	1	1	4	..	2	1	3	1	3	3	1	2	4	1	1	0	1	1	2	2	2	1	1	1	42	40	.512	16
Minnesota	0	1	0	0	0	1	1	0	2	1	0	3	1	0	2	..	1	0	1	2	0	0	2	1	0	1	0	20	62	.244	38
Dallas	0	0	1	0	0	..	1	1	0	1	0	0	0	0	0	5	0	0	0	0	0	1	2	0	0	0	1	13	69	.159	45

PACIFIC DIVISION

	Atl.	Bos.	Char.	Chi.	Cle.	Dal.	Den.	Det.	G.S.	Hou.	Ind.	L.A.C.	L.A.L.	Mia.	Mil.	Min.	N.J.	N.Y.	Orl.	Phi.	Pho.	Por.	Sac.	S.A.	Sea.	Uta.	Was.	W	L	Pct.	GB
Seattle	1	2	2	1	1	4	2	1	4	2	1	4	5	1	2	4	1	1	1	2	3	4	5	4	..	3	2	63	19	.768	..
Phoenix	1	1	0	1	2	4	3	1	3	2	1	5	2	2	2	4	2	1	1	2	..	3	4	3	2	2	2	56	26	.683	7
Golden State	2	1	2	0	0	4	3	2	..	0	1	4	5	2	2	2	0	1	1	2	3	4	2	1	3	2	1	50	32	.610	13
Portland	1	2	2	0	3	3	2	2	0	1	3	5	2	1	4	2	0	0	2	2	2	..	4	1	1	1	1	47	35	.573	16
L.A. Lakers	1	1	0	1	1	4	1	2	0	1	2	3	..	1	2	3	0	0	2	1	3	0	1	0	0	2	1	33	49	.402	30
Sacramento	0	1	1	1	0	2	2	1	1	0	0	2	4	1	1	2	1	0	0	2	1	1	..	1	0	1	2	28	54	.341	35
L.A. Clippers	1	1	1	0	0	4	1	1	1	0	0	..	2	1	1	1	1	1	0	1	1	0	2	3	1	1	1	27	55	.329	36

TEAM STATISTICS

OFFENSIVE

	G	FGM	FGA	Pct.	FTM	FTA	Pct.	REBOUNDS Off.	Def.	Tot.	Ast.	PF	Dq.	Stl.	TO	Blk.	SCORING Pts.	Avg.
Phoenix	82	3429	7080	.484	1674	2301	.728	1220	2453	3673	2261	1639	8	745	1305	460	8876	108.2
Golden State	82	3512	7145	.492	1529	2304	.664	1183	2396	3579	2198	1789	18	804	1433	511	8844	107.9
Portland	82	3371	7427	.454	1781	2396	.743	1302	2460	3762	2070	1827	5	744	1210	409	8795	107.3
Charlotte	82	3382	7100	.476	1632	2135	.764	1019	2475	3494	2214	1747	17	724	1266	394	8732	106.5
Seattle	82	3338	6901	.484	1769	2374	.745	1148	2233	3381	2112	1914	16	1053	1262	365	8687	105.9
Orlando	82	3341	6883	.485	1590	2346	.678	1177	2356	3533	2070	1713	10	683	1327	456	8666	105.7
Miami	82	3197	6896	.464	1744	2223	.785	1235	2407	3642	1856	2024	26	643	1315	374	8475	103.4
New Jersey	82	3169	7115	.445	1900	2495	.762	1300	2556	3856	1900	1693	9	696	1196	576	8461	103.2
L.A. Clippers	82	3343	7163	.467	1509	2128	.709	1120	2410	3530	2169	1769	18	807	1474	421	8447	103.0
Utah	82	3207	6729	.477	1761	2379	.740	1059	2385	3444	2179	1988	13	751	1191	364	8354	101.9
Atlanta	82	3247	7039	.461	1556	2070	.752	1250	2423	3673	2056	1625	5	915	1252	449	8318	101.4
Cleveland	82	3133	6731	.465	1736	2254	.770	1090	2353	3443	2049	1701	15	705	1136	426	8296	101.2
Houston	82	3197	6733	.475	1469	1978	.743	926	2619	3545	2087	1646	7	717	1338	485	8292	101.1
Sacramento	82	3179	7027	.452	1676	2292	.731	1122	2349	3471	2029	1979	27	669	1333	355	8291	101.1
Indiana	82	3167	6516	.486	1762	2387	.738	1130	2409	3539	2055	1974	19	706	1440	457	8280	101.0
Boston	82	3333	7057	.472	1463	2003	.730	1037	2380	3417	1928	1849	19	674	1242	440	8267	100.8
L.A. Lakers	82	3291	7316	.450	1410	1967	.717	1260	2204	3464	1983	1877	13	751	1197	461	8233	100.4
Washington	82	3195	6826	.468	1618	2162	.748	1071	2189	3260	1823	1715	9	701	1403	321	8229	100.4
Denver	82	3156	6781	.465	1739	2423	.718	1105	2557	3662	1763	1926	19	679	1422	686	8221	100.3
San Antonio	82	3178	6688	.475	1597	2151	.742	1189	2597	3786	1896	1662	4	561	1198	450	8202	100.0
New York	82	3098	6735	.460	1564	2097	.746	1175	2542	3717	2067	2001	23	752	1360	385	8076	98.5
Philadelphia	82	3103	6819	.455	1509	2112	.714	1012	2394	3406	1827	1488	7	663	1368	525	8033	98.0
Chicago	82	3245	6815	.476	1310	1859	.705	1143	2391	3534	2102	1750	11	740	1306	354	8033	98.0
Milwaukee	82	3044	6807	.447	1530	2181	.702	1126	2154	3280	1946	1821	19	800	1343	407	7949	96.9
Detroit	82	3169	7017	.452	1253	1715	.731	1027	2320	3347	1767	1935	23	602	1236	309	7949	96.9
Minnesota	82	2985	6535	.457	1777	2303	.772	990	2343	3333	1967	2016	20	600	1478	440	7930	96.7
Dallas	82	3055	7070	.432	1450	1942	.747	1271	2150	3421	1629	2007	13	767	1393	299	7801	95.1

DEFENSIVE

	FGM	FGA	Pct.	FTM	FTA	Pct.	REBOUNDS Off.	Def.	Tot.	Ast.	PF	Dq.	Stl.	TO	Blk.	SCORING Pts.	Avg.	Dif.
New York	2783	6451	.431	1684	2341	.719	1016	2245	3261	1677	1897	22	677	1420	333	7503	91.5	+7.0
San Antonio	3066	6880	.446	1349	1875	.719	1089	2153	3242	1769	1791	16	632	1020	346	7771	94.8	+5.2
Chicago	3029	6542	.463	1470	1987	.740	985	2240	3225	1840	1725	13	730	1335	374	7780	94.9	+3.1
Atlanta	3163	6954	.455	1285	1732	.742	1157	2358	3515	1897	1722	13	641	1465	338	7886	96.2	+5.2
Houston	3152	7166	.440	1377	1871	.736	1138	2434	3572	1901	1743	13	767	1221	312	7938	96.8	+4.3
Seattle	2928	6459	.453	1760	2374	.741	1084	2191	3275	1808	1884	8	686	1666	421	7942	96.9	+9.0
Cleveland	3131	6741	.464	1446	1967	.735	1059	2335	3394	2006	1797	12	628	1293	461	7966	97.1	+4.1
Indiana	2978	6614	.450	1768	2422	.730	1132	2153	3285	1902	1986	23	826	1340	389	7997	97.5	+3.5
Utah	2973	6641	.448	1773	2444	.725	1100	2327	3427	1806	1922	15	593	1318	459	8008	97.7	+4.2
Denver	3065	7000	.438	1770	2349	.750	1118	2331	3449	1745	1957	18	725	1245	502	8099	98.8	+1.5
Miami	3036	6641	.457	1889	2527	.748	1074	2266	3340	1821	1946	23	689	1314	438	8256	100.7	+2.7
New Jersey	3266	7125	.458	1514	2038	.743	1142	2528	3670	1919	1901	25	715	1248	582	8281	101.0	+2.2
Orlando	3263	7135	.457	1525	2047	.745	1197	2305	3502	2103	1844	16	756	1228	442	8283	101.8	+3.9
Milwaukee	3255	6625	.491	1684	2284	.737	1086	2495	3581	2092	1777	13	768	1416	420	8480	103.4	-6.5
Phoenix	3379	7135	.474	1438	1998	.720	1086	2247	3333	2154	1870	16	748	1254	437	8479	103.4	+4.8
Minnesota	3244	6874	.472	1783	2451	.727	1102	2296	3398	2108	1855	21	824	1164	549	8498	103.6	-6.9
Dallas	3212	6508	.494	1841	2498	.737	1101	2503	3604	1970	1649	7	782	1428	507	8514	103.8	-8.7
Portland	3311	7057	.469	1661	2216	.750	1016	2481	3497	2094	1944	15	654	1391	393	8579	104.6	+2.7
Detroit	3255	6878	.473	1805	2451	.736	1191	2590	3781	2097	1602	9	721	1169	368	8587	104.7	-7.8
L.A. Lakers	3337	7008	.476	1683	2346	.717	1284	2533	3817	2163	1659	10	664	1344	427	8585	104.7	-4.3
Boston	3357	7034	.477	1673	2218	.754	1131	2508	3639	2089	1738	12	690	1273	414	8618	105.1	-4.3
Philadelphia	3549	7338	.484	1297	1744	.744	1202	2607	3809	2357	1729	10	806	1190	385	8658	105.6	-7.6
Golden State	3428	7332	.468	1540	2108	.731	1324	2408	3732	2184	1870	18	842	1426	408	8701	106.1	+1.8
Charlotte	3463	7359	.471	1507	2036	.740	1217	2467	3684	2116	1761	12	629	1260	430	8750	106.7	-0.2
Sacramento	3360	7017	.479	1767	2448	.722	1189	2574	3763	2052	1895	14	746	1341	498	8764	106.9	-5.8
Washington	3569	7026	.508	1444	1996	.723	1119	2632	3751	2113	1823	8	815	1291	470	8834	107.7	-7.3
L.A. Clippers	3512	7421	.473	1584	2209	.717	1348	2568	3916	2220	1788	11	898	1364	476	8916	108.7	-5.7
Avgs.	3225	6924	.466	1604	2184	.734	1137	2389	3526	2000	1818	15	728	1312	429	8324	101.5	...

HOME/ROAD

	Home	Road	Total		Home	Road	Total
Atlanta	36-5	21-20	57-25	Milwaukee	11-30	9-32	20-62
Boston	18-23	14-27	32-50	Minnesota	13-28	7-34	20-62
Charlotte	28-13	13-28	41-41	New Jersey	29-12	16-25	45-37
Chicago	31-10	24-17	55-27	New York	32-9	25-16	57-25
Cleveland	31-10	16-25	47-35	Orlando	31-10	19-22	50-32
Dallas	6-35	7-34	13-69	Philadelphia	15-26	10-31	25-57
Denver	28-13	14-27	42-40	Phoenix	36-5	20-21	56-26
Detroit	10-31	10-31	20-62	Portland	30-11	17-24	47-35
Golden State	29-12	21-20	50-32	Sacramento	20-21	8-33	28-54
Houston	35-6	23-18	58-24	San Antonio	32-9	23-18	55-27
Indiana	29-12	18-23	47-35	Seattle	37-4	26-15	63-19
L.A. Clippers	17-24	10-31	27-55	Utah	33-8	20-21	53-29
L.A. Lakers	21-20	12-29	33-49	Washington	17-24	7-34	24-58
Miami	22-19	20-21	42-40	Totals	677-430	430-677	1107-1107

1993-94

POINTS
(minimum 70 games or 1,400 points)

	G	FGM	FTM	Pts.	Avg.
David Robinson, San Antonio . . .80		840	693	2383	29.8
Shaquille O'Neal, Orlando 81		953	471	2377	29.3
Hakeem Olajuwon, Houston 80		894	388	2184	27.3
Dominique Wilkins, Atl.-L.A. Clip.74		698	442	1923	26.0
Karl Malone, Utah 82		772	511	2063	25.2
Patrick Ewing, New York 79		745	445	1939	24.5
Mitch Richmond, Sacramento . .78		635	426	1823	23.4
Scottie Pippen, Chicago 72		627	270	1587	22.0
Charles Barkley, Phoenix 65		518	318	1402	21.6
Glen Rice, Miami 81		663	250	1708	21.1

REBOUNDS
(minimum 70 games or 800 rebounds)

	G	Off.	Def.	Tot.	Avg.
Dennis Rodman, San Antonio . . .79		453	914	1367	17.3
Shaquille O'Neal, Orlando 81		384	688	1072	13.2
Kevin Willis, Atlanta 80		335	628	963	12.0
Hakeem Olajuwon, Houston 80		229	726	955	11.9
Olden Polynice, Detroit-Sac. 68		299	510	809	11.9
Dikembe Mutombo, Denver 82		286	685	971	11.8
Charles Oakley, New York 82		349	616	965	11.8
Karl Malone, Utah 82		235	705	940	11.5
Derrick Coleman, New Jersey . . .77		262	608	870	11.3
Patrick Ewing, New York 79		219	666	885	11.2

FIELD GOALS
(minimum 300 made)

	FGM	FGA	Pct.
Shaquille O'Neal, Orlando 953		1591	.599
Dikembe Mutombo, Denver 365		642	.569
Otis Thorpe, Houston 449		801	.561
Chris Webber, Golden State 572		1037	.552
Shawn Kemp, Seattle 533		990	.538
Loy Vaught, L.A. Clippers 373		695	.537
Cedric Ceballos, Phoenix 425		795	.535
Rik Smits, Indiana 493		923	.534
Dale Davis, Indiana 308		582	.529
Hakeem Olajuwon, Houston 894		1694	.528
John Stockton, Utah 458		868	.528

STEALS
(minimum 70 games or 125 steals)

	G	No.	Avg.
Nate McMillan, Seattle 73		216	2.96
Scottie Pippen, Chicago 72		211	2.93
Mookie Blaylock, Atlanta 81		212	2.62
John Stockton, Utah .82		199	2.43
Eric Murdock, Milwaukee 82		197	2.40
Anfernee Hardaway, Orlando 82		190	2.32
Gary Payton, Seattle .82		188	2.29
Tom Gugliotta, Washington 78		172	2.21
Latrell Sprewell, Golden State 82		180	2.20
Dee Brown, Boston 77		156	2.03

BLOCKED SHOTS
(minimum 70 games or 100 blocked shots)

	G	No.	Avg.
Dikembe Mutombo, Denver 82		336	4.10
Hakeem Olajuwon, Houston 80		297	3.71
David Robinson, San Antonio 80		265	3.31
Alonzo Mourning, Charlotte 60		188	3.13
Shawn Bradley, Philadelphia 49		147	3.00
Shaquille O'Neal, Orlando 81		231	2.85
Patrick Ewing, New York 79		217	2.75
Oliver Miller, Phoenix 69		156	2.26
Chris Webber, Golden State 76		164	2.16
Shawn Kemp, Seattle 79		166	2.10

FREE THROWS
(minimum 125 made)

	FTM	FTA	Pct.
Mahmoud Abdul-Rauf, Denver 219		229	.956
Reggie Miller, Indiana 403		444	.908
Ricky Pierce, Seattle 189		211	.896
Sedale Threatt, L.A. Lakers 138		155	.890
Mark Price, Cleveland 238		268	.888
Glen Rice, Miami 250		284	.880
Jeff Hornacek, Philadelphia-Utah 260		296	.878
Scott Skiles, Orlando 195		222	.878
Terry Porter, Portland 204		234	.872
Kenny Smith, Houston 135		155	.871

3-POINT FIELD GOALS
(minimum 50 made)

	FGA	FGM	Pct.
Tracy Murray, Portland 109		50	.459
B.J. Armstrong, Chicago 135		60	.444
Reggie Miller, Indiana 292		123	.421
Steve Kerr, Chicago .124		52	.419
Scott Skiles, Orlando 165		68	.412
Eric Murdock, Milwaukee 168		69	.411
Mitch Richmond, Sacramento 312		127	.407
Kenny Smith, Houston 220		89	.405
Dell Curry, Charlotte 378		152	.402
Hubert Davis, New York 132		53	.402

ASSISTS
(minimum 70 games or 400 assists)

	G	No.	Avg.
John Stockton, Utah .82		1031	12.6
Muggsy Bogues, Charlotte 77		780	10.1
Mookie Blaylock, Atlanta 81		789	9.7
Kenny Anderson, New Jersey 82		784	9.6
Kevin Johnson, Phoenix 67		637	9.5
Rod Strickland, Portland 82		740	9.0
Sherman Douglas, Boston 78		683	8.8
Mark Jackson, L.A. Clippers 79		678	8.6
Mark Price, Cleveland 76		589	7.8
Micheal Williams, Minnesota 71		512	7.2

1993-94

ATLANTA HAWKS

	G	Min.	FGM	FGA	Pct.	FTM	FTA	Pct.	REBOUNDS Off.	Def.	Tot.	Ast.	PF	Dq.	Stl.	TO	Blk.	SCORING Pts.	Avg.	Hi.
Dominique Wilkins* . . 49		1687	430	996	.432	275	322	.854	119	186	305	114	87	0	63	120	22	1196	24.4	39
Kevin Willis. 80		2867	627	1257	.499	268	376	.713	335	628	963	150	250	2	79	188	38	1522	19.0	34
Danny Manning†. 26		925	177	372	.476	54	83	.651	49	120	169	85	93	0	46	86	25	408	15.7	24
Danny Manning‡. 68		2520	586	1201	.488	228	341	.669	131	334	465	261	260	2	99	233	82	1403	20.6	43
Stacey Augmon. 82		2605	439	861	.510	333	436	.764	178	216	394	187	179	0	149	147	45	1211	14.8	27
Mookie Blaylock 81		2915	444	1079	.411	116	159	.730	117	307	424	789	144	0	212	196	44	1004	12.4	28
Craig Ehlo. 82		2147	316	708	.446	112	154	.727	71	208	279	273	161	0	136	130	26	744	9.1	21
Duane Ferrell 72		1155	184	379	.485	144	184	.783	62	67	129	65	85	0	44	64	16	512	7.1	24
Andrew Lang 82		1608	215	458	.469	73	106	.689	126	187	313	51	192	2	38	81	87	503	6.1	20
Adam Keefe 63		763	96	213	.451	81	111	.730	77	124	201	34	80	0	20	60	9	273	4.3	14
Jon Koncak. 82		1823	159	369	.431	24	36	.667	83	282	365	102	236	1	63	44	125	342	4.2	12

	G	Min.	FGM	FGA	Pct.	FTM	FTA	Pct.	Off.	Def.	Tot.	Ast.	PF	Dq.	Stl.	TO	Blk.	Pts.	Avg.	Hi.
Ennis Whatley	82	1004	120	236	.508	52	66	.788	22	77	99	181	93	0	59	78	2	292	3.6	14
Doug Edwards	16	107	17	49	.347	9	16	.563	7	11	18	8	9	0	2	6	5	43	2.7	11
Paul Graham	21	128	21	57	.368	13	17	.765	4	8	12	13	11	0	4	5	5	55	2.6	11
Ricky Grace	3	8	2	3	.667	0	2	.000	0	1	1	3	0	0	0	0	0	4	1.3	4
John Bagley	3	13	0	2	.000	2	2	1.000	0	1	1	3	2	0	0	0	0	2	0.7	2

3-pt. FG: Atlanta 268-830 (.323)—Wilkins* 61-198 (.308); Willis 9-24 (.375); Manning† 1-3 (.333); Manning‡ 3-17 (.176); Augmon 1-7 (.143); Blaylock 114-341 (.334); Ehlo 77-221 (.348); Ferrell 1-9 (.111); Lang 1-4 (.250); Koncak 0-3 (.000); Whatley 0-6 (.000); Graham 3-13 (.231); Edwards 0-1 (.000). Opponents 275-872 (.315).

BOSTON CELTICS

	G	Min.	FGM	FGA	Pct.	FTM	FTA	Pct.	Off.	Def.	Tot.	Ast.	PF	Dq.	Stl.	TO	Blk.	Pts.	Avg.	Hi.
Dee Brown	77	2867	490	1021	.480	182	219	.831	63	237	300	347	207	3	156	126	47	1192	15.5	40
Dino Radja	80	2303	491	942	.521	226	301	.751	191	386	577	114	276	2	70	149	67	1208	15.1	36
Sherman Douglas	78	2789	425	919	.462	177	276	.641	70	123	193	683	171	2	89	233	11	1040	13.3	27
Robert Parish	74	1987	356	725	.491	154	208	.740	141	401	542	82	190	3	42	108	96	866	11.7	26
Kevin Gamble	75	1880	368	804	.458	103	126	.817	41	118	159	149	134	0	57	77	22	864	11.5	26
Xavier McDaniel	82	1971	387	839	.461	144	213	.676	142	258	400	126	193	0	48	116	39	928	11.3	26
Rick Fox	82	2096	340	728	.467	174	230	.757	105	250	355	217	244	4	81	158	52	887	10.8	33
Tony Harris	5	88	9	31	.290	23	25	.920	3	7	10	8	8	0	4	6	0	44	8.8	22
Acie Earl	74	1149	151	372	.406	108	160	.675	85	162	247	12	178	5	24	72	53	410	5.5	15
Ed Pinckney	76	1524	151	289	.522	92	125	.736	160	318	478	62	131	0	58	62	44	394	5.2	21
Jimmy Oliver	44	540	89	214	.416	25	33	.758	8	38	46	33	39	0	16	21	1	216	4.9	21
Alaa Abdelnaby	13	159	24	55	.436	16	25	.640	12	34	46	3	20	0	2	17	3	64	4.9	12
Todd Lichti†	4	48	6	14	.429	7	14	.500	2	6	8	6	4	0	5	3	1	19	4.8	6
Todd Lichti‡	13	126	20	51	.392	16	25	.640	8	14	22	11	16	0	7	5	1	58	4.5	11
Chris Corchiani	51	467	40	94	.426	26	38	.684	8	36	44	86	47	0	22	38	2	117	2.3	14
Matt Wenstrom	11	37	6	10	.600	6	10	.600	6	6	12	0	7	0	0	4	2	18	1.6	5

3-pt. FG: Boston 138-477 (.289)—Brown 30-96 (.313); Radja 0-1 (.000); Douglas 13-56 (.232); Gamble 25-103 (.243); McDaniel 10-41 (.244); Fox 33-100 (.330); Harris 3-9 (.333); Earl 0-1 (.000); Oliver 13-32 (.406); Lichti† 0-0; Lichti‡ 2-2 (1.000); Corchiani 11-38 (.289). Opponents 231-665 (.347).

CHARLOTTE HORNETS

	G	Min.	FGM	FGA	Pct.	FTM	FTA	Pct.	Off.	Def.	Tot.	Ast.	PF	Dq.	Stl.	TO	Blk.	Pts.	Avg.	Hi.
Alonzo Mourning	60	2018	427	845	.505	433	568	.762	177	433	610	86	207	3	27	199	188	1287	21.5	39
Larry Johnson	51	1757	346	672	.515	137	197	.695	143	305	448	184	131	0	29	116	14	834	16.4	31
Dell Curry	82	2173	533	1171	.455	117	134	.873	71	191	262	221	161	0	98	120	27	1335	16.3	30
Hersey Hawkins	82	2648	395	859	.460	312	362	.862	89	288	377	216	167	2	135	158	22	1180	14.4	41
Johnny Newman*	18	429	91	174	.523	48	59	.814	21	37	58	29	44	1	18	28	5	234	13.0	27
Eddie Johnson	73	1460	339	738	.459	99	127	.780	80	144	224	125	143	2	36	84	8	836	11.5	32
Muggsy Bogues	77	2746	354	751	.471	125	155	.806	78	235	313	780	147	1	133	171	2	835	10.8	24
Marty Conlon*	16	378	66	109	.606	31	38	.816	34	55	89	28	36	1	5	23	7	163	10.2	17
Frank Brickowski†	28	653	117	233	.502	47	63	.746	32	93	125	57	77	3	28	56	11	282	10.1	26
Frank Brickowski‡	71	2094	368	754	.488	195	254	.768	85	319	404	222	242	6	80	181	27	935	13.2	32
Kenny Gattison	77	1644	233	445	.524	126	195	.646	105	253	358	95	229	3	59	79	46	592	7.7	18
David Wingate	50	1005	136	283	.481	34	51	.667	30	104	134	104	85	0	42	53	6	310	6.2	16
Scott Burrell	51	767	98	234	.419	46	70	.657	46	86	132	62	88	0	37	45	16	244	4.8	16
LeRon Ellis	50	680	88	182	.484	45	68	.662	70	118	188	24	83	1	17	21	25	221	4.4	15
Mike Gminski*	21	255	31	79	.392	11	14	.786	19	40	59	11	20	0	13	11	13	73	3.5	14
Tony Bennett	74	983	105	263	.399	11	15	.733	16	74	90	163	84	0	39	40	1	248	3.4	20
Tim Kempton*	9	103	9	26	.346	7	10	.700	6	8	14	6	25	0	4	4	1	25	2.8	6
Rumeal Robinson†	14	95	13	33	.394	3	9	.333	2	6	8	18	15	0	3	18	0	30	2.1	7
Rumeal Robinson‡	31	396	55	152	.362	13	29	.448	6	26	32	63	48	0	18	43	3	131	4.2	16
Steve Henson	3	17	1	2	.500	0	0	. . .	0	1	1	5	3	0	0	1	0	3	1.0	3
Lorenzo Williams*	1	19	0	1	.000	0	0	. . .	0	4	4	0	2	0	1	1	2	0	0.0	0

3-pt. FG: Charlotte 336-916 (.367)—Mourning 0-2 (.000); L. Johnson 5-21 (.238); Curry 152-378 (.402); Hawkins 78-235 (.332); Newman* 4-16 (.250); E. Johnson 59-150 (.393); Bogues 2-12 (.167); Conlon* 0-1 (.000); Brickowski† 1-2 (.500); Brickowski‡ 4-20 (.200); Wingate 4-12 (.333); Burrell 2-6 (.333); Bennett 27-75 (.360); Robinson† 1-5 (.200); Robinson‡ 8-20 (.400); Henson 1-1 (1.000). Opponents 317-916 (.346).

CHICAGO BULLS

	G	Min.	FGM	FGA	Pct.	FTM	FTA	Pct.	Off.	Def.	Tot.	Ast.	PF	Dq.	Stl.	TO	Blk.	Pts.	Avg.	Hi.
Scottie Pippen	72	2759	627	1278	.491	270	409	.660	173	456	629	403	227	1	211	232	58	1587	22.0	39
Horace Grant	70	2570	460	878	.524	137	230	.596	306	463	769	236	164	0	74	109	84	1057	15.1	31
B.J. Armstrong	82	2770	479	1007	.476	194	227	.855	28	142	170	323	147	1	80	131	9	1212	14.8	28
Toni Kukoc	75	1808	313	726	.431	156	210	.743	98	199	297	252	122	0	81	167	33	814	10.9	24
Steve Kerr	82	2036	287	577	.497	83	97	.856	26	105	131	210	97	0	75	57	3	709	8.6	20
Pete Myers	82	2030	253	556	.455	136	194	.701	54	127	181	245	195	1	78	136	22	650	7.9	26
Scott Williams	38	638	114	236	.483	60	98	.612	69	112	181	39	112	1	16	44	21	289	7.6	22
Luc Longley†	27	513	85	176	.483	34	45	.756	42	96	138	63	85	2	10	40	27	204	7.6	16
Luc Longley‡	76	1502	219	465	.471	90	125	.720	129	304	433	109	216	3	45	119	79	528	6.9	16
Bill Wennington	76	1371	235	482	.488	72	88	.818	117	236	353	70	214	4	43	75	29	542	7.1	19
Bill Cartwright	42	780	98	191	.513	39	57	.684	43	109	152	57	83	0	8	50	8	235	5.6	15

	G	Min.	FGM	FGA	Pct.	FTM	FTA	Pct.	Off.	Def.	Tot.	Ast.	PF	Dq.	Stl.	TO	Blk.	Pts.	Avg.	Hi.
									REBOUNDS									**SCORING**		
Stacey King*	31	537	68	171	.398	36	53	.679	50	82	132	39	64	1	18	43	12	172	5.5	15
Jo Jo English	36	419	56	129	.434	10	21	.476	9	36	45	38	61	0	8	36	10	130	3.6	9
Corie Blount	67	690	76	174	.437	46	75	.613	76	118	194	56	93	0	19	52	33	198	3.0	17
Dave Johnson	17	119	17	54	.315	13	21	.619	9	7	16	4	7	0	4	9	0	47	2.8	11
Will Perdue	43	397	47	112	.420	23	32	.719	40	86	126	34	61	0	8	42	11	117	2.7	11
John Paxson	27	343	30	68	.441	1	2	.500	3	17	20	33	18	0	7	6	2	70	2.6	10

3-pt. FG: Chicago 233-659 (.354)—Pippen 63-197 (.320); Grant 0-6 (.000); Armstrong 60-135 (.444); Kukoc 32-118 (.271); Kerr 52-124 (.419); Myers 8-29 (.276); Williams 1-5 (.200); Wennington 0-2 (.000); Longley‡ 0-1 (.000); King* 0-2 (.000); English 8-17 (.471); Johnson 0-1 (.000); Perdue 0-1 (.000); Paxson 9-22 (.409). Opponents 252-780 (.323).

CLEVELAND CAVALIERS

	G	Min.	FGM	FGA	Pct.	FTM	FTA	Pct.	Off.	Def.	Tot.	Ast.	PF	Dq.	Stl.	TO	Blk.	Pts.	Avg.	Hi.
									REBOUNDS									**SCORING**		
Mark Price	76	2386	480	1005	.478	238	268	.888	39	189	228	589	93	0	103	189	11	1316	17.3	32
Brad Daugherty	50	1838	296	606	.488	256	326	.785	128	380	508	149	145	1	41	110	36	848	17.0	28
Gerald Wilkins	82	2768	446	975	.457	194	250	.776	106	197	303	255	186	0	105	131	38	1170	14.3	38
John Williams	76	2660	394	825	.478	252	346	.728	207	368	575	193	219	3	78	139	130	1040	13.7	23
Larry Nance	33	909	153	314	.487	64	85	.753	77	150	227	49	96	1	27	38	55	370	11.2	22
Tyrone Hill	57	1447	216	398	.543	171	256	.668	184	315	499	46	193	5	53	78	35	603	10.6	25
Chris Mills	79	2022	284	677	.419	137	176	.778	134	267	401	128	232	3	54	89	50	743	9.4	22
Terrell Brandon	73	1548	230	548	.420	139	162	.858	38	121	159	277	108	0	84	111	16	606	8.3	22
Bobby Phills	72	1531	242	514	.471	113	157	.720	71	141	212	133	135	1	67	63	12	598	8.3	26
John Battle	51	814	130	273	.476	73	97	.753	7	32	39	83	66	0	22	41	1	338	6.6	26
Rod Higgins	36	547	71	163	.436	31	42	.738	25	57	82	36	53	1	25	21	14	195	5.4	20
Danny Ferry	70	965	149	334	.446	38	43	.884	47	94	141	74	113	0	28	41	22	350	5.0	21
Tim Kempton†	4	33	6	12	.500	2	6	.333	4	6	10	3	8	0	2	7	1	14	3.5	9
Tim Kempton‡	13	136	15	38	.395	9	16	.563	10	14	24	9	33	0	6	11	2	39	3.0	9
Gary Alexander†	7	43	7	12	.583	3	7	.429	6	6	12	1	7	0	3	7	0	17	2.4	8
Gary Alexander‡	11	55	8	14	.571	3	9	.333	7	8	15	2	10	0	3	8	0	22	2.0	8
Gerald Madkins	22	149	11	31	.355	8	10	.800	1	10	11	19	16	0	9	13	0	35	1.6	11
Jay Guidinger	32	131	16	32	.500	15	21	.714	15	18	33	3	23	0	4	16	5	47	1.5	7
Sedric Toney	12	64	2	12	.167	2	2	1.000	1	2	3	11	8	0	0	5	0	6	0.5	2

3-pt. FG: Cleveland 294-813 (.362)—Price 118-297 (.397); Wilkins 84-212 (.396); Hill 0-2 (.000); Mills 38-122 (.311); Brandon 7-32 (.219); Phills 1-12 (.083); Battle 5-19 (.263); Higgins 22-50 (.440); Ferry 14-51 (.275); Alexander† 0-0; Alexander‡ 3-9 (.333); Madkins 5-15 (.333); Toney 0-1 (.000). Opponents 258-729 (.354).

DALLAS MAVERICKS

	G	Min.	FGM	FGA	Pct.	FTM	FTA	Pct.	Off.	Def.	Tot.	Ast.	PF	Dq.	Stl.	TO	Blk.	Pts.	Avg.	Hi.
									REBOUNDS									**SCORING**		
Jim Jackson	82	3066	637	1432	.445	285	347	.821	169	219	388	374	161	0	87	334	25	1576	19.2	37
Jamal Mashburn	79	2896	561	1382	.406	306	438	.699	107	246	353	266	205	0	89	245	14	1513	19.2	37
Derek Harper*	28	893	130	342	.380	28	50	.560	10	45	55	98	46	0	45	54	4	325	11.6	33
Sean Rooks	47	1255	193	393	.491	150	210	.714	84	175	259	49	109	0	21	80	44	536	11.4	26
Tony Campbell†	41	835	164	384	.427	64	83	.771	48	78	126	51	75	0	30	55	14	398	9.7	22
Tony Campbell‡	63	1214	227	512	.443	94	120	.783	76	110	186	82	134	1	50	84	15	555	8.8	22
Doug Smith	79	1684	295	678	.435	106	127	.835	114	235	349	119	287	3	82	93	38	698	8.8	36
Tim Legler	79	1322	231	528	.438	142	169	.840	36	92	128	120	133	0	52	60	13	656	8.3	25
Fat Lever	81	1947	227	557	.408	75	98	.765	83	200	283	213	155	1	159	88	15	555	6.9	16
Randy White	18	320	45	112	.402	19	33	.576	30	53	83	11	46	0	10	18	10	115	6.4	17
Popeye Jones	81	1773	195	407	.479	78	107	.729	299	306	605	99	246	2	61	94	31	468	5.8	16
Lucious Harris	77	1165	162	385	.421	87	119	.731	45	112	157	106	117	0	49	78	10	418	5.4	20
Darren Morningstar*	22	363	38	81	.469	18	30	.600	31	49	80	15	69	1	14	19	2	94	4.3	11
Terry Davis	15	286	24	59	.407	8	12	.667	30	44	74	6	27	0	9	5	1	56	3.7	10
Lorenzo Williams†	34	678	48	103	.466	12	28	.429	92	117	209	23	87	0	15	21	41	108	3.2	11
Lorenzo Williams‡	38	716	49	110	.445	12	28	.429	95	122	217	25	92	0	18	22	46	110	2.9	11
Chucky Brown	1	10	1	1	1.000	1	1	1.000	0	1	1	0	2	0	0	0	0	3	3.0	3
Donald Hodge	50	428	46	101	.455	44	52	.846	46	49	95	32	66	1	15	30	13	136	2.7	12
Greg Dreiling	54	685	52	104	.500	27	38	.711	47	123	170	31	159	5	16	43	24	132	2.4	9
Morlon Wiley†	12	124	6	21	.286	0	0	...	0	6	6	16	17	0	13	11	0	14	1.2	5
Morlon Wiley‡	16	158	9	29	.310	0	0	...	0	10	10	23	21	0	15	17	0	21	1.3	5

3-pt. FG: Dallas 241-773 (.312)—Jackson 17-60 (.283); Mashburn 85-299 (.284); Harper* 37-105 (.352); Rooks 0-1 (.000); Campbell† 6-25 (.240); Campbell‡ 7-28 (.250); Smith 2-9 (.222); Legler 52-139 (.374); Lever 26-74 (.351); White 6-20 (.300); Jones 0-1 (.000); Harris 7-33 (.212); Williams‡ 0-1 (.000); Dreiling 1-1 (1.000); Wiley† 2-6 (.333); Wiley‡ 3-10 (.300). Opponents 249-688 (.362).

DENVER NUGGETS

	G	Min.	FGM	FGA	Pct.	FTM	FTA	Pct.	Off.	Def.	Tot.	Ast.	PF	Dq.	Stl.	TO	Blk.	Pts.	Avg.	Hi.
									REBOUNDS									**SCORING**		
Mahmoud Abdul-Rauf	80	2617	588	1279	.460	219	229	.956	27	141	168	362	150	1	82	151	10	1437	18.0	33
LaPhonso Ellis	79	2699	483	963	.502	242	359	.674	220	462	682	167	304	6	63	172	80	1215	15.4	29
Reggie Williams	82	2654	418	1014	.412	165	225	.733	98	294	392	300	288	3	117	163	66	1065	13.0	27
Bryant Stith	82	2853	365	811	.450	291	351	.829	119	230	349	199	165	0	116	131	16	1023	12.5	33
Dikembe Mutombo	82	2853	365	642	.569	256	439	.583	286	685	971	127	262	2	59	206	336	986	12.0	27
Robert Pack	62	1382	223	503	.443	179	236	.758	25	98	123	356	147	1	81	204	9	631	9.6	24
Rodney Rogers	79	1406	239	545	.439	127	189	.672	90	136	226	101	195	3	63	131	48	640	8.1	25
Brian Williams	80	1507	251	464	.541	137	211	.649	138	308	446	50	221	3	49	104	87	639	8.0	16

	G	Min.	FGM	FGA	Pct.	FTM	FTA	Pct.	REBOUNDS Off.	Def.	Tot.	Ast.	PF	Dq.	Stl.	TO	Blk.	SCORING Pts.	Avg.	Hi.
Mark Macon*	7	126	14	45	.311	8	10	.800	3	4	7	11	17	0	6	14	1	36	5.1	9
Tom Hammonds	74	877	115	230	.500	71	104	.683	62	137	199	34	91	0	20	41	12	301	4.1	17
Marcus Liberty*	3	11	4	7	.571	1	2	.500	0	5	5	2	5	0	0	2	0	9	3.0	4
Kevin Brooks	34	190	36	99	.364	9	10	.900	5	16	21	3	19	0	0	12	2	85	2.5	10
Adonis Jordan	6	79	6	23	.261	0	0	...	3	3	6	19	6	0	0	6	1	15	2.5	8
Mark Randall	28	155	17	50	.340	22	28	.786	9	13	22	11	18	0	8	10	3	58	2.1	8
Darnell Mee	38	285	28	88	.318	12	27	.444	17	18	35	16	34	0	15	18	13	73	1.9	10
Jim Farmer	4	29	2	6	.333	0	0	...	0	2	2	4	3	0	0	5	0	4	1.0	2
Roy Marble	5	32	2	12	.167	0	3	.000	3	5	8	1	1	0	0	3	2	4	0.8	2

3-pt. FG: Denver 170-597 (.285)—Abdul-Rauf 42-133 (.316); Ellis 7-23 (.304); R. Williams 64-230 (.278); Stith 2-9 (.222); Mutombo 0-1 (.000); Pack 6-29 (.207); Rogers 35-92 (.380); B. Williams 0-3 (.000); Macon* 0-3 (.000); Liberty* 0-1 (.000); Brooks 4-23 (.174); Jordan 3-10 (.300); Randall 2-14 (.143); Mee 5-24 (.208); Farmer 0-2 (.000). Opponents 208-717 (.290).

DETROIT PISTONS

	G	Min.	FGM	FGA	Pct.	FTM	FTA	Pct.	REBOUNDS Off.	Def.	Tot.	Ast.	PF	Dq.	Stl.	TO	Blk.	SCORING Pts.	Avg.	Hi.
Joe Dumars	69	2591	505	1118	.452	276	330	.836	35	116	151	261	118	0	63	159	4	1410	20.4	44
Terry Mills	80	2773	588	1151	.511	181	227	.797	193	479	672	177	309	6	64	153	62	1381	17.3	35
Isiah Thomas	58	1750	318	763	.417	181	258	.702	46	113	159	399	126	0	68	202	6	856	14.8	31
Olden Polynice*	37	1350	222	406	.547	42	92	.457	148	308	456	22	108	1	24	49	36	486	13.1	27
Sean Elliott	73	2409	360	791	.455	139	173	.803	68	195	263	197	174	3	54	129	27	885	12.1	27
Lindsey Hunter	82	2172	335	893	.375	104	142	.732	47	142	189	390	174	1	121	184	10	843	10.3	29
Bill Laimbeer	11	248	47	90	.522	11	13	.846	9	47	56	14	30	0	6	10	4	108	9.8	25
Allan Houston	79	1519	272	671	.405	89	108	.824	19	101	120	100	165	2	34	99	13	668	8.5	31
Greg Anderson	77	1624	201	370	.543	88	154	.571	183	388	571	51	234	4	55	94	68	491	6.4	23
David Wood	78	1182	119	259	.459	62	82	.756	104	135	239	51	201	3	39	35	19	322	4.1	14
Pete Chilcutt†	30	391	51	120	.425	10	13	.769	29	71	100	15	48	0	10	18	11	115	3.8	12
Pete Chilcutt‡	76	1365	203	448	.453	41	65	.631	129	242	371	86	164	2	53	74	39	450	5.9	15
Mark Macon†	35	370	55	139	.396	15	24	.625	15	19	34	40	56	0	33	26	0	127	3.6	11
Mark Macon‡	42	496	69	184	.375	23	34	.676	18	23	41	51	73	0	39	40	1	163	3.9	11
Ben Coleman	9	77	12	25	.480	4	8	.500	10	16	26	0	9	0	2	7	2	28	3.1	8
Marcus Liberty†	35	274	36	116	.310	18	37	.486	26	30	56	15	29	0	11	22	4	100	2.9	23
Marcus Liberty‡	38	285	40	123	.325	19	39	.487	26	35	61	17	34	0	11	24	4	109	2.9	23
Charles Jones	42	877	36	78	.462	19	34	.559	89	146	235	29	136	3	14	12	43	91	2.2	9
Tod Murphy*	7	57	6	12	.500	3	6	.500	4	5	9	3	8	0	2	1	0	15	2.1	5
Tracy Moore	3	10	2	3	.667	2	2	1.000	0	1	1	0	0	0	2	0	0	6	2.0	6
Dan O'Sullivan	13	56	4	12	.333	9	12	.750	2	8	10	3	7	0	3	9	0	17	1.3	6

3-pt. FG: Detroit 358-1041 (.344)—Dumars 124-320 (.388); Mills 24-73 (.329); Thomas 39-126 (.310); Polynice* 0-1 (.000); Elliott 26-87 (.299); Hunter 69-207 (.333); Laimbeer 3-9 (.333); Houston 35-117 (.299); Anderson 1-3 (.333); Wood 22-49 (.449); Chilcutt† 3-14 (.214); Chilcutt‡ 3-15 (.200); Macon† 2-7 (.286); Macon‡ 2-10 (.200); Liberty† 10-27 (.370); Liberty‡ 10-28 (.357); Jones 0-1 (.000). Opponents 272-814 (.334).

GOLDEN STATE WARRIORS

	G	Min.	FGM	FGA	Pct.	FTM	FTA	Pct.	REBOUNDS Off.	Def.	Tot.	Ast.	PF	Dq.	Stl.	TO	Blk.	SCORING Pts.	Avg.	Hi.
Latrell Sprewell	82	3533	613	1417	.433	353	456	.774	80	321	401	385	158	0	180	226	76	1720	21.0	41
Chris Webber	76	2438	572	1037	.552	189	355	.532	305	389	694	272	247	4	93	206	164	1333	17.5	36
Chris Mullin	62	2324	410	869	.472	165	219	.753	64	281	345	315	114	0	107	178	53	1040	16.8	32
Billy Owens	79	2738	492	971	.507	199	326	.610	230	410	640	326	269	5	83	214	60	1186	15.0	29
Avery Johnson	82	2332	356	724	.492	178	253	.704	41	135	176	433	160	0	113	172	8	890	10.9	23
Victor Alexander	69	1318	266	502	.530	68	129	.527	114	194	308	66	168	0	28	86	32	602	8.7	19
Chris Gatling	82	1296	271	461	.588	129	208	.620	143	254	397	41	223	5	40	84	63	671	8.2	21
Jeff Grayer	67	1096	191	363	.526	71	118	.602	76	115	191	62	103	0	33	63	13	455	6.8	20
Todd Lichti*	5	58	10	28	.357	9	11	.818	3	7	10	3	9	0	0	0	0	31	6.2	11
Keith Jennings	76	1097	138	342	.404	100	120	.833	16	73	89	218	62	0	65	74	0	432	5.7	17
Andre Spencer*	5	63	9	18	.500	3	4	.750	4	8	12	3	6	0	1	2	0	21	4.2	8
Josh Grant	53	382	59	146	.404	22	29	.759	27	62	89	24	62	0	18	30	8	157	3.0	16
Jud Buechler	36	218	42	84	.500	10	20	.500	13	19	32	16	24	0	8	12	1	106	2.9	18
Byron Houston	71	866	81	177	.458	33	54	.611	67	127	194	32	181	4	33	49	31	196	2.8	11
Dell Demps	2	11	2	6	.333	0	2	.000	0	0	0	1	1	0	2	1	0	4	2.0	2
Tod Murphy†	2	10	0	0	...	0	0	...	0	1	1	1	2	0	0	0	0	0	0.0	0
Tod Murphy‡	9	67	6	12	.500	3	6	.500	4	6	10	4	10	0	2	1	0	15	1.7	5

3-pt. FG: Golden State 291-859 (.339)—Sprewell 141-391 (.361); Webber 0-14 (.000); Mullin 55-151 (.364); Owens 3-15 (.200); Johnson 0-12 (.000); Alexander 2-13 (.154); Gatling 0-1 (.000); Grayer 2-12 (.167); Lichti* 2-2 (1.000); Jennings 56-151 (.371); Grant 17-61 (.279); Buechler 12-29 (.414); Houston 1-7 (.143). Opponents 305-869 (.351).

HOUSTON ROCKETS

	G	Min.	FGM	FGA	Pct.	FTM	FTA	Pct.	REBOUNDS Off.	Def.	Tot.	Ast.	PF	Dq.	Stl.	TO	Blk.	SCORING Pts.	Avg.	Hi.
Hakeem Olajuwon	80	3277	894	1694	.528	388	542	.716	229	726	955	287	289	4	128	271	297	2184	27.3	45
Otis Thorpe	82	2909	449	801	.561	251	382	.657	271	599	870	189	253	1	66	185	28	1149	14.0	40
Vernon Maxwell	75	2571	380	976	.389	143	191	.749	42	147	189	380	143	0	125	185	20	1023	13.6	35
Kenny Smith	78	2209	341	711	.480	135	155	.871	24	114	138	327	121	0	59	126	4	906	11.6	41
Chris Jent	3	78	13	26	.500	1	2	.500	4	11	15	7	13	1	0	5	0	31	10.3	15
Robert Horry	81	2370	322	702	.459	115	157	.732	128	312	440	231	186	0	119	137	75	803	9.9	30

1993-94

	G	Min.	FGM	FGA	Pct.	FTM	FTA	Pct.	REBOUNDS Off.	Def.	Tot.	Ast.	PF	Dq.	Stl.	TO	Blk.	SCORING Pts.	Avg.	Hi.
Mario Elie	67	1606	208	466	.446	154	179	.860	28	153	181	208	124	0	50	109	8	626	9.3	25
Sam Cassell	66	1122	162	388	.418	90	107	.841	25	109	134	192	136	1	59	94	7	440	6.7	23
Scott Brooks	73	1225	142	289	.491	74	85	.871	10	92	102	149	98	0	51	55	2	381	5.2	16
Carl Herrera	75	1292	142	310	.458	69	97	.711	101	184	285	37	159	0	32	69	26	353	4.7	15
Larry Robinson	6	55	10	20	.500	3	8	.375	4	6	10	6	8	0	7	10	0	25	4.2	9
Matt Bullard	65	725	78	226	.345	20	26	.769	23	61	84	64	67	0	14	28	6	226	3.5	17
Richard Petruska	22	92	20	46	.435	6	8	.750	9	22	31	1	15	0	2	15	3	53	2.4	12
Earl Cureton	2	30	2	8	.250	0	2	.000	4	8	12	0	4	0	0	1	0	4	2.0	4
Eric Riley	47	219	34	70	.486	20	37	.541	24	35	59	9	30	0	5	15	9	88	1.9	12

3-pt. FG: Houston 429-1285 (.334)—Olajuwon 8-19 (.421); Thorpe 0-2 (.000); Maxwell 120-403 (.298); Smith 89-220 (.405); Jent 4-11 (.364); Horry 44-136 (.324); Elie 56-167 (.335); Cassell 26-88 (.295); Brooks 23-61 (.377); Robinson 2-8 (.250); Bullard 50-154 (.325); Petruska 7-15 (.467); Riley 0-1 (.000). Opponents 257-841 (.306).

INDIANA PACERS

	G	Min.	FGM	FGA	Pct.	FTM	FTA	Pct.	REBOUNDS Off.	Def.	Tot.	Ast.	PF	Dq.	Stl.	TO	Blk.	SCORING Pts.	Avg.	Hi.
Reggie Miller	79	2638	524	1042	.503	403	444	.908	30	182	212	248	193	2	119	175	24	1574	19.9	38
Rik Smits	78	2113	493	923	.534	238	300	.793	135	348	483	156	281	11	49	151	82	1224	15.7	40
Derrick McKey	76	2613	355	710	.500	192	254	.756	129	273	402	327	248	1	111	228	49	911	12.0	30
Dale Davis	66	2292	308	582	.529	155	294	.527	280	438	718	100	214	1	48	102	106	771	11.7	28
Byron Scott	67	1197	256	548	.467	157	195	.805	19	91	110	133	80	0	62	103	9	696	10.4	21
Pooh Richardson	37	1022	160	354	.452	47	77	.610	28	82	110	237	78	0	32	88	3	370	10.0	24
Antonio Davis	81	1732	216	425	.508	194	302	.642	190	315	505	55	189	1	45	107	84	626	7.7	26
Haywoode Workman	65	1714	195	460	.424	93	116	.802	32	172	204	404	152	0	85	151	4	501	7.7	21
Malik Sealy	43	623	111	274	.405	59	87	.678	43	75	118	48	84	0	31	51	8	285	6.6	27
Vern Fleming	55	1053	147	318	.462	64	87	.736	27	96	123	173	98	1	40	87	6	358	6.5	19
Kenny Williams	68	982	191	391	.488	45	64	.703	93	112	205	52	99	0	24	45	49	427	6.3	25
Sam Mitchell	75	1084	140	306	.458	82	110	.745	71	119	190	65	152	1	33	50	9	362	4.8	14
Lester Conner	11	169	14	38	.368	3	6	.500	10	14	24	31	12	0	14	9	1	31	2.8	7
Gerald Paddio*	7	55	9	23	.391	1	2	.500	0	5	5	4	2	0	1	4	0	19	2.7	9
LaSalle Thompson	30	282	27	77	.351	16	30	.533	24	49	75	16	59	1	10	23	8	70	2.3	5
Scott Haskin	27	186	21	45	.467	13	19	.684	17	38	55	6	33	0	2	13	15	55	2.0	8

3-pt. FG: Indiana 184-500 (.368)—Miller 123-292 (.421); Smits 0-1 (.000); McKey 9-31 (.290); D. Davis 0-1 (.000); Scott 27-74 (.365); Richardson 3-12 (.250); A. Davis 0-1 (.000); Workman 18-56 (.321); Sealy 4-16 (.250); Fleming 0-4 (.000); Williams 0-4 (.000); Mitchell 0-5 (.000); Conner 0-3 (.000). Opponents 273-815 (.335).

LOS ANGELES CLIPPERS

	G	Min.	FGM	FGA	Pct.	FTM	FTA	Pct.	REBOUNDS Off.	Def.	Tot.	Ast.	PF	Dq.	Stl.	TO	Blk.	SCORING Pts.	Avg.	Hi.
Dominique Wilkins†	25	948	268	592	.453	167	200	.835	63	113	176	55	39	0	29	52	8	727	29.1	42
Dominique Wilkins‡	74	2635	698	1588	.440	442	522	.847	182	299	481	169	126	0	92	172	30	1923	26.0	42
Danny Manning*	42	1595	409	829	.493	174	258	.674	82	214	296	176	167	2	53	147	57	994	23.7	43
Ron Harper	75	2856	569	1335	.426	299	418	.715	129	331	460	344	167	0	144	242	54	1508	20.1	39
Loy Vaught	75	2118	373	695	.537	131	182	.720	218	438	656	74	221	5	76	96	22	877	11.7	29
Mark Jackson	79	2711	331	732	.452	167	211	.791	107	241	348	678	115	0	120	232	6	865	10.9	26
Mark Aguirre	39	859	163	348	.468	50	72	.694	28	88	116	104	98	2	21	70	8	403	10.3	24
Elmore Spencer	76	1930	288	540	.533	97	162	.599	96	319	415	75	208	3	30	168	127	673	8.9	28
Harold Ellis	49	923	159	292	.545	106	149	.711	94	59	153	31	97	0	73	43	2	424	8.7	29
Gary Grant	78	1533	253	563	.449	65	76	.855	42	100	142	291	139	1	119	136	12	588	7.5	26
Stanley Roberts	14	350	43	100	.430	18	44	.409	27	66	93	11	54	2	6	24	25	104	7.4	13
Charles Outlaw	37	871	98	167	.587	61	103	.592	81	131	212	36	94	1	36	31	37	257	6.9	19
John Williams	34	725	81	188	.431	24	36	.667	37	90	127	97	85	1	25	35	10	191	5.6	21
Terry Dehere	64	759	129	342	.377	61	81	.753	25	43	68	78	69	0	28	61	3	342	5.3	26
Tom Tolbert	49	640	74	177	.418	33	45	.733	36	72	108	30	61	0	13	39	15	187	3.8	17
Randy Woods	40	352	49	133	.368	20	35	.571	13	16	29	71	40	0	24	34	2	145	3.6	20
Henry James	12	75	16	42	.381	5	5	1.000	6	8	14	1	9	0	2	2	0	41	3.4	9
Bob Martin	53	535	40	88	.455	31	51	.608	36	81	117	17	106	1	8	29	33	111	2.1	10

3-pt. FG: L.A. Clippers 252-831 (.303)—Wilkins† 24-97 (.247); Wilkins‡ 85-295 (.288); Manning* 2-14 (.143); Harper 71-236 (.301); Vaught 0-5 (.000); Jackson 36-127 (.283); Aguirre 37-93 (.398); Spencer 0-2 (.000); Ellis 0-4 (.000); Grant 17-62 (.274); Outlaw 0-2 (.000); Williams 5-20 (.250); Dehere 23-57 (.404); Tolbert 6-16 (.375); Woods 27-78 (.346); James 4-18 (.222). Opponents 308-882 (.349).

LOS ANGELES LAKERS

	G	Min.	FGM	FGA	Pct.	FTM	FTA	Pct.	REBOUNDS Off.	Def.	Tot.	Ast.	PF	Dq.	Stl.	TO	Blk.	SCORING Pts.	Avg.	Hi.
Vlade Divac	79	2685	453	895	.506	208	303	.686	282	569	851	307	288	5	92	191	112	1123	14.2	33
Anthony Peeler	30	923	176	409	.430	57	71	.803	48	61	109	94	93	0	43	59	8	423	14.1	28
Nick Van Exel	81	2700	410	1049	.394	150	192	.781	47	191	238	466	154	1	85	145	8	1099	13.6	31
Elden Campbell	76	2253	373	808	.462	188	273	.689	167	352	519	86	241	2	64	98	146	934	12.3	29
Sedale Threatt	81	2278	411	852	.482	138	155	.890	28	125	153	344	186	1	110	106	19	965	11.9	32
Doug Christie	65	1515	244	562	.434	145	208	.697	93	142	235	136	186	2	89	140	28	671	10.3	33
James Worthy	80	1597	340	838	.406	100	135	.741	48	133	181	154	80	0	45	97	18	812	10.2	31
Trevor Wilson*	5	126	19	39	.487	13	25	.520	12	16	28	12	17	0	5	6	1	51	10.2	16
George Lynch	71	1762	291	573	.508	99	166	.596	220	190	410	96	177	1	102	87	27	681	9.6	30
Sam Bowie	25	556	75	172	.436	72	83	.867	27	104	131	47	65	0	4	43	28	223	8.9	21

1993-94

	G	Min.	FGM	FGA	Pct.	FTM	FTA	Pct.	REBOUNDS Off.	Def.	Tot.	Ast.	PF	Dq.	Stl.	TO	Blk.	SCORING Pts.	Avg.	Hi.
Tony Smith	73	1617	272	617	.441	85	119	.714	106	89	195	148	128	1	59	76	14	645	8.8	25
Reggie Jordan	23	259	44	103	.427	35	51	.686	46	21	67	26	26	0	14	14	5	125	5.4	28
James Edwards	45	469	78	168	.464	54	79	.684	11	54	65	22	90	0	4	30	3	210	4.7	16
Kurt Rambis	50	635	59	114	.518	46	71	.648	84	105	189	32	89	0	22	26	23	164	3.3	13
Dan Schayes†	13	133	14	38	.368	8	10	.800	15	19	34	8	18	0	5	9	2	36	2.8	11
Dan Schayes‡	36	363	28	84	.333	29	32	.906	31	48	79	13	45	0	10	23	10	85	2.4	11
Antonio Harvey	27	247	29	79	.367	12	26	.462	26	33	59	5	39	0	8	17	19	70	2.6	16

3-pt. FG: L.A. Lakers 241-803 (.300)—Divac 9-47 (.191); Peeler 14-63 (.222); Van Exel 123-364 (.338); Campbell 0-2 (.000); Threatt 5-33 (.152); Christie 39-119 (.328); Worthy 32-111 (.288); Lynch 0-5 (.000); Bowie 1-4 (.250); Smith 16-50 (.320); Jordan 2-4 (.500); Rambis 0-1 (.000). Opponents 228-723 (.315).

MIAMI HEAT

	G	Min.	FGM	FGA	Pct.	FTM	FTA	Pct.	REBOUNDS Off.	Def.	Tot.	Ast.	PF	Dq.	Stl.	TO	Blk.	SCORING Pts.	Avg.	Hi.
Glen Rice	81	2999	663	1421	.467	250	284	.880	76	358	434	184	186	0	110	130	32	1708	21.1	40
Steve Smith	78	2776	491	1076	.456	273	327	.835	156	196	352	394	217	6	84	202	35	1346	17.3	32
Rony Seikaly	72	2410	392	803	.488	304	422	.720	244	496	740	136	279	8	59	195	100	1088	15.1	36
Grant Long	69	2201	300	672	.446	187	238	.786	190	305	495	170	244	5	89	125	26	788	11.4	24
Harold Miner	63	1358	254	532	.477	149	180	.828	75	81	156	95	132	0	31	95	13	661	10.5	28
Brian Shaw	77	2037	278	667	.417	64	89	.719	104	246	350	385	195	1	71	173	21	693	9.0	27
Bimbo Coles	76	1726	233	519	.449	102	131	.779	50	109	159	263	132	0	75	107	12	588	7.7	19
John Salley	76	1910	208	436	.477	164	225	.729	132	275	407	135	260	4	56	94	78	582	7.7	21
Matt Geiger	72	1199	202	352	.574	116	149	.779	119	184	303	32	201	2	36	61	29	521	7.2	23
Willie Burton	53	697	124	283	.438	120	158	.759	50	86	136	39	96	0	18	54	20	371	7.0	28
Keith Askins	37	319	36	88	.409	9	10	.900	33	49	82	13	57	0	11	21	1	85	2.3	13
Alec Kessler	15	66	11	25	.440	6	8	.750	4	6	10	2	14	0	1	5	1	33	2.2	5
Morlon Wiley*	4	34	3	8	.375	0	0	...	0	4	4	7	4	0	2	6	0	7	1.8	4
Gary Alexander*	4	12	1	2	.500	0	2	.000	1	2	3	1	3	0	0	1	0	2	0.5	2
Manute Bol*	8	61	1	12	.083	0	0	...	1	10	11	0	4	0	0	5	6	2	0.3	2

3-pt. FG: Miami 337-997 (.338)—Rice 132-346 (.382); Smith 91-262 (.347); Seikaly 0-2 (.000); Long 1-6 (.167); Miner 4-6 (.667); Shaw 73-216 (.338); Coles 20-99 (.202); Salley 2-3 (.667); Geiger 1-5 (.200); Burton 3-15 (.200); Askins 4-21 (.190); Kessler 5-9 (.556); Wiley* 1-4 (.250); Bol* 0-3 (.000). Opponents 295-892 (.331).

MILWAUKEE BUCKS

	G	Min.	FGM	FGA	Pct.	FTM	FTA	Pct.	REBOUNDS Off.	Def.	Tot.	Ast.	PF	Dq.	Stl.	TO	Blk.	SCORING Pts.	Avg.	Hi.
Eric Murdock	82	2533	477	1019	.468	234	288	.813	91	170	261	546	189	2	197	206	12	1257	15.3	32
Frank Brickowski*	43	1441	251	521	.482	148	191	.775	53	226	279	165	165	3	52	125	16	653	15.2	32
Vin Baker	82	2560	435	869	.501	234	411	.569	277	344	621	163	231	3	60	162	114	1105	13.5	29
Todd Day	76	2127	351	845	.415	231	331	.698	115	195	310	138	221	4	103	129	52	966	12.7	27
Ken Norman	82	2539	412	919	.448	92	183	.503	169	331	500	222	209	2	58	150	46	979	11.9	37
Blue Edwards	82	2322	382	800	.478	151	189	.799	104	225	329	171	235	1	83	146	27	953	11.6	28
Anthony Avent*	33	695	92	228	.404	61	79	.772	60	94	154	33	60	0	16	43	20	245	7.4	19
Derek Strong	67	1131	141	341	.413	159	206	.772	109	172	281	48	69	1	38	61	14	444	6.6	22
Jon Barry	72	1242	158	382	.414	97	122	.795	36	110	146	168	110	0	102	83	17	445	6.2	23
Lee Mayberry	82	1472	167	402	.415	58	84	.690	26	75	101	215	114	0	46	97	4	433	5.3	19
Brad Lohaus	67	962	102	281	.363	20	29	.690	33	117	150	62	142	3	30	58	55	270	4.0	21
Joe Courtney†	19	177	27	70	.386	9	15	.600	14	15	29	6	21	0	7	11	6	65	3.4	10
Joe Courtney‡	52	345	67	148	.453	32	47	.681	28	28	56	15	44	0	10	21	12	168	3.2	13
Greg Foster	3	19	4	7	.571	2	2	1.000	0	3	3	0	3	0	0	1	1	10	3.3	8
Anthony Cook†	23	203	26	53	.491	10	25	.400	20	36	56	4	22	30	3	11	12	62	2.7	14
Anthony Cook‡	25	203	26	54	.481	10	25	.400	20	36	56	4	22	0	3	12	14	62	2.5	14
Dan Schayes*	23	230	14	46	.304	21	22	.955	16	29	45	5	27	0	5	14	8	49	2.1	11
Mike Gminski†	8	54	5	24	.208	3	4	.750	3	12	15	0	3	0	0	2	3	13	1.6	10
Mike Gminski‡	29	309	36	103	.350	14	18	.778	22	52	74	11	23	0	13	13	16	86	3.0	14

3-pt. FG: Milwaukee 331-1019 (.325)—Murdock 69-168 (.411); Brickowski* 3-18 (.167); Baker 1-5 (.200); Day 33-148 (.223); Norman 63-189 (.333); Edwards 38-106 (.358); Strong 3-13 (.231); Barry 32-115 (.278); Mayberry 41-119 (.345); Lohaus 46-134 (.343); Courtney† 2-3 (.667); Courtney‡ 2-3 (.667); Cook† 0-1 (.000); Cook‡ 0-1 (.000). Opponents 286-789 (.362).

MINNESOTA TIMBERWOLVES

	G	Min.	FGM	FGA	Pct.	FTM	FTA	Pct.	REBOUNDS Off.	Def.	Tot.	Ast.	PF	Dq.	Stl.	TO	Blk.	SCORING Pts.	Avg.	Hi.
Christian Laettner	70	2428	396	883	.448	375	479	.783	160	442	602	307	264	6	87	259	86	1173	16.8	29
J.R. Rider	79	2415	522	1115	.468	215	265	.811	118	197	315	202	194	0	54	218	28	1313	16.6	32
Doug West	72	2182	434	891	.487	187	231	.810	61	170	231	172	236	3	65	137	24	1056	14.7	30
Micheal Williams	71	2206	314	687	.457	333	397	.839	67	154	221	512	193	3	118	203	24	971	13.7	33
Stacey King†	18	516	78	170	.459	57	83	.687	40	69	109	19	57	0	13	40	30	213	11.8	21
Stacey King‡	49	1053	146	341	.428	93	136	.684	90	151	241	58	121	1	31	83	42	385	7.9	21
Chuck Person	77	2029	356	843	.422	82	108	.759	55	198	253	185	164	0	45	121	12	894	11.6	28
Thurl Bailey	79	1297	232	455	.510	119	149	.799	66	149	215	54	93	0	20	58	58	583	7.4	20
Luc Longley*	49	989	134	289	.464	56	80	.700	87	208	295	46	131	1	35	79	58	324	6.6	14
Chris Smith	80	1617	184	423	.435	95	141	.674	15	107	122	285	131	1	38	101	18	473	5.9	25
Marlon Maxey	55	626	89	167	.533	70	98	.714	75	124	199	10	113	1	16	40	33	248	4.5	14
Mike Brown	82	1921	111	260	.427	77	118	.653	119	328	447	72	218	4	51	75	29	299	3.6	10

	G	Min.	FGM	FGA	Pct.	FTM	FTA	Pct.	REBOUNDS Off.	Def.	Tot.	Ast.	PF	Dq.	Stl.	TO	Blk.	SCORING Pts.	Avg.	Hi.
Andres Guibert	5	33	6	20	.300	3	6	.500	10	6	16	2	6	0	0	6	1	15	3.0	10
Tellis Frank	67	959	67	160	.419	54	76	.711	83	137	220	57	163	1	35	49	35	188	2.8	19
Corey Williams	4	46	5	13	.385	1	1	1.000	1	5	6	6	6	0	2	2	0	11	2.8	5
Stanley Jackson	17	92	17	33	.515	3	3	1.000	12	15	27	16	13	0	5	10	0	38	2.2	8
Brian Davis	68	374	40	126	.317	50	68	.735	21	34	55	22	34	0	16	19	4	131	1.9	11

3-pt. FG: Minnesota 183-557 (.329)—Laettner 6-25 (.240); Rider 54-150 (.360); West 1-8 (.125); M. Williams 10-45 (.222); King† 0-0; King‡ 0-2 (.000); Person 100-272 (.368); Bailey 0-2 (.000); Longley* 0-1 (.000); Smith 10-39 (.256); Maxey 0-2 (.000); Brown 0-2 (.000); Frank 0-2 (.000); C. Williams 0-1 (.000); Jackson 1-5 (.200); Davis 1-3 (.333). Opponents 227-738 (.308).

NEW JERSEY NETS

	G	Min.	FGM	FGA	Pct.	FTM	FTA	Pct.	REBOUNDS Off.	Def.	Tot.	Ast.	PF	Dq.	Stl.	TO	Blk.	SCORING Pts.	Avg.	Hi.
Derrick Coleman	77	2778	541	1209	.447	439	567	.774	262	608	870	262	209	2	68	208	142	1559	20.2	36
Kenny Anderson	82	3135	576	1381	.417	346	423	.818	89	233	322	784	201	0	158	266	15	1538	18.8	45
Kevin Edwards	82	2727	471	1028	.458	167	217	.770	94	187	281	232	150	0	120	135	34	1144	14.0	28
Armon Gilliam	82	1969	348	682	.510	274	361	.759	197	303	500	69	129	0	38	106	61	970	11.8	27
Chris Morris	50	1349	203	454	.447	85	118	.720	91	137	228	83	120	2	55	52	49	544	10.9	27
Johnny Newman†	63	1268	222	490	.453	134	166	.807	65	57	122	43	152	2	51	62	22	598	9.5	24
Johnny Newman‡	81	1697	313	664	.471	182	225	.809	86	94	180	72	196	3	69	90	27	832	10.3	27
Benoit Benjamin	77	1817	283	589	.480	152	214	.710	135	364	499	44	198	0	35	97	90	718	9.3	26
Rumeal Robinson*	17	301	42	119	.353	10	20	.500	4	20	24	45	33	0	15	25	3	101	5.9	16
P.J. Brown	79	1950	167	402	.415	115	152	.757	188	305	493	93	177	1	71	72	93	450	5.7	13
Jayson Williams	70	877	125	293	.427	72	119	.605	109	154	263	26	140	1	17	35	36	322	4.6	19
Ron Anderson*	11	176	15	43	.349	10	12	.833	8	18	26	6	9	0	5	1	2	44	4.0	10
Rex Walters	48	386	60	115	.522	28	34	.824	6	32	38	71	41	0	15	30	3	162	3.4	12
David Wesley	60	542	64	174	.368	44	53	.830	10	34	44	123	47	0	38	52	4	183	3.1	12
Dwayne Schintzius	30	319	29	84	.345	10	17	.588	26	63	89	13	49	1	7	13	17	68	2.3	10
Rick Mahorn	28	226	23	47	.489	13	20	.650	16	38	54	5	38	0	3	7	5	59	2.1	7
Dave Jamerson†	4	10	0	5	.000	1	2	.500	0	3	3	1	0	0	0	1	0	1	0.3	1
Dave Jamerson‡	5	14	0	7	.000	2	3	.667	0	4	4	1	0	0	0	1	0	2	0.4	1

3-pt. FG: New Jersey 223-683 (.327)—Coleman 38-121 (.314); K. Anderson 40-132 (.303); Edwards 35-99 (.354); Gilliam 0-1 (.000); Morris 53-147 (.361); Newman† 20-74 (.270); Newman‡ 24-90 (.267); Robinson* 7-15 (.467); Brown 1-6 (.167); R. Anderson* 4-12 (.333); Walters 14-28 (.500); Wesley 11-47 (.234); Mahorn 0-1 (.000). Opponents 235-739 (.318).

NEW YORK KNICKERBOCKERS

	G	Min.	FGM	FGA	Pct.	FTM	FTA	Pct.	REBOUNDS Off.	Def.	Tot.	Ast.	PF	Dq.	Stl.	TO	Blk.	SCORING Pts.	Avg.	Hi.
Patrick Ewing	79	2972	745	1503	.496	445	582	.765	219	666	885	179	275	3	90	260	217	1939	24.5	44
John Starks	59	2057	410	977	.420	187	248	.754	37	148	185	348	191	4	95	184	6	1120	19.0	39
Charles Oakley	82	2932	363	760	.478	243	313	.776	349	616	965	218	293	4	110	193	18	969	11.8	24
Hubert Davis	56	1333	238	505	.471	85	103	.825	23	44	67	165	118	0	40	76	4	614	11.0	32
Charles Smith	43	1105	176	397	.443	87	121	.719	66	99	165	50	144	4	26	64	45	447	10.4	25
Derek Harper†	54	1311	173	402	.430	84	113	.743	10	76	86	236	117	0	80	81	4	466	8.6	22
Derek Harper‡	82	2204	303	744	.407	112	163	.687	20	121	141	334	163	0	125	135	8	791	9.6	33
Greg Anthony	80	1994	225	571	.394	130	168	.774	43	146	189	365	163	1	114	127	13	628	7.9	19
Doc Rivers	19	499	55	127	.433	14	22	.636	4	35	39	100	44	0	25	29	5	143	7.5	15
Rolando Blackman	55	969	161	369	.436	48	53	.906	23	70	93	76	100	0	25	44	6	400	7.3	19
Anthony Mason	73	1903	206	433	.476	116	161	.720	158	269	427	151	190	2	31	107	9	528	7.2	20
Tony Campbell*	22	379	63	128	.492	30	37	.811	28	32	60	31	59	1	20	29	1	157	7.1	14
Anthony Bonner	73	1402	162	288	.563	50	105	.476	150	194	344	88	175	3	76	89	13	374	5.1	17
Herb Williams	70	774	103	233	.442	27	42	.643	56	126	182	28	108	1	18	39	43	233	3.3	15
Eric Anderson	11	39	7	17	.412	5	14	.357	6	11	17	2	9	0	0	2	1	21	1.9	4
Corey Gaines	18	78	9	20	.450	13	15	.867	3	10	13	30	12	0	2	5	0	33	1.8	7
Gerald Paddio*	3	8	2	5	.400	0	0	...	0	0	0	0	3	0	0	0	0	4	1.3	4

3-pt. FG: New York 316-908 (.348)—Ewing 4-14 (.286); Starks 113-337 (.335); Oakley 0-3 (.000); Davis 53-132 (.402); Smith 8-16 (.500); Harper† 36-98 (.367); Harper‡ 73-203 (.360); Anthony 48-160 (.300); Rivers 19-52 (.365); Blackman 30-84 (.357); Mason 0-1 (.000); Campbell* 1-3 (.333); Williams 0-1 (.000); Anderson 2-2 (1.000); Gaines 2-5 (.400). Opponents 253-825 (.307).

ORLANDO MAGIC

	G	Min.	FGM	FGA	Pct.	FTM	FTA	Pct.	REBOUNDS Off.	Def.	Tot.	Ast.	PF	Dq.	Stl.	TO	Blk.	SCORING Pts.	Avg.	Hi.
Shaquille O'Neal	81	3224	953	1591	.599	471	850	.554	384	688	1072	195	281	3	76	222	231	2377	29.3	53
Anfernee Hardaway	82	3015	509	1092	.466	245	330	.742	192	247	439	544	205	2	190	292	51	1313	16.0	32
Nick Anderson	81	2811	504	1054	.478	168	250	.672	113	363	476	294	148	1	134	165	33	1277	15.8	36
Dennis Scott	82	2283	384	949	.405	123	159	.774	54	164	218	216	161	0	81	93	32	1046	12.8	32
Scott Skiles	82	2303	276	644	.429	195	222	.878	42	147	189	503	171	1	47	193	2	815	9.9	27
Donald Royal	74	1357	174	347	.501	199	269	.740	94	154	248	61	121	1	50	76	16	547	7.4	18
Jeff Turner	68	1536	199	426	.467	35	45	.778	79	192	271	60	239	1	23	75	11	451	6.6	22
Larry Krystkowiak	34	682	71	148	.480	31	39	.795	38	85	123	35	74	0	14	29	4	173	5.1	14
Anthony Bowie	70	948	139	289	.481	41	49	.837	29	91	120	102	81	0	32	58	12	320	4.6	16
Anthony Avent†	41	676	58	170	.341	28	44	.636	84	100	184	32	87	0	17	42	11	144	3.5	13
Anthony Avent‡	74	1371	150	398	.377	89	123	.724	144	194	338	65	147	0	33	85	31	389	5.3	19
Litterial Green	29	126	22	57	.386	28	37	.757	6	6	12	9	16	0	6	13	1	73	2.5	16
Todd Lichti*	4	20	4	9	.444	0	0	...	3	1	4	2	3	0	2	2	0	8	2.0	6
Geert Hammink	1	3	1	3	.333	0	0	...	1	0	1	1	1	0	0	0	0	2	2.0	2
Tree Rollins	45	384	29	53	.547	18	30	.600	33	63	96	9	55	1	7	13	35	76	1.7	8

	G	Min.	FGM	FGA	Pct.	FTM	FTA	Pct.	Off.	Def.	Tot.	Ast.	PF	Dq.	Stl.	TO	Blk.	Pts.	Avg.	Hi.
									REBOUNDS									SCORING		
Greg Kite	29	309	13	35	.371	8	22	.364	22	48	70	4	61	0	2	17	12	34	1.2	4
Keith Tower.	11	32	4	9	.444	0	0	. . .	0	6	6	1	6	0	0	0	0	8	0.7	4
Lorenzo Williams*	3	19	1	6	.167	0	0	. . .	3	1	4	2	3	0	2	0	3	2	0.7	2
Anthony Cook*	2	2	0	1	.000	0	0	. . .	0	0	0	0	0	0	1	2	0	0	0.0	0

3-pt. FG: Orlando 394-1137 (.347)—O'Neal 0-2 (.000); Hardaway 50-187 (.267); Anderson 101-314 (.322); Scott 155-388 (.399); Skiles 68-165 (.412); Royal 0-2 (.000); Turner 18-55 (.327); Krystkowiak 0-1 (.000); Bowie 1-18 (.056); Green 1-4 (.250); Williams* 0-1 (.000). Opponents 296-847 (.349).

PHILADELPHIA 76ERS

	G	Min.	FGM	FGA	Pct.	FTM	FTA	Pct.	Off.	Def.	Tot.	Ast.	PF	Dq.	Stl.	TO	Blk.	Pts.	Avg.	Hi.
									REBOUNDS									SCORING		
Clarence Weatherspoon	82	3147	602	1246	.483	298	430	.693	254	578	832	192	152	0	100	195	116	1506	18.4	31
Jeff Malone†	27	903	187	389	.481	76	94	.809	23	61	84	59	46	0	14	28	0	454	16.8	32
Jeff Malone‡	77	2560	525	1081	.486	205	247	.830	51	148	199	125	123	0	40	85	5	1262	16.4	32
Jeff Hornacek*	53	1994	325	715	.455	178	204	.873	41	171	212	315	115	0	95	138	10	880	16.6	36
Dana Barros	81	2519	412	878	.469	116	145	.800	28	168	196	424	96	0	107	167	5	1075	13.3	28
Orlando Woolridge . . .	74	1955	364	773	.471	208	302	.689	103	195	298	139	186	1	41	142	56	937	12.7	29
Shawn Bradley	49	1385	201	491	.409	102	168	.607	98	208	306	98	170	3	45	148	147	504	10.3	25
Tim Perry	80	2336	272	625	.435	102	176	.580	117	287	404	94	154	1	60	80	82	719	9.0	31
Johnny Dawkins	72	1343	177	423	.418	84	100	.840	28	95	123	263	74	0	63	111	5	475	6.6	21
Moses Malone	55	618	102	232	.440	90	117	.769	106	120	226	34	52	0	11	59	17	294	5.3	18
Eric Leckner	71	1163	139	286	.486	84	130	.646	75	207	282	86	190	2	18	86	34	362	5.1	16
Isaac Austin	14	201	29	66	.439	14	23	.609	25	44	69	17	29	0	5	17	10	72	5.1	10
Greg Graham	70	889	122	305	.400	92	110	.836	21	65	86	66	54	0	61	65	4	338	4.8	16
Sean Green*	35	332	63	182	.346	13	18	.722	10	24	34	16	21	0	18	27	6	149	4.3	13
Warren Kidd	68	884	100	169	.592	47	86	.547	76	157	233	19	129	0	19	44	23	247	3.6	14
Bill Edwards	3	44	2	18	.111	2	5	.400	5	9	14	4	6	0	3	4	1	6	2.0	4
Manute Bol†	4	49	3	7	.429	0	0	. . .	2	4	6	0	8	0	2	0	9	6	1.5	2
Manute Bol‡	14	116	4	19	.211	0	0	. . .	3	15	18	1	13	0	2	5	16	8	0.6	2
Mike Curry	10	43	3	14	.214	3	4	.750	0	1	1	6	0	1	3	0	0	9	0.9	3

3-pt. FG: Philadelphia 318-942 (.338)—Weatherspoon 4-17 (.235); J. Malone† 4-6 (.667); J. Malone‡ 7-12 (.583); Hornacek* 52-166 (.313); Barros 135-354 (.381); Woolridge 1-14 (.071); Bradley 0-3 (.000); Perry 73-200 (.365); Dawkins 37-105 (.352); M. Malone 0-1 (.000); Leckner 0-2 (.000); Austin 0-1 (.000); Graham 2-25 (.080); Green* 10-41 (.244); Edwards 0-5 (.000); Curry 0-2 (.000); Bol† 0-0; Bol‡ 0-3 (.000). Opponents 263-795 (.331).

PHOENIX SUNS

	G	Min.	FGM	FGA	Pct.	FTM	FTA	Pct.	Off.	Def.	Tot.	Ast.	PF	Dq.	Stl.	TO	Blk.	Pts.	Avg.	Hi.
									REBOUNDS									SCORING		
Charles Barkley	65	2298	518	1046	.495	318	452	.704	198	529	727	296	160	1	101	206	37	1402	21.6	38
Kevin Johnson	67	2449	477	980	.487	380	464	.819	55	112	167	637	127	1	125	235	10	1340	20.0	42
Cedric Ceballos	53	1602	425	795	.535	160	221	.724	153	191	344	91	124	0	59	93	23	1010	19.1	40
Dan Majerle	80	3207	476	1138	.418	176	238	.739	120	229	349	275	153	0	129	137	43	1320	16.5	35
A.C. Green	82	2825	465	926	.502	266	362	.735	275	478	753	137	142	0	70	100	38	1204	14.7	35
Oliver Miller	69	1786	277	455	.609	80	137	.584	140	336	476	244	230	1	83	164	156	636	9.2	32
Danny Ainge	68	1555	224	537	.417	78	94	.830	28	103	131	180	140	0	57	81	8	606	8.9	34
Mark West	82	1236	162	286	.566	58	116	.500	112	183	295	33	214	4	31	74	109	382	4.7	21
Frank Johnson	70	875	134	299	.448	54	69	.783	29	53	82	148	120	0	41	65	1	324	4.6	26
Joe Kleine	74	848	125	256	.488	30	39	.769	50	143	193	45	118	1	14	35	19	285	3.9	14
Elliot Perry	27	432	42	113	.372	21	28	.750	12	27	39	125	36	0	25	43	1	105	3.9	10
Joe Courtney*	33	168	40	78	.513	23	32	.719	14	13	27	9	23	0	3	10	6	103	3.1	13
Jerrod Mustaf	33	196	30	84	.357	13	22	.591	20	35	55	8	29	0	4	10	5	73	2.2	11
Duane Cooper	23	136	18	41	.439	11	15	.733	2	7	9	28	12	0	3	20	0	48	2.1	8
Negele Knight*	1	8	1	4	.250	0	0	. . .	0	0	0	1	0	0	0	1	0	2	2.0	2
Malcolm Mackey	22	69	14	37	.378	4	8	.500	12	12	24	1	9	0	0	2	3	32	1.5	6
Skeeter Henry	4	15	1	5	.200	2	4	.500	0	2	2	4	1	0	1	0	0	4	1.0	2

3-pt. FG: Phoenix 344-1042 (.330)—Barkley 48-178 (.270); K. Johnson 6-27 (.222); Ceballos 0-9 (.000); Majerle 192-503 (.382); Green 8-35 (.229); Miller 2-9 (.222); Ainge 80-244 (.328); F. Johnson 2-12 (.167); Kleine 5-11 (.455); Perry 0-3 (.000); Cooper 1-7 (.143); Mackey 0-2 (.000); Henry 0-2 (.000). Opponents 283-863 (.328).

PORTLAND TRAIL BLAZERS

	G	Min.	FGM	FGA	Pct.	FTM	FTA	Pct.	Off.	Def.	Tot.	Ast.	PF	Dq.	Stl.	TO	Blk.	Pts.	Avg.	Hi.
									REBOUNDS									SCORING		
Cliff Robinson	82	2853	641	1404	.457	352	460	.765	164	386	550	159	263	0	118	169	111	1647	20.1	34
Clyde Drexler	68	2334	473	1105	.428	286	368	.777	154	291	445	333	202	2	98	167	34	1303	19.2	34
Rod Strickland	82	2889	528	1093	.483	353	471	.749	122	248	370	740	171	0	147	257	24	1411	17.2	30
Terry Porter	77	2074	348	836	.416	204	234	.872	45	170	215	401	132	0	79	166	18	1010	13.1	36
Harvey Grant	77	2112	356	774	.460	84	131	.641	109	242	351	107	179	1	70	56	49	798	10.4	29
Buck Williams	81	2636	291	524	.555	201	296	.679	315	528	843	80	239	1	58	111	47	783	9.7	22
Tracy Murray	66	820	167	355	.470	50	72	.694	43	68	111	31	76	0	21	37	20	434	6.6	22
Jerome Kersey	78	1276	203	469	.433	101	135	.748	130	201	331	75	213	1	71	63	49	508	6.5	24
Mark Bryant	79	1441	185	384	.482	72	104	.692	117	198	315	37	187	0	32	66	29	442	5.6	17
James Robinson	58	673	104	285	.365	45	67	.672	34	44	78	68	69	0	30	52	15	276	4.8	20
Jaren Jackson	29	187	34	87	.391	12	14	.857	6	11	17	27	20	0	4	14	2	80	2.8	11
Chris Dudley	6	86	6	25	.240	2	4	.500	16	8	24	5	18	0	4	2	3	14	2.3	7
Reggie Smith	43	316	29	72	.403	18	38	.474	40	59	99	4	47	0	12	12	6	76	1.8	6
Kevin Thompson	14	58	6	14	.429	1	2	.500	7	6	13	3	11	0	0	5	2	13	0.9	4

3-pt. FG: Portland 272-770 (.353)—C. Robinson 13-53 (.245); Drexler 71-219 (.324); Strickland 2-10 (.200); Porter 110-282 (.390); Grant 2-7 (.286); Williams 0-1 (.000); Murray 50-109 (.459); Kersey 1-8 (.125); Bryant 0-1 (.000); J. Robinson 23-73 (.315); Jackson 0-6 (.000); Thompson 0-1 (.000). Opponents 296-830 (.357).

SACRAMENTO KINGS

	G	Min.	FGM	FGA	Pct.	FTM	FTA	Pct.	Off.	Def.	Tot.	Ast.	PF	Dq.	Stl.	TO	Blk.	Pts.	Avg.	Hi.
Mitch Richmond	78	2897	635	1428	.445	426	511	.834	70	216	286	313	211	3	103	216	17	1823	23.4	40
Wayman Tisdale	79	2557	552	1102	.501	215	266	.808	159	401	560	139	290	4	37	124	52	1319	16.7	32
Lionel Simmons	75	2702	436	996	.438	251	323	.777	168	394	562	305	189	2	104	183	50	1129	15.1	33
Spud Webb	79	2567	373	810	.460	204	251	.813	44	178	222	528	182	1	93	168	23	1005	12.7	32
Walt Williams	57	1356	226	580	.390	148	233	.635	71	164	235	132	200	6	52	145	23	638	11.2	32
Olden Polynice†	31	1052	124	256	.484	55	99	.556	151	202	353	19	81	1	18	29	31	303	9.8	23
Olden Polynice‡	68	2402	346	662	.523	97	191	.508	299	510	809	41	189	2	42	78	67	789	11.6	27
Trevor Wilson†	52	1095	168	349	.481	79	141	.560	108	137	245	60	106	0	33	87	10	415	8.0	25
Trevor Wilson‡	57	1221	187	388	.482	92	166	.554	120	153	273	72	123	0	38	93	11	466	8.2	25
Pete Chilcutt*	46	974	152	328	.463	31	52	.596	100	171	271	71	116	2	43	56	28	335	7.3	15
Bobby Hurley	19	499	54	146	.370	24	30	.800	6	28	34	115	28	0	13	48	1	134	7.1	15
Andre Spencer†	23	286	43	100	.430	52	73	.712	26	35	61	19	37	0	18	19	5	138	6.0	18
Andre Spencer‡	28	349	52	118	.441	55	77	.714	30	43	73	22	43	0	19	21	7	159	5.7	18
LaBradford Smith†	59	829	116	288	.403	48	64	.750	29	47	76	104	88	2	37	49	4	301	5.1	17
LaBradford Smith‡	66	877	124	306	.405	63	84	.750	34	50	84	109	96	2	40	50	5	332	5.0	17
Randy Brown	61	1041	110	251	.438	53	87	.609	40	72	112	133	132	2	63	75	14	273	4.5	12
Duane Causwell	41	674	71	137	.518	40	68	.588	68	118	186	11	109	2	19	33	49	182	4.4	15
Mike Peplowski	55	667	76	141	.539	24	44	.545	49	120	169	24	131	2	17	34	25	176	3.2	14
Jim Les	18	169	13	34	.382	11	13	.846	5	8	13	39	16	0	7	11	1	45	2.5	11
Evers Burns	23	143	22	55	.400	12	23	.522	13	17	30	9	33	0	6	7	3	56	2.4	12
Randy Breuer	27	247	8	26	.308	3	14	.214	15	41	56	8	30	0	6	9	19	19	0.7	5

3-pt. FG: Sacramento 257-729 (.353)—Richmond 127-312 (.407); Simmons 6-17 (.353); Webb 55-164 (.335); Williams 38-132 (.288); Polynice† 0-1 (.000); Polynice‡ 0-2 (.000); Wilson† 0-2 (.000); Wilson‡ 0-2 (.000); Chilcutt* 0-1 (.000); Hurley 2-16 (.125); Smith† 21-60 (.350); Smith‡ 21-60 (.350); Brown 0-4 (.000); Peplowski 0-1 (.000); Les 8-18 (.444); Breuer 0-1 (.000). Opponents 277-771 (.359).

SAN ANTONIO SPURS

	G	Min.	FGM	FGA	Pct.	FTM	FTA	Pct.	Off.	Def.	Tot.	Ast.	PF	Dq.	Stl.	TO	Blk.	Pts.	Avg.	Hi.
David Robinson	80	3241	840	1658	.507	693	925	.749	241	614	855	381	228	3	139	253	265	2383	29.8	71
Dale Ellis	77	2590	478	967	.494	83	107	.776	70	185	255	80	141	0	66	75	11	1170	15.2	32
Willie Anderson	80	2488	394	837	.471	145	171	.848	68	174	242	347	187	1	71	153	46	955	11.9	33
Vinny Del Negro	77	1949	309	634	.487	140	170	.824	27	134	161	320	168	0	64	102	1	773	10.0	24
Negele Knight†	64	1430	224	471	.476	141	174	.810	28	75	103	197	120	0	34	94	10	593	9.3	23
Negele Knight‡	65	1438	225	475	.474	141	174	.010	28	75	103	197	121	0	34	94	11	595	9.2	23
J.R. Reid	70	1344	260	530	.491	107	153	.699	91	129	220	73	165	0	43	84	25	627	9.0	24
Terry Cummings	59	1133	183	428	.428	63	107	.589	132	165	297	50	137	0	31	59	13	429	7.3	22
Antoine Carr	34	465	78	160	.488	42	58	.724	12	39	51	15	75	0	9	15	22	198	5.8	15
Lloyd Daniels	65	980	140	372	.376	46	64	.719	45	66	111	94	69	0	29	60	16	370	5.7	18
Dennis Rodman	79	2989	156	292	.534	53	102	.520	453	914	1367	184	229	0	52	138	32	370	4.7	14
Sleepy Floyd	53	737	70	209	.335	52	78	.667	10	60	70	101	71	0	12	61	8	200	3.8	19
Chuck Nevitt	1	1	0	0	...	3	6	.500	1	0	1	0	1	0	0	1	0	3	3.0	3
Jack Haley	28	94	21	48	.438	17	21	.810	6	18	24	1	18	0	0	10	0	59	2.1	8
Chris Whitney	40	339	25	82	.305	12	15	.800	5	24	29	53	53	0	11	37	1	72	1.8	11

3-pt. FG: San Antonio 249-714 (.349)—Robinson 10-29 (.345); Ellis 131-332 (.395); Anderson 22-68 (.324); Del Negro 15-43 (.349); Knight† 4-21 (.190); Knight‡ 4-21 (.190); Reid 0-3 (.000); Cummings 0-2 (.000); Carr 0-1 (.000); Daniels 44-125 (.352); Rodman 5-24 (.208); Floyd 8-36 (.222); Whitney 10-30 (.333). Opponents 290-871 (.333).

SEATTLE SUPERSONICS

	G	Min.	FGM	FGA	Pct.	FTM	FTA	Pct.	Off.	Def.	Tot.	Ast.	PF	Dq.	Stl.	TO	Blk.	Pts.	Avg.	Hi.
Shawn Kemp	79	2597	533	990	.538	364	491	.741	312	539	851	207	312	11	142	259	166	1431	18.1	32
Gary Payton	82	2881	584	1159	.504	166	279	.595	105	164	269	494	227	0	188	173	19	1349	16.5	32
Detlef Schrempf	81	2728	445	903	.493	300	390	.769	144	310	454	275	273	3	73	173	9	1212	15.0	27
Ricky Pierce	51	1022	272	577	.471	189	211	.896	29	54	83	91	84	0	42	64	5	739	14.5	28
Kendall Gill	79	2435	429	969	.443	215	275	.782	91	177	268	275	194	1	151	143	32	1111	14.1	29
Sam Perkins	81	2170	341	779	.438	218	272	.801	120	246	366	111	197	0	67	103	31	999	12.3	28
Vincent Askew	80	1690	273	567	.481	175	211	.829	60	124	184	194	145	0	73	70	19	727	9.1	19
Nate McMillan	73	1887	177	396	.447	31	55	.564	50	233	283	387	201	1	216	126	22	437	6.0	19
Michael Cage	82	1708	171	314	.545	36	74	.486	164	280	444	45	179	0	77	51	38	378	4.6	12
Chris King	15	86	19	48	.396	15	26	.577	5	10	15	11	12	0	4	12	0	55	3.7	15
Alphonso Ford	6	16	7	13	.538	1	2	.500	0	0	0	1	2	0	2	1	0	16	2.7	5
Ervin Johnson	45	280	44	106	.415	29	46	.630	48	70	118	7	45	0	10	24	22	117	2.6	12
Steve Scheffler	35	152	28	46	.609	19	20	.950	11	15	26	6	25	0	7	8	0	75	2.1	11
Rich King	27	78	15	34	.441	9	22	.500	9	11	20	8	18	0	1	7	2	41	1.5	5

3-pt. FG: Seattle 242-722 (.335)—Kemp 1-4 (.250); Payton 15-54 (.278); Schrempf 22-68 (.324); Pierce 6-32 (.188); Gill 38-120 (.317); Perkins 99-270 (.367); Askew 6-31 (.194); McMillan 52-133 (.391); Cage 0-1 (.000); C. King 2-7 (.286); Ford 1-1 (1.000); R. King 0-1 (.000). Opponents 326-946 (.345).

1993-94

UTAH JAZZ

	G	Min.	FGM	FGA	Pct.	FTM	FTA	Pct.	Off.	Def.	Tot.	Ast.	PF	Dq.	Stl.	TO	Blk.	Pts.	Avg.	Hi.
Karl Malone	82	3329	772	1552	.497	511	736	.694	235	705	940	328	268	2	125	234	126	2063	25.2	38
Jeff Malone*	50	1657	338	692	.488	129	153	.843	28	87	115	66	77	0	26	57	5	808	16.2	27
John Stockton	82	2969	458	868	.528	272	338	.805	72	186	258	1031	236	3	199	266	22	1236	15.1	31
Jeff Hornacek†	27	826	147	289	.509	82	92	.891	19	48	67	104	71	0	32	33	3	394	14.6	28
Jeff Hornacek‡	80	2820	472	1004	.470	260	296	.878	60	219	279	419	186	0	127	171	13	1274	15.9	36
Tom Chambers	80	1838	329	748	.440	221	281	.786	87	239	326	79	232	2	40	89	32	893	11.2	26
Felton Spencer	79	2210	256	507	.505	165	272	.607	235	423	658	43	304	5	41	127	67	677	8.6	22
Tyrone Corbin	82	2149	268	588	.456	117	144	.813	150	239	389	122	212	0	99	92	24	659	8.0	20
Jay Humphries	75	1619	233	535	.436	57	76	.750	35	92	127	219	168	0	65	95	11	561	7.5	25
David Benoit	55	1070	139	361	.385	68	88	.773	89	171	260	23	115	0	23	37	37	358	6.5	18
Bryon Russell	67	1121	135	279	.484	62	101	.614	61	120	181	54	138	0	68	55	19	334	5.0	15
Stephen Howard	9	53	10	17	.588	11	16	.688	10	6	16	1	13	0	1	6	3	31	3.4	9
Walter Bond	56	559	63	156	.404	31	40	.775	20	41	61	31	90	1	16	17	12	176	3.1	13
Chad Gallagher	2	3	3	3	1.000	0	0	...	0	0	0	0	2	0	0	0	0	6	3.0	4
John Crotty	45	313	45	99	.455	31	36	.861	11	20	31	77	36	0	15	27	1	132	2.9	14
Darren Morningstar†	1	4	1	1	1.000	0	0	...	0	1	1	0	1	0	0	0	0	2	2.0	2
Darren Morningstar‡	23	367	39	82	.476	18	30	.600	31	50	81	15	70	1	14	19	2	96	4.2	11
Luther Wright	15	92	8	23	.348	3	4	.750	6	4	10	0	21	0	1	6	2	19	1.3	4
Dave Jamerson*	1	4	0	2	.000	1	1	1.000	0	1	1	0	0	0	0	0	0	1	1.0	1
Aaron Williams	6	12	2	8	.250	0	1	.000	1	2	3	1	4	0	0	1	0	4	0.7	2
Sean Green†	1	2	0	1	.000	0	0	...	0	0	0	0	0	0	0	0	0	0	0.0	0
Sean Green‡	36	334	63	183	.344	13	18	.722	10	24	34	16	21	0	18	27	6	149	4.1	13

3-pt. FG: Utah 179-559 (.320)—K. Malone 8-32 (.250); J. Malone* 3-6 (.500); Stockton 48-149 (.322); Hornacek† 18-42 (.429); Hornacek‡ 70-208 (.337); Chambers 14-45 (.311); Corbin 6-29 (.207); Humphries 38-96 (.396); Benoit 12-59 (.203); Russell 2-22 (.091); Green† 0-0; Green‡ 10-41 (.244); Bond 19-54 (.352); Crotty 11-24 (.458); Wright 0-1 (.000). Opponents 289-967 (.299).

WASHINGTON BULLETS

	G	Min.	FGM	FGA	Pct.	FTM	FTA	Pct.	Off.	Def.	Tot.	Ast.	PF	Dq.	Stl.	TO	Blk.	Pts.	Avg.	Hi.
Don MacLean	75	2487	517	1030	.502	328	398	.824	140	327	467	160	169	0	47	152	22	1365	18.2	38
Rex Chapman	60	2025	431	865	.498	168	206	.816	57	89	146	185	83	0	59	117	8	1094	18.2	39
Tom Gugliotta	78	2795	540	1159	.466	213	311	.685	189	539	728	276	174	0	172	247	51	1333	17.1	32
Michael Adams	70	2337	285	698	.408	224	270	.830	37	146	183	480	140	0	96	167	6	849	12.1	29
Calbert Cheaney	65	1604	327	696	.470	124	161	.770	88	102	190	126	148	0	63	108	10	779	12.0	31
Pervis Ellison	47	1178	137	292	.469	70	97	.722	77	165	242	70	140	3	25	73	50	344	7.3	25
Mitchell Butler	75	1321	207	418	.466	104	180	.578	106	119	225	77	131	1	54	87	20	518	6.9	26
Kevin Duckworth	69	1485	184	441	.417	88	132	.667	103	222	325	56	223	2	37	101	35	456	6.6	18
Brent Price	65	1035	141	326	.433	68	87	.782	31	59	90	213	114	1	55	119	2	400	6.2	19
Gheorghe Muresan	54	650	128	235	.545	48	71	.676	66	126	192	18	120	1	28	54	48	304	5.6	21
Ron Anderson†	10	180	20	43	.465	9	11	.818	8	19	27	11	7	0	3	9	1	52	5.2	9
Ron Anderson‡	21	356	35	86	.407	19	23	.826	16	37	53	17	16	0	8	10	3	96	4.6	10
Marty Conlon†	14	201	29	56	.518	12	15	.800	19	31	50	6	33	0	4	10	1	70	5.0	16
Marty Conlon‡	30	579	95	165	.576	43	53	.811	53	86	139	34	69	1	9	33	8	233	7.8	17
Kenny Walker	73	1397	132	274	.482	87	125	.696	118	171	289	33	156	1	26	44	59	351	4.8	19
LaBradford Smith*	7	48	8	18	.444	15	20	.750	5	3	8	5	8	0	3	1	1	31	4.4	16
Larry Stewart	3	35	3	8	.375	7	10	.700	1	6	7	2	4	0	2	2	1	13	4.3	8
Gerald Paddio†	8	74	11	32	.344	8	14	.571	5	6	11	7	4	0	3	2	0	30	3.8	9
Gerald Paddio‡	18	137	22	60	.367	9	16	.563	5	11	16	11	9	0	4	6	0	53	2.9	9
Doug Overton	61	749	87	216	.403	43	52	.827	19	50	69	92	48	0	21	54	1	218	3.6	12
Andrew Gaze	7	70	8	17	.471	2	2	1.000	1	6	7	5	9	0	2	3	1	22	3.1	6
Tito Horford	3	28	0	2	.000	0	0	...	1	2	3	0	3	0	1	1	3	0	0.0	0
Manute Bol*	2	6	0	0	...	0	0	...	0	1	1	1	1	0	0	0	1	0	0.0	0

3-pt. FG: Washington 221-744 (.297)—MacLean 3-21 (.143); Chapman 64-165 (.388); Gugliotta 40-148 (.270); Adams 55-191 (.288); Cheaney 1-23 (.043); Ellison 0-3 (.000); Butler 0-5 (.000); Price 50-150 (.333); Anderson† 3-14 (.214); Anderson‡ 7-26 (.269); Conlon† 0-1 (.000); Conlon‡ 0-2 (.000); Walker 0-3 (.000); Paddio† 0-1 (.000); Paddio‡ 0-1 (.000); Overton 1-11 (.091); Gaze 4-8 (.500). Opponents 252-723 (.349).

* Finished season with another team. † Totals with this team only. ‡ Totals with all teams.

EASTERN CONFERENCE

FIRST ROUND

Atlanta 3, Miami 2
Apr. 28—Thur.	Miami 93 at Atlanta	.88
Apr. 30—Sat.	Miami 86 at Atlanta	.104
May 3—Tue.	Atlanta 86 at Miami	.90
May 5—Thur.	Atlanta 103 at Miami	.89
May 8—Sun.	Miami 91 at Atlanta	.102

New York 3, New Jersey 1
Apr. 29—Fri.	New Jersey 80 at New York	.91
May 1—Sun.	New Jersey 81 at New York	.90
May 4—Wed.	New York 92 at New Jersey	*93
May 6—Fri.	New York 102 at New Jersey	.92

Chicago 3, Cleveland 0
Apr. 29—Fri.	Cleveland 96 at Chicago	.104
May 1—Sun.	Cleveland 96 at Chicago	.105
May 3—Tue.	Chicago 95 at Cleveland	*92

Indiana 3, Orlando 0
Apr. 28—Thur.	Indiana 89 at Orlando	.88
Apr. 30—Sat.	Indiana 103 at Orlando	.101
May 2—Mon.	Orlando 86 at Indiana	.99

SEMIFINALS

New York 4, Chicago 3
May 8—Sun.	Chicago 86 at New York	.90
May 11—Wed.	Chicago 91 at New York	.96
May 13—Fri.	New York 102 at Chicago	.104
May 15—Sun.	New York 83 at Chicago	.95
May 18—Wed.	Chicago 86 at New York	.87
May 20—Fri.	New York 79 at Chicago	.93
May 22—Sun.	Chicago 77 at New York	.87

Indiana 4, Atlanta 2
May 10—Tue.	Indiana 96 at Atlanta	.85
May 12—Thur.	Indiana 69 at Atlanta	.92
May 14—Sat.	Atlanta 81 at Indiana	.101
May 15—Sun.	Atlanta 86 at Indiana	.102
May 17—Tue.	Indiana 76 at Atlanta	.88
May 19—Thur.	Atlanta 79 at Indiana	.98

FINALS

New York 4, Indiana 3
May 24—Tue.	Indiana 89 at New York	.100
May 26—Thur.	Indiana 78 at New York	.89
May 28—Sat.	New York 68 at Indiana	.88
May 30—Mon.	New York 77 at Indiana	.83
June 1—Wed.	Indiana 93 at New York	.86
June 3—Fri.	New York 98 at Indiana	.91
June 5—Sun.	Indiana 90 at New York	.94

WESTERN CONFERENCE

FIRST ROUND

Denver 3, Seattle 2
Apr. 28—Thur.	Denver 82 at Seattle	.106
Apr. 30—Sat.	Denver 87 at Seattle	.97
May 2—Mon.	Seattle 93 at Denver	.110
May 5—Thur.	Seattle 85 at Denver	*94
May 7—Sat.	Denver 98 at Seattle	*94

Houston 3, Portland 1
Apr. 29—Fri.	Portland 104 at Houston	.114
May 1—Sun.	Portland 104 at Houston	.115
May 3—Tue.	Houston 115 at Portland	.118
May 6—Fri.	Houston 92 at Portland	.89

Phoenix 3, Golden State 0
Apr. 29—Fri.	Golden State 104 at Phoenix	.111
May 1—Sun.	Golden State 111 at Phoenix	.117
May 4—Wed.	Phoenix 140 at Golden State	.133

Utah 3, San Antonio 1
Apr. 28—Thur.	Utah 89 at San Antonio	.106
Apr. 30—Sat.	Utah 96 at San Antonio	.84
May 3—Tue.	San Antonio 72 at Utah	.105
May 5—Thur.	San Antonio 90 at Utah	.95

SEMIFINALS

Houston 4, Phoenix 3
May 8—Sun.	Phoenix 91 at Houston	.87
May 11—Wed.	Phoenix 124 at Houston	*117
May 13—Fri.	Houston 118 at Phoenix	.102
May 15—Sun.	Houston 107 at Phoenix	.96
May 17—Tue.	Phoenix 86 at Houston	.109
May 19—Thur.	Houston 89 at Phoenix	.103
May 21—Sat.	Phoenix 94 at Houston	.104

Utah 4, Denver 3
May 10—Tue.	Denver 91 at Utah	.100
May 12—Thur.	Denver 94 at Utah	.104
May 14—Sat.	Utah 111 at Denver	*109
May 15—Sun.	Utah 82 at Denver	.83
May 17—Tue.	Denver 109 at Utah	**101
May 19—Thur.	Utah 91 at Denver	.94
May 21—Sat.	Denver 81 at Utah	.91

FINALS

Houston 4, Utah 1
May 23—Mon.	Utah 88 at Houston	.100
May 25—Wed.	Utah 99 at Houston	.104
May 27—Fri.	Houston 86 at Utah	.95
May 29—Sun.	Houston 80 at Utah	.78
May 31—Tue.	Utah 83 at Houston	.94

NBA FINALS

Houston 4, New York 3
June 8—Wed.	New York 78 at Houston	.85
June 10—Fri.	New York 91 at Houston	.83
June 12—Sun.	Houston 93 at New York	.89
June 15—Wed.	Houston 82 at New York	.91
June 17—Fri.	Houston 84 at New York	.91
June 19—Sun.	New York 84 at Houston	.86
June 22—Wed.	New York 84 at Houston	.90

*Denotes number of overtime periods.

1993-84

1992-93 NBA CHAMPION CHICAGO BULLS
Front row (from left): supervisor of European scouting Ivica Dukan, scout/special assistant Jim Stack, scout/special assistant Clarence Gaines Jr., vice president/basketball operations Jerry Krause, assistant coach Jim Cleamons, head coach Phil Jackson, assistant coach John Bach, assistant coach Tex Winter, trainer Chip Schaefer, strength and conditioning assistant Erik Helland, strength and conditioning consultant Al Vermeil, equipment manager John Ligmanowski. Back row (from left): B.J. Armstrong, John Paxson, Michael Jordan, Scottie Pippen, Scott Williams, Stacey King, Will Perdue, Bill Cartwright, Horace Grant, Ed Nealy, Rodney McCray, Trent Tucker, Darrell Walker, Corey Williams.

FINAL STANDINGS

ATLANTIC DIVISION

	Atl.	Bos.	Char.	Chi.	Cle.	Dal.	Den.	Det.	G.S.	Hou.	Ind.	L.A.C.	L.A.L.	Mia.	Mil.	Min.	N.J.	N.Y.	Orl.	Phi.	Pho.	Por.	Sac.	S.A.	Sea.	Uta.	Was.	W	L	Pct.	GB
New York	2	4	3	3	3	2	1	2	2	1	3	0	2	5	3	2	3	..	2	5	1	1	2	2	1	1	4	60	22	.732	..
Boston	2	..	3	1	3	2	2	1	2	1	2	1	1	3	2	4	1	3	4	0	2	1	1	0	0	4		48	34	.585	12
New Jersey	3	0	2	0	2	2	1	1	1	1	1	2	2	3	4	1	..	1	3	3	1	0	2	1	1	1	4	43	39	.524	17
Orlando	3	2	1	1	2	1	2	1	1	1	2	1	1	2	2	2	2	2	..	3	0	2	2	0	0	1	4	41	41	.500	19
Miami	1	1	2	1	2	2	2	3	0	0	2	2	2	..	2	2	2	0	3	1	0	1	1	1	1	0	2	36	46	.439	24
Philadelphia	1	1	0	2	0	1	1	1	1	0	1	1	0	3	2	2	2	0	2	..	0	0	1	0	1	0	3	26	56	.317	34
Washington	2	1	0	0	1	1	0	0	1	1	1	0	0	3	3	1	1	1	0	1	0	1	1	1	0	1	..	22	60	.268	38

CENTRAL DIVISION

	Atl.	Bos.	Char.	Chi.	Cle.	Dal.	Den.	Det.	G.S.	Hou.	Ind.	L.A.C.	L.A.L.	Mia.	Mil.	Min.	N.J.	N.Y.	Orl.	Phi.	Pho.	Por.	Sac.	S.A.	Sea.	Uta.	Was.	W	L	Pct.	GB
Chicago	2	3	3	..	2	2	1	3	2	0	5	2	0	3	4	2	4	1	3	2	1	2	2	0	2	2	4	57	25	.695	..
Cleveland	5	1	3	3	..	2	1	3	2	1	4	1	2	2	4	2	2	1	2	4	2	0	1	1	1	1	3	54	28	.659	3
Charlotte	2	1	..	2	1	2	1	4	2	0	0	1	1	2	3	2	2	1	3	4	0	1	2	1	1	1	4	44	38	.537	13
Atlanta	..	2	3	2	0	1	2	2	2	1	2	1	1	3	3	2	1	2	1	3	0	1	1	2	1	2	2	43	39	.524	14
Indiana	2	2	5	0	0	1	1	2	2	0	..	1	1	2	2	1	3	1	2	3	1	1	2	1	2	0	3	41	41	.500	16
Detroit	3	3	1	1	2	1	1	..	0	1	3	1	1	1	2	1	3	2	3	3	0	1	2	0	0	0	4	40	42	.488	17
Milwaukee	2	2	1	1	1	2	1	2	1	1	3	0	1	2	..	1	0	1	2	2	0	0	1	0	0	0	1	28	54	.341	29

MIDWEST DIVISION

	Atl.	Bos.	Char.	Chi.	Cle.	Dal.	Den.	Det.	G.S.	Hou.	Ind.	L.A.C.	L.A.L.	Mia.	Mil.	Min.	N.J.	N.Y.	Orl.	Phi.	Pho.	Por.	Sac.	S.A.	Sea.	Uta.	Was.	W	L	Pct.	GB
Houston	1	1	2	2	1	4	3	1	2	..	2	4	3	2	1	4	1	1	1	2	2	1	4	4	1	4	1	55	27	.671	..
San Antonio	0	1	1	2	1	5	4	2	1	1	1	4	2	1	2	4	1	0	2	2	1	2	2	..	3	3	1	49	33	.598	6
Utah	0	2	1	0	1	5	3	2	1	1	2	2	3	2	2	4	1	1	2	1	2	2	3	2	..	1	47	35	.573	8
Denver	0	0	1	1	1	5	..	1	3	2	1	2	1	0	1	3	1	1	0	1	1	3	1	1	2	2	36	46	.439	19
Minnesota	0	0	0	0	0	4	2	1	1	2	1	0	1	0	1	..	1	0	0	0	0	1	1	1	0	1	1	19	63	.232	36
Dallas	1	0	0	0	0	..	1	1	0	1	1	0	1	0	0	1	1	0	0	1	1	0	0	0	1	0	1	11	71	.134	44

PACIFIC DIVISION

	Atl.	Bos.	Char.	Chi.	Cle.	Dal.	Den.	Det.	G.S.	Hou.	Ind.	L.A.C.	L.A.L.	Mia.	Mil.	Min.	N.J.	N.Y.	Orl.	Phi.	Pho.	Por.	Sac.	S.A.	Sea.	Uta.	Was.	W	L	Pct.	GB
Phoenix	2	2	2	1	0	4	3	2	4	2	1	2	5	2	2	4	1	1	2	2	..	3	5	3	2	3	2	62	20	.756	..
Seattle	1	2	1	0	1	3	3	2	4	3	0	4	4	1	2	4	1	1	2	1	3	3	4	1	..	2	2	55	27	.671	7
Portland	0	0	0	2	4	3	1	5	3	1	3	2	1	2	3	2	1	0	2	2	..	5	2	2	2	1	51	31	.622	11
L.A. Clippers	1	1	1	0	1	4	2	1	3	0	1	..	3	0	2	4	0	2	1	1	3	2	3	0	1	2	2	41	41	.500	21
L.A. Lakers	1	1	1	2	0	3	3	1	4	1	1	2	..	0	1	3	0	0	1	2	0	3	3	2	1	1	2	39	43	.476	23
Golden State	0	0	0	0	0	4	1	2	..	2	0	2	1	2	1	3	1	0	1	1	1	0	4	3	1	3	1	34	48	.415	28
Sacramento	1	1	0	0	1	4	1	0	1	0	0	2	2	1	1	3	0	0	0	1	0	0	..	2	1	2	1	25	57	.305	37

OFFENSIVE

	G	FGM	FGA	Pct.	FTM	FTA	Pct.	REBOUNDS Off.	Def.	Tot.	Ast.	PF	Dq.	Stl.	TO	Blk.	SCORING Pts.	Avg.
Phoenix	82	3494	7093	.493	1912	2539	.753	1141	2510	3651	2087	1739	10	752	1359	455	9298	113.4
Charlotte	82	3512	7210	.487	1831	2374	.771	1095	2508	3603	2161	1790	15	639	1325	473	9030	110.1
Golden State	82	3474	7212	.482	1768	2465	.717	1219	2384	3603	2010	2056	29	693	1451	383	9014	109.9
Portland	82	3361	7343	.458	1901	2551	.745	1226	2507	3733	1969	1892	14	770	1215	425	8898	108.5
Seattle	82	3473	7140	.486	1720	2259	.761	1222	2254	3476	1906	1971	27	944	1267	409	8884	108.3
Sacramento	82	3360	7264	.463	1865	2447	.762	1137	2281	3418	2075	2085	35	768	1364	348	8847	107.9
Indiana	82	3371	7022	.480	1837	2399	.766	1220	2455	3675	2144	2045	17	615	1256	403	8836	107.8
Cleveland	82	3425	6887	.497	1699	2119	.802	929	2496	3425	2349	1580	10	615	1120	536	8832	107.7
Atlanta	82	3392	7272	.466	1648	2221	.742	1290	2344	3634	2084	1807	12	806	1339	278	8814	107.5
L.A. Clippers	82	3544	7329	.484	1562	2177	.718	1183	2360	3543	2242	1920	30	847	1338	491	8783	107.1
Utah	82	3336	6828	.489	1907	2491	.766	1041	2463	3504	2177	1965	15	746	1270	344	8709	106.2
Orlando	82	3257	6708	.486	1821	2495	.730	1040	2566	3606	1952	1925	30	542	1429	467	8652	105.5
San Antonio	82	3311	6762	.490	1794	2346	.765	919	2542	3461	2012	1844	17	582	1227	514	8652	105.5
Denver	82	3352	7282	.460	1784	2360	.756	1266	2564	3830	1735	2039	25	651	1413	565	8626	105.2
Chicago	82	3475	7205	.482	1431	1952	.733	1290	2283	3573	2133	1804	13	783	1103	410	8625	105.2
Philadelphia	82	3225	7075	.456	1776	2329	.786	1031	2431	3462	2038	1604	9	672	1362	566	8556	104.3
L.A. Lakers	82	3309	6994	.473	1741	2304	.756	1103	2288	3391	2013	1778	9	782	1266	431	8546	104.2
Houston	82	3280	6744	.486	1584	2090	.758	985	2532	3517	2115	1699	11	682	1295	543	8531	104.0
Boston	82	3453	7093	.487	1486	1912	.777	1076	2436	3512	1999	1862	13	647	1174	458	8502	103.7
Miami	82	3127	6850	.456	1908	2476	.771	1134	2384	3518	1688	2011	37	609	1287	350	8495	103.6
New Jersey	82	3272	7084	.462	1732	2258	.767	1291	2506	3797	1872	1892	19	693	1355	526	8431	102.8
Milwaukee	82	3268	6924	.472	1544	2081	.742	1050	2113	3163	2084	1978	15	863	1363	393	8392	102.3
Washington	82	3302	7065	.467	1575	2107	.748	1031	2317	3348	2110	1795	10	673	1323	359	8353	101.9
New York	82	3209	6898	.465	1717	2316	.741	1150	2660	3810	2125	2111	20	680	1296	372	8328	101.6
Detroit	82	3267	7211	.453	1426	1957	.729	1293	2315	3608	1941	1747	16	580	1152	249	8252	100.6
Dallas	82	3164	7271	.435	1530	2171	.705	1234	2265	3499	1683	2302	38	649	1459	355	8141	99.3
Minnesota	82	3043	6529	.466	1794	2247	.798	940	2204	3144	2001	2028	32	649	1422	455	8046	98.1

DEFENSIVE

	FGM	FGA	Pct.	FTM	FTA	Pct.	REBOUNDS Off.	Def.	Tot.	Ast.	PF	Dq.	Stl.	TO	Blk.	SCORING Pts.	Avg.	Dif.
New York	2822	6621	.426	1949	2582	.755	1031	2325	3356	1658	2010	26	657	1360	384	7823	95.4	+6.2
Chicago	3139	6622	.474	1584	2033	.779	1039	2265	3304	1918	1731	15	595	1372	357	8109	98.9	+6.3
Houston	3255	7129	.457	1432	1877	.763	1167	2295	3462	1965	1793	22	717	1228	327	8184	99.8	+4.2
Cleveland	3370	7229	.466	1334	1742	.766	1115	2379	3494	2109	1828	19	610	1203	365	8303	101.3	+6.4
Seattle	3143	6707	.469	1746	2299	.759	1075	2220	3295	1835	1853	19	655	1516	406	8304	101.3	+7.0
New Jersey	3231	6945	.465	1665	2248	.741	1102	2345	3447	1786	1881	16	780	1304	416	8328	101.6	+1.2
Detroit	3321	6906	.481	1463	1987	.736	1099	2442	3541	2048	1804	16	623	1219	363	8366	102.0	-1.4
Boston	3232	6980	.463	1749	2269	.771	1094	2378	3472	1971	1676	14	637	1181	386	8429	102.8	+0.9
San Antonio	3290	7177	.458	1583	2051	.772	1082	2388	3470	1905	1998	33	655	1131	373	8433	102.8	+2.7
Utah	3258	6970	.467	1743	2343	.744	1120	2314	3434	1928	1970	20	648	1291	468	8531	104.0	+2.2
Orlando	3307	7255	.456	1682	2306	.729	1166	2271	3437	2091	1975	27	715	1119	401	8544	104.2	+1.3
Miami	3232	6791	.476	1860	2416	.770	1032	2424	3456	1965	2053	20	656	1304	426	8589	104.7	-1.1
Portland	3337	7125	.468	1692	2226	.760	1022	2527	3549	2059	2089	29	649	1404	452	8643	105.4	+3.1
L.A. Lakers	3438	7116	.483	1529	2050	.746	1158	2411	3569	2130	1872	12	686	1334	384	8650	105.5	-1.3
Minnesota	3323	6814	.488	1830	2413	.758	1122	2331	3453	2144	1875	20	734	1231	494	8684	105.9	-7.8
Indiana	3262	6955	.469	1957	2635	.743	1189	2345	3534	1987	1979	28	693	1178	387	8697	106.1	+1.7
Milwaukee	3303	6843	.483	1823	2437	.748	1269	2398	3667	2087	1810	14	773	1476	456	8698	106.1	-3.8
Phoenix	3500	7307	.479	1502	2078	.723	1118	2316	3434	2107	2041	24	708	1328	512	8752	106.7	+6.7
L.A. Clippers	3311	7051	.470	1857	2434	.763	1179	2437	3616	1970	1772	12	765	1445	453	8754	106.8	+0.3
Denver	3324	7214	.461	1899	2517	.754	1159	2505	3664	1890	1983	20	750	1340	503	8760	106.9	-1.7
Atlanta	3509	7074	.496	1586	2092	.758	1080	2413	3493	2189	1881	16	735	1363	363	8885	108.4	-0.9
Washington	3557	7214	.493	1577	2106	.749	1135	2555	3690	2062	1818	14	718	1279	425	8930	108.9	-7.0
Philadelphia	3666	7548	.486	1417	1878	.755	1258	2634	3892	2406	1790	13	781	1290	491	9029	110.1	-5.8
Charlotte	3634	7698	.472	1548	2080	.744	1350	2403	3753	2277	1923	26	599	1245	438	9050	110.4	-0.3
Golden State	3471	7197	.482	1881	2492	.755	1174	2345	3519	2098	1993	23	824	1350	457	9095	110.9	-1.0
Sacramento	3420	7024	.487	2054	2711	.758	1138	2562	3700	2073	2010	22	767	1466	551	9107	111.1	-3.2
Dallas	3401	6783	.501	2351	3071	.766	1063	2740	3803	2047	1861	8	802	1273	520	9387	114.5	-15.2
Avgs.	3335	7048	.473	1715	2273	.755	1131	2406	3537	2026	1899	20	701	1305	428	8632	105.3	...

HOME/ROAD

	Home	Road	Total		Home	Road	Total
Atlanta	25-16	18-23	43-39	Milwaukee	18-23	10-31	28-54
Boston	28-13	20-21	48-34	Minnesota	11-30	8-33	19-63
Charlotte	22-19	22-19	44-38	New Jersey	26-15	17-24	43-39
Chicago	31-10	26-15	57-25	New York	37-4	23-18	60-22
Cleveland	35-6	19-22	54-28	Orlando	27-14	14-27	41-41
Dallas	7-34	4-37	11-71	Philadelphia	15-26	11-30	26-56
Denver	28-13	8-33	36-46	Phoenix	35-6	27-14	62-20
Detroit	28-13	12-29	40-42	Portland	30-11	21-20	51-31
Golden State	19-22	15-26	34-48	Sacramento	16-25	9-32	25-57
Houston	31-10	24-17	55-27	San Antonio	31-10	18-23	49-33
Indiana	27-14	14-27	41-41	Seattle	33-8	22-19	55-27
L.A. Clippers	27-14	14-27	41-41	Utah	28-13	19-22	47-35
L.A. Lakers	20-21	19-22	39-43	Washington	15-26	7-34	22-60
Miami	26-15	10-31	36-46	Totals	676-431	431-676	1107-1107

1992-93

POINTS

(minimum 70 games or 1,400 points)

	G	FGM	FTM	Pts.	Avg.
Michael Jordan, Chicago	.78	992	476	2541	32.6
Dominique Wilkins, Atlanta	.71	741	519	2121	29.9
Karl Malone, Utah	.82	797	619	2217	27.0
Hakeem Olajuwon, Houston	.82	848	444	2140	26.1
Charles Barkley, Phoenix	.76	716	445	1944	25.6
Patrick Ewing, New York	.81	779	400	1959	24.2
Joe Dumars, Detroit	.77	677	343	1809	23.5
David Robinson, San Antonio	.82	676	561	1916	23.4
Shaquille O'Neal, Orlando	.81	733	427	1893	23.4
Danny Manning, L.A. Clippers	.79	702	388	1800	22.8

FIELD GOALS

(minimum 300 made)

	FGM	FGA	Pct.
Cedric Ceballos, Phoenix	.381	662	.576
Brad Daugherty, Cleveland	.520	911	.571
Dale Davis, Indiana	.304	535	.568
Shaquille O'Neal, Orlando	.733	1304	.562
Otis Thorpe, Houston	.385	690	.558
Karl Malone, Utah	.797	1443	.552
Larry Nance, Cleveland	.533	971	.549
Frank Brickowski, Milwaukee	.456	836	.545
Larry Stewart, Washington	.306	564	.543
Antoine Carr, San Antonio	.379	705	.538

FREE THROWS

(minimum 125 made)

	FTM	FTA	Pct.
Mark Price, Cleveland	.289	305	.948
Mahmoud Abdul-Rauf, Denver	.217	232	.935
Eddie Johnson, Seattle	.234	257	.911
Micheal Williams, Minnesota	.419	462	.907
Scott Skiles, Orlando	.289	324	.892
Ricky Pierce, Seattle	.313	352	.889
Reggie Miller, Indiana	.427	485	.880
Kenny Smith, Houston	.195	222	.878
Drazen Petrovic, New Jersey	.315	362	.870
Reggie Lewis, Boston	.326	376	.867

ASSISTS

(minimum 70 games or 400 assists)

	G	No.	Avg.
John Stockton, Utah	.82	987	12.0
Tim Hardaway, Golden State	.66	699	10.6
Scott Skiles, Orlando	.78	735	9.4
Mark Jackson, L.A. Clippers	.82	724	8.8
Muggsy Bogues, Charlotte	.81	711	8.8
Micheal Williams, Minnesota	.76	661	8.7
Isiah Thomas, Detroit	.79	671	8.5
Mookie Blaylock, Atlanta	.80	671	8.4
Kenny Anderson, New Jersey	.55	449	8.2
Mark Price, Cleveland	.75	602	8.0

REBOUNDS

(minimum 70 games or 800 rebounds)

	G	Off.	Def.	Tot.	Avg.
Dennis Rodman, Detroit	.62	367	765	1132	18.3
Shaquille O'Neal, Orlando	.81	342	780	1122	13.9
Dikembe Mutombo, Denver	.82	344	726	1070	13.0
Hakeem Olajuwon, Houston	.82	283	785	1068	13.0
Kevin Willis, Atlanta	.80	335	693	1028	12.9
Charles Barkley, Phoenix	.76	237	691	928	12.2
Patrick Ewing, New York	.81	191	789	980	12.1
Rony Seikaly, Miami	.72	259	587	846	11.8
David Robinson, San Antonio	.82	229	727	956	11.7
Karl Malone, Utah	.82	227	692	919	11.2
Derrick Coleman, New Jersey	.76	247	605	852	11.2

STEALS

(minimum 70 games or 125 steals)

	G	No.	Avg.
Michael Jordan, Chicago	.78	221	2.83
Mookie Blaylock, Atlanta	.80	203	2.54
John Stockton, Utah	.82	199	2.43
Nate McMillan, Seattle	.73	173	2.37
Alvin Robertson, Milwaukee-Detroit	.69	155	2.25
Ron Harper, L.A. Clippers	.80	177	2.21
Eric Murdock, Milwaukee	.79	174	2.20
Micheal Williams, Minnesota	.76	165	2.17
Gary Payton, Seattle	.82	177	2.16
Scottie Pippen, Chicago	.81	173	2.14

BLOCKED SHOTS

(minimum 70 games or 100 blocked shots)

	G	No.	Avg.
Hakeem Olajuwon, Houston	.82	342	4.17
Shaquille O'Neal, Orlando	.81	286	3.53
Dikembe Mutombo, Denver	.82	287	3.50
Alonzo Mourning, Charlotte	.78	271	3.47
David Robinson, San Antonio	.82	264	3.22
Larry Nance, Cleveland	.77	198	2.57
Pervis Ellison, Washington	.49	108	2.20
Manute Bol, Philadelphia	.58	119	2.05
Clifford Robinson, Portland	.82	163	1.99
Patrick Ewing, New York	.81	161	1.99

3-POINT FIELD GOALS

(minimum 50 made)

	FGA	FGM	Pct.
B.J. Armstrong, Chicago	.139	63	.453
Chris Mullin, Golden State	.133	60	.451
Drazen Petrovic, New Jersey	.167	75	.449
Kenny Smith, Houston	.219	96	.438
Jim Les, Sacramento	.154	66	.429
Mark Price, Cleveland	.293	122	.416
Terry Porter, Portland	.345	143	.414
Danny Ainge, Phoenix	.372	150	.403
Dennis Scott, Orlando	.268	108	.403
Steve Smith, Miami	.132	53	.402

INDIVIDUAL STATISTICS, TEAM BY TEAM

ATLANTA HAWKS

	G	Min.	FGM	FGA	Pct.	FTM	FTA	Pct.	Off.	Def.	Tot.	Ast.	PF	Dq.	Stl.	TO	Blk.	Pts.	Avg.	Hi.
Dominique Wilkins	71	2647	741	1584	.468	519	627	.828	187	295	482	227	116	0	70	184	27	2121	29.9	48
Kevin Willis	80	2878	616	1218	.506	196	300	.653	335	693	1028	165	264	1	68	213	41	1435	17.9	35
Stacey Augmon	73	2112	397	792	.501	227	307	.739	141	146	287	170	141	1	91	157	16	1021	14.0	27
Mookie Blaylock	80	2820	414	964	.429	123	169	.728	89	191	280	671	156	0	203	187	23	1069	13.4	30
Duane Ferrell	82	1736	327	696	.470	176	226	.779	97	94	191	132	160	1	59	103	17	839	10.2	27
Paul Graham	80	1508	256	560	.457	96	131	.733	61	129	190	164	185	0	86	120	6	650	8.1	29
Travis Mays	49	787	129	309	.417	54	82	.659	20	33	53	72	59	0	21	51	3	341	7.0	23
Adam Keefe	82	1549	188	376	.500	166	237	.700	171	261	432	80	195	1	57	100	16	542	6.6	30
Steve Henson	53	719	71	182	.390	34	40	.850	12	43	55	155	85	0	30	52	1	213	4.0	14
Jon Koncak	78	1975	124	267	.464	24	50	.480	100	327	427	140	264	6	75	52	100	275	3.5	15
Blair Rasmussen	22	283	30	80	.375	9	13	.692	20	35	55	5	61	2	5	12	10	71	3.2	12
Greg Foster†	33	205	44	95	.463	13	18	.722	24	32	56	10	41	0	3	16	9	101	3.1	12

(The table above has column groupings: REBOUNDS spans Off./Def./Tot., and SCORING spans Pts./Avg./Hi.)

(Side margin: 1992-93)

	G	Min.	FGM	FGA	Pct.	FTM	FTA	Pct.	Off.	Def.	Tot.	Ast.	PF	Dq.	Stl.	TO	Blk.	Pts.	Avg.	Hi.
Greg Foster‡ 43	298	55	120	.458	15	21	.714	32	51	83	21	58	0	3	25	14	125	2.9	12
Morlon Wiley* 25	354	26	81	.321	5	8	.625	9	26	35	81	49	0	26	29	2	72	2.9	8
Randy Breuer 12	107	15	31	.484	2	5	.400	10	18	28	6	12	0	2	5	3	32	2.7	11
Jeff Sanders 9	120	10	25	.400	4	8	.500	12	17	29	6	16	0	8	11	1	24	2.7	6
Alex Stivrins* 5	15	4	9	.444	0	0	...	2	3	5	0	0	0	0	0	1	8	1.6	2
Andre Spencer* 3	15	0	3	.000	0	0	...	0	1	1	0	3	0	2	2	0	0	0.0	0

3-pt. FG: Atlanta 382-1076 (.355)—Wilkins 120-316 (.380); Willis 7-29 (.241); Augmon 0-4 (.000); Blaylock 118-315 (.375); Ferrell 9-36 (.250); Graham 42-141 (.298); Mays 29-84 (.345); Keefe 0-1 (.000); Henson 37-80 (.463); Koncak 3-8 (.375); Rasmussen 2-6 (.333); Foster† 0-4 (.000); Foster‡ 0-4 (.000); Wiley* 15-51 (.294); Stivrins* 0-1 (.000). Opponents 281-833 (.337).

BOSTON CELTICS

	G	Min.	FGM	FGA	Pct.	FTM	FTA	Pct.	Off.	Def.	Tot.	Ast.	PF	Dq.	Stl.	TO	Blk.	Pts.	Avg.	Hi.
Reggie Lewis 80	3144	663	1410	.470	326	376	.867	88	259	347	298	248	1	118	133	77	1666	20.8	37
Xavier McDaniel 82	2215	457	924	.495	191	241	.793	168	321	489	163	249	4	72	171	51	1111	13.5	30
Kevin Gamble 82	2541	459	906	.507	123	149	.826	46	200	246	226	185	1	86	81	37	1093	13.3	31
Robert Parish 79	2146	416	777	.535	162	235	.689	246	494	740	61	201	3	57	120	107	994	12.6	24
Dee Brown 80	2254	328	701	.468	192	242	.793	45	201	246	461	203	2	138	136	32	874	10.9	25
Kevin McHale 71	1656	298	649	.459	164	195	.841	95	263	358	73	126	0	16	92	59	762	10.7	23
Alaa Abdelnaby† 63	1152	219	417	.525	76	100	.760	114	186	300	17	165	0	19	84	22	514	8.2	26
Alaa Abdelnaby‡ 75	1311	245	473	.518	88	116	.759	126	211	337	27	189	0	25	97	26	578	7.7	26
Sherman Douglas 79	1932	264	530	.498	84	150	.560	65	97	162	508	166	1	49	161	10	618	7.8	24
Rick Fox 71	1082	184	380	.484	81	101	.802	55	104	159	113	133	1	61	77	21	453	6.4	19
Kenny Battle 3	29	6	13	.462	2	2	1.000	7	4	11	2	2	0	1	2	0	14	4.7	10
Ed Pinckney 7	151	10	24	.417	12	13	.923	14	29	43	1	13	0	4	8	7	32	4.6	10
Marcus Webb 9	51	13	25	.520	13	21	.619	5	5	10	2	11	0	1	5	2	39	4.3	13
Joe Kleine 78	1129	108	267	.404	41	58	.707	113	233	346	39	123	0	17	37	17	257	3.3	11
Bart Kofoed 7	41	3	13	.231	11	14	.786	0	1	1	10	1	0	2	3	1	17	2.4	10
John Bagley 10	97	9	25	.360	5	6	.833	1	6	7	20	11	0	2	17	0	23	2.3	9
Lorenzo Williams† . . . 22	151	16	31	.516	2	7	.286	13	31	44	5	23	0	4	6	14	34	1.5	4
Lorenzo Williams‡ . . . 27	179	17	36	.472	2	7	.286	17	38	55	5	29	0	5	8	17	36	1.3	4
Joe Wolf* 2	9	0	1	.000	1	2	.500	1	2	3	0	2	0	0	2	1	1	0.5	1

3-pt. FG: Boston 110-383 (.287)—Lewis 14-60 (.233); McDaniel 6-22 (.273); Gamble 52-139 (.374); Brown 26-82 (.317); McHale 2-18 (.111); Abdelnaby† 0-0; Abdelnaby‡ 0-1 (.000); Douglas 6-29 (.207); Fox 4-23 (.174); Battle 0-1 (.000); Webb 0-1 (.000); Kleine 0-6 (.000); Kofoed 0-1 (.000); Bagley 0-1 (.000). Opponents 216-650 (.332).

CHARLOTTE HORNETS

	G	Min.	FGM	FGA	Pct.	FTM	FTA	Pct.	Off.	Def.	Tot.	Ast.	PF	Dq.	Stl.	TO	Blk.	Pts.	Avg.	Hi.
Larry Johnson 82	3323	728	1385	.526	336	438	.767	281	583	864	353	187	0	53	227	27	1810	22.1	36
Alonzo Mourning 78	2644	572	1119	.511	495	634	.781	263	542	805	76	286	6	27	236	271	1639	21.0	37
Kendall Gill 69	2430	463	1032	.449	224	290	.772	120	220	340	268	191	2	98	174	96	1167	16.9	27
Dell Curry 80	2094	498	1102	.452	136	157	.866	51	235	286	180	150	1	87	129	23	1227	15.3	33
Johnny Newman 64	1471	279	534	.522	194	240	.808	72	71	143	117	154	1	45	90	19	764	11.9	30
Muggsy Bogues 81	2833	331	730	.453	140	168	.833	51	247	298	711	179	0	161	154	5	808	10.0	20
J.R. Reid* 17	295	42	98	.429	43	58	.741	20	50	70	24	49	1	11	24	5	127	7.5	15
Kenny Gattison 75	1475	203	384	.529	102	169	.604	108	245	353	68	237	3	48	64	55	508	6.8	19
David Wingate 72	1471	180	336	.536	79	107	.738	49	125	174	183	135	1	66	89	9	440	6.1	23
Tony Bennett 75	857	110	260	.423	30	41	.732	12	51	63	136	110	0	30	50	0	276	3.7	14
Mike Gminski 34	251	42	83	.506	9	10	.900	34	51	85	7	28	0	1	11	9	93	2.7	12
Tom Hammonds* 19	142	19	45	.422	5	8	.625	5	26	31	8	20	0	0	3	4	43	2.3	9
Kevin Lynch 40	324	30	59	.508	26	38	.684	12	23	35	25	44	0	11	24	6	86	2.2	11
Sidney Green† 24	127	14	40	.350	12	16	.750	14	33	47	5	16	0	1	8	2	40	1.7	8
Sidney Green‡ 39	329	34	89	.382	25	31	.806	32	86	118	24	37	1	6	20	5	93	2.4	9
Lorenzo Williams* 2	18	1	3	.333	0	0	...	3	6	9	0	4	0	0	2	2	2	1.0	2

3-pt. FG: Charlotte 175-537 (.326)—Johnson 18-71 (.254); Mourning 0-3 (.000); Gill 17-62 (.274); Curry 95-237 (.401); Newman 12-45 (.267); Bogues 6-26 (.231); Reid* 0-1 (.000); Gattison 0-3 (.000); Wingate 1-6 (.167); Bennett 26-80 (.325); Green† 0-2 (.000); Green‡ 0-2 (.000); Lynch 0-1 (.000). Opponents 234-753 (.311).

CHICAGO BULLS

	G	Min.	FGM	FGA	Pct.	FTM	FTA	Pct.	Off.	Def.	Tot.	Ast.	PF	Dq.	Stl.	TO	Blk.	Pts.	Avg.	Hi.
Michael Jordan 78	3067	992	2003	.495	476	569	.837	135	387	522	428	188	0	221	207	61	2541	32.6	64
Scottie Pippen 81	3123	628	1327	.473	232	350	.663	203	418	621	507	219	3	173	246	73	1510	18.6	39
Horace Grant 77	2745	421	829	.508	174	281	.619	341	388	729	201	218	4	89	110	96	1017	13.2	30
B.J. Armstrong 82	2492	408	818	.499	130	151	.861	27	122	149	330	169	0	66	83	6	1009	12.3	28
Scott Williams 71	1369	166	356	.466	90	126	.714	168	283	451	68	230	3	55	73	66	422	5.9	15
Bill Cartwright 63	1253	141	343	.411	72	98	.735	83	150	233	83	154	1	20	62	10	354	5.6	17
Stacey King 76	1059	160	340	.471	86	122	.705	105	102	207	71	128	0	26	70	20	408	5.4	19
Trent Tucker 69	909	143	295	.485	18	22	.818	16	55	71	82	65	0	24	18	6	356	5.2	24
Will Perdue 72	998	137	246	.557	67	111	.604	103	184	287	74	139	2	22	74	47	341	4.7	17
John Paxson 59	1030	105	233	.451	17	20	.850	9	39	48	136	99	0	38	31	2	246	4.2	14
Rodney McCray 64	1019	92	204	.451	36	52	.692	53	105	158	81	99	0	12	53	15	222	3.5	15
Ricky Blanton 2	13	3	7	.429	0	0	...	2	1	3	1	1	0	2	1	0	6	3.0	4

	G	Min.	FGM	FGA	Pct.	FTM	FTA	Pct.	Off.	Def.	Tot.	Ast.	PF	Dq.	Stl.	TO	Blk.	Pts.	Avg.	Hi.
Darrell Walker†	28	367	31	77	.403	10	20	.500	18	21	39	44	51	0	23	12	2	72	2.6	10
Darrell Walker‡	37	511	34	96	.354	12	26	.462	22	36	58	53	63	0	33	25	2	80	2.2	10
Corey Williams	35	242	31	85	.365	18	22	.818	19	12	31	23	24	0	4	11	2	81	2.3	10
Joe Courtney*	5	34	4	9	.444	3	4	.750	2	0	2	1	9	0	2	3	1	11	2.2	5
Ed Nealy†	11	79	10	23	.435	2	2	1.000	4	12	16	2	6	0	3	2	1	23	2.1	8
Ed Nealy‡	41	308	26	69	.377	9	12	.750	12	52	64	15	41	0	12	7	2	69	1.7	8
JoJo English	6	31	3	10	.300	0	2	.000	2	4	6	1	5	0	3	4	2	6	1.0	2

3-pt. FG: Chicago 244-669 (.365)—Jordan 81-230 (.352); Pippen 22-93 (.237); Grant 1-5 (.200); Armstrong 63-139 (.453); S. Williams 0-7 (.000); King 2-6 (.333); Tucker 52-131 (.397); Perdue 0-1 (.000); Paxson 19-41 (.463); McCray 2-5 (.400); C. Williams 1-3 (.333); Walker† 0-0; Walker‡ 0-1 (.000); Nealy† 1-5 (.200); Nealy‡ 8-27 (.296); English 0-3 (.000). Opponents 247-685 (.361).

CLEVELAND CAVALIERS

	G	Min.	FGM	FGA	Pct.	FTM	FTA	Pct.	Off.	Def.	Tot.	Ast.	PF	Dq.	Stl.	TO	Blk.	Pts.	Avg.	Hi.
Brad Daugherty	71	2691	520	911	.571	391	492	.795	164	562	726	312	174	0	53	150	56	1432	20.2	37
Mark Price	75	2380	477	986	.484	289	305	.948	37	164	201	602	105	0	89	196	11	1365	18.2	39
Larry Nance	77	2753	533	971	.549	202	247	.818	184	484	668	223	223	3	54	107	198	1268	16.5	30
Craig Ehlo	82	2559	385	785	.490	86	120	.717	133	290	403	254	170	0	104	124	22	949	11.6	24
Gerald Wilkins	80	2079	361	797	.453	152	181	.840	74	140	214	183	154	1	78	94	18	890	11.1	28
John Williams	67	2055	263	560	.470	212	296	.716	127	288	415	152	171	2	48	116	105	738	11.0	27
Terrell Brandon	82	1622	297	621	.478	118	143	.825	37	142	179	302	122	1	79	107	27	725	8.8	21
Mike Sanders	53	1189	197	396	.497	59	78	.756	52	118	170	75	150	2	39	57	30	454	8.6	19
Danny Ferry	76	1461	220	459	.479	99	113	.876	81	198	279	137	171	1	29	83	49	573	7.5	18
John Battle	41	497	83	200	.415	56	72	.778	4	25	29	54	39	0	9	22	5	223	5.4	17
Bobby Phills	31	139	38	82	.463	15	25	.600	6	11	17	10	19	0	10	18	2	93	3.0	9
Jerome Lane	21	149	27	54	.500	5	20	.250	24	29	53	17	32	0	12	7	3	59	2.8	8
Steve Kerr*	5	41	5	10	.500	2	2	1.000	0	7	7	11	2	0	2	2	0	12	2.4	4
Jay Guidinger	32	215	19	55	.345	13	25	.520	26	38	64	17	48	0	9	10	10	51	1.6	9

3-pt. FG: Cleveland 283-742 (.381)—Daugherty 1-2 (.500); Price 122-293 (.416); Nance 0-4 (.000); Ehlo 93-244 (.381); Wilkins 16-58 (.276); Brandon 13-42 (.310); Sanders 1-4 (.250); Ferry 34-82 (.415); Battle 1-6 (.167); Phills 2-5 (.400); Kerr* 0-2 (.000). Opponents 229-695 (.329).

DALLAS MAVERICKS

	G	Min.	FGM	FGA	Pct.	FTM	FTA	Pct.	Off.	Def.	Tot.	Ast.	PF	Dq.	Stl.	TO	Blk.	Pts.	Avg.	Hi.
Derek Harper	62	2108	393	939	.419	239	316	.756	42	81	123	334	145	1	80	136	16	1126	18.2	35
Jim Jackson	28	938	184	466	.395	68	92	.739	42	80	122	131	80	0	40	115	11	457	16.3	32
Sean Rooks	72	2087	368	747	.493	234	389	.602	196	340	536	95	204	2	38	160	81	970	13.5	26
Terry Davis	75	2462	393	863	.455	167	281	.594	259	442	701	68	199	3	36	160	28	955	12.7	35
Doug Smith	61	1524	289	666	.434	56	74	.757	96	232	328	104	280	12	48	115	52	634	10.4	27
Randy White	64	1433	235	540	.435	138	184	.750	154	216	370	49	226	4	63	108	45	618	9.7	31
Tim Legler†	30	630	104	238	.437	57	71	.803	25	33	58	46	63	0	24	28	6	287	9.6	20
Tim Legler‡	33	635	105	241	.436	57	71	.803	25	34	59	46	63	0	24	28	6	289	8.8	20
Mike Iuzzolino	70	1769	221	478	.462	114	149	.765	31	109	140	328	101	0	49	129	6	610	8.7	23
Walter Bond	74	1578	227	565	.402	129	167	.772	52	144	196	122	223	3	75	112	18	590	8.0	25
Tracy Moore	39	510	103	249	.414	53	61	.869	23	29	52	47	54	0	21	32	4	282	7.2	20
Dexter Cambridge	53	885	151	312	.484	68	99	.687	88	79	167	58	128	1	24	63	6	370	7.0	16
Brian Howard	68	1295	183	414	.442	72	94	.766	66	146	212	67	217	8	55	68	34	439	6.5	18
Morlon Wiley†	33	641	70	173	.405	12	18	.667	20	36	56	100	78	2	39	51	1	191	5.8	15
Morlon Wiley‡	58	995	96	254	.378	17	26	.654	29	62	91	181	127	2	65	80	3	263	4.5	15
Lamont Strothers	9	138	20	61	.328	8	10	.800	8	6	14	13	13	0	8	15	0	50	5.6	10
Donald Hodge	79	1267	161	400	.403	71	104	.683	93	201	294	75	204	2	33	90	37	393	5.0	14
Walter Palmer	20	124	27	57	.474	6	9	.667	12	32	44	5	29	0	1	10	5	60	3.0	18
Radisav Curcic	20	166	16	41	.390	26	36	.722	17	32	49	12	30	0	7	8	2	58	2.9	11
Steve Bardo	23	175	19	62	.306	12	17	.706	10	27	37	29	28	0	8	17	3	51	2.2	6

3-pt. FG: Dallas 283-837 (.338)—Harper 101-257 (.393); Jackson 21-73 (.288); Rooks 0-2 (.000); Davis 2-8 (.250); Smith 0-4 (.000); White 10-42 (.238); Legler† 22-65 (.338); Legler‡ 22-65 (.338); Iuzzolino 54-144 (.375); Bond 7-42 (.167); Moore 23-67 (.343); Cambridge 0-4 (.000); Howard 1-7 (.143); Wiley† 39-103 (.379); Wiley‡ 54-154 (.351); Strothers 2-13 (.154); Bardo 1-6 (.167). Opponents 234-653 (.358).

DENVER NUGGETS

	G	Min.	FGM	FGA	Pct.	FTM	FTA	Pct.	Off.	Def.	Tot.	Ast.	PF	Dq.	Stl.	TO	Blk.	Pts.	Avg.	Hi.
Mahmoud Abdul-Rauf	81	2710	633	1407	.450	217	232	.935	51	174	225	344	179	0	84	187	8	1553	19.2	32
Reggie Williams	79	2722	535	1167	.458	238	296	.804	132	296	428	295	284	6	126	194	76	1341	17.0	35
LaPhonso Ellis	82	2749	483	958	.504	237	317	.748	274	470	744	151	293	8	72	153	111	1205	14.7	27
Dikembe Mutombo	82	3029	398	781	.510	335	492	.681	344	726	1070	147	284	5	43	216	287	1131	13.8	27
Robert Pack	77	1579	285	606	.470	239	311	.768	52	108	160	335	182	1	81	185	10	810	10.5	27
Bryant Stith	39	865	124	278	.446	99	119	.832	39	85	124	49	82	0	24	44	5	347	8.9	24
Marcus Liberty	78	1585	252	620	.406	102	156	.654	131	204	335	105	143	0	64	79	21	628	8.1	25
Mark Macon	48	1141	158	381	.415	42	60	.700	33	70	103	126	135	2	69	72	3	358	7.5	18
Todd Lichti	48	752	124	276	.449	81	102	.794	35	67	102	52	60	0	28	49	11	331	6.9	24
Tom Hammonds†	35	571	86	176	.489	33	54	.611	33	63	96	16	57	0	18	31	8	205	5.9	18
Tom Hammonds‡	54	713	105	221	.475	38	62	.613	38	89	127	24	77	0	18	34	12	248	4.6	18
Gary Plummer	60	737	106	228	.465	69	95	.726	53	120	173	40	141	1	14	78	11	281	4.7	20

	G	Min.	FGM	FGA	Pct.	FTM	FTA	Pct.	Off.	Def.	Tot.	Ast.	PF	Dq.	Stl.	TO	Blk.	Pts.	Avg.	Hi.
									REBOUNDS									SCORING		
Kevin Brooks	55	571	93	233	.399	35	40	.875	22	59	81	34	46	0	10	39	2	227	4.1	16
Scott Hastings	76	670	57	112	.509	40	55	.727	44	93	137	34	115	1	12	29	8	156	2.1	10
Robert Werdann	28	149	18	59	.305	17	31	.548	23	29	52	7	38	1	6	12	4	53	1.9	6

3-pt. FG: Denver 138-454 (.304)—Abdul-Rauf 70-197 (.355); Williams 33-122 (.270); Ellis 2-13 (.154); Pack 1-8 (.125); Stith 0-4 (.000); Liberty 22-59 (.373); Macon 0-6 (.000); Lichti 2-6 (.333); Plummer 0-3 (.000); Hammondst 0-1 (.000); Hammonds‡ 0-1 (.000); Brooks 6-26 (.231); Hastings 2-8 (.250); Werdann 0-1 (.000). Opponents 222-647 (.343).

DETROIT PISTONS

	G	Min.	FGM	FGA	Pct.	FTM	FTA	Pct.	Off.	Def.	Tot.	Ast.	PF	Dq.	Stl.	TO	Blk.	Pts.	Avg.	Hi.
									REBOUNDS									SCORING		
Joe Dumars	77	3094	677	1454	.466	343	397	.864	63	85	148	308	141	0	78	138	7	1809	23.5	43
Isiah Thomas	79	2922	526	1258	.418	278	377	.737	71	161	232	671	222	2	123	284	18	1391	17.6	43
Terry Mills	81	2183	494	1072	.461	201	254	.791	176	296	472	111	282	6	44	142	50	1199	14.8	41
Orlando Woolridge* .	50	1477	271	566	.479	113	168	.673	84	92	176	112	114	1	26	73	25	655	13.1	36
Mark Aguirre......	51	1056	187	422	.443	99	129	.767	43	109	152	105	101	1	16	68	7	503	9.9	29
Alvin Robertsont	30	941	108	249	.434	40	58	.690	60	72	132	107	98	1	65	56	9	279	9.3	26
Alvin Robertson‡ ...	69	2006	247	539	.458	84	128	.656	107	162	269	263	218	1	155	133	18	618	9.0	26
Bill Laimbeer......	79	1933	292	574	.509	93	104	.894	110	309	419	127	212	4	46	59	40	687	8.7	24
Dennis Rodman	62	2410	183	429	.427	87	163	.534	367	765	1132	102	201	0	48	103	45	468	7.5	18
Olden Polynice	67	1299	210	429	.490	66	142	.465	181	237	418	29	126	0	31	54	21	486	7.3	27
Gerald Glasst	56	777	134	312	.429	21	33	.636	60	79	139	68	98	1	30	30	18	296	5.3	22
Gerald Glass‡	60	848	142	339	.419	25	39	.641	61	81	142	77	104	1	33	35	18	316	5.3	22
Melvin Newbern	33	311	42	113	.372	34	60	.567	19	18	37	57	42	0	23	32	1	119	3.6	20
Danny Young	65	836	69	167	.413	28	32	.875	13	34	47	119	36	0	31	30	5	188	2.9	15
Mark Randallt......	35	240	40	79	.506	16	26	.615	27	28	55	10	32	0	4	16	2	97	2.8	12
Mark Randall‡......	37	248	40	80	.500	16	26	.615	27	28	55	11	33	0	4	17	2	97	2.6	12
Isaiah Morris	25	102	26	57	.456	3	4	.750	6	6	12	4	14	0	3	8	1	55	2.2	10
Jeff Ruland	11	55	5	11	.455	2	4	.500	9	9	18	2	16	0	2	6	0	12	1.1	4
Darrell Walker*......	9	144	3	19	.158	2	6	.333	4	15	19	9	12	0	10	13	0	8	0.9	3

3-pt. FG: Detroit 292-908 (.322)—Dumars 112-299 (.375); Thomas 61-198 (.308); Mills 10-36 (.278); Woolridge* 0-9 (.000); Aguirre 30-83 (.361); Robertsont 23-67 (.343); Robertson‡ 40-122 (.328); Laimbeer 10-27 (.370); Rodman 15-73 (.205); Polynice 0-1 (.000); Glass| 7-31 (.226); Glass‡ 7-31 (.226); Newbern 1-8 (.125); Randallt 1-7 (.143); Randall‡ 1-8 (.125); Young 22-68 (.324); Walker* 0-1 (.000). Opponents 261-769 (.339).

GOLDEN STATE WARRIORS

	G	Min.	FGM	FGA	Pct.	FTM	FTA	Pct.	Off.	Def.	Tot.	Ast.	PF	Dq.	Stl.	TO	Blk.	Pts.	Avg.	Hi.
									REBOUNDS									SCORING		
Chris Mullin	46	1902	474	930	.510	183	226	.810	42	190	232	166	76	0	68	139	41	1191	25.9	46
Tim Hardaway.......	66	2609	522	1168	.447	273	367	.744	60	203	263	699	152	0	116	220	12	1419	21.5	41
Sarunas Marciulionis.	30	836	178	328	.543	162	213	.761	40	57	97	105	92	1	51	76	2	521	17.4	34
Billy Owens........	37	1201	247	493	.501	117	183	.639	108	156	264	144	105	1	35	106	28	612	16.5	30
Latrell Sprewell......	77	2741	449	968	.464	211	283	.746	79	192	271	295	166	2	126	203	52	1182	15.4	36
Victor Alexander	72	1753	344	667	.516	111	162	.685	132	288	420	93	218	2	34	120	53	809	11.2	29
Andre Spencert	17	407	73	160	.456	41	54	.759	38	42	80	24	61	0	15	24	7	187	11.0	24
Andre Spencer‡	20	422	73	163	.448	41	54	.759	38	43	81	24	64	0	17	26	7	187	9.4	24
Chris Gatling	70	1248	249	462	.539	150	207	.725	129	191	320	40	197	2	44	102	53	648	9.3	29
Jeff Grayer	48	1025	165	353	.467	91	136	.669	71	86	157	70	120	1	31	54	8	423	8.8	24
Tyrone Hill	74	2070	251	494	.508	138	221	.624	255	499	754	68	320	8	41	92	40	640	8.6	24
Keith Jennings	8	136	25	42	.595	14	18	.778	2	9	11	23	18	0	4	7	0	69	8.6	22
Rod Higgins	29	591	96	215	.447	35	47	.745	23	45	68	66	54	0	13	64	5	240	8.3	19
Jud Buechler........	70	1287	176	403	.437	65	87	.747	81	114	195	94	98	0	47	55	19	437	6.2	19
Byron Houston	79	1274	145	325	.446	129	194	.665	119	196	315	69	253	12	44	87	43	421	5.3	18
Paul Pressey.......	18	296	29	66	.439	21	27	.778	8	23	31	30	36	0	11	23	5	79	4.4	8
Pat Durham	5	78	6	25	.240	9	12	.750	5	9	14	4	6	0	1	7	1	21	4.2	12
Joe Courtneyt	7	70	9	23	.391	4	5	.800	2	15	17	2	8	0	3	3	4	22	3.1	10
Joe Courtney‡......	12	104	13	32	.406	7	9	.778	4	15	19	3	17	0	5	6	5	33	2.8	10
Alton Lister	20	174	19	42	.452	7	13	.538	15	29	44	5	40	0	0	18	9	45	2.3	8
Ed Nealy*..........	30	229	16	46	.348	7	10	.700	8	40	48	13	35	0	9	5	1	46	1.5	6
Barry Stevens.......	2	6	1	2	.500	0	0	...	0	1	1	0	0	0	0	0	0	2	1.0	2

3-pt. FG: Golden State 298-852 (.350)—Mullin 60-133 (.451); Hardaway 102-309 (.330); Marciulionis 3-15 (.200); Owens 1-11 (.091); Sprewell 73-198 (.369); Alexander 10-22 (.455); Spencert 0-2 (.000); Spencer‡ 0-2 (.000); Gatling 0-6 (.000); Grayer 2-14 (.143); Hill 0-4 (.000); Jennings 5-9 (.556); Higgins 13-37 (.351); Buechler 20-59 (.339); Houston 2-7 (.286); Pressey 0-4 (.000); Nealy* 7-22 (.318). Opponents 272-794 (.343).

HOUSTON ROCKETS

	G	Min.	FGM	FGA	Pct.	FTM	FTA	Pct.	Off.	Def.	Tot.	Ast.	PF	Dq.	Stl.	TO	Blk.	Pts.	Avg.	Hi.
									REBOUNDS									SCORING		
Hakeem Olajuwon	82	3242	848	1603	.529	444	570	.779	283	785	1068	291	305	5	150	262	342	2140	26.1	45
Vernon Maxwell	71	2251	349	858	.407	164	228	.719	29	192	221	297	124	1	86	140	8	982	13.8	30
Kenny Smith	82	2422	387	744	.520	195	222	.878	28	132	160	446	110	0	80	163	7	1065	13.0	30
Otis Thorpe.........	72	2357	385	690	.558	153	256	.598	219	370	589	181	234	3	43	151	19	923	12.8	24
Robert Horry........	79	2330	323	680	.474	143	200	.715	113	279	392	191	210	1	80	156	83	801	10.1	29
Carl Herrera	81	1800	240	444	.541	125	176	.710	148	306	454	61	190	1	47	92	35	605	7.5	21
Matt Bullard	79	1356	213	494	.431	58	74	.784	66	156	222	110	129	0	30	57	11	575	7.3	28
Sleepy Floyd	52	867	124	305	.407	81	102	.794	14	72	86	132	59	0	32	68	6	345	6.6	28
Scott Brooks........	82	1516	183	385	.475	112	135	.830	22	77	99	243	136	0	79	72	3	519	6.3	16

	G	Min.	FGM	FGA	Pct.	FTM	FTA	Pct.	Off.	Def.	Tot.	Ast.	PF	Dq.	Stl.	TO	Blk.	Pts.	Avg.	Hi.
Winston Garland	66	1004	152	343	.443	81	89	.910	32	76	108	138	116	0	39	67	4	391	5.9	16
Kennard Winchester	39	340	61	139	.439	17	22	.773	17	32	49	13	40	0	10	15	10	143	3.7	15
Terry Teagle	2	25	2	7	.286	1	2	.500	0	3	3	2	1	0	0	1	0	5	2.5	3
Mark Acres*	6	23	2	9	.222	1	2	.500	2	4	6	0	2	0	0	2	0	6	1.0	3
Tree Rollins	42	247	11	41	.268	9	12	.750	12	48	60	10	43	0	6	9	15	31	0.7	4

3-pt. FG: Houston 387-1073 (.361)—Olajuwon 0-8 (.000); Maxwell 120-361 (.332); Smith 96-219 (.438); Thorpe 0-2 (.000); Horry 12-47 (.255); Herrera 0-2 (.000); Bullard 91-243 (.374); Floyd 16-56 (.286); Brooks 41-99 (.414); Garland 6-13 (.462); Winchester 4-19 (.211); Acres* 1-2 (.500); Rollins 0-2 (.000). Opponents 242-730 (.332).

INDIANA PACERS

	G	Min.	FGM	FGA	Pct.	FTM	FTA	Pct.	Off.	Def.	Tot.	Ast.	PF	Dq.	Stl.	TO	Blk.	Pts.	Avg.	Hi.
Reggie Miller	82	2954	571	1193	.479	427	485	.880	67	191	258	262	182	0	120	145	26	1736	21.2	57
Detlef Schrempf	82	3098	517	1085	.476	525	653	.804	210	570	780	493	305	3	79	243	27	1567	19.1	36
Rik Smits	81	2072	494	1017	.486	167	228	.732	126	306	432	121	285	5	27	147	75	1155	14.3	37
Pooh Richardson	74	2396	337	703	.479	92	124	.742	63	204	267	573	132	1	94	167	12	769	10.4	30
Vern Fleming	75	1503	280	554	.505	143	197	.726	63	106	169	224	126	1	63	121	9	710	9.5	31
Dale Davis	82	2264	304	535	.568	119	225	.529	291	432	723	69	274	5	63	79	148	727	8.9	20
Sam Mitchell	81	1402	215	483	.445	150	185	.811	93	155	248	76	207	1	23	51	10	584	7.2	20
George McCloud	78	1500	216	525	.411	75	102	.735	60	145	205	192	165	0	53	107	11	565	7.2	24
Kenny Williams	57	844	150	282	.532	48	68	.706	102	126	228	38	87	1	21	28	45	348	6.1	18
Malik Sealy	58	672	136	319	.426	51	74	.689	60	52	112	47	74	0	36	58	7	330	5.7	16
Sean Green	13	81	28	55	.509	3	4	.750	4	5	9	7	11	0	2	9	1	62	4.8	17
LaSalle Thompson	63	730	104	213	.488	29	39	.744	55	123	178	34	137	0	29	47	24	237	3.8	14
Greg Dreiling	43	239	19	58	.328	8	15	.533	26	40	66	8	60	0	5	9	8	46	1.1	6

3-pt. FG: Indiana 257-789 (.326)—Miller 167-419 (.399); Schrempf 8-52 (.154); Richardson 3-29 (.103); Fleming 7-36 (.194); Mitchell 4-23 (.174); McCloud 58-181 (.320); Williams 0-3 (.000); Sealy 7-31 (.226); Green 3-10 (.300); Thompson 0-1 (.000); Dreiling 0-4 (.000). Opponents 216-706 (.306).

LOS ANGELES CLIPPERS

	G	Min.	FGM	FGA	Pct.	FTM	FTA	Pct.	Off.	Def.	Tot.	Ast.	PF	Dq.	Stl.	TO	Blk.	Pts.	Avg.	Hi.
Danny Manning	79	2761	702	1379	.509	388	484	.802	198	322	520	207	323	8	108	230	101	1800	22.8	36
Ron Harper	80	2970	542	1203	.451	307	399	.769	117	308	425	360	212	1	177	222	73	1443	18.0	36
Ken Norman	76	2477	498	975	.511	130	220	.595	209	362	571	165	156	0	59	125	58	1137	15.0	34
Michael Jackson	82	3117	459	945	.486	241	300	.803	129	259	388	724	158	0	136	220	12	1181	14.4	27
Stanley Roberts	77	1816	375	711	.527	120	246	.488	181	297	478	59	332	15	34	121	141	870	11.3	27
Loy Vaught	79	1653	313	616	.508	116	155	.748	164	328	492	54	172	2	55	83	39	743	9.4	27
John Williams	74	1638	205	477	.430	70	129	.543	88	228	316	142	188	1	83	79	23	492	6.6	17
Gary Grant	74	1624	210	476	.441	55	74	.743	27	112	139	353	168	2	106	129	9	486	6.6	18
Kiki Vandeweghe	41	494	92	203	.453	58	66	.879	12	36	48	25	45	0	13	20	7	254	6.2	24
Jaren Jackson	34	350	53	128	.414	23	27	.852	19	20	39	35	45	1	19	17	5	131	3.9	14
Elmore Spencer	44	280	44	82	.537	16	32	.500	17	45	62	8	54	0	8	26	18	104	2.4	8
Lester Conner	31	422	28	62	.452	18	19	.947	16	33	49	65	39	0	34	21	4	74	2.4	11
Randy Woods	41	174	23	66	.348	19	26	.731	6	8	14	40	26	0	14	16	1	68	1.7	8
Alex Stivrins*	1	1	0	1	.000	0	0	...	0	0	0	0	0	0	0	0	0	0	0.0	0
Duane Washington	4	28	0	5	.000	0	0	...	0	2	2	5	2	0	1	2	0	0	0.0	0

3-pt. FG: L.A. Clippers 133-491 (.271)—Manning 8-30 (.267); Harper 52-186 (.280); Norman 10-38 (.263); M. Jackson 22-82 (.268); Vaught 1-4 (.250); Williams 12-53 (.226); Grant 11-42 (.262); Vandeweghe 12-37 (.324); J. Jackson 2-5 (.400); Woods 3-14 (.214). Opponents 275-790 (.348).

LOS ANGELES LAKERS

	G	Min.	FGM	FGA	Pct.	FTM	FTA	Pct.	Off.	Def.	Tot.	Ast.	PF	Dq.	Stl.	TO	Blk.	Pts.	Avg.	Hi.
Sedale Threatt	82	2893	522	1028	.508	177	215	.823	47	226	273	564	248	1	142	173	11	1235	15.1	32
James Worthy	82	2359	510	1142	.447	171	211	.810	73	174	247	278	87	0	92	137	27	1221	14.9	30
Byron Scott	58	1677	296	659	.449	156	184	.848	27	107	134	157	98	0	55	70	13	792	13.7	29
Sam Perkins*	49	1589	242	527	.459	184	222	.829	111	268	379	128	139	0	40	76	51	673	13.7	26
A.C. Green	82	2819	379	706	.537	277	375	.739	287	424	711	116	149	0	88	116	39	1051	12.8	30
Vlade Divac	82	2525	397	819	.485	235	341	.689	220	509	729	232	311	7	128	214	140	1050	12.8	28
Anthony Peeler	77	1656	297	634	.468	162	206	.786	64	115	179	166	193	0	60	123	14	802	10.4	25
Elden Campbell	79	1551	238	520	.458	130	204	.637	127	205	332	48	165	0	59	69	100	606	7.7	21
James Edwards	52	617	122	270	.452	84	118	.712	30	70	100	41	122	0	10	51	7	328	6.3	17
Doug Christie	23	332	45	106	.425	50	66	.758	24	27	51	53	53	0	22	50	5	142	6.2	17
Tony Smith	55	752	133	275	.484	62	82	.756	46	41	87	63	72	1	50	40	7	330	6.0	20
Benoit Benjamin†	28	306	52	108	.481	22	37	.595	24	72	96	10	61	0	14	36	13	126	4.5	17
Benoit Benjamin‡	59	754	133	271	.491	69	104	.663	51	158	209	22	134	0	31	78	48	335	5.7	18
Duane Cooper	65	645	62	158	.392	25	35	.714	13	37	50	150	66	0	18	69	2	156	2.4	9
Alex Blackwell	27	109	14	42	.333	6	8	.750	10	13	23	7	14	0	4	5	2	34	1.3	8

3-pt. FG: L.A. Lakers 187-626 (.299)—Threatt 14-53 (.264); Worthy 30-111 (.270); Scott 44-135 (.326); Perkins* 5-29 (.172); Green 16-46 (.348); Divac 21-75 (.280); Peeler 46-118 (.390); Campbell 0-3 (.000); Christie 2-12 (.167); Smith 2-11 (.182); Cooper 7-30 (.233); Blackwell 0-3 (.000). Opponents 245-726 (.337).

MIAMI HEAT

	G	Min.	FGM	FGA	Pct.	FTM	FTA	Pct.	Off.	Def.	Tot.	Ast.	PF	Dq.	Stl.	TO	Blk.	Pts.	Avg.	Hi.
Glen Rice	82	3082	582	1324	.440	242	295	.820	92	332	424	180	201	0	92	157	25	1554	19.0	45
Rony Seikaly	72	2456	417	868	.480	397	540	.735	259	587	846	100	260	3	38	203	83	1232	17.1	30
Steve Smith	48	1610	279	619	.451	155	197	.787	56	141	197	267	148	3	50	129	16	746	16.0	31
Grant Long	76	2728	397	847	.469	261	341	.765	197	371	568	182	264	8	104	133	31	1061	14.0	31
Kevin Edwards	40	1134	216	462	.468	119	141	.844	48	73	121	120	69	0	68	75	12	556	13.9	26
Bimbo Coles	81	2232	318	686	.464	177	220	.805	58	108	166	373	199	4	80	108	11	855	10.6	25
Harold Miner	73	1383	292	615	.475	163	214	.762	74	73	147	73	130	2	34	92	8	750	10.3	27
John Salley	51	1422	154	307	.502	115	144	.799	113	200	313	83	192	7	32	101	70	423	8.3	23
Willie Burton	26	451	54	141	.383	91	127	.717	22	48	70	16	58	0	13	50	16	204	7.8	23
Brian Shaw	68	1603	197	501	.393	61	78	.782	70	187	257	235	163	2	48	96	19	498	7.3	32
Matt Geiger	48	554	76	145	.524	62	92	.674	46	74	120	14	123	6	15	36	18	214	4.5	18
Alec Kessler	40	415	57	122	.467	36	47	.766	25	66	91	14	63	0	4	21	12	155	3.9	17
Keith Askins	69	935	88	213	.413	29	40	.725	74	124	198	31	141	2	31	37	29	227	3.3	14

3-pt. FG: Miami 333-940 (.354)—Rice 148-386 (.383); Seikaly 1-8 (.125); Smith 53-132 (.402); Long 6-26 (.231); Edwards 5-17 (.294); Coles 42-137 (.307); Miner 3-9 (.333); Burton 5-15 (.333); Shaw 43-130 (.331); Geiger 0-4 (.000); Kessler 5-11 (.455); Askins 22-65 (.338). Opponents 265-781 (.339).

MILWAUKEE BUCKS

	G	Min.	FGM	FGA	Pct.	FTM	FTA	Pct.	Off.	Def.	Tot.	Ast.	PF	Dq.	Stl.	TO	Blk.	Pts.	Avg.	Hi.
Blue Edwards	82	2729	554	1083	.512	237	300	.790	123	259	382	214	242	1	129	175	45	1382	16.9	36
Frank Brickowski	66	2075	456	836	.545	195	268	.728	120	285	405	196	235	8	80	202	44	1115	16.9	32
Eric Murdock	79	2437	438	936	.468	231	296	.780	95	189	284	603	177	2	174	207	7	1138	14.4	30
Todd Day	71	1931	358	828	.432	213	297	.717	144	147	291	117	222	1	75	118	48	983	13.8	30
Anthony Avent	82	2285	347	802	.433	112	172	.651	180	332	512	91	237	0	57	140	73	806	9.8	28
Brad Lohaus	80	1766	283	614	.461	73	101	.723	59	217	276	127	178	1	47	93	74	724	9.1	34
Alvin Robertson*	39	1065	139	290	.479	44	70	.629	47	90	137	156	120	0	90	77	9	339	8.7	20
Fred Roberts	79	1488	226	428	.528	135	169	.799	91	146	237	118	138	0	57	67	27	599	7.6	22
Derek Strong	23	339	42	92	.457	68	85	.800	40	75	115	14	20	0	11	13	1	156	6.8	20
Orlando Woolridge†	8	78	18	33	.545	7	9	.778	3	6	9	3	8	0	1	6	2	43	5.4	10
Orlando Woolridge‡	58	1555	289	599	.482	120	177	.678	87	98	185	115	122	1	27	79	27	698	12.0	36
Alaa Abdelnaby*	12	159	26	56	.464	12	16	.750	12	25	37	10	24	0	6	13	4	64	5.3	12
Lee Mayberry	82	1503	171	375	.456	39	68	.574	26	92	118	273	148	1	59	85	7	424	5.2	17
Dan Schayes	70	1124	105	263	.399	112	137	.818	72	177	249	78	148	1	36	65	36	322	4.6	20
Moses Malone	11	104	13	42	.310	24	31	.774	22	24	46	7	6	0	1	10	8	50	4.5	12
Jon Barry	47	520	76	206	.369	33	49	.673	10	33	43	68	57	0	35	42	3	206	4.4	18
Alex Stivrins*	3	25	4	11	.364	3	4	.750	3	3	6	2	4	0	1	2	0	11	3.7	9
Alan Ogg*	3	26	3	9	.333	2	2	1.000	1	5	6	4	6	0	1	3	3	8	2.7	4
Anthony Pullard	8	37	8	18	.444	1	3	.333	2	6	8	2	5	0	2	5	2	17	2.1	6
Dan O'Sullivan†	3	7	1	2	.500	3	4	.750	0	2	2	1	3	0	1	0	0	5	1.7	5
Dan O'Sullivan‡	6	17	3	5	.600	3	4	.750	2	4	6	1	4	0	1	0	0	9	1.5	5

3-pt. FG: Milwaukee 312-936 (.333)—Edwards 37-106 (.349); Brickowski 8-26 (.308); Murdock 31-119 (.261); Day 54-184 (.293); Avent 0-2 (.000); Lohaus 85-230 (.370); Robertson* 17-55 (.309); Roberts 12-29 (.414); Strong 4-8 (.500); Woolridge† 0-0; Woolridge‡ 0-9 (.000); Abdelnaby* 0-1 (.000); Mayberry 43-110 (.391); Schayes 0-3 (.000); Barry 21-63 (.333). Opponents 269-783 (.344).

MINNESOTA TIMBERWOLVES

	G	Min.	FGM	FGA	Pct.	FTM	FTA	Pct.	Off.	Def.	Tot.	Ast.	PF	Dq.	Stl.	TO	Blk.	Pts.	Avg.	Hi.
Doug West	80	3104	646	1249	.517	249	296	.841	89	158	247	235	279	1	85	165	21	1543	19.3	39
Christian Laettner	81	2823	503	1061	.474	462	553	.835	171	537	708	223	290	4	105	275	83	1472	18.2	35
Chuck Person	78	2985	541	1248	.433	109	168	.649	98	335	433	343	198	2	67	219	30	1309	16.8	37
Micheal Williams	76	2661	353	791	.446	419	462	.907	84	189	273	661	268	7	165	227	23	1151	15.1	31
Thurl Bailey	70	1276	203	446	.455	119	142	.838	53	162	215	61	88	0	20	60	47	525	7.5	23
Bob McCann	79	1536	200	410	.488	95	152	.625	92	190	282	68	202	2	51	79	58	495	6.3	18
Luc Longley	55	1045	133	292	.455	53	74	.716	71	169	240	51	169	4	47	88	77	319	5.8	19
Marlon Maxey	43	520	93	169	.550	45	70	.643	66	98	164	12	75	0	11	38	18	231	5.4	24
Gerald Glass	4	71	8	27	.296	4	6	.667	1	2	3	9	6	0	3	5	0	20	5.0	10
Chris Smith	80	1266	125	289	.433	95	120	.792	32	64	96	196	96	1	48	68	16	347	4.3	24
Felton Spencer	71	1296	105	226	.465	83	127	.654	134	190	324	17	243	10	23	70	66	293	4.1	13
Gundars Vetra	13	89	19	40	.475	4	6	.667	4	4	8	6	12	0	2	2	0	45	3.5	17
Lance Blanks	61	642	65	150	.433	20	32	.625	18	50	68	72	61	1	16	31	5	161	2.6	15
Brad Sellers	54	533	49	130	.377	37	39	.949	27	56	83	46	40	0	6	27	11	135	2.5	13
Mark Randall*	2	8	0	1	.000	0	0	...	0	0	0	1	1	0	0	1	0	0	0.0	0

3-pt. FG: Minnesota 166-569 (.292)—West 2-23 (.087); Laettner 4-40 (.100); Person 118-332 (.355); Williams 26-107 (.243); McCann 0-2 (.000); Maxey 0-1 (.000); Glass 0-2 (.000); Smith 2-14 (.143); Vetra 3-3 (1.000); Blanks 11-43 (.256); Sellers 0-1 (.000); Randall* 0-1 (.000). Opponents 208-578 (.360).

NEW JERSEY NETS

	G	Min.	FGM	FGA	Pct.	FTM	FTA	Pct.	Off.	Def.	Tot.	Ast.	PF	Dq.	Stl.	TO	Blk.	Pts.	Avg.	Hi.
Drazen Petrovic	70	2660	587	1134	.518	315	362	.870	42	148	190	247	237	5	94	204	13	1564	22.3	44
Derrick Coleman	76	2759	564	1226	.460	421	521	.808	247	605	852	276	210	1	92	243	126	1572	20.7	35
Kenny Anderson	55	2010	370	850	.435	180	232	.776	51	175	226	449	140	1	96	153	11	927	16.9	31
Chris Morris	77	2302	436	907	.481	197	248	.794	227	227	454	106	171	2	144	119	52	1086	14.1	32
Sam Bowie	79	2092	287	638	.450	141	181	.779	158	398	556	127	226	3	32	120	128	717	9.1	27
Rumeal Robinson	80	1585	270	638	.423	112	195	.574	49	110	159	323	169	2	96	140	12	672	8.4	28
Bernard King	32	430	91	177	.514	39	57	.684	35	41	76	18	53	0	11	21	3	223	7.0	24

	G	Min.	FGM	FGA	Pct.	FTM	FTA	Pct.	REBOUNDS Off.	Def.	Tot.	Ast.	PF	Dq.	Stl.	TO	Blk.	SCORING Pts.	Avg.	Hi.
Rafael Addison	68	1164	182	411	.443	57	70	.814	45	87	132	53	125	0	23	64	11	428	6.3	21
Chucky Brown	77	1186	160	331	.483	71	98	.724	88	144	232	51	112	0	20	56	24	391	5.1	19
Jayson Williams	12	139	21	46	.457	7	18	.389	22	19	41	0	24	0	4	8	4	49	4.1	11
Rick Mahorn	74	1077	101	214	.472	88	110	.800	93	186	279	33	156	0	19	58	31	291	3.9	14
Maurice Cheeks	35	510	51	93	.548	24	27	.889	5	37	42	107	35	0	33	33	2	126	3.6	14
Chris Dudley	71	1398	94	266	.353	57	110	.518	215	298	513	16	195	5	17	54	103	245	3.5	12
Tate George	48	380	51	135	.378	20	24	.833	9	18	27	59	25	0	10	31	3	122	2.5	11
Dwayne Schintzius	5	35	2	7	.286	3	3	1.000	2	6	8	2	4	0	2	0	2	7	1.4	3
Dan O'Sullivan*	3	10	2	3	.667	0	0	...	2	2	4	0	1	0	0	0	0	4	1.3	2
Doug Lee	5	33	2	7	.286	0	0	...	0	2	2	5	7	0	0	3	1	5	1.0	5
Dave Hoppen	2	10	1	1	1.000	0	0	...	0	2	2	0	2	0	0	0	0	2	1.0	2

3-pt. FG: New Jersey 155-488 (.318)—Petrovic 75-167 (.449); Coleman 23-99 (.232); Anderson 7-25 (.280); Morris 17-76 (.224); Bowie 2-6 (.333); Robinson 20-56 (.357); King 2-7 (.286); Addison 7-34 (.206); Brown 0-5 (.000); Mahorn 1-3 (.333); Cheeks 0-2 (.000); George 0-5 (.000); Lee 1-3 (.333). Opponents 201-618 (.325).

NEW YORK KNICKERBOCKERS

	G	Min.	FGM	FGA	Pct.	FTM	FTA	Pct.	REBOUNDS Off.	Def.	Tot.	Ast.	PF	Dq.	Stl.	TO	Blk.	SCORING Pts.	Avg.	Hi.
Patrick Ewing	81	3003	779	1550	.503	400	556	.719	191	789	980	151	286	2	74	265	161	1959	24.2	43
John Starks	80	2477	513	1199	.428	263	331	.795	54	150	204	404	234	3	91	173	12	1397	17.5	39
Charles Smith	81	2172	358	764	.469	287	367	.782	170	262	432	142	254	4	48	155	96	1003	12.4	36
Anthony Mason	81	2482	316	629	.502	199	292	.682	231	409	640	170	240	2	43	137	19	831	10.3	30
Rolando Blackman	60	1434	239	539	.443	71	90	.789	23	79	102	157	129	1	22	65	10	580	9.7	23
Doc Rivers	77	1886	216	494	.437	133	162	.821	26	166	192	405	215	2	123	114	9	604	7.8	24
Tony Campbell	58	1062	194	396	.490	59	87	.678	59	96	155	62	150	0	34	51	5	449	7.7	28
Charles Oakley	82	2230	219	431	.508	127	176	.722	288	420	708	126	289	5	85	124	15	565	6.9	18
Greg Anthony	70	1699	174	419	.415	107	159	.673	42	128	170	398	141	0	113	104	12	459	6.6	23
Hubert Davis	50	815	110	251	.438	43	54	.796	13	43	56	83	71	1	22	45	4	269	5.4	22
Bo Kimble	9	55	14	33	.424	3	8	.375	3	8	11	5	10	0	1	6	0	33	3.7	11
Herb Williams	55	571	72	175	.411	14	21	.667	44	102	146	19	78	0	21	22	28	158	2.9	14
Eric Anderson	16	44	5	18	.278	11	13	.846	6	8	14	3	14	0	3	5	1	21	1.3	4

3-pt. FG: New York 193-604 (.320)—Ewing 1-7 (.143); Starks 108-336 (.321); Smith 0-2 (.000); Blackman 31-73 (.425); Rivers 39-123 (.317); Campbell 2-5 (.400); Oakley 0-1 (.000); Anthony 4-30 (.133); Davis 6-19 (.316); Kimble 2-8 (.250). Opponents 230-753 (.305).

ORLANDO MAGIC

	G	Min.	FGM	FGA	Pct.	FTM	FTA	Pct.	REBOUNDS Off.	Def.	Tot.	Ast.	PF	Dq.	Stl.	TO	Blk.	SCORING Pts.	Avg.	Hi.
Shaquille O'Neal	81	3071	733	1304	.562	427	721	.592	342	780	1122	152	321	8	60	307	286	1893	23.4	46
Nick Anderson	79	2920	594	1324	.449	298	402	.741	122	355	477	265	200	1	128	164	56	1574	19.9	50
Dennis Scott	54	1759	329	763	.431	92	117	.786	38	148	186	136	131	3	57	104	18	858	15.9	41
Scott Skiles	78	3086	416	891	.467	289	324	.892	52	238	290	735	244	4	86	267	2	1201	15.4	32
Donald Royal	77	1636	194	391	.496	318	390	.815	116	179	295	80	179	4	36	113	25	706	9.2	28
Tom Tolbert	72	1838	226	454	.498	122	168	.726	133	279	412	91	192	4	33	124	21	583	8.1	24
Anthony Bowie	77	1761	268	569	.471	67	84	.798	36	158	194	175	131	0	54	84	14	618	8.0	23
Jeff Turner	75	1479	231	437	.529	56	70	.800	74	178	252	107	192	2	19	66	9	528	7.0	23
Terry Catledge	21	262	36	73	.493	27	34	.794	18	28	46	5	31	1	4	25	1	99	4.7	12
Chris Corchiani*	9	102	13	23	.565	16	21	.762	1	6	7	16	17	0	6	8	0	42	4.7	12
Brian Williams	21	240	40	78	.513	16	20	.800	24	32	56	5	48	2	14	25	17	96	4.6	14
Litterial Green	52	626	87	198	.439	60	96	.625	11	23	34	116	70	0	23	42	4	235	4.5	12
Steve Kerr†	47	440	48	112	.429	20	22	.909	5	33	38	59	34	0	8	25	1	122	2.6	12
Steve Kerr‡	52	481	53	122	.434	22	24	.917	5	40	45	70	36	0	10	27	1	134	2.6	12
Howard Wright	4	10	4	5	.800	0	2	.000	1	1	2	0	0	0	0	0	0	8	2.0	8
Greg Kite	64	640	38	84	.452	13	24	.542	66	127	193	10	133	1	13	35	12	89	1.4	10
Lorenzo Williams*	3	10	0	2	.000	0	0	...	1	1	2	0	2	0	1	0	1	0	0.0	0

3-pt. FG: Orlando 317-889 (.357)—O'Neal 0-2 (.000); Anderson 88-249 (.353); Scott 108-268 (.403); Skiles 80-235 (.340); Royal 0-3 (.000); Tolbert 9-28 (.321); Bowie 15-48 (.313); Turner 10-17 (.588); Corchiani* 0-3 (.000); B. Williams 0-1 (.000); Green 1-10 (.100); Kerr† 6-24 (.250); Kerr‡ 6-24 (.250); Kite 0-1 (.000). Opponents 248-754 (.329).

PHILADELPHIA 76ERS

	G	Min.	FGM	FGA	Pct.	FTM	FTA	Pct.	REBOUNDS Off.	Def.	Tot.	Ast.	PF	Dq.	Stl.	TO	Blk.	SCORING Pts.	Avg.	Hi.
Hersey Hawkins	81	2977	551	1172	.470	419	487	.860	91	255	346	317	189	0	137	180	30	1643	20.3	40
Jeff Hornacek	79	2860	582	1239	.470	250	289	.865	84	258	342	548	203	2	131	222	21	1511	19.1	39
Clarence Weatherspoon	82	2654	494	1053	.469	291	408	.713	179	410	589	147	188	1	85	176	67	1280	15.6	30
Armon Gilliam	80	1742	359	774	.464	274	325	.843	136	336	472	116	123	0	37	157	54	992	12.4	32
Thomas Jordan	4	106	18	41	.439	8	17	.471	5	14	19	3	14	0	3	12	5	44	11.0	18
Tim Perry	81	2104	287	613	.468	147	207	.710	154	255	409	126	159	0	40	123	91	731	9.0	21
Johnny Dawkins	74	1598	258	590	.437	113	142	.796	33	103	136	339	91	0	80	121	4	655	8.9	28
Ron Anderson	69	1263	225	544	.414	72	89	.809	62	122	184	93	75	0	31	63	5	561	8.1	25
Kenny Payne	13	154	38	90	.422	4	4	1.000	4	20	24	18	15	0	5	7	2	84	6.5	21
Eddie Lee Wilkins	26	192	55	97	.567	48	78	.615	14	26	40	2	34	1	7	11	1	158	6.1	18
Andrew Lang	73	1861	149	351	.425	87	114	.763	136	300	436	79	261	4	46	89	141	386	5.3	18
Charles Shackleford	48	568	80	164	.488	31	49	.633	65	140	205	26	92	1	13	36	25	191	4.0	15
Greg Grant	72	996	77	220	.350	20	31	.645	24	43	67	206	73	0	43	54	1	194	2.7	15
Manute Bol	58	855	52	127	.409	12	19	.632	44	149	193	18	87	0	14	50	119	126	2.2	18

3-pt. FG: Philadelphia 330-941 (.351)—Hawkins 122-307 (.397); Hornacek 97-249 (.390); Weatherspoon 1-4 (.250); Gilliam 0-1 (.000); Perry 10-49 (.204); Dawkins 26-84 (.310); Anderson 39-120 (.325); Payne 4-18 (.222); Wilkins 0-2 (.000); Lang 1-5 (.200); Shackleford 0-2 (.000); Grant 20-68 (.294); Bol 10-32 (.313). Opponents 280-782 (.358).

1992-93

PHOENIX SUNS

	G	Min.	FGM	FGA	Pct.	FTM	FTA	Pct.	Off.	Def.	Tot.	Ast.	PF	Dq.	Stl.	TO	Blk.	Pts.	Avg.	Hi.
									REBOUNDS									SCORING		
Charles Barkley	76	2859	716	1376	.520	445	582	.765	237	691	928	385	196	0	119	233	74	1944	25.6	44
Dan Majerle	82	3199	509	1096	.464	203	261	.778	120	263	383	311	180	0	138	133	33	1388	16.9	30
Kevin Johnson	49	1643	282	565	.499	226	276	.819	30	74	104	384	100	0	85	151	19	791	16.1	32
Richard Dumas	48	1320	302	576	.524	152	215	.707	100	123	223	60	127	0	85	92	39	757	15.8	32
Cedric Ceballos	74	1607	381	662	.576	187	258	.725	172	236	408	77	103	1	54	106	28	949	12.8	40
Tom Chambers	73	1723	320	716	.447	241	288	.837	96	249	345	101	212	2	43	92	23	892	12.2	28
Danny Ainge	80	2163	337	730	.462	123	145	.848	49	165	214	260	175	3	69	113	8	947	11.8	33
Negele Knight	52	888	124	317	.391	67	86	.779	28	36	64	145	66	1	23	73	4	315	6.1	22
Oliver Miller	56	1069	121	255	.475	71	100	.710	70	205	275	118	145	0	38	108	100	313	5.6	19
Mark West	82	1558	175	285	.614	86	166	.518	153	305	458	29	243	3	16	93	103	436	5.3	16
Jerrod Mustaf	32	336	57	130	.438	33	53	.623	29	54	83	10	40	0	14	22	11	147	4.6	16
Frank Johnson	77	1122	136	312	.436	59	76	.776	41	72	113	186	112	0	60	80	8	332	4.3	22
Alex Stivrins†	10	35	11	18	.611	0	0	...	2	6	8	1	7	0	1	5	1	22	2.2	12
Alex Stivrins‡	19	76	19	39	.487	3	4	.750	7	12	19	3	11	0	2	7	2	41	2.2	12
Tim Kempton	30	167	19	48	.396	18	31	.581	12	27	39	19	30	0	4	16	4	56	1.9	13
Kurt Rambis*	5	41	4	7	.571	1	2	.500	2	4	6	1	3	0	3	6	0	9	1.8	7

3-pt. FG: Phoenix 398-1095 (.363)—Barkley 67-220 (.305); Majerle 167-438 (.381); K. Johnson 1-8 (.125); Dumas 1-3 (.333); Ceballos 0-2 (.000); Chambers 11-28 (.393); Ainge 150-372 (.403); Knight 0-7 (.000); Miller 0-3 (.000); Mustaf 0-1 (.000); F. Johnson 1-12 (.083); Stivrins† 0-1 (.000); Stivrins‡ 0-2 (.000). Opponents 250-750 (.333).

PORTLAND TRAIL BLAZERS

	G	Min.	FGM	FGA	Pct.	FTM	FTA	Pct.	Off.	Def.	Tot.	Ast.	PF	Dq.	Stl.	TO	Blk.	Pts.	Avg.	Hi.
									REBOUNDS									SCORING		
Clyde Drexler	49	1671	350	816	.429	245	292	.839	126	183	309	278	159	1	95	115	37	976	19.9	36
Clifford Robinson	82	2575	632	1336	.473	287	416	.690	165	377	542	182	287	6	98	173	163	1570	19.1	40
Terry Porter	81	2883	503	1108	.454	327	388	.843	58	258	316	419	122	0	101	199	10	1476	18.2	40
Rod Strickland	78	2474	396	816	.485	273	381	.717	120	217	337	559	153	1	131	199	24	1069	13.7	25
Jerome Kersey	65	1719	281	642	.438	116	183	.634	126	280	406	121	181	2	80	84	41	686	10.6	23
Kevin Duckworth	74	1762	301	688	.438	127	174	.730	118	269	387	70	222	1	45	87	39	729	9.9	27
Mario Elie	82	1757	240	524	.458	183	214	.855	59	157	216	177	145	0	74	89	20	708	8.6	19
Buck Williams	82	2498	270	528	.511	138	214	.645	232	458	690	75	270	0	81	101	61	678	8.3	17
Mark Bryant	80	1396	186	370	.503	104	148	.703	132	192	324	41	226	1	37	65	23	476	6.0	19
Tracy Murray	48	495	108	260	.415	35	40	.875	40	43	83	11	59	0	8	31	5	272	5.7	20
Dave Johnson	42	356	57	149	.383	40	59	.678	18	30	48	13	23	0	8	28	1	157	3.7	14
Joe Wolf†	21	156	20	43	.465	12	14	.857	13	32	45	5	22	0	7	5	0	52	2.5	10
Joe Wolf‡	23	165	20	44	.455	13	16	.813	14	34	48	5	24	0	7	7	1	53	2.3	10
Delaney Rudd	15	95	7	36	.194	11	14	.786	4	5	9	17	7	0	1	11	0	26	1.7	11
Reggie Smith	23	68	10	27	.370	3	14	.214	15	6	21	1	16	0	4	4	1	23	1.0	4

3-pt. FG: Portland 275-843 (.327)—Drexler 31-133 (.233); Robinson 19-77 (.247); Porter 143-345 (.414); Strickland 4-30 (.133); Kersey 8-28 (.286); Duckworth 0-2 (.000); Elie 45-129 (.349); Williams 0-1 (.000); Bryant 0-1 (.000); Murray 21-70 (.300); Johnson 3-14 (.214); Wolf† 0-1 (.000); Wolf‡ 0-1 (.000); Rudd 1-11 (.091); Smith 0-1 (.000). Opponents 277-811 (.342).

SACRAMENTO KINGS

	G	Min.	FGM	FGA	Pct.	FTM	FTA	Pct.	Off.	Def.	Tot.	Ast.	PF	Dq.	Stl.	TO	Blk.	Pts.	Avg.	Hi.
									REBOUNDS									SCORING		
Mitch Richmond	45	1728	371	782	.474	197	233	.845	18	136	154	221	137	3	53	130	9	987	21.9	35
Lionel Simmons	69	2502	468	1055	.444	298	364	.819	156	339	495	312	197	4	95	196	38	1235	17.9	35
Walt Williams	59	1673	358	823	.435	224	302	.742	115	150	265	178	209	6	66	179	29	1001	17.0	40
Wayman Tisdale	76	2283	544	1068	.509	175	231	.758	127	373	500	108	277	8	52	117	47	1263	16.6	40
Spud Webb	69	2335	342	789	.433	279	328	.851	44	149	193	481	177	0	104	194	6	1000	14.5	34
Anthony Bonner	70	1764	229	497	.461	143	241	.593	188	267	455	96	183	1	86	105	17	601	8.6	23
Rod Higgins	69	1425	199	483	.412	130	151	.861	66	127	193	119	141	0	51	63	29	571	8.3	26
Duane Causwell	55	1211	175	321	.545	103	165	.624	112	191	303	35	192	7	32	58	87	453	8.2	20
Randy Brown	75	1726	225	486	.463	115	157	.732	75	137	212	196	206	4	108	120	34	567	7.6	27
Henry James*	8	79	20	45	.444	17	20	.850	6	4	10	1	9	0	3	7	0	60	7.5	20
Pete Chilcutt	59	834	165	340	.485	32	46	.696	80	114	194	64	102	2	22	54	21	362	6.1	19
Marty Conlon	46	467	81	171	.474	57	81	.704	48	75	123	37	43	0	13	28	5	219	4.8	19
Jim Les	73	880	110	259	.425	42	50	.840	20	69	89	169	81	0	40	48	7	328	4.5	14
Vincent Askew*	9	76	8	17	.471	11	15	.733	7	4	11	5	11	0	2	8	1	27	3.0	9
Kurt Rambis†	67	781	63	122	.516	42	63	.667	75	146	221	52	119	0	40	36	18	168	2.5	10
Kurt Rambis‡	72	822	67	129	.519	43	65	.662	77	150	227	53	122	0	43	42	18	177	2.5	10
Stan Kimbrough	3	15	2	6	.333	0	0	...	0	0	0	1	1	0	1	0	0	5	1.7	5

3-pt. FG: Sacramento 262-788 (.332)—Richmond 48-130 (.369); Simmons 1-11 (.091); Williams 61-191 (.319); Tisdale 0-2 (.000); Webb 37-135 (.274); Bonner 0-7 (.000); Higgins 43-133 (.323); Causwell 0-1 (.000); Brown 2-6 (.333); James* 3-10 (.300); Conlon 0-4 (.000); Les 66-154 (.429); Rambis† 0-2 (.000); Rambis‡ 0-2 (.000); Kimbrough 1-2 (.500). Opponents 213-680 (.313).

SAN ANTONIO SPURS

	G	Min.	FGM	FGA	Pct.	FTM	FTA	Pct.	Off.	Def.	Tot.	Ast.	PF	Dq.	Stl.	TO	Blk.	Pts.	Avg.	Hi.
									REBOUNDS									SCORING		
David Robinson	82	3211	676	1348	.501	561	766	.732	229	727	956	301	239	5	127	241	264	1916	23.4	52
Sean Elliott	70	2604	451	918	.491	268	337	.795	85	237	322	265	132	1	68	152	28	1207	17.2	41
Dale Ellis	82	2731	545	1092	.499	157	197	.797	81	231	312	107	179	0	78	111	18	1366	16.7	33
Antoine Carr	71	1947	379	705	.538	174	224	.777	107	281	388	97	264	5	35	96	87	932	13.1	27
J.R. Reid†	66	1592	241	497	.485	171	222	.770	100	286	386	56	217	2	36	101	26	653	9.9	29
J.R. Reid‡	83	1887	283	595	.476	214	280	.764	120	336	456	80	266	3	47	125	31	780	9.4	29
Lloyd Daniels	77	1573	285	644	.443	72	99	.727	86	130	216	148	144	0	38	102	30	701	9.1	26
Avery Johnson	75	2030	256	510	.502	144	182	.791	20	126	146	561	141	0	85	145	16	656	8.7	23

– 417 –

	G	Min.	FGM	FGA	Pct.	FTM	FTA	Pct.	REBOUNDS Off.	Def.	Tot.	Ast.	PF	Dq.	Stl.	TO	Blk.	SCORING Pts.	Avg.	Hi.
Vinny Del Negro	73	1526	218	430	.507	101	117	.863	19	144	163	291	146	0	44	92	1	543	7.4	24
Willie Anderson	38	560	80	186	.430	22	28	.786	7	50	57	79	52	0	14	44	6	183	4.8	18
Sam Mack	40	267	47	118	.398	45	58	.776	18	30	48	15	44	0	14	22	5	142	3.6	11
Sidney Green*	15	202	20	49	.408	13	15	.867	18	53	71	19	21	1	5	12	3	53	3.5	9
Terry Cummings	8	76	11	29	.379	5	10	.500	6	13	19	4	17	0	1	2	1	27	3.4	7
David Wood	64	598	52	117	.444	46	55	.836	38	59	97	34	93	1	13	29	12	155	2.4	12
Matt Othick	4	39	3	5	.600	0	2	.000	1	1	2	7	7	0	1	4	0	8	2.0	6
William Bedford	16	66	9	27	.333	6	12	.500	1	9	10	0	15	0	0	1	1	25	1.6	6
Larry Smith	66	833	38	87	.437	9	22	.409	103	165	268	28	133	2	23	39	16	85	1.3	6

3-pt. FG: San Antonio 236-692 (.341)—Robinson 3-17 (.176); Elliott 37-104 (.356); Ellis 119-297 (.401); Carr 0-5 (.000); Reid† 0-4 (.000); Reid‡ 0-5 (.000); Daniels 59-177 (.333); Johnson 0-8 (.000); Del Negro 6-24 (.250); Anderson 1-8 (.125); Mack 3-22 (.136); Wood 5-21 (.238); Othick 2-4 (.500); Bedford 1-1 (1.000). Opponents 270-747 (.361).

SEATTLE SUPERSONICS

	G	Min.	FGM	FGA	Pct.	FTM	FTA	Pct.	REBOUNDS Off.	Def.	Tot.	Ast.	PF	Dq.	Stl.	TO	Blk.	SCORING Pts.	Avg.	Hi.
Ricky Pierce	77	2218	524	1071	.489	313	352	.889	58	134	192	220	167	0	100	160	7	1403	18.2	33
Shawn Kemp	78	2582	515	1047	.492	358	503	.712	287	546	833	155	327	13	119	217	146	1388	17.8	35
Eddie Johnson	82	1869	463	991	.467	234	257	.911	124	148	272	135	173	0	36	134	4	1177	14.4	29
Gary Payton	82	2548	476	963	.494	151	196	.770	95	186	281	399	250	1	177	148	21	1110	13.5	31
Derrick McKey	77	2439	387	780	.496	220	297	.741	121	206	327	197	208	5	105	152	58	1034	13.4	30
Sam Perkins†	30	762	139	272	.511	66	83	.795	52	93	145	28	86	0	20	32	31	344	11.5	21
Sam Perkins‡	79	2351	381	799	.477	250	305	.820	163	361	524	156	225	0	60	108	82	1036	13.1	26
Dana Barros	69	1243	214	474	.451	49	59	.831	18	89	107	151	78	0	63	58	3	541	7.8	26
Nate McMillan	73	1977	213	459	.464	95	134	.709	84	222	306	384	240	6	173	139	33	546	7.5	26
Benoit Benjamin*	31	448	81	163	.497	47	67	.701	27	86	113	12	73	0	17	42	35	209	6.7	18
Michael Cage	82	2156	219	416	.526	61	130	.469	268	391	659	69	183	0	76	59	46	499	6.1	15
Vincent Askew†	64	1053	144	292	.493	94	134	.701	55	95	150	117	124	2	38	61	18	384	6.0	16
Vincent Askew‡	73	1129	152	309	.492	105	149	.705	62	99	161	122	135	2	40	69	19	411	5.6	16
Gerald Paddio	41	307	71	159	.447	14	21	.667	17	33	50	33	24	0	14	16	6	158	3.9	12
Steve Scheffler	29	166	25	48	.521	16	24	.667	15	21	36	5	37	0	6	5	1	66	2.3	10
Rich King	3	12	2	5	.400	2	2	1.000	1	4	5	1	1	0	0	3	0	6	2.0	4

3-pt. FG: Seattle 218-610 (.357)—Pierce 42-113 (.372); Kemp 0-4 (.000); Johnson 17-56 (.304); Payton 7-34 (.206); McKey 40-112 (.357); Perkins† 19-42 (.452); Perkins‡ 24-71 (.338); Barros 64-169 (.379); McMillan 25-65 (.385); Cage 0-1 (.000); Askew† 2-6 (.333); Askew‡ 2-6 (.333); Paddio 2-8 (.250). Opponents 272-808 (.337).

UTAH JAZZ

	G	Min.	FGM	FGA	Pct.	FTM	FTA	Pct.	REBOUNDS Off.	Def.	Tot.	Ast.	PF	Dq.	Stl.	TO	Blk.	SCORING Pts.	Avg.	Hi.
Karl Malone	82	3099	797	1443	.552	619	836	.740	227	692	919	308	261	2	124	240	85	2217	27.0	42
Jeff Malone	79	2558	595	1205	.494	236	277	.852	31	142	173	128	117	0	42	125	4	1429	18.1	40
John Stockton	82	2863	437	899	.486	293	367	.798	64	173	237	987	224	2	199	266	21	1239	15.1	32
Tyrone Corbin	82	2555	385	766	.503	180	218	.826	194	325	519	173	252	3	108	108	32	950	11.6	24
Jay Humphries	78	2034	287	659	.436	101	130	.777	40	103	143	317	236	3	101	132	11	690	8.8	20
David Benoit	82	1712	258	592	.436	114	152	.750	116	276	392	43	201	2	45	90	43	664	8.1	23
Larry Krystkowiak	71	1362	198	425	.466	117	147	.796	74	205	279	68	181	1	42	62	13	513	7.2	21
Mike Brown	82	1551	176	409	.430	113	164	.689	147	244	391	64	190	1	32	95	23	465	5.7	17
James Donaldson	6	94	8	14	.571	5	9	.556	6	23	29	1	13	0	1	4	7	21	3.5	8
Henry James†	2	9	1	6	.167	5	6	.833	1	0	1	0	0	0	0	0	0	7	3.5	7
Henry James‡	10	88	21	51	.412	22	26	.846	7	4	11	1	9	0	3	7	0	67	6.7	20
Mark Eaton	64	1104	71	130	.546	35	50	.700	73	191	264	17	143	0	18	43	79	177	2.8	10
Isaac Austin	46	306	50	112	.446	29	44	.659	38	41	79	6	60	1	8	23	14	129	2.8	8
John Crotty	40	243	37	72	.514	26	38	.684	4	13	17	55	29	0	11	30	0	102	2.6	14
Stephen Howard	49	260	35	93	.376	34	53	.642	26	34	60	10	58	0	15	23	12	104	2.1	12
Tim Legler*	3	5	1	3	.333	0	0	...	0	1	1	0	0	0	0	0	0	2	0.7	2

3-pt. FG: Utah 130-414 (.314)—K. Malone 4-20 (.200); J. Malone 3-9 (.333); Stockton 72-187 (.385); Corbin 0-5 (.000); Humphries 15-75 (.200); Benoit 34-98 (.347); Krystkowiak 0-1 (.000); James† 0-3 (.000); James‡ 3-13 (.231); Brown 0-1 (.000); Austin 0-1 (.000); Crotty 2-14 (.143). Opponents 272-836 (.325).

WASHINGTON BULLETS

	G	Min.	FGM	FGA	Pct.	FTM	FTA	Pct.	REBOUNDS Off.	Def.	Tot.	Ast.	PF	Dq.	Stl.	TO	Blk.	SCORING Pts.	Avg.	Hi.
Harvey Grant	72	2667	560	1149	.487	218	300	.727	133	279	412	205	168	0	72	90	44	1339	18.6	41
Pervis Ellison	49	1701	341	655	.521	170	242	.702	138	295	433	117	154	3	45	110	108	852	17.4	28
Michael Adams	70	2499	365	831	.439	237	277	.856	52	188	240	526	146	0	100	175	4	1035	14.8	29
Tom Gugliotta	81	2795	484	1135	.426	181	281	.644	219	562	781	306	195	0	134	230	35	1187	14.7	39
Rex Chapman	60	1300	287	602	.477	132	163	.810	19	69	88	116	119	1	38	79	10	749	12.5	37
Larry Stewart	81	1823	306	564	.543	184	253	.727	154	229	383	146	191	1	47	153	29	796	9.8	32
LaBradford Smith	69	1546	261	570	.458	109	127	.858	26	80	106	186	178	2	58	103	9	639	9.3	37
Doug Overton	45	990	152	323	.471	59	81	.728	25	81	106	157	81	0	31	72	6	366	8.1	21
Steve Burtt	4	35	10	26	.385	8	10	.800	2	1	3	6	5	0	2	4	0	29	7.3	13
Don MacLean	62	674	157	361	.435	90	111	.811	33	89	122	39	82	0	11	42	4	407	6.6	24
Buck Johnson	73	1287	193	403	.479	78	117	.730	78	117	195	89	187	2	36	70	18	478	6.5	29
Byron Irvin	4	45	9	18	.500	3	6	.500	2	2	4	2	5	0	1	4	0	22	5.5	18
Mark Acres†	12	246	24	40	.600	10	14	.714	24	37	61	5	32	0	3	11	6	58	4.8	12
Mark Acres‡	18	269	26	49	.531	11	16	.688	26	41	67	5	34	0	3	13	6	64	3.6	12
Brent Price	68	859	100	279	.358	54	68	.794	28	75	103	154	90	0	56	85	3	262	3.9	22
Larry Robinson	4	33	6	16	.375	3	5	.600	1	2	3	0	0	1	1	1	1	15	3.8	9

	G	Min.	FGM	FGA	Pct.	FTM	FTA	Pct.	REBOUNDS Off.	Def.	Tot.	Ast.	PF	Dq.	Stl.	TO	Blk.	SCORING Pts.	Avg.	Hi.
Greg Foster*........	10	93	11	25	.440	2	3	.667	8	19	27	11	17	0	0	9	5	24	2.4	6
Chris Corchianit......	1	3	1	1	1.000	0	0	...	0	0	0	0	1	0	0	0	0	2	2.0	2
Chris Corchianit.....	10	105	14	24	.583	16	21	.762	1	6	7	16	18	0	6	8	0	44	4.4	12
Alan Oggt...........	3	3	2	4	.500	1	2	.500	2	2	4	0	0	0	0	0	0	5	1.7	2
Alan Ogg‡..........	6	29	5	13	.385	3	4	.750	3	7	10	4	6	0	1	3	3	13	2.2	4
Charles Jones.......	67	1206	33	63	.524	22	38	.579	87	190	277	42	144	1	38	38	77	88	1.3	8

3-pt. FG: Washington 174-578 (.301)—Grant 1-10 (.100); Ellison 0-4 (.000); Adams 68-212 (.321); Gugliotta 38-135 (.281); Chapman 43-116 (.371); Stewart 0-2 (.000); Smith 8-23 (.348); Overton 3-13 (.231); Burtt 1-3 (.333); MacLean 3-6 (.500); Johnson 0-3 (.000); Irvin 1-1 (1.000); Acres† 0-0; Acres‡ 1-2 (.500); Price 8-48 (.167); Robinson 0-1 (.000); Corchianit 0-0; Corchiani‡ 0-3 (.000); Jones 0-1 (.000). Opponents 239-712 (.336).

* Finished season with another team   † Totals with this team only.   ‡ Totals with all teams.

PLAYOFF RESULTS

EASTERN CONFERENCE
FIRST ROUND

New York 3, Indiana 1
Apr. 30—Fri.	Indiana 104 at New York	107
May 2—Sun.	Indiana 91 at New York	101
May 4—Tue.	New York 93 at Indiana	116
May 6—Thur.	New York 109 at Indiana	*100

Chicago 3, Atlanta 0
Apr. 30—Fri.	Atlanta 90 at Chicago	114
May 2—Sun.	Atlanta 102 at Chicago	117
May 4—Tue.	Chicago 98 at Atlanta	88

Cleveland 3, New Jersey 2
Apr. 29—Thur.	New Jersey 98 at Cleveland	114
May 1—Sat.	New Jersey 101 at Cleveland	99
May 5—Wed.	Cleveland 93 at New Jersey	84
May 7—Fri.	Cleveland 79 at New Jersey	96
May 9—Sun.	New Jersey 89 at Cleveland	99

Charlotte 3, Boston 1
Apr. 29—Thur.	Charlotte 101 at Boston	112
May 1—Sat.	Charlotte 99 at Boston	**98
May 3—Mon.	Boston 89 at Charlotte	119
May 5—Wed.	Boston 103 at Charlotte	104

SEMIFINALS

New York 4, Charlotte 1
May 9—Sun.	Charlotte 95 at New York	111
May 12—Wed.	Charlotte 101 at New York	*105
May 14—Fri.	New York 106 at Charlotte	**110
May 16—Sun.	New York 94 at Charlotte	92
May 18—Tue.	Charlotte 101 at New York	105

Chicago 4, Cleveland 0
May 11—Tue.	Cleveland 84 at Chicago	91
May 13—Thur.	Cleveland 85 at Chicago	104
May 15—Sat.	Chicago 96 at Cleveland	90
May 17—Mon.	Chicago 103 at Cleveland	101

FINALS

Chicago 4, New York 2
May 23—Sun.	Chicago 90 at New York	98
May 25—Tue.	Chicago 91 at New York	96
May 29—Sat.	New York 83 at Chicago	103
May 31—Mon.	New York 95 at Chicago	105
June 2—Wed.	Chicago 97 at New York	94
June 4—Fri.	New York 88 at Chicago	96

WESTERN CONFERENCE
FIRST ROUND

Phoenix 3, L.A. Lakers 2
Apr. 30—Fri.	L.A. Lakers 107 at Phoenix	103
May 2—Sun.	L.A. Lakers 86 at Phoenix	81
May 4—Tue.	Phoenix 107 at L.A. Lakers	102
May 6—Thur.	Phoenix 101 at L.A. Lakers	86
May 9—Sun.	L.A. Lakers 104 at Phoenix	*112

Houston 3, L.A. Clippers 2
Apr. 29—Thur.	L.A. Clippers 94 at Houston	117
May 1—Sat.	L.A. Clippers 95 at Houston	83
May 3—Mon.	Houston 111 at L.A. Clippers	99
May 5—Wed.	Houston 90 at L.A. Clippers	93
May 8—Sat.	L.A. Clippers 80 at Houston	84

Seattle 3, Utah 2
Apr. 30—Fri.	Utah 85 at Seattle	99
May 2—Sun.	Utah 89 at Seattle	85
May 4—Tue.	Seattle 80 at Utah	90
May 6—Thur.	Seattle 93 at Utah	80
May 8—Sat.	Utah 92 at Seattle	99

San Antonio 3, Portland 1
Apr. 29—Thur.	San Antonio 87 at Portland	86
May 1—Sat.	San Antonio 96 at Portland	105
May 5—Wed.	Portland 101 at San Antonio	107
May 7—Fri.	Portland 97 at San Antonio	*100

SEMIFINALS

Phoenix 4, San Antonio 2
May 11—Tue.	San Antonio 89 at Phoenix	98
May 13—Thur.	San Antonio 103 at Phoenix	109
May 15—Sat.	Phoenix 96 at San Antonio	111
May 16—Sun.	Phoenix 103 at San Antonio	117
May 18—Tue.	San Antonio 97 at Phoenix	109
May 20—Thur.	Phoenix 102 at San Antonio	100

Seattle 4, Houston 3
May 10—Mon.	Houston 90 at Seattle	99
May 12—Wed.	Houston 100 at Seattle	111
May 15—Sat.	Seattle 79 at Houston	97
May 16—Sun.	Seattle 92 at Houston	103
May 18—Tue.	Houston 95 at Seattle	120
May 20—Thur.	Seattle 90 at Houston	103
May 22—Sat.	Houston 100 at Seattle	*103

FINALS

Phoenix 4, Seattle 3
May 24—Mon.	Seattle 91 at Phoenix	105
May 26—Wed.	Seattle 103 at Phoenix	99
May 28—Fri.	Phoenix 104 at Seattle	97
May 30—Sun.	Phoenix 101 at Seattle	120
June 1—Tue.	Seattle 114 at Phoenix	120
June 3—Thur.	Phoenix 102 at Seattle	118
June 5—Sat.	Seattle 110 at Phoenix	123

NBA FINALS

Chicago 4, Phoenix 2
June 9—Wed.	Chicago 100 at Phoenix	92
June 11—Fri.	Chicago 111 at Phoenix	108
June 13—Sun.	Phoenix 129 at Chicago	***121
June 16—Wed.	Phoenix 105 at Chicago	111
June 18—Fri.	Phoenix 108 at Chicago	98
June 20—Sun.	Chicago 99 at Phoenix	98

*Denotes number of overtime periods.

1991-92

1991-92 NBA CHAMPION CHICAGO BULLS

Front row (from left): Bobby Hansen, Stacey King, Will Perdue, Cliff Levingston, Scott Williams, Craig Hodges. Center row (from left): B.J. Armstrong, Michael Jordan, Horace Grant, Bill Cartwright, Scottie Pippen, John Paxson. Back row (from left): assistant coach Tex Winter, assistant coach Jim Cleamons, head coach Phil Jackson, assistant coach John Bach.

FINAL STANDINGS

ATLANTIC DIVISION

	Atl.	Bos.	Char.	Chi.	Cle.	Dal.	Den.	Det.	G.S.	Hou.	Ind.	L.A.C.	L.A.L.	Mia.	Mil.	Min.	N.J.	N.Y.	Orl.	Phi.	Pho.	Por.	Sac.	S.A.	Sea.	Uta.	Was.	W	L	Pct.	GB
Boston	1	..	3	1	3	1	1	4	1	1	2	2	2	3	2	0	2	3	5	3	1	1	2	1	2	1	3	51	31	.622	..
New York	2	2	4	0	2	2	2	1	1	3	2	0	4	3	2	3	4	..	3	1	1	0	2	2	2	2	4	51	31	.622	..
New Jersey	1	3	3	0	2	2	1	2	0	1	2	1	0	2	4	2	..	2	3	3	1	1	1	0	0	0	2	40	42	.488	11
Miami	2	2	3	0	1	1	2	2	1	0	1	0	0	..	4	2	2	2	3	1	0	0	2	1	1	1	5	38	44	.463	13
Philadelphia	2	1	1	1	0	2	0	1	1	1	2	1	0	4	1	2	2	1	2	..	0	1	1	1	2	0	5	35	47	.427	16
Washington	2	1	2	0	0	2	1	1	0	0	2	2	1	0	1	2	3	0	3	0	0	0	0	2	0	0	..	25	57	.305	26
Orlando	2	0	1	1	1	1	0	0	0	0	2	0	0	1	1	2	1	1	..	3	0	0	0	1	1	0	2	21	61	.256	30

CENTRAL DIVISION

	Atl.	Bos.	Char.	Chi.	Cle.	Dal.	Den.	Det.	G.S.	Hou.	Ind.	L.A.C.	L.A.L.	Mia.	Mil.	Min.	N.J.	N.Y.	Orl.	Phi.	Pho.	Por.	Sac.	S.A.	Sea.	Uta.	Was.	W	L	Pct.	GB
Chicago	5	3	4	..	3	2	2	4	1	1	3	2	1	4	3	2	4	4	3	3	1	2	2	1	2	1	4	67	15	.817	..
Cleveland	5	1	3	2	..	1	1	3	1	1	5	1	2	3	3	2	2	4	3	4	1	0	2	1	1	1	4	57	25	.695	10
Detroit	4	0	4	1	1	2	2	..	1	2	2	0	2	2	3	1	2	2	4	3	0	2	2	1	1	1	3	48	34	.585	19
Indiana	4	2	2	1	0	1	2	2	0	1	..	0	2	3	4	2	2	1	2	2	1	0	1	2	0	1	2	40	42	.488	27
Atlanta	..	3	2	0	0	2	2	1	1	2	1	1	0	2	3	2	3	2	2	2	0	1	0	1	1	2		38	44	.463	29
Charlotte	2	1	..	0	2	1	1	1	1	0	3	0	1	1	2	1	1	0	3	3	1	0	1	2	1	0	2	31	51	.378	36
Milwaukee	1	2	3	2	1	1	1	2	0	1	1	0	1	0	..	2	0	1	3	3	0	0	0	1	1	1	3	31	51	.378	36

MIDWEST DIVISION

	Atl.	Bos.	Char.	Chi.	Cle.	Dal.	Den.	Det.	G.S.	Hou.	Ind.	L.A.C.	L.A.L.	Mia.	Mil.	Min.	N.J.	N.Y.	Orl.	Phi.	Pho.	Por.	Sac.	S.A.	Sea.	Uta.	Was.	W	L	Pct.	GB
Utah	1	1	2	1	1	4	5	1	3	4	1	3	3	1	1	3	2	0	2	2	2	2	3	4	1	..	2	55	27	.671	..
San Antonio	2	1	0	1	1	5	4	1	2	2	0	2	3	1	1	6	2	1	1	1	2	3	..	3	1	0	2	47	35	.573	8
Houston	0	1	2	1	1	2	3	0	2	..	1	2	2	2	1	3	1	1	2	1	1	3	3	3	1	1	2	42	40	.512	13
Denver	0	1	1	0	1	2	..	0	0	2	0	0	1	0	1	2	1	0	2	2	1	1	2	1	1	1	1	24	58	.293	31
Dallas	0	1	1	0	1	..	3	0	0	4	1	1	0	1	3	0	1	0	2	0	1	0	0	1	0	1	0	22	60	.268	33
Minnesota	0	2	1	0	0	2	3	1	0	2	0	1	0	0	..	0	0	0	0	0	1	0	0	2	0	1	2	15	67	.183	40

PACIFIC DIVISION

	Atl.	Bos.	Char.	Chi.	Cle.	Dal.	Den.	Det.	G.S.	Hou.	Ind.	L.A.C.	L.A.L.	Mia.	Mil.	Min.	N.J.	N.Y.	Orl.	Phi.	Pho.	Por.	Sac.	S.A.	Sea.	Uta.	Was.	W	L	Pct.	GB
Portland	2	1	2	0	2	4	3	0	3	1	2	3	4	2	2	4	1	1	2	1	2	..	5	2	4	2	2	57	25	.695	..
Golden State	1	1	1	1	1	4	4	1	..	2	2	3	3	1	2	4	2	1	2	1	3	2	5	2	3	1	2	55	27	.671	2
Phoenix	0	1	1	1	2	3	2	2	3	1	2	2	4	1	1	4	1	1	2	2	..	3	4	3	3	2	2	53	29	.646	4
Seattle	1	0	1	0	1	4	3	1	2	3	2	3	4	1	1	4	2	0	1	0	2	1	4	1	..	3	2	47	35	.573	10
L.A. Clippers	1	0	2	0	1	3	4	2	2	2	2	..	2	2	2	4	1	0	2	1	3	2	2	2	2	1	0	45	37	.549	12
L.A. Lakers	2	0	1	1	0	4	3	0	2	2	0	3	..	2	1	3	2	2	2	2	2	1	4	1	1	1	1	43	39	.524	14
Sacramento	1	0	1	0	0	3	2	0	0	1	1	3	1	0	2	3	1	1	2	1	1	0	..	1	1	1	2	29	53	.354	28

TEAM STATISTICS

OFFENSIVE

	G	FGM	FGA	Pct.	FTM	FTA	Pct.	Off.	Def.	Tot.	Ast.	PF	Dq.	Stl.	TO	Blk.	Pts.	Avg.
								REBOUNDS									SCORING	
Golden State	82	3767	7427	.507	1944	2606	.746	1137	2376	3513	2064	2049	24	854	1353	375	9732	118.7
Indiana	82	3498	7079	.494	1868	2364	.790	1083	2564	3647	2398	2137	25	705	1402	393	9197	112.2
Phoenix	82	3553	7219	.492	1861	2397	.776	1088	2558	3646	2202	1852	14	673	1242	582	9194	112.1
Portland	82	3476	7352	.473	1858	2463	.754	1294	2549	3843	2065	1983	25	753	1328	410	9135	111.4
Chicago	82	3643	7168	.508	1587	2132	.744	1173	2439	3612	2279	1693	4	672	1088	480	9011	109.9
Charlotte	82	3613	7568	.477	1637	2168	.755	1164	2367	3531	2284	1819	14	822	1273	309	8980	109.5
Cleveland	82	3427	7025	.488	1819	2259	.805	1041	2450	3491	2260	1556	8	616	1073	621	8926	108.9
Utah	82	3379	6866	.492	1961	2490	.788	1097	2543	3640	2188	1746	11	715	1264	448	8877	108.3
Boston	82	3543	7196	.492	1549	1917	.808	1095	2583	3678	2072	1686	14	636	1165	484	8745	106.6
Seattle	82	3380	7128	.474	1772	2263	.783	1282	2257	3539	1877	1952	22	775	1323	448	8737	106.5
Atlanta	82	3492	7476	.467	1517	2074	.731	1288	2498	3786	2123	1771	8	793	1255	320	8711	106.2
New Jersey	82	3473	7580	.458	1471	2009	.732	1512	2392	3904	1937	1834	19	736	1392	615	8641	105.4
Milwaukee	82	3321	7216	.460	1596	2104	.759	1297	2172	3469	2018	1904	25	863	1350	317	8609	105.0
Miami	82	3256	7061	.461	1839	2329	.790	1187	2366	3553	1749	1819	14	670	1377	373	8608	105.0
Sacramento	82	3348	7189	.466	1615	2162	.747	1054	2354	3408	1957	1763	10	727	1360	618	8549	104.3
San Antonio	82	3377	7090	.476	1652	2246	.736	1229	2552	3781	2010	1799	14	729	1308	608	8524	104.0
L.A. Clippers	82	3347	7076	.473	1601	2223	.720	1132	2393	3525	2053	1873	15	824	1269	498	8440	102.9
Washington	82	3364	7301	.461	1521	1956	.778	1069	2345	3414	2011	1852	12	713	1254	422	8395	102.4
Houston	82	3273	6894	.475	1491	2020	.738	1074	2432	3506	2058	1769	23	656	1378	571	8366	102.0
Philadelphia	82	3187	6761	.471	1757	2267	.775	1058	2309	3367	1755	1582	8	692	1238	482	8358	101.9
Orlando	82	3220	7102	.453	1693	2268	.746	1171	2329	3500	1792	1977	24	643	1389	367	8330	101.6
New York	82	3312	6947	.477	1503	2049	.734	1185	2489	3674	2130	1905	15	634	1242	382	8328	101.6
Minnesota	82	3366	7342	.458	1379	1857	.743	1167	2168	3335	2025	1866	13	619	1157	526	8237	100.5
L.A. Lakers	82	3183	6977	.456	1744	2278	.766	1156	2196	3352	1803	1543	6	756	1089	400	8229	100.4
Denver	82	3262	7380	.442	1526	2067	.738	1350	2352	3702	1553	1984	17	773	1447	461	8176	99.7
Detroit	82	3191	6867	.465	1566	2108	.743	1210	2421	3631	1899	1646	3	546	1212	357	8113	98.9
Dallas	82	3120	7104	.439	1499	1999	.750	1194	2439	3633	1630	1867	15	536	1202	349	8007	97.6

DEFENSIVE

	FGM	FGA	Pct.	FTM	FTA	Pct.	Off.	Def.	Tot.	Ast.	PF	Dq.	Stl.	TO	Blk.	Pts.	Avg.	Dif.
							REBOUNDS									SCORING		
Detroit	3157	6973	.453	1421	1866	.762	1115	2255	3370	1894	1916	21	642	1117	373	7946	96.9	+2.0
New York	3082	6727	.458	1666	2172	.767	1014	2241	3255	1778	1803	19	669	1249	396	8009	97.7	+3.9
Chicago	3206	6970	.460	1525	1985	.760	1001	2171	3252	1841	1800	15	631	1288	352	8155	99.5	+10.4
San Antonio	3211	7098	.452	1587	2061	.770	1103	2362	3465	1882	1810	14	753	1252	463	8252	100.6	+3.4
L.A. Lakers	3408	7095	.480	1329	1744	.762	1234	2384	3618	2173	1831	22	594	1256	389	8319	101.5	-1.1
Utah	3292	7178	.459	1535	2056	.747	1146	2255	3401	1925	1958	24	646	1205	458	8353	101.9	+6.4
L.A. Clippers	3211	6997	.459	1706	2249	.759	1151	2445	3596	1784	7870	21	705	1396	432	8352	101.9	+1.0
Boston	3323	7293	.456	1601	2084	.768	1178	2333	3511	1923	1634	11	680	1114	414	8448	103.0	+3.6
Philadelphia	3449	7145	.483	1375	1772	.776	1171	2365	3536	2226	1766	11	686	1184	454	8462	103.2	-1.3
Cleveland	3496	7435	.470	1294	1683	.769	1236	2376	3612	2156	1874	9	649	1150	417	8479	103.4	+5.5
Houston	3391	7317	.463	1529	1985	.770	1232	2406	3638	2131	1673	13	743	1174	384	8507	103.7	-1.7
Portland	3249	7150	.454	1797	2367	.759	1097	2336	3433	1980	1957	23	688	1369	433	8539	104.1	+7.3
Seattle	3263	6864	.475	1848	2460	.751	1122	2228	3350	1832	1850	14	697	1320	479	8583	104.7	+1.8
Dallas	3314	7051	.470	1823	2368	.770	1157	2631	3788	1936	1735	19	723	1054	456	8634	105.3	-7.7
Phoenix	3429	7477	.459	1669	2207	.756	1218	2345	3563	1909	1931	11	659	1258	493	8707	106.2	+5.9
Milwaukee	3445	6911	.498	1638	2195	.746	1170	2319	3489	2118	1780	9	730	1420	473	8749	106.7	-1.7
Washington	3431	7474	.478	1687	2240	.753	1197	2636	3833	1902	1689	10	710	1325	450	8761	106.8	-4.4
New Jersey	3422	7175	.477	1775	2318	.766	1215	2355	3570	1789	1722	10	806	1343	484	8780	107.1	-1.7
Minnesota	3453	7116	.485	1738	2337	.744	1311	2534	3845	2088	1675	7	660	1215	574	8815	107.5	-7.0
Denver	3346	6967	.480	1943	2513	.773	1109	2530	3639	1811	1787	11	780	1393	593	8821	107.6	-7.9
Atlanta	3523	7342	.480	1537	2006	.766	1160	2545	3705	2168	1732	13	711	1253	393	8834	107.7	-1.5
Orlando	3426	7045	.486	1830	2437	.751	1107	2445	3552	2095	1895	16	791	1271	534	8897	108.5	-6.9
Miami	3529	7157	.493	1685	2242	.752	1134	2415	3549	2070	1968	21	731	1316	447	8953	109.2	-4.2
Indiana	3425	7312	.468	1976	2627	.752	1241	2325	3566	2165	1984	21	816	1247	386	9042	110.3	+1.9
Sacramento	3557	7420	.479	1728	2297	.752	1311	2639	3950	2128	1816	14	816	1357	530	9046	110.3	-6.0
Charlotte	3717	7495	.496	1661	2241	.741	1253	2581	3834	2366	1750	8	621	1392	524	9300	113.4	-3.9
Golden State	3616	7507	.482	1923	2563	.750	1324	2436	3760	2122	2021	15	794	1512	435	9412	114.8	+3.9
Avgs.	3384	7163	.472	1660	2188	.759	1177	2403	3581	2007	1823	15	709	1275	452	8635	105.3	...

HOME/ROAD

	Home	Road	Total		Home	Road	Total
Atlanta	23-18	15-26	38-44	Milwaukee	25-16	6-35	31-51
Boston	34-7	17-24	51-31	Minnesota	9-32	6-35	15-67
Charlotte	22-19	9-32	31-51	New Jersey	25-16	15-26	40-42
Chicago	36-5	31-10	67-15	New York	30-11	21-20	51-31
Cleveland	35-6	22-19	57-25	Orlando	13-28	8-33	21-61
Dallas	15-26	7-34	22-60	Philadelphia	23-18	12-29	35-47
Denver	18-23	6-35	24-58	Phoenix	36-5	17-24	53-29
Detroit	25-16	23-18	48-34	Portland	33-8	24-17	57-25
Golden State	31-10	24-17	55-27	Sacramento	21-20	8-33	29-53
Houston	28-13	14-27	42-40	San Antonio	31-10	16-25	47-35
Indiana	26-15	14-27	40-42	Seattle	28-13	19-22	47-35
L.A. Clippers	29-12	16-25	45-37	Utah	37-4	18-23	55-27
L.A. Lakers	24-17	19-22	43-39	Washington	14-27	11-30	25-57
Miami	28-13	10-31	38-44	Totals	699-408	408-699	1107-1107

1991-92

POINTS

(minimum 70 games or 1,400 points)

	G	FGM	FTM	Pts.	Avg.
Michael Jordan, Chicago	.80	943	491	2404	30.1
Karl Malone, Utah	.81	798	673	2272	28.0
Chris Mullin, Golden State	.81	830	350	2074	25.6
Clyde Drexler, Portland	.76	694	401	1903	25.0
Patrick Ewing, New York	.82	796	377	1970	24.0
Tim Hardaway, Golden State	.81	734	298	1893	23.4
David Robinson, San Antonio	.68	592	393	1578	23.2
Charles Barkley, Philadelphia	.75	622	454	1730	23.1
Mitch Richmond, Sacramento	.80	685	330	1803	22.5
Glen Rice, Miami	.79	672	266	1765	22.3

REBOUNDS

(minimum 70 games or 800 rebounds)

	G	Off.	Def.	Tot.	Avg.
Dennis Rodman, Detroit	.82	523	1007	1530	18.7
Kevin Willis, Atlanta	.81	418	840	1258	15.5
Dikembe Mutombo, Denver	.71	316	554	870	12.3
David Robinson, San Antonio	.68	261	568	829	12.2
Hakeem Olajuwon, Houston	.70	246	599	845	12.1
Rony Seikaly, Miami	.79	307	627	934	11.8
Greg Anderson, Denver	.82	337	604	941	11.5
Patrick Ewing, New York	.82	228	693	921	11.2
Karl Malone, Utah	.81	225	684	909	11.2
Charles Barkley, Philadelphia	.75	271	559	830	11.1

FIELD GOALS

(minimum 300 made)

	FGM	FGA	Pct.
Buck Williams, Portland	.340	563	.604
Otis Thorpe, Houston	.558	943	.592
Horace Grant, Chicago	.457	790	.578
Brad Daugherty, Cleveland	.576	1010	.570
Michael Cage, Seattle	.307	542	.566
Charles Barkley, Philadelphia	.622	1126	.552
David Robinson, San Antonio	.592	1074	.551
Danny Manning, L.A. Clippers	.650	1199	.542
Larry Nance, Cleveland	.556	1032	.539
Pervis Ellison, Washington	.547	1014	.539
Dennis Rodman, Detroit	.342	635	.539

STEALS

(minimum 70 games or 125 steals)

	G	No.	Avg.
John Stockton, Utah	.82	244	2.98
Micheal Williams, Indiana	.79	233	2.95
Alvin Robertson, Milwaukee	.82	210	2.56
Mookie Blaylock, New Jersey	.72	170	2.36
David Robinson, San Antonio	.68	158	2.32
Michael Jordan, Chicago	.80	182	2.28
Chris Mullin, Golden State	.81	173	2.14
Muggsy Bogues, Charlotte	.82	170	2.07
Sedale Threatt, L.A. Lakers	.82	168	2.05
Mark Macon, Denver	.76	154	2.03

FREE THROWS

(minimum 125 made)

	FTM	FTA	Pct.
Mark Price, Cleveland	.270	285	.947
Larry Bird, Boston	.150	162	.926
Ricky Pierce, Seattle	.417	455	.916
Jeff Malone, Utah	.256	285	.898
Rolando Blackman, Dallas	.239	266	.898
Scott Skiles, Orlando	.248	277	.895
Jeff Hornacek, Phoenix	.279	315	.886
Kevin Gamble, Boston	.139	157	.885
Johnny Dawkins, Philadelphia	.164	186	.882
Ron Anderson, Philadelphia	.143	163	.877

BLOCKED SHOTS

(minimum 70 games or 100 blocked shots)

	G	No.	Avg.
David Robinson, San Antonio	.68	305	4.49
Hakeem Olajuwon, Houston	.70	304	4.34
Larry Nance, Cleveland	.81	243	3.00
Patrick Ewing, New York	.82	245	2.99
Dikembe Mutombo, Denver	.71	210	2.96
Manute Bol, Philadelphia	.71	210	2.96
Duane Causwell, Sacramento	.80	215	2.69
Pervis Ellison, Washington	.66	177	2.68
Mark Eaton, Utah	.81	205	2.53
Andrew Lang, Phoenix	.81	201	2.48

ASSISTS

(minimum 70 games or 400 assists)

	G	No.	Avg.
John Stockton, Utah	.82	1126	13.7
Kevin Johnson, Phoenix	.78	836	10.7
Tim Hardaway, Golden State	.81	807	10.0
Muggsy Bogues, Charlotte	.82	743	9.1
Rod Strickland, San Antonio	.57	491	8.6
Mark Jackson, New York	.81	694	8.6
Pooh Richardson, Minnesota	.82	685	8.4
Micheal Williams, Indiana	.79	647	8.2
Michael Adams, Washington	.78	594	7.6
Mark Price, Cleveland	.72	535	7.4

3-POINT FIELD GOALS

(minimum 50 made)

	FGA	FGM	Pct.
Dana Barros, Seattle	.186	83	.446
Drazen Petrovic, New Jersey	.277	123	.444
Jeff Hornacek, Phoenix	.189	83	.439
Mike Iuzzolino, Dallas	.136	59	.434
Dale Ellis, Milwaukee	.329	138	.419
Craig Ehlo, Cleveland	.167	69	.413
John Stockton, Utah	.204	83	.407
Larry Bird, Boston	.128	52	.406
Dell Curry, Charlotte	.183	74	.404
Hersey Hawkins, Philadelphia	.229	91	.397

INDIVIDUAL STATISTICS, TEAM BY TEAM

ATLANTA HAWKS

								REBOUNDS									SCORING		
	G	Min.	FGM	FGA	Pct.	FTM	FTA	Pct.	Off.	Def.	Tot.	Ast.	PF	Dq.	Stl.	TO	Blk.	Pts.	Avg.	Hi.
Dominique Wilkins	42	1601	424	914	.464	294	352	.835	103	192	295	158	77	0	52	122	24	1179	28.1	52
Kevin Willis	81	2962	591	1224	.483	292	363	.804	418	840	1258	173	223	0	72	197	54	1480	18.3	32
Stacey Augmon	82	2505	440	899	.489	213	320	.666	191	229	420	201	161	0	124	181	27	1094	13.3	32
Rumeal Robinson	81	2220	423	928	.456	175	275	.636	64	155	219	446	178	0	105	206	24	1055	13.0	31
Duane Ferrell	66	1598.	331	632	.524	166	218	.761	105	105	210	92	134	0	49	99	17	839	12.7	27
Paul Graham	78	1718	305	682	.447	126	170	.741	72	159	231	175	193	3	96	91	21	791	10.1	24
Blair Rasmussen	81	1968	347	726	.478	30	40	.750	94	299	393	107	233	1	35	51	48	729	9.0	18
Alexander Volkov	77	1516	251	569	.441	125	198	.631	103	162	265	250	178	2	66	102	30	662	8.6	25
Travis Mays	2	32	6	14	.429	2	2	1.000	1	1	2	1	4	0	0	3	0	17	8.5	15
Maurice Cheeks	56	1086	115	249	.462	26	43	.605	29	66	95	185	73	0	83	36	0	259	4.6	11
Morlon Wiley†	41	767	71	160	.444	21	30	.700	22	51	73	166	73	0	43	52	3	177	4.3	12

	G	Min.	FGM	FGA	Pct.	FTM	FTA	Pct.	REBOUNDS Off.	Def.	Tot.	Ast.	PF	Dq.	Stl.	TO	Blk.	SCORING Pts.	Avg.	Hi.
Morlon Wiley‡	53	870	83	193	.430	24	35	.686	24	57	81	180	89	0	47	60	3	204	3.8	12
Jeff Sanders	12	117	20	45	.444	7	9	.778	9	17	26	9	15	0	5	5	3	47	3.9	9
Rodney Monroe	38	313	53	144	.368	19	23	.826	12	21	33	27	19	0	12	23	2	131	3.4	13
Jon Koncak	77	1489	111	284	.391	19	29	.655	62	199	261	132	207	2	50	54	67	241	3.1	11
Gary Leonard	5	13	4	6	.667	2	2	1.000	3	2	5	1	3	0	1	1	0	10	2.0	4

3-pt. FG: Atlanta 210-671 (.313)—Wilkins 37-128 (.289); Willis 6-37 (.162); Augmon 1-6 (.167); Robinson 34-104 (.327); Ferrell 11-33 (.333); Graham 55-141 (.390); Rasmussen 5-23 (.217); Volkov 35-110 (.318); Mays 3-6 (.500); Cheeks 3-6 (.500); Wiley† 14-38 (.368); Wiley‡ 14-42 (.333); Monroe 6-27 (.222); Koncak 0-12 (.000). Opponents 251-732 (.343).

BOSTON CELTICS

	G	Min.	FGM	FGA	Pct.	FTM	FTA	Pct.	REBOUNDS Off.	Def.	Tot.	Ast.	PF	Dq.	Stl.	TO	Blk.	SCORING Pts.	Avg.	Hi.
Reggie Lewis	82	3070	703	1397	.503	292	343	.851	117	277	394	185	258	4	125	136	105	1703	20.8	38
Larry Bird	45	1662	353	758	.466	150	162	.926	46	388	434	306	82	0	42	125	33	908	20.2	49
Robert Parish	79	2285	468	874	.535	179	232	.772	219	486	705	70	172	2	68	131	97	1115	14.1	31
Kevin McHale	56	1398	323	634	.509	134	163	.822	119	211	330	82	112	1	11	82	59	780	13.9	26
Kevin Gamble	82	2496	480	908	.529	139	157	.885	80	206	286	219	200	2	75	97	37	1108	13.5	34
Dee Brown	31	883	149	350	.426	60	78	.769	15	64	79	164	74	0	33	59	7	363	11.7	23
Brian Shaw*	17	436	70	164	.427	35	40	.875	11	58	69	89	29	0	12	32	10	175	10.3	24
Rick Fox	81	1535	241	525	.459	139	184	.755	73	147	220	126	230	3	78	123	30	644	8.0	31
Ed Pinckney	81	1917	203	378	.537	207	255	.812	252	312	564	62	158	1	70	73	56	613	7.6	17
Sherman Douglas†	37	654	101	222	.455	68	100	.680	12	45	57	153	68	0	21	60	9	271	7.3	20
Sherman Douglas‡	42	752	117	253	.462	73	107	.682	13	50	63	172	78	0	25	68	9	308	7.3	20
John Bagley	73	1742	223	506	.441	68	95	.716	38	123	161	480	123	1	57	148	4	524	7.2	18
Joe Kleine	70	991	144	293	.491	34	48	.708	94	202	296	32	99	0	23	27	14	326	4.7	15
Kevin Pritchard	11	136	16	34	.471	14	18	.778	1	10	11	30	17	0	3	11	4	46	4.2	10
Rickey Green	26	367	46	103	.447	13	18	.722	3	21	24	68	28	0	17	18	1	106	4.1	10
Larry Robinson	1	6	1	5	.200	0	0	...	2	0	2	1	3	0	0	1	0	2	2.0	2
Stojko Vrankovic	19	110	15	32	.469	7	12	.583	8	20	28	5	22	0	0	10	17	37	1.9	5
Kenny Battle*	8	46	3	4	.750	8	8	1.000	3	6	9	4	0	1	2	0	14	1.8	10
Tony Massenburg*	7	46	4	9	.444	2	4	.500	2	7	9	0	7	0	0	2	1	10	1.4	5

3-pt. FG: Boston 110-359 (.306)—Lewis 5-21 (.238); Bird 52-128 (.406); McHale 0-13 (.000); Gamble 9-31 (.290); Brown 5-22 (.227); Shaw* 0-7 (.000); Fox 23-70 (.329); Pinckney 0-1 (.000); Douglas† 1-9 (.111); Douglas‡ 1-10 (.100); Bagley 10-42 (.238); Kleine 4-8 (.500); Pritchard 0-3 (.000); Green 1-4 (.250). Opponents 201-652 (.308).

CHARLOTTE HORNETS

	G	Min.	FGM	FGA	Pct.	FTM	FTA	Pct.	REBOUNDS Off.	Def.	Tot.	Ast	PF	Dq.	Stl.	TO	Blk.	SCORING Pts.	Avg.	Hi.
Kendall Gill	79	2906	666	1427	.467	284	381	.745	165	237	402	329	237	1	154	180	46	1622	20.5	32
Larry Johnson	82	3047	616	1258	.490	339	409	.829	323	576	899	292	225	3	81	160	51	1576	19.2	34
Dell Curry	77	2020	504	1038	.486	127	152	.836	57	202	259	177	156	1	93	134	20	1209	15.7	29
Johnny Newman	55	1651	295	618	.477	236	308	.766	71	108	179	146	181	4	70	129	14	839	15.3	41
Kenny Gattison	82	2223	420	799	.529	196	285	.688	177	403	580	131	273	4	59	140	69	1042	12.7	24
Rex Chapman*	21	545	108	240	.450	36	53	.679	9	45	54	86	47	0	14	42	8	260	12.4	27
J.R. Reid	51	1257	213	435	.490	134	190	.705	96	221	317	81	159	0	49	84	23	560	11.0	23
Muggsy Bogues	82	2790	317	671	.472	94	120	.783	58	177	235	743	156	0	170	156	6	730	8.9	22
Anthony Frederick	66	852	161	370	.435	63	92	.685	75	69	144	71	91	0	40	58	26	389	5.9	21
Mike Gminski	35	499	90	199	.452	21	28	.750	37	81	118	31	37	0	11	20	16	202	5.8	22
Kevin Lynch	55	819	93	223	.417	35	46	.761	30	55	85	83	107	0	37	44	9	224	4.1	12
Eric Leckner	59	716	79	154	.513	38	51	.745	49	157	206	31	114	1	9	39	18	196	3.3	11
Ronnie Grandison	3	25	2	4	.500	6	10	.600	3	8	11	1	4	0	1	3	1	10	3.3	7
Michael Ansley†	2	13	3	7	.429	0	0	...	0	2	2	0	1	0	0	0	0	6	3.0	6
Michael Ansley‡	10	45	8	18	.444	5	6	.833	2	4	6	2	7	0	0	3	0	21	2.1	9
Elliot Perry†	40	371	43	114	.377	26	39	.667	12	20	32	64	26	0	25	37	2	113	2.8	12
Elliot Perry‡	50	437	49	129	.380	27	41	.659	14	25	39	78	36	0	34	50	3	126	2.5	12
Tony Massenburg*	3	13	0	3	.000	1	2	.500	1	3	4	0	2	0	1	4	0	1	0.3	1
Greg Grant*	13	57	0	8	.000	1	2	.500	1	3	4	18	3	0	8	5	0	1	0.1	1
Cedric Hunter	1	0	0	0	...	0	0	...	0	0	0	0	0	0	0	0	0	0	0.0	0

3-pt. FG: Charlotte 117-369 (.317)—Gill 6-25 (.240); Johnson 5-22 (.227); Curry 74-183 (.404); Newman 13-46 (.283); Gattison 0-2 (.000); Chapman* 8-27 (.296); Reid 0-3 (.000); Bogues 2-27 (.074); Frederick 4-17 (.235); Gminski 1-3 (.333); Lynch 3-8 (.375); Leckner 0-1 (.000); Perry† 1-5 (.200); Perry‡ 1-7 (.143). Opponents 205-632 (.324).

CHICAGO BULLS

	G	Min.	FGM	FGA	Pct.	FTM	FTA	Pct.	REBOUNDS Off.	Def.	Tot.	Ast.	PF	Dq.	Stl.	TO	Blk.	SCORING Pts.	Avg.	Hi.
Michael Jordan	80	3102	943	1818	.519	491	590	.832	91	420	511	489	201	1	182	200	75	2404	30.1	51
Scottie Pippen	82	3164	687	1359	.506	330	434	.760	185	445	630	572	242	2	155	253	93	1720	21.0	41
Horace Grant	81	2859	457	790	.578	235	317	.741	344	463	807	217	196	0	100	98	131	1149	14.2	28
B.J. Armstrong	82	1875	335	697	.481	104	129	.806	19	126	145	266	88	0	46	94	5	809	9.9	22
Bill Cartwright	64	1471	208	445	.467	96	159	.604	93	231	324	87	131	0	22	75	14	512	8.0	17
John Paxson	79	1946	257	487	.528	29	37	.784	21	75	96	241	142	0	49	44	9	555	7.0	16
Stacey King	79	1268	215	425	.506	119	158	.753	87	118	205	77	129	0	21	76	25	551	7.0	23
Will Perdue	77	1007	152	278	.547	45	91	.495	108	204	312	80	133	1	16	72	43	350	4.5	16
Craig Hodges	56	555	93	242	.384	16	17	.941	7	17	24	54	33	0	14	22	1	238	4.3	21
Cliff Levingston	79	1020	125	251	.498	60	96	.625	109	118	227	66	134	0	27	42	45	311	3.9	15
Scott Williams	63	690	83	172	.483	48	74	.649	90	157	247	50	122	0	13	35	36	214	3.4	12
Bobby Hansen†	66	769	75	169	.444	8	22	.364	15	58	73	68	128	0	26	28	3	165	2.5	13
Bobby Hansen‡	68	809	79	178	.444	8	22	.364	17	60	77	69	134	0	27	28	3	173	2.5	13
Mark Randall*	15	67	10	22	.455	6	8	.750	4	5	9	7	8	0	0	6	0	26	1.7	8

	G	Min.	FGM	FGA	Pct.	FTM	FTA	Pct.	Off.	Def.	Tot.	Ast.	PF	Dq.	Stl.	TO	Blk.	Pts.	Avg.	Hi.
Dennis Hopson*	2	10	1	2	.500	0	0	...	0	0	0	0	2	0	1	0	0	2	1.0	2
Rory Sparrow*	4	18	1	8	.125	0	0	...	0	1	1	4	2	0	2	0	3	0.8	3
Chuck Nevitt	4	9	1	3	.333	0	0	...	0	1	1	1	2	0	0	3	0	2	0.5	2

3-pt. FG: Chicago 138-454 (.304)—Jordan 27-100 (.270); Pippen 16-80 (.200); Grant 0-2 (.000); Armstrong 35-87 (.402); Paxson 12-44 (.273); King 2-5 (.400); Perdue 1-2 (.500); Hodges 36-96 (.375); Levingston 1-6 (.167); Williams 0-3 (.000); Hansen† 7-25 (.280); Hansen‡ 7-27 (.259); Randall* 0-2 (.000); Sparrow* 1-2 (.500). Opponents 218-657 (.332).

CLEVELAND CAVALIERS

	G	Min.	FGM	FGA	Pct.	FTM	FTA	Pct.	Off.	Def.	Tot.	Ast.	PF	Dq.	Stl.	TO	Blk.	Pts.	Avg.	Hi.
Brad Daugherty	73	2643	576	1010	.570	414	533	.777	191	569	760	262	190	1	65	185	78	1566	21.5	32
Mark Price	72	2138	438	897	.488	270	285	.947	38	135	173	535	113	0	94	159	12	1247	17.3	30
Larry Nance	81	2880	556	1032	.539	263	320	.822	213	457	670	232	200	2	80	87	243	1375	17.0	35
Craig Ehlo	63	2016	310	684	.453	87	123	.707	94	213	307	238	150	0	78	104	22	776	12.3	29
John Williams	80	2432	341	678	.503	270	359	.752	228	379	607	196	191	2	60	83	182	952	11.9	30
John Battle	76	1637	316	659	.480	145	171	.848	19	93	112	159	116	0	36	91	5	779	10.3	21
Mike Sanders†	21	552	81	139	.583	31	41	.756	27	61	88	42	75	1	22	16	9	194	9.2	23
Mike Sanders‡	31	633	92	161	.571	36	47	.766	27	69	96	53	83	1	24	22	10	221	7.1	23
Terrell Brandon	82	1605	252	601	.419	100	124	.806	49	113	162	316	107	0	81	136	22	605	7.4	19
Steve Kerr	48	847	121	237	.511	45	54	.833	14	64	78	110	29	0	27	31	10	319	6.6	24
Henry James	65	866	164	403	.407	61	76	.803	35	77	112	25	94	1	16	43	11	418	6.4	19
Danny Ferry	68	937	134	328	.409	61	73	.836	53	160	213	75	135	0	22	46	15	346	5.1	15
Winston Bennett*	52	831	79	209	.378	35	50	.700	62	99	161	38	121	1	19	33	9	193	3.7	11
Jimmy Oliver	27	252	39	98	.398	17	22	.773	9	18	27	20	22	0	9	9	2	96	3.6	11
John Morton*	4	54	3	12	.250	8	9	.889	3	4	7	5	3	0	1	4	0	14	3.5	7
Bobby Phills	10	65	12	28	.429	7	11	.636	4	4	8	4	3	0	3	8	1	31	3.1	11
Chucky Brown*	6	50	5	10	.500	5	8	.625	2	4	6	3	7	0	3	2	0	15	2.5	5

3-pt. FG: Cleveland 253-708 (.357)—Daugherty 0-2 (.000); Price 101-261 (.387); Nance 0-6 (.000); Ehlo 69-167 (.413); Williams 0-4 (.000); Battle 2-17 (.118); Brandon 1-23 (.043); Sanders† 1-3 (.333); Sanders‡ 1-3 (.333); Kerr 32-74 (.432); James 29-90 (.322); Ferry 17-48 (.354); Bennett* 0-1 (.000); Oliver 1-9 (.111); Morton* 0-1 (.000); Phills 0-2 (.000). Opponents 193-581 (.332).

DALLAS MAVERICKS

	G	Min.	FGM	FGA	Pct.	FTM	FTA	Pct.	Off.	Def.	Tot.	Ast.	PF	Dq.	Stl.	TO	Blk.	Pts.	Avg.	Hi.
Rolando Blackman	75	2527	535	1161	.461	239	266	.898	78	161	239	204	134	0	50	153	22	1374	18.3	31
Derek Harper	65	2252	448	1011	.443	198	261	.759	49	121	170	373	150	0	101	154	17	1152	17.7	38
Herb Williams	75	2040	367	851	.431	124	171	.725	106	348	454	94	189	2	35	114	98	859	11.5	26
Fat Lever	31	884	135	349	.387	60	80	.750	56	105	161	107	73	0	46	36	12	347	11.2	32
Terry Davis	68	2149	256	531	.482	181	285	.635	228	444	672	57	202	1	26	117	29	693	10.2	24
Mike Iuzzolino	52	1280	160	355	.451	107	128	.836	27	71	98	194	79	0	33	92	1	486	9.3	23
Rodney McCray	75	2106	271	622	.436	110	153	.719	149	319	468	219	180	2	48	115	30	677	9.0	24
Doug Smith	76	1707	291	702	.415	89	121	.736	129	262	391	129	259	5	62	97	34	671	8.8	25
Tracy Moore	42	782	130	325	.400	65	78	.833	31	51	82	48	97	0	32	44	4	355	8.5	19
Donald Hodge	51	1058	163	328	.497	100	150	.667	118	157	275	39	128	2	25	75	23	426	8.4	24
Randy White	65	1021	145	382	.380	124	162	.765	96	140	236	31	157	1	31	68	22	418	6.4	20
James Donaldson*	44	994	107	227	.471	59	84	.702	97	173	270	31	86	0	8	41	44	273	6.2	15
Brian Howard	27	318	54	104	.519	22	31	.710	17	34	51	14	55	2	11	15	8	131	4.9	14
Brad Davis	33	429	38	86	.442	11	15	.733	4	29	33	66	57	0	11	27	3	92	2.8	8
Brian Quinnett†	15	136	15	51	.294	8	12	.667	7	20	27	5	11	0	9	8	2	41	2.7	8
Brian Quinnett‡	39	326	43	124	.347	16	26	.615	16	35	51	12	32	0	16	16	8	115	2.9	14
Joao Vianna	1	9	1	2	.500	0	0	...	0	0	0	2	3	0	0	1	0	2	2.0	2
Tom Garrick†	6	63	4	17	.235	2	2	1.000	2	4	6	17	7	0	8	4	0	10	1.7	4
Tom Garrick‡	40	549	59	143	.413	18	26	.692	12	44	56	98	54	0	36	44	4	137	3.4	13

3-pt. FG: Dallas 268-797 (.336)—Blackman 65-169 (.385); Harper 58-186 (.312); Williams 1-6 (.167); Lever 17-52 (.327); T. Davis 0-5 (.000); Iuzzolino 59-136 (.434); McCray 25-85 (.294); Smith 0-11 (.000); Moore 30-84 (.357); White 4-27 (.148); Howard 1-2 (.500); Garrick† 0-1 (.000); Garrick‡ 1-4 (.250); B. Davis 5-18 (.278); Quinnett† 3-15 (.200); Quinnett‡ 13-41 (.317). Opponents 183-599 (.306).

DENVER NUGGETS

	G	Min.	FGM	FGA	Pct.	FTM	FTA	Pct.	Off.	Def.	Tot.	Ast.	PF	Dq.	Stl.	TO	Blk.	Pts.	Avg.	Hi.
Reggie Williams	81	2623	601	1277	.471	216	269	.803	145	260	405	235	270	4	148	173	68	1474	18.2	32
Dikembe Mutombo	71	2716	428	869	.493	321	500	.642	316	554	870	156	273	1	43	252	210	1177	16.6	39
Greg Anderson	82	2793	389	854	.456	167	268	.623	337	604	941	78	263	3	88	201	65	945	11.5	30
Winston Garland	78	2209	333	750	.444	171	199	.859	67	123	190	411	206	1	98	175	22	846	10.8	26
Mark Macon	76	2304	333	889	.375	135	185	.730	80	140	220	168	242	4	154	155	14	805	10.6	23
Mahmoud Abdul-Rauf	81	1538	356	845	.421	94	108	.870	22	92	114	192	130	0	44	117	4	837	10.3	29
Walter Davis	46	741	185	403	.459	82	94	.872	20	50	70	68	69	0	29	45	1	457	9.9	24
Marcus Liberty	75	1527	275	621	.443	131	180	.728	144	164	308	58	165	3	66	90	29	698	9.3	25
Todd Lichti	68	1176	173	376	.460	99	118	.839	36	82	118	74	131	0	43	72	12	446	6.6	17
Joe Wolf	67	1160	100	277	.361	53	66	.803	97	143	240	61	124	1	32	60	14	254	3.8	15
Jerome Lane*	9	141	10	40	.250	8	19	.421	22	22	44	13	18	0	2	10	1	28	3.1	10
Kevin Brooks	37	270	43	97	.443	17	21	.810	13	26	39	11	19	0	8	18	2	105	2.8	13
Steve Scheffler†	7	46	4	7	.571	4	6	.667	8	3	11	0	8	0	3	1	0	12	1.7	6
Steve Scheffler‡	11	61	6	9	.667	9	12	.750	10	4	14	0	10	0	3	1	1	21	1.9	7
Scott Hastings	40	421	17	50	.340	24	28	.857	30	68	98	26	56	0	10	22	15	58	1.5	10
Anthony Cook	22	115	15	25	.600	4	6	.667	13	21	34	2	10	0	5	3	4	34	1.5	7

3-pt. FG: Denver 126-418 (.301)—Williams 56-156 (.359); Anderson 0-4 (.000); Garland 9-28 (.321); Macon 4-30 (.133); Abdul-Rauf 31-94 (.330); Davis 5-16 (.313); Liberty 17-50 (.340); Lichti 1-9 (.111); Wolf 1-11 (.091); Brooks 2-11 (.182); Hastings 0-9 (.000). Opponents 186-532 (.350).

DETROIT PISTONS

	G	Min.	FGM	FGA	Pct.	FTM	FTA	Pct.	Off.	Def.	Tot.	Ast.	PF	Dq.	Stl.	TO	Blk.	Pts.	Avg.	Hi.
									REBOUNDS									SCORING		
Joe Dumars	82	3192	587	1311	.448	412	475	.867	82	106	188	375	145	0	71	193	12	1635	19.9	45
Isiah Thomas	78	2918	564	1264	.446	292	378	.772	68	179	247	560	194	2	118	252	15	1445	18.5	44
Orlando Woolridge . . .	82	2113	452	907	.498	241	353	.683	109	151	260	88	154	0	41	133	33	1146	14.0	34
Mark Aguirre.	75	1582	339	787	.431	158	230	.687	67	169	236	126	171	0	51	105	11	851	11.3	27
Dennis Rodman	82	3301	342	635	.539	84	140	.600	523	1007	1530	191	248	0	68	140	70	800	9.8	20
Bill Laimbeer.	81	2234	342	727	.470	67	75	.893	104	347	451	160	225	0	51	102	54	783	9.7	26
John Salley	72	1774	249	486	.512	186	260	.715	106	190	296	116	222	1	49	102	110	684	9.5	23
Darrell Walker.	74	1541	161	381	.423	65	105	.619	85	153	238	205	134	0	63	79	18	387	5.2	19
William Bedford	32	363	50	121	.413	14	22	.636	24	39	63	12	56	0	6	15	18	114	3.6	11
Gerald Henderson†	8	62	8	21	.381	5	5	1.000	0	6	6	5	8	0	3	4	0	24	3.0	8
Gerald Henderson‡ . . .	16	96	12	32	.375	9	11	.818	1	7	8	10	12	0	3	8	0	36	2.3	8
Brad Sellers	43	226	41	88	.466	20	26	.769	15	27	42	14	20	0	1	15	10	102	2.4	13
Lance Blanks	43	189	25	55	.455	8	11	.727	9	13	22	19	26	0	14	14	1	64	1.5	12
Charles Thomas	37	156	18	51	.353	10	15	.667	6	16	22	22	20	0	4	17	1	48	1.3	11
Bob McCann	26	129	13	33	.394	4	13	.308	12	18	30	6	23	0	6	7	4	30	1.2	10

3-pt. FG: Detroit 165-526 (.314)—Dumars 49-120 (.408); I. Thomas 25-86 (.291); Woolridge 1-9 (.111); Aguirre 15-71 (.211); Rodman 32-101 (.317); Laimbeer 32-85 (.376); Salley 0-3 (.000); Walker 0-10 (.000); Bedford 0-1 (.000); Henderson† 3-5 (.600); Henderson‡ 3-8 (.375); Sellers 0-1 (.000); Blanks 6-16 (.375); C. Thomas 2-17 (.118); McCann 0-1 (.000). Opponents 211-625 (.338).

GOLDEN STATE WARRIORS

	G	Min.	FGM	FGA	Pct.	FTM	FTA	Pct.	Off.	Def.	Tot.	Ast.	PF	Dq.	Stl.	TO	Blk.	Pts.	Avg.	Hi.
									REBOUNDS									SCORING		
Chris Mullin	81	3346	830	1584	.524	350	420	.833	127	323	450	286	171	1	173	202	62	2074	25.6	40
Tim Hardaway	81	3332	734	1592	.461	298	389	.766	81	229	310	807	208	1	164	267	13	1893	23.4	43
Sarunas Marciulionis .	72	2117	491	912	.538	376	477	.788	68	140	208	243	237	4	116	193	10	1361	18.9	35
Billy Owens.	80	2510	468	891	.525	204	312	.654	243	396	639	188	276	4	90	179	65	1141	14.3	30
Rod Higgins	25	535	87	211	.412	48	59	.814	30	55	85	22	75	2	15	15	13	255	10.2	23
Tyrone Hill	82	1886	254	487	.522	163	235	.694	182	411	593	47	315	7	73	106	43	671	8.2	20
Mario Elie	79	1677	221	424	.521	155	182	.852	69	158	227	174	159	3	68	83	15	620	7.8	27
Victor Alexander	80	1350	243	459	.529	103	149	.691	106	230	336	32	176	0	45	91	62	589	7.4	28
Vincent Askew	80	1496	193	379	.509	111	160	.694	89	144	233	188	128	1	47	84	23	498	6.2	16
Chris Gatling	54	612	117	206	.568	72	109	.661	75	107	182	16	101	0	31	44	36	306	5.7	18
Jaren Jackson	5	54	11	23	.478	4	6	.667	5	5	10	3	7	1	2	4	0	26	5.2	11
Alton Lister	26	293	44	79	.557	14	33	.424	21	71	92	14	61	0	5	20	16	102	3.9	15
Tom Tolbert	35	310	33	86	.384	22	40	.550	14	41	55	21	73	0	10	20	6	90	2.6	9
Kenny Battle†	8	46	8	13	.615	2	4	.500	1	6	7	4	6	0	1	2	2	18	2.3	6
Kenny Battle‡	16	92	11	17	.647	10	12	.833	4	12	16	4	10	0	2	4	2	32	2.0	10
Tony Massenburg†	7	22	5	8	.625	6	9	.667	4	8	12	0	10	0	0	3	0	16	2.3	6
Tony Massenburg‡ . .	18	90	10	25	.400	9	15	.600	7	18	25	0	21	0	1	9	1	29	1.6	9
Jud Buechler†	15	121	10	33	.303	9	12	.750	10	18	28	10	11	0	9	7	3	29	1.9	7
Jud Buechler‡	28	290	29	71	.408	12	21	.571	18	34	52	23	31	0	19	13	7	70	2.5	8
Jim Petersen.	27	169	18	40	.450	7	10	.700	12	33	45	9	35	0	5	5	6	43	1.6	11
Mike Smrek	2	3	0	0	. . .	0	0	. . .	0	1	1	0	0	0	0	0	0	0	0.0	0
Billy Thompson.	1	1	0	0	. . .	0	0	. . .	0	0	0	0	0	0	0	0	0	0	0.0	0

3-pt. FG: Golden State 254-763 (.333)—Mullin 64-175 (.366); Hardaway 127-376 (.338); Marciulionis 3-10 (.300); Owens 1-9 (.111); Higgins 33-95 (.347); Hill 0-1 (.000); Elie 23-70 (.329); Alexander 0-1 (.000); Askew 1-10 (.100); Gatling 0-4 (.000); Tolbert 2-8 (.250); Buechler† 0-1 (.000); Buechler‡ 0-1 (.000); Battle† 0-1 (.000); Battle‡ 0-1 (.000); Petersen 0-2 (.000). Opponents 257-776 (.331).

HOUSTON ROCKETS

	G	Min.	FGM	FGA	Pct.	FTM	FTA	Pct.	Off.	Def.	Tot.	Ast.	PF	Dq.	Stl.	TO	Blk.	Pts.	Avg.	Hi.
									REBOUNDS									SCORING		
Hakeem Olajuwon	70	2636	591	1177	.502	328	428	.766	246	599	845	157	263	7	127	187	304	1510	21.6	40
Otis Thorpe.	82	3056	558	943	.592	304	463	.657	285	577	862	250	307	7	52	237	37	1420	17.3	33
Vernon Maxwell	80	2700	502	1216	.413	206	267	.772	37	206	243	326	200	3	104	178	28	1372	17.2	35
Kenny Smith.	81	2735	432	910	.475	219	253	.866	34	143	177	562	112	0	104	227	7	1137	14.0	35
Sleepy Floyd	82	1662	286	704	.406	135	170	.794	34	116	150	239	128	0	57	128	21	744	9.1	31
Buck Johnson.	80	2202	290	633	.458	104	143	.727	95	217	312	158	234	2	72	104	49	685	8.6	20
Matt Bullard	80	1278	205	447	.459	38	50	.760	73	150	223	75	129	1	26	56	21	512	6.4	20
Avery Johnson†	49	772	103	222	.464	42	69	.609	8	37	45	166	46	0	40	65	6	251	5.1	22
Avery Johnson‡	69	1235	158	330	.479	66	101	.653	13	67	80	266	89	1	61	110	9	386	5.6	22
Carl Herrera	43	566	83	161	.516	25	44	.568	33	66	99	27	60	0	16	37	25	191	4.4	14
Dave Jamerson	48	378	79	191	.414	25	27	.926	22	21	43	33	39	0	17	24	0	191	4.0	16
John Turner	42	345	43	98	.439	31	59	.525	38	40	78	12	40	0	6	32	4	117	2.8	15
Larry Smith	45	800	50	92	.543	4	11	.364	107	149	256	33	121	3	21	44	7	104	2.3	15
Tree Rollins.	59	697	46	86	.535	26	30	.867	61	110	171	15	85	0	14	18	62	118	2.0	13
Gerald Henderson* . .	8	34	4	11	.364	4	6	.667	1	1	2	5	4	0	4	0	0	12	1.5	6
Kennard Winchester* . .	4	17	1	3	.333	0	0	. . .	0	0	0	0	1	0	0	0	0	2	0.5	0
Dan Godfread	1	2	0	0	. . .	0	0	. . .	0	0	0	0	0	0	0	0	0	0	0.0	0

3-pt. FG: Houston 329-959 (.343)—Olajuwon 0-1 (.000); Thorpe 0-7 (.000); Maxwell 162-473 (.342); K. Smith 54-137 (.394); Floyd 37-123 (.301); B. Johnson 1-9 (.111); Bullard 64-166 (.386); A. Johnson† 3-10 (.300); A. Johnson‡ 4-15 (.267); Herrera 0-1 (.000); Jamerson 8-28 (.286); L. Smith 0-1 (.000); Henderson* 0-3 (.000). Opponents 196-574 (.341).

INDIANA PACERS

	G	Min.	FGM	FGA	Pct.	FTM	FTA	Pct.	Off.	Def.	Tot.	Ast.	PF	Dq.	Stl.	TO	Blk.	Pts.	Avg.	Hi.
									REBOUNDS									SCORING		
Reggie Miller	82	3120	562	1121	.501	442	515	.858	82	236	318	314	210	1	105	157	26	1695	20.7	37
Chuck Person	81	2923	616	1284	.480	133	197	.675	114	312	426	382	247	5	68	216	18	1497	18.5	41

1991-92

	G	Min.	FGM	FGA	Pct.	FTM	FTA	Pct.	Off.	Def.	Tot.	Ast.	PF	Dq.	Stl.	TO	Blk.	Pts.	Avg.	Hi.
Detlef Schrempf	80	2605	496	925	.536	365	441	.828	202	568	770	312	286	4	62	191	37	1380	17.3	35
Micheal Williams	79	2750	404	824	.490	372	427	.871	73	209	282	647	262	7	233	240	22	1188	15.0	28
Rik Smits	74	1772	436	855	.510	152	193	.788	124	293	417	116	231	4	29	130	100	1024	13.8	31
Vern Fleming	82	1737	294	610	.482	132	179	.737	69	140	209	266	134	0	56	140	7	726	8.9	28
George McCloud	51	892	128	313	.409	50	64	.781	45	87	132	116	95	1	26	62	11	338	6.6	20
Dale Davis	64	1301	154	279	.552	87	152	.572	158	252	410	30	191	2	27	49	74	395	6.2	19
LaSalle Thompson	80	1299	168	359	.468	58	71	.817	98	283	381	102	207	0	52	98	34	394	4.9	16
Kenny Williams	60	565	113	218	.518	26	43	.605	64	65	129	40	99	0	20	22	41	252	4.2	23
Sean Green	35	256	62	158	.392	15	28	.536	22	20	42	22	31	0	13	27	6	141	4.0	15
Mike Sanders*	10	81	11	22	.500	5	6	.833	0	8	8	11	8	0	2	6	1	27	2.7	8
Greg Dreiling	60	509	43	87	.494	30	40	.750	22	74	96	25	123	1	10	31	16	117	2.0	15
Jerome Lane*	3	30	3	5	.600	0	6	.000	9	9	18	4	9	0	0	3	0	6	2.0	4
Randy Wittman	24	115	8	19	.421	1	2	.500	1	8	9	11	4	0	2	3	0	17	0.7	4

3-pt. FG: Indiana 333-940 (.354)—Miller 129-341 (.378); Person 132-354 (.373); Schrempf 23-71 (.324); M. Williams 8-33 (.242); Smits 0-2 (.000); Fleming 6-27 (.222); McCloud 32-94 (.340); Davis 0-1 (.000); Thompson 0-2 (.000); K. Williams 0-4 (.000); Green 2-10 (.200); Dreiling 1-1 (1.000). Opponents 216-640 (.338).

LOS ANGELES CLIPPERS

	G	Min.	FGM	FGA	Pct.	FTM	FTA	Pct.	Off.	Def.	Tot.	Ast.	PF	Dq.	Stl.	TO	Blk.	Pts.	Avg.	Hi.
Danny Manning	82	2904	650	1199	.542	279	385	.725	229	335	564	285	293	5	135	210	122	1579	19.3	34
Ron Harper	82	3144	569	1292	.440	292	398	.736	120	327	447	417	199	0	152	252	72	1495	18.2	30
Charles Smith	49	1310	251	539	.466	212	270	.785	95	206	301	56	159	2	41	69	98	714	14.6	30
Ken Norman	77	2009	402	821	.490	121	226	.535	158	290	448	125	145	0	53	100	66	929	12.1	27
Doc Rivers	59	1657	226	533	.424	163	196	.832	23	124	147	233	166	2	111	92	19	641	10.9	23
James Edwards	72	1437	250	538	.465	198	271	.731	55	147	202	53	236	1	24	72	33	698	9.7	26
Olden Polynice	76	1834	244	470	.519	125	201	.622	195	341	536	46	165	0	45	83	20	613	8.1	23
Gary Grant	78	2049	275	595	.462	44	54	.815	34	150	184	538	181	4	138	187	14	609	7.8	25
Loy Vaught	79	1687	271	551	.492	55	69	.797	160	352	512	71	165	1	37	66	31	601	7.6	23
Danny Young†	44	889	84	215	.391	47	53	.887	16	50	66	152	47	0	40	42	4	235	5.3	13
Danny Young‡	62	1023	100	255	.392	57	67	.851	16	59	75	172	53	0	46	47	4	280	4.5	13
Tony Brown*	22	254	39	89	.438	18	29	.621	9	19	28	16	31	0	12	14	1	103	4.7	13
Bo Kimble	34	277	44	111	.396	20	31	.645	13	19	32	17	37	0	10	15	6	112	3.3	15
Tharon Mayes†	3	40	2	5	.400	4	6	.667	0	1	1	3	9	0	2	3	1	9	3.0	5
Tharon Mayes‡	24	255	30	99	.303	24	36	.667	3	13	16	35	41	0	16	31	2	99	4.1	12
David Rivers	15	122	10	30	.333	10	11	.909	10	9	19	21	14	0	7	17	1	30	2.0	9
Lanard Copeland	10	48	7	23	.304	2	2	1.000	1	6	7	5	5	0	2	4	0	16	1.6	8
LeRon Ellis	29	103	17	50	.340	9	19	.474	12	12	24	1	11	0	6	11	9	43	1.5	6
Elliot Perry*	10	66	6	15	.400	1	2	.500	2	5	7	14	10	0	9	13	1	13	1.3	7

3-pt. FG: L.A. Clippers 145-502 (.289)—Manning 0-5 (.000); Harper 64-211 (.303); Smith 0-6 (.000); Norman 4-28 (.143); Do. Rivers 26-92 (.283); Edwards 0-1 (.000); Polynice 0-1 (.000); Grant 15-51 (.294); Vaught 4-5 (.800); Young† 20-60 (.333); Young‡ 23-70 (.329); Brown* 7-22 (.318); Kimble 4-13 (.308); Mayes† 1-2 (.500); Mayes‡ 15-41 (.366); Da. Rivers 0-1 (.000); Copeland 0-2 (.000); Perry* 0-2 (.000). Opponents 224-648 (.346).

LOS ANGELES LAKERS

	G	Min.	FGM	FGA	Pct.	FTM	FTA	Pct.	Off.	Def.	Tot.	Ast.	PF	Dq.	Stl.	TO	Blk.	Pts.	Avg.	Hi.
James Worthy	54	2108	504	1007	.447	166	204	.814	98	207	305	252	89	0	76	127	23	1075	19.9	37
Sam Perkins	63	2332	361	803	.450	304	372	.817	192	364	556	141	192	1	64	83	62	1041	16.5	29
Sedale Threatt	82	3070	509	1041	.489	202	243	.831	43	210	253	593	231	1	168	182	16	1240	15.1	42
Byron Scott	82	2679	460	1005	.458	244	291	.838	74	236	310	226	140	0	105	119	28	1218	14.9	31
A.C. Green	82	2902	382	803	.476	340	457	.744	306	456	762	117	141	0	91	111	36	1116	13.6	28
Vlade Divac	36	979	157	317	.495	86	112	.768	87	160	247	60	114	3	55	88	35	405	11.3	32
Terry Teagle	82	1602	364	805	.452	151	197	.766	91	92	183	113	148	0	66	114	9	880	10.7	28
Elden Campbell	81	1876	220	491	.448	138	223	.619	155	268	423	59	203	1	53	73	159	578	7.1	25
Tony Smith	63	820	113	283	.399	49	75	.653	31	45	76	109	91	0	39	50	8	275	4.4	18
Chucky Brown†	36	381	55	118	.466	25	41	.610	29	47	76	23	41	0	9	27	7	135	3.8	16
Chucky Brown‡	42	431	60	128	.469	30	49	.612	31	51	82	26	48	0	12	29	7	150	3.6	16
Cliff Robinson	9	78	11	27	.407	7	8	.875	7	12	19	9	4	0	5	7	0	29	3.2	10
Rory Sparrow†	42	471	57	143	.399	8	13	.615	3	24	27	79	55	0	12	31	5	124	3.0	12
Rory Sparrow‡	46	489	58	151	.384	8	13	.615	3	25	28	83	57	0	12	33	5	127	2.8	12
Jack Haley	49	394	31	84	.369	14	29	.483	31	64	95	7	75	0	7	25	8	76	1.6	11
Demetrius Calip	7	58	4	18	.222	2	3	.667	1	4	5	12	8	0	1	5	0	11	1.6	3
Keith Owens	20	80	9	32	.281	8	10	.800	8	7	15	3	11	0	5	2	4	26	1.3	8

3-pt. FG: L.A. Lakers 119-445 (.267)—Worthy 9-43 (.209); Perkins 15-69 (.217); Threatt 20-62 (.323); Scott 54-157 (.344); Green 12-56 (.214); Divac 5-19 (.263); Teagle 1-4 (.250); Campbell 0-2 (.000); Smith 0-11 (.000); Brown† 0-3 (.000); Brown‡ 0-3 (.000); Robinson 0-1 (.000); Sparrow† 2-13 (.154); Sparrow‡ 3-15 (.200); Calip 1-5 (.200). Opponents 174-596 (.292).

MIAMI HEAT

	G	Min.	FGM	FGA	Pct.	FTM	FTA	Pct.	Off.	Def.	Tot.	Ast.	PF	Dq.	Stl.	TO	Blk.	Pts.	Avg.	Hi.
Glen Rice	79	3007	672	1432	.469	266	318	.836	84	310	394	184	170	0	90	145	35	1765	22.3	46
Rony Seikaly	79	2800	463	947	.489	370	505	.733	307	627	934	109	278	2	40	216	121	1296	16.4	29
Grant Long	82	3063	440	890	.494	326	404	.807	259	432	691	225	248	2	139	185	40	1212	14.8	29
Steve Smith	61	1806	297	654	.454	95	127	.748	81	107	188	278	162	1	59	152	19	729	12.0	24
Willie Burton	68	1585	280	622	.450	196	245	.800	76	168	244	123	186	2	46	119	37	762	11.2	28
Kevin Edwards	81	1840	325	716	.454	162	191	.848	56	155	211	170	138	1	99	120	20	819	10.1	26
Bimbo Coles	81	1976	295	649	.455	216	262	.824	69	120	189	366	151	3	73	167	13	816	10.1	22
Sherman Douglas*	5	98	16	31	.516	5	7	.714	1	5	6	19	10	0	4	8	0	37	7.4	11
Brian Shaw†	46	987	139	349	.398	37	51	.725	39	96	135	161	86	0	45	67	12	321	7.0	20
Brian Shaw‡	63	1423	209	513	.407	72	91	.791	50	154	204	250	115	0	57	99	22	495	7.9	24

	G	Min.	FGM	FGA	Pct.	FTM	FTA	Pct.	REBOUNDS Off.	Def.	Tot.	Ast.	PF	Dq.	Stl.	TO	Blk.	SCORING Pts.	Avg.	Hi.
Alec Kessler	77	1197	158	·383	.413	94	115	.817	114	200	314	34	185	3	17	58	32	410	5.3	15
John Morton†	21	216	33	81	.407	24	29	.828	3	16	19	27	20	0	12	24	1	92	4.4	16
John Morton‡	25	270	36	93	.387	32	38	.842	6	20	26	32	23	0	13	28	1	106	4.2	16
Keith Askins	59	843	84	205	.410	26	37	.703	65	77	142	38	109	0	40	47	15	219	3.7	18
Alan Ogg	43	367	46	84	.548	16	30	.533	30	44	74	7	73	0	5	19	28	108	2.5	10
Milos Babic	9	35	6	13	.462	6	8	.750	2	9	11	6	0	0	1	5	0	18	2.0	6
Jon Sundvold	3	8	1	3	.333	0	0	...	0	0	0	2	2	0	0	0	0	3	1.0	3
Winston Bennett†	2	2	1	2	.500	0	0	...	1	0	1	0	1	0	0	0	0	2	1.0	2
Winston Bennett‡	54	833	80	211	.379	35	50	.700	63	99	162	38	122	1	19	33	9	195	3.6	14

3-pt. FG: Miami 257-751 (.342)—Rice 155-396 (.391); Seikaly 0-3 (.000); Long 6-22 (.273); Smith 40-125 (.320); Burton 6-15 (.400); Edwards 7-32 (.219); Coles 10-52 (.192); Douglas* 0-1 (.000); Shaw† 5-16 (.313); Shaw‡ 5-23 (.217); Morton† 2-15 (.133); Morton‡ 2-16 (.125); Askins 25-73 (.342); Bennett‡ 0-1 (.000); Sundvold 1-1 (1.000). Opponents 210-606 (.347).

MILWAUKEE BUCKS

	G	Min.	FGM	FGA	Pct.	FTM	FTA	Pct.	REBOUNDS Off.	Def.	Tot.	Ast.	PF	Dq.	Stl.	TO	Blk.	SCORING Pts.	Avg.	Hi.
Dale Ellis	81	2191	485	1034	.469	164	212	.774	92	161	253	104	151	0	57	119	18	1272	15.7	31
Moses Malone	82	2511	440	929	.474	396	504	.786	320	424	744	93	136	0	74	150	64	1279	15.6	30
Jay Humphries	71	2284	377	803	.469	195	249	.783	44	140	184	466	210	2	119	148	13	991	14.0	28
Alvin Robertson	82	2463	396	922	.430	151	198	.763	175	175	350	360	263	5	210	223	32	1010	12.3	30
Frank Brickowski	65	1556	306	584	.524	125	163	.767	97	247	344	122	223	11	60	112	23	740	11.4	26
Fred Roberts	80	1746	311	645	.482	128	171	.749	103	154	257	122	177	0	52	122	40	769	9.6	25
Jeff Grayer	82	1659	309	689	.448	102	153	.667	129	128	257	150	142	0	64	105	13	739	9.0	27
Larry Krystkowiak	79	1848	293	660	.444	128	169	.757	131	298	429	114	218	2	54	115	12	714	9.0	21
Brad Lohaus	70	1081	162	360	.450	27	41	.659	65	184	249	74	144	5	40	46	71	408	5.8	24
Dan Schayes	43	726	83	199	.417	74	96	.771	58	110	168	34	98	0	19	41	19	240	5.6	25
Lester Conner	81	1420	103	239	.431	81	115	.704	63	121	184	294	86	0	97	79	10	287	3.5	15
Steve Henson	50	386	52	144	.361	23	29	.793	17	24	41	82	50	0	15	40	1	150	3.0	17
Jerome Lane†	2	6	1	1	1.000	1	2	.500	1	3	4	0	1	0	0	1	0	3	1.5	3
Jerome Lane‡	14	177	14	46	.304	9	27	.333	32	34	66	17	28	0	2	14	1	37	2.6	10
Dave Popson	5	26	3	7	.429	1	2	.500	2	3	5	3	5	0	2	4	1	7	1.4	3

3-pt. FG: Milwaukee 371-1005 (.369)—Ellis 138-329 (.419); Malone 3-8 (.375); Humphries 42-144 (.292); Robertson 67-210 (.319); Brickowski 3-6 (.500); Roberts 19-37 (.514); Grayer 19-66 (.288); Krystkowiak 0-5 (.000); Lohaus 57-144 (.396); Conner 0-7 (.000); Henson 23-48 (.479); Popson 0-1 (.000). Opponents 221-603 (.367).

MINNESOTA TIMBERWOLVES

	G	Min.	FGM	FGA	Pct.	FTM	FTA	Pct.	REBOUNDS Off.	Def.	Tot.	Ast.	PF	Dq.	Stl.	TO	Blk.	SCORING Pts.	Avg.	Hi.
Tony Campbell	78	2441	527	1137	.464	240	299	.803	141	145	280	229	206	1	84	165	31	1307	16.8	36
Pooh Richardson	82	2922	587	1261	.466	123	178	.691	91	210	301	685	152	0	119	204	25	1350	16.5	27
Tyrone Corbin*	11	344	57	142	.401	44	53	.830	24	45	69	33	31	0	12	26	6	158	14.4	23
Doug West	80	2540	463	894	.518	186	231	.805	107	150	257	281	239	1	66	120	26	1116	14.0	28
Thurl Bailey†	71	1777	329	735	.448	171	215	.795	99	308	407	59	129	1	30	87	102	829	11.7	22
Thurl Bailey‡	84	2104	368	836	.440	215	270	.796	122	363	485	78	160	1	35	108	117	951	11.3	22
Gerald Glass	75	1822	383	871	.440	77	125	.616	107	153	260	175	171	0	66	103	30	859	11.5	31
Sam Mitchell	82	2151	307	725	.423	209	266	.786	158	315	473	94	230	3	53	97	39	825	10.1	24
Felton Spencer	61	1481	141	331	.426	123	178	.691	167	268	435	53	241	7	27	70	79	405	6.6	20
Randy Breuer	67	1176	161	344	.468	41	77	.532	98	183	281	89	117	0	27	41	99	363	5.4	18
Scott Brooks	82	1082	167	374	.447	51	63	.810	27	72	99	205	82	0	66	51	7	417	5.1	21
Tellis Frank	10	140	18	33	.545	10	15	.667	8	18	26	8	24	0	5	5	4	46	4.6	13
Luc Longley	66	991	114	249	.458	53	80	.663	67	190	257	53	157	0	35	83	64	281	4.3	20
Mark Randall†	39	374	58	127	.457	26	35	.743	35	27	62	26	31	0	12	19	3	145	3.7	14
Mark Randall‡	54	441	68	149	.456	32	43	.744	39	32	71	33	39	0	12	25	3	171	3.2	14
Myron Brown	4	23	4	6	.667	0	0	...	0	3	3	6	2	0	1	4	0	9	2.3	4
Tod Murphy	47	429	39	80	.488	19	34	.559	36	74	110	11	40	0	9	18	8	98	2.1	13
Tom Garrick*	15	112	11	33	.333	6	8	.750	2	7	9	18	14	0	7	10	3	29	1.9	7

3-pt. FG: Minnesota 126-394 (.320)—Campbell 13-37 (.351); Richardson 53-155 (.342); Corbin* 0-1 (.000); West 4-23 (.174); Bailey† 0-1 (.000); Bailey‡ 0-2 (.000); Glass 16-54 (.296); Mitchell 2-11 (.182); Breuer 0-1 (.000); Brooks 32-90 (.356); Randall† 3-14 (.214); Randall‡ 3-16 (.188); Brown 1-3 (.333); Murphy 1-2 (.500); Garrick* 1-2 (.500). Opponents 171-483 (.354).

NEW JERSEY NETS

	G	Min.	FGM	FGA	Pct.	FTM	FTA	Pct.	REBOUNDS Off.	Def.	Tot.	Ast.	PF	Dq.	Stl.	TO	Blk.	SCORING Pts.	Avg.	Hi.
Drazen Petrovic	82	3027	608	1315	.508	232	287	.808	97	161	258	252	248	3	105	215	11	1691	20.6	39
Derrick Coleman	65	2207	483	958	.504	300	393	.763	203	415	618	205	168	2	54	248	98	1289	19.8	38
Sam Bowie	71	2179	421	947	.445	212	280	.757	203	375	578	186	212	2	41	150	120	1062	15.0	34
Mookie Blaylock	72	2548	409	993	.432	126	177	.712	101	168	269	492	182	1	170	152	40	996	13.8	27
Chris Morris	77	2394	346	726	.477	165	231	.714	199	295	494	197	211	2	129	171	81	879	11.4	22
Terry Mills	82	1714	310	670	.463	114	152	.750	187	266	453	84	200	3	48	82	41	742	9.0	25
Kenny Anderson	64	1086	187	480	.390	73	98	.745	38	89	127	203	68	0	67	97	9	450	7.0	18
Tate George	70	1037	165	386	.427	87	106	.821	36	69	105	162	98	0	41	82	3	418	6.0	22
Rafael Addison	76	1175	187	432	.433	56	76	.737	65	100	165	68	109	1	28	46	28	444	5.8	19
Chris Dudley	82	1902	190	472	.403	80	171	.468	343	396	739	58	275	5	38	79	179	460	5.6	16
Jud Buechler*	2	29	4	8	.500	0	0	...	2	0	2	2	2	0	2	1	1	8	4.0	6
Doug Lee	46	307	50	116	.431	10	19	.526	17	18	35	22	39	0	11	12	1	120	2.6	9
Dave Feitl	34	175	33	77	.429	16	19	.842	21	40	61	6	22	0	2	19	3	82	2.4	8

3-pt. FG: New Jersey 224-670 (.334)—Petrovic 123-277 (.444); Coleman 23-76 (.303); Bowie 8-25 (.320); Blaylock 12-54 (.222); Morris 22-110 (.200); Mills 8-23 (.348); Anderson 3-13 (.231); George 1-6 (.167); Addison 14-49 (.286); Lee 10-37 (.270). Opponents 161-508 (.317).

1991-92

NEW YORK KNICKERBOCKERS

	G	Min.	FGM	FGA	Pct.	FTM	FTA	Pct.	Off.	Def.	Tot.	Ast.	PF	Dq.	Stl.	TO	Blk.	Pts.	Avg.	Hi.
Patrick Ewing	82	3150	796	1525	.522	377	511	.738	228	693	921	156	277	2	88	209	245	1970	24.0	45
John Starks	82	2118	405	902	.449	235	302	.778	45	146	191	276	231	4	103	150	18	1139	13.9	30
Xavier McDaniel	82	2344	488	1021	.478	137	192	.714	176	284	460	149	241	3	57	147	24	1125	13.7	37
Gerald Wilkins	82	2344	431	964	.447	116	159	.730	74	132	206	219	195	4	76	113	17	1016	12.4	28
Mark Jackson	81	2461	367	747	.491	171	222	.770	95	210	305	694	153	0	112	211	13	916	11.3	30
Anthony Mason	82	2198	203	399	.509	167	260	.642	216	357	573	106	229	0	46	101	20	573	7.0	17
Kiki Vandeweghe	67	956	188	383	.491	65	81	.802	31	57	88	57	87	0	15	27	8	467	7.0	25
Charles Oakley	82	2309	210	402	.522	86	117	.735	256	444	700	133	258	2	67	123	15	506	6.2	17
Greg Anthony	82	1510	161	435	.370	117	158	.741	33	103	136	314	170	0	59	98	9	447	5.5	20
Brian Quinnett*	24	190	28	73	.384	8	14	.571	9	15	24	7	21	0	7	8	6	74	3.1	14
Kennard Winchester†	15	64	12	27	.444	8	10	.800	6	9	15	8	4	0	2	2	2	33	2.2	4
Kennard Winchester‡	19	81	13	30	.433	8	10	.800	6	9	15	8	5	0	2	2	2	35	1.8	4
Carlton McKinney	2	9	2	9	.222	0	0	...	0	1	1	0	1	0	0	0	0	4	2.0	2
Tim McCormick	22	108	14	33	.424	14	21	.667	14	20	34	9	18	0	2	8	0	42	1.9	7
Patrick Eddie	4	13	2	9	.222	0	0	...	0	1	1	0	3	0	0	0	0	4	1.0	2
James Donaldson†	14	81	5	18	.278	2	2	1.000	2	17	19	2	17	0	0	7	5	12	0.9	2
James Donaldson‡	58	1075	112	245	.457	61	86	.709	99	190	289	33	103	0	8	48	49	285	4.9	15

3-pt. FG: New York 201-618 (.325)—Ewing 1-6 (.167); Starks 94-270 (.348); McDaniel 12-39 (.308); Wilkins 38-108 (.352); Jackson 11-43 (.256); Vande-weghe 26-66 (.394); Oakley 0-3 (.000); Anthony 8-55 (.145); Quinnett* 10-26 (.385); Winchester† 1-2 (.500); Winchester‡ 1-2 (.500). Opponents 179-606 (.295).

ORLANDO MAGIC

	G	Min.	FGM	FGA	Pct.	FTM	FTA	Pct.	Off.	Def.	Tot.	Ast.	PF	Dq.	Stl.	TO	Blk.	Pts.	Avg.	Hi.
Nick Anderson	60	2203	482	1042	.463	202	303	.667	98	286	384	163	132	0	97	126	33	1196	19.9	37
Dennis Scott	18	608	133	331	.402	64	71	.901	14	52	66	35	49	1	20	31	9	359	19.9	29
Terry Catledge	78	2430	457	922	.496	240	346	.694	257	292	549	109	196	2	58	138	16	1154	14.8	30
Anthony Bowie	52	1721	312	633	.493	117	136	.860	70	175	245	163	101	1	55	107	38	758	14.6	31
Scott Skiles	75	2377	359	868	.414	248	277	.895	36	166	202	544	188	0	74	233	5	1057	14.1	41
Jerry Reynolds	46	1159	197	518	.380	158	189	.836	47	102	149	151	69	0	63	96	17	555	12.1	30
Sam Vincent	39	885	150	349	.430	110	130	.846	19	82	101	148	55	1	35	72	4	411	10.5	35
Stanley Roberts	55	1118	236	446	.529	101	196	.515	113	223	336	39	221	7	22	78	83	573	10.4	24
Brian Williams	48	905	171	324	.528	95	142	.669	115	157	272	33	139	2	41	86	53	437	9.1	24
Sean Higgins†	32	580	123	262	.469	24	29	.828	27	67	94	37	52	0	14	37	6	276	8.6	29
Sean Higgins‡	38	616	127	277	.458	31	36	.861	29	73	102	41	58	0	16	41	6	291	7.7	29
Jeff Turner	75	1591	225	499	.451	79	114	.693	62	184	246	92	229	6	24	106	16	530	7.1	21
Otis Smith	55	877	116	318	.365	70	91	.769	40	76	116	57	85	1	36	62	13	310	5.6	22
Chris Corchiani	51	741	77	193	.399	91	104	.875	18	60	78	141	94	0	45	74	2	255	5.0	11
Greg Kite	72	1479	94	215	.437	40	68	.588	156	246	402	44	212	2	30	61	57	228	3.2	11
Mark Acres	68	926	78	151	.517	51	67	.761	97	155	252	22	140	1	25	33	15	208	3.1	13
Morlon Wiley*	9	90	9	28	.321	3	5	.600	2	5	7	13	13	0	4	8	0	21	2.3	7
Stephen Thompson*	1	15	1	3	.333	0	0	...	0	1	1	1	2	0	0	2	0	2	2.0	2

3-pt. FG: Orlando 197-608 (.324)—Anderson 30-85 (.353); Scott 29-89 (.326); Catledge 0-4 (.000); Bowie 17-44 (.386); Skiles 91-250 (.364); Reynolds 3-24 (.125); Vincent 1-13 (.077); Roberts 0-1 (.000); Higgins† 6-24 (.250); Higgins‡ 6-24 (.250); Turner 1-8 (.125); Smith 8-21 (.381); Corchiani 10-37 (.270); Kite 0-1 (.000); Acres 1-3 (.333); Wiley* 0-4 (.000). Opponents 215-609 (.353).

PHILADELPHIA 76ERS

	G	Min.	FGM	FGA	Pct.	FTM	FTA	Pct.	Off.	Def.	Tot.	Ast.	PF	Dq.	Stl.	TO	Blk.	Pts.	Avg.	Hi.
Charles Barkley	75	2881	622	1126	.552	454	653	.695	271	559	830	308	196	2	136	235	44	1730	23.1	38
Hersey Hawkins	81	3013	521	1127	.462	403	461	.874	53	218	271	248	174	0	157	189	43	1536	19.0	43
Armon Gilliam	81	2771	512	1001	.511	343	425	.807	234	426	660	118	176	1	51	166	85	1367	16.9	31
Ron Anderson	82	2432	469	1008	.465	143	163	.877	96	182	278	135	128	0	86	109	11	1123	13.7	34
Johnny Dawkins	82	2815	394	902	.437	164	186	.882	42	185	227	567	158	0	89	183	5	988	12.0	26
Charles Shackleford	72	1399	205	422	.486	63	95	.663	145	270	415	46	205	3	38	62	51	473	6.6	17
Mitchell Wiggins	49	569	88	229	.384	35	51	.686	43	51	94	22	67	0	20	25	1	211	4.3	19
Tharon Mayes*	21	215	28	94	.298	20	30	.667	3	12	15	32	32	0	14	28	1	90	4.3	12
Greg Grant†	55	834	99	217	.456	19	22	.864	13	52	65	199	73	0	37	41	2	224	4.1	15
Greg Grant‡	68	891	99	225	.440	20	24	.833	14	55	69	217	76	0	45	46	2	225	3.3	15
Jayson Williams	50	646	75	206	.364	56	88	.636	62	83	145	12	110	1	20	44	20	206	4.1	12
Jeff Ruland	13	209	20	38	.526	11	16	.688	16	31	47	5	45	0	7	20	4	51	3.9	9
Kenny Payne	49	353	65	145	.448	9	13	.692	13	41	54	17	34	0	16	19	8	144	2.9	24
Brian Oliver	34	279	33	100	.330	15	22	.682	10	20	30	20	33	0	10	24	2	81	2.4	12
Michael Ansley*	8	32	5	11	.455	5	6	.833	2	2	4	2	6	0	0	3	0	15	1.9	9
Manute Bol	71	1267	49	128	.383	12	26	.462	54	168	222	22	139	1	11	41	205	110	1.5	8
Dave Hoppen	11	40	2	7	.286	5	10	.500	1	9	10	2	6	0	0	3	0	9	0.8	5

3-pt. FG: Philadelphia 227-680 (.334)—Barkley 32-137 (.234); Hawkins 91-229 (.397); Gilliam 0-2 (.000); Anderson 42-127 (.331); Dawkins 36-101 (.356); Shackleford 0-1 (.000); Wiggins 0-1 (.000); Mayes* 14-39 (.359); Grant† 7-18 (.389); Grant‡ 7-18 (.389); Payne 5-12 (.417); Oliver 0-4 (.000); Bol 0-9 (.000). Opponents 189-615 (.307).

PHOENIX SUNS

	G	Min.	FGM	FGA	Pct.	FTM	FTA	Pct.	Off.	Def.	Tot.	Ast.	PF	Dq.	Stl.	TO	Blk.	Pts.	Avg.	Hi.
Jeff Hornacek	81	3078	635	1240	.512	279	315	.886	106	301	407	411	218	1	158	170	31	1632	20.1	35
Kevin Johnson	78	2899	539	1125	.479	448	555	.807	61	231	292	836	180	0	116	272	23	1536	19.7	44
Dan Majerle	82	2853	551	1153	.478	229	303	.756	148	335	483	274	158	0	131	102	43	1418	17.3	37
Tom Chambers	69	1948	426	989	.431	258	311	.830	86	315	401	142	196	1	57	103	37	1128	16.3	36
Tim Perry	80	2483	413	789	.523	153	215	.712	204	347	551	134	237	2	44	141	116	982	12.3	27
Andrew Lang	81	1965	248	475	.522	126	164	.768	170	376	546	43	306	8	48	87	201	622	7.7	21
Cedric Ceballos	64	725	176	365	.482	109	148	.736	60	92	152	50	52	0	16	71	11	462	7.2	27

– 428 –

	G	Min.	FGM	FGA	Pct.	FTM	FTA	Pct.	REBOUNDS Off.	Def.	Tot.	Ast.	PF	Dq.	Stl.	TO	Blk.	SCORING Pts.	Avg.	Hi.
Mark West	82	1436	196	310	.632	109	171	.637	134	238	372	22	239	2	14	82	81	501	6.1	16
Steve Burtt	31	356	74	160	.463	38	54	.704	10	24	34	59	58	0	16	33	4	187	6.0	23
Negele Knight	42	631	103	217	.475	33	48	.688	16	30	46	112	58	0	24	58	3	243	5.8	19
Jerrod Mustaf	52	545	92	193	.477	49	71	.690	45	100	145	45	59	0	21	51	16	233	4.5	19
Kurt Rambis	28	381	38	82	.463	14	18	.778	23	83	106	37	46	0	12	25	14	90	3.2	11
Ed Nealy	52	505	62	121	.512	16	24	.667	25	86	111	37	45	0	16	17	2	160	3.1	17

3-pt. FG: Phoenix 227-596 (.381)—Hornacek 83-189 (.439); Johnson 10-46 (.217); Majerle 87-228 (.382); Chambers 18-49 (.367); Perry 3-8 (.375); Lang 0-1 (.000); Ceballos 1-6 (.167); Burtt 1-6 (.167); Knight 4-13 (.308); Nealy 20-50 (.400). Opponents 180-586 (.307).

PORTLAND TRAIL BLAZERS

	G	Min.	FGM	FGA	Pct.	FTM	FTA	Pct.	REBOUNDS Off.	Def.	Tot.	Ast.	PF	Dq.	Stl.	TO	Blk.	SCORING Pts.	Avg.	Hi.
Clyde Drexler	76	2751	694	1476	.470	401	505	.794	166	334	500	512	229	2	138	240	70	1903	25.0	48
Terry Porter	82	2784	521	1129	.461	315	368	.856	51	204	255	477	155	1	127	188	12	1485	18.1	31
Jerome Kersey	77	2553	398	852	.467	174	262	.664	241	392	633	243	254	1	114	151	71	971	12.6	28
Clifford Robinson	82	2124	398	854	.466	219	330	.664	140	276	416	137	274	11	85	154	107	1016	12.4	22
Buck Williams	80	2519	340	563	.604	221	293	.754	260	444	704	108	244	4	62	130	41	901	11.3	23
Kevin Duckworth	82	2222	362	786	.461	156	226	.690	151	346	497	99	264	5	38	143	37	880	10.7	23
Danny Ainge	81	1595	299	676	.442	108	131	.824	40	108	148	202	148	0	73	70	13	784	9.7	27
Alaa Abdelnaby	71	934	178	361	.493	76	101	.752	81	179	260	30	132	1	25	66	16	432	6.1	20
Robert Pack	72	894	115	272	.423	102	127	.803	32	65	97	140	101	0	40	92	4	332	4.6	16
Mark Bryant	56	800	95	198	.480	40	60	.667	87	114	201	41	105	0	26	30	8	230	4.1	18
Ennis Whatley	23	209	21	51	.412	27	31	.871	6	15	21	34	12	0	14	14	3	69	3.0	12
Danny Young*	18	134	16	40	.400	10	14	.714	0	9	9	20	6	0	6	5	0	45	2.5	12
Lamont Strothers	4	17	4	12	.333	2	4	.500	1	0	1	1	2	0	1	2	1	10	2.5	7
Wayne Cooper	35	344	35	82	.427	7	11	.636	34	53	87	11	21	57	0	4	15	27	77	2.2	10

3-pt. FG: Portland 325-944 (.344)—Drexler 114-338 (.337); Porter 128-324 (.395); Kersey 1-8 (.125); Robinson 1-11 (.091); Williams 0-1 (.000); Duckworth 0-3 (.000); Ainge 78-230 (.339); Pack 0-10 (.000); Bryant 0-3 (.000); Whatley 0-4 (.000); Young* 3-10 (.300); Strothers 0-2 (.000). Opponents 244-805 (.303).

SACRAMENTO KINGS

	G	Min.	FGM	FGA	Pct.	FTM	FTA	Pct.	REBOUNDS Off.	Def.	Tot.	Ast.	PF	Dq.	Stl.	TO	Blk.	SCORING Pts.	Avg.	Hi.
Mitch Richmond	80	3095	685	1465	.468	330	406	.813	62	257	319	411	231	1	92	247	34	1803	22.5	37
Lionel Simmons	78	2895	527	1162	.454	281	365	.770	149	485	634	337	205	0	135	218	132	1336	17.1	33
Wayman Tisdale	72	2521	522	1043	.500	151	198	.763	135	334	469	106	248	3	55	124	79	1195	16.6	29
Spud Webb	77	2724	448	1006	.445	262	305	.859	30	193	223	547	193	1	125	229	24	1231	16.0	28
Carl Thomas	1	31	5	12	.417	1	2	.500	0	0	0	1	3	0	1	1	0	12	12.0	12
Dennis Hopson†	69	1304	275	591	.465	179	253	.708	105	101	206	102	113	0	66	100	39	741	10.7	26
Dennis Hopson‡	71	1314	276	593	.465	179	253	.708	105	101	206	102	115	0	67	100	39	743	10.5	26
Anthony Bonner	79	2287	294	658	.447	151	241	.627	192	293	485	125	194	0	94	133	26	740	9.4	21
Duane Causwell	80	2291	250	455	.549	136	222	.613	196	384	580	59	281	4	47	124	215	636	8.0	19
Bobby Hansen*	2	40	4	9	.444	0	0	...	2	2	4	1	6	0	1	0	0	8	4.0	6
Jim Les	62	712	74	192	.385	38	47	.809	11	52	63	143	58	0	31	42	3	231	3.7	17
Pete Chilcutt	69	817	113	250	.452	23	28	.821	78	109	187	38	70	0	32	41	17	251	3.6	19
Randy Brown	56	535	77	169	.456	38	58	.655	26	43	69	59	68	0	35	42	12	192	3.4	12
Dwayne Schintzius	33	400	50	117	.427	10	12	.833	43	75	118	20	67	1	6	19	28	110	3.3	12
Steve Scheffler*	4	15	2	2	1.000	5	6	.833	2	1	3	0	2	0	0	0	1	9	2.3	7
Stephen Thompson†	18	76	13	34	.382	3	8	.375	11	7	18	7	7	0	6	3	3	29	1.6	5
Stephen Thompson‡	19	91	14	37	.378	3	8	.375	11	8	19	8	9	0	6	5	3	31	1.6	5
Les Jepsen	31	87	9	24	.375	7	11	.636	12	18	30	1	17	0	1	3	5	25	0.8	4

3-pt. FG: Sacramento 238-675 (.353)—Richmond 103-268 (.384); Simmons 1-5 (.200); Tisdale 0-2 (.000); Webb 73-199 (.367); Thomas 1-2 (.500); Hopson† 12-47 (.255); Hopson‡ 12-47 (.255); Bonner 1-4 (.250); Causwell 0-1 (.000); Hansen* 0-2 (.000); Les 45-131 (.344); Chilcutt 2-2 (1.000); Brown 0-6 (.000); Schintzius 0-4 (.000); Thompson† 0-1 (.000); Thompson‡ 0-1 (.000); Jepsen 0-1 (.000). Opponents 204-616 (.331).

SAN ANTONIO SPURS

	G	Min.	FGM	FGA	Pct.	FTM	FTA	Pct.	REBOUNDS Off.	Def.	Tot.	Ast.	PF	Dq.	Stl.	TO	Blk.	SCORING Pts.	Avg.	Hi.
David Robinson	68	2564	592	1074	.551	393	561	.701	261	568	829	181	219	2	158	182	305	1578	23.2	39
Terry Cummings	70	2149	514	1053	.488	177	249	.711	247	384	631	102	210	4	58	115	34	1210	17.3	35
Sean Elliott	82	3120	514	1040	.494	285	331	.861	143	296	439	214	149	0	84	152	29	1338	16.3	33
Rod Strickland	57	2053	300	659	.455	182	265	.687	92	173	265	491	122	0	118	160	17	787	13.8	28
Willie Anderson	57	1889	312	685	.455	107	138	.775	62	238	300	302	151	2	54	140	51	744	13.1	36
Antoine Carr	81	1867	359	732	.490	162	212	.764	128	218	346	63	264	5	32	114	96	881	10.9	30
Vinnie Johnson	60	1350	202	499	.405	55	85	.647	67	115	182	145	93	0	41	74	14	478	8.0	17
Avery Johnson*	20	463	55	108	.509	24	32	.750	5	30	35	100	43	1	21	45	3	135	6.8	15
Trent Tucker	24	415	60	129	.465	16	20	.800	8	29	37	27	39	0	21	14	3	155	6.5	15
Tom Garrick*	19	374	44	93	.473	10	16	.625	8	33	41	63	33	0	21	30	1	98	5.2	13
Sidney Green	80	1127	147	344	.427	73	89	.820	92	250	342	36	148	0	29	62	11	367	4.6	13
Donald Royal	60	718	80	178	.449	92	133	.692	65	59	124	34	73	0	25	39	7	252	4.2	18
Greg Sutton	67	601	93	240	.388	34	45	.756	6	41	47	91	111	0	26	70	9	246	3.7	14
Jud Buechler*	11	140	15	30	.500	3	9	.333	6	16	22	11	18	0	8	5	3	33	3.0	8
Paul Pressey	56	759	60	161	.373	28	41	.683	22	73	95	142	86	0	29	64	19	151	2.7	11
Sean Higgins*	6	36	4	15	.267	7	7	1.000	2	6	8	4	6	0	2	4	0	15	2.5	7
Morlon Wiley*	3	13	3	5	.600	0	0	...	0	1	1	3	0	0	0	0	0	6	2.0	4
Tony Massenburg*	1	9	1	5	.200	0	0	...	1	0	1	0	0	0	0	0	0	2	2.0	2
Tom Copa	33	132	22	40	.550	4	13	.308	14	22	36	3	29	0	2	8	6	48	1.5	5
Steve Bardo	1	87	9	24	.375	7	11	.636	0	1	1	1	0	0	0	1	0	0	0.0	0

3-pt. FG: San Antonio 118-404 (.292)—Robinson 1-8 (.125); Cummings 5-13 (.385); Elliott 25-82 (.305); Strickland 5-15 (.333); Anderson 13-56 (.232); Carr 1-5 (.200); V. Johnson 19-60 (.317); A. Johnson* 1-5 (.200); Tucker 19-48 (.396); Garrick* 0-1 (.000); Sutton 26-89 (.292); Pressey 3-21 (.143); Higgins* 0-1 (.000). Opponents 243-700 (.347).

SEATTLE SUPERSONICS

	G	Min.	FGM	FGA	Pct.	FTM	FTA	Pct.	Off.	Def.	Tot.	Ast.	PF	Dq.	Stl.	TO	Blk.	Pts.	Avg.	Hi.
Ricky Pierce	78	2658	620	1306	.475	417	455	.916	93	140	233	241	213	2	86	189	20	1690	21.7	34
Eddie Johnson	81	2366	534	1164	.459	291	338	.861	118	174	292	161	199	0	55	130	11	1386	17.1	39
Shawn Kemp	64	1808	362	718	.504	270	361	.748	264	401	665	86	261	13	70	156	124	994	15.5	27
Derrick McKey	52	1757	285	604	.472	188	222	.847	95	173	268	120	142	2	61	114	47	777	14.9	29
Benoit Benjamin	63	1941	354	740	.478	171	249	.687	130	383	513	76	185	1	39	175	118	879	14.0	27
Gary Payton	81	2549	331	734	.451	99	148	.669	123	172	295	506	248	0	147	174	21	764	9.4	22
Michael Cage	82	2461	307	542	.566	106	171	.620	266	462	728	92	237	0	99	78	55	720	8.8	23
Dana Barros	75	1331	238	493	.483	60	79	.759	17	64	81	125	84	0	51	56	4	619	8.3	19
Nate McMillan	72	1652	177	405	.437	54	84	.643	92	160	252	359	218	4	129	112	29	435	6.0	20
Tony Brown†	35	401	63	160	.394	30	37	.811	23	33	56	32	51	0	18	21	4	168	4.8	12
Tony Brown‡	57	655	102	249	.410	48	66	.727	32	52	84	48	82	0	30	35	5	271	4.8	13
Quintin Dailey	11	98	9	37	.243	13	16	.813	2	10	12	4	6	0	5	10	1	31	2.8	13
Marty Conlon	45	381	48	101	.475	24	32	.750	33	36	69	12	40	0	9	27	7	120	2.7	17
Rich King	40	213	27	71	.380	34	45	.756	20	29	49	12	42	0	4	18	5	88	2.2	10
Bart Kofoed	44	239	25	53	.472	15	26	.577	6	20	26	51	26	0	2	20	2	66	1.5	15

3-pt. FG: Seattle 205-647 (.317)—Pierce 33-123 (.268); Johnson 27-107 (.252); Kemp 0-3 (.000); McKey 19-50 (.380); Benjamin 0-2 (.000); Payton 3-23 (.130); Cage 0-5 (.000); Barros 83-186 (.446); McMillan 27-98 (.276); Brown† 12-41 (.293); Brown‡ 19-63 (.302); Dailey 0-1 (.000); King 0-1 (.000); Kofoed 1-7 (.143). Opponents 209-621 (.337).

UTAH JAZZ

	G	Min.	FGM	FGA	Pct.	FTM	FTA	Pct.	Off.	Def.	Tot.	Ast.	PF	Dq.	Stl.	TO	Blk.	Pts.	Avg.	Hi.
Karl Malone	81	3054	798	1516	.526	673	865	.778	225	684	909	241	226	2	108	248	51	2272	28.0	44
Jeff Malone	81	2922	691	1353	.511	256	285	.898	49	184	233	180	126	1	56	140	5	1639	20.2	35
John Stockton	82	3002	453	939	.482	308	366	.842	68	202	270	1126	234	3	244	286	22	1297	15.8	27
Blue Edwards	81	2283	433	830	.522	113	146	.774	86	212	298	137	236	1	81	122	46	1018	12.6	30
Thurl Bailey*	13	327	39	101	.386	44	55	.800	23	55	78	19	31	0	5	21	15	122	9.4	21
Tyrone Corbin†	69	1863	246	488	.504	130	148	.878	139	264	403	107	162	1	70	71	14	622	9.0	21
Tyrone Corbin‡	80	2207	303	630	.481	174	201	.866	163	309	472	140	193	1	82	97	20	780	9.8	23
Mike Brown	82	1783	221	488	.453	190	285	.667	187	289	476	81	196	1	42	105	34	632	7.7	24
David Benoit	77	1161	175	375	.467	81	100	.810	105	191	296	34	124	0	19	71	44	434	5.6	15
Eric Murdock	50	478	76	183	.415	46	61	.754	21	33	54	92	52	0	30	50	7	203	4.1	12
Mark Eaton	81	2023	107	240	.446	52	87	.598	150	341	491	40	2239	2	36	60	205	266	3.3	14
Delaney Rudd	65	538	75	188	.399	32	42	.762	15	39	54	109	64	0	15	49	1	193	3.0	12
Corey Crowder	51	328	43	112	.384	15	18	.833	16	25	41	17	35	0	7	13	2	114	2.2	10
Isaac Austin	31	112	21	46	.457	19	30	.633	11	24	35	5	20	0	2	8	2	61	2.0	7
Bob Thornton	2	6	1	7	.143	2	2	1.000	2	0	2	0	1	0	0	0	0	4	2.0	4

3-pt. FG: Utah 158-458 (.345)—K. Malone 3-17 (.176); J. Malone 1-12 (.083); Stockton 83-204 (.407); Edwards 39-103 (.379); Bailey* 0-1 (.000); Corbin† 0-3 (.000); Corbin‡ 0-4 (.000); Brown 0-1 (.000); Benoit 3-14 (.214); Murdock 5-26 (.192); Rudd 11-47 (.234); Crowder 13-30 (.433). Opponents 234-695 (.337).

WASHINGTON BULLETS

	G	Min.	FGM	FGA	Pct.	FTM	FTA	Pct.	Off.	Def.	Tot.	Ast.	PF	Dq.	Stl.	TO	Blk.	Pts.	Avg.	Hi.
Pervis Ellison	66	2511	547	1014	.539	227	312	.728	217	523	740	190	222	2	62	196	177	1322	20.0	31
Michael Adams	78	2795	485	1233	.393	313	360	.869	58	252	310	594	162	1	145	212	9	1408	18.1	40
Harvey Grant	64	2388	489	1022	.478	176	220	.800	157	275	432	170	178	1	74	109	27	1155	18.0	33
Ledell Eackles	65	1463	355	759	.468	139	187	.743	39	139	178	125	145	1	47	75	7	856	13.2	40
Tom Hammonds	37	984	195	400	.488	50	82	.610	49	136	185	36	118	1	22	58	13	440	11.9	31
A.J. English	81	1665	366	846	.433	148	176	.841	74	94	168	143	160	1	32	89	9	886	10.9	27
Larry Stewart	76	2229	303	590	.514	188	233	.807	186	263	449	120	225	3	51	112	44	794	10.4	23
Rex Chapman†	1	22	5	12	.417	0	0	…	1	3	4	3	4	0	1	3	0	10	10.0	10
Rex Chapman‡	22	567	113	252	.448	36	53	.679	10	48	58	89	51	0	15	45	8	270	12.3	27
David Wingate	81	2127	266	572	.465	105	146	.719	80	189	269	247	162	1	123	124	21	638	7.9	18
Albert King	6	59	11	30	.367	7	8	.875	1	10	11	5	7	0	3	2	0	31	5.2	11
LaBradford Smith	48	708	100	246	.407	45	56	.804	30	51	81	99	98	0	44	63	1	247	5.1	17
Greg Foster	49	548	89	193	.461	35	49	.714	43	102	145	35	83	0	6	36	12	213	4.3	17
Andre Turner	70	871	111	261	.425	61	77	.792	17	73	90	177	59	0	57	84	2	284	4.1	15
Derek Strong	1	12	0	4	.000	3	4	.750	1	4	5	1	1	0	0	1	0	3	3.0	3
Ralph Sampson	10	108	9	29	.310	4	6	.667	11	19	30	4	14	1	3	10	8	22	2.2	7
Charles Jones	75	1365	33	90	.367	20	40	.500	105	212	317	62	214	0	43	39	92	86	1.1	6

3-pt. FG: Washington 146-537 (.272)—Ellison 1-3 (.333); Adams 125-386 (.324); Grant 1-8 (.125); Eackles 7-35 (.200); Hammonds 0-1 (.000); English 6-34 (.176); Stewart 0-3 (.000); Chapman† 0-2 (.000); Chapman‡ 8-29 (.276); Wingate 1-18 (.056); A. King 2-7 (.286); Smith 2-21 (.095); Foster 0-1 (.000); Turner 1-16 (.063); Sampson 0-2 (.000). Opponents 212-601 (.353).

* Finished season with another team. † Totals with this team only. ‡ Totals with all teams.

EASTERN CONFERENCE

FIRST ROUND

Chicago 3, Miami 0
Apr. 24—Fri.	Miami 94 at Chicago	113
Apr. 26—Sun.	Miami 90 at Chicago	120
Apr. 29—Wed.	Chicago 119 at Miami	114

Boston 3, Indiana 0
Apr. 23—Thur.	Indiana 113 at Boston	124
Apr. 25—Sat.	Indiana 112 at Boston	*119
Apr. 27—Mon.	Boston 102 at Indiana	98

Cleveland 3, New Jersey 1
Apr. 23—Thur.	New Jersey 113 at Cleveland	120
Apr. 25—Sat.	New Jersey 96 at Cleveland	118
Apr. 28—Tue.	Cleveland 104 at New Jersey	109
Apr. 30—Thur.	Cleveland 98 at New Jersey	89

New York 3, Detroit 2
Apr. 24—Fri.	Detroit 75 at New York	109
Apr. 26—Sun.	Detroit 89 at New York	88
Apr. 28—Tue.	New York 90 at Detroit	*87
May 1—Fri.	New York 82 at Detroit	86
May 3—Sun.	Detroit 87 at New York	94

SEMIFINALS

Cleveland 4, Boston 3
May 2—Sat.	Boston 76 at Cleveland	101
May 4—Mon.	Boston 104 at Cleveland	98
May 8—Fri.	Cleveland 107 at Boston	110
May 10—Sun.	Cleveland 114 at Boston	*112
May 13—Wed.	Boston 98 at Cleveland	114
May 15—Fri.	Cleveland 91 at Boston	122
May 17—Sun.	Boston 104 at Cleveland	122

Chicago 4, New York 3
May 5—Tue.	New York 94 at Chicago	89
May 7—Thur.	New York 78 at Chicago	86
May 9—Sat.	Chicago 94 at New York	86
May 10—Sun.	Chicago 86 at New York	93
May 12—Tue.	New York 88 at Chicago	96
May 14—Thur.	Chicago 86 at New York	100
May 17—Sun.	New York 81 at Chicago	110

FINALS

Chicago 4, Cleveland 2
May 19—Tue.	Cleveland 89 at Chicago	103
May 21—Thur.	Cleveland 107 at Chicago	81
May 23—Sat.	Chicago 105 at Cleveland	96
May 25—Mon.	Chicago 85 at Cleveland	99
May 27—Wed.	Cleveland 89 at Chicago	112
May 29—Fri.	Chicago 99 at Cleveland	94

WESTERN CONFERENCE

FIRST ROUND

Portland 3, L.A. Lakers 1
Apr. 23—Thur.	L.A. Lakers 102 at Portland	115
Apr. 25—Sat.	L.A. Lakers 79 at Portland	101
Apr. 29—Wed.	Portland 119 at L.A. Lakers	*121
May 3—Sun.	Portland 102, L.A. Lakers (at Las Vegas)	76

Utah 3, L.A. Clippers 2
Apr. 24—Fri.	L.A. Clippers 97 at Utah	115
Apr. 26—Sun.	L.A. Clippers 92 at Utah	103
Apr. 28—Tue.	Utah 88 at L.A. Clippers	98
May 3—Sun.	Utah 107, L.A. Clippers (at Anaheim, Calif.)	115
May 4—Mon.	L.A. Clippers 89 at Utah	98

Seattle 3, Golden State 1
Apr. 23—Thur.	Seattle 117 at Golden State	109
Apr. 25—Sat.	Seattle 101 at Golden State	115
Apr. 28—Tue.	Golden State 128 at Seattle	129
Apr. 30—Thur.	Golden State 116 at Seattle	119

Phoenix 3, San Antonio 0
Apr. 24—Fri.	San Antonio 111 at Phoenix	117
Apr. 26—Sun.	San Antonio 107 at Phoenix	119
Apr. 29—Wed.	Phoenix 101 at San Antonio	92

SEMIFINALS

Portland 4, Phoenix 1
May 5—Tue.	Phoenix 111 at Portland	113
May 7—Thur.	Phoenix 119 at Portland	126
May 9—Sat.	Portland 117 at Phoenix	124
May 11—Mon.	Portland 153 at Phoenix	**151
May 14—Thur.	Phoenix 106 at Portland	118

Utah 4, Seattle 1
May 6—Wed.	Seattle 100 at Utah	108
May 8—Fri.	Seattle 97 at Utah	103
May 10—Sun.	Utah 98 at Seattle	104
May 12—Tue.	Utah 89 at Seattle	83
May 14—Thur.	Seattle 100 at Utah	111

FINALS

Portland 4, Utah 2
May 16—Sat.	Utah 88 at Portland	113
May 19—Tue.	Utah 102 at Portland	119
May 22—Fri.	Portland 89 at Utah	97
May 24—Sun.	Portland 112 at Utah	121
May 26—Tue.	Utah 121 at Portland	*127
May 28—Thur.	Portland 105 at Utah	97

NBA FINALS

Chicago 4, Portland 2
June 3—Wed.	Portland 89 at Chicago	122
June 5—Fri.	Portland 115 at Chicago	*104
June 7—Sun.	Chicago 94 at Portland	84
June 10—Wed.	Chicago 88 at Portland	93
June 12—Fri.	Chicago 119 at Portland	106
June 14—Sun.	Portland 93 at Chicago	97

*Denotes number of overtime periods.

1991-92

1990-91

1990-91 NBA CHAMPION CHICAGO BULLS

Front row (from left): Craig Hodges, John Paxson, Horace Grant, Bill Cartwright, Scottie Pippen, Michael Jordan, B.J. Armstrong. Center row (from left): trainer Chip Schaefer, Cliff Levingston, Scott Williams, Will Perdue, Stacey King, Dennis Hopson, vice president of basketball operations Jerry Krause. Back row (from left): assistant coach Jim Cleamons, assistant coach Tex Winter, head coach Phil Jackson, assistant coach John Bach, scout Jim Stack, scout Clarence Gaines Jr.

FINAL STANDINGS

ATLANTIC DIVISION

	Atl.	Bos.	Char.	Chi.	Cle.	Dal.	Den.	Det.	G.S.	Hou.	Ind.	L.A.C.	L.A.L.	Mia.	Mil.	Min.	N.J.	N.Y.	Orl.	Phi.	Pho.	Por.	Sac.	S.A.	Sea.	Uta.	Was.	W	L	Pct.	GB
Boston	1	..	3	2	3	2	2	2	1	2	2	2	1	4	2	2	4	5	1	2	1	1	2	1	2	1	5	56	26	.683	..
Philadelphia	4	3	2	3	2	1	2	2	0	0	3	2	1	4	2	0	3	1	2	..	1	1	1	0	1	0	3	44	38	.537	12
New York	1	0	4	0	1	0	1	3	0	0	2	2	1	4	0	1	5	..	0	5	0	0	2	1	1	2	3	39	43	.476	17
Washington	2	1	2	1	3	0	1	1	2	1	2	2	0	2	1	1	3	2	1	2	0	0	0	0	0	0	..	30	52	.366	26
New Jersey	1	1	2	1	2	0	1	1	1	0	1	1	0	3	2	1	..	0	1	2	1	0	1	0	1	0	2	26	56	.317	30
Miami	0	1	2	0	1	2	2	1	0	0	2	2	0	..	0	0	3	1	1	1	0	0	1	0	0	1	3	24	58	.293	32

CENTRAL DIVISION

	Atl.	Bos.	Char.	Chi.	Cle.	Dal.	Den.	Det.	G.S.	Hou.	Ind.	L.A.C.	L.A.L.	Mia.	Mil.	Min.	N.J.	N.Y.	Orl.	Phi.	Pho.	Por.	Sac.	S.A.	Sea.	Uta.	Was.	W	L	Pct.	GB
Chicago	4	2	5	..	5	2	2	3	1	0	4	2	1	4	4	2	3	4	2	1	1	0	2	0	2	2	3	61	21	.744	..
Detroit	5	2	4	2	3	2	2	..	1	2	3	2	0	3	2	2	3	1	2	2	0	1	2	0	1	0	3	50	32	.610	11
Milwaukee	3	2	3	1	3	1	1	3	1	0	3	1	2	4	..	1	2	4	2	2	1	1	1	1	1	1	3	48	34	.585	13
Atlanta	..	3	1	1	3	2	1	0	1	4	2	1	4	2	1	3	3	1	0	0	1	2	2	1	1	2		43	39	.524	18
Indiana	1	2	5	1	4	0	2	2	1	1	..	1	0	2	2	1	3	2	1	1	0	2	1	1	2	2		41	41	.500	20
Cleveland	2	1	4	0	..	2	1	2	0	0	1	1	1	3	2	1	2	3	2	2	0	1	0	1	0	1	2	33	49	.402	28
Charlotte	4	1	..	0	1	1	0	1	1	0	0	1	2	2	1	2	0	2	2	0	0	2	1	0	0	2		26	56	.317	35

MIDWEST DIVISION

	Atl.	Bos.	Char.	Chi.	Cle.	Dal.	Den.	Det.	G.S.	Hou.	Ind.	L.A.C.	L.A.L.	Mia.	Mil.	Min.	N.J.	N.Y.	Orl.	Phi.	Pho.	Por.	Sac.	S.A.	Sea.	Uta.	Was.	W	L	Pct.	GB
San Antonio	0	1	1	2	2	4	4	2	2	3	1	2	1	2	1	4	2	1	3	2	3	2	3	..	3	2	2	55	27	.671	..
Utah	1	1	2	0	2	5	3	2	3	2	0	3	2	1	1	4	2	0	4	2	1	3	3	3		..	2	54	28	.659	1
Houston	1	0	2	2	2	3	5	0	2	..	1	2	1	2	2	5	2	3	2	3	0	3	2	2	1	1		52	30	.634	3
Orlando	1	1	0	0	0	4	3	0	2	2	1	3	0	1	0	2	1	2	..	0	2	0	2	1	1	1	1	31	51	.378	24
Minnesota	1	0	1	0	1	4	2	0	1	0	1	1	1	2	1	..	1	1	2	2	0	0	3	0	2	1	1	29	53	.354	26
Dallas	0	0	1	0	0	..	3	0	2	1	2	1	2	0	1	1	2	2	1	1	0	1	2	1	0	2		28	54	.341	27
Denver	1	0	2	0	1	1	..	0	1	0	0	0	0	0	1	3	1	1	2	0	0	0	3	1	0	1	1	20	62	.244	35

PACIFIC DIVISION

	Atl.	Bos.	Char.	Chi.	Cle.	Dal.	Den.	Det.	G.S.	Hou.	Ind.	L.A.C.	L.A.L.	Mia.	Mil.	Min.	N.J.	N.Y.	Orl.	Phi.	Pho.	Por.	Sac.	S.A.	Sea.	Uta.	Was.	W	L	Pct.	GB
Portland	1	1	2	2	2	3	4	1	3	4	2	3	3	2	1	4	2	2	4	1	2	..	3	2	4	3	2	63	19	.768	..
L.A. Lakers	1	1	2	1	1	2	4	2	3	3	2	4	..	2	0	3	2	1	4	1	3	2	4	3	3	2	2	58	24	.707	5
Phoenix	2	1	2	1	2	4	4	2	3	1	3	2	1	4	1	2	2	1	3	3	..	1	3	2	2	5		55	27	.671	8
Golden State	1	1	1	1	2	2	3	1	..	2	1	3	2	1	3	1	2	2	1	2	2	3	1	0	4			44	38	.537	19
Seattle	1	2	2	0	1	2	4	1	1	2	1	3	2	2	1	2	1	1	3	1	2	0	4	1	..		2	41	41	.500	22
L.A. Clippers	0	0	1	0	1	3	4	0	2	2	1	..	0	0	1	3	1	0	1	0	2	1	3	2	2	1	0	31	51	.378	32
Sacramento	0	0	0	0	1	2	1	0	3	1	0	2	0	1	1	1	1	0	2	1	1	2	..	1	1	1	2	25	57	.305	38

TEAM STATISTICS

OFFENSIVE

	G	FGM	FGA	Pct.	FTM	FTA	Pct.	REBOUNDS Off.	Def.	Tot.	Ast.	PF	Dq.	Stl.	TO	Blk.	SCORING Pts.	Avg.
Denver	82	3901	8868	.440	1726	2263	.763	1520	2530	4050	2005	2235	46	856	1332	406	9828	119.9
Golden State	82	3566	7346	.485	2162	2761	.783	1113	2306	3419	1954	2207	37	803	1359	378	9564	116.6
Portland	82	3577	7369	.485	1912	2538	.753	1202	2561	3763	2254	1975	19	724	1309	410	9407	114.7
Phoenix	82	3573	7199	.496	2064	2680	.770	1132	2598	3730	2209	1850	12	687	1302	535	9348	114.0
Indiana	82	3450	6994	.493	2010	2479	.811	1018	2376	3394	2181	2088	16	658	1355	357	9159	111.7
Boston	82	3695	7214	.512	1646	1997	.824	1088	2697	3785	2160	1695	12	672	1320	565	9145	111.5
Chicago	82	3632	7125	.510	1605	2111	.760	1148	2342	3490	2212	1751	7	822	1184	438	9024	110.0
Atlanta	82	3349	7223	.464	2034	2544	.800	1235	2420	3655	1864	1768	14	729	1231	374	9003	109.8
San Antonio	82	3409	6988	.488	1883	2459	.766	1131	2657	3788	2140	1896	22	670	1445	571	8782	107.1
Houston	82	3403	7287	.467	1631	2200	.741	1275	2508	3783	1906	1874	32	796	1402	409	8753	106.7
Seattle	82	3500	7117	.492	1608	2143	.750	1222	2173	3395	2042	1973	23	861	1404	380	8744	106.6
Milwaukee	82	3337	6948	.480	1796	2241	.801	1079	2162	3241	2075	2033	25	894	1321	330	8727	106.4
L.A. Lakers	82	3343	6911	.484	1805	2261	.798	1078	2440	3518	2091	1524	7	642	1203	384	8717	106.3
Orlando	82	3298	7256	.455	1818	2447	.743	1233	2429	3662	1809	1976	20	602	1391	306	8684	105.9
Philadelphia	82	3289	6925	.475	1868	2366	.790	984	2496	3480	1824	1629	11	678	1230	479	8641	105.4
Utah	82	3214	6537	.492	1951	2472	.789	867	2474	3341	2217	1796	14	652	1305	451	8527	104.0
L.A. Clippers	82	3391	7315	.464	1596	2273	.702	1246	2500	3746	2119	2043	23	725	1438	507	8491	103.5
New York	82	3308	6822	.485	1654	2147	.770	1053	2436	3489	2172	1764	8	638	1379	418	8455	103.1
New Jersey	82	3311	7459	.444	1658	2245	.739	1400	2348	3748	1782	1954	18	748	1423	600	8441	102.9
Charlotte	82	3286	7033	.467	1725	2214	.779	1027	2200	3227	2019	1946	23	759	1290	304	8428	102.8
Miami	82	3280	7139	.459	1649	2307	.715	1232	2302	3534	1904	2080	29	756	1551	387	8349	101.8
Cleveland	82	3259	6857	.475	1665	2176	.765	1011	2329	3340	2240	1672	12	643	1281	450	8343	101.7
Washington	82	3254	6868	.466	1478	2028	.729	1173	2390	3563	2081	1927	17	588	1359	468	8313	101.4
Detroit	82	3194	6875	.465	1686	2211	.763	1206	2452	3658	1825	1869	27	487	1181	367	8205	100.1
Dallas	82	3245	6890	.471	1512	1986	.761	984	2360	3344	1821	1840	14	581	1186	397	8195	99.9
Minnesota	82	3265	7276	.449	1531	2082	.735	1275	2113	3388	1885	1864	35	712	1062	440	8169	99.6
Sacramento	82	3086	6818	.453	1540	2105	.732	1027	2218	3245	1991	2075	28	631	1272	513	7928	96.7

DEFENSIVE

	FGM	FGA	Pct.	FTM	FTA	Pct.	REBOUNDS Off.	Def.	Tot.	Ast.	PF	Dq.	Stl.	TO	Blk.	SCORING Pts.	Avg.	Dif.
Detroit	3053	6743	.453	1674	2173	.770	1002	2274	3276	1736	1987	24	581	1127	289	7937	96.8	+3.3
I A. Lakers	3354	7262	.462	1278	1700	.752	1131	2187	3318	1998	1823	19	668	1175	334	8164	99.6	+6.7
Utah	3217	7011	.459	1615	2090	.773	1101	2278	3379	1858	1995	17	686	1254	409	8254	100.7	+3.3
Chicago	3267	6884	.475	1554	2017	.770	1062	2162	3224	2016	1826	17	633	1402	348	8278	101.0	+9.0
San Antonio	3265	7289	.448	1664	2187	.761	1122	2270	3392	1928	2008	31	801	1260	437	8412	102.6	+4.5
Houston	3337	7316	.456	1609	2086	.771	1242	2431	3673	1965	1786	20	711	1415	357	8466	103.2	+3.5
New York	3410	7162	.476	1471	1903	.773	1119	2336	3455	1999	1813	19	724	1239	368	8474	103.3	-0.2
Sacramento	3142	6687	.470	2045	2686	.761	1164	2543	3707	1912	1847	17	699	1312	448	8484	103.5	-6.8
Minnesota	3320	6778	.490	1680	2219	.757	1094	2379	3473	2142	1692	16	512	1238	511	8491	103.5	-3.9
Milwaukee	3290	6775	.486	1755	2312	.759	1108	2315	3423	2023	1912	17	704	1531	461	8524	104.0	+2.4
Cleveland	3459	7117	.486	1464	1916	.764	1097	2398	3495	2150	1895	20	710	1226	394	8545	104.2	-2.5
Dallas	3346	6945	.482	1700	2296	.740	1116	2489	3605	2025	1778	10	650	1147	400	8570	104.5	-4.6
Seattle	3285	6738	.488	1866	2459	.759	1107	2149	3256	1851	1820	20	729	1485	446	8643	105.4	+1.2
Philadelphia	3536	7432	.476	1388	1794	.774	1156	2519	3675	2220	1862	23	691	1177	391	8656	105.6	-0.2
Boston	3419	7559	.452	1639	2084	.786	1192	2204	3396	2052	1660	7	738	1127	381	8668	105.7	+5.8
Portland	3320	7275	.456	1819	2341	.777	1079	2354	3433	2048	2075	40	630	1397	352	8695	106.0	+8.7
Washington	3396	7280	.466	1763	2288	.771	1232	2473	3705	1861	1778	19	727	1254	492	8721	106.4	-5.0
L.A. Clippers	3337	7151	.467	1901	2529	.752	1115	2494	3609	1982	1887	23	773	1316	491	8774	107.0	-3.5
Phoenix	3462	7499	.462	1705	2244	.760	1195	2298	3493	1972	2059	24	682	1282	463	8811	107.5	+6.5
New Jersey	3374	7206	.468	1927	2493	.773	1287	2527	3814	1737	1896	18	831	1452	540	8811	107.5	-4.6
Miami	3335	6974	.478	1997	2603	.767	1176	2364	3540	2006	1960	13	853	1466	502	8840	107.8	-6.0
Charlotte	3408	6915	.493	1884	2441	.772	1151	2514	3665	2144	1841	19	675	1406	480	8858	108.0	-5.2
Atlanta	3568	7219	.494	1587	2069	.767	1080	2499	3579	2320	2034	29	688	1291	361	8940	109.0	+0.8
Orlando	3454	7232	.478	1879	2451	.767	1095	2500	3595	2118	1983	18	706	1215	654	9010	109.9	-4.0
Indiana	3577	7299	.490	1851	2490	.743	1202	2313	3515	2063	2037	21	729	1260	353	9191	112.1	-0.4
Golden State	3544	7349	.482	2121	2797	.758	1292	2480	3772	2164	2206	36	726	1534	437	9430	115.0	+1.6
Denver	4076	7962	.512	2377	3068	.775	1242	3067	4309	2492	1844	14	757	1527	525	10723	130.8	-10.9
Avgs.	3391	7150	.474	1749	2287	.765	1147	2401	3547	2029	1900	20	704	1315	431	8717	106.3	...

HOME/ROAD

	Home	Road	Total		Home	Road	Total
Atlanta	29-12	14-27	43-39	Milwaukee	33-8	15-26	48-34
Boston	35-6	21-20	56-26	Minnesota	21-20	8-33	29-53
Charlotte	17-24	9-32	26-56	New Jersey	20-21	6-35	26-56
Chicago	35-6	26-15	61-21	New York	21-20	18-23	39-43
Cleveland	23-18	10-31	33-49	Orlando	24-17	7-34	31-51
Dallas	20-21	8-33	28-54	Philadelphia	29-12	15-26	44-38
Denver	17-24	3-38	20-62	Phoenix	32-9	23-18	55-27
Detroit	32-9	18-23	50-32	Portland	36-5	27-14	63-19
Golden State	30-11	14-27	44-38	Sacramento	24-17	1-40	25-57
Houston	31-10	21-20	52-30	San Antonio	33-8	22-19	55-27
Indiana	29-12	12-29	41-41	Seattle	28-13	13-28	41-41
L.A. Clippers	23-18	8-33	31-51	Utah	36-5	18-23	54-28
L.A. Lakers	33-8	25-16	58-24	Washington	21-20	9-32	30-52
Miami	18-23	6-35	24-58	Totals	730-377	377-730	1107-1107

1990-91

POINTS
(minimum 70 games or 1,400 points)

	G	FGM	FTM	Pts.	Avg.
Michael Jordan, Chicago	.82	990	571	2580	31.5
Karl Malone, Utah	.82	847	684	2382	29.0
Bernard King, Washington	.64	713	383	1817	28.4
Charles Barkley, Philadelphia	.67	665	475	1849	27.6
Patrick Ewing, New York	.81	845	464	2154	26.6
Michael Adams, Denver	.66	560	465	1752	26.5
Dominique Wilkins, Atlanta	.81	770	476	2101	25.9
Chris Mullin, Golden State	.82	777	513	2107	25.7
David Robinson, San Antonio	.82	754	592	2101	25.6
Mitch Richmond, Golden State	.77	703	394	1840	23.9

REBOUNDS
(minimum 70 games or 800 rebounds)

	G	Off.	Def.	Tot.	Avg.
David Robinson, San Antonio	.82	335	728	1063	13.0
Dennis Rodman, Detroit	.82	361	665	1026	12.5
Charles Oakley, New York	.76	305	615	920	12.1
Karl Malone, Utah	.82	236	731	967	11.8
Patrick Ewing, New York	.81	194	711	905	11.2
Brad Daugherty, Cleveland	.76	177	653	830	10.9
Robert Parish, Boston	.81	271	585	856	10.6
Otis Thorpe, Houston	.82	287	559	846	10.3
Derrick Coleman, New Jersey	.74	269	490	759	10.3
Benoit Benjamin, L.A.C.-Seattle	.70	157	566	723	10.3

FIELD GOALS
(minimum 300 made)

	FGM	FGA	Pct.
Buck Williams, Portland	.358	595	.602
Robert Parish, Boston	.485	811	.598
Kevin Gamble, Boston	.548	933	.587
Charles Barkley, Philadelphia	.665	1167	.570
Vlade Divac, L.A. Lakers	.360	637	.565
Olden Polynice, Seattle-L.A. Clippers	.316	564	.560
Otis Thorpe, Houston	.549	988	.556
Kevin McHale, Boston	.504	912	.553
David Robinson, San Antonio	.754	1366	.552
John Paxson, Chicago	.317	578	.548

STEALS
(minimum 70 games or 125 steals)

	G	No.	Avg.
Alvin Robertson, Milwaukee	.81	246	3.04
John Stockton, Utah	.82	234	2.85
Michael Jordan, Chicago	.82	223	2.72
Tim Hardaway, Golden State	.82	214	2.61
Scottie Pippen, Chicago	.82	193	2.35
Mookie Blaylock, New Jersey	.72	169	2.35
Hersey Hawkins, Philadelphia	.80	178	2.23
Michael Adams, Denver	.66	147	2.23
Kevin Johnson, Phoenix	.77	163	2.12
Chris Mullin, Golden State	.82	173	2.11

FREE THROWS
(minimum 125 made)

	FTM	FTA	Pct.
Reggie Miller, Indiana	.551	600	.918
Jeff Malone, Utah	.231	252	.917
Ricky Pierce, Milwaukee-Seattle	.430	471	.913
Kelly Tripucka, Charlotte	.152	167	.910
Magic Johnson, L.A. Lakers	.519	573	.906
Scott Skiles, Orlando	.340	377	.902
Kiki Vandeweghe, New York	.259	288	.899
Jeff Hornacek, Phoenix	.201	224	.897
Eddie Johnson, Phoenix-Seattle	.229	257	.891
Larry Bird, Boston	.163	183	.891

BLOCKED SHOTS
(minimum 70 games or 100 blocked shots)

	G	No.	Avg.
Hakeem Olajuwon, Houston	.56	221	3.95
David Robinson, San Antonio	.82	320	3.90
Patrick Ewing, New York	.81	258	3.19
Manute Bol, Philadelphia	.82	247	3.01
Chris Dudley, New Jersey	.61	153	2.51
Larry Nance, Cleveland	.80	200	2.50
Mark Eaton, Utah	.80	188	2.35
Kevin McHale, Boston	.68	146	2.15
Pervis Ellison, Washington	.76	157	2.07
Benoit Benjamin, L.A. Clippers-Seattle	.70	145	2.07

ASSISTS
(minimum 70 games or 400 assists)

	G	No.	Avg.
John Stockton, Utah	.82	1164	14.2
Magic Johnson, L.A. Lakers	.79	989	12.5
Michael Adams, Denver	.66	693	10.5
Kevin Johnson, Phoenix	.77	781	10.1
Tim Hardaway, Golden State	.82	793	9.7
Isiah Thomas, Detroit	.48	446	9.3
Pooh Richardson, Minnesota	.82	734	9.0
Gary Grant, L.A. Clippers	.68	587	8.6
Sherman Douglas, Miami	.73	624	8.6
Scott Skiles, Orlando	.79	660	8.4

3-POINT FIELD GOALS
(minimum 50 made)

	FGA	FGM	Pct.
Jim Les, Sacramento	.154	71	.461
Trent Tucker, New York	.153	64	.418
Jeff Hornacek, Phoenix	.146	61	.418
Terry Porter, Portland	.313	130	.415
Scott Skiles, Orlando	.228	93	.408
Danny Ainge, Portland	.251	102	.406
Hersey Hawkins, Philadelphia	.270	108	.400
Larry Bird, Boston	.198	77	.389
Glen Rice, Miami	.184	71	.386
Tim Hardaway, Golden State	.252	97	.385

INDIVIDUAL STATISTICS, TEAM BY TEAM

ATLANTA HAWKS

	G	Min.	FGM	FGA	Pct.	FTM	FTA	Pct.	REBOUNDS Off.	Def.	Tot.	Ast.	PF	Dq.	Stl.	TO	Blk.	SCORING Pts.	Avg.	Hi.
Dominique Wilkins	81	3078	770	1640	.470	476	574	.829	261	471	732	265	156	0	123	201	65	2101	25.9	45
Doc Rivers	79	2586	444	1020	.435	221	262	.844	47	206	253	340	216	2	148	125	47	1197	15.2	36
John Battle	79	1863	397	862	.461	270	316	.854	34	125	159	217	145	0	45	113	6	1078	13.6	28
Spud Webb	75	2197	359	803	.447	231	266	.868	41	133	174	417	180	0	118	146	6	1003	13.4	32
Kevin Willis	80	2373	444	881	.504	159	238	.668	259	445	704	99	235	2	60	153	40	1051	13.1	29
Moses Malone	82	1912	280	598	.468	309	372	.831	271	396	667	68	134	0	30	137	74	869	10.6	25
Duane Ferrell	78	1165	174	356	.489	125	156	.801	97	82	179	55	151	3	33	78	27	475	6.1	20
Rumeal Robinson	47	674	108	242	.446	47	80	.588	20	51	71	132	65	0	32	76	8	265	5.6	19
Sidney Moncrief	72	1096	117	240	.488	82	105	.781	31	97	128	104	112	0	50	66	9	337	4.7	16
Tim McCormick	56	689	93	187	.497	66	90	.733	56	109	165	32	91	1	11	45	14	252	4.5	12
Jon Koncak	77	1931	140	321	.436	32	54	.593	101	274	375	124	265	6	74	50	76	313	4.1	20
Trevor Wilson	25	162	21	70	.300	13	26	.500	16	24	40	11	13	0	5	17	1	55	2.2	8
Howard Wright*	4	20	2	3	.667	1	1	1.000	1	5	6	0	3	0	2	0	1	5	1.3	3
Gary Leonard	4	9	0	0	...	2	4	.500	0	2	2	0	2	0	0	1	2	2	0.5	2

3-pt. FG: Atlanta 271-836 (.324)—Wilkins 85-249 (.341); Rivers 88-262 (.336); Battle 14-49 (.286); Webb 54-168 (.321); Willis 4-10 (.400); Malone 0-7 (.000); Ferrell 2-3 (.667); Robinson 2-11 (.182); Moncrief 21-64 (.328); McCormick 0-3 (.000); Koncak 1-8 (.125); Wilson 0-2 (.000). Opponents 217-621 (.349).

BOSTON CELTICS

	G	Min.	FGM	FGA	Pct.	FTM	FTA	Pct.	Off.	Def.	Tot.	Ast.	PF	Dq.	Stl.	TO	Blk.	Pts.	Avg.	Hi.
Larry Bird	60	2277	462	1017	.454	163	183	.891	53	456	509	431	118	0	108	187	58	1164	19.4	45
Reggie Lewis	79	2878	598	1219	.491	281	340	.826	119	291	410	201	234	1	98	147	85	1478	18.7	42
Kevin McHale	68	2067	504	912	.553	228	275	.829	145	335	480	126	194	2	25	140	146	1251	18.4	32
Kevin Gamble	82	2706	548	933	.587	185	227	.815	85	182	267	256	237	6	100	148	34	1281	15.6	33
Robert Parish	81	2441	485	811	.598	237	309	.767	271	585	856	66	197	1	66	153	103	1207	14.9	29
Brian Shaw	79	2772	442	942	.469	204	249	.819	104	266	370	602	206	1	105	223	34	1091	13.8	26
Dee Brown	82	1945	284	612	.464	137	157	.873	41	141	182	344	161	0	83	137	14	712	8.7	22
Ed Pinckney	70	1165	131	243	.539	104	116	.897	155	186	341	45	147	0	61	45	43	366	5.2	19
Michael Smith	47	389	95	200	.475	22	27	.815	21	35	56	43	27	0	6	37	2	218	4.6	23
Joe Kleine	72	850	102	218	.468	54	69	.783	71	173	244	21	108	0	15	53	14	258	3.6	18
Derek Smith	2	16	1	4	.250	3	4	.750	0	0	0	5	3	0	1	1	1	5	2.5	4
A.J. Wynder	6	39	3	12	.250	6	8	.750	1	2	3	8	1	0	1	4	0	12	2.0	4
Stojko Vrankovic	31	166	24	52	.462	10	18	.556	15	36	51	4	43	1	1	24	29	58	1.9	7
Dave Popson	19	64	13	32	.406	9	10	.900	7	7	14	2	12	0	1	6	2	35	1.8	10
Charles Smith	5	30	3	7	.429	3	5	.600	0	2	2	6	7	0	1	3	0	9	1.8	4

3-pt. FG: Boston 109-346 (.315)—Bird 77-198 (.389); Lewis 1-13 (.077); McHale 15-37 (.405); Gamble 0-7 (.000); Parish 0-1 (.000); Shaw 3-27 (.111); Brown 7-34 (.206); Pinckney 0-1 (.000); Kleine 0-2 (.000); D. Smith 0-1 (.000); Wynder 0-1 (.000). Opponents 191-611 (.313).

CHARLOTTE HORNETS

	G	Min.	FGM	FGA	Pct.	FTM	FTA	Pct.	Off.	Def.	Tot.	Ast.	PF	Dq.	Stl.	TO	Blk.	Pts.	Avg.	Hi.
Armon Gilliam*	25	949	195	380	.513	104	128	.813	86	148	234	27	65	1	34	64	21	494	19.8	39
Johnny Newman	81	2477	478	1017	.470	385	476	.809	94	160	254	188	278	7	100	189	17	1371	16.9	40
Rex Chapman	70	2100	410	922	.445	234	282	.830	45	146	191	250	167	1	73	131	16	1102	15.7	36
Mike Gminski†	50	1405	248	524	.473	75	95	.789	115	266	381	60	58	0	24	54	22	572	11.4	25
Mike Gminski‡	80	2196	357	808	.442	128	158	.810	186	396	582	93	99	0	40	85	56	844	10.6	25
J.R. Reid	80	2467	360	773	.466	182	259	.703	154	348	502	89	286	6	87	153	47	902	11.3	26
Kendall Gill	82	1944	376	836	.450	152	182	.835	105	158	263	303	186	0	104	163	39	906	11.0	28
Dell Curry	76	1515	337	715	.471	96	114	.842	47	152	199	166	125	0	75	80	25	802	10.6	26
Kenny Gattison	72	1552	243	457	.532	164	248	.661	136	243	379	44	211	3	48	102	67	650	9.0	19
Muggsy Bogues	81	2299	241	524	.460	86	108	.796	58	158	216	669	160	2	137	120	3	568	7.0	16
Kelly Tripucka	77	1289	187	412	.454	152	167	.910	46	130	176	159	130	0	33	92	13	541	7.0	23
Eric Leckner†	40	744	92	198	.465	46	84	.548	55	153	208	21	123	3	10	44	11	230	5.8	13
Eric Leckner‡	72	1122	131	294	.446	62	111	.559	82	213	295	39	192	4	14	69	22	324	4.5	13
Jeff Sanders	3	43	6	14	.429	1	2	.500	3	6	9	1	6	0	1	1	1	13	4.3	8
Randolph Keys	44	473	59	145	.407	19	33	.576	40	60	100	18	93	0	22	35	15	140	3.2	13
Scott Haffner	7	50	8	21	.381	1	2	.500	2	2	4	9	4	0	3	4	1	17	2.4	6
Dave Hoppen*	19	112	18	32	.563	8	10	.800	14	16	30	3	18	0	2	12	1	44	2.3	5
Earl Cureton	9	159	8	24	.333	1	3	.333	6	30	36	3	16	0	0	6	3	17	1.9	7
Steve Scheffler	39	227	20	39	.513	19	21	.905	21	24	45	9	20	0	6	4	2	59	1.5	6

3-pt. FG: Charlotte 131-417 (.314)—Newman 30-84 (.357); Chapman 48-148 (.324); Gminski† 1-6 (.167); Gminski‡ 2-14 (.143); Reid 0-2 (.000); Gill 2-14 (.143); Curry 32-86 (.372); Gattison 0-2 (.000); Bogues 0-12 (.000); Tripucka 15-45 (.333); Keys 3-14 (.214); Haffner 0-2 (.000); Hoppen* 0-1 (.000); Cureton 0-1 (.000). Opponents 158-500 (.316).

CHICAGO BULLS

	G	Min.	FGM	FGA	Pct.	FTM	FTA	Pct.	Off.	Def.	Tot.	Ast.	PF	Dq.	Stl.	TO	Blk.	Pts.	Avg.	Hi.
Michael Jordan	82	3034	990	1837	.539	571	671	.851	118	374	492	453	229	1	223	202	83	2580	31.5	46
Scottie Pippen	82	3014	600	1153	.520	240	340	.706	163	432	595	511	270	3	193	232	93	1461	17.8	43
Horace Grant	78	2641	401	733	.547	197	277	.711	266	393	659	178	203	2	95	92	69	1000	12.8	25
Bill Cartwright	79	2273	318	649	.490	124	178	.697	167	319	486	126	167	0	32	113	15	760	9.6	20
B.J. Armstrong	82	1731	304	632	.481	97	111	.874	25	124	149	301	118	0	70	107	4	720	8.8	19
John Paxson	82	1971	317	578	.548	34	41	.829	15	76	91	297	136	0	62	69	3	710	8.7	28
Stacey King	76	1198	156	334	.467	107	152	.704	72	136	208	65	134	0	24	91	42	419	5.5	16
Craig Hodges	73	843	146	344	.424	26	27	.963	10	32	42	97	74	0	34	35	2	362	5.0	20
Dennis Hopson	61	728	104	244	.426	55	83	.663	49	60	109	65	79	0	25	59	14	264	4.3	14
Will Perdue	74	972	116	235	.494	75	112	.670	122	214	336	47	147	1	23	75	57	307	4.1	15
Cliff Levingston	78	1013	127	282	.450	59	91	.648	99	126	225	56	143	0	29	50	43	314	4.0	14
Scott Williams	51	337	53	104	.510	20	28	.714	42	56	98	16	51	0	12	23	13	127	2.5	10

3-pt. FG: Chicago 155-424 (.366)—Jordan 29-93 (.312); Pippen 21-68 (.309); Grant 1-6 (.167); Armstrong 15-30 (.500); Paxson 42-96 (.438); King 0-2 (.000); Hodges 44-115 (.383); Hopson 1-5 (.200); Perdue 0-3 (.000); Levingston 1-4 (.250); Williams 1-2 (.500). Opponents 190-626 (.304).

CLEVELAND CAVALIERS

	G	Min.	FGM	FGA	Pct.	FTM	FTA	Pct.	Off.	Def.	Tot.	Ast.	PF	Dq.	Stl.	TO	Blk.	Pts.	Avg.	Hi.
Brad Daugherty	76	2946	605	1155	.524	435	579	.751	177	653	830	253	191	2	74	211	46	1645	21.6	38
Larry Nance	80	2927	635	1211	.524	265	330	.803	201	485	686	237	219	3	66	131	200	1537	19.2	34
Mark Price	16	571	97	195	.497	59	62	.952	8	37	45	166	23	0	42	56	2	271	16.9	26
John Williams	43	1293	199	430	.463	107	164	.652	111	179	290	100	126	2	36	63	69	505	11.7	23
Craig Ehlo	82	2766	344	773	.445	95	140	.679	142	246	388	376	209	0	121	160	34	832	10.1	24
Darnell Valentine	65	1841	230	496	.464	143	172	.831	37	135	172	351	170	2	98	126	12	609	9.4	28
Danny Ferry	81	1661	275	643	.428	124	152	.816	99	187	286	142	230	1	43	120	25	697	8.6	21
Chucky Brown	74	1485	263	502	.524	101	144	.701	78	135	213	80	130	0	26	94	24	627	8.5	21
Henry James	37	505	112	254	.441	52	72	.722	26	53	79	32	59	1	15	37	5	300	8.1	25

	G	Min.	FGM	FGA	Pct.	FTM	FTA	Pct.	Off.	Def.	Tot.	Ast.	PF	Dq.	Stl.	TO	Blk.	Pts.	Avg.	Hi.
Gerald Paddio	70	1181	212	506	.419	74	93	.796	38	80	118	90	71	0	20	71	6	504	7.2	24
John Morton	66	1207	120	274	.438	113	139	.813	41	62	103	243	112	1	61	107	18	357	5.4	21
Steve Kerr	57	905	99	223	.444	45	53	.849	5	32	37	131	52	0	29	40	4	271	4.8	13
Winston Bennett	27	334	40	107	.374	35	47	.745	30	34	64	28	50	0	8	20	2	115	4.3	23
Mike Woodson†	4	46	5	23	.217	1	1	1.000	1	1	2	5	7	0	0	5	1	11	2.8	9
Mike Woodson‡	15	171	26	77	.338	11	13	.846	3	10	13	15	18	0	5	12	5	64	4.3	16
Derrick Chievous	18	110	17	46	.370	9	16	.563	11	7	18	2	16	0	3	6	1	43	2.4	9
Milos Babic	12	52	6	19	.316	7	12	.583	6	3	9	4	7	0	1	5	1	19	1.6	5

3-pt. FG: Cleveland 160-479 (.334)—Daugherty 0-3 (.000); Nance 2-8 (.250); Price 18-53 (.340); Williams 0-1 (.000); Ehlo 49-149 (.329); Valentine 6-25 (.240); Ferry 23-77 (.299); Brown 0-4 (.000); James 24-60 (.400); Paddio 6-24 (.250); Morton 4-12 (.333); Kerr 28-62 (.452); Woodson† 0-1 (.000); Woodson‡ 1-7 (.143). Opponents 163-505 (.323).

DALLAS MAVERICKS

	G	Min.	FGM	FGA	Pct.	FTM	FTA	Pct.	Off.	Def.	Tot.	Ast.	PF	Dq.	Stl.	TO	Blk.	Pts.	Avg.	Hi.
Roy Tarpley	5	171	43	79	.544	16	18	.889	16	39	55	12	20	0	6	13	9	102	20.4	29
Rolando Blackman	80	2965	634	1316	.482	282	326	.865	63	193	256	301	153	0	69	159	19	1590	19.9	37
Derek Harper	77	2879	572	1226	.467	286	391	.731	59	174	233	548	222	1	147	177	14	1519	19.7	34
Herb Williams	60	1832	332	655	.507	83	130	.638	86	271	357	95	197	3	30	113	88	747	12.5	31
Rodney McCray	74	2561	336	679	.495	159	198	.803	153	407	560	259	203	3	70	129	51	844	11.4	23
James Donaldson	82	2800	327	615	.532	165	229	.721	201	526	727	69	181	0	34	146	93	819	10.0	25
Alex English	79	1748	322	734	.439	119	140	.850	108	146	254	105	141	0	40	101	25	763	9.7	27
Randy White	79	1901	265	665	.398	159	225	.707	173	331	504	63	308	6	81	131	44	695	8.8	24
Fat Lever	4	86	9	23	.391	11	14	.786	3	12	15	12	5	0	6	10	3	29	7.3	13
Kelvin Upshaw	48	514	104	231	.450	55	64	.859	20	35	55	86	77	0	28	39	5	270	5.6	19
Brad Davis	80	1426	159	373	.426	91	118	.771	13	105	118	230	212	1	45	77	17	431	5.4	15
Steve Alford	34	236	59	117	.504	26	31	.839	10	14	24	22	11	0	8	16	1	151	4.4	15
Jim Grandholm	26	168	30	58	.517	10	21	.476	20	30	50	8	33	0	2	11	8	79	3.0	10
John Shasky	57	510	51	116	.440	48	79	.608	58	76	134	11	75	0	14	27	20	150	2.6	13
Howard Wright†	3	8	2	3	.667	2	2	1.000	1	1	2	0	2	0	1	0	0	6	2.0	4
Howard Wright‡	15	164	19	47	.404	16	24	.667	12	33	45	3	28	0	4	11	5	54	3.6	13

3-pt. FG: Dallas 193-600 (.322)—Tarpley 0-1 (.000); Blackman 40-114 (.351); Harper 89-246 (.362); Williams 0-4 (.000); McCray 13-39 (.333); English 0-1 (.000); White 6-37 (.162); Lever 0-3 (.000); Upshaw 7-29 (.241); Davis 22-85 (.259); Alford 7-23 (.304); Grandholm 9-17 (.529); Wright† 0-1 (.000); Wright‡ 0-1 (.000). Opponents 178-583 (.305).

DENVER NUGGETS

	G	Min.	FGM	FGA	Pct.	FTM	FTA	Pct.	Off.	Def.	Tot.	Ast.	PF	Dq.	Stl.	TO	Blk.	Pts.	Avg.	Hi.
Michael Adams	66	2346	560	1421	.394	465	529	.879	58	198	256	693	162	1	147	240	6	1752	26.5	54
Orlando Woolridge	53	1823	490	983	.498	350	439	.797	141	220	361	119	145	2	69	152	23	1330	25.1	40
Walter Davis*	39	1044	316	667	.474	86	94	.915	52	71	123	84	108	2	62	63	3	728	18.7	41
Reggie Williams†	51	1542	323	728	.444	131	156	.840	116	131	247	87	189	7	93	76	30	820	16.1	28
Reggie Williams‡	73	1896	384	855	.449	166	197	.843	133	173	306	133	253	9	113	112	41	991	13.6	28
Mahmoud Abdul-Rauf	67	1505	417	1009	.413	84	98	.857	34	87	121	206	149	2	55	110	4	942	14.1	35
Todd Lichti	29	860	166	378	.439	59	69	.855	49	63	112	72	65	1	46	33	8	405	14.0	29
Blair Rasmussen	70	2325	405	885	.458	63	93	.677	170	508	678	70	307	15	52	81	132	875	12.5	25
Jim Farmer†	25	443	99	216	.458	46	63	.730	27	36	63	38	58	0	13	37	2	249	10.0	20
Jim Farmer‡	27	456	101	223	.453	48	65	.738	29	39	68	38	58	0	13	38	2	255	9.4	20
Corey Gaines	10	226	28	70	.400	22	26	.846	4	10	14	91	25	0	10	23	2	83	8.3	18
Jerome Lane	62	1383	202	461	.438	58	141	.411	280	298	578	123	192	1	51	105	14	463	7.5	22
Terry Mills*	17	279	56	120	.467	16	22	.727	31	57	88	16	44	0	16	18	9	128	7.5	15
Joe Wolf	74	1593	234	519	.451	69	83	.831	136	264	400	107	244	8	60	95	31	539	7.3	18
Marcus Liberty	76	1171	216	513	.421	58	92	.630	117	104	221	64	153	2	48	71	19	507	6.7	19
Kenny Battle†	40	682	95	196	.485	54	71	.761	62	61	123	47	83	0	41	36	12	243	6.1	18
Kenny Battle‡	56	945	133	282	.472	70	93	.753	83	93	176	62	108	0	60	53	18	339	6.1	23
Tim Legler	10	148	25	72	.347	5	6	.833	8	10	18	12	20	0	2	4	0	58	5.8	14
Anthony Cook	58	1121	118	283	.417	71	129	.550	134	192	326	26	100	1	35	50	72	307	5.3	14
Greg Anderson†	41	659	85	193	.440	44	87	.506	67	170	237	12	107	3	25	61	36	214	5.2	16
Greg Anderson‡	68	924	116	270	.430	60	115	.522	97	221	318	16	140	3	35	84	45	292	4.3	16
Craig Neal	10	125	14	35	.400	13	22	.591	2	14	16	37	26	1	4	19	0	44	4.4	14
Avery Johnson*	21	217	29	68	.426	21	32	.656	9	12	21	77	22	0	14	27	2	79	3.8	15
Anthony Mason	3	21	2	4	.500	6	8	.750	3	2	5	0	6	0	1	0	0	10	3.3	7
T.R. Dunn	17	217	21	47	.447	9	10	.900	22	20	42	24	30	0	12	7	1	52	3.1	12

3-pt. FG: Denver 300-1059 (.283)—Adams 167-564 (.296); Woolridge 0-4 (.000); Davis* 10-33 (.303); Williams† 43-131 (.328); Williams‡ 57-157 (.363); Abdul-Rauf 24-100 (.240); Lichti 14-47 (.298); Rasmussen 2-5 (.400); Farmer† 5-22 (.227); Farmer‡ 5-23 (.217); Gaines 5-21 (.238); Lane 1-4 (.250); Mills* 0-2 (.000); Wolf 2-15 (.133); Liberty 17-57 (.298); Battle† 3-22 (.136); Battle‡ 3-24 (.125); Legler 3-12 (.250); Cook 0-3 (.000); Neal 3-9 (.333); Anderson† 0-0; Anderson‡ 0-1 (.000); Johnson* 0-4 (.000); Dunn 1-4 (.250). Opponents 194-502 (.386).

DETROIT PISTONS

	G	Min.	FGM	FGA	Pct.	FTM	FTA	Pct.	Off.	Def.	Tot.	Ast.	PF	Dq.	Stl.	TO	Blk.	Pts.	Avg.	Hi.
Joe Dumars	80	3046	622	1292	.481	371	417	.890	62	125	187	443	135	0	89	189	7	1629	20.4	42
Isiah Thomas	48	1657	289	665	.435	179	229	.782	35	125	160	446	118	4	75	185	10	776	16.2	32
Mark Aguirre	78	2006	420	909	.462	240	317	.757	134	240	374	139	209	2	47	128	20	1104	14.2	30
James Edwards	72	1903	383	792	.484	215	295	.729	91	186	277	65	249	4	12	126	30	982	13.6	32
Vinnie Johnson	82	2390	406	936	.434	135	209	.646	110	170	280	271	166	0	75	118	15	958	11.7	32

	G	Min.	FGM	FGA	Pct.	FTM	FTA	Pct.	REBOUNDS Off.	Def.	Tot.	Ast.	PF	Dq.	Stl.	TO	Blk.	SCORING Pts.	Avg.	Hi.
Bill Laimbeer........	82	2668	372	778	.478	123	147	.837	173	564	737	157	242	3	38	98	56	904	11.0	25
Dennis Rodman.....	82	2747	276	560	.493	111	176	.631	361	665	1026	85	281	7	65	94	55	669	8.2	34
John Salley.........	74	1649	179	377	.475	186	256	.727	137	190	327	70	240	7	52	91	112	544	7.4	24
Gerald Henderson....	23	392	50	117	.427	16	21	.762	8	29	37	62	43	0	12	28	2	123	5.3	24
William Bedford....	60	562	106	242	.438	55	78	.705	55	76	131	32	76	0	2	32	36	272	4.5	20
John Long.........	25	256	35	85	.412	24	25	.960	9	23	32	18	17	0	9	14	2	96	3.8	14
Scott Hastings......	27	113	16	28	.571	13	13	1.000	14	14	28	7	23	0	0	7	0	48	1.8	7
Lance Blanks......	38	214	26	61	.426	10	14	.714	4	16	20	26	35	0	9	18	2	64	1.7	7
Tree Rollins........	37	202	14	33	.424	8	14	.571	13	29	42	4	35	0	2	15	20	36	1.0	6

3-pt. FG: Detroit 131-440 (.298)—Dumars 14-45 (.311); Thomas 19-65 (.292); Aguirre 24-78 (.308); Edwards 1-2 (.500); Johnson 11-34 (.324); Laimbeer 37-125 (.296); Rodman 6-30 (.200); Salley 0-1 (.000); Henderson 7-21 (.333); Bedford 5-13 (.385); Long 2-6 (.333); Hastings 3-4 (.750); Blanks 2-16 (.125). Opponents 157-504 (.312).

GOLDEN STATE WARRIORS

	G	Min.	FGM	FGA	Pct.	FTM	FTA	Pct.	REBOUNDS Off.	Def.	Tot.	Ast.	PF	Dq.	Stl.	TO	Blk.	SCORING Pts.	Avg.	Hi.
Chris Mullin........	82	3315	777	1449	.536	513	580	.884	141	302	443	329	176	2	173	245	63	2107	25.7	40
Mitch Richmond.....	77	3027	703	1424	.494	394	465	.847	147	305	452	238	207	0	126	230	34	1840	23.9	40
Tim Hardaway.....	82	3215	739	1551	.476	306	381	.803	87	245	332	793	228	7	214	270	12	1881	22.9	40
Sarunas Marciulionis..	50	987	183	365	.501	178	246	.724	51	67	118	85	136	4	62	75	4	545	10.9	23
Rod Higgins........	82	2024	259	559	.463	185	226	.819	109	245	354	113	198	2	52	65	37	776	9.5	24
Tom Tolbert.......	62	1371	183	433	.423	127	172	.738	87	188	275	76	195	4	35	80	38	500	8.1	19
Mario Elie†........	30	624	77	152	.507	74	87	.851	46	63	109	44	83	1	19	27	10	231	7.7	15
Mario Elie‡........	33	644	79	159	.497	75	89	.843	46	64	110	45	85	1	19	30	10	237	7.2	15
Alton Lister........	77	1552	188	393	.478	115	202	.569	121	362	483	93	282	4	20	106	90	491	6.4	19
Tyrone Hill........	74	1192	147	299	.492	96	152	.632	157	226	383	19	264	8	33	72	30	390	5.3	16
Vincent Askew....	7	85	12	25	.480	9	11	.818	7	4	11	13	21	1	2	6	0	33	4.7	10
Jim Petersen......	62	834	114	236	.483	50	76	.658	69	131	200	27	153	2	13	48	41	279	4.5	25
Kevin Pritchard....	62	773	88	229	.384	62	77	.805	16	49	65	81	104	1	30	59	8	243	3.9	15
Steve Johnson.....	24	228	34	63	.540	22	37	.595	18	39	57	17	50	1	4	25	4	90	3.8	11
Mike Smrek*......	5	25	6	11	.545	2	4	.500	3	4	7	1	9	0	2	2	0	14	2.8	4
Larry Robinson*....	24	170	24	59	.407	8	15	.533	15	8	23	11	23	0	9	16	1	56	2.3	7
Paul Mokeski.....	36	257	21	59	.356	12	15	.800	20	47	67	9	58	0	8	7	3	57	1.6	8
Les Jepsen........	21	105	11	36	.306	6	9	.667	17	20	37	1	16	0	1	3	3	28	1.3	5
Bart Kofoed.......	5	21	0	3	.000	3	6	.500	2	1	3	4	4	0	0	2	0	3	0.6	2

3-pt. FG: Golden State 270-801 (.337)—Mullin 40-133 (.301); Richmond 40-115 (.348); Hardaway 97-252 (.385); Marciulionis 1-6 (.167); Higgins 73-220 (.332); Tolbert 7-21 (.333); Elie† 3-8 (.375); Elie‡ 4-10 (.400); Lister 0-1 (.000); Petersen 1-4 (.250); Pritchard 5-31 (.161); Mokeski 3-9 (.333); Jepsen 0-1 (.000). Opponents 221-686 (.322).

HOUSTON ROCKETS

	G	Min.	FGM	FGA	Pct.	FTM	FTA	Pct.	REBOUNDS Off.	Def.	Tot.	Ast.	PF	Dq.	Stl.	TO	Blk.	SCORING Pts.	Avg.	Hi.
Hakeem Olajuwon....	56	2062	487	959	.508	213	277	.769	219	551	770	131	221	5	121	174	221	1187	21.2	39
Kenny Smith......	78	2699	522	1003	.520	287	340	.844	36	127	163	554	131	0	106	237	11	1380	17.7	38
Otis Thorpe........	82	3039	549	988	.556	334	480	.696	287	559	846	197	278	10	73	217	20	1435	17.5	35
Vernon Maxwell....	82	2870	504	1247	.404	217	296	.733	41	197	238	303	179	2	127	171	15	1397	17.0	51
Buck Johnson.......	73	2279	416	873	.477	157	216	.727	108	222	330	142	240	5	81	122	47	991	13.6	32
Sleepy Floyd......	82	1850	386	939	.411	185	246	.752	52	107	159	317	122	0	95	140	17	1005	12.3	40
David Wood.......	82	1421	148	349	.424	108	133	.812	107	139	246	94	236	4	58	89	16	432	5.3	27
Mike Woodson*.....	11	125	21	54	.389	10	12	.833	2	9	11	10	11	0	5	7	4	53	4.8	16
Kennard Winchester..	64	607	98	245	.400	35	45	.778	34	33	67	25	70	0	16	30	13	239	3.7	18
Larry Smith........	81	1923	128	263	.487	12	50	.240	302	407	709	88	265	6	83	93	22	268	3.3	12
Dave Jamerson....	37	202	43	113	.381	22	27	.815	9	21	30	27	24	0	6	20	1	113	3.1	12
Dave Feitl.........	52	372	52	140	.371	33	44	.750	29	71	100	8	52	0	3	25	12	137	2.6	12
Matt Bullard......	18	63	14	31	.452	11	17	.647	6	8	14	2	10	0	3	3	0	39	2.2	6
Adrian Caldwell.....	42	343	35	83	.422	7	17	.412	43	57	100	8	35	0	19	30	10	77	1.8	9

3-pt. FG: Houston 316-989 (.320)—Olajuwon 0-4 (.000); K. Smith 49-135 (.363); Thorpe 3-7 (.429); Maxwell 172-510 (.337); Johnson 2-15 (.133); Floyd 48-176 (.273); Wood 28-90 (.311); Woodson* 1-6 (.167); Winchester 8-20 (.400); Jamerson 5-19 (.263); Feitl 0-3 (.000); Bullard 0-3 (.000); Caldwell 0-1 (.000). Opponents 183-621 (.295).

INDIANA PACERS

	G	Min.	FGM	FGA	Pct.	FTM	FTA	Pct.	REBOUNDS Off.	Def.	Tot.	Ast.	PF	Dq.	Stl.	TO	Blk.	SCORING Pts.	Avg.	Hi.
Reggie Miller......	82	2972	596	1164	.512	551	600	.918	81	200	281	331	165	1	109	163	13	1855	22.6	40
Chuck Person......	80	2566	620	1231	.504	165	229	.721	121	296	417	238	221	1	56	184	17	1474	18.4	35
Detlef Schrempf.....	82	2632	432	831	.520	441	539	.818	178	482	660	301	262	3	58	175	22	1320	16.1	29
Vern Fleming.....	69	1929	356	671	.531	161	221	.729	83	131	214	369	116	0	76	137	13	877	12.7	31
Micheal Williams....	73	1706	261	523	.499	290	330	.879	49	127	176	348	202	1	150	150	17	813	11.1	29
Rik Smits..........	76	1690	342	705	.485	144	189	.762	116	241	357	84	246	3	24	86	111	828	10.9	31
LaSalle Thompson..	82	1946	276	565	.488	72	104	.692	154	409	563	147	265	4	63	168	63	625	7.6	19
Mike Sanders.....	80	1357	206	494	.417	47	57	.825	73	112	185	106	198	1	37	65	26	463	5.8	18
George McCloud.....	74	1070	131	351	.373	38	49	.776	35	83	118	150	141	1	40	91	11	343	4.6	18
Greg Dreiling........	73	1031	98	194	.505	63	105	.600	66	189	255	51	178	1	24	57	29	259	3.5	12
Kenny Williams.....	75	527	93	179	.520	34	50	.680	56	75	131	31	81	0	11	41	31	220	2.9	15
Randy Wittman......	41	355	35	79	.443	4	6	.667	6	27	33	25	9	0	10	10	4	74	1.8	12
Jawann Oldham.....	4	19	3	6	.500	0	0	...	0	3	3	0	1	0	0	0	6	6	1.5	6
Byron Dinkins†......	2	5	1	1	1.000	0	0	...	0	1	1	3	0	0	0	0	0	2	1.0	2
Byron Dinkins‡......	12	149	14	34	.412	8	9	.889	0	12	12	19	15	0	2	13	0	36	3.0	6

3-pt. FG: Indiana 249-749 (.332)—Miller 112-322 (.348); Person 69-203 (.340); Schrempf 15-40 (.375); Fleming 4-18 (.222); M. Williams 1-7 (.143); Thompson 1-5 (.200); Sanders 4-20 (.200); McCloud 43-124 (.347); Dreiling 0-2 (.000); K. Williams 0-3 (.000); Wittman 0-5 (.000). Opponents 186-609 (.305).

LOS ANGELES CLIPPERS

								REBOUNDS									SCORING		
	G	Min.	FGM	FGA	Pct.	FTM	FTA	Pct.	Off.	Def.	Tot.	Ast.	PF	Dq.	Stl.	TO	Blk.	Pts.	Avg.	Hi.
Charles Smith 74	2703	548	1168	.469	384	484	.793	216	392	608	134	267	4	81	165	145	1480	20.0	52
Ron Harper 39	1383	285	729	.391	145	217	.668	58	130	188	209	111	0	66	129	35	763	19.6	36
Ken Norman 70	2309	520	1037	.501	173	275	.629	177	320	497	159	192	0	63	139	63	1219	17.4	34
Danny Manning 73	2197	470	905	.519	219	306	.716	169	257	426	196	281	5	117	188	62	1159	15.9	31
Benoit Benjamin* 39	1337	229	465	.492	123	169	.728	95	374	469	74	110	1	26	138	91	581	14.9	27
Olden Polynice† 31	1132	151	261	.579	79	138	.572	106	177	283	26	98	1	17	35	13	381	12.3	30
Olden Polynice‡ 79	2092	316	564	.560	146	252	.579	220	333	553	42	192	1	43	88	32	778	9.8	30
Gary Grant 68	2105	265	587	.451	51	74	.689	69	140	209	587	192	4	103	210	12	590	8.7	24
Winston Garland 69	1702	221	519	.426	118	157	.752	46	152	198	317	189	3	97	116	10	564	8.2	21
Jeff Martin 74	1334	214	507	.422	68	100	.680	53	78	131	65	104	0	37	49	31	523	7.1	25
Bo Kimble 62	1004	159	418	.380	92	119	.773	42	77	119	76	158	2	30	77	8	429	6.9	27
Loy Vaught 73	1178	175	359	.487	49	74	.662	124	225	349	40	135	2	20	49	23	399	5.5	17
Tom Garrick 67	949	100	236	.424	60	79	.759	40	87	127	223	101	0	62	66	2	260	3.9	19
Ken Bannister 47	339	43	81	.531	25	65	.385	34	62	96	9	73	0	5	25	7	111	2.4	16
Greg Butler 9	37	5	19	.263	4	6	.667	8	8	16	1	9	0	0	4	0	14	1.6	5
Cedric Ball 7	26	3	8	.375	2	2	1.000	5	6	11	0	5	0	0	2	2	8	1.1	2
Mike Smrek† 10	70	3	16	.188	4	8	.500	4	15	19	3	18	1	1	1	3	10	1.0	4
Mike Smrek‡ 15	95	9	27	.333	6	12	.500	7	19	26	4	27	1	3	3	3	24	1.6	4

3-pt. FG: L.A. Clippers 113-434 (.260)—Smith 0-7 (.000); Harper 48-148 (.324); Norman 6-32 (.188); Manning 0-3 (.000); Polynice† 0-1 (.000); Polynice‡ 0-1 (.000); Grant 9-39 (.231); Garland 4-26 (.154); Martin 27-88 (.307); Kimble 19-65 (.292); Vaught 0-2 (.000); Garrick 0-22 (.000); Bannister 0-1 (.000). Opponents 199-593 (.336).

LOS ANGELES LAKERS

								REBOUNDS									SCORING		
	G	Min.	FGM	FGA	Pct.	FTM	FTA	Pct.	Off.	Def.	Tot.	Ast.	PF	Dq.	Stl.	TO	Blk.	Pts.	Avg.	Hi.
James Worthy 78	3008	716	1455	.492	212	266	.797	107	249	356	275	117	0	104	127	35	1670	21.4	36
Magic Johnson 79	2933	466	976	.477	519	573	.906	105	446	551	989	150	0	102	314	17	1531	19.4	34
Byron Scott 82	2630	501	1051	.477	118	148	.797	54	192	246	177	146	0	95	85	21	1191	14.5	32
Sam Perkins 73	2504	368	744	.495	229	279	.821	167	371	538	108	247	2	64	103	78	983	13.5	32
Vlade Divac 82	2310	360	637	.565	196	279	.703	205	461	666	92	247	3	106	146	127	921	11.2	25
Terry Teagle 82	1498	335	757	.443	145	177	.819	82	99	181	82	165	1	31	83	8	815	9.9	35
A.C. Green 82	2164	258	542	.476	223	302	.738	201	315	516	71	117	0	59	99	23	750	9.1	21
Mychal Thompson . . . 72	1077	113	228	.496	62	88	.705	74	154	228	21	112	0	23	47	23	288	4.0	19
Tony Smith 64	695	97	220	.441	40	57	.702	24	47	71	135	80	0	28	69	12	234	3.7	12
Larry Drew 48	496	54	125	.432	17	22	.773	5	29	34	118	40	0	15	49	1	139	2.9	11
Elden Campbell 52	380	56	123	.455	32	49	.653	40	56	96	10	71	1	11	16	38	144	2.8	12
Irving Thomas * 26	108	17	50	.340	12	21	.571	14	17	31	10	24	0	4	13	1	46	1.8	9
Tony Brown* 7	27	2	3	.667	0	0		0	4	4	3	8	0	0	4	0	5	0.7	3

3-pt. FG: L.A. Lakers 226-744 (.304)—Worthy 26-90 (.289); Johnson 80-250 (.320); Scott 71-219 (.324); Perkins 18-64 (.281); Divac 5-14 (.357); Teagle 0-9 (.000); Green 11-55 (.200); Thompson 0-2 (.000); Smith 0-7 (.000); Drew 14-33 (.424); Brown* 1-1 (1.000). Opponents 178-573 (.311).

MIAMI HEAT

								REBOUNDS									SCORING		
	G	Min.	FGM	FGA	Pct.	FTM	FTA	Pct.	Off.	Def.	Tot.	Ast.	PF	Dq.	Stl.	TO	Blk.	Pts.	Avg.	Hi.
Sherman Douglas 73	2562	532	1055	.504	284	414	.686	78	131	209	624	178	2	121	270	5	1352	18.5	42
Glen Rice 77	2646	550	1193	.461	171	209	.818	85	296	381	189	216	0	101	166	26	1342	17.4	37
Rony Seikaly 64	2171	395	822	.481	258	417	.619	207	502	709	95	213	2	51	205	86	1050	16.4	35
Kevin Edwards 79	2000	380	927	.410	171	213	.803	80	125	205	240	151	2	129	163	46	955	12.1	34
Willie Burton 76	1928	341	773	.441	229	293	.782	111	151	262	107	275	6	72	144	24	915	12.0	27
Grant Long 80	2514	276	561	.492	181	230	.787	225	343	568	176	295	10	119	156	43	734	9.2	22
Billy Thompson 73	1481	205	411	.499	89	124	.718	120	192	312	111	161	3	32	117	48	499	6.8	20
Alec Kessler 78	1259	199	468	.425	88	131	.672	115	221	336	31	189	1	17	108	26	486	6.2	21
Terry Davis 55	996	115	236	.487	69	124	.556	107	159	266	39	129	2	18	36	28	300	5.5	13
Bimbo Coles 82	1355	162	393	.412	71	95	.747	56	97	153	232	149	0	65	98	12	401	4.9	15
Milt Wagner 13	116	24	57	.421	9	11	.818	0	7	7	15	14	0	2	12	3	63	4.8	15
Jon Sundvold 24	225	43	107	.402	11	11	1.000	3	6	9	24	11	0	7	16	0	112	4.7	13
Keith Askins 39	266	34	81	.420	12	25	.480	30	38	68	19	46	0	16	11	13	86	2.2	10
Alan Ogg 31	261	24	55	.436	6	10	.600	15	34	49	2	53	1	6	8	27	54	1.7	11

3-pt. FG: Miami 140-464 (.302)—Douglas 4-31 (.129); Rice 71-184 (.386); Seikaly 2-6 (.333); Edwards 24-84 (.286); Burton 4-30 (.133); Long 1-6 (.167); Thompson 0-4 (.000); Kessler 0-4 (.000); Davis 1-2 (.500); Coles 6-34 (.176); Wagner 6-17 (.353); Sundvold 15-35 (.429); Askins 6-25 (.240); Ogg 0-2 (.000). Opponents 173-514 (.337).

MILWAUKEE BUCKS

								REBOUNDS									SCORING		
	G	Min.	FGM	FGA	Pct.	FTM	FTA	Pct.	Off.	Def.	Tot.	Ast.	PF	Dq.	Stl.	TO	Blk.	Pts.	Avg.	Hi.
Ricky Pierce* 46	1327	359	720	.499	282	311	.907	37	80	117	96	90	0	38	93	11	1037	22.5	37
Dale Ellis† 21	624	159	327	.486	58	82	.707	38	43	81	31	53	1	16	32	5	406	19.3	32
Dale Ellis‡ 51	1424	340	718	.474	120	166	.723	66	107	173	95	112	1	49	81	8	857	16.8	32
Jay Humphries 80	2726	482	960	.502	191	239	.799	57	163	220	538	237	2	129	151	7	1215	15.2	36
Alvin Robertson 81	2598	438	904	.485	199	263	.757	191	268	459	444	273	5	246	212	16	1098	13.6	31
Frank Brickowski 75	1912	372	706	.527	198	248	.798	129	297	426	131	255	4	86	160	43	942	12.6	32
Fred Roberts 82	2114	357	670	.533	170	209	.813	107	174	281	135	190	2	63	135	29	888	10.8	34
Dan Schayes 82	2228	298	597	.499	274	328	.835	174	361	535	98	264	4	55	106	61	870	10.6	21
Jack Sikma 77	1940	295	691	.427	166	197	.843	108	333	441	143	218	4	65	130	64	802	10.4	29
Jeff Grayer 82	1422	210	485	.433	101	147	.687	111	135	246	123	98	0	48	86	9	521	6.4	23

	G	Min.	FGM	FGA	Pct.	FTM	FTA	Pct.	Off.	Def.	Tot.	Ast.	PF	Dq.	Stl.	TO	Blk.	Pts.	Avg.	Hi.
Adrian Dantley 10	10	126	19	50	.380	18	26	.692	8	5	13	9	8	0	5	6	0	57	5.7	16
Brad Lohaus 81	81	1219	179	415	.431	37	54	.685	59	158	217	75	170	3	50	60	74	428	5.3	23
Steve Henson 68	68	690	79	189	.418	38	42	.905	14	37	51	131	83	0	32	43	0	214	3.1	16
Lester Conner† 39	39	519	38	96	.396	39	52	.750	10	45	55	107	37	0	48	31	1	115	2.9	13
Lester Conner‡ 74	74	1008	96	207	.464	68	94	.723	21	91	112	165	75	0	85	58	2	260	3.5	13
Greg Anderson* 26	26	247	27	73	.370	16	28	.571	26	49	75	3	29	0	8	22	9	70	2.7	12
Everette Stephens 3	3	6	2	3	.667	2	2	1.000	0	0	0	2	0	0	0	0	0	6	2.0	6
Frank Kornet 32	32	157	23	62	.371	7	13	.538	10	14	24	9	28	0	5	11	1	58	1.8	11

3-pt. FG: Milwaukee 257-753 (.341)—Pierce* 37-93 (.398); Ellis† 30-68 (.441); Ellis‡ 57-157 (.363); Humphries 60-161 (.373); Robertson 23-63 (.365); Brickowski 0-2 (.000); Roberts 4-25 (.160); Schayes 0-5 (.000); Sikma 46-135 (.341); Grayer 0-3 (.000); Dantley 1-3 (.333); Lohaus 33-119 (.277); Henson 18-54 (.333); Conner† 0-3 (.000); Conner‡ 0-5 (.000); Anderson* 0-1 (.000); Kornet 5-18 (.278). Opponents 189-574 (.329).

MINNESOTA TIMBERWOLVES

									REBOUNDS									SCORING		
	G	Min.	FGM	FGA	Pct.	FTM	FTA	Pct.	Off.	Def.	Tot.	Ast.	PF	Dq.	Stl.	TO	Blk.	Pts.	Avg.	Hi.
Tony Campbell 77	77	2893	652	1502	.434	358	446	.803	161	185	346	214	204	0	121	190	48	1678	21.8	34
Tyrone Corbin 82	82	3196	587	1311	.448	296	371	.798	185	404	589	347	257	3	162	209	53	1472	18.0	32
Pooh Richardson 82	82	3154	635	1350	.470	89	165	.539	82	204	286	734	114	0	131	174	13	1401	17.1	35
Sam Mitchell 82	82	3121	445	1010	.441	307	396	.775	188	332	520	133	338	13	66	104	57	1197	14.6	37
Felton Spencer 81	81	2099	195	381	.512	182	252	.722	272	369	641	25	337	14	48	77	121	572	7.1	23
Gerald Glass 51	51	606	149	340	.438	52	76	.684	54	48	102	42	76	2	28	41	9	352	6.9	32
Randy Breuer 73	73	1505	197	435	.453	35	79	.443	114	231	345	73	132	1	35	69	80	429	5.9	20
Scott Brooks 80	80	980	159	370	.430	61	72	.847	28	44	72	204	122	1	53	51	5	424	5.3	18
Tod Murphy 52	52	1063	90	227	.396	70	105	.667	92	163	255	60	101	1	25	32	20	251	4.8	13
Doug West 75	75	824	118	246	.480	58	84	.690	56	80	136	48	115	0	35	41	23	294	3.9	17
Richard Coffey 52	52	320	28	75	.373	12	22	.545	42	37	79	3	45	0	6	5	4	68	1.3	8
Bob Thornton 12	12	110	4	13	.308	8	10	.800	1	14	15	1	18	0	0	9	3	16	1.3	6
Dan Godfread 10	10	20	5	12	.417	3	4	.750	0	2	2	0	5	0	1	0	4	13	1.3	4
Jim Thomas 3	3	14	1	4	.250	0	0	—	0	0	0	1	0	0	1	1	0	2	0.7	2

3-pt. FG: Minnesota 108-381 (.283)—Campbell 16-61 (.262); Corbin 2-10 (.200); Richardson 42-128 (.328); Mitchell 0-9 (.000); Spencer 0-1 (.000); Glass 2-17 (.118); Brooks 45-135 (.333); Murphy 1-17 (.059); West 0-1 (.000); Coffey 0-1 (.000); Godfread 0-1 (.000). Opponents 171-505 (.339).

NEW JERSEY NETS

									REBOUNDS									SCORING		
	G	Min.	FGM	FGA	Pct.	FTM	FTA	Pct.	Off.	Def.	Tot.	Ast.	PF	Dq.	Stl.	TO	Blk.	Pts.	Avg.	Hi.
Reggie Theus 81	81	2955	583	1247	.468	292	343	.851	69	160	229	378	231	0	85	252	35	1510	18.6	36
Derrick Coleman 74	74	2602	514	1100	.467	323	442	.731	269	490	759	163	217	3	71	217	99	1364	18.4	42
Mookie Blaylock 72	72	2585	432	1039	.416	139	176	.790	67	182	249	441	180	0	169	207	40	1017	14.1	27
Chris Morris 79	79	2553	409	962	.425	179	244	.734	210	311	521	220	248	5	138	167	96	1042	13.2	32
Sam Bowie 62	62	1916	314	723	.434	169	231	.732	176	304	480	147	175	4	43	141	90	801	12.9	28
Drazen Petrovic† 43	43	882	211	422	.500	99	115	.861	41	51	92	66	111	0	37	69	1	543	12.6	27
Drazen Petrovic‡ 61	61	1015	243	493	.493	114	137	.832	51	59	110	86	132	0	43	81	1	623	10.2	27
Greg Anderson* 1	1	18	4	4	1.000	0	0	—	4	2	6	1	4	0	2	1	0	8	8.0	8
Derrick Gervin 56	56	743	164	394	.416	90	114	.789	40	70	110	30	88	0	19	45	19	425	7.6	34
Chris Dudley 61	61	1560	170	417	.408	94	176	.534	229	282	511	37	217	6	39	80	153	434	7.1	20
Jack Haley 78	78	1178	161	343	.469	112	181	.619	140	216	356	31	199	0	20	63	21	434	5.6	18
Terry Mills† 38	38	540	78	168	.464	31	44	.705	51	90	141	17	56	0	19	25	20	187	4.9	20
Terry Mills‡ 55	55	819	134	288	.465	47	66	.712	82	147	229	33	100	0	35	43	29	315	5.7	20
Roy Hinson 9	9	91	20	39	.513	1	3	.333	6	13	19	4	14	0	0	6	3	41	4.6	12
Lester Conner* 35	35	489	58	111	.523	29	42	.690	11	46	57	58	38	0	37	27	1	145	4.1	13
Tate George 56	56	594	80	193	.415	32	40	.800	19	28	47	104	58	0	25	42	5	192	3.4	18
Jud Buechler 74	74	859	94	226	.416	43	66	.652	61	80	141	51	79	0	33	26	15	232	3.1	12
Kurk Lee 48	48	265	19	71	.268	25	28	.893	7	23	30	34	39	0	11	20	2	66	1.4	8

3-pt. FG: New Jersey 161-586 (.275)—Theus 52-144 (.361); Coleman 13-38 (.342); Blaylock 14-91 (.154); Morris 45-179 (.251); Bowie 4-22 (.182); Petrovic † 22-59 (.373); Petrovic‡ 23-65 (.354); Gervin 7-28 (.250); Mills† 0-2 (.000); Mills‡ 0-4 (.000); Conner* 0-2 (.000); George 0-2 (.000); Buechler 1-4 (.250); Lee 3-15 (.200). Opponents 136-442 (.308).

NEW YORK KNICKERBOCKERS

									REBOUNDS									SCORING		
	G	Min.	FGM	FGA	Pct.	FTM	FTA	Pct.	Off.	Def.	Tot.	Ast.	PF	Dq.	Stl.	TO	Blk.	Pts.	Avg.	Hi.
Patrick Ewing 81	81	3104	845	1645	.514	464	623	.745	194	711	905	244	287	3	80	291	258	2154	26.6	50
Kiki Vandeweghe 75	75	2420	458	927	.494	259	288	.899	78	102	180	110	122	0	42	108	10	1226	16.3	29
Gerald Wilkins 68	68	2164	380	804	.473	169	206	.820	78	129	207	275	181	0	82	161	23	938	13.8	27
Charles Oakley 76	76	2739	307	595	.516	239	305	.784	305	615	920	204	288	4	62	215	17	853	11.2	24
Mark Jackson 72	72	1595	250	508	.492	117	160	.731	62	135	197	452	81	0	60	135	9	630	8.8	26
Maurice Cheeks 76	76	2147	241	483	.499	105	129	.814	22	151	173	435	138	0	128	108	10	592	7.8	27
John Starks 61	61	1173	180	410	.439	79	105	.752	30	101	131	204	137	1	59	74	17	466	7.6	25
Trent Tucker 65	65	1194	191	434	.440	17	27	.630	33	72	105	111	120	0	44	46	9	463	7.1	19
Brian Quinnett 68	68	1011	139	303	.459	26	36	.722	65	80	145	53	100	0	22	52	13	319	4.7	20
Jerrod Mustaf 62	62	825	106	228	.465	56	87	.644	51	118	169	36	109	0	15	61	14	268	4.3	13
Kenny Walker 54	54	771	83	191	.435	64	82	.780	63	94	157	13	92	0	18	30	30	230	4.3	13
Eddie Lee Wilkins 68	68	668	114	255	.447	51	90	.567	69	111	180	15	91	0	17	50	7	279	4.1	20
Stuart Gray 8	8	37	4	12	.333	3	3	1.000	2	8	10	0	6	0	0	2	1	11	1.4	4
Greg Grant 22	22	107	10	27	.370	5	6	.833	1	9	10	20	12	0	9	10	0	26	1.2	8

3-pt. FG: New York 185-558 (.332)—Ewing 0-6 (.000); Vandeweghe 51-141 (.362); G. Wilkins 9-43 (.209); Oakley 0-2 (.000); Jackson 13-51 (.255); Cheeks 5-20 (.250); Starks 27-93 (.290); Tucker 64-153 (.418); Quinnett 15-43 (.349); Mustaf 0-1 (.000); Walker 0-1 (.000); E. Wilkins 0-1 (.000); Grant 1-3 (.333). Opponents 183-545 (.336).

ORLANDO MAGIC

	G	Min.	FGM	FGA	Pct.	FTM	FTA	Pct.	Off.	Def.	Tot.	Ast.	PF	Dq.	Stl.	TO	Blk.	Pts.	Avg.	Hi.
Scott Skiles.........	79	2714	462	1039	.445	340	377	.902	57	213	270	660	192	2	89	252	4	1357	17.2	34
Dennis Scott........	82	2336	503	1183	.425	153	204	.750	62	173	235	134	203	1	62	127	25	1284	15.7	40
Terry Catledge......	51	1459	292	632	.462	161	258	.624	168	187	355	58	113	2	34	107	9	745	14.6	30
Nick Anderson	70	1971	400	857	.467	173	259	.668	92	294	386	106	145	0	74	113	44	990	14.1	31
Otis Smith	75	1885	407	902	.451	221	301	.734	176	213	389	169	190	1	85	140	35	1044	13.9	33
Jerry Reynolds	80	1843	344	793	.434	336	419	.802	88	211	299	203	123	0	95	172	56	1034	12.9	27
Jeff Turner	71	1683	259	532	.487	85	112	.759	108	255	363	97	234	5	29	126	10	609	8.6	28
Sam Vincent........	49	975	152	353	.431	99	120	.825	17	90	107	197	74	0	30	91	5	406	8.3	26
Michael Ansley.....	67	877	144	263	.548	91	127	.717	122	131	253	25	125	0	27	32	7	379	5.7	16
Howard Wright*.....	8	136	15	41	.366	13	21	.619	10	27	37	3	23	0	3	9	5	43	5.4	13
Greg Kite	82	2225	166	338	.491	63	123	.512	189	399	588	59	298	4	25	102	81	395	4.8	16
Mark Acres.........	68	1313	109	214	.509	66	101	.653	140	219	359	25	218	4	25	42	25	285	4.2	12
Morlon Wiley	34	350	45	108	.417	17	25	.680	4	13	17	73	37	1	24	34	0	113	3.3	17
Mark McNamara......	2	13	0	1	.000	0	0	...	0	4	4	0	1	0	0	0	0	0	0.0	0

3-pt. FG: Orlando 270-754 (.358)—Skiles 93-228 (.408); Scott 125-334 (.374); Catledge 0-5 (.000); Anderson 17-58 (.293); Smith 9-46 (.196); Reynolds 10-34 (.294); Turner 6-15 (.400); Vincent 3-19 (.158); Acres 1-3 (.333); Wiley 6-12 (.500). Opponents 223-674 (.331).

PHILADELPHIA 76ERS

	G	Min.	FGM	FGA	Pct.	FTM	FTA	Pct.	Off.	Def.	Tot.	Ast.	PF	Dq.	Stl.	TO	Blk.	Pts.	Avg.	Hi.
Charles Barkley......	67	2498	665	1167	.570	475	658	.722	258	422	680	284	173	2	110	210	33	1849	27.6	45
Hersey Hawkins	80	3110	590	1251	.472	479	550	.871	48	262	310	299	182	0	178	213	39	1767	22.1	39
Johnny Dawkins	4	124	26	41	.634	10	11	.909	0	16	16	28	4	0	3	8	0	63	15.8	25
Armon Gilliam†......	50	1695	292	621	.470	164	201	.816	134	230	364	78	120	1	35	110	32	748	15.0	29
Armon Gilliam‡......	75	2644	487	1001	.487	268	329	.815	220	378	598	105	185	2	69	174	53	1242	16.6	39
Ron Anderson.......	82	2340	512	1055	.485	165	198	.833	103	264	367	115	163	1	65	100	13	1198	14.6	28
Rickey Green	79	2248	334	722	.463	117	141	.830	33	104	137	413	130	0	57	108	6	793	10.0	27
Mike Gminski*......	30	791	109	284	.384	53	63	.841	71	130	201	33	41	0	16	31	34	272	9.1	19
Rick Mahorn........	80	2439	261	559	.467	189	240	.788	151	470	621	118	276	6	79	127	56	711	8.9	19
Andre Turner	70	1407	168	383	.439	64	87	.736	36	116	152	311	124	0	63	95	0	412	5.9	18
Brian Oliver........	73	800	111	272	.408	52	71	.732	18	62	80	88	76	0	34	50	4	279	3.8	19
Jayson Williams	52	508	72	161	.447	37	56	.661	41	70	111	16	92	1	9	40	6	182	3.5	17
Kenny Payne.......	47	444	68	189	.360	26	29	.897	17	49	66	16	43	0	10	21	6	166	3.5	15
Jim Farmer*.......	2	13	2	7	.286	2	2	1.000	2	3	5	0	0	0	1	0	0	6	3.0	6
Mario Elie*........	3	20	2	7	.286	1	2	.500	0	1	1	2	0	0	3	0	0	6	2.0	6
Manute Bol	82	1522	65	164	.396	24	41	.585	66	284	350	20	184	0	16	63	247	155	1.9	8
Dave Hoppen†	11	43	6	12	.500	8	12	.667	4	5	9	0	11	0	1	1	0	20	1.8	6
Dave Hoppen‡	30	155	24	44	.545	16	22	.727	18	21	39	3	29	0	3	13	1	64	2.1	6
Tony Harris........	6	41	4	16	.250	2	4	.500	0	1	1	0	5	0	1	3	0	10	1.7	5
Robert Reid	3	37	2	14	.143	0	0	...	2	7	9	4	3	0	1	3	3	4	1.3	4

3-pt. FG: Philadelphia 195-618 (.316)—Barkley 44-155 (.284); Hawkins 108-270 (.400); Dawkins 1-4 (.250); Gilliam† 0-2 (.000); Gilliam‡ 0-2 (.000); Anderson 9-43 (.209); Green 8-36 (.222); Gminski* 1-8 (.125); Mahorn 0-9 (.000); Turner 12-33 (.364); Oliver 5-18 (.278); Williams 1-2 (.500); Payne 4-18 (.222); Farmer* 0-1 (.000); Elie* 1-2 (.500); Bol 1-14 (.071); Hoppen† 0-1 (.000); Hoppen‡ 0-2 (.000); Harris 0-2 (.000). Opponents 196-660 (.297).

PHOENIX SUNS

	G	Min.	FGM	FGA	Pct.	FTM	FTA	Pct.	Off.	Def.	Tot.	Ast.	PF	Dq.	Stl.	TO	Blk.	Pts.	Avg.	Hi.
Kevin Johnson	77	2772	591	1145	.516	519	616	.843	54	217	271	781	174	0	163	269	11	1710	22.2	38
Tom Chambers	76	2475	556	1271	.437	379	459	.826	104	386	490	194	235	3	65	177	52	1511	19.9	39
Jeff Hornacek	80	2733	544	1051	.518	201	224	.897	74	247	321	409	185	1	111	130	16	1350	16.9	31
Xavier McDaniel†	66	2105	451	896	.503	144	198	.727	137	339	476	149	214	2	50	144	42	1046	15.8	34
Xavier McDaniel‡	81	2634	590	1186	.497	193	267	.723	173	384	557	187	264	2	76	184	46	1373	17.0	41
Dan Majerle	77	2281	397	821	.484	227	298	.762	168	250	418	216	162	0	106	114	40	1051	13.6	26
Eddie Johnson*	15	312	88	186	.473	21	29	.724	16	30	46	17	37	0	9	24	2	203	13.5	35
Cedric Ceballos.....	63	730	204	419	.487	110	166	.663	77	73	150	35	70	0	22	69	5	519	8.2	34
Mark West	82	1957	247	382	.647	135	206	.655	171	393	564	37	266	2	32	86	161	629	7.7	21
Kenny Battle*	16	263	38	86	.442	20	29	.690	21	32	53	15	25	0	19	17	6	96	6.0	23
Negele Knight	64	792	131	308	.425	71	118	.602	20	51	71	191	83	0	20	76	7	339	5.3	27
Andrew Lang	63	1152	109	189	.577	93	130	.715	113	190	303	27	168	2	17	45	127	311	4.9	16
Tim Perry	46	587	75	144	.521	43	70	.614	53	73	126	27	60	1	23	32	43	193	4.2	19
Ian Lockhart	1	2	1	1	1.000	2	2	1.000	0	0	0	0	0	0	0	0	0	4	4.0	4
Kurt Rambis	62	900	83	167	.497	60	85	.706	77	189	266	64	107	1	25	45	11	226	3.6	10
Joe Barry Carroll.....	11	96	13	36	.361	11	12	.917	3	21	24	11	18	0	1	12	8	37	3.4	8
Ed Nealy	55	573	45	97	.464	28	38	.737	44	107	151	36	46	0	24	19	4	123	2.2	9

3-pt. FG: Phoenix 138-432 (.319)—K. Johnson 9-44 (.205); Chambers 20-73 (.274); Hornacek 61-146 (.418); McDaniel† 0-5 (.000); McDaniel‡ 0-8 (.000); Majerle 30-86 (.349); E. Johnson* 6-21 (.286); Ceballos 1-6 (.167); Battle* 0-2 (.000); Knight 6-25 (.240); Lang 0-1 (.000); Perry 0-5 (.000); Rambis 0-2 (.000); Nealy 5-16 (.313). Opponents 182-584 (.312).

PORTLAND TRAIL BLAZERS

	G	Min.	FGM	FGA	Pct.	FTM	FTA	Pct.	Off.	Def.	Tot.	Ast.	PF	Dq.	Stl.	TO	Blk.	Pts.	Avg.	Hi.
Clyde Drexler	82	2852	645	1338	.482	416	524	.794	212	334	546	493	226	2	144	232	60	1767	21.5	39
Terry Porter	81	2665	486	944	.515	279	339	.823	52	230	282	649	151	2	158	189	12	1381	17.0	38
Kevin Duckworth.....	81	2511	521	1084	.481	240	311	.772	177	354	531	89	251	5	33	186	34	1282	15.8	27
Jerome Kersey	73	2359	424	887	.478	232	327	.709	169	312	481	227	251	4	101	149	76	1084	14.8	35
Clifford Robinson	82	1940	373	806	.463	205	314	.653	123	226	349	151	263	2	78	133	76	957	11.7	22

	G	Min.	FGM	FGA	Pct.	FTM	FTA	Pct.	REBOUNDS Off.	Def.	Tot.	Ast.	PF	Dq.	Stl.	TO	Blk.	SCORING Pts.	Avg.	Hi.
Buck Williams.......	80	2582	358	595	.602	217	308	.705	227	524	751	97	247	2	47	137	47	933	11.7	26
Danny Ainge.......	80	1710	337	714	.472	114	138	.826	45	160	205	285	195	2	63	100	13	890	11.1	20
Walter Davis†	32	439	87	195	.446	21	23	.913	19	39	58	41	42	0	18	25	0	196	6.1	16
Walter Davis‡	71	1483	403	862	.468	107	117	.915	71	110	181	125	150	2	80	88	3	924	13.0	41
Mark Bryant.......	53	781	99	203	.488	74	101	.733	65	125	190	27	120	0	15	33	12	272	5.1	20
Drazen Petrovic*...	18	133	32	71	.451	15	22	.682	10	8	18	20	21	0	6	12	0	80	4.4	11
Danny Young	75	897	103	271	.380	41	45	.911	22	53	75	141	49	0	50	50	7	283	3.8	21
Alaa Abdelnaby......	43	290	55	116	.474	25	44	.568	27	62	89	12	39	0	4	22	12	135	3.1	15
Wayne Cooper	67	746	57	145	.393	33	42	.786	54	134	188	22	120	0	7	22	61	147	2.2	13

3-pt. FG: Portland 341-904 (.377)—Drexler 61-191 (.319); Porter 130-313 (.415); Duckworth 0-2 (.000); Kersey 4-13 (.308); Robinson 6-19 (.316); Ainge 102-251 (.406); Davis† 1-3 (.333); Davis‡ 11-36 (.306); Bryant 0-1 (.000); Petrovic* 1-6 (.167); Young 36-104 (.346); Cooper 0-1 (.000). Opponents 236-730 (.323).

SACRAMENTO KINGS

	G	Min.	FGM	FGA	Pct.	FTM	FTA	Pct.	REBOUNDS Off.	Def.	Tot.	Ast.	PF	Dq.	Stl.	TO	Blk.	SCORING Pts.	Avg.	Hi.
Antoine Carr........	77	2527	628	1228	.511	295	389	.758	163	257	420	191	315	14	45	171	101	1551	20.1	41
Wayman Tisdale	33	1116	262	542	.483	136	170	.800	75	178	253	66	99	0	23	82	28	660	20.0	36
Lionel Simmons	79	2978	549	1301	.422	320	435	.736	193	504	697	315	249	0	113	230	85	1421	18.0	42
Travis Mays	64	2145	294	724	.406	255	331	.770	54	124	178	253	169	1	81	159	11	915	14.3	36
Rory Sparrow	80	2375	371	756	.491	58	83	.699	45	141	186	362	189	1	83	126	16	831	10.4	32
Anthony Bonner	34	750	103	230	.448	44	76	.579	59	102	161	49	62	0	39	41	5	250	7.4	18
Jim Les	55	1399	119	268	.444	86	103	.835	18	93	111	299	141	0	57	75	4	395	7.2	20
Duane Causwell	76	1719	210	413	.508	105	165	.636	141	250	391	69	225	4	49	96	148	525	6.9	22
Leon Wood.........	12	222	25	63	.397	19	21	.905	5	14	19	49	10	0	5	12	0	81	6.8	25
Bobby Hansen.......	36	811	96	256	.375	18	36	.500	33	63	96	90	72	1	20	34	5	229	6.4	18
Bill Wennington	77	1455	181	415	.436	74	94	.787	101	239	340	69	230	4	46	51	59	437	5.7	15
Anthony Frederick....	35	475	67	168	.399	43	60	.717	36	48	84	44	50	0	22	40	13	177	5.1	22
Rick Calloway	64	678	75	192	.391	55	79	.696	25	53	78	61	98	1	22	51	7	205	3.2	16
Steve Colter	19	251	23	56	.411	7	10	.700	5	21	26	37	27	0	11	11	1	58	3.1	17
Ralph Sampson	25	348	34	93	.366	5	19	.263	41	70	111	17	54	0	11	27	17	74	3.0	8
Eric Leckner*	32	378	39	96	.406	16	27	.593	27	60	87	18	69	1	4	25	11	94	2.9	10
Mike Higgins........	7	61	6	10	.600	4	7	.571	4	1	5	2	16	1	0	4	2	16	2.3	6
Tony Dawson	4	17	4	7	.571	0	0	...	2	0	2	0	0	0	0	1	0	9	2.3	4

3-pt. FG: Sacramento 216-578 (.374)—Carr 0-3 (.000); Tisdale 0-1 (.000); Simmons 3-11 (.273); Mays 72-197 (.365); Sparrow 31-78 (.397); Les 71-154 (.461); Wood 12-38 (.316); Hansen 19-69 (.275); Wennington 1-5 (.200); Calloway 0-2 (.000); Colter 5-14 (.357); Sampson 1-5 (.200); Dawson 1 1 (1.000). Opponents 155-491 (.316).

SAN ANTONIO SPURS

	G	Min.	FGM	FGA	Pct.	FTM	FTA	Pct.	REBOUNDS Off.	Def.	Tot.	Ast.	PF	Dq.	Stl.	TO	Blk.	SCORING Pts.	Avg.	Hi.
David Robinson	82	3095	754	1366	.552	592	777	.762	335	728	1063	208	264	5	127	270	320	2101	25.6	43
Terry Cummings	67	2195	503	1039	.484	164	240	.683	194	327	521	157	225	5	61	131	30	1177	17.6	31
Sean Elliott	82	3044	478	976	.490	325	402	.808	142	314	456	238	190	2	69	147	33	1301	15.9	34
Willie Anderson......	75	2592	453	991	.457	170	213	.798	68	283	351	358	226	4	79	167	46	1083	14.4	28
Rod Strickland	58	2076	314	651	.482	161	211	.763	57	162	219	463	125	0	117	156	11	800	13.8	27
Reggie Williams*	22	354	61	127	.480	35	41	.854	17	42	59	46	64	2	20	36	11	171	7.8	22
Paul Pressey	70	1683	201	426	.472	110	133	.827	50	126	176	271	174	1	63	130	32	528	7.5	18
Sidney Green	66	1099	177	384	.461	89	105	.848	98	215	313	52	172	0	32	89	13	443	6.7	19
David Wingate	25	563	53	138	.384	29	41	.707	24	51	75	46	66	0	19	42	5	136	5.4	15
Avery Johnson†	47	742	101	209	.483	38	55	.691	13	43	56	153	40	0	33	47	2	241	5.1	21
Avery Johnson‡	68	959	130	277	.469	59	87	.678	22	55	77	230	62	0	47	74	4	320	4.7	21
Clifford Lett	7	99	14	29	.483	6	9	.667	1	6	7	7	9	0	2	8	1	34	4.9	11
Sean Higgins	50	464	97	212	.458	28	33	.848	18	45	63	35	53	0	8	49	1	225	4.5	22
David Greenwood	63	1018	85	169	.503	69	94	.734	61	160	221	52	172	3	29	71	25	239	3.8	15
Dwayne Schintzius ..	42	398	68	155	.439	22	40	.550	28	93	121	17	64	0	2	34	29	158	3.8	16
Pete Myers*	8	103	10	23	.435	9	11	.818	2	16	18	14	14	0	3	14	3	29	3.6	8
Byron Dinkins*......	10	144	13	33	.394	8	9	.889	0	11	11	19	12	0	2	13	0	34	3.4	6
Tony Massenburg	35	277	27	60	.450	28	45	.622	23	35	58	4	26	0	4	13	9	82	2.3	19

3-pt. FG: San Antonio 81-297 (.273)—Robinson 1-7 (.143); Cummings 7-33 (.212); Elliott 20-64 (.313); Anderson 7-35 (.200); Strickland 11-33 (.333); Williams* 14-26 (.538); Pressey 16-57 (.281); Green 0-3 (.000); Wingate 1-9 (.111); Johnson† 1-5 (.200); Johnson‡ 1-9 (.111); Lett 0-1 (.000); Higgins 3-19 (.158); Greenwood 0-2 (.000); Schintzius 0-2 (.000); Myers 0-1 (.000). Opponents 218-704 (.310).

SEATTLE SUPERSONICS

	G	Min.	FGM	FGA	Pct.	FTM	FTA	Pct.	REBOUNDS Off.	Def.	Tot.	Ast.	PF	Dq.	Stl.	TO	Blk.	SCORING Pts.	Avg.	Hi.
Xavier McDaniel*	15	529	139	290	.479	49	69	.710	36	45	81	38	50	0	26	40	4	327	21.8	41
Ricky Pierce†	32	840	202	436	.463	148	160	.925	30	44	74	72	80	1	22	54	2	561	17.5	27
Ricky Pierce‡	78	2167	561	1156	.485	430	471	.913	67	124	191	168	170	1	60	147	13	1598	20.5	37
Eddie Johnson†	66	1773	455	936	.486	208	228	.912	91	134	225	94	144	0	49	98	7	1151	17.4	34
Eddie Johnson‡	81	2085	543	1122	.484	229	257	.891	107	164	271	111	181	0	58	122	9	1354	16.7	35
Derrick McKey	73	2503	438	847	.517	235	278	.845	172	251	423	169	220	2	91	158	56	1115	15.3	33
Shawn Kemp	81	2442	462	909	.508	288	436	.661	267	412	679	144	319	11	77	202	123	1214	15.0	31
Dale Ellis*..........	30	800	181	391	.463	62	84	.738	28	64	92	64	59	0	33	49	3	451	15.0	26
Benoit Benjamin†	31	899	157	313	.502	87	126	.690	62	192	254	45	74	0	28	97	54	401	12.9	28

								REBOUNDS									SCORING		
	G	Min.	FGM	FGA	Pct.	FTM	FTA	Pct.	Off.	Def.	Tot.	Ast.	PF	Dq.	Stl.	TO	Blk.	Pts.	Avg.	Hi.
Benoit Benjamin‡	70	2236	386	778	.496	210	295	.712	157	566	723	119	184	1	54	235	145	982	14.0	28
Sedale Threatt......	80	2066	433	835	.519	137	173	.792	25	74	99	273	191	0	113	138	8	1013	12.7	31
Olden Polynice*	48	960	165	303	.545	67	114	.588	114	156	270	16	94	0	26	53	19	397	8.3	27
Gary Payton	82	2244	259	575	.450	69	97	.711	108	135	243	528	249	3	165	180	15	588	7.2	19
Michael Cage	82	2141	226	445	.508	70	112	.625	177	381	558	89	194	0	85	83	58	522	6.4	17
Dana Barros	66	750	154	311	.495	78	85	.918	17	54	71	111	40	0	23	54	1	418	6.3	24
Quintin Dailey	30	299	73	155	.471	38	62	.613	11	21	32	16	25	0	7	19	1	184	6.1	29
Nate McMillan.......	78	1434	132	305	.433	57	93	.613	71	180	251	371	211	6	104	122	20	338	4.3	12
Dave Corzine........	28	147	17	38	.447	13	22	.591	10	23	33	4	18	0	5	2	5	47	1.7	10
Scott Meents	13	53	7	28	.250	2	4	.500	3	7	10	8	5	0	7	6	4	17	1.3	4

3-pt. FG: Seattle 136-427 (.319)—McDaniel* 0-3 (.000); Pierce† 9-23 (.391); Pierce‡ 46-116 (.397); Johnson† 33-99 (.333); Johnson‡ 39-120 (.325); McKey 4-19 (.211); Kemp 2-12 (.167); Ellis* 27-89 (.303); Threatt 10-35 (.286); Payton 1-13 (.077); Cage 0-3 (.000); Barros 32-81 (.395); Dailey 0-1 (.000); McMillan 17-48 (.354); Meents 1-1 (1.000). Opponents 207-633 (.327).

UTAH JAZZ

								REBOUNDS									SCORING		
	G	Min.	FGM	FGA	Pct.	FTM	FTA	Pct.	Off.	Def.	Tot.	Ast.	PF	Dq.	Stl.	TO	Blk.	Pts.	Avg.	Hi.
Karl Malone	82	3302	847	1608	.527	684	888	.770	236	731	967	270	268	2	89	244	79	2382	29.0	41
Jeff Malone.........	69	2466	525	1034	.508	231	252	.917	36	170	206	143	128	0	50	108	6	1282	18.6	43
John Stockton.......	82	3103	496	978	.507	363	434	.836	46	191	237	1164	233	1	234	298	16	1413	17.2	28
Thurl Bailey........	82	2486	399	872	.458	219	271	.808	101	306	407	124	160	0	53	130	91	1017	12.4	25
Blue Edwards	62	1611	244	464	.526	82	117	.701	51	150	201	108	203	4	57	105	29	576	9.3	25
Darrell Griffith	75	1005	174	445	.391	34	45	.756	17	73	90	37	100	1	42	48	7	430	5.7	24
Mark Eaton	80	2580	169	292	.579	71	112	.634	182	485	667	51	298	6	39	99	188	409	5.1	13
Mike Brown	82	1391	129	284	.454	132	178	.742	109	228	337	49	166	0	29	82	24	390	4.8	16
Delaney Rudd	82	874	124	285	.435	59	71	.831	14	52	66	216	92	0	36	102	2	324	4.0	11
Pat Cummings	4	26	4	6	.667	7	10	.700	3	2	5	0	8	0	0	2	0	15	3.8	10
Tony Brown†.......	23	267	28	77	.364	20	23	.870	24	15	39	13	39	0	4	12	0	78	3.4	10
Tony Brown‡........	30	294	30	80	.375	20	23	.870	24	19	43	16	47	0	4	16	0	83	2.8	10
Andy Toolson	47	470	50	124	.403	25	33	.758	32	35	67	31	58	0	14	24	2	137	2.9	13
Walter Palmer......	28	85	15	45	.333	10	15	.667	6	15	21	6	20	0	3	6	4	40	1.4	6
Chris Munk.........	11	29	3	7	.429	7	12	.583	5	9	14	1	5	0	1	5	2	13	1.2	4
Dan O'Sullivan	21	85	7	16	.438	7	11	.636	5	12	17	4	18	0	1	4	1	21	1.0	6

3-pt. FG: Utah 148-458 (.323)—K. Malone 4-14 (.286); J. Malone 1-6 (.167); Stockton 58-168 (.345); Bailey 0-3 (.000); Edwards 6-24 (.250); Griffith 48-138 (.348); Rudd 17-61 (.279); T. Brown† 2-11 (.182); T. Brown‡ 3-12 (.250); Toolson 12-32 (.375); Palmer 0-1 (.000). Opponents 205-667 (.307).

WASHINGTON BULLETS

								REBOUNDS									SCORING		
	G	Min.	FGM	FGA	Pct.	FTM	FTA	Pct.	Off.	Def.	Tot.	Ast.	PF	Dq.	Stl.	TO	Blk.	Pts.	Avg.	Hi.
Bernard King........	64	2401	713	1511	.472	383	485	.790	114	205	319	292	187	1	56	255	16	1817	28.4	52
Harvey Grant........	77	2842	609	1224	.498	185	249	.743	179	378	557	204	232	2	91	125	61	1405	18.2	34
Ledell Eackles.......	67	1616	345	762	.453	164	222	.739	47	81	128	136	121	0	47	115	10	868	13.0	33
John Williams.......	33	941	164	393	.417	73	97	.753	42	135	177	133	63	0	39	68	6	411	12.5	27
Pervis Ellison	76	1942	326	636	.513	139	214	.650	224	361	585	102	268	6	49	146	157	791	10.4	30
A.J. English.........	70	1443	251	572	.439	111	157	.707	66	81	147	177	127	1	25	114	15	616	8.8	31
Haywoode Workman..	73	2034	234	515	.454	101	133	.759	51	191	242	353	162	1	87	135	7	581	8.0	21
Darrell Walker.......	71	2305	230	535	.430	93	154	.604	140	358	498	459	199	2	78	154	33	553	7.8	22
Larry Robinson†.....	12	255	38	91	.418	7	12	.583	14	14	28	24	26	0	7	11	0	83	6.9	13
Larry Robinson‡.....	36	425	62	150	.413	15	27	.556	29	22	51	35	49	0	16	27	1	139	3.9	13
Mark Alarie.........	42	587	99	225	.440	41	48	.854	41	76	117	45	88	1	15	40	8	244	5.8	15
Tom Hammonds	70	1023	155	336	.461	57	79	.722	58	148	206	43	108	0	15	54	7	367	5.2	21
Byron Irvin	33	316	60	129	.465	50	61	.820	24	21	45	24	32	0	15	16	2	171	5.2	16
Greg Foster.........	54	606	97	211	.460	42	61	.689	52	99	151	37	112	1	12	45	22	236	4.4	12
Charles Jones	62	1499	67	124	.540	29	50	.580	119	240	359	48	199	2	51	46	124	163	2.6	10
Clinton Smith	5	45	2	4	.500	3	6	.500	2	2	4	4	3	0	1	1	0	7	1.4	2

3-pt. FG: Washington 55-284 (.194)—King 8-37 (.216); Grant 2-15 (.133); Eackles 14-59 (.237); Williams 10-41 (.244); Ellison 0-6 (.000); English 3-31 (.097); Workman 12-50 (.240); Walker 0-9 (.000); Robinson† 0-1 (.000); Robinson‡ 0-1 (.000); Alarie 5-21 (.238); Hammonds 0-4 (.000); Irvin 1-5 (.200); Foster 0-5 (.000). Opponents 166-555 (.299).

* Finished season with another team.   † Totals with this team only.   ‡ Totals with all teams.

EASTERN CONFERENCE

FIRST ROUND

Chicago 3, New York 0
Apr. 25—Thur. New York 85 at Chicago 126
Apr. 28—Sun. New York 79 at Chicago 89
Apr. 30—Tue. Chicago 103 at New York 94

Boston 3, Indiana 2
Apr. 26—Fri. Indiana 120 at Boston 127
Apr. 28—Sun. Indiana 130 at Boston 118
May 1—Wed. Boston 112 at Indiana 105
May 3—Fri. Boston 113 at Indiana 116
May 5—Sun. Indiana 121 at Boston 124

Detroit 3, Atlanta 2
Apr. 26—Fri. Atlanta 103 at Detroit 98
Apr. 28—Sun. Atlanta 88 at Detroit 101
Apr. 30—Tue. Detroit 103 at Atlanta 91
May 2—Thur. Detroit 111 at Atlanta 123
May 5—Sun. Atlanta 81 at Detroit 113

Philadelphia 3, Milwaukee 0
Apr. 25—Thur. Philadelphia 99 at Milwaukee 90
Apr. 27—Sat. Philadelphia 116 at Milwaukee *112
Apr. 30—Tue. Milwaukee 100 at Philadelphia 121

SEMIFINALS

Chicago 4, Philadelphia 1
May 4—Sat. Philadelphia 92 at Chicago 105
May 6—Mon. Philadelphia 100 at Chicago 112
May 10—Fri. Chicago 97 at Philadelphia 99
May 12—Sun. Chicago 101 at Philadelphia 85
May 14—Tue. Philadelphia 95 at Chicago 100

Detroit 4, Boston 2
May 7—Tue. Detroit 86 at Boston 75
May 9—Thur. Detroit 103 at Boston 109
May 11—Sat. Boston 115 at Detroit 83
May 13—Mon. Boston 97 at Detroit 104
May 15—Wed. Detroit 116 at Boston 111
May 17—Fri. Boston 113 at Detroit *117

FINALS

Chicago 4, Detroit 0
May 19—Sun. Detroit 83 at Chicago 94
May 21—Tue. Detroit 97 at Chicago 105
May 25—Sat. Chicago 113 at Detroit 107
May 27—Mon. Chicago 115 at Detroit 94

WESTERN CONFERENCE

FIRST ROUND

Portland 3, Seattle 2
Apr. 26—Fri. Seattle 102 at Portland 110
Apr. 28—Sun. Seattle 106 at Portland 115
Apr. 30—Tue. Portland 99 at Seattle 102
May 2—Thur. Portland 89 at Seattle 101
May 4—Sat. Seattle 107 at Portland 119

Golden State 3, San Antonio 1
Apr. 25—Thur. Golden State 121 at San Antonio 130
Apr. 27—Sat. Golden State 111 at San Antonio 98
May 1—Wed. San Antonio 106 at Golden State 109
May 3—Fri. San Antonio 97 at Golden State 110

L.A. Lakers 3, Houston 0
Apr. 25—Thur. Houston 92 at L.A. Lakers 94
Apr. 27—Sat. Houston 98 at L.A. Lakers 109
Apr. 30—Tue. L.A. Lakers 94 at Houston 90

Utah 3, Phoenix 1
Apr. 25—Thur. Utah 129 at Phoenix 90
Apr. 27—Sat. Utah 92 at Phoenix 102
Apr. 30—Tue. Phoenix 98 at Utah 107
May 2—Thur. Phoenix 93 at Utah 101

SEMIFINALS

L.A. Lakers 4, Golden State 1
May 5—Sun. Golden State 116 at L.A. Lakers 126
May 8—Wed. Golden State 125 at L.A. Lakers 124
May 10—Fri. L.A. Lakers 115 at Golden State 112
May 12—Sun. L.A. Lakers 123 at Golden State 107
May 14—Tue. Golden State 119 at L.A. Lakers *124

Portland 4, Utah 1
May 7—Tue. Utah 97 at Portland 117
May 9—Thur. Utah 116 at Portland 118
May 11—Sat. Portland 101 at Utah 107
May 12—Sun. Portland 104 at Utah 101
May 14—Tue. Utah 96 at Portland 103

FINALS

L.A. Lakers 4, Portland 2
May 18—Sat. L.A. Lakers 111 at Portland 106
May 21—Tue. L.A. Lakers 98 at Portland 109
May 24—Fri. Portland 92 at L.A. Lakers 106
May 26—Sun. Portland 95 at L.A. Lakers 116
May 28—Tue. L.A. Lakers 84 at Portland 95
May 30—Thur. Portland 90 at L.A. Lakers 91

NBA FINALS

Chicago 4, L.A. Lakers 1
June 2—Sun. L.A. Lakers 93 at Chicago 91
June 5—Wed. L.A. Lakers 86 at Chicago 107
June 7—Fri. Chicago 104 at L.A. Lakers *96
June 9—Sun. Chicago 97 at L.A. Lakers 82
June 12—Wed. Chicago 108 at L.A. Lakers 101

*Denotes number of overtime periods.

1990-91

1989-90

1989-90 NBA CHAMPION DETROIT PISTONS

Front row (from left): trainer Mike Abdenour, assistant to general manager Will Robinson, assistant coach Brendan Suhr, head coach Chuck Daly, managing partner William Davidson, general manager Jack McCloskey, CEO Thomas Wilson, legal counsel Oscar Feldman, assistant coach Brendan Malone, chief scout Stan Novak, announcer George Blaha. Back row (from left): Isiah Thomas, Joe Dumars, Mark Aguirre, David Greenwood, Bill Laimbeer, William Bedford, James Edwards, John Salley, Scott Hastings, Dennis Rodman, Ralph Lewis, Vinnie Johnson, Gerald Henderson.

FINAL STANDINGS

ATLANTIC DIVISION

	Atl.	Bos.	Char.	Chi.	Cle.	Dal.	Den.	Det.	G.S.	Hou.	Ind.	L.A.C.	L.A.L.	Mia.	Mil.	Min.	N.J.	N.Y.	Orl.	Phi.	Pho.	Por.	Sac.	S.A.	Sea.	Uta.	Was.	W	L	Pct.	GB
Philadelphia	2	2	2	2	2	1	1	3	1	1	4	2	1	5	3	1	4	3	2	..	1	1	1	1	1	1	5	53	29	.646	..
Boston	3	..	2	2	3	1	1	2	1	2	1	1	0	5	2	1	5	4	4	3	1	0	2	1	2	1	2	52	30	.634	1
New York	3	1	1	1	2	1	1	0	2	1	3	2	0	5	2	1	4	..	2	2	1	0	2	1	1	1	5	45	37	.549	8
Washington	2	3	2	1	1	1	1	0	1	1	1	1	3	1	1	3	0	4	1	0	1	1	0	0	0	1	..	31	51	.378	22
Miami	0	0	1	0	0	0	0	1	0	1	1	2	0	..	2	1	1	1	3	0	0	0	1	0	0	1	2	18	64	.220	35
New Jersey	2	1	1	1	0	0	0	0	0	1	0	0	0	4	0	1	..	1	1	1	0	0	1	0	0	0	2	17	65	.207	36

CENTRAL DIVISION

	Atl.	Bos.	Char.	Chi.	Cle.	Dal.	Den.	Det.	G.S.	Hou.	Ind.	L.A.C.	L.A.L.	Mia.	Mil.	Min.	N.J.	N.Y.	Orl.	Phi.	Pho.	Por.	Sac.	S.A.	Sea.	Uta.	Was.	W	L	Pct.	GB
Detroit	2	2	2	4	4	1	2	..	1	1	4	1	1	3	3	2	4	4	5	1	2	1	2	1	1	1	4	59	23	.720	..
Chicago	5	2	2	..	5	2	1	1	2	1	2	1	1	4	4	2	3	3	3	2	2	1	1	1	1	0	3	55	27	.671	4
Milwaukee	2	2	2	1	2	1	1	2	1	1	2	1	1	2	..	2	4	2	5	1	1	1	1	1	2	0	3	44	38	.537	15
Cleveland	3	1	1	0	..	0	0	1	1	0	3	1	1	4	3	1	4	2	4	2	1	1	2	1	1	1	3	42	40	.512	17
Indiana	3	1	3	2	0	2	1	1	1	1	..	0	0	3	3	1	4	1	4	0	1	1	1	1	1	1	3	42	40	.512	17
Atlanta	..	1	2	0	2	0	1	3	2	2	2	1	0	4	3	1	2	1	5	2	0	1	1	1	1	1	2	41	41	.500	18
Orlando	0	0	1	2	1	0	0	0	0	0	1	0	1	1	0	1	3	2	..	2	0	0	1	1	0	1	0	18	64	.220	41

MIDWEST DIVISION

	Atl.	Bos.	Char.	Chi.	Cle.	Dal.	Den.	Det.	G.S.	Hou.	Ind.	L.A.C.	L.A.L.	Mia.	Mil.	Min.	N.J.	N.Y.	Orl.	Phi.	Pho.	Por.	Sac.	S.A.	Sea.	Uta.	Was.	W	L	Pct.	GB
San Antonio	1	1	5	1	1	2	3	1	3	2	1	4	2	2	1	4	2	1	1	4	1	4	1	..	3	3	2	56	26	.683	..
Utah	1	1	5	2	1	3	4	1	2	2	1	4	2	1	2	5	2	1	1	1	2	3	2	3	1	..	2	55	27	.671	1
Dallas	2	1	3	0	2	..	2	1	3	4	2	3	0	2	1	4	2	1	2	1	1	0	3	3	2	1	1	47	35	.573	9
Denver	1	2	1	2	3	1	..	0	2	4	0	2	0	2	1	5	2	1	2	1	4	1	2	0	1	4	3	43	39	.524	13
Houston	0	0	4	1	2	1	1	2	1	..	2	2	1	2	1	1	2	1	2	1	4	2	2	3	1	4	1	41	41	.500	15
Minnesota	1	1	2	0	1	1	0	0	1	2	1	1	0	1	0	..	1	1	1	1	0	1	2	1	1	0	1	22	60	.268	34
Charlotte	0	0	..	0	1	1	3	0	2	1	1	2	0	1	0	2	1	1	0	1	0	1	0	0	0	0	0	19	63	.232	37

PACIFIC DIVISION

	Atl.	Bos.	Char.	Chi.	Cle.	Dal.	Den.	Det.	G.S.	Hou.	Ind.	L.A.C.	L.A.L.	Mia.	Mil.	Min.	N.J.	N.Y.	Orl.	Phi.	Pho.	Por.	Sac.	S.A.	Sea.	Uta.	Was.	W	L	Pct.	GB
L.A. Lakers	2	2	4	1	1	4	4	1	4	2	2	4	..	2	1	4	2	2	1	1	3	2	5	2	4	2	1	63	19	.768	..
Portland	1	2	4	1	1	4	2	1	2	3	1	5	3	1	3	2	2	2	1	3	2	..	4	3	3	2	1	59	23	.720	4
Phoenix	2	1	3	0	1	3	3	0	5	2	1	4	1	2	1	4	2	1	2	1	..	2	5	0	3	3	2	54	28	.659	9
Seattle	1	0	4	1	1	2	2	1	3	2	1	2	0	2	0	3	2	1	2	2	2	1	1	2	..	4	1	41	41	.500	22
Golden State	0	1	2	0	1	2	1	2	..	1	3	1	2	1	3	2	0	2	1	3	2	3	1	2	1	2	1	37	45	.451	26
L.A. Clippers	1	1	2	1	1	1	2	1	1	2	2	..	1	0	1	3	2	0	2	0	0	0	2	0	3	0	1	30	52	.366	33
Sacramento	1	0	3	1	0	1	0	0	2	0	1	3	0	1	1	2	1	0	1	1	0	0	..	0	2	1	1	23	59	.280	40

OFFENSIVE

	G	FGM	FGA	Pct.	FTM	FTA	Pct.	REBOUNDS Off.	Def.	Tot.	Ast.	PF	Dq.	Stl.	TO	Blk.	SCORING Pts.	Avg.
Golden State	82	3489	7208	.484	2313	2858	.809	915	2385	3300	1978	2010	22	756	1415	488	9534	116.3
Phoenix	82	3544	7139	.496	2159	2716	.795	1053	2651	3704	2109	1825	20	668	1275	501	9423	114.9
Denver	82	3716	8015	.464	1737	2201	.789	1169	2532	3701	2275	2047	31	814	1136	329	9397	114.6
Portland	82	3572	7547	.473	2031	2734	.743	1355	2552	3907	2085	2048	21	749	1356	364	9365	114.2
Orlando	82	3457	7525	.459	2060	2725	.756	1304	2465	3769	1993	1975	15	617	1407	294	9090	110.9
L.A. Lakers	82	3434	7010	.490	1902	2417	.787	1097	2460	3557	2232	1737	9	655	1226	445	9079	110.7
Philadelphia	82	3437	7028	.489	1976	2509	.788	1111	2406	3517	1932	1697	10	687	1209	365	9039	110.2
Boston	82	3563	7148	.498	1791	2153	.832	1066	2707	3773	2423	1717	13	539	1256	455	9023	110.0
Chicago	82	3531	7090	.498	1665	2140	.778	1075	2279	3354	2172	1906	15	814	1247	388	8977	109.5
Indiana	82	3381	6807	.497	1906	2335	.816	940	2388	3328	2023	1972	32	552	1342	350	8962	109.3
Atlanta	82	3417	7019	.487	1943	2544	.764	1273	2187	3460	1820	1871	19	717	1270	353	8901	108.5
New York	82	3434	7089	.484	1775	2349	.756	1187	2426	3613	2140	1828	15	714	1412	492	8879	108.3
Washington	82	3598	7581	.475	1599	2093	.764	1198	2450	3648	2214	1929	18	561	1201	424	8832	107.7
Seattle	82	3466	7243	.479	1606	2167	.741	1323	2255	3578	1874	2064	21	701	1336	335	8769	106.9
Utah	82	3330	6593	.505	1874	2484	.754	953	2501	3454	2212	2031	14	677	1410	491	8760	106.8
Houston	82	3483	7250	.480	1633	2267	.720	1217	2638	3855	2194	1934	23	809	1513	551	8752	106.7
San Antonio	82	3388	6997	.484	1888	2535	.745	1163	2474	3637	2037	1854	18	799	1399	554	8718	106.3
Milwaukee	82	3380	7146	.473	1722	2273	.758	1108	2246	3354	2046	2086	24	826	1315	326	8691	106.0
Detroit	82	3333	6980	.478	1713	2252	.761	1185	2458	3643	1996	1961	20	512	1233	418	8556	104.3
L.A. Clippers	82	3319	6853	.484	1815	2458	.738	1056	2362	3418	1978	1859	20	782	1547	507	8509	103.8
Cleveland	82	3214	6977	.461	1637	2201	.744	1128	2380	3508	2106	1666	16	645	1243	512	8411	102.6
Dallas	82	3246	6831	.475	1735	2261	.767	1042	2419	3461	1776	1733	13	664	1228	398	8384	102.2
Sacramento	82	3305	7056	.468	1515	1964	.771	952	2363	3315	2052	1863	17	546	1239	392	8341	101.7
Miami	82	3383	7345	.461	1393	2028	.687	1242	2313	3555	1957	2123	31	736	1557	388	8247	100.6
Charlotte	82	3270	7183	.455	1487	1967	.756	962	2211	3173	2080	1889	15	778	1226	262	8232	100.4
New Jersey	82	3157	7415	.426	1754	2350	.746	1363	2324	3687	1475	1952	16	774	1360	481	8208	100.1
Minnesota	82	3067	6876	.446	1596	2137	.747	1196	2053	3249	1844	1901	25	789	1197	344	7803	95.2

DEFENSIVE

	FGM	FGA	Pct.	FTM	FTA	Pct.	REBOUNDS Off.	Def.	Tot.	Ast.	PF	Dq.	Stl.	TO	Blk.	SCORING Pts.	Avg.	Dif.
Detroit	3043	6809	.447	1785	2342	.762	1040	2281	3321	1764	2072	29	606	1248	304	8057	98.3	+6.0
Minnesota	3081	6391	.482	1859	2420	.768	1050	2322	3372	1880	1748	11	570	1366	489	8150	99.4	-4.2
Utah	3164	6949	.455	1865	2452	.761	1100	2210	3310	1885	1910	19	736	1241	452	8367	102.0	+4.8
Dallas	3288	7013	.469	1627	2161	.753	1142	2398	3540	1961	1832	17	649	1238	388	8370	102.2	0.0
San Antonio	3269	7090	.461	1663	2169	.767	1125	2241	3366	1967	1919	20	760	1420	416	8432	102.8	+3.5
Cleveland	3418	7135	.479	1444	1898	.761	1134	2451	3585	2137	1893	19	680	1294	379	8436	102.9	-0.3
L.A. Lakers	3382	7247	.467	1584	2111	.750	1131	2243	3374	2009	1909	22	669	1200	428	8523	103.9	+6.8
Philadelphia	3417	7117	.480	1584	2054	.771	1113	2356	3469	2155	1945	16	636	1234	380	8630	105.2	+5.0
Houston	3399	7322	.464	1671	2256	.741	1175	2460	3635	2010	1819	10	790	1428	392	8632	105.3	+1.4
Seattle	3257	6704	.486	1992	2533	.766	1007	2204	3211	1862	1796	23	634	1303	406	8684	105.9	+1.0
Boston	3438	7383	.466	1648	2133	.773	1046	2318	3364	2078	1845	18	736	1003	356	8696	106.0	+4.0
Chicago	3361	6819	.493	1784	2392	.746	1068	2296	3364	2110	1742	17	665	1411	383	8710	106.2	+3.3
Sacramento	3384	7158	.473	1828	2324	.787	1146	2531	3677	2022	1740	14	704	1168	391	8756	106.8	-5.1
Milwaukee	3292	6871	.479	1990	2570	.774	1158	2405	3563	2023	1879	27	685	1506	444	8755	106.8	-0.8
New York	3497	7430	.471	1598	2100	.761	1249	2285	3534	2126	1869	30	719	1287	418	8763	106.9	+1.4
L.A. Clippers	3432	7207	.476	1737	2251	.772	1149	2367	3516	2092	1950	22	828	1364	429	8787	107.2	-3.4
Atlanta	3438	6935	.496	1760	2279	.772	1151	2236	3387	2144	1961	17	672	1294	389	8817	107.5	+1.0
Phoenix	3528	7588	.465	1585	2163	.733	1202	2335	3537	2125	2151	33	677	1254	395	8841	107.8	+7.1
Portland	3351	7227	.464	1917	2500	.767	1055	2357	3412	2026	2086	19	667	1489	432	8847	107.9	+6.3
New Jersey	3403	7020	.485	1906	2491	.765	1144	2590	3734	1871	1886	11	768	1419	478	8853	108.0	7.9
Charlotte	3438	6922	.497	1865	2380	.784	1063	2723	3786	2066	1754	11	638	1376	384	8873	108.2	-7.8
Indiana	3486	7225	.482	1804	2395	.753	1173	2297	3470	1945	2021	16	716	1189	321	8949	109.1	+0.2
Washington	3511	7403	.474	1845	2376	.777	1198	2503	3701	1952	1780	16	644	1200	430	9009	109.9	-2.2
Miami	3418	7010	.488	2050	2716	.755	1125	2467	3592	2076	1781	13	860	1473	477	9044	110.3	-9.7
Denver	3589	7334	.489	1939	2517	.770	1021	2846	3867	2073	1911	19	613	1514	462	9281	113.2	+1.4
Golden State	3766	8048	.468	1998	2633	.759	1495	2594	4089	2331	2219	24	817	1422	430	9791	119.4	-3.1
Orlando	3864	7757	.498	1897	2502	.758	1173	2569	3742	2333	2060	20	734	1216	556	9821	119.8	-8.9
Avgs.	3404	7146	.476	1786	2338	.764	1135	2403	3538	2038	1907	19	699	1317	415	8773	107.0	...

HOME/ROAD

	Home	Road	Total		Home	Road	Total
Atlanta	25-16	16-25	41-41	Milwaukee	27-14	17-24	44-38
Boston	30-11	22-19	52-30	Minnesota	17-24	5-36	22-60
Charlotte	13-28	6-35	19-63	New Jersey	13-28	4-37	17-65
Chicago	36-5	19-22	55-27	New York	29-12	16-25	45-37
Cleveland	27-14	15-26	42-40	Orlando	12-29	6-35	18-64
Dallas	30-11	17-24	47-35	Philadelphia	34-7	19-22	53-29
Denver	28-13	15-26	43-39	Phoenix	32-9	22-19	54-28
Detroit	35-6	24-17	59-23	Portland	35-6	24-17	59-23
Golden State	27-14	10-31	37-45	Sacramento	16-25	7-34	23-59
Houston	31-10	10-31	41-41	San Antonio	34-7	22-19	56-26
Indiana	28-13	14-27	42-40	Seattle	30-11	11-30	41-41
L.A. Clippers	20-21	10-31	30-52	Utah	36-5	19-22	55-27
L.A. Lakers	37-4	26-15	63-19	Washington	20-21	11-30	31-51
Miami	11-30	7-34	18-64	Totals	713-394	394-713	1107-1107

1989-90

INDIVIDUAL LEADERS

POINTS

(minimum 70 games or 1,400 points)

	G	FGM	FTM	Pts.	Avg.
Michael Jordan, Chicago	82	1034	593	2753	33.6
Karl Malone, Utah	82	914	696	2540	31.0
Patrick Ewing, New York	82	922	502	2347	28.6
Tom Chambers, Phoenix	81	810	557	2201	27.2
Dominique Wilkins, Atlanta	80	810	459	2138	26.7
Charles Barkley, Philadelphia	79	706	557	1989	25.2
Chris Mullin, Golden State	78	682	505	1956	25.1
Reggie Miller, Indiana	82	661	544	2016	24.6
Hakeem Olajuwon, Houston	82	806	382	1995	24.3
David Robinson, San Antonio	82	690	613	1993	24.3
Larry Bird, Boston	75	718	319	1820	24.3
Jeff Malone, Washington	75	781	257	1820	24.3

FIELD GOALS

(minimum 300 made)

	FGM	FGA	Pct.
Mark West, Phoenix	331	530	.625
Charles Barkley, Philadelphia	706	1177	.600
Robert Parish, Boston	505	871	.580
Karl Malone, Utah	914	1627	.562
Orlando Woolridge, L.A. Lakers	306	550	.556
Patrick Ewing, New York	922	1673	.551
Kevin McHale, Boston	648	1181	.549
James Worthy, L.A. Lakers	711	1298	.548
Otis Thorpe, Houston	547	998	.548
Buck Williams, Portland	413	754	.548

FREE THROWS

(minimum 125 made)

	FTM	FTA	Pct.
Larry Bird, Boston	319	343	.930
Eddie Johnson, Phoenix	188	205	.917
Walter Davis, Denver	207	227	.912
Joe Dumars, Detroit	297	330	.900
Kevin McHale, Boston	393	440	.893
Terry Porter, Portland	421	472	.892
Magic Johnson, L.A. Lakers	567	637	.890
Chris Mullin, Golden State	505	568	.889
Hersey Hawkins, Philadelphia	387	436	.888
Mark Price, Cleveland	300	338	.888

ASSISTS

(minimum 70 games or 400 assists)

	G	No.	Avg.
John Stockton, Utah	78	1134	14.5
Magic Johnson, L.A. Lakers	79	907	11.5
Kevin Johnson, Phoenix	74	846	11.4
Muggsy Bogues, Charlotte	81	867	10.7
Gary Grant, L.A. Clippers	44	442	10.0
Isiah Thomas, Detroit	81	765	9.4
Mark Price, Cleveland	73	666	9.1
Terry Porter, Portland	80	726	9.1
Tim Hardaway, Golden State	79	689	8.7
Darrell Walker, Washington	81	652	8.1

REBOUNDS

(minimum 70 games or 800 rebounds)

	G	Off.	Def.	Tot.	Avg.
Hakeem Olajuwon, Houston	82	299	850	1149	14.0
David Robinson, San Antonio	82	303	680	983	12.0
Charles Barkley, Philadelphia	79	361	548	909	11.5
Karl Malone, Utah	82	232	679	911	11.1
Patrick Ewing, New York	82	235	658	893	10.9
Rony Seikaly, Miami	74	253	513	766	10.4
Robert Parish, Boston	79	259	537	796	10.1
Michael Cage, Seattle	82	306	515	821	10.0
Moses Malone, Atlanta	81	364	448	812	10.0
Buck Williams, Portland	82	250	550	800	9.8

STEALS

(minimum 70 games or 125 steals)

	G	No.	Avg.
Michael Jordan, Chicago	82	227	2.77
John Stockton, Utah	78	207	2.65
Scottie Pippen, Chicago	82	211	2.57
Alvin Robertson, Milwaukee	81	207	2.56
Derek Harper, Dallas	82	187	2.28
Tyrone Corbin, Minnesota	82	175	2.13
Fat Lever, Denver	79	168	2.13
Hakeem Olajuwon, Houston	82	174	2.12
Lester Conner, New Jersey	82	172	2.10
Tim Hardaway, Golden State	79	165	2.09

BLOCKED SHOTS

(minimum 70 games or 100 blocked shots)

	G	No.	Avg.
Hakeem Olajuwon, Houston	82	376	4.59
Patrick Ewing, New York	82	327	3.99
David Robinson, San Antonio	82	319	3.89
Manute Bol, Golden State	75	238	3.17
Benoit Benjamin, L.A. Clippers	71	187	2.63
Mark Eaton, Utah	82	201	2.45
Charles Jones, Washington	81	197	2.43
Mark West, Phoenix	82	184	2.24
Rik Smits, Indiana	82	169	2.06
John Williams, Cleveland	82	167	2.04

3-POINT FIELD GOALS

(minimum 25 made)

	FGA	FGM	Pct.
Steve Kerr, Cleveland	144	73	.507
Craig Hodges, Chicago	181	87	.481
Drazen Petrovic, Portland	74	34	.459
Jon Sundvold, Miami	100	44	.440
Byron Scott, L.A. Lakers	220	93	.423
Hersey Hawkins, Philadelphia	200	84	.420
Craig Ehlo, Cleveland	248	104	.419
John Stockton, Utah	113	47	.416
Reggie Miller, Indiana	362	150	.414
Fat Lever, Denver	87	36	.414

INDIVIDUAL STATISTICS, TEAM BY TEAM

ATLANTA HAWKS

	G	Min.	FGM	FGA	Pct.	FTM	FTA	Pct.	Off.	Def.	Tot.	Ast.	PF	Dq.	Stl.	TO	Blk.	Pts.	Avg.	Hi.
Dominique Wilkins	80	2888	810	1672	.484	459	569	.807	217	304	521	200	141	0	126	174	47	2138	26.7	44
Moses Malone	81	2735	517	1077	.480	493	631	.781	364	448	812	130	158	0	47	232	84	1528	18.9	31
Doc Rivers	48	1526	218	480	.454	138	170	.812	47	153	200	264	151	2	116	98	22	598	12.5	24
Kevin Willis	81	2273	418	805	.519	168	246	.683	253	392	645	57	259	4	63	144	47	1006	12.4	30
John Battle	60	1477	275	544	.506	102	135	.756	27	72	99	154	115	0	28	89	3	654	10.9	27
Spud Webb	82	2184	294	616	.477	162	186	.871	38	163	201	477	185	0	105	141	12	751	9.2	26
John Long	48	1030	174	384	.453	46	55	.836	26	57	83	85	66	0	45	75	5	404	8.4	20
Kenny Smith†	33	674	98	204	.480	55	65	.846	7	30	37	142	45	0	22	47	1	255	7.7	22
Kenny Smith‡	79	2421	378	811	.466	161	196	.821	18	139	157	445	143	0	79	169	8	943	11.9	24
Antoine Carr*	44	803	128	248	.516	79	102	.775	50	99	149	53	128	4	15	54	34	335	7.6	21
Cliff Levingston	75	1706	216	424	.509	83	122	.680	113	206	319	80	216	2	55	49	41	516	6.9	21

	G	Min.	FGM	FGA	Pct.	FTM	FTA	Pct.	REBOUNDS Off.	Def.	Tot.	Ast.	PF	Dq.	Stl.	TO	Blk.	SCORING Pts.	Avg.	Hi.
Alexander Volkov	72	937	137	284	.482	70	120	.583	52	67	119	83	166	3	36	52	22	357	5.0	17
Wes Matthews	1	13	1	3	.333	2	2	1.000	0	0	0	5	0	0	0	0	0	4	4.0	4
Jon Koncak	54	977	78	127	.614	42	79	.532	58	168	226	23	182	4	38	47	34	198	3.7	12
Sedric Toney*	32	286	30	72	.417	21	25	.840	3	11	14	52	35	0	10	21	0	88	2.8	11
Roy Marble	24	162	16	58	.276	19	29	.655	15	9	24	11	16	0	7	14	1	51	2.1	7
Haywoode Workman	6	16	2	3	.667	2	2	1.000	0	3	3	2	3	0	3	0	0	6	1.0	4
Duane Ferrell	14	29	5	14	.357	2	6	.333	3	4	7	2	3	0	1	2	0	12	0.9	4
Mike Williams†	5	14	0	4	.000	0	0	...	0	1	1	0	2	0	0	0	0	0	0.0	0
Mike Williams‡	21	102	6	18	.333	3	6	.500	5	18	23	2	30	0	3	3	7	15	0.7	4

3-pt. FG: Atlanta 124-411 (.302)—Wilkins 59-183 (.322); Malone 1-9 (.111); Rivers 24-66 (.364); Willis 2-7 (.286); Battle 2-13 (.154); Webb 1-19 (.053); Long 10-29 (.345); Smith† 4-24 (.167); Smith‡ 26-83 (.313); Carr* 0-4 (.000); Levingston 1-5 (.200); Volkov 13-34 (.382); Matthews 0-1 (.000); Koncak 0-1 (.000); Toney* 7-13 (.538); Marble 0-2 (.000); Ferrell 0-1 (.000). Opponents 181-533 (.340).

BOSTON CELTICS

	G	Min.	FGM	FGA	Pct.	FTM	FTA	Pct.	REBOUNDS Off.	Def.	Tot.	Ast.	PF	Dq.	Stl.	TO	Blk.	SCORING Pts.	Avg.	Hi.
Larry Bird	75	2944	718	1517	.473	319	343	.930	90	622	712	562	173	2	106	243	61	1820	24.3	50
Kevin McHale	82	2722	648	1181	.549	393	440	.893	201	476	677	172	250	3	30	183	157	1712	20.9	34
Reggie Lewis	79	2522	540	1089	.496	256	317	.808	109	238	347	225	216	2	88	120	63	1340	17.0	34
Robert Parish	79	2396	505	871	.580	233	312	.747	259	537	796	103	189	2	38	169	69	1243	15.7	38
Dennis Johnson	75	2036	206	475	.434	118	140	.843	48	153	201	485	179	2	81	117	14	531	7.1	24
Jim Paxson	72	1283	191	422	.453	73	90	.811	24	53	77	137	115	0	33	54	5	460	6.4	18
Joe Kleine	81	1365	176	367	.480	83	100	.830	117	238	355	46	170	0	15	64	27	435	5.4	18
Kevin Gamble	71	990	137	301	.455	85	107	.794	42	70	112	119	77	1	28	44	8	362	5.1	18
Michael Smith	65	620	136	286	.476	53	64	.828	40	60	100	79	51	0	9	54	1	327	5.0	24
Ed Pinckney	77	1082	135	249	.542	92	119	.773	93	132	225	68	126	1	34	56	42	362	4.7	19
John Bagley	54	1095	100	218	.459	29	39	.744	26	63	89	296	77	0	40	90	4	230	4.3	14
Charles Smith	60	519	59	133	.444	53	76	.697	14	55	69	103	75	0	35	36	3	171	2.9	12
Kelvin Upshaw*	14	131	12	39	.308	4	6	.667	3	10	13	28	19	0	2	12	1	30	2.1	7

3-pt. FG: Boston 106-404 (.262)—Bird 65-195 (.333); McHale 23-69 (.333); Lewis 4-15 (.267); Johnson 1-24 (.042); Paxson 5-20 (.250); Kleine 0-4 (.000); Gamble 3-18 (.167); M. Smith 2-28 (.071); Pinckney 0-1 (.000); C. Smith 0-7 (.000); Upshaw* 2-5 (.400). Opponents 172-539 (.319).

CHARLOTTE HORNETS

	G	Min.	FGM	FGA	Pct.	FTM	FTA	Pct.	REBOUNDS Off.	Def.	Tot.	Ast.	PF	Dq.	Stl.	TO	Blk.	SCORING Pts.	Avg.	Hi.
Armòn Gilliam†	60	2159	432	819	.527	264	363	.727	185	344	529	91	184	4	63	166	46	1128	18.8	30
Armon Gilliam‡	76	2426	484	940	.515	303	419	.723	211	388	599	99	212	4	69	183	51	1271	16.7	30
Rex Chapman	54	1762	377	824	.408	144	192	.750	52	127	179	132	113	0	46	100	6	945	17.5	30
Dell Curry	67	1860	461	990	.466	96	104	.923	31	137	168	159	148	0	98	100	26	1070	16.0	30
Kelly Tripucka	79	2404	442	1029	.430	310	351	.883	82	240	322	224	220	1	75	176	16	1232	15.6	31
J.R. Reid	82	2757	358	814	.440	192	289	.664	199	492	691	101	292	7	92	172	54	908	11.1	25
Randolph Keys†	32	723	142	319	.445	40	58	.690	48	68	116	49	107	1	30	37	6	336	10.5	20
Randolph Keys‡	80	1615	293	678	.432	101	140	.721	100	153	253	88	224	1	68	84	8	701	8.8	22
Muggsy Bogues	81	2743	326	664	.491	106	134	.791	48	159	207	867	168	1	166	146	3	763	9.4	22
Kurt Rambis*	16	448	58	116	.500	30	55	.545	48	72	120	28	45	0	32	29	10	146	9.1	21
Micheal Williams†	22	303	58	109	.532	35	46	.761	11	20	31	77	39	0	22	28	1	151	6.9	17
Micheal Williams‡	28	329	60	119	.504	36	46	.783	12	20	32	81	39	0	22	33	1	156	5.6	17
Robert Reid†	60	1117	162	414	.391	50	78	.641	33	110	143	82	136	0	36	44	14	383	6.4	20
Robert Reid‡	72	1202	175	447	.391	54	86	.628	34	117	151	90	153	0	38	45	16	414	5.8	20
Kenny Gattison	63	941	148	269	.550	75	110	.682	75	122	197	39	150	1	35	67	31	372	5.9	18
Brian Rowsom	44	559	78	179	.436	68	83	.819	44	87	131	22	58	0	18	25	11	225	5.1	20
Richard Anderson	54	604	88	211	.417	18	23	.783	33	94	127	55	64	0	20	26	9	231	4.3	19
Dave Hoppen	10	135	16	41	.390	8	10	.800	19	17	36	6	26	0	2	8	1	40	4.0	8
Jerry Sichting*	34	469	50	119	.420	15	18	.833	3	16	19	92	39	0	16	22	2	118	3.5	12
Ralph Lewis†	3	20	4	6	.667	2	2	1.000	4	2	6	0	2	0	1	1	0	10	3.3	4
Ralph Lewis‡	7	26	4	7	.571	2	2	1.000	4	2	6	0	3	0	1	2	0	10	1.4	4
Andre Turner†	8	84	9	25	.360	4	4	1.000	1	2	3	20	5	0	7	8	0	22	2.8	8
Andre Turner‡	11	115	11	38	.289	4	4	1.000	4	4	8	23	6	0	8	12	0	26	2.4	8
Stuart Gray*	39	466	38	82	.463	25	39	.641	38	93	131	17	64	0	12	19	24	101	2.6	9
Terry Dozier	9	92	9	27	.333	4	8	.500	7	8	15	3	10	0	6	7	2	22	2.4	6
Michael Holton	16	109	14	26	.538	1	2	.500	1	1	2	16	19	0	1	13	0	29	1.8	10

3-pt. FG: Charlotte 205-611 (.336)—Gilliam† 0-2 (.000); Gilliam‡ 0-2 (.000); Chapman 47-142 (.331); Curry 52-147 (.354); Tripucka 38-104 (.365); J.R. Reid 0-5 (.000); Keys† 12-33 (.364); Keys‡ 14-43 (.326); Bogues 5-26 (.192); Rambis* 0-1 (.000); Williams† 0-3 (.000); Williams‡ 0-3 (.000); R. Reid† 9-29 (.310); R. Reid‡ 10-32 (.313); Gattison 1-1 (1.000); Rowsom 1-2 (.500); Anderson 37-100 (.370); Sichting* 3-12 (.250); Turner† 0-1 (.000); Turner‡ 0-2 (.000); Gray* 0-2 (.000); Dozier 0-1 (.000). Opponents 132-421 (.314).

CHICAGO BULLS

	G	Min.	FGM	FGA	Pct.	FTM	FTA	Pct.	REBOUNDS Off.	Def.	Tot.	Ast.	PF	Dq.	Stl.	TO	Blk.	SCORING Pts.	Avg.	Hi.
Michael Jordan	82	3197	1034	1964	.526	593	699	.848	143	422	565	519	241	0	227	247	54	2753	33.6	69
Scottie Pippen	82	3148	562	1150	.489	199	295	.675	150	397	547	444	298	6	211	278	101	1351	16.5	28
Horace Grant	80	2753	446	853	.523	179	256	.699	236	393	629	227	230	1	92	110	84	1071	13.4	23
Bill Cartwright	71	2160	292	598	.488	227	280	.811	137	328	465	145	243	6	38	123	34	811	11.4	24
John Paxson	82	2365	365	708	.516	56	68	.824	27	92	119	335	176	1	83	85	6	819	10.0	27
Stacey King	82	1777	267	530	.504	194	267	.727	169	215	384	87	215	0	38	119	58	728	8.9	24
Craig Hodges	63	1055	145	331	.438	30	33	.909	11	42	53	110	87	1	30	30	2	407	6.5	18
B.J. Armstrong	81	1291	190	392	.485	69	78	.885	19	83	102	199	105	0	46	83	6	452	5.6	20
Will Perdue	77	884	111	268	.414	72	104	.692	88	126	214	46	150	0	19	65	26	294	3.8	14

1989-90

	G	Min.	FGM	FGA	Pct.	FTM	FTA	Pct.	REBOUNDS Off.	Def.	Tot.	Ast.	PF	Dq.	Stl.	TO	Blk.	SCORING Pts.	Avg.	Hi.
Charlie Davis	53	429	58	158	.367	7	8	.875	25	56	81	18	52	0	10	20	8	130	2.5	8
Ed Nealy	46	503	37	70	.529	30	41	.732	46	92	138	28	67	0	16	17	4	104	2.3	10
Jack Haley*	11	58	9	20	.450	7	7	1.000	7	11	18	4	7	0	0	7	1	25	2.3	7
Clifford Lett	4	28	2	8	.250	0	0	...	0	0	0	1	8	0	0	2	0	4	1.0	2
Jeff Sanders	31	182	13	40	.325	2	4	.500	17	22	39	9	27	0	4	15	4	28	0.9	6

3-pt. FG: Chicago 250-669 (.374)—Jordan 92-245 (.376); Pippen 28-112 (.250); Paxson 33-92 (.359); King 0-1 (.000); Hodges 87-181 (.481); Armstrong 3-6 (.500); Perdue 0-5 (.000); Davis 7-25 (.280); Nealy 0-2 (.000). Opponents 204-581 (.351).

CLEVELAND CAVALIERS

	G	Min.	FGM	FGA	Pct.	FTM	FTA	Pct.	REBOUNDS Off.	Def.	Tot.	Ast.	PF	Dq.	Stl.	TO	Blk.	SCORING Pts.	Avg.	Hi.
Ron Harper*	7	262	61	138	.442	31	41	.756	19	29	48	49	25	1	14	18	9	154	22.0	36
Mark Price	73	2706	489	1066	.459	300	338	.888	66	185	251	666	89	0	114	214	5	1430	19.6	37
John Williams	82	2776	528	1070	.493	325	440	.739	220	443	663	168	214	2	86	143	167	1381	16.8	33
Brad Daugherty	41	1438	244	509	.479	202	287	.704	77	296	373	130	108	1	29	110	22	690	16.8	30
Larry Nance	62	2065	412	807	.511	186	239	.778	162	354	516	161	185	3	54	110	122	1011	16.3	31
Craig Ehlo	81	2894	436	940	.464	126	185	.681	147	292	439	371	226	2	126	161	23	1102	13.6	31
Randolph Keys*	48	892	151	359	.421	61	82	.744	52	85	137	39	117	0	38	47	2	365	7.6	22
Chucky Brown	75	1339	210	447	.470	125	164	.762	83	148	231	50	148	0	33	69	26	545	7.3	30
Reggie Williams*	32	542	91	239	.381	30	41	.732	17	43	60	38	79	2	22	32	10	218	6.8	17
Steve Kerr	78	1664	192	432	.444	63	73	.863	12	86	98	248	59	0	45	74	7	520	6.7	19
Winston Bennett	55	990	137	286	.479	64	96	.667	84	104	188	54	133	1	23	62	10	338	6.1	20
Chris Dudley*	37	684	79	203	.389	26	77	.338	88	115	203	20	83	1	19	48	41	184	5.0	15
Paul Mokeski	38	449	63	150	.420	25	36	.694	27	72	99	17	76	0	8	26	10	151	4.0	14
John Morton	37	402	48	161	.298	43	62	.694	7	25	32	67	30	0	18	51	4	146	3.9	14
Derrick Chievous†	14	99	15	42	.357	19	24	.792	7	8	15	4	11	0	3	5	1	49	3.5	12
Derrick Chievous‡	55	591	105	220	.477	80	111	.721	35	55	90	31	70	0	26	45	5	293	5.3	17
Tree Rollins	48	674	57	125	.456	11	16	.688	58	95	153	24	83	3	13	35	53	125	2.6	10
Gary Voce	1	4	1	3	.333	0	0	...	2	0	2	0	0	0	0	0	0	2	2.0	2

3-pt. FG: Cleveland 346-851 (.407)—Harper* 1-5 (.200); Price 152-374 (.406); Daugherty 0-2 (.000); Nance 1-1 (1.000); Ehlo 104-248 (.419); Keys* 2-10 (.200); Brown 0-7 (.000); R. Williams* 6-27 (.222); Kerr 73-144 (.507); Mokeski 0-1 (.000); Morton 7-30 (.233); Chievous† 0-1 (.000); Chievous‡ 3-9 (.333); Rollins 0-1 (.000). Opponents 156-500 (.312).

DALLAS MAVERICKS

	G	Min.	FGM	FGA	Pct.	FTM	FTA	Pct.	REBOUNDS Off.	Def.	Tot.	Ast.	PF	Dq.	Stl.	TO	Blk.	SCORING Pts.	Avg.	Hi.
Rolando Blackman	80	2934	626	1256	.498	287	340	.844	88	192	280	289	128	0	77	174	21	1552	19.4	35
Derek Harper	82	3007	567	1161	.488	250	315	.794	54	190	244	609	224	1	187	207	26	1473	18.0	42
Roy Tarpley	45	1648	314	696	.451	130	172	.756	189	400	589	67	160	0	79	117	70	758	16.8	27
Sam Perkins	76	2668	435	883	.493	330	424	.778	209	363	572	175	225	4	88	148	64	1206	15.9	45
Adrian Dantley	45	1300	231	484	.477	200	254	.787	78	94	172	80	99	0	20	75	7	662	14.7	30
James Donaldson	73	2265	258	479	.539	149	213	.700	155	475	630	57	129	0	22	119	47	665	9.1	21
Herb Williams	81	2199	295	665	.444	108	159	.679	76	315	391	119	243	4	51	106	106	700	8.6	21
Brad Davis	73	1292	179	365	.490	77	100	.770	12	81	93	242	151	2	47	86	9	470	6.4	25
Bill Wennington	60	814	105	234	.449	60	75	.800	64	134	198	41	144	2	20	50	21	270	4.5	14
Randy White	55	707	93	252	.369	50	89	.562	78	95	173	21	124	0	24	47	6	237	4.3	18
Steve Alford	41	302	63	138	.457	35	37	.946	2	23	25	39	22	0	15	16	3	168	4.1	16
Anthony Jones	66	650	72	194	.371	47	69	.681	33	49	82	29	77	0	32	42	16	195	3.0	13
Bob McCann†	10	62	7	21	.333	12	14	.857	4	8	12	6	7	0	2	6	2	26	2.6	8
Kelvin Upshaw*	3	4	1	3	.333	0	0	...	0	0	0	0	0	0	0	0	0	2	0.7	2
Mark Wade	1	3	0	0	...	0	0	...	0	0	0	2	0	0	0	0	0	0	0.0	0

3-pt. FG: Dallas 157-486 (.323)—Blackman 13-43 (.302); Harper 89-240 (.371); Tarpley 0-6 (.000); Perkins 6-28 (.214); Dantley 0-2 (.000); H. Williams 2-9 (.222); Davis 35-104 (.337); Wennington 0-4 (.000); White 1-14 (.071); Alford 7-22 (.318); Jones 4-13 (.308); Upshaw* 0-1 (.000). Opponents 175-587 (.298).

DENVER NUGGETS

	G	Min.	FGM	FGA	Pct.	FTM	FTA	Pct.	REBOUNDS Off.	Def.	Tot.	Ast.	PF	Dq.	Stl.	TO	Blk.	SCORING Pts.	Avg.	Hi.
Fat Lever	79	2832	568	1283	.443	271	337	.804	230	504	734	517	172	1	168	156	13	1443	18.3	31
Alex English	80	2211	635	1293	.491	161	183	.880	119	167	286	225	130	0	51	93	23	1433	17.9	38
Walter Davis	69	1635	497	1033	.481	207	227	.912	46	133	179	155	160	1	59	102	9	1207	17.5	36
Michael Adams	79	2690	398	989	.402	267	314	.850	49	176	225	495	133	0	121	141	3	1221	15.5	32
Blair Rasmussen	81	1995	445	895	.497	111	134	.828	174	420	594	82	300	10	40	75	104	1001	12.4	26
Joe Barry Carroll†	30	719	153	354	.432	52	70	.743	51	142	193	54	70	0	28	78	59	358	11.9	25
Joe Barry Carroll‡	76	1721	312	759	.411	137	177	.774	133	310	443	97	192	4	47	142	115	761	10.0	25
Dan Schayes	53	1194	163	330	.494	225	264	.852	117	225	342	61	200	7	41	72	45	551	10.4	28
Todd Lichti	79	1326	250	514	.486	130	174	.747	49	102	151	116	145	1	55	95	13	630	8.0	20
Bill Hanzlik	81	1605	179	396	.452	136	183	.743	67	140	207	186	249	7	78	87	29	500	6.2	19
Tim Kempton	71	1061	139	312	.490	77	114	.675	51	167	218	118	144	2	30	80	9	383	5.4	17
Jerome Lane	67	956	145	309	.469	44	120	.367	144	217	361	105	189	1	53	85	17	334	5.0	18
Eddie Hughes	60	892	83	202	.411	23	34	.676	15	55	70	116	87	0	48	39	1	209	3.5	17
Mike Higgins†	5	32	3	8	.375	7	8	.875	1	2	3	2	1	0	1	1	0	13	2.6	6
Mike Higgins‡	11	50	3	8	.375	8	10	.800	2	2	4	3	5	0	2	1	2	14	1.3	6
T.R. Dunn	65	657	44	97	.454	26	39	.667	56	82	138	43	67	1	41	19	4	114	1.8	12

3-pt. FG: Denver 228-677 (.337)—Lever 36-87 (.414); English 2-5 (.400); Davis 6-46 (.130); Adams 158-432 (.366); Rasmussen 0-1 (.000); Schayes 0-4 (.000); Carroll‡ 0-2 (.000); Lichti 0-14 (.000); Hanzlik 6-31 (.194); Kempton 0-1 (.000); Lane 0-5 (.000); Hughes 20-49 (.408); Dunn 0-2 (.000). Opponents 164-517 (.317).

DETROIT PISTONS

	G	Min.	FGM	FGA	Pct.	FTM	FTA	Pct.	Off.	Def.	Tot.	Ast.	PF	Dq.	Stl.	TO	Blk.	Pts.	Avg.	Hi.
									REBOUNDS									SCORING		
Isiah Thomas	81	2993	579	1322	.438	292	377	.775	74	234	308	765	206	0	139	322	19	1492	18.4	37
Joe Dumars	75	2578	508	1058	.480	297	330	.900	60	152	212	368	129	1	63	145	2	1335	17.8	34
James Edwards.....	82	2283	462	928	.498	265	354	.749	112	233	345	63	295	4	23	133	37	1189	14.5	32
Mark Aguirre........	78	2005	438	898	.488	192	254	.756	117	188	305	145	201	2	34	121	19	1099	14.1	31
Bill Laimbeer.......	81	2675	380	785	.484	164	192	.854	166	614	780	171	278	4	57	98	84	981	12.1	31
Vinnie Johnson......	82	1972	334	775	.431	131	196	.668	108	148	256	255	143	0	71	123	13	804	9.8	25
Dennis Rodman.....	82	2377	288	496	.581	142	217	.654	336	456	792	72	276	2	52	90	60	719	8.8	18
John Salley........	82	1914	209	408	.512	174	244	.713	154	285	439	67	282	7	51	97	153	593	7.2	21
William Bedford	42	246	54	125	.432	9	22	.409	15	43	58	4	39	0	3	21	17	118	2.8	13
Gerald Henderson†	46	335	42	83	.506	10	13	.769	8	23	31	61	36	0	8	16	2	108	2.3	13
Gerald Henderson‡ ...	57	464	53	109	.486	12	15	.800	11	32	43	74	50	0	16	24	2	135	2.4	13
David Greenwood ...	37	205	22	52	.423	16	29	.552	24	54	78	12	40	0	4	16	9	60	1.6	6
Stan Kimbrough ...	10	50	7	16	.438	2	2	1.000	4	3	7	5	4	0	4	4	0	16	1.6	4
Scott Hastings	40	166	10	33	.303	19	22	.864	7	25	32	8	31	0	3	7	3	42	1.1	9
Ralph Lewis*	4	6	0	1	.000	0	0	...	0	0	0	1	0	0	1	0	0	0	0.0	0

3-pt. FG: Detroit 177-541 (.327)—Thomas 42-136 (.309); Dumars 22-55 (.400); Edwards 0-3 (.000); Aguirre 31-93 (.333); Laimbeer 57-158 (.361); Johnson 5-34 (.147); Rodman 1-9 (.111); Salley 1-4 (.250); Bedford 1-6 (.167); Henderson† 14-31 (.452); Henderson‡ 17-38 (.447); Hastings 3-12 (.250). Opponents 186-558 (.333).

GOLDEN STATE WARRIORS

	G	Min.	FGM	FGA	Pct.	FTM	FTA	Pct.	Off.	Def.	Tot.	Ast.	PF	Dq.	Stl.	TO	Blk.	Pts.	Avg.	Hi.
									REBOUNDS									SCORING		
Chris Mullin	78	2830	682	1272	.536	505	568	.889	130	333	463	319	142	1	123	239	45	1956	25.1	39
Mitch Richmond	78	2799	640	1287	.497	406	469	.866	98	262	360	223	210	3	98	201	24	1720	22.1	32
Terry Teagle	82	2376	538	1122	.480	244	294	.830	114	253	367	155	231	3	91	144	15	1323	16.1	44
Tim Hardaway.......	79	2663	464	985	.471	211	276	.764	57	253	310	689	232	6	165	260	12	1162	14.7	28
Sarunas Marciulionis..	75	1695	289	557	.519	317	403	.787	84	137	221	121	230	5	94	137	7	905	12.1	33
Rod Higgins	82	1993	304	632	.481	234	285	.821	120	302	422	129	184	0	47	93	53	909	11.1	28
Tom Tolbert	70	1347	218	442	.493	175	241	.726	122	241	363	58	191	0	23	79	25	616	8.8	27
Kelvin Upshaw†	23	252	51	104	.490	24	31	.774	6	22	28	26	34	0	25	15	0	128	5.6	19
Kelvin Upshaw‡	40	387	64	146	.438	28	37	.757	9	32	41	54	53	0	27	27	1	160	4.0	19
Winston Garland*	51	891	108	288	.375	53	63	.841	31	80	111	157	77	1	48	81	5	270	5.3	13
Jim Petersen........	43	592	60	141	.426	52	73	.712	49	111	160	23	103	0	17	36	20	172	4.0	14
Marques Johnson ...	10	99	12	32	.375	14	17	.824	8	9	17	9	12	0	0	10	1	40	4.0	10
Alton Lister	3	40	4	8	.500	4	7	.571	5	3	8	2	8	0	1	0	0	12	4.0	7
Chris Welp	....	14	142	16	38	.421	18	23	.783	11	25	36	4	37	0	5	9	8	50	3.6	10
Chris Welp‡	27	198	23	61	.377	19	25	.760	18	30	48	9	58	0	6	15	8	65	2.4	10
Uwe Blab*	40	481	33	87	.379	17	31	.548	28	71	99	24	93	0	1	30	22	83	2.1	8
Manute Bol.........	75	1310	56	169	.331	25	49	.510	33	243	276	36	194	3	13	51	238	146	1.9	10
Mike Smrek	13	107	10	24	.417	1	6	.167	11	23	34	1	18	0	4	9	11	21	1.6	6
Leonard Taylor	10	37	0	6	.000	11	16	.688	4	8	12	1	4	0	0	5	0	11	1.1	3
John Shasky........	14	51	4	14	.286	2	6	.333	4	9	13	1	10	0	1	2	2	10	0.7	3

3-pt. FG: Golden State 243-750 (.324)—Mullin 87-234 (.372); Richmond 34-95 (.358); Teagle 3-14 (.214); Hardaway 23-84 (.274); Marciulionis 10-39 (.256); Higgins 67-193 (.347); Tolbert 5-18 (.278); Upshaw† 2-9 (.222); Upshaw‡ 4-15 (.267); Garland* 1-10 (.100); Petersen 0-1 (.000); Johnson 2-3 (.667); Lister 0-1 (.000); Bol 9-48 (.188); Taylor 0-1 (.000). Opponents 261-733 (.356).

HOUSTON ROCKETS

	G	Min.	FGM	FGA	Pct.	FTM	FTA	Pct.	Off.	Def.	Tot.	Ast.	PF	Dq.	Stl.	TO	Blk.	Pts.	Avg.	Hi.
									REBOUNDS									SCORING		
Hakeem Olajuwon	82	3124	806	1609	.501	382	536	.713	299	850	1149	234	314	6	174	316	376	1995	24.3	52
Otis Thorpe.........	82	2947	547	998	.548	307	446	.688	258	476	734	261	270	5	66	229	24	1401	17.1	33
Mitchell Wiggins	66	1852	416	853	.488	192	237	.810	133	153	286	104	165	0	85	87	1	1024	15.5	34
Buck Johnson.......	82	2832	504	1019	.495	205	270	.759	113	268	381	252	321	8	104	167	62	1215	14.8	30
Vernon Maxwell†	30	869	142	321	.442	77	116	.664	15	72	87	150	69	0	42	72	5	374	12.5	32
Vernon Maxwell‡	79	1987	275	627	.439	136	211	.645	50	178	228	296	148	0	84	143	10	714	9.0	32
Sleepy Floyd........	82	2630	362	803	.451	187	232	.806	46	152	198	600	159	0	94	204	11	1000	12.2	35
Mike Woodson	61	972	160	405	.395	62	86	.721	25	63	88	66	100	1	42	49	11	394	6.5	17
Derrick Chievous*....	41	492	90	178	.506	61	87	.701	28	47	75	27	59	0	23	40	4	244	6.0	17
John Lucas.........	49	938	109	291	.375	42	55	.764	19	71	90	238	59	0	45	85	2	286	5.8	16
Anthony Bowie	66	918	119	293	.406	40	54	.741	36	82	118	96	80	0	42	59	5	284	4.3	18
Byron Dinkins	33	362	44	109	.404	26	30	.867	13	27	40	75	30	0	19	37	2	115	3.5	12
Lewis Lloyd†	19	113	29	51	.569	9	16	.563	8	10	18	11	9	0	3	16	0	67	3.5	15
Lewis Lloyd‡	21	123	30	53	.566	9	16	.563	8	10	18	11	12	0	3	20	0	69	3.3	15
Larry Smith	74	1300	101	213	.474	20	55	.364	180	272	452	69	203	3	56	70	28	222	3.0	11
Adrian Caldwell......	51	331	42	76	.553	13	28	.464	36	73	109	7	69	0	11	32	18	97	1.9	11
Tim McCormick	18	116	10	29	.345	10	19	.526	8	19	27	3	24	0	3	10	1	30	1.7	6
Chuck Nevitt........	3	9	2	2	1.000	0	0	...	0	3	3	1	3	0	0	2	1	4	1.3	2

3-pt. FG: Houston 153-491 (.312)—Olajuwon 1-6 (.167); Thorpe 0-10 (.000); Wiggins 0-3 (.000); Johnson 2-17 (.118); Maxwell† 13-53 (.245); Maxwell‡ 28-105 (.267); Floyd 89-234 (.380); Woodson 12-41 (.293); Chievous* 3-8 (.375); Lucas 26-87 (.299); Bowie 6-21 (.286); Dinkins 1-9 (.111); Smith 0-2 (.000). Opponents 163-556 (.293).

INDIANA PACERS

	G	Min.	FGM	FGA	Pct.	FTM	FTA	Pct.	Off.	Def.	Tot.	Ast.	PF	Dq.	Stl.	TO	Blk.	Pts.	Avg.	Hi.
									REBOUNDS									SCORING		
Reggie Miller	82	3192	661	1287	.514	544	627	.868	95	200	295	311	175	1	110	122	18	2016	24.6	44
Chuck Person.......	77	2714	605	1242	.487	211	270	.781	126	319	445	230	217	1	53	170	20	1515	19.7	42
Detlef Schrempf	78	2573	424	822	.516	402	490	.820	149	471	620	247	271	6	59	180	16	1267	16.2	29

	G	Min.	FGM	FGA	Pct.	FTM	FTA	Pct.	Off.	Def.	Tot.	Ast.	PF	Dq.	Stl.	TO	Blk.	Pts.	Avg.	Hi.
									REBOUNDS									SCORING		
Rik Smits	82	2404	515	967	.533	241	297	.811	135	377	512	142	328	11	45	143	169	1271	15.5	34
Vern Fleming.	82	2876	467	919	.508	230	294	.782	118	204	322	610	213	1	92	206	10	1176	14.3	30
LaSalle Thompson . . .	82	2126	223	471	.473	107	134	.799	175	455	630	106	313	11	65	150	71	554	6.8	16
Mike Sanders	82	1531	225	479	.470	55	75	.733	78	152	230	89	220	1	43	79	23	510	6.2	19
Calvin Natt	14	164	20	31	.645	17	22	.773	10	25	35	9	14	0	1	5	0	57	4.1	16
Rickey Green	69	927	100	231	.433	43	51	.843	9	45	54	182	60	0	51	62	1	244	3.5	15
George McCloud.	44	413	45	144	.313	15	19	.789	12	30	42	45	56	0	19	36	3	118	2.7	13
Randy Wittman	61	544	62	122	.508	5	6	.833	4	26	30	39	21	0	7	23	4	130	2.1	14
Dyron Nix	20	109	14	39	.359	11	16	.688	8	18	26	5	15	0	3	7	1	39	2.0	8
Greg Dreiling	49	307	20	53	.377	25	34	.735	21	66	87	8	69	0	4	19	14	65	1.3	5

3-pt. FG: Indiana 294-770 (.382)—Miller 150-362 (.414); Person 94-253 (.372); Schrempf 17-48 (.354); Smits 0-1 (.000); Fleming 12-34 (.353); Thompson 1-5 (.200); Sanders 5-14 (.357); Green 1-11 (.091); McCloud 13-40 (.325); Wittman 1-2 (.500). Opponents 173-541 (.320).

LOS ANGELES CLIPPERS

	G	Min.	FGM	FGA	Pct.	FTM	FTA	Pct.	Off.	Def.	Tot.	Ast.	PF	Dq.	Stl.	TO	Blk.	Pts.	Avg.	Hi.
									REBOUNDS									SCORING		
Ron Harper†	28	1105	240	499	.481	151	190	.795	55	103	158	133	80	0	67	82	32	644	23.0	39
Ron Harper‡	35	1367	301	637	.473	182	231	.788	74	132	206	182	105	1	81	100	41	798	22.8	39
Charles Smith	78	2732	595	1145	.520	454	572	.794	177	347	524	114	294	6	86	162	119	1645	21.1	40
Danny Manning.	71	2269	440	826	.533	274	370	.741	142	280	422	187	261	4	91	188	39	1154	16.3	39
Ken Norman	70	2334	484	949	.510	153	242	.632	143	327	470	160	196	0	78	190	59	1128	16.1	35
Benoit Benjamin	71	2313	362	688	.526	235	321	.732	156	501	657	159	217	3	59	187	187	959	13.5	29
Gary Grant	44	1529	241	517	.466	88	113	.779	59	136	195	442	120	1	108	206	5	575	13.1	27
Reggie Williams*	5	133	21	57	.368	18	21	.857	8	7	15	10	7	0	9	9	1	60	12.0	24
Winston Garland†	28	871	122	285	.428	49	59	.831	20	83	103	146	75	0	30	77	5	304	10.9	23
Winston Garland‡	79	1762	230	573	.401	102	122	.836	51	163	214	303	152	1	78	158	10	574	7.3	23
Tom Garrick	73	1721	208	421	.494	88	114	.772	34	128	162	289	151	4	90	117	7	508	7.0	23
Jeff Martin	69	1351	170	414	.411	91	129	.705	78	81	159	44	97	0	41	47	16	433	6.3	20
Michael Young	45	459	92	194	.474	27	38	.711	36	50	86	24	47	0	25	15	3	219	4.9	27
Joe Wolf.	77	1325	155	392	.395	55	71	.775	63	169	232	62	129	0	30	77	24	370	4.8	19
David Rivers	52	724	80	197	.406	59	78	.756	30	55	85	155	53	0	31	88	0	219	4.2	15
Ken Bannister	52	589	77	161	.478	52	110	.473	39	73	112	18	92	1	17	44	7	206	4.0	15
Jim Les†	6	86	5	14	.357	11	13	.846	3	4	7	20	6	0	3	7	0	21	3.5	11
Jim Les‡	92	5	14	.357	13	17	.765	3	4	7	21	9	0	3	10	0	23	3.3	11		
Carlton McKinney	7	104	8	32	.250	2	4	.500	4	8	12	7	15	1	6	7	1	18	2.6	7
Steve Harris	15	93	14	40	.350	3	4	.750	5	5	10	1	9	0	7	5	1	31	2.1	8
Jay Edwards.	4	26	3	7	.429	1	3	.333	1	1	2	4	4	0	1	1	0	7	1.8	5
Torgeir Bryn	3	10	0	2	.000	4	6	.667	0	2	2	0	5	0	2	1	1	4	1.3	4
Andre Turner*.	3	31	2	13	.154	0	0	. . .	3	2	5	3	1	0	1	4	0	4	1.3	2

3-pt. FG: L.A. Clippers 56-230 (.243)—Harper† 13-46 (.283); Harper‡ 14-51 (.275); Smith 1-12 (.083); Manning 0-5 (.000); Norman 7-16 (.438); Benjamin 0-1 (.000); Grant 5-21 (.238); Williams* 0-5 (.000); Garland† 11-26 (.423); Garland‡ 12-36 (.333); Garrick 4-21 (.190); Martin 2-15 (.133); Young 8-26 (.308); Wolf 5-25 (.200); Rivers 0-5 (.000); Bannister 0-1 (.000); Les† 0-1 (.000); Les‡ 0-1 (.000); McKinney 0-1 (.000); Edwards 0-2 (.000); Turner* 0-1 (.000). Opponents 186-576 (.323).

LOS ANGELES LAKERS

	G	Min.	FGM	FGA	Pct.	FTM	FTA	Pct.	Off.	Def.	Tot.	Ast.	PF	Dq.	Stl.	TO	Blk.	Pts.	Avg.	Hi.
									REBOUNDS									SCORING		
Magic Johnson	79	2937	546	1138	.480	567	637	.890	128	394	522	907	167	1	132	289	34	1765	22.3	38
James Worthy.	80	2960	711	1298	.548	248	317	.782	160	318	478	288	190	0	99	160	49	1685	21.1	35
Byron Scott.	77	2593	472	1005	.470	160	209	.766	51	191	242	274	180	2	77	122	31	1197	15.5	33
A.C. Green	82	2709	385	806	.478	278	370	.751	262	450	712	90	207	0	66	116	50	1061	12.9	27
Orlando Woolridge . . .	62	1421	306	550	.556	176	240	.733	49	136	185	96	160	2	39	73	46	788	12.7	24
Mychal Thompson . . .	70	1883	281	562	.500	144	204	.706	173	304	477	43	207	0	33	79	73	706	10.1	24
Vlade Divac	82	1611	274	549	.499	153	216	.708	167	345	512	75	240	2	79	110	114	701	8.5	25
Michael Cooper.	80	1851	191	493	.387	83	94	.883	59	168	227	215	206	1	67	91	36	515	6.4	16
Larry Drew	80	1333	170	383	.444	46	60	.767	12	86	98	217	92	0	47	95	4	418	5.2	15
Jay Vincent†	24	200	41	78	.526	8	12	.667	7	19	26	10	29	0	8	19	3	90	3.8	16
Jay Vincent‡	41	459	86	183	.470	41	49	.837	20	42	62	18	52	0	18	33	5	215	5.2	19
Mark McNamara	33	190	38	86	.442	26	40	.650	22	41	63	3	31	1	2	21	1	102	3.1	15
Mel McCants.	13	65	8	26	.308	6	8	.750	1	5	6	2	11	0	3	1	0	22	1.7	4
Jawann Oldham†	3	9	2	3	.667	1	2	.500	0	1	1	1	3	0	0	1	0	5	1.7	3
Jawann Oldham‡	6	45	3	6	.500	3	7	.429	4	12	16	1	9	0	2	4	3	9	1.5	3
Steve Bucknall	18	75	9	33	.273	5	6	.833	5	2	7	10	10	0	2	11	1	23	1.3	4
Mike Higgins*.	6	18	0	0	. . .	1	2	.500	1	0	1	1	4	0	1	0	2	1	0.2	1

3-pt. FG: L.A. Lakers 309-841 (.367)—Johnson 106-276 (.384); Worthy 15-49 (.306); Scott 93-220 (.423); Green 13-46 (.283); Woolridge 0-5 (.000); Divac 0-5 (.000); Cooper 50-157 (.318); Drew 32-81 (.395); Vincent† 0-1 (.000); Vincent‡ 1-2 (.500); Bucknall 0-1 (.000). Opponents 175-519 (.337).

MIAMI HEAT

	G	Min.	FGM	FGA	Pct.	FTM	FTA	Pct.	Off.	Def.	Tot.	Ast.	PF	Dq.	Stl.	TO	Blk.	Pts.	Avg.	Hi.
									REBOUNDS									SCORING		
Rony Seikaly.	74	2409	486	968	.502	256	431	.594	253	513	766	78	258	8	78	236	124	1228	16.6	40
Sherman Douglas	81	2470	463	938	.494	224	326	.687	70	136	206	619	187	0	145	246	10	1155	14.3	37
Glen Rice	77	2311	470	1071	.439	91	124	.734	100	252	352	138	198	1	67	113	27	1048	13.6	28
Kevin Edwards	78	2211	395	959	.412	139	183	.760	77	205	282	252	149	1	125	180	33	938	12.0	33
Billy Thompson.	79	2142	375	727	.516	115	185	.622	238	313	551	166	237	1	54	156	89	867	11.0	29
Tellis Frank	77	1762	278	607	.458	179	234	.765	151	234	385	85	282	6	51	134	27	735	9.5	24
Grant Long	81	1856	257	532	.483	172	241	.714	156	246	402	96	300	11	91	139	38	686	8.5	22

1989-90

	G	Min.	FGM	FGA	Pct.	FTM	FTA	Pct.	REBOUNDS Off.	Def.	Tot.	Ast.	PF	Dq.	Stl.	TO	Blk.	SCORING Pts.	Avg.	Hi.
Jon Sundvold	63	867	148	363	.408	44	52	.846	15	56	71	102	69	0	25	52	0	384	6.1	18
Rory Sparrow	82	1756	210	510	.412	59	77	.766	37	101	138	298	140	0	49	99	4	487	5.9	21
Terry Davis	63	884	122	262	.466	54	87	.621	93	136	229	25	171	2	25	68	28	298	4.7	18
Pat Cummings	37	391	77	159	.484	21	37	.568	28	65	93	13	60	1	12	32	4	175	4.7	14
Scott Haffner	43	559	88	217	.406	17	25	.680	7	44	51	80	53	0	13	33	2	196	4.6	14
Jim Rowinski	14	112	14	32	.438	22	26	.846	17	12	29	5	19	0	1	10	2	50	3.6	11

3-pt. FG: Miami 88-300 (.293)—Seikaly 0-1 (.000); Douglas 5-31 (.161); Rice 17-69 (.246); Edwards 9-30 (.300); Thompson 2-4 (.500); Long 0-3 (.000); Sundvold 44-100 (.440); Sparrow 8-40 (.200); Davis 0-1 (.000); Haffner 3-21 (.143). Opponents 158-462 (.342).

MILWAUKEE BUCKS

	G	Min.	FGM	FGA	Pct.	FTM	FTA	Pct.	REBOUNDS Off.	Def.	Tot.	Ast.	PF	Dq.	Stl.	TO	Blk.	SCORING Pts.	Avg.	Hi.
Ricky Pierce	59	1709	503	987	.510	307	366	.839	64	103	167	133	158	2	50	129	7	1359	23.0	45
Jay Humphries	81	2818	496	1005	.494	224	285	.786	80	189	269	472	253	2	156	151	11	1237	15.3	29
Alvin Robertson	81	2599	476	946	.503	197	266	.741	230	329	559	445	280	2	207	217	17	1153	14.2	37
Jack Sikma	71	2250	344	827	.416	230	260	.885	109	383	492	229	244	5	76	139	48	986	13.9	30
Paul Pressey	57	1400	239	506	.472	144	190	.758	59	113	172	244	149	3	71	109	23	628	11.0	21
Fred Roberts	82	2235	330	666	.495	195	249	.783	107	204	311	147	210	5	56	130	25	857	10.5	27
Brad Lohaus†	52	1353	211	461	.458	54	77	.701	77	211	288	106	145	2	44	64	66	522	10.0	25
Brad Lohaus‡	80	1943	305	663	.460	75	103	.728	98	300	398	168	211	3	58	109	88	732	9.2	25
Greg Anderson	60	1291	219	432	.507	91	170	.535	112	261	373	24	176	3	32	80	54	529	8.8	28
Jeff Grayer	71	1427	224	487	.460	99	152	.651	94	123	217	107	125	0	48	82	10	548	7.7	18
Larry Krystkowiak	16	381	43	118	.364	26	33	.788	16	60	76	25	41	0	10	19	2	112	7.0	18
Randy Breuer*	30	554	86	186	.462	32	51	.627	43	84	127	13	63	0	9	28	33	204	6.8	18
Ben Coleman	22	305	46	97	.474	34	41	.829	31	56	87	12	54	0	7	26	7	126	5.7	17
Tony Brown	61	635	88	206	.427	38	56	.679	39	33	72	41	79	0	32	51	4	219	3.6	13
Mike Dunleavy	5	43	4	14	.286	7	8	.875	0	2	2	10	7	0	1	8	0	17	3.4	9
Jerry Sichting†	1	27	0	6	.000	3	4	.750	0	0	0	2	1	0	0	0	0	3	3.0	3
Jerry Sichting‡	35	496	50	125	.400	18	22	.818	3	16	19	94	40	0	16	22	2	121	3.5	12
Gerald Henderson*	11	129	11	26	.423	2	2	1.000	3	9	12	13	14	0	8	8	0	27	2.5	7
Frank Kornet	57	438	42	114	.368	24	39	.615	25	46	71	21	54	0	14	23	3	113	2.0	16
Tito Horford	35	236	18	62	.290	15	24	.625	19	40	59	2	33	0	5	14	16	51	1.5	6

3-pt. FG: Milwaukee 209-670 (.312)—Pierce 46-133 (.346); Humphries 21-70 (.300); Robertson 4-26 (.154); Sikma 68-199 (.342); Pressey 6-43 (.140); Roberts 2-11 (.182); Lohaus† 46-121 (.380); Lohaus‡ 47-137 (.343); Grayer 1-8 (.125); Krystkowiak 0-2 (.000); Coleman 0-1 (.000); Brown 5-20 (.250); Dunleavy 2-9 (.222); Sichting† 0-0; Sichting‡ 3-12 (.250); Henderson* 3-7 (.429); Kornet 5-20 (.250). Opponents 181-564 (.321).

MINNESOTA TIMBERWOLVES

	G	Min.	FGM	FGA	Pct.	FTM	FTA	Pct.	REBOUNDS Off.	Def.	Tot.	Ast.	PF	Dq.	Stl.	TO	Blk.	SCORING Pts.	Avg.	Hi.
Tony Campbell	82	3164	723	1581	.457	448	569	.787	209	242	451	213	260	7	111	251	31	1903	23.2	44
Tyrone Corbin	82	3011	521	1083	.481	161	209	.770	219	385	604	216	288	5	175	143	41	1203	14.7	36
Sam Mitchell	80	2414	372	834	.446	268	349	.768	180	282	462	89	301	7	66	96	54	1012	12.7	31
Pooh Richardson	82	2581	426	925	.461	63	107	.589	55	162	217	554	143	0	133	141	25	938	11.4	27
Randy Breuer†	51	1325	212	510	.416	94	142	.662	111	179	290	84	133	2	33	68	75	518	10.2	40
Randy Breuer‡	81	1879	298	696	.428	126	193	.653	154	263	417	97	196	2	42	96	108	722	8.9	40
Tod Murphy	82	2493	260	552	.471	144	203	.709	207	357	564	106	229	2	76	61	60	680	8.3	24
Brad Lohaus*	28	590	94	202	.465	21	26	.808	21	89	110	62	66	1	14	45	22	210	7.5	19
Scott Roth	71	1061	159	420	.379	150	201	.746	34	78	112	115	144	1	51	85	6	486	6.8	24
Donald Royal	66	746	117	255	.459	153	197	.777	69	68	137	43	107	0	32	81	8	387	5.9	23
Adrian Branch	11	91	25	61	.410	14	22	.636	8	12	20	4	14	0	6	8	0	65	5.9	14
Brad Sellers†	14	113	19	56	.339	9	12	.750	8	11	19	1	11	0	6	12	3	47	3.4	10
Brad Sellers‡	59	700	103	254	.406	58	73	.795	39	50	89	33	74	1	17	46	22	264	4.5	18
Doug West	52	378	53	135	.393	26	32	.813	24	46	70	18	61	0	10	31	6	135	2.6	23
Sidney Lowe	80	1744	73	229	.319	39	54	.722	41	122	163	337	114	0	73	63	4	187	2.3	22
Gary Leonard	22	127	13	31	.419	6	14	.429	10	17	27	1	26	0	3	8	9	32	1.5	6
Steve Johnson*	4	17	0	2	.000	0	0	—	0	3	3	1	4	0	0	6	0	0	0.0	0

3-pt. FG: Minnesota 73-294 (.248)—Campbell 9-54 (.167); Corbin 0-11 (.000); Mitchell 0-9 (.000); Richardson 23-83 (.277); Breuer† 0-1 (.000); Breuer‡ 0-1 (.000); Murphy 16-43 (.372); Lohaus* 1-16 (.063); Roth 18-52 (.346); Royal 0-1 (.000); Branch 1-1 (1.000); Sellers† 0-2 (.000); Sellers‡ 0-5 (.000); West 3-11 (.273); Lowe 2-9 (.222); Leonard 0-1 (.000). Opponents 129-391 (.330).

NEW JERSEY NETS

	G	Min.	FGM	FGA	Pct.	FTM	FTA	Pct.	REBOUNDS Off.	Def.	Tot.	Ast.	PF	Dq.	Stl.	TO	Blk.	SCORING Pts.	Avg.	Hi.
Dennis Hopson	79	2551	474	1093	.434	271	342	.792	113	166	279	151	183	1	100	168	51	1251	15.8	29
Roy Hinson	25	793	145	286	.507	86	99	.869	61	111	172	22	87	0	14	52	27	376	15.0	31
Chris Morris	80	2449	449	1065	.422	228	316	.722	194	228	422	143	219	1	130	185	79	1187	14.8	33
Sam Bowie	68	2207	347	834	.416	294	379	.776	206	484	690	91	211	5	38	125	121	998	14.7	29
Purvis Short	82	2213	432	950	.455	198	237	.835	101	147	248	145	202	2	66	119	20	1072	13.1	29
Derrick Gervin	21	339	92	197	.472	65	89	.730	29	36	65	8	47	0	20	12	7	251	12.0	25
Mookie Blaylock	50	1267	212	571	.371	63	81	.778	42	98	140	210	110	0	82	111	14	505	10.1	24
Joe Barry Carroll*	46	1002	159	405	.393	85	107	.794	82	168	250	43	122	4	19	64	56	403	8.8	22
Charles Shackleford	70	1557	247	535	.462	79	115	.687	180	299	479	56	183	1	40	116	35	573	8.2	23
Lester Conner	82	2355	237	573	.414	172	214	.804	90	175	265	385	182	0	172	138	8	648	7.9	18
Pete Myers†	28	543	74	180	.411	50	69	.725	23	45	68	100	70	0	20	58	9	198	7.1	16
Pete Myers‡	52	751	89	225	.396	66	100	.660	33	63	96	135	109	0	35	76	11	244	4.7	16
Chris Dudley†	27	672	67	152	.441	32	105	.305	86	134	220	19	81	1	22	36	31	166	6.1	14
Chris Dudley‡	64	1356	146	355	.411	58	182	.319	174	249	423	39	164	2	41	84	72	350	5.5	15
Jack Haley†	56	1026	129	327	.394	78	118	.661	108	174	282	22	163	1	18	65	11	336	6.0	19

	G	Min.	FGM	FGA	Pct.	FTM	FTA	Pct.	Off.	Def.	Tot.	Ast.	PF	Dq.	Stl.	TO	Blk.	Pts.	Avg.	Hi.
									REBOUNDS									SCORING		

	G	Min.	FGM	FGA	Pct.	FTM	FTA	Pct.	Off.	Def.	Tot.	Ast.	PF	Dq.	Stl.	TO	Blk.	Pts.	Avg.	Hi.
Jack Haley‡	67	1084	138	347	.398	85	125	.680	115	185	300	26	170	1	18	72	12	361	5.4	19
Jay Taylor	17	114	21	52	.404	6	9	.667	5	6	11	5	9	0	5	10	3	51	3.0	8
Jaren Jackson	28	160	25	69	.362	17	21	.810	16	8	24	13	16	0	13	18	1	67	2.4	13
Stanley Brundy	16	128	15	30	.500	7	18	.389	15	11	26	3	24	0	6	6	5	37	2.3	12
Leon Wood	28	200	16	49	.327	14	16	.875	1	11	12	47	16	0	6	8	0	50	1.8	11
Anthony Mason	21	108	14	40	.350	9	15	.600	11	23	34	7	20	0	2	11	2	37	1.8	8
Rick Carlisle	5	21	1	7	.143	0	0	...	0	0	0	5	7	0	1	4	1	2	0.4	2

3-pt. FG: New Jersey 140-506 (.277)—Hopson 32-101 (.317); Morris 61-193 (.316); Bowie 10-31 (.323); Short 10-35 (.286); Gervin 0-3 (.000); Blaylock 18-80 (.225); Carroll* 0-2 (.000); Shackleford 0-1 (.000); Conner 2-13 (.154); Myers† 0-6 (.000); Myers‡ 0-7 (.000); Haley† 0-1 (.000); Haley‡ 0-1 (.000); Taylor 3-13 (.231); Jackson 0-3 (.000); Wood 4-21 (.190); Carlisle 0-3 (.000). Opponents 141-420 (.336).

NEW YORK KNICKERBOCKERS

	G	Min.	FGM	FGA	Pct.	FTM	FTA	Pct.	Off.	Def.	Tot.	Ast.	PF	Dq.	Stl.	TO	Blk.	Pts.	Avg.	Hi.
Patrick Ewing	82	3165	922	1673	.551	502	648	.775	235	658	893	182	325	7	78	278	327	2347	28.6	51
Charles Oakley	61	2196	336	641	.524	217	285	.761	258	469	727	146	220	3	64	165	16	889	14.6	25
Gerald Wilkins	82	2609	472	1032	.457	208	259	.803	133	238	371	330	188	0	95	194	21	1191	14.5	30
Johnny Newman	80	2277	374	786	.476	239	299	.799	60	131	191	180	254	3	95	143	22	1032	12.9	30
Kiki Vandeweghe	22	563	102	231	.442	44	48	.917	15	38	53	41	28	0	15	26	3	258	11.7	24
Mark Jackson	82	2428	327	749	.437	120	165	.727	106	212	318	604	121	0	109	211	4	809	9.9	33
Rod Strickland*	51	1019	170	386	.440	83	130	.638	43	83	126	219	71	0	70	85	8	429	8.4	19
Trent Tucker	81	1725	253	606	.417	66	86	.767	57	117	174	173	159	0	74	73	8	667	8.2	21
Kenny Walker	68	1595	204	384	.531	125	173	.723	131	212	343	49	178	1	33	60	52	535	7.9	24
Maurice Cheeks†	31	753	92	159	.579	57	65	.877	11	62	73	151	32	0	42	36	5	244	7.9	20
Maurice Cheeks‡	81	2519	307	609	.504	171	202	.847	50	190	240	453	78	0	124	121	10	789	9.7	22
Eddie Lee Wilkins	79	972	141	310	.455	89	147	.605	114	151	265	16	152	1	18	73	18	371	4.7	14
Pete Myers*	24	208	15	45	.333	16	31	.516	10	18	28	35	39	0	15	18	2	46	1.9	9
Brian Quinnett	31	193	19	58	.328	2	3	.667	9	19	28	11	27	0	3	4	4	40	1.3	6
Stuart Gray†	19	94	4	17	.235	7	8	.875	2	12	14	2	26	0	3	5	2	15	0.8	2
Stuart Gray‡	58	560	42	99	.424	32	47	.681	40	105	145	19	90	0	15	24	26	116	2.0	9
Greg Butler	13	33	3	12	.250	0	2	.000	3	6	9	1	8	0	0	3	0	6	0.5	4

3-pt. FG: New York 236-710 (.332)—Ewing 1-4 (.250); Oakley 0-3 (.000); G. Wilkins 39-125 (.312); Newman 45-142 (.317); Vandeweghe 10-19 (.526); Jackson 35-131 (.267); Strickland* 6-21 (.286); Tucker 95-245 (.388); Walker 2-5 (.400); Cheeks† 3-7 (.429); Cheeks‡ 4-16 (.250); E. Wilkins 0-2 (.000); Myers* 0-1 (.000); Quinnett 0-2 (.000); Gray† 0-3 (.000); Gray‡ 0-5 (.000). Opponents 171-543 (.315).

ORLANDO MAGIC

	G	Min.	FGM	FGA	Pct.	FTM	FTA	Pct.	Off.	Def.	Tot.	Ast.	PF	Dq.	Stl.	TO	Blk.	Pts.	Avg.	Hi.
Terry Catledge	74	2462	546	1152	.474	341	486	.702	271	292	563	72	201	0	36	181	17	1435	19.4	49
Reggie Theus	76	2350	517	1178	.439	378	443	.853	75	146	221	407	194	1	60	226	12	1438	18.9	36
Otis Smith	65	1644	348	708	.492	169	222	.761	117	183	300	147	174	0	76	102	57	875	13.5	33
Jerry Reynolds	67	1817	309	741	.417	239	322	.742	91	232	323	180	162	1	93	139	64	858	12.8	34
Nick Anderson	81	1785	372	753	.494	186	264	.705	107	209	316	124	140	0	69	138	34	931	11.5	29
Sam Vincent	63	1657	258	564	.457	188	214	.879	37	157	194	354	108	1	65	132	20	705	11.2	29
Sidney Green	73	1860	312	667	.468	136	209	.651	166	422	588	99	231	4	50	119	26	761	10.4	36
Michael Ansley	72	1221	231	465	.497	164	227	.722	187	175	362	40	152	0	24	50	17	626	8.7	26
Scott Skiles	70	1460	190	464	.409	104	119	.874	23	136	159	334	126	0	36	90	4	536	7.7	23
Morlon Wiley	40	638	92	208	.442	28	38	.737	13	39	52	114	65	0	45	63	3	229	5.7	24
Jeff Turner	60	1105	132	308	.429	42	54	.778	52	175	227	53	161	4	23	61	12	308	5.1	18
Mark Acres	80	1691	138	285	.484	83	120	.692	154	277	431	67	248	4	36	70	25	362	4.5	18
Dave Corzine	6	79	11	29	.379	0	2	.000	7	11	18	2	7	0	2	8	0	22	3.7	12
Jawann Oldham*	3	36	1	3	.333	2	5	.400	4	11	15	0	6	0	2	3	3	4	1.3	3

3-pt. FG: Orlando 116-393 (.295)—Catledge 2-8 (.250); Theus 26-105 (.248); Smith 10-40 (.250); Reynolds 1-14 (.071); Anderson 1-17 (.059); Vincent 1-14 (.071); Green 1-3 (.333); Skiles 52-132 (.394); Wiley 17-46 (.370); Turner 2-10 (.200); Acres 3-4 (.750). Opponents 196-555 (.353).

PHILADELPHIA 76ERS

	G	Min.	FGM	FGA	Pct.	FTM	FTA	Pct.	Off.	Def.	Tot.	Ast.	PF	Dq.	Stl.	TO	Blk.	Pts.	Avg.	Hi.
Charles Barkley	79	3085	706	1177	.600	557	744	.749	361	548	909	307	250	2	148	243	50	1989	25.2	39
Hersey Hawkins	82	2856	522	1136	.460	387	436	.888	85	219	304	261	217	2	130	185	28	1515	18.5	31
Johnny Dawkins	81	2865	465	950	.489	210	244	.861	48	199	247	601	159	1	121	214	9	1162	14.3	30
Mike Gminski	81	2659	458	1002	.457	193	235	.821	196	491	687	128	136	0	43	98	102	1112	13.7	26
Ron Anderson	78	2089	379	841	.451	165	197	.838	81	214	295	143	143	0	72	78	13	926	11.9	30
Rick Mahorn	75	2271	313	630	.497	183	256	.715	167	401	568	98	251	2	44	104	103	811	10.8	27
Derek Smith	75	1405	261	514	.508	130	186	.699	62	110	172	109	198	2	35	85	20	668	8.9	20
Jay Vincent*	17	259	45	105	.429	33	37	.892	13	23	36	8	23	0	10	14	2	124	7.3	19
Scott Brooks	72	975	119	276	.431	50	57	.877	15	49	64	207	105	0	47	38	0	319	4.4	20
Kenny Payne	35	216	47	108	.435	16	18	.889	11	15	26	10	37	0	7	20	6	114	3.3	10
Lanard Copeland	23	110	31	68	.456	11	14	.786	4	6	10	9	12	0	1	19	1	74	3.2	8
Kurt Nimphius	38	314	38	91	.418	14	30	.467	22	39	61	6	45	0	4	12	18	90	2.4	9
Bob Thornton	56	592	48	112	.429	26	51	.510	45	88	133	10	105	1	20	35	12	123	2.2	11
Corey Gaines	9	81	4	12	.333	1	4	.250	1	4	5	26	11	0	4	10	0	10	1.1	4
Lewis Lloyd*	2	10	1	2	.500	0	0	...	0	0	0	0	3	0	0	4	0	2	1.0	2
Dexter Shouse	3	18	0	4	.000	0	0	...	0	0	0	2	1	0	1	2	1	0	0.0	0

3-pt. FG: Philadelphia 189-543 (.348)—Barkley 20-92 (.217); Hawkins 84-200 (.420); Dawkins 22-66 (.333); Gminski 3-17 (.176); Anderson 3-21 (.143); Mahorn 2-9 (.222); Smith 16-36 (.444); Vincent* 1-1 (1.000); Brooks 31-79 (.392); Payne 4-10 (.400); Copeland 1-5 (.200); Nimphius 0-1 (.000); Thornton 1-3 (.333); Gaines 1-2 (.500); Shouse 0-1 (.000). Opponents 212-573 (.370).

1989-90

PHOENIX SUNS

	G	Min.	FGM	FGA	Pct.	FTM	FTA	Pct.	Off.	Def.	Tot.	Ast.	PF	Dq.	Stl.	TO	Blk.	Pts.	Avg.	Hi.
									REBOUNDS									SCORING		
Tom Chambers	81	3046	810	1617	.501	557	647	.861	121	450	571	190	260	1	88	218	47	2201	27.2	60
Kevin Johnson	74	2782	578	1159	.499	501	598	.838	42	228	270	846	143	0	95	263	14	1665	22.5	44
Jeff Hornacek	67	2278	483	901	.536	173	202	.856	86	227	313	337	144	2	117	125	14	1179	17.6	30
Eddie Johnson	64	1811	411	907	.453	188	205	.917	69	177	246	107	174	4	32	108	10	1080	16.9	37
Dan Majerle	73	2244	296	698	.424	198	260	.762	144	286	430	188	177	5	100	82	32	809	11.1	32
Mark West	82	2399	331	530	.625	199	288	.691	212	516	728	45	277	5	36	126	184	861	10.5	20
Armon Gilliam*	16	267	52	121	.430	39	56	.696	26	44	70	8	28	0	6	17	5	143	8.9	22
Mike McGee	14	280	42	87	.483	10	21	.476	11	25	36	16	28	0	8	14	1	102	7.3	25
Kurt Rambis†	58	1456	132	257	.514	52	72	.722	108	297	405	107	163	0	68	75	27	316	5.4	16
Kurt Rambis‡	74	1904	190	373	.509	82	127	.646	156	369	525	135	208	0	100	104	37	462	6.2	21
Tim Perry	60	612	100	195	.513	53	90	.589	79	73	152	17	76	0	21	47	22	254	4.2	22
Kenny Battle	59	729	93	170	.547	55	82	.671	44	80	124	38	94	2	35	32	11	242	4.1	16
Andrew Lang	74	1011	97	174	.557	64	98	.653	83	188	271	21	171	1	22	41	133	258	3.5	16
Greg Grant	67	678	83	216	.384	39	59	.661	16	43	59	168	58	0	36	77	1	208	3.1	14
Tim Legler	11	83	11	29	.379	6	6	1.000	4	4	8	6	12	0	2	4	0	28	2.5	8
Mike Morrison	36	153	23	68	.338	24	30	.800	7	13	20	11	20	0	2	23	0	72	2.0	11
Micheal Williams*	6	26	2	10	.200	1	2	.500	1	0	1	4	0	0	0	5	0	5	0.8	2

3-pt. FG: Phoenix 176-543 (.324)—Chambers 24-86 (.279); K. Johnson 8-41 (.195); Hornacek 40-98 (.408); E. Johnson 70-184 (.380); Majerle 19-80 (.238); McGee 8-23 (.348); Rambis† 0-2 (.000); Rambis‡ 0-3 (.000); Perry 1-1 (1.000); Battle 1-4 (.250); Grant 3-16 (.188); Legler 0-1 (.000); Morrison 2-7 (.286). Opponents 200-563 (.355).

PORTLAND TRAIL BLAZERS

	G	Min.	FGM	FGA	Pct.	FTM	FTA	Pct.	Off.	Def.	Tot.	Ast.	PF	Dq.	Stl.	TO	Blk.	Pts.	Avg.	Hi.
									REBOUNDS									SCORING		
Clyde Drexler	73	2683	670	1357	.494	333	430	.774	208	299	507	432	222	1	145	191	51	1703	23.3	41
Terry Porter	80	2781	448	969	.462	421	472	.892	59	213	272	726	150	0	151	245	4	1406	17.6	31
Kevin Duckworth	82	2462	548	1146	.478	231	312	.740	184	325	509	91	271	2	36	171	34	1327	16.2	28
Jerome Kersey	82	2843	519	1085	.478	269	390	.690	251	439	690	188	304	7	121	144	63	1310	16.0	31
Buck Williams	82	2801	413	754	.548	288	408	.706	250	550	800	116	285	4	69	168	39	1114	13.6	24
Clifford Robinson	82	1565	298	751	.397	138	251	.550	110	198	308	72	226	4	53	129	53	746	9.1	22
Drazen Petrovic	77	967	207	427	.485	135	160	.844	50	61	111	116	134	0	23	96	2	583	7.6	24
Byron Irvin	50	488	96	203	.473	61	91	.670	30	44	74	47	40	0	28	39	1	258	5.2	23
Danny Young	82	1393	138	328	.421	91	112	.813	29	93	122	231	84	0	82	80	4	383	4.7	16
Wayne Cooper	79	1176	138	304	.454	25	39	.641	118	221	339	44	211	2	18	39	95	301	3.8	12
Mark Bryant	58	562	70	153	.458	28	50	.560	54	92	146	13	93	0	18	25	9	168	2.9	12
Robert Reid*	12	85	13	33	.394	4	8	.500	1	7	8	8	17	0	2	1	2	31	2.6	6
Nate Johnston†	15	74	14	37	.378	7	11	.636	11	10	21	1	11	1	3	5	7	35	2.3	8
Nate Johnston‡	21	87	18	48	.375	9	13	.692	13	10	23	1	11	1	3	6	8	46	2.2	8

3-pt. FG: Portland 190-565 (.336)—Drexler 30-106 (.283); Porter 89-238 (.374); Kersey 3-20 (.150); Williams 0-1 (.000); Robinson 12-44 (.273); Petrovic 34-74 (.459); Irvin 5-14 (.357); Young 16-59 (.271); Cooper 0-3 (.000); Reid* 1-3 (.333); Johnston† 0-3 (.000); Johnston‡ 1-4 (.250). Opponents 228-688 (.331).

SACRAMENTO KINGS

	G	Min.	FGM	FGA	Pct.	FTM	FTA	Pct.	Off.	Def.	Tot.	Ast.	PF	Dq.	Stl.	TO	Blk.	Pts.	Avg.	Hi.
									REBOUNDS									SCORING		
Wayman Tisdale	79	2937	726	1383	.525	306	391	.783	185	410	595	108	251	3	54	153	54	1758	22.3	40
Antoine Carr†	33	924	228	473	.482	158	196	.806	65	108	173	66	119	2	15	71	34	614	18.6	32
Antoine Carr‡	77	1727	356	721	.494	237	298	.795	115	207	322	119	247	6	30	125	68	949	12.3	32
Danny Ainge	75	2727	506	1154	.438	222	267	.831	69	257	326	453	238	2	113	185	18	1342	17.9	39
Rodney McCray	82	3238	537	1043	.515	273	348	.784	192	477	669	377	176	0	60	174	70	1358	16.6	30
Kenny Smith*	46	1747	280	607	.461	106	131	.809	11	109	120	303	98	0	57	122	7	688	15.0	24
Vinny Del Negro	76	1858	297	643	.462	135	155	.871	39	159	198	250	182	2	64	111	10	739	9.7	28
Harold Pressley	72	1603	240	566	.424	110	141	.780	94	215	309	149	148	0	58	88	36	636	8.8	24
Pervis Ellison	34	866	111	251	.442	49	78	.628	64	132	196	65	132	4	16	62	57	271	8.0	25
Sedric Toney†	32	682	57	178	.320	46	58	.793	11	35	46	122	71	1	23	52	0	176	5.5	16
Sedric Toney‡	64	968	87	250	.348	67	83	.807	14	46	60	174	106	1	33	73	0	264	4.1	16
Henry Turner	36	315	58	122	.475	40	65	.615	22	28	50	22	40	0	17	26	7	156	4.3	16
Ralph Sampson	26	417	48	129	.372	12	23	.522	11	73	84	28	66	1	14	34	22	109	4.2	16
Randy Allen	63	746	106	239	.444	23	43	.535	49	89	138	23	102	0	16	28	19	235	3.7	14
Greg Kite	71	1515	101	234	.432	27	54	.500	131	246	377	76	201	2	31	76	51	230	3.2	10
Mike Williams*	16	88	6	14	.429	3	6	.500	5	17	22	2	28	0	3	3	7	15	0.9	4
Michael Jackson	17	58	3	11	.273	4	6	.500	2	5	7	8	4	0	5	4	0	10	0.6	6
Greg Stokes	11	34	1	9	.111	2	2	1.000	2	3	5	0	8	0	0	3	0	4	0.4	2

3-pt. FG: Sacramento 216-649 (.333)—Tisdale 0-6 (.000); Carr† 0-3 (.000); Carr‡ 0-7 (.000); Ainge 108-289 (.374); McCray 11-42 (.262); Smith* 22-59 (.373); Del Negro 10-32 (.313); Pressley 46-148 (.311); Ellison 0-2 (.000); Toney† 16-50 (.320); Toney‡ 23-63 (.365); Turner 0-3 (.000); Sampson 1-4 (.250); Allen 0-7 (.000); Kite 1-1 (1.000); Williams* 0-1 (.000); Jackson 1-2 (.500). Opponents 160-507 (.316).

SAN ANTONIO SPURS

	G	Min.	FGM	FGA	Pct.	FTM	FTA	Pct.	Off.	Def.	Tot.	Ast.	PF	Dq.	Stl.	TO	Blk.	Pts.	Avg.	Hi.
									REBOUNDS									SCORING		
David Robinson	82	3002	690	1300	.531	613	837	.732	303	680	983	164	259	3	138	257	319	1993	24.3	41
Terry Cummings	81	2821	728	1532	.475	343	440	.780	226	451	677	219	286	1	110	202	52	1818	22.4	52
Willie Anderson	82	2788	532	1082	.492	217	290	.748	115	257	372	364	252	3	111	198	58	1288	15.7	28
Rod Strickland†	31	1121	173	370	.468	91	148	.615	47	86	133	249	89	3	57	85	6	439	14.2	21
Rod Strickland‡	82	2140	343	746	.454	174	278	.626	90	169	259	463	160	3	127	170	14	868	10.6	21
Maurice Cheeks*	56	1766	215	450	.478	114	137	.832	39	128	167	302	46	0	82	85	5	545	9.7	18
Sean Elliott	81	2032	311	647	.481	187	216	.866	127	170	297	154	172	0	45	112	14	810	10.0	24
Vernon Maxwell*	49	1118	133	306	.435	59	95	.621	35	106	141	146	79	0	42	71	5	340	6.9	16

	G	Min.	FGM	FGA	Pct.	FTM	FTA	Pct.	Off.	Def.	Tot.	Ast.	PF	Dq.	Stl.	TO	Blk.	Pts.	Avg.	Hi.
David Wingate.......	78	1856	220	491	.448	87	112	.777	62	133	195	208	154	2	89	127	18	527	6.8	19
Frank Brickowski.....	78	1438	211	387	.545	95	141	.674	89	238	327	105	226	4	66	93	37	517	6.6	16
Reggie Williams†	10	68	19	42	.452	4	6	.667	3	5	8	5	16	0	1	4	3	42	4.2	13
Reggie Williams‡	47	743	131	338	.388	52	68	.765	28	55	83	53	102	2	32	45	14	320	6.8	24
Zarko Paspalj	28	181	27	79	.342	18	22	.818	15	15	30	10	37	0	3	21	7	72	2.6	13
Caldwell Jones	72	885	67	144	.465	38	54	.704	76	154	230	20	146	2	20	48	27	173	2.4	11
Johnny Moore.......	53	516	47	126	.373	16	27	.593	16	36	52	82	55	0	32	39	3	118	2.2	11
Uwe Blab†	7	50	6	11	.545	3	6	.500	1	8	9	1	9	0	0	5	0	15	2.1	5
Uwe Blab‡	47	531	39	98	.398	20	37	.541	29	79	108	25	102	0	1	35	22	98	2.1	8
Jeff Lebo	4	32	2	7	.286	2	2	1.000	2	2	4	3	7	0	2	1	0	6	1.5	4
Chris Welp*	13	56	7	23	.304	1	2	.500	7	5	12	5	21	0	1	6	0	15	1.2	4

3-pt. FG: San Antonio 54-226 (.239)—Robinson 0-2 (.000); Cummings 19-59 (.322); Anderson 7-26 (.269); Strickland† 2-9 (.222); Strickland‡ 8-30 (.267); Cheeks* 1-9 (.111); Elliott 1-9 (.111); Maxwell* 15-52 (.288); Wingate 0-13 (.000); Brickowski 0-2 (.000); Williams† 0-5 (.000); Williams‡ 6-37 (.162); Paspalj 0-1 (.000); Jones 1-5 (.200); Moore 8-34 (.235). Opponents 231-624 (.370).

SEATTLE SUPERSONICS

	G	Min.	FGM	FGA	Pct.	FTM	FTA	Pct.	Off.	Def.	Tot.	Ast.	PF	Dq.	Stl.	TO	Blk.	Pts.	Avg.	Hi.
Dale Ellis...........	55	2033	502	1011	.497	193	236	.818	90	148	238	110	124	3	59	119	7	1293	23.5	53
Xavier McDaniel	69	2432	611	1233	.496	244	333	.733	165	282	447	171	231	2	73	187	36	1471	21.3	37
Derrick McKey	80	2748	468	949	.493	315	403	.782	170	319	489	187	247	2	87	192	81	1254	15.7	33
Sedale Threatt.......	65	1481	303	599	.506	130	157	.828	43	72	115	216	164	0	65	77	8	744	11.4	36
Michael Cage	82	2595	325	645	.504	148	212	.698	306	515	821	70	232	1	79	94	45	798	9.7	24
Dana Barros	81	1630	299	738	.405	89	110	.809	35	97	132	205	97	0	53	123	1	782	9.7	28
Quintin Dailey	30	491	97	240	.404	52	66	.788	18	33	51	34	63	0	12	34	0	247	8.2	22
Shawn Kemp	81	1120	203	424	.479	117	159	.736	146	200	346	26	204	5	47	107	70	525	6.5	20
Nate McMillan.......	82	2338	207	438	.473	98	153	.641	127	276	403	598	289	7	140	187	37	523	6.4	19
Jim Farmer	38	400	89	203	.438	57	80	.713	17	26	43	25	44	0	17	27	1	243	6.4	26
Steve Johnson†	21	242	48	90	.533	21	35	.600	19	31	50	16	52	0	3	25	5	117	5.6	13
Steve Johnson‡	25	259	48	92	.522	21	35	.600	19	34	53	17	56	0	3	31	5	117	4.7	13
Brad Sellers*	45	587	84	198	.424	49	61	.803	31	39	70	32	63	1	11	34	19	217	4.8	18
Olden Polynice	79	1085	156	289	.540	47	99	.475	128	172	300	15	187	0	25	35	21	360	4.6	18
Avery Johnson	53	575	55	142	.387	29	40	.725	21	22	43	162	55	0	26	48	1	140	2.6	12
Scott Meents	26	148	19	44	.432	17	23	.739	7	23	30	7	12	0	4	9	3	55	2.1	10

3-pt. FG: Seattle 231-650 (.355)—Ellis 96-256 (.375); McDaniel 5-17 (.294); McKey 3-23 (.130); Threatt 8-32 (.250); Barros 95-238 (.399); Dailey 1-5 (.200); Kemp 2-12 (.167); McMillan 11-31 (.355); Farmer 8-27 (.296); Sellers* 0-3 (.000); Polynice 1-2 (.500); A. Johnson 1-4 (.250). Opponents 178-520 (.342).

UTAH JAZZ

	G	Min.	FGM	FGA	Pct.	FTM	FTA	Pct.	Off.	Def.	Tot.	Ast.	PF	Dq.	Stl.	TO	Blk.	Pts.	Avg.	Hi.
Karl Malone	82	3122	914	1627	.562	696	913	.762	232	679	911	226	259	1	121	304	50	2540	31.0	61
John Stockton.......	78	2915	472	918	.514	354	432	.819	57	149	206	1134	233	2	207	272	18	1345	17.2	34
Thurl Bailey........	82	2583	470	977	.481	222	285	.779	116	294	410	137	175	2	32	139	100	1162	14.2	27
Darrell Griffith	82	1444	301	649	.464	51	78	.654	43	123	166	63	149	0	68	75	19	733	8.9	20
Blue Edwards	82	1889	286	564	.507	146	203	.719	69	182	251	145	280	2	76	152	36	727	8.9	22
Bobby Hansen.......	81	2174	265	568	.467	33	64	.516	66	163	229	149	194	2	52	79	11	617	7.6	23
Mike Brown	82	1397	177	344	.515	157	199	.789	111	262	373	47	187	0	32	88	28	512	6.2	22
Mark Eaton	82	2281	158	300	.527	79	118	.669	171	430	601	39	238	3	33	75	201	395	4.8	14
Eric Leckner	77	764	125	222	.563	81	109	.743	48	144	192	19	157	0	15	63	23	331	4.3	16
Delaney Rudd	77	850	111	259	.429	35	53	.660	12	43	55	177	81	0	22	88	1	273	3.5	18
Jose Ortiz..........	13	64	19	42	.452	3	5	.600	8	7	15	7	15	0	2	5	1	42	3.2	9
Jim Les*	1	6	0	0	—	2	4	.500	0	0	0	1	3	0	0	3	0	2	2.0	2
Nate Johnston*......	6	13	4	11	.364	2	2	1.000	0	2	2	0	0	0	1	1	1	11	1.8	5
Eric Johnson........	48	272	20	84	.238	13	17	.765	8	20	28	64	49	1	17	26	2	54	1.1	6
Raymond Brown	16	56	8	28	.286	0	2	.000	10	5	15	4	11	0	0	6	0	16	1.0	6

3-pt. FG: Utah 226-630 (.359)—Malone 16-43 (.372); Stockton 47-113 (.416); Bailey 0-8 (.000); Griffith 80-215 (.372); Edwards 9-30 (.300); Hansen 54-154 (.351); M. Brown 1-2 (.500); Rudd 16-56 (.286); Ortiz 1-2 (.500); Johnston* 1-1 (1.000); Johnson 1-6 (.167). Opponents 174-563 (.309).

WASHINGTON BULLETS

	G	Min.	FGM	FGA	Pct.	FTM	FTA	Pct.	Off.	Def.	Tot.	Ast.	PF	Dq.	Stl.	TO	Blk.	Pts.	Avg.	Hi.
Jeff Malone.........	75	2567	781	1592	.491	257	293	.877	54	152	206	243	116	1	48	125	6	1820	24.3	41
Bernard King........	82	2687	711	1459	.487	412	513	.803	129	275	404	376	230	1	51	248	7	1837	22.4	42
John Williams.......	18	632	130	274	.474	65	84	.774	27	109	136	84	33	0	21	43	9	327	18.2	29
Ledell Eackles	78	1696	413	940	.439	210	280	.750	74	101	175	182	157	0	50	143	4	1055	13.5	40
Mark Alarie	82	1893	371	785	.473	108	133	.812	151	223	374	142	219	2	60	101	39	860	10.5	20
Darrell Walker.......	81	2883	316	696	.454	138	201	.687	173	541	714	652	220	1	139	173	30	772	9.5	21
Harvey Grant........	81	1846	284	601	.473	96	137	.701	138	204	342	131	194	1	52	85	43	664	8.2	24
Tom Hammonds	61	805	129	295	.437	63	98	.643	61	107	168	51	98	0	11	46	14	321	5.3	17
Steve Colter	73	977	142	297	.478	77	95	.811	55	121	176	148	98	0	47	38	10	361	4.9	25
Mel Turpin.........	59	818	110	209	.526	56	71	.789	88	133	221	27	135	0	15	45	47	276	4.7	17
Ed Horton..........	45	374	80	162	.494	42	69	.609	59	49	108	19	63	1	9	39	5	202	4.5	18
Charles Jones.......	81	2240	94	185	.508	68	105	.648	145	359	504	139	296	10	50	76	197	256	3.2	14
Doug Roth	42	412	37	86	.430	7	14	.500	44	70	114	9	81	1	8	16	13	81	1.9	8

3-pt. FG: Washington 37-197 (.188)—Malone 1-6 (.167); King 3-23 (.130); Williams 2-18 (.111); Eackles 19-59 (.322); Alarie 10-49 (.204); Walker 2-21 (.095); Grant 0-8 (.000); Hammonds 0-1 (.000); Colter 0-5 (.000); Turpin 0-2 (.000); Horton 0-4 (.000); Roth 0-1 (.000). Opponents 142-474 (.300).

* Finished season with another team.   † Totals with this team only.   ‡ Totals with all teams.

EASTERN CONFERENCE

FIRST ROUND

New York 3, Boston 2
Apr. 26—Thur.	New York 105 at Boston	116
Apr. 28—Sat.	New York 128 at Boston	157
May 2—Wed.	Boston 99 at New York	102
May 4—Fri.	Boston 108 at New York	135
May 6—Sun.	New York 121 at Boston	114

Detroit 3, Indiana 0
Apr. 26—Thur.	Indiana 92 at Detroit	104
Apr. 28—Sat.	Indiana 87 at Detroit	100
May 1—Tue.	Detroit 108 at Indiana	96

Philadelphia 3, Cleveland 2
Apr. 26—Thur.	Cleveland 106 at Philadelphia	111
Apr. 29—Sun.	Cleveland 101 at Philadelphia	107
May 1—Tue.	Philadelphia 95 at Cleveland	122
May 3—Thur.	Philadelphia 96 at Cleveland	108
May 5—Sat.	Cleveland 97 at Philadelphia	113

Chicago 3, Milwaukee 1
Apr. 27—Fri.	Milwaukee 97 at Chicago	111
Apr. 29—Sun.	Milwaukee 102 at Chicago	109
May 1—Tue.	Chicago 112 at Milwaukee	119
May 3—Thur.	Chicago 110 at Milwaukee	86

SEMIFINALS

Chicago 4, Philadelphia 1
May 7—Mon.	Philadelphia 85 at Chicago	96
May 9—Wed.	Philadelphia 96 at Chicago	101
May 11—Fri.	Chicago 112 at Philadelphia	118
May 13—Sun.	Chicago 111 at Philadelphia	101
May 16—Wed.	Philadelphia 99 at Chicago	117

Detroit 4, New York 1
May 8—Tue.	New York 77 at Detroit	112
May 10—Thur.	New York 97 at Detroit	104
May 12—Sat.	Detroit 103 at New York	111
May 13—Sun.	Detroit 102 at New York	90
May 15—Tue.	New York 84 at Detroit	95

FINALS

Detroit 4, Chicago 3
May 20—Sun.	Chicago 77 at Detroit	86
May 22—Tue.	Chicago 93 at Detroit	102
May 26—Sat.	Detroit 102 at Chicago	107
May 28—Mon.	Detroit 101 at Chicago	108
May 30—Wed.	Chicago 83 at Detroit	97
June 1—Fri.	Detroit 91 at Chicago	109
June 3—Sun.	Chicago 74 at Detroit	93

WESTERN CONFERENCE

FIRST ROUND

L.A. Lakers 3, Houston 1
Apr. 27—Fri.	Houston 89 at L.A. Lakers	101
Apr. 29—Sun.	Houston 100 at L.A. Lakers	104
May 1—Tue.	L.A. Lakers 108 at Houston	114
May 3—Thur.	L.A. Lakers 109 at Houston	88

Phoenix 3, Utah 2
Apr. 27—Fri.	Phoenix 96 at Utah	113
Apr. 29—Sun.	Phoenix 105 at Utah	87
May 2—Wed.	Utah 105 at Phoenix	120
May 4—Fri.	Utah 105 at Phoenix	94
May 6—Sun.	Phoenix 104 at Utah	102

San Antonio 3, Denver 0
Apr. 26—Thur.	Denver 103 at San Antonio	119
Apr. 28—Sat.	Denver 120 at San Antonio	129
May 1—Tue.	San Antonio 131 at Denver	120

Portland 3, Dallas 0
Apr. 26—Thur.	Dallas 102 at Portland	109
Apr. 28—Sat.	Dallas 107 at Portland	114
May 1—Tue.	Portland 106 at Dallas	92

SEMIFINALS

Portland 4, San Antonio 3
May 5—Sat.	San Antonio 94 at Portland	107
May 8—Tue.	San Antonio 112 at Portland	122
May 10—Thur.	Portland 98 at San Antonio	121
May 12—Sat.	Portland 105 at San Antonio	115
May 15—Tue.	San Antonio 132 at Portland	**138
May 17—Thur.	Portland 97 at San Antonio	112
May 19—Sat.	San Antonio 105 at Portland	*108

Phoenix 4, L.A. Lakers 1
May 8—Tue.	Phoenix 104 at L.A. Lakers	102
May 10—Thur.	Phoenix 100 at L.A. Lakers	124
May 12—Sat.	L.A. Lakers 103 at Phoenix	117
May 13—Sun.	L.A. Lakers 101 at Phoenix	114
May 15—Tue.	Phoenix 106 at L.A. Lakers	103

FINALS

Portland 4, Phoenix 2
May 21—Mon.	Phoenix 98 at Portland	100
May 23—Wed.	Phoenix 107 at Portland	108
May 25—Fri.	Portland 89 at Phoenix	123
May 27—Sun.	Portland 107 at Phoenix	119
May 29—Tue.	Phoenix 114 at Portland	120
May 31—Thur.	Portland 112 at Phoenix	109

NBA FINALS

Detroit 4, Portland 1
June 5—Tue.	Portland 99 at Detroit	105
June 7—Thur.	Portland 106 at Detroit	*105
June 10—Sun.	Detroit 121 at Portland	106
June 12—Tue.	Detroit 112 at Portland	109
June 14—Thur.	Detroit 92 at Portland	90

*Denotes number of overtime periods.

1989-90

1988-89

1988-89 NBA CHAMPION DETROIT PISTONS

Front row (from left): Bill Laimbeer, John Long, head coach Chuck Daly, CEO Tom Wilson, owner William Davidson, general manager Jack McCloskey, legal counsel Oscar Feldman, John Salley, James Edwards, Rick Mahorn. Back row (from left): trainer Mike Abdenour, scouting director Stan Novak, assistant general manager Will Robinson, assistant coach Brendan Suhr, Micheal Williams, Vinnie Johnson, Fennis Dembo, Dennis Rodman, Mark Aguirre, Joe Dumars, Isiah Thomas, assistant coach Brendan Malone, announcer George Blaha.

FINAL STANDINGS

ATLANTIC DIVISION

	Atl.	Bos.	Char.	Chi.	Cle.	Dal.	Den.	Det.	G.S.	Hou.	Ind.	L.A.C.	L.A.L.	Mia.	Mil.	N.J.	N.Y.	Phi.	Pho.	Por.	Sac.	S.A.	Sea.	Uta.	Was.	W	L	Pct.	GB
New York	2	3	4	2	2	2	1	4	0	2	5	2	1	1	3	4	..	2	1	2	1	1	1	1	5	52	30	.634	..
Philadelphia	2	3	3	3	2	1	1	0	1	2	4	2	0	2	1	5	4	..	0	1	2	1	1	1	4	46	36	.561	6
Boston	1	..	6	1	1	1	1	1	1	1	2	2	1	2	2	5	3	3	0	1	2	2	0	1	2	42	40	.512	10
Washington	1	4	5	1	2	1	1	0	1	2	3	2	1	2	1	5	1	2	0	1	2	1	1	0	..	40	42	.488	12
New Jersey	1	1	4	2	0	1	1	0	0	0	3	1	1	1	1	..	2	1	1	0	1	1	2	0	1	26	56	.317	26
Charlotte	1	0	..	1	0	0	0	0	0	0	2	2	0	1	0	2	2	2	3	0	0	1	2	1	1	20	62	.244	32

CENTRAL DIVISION

	Atl.	Bos.	Char.	Chi.	Cle.	Dal.	Den.	Det.	G.S.	Hou.	Ind.	L.A.C.	L.A.L.	Mia.	Mil.	N.J.	N.Y.	Phi.	Pho.	Por.	Sac.	S.A.	Sea.	Uta.	Was.	W	L	Pct.	GB
Detroit	5	3	4	6	3	2	1	..	1	1	4	2	2	2	2	4	0	5	2	1	2	2	2	2	5	63	19	.768	..
Cleveland	2	4	4	6	..	2	2	3	1	1	5	1	0	2	3	4	2	3	2	2	2	1	1	1	2	57	25	.695	6
Atlanta	..	3	4	4	4	1	0	1	1	1	5	2	1	1	6	4	2	2	1	1	2	1	1	1	3	52	30	.634	11
Milwaukee	0	2	4	0	3	2	2	4	2	1	4	2	1	2	..	4	1	3	1	2	2	1	1	1	4	49	33	.598	14
Chicago	2	3	4	..	0	2	1	0	1	1	4	1	2	2	6	2	3	1	1	2	2	2	2	0	3	47	35	.573	16
Indiana	1	3	2	2	1	1	1	2	1	0	..	1	0	1	2	1	0	0	1	2	1	2	1	1	1	28	54	.341	35

MIDWEST DIVISION

	Atl.	Bos.	Char.	Chi.	Cle.	Dal.	Den.	Det.	G.S.	Hou.	Ind.	L.A.C.	L.A.L.	Mia.	Mil.	N.J.	N.Y.	Phi.	Pho.	Por.	Sac.	S.A.	Sea.	Uta.	Was.	W	L	Pct.	GB
Utah	1	1	1	2	1	2	3	0	2	4	1	3	3	5	1	2	1	1	2	4	3	5	1	..	2	51	31	.622	..
Houston	1	1	2	1	1	5	2	1	3	..	2	2	1	4	1	2	0	0	1	3	2	6	2	2	0	45	37	.549	6
Denver	2	1	2	1	0	3	..	1	3	4	1	2	5	0	1	1	1	1	1	2	3	3	2	3	1	44	38	.537	7
Dallas	1	1	2	0	0	..	3	0	1	1	3	0	6	0	1	0	1	0	1	2	2	5	2	4	1	38	44	.463	13
San Antonio	1	0	0	0	0	1	3	0	1	0	0	1	1	4	1	1	1	1	1	1	2	..	0	1	1	21	61	.256	30
Miami	1	0	1	0	0	0	1	0	0	2	1	3	0	..	0	1	1	0	0	1	2	0	1	0	0	15	67	.183	36

PACIFIC DIVISION

	Atl.	Bos.	Char.	Chi.	Cle.	Dal.	Den.	Det.	G.S.	Hou.	Ind.	L.A.C.	L.A.L.	Mia.	Mil.	N.J.	N.Y.	Phi.	Pho.	Por.	Sac.	S.A.	Sea.	Uta.	Was.	W	L	Pct.	GB
L.A. Lakers	1	1	2	0	2	4	3	0	3	3	2	5	..	4	1	1	1	2	3	5	5	3	4	1	1	57	25	.695	..
Phoenix	1	2	2	1	0	3	3	0	4	3	1	5	3	4	1	1	1	2	..	2	5	3	4	2	2	55	27	.671	2
Seattle	1	2	1	0	1	2	2	0	4	2	1	4	2	4	1	0	1	1	1	4	5	4	..	3	1	47	35	.573	10
Golden State	1	1	2	1	1	3	1	1	..	1	1	5	2	4	0	2	2	1	2	2	3	3	2	2	1	43	39	.524	14
Portland	1	1	2	0	0	2	2	1	4	1	0	5	0	4	0	2	0	1	3	..	3	4	2	0	1	39	43	.476	18
Sacramento	0	0	1	0	0	2	1	0	3	2	1	3	1	3	0	1	1	0	1	3	..	2	1	1	0	27	55	.329	30
L.A. Clippers	0	0	0	1	1	1	2	0	1	2	1	..	1	1	0	1	0	0	1	1	2	3	1	1	0	21	61	.256	36

OFFENSIVE

	G	FGM	FGA	Pct.	FTM	FTA	Pct.	REBOUNDS Off.	Def.	Tot.	Ast.	PF	Dq.	Stl.	TO	Blk.	SCORING Pts.	Avg.
Phoenix	82	3754	7545	.498	2051	2594	.791	1095	2619	3714	2280	1933	13	693	1279	416	9727	118.6
Denver	82	3813	8140	.468	1821	2314	.787	1206	2513	3719	2282	2088	26	811	1225	436	9675	118.0
New York	82	3701	7611	.486	1779	2366	.752	1322	2265	3587	2083	2053	16	900	1572	446	9567	116.7
Golden State	82	3730	7977	.468	1904	2384	.799	1323	2561	3884	2009	1946	21	831	1488	643	9558	116.6
L.A. Lakers	82	3584	7143	.502	2011	2508	.802	1094	2612	3706	2282	1672	2	724	1344	421	9406	114.7
Portland	82	3695	7795	.474	1789	2416	.740	1384	2381	3765	2212	2026	22	828	1435	388	9395	114.6
Seattle	82	3564	7478	.477	1775	2379	.746	1397	2238	3635	2083	2027	12	864	1403	494	9196	112.1
Philadelphia	82	3500	7201	.486	1970	2504	.787	1143	2356	3499	2110	1721	8	689	1214	354	9174	111.9
Atlanta	82	3412	7230	.472	2168	2709	.800	1372	2316	3688	1990	1880	14	817	1310	474	9102	111.0
Boston	82	3520	7143	.493	1840	2349	.783	1179	2442	3621	2189	1876	16	639	1336	418	8958	109.2
Milwaukee	82	3399	7167	.474	1955	2382	.821	1133	2272	3405	2071	1953	16	821	1305	323	8932	108.9
Cleveland	82	3466	6904	.502	1821	2438	.747	1033	2475	3508	2260	1592	5	791	1323	586	8923	108.8
Houston	82	3412	7196	.474	1909	2527	.755	1211	2554	3765	2016	2026	26	789	1569	501	8897	108.5
Washington	82	3519	7591	.464	1789	2318	.772	1254	2354	3608	2048	2054	17	694	1291	325	8879	108.3
Indiana	82	3385	6945	.487	1795	2275	.789	1065	2497	3562	2012	2105	48	563	1547	418	8767	106.9
Detroit	82	3395	6879	.494	1830	2379	.769	1154	2546	3700	2027	1939	15	522	1336	406	8740	106.6
Chicago	82	3448	6968	.495	1656	2106	.786	1018	2453	3471	2213	1855	17	722	1327	376	8726	106.4
L.A. Clippers	82	3526	7428	.475	1606	2220	.723	1156	2384	3540	2208	1937	17	815	1666	530	8712	106.2
San Antonio	82	3469	7409	.468	1651	2367	.698	1295	2181	3476	2037	2153	36	961	1712	423	8652	105.5
Sacramento	82	3362	7351	.457	1620	2104	.770	1141	2454	3595	1970	1877	28	624	1301	409	8651	105.5
Utah	82	3182	6595	.482	2110	2742	.770	1050	2607	3657	2108	1894	13	720	1532	583	8588	104.7
Charlotte	82	3426	7430	.461	1580	2060	.767	1138	2200	3338	2323	2068	20	705	1318	264	8566	104.5
New Jersey	82	3333	7226	.461	1653	2260	.731	1204	2419	3623	1793	1966	12	773	1449	431	8506	103.7
Dallas	82	3244	6917	.469	1785	2263	.789	1048	2397	3445	1867	1739	14	579	1233	476	8484	103.5
Miami	82	3221	7116	.453	1477	2103	.702	1309	2211	3520	1958	2124	38	744	1728	408	8016	97.8

DEFENSIVE

	FGM	FGA	Pct.	FTM	FTA	Pct.	REBOUNDS Off.	Def.	Tot.	Ast.	PF	Dq.	Stl.	TO	Blk.	SCORING Pts.	Avg.	Dif.
Utah	3113	7170	.434	1765	2342	.754	1220	2233	3453	1812	2086	26	779	1329	505	8176	99.7	+5.0
Detroit	3140	7022	.447	1826	2325	.785	1131	2188	3319	1855	2088	28	646	1225	341	8264	100.8	+5.8
Cleveland	3385	7346	.461	1358	1748	.777	1214	2283	3497	2043	1970	19	685	1429	363	8300	101.2	+7.6
Dallas	3422	7304	.469	1573	2090	.753	1231	2500	3731	2133	1869	11	660	1175	386	8583	104.7	-1.2
Chicago	3361	7098	.474	1603	2190	.773	1078	2300	3378	2099	1781	13	686	1255	348	8608	105.0	+1.4
Milwaukee	3301	6901	.478	1838	2369	.776	1094	2335	3429	2109	1935	14	707	1522	425	8636	105.3	+3.6
Atlanta	3363	7124	.472	1826	2329	.784	1261	2325	3586	2037	2109	23	687	1487	348	8699	106.1	+4.9
L.A. Lakers	3541	7540	.470	1542	2051	.752	1178	2222	3400	2157	1941	24	752	1263	432	8818	107.5	+7.2
Houston	3413	7290	.468	1806	2372	.761	1145	2428	3573	2015	2013	28	800	1455	439	8819	107.5	+1.0
Boston	3475	7183	.484	1780	2294	.776	1048	2222	3270	2124	1950	19	762	1191	387	8863	108.1	+1.1
Miami	3384	6928	.488	2021	2613	.773	1188	2366	3554	2062	1830	15	926	1543	553	8937	109.0	-11.2
Seattle	3437	7067	.486	1915	2489	.769	1188	2252	3440	1958	1881	15	670	1553	413	8958	109.2	+2.9
New Jersey	3560	7162	.497	1749	2286	.765	1030	2476	3506	2134	1834	14	744	1376	485	9027	110.1	-6.4
Washington	3486	7235	.482	1929	2510	.769	1132	2538	3670	2082	1921	19	655	1381	523	9056	110.4	-2.1
Philadelphia	3658	7296	.501	1565	2023	.774	1149	2412	3561	2281	2026	26	640	1269	445	9051	110.4	+1.5
Phoenix	3589	7736	.464	1737	2308	.753	1252	2458	3710	2166	2057	16	625	1368	427	9096	110.9	+7.7
Sacramento	3589	7420	.484	1747	2301	.759	1171	2604	3775	2107	1821	22	759	1284	442	9106	111.0	-5.5
Indiana	3453	7400	.467	2036	2606	.781	1288	2312	3600	2034	2029	15	836	1206	389	9109	111.1	-4.2
San Antonio	3486	7148	.488	2105	2714	.776	1256	2462	3718	2062	1938	21	915	1728	545	9249	112.8	-7.3
New York	3636	7358	.494	1834	2390	.767	1213	2326	3539	2292	1898	19	778	1688	433	9258	112.9	+3.8
Charlotte	3555	7113	.500	2040	2629	.776	1191	2621	3812	2061	1791	10	710	1425	441	9265	113.0	-8.5
Portland	3572	7322	.488	1933	2504	.772	1151	2391	3542	2073	1900	17	738	1569	358	9275	113.1	+1.5
L.A. Clippers	3747	7738	.484	1834	2400	.764	1342	2550	3892	2384	1882	17	933	1440	551	9525	116.2	-10.0
Denver	3701	7484	.495	1977	2683	.737	1136	2864	4000	2136	2001	21	665	1597	485	9536	116.3	+1.7
Golden State	3693	8000	.462	1916	2501	.766	1437	2639	4076	2215	1935	20	861	1554	485	9583	116.9	-0.3
Avgs.	3482	7295	.477	1814	2363	.768	1189	2412	3601	2097	1940	19	745	1412	438	8952	109.2	...

HOME/ROAD

	Home	Road	Total		Home	Road	Total
Atlanta	33-8	19-22	52-30	Miami	12-29	3-38	15-67
Boston	32-9	10-31	42-40	Milwaukee	31-10	18-23	49-33
Charlotte	12-29	8-33	20-62	New Jersey	17-24	9-32	26-56
Chicago	30-11	17-24	47-35	New York	35-6	17-24	52-30
Cleveland	37-4	20-21	57-25	Philadelphia	30-11	16-25	46-36
Dallas	24-17	14-27	38-44	Phoenix	35-6	20-21	55-27
Denver	35-6	9-32	44-38	Portland	28-13	11-30	39-43
Detroit	37-4	26-15	63-19	Sacramento	21-20	6-35	27-55
Golden State	29-12	14-27	43-39	San Antonio	18-23	3-38	21-61
Houston	31-10	14-27	45-37	Seattle	31-10	16-25	47-35
Indiana	20-21	8-33	28-54	Utah	34-7	17-24	51-31
L.A. Clippers	17-24	4-37	21-61	Washington	30-11	10-31	40-42
L.A. Lakers	35-6	22-19	57-25	Totals	694-331	331-694	1025-1025

1988-89

POINTS
(minimum 70 games or 1,400 points)

	G	FGM	FTM	Pts.	Avg.		G	FGM	FTM	Pts.	Avg.
Michael Jordan, Chicago	.81	966	674	2633	32.5	Terry Cummings, Milwaukee	.80	730	362	1829	22.9
Karl Malone, Utah	.80	809	703	2326	29.1	Patrick Ewing, New York	.80	727	361	1815	22.7
Dale Ellis, Seattle	.82	857	377	2253	27.5	Kelly Tripucka, Charlotte	.71	568	440	1606	22.6
Clyde Drexler, Portland	.78	829	438	2123	27.2	Kevin McHale, Boston	.78	661	436	1758	22.5
Chris Mullin, Golden State	.82	830	493	2176	26.5	Magic Johnson, L.A. Lakers	.77	579	513	1730	22.5
Alex English, Denver	.82	924	325	2175	26.5	Mitch Richmond, Golden State	.79	649	410	1741	22.0
Dominique Wilkins, Atlanta	.80	814	442	2099	26.2	Jeff Malone, Washington	.76	677	296	1651	21.7
Charles Barkley, Philadelphia	.79	700	602	2037	25.8	Chuck Person, Indiana	.80	711	243	1728	21.6
Tom Chambers, Phoenix	.81	774	509	2085	25.7	Eddie Johnson, Phoenix	.70	608	217	1504	21.5
Hakeem Olajuwon, Houston	.82	790	454	2034	24.8	Bernard King, Washington	.81	654	361	1674	20.7

FIELD GOALS
(minimum 300 made)

	FGM	FGA	Pct.		FGM	FGA	Pct.
Dennis Rodman, Detroit	.316	531	.595	Kevin McHale, Boston	.661	1211	.546
Charles Barkley, Philadelphia	.700	1208	.579	Otis Thorpe, Houston	.521	961	.542
Robert Parish, Boston	.596	1045	.570	Benoit Benjamin, L.A. Clippers	.491	907	.541
Patrick Ewing, New York	.727	1282	.567	Larry Nance, Cleveland	.496	920	.539
James Worthy, L.A. Lakers	.702	1282	.548	John Stockton, Utah	.497	923	.538

FREE THROWS
(minimum 125 made)

	FTM	FTA	Pct.
Magic Johnson, L.A. Lakers	.513	563	.911
Jack Sikma, Milwaukee	.266	294	.905
Scott Skiles, Indiana	.130	144	.903
Mark Price, Cleveland	.263	292	.901
Chris Mullin, Golden State	.493	553	.892
Kevin Johnson, Phoenix	.508	576	.882
Joe Kleine, Sacramento-Boston	.134	152	.882
Walter Davis, Denver	.175	199	.879
Mike Gminski, Philadelphia	.297	341	.871
Jeff Malone, Washington	.296	340	.871

STEALS
(minimum 70 games or 125 steals)

	G	No.	Avg.
John Stockton, Utah	.82	263	3.21
Alvin Robertson, San Antonio	.65	197	3.03
Michael Jordan, Chicago	.81	234	2.89
Fat Lever, Denver	.71	195	2.75
Clyde Drexler, Portland	.78	213	2.73
Hakeem Olajuwon, Houston	.82	213	2.60
Doc Rivers, Atlanta	.76	181	2.38
Ron Harper, Cleveland	.82	185	2.26
Winston Garland, Golden State	.79	175	2.22
Lester Conner, New Jersey	.82	181	2.21

ASSISTS
(minimum 70 games or 400 assists)

	G	No.	Avg.
John Stockton, Utah	.82	1118	13.6
Magic Johnson, L.A. Lakers	.77	988	12.8
Kevin Johnson, Phoenix	.81	991	12.2
Terry Porter, Portland	.81	770	9.5
Nate McMillan, Seattle	.75	696	9.3
Sleepy Floyd, Houston	.82	709	8.7
Mark Jackson, New York	.72	619	8.6
Mark Price, Cleveland	.75	631	8.4
Isiah Thomas, Detroit	.80	663	8.3
Michael Jordan, Chicago	.81	650	8.0

BLOCKED SHOTS
(minimum 70 games or 100 blocked shots)

	G	No.	Avg.
Manute Bol, Golden State	.80	345	4.31
Mark Eaton, Utah	.82	315	3.84
Patrick Ewing, New York	.80	281	3.51
Hakeem Olajuwon, Houston	.82	282	3.44
Larry Nance, Cleveland	.73	206	2.82
Benoit Benjamin, L.A. Clippers	.79	221	2.80
Wayne Cooper, Denver	.79	211	2.67
Mark West, Phoenix	.82	187	2.28
Alton Lister, Seattle	.82	180	2.20
Rik Smits, Indiana	.82	151	1.84

REBOUNDS
(minimum 70 games or 800 rebounds)

	G	Off.	Def.	Tot.	Avg.
Hakeem Olajuwon, Houston	.82	338	767	1105	13.5
Robert Parish, Boston	.80	342	654	996	12.5
Charles Barkley, Philadelphia	.79	403	583	986	12.5
Moses Malone, Atlanta	.81	386	570	956	11.8
Karl Malone, Utah	.80	259	594	853	10.7
Charles Oakley, New York	.82	343	518	861	10.5
Mark Eaton, Utah	.82	227	616	843	10.3
Otis Thorpe, Houston	.82	272	515	787	9.6
Bill Laimbeer, Detroit	.81	138	638	776	9.6
Michael Cage, Seattle	.80	276	489	765	9.6

3-POINT FIELD GOALS
(minimum 25 made)

	FGA	FGM	Pct.
Jon Sundvold, Miami	.92	48	.522
Dale Ellis, Seattle	.339	162	.478
Mark Price, Cleveland	.211	93	.441
Hersey Hawkins, Philadelphia	.166	71	.428
Craig Hodges, Phoenix-Chicago	.180	75	.417
Eddie Johnson, Phoenix	.172	71	.413
Ricky Berry, Sacramento	.160	65	.406
Harold Pressley, Sacramento	.295	119	.403
Reggie Miller, Indiana	.244	98	.402
Byron Scott, L.A. Lakers	.193	77	.399

1988-89

ATLANTA HAWKS

	G	Min.	FGM	FGA	Pct.	FTM	FTA	Pct.	Off.	Def.	Tot.	Ast.	PF	Dq.	Stl.	TO	Blk.	Pts.	Avg.	Hi.
Dominique Wilkins ...	80	2997	814	1756	.464	442	524	.844	256	297	553	211	138	0	117	181	52	2099	26.2	41
Moses Malone ...	81	2878	538	1096	.491	561	711	.789	386	570	956	112	154	0	79	245	100	1637	20.2	37
Reggie Theus ...	82	2517	497	1067	.466	285	335	.851	86	156	242	387	236	0	108	194	16	1296	15.8	32
Doc Rivers ...	76	2462	371	816	.455	247	287	.861	89	197	286	525	263	6	181	158	40	1032	13.6	32
John Battle ...	82	1672	287	628	.457	194	238	.815	30	110	140	197	125	0	42	104	9	779	9.5	21
Cliff Levingston ...	80	2184	300	568	.528	133	191	.696	194	304	498	75	270	4	97	105	70	734	9.2	23
Antoine Carr ...	78	1488	226	471	.480	130	152	.855	106	168	274	91	221	0	31	82	62	582	7.5	22
Jon Koncak ...	74	1531	141	269	.524	63	114	.553	147	306	453	56	238	4	54	60	98	345	4.7	16
Spud Webb ...	81	1219	133	290	.459	52	60	.867	21	102	123	284	104	0	70	83	6	319	3.9	21
Duane Ferrell ...	41	231	35	83	.422	30	44	.682	19	22	41	10	33	0	7	12	6	100	2.4	16
Ray Tolbert ...	50	341	40	94	.426	23	37	.622	31	57	88	16	55	0	13	35	13	103	2.1	9
Dudley Bradley ...	38	267	28	86	.326	8	16	.500	7	25	32	24	41	0	16	14	2	72	1.9	8
Pace Mannion† ...	5	18	2	6	.333	0	0	...	0	2	2	2	2	0	2	3	0	4	0.8	2
Pace Mannion‡ ...	10	32	4	8	.500	0	0	...	0	5	5	2	5	0	3	3	0	8	0.8	4

3-pt. FG: Atlanta 110-397 (.277)—Wilkins 29-105 (.276); Malone 0-12 (.000); Theus 17-58 (.293); Rivers 43-124 (.347); Battle 11-34 (.324); Levingston 1-5 (.200); Carr 0-1 (.000); Koncak 0-3 (.000); Webb 1-22 (.045); Bradley 8-31 (.258); Mannion† 0-2 (.000); Mannion‡ 0-2 (.000). Opponents 147-511 (.288).

BOSTON CELTICS

	G	Min.	FGM	FGA	Pct.	FTM	FTA	Pct.	Off.	Def.	Tot.	Ast.	PF	Dq.	Stl.	TO	Blk.	Pts.	Avg.	Hi.
Kevin McHale ...	78	2876	661	1211	.546	436	533	.818	223	414	637	172	223	2	26	196	97	1758	22.5	36
Larry Bird ...	6	189	49	104	.471	18	19	.947	1	36	37	29	18	0	6	11	5	116	19.3	29
Robert Parish ...	80	2840	596	1045	.570	294	409	.719	342	654	996	175	209	2	79	200	116	1486	18.6	34
Reggie Lewis ...	81	2657	604	1242	.486	284	361	.787	116	261	377	218	258	5	124	142	72	1495	18.5	39
Danny Ainge* ...	45	1349	271	589	.460	114	128	.891	37	117	154	215	108	0	52	82	1	714	15.9	45
Ed Pinckney† ...	29	678	95	176	.540	103	129	.798	60	88	148	44	77	1	29	38	23	293	10.1	22
Ed Pinckney‡ ...	80	2012	319	622	.513	280	350	.800	166	283	449	118	202	2	83	119	66	918	11.5	26
Dennis Johnson ...	72	2309	277	638	.434	160	195	.821	31	159	190	472	211	3	94	175	21	721	10.0	24
Brian Shaw ...	82	2301	297	686	.433	109	132	.826	119	257	376	472	211	1	78	188	27	703	8.6	31
Jim Paxson ...	57	1138	202	445	.454	84	103	.816	18	56	74	107	96	0	38	57	8	492	8.6	21
Kelvin Upshaw† ...	23	473	73	149	.490	14	20	.700	6	30	36	97	62	1	19	42	3	162	7.0	13
Kelvin Upshaw‡ ...	32	617	99	212	.467	18	26	.602	10	39	49	117	80	1	26	55	3	220	6.9	13
Joe Kleine† ...	28	498	59	129	.457	53	64	.828	49	88	137	32	66	0	15	37	5	171	6.1	16
Joe Kleine‡ ...	75	1411	175	432	.405	134	152	.882	124	254	378	67	192	2	33	104	23	484	6.5	19
Brad Lohaus* ...	48	738	117	270	.433	35	46	.761	47	95	142	49	101	1	21	49	26	269	5.6	18
Kevin Gamble ...	44	375	75	136	.551	35	55	.636	11	31	42	34	40	0	14	19	3	187	4.3	31
Otis Birdsong ...	13	108	18	36	.500	0	2	.000	4	9	13	9	10	0	3	12	1	37	2.8	11
Ronnie Grandison ...	72	528	59	142	.415	59	80	.738	47	45	92	42	71	0	18	36	3	177	2.5	15
Mark Acres ...	62	632	55	114	.482	26	48	.542	59	87	146	19	94	0	19	23	6	137	2.2	9
Ramon Rivas ...	28	91	12	31	.387	16	25	.640	9	15	24	3	21	0	4	9	1	40	1.4	8

3-pt. FG: Boston 78-309 (.252)—McHale 0-4 (.000); Lewis 3-22 (.136); Ainge* 58-155 (.374); Pinckney‡ 0-6 (.000); Johnson 7-50 (.140); Shaw 0-13 (.000); Paxson 4-24 (.167); Upshaw† 2-10 (.200); Upshaw‡ 4-15 (.267); Kleine† 0-1 (.000); Kleine‡ 0-2 (.000); Lohaus* 0-4 (.000); Gamble 2-11 (.182); Birdsong 1-3 (.333); Grandison 0-10 (.000); Acres 1-1 (1.000); Rivas 0-1 (.000). Opponents 133-459 (.290).

CHARLOTTE HORNETS

	G	Min.	FGM	FGA	Pct.	FTM	FTA	Pct.	Off.	Def.	Tot.	Ast.	PF	Dq.	Stl.	TO	Blk.	Pts.	Avg.	Hi.
Kelly Tripucka ...	71	2302	568	1215	.467	440	508	.866	79	188	267	224	196	0	88	236	16	1606	22.6	40
Rex Chapman ...	75	2219	526	1271	.414	155	195	.795	74	113	187	176	167	1	70	113	25	1267	16.9	37
Robert Reid ...	82	2152	519	1214	.428	152	196	.776	82	220	302	153	235	2	53	106	20	1207	14.7	28
Dell Curry ...	48	813	256	521	.491	40	46	.870	26	78	104	50	68	0	42	44	4	571	11.9	31
Kurt Rambis ...	75	2233	325	627	.518	182	248	.734	269	434	703	159	208	4	100	148	57	832	11.1	23
Michael Holton ...	67	1696	215	504	.427	120	143	.839	30	75	105	424	165	0	66	119	12	553	8.3	22
Brian Rowsom ...	34	517	80	162	.494	65	81	.802	56	81	137	24	69	1	10	18	12	226	6.6	17
Earl Cureton ...	82	2047	233	465	.501	66	123	.537	188	300	488	130	230	3	50	114	61	532	6.5	17
Dave Hoppen ...	77	1419	199	353	.564	101	139	.727	123	261	384	57	239	4	25	77	21	500	6.5	16
Tim Kempton ...	79	1341	171	335	.510	142	207	.686	91	213	304	102	215	3	41	121	14	484	6.1	21
Muggsy Bogues ...	79	1755	178	418	.426	66	88	.750	53	112	165	620	141	1	111	124	7	423	5.4	14
Rickey Green* ...	33	370	57	132	.432	13	14	.929	4	19	23	82	16	0	18	28	0	128	3.9	14
Ralph Lewis ...	42	336	58	121	.479	19	39	.487	35	26	61	15	28	0	11	24	3	136	3.2	17
Greg Kite† ...	12	213	16	30	.533	6	10	.600	15	38	53	7	43	1	4	12	8	38	3.2	6
Greg Kite‡ ...	70	942	65	151	.430	20	41	.488	81	162	243	36	161	1	27	58	54	150	2.1	9
Tom Tolbert ...	14	117	17	37	.459	6	12	.500	7	14	21	7	20	0	2	2	4	40	2.9	8
Sidney Lowe ...	14	250	8	25	.320	7	11	.636	6	28	34	93	28	0	14	9	0	23	1.6	5

3-pt. FG: Charlotte 134-430 (.312)—Tripucka 30-84 (.357); Chapman 60-191 (.314); Reid 17-52 (.327); Curry 19-55 (.345); Rambis 0-3 (.000); Holton 3-14 (.214); Rowsom 1-1 (1.000); Cureton 0-1 (.000); Hoppen 1-2 (.500); Kempton 0-1 (.000); Bogues 1-13 (.077); Green* 1-5 (.200); Lewis 1-3 (.333); Tolbert 0-3 (.000); Lowe 0-2 (.000). Opponents 115-399 (.288).

1988-89

CHICAGO BULLS

	G	Min.	FGM	FGA	Pct.	FTM	FTA	Pct.	Off.	Def.	Tot.	Ast.	PF	Dq.	Stl.	TO	Blk.	Pts.	Avg.	Hi.
Michael Jordan	81	3255	966	1795	.538	674	793	.850	149	503	652	650	247	2	234	290	65	2633	32.5	53
Scottie Pippen	73	2413	413	867	.476	201	301	.668	138	307	445	256	261	8	139	199	61	1048	14.4	31
Bill Cartwright	78	2333	365	768	.475	236	308	.766	152	369	521	90	234	2	21	190	41	966	12.4	23
Horace Grant	79	2809	405	781	.519	140	199	.704	240	441	681	168	251	1	86	128	62	950	12.0	25
Craig Hodges*	49	1112	187	394	.475	45	53	.849	21	63	84	138	82	0	41	52	4	490	10.0	23
Craig Hodges‡	59	1204	203	430	.472	48	57	.842	23	66	89	146	90	0	43	57	4	529	9.0	23
Sam Vincent	70	1703	274	566	.484	106	129	.822	34	156	190	335	124	0	53	142	10	656	9.4	23
John Paxson	78	1738	246	513	.480	31	36	.861	13	81	94	308	162	1	53	71	6	567	7.3	24
Brad Sellers	80	1732	231	476	.485	86	101	.851	85	142	227	99	176	2	35	72	69	551	6.9	32
Dave Corzine	81	1483	203	440	.461	71	96	.740	92	223	315	103	134	0	29	93	45	479	5.9	23
Charlie Davis	49	545	81	190	.426	19	26	.731	47	67	114	31	58	1	11	22	5	185	3.8	15
Jack Haley	51	289	37	78	.474	36	46	.783	21	50	71	10	56	0	11	26	0	110	2.2	12
Will Perdue	30	190	29	72	.403	8	14	.571	18	27	45	11	38	0	4	15	6	66	2.2	9
Anthony Jones*	8	65	5	15	.333	2	2	1.000	4	4	8	4	7	0	2	1	1	12	1.5	8
Ed Nealy*	13	94	5	7	.714	1	2	.500	4	19	23	6	23	0	3	1	1	11	0.8	2
Dominic Pressley†	3	17	1	6	.167	0	0	...	0	1	1	4	2	0	0	0	0	2	0.7	2
Dominic Pressley‡	13	124	9	31	.290	5	9	.556	3	12	15	26	11	0	4	11	0	23	1.8	4
David Wood	2	2	0	0	...	0	0	...	0	0	0	0	0	0	0	0	0	0	0.0	0

3-pt. FG: Chicago 174-530 (.328)—Jordan 27-98 (.276); Pippen 21-77 (.273); Grant 0-5 (.000); Hodges† 71-168 (.423); Hodges‡ 75-180 (.417); Vincent 2-17 (.118); Paxson 44-133 (.331); Sellers 3-6 (.500); Corzine 2-8 (.250); Davis 4-15 (.267); Jones* 0-1 (.000); Pressley† 0-2 (.000); Pressley‡ 0-2 (.000). Opponents 193-590 (.327).

CLEVELAND CAVALIERS

	G	Min.	FGM	FGA	Pct.	FTM	FTA	Pct.	Off.	Def.	Tot.	Ast.	PF	Dq.	Stl.	TO	Blk.	Pts.	Avg.	Hi.
Brad Daugherty	78	2821	544	1012	.538	386	524	.737	167	551	718	285	175	1	63	230	40	1475	18.9	36
Mark Price	75	2728	529	1006	.526	263	292	.901	48	178	226	631	98	0	115	212	7	1414	18.9	37
Ron Harper	82	2851	587	1149	.511	323	430	.751	122	287	409	434	224	1	185	230	74	1526	18.6	32
Larry Nance	73	2526	496	920	.539	267	334	.799	156	425	581	159	186	0	57	117	206	1259	17.2	33
John Williams	82	2125	356	700	.509	235	314	.748	173	304	477	108	188	1	77	102	134	948	11.6	27
Mike Sanders	82	2102	332	733	.453	97	135	.719	98	209	307	133	230	2	89	104	32	764	9.3	30
Craig Ehlo	82	1867	249	524	.475	71	117	.607	100	195	295	266	161	0	110	116	19	608	7.4	25
Darnell Valentine	77	1086	136	319	.426	91	112	.813	22	81	103	174	88	0	57	83	7	366	4.8	15
Randolph Keys	42	331	74	172	.430	20	29	.690	23	33	56	19	51	0	12	21	6	169	4.0	19
Chris Dudley	61	544	73	168	.435	39	107	.364	72	85	157	21	82	0	9	44	23	185	3.0	14
Phil Hubbard	31	191	28	63	.444	17	25	.680	14	26	40	11	20	0	6	9	0	73	2.4	9
Tree Rollins	60	583	62	138	.449	12	19	.632	38	101	139	19	89	0	11	22	38	136	2.3	8

3-pt. FG: Cleveland 170-474 (.359)—Daugherty 1-3 (.333); Price 93-211 (.441); Harper 29-116 (.250); Nance 0-4 (.000); Williams 1-4 (.250); Sanders 3-10 (.300); Ehlo 39-100 (.390); Valentine 3-14 (.214); Keys 1-10 (.100); Dudley 0-1 (.000); Rollins 0-1 (.000). Opponents 172-508 (.339).

DALLAS MAVERICKS

	G	Min.	FGM	FGA	Pct.	FTM	FTA	Pct.	Off.	Def.	Tot.	Ast.	PF	Dq.	Stl.	TO	Blk.	Pts.	Avg.	Hi.
Mark Aguirre*	44	1529	373	829	.450	178	244	.730	90	145	235	189	128	0	29	140	29	953	21.7	41
Adrian Dantley†	31	1081	212	459	.462	204	263	.776	64	89	153	78	87	0	20	82	7	628	20.3	34
Adrian Dantley‡	73	2422	470	954	.493	460	568	.810	117	200	317	171	186	1	43	163	13	1400	19.2	35
Rolando Blackman	78	2946	594	1249	.476	316	370	.854	70	203	273	288	137	0	65	165	20	1534	19.7	37
Derek Harper	81	2968	538	1127	.477	229	284	.806	46	182	228	570	219	3	172	205	41	1404	17.3	38
Roy Tarpley	19	591	131	242	.541	66	96	.688	77	141	218	17	70	2	28	45	30	328	17.3	35
Sam Perkins	78	2860	445	959	.464	274	329	.833	235	453	688	127	224	1	76	141	92	1171	15.0	30
Detlef Schrempf*	37	845	112	263	.426	127	161	.789	56	110	166	86	118	3	24	56	9	353	9.5	24
James Donaldson	53	1746	193	337	.573	95	124	.766	158	412	570	38	111	0	24	83	81	481	9.1	21
Herb Williams†	30	903	78	197	.396	43	68	.632	48	149	197	36	80	2	15	41	54	199	6.6	15
Herb Williams‡	76	2470	322	739	.436	133	194	.686	135	458	593	124	236	5	46	149	134	777	10.2	25
Brad Davis	78	1395	183	379	.483	99	123	.805	14	94	108	242	151	0	48	92	18	497	6.4	17
Terry Tyler	70	1057	169	360	.469	47	62	.758	74	135	209	40	90	0	24	51	39	386	5.5	20
Bill Wennington	65	1074	119	275	.433	61	82	.744	82	204	286	46	211	3	16	54	35	300	4.6	21
Anthony Jones†	25	131	24	64	.375	12	14	.857	10	10	20	13	13	0	9	4	2	64	2.6	8
Anthony Jones‡	33	196	29	79	.367	14	16	.875	14	14	28	17	20	0	11	5	3	76	2.3	8
Morlon Wiley	51	408	46	114	.404	13	16	.813	13	34	47	76	61	0	25	34	6	111	2.2	10
Uwe Blab	37	208	24	52	.462	20	25	.800	11	33	44	12	36	0	3	14	13	68	1.8	10
Steve Alford*	9	38	3	11	.273	1	2	.500	0	3	3	9	3	0	1	1	0	7	0.8	4

3-pt. FG: Dallas 211-681 (.310)—Aguirre* 29-99 (.293); Dantley† 0-1 (.000); Dantley‡ 0-1 (.000); Blackman 30-85 (.353); Harper 99-278 (.356); Tarpley 0-1 (.000); Perkins 7-38 (.184); Schrempf* 2-16 (.125); Williams† 0-2 (.000); Williams‡ 0-5 (.000); Davis 32-102 (.314); Tyler 1-9 (.111); Wennington 1-9 (.111); Jones† 4-15 (.267); Jones‡ 4-16 (.250); Wiley 6-24 (.250); Alford* 0-2 (.000). Opponents 166-515 (.322).

DENVER NUGGETS

	G	Min.	FGM	FGA	Pct.	FTM	FTA	Pct.	Off.	Def.	Tot.	Ast.	PF	Dq.	Stl.	TO	Blk.	Pts.	Avg.	Hi.
Alex English	82	2990	924	1881	.491	325	379	.858	148	178	326	383	174	0	66	198	12	2175	26.5	51
Fat Lever	71	2745	558	1221	.457	270	344	.785	187	475	662	559	178	1	195	157	20	1409	19.8	38
Michael Adams	77	2787	468	1082	.433	322	393	.819	71	212	283	490	149	0	166	180	11	1424	18.5	35
Walter Davis	81	1857	536	1076	.498	175	199	.879	41	110	151	190	187	1	72	132	5	1267	15.6	33

	G	Min.	FGM	FGA	Pct.	FTM	FTA	Pct.	REBOUNDS Off.	Def.	Tot.	Ast.	PF	Dq.	Stl.	TO	Blk.	SCORING Pts.	Avg.	Hi.
Dan Schayes	76	1918	317	607	.522	332	402	.826	142	358	500	105	320	8	42	160	81	969	12.8	37
Blair Rasmussen	77	1308	257	577	.445	69	81	.852	105	182	287	49	194	2	29	49	41	583	7.6	24
Wayne Cooper	79	1864	220	444	.495	79	106	.745	212	407	619	78	302	7	36	73	211	520	6.6	20
Jay Vincent*	5	95	13	38	.342	5	9	.556	2	16	18	5	11	0	1	5	1	32	6.4	12
David Greenwood†	29	491	62	148	.419	48	71	.676	48	116	164	41	78	3	17	36	28	172	5.9	17
David Greenwood‡	67	1403	167	395	.423	132	176	.750	140	262	402	96	201	5	47	91	52	466	7.0	23
Darwin Cook†	30	386	71	163	.436	17	22	.773	13	35	48	43	44	0	28	26	6	161	5.4	21
Darwin Cook‡	66	1143	218	478	.456	63	78	.808	34	73	107	127	121	0	71	88	10	507	7.7	21
Bill Hanzlik	41	701	66	151	.437	68	87	.782	18	75	93	86	82	1	25	53	5	201	4.9	22
Jerome Lane	54	550	109	256	.426	43	112	.384	87	113	200	60	105	1	20	50	4	261	4.8	18
Calvin Natt*	14	168	22	50	.440	22	31	.710	12	34	46	7	13	0	6	11	1	66	4.7	12
Elston Turner	78	1746	151	353	.428	33	56	.589	109	178	287	144	209	2	90	60	8	337	4.3	15
Eddie Hughes	26	224	28	64	.438	7	12	.583	6	13	19	35	30	0	17	11	2	70	2.7	9
Wayne Englestad	11	50	11	29	.379	6	10	.600	5	11	16	7	12	0	1	3	0	28	2.5	8

3-pt. FG: Denver 228-676 (.337)—English 2-8 (.250); Lever 23-66 (.348); Adams 166-466 (.356); Davis 20-69 (.290); Schayes 3-9 (.333); Cooper 1-4 (.250); Vincent* 1-2 (.500); Cook† 2-10 (.200); Cook‡ 8-41 (.195); Hanzlik 1-5 (.200); Lane 0-7 (.000); Natt* 0-1 (.000); Turner 2-7 (.286); ughes 7-22 (.318). Opponents 157-446 (.352).

DETROIT PISTONS

	G	Min.	FGM	FGA	Pct.	FTM	FTA	Pct.	REBOUNDS Off.	Def.	Tot.	Ast.	PF	Dq.	Stl.	TO	Blk.	SCORING Pts.	Avg.	Hi.
Adrian Dantley*	42	1341	258	495	.521	256	305	.839	53	111	164	93	99	1	23	81	6	772	18.4	35
Isiah Thomas	80	2924	569	1227	.464	287	351	.818	49	224	273	663	209	0	133	298	20	1458	18.2	37
Joe Dumars	69	2408	456	903	.505	260	306	.850	57	115	172	390	103	1	63	178	5	1186	17.2	42
Mark Aguirre†	36	1068	213	441	.483	110	149	.738	56	95	151	89	101	2	16	68	7	558	15.5	31
Mark Aguirre‡	80	2597	586	1270	.461	288	393	.733	146	240	386	278	229	2	45	208	36	1511	18.9	41
Vinnie Johnson	82	2073	462	996	.464	193	263	.734	109	146	255	242	155	0	74	105	17	1130	13.8	34
Bill Laimbeer	81	2640	449	900	.499	178	212	.840	138	638	776	177	259	2	51	129	100	1106	13.7	32
Dennis Rodman	82	2208	316	531	.595	97	155	.626	327	445	772	99	292	4	55	126	76	735	9.0	32
James Edwards	76	1254	211	422	.500	133	194	.686	68	163	231	49	226	1	11	72	31	555	7.3	18
Rick Mahorn	72	1795	203	393	.517	116	155	.748	141	355	496	59	206	1	40	97	66	522	7.3	19
John Salley	67	1458	166	333	.498	135	195	.692	134	201	335	75	197	3	40	100	72	467	7.0	19
Micheal Williams	49	358	47	129	.364	31	47	.660	9	18	27	70	44	0	13	42	3	127	2.6	11
John Long†	24	152	19	40	.475	11	13	.846	2	9	11	15	16	0	0	9	2	49	2.0	17
John Long‡	68	919	147	359	.409	70	76	.921	18	59	77	80	84	1	29	57	3	372	5.5	25
Darryl Dawkins	14	48	9	19	.474	9	18	.500	3	4	7	1	13	0	0	4	1	27	1.9	8
Steve Harris	3	7	1	4	.250	2	2	1.000	0	2	2	0	1	0	1	0	0	4	1.3	4
Fennis Dembo	31	74	14	42	.333	8	10	.800	8	15	23	5	15	0	1	7	0	36	1.2	8
Pace Mannion*	5	14	2	2	1.000	0	0	...	0	3	3	0	3	0	1	0	0	4	0.8	4
Jim Rowinski*	6	8	0	2	.000	4	4	1.000	0	2	2	0	1	0	0	0	0	4	0.7	4

3-pt. FG: Detroit 120-400 (.300)—Thomas 33-121 (.273); Dumars 14-29 (.483); Aguirre† 22-75 (.293); Aguirre‡ 51-174 (.293); Johnson 13-44 (.295); Laimbeer 30-86 (.349); Rodman 6-26 (.231); Edwards 0-2 (.000); Mahorn 0-2 (.000); Salley 0-2 (.000); Long‡ 8-20 (.400); Williams 2-9 (.222); Dembo 0-4 (.000). Opponents 158-554 (.285).

GOLDEN STATE WARRIORS

	G	Min.	FGM	FGA	Pct.	FTM	FTA	Pct.	REBOUNDS Off.	Def.	Tot.	Ast.	PF	Dq.	Stl.	TO	Blk.	SCORING Pts.	Avg.	Hi.
Chris Mullin	82	3093	830	1630	.509	493	553	.892	152	331	483	415	178	1	176	296	39	2176	26.5	47
Mitch Richmond	79	2717	649	1386	.468	410	506	.810	158	310	468	334	223	5	82	269	13	1741	22.0	47
Terry Teagle	66	1569	409	859	.476	182	225	.809	110	153	263	96	173	2	79	116	17	1002	15.2	36
Winston Garland	79	2661	466	1074	.434	203	251	.809	101	227	328	505	216	2	175	187	14	1145	14.5	31
Rod Higgins	81	1887	301	633	.476	188	229	.821	111	265	376	160	172	2	39	76	42	856	10.6	30
Otis Smith	80	1597	311	715	.435	174	218	.798	128	202	330	140	165	1	88	129	40	803	10.0	24
Ralph Sampson	61	1086	164	365	.449	62	95	.653	105	202	307	77	170	3	31	90	65	393	6.4	17
Steve Alford†	57	868	145	313	.463	49	59	.831	10	59	69	83	54	0	44	44	3	359	6.3	17
Steve Alford‡	66	906	148	324	.457	50	61	.820	10	62	72	92	57	0	45	45	3	366	5.5	17
Larry Smith	80	1897	219	397	.552	18	58	.310	272	380	652	118	248	2	61	110	54	456	5.7	18
John Starks	36	316	51	125	.408	34	52	.654	15	26	41	27	36	0	23	39	3	146	4.1	14
Manute Bol	80	1763	127	344	.369	40	66	.606	116	346	462	27	226	2	11	79	345	314	3.9	13
Tellis Frank	32	245	34	91	.374	39	51	.765	26	35	61	15	59	1	14	29	6	107	3.3	15
Ben McDonald	11	103	13	19	.684	9	15	.600	4	8	12	5	11	0	4	3	0	35	3.2	12
Shelton Jones*	2	13	3	5	.600	0	0	...	2	0	2	2	0	0	3	1	0	6	3.0	4
Jerome Whitehead*	5	42	3	6	.500	1	2	.500	0	5	5	2	8	0	1	2	0	7	1.4	5
Orlando Graham	7	22	3	10	.300	2	4	.500	8	3	11	0	6	0	0	2	0	8	1.1	2
John Stroeder†	4	20	2	5	.400	0	0	...	5	9	14	3	1	0	0	2	2	4	1.0	4
John Stroeder‡	5	22	2	5	.400	0	0	...	5	9	14	3	3	0	0	3	2	4	0.8	4

3-pt. FG: Golden State 194-629 (.308)—Mullin 23-100 (.230); Richmond 33-90 (.367); Teagle 2-12 (.167); Garland 10-43 (.233); Higgins 66-168 (.393); O. Smith 7-37 (.189); Sampson 3-8 (.375); Alford† 20-53 (.377); Alford‡ 20-55 (.364); Starks 10-26 (.385); Bol 20-91 (.220); Frank 0-1 (.000). Opponents 281-821 (.342).

HOUSTON ROCKETS

	G	Min.	FGM	FGA	Pct.	FTM	FTA	Pct.	REBOUNDS Off.	Def.	Tot.	Ast.	PF	Dq.	Stl.	TO	Blk.	SCORING Pts.	Avg.	Hi.
Hakeem Olajuwon	82	3024	790	1556	.508	454	652	.696	338	767	1105	149	329	10	213	275	282	2034	24.8	43
Otis Thorpe	82	3135	521	961	.542	328	450	.729	272	515	787	202	259	6	82	225	37	1370	16.7	37
Sleepy Floyd	82	2788	396	893	.443	261	309	.845	48	258	306	709	196	1	124	253	11	1162	14.2	37

	G	Min.	FGM	FGA	Pct.	FTM	FTA	Pct.	Off.	Def.	Tot.	Ast.	PF	Dq.	Stl.	TO	Blk.	Pts.	Avg.	Hi.
Mike Woodson	81	2259	410	936	.438	195	237	.823	51	143	194	206	195	1	89	136	18	1046	12.9	29
Buck Johnson	67	1850	270	515	.524	101	134	.754	114	172	286	126	213	4	64	110	35	642	9.6	24
Derrick Chievous	81	1539	277	634	.437	191	244	.783	114	142	256	77	161	1	48	136	11	750	9.3	27
Walter Berry†	40	799	146	270	.541	57	80	.713	54	98	152	57	114	1	19	49	35	350	8.8	18
Walter Berry‡	69	1355	254	501	.507	100	143	.699	86	181	267	77	183	1	29	89	48	609	8.8	26
Purvis Short	65	1157	198	480	.413	77	89	.865	65	114	179	107	116	1	44	70	13	482	7.4	26
Tim McCormick	81	1257	169	351	.481	87	129	.674	87	174	261	54	193	0	18	68	24	425	5.2	23
Frank Johnson	67	879	109	246	.443	75	93	.806	22	57	79	181	91	0	42	102	0	294	4.4	17
Allen Leavell	55	627	65	188	.346	44	60	.733	13	40	53	127	61	0	25	62	5	179	3.3	17
Bernard Thompson	23	222	20	59	.339	22	26	.846	9	19	28	13	33	0	13	19	1	62	2.7	10
Tony Brown*	14	91	14	45	.311	6	8	.750	7	8	15	5	14	0	3	7	0	36	2.6	14
Chuck Nevitt	43	228	27	62	.435	11	16	.688	17	47	64	3	51	1	5	22	29	65	1.5	8

3-pt. FG: Houston 164-523 (.314)—Olajuwon 0-10 (.000); Thorpe 0-2 (.000); Floyd 109-292 (.373); Woodson 31-89 (.348); B. Johnson 1-9 (.111); Chievous 5-24 (.208); Berry† 1-2 (.500); Berry‡ 1-2 (.500); Short 9-33 (.273); McCormick 0-4 (.000); F. Johnson 1-6 (.167); Leavell 5-41 (.122); Thompson 0-2 (.000); Brown* 2-9 (.222). Opponents 187-534 (.350).

INDIANA PACERS

	G	Min.	FGM	FGA	Pct.	FTM	FTA	Pct.	Off.	Def.	Tot.	Ast.	PF	Dq.	Stl.	TO	Blk.	Pts.	Avg.	Hi.
Chuck Person	80	3012	711	1453	.489	243	307	.792	144	372	516	289	280	12	83	308	18	1728	21.6	47
Reggie Miller	74	2536	398	831	.479	287	340	.844	73	219	292	227	170	2	93	143	29	1181	16.0	36
Wayman Tisdale*	48	1326	285	564	.505	198	250	.792	99	211	310	75	181	5	35	107	32	768	16.0	39
Detlef Schrempf†	32	1005	162	315	.514	146	189	.772	70	159	229	93	102	0	29	77	10	475	14.8	24
Detlef Schrempf‡	69	1850	274	578	.474	273	350	.780	126	269	395	179	220	3	53	133	19	828	12.0	24
Vern Fleming	76	2552	419	814	.515	243	304	.799	85	225	310	494	212	4	77	192	12	1084	14.3	26
Herb Williams*	46	1567	244	542	.450	90	126	.714	87	309	396	88	156	3	31	108	80	578	12.6	25
LaSalle Thompson†	33	1053	169	314	.538	75	93	.806	104	222	326	37	132	6	33	62	39	413	12.5	24
LaSalle Thompson‡	76	2329	416	850	.489	227	281	.808	224	494	718	81	285	12	79	179	94	1059	13.9	31
Rik Smits	82	2041	386	746	.517	184	255	.722	185	315	500	70	310	14	37	130	151	956	11.7	27
John Long*	44	767	128	319	.401	59	63	.937	16	50	66	65	68	1	29	48	1	323	7.3	25
Scott Skiles	80	1571	198	442	.448	130	144	.903	21	128	149	390	151	1	64	177	2	546	6.8	20
Randy Wittman†	33	704	80	169	.473	12	19	.632	20	34	54	79	31	0	13	20	2	173	5.2	17
Randy Wittman‡	64	1120	130	286	.455	28	41	.683	26	54	80	111	43	0	23	32	2	291	4.5	17
Anthony Frederick	46	313	63	125	.504	24	34	.706	26	26	52	20	59	0	14	34	6	152	3.3	19
John Morton	2	11	3	4	.750	0	0	...	0	0	0	1	2	0	0	1	0	6	3.0	6
Stuart Gray	72	783	72	153	.471	44	64	.688	84	161	245	29	128	0	11	48	21	188	2.6	14
Greg Dreiling	53	396	43	77	.558	43	64	.672	39	53	92	18	100	0	5	39	11	129	2.4	12
Everette Stephens	35	209	23	72	.319	17	22	.773	11	12	23	37	22	0	9	29	4	65	1.9	8
Sedric Toney	2	9	1	5	.200	0	1	.000	1	1	2	0	1	0	0	2	0	2	1.0	2

3-pt. FG: Indiana 202-615 (.328)—Person 63-205 (.307); Miller 98-244 (.402); Tisdale* 0-4 (.000); Schrempf† 5-19 (.263); Schrempf‡ 7-35 (.200); Fleming 3-23 (.130); Thompson† 0-0; Thompson‡ 0-1 (.000); Williams* 0-3 (.000); Smits 0-1 (.000); Long* 8-20 (.400); Skiles 20-75 (.267); Wittman† 1-2 (.500); Wittman‡ 3-6 (.500); Frederick 2-5 (.400); Gray 0-1 (.000); Stephens 2-10 (.200); Toney 0-3 (.000). Opponents 167-547 (.305).

LOS ANGELES CLIPPERS

	G	Min.	FGM	FGA	Pct.	FTM	FTA	Pct.	Off.	Def.	Tot.	Ast.	PF	Dq.	Stl.	TO	Blk.	Pts.	Avg.	Hi.
Ken Norman	80	3020	638	1271	.502	170	270	.630	245	422	667	277	223	2	106	206	66	1450	18.1	38
Danny Manning	26	950	177	358	.494	79	103	.767	70	101	171	81	89	1	44	93	25	434	16.7	29
Benoit Benjamin	79	2585	491	907	.541	317	426	.744	164	532	696	157	221	4	57	237	221	1299	16.4	34
Charles Smith	71	2161	435	878	.495	285	393	.725	173	292	465	103	273	6	68	146	89	1155	16.3	33
Quintin Dailey	69	1722	448	964	.465	217	286	.759	69	135	204	154	152	0	90	122	6	1114	16.1	36
Gary Grant	71	1924	361	830	.435	119	162	.735	80	158	238	506	170	1	144	258	9	846	11.9	31
Reggie Williams	63	1303	260	594	.438	92	122	.754	70	109	179	103	181	1	81	114	29	642	10.2	29
Ken Bannister	9	130	22	36	.611	30	53	.566	6	27	33	3	17	0	7	8	2	74	8.2	21
Norm Nixon	53	1318	153	370	.414	48	65	.738	13	65	78	339	69	0	46	118	0	362	6.8	18
Tom Garrick	71	1499	176	359	.490	102	127	.803	37	119	156	243	141	1	78	116	9	454	6.4	17
Joe Wolf	66	1450	170	402	.423	44	64	.688	83	188	271	113	152	1	32	94	16	386	5.8	17
Eric White†	37	434	62	119	.521	34	42	.810	34	36	70	17	39	0	10	26	1	158	4.3	24
Eric White‡	38	436	62	120	.517	34	42	.810	34	36	70	17	40	0	10	26	1	158	4.2	24
Ennis Whatley	8	90	12	33	.364	10	11	.909	2	14	16	22	15	0	7	11	1	34	4.3	11
Grant Gondrezick	27	244	38	95	.400	26	40	.650	15	21	36	34	36	0	13	17	1	105	3.9	17
Kevin Williams†	9	114	14	32	.438	6	8	.750	9	11	20	17	17	0	5	10	3	34	3.8	9
Kevin Williams‡	50	547	81	200	.405	46	59	.780	28	42	70	53	91	0	30	52	11	209	4.2	16
Dave Popson*	10	68	11	25	.440	1	2	.500	5	11	16	6	9	0	1	6	2	23	2.3	8
Greg Kite*	58	729	49	121	.405	14	31	.452	66	124	190	29	118	0	23	46	46	112	1.9	9
Rob Lock	20	110	9	32	.281	12	15	.800	14	18	32	4	15	0	3	13	4	30	1.5	6
Barry Sumpter	1	1	0	1	.000	0	0	...	0	0	0	0	0	0	0	0	0	0	0.0	0
Bob Rose	2	3	0	1	.000	0	0	...	1	1	2	0	0	0	0	0	0	0	0.0	0

3-pt. FG: L.A. Clippers 54-234 (.231)—Norman 4-21 (.190); Manning 1-5 (.200); Benjamin 0-2 (.000); Smith 0-3 (.000); Dailey 1-9 (.111); Grant 5-22 (.227); R. Williams 30-104 (.288); Bannister 0-1 (.000); Nixon 8-29 (.276); Garrick 0-13 (.000); Wolf 2-14 (.143); K. Williams† 0-0; K. Williams‡ 1-6 (.167); Gondrezick 3-11 (.273). Opponents 197-576 (.342).

LOS ANGELES LAKERS

	G	Min.	FGM	FGA	Pct.	FTM	FTA	Pct.	Off.	Def.	Tot.	Ast.	PF	Dq.	Stl.	TO	Blk.	Pts.	Avg.	Hi.
Magic Johnson	77	2886	579	1137	.509	513	563	.911	111	496	607	988	172	0	138	312	22	1730	22.5	40
James Worthy	81	2960	702	1282	.548	251	321	.782	169	320	489	288	175	0	108	182	56	1657	20.5	38
Byron Scott	74	2605	588	1198	.491	195	226	.863	72	230	302	231	181	1	114	157	27	1448	19.6	35
A.C. Green	82	2510	401	758	.529	282	359	.786	258	481	739	103	172	0	94	119	55	1088	13.3	33
Kareem Abdul-Jabbar	74	1695	313	659	.475	122	165	.739	103	231	334	74	196	1	38	95	85	748	10.1	21
Orlando Woolridge	74	1491	231	494	.468	253	343	.738	81	189	270	58	130	0	30	103	65	715	9.7	29
Mychal Thompson	80	1994	291	521	.559	156	230	.678	157	310	467	48	224	0	58	97	59	738	9.2	27
Michael Cooper	80	1943	213	494	.431	81	93	.871	33	158	191	314	186	0	72	94	32	587	7.3	18
Tony Campbell	63	787	158	345	.458	70	83	.843	53	77	130	47	108	0	37	62	6	388	6.2	19
David Rivers	47	440	49	122	.402	35	42	.833	13	30	43	106	50	0	23	61	9	134	2.9	10
Mark McNamara	39	318	32	64	.500	49	78	.628	38	62	100	10	51	0	4	24	3	113	2.9	10
Jeff Lamp	37	176	27	69	.391	4	5	.800	6	28	34	15	27	0	8	16	2	60	1.6	7

3-pt. FG: L.A. Lakers 227-667 (.340)—Johnson 59-188 (.314); Worthy 2-23 (.087); Scott 77-193 (.399); Green 4-17 (.235); Abdul-Jabbar 0-3 (.000); Woolridge 0-1 (.000); Thompson 0-1 (.000); Cooper 80-210 (.381); Campbell 2-21 (.095); Rivers 1-6 (.167); Lamp 2-4 (.500). Opponents 194-587 (.330).

MIAMI HEAT

	G	Min.	FGM	FGA	Pct.	FTM	FTA	Pct.	Off.	Def.	Tot.	Ast.	PF	Dq.	Stl.	TO	Blk.	Pts.	Avg.	Hi.
Kevin Edwards	79	2349	470	1105	.425	144	193	.746	85	177	262	349	154	0	139	246	27	1094	13.8	34
Rory Sparrow	80	2613	444	982	.452	94	107	.879	55	161	216	429	168	0	103	204	17	1000	12.5	29
Grant Long	82	2435	336	692	.486	304	406	.749	240	306	546	149	337	13	122	201	48	976	11.9	30
Rony Seikaly	78	1962	333	744	.448	181	354	.511	204	345	549	55	258	8	46	200	96	848	10.9	30
Billy Thompson	79	2273	349	716	.487	156	224	.696	241	331	572	176	260	8	56	189	105	854	10.8	30
Jon Sundvold	68	1338	307	675	.455	47	57	.825	18	69	87	137	78	0	27	87	1	709	10.4	28
Pat Cummings	53	1096	197	394	.500	72	97	.742	84	197	281	47	160	3	29	111	18	466	8.8	24
Sylvester Gray	55	1220	167	398	.420	105	156	.673	117	169	286	117	144	1	36	102	25	440	8.0	25
Pearl Washington	54	1065	164	387	.424	82	104	.788	49	74	123	226	101	0	73	122	4	411	7.6	21
Clinton Wheeler*	8	143	24	42	.571	8	10	.800	5	7	12	21	9	0	8	6	0	56	7.0	13
Anthony Taylor	21	368	60	151	.397	24	32	.750	11	23	34	43	37	0	22	20	5	144	6.9	21
Kelvin Upshaw*	9	144	26	63	.413	4	6	.667	4	9	13	20	18	0	7	13	0	57	6.3	13
John Shasky	65	944	121	248	.488	115	167	.689	96	136	232	22	94	0	14	46	13	357	5.5	19
Todd Mitchell*	22	320	41	88	.466	36	60	.600	17	30	47	20	49	0	15	29	2	118	5.4	15
Scott Hastings	75	1206	143	328	.436	91	107	.850	72	159	231	59	203	5	32	68	42	386	5.1	17
Craig Neal†	32	341	34	88	.386	13	21	.619	4	14	18	86	46	0	15	40	4	89	2.8	9
Craig Neal‡	53	500	45	123	.366	14	23	.609	7	22	29	118	70	0	24	54	4	114	2.2	9
Dave Popson†	7	38	5	15	.333	1	2	.500	7	4	11	2	8	0	0	4	1	11	1.6	4
Dave Popson‡	17	106	16	40	.400	2	4	.500	12	15	27	8	17	0	1	10	3	34	2.0	8

3-pt. FG: Miami 97-298 (.326)—Edwards 10-37 (.270); Sparrow 18-74 (.243); Long 0-5 (.000); Seikaly 1-4 (.250); Thompson 0-4 (.000); Sundvold 48-92 (.522); Cummings 0-2 (.000); Gray 1-4 (.250); Washington 1-14 (.071); Taylor 0-2 (.000); Upshaw* 1-5 (.200); Shasky 0-2 (.000); Hastings 9-28 (.321); Neal† 8-25 (.320); Neal‡ 10-34 (.294). Opponents 148-432 (.343).

MILWAUKEE BUCKS

	G	Min.	FGM	FGA	Pct.	FTM	FTA	Pct.	Off.	Def.	Tot.	Ast.	PF	Dq.	Stl.	TO	Blk.	Pts.	Avg.	Hi.
Terry Cummings	80	2824	730	1563	.467	362	460	.787	281	369	650	198	265	5	106	201	72	1829	22.9	38
Ricky Pierce	75	2078	527	1018	.518	255	297	.859	82	115	197	156	193	1	77	112	19	1317	17.6	29
Jack Sikma	80	2587	360	835	.431	266	294	.905	141	482	623	289	300	6	85	145	61	1068	13.4	30
Larry Krystkowiak	80	2472	362	766	.473	289	351	.823	198	412	610	107	219	0	93	147	9	1017	12.7	31
Paul Pressey	67	2170	307	648	.474	187	241	.776	73	189	262	439	221	2	119	184	44	813	12.1	25
Sidney Moncrief	62	1594	261	532	.491	205	237	.865	46	126	172	188	114	1	65	94	13	752	12.1	25
Jay Humphries	73	2220	345	714	.483	129	158	.816	70	119	189	405	187	1	142	160	5	844	11.6	24
Jeff Grayer	11	200	32	73	.438	17	20	.850	14	21	35	22	15	0	10	19	1	81	7.4	18
Fred Roberts	71	1251	155	319	.486	104	129	.806	68	141	209	66	126	0	36	80	23	417	5.9	19
Rickey Green†	30	501	72	132	.545	17	19	.895	7	39	46	105	19	0	22	33	2	163	5.4	14
Rickey Green‡	63	871	129	264	.489	30	33	.909	11	58	69	187	35	0	40	61	2	291	4.6	14
Randy Breuer	48	513	86	179	.480	28	51	.549	51	84	135	22	59	0	9	29	37	200	4.2	20
Mark Davis†	31	251	48	97	.495	26	32	.813	15	21	36	14	38	0	13	12	5	123	4.0	17
Mark Davis‡	33	258	49	102	.480	28	34	.824	16	21	37	14	39	0	13		5	127	3.8	17
Tony Brown†	29	274	36	73	.493	18	23	.783	15	14	29	21	28	0	12	10	4	92	3.2	15
Tony Brown‡	43	365	50	118	.424	24	31	.774	22	22	44	26	42	0	15	17	4	128	3.0	15
Paul Mokeski	74	690	59	164	.360	40	51	.784	63	124	187	36	153	0	29	35	21	165	2.2	8
Tito Horford	25	112	15	46	.326	12	19	.632	9	13	22	3	14	0	1	15	7	42	1.7	10
Andre Turner	4	13	3	6	.500	0	0	...	0	3	3	0	2	0	2	4	0	6	1.5	4
Mike Dunleavy	2	5	1	2	.500	0	0	...	0	0	0	0	0	0	0	0	0	3	1.5	3

3-pt. FG: Milwaukee 179-567 (.316)—Cummings 7-15 (.467); Pierce 8-36 (.222); Sikma 82-216 (.380); Krystkowiak 4-12 (.333); Pressey 12-55 (.218); Moncrief 25-73 (.342); Humphries 25-94 (.266); Grayer 0-2 (.000); Roberts 3-14 (.214); Green† 2-6 (.333); Green‡ 3-11 (.273); Davis† 1-9 (.111); Davis‡ 1-10 (.100); Brown† 2-7 (.286); Brown‡ 4-16 (.250); Mokeski 7-26 (.269); Dunleavy 1-2 (.500). Opponents 196-533 (.368).

1988-89

NEW JERSEY NETS

	G	Min.	FGM	FGA	Pct.	FTM	FTA	Pct.	REBOUNDS Off.	Def.	Tot.	Ast.	PF	Dq.	Stl.	TO	Blk.	SCORING Pts.	Avg.	Hi.
Roy Hinson........	82	2542	495	1027	.482	318	420	.757	152	370	522	71	298	3	34	165	121	1308	16.0	35
Chris Morris........	76	2096	414	905	.457	182	254	.717	188	209	397	119	250	4	102	190	60	1074	14.1	31
Joe Barry Carroll.....	64	1996	363	810	.448	176	220	.800	118	355	473	105	193	2	71	143	81	902	14.1	26
Mike McGee.......	80	2027	434	917	.473	77	144	.535	73	116	189	116	184	1	80	124	12	1038	13.0	33
Buck Williams......	74	2446	373	702	.531	213	320	.666	249	447	696	78	223	0	61	142	36	959	13.0	27
Dennis Hopson......	62	1551	299	714	.419	186	219	.849	91	111	202	103	150	0	70	102	30	788	12.7	32
Lester Conner.......	82	2532	309	676	.457	212	269	.788	100	255	355	604	132	1	181	181	5	843	10.3	20
Walter Berry*	29	556	108	231	.468	43	63	.683	32	83	115	20	69	0	10	40	13	259	8.9	26
John Bagley	68	1642	200	481	.416	89	123	.724	36	108	144	391	117	0	72	159	5	500	7.4	17
Keith Lee	57	840	109	258	.422	53	71	.746	73	186	259	42	138	1	20	53	33	271	4.8	16
Kevin Williams*	41	433	67	168	.399	40	51	.784	19	31	50	36	74	0	25	42	8	175	4.3	16
Bill Jones	37	307	50	102	.490	29	43	.674	20	27	47	20	38	0	17	18	6	129	3.5	14
Charles Shackleford .	60	484	83	168	.494	21	42	.500	50	103	153	21	71	0	15	27	18	187	3.1	13
Corey Gaines	32	337	27	64	.422	12	16	.750	3	16	19	67	27	0	15	20	1	67	2.1	18
Ron Cavenall........	5	16	2	3	.667	2	5	.400	0	2	2	0	2	0	0	2	2	6	1.2	6

3-pt. FG: New Jersey 187-568 (.329)—Hinson 0-2 (.000); Morris 64-175 (.366); McGee 93-255 (.365); B. Williams 0-3 (.000); Hopson 4-27 (.148); Conner 13-37 (.351); Bagley 11-54 (.204); Lee 0-2 (.000); K. Williams* 1-6 (.167); Jones 0-1 (.000); Shackleford 0-1 (.000); Gaines 1-5 (.200). Opponents 158-512 (.309).

NEW YORK KNICKERBOCKERS

	G	Min.	FGM	FGA	Pct.	FTM	FTA	Pct.	REBOUNDS Off.	Def.	Tot.	Ast.	PF	Dq.	Stl.	TO	Blk.	SCORING Pts.	Avg.	Hi.
Patrick Ewing	80	2896	727	1282	.567	361	484	.746	213	527	740	188	311	5	117	266	281	1815	22.7	45
Mark Jackson.......	72	2477	479	1025	.467	180	258	.698	106	235	341	619	163	1	139	226	7	1219	16.9	34
Johnny Newman	81	2336	455	957	.475	286	351	.815	93	113	206	162	259	4	111	153	23	1293	16.0	35
Gerald Wilkins.......	81	2414	462	1025	.451	186	246	.756	95	149	244	274	166	1	115	169	22	1161	14.3	30
Charles Oakley	82	2604	426	835	.510	197	255	.773	343	518	861	187	270	1	104	248	14	1061	12.9	27
Kiki Vandeweghe†	27	502	97	209	.464	51	56	.911	15	21	36	35	38	0	12	23	7	248	9.2	24
Kiki Vandeweghe‡....	45	934	200	426	.469	80	89	.899	26	45	71	69	78	0	19	41	11	499	11.1	28
Rod Strickland	81	1358	265	567	.467	172	231	.745	51	109	160	319	142	2	98	148	3	721	8.9	22
Trent Tucker	81	1824	263	579	.454	43	55	.782	55	121	176	132	163	0	88	59	6	687	8.5	25
Sidney Green	82	1277	194	422	.460	129	170	.759	157	237	394	76	172	0	47	125	18	517	6.3	15
Kenny Walker	79	1163	174	356	.489	66	85	.776	101	129	230	36	190	1	41	44	45	419	5.3	19
Eddie Lee Wilkins ...	71	584	114	245	.465	61	111	.550	72	76	148	7	110	1	10	56	16	289	4.1	12
Pete Myers†	29	230	25	61	.410	31	44	.705	12	11	23	46	41	0	17	19	2	81	2.8	8
Pete Myers‡	33	270	31	73	.425	33	48	.688	15	18	33	48	44	0	20	23	2	95	2.9	10
Greg Butler	33	140	20	48	.417	16	20	.800	9	19	28	2	28	0	1	17	2	56	1.7	7

3-pt. FG: New York 386-1147 (.337)—Ewing 0-6 (.000); Jackson 81-240 (.338); Newman 97-287 (.338); G. Wilkins 51-172 (.297); Oakley 12-48 (.250); Vandeweghe† 3-10 (.300); Vandeweghe‡ 19-48 (.396); Strickland 19-59 (.322); Tucker 118-296 (.399); Green 0-3 (.000); Walker 5-20 (.250); E. Wilkins 0-1 (.000); Myers† 0-2 (.000); Myers‡ 0-2 (.000); Butler 0-3 (.000). Opponents 152-534 (.285).

PHILADELPHIA 76ERS

	G	Min.	FGM	FGA	Pct.	FTM	FTA	Pct.	REBOUNDS Off.	Def.	Tot.	Ast.	PF	Dq.	Stl.	TO	Blk.	SCORING Pts.	Avg.	Hi.
Charles Barkley......	79	3088	700	1208	.579	602	799	.753	403	583	986	325	262	3	126	254	67	2037	25.8	43
Mike Gminski	82	2739	556	1166	.477	297	341	.871	213	556	769	138	142	0	46	129	106	1409	17.2	29
Ron Anderson.......	82	2618	566	1152	.491	196	229	.856	167	239	406	139	166	1	71	126	23	1330	16.2	30
Hersey Hawkins	79	2577	442	971	.455	241	290	.831	51	174	225	239	184	0	120	158	37	1196	15.1	32
Cliff Robinson	14	416	90	187	.481	32	44	.727	19	56	75	32	37	0	17	34	2	212	15.1	26
Maurice Cheeks	71	2298	336	696	.483	151	195	.774	39	144	183	554	114	0	105	116	17	824	11.6	24
Derek Smith†	36	695	105	220	.477	65	93	.699	31	55	86	68	100	3	24	44	15	279	7.8	18
Derek Smith‡	65	1295	216	496	.435	129	188	.686	61	106	167	128	164	4	43	88	23	568	8.7	27
Gerald Henderson....	65	986	144	348	.414	104	127	.819	17	51	68	140	121	1	42	73	3	425	6.5	20
Scott Brooks........	82	1372	156	371	.420	61	69	.884	19	75	94	306	116	0	69	65	3	428	5.2	18
Ben Coleman	58	703	117	241	.485	61	77	.792	49	128	177	17	120	0	10	48	18	295	5.1	15
Shelton Jones†	42	577	81	179	.453	50	67	.746	24	71	95	33	50	0	16	39	13	212	5.0	20
Shelton Jones‡	51	682	93	209	.445	58	80	.725	32	81	113	42	58	0	21	47	15	244	4.8	20
David Wingate	33	372	54	115	.470	27	34	.794	12	25	37	73	43	0	9	35	2	137	4.2	19
Pete Myers*	4	40	6	12	.500	2	4	.500	3	7	10	2	3	0	3	4	0	14	3.5	10
Chris Welp	72	843	99	222	.446	48	73	.658	59	134	193	29	176	0	23	42	41	246	3.4	12
Bob Thornton	54	449	47	111	.423	32	60	.533	36	56	92	15	87	0	8	23	7	127	2.4	16
Jim Rowinski†	3	7	1	2	.500	1	2	.500	1	2	3	0	0	0	0	0	0	3	1.0	2
Jim Rowinski‡	9	15	1	4	.250	5	6	.833	1	5	6	0	0	0	0	0	0	7	0.8	4

3-pt. FG: Philadelphia 204-646 (.316)—Barkley 35-162 (.216); Gminski 0-6 (.000); Anderson 2-11 (.182); Hawkins 71-166 (.428); Robinson 0-1 (.000); Cheeks 1-13 (.077); Smith† 4-16 (.250); Smith‡ 7-31 (.226); Henderson 33-107 (.308); Brooks 55-153 (.359); Jones† 0-1 (.000); Jones‡ 0-1 (.000); Wingate 2-6 (.333); Welp 0-1 (.000); Thornton 1-3 (.333). Opponents 170-495 (.343).

PHOENIX SUNS

	G	Min.	FGM	FGA	Pct.	FTM	FTA	Pct.	REBOUNDS Off.	Def.	Tot.	Ast.	PF	Dq.	Stl.	TO	Blk.	SCORING Pts.	Avg.	Hi.
Tom Chambers	81	3002	774	1643	.471	509	598	.851	143	541	684	231	271	2	87	231	55	2085	25.7	42
Eddie Johnson	70	2043	608	1224	.497	217	250	.868	91	215	306	162	198	0	47	122	7	1504	21.5	45
Kevin Johnson	81	3179	570	1128	.505	508	576	.882	46	294	340	991	226	1	135	322	24	1650	20.4	41

	G	Min.	FGM	FGA	Pct.	FTM	FTA	Pct.	REBOUNDS Off.	Def.	Tot.	Ast.	PF	Dq.	Stl.	TO	Blk.	SCORING Pts.	Avg.	Hi.
Armon Gilliam	74	2120	468	930	.503	240	323	.743	165	376	541	52	176	2	54	140	27	1176	15.9	41
Jeff Hornacek	78	2487	440	889	.495	147	178	.826	75	191	266	465	188	0	129	111	8	1054	13.5	32
Dan Majerle	54	1354	181	432	.419	78	127	.614	62	147	209	130	139	1	63	48	14	467	8.6	25
Tyrone Corbin	77	1655	245	454	.540	141	179	.788	176	222	398	118	222	2	82	92	13	631	8.2	30
Mark West	82	2019	243	372	.653	108	202	.535	167	384	551	39	273	4	35	103	187	594	7.2	24
Tim Perry	62	614	108	201	.537	40	65	.615	61	71	132	18	47	0	19	37	32	257	4.1	19
Craig Hodges*	10	92	16	36	.444	3	4	.750	2	3	5	8	8	0	2	5	0	39	3.9	9
Andrew Lang	62	526	60	117	.513	39	60	.650	54	93	147	9	112	1	17	28	48	159	2.6	21
Steve Kerr	26	157	20	46	.435	6	9	.667	3	14	17	24	12	0	7	6	0	54	2.1	7
Mark Davis*	2	7	1	5	.200	2	2	1.000	1	0	1	0	1	0	0	0	0	4	2.0	2
T.R. Dunn	34	321	12	35	.343	9	12	.750	30	30	60	25	35	0	12	6	1	33	1.0	4
Ed Nealy†	30	164	8	29	.276	3	7	.429	18	37	55	8	22	0	4	6	0	19	0.6	4
Ed Nealy‡	43	258	13	36	.361	4	9	.444	22	56	78	14	45	0	7	7	1	30	0.7	4
Kenny Gattison	2	9	0	1	.000	1	2	.500	0	1	1	0	2	0	0	0	0	1	0.5	1
Winston Crite	2	6	0	3	.000	0	0	...	1	0	1	0	1	0	0	1	0	0	0.0	0

3-pt. FG: Phoenix 168-481 (.349)—Chambers 28-86 (.326); E. Johnson 71-172 (.413); K. Johnson 2-22 (.091); Hornacek 27-81 (.333); Majerle 27-82 (.329); Corbin 0-2 (.000); Perry 1-4 (.250); Hodges* 4-12 (.333); Kerr 8-17 (.471); Davis* 0-1 (.000); Nealy† 0-2 (.000); Nealy‡ 0-2 (.000). Opponents 181-568 (.319).

PORTLAND TRAIL BLAZERS

	G	Min.	FGM	FGA	Pct.	FTM	FTA	Pct.	REBOUNDS Off.	Def.	Tot.	Ast.	PF	Dq.	Stl.	TO	Blk.	SCORING Pts.	Avg.	Hi.
Clyde Drexler	78	3064	829	1672	.496	438	548	.799	289	326	615	450	269	2	213	250	54	2123	27.2	50
Kevin Duckworth	79	2662	554	1161	.477	324	428	.757	246	389	635	60	300	6	56	200	49	1432	18.1	32
Terry Porter	81	3102	540	1146	.471	272	324	.840	85	282	367	770	187	1	146	248	8	1431	17.7	34
Jerome Kersey	76	2716	533	1137	.469	258	372	.694	246	383	629	243	277	6	137	167	84	1330	17.5	33
Kiki Vandeweghe*	18	432	103	217	.475	29	33	.879	11	24	35	34	40	0	7	18	4	251	13.9	28
Steve Johnson	72	1477	296	565	.524	129	245	.527	135	223	358	105	254	3	20	140	44	721	10.0	27
Sam Bowie	20	412	69	153	.451	28	49	.571	36	70	106	36	43	0	7	33	33	171	8.6	19
Adrian Branch	67	811	202	436	.463	87	120	.725	63	69	132	60	99	0	45	64	3	498	7.4	28
Danny Young	48	952	115	250	.460	50	64	.781	17	57	74	123	50	0	55	45	3	297	6.2	19
Richard Anderson	72	1082	145	348	.417	32	38	.842	62	169	231	98	100	1	44	54	12	371	5.2	20
Mark Bryant	56	803	120	247	.486	40	69	.580	65	114	179	33	144	3	20	41	7	280	5.0	17
Jerry Sichting	25	390	46	104	.442	7	8	.875	9	20	29	59	17	0	15	25	0	102	4.1	11
Brook Steppe	27	244	33	78	.423	32	37	.865	13	19	32	16	32	0	11	13	1	103	3.8	13
Caldwell Jones	72	1279	77	183	.421	48	61	.787	88	212	300	59	166	0	24	83	85	202	2.8	11
Clinton Wheeler†	20	211	21	45	.467	7	10	.700	12	7	19	33	17	0	19	18	0	49	2.5	8
Clinton Wheeler‡	28	354	45	87	.517	15	20	.750	17	14	31	54	26	0	27	24	0	105	3.8	13
Craig Neal*	21	159	11	35	.314	1	2	.500	3	8	11	32	24	0	9	14	0	25	1.2	4
Rolando Ferreira	12	34	1	18	.056	7	8	.875	4	9	13	1	7	0	0	6	1	9	0.8	2

3-pt. FG: Portland 216-645 (.335)—Drexler 27-104 (.260); Duckworth 0-2 (.000); Porter 79-219 (.361); Kersey 6-21 (.286); Vandeweghe* 16-38 (.421); Bowie 5-7 (.714); Branch 7-31 (.226); Young 17-50 (.340); Anderson 49-141 (.348); Sichting 3-12 (.250); Steppe 5-9 (.556); Jones 0-1 (.000); Wheeler† 0-1 (.000); Wheeler‡ 0-1 (.000); Neal* 2-9 (.222). Opponents 198-546 (.363).

SACRAMENTO KINGS

	G	Min.	FGM	FGA	Pct.	FTM	FTA	Pct.	REBOUNDS Off.	Def.	Tot.	Ast.	PF	Dq.	Stl.	TO	Blk.	SCORING Pts.	Avg.	Hi.
Danny Ainge†	28	1028	209	462	.452	91	112	.813	34	67	101	187	78	1	41	63	7	567	20.3	45
Danny Ainge‡	73	2377	480	1051	.457	205	240	.854	71	184	255	402	186	1	93	145	8	1281	17.5	45
Wayman Tisdale†	31	1108	247	472	.523	119	160	.744	88	211	299	53	109	2	20	65	20	613	19.8	34
Wayman Tisdale‡	79	2434	532	1036	.514	317	410	.773	187	422	609	128	290	7	55	172	52	1381	17.5	39
Kenny Smith*	81	3145	547	1183	.462	263	357	.737	49	177	226	621	173	0	102	249	7	1403	17.3	33
LaSalle Thompson*	43	1276	247	536	.461	152	188	.809	120	272	392	44	153	6	46	117	55	646	15.0	31
Rodney McCray	68	2435	340	729	.466	169	234	.722	143	371	514	293	121	0	57	168	36	854	12.6	29
Harold Pressley	80	2257	383	873	.439	96	123	.780	216	269	485	174	215	1	93	124	76	981	12.3	26
Ed Pinckney*	51	1334	224	446	.502	177	221	.801	106	195	301	74	125	1	54	81	43	625	12.3	26
Ricky Berry	64	1406	255	567	.450	131	169	.775	59	140	197	80	197	4	37	82	22	706	11.0	34
Jim Petersen	66	1633	278	606	.459	115	154	.747	121	292	413	81	236	8	47	147	68	671	10.2	25
Derek Smith*	29	600	111	276	.402	64	95	.674	30	51	81	60	64	1	19	44	8	289	10.0	27
Brad Lohaus†	29	476	93	216	.431	46	57	.807	37	77	114	17	60	0	9	28	30	233	8.0	29
Brad Lohaus‡	77	1214	210	486	.432	81	103	.786	84	172	256	66	161	1	30	77	56	502	6.5	29
Vinny Del Negro	80	1556	239	503	.475	85	100	.850	48	123	171	206	160	2	65	77	14	569	7.1	28
Joe Kleine*	47	913	116	303	.383	81	88	.920	75	166	241	35	126	2	18	67	18	313	6.7	19
Randy Wittman*	31	416	50	117	.427	16	22	.727	6	20	26	32	12	0	10	12	0	118	3.8	15
Randy Allen	7	43	8	19	.421	1	2	.500	3	4	7	0	7	0	1	2	1	17	2.4	6
Michael Jackson	14	70	9	24	.375	1	2	.500	1	3	4	11	12	0	3	4	0	21	1.5	4
Ben Gillery	24	84	6	19	.316	13	23	.565	7	16	23	2	29	0	2	5	4	25	1.0	5

3-pt. FG: Sacramento 307-824 (.373)—Ainge† 58-150 (.387); Ainge‡ 116-305 (.380); Tisdale† 0-0; Tisdale‡ 0-4 (.000); K. Smith* 46-128 (.359); Thompson* 0-1 (.000); McCray 5-22 (.227); Pressley 119-295 (.403); Pinckney* 0-6 (.000); Berry 65-160 (.406); Petersen 0-8 (.000); D. Smith* 3-15 (.200); Lohaus† 1-7 (.143); Lohaus‡ 1-11 (.091); Del Negro 6-20 (.300); Kleine* 0-1 (.000); Wittman* 2-4 (.500); Allen 0-1 (.000); Jackson 2-6 (.333). Opponents 181-573 (.316).

SAN ANTONIO SPURS

	G	Min.	FGM	FGA	Pct.	FTM	FTA	Pct.	REBOUNDS Off.	Def.	Tot.	Ast.	PF	Dq.	Stl.	TO	Blk.	SCORING Pts.	Avg.	Hi.
Willie Anderson	81	2738	640	1285	.498	224	289	.775	152	265	417	372	295	8	150	261	62	1508	18.6	36
Alvin Robertson	65	2287	465	962	.483	183	253	.723	157	227	384	393	259	6	197	231	36	1122	17.3	34
Johnny Dawkins	32	1083	177	400	.443	100	112	.893	32	69	101	224	64	0	55	111	0	454	14.2	30

	G	Min.	FGM	FGA	Pct.	FTM	FTA	Pct.	Off.	Def.	Tot.	Ast.	PF	Dq.	Stl.	TO	Blk.	Pts.	Avg.	Hi.
									REBOUNDS									**SCORING**		
Greg Anderson	82	2401	460	914	.503	207	403	.514	255	421	676	61	221	2	102	180	103	1127	13.7	29
Frank Brickowski	64	1822	337	654	.515	201	281	.715	148	258	406	131	252	10	102	165	35	875	13.7	27
Vernon Maxwell	79	2065	357	827	.432	181	243	.745	49	153	202	301	136	0	86	178	8	927	11.7	29
Darwin Cook*	36	757	147	315	.467	46	56	.821	21	38	59	84	77	0	43	62	4	346	9.6	19
Jay Vincent†	24	551	91	219	.416	35	51	.686	36	56	92	22	52	0	5	37	3	217	9.0	21
Jay Vincent‡	29	646	104	257	.405	40	60	.667	38	72	110	27	63	0	6	42	4	249	8.6	21
Anthony Bowie	18	438	72	144	.500	10	15	.667	25	31	56	29	43	1	18	22	4	155	8.6	24
Calvin Natt†	10	185	25	66	.379	35	48	.729	16	16	32	11	19	0	2	19	2	85	8.5	16
Calvin Natt‡	24	353	47	116	.405	57	79	.722	28	50	78	18	32	0	8	30	3	151	6.3	16
David Greenwood*	38	912	105	247	.425	84	105	.800	92	146	238	55	123	2	30	55	24	294	7.7	23
Albert King	46	791	141	327	.431	37	48	.771	33	107	140	79	97	2	27	74	7	327	7.1	20
Dallas Comegys	67	1119	166	341	.487	106	161	.658	112	122	234	30	160	2	42	85	63	438	6.5	21
Michael Anderson	36	730	73	175	.417	57	82	.695	44	45	89	153	64	0	44	84	3	204	5.7	21
Mike Smrek	43	623	72	153	.471	49	76	.645	42	87	129	12	102	2	13	48	58	193	4.5	15
Petur Gudmundsson	5	70	9	25	.360	3	4	.750	5	11	16	5	15	0	1	8	1	21	4.2	9
Shelton Jones*	7	92	9	25	.360	8	13	.615	6	10	16	7	8	0	2	7	2	26	3.7	7
Scott Roth†	47	464	52	143	.364	52	76	.684	20	36	56	48	55	0	19	33	4	158	3.4	14
Scott Roth‡	63	536	59	167	.353	60	87	.690	20	44	64	55	69	0	24	40	5	181	2.9	14
Jerome Whitehead†	52	580	69	176	.392	30	45	.667	49	80	129	17	107	1	22	22	4	168	3.2	12
Jerome Whitehead‡	57	622	72	182	.396	31	47	.660	49	85	134	19	115	1	23	24	4	175	3.1	12
Todd Mitchell†	2	33	2	9	.222	1	4	.250	1	2	3	1	2	0	1	4	0	5	2.5	5
Todd Mitchell‡	24	353	43	97	.443	37	64	.578	18	32	50	21	51	0	16	33	2	123	5.1	15
Keith Smart	2	12	0	2	.000	2	2	1.000	0	1	1	2	0	0	0	2	0	2	1.0	2
John Stroeder*	1	2	0	0	...	0	0	...	0	0	0	0	2	0	1	0	0	0	0.0	0

3-pt. FG: San Antonio 63-293 (.215)—W. Anderson 4-21 (.190); Robertson 9-45 (.200); Dawkins 0-4 (.000); G. Anderson 0-3 (.000); Brickowski 0-2 (.000); Maxwell 32-129 (.248); Cook* 6-31 (.194); Vincent† 0-1 (.000); Vincent‡ 1-3 (.333); Bowie 1-5 (.200); King 8-32 (.250); Comegys 0-2 (.000); Natt† 0-0; Natt‡ 0-1 (.000); M. Anderson 1-7 (.143); Roth† 2-10 (.200); Roth‡ 3-16 (.188); Smart 0-1 (.000). Opponents 172-532 (.323).

SEATTLE SUPERSONICS

	G	Min.	FGM	FGA	Pct.	FTM	FTA	Pct.	Off.	Def.	Tot.	Ast.	PF	Dq.	Stl.	TO	Blk.	Pts.	Avg.	Hi.
									REBOUNDS									**SCORING**		
Dale Ellis	82	3190	857	1710	.501	377	462	.816	156	186	342	164	197	0	108	218	22	2253	27.5	49
Xavier McDaniel	82	2385	677	1385	.489	312	426	.732	177	256	433	134	231	0	84	210	40	1677	20.5	39
Derrick McKey	82	2804	487	970	.502	301	375	.803	167	297	464	219	264	4	105	188	70	1305	15.9	34
Michael Cage	80	2536	314	630	.498	197	265	.743	276	489	765	126	184	1	92	124	52	825	10.3	24
Sedale Threatt	63	1220	235	476	.494	63	77	.818	31	86	117	238	155	0	83	77	4	544	8.6	21
Alton Lister	82	1806	271	543	.499	115	178	.646	207	338	545	54	310	3	28	117	180	657	8.0	20
Jerry Reynolds	56	737	149	357	.417	127	167	.760	49	51	100	62	58	0	53	57	26	428	7.6	25
Nate McMillan	75	2341	199	485	.410	119	189	.630	143	245	388	696	236	3	156	211	42	532	7.1	16
Russ Schoene	69	774	135	349	.387	46	57	.807	58	107	165	36	136	1	37	48	24	358	5.2	20
John Lucas	74	842	119	299	.398	54	77	.701	22	57	79	260	53	0	60	66	1	310	4.2	25
Greg Ballard	2	15	1	8	.125	4	4	1.000	2	5	7	0	3	0	0	0	0	6	3.0	4
Olden Polynice	80	835	91	180	.506	51	86	.593	98	108	206	21	164	0	37	46	30	233	2.9	12
Avery Johnson	43	291	29	83	.349	9	16	.563	11	13	24	73	34	0	21	18	3	68	1.6	10
Mike Champion	2	4	0	3	.000	0	0	...	0	0	0	0	2	0	1	0	0	0	0.0	0

3-pt. FG: Seattle 293-774 (.379)—Ellis 162-339 (.478); McDaniel 11-36 (.306); McKey 30-89 (.337); Cage 0-4 (.000); Threatt 11-30 (.367); Reynolds 3-15 (.200); McMillan 15-70 (.214); Schoene 42-110 (.382); Lucas 18-68 (.265); Ballard 0-1 (.000); Polynice 0-2 (.000); Johnson 1-9 (.111); Champion 0-1 (.000). Opponents 169-543 (.311).

UTAH JAZZ

	G	Min.	FGM	FGA	Pct.	FTM	FTA	Pct.	Off.	Def.	Tot.	Ast.	PF	Dq.	Stl.	TO	Blk.	Pts.	Avg.	Hi.
									REBOUNDS									**SCORING**		
Karl Malone	80	3126	809	1559	.519	703	918	.766	259	594	853	219	286	3	144	285	70	2326	29.1	44
Thurl Bailey	82	2777	615	1272	.483	363	440	.825	115	332	447	138	185	0	48	208	91	1595	19.5	33
John Stockton	82	3171	497	923	.538	390	452	.863	83	165	248	1118	241	3	263	308	14	1400	17.1	30
Darrell Griffith	82	2382	466	1045	.446	142	182	.780	77	253	330	130	175	0	86	141	22	1135	13.8	40
Bobby Hansen	46	964	140	300	.467	42	75	.560	29	99	128	50	105	0	37	43	6	341	7.4	20
Mark Eaton	82	2914	188	407	.462	132	200	.660	227	616	843	83	290	6	40	142	315	508	6.2	15
Mike Brown	66	1051	104	248	.419	92	130	.708	92	166	258	41	133	0	25	77	17	300	4.5	16
Eric Leckner	75	779	120	220	.545	79	113	.699	48	151	199	16	174	1	8	69	22	319	4.3	21
Jim Farmer	37	412	57	142	.401	29	41	.707	22	33	55	28	41	0	9	26	0	152	4.1	13
Jose Ortiz	51	327	55	125	.440	31	52	.596	30	28	58	11	40	0	8	36	7	141	2.8	15
Marc Iavaroni	77	796	72	163	.442	36	44	.818	41	91	132	32	99	0	11	52	13	180	2.3	10
Jim Les	82	781	40	133	.301	57	73	.781	23	64	87	215	88	0	27	88	5	138	1.7	10
Bart Kofoed	19	176	12	33	.364	6	11	.545	4	7	11	20	22	0	9	13	0	30	1.6	4
Scott Roth*	16	72	7	24	.292	8	11	.727	0	8	8	7	14	0	5	7	1	23	1.4	7
Eric White*	1	2	0	1	.000	0	0	...	0	0	0	1	0	0	0	0	0	0	0.0	0

3-pt. FG: Utah 114-380 (.300)—Malone 5-16 (.313); Bailey 2-5 (.400); Stockton 16-66 (.242); Griffith 61-196 (.311); Hansen 19-54 (.352); Farmer 9-20 (.450); Ortiz 0-1 (.000); Iavaroni 0-1 (.000); Les 1-14 (.071); Kofoed 0-1 (.000); Roth* 1-6 (.167). Opponents 185-606 (.305).

WASHINGTON BULLETS

	G	Min.	FGM	FGA	Pct.	FTM	FTA	Pct.	Off.	Def.	Tot.	Ast.	PF	Dq.	Stl.	TO	Blk.	Pts.	Avg.	Hi.
									REBOUNDS									**SCORING**		
Jeff Malone	76	2418	677	1410	.480	296	340	.871	55	124	179	219	155	0	39	165	14	1651	21.7	38
Bernard King	81	2559	654	1371	.477	361	440	.819	133	251	384	294	219	1	64	227	13	1674	20.7	41
John Williams	82	2413	438	940	.466	225	290	.776	158	415	573	356	213	1	142	157	70	1120	13.7	30
Ledell Eackles	80	1459	318	732	.434	272	346	.786	100	80	180	123	156	1	41	128	5	917	11.5	28

	G	Min.	FGM	FGA	Pct.	FTM	FTA	Pct.	REBOUNDS Off.	Def.	Tot.	Ast.	PF	Dq.	Stl.	TO	Blk.	SCORING Pts.	Avg.	Hi.
Terry Catledge........	79	2077	334	681	.490	153	254	.602	230	342	572	75	250	5	46	120	25	822	10.4	26
Darrell Walker........	79	2565	286	681	.420	142	184	.772	135	372	507	496	215	2	155	184	23	714	9.0	23
Steve Colter	80	1425	203	457	.444	125	167	.749	62	120	182	225	158	0	69	64	14	534	6.7	27
Mark Alarie.........	74	1141	206	431	.478	73	87	.839	103	152	255	63	160	1	25	62	22	498	6.7	22
Harvey Grant........	71	1193	181	390	.464	34	57	.596	75	88	163	79	147	2	35	28	29	396	5.6	14
Dave Feitl	57	828	116	266	.436	54	65	.831	69	133	202	36	136	0	17	65	18	286	5.0	14
Charles Jones	53	1154	60	125	.480	16	25	.640	77	180	257	42	187	4	39	39	76	136	2.6	9
Charles A. Jones.....	43	516	38	82	.463	33	53	.623	54	86	140	18	49	0	18	22	16	110	2.6	10
Dominic Pressley* ...	10	107	8	25	.320	5	9	.556	3	11	14	22	9	0	4	11	0	21	2.1	4

3-pt. FG: Washington 52-243 (.214)—Malone 1-19 (.053); King 5-30 (.167); Williams 19-71 (.268); Eackles 9-40 (.225); Catledge 1-5 (.200); Walker 0-9 (.000); Colter 3-25 (.120); Alarie 13-38 (.342); Grant 0-1 (.000); Feitl 0-1 (.000); C. Jones 0-1 (.000); C.A. Jones 1-3 (.333). Opponents 155-510 (.304).

* Finished season with another team. † Totals with this team only. ‡ Totals with all teams.

PLAYOFF RESULTS

EASTERN CONFERENCE

FIRST ROUND

New York 3, Philadelphia 0
Apr. 27—Thur. Philadelphia 96 at New York 102
Apr. 29—Sat. Philadelphia 106 at New York 107
May 2—Tue. New York 116 at Philadelphia *115

Detroit 3, Boston 0
Apr. 28—Fri. Boston 91 at Detroit 101
Apr. 30—Sun. Boston 95 at Detroit 102
May 2—Tue. Detroit 100 at Boston 85

Chicago 3, Cleveland 2
Apr. 28—Fri. Chicago 95 at Cleveland 88
Apr. 30—Sun. Chicago 88 at Cleveland 96
May 3—Wed. Cleveland 94 at Chicago 101
May 5—Fri. Cleveland 108 at Chicago *105
May 7—Sun. Chicago 101 at Cleveland 100

Milwaukee 3, Atlanta 2
Apr. 27—Thur. Milwaukee 92 at Atlanta 100
Apr. 29—Sat. Milwaukee 108 at Atlanta 98
May 2—Tue. Atlanta 113 at Milwaukee *117
May 5—Fri. Atlanta 113 at Milwaukee *106
May 7—Sun. Milwaukee 96 at Atlanta 92

SEMIFINALS

Chicago 4, New York 2
May 9—Tue. Chicago 120 at New York *109
May 11—Thur. Chicago 97 at New York 114
May 13—Sat. New York 88 at Chicago 111
May 14—Sun. New York 93 at Chicago 106
May 16—Tue. Chicago 114 at New York 121
May 19—Fri. New York 111 at Chicago 113

Detroit 4, Milwaukee 0
May 10—Wed. Milwaukee 80 at Detroit 85
May 12—Fri. Milwaukee 92 at Detroit 112
May 14—Sun. Detroit 110 at Milwaukee 90
May 15—Mon. Detroit 96 at Milwaukee 94

FINALS

Detroit 4, Chicago 2
May 21—Sun. Chicago 94 at Detroit 88
May 23—Tue. Chicago 91 at Detroit 100
May 27—Sat. Detroit 97 at Chicago 99
May 29—Mon. Detroit 86 at Chicago 80
May 31—Wed. Chicago 85 at Detroit 94
June 2—Fri. Detroit 103 at Chicago 94

WESTERN CONFERENCE

FIRST ROUND

L.A. Lakers 3, Portland 0
Apr. 27—Thur. Portland 108 at L.A. Lakers 128
Apr. 30—Sun. Portland 105 at L.A. Lakers 113
May 3—Wed. L.A. Lakers 116 at Portland 108

Golden State 3, Utah 0
Apr. 27—Thur. Golden State 123 at Utah 119
Apr. 29—Sat. Golden State 99 at Utah 91
May 2—Tue. Utah 106 at Golden State 120

Phoenix 3, Denver 0
Apr. 28—Fri Denver 103 at Phoenix 104
Apr. 30—Sun. Denver 114 at Phoenix 132
May 2—Tue. Phoenix 130 at Denver 121

Seattle 3, Houston 1
Apr. 28—Fri Houston 107 at Seattle 111
Apr. 30—Sun. Houston 97 at Seattle 109
May 3—Wed. Seattle 107 at Houston 126
May 5—Fri. Seattle 98 at Houston 96

SEMIFINALS

Phoenix 4, Golden State 1
May 6—Sat. Golden State 103 at Phoenix 130
May 9—Tue. Golden State 127 at Phoenix 122
May 11—Thur. Phoenix 113 at Golden State 104
May 13—Sat. Phoenix 135 at Golden State 99
May 16—Tue. Golden State 104 at Phoenix 116

L.A. Lakers 4, Seattle 0
May 7—Sun. Seattle 102 at L.A. Lakers 113
May 10—Wed. Seattle 108 at L.A. Lakers 130
May 12—Fri. L.A. Lakers 91 at Seattle 86
May 14—Sun. L.A. Lakers 97 at Seattle 95

FINALS

L.A. Lakers 4, Phoenix 0
May 20—Sat. Phoenix 119 at L.A. Lakers 127
May 23—Tue. Phoenix 95 at L.A. Lakers 101
May 26—Fri. L.A. Lakers 110 at Phoenix 107
May 28—Sun. L.A. Lakers 122 at Phoenix 117

NBA FINALS

Detroit 4, L.A. Lakers 0
June 6—Tue. L.A. Lakers 97 at Detroit 109
June 8—Thur. L.A. Lakers 105 at Detroit 108
June 11—Sun. Detroit 114 at L.A. Lakers 110
June 13—Tue. Detroit 105 at L.A. Lakers 97

*Denotes number of overtime periods.

1987-88

1987-88 NBA CHAMPION LOS ANGELES LAKERS

Front row (from left): owner Jerry Buss, Kurt Rambis, James Worthy, Kareem Abdul-Jabbar, Michael Cooper, Byron Scott, Magic Johnson, assistant coach Bill Bertka. Back row (from left): head coach Pat Riley, Wes Matthews, Billy Thompson, A.C. Green, Mike Smrek, Mychal Thompson, Jeff Lamp, Milt Wagner, assistant coach Randy Pfund, trainer Gary Vitti.

FINAL STANDINGS

ATLANTIC DIVISION

	Atl.	Bos.	Chi.	Cle.	Dal.	Den.	Det.	G.S.	Hou.	Ind.	L.A.C.	L.A.L.	Mil.	N.J.	N.Y.	Phi.	Pho.	Por.	Sac.	S.A.	Sea.	Uta.	Was.	W	L	Pct.	GB
Boston	4	..	3	2	2	0	3	2	1	5	2	0	3	5	5	4	2	2	2	2	1	2	5	57	25	.695	..
Washington	3	1	3	0	1	0	2	2	0	4	2	1	1	6	3	3	2	0	2	2	0	0	..	38	44	.463	19
New York	3	1	2	4	1	1	1	0	2	2	1	3	2	0	..	3	0	1	1	1	0	1	3	38	44	.463	19
Philadelphia	0	2	2	2	1	0	1	1	1	4	1	0	4	4	3	..	1	1	1	1	1	2	3	36	46	.439	21
New Jersey	0	1	1	1	1	0	0	1	0	2	0	2	2	..	3	2	1	0	1	1	0	1	0	19	63	.232	38

CENTRAL DIVISION

	Atl.	Bos.	Chi.	Cle.	Dal.	Den.	Det.	G.S.	Hou.	Ind.	L.A.C.	L.A.L.	Mil.	N.J.	N.Y.	Phi.	Pho.	Por.	Sac.	S.A.	Sea.	Uta.	Was.	W	L	Pct.	GB
Detroit	4	3	4	5	1	1	..	2	1	3	1	0	4	5	4	4	2	1	2	1	1	2	3	54	28	.659	..
Chicago	3	3	..	3	0	1	2	2	2	3	2	1	5	5	3	4	2	1	1	1	1	2	3	50	32	.610	4
Atlanta	..	2	2	5	2	1	2	2	1	4	2	0	3	5	3	6	1	0	1	2	2	1	3	50	32	.610	4
Milwaukee	3	3	1	4	0	1	2	2	0	3	2	2	..	3	3	2	1	1	2	1	1	4	3	42	40	.512	12
Cleveland	1	3	3	..	1	1	1	0	1	4	1	1	2	5	2	3	1	1	2	2	1	0	6	42	40	.512	12
Indiana	2	0	3	2	0	1	3	2	0	..	1	1	1	3	6	2	2	2	0	2	2	1	2	38	44	.463	16

MIDWEST DIVISION

	Atl.	Bos.	Chi.	Cle.	Dal.	Den.	Det.	G.S.	Hou.	Ind.	L.A.C.	L.A.L.	Mil.	N.J.	N.Y.	Phi.	Pho.	Por.	Sac.	S.A.	Sea.	Uta.	Was.	W	L	Pct.	GB
Denver	1	2	1	1	3	..	1	4	4	1	5	3	1	2	1	2	3	2	4	5	4	2	5	54	28	.659	..
Dallas	0	0	2	1	..	3	1	4	4	2	5	1	2	1	1	1	5	3	5	5	3	3	1	53	29	.646	1
Utah	1	0	0	2	3	4	0	4	3	1	4	1	1	1	1	0	3	4	5	3	4	..	2	47	35	.573	7
Houston	1	1	0	1	2	2	1	5	..	2	3	1	2	1	1	1	4	4	4	2	3	3	2	46	36	.561	8
San Antonio	0	0	1	0	1	1	1	2	4	0	5	0	1	1	1	1	3	0	3	..	3	3	0	31	51	.378	23
Sacramento	1	0	1	0	1	2	0	3	2	0	2	1	0	1	1	1	2	1	..	3	1	1	0	24	58	.293	30

PACIFIC DIVISION

	Atl.	Bos.	Chi.	Cle.	Dal.	Den.	Det.	G.S.	Hou.	Ind.	L.A.C.	L.A.L.	Mil.	N.J.	N.Y.	Phi.	Pho.	Por.	Sac.	S.A.	Sea.	Uta.	Was.	W	L	Pct.	GB
L.A. Lakers	2	2	1	1	4	2	2	6	4	1	5	..	0	2	2	2	5	3	4	5	4	4	1	62	20	.756	..
Portland	2	0	1	1	2	3	1	5	1	2	6	3	1	2	1	1	6	..	4	5	3	1	2	53	29	.646	9
Seattle	0	1	1	1	2	1	1	5	2	1	5	2	1	2	2	1	4	3	4	2	..	1	2	44	38	.537	18
Phoenix	1	0	0	1	0	2	0	4	1	0	4	1	1	1	2	1	..	0	3	2	2	2	0	28	54	.341	34
Golden State	0	0	0	2	1	1	0	..	0	0	3	0	0	2	0	1	2	1	2	3	1	1	0	20	62	.244	42
L.A. Clippers	0	0	0	1	0	0	1	3	2	1	..	1	0	0	0	1	2	0	3	0	1	1	0	17	65	.207	45

TEAM STATISTICS

OFFENSIVE

	G	FGM	FGA	Pct.	FTM	FTA	Pct.	REBOUNDS Off.	Def.	Tot.	Ast.	PF	Dq.	Stl.	TO	Blk.	SCORING Pts.	Avg.
Denver	82	3770	7961	.474	1841	2289	.804	1163	2442	3605	2300	1982	18	832	1186	401	9573	116.7
Portland	82	3661	7460	.491	2079	2701	.770	1251	2491	3742	2307	2091	21	726	1351	347	9518	116.1
San Antonio	82	3706	7559	.490	1769	2412	.733	1184	2335	3519	2344	1991	27	739	1418	468	9314	113.6
Boston	82	3599	6905	.521	1846	2300	.803	930	2440	3370	2448	1804	10	620	1304	415	9315	113.6

	G	FGM	FGA	Pct.	FTM	FTA	Pct.	Off.	Def.	Tot.	Ast.	PF	Dq.	Stl.	TO	Blk.	Pts.	Avg.
								REBOUNDS									SCORING	
L.A. Lakers....	82	3576	7078	.505	1956	2480	.789	1073	2491	3564	2347	1715	9	672	1318	404	9250	112.8
Seattle.......	82	3544	7443	.476	1826	2442	.748	1313	2314	3627	2146	2380	21	775	1376	447	9135	111.4
Dallas........	82	3413	7191	.475	1980	2510	.789	1341	2495	3836	1984	1734	14	645	1257	446	8960	109.3
Detroit.......	82	3461	7018	.493	1977	2612	.757	1181	2482	3663	2011	1957	20	588	1348	394	8957	109.2
Houston......	82	3465	7354	.471	1936	2483	.780	1239	2530	3769	1936	1865	17	712	1367	502	8935	109.0
Utah.........	82	3484	7092	.491	1802	2404	.750	1066	2553	3619	2407	1986	22	771	1481	627	8899	108.5
Phoenix......	82	3551	7302	.486	1681	2200	.764	1113	2379	3492	2332	2045	19	675	1413	353	8901	108.5
Sacramento ...	82	3458	7337	.471	1795	2324	.772	1232	2461	3693	2116	1895	14	582	1457	493	8855	108.0
Atlanta.......	82	3443	7102	.485	1873	2441	.767	1228	2379	3607	2062	2050	21	635	1225	537	8844	107.9
Golden State ..	82	3463	7404	.468	1754	2204	.796	1140	2252	3392	2005	2155	25	741	1395	283	8771	107.0
Milwaukee	82	3366	7079	.475	1832	2364	.775	1117	2335	3452	2194	1989	33	671	1275	380	8697	106.1
Philadelphia ...	82	3214	6785	.474	2087	2731	.764	1219	2307	3526	1897	1866	20	672	1433	465	8667	105.7
New York.....	82	3363	7232	.465	1750	2306	.759	1286	2194	3480	2012	2361	36	789	1518	445	8655	105.5
Washington ...	82	3355	7164	.468	1914	2476	.773	1229	2297	3526	1875	1922	16	698	1384	502	8653	105.5
Chicago......	82	3434	7015	.490	1685	2221	.759	1170	2459	3629	2149	1849	14	712	1263	475	8609	105.0
Indiana......	82	3436	7154	.480	1546	1982	.780	1078	2457	3535	1977	2038	20	619	1318	345	8581	104.6
Cleveland.....	82	3313	6755	.490	1813	2438	.744	1015	2289	3304	2070	1836	20	733	1439	526	8566	104.5
New Jersey ...	82	3208	6857	.468	1682	2308	.729	1075	2262	3337	1795	2042	27	727	1503	385	8235	100.4
L.A. Clippers ..	82	3190	7194	.443	1644	2305	.713	1191	2350	3541	1885	1908	18	721	1534	520	8103	98.8

DEFENSIVE

	FGM	FGA	Pct.	FTM	FTA	Pct.	Off.	Def.	Tot.	Ast.	PF	Dq.	Stl.	TO	Blk.	Pts.	Avg.	Dif.
							REBOUNDS									SCORING		
Chicago......	3276	6967	.470	1670	2205	.757	1023	2268	3291	2079	1880	27	597	1244	415	8330	101.6	+3.4
Cleveland.....	3383	7101	.476	1611	2044	.788	1159	2255	3414	1989	2021	26	692	1439	449	8504	103.7	+0.8
Detroit.......	3334	7134	.467	1751	2298	.762	1144	2276	3420	1964	2164	32	649	1328	406	8533	104.1	+5.1
Atlanta.......	3243	6885	.471	1927	2480	.777	1156	2353	3509	1976	2008	18	640	1322	353	8549	104.3	+3.6
Utah.........	3273	7283	.449	1905	2475	.770	1277	2444	3721	1991	2013	16	771	1467	472	8597	104.8	+3.7
Dallas........	3468	7385	.470	1499	1957	.766	1200	2233	3433	2240	1997	20	612	1228	436	8602	104.9	+4.4
Indiana......	3335	7060	.472	1858	2446	.760	1160	2500	3660	1933	1859	8	700	1269	407	8646	105.4	-0.8
Milwaukee	3344	7063	.473	1832	2410	.760	1172	2400	3572	2135	1952	22	621	1346	449	8653	105.5	+0.6
New York.....	3202	6710	.477	2177	2806	.776	1155	2284	3439	2005	1969	26	705	1631	447	8695	106.0	-0.5
Washington ...	3459	7235	.478	1670	2240	.744	1220	2364	3592	2134	1966	20	690	1384	527	8716	106.3	0.8
L.A. Lakers....	3551	7467	.476	1538	2020	.761	1175	2249	3424	2200	1940	20	732	1246	390	8771	107.0	+5.8
Philadelphia ...	3501	7063	.496	1640	2163	.758	1109	2225	3334	2217	2118	25	718	1280	441	8785	107.1	-1.4
Houston......	3454	7420	.465	1805	2352	.767	1261	2506	3767	1951	2012	17	737	1405	365	8821	107.6	+1.4
Boston.......	3497	7260	.402	1724	2240	.767	1122	2194	3316	2061	1989	25	734	1176	346	8828	107.7	+5.9
New Jersey....	3437	6918	.497	1895	2419	.783	1034	2461	3495	1993	1942	19	809	1433	522	8900	108.5	-8.1
L.A. Clippers ..	3513	7360	.477	1799	2309	.779	1241	2666	3907	2300	1912	13	842	1452	483	8949	109.1	-10.3
Seattle.......	3298	6798	.485	2240	2992	.749	1128	2306	3434	1964	1963	14	606	1533	423	8966	109.3	+2.1
Portland......	3492	7341	.476	2022	2632	.768	1153	2400	3553	2154	2135	31	648	1443	376	9147	111.5	+4.6
Denver.......	3608	7356	.490	1910	2508	.762	1179	2748	3927	2171	1989	24	621	1606	510	9239	112.7	+4.0
Phoenix......	3609	7248	.498	1922	2506	.767	1104	2416	3520	2225	1901	16	710	1296	441	9268	113.0	-4.5
Sacramento ...	3718	7465	.498	1771	2326	.761	1153	2424	3577	2176	1951	20	784	1195	533	9327	113.7	-5.7
Golden State ..	3627	7244	.501	2047	2700	.758	1209	2509	3718	2271	1811	10	747	1413	432	9453	115.3	-8.3
San Antonio ..	3851	7678	.502	1855	2390	.776	1292	2513	3805	2470	1969	13	690	1427	537	9/14	118.5	-4.9
Avgs........	3455	7193	.480	1829	2388	.766	1167	2391	3558	2113	1977	20	698	1372	442	8869	108.2	...

HOME/ROAD

	Home	Road	Total		Home	Road	Total
Atlanta........................	30-11	20-21	50-32	Milwaukee....................	30-11	12-29	42-40
Boston........................	36-5	21-20	57-25	New Jersey..................	16-25	3-38	19-63
Chicago.......................	30-11	20-21	50-32	New York.....................	29-12	9-32	38-44
Cleveland.....................	31-10	11-30	42-40	Philadelphia..................	27-14	9-32	36-46
Dallas........................	33-8	20-21	53-29	Phoenix......................	22-19	6-35	28-54
Denver........................	35-6	19-22	54-28	Portland....................	33-8	20-21	53-29
Detroit........................	34-7	20-21	54-28	Sacramento..................	19-22	5-36	24-58
Golden State	16-25	4-37	20-62	San Antonio..................	23-18	8-33	31-51
Houston.......................	31-10	15-26	46-36	Seattle.......................	32-9	12-29	44-38
Indiana.......................	25-16	13-28	38-44	Utah.........................	33-8	14-27	47-35
L.A. Clippers	14-27	3-38	17-65	Washington..................	25-16	13-28	38-44
L.A. Lakers	36-5	26-15	62-20	Totals.......................	640-303	303-640	943-943

INDIVIDUAL LEADERS

POINTS

(minimum 70 games or 1,400 points)

	G	FGM	FTM	Pts.	Avg.
Michael Jordan, Chicago	82	1069	723	2868	35.0
Dominique Wilkins, Atlanta	78	909	541	2397	30.7
Larry Bird, Boston	76	881	415	2275	29.9
Charles Barkley, Philadelphia ..	80	753	714	2264	28.3
Karl Malone, Utah	82	858	552	2268	27.7
Clyde Drexler, Portland	81	849	476	2185	27.0
Dale Ellis, Seattle	75	764	303	1938	25.8
Mark Aguirre, Dallas	77	746	388	1932	25.1
Alex English, Denver	80	843	314	2000	25.0

	G	FGM	FTM	Pts.	Avg.
Hakeem Olajuwon, Houston	79	712	381	1805	22.8
Kevin McHale, Boston	64	550	346	1446	22.6
Byron Scott, L.A. Lakers	81	710	272	1754	21.7
Reggie Theus, Sacramento ...	73	619	320	1574	21.6
Xavier McDaniel, Seattle	78	687	281	1669	21.4
Terry Cummings, Milwaukee ...	76	675	270	1621	21.3
Otis Thorpe, Sacramento	82	622	460	1704	20.8
Jeff Malone, Washington	80	648	335	1641	20.5
Tom Chambers, Seattle	82	611	419	1674	20.4
Moses Malone, Washington	79	531	543	1607	20.3
Patrick Ewing, New York	82	656	341	1653	20.2

1987-88

FIELD GOALS

(minimum 300 made)

	FGM	FGA	Pct.
Kevin McHale, Boston	.550	911	.604
Robert Parish, Boston	.442	750	.589
Charles Barkley, Philadelphia	.753	1283	.587
John Stockton, Utah	.454	791	.574
Walter Berry, San Antonio	.540	960	.563
Dennis Rodman, Detroit	.398	709	.561
Buck Williams, New Jersey	.466	832	.560
Cliff Levingston, Atlanta	.314	564	.557
Patrick Ewing, New York	.656	1183	.555
Mark West, Cleveland-Phoenix	.316	573	.551

FREE THROWS

(minimum 125 made)

	FTM	FTA	Pct.
Jack Sikma, Milwaukee	.321	348	.922
Larry Bird, Boston	.415	453	.916
John Long, Indiana	.166	183	.907
Mike Gminski, New Jersey-Philadelphia	.355	392	.906
Johnny Dawkins, San Antonio	.198	221	.896
Walter Davis, Phoenix	.205	231	.887
Chris Mullin, Golden State	.239	270	.885
Jeff Malone, Washington	.335	380	.882
Winston Garland, Golden State	.138	157	.879
Kiki Vandeweghe, Portland	.159	181	.878

ASSISTS

(minimum 70 games or 400 assists)

	G	No.	Avg.
John Stockton, Utah	.82	1128	13.8
Magic Johnson, L.A. Lakers	.72	858	11.9
Mark Jackson, New York	.82	868	10.6
Terry Porter, Portland	.82	831	10.1
Doc Rivers, Atlanta	.80	747	9.3
Nate McMillan, Seattle	.82	702	8.6
Isiah Thomas, Detroit	.81	678	8.4
Maurice Cheeks, Philadelphia	.79	635	8.0
Fat Lever, Denver	.82	639	7.8
Dennis Johnson, Boston	.77	598	7.8

REBOUNDS

(minimum 70 games or 800 rebounds)

	G	Off.	Def.	Tot.	Avg.
Michael Cage, L.A. Clippers	.72	371	567	938	13.03
Charles Oakley, Chicago	.82	326	740	1066	13.00
Hakeem Olajuwon, Houston	.79	302	657	959	12.1
Karl Malone, Utah	.82	277	709	986	12.0
Charles Barkley, Philadelphia	.80	385	566	951	11.9
Buck Williams, New Jersey	.70	298	536	834	11.9
Roy Tarpley, Dallas	.81	360	599	959	11.8
Moses Malone, Washington	.79	372	512	884	11.2
Otis Thorpe, Sacramento	.82	279	558	837	10.2
Bill Laimbeer, Detroit	.82	165	667	832	10.1

STEALS

(minimum 70 games or 125 steals)

	G	No.	Avg.
Michael Jordan, Chicago	.82	259	3.16
Alvin Robertson, San Antonio	.82	243	2.96
John Stockton, Utah	.82	242	2.95
Fat Lever, Denver	.82	223	2.72
Clyde Drexler, Portland	.81	203	2.51
Mark Jackson, New York	.82	205	2.50
Maurice Cheeks, Philadelphia	.79	167	2.11
Nate McMillan, Seattle	.82	169	2.06
Michael Adams, Denver	.82	168	2.05
Derek Harper, Dallas	.82	168	2.05
Hakeem Olajuwon, Houston	.79	162	2.05

BLOCKED SHOTS

(minimum 70 games or 100 blocked shots)

	G	No.	Avg.
Mark Eaton, Utah	.82	304	3.71
Benoit Benjamin, L.A. Clippers	.66	225	3.41
Patrick Ewing, New York	.82	245	2.99
Hakeem Olajuwon, Houston	.79	214	2.71
Manute Bol, Washington	.77	208	2.70
Larry Nance, Phoenix-Cleveland	.67	159	2.37
Jawann Oldham, Sacramento	.54	110	2.04
Herb Williams, Indiana	.75	146	1.95
John Williams, Cleveland	.77	145	1.88
Roy Hinson, Philadelphia-New Jersey	.77	140	1.82

3-POINT FIELD GOALS

(minimum 25 made)

	FGA	FGM	Pct.
Craig Hodges, Milwaukee-Phoenix	.175	86	.491
Mark Price, Cleveland	.148	72	.486
John Long, Indiana	.77	34	.442
Gerald Henderson, New York-Philadelphia	.163	69	.423
Kelly Tripucka, Utah	.74	31	.419
Danny Ainge, Boston	.357	148	.415
Larry Bird, Boston	.237	98	.414
Dale Ellis, Seattle	.259	107	.413
Trent Tucker, New York	.167	69	.413
Leon Wood, San Antonio-Atlanta	.127	52	.409

INDIVIDUAL STATISTICS, TEAM BY TEAM

ATLANTA HAWKS

	G	Min.	FGM	FGA	Pct.	FTM	FTA	Pct.	Off.	Def.	Tot.	Ast.	PF	Dq.	Stl.	TO	Blk.	Pts.	Avg.	Hi.
Dominique Wilkins	78	2948	909	1957	.464	541	655	.826	211	291	502	224	162	0	103	218	47	2397	30.7	51
Doc Rivers	80	2502	403	890	.453	319	421	.758	83	283	366	747	272	3	140	210	41	1134	14.2	37
Kevin Willis	75	2091	356	687	.518	159	245	.649	235	312	547	28	242	2	68	138	41	871	11.6	27
John Battle	67	1227	278	613	.454	141	188	.750	26	87	113	158	84	0	31	75	5	713	10.6	27
Randy Wittman	82	2412	376	787	.478	71	89	.798	39	131	170	302	117	0	50	82	18	823	10.0	20
Cliff Levingston	82	2135	314	564	.557	190	246	.772	228	276	504	71	287	5	52	94	84	819	10.0	29
Antoine Carr	80	1483	281	517	.544	142	182	.780	94	195	289	103	272	7	38	116	83	705	8.8	24
Spud Webb	82	1347	191	402	.475	107	131	.817	16	130	146	337	125	0	63	131	12	490	6.0	14
Jon Koncak	49	1073	98	203	.483	83	136	.610	103	230	333	19	161	1	36	53	56	279	5.7	25
Mike McGee*	11	117	22	52	.423	2	6	.333	4	12	16	13	6	0	5	7	0	51	4.6	18
Tree Rollins	76	1765	133	260	.512	70	80	.875	142	317	459	20	229	2	31	51	132	336	4.4	20
Leon Wood†	14	79	16	30	.533	7	8	.875	1	5	6	19	6	0	4	5	0	48	3.4	10
Leon Wood‡	52	909	136	312	.436	76	99	.768	17	40	57	174	50	0	26	39	1	400	7.7	27
Ennis Whatley	5	24	4	9	.444	3	4	.750	0	4	4	2	3	0	2	4	0	11	2.2	9
Scott Hastings	55	403	40	82	.488	25	27	.926	27	70	97	16	67	1	8	14	10	110	2.0	10
Chris Washburn†	29	174	22	49	.449	13	23	.565	19	36	55	3	19	0	4	10	8	57	2.0	8
Chris Washburn‡	37	260	36	81	.444	18	31	.581	28	47	75	6	29	0	5	17	8	90	2.4	10

3-pt. FG: Atlanta 85-282 (.301)—Wilkins 38-129 (.295); Rivers 9-33 (.273); Willis 0-2 (.000); Battle 16-41 (.390); Levingston 1-2 (.500); Carr 1-4 (.250); Webb 1-19 (.053); Koncak 0-2 (.000); McGee* 5-19 (.263); Wood† 9-19 (.474); Wood‡ 52-127 (.409); Hastings 5-12 (.417). Opponents 136-406 (.335).

1987-88

BOSTON CELTICS

	G	Min.	FGM	FGA	Pct.	FTM	FTA	Pct.	Off.	Def.	Tot.	Ast.	PF	Dq.	Stl.	TO	Blk.	Pts.	Avg.	Hi.
Larry Bird	76	2965	881	1672	.527	415	453	.916	108	595	703	467	157	0	125	213	57	2275	29.9	49
Kevin McHale	64	2390	550	911	.604	346	434	.797	159	377	536	171	179	1	27	141	92	1446	22.6	33
Danny Ainge	81	3018	482	982	.491	158	180	.878	59	190	249	503	203	1	115	153	17	1270	15.7	33
Robert Parish	74	2312	442	750	.589	177	241	.734	173	455	628	115	198	5	55	154	84	1061	14.3	26
Dennis Johnson	77	2670	352	803	.438	255	298	.856	62	178	240	598	204	0	93	195	29	971	12.6	24
Jim Paxson†	28	538	94	191	.492	54	61	.885	7	20	27	49	44	0	23	28	4	244	8.7	19
Jim Paxson‡	45	801	137	298	.460	68	79	.861	15	30	45	76	73	0	30	39	5	347	7.7	19
Fred Roberts	74	1032	161	330	.488	128	165	.776	60	102	162	81	118	0	16	68	15	450	6.1	20
Darren Daye	47	655	112	217	.516	59	87	.678	30	46	76	71	68	0	29	44	4	283	6.0	27
Reggie Lewis	49	405	90	193	.466	40	57	.702	28	35	63	26	54	0	16	30	15	220	4.5	14
Brad Lohaus	70	718	122	246	.496	50	62	.806	46	92	138	49	123	1	20	59	41	297	4.2	20
Jerry Sichting	24	370	44	82	.537	8	12	.667	5	16	21	60	30	0	14	14	0	98	4.1	17
Mark Acres	79	1151	108	203	.532	71	111	.640	105	165	270	42	198	2	29	54	27	287	3.6	19
Artis Gilmore†	47	521	58	101	.574	48	91	.527	54	94	148	12	94	0	10	39	18	164	3.5	15
Artis Gilmore‡	71	893	99	181	.547	67	128	.523	69	142	211	21	148	0	15	67	30	265	3.7	15
Conner Henry*	10	81	11	28	.393	9	10	.900	2	8	10	12	11	0	1	9	1	34	3.4	10
Dirk Minniefield†	61	868	83	173	.480	27	32	.844	22	53	75	190	107	0	44	77	3	196	3.2	16
Dirk Minniefield‡	72	1070	108	221	.489	41	55	.745	30	66	96	228	133	0	59	93	3	261	3.6	16
Greg Kite*	13	86	9	23	.391	1	6	.167	10	14	24	2	16	0	3	9	8	19	1.5	4

3-pt. FG: Boston 271-705 (.384)—Bird 98-237 (.414); Ainge 148-357 (.415); Parish 0-1 (.000); Johnson 12-46 (.261); Paxson† 2-13 (.154); Paxson‡ 5-21 (.238); Roberts 0-6 (.000); Daye 0-1 (.000); Lewis 0-4 (.000); Lohaus 3-13 (.231); Sichting 2-8 (.250); Henry* 3-8 (.375); Minniefield† 3-11 (.273); Minniefield‡ 4-16 (.250). Opponents 110-366 (.301).

CHICAGO BULLS

	G	Min.	FGM	FGA	Pct.	FTM	FTA	Pct.	Off.	Def.	Tot.	Ast.	PF	Dq.	Stl.	TO	Blk.	Pts.	Avg.	Hi.
Michael Jordan	82	3311	1069	1998	.535	723	860	.841	139	310	449	485	270	2	259	252	131	2868	35.0	59
Sam Vincent†	29	953	138	309	.447	99	107	.925	18	85	103	244	82	0	34	84	12	378	13.0	23
Sam Vincent‡	72	1501	210	461	.466	146	167	.868	35	117	152	381	145	0	55	136	16	573	8.0	23
Charles Oakley	82	2816	375	776	.483	261	359	.727	326	740	1066	248	272	2	68	241	28	1014	12.4	26
Dave Corzine	80	2328	344	715	.481	115	153	.752	170	357	527	154	149	1	36	109	95	804	10.1	21
Brad Sellers	82	2212	326	714	.457	124	157	.790	107	143	250	141	174	0	34	91	66	777	9.5	24
John Paxson	81	1888	287	582	.493	33	45	.733	16	88	104	303	154	2	49	64	1	640	7.9	22
Scottie Pippen	79	1650	261	564	.463	99	172	.576	115	183	298	169	214	3	91	131	52	625	7.9	24
Horace Grant	81	1827	254	507	.501	114	182	.626	155	292	447	89	221	3	51	86	53	622	7.7	20
Sedale Threatt*	45	701	132	263	.502	32	41	.780	12	43	55	107	71	0	27	44	3	298	6.6	26
Rory Sparrow†	55	992	112	274	.409	24	33	.727	14	56	70	162	72	1	37	52	3	250	4.5	19
Rory Sparrow‡	58	1044	117	293	.399	24	33	.727	15	57	72	167	79	1	41	58	3	260	4.5	19
Mike Brown	46	591	78	174	.448	41	71	.577	66	93	159	28	85	0	11	38	4	197	4.3	15
Artis Gilmore*	24	372	41	80	.513	19	37	.514	15	48	63	9	54	0	5	28	12	101	4.2	13
Elston Turner	17	98	8	30	.267	1	2	.500	8	2	10	9	5	0	8	10	0	17	1.0	4
Granville Walters	22	114	9	29	.310	0	2	.000	9	19	28	1	26	0	2	6	15	18	0.8	4
Tony White*	2	2	0	0	...	0	0	...	0	0	0	0	0	0	0	0	0	0	0.0	0

3-pt. FG: Chicago 56-243 (.230)—Jordan 7-53 (.132); Vincent† 3-8 (.375); Vincent‡ 8-21 (.381); Oakley 3-12 (.250); Corzine 1-9 (.111); Sellers 1-7 (.143); Paxson 33-95 (.347); Pippen 4-23 (.174); Grant 0-2 (.000); Threatt* 2-20 (.100); Sparrow† 2-12 (.167); Sparrow‡ 2-13 (.154); Brown 0-1 (.000); Waiters 0-1 (.000). Opponents 108-368 (.293).

CLEVELAND CAVALIERS

	G	Min.	FGM	FGA	Pct.	FTM	FTA	Pct.	Off.	Def.	Tot.	Ast.	PF	Dq.	Stl.	TO	Blk.	Pts.	Avg.	Hi.
Brad Daugherty	79	2957	551	1081	.510	378	528	.716	151	514	665	333	235	2	48	267	56	1480	18.7	44
Larry Nance†	27	906	160	304	.526	117	141	.830	74	139	213	84	90	3	18	49	63	437	16.2	29
Larry Nance‡	67	2383	487	920	.529	304	390	.779	193	414	607	207	242	10	63	155	159	1280	19.1	45
Mark Price	80	2626	493	974	.506	221	252	.877	54	126	180	480	119	1	99	184	12	1279	16.0	32
Ron Harper	57	1830	340	732	.464	196	278	.705	64	159	223	281	157	3	122	158	52	879	15.4	30
John Williams	77	2106	316	663	.477	211	279	.756	159	347	506	103	203	2	61	104	145	843	10.9	24
Dell Curry	79	1499	340	742	.458	79	101	.782	43	123	166	149	128	0	94	108	22	787	10.0	27
Mark West*	54	1183	182	316	.576	95	153	.621	83	198	281	50	158	2	25	91	79	459	8.5	17
Phil Hubbard	78	1631	237	485	.489	182	243	.749	117	164	281	81	167	1	50	118	7	656	8.4	25
Tyrone Corbin*	54	1148	158	322	.491	77	98	.786	79	141	220	56	128	2	42	66	15	393	7.3	23
Kevin Johnson*	52	1043	143	311	.460	92	112	.821	10	62	72	193	96	1	60	82	17	380	7.3	15
Craig Ehlo	79	1709	226	485	.466	89	132	.674	86	188	274	206	182	0	82	107	30	563	7.1	20
Mike Sanders†	24	417	71	132	.538	20	23	.870	10	37	47	26	58	1	13	23	5	162	6.8	20
Mike Sanders‡	59	883	153	303	.505	59	76	.776	38	71	109	56	131	1	31	50	9	365	6.2	29
Chris Dudley	55	513	65	137	.474	40	71	.563	74	70	144	23	87	2	13	31	19	170	3.1	14
Johnny Rogers	24	168	26	61	.426	10	13	.769	8	19	27	3	23	0	4	10	3	62	2.6	11
Kent Benson	2	12	2	2	1.000	1	2	.500	0	1	1	0	2	0	1	2	1	5	2.5	3
Kevin Henderson†	5	20	2	5	.400	5	12	.417	3	1	4	2	2	0	0	2	0	9	1.8	7
Kevin Henderson‡	17	190	21	53	.396	15	26	.577	9	12	21	23	26	0	8	17	0	57	3.4	14
Kannard Johnson*	4	12	1	3	.333	0	0	...	0	0	0	0	1	0	1	2	0	2	0.5	2

3-pt. FG: Cleveland 127-336 (.378)—Daugherty 0-2 (.000); Nance† 0-1 (.000); Nance‡ 2-6 (.333); Price 72-148 (.486); Harper 3-20 (.150); Williams 1-0 (.000); Curry 28-81 (.346); Hubbard 0-5 (.000); Corbin* 0-3 (.000); Ke. Johnson* 2-9 (.222); Ehlo 22-64 (.344); Sanders† 0-0; Sanders‡ 0-1 (.000); Rogers 0-2 (.000); Henderson† 0-0; Henderson‡ 0-1 (.000). Opponents 127-400 (.318).

DALLAS MAVERICKS

	G	Min.	FGM	FGA	Pct.	FTM	FTA	Pct.	Off.	Def.	Tot.	Ast.	PF	Dq.	Stl.	TO	Blk.	Pts.	Avg.	Hi.
Mark Aguirre........	77	2610	746	1571	.475	388	504	.770	182	252	434	278	223	1	70	203	57	1932	25.1	38
Rolando Blackman ...	71	2580	497	1050	.473	331	379	.873	82	164	246	262	112	0	64	144	18	1325	18.7	32
Derek Harper	82	3032	536	1167	.459	261	344	.759	71	175	246	634	164	0	168	190	35	1393	17.0	35
Sam Perkins........	75	2499	394	876	.450	273	332	.822	201	400	601	118	227	2	74	119	54	1066	14.2	26
Roy Tarpley........	81	2307	444	888	.500	205	277	.740	360	599	959	86	313	8	103	172	86	1093	13.5	29
Detlef Schrempf ...	82	1587	246	539	.456	201	266	.756	102	177	279	159	189	0	42	108	32	698	8.5	22
Brad Davis	75	1480	208	415	.501	91	108	.843	18	84	102	303	149	0	51	91	18	537	7.2	25
James Donaldson	81	2523	212	380	.558	147	189	.778	247	508	755	66	175	2	40	113	104	571	7.0	20
Uwe Blab	73	658	58	132	.439	46	65	.708	52	82	134	35	108	1	8	49	29	162	2.2	12
Bill Wennington ...	30	125	25	49	.510	12	19	.632	14	25	39	4	33	0	5	9	9	63	2.1	10
Steve Alford	28	197	21	55	.382	16	17	.941	3	20	23	23	23	0	17	12	3	59	2.1	10
Jim Farmer	30	157	26	69	.377	9	10	.900	9	7	16	18	16	0	3	22	1	61	2.0	8

3-pt. FG: Dallas 154-526 (.293)—Aguirre 52-172 (.302); Blackman 0-5 (.000); Harper 60-192 (.313); Perkins 5-30 (.167); Tarpley 0-5 (.000); Schrempf 5-32 (.156); Davis 30-74 (.405); Wennington 1-2 (.500); Alford 1-8 (.125); Farmer 0-6 (.000). Opponents 167-517 (.323).

DENVER NUGGETS

	G	Min.	FGM	FGA	Pct.	FTM	FTA	Pct.	Off.	Def.	Tot.	Ast.	PF	Dq.	Stl.	TO	Blk.	Pts.	Avg.	Hi.
Alex English	80	2818	843	1704	.495	314	379	.828	166	207	373	377	193	1	70	181	23	2000	25.0	37
Fat Lever..........	82	3061	643	1360	.473	248	316	.785	203	462	665	639	214	0	223	182	21	1546	18.9	32
Jay Vincent........	73	1755	446	958	.466	231	287	.805	80	229	309	143	198	1	46	137	26	1124	15.4	42
Michael Adams......	82	2778	416	927	.449	166	199	.834	40	183	223	503	138	0	168	144	16	1137	13.9	32
Dan Schayes........	81	2166	361	668	.540	407	487	.836	200	462	662	106	323	9	62	155	92	1129	13.9	32
Blair Rasmussen....	79	1779	435	884	.492	132	170	.776	130	307	437	78	241	2	22	73	81	1002	12.7	35
Calvin Natt	27	533	102	208	.490	54	73	.740	35	61	96	47	43	0	13	30	3	258	9.6	26
Wayne Cooper	45	865	118	270	.437	50	67	.746	98	172	270	30	145	3	12	59	94	286	6.4	23
Otis Smith*........	15	191	37	93	.398	21	28	.750	16	14	30	11	23	0	5	12	6	95	6.3	17
Mike Evans.........	56	656	139	307	.453	30	37	.811	9	39	48	81	78	0	34	43	6	344	6.1	29
Bill Hanzlik	77	1334	109	287	.380	129	163	.791	39	132	171	166	185	1	64	95	17	350	4.5	16
Andre Moore*.......	7	34	7	24	.292	6	6	1.000	5	7	12	5	4	0	2	3	1	20	2.9	10
Michael Brooks.....	16	133	20	49	.408	3	4	.750	19	25	44	13	21	1	4	12	1	43	2.7	10
T.R. Dunn..........	82	1534	70	156	.449	40	52	.769	110	130	240	87	152	0	101	26	11	180	2.2	10
Mo Martin..........	26	136	23	61	.377	10	21	.476	13	11	24	14	21	0	6	10	3	57	2.2	10
Brad Wright	2	7	1	5	.200	0	0	...	1	1	0	3	0	0	2	0	2	1.0	2

3-pt. FG: Denver 192-562 (.342)—English 0-6 (.000); Lever 12-57 (.211); Vincent 1-4 (.250); Schayes 0-2 (.000); Adams 139-379 (.367); Natt 0-1 (.000); Cooper 0-1 (.000); Evans 36-91 (.396); Hanzlik 3-16 (.188); Martin 1-4 (.250); Dunn 0-0 (.000). Opponents 113-377 (.300).

DETROIT PISTONS

	G	Min.	FGM	FGA	Pct.	FTM	FTA	Pct.	Off.	Def.	Tot.	Ast.	PF	Dq.	Stl.	TO	Blk.	Pts.	Avg.	Hi.
Adrian Dantley	69	2144	444	863	.514	492	572	.860	84	143	227	171	144	0	39	135	10	1380	20.0	45
Isiah Thomas	81	2927	621	1341	.463	305	394	.774	64	214	278	678	217	0	141	273	17	1577	19.5	42
Joe Dumars	82	2732	453	960	.472	251	308	.815	63	137	200	387	155	1	87	172	15	1161	14.2	25
Bill Laimbeer.......	82	2897	455	923	.493	187	214	.874	165	667	832	199	284	6	66	136	78	1110	13.5	30
Vinnie Johnson.....	82	1935	425	959	.443	147	217	.677	90	141	231	267	164	0	58	152	18	1002	12.2	27
Dennis Rodman	82	2147	398	709	.561	152	284	.535	318	397	715	110	273	5	75	156	45	953	11.6	30
Rick Mahorn	67	1963	276	481	.574	164	217	.756	159	406	565	60	262	4	43	119	42	717	10.7	34
John Salley........	82	2003	258	456	.566	185	261	.709	166	236	402	113	294	4	53	120	137	701	8.5	21
James Edwards†.....	26	328	48	101	.475	45	61	.738	22	55	77	5	57	0	2	22	5	141	5.4	16
James Edwards‡.....	69	1705	302	643	.470	210	321	.654	119	293	412	78	216	2	16	130	37	814	11.8	32
William Bedford ...	38	298	44	101	.436	13	23	.565	27	38	65	4	47	0	8	19	17	101	2.7	14
Darryl Dawkins†.....	2	7	1	2	.500	2	3	.667	0	0	0	1	4	0	0	3	1	4	2.0	4
Darryl Dawkins‡.....	6	33	2	9	.222	6	15	.400	2	3	5	2	14	0	0	7	2	10	1.7	4
Ralph Lewis	50	310	27	87	.310	29	48	.604	17	34	51	14	36	0	13	19	4	83	1.7	10
Ron Moore*	9	25	4	13	.308	2	4	.500	2	0	2	1	8	0	2	3	0	10	1.1	4
Chuck Nevitt.......	17	63	7	21	.333	3	6	.500	4	14	18	0	12	0	1	2	5	17	1.0	4
Walker Russell.....	1	1	0	1	.000	0	0	...	0	0	0	1	0	0	0	0	0	0	0.0	0

3-pt. FG: Detroit 58-202 (.287)—Dantley 0-2 (.000); Thomas 30-97 (.309); Dumars 4-19 (.211); Laimbeer 13-39 (.333); Johnson 5-24 (.208); Rodman 5-17 (.294); Mahorn 1-2 (.500); Edwards† 0-0; Edwards‡ 0-1 (.000); Lewis 0-1 (.000); Russell 0-1 (.000). Opponents 114-394 (.289).

GOLDEN STATE WARRIORS

	G	Min.	FGM	FGA	Pct.	FTM	FTA	Pct.	Off.	Def.	Tot.	Ast.	PF	Dq.	Stl.	TO	Blk.	Pts.	Avg.	Hi.
Sleepy Floyd*	18	680	132	301	.439	116	139	.835	26	65	91	178	46	0	27	67	2	381	21.2	37
Chris Mullin	60	2033	470	926	.508	239	270	.885	58	147	205	290	136	3	113	156	32	1213	20.2	38
Rod Higgins	68	2188	381	725	.526	273	322	.848	94	199	293	188	188	2	70	111	31	1054	15.5	41
Joe Barry Carroll ..	14	408	79	209	.378	59	74	.797	21	72	93	19	46	1	13	43	25	217	15.5	25
Ralph Sampson†.....	29	958	180	411	.438	86	111	.775	82	208	290	85	101	2	24	109	55	446	15.4	34
Ralph Sampson‡.....	48	1663	299	682	.438	149	196	.760	140	322	462	122	164	3	41	171	88	749	15.6	34
Otis Smith†........	57	1358	288	569	.506	157	201	.781	110	107	217	144	137	0	86	95	36	746	13.1	29
Otis Smith‡........	72	1549	325	662	.491	178	229	.777	126	121	247	155	160	0	91	107	42	841	11.7	29
Terry Teagle	47	958	248	546	.454	97	121	.802	41	40	81	61	95	0	32	80	4	594	12.6	28
Winston Garland ...	67	2122	340	775	.439	138	157	.879	68	159	227	429	188	2	116	167	7	831	12.4	27
Steve Harris†	44	885	189	401	.471	74	97	.763	41	64	105	70	74	0	42	50	6	452	10.3	24
Steve Harris‡	58	1084	223	487	.458	89	113	.788	53	73	126	87	89	0	50	56	8	535	9.2	24
Tellis Frank	78	1597	242	565	.428	150	207	.725	95	235	330	111	267	5	53	109	23	634	8.1	23
Ben McDonald	81	2039	258	552	.467	87	111	.784	133	202	335	138	246	4	39	93	8	612	7.6	22

	G	Min.	FGM	FGA	Pct.	FTM	FTA	Pct.	Off.	Def.	Tot.	Ast.	PF	Dq.	Stl.	TO	Blk.	Pts.	Avg.	Hi.
Dave Feitl	70	1128	182	404	.450	94	134	.701	83	252	335	53	146	1	15	87	9	458	6.5	20
Larry Smith	20	499	58	123	.472	11	27	.407	79	103	182	25	63	1	12	36	11	127	6.4	15
Tony White†	35	462	94	203	.463	30	41	.732	11	17	28	49	43	0	19	34	2	218	6.2	24
Tony White‡	49	581	111	249	.446	39	54	.722	12	19	31	59	57	0	20	47	2	261	5.3	24
Dave Hoppen†	36	607	80	172	.465	51	59	.864	54	113	167	30	84	1	13	35	6	211	5.9	17
Dave Hoppen‡	39	642	84	183	.459	54	62	.871	58	116	174	32	87	1	13	37	6	222	5.7	17
Dirk Minniefield*	11	202	25	48	.521	14	23	.609	8	13	21	38	26	0	15	16	0	65	5.9	11
Jerome Whitehead	72	1221	174	360	.483	59	82	.720	109	212	321	39	209	3	32	49	21	407	5.7	19
Chris Washburn*	8	86	14	32	.438	5	8	.625	9	11	20	3	10	0	1	7	0	33	4.1	10
Kevin Henderson*	12	170	19	48	.396	10	14	.714	6	11	17	21	24	0	8	15	0	48	4.0	14
Kermit Washington	6	56	7	14	.500	2	2	1.000	9	10	19	0	13	0	4	4	4	16	2.7	4
Mark Wade	11	123	3	20	.150	2	4	.500	3	12	15	34	13	0	7	13	1	8	0.7	4

3-pt. FG: Golden State 91-312 (.292)—Floyd* 1-20 (.050); Mullin 34-97 (.351); Higgins 19-39 (.487); Carroll 0-1 (.000); Sampson† 0-5 (.000); Sampson‡ 2-11 (.182); O. Smith† 13-41 (.317); O. Smith‡ 13-41 (.317); Teagle 1-9 (.111); Garland 13-39 (.333); Harris† 0-6 (.000); Harris‡ 0-7 (.000); Frank 0-1 (.000); McDonald 9-35 (.257); Feitl 0-4 (.000); L. Smith 0-1 (.000); White† 0-5 (.000); White‡ 0-6 (.000); Hoppen† 0-1 (.000); Hoppen‡ 0-1 (.000); Minniefield 1-5 (.200); Henderson* 0-1 (.000); Wade 0-2 (.000). Opponents 152-470 (.323).

HOUSTON ROCKETS

	G	Min.	FGM	FGA	Pct.	FTM	FTA	Pct.	Off.	Def.	Tot.	Ast.	PF	Dq.	Stl.	TO	Blk.	Pts.	Avg.	Hi.
Hakeem Olajuwon	79	2825	712	1385	.514	381	548	.695	302	657	959	163	324	7	162	243	214	1805	22.8	38
Ralph Sampson*	19	705	119	271	.439	63	85	.741	58	114	172	37	63	1	17	62	33	303	15.9	31
Purvis Short	81	1949	474	986	.481	206	240	.858	71	151	222	162	197	0	58	118	14	1159	14.3	33
Sleepy Floyd†	59	1834	288	668	.431	185	215	.860	51	154	205	366	144	1	68	156	10	774	13.1	27
Sleepy Floyd‡	77	2514	420	969	.433	301	354	.850	77	219	296	544	190	1	95	223	12	1155	15.0	37
Rodney McCray	81	2689	359	746	.481	288	367	.785	232	399	631	264	166	2	57	144	51	1006	12.4	24
Joe Barry Carroll†	63	1596	323	715	.452	113	151	.748	110	286	396	94	149	0	37	121	81	759	12.0	29
Joe Barry Carroll‡	77	2004	402	924	.435	172	225	.764	131	358	489	113	195	1	50	164	106	976	12.7	29
Allen Leavell	80	2150	291	666	.437	218	251	.869	22	126	148	405	162	1	124	130	9	819	10.2	26
Jim Petersen	69	1793	249	488	.510	114	153	.745	145	291	436	106	203	3	36	119	40	613	8.9	22
World B. Free	58	682	143	350	.409	80	100	.800	14	30	44	60	74	2	20	49	3	374	6.4	37
Robert Reid	62	980	165	356	.463	50	63	.794	38	87	125	67	118	0	27	41	5	393	6.3	21
Steve Harris*	14	199	34	86	.395	15	16	.938	12	9	21	17	15	0	8	6	2	83	5.9	17
Buck Johnson	70	879	155	298	.520	67	91	.736	77	91	168	49	127	0	30	54	20	378	5.4	19
Cedric Maxwell	71	848	80	171	.468	110	143	.769	74	105	179	60	75	0	22	54	12	270	3.8	23
Andre Turner	12	99	12	34	.353	10	14	.714	4	4	8	23	13	0	7	12	1	35	2.9	8
Richard Anderson*	12	53	11	26	.423	4	5	.800	9	8	17	4	4	0	1	1	0	32	2.7	7
Lester Conner	52	399	50	108	.463	32	41	.780	20	10	30	59	31	0	38	33	1	132	2.5	8

3-pt. FG: Houston 69-291 (.237)—Olajuwon 0-4 (.000); Sampson* 2-6 (.333); Short 5-21 (.238); Floyd† 13-52 (.250); Floyd‡ 14-72 (.194); McCray 0-4 (.000); Carroll† 0-1 (.000); Carroll‡ 0-2 (.000); Leavell 19-88 (.216); Petersen 1-6 (.167); Free 8-35 (.229); Reid 13-34 (.382); Harris* 0-1 (.000); Johnson 1-8 (.125); Maxwell 0-2 (.000); Turner 1-7 (.143); Anderson* 6-15 (.400); Conner 0-7 (.000). Opponents 108-393 (.275).

INDIANA PACERS

	G	Min.	FGM	FGA	Pct.	FTM	FTA	Pct.	Off.	Def.	Tot.	Ast.	PF	Dq.	Stl.	TO	Blk.	Pts.	Avg.	Hi.
Chuck Person	79	2807	575	1252	.459	132	197	.670	171	365	536	309	266	4	73	210	9	1341	17.0	35
Wayman Tisdale	79	2378	511	998	.512	246	314	.783	168	323	491	103	274	5	54	145	34	1268	16.1	32
Vern Fleming	80	2733	442	845	.523	227	283	.802	106	258	364	568	225	0	115	175	11	1111	13.9	30
Steve Stipanovich	80	2692	411	828	.496	254	314	.809	157	505	662	183	302	8	90	156	69	1079	13.5	26
John Long	81	2022	417	879	.474	166	183	.907	72	157	229	173	164	1	84	127	11	1034	12.8	32
Reggie Miller	82	1840	306	627	.488	149	186	.801	95	95	190	132	157	0	53	101	19	822	10.0	31
Herb Williams	75	1966	311	732	.425	126	171	.737	116	353	469	98	244	1	37	119	146	748	10.0	24
Ron Anderson	74	1097	217	436	.498	108	141	.766	89	127	216	78	98	0	41	73	6	542	7.3	25
Scott Skiles	51	760	86	209	.411	45	54	.833	11	55	66	180	97	0	22	76	3	223	4.4	16
Stuart Gray	74	807	90	193	.466	44	73	.603	70	180	250	44	152	1	11	50	32	224	3.0	15
Clinton Wheeler	59	513	62	132	.470	25	34	.735	19	21	40	103	37	0	36	52	2	149	2.5	18
Greg Dreiling	20	74	8	17	.471	18	26	.692	3	14	17	5	19	0	2	11	4	34	1.7	6
Brian Rowsom	4	16	0	6	.000	6	6	1.000	1	4	5	1	3	0	1	1	0	6	1.5	4

3-pt. FG: Indiana 163-485 (.336)—Person 59-177 (.333); Tisdale 0-2 (.000); Fleming 0-13 (.000); Stipanovich 3-15 (.200); Long 34-77 (.442); Williams 0-6 (.000); Miller 61-172 (.355); Anderson 0-2 (.000); Skiles 6-20 (.300); Gray 0-1 (.000). Opponents 118-368 (.321).

LOS ANGELES CLIPPERS

	G	Min.	FGM	FGA	Pct.	FTM	FTA	Pct.	Off.	Def.	Tot.	Ast.	PF	Dq.	Stl.	TO	Blk.	Pts.	Avg.	Hi.
Mike Woodson	80	2534	562	1263	.445	296	341	.868	64	126	190	273	210	1	109	186	26	1438	18.0	36
Michael Cage	72	2660	360	766	.470	326	474	.688	371	567	938	110	194	1	91	160	58	1046	14.5	26
Quintin Dailey	67	1282	328	755	.434	243	313	.776	62	92	154	109	128	1	69	123	4	901	13.4	33
Benoit Benjamin	66	2171	340	693	.491	180	255	.706	112	418	530	172	203	2	50	223	225	860	13.0	30
Eric White	17	352	66	124	.532	45	57	.789	31	31	62	9	32	0	7	21	3	178	10.5	20
Reggie Williams	35	857	152	427	.356	48	66	.727	55	63	118	58	108	1	29	63	21	365	10.4	34
Larry Drew	74	2024	328	720	.456	83	108	.769	21	98	119	383	114	0	65	152	0	765	10.3	27
Steve Burtt	19	312	62	138	.449	47	69	.681	6	21	27	38	56	0	10	40	5	171	9.0	17
Ken Norman	66	1435	241	500	.482	87	170	.512	100	163	263	78	123	0	44	103	34	569	8.6	31
Joe Wolf	42	1137	136	334	.407	45	54	.833	51	136	187	98	139	8	38	76	16	320	7.6	23
Kenny Fields	7	154	16	36	.444	20	26	.769	13	16	29	10	17	0	5	19	2	52	7.4	12
Darnell Valentine	79	1636	223	533	.418	101	136	.742	37	119	156	382	135	0	122	148	8	562	7.1	30
Claude Gregory	23	313	61	134	.455	12	36	.333	37	58	95	16	37	0	9	22	13	134	5.8	21
Norris Coleman	29	431	66	191	.346	20	36	.556	36	45	81	13	51	1	11	16	6	153	5.3	16

1987-88

	G	Min.	FGM	FGA	Pct.	FTM	FTA	Pct.	Off.	Def.	Tot.	Ast.	PF	Dq.	Stl.	TO	Blk.	Pts.	Avg.	Hi.
Greg Kite†	40	977	83	182	.456	39	73	.534	75	165	240	45	137	1	16	64	50	205	5.1	16
Greg Kite‡	53	1063	92	205	.449	40	79	.506	85	179	264	47	153	1	19	73	58	224	4.2	16
Tod Murphy	1	19	1	1	1.000	3	4	.750	1	1	2	2	2	0	1	0	0	5	5.0	5
Mike Phelps	2	23	3	7	.429	3	4	.750	0	2	2	3	1	0	5	2	0	9	4.5	7
Earl Cureton	69	1128	133	310	.429	33	63	.524	97	174	271	63	135	1	32	58	36	299	4.3	21
Lancaster Gordon	8	65	11	31	.355	6	6	1.000	2	2	4	7	8	0	1	4	2	28	3.5	8
Martin Nessley*	35	295	18	49	.367	7	14	.500	20	53	73	16	78	1	7	21	11	43	1.2	6

3-pt. FG: L.A. Clippers 79-317 (.249)—Woodson 18-78 (.231); Cage 0-1 (.000); Dailey 2-12 (.167); Benjamin 0-8 (.000); White 1-1 (1.000); Williams 13-58 (.224); Drew 26-90 (.289); Burtt 0-4 (.000); Norman 0-10 (.000); Wolf 3-15 (.200); Valentine 15-33 (.455); Gregory 0-1 (.000); Coleman 1-2 (.500); Kite† 0-1 (.000); Kite‡ 0-1 (.000); Cureton 0-3 (.000). Opponents 124-363 (.342).

LOS ANGELES LAKERS

	G	Min.	FGM	FGA	Pct.	FTM	FTA	Pct.	Off.	Def.	Tot.	Ast.	PF	Dq.	Stl.	TO	Blk.	Pts.	Avg.	Hi.
Byron Scott	81	3048	710	1348	.527	272	317	.858	76	257	333	335	204	2	155	161	27	1754	21.7	38
James Worthy	75	2655	617	1161	.531	242	304	.796	129	245	374	289	175	1	72	155	55	1478	19.7	38
Magic Johnson	72	2637	490	996	.492	417	489	.853	88	361	449	858	147	0	114	269	13	1408	19.6	39
Kareem Abdul-Jabbar	80	2308	480	903	.532	205	269	.762	118	360	478	135	216	1	48	159	92	1165	14.6	27
Mychal Thompson	80	2007	370	722	.512	185	292	.634	198	291	489	66	251	1	38	113	79	925	11.6	28
A.C. Green	82	2636	322	640	.503	293	379	.773	245	465	710	93	204	0	87	120	45	937	11.4	28
Tony Campbell	13	242	57	101	.564	28	39	.718	8	19	27	15	41	0	11	26	2	143	11.0	28
Michael Cooper	61	1793	189	482	.392	97	113	.858	50	178	228	289	136	1	66	101	26	532	8.7	21
Wes Matthews	51	706	114	248	.460	54	65	.831	16	50	66	138	65	0	25	69	3	289	5.7	18
Kurt Rambis	70	845	102	186	.548	73	93	.785	103	165	268	54	103	0	39	59	13	277	4.0	17
Milt Wagner	40	380	62	147	.422	26	29	.897	4	24	28	61	42	0	6	22	4	152	3.8	14
Ray Tolbert†	14	82	16	28	.571	10	13	.769	9	11	20	5	14	0	3	11	3	42	3.0	9
Ray Tolbert‡	25	259	35	69	.507	19	30	.633	23	32	55	10	39	0	8	21	5	89	3.6	9
Mike Smrek	48	421	44	103	.427	44	66	.667	27	58	85	8	105	3	7	30	42	132	2.8	12
Billy Thompson	9	38	3	13	.231	8	10	.800	2	7	9	1	11	0	1	6	0	14	1.6	4
Jeff Lamp	3	7	0	0	...	2	2	1.000	0	0	0	1	0	0	0	0	0	2	0.7	2

3-pt. FG: L.A. Lakers 142-478 (.297)—Scott 62-179 (.346); Worthy 2-16 (.125); Johnson 11-56 (.196); Abdul-Jabbar 0-1 (.000); M. Thompson 0-3 (.000); Green 0-2 (.000); Campbell 1-3 (.333); Cooper 57-178 (.320); Matthews 7-30 (.233); Wagner 2-10 (.200). Opponents 131-439 (.298).

MILWAUKEE BUCKS

	G	Min.	FGM	FGA	Pct.	FTM	FTA	Pct.	Off.	Def.	Tot.	Ast.	PF	Dq.	Stl.	TO	Blk.	Pts.	Avg.	Hi.
Terry Cummings	76	2629	675	1392	.485	270	406	.665	184	369	553	181	274	6	78	170	46	1621	21.3	36
Jack Sikma	82	2923	514	1058	.486	321	348	.922	195	514	709	279	316	11	93	157	80	1352	16.5	35
Ricky Pierce	37	965	248	486	.510	107	122	.877	30	53	83	73	94	0	21	57	7	606	16.4	29
Paul Pressey	75	2484	345	702	.491	285	357	.798	130	245	375	523	233	6	112	198	34	983	13.1	25
Randy Breuer	81	2258	390	788	.495	188	286	.657	191	360	551	103	198	3	46	107	107	968	12.0	33
Sidney Moncrief	56	1428	217	444	.489	164	196	.837	58	122	180	204	109	0	41	86	14	603	10.8	24
John Lucas	81	1766	281	631	.445	130	162	.802	29	130	159	392	102	1	88	125	3	743	9.2	25
Craig Hodges	43	983	155	345	.449	32	39	.821	12	34	46	109	80	1	30	49	0	397	9.2	22
Jerry Reynolds	62	1161	188	419	.449	119	154	.773	70	90	160	104	97	0	74	104	32	498	8.0	21
Larry Krystkowiak	50	1050	128	266	.481	103	127	.811	88	143	231	50	137	0	18	57	8	359	7.2	23
Paul Mokeski	60	848	100	210	.476	51	72	.708	70	151	221	22	194	5	27	49	27	251	4.2	14
Dave Hoppen*	3	35	4	11	.364	3	3	1.000	4	3	7	2	3	0	0	2	0	11	3.7	5
Pace Mannion	35	477	48	118	.407	25	37	.676	17	34	51	55	53	0	13	24	7	123	3.5	12
Jay Humphries†	18	252	20	54	.370	9	14	.643	5	18	23	41	23	0	20	19	1	49	2.7	9
Jay Humphries‡	68	1809	284	538	.528	112	153	.732	49	125	174	395	177	1	81	127	5	683	10.0	26
Charlie Davis*	5	39	6	18	.333	0	0	...	1	2	3	3	4	0	2	5	1	12	2.4	10
Conner Henry*	14	145	13	41	.317	4	7	.571	5	14	19	29	11	0	4	14	1	32	2.3	8
John Stroeder	41	271	29	79	.367	20	30	.667	24	47	71	20	48	0	3	24	12	78	1.9	10
Andre Moore†	3	16	2	3	.667	0	2	.000	1	1	2	1	2	0	0	1	0	4	1.3	2
Andre Moore‡	10	50	9	27	.333	6	8	.750	6	8	14	6	6	0	2	4	1	24	2.4	10
Rickie Winslow	7	45	3	13	.231	1	2	.500	3	4	7	2	9	0	1	4	0	7	1.0	5
Dudley Bradley*	2	5	0	1	.000	0	0	...	0	1	1	1	2	0	0	0	0	0	0.0	0

3-pt. FG: Milwaukee 133-410 (.324)—Cummings 1-3 (.333); Sikma 3-14 (.214); Pierce 3-14 (.214); Pressey 8-39 (.205); Moncrief 5-31 (.161); Hodges* 55-118 (.466); Lucas 51-151 (.338); Reynolds 3-7 (.429); Krystkowiak 0-3 (.000); Mokeski 0-4 (.000); Mannion 2-12 (.167); Humphries† 0-2 (.000); Humphries‡ 3-18 (.167); Davis* 0-2 (.000); Henry* 2-6 (.333); Stroeder 0-2 (.000); Winslow 0-1 (.000); Bradley* 0-1 (.000). Opponents 133-442 (.301).

NEW JERSEY NETS

	G	Min.	FGM	FGA	Pct.	FTM	FTA	Pct.	Off.	Def.	Tot.	Ast.	PF	Dq.	Stl.	TO	Blk.	Pts.	Avg.	Hi.
Buck Williams	70	2637	466	832	.560	346	518	.668	298	536	834	109	266	5	68	189	44	1279	18.3	30
Roy Hinson†	48	1747	330	658	.502	183	227	.806	106	242	348	72	185	3	45	106	72	843	17.6	27
Roy Hinson‡	77	2592	453	930	.487	272	351	.775	159	358	517	99	275	6	69	169	140	1178	15.3	27
Mike Gminski*	34	1194	215	474	.454	143	166	.861	82	238	320	55	78	0	28	83	33	573	16.9	27
Orlando Woolridge	19	622	110	247	.445	92	130	.708	31	60	91	71	73	2	13	48	20	312	16.4	29
Tim McCormick†	47	1513	277	510	.543	108	162	.667	97	226	323	92	159	2	18	76	15	662	14.1	27
Tim McCormick‡	70	2114	348	648	.537	145	215	.674	146	321	467	118	234	3	32	111	23	841	12.0	27
John Bagley	82	2774	393	896	.439	148	180	.822	61	196	257	479	162	0	110	201	10	981	12.0	31
Ben Coleman*	27	657	116	240	.483	65	84	.774	58	115	173	39	110	4	28	72	16	297	11.0	23
Otis Birdsong	67	1882	337	736	.458	47	92	.511	73	94	167	222	143	2	54	129	11	730	10.9	26
Dennis Hopson	61	1365	222	549	.404	131	177	.740	63	80	143	118	145	0	57	119	25	587	9.6	25
Pearl Washington	68	1379	245	547	.448	132	189	.698	54	64	118	206	163	2	91	114	4	633	9.3	27
Dudley Bradley†	63	1432	156	364	.429	74	97	.763	25	101	126	150	170	1	114	88	43	423	6.7	22

	G	Min.	FGM	FGA	Pct.	FTM	FTA	Pct.	Off.	Def.	Tot.	Ast.	PF	Dq.	Stl.	TO	Blk.	Pts.	Avg.	Hi.
									REBOUNDS									**SCORING**		
Dudley Bradley‡	65	1437	156	365	.427	74	97	.763	25	102	127	151	172	1	114	88	43	423	6.5	22
Adrian Branch	20	308	56	134	.418	20	23	.870	20	28	48	16	41	1	16	29	11	133	6.7	20
Dallas Comegys	75	1122	156	363	.430	106	150	.707	54	164	218	65	175	3	36	116	70	418	5.6	21
Jamie Waller	9	91	16	40	.400	10	18	.556	9	4	13	3	13	0	4	11	1	42	4.7	10
Mike O'Koren	4	52	9	16	.563	0	4	.000	1	3	4	2	2	0	3	0	2	18	4.5	8
Kevin McKenna	31	393	43	109	.394	24	25	.960	4	27	31	40	55	1	15	19	2	126	4.1	16
Duane Washington	15	156	18	42	.429	16	20	.800	5	17	22	34	23	0	12	9	0	54	3.6	18
Ricky Wilson*	6	47	7	11	.636	6	11	.545	1	0	1	6	6	0	6	4	0	21	3.5	9
Chris Engler	54	399	36	88	.409	31	35	.886	32	66	98	15	73	1	9	29	6	103	1.9	7
Johnny Moore†	1	10	0	1	.000	0	0	...	1	1	2	1	0	0	0	3	0	0	0.0	0
Johnny Moore‡	5	61	4	10	.400	0	0	...	2	4	6	12	1	0	3	7	0	8	1.6	8

3-pt. FG: New Jersey 137-455 (.301)—Williams 1-1 (1.000); Hinson† 0-1 (.000); Hinson‡ 0-2 (.000); Gminski* 0-2 (.000); Woolridge 0-2 (.000); McCormick† 0-2 (.000); McCormick‡ 0-2 (.000); Bagley 47-161 (.292); Coleman* 0-2 (.000); Birdsong 9-25 (.360); Hopson 12-45 (.267); P. Washington 11-49 (.224); Bradley† 37-101 (.366); Bradley‡ 37-102 (.363); Branch 1-5 (.200); Comegys 0-1 (.000); Waller 0-2 (.000); O'Koren 0-1 (.000); McKenna 16-50 (.320); Du. Washington 2-4 (.500); Wilson* 1-1 (1.000); Moore† 0-1 (.000); Moore‡ 0-1 (.000). Opponents 131-363 (.361).

NEW YORK KNICKERBOCKERS

	G	Min.	FGM	FGA	Pct.	FTM	FTA	Pct.	Off.	Def.	Tot.	Ast.	PF	Dq.	Stl.	TO	Blk.	Pts.	Avg.	Hi.
									REBOUNDS									**SCORING**		
Patrick Ewing	82	2546	656	1183	.555	341	476	.716	245	431	676	125	332	5	104	287	245	1653	20.2	42
Gerald Wilkins	81	2703	591	1324	.446	191	243	.786	106	164	270	326	183	1	90	212	22	1412	17.4	39
Mark Jackson	82	3249	438	1013	.432	206	266	.774	120	276	396	868	244	2	205	258	6	1114	13.6	33
Bill Cartwright	82	1676	287	528	.544	340	426	.798	127	257	384	85	234	4	43	135	43	914	11.1	23
Kenny Walker	82	2139	344	728	.473	138	178	.775	192	197	389	86	290	5	63	83	59	826	10.1	25
Johnny Newman	77	1589	270	620	.435	207	246	.841	87	72	159	62	204	5	72	103	11	773	10.0	29
Sidney Green	82	2049	258	585	.441	126	190	.663	221	421	642	93	318	9	65	148	32	642	7.8	20
Trent Tucker	71	1248	193	455	.424	51	71	.718	32	87	119	117	158	3	53	47	6	506	7.1	18
Pat Cummings	62	946	140	307	.456	59	80	.738	82	153	235	37	143	0	20	65	10	339	5.5	17
Ray Tolbert*	11	177	19	41	.463	9	17	.529	14	21	35	5	25	0	5	10	2	47	4.3	9
Tony White*	12	117	17	46	.370	9	13	.692	1	2	3	10	14	0	1	13	0	43	3.6	10
Chris McNealy	19	265	23	74	.311	21	31	.677	24	40	64	23	50	1	16	17	2	67	3.5	17
Rory Sparrow*	3	52	5	19	.263	0	0	...	1	1	2	5	7	0	4	6	0	10	3.3	6
Rick Carlisle	26	204	29	67	.433	10	11	.909	6	7	13	32	39	1	11	22	4	74	2.8	21
Sedric Toney	21	139	21	48	.438	10	11	.909	3	5	8	24	20	0	9	12	1	57	2.7	11
Billy Donovan	44	364	44	109	.404	17	21	.810	5	20	25	87	33	0	16	42	1	105	2.4	14
Bob Thornton*	7	85	6	19	.316	5	8	.625	5	8	13	4	23	0	2	8	0	17	2.4	6
Gerald Henderson*	6	69	5	14	.357	2	2	1.000	1	9	10	13	14	0	2	8	0	14	2.3	5
Louis Orr	29	180	10	50	.020	8	16	.500	13	21	34	9	27	0	6	14	0	40	1.4	5
Carey Scurry†	4	8	1	2	.500	0	0	...	1	2	3	1	3	0	2	2	1	2	0.5	2
Carey Scurry‡	33	455	55	118	.438	15	27	.692	30	54	84	50	81	0	49	43	23	140	4.2	13

3-pt. FG: New York 179-567 (.316)—Ewing 0-3 (.000); Wilkins 39-129 (.302); Jackson 32-126 (.254); Walker 0-1 (.000); Newman 26-93 (.280); Green 0-2 (.000); Tucker 69-167 (.413); Cummings 0-1 (.000); White* 0-1 (.000); Sparrow* 0-1 (.000); Carlisle 6-17 (.353); Toney 5-14 (.357); Donovan 0-7 (.000); Henderson* 2-4 (.500); Orr 0-1 (.000); Scurry† 0-0; Scurry‡ 3-8 (.375). Opponents 114-375 (.304).

PHILADELPHIA 76ERS

	G	Min.	FGM	FGA	Pct.	FTM	FTA	Pct.	Off.	Def.	Tot.	Ast.	PF	Dq.	Stl.	TO	Blk.	Pts.	Avg.	Hi.
									REBOUNDS									**SCORING**		
Charles Barkley	80	3170	753	1283	.587	714	951	.751	385	566	951	254	278	6	100	304	103	2264	28.3	47
Cliff Robinson	62	2110	483	1041	.464	210	293	.717	116	289	405	131	192	4	79	161	39	1178	19.0	32
Mike Gminski†	47	1767	290	652	.445	212	226	.938	163	331	494	84	98	0	36	94	85	792	16.9	30
Mike Gminski‡	81	2961	505	1126	.448	355	392	.906	245	569	814	139	176	0	64	177	118	1365	16.9	30
Maurice Cheeks	79	2871	428	865	.495	227	275	.825	59	194	253	635	116	0	167	160	22	1086	13.7	25
Roy Hinson*	29	845	123	272	.452	89	124	.718	53	116	169	27	90	3	24	63	68	335	11.6	22
David Wingate	61	1419	218	545	.400	99	132	.750	44	57	101	119	125	0	47	104	22	545	8.9	28
Gerald Henderson†	69	1436	189	439	.431	136	168	.810	26	71	97	218	173	0	67	125	5	581	8.4	18
Gerald Henderson‡	75	1505	194	453	.428	138	170	.812	27	80	107	231	187	0	69	133	5	595	7.9	18
Tim McCormick*	23	601	71	138	.514	37	53	.698	49	95	144	26	75	1	14	35	8	179	7.8	18
Andrew Toney	29	522	72	171	.421	58	72	.806	8	39	47	108	35	0	11	50	6	211	7.3	16
Albert King	72	1593	211	540	.391	78	103	.757	71	145	216	109	219	4	39	93	18	517	7.2	17
Ben Coleman†	43	841	110	213	.516	76	101	.752	58	119	177	23	120	1	15	55	25	296	6.9	16
Ben Coleman‡	70	1498	226	453	.499	141	185	.762	116	234	350	62	230	5	43	127	41	593	8.5	23
Dave Henderson	22	351	47	116	.405	32	47	.681	11	24	35	34	41	0	12	40	5	126	5.7	15
Chris Welp	10	132	18	31	.581	12	18	.667	11	13	24	5	20	0	5	9	5	48	4.8	18
Vincent Askew	14	234	22	74	.297	8	11	.727	6	16	22	33	12	0	10	12	6	52	3.7	9
Mark McNamara	42	581	52	133	.391	48	66	.727	66	91	157	18	67	0	4	26	12	152	3.6	17
Bob Thornton†	41	508	59	111	.532	29	47	.617	41	58	99	11	80	1	9	27	3	147	3.6	13
Bob Thornton‡	48	593	65	130	.500	34	55	.618	46	66	112	15	103	1	11	35	3	164	3.4	13
Steve Colter*	12	152	15	40	.375	7	9	.778	7	11	18	26	20	0	6	11	0	37	3.1	11
Danny Vranes	57	772	53	121	.438	15	35	.429	45	72	117	36	100	0	27	25	33	121	2.1	10

3-pt. FG: Philadelphia 152-471 (.323)—Barkley 44-157 (.280); Robinson 2-9 (.222); Gminski† 0-0; Gminski‡ 0-2 (.000); Cheeks 3-22 (.136); Hinson* 0-1 (.000); Wingate 10-40 (.250); G. Henderson† 67-159 (.421); G. Henderson‡ 69-163 (.423); Toney 9-27 (.333); King 17-49 (.347); Coleman† 0-1 (.000); Coleman‡ 0-3 (.000); D. Henderson 0-1 (.000); Thornton† 0-2 (.000); Thornton‡ 0-2 (.000); Vranes 0-3 (.000). Opponents 143-423 (.338).

PHOENIX SUNS

	G	Min.	FGM	FGA	Pct.	FTM	FTA	Pct.	Off.	Def.	Tot.	Ast.	PF	Dq.	Stl.	TO	Blk.	Pts.	Avg.	Hi.
									REBOUNDS									**SCORING**		
Larry Nance*	40	1477	327	616	.531	187	249	.751	119	275	394	123	152	7	45	106	96	843	21.1	45
Walter Davis	68	1951	488	1031	.473	205	231	.887	32	127	159	278	131	0	86	126	3	1217	17.9	35

	G	Min.	FGM	FGA	Pct.	FTM	FTA	Pct.	Off.	Def.	Tot.	Ast.	PF	Dq.	Stl.	TO	Blk.	Pts.	Avg.	Hi.
Eddie Johnson	73	2177	533	1110	.480	204	240	.850	121	197	318	180	190	0	33	139	9	1294	17.7	43
James Edwards*....	43	1377	254	542	.469	165	260	.635	97	238	335	73	159	2	14	108	32	673	15.7	32
Armon Gilliam...	55	1807	342	720	.475	131	193	.679	134	300	434	72	143	1	58	123	29	815	14.8	25
Jay Humphries*	50	1557	264	484	.545	103	139	.741	44	107	151	354	154	1	61	108	4	634	12.7	26
Kevin Johnson†	28	874	132	285	.463	85	99	.859	26	93	119	244	59	0	43	64	7	352	12.6	31
Kevin Johnson‡	80	1917	275	596	.461	177	211	.839	36	155	191	437	155	1	103	146	24	732	9.2	31
Mark West†	29	915	134	257	.521	75	132	.568	82	160	242	24	107	2	22	82	68	343	11.8	23
Mark West‡	83	2098	316	573	.551	170	285	.596	165	358	523	74	265	4	47	173	147	802	9.7	23
Craig Hodges†	23	462	87	178	.489	27	32	.844	7	25	32	44	38	0	16	28	2	232	10.1	19
Craig Hodges‡	66	1445	242	523	.463	59	71	.831	19	59	78	153	118	1	46	77	2	629	9.5	22
Jeff Hornacek	82	2243	306	605	.506	152	185	.822	71	191	262	540	151	0	107	156	10	781	9.5	21
Tyrone Corbin†	30	591	99	203	.488	33	40	.825	48	82	130	59	53	0	30	38	3	232	7.7	18
Tyrone Corbin‡	84	1739	257	525	.490	110	138	.797	127	223	350	115	181	2	72	104	18	625	7.4	23
Alvan Adams	82	1646	251	506	.496	108	128	.844	118	247	365	183	245	3	82	140	41	611	7.5	18
Mike Sanders*	35	466	82	171	.480	39	53	.736	28	34	62	30	73	0	18	27	4	203	5.8	19
Bernard Thompson	37	566	74	159	.465	43	60	.717	40	36	76	51	75	1	21	21	1	191	5.2	23
James Bailey	65	869	109	241	.452	70	89	.787	73	137	210	42	180	1	17	70	28	288	4.4	12
Bill Martin	10	101	16	51	.314	8	13	.615	9	18	27	6	16	0	5	9	0	40	4.0	10
Winston Crite	29	258	34	68	.500	19	25	.760	27	37	64	15	42	0	5	25	8	87	3.0	13
Ron Moore†	5	34	5	16	.313	4	4	1.000	0	6	6	0	13	0	3	1	0	14	2.8	6
Ron Moore‡	14	59	9	29	.310	6	8	.750	2	6	8	1	21	0	5	4	0	24	1.7	6
Jeff Cook	33	359	14	59	.237	23	28	.821	37	69	106	14	64	1	9	14	8	51	1.5	6

3-pt. FG: Phoenix 118-357 (.331)—Nance* 2-5 (.400); Davis 36-96 (.375); E. Johnson 24-94 (.255); Edwards* 0-1 (.000); Humphries* 3-16 (.188); K. Johnson† 3-15 (.200); K. Johnson‡ 5-24 (.208); West† 0-1 (.000); West‡ 0-1 (.000); Hodges† 31-57 (.544); Hodges‡ 86-175 (.491); Hornacek 17-58 (.293); Corbin† 1-3 (.333); Corbin‡ 1-6 (.167); Adams 1-2 (.500); Sanders* 0-1 (.000); Thompson 0-2 (.000); Bailey 0-4 (.000); Martin 0-1 (.000); Cook 0-1 (.000). Opponents 128-421 (.304).

PORTLAND TRAIL BLAZERS

REBOUNDS · SCORING

	G	Min.	FGM	FGA	Pct.	FTM	FTA	Pct.	Off.	Def.	Tot.	Ast.	PF	Dq.	Stl.	TO	Blk.	Pts.	Avg.	Hi.
Clyde Drexler	81	3060	849	1679	.506	476	587	.811	261	272	533	467	250	2	203	236	52	2185	27.0	42
Kiki Vandeweghe	37	1038	283	557	.508	159	181	.878	36	73	109	71	68	0	21	48	7	747	20.2	41
Jerome Kersey	79	2888	611	1225	.499	291	396	.735	211	446	657	243	302	8	127	161	65	1516	19.2	36
Kevin Duckworth	78	2223	450	907	.496	331	430	.770	224	352	576	66	280	5	31	177	32	1231	15.8	32
Steve Johnson	43	1050	258	488	.529	146	249	.586	84	158	242	57	151	4	17	122	32	662	15.4	36
Terry Porter	82	2991	462	890	.519	274	324	.846	65	313	378	831	204	1	150	244	16	1222	14.9	40
Richard Anderson†	62	1297	160	413	.387	54	72	.750	82	204	286	108	133	1	50	60	16	416	6.7	22
Richard Anderson‡	74	1350	171	439	.390	58	77	.753	91	212	303	112	137	1	51	61	16	448	6.1	22
Maurice Lucas	73	1191	168	373	.450	109	148	.736	101	214	315	94	188	0	33	73	10	445	6.1	18
Jim Paxson*	17	263	43	107	.402	14	18	.778	8	10	18	27	29	0	7	11	1	103	6.1	14
Michael Holton	82	1279	163	353	.462	107	129	.829	50	99	149	211	154	0	41	86	10	436	5.3	18
Caldwell Jones	79	1778	128	263	.487	78	106	.736	105	303	408	81	251	0	29	82	99	334	4.2	14
Jerry Sichting†	28	324	49	90	.544	9	11	.818	4	11	15	33	30	0	7	8	0	115	4.1	14
Jerry Sichting‡	52	694	93	172	.541	17	23	.739	9	27	36	93	60	0	21	22	0	213	4.1	17
Ronnie Murphy	18	89	14	49	.286	7	11	.636	5	6	11	6	14	0	5	8	1	36	2.0	11
Charles Jones	37	186	16	40	.400	19	33	.576	11	20	31	8	28	0	3	12	6	51	1.4	12
Nikita Wilson	15	54	7	23	.304	5	6	.833	2	9	11	3	7	0	0	5	0	19	1.3	3
Kevin Gamble	9	19	0	3	.000	0	0	...	2	1	3	1	2	0	2	2	0	0	0.0	0

3-pt. FG: Portland 117-380 (.308)—Drexler 11-52 (.212); Vandeweghe 22-58 (.379); Kersey 3-15 (.200); S. Johnson 0-1 (.000); Porter 24-69 (.348); Anderson† 42-135 (.311); Anderson‡ 48-150 (.320); Paxson* 3-8 (.375); Lucas 0-3 (.000); Holton 3-15 (.200); Ca. Jones 0-4 (.000); Sichting† 8-14 (.571); Sichting‡ 10-22 (.455); Murphy 1-4 (.250); Ch. Jones 0-1 (.000); Gamble 0-1 (.000). Opponents 141-462 (.305).

SACRAMENTO KINGS

REBOUNDS · SCORING

	G	Min.	FGM	FGA	Pct.	FTM	FTA	Pct.	Off.	Def.	Tot.	Ast.	PF	Dq.	Stl.	TO	Blk.	Pts.	Avg.	Hi.
Reggie Theus	73	2653	619	1318	.470	320	385	.831	72	160	232	463	173	0	59	234	16	1574	21.6	36
Otis Thorpe	82	3072	622	1226	.507	460	609	.755	279	558	837	266	264	3	62	228	56	1704	20.8	35
Mike McGee†	37	886	201	478	.421	74	96	.771	51	61	112	58	75	0	47	58	6	524	14.2	30
Mike McGee‡	48	1003	223	530	.421	76	102	.745	55	73	128	71	81	0	52	65	6	575	12.0	30
Kenny Smith	61	2170	331	694	.477	167	204	.819	40	98	138	434	140	1	92	184	8	841	13.8	30
Derek Smith	35	899	174	364	.478	87	113	.770	35	68	103	89	108	2	21	48	17	443	12.7	30
Joe Kleine	82	1999	324	686	.472	153	188	.814	179	400	579	93	228	1	28	107	59	801	9.8	23
Harold Pressley	80	2029	318	702	.453	130	164	.792	139	230	369	185	211	4	84	135	55	775	9.7	31
Franklin Edwards	16	414	54	115	.470	24	32	.750	4	15	19	92	10	0	10	47	1	132	8.3	19
LaSalle Thompson	69	1257	215	456	.471	118	164	.720	138	289	427	68	217	1	54	109	73	550	8.0	20
Conner Henry†	15	207	38	81	.469	26	30	.867	6	14	20	26	15	0	7	16	3	117	7.8	21
Conner Henry‡	39	433	62	150	.413	39	47	.830	13	36	49	67	37	0	12	39	5	183	4.7	21
Ed Pinckney	79	1177	179	343	.522	133	178	.747	94	136	230	66	118	0	39	77	32	491	6.2	24
Terry Tyler	74	1185	184	407	.452	41	64	.641	87	155	242	56	85	0	43	43	47	410	5.5	18
Jawann Oldham	54	946	119	250	.476	59	87	.678	82	222	304	33	143	2	12	62	110	297	5.5	19
Joe Arlauckas	9	85	14	43	.326	6	8	.750	6	7	13	8	16	0	3	4	4	34	3.8	17
Michael Jackson	58	760	64	171	.374	23	32	.719	17	42	59	179	81	0	20	58	5	157	2.7	11
Martin Nessley†	9	41	2	3	.667	1	4	.250	3	6	9	0	11	0	1	2	1	5	0.6	2
Martin Nessley‡	44	336	20	52	.385	8	18	.444	23	59	82	16	89	1	8	23	12	48	1.1	5

3-pt. FG: Sacramento 144-450 (.320)—Theus 16-59 (.271); Thorpe 0-6 (.000); McGee† 48-141 (.340); McGee‡ 53-160 (.331); K. Smith 12-39 (.308); D. Smith 8-23 (.348); Pressley 36-110 (.327); Edwards 0-2 (.000); Thompson 2-5 (.400); Henry† 15-31 (.484); Henry‡ 20-45 (.444); Pinckney 0-2 (.000); Tyler 1-7 (.143); Jackson 6-25 (.240). Opponents 120-370 (.324).

1987-88

SAN ANTONIO SPURS

	G	Min.	FGM	FGA	Pct.	FTM	FTA	Pct.	Off.	Def.	Tot.	Ast.	PF	Dq.	Stl.	TO	Blk.	Pts.	Avg.	Hi.
Alvin Robertson	82	2978	655	1408	.465	273	365	.748	165	333	498	557	300	4	243	251	69	1610	19.6	40
Walter Berry	73	1922	540	960	.563	192	320	.600	176	219	395	110	207	2	55	162	63	1272	17.4	31
Frank Brickowski...	70	2227	425	805	.528	268	349	.768	167	316	483	266	275	11	74	207	36	1119	16.0	34
Johnny Dawkins	65	2179	405	835	.485	198	221	.896	66	138	204	480	95	0	88	154	2	1027	15.8	30
Mike Mitchell	68	1501	378	784	.482	160	194	.825	54	144	198	68	101	0	31	52	13	919	13.5	36
Greg Anderson	82	1984	379	756	.501	198	328	.604	161	352	513	79	228	1	54	143	122	957	11.7	31
Leon Wood*	38	830	120	282	.426	69	91	.758	16	35	51	155	44	0	22	34	1	352	9.3	27
David Greenwood ...	45	1236	151	328	.460	83	111	.748	92	208	300	97	134	2	33	74	22	385	8.6	23
Jon Sundvold	52	1024	176	379	.464	43	48	.896	14	34	48	183	54	0	27	57	2	421	8.1	25
Ricky Wilson†	18	373	36	99	.364	23	29	.793	1	25	26	63	34	0	17	21	3	104	5.8	14
Ricky Wilson‡	24	420	43	110	.391	29	40	.725	2	25	27	69	40	0	23	25	3	125	5.2	14
Charlie Davis†	16	187	42	97	.433	7	10	.700	15	23	38	17	25	0	0	13	3	92	5.8	14
Charlie Davis‡	21	226	48	115	.417	7	10	.700	16	25	41	20	29	0	2	18	4	104	5.0	14
Petur Gudmundsson .	69	1017	139	280	.496	117	145	.807	93	230	323	86	197	5	18	103	61	395	5.7	21
Pete Myers	22	328	43	95	.453	26	39	.667	11	26	37	48	30	0	17	33	6	112	5.1	13
Kurt Nimphius......	72	919	128	257	.498	60	83	.723	62	91	153	53	141	2	22	49	56	316	4.4	25
Richard Rellford	4	42	5	8	.625	6	8	.750	2	5	7	1	3	0	0	4	3	16	4.0	8
Phil Zevenbergen ...	8	58	15	27	.556	0	2	.000	4	9	13	3	12	0	3	4	1	30	3.8	8
Nate Blackwell......	10	112	15	41	.366	5	6	.833	2	4	6	18	16	0	3	8	0	37	3.7	10
Ed Nealy	68	837	50	109	.459	41	63	.651	82	140	222	49	94	0	29	27	5	142	2.1	14
Johnny Moore*	4	51	4	9	.444	0	0	....	1	3	4	11	1	0	3	4	0	8	2.0	8

3-pt. FG: San Antonio 133-412 (.323)—Robertson 27-95 (.284); Brickowski 1-5 (.200); Dawkins 19-61 (.311); Mitchell 3-12 (.250); Anderson 1-5 (.200); Wood* 43-108 (.398); Greenwood 0-2 (.000); Sundvold 26-64 (.406); Wilson† 9-25 (.360); Wilson‡ 10-26 (.385); Davis† 1-15 (.067); Davis‡ 1-17 (.059); Gudmundsson 0-1 (.000); Myers 0-4 (.000); Nimphius 0-1 (.000); Blackwell 2-11 (.182); Nealy 1-2 (.500); Moore* 0-1 (.000). Opponents 157-450 (.349).

SEATTLE SUPERSONICS

	G	Min.	FGM	FGA	Pct.	FTM	FTA	Pct.	Off.	Def.	Tot.	Ast.	PF	Dq.	Stl.	TO	Blk.	Pts.	Avg.	Hi.
Dale Ellis..........	75	2790	764	1519	.503	303	395	.767	167	173	340	197	221	1	74	172	11	1938	25.8	47
Xavier McDaniel	78	2703	687	1407	.488	281	393	.715	206	312	518	263	230	2	96	223	52	1669	21.4	41
Tom Chambers	82	2680	611	1364	.448	419	519	.807	135	355	490	212	297	4	87	209	53	1674	20.4	46
Derrick McKey	82	1706	255	519	.491	173	224	.772	115	213	328	107	237	3	70	108	63	694	8.5	20
Nate McMillan.....	82	2453	235	496	.474	145	205	.707	117	221	338	702	238	1	169	189	47	624	7.6	21
Sedale Threatt†	26	354	84	162	.519	25	30	.833	11	22	33	53	29	0	33	19	5	194	7.5	31
Sedale Threatt‡....	71	1055	216	425	.508	57	71	.803	23	65	88	160	100	0	60	63	8	492	6.9	31
Kevin Williams	80	1084	199	450	.442	103	122	.844	61	66	127	96	207	1	62	68	7	502	6.3	21
Russ Schoene......	81	973	208	454	.458	51	63	.810	70	120	190	53	151	0	39	57	13	484	6.0	20
Alton Lister........	82	1812	173	343	.504	114	188	.606	200	427	627	58	319	8	27	90	140	461	5.6	19
Sam Vincent*	43	548	72	152	.474	46	60	.767	17	32	49	137	63	0	21	52	4	195	4.5	16
Olden Polynice	82	1080	118	254	.465	101	158	.639	122	208	330	33	215	1	32	81	26	337	4.1	15
Danny Young	77	949	89	218	.408	43	53	.811	18	57	75	218	69	0	52	37	2	243	3.2	13
Clemon Johnson.....	74	723	49	105	.467	22	32	.688	66	108	174	17	104	0	13	29	24	120	1.6	8

3-pt. FG: Seattle 221-638 (.346)—Ellis 107-259 (.413); McDaniel 14-50 (.280); Chambers 33-109 (.303); McKey 11-30 (.367); McMillan 9-24 (.375); Threatt† 1-7 (.143); Threatt‡ 3-27 (.111); Williams 1-7 (.143); Schoene 17-58 (.293); Lister 1-2 (.500); Vincent* 5-13 (.385); Polynice 0-2 (.000); Young 22-77 (.286). Opponents 130-400 (.325).

UTAH JAZZ

	G	Min.	FGM	FGA	Pct.	FTM	FTA	Pct.	Off.	Def.	Tot.	Ast.	PF	Dq.	Stl.	TO	Blk.	Pts.	Avg.	Hi.
Karl Malone	82	3198	858	1650	.520	552	789	.700	277	709	986	199	296	2	117	325	50	2268	27.7	41
Thurl Bailey.........	82	2804	633	1286	.492	337	408	.826	134	397	531	158	186	1	49	190	125	1604	19.6	41
John Stockton......	82	2842	454	791	.574	272	324	.840	54	183	237	1128	247	5	242	262	16	1204	14.7	27
Darrell Griffith......	52	1052	251	585	.429	59	92	.641	36	91	127	91	102	0	52	67	5	589	11.3	32
Bobby Hansen......	81	1796	316	611	.517	113	152	.743	64	123	187	175	193	2	65	91	5	777	9.6	28
Kelly Tripucka	49	976	139	303	.459	59	68	.868	30	87	117	105	68	1	34	68	4	368	7.5	25
Mark Eaton.........	82	2731	226	541	.418	119	191	.623	230	487	717	55	320	8	41	131	304	571	7.0	16
Mel Turpin	79	1401	199	389	.512	71	98	.724	88	148	236	32	157	2	26	71	68	470	5.9	22
Rickey Green	81	1116	157	370	.424	75	83	.904	14	66	80	300	83	0	57	94	1	393	4.9	18
Carey Scurry*	29	447	54	116	.466	27	39	.692	29	52	81	49	78	0	47	41	22	138	4.8	13
Marc Iavaroni	81	1238	143	308	.464	78	99	.788	94	174	268	67	162	1	23	83	25	364	4.5	17
Scott Roth	26	201	30	74	.405	22	30	.733	7	21	28	16	37	0	12	11	0	84	3.2	12
Eddie Hughes	11	42	5	13	.385	6	6	1.000	3	1	4	8	5	0	0	6	0	17	1.5	6
Darryl Dawkins*	4	26	1	7	.143	4	12	.333	2	3	5	1	10	0	0	4	1	6	1.5	3
Bart Kofoed.......	36	225	18	48	.375	8	13	.615	4	11	15	23	42	0	6	18	1	46	1.3	8

3-pt. FG: Utah 129-404 (.319)—Malone 0-5 (.000); Bailey 1-3 (.333); Stockton 24-67 (.358); Griffith 28-102 (.275); Hansen 32-97 (.330); Tripucka 31-74 (.419); Turpin 1-3 (.333); Green 4-19 (.211); Scurry* 3-8 (.375); Iavaroni 0-2 (.000); Roth 2-11 (.182); Hughes 1-6 (.167); Kofoed 2-7 (.286). Opponents 146-464 (.315).

WASHINGTON BULLETS

	G	Min.	FGM	FGA	Pct.	FTM	FTA	Pct.	Off.	Def.	Tot.	Ast.	PF	Dq.	Stl.	TO	Blk.	Pts.	Avg.	Hi.
Jeff Malone........	80	2655	648	1360	.476	335	380	.882	44	162	206	237	198	1	51	172	13	1641	20.5	47
Moses Malone	79	2692	531	1090	.487	543	689	.788	372	512	884	112	160	0	59	249	72	1607	20.3	36
Bernard King.......	69	2044	470	938	.501	247	324	.762	86	194	280	192	202	3	49	211	10	1188	17.2	34
John Williams......	82	2428	427	910	.469	188	256	.734	127	317	444	232	217	3	117	145	34	1047	12.8	28
Terry Catledge......	70	1610	296	585	.506	154	235	.655	180	217	397	63	172	0	33	101	9	746	10.7	27
Steve Colter†	56	1361	188	401	.469	86	109	.791	51	104	155	235	112	0	56	77	14	447	8.0	29
Steve Colter‡	68	1513	203	441	.460	75	95	.789	58	115	173	261	132	0	62	88	14	484	7.1	29

1987-88

	G	Min.	FGM	FGA	Pct.	FTM	FTA	Pct.	Off.	Def.	Tot.	Ast.	PF	Dq.	Stl.	TO	Blk.	Pts.	Avg.	Hi.
									REBOUNDS									SCORING		
Frank Johnson	75	1258	216	498	.434	121	149	.812	39	82	121	188	120	0	70	99	4	554	7.4	23
Darrell Walker	52	940	114	291	.392	82	105	.781	43	84	127	100	105	2	62	69	10	310	6.0	20
Mark Alarie	63	769	144	300	.480	35	49	.714	70	90	160	39	107	1	10	50	12	327	5.2	18
Muggsy Bogues	79	1628	166	426	.390	58	74	.784	35	101	136	404	138	1	127	101	3	393	5.0	16
Charles Jones	69	1313	72	177	.407	53	75	.707	106	219	325	59	226	5	53	57	113	197	2.9	11
Manute Bol	77	1136	75	165	.455	26	49	.531	72	203	275	13	160	0	11	35	208	176	2.3	13
Jay Murphy	9	46	8	23	.348	4	5	.800	4	12	16	1	5	0	0	5	0	20	2.2	5

3-pt. FG: Washington 29-138 (.210)—J. Malone 10-24 (.417); M. Malone 2-7 (.286); King 1-6 (.167); Williams 5-38 (.132); Catledge 0-2 (.000); Colter† 3-10 (.300); Colter‡ 3-10 (.300); Johnson 1-9 (.111); Walker 0-6 (.000); Alarie 4-18 (.222); Bogues 3-16 (.188); Jones 0-1 (.000); Bol 0-1 (.000). Opponents 128-390 (.328).

* Finished season with another team. † Totals with this team only. ‡ Totals with all teams.

PLAYOFF RESULTS

EASTERN CONFERENCE

FIRST ROUND

Boston 3, New York 1
Apr. 29—Fri.	New York 92 at Boston	112
May 1—Sun.	New York 102 at Boston	128
May 4—Wed.	Boston 100 at New York	109
May 6—Fri.	Boston 102 at New York	94

Detroit 3, Washington 2
Apr. 28—Thur.	Washington 87 at Detroit	96
Apr. 30—Sat.	Washington 101 at Detroit	102
May 2—Mon.	Detroit 106 at Washington	*114
May 4—Wed.	Detroit 103 at Washington	106
May 8—Sun.	Washington 78 at Detroit	99

Chicago 3, Cleveland 2
Apr. 28—Thur.	Cleveland 93 at Chicago	104
May 1—Sun.	Cleveland 101 at Chicago	106
May 3—Tue.	Chicago 102 at Cleveland	110
May 5—Thur.	Chicago 91 at Cleveland	97
May 8—Sun.	Cleveland 101 at Chicago	107

Atlanta 3, Milwaukee 2
Apr. 29—Fri.	Milwaukee 107 at Atlanta	110
May 1—Sun.	Milwaukee 97 at Atlanta	104
May 4—Wed.	Atlanta 115 at Milwaukee	123
May 6—Fri.	Atlanta 99 at Milwaukee	105
May 8—Sun.	Milwaukee 111 at Atlanta	121

SEMIFINALS

Boston 4, Atlanta 3
May 11—Wed.	Atlanta 101 at Boston	110
May 13—Fri.	Atlanta 97 at Boston	108
May 15—Sun.	Boston 92 at Atlanta	110
May 16—Mon.	Boston 109 at Atlanta	118
May 18—Wed.	Atlanta 112 at Boston	104
May 20—Fri.	Boston 102 at Atlanta	100
May 22—Sun.	Atlanta 116 at Boston	118

Detroit 4, Chicago 1
May 10—Tue.	Chicago 82 at Detroit	93
May 12—Thur.	Chicago 105 at Detroit	95
May 14—Sat.	Detroit 101 at Chicago	79
May 15—Sun.	Detroit 96 at Chicago	77
May 18—Wed.	Chicago 95 at Detroit	102

FINALS

Detroit 4, Boston 2
May 25—Wed.	Detroit 104 at Boston	96
May 26—Thur.	Detroit 115 at Boston	**119
May 28—Sat.	Boston 94 at Detroit	98
May 30—Mon.	Boston 79 at Detroit	78
June 1—Wed.	Detroit 102 at Boston	*96
June 3—Fri.	Boston 90 at Detroit	95

WESTERN CONFERENCE

FIRST ROUND

L.A. Lakers 3, San Antonio 0
Apr. 29—Fri.	San Antonio 110 at L.A. Lakers	122
May 1—Sun.	San Antonio 112 at L.A. Lakers	130
May 3—Tue.	L.A. Lakers 109 at San Antonio	107

Denver 3, Seattle 2
Apr. 29—Fri.	Seattle 123 at Denver	126
May 1—Sun.	Seattle 111 at Denver	91
May 3—Tue.	Denver 125 at Seattle	114
May 5—Thur.	Denver 117 at Seattle	127
May 7—Sat.	Seattle 96 at Denver	115

Dallas 3, Houston 1
Apr. 28—Thur.	Houston 110 at Dallas	120
Apr. 30—Sat.	Houston 119 at Dallas	108
May 3—Tue.	Dallas 93 at Houston	92
May 5—Thur.	Dallas 107 at Houston	97

Utah 3, Portland 1
Apr. 28—Thur.	Utah 96 at Portland	108
Apr. 30—Sat.	Utah 114 at Portland	105
May 4—Wed.	Portland 108 at Utah	113
May 6—Fri.	Portland 96 at Utah	111

SEMIFINALS

L.A. Lakers 4, Utah 3
May 8—Sun.	Utah 91 at L.A. Lakers	110
May 10—Tue.	Utah 101 at L.A. Lakers	97
May 13—Fri.	L.A. Lakers 89 at Utah	96
May 15—Sun.	L.A. Lakers 113 at Utah	100
May 17—Sun.	Utah 109 at L.A. Lakers	111
May 19—Thur.	L.A. Lakers 80 at Utah	108
May 21—Sat.	Utah 98 at L.A. Lakers	109

Dallas 4, Denver 2
May 10—Tue.	Dallas 115 at Denver	126
May 12—Thur.	Dallas 112 at Denver	108
May 14—Sat.	Denver 107 at Dallas	105
May 15—Sun.	Denver 103 at Dallas	124
May 17—Sun.	Dallas 110 at Denver	106
May 19—Thur.	Denver 95 at Dallas	108

FINALS

L.A. Lakers 4, Dallas 3
May 23—Mon.	Dallas 98 at L.A. Lakers	113
May 25—Wed.	Dallas 101 at L.A. Lakers	123
May 27—Fri.	L.A. Lakers 94 at Dallas	106
May 29—Sun.	L.A. Lakers 104 at Dallas	118
May 31—Tue.	Dallas 102 at L.A. Lakers	119
June 2—Thur.	L.A. Lakers 103 at Dallas	105
June 4—Sat.	Dallas 102 at L.A. Lakers	117

NBA FINALS

L.A. Lakers 4, Detroit 3
June 7—Tue.	Detroit 105 at L.A. Lakers	93
June 9—Thur.	Detroit 96 at L.A. Lakers	108
June 12—Sun.	L.A. Lakers 99 at Detroit	86
June 14—Tue.	L.A. Lakers 86 at Detroit	111
June 16—Thur.	L.A. Lakers 94 at Detroit	104
June 19—Sun.	Detroit 102 at L.A. Lakers	103
June 21—Tue.	Detroit 105 at L.A. Lakers	108

*Denotes number of overtime periods.

1987-88

1986-87

1986-87 NBA CHAMPION LOS ANGELES LAKERS
Front row (from left): owner Jerry Buss, Kurt Rambis, James Worthy, Kareem Abdul-Jabbar, Michael Cooper, Byron Scott, Magic Johnson, assistant coach Bill Bertka. Back row (from left): head coach Pat Riley, Wes Matthews, Billy Thompson, A.C. Green, Mike Smrek, Mychal Thompson, Adrian Branch, assistant coach Randy Pfund, trainer Gary Vitti.

FINAL STANDINGS

ATLANTIC DIVISION

	Atl.	Bos.	Chi.	Cle.	Dal.	Den.	Det.	G.S.	Hou.	Ind.	L.A.C.	L.A.L.	Mil.	N.J.	N.Y.	Phi.	Pho.	Por.	Sac	S.A.	Sea.	Uta.	Was.	W	L	Pct.	GB
Boston	3	..	6	3	2	2	3	2	2	5	2	0	3	4	4	3	2	2	2	2	2	1	4	59	23	.720	..
Philadelphia	3	3	3	4	0	2	0	1	2	4	2	0	3	3	3	..	1	2	2	1	2	1	3	45	37	.549	14
Washington	0	2	3	4	1	1	3	2	1	2	2	1	1	4	4	3	2	1	1	2	1	1	..	42	40	.512	17
New York	1	2	2	1	0	0	0	0	1	2	2	0	2	1	..	3	1	0	2	1	0	1	2	24	58	.293	35
New Jersey	0	2	2	2	0	0	1	0	1	1	1	0	2	..	5	3	1	0	0	0	0	1	2	24	58	.293	35

CENTRAL DIVISION

	Atl.	Bos.	Chi.	Cle.	Dal.	Den.	Det.	G.S.	Hou.	Ind.	L.A.C.	L.A.L.	Mil.	N.J.	N.Y.	Phi.	Pho.	Por.	Sac	S.A.	Sea.	Uta.	Was.	W	L	Pct.	GB
Atlanta	..	3	4	4	2	2	3	1	1	3	2	1	3	5	5	3	1	1	2	2	2	2	5	57	25	.695	..
Detroit	3	2	3	5	1	2	..	1	1	3	2	1	3	5	6	5	1	0	1	1	2	1	3	52	30	.634	5
Milwaukee	3	3	2	5	0	1	3	2	2	4	2	1	..	4	4	2	2	0	2	1	2	1	4	50	32	.610	7
Indiana	3	1	2	3	2	1	3	2	0	..	2	0	2	5	3	2	1	0	1	2	1	1	4	41	41	.500	16
Chicago	2	0	..	5	1	1	3	0	0	3	2	0	4	3	4	3	1	1	1	2	0	3	0	40	42	.488	17
Cleveland	2	2	1	..	0	1	1	1	0	3	2	0	1	4	4	2	1	1	1	1	1	0	2	31	51	.378	26

MIDWEST DIVISION

	Atl.	Bos.	Chi.	Cle.	Dal.	Den.	Det.	G.S.	Hou.	Ind.	L.A.C.	L.A.L.	Mil.	N.J.	N.Y.	Phi.	Pho.	Por.	Sac	S.A.	Sea.	Uta.	Was.	W	L	Pct.	GB
Dallas	0	0	1	2	..	4	1	5	3	0	5	3	2	2	2	2	3	2	5	4	5	3	1	55	27	.671	..
Utah	0	1	2	2	3	4	1	3	3	1	3	2	1	1	1	1	1	2	5	4	2	..	1	44	38	.537	11
Houston	1	0	1	2	3	3	1	1	..	2	4	1	0	1	1	0	3	2	5	5	1	3	1	42	40	.512	13
Denver	0	0	1	1	2	..	0	4	3	1	2	0	1	2	2	0	3	3	2	5	2	2	1	37	45	.451	18
Sacramento	0	0	1	1	1	4	1	1	1	1	4	0	0	2	0	0	3	2	..	3	2	1	1	29	53	.354	26
San Antonio	0	0	1	1	2	1	1	1	1	0	4	1	1	1	2	1	3	1	3	..	1	2	0	28	54	.341	27

PACIFIC DIVISION

	Atl.	Bos.	Chi.	Cle.	Dal.	Den.	Det.	G.S.	Hou.	Ind.	L.A.C.	L.A.L.	Mil.	N.J.	N.Y.	Phi.	Pho.	Por.	Sac	S.A.	Sea.	Uta.	Was.	W	L	Pct.	GB
L.A. Lakers	1	2	2	2	5	1	4	4	2	6		..	1	2	2	2	5	5	5	4	4	3	1	65	17	.793	..
Portland	1	0	1	1	3	2	2	2	3	2	6	1	2	2	2	0	4	..	3	4	4	3	1	49	33	.598	16
Golden State	1	0	2	1	0	1	1	..	4	0	6	2	0	2	2	1	1	4	4	4	2	0		42	40	.512	23
Seattle	0	0	0	1	3	0	2	4	1	4	2	0	2	2	0	0	5	2	3	4	..	3	1	39	43	.476	26
Phoenix	1	0	1	1	2	2	1	5	2	1	5	1	0	1	1	1	..	2	2	2	1	4	0	36	46	.439	29
L.A. Clippers	0	0	0	0	0	3	0	0	1	0	..	0	0	1	0	0	1	0	1	1	2	2	0	12	70	.146	53

OFFENSIVE

	G	FGM	FGA	Pct.	FTM	FTA	Pct.	REBOUNDS Off.	Def.	Tot.	Ast.	PF	Dq.	Stl.	TO	Blk.	SCORING Pts.	Avg.
Portland	82	3650	7249	.504	2269	2928	.775	1180	2413	3593	2359	2082	37	767	1546	387	9667	117.9
L.A. Lakers	82	3740	7245	.516	2012	2550	.789	1127	2515	3642	2428	1853	11	728	1358	482	9656	117.8
Dallas	82	3594	7373	.487	2148	2717	.791	1219	2494	3713	2017	1873	15	688	1205	424	9567	116.7
Denver	82	3744	7951	.471	1975	2568	.769	1294	2368	3662	2317	2184	22	754	1216	421	9569	116.7
Seattle	82	3593	7451	.482	1948	2571	.758	1373	2395	3768	2184	2224	33	705	1509	450	9325	113.7
Boston	82	3645	7051	.517	1740	2153	.808	933	2585	3518	2421	1710	15	561	1300	526	9237	112.6
Golden State	82	3551	7412	.479	1970	2526	.780	1193	2351	3544	2083	2138	18	715	1354	321	9188	112.0
Detroit	82	3544	7237	.490	1991	2602	.765	1245	2649	3894	2021	2078	21	643	1417	436	9118	111.2
Phoenix	82	3575	7190	.497	1900	2499	.760	1113	2366	3479	2354	2047	15	703	1498	397	9111	111.1
Sacramento	82	3522	7413	.475	1974	2479	.796	1282	2441	3723	2185	2007	31	513	1403	397	9095	110.9
Milwaukee	82	3457	7282	.475	1953	2549	.766	1119	2322	3441	2044	2180	35	845	1260	393	9052	110.4
Atlanta	82	3435	7141	.481	2019	2661	.759	1350	2478	3828	2077	2152	19	700	1279	511	9024	110.0
New Jersey	82	3374	7083	.476	2000	2607	.767	1169	2409	3578	1991	2353	56	643	1617	397	8893	108.5
San Antonio	82	3532	7456	.474	1701	2292	.742	1285	2347	3632	2220	1930	12	786	1406	325	8882	108.3
Utah	82	3485	7514	.464	1735	2389	.726	1194	2456	3650	2240	2040	13	835	1403	628	8844	107.9
Houston	82	3465	7262	.477	1746	2355	.741	1190	2481	3671	2227	1973	28	654	1384	555	8765	106.9
Philadelphia	82	3335	6792	.491	1977	2617	.753	1178	2327	3505	1943	1774	15	768	1519	540	8729	106.5
Indiana	82	3454	7324	.472	1696	2170	.782	1132	2464	3596	2170	2097	36	697	1276	311	8698	106.1
Washington	82	3356	7397	.454	1935	2531	.765	1305	2315	3620	1750	1775	5	755	1301	685	8690	106.0
Chicago	82	3382	7155	.473	1754	2254	.778	1248	2400	3648	2143	1922	16	677	1257	438	8596	104.8
L.A. Clippers	82	3311	7332	.452	1866	2515	.742	1231	2137	3368	1971	2004	30	751	1493	432	8566	104.5
Cleveland	82	3349	7122	.470	1779	2554	.697	1257	2420	3677	1912	1853	20	672	1619	559	8558	104.4
New York	82	3329	7023	.474	1725	2362	.730	1108	2162	3270	1941	2028	21	704	1420	396	8508	103.8

DEFENSIVE

	FGM	FGA	Pct.	FTM	FTA	Pct.	REBOUNDS Off.	Def.	Tot.	Ast.	PF	Dq.	Stl.	TO	Blk.	SCORING Pts.	Avg.	Dif.
Atlanta	3158	6998	.451	1987	2598	.765	1196	2277	3473	1917	2034	21	619	1314	385	8431	102.8	+7.2
Chicago	3337	6910	.483	1734	2255	.769	1027	2317	3344	2028	1844	20	583	1269	492	8523	103.9	+0.9
Houston	3348	7225	.463	1887	2422	.779	1167	2364	3531	2126	1922	13	721	1366	368	8683	105.9	+1.0
Boston	3470	7500	.463	1628	2148	.758	1237	2287	3524	2060	1911	14	722	1156	338	8692	106.0	+6.6
Milwaukee	3247	6906	.470	2117	2796	.757	1191	2477	3668	2014	2024	27	659	1551	460	8731	106.5	+3.9
Philadelphia	3537	7204	.491	1552	2049	.757	1214	2202	3416	2202	1982	30	813	1372	446	8745	106.6	-0.1
Indiana	3344	6969	.480	1960	2584	.759	1117	2584	3701	2019	1852	14	660	1416	472	8751	106.7	-0.6
Washington	3522	7453	.473	1654	2183	.758	1334	2483	3817	2144	1938	14	699	1439	548	8802	107.3	-1.3
Utah	3347	7338	.456	1974	2564	.770	1310	2637	3947	2011	1992	22	718	1579	457	8811	107.5	+0.4
Detroit	3376	7307	.462	1951	2608	.748	1143	2339	3482	2029	2067	28	670	1294	472	8836	107.8	+3.4
Cleveland	3556	7441	.478	1664	2209	.753	1254	2396	3650	2056	2076	23	810	1398	479	8817	108.2	-3.8
L.A. Lakers	3520	7531	.467	1731	2265	.764	1280	2174	3454	2212	2004	16	721	1370	404	8893	108.5	+9.3
New York	3500	7142	.490	1928	2534	.761	1331	2448	3779	2152	1950	19	761	1417	400	9022	110.0	-6.2
Dallas	3586	7503	.478	1750	2293	.763	1254	2386	3640	2304	2136	26	571	1332	421	9050	110.4	+6.3
Seattle	3514	7329	.479	2166	2819	.768	1236	2278	3514	2023	2027	23	731	1342	409	9287	113.3	+0.4
San Antonio	3704	7310	.507	1786	2364	.755	1100	2461	3561	2375	1844	16	699	1417	463	9300	113.4	-5.1
Phoenix	3623	7336	.494	1942	2570	.756	1235	2355	3590	2246	2034	20	799	1428	435	9311	113.5	-2.4
New Jersey	3418	7125	.480	2353	3018	.780	1129	2352	3481	1958	2126	33	814	1357	566	9307	113.5	-5.0
Sacramento	3656	7469	.489	1922	2500	.769	1160	2355	3515	2154	2068	21	707	1210	487	9359	114.1	-3.2
Golden State	3615	7339	.493	1995	2665	.749	1249	2481	3730	2174	2052	38	688	1412	450	9380	114.4	-2.4
Portland	3649	7523	.485	1996	2589	.771	1208	2279	3487	2189	2228	42	735	1504	473	9410	114.8	+3.1
L.A. Clippers	3759	7254	.518	1875	2515	.746	1187	2643	3830	2416	2021	19	806	1533	534	9503	115.9	-11.4
Denver	3636	7343	.495	2255	2901	.777	1166	2720	3886	2189	2145	25	558	1564	452	9640	117.6	-0.9
Avgs.	3497	7281	.480	1905	2498	.763	1205	2404	3610	2130	2012	23	707	1393	453	9015	109.9	...

HOME/ROAD

	Home	Road	Total		Home	Road	Total
Atlanta	35-6	22-19	57-25	Milwaukee	32-9	18-23	50-32
Boston	39-2	20-21	59-23	New Jersey	19-22	5-36	24-58
Chicago	29-12	11-30	40-42	New York	18-23	6-35	24-58
Cleveland	25-16	6-35	31-51	Philadelphia	28-13	17-24	45-37
Dallas	35-6	20-21	55-27	Phoenix	26-15	10-31	36-46
Denver	27-14	10-31	37-45	Portland	34-7	15-26	49-33
Detroit	32-9	20-21	52-30	Sacramento	20-21	9-32	29-53
Golden State	25-16	17-24	42-40	San Antonio	21-20	7-34	28-54
Houston	25-16	17-24	42-40	Seattle	25-16	14-27	39-43
Indiana	28-13	13-28	41-41	Utah	31-10	13-28	44-38
L.A. Clippers	9-32	3-38	12-70	Washington	27-14	15-26	42-40
L.A. Lakers	37-4	28-13	65-17	Totals	627-316	316-627	943-943

1986-87

INDIVIDUAL LEADERS

POINTS
(minimum 70 games or 1,400 points)

	G	FGM	FTM	Pts.	Avg.		G	FGM	FTM	Pts.	Avg.
Michael Jordan, Chicago	82	1098	833	3041	37.1	Walter Davis, Phoenix	79	779	288	1867	23.6
Dominique Wilkins, Atlanta	79	828	607	2294	29.0	Hakeem Olajuwon, Houston	75	677	400	1755	23.4
Alex English, Denver	82	965	411	2345	28.6	Tom Chambers, Seattle	82	660	535	1909	23.3
Larry Bird, Boston	74	786	414	2076	28.1	Xavier McDaniel, Seattle	82	806	275	1890	23.0
Kiki Vandeweghe, Portland	79	808	467	2122	26.9	Charles Barkley, Philadelphia	68	557	429	1564	23.0
Kevin McHale, Boston	77	790	428	2008	26.1	Ron Harper, Cleveland	82	734	386	1874	22.9
Mark Aguirre, Dallas	80	787	429	2056	25.7	Larry Nance, Phoenix	69	585	381	1552	22.5
Dale Ellis, Seattle	82	785	385	2041	24.9	Jeff Malone, Washington	80	689	376	1758	22.0
Moses Malone, Washington	73	595	570	1760	24.1	Clyde Drexler, Portland	82	707	357	1782	21.7
Magic Johnson, L.A. Lakers	80	683	535	1909	23.9	Karl Malone, Utah	82	728	323	1779	21.7

FIELD GOALS
(minimum 300 made)

	FGM	FGA	Pct.		FGM	FGA	Pct.
Kevin McHale, Boston	790	1307	.604	Buck Williams, New Jersey	521	936	.557
Artis Gilmore, San Antonio	346	580	.597	Robert Parish, Boston	588	1057	.556
Charles Barkley, Philadelphia	557	937	.594	Steve Johnson, Portland	494	889	.556
James Donaldson, Dallas	311	531	.586	Rodney McCray, Houston	432	783	.552
Kareem Abdul-Jabbar, L.A. Lakers	560	993	.564	Larry Nance, Phoenix	585	1062	.551

FREE THROWS
(minimum 125 made)

	FTM	FTA	Pct.
Larry Bird, Boston	414	455	.910
Danny Ainge, Boston	148	165	.897
Bill Laimbeer, Detroit	245	274	.894
Byron Scott, L.A. Lakers	224	251	.892
Craig Hodges, Milwaukee	131	147	.891
John Long, Indiana	219	246	.890
Kiki Vandeweghe, Portland	467	527	.886
Jeff Malone, Washington	376	425	.885
Rolando Blackman, Dallas	419	474	.884
Ricky Pierce, Milwaukee	387	440	.880

STEALS
(minimum 70 games or 125 steals)

	G	No.	Avg.
Alvin Robertson, San Antonio	81	260	3.21
Michael Jordan, Chicago	82	236	2.88
Maurice Cheeks, Philadelphia	68	180	2.65
Ron Harper, Cleveland	82	209	2.55
Clyde Drexler, Portland	82	204	2.49
Fat Lever, Denver	82	201	2.45
Derek Harper, Dallas	77	167	2.17
John Stockton, Utah	82	177	2.16
Doc Rivers, Atlanta	82	171	2.09
Terry Porter, Portland	80	159	1.99

ASSISTS
(minimum 70 games or 400 assists)

	G	No.	Avg.
Magic Johnson, L.A. Lakers	80	977	12.2
Sleepy Floyd, Golden State	82	848	10.3
Isiah Thomas, Detroit	81	813	10.0
Doc Rivers, Atlanta	82	823	10.0
Terry Porter, Portland	80	715	8.9
Reggie Theus, Sacramento	79	692	8.8
Nate McMillan, Seattle	71	583	8.2
John Stockton, Utah	82	670	8.2
Fat Lever, Denver	82	654	8.0
Maurice Cheeks, Philadelphia	68	538	7.9

BLOCKED SHOTS
(minimum 70 games or 100 blocked shots)

	G	No.	Avg.
Mark Eaton, Utah	79	321	4.06
Manute Bol, Washington	82	302	3.68
Hakeem Olajuwon, Houston	75	254	3.39
Benoit Benjamin, L.A. Clippers	72	187	2.60
Alton Lister, Seattle	75	180	2.40
Patrick Ewing, New York	63	147	2.33
Kevin McHale, Boston	77	172	2.23
Larry Nance, Phoenix	69	148	2.14
Roy Hinson, Philadelphia	76	161	2.12
Charles Jones, Washington	79	165	2.09

REBOUNDS
(minimum 70 games or 800 rebounds)

	G	Off.	Def.	Tot.	Avg.
Charles Barkley, Philadelphia	68	390	604	994	14.6
Charles Oakley, Chicago	82	299	775	1074	13.1
Buck Williams, New Jersey	82	322	701	1023	12.5
James Donaldson, Dallas	82	295	678	973	11.9
Bill Laimbeer, Detroit	82	243	712	955	11.6
Michael Cage, L.A. Clippers	80	354	568	922	11.5
Larry Smith, Golden State	80	366	551	917	11.5
Hakeem Olajuwon, Houston	75	315	543	858	11.4
Moses Malone, Washington	73	340	484	824	11.3
Robert Parish, Boston	80	254	597	851	10.6

3-POINT FIELD GOALS
(minimum 25 made)

	FGA	FGM	Pct.
Kiki Vandeweghe, Portland	81	39	.481
Detlef Schrempf, Dallas	69	33	.478
Danny Ainge, Boston	192	85	.443
Byron Scott, L.A. Lakers	149	65	.436
Trent Tucker, New York	161	68	.422
Kevin McKenna, New Jersey	124	52	.419
Larry Bird, Boston	225	90	.400
Michael Cooper, L.A. Lakers	231	89	.385
Sleepy Floyd, Golden State	190	73	.384
Mike McGee, Atlanta	229	86	.376

1986-87

ATLANTA HAWKS

	G	Min.	FGM	FGA	Pct.	FTM	FTA	Pct.	REBOUNDS Off.	Def.	Tot.	Ast.	PF	Dq.	Stl.	TO	Blk.	SCORING Pts.	Avg.	Hi.
Dominique Wilkins ...	79	2969	828	1787	.463	607	742	.818	210	284	494	261	149	0	117	215	51	2294	29.0	57
Kevin Willis........	81	2626	538	1003	.536	227	320	.709	321	528	849	62	313	4	65	173	61	1304	16.1	35
Doc Rivers........	82	2590	342	758	.451	365	441	.828	83	216	299	823	287	5	171	217	30	1053	12.8	27
Randy Wittman....	71	2049	398	792	.503	100	127	.787	30	94	124	211	107	0	39	88	16	900	12.7	30
Mike McGee........	76	1420	311	677	.459	80	137	.584	71	88	159	149	156	1	61	104	2	788	10.4	31
Cliff Levingston........	82	1848	251	496	.506	155	212	.731	219	314	533	40	261	4	48	72	68	657	8.0	19
Spud Webb........	33	532	71	162	.438	80	105	.762	6	54	60	167	65	1	34	70	2	223	6.8	17
John Battle........	64	804	144	315	.457	93	126	.738	16	44	60	124	76	0	29	60	5	381	6.0	27
Jon Koncak........	82	1684	169	352	.480	125	191	.654	153	340	493	31	262	2	52	92	76	463	5.6	15
Tree Rollins........	75	1764	171	313	.546	63	87	.724	155	333	488	22	240	1	43	61	140	405	5.4	14
Antoine Carr........	65	695	134	265	.506	73	103	.709	60	96	156	34	146	1	14	40	48	342	5.3	20
Gus Williams	33	481	53	146	.363	27	40	.675	8	32	40	139	53	0	17	54	5	138	4.2	12
Scott Hastings	40	256	23	68	.338	23	29	.793	16	54	70	13	35	0	10	13	7	71	1.8	7
Cedric Henderson* ..	6	10	2	5	.400	1	1	1.000	2	1	3	0	1	0	0	1	0	5	0.8	3
Mike Wilson†	2	2	0	2	.000	0	0	...	0	0	0	1	1	0	0	1	0	0	0.0	0
Mike Wilson‡	7	45	3	10	.300	2	2	1.000	1	3	4	7	10	0	1	5	0	8	1.1	4

3-pt. FG: Atlanta 135-425 (.318)—Wilkins 31-106 (.292); Willis 1-4 (.250); Rivers 4-21 (.190); Wittman 4-12 (.333); McGee 86-229 (.376); Levingston 0-3 (.000); Webb 1-6 (.167); Battle 0-10 (.000); Koncak 0-1 (.000); Carr 1-3 (.333); Williams 5-18 (.278); Hastings 2-12 (.167). Opponents 128-426 (.300).

BOSTON CELTICS

	G	Min.	FGM	FGA	Pct.	FTM	FTA	Pct.	REBOUNDS Off.	Def.	Tot.	Ast.	PF	Dq.	Stl.	TO	Blk.	SCORING Pts.	Avg.	Hi.
Larry Bird..........	74	3005	786	1497	.525	414	455	.910	124	558	682	566	185	3	135	240	70	2076	28.1	47
Kevin McHale	77	3060	790	1307	.604	428	512	.836	247	516	763	198	240	1	38	197	172	2008	26.1	38
Robert Parish	80	2995	588	1057	.556	227	309	.735	254	597	851	173	266	5	64	191	144	1403	17.5	34
Danny Ainge	71	2499	410	844	.486	148	165	.897	49	193	242	400	189	3	101	141	14	1053	14.8	35
Dennis Johnson	79	2933	423	953	.444	209	251	.833	45	216	261	594	201	0	87	177	38	1062	13.4	27
Jerry Sichting	78	1566	202	398	.508	37	42	.881	22	69	91	187	124	0	40	61	1	448	5.7	20
Fred Roberts........	73	1079	139	270	.515	124	153	.810	54	136	190	62	129	1	22	89	20	402	5.5	23
Darren Daye†	61	724	101	202	.500	34	65	.523	37	87	124	75	98	0	25	56	7	236	3.9	14
Darren Daye‡	62	731	101	202	.500	34	65	.523	37	88	125	76	100	0	25	57	7	236	3.8	14
Sam Vincent	46	374	60	136	.441	51	55	.927	5	22	27	59	33	0	13	33	1	171	3.7	10
Scott Wedman	6	78	9	27	.333	1	2	.500	3	6	9	6	6	0	2	3	2	20	3.3	9
Bill Walton	10	112	10	26	.385	8	15	.533	11	20	31	9	23	0	1	15	10	28	2.8	9
Conner Henry†	36	231	38	103	.369	10	17	.588	7	20	27	27	27	0	6	17	1	98	2.7	12
Conner Henry‡	54	323	46	136	.338	17	27	.630	7	27	34	35	34	0	9	26	1	122	2.3	12
Rick Carlisle	42	297	30	92	.326	15	20	.750	8	22	30	35	28	0	8	25	0	80	1.9	10
Greg Kite	74	745	47	110	.427	29	76	.382	61	108	169	27	148	2	17	34	46	123	1.7	10
David Thirdkill......	17	89	10	24	.417	5	16	.313	5	14	19	2	12	0	2	5	0	25	1.5	10
Andre Turner	3	18	2	5	.400	0	0	...	1	1	2	1	1	0	0	5	0	4	1.3	2

3-pt. FG: Boston 207-565 (.366)—Bird 90-225 (.400); McHale 0-4 (.000); Parish 0-1 (.000); Ainge 85-192 (.443); Johnson 7-62 (.113); Sichting 7-26 (.269); Roberts 0-3 (.000); Wedman 1-2 (.500); Henry† 12-31 (.387); Henry‡ 13-42 (.310); Carlisle 5-16 (.313); Kite 0-1 (.000); Thirdkill 0-1 (.000); Turner 0-1 (.000). Opponents 124-405 (.306).

CHICAGO BULLS

	G	Min.	FGM	FGA	Pct.	FTM	FTA	Pct.	REBOUNDS Off.	Def.	Tot.	Ast.	PF	Dq.	Stl.	TO	Blk.	SCORING Pts.	Avg.	Hi.
Michael Jordan	82	3281	1098	2279	.482	833	972	.857	166	264	430	377	237	0	236	272	125	3041	37.1	61
Charles Oakley	82	2980	468	1052	.445	245	357	.686	299	775	1074	296	315	4	85	299	36	1192	14.5	28
John Paxson........	82	2689	386	793	.487	106	131	.809	22	117	139	467	207	1	66	105	8	930	11.3	25
Gene Banks........	63	1822	249	462	.539	112	146	.767	115	193	308	170	173	3	52	113	17	610	9.7	24
Brad Sellers	80	1751	276	606	.455	126	173	.728	155	218	373	102	194	1	44	84	68	680	8.5	27
Dave Corzine.......	82	2287	294	619	.475	95	129	.736	199	341	540	209	202	1	38	114	87	683	8.3	26
Sedale Threatt†	40	778	131	273	.480	53	66	.803	8	43	51	177	88	0	42	42	9	315	7.9	21
Sedale Threatt‡	68	1446	239	534	.448	95	119	.798	26	82	108	259	164	0	74	89	13	580	8.5	27
Earl Cureton*	43	1105	129	276	.467	39	73	.534	113	114	227	70	102	2	15	45	26	297	6.9	18
Steve Colter*	27	473	49	142	.345	33	39	.846	9	33	42	94	38	0	19	32	6	131	4.9	14
Mike Brown	62	818	106	201	.527	46	72	.639	71	143	214	24	129	2	20	59	7	258	4.2	17
Elston Turner	70	936	112	252	.444	23	31	.742	34	81	115	102	97	1	30	31	4	248	3.5	14
Ben Poquette†	21	167	21	40	.525	9	11	.818	10	14	24	7	26	0	3	4	12	51	2.4	13
Ben Poquette‡	58	604	62	122	.508	40	50	.800	30	71	101	35	77	1	9	21	34	164	2.8	13
Pete Myers	29	155	19	52	.365	28	43	.651	8	9	17	21	25	0	14	10	2	66	2.3	13
Granville Waiters.....	44	534	40	93	.430	5	9	.556	38	49	87	22	83	1	10	16	31	85	1.9	6
Perry Young*	5	20	2	4	.500	1	2	.500	0	1	1	0	3	0	1	1	0	5	1.0	3
Fred Cofield	5	27	2	11	.182	0	0	...	1	4	5	4	1	0	2	1	0	4	0.8	4
Darren Daye*	1	7	0	0	...	0	0	...	1	1	1	2	0	1	0	0	0	0.0	0

3-pt. FG: Chicago 78-299 (.261)—Jordan 12-66 (.182); Oakley 11-30 (.367); Paxson 52-140 (.371); Banks 0-5 (.000); Sellers 2-10 (.200); Corzine 0-5 (.000); Threatt† 0-16 (.000); Threatt‡ 7-32 (.219); Cureton* 0-1 (.000); Colter* 0-9 (.000); Turner 1-8 (.125); Poquette† 0-1 (.000); Poquette‡ 0-1 (.000); Myers 0-6 (.000); Waiters 0-1 (.000); Cofield 0-1 (.000). Opponents 115-337 (.341).

1986-87

CLEVELAND CAVALIERS

	G	Min.	FGM	FGA	Pct.	FTM	FTA	Pct.	Off.	Def.	Tot.	Ast.	PF	Dq.	Stl.	TO	Blk.	Pts.	Avg.	Hi.
Ron Harper	82	3064	734	1614	.455	386	564	.684	169	223	392	394	247	3	209	345	84	1874	22.9	40
Brad Daugherty	80	2695	487	905	.538	279	401	.696	152	495	647	304	248	3	49	248	63	1253	15.7	33
John Williams	80	2714	435	897	.485	298	400	.745	222	407	629	154	197	0	58	139	167	1168	14.6	27
Phil Hubbard	68	2083	321	605	.531	162	272	.596	178	210	388	136	224	6	66	156	7	804	11.8	23
John Bagley	72	2182	312	732	.426	113	136	.831	55	197	252	379	114	0	91	163	7	768	10.7	24
Mark Price	67	1217	173	424	.408	95	114	.833	33	84	117	202	75	1	43	105	4	464	6.9	27
Mark West	78	1333	209	385	.543	89	173	.514	126	213	339	41	229	5	22	106	81	507	6.5	27
Craig Ehlo	44	890	99	239	.414	70	99	.707	55	106	161	92	80	0	40	61	30	273	6.2	26
Keith Lee	67	870	170	374	.455	72	101	.713	93	158	251	69	147	0	25	85	40	412	6.1	20
Mel Turpin	64	801	169	366	.462	55	77	.714	62	128	190	33	90	1	11	63	40	393	6.1	20
Johnny Newman	59	630	113	275	.411	66	76	.868	36	34	70	27	67	0	20	46	7	293	5.0	22
Tyrone Corbin†	32	438	43	117	.368	42	57	.737	36	60	96	17	48	0	17	20	2	129	4.0	14
Tyrone Corbin‡	63	1170	156	381	.409	91	124	.734	88	127	215	97	129	0	55	66	5	404	6.4	23
Scooter McCray	24	279	30	65	.462	20	41	.488	19	39	58	23	28	0	9	24	4	80	3.3	11
Ben Poquette*	37	437	41	82	.500	31	39	.795	20	57	77	28	51	1	6	17	22	113	3.1	10
Dirk Minniefield*	11	122	13	42	.310	1	4	.250	1	9	10	13	8	0	6	12	1	27	2.5	4

3-pt. FG: Cleveland 81-338 (.240)—Harper 20-94 (.213); Williams 0-1 (.000); Hubbard 0-4 (.000); Bagley 31-103 (.301); Price 23-70 (.329); West 0-2 (.000); Ehlo 5-29 (.172); Lee 0-1 (.000); Newman 1-22 (.045); Corbin† 1-4 (.250); Corbin‡ 1-4 (.250); Poquette* 0-3 (.000); Minniefield* 0-5 (.000). Opponents 95-342 (.278).

DALLAS MAVERICKS

	G	Min.	FGM	FGA	Pct.	FTM	FTA	Pct.	Off.	Def.	Tot.	Ast.	PF	Dq.	Stl.	TO	Blk.	Pts.	Avg.	Hi.
Mark Aguirre	80	2663	787	1590	.495	429	557	.770	181	246	427	254	243	4	84	217	30	2056	25.7	43
Rolando Blackman	80	2758	626	1264	.495	419	474	.884	96	182	278	266	142	0	64	174	21	1676	21.0	41
Derek Harper	77	2556	497	993	.501	160	234	.684	51	148	199	609	195	0	167	138	25	1230	16.0	31
Sam Perkins	80	2687	461	957	.482	245	296	.828	197	419	616	146	269	6	109	132	77	1186	14.8	29
James Donaldson	82	3028	311	531	.586	267	329	.812	295	678	973	63	191	0	51	104	136	889	10.8	23
Detlef Schrempf	81	1711	265	561	.472	193	260	.742	87	216	303	161	224	2	50	110	16	756	9.3	19
Roy Tarpley	75	1405	233	499	.467	94	139	.676	180	353	533	52	232	3	56	101	79	561	7.5	20
Brad Davis	82	1582	199	436	.456	147	171	.860	27	87	114	373	159	0	63	114	10	577	7.0	24
Al Wood	54	657	121	310	.390	109	139	.784	39	55	94	34	83	0	19	34	11	358	6.6	25
Bill Wennington	58	560	56	132	.424	45	60	.750	53	76	129	24	95	0	13	39	10	157	2.7	10
Dennis Nutt	25	91	16	40	.400	20	22	.909	1	7	8	16	6	0	7	10	0	52	2.3	11
Uwe Blab	30	160	20	51	.392	13	28	.464	11	25	36	13	33	0	4	15	9	53	1.8	7
Myron Jackson	8	22	2	9	.222	7	8	.875	1	2	3	6	1	0	1	5	0	11	1.4	3

3-pt. FG: Dallas 231-653 (.354)—Aguirre 53-150 (.353); Blackman 5-15 (.333); Harper 76-212 (.358); Perkins 19-54 (.352); Schrempf 33-69 (.478); Tarpley 1-3 (.333); Davis 32-106 (.302); Wood 7-25 (.280); Wennington 0-2 (.000); Nutt 5-17 (.294). Opponents 128-434 (.295).

DENVER NUGGETS

	G	Min.	FGM	FGA	Pct.	FTM	FTA	Pct.	Off.	Def.	Tot.	Ast.	PF	Dq.	Stl.	TO	Blk.	Pts.	Avg.	Hi.
Alex English	82	3085	965	1920	.503	411	487	.844	146	198	344	422	216	0	73	214	21	2345	28.6	46
Fat Lever	82	3054	643	1370	.469	244	312	.782	216	513	729	654	219	1	201	167	34	1552	18.9	36
Bill Hanzlik	73	1990	307	746	.412	316	402	.786	79	177	256	280	245	3	87	132	28	952	13.0	33
Darrell Walker	81	2020	358	742	.482	272	365	.745	157	170	327	282	229	0	120	187	37	988	12.2	39
Mike Evans	81	1567	334	729	.458	96	123	.780	36	92	128	185	149	1	79	107	12	817	10.1	27
Calvin Natt	1	20	4	10	.400	2	2	1.000	2	3	5	2	2	0	1	1	0	10	10.0	10
Blair Rasmussen	74	1421	268	570	.470	169	231	.732	183	282	465	60	224	6	24	79	58	705	9.5	24
Dan Schayes	76	1556	210	405	.519	229	294	.779	120	260	380	85	266	5	20	95	74	649	8.5	25
Wayne Cooper	69	1561	235	524	.448	79	109	.725	162	311	473	68	257	5	13	78	101	549	8.0	24
Mark Alarie	64	1110	217	443	.490	67	101	.663	73	141	214	74	138	1	22	56	28	503	7.9	21
T.R. Dunn	81	1932	118	276	.428	36	55	.655	91	174	265	147	160	0	100	33	21	272	3.4	12
Mo Martin	43	286	51	135	.378	42	66	.636	12	29	41	35	48	0	13	33	6	147	3.4	12
Otis Smith	28	168	33	79	.418	12	21	.571	17	17	34	22	30	0	1	19	1	78	2.8	12
Pete Williams	5	10	1	2	.500	0	0	...	0	1	1	1	1	0	0	1	0	2	0.4	2

3-pt. FG: Denver 106-391 (.271)—English 4-15 (.267); Lever 22-92 (.239); Hanzlik 22-80 (.275); Walker 0-4 (.000); Evans 53-169 (.314); Cooper 0-3 (.000); Alarie 2-9 (.222); Dunn 0-2 (.000); Martin 3-15 (.200); Smith 0-2 (.000). Opponents 113-361 (.313).

DETROIT PISTONS

	G	Min.	FGM	FGA	Pct.	FTM	FTA	Pct.	Off.	Def.	Tot.	Ast.	PF	Dq.	Stl.	TO	Blk.	Pts.	Avg.	Hi.
Adrian Dantley	81	2736	601	1126	.534	539	664	.812	104	228	332	162	193	1	63	181	7	1742	21.5	41
Isiah Thomas	81	3013	626	1353	.463	400	521	.768	82	237	319	813	251	5	153	343	20	1671	20.6	36
Vinnie Johnson	78	2166	533	1154	.462	158	201	.786	123	134	257	300	159	0	92	133	16	1228	15.7	30
Bill Laimbeer	82	2854	506	1010	.501	245	274	.894	243	712	955	151	283	4	72	120	69	1263	15.4	30
Joe Dumars	79	2439	369	749	.493	184	246	.748	50	117	167	352	194	1	83	171	5	931	11.8	24
Sidney Green	80	1792	256	542	.472	119	177	.672	196	457	653	62	197	0	41	127	50	631	7.9	22
Dennis Rodman	77	1155	213	391	.545	74	126	.587	163	169	332	56	166	1	38	93	48	500	6.5	21
Rick Mahorn	63	1278	144	322	.447	96	117	.821	93	282	375	38	221	4	32	73	50	384	6.1	17
John Salley	82	1463	163	290	.562	105	171	.614	108	188	296	54	256	5	44	74	125	431	5.3	28
Tony Campbell	40	332	57	145	.393	24	39	.615	21	37	58	19	40	0	12	34	1	138	3.5	17
Kurt Nimphius†	28	277	36	78	.462	24	32	.750	22	32	54	7	38	0	4	16	13	96	3.4	12

	G	Min.	FGM	FGA	Pct.	FTM	FTA	Pct.	Off.	Def.	Tot.	Ast.	PF	Dq.	Stl.	TO	Blk.	Pts.	Avg.	Hi.
									REBOUNDS									SCORING		
Kurt Nimphius‡	66	1088	155	330	.470	81	120	.675	80	107	187	25	156	1	20	63	54	391	5.9	22
Cozell McQueen	3	7	3	3	1.000	0	0	…	3	5	8	0	1	0	0	0	1	6	2.0	4
Chuck Nevitt	41	267	31	63	.492	14	24	.583	36	47	83	4	73	0	7	21	30	76	1.9	12
Jeff Taylor	12	44	6	10	.600	9	10	.900	1	3	4	3	4	0	2	8	1	21	1.8	6
John Schweitz	3	7	0	1	.000	0	0	…	0	1	1	0	2	0	2	0	0	0	0.0	0

3-pt. FG: Detroit 39-169 (.231)—Dantley 1-6 (.167); Thomas 19-98 (.194); Johnson 4-14 (.286); Laimbeer 6-21 (.286); Dumars 9-22 (.409); Green 0-2 (.000); Rodman 0-1 (.000); Salley 0-1 (.000); Campbell 0-3 (.000); Nimphius† 0-1 (.000); Nimphius‡ 0-4 (.000). Opponents 133-419 (.317).

GOLDEN STATE WARRIORS

	G	Min.	FGM	FGA	Pct.	FTM	FTA	Pct.	Off.	Def.	Tot.	Ast.	PF	Dq.	Stl.	TO	Blk.	Pts.	Avg.	Hi.
									REBOUNDS									SCORING		
Joe Barry Carroll	81	2724	690	1461	.472	340	432	.787	173	416	589	214	255	2	92	226	123	1720	21.2	43
Sleepy Floyd	82	3064	503	1030	.488	462	537	.860	56	212	268	848	199	1	146	280	18	1541	18.8	41
Purvis Short	34	950	240	501	.479	137	160	.856	55	82	137	86	103	1	45	68	7	621	18.3	34
Chris Mullin	82	2377	477	928	.514	269	326	.825	39	142	181	261	217	1	98	154	36	1242	15.1	32
Terry Teagle	82	1650	370	808	.458	182	234	.778	68	107	175	105	190	0	68	117	13	922	11.2	28
Larry Smith	80	2374	297	544	.546	113	197	.574	366	551	917	95	295	7	71	135	56	707	8.8	23
Rod Higgins	73	1497	214	412	.519	200	240	.833	72	165	237	96	145	0	40	76	21	631	8.6	26
Greg Ballard	82	1579	248	564	.440	68	91	.747	99	241	340	108	167	0	50	70	15	579	7.1	20
Ben McDonald	63	1284	164	360	.456	24	38	.632	63	120	183	84	200	5	27	43	8	353	5.6	20
Jerome Whitehead	73	937	147	327	.450	79	113	.699	110	152	262	24	175	1	16	50	12	373	5.1	15
Chris Washburn	35	385	57	145	.393	18	51	.353	36	65	101	16	51	0	6	39	8	132	3.8	17
Perry Moss	64	698	91	207	.440	49	69	.710	29	66	95	90	96	0	42	57	3	232	3.6	13
Clinton Smith	41	341	50	117	.427	27	36	.750	26	30	56	45	36	0	13	26	1	127	3.1	13
Kevin Henderson	5	45	3	8	.375	2	2	1.000	1	2	3	11	9	0	1	4	0	8	1.6	4

3-pt. FG: Golden State 116-364 (.319)—Floyd 73-190 (.384); Short 4-17 (.235); Mullin 19-63 (.302); Teagle 0-10 (.000); L. Smith 0-1 (.000); Higgins 3-17 (.176); Ballard 15-40 (.375); McDonald 1-8 (.125); Whitehead 0-1 (.000); Washburn 0-1 (.000); Moss 1-14 (.071); C. Smith 0-2 (.000). Opponents 155-460 (.337).

HOUSTON ROCKETS

	G	Min.	FGM	FGA	Pct.	FTM	FTA	Pct.	Off.	Def.	Tot.	Ast.	PF	Dq.	Stl.	TO	Blk.	Pts.	Avg.	Hi.
									REBOUNDS									SCORING		
Hakeem Olajuwon	75	2760	677	1332	.508	400	570	.702	315	543	858	220	294	8	140	228	254	1755	23.4	44
Ralph Sampson	43	1326	277	566	.489	118	189	.624	88	284	372	120	169	6	40	126	58	672	15.6	33
Rodney McCray	81	3136	432	783	.552	306	393	.779	190	388	578	434	172	2	88	208	53	1170	14.4	28
Robert Reid	75	2594	420	1006	.417	136	177	.768	47	242	289	323	232	2	75	104	21	1029	13.7	30
Lewis Lloyd	32	688	165	310	.532	65	86	.756	13	35	48	90	69	0	19	52	5	396	12.4	26
Jim Petersen	82	2403	386	755	.511	152	209	.727	177	380	557	127	268	5	43	152	102	924	11.3	28
Mitchell Wiggins	32	788	153	350	.437	49	65	.754	74	59	133	76	82	1	44	50	3	355	11.1	30
Steve Harris	74	1174	251	599	.419	111	130	.854	71	99	170	100	111	1	37	74	16	613	8.3	22
Allen Leavell	53	1175	147	358	.411	100	119	.840	14	47	61	224	126	1	53	64	10	412	7.8	21
Dirk Minniefield†	63	1478	205	440	.466	61	86	.709	28	102	130	335	166	2	66	145	6	482	7.7	20
Dirk Minniefield‡	74	1600	218	482	.452	62	90	.689	29	111	140	348	174	2	72	157	7	509	6.9	20
Cedric Maxwell†	46	836	103	188	.548	126	163	.773	72	112	184	75	76	0	13	48	5	332	7.2	17
Cedric Maxwell‡	81	1968	253	477	.530	303	391	.775	175	260	435	197	178	1	39	136	14	809	10.0	25
Buck Johnson	60	520	94	201	.468	40	58	.690	38	50	88	40	81	0	17	37	15	228	3.8	12
Dave Feitl	62	498	88	202	.436	53	71	.746	39	78	117	22	83	0	9	38	4	229	3.7	17
Richard Anderson	51	312	59	139	.424	22	29	.759	24	55	79	33	37	0	7	19	3	144	2.8	10
Conner Henry*	18	92	8	33	.242	7	10	.700	0	7	7	8	7	0	3	9	0	24	1.3	5

3-pt. FG: Houston 89-324 (.275)—Olajuwon 1-5 (.200); Sampson 0-3 (.000); McCray 0-9 (.000); Reid 53-162 (.327); Lloyd 1-7 (.143); Petersen 0-4 (.000); Wiggins 0-5 (.000); Harris 0-8 (.000); Leavell 18-57 (.316); Minniefield† 11-34 (.324); Minniefield‡ 11-39 (.282); Maxwell† 0-1 (.000); Maxwell‡ 0-1 (.000); Johnson 0-1 (.000); Feitl 0-1 (.000); Anderson 4-16 (.250); Henry* 1-11 (.091). Opponents 100-355 (.282).

INDIANA PACERS

	G	Min.	FGM	FGA	Pct.	FTM	FTA	Pct.	Off.	Def.	Tot.	Ast.	PF	Dq.	Stl.	TO	Blk.	Pts.	Avg.	Hi.
									REBOUNDS									SCORING		
Chuck Person	82	2956	635	1358	.468	222	297	.747	168	509	677	295	310	4	90	211	16	1541	18.8	42
John Long	80	2265	490	1170	.419	219	246	.890	75	142	217	258	167	1	96	153	8	1218	15.2	44
Herb Williams	74	2526	451	939	.480	199	269	.740	143	400	543	174	255	9	59	145	93	1101	14.9	32
Wayman Tisdale	81	2159	458	892	.513	258	364	.709	217	258	475	117	293	9	50	139	26	1174	14.5	35
Steve Stipanovich	81	2761	382	760	.503	307	367	.837	184	486	670	180	304	9	106	130	97	1072	13.2	30
Vern Fleming	82	2549	370	727	.509	238	302	.788	109	225	334	473	222	3	109	167	18	980	12.0	24
Clint Richardson	78	1396	218	467	.467	59	74	.797	51	92	143	241	106	0	49	85	7	501	6.4	22
Ron Anderson	63	721	139	294	.473	85	108	.787	73	78	151	54	65	0	31	55	3	363	5.8	27
Clark Kellogg	4	60	8	22	.364	3	4	.750	7	4	11	6	12	0	5	4	0	20	5.0	6
Kyle Macy	76	1250	164	341	.481	34	41	.829	25	88	113	197	136	0	59	58	7	376	4.9	18
Walker Russell	48	511	64	165	.388	27	37	.730	18	37	55	129	62	0	20	60	5	157	3.3	16
Michael Brooks	10	148	13	37	.351	7	10	.700	9	19	28	11	19	0	9	11	0	33	3.3	10
Stuart Gray	55	456	41	101	.406	28	39	.718	39	90	129	26	93	0	10	36	28	110	2.0	13
Peter Verhoeven	5	44	5	14	.357	0	0	…	2	5	7	2	11	1	2	0	1	10	2.0	4
Greg Dreiling	24	128	16	37	.432	10	12	.833	12	31	43	7	42	0	2	7	2	42	1.8	8

3-pt. FG: Indiana 94-316 (.297)—Person 49-138 (.355); Long 19-67 (.284); Williams 0-9 (.000); Tisdale 0-2 (.000); Stipanovich 1-4 (.250); Fleming 2-10 (.200); Richardson 6-17 (.353); Anderson 0-5 (.000); Kellogg 1-2 (.500); Macy 14-46 (.304); Russell 2-16 (.125). Opponents 103-345 (.299).

LOS ANGELES CLIPPERS

	G	Min.	FGM	FGA	Pct.	FTM	FTA	Pct.	REBOUNDS Off.	Def.	Tot.	Ast.	PF	Dq.	Stl.	TO	Blk.	SCORING Pts.	Avg.	Hi.
Mike Woodson	74	2126	494	1130	.437	240	290	.828	68	94	162	196	201	1	100	168	16	1262	17.1	37
Marques Johnson	10	302	68	155	.439	30	42	.714	9	24	33	28	24	0	12	17	5	166	16.6	31
Michael Cage	80	2922	457	878	.521	341	467	.730	354	568	922	131	221	1	99	171	67	1255	15.7	29
Cedric Maxwell*	35	1132	150	289	.519	177	228	.776	103	148	251	122	102	1	26	88	9	477	13.6	25
Larry Drew	60	1566	295	683	.432	139	166	.837	26	77	103	326	107	0	60	151	2	741	12.4	25
Benoit Benjamin	72	2230	320	713	.449	188	263	.715	134	452	586	135	251	7	60	184	187	828	11.5	28
Darnell Valentine	65	1759	275	671	.410	163	200	.815	38	112	150	447	148	3	116	167	10	726	11.2	24
Quintin Dailey	49	924	200	491	.407	119	155	.768	34	49	83	79	113	4	43	71	8	520	10.6	28
Rory White	68	1545	265	552	.480	94	144	.653	90	104	194	79	159	1	47	73	19	624	9.2	30
Kenny Fields†	44	861	153	344	.445	72	89	.809	63	83	146	60	120	2	31	52	11	381	8.7	22
Kenny Fields‡	48	883	159	352	.452	73	94	.777	63	85	148	61	123	2	32	53	11	394	8.2	22
Kurt Nimphius*	38	811	119	252	.472	57	88	.648	58	75	133	18	118	1	16	47	41	295	7.8	22
Earl Cureton†	35	868	114	234	.487	43	79	.544	99	126	225	52	86	0	18	35	30	271	7.7	23
Earl Cureton‡	78	1973	243	510	.476	82	152	.539	212	240	452	122	188	2	33	80	56	568	7.3	23
Lancaster Gordon	70	1130	221	545	.406	70	95	.737	64	62	126	139	106	1	61	102	13	526	7.5	33
Geoff Huston	19	428	55	121	.455	18	34	.529	6	11	17	101	28	0	14	45	0	129	6.8	17
Tim Kempton	66	936	97	206	.471	95	137	.693	70	124	194	53	162	6	38	49	12	289	4.4	18
Steffond Johnson	29	234	27	64	.422	20	38	.526	15	28	43	5	55	2	9	18	2	74	2.6	9
Dwayne Polee	1	6	1	4	.250	0	0	...	0	0	0	0	3	0	1	1	0	2	2.0	2

3-pt. FG: L.A. Clippers 78-348 (.224)—Woodson 34-123 (.276); M. Johnson 0-6 (.000); Cage 0-3 (.000); Drew 12-72 (.167); Benjamin 0-2 (.000); Valentine 13-56 (.232); Dailey 1-10 (.100); White 0-3 (.000); Fields† 3-12 (.250); Fields‡ 3-12 (.250); Nimphius* 0-3 (.000); Cureton† 0-1 (.000); Cureton‡ 0-2 (.000); Gordon 14-48 (.292); Huston 1-2 (.500); Kempton 0-1 (.000); S. Johnson 0-3 (.000); Polee 0-3 (.000). Opponents 110-320 (.344).

LOS ANGELES LAKERS

	G	Min.	FGM	FGA	Pct.	FTM	FTA	Pct.	REBOUNDS Off.	Def.	Tot.	Ast.	PF	Dq.	Stl.	TO	Blk.	SCORING Pts.	Avg.	Hi.
Magic Johnson	80	2904	683	1308	.522	535	631	.848	122	382	504	977	168	0	138	300	36	1909	23.9	46
James Worthy	82	2819	651	1207	.539	292	389	.751	158	308	466	226	206	0	108	168	83	1594	19.4	31
Kareem Abdul-Jabbar	78	2441	560	993	.564	245	343	.714	152	371	523	203	245	2	49	186	97	1366	17.5	30
Byron Scott	82	2729	554	1134	.489	224	251	.892	63	223	286	281	163	0	125	144	18	1397	17.0	33
A.C. Green	79	2240	316	587	.538	220	282	.780	210	405	615	84	171	0	70	102	80	852	10.8	26
Michael Cooper	82	2253	322	736	.438	126	148	.851	58	196	254	373	199	1	78	102	43	859	10.5	24
Mychal Thompson†	33	680	129	269	.480	75	101	.743	47	89	136	28	85	1	14		30	333	10.1	24
Mychal Thompson‡	82	1090	359	797	.450	210	297	.737	138	274	412	115	202	1	45	134	71	938	11.4	29
Kurt Rambis	78	1514	163	313	.521	120	157	.764	159	294	453	63	201	1	74	104	41	446	5.7	16
Billy Thompson	59	762	142	261	.544	48	74	.649	69	102	171	60	148	1	15	61	30	332	5.6	13
Adrian Branch	32	219	48	96	.500	42	54	.778	23	30	53	16	39	0	16	24	3	138	4.3	12
Wes Matthews	50	532	89	187	.476	29	36	.806	13	34	47	100	53	0	23	51	4	208	4.2	16
Frank Brickowski*	37	404	53	94	.564	40	59	.678	40	57	97	12	105	4	14	25	4	146	3.9	14
Mike Smrek	35	233	30	60	.500	16	25	.640	13	24	37	5	70	1	4	19	13	76	2.2	8

3-pt. FG: L.A. Lakers 164-447 (.367)—Johnson 8-39 (.205); Worthy 0-13 (.000); Abdul-Jabbar 1-3 (.333); Scott 65-149 (.436); Green 0-5 (.000); Cooper 89-231 (.385); M. Thompson† 0-1 (.000); M. Thompson‡ 1-2 (.500); B. Thompson 0-1 (.000); Branch 0-2 (.000); Matthews 1-3 (.333). Opponents 122-431 (.283).

MILWAUKEE BUCKS

	G	Min.	FGM	FGA	Pct.	FTM	FTA	Pct.	REBOUNDS Off.	Def.	Tot.	Ast.	PF	Dq.	Stl.	TO	Blk.	SCORING Pts.	Avg.	Hi.
Terry Cummings	82	2770	729	1426	.511	249	376	.662	214	486	700	229	296	3	129	172	81	1707	20.8	39
Ricky Pierce	79	2505	575	1077	.534	387	440	.880	117	149	266	144	222	0	64	120	24	1540	19.5	32
John Lucas	43	1358	285	624	.457	137	174	.787	29	96	125	290	82	0	71	89	6	753	17.5	29
Paul Pressey	61	2057	294	616	.477	242	328	.738	98	198	296	441	213	4	110	186	47	846	13.9	27
Jack Sikma	82	2536	390	842	.463	265	313	.847	208	614	822	203	328	14	88	160	90	1045	12.7	28
Sidney Moncrief	39	992	158	324	.488	136	162	.840	57	70	127	121	73	0	27	63	10	460	11.8	26
Craig Hodges	79	2147	315	682	.462	131	147	.891	48	92	140	240	189	3	76	124	7	846	10.8	27
Randy Breuer	76	1467	241	497	.485	118	202	.584	129	221	350	47	229	9	56	100	61	600	7.9	19
Jerry Reynolds	58	963	140	356	.393	118	184	.641	72	101	173	106	91	0	50	82	30	404	7.0	26
Junior Bridgeman	34	418	79	171	.462	16	20	.800	14	38	52	35	50	0	10	15	2	175	5.1	12
Don Collins	6	57	10	28	.357	5	7	.714	11	4	15	2	11	0	2	5	1	25	4.2	11
Scott Skiles	13	205	18	62	.290	10	12	.833	6	20	26	45	18	0	5	21	1	49	3.8	14
Mike Glenn	4	34	5	13	.385	5	7	.714	0	2	2	1	3	0	1	0	0	15	3.8	9
Keith Smith	42	461	57	150	.380	21	28	.750	13	19	32	43	74	0	25	30	3	138	3.3	15
Kenny Fields*	4	22	6	8	.750	1	5	.200	0	2	2	1	3	0	1	1	0	13	3.3	6
Dudley Bradley	68	900	76	213	.357	47	58	.810	31	71	102	66	118	2	105	34	8	212	3.1	12
Hank McDowell	7	70	8	17	.471	6	7	.857	9	10	19	2	14	0	2	3	0	22	3.1	8
Cedric Henderson†	2	6	2	3	.667	2	2	1.000	1	4	5	0	1	0	0	3	0	6	3.0	4
Cedric Henderson‡	8	16	4	8	.500	3	3	1.000	3	5	8	0	2	0	0	4	0	11	1.4	4
Paul Mokeski	62	626	52	129	.403	46	64	.719	45	93	138	22	126	0	18	22	13	150	2.4	11
Jerome Henderson	6	36	4	13	.308	4	4	1.000	2	5	7	0	12	0	1	6	1	12	2.0	7
Marvin Webster	15	102	10	19	.526	6	8	.750	12	14	26	3	17	0	3	8	7	27	1.8	11
Chris Engler*	5	48	3	12	.250	1	1	1.000	3	13	16	3	10	0	1	0	1	7	1.4	5

3-pt. FG: Milwaukee 185-572 (.323)—Cummings 0-3 (.000); Pierce 3-28 (.107); Lucas 46-126 (.365); Pressey 16-55 (.291); Sikma 0-2 (.000); Moncrief 8-31 (.258); Hodges 85-228 (.373); Reynolds 6-18 (.333); Bridgeman 1-6 (.167); Skiles 3-14 (.214); Smith 3-9 (.333); Bradley 13-50 (.260); Mokeski 0-1 (.000); Webster 1-1 (1.000). Opponents 120-415 (.289).

1986-87

NEW JERSEY NETS

	G	Min.	FGM	FGA	Pct.	FTM	FTA	Pct.	Off.	Def.	Tot.	Ast.	PF	Dq.	Stl.	TO	Blk.	Pts.	Avg.	Hi.
Orlando Woolridge . . . 75	75	2638	556	1067	.521	438	564	.777	118	249	367	261	243	4	54	213	86	1551	20.7	38
Buck Williams 82	82	2976	521	936	.557	430	588	.731	322	701	1023	129	315	8	78	280	91	1472	18.0	35
Mike Gminski 72	72	2272	433	947	.457	313	370	.846	192	438	630	99	159	0	52	129	69	1179	16.4	30
Tony Brown 77	77	2339	358	810	.442	152	206	.738	84	135	219	259	273	12	89	153	14	873	11.3	29
Ray Williams 32	32	800	131	290	.452	49	60	.817	26	49	75	185	111	4	38	94	9	318	9.9	25
Albert King 61	61	1291	244	573	.426	81	100	.810	82	132	214	103	177	5	34	103	28	582	9.5	22
Darryl Dawkins 6	6	106	20	32	.625	17	24	.708	9	10	19	2	25	0	2	15	3	57	9.5	14
Pearl Washington 72	72	1600	257	538	.478	98	125	.784	37	92	129	301	184	5	92	175	7	616	8.6	29
James Bailey 34	34	542	112	239	.469	58	80	.725	48	89	137	20	119	5	12	54	23	282	8.3	35
Leon Wood 76	76	1733	187	501	.373	123	154	.799	23	97	120	370	126	0	48	108	3	557	7.3	22
Kevin McKenna 56	56	942	153	337	.454	43	57	.754	21	56	77	93	141	0	54	53	7	401	7.2	20
Ben Coleman 68	68	1029	182	313	.581	88	121	.727	99	189	288	37	200	7	32	94	31	452	6.6	19
Otis Birdsong 7	7	127	19	42	.452	6	9	.667	3	4	7	17	16	0	3	9	0	44	6.3	17
Jeff Turner 76	76	1003	151	325	.465	76	104	.731	80	117	197	60	200	6	33	81	13	378	5.0	17
Pace Mannion 23	23	284	31	94	.330	18	31	.581	10	29	39	45	32	0	18	23	4	83	3.6	25
Chris Englert† 18	18	130	16	31	.516	8	12	.667	14	19	33	4	23	0	3	10	9	40	2.2	9
Chris Englert‡ 30	30	195	23	51	.451	12	16	.750	23	34	57	8	33	0	5	12	11	58	1.9	9
Mike Wilson* 5	5	43	3	8	.375	2	2	1.000	1	3	4	6	9	0	1	4	0	8	1.6	4

3-pt. FG: New Jersey 145-449 (.323)—Woolridge 1-8 (.125); B. Williams 0-1 (.000); Brown 5-20 (.250); R. Williams 7-28 (.250); King 13-32 (.406); Washington 4-24 (.167); Wood 60-200 (.300); McKenna 52-124 (.419); Coleman 0-1 (.000); Birdsong 0-1 (.000); Turner 0-1 (.000); Mannion 3-9 (.333). Opponents 118-366 (.322).

NEW YORK KNICKERBOCKERS

	G	Min.	FGM	FGA	Pct.	FTM	FTA	Pct.	Off.	Def.	Tot.	Ast.	PF	Dq.	Stl.	TO	Blk.	Pts.	Avg.	Hi.
Bernard King 6	6	214	52	105	.495	32	43	.744	13	19	32	19	14	0	2	15	0	136	22.7	31
Patrick Ewing 63	63	2206	530	1053	.503	296	415	.713	157	398	555	104	248	5	89	229	147	1356	21.5	43
Gerald Wilkins 80	80	2758	633	1302	.486	235	335	.701	120	174	294	354	165	0	88	214	18	1527	19.1	43
Bill Cartwright 58	58	1989	335	631	.531	346	438	.790	132	313	445	96	188	2	40	128	26	1016	17.5	32
Trent Tucker 70	70	1691	325	691	.470	77	101	.762	49	86	135	166	169	1	116	78	13	795	11.4	34
Gerald Henderson† . . 68	68	1890	273	624	.438	173	212	.816	44	122	166	439	191	1	95	157	11	738	10.9	24
Gerald Henderson‡ . . 74	74	2045	298	674	.442	190	230	.826	50	125	175	471	208	1	101	172	11	805	10.9	24
Kenny Walker 68	68	1719	285	581	.491	140	185	.757	118	220	338	75	236	7	49	75	49	710	10.4	26
Pat Cummings 49	49	1056	172	382	.450	79	110	.718	123	189	312	38	145	2	26	85	7	423	8.6	21
Rory Sparrow 80	80	1951	263	590	.446	71	89	.798	29	86	115	432	160	0	67	140	6	608	7.6	24
Louis Orr 65	65	1440	166	389	.427	125	172	.727	102	130	232	110	123	0	47	70	18	458	7.0	28
Eddie Lee Wilkins . . . 24	24	454	56	127	.441	27	58	.466	45	62	107	6	67	1	9	28	2	139	5.8	14
Chris McNealy 59	59	972	88	179	.492	52	80	.650	74	153	227	46	136	1	36	64	16	228	3.9	14
Jawann Oldham 44	44	776	71	174	.408	31	57	.544	51	128	179	19	95	1	22	48	71	173	3.9	13
Brad Wright 14	14	138	20	46	.435	12	28	.429	25	28	53	1	20	0	3	13	6	52	3.7	13
Stewart Granger 15	15	166	20	54	.370	9	11	.818	6	11	17	27	17	0	7	22	1	49	3.3	10
Bill Martin 8	8	68	9	25	.360	7	8	.875	2	5	7	0	5	0	4	7	2	25	3.1	6
Bob Thornton 33	33	282	29	67	.433	13	20	.650	18	38	56	8	48	0	4	24	3	71	2.2	11
McKinley Singleton . . 2	2	10	2	3	.667	0	0	—	0	0	0	1	1	0	0	0	0	4	2.0	2

3-pt. FG: New York 125-375 (.333)—Ewing 0-7 (.000); G. Wilkins 26-74 (.351); Tucker 68-161 (.422); Henderson† 19-74 (.257); Henderson‡ 19-77 (.247); Walker 0-4 (.000); Sparrow 11-42 (.262); Orr 1-5 (.200); E. Wilkins 0-1 (.000); Oldham 0-1 (.000); Wright 0-1 (.000); Granger 0-3 (.000); Thornton 0-1 (.000); Singleton 0-1 (.000). Opponents 94-358 (.263).

PHILADELPHIA 76ERS

	G	Min.	FGM	FGA	Pct.	FTM	FTA	Pct.	Off.	Def.	Tot.	Ast.	PF	Dq.	Stl.	TO	Blk.	Pts.	Avg.	Hi.
Charles Barkley 68	68	2740	557	937	.594	429	564	.761	390	604	994	331	252	5	119	322	104	1564	23.0	41
Julius Erving 60	60	1918	400	850	.471	191	235	.813	115	149	264	191	137	0	76	158	94	1005	16.8	38
Maurice Cheeks 68	68	2624	415	788	.527	227	292	.777	47	168	215	538	109	0	180	173	15	1061	15.6	31
Cliff Robinson 55	55	1586	338	729	.464	139	184	.755	86	221	307	89	150	1	86	123	30	815	14.8	35
Roy Hinson 76	76	2489	393	823	.478	273	360	.758	150	338	488	60	281	4	45	149	161	1059	13.9	28
Tim McCormick 81	81	2817	391	718	.545	251	349	.719	180	431	611	114	270	4	36	153	64	1033	12.8	27
Andrew Toney 52	52	1058	197	437	.451	133	167	.796	16	69	85	188	78	0	18	112	8	549	10.6	32
Sedale Threatt* 28	28	668	108	261	.414	42	53	.792	18	39	57	82	76	0	32	47	4	265	9.5	27
Jeff Ruland 5	5	116	19	28	.679	9	12	.750	12	16	28	10	13	0	0	10	4	47	9.4	19
David Wingate 77	77	1612	259	602	.430	149	201	.741	70	86	156	155	169	1	93	128	19	680	8.8	28
Steve Colter† 43	43	849	120	255	.471	49	68	.721	14	52	66	116	61	0	37	38	6	293	6.8	22
Steve Colter‡ 70	70	1322	169	397	.426	82	107	.766	23	85	108	210	99	0	56	70	12	424	6.1	22
World B. Free 20	20	285	39	123	.317	36	47	.766	5	14	19	30	26	0	5	18	4	116	5.8	12
Kenny Green 19	19	172	25	70	.357	14	19	.737	6	22	28	7	8	0	4	15	2	64	3.4	12
Mark McNamara 11	11	113	14	30	.467	7	19	.368	17	19	36	2	17	0	1	8	0	35	3.2	10
Jim Lampley 1	1	16	1	3	.333	1	2	.500	1	4	5	0	0	0	1	1	0	3	3.0	3
Danny Vranes 58	58	817	59	138	.428	21	45	.467	51	95	146	30	127	0	35	26	25	140	2.4	10

3-pt. FG: Philadelphia 88-340 (.259)—Barkley 21-104 (.202); Erving 14-53 (.264); Cheeks 4-17 (.235); Robinson 0-4 (.000); Hinson 0-1 (.000); McCormick 0-4 (.000); Toney 22-67 (.328); Threatt* 7-16 (.438); Wingate 13-52 (.250); Colter† 4-8 (.500); Colter‡ 4-17 (.235); Free 2-9 (.222); Vranes 1-5 (.200). Opponents 119-416 (.286).

PHOENIX SUNS

	G	Min.	FGM	FGA	Pct.	FTM	FTA	Pct.	Off.	Def.	Tot.	Ast.	PF	Dq.	Stl.	TO	Blk.	Pts.	Avg.	Hi.
Walter Davis	79	2646	779	1515	.514	288	334	.862	90	154	244	364	184	1	96	226	5	1867	23.6	45
Larry Nance	69	2569	585	1062	.551	381	493	.773	188	411	599	233	223	4	86	149	148	1552	22.5	35
James Edwards	14	304	57	110	.518	54	70	.771	20	40	60	19	42	1	6	15	7	168	12.0	16
Jay Humphries	82	2579	359	753	.477	200	260	.769	62	198	260	632	239	1	112	195	9	923	11.3	30
Alvan Adams	68	1690	311	618	.503	134	170	.788	94	247	338	223	207	3	62	139	37	756	11.1	25
Mike Sanders	82	1655	357	722	.494	143	183	.781	101	170	271	126	210	1	61	105	23	859	10.5	23
Ed Pinckney	80	2250	290	497	.584	257	348	.739	179	401	580	116	196	1	86	135	54	837	10.5	23
William Bedford	50	979	142	358	.397	50	86	.581	79	167	246	57	125	1	18	85	37	334	6.7	17
Rafael Addison	62	711	146	331	.441	51	64	.797	41	65	106	45	75	1	27	54	7	359	5.8	22
Grant Gondrezick	64	836	135	300	.450	75	107	.701	47	63	110	81	91	0	25	56	4	349	5.5	14
Jeff Hornacek	80	1561	159	350	.454	94	121	.777	41	143	184	361	130	0	70	153	5	424	5.3	14
Kenny Gattison	77	1104	148	311	.476	108	171	.632	87	183	270	36	178	1	24	88	33	404	5.2	29
Bernard Thompson	24	331	42	105	.400	27	33	.818	20	11	31	18	53	0	11	16	5	111	4.6	16
Nick Vanos	57	640	65	158	.411	38	59	.644	67	113	180	43	94	0	19	48	23	168	2.9	14

3-pt. FG: Phoenix 61-252 (.242)—Davis 21-81 (.259); Nance 1-5 (.200); Humphries 5-27 (.185); Adams 0-1 (.000); Sanders 2-17 (.118); Pinckney 0-2 (.000); Bedford 0-1 (.000); Addison 16-50 (.320); Gondrezick 4-17 (.235); Hornacek 12-43 (.279); Gattison 0-3 (.000); Thompson 0-3 (.000); Vanos 0-2 (.000). Opponents 123-395 (.311).

PORTLAND TRAIL BLAZERS

	G	Min.	FGM	FGA	Pct.	FTM	FTA	Pct.	Off.	Def.	Tot.	Ast.	PF	Dq.	Stl.	TO	Blk.	Pts.	Avg.	Hi.
Kiki Vandeweghe	79	3029	808	1545	.523	467	527	.886	86	165	251	220	137	0	52	139	17	2122	26.9	48
Clyde Drexler	82	3114	707	1408	.502	357	470	.760	227	291	518	566	281	7	204	253	71	1782	21.7	36
Steve Johnson	79	2345	494	889	.556	342	490	.698	194	372	566	155	340	16	49	276	76	1330	16.8	40
Sam Bowie	5	163	30	66	.455	20	30	.667	14	19	33	9	19	0	1	15	10	80	16.0	31
Terry Porter	80	2714	376	770	.488	280	334	.838	70	267	337	715	192	0	159	255	9	1045	13.1	24
Jerome Kersey	82	2088	373	733	.509	262	364	.720	201	295	496	194	328	5	122	149	77	1009	12.3	28
Jim Paxson	72	1798	337	733	.460	174	216	.806	41	98	139	237	134	0	76	108	12	874	12.1	22
Kenny Carr	49	1443	201	399	.504	126	169	.746	131	368	499	83	159	1	29	103	13	528	10.8	20
Kevin Duckworth†	51	753	112	228	.491	83	120	.692	63	129	192	23	165	3	16	74	18	307	6.0	18
Kevin Duckworth‡	65	875	130	273	.476	92	134	.687	76	147	223	29	192	3	21	78	21	352	5.4	18
Caldwell Jones	78	1578	111	224	.496	97	124	.782	114	341	455	64	227	5	23	87	77	319	4.1	15
Michael Holton	58	479	70	171	.409	44	55	.800	9	29	38	73	51	0	16	41	2	191	3.3	16
Perry Young†	4	52	4	17	.235	0	0	...	3	4	7	7	11	0	4	3	1	8	2.0	2
Perry Young‡	9	72	6	21	.286	1	2	.500	3	5	8	7	14	0	5	4	1	13	1.4	3
Walter Berry*	7	19	6	8	.750	1	1	1.000	4	3	7	1	8	0	2	0	0	13	1.9	7
Ron Rowan	7	16	4	9	.444	3	4	.750	1	0	1	1	1	0	4	3	0	12	1.7	4
Chris Engler*	7	17	4	8	.500	3	3	1.000	6	2	8	1	0	0	1	2	1	11	1.6	6
Joe Binion	11	51	4	10	.400	6	10	.600	8	10	18	1	5	0	2	3	2	14	1.3	5
Fernando Martin	24	146	9	31	.290	4	11	.364	8	20	28	9	24	0	7	20	1	22	0.9	6

3-pt. FG: Portland 98-339 (.289)—Vandeweghe 39-81 (.481); Drexler 11-47 (.234); Porter 13-60 (.217); Kersey 1-23 (.043); Paxson 26-98 (.265); Carr 0-2 (.000); Duckworth† 0-1 (.000); Duckworth‡ 0-1 (.000); Jones 0-2 (.000); Holton 7-23 (.304); Rowan 1-1 (1.000); Martin 0-1 (.000). Opponents 116-421 (.276).

SACRAMENTO KINGS

	G	Min.	FGM	FGA	Pct.	FTM	FTA	Pct.	Off.	Def.	Tot.	Ast.	PF	Dq.	Stl.	TO	Blk.	Pts.	Avg.	Hi.
Reggie Theus	79	2872	577	1223	.472	429	495	.867	86	180	266	692	208	3	78	289	16	1600	20.3	33
Otis Thorpe	82	2956	567	1050	.540	413	543	.761	259	560	819	201	292	11	46	189	60	1547	18.9	34
Eddie Johnson	81	2457	606	1309	.463	267	322	.829	146	207	353	251	218	4	42	163	19	1516	18.7	38
Derek Smith	52	1658	338	757	.446	178	228	.781	60	122	182	204	184	3	46	126	23	863	16.6	31
LaSalle Thompson	82	2166	362	752	.481	188	255	.737	237	450	687	122	290	6	69	143	126	912	11.1	27
Terry Tyler	82	1930	329	664	.495	101	140	.721	116	212	328	73	151	1	55	78	78	760	9.3	23
Joe Kleine	79	1658	256	543	.471	110	140	.786	173	310	483	71	213	2	35	90	30	622	7.9	22
Brook Steppe	34	665	95	199	.477	73	88	.830	21	40	61	81	56	0	18	54	3	266	7.8	24
Harold Pressley	67	913	134	317	.423	35	48	.729	68	108	176	120	96	1	40	63	21	310	4.6	19
Johnny Rogers	45	468	90	185	.486	9	15	.600	30	47	77	26	66	0	9	20	8	189	4.2	14
Othell Wilson	53	789	82	185	.443	43	54	.796	28	53	81	207	67	0	42	77	4	210	4.0	12
Franklin Edwards	8	122	9	32	.281	10	14	.714	2	8	10	29	7	0	5	17	0	28	3.5	10
Mark Olberding	76	1002	69	165	.418	116	131	.885	50	135	185	91	144	0	18	56	9	254	3.3	21
Bruce Douglas	8	98	7	24	.292	0	4	.000	5	9	14	17	9	0	9	9	0	14	1.8	6
Jerry Eaves	3	26	1	8	.125	2	2	1.000	1	0	1	0	6	0	1	2	0	4	1.3	4

3-pt. FG: Sacramento 77-307 (.251)—Theus 17-78 (.218); Thorpe 0-3 (.000); Johnson 37-118 (.314); Smith 9-33 (.273); Thompson 0-5 (.000); Tyler 1-3 (.333); Kleine 0-1 (.000); Steppe 3-9 (.333); Pressley 7-28 (.250); Rogers 0-5 (.000); Wilson 3-18 (.167); Edwards 0-4 (.000); Olberding 0-1 (.000); Douglas 0-1 (.000). Opponents 125-395 (.316).

SAN ANTONIO SPURS

	G	Min.	FGM	FGA	Pct.	FTM	FTA	Pct.	Off.	Def.	Tot.	Ast.	PF	Dq.	Stl.	TO	Blk.	Pts.	Avg.	Hi.
Alvin Robertson	81	2697	589	1264	.466	244	324	.753	186	238	424	421	264	2	260	243	35	1435	17.7	34
Walter Berry†	56	1567	401	758	.529	186	287	.648	132	170	302	104	188	2	36	153	40	988	17.6	29
Walter Berry‡	63	1586	407	766	.531	187	288	.649	136	173	309	105	196	2	38	153	40	1001	15.9	29
Mike Mitchell	40	922	208	478	.435	92	112	.821	38	65	103	38	68	0	19	51	9	509	12.7	34
Mychal Thompson*	49	1210	230	528	.436	144	196	.735	91	185	276	87	117	0	31	77	41	605	12.3	29
David Greenwood	79	2587	336	655	.513	241	307	.785	256	527	783	203	248	3	71	161	50	916	11.6	31
Artis Gilmore	82	2405	346	580	.597	242	356	.680	185	394	579	150	235	2	39	178	95	934	11.4	24
Jon Sundvold	76	1765	365	751	.486	70	84	.833	20	78	98	315	109	1	35	97	0	850	11.2	25
Johnny Dawkins	81	1682	334	764	.437	153	191	.801	56	113	169	290	118	0	67	120	3	835	10.3	28

1986-87

	G	Min.	FGM	FGA	Pct.	FTM	FTA	Pct.	Off.	Def.	Tot.	Ast.	PF	Dq.	Stl.	TO	Blk.	Pts.	Avg.	Hi.
									REBOUNDS									SCORING		
Tyrone Corbin*	31	732	113	264	.428	49	67	.731	52	67	119	80	81	0	38	46	3	275	8.9	23
Johnny Moore	55	1234	198	448	.442	56	70	.800	32	68	100	250	97	0	83	102	3	474	8.6	25
Larry Krystkowiak	68	1004	170	373	.456	110	148	.743	77	162	239	85	141	1	22	67	12	451	6.6	24
Anthony Jones†	49	744	119	289	.412	41	52	.788	39	56	95	66	68	0	32	38	18	286	5.8	24
Anthony Jones‡	65	858	133	322	.413	50	65	.769	40	64	104	73	79	0	42	49	19	323	5.0	24
Frank Brickowski†	7	83	10	30	.333	10	11	.909	8	11	19	5	13	0	6	7	2	30	4.3	11
Frank Brickowski‡	44	487	63	124	.508	50	70	.714	48	68	116	17	118	4	20	32	6	176	4.0	14
Ed Nealy	60	980	84	192	.438	51	69	.739	96	188	284	83	144	1	40	36	11	223	3.7	23
Kevin Duckworth*	14	122	18	45	.400	9	14	.643	13	18	31	6	27	0	5	4	3	45	3.2	11
Forrest McKenzie	6	42	7	28	.250	2	2	1.000	2	5	7	1	9	0	1	3	0	17	2.8	8
Mike Brittain	6	29	4	9	.444	1	2	.500	2	2	4	2	3	0	1	2	0	9	1.5	5

3-pt. FG: San Antonio 117-403 (.290)—Robertson 13-48 (.271); Berry† 0-3 (.000); Berry‡ 0-3 (.000); Mitchell 1-2 (.500); Thompson* 1-1 (1.000); Greenwood 3-6 (.500); Sundvold 50-149 (.336); Dawkins 14-47 (.298); Moore 22-79 (.278); Krystkowiak 1-12 (.083); Jones† 7-19 (.368); Jones‡ 7-20 (.350); Brickowski† 0-4 (.000); Brickowski‡ 0-4 (.000); Nealy 4-31 (.129); McKenzie 1-2 (.500). Opponents 106-379 (.280).

SEATTLE SUPERSONICS

	G	Min.	FGM	FGA	Pct.	FTM	FTA	Pct.	Off.	Def.	Tot.	Ast.	PF	Dq.	Stl.	TO	Blk.	Pts.	Avg.	Hi.
									REBOUNDS									SCORING		
Dale Ellis	82	3073	785	1520	.516	385	489	.787	187	260	447	238	267	2	104	238	32	2041	24.9	41
Tom Chambers	82	3018	660	1446	.456	535	630	.849	163	382	545	245	307	9	81	268	50	1909	23.3	42
Xavier McDaniel	82	3031	806	1583	.509	275	395	.696	338	367	705	207	300	4	115	234	52	1890	23.0	40
Alton Lister	75	2288	346	687	.504	179	265	.675	223	482	705	110	289	11	32	169	180	871	11.6	25
Gerald Henderson*	6	155	25	50	.500	17	18	.944	6	3	9	32	17	0	6	15	0	67	11.2	14
Eddie Johnson	24	508	85	186	.457	42	55	.764	11	35	46	115	36	0	12	41	1	217	9.0	22
Maurice Lucas	63	1120	175	388	.451	150	187	.802	88	219	307	65	171	1	34	75	21	500	7.9	22
Nate McMillan	71	1972	143	301	.475	87	141	.617	101	230	331	583	238	4	125	155	45	373	5.3	15
Kevin Williams	65	703	132	296	.446	55	66	.833	47	36	83	66	154	1	45	63	8	319	4.9	15
Danny Young	73	1482	132	288	.458	59	71	.831	23	90	113	353	72	0	74	85	3	352	4.8	17
Terence Stansbury	44	375	67	156	.429	31	50	.620	8	16	24	57	78	0	13	29	0	176	4.0	16
Clemon Johnson	78	1051	88	178	.494	70	110	.636	106	171	277	21	137	0	21	36	42	246	3.2	12
Mike Phelps	60	469	75	176	.426	31	44	.705	16	34	50	64	60	0	21	32	2	182	3.0	13
Russ Schoene	63	579	71	190	.374	29	46	.630	52	65	117	27	94	1	20	42	11	173	2.7	15
Curtis Kitchen	6	31	3	6	.500	3	4	.750	4	5	9	1	4	0	2	0	3	9	1.5	5

3-pt. FG: Seattle 191-571 (.335)—Ellis 86-240 (.358); Chambers 54-145 (.372); McDaniel 3-14 (.214); Lister 0-1 (.000); Henderson* 0-3 (.000); E. Johnson 5-15 (.333); Lucas 0-5 (.000); McMillan 0-7 (.000); Williams 0-7 (.000); Young 29-79 (.367); Stansbury 11-29 (.379); C. Johnson 0-2 (.000); Phelps 1-10 (.100); Schoene 2-13 (.154); Kitchen 0-1 (.000). Opponents 93-324 (.287).

UTAH JAZZ

	G	Min.	FGM	FGA	Pct.	FTM	FTA	Pct.	Off.	Def.	Tot.	Ast.	PF	Dq.	Stl.	TO	Blk.	Pts.	Avg.	Hi.
									REBOUNDS									SCORING		
Karl Malone	82	2857	728	1422	.512	323	540	.598	278	577	855	158	323	6	104	237	60	1779	21.7	38
Darrell Griffith	76	1843	463	1038	.446	149	212	.703	81	146	227	129	167	0	97	135	29	1142	15.0	38
Thurl Bailey	81	2155	463	1036	.447	190	236	.805	145	287	432	102	150	0	38	123	88	1116	13.8	29
Kelly Tripucka	79	1865	291	621	.469	197	226	.872	54	188	242	243	147	0	85	167	11	798	10.1	27
Bobby Hansen	72	1453	272	601	.453	136	179	.760	84	119	203	102	146	0	44	77	6	696	9.7	26
Rickey Green	81	2090	301	644	.467	172	208	.827	38	125	163	541	108	0	110	133	2	781	9.6	24
John Stockton	82	1858	231	463	.499	179	229	.782	32	119	151	670	224	1	177	164	14	648	7.9	21
Mark Eaton	79	2505	234	585	.400	140	213	.657	211	486	697	105	273	5	43	142	321	608	7.7	17
Carey Scurry	69	753	123	247	.498	94	134	.701	97	101	198	57	124	1	55	56	54	344	5.0	21
Dell Curry	67	636	139	326	.426	30	38	.789	30	48	78	58	86	0	27	44	4	325	4.9	20
Kent Benson	73	895	140	316	.443	47	58	.810	80	151	231	39	138	0	39	45	28	329	4.5	17
Marc Iavaroni	78	845	100	215	.465	78	116	.672	64	109	173	36	154	0	16	56	11	278	3.6	13

3-pt. FG: Utah 139-448 (.310)—Malone 0-7 (.000); Griffith 67-200 (.335); Bailey 0-2 (.000); Tripucka 19-52 (.365); Hansen 16-45 (.356); Green 7-19 (.368); Stockton 7-39 (.179); Scurry 4-13 (.308); Curry 17-60 (.283); Benson 2-7 (.286); Iavaroni 0-4 (.000). Opponents 143-451 (.317).

WASHINGTON BULLETS

	G	Min.	FGM	FGA	Pct.	FTM	FTA	Pct.	Off.	Def.	Tot.	Ast.	PF	Dq.	Stl.	TO	Blk.	Pts.	Avg.	Hi.
									REBOUNDS									SCORING		
Moses Malone	73	2488	595	1311	.454	570	692	.824	340	484	824	120	139	0	59	202	92	1760	24.1	50
Jeff Malone	80	2763	689	1509	.457	376	425	.885	50	168	218	298	154	0	75	182	13	1758	22.0	48
Jay Vincent	51	1386	274	613	.447	130	169	.769	69	141	210	85	127	0	40	77	17	678	13.3	33
Terry Catledge	78	2149	413	835	.495	199	335	.594	248	312	560	56	195	1	43	145	14	1025	13.1	32
John Williams	78	1773	283	624	.454	144	223	.646	130	236	366	191	173	1	128	122	30	718	9.2	21
Ennis Whatley	73	1816	246	515	.478	126	165	.764	58	136	194	392	172	0	92	138	10	618	8.5	20
Frank Johnson	18	399	59	128	.461	35	49	.714	10	20	30	58	31	0	21	31	0	153	8.5	18
Darwin Cook	82	1420	265	622	.426	82	103	.796	46	105	151	145	136	0	98	96	17	614	7.5	24
Michael Adams	63	1303	160	393	.407	105	124	.847	38	85	123	244	88	0	86	81	6	453	7.2	17
Dan Roundfield	36	669	90	220	.409	57	72	.792	64	106	170	39	77	0	11	49	16	238	6.6	22
Charles Jones	79	1609	118	249	.474	48	76	.632	144	212	356	80	252	2	67	77	165	284	3.6	12
Jay Murphy	21	141	31	72	.431	9	16	.563	17	22	39	5	21	0	3	6	2	71	3.4	8
Manute Bol	82	1552	103	231	.446	45	67	.672	84	278	362	11	189	1	20	61	302	251	3.1	10
Anthony Jones*	16	114	14	33	.424	9	13	.692	1	8	9	7	11	0	10	11	1	37	2.3	12
Mike O'Koren	15	123	16	42	.381	0	2	.000	6	8	14	13	10	0	2	6	0	32	2.1	8

3-pt. FG: Washington 43-218 (.197)—M. Malone 0-11 (.000); J. Malone 4-26 (.154); Vincent 0-3 (.000); Catledge 0-4 (.000); Williams 8-36 (.222); Whatley 0-2 (.000); Johnson 0-1 (.000); Cook 2-23 (.087); Adams 45-102 (.275); Roundfield 1-5 (.200); C. Jones 0-1 (.000); Bol 0-1 (.000); A. Jones 0-1 (.000); O'Koren 0-2 (.000). Opponents 104-358 (.291).

* Finished season with another team. † Totals with this team only. ‡ Totals with all teams.

1986-87

PLAYOFF RESULTS

EASTERN CONFERENCE

FIRST ROUND

Boston 3, Chicago 0
Apr. 23—Thur. Chicago 104 at Boston 108
Apr. 26—Sun. Chicago 96 at Boston 105
Apr. 28—Tue. Boston 105 at Chicago 94

Milwaukee 3, Philadelphia 2
Apr. 24—Fri. Philadelphia 104 at Milwaukee 107
Apr. 26—Sun. Philadelphia 125 at Milwaukee *122
Apr. 29—Wed. Milwaukee 121 at Philadelphia 120
May 1—Fri. Milwaukee 118 at Philadelphia 124
May 3—Sun. Philadelphia 89 at Milwaukee 102

Detroit 3, Washington 0
Apr. 24—Fri. Washington 92 at Detroit 106
Apr. 26—Sun. Washington 85 at Detroit 128
Apr. 29—Wed. Detroit 97 at Washington 96

Atlanta 3, Indiana 1
Apr. 24—Fri. Indiana 94 at Atlanta 110
Apr. 26—Sun. Indiana 93 at Atlanta 94
Apr. 29—Wed. Atlanta 87 at Indiana 96
May 1—Fri. Atlanta 101 at Indiana 97

SEMIFINALS

Detroit 4, Atlanta 1
May 3—Sun. Detroit 112 at Atlanta 111
May 5—Tue. Detroit 102 at Atlanta 115
May 8—Fri. Atlanta 99 at Detroit 108
May 10—Sun. Atlanta 88 at Detroit 89
May 13—Wed. Detroit 104 at Atlanta 96

Boston 4, Milwaukee 3
May 5—Tue. Milwaukee 98 at Boston 111
May 0—Wed. Milwaukee 124 at Boston 126
May 8—Fri. Boston 121 at Milwaukee *126
May 10—Sun. Boston 138 at Milwaukee **137
May 13—Wed. Milwaukee 129 at Boston 124
May 15—Fri. Boston 111 at Milwaukee 121
May 17—Sun. Milwaukee 113 at Boston 119

FINALS

Boston 4, Detroit 3
May 19—Tue. Detroit 91 at Boston 104
May 21—Thur. Detroit 101 at Boston 110
May 23—Sat. Boston 104 at Detroit 122
May 24—Sun. Boston 119 at Detroit 145
May 26—Tue. Detroit 107 at Boston 108
May 28—Thur. Boston 105 at Detroit 113
May 30—Sat. Detroit 114 at Boston 117

WESTERN CONFERENCE

FIRST ROUND

L.A. Lakers 3, Denver 0
Apr. 23—Thur. Denver 95 at L.A. Lakers 128
Apr. 25—Sat. Denver 127 at L.A. Lakers 139
Apr. 29—Wed. L.A. Lakers 140 at Denver 103

Golden State 3, Utah 2
Apr. 23—Thur. Golden State 85 at Utah 99
Apr. 25—Sat. Golden State 100 at Utah 103
Apr. 29—Wed. Utah 95 at Golden State 110
May 1—Fri. Utah 94 at Golden State 98
May 3—Sun. Golden State 118 at Utah 113

Houston 3, Portland 1
Apr. 24—Fri. Houston 125 at Portland 115
Apr. 26—Sun. Houston 98 at Portland 111
Apr. 28—Tue. Portland 108 at Houston 117
Apr. 30—Thur. Portland 101 at Houston 113

Seattle 3, Dallas 1
Apr. 23—Thur. Seattle 129 at Dallas 151
Apr. 25—Sat. Seattle 112 at Dallas 110
Apr. 28—Tue. Dallas 107 at Seattle 117
Apr. 30—Thur. Dallas 98 at Seattle 124

SEMIFINALS

Seattle 4, Houston 2
May 2—Sat. Seattle 111 at Houston *106
May 5—Tue. Seattle 99 at Houston 97
May 7—Thur. Houston 102 at Seattle 84
May 9—Sat. Houston 102 at Seattle 117
May 12—Tue. Seattle 107 at Houston 112
May 14—Thur. Houston 125 at Seattle **128

L.A. Lakers 4, Golden State 1
May 5—Tue. Golden State 116 at L.A. Lakers 125
May 7—Thur. Golden State 101 at L.A. Lakers 116
May 9—Sat. L.A. Lakers 133 at Golden State 108
May 10—Sun. L.A. Lakers 121 at Golden State 129
May 12—Tue. Golden State 106 at L.A. Lakers 118

FINALS

L.A. Lakers 4, Seattle 0
May 16—Sat. Seattle 87 at L.A. Lakers 92
May 19—Tue. Seattle 104 at L.A. Lakers 112
May 23—Sat. L.A. Lakers 122 at Seattle 121
May 25—Mon. L.A. Lakers 133 at Seattle 102

NBA FINALS

L.A. Lakers 4, Boston 2
June 2—Tue. Boston 113 at L.A. Lakers 126
June 4—Thur. Boston 122 at L.A. Lakers 141
June 7—Sun. L.A. Lakers 103 at Boston 109
June 9—Tue. L.A. Lakers 107 at Boston 106
June 11—Thur. L.A. Lakers 108 at Boston 123
June 14—Sun. Boston 93 at L.A. Lakers 106

*Denotes number of overtime periods.

1986-87

1985-86

1985-86 NBA CHAMPION BOSTON CELTICS

Front row (from left): Danny Ainge, Scott Wedman, vice chairman and treasurer Alan Cohen, executive vice president and general manager Jan Volk, president Red Auerbach, head coach K.C. Jones, chairman of the board Don Gaston, Larry Bird, Dennis Johnson. Back row (from left): equipment manager Wayne Lebeaux, team physician Dr. Thomas Silva, assistant coach Jimmy Rodgers, Sam Vincent, Rick Carlisle, Greg Kite, Robert Parish, Bill Walton, Kevin McHale, David Thirdkill, Jerry Sichting, assistant coach Chris Ford, trainer Ray Melchiorre.

FINAL STANDINGS

ATLANTIC DIVISION

	Atl.	Bos.	Chi.	Cle.	Dal.	Den.	Det.	G.S.	Hou.	Ind.	L.A.C.	L.A.L.	Mil.	N.J.	N.Y.	Phi.	Pho.	Por.	Sac.	S.A.	Sea.	Uta.	Was.	W	L	Pct.	GB
Boston	6	..	5	5	1	1	4	2	2	5	2	5	4	5	4	1	1	1	2	2	2	2	5	67	15	.817	..
Philadelphia	1	2	5	6	2	1	4	1	1	6	2	0	1	4	6	..	2	2	2	1	1	1	3	54	28	.659	13
New Jersey	2	2	3	3	0	1	2	1	3	0	1	2	5	..	2	2	2	2	1	0	2	2	2	39	43	.476	28
Washington	4	1	4	5	1	0	2	1	0	1	0	2	4	3	3	1	2	1	0	1	1	1	..	39	43	.476	28
New York	1	1	2	1	1	1	1	1	0	4	0	1	0	1	..	0	2	0	1	1	1	0	3	23	59	.280	44

CENTRAL DIVISION

	Atl.	Bos.	Chi.	Cle.	Dal.	Den.	Det.	G.S.	Hou.	Ind.	L.A.C.	L.A.L.	Mil.	N.J.	N.Y.	Phi.	Pho.	Por.	Sac.	S.A.	Sea.	Uta.	Was.	W	L	Pct.	GB
Milwaukee	3	0	5	5	2	0	4	2	2	4	1	0	..	4	6	4	1	2	2	2	2	2	4	57	25	.695	..
Atlanta	..	0	5	4	1	1	4	1	1	5	2	1	3	4	5	4	2	2	2	1	1	0	1	50	32	.610	7
Detroit	2	1	4	5	2	1	..	1	1	5	2	1	2	4	4	2	0	1	0	1	2	1	4	46	36	.561	11
Chicago	1	1	..	3	0	2	2	2	1	3	1	0	1	2	4	1	1	1	0	1	1	1	1	30	52	.366	27
Cleveland	2	1	3	..	1	1	1	0	0	3	1	1	1	3	4	0	2	0	2	1	1	0	1	29	53	.354	28
Indiana	1	1	3	2	0	0	1	1	0	..	2	0	2	2	2	2	1	0	0	1	2	0	5	26	56	.317	31

MIDWEST DIVISION

	Atl.	Bos.	Chi.	Cle.	Dal.	Den.	Det.	G.S.	Hou.	Ind.	L.A.C.	L.A.L.	Mil.	N.J.	N.Y.	Phi.	Pho.	Por.	Sac.	S.A.	Sea.	Uta.	Was.	W	L	Pct.	GB
Houston	1	0	1	2	5	3	1	5	..	2	3	1	0	1	2	1	3	3	4	5	3	3	2	51	31	.622	..
Denver	1	1	0	1	3	..	1	3	3	2	4	3	2	1	1	1	4	3	3	3	2	3	2	47	35	.573	4
Dallas	1	1	2	1	..	3	0	4	1	2	2	1	0	2	1	0	5	2	3	4	3	5	1	44	38	.537	7
Utah	2	0	1	2	1	3	1	3	3	2	2	0	0	0	2	1	4	3	4	4	3	..	1	42	40	.512	9
Sacramento	0	1	2	0	3	3	2	3	2	2	0	0	0	0	1	0	3	2	..	5	5	2	1	37	45	.451	14
San Antonio	1	0	1	1	2	3	1	3	1	1	4	1	0	1	1	1	2	4	1	..	2	2	2	35	47	.427	16

PACIFIC DIVISION

	Atl.	Bos.	Chi.	Cle.	Dal.	Den.	Det.	G.S.	Hou.	Ind.	L.A.C.	L.A.L.	Mil.	N.J.	N.Y.	Phi.	Pho.	Por.	Sac.	S.A.	Sea.	Uta.	Was.	W	L	Pct.	GB
L.A. Lakers	1	0	2	1	4	2	1	4	4	2	4	..	2	1	1	2	5	6	5	4	4	5	2	62	20	.756	..
Portland	0	1	1	2	3	2	1	5	2	2	4	0	0	2	0	4	3	..	1	5	2	0	0	40	42	.488	22
Phoenix	0	1	1	0	0	1	2	4	2	1	4	1	1	0	0	0	..	2	2	3	5	1	1	32	50	.390	30
L.A. Clippers	0	0	1	1	3	1	0	1	2	0	..	2	1	2	2	0	2	2	5	1	3	3	0	32	50	.390	30
Seattle	1	0	1	1	2	3	0	4	2	0	3	2	0	2	1	1	1	1	0	3	..	2	1	31	51	.378	31
Golden State	1	0	0	2	1	2	1	..	0	1	5	2	0	1	1	1	2	1	2	2	2	2	1	30	52	.366	32

TEAM STATISTICS

OFFENSIVE

	G	FGM	FGA	Pct.	FTM	FTA	Pct.	Off.	Def.	Tot.	Ast.	PF	Dq.	Stl.	TO	Blk.	Pts.	Avg.
L.A. Lakers	82	3834	7343	.522	1812	2329	.778	1101	2555	3656	2433	2031	8	693	1467	419	9618	117.3
Dallas	82	3631	7254	.501	2050	2643	.776	1059	2454	3513	2108	1733	17	605	1289	369	9453	115.3
Portland	82	3610	7281	.496	2142	2799	.765	1153	2316	3469	2180	2205	30	859	1529	356	9436	115.1
Denver	82	3705	7868	.471	1929	2416	.798	1223	2317	3540	2140	2164	23	826	1336	421	9410	114.8
Milwaukee	82	3601	7310	.493	2063	2701	.764	1189	2420	3609	2158	2210	34	805	1369	460	9390	114.5
Houston	82	3759	7671	.490	1776	2434	.730	1316	2434	3750	2318	1991	30	745	1374	551	9379	114.4
Detroit	82	3754	7750	.484	1800	2300	.783	1276	2461	3737	2319	2101	26	738	1343	340	9363	114.2
Boston	82	3718	7312	.508	1785	2248	.794	1054	2753	3807	2387	1756	15	641	1360	511	9359	114.1
Golden State	82	3650	7567	.482	1912	2517	.760	1271	2344	3615	2018	2032	37	751	1400	354	9299	113.4
San Antonio	82	3596	7104	.506	1882	2523	.746	1069	2413	3482	2260	2115	27	800	1624	390	9120	111.2
Philadelphia	82	3435	7058	.487	2130	2810	.758	1326	2378	3704	2017	1798	13	862	1595	490	9051	110.4
Phoenix	82	3518	6993	.503	1949	2683	.726	1034	2449	3483	2272	2260	29	773	1763	379	9023	110.0
Chicago	82	3476	7227	.481	1922	2499	.769	1280	2278	3558	2006	2166	34	609	1436	400	8962	109.3
New Jersey	82	3548	7301	.486	1810	2396	.755	1183	2483	3666	2128	2129	41	749	1575	345	8949	109.1
Sacramento	82	3538	7220	.490	1818	2338	.778	1135	2377	3512	2304	2134	19	602	1533	388	8924	108.8
L.A. Clippers	82	3388	7165	.473	2067	2683	.770	1159	2258	3417	1968	1931	23	694	1506	501	8907	108.6
Atlanta	82	3447	7029	.490	1979	2704	.732	1249	2405	3654	2025	2170	34	736	1483	434	8906	108.6
Utah	82	3453	7083	.488	1930	2694	.716	1068	2479	3547	2199	2038	14	717	1518	666	8871	108.2
Cleveland	82	3478	7239	.480	1748	2325	.752	1086	2455	3541	2064	2267	37	627	1411	436	8836	107.8
Seattle	82	3335	7059	.472	1815	2331	.779	1145	2256	3401	1977	2168	32	745	1435	295	8564	104.4
Indiana	82	3441	7150	.481	1614	2183	.739	1138	2613	3751	2159	2135	15	659	1515	381	8519	103.9
Washington	82	3311	7148	.463	1704	2286	.745	1066	2432	3498	1748	1796	15	626	1346	716	8442	103.0
New York	82	3239	7034	.460	1534	2237	.686	1081	2170	3251	1877	2213	47	714	1438	308	8094	98.7

DEFENSIVE

	FGM	FGA	Pct.	FTM	FTA	Pct.	Off.	Def.	Tot.	Ast.	PF	Dq.	Stl.	TO	Blk.	Pts.	Avg.	Dif.
New York	3192	6672	.478	2102	2744	.766	1166	2587	3753	2007	2018	25	701	1629	444	8554	104.3	-5.6
Seattle	3301	6774	.487	1913	2491	.768	1027	2308	3335	2038	2008	23	654	1467	406	8572	104.5	-0.1
Boston	3444	7476	.461	1617	2162	.748	1089	2317	3406	1924	1966	22	725	1258	341	8587	104.7	+9.4
Washington	3435	7360	.467	1649	2181	.756	1249	2591	3840	2014	1907	17	712	1373	454	8590	104.8	-1.8
Milwaukee	3286	7040	.467	1980	2674	.740	1169	2325	3494	1952	2139	26	633	1631	397	8649	105.5	+9.0
Atlanta	3360	7074	.475	1905	2508	.760	1202	2329	3531	1945	2129	30	697	1494	371	8712	106.2	+2.4
Indiana	3372	7123	.473	1975	2571	.768	1050	2479	3529	2057	1909	14	745	1315	445	8792	107.2	-3.3
Philadelphia	3615	7328	.493	1546	2041	.757	1189	2228	3417	2255	2187	41	802	1520	469	8858	108.0	+2.4
Utah	3470	7339	.473	1896	2483	.764	1208	2510	3718	1977	2221	35	752	1531	464	8901	108.5	-0.3
L.A. Lakers	3577	7450	.480	1778	2369	.751	1104	2226	3330	2235	1992	26	792	1330	359	8983	109.5	+7.8
Cleveland	3435	7239	.475	2115	2758	.767	1131	2494	3625	2122	1945	23	711	1331	364	9071	110.6	-2.8
New Jersey	3504	7124	.492	2008	2622	.766	1036	2369	3405	2019	2002	19	783	1523	390	9112	111.1	-2.0
Houston	3638	7402	.491	1802	2406	.749	1190	2389	3579	2196	1977	22	683	1464	386	9165	111.8	+2.6
Sacramento	3566	7225	.494	1971	2609	.755	1142	2339	3481	2118	2083	29	751	1409	478	9176	111.9	-3.1
Phoenix	3569	7307	.488	2041	2692	.758	1137	2265	3402	2149	2216	25	841	1515	466	9268	113.0	-3.0
Detroit	3620	7365	.492	1956	2589	.756	1180	2538	3718	2083	1977	25	662	1490	500	9267	113.0	+1.2
Chicago	3601	7138	.504	2002	2627	.762	1104	2362	3466	2170	2002	24	664	1298	491	9274	113.1	-3.8
San Antonio	3629	7365	.493	1916	2491	.769	1157	2304	3461	2269	2108	32	800	1519	453	9272	113.1	-1.9
Denver	3638	7404	.491	1967	2693	.730	1295	2732	4027	2106	2117	28	639	1741	484	9303	113.5	+1.3
Portland	3637	7249	.502	1992	2638	.755	1179	2362	3541	2254	2262	46	760	1645	426	9349	114.0	+1.1
Dallas	3864	7689	.503	1545	2049	.754	1219	2469	3688	2381	2196	33	617	1279	423	9363	114.2	+1.1
L.A. Clippers	3849	7588	.507	1704	2280	.747	1268	2458	3726	2469	2113	17	760	1396	457	9475	115.5	-6.9
Golden State	3863	7432	.520	1791	2401	.746	1170	2519	3689	2325	2069	18	692	1487	442	9582	116.9	-3.5
Avgs.	3542	7268	.487	1877	2482	.756	1159	2413	3572	2133	2067	26	721	1463	431	9038	110.2	...

HOME/ROAD

	Home	Road	Total		Home	Road	Total
Atlanta	34-7	16-25	50-32	Milwaukee	33-8	24-17	57-25
Boston	40-1	27-14	67-15	New Jersey	26-15	13-28	39-43
Chicago	22-19	8-33	30-52	New York	15-26	8-33	23-59
Cleveland	16-25	13-28	29-53	Philadelphia	31-10	23-18	54-28
Dallas	26-15	18-23	44-38	Phoenix	23-18	9-32	32-50
Denver	34-7	13-28	47-35	Portland	27-14	13-28	40-42
Detroit	31-10	15-26	46-36	Sacramento	25-16	12-29	37-45
Golden State	24-17	6-35	30-52	San Antonio	21-20	14-27	35-47
Houston	36-5	15-26	51-31	Seattle	24-17	7-34	31-51
Indiana	19-22	7-34	26-56	Utah	27-14	15-26	42-40
L.A. Clippers	22-19	10-31	32-50	Washington	26-15	13-28	39-43
L.A. Lakers	35-6	27-14	62-20	Totals	617-326	326-617	943-943

1985-86

POINTS

(minimum 70 games or 1,400 points)

	G	FGM	FTM	Pts.	Avg.		G	FGM	FTM	Pts.	Avg.
Dominique Wilkins, Atlanta	.78	888	577	2366	30.3	World B. Free, Cleveland	.75	652	379	1754	23.4
Alex English, Denver	.81	951	511	2414	29.8	Mark Aguirre, Dallas	.74	668	318	1670	22.6
Adrian Dantley, Utah	.76	818	630	2267	29.8	Jeff Malone, Washington	.80	735	322	1795	22.4
Larry Bird, Boston	.82	796	441	2115	25.8	Walter Davis, Phoenix	.70	624	257	1523	21.8
Purvis Short, Golden State	.64	633	351	1632	25.5	Rolando Blackman, Dallas	.82	677	404	1762	21.5
Kiki Vandeweghe, Portland	.79	719	523	1962	24.8	Kevin McHale, Boston	.68	561	326	1448	21.3
Moses Malone, Philadelphia	.74	571	617	1759	23.8	Joe Barry Carroll, Golden State	.79	650	377	1677	21.2
Hakeem Olajuwon, Houston	.68	625	347	1597	23.5	Isiah Thomas, Detroit	.77	609	365	1609	20.9
Mike Mitchell, San Antonio	.82	802	317	1921	23.4	Orlando Woolridge, Chicago	.70	540	364	1448	20.7
K. Abdul-Jabbar, L.A. Lakers	.79	755	336	1846	23.4	Marques Johnson, L.A. Clippers	.75	613	298	1525	20.3

FIELD GOALS

(minimum 300 made)

	FGM	FGA	Pct.		FGM	FGA	Pct.
Steve Johnson, San Antonio	.362	573	.632	Charles Barkley, Philadelphia	.595	1041	.572
Artis Gilmore, San Antonio	.423	684	.618	Kareem Abdul-Jabbar, L.A. Lakers	.755	1338	.564
Larry Nance, Phoenix	.582	1001	.581	Adrian Dantley, Utah	.818	1453	.563
James Worthy, L.A. Lakers	.629	1086	.579	Alton Lister, Milwaukee	.318	577	.551
Kevin McHale, Boston	.561	978	.574	Robert Parish, Boston	.530	966	.549

FREE THROWS

(minimum 125 made)

	FTM	FTA	Pct.
Larry Bird, Boston	.441	492	.896
Chris Mullin, Golden State	.189	211	.896
Mike Gminski, New Jersey	.351	393	.893
Jim Paxson, Portland	.217	244	.889
George Gervin, Chicago	.283	322	.879
Franklin Edwards, L.A. Clippers	.132	151	.874
Magic Johnson, L.A. Lakers	.378	434	.871
Kiki Vandeweghe, Portland	.523	602	.869
Jeff Malone, Washington	.322	371	.868
Brad Davis, Dallas	.198	228	.868

STEALS

(minimum 70 games or 125 steals)

	G	No.	Avg.
Alvin Robertson, San Antonio	.82	301	3.67
Micheal Ray Richardson, New Jersey	.47	125	2.66
Clyde Drexler, Portland	.75	197	2.63
Maurice Cheeks, Philadelphia	.82	207	2.52
Fat Lever, Denver	.78	178	2.28
Isiah Thomas, Detroit	.77	171	2.22
Charles Barkley, Philadelphia	.80	173	2.16
Paul Pressey, Milwaukee	.80	168	2.10
Larry Bird, Boston	.82	166	2.02
Darwin Cook, New Jersey	.79	156	1.97

ASSISTS

(minimum 70 games or 400 assists)

	G	No.	Avg.
Magic Johnson, L.A. Lakers	.72	907	12.6
Isiah Thomas, Detroit	.77	830	10.8
Reggie Theus, Sacramento	.82	788	9.6
John Bagley, Cleveland	.78	735	9.4
Maurice Cheeks, Philadelphia	.82	753	9.2
Sleepy Floyd, Golden State	.82	746	9.1
John Lucas, Houston	.65	571	8.8
Norm Nixon, L.A. Clippers	.67	576	8.6
Doc Rivers, Atlanta	.53	443	8.4
Clyde Drexler, Portland	.75	600	8.0

BLOCKED SHOTS

(minimum 70 games or 100 blocked shots)

	G	No.	Avg.
Manute Bol, Washington	.80	397	4.96
Mark Eaton, Utah	.80	369	4.61
Hakeem Olajuwon, Houston	.68	231	3.40
Wayne Cooper, Denver	.78	227	2.91
Benoit Benjamin, L.A. Clippers	.79	206	2.61
Jawann Oldham, Chicago	.52	134	2.58
Herb Williams, Indiana	.78	184	2.36
Tree Rollins, Atlanta	.74	167	2.26
Patrick Ewing, New York	.50	103	2.06
Kevin McHale, Boston	.68	134	1.97

REBOUNDS

(minimum 70 games or 800 rebounds)

	G	Off.	Def.	Tot.	Avg.
Bill Laimbeer, Detroit	.82	305	770	1075	13.1
Charles Barkley, Philadelphia	.80	354	672	1026	12.8
Buck Williams, New Jersey	.82	329	657	986	12.0
Moses Malone, Philadelphia	.74	339	533	872	11.8
Ralph Sampson, Houston	.79	258	621	879	11.1
Larry Smith, Golden State	.77	384	472	856	11.1
Larry Bird, Boston	.82	190	615	805	9.8
J. Donaldson, L.A. Clippers-Dal.	.83	171	624	795	9.6
LaSalle Thompson, Sacramento	.80	252	518	770	9.6
Robert Parish, Boston	.81	246	524	770	9.5

3-POINT FIELD GOALS

(minimum 25 made)

	FGA	FGM	Pct.
Craig Hodges, Milwaukee	.162	73	.451
Trent Tucker, New York	.91	41	.451
Ernie Grunfeld, New York	.61	26	.426
Larry Bird, Boston	.194	82	.423
World B. Free, Cleveland	.169	71	.420
Kyle Macy, Chicago	.141	58	.411
Michael Cooper, L.A. Lakers	.163	63	.387
Dale Ellis, Dallas	.173	63	.364
Mike McGee, L.A. Lakers	.114	41	.360
Leon Wood, Philadelphia-Washington	.114	41	.360
Kevin McKenna, Washington	.75	27	.360

INDIVIDUAL STATISTICS, TEAM BY TEAM

ATLANTA HAWKS

	G	Min.	FGM	FGA	Pct.	FTM	FTA	Pct.	Off.	Def.	Tot.	Ast.	PF	Dq.	Stl.	TO	Blk.	Pts.	Avg.	Hi.
Dominique Wilkins . . .	78	3049	888	1897	.468	577	705	.818	261	357	618	206	170	0	138	251	49	2366	30.3	57
Randy Wittman	81	2760	467	881	.530	104	135	.770	51	119	170	306	118	0	81	114	14	1043	12.9	24
Kevin Willis	82	2300	419	811	.517	172	263	.654	243	461	704	45	294	6	66	177	44	1010	12.3	39
Doc Rivers	53	1571	220	464	.474	172	283	.608	49	113	162	443	185	2	120	141	13	612	11.5	29
Eddie Johnson*	39	862	155	328	.473	79	110	.718	17	58	75	219	72	1	10	90	1	394	10.1	24
Cliff Levingston	81	1945	294	551	.534	164	242	.678	193	341	534	72	260	5	76	113	39	752	9.3	25
Ray Williams*	19	367	57	143	.399	41	48	.854	19	26	45	67	48	1	28	41	1	159	8.4	20
Jon Koncak	82	1695	263	519	.507	156	257	.607	171	296	467	55	296	10	37	111	69	682	8.3	21
Spud Webb	79	1229	199	412	.483	216	275	.785	27	96	123	337	164	1	82	159	5	616	7.8	23
Antoine Carr	17	258	49	93	.527	18	27	.667	16	36	52	14	51	1	7	14	15	116	6.8	14
Tree Rollins	74	1781	173	347	.499	69	90	.767	131	327	458	41	239	5	38	91	167	415	5.6	14
Johnny Davis†	27	402	46	107	.430	51	59	.864	2	17	19	112	32	0	13	38	0	144	5.3	17
Johnny Davis‡	66	1014	148	344	.430	118	138	.855	8	47	55	217	76	0	37	78	4	417	6.3	17
John Battle	64	639	101	222	.455	75	103	.728	12	50	62	74	80	0	23	47	3	277	4.3	22
Lorenzo Charles . .	36	273	49	88	.557	24	36	.667	13	26	39	8	37	0	2	18	6	122	3.4	12
Scott Hastings	62	650	65	159	.409	60	70	.857	44	80	124	26	118	2	14	40	8	193	3.1	12
Sedric Toney*	3	24	2	7	.286	1	1	1.000	0	2	2	6	0	1	3	0	5	1.7	5

3-pt. FG: Atlanta 33-166 (.199)—Wilkins 13-70 (.186); Wittman 5-16 (.313); Willis 0-6 (.000); Rivers 0-16 (.000); Johnson* 5-20 (.250); Levingston 0-1 (.000); Williams* 4-11 (.364); Koncak 0-1 (.000); Webb 2-11 (.182); Rollins 0-1 (.000); Davis† 1-2 (.500); Davis‡ 3-13 (.231); Battle 0-7 (.000); Hastings 3-4 (.750). Opponents 87-283 (.307).

BOSTON CELTICS

	G	Min.	FGM	FGA	Pct.	FTM	FTA	Pct.	Off.	Def.	Tot.	Ast.	PF	Dq.	Stl.	TO	Blk.	Pts.	Avg.	Hi.
Larry Bird	82	3113	796	1606	.496	441	492	.896	190	615	805	557	182	0	166	266	51	2115	25.8	50
Kevin McHale	68	2397	561	978	.574	326	420	.776	171	380	551	181	192	2	29	149	134	1448	21.3	34
Robert Parish	81	2567	530	966	.549	245	335	.731	246	524	770	145	215	3	65	187	116	1305	16.1	30
Dennis Johnson . .	78	2732	482	1060	.455	243	297	.818	69	199	268	456	206	3	110	173	35	1213	15.6	30
Danny Ainge	80	2407	353	701	.504	123	136	.904	47	188	235	405	204	4	94	129	7	855	10.7	27
Scott Wedman	79	1402	286	605	.473	45	68	.662	66	126	192	83	127	0	38	54	22	634	8.0	24
Bill Walton	80	1546	231	411	.562	144	202	.713	136	408	544	165	210	1	38	151	106	606	7.6	22
Jerry Sichting	82	1596	235	412	.570	61	66	.924	27	77	104	188	118	0	50	73	0	537	6.5	17
David Thirdkill	49	385	54	110	.491	55	88	.625	27	43	70	15	55	0	11	19	3	163	3.3	20
Sam Vincent	57	432	59	162	.364	65	70	.929	11	37	48	69	59	0	17	49	4	184	3.2	12
Sly Williams	6	54	5	21	.238	7	12	.583	7	8	15	2	15	0	1	7	1	17	2.8	7
Rick Carlisle	77	760	92	189	.487	15	23	.652	22	55	77	104	92	1	19	50	4	199	2.6	10
Greg Kite	64	464	34	91	.374	15	39	.385	35	93	128	17	81	1	3	32	28	83	1.3	8

3-pt. FG: Boston 138-393 (.351)—Bird 82-194 (.423); Johnson 6-42 (.143); Ainge 26-73 (.356); Wedman 17-48 (.354); Sichting 6-16 (.375); Thirdkill 0-1 (.000); Vincent 1-4 (.250); Williams 0-4 (.000); Carlisle 0-10 (.000); Kite 0-1 (.000). Opponents 82-304 (.270).

CHICAGO BULLS

	G	Min.	FGM	FGA	Pct.	FTM	FTA	Pct.	Off.	Def.	Tot.	Ast.	PF	Dq.	Stl.	TO	Blk.	Pts.	Avg.	Hi.
Michael Jordan	18	451	150	328	.457	105	125	.840	23	41	64	53	46	0	37	45	21	408	22.7	33
Orlando Woolridge . . .	70	2248	540	1090	.495	364	462	.788	150	200	350	213	186	2	49	174	47	1448	20.7	44
Quintin Dailey	35	723	203	470	.432	163	198	.823	20	48	68	67	86	0	22	67	5	569	16.3	38
George Gervin	82	2065	519	1100	.472	283	322	.879	78	137	215	144	210	4	49	161	23	1325	16.2	45
Sidney Green	80	2307	407	875	.465	262	335	.782	208	450	658	139	292	5	70	220	37	1076	13.5	31
Gene Banks	82	2139	356	688	.517	183	255	.718	178	182	360	251	212	4	81	139	10	895	10.9	38
Charles Oakley . . .	77	1772	281	541	.519	178	269	.662	255	409	664	133	250	9	68	175	30	740	9.6	35
Dave Corzine	67	1709	255	519	.491	127	171	.743	132	301	433	150	133	0	28	104	53	640	9.6	23
Kyle Macy	82	2426	286	592	.483	73	90	.811	41	137	178	446	201	1	81	117	1	703	8.6	22
Jawann Oldham . .	52	1276	167	323	.517	53	91	.582	112	194	306	37	206	6	28	86	134	387	7.4	17
Michael Holton†	24	447	73	155	.471	24	38	.632	10	20	30	48	40	1	23	23	0	171	7.1	21
Michael Holton‡ . .	28	512	77	175	.440	28	44	.636	11	22	33	55	47	1	25	27	0	183	6.5	21
John Paxson	75	1570	153	328	.466	74	92	.804	18	76	94	274	172	2	55	63	2	395	5.3	23
Rod Higgins†	5	81	9	23	.391	5	6	.833	3	4	7	5	11	0	4	2	3	23	4.6	7
Rod Higgins‡	30	332	39	106	.368	19	27	.704	14	37	51	24	49	0	9	13	11	98	3.3	11
Tony Brown	10	132	18	41	.439	9	13	.692	5	11	16	14	16	0	5	4	1	45	4.5	15
Mike Smrek	38	408	46	122	.377	16	29	.552	46	64	110	19	95	0	6	29	23	108	2.8	15
Billy McKinney	9	83	10	23	.435	2	2	1.000	1	4	5	13	9	0	3	2	0	22	2.4	4
Ron Brewer*	4	18	3	9	.333	1	1	1.000	0	0	0	1	0	0	2	0	7	1.8	7

3-pt. FG: Chicago 88-317 (.278)—Jordan 3-18 (.167); Woolridge 4-23 (.174); Dailey 0-8 (.000); Gervin 4-19 (.211); Green 0-8 (.000); Banks 0-19 (.000); Oakley 0-3 (.000); Corzine 3-12 (.250); Macy 58-141 (.411); Oldham 0-1 (.000); Holton† 1-10 (.100); Holton‡ 1-12 (.083); Paxson 15-50 (.300); Higgins† 0-1 (.000); Higgins‡ 1-9 (.111); Brown 0-2 (.000); Smrek 0-2 (.000). Opponents 70-233 (.300).

CLEVELAND CAVALIERS

	G	Min.	FGM	FGA	Pct.	FTM	FTA	Pct.	Off.	Def.	Tot.	Ast.	PF	Dq.	Stl.	TO	Blk.	Pts.	Avg.	Hi.
World B. Free	75	2535	652	1433	.455	379	486	.780	72	146	218	314	186	1	91	172	19	1754	23.4	43
Roy Hinson	82	2834	621	1167	.532	364	506	.719	167	472	639	102	316	7	62	188	112	1606	19.6	39

– 493 –

	G	Min.	FGM	FGA	Pct.	FTM	FTA	Pct.	REBOUNDS Off.	Def.	Tot.	Ast.	PF	Dq.	Stl.	TO	Blk.	SCORING Pts.	Avg.	Hi.
Mel Turpin	80	2292	456	838	.544	185	228	.811	182	374	556	55	260	6	65	134	106	1097	13.7	32
John Bagley	78	2472	366	865	.423	170	215	.791	76	199	275	735	165	1	122	239	10	911	11.7	24
Phil Hubbard	23	640	93	198	.470	76	112	.679	48	72	120	29	78	2	20	66	3	262	11.4	22
Eddie Johnson†	32	615	129	293	.440	33	45	.733	13	33	46	114	56	0	8	60	1	315	9.8	25
Eddie Johnson‡	71	1477	284	621	.457	112	155	.723	30	91	121	333	128	1	18	150	2	709	10.0	25
Edgar Jones	53	1011	187	370	.505	132	178	.742	71	136	207	45	142	0	30	64	38	513	9.7	24
Keith Lee	58	1197	177	380	.466	75	96	.781	116	235	351	67	204	9	29	78	37	431	7.4	25
Johnny Davis*	39	612	102	237	.430	67	79	.848	6	30	36	105	44	0	24	40	4	273	7.0	17
Dirk Minniefield	76	1131	167	347	.481	73	93	.785	43	88	131	269	165	1	65	108	1	417	5.5	20
Ron Brewer†	40	552	83	215	.386	33	37	.892	14	39	53	40	43	0	17	21	6	204	5.1	16
Ron Brewer‡	44	570	86	224	.384	34	38	.895	14	39	53	40	44	0	17	23	6	211	4.8	16
Ron Anderson*	17	207	37	74	.500	12	16	.750	5	21	26	8	20	0	1	6	0	86	5.1	14
Ben Poquette	81	1496	166	348	.477	72	100	.720	121	252	373	78	187	2	33	68	32	406	5.0	15
Lonnie Shelton	44	682	92	188	.489	14	16	.875	38	105	143	61	128	2	21	48	4	198	4.5	13
Mark West	67	1172	113	209	.541	54	103	.524	97	225	322	20	235	6	27	91	62	280	4.2	14
Ben McDonald	21	266	28	58	.483	5	8	.625	15	23	38	9	30	0	7	10	1	61	2.9	10
Ennis Whatley*	8	66	9	19	.474	4	7	.571	2	5	7	13	8	0	5	6	0	22	2.8	14

3-pt. FG: Cleveland 132-391 (.338)—Free 71-169 (.420); Hinson 0-4 (.000); Turpin 0-4 (.000); Bagley 9-37 (.243); Hubbard 0-1 (.000); Johnson† 24-65 (.369); Johnson‡ 29-85 (.341); Jones 7-23 (.304); Lee 2-9 (.222); Davis* 2-11 (.182); Minniefield 10-37 (.270); Brewer† 5-17 (.294); Brewer‡ 5-17 (.294); Anderson* 0-1 (.000); Poquette 2-10 (.200); Shelton 0-2 (.000); McDonald 0-1 (.000). Opponents 86-297 (.290).

DALLAS MAVERICKS

	G	Min.	FGM	FGA	Pct.	FTM	FTA	Pct.	REBOUNDS Off.	Def.	Tot.	Ast.	PF	Dq.	Stl.	TO	Blk.	SCORING Pts.	Avg.	Hi.
Mark Aguirre	74	2501	668	1327	.503	318	451	.705	177	268	445	339	229	6	62	252	14	1670	22.6	42
Rolando Blackman	82	2787	677	1318	.514	404	483	.836	88	203	291	271	138	0	79	189	25	1762	21.5	46
Sam Perkins	80	2626	458	910	.503	307	377	.814	195	490	685	153	212	2	75	145	94	1234	15.4	32
Jay Vincent	80	1994	442	919	.481	222	274	.810	107	261	368	180	193	2	66	145	21	1106	13.8	31
Derek Harper	79	2150	390	730	.534	171	229	.747	75	151	226	416	166	1	153	144	23	963	12.2	26
Brad Davis	82	1971	267	502	.532	198	228	.868	26	120	146	467	174	2	57	110	15	764	9.3	23
James Donaldson†	69	2241	213	375	.568	147	184	.799	143	521	664	84	156	0	23	85	110	573	8.3	20
James Donaldson‡	83	2682	256	459	.558	204	254	.803	171	624	795	96	189	0	28	123	139	716	8.6	20
Dale Ellis	72	1086	193	470	.411	59	82	.720	86	82	168	37	78	0	40	38	9	508	7.1	28
Kurt Nimphius*	13	280	37	72	.514	17	29	.586	23	37	60	14	38	1	3	13	12	91	7.0	20
Detlef Schrempf	64	969	142	315	.451	110	152	.724	70	128	198	88	166	1	23	84	10	397	6.2	23
Bill Wennington	56	562	72	153	.471	45	62	.726	32	100	132	21	83	0	11	21	22	189	3.4	15
Wallace Bryant*	9	154	11	30	.367	6	11	.545	9	24	33	11	26	2	3	7	2	28	3.1	7
Uwe Blab	48	409	44	94	.468	36	67	.537	25	66	91	17	65	0	3	28	12	124	2.6	14
Harold Keeling	20	75	17	39	.436	10	14	.714	3	3	6	10	9	0	7	7	0	44	2.2	7

3-pt. FG: Dallas 141-446 (.316)—Aguirre 16-56 (.286); Blackman 4-29 (.138); Perkins 11-33 (.333); Vincent 0-3 (.000); Harper 12-51 (.235); Davis 32-89 (.360); Ellis 63-173 (.364); Nimphius* 0-1 (.000); Schrempf 3-7 (.429); Wennington 0-4 (.000). Opponents 90-311 (.289).

DENVER NUGGETS

	G	Min.	FGM	FGA	Pct.	FTM	FTA	Pct.	REBOUNDS Off.	Def.	Tot.	Ast.	PF	Dq.	Stl.	TO	Blk.	SCORING Pts.	Avg.	Hi.
Alex English	81	3024	951	1888	.504	511	593	.862	192	213	405	320	235	1	73	249	29	2414	29.8	54
Calvin Natt	69	2007	469	930	.504	278	347	.801	125	311	436	164	143	0	58	130	13	1218	17.7	35
Fat Lever	78	2616	468	1061	.441	132	182	.725	136	284	420	584	204	3	178	210	15	1080	13.8	31
Wayne Cooper	78	2112	422	906	.466	174	219	.795	190	420	610	81	315	6	42	117	227	1021	13.1	32
Bill Hanzlik	79	1982	331	741	.447	318	405	.785	88	176	264	316	277	2	107	165	16	988	12.5	27
Mike Evans	81	1389	304	715	.425	126	149	.846	30	71	101	177	159	1	61	124	1	773	9.5	28
Dan Schayes	80	1654	221	440	.502	216	278	.777	154	285	439	79	298	7	42	105	63	658	8.2	25
Elston Turner	73	1324	165	379	.435	39	53	.736	64	137	201	165	150	1	70	80	6	369	5.1	16
T.R. Dunn	82	2401	172	379	.454	68	88	.773	143	234	377	171	228	1	155	51	16	412	5.0	12
Willie White	43	343	74	168	.440	19	23	.826	17	27	44	53	24	0	18	25	2	173	4.0	17
Blair Rasmussen	48	330	61	150	.407	31	39	.795	37	60	97	16	63	0	3	40	10	153	3.2	15
Pete Williams	53	573	67	111	.604	17	40	.425	47	99	146	14	68	1	19	19	23	151	2.8	16

3-pt. FG: Denver 71-305 (.233)—English 1-5 (.200); Natt 2-6 (.333); Lever 12-38 (.316); Cooper 3-7 (.429); Hanzlik 8-41 (.195); Evans 39-176 (.222); Schayes 0-1 (.000); Turner 0-9 (.000); Dunn 0-1 (.000); White 6-21 (.286). Opponents 60-262 (.229).

DETROIT PISTONS

	G	Min.	FGM	FGA	Pct.	FTM	FTA	Pct.	REBOUNDS Off.	Def.	Tot.	Ast.	PF	Dq.	Stl.	TO	Blk.	SCORING Pts.	Avg.	Hi.
Isiah Thomas	77	2790	609	1248	.488	365	462	.790	83	194	277	830	245	9	171	289	20	1609	20.9	39
Kelly Tripucka	81	2626	615	1236	.498	380	444	.856	116	232	348	265	167	0	93	183	10	1622	20.0	41
Bill Laimbeer	82	2891	545	1107	.492	266	319	.834	305	770	1075	146	291	4	59	133	65	1360	16.6	29
Vinnie Johnson	79	1978	465	996	.467	165	214	.771	119	107	226	269	180	2	80	88	23	1097	13.9	35
John Long	62	1176	264	548	.482	89	104	.856	47	51	98	82	92	0	41	59	13	620	10.0	28
Joe Dumars	82	1957	287	597	.481	190	238	.798	60	59	119	390	200	1	66	158	11	769	9.4	22
Earl Cureton	80	2017	285	564	.505	117	211	.555	198	306	504	137	239	3	58	150	58	687	8.6	25
Tony Campbell	82	1292	294	608	.484	58	73	.795	83	153	236	45	164	0	62	86	7	648	7.9	20
Kent Benson	72	1344	201	415	.484	66	83	.795	118	258	376	80	196	3	58	58	51	469	6.5	21
Rick Mahorn	80	1442	157	345	.455	81	119	.681	121	291	412	64	261	4	40	109	61	395	4.9	22
Chuck Nevitt†	25	101	12	32	.375	15	20	.750	10	15	25	5	29	0	2	7	17	39	1.6	8
Chuck Nevitt‡	29	126	15	43	.349	19	26	.731	13	19	32	7	35	0	4	12	19	49	1.7	8
Mike Gibson	32	161	20	51	.392	8	11	.727	15	25	40	5	35	0	8	6	4	48	1.5	9

	G	Min.	FGM	FGA	Pct.	FTM	FTA	Pct.	Off.	Def.	Tot.	Ast.	PF	Dq.	Stl.	TO	Blk.	Pts.	Avg.	Hi.
									REBOUNDS									SCORING		
Walker Russell 1	1	2	0	1	.000	0	0	. . .	0	0	0	1	0	0	0	0	0	0	0.0	0
Ron Crevier† 2	2	3	0	2	.000	0	2	.000	1	0	1	0	2	0	0	0	0	0	0.0	0
Ron Crevier† 3	3	4	0	3	.000	0	2	.000	1	0	1	0	2	0	0	0	0	0	0.0	0

3-pt. FG: Detroit 55-182 (.302)—Thomas 26-84 (.310); Tripucka 12-25 (.480); Laimbeer 4-14 (.286); Johnson 2-13 (.154); Long 3-16 (.188); Dumars 5-16 (.313); Cureton 0-2 (.000); Campbell 2-9 (.222); Benson 1-2 (.500); Mahorn 0-1 (.000). Opponents 71-258 (.275).

GOLDEN STATE WARRIORS

	G	Min.	FGM	FGA	Pct.	FTM	FTA	Pct.	Off.	Def.	Tot.	Ast.	PF	Dq.	Stl.	TO	Blk.	Pts.	Avg.	Hi.
									REBOUNDS									SCORING		
Purvis Short 64	64	2427	633	1313	.482	351	406	.865	126	203	329	237	229	5	92	184	22	1632	25.5	44
Joe Barry Carroll 79	79	2801	650	1404	.463	377	501	.752	193	477	670	176	277	13	101	275	143	1677	21.2	34
Sleepy Floyd 82	82	2764	510	1007	.506	351	441	.796	76	221	297	746	199	2	157	290	16	1410	17.2	32
Terry Teagle 82	82	2158	475	958	.496	211	265	.796	96	139	235	115	241	2	71	136	34	1165	14.2	33
Chris Mullin 55	55	1391	287	620	.463	189	211	.896	42	73	115	105	130	1	70	75	23	768	14.0	26
Larry Smith 77	77	2441	314	586	.536	112	227	.493	384	472	856	95	286	7	62	135	50	740	9.6	21
Greg Ballard 75	75	1792	272	570	.477	101	126	.802	132	285	417	83	174	0	65	54	8	662	8.8	25
Peter Thibeaux 42	42	531	100	233	.429	29	48	.604	28	47	75	28	82	1	23	39	15	231	5.5	18
Geoff Huston 82	82	1208	140	273	.513	63	92	.685	10	55	65	342	67	0	38	83	4	345	4.2	13
Lester Conner 36	36	413	51	136	.375	40	54	.741	25	37	62	43	23	0	24	15	1	144	4.0	11
Jerome Whitehead . . . 81	81	1079	126	294	.429	60	97	.619	94	234	328	19	176	2	18	64	19	312	3.9	18
Peter Verhoeven 61	61	749	90	167	.539	25	43	.581	65	95	160	29	141	3	29	30	17	206	3.4	16
Guy Williams 5	5	25	2	5	.400	3	6	.500	0	6	6	0	7	1	1	0	2	7	1.4	2
Ron Crevier* 1	1	1	0	1	.000	0	0	. . .	0	0	0	0	0	0	0	0	0	0	0.0	0

3-pt. FG: Golden State 87-278 (.313)—Short 15-49 (.306); Carroll 0-2 (.000); Floyd 39-119 (.328); Teagle 4-25 (.160); Mullin 5-27 (.185); Smith 0-1 (.000); Ballard 17-35 (.486); Thibeaux 2-5 (.400); Huston 2-6 (.333); Conner 2-7 (.286); Verhoeven 1-2 (.500). Opponents 65-229 (.284).

HOUSTON ROCKETS

	G	Min.	FGM	FGA	Pct.	FTM	FTA	Pct.	Off.	Def.	Tot.	Ast.	PF	Dq.	Stl.	TO	Blk.	Pts.	Avg.	Hi.
									REBOUNDS									SCORING		
Hakeem Olajuwon 68	68	2467	625	1188	.526	347	538	.645	333	448	781	137	271	9	134	195	231	1597	23.5	41
Ralph Sampson 79	79	2864	624	1280	.488	241	376	.641	258	621	879	283	308	12	99	285	129	1491	18.9	38
Lewis Lloyd 82	82	2444	592	1119	.529	199	236	.843	155	169	324	300	216	0	102	194	24	1386	16.9	38
John Lucas 65	65	2120	365	818	.446	231	298	.775	33	110	143	571	124	0	77	149	5	1006	15.5	31
Robert Reid 82	82	2157	409	881	.464	162	214	.757	67	234	301	222	231	3	91	96	16	986	12.0	25
Rodney McCray 82	82	2610	338	629	.537	171	222	.770	159	361	520	292	197	2	50	130	58	847	10.3	25
Allen Leavell 74	74	1190	212	458	.463	135	158	.854	6	61	67	234	120	1	58	88	8	583	7.9	28
Mitchell Wiggins 78	78	1198	222	489	.454	86	118	.729	87	72	159	101	155	1	59	62	5	531	6.8	22
Jim Petersen 82	82	1664	196	411	.477	113	160	.706	149	247	396	85	231	2	38	84	54	505	6.2	19
Steve Harris 57	57	482	103	233	.442	50	54	.926	25	32	57	50	75	0	21	34	4	257	4.5	16
Hank McDowell 22	22	204	24	42	.571	17	25	.680	12	37	49	6	25	0	1	10	3	65	3.0	8
Craig Ehlo 36	36	199	36	84	.429	23	29	.793	17	29	46	29	22	0	11	15	4	98	2.7	8
Granville Waiters 43	43	156	13	39	.333	1	6	.167	15	13	28	8	30	0	4	11	10	27	0.6	6

3-pt. FG: Houston 85-310 (.274)—Sampson 2-15 (.133); Lloyd 3-15 (.200); Lucas 45-146 (.308); Reid 6-33 (.182); McCray 0-3 (.000); Leavell 24-67 (.358); Wiggins 1-12 (.083); Petersen 0-3 (.000); Harris 1-5 (.200); McDowell 0-1 (.000); Ehlo 3-9 (.333); Waiters 0-1 (.000). Opponents 87-268 (.325).

INDIANA PACERS

	G	Min.	FGM	FGA	Pct.	FTM	FTA	Pct.	Off.	Def.	Tot.	Ast.	PF	Dq.	Stl.	TO	Blk.	Pts.	Avg.	Hi.
									REBOUNDS									SCORING		
Herb Williams 78	78	2770	627	1275	.492	294	403	.730	172	538	710	174	244	2	50	210	184	1549	19.9	40
Clark Kellogg 19	19	568	139	294	.473	53	69	.768	51	117	168	57	59	2	28	61	8	335	17.6	30
Wayman Tisdale 81	81	2277	516	1002	.515	160	234	.684	191	393	584	79	290	3	32	188	44	1192	14.7	32
Vern Fleming 80	80	2870	436	862	.506	263	353	.745	102	284	386	505	230	3	131	208	5	1136	14.2	27
Steve Stipanovich 79	79	2397	416	885	.470	242	315	.768	173	450	623	206	261	1	75	146	69	1076	13.6	25
Ron Anderson† 60	60	1469	273	554	.493	73	111	.658	125	123	248	136	105	0	55	76	6	621	10.4	28
Ron Anderson‡ 77	77	1676	310	628	.494	85	127	.669	130	144	274	144	125	0	56	82	6	707	9.2	28
Clint Richardson 82	82	2224	335	736	.455	123	147	.837	69	182	251	372	153	1	58	136	8	794	9.7	21
Bryan Warrick† 31	31	658	81	172	.471	53	67	.791	10	56	66	109	76	0	25	48	2	217	7.0	16
Bryan Warrick‡ 36	36	685	85	182	.467	54	68	.794	10	59	69	115	79	0	27	53	2	227	6.3	16
Terence Stansbury . . . 74	74	1331	191	441	.433	107	132	.811	29	110	139	206	200	2	59	139	8	498	6.7	22
Bill Martin 66	66	691	143	298	.480	46	54	.852	42	60	102	52	108	1	21	58	7	332	5.0	20
Bill Garnett 80	80	1197	112	239	.469	116	162	.716	106	169	275	95	174	0	39	91	22	340	4.3	13
Quinn Buckner 32	32	419	49	104	.471	19	27	.704	9	42	51	86	80	0	40	55	3	117	3.7	13
Dwayne McClain 45	45	461	69	180	.383	18	35	.514	14	16	30	60	61	0	38	40	4	157	3.5	15
Stuart Gray 67	67	423	54	108	.500	47	74	.635	45	73	118	15	94	0	8	32	11	155	2.3	11

3-pt. FG: Indiana 23-143 (.161)—Williams 1-12 (.083); Kellogg 4-13 (.308); Tisdale 0-2 (.000); Fleming 1-6 (.167); Stipanovich 2-10 (.200); Anderson† 2-8 (.250); Anderson‡ 2-9 (.222); Richardson 1-9 (.111); Warrick† 2-10 (.200); Warrick‡ 3-12 (.250); Stansbury 9-53 (.170); Martin 0-8 (.000); Garnett 0-2 (.000); Buckner 0-1 (.000); McClain 0-1 (.111). Opponents 73-275 (.265).

LOS ANGELES CLIPPERS

	G	Min.	FGM	FGA	Pct.	FTM	FTA	Pct.	Off.	Def.	Tot.	Ast.	PF	Dq.	Stl.	TO	Blk.	Pts.	Avg.	Hi.
									REBOUNDS									SCORING		
Derek Smith 11	11	339	100	181	.552	58	84	.690	20	21	41	31	35	2	9	33	13	259	23.5	36
Marques Johnson 75	75	2605	613	1201	.510	298	392	.760	156	260	416	283	214	2	107	183	50	1525	20.3	34
Norm Nixon 67	67	2138	403	921	.438	131	162	.809	45	135	180	576	143	0	84	190	3	979	14.6	33

	G	Min.	FGM	FGA	Pct.	FTM	FTA	Pct.	Off.	Def.	Tot.	Ast.	PF	Dq.	Stl.	TO	Blk.	Pts.	Avg.	Hi.
									REBOUNDS									SCORING		
Cedric Maxwell	76	2458	314	661	.475	447	562	.795	241	383	624	215	252	2	61	206	29	1075	14.1	27
Kurt Nimphius†	67	1946	314	622	.505	177	233	.760	129	264	393	48	229	7	30	107	93	805	12.0	26
Kurt Nimphius‡	80	2226	351	694	.506	194	262	.740	152	301	453	62	267	8	33	120	105	896	11.2	26
Rory White	75	1761	355	684	.519	164	222	.739	82	99	181	74	161	2	74	95	8	875	11.7	32
Benoit Benjamin	79	2088	324	661	.490	229	307	.746	161	439	600	79	286	5	64	145	206	878	11.1	28
James Donaldson*	14	441	43	84	.512	57	70	.814	28	103	131	12	33	0	5	38	29	143	10.2	17
Franklin Edwards	73	1491	262	577	.454	132	151	.874	24	62	86	259	87	0	89	137	4	657	9.0	28
Junior Bridgeman	58	1161	199	451	.441	106	119	.891	29	94	123	108	81	1	31	68	8	510	8.8	25
Michael Cage	78	1566	204	426	.479	113	174	.649	168	249	417	81	176	1	62	106	34	521	6.7	22
Darnell Valentine†	34	483	69	182	.379	59	75	.787	12	41	53	107	45	0	23	57	1	200	5.9	21
Darnell Valentine‡	62	1217	161	388	.415	130	175	.743	32	93	125	246	123	0	72	115	2	456	7.4	21
Jamaal Wilkes	13	195	26	65	.400	22	27	.815	13	16	29	15	19	0	7	16	2	75	5.8	15
Lancaster Gordon	60	704	130	345	.377	45	56	.804	24	44	68	60	91	1	33	62	10	312	5.2	22
Jay Murphy	14	100	16	45	.356	9	14	.643	7	8	15	3	12	0	4	5	3	41	2.9	7
Jim Thomas	6	69	6	15	.400	1	2	.500	3	5	8	12	12	0	5	9	1	13	2.2	5
Wallace Bryant†	8	64	4	18	.222	5	8	.625	8	12	20	4	12	0	2	2	3	13	1.6	5
Wallace Bryant‡	17	218	15	48	.313	11	19	.579	17	36	53	15	38	2	5	9	5	41	2.4	7
Jeff Cross	21	128	6	24	.250	14	25	.560	9	21	30	1	38	0	2	6	3	26	1.2	7
Ozell Jones	3	18	0	2	.000	0	0	...	0	2	2	0	5	0	2	3	1	0	0.0	0

3-pt. FG: L.A. Clippers 64-229 (.279)—Smith 1-2 (.500); Johnson 1-15 (.067); Nixon 42-121 (.347); Maxwell 0-3 (.000); Nimphius† 0-2 (.000); White 1-9 (.111); Benjamin 1-3 (.333); Edwards 1-9 (.111); Bridgeman 6-18 (.333); Cage 0-3 (.000); Valentine† 3-11 (.273); Valentine‡ 4-14 (.286); Wilkes 1-3 (.333); Gordon 7-28 (.250); Murphy 0-2 (.000). Opponents 73-261 (.280).

LOS ANGELES LAKERS

	G	Min.	FGM	FGA	Pct.	FTM	FTA	Pct.	Off.	Def.	Tot.	Ast.	PF	Dq.	Stl.	TO	Blk.	Pts.	Avg.	Hi.
									REBOUNDS									SCORING		
Kareem Abdul-Jabbar	79	2629	755	1338	.564	336	439	.765	133	345	478	280	248	2	67	203	130	1846	23.4	46
James Worthy	75	2454	629	1086	.579	242	314	.771	136	251	387	201	195	0	82	149	77	1500	20.0	37
Magic Johnson	72	2578	483	918	.526	378	434	.871	85	341	426	907	133	0	113	273	16	1354	18.8	34
Byron Scott	76	2190	507	989	.513	138	176	.784	55	134	189	164	167	0	85	110	15	1174	15.4	31
Maurice Lucas	77	1750	302	653	.462	180	230	.783	164	402	566	84	253	1	45	121	24	785	10.2	23
Michael Cooper	82	2269	274	606	.452	147	170	.865	44	200	244	466	238	2	89	151	43	758	9.2	20
Mike McGee	71	1213	252	544	.463	42	64	.656	51	89	140	83	131	0	53	70	7	587	8.3	34
Petur Gudmundsson	8	128	20	37	.541	18	27	.667	17	21	38	3	25	1	3	11	4	58	7.3	15
A.C. Green	82	1542	209	388	.539	102	167	.611	160	221	381	54	229	2	49	99	49	521	6.4	21
Mitch Kupchak	55	783	124	257	.482	84	112	.750	69	122	191	17	102	0	12	64	7	332	6.0	15
Kurt Rambis	74	1573	160	269	.595	88	122	.721	156	361	517	69	198	0	66	97	33	408	5.5	17
Larry Spriggs	43	471	88	192	.458	38	49	.776	28	53	81	49	78	0	18	54	9	214	5.0	18
Jerome Henderson	1	3	2	3	.667	0	0	...	0	1	1	0	1	0	0	0	0	4	4.0	4
Ronnie Lester	27	222	26	52	.500	15	19	.789	0	10	10	54	27	0	9	42	3	67	2.5	8
Chuck Nevitt*	4	25	3	11	.273	4	6	.667	3	4	7	2	6	0	2	5	2	10	2.5	4

3-pt. FG: L.A. Lakers 138-409 (.337)—Abdul-Jabbar 0-2 (.000); Worthy 0-13 (.000); Johnson 10-43 (.233); Scott 22-61 (.361); Lucas 1-2 (.500); Cooper 63-163 (.387); McGee 41-114 (.360); Green 1-6 (.167); Kupchak 0-1 (.000); Spriggs 0-1 (.000); Lester 0-3 (.000). Opponents 51-247 (.206).

MILWAUKEE BUCKS

	G	Min.	FGM	FGA	Pct.	FTM	FTA	Pct.	Off.	Def.	Tot.	Ast.	PF	Dq.	Stl.	TO	Blk.	Pts.	Avg.	Hi.
									REBOUNDS									SCORING		
Sidney Moncrief	73	2567	470	962	.489	498	580	.859	115	219	334	357	178	1	103	174	18	1471	20.2	35
Terry Cummings	82	2669	681	1438	.474	265	404	.656	222	472	694	193	283	4	121	191	51	1627	19.8	35
Paul Pressey	80	2704	411	843	.488	316	392	.806	127	272	399	623	247	4	168	240	71	1146	14.3	30
Ricky Pierce	81	2147	429	798	.538	266	310	.858	94	137	231	177	252	6	83	107	6	1127	13.9	32
Craig Hodges	66	1739	284	568	.500	75	86	.872	39	78	117	229	157	3	74	89	2	716	10.8	29
Alton Lister	81	1812	318	577	.551	160	266	.602	199	393	592	101	300	8	49	161	142	796	9.8	22
Randy Breuer	82	1792	272	570	.477	141	198	.712	159	299	458	114	214	2	50	122	116	685	8.4	19
Charlie Davis	57	873	188	397	.474	61	75	.813	60	110	170	55	113	1	26	50	7	440	7.7	26
Kenny Fields	78	1120	204	398	.513	91	132	.689	59	144	203	79	170	3	51	77	15	499	6.4	23
Jeff Lamp*	44	701	109	243	.449	55	64	.859	34	87	121	64	88	1	20	30	3	276	6.3	23
Mike Glenn	38	573	94	190	.495	47	49	.959	4	53	57	39	42	0	9	18	3	235	6.2	14
Jerry Reynolds	55	508	72	162	.444	58	104	.558	37	43	80	86	57	0	43	52	19	203	3.7	17
Paul Mokeski	45	521	59	139	.424	25	34	.735	36	103	139	30	92	1	6	25	6	143	3.2	12
Bryan Warrick*	5	27	4	10	.400	1	1	1.000	0	3	3	6	3	0	2	5	0	10	2.0	4
Derrick Rowland	2	9	1	3	.333	1	2	.500	0	1	1	1	1	0	0	0	0	3	1.5	2
Earl Jones	12	43	5	12	.417	3	4	.750	4	6	10	4	13	0	0	7	1	13	1.1	4

3-pt. FG: Milwaukee 125-382 (.327)—Moncrief 33-103 (.320); Cummings 0-2 (.000); Pressey 8-44 (.182); Pierce 3-23 (.130); Hodges 73-162 (.451); Lister 0-2 (.000); Breuer 0-1 (.000); Davis 3-24 (.125); Fields 0-4 (.000); Lamp* 3-13 (.231); Reynolds 1-2 (.500); Warrick* 1-2 (.500). Opponents 97-329 (.295).

NEW JERSEY NETS

	G	Min.	FGM	FGA	Pct.	FTM	FTA	Pct.	Off.	Def.	Tot.	Ast.	PF	Dq.	Stl.	TO	Blk.	Pts.	Avg.	Hi.
									REBOUNDS									SCORING		
Mike Gminski	81	2525	491	949	.517	351	393	.893	206	462	668	133	163	0	56	140	71	1333	16.5	41
Buck Williams	82	3070	500	956	.523	301	445	.676	329	657	986	131	294	9	73	244	96	1301	15.9	31
Otis Birdsong	77	2395	542	1056	.513	122	210	.581	88	114	202	261	228	8	85	179	17	1214	15.8	41
Micheal R. Richardson	47	1604	296	661	.448	141	179	.788	77	173	250	340	163	2	125	150	11	737	15.7	38
Darryl Dawkins	51	1207	284	441	.644	210	297	.707	85	166	251	77	227	10	16	124	59	778	15.3	27

	G	Min.	FGM	FGA	Pct.	FTM	FTA	Pct.	Off.	Def.	Tot.	Ast.	PF	Dq.	Stl.	TO	Blk.	Pts.	Avg.	Hi.
Albert King	73	1998	438	961	.456	167	203	.823	116	250	366	181	205	4	58	181	24	1047	14.3	34
Darwin Cook	79	1965	267	627	.426	84	111	.757	51	126	177	390	172	0	156	132	22	629	8.0	23
Mickey Johnson	79	1574	214	507	.422	183	233	.785	98	234	332	217	248	1	67	165	25	616	7.8	25
Kelvin Ransey	79	1504	231	505	.457	121	148	.818	34	82	116	252	128	0	51	114	4	586	7.4	21
Ray Williams†	5	63	10	32	.313	12	14	.857	35	51	86	9	12	0	5	9	0	32	6.4	13
Ray Williams‡	47	827	117	306	.382	115	126	.913	35	51	86	187	124	2	61	101	4	355	7.6	22
Mike O'Koren	67	1031	160	336	.476	23	39	.590	33	102	135	118	134	3	29	54	9	350	5.2	19
Jeff Turner	53	650	84	171	.491	58	78	.744	45	92	137	14	125	4	21	49	3	226	4.3	16
Bobby Cattage	29	185	28	83	.337	35	44	.795	15	19	34	4	23	0	6	13	0	92	3.2	12
Rod Higgins*	2	29	3	16	.188	0	0	...	3	5	8	1	6	0	1	2	4	6	3.0	4
Yvon Joseph	1	5	0	0	...	2	2	1.000	0	0	0	0	0	0	0	0	0	2	2.0	2

3-pt. FG: New Jersey 43-214 (.201)—Gminski 0-1 (.000); B. Williams 0-2 (.000); Birdsong 8-22 (.364); Richardson 4-27 (.148); Dawkins 0-1 (.000); King 4-23 (.174); Cook 11-53 (.208); Johnson 5-24 (.208); Ransey 3-24 (.125); R.Williams† 0-2 (.000); R. Williams‡ 6-19 (.316); O'Koren 7-27 (.259); Turner 0-1 (.000); Cattage 1-5 (.200); Higgins* 0-2 (.000). Opponents 96-316 (.304).

NEW YORK KNICKERBOCKERS

	G	Min.	FGM	FGA	Pct.	FTM	FTA	Pct.	Off.	Def.	Tot.	Ast.	PF	Dq.	Stl.	TO	Blk.	Pts.	Avg.	Hi.
Patrick Ewing	50	1771	386	814	.474	226	306	.739	124	327	451	102	191	7	54	172	103	998	20.0	37
Pat Cummings	31	1007	195	408	.478	97	139	.698	92	188	280	47	136	7	27	87	12	487	15.7	34
Gerald Wilkins	81	2025	437	934	.468	132	237	.557	92	116	208	161	155	0	68	157	9	1013	12.5	29
Louis Orr	74	2237	330	741	.445	218	278	.784	123	189	312	179	177	4	61	118	26	878	11.9	28
James Bailey	48	1245	202	443	.456	129	167	.772	102	232	334	50	207	12	33	99	40	533	11.1	31
Rory Sparrow	74	2344	345	723	.477	101	127	.795	50	120	170	472	182	1	85	154	14	796	10.8	27
Trent Tucker	77	1788	349	740	.472	79	100	.790	70	99	169	192	167	0	65	70	8	818	10.6	25
Darrell Walker	81	2023	324	753	.430	190	277	.686	100	120	220	337	216	1	146	192	36	838	10.3	28
Ken Bannister	70	1405	235	479	.491	131	249	.526	89	233	322	42	208	5	42	129	24	601	8.6	35
Bill Cartwright	2	36	3	7	.429	6	10	.600	2	8	10	5	6	0	1	6	1	12	6.0	11
Chris McNealy	30	627	70	144	.486	31	47	.660	62	141	203	41	88	2	38	35	12	171	5.7	17
Ernie Grunfeld	76	1402	148	355	.417	90	108	.833	42	164	206	119	192	2	39	50	13	412	5.4	15
Bob Thornton	71	1323	125	274	.456	86	162	.531	113	177	290	43	209	5	30	83	7	336	4.7	17
Ken Green	7	72	13	27	.481	5	9	.556	12	15	27	2	8	0	4	1	0	31	4.4	11
Fred Cofield	45	469	75	184	.408	12	20	.600	6	40	46	82	65	1	20	49	3	165	3.7	13
Butch Carter*	5	31	2	8	.250	1	1	1.000	2	1	3	3	6	0	1	6	0	5	1.0	3

3-pt. FG: New York 82-239 (.343)—Ewing 0-5 (.000); Cummings 0-2 (.000); Wilkins 7-25 (.280); Orr 0-4 (.000); Bailey 0-4 (.000); Sparrow 5-20 (.250); Tucker 41-91 (.451); Walker 0-10 (.000); Bannister 0-1 (.000); Grunfeld 26-61 (.426); Cofield 3-15 (.200); Carter* 0-1 (.000). Opponents 68-274 (.248).

PHILADELPHIA 76ERS

	G	Min.	FGM	FGA	Pct.	FTM	FTA	Pct.	Off.	Def.	Tot.	Ast.	PF	Dq.	Stl.	TO	Blk.	Pts.	Avg.	Hi.
Moses Malone	74	2706	571	1246	.458	617	784	.787	339	533	872	90	194	0	67	261	71	1759	23.8	42
Charles Barkley	80	2952	595	1041	.572	396	578	.685	354	672	1026	312	333	8	173	350	125	1603	20.0	36
Julius Erving	74	2474	521	1085	.480	289	368	.785	169	201	370	248	196	3	113	214	82	1340	18.1	31
Maurice Cheeks	82	3270	490	913	.537	282	335	.842	55	180	235	753	160	0	207	238	28	1266	15.4	31
Bob McAdoo	29	609	116	251	.462	62	81	.765	25	78	103	35	64	0	10	49	18	294	10.1	28
Sedale Threatt	70	1754	310	684	.453	75	90	.833	21	100	121	193	157	1	93	102	5	696	9.9	24
Paul Thompson	23	432	70	194	.361	37	43	.860	27	36	63	24	49	1	15	30	17	179	7.8	24
Terry Catledge	64	1092	202	431	.469	90	139	.647	107	165	272	21	127	0	31	69	8	494	7.7	30
Bobby Jones	70	1519	189	338	.559	114	145	.786	49	120	169	126	159	0	48	90	49	492	7.0	21
Leon Wood*	29	455	57	136	.419	27	34	.794	9	18	27	75	24	0	14	20	0	154	5.3	15
Kenny Green†	21	232	39	91	.429	14	23	.609	10	25	35	6	27	0	1	18	2	92	4.4	13
Kenny Green‡	41	453	83	192	.432	35	49	.714	27	46	73	9	53	0	5	35	9	201	4.9	20
Perry Moss†	60	852	95	239	.397	54	74	.730	25	65	90	89	106	0	50	61	12	249	4.2	14
Perry Moss‡	72	1012	116	292	.397	65	89	.730	34	81	115	108	132	1	56	79	15	304	4.2	14
Andrew Toney	6	84	11	36	.306	3	8	.375	2	3	5	12	8	0	2	7	0	25	4.2	8
Greg Stokes	31	350	56	119	.471	14	21	.667	27	30	57	17	56	0	14	19	11	126	4.1	16
Butch Carter†	4	36	5	16	.313	5	6	.833	0	1	1	1	8	0	0	1	0	15	3.8	9
Butch Carter‡	9	67	7	24	.292	6	7	.857	2	2	4	4	14	0	1	7	0	20	2.2	9
Clemon Johnson	75	1069	105	223	.471	51	81	.630	106	149	255	15	129	0	23	38	62	261	3.5	12
Voise Winters	4	17	3	13	.231	0	0	...	1	2	3	0	1	0	1	2	0	6	1.5	2
Michael Young	2	2	0	2	.000	0	0	...	0	0	0	0	0	0	0	0	0	0	0.0	0

3-pt. FG: Philadelphia 51-224 (.228)—Malone 0-1 (.000); Barkley 17-75 (.227); Erving 9-32 (.281); Cheeks 4-17 (.235); Threatt 1-24 (.042); Thompson 2-12 (.167); Catledge 0-4 (.000); Jones 0-1 (.000); Wood* 13-29 (.448); Moss† 5-25 (.200); Moss‡ 7-32 (.219); Toney 0-2 (.000); Stokes 0-1 (.000); Winters 0-1 (.000). Opponents 82-282 (.291).

PHOENIX SUNS

	G	Min.	FGM	FGA	Pct.	FTM	FTA	Pct.	Off.	Def.	Tot.	Ast.	PF	Dq.	Stl.	TO	Blk.	Pts.	Avg.	Hi.
Walter Davis	70	2239	624	1287	.485	257	305	.843	54	149	203	361	153	1	99	219	3	1523	21.8	43
Larry Nance	73	2484	582	1001	.581	310	444	.698	169	449	618	240	247	6	70	210	130	1474	20.2	44
James Edwards	52	1314	318	587	.542	212	302	.702	79	222	301	74	200	5	23	128	29	848	16.3	30
Jay Humphries	82	2733	352	735	.479	197	257	.767	56	204	260	526	222	1	132	190	9	905	11.0	27
Mike Sanders	82	1644	347	676	.513	208	257	.809	104	169	273	150	236	3	76	143	31	905	11.0	27
Alvan Adams	78	2005	341	679	.502	159	203	.783	148	329	477	324	272	7	103	206	46	841	10.8	28

	G	Min.	FGM	FGA	Pct.	FTM	FTA	Pct.	Off.	Def.	Tot.	Ast.	PF	Dq.	Stl.	TO	Blk.	Pts.	Avg.	Hi.
									REBOUNDS									SCORING		
Ed Pinckney	80	1602	255	457	.558	171	254	.673	95	213	308	90	190	3	71	148	37	681	8.5	27
Bernard Thompson	61	1281	195	399	.489	127	157	.809	58	83	141	132	151	0	51	90	10	517	8.5	19
Sedric Toney†	10	206	26	59	.441	20	30	.667	3	20	23	26	18	0	5	19	0	75	7.5	22
Sedric Toney‡	13	230	28	66	.424	21	31	.677	3	22	25	26	24	0	6	22	0	80	6.2	22
Charlie Pittman	69	1132	127	218	.583	99	141	.702	99	147	246	58	140	2	37	107	23	353	5.1	22
Georgi Glouchkov	49	772	84	209	.402	70	122	.574	31	132	163	32	124	0	26	76	25	239	4.9	13
Nick Vanos	11	202	23	72	.319	8	23	.348	21	39	60	16	34	0	2	20	5	54	4.9	13
Charles Jones	43	742	75	164	.457	50	98	.510	65	128	193	52	87	0	32	57	25	200	4.7	19
Devin Durrant	4	51	8	21	.381	1	4	.250	2	6	8	5	10	0	3	4	0	17	4.3	9
Rod Foster	48	704	85	218	.390	23	32	.719	9	49	58	121	77	0	22	61	1	202	4.2	13
Rick Robey	46	629	72	191	.377	33	48	.688	40	108	148	58	92	1	19	66	5	177	3.8	12
Michael Holton*	4	65	4	20	.200	4	6	.667	1	2	3	7	7	0	2	4	0	12	3.0	7

3-pt. FG: Phoenix 38-183 (.208)—Davis 18-76 (.237); Nance 0-8 (.000); Humphries 4-29 (.138); Sanders 3-15 (.200); Adams 0-2 (.000); Pinckney 0-2 (.000); Thompson 0-2 (.000); Toney† 3-10 (.300); Toney‡ 3-10 (.300); Glouchkov 1-1 (1.000); Jones 0-1 (.000); Foster 9-32 (.281); Robey 0-3 (.000); Holton* 0-2 (.000). Opponents 89-279 (.319).

PORTLAND TRAIL BLAZERS

	G	Min.	FGM	FGA	Pct.	FTM	FTA	Pct.	Off.	Def.	Tot.	Ast.	PF	Dq.	Stl.	TO	Blk.	Pts.	Avg.	Hi.
									REBOUNDS									SCORING		
Kiki Vandeweghe	79	2791	719	1332	.540	523	602	.869	92	124	216	187	161	0	54	177	17	1962	24.8	38
Clyde Drexler	75	2576	542	1142	.475	293	381	.769	171	250	421	600	270	8	197	282	46	1389	18.5	41
Mychal Thompson	82	2569	503	1011	.498	198	309	.641	181	427	608	176	267	5	76	196	35	1204	14.7	30
Jim Paxson	75	1931	372	792	.470	217	244	.889	42	106	148	278	156	3	94	112	5	981	13.1	33
Sam Bowie	38	1132	167	345	.484	114	161	.708	93	234	327	99	142	4	21	88	96	448	11.8	24
Kenny Carr	55	1557	232	466	.498	149	217	.687	146	346	492	70	203	5	38	106	30	613	11.1	27
Darnell Valentine*	28	734	92	206	.447	71	100	.710	20	52	72	139	78	0	49	58	1	256	9.1	18
Steve Colter	81	1868	272	597	.456	135	164	.823	41	136	177	257	188	0	113	115	10	706	8.7	26
Jerome Kersey	79	1217	258	470	.549	156	229	.681	137	156	293	83	208	2	85	113	32	672	8.5	22
Terry Porter	79	1214	212	447	.474	125	155	.806	35	82	117	198	136	0	81	106	1	562	7.1	24
Caldwell Jones	80	1437	126	254	.496	124	150	.827	105	250	355	74	244	2	38	102	61	376	4.7	21
Ken Johnson	64	815	113	214	.528	37	85	.435	90	153	243	19	147	1	13	59	22	263	4.1	15
Brian Martin†	5	14	2	5	.400	0	2	.000	0	0	0	0	5	0	0	0	0	4	0.8	2
Brian Martin‡	8	21	3	7	.429	0	2	.000	1	3	4	0	7	0	0	2	1	6	0.8	2

3-pt. FG: Portland 74-275 (.269)—Vandeweghe 1-8 (.125); Drexler 12-60 (.200); Paxson 20-62 (.323); Carr 0-4 (.000); Valentine* 1-3 (.333); Colter 27-83 (.325); Kersey 0-6 (.000); Porter 13-42 (.310); Jones 0-7 (.000). Opponents 83-248 (.335).

SACRAMENTO KINGS

	G	Min.	FGM	FGA	Pct.	FTM	FTA	Pct.	Off.	Def.	Tot.	Ast.	PF	Dq.	Stl.	TO	Blk.	Pts.	Avg.	Hi.
									REBOUNDS									SCORING		
Eddie Johnson	82	2514	623	1311	.475	280	343	.816	173	246	419	214	237	0	54	191	17	1530	18.7	38
Reggie Theus	82	2919	546	1137	.480	405	490	.827	73	231	304	788	231	3	112	327	20	1503	18.3	37
Mike Woodson	81	2417	510	1073	.475	242	289	.837	94	132	226	197	215	1	92	145	37	1264	15.6	39
LaSalle Thompson	80	2377	411	794	.518	202	276	.732	252	518	770	168	295	8	71	184	109	1024	12.8	25
Larry Drew	75	1971	376	776	.485	128	161	.795	25	100	125	338	134	0	66	133	2	890	11.9	26
Otis Thorpe	75	1675	289	492	.587	164	248	.661	137	283	420	84	233	3	55	123	34	742	9.9	28
Terry Tyler	71	1651	295	649	.455	84	112	.750	109	204	313	94	159	0	64	94	108	674	9.5	26
Mark Olberding	81	2157	225	403	.558	162	210	.771	113	310	423	266	276	3	43	148	23	612	7.6	17
Joe Kleine	80	1180	160	344	.465	94	130	.723	113	260	373	46	224	1	24	107	34	414	5.2	14
Carl Henry	28	149	31	67	.463	12	17	.706	8	11	19	4	11	0	5	9	0	78	2.8	10
Michael Adams	18	139	16	44	.364	8	12	.667	2	4	6	22	9	0	9	11	1	40	2.2	10
Mike Bratz	33	269	26	70	.371	14	18	.778	2	21	23	39	43	0	13	17	0	70	2.1	10
Rich Kelley	37	324	28	49	.571	18	22	.818	29	52	81	43	62	0	10	22	3	74	2.0	8
David Cooke	6	38	2	11	.182	5	10	.500	5	5	10	1	5	0	4	2	0	9	1.5	3

3-pt. FG: Sacramento 30-134 (.224)—Johnson 4-20 (.200); Theus 6-35 (.171); Woodson 2-13 (.154); Thompson 0-1 (.000); Drew 10-31 (.323); Tyler 0-3 (.000); Olberding 0-2 (.000); Henry 4-10 (.400); Adams 0-3 (.000); Bratz 4-14 (.286); Kelley 0-2 (.000). Opponents 73-281 (.260).

SAN ANTONIO SPURS

	G	Min.	FGM	FGA	Pct.	FTM	FTA	Pct.	Off.	Def.	Tot.	Ast.	PF	Dq.	Stl.	TO	Blk.	Pts.	Avg.	Hi.
									REBOUNDS									SCORING		
Mike Mitchell	82	2970	802	1697	.473	317	392	.809	134	275	409	188	175	0	56	184	25	1921	23.4	44
Alvin Robertson	82	2878	562	1093	.514	260	327	.795	184	332	516	448	296	4	301	256	40	1392	17.0	41
Artis Gilmore	71	2395	423	684	.618	338	482	.701	166	434	600	102	239	3	39	186	108	1184	16.7	33
Steve Johnson	71	1828	362	573	.632	259	373	.694	143	319	462	95	291	13	44	191	66	983	13.8	31
Johnny Moore	28	856	150	303	.495	59	86	.686	25	61	86	252	78	0	70	81	6	363	13.0	30
Jeff Lamp†	30	620	136	271	.502	56	69	.812	19	60	79	53	67	0	19	38	1	332	11.1	25
Jeff Lamp‡	74	1321	245	514	.477	111	133	.835	53	147	200	117	155	1	39	68	4	608	8.2	25
Wes Matthews	75	1853	320	603	.531	173	211	.820	30	101	131	476	168	1	87	232	32	817	10.9	29
David Greenwood	68	1910	198	388	.510	142	184	.772	151	380	531	90	207	3	37	113	52	538	7.9	27
Jon Sundvold	70	1150	220	476	.462	39	48	.813	22	58	80	261	110	0	34	85	0	500	7.1	18
Ray Williams*	23	397	50	131	.382	62	64	.969	13	24	37	111	64	1	28	51	3	164	7.1	22
Alfredrick Hughes	68	866	152	372	.409	49	84	.583	49	64	113	61	79	0	26	63	5	356	5.2	23
Jeff Wilkins†	27	522	51	134	.381	28	46	.609	34	93	127	18	71	1	8	20	10	130	4.8	13
Jeff Wilkins‡	75	1126	147	374	.393	58	93	.624	74	198	272	46	157	1	11	52	21	352	4.7	15
Marc Iavaroni*	42	669	74	163	.454	43	67	.642	42	90	132	53	109	0	22	51	14	191	4.5	17
Rod Higgins*	11	128	18	40	.450	11	16	.688	5	19	24	12	21	0	2	5	3	47	4.3	11

1985-86

	G	Min.	FGM	FGA	Pct.	FTM	FTA	Pct.	Off.	Def.	Tot.	Ast.	PF	Dq.	Stl.	TO	Blk.	Pts.	Avg.	Hi.
									REBOUNDS									SCORING		
Tyrone Corbin	16	174	27	64	.422	10	14	.714	11	14	25	11	21	0	11	12	2	64	4.0	12
Jeff Cook*	34	356	28	67	.418	26	41	.634	31	50	81	21	64	0	13	11	11	82	2.4	9
Mike Brittain	32	219	22	43	.512	10	19	.526	10	39	49	5	54	1	3	20	12	54	1.7	7
Ennis Whatley†	2	14	1	2	.500	0	0	...	0	0	0	3	1	0	0	4	0	2	1.0	2
Ennis Whatley‡	14	107	15	35	.429	5	10	.500	4	10	14	23	10	0	5	10	1	35	2.5	14

3-pt. FG: San Antonio 46-196 (.235)—Mitchell 0-12 (.000); Robertson 8-29 (.276); Gilmore 0-1 (.000); Moore 4-22 (.182); Lamp† 4-17 (.235); Lamp‡ 7-30 (.233); Matthews 4-25 (.160); Greenwood 0-1 (.000); Sundvold 21-60 (.350); Williams* 2-6 (.333); Hughes 3-17 (.176); Iavaroni* 0-2 (.000); Higgins* 0-2 (.000); Corbin 0-1 (.000); Cook* 0-1 (.000). Opponents 98-322 (.304).

SEATTLE SUPERSONICS

	G	Min.	FGM	FGA	Pct.	FTM	FTA	Pct.	Off.	Def.	Tot.	Ast.	PF	Dq.	Stl.	TO	Blk.	Pts.	Avg.	Hi.
									REBOUNDS									SCORING		
Tom Chambers	66	2019	432	928	.466	346	414	.836	126	305	431	132	248	6	55	194	37	1223	18.5	32
Xavier McDaniel	82	2706	576	1176	.490	250	364	.687	307	348	655	193	305	8	101	248	37	1404	17.1	36
Jack Sikma	80	2790	508	1100	.462	355	411	.864	146	602	748	301	293	4	92	214	73	1371	17.1	38
Gerald Henderson	82	2568	434	900	.482	185	223	.830	89	98	187	487	230	2	138	184	11	1071	13.1	26
Al Wood	78	1749	355	817	.435	187	239	.782	80	164	244	114	171	2	57	107	19	902	11.6	27
Tim McCormick	77	1705	253	444	.570	174	244	.713	140	263	403	83	219	4	19	110	28	681	8.8	21
Ricky Sobers	78	1279	240	541	.444	110	125	.880	29	70	99	180	139	1	44	85	2	603	7.7	23
Danny Young	82	1901	227	449	.506	90	106	.849	29	91	120	303	113	0	110	92	9	568	6.9	20
Mike Phelps	70	880	117	286	.409	44	74	.595	29	60	89	71	86	0	45	62	1	279	4.0	18
Danny Vranes	80	1569	131	284	.461	39	75	.520	115	166	281	68	218	3	63	58	31	301	3.8	13
Frank Brickowski	40	311	30	58	.517	18	27	.667	16	38	54	21	74	2	11	23	7	78	2.0	11
David Pope	11	74	9	20	.450	2	4	.500	6	5	11	4	11	0	2	2	1	21	1.9	16
Rod Higgins*	12	94	9	27	.333	3	5	.600	3	9	12	6	11	0	2	4	1	22	1.8	7
Alex Stivrins	3	14	1	4	.250	1	4	.250	3	0	3	1	2	0	0	3	0	3	1.0	2
George Johnson	41	264	12	23	.522	11	16	.688	26	34	60	13	46	0	6	14	37	35	0.9	5
Brian Martin*	3	7	1	2	.500	0	0	...	1	3	4	0	2	0	2	1	2	2	0.7	2

3-pt. FG: Seattle 79-300 (.263)—Chambers 13-48 (.271); McDaniel 2-10 (.200); Sikma 0-13 (.000); Henderson 18-52 (.346); Wood 5-37 (.135); McCormick 1-2 (.500); Sobers 13-43 (.302); Young 24-74 (.324); Phelps 1-12 (.083); Vranes 0-4 (.000); Pope 1-1 (1.000); Higgins* 1-4 (.250). Opponents 57-224 (.254).

UTAH JAZZ

	G	Min.	FGM	FGA	Pct.	FTM	FTA	Pct.	Off.	Def.	Tot.	Ast.	PF	Dq.	Stl.	TO	Blk.	Pts.	Avg.	Hi.
									REBOUNDS									SCORING		
Adrian Dantley	76	2744	818	1453	.563	630	796	.791	178	217	395	264	206	2	64	231	4	2267	29.8	47
Karl Malone	81	2475	504	1016	.496	195	405	.481	174	544	718	236	295	2	105	279	44	1203	14.9	29
Thurl Bailey	82	2358	483	1077	.448	230	277	.830	148	345	493	153	160	0	42	144	114	1196	14.6	26
Rickey Green	80	2012	357	758	.471	213	250	.852	32	103	135	411	130	0	106	132	6	932	11.7	27
Bobby Hansen	82	2032	299	628	.476	95	132	.720	82	162	244	193	205	1	74	126	9	710	8.7	25
Mark Eaton	80	2551	277	589	.470	122	202	.604	172	503	675	101	282	5	33	157	369	676	8.5	20
John Stockton	82	1935	228	466	.489	172	205	.839	33	146	179	610	227	2	157	168	10	630	7.7	19
Carey Scurry	78	1168	142	301	.472	78	126	.619	97	145	242	85	171	2	78	96	66	363	4.7	15
Jeff Wilkins*	48	604	96	240	.400	30	47	.638	40	105	145	28	86	0	3	32	11	222	4.6	16
Pace Mannion	57	673	97	214	.453	53	82	.646	26	56	82	55	68	0	32	41	5	255	4.5	19
Marc Iavaroni†	26	345	36	81	.444	33	48	.688	21	56	77	29	54	0	10	21	3	105	4.0	10
Marc Iavaroni‡	68	1014	110	244	.451	76	115	.661	63	146	209	82	163	0	32	72	17	296	4.4	17
Fred Roberts	58	469	74	167	.443	67	87	.770	31	49	80	27	72	0	8	53	6	216	3.7	21
Jeff Cook†	2	17	3	6	.500	1	1	1.000	2	3	5	0	1	0	0	3	0	7	3.5	7
Jeff Cook‡	36	373	31	73	.425	27	42	.643	33	53	86	21	65	0	13	14	11	89	2.5	9
Steve Hayes	58	397	39	87	.448	11	36	.306	32	45	77	7	81	0	5	16	19	89	1.5	10

3-pt. FG: Utah 35-169 (.207)—Dantley 1-11 (.091); Malone 0-2 (.000); Bailey 0-7 (.000); Green 5-29 (.172); Hansen 17-50 (.340); Stockton 2-15 (.133); Scurry 1-11 (.091); Mannion 8-42 (.190); Roberts 1-2 (.500). Opponents 65-251 (.259).

WASHINGTON BULLETS

	G	Min.	FGM	FGA	Pct.	FTM	FTA	Pct.	Off.	Def.	Tot.	Ast.	PF	Dq.	Stl.	TO	Blk.	Pts.	Avg.	Hi.
									REBOUNDS									SCORING		
Jeff Malone	80	2992	735	1522	.483	322	371	.868	66	222	288	191	180	2	70	168	12	1795	22.4	43
Jeff Ruland	30	1114	212	383	.554	145	200	.725	107	213	320	159	100	1	23	121	25	569	19.0	30
Cliff Robinson	78	2563	595	1255	.474	269	353	.762	180	500	680	186	217	2	98	206	44	1460	18.7	38
Gus Williams	77	2284	434	1013	.428	138	188	.734	52	114	166	453	113	0	96	160	15	1036	13.5	33
Frank Johnson	14	402	69	154	.448	38	54	.704	7	21	28	76	30	0	11	29	1	176	12.6	27
Dan Roundfield	79	2321	322	660	.488	273	362	.754	210	432	642	167	194	1	36	187	51	917	11.6	29
Leon Wood†	39	743	127	330	.385	96	121	.793	16	47	63	107	46	0	20	67	0	378	9.7	30
Leon Wood‡	68	1198	184	466	.395	123	155	.794	25	65	90	182	70	0	34	87	0	532	7.8	30
Darren Daye	64	1075	198	399	.496	159	237	.671	71	112	183	109	121	0	46	98	11	556	8.7	22
Freeman Williams	9	110	25	67	.373	12	17	.706	4	8	12	7	10	0	7	13	1	69	7.7	17
Tom McMillen	56	863	131	285	.460	64	79	.810	44	69	113	35	85	0	9	34	10	326	5.8	21
Kevin McKenna	30	430	61	166	.367	25	30	.833	9	27	36	23	54	1	29	18	2	174	5.8	25
Kenny Green*	20	221	44	101	.436	21	26	.808	17	21	38	3	26	0	4	17	7	109	5.5	20
Perry Moss*	12	160	21	53	.396	11	15	.733	9	16	25	19	26	1	6	18	3	55	4.6	14
Charles Jones	81	1609	129	254	.508	54	86	.628	122	199	321	76	235	2	57	71	133	312	3.9	17
Manute Bol	80	2090	128	278	.460	42	86	.488	123	354	477	23	255	5	28	65	397	298	3.7	18
Dudley Bradley	70	842	73	209	.349	32	56	.571	24	71	95	107	101	0	85	44	3	195	2.8	17

1985-86

	G	Min.	FGM	FGA	Pct.	FTM	FTA	Pct.	REBOUNDS			Ast.	PF	Dq.	Stl.	TO	Blk.	SCORING		
									Off.	Def.	Tot.							Pts.	Avg.	Hi.
Ennis Whatley*.......	4	27	5	14	.357	1	3	.333	2	5	7	7	1	0	0	0	1	11	2.8	5
George Johnson	2	7	1	3	.333	2	2	1.000	1	1	2	0	1	0	0	1	0	4	2.0	4
Claude Gregory.......	2	2	1	2	.500	0	0	...	2	0	2	0	1	0	1	2	0	2	1.0	2

3-pt. FG: Washington 116-408 (.284)—Malone 3-17 (.176); Ruland 0-4 (.000); Robinson 1-4 (.250); G. Williams 30-116 (.259); F. Johnson 0-3 (.000); Roundfield 0-6 (.000); Wood† 28-85 (.329); Wood‡ 41-114 (.360); Daye 1-3 (.333); F. Williams 7-14 (.500); McMillen 0-3 (.000); McKenna 27-75 (.360); Green* 0-1 (.000); Moss* 2-7 (.286); Jones 0-1 (.000); Bol 0-1 (.000); Bradley 17-68 (.250). Opponents 71-259 (.274).

* Finished season with another team. † Totals with this team only. ‡ Totals with all teams.

PLAYOFF RESULTS

EASTERN CONFERENCE

FIRST ROUND

Boston 3, Chicago 0
Apr. 17—Thur.	Chicago 104 at Boston	123
Apr. 20—Sun.	Chicago 131 at Boston	**135
Apr. 22—Tue.	Boston 122 at Chicago	104

Milwaukee 3, New Jersey 0
Apr. 18—Fri.	New Jersey 107 at Milwaukee	119
Apr. 20—Sun.	New Jersey 97 at Milwaukee	111
Apr. 22—Tue.	Milwaukee 118 at New Jersey	113

Philadelphia 3, Washington 2
Apr. 18—Fri.	Washington 95 at Philadelphia	94
Apr. 20—Sun.	Washington 97 at Philadelphia	102
Apr. 22—Tue.	Philadelphia 91 at Washington	86
Apr. 24—Thur.	Philadelphia 111 at Washington	116
Apr. 27—Sun.	Washington 109 at Philadelphia	134

Atlanta 3, Detroit 1
Apr. 17—Thur.	Detroit 122 at Atlanta	140
Apr. 19—Sat.	Detroit 125 at Atlanta	137
Apr. 22—Tue.	Atlanta 97 at Detroit	106
Apr. 25—Fri.	Atlanta 114 at Detroit	**113

SEMIFINALS

Boston 4, Atlanta 1
Apr. 27—Sun.	Atlanta 91 at Boston	103
Apr. 29—Tue.	Atlanta 108 at Boston	119
May 2—Fri.	Boston 111 at Atlanta	107
May 4—Sun.	Boston 94 at Atlanta	106
May 6—Tue.	Atlanta 99 at Boston	132

Milwaukee 4, Philadelphia 3
Apr. 29—Tue.	Philadelphia 118 at Milwaukee	112
May 1—Thur.	Philadelphia 107 at Milwaukee	119
May 3—Sat.	Milwaukee 103 at Philadelphia	107
May 5—Mon.	Milwaukee 109 at Philadelphia	104
May 7—Wed.	Philadelphia 108 at Milwaukee	113
May 9—Fri.	Milwaukee 108 at Philadelphia	126
May 11—Sun.	Philadelphia 112 at Milwaukee	113

FINALS

Boston 4, Milwaukee 0
May 13—Tue.	Milwaukee 96 at Boston	128
May 15—Thur.	Milwaukee 111 at Boston	122
May 17—Sat.	Boston 111 at Milwaukee	107
May 18—Sun.	Boston 111 at Milwaukee	98

WESTERN CONFERENCE

FIRST ROUND

L.A. Lakers 3, San Antonio 0
Apr. 17—Thur.	San Antonio 88 at L.A. Lakers	135
Apr. 19—Sat.	San Antonio 94 at L.A. Lakers	122
Apr. 23—Wed.	L.A. Lakers 114 at San Antonio	94

Houston 3, Sacramento 0
Apr. 17—Thur.	Sacramento 87 at Houston	107
Apr. 19—Sat.	Sacramento 103 at Houston	111
Apr. 22—Tue.	Houston 113 at Sacramento	98

Denver 3, Portland 1
Apr. 18—Fri.	Portland 126 at Denver	133
Apr. 20—Sun.	Portland 108 at Denver	106
Apr. 22—Tue.	Denver 115 at Portland	104
Apr. 24—Thur.	Denver 116 at Portland	112

Dallas 3, Utah 1
Apr. 18—Fri.	Utah 93 at Dallas	101
Apr. 20—Sun.	Utah 106 at Dallas	113
Apr. 23—Wed.	Dallas 98 at Utah	100
Apr. 25—Fri.	Dallas 117 at Utah	113

SEMIFINALS

L.A. Lakers 4, Dallas 2
Apr. 27—Sun.	Dallas 116 at L.A. Lakers	130
Apr. 30—Wed.	Dallas 113 at L.A. Lakers	117
May 2—Fri.	L.A. Lakers 108 at Dallas	110
May 4—Sun.	L.A. Lakers 118 at Dallas	120
May 6—Tue.	Dallas 113 at L.A. Lakers	116
May 8—Thur.	L.A. Lakers 120 at Dallas	107

Houston 4, Denver 2
Apr. 26—Sat.	Denver 119 at Houston	126
Apr. 29—Tue.	Denver 101 at Houston	119
May 2—Fri.	Houston 115 at Denver	116
May 4—Sun.	Houston 111 at Denver	*114
May 6—Tue.	Denver 103 at Houston	131
May 8—Thur.	Houston 126 at Denver	**122

FINALS

Houston 4, L.A. Lakers 1
May 10—Sat.	Houston 107 at L.A. Lakers	119
May 13—Tue.	Houston 112 at L.A. Lakers	102
May 16—Fri.	L.A. Lakers 109 at Houston	117
May 18—Sun.	L.A. Lakers 95 at Houston	105
May 21—Wed.	Houston 114 at L.A. Lakers	112

NBA FINALS

Boston 4, Houston 2
May 26—Mon.	Houston 100 at Boston	112
May 29—Thur.	Houston 95 at Boston	117
June 1—Sun.	Boston 104 at Houston	106
June 3—Tue.	Boston 106 at Houston	103
June 5—Thur.	Boston 96 at Houston	111
June 8—Sun.	Houston 97 at Boston	114

*Denotes number of overtime periods.

1985-86

1984-85

1984-85 NBA CHAMPION LOS ANGELES LAKERS
Front row (from left): owner Dr. Jerry Buss, Mike McGee, Kurt Rambis, Jamaal Wilkes, Kareem Abdul-Jabbar, Bob McAdoo, Magic Johnson, Michael Cooper, assistant coach Bill Bertka. Back row (from left): head coach Pat Riley, Byron Scott, Larry Spriggs, James Worthy, Mitch Kupchak, Ronnie Lester, assistant coach Dave Wohl, trainer Gary Vitti.

FINAL STANDINGS

ATLANTIC DIVISION

	Atl.	Bos.	Chi.	Cle.	Dal.	Den.	Det.	G.S.	Hou.	Ind.	K.C.	L.A.C.	L.A.L.	Mil.	N.J.	N.Y.	Phi.	Pho.	Por.	S.A.	Sea.	Uta.	Was.	W	L	Pct.	GB
Boston	4	..	4	6	2	1	4	2	2	5	2	2	1	1	5	6	3	2	1	2	1	2	5	63	19	.768	..
Philadelphia	5	3	5	2	1	1	5	2	1	5	1	2	1	3	4	4	..	2	2	1	2	2	4	58	24	.707	5
New Jersey	3	1	4	3	1	0	5	1	1	3	0	2	0	3	..	6	2	1	0	0	2	0	4	42	40	.512	21
Washington	3	1	2	3	1	0	3	1	2	4	1	1	1	2	2	6	2	1	1	2	0	1	..	40	42	.488	23
New York	3	0	2	3	0	1	2	1	0	4	1	1	0	0	0	..	2	0	0	1	2	1	0	24	58	.293	39

CENTRAL DIVISION

	Atl.	Bos.	Chi.	Cle.	Dal.	Den.	Det.	G.S.	Hou.	Ind.	K.C.	L.A.C.	L.A.L.	Mil.	N.J.	N.Y.	Phi.	Pho.	Por.	S.A.	Sea.	Uta.	Was.	W	L	Pct.	GB
Milwaukee	4	4	3	5	1	1	3	2	2	5	2	2	1	..	3	5	3	1	2	2	2	2	4	59	23	.720	..
Detroit	5	2	3	4	2	2	..	2	1	6	1	1	1	3	1	3	1	2	1	1	1	0	3	46	36	.561	13
Chicago	3	2	..	2	2	1	3	1	0	2	2	2	1	3	2	4	0	1	1	2	0	3		38	44	.463	21
Cleveland	3	0	4	..	1	0	1	0	4	2	2	0	1	2	3	4	1	1	1	1	1	3		36	46	.439	23
Atlanta	..	1	3	3	0	0	1	2	0	6	0	2	0	2	3	3	0	2	0	0	1	2	3	34	48	.415	25
Indiana	0	1	4	2	0	0	0	2	1	..	1	0	1	1	2	2	1	0	0	1	0	2	1	22	60	.268	37

MIDWEST DIVISION

	Atl.	Bos.	Chi.	Cle.	Dal.	Den.	Det.	G.S.	Hou.	Ind.	K.C.	L.A.C.	L.A.L.	Mil.	N.J.	N.Y.	Phi.	Pho.	Por.	S.A.	Sea.	Uta.	Was.	W	L	Pct.	GB
Denver	2	1	1	2	4	..	0	5	2	2	4	2	2	1	2	1	1	4	4	3	3	4	2	52	30	.634	..
Houston	2	0	2	2	4	4	1	3	..	1	5	2	1	0	1	2	1	4	3	4	3	3	0	48	34	.585	4
Dallas	2	0	0	1	..	2	0	4	2	2	5	3	1	1	1	2	1	2	4	4	5	1	1	44	38	.537	8
Utah	0	0	2	1	5	2	2	4	3	0	4	2	1	0	2	1	0	2	2	5	2	..	1	41	41	.500	11
San Antonio	2	0	1	1	2	3	1	4	2	1	4	3	2	0	2	1	1	4	2	..	4	1	0	41	41	.500	11
Kansas City	2	0	0	0	1	2	1	3	1	1	..	3	0	0	2	1	1	2	3	2	3	2	1	31	51	.378	21

PACIFIC DIVISION

	Atl.	Bos.	Chi.	Cle.	Dal.	Den.	Det.	G.S.	Hou.	Ind.	K.C.	L.A.C.	L.A.L.	Mil.	N.J.	N.Y.	Phi.	Pho.	Por.	S.A.	Sea.	Uta.	Was.	W	L	Pct.	GB
L.A. Lakers	2	1	1	2	4	3	1	5	4	1	5	6	..	1	2	2	1	5	5	3	3	4	1	62	20	.756	..
Portland	2	1	1	1	1	1	1	4	2	2	2	5	1	0	2	2	0	3	..	3	4	3	1	42	40	.512	20
Phoenix	0	0	1	1	3	1	0	4	1	2	3	2	1	1	1	2	0	..	3	1	5	3	1	36	46	.439	26
Seattle	1	1	0	1	0	2	1	3	2	2	4	3	0	0	0	0	1	2	1	..	3	2	1	31	51	.378	31
L.A. Clippers	0	0	0	0	2	3	1	4	3	2	2	..	0	0	0	1	0	4	1	2	2	3	1	31	51	.378	31
Golden State	0	0	1	1	1	0	0	..	2	0	2	2	1	0	1	1	0	2	2	1	3	1	1	22	60	.268	40

TEAM STATISTICS

OFFENSIVE

	G	FGM	FGA	Pct.	FTM	FTA	Pct.	Off.	Def.	Tot.	Ast.	PF	Dq.	Stl.	TO	Blk.	Pts.	Avg.
								Off.	Def.	Tot.							Pts.	Avg.
Denver	82	3876	7976	.486	2016	2568	.785	1331	2303	3634	2266	2152	18	894	1382	424	9841	120.0
L.A. Lakers	82	3952	7254	.545	1702	2232	.763	1063	2550	3613	2575	1931	7	695	1537	481	9696	118.2
Detroit	82	3840	7999	.480	1783	2262	.788	1403	2534	3937	2302	2076	21	691	1341	397	9508	116.0
Portland	82	3708	7374	.503	2002	2667	.751	1202	2298	3500	2225	1957	21	821	1481	516	9469	115.5
San Antonio	82	3698	7202	.513	1961	2571	.763	1127	2470	3597	2316	2180	23	757	1542	443	9412	114.8
Boston	82	3721	7325	.508	1860	2307	.806	1116	2630	3746	2287	1781	17	645	1332	414	9412	114.8
Kansas City	82	3664	7275	.504	2022	2595	.779	1167	2327	3494	2342	2169	19	661	1593	300	9413	114.8
Philadelphia	82	3443	6992	.492	2316	2883	.803	1301	2364	3665	1999	1971	11	817	1575	534	9261	112.9
Dallas	82	3560	7280	.489	1844	2324	.793	1095	2345	3440	2152	1796	12	575	1184	335	9116	111.2
Houston	82	3748	7440	.504	1581	2261	.699	1325	2395	3720	2239	2033	27	683	1605	597	9118	111.2
Milwaukee	82	3564	7256	.491	1873	2473	.757	1256	2353	3609	2164	2239	37	689	1382	486	9090	110.9
Golden State	82	3498	7555	.463	1944	2531	.768	1327	2139	3466	1759	2136	28	803	1460	284	9052	110.4
New Jersey	82	3646	7445	.490	1631	2237	.729	1233	2325	3558	2163	2011	33	772	1355	415	8975	109.5
Utah	82	3478	7302	.476	1878	2434	.772	1081	2554	3635	2143	1961	16	712	1575	697	8937	109.0
Chicago	82	3453	6909	.500	1981	2526	.784	1074	2366	3440	1992	2071	21	622	1463	468	8916	108.7
Cleveland	82	3470	7364	.471	1867	2491	.749	1203	2445	3648	2096	2173	41	622	1387	472	8903	108.6
Indiana	82	3489	7324	.476	1871	2516	.744	1198	2623	3821	1945	2237	25	625	1622	366	8879	108.3
Phoenix	82	3507	7144	.491	1757	2280	.771	1026	2425	3451	2335	2034	13	727	1583	349	8858	108.0
L.A. Clippers	82	3527	7119	.495	1674	2208	.758	1163	2434	3597	1934	1840	14	534	1587	497	8784	107.1
Atlanta	82	3444	7119	.484	1782	2371	.752	1161	2345	3506	2009	2047	28	665	1475	541	8743	106.6
Washington	82	3534	7383	.479	1478	1989	.743	1012	2395	3407	2088	1869	26	709	1282	393	8655	105.5
New York	82	3435	7101	.484	1706	2350	.726	1116	2102	3218	1999	2398	48	754	1458	267	8627	105.2
Seattle	82	3277	6910	.474	1777	2305	.771	1019	2287	3306	2185	1974	18	649	1493	343	8376	102.1

DEFENSIVE

	FGM	FGA	Pct.	FTM	FTA	Pct.	Off.	Def.	Tot.	Ast.	PF	Dq.	Stl.	TO	Blk.	Pts.	Avg.	Dif.
Milwaukee	3214	6972	.461	2020	2700	.748	1236	2293	3529	1904	2104	33	642	1562	389	8528	104.0	+6.9
Washington	3494	7179	.487	1623	2172	.747	1119	2673	3792	1988	1833	7	630	1467	397	8677	105.8	-0.3
Seattle	3520	7142	.493	1703	2212	.770	1113	2379	3492	2220	2020	13	732	1383	458	8822	107.6	-5.5
Boston	3642	7642	.477	1512	1922	.787	1105	2287	3392	2041	1964	20	641	1222	315	8867	108.1	+6.7
Atlanta	3504	7267	.482	1808	2384	.758	1332	2411	3743	2087	1972	22	674	1488	373	8862	108.1	-1.5
Philadelphia	3494	7157	.488	1857	2397	.775	1183	2173	3356	2139	2209	32	753	1534	391	8925	108.8	+4.1
Dallas	3626	7200	.504	1588	2080	.763	1062	2470	3532	2113	2066	17	572	1340	430	8938	109.0	+2.2
Utah	3532	7604	.464	1810	2375	.762	1360	2645	4005	2069	2076	21	806	1606	443	8946	109.1	-0.1
New Jersey	3514	7040	.499	1849	2454	.753	1084	2405	3489	1975	1933	22	680	1496	352	8956	109.2	+0.3
Houston	3500	7274	.481	1887	2425	.778	1159	2222	3381	2117	1903	22	773	1495	455	8977	109.5	+1.7
Chicago	3521	7210	.488	1852	2394	.774	1137	2260	3397	2045	2040	25	668	1323	447	8985	109.6	-0.9
New York	3329	6732	.495	2282	3006	.759	1219	2401	3620	2143	2038	17	667	1589	446	9007	109.8	-4.6
Phoenix	3605	7309	.493	1756	2295	.765	1125	2416	3541	2181	2019	25	771	1468	410	9031	110.1	-2.1
L.A. Lakers	3665	7639	.480	1679	2244	.748	1248	2078	3326	2313	1905	18	756	1365	370	9093	110.9	+7.3
Cleveland	3547	7415	.478	1965	2554	.769	1210	2451	3661	2215	2101	23	612	1357	429	9129	111.3	-2.7
L.A. Clippers	3737	7630	.490	1604	2115	.758	1248	2282	3530	2264	1887	14	770	1242	422	9152	111.6	-4.5
Portland	3697	7494	.493	1737	2269	.766	1268	2336	3604	2235	2160	29	726	1607	459	9190	112.1	+3.4
Detroit	3700	7457	.496	1826	2404	.760	1109	2563	3672	2107	2017	30	642	1486	508	9304	113.5	+2.5
San Antonio	3644	7348	.496	1977	2548	.776	1136	2265	3401	2283	2154	26	749	1489	472	9337	113.9	+0.9
Indiana	3628	7332	.495	2068	2707	.764	1098	2583	3681	2242	2072	25	777	1424	523	9388	114.5	-6.2
Kansas City	3805	7461	.510	1957	2546	.769	1166	2267	3433	2344	2205	30	761	1424	512	9632	117.5	-2.7
Denver	3775	7379	.512	2027	2648	.765	1181	2628	3809	2154	2178	28	670	1744	589	9641	117.6	+2.4
Golden State	3839	7165	.536	1919	2530	.758	1101	2521	3622	2336	2180	25	650	1583	469	9654	117.7	-7.3
Avgs.	3588	7306	.491	1839	2408	.764	1174	2382	3566	2153	2045	23	701	1465	436	9089	110.8	...

HOME/ROAD

	Home	Road	Total		Home	Road	Total
Atlanta	19-22	15-26	34-48	L.A. Lakers	36-5	26-15	62-20
Boston	35-6	28-13	63-19	Milwaukee	36-5	23-18	59-23
Chicago	26-15	12-29	38-44	New Jersey	27-14	15-26	42-40
Cleveland	20-21	16-25	36-46	New York	19-22	5-36	24-58
Dallas	24-17	20-21	44-38	Philadelphia	34-7	24-17	58-24
Denver	34-7	18-23	52-30	Phoenix	26-15	10-31	36-46
Detroit	26-15	20-21	46-36	Portland	30-11	12-29	42-40
Golden State	17-24	5-36	22-60	San Antonio	30-11	11-30	41-41
Houston	29-12	19-22	48-34	Seattle	20-21	11-30	31-51
Indiana	16-25	6-35	22-60	Utah	26-15	15-26	41-41
Kansas City	23-18	8-33	31-51	Washington	28-13	12-29	40-42
L.A. Clippers	20-21	11-30	31-51	Totals	601-342	342-601	943-943

POINTS

(minimum 70 games or 1,400 points)

	G	FGM	FTM	Pts.	Avg.		G	FGM	FTM	Pts.	Avg.
Bernard King, New York	55	691	426	1809	32.9	Calvin Natt, Denver	78	685	447	1817	23.3
Larry Bird, Boston	80	918	403	2295	28.7	Eddie Johnson, Kansas City	82	769	325	1876	22.9
Michael Jordan, Chicago	82	837	630	2313	28.2	Orlando Woolridge, Chicago	77	679	409	1767	22.9
Purvis Short, Golden State	78	819	501	2186	28.0	Darrell Griffith, Utah	78	728	216	1764	22.6
Alex English, Denver	81	939	383	2262	27.9	World B. Free, Cleveland	71	609	308	1597	22.5
Dominique Wilkins, Atlanta	81	853	486	2217	27.4	Kiki Vandeweghe, Portland	72	618	369	1616	22.4
Adrian Dantley, Utah	55	512	438	1462	26.6	Mike Mitchell, San Antonio	82	775	269	1824	22.2
Mark Aguirre, Dallas	80	794	440	2055	25.7	Ralph Sampson, Houston	82	753	303	1809	22.1
Moses Malone, Philadelphia	79	602	737	1941	24.6	Derek Smith, L.A. Clippers	80	682	400	1767	22.1
Terry Cummings, Milwaukee	79	759	343	1861	23.6	K. Abdul-Jabbar, L.A. Lakers	79	723	289	1735	22.0

FIELD GOALS

(minimum 300 made)

	FGM	FGA	Pct.		FGM	FGA	Pct.
James Donaldson, L.A. Clippers	351	551	.637	James Worthy, L.A. Lakers	610	1066	.572
Artis Gilmore, San Antonio	532	854	.623	Kevin McHale, Boston	605	1062	.570
Otis Thorpe, Kansas City	411	685	.600	Maurice Cheeks, Philadelphia	422	741	.570
Kareem Abdul-Jabbar, L.A. Lakers	723	1207	.599	Magic Johnson, L.A. Lakers	504	899	.561
Larry Nance, Phoenix	515	877	.587	Orlando Woolridge, Chicago	679	1225	.554

FREE THROWS

(minimum 125 made)

	FTM	FTA	Pct.
Kyle Macy, Phoenix	127	140	.907
Kiki Vandeweghe, Portland	369	412	.896
Brad Davis, Dallas	158	178	.888
Kelly Tripucka, Detroit	255	288	.885
Alvan Adams, Phoenix	250	283	.883
Larry Bird, Boston	403	457	.882
Junior Bridgeman, L.A. Clippers	181	206	.879
Maurice Cheeks, Philadelphia	175	199	.879
Eddie Johnson, Kansas City	325	373	.871
Rickey Green, Utah	232	267	.869

STEALS

(minimum 70 games or 125 steals)

	G	No.	Avg.
Micheal Ray Richardson, New Jersey	82	243	2.96
Johnny Moore, San Antonio	82	229	2.79
Fat Lever, Denver	82	202	2.46
Michael Jordan, Chicago	82	196	2.39
Doc Rivers, Atlanta	69	163	2.36
Isiah Thomas, Detroit	81	187	2.31
Gus Williams, Washington	79	178	2.25
Clyde Drexler, Portland	80	177	2.21
Maurice Cheeks, Philadelphia	78	169	2.17
Lester Conner, Golden State	79	161	2.04

ASSISTS

(minimum 70 games or 400 assists)

	G	No.	Avg.
Isiah Thomas, Detroit	81	1123	13.9
Magic Johnson, L.A. Lakers	77	968	12.6
Johnny Moore, San Antonio	82	816	10.0
Norm Nixon, L.A. Clippers	81	711	8.8
John Bagley, Cleveland	81	697	8.6
Micheal Ray Richardson, New Jersey	82	669	8.2
Reggie Theus, Kansas City	82	656	8.0
Eddie Johnson, Atlanta	73	566	7.8
Rickey Green, Utah	77	597	7.8
Gus Williams, Washington	79	608	7.7

BLOCKED SHOTS

(minimum 70 games or 100 blocked shots)

	G	No.	Avg.
Mark Eaton, Utah	82	456	5.56
Hakeem Olajuwon, Houston	82	220	2.68
Sam Bowie, Portland	76	203	2.67
Wayne Cooper, Denver	80	197	2.46
Tree Rollins, Atlanta	70	167	2.39
Roy Hinson, Cleveland	76	173	2.28
Artis Gilmore, San Antonio	81	173	2.14
Bill Walton, L.A. Clippers	67	140	2.09
Alton Lister, Milwaukee	81	167	2.06
Kareem Abdul-Jabbar, L.A. Lakers	79	162	2.05

REBOUNDS

(minimum 70 games or 800 rebounds)

	G	Off.	Def.	Tot.	Avg.
Moses Malone, Philadelphia	79	385	646	1031	13.1
Bill Laimbeer, Detroit	82	295	718	1013	12.4
Buck Williams, New Jersey	82	323	682	1005	12.3
Hakeem Olajuwon, Houston	82	440	534	974	11.9
Mark Eaton, Utah	82	207	720	927	11.3
Larry Smith, Golden State	80	405	464	869	10.9
Robert Parish, Boston	79	263	577	840	10.6
Larry Bird, Boston	80	164	678	842	10.5
LaSalle Thompson, Kansas City	82	274	580	854	10.4
Artis Gilmore, San Antonio	81	231	615	846	10.4

3-POINT FIELD GOALS

(minimum 25 made)

	FGA	FGM	Pct.
Byron Scott, L.A. Lakers	60	26	.433
Larry Bird, Boston	131	56	.427
Brad Davis, Dallas	115	47	.409
Trent Tucker, New York	72	29	.403
Dale Ellis, Dallas	109	42	.385
Andrew Toney, Philadelphia	105	39	.371
World B. Free, Cleveland	193	71	.368
Mike Evans, Denver	157	57	.363
Darrell Griffith, Utah	257	92	.358
Don Buse, Kansas City	87	31	.356

1984-85

ATLANTA HAWKS

	G	Min.	FGM	FGA	Pct.	FTM	FTA	Pct.	Off.	Def.	Tot.	Ast.	PF	Dq.	Stl.	TO	Blk.	Pts.	Avg.	Hi.
									REBOUNDS									**SCORING**		
Dominique Wilkins . . .	81	3023	853	1891	.451	486	603	.806	226	331	557	200	170	0	135	225	54	2217	27.4	48
Eddie Johnson	73	2367	453	946	.479	265	332	.798	38	154	192	566	184	1	43	244	7	1193	16.3	34
Doc Rivers	69	2126	334	701	.476	291	378	.770	66	148	214	410	250	7	163	176	53	974	14.1	30
Sly Williams	34	867	167	380	.439	79	123	.642	45	123	168	94	83	1	28	78	8	417	12.3	22
Randy Wittman	41	1168	187	352	.531	30	41	.732	16	57	73	125	58	0	28	57	7	406	9.9	28
Cliff Levingston	74	2017	291	552	.527	145	222	.653	230	336	566	104	231	3	70	133	69	727	9.8	22
Kevin Willis	82	1785	322	690	.467	119	181	.657	177	345	522	36	226	4	31	104	49	765	9.3	24
Mike Glenn	60	1126	228	388	.588	62	76	.816	20	61	81	122	74	0	27	55	0	518	8.6	21
Antoine Carr	62	1195	198	375	.528	101	128	.789	79	153	232	80	219	4	29	108	78	499	8.0	17
Tree Rollins	70	1750	186	339	.549	67	93	.720	113	329	442	52	213	6	35	80	167	439	6.3	19
Charlie Criss	4	115	7	17	.412	4	6	.667	2	12	14	22	5	0	3	11	0	18	4.5	8
Walker Russell	21	377	34	63	.540	14	17	.824	8	32	40	66	37	1	17	40	4	83	4.0	10
Scott Hastings	64	825	89	188	.473	63	81	.778	59	100	159	46	135	1	24	50	23	241	3.8	16
Jerry Eaves	3	37	3	6	.500	5	6	.833	0	0	0	4	6	0	0	4	0	11	3.7	6
Rickey Brown	69	814	78	192	.406	39	68	.574	76	147	223	25	117	0	19	51	22	195	2.8	12
Stewart Granger	9	92	6	17	.353	4	8	.500	1	5	6	12	13	0	2	12	0	16	1.8	5
Sidney Lowe†	15	159	8	20	.400	8	8	1.000	4	11	15	42	23	0	11	11	0	24	1.6	6
Sidney Lowe‡	21	190	10	27	.370	8	8	1.000	4	12	16	50	28	0	11	13	0	28	1.3	6
Leo Rautins	4	12	0	2	.000	0	0	. . .	1	1	2	3	3	0	0	1	0	0	0.0	0

3-pt. FG: Atlanta 73-235 (.311)—Wilkins 25-81 (.309); Johnson 22-72 (.306); Rivers 15-36 (.417); Williams 4-15 (.267); Wittman 2-7 (.286); Levingston 0-2 (.000); Willis 2-9 (.222); Glenn 0-2 (.000); Carr 2-6 (.333); Criss 0-2 (.000); Russell 1-1 (1.000); Granger 0-1 (.000); Lowe† 0-1 (.000); Lowe‡ 0-1 (.000). Opponents 46-212 (.217).

BOSTON CELTICS

	G	Min.	FGM	FGA	Pct.	FTM	FTA	Pct.	Off.	Def.	Tot.	Ast.	PF	Dq.	Stl.	TO	Blk.	Pts.	Avg.	Hi.
									REBOUNDS									**SCORING**		
Larry Bird	80	3161	918	1760	.522	403	457	.882	164	678	842	531	208	0	129	248	98	2295	28.7	60
Kevin McHale	79	2653	605	1062	.570	355	467	.760	229	483	712	141	234	3	28	157	120	1565	19.8	56
Robert Parish	79	2850	551	1016	.542	292	393	.743	263	577	840	125	223	2	56	186	101	1394	17.6	38
Dennis Johnson	80	2976	493	1066	.462	261	306	.853	91	226	317	543	224	2	96	212	39	1254	15.7	29
Danny Ainge	75	2564	419	792	.529	118	136	.868	76	192	268	399	228	4	122	149	6	971	12.9	26
Cedric Maxwell	57	1495	201	377	.533	231	278	.831	98	144	242	102	140	2	36	98	15	633	11.1	30
Scott Wedman	78	1127	220	460	.478	42	55	.764	57	102	159	94	111	0	23	47	10	499	6.4	31
Ray Williams	23	459	55	143	.385	31	46	.674	16	41	57	90	56	1	30	42	5	147	6.4	16
M.L. Carr	47	397	62	149	.416	17	17	1.000	21	22	43	24	44	0	21	24	6	150	3.2	13
Carlos Clark	62	562	64	152	.421	41	53	.774	29	40	69	48	66	0	35	42	2	169	2.7	12
Quinn Buckner	75	858	74	193	.383	32	50	.640	26	61	87	148	142	0	63	67	2	180	2.4	13
Rick Carlisle	38	179	26	67	.388	15	17	.882	8	13	21	25	21	0	3	19	0	67	1.8	8
Greg Kite	55	424	33	88	.375	22	32	.688	38	51	89	17	84	3	3	29	10	88	1.6	14

3-pt. FG: Boston 110-309 (.356)—Bird 56-131 (.427); McHale 0-6 (.000); Johnson 7-26 (.269); Ainge 15-56 (.268); Maxwell 0-2 (.000); Wedman 17-34 (.500); Williams 6-23 (.261); Carr 9-23 (.391); Clark 0-5 (.000); Buckner 0-1 (.000); Carlisle 0-2 (.000). Opponents 71-269 (.264).

CHICAGO BULLS

	G	Min.	FGM	FGA	Pct.	FTM	FTA	Pct.	Off.	Def.	Tot.	Ast.	PF	Dq.	Stl.	TO	Blk.	Pts.	Avg.	Hi.
									REBOUNDS									**SCORING**		
Michael Jordan	82	3144	837	1625	.515	630	746	.845	167	367	534	481	285	4	196	291	69	2313	28.2	49
Orlando Woolridge . . .	77	2816	679	1225	.554	409	521	.785	158	277	435	135	185	0	58	178	38	1767	22.9	37
Quintin Dailey	79	2101	525	1111	.473	205	251	.817	57	151	208	191	192	0	71	154	5	1262	16.0	30
Steve Johnson	74	1659	281	516	.545	181	252	.718	146	291	437	64	265	7	37	151	62	743	10.0	31
Dave Corzine	82	2062	276	568	.486	149	200	.745	130	292	422	140	189	2	32	124	64	701	8.5	23
David Greenwood	61	1523	152	332	.458	67	94	.713	108	280	388	78	190	1	34	63	18	371	6.1	20
Sidney Green	48	740	108	250	.432	79	98	.806	72	174	246	29	102	0	11	68	14	295	6.1	16
Wes Matthews	78	1523	191	386	.495	59	85	.694	16	51	67	354	133	0	73	124	12	443	5.7	21
Ennis Whatley	70	1385	140	313	.447	68	86	.791	34	67	101	381	141	1	66	144	10	349	5.0	12
Rod Higgins	68	942	119	270	.441	60	90	.667	55	92	147	73	91	0	21	49	13	308	4.5	15
Jawann Oldham	63	993	89	192	.464	34	50	.680	79	157	236	31	166	3	11	58	127	212	3.4	12
Caldwell Jones	42	885	53	115	.461	36	47	.766	49	162	211	34	125	3	12	40	31	142	3.4	16
Charles Jones*	3	29	2	4	.500	4	6	.667	2	4	6	1	6	0	0	4	5	8	2.7	4
Chris Engler*	3	3	1	2	.500	0	0	. . .	1	2	3	1	0	0	0	1	0	2	0.7	2

3-pt. FG: Chicago 29-161 (.180)—Jordan 9-52 (.173); Woolridge 0-5 (.000); Dailey 7-30 (.233); Johnson 0-3 (.000); Corzine 0-1 (.000); Greenwood 0-1 (.000); Green 0-4 (.000); Matthews 2-16 (.125); Whatley 1-9 (.111); Higgins 10-37 (.270); Oldham 0-1 (.000); Ca. Jones 0-2 (.000). Opponents 91-292 (.312).

CLEVELAND CAVALIERS

	G	Min.	FGM	FGA	Pct.	FTM	FTA	Pct.	Off.	Def.	Tot.	Ast.	PF	Dq.	Stl.	TO	Blk.	Pts.	Avg.	Hi.
									REBOUNDS									**SCORING**		
World B. Free	71	2249	609	1328	.459	308	411	.749	61	150	211	320	163	0	75	139	16	1597	22.5	45
Phil Hubbard	76	2249	415	822	.505	371	494	.751	214	265	479	114	258	8	81	178	9	1201	15.8	37
Roy Hinson	76	2344	465	925	.503	271	376	.721	186	410	596	68	311	13	51	171	173	1201	15.8	32
Johnny Davis	76	1920	337	791	.426	255	300	.850	35	84	119	426	136	1	43	152	4	941	12.4	33
Mel Turpin	79	1949	363	711	.511	109	139	.784	155	297	452	36	211	3	38	118	87	835	10.6	24
Paul Thompson*	33	715	148	354	.418	45	53	.849	36	80	116	58	77	1	41	42	20	347	10.5	24
John Bagley	81	2401	338	693	.488	125	167	.749	54	237	291	697	132	0	129	207	5	804	9.9	35
Edgar Jones†	26	447	86	184	.467	41	60	.683	34	75	109	11	71	1	11	33	11	213	8.2	15

								REBOUNDS									SCORING		
	G	Min.	FGM	FGA	Pct.	FTM	FTA	Pct.	Off.	Def.	Tot.	Ast.	PF	Dq.	Stl.	TO	Blk.	Pts.	Avg.	Hi.
Edgar Jones‡ 44	769	130	275	.473	82	111	.739	50	121	171	29	123	2	20	61	29	342	7.8	15
Mike Wilson* 11	175	27	54	.500	23	30	.767	10	8	18	24	14	0	10	15	3	77	7.0	13
Ben Poquette 79	1656	210	457	.460	109	137	.796	148	325	473	79	220	3	47	70	58	532	6.7	22
Lonnie Shelton 57	1244	158	363	.435	51	77	.662	82	185	267	96	187	3	44	74	18	367	6.4	16
Jeff Cook* 18	440	46	105	.438	17	27	.630	41	63	104	23	53	0	5	16	9	109	6.1	14
Ron Anderson. 36	520	84	195	.431	41	50	.820	39	49	88	34	40	0	9	34	7	210	5.8	27
Mark West† 65	882	106	193	.549	41	85	.482	89	161	250	15	193	7	13	57	48	253	3.9	16
Mark West‡ 66	888	106	194	.546	43	87	.494	90	161	251	15	197	7	13	59	49	255	3.9	16
Kevin Williams 46	413	58	134	.433	47	64	.734	19	44	63	61	86	1	22	49	4	163	3.5	13
Geoff Huston 8	93	12	25	.480	2	3	.667	0	1	1	23	8	0	0	8	0	26	3.3	10
Robert Smith 7	48	4	17	.235	8	10	.800	0	4	4	7	6	0	2	3	0	16	2.3	7
Campy Russell 3	24	2	7	.286	2	3	.667	0	5	5	3	3	0	0	5	0	6	2.0	4
Butch Graves 4	11	2	6	.333	1	5	.200	0	2	2	1	4	0	1	1	0	5	1.3	3

3-pt. FG: Cleveland 96-335 (.287)—Free 71-193 (.368); Hubbard 0-4 (.000); Hinson 0-3 (.000); Davis 12-46 (.261); Thompson* 6-23 (.261); Bagley 3-26 (.115); Jones† 0-3 (.000); Jones‡ 0-4 (.000); Poquette 3-17 (.176); Shelton 0-5 (.000); Cook* 0-1 (.000); Anderson 1-2 (.500); West† 0-1 (.000); West‡ 0-1 (.000); Williams 0-5 (.000); Smith 0-4 (.000); Russell 0-1 (.000); Graves 0-1 (.000). Opponents 70-253 (.277).

DALLAS MAVERICKS

								REBOUNDS									SCORING		
	G	Min.	FGM	FGA	Pct.	FTM	FTA	Pct.	Off.	Def.	Tot.	Ast.	PF	Dq.	Stl.	TO	Blk.	Pts.	Avg.	Hi.
Mark Aguirre. 80	2699	794	1569	.506	440	580	.759	188	289	477	249	250	3	60	253	24	2055	25.7	49
Rolando Blackman . . . 81	2834	625	1230	.508	342	413	.828	107	193	300	289	96	0	61	162	16	1598	19.7	36
Jay Vincent. 79	2543	545	1138	.479	351	420	.836	185	519	704	169	226	0	48	170	22	1441	18.2	39
Sam Perkins 82	2317	347	736	.471	200	244	.820	189	416	605	135	236	1	63	102	63	903	11.0	29
Brad Davis 82	2539	310	614	.505	158	178	.888	39	154	193	581	219	1	91	123	10	825	10.1	19
Derek Harper 82	2218	329	633	.520	111	154	.721	47	152	199	360	194	1	144	123	37	790	9.6	22
Dale Ellis. 72	1314	274	603	.454	77	104	.740	100	138	238	56	131	1	46	58	7	667	9.3	29
Kurt Nimphius. 82	2010	196	434	.452	108	140	.771	136	272	408	183	262	4	30	95	126	500	6.1	16
Wallace Bryant 56	860	67	148	.453	30	44	.682	74	167	241	84	110	1	21	46	24	164	2.9	14
Tom Sluby 31	151	30	58	.517	13	21	.619	5	7	12	16	18	0	3	11	0	73	2.4	8
Charlie Sitton 43	304	39	94	.415	13	25	.520	24	36	60	26	50	0	7	19	6	91	2.1	8
Howard Carter. 11	66	4	23	.174	1	1	1.000	1	2	3	4	4	0	1	8	0	9	0.8	3

3-pt. FG: Dallas 152-443 (.343)—Aguirre 27-85 (.318); Blackman 6-20 (.300); Vincent 0-4 (.000); Perkins 9-36 (.250); Davis 47-115 (.409); Harper 21-61 (.344); Ellis 42-109 (.385); Nimphius 0-6 (.000); Sluby 0-2 (.000); Sitton 0-2 (.000); Carter 0-3 (.000). Opponents 98-318 (.308).

DENVER NUGGETS

								REBOUNDS									SCORING		
	G	Min.	FGM	FGA	Pct.	FTM	FTA	Pct.	Off.	Def.	Tot.	Ast.	PF	Dq.	Stl.	TO	Blk.	Pts.	Avg.	Hi.
Alex English 81	2924	939	1812	.518	383	462	.829	203	255	458	344	259	1	101	251	46	2262	27.9	45
Calvin Natt 78	2657	685	1255	.546	447	564	.793	209	401	610	238	182	1	75	190	33	1817	23.3	37
Fat Lever. 82	2559	424	985	.430	197	256	.770	147	264	411	613	226	1	202	203	30	1051	12.8	26
Dan Issel 77	1684	363	791	.459	257	319	.806	80	251	331	137	171	1	65	93	31	984	12.8	27
Wayne Cooper 80	2031	404	856	.472	161	235	.685	229	402	631	86	304	2	28	149	197	969	12.1	26
Mike Evans 71	1437	323	661	.489	113	131	.863	26	93	119	231	174	2	65	130	12	816	10.1	34
Bill Hanzlik 80	1673	220	522	.421	180	238	.756	88	119	207	210	291	5	84	115	26	621	7.8	17
T.R. Dunn 81	2290	175	358	.489	84	116	.724	169	216	385	153	213	3	140	65	14	434	5.4	15
Elston Turner 61	1491	101	388	.466	61	66	.785	88	128	216	158	152	0	96	70	7	414	5.1	13
Dan Schayes. 56	542	60	129	.465	79	97	.814	48	96	144	38	98	2	20	44	25	199	3.6	23
Joe Kopicki 42	308	50	95	.526	43	54	.796	29	57	86	29	58	0	13	28	1	145	3.5	14
Willie White 39	234	52	124	.419	21	31	.677	15	21	36	29	24	0	5	30	2	129	3.3	21

3-pt. FG: Denver 73-235 (.311)—English 1-5 (.200); Natt 0-3 (.000); Lever 6-24 (.250); Issel 1-7 (.143); Cooper 0-2 (.000); Evans 57-157 (.363); Hanzlik 1-15 (.067); Dunn 0-2 (.000); Turner 1-6 (.167); Kopicki 2-3 (.667); White 4-11 (.364). Opponents 64-254 (.252).

DETROIT PISTONS

								REBOUNDS									SCORING		
	G	Min.	FGM	FGA	Pct.	FTM	FTA	Pct.	Off.	Def.	Tot.	Ast.	PF	Dq.	Stl.	TO	Blk.	Pts.	Avg.	Hi.
Isiah Thomas 81	3089	646	1410	.458	399	493	.809	114	247	361	1123	288	8	187	302	25	1720	21.2	38
Kelly Tripucka 55	1675	396	831	.477	255	288	.885	66	152	218	135	118	1	49	118	14	1049	19.1	45
Bill Laimbeer. 82	2892	595	1177	.506	244	306	.797	295	718	1013	154	308	4	69	129	71	1438	17.5	35
John Long 66	1820	431	885	.487	106	123	.862	81	109	190	130	139	0	71	98	14	973	14.7	28
Vinnie Johnson. 82	2093	428	942	.454	190	247	.769	134	118	252	325	205	2	71	135	20	1051	12.8	28
Terry Tyler 82	2004	422	855	.494	106	148	.716	148	275	423	63	192	0	49	76	90	950	11.6	28
Dan Roundfield 56	1492	236	505	.467	139	178	.781	175	278	453	102	147	0	26	123	54	611	10.9	27
Kent Benson 72	1401	201	397	.506	76	94	.809	103	221	324	93	207	4	53	68	44	478	6.6	15
Earl Cureton 81	1642	207	428	.484	82	144	.569	169	250	419	83	216	1	56	114	42	496	6.1	18
Tony Campbell 56	625	130	262	.496	56	70	.800	41	48	89	24	107	1	28	69	3	316	5.6	17
Brook Steppe 54	486	83	178	.466	87	104	.837	25	32	57	36	61	0	16	43	4	253	4.7	13
David Thirdkill* 10	115	12	23	.522	5	11	.455	4	4	8	1	16	0	3	12	2	29	2.9	8
Major Jones 47	418	48	87	.552	33	51	.647	48	80	128	15	58	0	9	35	14	129	2.7	15
Lorenzo Romar† 5	35	2	8	.250	5	5	1.000	0	0	0	10	5	0	4	5	0	9	1.8	5
Lorenzo Romar‡ 9	51	3	16	.188	5	5	1.000	0	0	0	12	7	0	4	5	0	11	1.2	5
Terry Teagle* 2	5	1	2	.500	0	0	. . .	0	0	0	2	2	0	0	1	0	2	1.0	2
Sidney Lowe* 6	31	2	7	.286	0	0	. . .	0	1	1	8	5	0	0	2	0	4	0.7	4
Dale Wilkinson* 2	7	0	2	.000	0	0	. . .	1	0	1	0	2	0	0	0	0	0	0.0	0

3-pt. FG: Detroit 45-199 (.226)—Thomas 29-113 (.257); Tripucka 2-5 (.400); Laimbeer 4-18 (.222); Long 5-15 (.333); Johnson 5-27 (.185); Tyler 0-8 (.000); Roundfield 0-2 (.000); Benson 0-3 (.000); Cureton 0-3 (.000); Campbell 0-1 (.000); Steppe 0-1 (.000); Thirdkill* 0-1 (.000); Romar† 0-2 (.000); Romar‡ 0-3 (.000). Opponents 78-249 (.313).

1984-85

GOLDEN STATE WARRIORS

	G	Min.	FGM	FGA	Pct.	FTM	FTA	Pct.	Off.	Def.	Tot.	Ast.	PF	Dq.	Stl.	TO	Blk.	Pts.	Avg.	Hi.
									REBOUNDS									SCORING		
Purvis Short	78	3081	819	1780	.460	501	613	.817	157	241	398	234	255	4	116	241	27	2186	28.0	59
Sleepy Floyd	82	2873	610	1372	.445	336	415	.810	62	140	202	406	226	1	134	251	41	1598	19.5	33
Mickey Johnson	66	1565	304	714	.426	260	316	.823	149	247	396	149	221	5	70	142	35	875	13.3	27
Jerome Whitehead	79	2536	421	825	.510	184	235	.783	219	403	622	53	322	8	45	141	43	1026	13.0	27
Larry Smith	80	2497	366	690	.530	155	256	.605	405	464	869	96	285	5	78	160	54	887	11.1	21
Terry Teagle†	19	344	73	135	.541	25	35	.714	22	21	43	14	34	0	13	14	5	173	9.1	24
Terry Teagle‡	21	349	74	137	.540	25	35	.714	22	21	43	14	36	0	13	15	5	175	8.3	24
Lester Conner	79	2258	246	546	.451	144	192	.750	87	159	246	369	136	1	161	138	13	640	8.1	21
Chuck Aleksinas	74	1114	161	337	.478	55	75	.733	87	183	270	36	171	1	15	72	15	377	5.1	15
Mike Bratz	56	746	106	250	.424	69	82	.841	11	47	58	122	76	1	47	54	4	287	5.1	19
Peter Thibeaux	51	461	94	195	.482	43	67	.642	29	40	69	17	85	1	11	34	17	231	4.5	22
Othell Wilson	74	1260	134	291	.460	54	76	.711	35	96	131	217	122	0	77	95	12	325	4.4	15
Steve Burtt	47	418	72	188	.383	53	77	.688	10	18	28	20	76	0	21	33	4	197	4.2	14
Gary Plummer	66	702	92	232	.397	65	92	.707	54	80	134	26	127	1	15	50	14	250	3.8	16

3-pt. FG: Golden State 112-397 (.282)—Short 47-150 (.313); Floyd 42-143 (.294); Johnson 7-30 (.233); Teagle† 2-4 (.500); Teagle‡ 2-4 (.500); Conner 4-20 (.200); Aleksinas 0-1 (.000); Bratz 6-26 (.231); Thibeaux 0-2 (.000); Wilson 3-16 (.188); Burtt 0-1 (.000); Plummer 1-4 (.250). Opponents 57-220 (.259).

HOUSTON ROCKETS

	G	Min.	FGM	FGA	Pct.	FTM	FTA	Pct.	Off.	Def.	Tot.	Ast.	PF	Dq.	Stl.	TO	Blk.	Pts.	Avg.	Hi.
									REBOUNDS									SCORING		
Ralph Sampson	82	3086	753	1499	.502	303	448	.676	227	626	853	224	306	10	81	326	168	1809	22.1	43
Hakeem Olajuwon	82	2914	677	1258	.538	338	551	.613	440	534	974	111	344	10	99	234	220	1692	20.6	42
Rodney McCray	82	3001	476	890	.535	231	313	.738	201	338	539	355	215	2	90	178	75	1183	14.4	25
Lewis Lloyd	82	2128	457	869	.526	161	220	.732	98	133	231	280	196	1	73	177	28	1077	13.1	28
John Lucas	47	1158	206	446	.462	103	129	.798	21	64	85	318	78	0	62	102	2	536	11.4	28
Mitchell Wiggins	82	1575	318	657	.484	96	131	.733	110	125	235	119	195	1	83	90	13	738	9.0	23
Robert Reid	82	1763	312	648	.481	88	126	.698	81	192	273	171	196	1	48	101	22	713	8.7	23
Lionel Hollins	80	1950	249	540	.461	108	136	.794	33	140	173	417	187	1	78	170	10	609	7.6	23
Allen Leavell	42	536	88	209	.421	44	57	.772	8	29	37	102	61	0	23	51	4	228	5.4	18
Larry Micheaux†	39	394	74	122	.607	17	26	.654	44	55	99	17	49	0	12	28	14	165	4.2	14
Larry Micheaux‡	57	565	91	157	.580	29	43	.674	62	81	143	30	75	0	20	36	21	211	3.7	16
Jim Petersen	60	714	70	144	.486	50	66	.758	44	103	147	29	125	1	14	71	32	190	3.2	13
Craig Ehlo	45	189	34	69	.493	19	30	.633	8	17	25	26	26	0	11	22	3	87	1.9	10
Phil Ford	25	290	14	47	.298	16	18	.889	3	24	27	61	33	0	6	17	1	44	1.8	8
Hank McDowell	34	132	20	42	.476	7	10	.700	7	15	22	9	22	0	3	8	5	47	1.4	6

3-pt. FG: Houston 41-186 (.220)—Sampson 0-6 (.000); McCray 0-6 (.000); Lloyd 2-8 (.250); Lucas 21-66 (.318); Wiggins 6-23 (.261); Reid 1-16 (.063); Hollins 3-13 (.231); Leavell 8-37 (.216); Micheaux† 0-3 (.000); Micheaux‡ 0-3 (.000); Ehlo 0-3 (.000); Ford 0-4 (.000); McDowell 0-1 (.000). Opponents 90-258 (.349).

INDIANA PACERS

	G	Min.	FGM	FGA	Pct.	FTM	FTA	Pct.	Off.	Def.	Tot.	Ast.	PF	Dq.	Stl.	TO	Blk.	Pts.	Avg.	Hi.
									REBOUNDS									SCORING		
Clark Kellogg	77	2449	562	1112	.505	301	396	.760	224	500	724	244	247	2	86	231	26	1432	18.6	37
Herb Williams	75	2557	575	1211	.475	224	341	.657	154	480	634	252	218	1	54	265	134	1375	18.3	33
Vern Fleming	80	2486	433	922	.470	260	339	.767	148	175	323	247	232	4	99	197	8	1126	14.1	29
Steve Stipanovich	82	2315	414	871	.475	297	372	.798	141	473	614	199	265	4	71	184	78	1126	13.7	34
Jim Thomas	80	2059	347	726	.478	183	234	.782	74	187	261	234	195	2	76	131	5	885	11.1	26
Jerry Sichting	70	1808	325	624	.521	112	128	.875	24	90	114	264	116	0	47	102	4	771	11.0	28
Terence Stansbury	74	1278	210	458	.459	102	126	.810	39	75	114	127	205	2	47	80	12	526	7.1	25
Tony Brown	82	1586	214	465	.460	116	171	.678	146	142	288	159	212	3	59	116	12	544	6.6	25
Bill Garnett	65	1123	149	310	.481	120	174	.690	98	188	286	67	196	3	28	92	15	418	6.4	21
Greg Kelser	10	114	21	53	.396	20	28	.714	6	13	19	13	16	0	7	12	0	62	6.2	19
Devin Durrant	59	756	114	274	.416	72	102	.706	49	75	124	80	106	0	19	77	10	300	5.1	17
Granville Waiters	62	703	85	190	.447	29	50	.580	57	113	170	30	107	2	16	55	44	199	3.2	14
Stuart Gray	52	391	35	92	.380	32	47	.681	29	94	123	15	82	1	9	51	14	102	2.0	7
Tracy Jackson	1	12	1	3	.333	0	0	...	1	0	1	4	1	0	2	1	0	2	2.0	2
Kent Edelin	10	143	4	13	.308	3	8	.375	8	18	26	10	39	1	5	3	4	11	1.1	2

3-pt. FG: Indiana 30-155 (.194)—Kellogg 7-14 (.500); Williams 1-9 (.111); Fleming 0-4 (.000); Stipanovich 1-11 (.091); Thomas 8-42 (.190); Sichting 9-37 (.243); Stansbury 4-25 (.160); Brown 0-6 (.000); Garnett 0-2 (.000); Kelser 0-1 (.000); Durrant 0-3 (.000); Waiters 0-1 (.000). Opponents 64-200 (.320).

KANSAS CITY KINGS

	G	Min.	FGM	FGA	Pct.	FTM	FTA	Pct.	Off.	Def.	Tot.	Ast.	PF	Dq.	Stl.	TO	Blk.	Pts.	Avg.	Hi.
									REBOUNDS									SCORING		
Eddie Johnson	82	3029	769	1565	.491	325	373	.871	151	256	407	273	237	2	83	225	22	1876	22.9	40
Mike Woodson	78	1998	530	1068	.496	264	330	.800	69	129	198	143	216	1	117	139	28	1329	17.0	35
Reggie Theus	82	2543	501	1029	.487	334	387	.863	106	164	270	656	250	0	95	307	18	1341	16.4	32
Larry Drew	72	2373	457	913	.501	154	194	.794	39	125	164	484	147	0	93	179	8	1075	14.9	30
Otis Thorpe	82	1918	411	685	.600	230	371	.620	187	369	556	111	256	2	34	187	37	1052	12.8	31
LaSalle Thompson	82	2458	369	695	.531	227	315	.721	274	580	854	130	328	4	98	202	128	965	11.8	26
Mark Olberding	81	2277	265	528	.502	293	352	.832	139	374	513	243	298	8	56	185	11	823	10.2	26
Billy Knight*	16	189	31	69	.449	13	16	.813	10	12	22	21	14	0	2	13	1	76	4.8	12

	G	Min.	FGM	FGA	Pct.	FTM	FTA	Pct.	Off.	Def.	Tot.	Ast.	PF	Dq.	Stl.	TO	Blk.	Pts.	Avg.	Hi.
Joe Meriweather	76	1061	121	243	.498	96	124	.774	94	169	263	27	181	1	17	50	28	339	4.5	20
Don Buse	65	939	82	203	.404	23	30	.767	21	40	61	203	75	0	38	45	1	218	3.4	17
Ed Nealy	22	225	26	44	.591	10	19	.526	15	29	44	18	26	0	3	12	1	62	2.8	11
Mark McNamara†	33	210	28	58	.483	23	44	.523	24	33	57	6	22	0	5	13	7	79	2.4	13
Mark McNamara‡	45	273	40	76	.526	32	62	.516	31	43	74	6	27	0	7	19	8	112	2.5	13
Peter Verhoeven	54	366	51	108	.472	21	25	.840	28	35	63	17	85	1	15	20	7	123	2.3	10
Dane Suttle	6	24	6	13	.462	2	2	1.000	0	3	3	2	3	0	1	1	0	14	2.3	6
David Pope	22	129	17	53	.321	7	13	.538	9	9	18	5	30	0	3	7	3	41	1.9	11
Kenny Natt†	4	16	0	1	.000	0	0	. . .	1	0	1	3	1	0	1	0	0	0	0.0	0
Kenny Natt‡	8	29	2	6	.333	2	4	.500	2	1	3	3	3	0	2	3	0	6	0.8	4

3-pt. FG: Kansas City 63-238 (.265)—Johnson 13-54 (.241); Woodson 5-21 (.238); Theus 5-38 (.132); Drew 7-28 (.250); Thorpe 0-2 (.000); Olberding 0-3 (.000); Knight* 1-1 (1.000); Meriweather 1-2 (.500); Suttle 0-1 (.000); Pope 0-1 (.000). Opponents 65-259 (.251).

LOS ANGELES CLIPPERS

	G	Min.	FGM	FGA	Pct.	FTM	FTA	Pct.	Off.	Def.	Tot.	Ast.	PF	Dq.	Stl.	TO	Blk.	Pts.	Avg.	Hi.
Derek Smith	80	2762	682	1271	.537	400	504	.794	174	253	427	216	317	8	77	230	52	1767	22.1	41
Norm Nixon	81	2894	596	1281	.465	170	218	.780	55	163	218	711	175	2	95	273	4	1395	17.2	39
Marques Johnson . . .	72	2448	494	1094	.452	190	260	.731	188	240	428	248	193	2	72	176	30	1181	16.4	32
Junior Bridgeman . . .	80	2042	460	990	.465	181	206	.879	55	175	230	171	128	0	47	116	18	1115	13.9	30
James Donaldson . . .	82	2392	351	551	.637	227	303	.749	168	500	668	48	217	1	28	206	130	929	11.3	24
Bill Walton	67	1647	269	516	.521	138	203	.680	168	432	600	156	184	0	50	174	140	676	10.1	23
Michael Cage	75	1610	216	398	.543	101	137	.737	126	266	392	51	164	1	41	81	32	533	7.1	22
Franklin Edwards . . .	16	198	36	66	.545	19	24	.792	3	11	14	38	10	0	17	17	0	91	5.7	12
Rory White	80	1106	144	279	.516	90	130	.692	94	101	195	34	115	0	35	87	20	378	4.7	15
Lancaster Gordon . . .	63	682	110	287	.383	37	49	.755	26	35	61	88	61	0	33	69	6	259	4.1	22
Bryan Warrick	58	713	85	173	.491	44	57	.772	10	48	58	153	85	0	23	70	6	215	3.7	18
Harvey Catchings	70	1049	72	149	.483	59	89	.663	89	173	262	14	162	0	15	55	57	203	2.9	11
Dale Wilkinson†	10	38	4	14	.286	6	7	.857	1	2	3	2	8	0	0	4	0	14	1.4	8
Dale Wilkinson‡	12	45	4	16	.250	6	7	.857	1	3	4	2	10	0	0	4	0	14	1.2	8
Jay Murphy	23	149	8	50	.160	12	21	.571	6	35	41	4	21	0	1	8	2	28	1.2	6

3-pt. FG: L.A. Clippers 56-188 (.298)—Smith 3-19 (.158); Nixon 33-99 (.333); Johnson 3-13 (.231); Bridgeman 14-39 (.359); Walton 0-2 (.000); Gordon 2-9 (.222); Warrick 1-4 (.250); Catchings 0-1 (.000); Wilkinson† 0-1 (.000); Wilkinson‡ 0-1 (.000); Murphy 0-1 (.000). Opponents 74-263 (.281).

LOS ANGELES LAKERS

	G	Min.	FGM	FGA	Pct.	FTM	FTA	Pct.	Off.	Def.	Tot.	Ast.	PF	Dq.	Stl.	TO	Blk.	Pts.	Avg.	Hi.
Kareem Abdul-Jabbar .	79	2630	723	1207	.599	289	395	.732	162	460	622	249	238	3	63	197	162	1735	22.0	40
Magic Johnson	77	2781	504	899	.561	391	464	.843	90	386	476	968	155	0	113	305	25	1406	18.3	39
James Worthy	80	2696	610	1066	.572	190	245	.776	169	342	511	201	196	0	87	198	67	1410	17.6	32
Byron Scott	81	2305	541	1003	.539	187	228	.820	57	153	210	244	197	1	100	138	17	1295	16.0	30
Bob McAdoo	66	1254	284	546	.520	122	162	.753	79	216	295	67	170	0	18	95	53	690	10.5	22
Mike McGee	76	1170	329	612	.538	94	160	.588	97	68	165	71	147	1	39	81	7	774	10.2	41
Michael Cooper	82	2189	276	593	.465	115	133	.865	56	199	255	429	208	0	93	156	49	702	8.6	19
Jamaal Wilkes	42	761	148	303	.488	51	66	.773	35	59	94	41	65	0	19	49	3	347	8.3	24
Larry Spriggs	75	1292	194	354	.548	112	146	.767	77	150	227	132	195	2	47	115	13	500	6.7	20
Mitch Kupchak	58	716	123	244	.504	60	91	.659	68	116	184	21	104	0	19	48	20	306	5.3	29
Kurt Rambis	82	1617	181	327	.554	68	103	.660	164	364	528	69	211	0	82	97	47	430	5.2	18
Ronnie Lester	32	278	34	82	.415	21	31	.677	4	22	26	80	25	0	15	32	3	89	2.8	15
Chuck Nevitt	11	59	5	17	.294	2	8	.250	5	15	20	3	20	0	0	10	15	12	1.1	4
Earl Jones	2	7	0	1	.000	0	0	. . .	0	0	0	0	0	0	0	1	0	0	0.0	0

3-pt. FG: L.A. Lakers 90-295 (.305)—Abdul-Jabbar 0-1 (.000); Johnson 7-37 (.189); Worthy 0-7 (.000); Scott 26-60 (.433); McAdoo 0-1 (.000); McGee 22-61 (.361); Cooper 35-123 (.285); Wilkes 0-1 (.000); Spriggs 0-3 (.000); Lester 0-1 (.000). Opponents 84-297 (.283).

MILWAUKEE BUCKS

	G	Min.	FGM	FGA	Pct.	FTM	FTA	Pct.	Off.	Def.	Tot.	Ast.	PF	Dq.	Stl.	TO	Blk.	Pts.	Avg.	Hi.
Terry Cummings	79	2722	759	1532	.495	343	463	.741	244	472	716	228	264	4	117	190	67	1861	23.6	39
Sidney Moncrief	73	2734	561	1162	.483	454	548	.828	149	242	391	382	197	1	117	184	39	1585	21.7	35
Paul Pressey	80	2876	480	928	.517	317	418	.758	149	280	429	543	258	4	129	247	56	1284	16.1	30
Craig Hodges	82	2496	359	732	.490	106	130	.815	74	112	186	349	262	8	96	135	1	871	10.6	21
Alton Lister	81	2091	322	598	.538	154	262	.588	219	428	647	127	287	5	49	183	167	798	9.9	30
Ricky Pierce	44	882	165	307	.537	102	124	.823	49	68	117	94	117	0	34	63	5	433	9.8	24
Mike Dunleavy	19	433	64	135	.474	25	29	.862	6	25	31	85	55	1	15	40	3	169	8.9	16
Paul Thompson†	16	227	41	105	.390	24	34	.706	21	21	42	20	42	0	15	15	5	106	6.6	16
Paul Thompson‡	49	942	189	459	.412	69	87	.793	57	101	158	78	119	1	56	57	25	453	9.2	24
Paul Mokeski	79	1586	205	429	.478	81	116	.698	107	303	410	99	266	6	28	85	35	491	6.2	21
Charlie Davis†	57	746	151	346	.436	48	58	.828	57	92	149	50	110	1	21	52	5	351	6.2	25
Charlie Davis‡	61	774	153	356	.430	51	62	.823	59	94	153	51	113	1	22	54	5	358	5.9	25
Kevin Grevey	78	1182	190	424	.448	88	107	.822	27	76	103	94	85	1	30	55	2	476	6.1	23
Randy Breuer	78	1083	162	317	.511	89	127	.701	92	164	256	40	179	4	21	63	82	413	5.3	18
Kenny Fields	51	535	84	191	.440	27	36	.750	41	43	84	38	84	2	9	32	10	195	3.8	21
Larry Micheaux*	18	171	17	35	.486	12	17	.706	18	26	44	13	26	0	8	8	7	46	2.6	16

1984-85

	G	Min.	FGM	FGA	Pct.	FTM	FTA	Pct.	Off.	Def.	Tot.	Ast.	PF	Dq.	Stl.	TO	Blk.	Pts.	Avg.	Hi.
Mark West*	1	6	0	1	.000	2	2	1.000	1	0	1	0	4	0	0	2	1	2	2.0	5
David Thirdkill*	6	16	3	4	.750	1	2	.500	1	1	2	0	1	0	0	0	0	7	1.2	5
Lorenzo Romar*	4	16	1	8	.125	0	0	...	0	0	0	2	2	0	0	0	0	2	0.5	2
Chris Engler†	1	3	0	2	.000	0	0	...	1	0	1	0	0	0	0	0	1	0	0.0	0
Chris Engler‡	11	82	8	20	.400	5	9	.556	12	18	30	0	5	0	2	2	5	21	1.9	14

3-pt. FG: Milwaukee 89-294 (.303)—Cummings 0-1 (.000); Moncrief 9-33 (.273); Pressey 7-20 (.350); Hodges 47-135 (.348); Lister 0-1 (.000); Pierce 1-4 (.250); Dunleavy 16-47 (.340); Thompson† 0-7 (.000); Thompson‡ 6-30 (.200); Mokeski 0-2 (.000); Davis† 1-10 (.100); Davis‡ 1-10 (.100); Grevey 8-33 (.242); Romar* 0-1 (.000). Opponents 80-308 (.260).

NEW JERSEY NETS

	G	Min.	FGM	FGA	Pct.	FTM	FTA	Pct.	Off.	Def.	Tot.	Ast.	PF	Dq.	Stl.	TO	Blk.	Pts.	Avg.	Hi.
Otis Birdsong	56	1842	495	968	.511	161	259	.622	60	88	148	232	145	1	84	117	7	1155	20.6	42
Micheal R. Richardson	82	3127	690	1470	.469	240	313	.767	156	301	457	669	277	3	243	249	22	1649	20.1	36
Buck Williams	82	3182	577	1089	.530	336	538	.625	323	682	1005	167	293	7	63	238	110	1491	18.2	33
Darryl Dawkins	39	972	192	339	.566	143	201	.711	55	126	181	45	171	11	14	93	35	527	13.5	30
Mike Gminski	81	2418	380	818	.465	276	328	.841	229	404	633	158	135	0	38	136	92	1036	12.8	28
Albert King	42	860	226	460	.491	85	104	.817	70	89	159	58	110	0	41	65	9	537	12.8	28
Ron Brewer†	11	245	49	84	.583	16	18	.889	8	10	18	11	15	0	5	5	5	114	10.4	17
Ron Brewer‡	20	326	62	118	.525	23	25	.920	9	12	21	17	23	0	6	9	6	147	7.4	17
Mike O'Koren	43	1119	194	393	.494	42	67	.627	46	120	166	102	115	1	32	51	16	438	10.2	27
Kelvin Ransey	81	1689	300	654	.459	122	142	.859	40	90	130	355	134	0	87	113	7	724	8.9	24
Darwin Cook	58	1063	212	453	.468	47	54	.870	21	71	92	160	96	0	74	75	10	473	8.2	22
Jeff Turner	72	1429	171	377	.454	79	92	.859	88	130	218	108	243	8	29	90	7	421	5.8	14
Kevin McKenna	29	535	61	134	.455	38	43	.884	20	29	49	58	63	0	30	32	7	165	5.7	17
Wayne Sappleton	33	298	41	87	.471	14	34	.412	28	47	75	7	50	0	7	21	4	96	2.9	9
Mike Wilson†	8	92	9	23	.391	4	6	.667	4	9	13	11	7	0	4	5	2	22	2.8	8
Mike Wilson‡	19	267	36	77	.468	27	36	.750	14	17	31	35	21	0	14	20	5	99	5.2	13
Chris Engler*	7	76	7	16	.438	5	9	.556	10	17	27	0	4	0	2	1	4	19	2.7	14
George Johnson	65	800	42	79	.532	22	27	.815	74	111	185	22	151	2	19	39	78	107	1.6	7
Tom LaGarde	1	8	0	1	.000	1	2	.500	1	1	2	0	2	0	0	1	0	1	1.0	1

3-pt. FG: New Jersey 52-224 (.232)—Birdsong 4-21 (.190); Richardson 29-115 (.252); Williams 1-4 (.250); Dawkins 0-1 (.000); Gminski 0-1 (.000); King 0-8 (.000); Brewer† 0-2 (.000); Brewer‡ 0-2 (.000); O'Koren 8-21 (.381); Ransey 2-11 (.182); Cook 2-23 (.087); Turner 0-3 (.000); McKenna 5-13 (.385); Johnson 1-1 (1.000). Opponents 79-262 (.302).

NEW YORK KNICKERBOCKERS

	G	Min.	FGM	FGA	Pct.	FTM	FTA	Pct.	Off.	Def.	Tot.	Ast.	PF	Dq.	Stl.	TO	Blk.	Pts.	Avg.	Hi.
Bernard King	55	2063	691	1303	.530	426	552	.772	114	203	317	204	191	3	71	204	15	1809	32.9	60
Pat Cummings	63	2069	410	797	.514	177	227	.780	139	379	518	109	247	6	50	166	17	997	15.8	34
Darrell Walker	82	2489	430	989	.435	243	347	.700	128	150	278	408	244	2	167	204	21	1103	13.5	31
Louis Orr	79	2452	372	766	.486	262	334	.784	171	220	391	134	195	1	100	138	27	1007	12.7	28
Rory Sparrow	79	2292	326	662	.492	122	141	.865	38	131	169	557	200	2	81	150	9	781	9.9	21
Trent Tucker	77	1819	293	606	.483	38	48	.792	74	114	188	199	195	0	75	64	15	653	8.5	27
Butch Carter	69	1279	214	476	.450	109	134	.813	36	59	95	167	151	1	57	109	5	548	7.9	22
Ken Bannister	75	1404	209	445	.470	91	192	.474	108	222	330	39	279	16	38	141	40	509	6.8	24
Ernie Grunfeld	69	1061	188	384	.490	77	104	.740	41	110	151	105	129	2	50	40	7	455	6.6	30
Eddie Lee Wilkins	54	917	116	233	.498	66	122	.541	86	176	262	16	155	3	21	64	16	298	5.5	24
James Bailey	74	1297	156	349	.447	73	108	.676	122	222	344	39	286	10	30	100	50	385	5.2	18
Truck Robinson	2	35	2	5	.400	0	2	.000	6	3	9	3	3	0	2	5	3	4	2.0	4
Ron Cavenall	53	653	28	86	.326	22	39	.564	53	113	166	19	123	2	12	45	42	78	1.5	7

3-pt. FG: New York 51-198 (.258)—King 1-10 (.100); Cummings 0-4 (.000); Walker 0-17 (.000); Orr 1-10 (.100); Sparrow 7-31 (.226); Tucker 29-72 (.403); Carter 11-43 (.256); Grunfeld 2-8 (.250); Wilkins 0-2 (.000); Bailey 0-1 (.000). Opponents 67-229 (.293).

PHILADELPHIA 76ERS

	G	Min.	FGM	FGA	Pct.	FTM	FTA	Pct.	Off.	Def.	Tot.	Ast.	PF	Dq.	Stl.	TO	Blk.	Pts.	Avg.	Hi.
Moses Malone	79	2957	602	1284	.469	737	904	.815	385	646	1031	130	216	0	67	286	123	1941	24.6	51
Julius Erving	78	2535	610	1236	.494	338	442	.765	172	242	414	233	199	0	135	208	109	1561	20.0	35
Andrew Toney	70	2237	450	914	.492	306	355	.862	35	142	177	363	211	1	65	224	24	1245	17.8	43
Charles Barkley	82	2347	427	783	.545	293	400	.733	266	437	703	155	301	5	95	209	80	1148	14.0	29
Maurice Cheeks	78	2616	422	741	.570	175	199	.879	54	163	217	497	184	0	169	155	24	1025	13.1	25
Bobby Jones	80	1633	207	385	.538	186	216	.861	105	192	297	155	183	2	84	118	50	600	7.5	17
Clint Richardson	74	1531	183	404	.453	76	89	.854	60	95	155	157	143	0	37	78	15	443	6.0	18
Sedale Threatt	82	1304	188	416	.452	66	90	.733	21	78	99	175	171	2	80	90	16	446	5.4	19
George Johnson	55	756	107	263	.407	49	56	.875	48	116	164	38	99	0	31	49	16	264	4.8	21
Clemon Johnson	58	875	117	235	.498	36	49	.735	92	129	221	33	112	0	15	43	44	270	4.7	12
Leon Wood	38	269	50	134	.373	18	26	.692	3	15	18	45	17	0	8	25	0	122	3.2	16
Samuel Williams	46	488	58	148	.392	28	47	.596	38	68	106	11	92	1	26	44	26	144	3.1	10
Marc Iavaroni*	12	156	12	31	.387	6	6	1.000	11	18	29	6	24	0	4	16	3	30	2.5	6
Steve Hayes	11	101	10	18	.556	2	4	.500	11	23	34	1	19	0	1	2	4	22	2.0	5

3-pt. FG: Philadelphia 59-224 (.263)—Malone 0-2 (.000); Erving 3-14 (.214); Toney 39-105 (.371); Barkley 1-6 (.167); Cheeks 6-26 (.231); Jones 0-4 (.000); Richardson 1-3 (.333); Threatt 4-22 (.182); G. Johnson 1-10 (.100); C. Johnson 0-1 (.000); Wood 4-30 (.133); Williams 0-1 (.000). Opponents 80-311 (.257).

PHOENIX SUNS

	G	Min.	FGM	FGA	Pct.	FTM	FTA	Pct.	REBOUNDS Off.	Def.	Tot.	Ast.	PF	Dq.	Stl.	TO	Blk.	SCORING Pts.	Avg.	Hi.
Larry Nance	61	2202	515	877	.587	180	254	.709	195	341	536	159	185	2	88	136	104	1211	19.9	44
Walter Davis	23	570	139	309	.450	64	73	.877	6	29	35	98	42	0	18	50	0	345	15.0	22
James Edwards	70	1787	384	766	.501	276	370	.746	95	292	387	153	237	5	26	162	52	1044	14.9	30
Alvan Adams	82	2136	476	915	.520	250	283	.883	153	347	500	308	254	2	115	197	48	1202	14.7	36
Maurice Lucas	63	1670	346	727	.476	150	200	.750	138	419	557	145	183	0	39	151	17	842	13.4	28
Kyle Macy	65	2018	282	582	.485	127	140	.907	33	146	179	380	128	0	85	111	3	714	11.0	30
Mike Sanders	21	418	85	175	.486	45	59	.763	38	51	89	29	59	0	23	34	4	215	10.2	21
Jay Humphries	80	2062	279	626	.446	141	170	.829	32	132	164	350	209	2	107	167	8	703	8.8	26
Rod Foster	79	1318	286	636	.450	83	110	.755	27	53	80	186	171	1	61	117	0	696	8.8	24
Charles Jones	78	1565	236	454	.520	182	281	.648	139	255	394	128	149	0	45	143	61	654	8.4	27
Michael Holton	74	1761	257	576	.446	96	118	.814	30	102	132	198	141	0	59	123	6	624	8.4	25
Charlie Pittman	68	1001	107	227	.471	109	146	.747	90	137	227	69	144	1	20	100	21	323	4.8	20
Alvin Scott	77	1238	111	259	.429	53	74	.716	46	115	161	127	125	0	39	60	25	276	3.6	10
Michael Young	2	11	2	6	.333	0	0	...	1	1	2	0	0	0	0	0	0	4	2.0	4
Rick Robey	4	48	2	9	.222	1	2	.500	3	5	8	5	7	0	2	8	0	5	1.3	3

3-pt. FG: Phoenix 87-307 (.283)—Nance 1-2 (.500); Davis 3-10 (.300); Edwards 0-3 (.000); Lucas 0-4 (.000); Macy 23-85 (.271); Humphries 4-20 (.200); Foster 41-126 (.325); Jones 0-4 (.000); Holton 14-45 (.311); Pittman 0-2 (.000); Scott 1-5 (.200); Young 0-1 (.000). Opponents 65-224 (.290).

PORTLAND TRAIL BLAZERS

	G	Min.	FGM	FGA	Pct.	FTM	FTA	Pct.	REBOUNDS Off.	Def.	Tot.	Ast.	PF	Dq.	Stl.	TO	Blk.	SCORING Pts.	Avg.	Hi.
Kiki Vandeweghe	72	2502	618	1158	.534	369	412	.896	74	154	228	106	116	0	37	116	22	1616	22.4	47
Mychal Thompson	79	2616	572	1111	.515	307	449	.684	211	407	618	205	216	0	78	231	104	1451	18.4	33
Jim Paxson	68	2253	508	988	.514	196	248	.790	69	153	222	264	115	0	101	108	5	1218	17.9	40
Clyde Drexler	80	2555	573	1161	.494	223	294	.759	217	259	476	441	265	3	177	223	68	1377	17.2	37
Darnell Valentine	75	2278	321	679	.473	230	290	.793	54	165	219	522	189	1	143	194	5	872	11.6	26
Kenny Carr	48	1120	190	363	.523	118	164	.720	90	233	323	56	141	0	25	100	17	498	10.4	30
Sam Bowie	76	2216	299	558	.537	160	225	.711	207	449	656	215	278	9	55	172	203	758	10.0	27
Steve Colter	78	1462	216	477	.453	98	130	.754	40	110	150	243	142	0	75	112	9	556	7.1	35
Jerome Kersey	77	958	178	372	.478	117	181	.646	95	111	206	63	147	1	49	66	29	473	6.1	21
Audie Norris	78	1117	133	245	.543	135	203	.665	90	160	250	47	221	7	42	100	33	401	5.1	20
Bernard Thompson	59	535	79	212	.373	39	51	.765	37	39	76	52	79	0	31	35	10	197	3.3	13
Tom Scheffler	39	268	21	51	.412	10	20	.500	18	58	76	11	48	0	8	15	11	52	1.3	10

3-pt. FG: Portland 51-202 (.252)—Vandeweghe 11-33 (.333); Paxson 6-39 (.154); Drexler 8-37 (.216); Valentine 0-2 (.000); Carr 0-3 (.000); Colter 26 74 (.351); Kersey 0-3 (.000); Norris 0-3 (.000); B. Thompson 0-8 (.000). Opponents 59-232 (.254).

SAN ANTONIO SPURS

	G	Min.	FGM	FGA	Pct.	FTM	FTA	Pct.	REBOUNDS Off.	Def.	Tot.	Ast.	PF	Dq.	Stl.	TO	Blk.	SCORING Pts.	Avg.	Hi.
Mike Mitchell	82	2853	775	1558	.497	269	346	.777	145	272	417	151	219	1	61	144	27	1824	22.2	40
George Gervin	72	2091	600	1182	.508	324	384	.844	79	155	234	178	208	2	66	198	48	1524	21.2	47
Artis Gilmore	81	2756	532	854	.623	484	646	.749	231	615	846	131	306	4	40	241	173	1548	19.1	35
Johnny Moore	82	2689	416	910	.457	189	248	.762	94	284	378	816	247	3	229	236	18	1046	12.8	27
Gene Banks	82	2091	289	493	.586	199	257	.774	133	312	445	234	220	3	65	140	13	778	9.5	32
Alvin Robertson	79	1685	299	600	.498	124	169	.734	116	149	265	275	217	1	127	167	24	726	9.2	27
David Thirdkill†	2	52	5	11	.455	5	6	.833	5	2	7	3	5	0	2	2	1	15	7.5	9
David Thirdkill‡	18	183	20	38	.526	11	19	.579	10	7	17	4	22	0	5	14	3	51	2.8	9
Edgar Jones	18	322	44	91	.484	41	51	.804	16	46	62	18	52	1	9	28	18	129	7.2	15
Marc Iavaroni†	57	1178	150	323	.464	81	122	.664	84	191	275	113	193	5	31	103	32	381	6.7	17
Marc Iavaroni‡	69	1334	162	354	.458	87	128	.680	95	209	304	119	217	5	35	119	35	411	6.0	17
John Paxson	78	1259	196	385	.509	84	100	.840	19	49	68	215	117	0	45	81	3	486	6.2	21
Billy Knight†	52	611	125	285	.439	51	57	.895	40	56	96	59	48	0	14	57	1	311	6.0	21
Billy Knight‡	68	800	156	354	.441	64	73	.877	50	68	118	80	62	0	16	70	2	387	5.7	21
Fred Roberts*	22	305	44	98	.449	29	38	.763	10	25	35	22	45	0	10	21	12	117	5.3	12
Jeff Cook†	54	848	92	174	.529	30	37	.811	81	129	210	39	150	2	25	32	14	214	4.0	13
Jeff Cook‡	72	1288	138	279	.495	47	64	.734	122	192	314	62	203	2	30	48	23	323	4.5	14
Ozell Jones	67	888	106	180	.589	33	83	.398	65	173	238	56	139	1	30	61	57	245	3.7	19
Ron Brewer*	9	81	13	34	.382	7	7	1.000	1	2	3	6	8	0	1	4	1	33	3.7	6
Mark McNamara*	12	63	12	18	.667	9	18	.500	7	10	17	0	5	0	2	6	1	33	2.8	9
Linton Townes	1	8	0	6	.000	2	2	1.000	1	0	1	0	1	0	0	0	0	2	2.0	2

3-pt. FG: San Antonio 55-202 (.272)—Mitchell 5-23 (.217); Gervin 0-10 (.000); Gilmore 0-2 (.000); Moore 25-89 (.281); Banks 1-3 (.333); Robertson 4-11 (.364); Thirdkill† 0-0; Thirdkill‡ 0-1 (.000); E. Jones 0-1 (.000); Iavaroni† 0-4 (.000); Iavaroni‡ 0-4 (.000); Paxson 10-34 (.294); Knight† 10-24 (.417); Knight‡ 11-25 (.440); Cook† 0-0; Cook‡ 0-1 (.000); O. Jones 0-1 (.000). Opponents 72-242 (.298).

SEATTLE SUPERSONICS

	G	Min.	FGM	FGA	Pct.	FTM	FTA	Pct.	Off.	Def.	Tot.	Ast.	PF	Dq.	Stl.	TO	Blk.	Pts.	Avg.	Hi.
									REBOUNDS									SCORING		
Tom Chambers	81	2923	629	1302	.483	475	571	.832	164	415	579	209	312	4	70	260	57	1739	21.5	38
Jack Sikma	68	2402	461	943	.489	335	393	.852	164	559	723	285	239	1	83	160	91	1259	18.5	34
Al Wood	80	2545	515	1061	.485	166	214	.776	99	180	279	236	187	3	84	120	52	1203	15.0	35
Gerald Henderson	79	2648	427	891	.479	199	255	.780	71	119	190	559	196	1	140	231	9	1062	13.4	31
Ricky Sobers	71	1490	280	628	.446	132	162	.815	27	76	103	252	156	0	49	158	9	700	9.9	26
Tim McCormick	78	1584	269	483	.557	188	263	.715	146	252	398	78	207	2	18	114	33	726	9.3	29
Danny Vranes	76	2163	186	402	.463	67	127	.528	154	282	436	152	256	4	76	119	57	440	5.8	24
Joe Cooper	3	45	7	15	.467	3	6	.500	3	6	9	2	7	1	2	0	1	17	5.7	14
Jon Sundvold	73	1150	170	400	.425	48	59	.814	17	53	70	206	87	0	36	85	1	400	5.5	24
Frank Brickowski	78	1115	150	305	.492	85	127	.669	76	184	260	100	171	1	34	100	15	385	4.9	22
Cory Blackwell	60	551	87	237	.367	28	55	.509	42	54	96	26	55	0	25	44	3	202	3.4	11
John Schweitz	19	110	25	74	.338	7	10	.700	6	15	21	18	12	0	0	14	1	57	3.0	11
Reggie King	60	860	63	149	.423	41	59	.695	44	78	122	53	74	1	28	42	11	167	2.8	13
Scooter McCray	6	93	6	10	.600	3	4	.750	6	11	17	7	13	0	1	10	3	15	2.5	5
Danny Young	3	26	2	10	.200	0	0	...	0	3	3	2	2	0	3	2	0	4	1.3	4

3-pt. FG: Seattle 45-185 (.243)—Chambers 6-22 (.273); Sikma 2-10 (.200); Wood 7-33 (.212); Henderson 9-38 (.237); Sobers 8-28 (.286); McCormick 0-1 (.000); Vranes 1-4 (.250); Sundvold 12-38 (.316); Brickowski 0-4 (.000); Blackwell 0-2 (.000); Schweitz 0-4 (.000); Young 0-1 (.000). Opponents 79-253 (.312).

UTAH JAZZ

	G	Min.	FGM	FGA	Pct.	FTM	FTA	Pct.	Off.	Def.	Tot.	Ast.	PF	Dq.	Stl.	TO	Blk.	Pts.	Avg.	Hi.
									REBOUNDS									SCORING		
Adrian Dantley	55	1971	512	964	.531	438	545	.804	148	175	323	186	175	0	57	171	8	1462	26.6	42
Darrell Griffith	78	2776	728	1593	.457	216	298	.725	124	220	344	243	178	1	133	247	30	1764	22.6	41
John Drew	19	463	107	260	.412	94	122	.770	36	46	82	35	65	0	22	42	2	308	16.2	38
Thurl Bailey	80	2481	507	1034	.490	197	234	.842	153	372	525	138	215	2	51	152	105	1212	15.2	27
Rickey Green	77	2431	381	798	.477	232	267	.869	37	152	189	597	131	0	132	177	3	1000	13.0	31
Mark Eaton	82	2813	302	673	.449	190	267	.712	207	720	927	124	312	5	36	206	456	794	9.7	20
Fred Roberts†	52	873	164	320	.513	121	144	.840	68	83	151	65	96	0	18	68	10	450	8.7	25
Fred Roberts‡	74	1178	208	418	.498	150	182	.824	78	108	186	87	141	0	28	89	22	567	7.7	25
Jeff Wilkins	79	1505	285	582	.490	61	80	.763	78	288	366	81	173	0	35	91	18	631	8.0	22
John Stockton	82	1490	157	333	.471	142	193	.736	26	79	105	415	203	3	109	150	11	458	5.6	19
Bobby Hansen	54	646	110	225	.489	40	72	.556	20	50	70	75	88	0	25	49	1	261	4.8	22
Rich Kelley	77	1276	103	216	.477	84	112	.750	118	232	350	120	227	5	42	124	30	290	3.8	16
Mitchell Anderson	44	457	61	149	.409	27	45	.600	29	53	82	21	70	0	29	32	9	149	3.4	11
Pace Mannion	34	190	27	63	.429	16	23	.696	12	11	23	27	17	0	16	18	3	70	2.1	8
Kenny Natt*	4	13	2	5	.400	2	4	.500	1	1	2	0	2	0	1	3	0	6	1.5	4
Billy Paultz	62	370	32	87	.368	18	28	.643	24	72	96	16	51	0	6	30	11	82	1.3	10

3-pt. FG: Utah 103-307 (.336)—Griffith 92-257 (.358); Drew 0-4 (.000); Bailey 1-1 (1.000); Green 6-20 (.300); Roberts† 1-1 (1.000); Roberts‡ 1-1 (1.000); Wilkins 0-1 (.000); Stockton 2-11 (.182); Hansen 1-7 (.143); Kelley 0-2 (.000); Anderson 0-2 (.000); Mannion 0-1 (.000). Opponents 72-280 (.257).

WASHINGTON BULLETS

	G	Min.	FGM	FGA	Pct.	FTM	FTA	Pct.	Off.	Def.	Tot.	Ast.	PF	Dq.	Stl.	TO	Blk.	Pts.	Avg.	Hi.
									REBOUNDS									SCORING		
Gus Williams	79	2960	638	1483	.430	251	346	.725	72	123	195	608	159	1	178	213	32	1578	20.0	37
Jeff Malone	76	2613	605	1213	.499	211	250	.844	60	146	206	184	176	1	52	107	9	1436	18.9	40
Jeff Ruland	37	1436	250	439	.569	200	292	.685	127	283	410	162	128	2	31	159	27	700	18.9	31
Cliff Robinson	60	1870	422	896	.471	158	213	.742	141	405	546	149	187	4	51	161	47	1003	16.7	32
Greg Ballard	82	2664	469	978	.480	120	151	.795	150	381	531	208	221	0	100	106	33	1072	13.1	31
Frank Johnson	46	925	175	358	.489	72	96	.750	23	40	63	143	72	0	43	59	3	428	9.3	21
Tom McMillen	69	1547	252	534	.472	112	135	.830	64	146	210	52	163	3	8	44	17	616	8.9	37
Darren Daye	80	1573	258	504	.512	178	249	.715	93	179	272	240	164	1	53	134	19	695	8.7	21
Rick Mahorn	77	2072	206	413	.499	71	104	.683	150	458	608	121	308	11	59	133	104	483	6.3	25
Charles Jones†	28	638	65	123	.528	36	52	.692	69	109	178	25	101	3	22	21	74	166	5.9	15
Charles Jones‡	31	667	67	127	.528	40	58	.690	71	113	184	26	107	3	22	25	79	174	5.6	15
Dudley Bradley	73	1232	142	299	.475	54	79	.684	34	100	134	173	152	0	96	84	21	358	4.9	22
Guy Williams	21	119	29	63	.460	2	5	.400	15	12	27	9	17	0	5	8	2	61	2.9	13
Don Collins	11	91	12	34	.353	8	9	.889	10	9	19	7	5	0	7	8	4	32	2.9	7
Charlie Davis`	4	28	2	10	.200	3	4	.750	2	2	4	1	3	0	1	2	0	7	1.8	5
Tom Sewell	21	87	9	36	.250	2	4	.500	2	2	4	6	13	0	3	7	1	20	1.0	4

3-pt. FG: Washington 109-398 (.274)—Gus Williams 51-176 (.290); Malone 15-72 (.208); Ruland 0-2 (.000); Robinson 1-3 (.333); Ballard 14-46 (.304); Johnson 6-17 (.353); McMillen 0-5 (.000); Daye 1-7 (.143); Bradley 20-64 (.313); Guy Williams 1-4 (.250); Sewell 0-2 (.000). Opponents 66-232 (.284).

* Finished season with another team. † Totals with this team only. ‡ Totals with all teams.

1984-85

EASTERN CONFERENCE

FIRST ROUND

Boston 3, Cleveland 1
Apr. 18—Thur. Cleveland 123 at Boston 126
Apr. 20—Sat.   Cleveland 106 at Boston 108
Apr. 23—Tue.   Boston 98 at Cleveland 105
Apr. 25—Thur. Boston 117 at Cleveland 115

Milwaukee 3, Chicago 1
Apr. 19—Fri.   Chicago 100 at Milwaukee 109
Apr. 21—Sun.   Chicago 115 at Milwaukee 122
Apr. 24—Wed.   Milwaukee 107 at Chicago 109
Apr. 26—Fri.   Milwaukee 105 at Chicago 97

Philadelphia 3, Washington 1
Apr. 17—Wed.   Washington 97 at Philadelphia 104
Apr. 21—Sun.   Washington 94 at Philadelphia 113
Apr. 24—Wed.   Philadelphia 100 at Washington 118
Apr. 26—Fri.   Philadelphia 106 at Washington 98

Detroit 3, New Jersey 0
Apr. 18—Thur. New Jersey 105 at Detroit 125
Apr. 21—Sun.   New Jersey 111 at Detroit 121
Apr. 24—Wed.   Detroit 116 at New Jersey 115

SEMIFINALS

Boston 4, Detroit 2
Apr. 28—Sun.   Detroit 99 at Boston 133
Apr. 30—Tue.   Detroit 114 at Boston 121
May 2—Thur.   Boston 117 at Detroit 125
May 5—Sun.   Boston 99 at Detroit 102
May 8—Wed.   Detroit 123 at Boston 130
May 10—Fri.   Boston 123 at Detroit 113

Philadelphia 4, Milwaukee 0
Apr. 28—Sun.   Philadelphia 127 at Milwaukee   105
Apr. 30—Tue.   Philadelphia 112 at Milwaukee 108
May 3—Fri.   Milwaukee 104 at Philadelphia 109
May 5—Sun.   Milwaukee 112 at Philadelphia 121

FINALS

Boston 4, Philadelphia 1
May 12—Sun.   Philadelphia 93 at Boston 108
May 14—Tue.   Philadelphia 98 at Boston 106
May 18—Sat.   Boston 105 at Philadelphia 94
May 19—Sun.   Boston 104 at Philadelphia 115
May 22—Wed.   Philadelphia 100 at Boston 102

WESTERN CONFERENCE

FIRST ROUND

L.A. Lakers 3, Phoenix 0
Apr. 18—Thur. Phoenix 114 at L.A. Lakers 142
Apr. 20—Sat.   Phoenix 130 at L.A. Lakers 147
Apr. 23—Tue.   L.A. Lakers 119 at Phoenix 103

Denver 3, San Antonio 2
Apr. 18—Thur. San Antonio 111 at Denver 141
Apr. 20—Sat.   San Antonio 113 at Denver 111
Apr. 23—Tue.   Denver 115 at San Antonio 112
Apr. 26—Fri.   Denver 111 at San Antonio 116
Apr. 28—Sun.   San Antonio 99 at Denver 126

Utah 3, Houston 2
Apr. 19—Fri.   Utah 115 at Houston 101
Apr. 21—Sun.   Utah 96 at Houston 122
Apr. 24—Wed.   Houston 104 at Utah 112
Apr. 26—Fri.   Houston 96 at Utah 94
Apr. 28—Sun.   Utah 104 at Houston 97

Portland 3, Dallas 1
Apr. 18—Thur. Portland 131 at Dallas **139
Apr. 20—Sat.   Portland 124 at Dallas *121
Apr. 23—Tue.   Dallas 109 at Portland 122
Apr. 25—Thur. Dallas 113 at Portland 115

SEMIFINALS

L.A. Lakers 4, Portland 1
Apr. 27—Sat.   Portland 101 at L.A. Lakers 125
Apr. 30—Tue.   Portland 118 at L.A. Lakers 134
May 3—Fri.   L.A. Lakers 130 at Portland 126
May 5—Sun.   L.A. Lakers 107 at Portland 115
May 7—Tue.   Portland 120 at L.A. Lakers 139

Denver 4, Utah 1
Apr. 30—Tue.   Utah 113 at Denver 130
May 2—Thur.   Utah 123 at Denver *131
May 4—Sat.   Denver 123 at Utah 131
May 5—Sun.   Denver 125 at Utah 118
May 7—Tue.   Utah 104 at Denver 116

FINALS

L.A. Lakers 4, Denver 1
May 11—Sat.   Denver 122 at L.A. Lakers 139
May 14—Tue.   Denver 136 at L.A. Lakers 114
May 17—Fri.   L.A. Lakers 136 at Denver 118
May 19—Sun.   L.A. Lakers 120 at Denver 116
May 22—Wed.   Denver 109 at L.A. Lakers 153

NBA FINALS

L.A. Lakers 4, Boston 2
May 27—Mon.   L.A. Lakers 114 at Boston 148
May 30—Thur.   L.A. Lakers 109 at Boston 102
June 2—Sun.   Boston 111 at L.A. Lakers 136
June 5—Wed.   Boston 107 at L.A. Lakers 105
June 7—Fri.   Boston 111 at L.A. Lakers 120
June 9—Sun.   L.A. Lakers 111 at Boston 100

*Denotes number of overtime periods.

1984-85

1983-84

1983-84 NBA CHAMPION BOSTON CELTICS

Front row (from left): Quinn Buckner, Cedric Maxwell, vice chairman of the board Paul Dupee, chairman of the board Don Gaston, president and general manager Red Auerbach, head coach K.C. Jones, vice chairman of the board Alan Cohen, Larry Bird, M.L. Carr. Back row (from left): team physician Dr. Thomas Silva, assistant coach Jimmy Rodgers, Gerald Henderson, Scott Wedman, Greg Kite, Robert Parish, Kevin McHale, Dennis Johnson, Danny Ainge, Carlos Clark, assistant coach Chris Ford, trainer Ray Melchiorre.

FINAL STANDINGS

ATLANTIC DIVISION

	Atl.	Bos.	Chi.	Cle.	Dal.	Den.	Det.	G.S.	Hou.	Ind.	K.C.	L.A.	Mil.	N.J.	N.Y.	Phi.	Pho.	Por.	S.A.	S.D.	Sea.	Uta.	Was.	W	L	Pct.	GB
Boston 5	..	5	6	2	2	4	2	1	5	2	0	5	4	3	2	2	2	2	1	2	1	4	62	20	.756	..
Philadelphia ..1	4	3	4	1	1	3	1	2	5	2	1	4	3	4	..	1	1	2	2	1	2	4	52	30	.634	10
New York 1	3	4	5	2	1	2	1	2	4	2	2	1	3	...	2	1	0	2	2	1	2	4	47	35	.573	15
New Jersey ..3	2	4	3	1	1	4	1	2	5	0	1	2	..	3	3	2	0	0	2	1	1	4	45	37	.549	17
Washington ..2	2	4	1	2	2	3	0	2	4	0	1	1	2	2	2	0	1	1	1	1	..	35	47	.427	27

CENTRAL DIVISION

	Atl.	Bos.	Chi.	Cle.	Dal.	Den.	Det.	G.S.	Hou.	Ind.	K.C.	L.A.	Mil.	N.J.	N.Y.	Phi.	Pho.	Por.	S.A.	S.D.	Sea.	Uta.	Was.	W	L	Pct.	GB
Milwaukee ...3	1	4	5	2	1	2	2	1	5	2	0	..	4	4	2	2	1	1	1	1	1	5	50	32	.610	..
Detroit 4	2	5	5	2	1	..	1	1	4	1	1	3	1	4	3	2	1	1	2	1	1	3	49	33	.598	1
Atlanta	0	4	3	1	0	2	1	1	4	0	0	3	3	4	5	1	0	1	1	1	1	4	40	42	.488	10
Cleveland 3	0	4	..	1	0	1	1	1	2	0	0	1	2	1	2	1	1	1	1	1	0	4	28	54	.341	22
Chicago 2	0	..	2	1	0	1	2	0	3	1	0	2	2	2	2	1	2	0	1	0	1	2	27	55	.329	23
Indiana 2	1	3	4	0	2	2	0	1	..	0	1	1	1	2	0	1	1	0	1	1	1	1	26	56	.317	24

MIDWEST DIVISION

	Atl.	Bos.	Chi.	Cle.	Dal.	Den.	Det.	G.S.	Hou.	Ind.	K.C.	L.A.	Mil.	N.J.	N.Y.	Phi.	Pho.	Por.	S.A.	S.D.	Sea.	Uta.	Was.	W	L	Pct.	GB
Utah 1	1	1	2	2	3	1	4	5	1	3	1	1	1	0	0	4	4	2	3	4	..	1	45	37	.549	..
Dallas 1	0	1	1	..	4	0	4	4	2	3	3	0	1	0	1	3	2	4	4	1	4	0	43	39	.524	2
Kansas City ..2	0	1	2	3	2	1	1	4	2	..	0	0	2	0	0	2	2	5	3	1	3	2	38	44	.463	7
Denver 2	0	2	2	2	..	1	2	4	0	4	1	1	1	1	2	1	3	3	2	3	0	38	44	.463	7
San Antonio ..1	0	2	1	2	3	1	2	4	2	1	3	1	2	0	0	0	1	..	4	2	4	1	37	45	.451	8
Houston 1	1	2	1	2	2	1	3	..	1	2	1	1	0	0	0	2	1	2	2	3	1	0	29	53	.354	16

PACIFIC DIVISION

	Atl.	Bos.	Chi.	Cle.	Dal.	Den.	Det.	G.S.	Hou.	Ind.	K.C.	L.A.	Mil.	N.J.	N.Y.	Phi.	Pho.	Por.	S.A.	S.D.	Sea.	Uta.	Was.	W	L	Pct.	GB
Los Angeles ..2	2	2	2	2	4	1	3	4	1	5	..	2	1	0	1	3	5	2	4	3	4	1	54	28	.659	..
Portland 2	0	0	1	3	4	1	4	4	1	3	1	1	2	2	1	4	..	4	4	4	1	1	48	34	.585	6
Seattle 1	0	2	1	4	3	1	2	2	1	4	3	1	1	1	1	4	2	3	3	..	1	1	42	40	.512	12
Phoenix 1	0	1	1	2	3	0	5	3	1	3	3	0	0	1	1	..	2	5	4	2	1	2	41	41	.500	13
Golden State .1	0	0	1	1	3	1	..	2	2	4	3	0	1	1	1	2	3	3	4	1	2	37	45	.451	17
San Diego ...1	1	1	1	1	2	0	3	3	1	2	2	1	0	0	0	2	2	1	..	3	2	1	30	52	.366	24

TEAM STATISTICS

OFFENSIVE

	G	FGM	FGA	Pct.	FTM	FTA	Pct.	REBOUNDS Off.	Def.	Tot.	Ast.	PF	Dq.	Stl.	TO	Blk.	SCORING Pts.	Avg.
Denver.......	82	3935	7983	.493	2200	2690	.818	1133	2444	3577	2482	2279	29	711	1344	352	10147	123.7
San Antonio ...	82	3909	7721	.506	1965	2604	.755	1230	2528	3758	2361	2146	37	685	1447	491	9862	120.3
Detroit	82	3798	7910	.480	1974	2547	.775	1427	2434	3861	2256	2177	30	697	1310	417	9602	117.1
Los Angeles ...	82	3854	7250	.532	1712	2272	.754	1095	2499	3594	2455	2054	12	726	1578	478	9478	115.6

	G	FGM	FGA	Pct.	FTM	FTA	Pct.	Off.	Def.	Tot.	Ast.	PF	Dq.	Stl.	TO	Blk.	Pts.	Avg.
								REBOUNDS									**SCORING**	
Utah........	82	3606	7242	.498	2115	2708	.781	1096	2522	3618	2230	1978	16	695	1510	604	9428	115.0
Portland.....	82	3632	7189	.505	1988	2637	.754	1251	2194	3445	2082	2134	16	814	1483	397	9277	113.1
Boston......	82	3616	7235	.500	1907	2407	.792	1159	2538	3697	2122	1949	25	673	1420	430	9194	112.1
Phoenix.....	82	3677	7220	.509	1673	2204	.759	1066	2298	3364	2214	2147	13	693	1451	388	9101	111.0
San Diego ...	82	3634	7325	.496	1785	2424	.736	1307	2382	3689	1981	2020	20	567	1515	385	9077	110.7
Houston.....	82	3729	7533	.495	1583	2139	.740	1200	2483	3683	2204	2317	52	621	1562	515	9071	110.6
Dallas.......	82	3618	7235	.500	1774	2350	.755	1090	2265	3355	2164	1906	21	579	1303	360	9052	110.4
New Jersey ...	82	3614	7258	.498	1742	2488	.700	1221	2313	3534	2148	2243	46	814	1608	499	9019	110.0
Kansas City ..	82	3516	7230	.486	1939	2495	.777	1144	2273	3417	2229	2200	33	715	1504	383	9023	110.0
Golden State ..	82	3519	7534	.467	1915	2577	.743	1390	2171	3561	1837	2108	23	830	1518	348	9008	109.9
Seattle......	82	3460	7083	.488	1918	2460	.780	1064	2332	3396	2233	1884	24	636	1360	350	8865	108.1
Philadelphia ..	82	3384	6833	.495	2041	2706	.754	1181	2382	3563	2032	2040	13	807	1628	653	8838	107.8
New York.....	82	3386	6837	.495	1944	2510	.775	1088	2230	3318	2041	2281	27	803	1587	360	8763	106.9
Milwaukee ...	82	3432	6970	.492	1743	2354	.740	1135	2385	3520	2113	2167	35	642	1415	489	8666	105.7
Indiana......	82	3447	7130	.483	1624	2119	.766	1002	2398	3400	2169	2061	20	834	1525	398	8566	104.5
Chicago......	82	3305	6972	.474	1871	2508	.746	1141	2300	3441	2095	2196	48	687	1578	454	8501	103.7
Washington ...	82	3344	6907	.484	1664	2201	.756	1027	2387	3414	2192	1989	37	556	1448	320	8423	102.7
Cleveland.....	82	3362	7232	.465	1619	2178	.743	1213	2388	3601	1930	2206	38	630	1332	375	8386	102.3
Atlanta.......	82	3230	6809	.474	1838	2414	.761	1112	2232	3344	1827	2091	35	626	1329	558	8321	101.5

DEFENSIVE

	FGM	FGA	Pct.	FTM	FTA	Pct.	Off.	Def.	Tot.	Ast.	PF	Dq.	Stl.	TO	Blk.	Pts.	Avg.	Dif.
							REBOUNDS										**SCORING**	
Milwaukee	3207	7033	.456	1869	2489	.751	1252	2235	3487	1959	2093	32	653	1404	319	8325	101.5	+4.2
Atlanta.......	3277	6845	.479	1834	2380	.771	1191	2410	3601	2026	2087	21	579	1409	424	8427	102.8	-1.3
New York.....	3260	6687	.488	1876	2474	.758	1045	2171	3216	2049	2197	31	721	1683	397	8448	103.0	+3.9
Philadelphia ..	3427	7136	.480	1757	2367	.742	1235	2237	3472	2062	2237	42	805	1559	483	8658	105.6	+2.2
Boston.......	3463	7372	.470	1659	2143	.774	1101	2227	3328	1957	2090	29	703	1329	328	8656	105.6	+6.5
Washington ...	3465	7086	.489	1693	2218	.763	1037	2381	3418	2038	2021	24	706	1277	492	8660	105.6	-2.9
Cleveland.....	3373	6930	.487	1939	2541	.763	983	2405	3388	2141	1906	21	579	1224	395	8735	106.5	-4.2
Seattle	3585	7337	.489	1655	2168	.763	1167	2404	3571	2278	2097	19	663	1330	388	8879	108.3	-0.2
Chicago	3502	7082	.494	1885	2471	.763	1125	2388	3513	2235	2110	35	786	1513	514	8926	108.9	-5.2
New Jersey ..	3422	6974	.491	2037	2675	.761	1097	2307	3404	1913	2161	30	781	1674	416	8929	108.9	+1.1
Indiana......	3552	7175	.495	1828	2415	.757	1194	2564	3758	2117	1930	15	761	1587	444	8961	109.3	-4.8
Portland......	3566	6943	.514	1797	2366	.760	1059	2185	3244	2119	2184	23	649	1633	440	8986	109.6	+3.5
Dallas........	3633	7282	.499	1688	2198	.768	1180	2346	3526	2131	2213	23	632	1386	417	9017	110.0	+0.4
Phoenix	3509	7061	.497	1956	2540	.770	1065	2333	3398	2059	2038	24	675	1480	298	9028	110.1	+0.9
Kansas City....	3601	7169	.502	1909	2510	.761	1126	2387	3513	2108	2191	30	660	1584	493	9144	111.5	-1.5
Los Angeles ..	3672	7600	.483	1763	2346	.751	1253	2154	3407	2261	1973	28	797	1443	376	9170	111.8	+3.8
Golden State...	3725	7210	.517	1801	2377	.758	1211	2513	3724	2150	2246	31	691	1694	494	9287	113.3	-3.4
Detroit.......	3657	7369	.496	1941	2577	.753	1163	2457	3620	2193	2187	46	621	1480	527	9308	113.3	+3.6
Houston......	3583	7412	.483	2116	2803	.755	1197	2458	3655	2023	1916	19	782	1421	426	9324	113.7	-3.1
Utah........	3745	7872	.476	1799	2414	.745	1458	2461	3919	2237	2194	31	747	1438	466	9335	113.8	+1.2
San Diego.....	3771	7406	.509	1749	2233	.783	1112	2163	3275	2370	2043	25	727	1242	458	9344	114.0	-3.3
San Antonio ..	3996	7910	.505	1840	2427	.758	1293	2455	3748	2518	2187	39	652	1427	464	9884	120.5	-0.2
Denver.......	4016	7747	.518	2143	2860	.749	1228	2737	3965	2453	2272	32	671	1538	545	10237	124.8	-1.1
Avgs........	3566	7245	.492	1849	2434	.760	1164	2364	3528	2148	2112	28	697	1468	435	9029	110.1	...

HOME/ROAD

	Home	Road	Total		Home	Road	Total
Atlanta..................	31-10	9-32	40-42	Milwaukee	30-11	20-21	50-32
Boston..................	33-8	29-12	62-20	New Jersey	29-12	16-25	45-37
Chicago.................	18-23	9-32	27-55	New York.................	29-12	18-23	47-35
Cleveland...............	23-18	5-36	28-54	Philadelphia	32-9	20-21	52-30
Dallas..................	31-10	12-29	43-39	Phoenix	31-10	10-31	41-41
Denver..................	27-14	11-30	38-44	Portland.................	33-8	15-26	48-34
Detroit..................	30-11	19-22	49-33	San Antonio	28-13	9-32	37-45
Golden State	27-14	10-31	37-45	San Diego	25-16	5-36	30-52
Houston.................	21-20	8-33	29-53	Seattle..................	32-9	10-31	42-40
Indiana.................	20-21	6-35	26-56	Utah	31-10	14-27	45-37
Kansas City	26-15	12-29	38-44	Washington	25-16	10-31	35-47
Los Angeles..............	28-13	26-15	54-28	Totals	640-303	303-640	943-943

1983-84

INDIVIDUAL LEADERS

POINTS

(minimum 70 games or 1,400 points)

	G	FGM	FTM	Pts.	Avg.		G	FGM	FTM	Pts.	Avg.
Adrian Dantley, Utah	79	802	813	2418	30.6	Moses Malone, Philadelphia ...	71	532	545	1609	22.7
Mark Aguirre, Dallas	79	925	465	2330	29.5	Rolando Blackman, Dallas	81	721	372	1815	22.4
Kiki Vandeweghe, Denver	78	895	494	2295	29.4	Julius Erving, Philadelphia	77	678	364	1727	22.4
Alex English, Denver	82	907	352	2167	26.4	World B. Free, Cleveland	75	626	395	1669	22.3
Bernard King, New York	77	795	437	2027	26.3	Jeff Ruland, Washington	75	599	466	1665	22.2
George Gervin, San Antonio ...	76	765	427	1967	25.9	Eddie Johnson, Kansas City ...	82	753	268	1794	21.9
Larry Bird, Boston	79	758	374	1908	24.2	Dominique Wilkins, Atlanta	81	684	382	1750	21.6
Mike Mitchell, San Antonio ...	79	779	275	1839	23.3	Kareem Abdul-Jabbar, L.A.	80	716	285	1717	21.5
Terry Cummings, San Diego ...	81	737	380	1854	22.9	Isiah Thomas, Detroit	82	669	388	1748	21.3
Purvis Short, Golden State	79	714	353	1803	22.8	Kelly Tripucka, Detroit	76	595	426	1618	21.3

FIELD GOALS
(minimum 300 made)

	FGM	FGA	Pct.
Artis Gilmore, San Antonio	.351	556	.631
James Donaldson, San Diego	.360	604	.596
Mike McGee, Los Angeles	.347	584	.594
Darryl Dawkins, New Jersey	.507	855	.593
Calvin Natt, Portland	.500	857	.583
Jeff Ruland, Washington	.599	1035	.579
Kareem Abdul-Jabbar, Los Angeles	.716	1238	.578
Larry Nance, Phoenix	.601	1044	.576
Bernard King, New York	.795	1391	.572
Bob Lanier, Milwaukee	.392	685	.572

FREE THROWS
(minimum 125 made)

	FTM	FTA	Pct.
Larry Bird, Boston	.374	421	.888
John Long, Detroit	.243	275	.884
Bill Laimbeer, Detroit	.316	365	.866
Walter Davis, Phoenix	.233	270	.863
Ricky Pierce, San Diego	.149	173	.861
Adrian Dantley, Utah	.813	946	.859
Billy Knight, Kansas City	.243	283	.859
Jack Sikma, Seattle	.411	480	.856
Kiki Vandeweghe, Denver	.494	580	.852
Dennis Johnson, Boston	.281	330	.852

ASSISTS
(minimum 70 games or 400 assists)

	G	No.	Avg.
Magic Johnson, Los Angeles	.67	875	13.1
Isiah Thomas, Detroit	.82	914	11.2
Norm Nixon, San Diego	.82	914	11.2
John Lucas, San Antonio	.63	673	10.7
Johnny Moore, San Antonio	.59	566	9.6
Rickey Green, Utah	.81	748	9.2
Gus Williams, Seattle	.80	675	8.4
Ennis Whatley, Chicago	.80	662	8.3
Larry Drew, Kansas City	.73	558	7.6
Brad Davis, Dallas	.81	561	6.9

REBOUNDS
(minimum 70 games or 800 rebounds)

	G	Off.	Def.	Tot.	Avg.
Moses Malone, Philadelphia	.71	352	598	950	13.4
Buck Williams, New Jersey	.81	355	645	1000	12.3
Jeff Ruland, Washington	.75	265	657	922	12.3
Bill Laimbeer, Detroit	.82	329	674	1003	12.2
Ralph Sampson, Houston	.82	293	620	913	11.1
Jack Sikma, Seattle	.82	225	686	911	11.1
Robert Parish, Boston	.80	243	614	857	10.7
Cliff Robinson, Cleveland	.73	156	597	753	10.3
Larry Bird, Boston	.79	181	615	796	10.1
David Greenwood, Chicago	.78	214	572	786	10.1

STEALS
(minimum 70 games or 125 steals)

	G	No.	Avg.
Rickey Green, Utah	.81	215	2.65
Isiah Thomas, Detroit	.82	204	2.49
Gus Williams, Seattle	.80	189	2.36
Maurice Cheeks, Philadelphia	.75	171	2.28
Magic Johnson, Los Angeles	.67	150	2.24
T.R. Dunn, Denver	.80	173	2.16
Ray Williams, New York	.76	162	2.13
Darwin Cook, New Jersey	.82	164	2.00
Lester Conner, Golden State	.82	162	1.98
Julius Erving, Philadelphia	.77	141	1.83

BLOCKED SHOTS
(minimum 70 games or 100 blocked shots)

	G	No.	Avg.
Mark Eaton, Utah	.82	351	4.28
Tree Rollins, Atlanta	.77	277	3.60
Ralph Sampson, Houston	.82	197	2.40
Larry Nance, Phoenix	.82	173	2.11
Artis Gilmore, San Antonio	.64	132	2.06
Roy Hinson, Cleveland	.80	145	1.81
LaSalle Thompson, Kansas City	.80	145	1.81
Julius Erving, Philadelphia	.77	139	1.81
Kareem Abdul-Jabbar, Los Angeles	.80	143	1.79
Joe Barry Carroll, Golden State	.80	142	1.78

3-POINT FIELD GOALS
(minimum 25 made)

	FGA	FGM	Pct.
Darrell Griffith, Utah	.252	91	.361
Mike Evans, Denver	.89	32	.360
Johnny Moore, San Antonio	.87	28	.322
Michael Cooper, Los Angeles	.121	38	.314
Ray Williams, New York	.81	25	.309
Ricky Sobers, Washington	.111	29	.261

INDIVIDUAL STATISTICS, TEAM BY TEAM
ATLANTA HAWKS

	G	Min.	FGM	FGA	Pct.	FTM	FTA	Pct.	Off.	Def.	Tot.	Ast.	PF	Dq.	Stl.	TO	Blk.	Pts.	Avg.	Hi.
									REBOUNDS									SCORING		
Dominique Wilkins	81	2961	684	1429	.479	382	496	.770	254	328	582	126	197	1	117	215	87	1750	21.6	39
Dan Roundfield	73	2610	503	1038	.485	374	486	.770	206	515	721	184	221	2	61	205	74	1380	18.9	37
Eddie Johnson	67	1893	353	798	.442	164	213	.770	31	115	146	374	155	2	58	173	7	886	13.2	29
Johnny Davis	75	2079	354	800	.443	217	256	.848	53	86	139	326	146	0	62	134	6	925	12.3	29
Doc Rivers	81	1938	250	541	.462	255	325	.785	72	148	220	314	286	8	127	174	30	757	9.3	21
Tree Rollins	77	2351	274	529	.518	118	190	.621	200	393	593	62	297	9	35	101	277	666	8.6	22
Mike Glenn	81	1503	312	554	.563	56	70	.800	17	87	104	171	146	1	46	63	5	681	8.4	24
Wes Matthews*	6	96	16	30	.533	18	22	.818	1	3	4	21	13	0	5	10	1	50	8.3	15
Sly Williams	13	258	34	114	.298	36	46	.783	19	31	50	16	33	0	14	18	1	105	8.1	16
Randy Wittman	78	1071	160	318	.503	28	46	.609	14	57	71	71	82	0	17	32	0	350	4.5	14
Scott Hastings	68	1135	111	237	.468	82	104	.788	96	174	270	46	220	7	40	66	36	305	4.5	16
Rickey Brown	68	785	94	201	.468	48	65	.738	67	114	181	29	161	4	18	53	23	236	3.5	11
Armond Hill	15	181	14	46	.304	17	21	.810	2	8	10	35	30	1	7	14	0	45	3.0	8
John Pinone	7	65	7	13	.538	6	10	.600	0	10	10	3	11	0	2	5	1	20	2.9	6
Charlie Criss†	9	108	9	22	.409	5	5	1.000	3	8	11	21	4	0	3	6	0	23	2.6	6
Charlie Criss‡	15	215	20	52	.385	12	16	.750	5	15	20	38	11	0	8	10	0	53	3.5	8
Billy Paultz	40	486	36	88	.409	17	33	.515	35	78	113	18	57	0	8	22	7	89	2.2	9
Mark Landsberger	35	335	19	51	.373	15	26	.577	42	77	119	10	32	0	6	21	3	53	1.5	7

3-pt. FG: Atlanta 23-106 (.217)—Wilkins 0-11 (.000); Roundfield 0-11 (.000); Johnson 16-43 (.372); Davis 0-8 (.000); Rivers 2-12 (.167); Glenn 1-2 (.500); Matthews* 0-1 (.000); Williams 1-9 (.111); Wittman 2-5 (.400); Hastings 1-4 (.250); Criss† 0-0; Criss‡ 1-6 (.167). Opponents 39-185 (.211).

BOSTON CELTICS

	G	Min.	FGM	FGA	Pct.	FTM	FTA	Pct.	REBOUNDS Off.	Def.	Tot.	Ast.	PF	Dq.	Stl.	TO	Blk.	SCORING Pts.	Avg.	Hi.
Larry Bird	79	3028	758	1542	.492	374	421	.888	181	615	796	520	197	0	144	237	69	1908	24.2	41
Robert Parish	80	2867	623	1140	.546	274	368	.745	243	614	857	139	266	7	55	184	116	1520	19.0	36
Kevin McHale	82	2577	587	1055	.556	336	439	.765	208	402	610	104	243	5	23	150	126	1511	18.4	33
Dennis Johnson	80	2665	384	878	.437	281	330	.852	87	193	280	338	251	6	93	172	57	1053	13.2	26
Cedric Maxwell	80	2502	317	596	.532	320	425	.753	201	260	461	205	224	4	63	203	24	955	11.9	24
Gerald Henderson	78	2088	376	718	.524	136	177	.768	68	79	147	300	209	1	117	161	14	908	11.6	22
Danny Ainge	71	1154	166	361	.460	46	56	.821	29	87	116	162	143	2	41	70	4	384	5.4	18
Scott Wedman	68	916	148	333	.444	29	35	.829	41	98	139	67	107	0	27	43	7	327	4.8	19
Quinn Buckner	79	1249	138	323	.427	48	74	.649	41	96	137	214	187	0	84	100	3	324	4.1	16
M.L. Carr	60	585	70	171	.409	42	48	.875	26	49	75	49	67	0	17	46	4	185	3.1	22
Greg Kite	35	197	30	66	.455	5	16	.313	27	35	62	7	42	0	1	20	5	65	1.9	13
Carlos Clark	31	127	19	52	.365	16	18	.889	7	10	17	17	13	0	8	12	1	54	1.7	6

3-pt. FG: Boston 55-229 (.240)—Bird 18-73 (.247); McHale 1-3 (.333); Johnson 4-32 (.125); Maxwell 1-6 (.167); Henderson 20-57 (.351); Ainge 6-22 (.273); Wedman 2-13 (.154); Buckner 0-6 (.000); Carr 3-15 (.200); Clark 0-2 (.000). Opponents 71-219 (.324).

CHICAGO BULLS

	G	Min.	FGM	FGA	Pct.	FTM	FTA	Pct.	REBOUNDS Off.	Def.	Tot.	Ast.	PF	Dq.	Stl.	TO	Blk.	SCORING Pts.	Avg.	Hi.
Orlando Woolridge	75	2544	570	1086	.525	303	424	.715	130	239	369	136	253	6	71	188	60	1444	19.3	33
Quintin Dailey	82	2449	583	1229	.474	321	396	.811	61	174	235	254	218	4	109	220	11	1491	18.2	44
Mitchell Wiggins	82	2123	399	890	.448	213	287	.742	138	190	328	187	278	8	106	139	11	1018	12.4	28
Dave Corzine	82	2674	385	824	.467	231	275	.840	169	406	575	202	227	3	58	175	120	1004	12.2	29
David Greenwood	78	2718	369	753	.490	213	289	.737	214	572	786	139	265	9	67	149	72	951	12.2	32
Steve Johnson†	31	594	113	198	.571	64	110	.582	68	98	166	18	119	8	15	59	21	290	9.4	23
Steve Johnson‡	81	1487	302	540	.559	165	287	.575	162	256	418	81	307	15	37	164	69	769	9.5	24
Reggie Theus*	31	601	92	237	.388	84	108	.778	21	25	46	142	78	2	21	59	3	271	8.7	22
Ennis Whatley	80	2159	261	556	.469	146	200	.730	63	134	197	662	223	4	119	268	17	668	8.4	21
Rod Higgins	78	1577	193	432	.447	113	156	.724	87	119	206	116	161	0	49	76	29	500	6.4	18
Ronnie Lester	43	687	78	188	.415	75	117	.862	20	26	46	168	59	1	30	72	6	232	5.4	16
Sidney Green	49	667	100	228	.439	55	77	.714	58	116	174	25	128	1	18	60	17	255	5.2	18
Wallace Bryant	29	317	52	133	.391	14	33	.424	37	43	80	13	48	0	9	16	11	118	4.1	18
Jawann Oldham	64	870	110	218	.505	39	66	.591	75	158	233	33	139	2	15	83	76	259	4.0	15

3-pt. FG: Chicago 20-117 (.171)—Woolridge 1-2 (.500); Dailey 4-32 (.125); Wiggins 7-29 (.241); Corzine 3-9 (.333); Greenwood 0-1 (.000); Theus* 3-15 (.200); Whatley 0-2 (.000); Higgins 1-22 (.045); Lester 1-5 (.200). Opponents 37-182 (.203).

CLEVELAND CAVALIERS

	G	Min.	FGM	FGA	Pct.	FTM	FTA	Pct.	REBOUNDS Off.	Def.	Tot.	Ast.	PF	Dq.	Stl.	TO	Blk.	SCORING Pts.	Avg.	Hi.
World B. Free	75	2375	626	1407	.445	395	504	.784	89	128	217	226	214	2	94	154	8	1669	22.3	40
Cliff Robinson	73	2402	533	1185	.450	234	334	.701	156	597	753	185	195	2	51	187	32	1301	17.8	32
Phil Hubbard	80	1799	321	628	.511	221	299	.739	172	208	380	86	244	3	71	115	6	863	10.8	31
Lonnie Shelton	79	2101	371	779	.476	107	140	.764	140	241	381	179	279	9	76	165	55	850	10.8	33
Geoff Huston	77	2041	348	699	.498	110	154	.714	32	64	96	413	126	0	38	145	1	808	10.5	24
Paul Thompson	82	1731	309	662	.467	115	149	.772	120	192	312	122	192	2	70	73	37	742	9.0	26
John Bagley	76	1712	257	607	.423	157	198	.793	49	107	150	333	113	1	78	170	4	673	8.9	26
Jeff Cook	81	1950	188	387	.486	94	130	.723	174	310	484	123	282	7	68	91	47	471	5.8	18
Roy Hinson	80	1458	184	371	.496	69	117	.590	175	324	499	69	306	11	31	109	145	437	5.5	22
Stewart Granger	56	738	97	226	.429	53	70	.757	8	47	55	134	97	0	24	57	0	251	4.5	16
John Garris	33	267	52	102	.510	27	34	.794	35	42	77	10	40	0	8	11	6	131	4.0	20
Ben Poquette	51	858	75	171	.439	34	43	.791	57	125	182	49	114	1	20	28	33	185	3.6	10
Geoff Crompton	7	23	1	8	.125	3	6	.500	6	3	9	1	4	0	1	4	1	5	0.7	2

3-pt. FG: Cleveland 43-164 (.262)—Free 22-69 (.319); Robinson 1-2 (.500); Hubbard 0-1 (.000); Shelton 1-5 (.200); Huston 2-11 (.182); Thompson 9-39 (.231); Bagley 2-17 (.118); Cook 1-2 (.500); Granger 4-13 (.308); Poquette 1-5 (.200). Opponents 50-190 (.263).

DALLAS MAVERICKS

	G	Min.	FGM	FGA	Pct.	FTM	FTA	Pct.	REBOUNDS Off.	Def.	Tot.	Ast.	PF	Dq.	Stl.	TO	Blk.	SCORING Pts.	Avg.	Hi.
Mark Aguirre	79	2900	925	1765	.524	465	621	.749	161	308	469	358	246	5	80	285	22	2330	29.5	46
Rolando Blackman	81	3025	721	1320	.546	372	458	.812	124	249	373	288	127	0	56	169	37	1815	22.4	43
Pat Cummings	80	2492	452	915	.494	141	190	.742	151	507	658	158	282	2	64	146	23	1045	13.1	28
Brad Davis	81	2665	345	651	.530	199	238	.836	41	146	187	561	218	4	94	166	13	896	11.1	24
Jay Vincent	61	1421	252	579	.435	168	215	.781	81	166	247	114	159	1	30	113	10	672	11.0	33
Dale Ellis	67	1059	225	493	.456	87	121	.719	106	144	250	56	118	0	41	78	9	549	8.2	31
Kurt Nimphius	82	2284	272	523	.520	101	162	.623	182	331	513	176	283	5	41	98	144	646	7.9	24
Derek Harper	82	1712	200	451	.443	66	98	.673	53	119	172	239	143	0	95	111	21	469	5.7	19
Bill Garnett	80	1529	141	299	.472	129	176	.733	123	208	331	128	217	4	44	68	66	411	5.1	13
Jim Spanarkel	7	54	7	16	.438	9	13	.692	5	2	7	5	8	0	6	4	0	24	3.4	8
Elston Turner	47	536	54	150	.360	28	34	.824	42	51	93	59	40	0	26	29	0	137	2.9	12
Roger Phegley†	10	76	9	31	.290	2	2	1.000	2	7	9	9	10	0	1	5	0	21	2.1	9
Roger Phegley‡	13	87	11	35	.314	4	4	1.000	2	9	11	11	11	0	1	6	0	28	2.2	9
Mark West	34	202	15	42	.357	7	23	.304	19	27	46	13	55	0	1	12	15	37	1.1	6

3-pt. FG: Dallas 42-184 (.228)—Aguirre 15-56 (.268); Blackman 1-11 (.091); Cummings 0-2 (.000); Davis 7-38 (.184); Vincent 0-1 (.000); Ellis 12-29 (.414); Nimphius 1-4 (.250); Harper 3-26 (.115); Garnett 0-2 (.000); Spanarkel 1-2 (.500); Turner 1-9 (.111); Phegley† 1-4 (.250); Phegley‡ 2-5 (.400). Opponents 63-222 (.284).

1983-84

DENVER NUGGETS

	G	Min.	FGM	FGA	Pct.	FTM	FTA	Pct.	Off.	Def.	Tot.	Ast.	PF	Dq.	Stl.	TO	Blk.	Pts.	Avg.	Hi.
Kiki Vandeweghe	78	2734	895	1603	.558	494	580	.852	84	289	373	238	187	1	53	156	50	2295	29.4	51
Alex English	82	2870	907	1714	.529	352	427	.824	216	248	464	406	252	3	83	222	95	2167	26.4	47
Dan Issel	76	2076	569	1153	.493	364	428	.850	112	401	513	173	182	2	60	122	44	1506	19.8	37
Rob Williams	79	1924	309	671	.461	171	209	.818	54	140	194	464	268	4	84	169	5	804	10.2	24
Richard Anderson	78	1380	272	638	.426	116	150	.773	136	270	406	193	183	0	46	109	28	663	8.5	23
Mike Evans	78	1687	243	564	.431	111	131	.847	23	115	138	288	175	2	61	117	4	629	8.1	31
Dan Schayes	82	1420	183	371	.493	215	272	.790	145	288	433	91	308	5	32	119	60	581	7.1	26
Howard Carter	55	688	145	316	.459	47	61	.770	38	48	86	71	81	0	19	42	4	342	6.2	25
T.R. Dunn	80	2705	174	370	.470	106	145	.731	195	379	574	228	233	5	173	97	32	454	5.7	14
Bill Hanzlik	80	1469	132	306	.431	167	207	.807	66	139	205	252	255	6	68	109	19	434	5.4	19
Anthony Roberts	19	197	34	91	.374	13	18	.722	20	31	51	13	43	1	5	17	1	81	4.3	14
Keith Edmonson†	15	101	23	47	.489	18	25	.720	6	12	18	7	16	0	4	16	1	64	4.3	30
Keith Edmonson‡	55	622	158	321	.492	94	126	.746	46	42	88	34	83	1	26	61	7	410	7.5	30
Kenny Dennard	43	413	36	99	.364	15	24	.625	37	64	101	45	83	0	23	29	8	90	2.1	7
Dave Robisch*	19	141	13	40	.325	11	13	.846	1	20	21	13	13	0	0	11	1	37	1.9	9

3-pt. FG: Denver 77-255 (.302)—Vandeweghe 11-30 (.367); English 1-7 (.143); Issel 4-19 (.211); Williams 15-47 (.319); Anderson 3-19 (.158); Evans 32-89 (.360); Schayes 0-2 (.000); Carter 5-19 (.263); Dunn 0-1 (.000); Hanzlik 3-12 (.250); Dennard 3-10 (.300). Opponents 62-205 (.302).

DETROIT PISTONS

	G	Min.	FGM	FGA	Pct.	FTM	FTA	Pct.	Off.	Def.	Tot.	Ast.	PF	Dq.	Stl.	TO	Blk.	Pts.	Avg.	Hi.
Isiah Thomas	82	3007	669	1448	.462	388	529	.733	103	224	327	914	324	8	204	307	33	1748	21.3	47
Kelly Tripucka	76	2493	595	1296	.459	426	523	.815	119	187	306	293	190	0	65	190	17	1618	21.3	44
Bill Laimbeer	82	2864	553	1044	.530	316	365	.866	329	674	1003	149	273	4	49	151	84	1422	17.3	33
John Long	82	2514	545	1155	.472	243	275	.884	139	150	289	205	199	1	93	143	18	1334	16.3	41
Vinnie Johnson	82	1909	426	901	.473	207	275	.753	130	107	237	271	196	1	44	135	19	1063	13.0	28
Terry Tyler	82	1602	313	691	.453	94	132	.712	104	181	285	76	151	1	63	78	59	722	8.8	20
Cliff Levingston	80	1746	229	436	.525	125	186	.672	234	311	545	109	281	7	44	77	78	583	7.3	22
Kent Benson	82	1734	248	451	.550	83	101	.822	117	292	409	130	230	4	71	79	53	579	7.1	23
Ray Tolbert	49	475	64	121	.529	23	45	.511	45	53	98	26	88	1	12	26	20	151	3.1	10
Earl Cureton	73	907	81	177	.458	31	59	.525	86	201	287	36	143	3	24	55	31	193	2.6	13
Walker Russell	16	119	14	42	.333	12	13	.923	6	13	19	22	25	0	4	9	0	41	2.6	10
Lionel Hollins	32	216	24	63	.381	11	13	.846	4	18	22	62	26	0	13	24	1	59	1.8	8
David Thirdkill	46	291	31	72	.431	15	31	.484	9	22	31	27	44	0	10	19	3	77	1.7	9
Ken Austin	7	28	6	13	.462	0	0	...	2	1	3	1	7	0	1	3	1	12	1.7	6

3-pt. FG: Detroit 32-141 (.227)—Thomas 22-65 (.338); Tripucka 2-17 (.118); Laimbeer 0-11 (.000); Long 1-5 (.200); Johnson 4-19 (.211); Tyler 2-13 (.154); Levingston 0-3 (.000); Benson 0-1 (.000); Tolbert 0-1 (.000); Cureton 0-1 (.000); Russell 1-2 (.500); Hollins 0-2 (.000); Thirdkill 0-1 (.000). Opponents 53-202 (.262).

GOLDEN STATE WARRIORS

	G	Min.	FGM	FGA	Pct.	FTM	FTA	Pct.	Off.	Def.	Tot.	Ast.	PF	Dq.	Stl.	TO	Blk.	Pts.	Avg.	Hi.
Purvis Short	79	2945	714	1509	.473	353	445	.793	184	254	438	246	252	2	103	228	11	1803	22.8	57
Joe Barry Carroll	80	2962	663	1390	.477	313	433	.723	235	401	636	198	244	9	103	268	142	1639	20.5	32
Sleepy Floyd	77	2555	484	1045	.463	315	386	.816	87	184	271	269	216	0	103	196	31	1291	16.8	35
Mickey Johnson	78	2122	359	852	.421	339	432	.785	198	320	518	219	290	3	101	216	30	1062	13.6	40
Lester Conner	82	2573	360	730	.493	186	259	.718	132	173	305	401	176	1	162	143	12	907	11.1	24
Larry Smith	75	2091	244	436	.560	94	168	.560	282	390	672	72	274	6	61	124	22	582	7.8	25
Don Collins	61	957	187	387	.483	65	89	.730	62	67	129	67	119	1	43	80	14	440	7.2	22
Mike Bratz	82	1428	213	521	.409	120	137	.876	41	102	143	252	155	0	84	109	6	561	6.8	23
Ron Brewer*	13	210	27	58	.466	11	17	.647	5	8	13	6	10	0	6	7	5	65	5.0	10
Samuel Williams*	7	59	11	26	.423	6	7	.857	4	9	13	2	6	0	6	3	3	28	4.0	11
Russell Cross	45	354	64	112	.571	38	91	.418	35	47	82	22	58	0	12	19	7	166	3.7	15
Darren Tillis	72	730	108	254	.425	41	63	.651	75	109	184	24	176	1	12	51	60	257	3.6	15
Pace Mannion	57	469	50	126	.397	18	23	.783	23	36	59	47	63	0	25	23	2	121	2.1	14
Lorenzo Romar*	3	15	2	5	.400	2	4	.500	0	1	1	1	0	0	0	0	0	6	2.0	4
Chris Engler	46	360	33	83	.398	14	23	.609	27	70	97	11	68	0	9	24	3	80	1.7	10

3-pt. FG: Golden State 55-226 (.243)—Short 22-72 (.306); Carroll 0-1 (.000); Floyd 8-45 (.178); Johnson 5-29 (.172); Conner 1-6 (.167); Collins 1-5 (.200); Bratz 15-51 (.294); Brewer* 0-1 (.000); Tillis 0-2 (.000); Mannion 3-13 (.231); Romar* 0-1 (.000). Opponents 36-171 (.211).

HOUSTON ROCKETS

	G	Min.	FGM	FGA	Pct.	FTM	FTA	Pct.	Off.	Def.	Tot.	Ast.	PF	Dq.	Stl.	TO	Blk.	Pts.	Avg.	Hi.
Ralph Sampson	82	2693	716	1369	.523	287	434	.661	293	620	913	163	339	16	70	294	197	1720	21.0	41
Lewis Lloyd	82	2578	610	1182	.516	235	298	.789	128	167	295	321	211	4	102	245	44	1458	17.8	36
Robert Reid	64	1936	406	857	.474	81	123	.659	97	244	341	217	243	5	88	92	30	895	14.0	32
Allen Leavell	82	2009	349	731	.477	238	286	.832	31	86	117	459	199	2	107	184	12	947	11.5	28
Rodney McCray	79	2081	335	672	.499	182	249	.731	173	277	450	176	205	1	53	120	54	853	10.8	28
Caldwell Jones	81	2506	318	633	.502	164	196	.837	168	414	582	156	335	7	46	158	80	801	9.9	24
James Bailey	73	1174	254	517	.491	138	192	.719	104	190	294	79	197	8	33	101	40	646	8.8	27
Phil Ford	81	2020	236	470	.502	98	117	.838	28	109	137	410	243	7	59	135	8	572	7.1	18
Elvin Hayes	81	994	158	389	.406	86	132	.652	87	173	260	71	123	1	16	82	28	402	5.0	22
Terry Teagle	68	616	148	315	.470	37	44	.841	28	50	78	63	81	1	13	62	4	340	5.0	27
Wally Walker	58	612	118	241	.490	6	18	.333	26	66	92	55	65	0	17	33	4	244	4.2	18
Craig Ehlo	7	63	11	27	.407	1	1	1.000	4	5	9	6	13	0	3	3	0	23	3.3	14
Major Jones	57	473	70	130	.538	30	49	.612	33	82	115	28	63	0	14	30	14	170	3.0	13

3-pt. FG: Houston 30-154 (.195)—Sampson 1-4 (.250); Lloyd 3-13 (.231); Reid 2-8 (.250); Leavell 11-71 (.155); McCray 1-4 (.250); C. Jones 1-3 (.333); Bailey 0-1 (.000); Ford 2-15 (.133); Hayes 0-2 (.000); Teagle 7-27 (.259); Walker 2-6 (.333). Opponents 42-157 (.268).

INDIANA PACERS

	G	Min.	FGM	FGA	Pct.	FTM	FTA	Pct.	REBOUNDS Off.	Def.	Tot.	Ast.	PF	Dq.	Stl.	TO	Blk.	SCORING Pts.	Avg.	Hi.
Clark Kellogg	79	2676	619	1193	.519	261	340	.768	230	489	719	234	242	2	121	218	28	1506	19.1	37
Herb Williams	69	2279	411	860	.478	207	295	.702	154	400	554	215	193	4	60	207	108	1029	14.9	32
Butch Carter	73	2045	413	862	.479	136	178	.764	70	83	153	206	211	1	128	141	13	977	13.4	42
George Johnson	81	2073	411	884	.465	223	270	.826	139	321	460	195	256	3	82	186	49	1056	13.0	32
Steve Stipanovich	81	2426	392	816	.480	183	243	.753	116	446	562	170	303	4	73	161	67	970	12.0	29
Jerry Sichting	80	2497	397	746	.532	117	135	.867	44	127	171	457	179	0	90	144	8	917	11.5	29
Brook Steppe	61	857	148	314	.471	134	161	.832	43	79	122	79	93	0	34	83	6	430	7.0	21
Jim Thomas	72	1219	187	403	.464	80	110	.727	59	90	149	130	115	1	60	69	6	455	6.3	21
Kevin McKenna	61	923	152	371	.410	80	98	.816	30	65	95	114	133	3	46	62	5	387	6.3	21
Leroy Combs	48	446	81	163	.497	56	91	.615	19	37	56	38	49	0	23	46	18	218	4.5	17
Sidney Lowe	78	1238	107	259	.413	108	139	.777	30	92	122	269	112	0	93	106	5	324	4.2	11
Granville Waiters	78	1040	123	238	.517	31	51	.608	64	163	227	60	164	2	24	65	85	277	3.6	12
Tracy Jackson	2	10	1	4	.250	4	4	1.000	1	0	1	0	3	0	0	1	0	6	3.0	4
Bruce Kuczenski†	5	51	5	17	.294	4	4	1.000	3	6	9	2	8	0	0	8	0	14	2.8	6
Bruce Kuczenski‡	15	119	10	37	.270	8	12	.667	7	16	23	8	18	0	1	15	1	28	1.9	6

3-pt. FG: Indiana 48-207 (.232)—Kellogg 7-21 (.333); Williams 0-4 (.000); Carter 15-46 (.326); Johnson 11-47 (.234); Stipanovich 3-16 (.188); Sichting 6-20 (.300); Steppe 0-3 (.000); Thomas 1-11 (.091); McKenna 3-17 (.176); Combs 0-3 (.000); Lowe 2-18 (.111); Waiters 0-1 (.000). Opponents 29-146 (.199).

KANSAS CITY KINGS

	G	Min.	FGM	FGA	Pct.	FTM	FTA	Pct.	REBOUNDS Off.	Def.	Tot.	Ast.	PF	Dq.	Stl.	TO	Blk.	SCORING Pts.	Avg.	Hi.
Eddie Johnson	82	2920	753	1552	.485	268	331	.810	165	290	455	296	266	4	76	213	21	1794	21.9	40
Larry Drew	73	2463	474	1026	.462	243	313	.776	33	113	146	558	170	0	121	194	10	1194	16.4	29
Reggie Theus†	30	897	170	388	.438	130	173	.751	29	54	83	210	93	1	29	97	9	474	15.8	36
Reggie Theus‡	61	1498	262	625	.419	214	281	.762	50	79	129	352	171	3	50	156	12	745	12.2	36
Mike Woodson	71	1838	389	816	.477	247	302	.818	62	113	175	175	174	2	83	115	28	1027	14.5	33
Billy Knight	75	1885	358	729	.491	243	283	.859	89	166	255	160	122	0	54	155	6	963	12.8	33
LaSalle Thompson	80	1915	333	637	.523	160	223	.717	260	449	709	86	327	8	71	168	145	826	10.3	28
Steve Johnson*	50	893	189	342	.553	101	177	.571	94	158	252	63	188	7	22	105	48	479	9.6	24
Mark Olberding	81	2160	249	504	.494	261	318	.821	119	326	445	192	291	2	50	166	28	759	9.4	26
Joe Meriweather	73	1501	193	363	.532	94	123	.764	111	242	353	51	247	8	35	83	61	480	6.6	18
Dane Suttle	40	469	109	214	.509	40	47	.851	21	25	46	46	46	0	20	32	0	258	6.5	26
Dave Robisch†	8	162	18	48	.375	11	13	.846	12	17	29	6	15	0	3	0	1	47	5.9	9
Dave Robisch‡	31	340	35	96	.365	22	26	.846	15	43	58	20	36	1	3	12	2	92	3.0	9
Don Buse	76	1327	150	352	.426	63	80	.788	29	87	116	303	62	0	86	87	1	381	5.0	15
Kevin Loder*	10	133	19	43	.442	9	13	.692	7	11	18	14	15	0	3	11	5	48	4.8	13
Larry Micheaux	39	332	49	90	.544	21	39	.538	40	73	113	19	46	0	21	21	11	119	3.1	15
Ed Nealy	71	960	63	126	.500	48	60	.800	73	149	222	50	138	1	41	33	9	174	2.5	11

3-pt. FG: Kansas City 52-189 (.275)—E. Johnson 20-64 (.313); Drew 3-10 (.300); Theus† 4-27 (.148); Theus‡ 7-42 (.167); Woodson 2-8 (.250); Knight 4-14 (.286); Olberding 0-1 (.000); Suttle 0-3 (.000); Buse 18-59 (.305); Loder* 1-3 (.333). Opponents 33-164 (.201).

LOS ANGELES LAKERS

	G	Min.	FGM	FGA	Pct.	FTM	FTA	Pct.	REBOUNDS Off.	Def.	Tot.	Ast.	PF	Dq.	Stl.	TO	Blk.	SCORING Pts.	Avg.	Hi.
Kareem Abdul-Jabbar	80	2622	716	1238	.578	285	394	.723	169	418	587	211	211	1	55	221	143	1717	21.5	35
Magic Johnson	67	2567	441	780	.565	290	358	.810	99	392	491	875	169	1	150	306	49	1178	17.6	33
Jamaal Wilkes	75	2507	542	1055	.514	208	280	.743	130	210	340	214	205	0	72	137	41	1294	17.3	31
James Worthy	82	2415	495	890	.556	195	257	.759	157	358	515	207	244	5	77	181	70	1185	14.5	37
Bob McAdoo	70	1456	352	748	.471	212	264	.803	82	207	289	74	182	0	42	127	50	916	13.1	32
Byron Scott	74	1637	334	690	.484	112	139	.806	50	114	164	177	174	0	81	116	19	788	10.6	32
Mike McGee	77	1425	347	584	.594	61	113	.540	117	76	193	81	176	0	49	111	6	757	9.8	33
Michael Cooper	82	2387	273	549	.497	155	185	.838	53	209	262	482	267	3	113	148	67	739	9.0	20
Calvin Garrett	41	478	78	152	.513	30	39	.769	24	47	71	31	62	2	12	34	2	188	4.6	16
Swen Nater	69	829	124	253	.490	63	91	.692	81	183	264	27	150	0	25	68	7	311	4.5	19
Kurt Rambis	47	743	63	113	.558	42	66	.636	82	184	266	34	108	0	30	56	14	168	3.6	10
Larry Spriggs	38	363	44	82	.537	36	50	.720	16	45	61	30	55	0	12	34	4	124	3.3	18
Mitch Kupchak	34	324	41	108	.380	22	34	.647	35	52	87	7	46	0	4	22	6	104	3.1	12
Eddie Jordan†	3	27	4	8	.500	1	2	.500	0	4	4	5	5	0	4	8	0	9	3.0	4
Eddie Jordan‡	16	210	17	49	.347	8	12	.667	3	14	17	44	37	0	25	26	0	42	2.6	8

3-pt. FG: L.A. Lakers 58-226 (.257)—Abdul-Jabbar 0-1 (.000); Johnson 6-29 (.207); Wilkes 2-8 (.250); Worthy 0-6 (.000); McAdoo 0-5 (.000); Scott 8-34 (.235); McGee 2-12 (.167); Cooper 38-121 (.314); Garrett 2-6 (.333); Nater 0-1 (.000); Spriggs 0-2 (.000); Kupchak 0-1 (.000); Jordan‡ 0-3 (.000). Opponents 63-223 (.283).

MILWAUKEE BUCKS

	G	Min.	FGM	FGA	Pct.	FTM	FTA	Pct.	REBOUNDS Off.	Def.	Tot.	Ast.	PF	Dq.	Stl.	TO	Blk.	SCORING Pts.	Avg.	Hi.
Sidney Moncrief	79	3075	560	1125	.498	529	624	.848	215	313	528	358	204	2	108	217	27	1654	20.9	43
Marques Johnson	74	2715	646	1288	.502	241	340	.709	173	307	480	315	194	1	115	180	45	1535	20.7	36
Junior Bridgeman	81	2431	509	1094	.465	196	243	.807	80	252	332	265	224	2	53	148	14	1220	15.1	31
Bob Lanier	72	2007	392	685	.572	194	274	.708	141	314	455	186	228	8	58	163	51	978	13.6	25
Mike Dunleavy	17	404	70	127	.551	32	40	.800	6	22	28	78	51	0	12	36	1	191	11.2	17
Paul Pressey	81	1730	276	528	.523	120	200	.600	102	180	282	252	241	6	86	157	50	674	8.3	21
Alton Lister	82	1955	256	512	.500	114	182	.626	156	447	603	110	327	11	41	153	140	626	7.6	19
Nate Archibald	46	1038	136	279	.487	64	101	.634	16	60	76	160	74	0	33	78	0	340	7.4	16
Kevin Grevey	64	923	178	395	.451	75	84	.893	30	51	81	75	95	0	27	45	4	446	7.0	25

1983-84

	G	Min.	FGM	FGA	Pct.	FTM	FTA	Pct.	REBOUNDS Off.	Def.	Tot.	Ast.	PF	Dq.	Stl.	TO	Blk.	SCORING Pts.	Avg.	Hi.
Lorenzo Romar†	65	1007	159	346	.460	65	90	.722	21	71	92	192	76	0	55	63	8	387	6.0	17
Lorenzo Romar‡	68	1022	161	351	.459	67	94	.713	21	72	93	193	77	0	55	63	8	393	5.8	17
Charlie Criss*	6	107	11	30	.367	7	11	.636	2	7	9	17	7	0	5	4	0	30	5.0	8
Paul Mokeski	68	838	102	213	.479	50	72	.694	51	115	166	44	168	1	11	44	29	255	3.8	14
Randy Breuer	57	472	68	177	.384	32	46	.696	48	61	109	17	98	1	11	35	38	168	2.9	10
Harvey Catchings	69	1156	61	153	.399	22	42	.524	89	182	271	43	172	3	25	57	81	144	2.1	8
Rory White*	8	45	7	17	.412	2	5	.400	5	3	8	1	3	0	2	5	1	16	2.0	8
Linton Townes*	2	2	1	1	1.000	0	0	...	0	0	0	0	1	0	0	0	0	2	1.0	2

3-pt. FG: Milwaukee 59-232 (.254)—Moncrief 5-18 (.278); Johnson 2-13 (.154); Bridgeman 6-31 (.194); Lanier 0-3 (.000); Dunleavy 19-45 (.422); Pressey 2-9 (.222); Archibald 4-18 (.222); Grevey 15-53 (.283); Romar† 4-32 (.125); Romar‡ 4-33 (.121); Criss* 1-6 (.167); Mokeski 1-3 (.333); Catchings 0-1 (.000). Opponents 42-203 (.207).

NEW JERSEY NETS

	G	Min.	FGM	FGA	Pct.	FTM	FTA	Pct.	REBOUNDS Off.	Def.	Tot.	Ast.	PF	Dq.	Stl.	TO	Blk.	SCORING Pts.	Avg.	Hi.
Otis Birdsong	69	2168	583	1147	.508	194	319	.608	74	96	170	266	180	2	86	170	17	1365	19.8	38
Darryl Dawkins	81	2417	507	855	.593	341	464	.735	159	382	541	123	386	22	60	231	136	1357	16.8	36
Buck Williams	81	3003	495	926	.535	284	498	.570	355	645	1000	130	298	3	81	237	125	1274	15.7	27
Albert King	79	2103	465	946	.492	232	295	.786	125	263	388	203	258	6	91	208	33	1165	14.7	31
Micheal R. Richardson	48	1285	243	528	.460	76	108	.704	56	116	172	214	156	4	103	118	20	576	12.0	25
Kelvin Ransey	80	1937	304	700	.434	145	183	.792	28	99	127	483	182	2	91	141	6	760	9.5	21
Darwin Cook	82	1870	304	687	.443	95	126	.754	51	105	156	356	184	3	164	142	36	714	8.7	21
Mike Gminski	82	1655	237	462	.513	147	184	.799	161	272	433	92	162	0	37	120	70	621	7.6	18
Mike O'Koren	73	1191	186	385	.483	53	87	.609	71	104	175	95	148	3	34	75	11	430	5.9	20
Reggie Johnson	72	818	127	256	.496	92	126	.730	53	85	138	40	141	1	24	59	18	346	4.8	14
Bill Willoughby	67	936	124	258	.481	55	63	.873	75	118	193	56	106	0	23	53	24	303	4.5	15
Foots Walker	34	378	32	90	.356	24	27	.889	8	23	31	81	37	0	20	31	3	90	2.6	10
Bruce Kuczenski*	7	28	4	12	.333	3	6	.500	3	5	8	4	3	0	0	2	0	11	1.6	3
Mark Jones	6	16	3	6	.500	1	2	.500	0	2	2	5	2	0	0	2	0	7	1.2	4

3-pt. FG: New Jersey 49-232 (.211)—Birdsong 5-20 (.250); Dawkins 2-5 (.400); Williams 0-4 (.000); King 3-22 (.136); Richardson 14-58 (.241); Ransey 7-32 (.219); Cook 11-46 (.239); Gminski 0-3 (.000); O'Koren 5-28 (.179); Johnson 0-1 (.000); Willoughby 0-7 (.000); Walker 2-5 (.400); Jones 0-1 (.000). Opponents 48-181 (.265).

NEW YORK KNICKERBOCKERS

	G	Min.	FGM	FGA	Pct.	FTM	FTA	Pct.	REBOUNDS Off.	Def.	Tot.	Ast.	PF	Dq.	Stl.	TO	Blk.	SCORING Pts.	Avg.	Hi.
Bernard King	77	2667	795	1391	.572	437	561	.779	123	271	394	164	273	2	75	197	17	2027	26.3	50
Bill Cartwright	77	2487	453	808	.561	404	502	.805	195	454	649	107	262	4	44	200	97	1310	17.0	38
Ray Williams	76	2230	418	939	.445	263	318	.827	67	200	267	449	274	5	162	219	26	1124	14.8	36
Truck Robinson	65	2135	284	581	.489	133	206	.646	171	374	545	94	217	6	43	160	27	701	10.8	31
Rory Sparrow	79	2436	350	738	.474	108	131	.824	48	141	189	539	230	4	100	210	8	818	10.4	24
Louis Orr	78	1640	262	572	.458	173	211	.820	101	127	228	61	142	0	66	95	17	697	8.9	25
Darrell Walker	82	1324	216	518	.417	208	263	.791	74	93	167	284	202	1	127	194	15	644	7.9	20
Trent Tucker	63	1228	225	450	.500	25	33	.758	43	87	130	138	124	0	63	54	8	481	7.6	20
Ernie Grunfeld	76	1119	166	362	.459	64	83	.771	24	97	121	108	151	0	43	71	7	398	5.2	16
Rudy Macklin	8	65	12	30	.400	11	13	.846	5	6	11	3	17	0	1	6	0	35	4.4	10
Marvin Webster	76	1290	112	239	.469	66	117	.564	146	220	366	53	187	2	34	85	100	290	3.8	13
Eric Fernsten	32	402	29	52	.558	25	34	.735	29	57	86	11	49	0	16	19	8	83	2.6	11
Len Elmore	65	832	64	157	.408	27	38	.711	62	103	165	30	153	3	29	46	30	155	2.4	8

3-pt. FG: New York 47-165 (.285)—King 0-4 (.000); Cartwright 0-1 (.000); Williams 25-81 (.309); Sparrow 10-39 (.256); Walker 4-15 (.267); Tucker 6-16 (.375); Grunfeld 2-9 (.222). Opponents 52-189 (.275).

PHILADELPHIA 76ERS

	G	Min.	FGM	FGA	Pct.	FTM	FTA	Pct.	REBOUNDS Off.	Def.	Tot.	Ast.	PF	Dq.	Stl.	TO	Blk.	SCORING Pts.	Avg.	Hi.
Moses Malone	71	2613	532	1101	.483	545	727	.750	352	598	950	96	188	0	71	250	110	1609	22.7	38
Julius Erving	77	2683	678	1324	.512	364	483	.754	190	342	532	309	217	3	141	230	139	1727	22.4	42
Andrew Toney	78	2556	593	1125	.527	390	465	.839	57	136	193	373	251	1	70	297	23	1588	20.4	40
Maurice Cheeks	75	2494	386	702	.550	170	232	.733	44	161	205	478	196	1	171	182	20	950	12.7	24
Bobby Jones	75	1761	226	432	.523	167	213	.784	92	231	323	187	199	1	107	101	103	619	8.3	19
Clint Richardson	69	1571	221	473	.467	79	103	.767	62	103	165	155	145	0	49	100	23	521	7.6	17
Wes Matthews†	14	292	45	101	.446	9	14	.643	6	17	23	62	32	0	11	30	2	100	7.1	18
Wes Matthews‡	20	388	61	131	.466	27	36	.750	7	20	27	83	45	0	16	40	3	150	7.5	18
Samuel Williams†	70	1375	193	405	.477	86	133	.647	117	209	326	60	203	3	62	96	103	472	6.7	18
Samuel Williams‡	77	1434	204	431	.473	92	140	.657	121	218	339	62	209	3	68	99	106	500	6.5	18
Clemon Johnson	80	1721	193	412	.468	69	113	.611	131	267	398	55	205	1	35	95	65	455	5.7	16
Marc Iavaroni	78	1532	149	322	.463	97	131	.740	91	219	310	95	222	1	36	124	55	395	5.1	12
Franklin Edwards	60	654	84	221	.380	34	48	.708	12	47	59	90	78	1	31	46	5	202	3.4	16
Sedale Threatt	45	464	62	148	.419	23	28	.821	11	23	40	41	65	1	13	33	2	148	3.3	12
Leo Rautins	28	196	21	58	.362	6	10	.600	9	24	33	29	31	0	9	19	2	48	1.7	13
Bruce Kuczenski*	3	40	1	8	.125	1	2	.500	1	5	6	2	7	0	1	5	1	3	1.0	3
Charles Jones	1	3	0	1	.000	1	4	.250	0	0	0	1	1	0	1	0	0	1	1.0	1

3-pt. FG: Philadelphia 29-107 (.271)—Malone 0-4 (.000); Erving 7-21 (.333); Toney 12-38 (.316); Cheeks 8-20 (.400); B. Jones 0-1 (.000); Richardson 0-4 (.000); Matthews† 1-7 (.143); Matthews‡ 1-8 (.125); Williams† 0-1 (.000); Williams‡ 0-1 (.000); Iavaroni 0-2 (.000); Edwards 0-1 (.000); Threatt 1-8 (.125). Opponents 47-207 (.227).

PHOENIX SUNS

	G	Min.	FGM	FGA	Pct.	FTM	FTA	Pct.	Off.	Def.	Tot.	Ast.	PF	Dq.	Stl.	TO	Blk.	Pts.	Avg.	Hi.
Walter Davis	78	2546	652	1274	.512	233	270	.863	38	164	202	429	202	0	107	213	12	1557	20.0	43
Larry Nance	82	2899	601	1044	.576	249	352	.707	227	451	678	214	274	5	86	177	173	1451	17.7	36
Maurice Lucas	75	2309	451	908	.497	293	383	.765	208	517	725	203	235	2	55	177	39	1195	15.9	29
James Edwards	72	1897	438	817	.536	183	254	.720	108	240	348	184	254	3	23	140	30	1059	14.7	33
Kyle Macy	82	2402	357	713	.501	95	114	.833	49	137	186	353	181	0	123	116	6	832	10.1	26
Alvan Adams	70	1452	269	582	.462	132	160	.825	118	201	319	219	195	1	73	117	32	670	9.6	26
Rod Foster	80	1424	260	580	.448	122	155	.787	39	81	120	172	193	0	54	108	9	664	8.3	27
Rory White*	22	308	69	144	.479	24	42	.571	30	32	62	14	25	0	13	18	2	162	7.4	18
Paul Westphal	59	865	144	313	.460	117	142	.824	8	35	43	148	69	0	41	77	6	412	7.0	22
Rick Robey	61	856	140	257	.545	61	88	.693	80	118	198	65	120	0	20	77	14	342	5.6	20
Charlie Pittman	69	989	126	209	.603	69	101	.683	76	138	214	70	129	1	16	81	22	321	4.7	18
Mike Sanders	50	586	97	203	.478	29	42	.690	40	63	103	44	101	0	23	44	12	223	4.5	14
Alvin Scott	65	735	55	124	.444	56	72	.778	29	71	100	48	85	0	19	42	20	167	2.6	9
Johnny High	29	512	18	52	.346	10	29	.345	16	50	66	51	84	1	40	38	11	46	1.6	6

3-pt. FG: Phoenix 74-291 (.254)—Davis 20-87 (.230); Nance 0-7 (.000); Lucas 0-5 (.000); Edwards 0-1 (.000); Macy 23-70 (.329); Adams 0-4 (.000); Foster 22-84 (.262); Westphal 7-26 (.269); Robey 1-1 (1.000); Pittman 0-2 (.000); Scott 1-2 (.500); High 0-2 (.000). Opponents 54-219 (.247).

PORTLAND TRAIL BLAZERS

	G	Min.	FGM	FGA	Pct.	FTM	FTA	Pct.	Off.	Def.	Tot.	Ast.	PF	Dq.	Stl.	TO	Blk.	Pts.	Avg.	Hi.
Jim Paxson	81	2686	680	1322	.514	345	410	.841	68	105	173	251	165	0	122	142	10	1722	21.3	41
Calvin Natt	79	2638	500	857	.583	275	345	.797	166	310	476	179	218	3	69	166	22	1277	16.2	33
Mychal Thompson	79	2648	487	929	.524	266	399	.667	235	453	688	308	237	2	84	235	108	1240	15.7	28
Kenny Carr	82	2455	518	923	.561	247	367	.673	208	434	642	157	274	3	68	202	33	1283	15.6	31
Darnell Valentine	68	1893	251	561	.447	194	246	.789	49	78	127	395	179	1	107	149	6	696	10.2	24
Wayne Cooper	81	1662	304	663	.459	185	230	.804	176	300	476	76	247	2	26	110	106	793	9.8	26
Fat Lever	81	2010	313	701	.447	159	214	.743	96	122	218	372	178	1	135	125	31	788	9.7	28
Clyde Drexler	82	1408	252	559	.451	123	169	.728	112	123	235	153	209	2	107	123	29	628	7.7	21
Jeff Lamp	64	660	128	261	.490	60	67	.896	23	40	63	51	67	0	22	52	4	318	5.0	19
Audie Norris	79	1157	124	246	.504	104	149	.698	82	175	257	76	231	2	30	114	34	352	4.5	12
Peter Verhoeven	43	327	50	100	.500	17	25	.680	27	34	61	20	75	0	22	21	11	117	2.7	9
Eddie Jordan*	13	183	13	41	.317	7	10	.700	3	10	13	39	32	0	21	18	0	33	2.5	8
Tom Piotrowski	18	78	12	26	.462	6	6	1.000	6	11	17	5	22	0	1	6	3	30	1.7	10

3-pt. FG: Portland 25-129 (.194)—Paxson 17-59 (.288); Natt 2-17 (.118); Thompson 0-2 (.000); Carr 0-5 (.000); Valentine 0-3 (.000); Cooper 0-7 (.000); Lever 3-15 (.200); Drexler 1-4 (.250); Lamp 2-13 (.154); Vorhoeven 0-1 (.000); Jordan* 0-3 (.000). Opponents 57-208 (.274).

SAN ANTONIO SPURS

	G	Min.	FGM	FGA	Pct.	FTM	FTA	Pct.	Off.	Def.	Tot.	Ast.	PF	Dq.	Stl.	TO	Blk.	Pts.	Avg.	Hi.
George Gervin	76	2584	765	1561	.490	427	507	.842	106	207	313	220	219	3	79	224	47	1967	25.9	44
Mike Mitchell	79	2853	779	1597	.488	275	353	.779	188	382	570	93	251	6	62	141	73	1839	23.3	47
Artis Gilmore	64	2034	351	556	.631	280	390	.718	213	449	662	70	229	4	36	149	132	982	15.3	30
Gene Banks	80	2600	424	747	.568	200	270	.741	204	378	582	254	256	5	105	166	23	1049	13.1	28
John Lucas	63	1807	275	595	.462	120	157	.764	23	157	180	673	123	1	92	147	5	689	10.9	29
Edgar Jones	81	1770	322	644	.500	176	242	.727	143	306	449	65	208	7	64	125	107	826	10.2	22
Johnny Moore	59	1650	231	518	.446	105	139	.755	37	141	178	566	168	2	123	143	20	595	10.1	24
Ron Brewer†	40	782	152	345	.441	41	50	.820	17	33	50	44	54	0	18	33	16	348	8.7	23
Ron Brewer‡	53	992	179	403	.444	52	67	.776	22	41	63	50	64	0	24	40	21	413	7.8	23
Keith Edmonson*	40	521	135	274	.493	76	101	.752	40	30	70	27	67	1	22	45	6	346	8.7	22
Fred Roberts	79	1531	214	399	.536	144	172	.837	102	202	304	98	219	4	52	100	38	573	7.3	17
Mark McNamara	70	1037	157	253	.621	74	157	.471	137	180	317	31	138	2	14	89	12	388	5.5	22
Kevin Williams	19	200	25	58	.431	25	32	.781	4	9	13	43	42	1	8	22	4	75	3.9	10
John Paxson	49	458	61	137	.445	16	26	.615	4	29	33	149	47	0	10	32	2	142	2.9	25
Dave Batton	4	31	5	10	.500	0	0	...	1	3	4	3	5	0	0	4	3	10	2.5	6
Roger Phegley*	3	11	2	4	.500	2	2	1.000	0	2	2	2	1	0	1	0	0	7	2.3	7
Dave Robisch*	4	37	4	8	.500	0	0	...	2	6	8	1	8	1	0	1	0	8	2.0	6
Bob Miller	2	8	2	3	.667	0	0	...	2	3	5	1	5	0	0	0	1	4	2.0	4
Darrell Lockhart	2	14	2	2	1.000	0	0	...	0	3	3	0	5	0	0	2	0	4	2.0	4
Brant Weidner	8	38	2	9	.222	4	4	1.000	4	7	11	0	5	0	0	2	2	8	1.0	2
Steve Lingenfelter	3	14	1	1	1.000	0	2	.000	3	1	4	1	6	0	0	1	0	2	0.7	2

3-pt. FG: San Antonio 79-263 (.300)—Gervin 10-24 (.417); Mitchell 6-14 (.429); Gilmore 0-3 (.000); Banks 1-6 (.167); Lucas 19-69 (.275); Jones 6-19 (.316); Moore 28-87 (.322); Brewer† 3-13 (.231); Brewer‡ 3-14 (.214); Roberts 1-4 (.250); Williams 0-1 (.000); Paxson 4-22 (.182); Phegley* 1-1 (1.000). Opponents 52-216 (.241).

SAN DIEGO CLIPPERS

	G	Min.	FGM	FGA	Pct.	FTM	FTA	Pct.	Off.	Def.	Tot.	Ast.	PF	Dq.	Stl.	TO	Blk.	Pts.	Avg.	Hi.
Terry Cummings	81	2907	737	1491	.494	380	528	.720	323	454	777	139	298	6	92	218	57	1854	22.9	37
Norm Nixon	82	3053	587	1270	.462	206	271	.760	56	147	203	914	180	1	94	257	4	1391	17.0	35
Bill Walton	55	1476	288	518	.556	92	154	.597	132	345	477	183	153	1	45	177	88	668	12.1	25
James Donaldson	82	2525	360	604	.596	249	327	.761	165	484	649	90	214	1	40	171	139	969	11.8	24
Michael Brooks	47	1405	213	445	.479	104	151	.689	142	200	342	88	125	1	50	78	14	530	11.3	31
Greg Kelser	80	1783	313	603	.519	250	356	.702	188	203	391	91	249	3	68	195	31	878	11.0	37
Ricky Pierce	69	1280	268	570	.470	149	173	.861	59	76	135	60	143	1	27	81	13	685	9.9	30
Derek Smith	61	1297	238	436	.546	123	163	.755	54	116	170	82	165	2	33	78	22	600	9.8	26

	G	Min.	FGM	FGA	Pct.	FTM	FTA	Pct.	Off.	Def.	Tot.	Ast.	PF	Dq.	Stl.	TO	Blk.	Pts.	Avg.	Hi.
Craig Hodges	76	1571	258	573	.450	66	88	.750	22	64	86	116	166	2	58	85	1	592	7.8	22
Jerome Whitehead	70	921	144	294	.490	88	107	.822	94	151	245	19	159	2	17	59	12	376	5.4	19
Billy McKinney	80	843	136	305	.446	39	46	.848	7	47	54	161	84	0	27	48	0	311	3.9	13
Hank McDowell	57	611	85	197	.431	38	56	.679	63	92	155	37	77	0	14	49	2	208	3.6	15
Linton Townes†	2	17	3	7	.429	0	0	...	0	1	1	1	3	0	1	1	2	6	3.0	6
Linton Townes‡	4	19	4	8	.500	0	0	...	0	1	1	1	4	0	1	1	2	8	2.0	6
Rory White†	6	19	4	9	.444	0	0	...	2	2	4	0	3	0	0	1	0	8	1.3	4
Rory White‡	36	372	80	170	.471	26	47	.553	37	37	74	15	31	0	15	24	3	186	5.2	18
Hutch Jones	4	18	0	3	.000	1	4	.250	0	0	0	0	0	0	1	2	0	1	0.3	1
Kevin Loder†	1	4	0	0	...	0	0	...	0	0	0	0	1	0	0	0	0	0	0.0	0
Kevin Loder‡	11	137	19	43	.442	9	13	.692	7	11	18	14	16	0	3	11	5	48	4.4	13

3-pt. FG: San Diego 24-128 (.188)—Cummings 0-3 (.000); Nixon 11-46 (.239); Walton 0-2 (.000); Brooks 0-5 (.000); Kelser 2-6 (.333); Pierce 0-9 (.000); Smith 1-6 (.167); Hodges 10-46 (.217); Loder† 0-0; Loder‡ 1-3 (.333); McKinney 0-2 (.000); McDowell 0-3 (.000). Opponents 53-187 (.283).

SEATTLE SUPERSONICS

	G	Min.	FGM	FGA	Pct.	FTM	FTA	Pct.	Off.	Def.	Tot.	Ast.	PF	Dq.	Stl.	TO	Blk.	Pts.	Avg.	Hi.
Jack Sikma	82	2993	576	1155	.499	411	480	.856	225	686	911	327	301	6	95	236	92	1563	19.1	35
Gus Williams	80	2818	598	1306	.458	297	396	.750	67	137	204	675	151	0	189	232	25	1497	18.7	37
Tom Chambers	82	2570	554	1110	.499	375	469	.800	219	313	532	133	309	8	47	192	51	1483	18.1	34
Al Wood	81	2236	467	945	.494	223	271	.823	94	181	275	166	207	1	64	126	32	1160	14.3	29
David Thompson	19	349	89	165	.539	62	73	.849	18	26	44	13	30	0	10	27	13	240	12.6	32
Fred Brown	71	1129	258	506	.510	77	86	.895	14	48	62	194	84	0	49	70	2	602	8.5	27
Danny Vranes	80	2174	258	495	.521	153	236	.648	150	245	395	132	263	4	51	121	54	669	8.4	20
Reggie King	77	2086	233	448	.520	136	206	.660	134	336	470	179	159	2	54	127	24	602	7.8	20
Jon Sundvold	73	1284	217	488	.445	64	72	.889	23	68	91	239	81	0	29	81	1	507	6.9	24
Steve Hawes	79	1153	114	237	.481	62	78	.795	50	170	220	99	144	2	24	52	16	291	3.7	14
Scooter McCray	47	520	47	121	.388	35	50	.700	45	70	115	44	73	1	11	34	19	129	2.7	13
Clay Johnson	25	176	20	50	.400	14	22	.636	6	6	12	14	24	0	8	12	2	55	2.2	9
Charles Bradley	8	39	3	7	.429	5	7	.714	0	3	3	5	6	0	0	8	1	11	1.4	6
Steve Hayes	43	253	26	50	.520	5	14	.357	19	43	62	13	52	0	5	13	18	57	1.3	6

3-pt. FG: Seattle 27-140 (.193)—Sikma 0-2 (.000); Williams 4-25 (.160); Chambers 0-12 (.000); Wood 3-21 (.143); Thompson 0-1 (.000); Brown 9-34 (.265); Vranes 0-1 (.000); King 0-2 (.000); Sundvold 9-37 (.243); Hawes 1-4 (.250); Johnson 1-1 (1.000). Opponents 54-228 (.237).

UTAH JAZZ

	G	Min.	FGM	FGA	Pct.	FTM	FTA	Pct.	Off.	Def.	Tot.	Ast.	PF	Dq.	Stl.	TO	Blk.	Pts.	Avg.	Hi.
Adrian Dantley	79	2984	802	1438	.558	813	946	.859	179	269	448	310	201	0	61	263	4	2418	30.6	47
Darrell Griffith	82	2650	697	1423	.490	151	217	.696	95	243	338	283	202	1	114	243	23	1636	20.0	36
John Drew	81	1797	511	1067	.479	402	517	.778	146	192	338	135	208	1	88	192	2	1430	17.7	42
Rickey Green	81	2768	439	904	.486	192	234	.821	56	174	230	748	155	1	215	172	13	1072	13.2	45
Thurl Bailey	81	2009	302	590	.512	88	117	.752	115	349	464	129	193	1	38	105	122	692	8.5	22
Jeff Wilkins	81	1734	249	520	.479	134	182	.736	109	346	455	73	205	1	27	109	42	632	7.8	22
Mark Eaton	82	2139	194	416	.466	73	123	.593	148	447	595	113	303	4	25	98	351	461	5.6	17
Rich Kelley	75	1674	132	264	.500	124	162	.765	140	350	490	157	273	6	55	148	29	388	5.2	14
Jerry Eaves	80	1034	132	293	.451	92	132	.697	29	56	85	200	90	0	33	93	5	356	4.5	21
Bobby Hansen	55	419	65	145	.448	18	28	.643	13	35	48	44	62	0	15	35	4	148	2.7	15
Mitchell Anderson	48	311	55	130	.423	12	29	.414	38	25	63	22	28	0	15	20	9	122	2.5	15
Tom Boswell	38	261	28	52	.538	16	21	.762	28	36	64	16	58	1	9	13	0	73	1.9	15

3-pt. FG: Utah 101-317 (.319)—Dantley 1-4 (.250); Griffith 91-252 (.361); Drew 6-22 (.273); Green 2-17 (.118); Wilkins 0-3 (.000); Eaton 0-1 (.000); Eaves 0-6 (.000); Hansen 0-8 (.000); Anderson 0-3 (.000); Boswell 1-1 (1.000). Opponents 46-208 (.221).

WASHINGTON BULLETS

	G	Min.	FGM	FGA	Pct.	FTM	FTA	Pct.	Off.	Def.	Tot.	Ast.	PF	Dq.	Stl.	TO	Blk.	Pts.	Avg.	Hi.
Jeff Ruland	75	3082	599	1035	.579	466	636	.733	265	657	922	296	285	8	68	342	72	1665	22.2	38
Ricky Sobers	81	2624	508	1115	.456	221	264	.837	51	128	179	377	278	10	117	222	17	1266	15.6	29
Greg Ballard	82	2701	510	1061	.481	166	208	.798	140	348	488	290	214	1	94	142	35	1188	14.5	33
Jeff Malone	81	1976	408	918	.444	142	172	.826	57	98	155	151	162	1	23	110	13	982	12.1	30
Frank Johnson	82	2686	392	840	.467	187	252	.742	58	126	184	567	174	1	96	191	6	982	12.0	28
Tom McMillen	62	1294	222	447	.497	127	156	.814	64	135	199	73	162	0	14	70	17	572	9.2	27
Rick Mahorn	82	2701	307	605	.507	125	192	.651	169	569	738	131	358	14	62	142	123	739	9.0	21
Darren Daye	75	1174	180	408	.441	95	1333	.071	90	98	188	176	154	0	38	96	12	455	6.1	16
Charlie Davis	46	467	103	218	.472	24	39	.615	34	69	103	30	58	1	14	36	10	231	5.0	14
Joe Kopicki	59	678	64	132	.485	91	112	.813	64	102	166	46	71	0	15	39	5	220	3.7	19
DeWayne Scales	2	13	3	5	.600	0	2	.000	0	3	3	0	1	0	1	2	0	6	3.0	6
Bryan Warrick	32	254	27	66	.409	8	16	.500	5	17	22	43	37	0	9	20	3	63	2.0	12
Mike Gibson	32	229	21	55	.382	11	17	.647	29	37	66	9	30	1	5	14	7	53	1.7	8
Mike Wilson	6	26	0	2	.000	1	2	.500	1	0	1	3	5	0	0	3	0	1	0.2	1

3-pt. FG: Washington 71-282 (.252)—Ruland 1-7 (.143); Sobers 29-111 (.261); Ballard 2-15 (.133); Malone 24-74 (.324); Johnson 11-43 (.256); McMillen 1-6 (.167); Daye 0-6 (.000); Davis 1-9 (.111); Kopicki 1-7 (.143); Warrick 1-3 (.333); Wilson 0-1 (.000). Opponents 37-172 (.215).

* Finished season with another team. † Totals with this team only. ‡ Totals with all teams.

EASTERN CONFERENCE

FIRST ROUND

Boston 3, Washington 1

Apr. 17—Tue.	Washington 83 at Boston	.91
Apr. 19—Thur.	Washington 85 at Boston	.88
Apr. 21—Sat.	Boston 108 at Washington	*111
Apr. 24—Tue.	Boston 99 at Washington	.96

Milwaukee 3, Atlanta 2

Apr. 17—Tue.	Atlanta 89 at Milwaukee	.105
Apr. 19—Thur.	Atlanta 87 at Milwaukee	.101
Apr. 21—Sat.	Milwaukee 94 at Atlanta	.103
Apr. 24—Tue.	Milwaukee 97 at Atlanta	.100
Apr. 26—Thur.	Atlanta 89 at Milwaukee	.118

New York 3, Detroit 2

Apr. 17—Tue.	New York 94 at Detroit	.93
Apr. 19—Thur.	New York 105 at Detroit	.113
Apr. 22—Sun.	Detroit 113 at New York	.120
Apr. 25—Wed.	Detroit 119 at New York	.112
Apr. 27—Fri.	New York 127 at Detroit	*123

New Jersey 3, Philadelphia 2

Apr. 18—Wed.	New Jersey 116 at Philadelphia	.101
Apr. 20—Fri.	New Jersey 116 at Philadelphia	.102
Apr. 22—Sun.	Philadelphia 108 at New Jersey	.100
Apr. 24—Tue.	Philadelphia 110 at New Jersey	.102
Apr. 26—Thur.	New Jersey 101 at Philadelphia	.98

SEMIFINALS

Boston 4, New York 3

Apr. 29—Sun.	New York 92 at Boston	.110
May 2—Wed.	New York 102 at Boston	.116
May 4—Fri.	Boston 92 at New York	.100
May 6—Sun.	Boston 113 at New York	.118
May 9—Wed.	New York 99 at Boston	.121
May 11—Fri.	Boston 104 at New York	.106
May 13—Sun.	New York 104 at Boston	.121

Milwaukee 4, New Jersey 2

Apr. 29—Sun.	New Jersey 106 at Milwaukee	.100
May 1—Tue.	New Jersey 94 at Milwaukee	.98
May 3—Thur.	Milwaukee 100 at New Jersey	.93
May 5—Sat.	Milwaukee 99 at New Jersey	.106
May 8—Tue.	New Jersey 82 at Milwaukee	.04
May 10—Thur.	Milwaukee 98 at New Jersey	.97

FINALS

Boston 4, Milwaukee 1

May 15—Tue.	Milwaukee 96 at Boston	.119
May 17—Thur.	Milwaukee 110 at Boston	.125
May 19—Sat.	Boston 109 at Milwaukee	.100
May 21—Mon.	Boston 113 at Milwaukee	.122
May 23—Wed.	Milwaukee 108 at Boston	.115

WESTERN CONFERENCE

FIRST ROUND

Utah 3, Denver 2

Apr. 17—Tue.	Denver 121 at Utah	.123
Apr. 19—Thur.	Denver 132 at Utah	.116
Apr. 22—Sun.	Utah 117 at Denver	.121
Apr. 24—Tue.	Utah 129 at Denver	.124
Apr. 26—Thur.	Denver 111 at Utah	.127

Dallas 3, Seattle 2

Apr. 17—Tue.	Seattle 86 at Dallas	.88
Apr. 19—Thur.	Seattle 95 at Dallas	.92
Apr. 21—Sat.	Dallas 94 at Seattle	.104
Apr. 24—Tue.	Dallas 107 at Seattle	.96
Apr. 26—Thur.	Seattle 104 at Dallas	*105

Phoenix 3, Portland 2

Apr. 18—Wed.	Phoenix 113 at Portland	.106
Apr. 20—Fri.	Phoenix 116 at Portland	.122
Apr. 22—Sun.	Portland 103 at Phoenix	.106
Apr. 24—Tue.	Portland 113 at Phoenix	.110
Apr. 26—Thur.	Phoenix 117 at Portland	.105

Los Angeles 3, Kansas City 0

Apr. 18—Wed.	Kansas City 105 at Los Angeles	.116
Apr. 20—Fri.	Kansas City 102 at Los Angeles	.109
Apr. 22—Sun.	Los Angeles 108 at Kansas City	.102

SEMIFINALS

Los Angeles 4, Dallas 1

Apr. 28—Sat.	Dallas 91 at Los Angeles	.134
May 1—Tue.	Dallas 101 at Los Angeles	.117
May 4—Fri.	Los Angeles 115 at Dallas	.125
May 6—Sun.	Los Angeles 122 at Dallas	*115
May 8—Tue.	Dallas 99 at Los Angeles	.115

Phoenix 4, Utah 2

Apr. 29—Sun.	Phoenix 95 at Utah	.105
May 2—Wed.	Phoenix 102 at Utah	.97
May 4—Fri.	Utah 94 at Phoenix	.106
May 6—Sun.	Utah 110 at Phoenix	*111
May 8—Tue.	Phoenix 106 at Utah	.118
May 10—Thur.	Utah 82 at Phoenix	.102

FINALS

Los Angeles 4, Phoenix 2

May 12—Sat.	Phoenix 94 at Los Angeles	.110
May 15—Tue.	Phoenix 102 at Los Angeles	.118
May 18—Fri.	Los Angeles 127 at Phoenix	*135
May 20—Sun.	Los Angeles 126 at Phoenix	.115
May 23—Wed.	Phoenix 126 at Los Angeles	.121
May 25—Fri.	Los Angeles 99 at Phoenix	.97

NBA FINALS

Boston 4, Los Angeles 3

May 27—Sun.	Los Angeles 115 at Boston	.109
May 31—Thur.	Los Angeles 121 at Boston	*124
June 3—Sun.	Boston 104 at Los Angeles	.137
June 6—Wed.	Boston 129 at Los Angeles	*125
June 8—Fri.	Los Angeles 103 at Boston	.121
June 10—Sun.	Boston 108 at Los Angeles	.119
June 12—Tue.	Los Angeles 102 at Boston	.111

*Denotes number of overtime periods.

1983-84

1982-83 NBA CHAMPION PHILADELPHIA 76ERS

Front row (from left): Maurice Cheeks, Bobby Jones, Earl Cureton, Julius Erving, Reggie Johnson, Clint Richardson, Franklin Edwards. Back row (from left): trainer Al Domenico, director of player personnel Jack McMahon, assistant coach Matt Goukas, head coach Billy Cunningham, Clemon Johnson, Mark McNamara, Moses Malone, Marc Iavaroni, Andrew Toney, general manager Pat Williams, conditioning coach John Kilbourne, owner Harold Katz, assistant general manager John Nash.

FINAL STANDINGS

ATLANTIC DIVISION

	Atl.	Bos.	Chi.	Cle.	Dal.	Den.	Det.	G.S.	Hou.	Ind.	K.C.	L.A.	Mil.	N.J.	N.Y.	Phi.	Pho.	Por.	S.A.	S.D.	Sea.	Uta.	Was.	W	L	Pct.	GB
Philadelphia	4	3	5	5	2	2	6	2	2	4	2	2	5	3	5	..	2	0	1	2	2	2	4	65	17	.793	..
Boston	5	..	3	5	2	2	3	1	2	4	1	2	3	5	3	3	2	1	2	1	1	2	3	56	26	.683	9
New Jersey	4	1	4	6	2	1	2	2	1	6	1	1	2	..	4	3	1	1	0	1	2	1	3	49	33	.598	16
New York	2	3	4	5	2	2	5	1	2	3	1	0	2	2	..	1	0	1	2	0	1	1	4	44	38	.537	21
Washington	2	3	5	2	2	1	2	0	1	5	0	1	3	3	2	2	2	1	0	2	1	2	..	42	40	.512	23

CENTRAL DIVISION

	Atl.	Bos.	Chi.	Cle.	Dal.	Den.	Det.	G.S.	Hou.	Ind.	K.C.	L.A.	Mil.	N.J.	N.Y.	Phi.	Pho.	Por.	S.A.	S.D.	Sea.	Uta.	Was.	W	L	Pct.	GB
Milwaukee	4	3	5	5	2	0	3	1	2	5	1	0	..	3	4	1	1	2	2	2	0	2	3	51	31	.622	..
Atlanta	..	1	5	6	1	1	3	0	2	6	0	0	1	2	3	2	1	1	0	1	1	2	4	43	39	.524	8
Detroit	3	3	4	5	0	0	..	2	2	4	0	0	3	3	1	0	1	1	1	1	0	0	3	37	45	.451	14
Chicago	1	2	..	5	1	1	2	2	1	4	0	0	1	2	1	1	0	1	0	1	0	1	1	28	54	.341	23
Cleveland	0	1	1	..	2	0	1	2	2	5	1	0	1	0	1	0	0	1	0	1	1	0	3	23	59	.280	28
Indiana	0	1	2	1	0	1	2	1	0	..	1	0	1	0	3	1	1	0	0	1	1	2	1	20	62	.244	31

MIDWEST DIVISION

	Atl.	Bos.	Chi.	Cle.	Dal.	Den.	Det.	G.S.	Hou.	Ind.	K.C.	L.A.	Mil.	N.J.	N.Y.	Phi.	Pho.	Por.	S.A.	S.D.	Sea.	Uta.	Was.	W	L	Pct.	GB
San Antonio	2	0	2	2	4	4	1	4	5	2	3	4	0	2	0	1	2	3	..	4	1	5	2	53	29	.646	..
Denver	1	0	1	2	3	..	2	4	5	1	3	1	2	1	0	0	4	2	2	3	3	4	1	45	37	.549	8
Kansas City	2	1	2	1	3	3	2	4	5	1	..	1	1	1	1	0	1	2	3	4	1	4	2	45	37	.549	8
Dallas	1	0	1	0	..	3	2	3	5	2	3	2	0	0	0	0	2	3	2	5	2	2	0	38	44	.463	15
Utah	0	0	1	2	4	2	2	2	6	0	2	1	0	1	1	0	0	2	1	3	0	..	0	30	52	.366	23
Houston	0	0	1	0	1	1	0	2	..	2	1	0	0	1	0	0	0	0	1	2	1	0	1	14	68	.171	39

PACIFIC DIVISION

	Atl.	Bos.	Chi.	Cle.	Dal.	Den.	Det.	G.S.	Hou.	Ind.	K.C.	L.A.	Mil.	N.J.	N.Y.	Phi.	Pho.	Por.	S.A.	S.D.	Sea.	Uta.	Was.	W	L	Pct.	GB
Los Angeles	2	0	2	2	3	4	2	5	5	2	4	..	2	1	2	0	3	3	1	5	5	4	1	58	24	.707	..
Phoenix	1	0	2	2	3	1	1	4	5	1	4	3	1	1	2	0	..	5	3	4	5	5	0	53	29	.646	5
Seattle	1	1	2	1	3	2	2	3	4	1	4	1	2	0	1	0	1	3	4	6	..	5	1	48	34	.585	10
Portland	1	1	1	1	2	3	1	4	5	2	3	3	0	1	1	2	1	..	2	5	3	3	1	46	36	.561	12
Golden State	2	1	0	0	2	1	0	..	3	1	1	1	1	0	1	0	2	2	1	3	3	3	2	30	52	.366	28
San Diego	1	1	1	1	0	2	1	3	3	1	1	1	0	1	2	0	2	1	1	..	0	2	0	25	57	.305	33

TEAM STATISTICS

OFFENSIVE

	G	FGM	FGA	Pct.	FTM	FTA	Pct.	REBOUNDS Off.	Def.	Tot.	Ast.	PF	Dq.	Stl.	TO	Blk.	SCORING Pts.	Avg.
Denver	82	3951	7999	.494	2179	2696	.808	1214	2524	3738	2336	2091	16	789	1496	352	10105	123.2
Los Angeles	82	3964	7512	.528	1495	2031	.736	1235	2433	3668	2519	1931	10	844	1584	479	9433	115.0
San Antonio	82	3697	7340	.504	1887	2468	.765	1232	2599	3831	2261	2095	26	675	1504	469	9375	114.3
Kansas City	82	3719	7485	.497	1839	2530	.727	1256	2407	3663	2155	2432	28	765	1691	409	9328	113.8
Dallas	82	3674	7550	.487	1852	2462	.752	1296	2381	3677	2227	2067	35	552	1348	348	9243	112.7
Detroit	82	3623	7602	.477	1921	2588	.742	1312	2477	3789	2108	2122	31	679	1557	572	9239	112.7
Boston	82	3711	7547	.492	1730	2348	.737	1273	2532	3805	2216	2062	23	789	1541	521	9191	112.1
Philadelphia	82	3600	7212	.499	1966	2650	.742	1334	2596	3930	2016	2041	11	812	1627	577	9191	112.1
Chicago	82	3537	7373	.480	1983	2690	.737	1267	2527	3794	2086	2192	32	666	1743	400	9102	111.0
Seattle	82	3597	7277	.494	1796	2459	.730	1152	2569	3721	2278	1969	21	677	1533	437	9019	110.0
Utah	82	3525	7342	.480	1844	2440	.756	1093	2550	3643	2176	2017	34	758	1683	595	8938	109.0
Indiana	82	3707	7723	.480	1447	1910	.758	1299	2294	3593	2150	2086	27	755	1535	411	8911	108.7
San Diego	82	3625	7634	.475	1589	2195	.724	1394	2108	3502	2087	2284	48	820	1600	408	8903	108.6
Golden State	82	3627	7508	.483	1620	2199	.737	1281	2284	3565	1964	2138	32	856	1606	430	8908	108.6
Portland	82	3459	7124	.486	1855	2512	.738	1180	2380	3560	2030	1960	23	749	1495	384	8808	107.4
Phoenix	82	3555	7158	.497	1626	2189	.743	1094	2518	3612	2300	2062	22	749	1545	495	8776	107.0
Milwaukee	82	3486	7133	.489	1731	2299	.753	1095	2477	3572	2116	2131	38	662	1447	532	8740	106.6
New Jersey	82	3510	7140	.492	1622	2301	.705	1266	2427	3693	2143	2166	44	911	1873	592	8672	105.8
Atlanta	82	3352	7146	.469	1586	2111	.751	1139	2433	3572	1945	2022	22	573	1424	665	8335	101.6
New York	82	3272	6793	.482	1621	2282	.710	1080	2263	3343	2034	2180	30	701	1509	378	8198	100.0
Houston	82	3338	7446	.448	1402	1934	.725	1206	2260	3466	1931	2131	22	646	1571	422	8145	99.3
Washington	82	3306	7059	.468	1452	2059	.705	1099	2430	3529	2046	1958	41	733	1588	400	8134	99.2
Cleveland	82	3252	6995	.465	1430	1983	.721	1173	2414	3587	1738	2236	56	617	1538	290	7964	97.1

DEFENSIVE

	FGM	FGA	Pct.	FTM	FTA	Pct.	REBOUNDS Off.	Def.	Tot.	Ast.	PF	Dq.	Stl.	TO	Blk.	SCORING Pts.	Avg.	Dif.
New York	3132	6592	.475	1695	2260	.750	1073	2337	3410	1873	2116	36	694	1682	399	7997	97.5	+2.5
Washington	3299	7044	.468	1510	2084	.725	1114	2514	3628	1871	1975	27	698	1543	555	8145	99.3	-0.1
Phoenix	3305	7265	.455	1707	2268	.753	1210	2326	3536	1988	2039	30	712	1560	343	8361	102.0	+5.0
Milwaukee	3338	7318	.456	1665	2243	.742	1303	2343	3646	2043	2145	25	623	1523	300	8379	102.2	+4.4
Atlanta	3383	7201	.470	1608	2235	.719	1303	2571	3874	1927	1981	21	656	1468	388	8413	102.6	-1.0
New Jersey	3327	6962	.478	1746	2370	.737	1102	2176	3278	1978	2129	32	860	1871	495	8445	103.0	+2.8
Philadelphia	3442	7470	.461	1624	2253	.721	1325	2263	3588	2089	2246	54	755	1590	511	8562	104.4	+7.7
Cleveland	3381	6911	.489	1780	2396	.743	974	2382	3356	2005	1830	14	621	1275	431	8574	104.6	-7.5
Portland	3503	7211	.486	1572	2046	.768	1126	2364	3490	2072	2232	32	658	1546	500	8633	105.3	+2.1
Boston	3477	7401	.470	1750	2307	.759	1186	2393	3579	2027	2137	40	699	1607	340	8752	106.7	+5.4
Seattle	3546	7703	.460	1615	2184	.739	1314	2397	3711	2146	2152	23	726	1443	360	8756	106.8	+3.2
Los Angeles	3734	7617	.490	1455	2008	.725	1294	2166	3460	2389	1863	14	766	1562	380	8978	109.5	+5.5
San Antonio	3654	7531	.485	1716	2239	.766	1160	2263	3423	2329	2199	37	654	1430	457	9075	110.7	+3.6
Houston	3641	7244	.503	1781	2375	.750	1198	2710	3908	2252	1933	13	772	1504	406	9096	110.9	-11.6
Kansas City	3531	7260	.487	2107	2885	.730	1250	2403	3653	1997	2245	37	809	1716	439	9209	112.3	+1.5
Golden State	3706	7260	.510	1751	2391	.732	1249	2495	3744	2170	2026	23	758	1090	480	9205	112.3	-3.7
Dallas	3758	7481	.502	1708	2347	.728	1217	2433	3650	2291	2227	39	607	1383	562	9277	113.1	-0.4
Detroit	3802	7679	.495	1647	2287	.720	1266	2594	3860	2252	2326	43	761	1580	561	9272	113.1	-0.4
Utah	3794	7932	.478	1646	2288	.719	1439	2671	4110	2202	2102	18	826	1601	448	9282	113.2	-4.2
San Diego	3652	6910	.529	1963	2626	.748	1095	2365	3460	2105	1962	22	789	1723	519	9299	113.4	-4.8
Indiana	3768	7284	.517	1815	2413	.752	1206	2564	3770	2237	1886	17	761	1643	439	9391	114.5	-5.8
Chicago	3816	7712	.495	1825	2438	.749	1197	2456	3653	2230	2266	39	845	1462	633	9503	115.9	-4.9
Denver	4098	8120	.505	1787	2393	.747	1369	2697	4066	2389	2356	36	728	1636	611	10054	122.6	+0.6
Avgs.	3569	7352	.485	1716	2319	.740	1216	2430	3646	2124	2103	29	729	1567	459	8898	108.5	...

HOME/ROAD

	Home	Road	Total		Home	Road	Total
Atlanta	26-15	17-24	43-39	Milwaukee	31-10	20-21	51-31
Boston	33-8	23-18	56-26	New Jersey	30-11	19-22	49-33
Chicago	18-23	10-31	28-54	New York	26-15	18-23	44-38
Cleveland	15-26	8-33	23-59	Philadelphia	35-6	30-11	65-17
Dallas	23-18	15-26	38-44	Phoenix	32-9	21-20	53-29
Denver	29-12	16-25	45-37	Portland	31-10	15-26	46-36
Detroit	23-18	14-27	37-45	San Antonio	31-10	22-19	53-29
Golden State	21-20	9-32	30-52	San Diego	18-23	7-34	25-57
Houston	9-32	5-36	14-68	Seattle	29-12	19-22	48-34
Indiana	14-27	6-35	20-62	Utah	21-20	9-32	30-52
Kansas City	30-11	15-26	45-37	Washington	27-14	15-26	42-40
Los Angeles	33-8	25-16	58-24	Totals	585-358	358-585	943-943

1982-83

POINTS
(minimum 70 games or 1,400 points)

	G	FGM	FTM	Pts.	Avg.		G	FGM	FTM	Pts.	Avg.
Alex English, Denver	.82	959	406	2326	28.4	Larry Bird, Boston	.79	747	351	1867	23.6
Kiki Vandeweghe, Denver	.82	841	489	2186	26.7	Isiah Thomas, Detroit	.81	725	368	1854	22.9
Kelly Tripucka, Detroit	.58	565	392	1536	26.5	Sidney Moncrief, Milwaukee	.76	606	499	1712	22.5
George Gervin, San Antonio	.78	757	517	2043	26.2	Darrell Griffith, Utah	.77	752	167	1709	22.2
Moses Malone, Philadelphia	.78	654	600	1908	24.5	Bernard King, New York	.68	603	280	1486	21.9
Mark Aguirre, Dallas	.81	767	429	1979	24.4	Kareem Abdul-Jabbar, L.A.	.79	722	278	1722	21.8
Joe Barry Carroll, Golden State	.79	785	337	1907	24.1	Jim Paxson, Portland	.81	682	388	1756	21.7
World B. Free, Golden State-Cle.	.73	649	430	1743	23.9	Dan Issel, Denver	.80	661	400	1726	21.6
Reggie Theus, Chicago	.82	749	434	1953	23.8	Marques Johnson, Milwaukee	.80	723	264	1714	21.4
Terry Cummings, San Diego	.70	684	292	1660	23.7	Purvis Short, Golden State	.67	589	255	1437	21.4

FIELD GOALS
(minimum 300 made)

	FGM	FGA	Pct.		FGM	FGA	Pct.
Artis Gilmore, San Antonio	.556	888	.626	Orlando Woolridge, Chicago	.361	622	.580
Steve Johnson, Kansas City	.371	595	.624	James Worthy, Los Angeles	.447	772	.579
Darryl Dawkins, New Jersey	.401	669	.599	Brad Davis, Dallas	.359	628	.572
Kareem Abdul-Jabbar, Los Angeles	.722	1228	.588	Bill Cartwright, New York	.455	804	.566
Buck Williams, New Jersey	.536	912	.588	Jeff Ruland, Washington	.580	1051	.552

FREE THROWS
(minimum 125 made)

	FTM	FTA	Pct.
Calvin Murphy, Houston	.138	150	.920
Kiki Vandeweghe, Denver	.489	559	.875
Kyle Macy, Phoenix	.129	148	.872
George Gervin, San Antonio	.517	606	.853
Adrian Dantley, Utah	.210	248	.847
Kelly Tripucka, Detroit	.392	464	.845
Brad Davis, Dallas	.186	220	.845
Billy Knight, Indiana	.343	408	.841
Larry Bird, Boston	.351	418	.840
Jack Sikma, Seattle	.400	478	.837

STEALS
(minimum 70 games or 125 steals)

	G	No.	Avg.
Micheal Ray Richardson, Golden St.-New Jersey	.64	182	2.84
Rickey Green, Utah	.78	220	2.82
Johnny Moore, San Antonio	.77	194	2.52
Isiah Thomas, Detroit	.81	199	2.46
Darwin Cook, New Jersey	.82	194	2.37
Maurice Cheeks, Philadelphia	.79	184	2.33
Gus Williams, Seattle	.80	182	2.28
Magic Johnson, Los Angeles	.79	176	2.23
Allen Leavell, Houston	.79	165	2.09
Fat Lever, Portland	.81	153	1.89

ASSISTS
(minimum 70 games or 400 assists)

	G	No.	Avg.
Magic Johnson, Los Angeles	.79	829	10.5
Johnny Moore, San Antonio	.77	753	9.8
Rickey Green, Utah	.78	697	8.9
Larry Drew, Kansas City	.75	610	8.1
Frank Johnson, Washington	.68	549	8.1
Gus Williams, Seattle	.80	643	8.0
Ray Williams, Kansas City	.72	569	7.9
Isiah Thomas, Detroit	.81	634	7.8
Norm Nixon, Los Angeles	.79	566	7.2
Brad Davis, Dallas	.79	565	7.2

BLOCKED SHOTS
(minimum 70 games or 100 blocked shots)

	G	No.	Avg.
Tree Rollins, Atlanta	.80	343	4.29
Bill Walton, San Diego	.33	119	3.61
Mark Eaton, Utah	.81	275	3.40
Larry Nance, Phoenix	.82	217	2.65
Artis Gilmore, San Antonio	.82	192	2.34
Kevin McHale, Boston	.82	192	2.34
Alton Lister, Milwaukee	.80	177	2.21
Herb Williams, Indiana	.78	171	2.19
Kareem Abdul-Jabbar, Los Angeles	.79	170	2.15
Moses Malone, Philadelphia	.78	157	2.01

REBOUNDS
(minimum 70 games or 800 rebounds)

	G	Off.	Def.	Tot.	Avg.
Moses Malone, Philadelphia	.78	445	749	1194	15.3
Buck Williams, New Jersey	.82	365	662	1027	12.5
Bill Laimbeer, Detroit	.82	282	711	993	12.1
Artis Gilmore, San Antonio	.82	299	685	984	12.0
Dan Roundfield, Atlanta	.77	259	621	880	11.4
Jack Sikma, Seattle	.75	213	645	858	11.4
Cliff Robinson, Cleveland	.77	190	666	856	11.1
Jeff Ruland, Washington	.79	293	578	871	11.0
Larry Bird, Boston	.79	193	677	870	11.0
Terry Cummings, San Diego	.70	303	441	744	10.6

3-POINT FIELD GOALS
(minimum 25 made)

	FGA	FGM	Pct.
Mike Dunleavy, San Antonio	.194	67	.345
Darrell Griffith, Utah	.132	38	.288
Isiah Thomas, Detroit	.125	36	.288
Allen Leavell, Houston	.175	42	.240

ATLANTA HAWKS

	G	Min.	FGM	FGA	Pct.	FTM	FTA	Pct.	REBOUNDS Off.	Def.	Tot.	Ast.	PF	Dq.	Stl.	TO	Blk.	SCORING Pts.	Avg.	Hi.
Dan Roundfield	77	2811	561	1193	.470	337	450	.749	259	621	880	225	239	1	60	245	115	1464	19.0	36
Dominique Wilkins	82	2697	601	1220	.493	230	337	.682	226	252	478	129	210	1	84	180	63	1434	17.5	34
Eddie Johnson	61	1813	389	858	.453	186	237	.785	26	98	124	318	138	2	61	156	6	978	16.0	32
Johnny Davis	53	1465	258	567	.455	164	206	.796	37	91	128	315	100	0	43	114	7	685	12.9	31
Rory Sparrow*	49	1548	264	512	.516	84	113	.743	39	102	141	238	162	2	70	126	1	615	12.6	30
Tom McMillen	61	1364	198	424	.467	108	133	.812	57	160	217	76	143	2	17	80	24	504	8.3	26
Tree Rollins	80	2472	261	512	.510	98	135	.726	210	533	743	75	294	7	49	95	343	620	7.8	22
Mike Glenn	73	1124	230	444	.518	74	89	.831	16	74	90	125	132	0	30	52	9	534	7.3	25
Wes Matthews	64	1187	171	424	.403	86	112	.768	25	66	91	249	129	0	60	123	8	442	6.9	26
Rudy Macklin	73	1171	170	360	.472	101	131	.771	85	105	190	71	189	4	41	89	10	441	6.0	19
Steve Hawes*	46	860	91	244	.373	46	62	.742	53	175	228	59	110	2	29	73	8	230	5.0	20
Rickey Brown†	26	305	49	104	.471	25	40	.625	35	53	88	9	46	1	5	22	5	123	4.7	16
Rickey Brown‡	76	1048	167	349	.479	65	105	.619	91	175	266	25	172	1	13	82	26	399	5.3	21
Randy Smith†	15	142	29	66	.439	13	14	.929	2	6	8	14	17	0	2	9	0	71	4.7	18
Randy Smith‡	80	1406	273	565	.483	114	131	.870	37	59	96	206	139	1	56	98	0	663	8.3	29
Keith Edmonson	32	309	48	139	.345	16	27	.593	20	19	39	22	41	0	11	20	6	112	3.5	14
Sam Pellom*	2	9	2	6	.333	0	0	...	0	0	0	1	0	0	0	0	0	4	2.0	4
George Johnson	37	461	25	57	.439	14	19	.737	44	73	117	17	69	0	10	19	59	64	1.7	6
Scott Hastings†	10	42	5	16	.313	4	6	.667	5	5	10	2	3	0	1	3	1	14	1.4	4
Scott Hastings‡	31	140	13	38	.342	11	20	.550	15	26	41	3	34	0	6	9	1	37	1.2	4

3-pt. FG: Atlanta 45-188 (.239)—Roundfield 5-27 (.185); Wilkins 2-11 (.182); E. Johnson 14-41 (.341); Davis 5-18 (.278); Sparrow* 3-15 (.200); McMillen 0-1 (.000); Rollins 0-1 (.000); Glenn 0-1 (.000); Matthews 14-48 (.292); Macklin 0-4 (.000); Hawes* 2-14 (.143); Brown† 0-1 (.000); Brown‡ 0-3 (.000); Smith† 0-2 (.000); Smith‡ 3-18 (.167); Edmonson 0-2 (.000); Hastings† 0-2 (.000); Hastings‡ 0-3 (.000). Opponents 39-166 (.235).

BOSTON CELTICS

	G	Min.	FGM	FGA	Pct.	FTM	FTA	Pct.	REBOUNDS Off.	Def.	Tot.	Ast.	PF	Dq.	Stl.	TO	Blk.	SCORING Pts.	Avg.	Hi.
Larry Bird	79	2982	747	1481	.504	351	418	.840	193	677	870	458	197	0	148	240	71	1867	23.6	53
Robert Parish	78	2459	619	1125	.550	271	388	.698	260	567	827	141	222	4	79	185	148	1509	19.3	36
Kevin McHale	82	2345	483	893	.541	193	269	.717	215	338	553	104	241	3	34	159	192	1159	14.1	30
Cedric Maxwell	79	2252	331	663	.499	280	345	.812	185	237	422	186	202	3	65	165	39	942	11.9	30
Nate Archibald	66	1811	235	553	.425	220	296	.743	25	66	91	409	110	1	38	163	4	695	10.5	23
Danny Ainge	80	2048	357	720	.496	72	97	.742	83	131	214	251	259	2	109	98	6	791	9.9	24
Gerald Henderson	82	1551	286	618	.463	96	133	.722	57	67	124	195	190	6	95	128	3	671	8.2	22
Quinn Buckner	72	1565	248	561	.442	74	117	.632	62	125	187	275	195	2	108	159	5	570	7.9	20
Scott Wedman†	40	503	94	205	.459	20	30	.667	29	45	74	31	83	1	20	32	6	209	5.2	14
Scott Wedman‡	75	1793	374	788	.475	85	107	.794	98	184	282	117	228	6	43	126	17	843	11.2	30
M.L. Carr	77	883	135	315	.429	60	81	.741	51	86	137	71	140	0	48	79	10	333	4.3	17
Rick Robey	59	855	100	214	.467	45	78	.577	79	140	219	65	131	1	13	72	8	245	4.2	18
Charles Bradley	51	532	69	176	.392	46	90	.511	30	48	78	28	84	0	32	42	27	184	3.6	14
Darren Tillis*	15	44	7	23	.304	2	6	.333	4	5	9	2	8	0	0	4	2	16	1.1	4

3-pt. FG: Boston 39-186 (.210)—Bird 22-77 (.286); Parish 0-1 (.000); McHale 0-1 (.000); Maxwell 0-1 (.000); Archibald 5-24 (.208); Ainge 5-29 (.172); Henderson 3-16 (.188); Buckner 0-4 (.000); Wedman† 1-10 (.100); Wedman‡ 10-32 (.313); Carr 3-19 (.158); Bradley 0-3 (.000); Tillis* 0-1 (.000). Opponents 48-180 (.267).

CHICAGO BULLS

	G	Min.	FGM	FGA	Pct.	FTM	FTA	Pct.	REBOUNDS Off.	Def.	Tot.	Ast.	PF	Dq.	Stl.	TO	Blk.	SCORING Pts.	Avg.	Hi.
Reggie Theus	82	2856	749	1567	.478	434	542	.801	91	209	300	484	281	6	143	321	17	1953	23.8	46
Orlando Woolridge	57	1627	361	622	.580	217	340	.638	122	176	298	97	177	1	38	157	44	939	16.5	34
Quintin Dailey	76	2081	470	1008	.466	206	282	.730	87	173	260	280	248	7	72	205	10	1151	15.1	30
Dave Corzine	82	2496	457	920	.497	232	322	.720	243	474	717	154	242	4	47	228	109	1146	14.0	35
Rod Higgins	82	2196	313	698	.448	209	264	.792	159	207	366	175	248	3	66	127	65	848	10.3	25
David Greenwood	79	2355	312	686	.455	165	233	.708	217	548	765	151	261	5	54	154	90	789	10.0	27
Mark Olberding	80	1817	251	522	.481	194	248	.782	108	250	358	131	246	3	50	152	9	698	8.7	28
Ronnie Lester	65	1437	202	446	.453	124	171	.725	46	126	172	332	121	2	51	134	6	528	8.1	21
Tracy Jackson	78	1309	199	426	.467	92	126	.730	87	92	179	105	132	0	64	83	11	492	6.3	17
Jawann Oldham	16	171	31	58	.534	12	22	.545	18	29	47	5	30	1	5	13	13	74	4.6	17
Dwight Jones*	49	673	86	193	.446	47	75	.627	56	139	195	40	90	0	18	66	14	219	4.5	19
Dudley Bradley	58	683	82	159	.516	36	45	.800	27	78	105	106	91	0	49	59	10	201	3.5	19
Mike Bratz	15	140	14	42	.333	10	13	.769	3	16	19	23	20	0	7	14	0	39	2.6	10
Larry Spriggs	9	39	8	20	.400	5	7	.714	2	7	9	3	3	0	1	2	2	21	2.3	6
Larry Kenon*	5	25	2	6	.333	0	0	...	1	3	4	0	2	0	1	2	0	4	0.8	2

3-pt. FG: Chicago 45-209 (.215)—Theus 21-91 (.231); Woolridge 0-3 (.000); Dailey 5-25 (.200); Corzine 0-2 (.000); Higgins 13-41 (.317); Greenwood 0-4 (.000); Olberding 2-12 (.167); Lester 0-5 (.000); Jackson 2-13 (.154); Bradley 1-5 (.200); Bratz 1-8 (.125). Opponents 46-176 (.261).

1982-83

CLEVELAND CAVALIERS

	G	Min.	FGM	FGA	Pct.	FTM	FTA	Pct.	Off.	Def.	Tot.	Ast.	PF	Dq.	Stl.	TO	Blk.	Pts.	Avg.	Hi.
World B. Free†	54	1938	485	1059	.458	324	434	.747	70	87	157	201	175	3	82	159	12	1309	24.2	37
World B. Free‡	73	2638	649	1423	.456	430	583	.738	92	109	201	290	241	4	97	209	15	1743	23.9	38
Scott Wedman*	35	1290	280	583	.480	65	77	.844	69	139	208	86	145	5	23	94	11	634	18.1	30
Cliff Robinson	77	2601	587	1230	.477	213	301	.708	190	666	856	145	272	7	61	224	58	1387	18.0	40
James Edwards*	15	382	73	150	.487	38	61	.623	37	59	96	13	61	3	7	30	14	184	12.3	25
Geoff Huston	80	2716	401	832	.482	168	245	.686	41	118	159	487	215	1	74	195	4	974	12.2	31
Ron Brewer*	21	563	98	245	.400	44	51	.863	9	28	37	27	27	0	20	25	6	240	11.4	33
Phil Hubbard	82	1953	288	597	.482	204	296	.689	222	249	471	89	271	11	87	158	8	780	9.5	22
Larry Kenon†	32	624	100	212	.472	35	46	.761	52	65	117	34	49	0	21	39	9	235	7.3	22
Larry Kenon‡	48	770	119	257	.463	42	57	.737	66	81	147	39	64	0	23	47	9	280	5.8	22
Jeff Cook†	30	782	87	162	.537	38	50	.760	75	131	206	44	92	3	27	49	18	212	7.1	14
Jeff Cook‡	75	1333	148	304	.487	79	104	.760	119	216	335	102	181	3	39	105	31	375	5.0	14
Carl Nicks	9	148	26	59	.441	11	17	.647	8	18	26	11	17	0	6	11	0	63	7.0	22
Bob Wilkerson	77	1702	213	511	.417	93	124	.750	62	180	242	189	157	0	68	160	16	519	6.7	21
John Bagley	68	990	161	373	.432	64	84	.762	17	79	96	167	74	0	54	118	5	386	5.7	29
Paul Mokeski*	23	539	55	121	.455	16	26	.615	47	91	138	26	85	6	12	27	23	126	5.5	13
Bruce Flowers	53	699	110	206	.534	41	53	.774	71	109	180	47	99	2	19	43	12	261	4.9	14
Sam Lacey	60	1232	111	264	.420	29	37	.784	62	169	231	118	209	3	29	98	25	253	4.2	16
Darren Tillis†	37	482	69	158	.437	14	22	.636	37	84	121	16	86	3	8	18	28	152	4.1	22
Darren Tillis‡	52	526	76	181	.420	16	28	.571	41	89	130	18	76	3	8	22	30	168	3.2	22
Steve Hayes	65	1058	104	217	.479	29	51	.569	102	134	236	36	215	9	17	49	41	237	3.6	15
Dave Magley	14	56	4	16	.250	4	8	.500	2	8	10	2	5	0	2	2	0	12	0.9	4

3-pt. FG: Cleveland 30-120 (.250)—Free† 15-42 (.357); Free‡ 15-45 (.333); Wedman* 9-22 (.409); Huston 4-12 (.333); Brewer* 0-3 (.000); Hubbard 0-2 (.000); Kenon† 0-1 (.000); Kenon‡ 0-1 (.000); Cook† 0-1 (.000); Cook‡ 0-3 (.000); Nicks 0-1 (.000); Wilkerson 0-4 (.000); Bagley 0-14 (.000); Flowers 0-2 (.000); Lacey 2-9 (.222); Hayes 0-1 (.000); Tillis† 0-0; Tillis‡ 0-1 (.000); Magley 0-1 (.000). Opponents 32-146 (.219).

DALLAS MAVERICKS

	G	Min.	FGM	FGA	Pct.	FTM	FTA	Pct.	Off.	Def.	Tot.	Ast.	PF	Dq.	Stl.	TO	Blk.	Pts.	Avg.	Hi.
Mark Aguirre	81	2784	767	1589	.483	429	589	.728	191	317	508	332	247	5	80	261	26	1979	24.4	44
Jay Vincent	81	2726	622	1272	.489	269	343	.784	217	375	592	212	295	4	70	188	45	1513	18.7	32
Rolando Blackman	75	2349	513	1042	.492	297	381	.780	108	185	293	185	116	0	37	118	29	1326	17.7	38
Pat Cummings	81	2317	433	878	.493	148	196	.755	225	443	668	144	296	9	57	162	35	1014	12.5	27
Brad Davis	79	2323	359	628	.572	186	220	.845	34	164	198	565	176	2	80	143	11	915	11.6	21
Kelvin Ransey	76	1607	343	746	.460	152	199	.764	44	103	147	280	109	1	58	129	4	840	11.1	35
Bill Garnett	75	1411	170	319	.533	129	174	.741	141	265	406	103	245	3	48	81	70	469	6.3	15
Jim Spanarkel	48	722	91	197	.462	88	113	.779	27	57	84	78	59	0	27	55	3	272	5.7	18
Kurt Nimphius	81	1515	174	355	.490	77	140	.550	157	247	404	115	287	11	24	66	111	426	5.3	20
Elston Turner	59	879	96	238	.403	20	30	.667	68	84	152	88	75	0	47	59	0	214	3.6	14
Scott Lloyd	15	206	19	50	.380	11	17	.647	19	27	46	21	24	0	6	6	6	49	3.3	12
Corny Thompson	44	520	43	137	.314	36	46	.783	41	79	120	34	92	0	12	31	7	122	2.8	9
Allan Bristow	37	371	44	99	.444	10	14	.714	24	35	59	70	46	0	6	31	1	104	2.8	10

3-pt. FG: Dallas 43-185 (.232)—Aguirre 16-76 (.211); Vincent 0-3 (.000); Blackman 3-15 (.200); Cummings 0-1 (.000); Davis 11-43 (.256); Ransey 2-16 (.125); Garnett 0-3 (.000); Spanarkel 2-10 (.200); Nimphius 1-1 (1.000); Turner 2-3 (.667); Lloyd 0-1 (.000); Bristow 6-13 (.462). Opponents 53-202 (.262).

DENVER NUGGETS

	G	Min.	FGM	FGA	Pct.	FTM	FTA	Pct.	Off.	Def.	Tot.	Ast.	PF	Dq.	Stl.	TO	Blk.	Pts.	Avg.	Hi.
Alex English	82	2988	959	1857	.516	406	490	.829	263	338	601	397	235	1	116	263	126	2326	28.4	45
Kiki Vandeweghe	82	2909	841	1537	.547	489	559	.875	124	313	437	203	198	0	66	177	38	2186	26.7	49
Dan Issel	80	2431	661	1296	.510	400	479	.835	151	445	596	223	227	0	83	174	43	1726	21.6	38
Billy McKinney	68	1559	266	546	.487	136	167	.814	21	100	121	288	142	0	39	101	5	668	9.8	30
Dan Schayes†	32	646	111	235	.472	71	100	.710	63	123	186	40	109	1	15	58	30	293	9.2	18
Dan Schayes‡	82	2284	342	749	.457	228	295	.773	200	435	635	205	325	8	54	253	98	912	11.1	28
T.R. Dunn	82	2640	254	527	.482	119	163	.730	231	384	615	189	218	2	147	113	25	627	7.6	20
Rob Williams	74	1443	191	468	.408	131	174	.753	37	99	136	361	221	4	89	185	12	515	7.0	18
Mike Evans	42	695	115	243	.473	33	41	.805	4	54	58	113	94	3	23	71	3	263	6.3	16
Bill Hanzlik	82	1547	187	437	.428	125	160	.781	80	156	236	268	220	0	75	144	15	500	6.1	18
Dave Robisch	61	711	96	251	.382	92	118	.780	34	117	151	53	61	0	10	45	9	284	4.7	15
Glen Gondrezick	76	1130	134	294	.456	82	114	.719	108	193	301	100	161	0	80	49	9	350	4.6	16
Rich Kelley*	38	565	59	141	.418	55	70	.786	61	111	172	59	115	3	21	53	18	173	4.6	10
Dwight Anderson	5	33	7	14	.500	7	10	.700	0	2	2	3	7	0	1	5	0	21	4.2	9
Jim Ray	45	433	70	153	.458	33	51	.647	37	89	126	39	83	2	24	50	19	173	3.8	11

3-pt. FG: Denver 24-126 (.190)—English 2-12 (.167); Vandeweghe 15-51 (.294); Issel 4-19 (.211); Schayes† 0-0; Schayes‡ 0-1 (.000); McKinney 0-7 (.000); Dunn 0-1 (.000); Williams 2-15 (.133); Evans 0-9 (.000); Hanzlik 1-7 (.143); Robisch 0-1 (.000); Gondrezick 0-3 (.000); Ray 0-1 (.000). Opponents 71-253 (.281).

DETROIT PISTONS

	G	Min.	FGM	FGA	Pct.	FTM	FTA	Pct.	Off.	Def.	Tot.	Ast.	PF	Dq.	Stl.	TO	Blk.	Pts.	Avg.	Hi.
Kelly Tripucka	58	2252	565	1156	.489	392	464	.845	126	138	264	237	157	0	67	187	20	1536	26.5	56
Isiah Thomas	81	3093	725	1537	.472	368	518	.710	105	223	328	634	318	8	199	326	29	1854	22.9	46
Vinnie Johnson	82	2511	520	1013	.513	245	315	.778	167	186	353	301	263	2	93	152	49	1296	15.8	33
Bill Laimbeer	82	2871	436	877	.497	245	310	.790	282	711	993	263	320	9	51	176	118	1119	13.6	30
Terry Tyler	82	2543	421	880	.478	146	196	.745	180	360	540	157	221	3	103	120	160	990	12.1	32

	G	Min.	FGM	FGA	Pct.	FTM	FTA	Pct.	Off.	Def.	Tot.	Ast.	PF	Dq.	Stl.	TO	Blk.	Pts.	Avg.	Hi.
John Long 70	70	1485	312	692	.451	111	146	.760	56	124	180	105	130	1	44	144	12	737	10.5	29
Kent Benson 21	21	599	85	182	.467	38	50	.760	53	102	155	49	61	0	14	35	17	208	9.9	18
Edgar Jones* 49	49	1036	145	294	.493	117	172	.680	80	191	271	69	160	5	28	103	77	409	8.3	19
Scott May 9	9	155	21	50	.420	17	21	.810	10	16	26	12	24	1	5	13	2	59	6.6	11
Cliff Levingston 62	62	879	131	270	.485	84	147	.571	104	128	232	52	125	2	23	73	36	346	5.6	24
Ray Tolbert† 28	28	395	57	124	.460	28	59	.475	26	65	91	19	56	0	10	32	23	142	5.1	20
Ray Tolbert‡ 73	73	1107	157	314	.500	52	103	.505	72	170	242	50	153	1	26	83	47	366	5.0	20
Tom Owens. 49	49	725	81	192	.422	45	66	.682	66	120	186	44	115	0	12	48	14	207	4.2	12
James Wilkes 9	9	129	11	34	.324	12	15	.800	9	10	19	10	22	0	3	5	1	34	3.8	8
Walker Russell 68	68	757	67	184	.364	47	58	.810	19	54	73	131	71	0	16	92	1	183	2.7	16
Ricky Pierce 39	39	265	33	88	.375	18	32	.563	15	20	35	14	42	0	8	18	4	85	2.2	13
Jim Smith. 4	4	18	3	4	.750	2	4	.500	0	5	5	0	4	0	0	0	0	8	2.0	5
James Johnstone† . . . 16	16	137	9	20	.450	6	15	.400	11	19	30	10	24	0	2	11	6	24	1.5	4
James Johnstone‡ . . . 23	23	191	11	30	.367	9	20	.450	15	31	46	11	33	0	3	15	7	31	1.3	4
Jim Zoet. 7	7	30	1	5	.200	0	0	...	3	5	8	1	9	0	1	4	3	2	0.3	2

3-pt. FG: Detroit 72-272 (.265)—Tripucka 14-37 (.378); Thomas 36-125 (.288); Johnson 11-40 (.275); Laimbeer 2-13 (.154); Tyler 2-15 (.133); Long 2-7 (.286); Benson 0-1 (.000); Jones* 2-6 (.333); Levingston 0-1 (.000); Tolbert† 0-1 (.000); Tolbert‡ 0-3 (.000); Wilkes 0-1 (.000); Russell 2-18 (.111); Pierce 1-7 (.143). Opponents 21-182 (.115).

GOLDEN STATE WARRIORS

	G	Min.	FGM	FGA	Pct.	FTM	FTA	Pct.	Off.	Def.	Tot.	Ast.	PF	Dq.	Stl.	TO	Blk.	Pts.	Avg.	Hi.
Joe Barry Carroll. 79	79	2988	785	1529	.513	337	469	.719	220	468	688	169	260	7	108	285	155	1907	24.1	52
World B. Free* 19	19	700	164	364	.451	106	149	.711	22	22	44	89	66	1	15	50	3	434	22.8	38
Purvis Short 67	67	2397	589	1209	.487	255	308	.828	145	209	354	228	242	3	94	194	14	1437	21.4	40
Mickey Johnson† 30	30	899	162	359	.451	141	170	.829	88	157	245	100	131	6	25	105	23	466	15.5	28
Mickey Johnson‡ 78	78	2053	391	921	.425	312	380	.821	163	331	494	255	288	10	82	238	46	1097	14.1	32
Micheal R. Richardson* 33	33	1074	176	427	.412	55	87	.632	45	100	145	245	124	2	101	137	9	411	12.5	31
Sleepy Floyd† 33	33	754	134	311	.431	112	135	.830	40	55	95	71	78	2	39	66	8	386	11.7	28
Sleepy Floyd‡ 76	76	1248	226	527	.429	150	180	.833	56	81	137	138	134	3	58	106	17	612	8.1	28
Ron Brewer† 53	53	1401	246	562	.438	98	119	.824	50	57	107	69	96	0	70	72	19	597	11.3	28
Ron Brewer‡ 74	74	1964	344	807	.426	142	170	.835	59	85	144	96	123	0	90	97	25	837	11.3	33
Lewis Lloyd 73	73	1350	293	566	.518	100	139	.719	77	183	260	130	109	0	61	118	31	687	9.4	30
Samuel Williams 75	75	1533	252	479	.526	123	171	.719	153	240	393	45	244	4	71	101	89	627	8.4	26
Larry Smith 49	49	1433	180	306	.588	53	99	.535	209	276	485	46	186	5	36	83	20	413	8.4	23
Lorenzo Romar. 82	82	2130	266	572	.465	78	105	.743	23	115	138	455	142	0	98	141	5	620	7.6	22
Joe Hassett. 6	6	139	19	44	.432	0	0	...	3	8	11	21	14	0	2	9	0	39	6.5	10
Rickey Brown* 50	50	743	118	245	.482	40	65	.615	56	122	178	16	126	0	8	60	21	276	5.5	21
Lester Conner 75	75	1416	145	303	.479	79	113	.699	69	152	221	253	141	1	116	99	7	369	4.9	16
Larry Kenon* 11	11	121	17	39	.436	7	11	.636	13	13	26	5	13	0	1	6	0	41	3.7	12
Terry Duerod. 5	5	49	9	19	.474	0	0	...	0	3	3	5	5	0	2	9	1	18	3.6	8
Hank McDowell*. 14	14	130	13	29	.448	14	18	.778	15	15	30	4	26	0	2	8	4	40	2.9	12
Derek Smith 27	27	154	21	51	.412	17	25	.680	10	28	38	2	40	0	0	11	4	59	2.2	10
Chris Engler 54	54	369	38	94	.404	5	16	.313	43	61	104	11	95	1	7	24	17	81	1.5	8

3-pt. FG: Golden State 34-150 (.227)—Carroll 0-3 (.000); Free* 0-3 (.000); Short 4-15 (.267); Johnson† 1-17 (.059); Johnson‡ 3-36 (.083); Richardson* 4-31 (.129); Floyd† 6-11 (.545); Floyd‡ 10-25 (.400); Brewer† 7-15 (.467); Brewer‡ 7-18 (.389); Lloyd 1-4 (.250); Williams 0-1 (.000); Romar 10-33 (.303); Hassett 1-9 (.111); Brown* 0-2 (.000); Conner 0-4 (.000); D. Smith 0-2 (.000). Opponents 42-167 (.251).

HOUSTON ROCKETS

	G	Min.	FGM	FGA	Pct.	FTM	FTA	Pct.	Off.	Def.	Tot.	Ast.	PF	Dq.	Stl.	TO	Blk.	Pts.	Avg.	Hi.
Allen Leavell 79	79	2602	439	1059	.415	247	297	.832	64	131	195	530	215	0	165	198	14	1167	14.8	42
James Bailey† 69	69	1715	376	756	.497	224	320	.700	168	300	468	65	256	7	42	190	59	976	14.1	34
James Bailey‡ 75	75	1765	385	774	.497	226	322	.702	171	303	474	67	271	7	43	196	60	996	13.3	34
Elvin Hayes. 81	81	2302	424	890	.476	196	287	.683	199	417	616	158	232	2	50	200	81	1046	12.9	35
Calvin Murphy 64	64	1423	337	754	.447	138	150	.920	34	40	74	158	163	3	59	89	4	816	12.8	32
Terry Teagle 73	73	1708	332	776	.428	97	125	.696	74	120	194	150	171	0	53	137	18	761	10.4	34
Joe Bryant 81	81	2055	344	768	.448	116	165	.703	88	189	277	186	258	4	82	177	30	812	10.0	28
Wally Walker. 82	82	2251	362	806	.449	72	116	.621	137	236	373	199	202	3	37	144	22	797	9.7	23
Caldwell Jones 82	82	2440	307	677	.453	162	206	.786	222	446	668	138	278	2	46	171	131	776	9.5	29
Major Jones 60	60	878	142	311	.457	56	102	.549	114	149	263	39	104	0	22	83	22	340	5.7	21
Tom Henderson 51	51	789	107	263	.407	45	57	.789	18	51	69	138	57	0	37	50	2	259	5.1	17
Chuck Nevitt. 6	6	64	11	15	.733	1	4	.250	6	11	17	0	14	0	1	7	12	23	3.8	8
Billy Paultz* 57	57	695	89	200	.446	26	57	.456	54	113	167	57	95	0	12	41	12	204	3.6	12
Jeff Taylor. 44	44	774	64	160	.400	30	46	.652	25	53	78	110	82	1	40	60	15	158	3.6	12
Calvin Garrett 4	4	34	4	11	.364	2	2	1.000	3	4	7	3	4	0	0	3	0	10	2.5	4

3-pt. FG: Houston 67-271 (.247)—Leavell 42-175 (.240); Bailey† 0-1 (.000); Bailey‡ 0-1 (.000); Hayes 2-4 (.500); Murphy 4-14 (.286); Teagle 10-29 (.345); Bryant 8-36 (.222); Walker 1-4 (.250); C. Jones 0-2 (.000); M. Jones 0-2 (.000); Henderson 0-2 (.000); Taylor 0-1 (.000); Garrett 0-1 (.000). Opponents 33-125 (.264).

INDIANA PACERS

	G	Min.	FGM	FGA	Pct.	FTM	FTA	Pct.	Off.	Def.	Tot.	Ast.	PF	Dq.	Stl.	TO	Blk.	Pts.	Avg.	Hi.
Clark Kellogg 81	81	2761	680	1420	.479	261	352	.741	340	520	860	223	298	6	141	217	43	1625	20.1	36
Billy Knight. 80	80	2262	512	984	.520	343	408	.841	152	172	324	192	143	0	66	193	8	1370	17.1	41
Herb Williams. 78	78	2513	580	1163	.499	155	220	.705	151	432	583	262	230	4	54	229	171	1315	16.9	34
George Johnson 82	82	2297	409	858	.477	126	172	.733	176	369	545	220	279	6	77	242	53	951	11.6	25

	G	Min.	FGM	FGA	Pct.	FTM	FTA	Pct.	Off.	Def.	Tot.	Ast.	PF	Dq.	Stl.	TO	Blk.	Pts.	Avg.	Hi.
									REBOUNDS									SCORING		
Butch Carter	81	1716	354	706	.501	124	154	.805	62	88	150	194	207	5	78	118	13	849	10.5	42
Clemon Johnson*	51	1216	208	399	.521	77	122	.631	115	204	319	115	137	2	51	88	63	493	9.7	22
Jerry Sichting	78	2435	316	661	.478	92	107	.860	33	122	155	433	185	0	104	138	2	727	9.3	18
Russ Schoene†	31	520	101	228	.443	40	55	.727	44	57	101	27	74	1	12	35	14	243	7.8	15
Russ Schoene‡	77	1222	207	435	.476	61	83	.735	96	159	255	59	192	3	25	81	23	476	6.2	25
Bradley Branson	62	680	131	308	.425	76	108	.704	73	100	173	46	81	0	27	45	26	338	5.5	30
Marty Byrnes	80	1436	157	374	.420	71	95	.747	75	116	191	179	149	1	41	73	6	391	4.9	17
John Duren	82	1433	163	360	.453	43	54	.796	38	69	107	200	203	2	66	96	5	369	4.5	14
Jose Slaughter	63	515	89	238	.374	38	59	.644	34	34	68	52	93	0	36	42	7	225	3.6	11
Guy Morgan	8	46	7	24	.292	1	4	.250	6	11	17	7	7	0	2	2	0	15	1.9	8

3-pt. FG: Indiana 50-236 (.212)—Kellogg 4-18 (.222); Knight 3-19 (.158); Williams 0-7 (.000); G. Johnson 7-38 (.184); Carter 17-51 (.333); C. Johnson* 0-1 (.000); Sichting 3-18 (.167); Schoene† 1-3 (.333); Schoene‡ 1-4 (.250); Branson 0-1 (.000); Byrnes 6-26 (.231); Duren 0-13 (.000); Slaughter 9-41 (.220). Opponents 40-142 (.282).

KANSAS CITY KINGS

	G	Min.	FGM	FGA	Pct.	FTM	FTA	Pct.	Off.	Def.	Tot.	Ast.	PF	Dq.	Stl.	TO	Blk.	Pts.	Avg.	Hi.
									REBOUNDS									SCORING		
Larry Drew	75	2690	599	1218	.492	310	378	.820	44	163	207	610	207	1	126	272	10	1510	20.1	33
Eddie Johnson	82	2933	677	1370	.494	247	317	.779	191	310	501	216	259	3	70	181	20	1621	19.8	39
Mike Woodson	81	2426	584	1154	.506	298	377	.790	84	164	248	254	203	0	137	174	59	1473	18.2	40
Ray Williams	72	2170	419	1068	.392	256	333	.769	93	234	327	569	248	3	120	335	26	1109	15.4	36
Steve Johnson	79	1544	371	595	.624	186	324	.574	140	258	398	95	323	9	40	180	83	928	11.7	27
Reggie Johnson*	50	992	178	355	.501	73	100	.730	75	126	201	48	150	2	18	69	26	430	8.6	18
Joe Meriweather	78	1706	258	453	.570	102	163	.626	150	274	424	64	285	4	47	118	86	618	7.9	21
LaSalle Thompson . . .	71	987	147	287	.512	89	137	.650	133	242	375	33	186	1	40	96	61	383	5.4	16
Kevin Loder	66	818	138	300	.460	53	80	.663	37	88	125	72	98	0	29	64	8	334	5.1	25
Reggie King	58	995	104	225	.462	73	96	.760	91	149	240	58	94	1	28	65	11	281	4.8	17
Ed Nealy	82	1643	147	247	.595	70	114	.614	170	315	485	62	247	4	68	51	12	364	4.4	16
Brook Steppe	62	606	84	176	.477	76	100	.760	25	48	73	68	92	0	26	55	3	245	4.0	16
Kenny Dennard	22	224	11	34	.324	6	9	.667	20	32	52	6	27	0	16	5	1	28	1.3	6
Leon Douglas	5	46	2	3	.667	0	2	.000	3	4	7	0	13	0	0	1	3	4	0.8	4

3-pt. FG: Kansas City 51-215 (.237)—Drew 2-16 (.125); E. Johnson 20-71 (.282); Woodson 7-33 (.212); Williams 15-74 (.203); R. Johnson* 1-4 (.250); Thompson 0-1 (.000); Loder 5-9 (.556); Steppe 1-7 (.143). Opponents 40-188 (.213).

LOS ANGELES LAKERS

	G	Min.	FGM	FGA	Pct.	FTM	FTA	Pct.	Off.	Def.	Tot.	Ast.	PF	Dq.	Stl.	TO	Blk.	Pts.	Avg.	Hi.
									REBOUNDS									SCORING		
Kareem Abdul-Jabbar .	79	2554	722	1228	.588	278	371	.749	167	425	592	200	220	1	61	200	170	1722	21.8	38
Jamaal Wilkes	80	2552	684	1290	.530	203	268	.757	146	197	343	182	221	0	65	150	17	1571	19.6	36
Magic Johnson	79	2907	511	933	.548	304	380	.800	214	469	683	829	200	1	176	301	47	1326	16.8	36
Norm Nixon	79	2711	533	1123	.475	125	168	.744	61	144	205	566	176	1	104	237	4	1191	15.1	27
Bob McAdoo	47	1019	292	562	.520	119	163	.730	76	171	247	39	153	2	40	68	40	703	15.0	26
James Worthy	77	1970	447	772	.579	138	221	.624	157	242	399	132	221	2	91	178	64	1033	13.4	28
Steve Mix†	1	17	4	10	.400	1	1	1.000	1	0	1	2	1	0	0	0	0	9	9.0	9
Steve Mix‡	58	809	137	283	.484	75	88	.852	38	99	137	70	71	0	33	45	3	350	6.0	20
Michael Cooper	82	2148	266	497	.535	102	130	.785	82	192	274	315	208	0	115	128	50	639	7.8	20
Kurt Rambis	78	1806	235	413	.569	114	166	.687	164	367	531	90	233	2	105	145	63	584	7.5	21
Dwight Jones†	32	491	62	132	.470	32	48	.667	28	86	114	22	82	0	13	35	9	156	4.9	14
Dwight Jones‡	81	1164	148	325	.455	79	123	.642	84	225	309	62	172	0	31	101	23	375	4.6	19
Mike McGee	39	381	69	163	.423	17	23	.739	33	20	53	26	50	1	11	27	5	156	4.0	19
Clay Johnson	48	447	53	135	.393	38	48	.792	40	29	69	24	62	0	22	25	4	144	3.0	13
Eddie Jordan	35	333	40	132	.303	11	17	.647	8	18	26	80	52	0	31	54	1	94	2.7	12
Mark Landsberger	39	356	43	102	.422	12	25	.480	55	73	128	12	48	0	8	20	4	98	2.5	8
Billy Ray Bates†	4	27	2	16	.125	1	2	.500	1	0	1	0	1	0	1	0	0	5	1.3	3
Billy Ray Bates‡	19	304	55	145	.379	11	22	.500	11	8	19	14	19	0	14	12	3	123	6.5	17
Joe Cooper*	2	11	1	4	.250	0	0	. . .	2	0	2	0	3	0	1	3	1	2	1.0	2

3-pt. FG: L.A. Lakers 10-96 (.104)—Abdul-Jabbar 0-2 (.000); Wilkes 0-6 (.000); M. Johnson 0-21 (.000); Nixon 0-13 (.000); McAdoo 0-1 (.000); Worthy 1-4 (.250); Mix† 0-0; Mix‡ 1-4 (.250); M. Cooper 5-21 (.238); Rambis 0-2 (.000); Jones† 0-1 (.000); Jones‡ 0-1 (.000); McGee 1-7 (.143); C. Johnson 0-2 (.000); Jordan 3-16 (.188); Bates† 0-0; Bates‡ 2-5 (.400). Opponents 55-212 (.259).

MILWAUKEE BUCKS

	G	Min.	FGM	FGA	Pct.	FTM	FTA	Pct.	Off.	Def.	Tot.	Ast.	PF	Dq.	Stl.	TO	Blk.	Pts.	Avg.	Hi.
									REBOUNDS									SCORING		
Sidney Moncrief	76	2710	606	1156	.524	499	604	.826	192	245	437	300	180	1	113	197	23	1712	22.5	42
Marques Johnson	80	2853	723	1420	.509	264	359	.735	196	366	562	363	211	0	100	196	56	1714	21.4	39
Junior Bridgeman . . .	70	1855	421	856	.492	164	196	.837	44	202	246	207	155	0	40	122	9	1007	14.4	31
Mickey Johnson*	6	153	30	66	.455	7	9	.778	9	16	25	11	22	0	1	12	2	67	11.2	17
Bob Lanier	39	978	163	332	.491	91	133	.684	58	142	200	105	125	2	34	82	24	417	10.7	26
Brian Winters	57	1361	255	587	.434	73	85	.859	35	75	110	156	132	2	45	81	4	605	10.6	30
Alton Lister	80	1885	272	514	.529	130	242	.537	168	400	568	111	328	18	50	186	177	674	8.4	27
Dave Cowens	40	1014	136	306	.444	52	63	.825	73	201	274	82	137	4	30	44	15	324	8.1	16
Phil Ford†	70	1447	193	410	.471	90	113	.796	18	78	96	252	168	2	46	113	3	477	6.8	21
Phil Ford‡	77	1610	213	445	.479	97	123	.789	18	85	103	290	190	2	52	134	3	524	6.8	21
Paul Pressey	79	1528	213	466	.457	105	176	.597	83	198	281	207	174	2	99	162	47	532	6.7	23
Charlie Criss	66	922	169	375	.451	68	76	.895	14	65	79	127	44	0	27	44	0	412	6.2	20

1982-83

	G	Min.	FGM	FGA	Pct.	FTM	FTA	Pct.	REBOUNDS Off.	Def.	Tot.	Ast.	PF	Dq.	Stl.	TO	Blk.	SCORING Pts.	Avg.	Hi.
Steve Mix*	57	792	133	273	.487	74	87	.851	37	99	136	68	70	0	33	45	3	341	6.0	20
Harvey Catchings	74	1554	90	197	.457	62	92	.674	132	276	408	77	224	4	26	83	148	242	3.3	12
Armond Hill	14	169	14	26	.538	18	22	.818	5	15	20	27	20	0	9	13	0	46	3.3	10
Paul Mokeski†	50	589	64	139	.460	34	42	.810	29	93	122	23	138	3	9	40	21	162	3.2	10
Paul Mokeski‡	73	1128	119	260	.458	50	68	.735	76	184	260	49	223	9	21	67	44	288	3.9	13
Sam Pellom†	4	20	4	10	.400	0	0	...	2	6	8	0	3	0	0	2	0	8	2.0	4
Sam Pellom‡	6	29	6	16	.375	0	0	...	2	6	8	1	3	0	0	2	0	12	2.0	4

3-pt. FG: Milwaukee 37-169 (.219)—Moncrief 1-10 (.100); Ma. Johnson 4-20 (.200); Bridgeman 1-13 (.077); Mi. Johnson* 0-2 (.000); Lanier 0-1 (.000); Winters 22-68 (.324); Cowens 0-2 (.000); Ford† 1-8 (.125); Ford‡ 1-9 (.111); Pressey 1-9 (.111); Criss 6-31 (.194); Mix* 1-4 (.250); Mokeski† 0-1 (.000); Mokeski‡ 0-1 (.000). Opponents 38-209 (.182).

NEW JERSEY NETS

	G	Min.	FGM	FGA	Pct.	FTM	FTA	Pct.	REBOUNDS Off.	Def.	Tot.	Ast.	PF	Dq.	Stl.	TO	Blk.	SCORING Pts.	Avg.	Hi.
Buck Williams	82	2961	536	912	.588	324	523	.620	365	662	1027	125	270	4	91	246	110	1396	17.0	30
Albert King	79	2447	582	1226	.475	176	227	.775	157	299	456	291	278	5	95	245	41	1346	17.0	31
Otis Birdsong	62	1885	426	834	.511	82	145	.566	53	97	150	239	155	0	85	114	16	936	15.1	29
Mickey Johnson*	42	1001	199	496	.401	164	201	.816	66	158	224	144	135	4	56	121	21	564	13.4	32
Darwin Cook	82	2625	443	986	.449	186	242	.769	73	167	240	448	213	2	194	238	48	1080	13.2	24
Micheal R. Richardson†31	1002	170	388	.438	51	76	.671	68	82	150	187	116	2	81	107	15	395	12.7	27		
Micheal R. Richardson‡64	2076	346	815	.425	106	163	.650	113	182	295	432	240	4	182	244	24	806	12.6	31		
Darryl Dawkins	81	2093	401	669	.599	166	257	.646	127	293	420	114	379	23	67	281	152	968	12.0	25
Mike Gminski	80	1255	213	426	.500	175	225	.778	154	228	382	61	118	0	35	126	116	601	7.5	18
Mike O'Koren	46	803	136	259	.525	34	48	.708	42	72	114	82	67	0	42	62	11	308	6.7	23
Phil Ford*	7	163	20	35	.571	7	10	.700	0	7	7	38	22	0	6	21	0	47	6.7	11
Sleepy Floyd*	43	494	92	216	.426	38	45	.844	16	26	42	67	56	1	19	40	9	226	5.3	13
Foots Walker	79	1388	114	250	.456	116	149	.779	30	106	136	264	134	1	78	104	3	346	4.4	15
Len Elmore	74	975	97	244	.398	54	84	.643	81	157	238	39	125	2	44	83	38	248	3.4	13
James Bailey*	6	50	9	18	.500	2	2	1.000	3	3	6	2	15	0	1	6	1	20	3.3	6
Eddie Phillips	48	416	56	138	.406	40	59	.678	27	50	77	29	58	0	14	50	8	152	3.2	12
Bill Willoughby†	10	84	11	29	.379	2	2	1.000	2	9	11	8	16	0	1	5	1	24	2.4	6
Bill Willoughby‡	62	1146	147	324	.454	43	55	.782	63	138	201	64	139	0	25	61	17	343	5.5	18
Jan van Breda Kolff	13	63	5	14	.357	5	6	.833	2	11	13	5	9	0	2	3	2	15	1.2	4

3-pt. FG: New Jersey 30-149 (.201)—Williams 0-4 (.000); King 6-23 (.261); Birdsong 2-6 (.333); Johnson* 2-17 (.118); Cook 8-38 (.211); Richardson† 4-20 (.200); Richardson‡ 8-51 (.157); Gminski 0-1 (.000); O'Koren 2-9 (.222); Ford* 0-1 (.000); Floyd* 4-14 (.286); Walker 2-12 (.167); Elmore 0 1 (.000); Phillips 0-2 (.000); Willoughby† 0-1 (.000); Willoughby‡ 6-14 (.429). Opponents 45-208 (.216).

NEW YORK KNICKERBOCKERS

	G	Min.	FGM	FGA	Pct.	FTM	FTA	Pct.	REBOUNDS Off.	Def.	Tot.	Ast.	PF	Dq.	Stl.	TO	Blk.	SCORING Pts.	Avg.	Hi.
Bernard King	68	2207	603	1142	.528	280	388	.722	99	227	326	195	233	5	90	197	13	1486	21.9	43
Bill Cartwright	82	2468	455	804	.566	380	511	.744	185	405	590	136	315	7	41	204	127	1290	15.7	32
Sly Williams	68	1385	314	647	.485	176	259	.680	94	196	290	133	166	3	73	133	3	806	11.9	23
Paul Westphal	80	1978	318	693	.459	148	184	.804	19	96	115	439	180	1	87	196	16	798	10.0	25
Rory Sparrow†	32	880	128	298	.430	63	86	.733	22	67	89	159	93	2	37	71	4	321	10.0	24
Rory Sparrow‡	81	2428	392	810	.484	147	199	.739	61	169	230	397	255	4	107	197	5	936	11.6	30
Truck Robinson	81	2426	326	706	.462	118	201	.587	199	458	657	145	241	4	57	190	24	770	9.5	26
Louis Orr	82	1666	274	593	.462	140	175	.800	94	134	228	94	134	0	64	93	24	688	8.4	28
Trent Tucker	78	1830	299	647	.462	43	64	.672	75	141	216	195	235	1	56	70	6	655	8.4	27
Ed Sherod	64	1624	171	421	.406	52	80	.650	43	106	149	311	112	2	96	104	14	395	6.2	20
Marvin Webster	82	1472	168	331	.508	106	180	.589	176	267	443	49	210	3	35	102	131	442	5.4	22
Ernie Grunfeld	77	1422	167	377	.443	81	98	.827	42	121	163	136	172	1	40	84	10	415	5.4	14
Vince Taylor	31	321	37	102	.363	21	32	.656	19	17	36	41	54	1	20	30	2	95	3.1	12
Mike Davis	8	28	4	10	.400	6	10	.600	3	7	10	0	4	0	0	4	4	14	1.8	5
Scott Hastings*	21	98	8	22	.364	7	14	.500	10	21	31	1	31	0	5	6	0	23	1.1	4

3-pt. FG: New York 33-131 (.252)—King 0-6 (.000); Williams 2-19 (.105); Westphal 14-48 (.292); Sparrow† 2-7 (.286); Sparrow‡ 5-22 (.227); Orr 0-2 (.000); Tucker 14-30 (.467); Sherod 1-13 (.077); Webster 0-1 (.000); Grunfeld 0-4 (.000); Hastings* 0-1 (.000). Opponents 38-166 (.229).

PHILADELPHIA 76ERS

	G	Min.	FGM	FGA	Pct.	FTM	FTA	Pct.	REBOUNDS Off.	Def.	Tot.	Ast.	PF	Dq.	Stl.	TO	Blk.	SCORING Pts.	Avg.	Hi.
Moses Malone	78	2922	654	1305	.501	600	788	.761	445	749	1194	101	206	0	89	264	157	1908	24.5	38
Julius Erving	72	2421	605	1170	.517	330	435	.759	173	318	491	263	202	1	112	196	131	1542	21.4	44
Andrew Toney	81	2474	626	1250	.501	324	411	.788	42	183	225	365	255	0	80	271	17	1598	19.7	42
Maurice Cheeks	79	2465	404	745	.542	181	240	.754	53	156	209	543	182	0	184	179	31	990	12.5	32
Bobby Jones	74	1749	250	460	.543	165	208	.793	102	242	344	142	199	4	85	109	91	665	9.0	17
Clint Richardson	77	1755	259	559	.463	71	111	.640	98	149	247	168	164	0	71	99	18	589	7.6	18
Clemon Johnson†	32	698	91	182	.500	34	58	.586	75	130	205	24	84	1	16	36	29	216	6.8	13
Clemon Johnson‡	83	1914	299	581	.515	111	180	.617	190	334	524	139	221	3	67	124	92	709	8.5	22
Franklin Edwards	81	1266	228	483	.472	86	113	.761	23	62	85	221	119	0	81	110	6	542	6.7	18
Reggie Johnson†	29	549	69	154	.448	22	30	.733	32	58	90	23	82	1	8	35	17	160	5.5	16
Reggie Johnson‡	79	1541	247	509	.485	95	130	.731	107	184	291	71	232	3	26	104	43	590	7.5	18
Marc Iavaroni	80	1612	163	353	.462	78	113	.690	117	212	329	83	238	0	32	133	44	404	5.1	19
Russ Schoene*	46	702	106	207	.512	21	28	.750	52	102	154	32	118	2	13	46	9	233	5.1	25

	G	Min.	FGM	FGA	Pct.	FTM	FTA	Pct.	Off.	Def.	Tot.	Ast.	PF	Dq.	Stl.	TO	Blk.	Pts.	Avg.	Hi.
Earl Cureton	73	987	108	258	.419	33	67	.493	84	185	269	43	144	1	37	76	24	249	3.4	19
Mark McNamara	36	182	29	64	.453	20	45	.444	34	42	76	7	42	1	3	36	3	78	2.2	7
Mitchell Anderson*	13	48	8	22	.364	1	3	.333	4	8	12	1	6	0	1	5	0	17	1.3	8

3-pt. FG: Philadelphia 25-109 (.229)—Malone 0-1 (.000); Erving 2-7 (.286); Toney 22-76 (.289); Cheeks 1-6 (.167); Jones 0-1 (.000); C. Johnson‡ 0-1 (.000); Richardson 0-6 (.000); R. Johnson† 0-0; R. Johnson‡ 1-4 (.250); Edwards 0-8 (.000); Iavaroni 0-2 (.000); Schoene* 0-1 (.000); Anderson* 0-1 (.000). Opponents 54-249 (.217).

PHOENIX SUNS

	G	Min.	FGM	FGA	Pct.	FTM	FTA	Pct.	Off.	Def.	Tot.	Ast.	PF	Dq.	Stl.	TO	Blk.	Pts.	Avg.	Hi.
Walter Davis	80	2491	665	1289	.516	184	225	.818	63	134	197	397	186	2	117	188	12	1521	19.0	38
Larry Nance	82	2914	588	1069	.550	193	287	.672	239	471	710	197	254	4	99	190	217	1370	16.7	31
Maurice Lucas	77	2586	495	1045	.474	278	356	.781	201	598	799	219	274	5	56	221	43	1269	16.5	33
Alvan Adams	80	2447	477	981	.486	180	217	.829	161	387	548	376	287	7	114	242	74	1135	14.2	30
Dennis Johnson	77	2551	398	861	.462	292	369	.791	92	243	335	388	204	1	97	204	39	1093	14.2	27
Kyle Macy	82	1836	328	634	.517	129	148	.872	41	124	165	278	130	0	64	90	8	808	9.9	25
James Edwards†	16	285	55	113	.487	31	47	.660	19	40	59	27	49	2	5	19	5	141	8.8	17
James Edwards‡	31	667	128	263	.487	69	108	.639	56	99	155	40	110	5	12	49	19	325	10.5	26
Rory White	65	626	127	234	.543	70	109	.642	47	58	105	30	54	0	16	51	2	324	5.0	16
Alvin Scott	81	1139	124	259	.479	81	110	.736	60	164	224	97	133	0	48	64	31	329	4.1	14
David Thirdkill	49	521	74	170	.435	45	78	.577	28	44	72	36	93	1	19	48	4	194	4.0	15
Jeff Cook*	45	551	61	142	.430	41	54	.759	44	85	129	58	89	0	12	56	13	163	3.6	12
Johnny High	82	1155	100	217	.461	63	136	.463	45	105	150	153	205	0	85	106	34	264	3.2	14
Charlie Pittman	28	170	19	40	.475	25	37	.676	13	18	31	7	41	0	2	22	7	63	2.3	10
Joel Kramer	54	458	44	104	.423	14	16	.875	41	47	88	37	63	0	15	22	6	102	1.9	8

3-pt. FG: Phoenix 40-158 (.253)—Davis 7-23 (.304); Nance 1-3 (.333); Lucas 1-3 (.333); Adams 1-3 (.333); Johnson 5-31 (.161); Macy 23-76 (.303); White 0-1 (.000); Scott 0-2 (.000); Thirdkill 1-7 (.143); Cook* 0-2 (.000); High 1-5 (.200); Pittman 0-1 (.000); Kramer 0-1 (.000). Opponents 44-199 (.221).

PORTLAND TRAIL BLAZERS

	G	Min.	FGM	FGA	Pct.	FTM	FTA	Pct.	Off.	Def.	Tot.	Ast.	PF	Dq.	Stl.	TO	Blk.	Pts.	Avg.	Hi.
Jim Paxson	81	2740	682	1323	.515	388	478	.812	68	106	174	231	160	0	140	156	17	1756	21.7	35
Calvin Natt	80	2879	644	1187	.543	339	428	.792	214	385	599	171	184	2	63	203	29	1630	20.4	34
Mychal Thompson	80	3017	505	1033	.489	249	401	.621	183	570	753	380	213	1	68	281	110	1259	15.7	26
Darnell Valentine	47	1298	209	460	.454	169	213	.793	34	83	117	293	139	1	101	131	5	587	12.5	24
Kenny Carr	82	2331	362	717	.505	255	360	.697	182	407	589	116	306	10	62	185	42	981	12.0	28
Wayne Cooper	80	2099	320	723	.443	135	197	.685	214	397	611	116	318	5	27	162	136	775	9.7	23
Fat Lever	81	2020	256	594	.431	116	159	.730	85	140	225	426	179	2	153	137	15	633	7.8	19
Don Buse	41	643	72	182	.396	41	46	.891	19	35	54	115	60	0	44	25	2	194	4.7	20
Linton Townes	55	516	105	234	.449	28	38	.737	30	35	65	31	81	0	19	33	5	247	4.5	20
Jeff Lamp	59	690	107	252	.425	42	52	.808	25	51	76	58	67	0	20	38	3	257	4.4	14
Peter Verhoeven	48	527	87	171	.509	21	31	.677	44	52	96	32	95	2	18	40	9	195	4.1	16
Jeff Judkins	34	309	39	88	.443	25	30	.833	18	25	43	17	39	0	15	17	2	105	3.1	9
Hank McDowell†	42	375	45	97	.464	33	43	.767	39	50	89	20	58	0	6	32	7	123	2.9	11
Hank McDowell‡	56	505	58	126	.460	47	61	.770	54	65	119	24	84	0	8	40	11	163	2.9	12
Audie Norris	30	311	26	63	.413	14	30	.467	25	44	69	24	61	0	13	33	2	66	2.2	8

3-pt. FG: Portland 35-150 (.233)—Paxson 4-25 (.160); Natt 3-20 (.150); Thompson 0-1 (.000); Valentine 0-1 (.000); Carr 2-6 (.333); Cooper 0-5 (.000); Lever 5-15 (.333); Buse 9-35 (.257); Townes 9-25 (.360); Lamp 1-6 (.167); Verhoeven 0-1 (.000); Judkins 2-8 (.250); McDowell† 0-2 (.000); McDowell‡ 0-2 (.000). Opponents 55-188 (.293).

SAN ANTONIO SPURS

	G	Min.	FGM	FGA	Pct.	FTM	FTA	Pct.	Off.	Def.	Tot.	Ast.	PF	Dq.	Stl.	TO	Blk.	Pts.	Avg.	Hi.
George Gervin	78	2830	757	1553	.487	517	606	.853	111	246	357	264	243	5	88	247	67	2043	26.2	47
Mike Mitchell	80	2803	686	1342	.511	219	289	.758	188	349	537	98	248	6	57	126	52	1591	19.9	43
Artis Gilmore	82	2797	556	888	.626	367	496	.740	299	685	984	126	273	4	40	254	192	1479	18.0	40
Gene Banks	81	2722	505	919	.550	196	278	.705	222	390	612	279	229	3	78	171	21	1206	14.9	43
Johnny Moore	77	2552	394	841	.468	148	199	.744	65	212	277	753	247	2	194	226	32	941	12.2	29
Edgar Jones†	28	622	92	185	.497	84	114	.737	56	121	177	20	107	5	14	43	31	268	9.6	25
Edgar Jones‡	77	1658	237	479	.495	201	286	.703	136	312	448	89	267	10	42	146	108	677	8.8	25
Mike Dunleavy	79	1619	213	510	.418	120	154	.779	18	116	134	437	210	1	74	160	4	613	7.8	24
Mike Sanders	26	393	76	157	.484	31	43	.721	31	63	94	19	57	0	18	28	6	183	7.0	16
Bill Willoughby*	52	1062	136	295	.461	41	53	.774	61	129	190	56	123	0	24	56	16	319	6.1	18
Roger Phegley	62	599	120	267	.449	43	56	.768	39	45	84	60	92	0	30	49	8	286	4.6	18
Billy Paultz†	7	125	12	27	.444	1	2	.500	10	23	33	4	14	0	5	6	6	25	3.6	8
Billy Paultz‡	64	820	101	227	.445	27	59	.458	64	136	200	61	109	0	17	47	18	229	3.6	12
Paul Griffin	53	956	60	116	.517	53	76	.697	77	139	216	86	153	0	33	68	25	173	3.3	14
Oliver Robinson	35	147	35	97	.361	30	45	.667	6	11	17	21	18	0	4	13	2	101	2.9	8
Ed Rains	34	292	33	83	.398	29	43	.674	25	19	44	22	35	0	10	25	1	95	2.8	13
Geoff Crompton	14	148	14	34	.412	3	5	.600	18	30	48	7	25	0	3	5	5	31	2.2	8
Robert Smith†	7	25	5	11	.455	2	2	1.000	0	3	3	6	0	0	1	3	0	12	1.7	6
Robert Smith‡	12	68	7	24	.292	9	10	.900	1	5	6	8	13	0	5	6	0	23	1.9	6
James Johnstone*	7	54	2	10	.200	3	5	.600	4	12	16	1	9	0	1	4	1	7	1.0	4
Coby Dietrick	8	34	1	5	.200	0	2	.000	2	6	8	6	0	1	1	0	2	0.3	2

3-pt. FG: San Antonio 94-308 (.305)—Gervin 12-33 (.364); Mitchell 0-3 (.000); Gilmore 0-6 (.000); Banks 0-5 (.000); Moore 5-22 (.227); Jones† 0-3 (.000); Jones‡ 2-9 (.222); Dunleavy 67-194 (.345); Sanders 0-2 (.000); Willoughby* 6-13 (.462); Phegley 3-14 (.214); Robinson 1-11 (.091); Rains 0-1 (.000); Smith† 0-1 (.000); Smith‡ 0-2 (.000). Opponents 51-201 (.254).

SAN DIEGO CLIPPERS

	G	Min.	FGM	FGA	Pct.	FTM	FTA	Pct.	REBOUNDS Off.	Def.	Tot.	Ast.	PF	Dq.	Stl.	TO	Blk.	SCORING Pts.	Avg.	Hi.
Terry Cummings	70	2531	684	1309	.523	292	412	.709	303	441	744	177	294	10	129	204	62	1660	23.7	39
Tom Chambers	79	2665	519	1099	.472	353	488	.723	218	301	519	192	333	15	79	234	57	1391	17.6	37
Bill Walton	33	1099	200	379	.528	65	117	.556	75	248	323	120	113	0	34	105	119	465	14.1	30
Lionel Hollins	56	1844	313	717	.437	129	179	.721	30	98	128	373	155	2	111	198	14	758	13.5	25
Michael Brooks	82	2457	402	830	.484	193	277	.697	239	282	521	262	297	6	112	177	39	1002	12.2	32
Al Wood	76	1822	343	740	.464	124	161	.770	96	140	236	134	188	5	55	111	36	825	10.9	27
Craig Hodges	76	2022	318	704	.452	94	130	.723	53	69	122	275	192	3	82	161	4	750	9.9	24
Randy Smith*	65	1264	244	499	.489	101	117	.863	35	53	88	192	122	1	54	89	0	592	9.1	29
Jerome Whitehead	46	905	164	306	.536	72	87	.828	105	156	261	42	139	2	21	65	15	400	8.7	29
Lowes Moore	37	642	81	190	.426	42	56	.750	15	40	55	73	72	1	22	46	1	210	5.7	19
Joe Cooper†	13	275	31	59	.525	11	20	.550	36	35	71	15	39	0	8	23	19	73	5.6	14
Joe Cooper‡	20	333	37	72	.514	16	29	.552	42	44	86	17	49	0	9	32	20	90	4.5	14
Richard Anderson	78	1274	174	431	.404	48	69	.696	111	161	272	120	170	2	57	93	26	403	5.2	21
Hutch Jones	9	85	17	37	.459	6	6	1.000	10	7	17	4	14	0	3	6	0	40	4.4	12
Jim Brogan	58	466	91	213	.427	34	43	.791	33	29	62	66	79	0	26	43	9	219	3.8	14
Bob Gross	27	373	35	82	.427	12	19	.632	32	34	66	34	69	1	22	24	7	83	3.1	9
Swen Nater	7	51	6	20	.300	4	4	1.000	2	11	13	1	1	0	1	3	0	16	2.3	4
Robert Smith*	5	43	2	13	.154	7	8	.875	1	2	3	6	7	0	4	3	0	11	2.2	6
John Douglas	3	12	1	6	.167	2	2	1.000	0	1	1	1	0	0	0	0	0	5	1.7	3

3-pt. FG: San Diego 64-262 (.244)—Cummings 0-1 (.000); Chambers 0-8 (.000); Hollins 3-21 (.143); Brooks 5-15 (.333); Wood 15-50 (.300); Hodges 20-90 (.222); Ra. Smith* 3-16 (.188); Moore 6-23 (.261); Anderson 7-19 (.368); Brogan 3-13 (.231); Gross 1-3 (.333); Ro. Smith* 0-1 (.000); Douglas 1-2 (.500). Opponents 32-130 (.246).

SEATTLE SUPERSONICS

	G	Min.	FGM	FGA	Pct.	FTM	FTA	Pct.	REBOUNDS Off.	Def.	Tot.	Ast.	PF	Dq.	Stl.	TO	Blk.	SCORING Pts.	Avg.	Hi.
Gus Williams	80	2761	660	1384	.477	278	370	.751	72	133	205	643	117	0	182	230	26	1600	20.0	38
Jack Sikma	75	2564	484	1043	.464	400	478	.837	213	645	858	233	263	4	87	190	65	1368	18.2	31
David Thompson	75	2155	445	925	.481	298	380	.784	96	174	270	222	142	0	47	163	33	1190	15.9	38
Lonnie Shelton	82	2572	437	813	.470	141	187	.764	158	337	495	237	310	8	75	172	72	1016	12.4	23
Fred Brown	80	1432	371	714	.520	58	72	.806	32	65	97	242	98	0	59	110	13	814	10.2	28
James Donaldson	82	1789	289	496	.583	150	218	.688	131	370	501	97	171	1	19	132	101	728	8.9	29
Greg Kelser	80	1507	247	450	.549	173	257	.673	158	245	403	97	243	5	52	149	35	667	8.3	30
Danny Vranes	82	2054	226	429	.527	115	209	.550	177	248	425	120	254	2	53	102	49	567	6.9	21
Phil Smith	79	1238	175	400	.438	101	133	.759	27	103	130	216	113	0	44	102	8	454	5.7	18
Steve Hawes†	31	556	72	146	.493	23	32	.719	28	105	133	36	79	0	9	34	6	170	5.5	16
Steve Hawes‡	77	1416	163	390	.418	69	94	.734	81	280	361	95	189	2	38	107	14	400	5.2	20
Ray Tolbert*	45	712	100	190	.526	24	44	.545	46	105	151	31	97	1	16	51	24	224	5.0	13
Mark Radford	54	439	84	172	.488	30	73	.411	12	35	47	104	78	0	34	74	4	202	3.7	22
John Greig	9	26	7	13	.538	5	6	.833	2	4	6	0	4	0	0	2	1	19	2.1	8

3-pt. FG: Seattle 29-138 (.210)—Williams 2-43 (.047); Sikma 0-8 (.000); Thompson 2-10 (.200); Shelton 1-6 (.167); Brown 14-32 (.438); Kelser 0-3 (.000); Vranes 0-1 (.000); Smith 3-8 (.375); Hawes† 3-7 (.429); Hawes‡ 5-21 (.238); Tolbert* 0-2 (.000); Radford 4-18 (.222). Opponents 49-197 (.249).

UTAH JAZZ

	G	Min.	FGM	FGA	Pct.	FTM	FTA	Pct.	REBOUNDS Off.	Def.	Tot.	Ast.	PF	Dq.	Stl.	TO	Blk.	SCORING Pts.	Avg.	Hi.
Adrian Dantley	22	887	233	402	.580	210	248	.847	58	82	140	105	62	2	20	81	0	676	30.7	57
Darrell Griffith	77	2787	752	1554	.484	167	246	.679	100	204	304	270	184	0	138	252	33	1709	22.2	38
John Drew	44	1206	318	671	.474	296	392	.755	98	137	235	97	152	8	35	135	7	932	21.2	40
Rickey Green	78	2783	464	942	.493	185	232	.797	62	161	223	697	154	0	220	222	4	1115	14.3	28
Dan Schayes*	50	1638	231	514	.449	157	195	.805	137	312	449	165	216	7	39	195	68	619	12.4	28
Jeff Wilkins	81	2307	389	816	.477	156	200	.780	154	442	596	132	251	4	41	186	42	934	11.5	35
Ben Poquette	75	2331	329	697	.472	166	221	.751	155	366	521	168	264	5	64	100	116	825	11.0	30
Jerry Eaves	82	1588	280	575	.487	200	247	.810	34	88	122	210	116	0	51	152	3	761	9.3	35
Mitchell Anderson†	52	1154	182	357	.510	99	172	.576	115	167	282	66	147	1	62	74	21	463	8.9	21
Mitchell Anderson‡	65	1202	190	379	.501	100	175	.571	119	175	294	67	153	1	63	79	21	480	7.4	21
Rich Kelley†	32	780	71	152	.467	87	105	.829	70	162	232	79	106	1	33	65	21	229	7.2	18
Rich Kelley‡	70	1345	130	293	.444	142	175	.811	131	273	404	138	221	4	54	118	39	402	5.7	18
Freeman Williams	18	210	36	101	.356	18	25	.720	3	14	17	10	30	0	6	12	1	92	5.1	23
Mark Eaton	81	1528	146	353	.414	59	90	.656	86	376	462	112	257	6	24	140	275	351	4.3	16
Kenny Natt	22	210	38	73	.521	9	14	.643	6	16	22	28	36	0	5	22	0	85	3.9	16
Rickey Williams	44	346	56	135	.415	35	53	.660	15	23	38	37	42	0	20	38	4	147	3.3	13

3-pt. FG: Utah 44-183 (.240)—Griffith 38-132 (.288); Drew 0-5 (.000); Green 2-13 (.154); Schayes* 0-1 (.000); Wilkins 0-3 (.000); Poquette 1-5 (.200); Eaves 1-8 (.125); Anderson† 0-3 (.000); Anderson‡ 0-4 (.000); F. Williams 2-7 (.286); Eaton 0-1 (.000); Natt 0-2 (.000); R. Williams 0-3 (.000). Opponents 48-199 (.241).

WASHINGTON BULLETS

	G	Min.	FGM	FGA	Pct.	FTM	FTA	Pct.	REBOUNDS Off.	Def.	Tot.	Ast.	PF	Dq.	Stl.	TO	Blk.	SCORING Pts.	Avg.	Hi.
Jeff Ruland	79	2862	580	1051	.552	375	544	.689	293	578	871	234	312	12	74	297	77	1536	19.4	37
Greg Ballard	78	2840	603	1274	.473	182	233	.781	123	385	508	262	176	2	135	157	25	1401	18.0	37
Ricky Sobers	41	1438	234	534	.438	154	185	.832	35	67	102	218	158	3	61	147	14	645	15.7	29
Frank Johnson	68	2324	321	786	.408	196	261	.751	46	132	178	549	170	1	110	238	6	852	12.5	36
Don Collins	65	1575	332	635	.523	101	136	.743	116	94	210	132	166	1	87	146	30	765	11.8	31
Rick Mahorn	82	3023	376	768	.490	146	254	.575	171	608	779	115	335	13	86	170	148	898	11.0	27
Spencer Haywood	38	775	125	312	.401	63	87	.724	77	106	183	30	94	2	12	67	27	313	8.2	21
Billy Ray Bates*	15	277	53	129	.411	10	20	.500	10	8	18	14	18	0	13	12	3	118	7.9	17
Charlie Davis	74	1161	251	534	.470	56	89	.629	83	130	213	73	122	0	32	91	22	560	7.6	33
Kevin Grevey	41	756	114	294	.388	54	69	.783	18	31	49	49	61	0	18	27	7	297	7.2	24
Kevin Porter	11	210	21	40	.525	5	6	.833	2	3	5	46	30	0	10	21	0	47	4.3	7
John Lucas	35	386	62	131	.473	21	42	.500	8	21	29	102	18	0	25	47	1	145	4.1	14
John Cox	7	78	13	37	.351	3	6	.500	7	3	10	6	16	0	0	9	1	29	4.1	10
Bryan Warrick	43	727	65	171	.380	42	57	.737	15	54	69	126	103	5	21	71	8	172	4.0	14
Joe Kopicki	17	201	23	51	.451	21	25	.840	18	44	62	9	21	0	9	8	2	67	3.9	16
Dave Batton	54	558	85	191	.445	8	17	.471	45	74	119	29	56	0	15	28	13	178	3.3	15
Joe Cooper*	5	47	5	9	.556	5	9	.556	4	9	13	2	7	0	0	6	0	15	3.0	5
Carlos Terry	55	514	39	106	.368	10	15	.667	27	72	99	46	79	1	24	20	13	88	1.6	15
Steve Lingenfelter	7	53	4	6	.667	0	4	.000	1	11	12	4	16	1	1	5	3	8	1.1	4

3-pt. FG: Washington 70-237 (.295)—Ruland 1-3 (.333); Ballard 13-37 (.351); Sobers 23-55 (.418); Johnson 14-61 (.230); Collins 0-6 (.000); Mahorn 0-3 (.000); Haywood 0-1 (.000); Bates* 2-5 (.400); Davis 2-10 (.200); Grevey 15-38 (.395); Lucas 0-5 (.000); Cox 0-2 (.000); Warrick 0-5 (.000); Kopicki 0-1 (.000); Batton 0-3 (.000); Terry 0-2 (.000). Opponents 37-163 (.227).

* Finished season with another team. † Totals with this team only. ‡ Totals with all teams.

PLAYOFF RESULTS

EASTERN CONFERENCE

FIRST ROUND
New York 2, New Jersey 0
| Apr. 20—Wed. | New York 118 at New Jersey | . . . . .107 |
| Apr. 21—Thur. | New Jersey 99 at New York | . . . . .105 |

Boston 2, Atlanta 1
Apr. 19—Tue.	Atlanta 95 at Boston	103
Apr. 22—Fri.	Boston 93 at Atlanta	95
Apr. 24—Sun.	Atlanta 79 at Boston	98

SEMIFINALS
Philadelphia 4, New York 0
Apr. 24—Sun.	New York 102 at Philadelphia	112
Apr. 27—Wed.	New York 91 at Philadelphia	98
Apr. 30—Sat.	Philadelphia 107 at New York	105
May 1—Sun.	Philadelphia 105 at New York	102

Milwaukee 4, Boston 0
Apr. 27—Wed.	Milwaukee 116 at Boston	95
Apr. 29—Fri.	Milwaukee 95 at Boston	91
May 1—Sun.	Boston 99 at Milwaukee	107
May 2—Mon.	Boston 93 at Milwaukee	107

FINALS
Philadelphia 4, Milwaukee 1
May 8—Sun.	Milwaukee 109 at Philadelphia	. . . .*111
May 11—Wed.	Milwaukee 81 at Philadelphia	87
May 14—Sat.	Philadelphia 104 at Milwaukee	96
May 15—Sun.	Philadelphia 94 at Milwaukee	100
May 18—Wed.	Milwaukee 103 at Philadelphia	115

WESTERN CONFERENCE

FIRST ROUND
Portland 2, Seattle 0
| Apr. 20—Wed. | Portland 108 at Seattle | . . . . .97 |
| Apr. 22—Fri. | Seattle 96 at Portland | . . . . .105 |

Denver 2, Phoenix 1
Apr. 19—Tue.	Denver 108 at Phoenix	121
Apr. 21—Thur.	Phoenix 99 at Denver	113
Apr. 24—Sun.	Denver 117 at Phoenix	. . . .*112

SEMIFINALS
Los Angeles 4, Portland 1
Apr. 24—Sun.	Portland 97 at Los Angeles	118
Apr. 26—Tue.	Portland 106 at Los Angeles	112
Apr. 29—Fri.	Los Angeles 115 at Portland	. . . .*109
May 1—Sun.	Los Angeles 95 at Portland	108
May 3—Tue.	Portland 108 at Los Angeles	116

San Antonio 4, Denver 1
Apr. 26—Tue.	Denver 133 at San Antonio	152
Apr. 27—Wed.	Denver 109 at San Antonio	126
Apr. 29—Fri.	San Antonio 127 at Denver	. . . .*126
May 2—Mon.	San Antonio 114 at Denver	124
May 4—Wed.	Denver 105 at San Antonio	145

FINALS
Los Angeles 4, San Antonio 2
May 8—Sun.	San Antonio 107 at Los Angeles	119
May 10—Tue.	San Antonio 122 at Los Angeles	113
May 13—Fri.	Los Angeles 113 at San Antonio	100
May 15—Sun.	Los Angeles 129 at San Antonio	121
May 18—Wed.	San Antonio 117 at Los Angeles	112
May 20—Fri.	Los Angeles 101 at San Antonio	100

NBA FINALS
Philadelphia 4, Los Angeles 0
May 22—Sun.	Los Angeles 107 at Philadelphia	113
May 26—Thur.	Los Angeles 93 at Philadelphia	103
May 29—Sun.	Philadelphia 111 at Los Angeles	94
May 31—Tue.	Philadelphia 115 at Los Angeles	108

*Denotes number of overtime periods.

1981-82

1981-82 NBA CHAMPION LOS ANGELES LAKERS

Front row (from left): owner Dr. Jerry Buss, Jim Brewer, Kurt Rambis, Jamaal Wilkes, Kareem Abdul-Jabbar, Michael Cooper, Norm Nixon, Magic Johnson, general manager Bill Sharman. Back row (from left): head coach Pat Riley, assistant coach Bill Bertka, Eddie Jordan, Kevin McKenna, Mitch Kupchak, Bob McAdoo, Mark Landsberger, Mike McGee, assistant coach Mike Thibault, trainer Jack Curran.

FINAL STANDINGS

ATLANTIC DIVISION

	Atl.	Bos.	Chi.	Cle.	Dal.	Den.	Det.	G.S.	Hou.	Ind.	K.C.	L.A.	Mil.	N.J.	N.Y.	Phi.	Pho.	Por.	S.A.	S.D.	Sea.	Uta.	Was.	W	L	Pct.	GB
Boston 5	..	4	5	2	1	6	1	1	4	2	1	3	5	5	4	1	1	2	2	0	2	6		63	19	.768	..
Philadelphia ..3	2	5	5	2	1	3	2	1	6	2	1	2	3	5	..	1	2	0	2	2	6			58	24	.707	5
New Jersey ..2	1	4	6	0	1	4	1	1	2	1	1	..	4	3	2	1	1	2	0	2	4	44		38	.537	19
Washington ..4	0	4	5	1	0	4	1	0	5	2	0	2	2	5	0	1	2	1	2	1	1	..	43	39	.524	20
New York 1	1	2	6	1	1	3	1	1	2	0	2	3	2	..	1	0	1	0	2	0	2	1	33	49	.402	30

CENTRAL DIVISION

	Atl.	Bos.	Chi.	Cle.	Dal.	Den.	Det.	G.S.	Hou.	Ind.	K.C.	L.A.	Mil.	N.J.	N.Y.	Phi.	Pho.	Por.	S.A.	S.D.	Sea.	Uta.	Was.	W	L	Pct.	GB
Milwaukee ...3	3	5	6	1	1	4	0	1	6	1	2	..	4	3	4	1	2	1	2	0	2	3	55	27	.671	..
Atlanta	1	2	4	1	1	2	0	2	4	1	0	3	3	5	3	1	2	1	1	1	2	2	42	40	.512	13
Detroit 4	0	6	5	1	1	..	2	2	2	2	0	2	2	3	2	0	0	0	2	1	1	1	39	43	.476	16
Indiana 2	1	3	5	1	2	4	0	0	..	1	0	0	4	3	0	1	1	2	2	1	1	1	35	47	.427	20
Chicago 3	2	..	5	1	0	0	1	3	1	2	1	2	3	1	0	1	0	1	2	1	1	2	34	48	.415	21
Cleveland 2	0	1	..	2	0	1	1	1	1	1	0	0	0	0	0	0	1	0	1	0	2	1	15	67	.183	40

MIDWEST DIVISION

	Atl.	Bos.	Chi.	Cle.	Dal.	Den.	Det.	G.S.	Hou.	Ind.	K.C.	L.A.	Mil.	N.J.	N.Y.	Phi.	Pho.	Por.	S.A.	S.D.	Sea.	Uta.	Was.	W	L	Pct.	GB
San Antonio ..1	0	1	2	5	4	2	2	3	0	5	3	1	1	2	2	1	2	..	3	4	3	1	48	34	.585	..
Denver 1	1	1	2	5	..	1	3	5	0	4	1	1	1	1	1	2	2	2	5	2	3	2	46	36	.561	2
Houston 0	1	1	4	1	0	4	..	2	3	1	1	1	1	1	3	4	3	4	2	6	2	46	36	.561	2
Kansas City ..1	0	1	1	2	2	0	2	3	1	..	1	1	1	2	0	2	0	1	4	2	3	0	30	52	.366	18
Dallas 1	0	1	0	..	1	1	0	2	1	4	1	1	2	1	0	2	2	1	2	1	3	1	28	54	.341	20
Utah 0	0	1	0	3	3	1	2	0	1	3	0	0	0	0	0	2	1	3	4	0	..	1	25	57	.305	23

PACIFIC DIVISION

	Atl.	Bos.	Chi.	Cle.	Dal.	Den.	Det.	G.S.	Hou.	Ind.	K.C.	L.A.	Mil.	N.J.	N.Y.	Phi.	Pho.	Por.	S.A.	S.D.	Sea.	Uta.	Was.	W	L	Pct.	GB
Los Angeles ..2	1	0	2	4	4	2	3	4	2	4	..	0	1	0	1	4	5	2	5	4	5	2	57	25	.695	..
Seattle 1	2	1	2	4	3	1	5	3	1	3	2	2	2	2	0	3	3	1	5	..	5	1	52	30	.634	5
Phoenix 1	1	2	2	3	3	2	2	2	1	3	2	1	0	2	1	..	3	4	4	3	3	1	46	36	.561	11
Golden State ..2	1	2	1	5	2	0	..	1	2	3	3	2	1	0	4	2	3	5	1	3	1	45	37	.549	12
Portland 0	1	1	3	3	2	4	1	1	5	1	0	1	1	0	3	..	3	4	3	4	0	42	40	.512	15
San Diego ...1	0	0	1	3	0	0	1	1	0	1	1	0	0	0	0	2	2	2	..	1	1	0	17	65	.207	40

TEAM STATISTICS

OFFENSIVE

	G	FGM	FGA	Pct.	FTM	FTA	Pct.	REBOUNDS Off.	Def.	Tot.	Ast.	PF	Dq.	Stl.	TO	Blk.	SCORING Pts.	Avg.
Denver	82	3980	7656	.520	2371	2978	.796	1149	2443	3592	2272	2131	18	664	1470	368	10371	126.5
Los Angeles	82	3919	7585	.517	1549	2161	.717	1258	2505	3763	2356	1999	11	848	1468	517	9400	114.6
San Antonio	82	3698	7613	.486	1812	2335	.776	1253	2537	3790	2257	2217	28	600	1293	555	9272	113.1
Boston	82	3657	7334	.499	1817	2457	.740	1253	2489	3742	2126	2014	21	652	1452	568	9180	112.0
Philadelphia	82	3616	6974	.518	1846	2471	.747	1031	2389	3420	2264	2183	18	856	1474	622	9119	111.2
Detroit	82	3561	7391	.482	1938	2581	.751	1298	2345	3643	2027	2160	16	741	1629	564	9112	111.1
Utah	82	3679	7446	.494	1714	2282	.751	1147	2362	3509	1895	2196	20	700	1435	357	9094	110.9
Golden State	82	3646	7349	.496	1709	2382	.717	1282	2452	3734	1820	2225	32	685	1424	391	9092	110.9
Portland	82	3629	7187	.505	1719	2387	.720	1142	2355	3497	2054	2012	22	706	1390	367	9006	109.8
San Diego	82	3552	7101	.500	1693	2341	.723	1131	2196	3327	1878	2353	58	636	1570	299	8896	108.5
Milwaukee	82	3544	7015	.505	1753	2329	.753	1167	2415	3582	2233	2281	30	763	1589	455	8890	108.4
Seattle	82	3505	7178	.488	1747	2362	.740	1103	2544	3647	2103	2057	26	691	1351	460	8795	107.3
Kansas City	82	3604	7284	.495	1551	2158	.719	1086	2276	3362	2056	2359	50	743	1507	402	8785	107.1
New Jersey	82	3501	7227	.484	1714	2354	.728	1194	2320	3514	2096	2295	33	918	1650	481	8746	106.7
Chicago	82	3369	6728	.501	1951	2545	.767	1125	2525	3650	2043	2008	16	580	1636	483	8743	106.6
New York	82	3523	7178	.491	1603	2171	.738	1168	2273	3441	2075	2195	18	719	1486	337	8707	106.2
Phoenix	82	3508	7140	.491	1635	2157	.758	1123	2517	3640	2223	2029	34	753	1528	429	8705	106.2
Houston	82	3504	7366	.476	1622	2225	.729	1403	2284	3687	1977	1871	9	648	1321	429	8680	105.9
Dallas	82	3390	7224	.469	1740	2366	.735	1213	2228	3441	2117	2193	40	566	1317	313	8575	104.6
Washington	82	3400	7168	.474	1626	2105	.772	1047	2583	3630	1983	2072	32	643	1390	397	8485	103.6
Cleveland	82	3405	7334	.464	1628	2179	.747	1190	2170	3360	1871	2193	35	634	1319	357	8463	103.2
Indiana	82	3332	7164	.465	1612	2176	.741	1141	2372	3513	1897	2041	23	753	1393	494	8379	102.2
Atlanta	82	3210	6776	.474	1833	2387	.768	1135	2368	3503	1815	2268	29	608	1343	485	8281	101.0

DEFENSIVE

	FGM	FGA	Pct.	FTM	FTA	Pct.	REBOUNDS Off.	Def.	Tot.	Ast.	PF	Dq.	Stl.	TO	Blk.	SCORING Pts.	Avg.	Dif.
Atlanta	3150	6709	.470	1891	2482	.762	1135	2388	3523	1871	2179	21	578	1444	434	8237	100.5	+0.5
Washington	3362	7229	.465	1645	2237	.735	1110	2516	3626	1889	1907	18	624	1325	543	8413	102.6	+1.0
Phoenix	3350	7186	.466	1671	2215	.754	1158	2366	3524	1949	2064	18	775	1391	360	8422	102.7	+3.5
Milwaukee	3297	7066	.467	1790	2470	.725	1172	2155	3327	2016	2189	25	720	1538	350	8441	102.9	+5.5
Seattle	3411	7407	.461	1586	2183	.727	1241	2420	3661	1994	2150	26	660	1405	311	8456	103.1	+4.2
Indiana	3470	7062	.491	1558	2133	.730	1204	2598	3802	2053	2016	14	678	1517	397	8532	104.0	-1.8
Philadelphia	3371	7083	.476	1852	2496	.742	1289	2344	3633	1965	2216	44	702	1615	470	8649	105.5	+5.7
Boston	3490	7429	.470	1638	2172	.754	1193	2247	3440	1972	2240	31	681	1432	367	8657	105.6	+6.4
Houston	3566	7180	.497	1503	2011	.747	1170	2304	3474	2128	2047	36	678	1341	353	8683	105.9	.0
New Jersey	3343	6934	.482	1946	2597	.749	1142	2346	3488	1931	2164	22	832	1809	539	8690	106.0	+0.7
Chicago	3659	7388	.495	1533	2053	.747	1134	2225	3359	2043	2220	25	807	1257	469	8909	108.6	-2.0
New York	3541	7018	.505	1793	2369	.757	1125	2366	3491	2089	2017	27	703	1462	358	8926	108.9	-2.7
Dallas	3530	6953	.508	1847	2491	.741	1108	2361	3469	1984	2243	23	643	1370	509	8938	109.0	-4.4
Portland	3637	7293	.499	1629	2149	.758	1221	2367	3588	2114	2142	31	708	1452	427	8957	109.2	+0.6
Los Angeles	3745	7679	.488	1433	2008	.714	1275	2255	3530	2319	2004	25	718	1483	435	9001	109.8	+4.8
Golden State	3555	7250	.490	1857	2466	.753	1112	2407	3519	2079	2156	26	661	1368	393	9007	109.8	+1.1
Kansas City	3493	6984	.500	2005	2653	.756	1171	2552	3723	1853	2136	30	707	1609	450	9039	110.2	-3.1
San Antonio	3566	7385	.483	1893	2497	.758	1151	2434	3585	2036	2179	30	611	1352	429	9083	110.8	+2.3
Cleveland	3608	7044	.512	1906	2529	.754	1125	2529	3654	2169	2071	17	655	1405	480	9161	111.7	-8.5
Detroit	3749	7362	.509	1648	2211	.745	1159	2434	3593	2191	2383	40	782	1637	581	9187	112.0	-0.9
San Diego	3739	7105	.526	1988	2647	.751	1033	2276	3309	2129	2124	19	772	1334	487	9502	115.9	-7.4
Utah	3835	7530	.509	1837	2466	.745	1253	2599	3852	2148	2052	23	663	1413	420	9558	116.6	-5.7
Denver	4265	8142	.524	1734	2354	.737	1358	2459	3817	2516	2453	48	749	1476	569	10328	126.0	+0.5
Avgs.	3554	7236	.491	1747	2343	.746	1176	2389	3565	2063	2146	27	700	1454	440	8904	108.6	...

HOME/ROAD

	Home	Road	Total		Home	Road	Total
Atlanta	24-17	18-23	42-40	New Jersey	25-16	19-22	44-38
Boston	35-6	28-13	63-19	New York	19-22	14-27	33-49
Chicago	22-19	12-29	34-48	Philadelphia	32-9	26-15	58-24
Cleveland	9-32	6-35	15-67	Phoenix	31-10	15-26	46-36
Dallas	16-25	12-29	28-54	Portland	27-14	15-26	42-40
Denver	29-12	17-24	46-36	San Antonio	29-12	19-22	48-34
Detroit	23-18	16-25	39-43	San Diego	11-30	6-35	17-65
Golden State	28-13	17-24	45-37	Seattle	31-10	21-20	52-30
Houston	25-16	21-20	46-36	Utah	18-23	7-34	25-57
Indiana	25-16	10-31	35-47	Washington	22-19	21-20	43-39
Kansas City	23-18	7-34	30-52	Totals	565-378	378-565	943-943
Los Angeles	30-11	27-14	57-25				
Milwaukee	31-10	24-17	55-27				

1981-82

POINTS
(minimum 70 games or 1,400 points)

	G	FGM	FTM	Pts.	Avg.		G	FGM	FTM	Pts.	Avg.
George Gervin, San Antonio	79	993	555	2551	32.3	Larry Bird, Boston	77	711	328	1761	22.9
Moses Malone, Houston	81	945	630	2520	31.1	John Long, Detroit	69	637	238	1514	21.9
Adrian Dantley, Utah	81	904	648	2457	30.3	Kelly Tripucka, Detroit	82	636	495	1772	21.6
Alex English, Denver	82	855	372	2082	25.4	Kiki Vandeweghe, Denver	82	706	347	1760	21.5
Julius Erving, Philadelphia	81	780	411	1974	24.4	Jay Vincent, Dallas	81	719	293	1732	21.4
Kareem Abdul-Jabbar, L.A.	76	753	312	1818	23.9	Jamaal Wilkes, Los Angeles	82	744	246	1734	21.1
Gus Williams, Seattle	80	773	320	1875	23.4	Mychal Thompson, Portland	79	681	280	1642	20.8
Bernard King, Golden State	79	740	352	1833	23.2	Mike Mitchell, Cleveland-S.A.	84	753	220	1726	20.5
Dan Issel, Denver	81	651	546	1852	22.9	Ray Williams, New Jersey	82	639	387	1674	20.4
World B. Free, Golden State	78	650	479	1789	22.9	Robert Parish, Boston	80	669	252	1590	19.9

FIELD GOALS
(minimum 300 made)

	FGM	FGA	Pct.		FGM	FGA	Pct.
Artis Gilmore, Chicago	546	837	.652	Adrian Dantley, Utah	904	1586	.570
Steve Johnson, Kansas City	395	644	.613	Bernard King, Golden State	740	1307	.566
Buck Williams, New Jersey	513	881	.582	Bobby Jones, Philadelphia	416	737	.564
Kareem Abdul-Jabbar, Los Angeles	753	1301	.579	Bill Cartwright, New York	390	694	.562
Calvin Natt, Portland	515	894	.576	Jeff Ruland, Washington	420	749	.561

FREE THROWS
(minimum 125 made)

	FTM	FTA	Pct.
Kyle Macy, Phoenix	152	169	.899
Charlie Criss, Atlanta-San Diego	141	159	.887
John Long, Detroit	238	275	.865
George Gervin, San Antonio	555	642	.864
Larry Bird, Boston	328	380	.863
James Silas, Cleveland	246	286	.860
Kiki Vandeweghe, Denver	347	405	.857
Mike Newlin, New York	126	147	.857
Jack Sikma, Seattle	447	523	.855
Kevin Grevey, Washington	165	193	.855

STEALS
(minimum 70 games or 125 steals)

	G	No.	Avg.
Magic Johnson, Los Angeles	78	208	2.67
Maurice Cheeks, Philadelphia	79	209	2.65
Micheal Ray Richardson, New York	82	213	2.60
Quinn Buckner, Milwaukee	70	174	2.49
Ray Williams, New Jersey	82	199	2.43
Rickey Green, Utah	81	185	2.28
Gus Williams, Seattle	80	172	2.15
Isiah Thomas, Detroit	72	150	2.08
Johnny Moore, San Antonio	70	163	2.06
Don Buse, Indiana	82	164	2.00

ASSISTS
(minimum 70 games or 400 assists)

	G	No.	Avg.
Johnny Moore, San Antonio	79	762	9.7
Magic Johnson, Los Angeles	78	743	9.5
Maurice Cheeks, Philadelphia	79	667	8.4
Nate Archibald, Boston	68	541	8.0
Norm Nixon, Los Angeles	82	652	8.0
Isiah Thomas, Detroit	72	565	7.9
Rickey Green, Utah	81	630	7.8
Geoff Huston, Cleveland	78	590	7.6
Kelvin Ransey, Portland	78	555	7.1
Micheal Ray Richardson, New York	82	572	7.0

BLOCKED SHOTS
(minimum 70 games or 100 blocked shots)

	G	No.	Avg.
George Johnson, San Antonio	75	234	3.12
Tree Rollins, Atlanta	79	224	2.84
Kareem Abdul-Jabbar, Los Angeles	76	207	2.72
Artis Gilmore, Chicago	82	221	2.70
Robert Parish, Boston	80	192	2.40
Kevin McHale, Boston	82	185	2.26
Herb Williams, Indiana	82	178	2.17
Terry Tyler, Detroit	82	160	1.95
Caldwell Jones, Philadelphia	81	146	1.80
Julius Erving, Philadelphia	81	141	1.74

REBOUNDS
(minimum 70 games or 800 rebounds)

	G	Off.	Def.	Tot.	Avg.
Moses Malone, Houston	81	558	630	1188	14.7
Jack Sikma, Seattle	82	223	815	1038	12.7
Buck Williams, New Jersey	82	347	658	1005	12.3
Mychal Thompson, Portland	79	258	663	921	11.7
Maurice Lucas, New York	80	274	629	903	11.3
Larry Smith, Golden State	74	279	534	813	11.0
Larry Bird, Boston	77	200	637	837	10.9
Robert Parish, Boston	80	288	578	866	10.8
Artis Gilmore, Chicago	82	224	611	835	10.2
Truck Robinson, Phoenix	74	202	519	721	9.7

3-POINT FIELD GOALS
(minimum 25 made)

	FGA	FGM	Pct.
Campy Russell, New York	57	25	.439
Andrew Toney, Philadelphia	59	25	.424
Kyle Macy, Phoenix	100	39	.390
Brian Winters, Milwaukee	93	36	.387
Don Buse, Indiana	189	73	.386
Mike Dunleavy, Houston	86	33	.384
Mark Aguirre, Dallas	71	25	.352
Kevin Grevey, Washington	82	28	.341
Mike Bratz, San Antonio	138	46	.333
Joe Hassett, Golden State	214	71	.332

(vertical text: 1981-82)

INDIVIDUAL STATISTICS, TEAM BY TEAM

ATLANTA HAWKS

	G	Min.	FGM	FGA	Pct.	FTM	FTA	Pct.	REBOUNDS Off.	Def.	Tot.	Ast.	PF	Dq.	Stl.	TO	Blk.	SCORING Pts.	Avg.	Hi.
Dan Roundfield	61	2217	424	910	.466	285	375	.760	227	494	721	162	210	3	64	183	93	1134	18.6	35
John Drew	70	2040	465	957	.486	364	491	.741	169	206	375	96	250	6	64	178	3	1298	18.5	35

	G	Min.	FGM	FGA	Pct.	FTM	FTA	Pct.	Off.	Def.	Tot.	Ast.	PF	Dq.	Stl.	TO	Blk.	Pts.	Avg.	Hi.
Eddie Johnson	68	2314	455	1011	.450	294	385	.764	63	128	191	358	188	1	102	186	16	1211	17.8	35
Rory Sparrow	82	2610	366	730	.501	124	148	.838	53	171	224	424	240	2	87	145	13	857	10.5	22
Tom McMillen	73	1792	291	572	.509	140	170	.824	102	234	336	129	202	1	25	124	24	723	9.9	26
Steve Hawes	49	1317	178	370	.481	96	126	.762	89	231	320	142	156	4	36	87	34	456	9.3	19
Charlie Criss*	27	552	84	210	.400	65	73	.890	6	32	38	75	40	0	23	30	2	235	8.7	31
Mike Glenn	49	833	158	291	.543	59	67	.881	5	56	61	87	80	0	26	27	3	376	7.7	26
Rudy Macklin	79	1516	210	484	.434	134	173	.775	113	150	263	47	225	5	40	112	20	554	7.0	30
Wes Matthews	47	837	131	298	.440	60	79	.759	19	39	58	139	129	3	53	63	2	324	6.9	27
Jim McElroy	20	349	52	125	.416	29	36	.806	6	11	17	39	44	0	8	22	3	134	6.7	16
Tree Rollins	79	2018	202	346	.584	79	129	.612	168	443	611	59	285	4	35	79	224	483	6.1	26
Freeman Williams†	23	189	42	110	.382	22	26	.846	2	10	12	19	18	0	6	18	0	110	4.8	15
Freeman Williams‡	60	997	276	623	.443	140	166	.843	23	39	62	86	103	1	29	107	0	720	12.0	32
Al Wood*	19	238	36	105	.343	20	28	.714	22	22	44	11	34	0	9	11	1	92	4.8	17
Sam Pellom	69	1037	114	251	.454	61	79	.772	90	139	229	28	164	0	29	57	47	289	4.2	17
Craig Shelton	4	21	2	6	.333	1	2	.500	1	2	3	0	3	0	1	0	0	5	1.3	4

3-pt. FG: Atlanta 28-128 (.219)—Roundfield 1-5 (.200); Drew 4-12 (.333); Johnson 7-30 (.233); Sparrow 1-15 (.067); McMillen 1-3 (.333); Hawes 4-10 (.400); Criss* 2-8 (.250); Glenn 1-2 (.500); Macklin 0-3 (.000); Matthews 2-8 (.250); McElroy 1-5 (.200); Williams† 4-20 (.200); Williams‡ 28-94 (.298); Wood* 0-6 (.000); Pellom 0-1 (.000). Opponents 46-186 (.247).

BOSTON CELTICS

	G	Min.	FGM	FGA	Pct.	FTM	FTA	Pct.	Off.	Def.	Tot.	Ast.	PF	Dq.	Stl.	TO	Blk.	Pts.	Avg.	Hi.
Larry Bird	77	2923	711	1414	.503	328	380	.863	200	637	837	447	244	0	143	254	66	1761	22.9	40
Robert Parish	80	2534	669	1235	.542	252	355	.710	288	578	866	140	267	5	68	221	192	1590	19.9	37
Cedric Maxwell	78	2590	397	724	.548	357	478	.747	218	281	499	183	263	6	79	174	49	1151	14.8	31
Kevin McHale	82	2332	465	875	.531	187	248	.754	191	365	556	91	264	1	30	137	185	1117	13.6	28
Nate Archibald	68	2167	308	652	.472	236	316	.747	25	91	116	541	131	1	52	178	3	858	12.6	26
Gerald Henderson	82	1844	353	705	.501	125	172	.727	47	105	152	252	199	3	82	150	11	833	10.2	27
M.L. Carr	56	1296	184	409	.450	82	116	.707	56	94	150	128	136	2	67	63	21	455	8.1	22
Rick Robey	80	1186	185	375	.493	84	157	.535	114	181	295	68	183	2	27	92	14	454	5.7	17
Chris Ford	76	1591	188	450	.418	39	56	.696	52	56	108	142	143	0	42	52	10	435	5.7	15
Danny Ainge	53	564	79	221	.357	56	65	.862	25	31	56	87	86	1	37	53	3	219	4.1	17
Terry Duerod	21	146	34	77	.442	4	12	.333	6	9	15	12	9	0	3	2	1	72	3.4	12
Charles Bradley	51	339	55	122	.451	42	62	.677	12	26	38	22	61	0	14	37	6	152	3.0	10
Tracy Jackson*	11	66	10	26	.385	6	10	.600	7	5	12	5	5	0	3	6	0	26	2.4	4
Eric Fernsten	43	202	19	49	.388	19	30	.633	12	30	42	8	23	0	5	13	7	57	1.3	6

3-pt. FG: Boston 49-184 (.266)—Bird 11-52 (.212); Maxwell 0-3 (.000); Archibald 6-16 (.375); Henderson 2-12 (.167); Carr 5-17 (.294); Robey 0-2 (.000); Ford 20-63 (.317); Ainge 5-17 (.294); Duerod 0-1 (.000); Bradley 0-1 (.000). Opponents 39-203 (.192).

CHICAGO BULLS

	G	Min.	FGM	FGA	Pct.	FTM	FTA	Pct.	Off.	Def.	Tot.	Ast.	PF	Dq.	Stl.	TO	Blk.	Pts.	Avg.	Hi.
Artis Gilmore	82	2796	546	837	.652	424	552	.768	224	611	835	136	287	4	49	227	221	1517	18.5	39
Reggie Theus	82	2838	560	1194	.469	363	449	.808	115	197	312	476	243	1	87	277	16	1508	18.4	36
David Greenwood	82	2914	480	1014	.473	240	291	.825	192	594	786	262	292	1	70	180	92	1200	14.6	35
Ricky Sobers	80	1938	363	801	.453	195	254	.768	37	105	142	301	238	6	73	217	18	940	11.8	28
Ronnie Lester	75	2252	329	657	.501	208	256	.813	75	138	213	362	158	2	80	185	14	870	11.6	27
Dwight Jones	78	2040	303	572	.530	172	238	.723	156	351	507	114	217	0	49	155	36	779	10.0	21
Orlando Woolridge	75	1188	202	394	.513	144	206	.699	82	145	227	81	152	1	23	107	24	548	7.3	24
Larry Kenon	60	1036	192	412	.466	50	88	.568	72	108	180	65	71	0	30	82	7	434	7.2	22
James Wilkes	57	862	128	266	.481	58	80	.725	62	97	159	64	112	0	30	62	18	314	5.5	20
Ray Blume	49	546	102	222	.459	18	28	.643	14	27	41	68	57	0	23	54	2	226	4.6	18
Tracy Jackson†	38	412	69	146	.473	32	39	.821	28	23	51	22	43	0	11	18	3	170	4.5	17
Tracy Jackson‡	49	478	79	172	.459	38	49	.776	35	28	63	27	48	0	14	24	3	196	4.0	17
Jackie Robinson	3	29	3	9	.333	4	4	1.000	3	0	3	0	1	0	0	1	0	10	3.3	6
Coby Dietrick	74	999	92	200	.460	38	54	.704	63	125	188	87	131	1	49	44	30	222	3.0	12
Roger Burkman	6	30	0	4	.000	5	6	.833	2	4	6	5	6	0	6	3	2	5	0.8	2

3-pt. FG: Chicago 54-213 (.254)—Gilmore 1-1 (1.000); Theus 25-100 (.250); Greenwood 0-3 (.000); Sobers 19-76 (.250); Lester 4-8 (.500); Jones 1-1 (1.000); Woolridge 0-3 (.000); Wilkes 0-1 (.000); Blume 0-1 (.222); Dietrick 0-1 (.000); Burkman 0-1 (.000). Opponents 58-194 (.299).

CLEVELAND CAVALIERS

	G	Min.	FGM	FGA	Pct.	FTM	FTA	Pct.	Off.	Def.	Tot.	Ast.	PF	Dq.	Stl.	TO	Blk.	Pts.	Avg.	Hi.
Mike Mitchell*	27	973	229	504	.454	72	100	.720	71	70	141	39	77	0	27	55	15	530	19.6	36
Ron Brewer†	47	1724	387	833	.465	134	172	.779	42	69	111	121	114	0	59	91	23	913	19.4	32
Ron Brewer‡	72	2319	569	1194	.477	211	260	.812	55	106	161	188	151	0	82	125	30	1357	18.8	44
James Edwards	77	2539	528	1033	.511	232	339	.684	189	392	581	123	347	17	24	162	117	1288	16.7	31
Cliff Robinson†	30	946	196	435	.451	97	133	.729	91	196	287	49	102	3	42	63	43	489	16.3	34
Cliff Robinson‡	68	2175	518	1143	.453	222	313	.709	174	435	609	120	222	4	88	149	103	1258	18.5	38
Kenny Carr*	46	1482	271	524	.517	145	220	.659	114	280	394	63	180	0	58	112	16	688	15.0	32
Lowes Moore	4	70	19	38	.500	6	8	.750	1	3	4	15	15	1	6	5	1	45	11.3	20
James Silas	67	1447	251	573	.438	246	286	.860	26	83	109	222	109	0	40	107	6	748	11.2	31
Bob Wilkerson	65	1805	284	679	.418	145	185	.784	60	190	250	237	188	3	92	138	25	716	11.0	28
Scott Wedman	54	1638	260	589	.441	66	90	.733	128	176	304	133	189	4	73	73	14	591	10.9	28
Phil Hubbard†	31	735	119	255	.467	85	117	.726	86	115	201	24	116	2	27	62	3	323	10.4	21
Phil Hubbard‡	83	1839	326	665	.490	191	280	.682	187	286	473	91	292	3	65	161	19	843	10.2	21

	G	Min.	FGM	FGA	Pct.	FTM	FTA	Pct.	REBOUNDS Off.	Def.	Tot.	Ast.	PF	Dq.	Stl.	TO	Blk.	SCORING Pts.	Avg.	Hi.
Geoff Huston 78	78	2409	325	672	.484	153	200	.765	53	97	150	590	169	1	70	171	11	806	10.3	26
Reggie Johnson* 23	23	617	94	175	.537	35	44	.795	43	82	125	22	73	1	6	24	17	223	9.7	19
Roger Phegley* 27	27	566	104	214	.486	36	45	.800	28	43	71	53	61	0	16	33	2	248	9.2	18
Bill Laimbeer*....... 50	50	894	119	253	.470	93	120	.775	124	153	277	45	170	3	22	61	30	334	6.7	30
Richard Washington . . 18	18	313	50	115	.435	9	15	.600	32	43	75	15	51	0	8	35	2	109	6.1	12
Bradley Branson 10	10	176	21	52	.404	11	12	.917	14	19	33	6	17	0	5	13	4	53	5.3	13
Mike Evans† 8	8	74	11	35	.314	5	8	.625	2	8	10	20	10	0	4	11	0	27	3.4	12
Mike Evans‡ 22	22	270	35	86	.407	13	20	.650	5	17	22	42	36	1	13	26	0	83	3.8	12
Paul Mokeski† 28	28	345	35	82	.427	23	30	.767	24	62	86	11	68	0	20	16	17	93	3.3	11
Paul Mokeski‡ 67	67	868	84	193	.435	48	63	.762	59	149	208	35	171	2	33		40	216	3.2	11
Keith Herron 30	30	269	39	106	.368	7	8	.875	10	11	21	23	25	0	8	12	2	85	2.8	12
Mickey Dillard....... 33	33	221	29	79	.367	15	23	.652	6	9	15	34	40	0	8	17	2	73	2.2	8
Mel Bennett 3	3	23	2	4	.500	1	6	.167	1	2	3	0	2	0	1	4	0	5	1.7	4
Kevin Restani† 34	34	338	23	60	.383	7	12	.583	31	46	77	15	40	0	10	14	7	53	1.6	10
Kevin Restani‡ 47	47	483	32	88	.364	10	16	.625	39	73	112	22	56	0	11	20	11	74	1.6	10
Don Ford 21	21	201	9	24	.375	5	6	.833	14	21	35	11	30	0	8	15	0	23	1.1	6

3-pt. FG: Cleveland 25-137 (.182)—Mitchell* 0-6 (.000); Brewer† 5-21 (.238); Brewer‡ 8-31 (.258); Edwards 0-4 (.000); Robinson† 0-1 (.000); Robinson‡ 0-4 (.000); Carr* 1-9 (.111); Moore 1-5 (.200); Silas 0-5 (.000); Wilkerson 3-18 (.167); Wedman 5-23 (.217); Hubbard† 0-1 (.000); Hubbard‡ 0-4 (.000); Huston 3-10 (.300); Phegley* 4-13 (.308); Laimbeer* 3-6 (.500); Washington 0-2 (.000); Evans† 0-4 (.000); Evans‡ 0-6 (.000); Mokeski† 0-2 (.000); Mokeski‡ 0-3 (.000); Herron 0-1 (.000); Dillard 0-4 (.000); Restani† 0-1 (.000); Restani‡ 0-2 (.000); Ford 0-1 (.000). Opponents 39-131 (.298).

DALLAS MAVERICKS

	G	Min.	FGM	FGA	Pct.	FTM	FTA	Pct.	REBOUNDS Off.	Def.	Tot.	Ast.	PF	Dq.	Stl.	TO	Blk.	SCORING Pts.	Avg.	Hi.
Jay Vincent......... 81	81	2626	719	1448	.497	293	409	.716	182	383	565	176	308	8	89	194	22	1732	21.4	41
Mark Aguirre........ 51	51	1468	381	820	.465	168	247	.680	89	160	249	164	152	0	37	135	22	955	18.7	42
Rolando Blackman ... 82	82	1979	439	855	.513	212	276	.768	97	157	254	105	122	0	46	113	30	1091	13.3	27
Brad Davis 82	82	2614	397	771	.515	185	230	.804	35	191	226	509	218	5	73	159	6	993	12.1	32
Jim Spanarkel....... 82	82	1755	270	564	.479	279	327	.853	99	111	210	206	140	0	86	111	9	827	10.1	24
Wayne Cooper 76	76	1818	281	669	.420	119	160	.744	200	350	550	115	285	10	37	88	106	682	9.0	22
Elston Turner 80	80	1996	282	639	.441	97	138	.703	143	158	301	189	182	1	75	116	2	661	8.3	19
Allan Bristow 82	82	2035	218	499	.437	134	104	.017	119	220	330	448	222	2	65	165	6	573	7.0	16
Tom LaGarde 47	47	909	113	269	.420	86	166	.518	63	147	210	49	138	3	17	82	17	312	6.6	18
Kurt Nimphius 63	63	1085	137	297	.461	63	108	.583	92	203	295	61	190	5	17	56	82	337	5.3	20
Scott Lloyd 74	74	1047	108	285	.379	69	91	.758	60	103	163	67	175	6	15	59	7	287	3.9	15
Ollie Mack.......... 13	13	150	19	59	.322	6	8	.750	8	10	18	14	6	0	5	4	1	44	3.4	12
Clarence Kea........ 35	35	248	26	49	.531	29	42	.690	20	35	61	14	55	0	4	16	3	81	2.3	10

3-pt. FG: Dallas 55-190 (.289)—Vincent 1-4 (.250); Aguirre 25-71 (.352); Blackman 1-4 (.250); Davis 14-49 (.286); Spanarkel 8-24 (.333); Cooper 1-8 (.125); Turner 0-4 (.000); Bristow 3-18 (.167); LaGarde 0-2 (.000); Lloyd 2-4 (.500); Mack 0-2 (.000). Opponents 31-138 (.225).

DENVER NUGGETS

	G	Min.	FGM	FGA	Pct.	FTM	FTA	Pct.	REBOUNDS Off.	Def.	Tot.	Ast.	PF	Dq.	Stl.	TO	Blk.	SCORING Pts.	Avg.	Hi.
Alex English 82	82	3015	855	1553	.551	372	443	.840	210	348	558	433	261	2	87	261	120	2082	25.4	38
Dan Issel 81	81	2472	651	1236	.527	546	655	.834	174	434	608	179	245	4	67	169	55	1852	22.9	39
Kiki Vandeweghe 82	82	2775	706	1200	.500	347	405	.857	149	312	461	247	217	1	52	189	29	1760	21.5	40
David Thompson..... 61	61	1246	313	644	.486	276	339	.814	57	91	148	117	149	1	34	142	29	906	14.9	41
Dave Robisch 12	12	257	48	106	.453	48	55	.873	14	49	63	32	29	0	3	13	4	144	12.0	18
Billy McKinney 81	81	1963	369	699	.528	137	170	.806	29	113	142	338	186	0	69	115	16	875	10.8	26
Glen Gondrezick 80	80	1699	250	495	.505	160	217	.737	140	283	423	152	229	0	92	100	36	660	8.3	24
T.R. Dunn 82	82	2259	258	504	.512	153	215	.712	211	348	559	188	210	1	135	123	36	669	8.2	23
Kenny Higgs 76	76	1696	202	468	.432	161	197	.817	23	121	144	395	263	8	72	156	6	569	7.5	27
Cedrick Hordges 77	77	1372	204	414	.493	116	199	.583	119	276	395	65	230	1	26	111	19	527	6.8	19
John Roche 39	39	501	68	150	.453	28	38	.737	4	19	23	89	40	0	15	29	2	187	4.8	24
Jim Ray 40	40	262	51	116	.440	21	36	.583	18	47	65	26	59	0	10	37	16	124	3.1	11
David Burns† 6	6	53	5	11	.455	6	9	.667	1	2	3	11	13	0	2	8	0	16	2.7	7
David Burns‡ 9	9	87	7	16	.438	9	15	.600	1	4	5	15	17	0	3	13	0	23	2.6	7

3-pt. FG: Denver 40-149 (.268)—English 0-8 (.000); Issel 4-6 (.667); Vandeweghe 1-13 (.077); Thompson 4-14 (.286); McKinney 0-17 (.000); Gondrezick 0-3 (.000); Dunn 0-1 (.000); Higgs 4-21 (.190); Hordges 3-13 (.231); Roche 23-52 (.442); Ray 1-1 (1.000). Opponents 64-227 (.282).

DETROIT PISTONS

	G	Min.	FGM	FGA	Pct.	FTM	FTA	Pct.	REBOUNDS Off.	Def.	Tot.	Ast.	PF	Dq.	Stl.	TO	Blk.	SCORING Pts.	Avg.	Hi.
John Long 69	69	2211	637	1294	.492	238	275	.865	95	162	257	148	173	0	65	167	25	1514	21.9	41
Kelly Tripucka 82	82	3077	636	1281	.496	495	621	.797	219	224	443	270	241	0	89	280	16	1772	21.6	49
Isiah Thomas 72	72	2433	453	1068	.424	302	429	.704	57	152	209	565	253	2	150	299	17	1225	17.0	34
Bill Laimbeer† 30	30	935	146	283	.516	91	112	.813	110	230	340	55	126	2	17	60	34	384	12.8	24
Bill Laimbeer‡....... 80	80	1829	265	536	.494	184	232	.793	234	383	617	100	296	5	39	121	64	718	9.0	30
Kent Benson 75	75	2467	405	802	.505	127	158	.804	219	434	653	159	214	2	66	160	98	940	12.5	27
Phil Hubbard*....... 52	52	1104	207	410	.505	106	163	.650	101	171	272	67	176	1	38	99	16	520	10.0	20
Terry Tyler 82	82	1989	336	643	.523	142	192	.740	154	339	493	126	182	1	77	121	160	815	9.9	22
Greg Kelser* 11	11	183	35	86	.407	27	41	.659	13	26	39	12	32	0	5	22	7	97	8.8	14
Edgar Jones 48	48	802	142	259	.548	90	129	.698	70	137	207	40	149	3	28	66	92	375	7.8	25
Vinnie Johnson† 67	67	1191	208	422	.493	98	130	.754	75	69	144	160	93	0	50	91	23	517	7.7	20
Vinnie Johnson‡ 74	74	1295	217	444	.489	107	142	.754	82	77	159	171	100	0	56	96	25	544	7.4	20

	G	Min.	FGM	FGA	Pct.	FTM	FTA	Pct.	Off.	Def.	Tot.	Ast.	PF	Dq.	Stl.	TO	Blk.	Pts.	Avg.	Hi.
Kenny Carr†	28	444	77	168	.458	53	82	.646	53	84	137	23	69	0	6	40	6	207	7.4	16
Kenny Carr‡	74	1926	348	692	.503	198	302	.656	167	364	531	86	249	0	64	152	22	895	12.1	32
Steve Hayes†	26	412	46	93	.495	25	41	.610	32	68	100	24	54	0	3	17	18	117	4.5	9
Steve Hayes‡	35	487	54	111	.486	32	53	.604	39	78	117	28	71	0	7	19	20	140	4.0	10
Alan Hardy	38	310	62	136	.456	18	29	.621	14	20	34	20	32	0	9	20	4	142	3.7	13
Ron Lee	81	1467	88	246	.358	84	119	.706	35	120	155	312	221	3	116	123	20	278	3.4	11
Paul Mokeski*	39	523	49	111	.441	25	33	.758	35	87	122	24	103	2	13	39	23	123	3.2	9
Jeff Judkins	30	251	31	81	.383	16	26	.615	14	20	34	14	33	0	6	9	5	79	2.6	8
Glenn Hagan	4	25	3	7	.429	1	1	1.000	2	2	4	8	7	0	3	1	0	7	1.8	5
Larry Wright	1	6	0	1	.000	0	0	...	0	0	0	0	2	0	0	1	0	0	0.0	0

3-pt. FG: Detroit 52-213 (.244)—Long 2-15 (.133); Tripucka 5-22 (.227); Thomas 17-59 (.288); Laimbeer† 1-7 (.143); Laimbeer‡ 4-13 (.308); Benson 3-11 (.273); Hubbard* 0-3 (.000); Tyler 1-4 (.250); Kelser* 0-3 (.000); Jones 1-2 (.500); Johnson† 3-11 (.273); Johnson‡ 3-12 (.250); Carr† 0-1 (.000); Carr‡ 1-10 (.100); Hardy 0-5 (.000); Lee 18-59 (.305); Mokeski* 0-1 (.000); Judkins 1-10 (.100). Opponents 41-175 (.234).

GOLDEN STATE WARRIORS

	G	Min.	FGM	FGA	Pct.	FTM	FTA	Pct.	Off.	Def.	Tot.	Ast.	PF	Dq.	Stl.	TO	Blk.	Pts.	Avg.	Hi.
Bernard King	79	2861	740	1307	.566	352	499	.705	140	329	469	282	285	6	78	267	23	1833	23.2	45
World B. Free	78	2796	650	1452	.448	479	647	.740	118	130	248	419	222	1	71	208	8	1789	22.9	37
Joe Barry Carroll	76	2627	527	1016	.519	235	323	.728	210	423	633	64	265	8	64	206	127	1289	17.0	33
Purvis Short	76	1782	456	935	.488	177	221	.801	123	143	266	209	220	3	65	122	10	1095	14.4	35
Larry Smith	74	2213	220	412	.534	88	159	.553	279	534	813	83	291	7	65	105	54	528	7.1	20
Lorenzo Romar	79	1259	203	403	.504	79	96	.823	12	86	98	226	103	0	60	89	13	488	6.2	17
Samuel Williams	59	1073	154	277	.556	49	89	.551	91	217	308	38	156	0	45	64	76	357	6.1	23
Rickey Brown	82	1260	192	418	.459	86	122	.705	136	228	364	19	243	4	36	84	29	470	5.7	20
Joe Hassett	68	787	144	382	.377	31	37	.838	13	40	53	104	94	1	30	36	3	390	5.7	20
Mike Gale	75	1793	185	373	.496	51	65	.785	37	152	189	261	173	1	121	126	28	421	5.6	14
Sonny Parker	71	899	116	245	.473	48	72	.667	73	104	177	89	101	0	39	51	11	280	3.9	15
Lewis Lloyd	16	95	25	45	.556	7	11	.636	9	7	16	6	20	0	5	14	1	57	3.6	11
Hank McDowell	30	335	34	84	.405	27	41	.659	41	59	100	20	52	1	6	21	8	95	3.2	9

3-pt. FG: Golden State 91-325 (.280)—King 1-5 (.200); Free 10-56 (.179); Carroll 0-1 (.000); Short 6-28 (.214); Smith 0-1 (.000); Romar 3-15 (.200); Hassett 71-214 (.332); Gale 0-5 (.000). Opponents 40-172 (.233).

HOUSTON ROCKETS

	G	Min.	FGM	FGA	Pct.	FTM	FTA	Pct.	Off.	Def.	Tot.	Ast.	PF	Dq.	Stl.	TO	Blk.	Pts.	Avg.	Hi.
Moses Malone	81	3398	945	1822	.519	630	827	.762	558	630	1188	142	208	0	76	294	125	2520	31.1	53
Elvin Hayes	82	3032	519	1100	.472	280	422	.664	267	480	747	144	287	4	62	208	104	1318	16.1	31
Robert Reid	77	2913	437	958	.456	160	214	.748	175	336	511	314	297	2	115	157	48	1035	13.4	29
Allen Leavell	79	2150	370	793	.467	115	135	.852	49	119	168	457	182	2	150	153	15	864	10.9	32
Calvin Murphy	64	1204	277	648	.427	100	110	.909	20	41	61	163	142	0	43	82	1	655	10.2	33
Bill Willoughby	69	1475	240	464	.517	56	77	.727	107	157	264	75	146	1	31	78	59	539	7.8	19
Mike Dunleavy	70	1315	206	450	.458	75	106	.708	24	80	104	227	161	0	45	80	3	520	7.4	19
Tom Henderson	75	1721	183	403	.454	105	150	.700	33	105	138	306	120	0	55	105	7	471	6.3	19
Major Jones	60	746	113	213	.531	42	77	.545	80	122	202	25	100	0	20	50	29	268	4.5	15
Calvin Garrett	51	858	105	242	.434	17	26	.654	27	67	94	76	94	0	32	38	6	230	4.5	18
Larry Spriggs	4	37	7	11	.636	0	2	.000	2	4	6	4	7	0	2	4	0	14	3.5	8
Billy Paultz	65	807	89	226	.394	34	65	.523	54	126	180	41	99	0	15	45	22	212	3.3	12
Jawann Oldham	22	124	13	36	.361	8	14	.571	7	17	24	3	28	0	2	6	10	34	1.5	5

3-pt. FG: Houston 50-176 (.284)—Malone 0-6 (.000); Hayes 0-5 (.000); Reid 1-10 (.100); Leavell 9-31 (.290); Murphy 1-16 (.063); Willoughby 3-7 (.429); Dunleavy 33-86 (.384); Henderson 0-2 (.000); Jones 0-3 (.000); Garrett 3-10 (.300). Opponents 48-202 (.238).

INDIANA PACERS

	G	Min.	FGM	FGA	Pct.	FTM	FTA	Pct.	Off.	Def.	Tot.	Ast.	PF	Dq.	Stl.	TO	Blk.	Pts.	Avg.	Hi.
Johnny Davis	82	2664	538	1153	.467	315	394	.799	72	106	178	346	176	1	76	186	11	1396	17.0	34
Billy Knight	81	1803	378	764	.495	233	282	.826	97	160	257	118	132	0	63	137	14	998	12.3	34
Mike Bantom*	39	1037	178	406	.438	101	153	.660	87	127	214	68	139	5	38	85	24	458	11.7	28
Herb Williams	82	2277	407	854	.477	126	188	.670	175	430	605	139	200	0	53	137	178	942	11.5	26
Louis Orr	80	1951	357	719	.497	203	254	.799	127	204	331	134	182	1	56	137	26	918	11.5	24
Tom Owens	74	1599	299	636	.470	181	226	.801	142	230	372	127	259	7	41	137	37	780	10.5	26
Don Buse	82	2529	312	685	.455	100	123	.813	46	177	223	407	176	0	164	95	27	797	9.7	23
Clemon Johnson	79	1979	312	641	.487	123	189	.651	184	387	571	127	241	3	60	138	112	747	9.5	20
Butch Carter	75	1035	188	402	.468	58	70	.829	30	49	79	60	110	0	34	54	11	442	5.9	20
George Johnson	59	720	120	291	.412	60	80	.750	72	145	217	40	147	2	36	68	25	300	5.1	15
George McGinnis	76	1341	141	378	.373	72	159	.453	93	305	398	204	198	4	96	131	28	354	4.7	17
Jerry Sichting	51	800	91	194	.469	29	38	.763	14	41	55	117	63	0	33	42	1	212	4.2	16
Raymond Townsend	14	95	11	41	.268	11	20	.550	2	11	13	10	18	0	3	6	0	35	2.5	6

3-pt. FG: Indiana 103-316 (.326)—Davis 5-27 (.185); Knight 9-32 (.281); Bantom* 1-3 (.333); Williams 2-7 (.286); Orr 1-8 (.125); Owens 1-2 (.500); Buse 73-189 (.386); Carter 8-25 (.320); G. Johnson 0-2 (.000); McGinnis 0-3 (.000); Sichting 1-9 (.111); Townsend 2-9 (.222). Opponents 34-183 (.186).

KANSAS CITY KINGS

	G	Min.	FGM	FGA	Pct.	FTM	FTA	Pct.	Off.	Def.	Tot.	Ast.	PF	Dq.	Stl.	TO	Blk.	Pts.	Avg.	Hi.
Cliff Robinson*	38	1229	322	708	.455	125	180	.694	83	239	322	71	120	1	46	86	60	769	20.2	38
Mike Woodson†	76	2186	508	1001	.507	198	254	.780	97	137	234	206	199	2	135	144	33	1221	16.1	28
Mike Woodson‡	83	2331	538	1069	.503	221	286	.773	102	145	247	222	220	3	142	153	35	1304	15.7	28
Steve Johnson	78	1741	395	644	.613	212	330	.642	152	307	459	91	372	25	39	197	89	1002	12.8	33
Ernie Grunfeld	81	1892	420	822	.511	188	229	.821	55	127	182	276	191	0	72	148	39	1030	12.7	26
Reggie Johnson†	31	783	163	293	.556	51	72	.708	54	135	189	31	117	4	20	50	27	377	12.2	27
Reggie Johnson‡	75	1904	351	662	.530	118	156	.756	140	311	451	73	257	5	33	100	60	820	10.9	27
Reggie King	80	2609	383	752	.509	201	285	.705	162	361	523	173	221	6	84	155	29	967	12.1	33
Larry Drew	81	1973	358	757	.473	150	189	.794	30	119	149	419	150	0	110	174	1	874	10.8	28
Phil Ford	72	1952	285	649	.439	136	166	.819	24	81	105	451	160	0	63	194	1	713	9.9	24
Eddie Johnson	74	1517	295	643	.459	99	149	.664	128	194	322	109	210	6	50	97	14	690	9.3	23
Kevin Loder	71	1139	208	448	.464	77	107	.720	69	126	195	88	147	0	35	68	30	493	6.9	25
Joe Meriweather	18	380	47	91	.516	31	40	.775	25	63	88	17	68	1	13	25	21	125	6.9	18
Kenny Dennard	30	607	62	121	.512	26	40	.650	47	86	133	42	81	0	35	35	8	150	5.0	13
John Lambert*	42	493	60	139	.432	21	28	.750	36	91	127	24	80	0	12	38	10	142	3.4	13
Sam Lacey*	2	20	3	5	.600	0	2	.000	0	4	4	4	2	0	2	2	1	6	3.0	6
Leon Douglas	63	1093	70	140	.500	32	80	.400	111	179	290	35	210	5	15	55	38	172	2.7	15
Charles Whitney	23	266	25	71	.352	4	7	.571	13	27	40	19	31	0	12	14	1	54	2.3	9

3-pt. FG: Kansas City 26-130 (.200)—Robinson* 0-3 (.000); Woodson† 7-24 (.292); Woodson‡ 7-25 (.280); Grunfield 2-14 (.143); R. Johnson† 0-1 (.000); R. Johnson‡ 0-1 (.000); Drew 8-27 (.296); Ford 7-32 (.219); E. Johnson 1-11 (.091); Loder 0-11 (.000); Lambert* 1-6 (.167); Whitney 0-1 (.000). Opponents 48-158 (.304).

LOS ANGELES LAKERS

	G	Min.	FGM	FGA	Pct.	FTM	FTA	Pct.	Off.	Def.	Tot.	Ast.	PF	Dq.	Stl.	TO	Blk.	Pts.	Avg.	Hi.
Kareem Abdul-Jabbar	76	2677	753	1301	.579	312	442	.706	172	487	659	225	224	0	63	230	207	1818	23.9	41
Jamaal Wilkes	82	2906	744	1417	.525	246	336	.732	153	240	393	143	240	1	89	164	24	1734	21.1	36
Magic Johnson	78	2991	556	1036	.537	329	433	.760	252	499	751	743	223	1	208	286	34	1447	18.6	40
Norm Nixon	82	3024	628	1274	.493	181	224	.808	38	138	176	652	264	3	132	238	7	1440	17.6	28
Mitch Kupchak	26	821	153	267	.573	65	98	.663	64	146	210	33	80	1	12	43	10	371	14.3	25
Michael Cooper	76	2197	383	741	.517	139	171	.813	84	185	269	230	216	1	120	151	61	907	11.9	31
Bob McAdoo	41	746	151	330	.458	90	126	.714	45	114	159	32	109	1	22	51	36	392	9.6	30
Mike McGee	39	352	80	172	.465	31	53	.585	34	15	49	16	59	0	18	34	3	191	4.9	27
Kurt Rambis	64	1131	118	228	.518	59	117	.504	116	232	348	56	167	2	60	77	76	295	4.6	16
Mark Landsberger	75	1134	144	329	.438	33	65	.508	164	237	401	32	134	0	10	49	7	321	4.3	17
Eddie Jordan	58	608	80	208	.428	43	54	.796	4	39	43	131	98	0	62	66	1	222	3.8	17
Clay Johnson	7	65	11	20	.550	3	6	.500	8	4	12	7	13	0	3	7	3	25	3.6	14
Jim Brewer	71	966	81	175	.463	7	19	.368	106	158	264	42	127	1	39	37	46	170	2.4	10
Kevin McKenna	36	237	28	87	.322	11	17	.647	18	11	29	14	45	0	10	20	2	67	1.9	8

3-pt. FG: L.A. Lakers 13-94 (.138)—Abdul-Jabbar 0-3 (.000); Wilkes 0-4 (.000); M. Johnson 6-29 (.207); Nixon 3-12 (.250); Cooper 2-17 (.118); McAdoo 0-5 (.000); McGee 0-4 (.000); Rambis 0-1 (.000); Landsberger 0-2 (.000); Jordan 1-9 (.111); Brewer 1-6 (.167); McKenna 0-2 (.000). Opponents 78-213 (.366).

MILWAUKEE BUCKS

	G	Min.	FGM	FGA	Pct.	FTM	FTA	Pct.	Off.	Def.	Tot.	Ast.	PF	Dq.	Stl.	TO	Blk.	Pts.	Avg.	Hi.
Sidney Moncrief	80	2980	556	1063	.523	468	573	.817	221	313	534	382	206	3	138	208	22	1581	19.8	39
Marques Johnson	60	1900	404	760	.532	182	260	.700	153	211	364	213	142	1	59	145	35	990	16.5	32
Brian Winters	61	1829	404	806	.501	123	156	.788	51	119	170	253	187	1	57	118	9	967	15.9	42
Bob Lanier	74	1986	407	729	.558	182	242	.752	92	296	388	219	211	3	72	166	56	996	13.5	29
Mickey Johnson	76	1934	372	757	.491	233	291	.801	133	321	454	215	240	4	72	191	45	978	12.9	35
Quinn Buckner	70	2156	396	822	.482	110	168	.655	77	173	250	328	218	2	174	180	3	906	12.9	27
Junior Bridgeman	41	924	209	433	.483	89	103	.864	37	88	125	109	91	0	28	64	3	511	12.5	31
Scott May	65	1187	212	417	.508	159	193	.824	85	133	218	133	151	2	50	92	6	583	9.0	27
Robert Smith	17	316	52	110	.473	10	12	.833	1	13	14	44	35	0	10	14	1	116	6.8	15
Pat Cummings	78	1132	219	430	.509	67	91	.736	61	184	245	99	227	6	22	108	8	505	6.5	20
Bob Dandridge	11	174	21	55	.382	10	17	.588	4	13	17	13	25	0	5	11	2	52	4.7	11
Alton Lister	80	1186	149	287	.519	64	123	.520	108	279	387	84	239	4	18	129	118	362	4.5	18
Kevin Stacom	7	90	14	34	.412	1	2	.500	2	5	7	7	6	0	1	9	0	30	4.3	10
Mike Evans*	14	196	24	51	.471	8	12	.667	3	9	12	22	26	1	9	15	0	56	4.0	12
Harvey Catchings	80	1603	94	224	.420	41	69	.594	129	227	356	97	237	3	42	94	135	229	2.9	9
Geoff Crompton	35	203	11	32	.344	6	15	.400	10	31	41	13	39	0	6	17	12	28	0.8	4
Brad Holland†	1	9	0	5	.000	0	2	.000	0	0	0	2	1	0	0	1	0	0	0.0	0
Brad Holland‡	14	194	27	78	.346	3	6	.500	6	7	13	18	13	0	11	8	1	57	4.1	12

3-pt. FG: Milwaukee 49-164 (.299)—Moncrief 1-14 (.071); Ma. Johnson 0-4 (.000); Winters 36-93 (.387); Lanier 0-2 (.000); Mi. Johnson 1-7 (.143); Buckner 4-15 (.267); Bridgeman 4-9 (.444); May 0-4 (.000); Smith 2-10 (.200); Cummings 0-2 (.000); Stacom 1-2 (.500); Holland‡ 0-3 (.000); Evans* 0-2 (.000). Opponents 57-224 (.254).

NEW JERSEY NETS

	G	Min.	FGM	FGA	Pct.	FTM	FTA	Pct.	Off.	Def.	Tot.	Ast.	PF	Dq.	Stl.	TO	Blk.	Pts.	Avg.	Hi.
Ray Williams	82	2732	639	1383	.462	387	465	.832	117	208	325	488	302	9	199	290	43	1674	20.4	52
Buck Williams	82	2825	513	881	.582	242	388	.624	347	658	1005	107	285	5	84	235	84	1268	15.5	29
Otis Birdsong	37	1025	225	480	.469	74	127	.583	30	67	97	124	74	0	30	64	5	524	14.2	37

	G	Min.	FGM	FGA	Pct.	FTM	FTA	Pct.	Off.	Def.	Tot.	Ast.	PF	Dq.	Stl.	TO	Blk.	Pts.	Avg.	Hi.
Albert King	76	1694	391	812	.482	133	171	.778	105	207	312	142	261	4	64	180	36	918	12.1	24
Mike Woodson*	7	145	30	68	.441	23	32	.719	5	8	13	16	21	1	7	9	2	83	11.9	19
Mike O'Koren	80	2018	383	778	.492	135	189	.714	111	194	305	192	175	0	83	147	13	909	11.4	25
Darwin Cook.	82	2090	387	803	.482	118	162	.728	52	103	155	319	196	2	146	175	24	899	11.0	29
Len Elmore	81	2100	300	652	.460	135	170	.794	167	274	441	100	280	6	92	136	92	735	9.1	25
James Bailey†	67	1288	230	440	.523	133	213	.624	110	233	343	52	228	3	39	120	76	593	8.9	22
James Bailey‡	77	1468	261	505	.517	137	224	.612	127	264	391	65	270	5	42	139	83	659	8.6	22
Foots Walker.	77	1861	156	378	.413	141	194	.727	31	119	150	398	179	1	120	107	6	456	5.9	18
Mike Gminski	64	740	119	270	.441	97	118	.822	70	116	186	41	69	0	17	56	48	335	5.2	20
Ray Tolbert*	12	115	20	44	.455	4	8	.500	11	16	27	8	19	0	4	12	2	44	3.7	11
Jan van Breda Kolff. . .	41	452	41	82	.500	62	76	.816	17	31	48	32	63	1	12	29	13	144	3.5	12
Sam Lacey†	54	650	64	149	.430	27	35	.771	20	83	103	73	137	1	20	54	37	155	2.9	10
Sam Lacey‡	56	670	67	154	.435	27	37	.730	20	87	107	77	139	1	22	56	38	161	2.9	10
David Burns*	3	34	2	5	.400	3	6	.500	0	2	2	4	0	1	5	0	0	7	2.3	4
Joe Cooper	1	11	1	2	.500	0	0	. . .	1	1	2	0	2	0	0	1	0	2	2.0	2

3-pt. FG: New Jersey 30-146 (.205)—R. Williams 9-54 (.167); B. Williams 0-1 (.000); Birdsong 0-10 (.000); King 3-13 (.231); Woodson* 0-1 (.000); O'Koren 8-23 (.348); Cook 7-31 (.226); Walker 3-9 (.333); Tolbert* 0-1 (.000); van Breda Kolff 0-2 (.000); Lacey† 0-1 (.000); Lacey‡ 0-1 (.000). Opponents 58-187 (.310).

NEW YORK KNICKERBOCKERS

	G	Min.	FGM	FGA	Pct.	FTM	FTA	Pct.	Off.	Def.	Tot.	Ast.	PF	Dq.	Stl.	TO	Blk.	Pts.	Avg.	Hi.
Micheal Ray Richardson	82	3044	619	1343	.461	212	303	.700	177	388	565	572	317	3	213	291	41	1469	17.9	33
Maurice Lucas	80	2671	505	1001	.504	253	349	.725	274	629	903	179	309	4	68	173	70	1263	15.8	35
Bill Cartwright.	72	2060	390	694	.562	257	337	.763	116	305	421	87	208	2	48	166	65	1037	14.4	31
Campy Russell	77	2358	410	858	.478	228	294	.776	86	150	236	284	221	1	77	195	12	1073	13.9	29
Sly Williams	60	1521	349	628	.556	131	173	.757	100	127	227	142	153	0	77	114	16	831	13.9	34
Paul Westphal.	18	451	86	194	.443	36	47	.766	9	13	22	100	61	1	19	47	8	210	11.7	19
Randy Smith.	82	2033	348	748	.465	122	151	.808	53	102	155	255	199	1	91	124	1	821	10.0	26
Mike Newlin	76	1507	286	615	.465	126	147	.857	36	55	91	170	194	2	33	104	3	705	9.3	31
Marvin Webster	82	1883	199	405	.491	108	170	.635	184	306	490	99	211	2	22	90	90	506	6.2	20
Toby Knight	40	550	102	183	.557	17	25	.680	33	49	82	23	74	0	14	21	11	221	5.5	19
Reggie Carter	75	923	119	280	.425	64	80	.800	35	60	95	130	124	1	36	78	6	302	4.0	12
Alex Bradley	39	331	54	103	.524	29	48	.604	31	34	65	11	37	0	12	28	5	137	3.5	17
Hollis Copeland	18	118	16	38	.421	5	6	.833	3	2	5	9	19	0	4	4	2	37	2.1	7
Larry Demic	48	356	39	83	.470	14	39	.359	29	50	79	14	65	1	4	26	6	92	1.9	11
DeWayne Scales	3	24	1	5	.200	1	2	.500	2	3	5	0	3	0	1	2	1	3	1.0	2

3-pt. FG: New York 58-214 (.271)—Richardson 19-101 (.188); Lucas 0-3 (.000); Russell 25-57 (.439); Williams 2-9 (.222); Westphal 2-8 (.250); Smith 3-11 (.273); Newlin 7-23 (.304); Bradley 0-1 (.000); Demic 0-1 (.000). Opponents 51-168 (.304).

PHILADELPHIA 76ERS

	G	Min.	FGM	FGA	Pct.	FTM	FTA	Pct.	Off.	Def.	Tot.	Ast.	PF	Dq.	Stl.	TO	Blk.	Pts.	Avg.	Hi.
Julius Erving.	81	2789	780	1428	.546	411	539	.763	220	337	557	319	229	1	161	214	141	1974	24.4	38
Andrew Toney.	77	1909	511	979	.522	227	306	.742	43	91	134	283	269	5	64	214	17	1274	16.5	46
Bobby Jones.	76	2181	416	737	.564	263	333	.790	109	284	393	189	211	3	99	145	112	1095	14.4	25
Maurice Cheeks	79	2498	352	676	.521	171	220	.777	51	197	248	667	247	0	209	184	33	881	11.2	27
Lionel Hollins	81	2257	380	797	.477	132	188	.702	35	152	187	316	198	1	103	146	20	894	11.0	25
Darryl Dawkins	48	1124	207	367	.564	114	164	.695	68	237	305	55	193	5	19	96	55	528	11.0	22
Mike Bantom†	43	979	156	306	.510	67	114	.588	87	139	226	46	133	0	25	64	37	380	8.8	22
Mike Bantom‡.	82	2016	334	712	.469	168	267	.629	174	266	440	114	272	5	63	149	61	838	10.2	28
Caldwell Jones	81	2446	231	465	.497	179	219	.817	164	544	708	100	301	3	38	155	146	641	7.9	20
Steve Mix	75	1235	202	399	.506	136	172	.791	92	133	225	93	86	0	42	67	17	541	7.2	21
Earl Cureton	66	956	149	306	.487	51	94	.543	90	180	270	32	142	0	31	44	27	349	5.3	23
Clint Richardson	77	1040	140	310	.452	69	88	.784	55	63	118	109	109	0	36	79	9	351	4.6	12
Franklin Edwards.	42	291	65	150	.433	20	27	.741	10	17	27	45	37	0	16	24	5	150	3.6	17
Ollie Johnson	26	150	27	54	.500	6	7	.857	7	15	22	10	28	0	13	13	3	61	2.3	8

3-pt. FG: Philadelphia 41-139 (.295)—Erving 3-11 (.273); Toney 25-59 (.424); B. Jones 0-3 (.000); Cheeks 6-22 (.273); Hollins 2-16 (.125); Dawkins 0-2 (.000); Bantom† 1-3 (.333); Bantom‡ 2-6 (.333); C. Jones 0-3 (.000); Mix 1-4 (.250); Cureton 0-2 (.000); Richardson 2-2 (1.000); Edwards 0-9 (.000); Johnson 1-3 (.333). Opponents 55-212 (.259).

PHOENIX SUNS

	G	Min.	FGM	FGA	Pct.	FTM	FTA	Pct.	Off.	Def.	Tot.	Ast.	PF	Dq.	Stl.	TO	Blk.	Pts.	Avg.	Hi.
Dennis Johnson	80	2937	577	1228	.470	399	495	.806	142	268	410	369	253	6	105	233	55	1561	19.5	37
Truck Robinson.	74	2745	579	1128	.513	256	371	.687	202	519	721	179	215	2	42	202	28	1414	19.1	38
Alvan Adams.	79	2393	507	1027	.494	182	233	.781	138	448	586	356	269	7	114	196	78	1196	15.1	32
Walter Davis.	55	1182	350	669	.523	91	111	.820	21	82	103	162	104	1	46	112	3	794	14.4	28
Kyle Macy.	82	2845	486	945	.514	152	169	.899	78	183	261	384	185	1	143	125	9	1163	14.2	31
Rich Kelley	81	1892	236	505	.467	167	223	.749	168	329	497	293	292	14	64	244	71	639	7.9	23
Larry Nance	80	1186	227	436	.521	75	117	.641	95	161	256	82	169	2	42	104	71	529	6.6	29
Alvin Scott	81	1740	189	380	.497	108	148	.730	97	197	294	149	169	0	59	98	70	486	6.0	17
Jeff Cook	76	1298	151	358	.422	89	134	.664	112	189	301	100	174	1	37	80	23	391	5.1	16

REBOUNDS SCORING

	G	Min.	FGM	FGA	Pct.	FTM	FTA	Pct.	Off.	Def.	Tot.	Ast.	PF	Dq.	Stl.	TO	Blk.	Pts.	Avg.	Hi.
									|REBOUNDS									|SCORING		
Dudley Bradley	64	937	125	281	.445	74	100	.740	30	57	87	80	115	0	78	71	10	325	5.1	20
Joel Kramer	56	549	55	133	.414	33	42	.786	36	72	108	51	62	0	19	26	11	143	2.6	9
John McCullough	8	23	9	13	.692	3	5	.600	1	3	4	3	3	0	2	3	0	21	2.6	7
Craig Dykema	32	103	17	37	.459	7	9	.778	3	9	12	15	19	0	2	7	0	43	1.3	6

3-pt. FG: Phoenix 54-174 (.310)—Johnson 8-42 (.190); Robinson 1-1 (1.000); Adams 0-1 (.000); Davis 3-16 (.188); Macy 39-100 (.390); Kelley 0-1 (.000); Nance 0-1 (.000); Scott 0-2 (.000); Cook 0-2 (.000); Bradley 1-4 (.250); Dykema 2-4 (.500). Opponents 51-200 (.255).

PORTLAND TRAIL BLAZERS

	G	Min.	FGM	FGA	Pct.	FTM	FTA	Pct.	REBOUNDS Off.	Def.	Tot.	Ast.	PF	Dq.	Stl.	TO	Blk.	SCORING Pts.	Avg.	Hi.
Mychal Thompson	79	3129	681	1303	.523	280	446	.628	258	663	921	319	233	2	69	245	107	1642	20.8	38
Jim Paxson	82	2756	662	1258	.526	220	287	.767	75	146	221	276	159	0	129	144	12	1552	18.9	33
Calvin Natt	75	2599	515	894	.576	294	392	.750	193	420	613	150	175	1	62	140	36	1326	17.7	34
Kelvin Ransey	78	2418	504	1095	.460	242	318	.761	39	147	186	555	169	1	97	229	4	1253	16.1	33
Billy Ray Bates	75	1229	327	692	.473	166	211	.787	53	55	108	111	100	0	61	93	5	832	11.1	29
Bob Gross	59	1377	173	322	.537	78	104	.750	101	158	259	125	162	2	75	88	41	427	7.2	18
Mike Harper	68	1433	184	370	.497	96	153	.627	127	212	339	54	229	7	55	92	82	464	6.8	20
Darnell Valentine	82	1387	187	453	.413	152	200	.760	48	101	149	270	187	1	94	127	3	526	6.4	20
Kermit Washington	20	418	38	78	.487	24	41	.585	40	77	117	29	56	0	9	19	16	100	5.0	17
Peter Verhoeven	71	1207	149	296	.503	51	72	.708	106	148	254	52	215	4	42	55	22	349	4.9	28
Jeff Lamp	54	617	100	196	.510	50	61	.820	24	40	64	28	83	0	16	45	1	250	4.6	21
Petur Gudmundsson	68	845	83	166	.500	52	76	.684	51	135	186	59	163	2	13	73	30	219	3.2	18
Kevin Kunnert	21	237	20	48	.417	9	17	.529	20	46	66	18	51	1	3	18	6	49	2.3	9
Carl Bailey	1	7	1	1	1.000	0	0	—	0	0	0	2	0	0	2	0	2	2.0	2
Dennis Awtrey	10	121	5	15	.333	5	9	.556	7	7	14	8	28	1	1	6	2	15	1.5	5

3-pt. FG: Portland 29-140 (.207)—Paxson 8-35 (.229); Natt 2-8 (.250); Ransey 3-38 (.079); Bates 12-41 (.293); Gross 3-6 (.500); Harper 0-1 (.000); Valentine 0-9 (.000); Lamp 0-1 (.000); Gudmundsson 1-1 (1.000). Opponents 54-206 (.262).

SAN ANTONIO SPURS

	G	Min.	FGM	FGA	Pct.	FTM	FTA	Pct.	REBOUNDS Off.	Def.	Tot.	Ast.	PF	Dq.	Stl.	TO	Blk.	SCORING Pts.	Avg.	Hi.
George Gervin	79	2817	993	1987	.500	555	642	.864	138	254	392	187	215	2	77	210	45	2551	32.3	50
Mike Mitchell†	57	2090	524	973	.539	148	202	.733	173	276	449	43	200	4	33	98	28	1196	21.0	45
Mike Mitchell‡	84	3063	753	1477	.510	220	302	.728	244	346	590	82	277	4	60	153	43	1726	20.5	45
Ron Brewer*	25	595	182	361	.504	77	88	.875	13	37	50	67	37	0	23	34	7	444	17.8	44
Mark Olberding	68	2098	333	705	.472	273	338	.808	118	321	439	202	253	5	57	139	29	941	13.8	30
Reggie Johnson*	21	504	94	194	.485	32	40	.800	43	94	137	20	67	0	7	26	16	220	10.5	20
Dave Corzine	82	2189	336	648	.519	159	213	.746	211	418	629	130	235	3	33	139	126	832	10.1	25
Gene Banks	80	1700	311	652	.477	145	212	.684	157	254	411	147	199	2	55	106	17	767	9.6	23
Johnny Moore	79	2294	309	667	.463	122	182	.670	62	213	275	762	254	6	163	175	12	741	9.4	27
Mike Bratz	81	1616	230	565	.407	119	152	.783	40	126	166	438	183	0	65	139	11	625	7.7	28
Roger Phegley†	54	617	129	293	.440	49	64	.766	33	50	83	61	91	0	20	33	6	308	5.7	17
Roger Phegley‡	81	1183	233	507	.460	85	109	.780	61	93	154	114	152	0	36	66	8	556	6.9	18
Ed Rains	49	637	77	177	.435	38	64	.594	37	43	80	40	74	0	18	25	2	192	3.9	21
Paul Griffin	23	459	32	66	.485	24	37	.649	29	66	95	54	67	0	20	40	8	88	3.8	16
Rich Yonakor	10	70	14	26	.538	5	7	.714	13	14	27	3	7	0	1	2	2	33	3.3	11
George Johnson	75	1578	91	195	.467	43	64	.672	152	302	454	79	259	6	20	92	234	225	3.0	10
Steve Hayes*	9	75	8	18	.444	7	12	.583	7	10	17	4	17	0	1	2	2	23	2.6	10
Kevin Restani*	13	145	9	28	.321	3	4	.750	8	27	35	7	16	0	1	6	4	21	1.6	6
John Lambert†	21	271	26	58	.448	13	14	.929	19	32	51	13	43	0	6	10	6	65	3.1	10
John Lambert‡	63	764	86	197	.437	34	42	.810	55	123	178	37	123	0	18	48	16	207	3.3	13

3-pt. FG: San Antonio 64-252 (.254)—Gervin 10-36 (.278); Mitchell† 0-1 (.000); Mitchell‡ 0-7 (.000); Brewer* 3-10 (.300); Olberding 2-12 (.167); Corzine 1-4 (.250); Banks 0-8 (.000); Moore 1-21 (.048); Bratz 46-138 (.333); Phegley† 1-18 (.056); Phegley‡ 5-31 (.161); Rains 0-2 (.000); Lambert† 0-1 (.000); Lambert‡ 1-7 (.143); Restani* 0-1 (.000). Opponents 58-199 (.291).

SAN DIEGO CLIPPERS

	G	Min.	FGM	FGA	Pct.	FTM	FTA	Pct.	REBOUNDS Off.	Def.	Tot.	Ast.	PF	Dq.	Stl.	TO	Blk.	SCORING Pts.	Avg.	Hi.
Tom Chambers	81	2682	554	1056	.525	284	458	.620	211	350	561	146	341	17	58	220	46	1392	17.2	39
Freeman Williams*	37	808	234	513	.456	118	140	.843	21	29	50	67	85	1	23	89	0	610	16.5	32
Michael Brooks	82	2750	537	1066	.504	202	267	.757	207	417	624	236	285	7	113	197	39	1276	15.6	37
Jerome Whitehead	72	2214	406	726	.559	184	241	.763	231	433	664	102	290	16	48	141	44	996	13.8	31
Phil Smith*	48	1446	253	575	.440	123	168	.732	34	83	117	233	151	0	45	116	19	634	13.2	30
Charlie Criss†	28	840	138	288	.479	76	86	.884	7	37	44	112	56	0	21	52	4	360	12.9	34
Charlie Criss‡	55	1392	222	498	.446	141	159	.887	13	69	82	187	96	0	44	82	6	595	10.8	34
Al Wood†	29	692	143	276	.518	73	91	.802	29	61	90	47	74	4	22	60	8	362	12.5	29
Al Wood‡	48	930	179	381	.470	93	119	.782	51	83	134	58	108	4	31	71	9	454	9.5	29
Swen Nater	21	575	101	175	.577	59	79	.747	46	146	192	30	64	1	6	48	9	262	12.5	20
Joe Bryant	75	1998	341	701	.486	194	247	.785	79	195	274	189	250	1	78	183	29	884	11.8	32
Brian Taylor	41	1274	165	328	.503	90	110	.818	26	70	96	229	113	1	47	82	9	443	10.8	32
Michael Wiley	61	1013	203	359	.565	98	141	.695	67	115	182	52	127	1	40	71	16	504	8.3	28
John Douglas	64	1031	181	389	.465	67	102	.657	27	63	90	146	147	2	48	92	9	447	7.0	28
Jim Brogan	63	1027	165	364	.453	61	84	.726	61	59	120	156	123	2	49	83	13	400	6.3	24

	G	Min.	FGM	FGA	Pct.	FTM	FTA	Pct.	Off.	Def.	Tot.	Ast.	PF	Dq.	Stl.	TO	Blk.	Pts.	Avg.	Hi.
									REBOUNDS									SCORING		
Armond Hill†	19	480	34	89	.382	22	32	.688	6	21	27	81	51	0	16	52	3	90	4.7	13
Armond Hill‡	40	723	53	126	.421	39	55	.709	12	40	52	106	88	0	21	66	5	145	3.6	13
Ron Davis	7	67	10	25	.400	3	6	.500	7	6	13	4	8	0	0	5	0	23	3.3	16
Jim Smith	72	858	86	169	.509	39	85	.459	72	110	182	46	185	5	22	47	51	211	2.9	13
Rock Lee	2	10	1	2	.500	0	4	.000	0	1	1	2	3	0	0	0	0	2	1.0	2

3-pt. FG: San Diego 99-338 (.293)—Chambers 0-2 (.000); Williams* 24-74 (.324); Brooks 0-7 (.000); P. Smith* 5-24 (.208); Criss† 8-21 (.381); Criss‡ 10-29 (.345); Wood† 3-18 (.167); Wood‡ 3-24 (.125); Nater 1-1 (1.000); Bryant 8-30 (.267); Taylor 23-63 (.365); Wiley 0-5 (.000); Douglas 18-59 (.305); Brogan 9-32 (.281); Hill† 0-2 (.000); Hill‡ 0-2 (.000). Opponents 36-146 (.247).

SEATTLE SUPERSONICS

	G	Min.	FGM	FGA	Pct.	FTM	FTA	Pct.	Off.	Def.	Tot.	Ast.	PF	Dq.	Stl.	TO	Blk.	Pts.	Avg.	Hi.
									REBOUNDS									SCORING		
Gus Williams	80	2876	773	1592	.486	320	436	.734	92	152	244	549	163	0	172	197	36	1875	23.4	42
Jack Sikma	82	3049	581	1212	.479	447	523	.855	223	815	1038	277	268	5	102	213	107	1611	19.6	39
Lonnie Shelton	81	2667	508	1046	.486	188	240	.783	161	348	509	252	317	12	99	199	43	1204	14.9	37
Fred Brown	82	1785	393	863	.455	111	129	.860	42	98	140	238	111	0	69	96	4	922	11.2	24
Wally Walker	70	1965	302	629	.480	90	134	.672	108	197	305	218	215	2	36	111	28	694	9.9	24
Phil Smith†	26	596	87	186	.468	40	55	.727	17	52	69	74	62	0	22	39	8	214	8.2	17
Phil Smith‡	74	2042	340	761	.447	163	223	.731	51	135	186	307	213	0	67	155	27	848	11.5	30
James Donaldson	82	1710	255	419	.609	151	240	.629	138	352	490	51	186	2	27	115	139	661	8.1	23
James Bailey*	10	180	31	65	.477	4	11	.364	17	31	48	13	42	2	3	19	7	66	6.6	12
Bill Hanzlik	81	1974	167	357	.468	138	176	.784	99	167	266	183	250	3	81	106	30	472	5.8	25
Danny Vranes	77	1075	143	262	.546	89	148	.601	71	127	198	56	150	0	28	68	21	375	4.9	15
Greg Kelser†	49	558	81	185	.438	78	119	.655	67	87	154	45	99	0	13	62	14	240	4.9	19
Greg Kelser‡	60	741	116	271	.428	105	160	.656	80	113	193	57	131	0	18	84	21	337	5.6	19
John Johnson	14	187	22	45	.489	15	20	.750	3	15	18	29	20	0	4	17	3	59	4.2	8
Vinnie Johnson*	7	104	9	22	.409	9	12	.750	7	8	15	11	8	0	6	5	2	27	3.9	9
Ray Tolbert†	52	492	80	158	.506	15	27	.556	39	60	99	25	64	0	8	33	14	175	3.4	11
Ray Tolbert‡	64	607	100	202	.495	19	35	.543	50	76	126	33	83	0	12	45	16	219	3.4	11
Mark Radford	43	369	54	100	.540	35	69	.507	13	16	29	57	65	0	16	42	2	145	3.4	15
Armond Hill*	21	243	19	37	.514	17	23	.739	6	19	25	37	37	0	5	14	2	55	2.6	11

3-pt. FG: Seattle 38-153 (.248)—Williams 9-40 (.225); Sikma 2-13 (.154); Shelton 0-8 (.000); Brown 25-77 (.325); Walker 0-2 (.000); Smith† 0-3 (.000); Smith‡ 5-27 (.185); Hanzlik 0-4 (.000); Kelser‡ 0-3 (.000); Vranes 0-1 (.000); V. Johnson* 0-1 (.000); Tolbert† 0-1 (.000); Tolbert‡ 0-2 (.000); Radford 2-3 (.667). Opponents 48-201 (.239).

UTAH JAZZ

	G	Min.	FGM	FGA	Pct.	FTM	FTA	Pct.	Off.	Def.	Tot.	Ast.	PF	Dq.	Stl.	TO	Blk.	Pts.	Avg.	Hi.
									REBOUNDS									SCORING		
Adrian Dantley	81	3222	904	1586	.570	648	818	.792	231	283	514	324	252	1	95	299	14	2457	30.3	53
Darrell Griffith	80	2597	689	1429	.482	189	271	.697	128	177	305	187	213	0	95	193	34	1582	19.8	39
Rickey Green	81	2822	500	1015	.493	202	264	.765	85	158	243	630	183	0	185	198	9	1202	14.8	35
Jeff Wilkins	82	2274	314	718	.437	137	176	.778	120	491	611	90	248	4	32	134	77	765	9.3	37
Dan Schayes	82	1623	252	524	.481	140	185	.757	131	296	427	146	292	4	46	151	72	644	7.9	22
Carl Nicks	80	1322	252	555	.454	85	150	.567	67	94	161	89	184	0	66	101	4	589	7.4	19
Ben Poquette	82	1698	220	428	.514	97	120	.808	117	294	411	94	235	4	51	69	65	540	6.6	20
Bill Robinzine	56	651	131	294	.446	61	75	.813	56	88	144	49	156	5	37	83	5	323	5.8	18
James Hardy	82	1814	179	369	.485	64	93	.688	153	317	470	110	192	2	58	78	67	422	5.1	19
John Duren	79	1056	121	268	.451	27	37	.730	14	70	84	157	143	0	20	72	4	272	3.4	16
Howard Wood	42	342	55	120	.458	34	52	.654	22	43	65	9	37	0	8	15	6	144	3.4	16
Bobby Cattage	49	337	60	135	.444	30	41	.732	22	51	73	7	58	0	7	18	0	150	3.1	15
Sam Worthen	5	22	2	5	.400	0	0	...	1	0	1	3	3	0	0	2	0	4	0.8	4

3-pt. FG: Utah 22-97 (.227)—Dantley 1-3 (.333); Griffith 15-52 (.288); Green 0-8 (.000); Wilkins 0-3 (.000); Schayes 0-1 (.000); Nicks 0-5 (.000); Poquette 3-10 (.300); Hardy 0-1 (.000); Duren 3-11 (.273); Wood 0-1 (.000); Cattage 0-2 (.000). Opponents 51-200 (.255).

WASHINGTON BULLETS

	G	Min.	FGM	FGA	Pct.	FTM	FTA	Pct.	Off.	Def.	Tot.	Ast.	PF	Dq.	Stl.	TO	Blk.	Pts.	Avg.	Hi.
									REBOUNDS									SCORING		
Greg Ballard	79	2946	621	1307	.475	235	283	.830	136	497	633	250	204	0	137	119	22	1486	18.8	33
Jeff Ruland	82	2214	420	749	.561	342	455	.752	253	509	762	134	319	7	44	237	58	1183	14.4	28
Spencer Haywood	76	2086	395	829	.476	219	260	.842	144	278	422	64	249	6	45	175	68	1009	13.3	27
Kevin Grevey	71	2164	376	857	.439	165	193	.855	57	138	195	149	151	1	44	96	23	945	13.3	26
Rick Mahorn	80	2664	414	816	.507	148	234	.632	149	555	704	150	349	12	57	162	138	976	12.2	26
Frank Johnson	79	2027	336	812	.414	153	204	.750	34	113	147	380	196	1	76	160	7	842	10.7	27
Don Collins	79	1609	334	653	.511	121	169	.716	101	95	196	148	195	3	89	135	24	790	10.0	32
John Lucas	79	1940	263	618	.426	138	176	.784	40	126	166	551	105	0	95	156	6	666	8.4	24
Brad Holland*	13	185	27	73	.370	3	4	.750	6	7	13	16	12	0	11	7	1	57	4.4	12
Charlie Davis	54	575	88	184	.478	30	37	.811	54	79	133	31	89	0	10	43	13	206	3.8	20
Jim Chones	59	867	74	171	.433	36	46	.783	39	146	185	64	114	1	15	41	32	184	3.1	19
Garry Witts	46	493	49	84	.583	33	40	.825	29	33	62	38	74	1	17	35	4	132	2.9	13
Carlos Terry	13	60	3	15	.200	3	4	.750	5	7	12	8	15	0	3	5	1	9	0.7	2

3-pt. FG: Washington 59-236 (.250)—Ballard 9-22 (.409); Ruland 1-3 (.333); Haywood 0-3 (.000); Grevey 28-82 (.341); Mahorn 0-3 (.000); Johnson 17-79 (.215); Collins 1-12 (.083); Lucas 2-22 (.091); Holland* 0-3 (.000); Davis 0-2 (.000); Witts 1-2 (.500); Terry 0-3 (.000). Opponents 44-183 (.240).

* Finished season with another team. † Totals with this team only. ‡ Totals with all teams.

1981-82

EASTERN CONFERENCE

FIRST ROUND

Philadelphia 2, Atlanta 0
Apr. 21—Wed.	Atlanta 76 at Philadelphia	111
Apr. 23—Fri.	Philadelphia 98 at Atlanta	*95

Washington 2, New Jersey 0
Apr. 20—Tue.	Washington 96 at New Jersey	83
Apr. 23—Fri.	New Jersey 92 at Washington	103

SEMIFINALS

Boston 4, Washington 1
Apr. 25—Sun.	Washington 91 at Boston	109
Apr. 28—Wed.	Washington 103 at Boston	102
May 1—Sat.	Boston 92 at Washington	83
May 2—Sun.	Boston 103 at Washington	*99
May 5—Wed.	Washington 126 at Boston	**131

Philadelphia 4, Milwaukee 2
Apr. 25—Sun.	Milwaukee 122 at Philadelphia	125
Apr. 28—Wed.	Milwaukee 108 at Philadelphia	120
May 1—Sat.	Philadelphia 91 at Milwaukee	92
May 2—Sun.	Philadelphia 100 at Milwaukee	93
May 5—Wed.	Milwaukee 110 at Philadelphia	98
May 7—Fri.	Philadelphia 102 at Milwaukee	90

FINALS

Philadelphia 4, Boston 3
May 9—Sun.	Philadelphia 81 at Boston	121
May 12—Wed.	Philadelphia 121 at Boston	113
May 15—Sat.	Boston 97 at Philadelphia	99
May 16—Sun.	Boston 94 at Philadelphia	119
May 19—Wed.	Philadelphia 85 at Boston	114
May 21—Fri.	Boston 88 at Philadelphia	75
May 23 —Sun.	Philadelphia 120 at Boston	106

WESTERN CONFERENCE

FIRST ROUND

Seattle 2, Houston 1
Apr. 21—Wed.	Houston 87 at Seattle	102
Apr. 23—Fri.	Seattle 70 at Houston	91
Apr. 25—Sun.	Houston 83 at Seattle	104

Phoenix 2, Denver 1
Apr. 20—Tue.	Phoenix 113 at Denver	129
Apr. 23—Fri.	Denver 110 at Phoenix	126
Apr. 24—Sat.	Phoenix 124 at Denver	119

SEMIFINALS

Los Angeles 4, Phoenix 0
Apr. 27—Tue.	Phoenix 96 at Los Angeles	115
Apr. 28—Wed.	Phoenix 98 at Los Angeles	117
Apr. 30—Fri.	Los Angeles 114 at Phoenix	106
May 2—Sun.	Los Angeles 112 at Phoenix	107

San Antonio 4, Seattle 1
Apr. 27—Tue.	San Antonio 95 at Seattle	93
Apr. 28—Wed.	San Antonio 99 at Seattle	114
Apr. 30—Fri.	Seattle 97 at San Antonio	99
May 2—Sun.	Seattle 113 at San Antonio	115
May 5—Wed.	San Antonio 109 at Seattle	103

FINALS

Los Angeles 4, San Antonio 0
May 9—Sun.	San Antonio 117 at Los Angeles	128
May 11—Tue.	San Antonio 101 at Los Angeles	110
May 14 Fri.	Los Angeles 118 at San Antonio	108
May 15—Sat.	Los Angeles 128 at San Antonio	123

NBA FINALS

Los Angeles 4, Philadelphia 2
May 27—Thur.	Los Angeles 124 at Philadelphia	117
May 30—Sun.	Los Angeles 94 at Philadelphia	110
June 1—Tue.	Philadelphia 108 at Los Angeles	129
June 3—Thur.	Philadelphia 101 at Los Angeles	111
June 6—Sun.	Los Angeles 102 at Philadelphia	135
June 8—Tue.	Philadelphia 104 at Los Angeles	114

*Denotes number of overtime periods.

1981-82

1980-81 NBA CHAMPION BOSTON CELTICS

Front row (from left): Chris Ford, Cedric Maxwell, president and general manager Red Auerbach, head coach Bill Fitch, chairman of the board Harry T. Mangurian Jr., Larry Bird, Nate Archibald. Back row (from left): assistant coach K.C. Jones, Wayne Kreklow, M.L. Carr, Rick Robey, Robert Parish, Kevin McHale, Eric Fernsten, Gerald Henderson, assistant coach Jimmy Rodgers, trainer Ray Melchiorre.

FINAL STANDINGS

ATLANTIC DIVISION

	Atl.	Bos.	Chi.	Cle.	Dal.	Den.	Det.	G.S.	Hou.	Ind.	K.C.	L.A.	Mil.	N.J.	N.Y.	Phi.	Pho.	Por.	S.A.	S.D.	Sea.	Uta.	Was.	W	L	Pct.	GB
Boston	4	..	5	4	2	2	4	1	2	3	1	2	3	6	5	3	2	2	2	2	2	2	4	62	20	.756	..
Philadelphia	5	3	4	6	2	1	4	2	2	6	2	1	2	5	3	..	1	1	2	2	1	1	5	62	20	.756	..
New York	4	1	3	5	1	2	5	0	2	2	1	0	3	6	..	3	1	1	0	2	2	2	4	50	32	.610	12
Washington	4	1	1	2	2	2	5	1	2	2	1	1	0	3	2	2	1	0	1	2	1	2	..	39	43	.476	23
New Jersey	2	0	2	3	1	1	3	1	0	1	0	0	..	0	1	1	2	0	0	1	1		3	24	58	.293	38

CENTRAL DIVISION

	Atl.	Bos.	Chi.	Cle.	Dal.	Den.	Det.	G.S.	Hou.	Ind.	K.C.	L.A.	Mil.	N.J.	N.Y.	Phi.	Pho.	Por.	S.A.	S.D.	Sea.	Uta.	Was.	W	L	Pct.	GB
Milwaukee	5	3	3	6	2	1	5	1	2	4	1	2	..	5	3	3	1	2	1	2	2	2	4	60	22	.732	..
Chicago	4	1	..	5	1	1	5	1	1	3	2	1	3	3	3	2	0	0	0	1	1	2	5	45	37	.549	15
Indiana	5	3	2	4	2	1	4	1	1	..	2	0	2	5	3	0	1	0	2	1	0	1	4	44	38	.537	16
Atlanta	..	2	2	1	2	1	4	2	1	1	1	0	1	3	2	1	0	1	1	1	1	2	1	31	51	.378	29
Cleveland	5	1	1	..	2	1	3	1	0	2	0	0	0	3	0	1	1	1	0	1			4	28	54	.341	32
Detroit	2	1	1	3	2	0	..	0	1	2	1	0	1	3	1	1	0	0	0	1	0	0	1	21	61	.256	39

MIDWEST DIVISION

	Atl.	Bos.	Chi.	Cle.	Dal.	Den.	Det.	G.S.	Hou.	Ind.	K.C.	L.A.	Mil.	N.J.	N.Y.	Phi.	Pho.	Por.	S.A.	S.D.	Sea.	Uta.	Was.	W	L	Pct.	GB
San Antonio	1	0	2	1	5	4	2	4	3	0	4	3	1	2	2	0	2	3	..	4	3	5	1	52	30	.634	..
Kansas City	1	1	0	2	6	2	1	0	4	0	..	0	1	2	1	0	3	3	2	3	2	5	1	40	42	.488	12
Houston	1	0	1	2	6	4	1	2	..	1	2	2	0	2	0	0	1	3	3	1	4	4	0	40	42	.488	12
Denver	1	0	1	1	3	..	2	3	2	1	4	3	1	1	0	1	1	2	2	3	3	2	0	37	45	.451	15
Utah	0	1	0	1	5	4	2	1	2	1	1	2	0	1	0	0	0	3	1	2	1	..	0	28	54	.341	24
Dallas	0	0	1	0	..	3	0	2	0	0	0	0	0	1	1	0	1	1	2	1	1	1	0	15	67	.183	37

PACIFIC DIVISION

	Atl.	Bos.	Chi.	Cle.	Dal.	Den.	Det.	G.S.	Hou.	Ind.	K.C.	L.A.	Mil.	N.J.	N.Y.	Phi.	Pho.	Por.	S.A.	S.D.	Sea.	Uta.	Was.	W	L	Pct.	GB
Phoenix	2	0	2	1	4	4	2	4	4	1	2	4	1	1	1	1	..	3	3	6	5	5	1	57	25	.695	..
Los Angeles	2	0	1	2	5	2	2	5	3	2	5	..	0	2	2	1	2	3	2	3	6	3	1	54	28	.659	3
Portland	1	0	2	1	4	3	2	4	2	2	3	0	0	1	1	3	..	2	4	4	2	2	4	45	37	.549	12
Golden State	0	1	1	3	2	2	..	3	1	5	1	1	1	2	0	2	2	1	2	3	4	1		39	43	.476	18
San Diego	1	0	1	1	3	2	1	4	4	1	2	3	0	2	0	0	0	2	1	..	5	3	0	36	46	.439	21
Seattle	1	1	1	2	4	2	2	3	1	2	3	0	0	1	0	0	1	2	2	1	..	4	1	34	48	.415	23

TEAM STATISTICS

OFFENSIVE

	G	FGM	FGA	Pct.	FTM	FTA	Pct.	REBOUNDS Off.	Def.	Tot.	Ast.	PF	Dq.	Stl.	TO	Blk.	SCORING Pts.	Avg.
Denver	82	3784	7960	.475	2388	3051	.783	1325	2497	3822	2030	2108	24	720	1444	380	9986	121.8
Milwaukee	82	3722	7472	.498	1802	2340	.770	1261	2408	3669	2319	2198	27	862	1581	530	9276	113.1
San Antonio	82	3571	7276	.491	2052	2668	.769	1304	2582	3886	2048	2114	25	685	1533	643	9209	112.3
Philadelphia	82	3636	7073	.514	1865	2427	.768	1091	2618	3709	2369	2061	21	857	1702	591	9156	111.7
Los Angeles	82	3780	7382	.512	1540	2113	.729	1165	2491	3656	2363	1955	17	808	1557	551	9117	111.2
Portland	82	3741	7535	.496	1573	2191	.718	1243	2388	3631	2244	2034	30	769	1518	480	9080	110.7
Phoenix	82	3587	7326	.490	1810	2430	.745	1234	2490	3724	2205	1996	13	876	1733	416	9019	110.0
Boston	82	3581	7099	.504	1781	2369	.752	1155	2424	3579	2202	1990	22	683	1577	594	9008	109.9
Golden State	82	3560	7284	.489	1826	2513	.727	1403	2366	3769	2026	2158	36	611	1547	301	9006	109.8
Chicago	82	3457	6903	.501	1985	2563	.774	1227	2475	3702	1925	2058	15	729	1672	514	8937	109.0
Houston	82	3573	7335	.487	1711	2223	.770	1216	2347	3563	2099	1901	8	705	1451	390	8878	108.3
New York	82	3505	7255	.483	1783	2386	.747	1137	2205	3342	1976	1917	12	861	1461	314	8849	107.9
Indiana	82	3491	7245	.482	1815	2540	.715	1325	2267	3592	2091	2006	26	833	1491	484	8827	107.6
New Jersey	82	3477	7314	.475	1780	2371	.751	1092	2374	3466	2068	2204	35	750	1664	438	8768	106.9
Kansas City	82	3572	7151	.500	1576	2206	.714	1037	2450	3487	2271	2092	23	719	1448	385	8769	106.9
San Diego	82	3477	7283	.477	1651	2246	.735	1169	2144	3313	2098	2078	21	764	1407	292	8737	106.5
Cleveland	82	3556	7609	.467	1486	1909	.778	1258	2243	3501	2007	1995	31	632	1396	322	8670	105.7
Washington	82	3549	7517	.472	1499	2072	.723	1155	2533	3688	2151	1895	21	641	1422	392	8662	105.6
Atlanta	82	3291	6866	.479	2012	2590	.777	1201	2224	3425	1846	2276	54	749	1605	469	8604	104.9
Seattle	82	3343	7145	.468	1813	2376	.763	1167	2434	3601	1945	1986	23	628	1524	438	8531	104.0
Dallas	82	3204	6928	.462	1868	2487	.751	1109	2177	3286	1984	2008	32	561	1439	214	8322	101.5
Utah	82	3332	6825	.488	1595	2080	.767	962	2325	3287	1948	2110	39	637	1423	386	8301	101.2
Detroit	82	3236	6986	.463	1689	2330	.725	1201	2111	3312	1819	2125	35	884	1759	492	8174	99.7

DEFENSIVE

	FGM	FGA	Pct.	FTM	FTA	Pct.	REBOUNDS Off.	Def.	Tot.	Ast.	PF	Dq.	Stl.	TO	Blk.	SCORING Pts.	Avg.	Dif.
Philadelphia	3307	7337	.451	1850	2487	.744	1286	2287	3573	2033	2044	32	818	1642	379	8512	103.8	+7.9
Boston	3372	7206	.462	1752	2277	.769	1192	2174	3366	1890	2059	33	736	1473	351	8526	104.0	+5.9
Phoenix	3368	7221	.466	1762	2383	.739	1160	2284	3444	1970	2116	26	912	1752	401	8567	104.5	+5.5
Washington	3518	7491	.470	1588	2161	.735	1204	2638	3842	2060	1888	13	739	1410	469	8661	105.6	0.0
Seattle	3453	7421	.465	1718	2323	.740	1247	2357	3604	2044	2044	23	747	1348	387	8666	105.7	-1.7
Milwaukee	3311	7220	.459	2023	2701	.749	1265	2209	3474	2033	2050	25	735	1670	400	8680	105.9	+7.2
Detroit	3499	6869	.509	1663	2217	.750	1090	2396	3486	2033	2095	20	793	1797	505	8692	106.0	6.3
Indiana	3457	7071	.489	1757	2290	.767	1246	2407	3653	2113	2064	27	695	1655	439	8712	106.2	+1.4
New York	3555	7092	.501	1563	2082	.751	1147	2457	3604	2088	1994	14	689	1660	452	8716	106.3	+1.6
Kansas City	3424	7117	.481	1889	2500	.756	1138	2510	3648	1867	2015	20	717	1520	383	8768	106.9	0.0
Chicago	3527	7209	.489	1669	2211	.755	1145	2096	3241	1950	2135	42	784	1502	441	8775	107.0	+2.0
Utah	3430	7018	.489	1879	2472	.760	1154	2440	3594	1985	1855	24	596	1303	406	8784	107.1	-5.9
Los Angeles	3581	7701	.465	1598	2158	.741	1378	2274	3652	2280	1869	11	754	1473	357	8802	107.3	+3.9
Houston	3617	7341	.493	1568	2108	.744	1177	2367	3544	2191	1977	18	689	1430	367	8851	107.9	+0.4
Atlanta	3401	6867	.495	2024	2641	.766	1207	2318	3525	1935	2209	30	748	1685	555	8858	108.0	-3.1
San Diego	3508	6951	.505	1818	2433	.747	1091	2377	3468	2097	2006	19	683	1553	392	8867	108.1	-1.6
San Antonio	3581	7582	.472	1766	2387	.740	1214	2177	3391	2200	2108	37	700	1422	481	8973	109.4	+2.9
Portland	3584	7351	.488	1805	2377	.759	1249	2419	3668	2109	1932	30	802	1575	422	9007	109.8	+0.9
Dallas	3622	7060	.513	1731	2297	.754	1173	2498	3671	2098	2187	31	713	1433	480	9011	109.9	-8.4
Cleveland	3608	7174	.503	1800	2395	.752	1158	2499	3657	2166	1956	21	681	1474	454	9068	110.6	-4.9
Golden State	3631	7204	.504	1804	2411	.748	1137	2210	3347	2223	2093	19	714	1385	386	9103	111.0	-1.2
New Jersey	3612	7159	.505	2010	2663	.755	1059	2499	3558	2144	2092	23	815	1637	502	9262	113.0	-6.1
Denver	4059	8017	.506	1863	2507	.743	1320	2680	4000	2529	2387	52	704	1555	547	10025	122.3	-0.5
Avgs.	3523	7251	.486	1778	2369	.751	1193	2373	3566	2088	2055	26	738	1537	436	8865	108.1	...

HOME/ROAD

	Home	Road	Total		Home	Road	Total
Atlanta	20-21	11-30	31-51	Milwaukee	34-7	26-15	60-22
Boston	35-6	27-14	62-20	New Jersey	16-25	8-33	24-58
Chicago	26-15	19-22	45-37	New York	28-13	22-19	50-32
Cleveland	20-21	8-33	28-54	Philadelphia	37-4	25-16	62-20
Dallas	11-30	4-37	15-67	Phoenix	36-5	21-20	57-25
Denver	23-18	14-27	37-45	Portland	30-11	15-26	45-37
Detroit	14-27	7-34	21-61	San Antonio	34-7	18-23	52-30
Golden State	26-15	13-28	39-43	San Diego	22-19	14-27	36-46
Houston	25-16	15-26	40-42	Seattle	22-19	12-29	34-48
Indiana	27-14	17-24	44-38	Utah	20-21	8-33	28-54
Kansas City	24-17	16-25	40-42	Washington	26-15	13-28	39-43
Los Angeles	30-11	24-17	54-28	Totals	586-357	357-586	943-943

1980-81

POINTS
(minimum 70 games or 1,400 points)

	G	FGM	FTM	Pts.	Avg.		G	FGM	FTM	Pts.	Avg.
Adrian Dantley, Utah	.80	909	632	2452	30.7	Jamaal Wilkes, Los Angeles	.81	786	254	1827	22.6
Moses Malone, Houston	.80	806	609	2222	27.8	Bernard King, Golden State	.81	731	307	1771	21.9
George Gervin, San Antonio	.82	850	512	2221	27.1	Dan Issel, Denver	.80	614	519	1749	21.9
Kareem Abdul-Jabbar, L.A.	.80	836	423	2095	26.2	John Drew, Atlanta	.67	500	454	1454	21.7
David Thompson, Denver	.77	734	489	1967	25.5	Mike Newlin, New Jersey	.79	632	414	1688	21.4
Julius Erving, Philadelphia	.82	794	422	2014	24.6	Larry Bird, Boston	.82	719	283	1741	21.2
Otis Birdsong, Kansas City	.71	710	317	1747	24.6	Darrell Griffith, Utah	.81	716	229	1671	20.6
Mike Mitchell, Cleveland	.82	853	302	2012	24.5	Marques Johnson, Milwaukee	.76	636	269	1541	20.3
World B. Free, Golden State	.65	516	528	1565	24.1	Bill Cartwright, New York	.82	619	408	1646	20.1
Alex English, Denver	.81	768	390	1929	23.8	Ray Williams, New York	.79	616	312	1560	19.7

FIELD GOALS
(minimum 300 made)

	FGM	FGA	Pct.		FGM	FGA	Pct.
Artis Gilmore, Chicago	.547	816	.670	Kermit Washington, Portland	.325	571	.569
Darryl Dawkins, Philadelphia	.423	697	.607	Adrian Dantley, Utah	.909	1627	.559
Bernard King, Golden State	.731	1244	.588	Bill Cartwright, New York	.619	1118	.554
Cedric Maxwell, Boston	.441	750	.588	Swen Nater, San Diego	.517	935	.553
Kareem Abdul-Jabbar, Los Angeles	.836	1457	.574	Marques Johnson, Milwaukee	.636	1153	.552

FREE THROWS
(minimum 125 made)

	FTM	FTA	Pct.
Calvin Murphy, Houston	.206	215	.958
Ricky Sobers, Chicago	.231	247	.935
Mike Newlin, New Jersey	.414	466	.888
Jim Spanarkel, Dallas	.375	423	.887
Junior Bridgeman, Milwaukee	.213	241	.884
John Long, Detroit	.160	184	.870
Charlie Criss, Atlanta	.185	214	.864
Larry Bird, Boston	.283	328	.863
Billy McKinney, Utah-Denver	.162	188	.862
Billy Ray Bates, Portland	.170	199	.854

STEALS
(minimum 70 games or 125 steals)

	G	No.	Avg.
Magic Johnson, Los Angeles	.37	127	3.43
Micheal Ray Richardson, New York	.79	232	2.94
Quinn Buckner, Milwaukee	.82	197	2.40
Maurice Cheeks, Philadelphia	.81	193	2.38
Ray Williams, New York	.79	185	2.34
Dudley Bradley, Indiana	.82	186	2.27
Julius Erving, Philadelphia	.82	173	2.11
Ron Lee, Detroit	.82	166	2.02
Robert Reid, Houston	.82	163	1.99
Larry Bird, Boston	.82	161	1.96

ASSISTS
(minimum 70 games or 400 assists)

	G	No.	Avg.
Kevin Porter, Washington	.81	734	9.1
Norm Nixon, Los Angeles	.79	696	8.8
Phil Ford, Kansas City	.66	580	8.8
Micheal Ray Richardson, New York	.79	627	7.9
Nate Archibald, Boston	.80	618	7.7
John Lucas, Golden State	.66	464	7.0
Kelvin Ransey, Portland	.80	555	6.9
Maurice Cheeks, Philadelphia	.81	560	6.9
Johnny Davis, Indiana	.76	480	6.3
Kenny Higgs, Denver	.72	408	5.7

BLOCKED SHOTS
(minimum 70 games or 100 blocked shots)

	G	No.	Avg.
George Johnson, San Antonio	.82	278	3.39
Tree Rollins, Atlanta	.40	117	2.93
Kareem Abdul-Jabbar, Los Angeles	.80	228	2.85
Robert Parish, Boston	.82	214	2.61
Artis Gilmore, Chicago	.82	198	2.41
Harvey Catchings, Milwaukee	.77	184	2.39
Terry Tyler, Detroit	.82	180	2.20
Mychal Thompson, Portland	.79	170	2.15
Ben Poquette, Utah	.82	174	2.12
Elvin Hayes, Washington	.81	171	2.11

REBOUNDS
(minimum 70 games or 800 rebounds)

	G	Off.	Def.	Tot.	Avg.
Moses Malone, Houston	.80	474	706	1180	14.8
Swen Nater, San Diego	.82	295	722	1017	12.4
Larry Smith, Golden State	.82	433	561	994	12.1
Larry Bird, Boston	.82	191	704	895	10.9
Jack Sikma, Seattle	.82	184	668	852	10.4
Kenny Carr, Cleveland	.81	260	575	835	10.3
Kareem Abdul-Jabbar, L.A.	.80	197	624	821	10.3
Artis Gilmore, Chicago	.82	220	608	828	10.1
Caldwell Jones, Philadelphia	.81	200	613	813	10.0
Elvin Hayes, Washington	.81	235	554	789	9.7

3-POINT FIELD GOALS
(minimum 25 made)

	FGA	FGM	Pct.
Brian Taylor, San Diego	.115	44	.383
Joe Hassett, Dallas-Golden State	.156	53	.340
Freeman Williams, San Diego	.141	48	.340
Mike Bratz, Cleveland	.169	57	.337
Henry Bibby, San Diego	.95	32	.337
Kevin Grevey, Washington	.136	45	.331
Chris Ford, Boston	.109	36	.330
Scott Wedman, Kansas City	.77	25	.325

INDIVIDUAL STATISTICS, TEAM BY TEAM

ATLANTA HAWKS

									REBOUNDS									SCORING		
	G	Min.	FGM	FGA	Pct.	FTM	FTA	Pct.	Off.	Def.	Tot.	Ast.	PF	Dq.	Stl.	TO	Blk.	Pts.	Avg.	Hi.
John Drew	67	2075	500	1096	.456	454	577	.787	145	238	383	79	264	9	98	194	15	1454	21.7	47
Eddie Johnson	75	2693	573	1136	.504	279	356	.784	60	119	179	407	188	2	126	197	11	1431	19.1	40
Dan Roundfield	63	2128	426	808	.527	256	355	.721	231	403	634	161	258	8	76	178	119	1108	17.6	29
Don Collins*	47	1184	230	530	.434	137	162	.846	96	91	187	115	166	5	69	107	11	597	12.7	25
Wes Matthews†	34	1105	161	330	.488	103	123	.837	16	56	72	212	122	1	61	112	7	425	12.5	26
Wes Matthews‡	79	2266	385	779	.494	202	252	.802	46	93	139	411	242	2	107	261	17	977	12.4	26
Steve Hawes	74	2309	333	637	.523	222	278	.799	165	396	561	168	289	13	73	161	32	889	12.0	32

	G	Min.	FGM	FGA	Pct.	FTM	FTA	Pct.	REBOUNDS Off.	Def.	Tot.	Ast.	PF	Dq.	Stl.	TO	Blk.	SCORING Pts.	Avg.	Hi.
Charlie Criss	66	1708	220	485	.454	185	214	.864	26	74	100	283	87	0	61	134	3	626	9.5	21
Tom McMillen	79	1564	253	519	.487	80	108	.741	96	199	295	72	165	0	23	81	25	587	7.4	21
Tree Rollins	40	1044	116	210	.552	46	57	.807	102	184	286	35	151	7	29	57	117	278	7.0	13
Sam Pellom	77	1472	186	380	.489	81	116	.698	122	234	356	48	228	6	50	99	92	453	5.9	20
Armond Hill*	24	624	39	116	.336	42	50	.840	10	41	51	118	60	0	26	58	3	120	5.0	14
Craig Shelton	55	586	100	219	.457	35	58	.603	59	79	138	27	128	1	18	61	5	235	4.3	22
Jim McElroy	54	680	78	202	.386	48	59	.814	10	38	48	84	62	0	20	79	9	205	3.8	12
Tom Burleson	31	363	41	99	.414	20	41	.488	44	50	94	12	73	2	8	24	19	102	3.3	12
Art Collins	29	395	35	99	.354	24	36	.667	19	22	41	25	35	0	11	32	1	94	3.2	15

3-pt. FG: Atlanta 10-82 (.122)—Drew 0-7 (.000); Johnson 6-20 (.300); Roundfield 0-1 (.000); D. Collins* 0-3 (.000); Matthews† 0-6 (.000); Matthews‡ 5-21 (.238); Hawes 1-4 (.250); Criss 1-21 (.048); McMillen 1-6 (.167); Rollins 0-1 (.000); Pellom 0-1 (.000); Hill* 0-1 (.000); Shelton 0-1 (.000); McElroy 1-8 (.125); A. Collins 0-2 (.000). Opponents 32-152 (.211).

BOSTON CELTICS

	G	Min.	FGM	FGA	Pct.	FTM	FTA	Pct.	REBOUNDS Off.	Def.	Tot.	Ast.	PF	Dq.	Stl.	TO	Blk.	SCORING Pts.	Avg.	Hi.
Larry Bird	82	3239	719	1503	.478	283	328	.863	191	704	895	451	239	2	161	289	63	1741	21.2	36
Robert Parish	82	2298	635	1166	.545	282	397	.710	245	532	777	144	310	9	81	191	214	1552	18.9	40
Cedric Maxwell	81	2730	441	750	.588	352	450	.782	222	303	525	219	256	5	79	180	68	1234	15.2	34
Nate Archibald	80	2820	382	766	.499	342	419	.816	36	140	176	618	201	1	75	265	18	1106	13.8	26
Kevin McHale	82	1645	355	666	.533	108	159	.679	155	204	359	55	260	3	27	110	151	818	10.0	23
Rick Robey	82	1569	298	547	.545	144	251	.574	132	258	390	126	204	0	38	141	19	740	9.0	24
Chris Ford	82	2723	314	707	.444	64	87	.736	72	91	163	295	212	2	100	127	23	728	8.9	23
Gerald Henderson	82	1608	261	579	.451	113	157	.720	43	89	132	213	177	0	79	160	12	636	7.8	19
M.L. Carr	41	655	97	216	.449	53	67	.791	26	57	83	56	74	0	30	47	18	248	6.0	25
Terry Duerod†	32	114	30	73	.411	13	14	.929	2	3	5	6	8	0	5	10	0	79	2.5	12
Terry Duerod‡	50	451	104	234	.444	31	41	.756	17	27	44	36	27	0	17	35	4	247	4.9	22
Eric Fernsten	45	279	38	79	.481	20	30	.667	29	33	62	10	29	0	6	20	7	96	2.1	9
Wayne Kreklow	25	100	11	47	.234	7	10	.700	2	10	12	9	20	0	2	10	1	30	1.2	4

3-pt. FG: Boston 65-241 (.270)—Bird 20-74 (.270); Parish 0-1 (.000); Maxwell 0-1 (.000); Archibald 0-9 (.000); McHale 0-2 (.000); Robey 0-1 (.000); Ford 36-109 (.330); Henderson 1-16 (.063); Carr 1-14 (.071); Duerod† 6-10 (.600); Duerod‡ 8-16 (.500); Kreklow 1-4 (.250). Opponents 30-139 (.210).

CHICAGO BULLS

	G	Min.	FGM	FGA	Pct.	FTM	FTA	Pct.	REBOUNDS Off.	Def.	Tot.	Ast.	PF	Dq.	Stl.	TO	Blk.	SCORING Pts.	Avg.	Hi.
Reggie Theus	82	2820	543	1097	.495	445	550	.809	124	163	287	426	258	1	122	259	20	1549	18.9	32
Artis Gilmore	82	2832	547	816	.670	375	532	.705	220	608	828	172	295	2	47	236	198	1469	17.9	31
David Greenwood	82	2710	481	989	.486	217	290	.748	243	481	724	218	282	5	77	192	124	1179	14.4	28
Larry Kenon	77	2161	454	946	.480	180	245	.735	179	219	398	120	160	2	75	161	18	1088	14.1	32
Ricky Sobers	71	1803	355	769	.462	231	247	.935	46	98	144	284	225	3	98	206	17	958	13.5	27
Bob Wilkerson	80	2238	330	715	.462	137	163	.840	86	196	282	272	170	0	102	175	23	798	10.0	28
Dwight Jones	81	1574	245	507	.483	125	161	.776	127	274	401	99	200	1	40	126	36	615	7.6	29
Scott May	63	815	165	338	.488	113	149	.758	62	93	155	63	83	0	35	71	7	443	7.0	20
Coby Dietrick	82	1243	146	320	.456	77	111	.694	79	186	265	118	176	1	48	88	53	371	4.5	16
James Wilkes	48	540	85	184	.462	29	46	.630	36	60	96	30	86	0	25	34	12	199	4.1	21
Ronnie Lester	8	83	10	24	.417	10	11	.909	3	3	6	7	5	0	2	9	0	30	3.8	9
Sam Worthen	64	945	95	192	.495	45	60	.750	22	93	115	115	115	0	57	91	6	235	3.7	18
Ollie Mack*	3	16	1	6	.167	1	2	.500	0	1	1	1	3	0	1	0	0	3	1.0	2

3-pt. FG: Chicago 38-179 (.212)—Theus 18-90 (.200); Greenwood 0-2 (.000); Sobers 17-66 (.258); Wilkerson 1-10 (.100); Dietrick 2-6 (.333); Wilkes 0-1 (.000); Worthen 0-4 (.000). Opponents 52-223 (.233).

CLEVELAND CAVALIERS

	G	Min.	FGM	FGA	Pct.	FTM	FTA	Pct.	REBOUNDS Off.	Def.	Tot.	Ast.	PF	Dq.	Stl.	TO	Blk.	SCORING Pts.	Avg.	Hi.
Mike Mitchell	82	3194	853	1791	.476	302	385	.784	215	287	502	139	199	0	63	175	52	2012	24.5	42
Kenny Carr	81	2615	469	918	.511	292	409	.714	260	575	835	192	296	3	76	231	42	1230	15.2	31
Randy Smith	82	2199	486	1043	.466	221	271	.815	46	147	193	357	132	0	113	195	14	1194	14.6	33
Roger Phegley	82	2269	474	965	.491	224	267	.839	90	156	246	184	262	7	65	165	15	1180	14.4	30
Mike Bratz	80	2595	319	817	.390	107	132	.811	66	132	198	452	194	1	136	162	17	802	10.0	22
Richard Washington†	69	1505	289	630	.459	102	136	.750	133	236	369	113	246	3	41	108	54	681	9.9	24
Richard Washington‡	81	1812	340	747	.455	119	159	.748	158	295	453	129	273	3	46	129	61	800	10.0	24
Bill Laimbeer	81	2460	337	670	.503	117	153	.765	266	427	693	216	332	14	56	132	78	791	9.8	26
Dave Robisch*	11	372	37	98	.378	29	36	.806	27	58	85	44	21	0	7	14	6	103	9.4	17
Robert Smith	1	20	2	5	.400	4	4	1.000	1	2	3	3	6	1	0	3	0	8	8.0	8
Geoff Huston†	25	542	76	153	.497	22	27	.815	12	27	39	117	35	0	13	31	1	174	7.0	19
Geoff Huston‡	81	2434	461	942	.489	150	212	.708	45	93	138	394	148	1	58	179	7	1073	13.2	29
Bill Robinzine*	8	84	14	32	.438	5	8	.625	4	9	13	5	19	1	4	10	0	33	4.1	10
Don Ford	64	996	100	224	.446	22	24	.917	74	90	164	84	100	1	15	49	12	222	3.5	14
Chad Kinch*	29	247	38	96	.396	4	5	.800	7	17	24	35	24	0	9	22	5	80	2.8	10
Mack Calvin	21	128	13	39	.333	25	35	.714	2	10	12	28	13	0	5	17	0	52	2.5	6
Walter Jordan	30	207	29	75	.387	10	17	.588	23	19	42	11	35	0	11	17	5	68	2.3	8
John Lambert*	3	8	3	5	.600	0	0	...	1	2	3	3	2	0	0	2	0	6	2.0	4
Kim Hughes†	45	331	16	45	.356	0	0	...	29	48	77	24	73	0	17	33	21	32	0.7	6
Kim Hughes‡	53	490	27	70	.386	1	2	.500	48	79	127	35	106	2	28	44	35	55	1.0	6

– 547 –

	G	Min.	FGM	FGA	Pct.	FTM	FTA	Pct.	REBOUNDS Off.	Def.	Tot.	Ast.	PF	Dq.	Stl.	TO	Blk.	SCORING Pts.	Avg.	Hi.
Jerome Whitehead* ...3	8	1	3	.333	0	0	...	2	1	3	0	6	0	1	0	0	2	0.7	2

3-pt. FG: Cleveland 72-249 (.289)—Mitchell 4-9 (.444); Carr 0-4 (.000); Ra. Smith 1-28 (.036); Phegley 8-28 (.286); Bratz 57-169 (.337); Washington† 1-2 (.500); Washington‡ 1-2 (.500); Huston† 0-1 (.000); Huston‡ 1-5 (.200); Ford 0-3 (.000); Calvin 1-5 (.200). Opponents 52-168 (.310).

DALLAS MAVERICKS

	G	Min.	FGM	FGA	Pct.	FTM	FTA	Pct.	REBOUNDS Off.	Def.	Tot.	Ast.	PF	Dq.	Stl.	TO	Blk.	SCORING Pts.	Avg.	Hi.
Geoff Huston*.......56	1892	385	789	.488	128	185	.692	33	66	99	277	113	1	45	148	6	899	16.1	29
Jim Spanarkel.....82	2317	404	866	.467	375	423	.887	142	155	297	232	230	3	117	172	20	1184	14.4	28
Bill Robinzine† .70	1932	378	794	.476	213	273	.780	164	356	520	113	256	5	71	177	9	970	13.9	26
Bill Robinzine‡ .78	2016	392	826	.475	218	281	.776	168	365	533	118	275	6	75	187	9	1002	12.8	26
Tom LaGarde .82	2670	417	888	.470	288	444	.649	177	488	665	237	293	6	35	206	45	1122	13.7	26
Brad Davis 56	1686	230	410	.561	163	204	.799	29	122	151	385	156	2	52	123	11	626	11.2	31
Richard Washington* .11	307	51	117	.436	17	23	.739	25	59	84	16	37	0	5	21	7	119	10.8	24
Ollie Mack†.........62	1666	278	600	.463	79	123	.642	92	137	229	162	114	0	55	70	7	635	10.2	28
Ollie Mack‡.....65	1682	279	606	.460	80	125	.640	92	138	230	163	117	0	56	70	7	638	9.8	28
Terry Duerod*.......18	337	74	161	.460	18	27	.667	15	24	39	30	19	0	12	25	4	168	9.3	22
Scott Lloyd 72	2186	245	547	.448	147	205	.717	161	293	454	159	269	8	34	145	25	637	8.8	28
Abdul Jeelani ..66	1108	187	440	.425	179	220	.814	83	147	230	65	123	2	44	87	31	553	8.4	31
Joe Hassett*........17	280	59	142	.415	10	13	.769	11	14	25	18	21	0	5	11	0	138	8.1	15
Marty Byrnes 72	1360	216	451	.479	120	157	.764	74	103	177	113	126	0	29	61	17	561	7.8	25
Clarence Kea...16	199	37	81	.457	43	62	.694	28	39	67	5	44	2	6	16	1	117	7.3	22
Winford Boynes 44	757	121	313	.387	45	55	.818	24	51	75	37	79	1	23	69	16	287	6.5	22
Jerome Whitehead* ...7	118	16	38	.421	5	11	.455	8	20	28	2	16	0	4	11	1	37	5.3	14
Stan Pietkiewicz† .36	431	55	133	.414	11	14	.786	13	28	41	75	26	0	15	17	2	140	3.9	10
Stan Pietkiewicz‡ .42	461	57	138	.413	11	14	.786	13	29	42	77	28	0	15	22	2	144	3.4	10
Chad Kinch†........12	106	14	45	.311	10	13	.769	0	9	9	10	9	0	2	8	1	38	3.2	7
Chad Kinch‡........41	353	52	141	.369	14	18	.778	7	26	33	45	33	0	11	30	6	118	2.9	10
Darrell Allums 22	276	23	67	.343	13	22	.591	19	46	65	25	51	2	5	23	8	59	2.7	11
Ralph Drollinger 6	67	7	14	.500	1	4	.250	5	14	19	14	16	0	1	13	2	15	2.5	8
Austin Carr*......8	77	7	28	.250	2	4	.500	4	5	9	9	10	0	1	9	0	16	2.0	5
Monti Davis†........1	8	0	4	.000	1	5	.200	2	1	3	0	0	0	0	0	1	1	1.0	1
Monti Davis‡ 2	10	1	5	.200	1	5	.200	2	2	4	0	0	0	0	1	1	3	1.5	2

3-pt. FG: Dallas 46-165 (.279)—Huston* 1-4 (.250); Spanarkel 1-10 (.100); Robinzine† 1-6 (.167); Robinzine‡ 1-6 (.167); B. Davis 3-17 (.176); Mack† 0-9 (.000); Mack‡ 0-9 (.000); Duerod* 2-6 (.333); Lloyd 0-2 (.000); Jeelani 0-1 (.000); Hassett† 10-40 (.250); Byrnes 9-20 (.450); Kea 0-1 (.000); Pietkiewicz† 19-48 (.396); Pietkiewicz‡ 19-48 (.396); Allums 0-1 (.000). Opponents 36-137 (.263).

DENVER NUGGETS

	G	Min.	FGM	FGA	Pct.	FTM	FTA	Pct.	REBOUNDS Off.	Def.	Tot.	Ast.	PF	Dq.	Stl.	TO	Blk.	SCORING Pts.	Avg.	Hi.
David Thompson.....77	2620	734	1451	.506	489	615	.795	107	180	287	231	231	3	53	250	60	1967	25.5	44
Alex English 81	3093	768	1555	.494	390	459	.850	273	373	646	290	255	2	106	241	100	1929	23.8	42
Dan Issel 80	2641	614	1220	.503	519	684	.759	229	447	676	158	249	6	83	130	53	1749	21.9	37
Kiki Vandeweghe...51	1376	229	537	.426	130	159	.818	86	184	270	94	116	0	29	86	24	588	11.5	30
Billy McKinney† 49	1134	203	412	.493	118	140	.843	24	86	110	203	124	0	61	88	7	525	10.7	21
Billy McKinney‡ 84	2166	327	645	.507	162	188	.862	36	148	184	360	231	3	99	158	11	818	9.7	21
Dave Robisch† 73	1744	293	642	.456	171	211	.810	130	284	414	129	152	0	30	69	28	757	10.4	27
Dave Robisch‡ 84	2116	330	740	.446	200	247	.810	157	342	499	173	173	0	37	83	34	860	10.2	27
John Roche 26	611	82	179	.458	58	77	.753	5	32	37	140	44	0	17	52	8	231	8.9	30
Cedrick Hordges.....68	1599	221	480	.460	130	186	.699	120	338	458	104	226	4	33	120	19	572	8.4	21
Kenny Higgs 72	1689	209	474	.441	140	172	.814	24	121	145	408	243	5	101	166	6	562	7.8	21
Carl Nicks*.........27	493	65	149	.436	35	59	.593	13	36	49	80	52	0	28	63	2	165	6.1	17
Glen Gondrezick 73	1077	155	329	.471	112	137	.818	136	171	307	83	185	2	91	69	20	422	5.8	27
T.R. Dunn 82	1427	146	354	.412	79	121	.653	133	168	301	81	141	0	66	56	29	371	4.5	16
Ron Valentine 24	123	37	98	.378	9	19	.474	10	20	30	7	23	0	7	16	4	84	3.5	9
Kim Hughes*........8	159	11	25	.440	1	2	.500	19	31	50	11	33	2	11	11	14	23	2.9	6
Jim Ray 18	148	15	49	.306	7	10	.700	13	24	37	11	31	0	4	13	4	37	2.1	7
Jawann Oldham 4	21	2	6	.333	0	0	...	3	2	5	0	3	0	0	2	2	4	1.0	2

3-pt. FG: Denver 30-145 (.207)—Thompson 10-39 (.256); English 3-5 (.600); Issel 2-12 (.167); Vandeweghe 0-7 (.000); McKinney† 1-10 (.100); McKinney‡ 2-12 (.167); Roche 9-27 (.333); Hordges 0-3 (.000); Higgs 4-34 (.118); Nicks* 0-1 (.000); Gondrezick 0-2 (.000); Dunn 0-2 (.000); Valentine 1-2 (.500); Ray 0-1 (.000). Opponents 44-162 (.272).

DETROIT PISTONS

	G	Min.	FGM	FGA	Pct.	FTM	FTA	Pct.	REBOUNDS Off.	Def.	Tot.	Ast.	PF	Dq.	Stl.	TO	Blk.	SCORING Pts.	Avg.	Hi.
John Long 59	1750	441	957	.461	160	184	.870	95	102	197	106	164	3	95	151	22	1044	17.7	40
Kent Benson........59	1956	364	770	.473	196	254	.772	124	276	400	172	184	1	72	190	67	924	15.7	27
Phil Hubbard.......80	2289	433	880	.492	294	426	.690	236	350	586	150	317	14	80	229	20	1161	14.5	29
Keith Herron......80	2270	432	954	.453	228	267	.854	98	113	211	148	154	1	91	153	26	1094	13.7	29
Terry Tyler 82	2549	476	895	.532	148	250	.592	198	369	567	136	215	2	112	163	180	1100	13.4	31
Greg Kelser........25	654	120	285	.421	68	106	.642	53	67	120	45	89	0	34	78	29	308	12.3	33
Bob McAdoo*.......6	168	30	82	.366	12	20	.600	9	32	41	20	16	0	8	18	7	72	12.0	16
Wayne Robinson.....81	1592	234	509	.460	175	240	.729	117	177	294	112	186	2	46	149	24	643	7.9	19
Larry Wright........45	997	140	303	.462	53	66	.803	26	62	88	153	114	1	42	74	7	335	7.4	19
Paul Mokeski 80	1815	224	458	.489	120	200	.600	141	277	418	135	267	7	38	160	73	568	7.1	18

	G	Min.	FGM	FGA	Pct.	FTM	FTA	Pct.	Off.	Def.	Tot.	Ast.	PF	Dq.	Stl.	TO	Blk.	Pts.	Avg.	Hi.
Larry Drew	76	1581	197	484	.407	106	133	.797	24	96	120	249	125	0	88	166	7	504	6.6	23
Ron Lee	82	1829	113	323	.350	113	156	.724	65	155	220	362	260	4	166	173	29	341	4.2	15
Tony Fuller	15	248	24	66	.364	12	16	.750	13	29	42	28	25	0	10	23	1	60	4.0	9
Ed Lawrence	3	19	5	8	.625	2	4	.500	2	2	4	1	6	0	1	1	0	12	4.0	6
Norman Black	3	28	3	10	.300	2	8	.250	0	2	2	2	2	0	1	1	0	8	2.7	4
Lee Johnson†	2	10	0	2	.000	0	0	...	0	2	2	0	1	0	0	0	0	0	0.0	0
Lee Johnson‡	12	90	7	25	.280	0	0	...	6	16	22	1	18	0	0	7	5	14	1.2	6

3-pt. FG: Detroit 13-84 (.155)—Long 2-11 (.182); Benson 0-4 (.000); Hubbard 1-3 (.333); Herron 2-11 (.182); Tyler 0-8 (.000); Kelser 0-2 (.000); Robinson 0-6 (.000); Wright 2-7 (.286); Mokeski 0-1 (.000); Drew 4-17 (.235); Lee 2-13 (.154); Fuller 0-1 (.000). Opponents 31-127 (.244).

GOLDEN STATE WARRIORS

	G	Min.	FGM	FGA	Pct.	FTM	FTA	Pct.	Off.	Def.	Tot.	Ast.	PF	Dq.	Stl.	TO	Blk.	Pts.	Avg.	Hi.
World B. Free	65	2370	516	1157	.446	528	649	.814	48	111	159	361	183	1	85	195	11	1565	24.1	39
Bernard King	81	2914	731	1244	.588	307	437	.703	178	373	551	287	304	5	72	265	34	1771	21.9	50
Joe Barry Carroll	82	2919	616	1254	.491	315	440	.716	274	485	759	117	313	10	50	243	121	1547	18.9	46
Purvis Short	79	2309	549	1157	.475	168	205	.820	151	240	391	249	244	3	78	143	19	1269	16.1	45
Larry Smith	82	2578	304	594	.512	177	301	.588	433	561	994	93	316	10	70	146	63	785	9.6	23
Joe Hassett†	24	434	84	198	.424	7	8	.875	13	30	43	56	44	0	8	11	2	218	9.1	23
Joe Hassett‡	41	714	143	340	.421	17	21	.810	24	44	68	74	65	0	13	22	2	356	8.7	23
John Lucas	66	1919	222	506	.439	107	145	.738	34	120	154	464	140	1	83	185	2	555	8.4	23
Sonny Parker	73	1317	191	388	.492	94	128	.734	101	93	194	106	112	0	67	84	13	476	6.5	18
Rudy White*	4	43	9	18	.500	4	4	1.000	0	0	0	2	7	0	4	3	0	22	5.5	12
Lorenzo Romar	53	726	87	211	.412	43	63	.683	10	46	56	136	64	0	27	52	3	219	4.1	14
Rickey Brown	45	580	83	162	.512	16	21	.762	52	114	166	21	103	4	9	31	14	182	4.0	15
Billy Reid	59	597	84	185	.454	22	39	.564	27	33	60	71	111	0	33	78	5	190	3.2	14
Phil Chenier	9	82	11	33	.333	6	6	1.000	1	7	8	7	10	0	0	4	0	29	3.2	6
Clifford Ray	66	838	64	152	.421	29	62	.468	73	144	217	52	194	2	24	74	13	157	2.4	18
Bill Mayfield	7	54	8	18	.444	1	2	.500	7	2	9	1	8	0	0	3	1	17	2.4	6
Tom Abernethy*	10	39	1	3	.333	2	3	.667	1	7	8	1	5	0	1	2	0	4	0.4	2
John Mengelt	2	11	0	4	.000	0	0	...	0	0	0	2	0	0	0	0	0	0	0.0	0

3-pt. FG: Golden State 60-210 (.286)—Free 5-31 (.161); King 2-6 (.333); Carroll 0-2 (.000); Short 3-17 (.176); Hassett† 43-116 (.371); Hassett‡ 53-156 (.340); Lucas 4-24 (.167); Romar 2-6 (.333); Reid 0-5 (.000); Chenier 1-3 (.333). Opponents 37-100 (.201).

HOUSTON ROCKETS

	G	Min.	FGM	FGA	Pct.	FTM	FTA	Pct.	Off.	Def.	Tot.	Ast.	PF	Dq.	Stl.	TO	Blk.	Pts.	Avg.	Hi.
Moses Malone	80	3245	806	1545	.522	609	804	.757	474	706	1180	141	223	0	83	308	150	2222	27.8	51
Calvin Murphy	76	2014	528	1074	.492	206	215	.958	33	54	87	222	209	0	111	129	6	1266	16.7	42
Robert Reid	82	2963	536	1113	.482	229	303	.756	164	419	583	344	325	4	163	198	66	1301	15.9	34
Rudy Tomjanovich	52	1264	263	563	.467	65	82	.793	78	130	208	81	121	0	19	58	6	603	11.6	25
Mike Dunleavy	74	1609	310	632	.491	156	186	.839	28	90	118	268	165	1	64	137	2	777	10.5	48
Allen Leavell	79	1686	258	548	.471	124	149	.832	30	104	134	384	160	1	97	189	15	642	8.1	24
Billy Paultz	81	1659	262	517	.507	75	153	.490	111	280	391	105	182	1	28	89	72	599	7.4	20
Bill Willoughby	55	1145	150	287	.523	49	64	.766	74	153	227	64	102	0	18	74	31	349	6.3	21
Calvin Garrett	70	1638	188	415	.453	50	62	.806	85	179	264	132	167	0	50	90	10	427	6.1	22
Tom Henderson	66	1411	137	332	.413	78	95	.821	30	74	104	307	111	1	53	93	4	352	5.3	16
Major Jones	68	1003	117	252	.464	64	101	.634	96	138	234	41	112	0	18	57	23	298	4.4	18
John Stroud	9	88	11	34	.324	3	4	.750	7	6	13	9	7	0	1	4	0	25	2.8	11
Lee Johnson*	10	80	7	23	.304	3	5	.600	6	14	20	1	17	0	0	7	5	17	1.7	6

3-pt. FG: Houston 21-118 (.178)—Malone 1-3 (.333); Murphy 4-17 (.235); Reid 0-4 (.000); Tomjanovich 12-51 (.235); Dunleavy 1-16 (.063); Leavell 2-17 (.118); Paultz 0-3 (.000); Garrett 1-3 (.333); Henderson 0-3 (.000); Jones 0-1 (.000). Opponents 49-171 (.287).

INDIANA PACERS

	G	Min.	FGM	FGA	Pct.	FTM	FTA	Pct.	Off.	Def.	Tot.	Ast.	PF	Dq.	Stl.	TO	Blk.	Pts.	Avg.	Hi.
Billy Knight	82	2385	546	1025	.533	341	410	.832	191	219	410	157	155	1	84	177	12	1436	17.5	52
James Edwards	81	2375	511	1004	.509	244	347	.703	191	380	571	212	304	7	32	164	128	1266	15.6	39
Johnny Davis	72	2536	426	917	.465	238	299	.796	56	114	170	480	179	2	95	167	14	1094	14.4	30
Mike Bantom	76	2375	431	882	.489	199	281	.708	150	277	427	240	284	9	80	197	85	1061	14.0	29
George McGinnis	69	1845	348	768	.453	207	385	.538	164	364	528	210	242	3	99	221	28	903	13.1	27
George Johnson	43	930	182	394	.462	93	122	.762	99	179	278	86	120	1	47	85	23	457	10.6	26
Louis Orr	82	1787	348	709	.491	163	202	.807	172	189	361	132	153	0	55	123	25	859	10.5	22
Dudley Bradley	82	1867	265	559	.474	125	178	.702	70	123	193	188	236	2	186	122	37	657	8.0	20
Clemon Johnson	81	1643	235	466	.504	112	189	.593	173	295	468	144	185	1	44	121	119	582	7.2	17
Don Buse	58	1095	114	287	.397	50	65	.769	19	65	84	140	61	0	74	38	8	297	5.1	13
Kenny Natt	19	149	25	77	.325	7	11	.636	9	6	15	10	18	0	5	10	1	59	3.1	15
Jerry Sichting	47	450	34	95	.358	25	32	.781	11	32	43	70	38	0	23	28	1	93	2.0	12
Tom Abernethy†	29	259	24	56	.429	11	19	.579	19	21	40	18	29	0	6	6	3	59	2.0	6
Tom Abernethy‡	39	298	25	59	.424	13	22	.591	20	28	48	19	34	0	7	8	3	63	1.6	6
Dick Miller*	5	34	2	6	.333	0	0	...	1	3	4	4	2	0	3	4	0	4	0.8	2

3-pt. FG: Indiana 30-169 (.178)—Knight 3-19 (.158); Edwards 0-3 (.000); Davis 4-33 (.121); Bantom 0-6 (.000); McGinnis 0-7 (.000); G. Johnson 0-5 (.000); Orr 0-6 (.000); Bradley 2-16 (.125); C. Johnson 0-1 (.000); Buse 19-58 (.328); Natt 2-8 (.250); Sichting 0-5 (.000); Abernethy† 0-1 (.000); Abernethy‡ 0-1 (.000); Miller* 0-1 (.000). Opponents 41-179 (.229).

1980-81

KANSAS CITY KINGS

	G	Min.	FGM	FGA	Pct.	FTM	FTA	Pct.	Off.	Def.	Tot.	Ast.	PF	Dq.	Stl.	TO	Blk.	Pts.	Avg.	Hi.
Otis Birdsong	71	2593	710	1306	.544	317	455	.697	119	139	258	233	172	2	93	173	18	1747	24.6	42
Scott Wedman	81	2902	685	1437	.477	140	204	.686	128	305	433	226	294	4	97	161	46	1535	19.0	41
Phil Ford	66	2287	424	887	.478	294	354	.831	26	102	128	580	190	3	99	241	6	1153	17.5	38
Reggie King	81	2743	472	867	.544	264	386	.684	235	551	786	122	227	2	102	164	41	1208	14.9	33
Joe Meriweather	74	1514	206	415	.496	148	213	.695	126	267	393	77	219	4	27	125	80	560	7.6	24
Ernie Grunfeld	79	1584	260	486	.535	75	101	.743	31	175	206	205	155	1	60	88	15	595	7.5	30
Charles Whitney	47	782	149	306	.487	50	65	.769	29	77	106	68	98	0	47	48	6	350	7.4	20
Sam Lacey	82	2228	237	536	.442	92	117	.786	131	453	584	399	302	5	95	182	120	567	6.9	16
Jo Jo White	13	236	36	82	.439	11	18	.611	3	18	21	37	21	0	11	18	1	83	6.4	12
Leon Douglas	79	1356	185	323	.573	102	186	.548	150	234	384	69	251	2	25	90	38	472	6.0	17
Frankie Sanders	23	186	34	77	.442	20	22	.909	6	15	21	17	20	0	16	21	1	88	3.8	13
Gus Gerard*	16	123	19	51	.373	19	29	.655	13	16	29	6	24	0	3	7	6	57	3.6	9
Lloyd Walton	61	821	90	218	.413	26	33	.788	13	35	48	208	45	0	32	80	2	206	3.4	18
John Lambert†	43	475	65	160	.406	18	23	.783	27	63	90	24	74	0	12	17	5	148	3.4	12
John Lambert‡	46	483	68	165	.412	18	23	.783	27	63	90	27	76	0	12	19	5	154	3.3	12

3-pt. FG: Kansas City 49-168 (.292)—Birdsong 10-35 (.286); Wedman 25-77 (.325); Ford 11-36 (.306); Whitney 2-6 (.333); Lacey 1-5 (.200); Douglas 0-3 (.000); Gerard* 0-3 (.000); Walton 0-1 (.000); Lambert† 0-2 (.000); Lambert‡ 0-2 (.000). Opponents 31-153 (.203).

LOS ANGELES LAKERS

	G	Min.	FGM	FGA	Pct.	FTM	FTA	Pct.	Off.	Def.	Tot.	Ast.	PF	Dq.	Stl.	TO	Blk.	Pts.	Avg.	Hi.
Kareem Abdul-Jabbar	80	2976	836	1457	.574	423	552	.766	197	624	821	272	244	4	59	249	228	2095	26.2	42
Jamaal Wilkes	81	3028	786	1495	.526	254	335	.758	146	289	435	235	223	1	121	207	29	1827	22.6	34
Magic Johnson	37	1371	312	587	.532	171	225	.760	101	219	320	317	100	0	127	143	27	798	21.6	41
Norm Nixon	79	2962	576	1210	.476	196	252	.778	64	168	232	696	226	2	146	285	11	1350	17.1	30
Jim Chones	82	2562	378	751	.503	126	193	.653	180	477	657	153	324	4	39	159	96	882	10.8	23
Michael Cooper	81	2625	321	654	.491	117	149	.785	121	215	336	332	249	4	133	164	78	763	9.4	20
Mark Landsberger	69	1086	164	327	.502	62	116	.534	152	225	377	27	135	0	19	65	6	390	5.7	22
Butch Carter	54	672	114	247	.462	70	95	.737	34	31	65	52	99	0	23	50	1	301	5.6	16
Eddie Jordan†	60	987	120	279	.430	63	95	.663	25	55	80	195	136	0	74	120	7	306	5.1	18
Eddie Jordan‡	74	1226	150	352	.426	87	127	.685	30	68	98	241	165	0	98	143	8	393	5.3	18
Brad Holland	41	295	47	111	.423	35	49	.714	9	20	29	23	44	0	21	31	1	130	3.2	10
Jim Brewer	78	1107	107	197	.543	15	40	.375	127	154	281	55	158	2	43	48	58	229	2.9	14
Alan Hardy	22	111	22	59	.373	7	10	.700	8	11	19	3	13	0	1	11	9	51	2.3	8
Myles Patrick	3	9	2	5	.400	1	2	.500	1	1	2	1	3	0	0	1	0	5	1.7	3
Tony Jackson	2	14	1	3	.333	0	0	...	0	2	2	2	1	0	2	0	0	2	1.0	2

3-pt. FG: L.A. Lakers 17-94 (.181)—Abdul-Jabbar 0-1 (.000); Wilkes 1-13 (.077); Johnson 3-17 (.176); Nixon 2-12 (.167); Chones 0-4 (.000); Cooper 4-19 (.211); Landsberger 0-1 (.000); Carter 3-10 (.300); Jordan† 3-12 (.250); Jordan‡ 6-22 (.273); Holland 1-3 (.333); Brewer 0-2 (.000). Opponents 42-184 (.228).

MILWAUKEE BUCKS

	G	Min.	FGM	FGA	Pct.	FTM	FTA	Pct.	Off.	Def.	Tot.	Ast.	PF	Dq.	Stl.	TO	Blk.	Pts.	Avg.	Hi.
Marques Johnson	76	2542	636	1153	.552	269	381	.706	225	293	518	346	196	1	115	190	41	1541	20.3	40
Junior Bridgeman	77	2215	537	1102	.487	213	241	.884	78	211	289	234	182	2	88	150	28	1290	16.8	34
Bob Lanier	67	1753	376	716	.525	208	277	.751	128	285	413	179	184	0	73	139	81	961	14.3	29
Sidney Moncrief	80	2417	400	739	.541	320	398	.804	186	220	406	264	156	1	90	145	37	1122	14.0	27
Quinn Buckner	82	2384	471	956	.493	149	203	.734	88	210	298	384	271	3	197	236	3	1092	13.3	31
Mickey Johnson	82	2118	379	846	.448	262	332	.789	183	362	545	286	256	4	94	230	71	1023	12.5	23
Brian Winters	69	1771	331	697	.475	119	137	.869	32	108	140	229	185	2	70	136	10	799	11.6	26
Pat Cummings	74	1084	248	460	.539	99	140	.707	97	195	292	62	192	4	31	114	19	595	8.0	30
Mike Evans	71	911	134	291	.460	50	64	.781	22	65	87	167	114	0	34	77	4	320	4.5	16
Harvey Catchings	77	1635	134	300	.447	59	92	.641	154	319	473	99	284	7	33	105	184	327	4.2	14
Len Elmore	72	925	76	212	.358	54	75	.720	68	140	208	69	178	3	37	44	52	206	2.9	12

3-pt. FG: Milwaukee 30-131 (.229)—Ma. Johnson 0-9 (.000); Bridgeman 3-21 (.143); Lanier 1-1 (1.000); Moncrief 2-9 (.222); Buckner 1-6 (.167); Mi. Johnson 3-18 (.167); Winters 18-51 (.353); Cummings 0-2 (.000); Evans 2-14 (.143). Opponents 35-199 (.176).

NEW JERSEY NETS

	G	Min.	FGM	FGA	Pct.	FTM	FTA	Pct.	Off.	Def.	Tot.	Ast.	PF	Dq.	Stl.	TO	Blk.	Pts.	Avg.	Hi.
Mike Newlin	79	2911	632	1272	.497	414	466	.888	78	141	219	299	237	2	87	248	9	1688	21.4	43
Cliff Robinson	63	1822	525	1070	.491	178	248	.718	120	361	481	105	216	6	58	182	52	1229	19.5	38
Maurice Lucas	68	2162	404	835	.484	191	254	.752	153	422	575	173	260	3	57	176	59	999	14.7	39
Mike Gminski	56	1579	291	688	.423	155	202	.767	137	282	419	72	127	1	54	128	100	737	13.2	31
Darwin Cook	81	1980	383	819	.468	132	180	.733	96	140	236	297	197	4	141	176	36	904	11.2	35
Mike O'Koren	79	2473	365	751	.486	135	212	.637	179	299	478	252	243	8	86	146	27	870	11.0	28
Bob McAdoo†	10	153	38	75	.507	17	21	.810	8	18	26	10	22	0	9	14	6	93	9.3	17
Bob McAdoo‡	16	321	68	157	.433	29	41	.707	17	50	67	30	38	0	17	32	13	165	10.3	17
Edgar Jones	60	950	189	357	.529	146	218	.670	92	171	263	43	185	4	36	101	81	524	8.7	27
Bob Elliott	73	1320	214	419	.511	121	202	.599	104	157	261	129	175	3	34	119	16	550	7.5	22
Lowes Moore	71	1406	212	478	.444	69	92	.750	43	125	168	228	179	1	61	108	17	497	7.0	19
Eddie Jordan*	14	239	30	73	.411	24	32	.750	5	13	18	46	29	0	24	23	1	87	6.2	14
Foots Walker	41	1172	72	169	.426	88	111	.793	22	80	102	253	105	0	52	85	1	234	5.7	25

	G	Min.	FGM	FGA	Pct.	FTM	FTA	Pct.	Off.	Def.	Tot.	Ast.	PF	Dq.	Stl.	TO	Blk.	Pts.	Avg.	Hi.
Jan van Breda Kolff	78	1426	100	245	.408	98	117	.838	48	154	202	129	214	3	38	108	50	300	3.8	11
Rory Sparrow	15	212	22	63	.349	12	16	.750	7	11	18	32	15	0	13	18	3	56	3.7	14

3-pt. FG: New Jersey 34-138 (.246)—Newlin 10-30 (.333); Robinson 1-1 (1.000); Lucas 0-2 (.000); Gminski 0-1 (.000); Cook 6-25 (.240); O'Koren 5-18 (.278); McAdoo† 0-1 (.000); McAdoo‡ 0-1 (.000); Jones 0-4 (.000); Elliott 1-2 (.500); Moore 4-27 (.148); Jordan* 3-10 (.300); Walker 2-9 (.222); van Breda Kolff 2-8 (.250). Opponents 28-130 (.215).

NEW YORK KNICKERBOCKERS

	G	Min.	FGM	FGA	Pct.	FTM	FTA	Pct.	Off.	Def.	Tot.	Ast.	PF	Dq.	Stl.	TO	Blk.	Pts.	Avg.	Hi.
Bill Cartwright	82	2925	619	1118	.554	408	518	.788	161	452	613	111	259	2	48	200	83	1646	20.1	33
Ray Williams	79	2742	616	1335	.461	312	382	.817	122	199	321	432	270	4	185	235	37	1560	19.7	42
Micheal R. Richardson	79	3175	523	1116	.469	224	338	.663	173	372	545	627	258	2	232	302	35	1293	16.4	28
Campy Russell	79	2865	508	1095	.464	268	343	.781	109	244	353	257	248	2	99	212	8	1292	16.4	36
Sly Williams	67	1976	349	708	.493	185	268	.690	159	257	416	180	199	0	116	141	18	885	13.2	27
Mike Glenn	82	1506	285	511	.558	98	110	.891	27	61	88	108	126	0	72	62	5	672	8.2	29
Marvin Webster	82	1708	159	341	.466	104	163	.638	162	303	465	72	187	2	27	103	97	423	5.2	16
DeWayne Scales	44	484	94	225	.418	26	39	.667	47	85	132	10	54	0	12	30	4	215	4.9	20
Mike Woodson	81	949	165	373	.442	49	64	.766	33	64	97	75	95	0	36	54	12	380	4.7	25
Larry Demic	76	964	128	254	.504	58	92	.630	114	129	243	28	153	0	12	58	13	314	4.1	17
Reggie Carter	60	536	59	179	.330	51	69	.739	30	39	69	76	68	0	22	38	2	169	2.8	11

3-pt. FG: New York 56-236 (.237)—Cartwright 0-1 (.000); R. Williams 16-68 (.235); Richardson 23-102 (.225); Russell 8-26 (.308); S. Williams 2-8 (.250); Glenn 4-11 (.364); Webster 1-4 (.250); Scales 1-6 (.167); Woodson 1-5 (.200); Demic 0-2 (.000); Carter 0-3 (.000). Opponents 43-172 (.250).

PHILADELPHIA 76ERS

	G	Min.	FGM	FGA	Pct.	FTM	FTA	Pct.	Off.	Def.	Tot.	Ast.	PF	Dq.	Stl.	TO	Blk.	Pts.	Avg.	Hi.
Julius Erving	82	2874	794	1524	.521	422	536	.787	244	413	657	364	233	0	173	266	147	2014	24.6	45
Darryl Dawkins	76	2088	423	697	.607	219	304	.720	106	439	545	109	316	9	38	220	112	1065	14.0	26
Bobby Jones	81	2046	407	755	.539	282	347	.813	142	293	435	226	226	2	95	149	74	1096	13.5	26
Andrew Toney	76	1768	399	806	.495	161	226	.712	32	111	143	273	234	5	59	219	10	968	12.9	35
Doug Collins	12	329	62	126	.492	24	29	.828	6	23	29	42	23	0	7	22	4	148	12.3	19
Steve Mix	72	1327	288	575	.501	200	240	.833	105	159	264	114	107	0	59	88	18	776	10.8	28
Lionel Hollins	82	2154	327	696	.470	125	171	.731	47	144	191	352	205	2	104	207	18	781	9.5	23
Maurice Cheeks	81	2415	310	581	.534	140	178	.787	67	178	245	560	231	1	193	174	39	763	9.4	27
Caldwell Jones	81	2639	218	485	.449	148	193	.767	200	613	813	122	271	2	53	168	134	584	7.2	15
Clint Richardson	77	1313	227	464	.489	84	108	.778	83	93	176	152	102	0	36	110	10	538	7.0	19
Ollie Johnson	40	372	87	158	.551	27	31	.871	8	47	55	30	45	0	20	25	2	202	5.1	20
Earl Cureton	52	528	93	205	.454	33	64	.516	51	104	155	25	68	0	20	29	23	219	4.2	16
Monti Davis*	1	2	1	1	1.000	0	0	...	0	1	1	0	0	0	0	0	0	2	2.0	2

3-pt. FG: Philadelphia 19-84 (.226)—Erving 4-18 (.222); B. Jones 0-3 (.000); Toney 9-29 (.310); Mix 0-3 (.000); Hollins 2-15 (.133); Cheeks 3-8 (.375); Richardson 0-1 (.000); Johnson 1-6 (.167); Cureton 0-1 (.000). Opponents 48-200 (.240).

PHOENIX SUNS

	G	Min.	FGM	FGA	Pct.	FTM	FTA	Pct.	Off.	Def.	Tot.	Ast.	PF	Dq.	Stl.	TO	Blk.	Pts.	Avg.	Hi.
Truck Robinson	82	3088	647	1280	.505	249	396	.629	216	573	789	206	220	1	68	250	38	1543	18.8	40
Dennis Johnson	79	2615	532	1220	.436	411	501	.820	160	203	363	291	244	2	136	208	61	1486	18.8	39
Walter Davis	78	2182	593	1101	.539	209	250	.836	63	137	200	302	192	3	97	222	12	1402	18.0	32
Alvan Adams	75	2054	458	870	.526	199	259	.768	157	389	546	344	226	2	106	226	69	1115	14.9	31
Jeff Cook	79	2192	286	616	.464	100	155	.645	170	297	467	201	236	3	82	146	54	672	8.5	16
Johnny High	81	1750	246	576	.427	183	264	.693	89	139	228	202	251	2	129	188	26	677	8.4	20
Kyle Macy	82	1469	272	532	.511	107	119	.899	44	88	132	160	120	0	76	95	5	663	8.1	21
Rich Kelley	81	1686	196	387	.506	175	231	.758	131	310	441	282	210	0	79	209	63	567	7.0	17
Alvin Scott	82	1423	173	348	.497	97	127	.764	101	167	268	114	124	0	60	77	70	444	5.4	14
Joel Kramer	82	1065	136	258	.527	63	91	.692	77	155	232	88	132	0	35	67	17	335	4.1	17
Mike Niles	44	231	48	138	.348	17	37	.459	26	32	58	15	41	0	8	25	1	115	2.6	10

3-pt. FG: Phoenix 35-161 (.217)—Johnson 11-51 (.216); Davis 7-17 (.412); Cook 0-5 (.000); High 2-24 (.083); Macy 12-51 (.235); Kelley 0-2 (.000); Scott 1-6 (.167); Kramer 0-1 (.000); Niles 2-4 (.500). Opponents 69-209 (.330).

PORTLAND TRAIL BLAZERS

	G	Min.	FGM	FGA	Pct.	FTM	FTA	Pct.	Off.	Def.	Tot.	Ast.	PF	Dq.	Stl.	TO	Blk.	Pts.	Avg.	Hi.
Jim Paxson	79	2701	585	1092	.536	182	248	.734	74	137	211	299	172	1	140	131	9	1354	17.1	32
Mychal Thompson	79	2790	569	1151	.494	207	323	.641	223	463	686	284	260	5	62	241	170	1345	17.0	33
Kelvin Ransey	80	2431	525	1162	.452	164	219	.749	42	153	195	555	201	1	88	232	9	1217	15.2	35
Billy Ray Bates	77	1560	439	902	.487	170	199	.854	71	86	157	196	120	0	82	149	6	1062	13.8	40
Calvin Natt	74	2111	395	794	.497	200	283	.707	149	282	431	159	188	2	73	163	18	994	13.4	29
Kermit Washington	73	2120	325	571	.569	181	288	.628	236	450	686	149	258	5	85	144	86	831	11.4	27
Tom Owens	79	1843	322	630	.511	191	250	.764	165	291	456	140	273	10	36	130	47	835	10.6	27
Bob Gross	82	1934	253	479	.528	135	159	.849	126	202	328	251	238	5	90	151	67	641	7.8	17
Ron Brewer*	29	548	95	246	.386	26	34	.765	13	20	33	55	42	0	34	38	9	217	7.5	26
Kevin Kunnert	55	842	101	216	.468	42	54	.778	98	189	287	67	143	1	17	50	32	244	4.4	19
Mike Gale†	42	476	71	145	.490	36	42	.857	9	38	47	70	61	0	39	38	5	179	4.3	19
Mike Gale‡	77	1112	157	309	.508	55	68	.809	16	83	99	169	117	0	94	77	7	371	4.8	19

	G	Min.	FGM	FGA	Pct.	FTM	FTA	Pct.	REBOUNDS Off.	Def.	Tot.	Ast.	PF	Dq.	Stl.	TO	Blk.	SCORING Pts.	Avg.	Hi.
Roy Hamilton 1	1	5	1	3	.333	1	2	.500	2	1	3	0	1	0	0	1	0	3	3.0	3
Mike Harper 55	55	461	56	136	.412	37	85	.435	28	65	93	17	73	0	23	32	20	149	2.7	12
Geoff Crompton 6	6	33	4	8	.500	1	5	.200	7	11	18	2	4	0	0	5	2	9	1.5	6

3-pt. FG: Portland 25-148 (.169)—Paxson 2-30 (.067); Thompson 0-1 (.000); Ransey 3-31 (.097); Bates 14-54 (.259); Natt 4-8 (.500); Washington 0-1 (.000); Owens 0-4 (.000); Gross 0-9 (.000); Brewer* 1-3 (.333); Gale† 1-4 (.250); Gale‡ 2-7 (.286); Harper 0-3 (.000). Opponents 34-149 (.228).

SAN ANTONIO SPURS

	G	Min.	FGM	FGA	Pct.	FTM	FTA	Pct.	REBOUNDS Off.	Def.	Tot.	Ast.	PF	Dq.	Stl.	TO	Blk.	SCORING Pts.	Avg.	Hi.
George Gervin. 82	82	2765	850	1729	.492	512	620	.826	126	293	419	260	212	4	94	251	56	2221	27.1	49
James Silas 75	75	2055	476	997	.477	374	440	.850	44	187	231	285	129	0	51	159	12	1326	17.7	34
Mark Olberding 82	82	2408	348	685	.508	315	380	.829	146	325	471	277	307	6	75	202	31	1012	12.3	28
Dave Corzine. 82	82	1960	366	747	.490	125	175	.714	228	408	636	117	212	0	42	131	99	857	10.5	24
Reggie Johnson 79	79	1716	340	682	.499	128	193	.663	132	226	358	78	283	8	45	130	48	808	10.2	27
Ron Brewer† 46	46	904	180	385	.468	65	80	.813	21	32	53	93	53	0	27	54	25	425	9.2	20
Ron Brewer‡ 75	75	1452	275	631	.436	91	114	.798	34	52	86	148	95	0	61	92	34	642	8.6	26
John Shumate* 22	22	519	56	128	.438	53	73	.726	33	54	87	24	46	0	21	41	9	165	7.5	15
Johnny Moore 82	82	1578	249	520	.479	105	172	.610	58	138	196	373	178	0	120	154	22	604	7.4	22
Kevin Restani 64	64	999	192	369	.520	62	88	.705	71	103	174	81	103	0	16	68	14	449	7.0	22
Paul Griffin 82	82	1930	166	325	.511	170	253	.672	184	321	505	249	207	3	77	132	38	502	6.1	12
Michael Wiley 33	33	271	76	138	.551	36	48	.750	22	42	64	11	38	1	8	28	6	188	5.7	17
Mike Gale* 35	35	636	86	164	.524	19	26	.731	7	45	52	99	56	0	55	39	2	192	5.5	15
George Johnson 82	82	1935	164	347	.473	80	109	.734	215	387	602	92	273	3	47	110	278	408	5.0	15
Gus Gerard† 11	11	129	22	60	.367	8	11	.727	17	21	38	9	17	0	7	8	3	52	4.7	12
Gus Gerard‡ 27	27	252	41	111	.369	27	40	.675	30	37	67	15	41	0	10	15	9	109	4.0	12

3-pt. FG: San Antonio 15-85 (.176)—Gervin 9-35 (.257); Silas 0-2 (.000); Olberding 1-7 (.143); Corzine 0-3 (.000); R. Johnson 0-1 (.000); Brewer† 0-4 (.000); Brewer‡ 1-7 (.143); Moore 1-19 (.053); Restani 3-8 (.375); Wiley 0-2 (.000); Gale* 1-3 (.333); Gerard† 0-1 (.000); Gerard‡ 0-4 (.000). Opponents 45-168 (.268).

SAN DIEGO CLIPPERS

	G	Min.	FGM	FGA	Pct.	FTM	FTA	Pct.	REBOUNDS Off.	Def.	Tot.	Ast.	PF	Dq.	Stl.	TO	Blk.	SCORING Pts.	Avg.	Hi.
Freeman Williams 82	82	1976	642	1381	.465	253	297	.852	75	54	129	164	157	0	91	166	5	1585	19.3	41
Phil Smith. 76	76	2378	519	1057	.491	237	313	.757	49	107	156	372	231	1	84	176	18	1279	16.8	35
Swen Nater. 82	82	2809	517	935	.553	244	307	.795	295	722	1017	199	295	8	49	211	46	1278	15.6	30
Michael Brooks 82	82	2479	488	1018	.479	226	320	.706	210	232	442	208	234	2	99	163	31	1202	14.7	35
Joe Bryant 82	82	2359	379	791	.479	193	244	.791	146	294	440	189	264	4	72	176	34	953	11.6	34
Brian Taylor 80	80	2312	310	591	.525	146	185	.789	58	93	151	440	212	0	118	111	23	810	10.1	31
Sidney Wicks 49	49	1083	125	286	.437	76	150	.507	79	144	223	111	168	3	40	94	40	326	6.7	18
Ron Davis. 64	64	817	139	314	.443	94	158	.595	47	72	119	47	98	0	36	61	11	374	5.8	18
Gar Heard 78	78	1631	149	396	.376	79	101	.782	120	228	348	122	196	0	104	81	72	377	4.8	16
Henry Bibby 73	73	1112	118	306	.386	67	98	.684	25	49	74	200	85	0	47	76	2	335	4.6	18
Jerome Whitehead† . . 38	38	562	66	139	.475	23	45	.511	48	135	183	24	100	2	15	45	8	155	4.1	16
Jerome Whitehead‡ . . 48	48	688	83	180	.461	28	56	.500	58	156	214	26	122	2	20	56	9	194	4.0	16
Wally Rank 25	25	153	21	57	.368	13	28	.464	17	13	30	17	33	1	7	26	1	55	2.2	6
Tony Price 5	5	29	2	7	.286	0	0	. . .	0	0	0	3	3	0	2	2	1	4	0.8	2
Stan Pietkiewicz* 6	6	30	2	5	.400	0	0	. . .	0	1	1	2	2	0	0	5	0	4	0.7	2

3-pt. FG: San Diego 132-407 (.324)—Williams 48-141 (.340); Smith 4-18 (.222); Brooks 0-6 (.000); Bryant 2-15 (.133); Taylor 44-115 (.383); Wicks 0-1 (.000); Davis 2-8 (.250); Heard 0-7 (.000); Bibby 32-95 (.337); Whitehead† 0-1 (.000); Whitehead‡ 0-1 (.000). Opponents 33-153 (.216).

SEATTLE SUPERSONICS

	G	Min.	FGM	FGA	Pct.	FTM	FTA	Pct.	REBOUNDS Off.	Def.	Tot.	Ast.	PF	Dq.	Stl.	TO	Blk.	SCORING Pts.	Avg.	Hi.
Jack Sikma. 82	82	2920	595	1311	.454	340	413	.823	184	668	852	248	282	5	78	201	93	1530	18.7	38
Paul Westphal. 36	36	1078	221	500	.442	153	184	.832	11	57	68	148	70	0	46	78	14	601	16.7	32
Fred Brown. 78	78	1986	505	1035	.488	173	208	.832	53	122	175	233	141	0	88	131	13	1206	15.5	28
James Bailey. 82	82	2539	444	889	.499	256	361	.709	192	415	607	98	332	11	74	219	143	1145	14.0	27
Vinnie Johnson 81	81	2311	419	785	.534	214	270	.793	193	173	366	341	198	0	78	216	20	1053	13.0	31
Lonnie Shelton 14	14	440	73	174	.420	36	55	.655	31	47	78	35	48	0	22	41	3	182	13.0	30
John Johnson 80	80	2324	373	866	.431	173	214	.808	135	227	362	312	202	2	57	230	25	919	11.5	26
Wally Walker 82	82	1796	290	626	.463	109	169	.645	105	210	315	122	168	1	53	115	15	689	8.4	21
Bill Hanzlik 74	74	1259	138	289	.478	119	150	.793	67	86	153	111	168	1	58	84	20	396	5.4	17
James Donaldson 68	68	980	129	238	.542	101	170	.594	107	202	309	42	79	0	8	68	74	359	5.3	20
Armond Hill† 51	51	1114	78	219	.356	99	122	.811	31	77	108	174	147	3	40	69	8	255	5.0	17
Armond Hill‡ 75	75	1738	117	335	.349	141	172	.820	41	118	159	292	207	3	66	127	11	375	5.0	17
Rudy White† 12	12	165	14	47	.298	11	12	.917	1	10	11	18	16	0	5	9	1	39	3.3	13
Rudy White‡ 16	16	208	23	65	.354	15	16	.938	1	10	11	20	23	0	9	12	1	61	3.8	13
Dennis Awtrey. 47	47	607	44	93	.473	14	20	.700	33	75	108	54	85	0	12	33	8	102	2.2	8
Jacky Dorsey 29	29	253	20	70	.286	13	25	.520	23	65	88	9	47	0	9	14	1	53	1.8	8
John Shumate† 2	2	8	0	3	.000	2	3	.667	1	0	1	0	3	0	0	1	0	2	1.0	2
John Shumate‡ 24	24	527	56	131	.427	55	76	.724	34	54	88	24	49	0	21	42	9	167	7.0	15

3-pt. FG: Seattle 32-117 (.274)—Sikma 0-5 (.000); Westphal 6-25 (.240); Brown 23-64 (.359); Bailey 1-2 (.500); V. Johnson 1-5 (.200); J. Johnson 0-1 (.000); Walker 0-3 (.000); Hanzlik 1-5 (.200); Hill† 0-6 (.000); Hill‡ 0-7 (.000); White† 0-1 (.000); White‡ 0-1 (.000). Opponents 42-157 (.268).

1980-81

UTAH JAZZ

	G	Min.	FGM	FGA	Pct.	FTM	FTA	Pct.	REBOUNDS Off.	Def.	Tot.	Ast.	PF	Dq.	Stl.	TO	Blk.	SCORING Pts.	Avg.	Hi.
Adrian Dantley	80	3417	909	1627	.559	632	784	.806	192	317	509	322	245	1	109	282	18	2452	30.7	55
Darrell Griffith	81	2867	716	1544	.464	229	320	.716	79	209	288	194	219	0	106	231	50	1671	20.6	38
Ben Poquette	82	2808	324	614	.528	126	162	.778	160	469	629	161	342	18	67	122	174	777	9.5	20
Rickey Green	47	1307	176	366	.481	70	97	.722	30	86	116	235	123	2	75	83	1	422	9.0	20
Allan Bristow	82	2001	271	611	.444	166	198	.838	103	327	430	383	190	1	63	171	3	713	8.7	18
Billy McKinney*	35	1032	124	233	.532	44	48	.917	12	62	74	157	107	3	38	70	4	293	8.4	21
Ron Boone	52	1146	160	371	.431	75	94	.798	17	67	84	161	126	0	33	111	8	406	7.8	18
Wayne Cooper	71	1420	213	471	.452	62	90	.689	166	274	440	52	219	8	18	77	51	489	6.9	22
Carl Nickst	40	616	107	210	.510	36	67	.537	24	37	61	69	89	0	32	53	1	250	6.3	24
Carl Nickst	67	1109	172	359	.479	71	126	.563	37	73	110	149	141	0	60	116	3	415	6.2	24
James Hardy	23	509	52	111	.468	11	20	.550	39	94	133	36	58	2	21	23	20	115	5.0	13
Jeff Wilkins	56	1058	117	260	.450	27	40	.675	62	212	274	40	169	3	32	59	46	261	4.7	22
Jeff Judkins	62	666	92	216	.426	45	51	.882	29	64	93	59	84	0	16	30	2	238	3.8	13
Mel Bennett	28	313	26	60	.433	53	81	.654	33	60	93	15	56	0	3	31	11	105	3.8	12
Brett Vroman	11	93	10	27	.370	14	19	.737	7	18	25	9	26	1	5	9	5	34	3.1	9
John Duren	40	458	33	101	.327	5	9	.556	8	27	35	54	54	0	18	37	2	71	1.8	10
Dick Millert	3	19	2	3	.667	0	0	...	1	2	3	1	3	0	1	4	0	4	1.3	4
Dick Millert	8	53	4	9	.444	0	0	...	2	5	7	5	5	0	4	8	0	8	1.0	4

3-pt. FG: Utah 42-163 (.258)—Dantley 2-7 (.286); Griffith 10-52 (.192); Poquette 3-6 (.500); Green 0-1 (.000); Bristow 5-18 (.278); McKinney* 1-2 (.500); Boone 11-39 (.282); Cooper 1-3 (.333); Nickst 0-3 (.000); Nickst 0-4 (.000); Judkins 9-28 (.321); Bennett 0-2 (.000); Vroman 0-1 (.000); Duren 0-1 (.000); Millert 0-0; Millert 0-1 (.000). Opponents 45-147 (.306).

WASHINGTON BULLETS

	G	Min.	FGM	FGA	Pct.	FTM	FTA	Pct.	REBOUNDS Off.	Def.	Tot.	Ast.	PF	Dq.	Stl.	TO	Blk.	SCORING Pts.	Avg.	Hi.
Elvin Hayes	81	2931	584	1296	.451	271	439	.617	235	554	789	98	300	6	68	189	171	1439	17.8	34
Kevin Grevey	75	2616	500	1103	.453	244	290	.841	67	152	219	300	161	1	68	144	17	1289	17.2	36
Greg Ballard	82	2610	549	1186	.463	166	196	.847	167	413	580	195	194	1	118	117	39	1271	15.5	38
Kevin Porter	81	2577	446	859	.519	191	247	.773	35	89	124	734	257	4	110	251	10	1086	13.4	31
Mitch Kupchak	82	1934	392	747	.525	240	340	.706	198	371	569	62	195	1	36	161	26	1024	12.5	30
Wes Matthews*	45	1161	224	449	.499	99	129	.767	30	37	67	199	120	1	46	149	10	552	12.3	24
Bob Dandridge	23	545	101	237	.426	28	39	.718	19	64	83	60	54	1	16	33	9	230	10.0	27
Don Collinst	34	661	130	281	.463	74	110	.673	33	48	81	75	93	1	35	67	14	334	9.8	27
Don Collinst	81	1845	360	811	.444	211	272	.776	129	139	268	190	259	6	104	174	25	931	11.5	27
Wes Unseld	63	2032	225	429	.524	55	86	.640	207	466	673	170	171	1	52	97	38	507	8.0	22
Carlos Terry	26	504	80	160	.500	28	42	.667	43	73	116	70	68	1	27	57	13	188	7.2	16
Austin Carrt	39	580	80	206	.388	32	50	.640	18	34	52	49	43	0	14	32	2	192	4.9	17
Austin Carrt	47	657	87	234	.372	34	54	.630	22	39	61	58	53	0	15	41	2	208	4.4	17
Anthony Roberts	26	350	54	144	.375	19	29	.655	18	50	68	20	52	0	11	28	0	127	4.9	18
Rick Mahorn	52	696	111	219	.507	27	40	.675	67	148	215	25	134	3	21	38	44	249	4.8	28
John Williamson	9	112	18	56	.321	5	6	.833	0	7	7	17	13	0	4	12	1	42	4.7	12
Andre McCarter	43	448	51	135	.378	18	24	.750	16	23	39	73	36	0	14	24	0	122	2.8	14
Dave Britton	2	9	2	3	.667	0	0	...	0	2	2	3	2	0	1	2	0	4	2.0	2
Keith McCord	2	9	2	4	.500	0	0	...	1	1	2	1	0	0	0	2	0	4	2.0	2
Lewis Brown	2	5	0	3	.000	2	5	.400	1	1	2	0	2	0	0	1	0	2	1.0	2

3-pt. FG: Washington 65-241 (.270)—Hayes 0-10 (.000); Grevey 45-136 (.331); Ballard 7-32 (.219); Porter 3-12 (.250); Kupchak 0-1 (.000); Matthews* 5-15 (.333); Dandridge 0-1 (.000); Collinst 0-3 (.000); Collinst 0-6 (.000); Unseld 2-4 (.500); Terry 0-6 (.000); Carrt 0-7 (.000); Carrt 0-7 (.000); Williamson 1-6 (.167); McCarter 2-8 (.250). Opponents 37-176 (.210).

* Finished season with another team. † Totals with this team only. ‡ Totals with all teams.

EASTERN CONFERENCE

FIRST ROUND

Chicago 2, New York 0
Mar. 31—Tue.   Chicago 90 at New York 80
Apr. 3—Fri.   New York 114 at Chicago *115

Philadelphia 2, Indiana 0
Mar. 31—Tue.   Indiana 108 at Philadelphia 124
Apr. 2—Thur.   Philadelphia 96 at Indiana 85

SEMIFINALS

Philadelphia 4, Milwaukee 3
Apr. 5—Sun.   Milwaukee 122 at Philadelphia 125
Apr. 7—Tue.   Milwaukee 109 at Philadelphia 99
Apr. 10—Fri.   Philadelphia 108 at Milwaukee 103
Apr. 12—Sun.   Philadelphia 98 at Milwaukee 109
Apr. 15—Wed.   Milwaukee 99 at Philadelphia 116
Apr. 17—Fri.   Philadelphia 86 at Milwaukee 109
Apr. 19—Sun.   Milwaukee 98 at Philadelphia 99

Boston 4, Chicago 0
Apr. 5—Sun.   Chicago 109 at Boston 121
Apr. 7—Tue.   Chicago 97 at Boston 106
Apr. 10—Fri.   Boston 113 at Chicago 107
Apr. 12—Sun.   Boston 109 at Chicago 103

FINALS

Boston 4, Philadelphia 3
Apr. 21—Tue.   Philadelphia 105 at Boston 104
Apr. 22—Wed.   Philadelphia 99 at Boston 118
Apr. 24—Fri.   Boston 100 at Philadelphia 110
Apr. 26—Sun.   Boston 105 at Philadelphia 107
Apr. 29—Wed.   Philadelphia 109 at Boston 111
May 1—Fri.   Boston 100 at Philadelphia 98
May 3—Sun.   Philadelphia 90 at Boston 91

FINALS

WESTERN CONFERENCE

Boston 4, Ppr

FIRST ROUND

Houston 2, Los Angeles 1
Apr. 1—Wed.   Houston 111 at Los Angeles 107
Apr. 3—Fri.   Los Angeles 111 at Houston 106
Apr. 5—Sun.   Houston 89 at Los Angeles 86

Kansas City 2, Portland 1
Apr. 1—Wed.   Kansas City 98 at Portland *97
Apr. 3—Fri.   Portland 124 at Kansas City *119
Apr. 5—Sun.   Kansas City 104 at Portland 95

SEMIFINALS

Kansas City 4, Phoenix 3
Apr. 7—Tue.   Kansas City 80 at Phoenix 102
Apr. 8—Wed.   Kansas City 88 at Phoenix 83
Apr. 10—Fri.   Phoenix 92 at Kansas City 93
Apr. 12—Sun.   Phoenix 95 at Kansas City 102
Apr. 15—Wed.   Kansas City 89 at Phoenix 101
Apr. 17—Fri.   Phoenix 81 at Kansas City 76
Apr. 19—Sun.   Kansas City 95 at Phoenix 88

Houston 4, San Antonio 3
Apr. 7—Tue.   Houston 107 at San Antonio 98
Apr. 8—Wed.   Houston 113 at San Antonio 125
Apr. 10—Fri.   San Antonio 99 at Houston 112
Apr. 12—Sun.   San Antonio 114 at Houston 112
Apr. 14—Tue.   Houston 123 at San Antonio 117
Apr. 15—Wed.   San Antonio 101 at Houston 96
Apr. 17—Fri.   Houston 105 at San Antonio 100

FINALS

Houston 4, Kansas City 1
Apr. 21—Tue.   Houston 97 at Kansas City 78
Apr. 22—Wed.   Houston 79 at Kansas City 88
Apr. 24—Fri.   Kansas City 88 at Houston 92
Apr. 26—Sun.   Kansas City 89 at Houston 100
Apr. 29—Wed.   Houston 97 at Kansas City 88

NBA FINALS

Boston 4, Houston 2
May 5—Tue.   Houston 95 at Boston 98
May 7—Thur.   Houston 92 at Boston 90
May 9—Sat.   Boston 94 at Houston 71
May 10—Sun.   Boston 86 at Houston 91
May 12—Tue.   Houston 80 at Boston 109
May 14—Thur.   Boston 102 at Houston 91

*Denotes number of overtime periods.

1980-81

1979-80

1979-80 NBA CHAMPION LOS ANGELES LAKERS
Front row (from left): chairman of the board Dr. Jerry Buss, Spencer Haywood, Jamaal Wilkes, Kareem Abdul-Jabbar, Magic Johnson, Jim Chones, general manager Bill Sharman. Back row (from left): head coach Paul Westhead, Dutch Loo, Brad Holland, Mark Landsberger, Marty Byrnes, Michael Cooper, Norm Nixon, trainer Jack Curran, assistant coach Pat Riley.

FINAL STANDINGS

ATLANTIC DIVISION

	Atl.	Bos.	Chi.	Cle.	Den.	Det.	G.S.	Hou.	Ind.	K.C.	L.A.	Mil.	N.J.	N.Y.	Phi.	Pho.	Por.	S.A.	S.D.	Sea.	Uta.	Was.	W	L	Pct.	GB
Boston 4	..	2	4	2	6	2	6	4	1	0	2	5	5	3	1	2	4	2	0	2	4	61	21	.744	..
Philadelphia ..2	3	1	5	2	5	2	4	5	1	1	2	5	6	..	1	2	4	1	1	1	5	59	23	.720	2
Washington ..3	2	2	3	1	4	2	4	2	0	1	1	3	3	1	0	1	2	1	1	2	..	39	43	.476	22
New York 2	1	2	3	1	4	2	3	2	1	0	1	4	..	0	2	2	4	1	0	1	3	39	43	.476	22
New Jersey ...2	1	1	3	1	4	0	3	4	1	0	1	..	2	1	1	0	3	1	1	1	3	34	48	.415	27

CENTRAL DIVISION

	Atl.	Bos.	Chi.	Cle.	Den.	Det.	G.S.	Hou.	Ind.	K.C.	L.A.	Mil.	N.J.	N.Y.	Phi.	Pho.	Por.	S.A.	S.D.	Sea.	Uta.	Was.	W	L	Pct.	GB
Atlanta	2	1	4	1	6	2	2	4	0	1	1	4	4	4	1	2	5	1	0	2	3	50	32	.610	..
Houston 4	0	1	4	1	5	1	..	4	0	0	1	3	3	2	1	1	3	2	1	2	2	41	41	.500	9
San Antonio ..1	2	2	2	1	4	2	3	4	1	0	2	3	2	2	1	1	..	2	1	1	4	41	41	.500	9
Cleveland 2	2	0	..	1	6	2	2	2	2	1	0	3	3	1	1	0	4	1	0	1	3	37	45	.451	13
Indiana 2	2	2	4	1	5	1	2	..	1	0	0	2	4	1	0	2	2	1	0	1	4	37	45	.451	13
Detroit 0	0	1	0	1	..	1	1	1	0	0	1	2	2	1	0	0	2	0	0	1	2	16	66	.195	34

MIDWEST DIVISION

	Atl.	Bos.	Chi.	Cle.	Den.	Det.	G.S.	Hou.	Ind.	K.C.	L.A.	Mil.	N.J.	N.Y.	Phi.	Pho.	Por.	S.A.	S.D.	Sea.	Uta.	Was.	W	L	Pct.	GB
Milwaukee ...1	0	5	2	3	1	6	1	2	3	3	..	1	1	0	4	5	0	4	2	4	1	49	33	.598	..
Kansas City ..2	1	3	0	6	2	3	2	1	..	2	3	1	1	1	1	1	5	3	6	2	47	35	.573	2
Denver 1	0	4	1	..	1	3	1	1	0	1	3	1	1	0	1	2	1	3	1	3	1	30	52	.366	19
Chicago 1	0	..	2	2	1	4	1	0	3	1	1	1	1	0	1	3	0	4	2	2	0	30	52	.366	19
Utah 0	0	4	1	3	1	3	0	1	0	0	2	1	1	1	0	3	1	1	1	..	0	24	58	.293	25

PACIFIC DIVISION

	Atl.	Bos.	Chi.	Cle.	Den.	Det.	G.S.	Hou.	Ind.	K.C.	L.A.	Mil.	N.J.	N.Y.	Phi.	Pho.	Por.	S.A.	S.D.	Sea.	Uta.	Was.	W	L	Pct.	GB
Los Angeles ..1	2	5	1	5	2	5	2	2	4	..	3	2	2	1	3	2	2	5	4	6	1	60	22	.732	..
Seattle 2	2	4	2	5	2	6	1	2	3	2	4	1	2	1	2	5	1	3	..	5	1	56	26	.683	4
Phoenix 1	1	5	1	5	2	4	1	2	5	3	2	1	0	1	..	6	1	2	4	6	2	55	27	.671	5
Portland 0	0	3	2	4	2	4	1	0	5	4	1	2	0	0	0	..	1	4	1	3	1	38	44	.463	22
San Diego 1	0	2	1	3	2	3	0	1	1	1	2	1	1	1	4	2	0	..	3	5	1	35	47	.427	25
Golden State ..0	0	2	0	3	1	..	1	1	3	1	0	2	0	0	2	2	0	3	0	3	0	24	58	.293	36

TEAM STATISTICS

OFFENSIVE

								REBOUNDS								SCORING	
	G	FGM	FGA	Pct.	FTM	FTA	Pct.	Off.	Def.	Tot.	Ast.	PF	Dq.	Stl.	TO	Blk.	Pts.	Avg.
San Antonio ... 82	3856	7738	.498	2024	2528	.801	1153	2515	3668	2326	2103	29	771	1589	333	9788	119.4
Los Angeles ... 82	3898	7368	.529	1622	2092	.775	1085	2653	3738	2413	1784	15	774	1639	546	9438	115.1

	G	FGM	FGA	Pct.	FTM	FTA	Pct.	REBOUNDS Off.	Def.	Tot.	Ast.	PF	Dq.	Stl.	TO	Blk.	SCORING Pts.	Avg.
Cleveland	82	3811	8041	.474	1702	2205	.772	1307	2381	3688	2108	1934	18	764	1370	342	9360	114.1
New York	82	3802	7672	.496	1698	2274	.747	1236	2303	3539	2265	2168	33	881	1613	457	9344	114.0
Boston	82	3617	7387	.490	1907	2449	.779	1227	2457	3684	2198	1974	19	809	1539	308	9303	113.5
Indiana	82	3639	7689	.473	1753	2333	.751	1398	2326	3724	2148	1973	37	900	1517	530	9119	111.2
Phoenix	82	3570	7235	.493	1906	2466	.773	1071	2458	3529	2283	1853	9	908	1629	344	9114	111.1
Houston	82	3599	7496	.480	1782	2326	.766	1394	2217	3611	2149	1927	11	782	1565	373	9084	110.8
Milwaukee	82	3685	7553	.488	1605	2102	.764	1245	2396	3641	2277	1937	12	778	1496	510	9025	110.1
Philadelphia	82	3523	7156	.492	1876	2431	.772	1187	2635	3822	2226	1860	17	792	1708	652	8949	109.1
Detroit	82	3643	7596	.480	1590	2149	.740	1226	2415	3641	1950	2069	47	783	1742	562	8933	108.9
Seattle	82	3554	7565	.470	1730	2253	.768	1380	2550	3930	2043	1865	27	750	1496	428	8897	108.5
New Jersey	82	3456	7504	.461	1882	2406	.782	1229	2535	3764	2094	2181	38	869	1702	581	8879	108.3
Denver	82	3462	7470	.463	1871	2539	.737	1311	2524	3835	2079	1917	24	746	1533	404	8878	108.3
Kansas City	82	3582	7489	.478	1671	2250	.743	1187	2429	3616	2123	2135	20	863	1439	356	8860	108.0
San Diego	82	3524	7494	.470	1595	2167	.736	1294	2308	3602	1688	1896	24	664	1443	288	8820	107.6
Chicago	82	3362	6943	.484	2019	2592	.779	1115	2465	3580	2152	2146	26	704	1684	392	8813	107.5
Washington	82	3574	7796	.458	1552	2048	.758	1334	2723	4057	2201	1893	24	530	1380	443	8773	107.0
Atlanta	82	3261	7027	.464	2038	2645	.771	1369	2406	3775	1913	2293	46	782	1495	539	8573	104.5
Golden State	82	3527	7318	.482	1914	2437	.738	1155	2437	3592	2028	2082	28	779	1492	339	8493	103.6
Portland	82	3408	7167	.476	1560	2100	.743	1295	2408	3703	1898	1956	23	708	1552	472	8402	102.5
Utah	82	3382	6817	.496	1571	1943	.809	967	2359	3326	2005	2006	33	656	1543	362	8394	102.4

DEFENSIVE

	FGM	FGA	Pct.	FTM	FTA	Pct.	REBOUNDS Off.	Def.	Tot.	Ast.	PF	Dq.	Stl.	TO	Blk.	SCORING Pts.	Avg.	Dif.
Atlanta	3144	6872	.458	2000	2616	.765	1261	2339	3600	1758	2171	35	682	1660	554	8334	101.6	+2.9
Portland	3349	7008	.478	1716	2281	.752	1138	2358	3496	2008	1880	23	756	1450	395	8469	103.3	-0.8
Seattle	3408	7424	.459	1640	2147	.764	1203	2409	3612	2016	1997	24	728	1519	393	8515	103.8	+4.7
Philadelphia	3444	7561	.455	1640	2145	.765	1318	2352	3670	2089	2100	39	876	1561	388	8603	104.9	+4.2
Kansas City	3328	6992	.476	1906	2497	.763	1140	2644	3784	1778	2072	17	695	1762	425	8603	104.9	+3.1
Boston	3439	7313	.470	1712	2222	.770	1168	2294	3462	1867	2059	34	686	1635	419	8664	105.7	+7.8
Milwaukee	3456	7487	.462	1714	2275	.753	1360	2293	3653	2154	1912	15	717	1638	358	8702	106.1	+4.0
Phoenix	3563	7480	.476	1593	2119	.752	1216	2447	3663	2026	2051	32	882	1663	389	8819	107.5	+3.6
Golden State	3438	6975	.493	1905	2544	.749	1056	2564	3620	2091	1785	14	720	1486	361	8853	108.0	-4.4
Utah	3559	7182	.496	1702	2205	.772	1159	2288	3447	1997	1782	15	710	1274	398	8887	108.4	-6.0
Los Angeles	3723	7921	.470	1430	1884	.759	1312	2242	3554	2324	1860	27	797	1420	382	8954	109.2	+5.9
New Jersey	3480	7427	.469	1957	2572	.761	1285	2596	3881	2189	2042	27	849	1692	514	8975	109.5	-1.2
Washington	3615	7771	.465	1696	2184	.777	1197	2672	3869	2120	1901	24	734	1222	519	8982	109.5	-2.5
Chicago	3585	7222	.496	1811	2358	.768	1159	2345	3504	2109	2203	38	846	1543	498	9035	110.2	-2.7
Houston	3658	7382	.496	1696	2153	.788	1290	2317	3607	2223	2049	29	778	1597	428	9070	110.6	+0.2
San Diego	3752	7508	.500	1613	2086	.773	1222	2487	3709	2012	1889	16	764	1391	408	9160	111.7	-4.1
Indiana	3693	7545	.489	1734	2295	.756	1394	2552	3946	2323	2028	26	738	1758	470	9176	111.9	-0.7
Denver	3736	7591	.492	1698	2235	.760	1197	2587	3784	2289	2033	22	812	1438	455	9240	112.7	-4.4
Cleveland	3811	7610	.501	1645	2150	.765	1230	2638	3868	2208	2033	30	708	1667	490	9332	113.8	+0.3
New York	3707	7492	.495	1969	2556	.770	1293	2432	3725	2143	2042	31	813	1694	390	9438	115.1	-1.1
Detroit	3847	7761	.496	1858	2405	.773	1319	2572	3891	2306	1871	14	874	1583	470	9609	117.2	-8.3
San Antonio	4000	7997	.500	1731	2283	.758	1248	2472	3720	2537	2192	28	828	1513	457	9819	119.7	-0.3
Avgs.	3579	7433	.482	1744	2282	.764	1235	2450	3685	2117	1998	25	772	1553	435	8965	109.3	...

HOME/ROAD

	Home	Road	Total		Home	Road	Total
Atlanta	32-9	18-23	50-32	New Jersey	22-19	12-29	34-48
Boston	35-6	26-15	61-21	New York	25-16	14-27	39-43
Chicago	21-20	9-32	30-52	Philadelphia	36-5	23-18	59-23
Cleveland	28-13	9-32	37-45	Phoenix	36-5	19-22	55-27
Denver	24-17	6-35	30-52	Portland	26-15	12-29	38-44
Detroit	13-28	3-38	16-66	San Antonio	27-14	14-27	41-41
Golden State	15-26	9-32	24-58	San Diego	24-17	11-30	35-47
Houston	29-12	12-29	41-41	Seattle	33-8	23-18	56-26
Indiana	26-15	11-30	37-45	Utah	17-24	7-34	24-58
Kansas City	30-11	17-24	47-35	Washington	24-17	15-26	39-43
Los Angeles	37-4	23-18	60-22	Totals	588-314	314-588	902-902
Milwaukee	28-13	21-20	49-33				

INDIVIDUAL LEADERS

POINTS

(minimum 70 games or 1,400 points)

	G	FGM	FTM	Pts.	Avg.
George Gervin, San Antonio	78	1024	505	2585	33.1
World B. Free, San Diego	68	737	572	2055	30.2
Adrian Dantley, Utah	68	730	443	1903	28.0
Julius Erving, Philadelphia	78	838	420	2100	26.9
Moses Malone, Houston	82	778	563	2119	25.8
Kareem Abdul-Jabbar, L.A.	82	835	364	2034	24.8
Dan Issel, Denver	82	715	517	1951	23.8
Elvin Hayes, Washington	81	761	334	1859	23.0
Otis Birdsong, Kansas City	82	781	286	1858	22.7
Mike Mitchell, Cleveland	82	775	270	1820	22.2
Gus Williams, Seattle	82	739	331	1816	22.1
Paul Westphal, Phoenix	82	692	382	1792	21.9
Bill Cartwright, New York	82	665	451	1781	21.7
Marques Johnson, Milwaukee	77	689	291	1671	21.7
Walter Davis, Phoenix	75	657	299	1613	21.5
Larry Bird, Boston	82	693	301	1745	21.3
Ray Williams, New York	82	687	333	1714	20.9
Mike Newlin, New Jersey	78	611	367	1634	20.9
Reggie Theus, Chicago	82	566	500	1660	20.2
Larry Kenon, San Antonio	78	647	270	1565	20.1

FIELD GOALS

(minimum 300 made)

	FGM	FGA	Pct.
Cedric Maxwell, Boston	.457	750	.609
Kareem Abdul-Jabbar, Los Angeles	.835	1383	.604
Artis Gilmore, Chicago	.305	513	.595
Adrian Dantley, Utah	.730	1267	.576
Tom Boswell, Denver-Utah	.346	613	.564
Walter Davis, Phoenix	.657	1166	.563
Swen Nater, San Diego	.443	799	.554
Kermit Washington, Portland	.421	761	.553
Bill Cartwright, New York	.665	1215	.547
Marques Johnson, Milwaukee	.689	1267	.544

FREE THROWS

(minimum 125 made)

	FTM	FTA	Pct.
Rick Barry, Houston	.143	153	.935
Calvin Murphy, Houston	.271	302	.897
Ron Boone, Los Angeles-Utah	.175	196	.893
James Silas, San Antonio	.339	382	.887
Mike Newlin, New Jersey	.367	415	.884
Roger Phegley, Washington-New Jersey	.177	203	.872
Terry Furlow, Atlanta-Utah	.171	196	.872
Mike Bratz, Phoenix	.141	162	.870
Kevin Grevey, Washington	.216	249	.867
Johnny Roche, Denver	.175	202	.866

ASSISTS

(minimum 70 games or 400 assists)

	G	No.	Avg.
Micheal Ray Richardson, New York	.82	832	10.2
Nate Archibald, Boston	.80	671	8.4
Foots Walker, Cleveland	.76	607	8.0
Norm Nixon, Los Angeles	.82	642	7.8
John Lucas, Golden State	.80	602	7.5
Phil Ford, Kansas City	.82	610	7.4
Magic Johnson, Los Angeles	.77	563	7.3
Maurice Cheeks, Philadelphia	.79	556	7.0
Eddie Jordan, New Jersey	.82	557	6.8
Kevin Porter, Washington	.70	457	6.5

REBOUNDS

(minimum 70 games or 800 rebounds)

	G	Off.	Def.	Tot.	Avg.
Swen Nater, San Diego	.81	352	864	1216	15.0
Moses Malone, Houston	.82	573	617	1190	14.5
Wes Unseld, Washington	.82	334	760	1094	13.3

	G	Off.	Def.	Tot.	Avg.
Caldwell Jones, Philadelphia	.80	219	731	950	11.9
Jack Sikma, Seattle	.82	198	710	908	11.1
Elvin Hayes, Washington	.81	269	627	896	11.1
Robert Parish, Golden State	.72	247	536	783	10.9
Kareem Abdul-Jabbar, L.A.	.82	190	696	886	10.8
Kermit Washington, Portland	.80	325	517	842	10.5
Larry Bird, Boston	.82	216	636	852	10.4

STEALS

(minimum 70 games or 125 steals)

	G	No.	Avg.
Micheal Ray Richardson, New York	.82	265	3.23
Eddie Jordan, New Jersey	.82	223	2.72
Dudley Bradley, Indiana	.82	211	2.57
Gus Williams, Seattle	.82	200	2.44
Magic Johnson, Los Angeles	.77	187	2.43
Maurice Cheeks, Philadelphia	.79	183	2.32
Julius Erving, Philadelphia	.78	170	2.18
Sonny Parker, Golden State	.82	173	2.11
Ray Williams, New York	.82	167	2.04
Foots Walker, Cleveland	.76	155	2.04

BLOCKED SHOTS

(minimum 70 games or 100 blocked shots)

	G	No.	Avg.
Kareem Abdul-Jabbar, Los Angeles	.82	280	3.41
George Johnson, New Jersey	.81	258	3.19
Tree Rollins, Atlanta	.82	244	2.98
Terry Tyler, Detroit	.82	220	2.68
Elvin Hayes, Washington	.81	189	2.33
Harvey Catchings, Milwaukee	.72	162	2.25
Caldwell Jones, Philadelphia	.80	162	2.03
Ben Poquette, Utah	.82	162	1.98
Joe Meriweather, New York	.65	120	1.85
Julius Erving, Philadelphia	.78	140	1.79

3-POINT FIELD GOALS

(minimum 25 made)

	FGA	FGM	Pct.
Fred Brown, Seattle	.88	39	.443
Chris Ford, Boston	.164	70	.427
Larry Bird, Boston	.143	58	.406
Johnny Roche, Denver	.129	49	.380
Brian Taylor, San Diego	.239	90	.377
Brian Winters, Milwaukee	.102	38	.373
Kevin Grevey, Washington	.92	34	.370
Joe Hassett, Indiana	.198	69	.348
Rick Barry, Houston	.221	73	.330
Freeman Williams, San Diego	.128	42	.328

1979-80

INDIVIDUAL STATISTICS, TEAM BY TEAM

ATLANTA HAWKS

	G	Min.	FGM	FGA	Pct.	FTM	FTA	Pct.	Off.	Def.	Tot.	Ast.	PF	Dq.	Stl.	TO	Blk.	Pts.	Avg.	Hi.
										REBOUNDS								SCORING		
John Drew	80	2306	535	1182	.453	489	646	.757	203	268	471	101	313	10	91	240	23	1559	19.5	40
Eddie Johnson	79	2622	590	1212	.487	280	338	.828	95	105	200	370	216	2	120	189	24	1465	18.5	36
Dan Roundfield	81	2588	502	1007	.499	330	465	.710	293	544	837	184	317	6	101	233	139	1334	16.5	31
Steve Hawes	82	1885	304	605	.502	150	182	.824	148	348	496	144	205	4	74	121	29	761	9.3	24
Tree Rollins	82	2123	287	514	.558	157	220	.714	283	491	774	76	322	12	54	99	244	731	8.9	20
Tom McMillen	53	1071	191	382	.500	81	107	.757	70	150	220	62	126	2	36	64	14	463	8.7	24
Terry Furlow*	21	404	66	161	.410	44	51	.863	23	19	42	72	19	0	19	34	9	177	8.4	22
Charlie Criss	81	1794	249	578	.431	172	212	.811	27	89	116	246	133	0	74	130	4	671	8.3	26
Armond Hill	79	2092	177	431	.411	124	146	.849	31	107	138	424	261	7	107	171	8	479	6.1	17
Jack Givens	82	1254	182	473	.385	106	128	.828	114	128	242	59	132	1	51	59	19	470	5.7	20
Jim McElroy†	31	516	66	171	.386	37	53	.698	20	29	49	65	45	1	21	43	5	171	5.5	20
Jim McElroy‡	67	1528	228	527	.433	132	172	.767	32	67	99	227	123	2	46	131	19	593	8.9	33
John Brown†	28	361	37	98	.378	34	44	.773	21	41	62	14	66	0	3	24	4	108	3.9	12
John Brown‡	32	385	37	105	.352	38	48	.792	26	45	71	18	70	0	3	29	4	112	3.5	12
Sam Pellom	44	373	44	108	.407	21	30	.700	28	64	92	18	70	0	12	18	12	109	2.5	10
Ron Lee	30	364	29	91	.319	9	17	.529	11	22	33	67	65	1	15	33	4	67	2.2	8
Rick Wilson	5	59	2	14	.143	4	6	.667	2	1	3	11	3	0	4	8	1	8	1.6	3

3-pt. FG: Atlanta 13-75 (.173)—Drew 0-7 (.000); Johnson 5-13 (.385); Roundfield 0-4 (.000); Hawes 3-8 (.375); McMillen 0-1 (.000); Furlow* 1-9 (.111); Criss 1-17 (.059); Hill 1-4 (.250); Givens 0-2 (.000); McElroy† 2-7 (.286); McElroy‡ 5-21 (.238); Lee 0-3 (.000). Opponents 46-183 (.251).

BOSTON CELTICS

	G	Min.	FGM	FGA	Pct.	FTM	FTA	Pct.	Off.	Def.	Tot.	Ast.	PF	Dq.	Stl.	TO	Blk.	Pts.	Avg.	Hi.
									REBOUNDS									**SCORING**		
Larry Bird	82	2955	693	1463	.474	301	360	.836	216	636	852	370	279	4	143	263	53	1745	21.3	45
Cedric Maxwell	80	2744	457	750	.609	436	554	.787	284	420	704	199	266	6	76	230	61	1350	16.9	29
Dave Cowens	66	2159	422	932	.453	95	122	.779	126	408	534	206	216	2	69	108	61	940	14.2	32
Nate Archibald	80	2864	383	794	.482	361	435	.830	59	138	197	671	218	2	106	242	10	1131	14.1	29
Rick Robey	82	1918	379	727	.521	184	269	.684	209	321	530	92	244	2	53	151	15	942	11.5	27
Pete Maravich†	26	442	123	249	.494	50	55	.909	10	28	38	29	49	1	9	37	2	299	11.5	31
Pete Maravich‡	43	964	244	543	.449	91	105	.867	17	61	78	83	79	1	24	82	6	589	13.7	31
Chris Ford	73	2115	330	709	.465	86	114	.754	77	104	181	215	178	0	111	105	27	816	11.2	27
M.L. Carr	82	1994	362	763	.474	178	241	.739	106	224	330	156	214	1	120	143	36	914	11.1	25
Gerald Henderson . . .	76	1061	191	382	.500	89	129	.690	37	46	83	147	96	0	45	109	15	473	6.2	17
Jeff Judkins	65	674	139	276	.504	62	76	.816	32	34	66	47	91	0	29	49	5	351	5.4	17
Eric Fernsten	56	431	71	153	.464	33	52	.635	40	56	96	28	43	0	17	20	12	175	3.1	11
Don Chaney	60	523	67	189	.354	32	42	.762	31	42	73	38	80	1	31	33	11	167	2.8	8

3-pt. FG: Boston 162-422 (.384)—Bird 58-143 (.406); Cowens 1-12 (.083); Archibald 4-18 (.222); Robey 0-1 (.000); Maravich† 3-4 (.750); Maravich‡ 10-15 (.667); Ford 70-164 (.427); Carr 12-41 (.293); Henderson 2-6 (.333); Judkins 11-27 (.407); Chaney 1-6 (.167). Opponents 74-259 (.286).

CHICAGO BULLS

	G	Min.	FGM	FGA	Pct.	FTM	FTA	Pct.	Off.	Def.	Tot.	Ast.	PF	Dq.	Stl.	TO	Blk.	Pts.	Avg.	Hi.
									REBOUNDS									**SCORING**		
Reggie Theus	82	3029	566	1172	.483	500	597	.838	143	186	329	515	262	4	114	348	20	1660	20.2	33
Artis Gilmore	48	1568	305	513	.595	245	344	.712	108	324	432	133	167	5	29	133	59	855	17.8	32
David Greenwood . . .	82	2791	498	1051	.474	337	416	.810	223	550	773	182	313	8	60	210	129	1334	16.3	31
Ricky Sobers	82	2673	470	1002	.469	200	239	.837	75	167	242	426	294	4	136	282	17	1161	14.2	33
Scott May	54	1298	264	587	.450	144	172	.837	78	140	218	104	126	2	45	77	5	672	12.4	26
Dwight Jones†	53	1170	207	387	.535	119	165	.721	83	213	296	90	159	0	24	102	37	533	10.1	24
Dwight Jones‡	74	1448	257	506	.508	146	201	.726	114	254	368	101	207	0	28	122	42	660	8.9	24
Sam Smith	30	496	97	230	.422	57	63	.905	22	32	54	42	54	0	25	33	7	259	8.6	22
Mark Landsberger* . . .	54	1136	183	346	.529	87	166	.524	157	293	450	32	113	1	23	75	17	453	8.4	25
Ollie Mack†	23	526	77	149	.517	29	33	.879	25	24	49	33	34	0	20	26	3	183	8.0	18
Ollie Mack‡	50	681	98	199	.492	38	51	.745	32	39	71	53	50	0	24	35	3	234	4.7	18
Ollie Johnson	79	1535	262	527	.497	82	93	.882	50	113	163	161	165	0	59	96	24	607	7.7	21
Coby Dietrick	79	1830	227	500	.454	90	118	.763	101	262	363	216	230	2	89	112	51	545	6.9	19
John Mengelt	36	387	90	166	.542	39	49	.796	3	20	23	38	54	0	10	36	0	219	6.1	21
Del Beshore	68	869	88	250	.352	58	87	.667	16	47	63	139	105	0	58	104	5	244	3.6	15
Dennis Awtrey	26	560	27	60	.450	32	50	.640	29	86	115	40	66	0	12	27	15	86	3.3	9
Roger Brown	4	37	1	3	.333	0	0	. . .	2	8	10	1	4	0	0	3	2	2	0.5	2

3-pt. FG: Chicago 70-275 (.255)—Theus 28-105 (.267); Greenwood 1-7 (.143); Sobers 21-68 (.309); May 0-4 (.000); Smith 8-35 (.229); Mack† 0-4 (.000); Mack‡ 0-5 (.000); Johnson 1-11 (.091); Dietrick 1-9 (.111); Mengelt 0-6 (.000); Beshore 10-26 (.385). Opponents 54-199 (.271).

CLEVELAND CAVALIERS

	G	Min.	FGM	FGA	Pct.	FTM	FTA	Pct.	Off.	Def.	Tot.	Ast.	PF	Dq.	Stl.	TO	Blk.	Pts.	Avg.	Hi.
									REBOUNDS									**SCORING**		
Mike Mitchell	82	2802	775	1482	.523	270	343	.787	206	385	591	93	259	4	70	172	77	1820	22.2	46
Campy Russell	41	1331	284	630	.451	178	239	.745	76	149	225	173	113	1	72	148	20	747	18.2	33
Randy Smith	82	2677	599	1326	.452	233	283	.823	93	163	256	363	190	1	125	200	7	1441	17.6	36
Dave Robisch	82	2670	489	940	.520	277	329	.842	225	433	658	192	211	2	53	138	53	1255	15.3	36
Kenny Carr†	74	1781	371	752	.493	171	261	.655	194	377	571	76	240	3	64	145	51	913	12.3	32
Kenny Carr‡	79	1838	378	768	.492	173	263	.658	199	389	588	77	246	3	66	154	52	929	11.8	32
Austin Carr	77	1595	390	839	.465	127	172	.738	81	84	165	150	120	0	39	108	3	909	11.8	32
Foots Walker	76	2422	258	568	.454	195	243	.802	78	209	287	607	202	2	155	157	12	712	9.4	23
Bobby Smith*	8	135	33	72	.458	7	8	.875	2	12	14	7	21	0	3	9	2	74	9.3	17
Don Ford†	21	419	65	144	.451	22	25	.880	21	66	87	29	45	0	11	21	6	153	7.3	17
Don Ford‡	73	999	131	274	.478	45	53	.849	44	141	185	65	131	0	22	51	21	308	4.2	17
Bill Willoughby	78	1447	219	457	.479	96	127	.756	122	207	329	72	189	0	32	68	62	535	6.9	20
John Lambert	74	1324	165	400	.413	73	101	.723	138	214	352	56	203	4	47	64	42	403	5.4	18
Willie Smith	62	1051	121	315	.384	40	52	.769	56	65	121	259	110	1	75	95	1	299	4.8	14
Walt Frazier	3	27	4	11	.364	2	2	1.000	1	2	3	8	2	0	2	4	1	10	3.3	6
Earl Tatum	33	225	36	94	.383	11	19	.579	11	15	26	20	29	0	16	17	5	85	2.6	11
Butch Lee*	3	24	2	11	.182	0	1	.000	3	0	3	3	0	0	0	3	0	4	1.3	2

3-pt. FG: Cleveland 36-187 (.193)—Mitchell 0-6 (.000); Russell 1-9 (.111); R. Smith 10-53 (.189); Robisch 0-3 (.000); K. Carr† 0-4 (.000); K. Carr‡ 0-4 (.000); A. Carr 2-6 (.333); Walker 1-9 (.111); B. Smith* 1-5 (.200); Ford† 1-2 (.500); Ford‡ 1-3 (.333); Willoughby 1-9 (.111); Lambert 0-3 (.000); W. Smith 17-71 (.239); Frazier 0-1 (.000); Tatum 2-6 (.333). Opponents 65-223 (.291).

DENVER NUGGETS

	G	Min.	FGM	FGA	Pct.	FTM	FTA	Pct.	Off.	Def.	Tot.	Ast.	PF	Dq.	Stl.	TO	Blk.	Pts.	Avg.	Hi.
									REBOUNDS									**SCORING**		
Dan Issel	82	2938	715	1416	.505	517	667	.775	236	483	719	198	190	1	88	163	54	1951	23.8	47
David Thompson	39	1239	289	617	.468	254	335	.758	56	118	174	124	106	0	39	116	38	839	21.5	49
Alex English†	24	875	207	427	.485	96	126	.762	102	123	225	82	78	0	28	90	29	512	21.3	40
Alex English‡	78	2401	553	1113	.497	210	266	.789	269	336	605	224	206	0	73	214	62	1318	16.9	40
George McGinnis* . . .	45	1424	268	584	.459	166	307	.541	134	328	462	221	187	8	69	188	17	703	15.6	43
Bob Wilkerson	75	2381	430	1030	.417	166	222	.748	85	231	316	243	194	1	93	193	27	1033	13.8	31

	G	Min.	FGM	FGA	Pct.	FTM	FTA	Pct.	Off.	Def.	Tot.	Ast.	PF	Dq.	Stl.	TO	Blk.	Pts.	Avg.	Hi.
John Roche	82	2286	354	741	.478	175	202	.866	24	91	115	405	139	0	82	159	12	932	11.4	33
Tom Boswell*	18	522	72	135	.533	58	70	.829	40	74	114	46	56	1	5	39	8	203	11.3	24
George Johnson	75	1938	309	649	.476	148	189	.783	190	394	584	157	260	4	84	148	67	768	10.2	30
Charlie Scott	69	1860	276	668	.413	85	118	.720	51	115	166	250	197	3	47	163	23	639	9.3	30
Anthony Roberts	23	486	69	181	.381	39	60	.650	54	55	109	20	52	1	13	28	3	177	7.7	18
Glen Gondrezick	59	1020	148	286	.517	92	121	.760	107	152	259	81	119	0	68	58	16	390	6.6	20
Gary Garland	78	1106	155	356	.435	18	26	.692	50	88	138	145	80	1	54	73	4	334	4.3	17
Bo Ellis	48	502	61	136	.449	40	53	.755	51	65	116	30	67	1	10	24	24	162	3.4	12
Kim Hughes	70	1208	102	202	.505	15	41	.366	125	201	326	74	184	3	66	50	77	219	3.1	14
Arvid Kramer	8	45	7	22	.318	2	2	1.000	6	6	12	3	8	0	0	5	5	16	2.0	10

3-pt. FG: Denver 83-255 (.325)—Issel 4-12 (.333); Thompson 7-19 (.368); English† 2-3 (.667); English‡ 2-6 (.333); McGinnis* 1-7 (.143); Wilkerson 7-34 (.206); Roche 49-129 (.380); Boswell* 1-2 (.500); Johnson 2-9 (.222); Scott 2-11 (.182); Roberts 0-1 (.000); Gondrezick 2-6 (.333); Garland 6-19 (.316); Ellis 0-3 (.000). Opponents 70-214 (.327).

DETROIT PISTONS

									REBOUNDS									SCORING		
	G	Min.	FGM	FGA	Pct.	FTM	FTA	Pct.	Off.	Def.	Tot.	Ast.	PF	Dq.	Stl.	TO	Blk.	Pts.	Avg.	Hi.
Bob Lanier*	37	1392	319	584	.546	164	210	.781	108	265	373	122	130	2	38	113	60	802	21.7	34
Bob McAdoo	58	2097	492	1025	.480	235	322	.730	100	367	467	200	178	3	73	238	65	1222	21.1	37
John Long	69	2364	588	1164	.505	160	194	.825	152	185	337	206	221	4	129	206	26	1337	19.4	38
Greg Kelser	50	1233	280	593	.472	146	203	.719	124	152	276	108	176	5	60	140	34	709	14.2	34
Terry Tyler	82	2670	430	925	.465	143	187	.765	228	399	627	129	237	3	107	175	220	1005	12.3	29
Kent Benson†	17	502	86	187	.460	33	44	.750	30	90	120	51	68	3	19	51	18	206	12.1	26
Kent Benson‡	73	1891	299	618	.484	99	141	.702	126	327	453	178	246	4	73	157	92	698	9.6	26
Jim McElroy*	36	1012	162	356	.455	95	119	.798	12	38	50	162	78	1	25	88	14	422	11.7	33
Eric Money†	55	1467	259	510	.508	81	104	.779	28	69	97	238	135	3	53	143	10	599	10.9	26
Eric Money‡	61	1549	273	546	.500	83	106	.783	31	73	104	254	146	3	53	155	11	629	10.3	26
John Shumate*	9	228	65	121	.538	17	25	.680	18	52	70	9	16	0	9	14	5	87	9.7	20
Terry Duerod	67	1331	282	598	.472	45	66	.682	29	69	98	117	102	0	41	79	11	624	9.3	28
Phil Hubbard	64	1189	210	451	.466	165	220	.750	114	206	320	70	202	9	48	120	10	585	9.1	30
Leon Douglas	70	1782	221	455	.486	126	195	.676	171	330	501	124	249	10	30	127	62	567	8.1	26
Ron Lee†	31	803	84	214	.393	35	53	.660	29	61	90	174	107	4	84	68	10	226	7.3	23
Ron Lee‡	61	1167	113	305	.370	44	70	.629	40	83	123	241	172	5	99	101	17	292	4.8	23
Roy Hamilton	72	1116	115	287	.401	103	150	.687	45	62	107	192	82	0	48	118	5	333	4.6	17
Earl Evans	36	381	63	140	.450	24	42	.571	26	49	75	37	64	0	14	36	1	157	4.4	16
Jackie Robinson	7	51	9	17	.529	9	11	.818	3	2	5	0	8	0	3	2	3	27	3.9	10
Steve Malovic†	10	162	8	25	.320	10	14	.714	9	19	28	14	16	0	2	9	5	26	2.6	9
Steve Malovic‡	39	445	31	67	.463	18	27	.667	36	50	86	26	51	0	8	23	6	80	2.1	9

3-pt. FG: Detroit 57-219 (.260)—Lanier* 0-5 (.000); McAdoo 3-24 (.125); Long 1-12 (.083); Kelser 3-15 (.200); Tyler 2-12 (.167); Benson† 1-4 (.250); Benson‡ 1-5 (.200); McElroy* 3-14 (.214); Duerod 15-53 (.283); Hubbard 0-2 (.000); Douglas 0-1 (.000); Lee† 22-56 (.393); Lee‡ 22-59 (.373); Hamilton 0-2 (.000); Evans 7-18 (.389); Robinson 0-1 (.000). Opponents 57-206 (.277).

GOLDEN STATE WARRIORS

									REBOUNDS									SCORING		
	G	Min.	FGM	FGA	Pct.	FTM	FTA	Pct.	Off.	Def.	Tot.	Ast.	PF	Dq.	Stl.	TO	Blk.	Pts.	Avg.	Hi.
Robert Parish	72	2119	510	1006	.507	203	284	.715	247	536	783	122	248	6	58	225	115	1223	17.0	29
Purvis Short	62	1636	461	916	.503	134	165	.812	119	197	316	123	186	4	63	122	9	1056	17.0	37
Phil Smith	51	1552	325	685	.474	135	171	.789	28	118	146	187	154	1	62	121	15	792	15.5	29
Sonny Parker	82	2849	483	988	.489	237	302	.785	166	298	464	254	195	2	173	163	32	1203	14.7	36
John Lucas	80	2763	388	830	.467	222	289	.768	61	159	220	602	196	2	138	184	9	1010	12.6	27
Wayne Cooper	79	1781	367	750	.489	136	181	.751	202	305	507	42	246	5	20	140	79	871	11.0	30
Jo Jo White	78	2052	336	706	.476	97	114	.851	42	139	181	239	186	0	88	157	13	770	9.9	21
Clifford Ray	81	1683	203	383	.530	84	149	.564	122	344	466	183	266	6	51	155	32	490	6.0	19
Raymond Townsend	75	1159	171	421	.406	60	84	.714	33	56	89	116	113	0	60	65	4	406	5.4	17
Tom Abernethy	67	1222	153	318	.481	56	82	.683	62	129	191	87	118	0	35	39	12	362	5.4	20
Darnell Hillman	49	708	82	179	.458	34	68	.500	59	121	180	47	128	2	21	59	24	198	4.0	19
Lynbert Johnson	9	53	12	30	.400	3	5	.600	6	8	14	2	11	0	1	4	0	27	3.0	6
John Coughran	24	160	29	81	.358	8	14	.571	2	17	19	12	24	0	7	13	1	68	2.8	11
Bubba Wilson	15	143	7	25	.280	3	6	.500	6	10	16	12	11	0	2	8	0	17	1.1	4

3-pt. FG: Golden State 27-121 (.223)—Parish 0-1 (.000); Short 0-6 (.000); Smith 7-22 (.318); Parker 0-2 (.000); Lucas 12-42 (.286); Cooper 1-4 (.250); White 1-6 (.167); Ray 0-2 (.000); Townsend 4-26 (.154); Abernethy 0-1 (.000); Coughran 2-9 (.222). Opponents 72-219 (.329).

HOUSTON ROCKETS

									REBOUNDS									SCORING		
	G	Min.	FGM	FGA	Pct.	FTM	FTA	Pct.	Off.	Def.	Tot.	Ast.	PF	Dq.	Stl.	TO	Blk.	Pts.	Avg.	Hi.
Moses Malone	82	3140	778	1549	.502	563	783	.719	573	617	1190	147	210	0	80	300	107	2119	25.8	45
Calvin Murphy	76	2676	624	1267	.493	271	302	.897	68	82	150	299	269	3	143	162	9	1520	20.0	38
Rudy Tomjanovich	62	1834	370	778	.476	118	147	.803	132	226	358	109	161	2	32	98	10	880	14.2	27
Robert Reid	76	2304	419	861	.487	153	208	.736	140	301	441	244	281	2	132	164	57	991	13.0	31
Rick Barry	72	1816	325	771	.422	143	153	.935	53	183	236	268	182	0	80	152	28	866	12.0	30
Allen Leavell	77	2123	330	656	.503	180	221	.814	57	127	184	417	197	1	127	205	28	843	10.9	22
Billy Paultz†	37	980	138	292	.473	43	82	.524	92	173	265	70	86	0	22	57	39	319	8.6	28
Billy Paultz‡	84	2193	327	675	.486	109	182	.599	187	399	586	188	213	3	69	115	84	763	9.1	28
Mike Dunleavy	51	1036	148	319	.464	111	134	.828	26	74	100	210	120	2	40	110	4	410	8.0	31
Dwight Jones*	21	278	50	119	.420	27	36	.750	31	41	72	11	48	0	4	20	5	127	6.0	23

1979-80

	G	Min.	FGM	FGA	Pct.	FTM	FTA	Pct.	Off.	Def.	Tot.	Ast.	PF	Dq.	Stl.	TO	Blk.	Pts.	Avg.	Hi.
Tom Henderson	66	1551	154	323	.477	56	77	.727	34	77	111	274	107	1	55	102	4	364	5.5	19
Major Jones	82	1545	188	392	.480	61	108	.565	147	234	381	67	186	0	50	112	67	438	5.3	17
Rudy White	9	106	13	24	.542	10	13	.769	0	9	9	5	8	0	5	8	0	36	4.0	11
John Shumate*	29	332	34	64	.531	33	44	.750	25	54	79	23	39	0	8	27	9	101	3.5	12
Paul Mokeski	12	113	11	33	.333	7	9	.778	14	15	29	2	24	0	1	10	6	29	2.4	6
Alonzo Bradley	22	96	17	48	.354	6	9	.667	2	4	6	3	9	0	3	8	0	41	1.9	8

3-pt. FG: Houston 104-379 (.274)—Malone 0-6 (.000); Murphy 1-25 (.040); Tomjanovich 22-79 (.278); Reid 0-3 (.000); Barry 73-221 (.330); Leavell 3-19 (.158); Dunleavy 3-20 (.150); Henderson 0-2 (.000); M. Jones 1-3 (.333); Bradley 1-1 (1.000). Opponents 58-215 (.270).

INDIANA PACERS

	G	Min.	FGM	FGA	Pct.	FTM	FTA	Pct.	Off.	Def.	Tot.	Ast.	PF	Dq.	Stl.	TO	Blk.	Pts.	Avg.	Hi.
Mickey Johnson	82	2647	588	1271	.463	385	482	.799	258	423	681	344	291	11	153	286	112	1566	19.1	41
Johnny Davis	82	2912	496	1159	.428	304	352	.864	102	124	226	440	178	0	110	202	23	1300	15.9	32
James Edwards	82	2314	528	1032	.512	231	339	.681	179	399	578	127	324	12	55	131	104	1287	15.7	35
Alex English*	54	1526	346	686	.504	114	140	.814	167	213	380	142	128	0	45	124	33	806	14.9	37
George McGinnis†	28	784	132	302	.437	104	181	.575	88	149	237	112	116	4	32	93	6	369	13.2	31
George McGinnis‡	73	2208	400	886	.451	270	448	.603	222	477	699	333	303	12	101	281	23	1072	14.7	43
Billy Knight	75	1910	385	722	.533	212	262	.809	136	225	361	155	96	0	82	132	9	986	13.1	44
Mike Bantom	77	2330	384	760	.505	139	209	.665	192	264	456	279	268	7	85	189	49	908	11.8	27
Dudley Bradley	82	2027	275	609	.452	136	174	.782	69	154	223	252	194	1	211	166	48	688	8.4	22
Joe Hassett	74	1135	215	509	.422	24	29	.828	35	59	94	104	85	0	46	45	8	523	7.1	23
Clemon Johnson	79	1541	199	396	.503	74	117	.632	145	249	394	115	211	2	48	78	121	472	6.0	22
Phil Chenier†	23	380	52	135	.385	18	26	.692	9	26	35	47	29	0	15	26	10	124	5.4	14
Phil Chenier‡	43	850	136	349	.390	49	67	.731	19	59	78	89	55	0	33	55	15	326	7.6	22
Ron Carter	13	117	15	37	.405	2	7	.286	5	14	19	9	19	0	2	10	3	32	2.5	6
Tony Zeno	8	59	6	21	.286	2	2	1.000	3	11	14	1	13	0	4	9	3	14	1.8	4
Brad Davis*	5	43	2	7	.286	3	4	.750	0	2	2	5	7	0	3	3	0	7	1.4	5
John Kuester	24	100	12	34	.353	5	7	.714	3	11	14	16	8	0	7	5	1	29	1.2	6
Corky Calhoun	7	30	4	9	.444	0	2	.000	7	3	10	0	6	0	2	1	0	8	1.1	2

3-pt. FG: Indiana 88-314 (.280)—M. Johnson 5-32 (.156); J. Davis 4-42 (.095); Edwards 0-1 (.000); English* 0-3 (.000); McGinnis† 1-8 (.125); McGinnis‡ 2-15 (.133); Knight 4-15 (.267); Bantom 1-3 (.333); Bradley 2-5 (.400); Hassett 69-198 (.348); Chenier† 2-6 (.333); Chenier‡ 5-12 (.417); Kuester 0-1 (.000). Opponents 56-228 (.246).

KANSAS CITY KINGS

	G	Min.	FGM	FGA	Pct.	FTM	FTA	Pct.	Off.	Def.	Tot.	Ast.	PF	Dq.	Stl.	TO	Blk.	Pts.	Avg.	Hi.
Otis Birdsong	82	2885	781	1546	.505	286	412	.694	170	161	331	202	226	2	136	179	22	1858	22.7	49
Scott Wedman	68	2347	569	1112	.512	145	181	.801	114	272	386	145	230	1	84	112	45	1290	19.0	45
Phil Ford	82	2621	489	1058	.462	346	423	.818	29	143	172	610	208	0	136	282	4	1328	16.2	35
Bill Robinzine	81	1917	362	723	.501	200	274	.730	184	342	526	62	311	5	106	148	23	925	11.4	28
Sam Lacey	81	2412	303	677	.448	137	185	.741	172	473	645	460	307	8	111	211	109	743	9.2	24
Reggie King	82	2052	257	499	.515	159	219	.726	184	382	566	106	230	2	69	100	31	673	8.2	21
Mike Green	21	459	69	159	.434	24	42	.571	35	78	113	28	55	0	13	36	21	162	7.7	21
Billy McKinney	76	1333	206	459	.449	107	133	.805	20	66	86	248	87	0	58	89	5	520	6.8	26
Ernie Grunfeld	80	1397	186	420	.443	101	131	.771	87	145	232	109	151	1	56	81	9	474	5.9	18
Marlon Redmond	24	298	59	138	.428	24	34	.706	18	34	52	19	27	0	4	19	9	142	5.9	19
Gus Gerard	73	869	159	348	.457	66	100	.660	77	100	177	43	96	1	41	49	26	385	5.3	25
Len Elmore	58	915	104	242	.430	51	74	.689	74	183	257	64	154	0	41	67	39	259	4.5	23
Tom Burleson	37	272	36	104	.346	23	40	.575	23	49	72	20	49	0	8	25	13	95	2.6	12
Terry Crosby	4	28	2	4	.500	2	2	1.000	0	1	1	7	4	0	5	0	0	6	1.5	4

3-pt. FG: Kansas City 25-114 (.219)—Birdsong 10-36 (.278); Wedman 7-22 (.318); Ford 4-23 (.174); Robinzine 1-2 (.500); Lacey 0-1 (.000); King 0-1 (.000); Green 0-2 (.000); McKinney 1-10 (.100); Grunfeld 1-2 (.500); Redmond 0-9 (.000); Gerard 1-3 (.333); Burleson 0-3 (.000). Opponents 41-172 (.238).

LOS ANGELES LAKERS

	G	Min.	FGM	FGA	Pct.	FTM	FTA	Pct.	Off.	Def.	Tot.	Ast.	PF	Dq.	Stl.	TO	Blk.	Pts.	Avg.	Hi.
Kareem Abdul-Jabbar	82	3143	835	1383	.604	364	476	.765	190	696	886	371	216	2	81	297	280	2034	24.8	42
Jamaal Wilkes	82	3111	726	1358	.535	189	234	.808	176	349	525	250	220	1	129	157	28	1644	20.0	30
Magic Johnson	77	2795	503	949	.530	374	462	.810	166	430	596	563	218	1	187	305	41	1387	18.0	31
Norm Nixon	82	3226	624	1209	.516	197	253	.779	52	177	229	642	241	1	147	288	14	1446	17.6	30
Jim Chones	82	2394	372	760	.489	125	169	.740	143	421	564	151	271	5	56	175	65	869	10.6	23
Spencer Haywood	76	1544	288	591	.487	159	206	.772	132	214	346	93	197	2	35	134	57	736	9.7	25
Michael Cooper	82	1973	303	578	.524	111	143	.776	101	128	229	221	215	3	86	142	38	722	8.8	20
Mark Landsberger†	23	374	66	137	.482	29	56	.518	69	94	163	14	27	0	10	25	5	161	7.0	14
Mark Landsberger‡	77	1510	249	483	.516	116	222	.523	226	387	613	46	140	1	33	100	22	614	8.0	25
Ron Boone*	6	106	14	40	.350	6	7	.857	7	4	11	7	13	0	5	13	0	34	5.7	10
Kenny Carr*	5	57	7	16	.438	2	2	1.000	5	12	17	1	6	0	2	9	1	16	3.2	6
Don Ford*	52	580	66	130	.508	23	28	.821	23	75	98	36	86	0	11	30	15	155	3.0	15
Brad Holland	38	197	44	104	.423	15	16	.938	4	13	17	22	24	0	15	13	1	106	2.8	14
Marty Byrnes	32	194	25	50	.500	13	15	.867	9	18	27	13	32	0	5	22	1	63	2.0	11
Ollie Mack*	27	155	21	50	.420	9	18	.500	7	15	22	20	16	0	4	9	0	51	1.9	10
Butch Lee†	11	31	4	13	.308	6	7	.857	4	4	8	9	2	0	1	7	0	14	1.3	4
Butch Lee‡	14	55	6	24	.250	6	8	.750	7	4	11	12	2	0	1	10	0	18	1.3	4

3-pt. FG: L.A. Lakers 20-100 (.200)—Abdul-Jabbar 0-1 (.000); Wilkes 3-17 (.176); Johnson 7-31 (.226); Nixon 1-8 (.125); Chones 0-2 (.000); Haywood 1-4 (.250); Cooper 5-20 (.250); Ford* 0-1 (.000); Holland 3-15 (.200); Mack* 0-1 (.000). Opponents 78-274 (.285).

MILWAUKEE BUCKS

	G	Min.	FGM	FGA	Pct.	FTM	FTA	Pct.	REBOUNDS Off.	Def.	Tot.	Ast.	PF	Dq.	Stl.	TO	Blk.	SCORING Pts.	Avg.	Hi.
Marques Johnson	77	2686	689	1267	.544	291	368	.791	217	349	566	273	173	0	100	185	70	1671	21.7	37
Junior Bridgeman	81	2316	594	1243	.478	230	266	.865	104	197	301	237	216	3	94	172	20	1423	17.6	35
Brian Winters	80	2623	535	1116	.479	184	214	.860	48	175	223	362	208	0	101	186	28	1292	16.2	34
Bob Lanier†	26	739	147	283	.519	113	144	.785	44	135	179	62	70	1	36	49	29	408	15.7	32
Bob Lanier‡	63	2131	466	867	.537	277	354	.782	152	400	552	184	200	3	74	162	89	1210	19.2	34
Dave Meyers........	79	2204	399	830	.481	156	246	.634	140	308	448	225	218	3	72	182	40	955	12.1	28
Quinn Buckner	67	1690	306	655	.467	105	143	.734	69	169	238	383	202	1	135	149	4	719	10.7	40
Kent Benson*	56	1389	213	431	.494	66	97	.680	96	237	333	127	178	1	54	106	74	492	8.8	19
Sidney Moncrief	77	1557	211	451	.468	232	292	.795	154	184	338	133	106	0	72	117	16	654	8.5	23
Pat Cummings	71	900	187	370	.505	94	123	.764	81	157	238	53	141	0	22	74	17	468	6.6	30
Richard Washington .	75	1092	197	421	.468	46	76	.605	95	181	276	55	166	2	26	63	48	440	5.9	20
Lloyd Walton........	76	1243	110	242	.455	49	71	.690	33	58	91	285	68	0	43	112	2	270	3.6	18
Harvey Catchings	72	1366	97	244	.398	39	62	.629	164	246	410	82	191	1	23	68	162	233	3.2	12

3-pt. FG: Milwaukee 50-155 (.323)—Johnson 2-9 (.222); Bridgeman 5-27 (.185); Winters 38-102 (.373); Lanier† 1-1 (1.000); Lanier‡ 1-6 (.167); Meyers 1-5 (.200); Buckner 2-5 (.400); Benson* 0-1 (.000); Moncrief 0-1 (.000); Walton 1-3 (.333); Catchings 0-1 (.000). Opponents 76-305 (.249).

NEW JERSEY NETS

	G	Min.	FGM	FGA	Pct.	FTM	FTA	Pct.	REBOUNDS Off.	Def.	Tot.	Ast.	PF	Dq.	Stl.	TO	Blk.	SCORING Pts.	Avg.	Hi.
Mike Newlin	78	2510	611	1329	.460	367	415	.884	101	163	264	314	195	1	115	231	4	1634	20.9	52
Calvin Natt*	53	2046	421	879	.479	199	280	.711	173	340	513	112	148	1	78	133	22	1042	19.7	33
John Williamson* ...	28	771	206	461	.447	76	88	.864	24	30	54	87	71	1	26	43	9	496	17.7	32
Maurice Lucas†	22	708	128	261	.490	79	102	.775	58	154	212	83	82	1	19	70	27	335	15.2	32
Maurice Lucas‡	63	1884	371	813	.456	179	239	.749	143	394	537	208	223	2	42	218	62	923	14.7	32
Cliff Robinson	70	1661	391	833	.469	168	242	.694	174	332	506	98	178	1	61	137	34	951	13.6	45
Eddie Jordan.......	82	2657	437	1017	.430	201	258	.779	62	208	270	557	238	7	223	258	27	1087	13.3	28
Roger Phegley†	28	541	126	260	.485	73	83	.880	26	44	70	32	52	0	15	49	4	327	11.7	26
Roger Phegley‡	78	1512	350	733	.477	177	203	.872	75	110	185	102	158	1	34	119	7	881	11.3	35
Rich Kelley*	57	1466	186	399	.466	197	250	.788	156	241	397	128	215	5	50	152	79	569	10.0	26
Winford Boynes	64	1102	221	467	.473	104	136	.765	51	82	133	95	132	1	59	96	19	546	8.5	32
George Johnson	81	2119	248	543	.457	89	126	.706	192	410	602	173	312	7	53	199	258	585	7.2	22
Jan van Breda Kolff. .	82	2399	212	458	.463	130	155	.839	103	326	429	247	307	11	100	158	76	561	6.8	18
Bob Elliott.........	54	722	101	228	.443	104	152	.684	67	118	185	53	97	0	29	88	14	307	5.7	18
Robert Smith†	59	736	113	254	.445	75	87	.862	17	59	76	85	102	1	22	52	4	309	5.2	17
Robert Smith‡	65	809	118	269	.439	80	92	.870	20	59	79	92	105	1	26	53	4	324	5.0	17
Ralph Simpson......	8	81	18	47	.383	5	10	.500	6	5	11	14	3	0	9	12	0	41	5.1	12
Phil Jackson........	16	194	29	46	.630	7	10	.700	12	12	24	12	35	1	5	9	4	65	4.1	14
Tim Bassett*	7	92	8	22	.364	8	12	.667	7	11	18	4	14	0	5	4	0	24	3.4	11

3-pt. FG: New Jersey 85-298 (.285)—Newlin 45-152 (.296); Natt* 1-5 (.200); Williamson* 8-19 (.421); Lucas† 0-4 (.000); Lucas‡ 2-9 (.222); Robinson 1-4 (.250); Jordan 12-48 (.250); Phegley† 2-4 (.500); Phegley‡ 4-9 (.444); Kelley* 0-3 (.000); Boynes 0-4 (.000); Johnson 0-1 (.000); van Breda Kolff 7-20 (.350); Elliott 1-4 (.250); Smith† 8-26 (.308); Smith‡ 8-26 (.308); Simpson 0-2 (.000); Jackson 0-2 (.000). Opponents 58-208 (.279).

NEW YORK KNICKERBOCKERS

	G	Min.	FGM	FGA	Pct.	FTM	FTA	Pct.	REBOUNDS Off.	Def.	Tot.	Ast.	PF	Dq.	Stl.	TO	Blk.	SCORING Pts.	Avg.	Hi.
Bill Cartwright.......	82	3150	665	1215	.547	451	566	.797	194	532	726	165	279	2	48	222	101	1781	21.7	37
Ray Williams........	82	2582	687	1384	.496	333	423	.787	149	263	412	512	295	5	167	256	24	1714	20.9	39
Toby Knight	81	2945	669	1265	.529	211	261	.808	201	292	493	150	302	4	117	163	86	1549	19.1	34
Micheal Ray Richardson	82	3060	502	1063	.472	223	338	.660	151	388	539	832	260	3	265	359	35	1254	15.3	28
Joe Meriweather	65	1565	252	477	.528	78	121	.645	122	228	350	66	239	8	37	112	120	582	9.0	24
Earl Monroe	51	633	161	352	.457	56	64	.875	16	20	36	67	46	0	21	28	3	378	7.4	25
Larry Demic	82	1872	230	528	.436	110	183	.601	195	288	483	64	306	10	56	168	30	570	7.0	19
Mike Glenn	75	800	188	364	.516	63	73	.863	21	45	66	85	79	0	35	38	7	441	5.9	19
Hollis Copeland......	75	1142	182	368	.495	63	86	.733	70	86	156	80	154	0	61	84	25	427	5.7	19
Sly Williams	57	556	104	267	.390	58	90	.644	65	56	121	36	73	0	19	49	8	266	4.7	21
Marvin Webster	20	298	38	79	.481	12	16	.750	28	52	80	9	39	1	3	20	11	88	4.4	13
Jim Cleamons*	22	254	30	69	.435	12	15	.800	10	9	19	40	13	0	13	17	2	75	3.4	13
Geoff Huston	71	923	94	241	.390	28	38	.737	14	44	58	159	83	0	39	73	5	219	3.1	14

3-pt. FG: New York 42-191 (.220)—R. Williams 7-37 (.189); Knight 0-2 (.000); Richardson 27-110 (.245); Meriweather 0-1 (.000); Glenn 2-10 (.200); Copeland 0-2 (.000); S. Williams 0-4 (.000); Cleamons* 3-8 (.375); Huston 3-17 (.176). Opponents 55-198 (.278).

PHILADELPHIA 76ERS

	G	Min.	FGM	FGA	Pct.	FTM	FTA	Pct.	REBOUNDS Off.	Def.	Tot.	Ast.	PF	Dq.	Stl.	TO	Blk.	SCORING Pts.	Avg.	Hi.
Julius Erving........	78	2812	838	1614	.519	420	534	.787	215	361	576	355	208	0	170	284	140	2100	26.9	44
Darryl Dawkins	80	2541	494	946	.522	190	291	.653	197	496	693	149	328	8	49	230	142	1178	14.7	34
Doug Collins........	36	963	191	410	.466	113	124	.911	29	65	94	100	76	0	30	82	7	495	13.8	33
Bobby Jones	81	2125	398	748	.532	257	329	.781	152	298	450	146	223	3	102	146	118	1053	13.0	26
Lionel Hollins†	27	796	130	313	.415	67	87	.770	24	45	69	112	68	0	46	68	9	329	12.2	26

	G	Min.	FGM	FGA	Pct.	FTM	FTA	Pct.	REBOUNDS Off.	Def.	Tot.	Ast.	PF	Dq.	Stl.	TO	Blk.	SCORING Pts.	Avg.	Hi.
Lionel Hollins‡	47	1209	212	526	.403	101	140	.721	29	60	89	162	103	0	76	128	10	528	11.2	26
Steve Mix	81	1543	363	703	.516	207	249	.831	114	176	290	149	114	0	67	132	9	937	11.6	25
Maurice Cheeks	79	2623	357	661	.540	180	231	.779	75	199	274	556	197	1	183	216	32	894	11.3	24
Henry Bibby	82	2035	251	626	.401	226	286	.790	65	143	208	307	161	0	62	147	6	739	9.0	21
Caldwell Jones	80	2771	232	532	.436	124	178	.697	219	731	950	164	298	5	43	218	162	588	7.4	20
Clint Richardson	52	988	159	348	.457	28	45	.622	55	68	123	107	97	0	24	64	15	347	6.7	24
Jim Spanarkel	40	442	72	153	.471	54	65	.831	27	27	54	51	58	0	12	57	6	198	5.0	19
Eric Money*	6	82	14	36	.389	2	2	1.000	3	4	7	16	11	0	0	12	1	30	5.0	10
Bernard Toone	23	124	23	64	.359	8	10	.800	12	22	34	12	20	0	4	16	5	55	2.4	8
Al Skinner	2	10	1	2	.500	0	0		0	0	0	2	1	0	0	2	0	2	1.0	2

3-pt. FG: Philadelphia 27-125 (.216)—Erving 4-20 (.200); Dawkins 0-6 (.000); Collins 0-1 (.000); B. Jones 0-3 (.000); Hollins† 2-10 (.200); Hollins‡ 3-20 (.150); Mix 4-10 (.400); Cheeks 4-9 (.444); Bibby 11-52 (.212); C. Jones 0-2 (.000); Richardson 1-3 (.333); Spanarkel 0-2 (.000); Toone 1-7 (.143). Opponents 75-277 (.271).

PHOENIX SUNS

	G	Min.	FGM	FGA	Pct.	FTM	FTA	Pct.	REBOUNDS Off.	Def.	Tot.	Ast.	PF	Dq.	Stl.	TO	Blk.	SCORING Pts.	Avg.	Hi.
Paul Westphal	82	2665	692	1317	.525	382	443	.862	46	141	187	416	162	0	119	207	35	1792	21.9	49
Walter Davis	75	2309	657	1166	.563	299	365	.819	75	197	272	337	202	2	114	242	19	1613	21.5	40
Truck Robinson	82	2710	545	1064	.512	325	487	.667	213	557	770	142	262	2	58	251	59	1415	17.3	34
Alvan Adams	75	2168	468	875	.535	188	236	.797	158	451	609	322	237	4	108	218	55	1124	15.0	32
Mike Bratz	82	1589	269	687	.392	141	162	.870	50	117	167	223	165	0	93	135	9	700	8.5	21
Don Buse	81	2499	261	589	.443	85	128	.664	70	163	233	320	111	0	132	91	10	626	7.7	17
Rich Kelley†	23	373	43	85	.506	47	60	.783	44	74	118	50	58	0	28	46	17	133	5.8	10
Rich Kelley‡	80	1839	229	484	.473	244	310	.787	200	315	515	178	273	5	78	198	96	702	8.8	26
Jeff Cook	66	904	129	275	.469	104	129	.806	90	151	241	84	102	0	28	71	18	362	5.5	16
Johnny High	82	1121	144	323	.446	120	178	.674	69	104	173	119	172	1	71	123	15	409	5.0	18
Gar Heard	82	1403	171	410	.417	64	86	.744	118	262	380	97	177	0	84	88	49	406	5.0	18
Alvin Scott	79	1303	127	301	.422	95	122	.779	89	139	228	98	101	0	47	92	53	350	4.4	10
Joel Kramer	54	711	67	143	.469	56	70	.800	49	102	151	75	104	0	26	51	5	190	3.5	13

3-pt. FG: Phoenix 68-280 (.243)—Westphal 26-93 (.280); Davis 0-4 (.000); Adams 0-2 (.000); Kelley† 0-0; Kelley‡ 0-3 (.000); Bratz 21-86 (.244); Buse 19-79 (.241); Cook 0-3 (.000); High 1-7 (.143); Heard 0-2 (.000); Scott 1-3 (.333); Kramer 0-1 (.000). Opponents 100-297 (.337).

PORTLAND TRAIL BLAZERS

	G	Min.	FGM	FGA	Pct.	FTM	FTA	Pct.	REBOUNDS Off.	Def.	Tot.	Ast.	PF	Dq.	Stl.	TO	Blk.	SCORING Pts.	Avg.	Hi.
Calvin Natt†	25	811	201	419	.480	107	139	.770	66	112	178	57	57	0	24	65	12	511	20.4	39
Calvin Natt‡	78	2857	622	1298	.479	306	419	.730	239	452	691	169	205	1	102	198	34	1553	19.9	39
Tom Owens	76	2337	518	1008	.514	213	283	.753	189	384	573	194	270	5	45	174	53	1250	16.4	32
Ron Brewer	82	2815	548	1182	.464	184	219	.840	54	160	214	216	154	0	98	167	48	1286	15.7	33
Maurice Lucas*	41	1176	243	552	.440	100	137	.730	85	240	325	125	141	1	23	148	35	588	14.3	30
Kermit Washington	80	2657	421	761	.553	231	360	.642	325	517	842	167	307	8	73	170	131	1073	13.4	27
Billy Ray Bates	16	235	72	146	.493	28	39	.718	13	16	29	31	26	0	14	20	2	180	11.3	26
Lionel Hollins*	20	413	82	213	.385	34	53	.642	5	15	20	50	35	0	30	60	1	199	10.0	24
Abdul Jeelani	77	1286	288	565	.510	161	204	.789	114	156	270	95	155	0	40	117	40	737	9.6	28
Larry Steele	16	446	62	146	.425	22	27	.815	13	32	45	67	53	0	25	33	1	146	9.1	18
Bob Gross	62	1581	221	472	.468	95	114	.833	84	165	249	228	179	3	60	166	47	538	8.7	22
Dave Twardzik	67	1594	183	394	.464	197	252	.782	52	104	156	273	149	2	77	131	1	567	8.5	23
Kevin Kunnert	18	302	50	114	.439	26	43	.605	37	75	112	29	59	1	7	41	22	126	7.0	16
T.R. Dunn	82	1841	240	551	.436	84	111	.757	132	192	324	147	145	1	102	91	31	564	6.9	23
Jim Paxson	72	1270	189	460	.411	64	90	.711	25	84	109	144	97	0	48	93	5	443	6.2	21
Jim Brewer	67	1016	90	184	.489	14	29	.483	101	156	257	75	129	2	42	47	43	194	2.9	17

3-pt. FG: Portland 26-132 (.197)—Natt† 2-4 (.500); Natt‡ 3-9 (.333); Owens 1-2 (.500); R. Brewer 6-32 (.188); Lucas* 2-5 (.400); Washington 0-3 (.000); Bates 8-19 (.421); Hollins* 1-10 (.100); Jeelani 0-6 (.000); Steele 0-4 (.000); Gross 1-10 (.100); Twardzik 4-7 (.571); Dunn 0-3 (.000); Paxson 1-22 (.045); J. Brewer 0-5 (.000). Opponents 55-186 (.296).

SAN ANTONIO SPURS

	G	Min.	FGM	FGA	Pct.	FTM	FTA	Pct.	REBOUNDS Off.	Def.	Tot.	Ast.	PF	Dq.	Stl.	TO	Blk.	SCORING Pts.	Avg.	Hi.
George Gervin	78	2934	1024	1940	.528	505	593	.852	154	249	403	202	208	0	110	254	79	2585	33.1	55
Larry Kenon	78	2798	647	1333	.485	270	345	.783	258	517	775	231	192	0	111	232	18	1565	20.1	51
James Silas	77	2293	513	999	.514	339	382	.887	45	122	167	347	206	2	61	192	14	1365	17.7	35
John Shumate†	27	777	138	263	.525	115	147	.782	65	149	214	52	71	1	23	50	31	391	14.5	29
John Shumate‡	65	1337	207	392	.528	165	216	.764	108	255	363	84	126	1	40	91	45	579	8.9	29
Kevin Restani	82	1966	369	727	.508	131	161	.814	142	244	386	189	186	0	54	129	12	874	10.7	24
Mark Olberding	75	2111	291	609	.478	210	264	.795	83	335	418	327	274	7	67	180	22	792	10.6	22
Billy Paultz*	47	1213	189	381	.496	66	100	.660	95	226	321	118	127	3	47	58	45	444	9.4	26
Mike Gale	67	1474	171	377	.454	97	120	.808	34	118	152	312	134	2	123	115	13	441	6.6	22
Paul Griffin	82	1812	173	313	.553	174	240	.725	154	284	438	250	306	9	81	131	53	520	6.3	18
Mike Evans	79	1246	208	464	.448	58	85	.682	29	78	107	230	194	2	60	128	9	486	6.2	21
Wiley Peck	52	628	73	169	.432	34	55	.618	66	117	183	33	100	2	17	48	23	180	3.5	13
Harry Davis	4	30	6	12	.500	1	2	.500	2	4	6	0	8	0	1	3	0	13	3.3	9
Irv Kiffin	26	212	32	96	.333	18	25	.720	12	28	40	19	43	0	10	30	2	82	3.2	12
Sylvester Norris	17	189	18	43	.419	4	6	.667	10	33	43	6	41	1	3	19	12	40	2.4	8
Tim Bassett†	5	72	4	12	.333	2	3	.667	4	11	15	10	13	0	3	5	0	10	2.0	4
Tim Bassett‡	12	164	12	34	.353	10	15	.667	11	22	33	14	27	0	8	9	0	34	2.8	11

1979-80

3-pt. FG: San Antonio 52-206 (.252)—Gervin 32-102 (.314); Kenon 1-9 (.111); Silas 0-4 (.000); Shumate† 0-1 (.000); Shumate‡ 0-1 (.000); Restani 5-29 (.172); Olberding 0-3 (.000); Paultz* 0-1 (.000); Gale 2-13 (.154); Evans 12-42 (.286); Peck 0-2 (.000). Opponents 88-288 (.306).

SAN DIEGO CLIPPERS

								REBOUNDS								SCORING		
	G	Min.	FGM	FGA	Pct.	FTM	FTA	Pct.	Off.	Def.	Tot.	Ast.	PF	Dq.	Stl.	TO	Blk.	Pts.	Avg.	Hi.
World B. Free	68	2585	737	1556	.474	572	760	.753	129	109	238	283	195	0	81	228	32	2055	30.2	49
Freeman Williams	82	2118	645	1343	.480	194	238	.815	103	89	192	166	145	0	72	171	9	1526	18.6	51
Bill Walton	14	337	81	161	.503	32	54	.593	28	98	126	34	37	0	8	37	38	194	13.9	28
Brian Taylor	78	2754	418	895	.467	130	162	.802	76	112	188	335	246	6	147	141	25	1056	13.5	28
Swen Nater	81	2860	443	799	.554	196	273	.718	352	864	1216	233	259	3	45	257	37	1082	13.4	28
Bobby Smith†	70	1988	352	819	.430	93	107	.869	92	153	245	93	188	4	59	72	15	819	11.7	23
Bobby Smith‡	78	2123	385	891	.432	100	115	.870	94	165	259	100	209	4	62	81	17	893	11.4	23
Joe Bryant	81	2328	294	682	.431	161	217	.742	171	345	516	144	258	4	102	170	39	754	9.3	23
Sidney Wicks	71	2146	210	496	.423	83	152	.546	138	271	409	213	241	5	76	167	52	503	7.1	17
Nick Weatherspoon	57	1124	164	378	.434	63	91	.692	83	125	208	54	136	1	34	86	17	391	6.9	23
Stan Pietkiewicz	50	577	91	179	.508	37	46	.804	26	19	45	94	52	1	25	51	4	228	4.6	20
Bob Carrington	10	134	15	37	.405	6	8	.750	6	7	13	3	18	0	4	5	1	36	3.6	9
Jerome Whitehead*	18	225	27	45	.600	5	18	.278	29	41	70	6	32	0	1	8	6	59	3.3	11
Marvin Barnes	20	287	24	60	.400	16	32	.500	34	43	77	18	52	0	5	18	12	64	3.2	8
Steve Malovic*	28	277	23	42	.548	7	9	.778	27	31	58	12	35	0	5	14	1	53	1.9	6
John Olive	1	15	0	2	.000	0	0	—	0	1	1	0	2	0	0	2	0	0	0.0	0

3-pt. FG: San Diego 177-543 (.326)—Free 9-25 (.360); Williams 42-128 (.328); Taylor 90-239 (.377); Nater 0-2 (.000); Smith† 22-76 (.289); Smith‡ 23-81 (.284); Bryant 5-34 (.147); Wicks 0-1 (.000); Pietkiewicz 9-36 (.250); Carrington 0-2 (.000). Opponents 43-187 (.230).

SEATTLE SUPERSONICS

								REBOUNDS								SCORING		
	G	Min.	FGM	FGA	Pct.	FTM	FTA	Pct.	Off.	Def.	Tot.	Ast.	PF	Dq.	Stl.	TO	Blk.	Pts.	Avg.	Hi.
Gus Williams	82	2969	739	1533	.482	331	420	.788	127	148	275	397	160	1	200	181	37	1816	22.1	41
Dennis Johnson	81	2937	574	1361	.422	380	487	.780	173	241	414	332	267	6	144	227	82	1540	19.0	36
Jack Sikma	82	2793	470	909	.475	235	292	.805	198	710	908	279	232	5	68	202	77	1175	14.3	32
Lonnie Shelton	76	2243	425	802	.530	184	241	.763	199	383	582	145	292	11	92	169	79	1035	13.6	30
Fred Brown	80	1701	404	843	.479	113	135	.837	35	120	155	174	117	0	65	105	17	960	12.0	27
John Johnson	81	2533	377	772	.488	161	201	.801	163	263	426	424	213	1	76	247	35	915	11.3	22
Tom LaGarde	82	1164	146	306	.477	90	137	.657	127	185	312	91	206	2	19	97	34	382	4.7	13
Wally Walker	70	844	139	274	.507	48	04	.750	04	100	170	53	102	0	21	60	4	326	4.7	14
James Bailey	67	726	122	271	.450	68	101	.673	71	126	197	28	116	1	21	79	54	312	4.7	23
Paul Silas	82	1595	113	299	.378	89	136	.654	204	232	436	66	120	0	25	83	5	315	3.8	14
Vinnie Johnson	38	325	45	115	.391	31	39	.795	19	36	55	54	40	0	19	42	4	121	3.2	12

3-pt. FG: Seattle 59-189 (.312)—Williams 7-36 (.194); D. Johnson 12-58 (.207); Sikma 0-1 (.000); Shelton 1-5 (.200); Brown 39-88 (.443); V. Johnson 0-1 (.000). Opponents 59-240 (.246).

UTAH JAZZ

								REBOUNDS								SCORING		
	G	Min.	FGM	FGA	Pct.	FTM	FTA	Pct.	Off.	Def.	Tot.	Ast.	PF	Dq.	Stl.	TO	Blk.	Pts.	Avg.	Hi.
Adrian Dantley	68	2674	730	1267	.576	443	526	.842	183	333	516	191	211	2	96	233	14	1903	28.0	50
Pete Maravich*	17	522	121	294	.412	41	50	.820	7	33	40	54	30	0	15	45	4	290	17.1	31
Terry Furlow†	55	1718	364	765	.476	127	145	.876	47	105	152	221	79	0	54	129	14	878	16.0	37
Terry Furlow‡	76	2122	430	926	.464	171	196	.872	70	124	194	293	98	0	73	163	23	1055	13.9	37
Ron Boone†	75	2286	391	875	.447	169	189	.894	50	166	216	302	219	3	92	184	3	970	12.9	35
Ron Boone‡	81	2392	405	915	.443	175	196	.893	54	173	227	309	232	3	97	197	3	1004	12.4	35
Allan Bristow	82	2304	377	705	.480	197	243	.811	170	342	512	341	211	2	88	179	6	953	11.6	31
Tom Boswell†	61	1555	274	478	.573	148	203	.729	106	222	328	115	214	8	24	142	29	700	11.5	25
Tom Boswell‡	79	2077	346	613	.564	206	273	.755	146	296	442	161	270	9	29	181	37	903	11.4	25
Bernard King	19	419	71	137	.518	34	63	.540	24	64	88	52	66	3	7	50	4	176	9.3	24
Ben Poquette	82	2349	296	566	.523	139	167	.832	124	436	560	131	283	8	45	103	162	731	8.9	27
Don Williams	77	1794	232	519	.447	42	60	.700	21	85	106	183	166	0	100	107	11	506	6.6	22
Mack Calvin	48	722	100	227	.441	105	117	.897	13	71	84	134	72	0	27	57	0	306	6.4	17
Brad Davis†	13	225	33	56	.589	10	12	.833	4	11	15	45	21	0	10	11	1	76	5.8	17
Brad Davis‡	18	268	35	63	.556	13	16	.813	4	13	17	50	28	0	13	14	1	83	4.6	17
James Hardy	76	1600	184	363	.507	51	66	.773	124	275	399	104	207	4	47	105	87	420	5.5	22
Paul Dawkins	57	776	141	300	.470	33	48	.688	42	83	125	77	112	0	33	76	9	316	5.5	30
John Gianelli	17	285	23	66	.348	9	16	.563	14	48	62	17	26	0	6	22	7	55	3.2	10
Robert Smith*	6	73	5	15	.333	5	5	1.000	3	0	3	7	3	0	4	1	0	15	2.5	5
Jerome Whitehead†	32	328	31	69	.449	5	17	.294	27	70	97	18	65	3	7	28	11	67	2.1	8
Jerome Whitehead‡	50	553	58	114	.509	10	35	.286	56	111	167	24	97	3	8	36	17	126	2.5	11
Andre Wakefield	8	47	6	15	.400	3	3	1.000	0	4	4	3	13	0	1	8	0	15	1.9	5
Carl Kilpatrick	2	6	1	2	.500	1	2	.500	1	3	4	0	1	0	0	0	0	3	1.5	3
Greg Deane	7	48	2	11	.182	5	7	.714	2	4	6	6	3	0	0	3	0	10	1.4	3
John Brown*	4	24	0	7	.000	4	4	1.000	5	4	9	4	0	0	0	5	0	4	1.0	2

3-pt. FG: Utah 59-185 (.319)—Dantley 0-2 (.000); Maravich* 7-11 (.636); Furlow† 23-73 (.315); Furlow‡ 24-82 (.293); Boone† 19-50 (.380); Boone‡ 19-50 (.380); Bristow 2-7 (.286); Boswell† 4-8 (.500); Boswell‡ 5-10 (.500); Poquette 0-2 (.000); Williams 0-12 (.000); Calvin 1-11 (.091); Davis† 0-1 (.000); Davis‡ 0-1 (.000); Hardy 1-2 (.500); Dawkins 1-5 (.200); Deane 1-1 (1.000). Opponents 67-211 (.318).

1979-80

WASHINGTON BULLETS

	G	Min.	FGM	FGA	Pct.	FTM	FTA	Pct.	Off.	Def.	Tot.	Ast.	PF	Dq.	Stl.	TO	Blk.	Pts.	Avg.	Hi.
									REBOUNDS									SCORING		
Elvin Hayes........	81	3183	761	1677	.454	334	478	.699	269	627	896	129	309	9	62	215	189	1859	23.0	43
Bob Dandridge	45	1457	329	729	.451	123	152	.809	63	183	246	178	112	1	29	123	36	783	17.4	31
Greg Ballard	82	2438	545	1101	.495	171	227	.753	240	398	638	159	197	2	90	133	36	1277	15.6	32
Kevin Grevey........	65	1818	331	804	.412	216	249	.867	80	107	187	177	158	0	56	102	16	912	14.0	32
John Williamson†	30	603	153	356	.430	40	50	.800	14	31	45	39	66	0	10	49	10	349	11.6	24
John Williamson‡	58	1374	359	817	.439	116	138	.841	38	61	99	126	137	1	36	92	19	845	14.6	32
Roger Phegley*	50	971	224	473	.474	104	120	.867	49	66	115	70	106	1	19	70	3	554	11.1	35
Phil Chenier*	20	470	84	214	.393	31	41	.756	10	33	43	42	26	0	18	29	5	202	10.1	22
Wes Unseld	82	2973	327	637	.513	139	209	.665	334	760	1094	366	249	5	65	153	61	794	9.7	24
Jim Cleamons†	57	1535	184	381	.483	72	98	.735	43	90	133	248	120	0	44	92	9	444	7.8	20
Jim Cleamons‡	79	1789	214	450	.476	84	113	.743	53	99	152	288	133	0	57	109	11	519	6.6	20
Larry Wright........	76	1286	229	500	.458	96	108	.889	40	82	122	222	144	3	49	108	18	558	7.3	25
Kevin Porter	70	1494	201	438	.459	110	137	.803	25	57	82	457	180	1	59	164	11	512	7.3	24
Mitch Kupchak	40	451	67	160	.419	52	75	.693	32	73	105	16	49	1	8	40	8	186	4.7	20
Lawrence Boston	13	125	24	52	.462	8	13	.615	19	20	39	2	25	0	4	8	2	56	4.3	15
Ron Behagen	6	64	9	23	.391	5	6	.833	6	8	14	7	14	0	0	4	4	23	3.8	9
Dave Corzine........	78	826	90	216	.417	45	68	.662	104	166	270	63	120	1	9	60	31	225	2.9	13
Gus Bailey	20	180	16	35	.457	5	13	.385	6	22	28	26	18	0	7	11	4	38	1.9	6
Steve Malovic*	1	6	0	0		1	4	.250	0	0	0	0	0	0	1	0	0	1	1.0	1

3-pt. FG: Washington 73-238 (.307)—Hayes 3-13 (.231); Dandridge 2-11 (.182); Ballard 16-47 (.340); Grevey 34-92 (.370); Williamson† 3-16 (.188); Williamson‡ 11-35 (.314); Phegley* 2-5 (.400); Chenier* 3-6 (.500); Unseld 1-2 (.500); Cleamons† 4-23 (.174); Cleamons‡ 7-31 (.226); Wright 4-16 (.250); Porter 0-4 (.000); Kupchak 0-2 (.000); Bailey 1-1 (1.000). Opponents 56-214 (.262).

* Finished season with another team. † Totals with this team only. ‡ Totals with all teams.

PLAYOFF RESULTS

EASTERN CONFERENCE

FIRST ROUND

Philadelphia 2, Washington 0
Apr. 2—Wed.	Washington 96 at Philadelphia	111
Apr. 4—Fri.	Philadelphia 112 at Washington	104

Houston 2, San Antonio 1
Apr. 2—Wed.	San Antonio 85 at Houston	95
Apr. 4—Fri.	Houston 101 at San Antonio	106
Apr. 6—Sun.	San Antonio 120 at Houston	141

SEMIFINALS

Boston 4, Houston 0
Apr. 9—Wed.	Houston 101 at Boston	119
Apr. 11—Fri.	Houston 75 at Boston	95
Apr. 13—Sun.	Boston 100 at Houston	81
Apr. 14—Mon.	Boston 138 at Houston	121

Philadelphia 4, Atlanta 1
Apr. 6—Sun.	Atlanta 104 at Philadelphia	107
Apr. 9—Wed.	Atlanta 92 at Philadelphia	99
Apr. 10—Thur.	Philadelphia 93 at Atlanta	105
Apr. 13—Sun.	Philadelphia 107 at Atlanta	83
Apr. 15—Tue.	Atlanta 100 at Philadelphia	105

FINALS

Philadelphia 4, Boston 1
Apr. 18—Fri.	Philadelphia 96 at Boston	93
Apr. 20—Sun.	Philadelphia 90 at Boston	96
Apr. 23—Wed.	Boston 97 at Philadelphia	99
Apr. 24—Thur.	Boston 90 at Philadelphia	102
Apr. 27—Sun.	Philadelphia 105 at Boston	94

WESTERN CONFERENCE

FIRST ROUND

Phoenix 2, Kansas City 1
Apr. 2—Wed.	Kansas City 93 at Phoenix	96
Apr. 4—Fri.	Phoenix 96 at Kansas City	106
Apr. 6—Sun.	Kansas City 99 at Phoenix	114

Seattle 2, Portland 1
Apr. 2—Wed.	Portland 110 at Seattle	120
Apr. 4—Fri.	Seattle 95 at Portland	*105
Apr. 6—Sun.	Portland 86 at Seattle	103

SEMIFINALS

Los Angeles 4, Phoenix 1
Apr. 8—Tue.	Phoenix 110 at Los Angeles	*119
Apr. 9—Wed.	Phoenix 128 at Los Angeles	*131
Apr. 11—Fri.	Los Angeles 108 at Phoenix	105
Apr. 13—Sun.	Los Angeles 101 at Phoenix	127
Apr. 15—Tue.	Phoenix 101 at Los Angeles	126

Seattle 4, Milwaukee 3
Apr. 8—Tue.	Milwaukee 113 at Seattle	*114
Apr. 9—Wed.	Milwaukee 114 at Seattle	*112
Apr. 11—Fri.	Seattle 91 at Milwaukee	95
Apr. 13—Sun.	Seattle 112 at Milwaukee	107
Apr. 15—Tue.	Milwaukee 108 at Seattle	97
Apr. 18—Fri.	Seattle 86 at Milwaukee	85
Apr. 20—Sun.	Milwaukee 94 at Seattle	98

FINALS

Los Angeles 4, Seattle 1
Apr. 22—Tue.	Seattle 108 at Los Angeles	107
Apr. 23—Wed.	Seattle 99 at Los Angeles	108
Apr. 25—Fri.	Los Angeles 104 at Seattle	100
Apr. 27—Sun.	Los Angeles 98 at Seattle	93
Apr. 30—Wed.	Seattle 105 at Los Angeles	111

NBA FINALS

Los Angeles 4, Philadelphia 2
May 4—Sun.	Philadelphia 102 at Los Angeles	109
May 7—Wed.	Philadelphia 107 at Los Angeles	104
May 10—Sat.	Los Angeles 111 at Philadelphia	101
May 11—Sun.	Los Angeles 102 at Philadelphia	105
May 14—Wed.	Philadelphia 103 at Los Angeles	108
May 16—Fri.	Los Angeles 123 at Philadelphia	107

*Denotes number of overtime periods.

1979-80

1978-79

1978-79 NBA CHAMPION SEATTLE SUPERSONICS
Front row (from left): trainer Frank Furtado, Dick Snyder, Jackie Robinson, Fred Brown, Joe Hassett, Dennis Johnson, Gus Williams. Center row (from left): head coach Lenny Wilkens, Dennis Awtrey, Tom LaGarde, John Johnson, Lonnie Shelton, Paul Silas, scout Mike Uporsky, assistant coach Les Habegger. Back row (from left): Jack Sikma, general manager Zollie Volchok. Not pictured: Wally Walker.

FINAL STANDINGS

ATLANTIC DIVISION

	Atl.	Bos.	Chi.	Cle.	Den.	Det.	G.S.	Hou.	Ind.	K.C.	L.A.	Mil.	N.J.	N.O.	N.Y	Phi.	Pho.	Por.	S.A.	S.D.	Sea.	Was.	W	L	Pct.	GB
Washington . .2	4	3	4	3	3	2	2	3	0	2	3	3	4	3	1	3	1	3	3	2	..	54	28	.659	..
Philadelphia . .2	2	3	2	3	3	1	4	2	2	3	2	2	2	2	..	1	1	3	3	1	3	47	35	.573	7
New Jersey . . .2	3	2	1	0	4	3	1	2	1	2	2	..	3	1	2	3	2	0	2	0	1	37	45	.451	17
New York 2	1	1	2	1	3	1	0	2	1	0	3	3	2	..	2	0	1	1	2	2	1	31	51	.378	23
Boston 2	..	1	2	1	2	2	1	3	1	1	1	1	2	3	2	0	1	0	1	2	0	29	53	.354	25

CENTRAL DIVISION

	Atl.	Bos.	Chi.	Cle.	Den.	Det.	G.S.	Hou.	Ind.	K.C.	L.A.	Mil.	N.J.	N.O.	N.Y	Phi.	Pho.	Por.	S.A.	S.D.	Sea.	Was.	W	L	Pct.	GB
San Antonio . .1	4	3	4	1	3	3	1	1	3	2	3	4	2	3	1	1	1	..	4	2	1	48	34	.585	..
Houston 1	3	2	2	3	2	2	..	0	3	2	2	3	4	4	0	2	3	3	2	2	2	47	35	.573	1
Atlanta	2	3	3	3	3	1	3	1	2	1	3	2	2	2	2	2	2	3	3	1	2	46	36	.561	2
Detroit 1	2	2	3	2	..	1	2	2	2	2	2	0	2	1	1	0	1	1	2	0	1	30	52	.366	18
Cleveland 1	2	3	..	1	1	2	2	1	1	2	1	3	2	2	0	0	0	2	2	0	0	30	52	.366	18
New Orleans . .2	2	2	2	1	2	1	0	1	1	2	1	1	..	2	2	1	1	2	0	0	0	26	56	.317	22

MIDWEST DIVISION

	Atl.	Bos.	Chi.	Cle.	Den.	Det.	G.S.	Hou.	Ind.	K.C.	L.A.	Mil.	N.J.	N.O.	N.Y	Phi.	Pho.	Por.	S.A.	S.D.	Sea.	Was.	W	L	Pct.	GB
Kansas City . . .2	3	4	3	3	2	2	1	3	..	2	2	3	3	2	2	2	1	1	2	2	3	48	34	.585	..
Denver 1	3	2	2	..	2	4	1	3	1	3	2	4	3	3	0	3	1	3	2	3	1	47	35	.573	1
Milwaukee . . .0	3	3	3	2	1	2	2	2	2	1	..	2	3	1	2	2	1	1	2	1	1	38	44	.463	10
Indiana 3	1	2	3	1	2	2	4	..	1	0	2	1	2	2	2	2	3	3	1	0	1	38	44	.463	10
Chicago 1	2	..	1	2	2	3	2	2	0	1	1	2	2	3	1	1	4	0	0	0	1	31	51	.378	17

PACIFIC DIVISION

	Atl.	Bos.	Chi.	Cle.	Den.	Det.	G.S.	Hou.	Ind.	K.C.	L.A.	Mil.	N.J.	N.O.	N.Y	Phi.	Pho.	Por.	S.A.	S.D.	Sea.	Was.	W	L	Pct.	GB
Seattle 3	2	4	2	1	3	1	2	4	2	2	2	4	3	2	3	3	2	2	..	2	52	30	.634	..
Phoenix 1	4	3	4	1	4	3	2	2	2	2	2	0	3	4	3	..	3	3	2	1	1	50	32	.610	2
Los Angeles . .3	3	3	2	1	2	3	1	4	2	..	3	2	2	3	1	2	2	2	2	2	2	47	35	.573	5
Portland 2	3	0	4	3	3	2	1	1	3	2	2	2	3	3	2	1	..	2	2	1	3	45	37	.549	7
San Diego 1	3	4	2	2	2	3	1	3	2	2	3	2	4	2	1	2	2	0	..	2	0	43	39	.524	9
Golden State . .3	1	1	1	0	3	..	2	2	2	1	2	1	3	3	3	1	2	1	3	2	1	38	44	.463	14

TEAM STATISTICS

OFFENSIVE

								REBOUNDS									SCORING	
	G	FGM	FGA	Pct.	FTM	FTA	Pct.	Off.	Def.	Tot.	Ast.	PF	Dq.	Stl.	TO	Blk.	Pts.	Avg.
San Antonio . . .82	3927	7760	.506	1926	2423	.795	1096	2619	3715	2313	2071	25	829	1652	509	9780	119.3
Phoenix 82	3847	7516	.512	1765	2299	.768	1083	2379	3462	2500	1944	19	915	1760	337	9459	115.4

	G	FGM	FGA	Pct.	FTM	FTA	Pct.	Off.	Def.	Tot.	Ast.	PF	Dq.	Stl.	TO	Blk.	Pts.	Avg.
								REBOUNDS									SCORING	
Washington	82	3819	7873	.485	1785	2428	.735	1309	2768	4077	2169	1804	18	614	1420	401	9423	114.9
Milwaukee	82	3906	7773	.503	1541	2021	.762	1157	2370	3527	2562	2106	25	862	1574	435	9353	114.1
Houston	82	3726	7498	.497	1845	2330	.792	1256	2504	3760	2302	2001	19	632	1510	286	9297	113.4
Kansas City	82	3764	7644	.492	1746	2392	.730	1191	2404	3595	2239	2419	53	825	1631	390	9274	113.1
San Diego	82	3721	7706	.483	1836	2471	.743	1392	2413	3805	1539	2127	43	703	1623	392	9278	113.1
Los Angeles	82	3827	7397	.517	1606	2088	.769	949	2557	3506	2338	1851	16	793	1569	500	9260	112.9
Denver	82	3517	7311	.481	2046	2841	.720	1307	2596	3903	2166	2106	45	673	1666	416	9080	110.7
Detroit	82	3708	7802	.475	1607	2242	.717	1303	2380	3683	2092	2141	37	847	1599	550	9023	110.0
Philadelphia	82	3584	7338	.488	1815	2411	.753	1149	2712	3861	2253	2072	26	779	1771	599	8983	109.5
Atlanta	82	3505	7410	.473	1940	2534	.766	1381	2341	3722	1938	2424	72	801	1523	596	8950	109.1
Indiana	82	3575	7525	.475	1759	2317	.759	1225	2530	3755	2005	2093	41	687	1536	416	8909	108.6
Portland	82	3541	7338	.483	1806	2362	.765	1256	2435	3691	1946	2187	49	776	1658	512	8888	108.4
New Orleans	82	3517	7511	.468	1848	2409	.767	1234	2676	3910	2079	1940	27	760	1764	559	8882	108.3
Boston	82	3527	7347	.480	1820	2321	.784	1119	2396	3515	1995	1977	39	710	1713	283	8874	108.2
New Jersey	82	3464	7523	.460	1904	2613	.729	1241	2370	3611	1907	2329	43	853	1861	619	8832	107.7
New York	82	3676	7554	.487	1478	2111	.700	1200	2430	3630	2121	2154	34	699	1605	397	8830	107.7
Seattle	82	3504	7484	.468	1732	2298	.754	1310	2591	3901	1973	1914	23	690	1586	398	8740	106.6
Cleveland	82	3556	7602	.468	1620	2103	.770	1229	2256	3485	1796	2027	21	688	1376	334	8732	106.5
Golden State	82	3627	7453	.487	1367	1872	.730	1169	2513	3682	2064	2023	25	774	1500	420	8621	105.1
Chicago	82	3478	7108	.489	1632	2184	.747	1224	2544	3768	2169	1970	30	576	1813	324	8588	104.7

DEFENSIVE

	FGM	FGA	Pct.	FTM	FTA	Pct.	Off.	Def.	Tot.	Ast.	PF	Dq.	Stl.	TO	Blk.	Pts.	Avg.	Dif.
							REBOUNDS									SCORING		
Seattle	3475	7509	.463	1567	2108	.743	1156	2453	3609	1910	2057	27	755	1493	407	8517	103.9	+2.7
Golden State	3493	7255	.481	1604	2155	.744	1147	2533	3680	2094	1854	20	637	1580	362	8590	104.8	+0.3
Portland	3448	7059	.488	1889	2501	.755	1080	2350	3430	1963	2206	48	797	1650	422	8785	107.1	+1.3
Atlanta	3367	7064	.477	2045	2727	.750	1176	2440	3616	1928	2135	45	646	1799	559	8779	107.1	+2.0
Philadelphia	3542	7626	.464	1747	2331	.749	1252	2506	3758	2094	2128	35	795	1627	353	8831	107.7	+1.8
Chicago	3682	7408	.497	1549	2029	.763	1095	2377	3472	2146	2093	38	844	1468	503	8913	108.7	-4.0
Denver	3631	7616	.477	1713	2277	.752	1218	2429	3647	2173	2262	56	738	1529	471	8975	109.5	+1.2
Washington	3804	8011	.475	1406	1897	.741	1178	2541	3719	2180	2144	37	726	1338	434	9014	109.9	+5.0
Los Angeles	3797	7848	.484	1415	1931	.733	1288	2486	3774	2234	1958	28	737	1542	359	9009	109.9	+3.0
Kansas City	3434	7061	.486	2170	2897	.749	1156	2547	3703	1776	2223	41	678	1879	435	9038	110.2	+2.9
Indiana	3586	7499	.478	1868	2416	.773	1299	2605	3904	2178	2091	30	677	1618	437	9040	110.2	-1.6
Cleveland	3600	7150	.503	1837	2423	.758	1123	2587	3710	2062	2001	21	658	1557	503	9037	110.2	-3.7
New York	3600	7457	.483	1907	2506	.761	1225	2489	3714	2114	1961	29	751	1558	378	9107	111.1	-3.4
Phoenix	3775	7626	.495	1606	2127	.755	1238	2424	3662	2091	2144	33	890	1841	402	9156	111.7	+3.7
Milwaukee	3676	7505	.490	1819	2415	.753	1229	2437	3666	2301	1928	17	763	1748	462	9171	111.8	+2.3
New Jersey	3507	7306	.480	2160	2861	.755	1234	2667	3901	2185	2208	37	861	1919	492	9174	111.9	-4.2
Houston	3795	7625	.498	1627	2211	.736	1186	2315	3501	2278	2055	43	660	1400	431	9217	112.4	+1.0
Detroit	3755	7623	.493	1732	2295	.755	1301	2628	3929	2197	1914	21	666	1744	504	9242	112.7	-2.7
Boston	3855	7593	.508	1578	2079	.759	1122	2453	3575	2170	2025	25	717	1603	438	9288	113.3	-5.1
San Antonio	3798	7970	.477	1759	2343	.751	1297	2531	3828	2232	2168	41	788	1700	405	9355	114.1	+5.2
New Orleans	3864	8039	.481	1666	2246	.742	1486	2664	4150	2264	2061	28	955	1600	566	9394	114.6	-6.3
San Diego	3832	7801	.491	1760	2295	.767	1294	2322	3616	1896	2064	30	747	1517	350	9424	114.9	-1.8
Avgs.	3651	7522	.485	1747	2321	.753	1217	2490	3707	2112	2076	33	749	1623	440	9048	110.3	...

HOME/ROAD

	Home	Road	Total
Atlanta	34-7	12-29	46-36
Boston	21-20	8-33	29-53
Chicago	19-22	12-29	31-51
Cleveland	20-21	10-31	30-52
Denver	29-12	18-23	47-35
Detroit	22-19	8-33	30-52
Golden State	23-18	15-26	38-44
Houston	30-11	17-24	47-35
Indiana	25-16	13-28	38-44
Kansas City	32-9	16-25	48-34
Los Angeles	31-10	16-25	47-35
Milwaukee	28-13	10-31	38-44
New Jersey	25-16	12-29	37-45
New Orleans	22-19	4-37	26-56
New York	23-18	8-33	31-51
Philadelphia	31-10	16-25	47-35
Phoenix	32-9	18-23	50-32
Portland	33-8	12-29	45-37
San Antonio	29-12	19-22	48-34
San Diego	29-12	14-27	43-39
Seattle	31-10	21-20	52-30
Washington	31-10	23-18	54-28
Totals	600-302	302-600	902-902

INDIVIDUAL LEADERS

POINTS

(minimum 70 games or 1,400 points)

	G	FGM	FTM	Pts.	Avg.
George Gervin, San Antonio	80	947	471	2365	29.6
World B. Free, San Diego	78	795	654	2244	28.8
Marques Johnson, Milwaukee	77	820	332	1972	25.6
Moses Malone, Houston	82	716	599	2031	24.8
Bob McAdoo, New York-Boston	60	596	295	1487	24.8
Paul Westphal, Phoenix	81	801	339	1941	24.0
David Thompson, Denver	76	693	439	1825	24.0
Kareem Abdul-Jabbar, L.A.	80	777	349	1903	23.8
Artis Gilmore, Chicago	82	753	434	1940	23.7
Walter Davis, Phoenix	79	764	340	1868	23.6
Julius Erving, Philadelphia	78	715	373	1803	23.1
John Drew, Atlanta	79	650	495	1795	22.7
George McGinnis, Denver	76	603	509	1715	22.6
John Williamson, New Jersey	74	635	373	1643	22.2
Larry Kenon, San Antonio	81	748	295	1791	22.1
Campy Russell, Cleveland	74	603	417	1623	21.9
Elvin Hayes, Washington	82	720	349	1789	21.8
Otis Birdsong, Kansas City	82	741	296	1778	21.7
Bernard King, New Jersey	82	710	349	1769	21.6
Truck Robinson, N.O.-Phoenix	69	566	324	1456	21.1

FIELD GOALS
(minimum 300 made)

	FGM	FGA	Pct.
Cedric Maxwell, Boston	.472	808	.584
Kareem Abdul-Jabbar, Los Angeles	.777	1347	.577
Wes Unseld, Washington	.346	600	.577
Artis Gilmore, Chicago	.753	1310	.575
Swen Nater, San Diego	.357	627	.569
Kermit Washington, San Diego	.350	623	.562
Walter Davis, Phoenix	.764	1362	.561
Marques Johnson, Milwaukee	.820	1491	.550
Tom Owens, Portland	.600	1095	.548
Bill Robinzine, Kansas City	.459	837	.548

FREE THROWS
(minimum 125 made)

	FTM	FTA	Pct.
Rick Barry, Houston	.160	169	.947
Calvin Murphy, Houston	.246	265	.928
Fred Brown, Seattle	.183	206	.888
Robert Smith, Denver	.159	180	.883
Ricky Sobers, Indiana	.298	338	.882
Jo Jo White, Boston-Golden State	.139	158	.880
Dave Twardzik, Portland	.261	299	.873
Mike Newlin, Houston	.212	243	.872
Mike Dunleavy, Houston	.159	184	.864
Brian Winters, Milwaukee	.237	277	.856

ASSISTS
(minimum 70 games or 400 assists)

	G	No.	Avg.
Kevin Porter, Detroit	.82	1099	13.4
John Lucas, Golden State	.82	762	9.3
Norm Nixon, Los Angeles	.82	737	9.0
Phil Ford, Kansas City	.79	681	8.6
Paul Westphal, Phoenix	.81	529	6.5
Rick Barry, Houston	.80	502	6.3
Ray WIllIams, New York	.81	504	6.2
Tom Henderson, Washington	.70	419	6.0
Armond Hill, Atlanta	.82	480	5.9
Quinn Buckner, Milwaukee	.81	468	5.8

REBOUNDS
(minimum 70 games or 800 rebounds)

	G	Off.	Def.	Tot.	Avg.
Moses Malone, Houston	.82	587	857	1444	17.6
Rich Kelley, New Orleans	.80	303	723	1026	12.8
Kareem Abdul-Jabbar, L.A.	.80	207	818	1025	12.8
Artis Gilmore, Chicago	.82	293	750	1043	12.7
Jack Sikma, Seattle	.82	232	781	1013	12.4
Elvin Hayes, Washington	.82	312	682	994	12.1
Robert Parish, Golden State	.76	265	651	916	12.1
Truck Robinson, N.O.-Phoenix	.69	195	607	802	11.6
George McGinnis, Denver	.76	256	608	864	11.4
Dan Roundfield, Atlanta	.80	326	539	865	10.8

STEALS
(minimum 70 games or 125 steals)

	G	No.	Avg.
M.L. Carr, Detroit	.80	197	2.46
Eddie Jordan, New Jersey	.82	201	2.45
Norm Nixon, Los Angeles	.82	201	2.45
Foots Walker, Cleveland	.55	130	2.36
Phil Ford, Kansas City	.79	174	2.20
Randy Smith, San Diego	.82	177	2.16
Maurice Cheeks, Philadelphia	.82	174	2.12
Gus Williams, Seattle	.76	158	2.08
Kevin Porter, Detroit	.82	158	1.93
Quinn Buckner, Milwaukee	.81	156	1.93

BLOCKED SHOTS
(minimum 70 games or 100 blocked shots)

	G	No.	Avg.
Kareem Abdul-Jabbar, Los Angeles	.80	316	3.95
George Johnson, New Jersey	.78	253	3.24
Tree Rollins, Atlanta	.81	254	3.14
Robert Parish, Golden State	.76	217	2.86
Terry Tyler, Detroit	.82	201	2.45
Elvin Hayes, Washington	.82	190	2.32
Dan Roundfield, Atlanta	.80	176	2.20
Rich Kelley, New Orleans	.80	166	2.08
Caldwell Jones, Philadelphia	.78	157	2.01
Artis Gilmore, Chicago	.82	156	1.90

1978-79

INDIVIDUAL STATISTICS, TEAM BY TEAM

ATLANTA HAWKS

									REBOUNDS									SCORING		
	G	Min.	FGM	FGA	Pct.	FTM	FTA	Pct.	Off.	Def.	Tot.	Ast.	PF	Dq.	Stl.	TO	Blk.	Pts.	Avg.	Hi.
John Drew	79	2410	650	1375	.473	495	677	.731	225	297	522	119	332	19	128	211	16	1795	22.7	50
Eddie Johnson	78	2413	501	982	.510	243	292	.832	65	105	170	360	241	6	121	213	11	1245	16.0	30
Dan Roundfield	80	2539	462	916	.504	300	420	.714	326	539	865	131	358	16	87	209	176	1224	15.3	38
Steve Hawes	81	2205	372	756	.492	108	132	.818	190	401	591	184	264	1	79	145	47	852	10.5	27
Armond Hill	82	2527	296	682	.434	246	288	.854	41	123	164	480	292	8	102	202	16	838	10.2	26
Terry Furlow†	29	576	113	235	.481	60	70	.857	32	39	71	81	42	0	18	47	13	286	9.9	30
Terry Furlow‡	78	1686	388	804	.483	163	195	.836	76	91	167	184	122	1	58	134	30	939	12.0	30
Tree Rollins	81	1900	297	555	.535	89	141	.631	219	369	588	49	328	19	46	87	254	683	8.4	24
Jack Givens	74	1347	234	564	.415	102	135	.756	98	116	214	83	121	0	72	75	17	570	7.7	22
Butch Lee*	49	997	144	313	.460	88	117	.752	11	48	59	169	88	0	56	96	1	376	7.7	21
Tom McMillen	82	1392	232	498	.466	106	119	.891	131	201	332	69	211	2	15	87	32	570	7.0	22
Charlie Criss	54	879	109	289	.377	67	86	.779	19	41	60	138	70	0	41	79	3	285	5.3	17
Rick Wilson	61	589	81	197	.411	24	44	.545	20	56	76	72	66	1	30	41	8	186	3.0	10
Keith Herron	14	81	14	48	.292	12	13	.923	4	6	10	3	11	0	6	5	2	40	2.9	7

BOSTON CELTICS

									REBOUNDS									SCORING		
	G	Min.	FGM	FGA	Pct.	FTM	FTA	Pct.	Off.	Def.	Tot.	Ast.	PF	Dq.	Stl.	TO	Blk.	Pts.	Avg.	Hi.
Bob McAdoo†	20	637	167	334	.500	77	115	.670	36	105	141	40	55	1	12	64	20	411	20.6	42
Bob McAdoo‡	60	2231	596	1127	.529	295	450	.656	130	390	520	168	189	3	74	217	67	1487	24.8	45
Cedric Maxwell	80	2969	472	808	.584	574	716	.802	272	519	791	228	266	4	98	273	74	1518	19.0	35
Dave Cowens	68	2517	488	1010	.483	151	187	.807	152	500	652	242	263	16	76	174	51	1127	16.6	32
Chris Ford†	78	2629	525	1107	.474	165	219	.753	115	141	256	369	200	2	114	200	24	1215	15.6	34
Chris Ford‡	81	2737	538	1142	.471	172	227	.758	124	150	274	374	209	3	115	210	25	1248	15.4	34
Billy Knight*	40	1119	219	436	.502	118	146	.808	41	132	173	66	86	1	31	129	3	556	13.9	37
Jo Jo White*	47	1455	255	596	.428	79	89	.888	22	106	128	214	100	1	54	142	4	589	12.5	28
Rick Robey†	36	914	182	378	.481	84	103	.816	88	171	259	79	121	3	23	75	3	448	12.4	27

	G	Min.	FGM	FGA	Pct.	FTM	FTA	Pct.	Off.	Def.	Tot.	Ast.	PF	Dq.	Stl.	TO	Blk.	Pts.	Avg.	Hi.
									REBOUNDS									SCORING		
Rick Robey‡	79	1763	322	673	.478	174	224	.777	168	345	513	132	232	4	48	164	15	818	10.4	28
Nate Archibald	69	1662	259	573	.452	242	307	.788	25	78	103	324	132	2	55	197	6	760	11.0	25
Jeff Judkins	81	1521	295	587	.503	119	146	.815	70	121	191	145	184	1	81	109	12	709	8.8	29
Marvin Barnes	38	796	133	271	.491	43	66	.652	57	120	177	53	144	3	38	68	39	309	8.1	29
Curtis Rowe	53	1222	151	346	.436	52	75	.693	79	163	242	69	105	2	15	88	13	354	6.7	21
Earl Tatum*	3	38	8	20	.400	4	5	.800	1	3	4	1	7	0	0	3	1	20	6.7	11
Earl Williams	20	273	54	123	.439	14	24	.583	41	64	105	12	41	0	12	20	9	122	6.1	27
Don Chaney	65	1074	174	414	.420	36	42	.857	63	78	141	75	167	3	72	65	11	384	5.9	20
Frankie Sanders†	24	216	55	119	.462	22	27	.815	22	29	51	17	25	0	7	23	3	132	5.5	14
Frankie Sanders‡	46	479	105	246	.427	54	68	.794	35	75	110	52	69	1	21	55	6	264	5.7	16
Kevin Stacom†	24	260	52	133	.391	13	19	.684	10	14	24	35	18	0	15	26	0	117	4.9	15
Kevin Stacom‡	68	831	128	342	.374	44	60	.733	30	55	85	112	47	0	29	80	1	300	4.4	16
Tom Barker*	12	131	21	48	.438	11	15	.733	12	18	30	6	26	0	4	13	4	53	4.4	14
Dennis Awtrey*	23	247	17	44	.386	16	20	.800	13	34	47	20	37	0	3	21	6	50	2.2	7

CHICAGO BULLS

	G	Min.	FGM	FGA	Pct.	FTM	FTA	Pct.	Off.	Def.	Tot.	Ast.	PF	Dq.	Stl.	TO	Blk.	Pts.	Avg.	Hi.
									REBOUNDS									SCORING		
Artis Gilmore	82	3265	753	1310	.575	434	587	.739	293	750	1043	274	280	2	50	310	156	1940	23.7	41
Reggie Theus	82	2753	537	1119	.480	264	347	.761	92	136	228	429	270	2	93	303	18	1338	16.3	30
Mickey Johnson	82	2594	496	1105	.449	273	329	.830	193	434	627	380	286	9	88	312	59	1265	15.4	33
Wilbur Holland	82	2483	445	940	.473	141	176	.801	78	176	254	330	240	9	122	185	12	1031	12.6	32
John Mengelt	75	1705	338	689	.491	150	182	.824	25	93	118	187	148	1	46	120	4	826	11.0	26
Ollie Johnson	71	1734	281	540	.520	88	110	.800	58	169	227	163	182	2	54	114	33	650	9.2	24
Mark Landsberger	80	1959	278	585	.475	91	194	.469	292	450	742	68	125	0	27	149	22	647	8.1	21
John Brown	77	1265	152	317	.479	84	98	.857	83	155	238	104	180	5	18	89	10	388	5.0	14
Scott May	37	403	59	136	.434	30	40	.750	14	50	64	39	51	0	22	51	1	148	4.0	15
Charles Dudley	43	684	45	125	.360	28	42	.667	25	61	86	116	82	0	32	64	1	118	2.7	14
Steve Sheppard*	22	203	24	51	.471	12	19	.632	16	12	28	15	16	0	5	21	0	60	2.7	11
Tate Armstrong	26	259	28	70	.400	10	13	.769	7	13	20	31	22	0	10	21	0	66	2.5	8
Scott Lloyd†	67	465	42	120	.350	27	47	.574	48	45	93	32	86	0	9	43	8	111	1.7	11
Scott Lloyd‡	72	496	42	122	.344	27	47	.574	49	47	96	32	92	0	10	51	8	111	1.5	11
Andre Wakefield*	2	8	0	1	.000	0	0	...	0	0	0	1	2	0	0	0	0	0	0.0	0

CLEVELAND CAVALIERS

	G	Min.	FGM	FGA	Pct.	FTM	FTA	Pct.	Off.	Def.	Tot.	Ast.	PF	Dq.	Stl.	TO	Blk.	Pts.	Avg.	Hi.
									REBOUNDS									SCORING		
Campy Russell	74	2859	603	1268	.476	417	523	.797	147	356	503	348	222	2	98	259	25	1623	21.9	41
Austin Carr	82	2714	551	1161	.475	292	358	.816	155	135	290	217	210	1	77	175	14	1394	17.0	30
Jim Chones	82	2850	472	1073	.440	158	215	.735	260	582	842	181	278	4	47	187	102	1102	13.4	28
Terry Furlow*	49	1110	275	569	.483	103	125	.824	44	52	96	103	80	1	40	87	17	653	13.3	25
Butch Lee†	33	782	146	321	.455	87	113	.770	22	45	67	126	58	0	30	58	0	379	11.5	22
Butch Lee‡	82	1779	290	634	.457	175	230	.761	33	93	126	295	146	0	86	154	1	755	9.2	22
Bobby Smith	72	1650	361	784	.460	83	106	.783	77	129	206	121	188	2	43	75	7	805	11.2	23
Walt Frazier	12	279	54	122	.443	21	27	.778	7	13	20	32	22	0	13	22	2	129	10.8	18
Mike Mitchell	80	1576	362	706	.513	131	178	.736	127	202	329	60	215	6	51	102	29	855	10.7	32
Foots Walker	55	1753	208	448	.464	137	175	.783	59	139	198	321	153	0	130	127	18	553	10.1	26
Elmore Smith	24	332	69	130	.531	18	26	.692	45	61	106	13	60	0	7	42	16	156	6.5	16
Kenny Higgs	68	1050	127	279	.455	85	111	.766	18	84	102	141	176	2	66	47	11	339	5.0	21
John Lambert	70	1030	148	329	.450	35	55	.636	116	174	290	43	163	0	25	65	29	331	4.7	16
Jim Brewer*	55	1301	114	259	.440	23	48	.479	125	245	370	74	136	2	48	78	56	251	4.6	14
Harry Davis	40	394	66	153	.431	30	43	.698	27	39	66	16	66	1	13	23	8	162	4.1	12

DENVER NUGGETS

	G	Min.	FGM	FGA	Pct.	FTM	FTA	Pct.	Off.	Def.	Tot.	Ast.	PF	Dq.	Stl.	TO	Blk.	Pts.	Avg.	Hi.
									REBOUNDS									SCORING		
David Thompson	76	2670	693	1353	.512	439	583	.753	109	165	274	225	180	2	70	186	82	1825	24.0	44
George McGinnis	76	2552	603	1273	.474	509	765	.665	256	608	864	283	321	16	129	346	52	1715	22.6	41
Dan Issel	81	2742	532	1030	.517	316	419	.754	240	498	738	255	233	6	61	171	46	1380	17.0	29
Charlie Scott	79	2617	393	854	.460	161	215	.749	54	156	210	428	284	12	78	255	30	947	12.0	28
Bob Wilkerson	80	2425	396	869	.456	119	173	.688	100	314	414	284	190	0	118	196	21	911	11.4	26
Tom Boswell	79	2201	321	603	.532	198	284	.697	248	290	538	242	263	4	50	185	51	840	10.6	22
Anthony Roberts	63	1236	211	498	.424	76	110	.691	106	152	258	107	142	2	20	65	2	498	7.9	18
Robert Smith	82	1479	184	436	.422	159	180	.883	41	105	146	208	165	1	58	95	13	527	6.4	19
Bo Ellis	42	268	42	92	.457	29	36	.806	17	45	62	10	45	0	10	22	13	113	2.7	10
Kim Hughes	81	1086	98	182	.538	18	45	.400	112	223	335	74	215	2	56	78	102	214	2.6	14
Phil Hicks	20	128	18	43	.419	3	5	.600	13	15	28	8	20	0	5	13	0	39	2.0	15
John Kuester	33	212	16	52	.308	13	14	.929	5	8	13	37	29	1	18	20	1	45	1.4	8
Geoff Crompton	20	88	10	26	.385	6	12	.500	6	17	23	5	19	0	0	12	3	26	1.3	6

DETROIT PISTONS

	G	Min.	FGM	FGA	Pct.	FTM	FTA	Pct.	Off.	Def.	Tot.	Ast.	PF	Dq.	Stl.	TO	Blk.	Pts.	Avg.	Hi.
									REBOUNDS									SCORING		
Bob Lanier	53	1835	489	950	.515	275	367	.749	164	330	494	140	181	5	50	175	75	1253	23.6	38
M.L. Carr	80	3207	587	1143	.514	323	435	.743	219	370	589	262	279	2	197	255	46	1497	18.7	36

	G	Min.	FGM	FGA	Pct.	FTM	FTA	Pct.	REBOUNDS			Ast.	PF	Dq.	Stl.	TO	Blk.	SCORING		
									Off.	Def.	Tot.							Pts.	Avg.	Hi.
John Long	82	2498	581	1240	.469	157	190	.826	127	139	266	121	224	1	102	137	19	1319	16.1	28
Kevin Porter	82	3064	534	1110	.481	192	266	.722	62	147	209	1099	302	5	158	337	5	1260	15.4	32
Terry Tyler	82	2560	456	946	.482	144	219	.658	211	437	648	89	254	3	104	141	201	1056	12.9	32
Leon Douglas	78	2215	342	698	.490	208	328	.634	248	416	664	74	319	13	39	190	55	892	11.4	24
Chris Ford*	3	108	13	35	.371	7	8	.875	9	9	18	5	9	1	1	10	1	33	11.0	22
Earl Tatum†	76	1195	272	607	.448	48	66	.727	40	81	121	72	158	3	78	85	33	592	7.8	20
Earl Tatum‡	79	1233	280	627	.447	52	71	.732	41	84	125	73	165	3	78	88	34	612	7.7	20
Ben Poquette	76	1337	198	464	.427	111	142	.782	99	237	336	57	198	4	38	65	98	507	6.7	28
Rickey Green	27	431	67	177	.379	45	67	.672	15	25	40	63	37	0	25	44	1	179	6.6	17
Otis Howard†	11	91	19	45	.422	11	23	.478	13	21	34	4	16	0	2	5	2	49	4.5	16
Otis Howard‡	14	113	24	56	.429	11	23	.478	18	23	41	5	24	0	2	7	2	59	4.2	16
Robert Hawkins	4	28	6	16	.375	6	6	1.000	3	3	6	4	7	0	5	2	0	18	4.5	10
Essie Hollis	25	154	30	75	.400	9	12	.750	21	24	45	6	28	0	11	14	1	69	2.8	10
Larry McNeill	11	46	9	20	.450	11	12	.917	3	7	10	3	7	0	0	4	0	29	2.6	19
Andre Wakefield†	71	578	62	176	.352	48	69	.696	25	51	76	69	68	0	19	71	2	172	2.4	17
Andre Wakefield‡	73	586	62	177	.350	48	69	.696	25	51	76	70	70	0	19	73	2	172	2.4	17
Jim Brewer†	25	310	27	60	.450	3	15	.200	34	71	105	13	38	0	13	19	10	57	2.3	7
Jim Brewer‡	80	1611	141	319	.442	26	63	.413	159	316	475	87	174	2	61	97	66	308	3.9	14
Steve Sheppard†	20	76	12	25	.480	8	15	.533	9	10	19	4	10	0	3	4	1	32	1.6	15
Steve Sheppard‡	42	279	36	76	.474	20	34	.588	25	22	47	19	26	0	8	25	1	92	2.2	15
Gus Gerard*	2	6	1	3	.333	1	2	.500	1	0	1	0	0	0	2	0	0	3	1.5	3
Dennis Boyd	5	40	3	12	.250	0	0	...	0	2	2	7	5	0	6	0	0	6	1.2	2
Ron Behagen*	1	1	0	0	...	0	0	...	0	0	0	0	1	0	0	1	0	0	0.0	0

GOLDEN STATE WARRIORS

	G	Min.	FGM	FGA	Pct.	FTM	FTA	Pct.	REBOUNDS			Ast.	PF	Dq.	Stl.	TO	Blk.	SCORING		
									Off.	Def.	Tot.							Pts.	Avg.	Hi.
Phil Smith	59	2288	489	977	.501	194	255	.761	48	164	212	261	159	3	101	170	23	1172	19.9	37
Robert Parish	76	2411	554	1110	.499	196	281	.698	265	651	916	115	303	10	100	233	217	1304	17.2	33
John Lucas	82	3095	530	1146	.462	264	321	.822	65	182	247	762	229	1	152	255	9	1324	16.1	35
Sonny Parker	79	2893	512	1019	.502	175	222	.788	164	280	444	291	187	0	144	193	33	1199	15.2	28
Jo Jo White†	29	883	149	314	.475	60	69	.870	20	52	72	133	73	0	26	70	3	358	12.3	30
Jo Jo White‡	76	2338	404	910	.444	139	158	.880	42	158	200	347	173	1	80	212	7	947	12.5	30
Purvis Short	75	1703	369	771	.479	57	85	.671	127	220	347	97	233	6	54	111	12	795	10.6	27
Nate Williams	81	1299	284	567	.501	102	117	.872	68	139	207	61	169	0	55	93	5	670	8.3	27
Clifford Ray	82	1917	231	439	.526	106	190	.558	213	395	608	136	264	4	47	153	50	568	6.9	21
Tom Abernethy	70	1219	176	342	.515	70	94	.745	74	142	216	79	133	1	39	32	13	422	6.0	21
Raymond Townsend	65	771	127	289	.439	50	68	.735	11	44	55	91	70	0	27	51	6	304	4.7	24
Wesley Cox	31	360	53	123	.431	40	92	.435	18	45	63	11	68	0	13	44	5	146	4.7	16
Wayne Cooper	65	795	128	293	.437	41	61	.672	90	190	280	21	118	0	7	52	44	297	4.6	22
Tony Robertson	12	74	15	40	.375	6	9	.667	6	4	10	4	10	0	8	8	0	36	3.0	8
Ray Epps	13	72	10	23	.435	6	8	.750	0	5	5	2	7	0	1	2	0	26	2.0	10

HOUSTON ROCKETS

	G	Min.	FGM	FGA	Pct.	FTM	FTA	Pct.	REBOUNDS			Ast.	PF	Dq.	Stl.	TO	Blk.	SCORING		
									Off.	Def.	Tot.							Pts.	Avg.	Hi.
Moses Malone	82	3390	716	1325	.540	599	811	.739	587	857	1444	147	223	0	79	326	119	2031	24.8	45
Calvin Murphy	82	2941	707	1424	.496	246	265	.928	78	95	173	351	288	5	117	187	6	1660	20.2	38
Rudy Tomjanovich	74	2641	620	1200	.517	168	221	.760	170	402	572	137	186	0	44	138	18	1408	19.0	33
Rick Barry	80	2566	461	1000	.461	160	169	.947	40	237	277	502	195	0	95	198	38	1082	13.5	38
Robert Reid	82	2259	382	777	.492	131	186	.704	129	354	483	230	302	7	75	131	48	895	10.9	21
Mike Newlin	76	1828	283	581	.487	212	243	.872	51	119	170	291	218	3	51	175	79	778	10.2	24
Mike Dunleavy	74	1486	215	425	.506	159	184	.864	28	100	128	324	168	2	56	130	5	589	8.0	22
Dwight Jones	81	1215	181	395	.458	96	132	.727	110	218	328	57	204	1	34	102	26	458	5.7	16
Donald Watts	61	1046	92	227	.405	41	67	.612	35	68	103	243	143	1	73	71	14	225	3.7	16
Alonzo Bradley	34	245	37	88	.420	22	33	.667	13	33	46	17	33	0	5	17	1	96	2.8	17
Jacky Dorsey	20	108	24	43	.558	8	16	.500	12	11	23	2	25	0	1	8	2	56	2.8	8
E.C. Coleman	6	39	5	7	.714	1	1	1.000	1	6	7	1	11	0	2	0	0	11	1.8	9
Tom Barker*	5	16	3	6	.500	2	2	1.000	2	4	6	0	5	0	0	1	0	8	1.6	4

INDIANA PACERS

	G	Min.	FGM	FGA	Pct.	FTM	FTA	Pct.	REBOUNDS			Ast.	PF	Dq.	Stl.	TO	Blk.	SCORING		
									Off.	Def.	Tot.							Pts.	Avg.	Hi.
Johnny Davis	79	2971	565	1240	.456	314	396	.793	70	121	191	453	177	1	95	214	22	1444	18.3	35
Ricky Sobers	81	2825	553	1194	.463	298	338	.882	118	183	301	450	315	8	138	304	23	1404	17.3	34
James Edwards	82	2546	534	1065	.501	298	441	.676	179	514	693	92	363	16	60	162	109	1366	16.7	36
Alex English	81	2696	563	1102	.511	173	230	.752	253	402	655	271	214	3	70	196	78	1299	16.0	32
Mike Bantom	81	2528	482	1036	.465	227	338	.672	225	425	650	223	316	8	99	193	62	1191	14.7	29
Billy Knight†	39	976	222	399	.556	131	150	.873	53	121	174	86	74	0	32	96	5	575	14.7	37
Billy Knight‡	79	2095	441	835	.528	249	296	.841	94	253	347	152	160	1	63	225	8	1131	14.3	37
Rick Robey*	43	849	140	295	.475	90	121	.744	80	174	254	53	111	1	25	89	12	370	8.6	28
Corky Calhoun	81	1332	153	335	.457	72	86	.837	64	174	238	104	189	1	37	56	19	378	4.7	19
Len Elmore	80	1264	139	342	.406	56	78	.718	115	287	402	75	183	3	62	73	79	334	4.2	17
Kevin Stacom*	44	571	76	209	.364	31	41	.756	20	41	61	77	29	0	14	54	1	183	4.2	16

	G	Min.	FGM	FGA	Pct.	FTM	FTA	Pct.	Off.	Def.	Tot.	Ast.	PF	Dq.	Stl.	TO	Blk.	Pts.	Avg.	Hi.
									REBOUNDS									SCORING		
Wayne Radford	52	649	83	175	.474	36	45	.800	25	43	68	57	61	0	30	45	1	202	3.9	15
Steve Green	39	265	42	89	.472	20	34	.588	22	30	52	21	39	0	11	17	3	104	2.7	13
Brad Davis†	22	233	23	44	.523	13	19	.684	1	15	16	43	22	0	14	11	2	59	2.7	11
Brad Davis‡	27	298	31	55	.564	16	23	.696	1	16	17	52	32	0	16	17	2	78	2.9	11

KANSAS CITY KINGS

	G	Min.	FGM	FGA	Pct.	FTM	FTA	Pct.	Off.	Def.	Tot.	Ast.	PF	Dq.	Stl.	TO	Blk.	Pts.	Avg.	Hi.
									REBOUNDS									SCORING		
Otis Birdsong	82	2839	741	1456	.509	296	408	.725	176	178	354	281	255	2	125	200	17	1778	21.7	39
Scott Wedman	73	2498	561	1050	.534	216	271	.797	135	251	386	144	239	4	76	106	30	1338	18.3	35
Phil Ford	79	2723	467	1004	.465	326	401	.813	33	149	182	681	245	3	174	323	6	1260	15.9	33
Bill Robinzine	82	2179	459	837	.548	180	246	.732	218	420	638	104	367	16	105	179	15	1098	13.4	32
Sam Lacey	82	2627	350	697	.502	167	226	.739	179	523	702	430	309	11	106	245	141	867	10.6	26
Billy McKinney	78	1242	240	477	.503	129	162	.796	20	65	85	253	121	0	58	124	3	609	7.8	30
Tom Burleson	56	927	157	342	.459	121	169	.716	84	197	281	50	183	3	26	64	58	435	7.8	18
Marlon Redmond*	49	736	162	375	.432	31	50	.620	57	51	108	57	93	2	28	56	16	355	7.2	18
Darnell Hillman	78	1618	211	428	.493	125	224	.558	138	293	431	91	228	11	50	134	66	547	7.0	16
Bob Nash	82	1307	227	522	.435	69	86	.802	76	130	206	71	135	0	29	82	15	523	6.4	24
Ron Behagen†	9	126	23	50	.460	8	11	.727	11	20	31	5	27	0	2	6	1	54	6.0	12
Ron Behagen‡	15	165	28	62	.452	10	13	.769	13	29	42	7	36	0	4	11	1	66	4.4	12
Lucius Allen	31	413	69	174	.397	19	33	.576	14	32	46	44	52	0	21	30	6	157	5.1	16
Gus Gerard†	56	459	83	191	.435	49	89	.551	39	58	97	21	74	1	18	36	13	215	3.8	11
Gus Gerard‡	58	465	84	194	.433	50	91	.549	40	58	98	21	74	14	20	36	13	218	3.8	11
Richard Washington	18	161	14	41	.341	10	16	.625	11	37	48	7	31	0	7	15	3	38	2.1	12

LOS ANGELES LAKERS

	G	Min.	FGM	FGA	Pct.	FTM	FTA	Pct.	Off.	Def.	Tot.	Ast.	PF	Dq.	Stl.	TO	Blk.	Pts.	Avg.	Hi.
									REBOUNDS									SCORING		
Kareem Abdul-Jabbar	80	3157	777	1347	.577	349	474	.736	207	818	1025	431	230	3	76	282	316	1903	23.8	40
Jamaal Wilkes	82	2915	626	1242	.504	272	362	.751	164	445	609	227	275	2	134	224	27	1524	18.6	31
Adrian Dantley	60	1775	374	733	.510	292	342	.854	131	211	342	138	162	0	63	155	12	1040	17.3	40
Norm Nixon	82	3145	623	1149	.542	158	204	.775	48	183	231	737	250	6	201	231	17	1404	17.1	29
Lou Hudson	78	1686	329	636	.517	110	124	.887	64	76	140	141	133	1	58	99	17	768	9.8	23
Ron Boone	82	1583	259	569	.455	90	104	.865	53	92	145	154	171	1	66	147	11	608	7.4	18
Kenny Carr	72	1149	225	450	.500	83	137	.606	70	222	292	60	152	0	38	116	31	533	7.4	17
Don Ford	79	1540	228	450	.507	72	89	.809	83	185	268	101	177	2	51	93	25	528	6.7	22
Jim Price	75	1207	171	344	.497	55	79	.696	26	97	123	218	128	0	66	100	12	397	5.3	19
Dave Robisch	80	1219	150	336	.446	86	115	.748	82	203	285	97	108	0	20	53	25	386	4.8	15
Brad Davis*	5	65	8	11	.727	3	4	.750	0	1	1	9	10	0	2	6	0	19	3.8	9
Ron Carter	46	332	54	124	.435	36	54	.667	21	24	45	25	54	1	17	40	7	144	3.1	14
Michael Cooper	3	7	3	6	.500	0	0	...	0	0	0	0	1	0	1	1	0	6	2.0	4

MILWAUKEE BUCKS

	G	Min.	FGM	FGA	Pct.	FTM	FTA	Pct.	Off.	Def.	Tot.	Ast.	PF	Dq.	Stl.	TO	Blk.	Pts.	Avg.	Hi.
									REBOUNDS									SCORING		
Marques Johnson	77	2779	820	1491	.550	332	437	.760	212	374	586	234	186	1	116	170	89	1972	25.6	40
Brian Winters	79	2575	662	1343	.493	237	277	.856	48	129	177	383	243	1	83	257	40	1561	19.8	37
Junior Bridgeman	82	1963	540	1067	.506	189	228	.829	113	184	297	163	184	2	88	138	41	1269	15.5	37
Kent Benson	82	2132	413	798	.518	180	245	.735	187	397	584	204	280	4	89	156	81	1006	12.3	28
Ernie Grunfeld	82	1778	326	661	.493	191	251	.761	124	236	360	216	220	3	58	141	15	843	10.3	27
Quinn Buckner	81	1757	251	553	.454	79	125	.632	57	153	210	468	224	1	156	208	17	581	7.2	19
John Gianelli	82	2057	256	527	.486	72	102	.706	122	286	408	160	196	4	44	106	67	584	7.1	16
Kevin Restani	81	1598	262	529	.495	51	73	.699	141	244	385	122	155	0	30	96	27	575	7.1	22
George Johnson	67	1157	165	342	.482	84	117	.718	106	254	360	81	187	5	75	100	49	414	6.2	20
Lloyd Walton	75	1381	157	327	.480	61	90	.678	34	70	104	356	103	0	72	123	9	375	5.0	20
Sam Smith	16	125	19	47	.404	18	24	.750	0	9	9	16	12	0	8	8	7	56	3.5	10
Otis Howard*	3	22	5	11	.455	0	0	...	5	2	7	1	8	0	0	2	0	10	3.3	6
Norm Van Lier	38	555	30	77	.390	47	52	.904	8	32	40	158	108	4	43	49	3	107	2.8	16
Del Beshore	1	1	0	0	...	0	0	...	0	0	0	0	0	0	0	0	0	0	0.0	0

NEW JERSEY NETS

	G	Min.	FGM	FGA	Pct.	FTM	FTA	Pct.	Off.	Def.	Tot.	Ast.	PF	Dq.	Stl.	TO	Blk.	Pts.	Avg.	Hi.
									REBOUNDS									SCORING		
John Williamson	74	2451	635	1367	.465	373	437	.854	53	143	196	255	215	3	89	233	12	1643	22.2	48
Bernard King	82	2859	710	1359	.522	349	619	.564	251	418	669	295	326	10	118	323	39	1769	21.6	41
Eric Money*	47	1434	325	676	.481	136	183	.743	15	70	125	249	132	0	74	166	10	786	16.7	40
Eddie Jordan	82	2260	401	960	.418	213	274	.777	74	141	215	365	209	0	201	244	40	1015	12.4	29
Winford Boynes	69	1176	256	595	.430	133	169	.787	60	95	155	75	117	1	43	119	7	645	9.3	29
Bob Elliott	14	282	41	73	.562	41	56	.732	16	40	56	22	34	2	6	26	4	123	8.8	16
Wilson Washington	62	1139	218	434	.502	66	104	.635	88	206	294	47	186	5	31	98	67	502	8.1	16
Al Skinner*	23	334	55	125	.440	72	82	.878	12	30	42	49	53	0	22	38	2	182	7.9	19
Ralph Simpson†	32	527	87	237	.367	48	71	.676	19	42	61	68	30	0	12	53	4	222	6.9	17
Ralph Simpson‡	68	979	174	433	.402	76	111	.685	35	61	96	126	57	0	37	100	5	424	6.2	20
Jan van Breda Kolff	80	1998	196	423	.463	146	183	.798	108	274	382	180	235	4	85	135	74	538	6.7	25
George Johnson	78	2058	206	483	.427	105	138	.761	201	415	616	88	315	8	68	178	253	517	6.6	25
Phil Jackson	59	1070	144	303	.475	86	105	.819	59	119	178	85	168	7	45	78	22	374	6.3	20

	G	Min.	FGM	FGA	Pct.	FTM	FTA	Pct.	Off.	Def.	Tot.	Ast.	PF	Dq.	Stl.	TO	Blk.	Pts.	Avg.	Hi.
Harvey Catchings† . . .	32	659	74	175	.423	47	61	.770	71	133	204	30	90	2	15	51	56	195	6.1	16
Harvey Catchings‡ . .	56	948	102	243	.420	60	78	.769	101	201	302	48	132	3	23	88	91	264	4.7	16
Tim Bassett	82	1508	116	313	.371	89	131	.679	174	244	418	99	219	1	44	103	29	321	3.9	16

NEW ORLEANS JAZZ

	G	Min.	FGM	FGA	Pct.	FTM	FTA	Pct.	Off.	Def.	Tot.	Ast.	PF	Dq.	Stl.	TO	Blk.	Pts.	Avg.	Hi.
Truck Robinson*	43	1781	397	819	.485	245	339	.723	139	438	577	74	130	1	29	143	63	1039	24.2	51
Spencer Haywood† . . .	34	1338	346	696	.497	124	146	.849	106	221	327	71	128	6	30	113	53	816	24.0	33
Spencer Haywood‡ . .	68	2361	595	1205	.494	231	292	.791	172	361	533	127	236	8	40	200	82	1421	20.9	46
Pete Maravich	49	1824	436	1035	.421	233	277	.841	33	88	121	243	104	2	60	200	18	1105	22.6	41
Jim McElroy	79	2698	539	1097	.491	259	340	.762	61	154	215	453	183	1	148	237	49	1337	16.9	40
Rich Kelley	80	2705	440	870	.506	373	458	.814	303	723	1026	285	309	8	126	288	166	1253	15.7	30
Gail Goodrich	74	2130	382	850	.449	174	204	.853	68	115	183	357	177	1	90	185	13	938	12.7	26
Aaron James.	73	1417	311	630	.494	105	140	.750	97	151	248	78	202	1	28	111	21	727	10.0	29
James Hardy	68	1456	196	426	.460	61	88	.693	121	189	310	65	133	1	52	93	61	453	6.7	19
Ron Lee†	17	398	45	124	.363	24	37	.649	21	34	55	73	44	1	38	49	2	114	6.7	14
Ron Lee‡	60	1346	218	507	.430	98	141	.695	63	105	168	205	182	3	107	165	6	534	8.9	24
Joe Meriweather*	36	640	84	187	.449	51	78	.654	62	122	184	31	105	2	17	45	41	219	6.1	24
Marty Byrnes†	36	530	78	166	.470	33	54	.611	41	53	94	43	42	0	12	40	8	189	5.3	16
Marty Byrnes‡	79	1264	187	389	.481	106	154	.688	90	101	191	104	111	0	27	119	10	480	6.1	16
Ira Terrell*	31	572	63	144	.438	27	38	.711	34	75	109	26	73	0	15	36	22	153	4.9	12
Paul Griffin	77	1398	106	223	.475	91	147	.619	126	265	391	138	198	3	54	117	36	303	3.9	14
Tommy Green	59	809	92	237	.388	48	63	.762	20	48	68	140	111	0	61	89	6	232	3.9	16
Gus Bailey	2	9	2	7	.286	0	0	. . .	2	0	2	2	1	0	0	1	0	4	2.0	2

NEW YORK KNICKERBOCKERS

	G	Min.	FGM	FGA	Pct.	FTM	FTA	Pct.	Off.	Def.	Tot.	Ast.	PF	Dq.	Stl.	TO	Blk.	Pts.	Avg.	Hi.
Bob McAdoo*	40	1594	429	793	.541	218	335	.651	94	285	379	128	134	2	62	153	47	1076	26.9	45
Spencer Haywood* . .	34	1023	249	509	.489	107	146	.733	66	140	206	56	108	2	10	87	29	605	17.8	46
Ray Williams.	81	2370	575	1257	.457	251	313	.802	104	187	291	504	274	4	128	285	19	1401	17.3	37
Toby Knight	82	2667	609	1174	.519	145	206	.704	201	347	548	124	309	7	61	163	60	1363	16.6	43
Earl Monroe	64	1393	329	699	.471	129	154	.838	26	48	74	189	123	0	48	98	6	787	12.3	34
Marvin Webster	60	2027	264	558	.473	150	262	.573	198	457	655	172	183	6	24	170	112	678	11.3	23
Jim Cleamons	79	2390	311	657	.473	130	171	.760	65	160	225	376	147	1	73	142	11	752	9.5	24
Joe Meriweather†	41	1053	158	313	.505	75	109	.688	81	144	225	40	178	8	23	85	53	391	9.5	22
Joe Meriweather‡ . . .	77	1693	242	500	.484	126	187	.674	143	266	409	79	283	10	40	130	94	610	7.9	24
Mike Glenn	75	1171	263	486	.541	57	63	.905	28	54	82	136	113	0	37	64	6	583	7.8	31
Micheal Ray Richardson	72	1218	200	483	.414	69	128	.539	78	155	233	213	188	2	100	141	18	469	6.5	19
Glen Gondrezick	75	1602	161	326	.494	55	97	.567	147	277	424	106	226	1	98	95	18	377	5.0	16
Tom Barker†	22	329	44	102	.431	14	20	.700	31	52	83	9	45	0	6	20	7	102	4.6	13
Tom Barker‡	39	476	68	156	.436	27	37	.730	45	74	119	15	76	0	10	34	11	163	4.2	14
John Rudd	58	723	59	133	.444	66	93	.710	69	98	167	35	95	1	17	59	8	184	3.2	17
Butch Beard	7	85	11	26	.423	0	0	. . .	1	9	10	19	13	0	7	10	0	22	3.1	6
Ron Behagen*	5	38	5	12	.417	2	2	1.000	2	9	11	2	8	0	2	4	0	12	2.4	6
Greg Bunch	12	97	9	26	.346	10	12	.833	9	8	17	4	10	0	3	5	3	28	2.3	7

PHILADELPHIA 76ERS

	G	Min.	FGM	FGA	Pct.	FTM	FTA	Pct.	Off.	Def.	Tot.	Ast.	PF	Dq.	Stl.	TO	Blk.	Pts.	Avg.	Hi.
Julius Erving.	78	2802	715	1455	.491	373	501	.745	198	366	564	357	207	0	133	315	100	1803	23.1	37
Doug Collins	47	1595	358	717	.499	201	247	.814	36	87	123	191	139	1	52	131	20	917	19.5	32
Darryl Dawkins	78	2035	430	831	.517	158	235	.672	123	508	631	128	295	5	32	197	143	1018	13.1	30
Henry Bibby	82	2538	368	869	.423	266	335	.794	72	172	244	371	199	0	72	19/	7	1002	12.2	27
Bobby Jones.	80	2304	378	704	.537	209	277	.755	199	332	531	201	245	2	107	165	96	965	12.1	33
Eric Money†	23	545	119	217	.548	34	54	.630	15	22	37	82	70	2	13	69	2	272	11.8	21
Eric Money‡	69	1979	444	893	.497	170	237	.717	70	92	162	331	202	2	87	235	12	1058	15.3	40
Caldwell Jones	78	2171	302	637	.474	121	162	.747	177	570	747	151	303	10	39	156	157	725	9.3	22
Steve Mix	74	1269	265	493	.538	161	201	.801	109	184	293	121	112	0	57	100	16	691	9.3	34
Maurice Cheeks	82	2409	292	572	.510	101	140	.721	63	191	254	431	198	2	174	193	12	685	8.4	27
Joe Bryant	70	1064	205	478	.429	123	170	.724	96	163	259	103	171	1	49	114	9	533	7.6	27
Ralph Simpson*	37	452	87	196	.444	28	40	.700	16	19	35	58	27	8	25	47	1	202	5.5	20
Al Skinner†	22	309	36	89	.404	27	32	.844	15	29	44	40	61	2	18	34	1	99	4.5	22
Al Skinner‡	45	643	91	214	.425	99	114	.868	27	59	86	89	114	2	40	72	3	281	6.2	22
Harvey Catchings* . .	25	289	28	68	.412	13	17	.765	30	68	98	18	42	1	8	37	35	69	2.8	12
Marlon Redmond†	4	23	1	12	.083	0	0	. . .	0	1	1	1	3	0	0	1	0	2	0.5	2
Marlon Redmond‡ . . .	53	759	163	387	.421	31	50	.620	57	52	109	58	96	2	28	57	16	357	6.7	18

PHOENIX SUNS

	G	Min.	FGM	FGA	Pct.	FTM	FTA	Pct.	Off.	Def.	Tot.	Ast.	PF	Dq.	Stl.	TO	Blk.	Pts.	Avg.	Hi.
Paul Westphal.	81	2641	801	1496	.535	339	405	.837	35	124	159	529	159	1	111	232	26	1941	24.0	43
Walter Davis	79	2437	764	1362	.561	340	409	.831	111	262	373	339	250	50	147	293	26	1868	23.6	42
Alvan Adams.	77	2364	569	1073	.530	231	289	.799	220	485	705	360	246	4	110	279	63	1369	17.8	33
Truck Robinson†	26	756	169	333	.508	79	123	.642	56	169	225	39	76	1	17	90	12	417	16.0	28

	G	Min.	FGM	FGA	Pct.	FTM	FTA	Pct.	Off.	Def.	Tot.	Ast.	PF	Dq.	Stl.	TO	Blk.	Pts.	Avg.	Hi.
Truck Robinson‡	69	2537	566	1152	.491	324	462	.701	195	607	802	113	206	2	46	233	75	1456	21.1	51
Ron Lee*	43	948	173	383	.452	74	104	.712	42	71	113	132	138	2	69	116	4	420	9.8	24
Mike Bratz	77	1297	242	533	.454	139	170	.818	55	86	141	179	151	0	64	135	7	623	8.1	20
Don Buse	82	2544	285	576	.495	70	91	.769	44	173	217	356	149	0	156	96	18	640	7.8	21
Marty Byrnes*	43	734	109	223	.489	73	100	.730	49	48	97	61	69	0	15	79	2	291	6.8	16
Alvin Scott	81	1737	212	396	.535	120	168	.714	104	256	360	126	139	2	80	99	62	544	6.7	18
Gar Heard	63	1213	162	367	.441	71	103	.689	98	253	351	60	141	1	53	60	57	395	6.3	18
Joel Kramer	82	1401	181	370	.489	125	176	.710	134	203	337	92	224	2	45	98	23	487	5.9	18
Ted McClain	36	465	62	132	.470	42	46	.913	25	44	69	60	51	0	19	54	0	166	4.6	16
Bayard Forrest	75	1243	118	272	.434	62	115	.539	110	205	315	167	151	1	29	107	37	298	4.0	15

PORTLAND TRAIL BLAZERS

	G	Min.	FGM	FGA	Pct.	FTM	FTA	Pct.	Off.	Def.	Tot.	Ast.	PF	Dq.	Stl.	TO	Blk.	Pts.	Avg.	Hi.
Maurice Lucas	69	2462	568	1208	.470	270	345	.783	192	524	716	215	254	3	66	233	81	1406	20.4	46
Tom Owens	82	2791	600	1095	.548	320	403	.794	263	477	740	301	329	15	59	247	58	1520	18.5	37
Lionel Hollins	64	1967	402	886	.454	172	221	.778	32	117	149	325	199	3	114	223	24	976	15.3	33
Mychal Thompson	73	2144	460	938	.490	154	269	.572	198	406	604	176	270	10	67	205	134	1074	14.7	37
Ron Brewer	81	2454	434	878	.494	210	256	.820	88	141	229	165	181	3	102	153	79	1078	13.3	30
Dave Twardzik	64	1570	203	381	.533	261	299	.873	39	80	119	176	185	5	84	127	4	667	10.4	23
Bob Gross	53	1441	209	443	.472	96	119	.807	106	144	250	184	161	4	70	121	47	514	9.7	19
T.R. Dunn	80	1828	246	549	.448	122	158	.772	145	199	344	103	166	1	86	93	23	614	7.7	18
Larry Steele	72	1488	203	483	.420	112	136	.824	58	113	171	142	208	4	74	96	10	518	7.2	29
Willie Smith	13	131	23	44	.523	12	17	.706	7	6	13	17	19	0	10	14	1	58	4.5	14
Ira Terrell†	18	160	30	54	.556	8	15	.533	10	27	37	15	27	0	7	17	6	68	3.8	11
Ira Terrell‡	49	732	93	198	.470	35	53	.660	44	102	146	41	100	0	22	53	28	221	4.5	12
Jim McMillian	23	278	33	74	.446	17	21	.810	16	23	39	33	18	0	10	16	3	83	3.6	12
Clemon Johnson	74	794	102	217	.470	36	74	.486	83	143	226	78	121	1	23	65	36	240	3.2	8
Kim Anderson	21	224	24	77	.312	15	28	.536	17	28	45	15	42	0	4	22	5	63	3.0	10
Lloyd Neal	4	48	4	11	.364	1	1	1.000	2	7	9	1	7	0	0	6	1	9	2.3	5

SAN ANTONIO SPURS

	G	Min.	FGM	FGA	Pct.	FTM	FTA	Pct.	Off.	Def.	Tot.	Ast.	PF	Dq.	Stl.	TO	Blk.	Pts.	Avg.	Hi.
George Gervin	80	2888	947	1749	.541	471	570	.826	142	258	400	219	275	5	137	286	91	2365	29.6	52
Larry Kenon	81	2947	748	1484	.504	295	349	.845	260	530	790	335	192	1	154	300	19	1791	22.1	39
James Silas	79	2171	466	922	.505	334	402	.831	35	148	183	273	215	1	76	199	20	1266	16.0	31
Billy Paultz	79	2122	399	758	.526	114	194	.588	169	456	625	178	204	4	35	157	125	912	11.5	28
Mark Olberding	80	1885	261	551	.474	233	290	.803	96	333	429	211	282	2	53	163	18	755	9.4	25
Mike Gale	82	2121	284	612	.464	91	108	.843	40	146	186	374	192	1	152	153	40	659	8.0	19
Mike Green	76	1641	235	477	.493	101	144	.701	131	223	354	116	230	3	37	89	122	571	7.5	21
Coby Dietrick	76	1487	209	400	.523	79	99	.798	88	227	315	198	206	7	72	92	38	497	6.5	16
Allan Bristow	74	1324	174	354	.492	124	149	.832	80	167	247	231	154	0	56	108	15	472	6.4	19
Frankie Sanders*	22	263	50	127	.394	32	41	.780	13	46	59	35	44	1	14	32	3	132	6.0	16
Louie Dampier	70	760	123	251	.490	29	39	.744	15	48	63	124	42	0	35	39	8	275	3.9	18
Glenn Mosley	26	221	31	75	.413	23	38	.605	27	37	64	19	35	0	8	20	10	85	3.3	11

SAN DIEGO CLIPPERS

	G	Min.	FGM	FGA	Pct.	FTM	FTA	Pct.	Off.	Def.	Tot.	Ast.	PF	Dq.	Stl.	TO	Blk.	Pts.	Avg.	Hi.
World B. Free	78	2954	795	1653	.481	654	865	.756	127	174	301	340	253	8	111	297	35	2244	28.8	49
Randy Smith	82	3111	693	1523	.455	292	359	.813	102	193	295	395	177	1	177	255	5	1678	20.5	37
Nick Weatherspoon	82	2642	479	998	.480	176	238	.739	179	275	454	135	287	6	80	184	37	1134	13.8	38
Kermit Washington	82	2764	350	623	.562	227	330	.688	296	504	800	125	317	11	85	185	121	927	11.3	29
Swen Nater	79	2006	357	627	.569	132	165	.800	218	483	701	140	244	6	38	170	29	846	10.7	22
Freeman Williams	72	1195	335	683	.490	76	98	.776	48	50	98	83	88	0	42	99	2	746	10.4	26
Sidney Wicks	79	2022	312	676	.462	147	226	.650	159	246	405	126	274	4	70	180	36	771	9.8	22
Connie Norman	22	323	71	165	.430	19	23	.826	13	19	32	24	35	0	10	22	3	161	7.3	21
Kevin Kunnert	81	1684	234	501	.467	56	85	.659	202	367	569	113	309	7	45	141	118	524	6.5	16
Brian Taylor	20	212	30	83	.361	16	18	.889	13	13	26	20	34	0	24	17	0	76	3.8	13
Bob Bigelow	29	413	36	90	.400	13	21	.619	15	31	46	25	37	0	12	18	2	85	2.9	11
John Olive	34	189	13	40	.325	18	23	.783	3	16	19	3	32	0	4	13	0	44	1.3	7
Jerome Whitehead	31	152	15	34	.441	8	18	.444	16	34	50	7	29	0	3	11	4	38	1.2	6
Stan Pietkiewicz	4	32	1	8	.125	2	2	1.000	0	6	6	3	5	0	1	1	0	4	1.0	2
Scott Lloyd*	5	31	0	2	.000	0	0	...	1	2	3	0	6	0	1	8	0	0	0.0	0

SEATTLE SUPERSONICS

	G	Min.	FGM	FGA	Pct.	FTM	FTA	Pct.	Off.	Def.	Tot.	Ast.	PF	Dq.	Stl.	TO	Blk.	Pts.	Avg.	Hi.
Gus Williams	76	2266	606	1224	.495	245	316	.775	111	134	245	307	162	3	158	190	29	1457	19.2	38
Dennis Johnson	80	2717	482	1110	.434	306	392	.781	146	228	374	280	209	2	100	191	97	1270	15.9	30
Jack Sikma	82	2958	476	1034	.460	329	404	.814	232	781	1013	261	295	4	82	253	67	1281	15.6	30
Fred Brown	77	1961	446	951	.469	183	206	.888	38	134	172	260	142	0	119	164	23	1075	14.0	28
Lonnie Shelton	76	2158	446	859	.519	131	189	.693	182	286	468	110	266	7	76	188	75	1023	13.5	28
John Johnson	82	2386	356	821	.434	190	250	.760	127	285	412	358	245	2	59	254	25	902	11.0	21
Tom LaGarde	23	575	98	181	.541	57	95	.600	61	129	190	32	75	2	6	47	18	253	11.0	32

	G	Min.	FGM	FGA	Pct.	FTM	FTA	Pct.	Off.	Def.	Tot.	Ast.	PF	Dq.	Stl.	TO	Blk.	Pts.	Avg.	Hi.
									REBOUNDS									SCORING		
Wally Walker........	60	969	167	343	.487	58	96	.604	66	111	177	69	127	0	12	68	26	392	6.5	19
Paul Silas..........	82	1957	170	402	.423	116	194	.598	259	316	575	115	177	3	31	98	19	456	5.6	16
Lars Hansen........	15	205	29	57	.509	18	31	.581	22	37	59	14	28	0	1	9	1	76	5.1	19
Joe Hassett.........	55	463	100	211	.474	23	23	1.000	13	32	45	42	58	0	14	32	4	223	4.1	18
Jackie Robinson.....	12	105	19	41	.463	8	15	.533	9	10	19	13	9	0	5	11	1	46	3.8	10
Dick Snyder	56	536	81	187	.433	43	51	.843	15	33	48	63	52	0	14	36	6	205	3.7	16
Dennis Awtrey†......	40	499	27	63	.429	25	36	.694	29	75	104	49	69	0	13	31	7	79	2.0	8
Dennis Awtrey‡......	63	746	44	107	.411	41	56	.732	42	109	151	69	106	0	16	52	13	129	2.0	8

WASHINGTON BULLETS

	G	Min.	FGM	FGA	Pct.	FTM	FTA	Pct.	Off.	Def.	Tot.	Ast.	PF	Dq.	Stl.	TO	Blk.	Pts.	Avg.	Hi.
									REBOUNDS									SCORING		
Elvin Hayes.........	82	3105	720	1477	.487	349	534	.654	312	682	994	143	308	5	75	235	190	1789	21.8	36
Bob Dandridge	78	2629	629	1260	.499	331	401	.825	109	338	447	365	259	4	71	222	57	1589	20.4	38
Kevin Grevey........	65	1856	418	922	.453	173	224	.772	90	142	232	153	159	1	46	120	14	1009	15.5	28
Mitch Kupchak	66	1604	369	685	.539	223	300	.743	152	278	430	88	141	0	23	120	23	961	14.6	32
Wes Unseld	77	2406	346	600	.577	151	235	.643	274	556	830	315	204	2	71	156	37	843	10.9	28
Tom Henderson	70	2081	299	641	.466	156	195	.800	51	112	163	419	123	0	87	148	10	754	10.8	24
Larry Wright........	73	1658	276	589	.469	125	168	.744	48	92	140	298	166	3	69	119	13	677	9.3	30
Charles Johnson....	82	1819	342	786	.435	67	79	.848	70	132	202	177	161	0	95	87	6	751	9.2	28
Greg Ballard	82	1552	260	559	.465	119	172	.692	143	307	450	116	167	3	58	97	30	639	7.8	24
Phil Chenier	27	385	69	158	.437	18	28	.643	3	17	20	31	28	0	4	31	5	156	5.8	20
Dave Corzine.......	59	532	63	118	.534	49	63	.778	52	95	147	49	67	0	10	53	14	175	3.0	15
Roger Phegley	29	153	28	78	.359	24	29	.828	5	17	22	15	21	0	5	17	2	80	2.8	14

* Finished season with another team. † Totals with this team only. ‡ Totals with all teams.

PLAYOFF RESULTS

EASTERN CONFERENCE

FIRST ROUND

Philadelphia 2, New Jersey 0
Apr. 11—Wed.   New Jersey 114 at Philadelphia 122
Apr. 13—Fri.   Philadelphia 111 at New Jersey 101

Atlanta 2, Houston 0
Apr. 11—Wed.   Atlanta 109 at Houston 106
Apr. 13—Fri.   Houston 91 at Atlanta 100

SEMIFINALS

Washington 4, Atlanta 3
Apr. 15—Sun.   Atlanta 89 at Washington 103
Apr. 17—Tue.   Atlanta 107 at Washington 99
Apr. 20—Fri.   Washington 89 at Atlanta 77
Apr. 22—Sun.   Washington 120 at Atlanta *118
Apr. 24—Tue.   Atlanta 107 at Washington 103
Apr. 26—Thur. Washington 86 at Atlanta 104
Apr. 29—Sun.   Atlanta 94 at Washington 100

San Antonio 4, Philadelphia 3
Apr. 15—Sun.   Philadelphia 106 at San Antonio 119
Apr. 17—Tue.   Philadelphia 120 at San Antonio 121
Apr. 20—Fri.   San Antonio 115 at Philadelphia 123
Apr. 22—Sun.   San Antonio 115 at Philadelphia 112
Apr. 26—Thur. Philadelphia 120 at San Antonio 97
Apr. 29—Sun.   San Antonio 90 at Philadelphia 92
May 2—Wed.   Philadelphia 108 at San Antonio 111

FINALS

Washington 4, San Antonio 3
May 4—Fri.   San Antonio 118 at Washington 97
May 6—Sun.   San Antonio 95 at Washington 115
May 9—Wed.   Washington 114 at San Antonio 116
May 11—Fri.   Washington 102 at San Antonio 118
May 13—Sun.   San Antonio 103 at Washington 107
May 16—Wed.   Washington 108 at San Antonio 100
May 18—Fri.   San Antonio 105 at Washington 107

WESTERN CONFERENCE

FIRST ROUND

Phoenix 2, Portland 1
Apr. 10—Tue.   Portland 103 at Phoenix 107
Apr. 13—Fri.   Phoenix 92 at Portland 96
Apr. 15—Sun.   Portland 91 at Phoenix 101

Los Angeles 2, Denver 1
Apr. 10—Tue.   Los Angeles 105 at Denver 110
Apr. 13—Fri.   Denver 109 at Los Angeles 121
Apr. 15—Sun.   Los Angeles 112 at Denver 111

SEMIFINALS

Seattle 4, Los Angeles 1
Apr. 17—Tue.   Los Angeles 101 at Seattle 112
Apr. 18—Wed.   Los Angeles 103 at Seattle *108
Apr. 20—Fri.   Seattle 112 at Los Angeles *118
Apr. 22—Sun.   Seattle 117 at Los Angeles 115
Apr. 25—Wed.   Los Angeles 100 at Seattle 106

Phoenix 4, Kansas City 1
Apr. 17—Tue.   Kansas City 99 at Phoenix 102
Apr. 20—Fri.   Phoenix 91 at Kansas City 111
Apr. 22—Sun.   Kansas City 93 at Phoenix 108
Apr. 25—Wed.   Phoenix 108 at Kansas City 94
Apr. 27—Fri.   Kansas City 99 at Phoenix 120

FINALS

Seattle 4, Phoenix 3
May 1—Tue.   Phoenix 93 at Seattle 108
May 4—Fri.   Phoenix 97 at Seattle 103
May 6—Sun.   Seattle 103 at Phoenix 113
May 8—Tue.   Seattle 91 at Phoenix 100
May 11—Fri.   Phoenix 99 at Seattle 93
May 13—Sun.   Seattle 106 at Phoenix 105
May 17—Thur. Phoenix 110 at Seattle 114

NBA FINALS

Seattle 4, Washington 1
May 20—Sun.   Seattle 97 at Washington 99
May 24—Thur. Seattle 92 at Washington 82
May 27—Sun.   Washington 95 at Seattle 105
May 29—Tue.   Washington 112 at Seattle *114
June 1—Fri.   Seattle 97 at Washington 93
*Denotes number of overtime periods.

1977-78

1977-78 NBA CHAMPION WASHINGTON BULLETS

Front row (from left): general manager Bob Ferry, head coach Dick Motta, Larry Wright, Phil Chenier, Tom Henderson, Phil Walker, owner Abe Pollin, vice president Jerry Sachs. Back row (from left): assistant coach Bernie Bickerstaff, Kevin Grevey, Greg Ballard, Elvin Hayes, Wes Unseld, Mitch Kupchak, Joe Pace, Bob Dandridge, trainer John Lally. Inset: Charles Johnson.

FINAL STANDINGS

ATLANTIC DIVISION

	Atl.	Bos.	Buf.	Chi.	Cle.	Den.	Det.	G.S.	Hou.	Ind.	K.C.	L.A.	Mil.	N.J.	N.O.	N.Y.	Phi.	Pho.	Por.	S.A.	Sea.	Was.	W	L	Pct.	GB
Philadelphia	.2	4	3	1	3	3	4	3	2	2	3	2	2	4	2	3	..	2	2	3	3	2	55	27	.671	..
New York	.2	2	1	3	1	3	3	2	2	3	4	1	1	3	3	..	1	1	1	2	2	2	43	39	.524	12
Boston	.2	..	3	1	1	1	1	2	2	2	2	1	3	3	2	2	0	2	1	0	0	1	32	50	.390	23
Buffalo	.1	1	..	3	1	1	1	0	3	1	1	1	1	2	2	3	1	0	1	1	1	1	27	55	.329	28
New Jersey	.1	1	2	2	1	1	1	1	2	2	2	0	1	..	0	1	0	2	0	0	2	2	24	58	.293	31

CENTRAL DIVISION

	Atl.	Bos.	Buf.	Chi.	Cle.	Den.	Det.	G.S.	Hou.	Ind.	K.C.	L.A.	Mil.	N.J.	N.O.	N.Y.	Phi.	Pho.	Por.	S.A.	Sea.	Was.	W	L	Pct.	GB
San Antonio	.3	4	3	2	4	1	2	1	3	3	4	2	2	4	3	2	1	2	2	..	2	2	52	30	.634	..
Washington	.3	3	3	1	2	1	2	2	3	1	2	2	1	2	4	2	2	2	1	2	3	..	44	38	.537	8
Cleveland	.3	3	3	1	..	3	2	2	2	2	2	2	3	3	2	3	1	1	0	0	3	2	43	39	.524	9
Atlanta	..	2	3	1	1	1	2	1	3	3	2	3	2	3	2	2	2	3	1	1	2	1	41	41	.500	11
New Orleans	.2	2	2	2	2	1	1	4	3	2	2	1	1	4	..	1	2	1	3	1	2	0	39	43	.476	13
Houston	.1	2	1	1	2	0	1	1	..	3	2	1	1	2	1	2	2	1	2	1	0	1	28	54	.341	24

MIDWEST DIVISION

	Atl.	Bos.	Buf.	Chi.	Cle.	Den.	Det.	G.S.	Hou.	Ind.	K.C.	L.A.	Mil.	N.J.	N.O.	N.Y.	Phi.	Pho.	Por.	S.A.	Sea.	Was.	W	L	Pct.	GB
Denver	.3	3	3	2	1	..	2	2	3	2	2	3	3	3	3	1	1	2	3	2	1	3	48	34	.585	..
Milwaukee	.2	1	3	3	1	2	2	3	4	4	1	..	3	2	3	1	1	1	2	1	3	4	44	38	.537	4
Chicago	.3	3	1	..	3	2	2	1	3	3	0	2	1	1	2	1	3	2	1	2	2	2	40	42	.488	8
Detroit	.2	3	3	2	2	2	..	2	3	1	1	2	2	3	3	0	0	2	1	1	1	2	38	44	.463	10
Indiana	.1	1	3	1	1	2	3	1	1	..	2	1	0	2	2	1	2	1	1	1	1	3	31	51	.378	17
Kansas City	.1	2	2	4	2	2	3	1	2	2	..	2	0	2	2	0	1	0	0	0	1	2	31	51	.378	17

PACIFIC DIVISION

	Atl.	Bos.	Buf.	Chi.	Cle.	Den.	Det.	G.S.	Hou.	Ind.	K.C.	L.A.	Mil.	N.J.	N.O.	N.Y.	Phi.	Pho.	Por.	S.A.	Sea.	Was.	W	L	Pct.	GB
Portland	.3	3	3	3	4	1	3	3	2	3	4	4	3	3	1	3	2	3	..	2	3	2	58	24	.707	..
Phoenix	.1	2	4	2	2	2	2	2	3	3	4	3	3	2	3	3	1	..	1	2	2	2	49	33	.598	9
Seattle	.1	4	3	2	1	3	3	2	4	3	3	3	2	2	1	1	2	1	2	..	1	4	47	35	.573	11
Los Angeles	.1	2	3	2	2	1	2	4	3	3	2	..	3	4	2	3	2	1	0	2	1	2	45	37	.549	13
Golden State	.3	2	3	3	2	2	2	..	2	3	3	0	2	3	0	2	1	2	1	3	2	2	43	39	.524	15

TEAM STATISTICS

OFFENSIVE

	G	FGM	FGA	Pct.	FTM	FTA	Pct.	REBOUNDS Off.	Def.	Tot.	Ast.	PF	Dq.	Stl.	TO	Blk.	SCORING Pts.	Avg.
Philadelphia	82	3628	7471	.486	2153	2863	.752	1299	2694	3993	2220	2188	20	800	1752	548	9409	114.7
San Antonio	82	3794	7594	.500	1797	2234	.804	1030	2594	3624	2240	1871	16	797	1665	553	9385	114.5
New York	82	3815	7822	.488	1670	2225	.751	1180	2689	3869	2338	2193	26	818	1764	442	9300	113.4
Milwaukee	82	3801	7883	.482	1612	2220	.726	1239	2480	3719	2306	2038	23	867	1680	472	9214	112.4

	G	FGM	FGA	Pct.	FTM	FTA	Pct.	REBOUNDS Off.	Def.	Tot.	Ast.	PF	Dq.	Stl.	TO	Blk.	SCORING Pts.	Avg.
Phoenix	82	3731	7836	.476	1749	2329	.751	1166	2579	3745	2338	1956	16	1059	1766	372	9211	112.3
Denver	82	3548	7441	.477	2068	2705	.765	1177	2736	3913	2187	2116	20	824	1748	422	9164	111.8
Los Angeles	82	3734	7672	.487	1576	2095	.752	1136	2647	3783	2229	1964	18	802	1548	409	9044	110.3
Washington	82	3580	7772	.461	1887	2655	.711	1349	2815	4164	1948	1879	25	668	1613	386	9047	110.3
Kansas City	82	3601	7731	.466	1775	2262	.785	1208	2632	3840	1992	2228	37	794	1690	370	8977	109.5
Detroit	82	3552	7424	.478	1832	2490	.736	1229	2601	3830	1840	1980	29	866	1858	330	8936	109.0
Indiana	82	3500	7783	.450	1904	2564	.743	1386	2624	4010	1982	2230	53	808	1642	456	8904	108.6
Portland	82	3556	7367	.483	1717	2259	.760	1187	2686	3873	2067	2068	30	798	1625	390	8829	107.7
New Orleans	82	3568	7717	.462	1690	2331	.725	1309	2907	4216	2079	1938	35	662	1694	514	8826	107.6
New Jersey	82	3547	8004	.443	1652	2304	.717	1306	2595	3901	1879	2312	72	857	1774	631	8746	106.7
Golden State	82	3574	7654	.467	1550	2081	.745	1183	2629	3812	2097	2113	29	873	1518	405	8698	106.1
Boston	82	3494	7635	.458	1682	2159	.779	1235	2850	4085	1969	2033	32	643	1652	295	8670	105.7
Buffalo	82	3413	7323	.466	1808	2314	.781	1083	2538	3621	1975	2017	31	650	1575	327	8634	105.3
Seattle	82	3445	7715	.447	1675	2352	.712	1456	2601	4057	1799	2008	24	782	1636	429	8565	104.5
Cleveland	82	3496	7707	.454	1569	2116	.741	1187	2676	3863	1740	1832	15	692	1382	455	8561	104.4
Chicago	82	3330	7041	.473	1863	2471	.754	1248	2577	3825	2119	1930	30	665	1667	322	8523	103.9
Houston	82	3523	7691	.458	1467	1896	.774	1301	2421	3722	1942	2025	32	683	1376	319	8513	103.8
Atlanta	82	3335	7253	.460	1836	2316	.793	1160	2359	3519	1901	2470	80	916	1592	408	8506	103.7

DEFENSIVE

	FGM	FGA	Pct.	FTM	FTA	Pct.	REBOUNDS Off.	Def.	Tot.	Ast.	PF	Dq.	Stl.	TO	Blk.	SCORING Pts.	Avg.	Dif.
Portland	3289	7318	.449	1747	2282	.766	1187	2523	3710	1818	2093	36	748	1624	390	8325	101.5	+6.2
Seattle	3384	7377	.459	1670	2203	.758	1121	2600	3721	1956	2067	26	735	1646	410	8438	102.9	+1.6
Cleveland	3474	7620	.456	1574	2113	.745	1214	2779	3993	1915	1952	16	690	1475	446	8522	103.9	+0.5
Atlanta	3162	6671	.474	2193	2930	.748	1160	2606	3766	1774	2122	36	750	1980	484	8517	103.9	-0.2
Chicago	3565	7273	.490	1466	1980	.740	1065	2367	3432	2076	2199	46	777	1479	451	8596	104.8	-0.9
Golden State	3425	7368	.465	1820	2408	.756	1185	2794	3979	2037	1975	21	728	1738	408	8670	105.7	+0.4
Los Angeles	3648	7880	.463	1529	2050	.746	1365	2599	3964	2073	1919	30	756	1570	379	8825	107.6	+2.7
Boston	3539	7761	.456	1752	2278	.769	1142	2575	3717	1981	1871	24	763	1412	374	8830	107.7	-2.0
Houston	3571	7404	.482	1699	2238	.759	1195	2525	3720	1990	1752	18	605	1410	360	8841	107.8	-4.0
Phoenix	3578	7622	.469	1749	2319	.754	1202	2743	3945	1988	2178	41	937	1969	372	8905	108.6	+3.7
Buffalo	3623	7609	.476	1695	2250	.753	1178	2587	3765	2137	2003	25	722	1476	375	8941	109.0	-3.7
Washington	3767	8065	.467	1437	1895	.758	1166	2683	3849	2144	2312	50	770	1437	427	8971	109.4	+0.0
New Orleans	3659	7938	.461	1661	2213	.751	1273	2747	4020	2084	2062	28	851	1511	476	8979	109.5	-1.9
Philadelphia	3592	7788	.461	1803	2435	.740	1363	2473	3836	2095	2287	50	823	1709	346	8987	109.6	+5.1
Detroit	3688	7706	.479	1662	2177	.763	1244	2494	3738	2105	2088	27	902	1719	395	9038	110.2	-1.2
Denver	3678	7799	.472	1740	2305	.730	1267	2546	3813	2248	2220	49	877	1620	524	9096	110.9	+0.9
Indiana	3634	7663	.474	1841	2455	.750	1350	2793	4143	2259	2135	39	727	1762	466	9109	111.1	-2.5
San Antonio	3808	8063	.472	1494	1996	.748	1345	2576	3921	2145	2059	25	837	1662	379	9110	111.1	+3.4
Kansas City	3564	7521	.474	2004	2635	.761	1232	2684	3916	1928	2088	18	796	1694	408	9132	111.4	-1.9
New Jersey	3544	7620	.465	2135	2830	.754	1312	2996	4308	2073	1999	29	852	1864	560	9223	112.5	-5.8
Milwaukee	3715	7728	.481	1832	2404	.762	1234	2617	3851	2248	2019	28	790	1783	468	9262	113.0	-0.6
New York	3658	7742	.472	2029	2785	.729	1254	2623	3877	2113	1989	31	879	1677	357	9345	114.0	-0.6
Avgs.	3571	7615	.469	1751	2329	.752	1230	2633	3863	2054	2063	32	787	1646	421	8894	108.5	...

HOME/ROAD

	Home	Road	Total		Home	Road	Total
Atlanta	29-12	12-29	41-41	Milwaukee	28-13	16-25	44-38
Boston	24-17	8-33	32-50	New Jersey	18-23	6-35	24-58
Buffalo	20-21	7-34	27-55	New Orleans	27-14	12-29	39-43
Chicago	29-12	11-30	40-42	New York	29-12	14-27	43-39
Cleveland	27-14	16-25	43-39	Philadelphia	37-4	18-23	55-27
Denver	33-8	15-26	48-34	Phoenix	34-7	15-26	49-33
Detroit	24-17	14-27	38-44	Portland	36-5	22-19	58-24
Golden State	30-11	13-28	43-39	San Antonio	32-9	20-21	52-30
Houston	21-20	7-34	28-54	Seattle	31-10	16-25	47-35
Indiana	21-20	10-31	31-51	Washington	29-12	15-26	44-38
Kansas City	22-19	9-32	31-51	Totals	610-292	292-610	902-902
Los Angeles	29-12	16-25	45-37				

INDIVIDUAL LEADERS

POINTS

(minimum 70 games or 1,400 points)

	G	FGM	FTM	Pts.	Avg.		G	FGM	FTM	Pts.	Avg.
George Gervin, San Antonio	82	864	504	2232	27.21	John Williamson, Ind.-N.J.	75	723	331	1777	23.7
David Thompson, Denver	80	826	520	2172	27.15	John Drew, Atlanta	70	593	437	1623	23.2
Bob McAdoo, New York	79	814	469	2097	26.5	Rick Barry, Golden State	82	760	378	1898	23.1
Kareem Abdul-Jabbar, L.A.	62	663	274	1600	25.8	Artis Gilmore, Chicago	82	704	471	1879	22.9
Calvin Murphy, Houston	76	852	245	1949	25.6	Truck Robinson, New Orleans	82	748	366	1862	22.7
Paul Westphal, Phoenix	80	809	396	2014	25.2	Adrian Dantley, Indiana-L.A.	79	578	541	1697	21.5
Randy Smith, Buffalo	82	789	443	2021	24.6	Dan Issel, Denver	82	659	428	1746	21.3
Bob Lanier, Detroit	63	622	298	1542	24.5	Larry Kenon, San Antonio	81	698	276	1672	20.6
Walter Davis, Phoenix	81	786	387	1959	24.2	Julius Erving, Philadelphia	74	611	306	1528	20.6
Bernard King, New Jersey	79	798	313	1909	24.2	George McGinnis, Philadelphia	78	588	411	1587	20.3

1977-78

FIELD GOALS

(minimum 300 made)

	FGM	FGA	Pct.
Bobby Jones, Denver	.440	761	.578
Darryl Dawkins, Philadelphia	.332	577	.575
Artis Gilmore, Chicago	.704	1260	.559
Kareem Abdul-Jabbar, Los Angeles	.663	1205	.550
Alex English, Milwaukee	.343	633	.542
Bob Lanier, Detroit	.622	1159	.537
George Gervin, San Antonio	.864	1611	.536
Billy Paultz, San Antonio	.518	979	.529
Bob Gross, Portland	.381	720	.529
Walter Davis, Phoenix	.786	1494	.526

REBOUNDS

(minimum 70 games or 800 rebounds)

	G	Off.	Def.	Tot.	Avg.
Truck Robinson, New Orleans	.82	298	990	1288	15.7
Moses Malone, Houston	.59	380	506	886	15.0
Dave Cowens, Boston	.77	248	830	1078	14.0
Elvin Hayes, Washington	.81	335	740	1075	13.3
Swen Nater, Buffalo	.78	278	751	1029	13.2
Artis Gilmore, Chicago	.82	318	753	1071	13.1
Kareem Abdul-Jabbar, L.A.	.62	186	615	801	12.9
Bob McAdoo, New York	.79	236	774	1010	12.8
Marvin Webster, Seattle	.82	361	674	1035	12.6
Wes Unseld, Washington	.80	286	669	955	11.9

FREE THROWS

(minimum 125 made)

	FTM	FTA	Pct.
Rick Barry, Golden State	.378	409	.924
Calvin Murphy, Houston	.245	267	.918
Fred Brown, Seattle	.176	196	.898
Mike Newlin, Houston	.152	174	.874
Pete Maravich, New Orleans	.240	276	.870
Scott Wedman, Kansas City	.221	254	.870
John Havlicek, Boston	.230	269	.855
Ron Boone, Kansas City	.322	377	.854
Larry Kenon, San Antonio	.276	323	.854
Walt Frazier, Cleveland	.153	180	.850

STEALS

(minimum 70 games or 125 steals)

	G	No.	Avg.
Ron Lee, Phoenix	.82	225	2.74
Gus Williams, Seattle	.79	185	2.34
Quinn Buckner, Milwaukee	.82	188	2.29
Mike Gale, San Antonio	.70	159	2.27
Don Buse, Phoenix	.82	185	2.26
Foots Walker, Cleveland	.81	176	2.17
Ricky Sobers, Indiana	.79	170	2.15
Randy Smith, Buffalo	.82	172	2.10
Chris Ford, Detroit	.82	166	2.02
Wilbur Holland, Chicago	.82	164	2.00

ASSISTS

(minimum 70 games or 400 assists)

	G	No.	Avg.
Kevin Porter, Detroit-New Jersey	.82	837	10.2
John Lucas, Houston	.82	768	9.4
Ricky Sobers, Indiana	.79	584	7.4
Norm Nixon, Los Angeles	.81	553	6.8
Norm Van Lier, Chicago	.78	531	6.8
Henry Bibby, Philadelphia	.82	464	5.7
Foots Walker, Cleveland	.81	453	5.6
Randy Smith, Buffalo	.82	458	5.6
Quinn Buckner, Milwaukee	.82	456	5.6
Paul Westphal, Phoenix	.80	437	5.5

BLOCKED SHOTS

(minimum 70 games or 100 blocked shots)

	G	No.	Avg.
George Johnson, New Jersey	.81	274	3.38
Kareem Abdul-Jabbar, Los Angeles	.62	185	2.98
Tree Rollins, Atlanta	.80	218	2.73
Bill Walton, Portland	.58	146	2.52
Billy Paultz, San Antonio	.80	194	2.43
Artis Gilmore, Chicago	.82	181	2.21
Joe Meriweather, New Orleans	.54	118	2.19
Elmore Smith, Cleveland	.81	176	2.17
Marvin Webster, Seattle	.82	162	1.98
Elvin Hayes, Washington	.81	159	1.96

1977-78

INDIVIDUAL STATISTICS, TEAM BY TEAM

ATLANTA HAWKS

	G	Min.	FGM	FGA	Pct.	FTM	FTA	Pct.	Off.	Def.	Tot.	Ast.	PF	Dq.	Stl.	TO	Blk.	Pts.	Avg.	Hi.
									REBOUNDS									SCORING		
John Drew	70	2203	593	1236	.480	437	575	.760	213	298	511	141	247	8	119	210	27	1623	23.2	48
Steve Hawes	75	2325	387	854	.453	175	214	.818	180	510	690	190	230	4	78	148	57	949	12.7	27
Charlie Criss	77	1935	319	751	.425	236	296	.797	24	97	121	294	143	0	108	150	5	874	11.4	30
Ron Behagen*	26	571	117	249	.470	51	70	.729	53	120	173	34	97	3	30	58	12	285	11.0	22
Eddie Johnson	79	1875	332	686	.484	164	201	.816	51	102	153	235	232	4	100	168	4	828	10.5	29
Tom McMillen	68	1683	280	568	.493	116	145	.800	151	265	416	84	233	8	33	109	16	676	9.9	23
Armond Hill	82	2530	304	732	.415	189	223	.848	59	172	231	427	302	15	151	240	15	797	9.7	21
Ken Charles	21	520	73	184	.397	42	50	.840	6	18	24	82	53	0	25	37	5	188	9.0	17
Ollie Johnson	82	1704	292	619	.472	111	130	.854	89	171	260	120	180	2	80	107	36	695	8.5	22
Tree Rollins	80	1795	253	520	.487	104	148	.703	179	373	552	79	326	16	57	121	218	610	7.6	21
John Brown	75	1594	192	405	.474	165	200	.825	137	166	303	105	280	18	55	116	8	549	7.3	27
Tony Robertson	63	929	168	381	.441	37	53	.698	15	55	70	103	133	2	74	88	5	373	5.9	18
Claude Terry	27	166	25	68	.368	9	11	.818	3	12	15	7	14	0	6	8	0	59	2.2	6

BOSTON CELTICS

	G	Min.	FGM	FGA	Pct.	FTM	FTA	Pct.	Off.	Def.	Tot.	Ast.	PF	Dq.	Stl.	TO	Blk.	Pts.	Avg.	Hi.
									REBOUNDS									SCORING		
Dave Cowens	77	3215	598	1220	.490	239	284	.842	248	830	1078	351	297	5	102	217	67	1435	18.6	36
Charlie Scott*	31	1080	210	485	.433	84	118	.712	24	77	101	143	97	2	51	105	6	504	16.3	30
John Havlicek	82	2797	546	1217	.449	230	269	.855	93	239	332	328	185	2	90	204	22	1322	16.1	32
Jo Jo White	46	1641	289	690	.419	103	120	.858	53	127	180	209	109	2	49	117	7	681	14.8	27
Dave Bing	80	2256	422	940	.449	244	296	.824	76	136	212	300	247	2	79	216	18	1088	13.6	30
Sidney Wicks	81	2413	433	927	.467	217	329	.660	223	450	673	171	318	9	67	226	46	1083	13.4	35
Kermit Washington†	32	866	137	263	.521	102	136	.750	105	230	335	42	114	2	28	64	40	376	11.8	18
Kermit Washington‡	57	1617	247	507	.487	170	246	.691	215	399	614	72	188	3	47	107	64	664	11.6	22
Kevin Stacom	55	1006	206	484	.426	54	71	.761	26	80	106	111	60	0	28	69	3	466	8.5	22
Cedric Maxwell	72	1213	170	316	.538	188	250	.752	138	241	379	68	151	2	53	122	48	528	7.3	21
Tom Boswell	65	1149	185	357	.518	93	123	.756	117	171	288	71	204	5	25	95	14	463	7.1	22

	G	Min.	FGM	FGA	Pct.	FTM	FTA	Pct.	REBOUNDS Off.	Def.	Tot.	Ast.	PF	Dq.	Stl.	TO	Blk.	SCORING Pts.	Avg.	Hi.
Curtis Rowe	51	911	123	273	.451	66	89	.742	74	129	203	45	94	1	14	76	8	312	6.1	20
Don Chaney†	42	702	91	233	.391	33	39	.846	36	69	105	49	93	0	36	50	10	215	5.1	17
Don Chaney‡	51	835	104	269	.387	38	45	.844	40	76	116	66	107	0	44	61	13	246	4.8	17
Zaid Abdul-Aziz*	2	24	3	13	.231	2	3	.667	6	9	15	3	4	0	1	3	1	8	4.0	6
Ernie DiGregorio†	27	274	47	109	.431	12	13	.923	2	25	27	66	22	0	12	47	1	106	3.9	24
Ernie DiGregorio‡	52	606	88	209	.421	28	33	.848	7	43	50	137	44	0	18	93	1	204	3.9	24
Fred Saunders*	26	243	30	91	.330	14	17	.824	11	26	37	11	34	0	7	20	4	74	2.8	12
Bob Bigelow†	4	17	3	12	.250	0	0	...	1	3	4	0	1	0	0	0	0	6	1.5	4
Bob Bigelow‡	5	24	4	13	.308	0	0	...	3	6	9	0	3	0	0	0	0	8	1.6	4
Jim Ard*	1	9	0	1	.000	1	2	.500	1	3	4	1	1	0	0	0	0	1	1.0	1
Steve Kuberski	3	14	1	4	.250	0	0	...	1	5	6	0	2	0	1	2	0	2	0.7	2

BUFFALO BRAVES

	G	Min.	FGM	FGA	Pct.	FTM	FTA	Pct.	REBOUNDS Off.	Def.	Tot.	Ast.	PF	Dq.	Stl.	TO	Blk.	SCORING Pts.	Avg.	Hi.
Randy Smith	82	3314	789	1697	.465	443	554	.800	110	200	310	458	224	2	172	286	11	2021	24.6	40
Billy Knight	53	2155	457	926	.494	301	372	.809	126	257	383	161	137	0	82	167	13	1215	22.9	41
Swen Nater	78	2778	501	994	.504	208	272	.765	278	751	1029	216	274	3	40	225	47	1210	15.5	35
John Shumate*	18	590	75	151	.497	74	99	.747	32	96	128	58	58	1	14	46	9	224	12.4	26
Larry McNeill†	37	873	156	338	.462	130	156	.833	78	110	188	45	100	1	18	60	10	442	11.9	31
Larry McNeill‡	46	940	162	356	.455	145	175	.829	80	122	202	47	114	1	18	67	11	469	10.2	31
Marvin Barnes†	48	1377	226	543	.416	114	153	.745	107	241	348	117	198	7	57	107	72	566	11.8	27
Marvin Barnes‡	60	1646	279	661	.422	128	182	.703	135	304	439	136	241	9	64	136	83	686	11.4	27
William Averitt†	34	676	129	296	.436	64	96	.667	10	40	50	128	86	2	22	88	8	322	9.5	24
William Averitt‡	55	1085	198	484	.409	100	141	.709	17	66	83	196	123	3	39	143	9	496	9.0	32
Mike Glenn	56	947	195	370	.527	51	65	.785	14	65	79	78	98	0	35	50	5	441	7.9	25
Chuck Williams	73	2002	208	436	.477	114	138	.826	29	108	137	317	137	0	48	156	4	530	7.3	22
Wil Jones	79	1711	226	514	.440	84	119	.706	106	228	334	116	255	7	70	137	43	536	6.8	18
Bill Willoughby	56	1079	156	363	.430	64	80	.800	76	143	219	38	131	2	24	56	47	376	6.7	20
Jim McDaniels	42	694	100	234	.427	36	42	.857	46	135	181	44	112	3	4	50	37	236	5.6	26
Ted McClain*	41	727	81	184	.440	50	63	.794	11	64	75	123	88	2	42	68	2	212	5.2	17
Gus Gerard*	10	85	16	40	.400	11	15	.733	6	8	14	9	13	0	2	7	3	43	4.3	13
Gary Brokaw	13	130	18	43	.419	18	24	.750	3	9	12	20	11	0	3	12	5	54	4.2	16
Scott Lloyd†	56	566	68	160	.425	43	58	.741	45	74	119	35	83	1	11	36	9	179	3.2	10
Scott Lloyd‡	70	678	80	193	.415	49	68	.721	52	93	145	44	105	1	14	43	14	209	3.0	10
Eddie Owens	8	63	9	21	.429	3	6	.500	5	5	10	5	9	0	1	3	0	21	2.6	8
Larry Johnson	4	38	3	13	.231	0	2	.000	1	4	5	7	3	0	5	3	2	6	1.5	6

CHICAGO BULLS

	G	Min.	FGM	FGA	Pct.	FTM	FTA	Pct.	REBOUNDS Off.	Def.	Tot.	Ast.	PF	Dq.	Stl.	TO	Blk.	SCORING Pts.	Avg.	Hi.
Artis Gilmore	82	3067	704	1260	.559	471	669	.704	318	753	1071	263	261	4	42	366	181	1879	22.9	38
Mickey Johnson	81	2870	561	1215	.462	362	446	.812	218	520	738	267	317	8	92	270	68	1484	18.3	39
Wilbur Holland	82	2884	569	1285	.443	223	279	.799	105	189	294	313	258	4	164	223	14	1361	16.6	36
Scott May	55	1802	280	617	.454	175	216	.810	118	214	332	114	170	4	50	125	6	735	13.4	27
John Mengelt	81	1767	325	675	.481	184	238	.773	41	88	129	232	169	0	51	124	4	834	10.3	27
Cazzie Russell	36	789	133	304	.438	49	57	.860	31	52	83	61	63	1	19	35	4	315	8.8	24
Norm Van Lier	78	2524	200	477	.419	172	229	.751	86	198	284	531	279	9	144	200	5	572	7.3	23
Mark Landsberger	62	926	127	251	.506	91	157	.580	110	191	301	41	78	0	21	69	6	345	5.6	25
Nick Weatherspoon	41	611	86	194	.443	37	42	.881	57	68	125	32	74	0	19	49	10	209	5.1	17
Tate Armstrong	66	716	131	280	.468	22	27	.815	24	44	68	74	42	0	23	58	0	284	4.3	22
Steve Sheppard	64	698	119	262	.454	37	56	.661	67	64	131	43	72	0	14	46	3	275	4.3	22
Derrek Dickey†	25	220	27	68	.397	14	19	.737	15	33	48	10	27	0	4	23	2	68	2.7	11
Derrek Dickey‡	47	493	87	198	.439	30	36	.833	36	61	97	21	56	0	14	40	4	204	4.3	18
Tom Boerwinkle	22	227	23	50	.460	10	13	.769	14	45	59	44	36	0	3	26	4	56	2.5	10
Cliff Pondexter	44	534	37	85	.435	14	20	.700	36	94	130	87	66	0	19	30	15	88	2.0	14
Jim Ard†	14	116	8	16	.500	2	3	.667	8	24	32	7	18	0	0	14	0	18	1.3	4
Jim Ard‡	15	125	8	17	.471	3	5	.600	9	27	36	8	19	0	0	14	0	19	1.3	4
Glenn Hansen*	2	4	0	2	.000	0	0	...	0	0	0	0	0	0	0	1	0	0	0.0	0

CLEVELAND CAVALIERS

	G	Min.	FGM	FGA	Pct.	FTM	FTA	Pct.	REBOUNDS Off.	Def.	Tot.	Ast.	PF	Dq.	Stl.	TO	Blk.	SCORING Pts.	Avg.	Hi.
Campy Russell	72	2520	523	1168	.448	352	469	.751	154	304	458	278	193	3	88	206	12	1398	19.4	38
Walt Frazier	51	1664	336	714	.471	153	180	.850	54	155	209	209	124	1	77	113	13	825	16.2	29
Jim Chones	82	2906	525	1113	.472	180	250	.720	219	625	844	131	235	4	52	184	58	1230	15.0	31
Elmore Smith	81	1996	402	809	.497	205	309	.663	178	500	678	57	241	4	50	141	176	1009	12.5	32
Austin Carr	82	2186	414	945	.438	183	225	.813	76	111	187	225	168	1	68	146	19	1011	12.3	30
Bobby Smith	82	1581	369	840	.439	108	135	.800	65	142	207	91	155	1	38	81	21	846	10.3	30
Foots Walker	81	2496	287	641	.448	159	221	.719	76	218	294	453	218	0	176	181	24	733	9.0	20
Terry Furlow	53	827	192	443	.433	88	99	.889	47	60	107	72	67	0	21	77	14	472	8.9	23
Jim Brewer	80	1798	175	390	.449	46	100	.460	182	313	495	98	178	1	60	103	48	396	5.0	20
Dick Snyder	58	660	112	252	.444	56	64	.875	9	40	49	56	74	0	23	48	19	280	4.8	17
John Lambert	76	1075	142	336	.423	27	48	.563	125	199	324	38	169	0	27	62	50	311	4.1	16
Eddie Jordan*	22	171	19	56	.339	12	16	.750	2	9	11	32	10	0	12	14	1	50	2.3	11

1977-78

DENVER NUGGETS

	G	Min.	FGM	FGA	Pct.	FTM	FTA	Pct.	Off.	Def.	Tot.	Ast.	PF	Dq.	Stl.	TO	Blk.	Pts.	Avg.	Hi.
									REBOUNDS									SCORING		
David Thompson	80	3025	826	1584	.521	520	668	.778	156	234	390	362	213	1	92	245	99	2172	27.2	73
Dan Issel	82	2851	659	1287	.512	428	547	.782	253	577	830	304	279	5	100	259	41	1746	21.3	40
Bobby Jones	75	2440	440	761	.578	208	277	.751	164	472	636	252	221	2	137	194	126	1088	14.5	29
Brian Taylor	39	1222	182	403	.452	88	115	.765	30	68	98	132	120	1	71	77	9	452	11.6	23
Bob Wilkerson	81	2780	382	936	.408	157	210	.748	98	376	474	439	275	3	126	294	21	921	11.4	24
Anthony Roberts	82	1598	311	736	.423	153	212	.722	135	216	351	105	212	1	40	118	7	775	9.5	27
Darnell Hillman†	33	746	104	209	.498	49	81	.605	73	166	239	53	130	4	14	66	37	257	7.8	16
Darnell Hillman‡	78	1966	340	710	.479	167	286	.584	199	378	577	102	290	11	63	175	81	847	10.9	28
Jim Price*	49	1090	141	293	.481	51	66	.773	30	129	159	158	118	0	69	101	4	333	6.8	22
Mack Calvin	77	988	147	333	.441	173	206	.840	11	73	84	148	87	0	46	108	5	467	6.1	20
Ralph Simpson†	32	584	73	230	.317	31	40	.775	26	49	75	72	42	0	43	48	4	177	5.5	21
Ralph Simpson‡	64	1323	216	576	.375	85	104	.817	53	104	157	159	90	1	75	126	7	517	8.1	23
Bo Ellis	78	1213	133	320	.416	72	104	.692	114	190	304	73	208	2	49	99	47	338	4.3	13
Tom LaGarde	77	868	96	237	.405	114	150	.760	75	139	214	47	146	1	17	101	17	306	4.0	14
Robert Smith	45	378	50	97	.515	21	24	.875	6	30	36	39	52	0	18	20	3	121	2.7	10
Jacky Dorsey*	7	37	3	12	.250	3	5	.600	5	15	20	2	9	0	2	3	2	9	1.3	3
Norm Cook	2	10	1	3	.333	0	0		1	2	3	1	4	0	0	0	0	2	1.0	2

DETROIT PISTONS

	G	Min.	FGM	FGA	Pct.	FTM	FTA	Pct.	Off.	Def.	Tot.	Ast.	PF	Dq.	Stl.	TO	Blk.	Pts.	Avg.	Hi.
									REBOUNDS									SCORING		
Bob Lanier	63	2311	622	1159	.537	298	386	.772	197	518	715	216	185	2	82	225	93	1542	24.5	41
Eric Money	76	2557	600	1200	.500	214	298	.718	90	119	209	356	237	5	123	322	12	1414	18.6	39
John Shumate†	62	2170	316	622	.508	326	409	.797	125	429	554	122	142	1	76	186	43	958	15.5	31
John Shumate‡	80	2760	391	773	.506	400	508	.787	157	525	682	180	200	2	90	232	52	1182	14.8	31
M.L. Carr	79	2556	390	857	.455	200	271	.738	202	355	557	185	243	4	147	210	27	980	12.4	28
Jim Price†	34	839	153	363	.421	84	103	.816	27	74	101	102	82	0	45	74	5	390	11.5	26
Jim Price‡	83	1929	294	656	.448	135	169	.799	57	203	260	260	200	0	114	175	9	723	8.7	26
Leon Douglas	79	1993	321	667	.481	221	345	.641	181	401	582	112	295	6	57	197	48	863	10.9	28
Ralph Simpson*	32	739	143	346	.413	54	64	.844	27	55	82	87	48	1	32	78	3	340	10.6	23
Chris Ford	82	2582	374	777	.481	113	154	.734	117	151	268	381	182	2	166	232	17	861	10.5	25
Marvin Barnes*	12	269	53	118	.449	14	29	.483	28	63	91	19	43	2	7	29	11	120	10.0	15
Gus Gerard†	47	805	154	355	.434	64	93	.688	49	97	146	44	96	1	34	54	22	372	7.9	20
Gus Gerard‡	57	890	170	395	.430	75	108	.694	55	105	160	53	109	1	36	61	25	415	7.3	20
Al Skinner†	69	1274	181	387	.468	123	159	.774	53	119	172	113	208	4	52	132	15	485	7.0	27
Al Skinner‡	77	1551	222	488	.455	162	203	.798	67	157	224	146	242	6	65	161	20	606	7.9	28
Jim Bostic	4	48	12	22	.545	2	5	.400	8	8	16	3	5	0	0	3	0	26	6.5	12
Willie Norwood*	16	260	34	82	.415	20	29	.690	27	27	54	14	45	0	13	17	3	88	5.5	13
Al Eberhard	37	576	71	160	.444	41	61	.672	37	65	102	26	64	0	13	23	4	183	4.9	20
Kevin Porter*	8	127	14	31	.452	9	13	.692	5	10	15	36	18	0	5	12	0	37	4.6	14
Ben Poquette	52	626	95	225	.422	42	60	.700	50	95	145	20	69	1	10	40	22	232	4.5	18
Howard Porter*	8	107	16	43	.372	4	7	.571	5	12	17	2	15	0	3	5	5	36	4.5	10
Wayman Britt	7	16	3	10	.300	3	4	.750	1	3	4	2	3	0	1	1	0	9	1.3	4

GOLDEN STATE WARRIORS

	G	Min.	FGM	FGA	Pct.	FTM	FTA	Pct.	Off.	Def.	Tot.	Ast.	PF	Dq.	Stl.	TO	Blk.	Pts.	Avg.	Hi.
									REBOUNDS									SCORING		
Rick Barry	82	3024	760	1686	.451	378	409	.924	75	374	449	446	188	1	158	224	45	1898	23.1	55
Phil Smith	82	2940	648	1373	.472	316	389	.812	100	200	300	393	219	2	108	266	27	1612	19.7	33
Robert Parish	82	1969	430	911	.472	165	264	.625	211	469	680	95	291	10	79	201	123	1025	12.5	28
Sonny Parker	82	2069	406	783	.519	122	173	.705	167	222	389	155	186	0	135	128	36	934	11.4	26
Nate Williams†	46	815	222	510	.435	70	84	.833	38	76	114	40	120	2	36	58	22	514	11.2	27
Nate Williams‡	73	1249	312	724	.431	101	121	.835	65	139	204	74	181	3	57	83	34	725	9.9	27
Clifford Ray	79	2268	272	476	.571	148	243	.609	236	522	758	147	291	9	74	150	90	692	8.8	21
E.C. Coleman	72	1801	212	446	.475	40	55	.727	117	259	376	100	253	4	66	95	23	464	6.4	18
Charles Johnson*	32	492	96	235	.409	7	10	.700	23	39	62	48	53	0	31	23	4	199	6.2	23
Derrek Dickey*	22	273	60	130	.462	16	17	.941	21	28	49	11	29	0	10	17	2	136	6.2	18
Charles Dudley	78	1660	127	249	.510	138	195	.708	86	201	287	409	181	0	68	163	2	392	5.0	14
Wesley Cox	43	453	69	173	.399	58	100	.580	42	101	143	12	82	1	21	36	10	196	4.6	23
Rickey Green	76	1098	143	375	.381	54	90	.600	49	67	116	149	95	0	58	79	1	340	4.5	22
Ricky Marsh	60	851	123	289	.426	23	33	.697	16	59	75	90	111	0	29	50	19	269	4.5	23
Larry McNeill*	9	67	6	18	.333	15	19	.789	2	12	14	2	14	0	0	7	1	27	3.0	6

HOUSTON ROCKETS

	G	Min.	FGM	FGA	Pct.	FTM	FTA	Pct.	Off.	Def.	Tot.	Ast.	PF	Dq.	Stl.	TO	Blk.	Pts.	Avg.	Hi.
									REBOUNDS									SCORING		
Calvin Murphy	76	2900	852	1737	.491	245	267	.918	57	107	164	259	241	4	112	173	3	1949	25.6	57
Rudy Tomjanovich	23	849	217	447	.485	61	81	.753	40	98	138	32	63	0	15	38	5	495	21.5	35
Moses Malone	59	2107	413	828	.499	318	443	.718	380	506	886	31	179	3	48	220	76	1144	19.4	39
Mike Newlin	45	1181	216	495	.436	152	174	.874	36	84	120	203	128	1	52	120	9	584	13.0	27
John Lucas	82	2933	412	947	.435	193	250	.772	51	204	255	768	208	1	160	213	9	1017	12.4	28
Dwight Jones	82	2476	346	777	.445	181	233	.777	215	426	641	109	265	2	77	165	39	873	10.6	22
Kevin Kunnert	80	2152	368	842	.437	93	135	.689	262	431	693	97	315	13	44	141	90	829	10.4	27

Bob Lanier averaged 24.5 points per game for the Detroit Pistons in 1977-78 in the middle of a 14-year Hall of Fame career.

	G	Min.	FGM	FGA	Pct.	FTM	FTA	Pct.	REBOUNDS Off.	Def.	Tot.	Ast.	PF	Dq.	Stl.	TO	Blk.	SCORING Pts.	Avg.	Hi.
Robert Reid	80	1849	261	574	.455	63	96	.656	111	248	359	121	277	8	67	81	51	585	7.3	29
Alonzo Bradley	43	798	130	304	.428	43	59	.729	24	75	99	54	83	1	16	55	6	303	7.0	20
Ron Behagen*	3	33	7	11	.636	0	1	.000	2	5	7	2	6	0	0	3	0	14	4.7	8
Ed Ratleff	68	1163	130	310	.419	39	47	.830	56	106	162	153	109	0	60	67	22	299	4.4	16
Mike Dunleavy†	11	102	17	43	.395	11	16	.688	1	8	9	22	12	0	8	9	1	45	4.1	9
Mike Dunleavy‡	15	119	20	50	.400	13	18	.722	1	9	10	28	12	0	9	12	1	53	3.5	9
C.J. Kupec	49	626	84	197	.426	27	33	.818	27	64	91	50	54	0	10	24	3	195	4.0	14
John Johnson*	1	11	1	4	.250	2	3	.667	2	1	3	1	3	0	0	3	0	4	4.0	4
Zaid Abdul-Aziz†	14	134	20	47	.426	15	20	.750	13	22	35	7	25	0	2	8	2	55	3.9	8
Zaid Abdul-Aziz‡	16	158	23	60	.383	17	23	.739	19	31	50	10	29	0	3	11	3	63	3.9	8
Rudy White	21	219	31	85	.365	14	18	.778	8	13	21	22	24	0	8	22	0	76	3.6	10
Robin Jones	12	66	11	20	.550	4	10	.400	5	9	14	2	16	0	1	7	1	26	2.2	6
Larry Moffett	20	110	5	17	.294	6	10	.600	10	11	21	7	16	0	2	8	2	16	0.8	6
Phil Bond	7	21	2	6	.333	0	0	...	1	3	4	2	1	0	1	2	0	4	0.6	2

INDIANA PACERS

	G	Min.	FGM	FGA	Pct.	FTM	FTA	Pct.	REBOUNDS Off.	Def.	Tot.	Ast.	PF	Dq.	Stl.	TO	Blk.	SCORING Pts.	Avg.	Hi.
Adrian Dantley*	23	948	201	403	.499	207	263	.787	94	122	216	65	76	1	48	67	17	609	26.5	37
John Williamson*	42	1449	335	795	.421	134	161	.832	34	86	120	132	131	4	47	127	0	804	19.1	43
Ricky Sobers	79	3019	553	1221	.453	330	400	.825	92	235	327	584	308	10	170	352	23	1436	18.2	31
James Edwards†	58	1682	350	777	.450	192	296	.649	153	282	435	56	233	9	36	112	50	892	15.4	33
James Edwards‡	83	2405	495	1093	.453	272	421	.646	197	418	615	85	322	12	53	169	78	1262	15.2	33
Mike Bantom	82	2775	502	1047	.479	254	342	.743	184	426	610	238	333	13	100	218	50	1258	15.3	38
Earl Tatum†	57	1859	357	773	.462	108	137	.788	56	149	205	226	172	4	103	131	30	822	14.4	25
Earl Tatum‡	82	2522	510	1087	.469	153	196	.781	79	216	295	296	257	5	140	184	40	1173	14.3	25
Dan Roundfield	79	2423	421	861	.489	218	300	.727	275	527	802	196	297	4	81	194	149	1060	13.4	36
Ron Behagen†	51	1131	222	544	.408	128	176	.727	146	187	333	65	160	1	32	113	19	572	11.2	24
Ron Behagen‡	80	1735	346	804	.430	179	247	.725	201	312	513	101	263	4	62	174	31	871	10.9	24
Dave Robisch*	23	598	73	181	.403	50	64	.781	47	126	173	49	59	1	20	34	15	196	8.5	16
Bob Carrington†	35	621	96	197	.487	58	74	.784	28	34	62	62	73	1	22	52	11	250	7.1	17
Bob Carrington‡	72	1653	253	589	.430	130	171	.760	70	104	174	117	205	6	65	118	23	636	8.8	28
Len Elmore	69	1327	142	386	.368	88	132	.667	139	281	420	80	174	4	74	73	71	372	5.4	19
Michael Flynn	71	955	120	267	.449	55	97	.567	47	70	117	142	52	0	41	75	10	295	4.2	14
Johnny Neumann	20	216	35	86	.407	13	18	.722	5	9	14	27	24	0	6	22	1	83	4.2	15
Steve Green	44	449	56	128	.438	39	56	.696	31	40	71	30	67	0	14	23	2	151	3.4	13
Bobby Wilson	12	86	14	36	.389	2	3	.667	6	6	12	8	16	0	2	6	1	30	2.5	12
Mel Bennett	31	285	23	81	.284	28	45	.622	49	44	93	22	54	1	11	30	7	74	2.4	8
Willie Smith	1	7	0	0	...	0	0	...	0	0	0	1	1	0	0	0	0	0	0.0	0

KANSAS CITY KINGS

	G	Min.	FGM	FGA	Pct.	FTM	FTA	Pct.	Off.	Def.	Tot.	Ast.	PF	Dq.	Stl.	TO	Blk.	Pts.	Avg.	Hi.
Ron Boone	82	2653	563	1271	.443	322	377	.854	112	157	269	311	233	3	105	303	11	1448	17.7	40
Scott Wedman	81	2961	607	1192	.509	221	254	.870	144	319	463	201	242	2	99	158	22	1435	17.7	35
Otis Birdsong	73	1878	470	955	.492	216	310	.697	70	105	175	174	179	1	74	145	12	1156	15.8	37
Richard Washington	78	2231	425	891	.477	150	199	.754	188	466	654	118	324	12	74	191	73	1000	12.8	29
Lucius Allen	77	2147	373	846	.441	174	220	.791	66	163	229	360	180	0	93	217	28	920	11.9	30
Bill Robinzine	82	1748	305	677	.451	206	271	.760	173	366	539	72	281	5	74	172	11	816	10.0	28
Sam Lacey	77	2131	265	590	.449	134	187	.717	155	487	642	300	264	7	120	186	108	664	8.6	24
Tom Burleson	76	1525	228	525	.434	197	248	.794	170	312	482	131	259	6	62	123	81	653	8.6	20
Bob Nash	66	800	157	304	.516	50	69	.725	75	94	169	46	75	0	27	47	18	364	5.5	33
John Kuester	78	1215	145	319	.455	87	105	.829	19	95	114	252	143	1	58	97	1	377	4.8	21
Kevin Restani†	46	463	59	139	.424	9	11	.818	32	62	94	21	37	0	5	15	4	127	2.8	10
Kevin Restani‡	54	547	72	167	.431	9	13	.692	36	72	108	30	41	0	5	17	5	153	2.8	10
Bob Bigelow*	1	7	1	1	1.000	0	0	...	2	3	5	0	2	0	0	0	0	2	2.0	2
Louie Nelson*	8	53	3	14	.214	9	11	.818	1	2	3	5	5	0	2	8	1	15	1.9	4
Andre McCarter	1	9	0	2	.000	0	0	...	0	1	1	0	1	0	0	0	0	0	0.0	0
Glenn Hansen†	3	9	0	5	.000	0	0	...	1	0	1	1	3	0	1	0	0	0	0.0	0
Glenn Hansen‡	5	13	0	7	.000	0	0	...	1	0	1	1	3	0	1	1	0	0	0.0	0

LOS ANGELES LAKERS

	G	Min.	FGM	FGA	Pct.	FTM	FTA	Pct.	Off.	Def.	Tot.	Ast.	PF	Dq.	Stl.	TO	Blk.	Pts.	Avg.	Hi.
Kareem Abdul-Jabbar	62	2265	663	1205	.550	274	350	.783	186	615	801	269	182	1	103	208	185	1600	25.8	43
Adrian Dantley†	56	1985	377	725	.520	334	417	.801	171	233	404	188	157	1	70	161	7	1088	19.4	37
Adrian Dantley‡	79	2933	578	1128	.512	541	680	.796	265	355	620	253	233	2	118	228	24	1697	21.5	37
James Edwards*	25	723	145	316	.459	80	125	.640	44	136	180	29	89	3	16	57	28	370	14.8	32
Earl Tatum*	25	663	153	314	.487	45	59	.763	23	67	90	70	85	1	37	53	10	351	14.0	25
Lou Hudson	82	2283	493	992	.497	137	177	.774	80	108	188	193	196	0	94	150	14	1123	13.7	30
Norm Nixon	81	2779	496	998	.497	115	161	.714	41	198	239	553	259	3	138	251	7	1107	13.7	28
Jamaal Wilkes	51	1490	277	630	.440	106	148	.716	113	267	380	182	162	1	77	107	22	660	12.9	29
Charlie Scott†	48	1393	225	509	.442	110	142	.775	38	110	148	235	155	4	59	133	11	560	11.7	24
Charlie Scott‡	79	2473	435	994	.438	194	260	.746	62	187	249	378	252	6	110	238	17	1064	13.5	30
Kermit Washington*	25	751	110	244	.451	68	110	.618	110	169	279	30	74	1	19	53	24	288	11.5	22
Don Ford	79	1945	272	576	.472	68	90	.756	106	247	353	142	210	1	68	88	46	612	7.7	22
Tom Abernethy	73	1317	201	404	.498	91	111	.820	105	160	265	101	122	1	55	50	22	493	6.8	24
Kenny Carr	52	733	134	302	.444	55	85	.647	53	155	208	26	127	0	18	89	14	323	6.2	15
Dave Robisch†	55	679	104	249	.418	50	65	.769	53	126	179	40	71	0	19	37	14	258	4.7	16
Dave Robisch‡	78	1277	177	430	.412	100	129	.775	100	252	352	88	130	1	39	71	29	454	5.8	16
Ernie DiGregorio*	25	332	41	100	.410	16	20	.800	5	18	23	71	22	0	6	46	0	98	3.9	11
Don Chaney*	9	133	13	36	.361	5	6	.833	4	7	11	17	14	0	8	11	3	31	3.4	11
Brad Davis	33	334	30	72	.417	22	29	.759	4	31	35	83	39	1	15	35	2	82	2.5	10

MILWAUKEE BUCKS

	G	Min.	FGM	FGA	Pct.	FTM	FTA	Pct.	Off.	Def.	Tot.	Ast.	PF	Dq.	Stl.	TO	Blk.	Pts.	Avg.	Hi.
Brian Winters	80	2751	674	1457	.463	246	293	.840	87	163	250	393	239	4	124	236	27	1594	19.9	37
Marques Johnson	80	2765	628	1204	.522	301	409	.736	292	555	847	190	221	3	92	175	103	1557	19.5	32
Dave Meyers	80	2416	432	938	.461	314	435	.722	144	393	537	241	240	2	86	213	46	1178	14.7	34
Junior Bridgeman	82	1876	476	947	.503	166	205	.810	114	176	290	175	202	1	72	176	30	1118	13.6	35
Alex English	82	1552	343	633	.542	104	143	.727	144	251	395	129	178	1	41	137	55	790	9.6	21
Quinn Buckner	82	2072	314	671	.468	131	203	.645	78	169	247	456	287	6	188	228	19	759	9.3	27
John Gianelli	82	2327	307	629	.488	79	123	.642	166	343	509	192	189	4	54	147	92	693	8.5	21
Kent Benson	69	1288	220	473	.465	92	141	.652	89	206	295	99	177	1	69	119	54	532	7.7	21
Ernie Grunfeld	73	1261	204	461	.443	94	143	.657	70	124	194	145	150	1	54	98	19	502	6.9	22
Lloyd Walton	76	1264	154	344	.448	54	83	.651	26	50	76	253	94	0	77	107	13	362	4.8	14
Kevin Restani*	8	84	13	28	.464	0	2	.000	4	10	14	9	4	0	0	2	1	26	3.3	8
Jim Eakins†	17	155	14	34	.412	21	26	.808	28	17	45	12	25	0	4	9	7	49	2.9	9
Jim Eakins‡	33	406	44	86	.512	50	60	.833	29	46	75	29	71	0	7	33	17	138	4.2	10
Rich Laurel	10	57	10	31	.323	4	4	1.000	6	4	10	3	10	0	3	4	1	24	2.4	8
Scott Lloyd*	14	112	12	33	.364	6	10	.600	7	19	26	9	22	0	3	7	5	30	2.1	5

NEW JERSEY NETS

	G	Min.	FGM	FGA	Pct.	FTM	FTA	Pct.	Off.	Def.	Tot.	Ast.	PF	Dq.	Stl.	TO	Blk.	Pts.	Avg.	Hi.
John Williamson†	33	1282	388	854	.454	197	230	.857	32	75	107	82	105	2	47	101	10	973	29.5	50
John Williamson‡	75	2731	723	1649	.438	331	391	.847	66	161	227	214	236	6	94	228	10	1777	23.7	50
Bernard King	79	3092	798	1665	.479	313	462	.677	265	486	751	193	302	5	122	311	36	1909	24.2	44
Kevin Porter†	74	2686	481	1024	.470	235	307	.765	48	151	199	801	265	6	118	348	15	1197	16.2	40
Kevin Porter‡	82	2813	495	1055	.469	244	320	.763	53	161	214	837	283	6	123	360	15	1234	15.0	40
Al Skinner*	8	277	41	101	.406	39	44	.886	14	38	52	33	34	2	13	29	5	121	15.1	28
Darnell Hillman*	45	1220	236	501	.471	118	205	.576	126	212	338	49	160	7	49	109	44	590	13.1	28
Howard Porter†	55	1216	293	592	.495	120	148	.811	95	167	262	40	119	0	26	50	33	706	12.8	29
Howard Porter‡	63	1323	309	635	.487	124	155	.800	100	179	279	42	134	0	29	55	38	742	11.8	29

	G	Min.	FGM	FGA	Pct.	FTM	FTA	Pct.	REBOUNDS Off.	Def.	Tot.	Ast.	PF	Dq.	Stl.	TO	Blk.	SCORING Pts.	Avg.	Hi.
Robert Hawkins	15	343	69	150	.460	25	29	.862	21	29	50	37	51	1	22	43	13	163	10.9	25
Bob Carrington*	37	1032	157	392	.401	72	97	.742	42	70	112	55	132	5	43	66	12	386	10.4	28
Eddie Jordan†	51	1042	196	482	.407	119	151	.788	33	75	108	145	84	0	114	92	18	511	10.0	30
Eddie Jordan‡	73	1213	215	538	.400	131	167	.784	35	84	119	177	94	0	126	106	19	561	7.7	30
Wilson Washington†	24	523	92	187	.492	26	47	.553	48	94	142	9	72	2	17	53	35	210	8.8	19
Wilson Washington‡	38	561	100	206	.485	29	53	.547	50	106	156	10	75	2	18	63	37	229	6.0	19
George Johnson	81	2411	285	721	.395	133	185	.719	245	534	779	111	339	20	78	221	274	703	8.7	24
Louie Nelson†	25	353	82	197	.416	48	73	.658	12	37	49	29	28	0	20	40	35	212	8.5	22
Louie Nelson‡	33	406	85	211	.403	57	84	.679	13	39	52	34	33	0	22	48	7	227	6.9	22
William Averitt*	21	409	69	188	.367	36	45	.800	7	26	33	68	37	1	17	55	1	174	8.3	32
Mark Crow	15	154	35	80	.438	14	20	.700	14	13	27	8	24	0	5	12	1	84	5.6	16
Tim Bassett	65	1474	149	384	.388	50	97	.515	142	262	404	63	181	5	62	80	33	348	5.4	17
Jan van Breda Kolff	68	1419	107	292	.366	87	123	.707	66	178	244	105	192	7	52	73	46	301	4.4	13
Dave Wohl	10	118	12	34	.353	11	12	.917	1	3	4	13	24	0	3	16	0	35	3.5	17
Kim Hughes	56	854	57	160	.356	9	29	.310	95	145	240	38	163	9	49	57	49	123	2.2	13

NEW ORLEANS JAZZ

	G	Min.	FGM	FGA	Pct.	FTM	FTA	Pct.	REBOUNDS Off.	Def.	Tot.	Ast.	PF	Dq.	Stl.	TO	Blk.	SCORING Pts.	Avg.	Hi.
Pete Maravich	50	2041	556	1253	.444	240	276	.870	49	129	178	335	116	1	101	248	8	1352	27.0	42
Truck Robinson	82	3638	748	1683	.444	366	572	.640	298	990	1288	171	265	5	73	301	79	1862	22.7	39
Gail Goodrich	81	2553	520	1050	.495	264	332	.795	75	102	177	388	186	0	82	205	22	1304	16.1	38
Aaron James	80	2118	428	861	.497	117	157	.745	163	258	421	112	254	5	36	130	22	973	12.2	30
Rich Kelley	82	2119	304	602	.505	225	289	.779	249	510	759	233	293	6	89	225	129	833	10.2	33
Jim McElroy	74	1760	287	607	.473	123	167	.737	44	104	148	292	110	0	58	141	34	697	9.4	27
Joe Meriweather	54	1277	194	411	.472	87	133	.654	135	237	372	58	188	8	18	94	118	475	8.8	21
Nate Williams*	27	434	90	214	.421	31	37	.838	27	63	90	34	61	1	21	25	12	211	7.8	23
Donald Watts†	39	775	109	286	.381	62	103	.602	39	59	98	161	96	0	55	76	17	280	7.2	26
Donald Watts‡	71	1584	219	558	.392	92	156	.590	60	119	179	294	184	1	108	168	31	530	7.5	26
Paul Griffin	82	1853	160	358	.447	112	157	.713	157	353	510	172	228	6	88	150	45	432	5.3	15
Fred Saunders†	30	400	69	143	.483	12	19	.632	27	47	74	35	72	3	14	22	10	150	5.0	18
Fred Saunders‡	56	643	99	234	.423	26	36	.722	38	73	111	46	106	3	21	42	14	224	4.0	18
Freddie Boyd	21	363	44	110	.400	14	22	.636	2	17	19	48	23	0	9	20	3	102	4.9	14
Gus Bailey	48	449	59	139	.424	37	67	.552	44	38	82	40	46	0	18	33	15	155	3.2	20

NEW YORK KNICKERBOCKERS

	G	Min.	FGM	FGA	Pct.	FTM	FTA	Pct.	REBOUNDS Off.	Def.	Tot.	Ast.	PF	Dq.	Stl.	TO	Blk.	SCORING Pts.	Avg.	Hi.
Bob McAdoo	79	3182	814	1564	.520	469	645	.727	236	774	1010	298	297	6	105	346	126	2097	26.5	40
Earl Monroe	76	2369	556	1123	.495	242	291	.832	47	135	182	361	189	0	60	179	19	1354	17.8	37
Lonnie Shelton	82	2319	508	988	.514	203	276	.736	204	376	580	195	350	11	109	228	112	1219	14.9	41
Spencer Haywood	67	1765	412	852	.484	96	135	.711	141	301	442	126	188	1	37	140	72	920	13.7	37
Butch Beard	79	1979	308	614	.502	129	160	.806	76	188	264	339	201	2	117	154	3	745	9.4	32
Ray Williams	81	1550	305	689	.443	146	207	.705	85	124	209	363	211	4	108	242	15	756	9.3	29
Jim McMillian	81	1977	288	623	.462	115	134	.858	80	209	289	205	116	0	76	104	17	691	8.5	24
Jim Cleamons	79	2009	215	448	.480	81	103	.786	69	143	212	283	142	1	68	113	17	511	6.5	18
Toby Knight	80	1169	222	465	.477	63	97	.649	121	200	321	38	211	1	50	97	28	507	6.3	22
Glen Gondrezick	72	1017	131	339	.386	83	121	.686	92	158	250	83	181	0	56	82	18	345	4.8	17
Phil Jackson	63	654	55	115	.478	43	56	.768	29	81	110	46	106	0	31	47	15	153	2.4	16
Luther Burden	2	15	1	2	.500	0	0	...	0	0	0	1	1	0	1	0	0	2	1.0	2

PHILADELPHIA 76ERS

	G	Min.	FGM	FGA	Pct.	FTM	FTA	Pct.	REBOUNDS Off.	Def.	Tot.	Ast.	PF	Dq.	Stl.	TO	Blk.	SCORING Pts.	Avg.	Hi.
Julius Erving	74	2429	611	1217	.502	306	362	.845	179	302	481	279	207	0	135	238	97	1528	20.6	43
George McGinnis	78	2533	588	1270	.463	411	574	.716	282	528	810	294	287	6	137	312	27	1587	20.3	37
Doug Collins	79	2770	643	1223	.526	267	329	.812	87	143	230	320	228	2	128	250	25	1553	19.7	37
World B. Free	76	2050	390	857	.455	411	562	.731	92	120	212	306	199	0	68	200	41	1191	15.7	29
Darryl Dawkins	70	1722	332	577	.575	156	220	.709	117	438	555	85	268	5	34	123	125	820	11.7	23
Steve Mix	82	1819	291	560	.520	175	220	.795	96	201	297	174	158	1	87	131	3	757	9.2	27
Henry Bibby	82	2518	286	659	.434	171	219	.781	62	189	251	464	207	0	91	153	6	743	9.1	22
Joe Bryant	81	1236	190	436	.436	111	144	.771	103	177	280	129	185	1	56	115	24	491	6.1	28
Caldwell Jones	81	2466	169	359	.471	96	153	.627	165	405	570	92	281	4	26	128	127	434	5.4	18
Ted McClain†	29	293	42	96	.438	7	10	.700	9	28	37	34	36	0	16	22	4	91	3.1	16
Ted McClain‡	70	1020	123	280	.439	57	73	.781	20	92	112	157	124	2	58	90	6	303	4.3	17
Harvey Catchings	61	748	70	178	.393	34	55	.618	105	145	250	34	124	1	20	44	67	174	2.9	10
Glenn Mosley	6	21	5	13	.385	3	7	.429	0	5	5	2	5	0	0	5	0	13	2.2	6
Mike Dunleavy*	4	17	3	7	.429	2	2	1.000	0	1	1	6	0	0	1	3	0	8	2.0	4
Wilson Washington*	14	38	8	19	.421	3	6	.500	2	12	14	1	3	0	1	10	2	19	1.4	4

1977-78

PHOENIX SUNS

	G	Min.	FGM	FGA	Pct.	FTM	FTA	Pct.	Off.	Def.	Tot.	Ast.	PF	Dq.	Stl.	TO	Blk.	Pts.	Avg.	Hi.
										REBOUNDS									SCORING	
Paul Westphal	80	2481	809	1568	.516	396	487	.813	41	123	164	437	162	0	138	280	31	2014	25.2	48
Walter Davis	81	2590	786	1494	.526	387	466	.830	158	326	484	273	242	2	113	283	20	1959	24.2	40
Alvan Adams	70	1914	434	895	.485	214	293	.730	158	407	565	225	242	8	86	234	63	1082	15.5	35
Ron Lee	82	1928	417	950	.439	170	228	.746	95	159	254	305	257	3	225	221	17	1004	12.2	30
Don Buse	82	2547	287	626	.458	112	136	.824	59	190	249	391	144	0	185	124	14	686	8.4	19
Gar Heard	80	2099	265	625	.424	90	147	.612	166	486	652	132	213	0	129	120	101	620	7.8	24
Alvin Scott	81	1538	180	369	.488	132	191	.691	135	222	357	88	158	0	52	85	40	492	6.1	16
Curtis Perry	45	818	110	243	.453	51	65	.785	87	163	250	48	120	2	34	63	22	271	6.0	18
Mike Bratz	80	933	159	395	.403	56	68	.824	42	73	115	123	104	1	39	89	5	374	4.7	16
Bayard Forrest	64	887	111	238	.466	49	103	.476	84	166	250	129	105	0	23	84	34	271	4.2	23
Greg Griffin	36	422	61	169	.361	23	36	.639	44	59	103	24	56	0	16	39	0	145	4.0	15
Dennis Awtrey	81	1623	112	264	.424	69	109	.633	97	205	302	163	153	0	19	127	25	293	3.6	16

PORTLAND TRAIL BLAZERS

	G	Min.	FGM	FGA	Pct.	FTM	FTA	Pct.	Off.	Def.	Tot.	Ast.	PF	Dq.	Stl.	TO	Blk.	Pts.	Avg.	Hi.
										REBOUNDS									SCORING	
Bill Walton	58	1929	460	882	.522	177	246	.720	118	648	766	291	145	3	60	206	146	1097	18.9	34
Maurice Lucas	68	2119	453	989	.458	207	270	.767	186	435	621	173	221	3	61	192	56	1113	16.4	35
Lionel Hollins	81	2741	531	1202	.442	223	300	.743	81	196	277	380	268	4	157	241	29	1285	15.9	38
Bob Gross	72	2163	381	720	.529	152	190	.800	180	220	400	254	234	5	100	179	52	914	12.7	27
Lloyd Neal	61	1174	272	540	.504	127	177	.718	116	257	373	81	128	0	29	96	21	671	11.0	35
Johnny Davis	82	2188	343	756	.454	188	227	.828	65	108	173	217	173	0	81	151	14	874	10.7	23
Tom Owens	82	1714	313	639	.490	206	278	.741	195	346	541	160	263	7	33	152	37	832	10.1	27
Dave Twardzik	75	1820	242	409	.592	183	234	.782	36	98	134	244	186	2	107	158	4	667	8.9	22
Larry Steele	65	1132	210	447	.470	100	122	.820	34	79	113	87	138	2	59	66	5	520	8.0	21
Jacky Dorsey†	4	51	9	19	.474	7	11	.636	6	4	10	3	8	0	0	3	1	25	6.3	9
Jacky Dorsey‡	11	88	12	31	.387	10	16	.625	11	19	30	5	17	0	2	6	3	34	3.1	9
Willie Norwood†	19	351	40	99	.404	30	46	.652	22	43	65	19	56	1	18	39	0	110	5.8	14
Willie Norwood‡	35	611	74	181	.409	50	75	.667	49	70	119	33	101	1	31	56	3	198	5.7	14
Corky Calhoun	79	1370	175	365	.479	66	76	.868	73	142	215	87	141	3	42	64	15	416	5.3	24
Wally Walker*	9	101	19	41	.463	5	8	.625	7	10	17	8	13	0	2	11	0	43	4.8	12
T.R. Dunn	63	768	100	240	.417	37	56	.661	63	84	147	45	74	0	46	35	8	237	3.8	13
Dale Schlueter	10	109	8	19	.421	9	18	.500	5	16	21	18	20	0	3	15	2	25	2.5	10

SAN ANTONIO SPURS

	G	Min.	FGM	FGA	Pct.	FTM	FTA	Pct.	Off.	Def.	Tot.	Ast.	PF	Dq.	Stl.	TO	Blk.	Pts.	Avg.	Hi.
										REBOUNDS									SCORING	
George Gervin	82	2857	864	1611	.536	504	607	.830	118	302	420	302	255	3	136	306	110	2232	27.2	63
Larry Kenon	81	2869	698	1426	.489	276	323	.854	245	528	773	268	209	2	115	279	24	1672	20.6	42
Billy Paultz	80	2479	518	979	.529	230	306	.752	172	503	675	213	222	3	42	167	194	1266	15.8	29
Louie Dampier	82	2037	336	660	.509	76	101	.752	24	98	122	285	84	0	87	95	13	748	9.1	21
Mike Gale	70	2091	275	581	.473	87	100	.870	57	166	223	376	170	2	159	176	25	637	9.1	22
Mark Olberding	79	1773	231	480	.481	184	227	.811	104	269	373	131	235	1	45	118	26	646	8.2	22
Allan Bristow	82	1481	257	538	.478	152	208	.731	99	158	257	194	150	0	69	146	4	666	8.1	27
Mike Green†	63	1132	195	427	.457	86	111	.775	108	196	304	66	167	1	24	83	87	476	7.6	20
Mike Green‡	72	1382	238	514	.463	107	142	.754	130	229	359	76	193	1	30	105	100	583	8.1	20
Coby Dietrick	79	1876	250	543	.460	89	114	.781	73	285	358	217	231	4	81	144	55	589	7.5	18
Jim Eakins*	16	251	30	52	.577	29	34	.853	17	29	46	17	46	0	3	24	10	89	5.6	10
Dennis Layton	41	498	85	168	.506	12	13	.923	4	28	32	108	51	0	21	59	4	182	4.4	14
James Silas	37	311	43	97	.443	60	73	.822	4	19	23	38	29	0	11	30	1	146	3.9	15
Scott Sims	12	95	10	26	.385	10	15	.667	5	8	13	20	16	0	3	19	0	30	2.5	11
George Karl	4	30	2	6	.333	2	2	1.000	0	5	5	5	6	0	1	4	0	6	1.5	4

SEATTLE SUPERSONICS

	G	Min.	FGM	FGA	Pct.	FTM	FTA	Pct.	Off.	Def.	Tot.	Ast.	PF	Dq.	Stl.	TO	Blk.	Pts.	Avg.	Hi.
										REBOUNDS									SCORING	
Gus Williams	79	2572	602	1335	.451	227	278	.817	83	173	256	290	198	2	185	189	41	1431	18.1	37
Fred Brown	72	1965	508	1042	.488	176	196	.898	61	127	188	240	145	0	110	164	25	1192	16.6	37
Marvin Webster	82	2910	427	851	.502	290	461	.629	361	674	1035	203	262	8	48	257	162	1144	14.0	26
Dennis Johnson	81	2209	367	881	.417	297	406	.732	152	142	294	230	213	2	118	164	51	1031	12.7	27
Mike Green*	9	250	43	87	.494	21	31	.677	22	33	55	10	26	0	6	22	13	107	11.9	20
Jack Sikma	82	2238	342	752	.455	192	247	.777	196	482	678	134	300	6	68	186	40	876	10.7	28
John Johnson†	76	1812	341	820	.416	131	174	.753	100	207	307	210	194	0	43	166	19	813	10.7	26
John Johnson‡	77	1823	342	824	.415	133	177	.751	102	208	310	211	197	0	43	169	19	817	10.6	26
Bruce Seals	73	1322	230	551	.417	111	175	.634	62	164	226	81	210	4	41	103	33	571	7.8	28
Donald Watts*	32	809	110	272	.404	30	53	.566	21	60	81	133	88	1	53	92	14	250	7.8	18
Wally Walker†	68	1003	185	420	.440	70	112	.625	80	122	202	69	125	1	24	66	10	440	6.5	18
Wally Walker‡	77	1104	204	461	.443	75	120	.625	87	132	219	77	138	1	26	77	10	483	6.3	18
Paul Silas	82	2172	187	464	.403	109	186	.586	289	377	666	145	182	0	65	152	16	483	5.9	17
Joe Hassett	48	404	91	205	.444	10	12	.833	14	22	36	41	45	0	21	34	0	192	4.0	14
Al Fleming	20	97	15	31	.484	10	17	.588	13	17	30	7	16	0	0	16	5	40	2.0	8
Willie Wise	2	10	0	3	.000	1	4	.250	2	1	3	0	2	0	0	0	0	1	0.5	1
Dean Tolson	1	7	0	1	.000	0	0	...	0	0	0	2	2	0	0	1	0	0	0.0	0

WASHINGTON BULLETS

	G	Min.	FGM	FGA	Pct.	FTM	FTA	Pct.	REBOUNDS Off.	Def.	Tot.	Ast.	PF	Dq.	Stl.	TO	Blk.	SCORING Pts.	Avg.	Hi.
Elvin Hayes	81	3246	636	1409	.451	326	514	.634	335	740	1075	149	313	7	96	229	159	1598	19.7	37
Bob Dandridge	75	2777	560	1190	.471	330	419	.788	137	305	442	287	262	6	101	241	44	1450	19.3	37
Mitch Kupchak	67	1759	393	768	.512	280	402	.697	162	298	460	71	196	1	28	184	42	1066	15.9	32
Kevin Grevey	81	2121	505	1128	.448	243	308	.789	124	166	290	155	203	4	61	159	17	1253	15.5	43
Phil Chenier	36	937	200	451	.443	109	138	.790	15	87	102	73	54	0	36	67	9	509	14.1	28
Tom Henderson	75	2315	339	784	.432	179	240	.746	66	127	193	406	131	0	93	195	15	857	11.4	24
Larry Wright	70	1466	283	570	.496	76	107	.710	31	71	102	260	195	3	68	134	15	642	9.2	43
Charles Johnson†	39	807	141	346	.408	42	51	.824	20	73	93	82	76	0	31	50	1	324	8.3	29
Charles Johnson‡	71	1299	237	581	.408	49	61	.803	43	112	155	130	129	0	62	73	5	523	7.4	29
Wes Unseld	80	2644	257	491	.523	93	173	.538	286	669	955	326	234	2	98	173	45	607	7.6	25
Greg Ballard	76	936	142	334	.425	88	114	.772	102	164	266	62	90	1	30	64	13	372	4.9	19
Phil Walker	40	384	57	161	.354	64	96	.667	21	31	52	54	39	0	14	62	5	178	4.5	23
Joe Pace	49	438	67	140	.479	57	93	.613	50	84	134	23	86	1	12	44	21	191	3.9	18

* Finished season with another team. † Totals with this team only. ‡ Totals with all teams.

PLAYOFF RESULTS

EASTERN CONFERENCE

FIRST ROUND
New York 2, Cleveland 0
Apr. 12—Wed.	New York 132 at Cleveland	114
Apr. 14—Fri.	Cleveland 107 at New York	109

Washington 2, Atlanta 0
Apr. 12—Wed.	Atlanta 94 at Washington	103
Apr. 14—Fri.	Washington 107 at Atlanta	*103

SEMIFINALS
Philadelphia 4, New York 0
Apr. 16—Sun.	New York 90 at Philadelphia	130
Apr. 18—Tue.	New York 100 at Philadelphia	119
Apr. 20—Thur.	Philadelphia 137 at New York	126
Apr. 23—Sun.	Philadelphia 112 at New York	107

Washington 4, San Antonio 2
Apr. 16—Sun.	Washington 103 at San Antonio	114
Apr. 18—Tue.	Washington 121 at San Antonio	117
Apr. 21—Fri.	San Antonio 105 at Washington	118
Apr. 23—Sun.	San Antonio 95 at Washington	98
Apr. 25—Tue.	Washington 105 at San Antonio	116
Apr. 28—Fri.	San Antonio 100 at Washington	103

FINALS
Washington 4, Philadelphia 2
Apr. 30—Sun.	Washington 122 at Philadelphia	117
May 3—Wed.	Washington 104 at Philadelphia	110
May 5—Fri.	Philadelphia 108 at Washington	123
May 7—Sun.	Philadelphia 105 at Washington	121
May 10—Wed.	Washington 94 at Philadelphia	107
May 12—Fri.	Philadelphia 99 at Washington	101

WESTERN CONFERENCE

FIRST ROUND
Milwaukee 2, Phoenix 0
Apr. 11—Tue.	Milwaukee 111 at Phoenix	103
Apr. 14—Fri.	Phoenix 90 at Milwaukee	94

Seattle 2, Los Angeles 1
Apr. 12—Wed.	Los Angeles 90 at Seattle	102
Apr. 14—Fri.	Seattle 99 at Los Angeles	105
Apr. 16—Sun.	Los Angeles 102 at Seattle	111

SEMIFINALS
Seattle 4, Portland 2
Apr. 18—Tue.	Seattle 104 at Portland	95
Apr. 21—Fri.	Seattle 93 at Portland	96
Apr. 23—Sun.	Portland 84 at Seattle	99
Apr. 26—Wed.	Portland 98 at Seattle	100
Apr. 30—Sun.	Seattle 89 at Portland	113
May 1—Mon.	Portland 94 at Seattle	105

Denver 4, Milwaukee 3
Apr. 18—Tue.	Milwaukee 103 at Denver	119
Apr. 21—Fri.	Milwaukee 111 at Denver	127
Apr. 23—Sun.	Denver 112 at Milwaukee	143
Apr. 25—Tue.	Denver 118 at Milwaukee	104
Apr. 28—Fri.	Milwaukee 117 at Denver	112
Apr. 30—Sun.	Denver 91 at Milwaukee	119
May 3—Wed.	Milwaukee 110 at Denver	116

FINALS
Seattle 4, Denver 2
May 5—Fri.	Seattle 107 at Denver	116
May 7—Sun.	Seattle 121 at Denver	111
May 10—Wed.	Denver 91 at Seattle	105
May 12—Fri.	Denver 94 at Seattle	100
May 14—Sun.	Seattle 114 at Denver	123
May 17—Wed.	Denver 108 at Seattle	123

NBA FINALS
Washington 4, Seattle 3
May 21—Sun.	Washington 102 at Seattle	106
May 25—Thur.	Seattle 98 at Washington	106
May 28—Sun.	Seattle 93 at Washington	92
May 30—Tue.	Washington 120 at Seattle	*116
June 2—Fri.	Washington 94 at Seattle	98
June 4—Sun.	Seattle 82 at Washington	117
June 7—Wed.	Washington 105 at Seattle	99

*Denotes number of overtime periods.

1977-78

1976-77 NBA CHAMPION PORTLAND TRAIL BLAZERS
Front row (from left): president Larry Weinberg, general manager Harry Glickman, Herm Gilliam, Dave Twardzik, Johnny Davis, Lionel Hollins, head coach Jack Ramsay, assistant coach Jack McKinney. Center row (from left): Lloyd Neal, Larry Steele, Corky Calhoun, Bill Walton, Maurice Lucas, Wally Walker, Robin Jones, Bob Gross. Back row (from left): radio announcer Bill Schonley, team physician Dr. Robert Cook, trainer Ron Culp, promotions director Wallace Scales, team dentist Dr. Larry Mudrick, business manager George Rickles, administrative assistant Berlyn Hodges.

FINAL STANDINGS

ATLANTIC DIVISION

	Atl.	Bos.	Buf.	Chi.	Cle.	Den.	Det.	G.S.	Hou.	Ind.	K.C.	L.A.	Mil.	N.O.	N.Y.K.	N.Y.N.	Phi.	Pho.	Por.	S.A.	Sea.	Was.	W	L	Pct.	GB
Philadelphia	3	3	2	2	3	3	2	1	3	2	3	2	2	4	3	3	..	1	2	1	2	3	50	32	.610	..
Boston	4	..	3	2	1	3	2	1	2	1	3	2	3	2	2	3	1	2	1	4	2	0	44	38	.537	6
N.Y. Knicks	3	2	3	2	2	2	2	3	2	2	0	3	3	1	..	2	1	2	1	1	1	2	40	42	.488	10
Buffalo	0	1	..	1	2	2	3	0	1	1	0	1	3	3	1	2	2	3	1	0	3	0	30	52	.366	20
N.Y. Nets	1	1	2	1	1	1	1	1	1	2	0	0	0	1	2	..	2	1	2	0	1	1	22	60	.268	28

CENTRAL DIVISION

	Atl.	Bos.	Buf.	Chi.	Cle.	Den.	Det.	G.S.	Hou.	Ind.	K.C.	L.A.	Mil.	N.O.	N.Y.K.	N.Y.N.	Phi.	Pho.	Por.	S.A.	Sea.	Was.	W	L	Pct.	GB
Houston	3	2	3	3	3	0	2	1	..	4	2	2	3	2	2	1	3	3	2	3	3	3	49	33	.598	..
Washington	3	4	4	2	3	2	3	1	1	4	2	0	3	2	2	3	1	3	2	2	1	..	48	34	.585	1
San Antonio	0	0	4	1	2	2	2	2	2	2	3	1	1	3	3	3	3	3	2	..	3	2	44	38	.537	5
Cleveland	2	3	2	1	..	2	1	2	1	2	3	2	4	2	2	3	1	2	2	2	3	1	43	39	.524	6
New Orleans	3	2	1	0	2	1	1	3	2	2	2	0	2	..	3	2	0	3	2	1	1	2	35	47	.427	14
Atlanta	..	0	4	2	2	2	0	0	1	0	1	2	2	1	1	3	1	0	3	4	1	1	31	51	.378	18

MIDWEST DIVISION

	Atl.	Bos.	Buf.	Chi.	Cle.	Den.	Det.	G.S.	Hou.	Ind.	K.C.	L.A.	Mil.	N.O.	N.Y.K.	N.Y.N.	Phi.	Pho.	Por.	S.A.	Sea.	Was.	W	L	Pct.	GB
Denver	2	1	2	3	2	..	3	2	3	3	3	2	3	3	2	3	1	3	2	1	4	2	50	32	.610	..
Chicago	2	2	3	..	3	1	2	2	1	2	2	3	3	4	2	2	2	0	3	2	1	1	44	38	.537	6
Detroit	4	2	1	2	3	1	..	3	2	2	4	1	3	3	1	3	2	2	1	1	1	1	44	38	.537	6
Kansas City	2	1	3	2	1	1	0	3	2	2	..	1	2	2	4	4	1	3	2	1	1	2	40	42	.488	10
Indiana	4	2	3	2	1	1	2	0	0	..	2	1	2	2	2	4	2	0	0	2	2	0	36	46	.439	14
Milwaukee	2	1	1	1	0	1	1	3	1	2	2	1	..	1	1	3	1	1	2	3	1	1	30	52	.366	20

PACIFIC DIVISION

	Atl.	Bos.	Buf.	Chi.	Cle.	Den.	Det.	G.S.	Hou.	Ind.	K.C.	L.A.	Mil.	N.O.	N.Y.K.	N.Y.N.	Phi.	Pho.	Por.	S.A.	Sea.	Was.	W	L	Pct.	GB
Los Angeles	2	1	3	1	2	2	3	2	2	3	3	..	3	3	1	4	2	3	3	3	3	4	53	29	.646	..
Portland	1	3	3	4	2	2	2	3	1	4	2	1	2	2	3	3	2	3	..	2	3	1	49	33	.598	4
Golden State	4	3	3	2	2	2	1	..	2	4	1	2	1	1	1	3	3	4	1	2	1	3	46	36	.561	7
Seattle	2	2	1	2	1	0	3	3	1	2	3	1	3	3	2	3	2	1	1	1	..	3	40	42	.488	13
Phoenix	4	2	1	2	1	1	2	0	1	2	1	1	3	1	2	2	2	..	1	1	3	1	34	48	.415	19

TEAM STATISTICS

OFFENSIVE

	G	FGM	FGA	Pct.	FTM	FTA	Pct.	Off.	Def.	Tot.	Ast.	PF	Dq.	Stl.	TO	Blk.	Pts.	Avg.
								REBOUNDS									SCORING	
San Antonio . . .	82	3711	7657	.485	2010	2522	.797	1110	2550	3660	2115	1966	35	857	1770	499	9432	115.0
Denver	82	3590	7471	.481	2053	2783	.738	1288	2700	3988	2262	2142	29	953	2011	471	9233	112.6
Portland	82	3623	7537	.481	1917	2515	.762	1260	2703	3963	1990	2220	38	868	1757	492	9163	111.7
Golden State . .	82	3724	7832	.475	1649	2172	.759	1300	2639	3939	2120	2058	24	904	1624	432	9097	110.9
Philadelphia . .	82	3511	7322	.480	2012	2732	.736	1293	2752	4045	1966	2074	18	814	1915	561	9034	110.2
Detroit	82	3764	7792	.483	1442	1960	.736	1169	2495	3664	2004	2200	39	877	1718	459	8970	109.4
N.Y. Knicks. . . .	82	3659	7530	.486	1587	2078	.764	974	2680	3654	1956	2007	16	714	1680	304	8905	108.6
Milwaukee	82	3668	7840	.468	1553	2072	.750	1220	2519	3739	1970	2094	27	790	1648	342	8889	108.4
Kansas City . .	82	3561	7733	.460	1706	2140	.797	1222	2593	3815	1982	2173	36	849	1576	386	8828	107.7
Los Angeles . . .	82	3663	7657	.478	1437	1941	.740	1177	2628	3805	2057	1867	14	801	1538	445	8763	106.9
Indiana	82	3522	7840	.449	1714	2297	.746	1409	2584	3993	2009	2030	37	924	1609	458	8758	106.8
Houston	82	3535	7325	.483	1656	2103	.787	1254	2632	3886	1913	2132	35	616	1600	411	8726	106.4
Washington . . .	82	3514	7479	.470	1622	2264	.716	1185	2758	3943	1935	1940	19	642	1677	433	8650	105.5
Buffalo	82	3366	7475	.450	1880	2492	.754	1213	2623	3836	1883	1842	15	683	1699	392	8612	105.0
Phoenix	82	3406	7249	.470	1791	2345	.764	1059	2493	3552	2100	2089	24	750	1830	346	8603	104.9
New Orleans. .	82	3443	7602	.453	1688	2183	.773	1249	2828	4077	1854	2099	32	613	1706	357	8574	104.6
Boston	82	3462	7775	.445	1648	2181	.756	1241	2966	4207	2010	2039	49	506	1673	263	8572	104.5
Seattle	82	3439	7639	.450	1646	2386	.690	1355	2433	3788	1772	2198	23	932	1759	503	8524	104.0
Atlanta	82	3279	7176	.457	1836	2451	.749	1244	2512	3756	1882	2302	71	733	1779	330	8394	102.4
Cleveland	82	3451	7688	.449	1468	1993	.737	1312	2563	3875	1845	1951	24	579	1356	472	8370	102.1
Chicago	82	3249	7186	.452	1613	2159	.747	1292	2705	3997	1989	1871	26	699	1552	364	8111	98.9
N.Y. Nets	82	3096	7222	.429	1673	2274	.736	1157	2547	3704	1422	2187	43	802	1630	435	7865	95.9

DEFENSIVE

	FGM	FGA	Pct.	FTM	FTA	Pct.	Off.	Def.	Tot.	Ast.	PF	Dq.	Stl.	TO	Blk.	Pts.	Avg.	Dif.
							REBOUNDS									SCORING		
Chicago	3306	7095	.466	1425	1907	.747	1055	2559	3614	1917	2166	51	723	1598	460	8037	98.0	+0.9
Cleveland . . .	3265	7268	.449	1748	2325	.752	1202	2711	3913	1736	1908	23	660	1542	389	8278	101.0	+1.1
N.Y. Nets	3279	7074	.464	1863	2488	.749	1149	2907	4006	1910	1970	21	778	1735	512	8421	102.7	-6.8
Los Angeles . . .	3515	7781	.452	1510	1990	.759	1348	2625	3973	1900	1816	21	763	1599	362	8540	104.1	+2.8
Phoenix	3320	7192	.462	1903	2525	.754	1180	2594	3774	1856	2325	39	897	1835	440	8543	104.2	+0.7
Washington . . .	3552	7751	.458	1462	1943	.752	1167	2565	3732	1893	2088	31	815	1506	348	8566	104.5	+1.0
Houston	3424	7356	.465	1746	2252	.775	1121	2232	3353	1883	1978	27	547	1395	350	8594	104.8	+1.6
Seattle	3394	7339	.462	1863	2474	.753	1257	2851	3908	2040	2104	24	726	1005	476	8651	105.5	-1.5
Philadelphia . .	3575	7920	.451	1561	2074	.753	1416	2448	3864	2012	2232	44	823	1769	371	8711	106.2	+4.0
Portland	3408	7404	.460	1889	2514	.751	1197	2510	3707	1817	2242	37	840	1765	478	8705	106.2	+5.5
Atlanta	3409	7137	.478	1909	2527	.755	1121	2533	3654	2020	2174	44	803	1692	442	8727	106.4	-4.0
Boston	3559	7904	.450	1616	2180	.741	1110	2753	3863	1918	1954	24	699	1369	349	8734	106.5	-2.0
Kansas City . .	3422	7244	.472	1912	2513	.761	1097	2739	3836	1744	2030	35	722	1755	392	8756	106.8	+0.9
New Orleans. .	3486	7712	.452	1833	2448	.749	1318	2781	4099	1748	2125	35	835	1615	361	8805	107.4	-2.8
Denver	3585	7743	.463	1635	2231	.733	1269	2481	3750	2082	2285	41	941	1944	470	8805	107.4	+5.2
Golden State. .	3567	7584	.470	1699	2282	.745	1256	2640	3896	2114	1939	26	757	1778	420	8833	107.7	+3.2
N.Y. Knicks. . . .	3577	7610	.470	1752	2327	.753	1163	2716	3879	1847	2008	20	793	1612	412	8906	108.6	0.0
Indiana	3599	7629	.472	1705	2252	.757	1378	2770	4148	2097	2043	23	715	1792	466	8903	108.6	-1.8
Buffalo	3786	7917	.478	1404	1859	.755	1268	2721	3989	2192	2129	31	729	1607	446	8976	109.5	-4.5
Detroit	3561	7539	.472	1933	2543	.760	1317	2637	3954	1952	1827	15	793	1828	381	9055	110.4	-1.0
Milwaukee . . .	3712	7753	.479	1721	2330	.739	1265	2613	3878	2193	2193	22	736	1644	410	9145	111.5	-3.1
San Antonio . .	3955	8075	.490	1512	2059	.734	1329	2687	4016	2159	2189	40	811	1822	420	9382	114.4	+0.6
Avgs.	3511	7547	.465	1709	2275	.751	1227	2632	3858	1956	2067	31	768	1687	416	8731	106.5	. . .

HOME/ROAD

	Home	Road	Total		Home	Road	Total
Atlanta.	19-22	12-29	31-51	Milwaukee	24-17	6-35	30-52
Boston.	28-13	16-25	44-38	New Orleans	26-15	9-32	35-47
Buffalo.	23-18	7-34	30-52	New York Knicks	26-15	14-27	40-42
Chicago.	31-10	13-28	44-38	New York Nets.	10-31	12-29	22-60
Cleveland.	29-12	14-27	43-39	Philadelphia.	32-9	18-23	50-32
Denver.	36-5	14-27	50-32	Phoenix.	26-15	8-33	34-48
Detroit.	30-11	14-27	44-38	Portland	35-6	14-27	49-33
Golden State	29-12	17-24	46-36	San Antonio.	31-10	13-28	44-38
Houston	34-7	15-26	49-33	Seattle.	27-14	13-28	40-42
Indiana	25-16	11-30	36-46	Washington	32-9	16-25	48-34
Kansas City	28-13	12-29	40-42	Totals.	618-284	284-618	902-902
Los Angeles.	37-4	16-25	53-29				

1976-77

POINTS

(minimum 70 games or 1,400 points)

	G	FGM	FTM	Pts.	Avg.		G	FGM	FTM	Pts.	Avg.
Pete Maravich, New Orleans	73	886	501	2273	31.1	Ron Boone, Kansas City	82	747	324	1818	22.2
Billy Knight, Indiana	78	831	413	2075	26.6	Larry Kenon, San Antonio	78	706	293	1705	21.9
Kareem Abdul-Jabbar, L.A.	82	888	376	2152	26.2	Rick Barry, Golden State	79	682	359	1723	21.8
David Thompson, Denver	82	824	477	2125	25.9	Julius Erving, Philadelphia	82	685	400	1770	21.6
Bob McAdoo, Buf.-N.Y. Knicks	72	740	381	1861	25.8	Rudy Tomjanovich, Houston	81	733	287	1753	21.6
Bob Lanier, Detroit	64	678	260	1616	25.3	George McGinnis, Philadelphia	79	659	372	1690	21.4
John Drew, Atlanta	74	689	412	1790	24.2	Paul Westphal, Phoenix	81	682	362	1726	21.3
Elvin Hayes, Washington	82	760	422	1942	23.7	John Williamson, N.Y. Nets-Ind.	72	618	259	1495	20.8
George Gervin, San Antonio	82	726	443	1895	23.1	Bob Dandridge, Milwaukee	70	585	283	1453	20.8
Dan Issel, Denver	79	660	445	1765	22.3	Randy Smith, Buffalo	82	702	294	1698	20.7

FIELD GOALS

(minimum 300 made)

	FGM	FGA	Pct.
Kareem Abdul-Jabbar, Los Angeles	888	1533	.579
Mitch Kupchak, Washington	341	596	.572
Bobby Jones, Denver	501	879	.570
George Gervin, San Antonio	726	1335	.544
Bob Lanier, Detroit	678	1269	.534
Bob Gross, Portland	376	711	.529
Bill Walton, Portland	491	930	.528
Swen Nater, Milwaukee	383	725	.528
Joe Meriweather, Atlanta	319	607	.526
Artis Gilmore, Chicago	570	1091	.522

REBOUNDS

(minimum 70 games or 800 rebounds)

	G	Off.	Def.	Tot.	Avg.
Bill Walton, Portland	65	211	723	934	14.4
Kareem Abdul-Jabbar, L.A.	82	266	824	1090	13.3
Moses Malone, Buffalo-Houston	82	437	635	1072	13.1
Artis Gilmore, Chicago	82	313	757	1070	13.0
Bob McAdoo, Buf.-N.Y. Knicks	72	199	727	926	12.9
Elvin Hayes, Washington	82	289	740	1029	12.5
Swen Nater, Milwaukee	72	266	599	865	12.0
George McGinnis, Philadelphia	79	324	587	911	11.5
Maurice Lucas, Portland	79	271	628	899	11.4
Larry Kenon, San Antonio	78	282	597	879	11.3

FREE THROWS

(minimum 125 made)

	FTM	FTA	Pct.
Ernie DiGregorio, Buffalo	138	146	.945
Rick Barry, Golden State	359	392	.916
Calvin Murphy, Houston	272	307	.886
Mike Newlin, Houston	269	304	.885
Fred Brown, Seattle	168	190	.884
Dick Van Arsdale, Phoenix	145	166	.873
Jo Jo White, Boston	333	383	.869
Junior Bridgeman, Milwaukee	197	228	.864
Cazzie Russell, Los Angeles	188	219	.858
Jan van Breda Kolff, N.Y. Nets	195	228	.855

STEALS

(minimum 70 games or 125 steals)

	G	No.	Avg.
Don Buse, Indiana	81	281	3.47
Brian Taylor, Kansas City	72	199	2.76
Donald Watts, Seattle	79	214	2.71
Quinn Buckner, Milwaukee	79	192	2.43
Mike Gale, San Antonio	82	191	2.33
Bobby Jones, Denver	82	186	2.27
Chris Ford, Detroit	82	179	2.18
Rick Barry, Golden State	79	172	2.18
Lionel Hollins, Portland	76	166	2.18
Randy Smith, Buffalo	82	176	2.15

ASSISTS

(minimum 70 games or 400 assists)

	G	No.	Avg.
Don Buse, Indiana	81	685	8.5
Donald Watts, Seattle	79	630	8.0
Norm Van Lier, Chicago	82	636	7.8
Kevin Porter, Detroit	81	592	7.3
Tom Henderson, Atlanta-Washington	87	598	6.9
Rick Barry, Golden State	79	475	6.0
Jo Jo White, Boston	82	492	6.0
Mike Gale, San Antonio	82	473	5.8
Paul Westphal, Phoenix	81	459	5.7
John Lucas, Houston	82	463	5.7

BLOCKED SHOTS

(minimum 70 games or 100 blocked shots)

	G	No.	Avg.
Bill Walton, Portland	65	211	3.25
Kareem Abdul-Jabbar, Los Angeles	82	261	3.18
Elvin Hayes, Washington	82	220	2.68
Artis Gilmore, Chicago	82	203	2.48
Caldwell Jones, Philadelphia	82	200	2.44
George Johnson, Golden State-Buffalo	78	177	2.27
Moses Malone, Buffalo-Houston	82	181	2.21
Dan Roundfield, Indiana	61	131	2.15
Billy Paultz, San Antonio	82	173	2.11
Elmore Smith, Milwaukee-Cleveland	70	144	2.06

1976-77

INDIVIDUAL STATISTICS, TEAM BY TEAM

ATLANTA HAWKS

	G	Min.	FGM	FGA	Pct.	FTM	FTA	Pct.	REBOUNDS Off.	Def.	Tot.	Ast.	PF	Dq.	Stl.	TO	Blk.	SCORING Pts.	Avg.	Hi.
John Drew	74	2688	689	1416	.487	412	577	.714	280	395	675	133	275	9	102	...	29	1790	24.2	42
Truck Robinson†	36	1449	310	648	.478	186	241	.772	133	329	462	97	130	3	38	...	20	806	22.4	34
Truck Robinson‡	77	2777	574	1200	.478	314	430	.730	252	576	828	142	253	3	66	...	38	1462	19.0	34
Lou Hudson	58	1745	413	905	.456	142	169	.840	48	81	129	155	160	2	67	...	19	968	16.7	39
Tom Henderson*	46	1568	196	453	.433	126	168	.750	18	106	124	386	74	0	79	...	8	518	11.3	27
Ken Charles	82	2487	354	855	.414	205	256	.801	41	127	168	295	240	4	141	...	45	913	11.1	27
Joe Meriweather	74	2068	319	607	.526	182	255	.714	216	380	596	82	324	21	41	...	82	820	11.1	27
Claude Terry†	12	241	47	87	.540	18	21	.857	8	10	18	25	21	0	9	...	1	112	9.3	22
Claude Terry‡	45	545	96	191	.503	36	44	.818	12	34	46	58	48	0	20	...	1	228	5.1	22
Steve Hawes	44	945	147	305	.482	67	88	.761	78	183	261	63	144	4	36	...	24	361	8.2	19
Tom Barker	59	1354	182	436	.417	112	164	.683	111	290	401	60	223	11	33	...	41	476	8.1	21
Armond Hill	81	1825	175	439	.399	139	174	.799	39	104	143	403	245	8	85	...	6	489	6.0	26
John Brown	77	1405	160	350	.457	121	150	.807	75	161	236	103	217	7	46	...	7	441	5.7	20

	G	Min.	FGM	FGA	Pct.	FTM	FTA	Pct.	REBOUNDS Off.	Def.	Tot.	Ast.	PF	Dq.	Stl.	TO	Blk.	SCORING Pts.	Avg.	Hi.
Randy Denton	45	700	103	256	.402	33	47	.702	81	137	218	33	100	1	14	...	16	239	5.3	25
Bill Willoughby	39	549	75	169	.444	43	63	.683	65	105	170	13	64	1	19	...	23	193	4.9	16
Mike Sojourner	51	551	95	203	.468	41	57	.719	49	97	146	21	66	0	15	...	9	231	4.5	18
Ron Davis	7	67	8	35	.229	4	13	.308	2	5	7	2	9	0	7	...	0	20	2.9	6
Henry Dickerson	6	63	6	12	.500	5	8	.625	0	2	2	11	13	0	1	...	0	17	2.8	6

BOSTON CELTICS

	G	Min.	FGM	FGA	Pct.	FTM	FTA	Pct.	REBOUNDS Off.	Def.	Tot.	Ast.	PF	Dq.	Stl.	TO	Blk.	SCORING Pts.	Avg.	Hi.
Jo Jo White	82	3333	638	1488	.429	333	383	.869	87	296	383	492	193	5	118	...	22	1609	19.6	41
Charlie Scott	43	1581	326	734	.444	129	173	.746	52	139	191	196	155	3	60	...	12	781	18.2	31
John Havlicek	79	2913	580	1283	.452	235	288	.816	109	273	382	400	208	4	84	...	18	1395	17.7	33
Dave Cowens	50	1888	328	756	.434	162	198	.818	147	550	697	248	181	7	46	...	49	818	16.4	33
Sidney Wicks	82	2642	464	1012	.458	310	464	.668	268	556	824	169	331	14	64	...	61	1238	15.1	25
Curtis Rowe	79	2190	315	632	.498	170	240	.708	188	375	563	107	215	3	24	...	47	800	10.1	22
Tom Boswell	70	1083	175	340	.515	96	135	.711	111	195	306	85	237	9	27	...	8	446	6.4	22
Fred Saunders	68	1051	184	395	.466	35	53	.660	73	150	223	85	191	3	26	...	7	403	5.9	21
Kevin Stacom	79	1051	179	438	.409	46	58	.793	40	57	97	117	65	0	19	...	3	404	5.1	16
Steve Kuberski	76	860	131	312	.420	63	83	.759	76	133	209	39	89	0	7	...	5	325	4.3	16
Jim Ard	63	969	96	254	.378	49	76	.645	77	219	296	53	128	1	18	...	28	241	3.8	14
Norm Cook	25	138	27	72	.375	9	17	.529	10	17	27	5	27	0	10	...	3	63	2.5	10
Bobby Wilson	25	131	19	59	.322	11	13	.846	3	6	9	14	19	0	3	...	0	49	2.0	10

BUFFALO BRAVES

	G	Min.	FGM	FGA	Pct.	FTM	FTA	Pct.	REBOUNDS Off.	Def.	Tot.	Ast.	PF	Dq.	Stl.	TO	Blk.	SCORING Pts.	Avg.	Hi.
Bob McAdoo*	20	767	182	400	.455	110	158	.696	66	198	264	65	74	1	16	...	34	474	23.7	42
Randy Smith	82	3094	702	1504	.467	294	386	.762	134	323	457	441	264	2	176	...	8	1698	20.7	41
Adrian Dantley	77	2816	544	1046	.520	476	582	.818	251	336	587	144	215	2	91	...	15	1564	20.3	39
John Shumate	74	2601	407	810	.502	302	450	.671	163	538	701	159	197	1	90	...	84	1116	15.1	26
Ernie DiGregorio	81	2267	365	875	.417	138	146	.945	52	132	184	378	150	1	57	...	3	868	10.7	36
Johnny Neumann*	4	49	15	34	.441	5	6	.833	5	4	9	4	7	0	3	...	2	35	8.8	21
William Averitt	75	1136	234	619	.378	121	169	.716	20	58	78	134	127	2	30	...	5	589	7.9	26
George Johnson†	39	1055	125	279	.448	46	67	.687	117	283	400	78	141	6	22	...	104	296	7.6	16
George Johnson‡	78	1652	190	420	.462	71	98	.724	204	407	611	104	246	8	37	...	177	467	6.0	16
Don Adams	77	1710	216	526	.411	129	173	.746	130	241	371	150	201	0	74	...	16	561	7.3	28
John Gianelli†	57	1283	171	397	.431	55	77	.714	94	203	297	57	117	0	21	...	70	397	7.0	16
John Gianelli‡	76	1913	257	579	.444	90	125	.720	154	321	475	83	171	0	35	...	98	604	7.9	19
Gus Gerard†	41	592	100	244	.410	40	61	.656	51	66	117	43	91	0	23	...	32	240	5.9	18
Gus Gerard‡	65	1048	201	454	.443	78	117	.667	89	128	217	92	164	1	44	...	62	480	7.4	21
Tom McMillen*	20	270	45	92	.489	26	36	.722	29	43	72	16	29	0	1	...	2	116	5.8	19
Jim Price*	20	333	44	104	.423	17	20	.850	5	29	34	38	52	0	25	...	5	105	5.3	17
Fred Foster	59	689	99	247	.401	30	44	.682	33	43	76	48	92	0	16	...	0	228	3.9	14
Zaid Abdul-Aziz	22	195	25	74	.338	33	43	.767	41	49	90	7	21	0	3	...	9	83	3.8	16
Claude Terry*	33	304	49	104	.471	18	23	.783	4	24	28	33	27	0	11	...	0	116	3.5	14
Chuck Williams†	44	556	43	117	.368	38	48	.792	18	49	67	88	34	0	24	...	3	124	2.8	8
Chuck Williams‡	65	867	78	210	.371	68	87	.782	26	75	101	132	60	0	32	...	3	224	3.4	14
Clyde Mayes*	2	7	0	3	.000	2	3	.667	0	3	3	0	2	0	0	...	0	2	1.0	2
Moses Malone*	2	6	0	0	...	0	0	...	0	1	1	0	1	0	0	...	0	0	0.0	0

CHICAGO BULLS

	G	Min.	FGM	FGA	Pct.	FTM	FTA	Pct.	REBOUNDS Off.	Def.	Tot.	Ast.	PF	Dq.	Stl.	TO	Blk.	SCORING Pts.	Avg.	Hi.
Artis Gilmore	82	2877	570	1091	.522	387	586	.660	313	757	1070	199	266	4	44	...	203	1527	18.6	42
Mickey Johnson	81	2847	538	1205	.446	324	407	.796	297	531	828	195	315	10	103	...	64	1400	17.3	37
Wilbur Holland	79	2453	509	1120	.454	158	192	.823	78	175	253	253	201	3	169	...	16	1176	14.9	30
Scott May	72	2369	431	955	.451	188	227	.828	141	296	437	145	185	2	78	...	17	1050	14.6	25
Bob Love*	14	496	68	201	.338	35	46	.761	38	35	73	23	47	1	8	...	2	171	12.2	22
Norm Van Lier	82	3097	300	729	.412	238	306	.778	108	262	370	636	268	3	129	...	16	838	10.2	27
John Mengelt	61	1178	209	458	.456	89	113	.788	29	81	110	114	102	2	37	...	4	507	8.3	26
Jack Marin	54	869	167	359	.465	31	39	.795	27	64	91	62	85	0	13	...	6	365	6.8	18
Paul McCracken	9	119	18	47	.383	11	18	.611	6	10	16	14	17	0	6	...	0	47	5.2	13
John Laskowski	47	562	75	212	.354	27	30	.900	16	47	63	44	22	0	32	...	2	177	3.8	15
Tom Boerwinkle	82	1070	134	273	.491	34	63	.540	101	211	312	189	147	0	19	...	19	302	3.7	19
Cliff Pondexter	78	996	107	257	.416	42	65	.646	77	159	236	41	82	0	34	...	11	256	3.3	12
Tom Kropp	53	480	73	152	.480	28	41	.683	21	26	47	39	77	1	18	...	1	174	3.3	18
Eric Fernsten	5	61	3	15	.200	8	11	.727	9	7	16	6	9	0	1	...	3	14	2.8	5
Phil Hicks†	35	255	41	87	.471	11	13	.846	25	40	65	23	36	0	7	...	0	93	2.7	12
Phil Hicks‡	37	262	41	89	.461	11	13	.846	26	40	66	24	37	0	8	...	0	93	2.5	12
Keith Starr	17	65	6	24	.250	2	2	1.000	6	4	10	6	11	0	1	...	0	14	0.8	4
Willie Smith	2	11	0	1	.000	0	0	...	0	0	0	0	1	0	0	...	0	0	0.0	0

1976-77

CLEVELAND CAVALIERS

	G	Min.	FGM	FGA	Pct.	FTM	FTA	Pct.	REBOUNDS Off.	Def.	Tot.	Ast.	PF	Dq.	Stl.	TO	Blk.	SCORING Pts.	Avg.	Hi.
Campy Russell	70	2109	435	1003	.434	288	370	.778	144	275	419	189	196	3	70	...	24	1158	16.5	36
Austin Carr	82	2409	558	1221	.457	213	268	.795	120	120	240	220	221	3	57	...	10	1329	16.2	42
Bobby Smith	81	2135	513	1149	.446	148	181	.818	92	225	317	152	211	3	61	...	30	1174	14.5	34
Jim Chones	82	2378	450	972	.463	155	212	.731	208	480	688	104	258	3	32	...	77	1055	12.9	24
Jim Cleamons	60	2045	257	592	.434	112	148	.757	99	174	273	308	126	0	66	...	23	626	10.4	25
Dick Snyder	82	1685	316	693	.456	127	149	.852	47	102	149	160	177	2	45	...	30	759	9.3	18
Elmore Smith†	36	675	128	254	.504	56	108	.519	62	169	231	13	98	2	16	...	75	312	8.7	30
Elmore Smith‡	70	1464	241	507	.475	117	213	.549	114	325	439	43	207	4	35	...	144	599	8.6	30
Jim Brewer	81	2672	296	657	.451	97	178	.545	275	487	762	195	214	3	94	...	82	689	8.5	20
Gary Brokaw†	39	596	112	240	.467	58	82	.707	12	47	59	117	79	2	14	...	13	282	7.2	21
Gary Brokaw‡	80	1487	242	564	.429	163	219	.744	22	101	123	228	164	2	36	...	36	647	8.1	27
Foots Walker	62	1216	157	349	.450	89	115	.774	55	105	160	254	124	1	83	...	4	403	6.5	23
Nate Thurmond	49	997	100	246	.407	68	106	.642	121	253	374	83	128	2	16	...	81	268	5.5	13
Rowland Garrett*	29	215	40	93	.430	18	22	.818	10	30	40	7	30	0	7	...	3	98	3.4	12
John Lambert	63	555	67	157	.427	25	36	.694	62	92	154	31	75	0	16	...	18	159	2.5	11
Mo Howard*	9	28	8	15	.533	5	6	.833	2	3	5	5	7	0	1	...	2	21	2.3	8
Chuckie Williams	22	65	14	47	.298	9	12	.750	3	1	4	7	7	0	1	...	0	37	1.7	6

DENVER NUGGETS

	G	Min.	FGM	FGA	Pct.	FTM	FTA	Pct.	REBOUNDS Off.	Def.	Tot.	Ast.	PF	Dq.	Stl.	TO	Blk.	SCORING Pts.	Avg.	Hi.
David Thompson	82	3001	824	1626	.507	477	623	.766	138	196	334	337	236	1	114	...	53	2125	25.9	44
Dan Issel	79	2507	660	1282	.515	445	558	.797	211	485	696	177	246	7	91	...	29	1765	22.3	40
Bobby Jones	82	2419	501	879	.570	236	329	.717	174	504	678	264	238	3	186	...	162	1238	15.1	27
Mack Calvin†	29	625	100	225	.444	123	144	.854	19	30	49	115	53	0	27	...	1	323	11.1	26
Mack Calvin‡	76	1438	220	544	.404	287	338	.849	36	60	96	240	127	0	61	...	3	727	9.6	26
Gus Gerard*	24	456	101	210	.481	38	56	.679	38	62	100	49	73	1	21	...	30	240	10.0	21
Willie Wise	75	1403	237	513	.462	142	218	.651	76	177	253	142	180	2	60	...	18	616	8.2	20
Ted McClain	72	2002	245	551	.445	99	133	.744	52	177	229	324	255	9	106	...	13	589	8.2	18
Jim Price†	55	1384	188	422	.445	59	74	.797	41	143	184	208	181	3	96	...	14	435	7.9	20
Jim Price‡	81	1828	253	567	.446	83	103	.806	50	181	231	261	247	3	128	...	20	589	7.3	20
Paul Silas	81	1959	206	572	.360	170	225	.756	236	370	606	132	183	0	58	...	23	582	7.2	20
Marvin Webster	80	1276	198	400	.495	143	220	.650	152	332	484	62	149	2	23	...	118	539	6.7	17
Chuck Williams*	21	311	35	93	.376	30	39	.769	8	26	34	44	26	0	8	...	0	100	4.8	14
Byron Beck	53	480	107	246	.435	36	44	.818	45	51	96	33	59	1	15	...	1	250	4.7	16
Roland Taylor	79	1548	132	314	.420	37	65	.569	90	121	211	288	202	0	132	...	9	301	3.8	11
Monte Towe	51	409	56	138	.406	18	25	.720	8	26	34	87	61	0	16	...	0	130	2.5	8

DETROIT PISTONS

	G	Min.	FGM	FGA	Pct.	FTM	FTA	Pct.	REBOUNDS Off.	Def.	Tot.	Ast.	PF	Dq.	Stl.	TO	Blk.	SCORING Pts.	Avg.	Hi.
Bob Lanier	64	2446	678	1269	.534	260	318	.818	200	545	745	214	174	0	70	...	126	1616	25.3	40
M.L. Carr	82	2643	443	931	.476	205	279	.735	211	420	631	181	287	8	165	...	58	1091	13.3	29
Howard Porter	78	2200	465	962	.483	103	120	.858	155	303	458	53	202	0	50	...	73	1033	13.2	27
Chris Ford	82	2539	437	918	.476	131	170	.771	96	174	270	337	192	1	179	...	26	1005	12.3	33
Ralph Simpson	77	1597	356	834	.427	138	195	.708	48	133	181	180	100	0	68	...	5	850	11.0	25
Eric Money	73	1586	329	631	.521	90	114	.789	43	81	124	243	199	3	91	...	14	748	10.2	32
Marvin Barnes	53	989	202	452	.447	106	156	.679	69	184	253	45	139	1	38	...	33	510	9.6	33
Kevin Porter	81	2117	310	605	.512	97	133	.729	28	70	98	592	271	8	88	...	8	717	8.9	28
Leon Douglas	82	1626	245	512	.479	127	229	.555	181	345	526	68	294	10	44	...	81	617	7.5	30
Al Eberhard	68	1219	181	380	.476	109	138	.790	76	145	221	50	197	4	45	...	15	471	6.9	24
George Trapp	6	68	15	29	.517	3	4	.750	4	6	10	3	13	0	0	...	1	33	5.5	15
Phil Sellers	44	329	73	190	.384	52	72	.722	19	22	41	25	56	0	22	...	0	198	4.5	17
Cornelius Cash	6	49	9	23	.391	3	6	.500	8	8	16	1	8	0	2	...	1	21	3.5	11
Roger Brown	43	322	21	56	.375	18	26	.692	31	59	90	12	68	4	15	...	18	60	1.4	10

GOLDEN STATE WARRIORS

	G	Min.	FGM	FGA	Pct.	FTM	FTA	Pct.	REBOUNDS Off.	Def.	Tot.	Ast.	PF	Dq.	Stl.	TO	Blk.	SCORING Pts.	Avg.	Hi.
Rick Barry	79	2904	682	1551	.440	359	392	.916	73	349	422	475	194	2	172	...	58	1723	21.8	42
Phil Smith	82	2880	631	1318	.479	295	376	.785	101	231	332	328	227	0	98	...	29	1557	19.0	51
Jamaal Wilkes	76	2579	548	1147	.478	247	310	.797	155	423	578	211	222	1	127	...	16	1343	17.7	32
Gus Williams	82	1930	325	701	.464	112	150	.747	72	161	233	292	218	4	121	...	19	762	9.3	26
Robert Parish	77	1384	288	573	.503	121	171	.708	201	342	543	74	224	7	55	...	94	697	9.1	30
Clifford Ray	77	2018	263	450	.584	105	199	.528	199	416	615	112	242	5	74	...	81	631	8.2	23
Derrek Dickey	49	856	158	345	.458	45	61	.738	100	140	240	63	101	1	20	...	11	361	7.4	20
Charles Dudley	79	1682	220	421	.523	129	203	.635	119	177	296	347	169	0	67	...	6	569	7.2	19
Charles Johnson	79	1196	255	583	.437	49	69	.710	50	91	141	91	134	1	77	...	7	559	7.1	22
Sonny Parker	65	889	154	292	.527	71	92	.772	85	88	173	59	77	0	53	...	26	379	5.8	20
Larry McNeill†	16	137	29	61	.475	28	31	.903	18	31	49	3	19	0	6	...	1	86	5.4	11
Larry McNeill‡	24	230	47	112	.420	52	61	.852	28	47	75	6	32	1	10	...	2	146	6.1	23
Dwight Davis	33	552	55	124	.444	49	72	.681	34	61	95	59	93	1	11	...	8	159	4.8	12

1976-77

| | | | | | | REBOUNDS | | | | | | | | | SCORING | | |
	G	Min.	FGM	FGA	Pct.	FTM	FTA	Pct.	Off.	Def.	Tot.	Ast.	PF	Dq.	Stl.	TO	Blk.	Pts.	Avg.	Hi.
George Johnson*	39	597	73	150	.487	25	31	.806	87	124	211	26	105	2	15	...	73	171	4.4	13
Marshall Rogers	26	176	43	116	.371	14	15	.933	6	5	11	10	33	0	8	...	3	100	3.8	10

HOUSTON ROCKETS

| | | | | | | REBOUNDS | | | | | | | | | SCORING | | |
	G	Min.	FGM	FGA	Pct.	FTM	FTA	Pct.	Off.	Def.	Tot.	Ast.	PF	Dq.	Stl.	TO	Blk.	Pts.	Avg.	Hi.
Rudy Tomjanovich	81	3130	733	1437	.510	287	342	.839	172	512	684	172	198	1	57	...	27	1753	21.6	40
Calvin Murphy	82	2764	596	1216	.490	272	307	.886	54	118	172	386	281	6	144	...	8	1464	17.9	34
Moses Malone†	80	2500	389	810	.480	305	440	.693	437	634	1071	89	274	3	67	...	181	1083	13.5	26
Moses Malone‡	82	2506	389	810	.480	305	440	.693	437	635	1072	89	275	3	67	...	181	1083	13.2	26
Mike Newlin	82	2119	387	850	.455	269	304	.885	53	151	204	320	226	2	60	...	3	1043	12.7	38
John Lucas	82	2531	388	814	.477	135	171	.789	55	164	219	463	174	0	125	...	19	911	11.1	25
Kevin Kunnert	81	2050	333	685	.486	93	126	.738	210	459	669	154	361	17	35	...	105	759	9.4	31
John Johnson	79	1738	319	696	.458	94	132	.712	75	191	266	163	199	1	47	...	24	732	9.3	30
Dwight Jones	74	1239	167	338	.494	101	126	.802	98	186	284	48	175	1	38	...	19	435	5.9	18
Ed Ratleff	37	533	70	161	.435	26	42	.619	24	53	77	43	45	0	20	...	6	166	4.5	12
Tom Owens	46	462	68	135	.504	52	76	.684	47	95	142	18	96	2	4	...	13	188	4.1	13
Rudy White	46	368	47	106	.443	15	25	.600	13	28	41	35	39	0	11	...	1	109	2.4	14
Eugene Kennedy	32	277	31	58	.534	3	8	.375	14	37	51	6	45	1	7	...	5	65	2.0	10
Dave Wohl*	14	62	7	17	.412	4	4	1.000	1	4	5	15	18	1	0	...	0	18	1.3	4
Phil Hicks*	2	7	0	2	.000	0	0	...	1	0	1	1	1	0	1	...	0	0	0.0	0

INDIANA PACERS

| | | | | | | REBOUNDS | | | | | | | | | SCORING | | |
	G	Min.	FGM	FGA	Pct.	FTM	FTA	Pct.	Off.	Def.	Tot.	Ast.	PF	Dq.	Stl.	TO	Blk.	Pts.	Avg.	Hi.
Billy Knight	78	3117	831	1687	.493	413	506	.816	223	359	582	260	197	0	117	...	19	2075	26.6	43
John Williamson†	30	1055	261	544	.480	98	125	.784	18	56	74	111	103	1	48	...	7	620	20.7	33
John Williamson‡	72	2481	618	1347	.459	259	329	.787	42	151	193	201	246	4	107	...	13	1495	20.8	37
Dan Roundfield	61	1645	342	734	.466	164	239	.686	179	339	518	69	243	8	61	...	131	848	13.9	33
Wil Jones	80	2709	438	1019	.430	166	223	.744	218	386	604	189	305	10	102	...	80	1042	13.0	26
Dave Robisch	80	1966	369	811	.455	213	256	.832	171	383	554	158	169	1	55	...	37	951	11.9	30
Darnell Hillman	82	2302	359	811	.443	161	244	.660	228	465	693	166	353	15	95	...	106	879	10.7	27
Michael Flynn	73	1324	250	573	.436	101	142	.711	76	11	87	179	106	0	57	...	6	601	8.2	24
Don Buse	81	2947	266	639	.416	114	145	.786	66	204	270	685	129	0	281	...	16	646	8.0	19
Freddie Lewis	32	552	81	199	.407	62	77	.805	17	30	47	56	58	0	18	...	2	224	7.0	20
Steve Green	70	918	183	424	.432	84	113	.743	79	90	177	46	157	2	46	...	12	450	6.4	24
Mel Bennett	67	911	101	294	.344	112	187	.599	110	127	237	70	155	0	37	...	33	314	4.7	19
Clyde Mayes*	2	21	3	7	.429	1	4	.250	4	3	7	3	5	0	0	...	2	7	3.5	4
Len Elmore	6	46	7	17	.412	4	5	.800	7	8	15	2	11	0	0	...	4	18	3.0	7
Jerome Anderson	27	164	26	59	.441	14	20	.700	9	3	12	10	26	0	6	...	2	66	2.4	14
Rudy Hackett†	5	38	3	8	.375	6	9	.667	3	7	10	3	7	0	0	...	1	12	2.4	3
Rudy Hackett‡	6	46	3	10	.300	8	14	.571	4	9	13	3	8	0	0	...	1	14	2.3	3
Darrell Elston	5	40	2	14	.143	1	2	.500	1	5	6	2	6	0	1	...	0	5	1.0	5

KANSAS CITY KINGS

| | | | | | | REBOUNDS | | | | | | | | | SCORING | | |
	G	Min.	FGM	FGA	Pct.	FTM	FTA	Pct.	Off.	Def.	Tot.	Ast.	PF	Dq.	Stl.	TO	Blk.	Pts.	Avg.	Hi.
Ron Boone	82	3021	747	1577	.474	324	384	.844	128	193	321	338	258	1	119	...	19	1818	22.2	43
Brian Taylor	72	2488	501	995	.504	225	275	.818	88	150	238	320	206	1	199	...	16	1227	17.0	38
Scott Wedman	81	2743	521	1133	.460	206	241	.855	187	319	506	227	226	3	100	...	23	1248	15.4	38
Richard Washington	82	2265	446	1034	.431	177	254	.697	201	497	698	85	324	13	63	...	90	1069	13.0	30
Sam Lacey	82	2595	327	774	.422	215	282	.762	189	545	734	386	292	9	119	...	133	869	10.6	28
Bill Robinzine	75	1594	307	677	.453	159	216	.736	164	310	474	95	283	7	86	...	13	773	10.3	27
Ollie Johnson	81	1386	218	446	.489	101	115	.878	68	144	212	105	169	1	43	...	21	537	6.6	18
Jim Eakins	82	1338	151	336	.449	188	222	.847	112	249	361	119	195	1	29	...	49	490	6.0	23
Andre McCarter	59	725	119	257	.463	32	45	.711	16	39	55	99	63	0	23	...	0	270	4.6	22
Mike Barr	73	1224	122	279	.437	41	57	.719	33	97	130	175	96	0	52	...	18	285	3.9	14
Glenn Hansen	41	289	67	155	.432	23	32	.719	28	31	59	25	44	0	13	...	3	157	3.8	13
Bob Bigelow	29	162	35	70	.500	15	17	.882	8	19	27	8	17	0	3	...	1	85	2.9	11

LOS ANGELES LAKERS

| | | | | | | REBOUNDS | | | | | | | | | SCORING | | |
	G	Min.	FGM	FGA	Pct.	FTM	FTA	Pct.	Off.	Def.	Tot.	Ast.	PF	Dq.	Stl.	TO	Blk.	Pts.	Avg.	Hi.
Kareem Abdul-Jabbar	82	3016	888	1533	.579	376	536	.701	266	824	1090	319	262	4	101	...	261	2152	26.2	40
Cazzie Russell	82	2583	578	1179	.490	188	219	.858	86	208	294	210	163	1	86	...	7	1344	16.4	35
Lucius Allen	78	2482	472	1035	.456	195	252	.774	58	193	251	405	183	0	116	...	19	1139	14.6	30
Kermit Washington	53	1342	191	380	.503	132	187	.706	182	310	492	48	183	1	43	...	52	514	9.7	20
Earl Tatum	68	1249	283	607	.466	72	100	.720	83	153	236	118	168	1	85	...	22	638	9.4	23
Mack Calvin*	12	207	27	82	.329	41	48	.854	6	10	16	21	16	0	11	...	1	95	7.9	20
Don Ford	82	1782	262	570	.460	73	102	.716	105	248	353	133	170	0	60	...	21	597	7.3	19
Bo Lamar	71	1165	228	561	.406	46	68	.676	30	62	92	177	73	0	59	...	3	502	7.1	22
Tom Abernethy	70	1378	169	349	.484	101	134	.754	113	178	291	98	118	1	49	...	10	439	6.3	19
Don Chaney	81	2408	213	522	.408	70	94	.745	120	210	330	308	224	4	140	...	33	496	6.1	16
Johnny Neumann†	59	888	146	363	.402	54	81	.667	19	44	63	137	127	2	28	...	8	346	5.9	24

	G	Min.	FGM	FGA	Pct.	FTM	FTA	Pct.	Off.	Def.	Tot.	Ast.	PF	Dq.	Stl.	TO	Blk.	Pts.	Avg.	Hi.
Johnny Neumann‡	63	937	161	397	.406	59	87	.678	24	48	72	141	134	2	31	...	10	381	6.0	24
C.J. Kupec	82	908	153	342	.447	78	101	.772	76	123	199	53	113	0	18	...	4	384	4.7	14
Cornell Warner	14	170	25	53	.472	4	6	.667	21	48	69	11	28	0	1	...	2	54	3.9	10
Allen Murphy	2	18	1	5	.200	3	7	.429	3	1	4	0	5	0	0	...	0	5	2.5	3
Marv Roberts	28	209	27	76	.355	4	6	.667	9	16	25	19	34	0	4	...	2	58	2.1	12

MILWAUKEE BUCKS

	G	Min.	FGM	FGA	Pct.	FTM	FTA	Pct.	Off.	Def.	Tot.	Ast.	PF	Dq.	Stl.	TO	Blk.	Pts.	Avg.	Hi.
Bob Dandridge	70	2501	585	1253	.467	283	367	.771	146	294	440	268	222	1	95	...	28	1453	20.8	37
Brian Winters	78	2717	652	1308	.498	205	242	.847	64	167	231	337	228	1	114	...	29	1509	19.3	43
Junior Bridgeman	82	2410	491	1094	.449	197	228	.864	129	287	416	205	221	3	82	...	26	1179	14.4	41
Swen Nater	72	1960	383	725	.528	172	228	.754	266	599	865	108	214	6	54	...	51	938	13.0	30
Dave Meyers	50	1262	179	383	.467	127	192	.661	122	219	341	86	152	4	42	...	32	485	9.7	31
Gary Brokaw*	41	891	130	324	.401	105	137	.766	10	54	64	111	85	0	22	...	23	365	8.9	27
Quinn Buckner	79	2095	299	689	.434	83	154	.539	91	173	264	372	291	5	192	...	21	681	8.6	21
Elmore Smith*	34	789	113	253	.447	61	105	.581	52	156	208	30	109	2	19	...	69	287	8.4	21
Fred Carter†	47	875	166	399	.416	58	77	.753	45	48	93	104	96	0	28	...	7	390	8.3	27
Fred Carter‡	61	1112	209	500	.418	68	96	.708	55	62	117	125	125	0	39	...	9	486	8.0	27
Jim Price*	6	111	21	41	.512	7	9	.778	4	9	13	15	14	0	7	...	1	49	8.2	20
Scott Lloyd	69	1025	153	324	.472	95	126	.754	81	129	210	33	158	5	21	...	13	401	5.8	22
Kevin Restani	64	1116	173	334	.518	12	24	.500	81	181	262	88	102	0	33	...	11	358	5.6	22
Alex English	60	648	132	277	.477	46	60	.767	68	100	168	25	78	0	17	...	18	310	5.2	21
Rowland Garrett†	33	383	66	146	.452	23	29	.793	27	45	72	20	50	0	14	...	7	155	4.7	12
Rowland Garrett‡	62	598	106	239	.444	41	51	.804	37	75	112	27	80	0	21	...	10	253	4.1	12
Lloyd Walton	53	678	88	188	.468	53	65	.815	15	36	51	141	52	0	40	...	2	229	4.3	13
Mickey Davis	19	165	29	68	.426	23	25	.920	11	18	29	20	11	0	6	...	4	81	4.3	9
Glenn McDonald	9	79	8	34	.235	3	4	.750	8	4	12	7	11	0	4	...	0	19	2.1	12

NEW ORLEANS JAZZ

	G	Min.	FGM	FGA	Pct.	FTM	FTA	Pct.	Off.	Def.	Tot.	Ast.	PF	Dq.	Stl.	TO	Blk.	Pts.	Avg.	Hi.
Pete Maravich	73	3041	886	2047	.433	501	600	.835	90	284	374	392	191	1	84	...	22	2273	31.1	68
Gail Goodrich	27	609	136	305	.446	68	85	.800	25	36	61	74	43	0	22	...	2	340	12.6	28
Nate Williams	79	1776	414	917	.451	146	194	.753	107	199	306	92	200	0	76	...	16	974	12.3	41
Aaron James	52	1059	238	486	.490	89	114	.781	56	130	186	55	127	1	20	...	5	565	10.9	36
Jim McElroy	73	2029	301	640	.470	169	217	.779	55	128	183	260	119	3	60	...	8	771	10.6	37
Freddie Boyd	47	1212	194	406	.478	79	98	.806	19	71	90	147	78	0	44	...	6	467	9.9	24
E.C. Coleman	77	2369	290	628	.462	82	112	.732	149	399	548	103	280	9	62	...	32	662	8.6	22
Ron Behagen	60	1170	213	509	.418	90	126	.714	144	287	431	83	166	1	41	...	19	516	8.6	24
Rich Kelley	76	1505	184	386	.477	156	197	.792	210	377	587	208	244	7	45	...	63	524	6.9	21
Bud Stallworth	40	526	126	272	.463	17	29	.586	19	52	71	23	76	1	19	...	11	269	6.7	26
Otto Moore	81	2084	193	477	.405	91	134	.679	170	466	636	181	231	3	54	...	117	477	5.9	17
Mo Howard†	23	317	56	117	.479	19	29	.655	15	19	34	37	44	0	16	...	6	131	5.7	17
Mo Howard‡	32	345	64	132	.485	24	35	.686	17	22	39	42	51	0	17	...	8	152	4.8	17
Paul Griffin	81	1645	140	256	.547	145	201	.721	167	328	495	167	241	6	50	...	43	425	5.2	17
Andy Walker	40	438	72	156	.462	36	47	.766	23	52	75	32	59	0	20	...	7	180	4.5	17

NEW YORK KNICKERBOCKERS

	G	Min.	FGM	FGA	Pct.	FTM	FTA	Pct.	Off.	Def.	Tot.	Ast.	PF	Dq.	Stl.	TO	Blk.	Pts.	Avg.	Hi.
Bob McAdoo†	52	2031	558	1045	.534	271	358	.757	133	529	662	140	188	2	61	...	65	1387	26.7	43
Bob McAdoo‡	72	2798	740	1445	.512	381	516	.738	199	727	926	205	262	3	77	...	99	1861	25.8	43
Earl Monroe	77	2656	613	1185	.517	307	366	.839	45	178	223	366	197	0	91	...	23	1533	19.9	37
Walt Frazier	76	2687	532	1089	.489	259	336	.771	52	241	293	403	194	0	132	...	9	1323	17.4	41
Spencer Haywood	31	1021	202	449	.450	109	131	.832	77	203	280	50	72	0	14	...	29	513	16.5	35
Lonnie Shelton	82	2104	398	836	.476	159	225	.707	220	413	633	149	363	10	125	...	98	955	11.6	31
John Gianelli*	19	630	86	182	.473	35	48	.729	60	118	178	26	54	0	14	...	28	207	10.9	19
Jim McMillian	67	2158	298	642	.464	67	86	.779	66	241	307	139	103	0	63	...	5	663	9.9	25
Tom McMillen†	56	1222	229	471	.486	70	87	.805	85	232	317	51	134	0	10	...	4	528	9.4	31
Tom McMillen‡	76	1492	274	563	.487	96	123	.780	114	275	389	67	163	0	11	...	6	644	8.5	31
Dennis Layton	56	765	134	277	.484	58	73	.795	11	36	47	154	87	0	21	...	6	326	5.8	24
Luther Burden	61	608	148	352	.420	51	85	.600	26	40	66	62	88	0	47	...	1	347	5.7	21
Neal Walk	11	135	28	57	.491	6	7	.857	5	22	27	6	22	0	4	...	3	62	5.6	17
Butch Beard	70	1082	148	293	.505	75	109	.688	50	113	163	144	137	0	57	...	5	371	5.3	18
Mel Davis*	22	342	41	110	.373	22	31	.710	30	70	100	24	45	0	9	...	1	104	4.7	13
Bill Bradley	67	1027	127	274	.464	34	42	.810	27	76	103	128	122	0	25	...	8	288	4.3	20
Phil Jackson	76	1033	102	232	.440	51	71	.718	75	154	229	85	184	4	33	...	18	255	3.4	19
Dean Meminger	32	254	15	36	.417	13	23	.565	12	14	26	29	17	0	8	...	1	43	1.3	10

NEW YORK NETS

	G	Min.	FGM	FGA	Pct.	FTM	FTA	Pct.	Off.	Def.	Tot.	Ast.	PF	Dq.	Stl.	TO	Blk.	Pts.	Avg.	Hi.
John Williamson*	42	1426	357	803	.445	161	204	.789	24	95	119	90	143	3	59	...	6	875	20.8	37
Nate Archibald	34	1277	250	560	.446	197	251	.785	22	58	80	254	77	1	59	...	11	697	20.5	34
Robert Hawkins	52	1481	406	909	.447	194	282	.688	67	87	154	93	163	2	77	...	26	1006	19.3	44
Mike Bantom†	33	114	224	474	.473	166	226	.735	101	184	285	50	120	4	28	...	28	614	18.6	32
Mike Bantom‡	77	1909	361	755	.478	224	310	.723	184	287	471	102	233	7	63	...	49	946	12.3	32
Al Skinner	79	2256	382	887	.431	231	292	.791	112	251	363	289	279	7	103	...	53	995	12.6	24
Rich Jones	34	877	134	348	.385	92	121	.760	48	146	194	46	109	2	38	...	11	360	10.6	20
Jan van Breda Kolff	72	2398	271	609	.445	195	228	.855	156	304	460	117	205	2	74	...	68	737	10.2	24
Bob Love†	13	228	49	106	.462	33	39	.846	15	23	38	4	23	0	1	...	2	131	10.1	20
Tim Bassett	76	2442	293	739	.396	101	177	.571	175	466	641	109	246	10	95	...	53	687	9.0	24
Mel Davis†	34	752	127	354	.359	42	60	.700	68	125	193	47	85	0	22	...	4	296	8.7	25
Mel Davis‡	56	1094	168	464	.362	64	91	.703	98	195	293	71	130	0	31	...	5	400	7.1	25
Larry McNeill*	8	93	18	51	.353	24	30	.800	10	16	26	3	13	1	4	...	1	60	7.5	23
Dave Wohl†	37	924	109	273	.399	57	85	.671	15	61	76	127	97	1	39	...	6	275	7.4	22
Dave Wohl‡	51	986	116	290	.400	61	89	.685	16	65	81	142	115	2	39	...	6	293	5.7	22
Jim Fox	71	1165	184	398	.462	95	114	.833	100	229	329	49	158	1	20	...	25	463	6.5	21
Chuck Terry	61	1075	128	318	.403	48	62	.774	43	100	143	39	120	0	58	...	10	304	5.0	19
Kim Hughes	81	2081	151	354	.427	19	69	.275	189	375	564	98	308	9	122	...	119	321	4.0	14
Mel Daniels	11	126	13	35	.371	13	23	.565	10	24	34	6	29	0	3	...	11	39	3.5	7
Earl Williams	1	7	0	2	.000	3	6	.500	1	1	2	1	2	0	0	...	1	3	3.0	3
Rudy Hackett*	1	8	0	2	.000	2	5	.400	1	2	3	0	1	0	0	...	0	2	2.0	2

PHILADELPHIA 76ERS

	G	Min.	FGM	FGA	Pct.	FTM	FTA	Pct.	Off.	Def.	Tot.	Ast.	PF	Dq.	Stl.	TO	Blk.	Pts.	Avg.	Hi.
Julius Erving	82	2940	685	1373	.499	400	515	.777	192	503	695	306	251	1	159	...	113	1770	21.6	40
George McGinnis	79	2769	659	1439	.458	372	546	.681	324	587	911	302	299	4	163	...	37	1690	21.4	37
Doug Collins	58	2037	426	823	.518	210	250	.840	64	131	195	271	174	2	70	...	15	1062	18.3	33
World B. Free	78	2253	467	1022	.457	334	464	.720	97	140	237	266	207	2	75	...	25	1268	16.3	39
Steve Mix	75	1958	288	551	.523	215	263	.817	127	249	370	152	107	0	90	...	20	791	10.5	37
Henry Bibby	81	2639	302	702	.430	221	282	.784	86	187	273	356	200	2	108	...	5	825	10.2	28
Fred Carter*	14	237	43	101	.426	10	19	.526	10	14	24	21	29	0	11	...	2	96	6.9	19
Caldwell Jones	82	2023	215	424	.507	64	116	.552	190	476	666	92	301	3	43	...	200	494	6.0	16
Darryl Dawkins	59	684	135	215	.628	40	79	.506	59	171	230	24	129	1	12	...	49	310	5.3	20
Mike Dunleavy	32	359	60	145	.414	34	45	.756	10	24	34	50	04	1	10	...	2	154	4.8	32
Joe Bryant	61	612	107	240	.446	53	70	.757	45	72	117	48	84	1	36	...	13	267	4.4	22
Jim Barnett	16	231	28	64	.438	10	18	.556	7	7	14	23	28	0	4	...	0	66	4.1	10
Harvey Catchings	53	864	62	123	.504	33	47	.702	64	170	234	30	130	1	23	...	78	157	3.0	16
Terry Furlow	32	174	34	100	.340	16	18	.889	18	21	39	19	11	0	7	...	2	84	2.6	13

PHOENIX SUNS

	G	Min.	FGM	FGA	Pct.	FTM	FTA	Pct.	Off.	Def.	Tot.	Ast.	PF	Dq.	Stl.	TO	Blk.	Pts.	Avg.	Hi.
Paul Westphal	81	2600	682	1317	.518	362	439	.825	57	133	190	459	171	1	134	...	21	1726	21.3	40
Alvan Adams	72	2278	522	1102	.474	252	334	.754	180	472	652	322	260	4	95	...	87	1296	18.0	47
Ricky Sobers	79	2005	414	834	.496	243	289	.841	82	152	234	238	258	3	93	...	14	1071	13.6	32
Curtis Perry	44	1391	179	414	.432	112	142	.789	149	246	395	79	163	3	49	...	28	470	10.7	20
Ron Lee	82	1849	347	786	.441	142	210	.676	99	200	299	263	276	10	156	...	33	836	10.2	33
Gar Heard	46	1363	173	457	.379	100	138	.725	120	320	440	89	139	2	55	...	55	446	9.7	28
Ira Terrell	78	1751	277	545	.508	111	176	.630	99	288	387	103	165	0	41	...	47	665	8.5	22
Dick Van Arsdale	78	1535	227	498	.456	145	166	.873	31	86	117	120	94	0	35	...	5	599	7.7	19
Keith Erickson	50	949	142	294	.483	37	50	.740	36	108	144	104	122	0	30	...	7	321	6.4	19
Tom Van Arsdale	77	1425	171	395	.433	102	145	.703	47	137	184	67	163	0	20	...	3	444	5.8	20
Dennis Awtrey	72	1760	160	373	.429	91	126	.722	111	245	356	182	170	1	23	...	31	411	5.7	17
Butch Feher	48	487	86	162	.531	76	99	.768	18	56	74	36	46	0	11	...	7	248	5.2	23
Dale Schlueter	39	337	26	72	.361	18	31	.581	30	50	80	38	62	0	8	...	8	70	1.8	7

PORTLAND TRAIL BLAZERS

	G	Min.	FGM	FGA	Pct.	FTM	FTA	Pct.	Off.	Def.	Tot.	Ast.	PF	Dq.	Stl.	TO	Blk.	Pts.	Avg.	Hi.
Maurice Lucas	79	2863	632	1357	.466	335	438	.765	271	628	899	229	294	6	83	...	56	1599	20.2	41
Bill Walton	65	2264	491	930	.528	228	327	.697	211	723	934	245	174	5	66	...	211	1210	18.6	30
Lionel Hollins	76	2224	452	1046	.432	215	287	.749	52	158	210	313	265	5	166	...	38	1119	14.7	43
Bob Gross	82	2232	376	711	.529	183	215	.851	173	221	394	242	255	7	107	...	57	935	11.4	25
Larry Steele	81	1680	326	652	.500	183	227	.806	71	117	188	172	216	3	118	...	13	835	10.3	28
Dave Twardzik	74	1937	263	430	.612	239	284	.842	75	127	202	247	228	6	128	...	15	765	10.3	28
Herm Gilliam	80	1665	326	744	.438	92	120	.767	64	137	201	170	168	1	76	...	6	744	9.3	23
Johnny Davis	79	1451	320	531	.441	166	209	.794	62	64	126	148	128	1	41	...	11	634	8.0	25
Lloyd Neal	58	955	160	340	.471	77	117	.658	87	168	255	58	148	0	8	...	35	397	6.8	20
Robin Jones	63	1065	139	299	.465	66	109	.606	103	193	296	80	124	3	37	...	38	344	5.5	21
Wally Walker	66	627	137	305	.449	67	100	.670	45	63	108	51	92	0	14	...	2	341	5.2	19
Corky Calhoun	70	743	85	183	.464	66	85	.776	40	104	144	35	123	1	24	...	8	236	3.4	16

1976-77

	G	Min.	FGM	FGA	Pct.	FTM	FTA	Pct.	Off.	Def.	Tot.	Ast.	PF	Dq.	Stl.	TO	Blk.	Pts.	Avg.	Hi.
									REBOUNDS									SCORING		
Clyde Mayes†	5	24	2	9	.222	0	0	...	6	0	6	0	5	0	0	...	2	4	0.8	2
Clyde Mayes‡	9	52	5	19	.263	3	7	.429	10	6	16	3	12	0	0	...	4	13	1.4	4

SAN ANTONIO SPURS

	G	Min.	FGM	FGA	Pct.	FTM	FTA	Pct.	Off.	Def.	Tot.	Ast.	PF	Dq.	Stl.	TO	Blk.	Pts.	Avg.	Hi.
									REBOUNDS									SCORING		
George Gervin	82	2705	726	1335	.544	443	532	.833	134	320	454	238	286	12	105	...	104	1895	23.1	42
Larry Kenon	78	2936	706	1435	.492	293	356	.823	282	597	879	229	190	0	167	...	60	1705	21.9	43
Billy Paultz	82	2694	521	1102	.473	238	320	.744	192	495	687	223	262	5	55	...	173	1280	15.6	31
Allan Bristow	82	2017	365	747	.489	206	258	.798	119	229	348	240	195	1	89	...	2	936	11.4	25
Mark Olberding	82	1949	301	598	.503	251	316	.794	162	287	449	119	277	6	59	...	29	853	10.4	23
Mike Gale	82	2598	353	754	.468	137	167	.820	54	219	273	473	224	3	191	...	50	843	10.3	24
James Silas	22	356	61	142	.430	87	107	.813	7	25	32	50	36	0	13	...	3	209	9.5	28
Mack Calvin*	35	606	93	237	.392	123	146	.842	11	20	31	104	58	0	23	...	1	309	8.8	24
Coby Dietrick	82	1772	285	620	.460	119	166	.717	111	261	372	148	267	8	88	...	57	689	8.4	24
Louie Dampier	80	1634	233	507	.460	64	86	.744	222	54	276	234	93	0	49	...	15	530	6.6	21
Louie Nelson	4	57	7	14	.500	4	7	.571	2	5	7	3	9	0	2	...	0	18	4.5	7
Henry Ward	27	171	34	90	.378	15	17	.882	10	23	33	6	30	0	6	...	5	83	3.1	16
George Karl	29	251	25	73	.342	29	42	.690	4	13	17	46	36	0	10	...	0	79	2.7	9
Mike D'Antoni	2	9	1	3	.333	1	2	.500	0	2	2	2	3	0	0	...	0	3	1.5	2

SEATTLE SUPERSONICS

	G	Min.	FGM	FGA	Pct.	FTM	FTA	Pct.	Off.	Def.	Tot.	Ast.	PF	Dq.	Stl.	TO	Blk.	Pts.	Avg.	Hi.
									REBOUNDS									SCORING		
Fred Brown	72	2098	534	1114	.479	168	190	.884	68	164	232	176	140	1	124	...	19	1236	17.2	42
Donald Watts	79	2627	428	1015	.422	172	293	.587	81	226	307	630	256	5	214	...	25	1028	13.0	37
Nick Weatherspoon†	51	1505	283	614	.461	86	136	.632	109	295	404	51	149	1	49	...	23	652	12.8	25
Nick Weatherspoon‡	62	1657	310	690	.449	91	144	.632	120	308	428	53	168	1	52	...	28	711	11.5	25
Leonard Gray*	25	643	114	262	.435	59	78	.756	23	84	107	55	84	1	27	...	13	287	11.5	23
Bruce Seals	81	1977	378	851	.444	138	195	.708	118	236	354	93	262	6	49	...	58	894	11.0	38
Mike Green	76	1928	290	658	.441	166	235	.706	191	312	503	120	201	1	45	...	129	746	9.8	31
Tom Burleson	82	1803	288	652	.442	220	301	.731	184	367	551	93	259	1	74	...	117	796	9.7	26
Dennis Johnson	81	1667	285	566	.504	179	287	.624	161	141	302	123	221	3	123	...	57	749	9.2	24
Willie Norwood	76	1647	216	461	.469	151	206	.733	127	165	292	99	191	1	62	...	6	583	7.7	21
Mike Bantom*	44	795	137	281	.488	58	84	.690	83	103	186	52	113	3	35	...	21	332	7.5	18
Bob Wilkerson	78	1552	221	573	.386	84	122	.689	96	162	258	171	136	0	72	...	8	526	6.7	20
Dean Tolson	60	587	137	242	.566	85	159	.535	73	84	157	27	83	0	32	...	21	359	6.0	19
Bob Love†	32	450	45	121	.372	41	47	.872	26	61	87	21	50	0	13	...	2	131	4.1	14
Bob Love‡	59	1174	162	428	.379	109	132	.826	79	119	198	48	120	1	22	...	6	433	7.3	22
Frank Oleynick	50	516	81	223	.363	39	53	.736	13	32	45	60	48	0	13	...	4	201	4.0	19
Norton Barnhill	4	10	2	6	.333	0	0	...	2	1	3	1	5	0	0	...	0	4	1.0	2

WASHINGTON BULLETS

	G	Min.	FGM	FGA	Pct.	FTM	FTA	Pct.	Off.	Def.	Tot.	Ast.	PF	Dq.	Stl.	TO	Blk.	Pts.	Avg.	Hi.
									REBOUNDS									SCORING		
Elvin Hayes	82	3364	760	1516	.501	422	614	.687	289	740	1029	158	312	1	87	...	220	1942	23.7	47
Phil Chenier	78	2842	654	1472	.444	270	321	.841	56	243	299	294	166	0	120	...	39	1578	20.2	38
Truck Robinson*	41	1328	264	522	.506	128	189	.677	119	247	366	45	123	0	28	...	18	656	16.0	33
Tom Henderson†	41	1223	175	373	.469	107	145	.738	25	90	115	212	74	0	59	...	9	457	11.1	23
Tom Henderson‡	87	2791	454	826	.449	223	313	.744	43	196	239	598	148	0	138	...	17	975	11.2	27
Dave Bing	64	1516	271	597	.454	136	176	.773	54	89	143	275	150	1	61	...	5	678	10.6	32
Mitch Kupchak	82	1513	341	596	.572	170	246	.691	183	311	494	62	204	3	22	...	34	852	10.4	26
Wes Unseld	82	2860	270	551	.490	100	166	.602	243	634	877	363	253	5	87	...	45	640	7.8	18
Larry Wright	78	1421	262	595	.440	88	115	.765	32	66	98	232	170	0	55	...	5	612	7.8	27
Kevin Grevey	76	1306	224	530	.423	79	119	.664	73	105	178	68	148	1	29	...	9	527	6.9	22
Leonard Gray†	58	996	144	330	.436	59	80	.738	61	125	186	69	189	8	31	...	18	347	6.0	18
Leonard Gray‡	83	1639	258	592	.436	118	158	.747	84	209	293	124	273	9	58	...	31	634	7.6	23
Nick Weatherspoon*	11	152	27	76	.355	5	8	.625	11	13	24	2	19	0	3	...	5	59	5.4	14
Bob Weiss	62	768	62	133	.466	29	37	.784	15	54	69	130	66	0	53	...	7	153	2.5	10
Joe Pace	30	119	24	55	.436	16	29	.552	16	18	34	4	29	0	2	...	17	64	2.1	12
Jimmy Jones	3	33	2	9	.222	2	4	.500	1	3	4	1	4	0	2	...	0	6	2.0	4
Mike Riordan	49	289	34	94	.362	11	15	.733	7	20	27	20	33	0	3	...	2	79	1.6	8

1976-77

* Finished season with another team. † Totals with this team only. ‡ Totals with all teams.

EASTERN CONFERENCE

FIRST ROUND

Boston 2, San Antonio 0
Apr. 12—Tue. San Antonio 94 at Boston 104
Apr. 15—Fri. Boston 113 at San Antonio 109

Washington 2, Cleveland 1
Apr. 13—Wed. Cleveland 100 at Washington 109
Apr. 15—Fri. Washington 83 at Cleveland 91
Apr. 17—Sun. Cleveland 98 at Washington 104

SEMIFINALS

Philadelphia 4, Boston 3
Apr. 17—Sun. Boston 113 at Philadelphia 111
Apr. 20—Wed. Boston 101 at Philadelphia 113
Apr. 22—Fri. Philadelphia 109 at Boston 100
Apr. 24—Sun. Philadelphia 119 at Boston 124
Apr. 27—Wed. Boston 91 at Philadelphia 110
Apr. 29—Fri. Philadelphia 108 at Boston 113
May 1—Sun. Boston 77 at Philadelphia 83

Houston 4, Washington 2
Apr. 19—Tue. Washington 111 at Houston 101
Apr. 21—Thur. Washington 118 at Houston *124
Apr. 24—Sun. Houston 90 at Washington 93
Apr. 26—Tue. Houston 107 at Washington 103
Apr. 29—Fri. Washington 115 at Houston 123
May 1—Sun. Houston 108 at Washington 103

FINALS

Philadelphia 4, Houston 2
May 5—Thur. Houston 117 at Philadelphia 128
May 8—Sun. Houston 97 at Philadelphia 106
May 11—Wed. Philadelphia 94 at Houston 118
May 13—Fri. Philadelphia 107 at Houston 95
May 15—Sun. Houston 118 at Philadelphia 115
May 17—Tue. Philadelphia 112 at Houston 109

WESTERN CONFERENCE

FIRST ROUND

Golden State 2, Detroit 1
Apr. 12—Tue. Detroit 95 at Golden State 90
Apr. 14—Thur. Golden State 138 at Detroit 108
Apr. 17—Sun. Detroit 101 at Golden State 109

Portland 2, Chicago 1
Apr. 12—Tue. Chicago 83 at Portland 96
Apr. 15—Fri. Portland 104 at Chicago 107
Apr. 17—Sun. Chicago 98 at Portland 106

SEMIFINALS

Los Angeles 4, Golden State 3
Apr. 20—Wed. Golden State 106 at Los Angeles 115
Apr. 22—Fri. Golden State 86 at Los Angeles 95
Apr. 24—Sun. Los Angeles 105 at Golden State 109
Apr. 26—Tue. Los Angeles 103 at Golden State 114
Apr. 29—Fri. Golden State 105 at Los Angeles 112
May 1—Sun. Los Angeles 106 at Golden State 115
May 4—Wed. Golden State 84 at Los Angeles 97

Portland 4, Denver 2
Apr. 20—Wed. Portland 101 at Denver 100
Apr. 22—Fri. Portland 110 at Denver 121
Apr. 24—Sun. Denver 106 at Portland 110
Apr. 26—Tue. Denver 96 at Portland 105
May 1—Sun. Portland 105 at Denver *114
May 2—Mon. Denver 92 at Portland 108

FINALS

Portland 4, Los Angeles 0
May 6—Fri. Portland 121 at Los Angeles 109
May 8—Sun. Portland 99 at Los Angeles 97
May 10—Tue. Los Angeles 97 at Portland 102
May 13—Fri. Los Angeles 101 at Portland 105

NBA FINALS

Portland 4, Philadelphia 2
May 22—Sun. Portland 101 at Philadelphia 107
May 26—Thur. Portland 89 at Philadelphia 107
May 29—Sun. Philadelphia 107 at Portland 129
May 31—Tue. Philadelphia 98 at Portland 130
June 3—Fri. Portland 110 at Philadelphia 104
June 5—Sun. Philadelphia 107 at Portland 109

*Denotes number of overtime periods.

1976-77

1975-76

1975-76 NBA CHAMPION BOSTON CELTICS

Front row (from left): Charlie Scott, Paul Silas, Dave Cowens, chairman of the board Irving Levin, head coach Tom Heinsohn, president Red Auerbach, captain John Havlicek, Jo Jo White, Don Nelson. Back row (from left): Dr. Tom Silva, assistant trainer Mark Volk, Kevin Stacom, Glenn McDonald, Tom Boswell, Jim Ard, Steve Kuberski, Jerome Anderson, trainer Frank Challant, Dr. Sam Kane. Inset: assistant coach and chief scout John Killilea.

FINAL STANDINGS

ATLANTIC DIVISION

	Atl.	Bos.	Buf.	Chi.	Cle.	Det.	G.S.	Hou.	K.C.	L.A.	Mil.	N.O.	N.Y.	Phi.	Pho.	Por.	Sea.	Was.	W	L	Pct.	GB
Boston 3	..	4	2	3	4	2	4	2	4	2	4	5	4	4	2	2	3	54	28	.659	..
Buffalo 3	3	..	3	3	1	1	3	4	2	3	4	4	3	3	2	2	2	46	36	.561	8
Philadelphia. . . 3	3	4	4	2	3	1	2	3	2	2	4	2	..	3	4	2	2	46	36	.561	8
New York 2	2	3	4	2	1	0	2	3	1	2	3	..	5	2	3	0	3	38	44	.463	16

CENTRAL DIVISION

	Atl.	Bos.	Buf.	Chi.	Cle.	Det.	G.S.	Hou.	K.C.	L.A.	Mil.	N.O.	N.Y.	Phi.	Pho.	Por.	Sea.	Was.	W	L	Pct.	GB
Cleveland. 5	2	2	4	..	2	1	2	1	2	4	4	3	3	4	3	4	3	4	49	33	.598	..
Washington . . . 5	2	3	4	2	2	1	4	3	3	2	3	2	3	4	2	3	..	48	34	.585	1
Houston 5	1	2	3	4	2	2	..	2	1	2	2	3	3	0	3	2	3	40	42	.488	9
New Orleans . . 4	1	1	2	3	3	2	4	3	1	2	..	2	1	1	3	1	4	38	44	.463	11
Atlanta.	2	2	2	2	1	2	4	2	1	2	2	3	2	0	2	1	1	29	53	.354	20

MIDWEST DIVISION

	Atl.	Bos.	Buf.	Chi.	Cle.	Det.	G.S.	Hou.	K.C.	L.A.	Mil.	N.O.	N.Y.	Phi.	Pho.	Por.	Sea.	Was.	W	L	Pct.	GB
Milwaukee 2	2	1	4	0	4	0	2	5	3	..	2	2	2	3	2	2	2	38	44	.463	..
Detroit. 3	0	3	4	2	..	0	2	5	1	3	1	3	1	1	2	3	2	36	46	.439	2
Kansas City . . . 2	2	0	6	3	2	1	2	..	2	2	1	1	1	3	0	2	1	31	51	.378	7
Chicago. 2	2	1	..	0	3	1	1	1	3	3	2	0	0	2	1	2	0	24	58	.293	14

PACIFIC DIVISION

	Atl.	Bos.	Buf.	Chi.	Cle.	Det.	G.S.	Hou.	K.C.	L.A.	Mil.	N.O.	N.Y.	Phi.	Pho.	Por.	Sea.	Was.	W	L	Pct.	GB
Golden State . . 2	2	3	4	3	5	..	2	4	5	5	2	4	3	4	4	4	3	59	23	.720	..
Seattle. 3	2	2	3	1	2	3	2	3	3	3	3	4	2	3	3	..	1	43	39	.524	16
Phoenix. 4	0	1	3	1	4	2	4	2	4	2	3	2	1	..	5	4	0	42	40	.512	17
Los Angeles. . . 3	0	2	2	2	4	2	3	3	..	2	3	3	2	3	3	1	4	40	42	.488	19
Portland 2	2	2	4	0	3	2	1	5	4	3	1	1	0	2	..	3	2	37	45	.451	22

TEAM STATISTICS

OFFENSIVE

	G	FGM	FGA	Pct.	FTM	FTA	Pct.	REBOUNDS Off.	Def.	Tot.	Ast.	PF	Dq.	Stl.	TO	Blk.	SCORING Pts.	Avg.
Golden State . . 82	82	3691	7982	.462	1620	2158	.751	1349	2912	4261	2041	2022	13	928	1613	416	9002	109.8
Buffalo 82	82	3481	7307	.476	1833	2368	.774	1002	2719	3721	2112	2017	22	720	1743	366	8795	107.3
Los Angeles . . . 82	82	3547	7622	.465	1670	2164	.772	1132	2870	4002	1939	2025	24	674	1612	528	8764	106.9
Philadelphia . . 82	82	3462	7752	.447	1811	2469	.733	1385	2685	4070	1658	2187	35	809	1729	367	8735	106.5
Seattle 82	82	3542	7730	.458	1642	2309	.711	1217	2498	3715	1935	2133	38	866	1615	355	8726	106.4
Houston 82	82	3546	7304	.485	1616	2046	.790	1059	2644	3703	2213	2045	36	656	1665	359	8708	106.2
Boston 82	82	3527	7901	.446	1654	2120	.780	1369	2972	4341	1980	2002	37	561	1609	260	8708	106.2

	G	FGM	FGA	Pct.	FTM	FTA	Pct.	REBOUNDS Off.	Def.	Tot.	Ast.	PF	Dq.	Stl.	TO	Blk.	SCORING Pts.	Avg.
Phoenix	82	3420	7251	.472	1780	2337	.762	1108	2558	3666	2083	2018	31	853	1852	349	8620	105.1
Detroit	82	3524	7598	.464	1557	2049	.760	1205	2545	3750	1751	2086	26	786	1619	332	8605	104.9
Portland	82	3417	7292	.469	1699	2350	.723	1116	2843	3959	2094	2091	35	776	1867	408	8533	104.1
New Orleans	82	3352	7491	.447	1831	2415	.758	1189	2779	3968	1765	2175	30	750	1659	343	8535	104.1
Kansas City	82	3341	7379	.453	1792	2335	.767	1133	2668	3801	1864	2056	44	751	1607	324	8474	103.3
Washington	82	3416	7234	.472	1595	2215	.720	1019	2812	3831	1823	1921	20	696	1672	485	8427	102.8
New York	82	3443	7555	.456	1532	1985	.772	1022	2723	3745	1660	2006	14	575	1403	259	8418	102.7
Atlanta	82	3301	7338	.450	1809	2467	.733	1225	2540	3765	1666	1983	39	790	1553	277	8411	102.6
Milwaukee	82	3456	7435	.465	1437	1952	.736	1094	2688	3782	1817	2041	30	715	1624	468	8349	101.8
Cleveland	82	3497	7709	.454	1346	1827	.737	1192	2588	3780	1844	1871	10	638	1330	397	8340	101.7
Chicago	82	3106	7499	.414	1651	2197	.751	1375	2726	4101	1704	1977	37	627	1413	255	7863	95.9

DEFENSIVE

	FGM	FGA	Pct.	FTM	FTA	Pct.	REBOUNDS Off.	Def.	Tot.	Ast.	PF	Dq.	Stl.	TO	Blk.	SCORING Pts.	Avg.	Dif.
Chicago	3246	6946	.467	1609	2137	.753	930	2809	3739	1669	2081	31	615	1485	461	8101	98.8	-2.9
Cleveland	3262	7188	.454	1610	2152	.748	1134	2792	3926	1728	1860	17	610	1579	325	8134	99.2	+2.5
Washington	3377	7636	.442	1482	1992	.744	1145	2687	3832	1705	1988	33	810	1510	338	8236	100.4	+2.4
Golden State	3437	7742	.444	1583	2150	.736	1288	2730	4018	2006	1946	22	743	1761	395	8457	103.1	+6.7
Milwaukee	3402	7624	.446	1664	2182	.763	1229	2604	3833	1897	1828	21	683	1503	325	8468	103.3	-1.5
New York	3407	7426	.459	1705	2274	.750	1068	2891	3959	1812	1954	31	608	1453	335	8519	103.9	-1.2
Boston	3489	7772	.449	1538	2074	.742	1037	2659	3696	1835	1895	25	650	1422	334	8516	103.9	+2.3
Phoenix	3444	7357	.468	1682	2265	.743	1143	2513	3656	1979	2163	41	912	1746	336	8570	104.5	+0.6
New Orleans	3396	7413	.458	1816	2464	.737	1182	2846	4028	1684	2162	40	777	1748	405	8608	105.0	-0.9
Portland	3405	7531	.452	1825	2333	.782	1121	2657	3778	1920	2128	29	917	1613	386	8635	105.3	-1.2
Atlanta	3529	7357	.480	1592	2102	.757	1186	2728	3914	1778	2177	30	779	1663	427	8650	105.5	-2.9
Detroit	3492	7479	.467	1707	2211	.772	1218	2690	3908	2014	1914	21	724	1671	437	8691	106.0	-1.1
Kansas City	3477	7454	.466	1753	2310	.759	1153	2778	3931	1825	2124	26	680	1639	321	8707	106.2	-2.9
Philadelphia	3467	7737	.448	1780	2334	.763	1435	2717	4152	1849	2151	37	730	1794	342	8714	106.3	+0.2
Buffalo	3558	7722	.461	1611	2156	.747	1183	2645	3828	2079	2137	38	729	1660	319	8727	106.4	+0.9
Seattle	3486	7464	.467	1777	2407	.738	1239	2713	3952	2109	2111	34	745	1852	388	8749	106.7	-0.3
Los Angeles	3592	7980	.450	1573	2140	.732	1384	2837	4221	2032	1987	22	775	1564	363	8757	106.8	+0.1
Houston	3603	7551	.477	1568	2072	.757	1116	2473	3589	2028	2050	23	684	1522	311	8771	107.0	-0.8
Avgs.	3448	7521	.458	1660	2209	.751	1177	2709	3887	1886	2036	29	732	1621	364	8556	104.3	...

HOME/ROAD

	Home	Road	Total		Home	Road	Total
Atlanta	20-21	9-32	29-53	Milwaukee	22-19	16-25	38-44
Boston	31-10	23-18	54-28	New Orleans	22-19	16-25	38-44
Buffalo	28-13	18-23	46-36	New York	24-17	14-27	38-44
Chicago	15-26	9-32	24-58	Philadelphia	34-7	12-29	46-36
Cleveland	29-12	20-21	49-33	Phoenix	27-14	15-26	42-40
Detroit	24-17	12-29	36-46	Portland	26-15	11-30	37-45
Golden State	36-5	23-18	59-23	Seattle	31-10	12-29	43-39
Houston	28-13	12-29	40-42	Washington	31-10	17-24	48-34
Kansas City	25-16	6-35	31-51	Totals	484-254	254-484	738-738
Los Angeles	31-10	9-32	40-42				

INDIVIDUAL LEADERS

POINTS

(minimum 70 games or 1,400 points)

	G	FGM	FTM	Pts.	Avg.
Bob McAdoo, Buffalo	78	934	559	2427	31.1
Kareem Abdul-Jabbar, L.A.	82	914	447	2275	27.7
Pete Maravich, New Orleans	62	604	396	1604	25.9
Nate Archibald, Kansas City	78	717	501	1935	24.8
Fred Brown, Seattle	76	742	273	1757	23.1
George McGinnis, Philadelphia	77	647	475	1769	23.0
Randy Smith, Buffalo	82	702	383	1787	21.8
John Drew, Atlanta	77	586	488	1660	21.6
Bob Dandridge, Milwaukee	73	650	271	1571	21.5
Calvin Murphy, Houston	82	675	372	1722	21.0
Rick Barry, Golden State	81	707	287	1701	21.0
Doug Collins, Philadelphia	77	614	372	1600	20.8
Earl Monroe, New York	76	647	280	1574	20.7
Paul Westphal, Phoenix	82	657	365	1679	20.5
Phil Smith, Golden State	82	659	323	1641	20.0
Phil Chenier, Washington	80	654	282	1590	19.9
Spencer Haywood, New York	78	605	339	1549	19.9
Elvin Hayes, Washington	80	649	287	1585	19.8
Gail Goodrich, Los Angeles	75	583	293	1459	19.5
Bob Love, Chicago	76	543	362	1448	19.1

FIELD GOALS

(minimum 300 made)

	FGM	FGA	Pct.
Wes Unseld, Washington	318	567	.56085
John Shumate, Phoenix-Buffalo	332	592	.56081
Jim McMillian, Buffalo	492	918	.536
Bob Lanier, Detroit	541	1017	.532
Kareem Abdul-Jabbar, Los Angeles	914	1728	.529
Elmore Smith, Milwaukee	498	962	.518
Rudy Tomjanovich, Houston	622	1202	.517
Doug Collins, Philadelphia	614	1196	.513
Ollie Johnson, Kansas City	348	678	.513
Mike Newlin, Houston	569	1123	.507

FREE THROWS

(minimum 125 made)

	FTM	FTA	Pct.
Rick Barry, Golden State	287	311	.923
Calvin Murphy, Houston	372	410	.907
Cazzie Russell, Los Angeles	132	148	.892
Bill Bradley, New York	130	148	.878
Fred Brown, Seattle	273	314	.869
Mike Newlin, Houston	385	445	.865
Jimmy Walker, Kansas City	231	267	.865
Jim McMillian, Buffalo	188	219	.858
Jack Marin, Buffalo-Chicago	161	188	.856
Keith Erickson, Phoenix	134	157	.854

1975-76

ASSISTS

(minimum 70 games or 400 assists)

	G	No.	Avg.
Donald Watts, Seattle	82	661	8.1
Nate Archibald, Kansas City	78	615	7.9
Calvin Murphy, Houston	82	596	7.3
Norm Van Lier, Chicago	76	500	6.6
Rick Barry, Golden State	81	496	6.1
Dave Bing, Washington	82	492	6.0
Randy Smith, Buffalo	82	484	5.9
Alvan Adams, Phoenix	80	450	5.6
Gail Goodrich, Los Angeles	75	421	5.6
Mike Newlin, Houston	82	457	5.6

STEALS

(minimum 70 games or 125 steals)

	G	No.	Avg.
Donald Watts, Seattle	82	261	3.18
George McGinnis, Philadelphia	77	198	2.57
Paul Westphal, Phoenix	82	210	2.56
Rick Barry, Golden State	81	202	2.49
Chris Ford, Detroit	82	178	2.17
Larry Steele, Portland	81	170	2.10
Phil Chenier, Washington	80	158	1.98
Norm Van Lier, Chicago	76	150	1.97
Steve Mix, Philadelphia	81	158	1.95
Fred Brown, Seattle	76	143	1.88

REBOUNDS

(minimum 70 games or 800 rebounds)

	G	Off.	Def.	Tot.	Avg.
Kareem Abdul-Jabbar, L.A.	82	272	1111	1383	16.9
Dave Cowens, Boston	78	335	911	1246	16.0
Wes Unseld, Washington	78	271	765	1036	13.3
Paul Silas, Boston	81	365	660	1025	12.7
Sam Lacey, Kansas City	81	218	806	1024	12.6
George McGinnis, Philadelphia	77	260	707	967	12.6
Bob McAdoo, Buffalo	78	241	724	965	12.4
Elmore Smith, Milwaukee	78	201	692	893	11.4
Spencer Haywood, New York	78	234	644	878	11.3
Elvin Hayes, Washington	80	210	668	878	11.0

BLOCKED SHOTS

(minimum 70 games or 100 blocked shots)

	G	No.	Avg.
Kareem Abdul-Jabbar, Los Angeles	82	338	4.12
Elmore Smith, Milwaukee	78	238	3.05
Elvin Hayes, Washington	80	202	2.53
Harvey Catchings, Philadelphia	75	164	2.19
George Johnson, Golden State	82	174	2.12
Bob McAdoo, Buffalo	78	160	2.05
Tom Burleson, Seattle	82	150	1.83
Otto Moore, New Orleans	81	136	1.68
Sam Lacey, Kansas City	81	134	1.65
Lloyd Neal, Portland	68	107	1.57

INDIVIDUAL STATISTICS, TEAM BY TEAM

ATLANTA HAWKS

								REBOUNDS									SCORING		
	G	Min.	FGM	FGA	Pct.	FTM	FTA	Pct.	Off.	Def.	Tot.	Ast.	PF	Dq.	Stl.	TO	Blk.	Pts.	Avg.	Hi.
John Drew	77	2351	586	1168	.502	488	656	.744	286	374	660	150	261	11	138	...	30	1660	21.6	42
Lou Hudson	81	2558	569	1205	.472	237	291	.814	104	196	300	214	241	3	124	...	17	1375	17.0	42
Tom Henderson	81	2900	469	1136	.413	216	305	.708	58	207	265	374	195	1	137	...	10	1154	14.2	33
Tom Van Arsdale	75	2026	346	785	.441	126	166	.759	35	151	186	146	202	5	57	...	7	818	10.9	26
Dwight Jones	66	1762	251	542	.463	163	219	.744	171	353	524	83	214	8	52	...	61	665	10.1	24
Mike Sojourner	67	1602	248	524	.473	80	119	.672	126	323	449	58	174	2	38	...	40	576	8.6	22
Connie Hawkins	74	1907	237	530	.447	136	191	.712	102	343	445	212	172	2	80	...	46	610	8.2	22
John Brown	75	1758	215	486	.442	162	209	.775	146	257	403	126	235	7	45	...	16	592	7.9	22
Dean Meminger	68	1418	155	379	.409	100	152	.658	65	86	151	222	116	0	54	...	8	410	6.0	27
Wilbur Holland	33	351	85	213	.399	22	34	.647	15	26	41	26	48	0	20	...	2	192	5.8	21
Bill Willoughby	62	870	113	284	.398	66	100	.660	103	185	288	31	87	0	37	...	29	292	4.7	20
Dennis DuVal	13	130	15	43	.349	6	9	.667	1	7	8	20	15	0	6	...	2	36	2.8	10
Jim Creighton	32	172	12	43	.279	7	16	.438	13	32	45	4	23	0	2	...	9	31	1.0	5

BOSTON CELTICS

								REBOUNDS									SCORING		
	G	Min.	FGM	FGA	Pct.	FTM	FTA	Pct.	Off.	Def.	Tot.	Ast.	PF	Dq.	Stl.	TO	Blk.	Pts.	Avg.	Hi.
Dave Cowens	78	3101	611	1305	.468	257	340	.756	335	911	1246	325	314	10	94	...	71	1479	19.0	39
Jo Jo White	82	3257	670	1492	.449	212	253	.838	61	252	313	445	183	2	107	...	20	1552	18.9	34
Charlie Scott	82	2913	588	1309	.449	267	335	.797	106	252	358	341	356	17	103	...	24	1443	17.6	32
John Havlicek	76	2598	504	1121	.450	281	333	.844	116	198	314	278	204	1	97	...	29	1289	17.0	38
Paul Silas	81	2662	315	740	.426	236	333	.709	365	660	1025	203	227	3	56	...	33	866	10.7	19
Don Nelson	75	943	175	379	.462	127	161	.789	56	126	182	77	115	0	14	...	7	477	6.4	27
Glenn McDonald	75	1019	191	456	.419	40	56	.714	56	79	135	68	123	0	39	...	20	422	5.6	18
Steve Kuberski†	60	882	128	274	.467	68	76	.895	86	148	234	44	123	1	11	...	11	324	5.4	20
Steve Kuberski‡	70	967	135	291	.464	71	79	.899	90	169	259	47	133	1	12	...	13	341	4.9	20
Kevin Stacom	77	1114	170	387	.439	68	91	.747	62	99	161	128	117	0	23	...	5	408	5.3	16
Jim Ard	81	853	107	294	.364	71	100	.710	96	193	289	48	141	2	12	...	36	285	3.5	18
Jerome Anderson	22	126	25	45	.556	11	16	.688	4	9	13	6	25	0	3	...	3	61	2.8	8
Tom Boswell	35	275	41	93	.441	14	24	.583	26	45	71	16	70	1	2	...	1	96	2.7	9
Ed Searcy	4	12	2	6	.333	2	2	1.000	0	0	0	1	4	0	0	...	0	6	1.5	2

BUFFALO BRAVES

								REBOUNDS									SCORING		
	G	Min.	FGM	FGA	Pct.	FTM	FTA	Pct.	Off.	Def.	Tot.	Ast.	PF	Dq.	Stl.	TO	Blk.	Pts.	Avg.	Hi.
Bob McAdoo	78	3328	934	1918	.487	559	734	.762	241	724	965	315	298	5	93	...	160	2427	31.1	52
Randy Smith	82	3167	702	1422	.494	383	469	.817	104	313	417	484	274	5	153	...	4	1787	21.8	37
Jim McMillian	74	2610	492	918	.536	188	219	.858	134	256	390	205	141	0	88	...	14	1172	15.8	35
John Shumate†	32	1046	146	254	.575	97	143	.678	82	232	314	65	83	1	38	...	18	389	12.2	25
John Shumate‡	75	1976	332	592	.561	212	326	.650	143	411	554	127	159	2	82	...	34	876	11.7	28
Ken Charles	81	2247	328	719	.456	161	205	.785	58	161	219	204	257	5	123	...	48	817	10.1	29

	G	Min.	FGM	FGA	Pct.	FTM	FTA	Pct.	Off.	Def.	Tot.	Ast.	PF	Dq.	Stl.	TO	Blk.	Pts.	Avg.	Hi.
									REBOUNDS									SCORING		
Gar Heard*	50	1527	207	492	.421	82	135	.607	138	373	511	126	183	0	66	...	55	496	9.9	20
Jack Marin*	12	278	41	94	.436	27	33	.818	10	30	40	23	30	0	7	...	6	109	9.1	23
Ernie DiGregorio	67	1364	182	474	.384	86	94	.915	15	97	112	265	158	1	37	...	1	450	6.7	22
Dick Gibbs	72	866	129	301	.429	77	93	.828	42	64	106	49	133	2	16	...	14	335	4.7	19
Tom McMillen	50	708	96	222	.432	41	54	.759	64	122	186	69	87	1	7	...	6	233	4.7	18
Bob Weiss	66	995	89	183	.486	35	48	.729	13	53	66	150	94	0	48	...	14	213	3.2	17
Don Adams	56	704	67	170	.394	40	57	.702	38	107	145	73	128	1	30	...	7	174	3.1	20
Dale Schlueter	71	773	61	122	.500	54	81	.667	58	166	224	80	141	1	13	...	17	176	2.5	9
Steve Kuberski*	10	85	7	17	.412	3	3	1.000	4	21	25	3	10	0	1	...	2	17	1.7	5
Jim Washington	1	7	0	1	.000	0	0	...	1	0	1	1	0	0	0	...	0	0	0.0	0

CHICAGO BULLS

	G	Min.	FGM	FGA	Pct.	FTM	FTA	Pct.	Off.	Def.	Tot.	Ast.	PF	Dq.	Stl.	TO	Blk.	Pts.	Avg.	Hi.
									REBOUNDS									SCORING		
Bob Love	76	2823	543	1391	.390	362	452	.801	191	319	510	145	233	3	63	...	10	1448	19.1	40
Mickey Johnson	81	2390	478	1033	.463	283	360	.786	279	479	758	130	292	8	93	...	66	1239	15.3	30
Norm Van Lier	76	3026	361	987	.366	235	319	.737	138	272	410	500	298	9	150	...	26	957	12.6	28
Jack Marin†	67	1631	302	718	.421	134	155	.865	59	153	212	118	134	0	38	...	5	738	11.0	34
Jack Marin‡	79	1909	343	812	.422	161	188	.856	69	183	252	141	164	0	45	...	11	847	10.7	34
Rowland Garrett*	14	324	57	131	.435	38	44	.864	27	48	75	7	32	0	8	...	4	152	10.9	22
Jerry Sloan	22	617	84	210	.400	55	78	.705	40	76	116	22	77	1	27	...	5	223	10.1	21
John Laskowski	71	1570	284	690	.412	87	120	.725	52	167	219	55	90	0	56	...	10	655	9.2	29
Tom Boerwinkle	74	2045	265	530	.500	118	177	.667	263	529	792	283	263	9	47	...	52	648	8.8	31
Bobby Wilson	58	856	197	489	.403	43	58	.741	32	62	94	52	96	1	25	...	2	437	7.5	28
Leon Benbow	76	1586	219	551	.397	105	140	.750	65	111	176	158	186	1	62	...	11	543	7.1	19
Cliff Pondexter	75	1326	156	380	.411	122	182	.670	113	268	381	90	134	4	28	...	26	434	5.8	22
Matt Guokas*	18	278	36	74	.486	9	11	.818	4	12	16	28	23	0	5	...	1	81	4.5	12
Nate Thurmond†	13	260	20	45	.444	8	18	.444	14	57	71	26	15	0	4	...	12	48	3.7	8
Steve Patterson†	52	782	69	182	.379	26	44	.591	73	127	200	71	82	1	13	...	11	164	3.2	13
Steve Patterson‡	66	918	84	220	.382	34	54	.630	80	148	228	80	93	1	16	...	16	202	3.1	13
Eric Fernsten†	33	260	33	84	.393	26	37	.703	25	44	69	19	20	0	7	...	14	92	2.8	8
Eric Fernsten‡	37	268	33	86	.384	26	37	.703	25	45	70	19	21	0	7	...	14	92	2.5	8
John Block	2	7	2	4	.500	0	2	.000	0	2	2	0	2	0	1	...	0	4	2.0	4

CLEVELAND CAVALIERS

	G	Min.	FGM	FGA	Pct.	FTM	FTA	Pct.	Off.	Def.	Tot.	Ast.	PF	Dq.	Stl.	TO	Blk.	Pts.	Avg.	Hi.
									REBOUNDS									SCORING		
Jim Chones	82	2741	563	1258	.448	172	260	.662	197	542	739	163	241	2	42	...	93	1298	15.8	29
Campy Russell	82	1961	483	1003	.482	266	344	.773	134	211	345	107	231	5	69	...	10	1232	15.0	35
Bobby Smith	81	2338	495	1121	.442	111	136	.816	83	258	341	155	231	0	58	...	36	1101	13.6	30
Dick Snyder	82	2274	441	881	.501	155	188	.824	50	148	198	220	215	0	59	...	33	1037	12.6	36
Jim Cleamons	82	2835	413	887	.466	174	218	.798	124	230	354	428	214	2	124	...	20	1000	12.2	29
Jim Brewer	82	2913	400	874	.458	140	214	.654	298	593	891	209	214	0	94	...	89	940	11.5	25
Austin Carr	65	1282	276	625	.442	106	134	.791	67	65	132	122	92	0	37	...	2	658	10.1	27
Butch Beard*	15	255	35	90	.389	27	37	.730	14	29	43	45	36	0	10	...	2	97	6.5	16
Foots Walker	81	1280	143	369	.388	84	108	.778	53	129	182	288	136	0	98	...	5	370	4.6	17
Nate Thurmond†	65	1133	122	292	.418	54	105	.514	101	243	344	68	145	1	18	...	86	298	4.6	15
Nate Thurmond‡	78	1393	142	337	.421	62	123	.504	115	300	415	94	160	1	22	...	98	346	4.4	15
Rowland Garrett†	41	216	51	127	.402	15	21	.714	18	24	42	10	36	0	17	...	3	117	2.9	15
Rowland Garrett‡	55	540	108	258	.419	53	65	.815	45	72	117	17	68	0	25	...	7	269	4.9	22
Steve Patterson*	14	136	15	38	.395	8	10	.800	7	21	28	9	11	0	3	...	5	38	2.7	8
John Lambert	54	333	49	110	.445	25	37	.676	37	65	102	16	54	0	8	...	12	123	2.3	10
Luke Witte	22	99	11	32	.344	9	15	.600	9	29	38	4	14	0	1	...	1	31	1.4	6
Eric Fernsten*	4	9	0	2	.000	0	0	...	0	1	1	0	1	0	0	...	0	0	0.0	0

DETROIT PISTONS

	G	Min.	FGM	FGA	Pct.	FTM	FTA	Pct.	Off.	Def.	Tot.	Ast.	PF	Dq.	Stl.	TO	Blk.	Pts.	Avg.	Hi.
									REBOUNDS									SCORING		
Bob Lanier	64	2363	541	1017	.532	284	370	.768	217	529	746	217	203	2	79	...	86	1366	21.3	41
Curtis Rowe	80	2998	514	1098	.468	252	342	.737	231	466	697	183	209	3	47	...	45	1280	16.0	29
Eric Money	80	2267	449	947	.474	145	180	.806	77	130	207	338	243	4	137	...	11	1043	13.0	26
Kevin Porter	19	687	99	235	.421	42	56	.750	14	30	44	193	83	3	35	...	3	240	12.6	23
John Mengelt	67	1105	264	540	.489	192	237	.810	27	88	115	108	138	1	40	...	5	720	10.7	32
Al Eberhard	81	2066	283	683	.414	191	229	.484	139	251	390	83	250	5	87	...	15	757	9.3	30
Howard Porter	75	1482	298	635	.469	73	97	.753	81	214	295	25	133	0	31	...	36	669	8.9	28
Chris Ford	82	2198	301	707	.426	83	115	.722	80	211	291	272	222	0	178	...	24	685	8.4	24
George Trapp	76	1091	278	602	.462	63	88	.716	79	150	229	50	167	3	33	...	23	619	8.1	27
Wali Jones*	1	19	4	11	.364	0	0	...	0	0	0	2	2	0	2	...	0	8	8.0	8
Archie Clark	79	1589	250	577	.433	100	116	.862	27	110	137	218	157	0	62	...	4	600	7.6	18
Harold Hairston	47	651	104	228	.456	65	112	.580	65	114	179	21	84	2	21	...	32	273	5.8	25
Earl Williams	46	562	73	152	.480	22	44	.500	103	148	251	18	81	0	22	...	20	168	3.7	13
Terry Thomas	28	136	28	65	.431	21	29	.724	15	21	36	3	21	1	4	...	2	77	2.8	18
Roger Brown	29	454	29	72	.403	14	18	.778	47	83	130	12	76	1	6	...	25	72	2.5	11
Henry Dickerson	17	112	9	29	.310	10	16	.625	3	0	3	8	17	1	2	...	1	28	1.6	11

1975-76

Golden State's Rick Barry led the NBA with a .923 free-throw percentage and averaged 21.0 points per game in the 1975-76 season.

GOLDEN STATE WARRIORS

	G	Min.	FGM	FGA	Pct.	FTM	FTA	Pct.	REBOUNDS Off.	Def.	Tot.	Ast.	PF	Dq.	Stl.	TO	Blk.	SCORING Pts.	Avg.	Hi.
Rick Barry	81	3122	707	1624	.435	287	311	.923	74	422	496	496	215	1	202	...	27	1701	21.0	41
Phil Smith	82	2793	659	1383	.477	323	410	.788	133	243	376	362	223	0	108	...	18	1641	20.0	51
Jamaal Wilkes	82	2716	617	1334	.463	227	294	.772	193	527	720	167	222	0	102	...	31	1461	17.8	34
Gus Williams	77	1728	365	853	.428	173	233	.742	62	97	159	240	143	2	140	...	26	903	11.7	27
Charles Johnson	81	1549	342	732	.467	60	79	.759	77	125	202	122	178	1	100	...	7	744	9.2	26
Clifford Ray	82	2184	212	404	.525	140	230	.609	270	506	776	149	247	2	78	...	83	564	6.9	20
Charles Dudley	82	1456	182	345	.528	157	245	.641	112	157	269	239	170	0	77	...	2	521	6.4	18
Derrek Dickey	79	1207	220	473	.465	62	79	.785	114	235	349	83	141	1	26	...	11	502	6.4	20
George Johnson	82	1745	165	341	.484	70	104	.673	200	427	627	82	275	6	51	...	174	400	4.9	16
Jeff Mullins	29	311	58	120	.483	23	29	.793	12	20	32	39	36	0	14	...	1	139	4.8	18
Dwight Davis	72	866	111	269	.413	78	113	.690	86	139	225	46	141	0	20	...	28	300	4.2	12
Robert Hawkins	32	153	53	104	.510	20	31	.645	16	14	30	16	31	0	10	...	8	126	3.9	15

HOUSTON ROCKETS

	G	Min.	FGM	FGA	Pct.	FTM	FTA	Pct.	REBOUNDS Off.	Def.	Tot.	Ast.	PF	Dq.	Stl.	TO	Blk.	SCORING Pts.	Avg.	Hi.
Calvin Murphy	82	2995	675	1369	.493	372	410	.907	52	157	209	596	294	3	151	...	6	1722	21.0	40
Mike Newlin	82	3065	569	1123	.507	385	445	.865	72	264	336	457	263	5	106	...	5	1523	18.6	34
Rudy Tomjanovich	79	2912	622	1202	.517	221	288	.767	167	499	666	188	206	1	42	...	19	1465	18.5	32
Kevin Kunnert	80	2335	465	954	.487	102	156	.654	267	520	787	155	315	14	57	...	105	1032	12.9	29
Ed Ratleff	72	2401	314	647	.485	168	206	.816	107	272	379	260	234	4	114	...	37	796	11.1	33
Joe Meriweather	81	2042	338	684	.494	154	239	.644	163	353	516	82	219	4	36	...	120	830	10.2	29
John Johnson†	67	1485	275	609	.452	97	128	.758	81	211	292	197	163	0	50	...	28	647	9.7	23
John Johnson‡	76	1697	316	697	.453	120	155	.774	94	238	332	217	194	1	57	...	36	752	9.9	23
Cliff Meely*	14	174	32	81	.395	9	16	.563	12	40	52	10	31	1	9	...	4	73	5.2	15
Ron Riley	65	1049	115	280	.411	38	56	.679	91	213	304	75	137	1	32	...	21	268	4.1	21
Dave Wohl	50	700	66	163	.405	38	49	.776	9	47	56	112	112	2	26	...	1	170	3.4	10
Rudy White	32	284	42	102	.412	18	25	.720	13	25	38	30	32	0	19	...	5	102	3.2	14
Gus Bailey	30	262	28	77	.364	14	28	.500	20	30	50	41	33	1	14	...	8	70	2.3	10
Steve Hawes*	6	51	5	13	.385	0	0	...	5	13	18	10	6	0	0	...	0	10	1.7	8

KANSAS CITY KINGS

	G	Min.	FGM	FGA	Pct.	FTM	FTA	Pct.	REBOUNDS Off.	Def.	Tot.	Ast.	PF	Dq.	Stl.	TO	Blk.	SCORING Pts.	Avg.	Hi.
Nate Archibald	78	3184	717	1583	.453	501	625	.802	67	146	213	615	169	0	126	...	15	1935	24.8	39
Jimmy Walker	73	2490	459	950	.483	231	267	.865	49	128	177	176	186	2	87	...	14	1149	15.7	32
Scott Wedman	82	2968	538	1181	.456	191	245	.780	199	407	606	199	280	8	103	...	36	1267	15.5	28
Sam Lacey	81	3083	409	1019	.401	217	286	.759	218	806	1024	378	286	7	132	...	134	1035	12.8	26
Ollie Johnson	81	2150	348	678	.513	125	149	.839	116	241	357	146	217	4	67	...	42	821	10.1	23
Larry McNeill	82	1613	295	610	.484	207	273	.758	157	353	510	72	244	2	51	...	32	797	9.7	25
Bill Robinzine	75	1327	229	499	.459	145	198	.732	128	227	355	60	290	19	80	...	8	603	8.0	21
Glenn Hansen	66	1145	173	420	.412	85	117	.726	77	110	187	67	144	1	47	...	13	431	6.5	26
Lee Winfield	22	214	32	66	.485	9	14	.643	8	16	24	19	14	0	10	...	6	73	3.3	14
Rick Roberson	74	709	73	180	.406	42	103	.408	74	159	233	53	126	1	18	...	17	188	2.5	13
Matt Guokas†	38	515	37	99	.374	9	16	.563	18	29	47	42	53	0	13	...	2	83	2.2	9
Matt Guokas‡	56	793	73	173	.422	18	27	.667	22	41	63	70	76	0	18	...	3	164	2.9	12
Len Kosmalski	9	93	8	20	.400	4	7	.571	9	16	25	12	11	0	3	...	4	20	2.2	11
Bob Bigelow	31	163	16	47	.340	24	33	.727	9	20	29	9	18	0	4	...	1	56	1.8	8
Mike D'Antoni	9	101	7	27	.259	2	2	1.000	4	10	14	16	18	0	10	...	0	16	1.8	6

LOS ANGELES LAKERS

	G	Min.	FGM	FGA	Pct.	FTM	FTA	Pct.	REBOUNDS Off.	Def.	Tot.	Ast.	PF	Dq.	Stl.	TO	Blk.	SCORING Pts.	Avg.	Hi.
Kareem Abdul-Jabbar	82	3379	914	1728	.529	447	636	.703	272	1111	1383	413	292	6	119	...	338	2275	27.7	48
Gail Goodrich	75	2646	583	1321	.441	293	346	.847	94	120	214	421	238	3	123	...	17	1459	19.5	37
Lucius Allen	76	2388	461	1004	.459	197	254	.776	64	150	214	357	241	2	101	...	20	1119	14.7	28
Cazzie Russell	74	1625	371	802	.463	132	148	.892	50	133	183	122	122	0	53	...	3	874	11.8	33
Donnie Freeman	64	1480	263	606	.434	163	199	.819	72	108	180	171	160	1	57	...	11	689	10.8	25
Don Ford	76	1838	311	710	.438	104	139	.748	118	215	333	111	186	3	50	...	14	726	9.6	25
Cornell Warner	81	2512	251	524	.479	89	128	.695	223	499	722	106	283	3	55	...	46	591	7.3	24
Pat Riley*	2	23	5	13	.385	1	3	.333	1	2	3	0	5	0	1	...	1	11	5.5	9
Corky Calhoun	76	1816	172	368	.467	65	83	.783	117	224	341	85	216	4	62	...	35	409	5.4	18
Ron Williams	9	158	17	43	.395	10	13	.769	2	17	19	21	15	0	3	...	0	44	4.9	12
Stu Lantz	53	853	85	204	.417	80	89	.899	28	71	99	76	105	1	27	...	3	250	4.7	19
Walt Wesley	1	7	1	2	.500	2	4	.500	0	1	1	1	2	0	0	...	0	4	4.0	4
Kermit Washington	36	492	39	90	.433	45	66	.682	51	114	165	20	76	0	11	...	26	123	3.4	14
Cliff Meely†	20	139	20	51	.392	24	32	.750	10	35	45	9	30	0	5	...	4	64	3.2	11
Cliff Meely‡	34	313	52	132	.394	33	48	.688	22	75	97	19	61	1	14	...	8	137	4.0	15
Jim McDaniels	35	242	41	102	.402	9	9	1.000	26	48	74	15	40	1	4	...	10	91	2.6	12
C.J. Kupec	16	55	10	40	.250	7	11	.636	4	19	23	5	7	0	3	...	0	27	1.7	6
John Roche	15	52	3	14	.214	2	4	.500	0	3	3	6	7	0	0	...	0	8	0.5	4

MILWAUKEE BUCKS

	G	Min.	FGM	FGA	Pct.	FTM	FTA	Pct.	REBOUNDS Off.	Def.	Tot.	Ast.	PF	Dq.	Stl.	TO	Blk.	SCORING Pts.	Avg.	Hi.
Bob Dandridge	73	2735	650	1296	.502	271	329	.824	171	369	540	206	263	5	111	...	38	1571	21.5	40
Brian Winters	78	2795	618	1333	.464	180	217	.829	66	183	249	366	240	0	124	...	25	1416	18.2	34
Elmore Smith	78	2809	498	962	.518	222	351	.632	201	692	893	97	268	7	78	...	238	1218	15.6	31
Jim Price	80	2525	398	958	.415	141	166	.849	74	187	261	395	264	3	148	...	32	937	11.7	26
Junior Bridgeman	81	1646	286	651	.439	128	161	.795	113	181	294	157	235	3	52	...	21	700	8.6	28
Gary Brokaw	75	1468	237	519	.457	159	227	.700	26	99	125	246	138	1	37	...	17	633	8.4	28
Dave Meyers	72	1589	198	472	.419	135	210	.643	121	324	445	100	145	0	72	...	25	531	7.4	28
Kevin Restani	82	1650	234	493	.475	24	42	.571	115	261	376	96	151	3	36	...	12	492	6.0	18
Clyde Mayes	65	948	114	248	.460	56	97	.577	97	166	263	37	154	7	9	...	42	284	4.4	19
Jon McGlocklin	33	336	63	148	.426	9	10	.900	3	14	17	38	18	0	8	...	0	135	4.1	12
Jim Fox	70	918	105	203	.517	62	79	.785	82	153	235	42	129	1	27	...	16	272	3.9	21
Mickey Davis	45	411	55	152	.362	50	63	.794	25	59	84	37	36	0	13	...	2	160	3.6	12

NEW ORLEANS JAZZ

	G	Min.	FGM	FGA	Pct.	FTM	FTA	Pct.	REBOUNDS Off.	Def.	Tot.	Ast.	PF	Dq.	Stl.	TO	Blk.	SCORING Pts.	Avg.	Hi.
Pete Maravich	62	2373	604	1316	.459	396	488	.811	46	254	300	332	197	3	87	...	23	1604	25.9	49
Nate Williams	81	1935	421	948	.444	197	239	.824	135	225	360	107	253	6	109	...	17	1039	12.8	33
Louie Nelson	66	2030	327	755	.433	169	230	.735	81	121	202	169	147	1	82	...	6	823	12.5	27
Ron Behagen	66	1733	308	691	.446	144	179	.804	190	363	553	139	222	6	67	...	26	760	11.5	27
Henry Bibby	79	1772	266	622	.428	200	251	.797	58	121	179	225	165	0	62	...	3	732	9.3	24
Bud Stallworth	56	1051	211	483	.437	85	124	.685	42	103	145	53	135	1	30	...	17	507	9.1	22
Otto Moore	81	2407	293	672	.436	144	226	.637	162	631	793	216	250	3	85	...	136	730	9.0	20
Aaron James	75	1346	262	594	.441	153	204	.750	93	156	249	59	172	1	33	...	6	677	9.0	24
Jim McElroy	51	1134	151	296	.510	81	110	.736	34	76	110	107	70	0	44	...	4	383	7.5	20
E.C. Coleman	67	1850	216	479	.451	59	89	.663	124	295	419	87	227	3	56	...	30	491	7.3	20
Rich Kelley	75	1346	184	379	.485	159	205	.776	193	335	528	155	209	5	52	...	60	527	7.0	20
Freddie Boyd†	30	584	72	165	.436	28	49	.571	4	26	30	78	54	0	27	...	7	172	5.7	18
Freddie Boyd‡	36	617	74	171	.433	29	51	.569	4	28	32	80	59	0	28	...	7	177	4.9	18
Mel Counts	30	319	37	91	.407	16	21	.762	27	73	100	38	74	1	16	...	8	90	3.0	16

NEW YORK KNICKERBOCKERS

	G	Min.	FGM	FGA	Pct.	FTM	FTA	Pct.	REBOUNDS Off.	Def.	Tot.	Ast.	PF	Dq.	Stl.	TO	Blk.	SCORING Pts.	Avg.	Hi.
Earl Monroe	76	2889	647	1354	.478	280	356	.787	48	225	273	304	209	1	111	...	22	1574	20.7	37
Spencer Haywood	78	2892	605	1360	.445	339	448	.757	234	644	878	92	255	1	53	...	80	1549	19.9	35
Walt Frazier	59	2427	470	969	.485	186	226	.823	79	321	400	351	163	1	106	...	9	1126	19.1	38
Bill Bradley	82	2709	392	906	.433	130	148	.878	47	187	234	247	256	2	68	...	18	914	11.1	25
John Gianelli	82	2332	325	687	.473	114	160	.713	187	365	552	115	194	1	25	...	62	764	9.3	24
Butch Beard†	60	1449	193	406	.475	117	155	.755	89	178	267	173	180	2	71	...	6	503	8.4	21
Butch Beard‡	75	1704	228	496	.460	144	192	.750	103	207	310	218	216	2	81	...	8	600	8.0	21
Neal Walk	82	1340	262	607	.432	79	99	.798	98	291	389	119	209	3	26	...	22	603	7.4	21
Phil Jackson	80	1461	185	387	.478	110	150	.733	80	263	343	105	275	3	41	...	20	480	6.0	17
Jim Barnett	71	1026	164	371	.442	90	114	.789	48	40	88	90	86	0	24	...	3	418	5.9	18
Mel Davis	42	408	76	193	.394	22	29	.759	43	105	148	31	56	0	16	...	5	174	4.1	20
Harthorne Wingo	57	533	72	163	.442	40	60	.667	46	61	107	18	59	0	19	...	8	184	3.2	13
Ken Mayfield	13	64	17	46	.370	3	3	1.000	1	7	8	4	18	0	0	...	0	37	2.8	8
Gene Short†	27	185	26	80	.325	19	30	.633	17	24	41	8	31	0	8	...	3	71	2.6	10
Gene Short‡	34	222	32	91	.352	20	32	.625	19	29	48	10	36	0	8	...	3	84	2.5	10
Dennis Bell	10	76	8	21	.381	3	7	.429	4	10	14	3	11	0	6	...	1	19	1.9	8
Larry Fogle	2	14	1	5	.200	0	0	...	1	2	3	0	4	0	1	...	0	2	1.0	2

1975-76

PHILADELPHIA 76ERS

	G	Min.	FGM	FGA	Pct.	FTM	FTA	Pct.	Off.	Def.	Tot.	Ast.	PF	Dq.	Stl.	TO	Blk.	Pts.	Avg.	Hi.
									REBOUNDS									SCORING		
George McGinnis	77	2946	647	1552	.417	475	642	.740	260	707	967	359	334	13	198	...	41	1769	23.0	39
Doug Collins........	77	2995	614	1196	.513	372	445	.836	126	181	307	191	249	2	110	...	24	1600	20.8	38
Fred Carter	82	2992	665	1594	.417	219	312	.702	113	186	299	372	286	5	137	...	13	1549	18.9	35
Steve Mix	81	3039	421	844	.499	287	351	.818	215	447	662	216	288	6	158	...	29	1129	13.9	33
Billy Cunningham	20	640	103	251	.410	68	88	.773	29	118	147	107	57	1	24	...	10	274	13.7	26
World B. Free	71	1121	239	533	.448	112	186	.602	64	61	125	104	107	0	37	...	6	590	8.3	29
Joe Bryant	75	1203	233	552	.422	92	147	.626	97	181	278	61	165	0	44	...	23	558	7.4	26
Connie Norman......	65	818	183	422	.434	20	24	.833	51	50	101	66	87	1	28	...	7	386	5.9	20
LeRoy Ellis	29	489	61	132	.462	17	28	.607	47	75	122	21	62	0	16	...	9	139	4.8	14
Clyde Lee	79	1421	123	282	.436	63	95	.663	164	289	453	59	188	0	23	...	27	309	3.9	14
Harvey Catchings	75	1731	103	242	.426	58	96	.604	191	329	520	63	262	6	21	...	164	264	3.5	13
Wali Jones†	16	157	19	38	.500	9	13	.692	0	9	9	31	25	0	4	...	0	47	2.9	10
Wali Jones‡	17	176	23	49	.469	9	13	.692	0	9	9	33	27	0	6	...	0	55	3.2	10
Darryl Dawkins	37	165	41	82	.500	8	24	.333	15	34	49	3	40	1	2	...	9	90	2.4	12
Jerry Baskerville	21	105	8	26	.308	10	16	.625	13	15	28	3	32	0	6	...	5	26	1.2	4
Freddie Boyd*........	6	33	2	6	.333	1	2	.500	0	2	2	2	5	0	1	...	0	5	0.8	2

PHOENIX SUNS

	G	Min.	FGM	FGA	Pct.	FTM	FTA	Pct.	Off.	Def.	Tot.	Ast.	PF	Dq.	Stl.	TO	Blk.	Pts.	Avg.	Hi.
									REBOUNDS									SCORING		
Paul Westphal.......	82	2960	657	1329	.494	365	440	.830	74	185	259	440	218	3	210	...	38	1679	20.5	39
Alvan Adams........	80	2656	629	1341	.469	261	355	.735	215	512	727	450	274	6	121	...	116	1519	19.0	35
Curtis Perry	71	2353	386	776	.497	175	239	.732	197	487	684	182	269	5	84	...	66	947	13.3	27
Dick Van Arsdale.....	58	1870	276	570	.484	195	235	.830	39	98	137	140	113	2	52	...	11	747	12.9	26
Gar Heard†	36	1220	185	409	.452	76	113	.673	109	249	358	64	120	2	51	...	41	446	12.4	27
Gar Heard‡	86	2747	392	901	.435	158	248	.637	247	622	869	190	303	2	117	...	96	942	11.0	27
John Shumate*......	43	930	186	338	.550	115	183	.628	61	179	240	62	76	1	44	...	16	487	11.3	28
Keith Erickson	74	1850	305	649	.470	134	157	.854	106	226	332	185	196	4	79	...	6	744	10.1	26
Ricky Sobers	78	1898	280	623	.449	158	192	.823	80	179	259	215	253	6	106	...	7	718	9.2	27
Nate Hawthorne	79	1144	182	423	.430	115	170	.676	86	123	209	46	147	0	33	...	15	479	6.1	25
Dennis Awtrey.......	74	1376	142	304	.467	75	109	.688	93	200	293	159	153	1	21	...	22	359	4.9	12
Pat Riley†	60	790	112	288	.389	54	74	.730	15	32	47	57	107	0	21	...	5	278	4.6	16
Pat Riley‡	62	813	117	301	.389	55	77	.714	16	34	50	57	112	0	22	...	6	289	4.7	16
Fred Saunders.......	17	146	28	64	.438	6	11	.545	11	26	37	13	23	0	5	...	1	62	3.6	12
Mike Bantom*	7	68	8	26	.308	5	5	1.000	7	16	23	3	13	1	2	...	2	21	3.0	9
Phil Lumpkin	34	370	22	65	.338	26	30	.867	7	16	23	48	26	0	15	...	0	70	2.1	10
John Wetzel	37	249	22	46	.478	20	24	.833	8	30	38	19	30	0	9	...	3	64	1.7	6

PORTLAND TRAIL BLAZERS

	G	Min.	FGM	FGA	Pct.	FTM	FTA	Pct.	Off.	Def.	Tot.	Ast.	PF	Dq.	Stl.	TO	Blk.	Pts.	Avg.	Hi.
									REBOUNDS									SCORING		
Sidney Wicks	79	3044	580	1201	.483	345	512	.674	245	467	712	244	250	5	77	...	53	1505	19.1	35
Geoff Petrie........	72	2557	543	1177	.461	277	334	.829	38	130	168	330	194	0	82	...	5	1363	18.9	34
Bill Walton	51	1687	345	732	.471	133	228	.583	132	549	681	220	144	3	49	...	82	823	16.1	36
Lloyd Neal	68	2320	435	904	.481	186	268	.694	145	440	585	118	254	4	53	...	107	1056	15.5	31
John Johnson*.......	9	212	41	88	.466	23	27	.852	13	27	40	20	31	1	7	...	8	105	11.7	21
Lionel Hollins	74	1891	314	738	.421	178	247	.721	39	136	175	306	235	5	131	...	28	800	10.8	25
Larry Steele	81	2382	322	651	.495	154	203	.759	77	215	292	324	289	8	170	...	19	798	9.9	30
Steve Hawes†	66	1360	194	390	.497	87	120	.725	166	313	479	105	163	5	44	...	25	475	7.2	23
Steve Hawes‡	72	1411	199	403	.494	87	120	.725	171	326	497	115	169	5	44	...	25	485	6.7	23
Bob Gross	76	1474	209	400	.523	97	142	.683	138	169	307	163	186	3	91	...	43	515	6.8	24
Steve Jones	64	819	168	380	.442	78	94	.830	13	62	75	63	96	0	17	...	6	414	6.5	23
LaRue Martin	63	889	109	302	.361	57	77	.740	68	243	311	72	126	1	6	...	23	275	4.4	18
Dan Anderson	52	614	88	181	.486	51	61	.836	15	47	62	85	58	0	20	...	2	227	4.4	17
Barry Clemens	49	443	70	143	.490	31	35	.886	27	43	70	33	57	0	27	...	7	171	3.5	20
Greg Lee...........	5	35	2	4	.500	2	2	1.000	0	2	2	11	6	0	2	...	0	6	1.2	4
Greg Smith..........	1	3	0	1	.000	0	0	...	0	0	0	2	0	0	0	...	0	0	0.0	0

SEATTLE SUPERSONICS

	G	Min.	FGM	FGA	Pct.	FTM	FTA	Pct.	Off.	Def.	Tot.	Ast.	PF	Dq.	Stl.	TO	Blk.	Pts.	Avg.	Hi.
									REBOUNDS									SCORING		
Fred Brown.........	76	2516	742	1522	.488	273	314	.869	111	206	317	207	186	0	143	...	18	1757	23.1	41
Tom Burleson	82	2647	496	1032	.481	291	388	.750	258	484	742	180	273	1	70	...	150	1283	15.6	35
Leonard Gray	66	2139	394	831	.474	126	169	.746	109	289	398	203	260	10	75	...	36	914	13.8	32
Donald Watts	82	2776	433	1015	.427	199	344	.578	112	253	365	661	270	3	261	...	16	1065	13.0	26
Bruce Seals........	81	2435	388	889	.436	181	267	.678	157	350	507	119	314	11	64	...	44	957	11.8	29
Herm Gilliam.......	81	1644	299	676	.442	90	116	.776	56	164	220	202	139	0	82	...	12	688	8.5	24
Mike Bantom†	66	1503	212	450	.471	131	194	.675	133	235	368	102	208	3	26	...	26	555	8.4	21
Mike Bantom‡.......	73	1571	220	476	.462	136	199	.683	140	251	391	105	221	4	28	...	28	576	7.9	21
Willie Norwood	64	1004	146	301	.485	152	203	.749	91	138	229	59	139	3	42	...	4	444	6.9	24
Frank Oleynick	52	650	127	316	.402	53	77	.688	10	35	45	53	62	0	21	...	6	307	5.9	22
Talvin Skinner	72	1224	132	285	.463	49	80	.613	89	175	264	67	116	1	50	...	7	313	4.3	16
Rod Derline........	49	339	73	181	.403	45	56	.804	8	19	27	26	22	0	11	...	1	191	3.9	16
Zaid Abdul-Aziz......	27	223	35	75	.467	16	29	.552	30	46	76	16	29	0	8	...	15	86	3.2	11

	G	Min.	FGM	FGA	Pct.	FTM	FTA	Pct.	Off.	Def.	Tot.	Ast.	PF	Dq.	Stl.	TO	Blk.	Pts.	Avg.	Hi.
John Hummer	29	364	32	67	.478	17	41	.415	21	56	77	25	71	5	6	...	9	81	2.8	14
Alvin Carlson	28	279	27	79	.342	18	29	.621	30	43	73	13	39	1	7	...	11	72	2.6	7
Gene Short*	7	37	6	11	.545	1	2	.500	2	5	7	2	5	0	0	...	0	13	1.9	6

WASHINGTON BULLETS

	G	Min.	FGM	FGA	Pct.	FTM	FTA	Pct.	Off.	Def.	Tot.	Ast.	PF	Dq.	Stl.	TO	Blk.	Pts.	Avg.	Hi.
Phil Chenier	80	2952	654	1355	.483	282	341	.827	84	236	320	255	186	2	158	...	45	1590	19.9	44
Elvin Hayes	80	2975	649	1381	.470	287	457	.628	210	668	878	121	293	5	104	...	202	1585	19.8	37
Dave Bing	82	2945	497	1113	.447	332	422	.787	94	143	237	492	262	0	118	...	23	1326	16.2	34
Truck Robinson	82	2055	354	779	.454	211	314	.672	139	418	557	113	239	3	42	...	107	919	11.2	29
Wes Unseld	78	2922	318	567	.561	114	195	.585	271	765	1036	404	203	3	84	...	59	750	9.6	25
Mike Riordan	78	1943	291	662	.440	71	96	.740	44	143	187	122	201	2	54	...	13	653	8.4	22
Nick Weatherspoon	64	1083	218	458	.476	96	137	.701	85	189	274	55	172	2	46	...	16	532	8.3	31
Clem Haskins	55	737	148	269	.550	54	65	.831	12	42	54	73	79	2	23	...	8	350	6.4	25
Jimmy Jones	64	1133	153	308	.497	72	94	.766	32	99	131	120	127	1	33	...	5	378	5.9	16
Kevin Grevey	56	504	79	213	.371	52	58	.897	24	36	60	27	65	0	13	...	3	210	3.8	19
Thomas Kozelko	67	584	48	99	.485	19	30	.633	19	63	82	33	74	0	19	...	4	115	1.7	15
Tom Kropp	25	72	7	30	.233	5	6	.833	5	10	15	8	20	0	2	...	0	19	0.8	5

* Finished season with another team. † Totals with this team only. ‡ Totals with all teams.

PLAYOFF RESULTS

EASTERN CONFERENCE

FIRST ROUND

Buffalo 2, Philadelphia 1
Apr. 15—Thur.	Buffalo 95 at Philadelphia	89
Apr. 16—Fri.	Philadelphia 131 at Buffalo	106
Apr. 18—Sun.	Buffalo 124 at Philadelphia	*123

SEMIFINALS

Boston 4, Buffalo 2
Apr. 21—Wed.	Buffalo 98 at Boston	107
Apr. 23—Fri.	Buffalo 96 at Boston	101
Apr. 25—Sun.	Boston 93 at Buffalo	90
Apr. 28—Wed.	Boston 122 at Buffalo	124
Apr. 30—Fri.	Buffalo 88 at Boston	99
May 2—Sun.	Boston 104 at Buffalo	100

Cleveland 4, Washington 3
Apr. 13—Tue.	Washington 100 at Cleveland	95
Apr. 15—Thur.	Cleveland 80 at Washington	79
Apr. 17—Sat.	Washington 76 at Cleveland	88
Apr. 21—Wed.	Cleveland 98 at Washington	109
Apr. 22—Thur.	Washington 91 at Cleveland	92
Apr. 26—Mon.	Cleveland 98 at Washington	*102
Apr. 29—Thur.	Washington 85 at Cleveland	87

FINALS

Boston 4, Cleveland 2
May 6—Thur.	Cleveland 99 at Boston	111
May 9—Sun.	Cleveland 89 at Boston	94
May 11—Tue.	Boston 78 at Cleveland	83
May 14—Fri.	Boston 87 at Cleveland	106
May 16—Sun.	Cleveland 94 at Boston	99
May 18—Tue.	Boston 94 at Cleveland	87

WESTERN CONFERENCE

FIRST ROUND

Detroit 2, Milwaukee 1
Apr. 13—Tue.	Detroit 107 at Milwaukee	110
Apr. 15—Thur.	Milwaukee 123 at Detroit	126
Apr. 18—Sun.	Detroit 107 at Milwaukee	104

SEMIFINALS

Golden State 4, Detroit 2
Apr. 20—Tue.	Detroit 103 at Golden State	127
Apr. 22—Thur.	Detroit 123 at Golden State	111
Apr. 24—Sat.	Golden State 113 at Detroit	106
Apr. 26—Mon.	Golden State 102 at Detroit	106
Apr. 28—Wed.	Detroit 109 at Golden State	128
Apr. 30—Fri.	Golden State 118 at Detroit	*116

Phoenix 4, Seattle 2
Apr. 13—Tue.	Phoenix 99 at Seattle	102
Apr. 15—Thur.	Phoenix 116 at Seattle	111
Apr. 18—Sun.	Seattle 91 at Phoenix	103
Apr. 20—Tue.	Seattle 114 at Phoenix	130
Apr. 25—Sun.	Phoenix 108 at Seattle	114
Apr. 27—Tue.	Seattle 112 at Phoenix	123

FINALS

Phoenix 4, Golden State 3
May 2—Sun.	Phoenix 103 at Golden State	128
May 5—Wed.	Phoenix 108 at Golden State	101
May 7—Fri.	Golden State 99 at Phoenix	91
May 9—Sun.	Golden State 129 at Phoenix	**133
May 12—Wed.	Phoenix 95 at Golden State	111
May 14—Fri.	Golden State 104 at Phoenix	105
May 16—Sun.	Phoenix 94 at Golden State	86

NBA FINALS

Boston 4, Phoenix 2
May 23—Sun.	Phoenix 87 at Boston	98
May 27—Thur.	Phoenix 90 at Boston	105
May 30—Sun.	Boston 98 at Phoenix	105
June 2—Wed.	Boston 107 at Phoenix	109
June 4—Fri.	Phoenix 126 at Boston	***128
June 6—Sun.	Boston 87 at Phoenix	80

*Denotes number of overtime periods.

1974-75

1974-75 NBA CHAMPION GOLDEN STATE WARRIORS
Front row (from left): Charles Johnson, Jeff Mullins, assistant coach Joe Roberts, head coach Al Attles, owner Franklin Mieuli, captain Rick Barry, Butch Beard, Phil Smith, trainer Dick D'Oliva. Back row (from left): assistant general manager Hal Childs, Charles Dudley, Bill Bridges, Clifford Ray, George Johnson, Derrek Dickey, Jamaal Wilkes, Steve Bracey, director of player personnel Bob Feerick, general manager Dick Vertlieb.

FINAL STANDINGS

ATLANTIC DIVISION

	Atl.	Bos.	Buf.	Chi.	Cle.	Det.	G.S.	Hou.	KC/O	L.A.	Mil.	N.O.	N.Y.	Phi.	Pho.	Por.	Sea.	Was.	W	L	Pct.	GB
Boston 4	..	5	3	3	3	3	1	4	2	4	4	4	7	5	3	4	2	2	60	22	.732	..
Buffalo 3	4	..	1	3	2	3	2	1	4	1	4	5	6	3	2	3	2	49	33	.598	11
New York. 4	2	3	1	3	2	1	3	2	4	1	2	..	4	3	2	2	1	40	42	.488	20
Philadelphia. . . 2	3	3	2	1	1	1	2	3	1	1	2	5	..	2	2	2	1	34	48	.415	26

CENTRAL DIVISION

	Atl.	Bos.	Buf.	Chi.	Cle.	Det.	G.S.	Hou.	KC/O	L.A.	Mil.	N.O.	N.Y.	Phi.	Pho.	Por.	Sea.	Was.	W	L	Pct.	GB
Washington. . . 5	2	2	3	5	3	3	5	3	3	4	7	3	3	3	3	3	..	60	22	.732	..
Houston 5	0	2	2	4	2	2	..	4	2	3	5	1	2	2	2	1	2	41	41	.500	19
Cleveland. . . . 4	1	1	2	..	2	2	4	2	2	1	6	1	3	2	2	2	3	40	42	.488	20
Atlanta.	0	1	0	3	2	1	2	2	2	2	3	0	2	4	1	3	3	31	51	.378	29
New Orleans . . 5	0	0	0	1	0	2	3	2	1	1	..	2	2	1	2	1	0	23	59	.280	37

MIDWEST DIVISION

	Atl.	Bos.	Buf.	Chi.	Cle.	Det.	G.S.	Hou.	KC/O	L.A.	Mil.	N.O.	N.Y.	Phi.	Pho.	Por.	Sea.	Was.	W	L	Pct.	GB
Chicago. 4	1	3	..	2	4	3	2	4	3	3	4	3	2	2	2	4	1	47	35	.573	..
K.C./Omaha. . . 2	2	3	5	2	6	2	0	..	3	6	2	2	1	3	3	1	1	44	38	.537	3
Detroit. 2	1	2	5	2	..	1	2	2	3	3	4	2	3	2	3	2	1	40	42	.488	7
Milwaukee. . . . 2	0	3	5	3	6	1	1	3	0	..	3	3	3	2	2	1	0	38	44	.463	9

PACIFIC DIVISION

	Atl.	Bos.	Buf.	Chi.	Cle.	Det.	G.S.	Hou.	KC/O	L.A.	Mil.	N.O.	N.Y.	Phi.	Pho.	Por.	Sea.	Was.	W	L	Pct.	GB
Golden State . . 3	3	1	1	2	3	..	2	2	5	3	2	3	3	5	5	4	1	48	34	.585	..
Seattle. 1	2	1	0	2	2	3	3	3	6	3	3	2	2	3	6	..	1	43	39	.524	5
Portland 3	0	2	2	2	1	3	2	1	5	2	2	2	2	6	..	2	1	38	44	.463	10
Phoenix. 0	1	1	2	2	2	3	2	1	4	2	3	1	2	..	1	4	1	32	50	.390	16
Los Angeles. . . 2	0	0	1	2	1	2	2	1	..	4	3	0	3	4	2	2	1	30	52	.366	18

TEAM STATISTICS

OFFENSIVE

	G	FGM	FGA	Pct.	FTM	FTA	Pct.	REBOUNDS Off.	Def.	Tot.	Ast.	PF	Dq.	Stl.	TO	Blk.	SCORING Pts.	Avg.
Golden State . . 82	3714	7981	.465	1470	1915	.768	1416	2854	4270	2076	2109	22	972	1716	365	8898	108.5
Buffalo. 82	3552	7469	.476	1735	2224	.780	1108	2735	3843	2063	1879	18	718	1710	456	8839	107.8
Boston. 82	3587	7825	.458	1560	1971	.791	1315	2949	4264	2159	1913	23	662	1625	288	8734	106.5
Atlanta. 82	3424	7824	.438	1772	2435	.728	1441	2653	4094	1878	1964	33	744	1550	227	8620	105.1
Washington . . . 82	3555	7697	.462	1475	1962	.752	1133	2764	3897	2005	1961	26	929	1594	409	8585	104.7
Houston 82	3448	7231	.477	1625	2034	.799	1177	2495	3672	2155	2068	30	746	1759	351	8521	103.9
Portland. 82	3414	7113	.480	1680	2265	.742	1049	2758	3807	2209	2055	29	755	1853	399	8508	103.8
Los Angeles . . . 82	3409	7577	.450	1641	2182	.752	1312	2763	4075	2091	2079	23	755	1785	423	8459	103.2
Seattle. 82	3488	7653	.456	1475	1970	.749	1142	2579	3721	1997	1977	27	837	1610	378	8451	103.1
New Orleans. . . 82	3301	7509	.440	1717	2247	.764	1144	2616	3760	1818	2222	34	725	1802	256	8319	101.5

	G	FGM	FGA	Pct.	FTM	FTA	Pct.	REBOUNDS Off.	Def.	Tot.	Ast.	PF	Dq.	Stl.	TO	Blk.	SCORING Pts.	Avg.
K.C./Omaha . . .	82	3257	7258	.449	1797	2190	.821	991	2745	3736	1853	1968	19	724	1542	347	8311	101.4
Phoenix	82	3381	7561	.447	1535	2082	.737	1349	2684	4033	1879	2090	45	664	1760	317	8297	101.2
Milwaukee . . .	82	3450	7367	.468	1354	1746	.775	1021	2766	3787	1932	1949	30	596	1540	400	8254	100.7
New York	82	3359	7464	.450	1518	1967	.772	981	2652	3633	1675	2001	22	652	1374	300	8236	100.4
Philadelphia . .	82	3325	7476	.445	1530	2043	.749	1200	2706	3906	1709	1974	34	576	1591	263	8180	99.8
Cleveland	82	3408	7371	.462	1301	1753	.742	1058	2502	3560	1903	1881	16	600	1462	348	8117	99.0
Detroit	82	3289	7053	.466	1533	1975	.776	1002	2515	3517	1916	1866	13	679	1557	380	8111	98.9
Chicago	82	3167	7085	.447	1711	2203	.777	1107	2786	3893	1840	1952	23	668	1482	379	8045	98.1

DEFENSIVE

	FGM	FGA	Pct.	FTM	FTA	Pct.	REBOUNDS Off.	Def.	Tot.	Ast.	PF	Dq.	Stl.	TO	Blk.	SCORING Pts.	Avg.	Dif.
Chicago	3167	7070	.448	1457	1900	.767	1008	2647	3655	1686	2168	37	625	1580	404	7791	95.0	+3.1
Washington . . .	3249	7415	.438	1499	1967	.762	1184	2819	4003	1811	2004	25	710	1842	259	7997	97.5	+7.2
Cleveland	3263	7243	.451	1621	2102	.771	1235	2694	3929	1746	1932	26	711	1618	277	8147	99.4	-0.4
Detroit	3409	7257	.470	1410	1793	.786	1104	2550	3654	2012	1875	24	663	1523	306	8228	100.3	-1.4
Milwaukee . . .	3371	7600	.444	1495	1910	.783	1153	2645	3798	1960	1704	11	660	1379	298	8237	100.5	+0.2
Boston	3432	7726	.444	1401	1882	.744	1060	2622	3682	1833	1869	24	599	1475	283	8265	100.8	+5.7
K.C./Omaha . . .	3410	7400	.461	1515	1972	.768	1060	2812	3872	1840	2029	25	606	1605	312	8335	101.6	-0.2
New York	3361	7357	.457	1615	2082	.776	1070	2856	3926	1668	1912	15	572	1493	369	8337	101.7	-1.3
Philadelphia . .	3445	7466	.461	1541	1979	.779	1167	2748	3915	1959	2036	26	742	1577	343	8431	102.8	-3.0
Houston	3429	7127	.481	1576	2127	.741	1036	2380	3416	2024	2063	37	750	1685	308	8434	102.9	+1.0
Portland	3379	7502	.450	1714	2178	.787	1207	2572	3779	2090	2085	34	927	1607	383	8472	103.3	+0.5
Phoenix	3356	7323	.458	1780	2350	.757	1112	2564	3676	2062	1992	20	870	1586	412	8492	103.6	-2.4
Seattle	3490	7606	.459	1560	2090	.746	1286	2754	4040	2188	1948	24	692	1755	349	8540	104.1	-1.0
Golden State . .	3481	7628	.456	1666	2209	.754	1185	2658	3843	2084	1855	17	794	1644	387	8628	105.2	+3.3
Buffalo	3575	7943	.450	1513	1943	.779	1295	2619	3914	2151	2030	31	730	1670	383	8663	105.6	+2.2
Atlanta	3563	7504	.475	1606	2098	.765	1169	2851	4020	1914	2265	33	746	1723	422	8732	106.5	-1.4
Los Angeles . .	3595	7914	.454	1603	2117	.757	1422	2807	4229	2239	2015	25	822	1606	442	8793	107.2	-4.0
New Orleans . . .	3553	7433	.478	1857	2465	.753	1193	2924	4117	1891	2126	33	783	1924	349	8963	109.3	-7.8
Avgs.	3418	7473	.457	1579	2065	.765	1164	2696	3859	1953	1995	26	722	1628	349	8416	102.6	. . .

HOME/ROAD

	Home	Road	Total		Home	Road	Total
Atlanta.	22-19	9-32	31-51	Milwaukee	25-16	13-28	38-44
Boston.	28-13	32-9	60-22	New Orleans	20-21	3-38	23-59
Buffalo.	30-11	19-22	49-33	New York.	23-18	17-24	40-42
Chicago.	29-12	18-23	47-35	Philadelphia.	20-21	14-27	34-40
Cleveland.	29-12	11-30	40-42	Phoenix.	22-19	10-31	32-50
Detroit.	26-15	14-27	40-42	Portland.	28-13	10-31	38-44
Golden State	31-10	17-24	48-34	Seattle.	24-17	19-22	43-39
Houston.	29-12	12-29	41-41	Washington	36-5	24-17	60-22
Kansas City/Omaha	29-12	15-26	44-38	Totals.	472-266	266-472	738-738
Los Angeles.	21-20	9-32	30-52				

INDIVIDUAL LEADERS

POINTS

(minimum 70 games or 1,400 points)

	G	FGM	FTM	Pts.	Avg.
Bob McAdoo, Buffalo	82	1095	641	2831	34.5
Rick Barry, Golden State	80	1028	394	2450	30.6
Kareem Abdul-Jabbar, Milw. . . .	65	812	325	1949	30.0
Nate Archibald, K.C./Omaha . .	82	759	652	2170	26.5
Charlie Scott, Phoenix	69	703	274	1680	24.3
Bob Lanier, Detroit	76	731	361	1823	24.0
Elvin Hayes, Washington	82	739	409	1887	23.0
Gail Goodrich, Los Angeles . . .	72	656	318	1630	22.6
Spencer Haywood, Seattle	68	608	309	1525	22.4
Fred Carter, Philadelphia	77	715	256	1686	21.9
Phil Chenier, Washington	77	690	301	1681	21.8
Sidney Wicks, Portland	82	692	394	1778	21.7
Pete Maravich, New Orleans . . .	79	655	390	1700	21.5
Walt Frazier, New York	78	672	331	1675	21.5
Fred Brown, Seattle	81	737	226	1700	21.0
Earl Monroe, New York	78	668	297	1633	20.9
Rudy Tomjanovich, Houston . .	81	694	289	1677	20.7
Bob Dandridge, Milwaukee	80	691	211	1593	19.9
Billy Cunningham, Philadelphia	80	609	345	1563	19.5
Chet Walker, Chicago	76	524	413	1461	19.2

FIELD GOALS

(minimum 300 made)

	FGM	FGA	Pct.
Don Nelson, Boston	423	785	.539
Butch Beard, Golden State	408	773	.528
Rudy Tomjanovich, Houston	694	1323	.525
Kareem Abdul-Jabbar, Milwaukee	812	1584	.513
Bob McAdoo, Buffalo	1095	2138	.512
Kevin Kunnert, Houston	346	676	.512
Bob Lanier, Detroit	731	1433	.510
Paul Westphal, Boston	342	670	.510
Dick Snyder, Cleveland	498	988	.504
Jim McMillian, Buffalo	347	695	.499

FREE THROWS

(minimum 125 made)

	FTM	FTA	Pct.
Rick Barry, Golden State	394	436	.904
Calvin Murphy, Houston	341	386	.883
Bill Bradley, New York	144	165	.873
Nate Archibald, Kansas City/Omaha	652	748	.872
Jim Price, Los Angeles-Milwaukee	169	194	.871
John Havlicek, Boston	289	332	.870
Mike Newlin, Houston	265	305	.869
Jack Marin, Buffalo	193	222	.869
Chet Walker, Chicago	413	480	.860
Jimmy Walker, Kansas City/Omaha	247	289	.855

1974-75

ASSISTS

(minimum 70 games or 400 assists)

	G	No.	Avg.
Kevin Porter, Washington	81	650	8.0
Dave Bing, Detroit	79	610	7.7
Nate Archibald, Kansas City/Omaha	82	557	6.8
Randy Smith, Buffalo	82	534	6.5
Pete Maravich, New Orleans	79	488	6.2
Rick Barry, Golden State	80	492	6.2
Donald Watts, Seattle	82	499	6.1
Walt Frazier, New York	78	474	6.1
Gail Goodrich, Los Angeles	72	420	5.8
Norm Van Lier, Chicago	70	403	5.8

STEALS

(minimum 70 games or 125 steals)

	G	No.	Avg.
Rick Barry, Golden State	80	228	2.85
Walt Frazier, New York	78	190	2.44
Larry Steele, Portland	76	183	2.41
Donald Watts, Seattle	82	190	2.32
Fred Brown, Seattle	81	187	2.31
Phil Chenier, Washington	77	176	2.29
Jerry Sloan, Chicago	78	171	2.19
Lucius Allen, Milwaukee-Los Angeles	66	136	2.06
Norm Van Lier, Chicago	70	139	1.99
Elvin Hayes, Washington	82	158	1.93

REBOUNDS

(minimum 70 games or 800 rebounds)

	G	Off.	Def.	Tot.	Avg.
Wes Unseld, Washington	73	318	759	1077	14.8
Dave Cowens, Boston	65	229	729	958	14.7
Sam Lacey, Kansas City/Omaha	81	228	921	1149	14.2
Bob McAdoo, Buffalo	82	307	848	1155	14.1
Kareem Abdul-Jabbar, Milw.	65	194	718	912	14.0
Happy Hairston, Los Angeles	74	304	642	946	12.8
Paul Silas, Boston	82	348	677	1025	12.5
Elvin Hayes, Washington	82	221	783	1004	12.2
Bob Lanier, Detroit	76	225	689	914	12.0
Curtis Perry, Phoenix	79	347	593	940	11.9

BLOCKED SHOTS

(minimum 70 games or 100 blocked shots)

	G	No.	Avg.
Kareem Abdul-Jabbar, Milwaukee	65	212	3.26
Elmore Smith, Los Angeles	74	216	2.92
Nate Thurmond, Chicago	80	195	2.44
Elvin Hayes, Washington	82	187	2.28
Bob Lanier, Detroit	76	172	2.26
Bob McAdoo, Buffalo	82	174	2.12
Sam Lacey, Kansas City/Omaha	81	168	2.07
Tom Burleson, Seattle	82	153	1.87
Gar Heard, Buffalo	67	120	1.79
Jim Chones, Cleveland	72	120	1.67

INDIVIDUAL STATISTICS, TEAM BY TEAM

ATLANTA HAWKS

	G	Min.	FGM	FGA	Pct.	FTM	FTA	Pct.	REBOUNDS Off.	Def.	Tot.	Ast.	PF	Dq.	Stl.	TO	Blk.	SCORING Pts.	Avg.	Hi.
Lou Hudson	11	380	97	225	.431	48	57	.842	14	33	47	40	33	1	13	...	2	242	22.0	36
Tom Van Arsdale†	73	2570	544	1269	.429	294	383	.768	70	179	249	207	231	5	78	...	3	1382	18.9	35
Tom Van Arsdale‡	82	2843	593	1385	.428	322	424	.759	77	201	278	223	257	5	91	...	3	1508	18.4	35
John Drew	78	2289	527	1230	.428	388	544	.713	357	479	836	138	274	4	119	...	39	1442	18.5	44
Herm Gilliam	60	1393	314	736	.427	94	113	.832	76	128	204	170	124	1	77	...	13	722	12.0	26
Mike Sojourner	73	2129	378	775	.488	95	146	.651	196	446	642	93	217	10	35	...	57	851	11.7	29
Tom Henderson	79	2131	367	893	.411	168	241	.697	51	161	212	314	149	0	105	...	7	902	11.4	32
John Brown	73	1986	315	684	.461	185	250	.740	180	254	434	133	228	7	54	...	15	815	11.2	28
Dwight Jones	75	2086	323	752	.430	132	183	.721	236	461	697	152	226	1	51	...	51	778	10.4	24
Dean Meminger	80	2177	233	500	.466	168	263	.639	84	130	214	397	160	0	118	...	11	634	7.9	26
Jim Washington*	38	905	114	259	.440	41	55	.745	52	141	193	68	86	2	23	...	13	269	7.1	19
Clyde Lee*	9	177	12	36	.333	32	39	.821	24	46	70	8	25	0	1	...	4	56	6.2	16
Bob Kauffman	73	797	113	261	.433	59	84	.702	67	115	182	81	103	1	19	...	4	285	3.9	17
John Wetzel	63	785	87	204	.426	68	77	.883	34	80	114	77	108	1	51	...	8	242	3.8	14

BOSTON CELTICS

	G	Min.	FGM	FGA	Pct.	FTM	FTA	Pct.	REBOUNDS Off.	Def.	Tot.	Ast.	PF	Dq.	Stl.	TO	Blk.	SCORING Pts.	Avg.	Hi.
Dave Cowens	65	2632	569	1199	.475	191	244	.783	229	729	958	296	243	7	87	...	73	1329	20.4	38
John Havlicek	82	3132	642	1411	.455	289	332	.870	154	330	484	432	231	2	110	...	16	1573	19.2	40
Jo Jo White	82	3220	658	1440	.457	186	223	.834	84	227	311	458	207	1	128	...	17	1502	18.3	33
Don Nelson	79	2052	423	785	.539	263	318	.827	127	342	469	181	239	2	32	...	15	1109	14.0	35
Paul Silas	82	2661	312	749	.417	244	344	.709	348	677	1025	224	229	3	60	...	22	868	10.6	22
Paul Westphal	82	1581	342	670	.510	119	156	.763	44	119	163	235	192	0	78	...	33	803	9.8	27
Don Chaney	82	2208	321	750	.428	133	165	.806	171	199	370	181	244	5	122	...	66	775	9.5	28
Phil Hankinson	3	24	6	11	.545	0	0	...	1	6	7	2	3	0	1	...	0	12	4.0	6
Jim Ard	59	719	89	266	.335	48	65	.738	59	140	199	40	96	2	13	...	32	226	3.8	19
Kevin Stacom	61	447	72	159	.453	29	33	.879	30	25	55	49	65	0	11	...	3	173	2.8	10
Ben Clyde	25	157	31	72	.431	7	9	.778	15	26	41	5	34	1	5	...	3	69	2.8	16
Glenn McDonald	62	395	70	182	.385	28	37	.757	20	48	68	24	58	0	8	...	5	168	2.7	14
Hank Finkel	62	518	52	129	.403	23	43	.535	33	79	112	32	72	0	7	...	3	127	2.0	10
Steve Downing	3	9	0	2	.000	0	2	.000	0	2	2	0	0	0	0	...	0	0	0.0	0

BUFFALO BRAVES

	G	Min.	FGM	FGA	Pct.	FTM	FTA	Pct.	REBOUNDS Off.	Def.	Tot.	Ast.	PF	Dq.	Stl.	TO	Blk.	SCORING Pts.	Avg.	Hi.
Bob McAdoo	82	3539	1095	2138	.512	641	796	.805	307	848	1155	179	278	3	92	...	174	2831	34.5	51
Randy Smith	82	3001	610	1261	.484	236	295	.800	95	249	344	534	247	2	137	...	3	1456	17.8	35
Jim McMillian	62	2132	347	695	.499	194	231	.840	127	258	385	156	129	0	69	...	15	888	14.3	28
Jack Marin	81	2147	380	836	.455	193	222	.869	104	259	363	133	238	7	51	...	16	953	11.8	26
Gar Heard	67	2148	318	819	.388	106	188	.564	185	481	666	190	242	2	106	...	120	742	11.1	24

Buffalo's Bob McAdoo led the NBA in scoring with a 34.5 average in 1974-75.

	G	Min.	FGM	FGA	Pct.	FTM	FTA	Pct.	REBOUNDS Off.	Def.	Tot.	Ast.	PF	Dq.	Stl.	TO	Blk.	SCORING Pts.	Avg.	Hi.
Ernie DiGregorio	31	712	103	234	.440	35	45	.778	6	39	45	151	62	0	19	...	0	241	7.8	33
Ken Charles	79	1690	240	515	.466	120	146	.822	68	96	164	171	165	0	87	...	20	600	7.6	19
Lee Winfield	68	1259	164	312	.526	49	68	.721	48	81	129	134	106	1	43	...	30	377	5.5	16
Jim Washington†	42	674	77	162	.475	21	38	.553	58	139	197	43	81	3	11	...	13	175	4.2	16
Jim Washington‡	80	1579	191	421	.454	62	93	.667	110	280	390	111	167	5	34	...	26	444	5.6	19
Dale Schlueter	76	962	92	178	.517	84	121	.694	78	186	264	104	163	0	18	...	42	268	3.5	13
Bob Weiss	76	1338	102	261	.391	54	67	.806	21	83	104	260	146	0	82	...	19	258	3.4	14
Paul Ruffner	22	103	22	47	.468	1	5	.200	12	10	22	7	22	0	3	...	3	45	2.0	8
Bernie Harris	11	25	2	11	.182	1	2	.500	2	6	8	1	0	0	0	...	1	5	0.5	2

CHICAGO BULLS

	G	Min.	FGM	FGA	Pct.	FTM	FTA	Pct.	REBOUNDS Off.	Def.	Tot.	Ast.	PF	Dq.	Stl.	TO	Blk.	SCORING Pts.	Avg.	Hi.
Bob Love	61	2401	539	1256	.429	264	318	.830	99	286	385	102	209	3	63	...	12	1342	22.0	39
Chet Walker	76	2452	524	1076	.487	413	480	.860	114	318	432	169	181	0	49	...	6	1461	19.2	39
Norm Van Lier	70	2590	407	970	.420	236	298	.792	86	242	328	403	246	5	139	...	14	1050	15.0	42
Jerry Sloan	78	2577	380	865	.439	193	258	.748	177	361	538	161	265	5	171	...	17	953	12.2	27
Rick Adelman*	12	340	43	104	.413	28	39	.718	6	20	26	35	31	0	16	...	1	114	9.5	16
John Block†	50	882	150	317	.473	105	134	.784	63	151	214	44	110	0	38	...	31	405	8.1	29
John Block‡	54	939	159	346	.460	114	144	.792	69	163	232	51	121	0	42	...	32	432	8.0	29
Nate Thurmond	80	2756	250	686	.364	132	224	.589	259	645	904	328	271	6	46	...	195	632	7.9	25
Rowland Garrett	70	1183	228	474	.481	77	97	.794	80	167	247	43	124	0	24	...	13	533	7.6	21
Matt Guokas	82	2089	255	500	.510	78	103	.757	24	115	139	178	154	1	45	...	17	588	7.2	20
Bill Hewitt	18	467	56	129	.434	14	23	.609	30	86	116	24	46	1	9	...	10	126	7.0	17
Bobby Wilson	48	425	115	225	.511	46	58	.793	13	34	52	36	54	1	22	...	1	276	5.8	20
Tom Boerwinkle	80	1175	132	271	.487	73	95	.768	105	275	380	272	163	0	25	...	45	337	4.2	17
Mickey Johnson	38	291	53	118	.449	37	58	.638	32	62	94	20	57	1	10	...	11	143	3.8	16
Leon Benbow	39	252	35	94	.372	15	18	.833	14	24	38	25	41	0	11	...	6	85	2.2	8

CLEVELAND CAVALIERS

	G	Min.	FGM	FGA	Pct.	FTM	FTA	Pct.	REBOUNDS Off.	Def.	Tot.	Ast.	PF	Dq.	Stl.	TO	Blk.	SCORING Pts.	Avg.	Hi.
Bobby Smith	82	2636	585	1212	.483	132	160	.825	108	299	407	229	227	1	80	...	26	1302	15.9	41
Jim Chones	72	2427	446	916	.487	152	224	.679	156	521	677	132	247	5	49	...	120	1044	14.5	28
Austin Carr	41	1081	252	538	.468	89	106	.840	51	56	107	154	57	0	48	...	2	593	14.5	34
Dick Snyder	82	2590	498	988	.504	165	195	.846	37	201	238	281	226	3	69	...	43	1161	14.2	30
Jim Cleamons	74	2691	369	768	.480	144	181	.796	97	232	329	381	194	0	84	...	21	882	11.9	29
Dwight Davis	78	1964	295	666	.443	176	245	.718	108	356	464	150	254	3	45	...	39	766	9.8	24
Jim Brewer	82	1991	291	639	.455	103	159	.648	205	304	509	128	150	2	77	...	43	685	8.4	26
Fred Foster	73	1136	217	521	.417	69	97	.711	56	54	110	103	130	1	22	...	2	503	6.9	23
Campy Russell	68	754	150	365	.411	124	165	.752	43	109	152	45	100	0	21	...	3	424	6.2	18
Steve Patterson	81	1269	161	387	.416	48	73	.658	112	217	329	93	128	1	21	...	20	370	4.6	23
Foots Walker	72	1070	111	275	.404	80	117	.684	47	99	146	192	126	0	80	...	7	302	4.2	18
Luke Witte	39	271	33	96	.344	19	31	.613	38	54	92	15	42	0	4	...	22	85	2.2	9

DETROIT PISTONS

	G	Min.	FGM	FGA	Pct.	FTM	FTA	Pct.	Off.	Def.	Tot.	Ast.	PF	Dq.	Stl.	TO	Blk.	Pts.	Avg.	Hi.
									REBOUNDS									SCORING		
Bob Lanier	76	2987	731	1433	.510	361	450	.802	225	689	914	350	237	1	75	...	172	1823	24.0	45
Dave Bing	79	3222	578	1333	.434	343	424	.809	86	200	286	610	222	3	116	...	26	1499	19.0	32
Curtis Rowe	82	2787	422	874	.483	171	227	.753	174	411	585	121	190	0	50	...	44	1015	12.4	26
John Mengelt	80	1995	336	701	.479	211	248	.851	38	153	191	201	198	2	72	...	4	883	11.0	33
Howard Porter†	41	1030	188	376	.500	59	70	.843	66	150	216	17	76	0	20	...	25	435	10.6	22
Howard Porter‡	58	1163	201	412	.488	66	79	.835	79	175	254	19	93	0	23	...	26	468	8.1	22
George Trapp	78	1472	288	652	.442	99	131	.756	71	205	276	63	210	1	37	...	14	675	8.7	24
Willie Norwood	24	347	64	123	.520	31	42	.738	31	57	88	16	51	0	23	...	0	159	6.6	18
Chris Ford	80	1962	206	435	.474	63	95	.663	93	176	269	230	187	0	113	...	26	475	5.9	18
Don Adams	51	1376	127	315	.403	45	78	.577	63	181	244	75	179	1	69	...	20	299	5.9	19
Eric Money	66	889	144	319	.451	31	45	.689	27	61	88	101	121	3	33	...	2	319	4.8	21
Jim Davis	79	1078	118	260	.454	85	117	.726	96	189	285	90	129	2	50	...	36	321	4.1	21
Jim Ligon	38	272	55	143	.385	16	25	.640	14	12	26	25	31	0	8	...	9	126	3.3	15
Al Eberhard	34	277	31	85	.365	17	21	.810	18	29	47	16	33	0	13	...	1	79	2.3	11
Otto Moore*	2	11	1	4	.250	1	2	.500	0	2	2	1	2	0	0	...	1	3	1.5	3

GOLDEN STATE WARRIORS

	G	Min.	FGM	FGA	Pct.	FTM	FTA	Pct.	Off.	Def.	Tot.	Ast.	PF	Dq.	Stl.	TO	Blk.	Pts.	Avg.	Hi.
									REBOUNDS									SCORING		
Rick Barry	80	3235	1028	2217	.464	394	436	.904	92	364	456	492	225	0	228	...	33	2450	30.6	55
Jamaal Wilkes	82	2515	502	1135	.442	160	218	.734	203	468	671	183	222	0	107	...	22	1164	14.2	31
Butch Beard	82	2521	408	773	.528	232	279	.832	116	200	316	345	297	9	132	...	11	1048	12.8	29
Charles Johnson	79	2171	394	957	.412	75	102	.735	134	177	311	233	204	2	138	...	8	863	10.9	25
Clifford Ray	82	2519	299	573	.522	171	284	.602	259	611	870	178	305	9	95	...	116	769	9.4	20
Jeff Mullins	66	1141	234	514	.455	71	87	.816	46	77	123	153	123	0	57	...	14	539	8.2	24
Derrek Dickey	80	1859	274	569	.482	66	99	.667	190	360	550	125	199	0	52	...	19	614	7.7	20
Phil Smith	74	1055	221	464	.476	127	158	.804	51	89	140	135	141	0	62	...	0	569	7.7	26
George Johnson	82	1439	152	319	.476	60	91	.659	217	357	574	67	206	1	32	...	136	364	4.4	16
Charles Dudley	67	756	102	217	.470	70	97	.722	61	84	145	103	105	1	40	...	2	274	4.1	15
Frank Kendrick	24	121	31	77	.403	18	22	.818	19	17	36	6	22	0	11	...	3	80	3.3	10
Steve Bracey	42	340	54	130	.415	25	38	.658	10	28	38	52	41	0	14	...	1	133	3.2	13
Bill Bridges†	15	108	15	36	.417	1	4	.250	18	22	40	4	19	0	4	...	0	31	2.1	8
Bill Bridges‡	32	415	35	93	.376	17	34	.500	64	70	134	31	65	1	11	...	5	87	2.7	15

HOUSTON ROCKETS

	G	Min.	FGM	FGA	Pct.	FTM	FTA	Pct.	Off.	Def.	Tot.	Ast.	PF	Dq.	Stl.	TO	Blk.	Pts.	Avg.	Hi.
									REBOUNDS									SCORING		
Rudy Tomjanovich	81	3134	694	1323	.525	289	366	.790	184	429	613	236	230	1	76	...	24	1677	20.7	41
Calvin Murphy	78	2513	557	1152	.484	341	386	.883	52	121	173	381	281	8	128	...	4	1455	18.7	45
Mike Newlin	79	2709	436	905	.482	265	305	.869	55	205	260	403	288	4	111	...	7	1137	14.4	37
Ed Ratleff	80	2563	392	851	.461	157	190	.826	185	274	459	259	231	5	146	...	51	941	11.8	31
Kevin Kunnert	75	1801	346	676	.512	116	169	.686	214	417	631	108	223	2	34	...	84	808	10.8	27
Zaid Abdul-Aziz	65	1450	235	538	.437	159	203	.783	154	334	488	84	128	1	37	...	74	629	9.7	26
Cliff Meely	48	753	156	349	.447	68	94	.723	55	109	164	45	117	4	21	...	21	380	7.9	21
Dave Wohl	75	1722	203	462	.439	79	106	.745	26	86	112	340	184	1	75	...	9	485	6.5	29
Ron Riley	77	1578	196	470	.417	71	97	.732	137	243	380	130	197	3	56	...	22	463	6.0	16
Steve Hawes	55	897	140	279	.502	45	55	.818	80	195	275	88	99	1	36	...	36	325	5.9	20
Owen Wells	33	214	42	100	.420	15	22	.682	12	23	35	22	38	0	9	...	3	99	3.0	12
Gus Bailey	47	446	51	126	.405	20	41	.488	23	59	82	59	52	0	17	...	16	122	2.6	14

KANSAS CITY/OMAHA KINGS

	G	Min.	FGM	FGA	Pct.	FTM	FTA	Pct.	Off.	Def.	Tot.	Ast.	PF	Dq.	Stl.	TO	Blk.	Pts.	Avg.	Hi.
									REBOUNDS									SCORING		
Nate Archibald	82	3244	759	1664	.456	652	748	.872	48	174	222	557	187	0	119	...	7	2170	26.5	51
Jimmy Walker	81	3122	553	1164	.475	247	289	.855	51	188	239	226	222	2	85	...	13	1353	16.7	32
Nate Williams*	50	1131	265	584	.454	97	118	.822	58	121	179	78	152	2	53	...	24	627	12.5	27
Sam Lacey	81	3378	392	917	.427	144	191	.754	228	921	1149	428	274	4	139	...	168	928	11.5	23
Scott Wedman	80	2554	375	806	.465	139	170	.818	202	288	490	129	270	2	81	...	27	889	11.1	26
Ron Behagen	81	2205	333	834	.399	199	264	.754	146	446	592	153	301	8	60	...	42	865	10.7	23
Larry McNeill	80	1749	296	645	.459	189	241	.784	149	348	497	73	229	1	69	...	27	781	9.8	26
Ollie Johnson†	30	508	64	130	.492	33	37	.892	27	39	66	30	69	0	17	...	13	161	5.4	15
Ollie Johnson‡	73	1667	203	429	.473	95	114	.833	87	156	243	110	172	1	59	...	33	501	6.9	20
Don Kojis	21	232	46	98	.469	20	30	.667	14	25	39	10	31	0	12	...	1	112	5.3	18
Ken Durrett*	21	175	32	78	.410	11	20	.550	14	26	40	8	30	0	5	...	4	75	3.6	9
Mike D'Antoni	67	759	69	173	.399	28	36	.778	13	64	77	107	106	0	67	...	12	166	2.5	14
Don May	29	139	27	54	.500	10	12	.833	4	9	13	5	21	0	4	...	2	64	2.2	12
Rick Adelman†	18	121	13	28	.464	4	5	.800	6	8	14	8	12	0	7	...	1	30	1.7	9
Rick Adelman‡	58	1074	123	291	.423	73	103	.709	25	70	95	112	101	1	70	...	8	319	5.5	16
Len Kosmalski	67	413	33	83	.398	24	29	.828	31	88	119	41	64	0	6	...	6	90	1.3	7

LOS ANGELES LAKERS

	G	Min.	FGM	FGA	Pct.	FTM	FTA	Pct.	REBOUNDS Off.	Def.	Tot.	Ast.	PF	Dq.	Stl.	TO	Blk.	SCORING Pts.	Avg.	Hi.
Gail Goodrich 72	72	2668	656	1429	.459	318	378	.841	96	123	219	420	214	1	102	. . .	6	1630	22.6	53
Jim Price* 9	9	339	75	167	.449	41	45	.911	17	26	43	63	36	1	21	. . .	3	191	21.2	27
Lucius Allen† 56	56	2011	443	1006	.440	207	269	.770	81	166	247	319	194	4	122	. . .	28	1093	19.5	39
Lucius Allen‡ 66	66	2353	511	1170	.437	238	306	.778	90	188	278	372	217	4	136	. . .	29	1260	19.1	39
Cazzie Russell 40	40	1055	264	580	.455	101	113	.894	34	81	115	109	56	0	27	. . .	2	629	15.7	30
Brian Winters 68	68	1516	359	810	.443	76	92	.826	39	99	138	195	168	1	74	. . .	18	794	11.7	30
Pat Riley 46	46	1016	219	523	.419	69	93	.742	25	60	85	121	128	0	36	. . .	4	507	11.0	38
Elmore Smith 74	74	2341	346	702	.493	112	231	.485	210	600	810	145	255	6	84	. . .	216	804	10.9	30
Happy Hairston 74	74	2283	271	536	.506	217	271	.801	304	642	946	173	218	2	52	. . .	11	759	10.3	21
Stu Lantz† 56	56	1430	189	446	.424	145	176	.824	81	89	170	158	134	1	44	. . .	10	523	9.3	26
Stu Lantz‡ 75	75	1783	228	561	.406	192	229	.838	88	106	194	188	162	1	56	. . .	12	648	8.6	26
Connie Hawkins 43	43	1026	139	324	.429	68	99	.687	54	144	198	120	116	1	51	. . .	23	346	8.0	24
Stan Love 30	30	431	85	194	.438	47	66	.712	31	66	97	26	69	1	16	. . .	13	217	7.2	18
Zelmo Beaty 69	69	1213	136	310	.439	108	135	.800	93	234	327	74	130	1	45	. . .	29	380	5.5	19
Corky Calhoun† 57	57	1270	120	286	.420	44	62	.710	95	141	236	75	160	1	49	. . .	23	284	5.0	13
Corky Calhoun‡ 70	70	1378	132	318	.415	58	77	.753	109	160	269	79	180	1	55	. . .	25	322	4.6	13
Kermit Washington . . 55	55	949	87	207	.420	72	122	.590	106	244	350	66	155	2	25	. . .	32	246	4.5	12
Bill Bridges* 17	17	307	20	57	.351	16	30	.533	46	48	94	27	46	1	7	. . .	5	56	3.3	15

MILWAUKEE BUCKS

	G	Min.	FGM	FGA	Pct.	FTM	FTA	Pct.	REBOUNDS Off.	Def.	Tot.	Ast.	PF	Dq.	Stl.	TO	Blk.	SCORING Pts.	Avg.	Hi.
Kareem Abdul-Jabbar . 65	65	2747	812	1584	.513	325	426	.763	194	718	912	264	205	2	65	. . .	212	1949	30.0	52
Bob Dandridge 80	80	3031	691	1460	.473	211	262	.805	142	409	551	243	330	7	122	. . .	48	1593	19.9	33
Lucius Allen* 10	10	342	68	164	.415	31	37	.838	9	22	31	53	23	0	14	. . .	1	167	16.7	23
Jim Price† 41	41	1531	242	550	.440	128	149	.859	45	110	155	223	146	0	90	. . .	21	612	14.9	43
Jim Price‡ 50	50	1870	317	717	.442	169	194	.871	62	136	198	286	182	1	111	. . .	24	803	16.1	43
George Thompson . . . 73	73	1983	306	691	.443	168	214	.785	50	131	181	225	203	5	66	. . .	6	780	10.7	24
Jon McGlocklin 79	79	1853	323	651	.496	63	72	.875	25	94	119	255	142	2	51	. . .	6	709	9.0	24
Gary Brokaw 73	73	1639	234	514	.455	126	184	.685	36	111	147	221	176	3	31	. . .	18	594	8.1	24
Cornell Warner 79	79	2519	248	541	.458	106	155	.684	238	574	812	127	267	8	49	. . .	54	602	7.6	19
Mickey Davis 75	75	1077	174	363	.479	78	88	.886	68	169	237	79	103	0	30	. . .	5	426	5.7	18
Kevin Restani 76	76	1755	188	427	.440	35	49	.714	131	272	403	119	172	1	36	. . .	19	411	5.4	18
Ron Williams 46	46	526	62	165	.376	24	29	.828	10	33	43	71	70	2	23	. . .	2	148	3.2	15
Steve Kuberski 59	59	517	62	159	.390	44	56	.786	52	71	123	35	59	0	11	. . .	3	168	2.8	10
Walt Wesley† 41	41	214	37	84	.440	14	23	.609	14	41	55	11	43	0	7	. . .	5	88	2.1	10
Walt Wesley‡ 45	45	247	42	93	.452	16	27	.593	18	45	63	12	51	0	7	. . .	5	100	2.2	10
Terry Driscoll 11	11	52	3	13	.231	1	2	.500	7	9	16	3	7	0	1	. . .	0	7	0.6	3
Dick Cunningham 2	2	8	0	0	. . .	0	0	. . .	0	2	2	1	1	0	0	. . .	0	0	0.0	0
Bob Rule 1	1	11	0	1	.000	0	0	. . .	0	0	0	2	2	0	0	. . .	0	0	0.0	0

NEW ORLEANS JAZZ

	G	Min.	FGM	FGA	Pct.	FTM	FTA	Pct.	REBOUNDS Off.	Def.	Tot.	Ast.	PF	Dq.	Stl.	TO	Blk.	SCORING Pts.	Avg.	Hi.
Pete Maravich 79	79	2853	655	1562	.419	390	481	.811	93	329	422	488	227	4	120	. . .	18	1700	21.5	47
Nate Williams† 35	35	814	209	404	.517	84	102	.824	44	114	158	67	99	1	44	. . .	6	502	14.3	28
Nate Williams‡ 85	85	1945	474	988	.480	181	220	.823	102	235	337	145	251	3	97	. . .	30	1129	13.3	28
Jim Barnett* 45	45	1238	215	480	.448	156	188	.830	45	83	128	137	109	1	35	. . .	16	586	13.0	30
Aaron James 76	76	1731	370	776	.477	147	189	.778	140	226	366	66	217	4	41	. . .	15	887	11.7	34
Louie Nelson 72	72	1898	307	679	.452	192	250	.768	75	121	196	178	186	1	65	. . .	6	806	11.2	29
Bud Stallworth 73	73	1668	298	710	.420	125	182	.687	78	168	246	46	208	4	59	. . .	11	721	9.9	24
Neal Walk* 37	37	851	151	358	.422	64	80	.800	73	189	262	101	122	3	30	. . .	20	366	9.9	23
Henry Bibby† 28	28	524	91	219	.416	68	93	.731	18	32	50	76	61	0	25	. . .	0	250	8.9	20
Henry Bibby‡ 75	75	1400	270	619	.436	137	189	.725	47	90	137	181	157	0	54	. . .	3	677	9.0	27
E.C. Coleman 77	77	2176	253	568	.445	116	166	.699	189	360	549	105	277	10	82	. . .	37	622	8.1	23
Ollie Johnson* 43	43	1159	139	299	.465	62	77	.805	60	117	177	80	103	1	42	. . .	20	340	7.9	20
Rick Roberson 16	16	339	48	108	.444	23	40	.575	39	79	118	23	49	0	7	. . .	8	119	7.4	20
Otto Moore† 40	40	1055	117	258	.453	45	67	.672	92	236	328	82	146	3	21	. . .	39	279	7.0	16
Otto Moore‡ 42	42	1066	118	262	.450	46	69	.667	92	238	330	83	148	3	21	. . .	40	282	6.7	16
Mel Counts 75	75	1421	217	495	.438	86	113	.761	102	339	441	182	196	0	49	. . .	43	520	6.9	20
John Block* 4	4	57	9	29	.310	9	10	.900	6	12	18	7	11	0	4	. . .	1	27	6.8	12
Toby Kimball 3	3	90	7	23	.304	6	7	.857	8	18	26	4	12	0	2	. . .	0	20	6.7	8
Stu Lantz* 19	19	353	39	115	.339	47	53	.887	7	17	24	30	28	0	12	. . .	2	125	6.6	22
Rick Adelman* 28	28	613	67	159	.421	41	59	.695	13	42	55	69	58	1	47	. . .	6	175	6.3	16
Walt Bellamy 1	1	14	2	2	1.000	2	2	1.000	0	5	5	0	2	0	0	. . .	0	6	6.0	6
Russ Lee 15	15	139	29	76	.382	7	14	.500	5	16	31	7	17	1	11	. . .	3	65	4.3	11
Bernie Fryer 31	31	432	47	106	.443	33	43	.767	16	30	46	52	54	0	22	. . .	0	127	4.1	17
Lamar Green 15	15	280	24	70	.343	9	20	.450	28	81	109	16	38	0	4	. . .	5	57	3.8	10
Ken Boyd 6	6	25	7	13	.538	5	11	.455	3	2	5	2	2	0	3	. . .	0	19	3.2	7

NEW YORK KNICKERBOCKERS

	G	Min.	FGM	FGA	Pct.	FTM	FTA	Pct.	REBOUNDS Off.	Def.	Tot.	Ast.	PF	Dq.	Stl.	TO	Blk.	SCORING Pts.	Avg.	Hi.
Walt Frazier	78	3204	672	1391	.483	331	400	.828	90	375	465	474	205	2	190	...	14	1675	21.5	43
Earl Monroe	78	2814	668	1462	.457	297	359	.827	56	271	327	270	200	0	108	...	29	1633	20.9	38
Bill Bradley	79	2787	452	1036	.436	144	165	.873	65	186	251	247	283	5	74	...	18	1048	13.3	32
Phil Jackson	78	2285	324	712	.455	193	253	.763	137	463	600	136	330	10	84	...	53	841	10.8	29
John Gianelli	80	2797	343	726	.472	135	195	.692	214	475	689	163	263	3	38	...	118	821	10.3	23
Henry Bibby*	47	876	179	400	.448	69	96	.719	29	58	87	105	96	0	29	...	3	427	9.1	27
Harthorne Wingo	82	1686	233	506	.460	141	187	.754	163	293	456	84	215	2	48	...	35	607	7.4	19
Jim Barnett†	28	538	70	172	.407	43	50	.860	15	36	51	39	51	0	12	...	0	183	6.5	22
Jim Barnett‡	73	1776	285	652	.437	199	238	.836	60	119	179	176	160	1	47	...	16	769	10.5	30
Mel Davis	62	903	154	395	.390	48	70	.686	70	251	321	54	105	0	16	...	8	356	5.7	24
Neal Walk†	30	274	47	115	.409	22	25	.880	18	59	77	22	55	0	7	...	3	116	3.9	12
Neal Walk‡	67	1125	198	473	.419	86	105	.819	91	248	339	123	177	3	37	...	23	482	7.2	23
Jesse Dark	47	401	74	157	.471	22	40	.550	15	22	37	30	48	0	3	...	1	170	3.6	13
Dennis Bell	52	465	68	181	.376	20	36	.556	48	57	105	25	54	0	22	...	9	156	3.0	20
Tom Riker	51	483	53	147	.361	46	82	.561	40	67	107	19	64	0	15	...	5	152	3.0	12
Howard Porter*	17	133	13	36	.361	7	9	.778	13	25	38	2	17	0	3	...	1	33	1.9	7
Greg Jackson*	5	27	4	10	.400	0	0	...	2	0	2	3	5	0	0	...	0	8	1.6	6
Dave Stallworth	7	57	5	18	.278	0	0	...	6	14	20	2	10	0	3	...	3	10	1.4	6

PHILADELPHIA 76ERS

	G	Min.	FGM	FGA	Pct.	FTM	FTA	Pct.	REBOUNDS Off.	Def.	Tot.	Ast.	PF	Dq.	Stl.	TO	Blk.	SCORING Pts.	Avg.	Hi.
Fred Carter	77	3046	715	1598	.447	256	347	.738	73	267	340	336	257	5	82	...	20	1686	21.9	37
Billy Cunningham	80	2859	609	1423	.428	345	444	.777	130	596	726	442	270	4	91	...	35	1563	19.5	38
Doug Collins	81	2820	561	1150	.488	331	392	.844	104	211	315	213	291	6	108	...	17	1453	17.9	39
Steve Mix	46	1748	280	582	.481	159	205	.776	155	345	500	99	175	6	79	...	21	719	15.6	36
Tom Van Arsdale*	9	273	49	116	.422	28	41	.683	7	22	29	16	26	0	13	...	0	126	14.0	21
LeRoy Ellis	82	2183	287	623	.461	72	99	.727	195	387	582	117	178	1	44	...	55	646	7.9	27
Freddie Boyd	66	1362	205	495	.414	55	115	.478	16	73	89	161	134	0	43	...	4	465	7.0	35
Allan Bristow	72	1101	163	393	.415	121	153	.791	111	143	254	99	101	0	25	...	2	447	6.2	23
Clyde Lee†	71	2279	164	391	.419	87	138	.630	264	423	687	97	260	9	29	...	16	415	5.8	19
Clyde Lee‡	80	2456	176	427	.412	119	177	.672	288	469	757	105	285	9	30	...	20	471	5.9	19
Don Smith	54	538	131	321	.408	21	21	1.000	14	16	30	47	45	0	20	...	3	283	5.2	19
Connie Norman	12	72	23	44	.523	2	3	.667	3	9	12	4	9	0	3	...	1	48	4.0	10
Ken Durrett†	27	270	35	88	.398	20	32	.625	21	41	62	10	42	0	4	...	4	90	3.3	9
Ken Durrett‡	48	445	67	166	.404	31	52	.596	35	67	102	18	72	0	9	...	8	165	3.4	9
John Tschogl	39	623	53	148	.358	13	22	.591	52	59	111	30	80	2	25	...	25	119	3.1	13
Walt Wesley*	4	33	5	9	.556	2	4	.500	4	4	8	1	8	0	0	...	0	12	3.0	10
Harvey Catchings	37	528	41	74	.554	16	25	.640	49	104	153	21	82	1	10	...	60	98	2.6	8
Perry Warbington	5	70	4	21	.190	2	2	1.000	2	6	8	16	16	0	0	...	0	10	2.0	4

PHOENIX SUNS

	G	Min.	FGM	FGA	Pct.	FTM	FTA	Pct.	REBOUNDS Off.	Def.	Tot.	Ast.	PF	Dq.	Stl.	TO	Blk.	SCORING Pts.	Avg.	Hi.
Charlie Scott	69	2592	703	1594	.441	274	351	.781	72	201	273	311	296	11	111	...	24	1680	24.3	41
Dick Van Arsdale	70	2419	421	895	.470	282	339	.832	52	137	189	195	177	2	81	...	11	1124	16.1	46
Curtis Perry	79	2688	437	917	.477	184	256	.719	347	593	940	186	288	10	108	...	78	1058	13.4	26
Mike Bantom	82	2239	418	907	.461	185	259	.714	211	342	553	159	273	8	62	...	47	1021	12.5	29
Keith Erickson	49	1469	237	557	.425	130	156	.833	70	173	243	170	150	3	50	...	12	604	12.3	29
Dennis Awtrey	82	2837	339	722	.470	132	195	.677	242	462	704	342	227	2	60	...	52	810	9.9	24
Gary Melchionni	68	1529	232	539	.430	114	141	.809	45	142	187	156	116	1	48	...	12	578	8.5	23
Fred Saunders	69	1059	176	406	.433	66	95	.695	82	171	253	80	151	3	41	...	15	418	6.1	21
Nate Hawthorne	50	618	118	287	.411	61	94	.649	34	58	92	39	94	0	30	...	21	297	5.9	20
Earl Williams	79	1040	163	394	.414	45	103	.437	156	300	456	95	146	0	28	...	32	371	4.7	22
Greg Jackson†	44	775	69	166	.416	36	62	.581	17	50	67	93	125	5	23	...	9	174	4.0	18
Greg Jackson‡	49	802	73	176	.415	36	62	.581	19	50	69	96	130	5	23	...	9	182	3.7	18
Jim Owens	41	432	56	145	.386	12	16	.750	7	36	43	49	27	0	16	...	2	124	3.0	12
Corky Calhoun*	13	108	12	32	.375	14	15	.933	14	19	33	4	20	0	6	...	2	38	2.9	13

PORTLAND TRAIL BLAZERS

	G	Min.	FGM	FGA	Pct.	FTM	FTA	Pct.	REBOUNDS Off.	Def.	Tot.	Ast.	PF	Dq.	Stl.	TO	Blk.	SCORING Pts.	Avg.	Hi.
Sidney Wicks	82	3162	692	1391	.497	394	558	.706	231	646	877	287	289	5	108	...	80	1778	21.7	36
Geoff Petrie	80	3109	602	1319	.456	261	311	.839	38	171	209	424	215	1	81	...	13	1465	18.3	37
John Johnson	80	2540	527	1082	.487	236	301	.784	162	339	501	240	249	3	75	...	39	1290	16.1	35
Bill Walton	35	1153	177	345	.513	94	137	.686	92	349	441	167	115	4	29	...	94	448	12.8	25
Lloyd Neal	82	2278	409	869	.471	189	295	.641	186	501	687	139	239	2	43	...	87	1007	12.3	29
Larry Steele	76	2389	265	484	.548	122	146	.836	96	140	226	287	254	6	183	...	16	652	8.6	23
LaRue Martin	81	1372	236	522	.452	99	142	.697	136	272	408	69	239	5	33	...	49	571	7.0	22
Lenny Wilkens	65	1161	134	305	.439	152	198	.768	38	82	120	235	96	1	77	...	9	420	6.5	20
Barry Clemens	77	952	168	355	.473	45	60	.750	33	128	161	76	139	0	68	...	2	381	4.9	24
Phil Lumpkin	48	792	86	190	.453	30	39	.769	10	49	59	177	80	1	20	...	3	202	4.2	14
Greg Smith	55	519	71	146	.486	32	48	.667	29	60	89	27	96	1	22	...	6	174	3.2	16
Dan Anderson	43	453	47	105	.448	26	30	.867	8	21	29	81	44	0	16	...	1	120	2.8	10

SEATTLE SUPERSONICS

	G	Min.	FGM	FGA	Pct.	FTM	FTA	Pct.	REBOUNDS Off.	Def.	Tot.	Ast.	PF	Dq.	Stl.	TO	Blk.	SCORING Pts.	Avg.	Hi.
Spencer Haywood	68	2529	608	1325	.459	309	381	.811	198	432	630	137	173	1	54	. . .	108	1525	22.4	40
Fred Brown	81	2669	737	1537	.480	226	272	.831	113	230	343	284	227	2	187	. . .	14	1700	21.0	40
Archie Clark	77	2481	455	919	.495	161	193	.834	59	176	235	433	188	4	110	. . .	5	1071	13.9	31
Leonard Gray	75	2280	378	773	.489	104	144	.722	133	345	478	163	292	9	63	. . .	24	860	11.5	33
Tom Burleson	82	1888	322	772	.417	182	265	.687	155	417	572	115	221	1	64	. . .	153	826	10.1	29
Jim Fox	75	1766	253	540	.469	170	212	.802	128	363	491	137	168	1	48	. . .	17	676	9.0	28
John Brisker	21	276	60	141	.426	42	49	.857	15	18	33	19	33	0	7	. . .	3	162	7.7	28
Donald Watts	82	2056	232	551	.421	93	153	.608	95	167	262	499	254	7	190	. . .	12	557	6.8	23
Rod Derline	58	666	142	332	.428	43	56	.768	12	47	59	45	47	0	23	. . .	4	327	5.6	20
Talvin Skinner	73	1574	142	347	.409	63	97	.649	135	209	344	85	161	0	49	. . .	17	347	4.8	22
Wardell Jackson	56	939	96	242	.397	51	71	.718	53	80	133	30	126	2	26	. . .	5	243	4.3	23
Kennedy McIntosh	6	101	6	29	.207	6	9	.667	6	9	15	7	12	0	4	. . .	3	18	3.0	6
Dean Tolson	19	87	16	37	.432	11	17	.647	12	10	22	5	12	0	4	. . .	6	43	2.3	14
John Hummer	43	568	41	108	.380	14	51	.275	28	76	104	38	63	0	8	. . .	7	96	2.2	13

WASHINGTON BULLETS

	G	Min.	FGM	FGA	Pct.	FTM	FTA	Pct.	REBOUNDS Off.	Def.	Tot.	Ast.	PF	Dq.	Stl.	TO	Blk.	SCORING Pts.	Avg.	Hi.
Elvin Hayes	82	3465	739	1668	.443	409	534	.766	221	783	1004	206	238	0	158	. . .	187	1887	23.0	39
Phil Chenier	77	2869	690	1533	.450	301	365	.825	74	218	292	248	158	3	176	. . .	58	1681	21.8	38
Mike Riordan	74	2191	520	1057	.492	98	117	.838	90	194	284	198	238	4	72	. . .	6	1138	15.4	39
Kevin Porter	81	2589	406	827	.491	131	186	.704	55	97	152	650	320	12	152	. . .	11	943	11.6	29
Wes Unseld	73	2904	273	544	.502	126	184	.685	318	759	1077	297	180	1	115	. . .	68	672	9.2	26
Nick Weatherspoon . . .	82	1347	256	562	.456	103	138	.746	132	214	346	51	212	2	65	. . .	21	615	7.5	24
Jimmy Jones	73	1424	207	400	.518	103	142	.725	36	101	137	162	190	0	76	. . .	10	517	7.1	24
Truck Robinson	76	995	191	393	.486	60	115	.522	94	207	301	40	132	0	36	. . .	32	442	5.8	18
Clem Haskins	70	702	115	290	.397	53	63	.841	29	51	80	79	73	0	23	. . .	6	283	4.0	18
Dick Gibbs	59	424	74	190	.389	48	64	.750	26	35	61	19	60	0	12	. . .	3	196	3.3	13
Thomas Kozelko	73	754	60	167	.359	31	36	.861	50	90	140	41	125	4	28	. . .	5	151	2.1	14
Dennis DuVal	37	137	24	65	.369	12	18	.667	8	15	23	14	34	0	16	. . .	2	60	1.6	5
Stan Washington	1	4	0	1	.000	0	0	. . .	0	0	0	0	1	0	0	. . .	0	0	0.0	0

* Finished season with another team.   † Totals with this team only.   ‡ Totals with all teams.

PLAYOFF RESULTS

EASTERN CONFERENCE

FIRST ROUND

Houston 2, New York 1
Apr. 8—Tue.	New York 84 at Houston	.99
Apr. 10—Thur.	Houston 96 at New York	106
Apr. 12—Sat.	New York 86 at Houston	118

SEMIFINALS

Boston 4, Houston 1
Apr. 14—Mon.	Houston 106 at Boston	123
Apr. 16—Wed.	Houston 100 at Boston	112
Apr. 19—Sat.	Boston 102 at Houston	117
Apr. 22—Tue.	Boston 122 at Houston	117
Apr. 24—Thur.	Houston 115 at Boston	128

Washington 4, Buffalo 3
Apr. 10—Thur.	Buffalo 113 at Washington	102
Apr. 12—Sat.	Washington 120 at Buffalo	106
Apr. 16—Wed.	Buffalo 96 at Washington	111
Apr. 18—Fri.	Washington 102 at Buffalo	108
Apr. 20—Sun.	Buffalo 93 at Washington	.97
Apr. 23—Wed.	Washington 96 at Buffalo	102
Apr. 25—Fri.	Buffalo 96 at Washington	115

FINALS

Washington 4, Boston 2
Apr. 27—Sun.	Washington 100 at Boston	.95
Apr. 30—Wed.	Boston 92 at Washington	117
May 3—Sat.	Washington 90 at Boston	101
May 7—Wed.	Boston 108 at Washington	119
May 9—Fri.	Washington 99 at Boston	103
May 11—Sun.	Boston 92 at Washington	.98

WESTERN CONFERENCE

FIRST ROUND

Seattle 2, Detroit 1
Apr. 8—Tue.	Detroit 77 at Seattle	.90
Apr. 10—Thur.	Seattle 106 at Detroit	122
Apr. 12—Sat.	Detroit 93 at Seattle	100

SEMIFINALS

Golden State 4, Seattle 2
Apr. 14—Mon.	Seattle 96 at Golden State	123
Apr. 16—Wed.	Seattle 100 at Golden State	.99
Apr. 17—Thur.	Golden State 105 at Seattle	.96
Apr. 19—Sat.	Golden State 94 at Seattle	111
Apr. 22—Tue.	Seattle 100 at Golden State	124
Apr. 24—Thur.	Golden State 105 at Seattle	.96

Chicago 4, Kansas City/Omaha 2
Apr. 9—Wed.	Kansas City/Omaha 89 at Chicago	.95
Apr. 13—Sun.	Chicago 95 at Kansas City/Omaha	102
Apr. 16—Wed.	Kansas City/Omaha 90 at Chicago	.93
Apr. 18—Fri.	Chicago 100 at Kansas City/Omaha	*104
Apr. 20—Sun.	Kansas City/Omaha 77 at Chicago	104
Apr. 23—Wed.	Chicago 101 at Kansas City/Omaha	.89

FINALS

Golden State 4, Chicago 3
Apr. 27—Sun.	Chicago 89 at Golden State	107
Apr. 30—Wed.	Golden State 89 at Chicago	.90
May 4—Sun.	Golden State 101 at Chicago	108
May 6—Tue.	Chicago 106 at Golden State	111
May 8—Thur.	Chicago 89 at Golden State	.79
May 11—Sun.	Golden State 86 at Chicago	.72
May 14—Wed.	Chicago 79 at Golden State	.83

NBA FINALS

Golden State 4, Washington 0
May 18—Sun.	Golden State 101 at Washington	.95
May 20—Tue.	Washington 91 at Golden State	.92
May 23—Fri.	Washington 101 at Golden State	109
May 25—Sun.	Golden State 96 at Washington	.95

*Denotes number of overtime periods.

1973-74

1973-74 NBA CHAMPION BOSTON CELTICS

Front row (from left): Jo Jo White, Don Chaney, John Havlicek, president and general manager Red Auerbach, chairman of the board Robert Schmertz, head coach Tom Heinsohn, Dave Cowens, Paul Silas, assistant coach John Killilea. Back row (from left): assistant trainer Mark Volk, team dentist Dr. Samuel Kane, Paul Westphal, Phil Hankinson, Steve Downing, Don Nelson, Hank Finkel, Steve Kuberski, Art Williams, team physician Dr. Thomas Silva, trainer Frank Challant.

FINAL STANDINGS

ATLANTIC DIVISION

	Atl.	Bos.	Buf.	Cap.	Chi.	Cle.	Det.	G.S.	Hou.	KC/O	L.A.	Mil.	N.Y.	Phi.	Pho.	Por.	Sea.	W	L	Pct.	GB
Boston	5	..	5	2	2	4	3	3	4	3	2	2	5	7	3	4	2	56	26	.683	..
New York.	5	2	4	3	2	5	3	3	2	3	2	2	..	4	3	2	4	49	33	.598	7
Buffalo	4	2	..	3	1	5	1	1	4	2	0	1	4	6	3	3	2	42	40	.512	14
Philadelphia. .	3	1	1	2	1	1	2	1	2	3	0	0	3	..	3	2	0	25	57	.305	31

CENTRAL DIVISION

	Atl.	Bos.	Buf.	Cap.	Chi.	Cle.	Det.	G.S.	Hou.	KC/O	L.A.	Mil.	N.Y.	Phi.	Pho.	Por.	Sea.	W	L	Pct.	GB
Capital.	4	4	3	..	1	6	2	3	4	3	2	1	3	4	2	3	2	47	35	.573	..
Atlanta.	..	1	2	4	1	4	0	1	5	1	4	1	1	3	1	2	4	35	47	.427	12
Houston	2	2	2	3	0	4	1	0	..	2	2	0	4	4	2	3	1	32	50	.390	15
Cleveland. . . .	3	2	1	1	0	..	2	0	4	0	3	0	1	5	1	4	2	29	53	.354	18

MIDWEST DIVISION

	Atl.	Bos.	Buf.	Cap.	Chi.	Cle.	Det.	G.S.	Hou.	KC/O	L.A.	Mil.	N.Y.	Phi.	Pho.	Por.	Sea.	W	L	Pct.	GB
Milwaukee. . .	3	2	3	3	3	4	4	3	4	7	2	..	2	4	5	6	4	59	23	.720	..
Chicago.	3	2	3	3	..	4	5	4	4	5	1	3	2	3	4	4	4	54	28	.659	5
Detroit.	4	1	3	2	2	2	..	5	3	4	4	3	1	2	6	5	5	52	30	.634	7
K.C./Omaha. .	3	1	2	1	2	4	2	3	2	..	1	0	1	1	4	4	2	33	49	.402	26

PACIFIC DIVISION

	Atl.	Bos.	Buf.	Cap.	Chi.	Cle.	Det.	G.S.	Hou.	KC/O	L.A.	Mil.	N.Y.	Phi.	Pho.	Por.	Sea.	W	L	Pct.	GB
Los Angeles. .	0	2	4	2	5	1	2	2	2	5	..	4	2	4	4	4	4	47	35	.573	..
Golden State .	3	1	3	1	2	4	1	..	4	3	4	3	1	3	5	3	3	44	38	.537	3
Seattle.	0	2	2	2	2	1	3	3	3	4	3	2	0	4	3	3	..	36	46	.439	11
Phoenix.	3	1	1	2	2	3	0	2	2	2	2	1	1	1	..	3	4	30	52	.366	17
Portland	2	0	1	1	2	0	1	4	1	2	3	0	2	2	3	..	3	27	55	.329	20

TEAM STATISTICS

OFFENSIVE

	G	FGM	FGA	Pct.	FTM	FTA	Pct.	REBOUNDS Off.	Def.	Tot.	Ast.	PF	Dq.	Stl.	TO	Blk.	SCORING Pts.	Avg.
Buffalo	82	3728	7763	.480	1699	2221	.765	1150	2830	3980	2165	1875	17	786	1828	600	9155	111.6
Golden State . .	82	3721	8020	.464	1569	2018	.778	1379	3035	4414	1989	1893	33	668	1667	450	9011	109.9
Los Angeles . . .	82	3536	7803	.453	1879	2443	.769	1365	2970	4335	2179	2032	26	794	1913	653	8951	109.2
Boston	82	3630	7969	.456	1677	2097	.800	1378	3074	4452	2187	1868	22	561	1796	305	8937	109.0
Atlanta	82	3602	7744	.465	1703	2264	.752	1240	2712	3952	1993	2073	33	758	1823	332	8907	108.6
Phoenix	82	3555	7726	.460	1737	2235	.777	1090	2723	3813	2052	2123	46	658	1666	305	8847	107.9
Houston	82	3564	7426	.480	1682	2071	.812	1063	2588	3651	2212	2104	36	727	1681	407	8810	107.4
Milwaukee	82	3726	7571	.492	1328	1741	.763	1133	2881	4014	2225	1864	26	726	1694	519	8780	107.1
Seattle	82	3584	8056	.445	1606	2095	.767	1323	2706	4029	2106	2074	31	689	1622	294	8774	107.0

	G	FGM	FGA	Pct.	FTM	FTA	Pct.	REBOUNDS Off.	Def.	Tot.	Ast.	PF	Dq.	Stl.	TO	Blk.	SCORING Pts.	Avg.
Portland	82	3585	7684	.467	1591	2112	.753	1254	2598	3852	2106	2050	23	797	1823	341	8761	106.8
Detroit	82	3453	7515	.459	1654	2164	.764	1200	2681	3881	1956	1930	19	793	1763	419	8560	104.4
Chicago	82	3292	7378	.446	1784	2314	.771	1143	2616	3759	1868	1874	17	764	1690	316	8368	102.0
K.C./Omaha	82	3369	7342	.459	1628	2104	.774	1112	2554	3666	1744	1916	22	796	1791	384	8366	102.0
Capital	82	3480	7886	.441	1393	1869	.745	1286	2887	4173	1770	1746	24	703	1568	441	8353	101.9
New York	82	3478	7483	.465	1350	1738	.777	959	2725	3684	1937	1884	14	554	1463	277	8306	101.3
Philadelphia	82	3331	7702	.432	1633	2118	.771	1182	2626	3808	1799	1964	25	756	1665	220	8295	101.2
Cleveland	82	3420	7782	.439	1381	1788	.772	1275	2492	3767	2048	1925	22	598	1545	293	8221	100.3

DEFENSIVE

	FGM	FGA	Pct.	FTM	FTA	Pct.	REBOUNDS Off.	Def.	Tot.	Ast.	PF	Dq.	Stl.	TO	Blk.	SCORING Pts.	Avg.	Dif.
New York	3292	7377	.446	1496	1974	.758	1042	2790	3832	1580	1792	13	479	1555	348	8080	98.5	+2.8
Chicago	3336	7246	.460	1425	1847	.772	1136	2734	3870	1830	2200	34	614	1880	406	8097	98.7	+3.3
Milwaukee	3311	7799	.425	1499	1969	.761	1269	2487	3756	1909	1707	12	719	1554	312	8121	99.0	+8.1
Detroit	3376	7499	.450	1475	1932	.763	1173	2632	3805	1980	1996	30	772	1822	410	8227	100.3	+4.1
Capital	3496	7760	.451	1239	1639	.756	1206	2915	4121	1900	1840	9	651	1651	350	8231	100.4	+1.5
Cleveland	3440	7342	.469	1696	2163	.784	1137	2802	3939	2120	1853	27	630	1654	343	8576	104.6	-4.3
Boston	3561	8047	.443	1494	1936	.772	1131	2604	3735	1934	1858	29	540	1599	309	8616	105.1	+3.9
K.C./Omaha	3580	7514	.476	1512	1950	.775	1210	2650	3860	1916	1907	22	723	1765	373	8672	105.8	-3.8
Golden State	3619	7995	.453	1563	2054	.761	1227	2702	3929	2027	1826	15	714	1477	465	8801	107.3	+2.6
Philadelphia	3600	7685	.468	1617	2066	.783	1311	3107	4418	1930	1991	23	755	1830	446	8817	107.5	-6.3
Houston	3551	7433	.478	1719	2337	.736	1162	2619	3781	2122	1994	29	707	1737	375	8821	107.6	-0.2
Los Angeles	3667	8364	.438	1546	2044	.756	1525	2786	4311	2061	2135	37	797	1719	430	8880	108.3	+0.9
Seattle	3554	7675	.463	1875	2427	.773	1173	2932	4105	2255	2012	34	730	1796	355	8983	109.5	-2.5
Atlanta	3573	7628	.468	1878	2386	.787	1142	2754	3896	2028	2128	40	823	1846	388	9024	110.0	-1.4
Phoenix	3648	7809	.467	1843	2356	.782	1220	2773	3993	2180	2003	25	810	1637	396	9139	111.5	-3.6
Portland	3664	7571	.484	1825	2299	.794	1197	2678	3875	2308	1961	20	866	1713	415	9153	111.6	-4.8
Buffalo	3786	8106	.467	1592	2013	.791	1271	2733	4004	2256	1992	37	798	1763	435	9164	111.8	-0.2
Avgs.	3533	7697	.459	1606	2082	.771	1208	2747	3955	2020	1953	26	713	1706	386	8671	105.7	...

HOME/ROAD/NEUTRAL

	Home	Road	Neutral	Total		Home	Road	Neutral	Total
Atlanta	23-18	12-25	0-4	35-47	Kansas City/Omaha	20-21	13-28	0-0	33-49
Boston	26-6	21-18	9-2	56-26	Los Angeles	30-11	17-24	0-0	47-35
Buffalo	19-13	17-21	6-6	42-40	Milwaukee	31-7	24-16	4-0	59-23
Capital	31-10	15-25	1-0	47-35	New York	28-13	21-19	0-1	49-33
Chicago	32-9	21-19	1-0	54-28	Philadelphia	14-23	9-30	2-4	25-57
Cleveland	18-23	11-28	0-2	29-53	Phoenix	24-17	6-34	0-1	30-52
Detroit	29-12	23-17	0-1	52-30	Portland	22-19	5-34	0-2	27-55
Golden State	23-18	20-20	1-0	44-38	Seattle	22-19	14-27	0-0	36-46
Houston	18-23	13-25	1-2	32-50	Totals	410-262	262-410	25-25	697-697

INDIVIDUAL LEADERS

POINTS

(minimum 70 games)

	G	FGM	FTM	Pts.	Avg.
Bob McAdoo, Buffalo	74	901	459	2261	30.6
Pete Maravich, Atlanta	76	819	469	2107	27.7
Kareem Abdul-Jabbar, Milw.	81	948	295	2191	27.0
Gail Goodrich, Los Angeles	82	784	508	2076	25.3
Rick Barry, Golden State	80	796	417	2009	25.1
Rudy Tomjanovich, Houston	80	788	385	1961	24.5
Geoff Petrie, Portland	73	740	291	1771	24.3
Spencer Haywood, Seattle	75	694	373	1761	23.5
John Havlicek, Boston	76	685	346	1716	22.6
Bob Lanier, Detroit	81	748	326	1822	22.5
Sidney Wicks, Portland	75	685	314	1684	22.5
Austin Carr, Cleveland	81	748	279	1775	21.9
Phil Chenier, Capital	76	697	274	1668	21.9
Bob Love, Chicago	82	731	323	1785	21.8
Elvin Hayes, Capital	81	689	357	1735	21.4
Fred Carter, Philadelphia	78	706	254	1666	21.4
Cazzie Russell, Golden State	82	738	208	1684	20.5
Walt Frazier, New York	80	674	295	1643	20.5
Calvin Murphy, Houston	81	671	310	1652	20.4
Tom Van Arsdale, Philadelphia	78	614	298	1526	19.6

FIELD GOALS

(minimum 560 attempted)

	FGM	FGA	Pct.
Bob McAdoo, Buffalo	901	1647	.547
Kareem Abdul-Jabbar, Milwaukee	948	1759	.539
Rudy Tomjanovich, Houston	788	1470	.536
Calvin Murphy, Houston	671	1285	.522
Butch Beard, Golden State	316	617	.512
Clifford Ray, Chicago	313	612	.511
Don Nelson, Boston	364	717	.508
Happy Hairston, Los Angeles	385	759	.507
Bob Lanier, Detroit	748	1483	.504
Bob Dandridge, Milwaukee	583	1158	.503

FREE THROWS

(minimum 160 attempted)

	FTM	FTA	Pct.
Ernie DiGregorio, Buffalo	174	193	.902
Rick Barry, Golden State	417	464	.899
Chet Walker, Chicago	439	502	.875
Jeff Mullins, Golden State	168	192	.875
Bill Bradley, New York	146	167	.874
Calvin Murphy, Houston	310	357	.868
Dick Snyder, Seattle	194	224	.866
Gail Goodrich, Los Angeles	508	588	.864
Fred Brown, Seattle	195	226	.863
Jim McMillian, Buffalo	325	379	.858

1973-74

ASSISTS

ASSISTS
(minimum 70 games)

	G	No.	Avg.
Ernie DiGregorio, Buffalo	.81	663	8.2
Calvin Murphy, Houston	.81	603	7.4
Lenny Wilkens, Cleveland	.74	522	7.1
Walt Frazier, New York	.80	551	6.9
Norm Van Lier, Chicago	.80	548	6.9
Dave Bing, Detroit	.81	555	6.9
Oscar Robertson, Milwaukee	.70	446	6.4
Rick Barry, Golden State	.80	484	6.1
John Havlicek, Boston	.76	447	5.9
Kevin Porter, Capital	.81	469	5.8

STEALS
(minimum 70 games)

	G	No.	Avg.
Larry Steele, Portland	.81	217	2.68
Steve Mix, Philadelphia	.82	212	2.59
Randy Smith, Buffalo	.82	203	2.48
Jerry Sloan, Chicago	.77	183	2.38
Rick Barry, Golden State	.80	169	2.11
Phil Chenier, Capital	.76	155	2.04
Norm Van Lier, Chicago	.80	162	2.03
Walt Frazier, New York	.80	161	2.01
Calvin Murphy, Houston	.81	157	1.94
Jim Price, Los Angeles	.82	157	1.91

REBOUNDS
(minimum 70 games)

	G	Off.	Def.	Tot.	Avg.
Elvin Hayes, Capital	.81	354	1109	1463	18.1
Dave Cowens, Boston	.80	264	993	1257	15.7
Bob McAdoo, Buffalo	.74	281	836	1117	15.1
Kareem Abdul-Jabbar, Milw.	.81	287	891	1178	14.5
Happy Hairston, Los Angeles	.77	335	705	1040	13.5
Sam Lacey, Kansas City/Omaha	.79	293	762	1055	13.4
Spencer Haywood, Seattle	.75	318	689	1007	13.4
Bob Lanier, Detroit	.81	269	805	1074	13.3
Clifford Ray, Chicago	.80	285	692	977	12.2
Gar Heard, Buffalo	.81	270	677	947	11.7

BLOCKED SHOTS
(minimum 70 games)

	G	No.	Avg.
Elmore Smith, Los Angeles	.81	393	4.85
Kareem Abdul-Jabbar, Milwaukee	.81	283	3.49
Bob McAdoo, Buffalo	.74	246	3.32
Bob Lanier, Detroit	.81	247	3.05
Elvin Hayes, Capital	.81	240	2.96
Gar Heard, Buffalo	.81	230	2.84
Sam Lacey, Kansas City/Omaha	.79	184	2.33
Clifford Ray, Chicago	.80	173	2.16
Spencer Haywood, Seattle	.75	106	1.41
Zaid Abdul-Aziz, Houston	.79	104	1.32

INDIVIDUAL STATISTICS, TEAM BY TEAM

ATLANTA HAWKS

	G	Min.	FGM	FGA	Pct.	FTM	FTA	Pct.	Off.	Def.	Tot.	Ast.	PF	Dq.	Stl.	TO	Blk.	Pts.	Avg.	Hi.
Pete Maravich	76	2903	819	1791	.457	469	568	.826	98	276	374	396	261	4	111	...	13	2107	27.7	42
Lou Hudson	65	2588	678	1356	.500	295	353	.836	126	224	350	213	205	3	160	...	29	1651	25.4	44
Herm Gilliam	62	2003	384	846	.454	106	134	.791	61	206	267	355	190	5	134	...	18	874	14.1	35
Walt Bellamy	77	2440	389	801	.486	233	383	.608	264	476	740	189	232	2	52	...	48	1011	13.1	34
Jim Washington	73	2519	297	612	.485	134	196	.684	207	528	735	156	249	5	49	...	74	728	10.0	23
John Brown	77	1715	277	632	.438	163	217	.751	177	264	441	114	239	10	29	...	16	717	9.3	25
Dwight Jones	74	1448	238	502	.474	116	156	.744	145	309	454	86	197	3	29	...	64	592	8.0	33
Steve Bracey	75	1463	241	520	.463	69	96	.719	26	120	146	231	157	0	60	...	5	551	7.3	25
John Wetzel	70	1232	107	252	.425	41	57	.719	39	131	170	138	147	1	73	...	19	255	3.6	17
Dale Schlueter	57	547	63	135	.467	38	50	.760	54	101	155	45	84	0	25	...	22	164	2.9	12
Tom Ingelsby	48	398	50	131	.382	29	37	.784	10	34	44	37	43	0	19	...	4	129	2.7	10
John Tschogl	64	499	59	166	.355	10	17	.588	33	43	76	33	69	0	17	...	20	128	2.0	14

BOSTON CELTICS

	G	Min.	FGM	FGA	Pct.	FTM	FTA	Pct.	Off.	Def.	Tot.	Ast.	PF	Dq.	Stl.	TO	Blk.	Pts.	Avg.	Hi.
John Havlicek	76	3091	685	1502	.456	346	416	.832	138	349	487	447	196	1	95	...	32	1716	22.6	34
Dave Cowens	80	3352	645	1475	.437	228	274	.832	264	993	1257	354	294	7	95	...	101	1518	19.0	35
Jo Jo White	82	3238	649	1445	.449	190	227	.837	100	251	351	448	185	1	105	...	25	1488	18.1	37
Paul Silas	82	2599	340	772	.440	264	337	.783	334	581	915	186	246	3	63	...	20	944	11.5	31
Don Nelson	82	1748	364	717	.508	215	273	.788	90	255	345	162	189	1	19	...	13	943	11.5	29
Don Chaney	81	2258	348	750	.464	149	180	.828	210	168	378	176	247	7	83	...	62	845	10.4	26
Paul Westphal	82	1165	238	475	.501	112	153	.732	49	94	143	171	173	1	39	...	34	588	7.2	28
Steve Kuberski	78	985	157	368	.427	86	111	.775	96	141	237	38	125	0	7	...	7	400	5.1	21
Phil Hankinson	28	163	50	103	.485	10	13	.769	22	28	50	4	18	0	3	...	1	110	3.9	13
Steve Downing	24	137	21	64	.328	22	38	.579	14	25	39	11	33	0	5	...	0	64	2.7	4
Art Williams	67	617	73	168	.435	27	32	.844	20	95	115	163	100	0	44	...	3	173	2.6	14
Hank Finkel	60	427	60	130	.462	28	43	.651	41	94	135	27	62	1	3	...	7	148	2.5	14

BUFFALO BRAVES

	G	Min.	FGM	FGA	Pct.	FTM	FTA	Pct.	Off.	Def.	Tot.	Ast.	PF	Dq.	Stl.	TO	Blk.	Pts.	Avg.	Hi.
Bob McAdoo	74	3185	901	1647	.547	459	579	.793	281	836	1117	170	252	...	88	...	246	2261	30.6	52
Jim McMillian	82	3322	600	1214	.494	325	379	.858	216	394	610	256	186	0	129	...	26	1525	18.6	48
Randy Smith	82	2745	531	1079	.492	205	288	.712	87	228	315	383	261	4	203	...	4	1267	15.5	32
Gar Heard	81	2889	524	1205	.435	191	294	.650	270	677	947	180	300	3	136	...	230	1239	15.3	36
Ernie DiGregorio	81	2910	530	1260	.421	174	193	.902	48	171	219	663	242	2	59	...	9	1234	15.2	32
Jack Marin†	27	680	145	266	.545	71	81	.877	30	92	122	46	93	3	23	...	18	361	13.4	24
Jack Marin‡	74	1782	355	709	.501	153	179	.855	59	169	228	167	213	5	46	...	26	863	11.7	26
Bob Kauffman	74	1304	171	366	.467	107	150	.713	97	229	326	142	155	0	37	...	18	449	6.1	16
Matt Guokas†	27	549	61	110	.555	10	20	.500	12	28	40	69	56	1	19	...	6	132	4.9	23
Matt Guokas‡	75	1871	195	396	.492	39	60	.650	31	90	121	238	150	3	54	...	21	429	5.7	23

	G	Min.	FGM	FGA	Pct.	FTM	FTA	Pct.	REBOUNDS Off.	Def.	Tot.	Ast.	PF	Dq.	Stl.	TO	Blk.	SCORING Pts.	Avg.	Hi.
Dave Wohl*	41	606	60	150	.400	42	60	.700	7	22	29	127	72	1	33	...	1	162	4.0	16
Ken Charles	59	693	88	185	.476	53	79	.671	25	40	65	54	91	0	31	...	10	229	3.9	16
Lee Winfield	36	433	37	105	.352	33	52	.635	19	24	43	47	42	0	15	...	5	107	3.0	9
Kevin Kunnert*	39	340	49	101	.485	11	16	.688	43	63	106	25	83	0	5	...	25	109	2.8	9
Mike Macaluso	30	112	19	44	.432	10	17	.588	10	15	25	3	31	0	7	...	1	48	1.6	8
Paul Ruffner	20	51	11	27	.407	8	13	.615	4	7	11	0	10	0	1	...	1	30	1.5	7
Jim Garvin	6	11	1	4	.250	0	0	...	1	4	5	0	1	0	0	...	0	2	0.3	2

CAPITAL BULLETS

	G	Min.	FGM	FGA	Pct.	FTM	FTA	Pct.	REBOUNDS Off.	Def.	Tot.	Ast.	PF	Dq.	Stl.	TO	Blk.	SCORING Pts.	Avg.	Hi.
Phil Chenier	76	2942	697	1607	.434	274	334	.820	114	274	388	239	135	0	155	...	67	1668	21.9	38
Elvin Hayes	81	3602	689	1627	.423	357	495	.721	354	1109	1463	163	252	1	86	...	240	1735	21.4	43
Mike Riordan	81	3230	577	1223	.472	136	174	.782	120	260	380	264	237	2	102	...	14	1290	15.9	33
Kevin Porter	81	2339	477	997	.478	180	249	.723	79	100	179	469	319	14	95	...	9	1134	14.0	28
Archie Clark	56	1786	315	675	.467	103	131	.786	44	97	141	285	122	0	59	...	6	733	13.1	28
Nick Weatherspoon	65	1216	199	483	.412	96	139	.691	133	264	397	38	179	1	48	...	16	494	7.6	19
Wes Unseld	56	1727	146	333	.438	36	55	.655	152	365	517	159	121	1	56	...	16	328	5.9	14
Louie Nelson	49	556	93	215	.433	53	73	.726	26	44	70	52	62	0	31	...	2	239	4.9	17
Dave Stallworth	45	458	75	187	.401	47	55	.855	52	73	125	25	61	0	28	...	4	197	4.4	19
Walt Wesley	39	400	71	151	.470	26	43	.605	63	73	136	14	74	1	9	...	20	168	4.3	20
Manny Leaks	53	845	79	232	.341	58	83	.699	94	150	244	25	95	1	10	...	39	216	4.1	19
Thomas Kozelko	49	573	59	133	.444	23	32	.719	52	72	124	25	82	3	21	...	7	141	2.9	15
Rich Rinaldi	7	48	3	22	.136	3	4	.750	2	5	7	10	7	0	3	...	1	9	1.3	3
Tom Patterson	2	8	0	1	.000	1	2	.500	1	1	2	2	0	0	0	...	0	1	0.5	1

CHICAGO BULLS

	G	Min.	FGM	FGA	Pct.	FTM	FTA	Pct.	REBOUNDS Off.	Def.	Tot.	Ast.	PF	Dq.	Stl.	TO	Blk.	SCORING Pts.	Avg.	Hi.
Bob Love	82	3292	731	1752	.417	323	395	.818	183	309	492	130	221	1	84	...	28	1785	21.8	43
Chet Walker	82	2661	572	1178	.486	439	502	.875	131	275	406	200	201	1	68	...	4	1583	19.3	39
Norm Van Lier	80	2863	427	1051	.406	288	370	.778	114	263	377	548	282	4	162	...	7	1142	14.3	30
Jerry Sloan	77	2860	412	921	.447	194	273	.711	150	406	556	149	273	3	183	...	10	1018	13.2	25
Howard Porter	73	1229	296	658	.450	92	115	.800	86	199	285	32	116	0	23	...	9	684	9.4	25
Clifford Ray	80	2632	313	612	.511	121	199	.608	285	692	977	246	281	5	58	...	173	747	9.3	24
Bob Weiss	79	1708	263	564	.466	142	170	.835	32	71	103	303	158	0	104	...	12	668	8.5	24
Rowland Garrett	41	373	68	184	.370	21	32	.656	31	39	70	11	43	0	5	...	9	157	3.8	16
Tom Boerwinkle	46	602	58	119	.487	42	60	.700	53	160	213	94	80	0	16	...	18	158	3.4	16
Rick Adelman	55	618	64	170	.376	54	76	.711	16	53	69	56	63	0	36	...	1	182	3.3	12
John Hummer*	18	186	23	46	.500	14	28	.500	13	24	37	13	30	0	3	...	1	60	3.3	12
Dennis Awtrey	68	756	65	123	.528	54	94	.574	49	125	174	86	128	3	22	...	14	184	2.7	10

CLEVELAND CAVALIERS

	G	Min.	FGM	FGA	Pct.	FTM	FTA	Pct.	REBOUNDS Off.	Def.	Tot.	Ast.	PF	Dq.	Stl.	TO	Blk.	SCORING Pts.	Avg.	Hi.
Austin Carr	81	3100	748	1682	.445	279	326	.856	139	150	289	305	189	2	92	...	14	1775	21.9	39
Lenny Wilkens	74	2483	462	994	.465	289	361	.801	80	197	277	522	165	2	97	...	17	1213	16.4	34
Bobby Smith	82	2612	536	1179	.455	139	169	.822	134	301	435	198	242	4	89	...	30	1211	14.8	34
Dwight Davis	76	2477	376	862	.436	197	274	.719	174	470	644	186	291	6	63	...	74	949	12.5	25
Steve Patterson	76	1910	262	599	.437	69	112	.616	223	396	619	165	193	3	48	...	58	593	7.8	22
Bob Rule	26	540	76	192	.396	34	46	.739	43	60	103	47	71	0	12	...	10	186	7.2	22
Jim Cleamons	81	1642	236	545	.433	93	133	.699	63	167	230	227	152	1	61	...	17	565	7.0	21
Jim Brewer	82	1862	210	548	.383	80	123	.650	207	317	524	149	192	1	46	...	35	500	6.1	18
Barry Clemens	71	913	163	346	.471	62	73	.849	42	124	166	80	136	2	36	...	2	388	5.5	18
Fred Foster	57	649	112	288	.389	54	64	.844	43	65	108	62	79	0	19	...	6	278	4.8	21
Luke Witte	57	728	105	243	.432	46	62	.742	80	147	227	41	91	0	8	...	22	256	4.5	17
Johnny Warren	69	790	132	291	.454	35	41	.854	42	86	128	62	117	1	27	...	6	299	4.3	24
Cornell Warner*	5	49	2	13	.154	4	4	1.000	5	12	17	4	7	0	0	...	2	8	1.6	4

DETROIT PISTONS

	G	Min.	FGM	FGA	Pct.	FTM	FTA	Pct.	REBOUNDS Off.	Def.	Tot.	Ast.	PF	Dq.	Stl.	TO	Blk.	SCORING Pts.	Avg.	Hi.
Bob Lanier	81	3047	748	1483	.504	326	409	.797	269	805	1074	343	273	7	110	...	247	1822	22.5	45
Dave Bing	81	3124	582	1336	.436	356	438	.813	108	173	281	555	216	1	109	...	17	1520	18.8	33
Curtis Rowe	82	2499	380	769	.494	118	169	.698	167	348	515	136	177	1	49	...	36	878	10.7	28
Don Adams	74	2298	303	742	.408	153	201	.761	133	315	448	141	242	2	110	...	12	759	10.3	25
George Trapp	82	1489	333	693	.481	99	134	.739	97	216	313	81	226	2	47	...	33	765	9.3	22
Stu Lantz	50	980	154	361	.427	139	163	.853	34	79	113	97	79	0	38	...	3	447	8.9	24
John Mengelt	77	1555	249	558	.446	182	229	.795	40	166	206	148	164	2	68	...	7	680	8.8	30
Willie Norwood	74	1178	247	484	.510	95	143	.664	95	134	229	58	156	2	60	...	9	589	8.0	29
Chris Ford	82	2059	264	595	.444	57	77	.740	109	195	304	279	159	1	148	...	14	585	7.1	24
Jim Davis	78	947	117	283	.413	90	139	.647	102	191	293	86	158	1	39	...	30	324	4.2	15
Bob Nash	35	281	41	115	.357	24	39	.615	31	43	74	14	35	0	3	...	10	106	3.0	16
Ben Kelso	46	298	35	96	.365	15	22	.682	15	16	31	18	45	0	12	...	1	85	1.8	8

1973-74

GOLDEN STATE WARRIORS

	G	Min.	FGM	FGA	Pct.	FTM	FTA	Pct.	Off.	Def.	Tot.	Ast.	PF	Dq.	Stl.	TO	Blk.	Pts.	Avg.	Hi.
									REBOUNDS									SCORING		
Rick Barry.........	80	2918	796	1746	.456	417	464	.899	103	437	540	484	265	4	169	...	40	2009	25.1	64
Cazzie Russell......	82	2574	738	1531	.482	208	249	.835	142	211	353	192	194	1	54	...	17	1684	20.5	49
Jeff Mullins.......	77	2498	541	1144	.473	168	192	.875	86	190	276	305	214	2	69	...	22	1250	16.2	32
Nate Thurmond.....	62	2463	308	694	.444	191	287	.666	249	629	878	165	179	4	41	...	179	807	13.0	31
Jim Barnett.......	77	1689	350	755	.464	184	226	.814	76	146	222	209	146	1	56	...	11	884	11.5	30
Butch Beard......	79	2134	316	617	.512	173	234	.739	136	253	389	300	241	11	105	...	9	805	10.2	30
Charles Johnson....	59	1051	194	468	.415	38	55	.691	49	126	175	102	111	1	62	...	7	426	7.2	20
George Johnson	66	1291	173	358	.483	59	107	.551	190	332	522	73	176	3	35	...	124	405	6.1	23
Clyde Lee	54	1642	129	284	.454	62	107	.579	188	410	598	68	179	3	27	...	17	320	5.9	14
Derrek Dickey......	66	930	115	233	.494	51	66	.773	123	216	339	54	112	1	17	...	15	281	4.3	17
Joe Ellis	50	515	61	190	.321	18	31	.581	37	85	122	37	76	2	33	...	9	140	2.8	17

HOUSTON ROCKETS

	G	Min.	FGM	FGA	Pct.	FTM	FTA	Pct.	Off.	Def.	Tot.	Ast.	PF	Dq.	Stl.	TO	Blk.	Pts.	Avg.	Hi.
									REBOUNDS									SCORING		
Rudy Tomjanovich ...	80	3227	788	1470	.536	385	454	.848	230	487	717	250	230	0	89	...	66	1961	24.5	42
Calvin Murphy......	81	2922	671	1285	.522	310	357	.868	51	137	188	603	310	8	157	...	4	1652	20.4	39
Mike Newlin	76	2591	510	1139	.448	380	444	.856	77	185	262	363	259	5	87	...	9	1400	18.4	36
Zaid Abdul-Aziz.....	79	2459	336	732	.459	193	240	.804	259	664	923	166	227	3	80	...	104	865	10.9	27
Jack Marin*	47	1102	210	443	.474	82	98	.837	29	77	106	121	120	2	23	...	8	502	10.7	26
Cliff Meely	77	1754	330	773	.427	90	140	.643	103	336	439	124	234	5	53	...	77	750	9.7	22
Ed Ratleff	81	1773	254	585	.434	103	129	.798	93	193	286	181	182	2	90	...	27	611	7.5	18
Dave Wohl†	26	449	61	127	.480	33	42	.786	4	13	17	109	64	2	43	...	1	155	6.0	18
Dave Wohl‡........	67	1055	121	277	.437	75	102	.735	11	35	46	236	136	3	76	...	2	317	4.7	18
Matt Guokas*	39	1007	93	203	.458	21	28	.750	17	43	60	133	73	1	27	...	14	207	5.3	14
E.C. Coleman	58	1075	128	250	.512	47	74	.635	81	171	252	76	162	4	37	...	20	303	5.2	19
Otto Moore*	13	313	32	69	.464	4	8	.500	20	64	84	18	37	2	10	...	18	68	5.2	14
Kevin Kunnert†	25	361	56	114	.491	10	17	.588	40	71	111	18	68	1	5	...	29	122	4.9	12
Kevin Kunnert‡	64	701	105	215	.488	21	33	.636	83	134	217	43	151	1	10	...	54	231	3.6	12
Jimmy Walker*.....	3	38	7	12	.583	0	1	.000	0	2	2	4	4	0	0	...	0	14	4.7	6
Ron Riley†	36	421	57	145	.393	10	14	.714	35	86	121	29	68	0	15	...	22	124	3.4	13
Ron Riley‡	48	591	81	202	.401	24	38	.632	48	129	177	37	95	0	18	...	24	186	3.9	15
George Johnson	26	238	23	51	.451	8	17	.471	20	41	61	9	46	1	8	...	8	54	2.1	8
Stan McKenzie	11	112	7	24	.292	6	8	.750	3	13	16	6	17	0	3	...	0	20	1.8	9
Paul McCracken	4	13	1	4	.250	0	0	...	1	5	6	2	3	0	0	...	0	2	0.5	2

KANSAS CITY/OMAHA KINGS

	G	Min.	FGM	FGA	Pct.	FTM	FTA	Pct.	Off.	Def.	Tot.	Ast.	PF	Dq.	Stl.	TO	Blk.	Pts.	Avg.	Hi.
									REBOUNDS									SCORING		
Jimmy Walker†......	72	2920	575	1228	.468	273	332	.822	39	163	202	303	166	0	81	...	9	1423	19.8	38
Jimmy Walker‡......	75	2958	582	1240	.469	273	333	.820	39	165	204	307	170	0	81	...	9	1437	19.2	38
Nate Archibald	35	1272	222	492	.451	173	211	.820	21	64	85	266	76	0	56	...	7	617	17.6	42
Nate Williams	82	2513	538	1165	.462	193	236	.818	118	226	344	182	290	5	149	...	34	1269	15.5	30
Sam Lacey	79	3107	467	982	.476	185	247	.749	293	762	1055	299	254	3	126	...	184	1119	14.2	26
Don Kojis	77	2091	400	836	.478	210	272	.772	126	257	383	110	157	2	77	...	15	1010	13.1	30
Ron Behagen	80	2059	357	827	.432	162	212	.764	188	379	567	134	291	9	56	...	37	876	11.0	27
Matt Guokas*	9	315	41	83	.494	8	12	.667	2	19	21	36	21	1	8	...	1	90	10.0	18
John Block	82	1777	275	634	.434	164	206	.796	129	260	389	94	229	2	68	...	35	714	8.7	27
Larry McNeill	54	516	106	220	.482	99	140	.707	60	86	146	24	76	0	35	...	6	311	5.8	21
Ron Riley*	12	170	24	57	.421	14	24	.583	13	43	56	8	27	0	3	...	2	62	5.2	15
Mike D'Antoni	52	989	107	266	.402	33	47	.702	24	69	93	123	112	0	75	...	15	247	4.8	15
Ken Durrett	45	462	86	176	.489	42	69	.609	28	50	78	19	68	0	13	...	5	214	4.8	24
Howie Komives......	44	830	78	192	.406	33	38	.868	10	33	43	97	83	0	32	...	3	189	4.3	18
Otto Moore†	65	633	88	171	.515	35	54	.648	60	140	200	47	62	0	16	...	31	211	3.2	15
Otto Moore‡	78	946	120	240	.500	39	62	.629	80	204	284	65	99	2	26	...	49	279	3.6	15
Ted Manakas........	5	45	4	10	.400	4	4	1.000	0	3	3	2	4	0	1	...	0	12	2.4	4
Justus Thigpen......	1	2	1	3	.333	0	0	...	1	0	1	0	0	0	0	...	0	2	2.0	2
Mike Ratliff.........	2	4	0	0	...	0	0	...	0	0	0	0	0	0	0	...	0	0	0.0	0

LOS ANGELES LAKERS

	G	Min.	FGM	FGA	Pct.	FTM	FTA	Pct.	Off.	Def.	Tot.	Ast.	PF	Dq.	Stl.	TO	Blk.	Pts.	Avg.	Hi.
									REBOUNDS									SCORING		
Gail Goodrich	82	3061	784	1773	.442	508	588	.864	95	155	250	427	227	3	126	...	12	2076	25.3	49
Jerry West	31	967	232	519	.447	165	198	.833	30	86	116	206	80	0	81	...	23	629	20.3	35
Jim Price	82	2628	538	1197	.449	187	234	.799	120	258	378	369	229	2	157	...	29	1263	15.4	31
Happy Hairston......	77	2634	385	759	.507	343	445	.771	335	705	1040	208	264	2	64	...	17	1113	14.5	29
Connie Hawkins†	71	2538	368	733	.502	173	224	.772	162	360	522	379	203	1	105	...	78	909	12.8	26
Connie Hawkins‡	79	2761	404	807	.501	191	251	.761	176	389	565	407	223	1	113	...	81	999	12.6	26
Elmore Smith	81	2922	434	949	.457	147	249	.590	204	702	906	150	309	8	71	...	393	1015	12.5	37
Pat Riley..........	72	1361	287	667	.430	110	144	.764	38	90	128	148	173	1	54	...	3	684	9.5	22
Bill Bridges	65	1812	216	513	.421	116	164	.707	193	306	499	148	219	3	58	...	31	548	8.4	28
Stan Love	51	698	119	278	.428	49	64	.766	54	116	170	48	132	3	28	...	20	287	5.6	21
Kermit Washington ...	45	400	73	151	.483	26	49	.531	62	85	147	19	77	0	21	...	18	172	3.8	18
Mel Counts........	45	499	61	167	.365	24	33	.727	56	90	146	54	85	2	20	...	23	146	3.2	16
Nate Hawthorne	33	229	38	93	.409	30	48	.625	16	16	32	23	33	1	9	...	6	106	3.2	13
Travis Grant	3	6	1	4	.250	1	3	.333	0	1	1	0	1	0	0	...	0	3	1.0	3

MILWAUKEE BUCKS

	G	Min.	FGM	FGA	Pct.	FTM	FTA	Pct.	Off.	Def.	Tot.	Ast.	PF	Dq.	Stl.	TO	Blk.	Pts.	Avg.	Hi.
									REBOUNDS									SCORING		
Kareem Abdul-Jabbar	81	3548	948	1759	.539	295	420	.702	287	891	1178	386	238	2	112	...	283	2191	27.0	44
Bob Dandridge	71	2521	583	1158	.503	175	214	.818	117	362	479	201	271	4	111	...	41	1341	18.9	32
Lucius Allen	72	2388	526	1062	.495	216	274	.788	89	202	291	374	215	2	137	...	22	1268	17.6	39
Oscar Robertson	70	2477	338	772	.438	212	254	.835	71	208	279	446	132	0	77	...	4	888	12.7	24
Jon McGlocklin	79	1910	329	693	.475	72	80	.900	33	106	139	241	128	1	43	...	7	730	9.2	29
Curtis Perry	81	2386	325	729	.446	78	134	.582	242	461	703	183	301	8	104	...	97	728	9.0	23
Ron Williams	71	1130	192	393	.489	60	68	.882	19	50	69	153	114	1	49	...	2	444	6.3	21
Cornell Warner†	67	1356	172	336	.512	81	110	.736	101	279	380	67	197	8	27	...	40	425	6.3	21
Cornell Warner‡	72	1405	174	349	.499	85	114	.746	106	291	397	71	204	8	27	...	42	433	6.0	21
Mickey Davis	73	1012	169	335	.504	93	112	.830	78	146	224	87	94	0	27	...	5	431	5.9	22
Terry Driscoll	64	697	88	187	.471	30	46	.652	73	126	199	54	121	0	21	...	16	206	3.2	15
Russ Lee	36	166	38	94	.404	11	16	.688	16	24	40	20	29	0	11	...	0	87	2.4	10
Dick Garrett†	15	87	11	35	.314	5	6	.833	5	9	14	9	15	0	3	...	1	27	1.8	8
Dick Garrett‡	40	326	43	126	.341	15	19	.789	15	25	40	23	56	0	10	...	1	101	2.5	14
Chuck Terry	7	32	4	12	.333	0	0	...	1	2	3	4	4	0	2	...	0	8	1.1	4
Dick Cunningham	8	45	3	6	.500	0	7	.000	1	15	16	0	5	0	2	...	2	6	0.8	4

NEW YORK KNICKERBOCKERS

	G	Min.	FGM	FGA	Pct.	FTM	FTA	Pct.	Off.	Def.	Tot.	Ast.	PF	Dq.	Stl.	TO	Blk.	Pts.	Avg.	Hi.
									REBOUNDS									SCORING		
Walt Frazier	80	3338	674	1429	.472	295	352	.838	120	416	536	551	212	2	161	...	15	1643	20.5	44
Dave DeBusschere	71	2699	559	1212	.461	164	217	.756	134	623	757	253	222	2	67	...	39	1282	18.1	41
Bill Bradley	82	2813	502	1112	.451	146	167	.874	59	194	253	242	278	2	42	...	21	1150	14.0	31
Earl Monroe	41	1194	240	513	.468	93	113	.823	22	99	121	110	97	0	34	...	19	573	14.0	29
Phil Jackson	82	2050	361	757	.477	191	246	.776	123	355	478	134	277	7	42	...	67	913	11.1	30
Willis Reed	19	500	84	184	.457	42	53	.792	47	94	141	30	49	0	12	...	21	210	11.1	25
Dean Meminger	78	2079	274	539	.508	103	160	.644	125	156	281	162	161	0	62	...	8	651	8.3	27
Henry Bibby	66	986	210	465	.452	73	88	.830	48	85	133	91	123	0	65	...	2	493	7.5	22
John Gianelli	70	1423	208	434	.479	92	121	.760	110	233	343	77	159	1	23	...	42	500	7.3	25
Jerry Lucas	73	1627	194	420	.462	67	96	.698	62	312	374	230	134	0	28	...	24	455	6.2	17
Dick Barnett	5	58	10	26	.385	2	3	.667	1	3	4	6	2	0	1	...	0	22	4.4	10
Harthorne Wingo	60	536	82	172	.477	48	76	.632	72	94	166	25	85	0	7	...	14	212	3.5	14
Dick Garrett*	25	239	32	91	.352	10	13	.769	10	16	26	14	41	0	7	...	1	74	3.0	14
Mel Davis	30	167	33	95	.347	12	16	.750	17	37	54	8	36	0	3	...	4	78	2.6	12
Tom Riker	17	57	13	29	.448	12	17	.706	9	6	15	3	6	0	0	...	0	38	2.2	11
Al McGuire	2	10	2	4	.500	0	0	...	0	2	2	1	2	0	0	...	0	4	2.0	2
Dennis Bell	1	4	0	1	.000	0	0	...	0	0	0	0	0	0	0	...	0	0	0.0	0

PHILADELPHIA 76ERS

	G	Min.	FGM	FGA	Pct.	FTM	FTA	Pct.	Off.	Def.	Tot.	Ast.	PF	Dq.	Stl.	TO	Blk.	Pts.	Avg.	Hi.
									REBOUNDS									SCORING		
Fred Carter	78	3044	706	1641	.430	254	358	.709	82	289	371	443	276	4	113	...	23	1666	21.4	35
Tom Van Arsdale	78	3041	614	1433	.428	298	350	.851	88	305	393	202	300	6	62	...	3	1526	19.6	35
Steve Mix	82	2969	495	1042	.475	228	288	.792	305	559	864	152	305	9	212	...	37	1218	14.9	38
Larry Jones	72	1876	263	622	.423	197	235	.838	71	113	184	230	116	0	85	...	18	723	10.0	22
LeRoy Ellis	81	2831	326	722	.452	147	196	.750	292	598	890	189	224	2	86	...	87	799	9.9	24
Freddie Boyd	75	1818	286	712	.402	141	195	.723	16	77	93	249	173	1	60	...	9	713	9.5	24
Doug Collins	25	436	72	194	.371	55	72	.764	7	39	46	40	65	1	13	...	2	199	8.0	17
Toby Kimball	75	1592	216	456	.474	127	185	.686	185	367	552	73	199	1	49	...	23	559	7.5	22
Don May	56	812	152	367	.414	89	102	.873	25	111	136	63	137	0	25	...	8	393	7.0	28
Larry Cannon	19	335	49	127	.386	19	28	.679	16	20	36	52	48	0	7	...	4	117	6.2	17
Allan Bristow	55	643	108	270	.400	42	57	.737	68	99	167	92	68	1	29	...	1	258	4.7	20
Rod Freeman	35	265	39	103	.379	28	41	.683	22	32	54	14	42	0	12	...	1	106	3.0	11
Luke Rackley	9	68	5	13	.385	8	11	.727	5	17	22	0	11	0	3	...	4	18	2.0	5

PHOENIX SUNS

	G	Min.	FGM	FGA	Pct.	FTM	FTA	Pct.	Off.	Def.	Tot.	Ast.	PF	Dq.	Stl.	TO	Blk.	Pts.	Avg.	Hi.
									REBOUNDS									SCORING		
Charlie Scott	52	2003	538	1171	.459	246	315	.781	64	158	222	271	194	6	99	...	22	1322	25.4	44
Dick Van Arsdale	78	2832	514	1028	.500	361	423	.853	66	155	221	324	241	2	96	...	17	1389	17.8	37
Neal Walk	82	2549	573	1245	.460	235	297	.791	235	602	837	331	255	9	73	...	57	1381	16.8	32
Keith Erickson	66	2033	393	824	.477	177	221	.801	94	320	414	205	193	3	63	...	20	963	14.6	40
Connie Hawkins*	8	223	36	74	.486	18	27	.667	14	29	43	28	20	0	8	...	3	90	11.3	21
Clem Haskins	81	1822	364	792	.460	171	203	.842	78	144	222	259	166	1	81	...	16	899	11.1	36
Mike Bantom	76	1982	314	787	.399	141	213	.662	172	347	519	163	289	15	50	...	47	769	10.1	26
Corky Calhoun	77	2207	268	581	.461	98	129	.760	115	292	407	135	253	4	71	...	30	634	8.2	25
Gary Melchionni	69	1251	202	439	.460	92	107	.860	46	96	142	142	85	1	41	...	9	496	7.2	23
Bill Chamberlain	28	367	57	130	.438	39	56	.696	33	47	80	37	74	2	20	...	12	153	5.5	19
Bob Christian	81	1244	140	288	.486	106	151	.702	85	254	339	98	191	3	19	...	32	386	4.8	21
Lamar Green	72	1103	129	317	.407	38	68	.559	85	265	350	43	150	1	32	...	38	296	4.1	14
Jim Owens	17	101	21	39	.538	11	14	.786	1	8	9	15	6	0	5	...	0	53	3.1	10
Joe Reaves	7	38	6	11	.545	4	11	.364	2	6	8	1	6	0	0	...	2	16	2.3	4

1973-74

PORTLAND TRAIL BLAZERS

	G	Min.	FGM	FGA	Pct.	FTM	FTA	Pct.	Off.	Def.	Tot.	Ast.	PF	Dq.	Stl.	TO	Blk.	Pts.	Avg.	Hi.
Geoff Petrie	73	2800	740	1537	.481	291	341	.853	64	144	208	315	199	2	84	...	15	1771	24.3	43
Sidney Wicks	75	2853	685	1492	.459	314	412	.762	196	488	684	326	214	2	90	...	63	1684	22.5	38
John Johnson	69	2287	459	990	.464	212	261	.812	160	355	515	284	221	1	69	...	29	1130	16.4	32
Rick Roberson	69	2060	364	797	.457	205	316	.649	251	450	701	133	252	4	65	...	55	933	13.5	37
Larry Steele	81	2648	325	680	.478	135	171	.789	89	221	310	323	295	10	217	...	32	785	9.7	28
Lloyd Neal	80	1517	246	502	.490	117	168	.696	150	344	494	89	190	0	45	...	73	609	7.6	22
Bernie Fryer	80	1674	226	491	.460	107	135	.793	60	99	159	279	187	1	92	...	10	559	7.0	27
Ollie Johnson	79	1718	209	434	.482	77	94	.819	116	208	324	167	179	2	60	...	30	495	6.3	23
Dennis Layton	22	327	55	112	.491	14	26	.538	7	26	33	51	45	0	9	...	1	124	5.6	19
Bob Verga	21	216	42	93	.452	20	32	.625	11	7	18	17	22	0	12	...	0	104	5.0	22
LaRue Martin	50	538	101	232	.435	42	66	.636	74	107	181	20	90	0	7	...	26	244	4.9	17
Charlie Davis	8	90	14	40	.350	3	4	.750	2	9	11	11	7	0	2	...	0	31	3.9	11
Greg Smith	67	878	99	228	.434	48	79	.608	65	124	189	78	126	1	41	...	6	246	3.7	12
Donald Sibley	28	124	20	56	.357	6	7	.857	9	16	25	13	23	0	4	...	1	46	1.6	8

SEATTLE SUPERSONICS

	G	Min.	FGM	FGA	Pct.	FTM	FTA	Pct.	Off.	Def.	Tot.	Ast.	PF	Dq.	Stl.	TO	Blk.	Pts.	Avg.	Hi.
Spencer Haywood	75	3039	694	1520	.457	373	458	.814	318	689	1007	240	198	2	65	...	106	1761	23.5	37
Dick Snyder	74	2670	572	1189	.481	194	224	.866	90	216	306	265	257	4	90	...	26	1338	18.1	41
Fred Brown	82	2501	578	1226	.471	195	226	.863	114	287	401	414	276	6	136	...	18	1351	16.5	58
John Brisker	35	717	178	396	.449	82	100	.820	59	87	146	56	70	0	28	...	6	438	12.5	47
Jim Fox	78	2179	322	673	.478	241	293	.823	244	470	714	227	247	5	56	...	21	885	11.3	29
Dick Gibbs	71	1528	302	700	.431	162	201	.806	91	132	223	79	195	1	39	...	18	766	10.8	30
John Hummer†	35	933	121	259	.467	45	96	.469	71	175	246	94	89	0	25	...	21	287	8.2	16
John Hummer‡	53	1119	144	305	.472	59	124	.476	84	199	283	107	119	0	28	...	22	347	6.5	16
Donald Watts	62	1424	198	510	.388	100	155	.645	72	110	182	351	207	8	115	...	13	496	8.0	24
Kennedy McIntosh	69	2056	223	573	.389	65	107	.607	111	250	361	94	178	4	52	...	29	511	7.4	22
Bud Stallworth	67	1019	188	479	.392	48	77	.623	51	123	174	33	129	0	21	...	12	424	6.3	23
Jim McDaniels	27	439	63	173	.364	23	43	.535	51	77	128	24	48	0	7	...	15	149	5.5	29
Walt Hazzard	49	571	76	180	.422	34	45	.756	18	39	57	122	78	0	26	...	6	186	3.8	24
Milt Williams	53	505	62	149	.416	41	63	.651	19	28	47	103	82	1	25	...	0	165	3.1	22
Vester Marshall	13	174	7	29	.241	3	7	.429	14	23	37	4	20	0	4	...	3	17	1.3	5

* Finished season with another team. † Totals with this team only. ‡ Totals with all teams.

PLAYOFF RESULTS

EASTERN CONFERENCE

SEMIFINALS

Boston 4, Buffalo 2
Mar. 30—Sat.	Buffalo 97 at Boston	107
Apr. 2—Tue.	Boston 105 at Buffalo	115
Apr. 3—Wed.	Buffalo 107 at Boston	120
Apr. 6—Sat.	Boston 102 at Buffalo	104
Apr. 9—Tue.	Buffalo 97 at Boston	100
Apr. 12—Fri.	Boston 106 at Buffalo	104

New York 4, Capital 3
Mar. 29—Fri.	Capital 91 at New York	102
Mar. 31—Sun.	New York 87 at Capital	99
Apr. 2—Tue.	Capital 88 at New York	79
Apr. 5—Fri.	New York 101 at Capital	*93
Apr. 7—Sun.	Capital 105 at New York	106
Apr. 10—Wed.	New York 92 at Capital	109
Apr. 12—Fri.	Capital 81 at New York	91

FINALS

Boston 4, New York 1
Apr. 14—Sun.	New York 88 at Boston	113
Apr. 16—Tue.	Boston 111 at New York	99
Apr. 19—Fri.	New York 103 at Boston	100
Apr. 21—Sun.	Boston 98 at New York	91
Apr. 24—Wed.	New York 94 at Boston	105

WESTERN CONFERENCE

SEMIFINALS

Milwaukee 4, Los Angeles 1
Mar. 29—Fri.	Los Angeles 95 at Milwaukee	99
Mar. 31—Sun.	Los Angeles 90 at Milwaukee	109
Apr. 2—Tue.	Milwaukee 96 at Los Angeles	98
Apr. 4—Thur.	Milwaukee 112 at Los Angeles	90
Apr. 7—Sun.	Los Angeles 92 at Milwaukee	114

Chicago 4, Detroit 3
Mar. 30—Sat.	Detroit 97 at Chicago	88
Apr. 1—Mon.	Chicago 108 at Detroit	103
Apr. 5—Fri.	Detroit 83 at Chicago	84
Apr. 7—Sun.	Chicago 87 at Detroit	102
Apr. 9—Tue.	Detroit 94 at Chicago	98
Apr. 11—Thur.	Chicago 88 at Detroit	92
Apr. 13—Sat.	Detroit 94 at Chicago	96

FINALS

Milwaukee 4, Chicago 0
Apr. 16—Tue.	Chicago 85 at Milwaukee	101
Apr. 18—Thur.	Milwaukee 113 at Chicago	111
Apr. 20—Sat.	Chicago 90 at Milwaukee	113
Apr. 22—Mon.	Milwaukee 115 at Chicago	99

NBA FINALS

Boston 4, Milwaukee 3
Apr. 28—Sun.	Boston 98 at Milwaukee	83
Apr. 30—Tue.	Boston 96 at Milwaukee	*105
May 3—Fri.	Milwaukee 83 at Boston	95
May 5—Sun.	Milwaukee 97 at Boston	89
May 7—Tue.	Boston 96 at Milwaukee	87
May 10—Fri.	Milwaukee 102 at Boston	**101
May 12—Sun.	Boston 102 at Milwaukee	87

*Denotes number of overtime periods.

1972-73

1972-73 NBA CHAMPION NEW YORK KNICKERBOCKERS
Front row (from left): Henry Bibby, Walt Frazier, president Ned Irish, chairman of the board Irving Mitchell Felt, general manager and coach Red Holzman, Earl Monroe, Dick Barnett. Back row (from left): Bill Bradley, Phil Jackson, John Gianelli, Dave DeBusschere, Willis Reed, Jerry Lucas, Tom Riker, Dean Meminger, trainer Danny Whalen.

FINAL STANDINGS

ATLANTIC DIVISION

	Atl.	Balt.	Bos.	Buf.	Chi.	Cle.	Det.	G.S.	Hou.	KC/O	L.A.	Mil.	N.Y.	Phi.	Pho.	Por.	Sea.	W	L	Pct.	GB
Boston	5	5	..	7	3	5	3	3	5	3	4	2	4	7	4	4	4	68	14	.829	..
New York	3	3	4	6	1	6	3	2	5	4	2	2	..	6	3	3	4	57	25	.695	11
Buffalo	1	1	0	..	2	1	1	0	1	1	0	0	1	7	1	2	2	21	61	.256	47
Philadelphia	0	1	0	1	0	0	1	0	1	1	0	1	1	..	0	1	1	9	73	.110	59

CENTRAL DIVISION

	Atl.	Balt.	Bos.	Buf.	Chi.	Cle.	Det.	G.S.	Hou.	KC/O	L.A.	Mil.	N.Y.	Phi.	Pho.	Por.	Sea.	W	L	Pct.	GB
Baltimore	4	..	1	5	0	8	2	3	5	3	1	2	3	5	2	4	4	52	30	.634	..
Atlanta	..	3	1	5	2	3	2	1	4	2	3	1	3	6	3	4	3	46	36	.561	6
Houston	4	2	1	5	0	3	3	1	..	0	1	1	1	5	2	2	2	33	49	.402	19
Cleveland	4	0	1	5	1	..	1	1	4	2	1	1	0	6	1	1	3	32	50	.390	20

MIDWEST DIVISION

	Atl.	Balt.	Bos.	Buf.	Chi.	Cle.	Det.	G.S.	Hou.	KC/O	L.A.	Mil.	N.Y.	Phi.	Pho.	Por.	Sea.	W	L	Pct.	GB
Milwaukee	3	2	2	4	4	3	5	5	3	6	3	..	2	3	5	5	5	60	22	.732	..
Chicago	2	4	1	2	..	3	3	3	4	5	1	2	3	4	4	5	5	51	31	.622	9
Detroit	2	2	1	3	4	3	..	2	1	3	1	2	1	3	4	6	2	40	42	.488	20
K.C./Omaha	2	1	1	3	2	2	3	2	4	..	1	1	0	3	3	4	4	36	46	.439	24

PACIFIC DIVISION

	Atl.	Balt.	Bos.	Buf.	Chi.	Cle.	Det.	G.S.	Hou.	KC/O	L.A.	Mil.	N.Y.	Phi.	Pho.	Por.	Sea.	W	L	Pct.	GB
Los Angeles	1	3	0	4	5	3	5	4	3	5	..	3	2	4	6	6	6	60	22	.732	..
Golden State	3	1	1	4	3	3	4	..	3	4	3	1	2	4	2	5	4	47	35	.573	13
Phoenix	1	2	0	3	2	3	2	4	2	3	1	1	1	4	..	5	4	38	44	.463	22
Seattle	1	0	0	2	1	1	4	3	2	2	0	1	0	3	2	4	..	26	56	.317	34
Portland	0	0	0	2	1	3	0	1	2	2	0	1	1	3	2	..	3	21	61	.256	39

TEAM STATISTICS

OFFENSIVE

	G	FGM	FGA	Pct.	FTM	FTA	Pct.	Reb.	Ast.	PF	Dq.	SCORING Pts.	SCORING Avg.
Houston	82	3772	8249	.457	1706	2152	.793	4060	1939	1949	25	9250	112.8
Boston	82	3811	8511	.448	1616	2073	.780	4802	2320	1805	19	9238	112.7
Atlanta	82	3700	8033	.461	1819	2482	.733	4174	2074	1916	30	9219	112.4
Los Angeles	82	3740	7819	.478	1679	2264	.742	4562	2302	1636	9	9159	111.7
Phoenix	82	3612	7942	.455	1931	2437	.792	4003	1944	2012	40	9155	111.6
Detroit	82	3666	7916	.463	1710	2294	.745	4105	1882	1812	10	9042	110.3
Golden State	82	3715	8163	.455	1493	1871	.798	4405	1985	1693	15	8923	108.8
Kansas City/Omaha	82	3621	7581	.478	1580	2036	.776	3628	2118	2054	33	8822	107.6

	G	FGM	FGA	Pct.	FTM	FTA	Pct.	Reb.	Ast.	PF	Dq.	SCORING Pts.	Avg.
Milwaukee	82	3759	7808	.481	1271	1687	.753	4245	2226	1763	13	8789	107.2
Portland	82	3588	7842	.458	1531	2129	.719	3928	2102	1970	33	8707	106.2
New York	82	3627	7764	.467	1356	1739	.780	3382	2187	1775	10	8610	105.0
Baltimore	82	3656	7883	.464	1294	1742	.743	4205	2051	1672	14	8606	105.0
Chicago	82	3480	7835	.444	1574	2073	.759	4000	2023	1881	26	8534	104.1
Philadelphia	82	3471	8264	.420	1598	2130	.750	4174	1688	1984	28	8540	104.1
Seattle	82	3447	7681	.449	1606	2080	.772	4161	1958	1877	24	8500	103.7
Buffalo	82	3536	7877	.449	1399	1966	.712	4158	2218	2034	40	8471	103.3
Cleveland	82	3431	7884	.435	1556	2084	.747	4063	2106	1941	21	8418	102.7

DEFENSIVE

	FGM	FGA	Pct.	FTM	FTA	Pct.	Reb.	Ast.	PF	Dq.	SCORING Pts.	Avg.	Dif.
New York	3291	7561	.435	1471	1961	.750	4100	1714	1781	18	8053	98.2	+6.8
Milwaukee	3385	8028	.422	1345	1783	.754	3916	1906	1601	13	8115	99.0	+8.2
Chicago	3343	7098	.471	1562	2080	.751	3915	1910	2002	38	8248	100.6	+3.5
Baltimore	3531	8010	.441	1269	1702	.746	4226	1852	1682	11	8331	101.6	+3.4
Los Angeles	3646	8409	.434	1167	1583	.737	4101	1963	1941	27	8459	103.2	+8.5
Boston	3513	8095	.434	1540	2032	.758	3958	1957	1821	23	8566	104.5	+8.2
Cleveland	3465	7673	.452	1707	2230	.765	4115	2311	1932	25	8637	105.3	-2.6
Golden State	3603	8163	.441	1463	1891	.774	4265	2034	1766	14	8669	105.7	+3.1
Seattle	3678	8093	.454	1628	2156	.755	4158	2145	1875	25	8984	109.6	-5.9
Detroit	3803	8064	.472	1418	1862	.762	4019	2263	1891	22	9024	110.0	+0.3
Kansas City/Omaha	3698	7640	.484	1665	2174	.766	3961	1885	1816	9	9061	110.5	-2.9
Atlanta	3758	8152	.461	1696	2193	.773	4147	2020	2104	35	9212	112.3	+0.1
Portland	3709	7780	.477	1800	2327	.774	4236	2271	1885	18	9218	112.4	-6.2
Buffalo	3745	7947	.471	1733	2299	.754	4278	2383	1822	23	9223	112.5	-9.2
Phoenix	3758	8005	.469	1744	2318	.752	4139	2166	2068	46	9260	112.9	-1.3
Houston	3824	8119	.471	1744	2290	.762	4338	2104	1902	22	9302	113.4	-0.6
Philadelphia	3882	8215	.473	1767	2358	.749	4683	2239	1885	21	9531	116.2	-12.1
Avgs.	3625	7944	.456	1572	2073	.758	4121	2066	1869	23	8823	107.6	...

HOME/ROAD/NEUTRAL

	Home	Road	Neutral	Total		Home	Road	Neutral	Total
Atlanta	28-13	17-23	1-0	46-36	Kansas City/Omaha	24-17	12-29	0-0	36-46
Baltimore	24-9	21-17	7-4	52-30	Los Angeles	30-11	28-11	2-0	60-22
Boston	33-6	32-8	3-0	68-14	Milwaukee	33-5	25-15	2-2	60-22
Buffalo	14-27	6-31	1-3	21-61	New York	35-6	21-18	1-1	57-25
Chicago	29-12	20-19	2-0	51-31	Philadelphia	5-26	2-36	2-11	9-73
Cleveland	20-21	10-27	2-2	32-50	Phoenix	22-19	15-25	1-0	38-44
Detroit	26-15	13-25	1-2	40-42	Portland	13-28	8-32	0-1	21-61
Golden State	27-14	18-20	2-1	47-35	Seattle	16-25	10-29	0-2	26-56
Houston	14-14	10-28	9-7	33-49	Totals	393-268	268-393	36-36	697-697

INDIVIDUAL LEADERS

POINTS

(minimum 70 games)

	G	FGM	FTM	Pts.	Avg.
Nate Archibald, K.C./Omaha	.80	1028	663	2719	34.0
Kareem Abdul-Jabbar, Milw.	.76	982	328	2292	30.2
Spencer Haywood, Seattle	.77	889	473	2251	29.2
Lou Hudson, Atlanta	.75	816	397	2029	27.1
Pete Maravich, Atlanta	.79	789	485	2063	26.1
Charlie Scott, Phoenix	.81	806	436	2048	25.3
Geoff Petrie, Portland	.79	836	298	1970	24.9
Gail Goodrich, Los Angeles	.76	750	314	1814	23.9
Bob Lanier, Detroit	.81	810	307	1927	23.8
Sidney Wicks, Portland	.80	761	384	1906	23.8
John Havlicek, Boston	.80	766	370	1902	23.8
Bob Love, Chicago	.82	774	347	1895	23.1
Dave Bing, Detroit	.82	692	456	1840	22.4
Rick Barry, Golden State	.82	737	358	1832	22.3
Elvin Hayes, Baltimore	.81	713	291	1717	21.2
Walt Frazier, New York	.78	681	286	1648	21.1
Austin Carr, Cleveland	.82	702	281	1685	20.5
Dave Cowens, Boston	.82	740	204	1684	20.5
Lenny Wilkens, Cleveland	.75	572	394	1538	20.5
Neal Walk, Phoenix	.81	678	279	1635	20.2
Bob Dandridge, Milwaukee	.73	638	198	1474	20.2

FIELD GOALS

(minimum 560 attempted)

	FGM	FGA	Pct.
Wilt Chamberlain, Los Angeles	.426	586	.727
Matt Guokas, Kansas City/Omaha	.322	565	.570
Kareem Abdul-Jabbar, Milwaukee	.982	1772	.554
Curtis Rowe, Detroit	.547	1053	.519
Jim Fox, Seattle	.316	613	.515
Jerry Lucas, New York	.312	608	.513
Mike Riordan, Baltimore	.652	1278	.510
Archie Clark, Baltimore	.302	596	.507
Bob Kauffman, Buffalo	.535	1059	.505
Walt Bellamy, Atlanta	.455	901	.505

FREE THROWS

(minimum 160 attempted)

	FTM	FTA	Pct.
Rick Barry, Golden State	.358	397	.902
Calvin Murphy, Houston	.239	269	.888
Mike Newlin, Houston	.327	369	.886
Jimmy Walker, Houston	.244	276	.884
Bill Bradley, New York	.169	194	.871
Cazzie Russell, Golden State	.172	199	.864
Dick Snyder, Seattle	.186	216	.861
Dick Van Arsdale, Phoenix	.426	496	.859
John Havlicek, Boston	.370	431	.858
Jack Marin, Houston	.248	292	.849

ASSISTS

(minimum 70 games)

	G	No.	Avg.
Nate Archibald, Kansas City/Omaha	80	910	11.4
Lenny Wilkens, Cleveland	75	628	8.4
Dave Bing, Detroit	82	637	7.8
Oscar Robertson, Milwaukee	73	551	7.6
Norm Van Lier, Chicago	80	567	7.1
Pete Maravich, Atlanta	79	546	6.9
John Havlicek, Boston	80	529	6.6
Herm Gilliam, Atlanta	76	482	6.3
Charlie Scott, Phoenix	81	495	6.1
Jo Jo White, Boston	82	498	6.1

REBOUNDS

(minimum 70 games)

	G	No.	Avg.
Wilt Chamberlain, Los Angeles	82	1526	18.6
Nate Thurmond, Golden State	79	1349	17.1
Dave Cowens, Boston	82	1329	16.2
Kareem Abdul-Jabbar, Milwaukee	76	1224	16.1
Wes Unseld, Baltimore	79	1260	15.9
Bob Lanier, Detroit	81	1205	14.9
Elvin Hayes, Baltimore	81	1177	14.5
Paul Silas, Boston	80	1039	13.0
Walt Bellamy, Atlanta	74	964	13.0
Spencer Haywood, Seattle	77	995	12.9

INDIVIDUAL STATISTICS, TEAM BY TEAM

ATLANTA HAWKS

	G	Min.	FGM	FGA	Pct.	FTM	FTA	Pct.	Reb.	Ast.	PF	Dq.	Pts.	Avg.
Lou Hudson	75	3027	816	1710	.477	397	481	.825	467	258	197	1	2029	27.1
Pete Maravich	79	3089	789	1788	.441	485	606	.800	346	546	245	1	2063	26.1
Walt Bellamy	74	2802	455	901	.505	283	526	.538	964	179	244	1	1193	16.1
Herm Gilliam	76	2741	471	1007	.468	123	150	.820	399	482	257	8	1065	14.0
George Trapp	77	1853	359	824	.436	150	194	.773	455	127	274	11	868	11.3
Jim Washington	75	2833	308	713	.432	163	224	.728	801	174	252	5	779	10.4
Steve Bracey	70	1050	192	395	.486	73	110	.664	107	125	125	0	457	6.5
Don Adams*	4	76	8	38	.211	7	8	.875	22	5	11	0	23	5.8
Jeff Halliburton*	24	238	50	116	.431	21	22	.955	26	28	29	0	121	5.0
Don May*	32	317	61	134	.455	22	31	.710	67	21	55	0	144	4.5
Bob Christian	55	759	85	155	.548	60	79	.759	305	47	11	2	230	4.2
John Wetzel	28	504	42	94	.447	14	17	.824	58	39	41	1	98	3.5
John Tschogl	10	94	14	40	.350	2	4	.500	21	6	25	0	30	3.0
Eddie Mast	42	447	50	118	.424	19	30	.633	136	37	50	0	119	2.8

BALTIMORE BULLETS

	G	Min.	FGM	FGA	Pct.	FTM	FTA	Pct.	Reb.	Ast.	PF	Dq.	Pts.	Avg.
Elvin Hayes	81	3347	713	1607	.444	291	434	.671	1177	127	232	3	1717	21.2
Phil Chenier	71	2776	602	1332	.452	194	244	.795	288	301	160	0	1398	19.7
Archie Clark	39	1477	302	596	.507	111	137	.810	129	275	111	1	715	18.3
Mike Riordan	82	3466	652	1278	.510	179	218	.821	404	426	216	0	1483	18.1
Wes Unseld	79	3085	421	854	.493	149	212	.703	1260	347	168	0	991	12.5
Mike Davis	13	283	50	118	.424	23	25	.920	35	19	45	4	123	9.5
Rich Rinaldi	33	646	116	284	.408	48	64	.750	68	48	40	0	280	8.5
Flynn Robinson†	38	583	119	260	.458	26	31	.839	55	77	60	0	264	6.9
Flynn Robinson‡	44	630	133	288	.462	32	39	.821	62	85	71	0	298	6.8
Kevin Porter	71	1217	205	451	.455	62	101	.614	72	237	206	5	472	6.6
Stan Love	72	995	190	436	.436	79	100	.790	300	46	175	0	459	6.4
Dave Stallworth	73	1217	180	435	.414	78	101	.772	236	112	139	1	438	6.0
John Tresvant	55	541	85	182	.467	41	59	.695	156	33	101	0	211	3.8
Tom Patterson	23	92	21	49	.429	13	16	.813	22	3	18	0	55	2.4
Terry Driscoll*	1	5	0	1	.000	0	0	...	3	0	1	0	0	0.0

BOSTON CELTICS

	G	Min.	FGM	FGA	Pct.	FTM	FTA	Pct.	Reb.	Ast.	PF	Dq.	Pts.	Avg.
John Havlicek	80	3367	766	1704	.450	370	431	.858	567	529	195	1	1902	23.8
Dave Cowens	82	3425	740	1637	.452	204	262	.779	1329	333	311	7	1684	20.5
Jo Jo White	82	3250	717	1655	.433	178	228	.781	414	498	185	2	1612	19.7
Paul Silas	80	2618	400	851	.470	266	380	.700	1039	251	197	1	1066	13.3
Don Chaney	79	2488	414	859	.482	210	267	.787	449	221	276	6	1038	13.1
Don Nelson	72	1425	309	649	.476	159	188	.846	315	102	155	1	777	10.8
Steve Kuberski	78	762	140	347	.403	65	84	.774	197	26	92	0	345	4.4
Paul Westphal	60	482	89	212	.420	67	86	.779	67	69	88	0	245	4.1
Art Williams	81	974	110	261	.421	43	56	.768	182	236	136	1	263	3.2
Hank Finkel	76	496	78	173	.451	28	52	.538	151	26	83	0	184	2.4
Tom Sanders	59	423	47	149	.315	23	35	.657	88	27	82	0	117	2.0
Mark Minor	4	20	1	4	.250	3	4	.750	4	2	5	0	5	1.3

BUFFALO BRAVES

	G	Min.	FGM	FGA	Pct.	FTM	FTA	Pct.	Reb.	Ast.	PF	Dq.	Pts.	Avg.
Elmore Smith	76	2829	600	1244	.482	188	337	.558	946	192	295	16	1388	18.3
Bob McAdoo	80	2562	585	1293	.452	271	350	.774	728	139	256	6	1441	18.0
Bob Kauffman	77	3049	535	1059	.505	280	359	.780	855	396	211	1	1350	17.5
Randy Smith	82	2603	511	1154	.443	192	264	.727	391	422	247	1	1214	14.8
Dick Garrett	78	1805	341	813	.419	96	110	.873	209	217	217	4	778	10.0
Dave Wohl†	56	1540	207	454	.456	79	100	.790	89	258	182	3	493	8.8

1972-73

	G	Min.	FGM	FGA	Pct.	FTM	FTA	Pct.	Reb.	Ast.	PF	Dq.	Pts.	Avg.
Dave Wohl‡	78	1933	254	568	.447	103	133	.774	109	326	227	3	611	7.8
John Hummer	66	1546	206	464	.444	115	205	.561	323	138	185	5	527	8.0
Fred Hilton	59	731	191	494	.387	41	53	.774	98	74	100	0	423	7.2
Howie Komives	67	1468	163	429	.380	85	98	.867	118	239	155	1	411	6.1
Walt Hazzard*	9	134	25	60	.417	3	6	.500	10	17	19	0	53	5.9
Bill Hewitt	73	1332	152	364	.418	41	74	.554	368	110	154	3	345	4.7
Cornell Warner*	4	47	8	17	.471	1	2	.500	15	6	6	0	17	4.3
Harold Fox	10	84	12	32	.375	7	8	.875	8	10	7	0	31	3.1

CHICAGO BULLS

	G	Min.	FGM	FGA	Pct.	FTM	FTA	Pct.	Reb.	Ast.	PF	Dq.	Pts.	Avg.
Bob Love	82	3033	774	1794	.431	347	421	.824	532	119	240	1	1895	23.1
Chet Walker	79	2455	597	1248	.478	376	452	.832	395	179	166	1	1570	19.9
Norm Van Lier	80	2882	474	1064	.445	166	211	.787	438	567	269	5	1114	13.9
Gar Heard†	78	1535	346	815	.425	115	177	.650	447	58	167	1	807	10.3
Gar Heard‡	81	1552	350	824	.425	116	178	.652	453	60	171	1	816	10.1
Jerry Sloan	69	2412	301	733	.411	94	133	.707	475	151	235	5	696	10.1
Bob Weiss	82	2086	279	655	.426	159	189	.841	148	295	151	1	717	8.7
Cliff Ray	73	2009	254	516	.492	117	189	.619	797	271	232	5	625	8.6
Kennedy McIntosh*	3	33	8	13	.615	0	2	.000	9	1	4	0	16	5.3
Howard Porter	43	407	98	217	.452	22	29	.759	118	16	52	1	218	5.1
Dennis Awtrey†	79	1650	143	298	.480	85	149	.570	433	222	226	6	371	4.7
Dennis Awtrey‡	82	1687	146	305	.479	86	153	.562	447	224	234	6	378	4.6
Jim King	65	785	116	263	.441	44	52	.846	76	81	76	0	276	4.2
Tom Boerwinkle	8	176	9	24	.375	12	20	.600	54	40	22	0	30	3.8
Rowland Garrett	35	211	52	118	.441	21	31	.677	61	8	29	0	125	3.6
Frank Russell	23	131	29	77	.377	16	18	.889	17	15	12	0	74	3.2

CLEVELAND CAVALIERS

	G	Min.	FGM	FGA	Pct.	FTM	FTA	Pct.	Reb.	Ast.	PF	Dq.	Pts.	Avg.
Austin Carr	82	3097	702	1575	.446	281	342	.822	369	279	185	1	1685	20.5
Lenny Wilkens	75	2973	572	1275	.449	394	476	.828	346	628	221	2	1538	20.5
John Johnson	82	2815	492	1143	.430	199	271	.734	552	309	246	3	1183	14.4
Rick Roberson	62	2127	307	709	.433	167	290	.576	693	134	249	5	781	12.6
Dwight Davis	81	2151	293	748	.392	176	222	.793	563	118	297	5	762	9.4
Bobby Smith	73	1068	268	603	.444	64	81	.790	199	108	80	0	600	8.2
Charlie Davis*	6	86	20	41	.488	4	7	.571	5	10	20	1	44	7.3
Barry Clemens	72	1119	209	405	.516	53	68	.779	211	115	136	0	471	6.5
Jim Cleamons	80	1392	192	423	.454	75	101	.743	167	205	108	0	459	5.7
Cornell Warner†	68	1323	166	404	.411	58	88	.659	507	66	172	3	390	5.7
Cornell Warner‡	72	1370	174	421	.413	59	90	.656	522	72	178	3	407	5.7
Johnny Warren	40	290	54	111	.486	18	19	.947	42	34	45	0	126	3.2
Walt Wesley*	12	110	14	47	.298	8	12	.667	38	7	21	0	36	3.0
Bob Rule†	49	440	60	157	.382	20	31	.645	106	37	66	1	140	2.9
Bob Rule‡	52	452	60	158	.380	20	31	.645	108	38	68	0	140	2.7
Steve Patterson	62	710	71	198	.359	34	65	.523	228	51	79	1	176	2.8
Dave Sorenson*	10	129	11	45	.244	5	11	.455	37	5	16	0	27	2.7

DETROIT PISTONS

	G	Min.	FGM	FGA	Pct.	FTM	FTA	Pct.	Reb.	Ast.	PF	Dq.	Pts.	Avg.
Bob Lanier	81	3150	810	1654	.490	307	397	.773	1205	260	278	4	1927	23.8
Dave Bing	82	3361	692	1545	.448	456	560	.814	298	637	229	1	1840	22.4
Curtis Rowe	81	3009	547	1053	.519	210	327	.642	760	172	191	0	1304	16.1
John Mengelt†	67	1435	294	583	.504	116	141	.823	159	128	124	0	704	10.5
John Mengelt‡	79	1647	320	651	.492	127	160	.794	181	153	148	0	767	9.7
Stu Lantz	51	1603	185	455	.407	120	150	.800	172	138	117	0	490	9.6
Don Adams†	70	1798	257	640	.402	138	176	.784	419	112	220	2	652	9.3
Don Adams‡	74	1874	265	678	.391	145	184	.788	441	117	231	2	675	9.1
Fred Foster	63	1460	243	627	.388	61	87	.701	183	94	150	0	547	8.7
Willie Norwood	79	1282	249	504	.494	154	225	.684	324	56	182	0	652	8.3
Chris Ford	74	1537	208	434	.479	60	93	.645	266	194	133	1	476	6.4
Jim Davis	73	771	131	257	.510	72	114	.632	261	56	126	2	334	4.6
Justus Thigpen	18	99	23	57	.404	0	0	...	9	8	18	0	46	2.6
Bob Nash	36	169	16	72	.222	11	17	.647	34	16	30	0	43	1.2
Erwin Mueller	21	80	9	31	.290	5	7	.714	14	7	13	0	23	1.1
Harvey Marlatt	7	26	2	4	.500	0	0	...	1	4	1	0	4	0.6

GOLDEN STATE WARRIORS

	G	Min.	FGM	FGA	Pct.	FTM	FTA	Pct.	Reb.	Ast.	PF	Dq.	Pts.	Avg.
Rick Barry	82	3075	737	1630	.452	358	397	.902	728	399	245	2	1832	22.3
Jeff Mullins	81	3005	651	1321	.493	143	172	.831	363	337	201	2	1445	17.8
Nate Thurmond	79	3419	517	1159	.446	315	439	.718	1349	280	240	2	1349	17.1
Cazzie Russell	80	2429	541	1182	.458	172	199	.864	350	187	171	0	1254	15.7
Jim Barnett	82	2215	394	844	.467	183	217	.843	255	301	150	1	971	11.8

1972-73

	G	Min.	FGM	FGA	Pct.	FTM	FTA	Pct.	Reb.	Ast.	PF	Dq.	Pts.	Avg.
													SCORING	
Joe Ellis.	74	1054	199	487	.409	69	93	.742	282	88	143	2	467	6.3
Clyde Lee.	66	1476	170	365	.466	74	131	.565	598	34	183	5	414	6.3
Ron Williams.	73	1016	180	409	.440	75	83	.904	81	114	108	0	435	6.0
Charles Johnson	70	887	171	400	.428	33	46	.717	132	118	105	0	375	5.4
Walt Hazzard†	46	629	82	196	.418	44	51	.863	78	112	91	1	208	4.5
Walt Hazzard‡	55	763	107	256	.418	47	57	.825	88	129	110	1	261	4.7
Bob Portman.	32	176	32	70	.457	20	26	.769	51	7	16	0	84	2.6
George Johnson	56	349	41	100	.410	7	17	.412	138	8	40	0	89	1.6

HOUSTON ROCKETS

	G	Min.	FGM	FGA	Pct.	FTM	FTA	Pct.	Reb.	Ast.	PF	Dq.	Pts.	Avg.
													SCORING	
Rudy Tomjanovich	81	2972	655	1371	.478	205	335	.612	938	178	225	1	1560	19.3
Jack Marin.	81	3019	624	1334	.468	248	292	.849	499	291	247	4	1496	18.5
Jimmy Walker	81	3079	605	1301	.465	244	276	.884	268	442	207	0	1454	18.0
Mike Newlin.	82	2658	534	1206	.443	327	369	.886	340	409	301	5	1395	17.0
Calvin Murphy.	77	1697	381	820	.465	239	269	.888	149	262	211	3	1001	13.0
Otto Moore.	82	2712	418	859	.487	127	211	.602	868	167	239	4	963	11.7
Zaid Abdul-Aziz	48	900	149	375	.397	119	162	.735	304	53	108	2	417	8.7
Cliff Meely.	82	1694	268	657	.408	92	137	.672	496	91	263	6	628	7.7
Paul McCracken.	24	305	44	89	.494	23	39	.590	51	17	32	0	111	4.6
Stan McKenzie†	26	187	35	83	.422	16	21	.762	34	15	28	0	86	3.3
Stan McKenzie‡	33	294	48	119	.403	30	37	.811	55	23	43	1	126	3.8
Greg Smith*	4	41	5	16	.313	0	0	…	8	5	8	0	10	2.5
George Johnson	19	169	20	39	.513	3	4	.750	45	3	33	0	43	2.3
Eric McWilliams.	44	245	34	98	.347	18	37	.486	60	5	46	0	86	2.0
Dick Gibbs*	1	2	0	1	.000	0	0	…	0	1	1	0	0	0.0

KANSAS CITY/OMAHA KINGS

	G	Min.	FGM	FGA	Pct.	FTM	FTA	Pct.	Reb.	Ast.	PF	Dq.	Pts.	Avg.
													SCORING	
Nate Archibald	80	3681	1028	2106	.488	663	783	.847	223	910	207	2	2719	34.0
Sam Lacey.	79	2930	471	994	.474	126	178	.708	933	189	283	6	1068	13.5
Tom Van Arsdale*	49	1282	250	547	.457	110	140	.786	173	90	123	1	610	12.4
Nate Williams	80	1079	417	874	.477	106	133	.797	339	128	272	9	940	11.8
Matt Guokas	79	2846	322	565	.570	74	90	.822	245	403	190	0	718	9.1
John Block†	25	483	80	180	.444	64	76	.842	120	19	69	1	224	9.0
John Block‡	73	2041	391	886	.441	300	378	.794	562	113	242	5	1082	14.8
Don Kojis	77	1240	276	575	.480	106	137	.774	198	80	128	0	658	8.5
Ron Riley.	74	1634	273	634	.431	79	116	.681	507	76	226	3	625	8.4
Johnny Green	66	1245	190	317	.599	89	131	.679	361	59	185	7	469	7.1
John Mengelt*	12	212	26	68	.382	11	19	.579	22	25	24	0	63	5.3
Mike Ratliff	58	681	98	235	.417	45	84	.536	194	38	111	1	241	4.2
Toby Kimball	67	743	96	220	.436	44	67	.657	191	27	86	2	236	3.5
Dick Gibbs†	66	733	80	221	.362	47	63	.746	94	61	113	1	207	3.1
Dick Gibbs‡	67	735	80	222	.360	47	63	.746	94	62	114	1	207	3.1
Ken Durrett.	8	65	8	21	.381	6	8	.750	14	3	16	0	22	2.8
Sam Sibert.	5	26	4	13	.308	4	5	.800	4	0	4	0	12	2.4
Frank Schade	9	76	2	7	.286	6	6	1.000	6	10	12	0	10	1.1
Pete Cross*	3	24	0	4	.000	0	0	…	4	0	5	0	0	0.0

LOS ANGELES LAKERS

	G	Min.	FGM	FGA	Pct.	FTM	FTA	Pct.	Reb.	Ast.	PF	Dq.	Pts.	Avg.
													SCORING	
Gail Goodrich.	76	2697	750	1615	.464	314	374	.840	263	332	193	1	1814	23.9
Jerry West.	69	2460	618	1291	.479	339	421	.805	289	607	138	0	1575	22.8
Jim McMillian	81	2953	655	1431	.458	223	264	.845	447	221	176	0	1533	18.9
Happy Hairston	28	930	168	328	.482	140	178	.787	370	68	77	0	456	16.3
Wilt Chamberlain.	82	3542	426	586	.727	232	455	.510	1526	365	191	0	1084	13.2
Bill Bridges†	72	2491	286	597	.479	133	190	.700	782	196	261	3	705	9.8
Bill Bridges‡	82	2867	333	722	.461	179	255	.702	904	219	296	3	845	10.3
Keith Erickson	76	1920	299	696	.430	89	110	.809	337	242	190	3	687	9.0
Pat Riley.	55	801	167	390	.428	65	82	.793	65	81	126	0	399	7.3
Jim Price.	59	828	158	359	.440	60	73	.822	115	97	119	1	376	6.4
Flynn Robinson*.	6	47	14	28	.500	6	8	.750	7	8	11	0	34	5.7
Mel Counts†	59	611	127	278	.457	39	58	.672	237	62	98	1	293	5.0
Mel Counts‡	66	658	132	294	.449	39	58	.672	253	65	106	1	303	4.6
Travis Grant.	33	153	51	116	.440	23	26	.885	52	7	19	0	125	3.8
LeRoy Ellis*	10	156	11	40	.275	4	5	.800	33	3	13	0	26	2.6
John Trapp*	5	35	3	12	.250	7	10	.700	14	2	10	0	13	2.6
Bill Turner†	19	117	17	52	.327	4	7	.571	25	11	13	0	38	2.0
Bill Turner‡	21	125	19	58	.328	4	7	.571	27	11	16	0	42	2.0
Roger Brown	1	5	0	0	…	1	3	.333	0	0	1	0	1	1.0

1972-73

MILWAUKEE BUCKS

	G	Min.	FGM	FGA	Pct.	FTM	FTA	Pct.	Reb.	Ast.	PF	Dq.	SCORING Pts.	Avg.
Kareem Abdul-Jabbar	76	3254	982	1772	.554	328	460	.713	1224	379	208	0	2292	30.2
Bob Dandridge	73	2852	638	1353	.472	198	251	.789	600	207	279	2	1474	20.2
Lucius Allen	80	2693	547	1130	.484	143	200	.715	279	426	188	1	1237	15.5
Oscar Robertson	73	2737	446	983	.454	238	281	.847	360	551	167	0	1130	15.5
Jon McGlocklin	80	1951	351	699	.502	63	73	.863	158	236	119	0	765	9.6
Curtis Perry	67	2094	265	575	.461	83	126	.659	644	123	246	6	613	9.1
Terry Driscoll†	59	959	140	326	.429	43	62	.694	297	55	143	3	323	5.5
Terry Driscoll‡	60	964	140	327	.428	43	62	.694	300	55	144	3	323	5.4
Mickey Davis	74	1046	152	347	.438	76	92	.826	226	72	119	0	380	5.1
Wali Jones	27	419	59	145	.407	16	18	.889	29	56	39	0	134	5.0
Gary Gregor	9	88	11	33	.333	5	7	.714	32	9	9	0	27	3.0
Russ Lee	46	277	49	127	.386	32	43	.744	43	38	36	0	130	2.8
Dick Cunningham	72	692	64	156	.410	29	50	.580	208	34	94	0	157	2.2
Chuck Terry	67	693	55	162	.340	17	24	.708	145	40	116	1	127	1.9

NEW YORK KNICKERBOCKERS

	G	Min.	FGM	FGA	Pct.	FTM	FTA	Pct.	Reb.	Ast.	PF	Dq.	SCORING Pts.	Avg.
Walt Frazier	78	3181	681	1389	.490	286	350	.817	570	461	186	0	1648	21.1
Dave DeBusschere	77	2827	532	1224	.435	194	260	.746	787	259	215	1	1258	16.3
Bill Bradley	82	2998	575	1252	.459	169	194	.871	301	367	273	5	1319	16.1
Earl Monroe	75	2370	496	1016	.488	171	208	.822	245	288	195	1	1163	15.5
Willis Reed	69	1876	334	705	.474	92	124	.742	590	126	205	0	760	11.0
Jerry Lucas	71	2001	312	608	.513	80	100	.800	510	317	157	0	704	9.9
Phil Jackson	80	1393	245	553	.443	154	195	.790	344	94	218	2	644	8.1
Dean Meminger	80	1453	188	365	.515	81	129	.628	229	133	109	1	457	5.7
Henry Bibby	55	475	78	205	.380	73	86	.849	82	64	67	0	229	4.2
Dick Barnett	51	514	88	226	.389	16	30	.533	41	50	52	0	192	3.8
John Gianelli	52	516	79	175	.451	23	33	.697	150	25	72	0	181	3.5
Tom Riker	14	65	10	24	.417	15	24	.625	16	2	15	0	35	2.5
Harthorne Wingo	13	59	9	22	.409	2	6	.333	16	1	9	0	20	1.5
Luke Rackley	1	2	0	0	...	0	0	...	1	0	2	0	0	0.0

PHILADELPHIA 76ERS

	G	Min.	FGM	FGA	Pct.	FTM	FTA	Pct.	Reb.	Ast.	PF	Dq.	SCORING Pts.	Avg.
Fred Carter	81	2993	679	1614	.421	259	368	.704	485	349	252	8	1617	20.0
John Block*	48	1558	311	706	.441	236	302	.781	442	94	173	4	858	17.9
Tom Van Arsdale†	30	1029	195	496	.393	140	168	.833	185	62	101	1	530	17.7
Tom Van Arsdale‡	79	2311	445	1043	.427	250	308	.812	358	152	224	2	1140	14.4
Bill Bridges*	10	376	47	125	.376	46	65	.708	122	23	35	0	140	14.0
Kevin Loughery	32	955	169	427	.396	107	130	.823	113	148	104	0	445	13.9
LeRoy Ellis†	69	2444	410	929	.441	125	156	.801	744	136	186	2	945	13.7
LeRoy Ellis‡	79	2600	421	969	.434	129	161	.801	777	139	199	2	971	12.3
Don May†	26	602	128	290	.441	53	62	.855	143	43	80	1	309	11.9
Don May‡	58	919	189	424	.446	75	93	.806	210	64	135	1	453	7.8
Manny Leaks	82	2530	377	933	.404	144	200	.720	677	95	191	5	898	11.0
John Trapp†	39	854	168	408	.412	83	112	.741	186	47	140	4	419	10.7
John Trapp‡	44	889	171	420	.407	90	122	.738	200	49	150	4	432	9.8
Freddie Boyd	82	2351	362	923	.392	136	200	.680	210	301	184	1	860	10.5
Jeff Halliburton†	31	549	122	280	.436	50	66	.758	82	68	78	1	294	9.5
Jeff Halliburton‡	55	787	172	396	.434	71	88	.807	108	96	107	1	415	7.5
Dave Sorenson†	48	626	113	248	.456	59	79	.747	173	31	91	0	285	5.9
Dave Sorenson‡	58	755	124	293	.423	64	90	.711	210	36	107	0	312	5.4
Hal Greer	38	848	91	232	.392	32	39	.821	106	111	76	1	214	5.6
Dale Schlueter	78	1136	166	317	.524	86	123	.699	354	103	166	0	418	5.4
Mike Price	57	751	125	301	.415	38	47	.809	117	71	106	0	288	5.1
Dennis Awtrey*	3	37	3	7	.429	1	4	.250	14	2	8	0	7	2.3
Mel Counts*	7	47	5	16	.313	0	0	...	16	3	8	0	10	1.4
Luther Green	5	32	0	11	.000	3	9	.333	3	0	3	0	3	0.6
Bob Rule*	3	12	0	1	.000	0	0	...	2	1	2	0	0	0.0

PHOENIX SUNS

	G	Min.	FGM	FGA	Pct.	FTM	FTA	Pct.	Reb.	Ast.	PF	Dq.	SCORING Pts.	Avg.
Charlie Scott	81	3062	806	1809	.446	436	556	.784	342	495	306	5	2048	25.3
Neal Walk	81	3114	678	1455	.466	279	355	.786	1006	287	323	11	1635	20.2
Dick Van Arsdale	81	2979	532	1118	.476	426	496	.859	326	268	221	2	1490	18.4
Connie Hawkins	75	2768	441	920	.479	322	404	.797	641	304	229	5	1204	16.1
Clem Haskins	77	1581	339	731	.464	130	156	.833	173	203	143	2	808	10.5
Gus Johnson	21	417	69	181	.381	25	36	.694	136	31	55	0	163	7.8
Dennis Layton	65	990	187	434	.431	90	119	.756	77	139	127	2	464	7.1
Lamar Green	80	2048	224	520	.431	89	118	.754	746	89	263	10	537	6.7
Corky Calhoun	82	2025	211	450	.469	71	96	.740	338	76	214	2	493	6.0
Walt Wesley†	45	364	63	155	.406	18	34	.529	113	24	56	1	144	3.2
Walt Wesley‡	57	474	77	202	.381	26	46	.565	141	31	77	1	180	3.2
Scott English	29	196	36	93	.387	21	29	.724	44	15	38	0	93	3.2
Paul Stovall	25	211	26	76	.342	24	38	.632	61	13	37	0	76	3.0

1972-73

PORTLAND TRAIL BLAZERS

	G	Min.	FGM	FGA	Pct.	FTM	FTA	Pct.	Reb.	Ast.	PF	Dq.	Pts.	Avg.
Geoff Petrie.................	79	3134	836	1801	.464	298	383	.778	273	350	163	2	1970	24.9
Sidney Wicks...............	80	3152	761	1684	.452	384	531	.723	870	440	253	3	1906	23.8
Lloyd Neal.................	82	2723	455	921	.494	187	293	.638	967	146	305	6	1097	13.4
Ollie Johnson.............	78	2138	308	620	.497	156	206	.757	417	200	166	0	772	9.9
Charlie Davis†	69	1333	243	590	.412	126	161	.783	111	175	174	6	612	8.9
Charlie Davis‡	75	1419	263	631	.417	130	168	.774	116	185	194	7	656	8.7
Greg Smith†	72	1569	229	469	.488	75	128	.586	375	117	210	8	533	7.4
Greg Smith‡	76	1610	234	485	.482	75	128	.586	383	122	218	8	543	7.1
Rick Adelman	76	1822	214	525	.408	73	102	.716	157	294	155	2	501	6.6
Terry Dischinger	63	970	161	338	.476	64	96	.667	190	103	125	1	386	6.1
Larry Steele...............	66	1301	159	329	.483	71	89	.798	154	156	181	4	389	5.9
Stan McKenzie*............	7	107	13	36	.361	14	16	.875	21	8	15	1	40	5.7
Dave Wohl*................	22	393	47	114	.412	24	33	.727	20	68	45	0	118	5.4
LaRue Martin..............	77	996	145	366	.396	50	77	.649	358	42	162	0	340	4.4
Bill Smith.................	8	43	9	15	.600	5	8	.625	8	1	8	0	23	2.9
Bill Turner*...............	2	8	2	6	.333	0	0	...	2	0	3	0	4	2.0
Bob Davis.................	9	41	6	28	.214	4	6	.667	5	2	5	0	16	1.8

SEATTLE SUPERSONICS

	G	Min.	FGM	FGA	Pct.	FTM	FTA	Pct.	Reb.	Ast.	PF	Dq.	Pts.	Avg.
Spencer Haywood	77	3259	889	1868	.476	473	564	.839	995	196	213	2	2251	29.2
Dick Snyder...............	82	3060	473	1022	.463	186	216	.861	323	311	216	2	1132	13.8
Fred Brown................	79	2320	471	1035	.455	121	148	.818	318	438	226	5	1063	13.5
John Brisker..............	70	1633	352	809	.435	194	236	.822	319	150	169	1	898	12.8
Jim Fox...................	74	2439	316	613	.515	214	265	.808	827	176	239	6	846	11.4
Butch Beard...............	73	1403	191	435	.439	100	140	.714	174	247	139	0	482	6.6
Lee Winfield	53	1061	143	332	.431	62	108	.574	126	186	92	3	348	6.6
Bud Stallworth............	77	1225	198	522	.379	86	114	.754	225	58	138	0	482	6.3
Jim McDaniels.............	68	1095	154	386	.399	70	100	.700	345	78	140	4	378	5.6
Kennedy McIntosh†	56	1105	107	328	.326	40	65	.615	222	53	98	1	254	4.5
Kennedy McIntosh‡	59	1138	115	341	.337	40	67	.597	231	54	102	1	270	4.6
Joby Wright...............	77	931	133	270	.478	37	89	.416	218	36	164	0	303	3.9
Gar Heard*................	3	17	4	9	.444	1	1	1.000	6	2	4	0	9	3.0
Charles Dudley	12	99	10	23	.435	14	16	.875	6	16	15	0	34	2.8
Pete Cross†	26	133	6	21	.286	8	18	.444	57	11	24	0	20	0.8
Pete Cross‡	29	157	6	25	.240	8	18	.444	61	11	29	0	20	0.7

* Finished season with another team. † Totals with this team only. ‡ Totals with all teams.

PLAYOFF RESULTS

EASTERN CONFERENCE

SEMIFINALS

Boston 4, Atlanta 2

Apr. 1—Sun.	Atlanta 109 at Boston 134
Apr. 4—Wed.	Boston 126 at Atlanta 113
Apr. 6—Fri.	Atlanta 118 at Boston 105
Apr. 8—Sun.	Boston 94 at Atlanta 97
Apr. 11—Wed.	Atlanta 101 at Boston 108
Apr. 13—Fri.	Boston 121 at Atlanta 103

New York 4, Baltimore 1

Mar. 30—Fri.	Baltimore 83 at New York 95
Apr. 1—Sun.	Baltimore 103 at New York 123
Apr. 4—Wed.	New York 103 at Baltimore 96
Apr. 6 Fri.	New York 89 at Baltimore 97
Apr. 8—Sun.	Baltimore 99 at New York 109

FINALS

New York 4, Boston 3

Apr. 15—Sun.	New York 108 at Boston 134
Apr. 18—Wed.	Boston 96 at New York 129
Apr. 20—Fri.	New York 98 at Boston 91
Apr. 22—Sun.	Boston 110 at New York **117
Apr. 25—Wed.	New York 97 at Boston 98
Apr. 27—Fri.	Boston 110 at New York 100
Apr. 29—Sun.	New York 94 at Boston 78

WESTERN CONFERENCE

SEMIFINALS

Golden State 4, Milwaukee 2

Mar. 30—Fri.	Golden State 90 at Milwaukee 110
Apr. 1—Sun.	Golden State 95 at Milwaukee 92
Apr. 5—Thur.	Milwaukee 113 at Golden State 93
Apr. 7—Sat.	Milwaukee 97 at Golden State 102
Apr. 10—Tue.	Golden State 100 at Milwaukee 97
Apr. 13—Fri.	Milwaukee 86 at Golden State 100

Los Angeles 4, Chicago 3

Mar. 30—Fri.	Chicago 104 at Los Angeles *107
Apr. 1—Sun.	Chicago 93 at Los Angeles 108
Apr. 6—Fri.	Los Angeles 86 at Chicago 96
Apr. 8—Sun.	Los Angeles 94 at Chicago 98
Apr. 10—Tue.	Chicago 102 at Los Angeles 123
Apr. 13—Fri.	Los Angeles 93 at Chicago 101
Apr. 15—Sun.	Chicago 92 at Los Angeles 95

FINALS

Los Angeles 4, Golden State 1

Apr. 17—Tue.	Golden State 99 at Los Angeles 101
Apr. 19—Thur.	Golden State 93 at Los Angeles 104
Apr. 21—Sat.	Los Angeles 126 at Golden State 70
Apr. 23—Mon.	Los Angeles 109 at Golden State 117
Apr. 25—Wed.	Golden State 118 at Los Angeles 128

NBA FINALS

New York 4, Los Angeles 1

May 1—Tue.	New York 112 at Los Angeles 115
May 3—Thur.	New York 99 at Los Angeles 95
May 6—Sun.	Los Angeles 83 at New York 87
May 8—Tue.	Los Angeles 98 at New York 103
May 10—Thur.	New York 102 at Los Angeles 93

*Denotes number of overtime periods.

1971-72

1971-72 NBA CHAMPION LOS ANGELES LAKERS

Front row (from left): Jim McMillian, Jim Cleamons, Pat Riley, Wilt Chamberlain, head coach Bill Sharman, LeRoy Ellis, Willie McCarter, Ernie Killum, Flynn Robinson. Back row (from left): assistant coach K.C. Jones, Elgin Baylor, Keith Erickson, Gail Goodrich, Fred Hetzel, Roger Brown, Rick Roberson, Malkin Strong, Jerry West, Happy Hairston, trainer Frank O'Neill.

FINAL STANDINGS

ATLANTIC DIVISION

	Atl.	Balt.	Bos.	Buf.	Chi.	Cin.	Cle.	Det.	G.S.	Hou.	L.A.	Mil.	N.Y.	Phi.	Pho.	Por.	Sea.	W	L	Pct.	GB
Boston	4	2	..	6	3	4	5	5	2	5	1	2	3	6	3	4	3	56	26	.683	..
New York.....	1	4	3	5	2	2	5	4	3	5	1	3	..	3	1	3	3	48	34	.585	8
Philadelphia...	3	0	0	3	1	2	4	4	1	1	0	1	3	..	1	2	4	30	52	.366	26
Buffalo	2	3	0	..	1	3	4	2	1	0	0	0	1	3	0	2	0	22	60	.268	34

CENTRAL DIVISION

	Atl.	Balt.	Bos.	Buf.	Chi.	Cin.	Cle.	Det.	G.S.	Hou.	L.A.	Mil.	N.Y.	Phi.	Pho.	Por.	Sea.	W	L	Pct.	GB
Baltimore.....	4	..	2	3	1	4	1	3	1	3	1	0	2	4	4	3	2	38	44	.463	..
Atlanta........	..	2	0	4	0	3	4	3	3	1	0	2	3	3	3	4	1	36	46	.439	2
Cincinnati	3	2	2	3	1	..	6	2	2	0	1	0	2	2	2	2	0	30	52	.366	8
Cleveland.....	2	5	1	2	0	2	..	1	0	2	1	0	1	2	0	4	0	23	59	.280	15

MIDWEST DIVISION

	Atl.	Balt.	Bos.	Buf.	Chi.	Cin.	Cle.	Det.	G.S.	Hou.	L.A.	Mil.	N.Y.	Phi.	Pho.	Por.	Sea.	W	L	Pct.	GB
Milwaukee....	3	5	3	4	4	5	4	5	2	5	1	..	2	4	4	6	6	63	19	.768	..
Chicago......	5	4	2	3	..	3	4	5	3	5	1	2	3	4	5	6	2	57	25	.695	6
Phoenix......	2	1	3	4	1	3	4	4	3	3	2	2	4	4	..	6	3	49	33	.598	14
Detroit.......	2	2	0	4	1	3	3	..	0	3	1	1	1	1	2	2	0	26	56	.317	37

PACIFIC DIVISION

	Atl.	Balt.	Bos.	Buf.	Chi.	Cin.	Cle.	Det.	G.S.	Hou.	L.A.	Mil.	N.Y.	Phi.	Pho.	Por.	Sea.	W	L	Pct.	GB
Los Angeles...	5	4	4	4	3	4	3	4	5	5	..	4	4	5	4	6	5	69	13	.841	..
Golden State ..	2	4	3	3	3	4	5	..	5	1	2	2	4	2	4	4	51	31	.622	18
Seattle.......	4	3	3	4	3	5	4	4	2	3	1	0	2	1	2	6	..	47	35	.573	22
Houston......	4	2	0	4	1	4	2	3	1	..	1	0	0	4	1	4	3	34	48	.415	35
Portland	0	1	0	4	0	2	2	2	2	2	0	0	1	2	0	..	0	18	64	.220	51

TEAM STATISTICS

OFFENSIVE

	G	FGM	FGA	Pct.	FTM	FTA	Pct.	Reb.	Ast.	PF	Dq.	Pts.	Avg.
Los Angeles	82	3920	7998	.490	2080	2833	.734	4628	2232	1636	7	9920	121.0
Phoenix.	82	3599	7877	.457	2336	2999	.779	4301	1976	2026	20	9534	116.3
Boston	82	3819	8431	.453	1839	2367	.777	4462	2230	2030	36	9477	115.6
Milwaukee.	82	3813	7653	.498	1774	2399	.739	4269	1862	1862	29	9400	114.6
Philadelphia	82	3577	8057	.444	2049	2825	.725	4318	1920	2203	50	9203	112.2
Chicago.	82	3539	7853	.451	2039	2700	.755	4371	2087	1964	24	9117	111.2
Houston	82	3590	8277	.434	1813	2424	.748	4433	1777	1992	32	8993	109.7
Atlanta	82	3482	7570	.460	2018	2725	.741	1080	1897	1967	14	8982	109.5
Seattle	82	3461	7457	.464	2035	2659	.765	4123	1976	1738	18	8957	109.2
Detroit	82	3482	7665	.454	1981	2653	.747	3970	1687	1954	26	8945	109.1
Golden State	82	3477	7923	.439	1917	2500	.767	4450	1854	1840	16	8871	108.2

	G	FGM	FGA	Pct.	FTM	FTA	Pct.	Reb.	Ast.	PF	Dq.	SCORING Pts.	Avg.
Cincinnati	82	3444	7496	.459	1948	2578	.756	3754	2020	2079	40	8836	107.8
New York	82	3521	7673	.459	1743	2303	.757	3909	1985	1899	15	8785	107.1
Baltimore	82	3490	7748	.450	1804	2378	.759	4159	1816	1858	16	8784	107.1
Portland	82	3462	7840	.442	1835	2494	.736	3996	2090	1873	24	8759	106.8
Cleveland	82	3458	8074	.428	1758	2390	.736	4098	2060	1936	23	8674	105.8
Buffalo	82	3409	7560	.451	1549	2219	.698	3978	1759	2110	42	8367	102.0

DEFENSIVE

	FGM	FGA	Pct.	FTM	FTA	Pct.	Reb.	Ast.	PF	Dq.	SCORING Pts.	Avg.	Dif.
Chicago	3263	7189	.454	1914	2617	.731	3928	1853	2041	32	8440	102.9	+8.3
Milwaukee	3370	8025	.420	1745	2358	.740	3922	1843	1788	10	8485	103.5	+11.1
New York	3332	7513	.443	1920	2565	.749	4169	1626	1892	28	8584	104.7	+2.4
Golden State	3560	8082	.440	1688	2265	.745	4381	1968	1912	25	8808	107.4	+0.8
Baltimore	3545	7842	.452	1790	2412	.742	4244	1844	1869	28	8880	108.3	-1.2
Los Angeles	3699	8553	.432	1515	1972	.768	4290	1994	1997	29	8913	108.7	+12.3
Seattle	3619	8029	.451	1681	2248	.748	4183	2037	1975	29	8919	108.8	+0.4
Boston	3498	7886	.444	2089	2766	.755	4179	1798	1842	16	9085	110.8	+4.8
Phoenix	3568	7896	.452	1947	2658	.733	4009	1929	2182	45	9083	110.8	+5.5
Houston	3542	7817	.453	2037	2737	.744	4298	1945	1944	19	9121	111.2	-1.5
Atlanta	3601	7744	.465	1925	2530	.761	4004	1890	1996	25	9127	111.3	-1.8
Buffalo	3479	7557	.460	2167	2842	.762	4187	1918	1728	9	9125	111.3	-9.3
Cincinnati	3537	7588	.466	2093	2829	.740	4228	2028	1971	36	9167	111.8	-4.0
Cleveland	3653	7537	.485	1994	2611	.764	4034	2322	1937	24	9300	113.4	-7.6
Detroit	3822	8106	.472	1862	2474	.753	4377	2214	1931	25	9506	115.9	-6.8
Philadelphia	3614	7882	.459	2276	3063	.743	4427	2005	2059	33	9504	115.9	-3.7
Portland	3841	7906	.486	1875	2499	.750	4439	2312	1903	19	9557	116.5	-9.7
Avgs.	3561	7832	.455	1913	2556	.748	4018	1972	1939	25	9036	110.2	...

HOME/ROAD/NEUTRAL

	Home	Road	Neutral	Total		Home	Road	Neutral	Total
Atlanta	22-19	13-26	1-1	36-46	Houston	15-20	14-23	5-5	34-48
Baltimore	18-15	16-24	4-5	38-44	Los Angeles	36-5	31-7	2-1	69-13
Boston	32-9	21-16	3-1	56-26	Milwaukee	31-5	27-12	5-2	63-19
Buffalo	13-27	8-31	1-2	22-60	New York	27-14	20-19	1-1	48-34
Chicago	29-12	26-12	2-1	57-25	Philadelphia	14-23	14-26	2-3	30-52
Cincinnati	20-18	8-32	2-2	30-52	Phoenix	30-11	19-20	0-2	49-33
Cleveland	13-28	8-30	2-1	23-59	Portland	14-26	4-35	0-3	18-64
Detroit	16-25	9-30	1-1	26-56	Seattle	28-12	18-22	1-1	47-35
Golden State	27-8	21-20	3-3	51-31	Totals	385-277	277-385	35-35	697-697

INDIVIDUAL LEADERS

POINTS

(minimum 70 games)

	G	FGM	FTM	Pts.	Avg.
Kareem Abdul-Jabbar, Milw.	81	1159	504	2822	34.8
Nate Archibald, Cincinnati	76	734	677	2145	28.2
John Havlicek, Boston	82	897	458	2252	27.5
Spencer Haywood, Seattle	73	717	480	1914	26.2
Gail Goodrich, Los Angeles	82	826	475	2127	25.9
Bob Love, Chicago	79	819	399	2037	25.8
Jerry West, Los Angeles	77	735	515	1985	25.8
Bob Lanier, Detroit	80	834	388	2056	25.7
Elvin Hayes, Houston	82	832	399	2063	25.2
Archie Clark, Philadelphia-Balt.	77	712	514	1938	25.2
Lou Hudson, Atlanta	77	775	349	1899	24.7
Sidney Wicks, Portland	82	784	441	2009	24.5
Billy Cunningham, Philadelphia	75	658	428	1744	23.3
Walt Frazier, New York	77	669	450	1788	23.2
Jo Jo White, Boston	79	770	285	1825	23.1
Jack Marin, Baltimore	78	690	356	1736	22.3
Chet Walker, Chicago	78	619	481	1719	22.0
Jeff Mullins, Golden State	80	685	350	1720	21.5
Cazzie Russell, Golden State	79	689	315	1693	21.4
Nate Thurmond, Golden State	78	628	417	1673	21.4

FIELD GOALS

(minimum 700 attempted)

	FGM	FGA	Pct.
Wilt Chamberlain, Los Angeles	496	764	.649
Kareem Abdul-Jabbar, Milwaukee	1159	2019	.574
Walt Bellamy, Atlanta	593	1089	.545
Dick Snyder, Seattle	496	937	.529
Walt Frazier, New York	669	1307	.512
Jerry Lucas, New York	543	1060	.512
Jon McGlocklin, Milwaukee	374	733	.510
Chet Walker, Chicago	619	1225	.505
Lucius Allen, Milwaukee	441	874	.505
Lou Hudson, Atlanta	775	1540	.503

FREE THROWS

(minimum 350 attempted)

	FTM	FTA	Pct.
Jack Marin, Baltimore	356	398	.894
Calvin Murphy, Houston	349	392	.890
Gail Goodrich, Los Angeles	475	559	.850
Chet Walker, Chicago	481	568	.847
Dick Van Arsdale, Phoenix	529	626	.845
Stu Lantz, Houston	387	462	.838
John Havlicek, Boston	458	549	.834
Cazzie Russell, Golden State	315	378	.833
Stan McKenzie, Portland	315	379	.831
Jimmy Walker, Detroit	397	480	.827

ASSISTS

(minimum 70 games)

	G	No.	Avg.
Jerry West, Los Angeles	77	747	9.7
Lenny Wilkens, Seattle	80	766	9.6
Nate Archibald, Cincinnati	76	701	9.2
Archie Clark, Philadelphia-Baltimore	77	613	8.0
John Havlicek, Boston	82	614	7.5
Norm Van Lier, Cincinnati-Chicago	79	542	6.9
Billy Cunningham, Philadelphia	75	443	5.9
Jeff Mullins, Golden State	80	471	5.9
Walt Frazier, New York	77	446	5.8
Walt Hazzard, Buffalo	72	406	5.6

1971-72

REBOUNDS

(minimum 70 games)

	G	No.	Avg.		G	No.	Avg.
Wilt Chamberlain, Los Angeles	82	1572	19.2	Elmore Smith, Buffalo	78	1184	15.2
Wes Unseld, Baltimore	76	1336	17.6	Elvin Hayes, Houston	82	1197	14.6
Kareem Abdul-Jabbar, Milwaukee	81	1346	16.6	Clyde Lee, Golden State	78	1132	14.5
Nate Thurmond, Golden State	78	1252	16.1	Bob Lanier, Detroit	80	1132	14.2
Dave Cowens, Boston	79	1203	15.2	Bill Bridges, Atlanta-Philadelphia	78	1051	13.5

INDIVIDUAL STATISTICS, TEAM BY TEAM

ATLANTA HAWKS

	G	Min.	FGM	FGA	Pct.	FTM	FTA	Pct.	Reb.	Ast.	PF	Dq.	SCORING Pts.	Avg.
Lou Hudson	77	3042	775	1540	.503	349	430	.812	385	309	225	0	1899	24.7
Pete Maravich	66	2302	460	1077	.427	355	438	.811	256	393	207	0	1275	19.3
Walt Bellamy	82	3187	593	1089	.545	340	581	.585	1049	262	255	2	1526	18.6
Jim Washington†	67	2416	325	729	.446	201	256	.785	601	121	217	0	851	12.7
Jim Washington‡	84	2961	393	885	.444	256	323	.793	736	146	276	3	1042	12.4
Don Adams†	70	2030	307	779	.394	204	273	.747	494	137	259	5	818	11.7
Don Adams‡	73	2071	313	798	.392	205	275	.745	502	140	266	6	831	11.4
Herm Gilliam	82	2337	345	774	.446	145	173	.838	335	377	232	3	835	10.2
Bill Bridges*	14	546	51	134	.381	31	44	.705	190	40	50	1	133	9.5
Don May	75	1285	234	476	.492	126	164	.768	217	55	133	0	594	7.9
Milt Williams	10	127	23	53	.434	21	29	.724	4	20	18	0	67	6.7
George Trapp	60	890	144	388	.371	105	139	.755	183	51	144	2	393	6.6
John Vallely*	9	110	20	43	.465	13	20	.650	11	9	13	0	53	5.9
Tom Payne	29	227	45	103	.437	29	46	.630	69	15	40	0	119	4.1
Jeff Halliburton	37	228	61	133	.459	25	30	.833	37	20	50	1	147	4.0
Larry Siegfried†	21	335	25	77	.325	20	23	.870	32	52	32	0	70	3.3
Larry Siegfried‡	31	558	43	123	.350	32	37	.865	42	72	53	0	118	3.8
Bob Christian	56	485	66	142	.465	44	61	.721	181	28	77	0	176	3.1
Jim Davis*	11	119	8	33	.242	10	18	.556	36	8	14	0	26	2.4
Shaler Halimon	1	4	0	0	...	0	0	...	0	0	1	0	0	0.0

BALTIMORE BULLETS

	G	Min.	FGM	FGA	Pct.	FTM	FTA	Pct.	Reb.	Ast.	PF	Dq.	SCORING Pts.	Avg.
Archie Clark†	76	3243	701	1500	.467	507	656	.773	265	606	191	0	1909	25.1
Archie Clark‡	77	3285	712	1516	.470	514	667	.771	268	613	194	0	1938	25.2
Jack Marin	78	2927	690	1444	.478	356	398	.894	528	169	240	2	1736	22.3
Earl Monroe*	3	103	26	64	.406	13	18	.722	8	10	9	0	65	21.7
Wes Unseld	76	3171	409	822	.498	171	272	.629	1336	278	218	1	989	13.0
Phil Chenier	81	2481	407	981	.415	182	247	.737	268	205	191	2	996	12.3
Dave Stallworth†	64	1815	303	690	.439	123	153	.804	398	133	186	3	729	11.4
Dave Stallworth‡	78	2040	336	778	.432	152	188	.809	433	158	217	3	824	10.6
Mike Riordan†	54	1344	229	488	.469	84	123	.683	127	124	127	0	542	10.0
Mike Riordan‡	58	1377	233	499	.467	84	124	.677	128	126	129	0	550	9.5
Stan Love	74	1327	242	536	.451	103	140	.736	338	52	202	0	587	7.9
Fred Carter*	2	68	6	27	.222	3	9	.333	19	12	7	0	15	7.5
John Tresvant	65	1227	162	360	.450	121	148	.818	323	83	175	6	445	6.8
Gary Zeller	28	471	83	229	.362	22	35	.629	65	30	62	0	188	6.7
Kevin Loughery*	2	42	4	17	.235	5	8	.625	5	8	5	0	13	6.5
Gus Johnson	39	668	103	269	.383	43	63	.683	226	51	91	0	249	6.4
Terry Driscoll	40	313	40	104	.385	27	39	.692	109	23	53	0	107	2.7
Rich Rinaldi	39	159	42	104	.404	20	30	.667	18	15	25	0	104	2.7
Dorie Murrey	51	421	43	113	.381	24	39	.615	126	17	76	2	110	2.2

BOSTON CELTICS

	G	Min.	FGM	FGA	Pct.	FTM	FTA	Pct.	Reb.	Ast.	PF	Dq.	SCORING Pts.	Avg.
John Havlicek	82	3698	897	1957	.458	458	549	.834	672	614	183	1	2252	27.5
Jo Jo White	79	3261	770	1788	.431	285	343	.831	446	416	227	1	1825	23.1
Dave Cowens	79	3186	657	1357	.484	175	243	.720	1203	245	314	10	1489	18.8
Don Nelson	82	2086	389	811	.480	356	452	.788	453	192	220	3	1134	13.8
Don Chaney	79	2275	373	786	.475	197	255	.773	395	202	295	7	943	11.9
Tom Sanders	82	1631	215	524	.410	111	136	.816	353	98	257	7	541	6.6
Steve Kuberski	71	1128	185	444	.417	80	102	.784	320	46	130	1	450	6.3
Art Williams	81	1326	161	339	.475	90	119	.756	256	327	204	2	412	5.1
Hank Finkel	78	736	103	254	.406	43	74	.581	251	61	118	4	249	3.2
Clarence Glover	25	119	25	55	.455	15	32	.469	46	4	26	0	65	2.6
Garfield Smith	26	134	28	66	.424	6	31	.194	37	8	22	0	62	2.4
Rex Morgan	28	150	16	50	.320	23	31	.742	30	17	34	0	55	2.0

BUFFALO BRAVES

	G	Min.	FGM	FGA	Pct.	FTM	FTA	Pct.	Reb.	Ast.	PF	Dq.	SCORING Pts.	Avg.
Bob Kauffman	77	3205	558	1123	.497	341	429	.795	787	297	273	7	1457	18.9
Elmore Smith	78	3186	579	1275	.454	194	363	.534	1184	111	306	10	1352	17.3

	G	Min.	FGM	FGA	Pct.	FTM	FTA	Pct.	Reb.	Ast.	PF	Dq.	Pts.	Avg.
Walt Hazzard	72	2389	450	998	.451	237	303	.782	213	406	230	2	1137	15.8
Randy Smith	76	2094	432	896	.482	158	254	.622	368	189	202	2	1022	13.4
Fred Hilton	61	1349	309	795	.389	90	122	.738	156	116	145	0	708	11.6
Dick Garrett	73	1905	325	735	.442	136	157	.866	225	165	225	5	786	10.8
Mike Davis	62	1068	213	501	.425	138	180	.767	120	82	141	5	564	9.1
Jerry Chambers	26	369	78	180	.433	22	32	.688	67	23	39	0	178	6.8
Cornell Warner	62	1239	162	366	.443	58	78	.744	379	54	125	2	382	6.2
John Hummer	55	1186	113	290	.390	58	124	.468	229	72	178	4	284	5.2
Emmette Bryant	54	1223	101	220	.459	75	125	.600	127	206	167	5	277	5.1
Bill Hosket	44	592	89	181	.492	42	52	.808	123	38	79	0	220	5.0

CHICAGO BULLS

	G	Min.	FGM	FGA	Pct.	FTM	FTA	Pct.	Reb.	Ast.	PF	Dq.	Pts.	Avg.
Bob Love	79	3108	819	1854	.442	399	509	.784	518	125	235	2	2037	25.8
Chet Walker	78	2588	619	1225	.505	481	568	.847	473	178	171	0	1719	22.0
Jerry Sloan	82	3035	535	1206	.444	258	391	.660	691	211	309	8	1328	16.2
Norm Van Lier†	69	2140	306	671	.456	220	278	.791	299	491	207	4	832	12.1
Norm Van Lier‡	79	2415	334	761	.439	237	300	.790	357	542	239	5	905	11.5
Bob Weiss	82	2450	358	832	.430	212	254	.835	170	377	212	1	928	11.3
Cliff Ray	82	1872	222	445	.499	134	218	.615	869	254	296	5	578	7.0
Tom Boerwinkle	80	2022	219	500	.438	118	180	.656	897	281	253	4	556	7.0
Howard Porter	67	730	171	403	.424	59	77	.766	183	24	88	0	401	6.0
Jim Fox*	10	133	20	53	.377	20	28	.714	54	6	21	0	60	6.0
Jim King	73	1017	162	356	.455	89	113	.788	81	101	103	0	413	5.7
Jimmy Collins	19	134	26	71	.366	10	11	.909	12	10	11	0	62	3.3
Charlie Paulk*	7	60	8	28	.286	7	9	.778	15	4	7	0	23	3.3
Kennedy McIntosh	43	405	57	168	.339	21	44	.477	89	18	41	0	135	3.1
Jackie Dinkins	18	89	17	41	.415	11	20	.550	20	7	10	0	45	2.5

CINCINNATI ROYALS

	G	Min.	FGM	FGA	Pct.	FTM	FTA	Pct.	Reb.	Ast.	PF	Dq.	Pts.	Avg.
Nate Archibald	76	3272	734	1511	.486	677	824	.822	222	701	198	3	2145	28.2
Tom Van Arsdale	73	2598	550	1205	.456	299	396	.755	350	198	241	1	1399	19.2
Jim Fox†	71	2047	334	735	.454	207	269	.770	659	80	236	8	875	12.3
Jim Fox‡	81	2180	354	788	.449	227	297	.764	713	86	257	8	935	11.5
Nate Williams	81	2173	418	968	.432	127	172	.738	372	174	300	11	963	11.9
Sam Lacey	81	2832	410	972	.422	119	169	.704	968	173	284	6	939	11.6
John Mengelt	78	1438	287	605	.474	208	252	.825	148	146	163	0	782	10.0
Johnny Green	82	1914	331	582	.569	141	250	.564	560	120	238	5	803	9.8
Matt Guokas	61	1975	191	385	.496	64	83	.771	142	321	150	0	446	7.3
Norm Van Lier*	10	275	28	90	.311	17	22	.773	58	51	32	1	73	7.3
Jake Jones†	11	161	22	54	.407	13	21	.619	20	10	19	0	57	5.2
Jake Jones‡	17	202	28	72	.389	20	31	.645	26	12	22	0	76	4.5
Ken Durrett	19	233	31	79	.392	21	28	.750	39	14	41	0	83	4.4
Gil McGregor	42	532	66	182	.363	39	56	.696	148	18	120	4	171	4.1
Fred Taylor†	21	214	30	90	.333	11	19	.579	37	11	32	0	71	3.4
Fred Taylor‡	34	283	36	117	.308	15	32	.469	54	18	40	0	87	2.6
Darrall Imhoff*	9	76	10	29	.345	3	8	.375	27	2	22	1	23	2.6
Sid Catlett	9	40	2	9	.222	2	9	.222	4	1	3	0	6	0.7

CLEVELAND CAVALIERS

	G	Min.	FGM	FGA	Pct.	FTM	FTA	Pct.	Reb.	Ast.	PF	Dq.	Pts.	Avg.
Austin Carr	43	1539	381	894	.426	149	196	.760	150	148	99	0	911	21.2
John Johnson	82	3041	557	1286	.433	277	353	.785	631	415	268	2	1391	17.0
Butch Beard	68	2434	394	849	.464	260	342	.760	276	456	213	2	1048	15.4
Bobby Smith	82	2734	527	1190	.443	178	224	.795	502	247	222	3	1232	15.0
Rick Roberson	63	2207	304	688	.442	215	366	.587	801	109	251	7	823	13.1
Walt Wesley	82	2185	412	1006	.410	196	291	.674	711	76	245	4	1020	12.4
Charlie Davis	61	1144	229	569	.402	142	169	.840	92	123	143	3	600	9.8
Dave Sorenson	76	1162	213	475	.448	106	136	.779	301	81	120	1	532	7.0
Bobby Washington	69	967	123	309	.398	104	128	.813	129	223	135	1	350	5.1
Johnny Warren	68	969	144	345	.417	49	58	.845	133	91	92	0	337	5.0
Steve Patterson	65	775	94	263	.357	23	46	.500	228	54	80	0	211	3.2
Greg Howard	48	426	50	131	.382	39	51	.765	108	27	50	0	139	2.9
Luke Rackley*	9	65	11	25	.440	1	4	.250	21	3	3	0	23	2.6
Jackie Ridgle	32	107	19	44	.432	19	26	.731	15	7	15	0	57	1.8

DETROIT PISTONS

	G	Min.	FGM	FGA	Pct.	FTM	FTA	Pct.	Reb.	Ast.	PF	Dq.	Pts.	Avg.
Bob Lanier	80	3092	834	1690	.493	388	505	.768	1132	248	297	6	2056	25.7
Dave Bing	45	1936	369	891	.414	278	354	.785	186	317	138	3	1016	22.6
Jimmy Walker	78	3083	634	1386	.457	397	480	.827	231	315	198	2	1665	21.3
Curtis Rowe	82	2661	369	802	.460	192	287	.669	699	99	171	1	930	11.3
Terry Dischinger	79	2062	295	574	.514	156	200	.780	338	92	289	7	746	9.4

	G	Min.	FGM	FGA	Pct.	FTM	FTA	Pct.	Reb.	Ast.	PF	Dq.	Pts.	Avg.
Howie Komives	79	2071	262	702	.373	164	203	.808	172	291	196	0	688	8.7
Willie Norwood	78	1272	222	440	.505	140	215	.651	316	43	229	4	584	7.5
Bob Quick	18	204	39	82	.476	34	45	.756	51	11	29	0	112	6.2
Jim Davis†	52	684	121	251	.482	64	98	.653	196	38	106	1	306	5.9
Jim Davis‡	75	983	147	338	.435	100	154	.649	276	51	138	1	394	5.3
Harvey Marlatt	31	506	60	149	.403	36	42	.857	62	60	64	1	156	5.0
Steve Mix	8	104	15	47	.319	7	12	.583	23	4	7	0	37	4.6
Bill Hewitt	68	1203	131	277	.473	41	82	.500	370	71	134	1	303	4.5
Erwin Mueller	42	605	68	197	.345	43	74	.581	147	57	64	0	179	4.3
Isaiah Wilson	48	322	63	177	.356	41	56	.732	47	41	32	0	167	3.5

GOLDEN STATE WARRIORS

	G	Min.	FGM	FGA	Pct.	FTM	FTA	Pct.	Reb.	Ast.	PF	Dq.	Pts.	Avg.
Jeff Mullins	80	3214	685	1466	.467	350	441	.794	444	471	260	5	1720	21.5
Cazzie Russell	79	2902	689	1514	.455	315	378	.833	428	248	176	0	1693	21.4
Nate Thurmond	78	3362	628	1454	.432	417	561	.743	1252	230	214	1	1673	21.4
Jim Barnett	80	2200	374	915	.409	244	292	.836	250	309	189	0	992	12.4
Ron Williams	80	1932	291	614	.474	195	234	.833	147	308	232	1	777	9.7
Joe Ellis	78	1462	280	681	.411	95	132	.720	389	97	224	4	655	8.4
Clyde Lee	78	2674	256	544	.471	120	222	.541	1132	85	244	4	632	8.1
Bob Portman	61	553	89	221	.403	53	60	.883	133	26	69	0	231	3.8
Nick Jones	65	478	82	196	.418	51	61	.836	39	45	109	0	215	3.3
Bill Turner	62	597	71	181	.392	40	53	.755	131	22	67	1	182	2.9
Odis Allison	36	166	17	78	.218	33	61	.541	45	10	34	0	67	1.9
Vic Bartolome	38	165	15	59	.254	4	5	.800	60	3	22	0	34	0.9

HOUSTON ROCKETS

	G	Min.	FGM	FGA	Pct.	FTM	FTA	Pct.	Reb.	Ast.	PF	Dq.	Pts.	Avg.
Elvin Hayes	82	3461	832	1918	.434	399	615	.649	1197	270	233	1	2063	25.2
Stu Lantz	81	3097	557	1279	.435	387	462	.838	345	337	211	2	1501	18.5
Calvin Murphy	82	2538	571	1255	.455	349	392	.890	258	393	298	6	1491	18.2
Rudy Tomjanovich	78	2689	500	1010	.495	172	238	.723	923	117	193	2	1172	15.0
Cliff Meely	77	1815	315	776	.406	133	197	.675	507	119	254	9	763	9.9
Greg Smith†	54	1519	212	473	.448	70	110	.636	322	159	167	3	494	9.1
Greg Smith‡	82	2256	309	671	.461	111	168	.661	483	222	259	4	729	8.9
Mike Newlin	82	1495	256	618	.414	108	144	.750	228	135	233	6	620	7.6
Jim Davis*	12	180	18	54	.333	26	38	.684	44	5	18	0	62	5.2
Larry Siegfried*	10	223	18	46	.391	12	14	.857	10	20	21	0	48	4.8
Don Adams*	3	41	6	19	.316	1	2	.500	8	3	7	1	13	4.3
Dick Gibbs	64	757	90	265	.340	55	66	.833	140	51	127	0	235	3.7
Curtis Perry*	25	355	38	115	.330	12	24	.500	122	22	47	1	88	3.5
John Vallely†	40	256	49	128	.383	17	25	.680	21	28	37	0	115	2.9
John Vallely‡	49	366	69	171	.404	30	45	.667	32	37	50	0	168	3.4
Johnny Egan	38	437	42	104	.404	26	32	.813	26	51	55	0	110	2.9
McCoy McLemore†	17	147	19	43	.442	9	12	.750	39	10	15	1	47	2.8
McCoy McLemore‡	27	246	28	71	.394	20	24	.833	73	22	33	1	76	2.8
Dick Cunningham	63	720	67	174	.385	37	53	.698	243	57	76	0	171	2.7

LOS ANGELES LAKERS

	G	Min.	FGM	FGA	Pct.	FTM	FTA	Pct.	Reb.	Ast.	PF	Dq.	Pts.	Avg.
Gail Goodrich	82	3040	826	1695	.487	475	559	.850	295	365	210	0	2127	25.9
Jerry West	77	2973	735	1540	.477	515	633	.814	327	747	209	0	1985	25.8
Jim McMillian	80	3050	642	1331	.482	219	277	.791	522	209	209	0	1503	18.8
Wilt Chamberlain	82	3469	496	764	.649	221	524	.422	1572	329	196	0	1213	14.8
Happy Hairston	80	2748	368	798	.461	311	399	.779	1045	193	251	2	1047	13.1
Elgin Baylor	9	239	42	97	.433	22	27	.815	57	18	20	0	106	11.8
Flynn Robinson	64	1007	262	535	.490	111	129	.860	115	138	139	2	635	9.9
Pat Riley	67	926	197	441	.447	55	74	.743	127	75	110	0	449	6.7
John Trapp	58	759	139	314	.443	51	73	.699	180	42	130	3	329	5.7
Keith Erickson	15	262	40	83	.482	6	7	.857	39	35	26	0	86	5.7
LeRoy Ellis	74	1081	138	300	.460	66	95	.695	310	46	115	0	342	4.6
Jim Cleamons	38	201	35	100	.350	28	36	.778	39	35	21	0	98	2.6

MILWAUKEE BUCKS

	G	Min.	FGM	FGA	Pct.	FTM	FTA	Pct.	Reb.	Ast.	PF	Dq.	Pts.	Avg.
Kareem Abdul-Jabbar	81	3583	1159	2019	.574	504	732	.689	1346	370	235	1	2822	34.8
Bob Dandridge	80	2957	630	1264	.498	215	291	.739	613	249	297	7	1475	18.4
Oscar Robertson	64	2390	419	887	.472	276	330	.836	323	491	116	0	1114	17.4
Lucius Allen	80	2316	441	874	.505	198	259	.764	254	333	214	2	1080	13.5
Jon McGlocklin	80	2213	374	733	.510	109	126	.865	181	231	146	0	857	10.7
John Block	79	1524	233	530	.440	206	275	.749	410	95	213	4	672	8.5
Greg Smith*	28	737	97	198	.490	41	58	.707	161	63	92	1	235	8.4
Wali Jones	48	1030	144	354	.407	74	90	.822	75	141	112	0	362	7.5
Curtis Perry†	50	1471	143	371	.385	64	95	.674	471	78	214	13	350	7.0

	G	Min.	FGM	FGA	Pct.	FTM	FTA	Pct.	Reb.	Ast.	PF	Dq.	SCORING Pts.	Avg.
Curtis Perry‡	75	1826	181	486	.372	76	119	.639	593	100	261	14	438	5.8
Toby Kimball	74	971	107	229	.467	44	81	.543	312	60	137	0	258	3.5
McCoy McLemore*	10	99	9	28	.321	11	12	.917	34	12	18	0	29	2.9
Chuck Lowery	20	134	17	38	.447	11	18	.611	19	14	16	1	45	2.3
Bill Dinwiddie	23	144	16	57	.281	5	9	.556	32	9	23	0	37	1.6
Jeff Webb*	19	109	9	35	.257	11	13	.846	18	7	8	0	29	1.5
Barry Nelson	28	102	15	36	.417	5	10	.500	20	7	21	0	35	1.3

NEW YORK KNICKERBOCKERS

	G	Min.	FGM	FGA	Pct.	FTM	FTA	Pct.	Reb.	Ast.	PF	Dq.	SCORING Pts.	Avg.
Walt Frazier	77	3126	669	1307	.512	450	557	.808	513	446	185	0	1788	23.2
Jerry Lucas	77	2926	543	1060	.512	197	249	.791	1011	318	218	1	1283	16.7
Dave DeBusschere	80	3072	520	1218	.427	193	265	.728	901	291	219	1	1233	15.4
Bill Bradley	78	2780	504	1085	.465	169	199	.849	250	315	254	4	1177	15.1
Willis Reed	11	363	60	137	.438	27	39	.692	96	22	30	0	147	13.4
Dick Barnett	79	2256	401	918	.437	162	215	.753	153	198	229	4	964	12.2
Earl Monroe†	60	1234	261	598	.436	162	206	.786	92	132	130	1	684	11.4
Earl Monroe‡	63	1337	287	662	.434	175	224	.781	100	142	139	1	749	11.9
Phil Jackson	80	1273	205	466	.440	167	228	.732	326	72	224	4	577	7.2
Dave Stallworth*	14	225	33	88	.375	29	35	.829	35	25	31	0	95	6.8
Dean Meminger	78	1173	139	293	.474	79	140	.564	185	103	137	0	357	4.6
Luke Rackley†	62	618	92	215	.428	49	84	.583	187	18	104	0	233	3.8
Luke Rackley‡	71	683	103	240	.429	50	88	.568	208	21	107	0	256	3.6
Mike Price	6	40	5	14	.357	9	11	.818	6	6	10	0	19	3.2
Eddie Mast	40	270	39	112	.348	25	41	.610	73	10	39	0	103	2.6
Mike Riordan*	4	33	4	11	.364	0	1	.000	1	2	2	0	8	2.0
Eddie Miles	42	198	23	64	.359	16	18	.889	16	17	46	0	62	1.5
Greg Fillmore	10	67	7	27	.259	1	3	.333	15	3	17	0	15	1.5
Charlie Paulk†	28	151	16	60	.267	8	12	.667	49	7	24	0	40	1.4
Charlie Paulk‡	35	211	24	88	.273	15	21	.714	64	11	31	0	63	1.8

PHILADELPHIA 76ERS

	G	Min.	FGM	FGA	Pct.	FTM	FTA	Pct.	Reb.	Ast.	PF	Dq.	SCORING Pts.	Avg.
Archie Clark*	1	42	11	16	.688	7	11	.636	3	7	3	0	29	29.0
Billy Cunningham	75	2900	658	1428	.461	428	601	.712	918	443	295	12	1744	23.3
Bob Rule†	60	1987	410	934	.445	203	292	.605	479	110	162	4	1035	17.3
Bob Rule‡	76	2230	461	1058	.436	226	335	.675	534	116	189	4	1148	15.1
Fred Carter†	77	2147	440	991	.444	179	284	.630	307	199	235	4	1059	13.8
Fred Carter‡	79	2215	446	1018	.438	182	293	.621	326	211	242	4	1074	13.6
Bill Bridges†	64	2210	328	645	.509	191	272	.702	861	158	219	5	847	13.2
Bill Bridges‡	78	2756	379	779	.487	222	316	.703	1051	198	269	6	980	12.6
Kevin Loughery†	74	1829	337	792	.426	258	312	.827	178	188	208	3	932	12.6
Kevin Loughery‡	76	1771	341	809	.422	263	320	.822	183	196	213	3	945	12.4
Fred Foster	74	1699	347	837	.415	185	243	.761	276	90	184	3	879	11.9
Hal Greer	81	2410	389	866	.449	181	234	.774	271	316	268	10	959	11.8
Jim Washington*	17	545	68	156	.436	55	67	.821	135	25	59	3	191	11.2
Dave Wohl	79	1628	243	567	.429	156	206	.757	150	228	229	2	642	8.1
Lucious Jackson	63	1083	137	346	.396	92	133	.692	309	88	141	1	366	5.8
Al Henry	43	421	68	156	.436	51	73	.699	137	8	42	0	187	4.3
Dennis Awtrey	58	794	98	222	.441	49	76	.645	248	51	141	3	245	4.2
Jake Jones*	6	41	6	18	.333	7	10	.700	6	2	3	0	19	3.2
Barry Yates	24	144	31	83	.373	7	11	.636	40	7	14	0	69	2.9

PHOENIX SUNS

	G	Min.	FGM	FGA	Pct.	FTM	FTA	Pct.	Reb.	Ast.	PF	Dq.	SCORING Pts.	Avg.
Connie Hawkins	76	2798	571	1244	.459	456	565	.807	633	296	235	2	1598	21.0
Dick Van Arsdale	82	3096	545	1178	.463	529	626	.845	334	297	232	1	1619	19.7
Charlie Scott	6	177	48	113	.425	17	21	.810	23	26	19	0	113	18.8
Paul Silas	80	3082	485	1031	.470	433	560	.773	955	343	201	2	1403	17.5
Neal Walk	81	2142	506	1057	.479	256	344	.744	665	151	295	9	1268	15.7
Clem Haskins	79	2453	509	1054	.483	220	258	.853	270	290	194	1	1238	15.7
Dennis Layton	80	1849	304	717	.424	122	165	.739	164	247	219	0	730	9.1
Otto Moore	81	1624	260	597	.436	94	156	.603	540	88	212	2	614	7.6
Mel Counts	76	906	147	344	.427	101	140	.721	257	96	159	2	395	5.2
Lamar Green	67	991	133	298	.446	66	90	.733	348	45	134	1	332	5.0
Art Harris	21	145	23	70	.329	9	21	.429	13	18	26	0	55	2.6
Jeff Webb†	27	129	31	65	.477	5	10	.500	17	16	21	0	67	2.5
Jeff Webb‡	46	238	40	100	.400	16	23	.696	35	23	29	0	96	2.1
John Wetzel	51	419	31	82	.378	24	30	.800	65	56	71	0	86	1.7
Fred Taylor*	13	69	6	27	.222	4	13	.308	17	7	8	0	16	1.2

1971-72

PORTLAND TRAIL BLAZERS

	G	Min.	FGM	FGA	Pct.	FTM	FTA	Pct.	Reb.	Ast.	PF	Dq.	SCORING Pts.	Avg.
Sidney Wicks	82	3245	784	1837	.427	441	621	.710	943	350	186	1	2009	24.5
Geoff Petrie	60	2155	465	1115	.417	202	256	.789	133	248	108	0	1132	18.9
Stan McKenzie	82	2036	410	834	.492	315	379	.831	272	148	240	2	1135	13.8
Dale Schlueter	81	2693	353	672	.525	241	326	.739	860	285	277	3	947	11.7
Gary Gregor	82	2371	399	884	.451	114	151	.755	591	187	201	2	912	11.1
Rick Adelman	80	2445	329	753	.437	151	201	.751	229	413	209	2	809	10.1
Bill Smith	22	448	72	173	.416	38	64	.594	135	19	73	3	182	8.3
Charlie Yelverton	69	1227	206	530	.389	133	188	.707	201	81	145	2	545	7.9
Willie McCarter	39	612	103	257	.401	37	55	.673	43	45	58	0	243	6.2
Ron Knight	49	483	112	257	.436	31	62	.500	116	33	52	0	255	5.2
Larry Steele	72	1311	148	308	.481	70	97	.722	282	161	198	8	366	5.1
Jim Marsh	39	375	39	117	.333	41	59	.695	84	30	50	0	119	3.1
Darrall Imhoff†	40	404	42	103	.408	21	35	.600	107	50	76	1	105	2.6
Darrall Imhoff‡	49	480	52	132	.394	24	43	.558	134	52	98	2	128	2.6

SEATTLE SUPERSONICS

	G	Min.	FGM	FGA	Pct.	FTM	FTA	Pct.	Reb.	Ast.	PF	Dq.	SCORING Pts.	Avg.
Spencer Haywood	73	3167	717	1557	.461	480	586	.819	926	148	208	0	1914	26.2
Lenny Wilkens	80	2989	479	1027	.466	480	620	.774	338	766	209	4	1438	18.0
Dick Snyder	73	2534	496	937	.529	218	259	.842	228	283	200	3	1210	16.6
Zaid Abdul-Aziz	58	1780	322	751	.429	154	214	.720	654	124	178	1	798	13.8
Don Kojis	73	1857	322	687	.469	188	237	.793	335	82	168	1	832	11.4
Lee Winfield	81	2040	343	692	.496	175	262	.668	218	290	198	1	861	10.6
Jim McDaniels	12	235	51	123	.415	11	18	.611	82	9	26	0	113	9.4
Gar Heard	58	1499	190	474	.401	79	128	.617	442	55	126	2	459	7.9
Barry Clemens	82	1447	252	484	.521	76	90	.844	288	64	198	4	580	7.1
Bob Rule*	16	243	45	124	.363	23	43	.535	55	6	27	0	113	7.1
Pete Cross	74	1424	152	355	.428	103	140	.736	509	63	135	2	407	5.5
Fred Brown	33	359	59	180	.328	22	29	.759	37	60	44	0	140	4.2
Jake Ford	26	181	33	66	.500	26	33	.788	11	26	21	0	92	3.5

* Finished season with another team.   † Totals with this team only.   ‡ Totals with all teams.

PLAYOFF RESULTS

EASTERN CONFERENCE

SEMIFINALS

Boston 4, Atlanta 2

Mar. 29—Wed.	Atlanta 108 at Boston	126
Mar. 31—Fri.	Boston 104 at Atlanta	113
Apr. 2—Sun.	Atlanta 113 at Boston	136
Apr. 4—Tue.	Boston 110 at Atlanta	112
Apr. 7—Fri.	Atlanta 114 at Boston	124
Apr. 9—Sun.	Boston 127 at Atlanta	118

New York 4, Baltimore 2

Mar. 31—Fri.	New York 105 at Baltimore	*108
Apr. 2—Sun.	Baltimore 88 at New York	110
Apr. 4—Tue.	New York 103 at Baltimore	104
Apr. 6—Thur.	Baltimore 98 at New York	104
Apr. 9—Sun.	New York 106 at Baltimore	82
Apr. 11—Tue.	Baltimore 101 at New York	107

FINALS

New York 4, Boston 1

Apr. 13—Thur.	New York 116 at Boston	94
Apr. 16—Sun.	Boston 105 at New York	106
Apr. 19—Wed.	New York 109 at Boston	115
Apr. 21—Fri.	Boston 98 at New York	116
Apr. 23—Sun.	New York 111 at Boston	103

WESTERN CONFERENCE

SEMIFINALS

Milwaukee 4, Golden State 1

Mar. 28—Tue.	Golden State 117 at Milwaukee	106
Mar. 30—Thur.	Golden State 93 at Milwaukee	118
Apr. 1—Sat.	Milwaukee 122 at Golden State	94
Apr. 4—Tue.	Milwaukee 106 at Golden State	99
Apr. 6—Thur.	Golden State 100 at Milwaukee	108

Los Angeles 4, Chicago 0

Mar. 28—Tue.	Chicago 80 at Los Angeles	95
Mar. 30—Thur.	Chicago 124 at Los Angeles	131
Apr. 2—Sun.	Los Angeles 108 at Chicago	101
Apr. 4—Tue.	Los Angeles 108 at Chicago	97

FINALS

Los Angeles 4, Milwaukee 2

Apr. 9—Sun.	Milwaukee 93 at Los Angeles	72
Apr. 12—Wed.	Milwaukee 134 at Los Angeles	135
Apr. 14—Fri.	Los Angeles 108 at Milwaukee	105
Apr. 16—Sun.	Los Angeles 88 at Milwaukee	114
Apr. 18—Tue.	Milwaukee 90 at Los Angeles	115
Apr. 22—Sat.	Los Angeles 104 at Milwaukee	100

NBA FINALS

Los Angeles 4, New York 1

Apr. 26—Wed.	New York 114 at Los Angeles	92
Apr. 30—Sun.	New York 92 at Los Angeles	106
May 3—Wed.	Los Angeles 107 at New York	96
May 5—Fri.	Los Angeles 116 at New York	*111
May 7—Sun.	New York 100 at Los Angeles	114

*Denotes number of overtime periods.

1970-71

1970-71 NBA CHAMPION MILWAUKEE BUCKS
Front row (from left): Bob Boozer, Greg Smith, Bob Dandridge, Oscar Robertson, Kareem Abdul-Jabbar, Jon McGlocklin, Lucius Allen, head coach Larry Costello. Back row (from left): trainer Arnie Garber, Jeff Webb, Marv Winkler, Dick Cunningham, Bob Greacen, McCoy McLemore, assistant coach Tom Nissalke.

FINAL STANDINGS

ATLANTIC DIVISION

	Atl.	Balt.	Bos.	Buf.	Chi.	Cin.	Cle.	Det.	L.A.	Mil.	N.Y.	Phi.	Pho.	Por.	S.D.	S.F.	Sea.	W	L	Pct.	GB
New York..... 3	4	6	2	2	4	4	3	2	4	..	2	4	3	4	3	2	52	30	.634	..
Philadelphia... 2	3	2	4	2	5	3	3	2	1	4	..	3	4	3	3	3	47	35	.573	5
Boston 4	3	..	4	4	4	3	2	3	0	0	4	2	2	3	3	3	44	38	.537	8
Buffalo 1	1	0	..	0	0	5	1	2	0	2	0	1	6	1	1	1	22	60	.268	30

CENTRAL DIVISION

	Atl.	Balt.	Bos.	Buf.	Chi.	Cin.	Cle.	Det.	L.A.	Mil.	N.Y.	Phi.	Pho.	Por.	S.D.	S.F.	Sea.	W	L	Pct.	GB
Baltimore..... 3	..	3	3	2	3	4	2	2	1	2	3	3	2	4	2	3	42	40	.512	..
Atlanta........	3	2	3	1	2	4	0	3	1	3	4	1	2	2	2	3	36	46	.439	6
Cincinnati 4	3	2	4	0	..	5	1	1	1	2	1	1	4	1	2	1	33	49	.402	9
Cleveland..... 0	0	1	7	0	1	..	2	0	0	0	1	0	2	0	1	0	15	67	.183	27

MIDWEST DIVISION

	Atl.	Balt.	Bos.	Buf.	Chi.	Cin.	Cle.	Det.	L.A.	Mil.	N.Y.	Phi.	Pho.	Por.	S.D.	S.F.	Sea.	W	L	Pct.	GB
Milwaukee.... 4	4	5	4	5	4	4	5	4	..	1	4	4	3	4	6	5	66	16	.805	..
Chicago...... 4	3	1	4	..	4	4	3	2		3	3	3	3	6	4	3	51	31	.622	15
Phoenix...... 4	2	3	3	3	4	4	4	4	2	1	2	..	4	2	3	3	48	34	.585	18
Detroit....... 5	3	3	5	3	4	2	..	2	1	2	2	2	3	4	1	3	45	37	.549	21

PACIFIC DIVISION

	Atl.	Balt.	Bos.	Buf.	Chi.	Cin.	Cle.	Det.	L.A.	Mil.	N.Y.	Phi.	Pho.	Por.	S.D.	S.F.	Sea.	W	L	Pct.	GB
Los Angeles... 2	3	2	2	4	4	4	3	..	1	3	3	2	4	3	4	4	48	34	.585	..
San Francisco . 3	3	2	3	2	3	3	4	2	0	2	2	2	3	4	..	3	41	41	.500	7
San Diego 3	1	2	3	0	3	4	2	3	1	1	2	4	4	..	2	5	40	42	.488	8
Seattle....... 2	2	2	3	2	4	4	1	2	1	3	2	2	4	1	3	..	38	44	.463	10
Portland 2	2	2	6	1	0	10	1	0	1	1	0	0	..	0	1	2	29	53	.354	19

TEAM STATISTICS

OFFENSIVE

	G	FGM	FGA	Pct.	FTM	FTA	Pct.	Reb.	Ast.	PF	Dq.	SCORING Pts.	SCORING Avg.
Milwaukee........... 82	3972	7803	.509	1766	2379	.742	4344	2249	1847	15	9710	118.4
Boston 82	3804	8616	.442	2000	2648	.755	4833	2052	2138	43	9608	117.2
Cincinnati 82	3805	8374	.454	1901	2622	.725	4151	2022	2126	45	9511	116.0
Portland 82	3721	8562	.435	2025	2671	.758	4210	2227	2024	23	9467	115.5
Seattle 82	3664	8034	.456	2101	2790	.753	4456	2049	1917	20	9429	115.0
Los Angeles 82	3739	7857	.476	1933	2717	.711	4269	2205	1709	14	9411	114.8
Philadelphia 82	3608	8026	.450	2199	2967	.741	4437	1976	2168	34	9415	114.8

	G	FGM	FGA	Pct.	FTM	FTA	Pct.	Reb.	Ast.	PF	Dq.	SCORING Pts.	Avg.
Atlanta	82	3614	7779	.465	2120	2975	.713	4472	1906	1958	23	9348	114.0
Phoenix	82	3503	8021	.437	2327	3078	.756	4442	1927	2132	30	9333	113.8
San Diego	82	3547	8426	.421	2188	2921	.749	4686	1921	2128	39	9282	113.2
Baltimore	82	3684	8331	.442	1886	2500	.754	4550	1772	1966	20	9254	112.9
Chicago	82	3460	7660	.452	2150	2721	.790	4325	2142	1797	12	9070	110.6
Detroit	82	3468	7730	.449	2093	2808	.745	3923	1696	1969	18	9029	110.1
New York	82	3633	8076	.450	1760	2377	.740	4075	1779	1916	13	9026	110.1
San Francisco	82	3454	7709	.448	1875	2468	.760	4643	1893	1833	25	8783	107.1
Buffalo	82	3424	7860	.436	1805	2504	.721	4261	1962	2232	55	8653	105.5
Cleveland	82	3299	7778	.424	1775	2380	.746	3982	2065	2114	37	8373	102.1

DEFENSIVE

	FGM	FGA	Pct.	FTM	FTA	Pct.	Reb.	Ast.	PF	Dq.	SCORING Pts.	Avg.	Dif.
New York	3343	7752	.431	1928	2565	.752	4591	1509	1889	22	8614	105.0	+5.1
Chicago	3491	7709	.453	1658	2216	.748	4031	1914	2099	36	8640	105.4	+5.2
Milwaukee	3489	8224	.424	1727	2322	.744	4004	1923	1770	11	8705	106.2	+12.2
San Francisco	3583	8371	.428	1735	2318	.748	4305	1949	1882	16	8901	108.5	-1.4
Detroit	3525	7713	.457	2040	2703	.755	4292	1912	2087	30	9090	110.9	-0.8
Los Angeles	3796	8511	.446	1567	2107	.744	4552	2078	1951	23	9159	111.7	+3.1
Phoenix	3506	7828	.448	2165	2923	.741	4173	2069	2202	42	9177	111.9	+1.9
Buffalo	3486	7666	.455	2224	3018	.737	4447	1998	1956	25	9196	112.1	-6.6
Baltimore	3640	8164	.446	1926	2584	.745	4435	1862	1897	20	9206	112.3	+0.6
Philadelphia	3514	7806	.450	2260	3076	.735	4372	1970	2089	39	9288	113.3	+1.5
Cleveland	3476	7480	.465	2337	3024	.773	4175	2307	1899	15	9289	113.3	-11.2
San Diego	3639	8102	.449	2024	2745	.737	4345	2135	2141	41	9302	113.4	-0.2
Boston	3612	8211	.440	2214	2982	.742	4342	1910	1962	27	9438	115.1	+2.1
Atlanta	3801	8525	.446	1893	2515	.753	4279	1996	2074	30	9495	115.8	-1.8
Seattle	3803	8117	.469	1985	2679	.741	4156	1994	2062	20	9591	117.0	-2.0
Cincinnati	3795	8130	.467	2184	2991	.730	4675	2050	1979	37	9774	119.2	-3.2
Portland	3900	8333	.468	2037	2758	.739	4885	2267	2035	32	9837	120.0	-4.5
Avgs.	3612	8038	.449	1994	2678	.745	4356	1991	1998	27	9218	112.4	...

HOME/ROAD/NEUTRAL

	Home	Road	Neutral	Total		Home	Road	Neutral	Total
Atlanta	21-20	14-26	1-0	36-46	Milwaukee	34-2	28-13	4-1	66-16
Baltimore	24-13	16-25	2-2	42-40	New York	32-9	19-20	1-1	52-30
Boston	25-14	18-22	1-2	44-38	Philadelphia	24-15	21-18	2-2	47-35
Buffalo	14-23	6-30	2-7	22-60	Phoenix	27-14	19-20	2-0	48-34
Chicago	30-11	17-19	4-1	51-31	Portland	18-21	9-26	2-6	29-53
Cincinnati	17-16	11-28	5-5	33-49	San Diego	24-15	15-26	1-1	40-42
Cleveland	11-30	2-37	2-0	15-67	San Francisco	20-18	19-21	2-2	41-41
Detroit	24-17	20-19	1-1	45-37	Seattle	27-13	11-30	0-1	38-44
Los Angeles	30-11	17-22	1-1	48-34	Totals	402-262	262-402	33-33	697-697

INDIVIDUAL LEADERS

POINTS
(minimum 70 games)

	G	FGM	FTM	Pts.	Avg.
Kareem Abdul-Jabbar, Milw.	82	1063	470	2596	31.7
John Havlicek, Boston	81	892	554	2338	28.9
Elvin Hayes, San Diego	82	948	454	2350	28.7
Dave Bing, Detroit	82	799	615	2213	27.0
Lou Hudson, Atlanta	76	829	381	2039	26.8
Bob Love, Chicago	81	765	513	2043	25.2
Geoff Petrie, Portland	82	784	463	2031	24.8
Pete Maravich, Atlanta	81	738	404	1880	23.2
Billy Cunningham, Philadelphia	81	702	455	1859	23.0
Tom Van Arsdale, Cincinnati	82	749	377	1875	22.9
Chet Walker, Chicago	81	650	480	1780	22.0
Dick Van Arsdale, Phoenix	81	609	553	1771	21.9
Walt Frazier, New York	80	651	434	1736	21.7
Earl Monroe, Baltimore	81	663	406	1732	21.4
Archie Clark, Philadelphia	82	662	422	1746	21.3
Jo Jo White, Boston	75	693	215	1601	21.3
Willis Reed, New York	73	614	299	1527	20.9
Connie Hawkins, Phoenix	71	512	457	1481	20.9
Jeff Mullins, San Francisco	75	630	302	1562	20.8
Wilt Chamberlain, Los Angeles	82	668	360	1696	20.7

FIELD GOALS
(minimum 700 attempted)

	FGM	FGA	Pct.
Johnny Green, Cincinnati	.502	855	.587
Kareem Abdul-Jabbar, Milwaukee	1063	1843	.577
Wilt Chamberlain, Los Angeles	.668	1226	.545
Jon McGlocklin, Milwaukee	.574	1073	.535
Dick Snyder, Seattle	.645	1215	.531
Greg Smith, Milwaukee	.409	799	.512
Bob Dandridge, Milwaukee	.594	1167	.509
Wes Unseld, Baltimore	.424	846	.501
Jerry Lucas, San Francisco	.623	1250	.498
Archie Clark, Philadelphia	.662	1334	.496
Oscar Robertson, Milwaukee	.592	1193	.496

FREE THROWS
(minimum 350 attempted)

	FTM	FTA	Pct.
Chet Walker, Chicago	.480	559	.859
Oscar Robertson, Milwaukee	.385	453	.850
Ron Williams, San Francisco	.331	392	.844
Jeff Mullins, San Francisco	.302	358	.844
Dick Snyder, Seattle	.302	361	.837
Stan McKenzie, Portland	.331	396	.836
Jerry West, Los Angeles	.525	631	.832
Jimmy Walker, Detroit	.344	414	.831
Bob Love, Chicago	.513	619	.829
Calvin Murphy, San Diego	.356	434	.820

ASSISTS

ASSISTS
(minimum 70 games)

	G	No.	Avg.
Norm Van Lier, Cincinnati	82	832	10.2
Lenny Wilkens, Seattle	71	654	9.2
Oscar Robertson, Milwaukee	81	668	8.3
John Havlicek, Boston	81	607	7.5
Walt Frazier, New York	80	536	6.7
Walt Hazzard, Atlanta	82	514	6.3
Ron Williams, San Francisco	82	480	5.9
Nate Archibald, Cincinnati	82	450	5.5
Archie Clark, Philadelphia	82	440	5.4
Dave Bing, Detroit	82	408	5.0

REBOUNDS
(minimum 70 games)

	G	No.	Avg.
Wilt Chamberlain, Los Angeles	82	1493	18.2
Wes Unseld, Baltimore	74	1253	16.9
Elvin Hayes, San Diego	82	1362	16.6
Kareem Abdul-Jabbar, Milwaukee	82	1311	16.0
Jerry Lucas, San Francisco	80	1265	15.8
Bill Bridges, Atlanta	82	1233	15.0
Dave Cowens, Boston	81	1216	15.0
Tom Boerwinkle, Chicago	82	1133	13.8
Nate Thurmond, San Francisco	82	1128	13.8
Willis Reed, New York	73	1003	13.7

INDIVIDUAL STATISTICS, TEAM BY TEAM

ATLANTA HAWKS

SCORING

	G	Min.	FGM	FGA	Pct.	FTM	FTA	Pct.	Reb.	Ast.	PF	Dq.	Pts.	Avg.
Lou Hudson	76	3113	829	1713	.484	381	502	.759	386	257	186	0	2039	26.8
Pete Maravich	81	2926	738	1613	.458	404	505	.800	298	355	238	1	1880	23.2
Walt Hazzard	82	2877	517	1126	.459	315	415	.759	300	514	276	2	1349	16.5
Walt Bellamy	82	2908	433	879	.493	336	556	.604	1060	230	271	4	1202	14.7
Bill Bridges	82	3140	382	834	.458	211	330	.639	1233	240	317	7	975	11.9
Jerry Chambers	65	1168	237	526	.451	106	134	.791	245	61	119	0	580	8.9
Jim Davis	82	1864	241	503	.479	195	288	.677	546	108	253	5	677	8.3
Len Chappell†	42	451	71	161	.441	60	74	.811	151	16	63	2	202	4.8
Len Chappell‡	48	537	86	199	.432	71	88	.807	133	17	72	2	243	5.1
John Vallely	51	430	73	204	.358	45	59	.763	34	47	50	0	191	3.7
Bob Christian	54	524	55	127	.433	40	64	.625	177	30	118	0	150	2.8
Herb White	38	315	34	84	.405	22	39	.564	48	47	62	2	90	2.4
Bob Riley	7	39	4	9	.444	5	9	.556	12	1	5	0	13	1.9

BALTIMORE BULLETS

SCORING

	G	Min.	FGM	FGA	Pct.	FTM	FTA	Pct.	Reb.	Ast.	PF	Dq.	Pts.	Avg.
Earl Monroe	81	2843	663	1501	.442	406	506	.802	213	354	220	3	1732	21.4
Jack Marin	82	2920	626	1360	.460	290	342	.848	513	217	261	3	1542	18.8
Gus Johnson	66	2538	494	1090	.453	214	290	.738	1128	192	227	4	1202	18.2
Kevin Loughery	82	2260	481	1193	.403	275	331	.831	219	301	246	2	1237	15.1
Wes Unseld	74	2904	424	846	.501	199	303	.657	1253	293	235	2	1047	14.1
Fred Carter	77	1707	340	815	.417	119	183	.650	251	165	165	0	799	10.4
Eddie Miles	63	1541	252	591	.426	118	147	.803	167	110	119	0	622	9.9
John Tresvant†	67	1457	184	401	.459	139	195	.713	359	76	185	1	507	7.6
John Tresvant‡	75	1517	202	436	.463	146	205	.712	382	86	196	1	550	7.3
Al Tucker	31	276	52	115	.452	25	31	.806	73	7	33	0	129	4.2
George Johnson	24	337	41	100	.410	11	30	.367	114	10	63	1	93	3.9
Jim Barnes	11	100	15	28	.536	7	11	.636	16	8	23	0	37	3.4
Dorie Murrey†	69	696	77	172	.448	66	101	.653	214	31	146	4	220	3.2
Dorie Murrey‡	71	716	78	178	.438	75	112	.670	221	32	149	4	231	3.3
Dennis Stewart	2	6	1	4	.250	2	2	1.000	3	1	0	0	4	2.0
Gary Zeller	50	226	34	115	.296	15	28	.536	27	7	43	0	83	1.7

BOSTON CELTICS

SCORING

	G	Min.	FGM	FGA	Pct.	FTM	FTA	Pct.	Reb.	Ast.	PF	Dq.	Pts.	Avg.
John Havlicek	81	3678	892	1982	.450	554	677	.818	730	607	200	0	2338	28.9
Jo Jo White	75	2787	693	1494	.464	215	269	.799	376	361	255	5	1601	21.3
Dave Cowens	81	3076	550	1302	.422	273	373	.732	1216	228	350	15	1373	17.0
Don Nelson	82	2254	412	881	.468	317	426	.744	565	153	232	2	1141	13.9
Don Chaney	81	2289	348	766	.454	234	313	.748	463	235	288	11	930	11.5
Steve Kuberski	82	1867	313	745	.420	133	183	.727	538	78	198	1	759	9.3
Rich Johnson	1	13	4	5	.800	0	0	…	5	0	3	0	8	8.0
Hank Finkel	80	1234	214	489	.438	93	127	.732	343	79	196	5	521	6.5
Art Williams	74	1141	150	330	.455	60	83	.723	205	233	182	1	360	4.9
Bill Dinwiddie	61	717	123	328	.375	54	74	.730	209	34	90	1	300	4.9
Rex Morgan	34	266	41	102	.402	35	54	.648	61	22	58	2	117	3.4
Garfield Smith	37	281	42	116	.362	22	56	.393	95	9	53	0	106	2.9
Tom Sanders	17	121	16	44	.364	7	8	.875	17	11	25	0	39	2.3
Willie Williams*	16	56	6	32	.188	3	5	.600	10	2	8	0	15	0.9

BUFFALO BRAVES

SCORING

	G	Min.	FGM	FGA	Pct.	FTM	FTA	Pct.	Reb.	Ast.	PF	Dq.	Pts.	Avg.
Bob Kauffman	78	2778	616	1309	.471	359	485	.740	837	354	263	8	1591	20.4
Don May	76	2666	629	1336	.471	277	350	.791	567	150	219	4	1535	20.2
Dick Garrett	75	2375	373	902	.414	218	251	.869	295	264	290	9	964	12.9
Mike Davis	73	1617	317	744	.426	199	262	.760	187	153	220	7	833	11.4

1970-71

	G	Min.	FGM	FGA	Pct.	FTM	FTA	Pct.	Reb.	Ast.	PF	Dq.	SCORING Pts.	Avg.
John Hummer	81	2637	339	764	.444	235	405	.580	717	163	284	10	913	11.3
Herm Gilliam	80	2082	378	896	.422	142	189	.751	334	291	246	4	898	11.2
Emmette Bryant	73	2137	288	684	.421	151	203	.744	262	352	266	7	727	10.0
Bill Hosket	13	217	47	90	.522	11	17	.647	75	20	27	1	105	8.1
Cornell Warner	65	1293	156	376	.415	79	143	.552	452	53	140	2	391	6.0
Freddie Crawford*	15	203	36	106	.340	16	26	.615	35	24	18	0	88	5.9
George Wilson	46	713	92	269	.342	56	69	.812	230	48	99	1	240	5.2
Paul Long	30	213	57	120	.475	20	24	.833	31	25	23	0	134	4.5
Nate Bowman	44	483	58	148	.392	20	38	.526	173	41	91	2	136	3.1
Mike Silliman	36	366	36	79	.456	19	39	.487	62	23	37	0	91	2.5
Mike Lynn	5	25	2	7	.286	3	3	1.000	4	1	9	0	7	1.4

CHICAGO BULLS

	G	Min.	FGM	FGA	Pct.	FTM	FTA	Pct.	Reb.	Ast.	PF	Dq.	SCORING Pts.	Avg.
Bob Love	81	3482	765	1710	.447	513	619	.829	690	185	259	0	2043	25.2
Chet Walker	81	2927	650	1398	.465	480	559	.859	588	179	187	2	1780	22.0
Jerry Sloan	80	3140	592	1342	.441	278	389	.715	701	281	289	5	1462	18.3
Tom Boerwinkle	82	2370	357	736	.485	168	232	.724	1133	397	275	3	882	10.8
Jim Fox	82	1628	280	611	.458	239	321	.745	598	196	213	0	799	9.7
Bob Weiss	82	2237	278	659	.422	226	269	.840	189	387	216	1	782	9.5
Matt Guokas†	78	2208	206	418	.493	101	138	.732	157	342	189	1	513	6.6
Matt Guokas‡	79	2213	206	418	.493	101	138	.732	158	342	189	1	513	6.5
Jim King	55	645	100	228	.439	64	79	.810	68	78	55	0	264	4.8
Johnny Baum	62	543	123	293	.420	40	58	.690	125	31	55	0	286	4.6
Jimmy Collins	55	478	92	214	.430	35	45	.778	54	60	43	0	219	4.0
Paul Ruffner	10	60	15	35	.429	4	8	.500	16	2	10	0	34	3.4
Shaler Halimon*	2	23	1	8	.125	0	1	.000	2	4	5	0	2	1.0
A.W. Holt	6	14	1	8	.125	2	3	.667	4	0	1	0	4	0.7

CINCINNATI ROYALS

	G	Min.	FGM	FGA	Pct.	FTM	FTA	Pct.	Reb.	Ast.	PF	Dq.	SCORING Pts.	Avg.
Tom Van Arsdale	82	3146	749	1642	.456	377	523	.721	499	181	294	3	1875	22.9
Johnny Green	75	2147	502	855	.587	248	402	.617	656	89	233	7	1252	16.7
Norm Van Lier	82	3324	478	1138	.420	359	440	.816	583	832	343	12	1315	16.0
Nate Archibald	82	2867	486	1095	.444	336	444	.757	242	450	218	2	1308	16.0
Sam Lacey	81	2648	467	1117	.418	156	227	.687	913	117	270	8	1090	13.5
Flynn Robinson	71	1368	374	817	.458	195	228	.855	143	138	161	0	943	13.3
Charlie Paulk	68	1213	274	637	.430	79	131	.603	320	27	186	6	627	9.2
Darrall Imhoff	34	826	119	258	.461	37	73	.507	233	79	120	5	275	8.1
Fred Foster*	1	21	3	8	.375	1	3	.333	4	0	2	0	7	7.0
Connie Dierking*	1	23	3	16	.188	0	0	...	7	1	5	0	6	6.0
Bob Arnzen	55	594	128	277	.462	45	52	.865	152	24	54	0	301	5.5
Greg Hyder	77	1359	183	409	.447	51	71	.718	332	48	187	2	417	5.4
Moe Barr	31	145	25	62	.403	11	13	.846	20	28	27	0	61	2.0
Tom Black†	16	100	10	33	.303	6	15	.400	34	2	20	0	26	1.6
Tom Black‡	71	873	121	301	.402	57	88	.648	259	44	136	1	299	4.2
Willie Williams†	9	49	4	10	.400	0	0	...	13	6	6	0	8	0.9
Willie Williams‡	25	105	10	42	.238	3	5	.600	23	8	14	0	23	0.9

CLEVELAND CAVALIERS

	G	Min.	FGM	FGA	Pct.	FTM	FTA	Pct.	Reb.	Ast.	PF	Dq.	SCORING Pts.	Avg.
Walt Wesley	82	2425	565	1241	.455	325	473	.687	713	83	295	5	1455	17.7
John Johnson	67	2310	435	1032	.422	240	298	.805	453	323	251	3	1110	16.6
Bobby Smith	77	2332	495	1106	.448	178	234	.761	429	258	175	4	1168	15.2
McCoy McLemore*	58	1839	254	654	.388	170	220	.773	463	176	169	1	678	11.7
Johnny Warren	82	2610	380	899	.423	180	217	.829	344	347	299	13	940	11.5
Dave Sorenson	79	1940	353	794	.445	184	229	.803	486	163	181	3	890	11.3
Luke Rackley	74	1434	219	470	.466	121	190	.637	394	66	186	3	559	7.6
Bobby Washington	47	823	123	310	.397	104	140	.743	105	190	105	0	350	7.4
Len Chappell*	6	86	15	38	.395	11	14	.786	18	1	9	0	41	6.8
Bob Lewis	79	1852	179	484	.370	109	152	.717	206	244	176	1	467	5.9
Joe Cooke	73	725	134	341	.393	48	59	.814	114	93	135	2	316	4.3
Johnny Egan*	26	410	40	98	.408	25	28	.893	32	58	31	0	105	4.0
Cliff Anderson*	23	171	19	59	.322	41	60	.683	37	16	22	1	79	3.4
Larry Mikan	53	536	62	186	.333	34	55	.618	139	41	56	1	158	3.0
Gary Suiter	30	140	19	54	.352	4	9	.444	41	2	20	0	42	1.4
Gary Freeman†	11	47	7	12	.583	1	2	.500	8	4	4	0	15	1.4
Gary Freeman‡	52	382	69	134	.515	29	40	.725	106	35	67	0	167	3.2

DETROIT PISTONS

	G	Min.	FGM	FGA	Pct.	FTM	FTA	Pct.	Reb.	Ast.	PF	Dq.	SCORING Pts.	Avg.
Dave Bing	82	3065	799	1710	.467	615	772	.797	364	408	228	4	2213	27.0
Jimmy Walker	79	2765	524	1201	.436	344	414	.831	207	268	173	0	1392	17.6
Bob Lanier	82	2017	504	1108	.455	273	376	.726	665	146	272	4	1281	15.6

	G	Min.	FGM	FGA	Pct.	FTM	FTA	Pct.	Reb.	Ast.	PF	Dq.	Pts.	Avg.
Terry Dischinger	65	1855	304	568	.535	161	211	.763	339	113	189	2	769	11.8
Otto Moore	82	1926	310	696	.445	121	219	.553	700	88	182	0	741	9.0
Steve Mix	35	731	111	294	.378	68	89	.764	164	34	72	0	290	8.3
Howie Komives	82	1932	275	715	.385	121	151	.801	152	262	184	0	671	8.2
Bob Quick	56	1146	155	341	.455	138	176	.784	230	56	142	1	448	8.0
Bill Hewitt	62	1725	203	435	.467	69	120	.575	454	124	189	5	475	7.7
Erwin Mueller	52	1224	126	309	.408	60	108	.556	223	113	99	0	312	6.0
Terry Driscoll	69	1255	132	318	.415	108	154	.701	402	54	212	2	372	5.4
Harvey Marlatt	23	214	25	80	.313	15	18	.833	23	30	27	0	65	2.8

LOS ANGELES LAKERS

	G	Min.	FGM	FGA	Pct.	FTM	FTA	Pct.	Reb.	Ast.	PF	Dq.	Pts.	Avg.
Jerry West	69	2845	667	1351	.494	525	631	.832	320	655	180	0	1859	26.9
Wilt Chamberlain	82	3630	668	1226	.545	360	669	.538	1493	352	174	0	1696	20.7
Happy Hairston	80	2921	574	1233	.466	337	431	.782	797	168	256	2	1485	18.6
Gail Goodrich	79	2808	558	1174	.475	264	343	.770	260	380	258	3	1380	17.5
Keith Erickson	73	2272	369	783	.471	85	112	.759	404	223	241	4	823	11.3
Elgin Baylor	2	57	8	19	.421	4	6	.667	11	2	6	0	20	10.0
Jim McMillian	81	1747	289	629	.459	100	130	.769	330	133	122	1	678	8.4
Willie McCarter	76	1369	247	592	.417	46	77	.597	122	126	152	0	540	7.1
John Tresvant*	8	66	18	35	.514	7	10	.700	23	10	11	0	43	5.4
Rick Roberson	65	909	125	301	.415	88	143	.615	304	47	125	1	338	5.2
Pat Riley	54	506	105	254	.413	56	87	.644	54	72	84	0	266	4.9
Fred Hetzel	59	613	111	256	.434	60	77	.779	149	37	99	3	282	4.8
Ernie Killum	4	12	0	4	.000	1	1	1.000	2	0	1	0	1	0.3

MILWAUKEE BUCKS

	G	Min.	FGM	FGA	Pct.	FTM	FTA	Pct.	Reb.	Ast.	PF	Dq.	Pts.	Avg.
Kareem Abdul-Jabbar	82	3288	1063	1843	.577	470	681	.690	1311	272	264	4	2596	31.7
Oscar Robertson	81	3194	592	1193	.496	385	453	.850	462	668	203	0	1569	19.4
Bob Dandridge	79	2862	594	1167	.509	264	376	.702	632	277	287	4	1452	18.4
Jon McGlocklin	82	2891	574	1073	.535	144	167	.862	223	305	189	0	1292	15.8
Greg Smith	82	2428	409	799	.512	141	213	.662	589	227	284	5	959	11.7
Bob Boozer	80	1775	290	645	.450	148	181	.818	435	128	216	0	728	9.1
Lucius Allen	61	1102	170	308	.447	77	110	.700	152	161	108	0	433	7.1
McCoy McLemore†	28	415	49	133	.368	34	41	.829	105	30	66	1	132	4.7
McCoy McLemore‡	86	2254	303	787	.385	204	261	.782	568	206	235	2	810	9.4
Gary Freeman*	41	335	62	122	.508	28	38	.737	98	31	63	0	152	3.7
Marv Winkler	3	14	3	10	.300	2	2	1.000	4	2	3	0	8	2.7
Dick Cunningham	76	675	81	195	.415	39	59	.661	257	43	90	1	201	2.6
Bob Greacen	2	43	1	12	.083	3	7	.429	6	13	7	0	5	2.5
Bill Zopf	53	398	49	135	.363	20	36	.556	46	73	34	0	118	2.2
Jeff Webb	29	300	27	78	.346	11	15	.733	24	19	33	0	65	2.2

NEW YORK KNICKERBOCKERS

	G	Min.	FGM	FGA	Pct.	FTM	FTA	Pct.	Reb.	Ast.	PF	Dq.	Pts.	Avg.
Walt Frazier	80	3455	651	1317	.494	434	557	.779	544	536	240	1	1736	21.7
Willis Reed	73	2855	614	1330	.462	299	381	.785	1003	148	228	1	1527	20.9
Dave DeBusschere	81	2891	523	1243	.421	217	312	.696	901	220	237	2	1263	15.6
Dick Barnett	82	2843	540	1184	.456	193	278	.694	238	225	232	1	1273	15.5
Bill Bradley	78	2300	413	912	.453	144	175	.823	260	280	245	3	970	12.4
Dave Stallworth	81	1565	295	685	.431	169	230	.735	352	106	175	1	759	9.4
Cazzie Russell	57	1056	216	504	.429	92	119	.773	192	77	74	0	524	9.2
Mike Riordan	82	1320	162	388	.418	67	108	.620	109	121	151	0	391	4.8
Phil Jackson	71	771	118	263	.449	95	133	.714	238	31	169	4	331	4.7
Greg Fillmore	39	271	45	102	.441	13	27	.481	93	17	80	0	103	2.6
Eddie Mast	30	164	25	66	.379	11	20	.550	56	4	25	0	61	2.0
Mike Price	56	251	30	81	.370	24	34	.706	29	12	57	0	84	1.5
Milt Williams	5	13	1	1	1.000	2	3	.667	0	2	3	0	4	0.8

PHILADELPHIA 76ERS

	G	Min.	FGM	FGA	Pct.	FTM	FTA	Pct.	Reb.	Ast.	PF	Dq.	Pts.	Avg.
Billy Cunningham	81	3090	702	1519	.462	455	620	.734	946	395	328	5	1859	23.0
Archie Clark	82	3245	662	1334	.496	422	536	.787	391	440	217	2	1746	21.3
Hal Greer	81	3060	591	1371	.431	326	405	.805	364	369	289	4	1508	18.6
Jim Washington	78	2501	395	829	.476	259	340	.762	747	97	258	6	1049	13.4
Bailey Howell	82	1589	324	686	.472	230	315	.730	441	115	234	2	878	10.7
Wali Jones	41	962	168	418	.402	79	101	.782	64	128	110	1	415	10.1
Dennis Awtrey	70	1292	200	421	.475	104	157	.662	430	89	211	7	504	7.2
Lucious Jackson	79	1774	199	529	.376	131	189	.693	568	148	211	3	529	6.7
Connie Dierking†	53	714	122	306	.399	61	89	.685	227	59	109	1	305	5.8
Connie Dierking‡	54	737	125	322	.388	61	89	.685	234	60	114	1	311	5.8
Fred Foster†	66	888	145	360	.403	72	103	.699	147	61	113	3	362	5.5
Fred Foster‡	67	909	148	368	.402	73	106	.689	151	61	115	3	369	5.5

1970-71

	G	Min.	FGM	FGA	Pct.	FTM	FTA	Pct.	Reb.	Ast.	PF	Dq.	Pts.	Avg.
Freddie Crawford†	36	449	74	175	.423	32	72	.444	69	54	59	0	180	5.0
Freddie Crawford‡	51	652	110	281	.391	48	98	.490	104	78	77	0	268	5.3
Bud Ogden	27	133	24	66	.364	18	26	.692	20	17	21	0	66	2.4
Cliff Anderson†	5	27	1	6	.167	5	7	.714	11	4	7	0	7	1.4
Cliff Anderson‡	28	198	20	65	.308	46	67	.687	48	20	29	1	86	3.1
Al Henry	6	26	1	6	.167	5	7	.714	11	0	1	0	7	1.2
Matt Guokas*	1	5	0	0		0	0	...	1	0	0	0	0	0.0

PHOENIX SUNS

	G	Min.	FGM	FGA	Pct.	FTM	FTA	Pct.	Reb.	Ast.	PF	Dq.	Pts.	Avg.
Dick Van Arsdale	81	3157	609	1346	.452	553	682	.811	316	329	246	1	1771	21.9
Connie Hawkins	71	2662	512	1181	.434	457	560	.816	643	322	197	2	1481	20.9
Clem Haskins	82	2764	562	1277	.440	338	431	.784	324	383	207	2	1462	17.8
Neal Walk	82	2033	426	945	.451	205	268	.765	674	117	282	8	1057	12.9
Paul Silas	81	2944	338	789	.428	285	416	.685	1015	247	227	3	961	11.9
Mel Counts	80	1669	365	799	.457	149	198	.753	503	136	279	8	879	11.0
Art Harris	56	952	199	484	.411	69	113	.611	100	132	137	0	467	8.3
Lamar Green	68	1326	167	369	.453	64	106	.604	466	53	202	5	398	5.9
Fred Taylor	54	552	110	284	.387	78	125	.624	86	51	113	0	298	5.5
John Wetzel	70	1091	124	288	.431	83	101	.822	153	114	156	1	331	4.7
Greg Howard	44	426	68	173	.393	37	58	.638	119	26	67	0	173	3.9
Joe Thomas	39	204	23	86	.267	9	20	.450	43	17	19	0	55	1.4

PORTLAND TRAIL BLAZERS

	G	Min.	FGM	FGA	Pct.	FTM	FTA	Pct.	Reb.	Ast.	PF	Dq.	Pts.	Avg.
Geoff Petrie	82	3032	784	1770	.443	463	600	.772	280	390	196	1	2031	24.8
Jim Barnett	78	2371	559	1283	.436	326	402	.811	376	323	190	1	1444	18.5
LeRoy Ellis	74	2581	485	1095	.443	209	261	.801	907	235	258	5	1179	15.9
Stan McKenzie	82	2290	398	902	.441	331	396	.836	309	235	238	2	1127	13.7
Rick Adelman	81	2303	378	895	.422	267	369	.724	282	380	214	2	1023	12.6
Gary Gregor	44	1153	181	421	.430	59	89	.663	334	81	120	2	421	9.6
Shaler Halimon†	79	1629	300	775	.387	107	161	.665	415	211	178	1	707	8.9
Shaler Halimon‡	81	1652	301	783	.384	107	162	.660	417	215	183	1	709	8.8
Dale Schlueter	80	1823	257	527	.488	143	218	.656	629	192	265	4	657	8.2
Ed Manning	79	1558	243	559	.435	75	93	.806	411	111	198	3	561	7.1
Dorie Murrey*	2	20	1	6	.167	9	11	.818	7	1	3	0	11	5.5
Ron Knight	52	662	99	230	.430	19	38	.500	167	50	99	1	217	4.2
Bill Stricker	1	2	2	3	.667	0	0	...	0	0	1	0	4	4.0
Walt Gilmore	27	261	23	54	.426	12	26	.462	73	12	49	1	58	2.1
Claude English	18	70	11	42	.262	5	7	.714	20	6	15	0	27	1.5

SAN DIEGO ROCKETS

	G	Min.	FGM	FGA	Pct.	FTM	FTA	Pct.	Reb.	Ast.	PF	Dq.	Pts.	Avg.
Elvin Hayes	82	3633	948	2215	.428	454	676	.672	1362	186	225	1	2350	28.7
Stu Lantz	82	3102	585	1305	.448	519	644	.806	406	344	230	3	1689	20.6
Calvin Murphy	82	2020	471	1029	.458	356	434	.820	245	329	263	4	1298	15.8
Don Adams	82	2374	391	957	.409	155	212	.731	581	173	344	11	937	11.4
John Trapp	82	2080	322	766	.420	142	188	.755	510	138	337	16	786	9.6
John Block	73	1464	245	584	.420	212	270	.785	442	98	193	2	702	9.6
Larry Siegfried	53	1673	146	378	.386	130	153	.850	207	346	146	0	422	8.0
Rudy Tomjanovich	77	1062	168	439	.383	73	112	.652	381	73	124	0	409	5.3
Bernie Williams	56	708	112	338	.331	68	81	.840	85	113	76	1	292	5.2
Toby Kimball	80	1100	111	287	.387	51	108	.472	406	62	128	1	273	3.4
Curtis Perry	18	100	21	48	.438	11	20	.550	30	5	22	0	53	2.9
Johnny Egan†	36	414	27	80	.338	17	23	.739	31	54	40	0	71	2.0
Johnny Egan‡	62	824	67	178	.376	42	51	.824	63	112	71	0	176	2.8

SAN FRANCISCO WARRIORS

	G	Min.	FGM	FGA	Pct.	FTM	FTA	Pct.	Reb.	Ast.	PF	Dq.	Pts.	Avg.
Jeff Mullins	75	2909	630	1308	.482	302	358	.844	341	332	246	5	1562	20.8
Nate Thurmond	82	3351	623	1401	.445	395	541	.730	1128	257	192	1	1641	20.0
Jerry Lucas	80	3251	623	1250	.498	289	367	.787	1265	293	197	0	1535	19.2
Ron Williams	82	2809	426	977	.436	331	392	.844	244	480	301	9	1183	14.4
Joe Ellis	80	2275	356	898	.396	151	203	.744	511	161	287	6	863	10.8
Bob Portman	68	1395	221	483	.458	77	106	.726	321	67	130	0	519	7.6
Nick Jones	81	1183	225	523	.430	111	151	.735	110	113	192	2	561	6.9
Clyde Lee	82	1392	194	428	.453	111	199	.558	570	63	137	0	499	6.1
Adrian Smith	21	247	38	89	.427	35	41	.854	24	30	24	0	111	5.3
Levi Fontaine	35	210	53	145	.366	28	37	.757	15	22	27	0	134	3.8
Bill Turner	18	200	26	82	.317	13	20	.650	42	8	24	0	65	3.6
Al Attles	34	321	22	54	.407	24	41	.585	40	58	59	2	68	2.0
Ralph Ogden	32	162	17	71	.239	8	12	.667	32	9	17	0	42	1.3

1970-71

SEATTLE SUPERSONICS

	G	Min.	FGM	FGA	Pct.	FTM	FTA	Pct.	Reb.	Ast.	PF	Dq.	Pts.	Avg.
Bob Rule	4	142	47	98	.480	25	30	.833	46	7	14	0	119	29.8
Spencer Haywood	33	1162	260	579	.449	160	218	.734	396	48	84	1	680	20.6
Lenny Wilkens	71	2641	471	1125	.419	461	574	.803	319	654	201	3	1403	19.8
Dick Snyder	82	2824	645	1215	.531	302	361	.837	257	352	246	6	1592	19.4
Don Kojis	79	2143	454	1018	.446	249	320	.778	435	130	220	3	1157	14.6
Zaid Abdul-Aziz	61	1276	263	597	.441	139	188	.739	468	42	118	0	665	10.9
Lee Winfield	79	1605	334	716	.466	162	244	.664	193	225	135	1	830	10.5
Tom Meschery	79	1822	285	615	.463	162	216	.750	485	108	202	2	732	9.3
Pete Cross	79	2194	245	554	.442	140	203	.690	949	113	212	2	630	8.0
Barry Clemens	78	1286	247	526	.470	83	114	.728	243	92	169	1	577	7.4
Jake Ford	5	68	9	25	.360	16	22	.727	9	9	11	0	34	6.8
Gar Heard	65	1027	152	399	.381	82	125	.656	328	45	126	0	386	5.9
Rod Thorn	63	767	141	299	.472	69	102	.676	103	182	60	0	351	5.6
Tom Black*	55	773	111	268	.414	51	73	.699	225	42	116	1	273	5.0

* Finished season with another team.   † Totals with this team only.   ‡ Totals with all teams.

PLAYOFF RESULTS

EASTERN CONFERENCE

SEMIFINALS

New York 4, Atlanta 1
Mar. 25—Thur.	Atlanta 101 at New York	112
Mar. 27—Sat.	Atlanta 113 at New York	104
Mar. 28—Sun.	New York 110 at Atlanta	95
Mar. 30—Tue.	New York 113 at Atlanta	107
Apr. 1—Thur.	Atlanta 107 at New York	111

Baltimore 4, Philadelphia 3
Mar. 24—Wed.	Philadelphia 126 at Baltimore	112
Mar. 26—Fri.	Baltimore 119 at Philadelphia	107
Mar. 28—Sun.	Philadelphia 103 at Baltimore	111
Mar. 30—Tue.	Baltimore 120 at Philadelphia	105
Apr. 1—Thur.	Philadelphia 104 at Baltimore	103
Apr. 3—Sat.	Baltimore 94 at Philadelphia	98
Apr. 4—Sun.	Philadelphia 120 at Baltimore	128

FINALS

Baltimore 4, New York 3
Apr. 6—Tue.	Baltimore 111 at New York	112
Apr. 9—Fri.	Baltimore 88 at New York	107
Apr. 11—Sun.	New York 88 at Baltimore	114
Apr. 14—Wed.	New York 80 at Baltimore	101
Apr. 16—Fri.	Baltimore 84 at New York	89
Apr. 18—Sun.	New York 96 at Baltimore	113
Apr. 19—Mon.	Baltimore 93 at New York	91

WESTERN CONFERENCE

SEMIFINALS

Milwaukee 4, San Francisco 1
Mar. 27—Sat.	Milwaukee 107 at San Francisco	96
Mar. 29—Mon.	San Francisco 90, Milwaukee (at Madison, Wis.)	104
Mar. 30—Tue.	San Francisco 102, Milwaukee (at Madison, Wis.)	114
Apr. 1—Thur.	Milwaukee 104 at San Francisco	106
Apr. 4—Sun.	San Francisco 86, Milwaukee (at Madison, Wis.)	136

Los Angeles 4, Chicago 3
Mar. 24—Wed.	Chicago 99 at Los Angeles	100
Mar. 26—Fri.	Chicago 95 at Los Angeles	105
Mar. 28—Sun.	Los Angeles 90 at Chicago	106
Mar. 30—Tue.	Los Angeles 102 at Chicago	112
Apr. 1—Thur.	Chicago 86 at Los Angeles	115
Apr. 4—Sun.	Los Angeles 99 at Chicago	113
Apr. 6—Tue.	Chicago 98 at Los Angeles	109

FINALS

Milwaukee 4, Los Angeles 1
Apr. 9—Fri.	Los Angeles 85 at Milwaukee	106
Apr. 11—Sun.	Los Angeles 73 at Milwaukee	91
Apr. 14—Wed.	Milwaukee 107 at Los Angeles	118
Apr. 16—Fri.	Milwaukee 117 at Los Angeles	94
Apr. 18—Sun.	Los Angeles 98 at Milwaukee	116

NBA FINALS

Milwaukee 4, Baltimore 0
Apr. 21—Wed.	Baltimore 88 at Milwaukee	98
Apr. 25—Sun.	Milwaukee 102 at Baltimore	83
Apr. 28—Wed.	Baltimore 99 at Milwaukee	107
Apr. 30—Fri.	Milwaukee 118 at Baltimore	106

1970-71

1969-70 NBA CHAMPION NEW YORK KNICKERBOCKERS
Front row (from left): Johnny Warren, Don May, Walt Frazier, president Ned Irish, chairman of the board Irving Mitchell Felt, general manager Ed Donovan, Dick Barnett, Mike Riordan, Cazzie Russell. Back row (from left): head coach Red Holzman, Phil Jackson, Dave Stallworth, Dave DeBusschere, captain Willis Reed, Bill Hosket, Nate Bowman, Bill Bradley, chief scout Dick McGuire, trainer Dan Whelan.

FINAL STANDINGS

EASTERN DIVISION

	N.Y.	Mil.	Balt.	Phi.	Cin.	Bos.	Det.	Atl.	L.A.	Chi.	Pho.	Sea.	S.F.	S.D.	W	L	Pct.	GB
New York	..	4	5	5	5	3	6	2	4	6	6	4	5	5	60	22	.732	..
Milwaukee	2	..	3	5	5	6	6	3	3	2	6	5	4	6	56	26	.683	4
Baltimore	1	3	..	3	4	5	5	4	4	5	3	2	5	6	50	32	.610	10
Philadelphia	2	2	4	..	3	4	5	3	2	3	4	0	6	4	42	40	.512	18
Cincinnati	2	2	3	4	..	3	4	3	2	3	3	1	2	4	36	46	.439	24
Boston	4	1	2	2	3	..	4	0	2	3	2	5	2	4	34	48	.415	26
Detroit	1	1	2	1	2	3	..	3	3	3	3	3	3	3	31	51	.378	29

WESTERN DIVISION

	N.Y.	Mil.	Balt.	Phi.	Cin.	Bos.	Det.	Atl.	L.A.	Chi.	Pho.	Sea.	S.F.	S.D.	W	L	Pct.	GB
Atlanta	4	3	2	3	3	6	3	..	4	5	2	5	4	4	48	34	.585	..
Los Angeles	2	3	2	4	4	4	3	3	..	2	3	6	5	5	46	36	.561	2
Chicago	0	4	1	3	3	3	3	2	4	..	5	4	4	3	39	43	.476	9
Phoenix	0	0	3	2	3	4	3	4	4	2	..	4	3	7	39	43	.476	9
Seattle	2	1	4	6	5	1	3	2	0	3	3	..	4	2	36	46	.439	12
San Francisco . . .	1	2	1	0	4	4	3	3	2	2	3	3	..	2	30	52	.366	18
San Diego	1	0	0	2	2	2	3	2	2	4	0	4	5	..	27	55	.329	21

TEAM STATISTICS

	G	FGM	FGA	Pct.	FTM	FTA	Pct.	Reb.	Ast.	PF	Dq.	AVERAGE POINTS For	AVERAGE POINTS Agst.	AVERAGE POINTS Dif.
New York.	82	3803	7975	.477	1821	2484	.733	4006	2135	2016	10	115.0	105.9	+9.1
Milwaukee	82	3923	8041	.488	1895	2589	.732	4419	2168	1971	27	118.8	114.2	+4.6
Philadelphia.	82	3915	8345	.469	2168	2884	.752	4463	2127	2196	47	121.9	118.5	+3.4
Baltimore.	82	3925	8567	.458	2050	2652	.773	4679	1881	1896	21	120.7	118.6	+2.1
Los Angeles.	82	3668	7952	.461	1991	2641	.754	4154	2030	1896	41	113.7	111.8	+1.9
Atlanta.	82	3817	7907	.483	2012	2669	.754	4210	2142	2016	29	117.6	117.2	+0.4
Chicago.	82	3607	8133	.444	2209	2861	.772	4383	2133	1863	13	114.9	116.7	-1.8
Phoenix.	82	3676	7856	.468	2434	3270	.744	4183	2076	2183	33	119.3	121.1	-1.8
Boston	82	3645	8235	.443	2132	2711	.786	4336	1875	2320	41	114.9	116.8	-1.9
Seattle.	82	3709	8029	.462	2171	2851	.761	4312	2214	2175	42	116.9	119.5	-2.6
Cincinnati	82	3767	8271	.455	2082	2841	.733	4163	1992	2215	52	117.3	120.2	-2.9
San Diego	82	3866	8867	.436	2000	2728	.733	4786	2036	2096	17	118.7	121.8	-3.1
Detroit.	82	3565	7657	.466	2116	2881	.734	3831	1709	1930	22	112.8	116.1	-3.3
San Francisco	82	3555	8224	.432	2004	2646	.757	4772	1861	2050	32	111.1	115.6	-4.5
Avgs.	82	3746	8147	.460	2078	2765	.752	4336	2027	2059	30.5	116.7	. . .	. . .

HOME/ROAD/NEUTRAL

	Home	Road	Neutral	Total		Home	Road	Neutral	Total
Atlanta	25-13	18-16	5-5	48-34	Milwaukee	27-11	24-14	5-1	56-26
Baltimore	25-12	19-18	6-2	50-32	New York	30-11	27-10	3-1	60-22
Boston	16-21	13-27	5-0	34-48	Philadelphia	22-16	16-22	4-2	42-40
Chicago	23-10	9-25	7-8	39-43	Phoenix	22-15	12-25	5-3	39-43
Cincinnati	19-13	14-25	3-8	36-46	San Diego	21-17	4-33	2-5	27-55
Detroit	18-20	10-25	3-6	31-51	San Francisco	16-20	14-26	0-6	30-52
Los Angeles	27-14	17-21	2-1	46-36	Seattle	22-14	10-26	4-6	36-46
					Totals	313-207	207-313	54-54	574-574

INDIVIDUAL LEADERS

POINTS

(minimum 70 games)

	G	FGM	FTM	Pts.	Avg.
Jerry West, Los Angeles	74	831	647	2309	31.2
Kareem Abdul-Jabbar, Milw.	82	938	485	2361	28.8
Elvin Hayes, San Diego	82	914	428	2256	27.5
Billy Cunningham, Philadelphia	81	802	510	2114	26.1
Lou Hudson, Atlanta	80	830	371	2031	25.4
Connie Hawkins, Phoenix	81	709	577	1995	24.6
Bob Rule, Seattle	80	789	387	1965	24.6
John Havlicek, Boston	81	736	488	1960	24.2
Earl Monroe, Baltimore	82	695	532	1922	23.4
Dave Bing, Detroit	70	575	454	1604	22.9
Tom Van Arsdale, Cincinnati	71	620	381	1621	22.8
Jeff Mullins, San Francisco	74	656	320	1632	22.1
Hal Greer, Philadelphia	80	705	352	1762	22.0
Flynn Robinson, Milwaukee	81	663	439	1765	21.8
Willis Reed, New York	81	702	351	1755	21.7
Chet Walker, Chicago	78	596	483	1675	21.5
Dick Van Arsdale, Phoenix	77	592	459	1643	21.3
Joe Caldwell, Atlanta	82	674	379	1727	21.1
Bob Love, Chicago	82	640	442	1722	21.0
Walt Frazier, New York	77	600	409	1609	20.9

FIELD GOALS

(minimum 700 attempted in 70 games)

	FGM	FGA	Pct.
Johnny Green, Cincinnati	481	860	.559
Darrall Imhoff, Philadelphia	430	796	.540
Lou Hudson, Atlanta	830	1564	.531
Jon McGlocklin, Milwaukee	639	1206	.530
Dick Snyder, Phoenix-Seattle	456	863	.528
Jim Fox, Phoenix	413	788	.524
Kareem Abdul-Jabbar, Milwaukee	938	1810	.518
Walt Frazier, New York	600	1158	.518
Wes Unseld, Baltimore	526	1015	.518
Dick Van Arsdale, Phoenix	592	1166	.508

FREE THROWS

(minimum 350 attempted in 70 games)

	FTM	FTA	Pct.
Flynn Robinson, Milwaukee	439	489	.898
Chet Walker, Chicago	483	568	.850
Jeff Mullins, San Francisco	320	378	.847
John Havlicek, Boston	488	578	.844
Bob Love, Chicago	442	525	.842
Earl Monroe, Baltimore	532	641	.830
Jerry West, Los Angeles	647	785	.824
Lou Hudson, Atlanta	371	450	.824
Hal Greer, Philadelphia	352	432	.815
Gail Goodrich, Phoenix	488	604	.808

ASSISTS

(minimum 70 games)

	G	No.	Avg.
Lenny Wilkens, Seattle	75	683	9.1
Walt Frazier, New York	77	629	8.2
Clem Haskins, Chicago	82	624	7.6
Jerry West, Los Angeles	74	554	7.5
Gail Goodrich, Phoenix	81	605	7.5
Walt Hazzard, Atlanta	82	561	6.8
John Havlicek, Boston	81	550	6.8
Art Williams, San Diego	80	503	6.3
Norm Van Lier, Cincinnati	81	500	6.2
Dave Bing, Detroit	70	418	6.0

REBOUNDS

(minimum 70 games)

	G	No.	Avg.
Elvin Hayes, San Diego	82	1386	16.9
Wes Unseld, Baltimore	82	1370	16.7
Kareem Abdul-Jabbar, Milwaukee	82	1190	14.5
Bill Bridges, Atlanta	82	1181	14.4
Willis Reed, New York	81	1126	13.9
Gus Johnson, Baltimore	78	1086	13.9
Billy Cunningham, Philadelphia	81	1101	13.6
Tom Boerwinkle, Chicago	81	1016	12.5
Paul Silas, Phoenix	78	916	11.7
Clyde Lee, San Francisco	82	929	11.3

INDIVIDUAL STATISTICS, TEAM BY TEAM

ATLANTA HAWKS

	G	Min.	FGM	FGA	Pct.	FTM	FTA	Pct.	Reb.	Ast.	PF	Dq.	SCORING Pts.	SCORING Avg.
Lou Hudson	80	3091	830	1564	.531	371	450	.824	373	276	225	1	2031	25.4
Joe Caldwell	82	2857	674	1329	.507	379	551	.688	407	287	255	3	1727	21.1
Walt Bellamy†	23	855	141	287	.491	75	124	.605	310	88	97	2	357	15.5
Walt Bellamy‡	79	2028	351	671	.523	215	373	.576	707	143	260	5	917	11.6
Walt Hazzard	82	2757	493	1056	.467	267	330	.809	329	561	264	3	1253	15.3
Bill Bridges	82	3269	443	932	.475	331	451	.734	1181	345	292	6	1217	14.8
Jim Davis	82	2623	438	943	.464	240	318	.755	796	238	335	5	1116	13.6
Gary Gregor	81	1603	286	661	.433	88	113	.779	397	63	159	5	660	8.1
Butch Beard	72	941	183	392	.467	135	163	.828	140	121	124	0	501	7.0
Don Ohl	66	984	176	372	.473	58	72	.806	71	98	113	1	410	6.2
Dave Newmark	64	612	127	296	.429	59	77	.766	174	42	128	3	313	4.9
Grady O'Malley	24	113	21	60	.350	8	19	.421	26	10	12	0	50	2.1
Gene Tormohlen	2	11	2	4	.500	0	0	. . .	4	1	3	0	4	2.0
Richie Guerin	8	64	3	11	.273	1	1	1.000	2	12	9	0	7	0.9

The Lakers' "Mr. Clutch," Hall of Famer Jerry West, is 11th on the career scoring list with 25,192 points.

BALTIMORE BULLETS

	G	Min.	FGM	FGA	Pct.	FTM	FTA	Pct.	Reb.	Ast.	PF	Dq.	SCORING Pts.	Avg.
Earl Monroe	82	3051	695	1557	.446	532	641	.830	257	402	258	3	1922	23.4
Kevin Loughery	55	2037	477	1082	.441	253	298	.849	168	292	183	3	1207	21.9
Jack Marin	82	2947	666	1363	.489	286	339	.844	537	217	248	6	1618	19.7
Gus Johnson	78	2919	578	1282	.451	197	272	.724	1086	264	269	6	1353	17.3
Wes Unseld	82	3234	526	1015	.518	273	428	.638	1370	291	250	2	1325	16.2
Mike Davis	56	1330	260	586	.444	149	192	.776	128	111	174	1	669	11.9
Ray Scott	73	1393	257	605	.425	139	173	.803	457	114	147	0	653	8.9
LeRoy Ellis	72	1163	194	414	.469	86	116	.741	376	47	129	0	474	6.6
Eddie Miles†	3	52	7	10	.700	3	5	.600	4	4	8	0	17	5.7
Eddie Miles‡	47	1295	238	541	.440	133	175	.760	177	86	107	0	609	13.0
Fred Carter	76	1219	157	439	.358	80	116	.690	192	121	137	0	394	5.2
Al Tucker†	28	262	49	96	.510	33	42	.786	53	7	34	0	131	4.7
Al Tucker‡	61	819	146	285	.512	70	87	.805	166	38	86	0	362	5.9
Bob Quick*	15	67	14	28	.500	12	18	.667	12	3	9	0	40	2.7
Ed Manning*	29	161	32	66	.485	5	8	.625	35	2	33	0	69	2.4
Brian Heaney	14	70	13	24	.542	2	4	.500	4	6	17	0	28	2.0

BOSTON CELTICS

	G	Min.	FGM	FGA	Pct.	FTM	FTA	Pct.	Reb.	Ast.	PF	Dq.	SCORING Pts.	Avg.
John Havlicek	81	3369	736	1585	.464	488	578	.844	635	550	211	1	1960	24.2
Don Nelson	82	2224	461	920	.501	337	435	.775	601	148	238	3	1259	15.4
Bailey Howell	82	2078	399	931	.429	235	308	.763	550	120	261	4	1033	12.6
Larry Siegfried	78	2081	382	902	.424	220	257	.856	212	299	187	2	984	12.6
Jo Jo White	60	1328	309	684	.452	111	135	.822	169	145	132	1	729	12.2
Tom Sanders	57	1616	246	555	.443	161	183	.880	314	92	199	5	653	11.5
Hank Finkel	80	1866	310	683	.454	156	233	.670	613	103	292	13	776	9.7
Emmette Bryant	71	1617	210	520	.404	135	181	.746	269	231	201	5	555	7.8
Steve Kuberski	51	797	130	335	.388	64	92	.696	257	29	87	0	324	6.4
Jim Barnes	77	1049	178	434	.410	95	128	.742	350	52	229	4	451	5.9
Rich Johnson	65	898	167	361	.463	46	70	.657	208	32	155	3	380	5.8
Don Chaney	63	839	115	320	.359	82	109	.752	152	72	118	0	312	5.0
Rich Niemann	6	18	2	5	.400	2	2	1.000	6	2	10	0	6	1.0

CHICAGO BULLS

	G	Min.	FGM	FGA	Pct.	FTM	FTA	Pct.	Reb.	Ast.	PF	Dq.	SCORING Pts.	SCORING Avg.
Chet Walker	78	2726	596	1249	.477	483	568	.850	604	192	203	1	1675	21.5
Bob Love	82	3123	640	1373	.466	442	525	.842	712	148	260	2	1722	21.0
Clem Haskins	82	3214	668	1486	.450	332	424	.783	378	624	237	0	1668	20.3
Jerry Sloan	53	1822	310	737	.421	207	318	.651	372	165	179	3	827	15.6
Bob Weiss	82	2544	365	855	.427	213	253	.842	227	474	206	0	943	11.5
Tom Boerwinkle	81	2335	348	775	.449	150	226	.664	1016	229	255	4	846	10.4
Walt Wesley	72	1407	270	648	.417	145	219	.662	455	68	184	1	685	9.5
Al Tucker*	33	557	97	189	.513	37	45	.822	113	31	52	0	231	7.0
Shaler Halimon	38	517	96	244	.393	49	73	.671	68	69	58	0	241	6.3
Ed Manning†	38	616	87	255	.341	37	48	.771	197	34	89	1	211	5.6
Ed Manning‡	67	777	119	321	.371	42	56	.750	232	36	122	1	280	4.2
Bob Kauffman	64	775	94	221	.425	88	123	.715	211	76	117	1	276	4.3
Loy Petersen	31	231	33	90	.367	26	39	.667	26	23	22	0	92	3.0
Johnny Baum	3	13	3	11	.273	0	0	...	4	0	1	0	6	2.0

CINCINNATI ROYALS

	G	Min.	FGM	FGA	Pct.	FTM	FTA	Pct.	Reb.	Ast.	PF	Dq.	SCORING Pts.	SCORING Avg.
Oscar Robertson	69	2865	647	1267	.511	454	561	.809	422	558	175	1	1748	25.3
Tom Van Arsdale	71	2544	620	1376	.451	381	492	.774	463	155	247	3	1621	22.8
Connie Dierking	76	2448	521	1243	.419	230	306	.752	624	169	275	7	1272	16.7
Johnny Green	78	2278	481	860	.559	254	429	.592	841	112	268	6	1216	15.6
Fred Foster	74	2077	461	1026	.449	176	243	.724	310	107	209	2	1098	14.8
Jerry Lucas*	4	118	18	35	.514	5	7	.714	45	9	5	0	41	10.3
Norm Van Lier	81	2895	302	749	.403	166	224	.741	409	500	329	18	770	9.5
Luke Rackley	66	1256	190	423	.449	124	195	.636	378	56	204	5	504	7.6
Herm Gilliam	57	1161	179	441	.406	68	91	.747	215	178	163	6	426	7.5
Bill Turner†	69	1095	188	451	.417	118	157	.752	290	42	187	3	494	7.2
Bill Turner‡	72	1170	197	468	.421	123	167	.737	304	43	193	3	517	7.2
Adrian Smith*	32	453	60	148	.405	52	60	.867	33	45	56	0	172	5.4
Wally Anderzunas	44	370	65	166	.392	29	46	.630	82	9	47	1	159	3.6
Jim King†	31	286	34	83	.410	22	27	.815	46	42	39	0	90	2.9
Jim King‡	34	391	53	129	.411	33	41	.805	62	52	47	0	139	4.1
Bob Cousy	7	34	1	3	.333	3	3	1.000	5	10	11	0	5	0.7

DETROIT PISTONS

	G	Min.	FGM	FGA	Pct.	FTM	FTA	Pct.	Reb.	Ast.	PF	Dq.	SCORING Pts.	SCORING Avg.
Dave Bing	70	2334	575	1295	.444	454	580	.783	299	418	196	0	1604	22.9
Jimmy Walker	81	2869	666	1394	.478	355	440	.807	242	248	203	4	1687	20.8
Eddie Miles*	44	1243	231	531	.435	130	170	.765	173	82	99	0	592	13.5
Otto Moore	81	2523	383	805	.476	194	305	.636	900	104	232	3	960	11.9
Terry Dischinger	75	1754	342	650	.526	174	241	.722	369	106	213	5	858	11.4
Howie Komives	82	2418	363	878	.413	190	234	.812	193	312	247	2	916	11.2
Happy Hairston*	15	282	57	103	.553	45	63	.714	88	11	36	0	159	10.6
Erwin Mueller†	74	2284	287	614	.467	185	254	.728	469	199	186	1	759	10.3
Erwin Mueller‡	78	2353	300	646	.464	189	263	.719	483	205	192	1	789	10.1
Walt Bellamy*	56	1173	210	384	.547	140	249	.562	397	55	163	3	560	10.0
McCoy McLemore	73	1421	233	500	.466	119	145	.821	336	83	159	3	585	8.0
Bob Quick†	19	297	49	111	.441	37	53	.698	63	11	41	0	135	7.1
Bob Quick‡	34	364	63	139	.453	49	71	.690	75	14	50	0	175	5.1
Steve Mix	18	276	48	100	.480	23	39	.590	64	15	31	0	119	6.6
Bill Hewitt†	45	801	85	210	.405	38	63	.603	213	36	91	1	208	4.6
Bill Hewitt‡	65	1279	110	298	.369	54	94	.574	356	64	130	1	274	4.2
Paul Long	25	130	28	62	.452	27	38	.711	11	17	22	0	83	3.3
George Reynolds	10	44	8	19	.421	5	7	.714	14	12	10	0	21	2.1
Tom Workman	2	6	0	1	.000	0	0	...	0	0	1	0	0	0.0

LOS ANGELES LAKERS

	G	Min.	FGM	FGA	Pct.	FTM	FTA	Pct.	Reb.	Ast.	PF	Dq.	SCORING Pts.	SCORING Avg.
Jerry West	74	3106	831	1673	.497	647	785	.824	338	554	160	3	2309	31.2
Wilt Chamberlain	12	505	129	227	.568	70	157	.446	221	49	31	0	328	27.3
Elgin Baylor	54	2213	511	1051	.486	276	357	.773	559	292	132	1	1298	24.0
Happy Hairston†	55	2145	426	870	.490	281	350	.803	687	110	194	9	1133	20.6
Happy Hairston‡	70	2427	483	973	.496	326	413	.789	775	121	230	9	1292	18.5
Mel Counts	81	2193	434	1017	.427	156	201	.776	683	160	304	7	1024	12.6
Dick Garrett	73	2318	354	816	.434	138	162	.852	235	180	236	5	846	11.6
Keith Erickson	68	1755	258	563	.458	91	122	.746	304	209	175	3	607	8.9
Rick Roberson	74	2005	262	586	.447	120	212	.566	672	92	256	7	644	8.7
Willie McCarter	40	861	132	349	.378	43	60	.717	83	93	71	0	307	7.7
Johnny Egan	72	1627	215	491	.438	99	121	.818	104	216	171	2	529	7.3
John Tresvant†	20	221	47	88	.534	23	35	.657	63	17	40	0	117	5.9
John Tresvant‡	69	1499	264	595	.444	206	284	.725	425	112	204	4	734	10.6
Bill Hewitt*	20	478	25	88	.284	16	31	.516	141	28	39	0	66	3.3
Mike Lynn	44	403	44	133	.331	31	48	.646	64	30	87	4	119	2.7

MILWAUKEE BUCKS

	G	Min.	FGM	FGA	Pct.	FTM	FTA	Pct.	Reb.	Ast.	PF	Dq.	Pts.	Avg.
Kareem Abdul-Jabbar	82	3534	938	1810	.518	485	743	.653	1190	337	283	8	2361	28.8
Flynn Robinson	81	2762	663	1391	.477	439	489	.898	263	449	254	5	1765	21.8
Jon McGlocklin	82	2966	639	1206	.530	169	198	.854	252	303	164	0	1447	17.6
Bob Dandridge	81	2461	434	895	.485	199	264	.754	625	292	279	1	1067	13.2
Greg Smith	82	2368	339	664	.511	125	174	.718	712	156	304	8	803	9.8
Len Chappell	75	1134	243	523	.465	135	211	.640	276	56	127	1	621	8.3
Freddie Crawford	77	1331	243	506	.480	101	148	.682	184	225	181	1	587	7.6
Zaid Abdul-Aziz	80	1637	237	546	.434	119	185	.643	603	62	167	2	593	7.4
Guy Rodgers	64	749	68	191	.356	67	90	.744	74	213	73	1	203	3.2
John Arthurs	11	86	12	35	.343	11	15	.733	14	17	15	0	35	3.2
Bob Greacen	41	292	44	109	.404	18	28	.643	59	27	49	0	106	2.6
Sam Williams	11	44	11	24	.458	5	11	.455	7	3	5	0	27	2.5
Dick Cunningham	60	416	52	141	.369	22	33	.667	160	28	70	0	126	2.1

NEW YORK KNICKERBOCKERS

	G	Min.	FGM	FGA	Pct.	FTM	FTA	Pct.	Reb.	Ast.	PF	Dq.	Pts.	Avg.
Willis Reed	81	3089	702	1385	.507	351	464	.756	1126	161	287	2	1755	21.7
Walt Frazier	77	3040	600	1158	.518	409	547	.748	465	629	203	1	1609	20.9
Dick Barnett	82	2772	494	1039	.475	232	325	.714	221	298	220	0	1220	14.9
Dave DeBusschere	79	2627	488	1082	.451	176	256	.688	790	194	244	2	1152	14.6
Bill Bradley	67	2098	413	897	.460	145	176	.824	239	268	219	0	971	14.5
Cazzie Russell	78	1563	385	773	.498	124	160	.775	236	135	137	0	894	11.5
Dave Stallworth	82	1375	239	557	.429	161	225	.716	323	139	194	2	639	7.8
Mike Riordan	81	1677	255	549	.464	114	165	.691	194	201	192	1	624	7.7
Bill Hosket	36	235	46	91	.505	26	33	.788	63	17	36	0	118	3.3
Nate Bowman	81	744	98	235	.417	41	79	.519	257	46	189	2	237	2.9
Don May	37	238	39	101	.386	18	19	.947	52	17	42	0	96	2.6
Johnny Warren	44	272	44	108	.407	24	35	.686	40	30	53	0	112	2.5

PHILADELPHIA 76ERS

	G	Min.	FGM	FGA	Pct.	FTM	FTA	Pct.	Reb.	Ast.	PF	Dq.	Pts.	Avg.
Billy Cunningham	81	3194	802	1710	.469	510	700	.729	1101	352	331	15	2114	26.1
Hal Greer	80	3024	705	1551	.455	352	432	.815	376	405	300	8	1762	22.0
Archie Clark	76	2772	594	1198	.496	311	396	.785	301	380	201	2	1499	19.7
Darrall Imhoff	79	2474	430	796	.540	215	331	.650	754	211	294	7	1075	13.6
Jim Washington	79	2459	401	842	.476	204	273	.747	734	104	262	5	1006	12.7
Wali Jones	78	1740	366	851	.430	190	226	.841	173	276	210	2	922	11.8
Matt Guokas	80	1558	189	416	.454	106	149	.711	216	222	201	0	484	6.1
Fred Hetzel	63	757	156	323	.483	71	85	.835	207	44	110	3	383	6.1
Lucious Jackson	37	583	71	181	.392	60	81	.741	198	50	80	0	202	5.5
George Wilson	67	836	118	304	.388	122	172	.709	317	52	145	3	358	5.3
Bud Ogden	47	357	82	172	.477	27	39	.692	86	31	62	2	191	4.1
Dave Scholz	1	1	1	1	1.000	0	0	...	0	0	0	0	2	2.0

PHOENIX SUNS

	G	Min.	FGM	FGA	Pct.	FTM	FTA	Pct.	Reb.	Ast.	PF	Dq.	Pts.	Avg.
Connie Hawkins	81	3312	709	1447	.490	577	741	.779	846	391	287	4	1995	24.6
Dick Van Arsdale	77	2966	592	1166	.508	459	575	.798	264	338	282	5	1643	21.3
Gail Goodrich	81	3234	568	1251	.454	488	604	.808	340	605	251	3	1624	20.0
Jim Fox	81	2041	413	788	.524	218	283	.770	570	93	261	7	1044	12.9
Paul Silas	78	2836	373	804	.464	250	412	.607	916	214	266	5	996	12.8
Dick Snyder*	6	147	22	45	.489	7	8	.875	15	9	20	1	51	8.5
Jerry Chambers	79	1139	283	658	.430	91	125	.728	219	54	162	3	657	8.3
Neal Walk	82	1394	257	547	.470	155	242	.640	455	80	225	2	669	8.2
Art Harris†	76	1375	257	650	.395	82	125	.656	142	211	209	0	596	7.8
Art Harris‡	81	1553	285	723	.394	86	134	.642	161	231	220	0	656	8.1
Lamar Green	58	700	101	234	.432	41	70	.586	276	17	115	2	243	4.2
Stan McKenzie	58	525	81	206	.393	58	73	.795	93	52	67	1	220	3.8
Neil Johnson	28	136	20	60	.333	8	12	.667	47	12	38	0	48	1.7

SAN DIEGO ROCKETS

	G	Min.	FGM	FGA	Pct.	FTM	FTA	Pct.	Reb.	Ast.	PF	Dq.	Pts.	Avg.
Elvin Hayes	82	3665	914	2020	.452	428	622	.688	1386	162	270	5	2256	27.5
Don Kojis	56	1578	338	756	.447	181	241	.751	388	78	135	1	857	15.3
Jim Barnett	80	2105	450	998	.451	289	366	.790	305	287	222	3	1189	14.9
John Block	82	2152	453	1025	.442	287	367	.782	609	137	275	2	1193	14.5
Stu Lantz	82	2471	455	1027	.443	278	361	.770	255	287	238	2	1188	14.5
Bernie Williams	72	1228	251	641	.392	96	122	.787	155	165	124	0	598	8.3
Rick Adelman	35	717	96	247	.389	68	91	.747	81	113	90	0	260	7.4
Bobby Smith	75	1198	242	567	.427	66	96	.688	328	75	119	0	550	7.3
Toby Kimball	77	1622	218	508	.429	107	185	.578	621	95	187	1	543	7.1
John Trapp	70	1025	185	434	.426	72	104	.692	309	49	200	3	442	6.3
Art Williams	80	1545	189	464	.407	88	118	.746	292	503	168	0	466	5.8
Pat Riley	36	474	75	180	.417	40	55	.727	57	85	68	0	190	5.3

SCORING

1969-70

SAN FRANCISCO WARRIORS

	G	Min.	FGM	FGA	Pct.	FTM	FTA	Pct.	Reb.	Ast.	PF	Dq.	SCORING Pts.	SCORING Avg.
Jeff Mullins	74	2861	656	1426	.460	320	378	.847	382	360	240	4	1632	22.1
Nate Thurmond	43	1919	341	824	.414	261	346	.754	762	150	110	1	943	21.9
Jim King*	3	105	19	46	.413	11	14	.786	16	10	8	0	49	16.3
Joe Ellis	76	2380	501	1223	.410	200	270	.741	594	139	281	13	1202	15.8
Jerry Lucas†	63	2302	387	764	.507	195	248	.786	906	166	159	2	969	15.4
Jerry Lucas‡	67	2420	405	799	.507	200	255	.784	951	173	166	2	1010	15.1
Ron Williams	80	2435	452	1046	.432	277	337	.822	190	424	287	7	1181	14.8
Clyde Lee	82	2641	362	822	.440	178	300	.593	929	80	263	5	902	11.0
Bill Turner*	3	75	9	17	.529	5	10	.500	14	1	7	0	23	7.7
Bob Lewis	73	1353	213	557	.382	100	152	.658	157	194	170	0	526	7.2
Dave Gambee	73	951	185	464	.399	156	186	.839	244	55	172	0	526	7.2
Bob Portman	60	813	177	398	.445	66	85	.776	224	28	77	0	420	7.0
Adrian Smith†	45	634	93	268	.347	100	110	.909	49	87	66	0	286	6.4
Adrian Smith‡	77	1087	153	416	.368	152	170	.894	82	133	122	0	458	5.9
Al Attles	45	676	78	202	.386	75	113	.664	74	142	103	0	231	5.1
Dale Schlueter	63	685	82	167	.491	60	97	.619	231	25	108	0	224	3.6

SEATTLE SUPERSONICS

	G	Min.	FGM	FGA	Pct.	FTM	FTA	Pct.	Reb.	Ast.	PF	Dq.	SCORING Pts.	SCORING Avg.
Bob Rule	80	2959	789	1705	.463	387	542	.714	825	144	278	6	1965	24.6
Lenny Wilkens	75	2802	448	1066	.420	438	556	.788	378	683	212	5	1334	17.8
Bob Boozer	82	2549	493	1005	.491	263	320	.822	717	110	237	2	1249	15.2
Dick Snyder†	76	2290	434	818	.531	162	200	.810	308	333	257	7	1030	13.6
Dick Snyder‡	82	2437	456	863	.528	169	208	.813	323	342	277	8	1081	13.2
John Tresvant*	49	1278	217	507	.428	183	249	.735	362	95	164	4	617	12.6
Tom Meschery	80	2294	394	818	.482	196	248	.790	666	157	317	13	984	12.3
Art Harris*	5	178	28	73	.384	4	9	.444	19	20	11	0	60	12.0
Lucius Allen	81	1817	306	692	.442	182	249	.731	211	342	201	0	794	9.8
Barry Clemens	78	1487	270	595	.454	111	140	.793	316	116	188	1	651	8.3
Erwin Mueller*	4	69	13	32	.406	4	9	.444	14	6	6	0	30	7.5
Lee Winfield	64	771	138	288	.479	87	116	.750	98	102	95	0	363	5.7
Dorie Murrey	81	1079	153	343	.446	136	186	.731	357	76	191	4	442	5.5
Rod Thorn	19	105	20	45	.444	15	24	.625	16	17	8	0	55	2.9
Al Hairston	3	20	3	8	.375	1	1	1.000	5	6	3	0	7	2.3
Joe Kennedy	14	82	3	34	.088	2	2	1.000	20	7	7	0	8	0.6

* Finished season with another team.   † Totals with this team only.   ‡ Totals with all teams.

1969-70

PLAYOFF RESULTS

EASTERN DIVISION

SEMIFINALS

Milwaukee 4, Philadelphia 1

Mar. 25—Wed.	Philadelphia 118 at Milwaukee	125
Mar. 27—Fri.	Philadelphia 112 at Milwaukee	105
Mar. 30—Mon.	Milwaukee 156 at Philadelphia	120
Apr. 1—Wed.	Milwaukee 118 at Philadelphia	111
Apr. 3—Fri.	Philadelphia 106 at Milwaukee	115

New York 4, Baltimore 3

Mar. 26—Thur.	Baltimore 117 at New York	**120
Mar. 27—Fri.	New York 106 at Baltimore	99
Mar. 29—Sun.	Baltimore 127 at New York	113
Mar. 31—Tue.	New York 92 at Baltimore	102
Apr. 2—Thur.	Baltimore 80 at New York	101
Apr. 5—Sun.	New York 87 at Baltimore	96
Apr. 6—Mon.	Baltimore 114 at New York	127

FINALS

New York 4, Milwaukee 1

Apr. 11—Sat.	Milwaukee 102 at New York	110
Apr. 13—Mon.	Milwaukee 111 at New York	112
Apr. 17—Fri.	New York 96 at Milwaukee	101
Apr. 19—Sun.	New York 117 at Milwaukee	105
Apr. 20—Mon.	Milwaukee 96 at New York	132

WESTERN DIVISION

SEMIFINALS

Atlanta 4, Chicago 1

Mar. 25—Wed.	Chicago 111 at Atlanta	129
Mar. 28—Sat.	Chicago 104 at Atlanta	124
Mar. 31—Tue.	Atlanta 106 at Chicago	101
Apr. 3—Fri.	Atlanta 120 at Chicago	131
Apr. 5—Sun.	Chicago 107 at Atlanta	113

Los Angeles 4, Phoenix 3

Mar. 25—Wed.	Phoenix 112 at Los Angeles	128
Mar. 29—Sun.	Phoenix 104 at Los Angeles	101
Apr. 2—Thur.	Los Angeles 98 at Phoenix	112
Apr. 4—Sat.	Los Angeles 102 at Phoenix	112
Apr. 5—Sun.	Phoenix 121 at Los Angeles	138
Apr. 7—Tue.	Los Angeles 104 at Phoenix	93
Apr. 9—Thur.	Phoenix 94 at Los Angeles	129

FINALS

Los Angeles 4, Atlanta 0

Apr. 12—Sun.	Los Angeles 119 at Atlanta	115
Apr. 14—Tue.	Los Angeles 105 at Atlanta	94
Apr. 16—Thur.	Atlanta 114 at Los Angeles	*115
Apr. 19—Sun.	Atlanta 114 at Los Angeles	133

NBA FINALS

New York 4, Los Angeles 3

Apr. 24—Fri.	Los Angeles 112 at New York	124
Apr. 27—Mon.	Los Angeles 105 at New York	103
Apr. 29—Wed.	New York 111 at Los Angeles	*108
May 1—Fri.	New York 115 at Los Angeles	*121
May 4—Mon.	Los Angeles 100 at New York	107
May 6—Wed.	New York 113 at Los Angeles	135
May 8—Fri.	Los Angeles 99 at New York	113

*Denotes number of overtime periods.

1968-69

1968-69 NBA CHAMPION BOSTON CELTICS
Front row (from left): Don Nelson, Sam Jones, player/coach Bill Russell, president Jack Waldron, general manager Red Auerbach, John Havlicek, team physician Dr. Thomas Silva, Larry Siegfried. Back row (from left): trainer Joe DeLauri, Emmette Bryant, Don Chaney, Tom Sanders, Rich Johnson, Jim Barnes, Bailey Howell, Mal Graham.

FINAL STANDINGS

EASTERN DIVISION

	Balt.	Phi.	N.Y.	Bos.	Cin.	Det.	Mil.	L.A.	Atl.	S.F.	S.D.	Chi.	Sea.	Pho.	W	L	Pct.	GB
Baltimore	..	2	3	5	4	7	5	3	4	3	5	6	4	6	57	25	.695	..
Philadelphia 4	..		3	2	4	4	6	5	5	2	4	5	6	5	55	27	.671	2
New York 4	4	..		6	2	4	6	1	4	5	3	4	6	5	54	28	.659	3
Boston 2	5	1	..		5	5	5	2	3	3	4	4	3	6	48	34	.585	9
Cincinnati 3	3	4	2	..		3	5	2	2	3	2	5	3	4	41	41	.500	16
Detroit 0	3	3	1	4	..		2	3	0	2	3	3	4	4	32	50	.390	25
Milwaukee 1	0	0	1	1	4	..		1	2	3	4	1	3	6	27	55	.329	30

WESTERN DIVISION

	Balt.	Phi.	N.Y.	Bos.	Cin.	Det.	Mil.	L.A.	Atl.	S.F.	S.D.	Chi.	Sea.	Pho.	W	L	Pct.	GB
Los Angeles 3	1	5	4	4	3	5	..		4	4	7	4	5	6	55	27	.671	..
Atlanta 2	1	2	3	4	6	4	3	..		4	3	6	4	6	48	34	.585	7
San Francisco . . . 3	4	1	3	3	4	3	3	3	..		3	3	4	4	41	41	.500	14
San Diego 1	2	3	2	4	3	2	0	4	3	..		3	3	7	37	45	.451	18
Chicago 0	1	2	2	1	3	5	3	1	4	3	..		4	4	33	49	.402	22
Seattle 2	0	0	3	3	2	5	1	2	3	3	3	..		3	30	52	.366	25
Phoenix 0	1	1	0	2	2	2	0	0	2	1	2	3	..		16	66	.195	39

TEAM STATISTICS

	G	FGM	FGA	Pct.	FTM	FTA	Pct.	Reb.	Ast.	PF	Dq.	AVERAGE POINTS For	AVERAGE POINTS Agst.	AVERAGE POINTS Dif.
Boston 82		3583	8316	.431	1936	2657	.729	4840	1953	2073	27	111.0	105.4	+5.6
New York. 82		3588	7813	.459	1911	2596	.736	4246	2071	2175	35	110.8	105.2	+5.6
Philadelphia 82		3754	8274	.454	2238	3087	.725	4513	1914	2145	44	118.9	113.8	+5.1
Baltimore 82		3770	8567	.440	2002	2734	.732	4963	1682	2038	17	116.4	112.1	+4.3
Los Angeles 82		3574	7620	.469	2056	3161	.650	4749	2068	1773	16	112.2	108.1	+4.1
Atlanta 82		3605	7844	.460	1913	2785	.687	4599	2069	2082	28	111.3	109.4	+1.9
San Diego 82		3691	8631	.428	2074	3039	.682	5026	1925	2110	19	115.3	115.5	-0.2
Cincinnati 82		3565	7742	.460	2262	3012	.751	4525	1983	2031	29	114.5	115.6	-1.1
San Francisco 82		3414	8218	.415	2119	2949	.719	5109	1822	2087	43	109.1	110.7	-1.6
Chicago 82		3355	8021	.418	1877	2577	.728	4550	1597	2064	29	104.7	106.9	-2.2
Detroit 82		3609	7997	.451	2141	3025	.708	4471	1757	2105	24	114.1	117.3	-3.2
Seattle 82		3543	8149	.435	2105	2979	.707	4498	1927	2281	54	112.1	116.9	-4.8
Milwaukee 82		3537	8258	.428	1966	2638	.745	4727	1882	2187	50	110.2	115.4	-5.2
Phoenix 82		3541	8242	.430	2080	2950	.705	4508	1918	2086	30	111.7	120.5	-8.8
Avgs. 82		3581	8121	.441	2049	2871	.714	4666	1898	2088	31.8	112.3	. . .	. . .

HOME/ROAD/NEUTRAL

	Home	Road	Neutral	Total		Home	Road	Neutral	Total
Atlanta	28-12	18-21	2-1	48-34	New York	30-7	19-20	5-1	54-28
Baltimore	29-9	24-15	4-1	57-25	Philadelphia	26-8	24-16	5-3	55-27
Boston	24-12	21-19	3-3	48-34	Phoenix	11-26	4-28	1-12	16-66
Chicago	19-21	12-25	2-3	33-49	San Diego	25-16	8-25	4-4	37-45
Cincinnati	15-13	16-21	10-7	41-41	San Francisco	22-19	18-21	1-1	41-41
Detroit	21-17	7-30	4-3	32-50	Seattle	18-18	6-29	6-5	30-52
Los Angeles	32-9	21-18	2-0	55-27	Totals	315-206	206-315	53-53	574-574
Milwaukee	15-19	8-27	4-9	27-55					

INDIVIDUAL LEADERS

POINTS

	G	FGM	FTM	Pts.	Avg.
Elvin Hayes, San Diego	.82	930	467	2327	28.4
Earl Monroe, Baltimore	.80	809	447	2065	25.8
Billy Cunningham, Philadelphia	.82	739	556	2034	24.8
Bob Rule, Seattle	.82	776	413	1965	24.0
Oscar Robertson, Cincinnati	.79	656	643	1955	24.7
Gail Goodrich, Phoenix	.81	718	495	1931	23.8
Hal Greer, Philadelphia	.82	732	432	1896	23.1
Elgin Baylor, Los Angeles	.76	730	421	1881	24.8
Lenny Wilkens, Seattle	.82	644	547	1835	22.4
Don Kojis, San Diego	.81	687	446	1820	22.5
Kevin Loughery, Baltimore	.80	717	372	1806	22.6
Dave Bing, Detroit	.77	678	444	1800	23.4
Jeff Mullins, San Francisco	.78	697	381	1775	22.8
John Havlicek, Boston	.82	692	387	1771	21.6
Lou Hudson, Atlanta	.81	716	338	1770	21.9
Willis Reed, New York	.82	704	325	1733	21.1
Bob Boozer, Chicago	.79	661	394	1716	21.7
Dick Van Arsdale, Phoenix	.80	612	454	1678	21.0
Wilt Chamberlain, Los Angeles	.81	641	382	1664	20.5
Flynn Robinson, Chicago-Milw.	.83	625	412	1662	20.0

FIELD GOALS

(minimum 230 made)

	FGM	FGA	Pct.
Wilt Chamberlain, Los Angeles	.641	1099	.583
Jerry Lucas, Cincinnati	.555	1007	.551
Willis Reed, New York	.704	1351	.521
Terry Dischinger, Detroit	.264	513	.515
Walt Bellamy, New York-Detroit	.563	1103	.510
Joe Caldwell, Atlanta	.561	1106	.507
Walt Frazier, New York	.531	1052	.505
Tom Hawkins, Los Angeles	.230	461	.499
Lou Hudson, Atlanta	.716	1455	.492
Jon McGlocklin, Milwaukee	.662	1358	.487

FREE THROWS

(minimum 230 made)

	FTM	FTA	Pct.
Larry Siegfried, Boston	.336	389	.864
Jeff Mullins, San Francisco	.381	452	.843
Jon McGlocklin, Milwaukee	.246	292	.842
Flynn Robinson, Chicago-Milwaukee	.412	491	.839
Oscar Robertson, Cincinnati	.643	767	.838
Fred Hetzel, Milwaukee-Cincinnati	.299	357	.838
Jack Marin, Baltimore	.292	352	.830
Jerry West, Los Angeles	.490	597	.821
Bob Boozer, Chicago	.394	489	.806
Chet Walker, Philadelphia	.369	459	.804

ASSISTS

	G	No.	Avg.
Oscar Robertson, Cincinnati	.79	772	9.8
Lenny Wilkens, Seattle	.82	674	8.2
Walt Frazier, New York	.80	635	7.9
Guy Rodgers, Milwaukee	.81	561	6.9
Dave Bing, Detroit	.77	546	7.1
Art Williams, San Diego	.79	524	6.6
Gail Goodrich, Phoenix	.81	518	6.4
Walt Hazzard, Atlanta	.80	474	5.9
John Havlicek, Boston	.82	441	5.4
Jerry West, Los Angeles	.61	423	6.9

REBOUNDS

	G	No.	Avg.
Wilt Chamberlain, Los Angeles	.81	1712	21.1
Wes Unseld, Baltimore	.82	1491	18.2
Bill Russell, Boston	.77	1484	19.3
Elvin Hayes, San Diego	.82	1406	17.1
Nate Thurmond, San Francisco	.71	1402	19.7
Jerry Lucas, Cincinnati	.74	1360	18.4
Willis Reed, New York	.82	1191	14.5
Bill Bridges, Atlanta	.80	1132	14.2
Walt Bellamy, New York-Detroit	.88	1101	12.5
Billy Cunningham, Philadelphia	.82	1050	12.8

INDIVIDUAL STATISTICS, TEAM BY TEAM

ATLANTA HAWKS

	G	Min.	FGM	FGA	Pct.	FTM	FTA	Pct.	Reb.	Ast.	PF	Dq.	Pts.	Avg.
Lou Hudson	81	2869	716	1455	.492	338	435	.777	533	216	248	0	1770	21.9
Zelmo Beaty	72	2578	586	1251	.468	370	506	.731	798	131	272	7	1542	21.4
Joe Caldwell	81	2720	561	1106	.507	159	296	.537	303	320	231	1	1281	15.8
Bill Bridges	80	2930	351	775	.453	239	353	.677	1132	298	290	3	941	11.8
Don Ohl	76	1995	385	901	.427	147	208	.707	170	221	232	5	917	12.1
Walt Hazzard	80	2420	345	869	.397	208	294	.707	266	474	264	6	898	11.2
Paul Silas	79	1853	241	575	.419	204	333	.613	745	140	166	0	686	8.7
Jim Davis	78	1367	265	568	.467	154	231	.667	529	97	239	6	684	8.8
Richie Guerin	27	472	47	111	.423	57	74	.770	59	99	66		151	5.6
Skip Harlicka	26	218	41	90	.456	24	31	.774	16	37	29	0	106	4.1
Dennis Hamilton	25	141	37	67	.552	2	5	.400	29	8	19	0	76	3.0
George Lehmann	11	138	26	67	.388	8	12	.667	9	27	18	0	60	5.5
Dwight Waller	11	29	2	9	.222	3	7	.429	10	1	8	0	7	0.6

BALTIMORE BULLETS

SCORING

	G	Min.	FGM	FGA	Pct.	FTM	FTA	Pct.	Reb.	Ast.	PF	Dq.	Pts.	Avg.
Earl Monroe	80	3075	809	1837	.440	447	582	.768	280	392	261	1	2065	25.8
Kevin Loughery	80	3135	717	1636	.438	372	463	.803	266	384	299	3	1806	22.6
Jack Marin	82	2710	505	1109	.455	292	352	.830	608	231	275	4	1302	15.9
Wes Unseld	82	2970	427	897	.476	277	458	.605	1491	213	276	4	1131	13.8
Ray Scott	82	2168	386	929	.416	195	257	.759	722	133	212	1	967	11.8
Gus Johnson	49	1671	359	782	.459	160	223	.717	568	97	176	1	878	17.9
LeRoy Ellis	80	1603	229	527	.435	117	155	.755	510	73	168	0	575	7.2
Ed Manning	63	727	129	288	.448	35	54	.648	246	21	120	0	293	4.7
John Barnhill	30	504	76	175	.434	39	65	.600	53	71	63	0	191	6.4
Barry Orms	64	916	76	246	.309	29	60	.483	158	49	155	3	181	2.8
Bob Quick	28	154	30	73	.411	27	44	.614	25	12	14	0	87	3.1
Tom Workman	21	86	22	54	.407	9	15	.600	27	2	16	0	53	2.5
Bob Ferry	7	36	5	14	.357	3	6	.500	9	4	3	0	13	1.9

BOSTON CELTICS

SCORING

	G	Min.	FGM	FGA	Pct.	FTM	FTA	Pct.	Reb.	Ast.	PF	Dq.	Pts.	Avg.
John Havlicek	82	3174	692	1709	.405	387	496	.780	570	441	247	0	1771	21.6
Bailey Howell	78	2527	612	1257	.487	313	426	.735	685	137	285	3	1537	19.7
Sam Jones	70	1820	496	1103	.450	148	189	.783	265	182	121	0	1140	16.3
Larry Siegfried	79	2560	392	1031	.380	336	389	.864	282	370	222	0	1120	14.2
Don Nelson	82	1773	374	771	.485	201	259	.776	458	92	198	2	949	11.6
Tom Sanders	82	2184	364	847	.430	187	255	.733	574	110	293	9	915	11.2
Bill Russell	77	3291	279	645	.433	204	388	.526	1484	374	231	2	762	9.9
Emmette Bryant	80	1388	197	488	.404	65	100	.650	192	176	264	9	459	5.7
Jim Barnes†	49	595	92	202	.455	65	92	.707	194	27	107	2	249	5.1
Jim Barnes‡	59	606	115	261	.441	75	111	.676	224	28	122	2	305	5.2
Don Chaney	20	209	36	113	.319	8	20	.400	46	19	32	0	80	4.0
Rich Johnson	31	163	29	76	.382	11	23	.478	52	7	40	0	69	2.2
Mal Graham	22	103	13	55	.236	11	14	.786	24	14	27	0	37	1.7
Bud Olsen*	7	43	7	19	.368	0	6	.000	14	4	6	0	14	2.0

CHICAGO BULLS

SCORING

	G	Min.	FGM	FGA	Pct.	FTM	FTA	Pct.	Reb.	Ast.	PF	Dq.	Pts.	Avg.
Bob Boozer	79	2872	661	1375	.481	394	489	.806	614	156	218	2	1716	21.7
Clem Haskins	79	2874	537	1275	.421	282	361	.781	359	306	230	0	1356	17.2
Jerry Sloan	78	2939	488	1170	.417	333	447	.745	619	276	313	6	1309	16.8
Jim Washington	80	2705	440	1023	.430	241	356	.677	847	104	226	0	1121	14.0
Tom Boerwinkle	80	2365	318	831	.383	145	222	.653	889	178	317	11	781	9.8
Barry Clemens	75	1444	235	628	.374	82	125	.656	318	125	163	1	552	7.4
Dave Newmark	81	1159	185	475	.389	86	139	.619	347	58	205	7	456	5.6
Bob Weiss†	62	1236	153	385	.397	101	126	.802	135	172	150	0	407	6.6
Bob Weiss‡	77	1478	189	499	.379	128	160	.800	162	199	174	1	506	6.6
Flynn Robinson*	18	550	124	293	.423	95	114	.833	69	57	52	1	343	19.1
Erwin Mueller*	52	872	75	224	.335	46	90	.511	193	124	98	1	196	3.8
Bob Love†	35	315	69	166	.416	42	58	.724	86	14	37	0	180	5.1
Bob Love‡	49	542	108	272	.397	71	96	.740	150	17	59	0	287	5.9
Loy Petersen	38	299	44	109	.404	19	27	.704	41	25	39	0	107	2.8
Jim Barnes*	10	111	23	59	.390	10	19	.526	30	1	15	0	56	5.6
Ken Wilburn	4	14	3	8	.375	1	4	.250	3	1	1	0	7	1.8

CINCINNATI ROYALS

SCORING

	G	Min.	FGM	FGA	Pct.	FTM	FTA	Pct.	Reb.	Ast.	PF	Dq.	Pts.	Avg.
Oscar Robertson	79	3461	656	1351	.486	643	767	.838	502	772	231	2	1955	24.7
Tom Van Arsdale	77	3059	547	1233	.444	398	533	.747	356	208	300	6	1492	19.4
Jerry Lucas	74	3075	555	1007	.551	247	327	.755	1360	306	206	0	1357	18.3
Connie Dierking	82	2540	546	1232	.443	243	319	.762	739	222	305	9	1335	16.3
Adrian Smith	73	1336	243	562	.432	217	269	.807	105	127	166	1	703	9.6
Walt Wesley	82	1334	245	534	.459	134	207	.647	403	47	191	0	624	7.6
John Tresvant*	51	1681	239	531	.450	130	223	.583	419	103	193	5	608	11.9
Fred Hetzel†	31	685	140	287	.488	88	105	.838	140	29	94	3	368	11.9
Fred Hetzel‡	84	2276	456	1047	.436	299	357	.838	613	112	287	9	1211	14.4
Al Tucker†	28	626	126	265	.475	49	73	.671	122	19	75	2	301	10.8
Al Tucker‡	84	1885	361	809	.446	158	244	.648	439	74	186	2	880	10.5
Bill Dinwiddie	69	1028	124	352	.352	45	87	.517	242	55	146	0	293	4.2
Fred Foster	56	497	74	193	.383	43	66	.652	61	36	49	0	191	3.4

	G	Min.	FGM	FGA	Pct.	FTM	FTA	Pct.	Reb.	Ast.	PF	Dq.	Pts.	Avg.
Pat Frink	48	363	50	147	.340	23	29	.793	41	55	54	1	123	2.6
Zaid Abdul-Aziz*	20	108	18	43	.419	2	7	.286	31	4	17	0	38	1.9
Doug Sims	4	12	2	5	.400	0	0	...	4	0	4	0	4	1.0

DETROIT PISTONS

	G	Min.	FGM	FGA	Pct.	FTM	FTA	Pct.	Reb.	Ast.	PF	Dq.	Pts.	Avg.
Dave Bing	77	3039	678	1594	.425	444	623	.713	382	546	256	3	1800	23.4
Happy Hairston	81	2889	530	1131	.469	404	553	.731	959	109	255	3	1464	18.1
Eddie Miles	80	2252	441	983	.449	182	273	.667	283	180	201	0	1064	13.3
Walt Bellamy†	53	2023	359	701	.512	276	416	.663	716	99	197	4	994	18.8
Walt Bellamy‡	88	3159	563	1103	.510	401	618	.649	1101	176	320	5	1527	17.4
Jimmy Walker	69	1639	312	670	.466	182	229	.795	157	221	172	1	806	11.7
Howie Komives†	53	1726	272	665	.409	138	178	.775	204	266	178	1	682	12.9
Howie Komives‡	85	2562	379	974	.389	211	264	.799	299	403	274	1	969	11.4
Terry Dischinger	75	1456	264	513	.515	130	178	.730	323	93	230	5	658	8.8
Otto Moore	74	1605	241	544	.443	88	168	.524	524	68	182	2	570	7.7
Dave DeBusschere*	29	1092	189	423	.447	94	130	.723	353	63	111	1	472	16.3
McCoy McLemore†	50	910	141	356	.396	84	104	.808	236	44	113	3	366	7.3
McCoy McLemore‡	81	1620	282	722	.391	169	214	.790	404	94	186	4	733	9.0
Dave Gambee†	25	302	60	142	.423	49	62	.790	78	15	60	0	169	6.8
Dave Gambee‡	59	926	210	465	.452	159	195	.815	257	47	159	4	579	9.8
Jim Fox*	25	375	45	96	.469	34	53	.642	139	23	56	1	124	5.0
Sonny Dove	29	236	47	100	.470	24	36	.667	62	12	49	0	118	4.1
Rich Niemann*	16	123	20	47	.426	8	10	.800	41	9	30	0	48	3.0
Bud Olsen†	10	70	8	23	.348	4	12	.333	11	7	8	0	20	2.0
Bud Olsen‡	17	113	15	42	.357	4	18	.222	25	11	14	0	34	2.0
Cliff Williams	3	18	2	9	.222	0	0	...	3	2	7	0	4	1.3

LOS ANGELES LAKERS

	G	Min.	FGM	FGA	Pct.	FTM	FTA	Pct.	Reb.	Ast.	PF	Dq.	Pts.	Avg.
Elgin Baylor	76	3064	730	1632	.447	421	567	.743	805	408	204	0	1881	24.8
Wilt Chamberlain	81	3669	641	1099	.583	382	857	.446	1712	366	142	0	1664	20.5
Jerry West	61	2394	545	1156	.471	490	597	.821	262	423	156	1	1580	25.9
Mel Counts	77	1866	390	867	.450	178	221	.805	600	109	223	5	958	12.4
Johnny Egan	82	1805	246	597	.412	204	240	.850	147	215	206	1	696	8.5
Keith Erickson	77	1974	264	629	.420	120	175	.686	308	194	222	6	648	8.4
Bill Hewitt	75	1455	239	528	.453	61	106	.575	332	76	139	1	539	7.2
Tom Hawkins	74	1507	230	461	.499	62	151	.411	266	81	168	1	522	7.1
Freddie Crawford	81	1690	211	454	.465	83	154	.539	215	154	224	1	505	6.2
Cliff Anderson	35	289	44	108	.407	47	82	.573	44	31	58	0	135	3.9
Jay Carty	28	192	34	89	.382	8	11	.727	58	11	31	0	76	2.7

MILWAUKEE BUCKS

	G	Min.	FGM	FGA	Pct.	FTM	FTA	Pct.	Reb.	Ast.	PF	Dq.	Pts.	Avg.
Jon McGlocklin	80	2888	662	1358	.487	246	292	.842	343	312	186	1	1570	19.6
Flynn Robinson†	65	2066	501	1149	.436	317	377	.841	237	320	209	6	1319	20.3
Flynn Robinson‡	83	2616	625	1442	.433	412	491	.839	306	377	261	7	1662	20.0
Len Chappell	80	2207	459	1011	.454	250	339	.737	637	95	247	3	1168	14.6
Wayne Embry	78	2355	382	894	.427	259	390	.664	672	149	302	8	1023	13.1
Fred Hetzel*	53	1591	316	760	.416	211	252	.837	473	83	193	6	843	15.9
Guy Rodgers	81	2157	325	862	.377	184	232	.793	226	561	207	2	834	10.3
Greg Smith	79	2207	276	613	.450	91	155	.587	804	137	264	12	643	8.1
Dave Gambee*	34	624	150	323	.464	110	133	.827	179	32	99	4	410	12.1
Dick Cunningham	77	1236	141	332	.425	69	106	.651	438	58	166	2	351	4.6
Zaid Abdul-Aziz†	29	837	126	347	.363	68	106	.642	378	33	98	3	320	11.0
Zaid Abdul-Aziz‡	49	945	144	390	.369	70	113	.619	409	37	115	3	358	7.3
Sam Williams	55	628	78	228	.342	72	134	.537	109	61	106	1	228	4.1
Bob Love*	14	227	39	106	.368	29	38	.763	64	3	22	0	107	7.6
Bob Weiss*	15	242	36	114	.316	27	34	.794	27	27	24	1	99	6.6
Rich Niemann†	18	149	24	59	.407	11	15	.733	59	7	31	1	59	3.3
Rich Niemann‡	34	272	44	106	.415	19	25	.760	100	16	61	1	107	3.1
Charlie Paulk	17	217	19	84	.226	13	23	.565	78	3	26	0	51	3.0
Jay Miller	3	27	2	10	.200	5	7	.714	2	0	4	0	9	3.0
Bob Warlick*	3	22	1	8	.125	4	5	.800	1	1	3	0	6	2.0

NEW YORK KNICKERBOCKERS

	G	Min.	FGM	FGA	Pct.	FTM	FTA	Pct.	Reb.	Ast.	PF	Dq.	Pts.	Avg.
Willis Reed	82	3108	704	1351	.521	325	435	.747	1191	190	314	7	1733	21.1
Dick Barnett	82	2953	565	1220	.463	312	403	.774	251	291	239	4	1442	17.6
Walt Frazier	80	2949	531	1052	.505	341	457	.746	499	635	245	2	1403	17.5
Bill Bradley	82	2413	407	948	.429	206	253	.814	350	302	295	4	1020	12.4
Cazzie Russell	50	1645	362	804	.450	191	240	.796	209	115	140	1	915	18.3
Dave DeBusschere†	47	1851	317	717	.442	135	198	.682	535	128	179	5	769	16.4
Dave DeBusschere‡	76	2943	506	1140	.444	229	328	.698	888	191	290	6	1241	16.3
Walt Bellamy*	35	1136	204	402	.507	125	202	.619	385	77	123	1	533	15.2
Phil Jackson	47	924	126	294	.429	80	119	.672	246	43	168	6	332	7.1
Howie Komives*	32	836	107	309	.346	73	86	.849	95	137	96	0	287	9.0
Don May	48	560	81	223	.363	42	58	.724	114	35	64	0	204	4.3
Nate Bowman	67	607	82	226	.363	29	61	.475	220	53	142	4	193	2.9
Bill Hosket	50	351	53	123	.431	24	42	.571	94	19	77	0	130	2.6
Mike Riordan	54	397	49	144	.340	28	42	.667	57	46	93	1	126	2.3

PHILADELPHIA 76ERS

	G	Min.	FGM	FGA	Pct.	FTM	FTA	Pct.	Reb.	Ast.	PF	Dq.	Pts.	Avg.
Billy Cunningham	82	3345	739	1736	.426	556	754	.737	1050	287	329	10	2034	24.8
Hal Greer	82	3311	732	1595	.459	432	543	.796	435	414	294	8	1896	23.1
Chet Walker	82	2753	554	1145	.484	369	459	.804	640	144	244	0	1477	18.0
Archie Clark	82	2144	444	928	.478	219	314	.697	265	296	188	1	1107	13.5
Wali Jones	81	2340	432	1005	.430	207	256	.809	251	292	280	5	1071	13.2
Darrall Imhoff	82	2360	279	593	.470	194	325	.597	792	218	310	12	752	9.2
Lucious Jackson	25	840	145	332	.437	69	97	.711	286	54	102	3	359	14.4
Johnny Green	74	795	146	282	.518	57	125	.456	330	47	110	1	349	4.7
Matt Guokas	72	838	92	216	.426	54	81	.667	94	104	121	1	238	3.3
George Wilson†	38	552	81	182	.445	60	84	.714	216	32	87	1	222	5.8
George Wilson‡	79	1846	272	663	.410	153	235	.651	721	108	232	5	697	8.8
Shaler Halimon	50	350	88	196	.449	10	32	.313	86	18	34	0	186	3.7
Craig Raymond	27	177	22	64	.344	11	17	.647	68	8	46	2	55	2.0

PHOENIX SUNS

	G	Min.	FGM	FGA	Pct.	FTM	FTA	Pct.	Reb.	Ast.	PF	Dq.	Pts.	Avg.
Gail Goodrich	81	3236	718	1746	.411	495	663	.747	437	518	253	3	1931	23.8
Dick Van Arsdale	80	3388	612	1386	.442	454	644	.705	548	385	245	2	1678	21.0
Dick Snyder	81	2108	399	846	.472	185	255	.725	328	211	213	2	983	12.1
Gary Gregor	80	2182	400	963	.415	85	131	.649	711	96	249	2	885	11.1
Stan McKenzie	80	1569	264	618	.427	219	287	.763	251	123	191	3	747	9.3
Jim Fox†	51	1979	273	581	.470	157	214	.734	679	143	210	5	703	13.8
Jim Fox‡	76	2354	318	677	.470	191	267	.715	818	166	266	6	827	10.9
Bob Warlick†	63	975	212	501	.423	83	137	.606	151	131	119	0	507	8.0
Bob Warlick‡	66	997	213	509	.418	87	142	.613	152	132	122	0	513	7.8
George Wilson*	41	1294	191	481	.397	93	151	.616	505	76	145	4	475	11.6
Neil Johnson	80	1319	177	368	.481	110	177	.621	396	134	214	3	464	5.8
Dave Lattin	68	987	150	366	.410	109	172	.634	323	48	163	5	409	6.0
McCoy McLemore*	31	710	141	366	.385	85	110	.773	168	50	73	1	367	11.8
Rod Knowles	8	40	4	14	.286	1	3	.333	9	0	10	0	9	1.1
Ed Biedenbach	7	18	0	6	.000	4	6	.667	2	3	1	0	4	0.6

SAN DIEGO ROCKETS

	G	Min.	FGM	FGA	Pct.	FTM	FTA	Pct.	Reb.	Ast.	PF	Dq.	Pts.	Avg.
Elvin Hayes	82	3695	930	2082	.447	467	746	.626	1406	113	266	2	2327	28.4
Don Kojis	81	3130	687	1582	.434	446	596	.748	776	214	303	6	1820	22.5
John Block	78	2489	448	1061	.422	299	400	.748	703	141	249	0	1195	15.3
Jim Barnett	80	2346	465	1093	.425	233	310	.752	362	339	240	2	1163	14.5
Toby Kimball	76	1680	239	537	.445	117	250	.468	669	90	216	6	595	7.8
Stu Lantz	73	1378	220	482	.456	129	167	.772	236	99	178	1	569	7.8
Art Williams	79	1987	227	592	.383	105	149	.705	364	524	238	0	559	7.1
Pat Riley	56	1027	202	498	.406	90	134	.672	112	136	146	1	494	8.8
Rick Adelman	77	1448	177	449	.394	131	204	.642	216	238	158	1	485	6.3
Hank Finkel	35	332	49	111	.441	31	41	.756	107	21	53	1	129	3.7
John Trapp	25	142	29	80	.363	19	29	.655	49	5	38	0	77	3.1
Harry Barnes	22	126	18	64	.281	7	13	.538	26	5	25	0	43	2.0

SAN FRANCISCO WARRIORS

	G	Min.	FGM	FGA	Pct.	FTM	FTA	Pct.	Reb.	Ast.	PF	Dq.	Pts.	Avg.
Jeff Mullins	78	2916	697	1517	.459	381	452	.843	460	339	251	4	1775	22.8
Rudy LaRusso	75	2782	553	1349	.410	444	559	.794	624	159	268	9	1550	20.7
Nate Thurmond	71	3208	571	1394	.410	382	621	.615	1402	253	171	0	1524	21.5
Joe Ellis	74	1731	371	939	.395	147	201	.731	481	130	258	13	889	12.0
Clyde Lee	65	2237	268	674	.398	160	256	.625	897	82	225	1	696	10.7
Bill Turner	79	1486	222	535	.415	175	230	.761	380	67	231	6	619	7.8
Ron Williams	75	1472	238	567	.420	109	142	.768	178	247	176	3	585	7.8
Al Attles	51	1516	162	359	.451	95	149	.638	181	306	183	3	419	8.2
Jim King	46	1010	137	394	.348	78	108	.722	120	123	99	1	352	7.7
Bob Lewis	62	756	113	290	.390	83	113	.735	114	76	117	0	309	5.0
Dale Schlueter	31	559	68	157	.433	45	82	.549	216	30	81	3	181	5.8
Bob Allen	27	232	14	43	.326	20	36	.556	56	10	27	0	48	1.8

SCORING

SEATTLE SUPERSONICS

	G	Min.	FGM	FGA	Pct.	FTM	FTA	Pct.	Reb.	Ast.	PF	Dq.	Pts.	Avg.
Bob Rule	82	3104	776	1655	.469	413	606	.682	941	141	322	8	1965	24.0
Lenny Wilkens	82	3463	644	1462	.440	547	710	.770	511	674	294	8	1835	22.4
Tom Meschery	82	2673	462	1019	.453	220	299	.736	822	194	304	7	1144	14.0
Art Harris	80	2556	416	1054	.395	161	251	.641	301	258	326	14	993	12.4
Bob Kauffman	82	1660	219	496	.442	203	289	.702	484	83	252	8	641	7.8
Al Tucker*	56	1259	235	544	.432	109	171	.637	317	55	111	0	579	10.3
Joe Kennedy	72	1241	174	411	.423	98	124	.790	241	60	158	2	446	6.2
Tom Kron	76	1124	146	372	.392	96	137	.701	212	191	179	2	388	5.1
John Tresvant†	26	801	141	289	.488	72	107	.673	267	63	107	4	354	13.6
John Tresvant‡	77	2482	380	820	.463	202	330	.612	686	166	300	9	962	12.5
Rod Thorn	29	567	131	283	.463	71	97	.732	83	80	58	0	333	11.5
Dorie Murrey	38	465	75	194	.387	62	97	.639	149	21	81	1	212	5.6
Erwin Mueller†	26	483	69	160	.431	43	72	.597	104	62	45	0	181	7.0
Erwin Mueller†	78	1355	144	384	.375	89	162	.549	297	186	143	1	377	4.8
Al Hairston	39	274	38	114	.333	8	14	.571	36	38	35	0	84	2.2
Plummer Lott	23	160	17	66	.258	2	5	.400	30	7	9	0	36	1.6

SCORING

* Finished season with another team.   † Totals with this team only.   ‡ Totals with all teams.

PLAYOFF RESULTS

EASTERN DIVISION
SEMIFINALS

New York 4, Baltimore 0
Mar. 27—Thur.	New York 113 at Baltimore	101
Mar. 29—Sat.	Baltimore 91 at New York	107
Mar. 30—Sun.	New York 119 at Baltimore	116
Apr. 2—Wed.	Baltimore 108 at New York	115

Boston 4, Philadelphia 1
Mar. 26—Wed.	Boston 114 at Philadelphia	100
Mar. 28—Fri.	Philadelphia 103 at Boston	134
Mar. 30—Sun.	Boston 125 at Philadelphia	118
Apr. 1—Tue.	Philadelphia 119 at Boston	116
Apr. 4—Fri.	Boston 93 at Philadelphia	90

FINALS
Boston 4, New York 2
Apr. 6—Sun.	Boston 108 at New York	100
Apr. 9—Wed.	New York 97 at Boston	112
Apr. 10—Thur.	Boston 91 at New York	101
Apr. 13—Sun.	New York 96 at Boston	97
Apr. 14—Mon.	Boston 104 at New York	112
Apr. 18—Fri.	New York 105 at Boston	106

WESTERN DIVISION
SEMIFINALS

Los Angeles 4, San Francisco 2
Mar. 26—Wed.	San Francisco 99 at Los Angeles	94
Mar. 28—Fri.	San Francisco 107 at Los Angeles	101
Mar. 31—Mon.	Los Angeles 115 at San Francisco	98
Apr. 2—Wed.	Los Angeles 103 at San Francisco	88
Apr. 4—Fri.	San Francisco 98 at Los Angeles	103
Apr. 5—Sat.	Los Angeles 118 at San Francisco	78

Atlanta 4, San Diego 2
Mar. 27—Thur.	San Diego 98 at Atlanta	107
Mar. 29—Sat.	San Diego 114 at Atlanta	116
Apr. 1—Tue.	Atlanta 97 at San Diego	104
Apr. 4—Fri.	Atlanta 112 at San Diego	114
Apr. 6—Sun.	San Diego 101 at Atlanta	112
Apr. 7—Mon.	Atlanta 108 at San Diego	106

FINALS
Los Angeles 4, Atlanta 1
Apr. 11—Fri.	Atlanta 93 at Los Angeles	95
Apr. 13—Sun.	Atlanta 102 at Los Angeles	104
Apr. 15—Tue.	Los Angeles 80 at Atlanta	99
Apr. 17—Thur.	Los Angeles 100 at Atlanta	85
Apr. 20—Sun.	Atlanta 96 at Los Angeles	104

NBA FINALS

Boston 4, Los Angeles 3
Apr. 23—Wed.	Boston 118 at Los Angeles	120
Apr. 25—Fri.	Boston 112 at Los Angeles	118
Apr. 27—Sun.	Los Angeles 105 at Boston	111
Apr. 29—Tue.	Los Angeles 88 at Boston	89
May 1—Thur.	Boston 104 at Los Angeles	117
May 3—Sat.	Los Angeles 90 at Boston	99
May 5—Mon.	Boston 108 at Los Angeles	106

1968-69

1967-68

1967-68 NBA CHAMPION BOSTON CELTICS
Front row (from left): Sam Jones, Larry Siegfried, general manager Red Auerbach, chairman of the board Marvin Kratter, president Clarence Adams, player/coach Bill Russell, John Havlicek. Back row (from left): trainer Joe Delauri, Rick Weitzman, Tom Thacker, Tom Sanders, Bailey Howell, Wayne Embry, Don Nelson, Johnny Jones, Mal Graham.

FINAL STANDINGS

EASTERN DIVISION

	Phi.	Bos.	N.Y.	Det.	Cin.	Balt.	St.L.	L.A.	S.F.	Chi.	Sea.	S.D.	W	L	Pct.	GB
Philadelphia	..	4	5	7	5	8	5	5	4	6	7	6	62	20	.756	..
Boston	4	..	6	6	3	5	4	4	4	5	6	7	54	28	.659	8
New York	3	2	..	4	5	5	1	3	5	5	4	6	43	39	.524	19
Detroit	1	2	4	..	4	4	4	2	4	4	6	5	40	42	.488	22
Cincinnati	3	5	3	4	..	3	1	1	4	2	6	7	39	43	.476	23
Baltimore	0	3	3	4	5	..	2	3	2	2	5	7	36	46	.439	26

WESTERN DIVISION

	Phi.	Bos.	N.Y.	Det.	Cin.	Balt.	St.L.	L.A.	S.F.	Chi.	Sea.	S.D.	W	L	Pct.	GB
St. Louis	2	3	6	3	6	5	..	2	7	7	8	7	56	26	.683	..
Los Angeles	2	3	4	5	6	4	6	..	4	7	4	7	52	30	.634	4
San Francisco	3	3	2	3	3	5	1	4	..	6	7	6	43	39	.524	13
Chicago	1	2	2	3	5	5	1	1	2	..	3	4	29	53	.354	27
Seattle	0	1	3	1	1	2	0	4	1	5	..	5	23	59	.280	33
San Diego	1	0	1	2	0	0	1	1	2	4	3	..	15	67	.183	41

TEAM STATISTICS

	G	FGM	FGA	Pct.	FTM	FTA	Pct.	Reb.	Ast.	PF	Dq.	AVERAGE POINTS For	AVERAGE POINTS Agst.	AVERAGE POINTS Dif.
Philadelphia......	82	3965	8414	.471	2121	3338	.635	5914	2197	1851	23	122.6	114.0	+8.6
Los Angeles......	82	3827	8031	.477	2283	3143	.726	5225	1983	2152	30	121.2	115.6	+5.6
Boston	82	3686	8371	.440	2151	2983	.721	5666	1798	2147	26	116.1	112.0	+4.1
St. Louis	82	3504	7765	.451	2258	3111	.726	5325	1988	2046	36	113.0	110.3	+2.7
New York........	82	3682	8070	.456	2159	3042	.710	5122	1967	2364	25	116.1	114.3	+1.8
Baltimore........	82	3691	8428	.438	2245	2994	.750	5431	1534	2127	38	117.4	117.8	-0.4
San Francisco	82	3632	8587	.423	2334	3153	.740	6029	1901	2265	52	117.0	117.6	-0.6
Cincinnati	82	3679	7864	.468	2204	2892	.762	5129	2048	2016	29	116.6	117.4	-0.8
Detroit	82	3755	8386	.448	2215	3129	.708	5452	1700	2240	52	118.6	120.6	-2.0
Chicago.........	82	3488	8138	.429	2006	2718	.738	5117	1527	2130	42	109.5	113.5	-4.0
Seattle..........	82	3772	8593	.439	2188	3042	.719	5338	1998	2372	49	118.7	125.1	-6.4
San Diego	82	3466	8547	.406	2083	2929	.711	5418	1837	2188	27	112.4	121.0	-8.6
Avgs..........	82	3679	8266	.445	2187	3040	.719	5431	1873	2158	35.8	116.6	...	...

HOME/ROAD/NEUTRAL

	Home	Road	Neutral	Total		Home	Road	Neutral	Total
Baltimore	17-19	12-23	7-4	36-46	New York	20-17	21-16	2-6	43-39
Boston	28-9	20-16	6-3	54-28	Philadelphia	27-8	25-12	10-0	62-20
Chicago	11-22	12-23	6-8	29-53	St. Louis	25-7	22-13	9-6	56-26
Cincinnati	18-12	13-23	8-8	39-43	San Diego	8-33	4-26	3-8	15-67
Detroit	21-11	12-23	7-8	40-42	San Francisco	27-14	16-23	0-2	43-39
Los Angeles	30-11	18-19	4-0	52-30	Seattle	9-19	7-24	7-16	23-59
					Totals	241-182	182-241	69-69	492-492

INDIVIDUAL LEADERS

POINTS

	G	FGM	FTM	Pts.	Avg.
Dave Bing, Detroit	79	835	472	2142	27.1
Elgin Baylor, Los Angeles	77	757	488	2002	26.0
Wilt Chamberlain, Philadelphia	82	819	354	1992	24.3
Earl Monroe, Baltimore	82	742	507	1991	24.3
Hal Greer, Philadelphia	82	777	422	1976	24.1
Oscar Robertson, Cincinnati	65	660	576	1896	29.2
Walt Hazzard, Seattle	79	733	428	1894	24.0
Jerry Lucas, Cincinnati	82	707	346	1760	21.5
Zelmo Beaty, St. Louis	82	639	455	1733	21.1
Rudy LaRusso, San Francisco	79	602	522	1726	21.8
John Havlicek, Boston	82	666	368	1700	20.7
Willis Reed, New York	81	659	367	1685	20.8
Bob Boozer, Chicago	77	622	411	1655	21.5
Lenny Wilkens, St. Louis	82	546	546	1638	20.0
Bailey Howell, Boston	82	643	335	1621	19.8
Archie Clark, Los Angeles	81	628	356	1612	19.9
Sam Jones, Boston	73	621	311	1553	21.3
Jeff Mullins, San Francisco	79	610	273	1493	18.9
Bob Rule, Seattle	82	568	348	1484	18.1
Chet Walker, Philadelphia	82	539	387	1465	17.9

FIELD GOALS

(minimum 220 made)

	FGM	FGA	Pct.
Wilt Chamberlain, Philadelphia	819	1377	.595
Walt Bellamy, New York	511	944	.541
Jerry Lucas, Cincinnati	707	1361	.519
Jerry West, Los Angeles	476	926	.514
Len Chappell, Cincinnati-Detroit	235	458	.513
Oscar Robertson, Cincinnati	660	1321	.500
Tom Hawkins, Los Angeles	389	779	.499
Terry Dischinger, Detroit	394	797	.494
Don Nelson, Boston	312	632	.494
Henry Finkel, San Diego	242	492	.492

FREE THROWS

(minimum 220 made)

	FTM	FTA	Pct.
Oscar Robertson, Cincinnati	.576	660	.873
Larry Siegfried, Boston	.236	272	.868
Dave Gambee, San Diego	.321	379	.847
Fred Hetzel, San Francisco	.395	474	.833
Adrian Smith, Cincinnati	.320	386	.829
Sam Jones, Boston	.311	376	.827
Flynn Robinson, Cincinnati-Chicago	.288	351	.821
John Havlicek, Boston	.368	453	.812
Jerry West, Los Angeles	.391	482	.811
Cazzie Russell, New York	.282	349	.808

ASSISTS

	G	No.	Avg.
Wilt Chamberlain, Philadelphia	82	702	8.6
Lenny Wilkens, St. Louis	82	679	8.3
Oscar Robertson, Cincinnati	65	633	9.7
Dave Bing, Detroit	79	509	6.4
Walt Hazzard, Seattle	79	493	6.2
Art Williams, San Diego	79	391	5.0
Al Attles, San Francisco	67	300	5.8
John Havlicek, Boston	82	384	4.7
Guy Rodgers, Chicago-Cincinnati	79	380	4.8
Hal Greer, Philadelphia	82	372	4.5

REBOUNDS

	G	No.	Avg.
Wilt Chamberlain, Philadelphia	82	1952	23.8
Jerry Lucas, Cincinnati	82	1560	19.0
Bill Russell, Boston	78	1451	18.6
Clyde Lee, San Francisco	82	1141	13.9
Nate Thurmond, San Francisco	51	1121	22.0
Ray Scott, Baltimore	81	1111	13.7
Bill Bridges, St. Louis	82	1102	13.4
Dave DeBusschere, Detroit	80	1081	13.5
Willis Reed, New York	81	1073	13.2
Walt Bellamy, New York	82	961	11.7

1967-68

INDIVIDUAL STATISTICS, TEAM BY TEAM

BALTIMORE BULLETS

	G	Min.	FGM	FGA	Pct.	FTM	FTA	Pct.	Reb.	Ast.	PF	Dq.	SCORING Pts.	Avg.
Earl Monroe	82	3012	742	1637	.453	507	649	.781	465	349	282	3	1991	24.3
Ray Scott	81	2924	490	1189	.412	348	447	.779	1111	167	252	2	1328	16.4
Kevin Loughery	77	2297	458	1127	.406	305	392	.778	247	256	301	13	1221	15.9
Gus Johnson	60	2271	482	1033	.467	180	270	.667	782	159	223	7	1144	19.1
Jack Marin	82	2037	429	932	.460	250	314	.796	473	110	246	4	1108	13.5
LeRoy Ellis	78	2719	380	800	.475	207	286	.724	862	158	256	5	967	12.4
Don Ohl*	39	1096	232	536	.433	114	148	.770	113	84	91	0	578	14.8
Johnny Egan	67	930	163	415	.393	142	183	.776	112	134	127	0	468	7.0
Bob Ferry	59	841	128	311	.412	73	117	.624	186	61	92	0	329	5.6
Ed Manning	71	951	112	259	.432	60	99	.606	375	32	153	3	284	4.0
Stan McKenzie	50	653	73	182	.401	58	88	.659	121	24	98	1	204	4.1
Roland West	4	14	2	5	.400	0	0	...	5	0	3	0	4	1.0
Tom Workman†	1	10	0	2	.000	1	1	1.000	1	0	3	0	1	1.0
Tom Workman‡	20	95	19	40	.475	18	23	.783	25	3	17	0	56	2.8

BOSTON CELTICS

	G	Min.	FGM	FGA	Pct.	FTM	FTA	Pct.	Reb.	Ast.	PF	Dq.	SCORING Pts.	Avg.
John Havlicek	82	2921	666	1551	.429	368	453	.812	546	384	237	2	1700	20.7
Bailey Howell	82	2801	643	1336	.481	335	461	.727	805	133	285	4	1621	19.8
Sam Jones	73	2408	621	1348	.461	311	376	.827	357	216	181	0	1553	21.3

	G	Min.	FGM	FGA	Pct.	FTM	FTA	Pct.	Reb.	Ast.	PF	Dq.	Pts.	Avg.
													SCORING	
Bill Russell	78	2953	365	858	.425	247	460	.537	1451	357	242	2	977	12.5
Don Nelson	82	1498	312	632	.494	195	268	.728	431	103	178	1	819	10.0
Tom Sanders	78	1981	296	691	.428	200	255	.784	454	100	300	12	792	10.2
Larry Siegfried	62	1937	261	629	.415	236	272	.868	215	289	194	2	758	12.2
Wayne Embry	78	1088	193	483	.400	109	185	.589	321	52	174	1	495	6.3
Mal Graham	78	786	117	272	.430	56	88	.636	94	61	123	0	290	3.7
Tom Thacker	65	782	114	272	.419	43	84	.512	161	69	165	2	271	4.2
Johnny Jones	51	475	86	253	.340	42	68	.618	114	26	60	0	214	4.2
Rick Weitzman	25	75	12	46	.261	9	13	.692	10	8	8	0	33	1.3

CHICAGO BULLS

	G	Min.	FGM	FGA	Pct.	FTM	FTA	Pct.	Reb.	Ast.	PF	Dq.	Pts.	Avg.
													SCORING	
Bob Boozer	77	2988	622	1265	.492	411	535	.768	756	121	229	1	1655	21.5
Flynn Robinson†	73	2030	441	1000	.441	285	344	.828	268	214	180	1	1167	16.0
Flynn Robinson‡	75	2046	444	1010	.440	288	351	.821	272	219	184	1	1176	15.7
Jerry Sloan	77	2454	369	959	.385	289	386	.749	591	229	291	11	1027	13.3
Jim Washington	82	2525	418	915	.457	187	274	.682	825	113	233	1	1023	12.5
McCoy McLemore	76	2100	374	940	.398	215	276	.779	430	130	219	4	963	12.7
Keith Erickson	78	2257	377	940	.401	194	257	.755	423	267	276	15	948	12.2
Barry Clemens	78	1631	301	670	.449	123	170	.724	375	98	223	4	725	9.3
Clem Haskins	76	1477	273	650	.420	133	202	.658	227	165	175	1	679	8.9
Jim Barnes†	37	712	120	264	.455	74	103	.718	204	28	128	3	314	8.5
Jim Barnes‡	79	1425	221	499	.443	133	191	.696	415	55	262	7	575	7.3
Erwin Mueller*	35	815	91	235	.387	46	82	.561	167	76	78	1	228	6.5
Dave Schellhase	42	301	47	138	.341	20	38	.526	47	37	43	0	114	2.7
Reggie Harding	14	305	27	71	.380	17	33	.515	94	18	35	0	71	5.1
Guy Rodgers*	4	129	16	54	.296	9	11	.818	14	28	11	0	41	10.3
Craig Spitzer	10	44	8	21	.381	2	3	.667	24	0	4	0	18	1.8
Ken Wilburn	3	26	5	9	.556	1	4	.250	10	2	4	0	11	3.7
Jim Burns	3	11	2	7	.286	0	0	…	2	1	1	0	4	1.3

CINCINNATI ROYALS

	G	Min.	FGM	FGA	Pct.	FTM	FTA	Pct.	Reb.	Ast.	PF	Dq.	Pts.	Avg.
													SCORING	
Oscar Robertson	65	2765	660	1321	.500	576	660	.873	391	633	199	2	1896	29.2
Jerry Lucas	82	3619	707	1361	.519	346	445	.778	1560	251	243	3	1760	21.5
Connie Dierking	81	2637	544	1164	.467	237	310	.765	766	191	315	6	1325	16.4
Adrian Smith	82	2783	480	1035	.464	320	386	.829	185	272	259	6	1280	15.6
Happy Hairston*	48	1625	317	630	.503	203	296	.686	355	58	127	1	837	17.4
Bob Love	72	1068	193	455	.424	78	114	.684	209	55	141	1	464	6.4
Walt Wesley	66	918	188	404	.465	76	152	.500	281	34	168	2	452	6.8
Guy Rodgers†	75	1417	132	372	.355	98	122	.803	136	352	156	1	362	4.8
Guy Rodgers‡	79	1546	148	426	.347	107	133	.805	150	380	167	1	403	5.1
Bill Dinwiddie	67	871	141	358	.394	62	102	.608	237	31	122	2	344	5.1
John Tresvant†	30	802	121	270	.448	67	106	.632	169	46	105	3	309	10.3
John Tresvant‡	85	2473	396	867	.457	250	384	.651	709	160	344	18	1042	12.3
Tom Van Arsdale†	27	682	97	238	.408	87	116	.750	93	76	83	2	281	10.4
Tom Van Arsdale‡	77	1514	211	545	.387	188	252	.746	225	155	202	5	610	7.9
Gary Gray	44	276	49	134	.366	7	10	.700	23	26	48	0	105	2.4
Jim Fox*	31	244	32	79	.405	36	56	.643	95	12	34	0	100	3.2
Len Chappell*	10	65	15	30	.500	8	10	.800	15	5	6	0	38	3.8
Flynn Robinson*	2	16	3	10	.300	3	7	.429	4	5	4	0	9	4.5
Al Jackson	2	17	0	3	.000	0	0	…	0	1	6	0	0	0.0

DETROIT PISTONS

	G	Min.	FGM	FGA	Pct.	FTM	FTA	Pct.	Reb.	Ast.	PF	Dq.	Pts.	Avg.
													SCORING	
Dave Bing	79	3209	835	1893	.441	472	668	.707	373	509	254	2	2142	27.1
Dave DeBusschere	80	3125	573	1295	.442	289	435	.664	1081	181	304	3	1435	17.9
Eddie Miles	76	2303	561	1180	.475	282	369	.764	264	215	200	3	1404	18.5
Terry Dischinger	78	1936	394	797	.494	237	311	.762	483	114	247	6	1025	13.1
John Tresvant*	55	1671	275	597	.461	183	278	.658	540	114	239	15	733	13.3
Jimmy Walker	81	1585	289	733	.394	134	175	.766	135	226	204	1	712	8.8
Len Chappell†	57	999	220	428	.514	130	184	.707	346	48	113	1	570	10.0
Len Chappell‡	67	1064	235	458	.513	138	194	.711	361	53	119	1	608	9.1
Joe Strawder	73	2029	206	456	.452	139	215	.647	685	85	312	18	551	7.5
Happy Hairston†	26	892	164	357	.459	162	226	.717	262	37	72	0	490	18.8
Happy Hairston‡	74	2517	481	987	.487	365	522	.699	617	95	199	1	1327	17.9
Tom Van Arsdale*	50	832	114	307	.371	101	136	.743	132	79	119	3	329	6.6
George Patterson	59	559	44	133	.331	32	38	.842	159	51	85	0	120	2.0
Jim Fox†	24	380	34	82	.415	30	52	.577	135	17	51	0	98	4.1
Jim Fox‡	55	624	66	161	.410	66	108	.611	230	29	85	0	198	3.6
Paul Long	16	93	23	51	.451	11	15	.733	15	12	13	0	57	3.6
Sonny Dove	28	162	22	75	.293	12	26	.462	52	11	27	0	56	2.0
George Carter	1	5	1	2	.500	1	1	1.000	0	1	0	0	3	3.0

Dave Bing revved up the Pistons' offense, averaging 27.1 points in 1967-68 and exactly 27 three seasons later.

LOS ANGELES LAKERS

	G	Min.	FGM	FGA	Pct.	FTM	FTA	Pct.	Reb.	Ast.	PF	Dq.	SCORING Pts.	Avg.
Elgin Baylor	77	3029	757	1709	.443	488	621	.786	941	355	232	0	2002	26.0
Archie Clark	81	3039	628	1309	.480	356	481	.740	342	353	235	3	1612	19.9
Jerry West	51	1919	476	926	.514	391	482	.811	294	310	152	1	1343	26.3
Gail Goodrich	79	2057	395	812	.486	302	392	.770	199	205	228	2	1092	13.8
Mel Counts	82	1739	384	808	.475	190	254	.748	732	139	309	6	958	11.7
Tom Hawkins	78	2463	389	779	.499	125	229	.546	458	117	289	7	903	11.6
Darrall Imhoff	82	2271	293	613	.478	177	286	.619	893	206	264	3	763	9.3
Freddie Crawford†	38	756	159	330	.482	74	120	.617	112	95	104	1	392	10.3
Freddie Crawford‡	69	1182	224	507	.442	111	179	.620	195	141	171	1	559	8.1
Erwin Mueller†	39	973	132	254	.520	61	103	.592	222	78	86	2	325	8.3
Erwin Mueller‡	74	1788	223	489	.456	107	185	.578	389	154	164	3	553	7.5
Jim Barnes*	42	713	101	235	.430	59	88	.670	211	27	134	4	261	6.2
John Wetzel	38	434	52	119	.437	35	46	.761	84	51	55	0	139	3.7
Dennis Hamilton	44	378	54	108	.500	13	13	1.000	72	30	46	0	121	2.8
Cliff Anderson	18	94	7	29	.241	12	28	.429	11	17	18	1	26	1.4

NEW YORK KNICKERBOCKERS

	G	Min.	FGM	FGA	Pct.	FTM	FTA	Pct.	Reb.	Ast.	PF	Dq.	SCORING Pts.	SCORING Avg.
Willis Reed	81	2879	659	1346	.490	367	509	.721	1073	159	343	12	1685	20.8
Dick Barnett...............	81	2488	559	1159	.482	343	440	.780	238	242	222	0	1461	18.0
Cazzie Russell	82	2296	551	1192	.462	282	349	.808	374	195	223	2	1384	16.9
Walt Bellamy..............	82	2695	511	944	.541	350	529	.662	961	164	259	3	1372	16.7
Dick Van Arsdale	78	2348	316	725	.436	227	339	.670	424	230	225	0	859	11.0
Walt Frazier	74	1588	256	568	.451	154	235	.655	313	305	199	2	666	9.0
Howie Komives	78	1660	233	631	.369	132	161	.820	168	246	170	1	598	7.7
Phil Jackson	75	1093	182	455	.400	99	168	.589	338	55	212	3	463	6.2
Bill Bradley	45	874	142	341	.416	76	104	.731	113	137	138	2	360	8.0
Emmette Bryant............	77	968	112	291	.385	59	86	.686	133	134	173	0	283	3.7
Freddie Crawford*	31	426	65	177	.367	37	59	.627	83	46	67	0	167	5.4
Nate Bowman	42	272	52	134	.388	10	15	.667	113	20	69	0	114	2.7
Neil Johnson	43	286	44	106	.415	23	48	.479	75	33	63	0	111	2.6
Jim Caldwell................	2	7	0	1	.000	0	0	...	1	1	1	0	0	0.0

PHILADELPHIA 76ERS

	G	Min.	FGM	FGA	Pct.	FTM	FTA	Pct.	Reb.	Ast.	PF	Dq.	SCORING Pts.	SCORING Avg.
Wilt Chamberlain	82	3836	819	1377	.595	354	932	.380	1952	702	160	0	1992	24.3
Hal Greer..................	82	3263	777	1626	.478	422	549	.769	444	372	289	6	1976	24.1
Chet Walker	82	2623	539	1172	.460	387	533	.726	607	157	252	3	1465	17.9
Billy Cunningham............	74	2076	516	1178	.438	368	509	.723	562	187	260	3	1400	18.9
Wali Jones.................	77	2058	413	1040	.397	159	202	.787	219	245	225	5	985	12.8
Lucious Jackson	82	2570	401	927	.433	166	231	.719	872	139	287	6	968	11.8
Matt Guokas	82	1612	190	393	.483	118	152	.776	185	191	172	0	498	6.1
Bill Melchionni.............	71	758	146	336	.435	33	47	.702	104	105	75	0	325	4.6
Larry Costello	28	492	67	148	.453	67	81	.827	51	68	62	0	201	7.2
Johnny Green†	35	367	69	150	.460	39	83	.470	122	21	51	0	177	5.1
Johnny Green‡	77	1440	310	676	.459	139	295	.471	545	80	163	3	759	9.9
Ronald Filipek	19	73	18	47	.383	7	14	.500	25	7	12	0	43	2.3
Jim Reid....................	6	52	10	20	.500	1	5	.200	11	3	6	0	21	3.5

ST. LOUIS HAWKS

	G	Min.	FGM	FGA	Pct.	FTM	FTA	Pct.	Reb.	Ast.	PF	Dq.	SCORING Pts.	SCORING Avg.
Zelmo Beaty	82	3068	639	1310	.488	455	573	.794	959	174	295	6	1733	21.1
Lenny Wilkens..............	82	3169	546	1246	.438	546	711	.768	438	679	255	3	1638	20.0
Joe Caldwell...............	79	2641	564	1219	.463	165	290	.569	338	240	208	1	1293	16.4
Bill Bridges	82	3197	466	1009	.462	347	484	.717	1102	253	366	12	1279	15.6
Paul Silas	82	2652	399	871	.458	299	424	.705	958	162	243	4	1097	13.4
Dick Snyder................	75	1622	257	613	.419	129	167	.772	194	164	215	5	643	8.6
Lou Hudson.................	46	966	227	500	.454	120	164	.732	193	65	113	2	574	12.5
Don Ohl‡...................	31	823	161	355	.454	83	106	.783	62	73	93	1	405	13.1
Don Ohl‡...................	70	1919	393	891	.441	197	254	.776	175	157	184	1	983	14.0
Gene Tormohlen	77	714	98	262	.374	33	56	.589	226	68	94	0	229	3.0
George Lehmann............	55	497	59	172	.343	35	43	.814	44	93	54	0	153	2.8
Jim Davis	50	394	61	139	.439	25	64	.391	123	13	85	2	147	2.9
Tom Workman*	19	85	19	38	.500	17	22	.773	24	3	14	0	55	2.9
Jay Miller	8	52	8	31	.258	4	7	.571	7	1	11	0	20	2.5

SAN DIEGO ROCKETS

	G	Min.	FGM	FGA	Pct.	FTM	FTA	Pct.	Reb.	Ast.	PF	Dq.	SCORING Pts.	SCORING Avg.
Don Kojis	69	2548	530	1189	.446	300	413	.726	710	176	259	5	1360	19.7
Dave Gambee	80	1755	375	853	.440	321	379	.847	464	93	253	5	1071	13.4
John Block	52	1805	366	865	.423	316	394	.802	571	71	189	3	1048	20.2
Toby Kimball	81	2519	354	894	.396	181	306	.592	947	147	273	3	889	11.0
Jon McGlocklin	65	1876	316	757	.417	156	180	.867	199	178	117	0	788	12.1
John Barnhill	75	1883	295	700	.421	154	234	.658	173	259	143	1	744	9.9
Art Williams...............	79	1739	265	718	.369	113	165	.685	286	391	204	0	643	8.1
Pat Riley	80	1263	250	660	.379	128	202	.634	177	138	205	1	628	7.9
Hank Finkel	53	1116	242	492	.492	131	191	.686	375	72	175	5	615	11.6
Johnny Green*	42	1073	241	526	.458	100	212	.472	423	59	112	3	582	13.9
Jim Barnett	47	1068	179	456	.393	84	118	.712	155	134	101	0	442	9.4
Nick Jones.................	42	603	86	232	.371	55	69	.797	67	89	84	0	227	5.4
Charles Acton	23	195	29	74	.392	19	29	.655	47	11	35	0	77	3.3
Jim Ware.................	30	228	25	97	.258	23	34	.676	77	7	28	1	73	2.4
Tyrone Britt	11	84	13	34	.382	2	3	.667	15	12	10	0	28	2.5

SAN FRANCISCO WARRIORS

	G	Min.	FGM	FGA	Pct.	FTM	FTA	Pct.	Reb.	Ast.	PF	Dq.	SCORING Pts.	SCORING Avg.
Rudy LaRusso.............	79	2819	602	1389	.433	522	661	.790	741	182	337	14	1726	21.8
Jeff Mullins................	79	2805	610	1391	.439	273	344	.794	447	351	271	2	1493	18.9
Fred Hetzel	77	2394	533	1287	.414	395	474	.833	546	131	262	7	1461	19.0
Nate Thurmond	51	2222	382	929	.411	282	438	.644	1121	215	137	1	1046	20.5

	G	Min.	FGM	FGA	Pct.	FTM	FTA	Pct.	Reb.	Ast.	PF	Dq.	SCORING Pts.	Avg.
Clyde Lee	82	2699	373	894	.417	229	335	.684	1141	135	331	10	975	11.9
Jim King	54	1743	340	800	.425	217	268	.810	243	226	172	1	897	16.6
Al Attles	67	1992	252	540	.467	150	216	.694	276	390	284	9	654	9.8
Bob Warlick	69	1320	257	610	.421	97	171	.567	264	159	164	1	611	8.9
Joe Ellis	51	624	111	302	.368	32	50	.640	195	37	83	2	254	5.0
Bob Lewis	41	342	59	151	.391	61	79	.772	56	41	40	0	179	4.4
Bill Turner	42	482	68	157	.433	36	60	.600	155	16	74	1	172	4.1
Dave Lattin	44	257	37	102	.363	23	33	.697	104	14	94	4	97	2.2
George Lee	10	106	8	35	.229	17	24	.708	27	4	16	0	33	3.3

SEATTLE SUPERSONICS

	G	Min.	FGM	FGA	Pct.	FTM	FTA	Pct.	Reb.	Ast.	PF	Dq.	SCORING Pts.	Avg.
Walt Hazzard	79	2666	733	1662	.441	428	553	.774	332	493	246	3	1894	24.0
Bob Rule	82	2424	568	1162	.489	348	529	.658	776	99	316	10	1484	18.1
Tom Meschery	82	2857	473	1008	.469	244	345	.707	840	193	323	14	1190	14.5
Al Tucker	81	2368	437	989	.442	186	263	.707	605	111	262	6	1060	13.1
Rod Thorn	66	1668	377	835	.451	252	342	.737	265	230	117	1	1006	15.2
Bob Weiss	82	1614	295	686	.430	213	254	.839	150	342	137	0	803	9.8
Tom Kron	76	1794	277	699	.396	184	233	.790	355	281	231	4	738	9.7
Dorie Murrey	81	1494	211	484	.436	168	244	.689	600	68	273	7	590	7.3
George Wilson	77	1236	179	498	.359	109	155	.703	470	56	218	1	467	6.1
Bud Olsen	73	897	130	285	.456	17	62	.274	204	75	136	1	277	3.8
Henry Akin	36	259	46	137	.336	20	31	.645	57	14	48	1	112	3.1
Plummer Lott	44	478	46	148	.311	19	31	.613	93	36	65	1	111	2.5

* Finished season with another team.   † Totals with this team only.   ‡ Totals with all teams.

PLAYOFF RESULTS

EASTERN DIVISION

SEMIFINALS

Philadelphia 4, New York 2
Mar. 22—Fri.	New York 110 at Philadelphia	118
Mar. 23—Sat.	Philadelphia 117 at New York	128
Mar. 27—Wed.	New York 132 at Philadelphia	138
Mar. 30—Sat.	Philadelphia 98 at New York	107
Mar. 31—Sun.	New York 107 at Philadelphia	123
Apr. 1—Mon.	Philadelphia 113 at New York	97

Boston 4, Detroit 2
Mar. 24—Sun.	Detroit 116 at Boston	123
Mar. 25—Mon.	Boston 116 at Detroit	126
Mar. 27—Wed.	Detroit 109 at Boston	98
Mar. 28—Thur.	Boston 135 at Detroit	110
Mar. 31—Sun.	Detroit 96 at Boston	110
Apr. 1—Mon.	Boston 111 at Detroit	103

FINALS

Boston 4, Philadelphia 3
Apr. 5—Fri.	Boston 127 at Philadelphia	118
Apr. 10—Wed.	Philadelphia 115 at Boston	106
Apr. 11—Thur.	Boston 114 at Philadelphia	122
Apr. 14—Sun.	Philadelphia 110 at Boston	105
Apr. 15—Mon.	Boston 122 at Philadelphia	104
Apr. 17—Wed.	Philadelphia 106 at Boston	114
Apr. 19—Fri.	Boston 100 at Philadelphia	96

WESTERN DIVISION

SEMIFINALS

San Francisco 4, St. Louis 2
Mar. 22—Fri.	San Francisco 111 at St. Louis	106
Mar. 23—Sat.	San Francisco 103 at St. Louis	111
Mar. 26—Tue.	St. Louis 109 at San Francisco	124
Mar. 29—Fri.	St. Louis 107 at San Francisco	108
Mar. 31—Sun.	San Francisco 103 at St. Louis	129
Apr. 2—Tue.	St. Louis 106 at San Francisco	111

Los Angeles 4, Chicago 1
Mar. 24—Sun.	Chicago 101 at Los Angeles	109
Mar. 25—Mon.	Chicago 106 at Los Angeles	111
Mar. 27—Wed.	Los Angeles 98 at Chicago	104
Mar. 29—Fri.	Los Angeles 93 at Chicago	87
Mar. 31—Sun.	Chicago 99 at Los Angeles	122

FINALS

Los Angeles 4, San Francisco 0
Apr. 5—Fri.	San Francisco 105 at Los Angeles	133
Apr. 10—Wed.	San Francisco 112 at Los Angeles	115
Apr. 11—Thur.	Los Angeles 128 at San Francisco	124
Apr. 13—Sat.	Los Angeles 106 at San Francisco	100

NBA FINALS

Boston 4, Los Angeles 2
Apr. 21—Sun.	Los Angeles 101 at Boston	107
Apr. 24—Wed.	Los Angeles 123 at Boston	113
Apr. 26—Fri.	Boston 127 at Los Angeles	119
Apr. 28—Sun.	Boston 105 at Los Angeles	119
Apr. 30—Tue.	Los Angeles 117 at Boston	*120
May 2—Thur.	Boston 124 at Los Angeles	109

*Denotes number of overtime periods.

1966-67

1966-67 NBA CHAMPION PHILADELPHIA 76ERS
Front row (from left): Wilt Chamberlain, Dave Gambee, Lucious Jackson, Billy Cunningham, Chet Walker. Back row (from left): trainer Al Domenico, head coach Alex Hannum, Wali Jones, Bill Melchionni, Matt Guokas, Hal Greer, Larry Costello, owner Irv Kosloff, general manager Jack Ramsay.

FINAL STANDINGS

EASTERN DIVISION

	Phi.	Bos.	Cin.	N.Y.	Balt.	S.F.	St.L.	L.A.	Chi.	Det.	W	L	Pct.	GB
Philadelphia..........	..	4	8	8	8	7	8	8	8	9	68	13	.840	..
Boston 5	..	..	8	9	8	6	5	5	8	6	60	21	.741	8
Cincinnati 1	1	..	..	6	6	5	6	3	4	7	39	42	.481	29
New York..........1	0	3	..	2	7	5	4	5	6	5	36	45	.444	32
Baltimore..........1	1	3	2	..	2	4	2	3	2	20	61	.247	48

WESTERN DIVISION

San Francisco 2	3	4	4	7	..	5	6	6	7	44	37	.543	..
St. Louis 1	4	3	5	5	4	..	5	5	7	39	42	.481	5
Los Angeles........1	4	6	4	7	3	4	..	3	3	36	45	.444	8
Chicago...........1	1	5	3	6	3	4	6	..	4	33	48	.407	11
Detroit.............0	3	2	4	7	2	2	5	5	..	30	51	.370	14

TEAM STATISTICS

	G	FGM	FGA	Pct.	FTM	FTA	Pct.	Reb.	Ast.	PF	Dq.	AVERAGE POINTS For	AVERAGE POINTS Agst.	AVERAGE POINTS Dif.
Philadelphia.....81	3912	8103	.483	2319	3411	.680	5701	2138	1906	30	125.2	115.8	+9.4
Boston 81	3724	8325	.447	2216	2963	.748	5703	1962	2138	23	119.3	111.3	+8.0
San Francisco ...81	3814	8818	.433	2283	3021	.756	5974	1876	2120	48	122.4	119.5	+2.9
Los Angeles......81	3786	8466	.447	2192	2917	.751	5415	1906	2168	31	120.5	120.2	+0.3
Cincinnati 81	3654	8137	.449	2179	2806	.777	5198	1858	2073	25	117.1	117.4	-0.3
St. Louis 81	3547	8004	.443	2110	2979	.708	5219	1708	2173	40	113.6	115.2	-1.6
New York.......81	3637	8025	.453	2151	2980	.722	5178	1782	2110	29	116.4	119.4	-3.0
Chicago........81	3565	8505	.419	2037	2784	.732	5295	1827	2205	21	113.2	116.9	-3.7
Detroit.........81	3523	8542	.412	1969	2725	.723	5511	1465	2198	49	111.3	116.8	-5.5
Baltimore........81	3664	8578	.427	2025	2771	.731	5342	1652	2153	51	115.5	122.0	-6.5
Avgs..........81	3683	8350	.441	2148	2936	.732	5454	1817	2124	34.7	117.4	...	...

HOME/ROAD/NEUTRAL

	Home	Road	Neutral	Total		Home	Road	Neutral	Total
Baltimore	12-20	3-30	5-11	20-61	New York	20-15	9-24	7-6	36-45
Boston	27-4	25-11	8-6	60-21	Philadelphia	28-2	26-8	14-3	68-13
Chicago	17-19	9-17	7-12	33-48	St. Louis.	18-11	12-21	9-10	39-42
Cincinnati	20-11	12-24	7-7	39-42	San Francisco	18-10	11-19	15-8	44-37
Detroit	12-18	9-19	9-14	30-51	Totals	193-128	128-193	84-84	405-405
Los Angeles	21-18	12-20	3-7	36-45					

POINTS

	G	FGM	FTM	Pts.	Avg.
Rick Barry, San Francisco	78	1011	753	2775	35.6
Oscar Robertson, Cincinnati	79	838	736	2412	30.5
Wilt Chamberlain, Philadelphia	81	785	386	1956	24.1
Jerry West, Los Angeles	66	645	602	1892	28.7
Elgin Baylor, Los Angeles	70	711	440	1862	26.6
Hal Greer, Philadelphia	80	699	367	1765	22.1
John Havlicek, Boston	81	684	365	1733	21.4
Willis Reed, New York	78	635	358	1628	20.9
Bailey Howell, Boston	81	636	349	1621	20.0
Dave Bing, Detroit	80	664	273	1601	20.0
Sam Jones, Boston	72	638	318	1594	22.1
Chet Walker, Philadelphia	81	561	445	1567	19.3
Gus Johnson, Baltimore	73	620	271	1511	20.7
Walt Bellamy, New York	79	565	369	1499	19.0
Billy Cunningham, Philadelphia	81	556	383	1495	18.5
Lou Hudson, St. Louis	80	620	231	1471	18.4
Guy Rodgers, Chicago	81	538	383	1459	18.0
Jerry Lucas, Cincinnati	81	577	284	1438	17.8
Bob Boozer, Chicago	80	538	360	1436	18.0
Eddie Miles, Detroit	81	582	261	1425	17.6

FIELD GOALS

(minimum 220 made)

	FGM	FGA	Pct.
Wilt Chamberlain, Philadelphia	785	1150	.683
Walt Bellamy, New York	565	1084	.521
Bailey Howell, Boston	636	1242	.512
Oscar Robertson, Cincinnati	838	1699	.493
Willis Reed, New York	635	1298	.489
Chet Walker, Philadelphia	561	1150	.488
Bob Boozer, Chicago	538	1104	.487
Tom Hawkins, Los Angeles	275	572	.481
Happy Hairston, Cincinnati	461	962	.479
Dick Barnett, New York	454	949	.478

FREE THROWS

(minimum 220 made)

	FTM	FTA	Pct.
Adrian Smith, Cincinnati	343	380	.903
Rick Barry, San Francisco	753	852	.884
Jerry West, Los Angeles	602	686	.878
Oscar Robertson, Cincinnati	736	843	.873
Sam Jones, Boston	318	371	.857
Larry Siegfried, Boston	294	347	.847
Wali Jones, Philadelphia	223	266	.838
John Havlicek, Boston	365	441	.828
Kevin Loughery, Baltimore	340	412	.825
Elgin Baylor, Los Angeles	440	541	.813

ASSISTS

	G	No.	Avg.
Guy Rodgers, Chicago	81	908	11.2
Oscar Robertson, Cincinnati	79	845	10.7
Wilt Chamberlain, Philadelphia	81	630	7.8
Bill Russell, Boston	81	472	5.8
Jerry West, Los Angeles	66	447	6.8
Lenny Wilkens, St. Louis	78	442	5.7
Howard Komives, New York	65	401	6.2
K.C. Jones, Boston	78	389	5.0
Richie Guerin, St. Louis	80	345	4.3
Paul Neumann, San Francisco	78	342	4.4

REBOUNDS

	G	No.	Avg.
Wilt Chamberlain, Philadelphia	81	1957	24.2
Bill Russell, Boston	81	1700	21.0
Jerry Lucas, Cincinnati	81	1547	19.1
Nate Thurmond, San Francisco	65	1382	21.3
Bill Bridges, St. Louis	79	1190	15.1
Willis Reed, New York	78	1136	14.6
Darrall Imhoff, Los Angeles	81	1080	13.3
Walt Bellamy, New York	79	1064	13.5
LeRoy Ellis, Baltimore	81	970	12.0
Dave DeBusschere, Detroit	78	924	11.8

1966-67

INDIVIDUAL STATISTICS, TEAM BY TEAM

BALTIMORE BULLETS

	G	Min.	FGM	FGA	Pct.	FTM	FTA	Pct.	Reb.	Ast.	PF	Dq.	SCORING Pts.	Avg.
Gus Johnson	73	2626	620	1377	.450	271	383	.708	855	194	281	7	1511	20.7
Kevin Loughery	76	2577	520	1306	.398	340	412	.825	349	288	294	10	1380	18.2
LeRoy Ellis	81	2938	496	1166	.425	211	286	.738	970	170	258	3	1203	14.9
Don Ohl	58	2024	452	1002	.451	276	354	.780	189	168	1	1	1180	20.3
Johnny Egan	71	1743	267	624	.428	185	219	.845	180	275	190	3	719	10.1
Jack Marin	74	1323	283	632	.448	145	187	.775	313	75	199	6	711	9.6
Ray Scott†	27	969	206	463	.445	100	160	.625	356	76	83	1	512	19.0
Ray Scott†	72	2446	458	1144	.400	256	366	.699	760	160	225	2	1172	16.3
Johnny Green	61	948	203	437	.465	96	207	.464	394	57	139	7	502	8.2
John Barnhill	53	1214	187	447	.418	66	103	.641	157	136	80	0	440	8.3
Ben Warley	62	1037	125	312	.401	134	170	.788	325	51	176	6	384	6.2
Bob Ferry	51	991	132	315	.419	70	110	.636	258	92	97	0	334	6.5
Wayne Hightower*	43	746	103	308	.334	89	124	.718	241	36	110	5	295	6.9
Mel Counts*	25	343	65	167	.389	29	40	.725	155	30	81	2	159	6.4
Johnny Austin	4	61	5	22	.227	13	16	.813	7	4	12	0	23	5.8

BOSTON CELTICS

	G	Min.	FGM	FGA	Pct.	FTM	FTA	Pct.	Reb.	Ast.	PF	Dq.	SCORING Pts.	Avg.
John Havlicek	81	2602	684	1540	.444	365	441	.828	532	278	210	0	1733	21.4
Bailey Howell	81	2503	636	1242	.512	349	471	.741	677	103	296	4	1621	20.0
Sam Jones	72	2325	638	1406	.454	318	371	.857	338	217	191	1	1594	22.1
Bill Russell	81	3297	395	870	.454	285	467	.610	1700	472	258	4	1075	13.3
Larry Siegfried	73	1891	368	833	.442	294	347	.847	228	250	207	1	1030	14.1
Tom Sanders	81	1926	323	755	.428	178	218	.817	439	91	304	6	824	10.2
Don Nelson	79	1202	227	509	.446	141	190	.742	295	65	143	0	595	7.5
K.C. Jones	78	2446	182	459	.397	119	189	.630	239	389	273	7	483	6.2
Wayne Embry	72	729	147	359	.409	82	144	.569	294	42	137	0	376	5.2
Jim Barnett	48	383	78	211	.370	42	62	.677	53	41	61	0	198	4.1
Toby Kimball	38	222	35	97	.361	27	40	.675	146	13	42	0	97	2.6
Ron Watts	27	89	11	44	.250	16	23	.696	38	1	16	0	38	1.4

An Ohio high school standout and a three-time All-America selection at Ohio State, Jerry Lucas remained in his native state for his first six NBA seasons and was a major force along the front line for the Cincinnati Royals.

CHICAGO BULLS

	G	Min.	FGM	FGA	Pct.	FTM	FTA	Pct.	Reb.	Ast.	PF	Dq.	SCORING Pts.	Avg.
Guy Rodgers	81	3063	538	1377	.391	383	475	.806	346	908	243	1	1459	18.0
Bob Boozer	80	2451	538	1104	.487	360	461	.781	679	90	212	0	1436	18.0
Jerry Sloan	80	2942	525	1214	.432	340	427	.796	726	170	293	7	1390	17.4
Erwin Mueller	80	2136	422	957	.441	171	260	.658	497	131	223	2	1015	12.7
Don Kojis	78	1655	329	773	.426	134	222	.604	479	70	204	3	792	10.2
McCoy McLemore	79	1382	258	670	.385	210	272	.772	374	62	189	2	726	9.2
Jim Washington	77	1475	252	604	.417	88	159	.553	468	56	181	1	592	7.7
Keith Erickson	76	1454	235	641	.367	117	159	.736	339	119	199	2	587	7.7
Barry Clemens	60	986	186	444	.419	68	90	.756	201	39	143	1	440	7.3
Gerry Ward	76	1042	117	307	.381	87	138	.630	179	130	169	2	321	4.2
George Wilson†	43	448	77	193	.399	45	70	.643	163	15	73	0	199	4.6
George Wilson‡	55	573	85	234	.363	58	86	.674	206	15	92	0	228	4.1
Len Chappell*	19	179	40	89	.449	14	21	.667	38	12	31	0	94	4.9
Dave Schellhase	31	212	40	111	.360	14	22	.636	29	23	27	0	94	3.0
Nate Bowman	9	65	8	21	.381	6	8	.750	28	2	18	0	22	2.4

CINCINNATI ROYALS

	G	Min.	FGM	FGA	Pct.	FTM	FTA	Pct.	Reb.	Ast.	PF	Dq.	Pts.	Avg.
													SCORING	
Oscar Robertson	79	3468	838	1699	.493	736	843	.873	486	845	226	2	2412	30.5
Jerry Lucas	81	3558	577	1257	.459	284	359	.791	1547	268	280	2	1438	17.8
Adrian Smith	81	2636	502	1147	.438	343	380	.903	205	187	272	0	1347	16.6
Happy Hairston	79	2442	461	962	.479	252	382	.660	631	62	273	5	1174	14.9
Connie Dierking	77	1905	291	729	.399	134	180	.744	603	158	251	7	716	9.3
Flynn Robinson	76	1140	274	599	.457	120	154	.779	133	110	197	3	668	8.8
Jon McGlocklin	60	1194	217	493	.440	74	104	.712	164	93	84	0	508	8.5
Bob Love	66	1074	173	403	.429	93	147	.633	257	49	153	3	439	6.7
Walt Wesley	64	909	131	333	.393	52	123	.423	329	19	161	2	314	4.9
Len Chappell†	54	529	92	224	.411	39	60	.650	151	21	73	0	223	4.1
Len Chappell‡	73	708	132	313	.422	53	81	.654	189	33	104	0	317	4.3
Freddie Lewis	32	334	60	153	.392	29	41	.707	44	40	49	1	149	4.7
Jim Ware	33	201	30	97	.309	10	17	.588	69	6	35	0	70	2.1
George Wilson*	12	125	8	41	.195	13	16	.813	43	0	19	0	29	2.4

DETROIT PISTONS

	G	Min.	FGM	FGA	Pct.	FTM	FTA	Pct.	Reb.	Ast.	PF	Dq.	Pts.	Avg.
													SCORING	
Dave Bing	80	2762	664	1522	.436	273	370	.738	359	330	217	2	1601	20.0
Eddie Miles	81	2419	582	1363	.427	261	338	.772	298	181	216	2	1425	17.6
Dave DeBusschere	78	2897	531	1278	.415	361	512	.705	924	216	297	7	1423	18.2
Tom Van Arsdale	79	2134	347	887	.391	272	347	.784	341	193	241	3	966	12.2
Joe Strawder	79	2156	281	660	.426	188	262	.718	791	82	344	19	750	9.5
John Tresvant	68	1553	256	585	.438	164	234	.701	483	88	246	8	676	9.9
Ray Scott*	45	1477	252	681	.370	156	206	.757	404	84	132	1	660	14.7
Ron Reed	61	1248	223	600	.372	79	133	.594	423	81	145	2	525	8.6
Reggie Harding	74	1367	172	383	.449	63	103	.612	455	94	164	2	407	5.5
Wayne Hightower†	29	564	92	259	.355	64	86	.744	164	28	80	1	248	8.6
Wayne Hightower‡	72	1310	195	567	.344	153	210	.729	405	64	190	6	543	7.5
Charles Vaughn	50	680	85	226	.376	50	74	.676	67	75	54	0	220	4.4
Dorie Murrey	35	311	33	82	.402	32	54	.593	102	12	57	2	98	2.8
Bob Hogsett	7	22	5	16	.313	6	6	1.000	3	1	5	0	16	2.3

LOS ANGELES LAKERS

	G	Min.	FGM	FGA	Pct.	FTM	FTA	Pct.	Reb.	Ast.	PF	Dq.	Pts.	Avg.
													SCORING	
Jerry West	66	2670	645	1389	.464	602	686	.878	392	447	160	1	1892	28.7
Elgin Baylor	70	2706	711	1658	.429	440	541	.813	898	215	211	1	1862	26.6
Gail Goodrich	77	1780	352	776	.454	253	337	.751	251	210	294	3	957	12.4
Darrall Imhoff	81	2725	370	780	.474	127	207	.614	1080	222	281	7	867	10.7
Archie Clark	76	1763	331	732	.452	136	192	.708	218	205	193	1	798	10.5
Walt Hazzard	79	1642	301	706	.426	129	177	.729	231	323	203	1	731	9.3
Tom Hawkins	76	1798	275	572	.481	82	173	.474	434	83	207	1	632	8.3
Rudy LaRusso	45	1292	211	509	.415	156	224	.696	351	78	149	6	578	12.8
Jim Barnes	80	1398	217	497	.437	128	187	.684	450	47	266	5	562	7.0
Jerry Chambers	68	1015	224	496	.452	68	93	.731	208	44	143	0	516	7.6
Mel Counts†	31	517	112	252	.444	40	54	.741	189	22	102	4	264	8.5
Mel Counts‡	56	860	177	419	.422	69	94	.734	344	52	183	6	423	7.6
John Block	22	118	20	52	.385	24	34	.706	45	5	20	0	64	2.9
Hank Finkel	27	141	17	47	.362	7	12	.583	64	5	39	1	41	1.5

NEW YORK KNICKERBOCKERS

	G	Min.	FGM	FGA	Pct.	FTM	FTA	Pct.	Reb.	Ast.	PF	Dq.	Pts.	Avg.
													SCORING	
Willis Reed	78	2824	635	1298	.489	358	487	.735	1136	126	293	9	1628	20.9
Walt Bellamy	79	3010	565	1084	.521	369	580	.636	1064	206	275	5	1499	19.0
Dick Van Arsdale	79	2892	410	913	.449	371	509	.729	555	247	264	3	1191	15.1
Dick Barnett	67	1969	454	949	.478	231	295	.783	226	161	185	2	1139	17.0
Howie Komives	65	2282	402	995	.404	217	253	.858	183	401	213	1	1021	15.7
Dave Stallworth	76	1889	380	816	.466	229	320	.716	472	144	226	4	989	13.0
Cazzie Russell	77	1696	344	789	.436	179	228	.785	251	187	174	1	867	11.3
Emmette Bryant	63	1593	236	577	.409	74	114	.649	273	218	231	4	546	8.7
Henry Akin	50	453	83	230	.361	26	37	.703	120	25	82	0	192	3.8
Neil Johnson	51	522	59	171	.345	57	86	.663	167	38	102	0	175	3.4
Freddie Crawford	19	192	44	116	.379	24	38	.632	48	12	39	0	112	5.9
Wayne Molis	13	75	19	51	.373	7	13	.538	22	2	9	0	45	3.5
Dave Deutsch	19	93	6	36	.167	9	20	.450	21	15	17	0	21	1.1

PHILADELPHIA 76ERS

	G	Min.	FGM	FGA	Pct.	FTM	FTA	Pct.	Reb.	Ast.	PF	Dq.	Pts.	Avg.
													SCORING	
Wilt Chamberlain	81	3682	785	1150	.683	386	875	.441	1957	630	143	0	1956	24.1
Hal Greer	80	3086	699	1524	.459	367	466	.788	422	303	302	5	1765	22.1
Chet Walker	81	2691	561	1150	.488	445	581	.766	660	188	232	4	1567	19.3
Billy Cunningham	81	2168	556	1211	.459	383	558	.686	589	205	260	2	1495	18.5
Wali Jones	81	2249	423	982	.431	223	266	.838	265	303	246	6	1069	13.2

1966-67

	G	Min.	FGM	FGA	Pct.	FTM	FTA	Pct.	Reb.	Ast.	PF	Dq.	SCORING Pts.	Avg.
Lucious Jackson	81	2377	386	882	.438	198	261	.759	724	114	276	6	970	12.0
Dave Gambee	63	757	150	345	.435	107	125	.856	197	42	143	5	407	6.5
Larry Costello	49	976	130	293	.444	120	133	.902	103	140	141	2	380	7.8
Bill Melchionni	73	692	138	353	.391	39	60	.650	98	98	73	0	315	4.3
Matt Guokas	69	808	79	203	.389	49	81	.605	83	105	82	0	207	3.0
Bob Weiss	6	29	5	10	.500	2	5	.400	3	10	8	0	12	2.0

ST. LOUIS HAWKS

	G	Min.	FGM	FGA	Pct.	FTM	FTA	Pct.	Reb.	Ast.	PF	Dq.	SCORING Pts.	Avg.
Lou Hudson	80	2446	620	1328	.467	231	327	.706	435	95	277	3	1471	18.4
Bill Bridges	79	3130	503	1106	.455	367	523	.702	1190	222	325	12	1373	17.4
Lenny Wilkens	78	2974	448	1036	.432	459	583	.787	412	442	280	6	1355	17.4
Joe Caldwell	81	2256	458	1076	.426	200	308	.649	442	166	230	4	1116	13.8
Richie Guerin	80	2275	394	904	.436	304	416	.731	192	345	247	2	1092	13.7
Zelmo Beaty	48	1661	328	694	.473	197	260	.758	515	60	189	3	853	17.8
Rod Thorn	67	1166	233	524	.445	125	172	.727	160	118	88	0	591	8.8
Paul Silas	77	1570	207	482	.429	113	213	.531	669	74	208	4	527	6.8
Gene Tormohlen	63	1036	172	403	.427	50	84	.595	347	73	177	4	394	6.3
Dick Snyder	55	676	144	333	.432	46	61	.754	91	59	82	1	334	6.1
Tom Kron	32	221	27	87	.310	13	19	.684	36	46	35	0	67	2.1
Tom Hoover	17	129	13	31	.419	5	13	.385	36	8	35	1	31	1.8

SAN FRANCISCO WARRIORS

	G	Min.	FGM	FGA	Pct.	FTM	FTA	Pct.	Reb.	Ast.	PF	Dq.	SCORING Pts.	Avg.
Rick Barry	78	3175	1011	2240	.451	753	852	.884	714	282	258	1	2775	35.6
Nate Thurmond	65	2755	467	1068	.437	280	445	.629	1382	166	183	3	1214	18.7
Paul Neumann	78	2421	386	911	.424	312	390	.800	272	342	266	4	1084	13.9
Jeff Mullins	77	1835	421	919	.458	150	214	.701	388	226	195	5	992	12.9
Fred Hetzel	77	2123	373	932	.400	192	237	.810	639	111	228	3	938	12.2
Tom Meschery	72	1846	293	706	.415	175	244	.717	549	94	264	8	761	10.6
Jim King	67	1667	286	685	.418	174	221	.787	319	240	193	5	746	11.1
Clyde Lee	74	1247	205	503	.408	105	166	.633	551	77	168	5	515	7.0
Al Attles	69	1764	212	467	.454	88	151	.583	321	269	265	13	512	7.4
Bud Olsen	40	348	75	167	.449	23	58	.397	103	32	51	1	173	4.3
Joe Ellis	41	333	67	164	.409	19	25	.760	112	27	45	0	153	3.7
Bob Warlick	12	65	15	52	.288	6	11	.545	20	10	4	0	36	3.0
George Lee	1	5	3	4	.750	6	7	.857	0	0	0	0	12	12.0

* Finished season with another team.   † Totals with this team only.   ‡ Totals with all teams.

PLAYOFF RESULTS

EASTERN DIVISION

SEMIFINALS

Boston 3, New York 1
Mar. 21—Tue.	New York 110 at Boston	140
Mar. 25—Sat.	Boston 115 at New York	108
Mar. 26—Sun.	New York 123 at Boston	112
Mar. 28—Tue.	Boston 118 at New York	109

Philadelphia 3, Cincinnati 1
Mar. 21—Tue.	Cincinnati 120 at Philadelphia	116
Mar. 22—Wed.	Philadelphia 123 at Cincinnati	102
Mar. 24—Fri.	Cincinnati 106 at Philadelphia	121
Mar. 25—Sat.	Philadelphia 112 at Cincinnati	94

FINALS

Philadelphia 4, Boston 1
Mar. 31—Fri.	Boston 113 at Philadelphia	127
Apr. 2—Sun.	Philadelphia 107 at Boston	102
Apr. 5—Wed.	Boston 104 at Philadelphia	115
Apr. 9—Sun.	Philadelphia 117 at Boston	121
Apr. 11—Tue.	Boston 116 at Philadelphia	140

WESTERN DIVISION

SEMIFINALS

St. Louis 3, Chicago 0
Mar. 21—Tue.	Chicago 100 at St. Louis	114
Mar. 23—Thur.	St. Louis 113 at Chicago	107
Mar. 25—Sat.	Chicago 106 at St. Louis	119

San Francisco 3, Los Angeles 0
Mar. 21—Tue.	Los Angeles 108 at San Francisco	124
Mar. 23—Thur.	San Francisco 113 at Los Angeles	102
Mar. 26—Sun.	Los Angeles 115 at San Francisco	122

FINALS

San Francisco 4, St. Louis 2
Mar. 30—Thur.	St. Louis 115 at San Francisco	117
Apr. 1—Sat.	St. Louis 136 at San Francisco	143
Apr. 5—Wed.	San Francisco 109 at St. Louis	115
Apr. 8—Sat.	San Francisco 104 at St. Louis	109
Apr. 10—Mon.	St. Louis 102 at San Francisco	123
Apr. 12—Wed.	San Francisco 112 at St. Louis	107

NBA FINALS

Philadelphia 4, San Francisco 2
Apr. 14—Fri.	San Francisco 135 at Philadelphia	*141
Apr. 16—Sun.	San Francisco 95 at Philadelphia	126
Apr. 18—Tue.	Philadelphia 124 at San Francisco	130
Apr. 20—Thur.	Philadelphia 122 at San Francisco	108
Apr. 23—Sun.	San Francisco 117 at Philadelphia	109
Apr. 24—Mon.	Philadelphia 125 at San Francisco	122

*Denotes number of overtime periods.

1966-67

1965-66

1965-66 NBA CHAMPION BOSTON CELTICS
Front row (from left): John Havlicek, K.C. Jones, chairman of the board Marvin Kratter, head coach Red Auerbach, president John J. Waldron, Bill Russell. Back row (from left): Ron Bonham, Don Nelson, Tom Sanders, Mel Counts, John Thompson, Woody Sauldsberry, Willie Naulls, Sam Jones, Larry Siegfried, trainer Buddy LeRoux.

FINAL STANDINGS

EASTERN DIVISION

	Phi.	Bos.	Cin.	N.Y.	L.A.	Balt.	St.L.	S.F.	Det.	W	L	Pct.	GB
Philadelphia	..	6	6	8	8	5	7	8	7	55	25	.688	..
Boston	4	..	5	10	7	7	7	8	6	54	26	.675	1
Cincinnati	4	5	..	7	4	7	5	5	8	45	35	.563	10
New York	2	0	3	..	5	3	4	5	8	30	50	.375	25

WESTERN DIVISION

	Phi.	Bos.	Cin.	N.Y.	L.A.	Balt.	St.L.	S.F.	Det.	W	L	Pct.	GB
Los Angeles	2	3	6	5	..	6	8	7	8	45	35	.563	..
Baltimore	5	3	3	7	4	..	7	4	5	38	42	.475	7
St. Louis	3	3	5	6	2	3	..	6	8	36	44	.450	9
San Francisco	2	2	5	5	3	6	4	..	8	35	45	.438	10
Detroit	3	4	2	2	2	5	2	2	..	22	58	.275	23

TEAM STATISTICS

	G	FGM	FGA	Pct.	FTM	FTA	Pct.	Reb.	Ast.	PF	Dq.	AVERAGE POINTS For	AVERAGE POINTS Agst.	AVERAGE POINTS Dif.
Boston	80	3488	8367	.417	2038	2758	.739	5591	1795	2012	39	112.7	107.8	+4.9
Philadelphia	80	3650	8189	.446	2087	3141	.664	5652	1905	2095	39	117.3	112.7	+4.6
Los Angeles	80	3597	8109	.444	2363	3057	.773	5334	1936	2035	25	119.5	116.4	+3.1
Cincinnati	80	3610	8123	.444	2204	2906	.758	5559	1818	2033	24	117.8	116.6	+1.2
St. Louis	80	3379	7836	.431	2155	2870	.751	5167	1782	2179	47	111.4	112.0	-0.6
Baltimore	80	3599	8210	.438	2267	3186	.712	5542	1890	2199	52	118.3	119.5	-1.2
New York	80	3559	7910	.450	2217	3078	.720	5119	1896	2227	48	116.7	119.3	-2.6
San Francisco	80	3557	8512	.418	2129	2879	.739	5727	1872	2069	37	115.5	118.2	-2.7
Detroit	80	3475	8502	.409	1877	2734	.687	5427	1569	2016	27	110.3	117.2	-6.9
Avgs	80	3546	8195	.433	2149	2957	.727	5458	1829	2096	37.6	115.5	. . .	. . .

HOME/ROAD/NEUTRAL

	Home	Road	Neutral	Total		Home	Road	Neutral	Total
Baltimore	29-9	4-25	5-8	38-42	New York	20-14	4-30	6-6	30-50
Boston	26-5	19-18	9-3	54-26	Philadelphia	22-3	20-17	13-5	55-25
Cincinnati	25-6	11-23	9-6	45-35	St. Louis	22-10	6-22	8-12	36-44
Detroit	13-17	4-22	5-19	22-58	San Francisco	12-14	8-19	15-12	35-45
Los Angeles	28-11	13-21	4-3	45-35	Totals	197-89	89-197	74-74	360-360

POINTS

	G	FGM	FTM	Pts.	Avg.
Wilt Chamberlain, Philadelphia	.79	1074	501	2649	33.5
Jerry West, Los Angeles	.79	818	840	2476	31.3
Oscar Robertson, Cincinnati	.76	818	742	2378	31.3
Rick Barry, San Francisco	.80	745	569	2059	25.7
Walt Bellamy, Baltimore-N.Y.	.80	695	430	1820	22.8
Hal Greer, Philadelphia	.80	703	413	1819	22.7
Dick Barnett, New York	.75	631	467	1729	23.1
Jerry Lucas, Cincinnati	.79	690	317	1697	21.5
Zelmo Beaty, St. Louis	.80	616	424	1656	20.7
Sam Jones, Boston	.67	626	325	1577	23.5
Eddie Miles, Detroit	.80	634	298	1566	19.6
Don Ohl, Baltimore	.73	593	316	1502	20.6
Adrian Smith, Cincinnati	.80	531	408	1470	18.4
Guy Rodgers, San Francisco	.79	586	296	1468	18.6
Ray Scott, Detroit	.79	544	323	1411	17.9
Bailey Howell, Baltimore	.78	481	402	1364	17.5
Kevin Loughery, Baltimore	.74	526	297	1349	18.2
John Havlicek, Boston	.71	530	274	1334	18.8
Dave DeBusschere, Detroit	.79	524	249	1297	16.4
Lenny Wilkens, St. Louis	.69	411	422	1244	18.0

FIELD GOALS

(minimum 210 made)

	FGM	FGA	Pct.
Wilt Chamberlain, Philadelphia	1074	1990	.540
John Green, New York-Baltimore	358	668	.536
Walt Bellamy, Baltimore-New York	695	1373	.506
Al Attles, San Francisco	364	724	.503
Happy Hairston, Cincinnati	398	814	.489
Bailey Howell, Baltimore	481	986	.488
Bob Boozer, Los Angeles	365	754	.484
Oscar Robertson, Cincinnati	818	1723	.475
Jerry West, Los Angeles	818	1731	.473
Zelmo Beaty, St. Louis	616	1301	.473

FREE THROWS

(minimum 210 made)

	FTM	FTA	Pct.
Larry Siegfried, Boston	.274	311	.881
Rick Barry, San Francisco	.569	660	.862
Howard Komives, New York	.241	280	.861
Jerry West, Los Angeles	.840	977	.860
Adrian Smith, Cincinnati	.408	480	.850
Oscar Robertson, Cincinnati	.742	881	.842
Paul Neumann, San Francisco	.265	317	.836
Kevin Loughery, Baltimore	.297	358	.830
Richie Guerin, St. Louis	.362	446	.812
Hal Greer, Philadelphia	.413	514	.804

ASSISTS

	G	No.	Avg.
Oscar Robertson, Cincinnati	.76	847	11.1
Guy Rodgers, San Francisco	.79	846	10.7
K.C. Jones, Boston	.80	503	6.3
Jerry West, Los Angeles	.79	480	6.1
Lenny Wilkens, St. Louis	.69	429	6.2
Howard Komives, New York	.80	425	5.3
Wilt Chamberlain, Philadelphia	.79	414	5.2
Walt Hazzard, Los Angeles	.80	393	4.9
Richie Guerin, St. Louis	.80	388	4.9
Hal Greer, Philadelphia	.80	384	4.8

REBOUNDS

	G	No.	Avg.
Wilt Chamberlain, Philadelphia	.79	1943	24.6
Bill Russell, Boston	.78	1779	22.8
Jerry Lucas, Cincinnati	.79	1668	21.1
Nate Thurmond, San Francisco	.73	1312	18.0
Walt Bellamy, Baltimore-New York	.80	1254	15.7
Zelmo Beaty, St. Louis	.80	1086	13.6
Bill Bridges, St. Louis	.78	951	12.2
Dave DeBusschere, Detroit	.79	916	11.6
Willis Reed, New York	.76	883	11.6
Rick Barry, San Francisco	.80	850	10.6

BALTIMORE BULLETS

SCORING

	G	Min.	FGM	FGA	Pct.	FTM	FTA	Pct.	Reb.	Ast.	PF	Dq.	Pts.	Avg.
Don Ohl	73	2645	593	1334	.445	316	430	.735	280	290	208	1	1502	20.6
Bailey Howell	78	2328	481	986	.488	402	551	.730	773	155	306	12	1364	17.5
Kevin Loughery	74	2455	526	1264	.416	297	358	.830	227	356	273	8	1349	18.2
Johnny Green†	72	1437	315	589	.535	187	357	.524	571	96	162	3	817	11.3
Johnny Green‡	79	1645	358	668	.536	202	388	.521	645	107	183	3	918	11.6
Jim Barnes†	66	1928	308	728	.423	182	268	.679	683	85	250	10	798	12.1
Jim Barnes‡	73	2191	348	818	.425	212	310	.684	755	94	283	10	908	12.4
Red Kerr	71	1770	286	692	.413	209	272	.768	586	225	148	0	781	11.0
Gus Johnson	41	1284	273	661	.413	131	178	.736	546	114	136	3	677	16.5
Johnny Egan†	69	1586	254	558	.455	166	217	.765	181	259	163	1	674	9.8
Johnny Egan‡	76	1644	259	574	.451	173	227	.762	183	273	167	1	691	9.1
Bob Ferry	66	1229	188	457	.411	105	157	.669	334	111	134	1	481	7.3
Jerry Sloan	59	952	120	289	.415	98	139	.705	230	110	176	7	338	5.7
Ben Warley†	56	767	115	281	.409	64	97	.660	215	25	128	2	294	5.3
Ben Warley‡	57	773	116	284	.408	64	97	.660	217	25	129	2	296	5.2
Wayne Hightower	24	460	63	186	.339	57	78	.731	131	35	61	2	183	7.6
Walt Bellamy*	8	268	56	124	.452	40	67	.597	102	18	32	2	152	19.0
Willie Somerset	7	98	18	43	.419	9	11	.818	15	9	21	0	45	6.4
Gary Bradds	3	15	2	6	.333	3	4	.750	8	1	1	0	7	2.3
Thales McReynolds	5	28	1	12	.083	1	2	.500	6	1	0	0	3	0.6

BOSTON CELTICS

SCORING

	G	Min.	FGM	FGA	Pct.	FTM	FTA	Pct.	Reb.	Ast.	PF	Dq.	Pts.	Avg.
Sam Jones	67	2155	626	1335	.469	325	407	.799	347	216	170	0	1577	23.5
John Havlicek	71	2175	530	1328	.399	274	349	.785	423	210	158	1	1334	18.8

SCORING

	G	Min.	FGM	FGA	Pct.	FTM	FTA	Pct.	Reb.	Ast.	PF	Dq.	Pts.	Avg.
Bill Russell	78	3386	391	943	.415	223	405	.551	1779	371	221	4	1005	12.9
Larry Siegfried	71	1675	349	825	.423	274	311	.881	196	165	157	1	972	13.7
Tom Sanders	72	1896	349	816	.428	211	276	.764	508	90	317	19	909	12.6
Don Nelson	75	1765	271	618	.439	223	326	.684	403	79	187	1	765	10.2
Willie Naulls	71	1433	328	815	.402	104	131	.794	319	72	197	4	760	10.7
K.C. Jones	80	2710	240	619	.388	209	303	.690	304	503	243	4	689	8.6
Mel Counts	67	1021	221	549	.403	120	145	.828	432	50	207	5	562	8.4
Ron Bonham	39	312	76	207	.367	52	61	.852	35	11	29	0	204	5.2
Woody Sauldsberry	39	530	80	249	.321	11	22	.500	142	15	94	0	171	4.4
John Thompson	10	72	14	30	.467	4	6	.667	30	3	15	0	32	3.2
Sihugo Green	10	92	12	31	.387	8	16	.500	11	9	16	0	32	3.2
Ron Watts	1	3	1	2	.500	0	0	...	1	1	1	0	2	2.0

CINCINNATI ROYALS

SCORING

	G	Min.	FGM	FGA	Pct.	FTM	FTA	Pct.	Reb.	Ast.	PF	Dq.	Pts.	Avg.
Oscar Robertson	76	3493	818	1723	.475	742	881	.842	586	847	227	1	2378	31.3
Jerry Lucas	79	3517	690	1523	.453	317	403	.787	1668	213	274	5	1697	21.5
Adrian Smith	80	2982	531	1310	.405	408	480	.850	287	256	276	1	1470	18.4
Happy Hairston	72	1794	398	814	.489	220	321	.685	546	44	216	3	1016	14.1
Tom Hawkins	79	2123	273	604	.452	116	209	.555	575	99	274	4	662	8.4
Wayne Embry	80	1882	232	564	.411	141	234	.603	525	81	287	9	605	7.6
Jack Twyman	73	943	224	498	.450	95	117	.812	168	60	122	1	543	7.4
Jon McGlocklin	72	852	153	363	.421	62	79	.785	133	88	77	0	368	5.1
Connie Dierking	57	782	134	322	.416	50	82	.610	245	43	113	0	318	5.6
Tom Thacker	50	478	84	207	.406	15	38	.395	119	61	85	0	183	3.7
George Wilson	47	276	54	138	.391	27	42	.643	98	17	56	0	135	2.9
Art Heyman*	11	100	15	43	.349	10	17	.588	13	7	19	0	40	3.6
Bud Olsen*	4	36	3	8	.375	1	3	.333	13	2	4	0	7	1.8
Jay Arnette	3	14	1	6	.167	0	0	...	0	0	3	0	2	0.7

DETROIT PISTONS

SCORING

	G	Min.	FGM	FGA	Pct.	FTM	FTA	Pct.	Reb.	Ast.	PF	Dq.	Pts.	Avg.
Eddie Miles	80	2788	634	1418	.447	298	402	.741	302	221	203	2	1566	19.6
Ray Scott	79	2652	544	1309	.416	323	435	.743	755	238	209	1	1411	17.9
Dave DeBusschere	79	2696	524	1284	.408	249	378	.659	916	209	252	5	1297	16.4
Tom Van Arsdale	79	2041	312	834	.374	209	290	.721	309	205	251	1	833	10.5
Joe Strawder	79	2180	250	613	.408	176	256	.688	820	78	305	10	676	8.6
Don Kojis	60	783	182	439	.415	76	141	.539	260	42	94	0	440	7.3
Ron Reed	57	997	186	524	.355	54	100	.540	339	92	133	1	426	7.5
John Tresvant†	46	756	134	322	.416	115	158	.728	279	62	136	2	383	8.3
John Tresvant‡	61	969	171	400	.428	142	190	.747	364	72	179	2	484	7.9
Rod Thorn*	27	815	143	343	.417	90	123	.732	101	64	67	0	376	13.9
Joe Caldwell*	33	716	143	338	.423	60	88	.682	190	65	63	0	346	10.5
John Barnhill†	45	926	139	363	.383	59	98	.602	112	113	76	0	337	7.5
John Barnhill‡	76	1617	243	606	.401	113	184	.614	203	196	134	0	599	7.9
Bill Buntin	42	713	118	299	.305	88	143	.615	252	36	119	4	324	7.7
Charles Vaughn†	37	774	110	282	.390	60	82	.732	63	104	60	0	280	7.6
Charles Vaughn‡	56	1219	182	474	.384	106	144	.736	109	140	99	1	470	8.4
Donnis Butcher	15	285	45	96	.469	18	34	.529	33	30	40	1	108	7.2
Bob Warlick	10	78	11	38	.289	2	6	.333	16	10	8	0	24	2.4

LOS ANGELES LAKERS

SCORING

	G	Min.	FGM	FGA	Pct.	FTM	FTA	Pct.	Reb.	Ast.	PF	Dq.	Pts.	Avg.
Jerry West	79	3218	818	1731	.473	840	977	.860	562	480	243	1	2476	31.3
Rudy LaRusso	76	2316	410	897	.457	350	445	.787	660	165	261	9	1170	15.4
Walt Hazzard	80	2198	458	1003	.457	182	257	.708	219	393	224	0	1098	13.7
Elgin Baylor	65	1975	415	1034	.401	249	337	.739	621	224	157	0	1079	16.6
LeRoy Ellis	80	2219	393	927	.424	186	256	.727	735	74	232	3	972	12.2
Bob Boozer	78	1847	365	754	.484	225	289	.779	548	87	196	0	955	12.2
Jim King	76	1499	238	545	.437	94	115	.817	204	223	181	1	570	7.5
Gail Goodrich	65	1008	203	503	.404	103	149	.691	130	103	103	1	509	7.8
Darrall Imhoff	77	1413	151	337	.448	77	136	.566	509	113	234	7	379	4.9
Gene Wiley	67	1386	123	289	.426	43	76	.566	490	63	171	3	289	4.3
John Fairchild	30	171	23	89	.258	14	20	.700	45	11	33	0	60	2.0

1965-66

NEW YORK KNICKERBOCKERS

	G	Min.	FGM	FGA	Pct.	FTM	FTA	Pct.	Reb.	Ast.	PF	Dq.	Pts.	Avg.
Dick Barnett	75	2589	631	1344	.469	467	605	.772	310	259	235	6	1729	23.1
Walt Bellamy†	72	3084	639	1249	.512	390	622	.627	1152	217	262	7	1668	23.2
Walt Bellamy‡	80	3352	695	1373	.506	430	689	.624	1254	235	294	9	1820	22.8
Willis Reed	76	2537	438	1009	.434	302	399	.757	883	91	323	13	1178	15.5
Howie Komives	80	2612	436	1116	.391	241	280	.861	281	425	278	5	1113	13.9
Dave Stallworth	80	1893	373	820	.455	258	376	.686	492	186	237	4	1004	12.6
Dick Van Arsdale	79	2289	359	838	.428	251	351	.715	376	184	235	5	969	12.3
Emmette Bryant	71	1193	212	449	.472	74	101	.733	170	216	215	4	498	7.0
Barry Clemens	70	877	161	391	.412	54	78	.692	183	67	113	0	376	5.4
Tom Gola	74	1127	122	271	.450	82	105	.781	289	191	207	3	326	4.4
Len Chappell	46	545	100	238	.420	46	78	.590	127	26	64	1	246	5.3
Jim Barnes*	7	263	40	90	.444	30	42	.714	72	9	33	0	110	15.7
Johnny Green*	7	208	43	79	.544	15	31	.484	74	11	21	0	101	14.4
Johnny Egan*	7	58	5	16	.313	7	10	.700	2	14	4	0	17	2.4

PHILADELPHIA 76ERS

	G	Min.	FGM	FGA	Pct.	FTM	FTA	Pct.	Reb.	Ast.	PF	Dq.	Pts.	Avg.
Wilt Chamberlain	79	3737	1074	1990	.540	501	976	.513	1943	414	171	0	2649	33.5
Hal Greer	80	3326	703	1580	.445	413	514	.804	473	384	315	6	1819	22.7
Chet Walker	80	2603	443	982	.451	335	468	.716	636	201	238	3	1221	15.3
Billy Cunningham	80	2134	431	1011	.426	281	443	.634	599	207	301	12	1143	14.3
Wali Jones	80	2196	296	799	.370	128	172	.744	169	273	250	6	720	9.0
Lucious Jackson	79	1966	246	614	.401	158	214	.738	676	132	216	2	650	8.2
Dave Gambee	72	1068	168	437	.384	159	187	.850	273	71	189	3	495	6.9
Al Bianchi	78	1312	214	560	.382	66	98	.673	134	134	232	4	494	6.3
Gerry Ward	65	838	67	189	.354	39	60	.650	89	80	163	3	173	2.7
Art Heyman†	6	20	3	9	.333	4	5	.800	4	4	4	0	10	1.7
Art Heyman‡	17	120	18	52	.346	14	22	.636	17	11	23	0	50	2.9
Bob Weiss	7	30	3	9	.333	0	0	. . .	7	4	10	0	6	0.9
Jesse Branson	5	14	1	6	.167	3	4	.750	9	1	4	0	5	1.0
Ben Warley*	1	6	1	3	.333	0	0	. . .	2	0	1	0	2	2.0

ST. LOUIS HAWKS

	G	Min.	FGM	FGA	Pct.	FTM	FTA	Pct.	Reb.	Ast.	PF	Dq.	Pts.	Avg.
Zelmo Beaty	80	3072	616	1301	.473	424	559	.758	1086	125	344	15	1656	20.7
Lenny Wilkens	69	2692	411	954	.431	422	532	.793	322	429	248	4	1244	18.0
Richie Guerin	80	2363	414	998	.415	362	446	.812	314	388	256	4	1190	14.9
Cliff Hagan	74	1851	419	942	.445	176	206	.854	234	164	177	1	1014	13.7
Bill Bridges	78	2677	377	927	.407	257	364	.706	951	208	333	11	1011	13.0
Joe Caldwell†	46	1141	268	600	.447	119	166	.717	246	61	140	3	655	14.2
Joe Caldwell‡	79	1857	411	938	.438	179	254	.705	436	126	203	3	1001	12.7
Rod Thorn†	46	924	163	385	.423	78	113	.690	109	81	77	0	404	8.8
Rod Thorn‡	73	1739	306	728	.420	168	236	.712	210	145	144	0	780	10.7
Jim Washington	65	1104	158	393	.402	68	120	.567	353	43	176	4	384	5.9
Gene Tormohlen	71	775	144	324	.444	54	82	.659	314	60	138	3	342	4.8
John Barnhill*	31	691	104	243	.428	54	86	.628	91	83	58	0	262	8.5
Jeff Mullins	44	587	113	296	.382	29	36	.806	69	66	68	1	255	5.8
Charles Vaughn*	19	445	72	192	.375	46	62	.742	46	36	39	1	190	10.0
Paul Silas	46	586	70	173	.405	35	61	.574	236	22	72	0	175	3.8
John Tresvant*	15	213	37	78	.474	27	32	.844	85	10	43	0	101	6.7
Mike Farmer	9	79	13	30	.433	4	5	.800	18	6	10	0	30	3.3

SAN FRANCISCO WARRIORS

	G	Min.	FGM	FGA	Pct.	FTM	FTA	Pct.	Reb.	Ast.	PF	Dq.	Pts.	Avg.
Rick Barry	80	2990	745	1698	.439	569	660	.862	850	173	297	2	2059	25.7
Guy Rodgers	79	2902	586	1571	.373	296	407	.727	421	846	241	6	1468	18.6
Nate Thurmond	73	2891	454	1119	.406	280	428	.654	1312	111	223	7	1188	16.3
Tom Meschery	80	2383	401	895	.448	224	293	.765	716	81	285	7	1026	12.8
Paul Neumann	66	1729	343	817	.420	265	317	.836	208	184	174	0	951	14.4
Al Attles	79	2053	364	724	.503	154	252	.611	322	225	265	7	882	11.2
McCoy McLemore	80	1467	225	528	.426	142	191	.743	488	55	197	4	592	7.4
Fred Hetzel	56	722	160	401	.399	63	92	.685	290	27	121	2	383	6.8
Gary Phillips	67	867	106	303	.350	54	87	.621	134	113	97	0	266	4.0
Keith Erickson	64	646	95	267	.356	43	65	.662	162	38	91	1	233	3.6

	G	Min.	FGM	FGA	Pct.	FTM	FTA	Pct.	Reb.	Ast.	PF	Dq.	Pts.	Avg.
Bud Olsen†	55	566	78	185	.422	38	85	.447	179	18	77	1	194	3.5
Bud Olsen‡	59	602	81	193	.420	39	88	.443	192	20	81	1	201	3.4
Will Frazier	2	9	0	4	.000	1	2	.500	5	1	1	0	1	0.5

* Finished season with another team.   † Totals with this team only.   ‡ Totals with all teams.

PLAYOFF RESULTS

EASTERN DIVISION

SEMIFINALS
Boston 3, Cincinnati 2
Mar. 23—Wed.	Cincinnati 107 at Boston	103
Mar. 26—Sat.	Boston 132 at Cincinnati	125
Mar. 27—Sun.	Cincinnati 113 at Boston	107
Mar. 30—Wed.	Boston 120 at Cincinnati	103
Apr. 1—Fri.	Cincinnati 103 at Boston	112

FINALS
Boston 4, Philadelphia 1
Apr. 3—Sun.	Boston 115 at Philadelphia	96
Apr. 6—Wed.	Philadelphia 93 at Boston	114
Apr. 7—Thur.	Boston 105 at Philadelphia	111
Apr. 10—Sun.	Philadelphia 108 at Boston	*114
Apr. 12—Tue.	Boston 120 at Philadelphia	112

WESTERN DIVISION

SEMIFINALS
St. Louis 3, Baltimore 0
Mar. 24—Thur.	St. Louis 113 at Baltimore	111
Mar. 27—Sun.	St. Louis 105 at Baltimore	100
Mar. 30—Wed.	Baltimore 112 at St. Louis	121

FINALS
Los Angeles 4, St. Louis 3
Apr. 1—Fri.	St. Louis 106 at Los Angeles	129
Apr. 3—Sun.	St. Louis 116 at Los Angeles	125
Apr. 6—Wed.	Los Angeles 113 at St. Louis	120
Apr. 9—Sat.	Los Angeles 107 at St. Louis	95
Apr. 10—Sun.	St. Louis 112 at Los Angeles	100
Apr. 13—Wed.	Los Angeles 127 at St. Louis	131
Apr. 15—Fri.	St. Louis 121 at Los Angeles	130

NBA FINALS
Boston 4, Los Angeles 3
Apr. 17—Sun.	Los Angeles 133 at Boston	*129
Apr. 19—Tue.	Los Angeles 109 at Boston	129
Apr. 20—Wed.	Boston 120 at Los Angeles	106
Apr. 22—Fri.	Boston 122 at Los Angeles	117
Apr. 24—Sun.	Los Angeles 121 at Boston	117
Apr. 26—Tue.	Boston 115 at Los Angeles	123
Apr. 28—Thur.	Los Angeles 93 at Boston	95

*Denotes number of overtime periods.

1965-66

1964-65

1964-65 NBA CHAMPION BOSTON CELTICS

Front row (from left): K.C. Jones, Tom Heinsohn, president Lou Pieri, head coach Red Auerbach, Bill Russell, Sam Jones. Back row (from left): Ron Bonham, Larry Siegfried, Willie Naulls, Mel Counts, John Thompson, Tom Sanders, John Havlicek, trainer Buddy LeRoux.

FINAL STANDINGS

EASTERN DIVISION

	Bos.	Cin.	Phi.	N.Y.	L.A.	St.L.	Balt.	Det.	S.F.	W	L	Pct.	GB
Boston...................	..	8	5	7	7	9	7	10	9	62	18	.775	..
Cincinnati..............	2	..	6	8	6	8	4	6	8	48	32	.600	14
Philadelphia...........	5	4	..	5	3	5	6	6	6	40	40	.500	22
New York..............	3	2	5	..	0	1	8	5	7	31	49	.388	31

WESTERN DIVISION

	Bos.	Cin.	Phi.	N.Y.	L.A.	St.L.	Balt.	Det.	S.F.	W	L	Pct.	GB
Los Angeles.............	3	4	7	10	..	4	6	7	8	49	31	.613	..
St. Louis...............	1	2	5	9	6	..	5	7	10	45	35	.563	4
Baltimore.............	3	6	4	2	4	5	..	6	7	37	43	.463	12
Detroit.................	0	4	4	5	3	3	4	..	8	31	49	.388	18
San Francisco...........	1	2	4	3	2	0	3	2	..	17	63	.213	32

TEAM STATISTICS

	G	FGM	FGA	Pct.	FTM	FTA	Pct.	Reb.	Ast.	PF	Dq.	AVERAGE POINTS For	AVERAGE POINTS Agst.	AVERAGE POINTS Dif.
Boston	80	3567	8609	.414	1890	2587	.731	5748	1772	2065	36	112.8	104.5	+8.3
St. Louis	80	3269	7710	.424	2168	2947	.736	5208	1691	2069	26	108.8	105.8	+3.0
Cincinnati	80	3482	7797	.447	2170	2866	.757	5387	1843	1992	30	114.2	111.9	+2.3
Los Angeles.....	80	3336	7628	.437	2276	2984	.763	5231	1601	1998	28	111.9	109.9	+2.0
Philadelphia.....	80	3391	8028	.422	2221	3011	.738	5246	1692	2096	53	112.5	112.7	-0.2
Baltimore.......	80	3421	7734	.442	2245	3144	.714	5298	1676	2119	41	113.6	115.8	-2.2
Detroit.........	80	3467	8297	.418	1747	2537	.689	5394	1609	2058	35	108.5	111.9	-3.4
New York.......	80	3339	7834	.426	1915	2684	.713	5206	1550	2283	40	107.4	111.1	-3.7
San Francisco	80	3323	8245	.403	1819	2844	.640	5715	1653	2002	34	105.8	112.0	-6.2
Avgs..........	80	3399	7987	.426	2050	2845	.721	5381	1676	2076	35.9	110.6	...	...

HOME/ROAD/NEUTRAL

	Home	Road	Neutral	Total		Home	Road	Neutral	Total
Baltimore.............	23-14	12-19	2-10	37-43	New York.............	15-20	9-21	7-8	31-49
Boston...............	27-3	27-11	8-4	62-18	Philadelphia..........	13-12	9-21	18-7	40-40
Cincinnati............	25-7	17-21	6-4	48-32	St. Louis.............	26-14	15-17	4-4	45-35
Detroit..............	13-17	11-20	7-12	31-49	San Francisco.........	10-26	5-31	2-6	17-63
Los Angeles..........	25-13	21-16	3-2	49-31	Totals	178-125	125-178	57-57	360-360

POINTS

	G	FGM	FTM	Pts.	Avg.
Wilt Chamberlain, S.F.-Phil.	.73	1063	408	2534	34.7
Jerry West, Los Angeles	.74	822	648	2292	31.0
Oscar Robertson, Cincinnati	.75	807	665	2279	30.4
Sam Jones, Boston	.80	821	428	2070	25.9
Elgin Baylor, Los Angeles	.74	763	483	2009	27.1
Walt Bellamy, Baltimore	.80	733	515	1981	24.8
Willis Reed, New York	.80	629	302	1560	19.5
Bailey Howell, Baltimore	.80	515	504	1534	19.2
Terry Dischinger, Detroit	.80	568	320	1456	18.2
Don Ohl, Baltimore	.77	568	284	1420	18.4
Gus Johnson, Baltimore	.76	577	261	1415	18.6
Jerry Lucas, Cincinnati	.66	558	298	1414	21.4
Hal Greer, Philadelphia	.70	539	335	1413	20.2
John Havlicek, Boston	.75	570	235	1375	18.3
Zelmo Beaty, St. Louis	.80	505	341	1351	16.9
Dave DeBusschere, Detroit	.79	508	306	1322	16.7
Lenny Wilkens, St. Louis	.78	434	416	1284	16.5
Nate Thurmond, San Francisco	.77	519	235	1273	16.5
Adrian Smith, Cincinnati	.80	463	284	1210	15.1
Jim Barnes, New York	.75	454	251	1159	15.5

FIELD GOALS

(minimum 220 made)

	FGM	FGA	Pct.
Wilt Chamberlain, San Francisco-Philadelphia	.1063	2083	.510
Walt Bellamy, Baltimore	.733	1441	.509
Jerry Lucas, Cincinnati	.558	1121	.498
Jerry West, Los Angeles	.822	1655	.497
Bailey Howell, Baltimore	.515	1040	.495
Terry Dischinger, Detroit	.568	1153	.493
John Egan, New York	.258	529	.488
Zelmo Beaty, St. Louis	.505	1047	.482
Oscar Robertson, Cincinnati	.807	1681	.480
Paul Neumann, Philadelphia-San Francisco	.365	772	.473

FREE THROWS

(minimum 210 made)

	FTM	FTA	Pct.
Larry Costello, Philadelphia	.243	277	.877
Oscar Robertson, Cincinnati	.665	793	.839
Howard Komives, New York	.212	254	.835
Adrian Smith, Cincinnati	.284	342	.830
Jerry West, Los Angeles	.648	789	.821
Sam Jones, Boston	.428	522	.820
Bob Pettit, St. Louis	.332	405	.820
Jerry Lucas, Cincinnati	.298	366	.814
Dave Gambee, Philadelphia	.299	368	.813
Hal Greer, Philadelphia	.335	413	.811

ASSISTS

	G	No.	Avg.
Oscar Robertson, Cincinnati	.75	861	11.5
Guy Rodgers, San Francisco	.79	565	7.2
K.C. Jones, Boston	.78	437	5.6
Lenny Wilkens, St. Louis	.78	431	5.5
Bill Russell, Boston	.78	410	5.3
Jerry West, Los Angeles	.74	364	4.9
Hal Greer, Philadelphia	.70	313	4.5
Kevin Loughery, Baltimore	.80	296	3.7
Elgin Baylor, Los Angeles	.74	280	3.8
Larry Costello, Philadelphia	.64	275	4.3

REBOUNDS

	G	No.	Avg.
Bill Russell, Boston	.78	1878	24.1
Wilt Chamberlain, San Francisco-Philadelphia	.73	1673	22.9
Nate Thurmond, San Francisco	.77	1395	18.1
Jerry Lucas, Cincinnati	.66	1321	20.0
Willis Reed, New York	.80	1175	14.7
Walt Bellamy, Baltimore	.80	1166	14.6
Gus Johnson, Baltimore	.76	988	13.0
Lucious Jackson, Philadelphia	.76	980	12.9
Zelmo Beaty, St. Louis	.80	966	12.1
Elgin Baylor, Los Angeles	.74	950	12.8

INDIVIDUAL STATISTICS, TEAM BY TEAM

BALTIMORE BULLETS

	G	Min.	FGM	FGA	Pct.	FTM	FTA	Pct.	Reb.	Ast.	PF	Dq.	SCORING Pts.	Avg.
Walt Bellamy	80	3301	733	1441	.509	515	752	.685	1166	191	260	2	1981	24.8
Bailey Howell	80	2975	515	1040	.495	504	629	.801	869	208	345	10	1534	19.2
Don Ohl	77	2821	568	1297	.438	284	388	.732	336	250	274	7	1420	18.4
Gus Johnson	76	2899	577	1379	.418	261	386	.676	988	270	258	4	1415	18.6
Kevin Loughery	80	2417	406	957	.424	212	281	.754	235	296	320	13	1024	12.8
Bob Ferry	77	1280	143	338	.423	122	199	.613	355	60	156	2	408	5.3
Wali Jones	77	1250	154	411	.375	99	136	.728	140	200	196	1	407	5.3
Sihugo Green	70	1086	152	368	.413	101	161	.627	169	140	134	1	405	5.8
Wayne Hightower†	27	510	60	174	.345	62	81	.765	173	16	61	1	182	6.7
Wayne Hightower‡	75	1547	196	570	.344	195	254	.768	420	54	204	2	587	7.8
Gary Bradds	41	335	46	111	.414	45	63	.714	84	19	36	0	137	3.3
Charles Hardnett	20	200	25	80	.313	23	39	.590	77	2	37	0	73	3.7
Al Butler	25	172	24	73	.329	11	15	.733	21	12	25	0	59	2.4
Les Hunter	24	114	18	64	.281	6	14	.429	50	11	16	0	42	1.8
Gary Hill†	3	15	0	1	.000	0	0	...	1	1	1	0	0	0.0
Gary Hill‡	12	103	10	36	.278	7	14	.500	16	7	11	0	27	2.3

BOSTON CELTICS

	G	Min.	FGM	FGA	Pct.	FTM	FTA	Pct.	Reb.	Ast.	PF	Dq.	SCORING Pts.	Avg.
Sam Jones	80	2885	821	1818	.452	428	522	.820	411	223	176	0	2070	25.9
John Havlicek	75	2169	570	1420	.401	235	316	.744	371	199	200	2	1375	18.3
Bill Russell	78	3466	429	980	.438	244	426	.573	1878	410	204	1	1102	14.1
Tom Sanders	80	2459	374	871	.429	193	259	.745	661	92	318	15	941	11.8
Tom Heinsohn	67	1706	365	954	.383	182	229	.795	399	157	252	5	912	13.6
Willie Naulls	71	1465	302	786	.384	143	176	.813	336	72	225	5	747	10.5
K.C. Jones	78	2434	253	639	.396	143	227	.630	318	437	263	5	649	8.3
Larry Siegfried	72	996	173	417	.415	109	140	.779	134	119	108	1	455	6.3
Ron Bonham	37	369	91	220	.414	92	112	.821	78	19	33	0	274	7.4
Mel Counts	54	572	100	272	.368	58	74	.784	265	19	134	1	258	4.8
John Thompson	64	699	84	209	.402	62	105	.590	230	16	141	1	230	3.6
Bob Nordmann	3	25	3	5	.600	0	0	...	8	3	5	0	6	2.0
Gerry Ward	3	30	2	18	.111	1	1	1.000	5	6	6	0	5	1.7

1964-65

CINCINNATI ROYALS

	G	Min.	FGM	FGA	Pct.	FTM	FTA	Pct.	Reb.	Ast.	PF	Dq.	Pts.	Avg.
Oscar Robertson	75	3421	807	1681	.480	665	793	.839	674	861	205	2	2279	30.4
Jerry Lucas	66	2864	558	1121	.498	298	366	.814	1321	157	214	1	1414	21.4
Adrian Smith	80	2745	463	1016	.456	284	342	.830	220	240	199	2	1210	15.1
Jack Twyman	80	2236	479	1081	.443	198	239	.828	383	137	239	4	1156	14.5
Wayne Embry	74	2243	352	772	.456	239	371	.644	741	92	297	10	943	12.7
Bud Olsen	79	1372	224	512	.438	144	195	.738	333	84	203	5	592	7.5
Tom Hawkins	79	1864	220	538	.409	116	204	.569	475	80	240	4	556	7.0
Happy Hairston	61	736	131	351	.373	110	165	.667	293	27	95	0	372	6.1
Jay Arnette	63	662	91	245	.371	56	75	.747	62	68	125	1	238	3.8
Arlen Bockhorn	19	424	60	157	.382	28	39	.718	55	45	52	1	148	7.8
Tom Thacker	55	470	56	168	.333	23	47	.489	127	41	64	0	135	2.5
George Wilson	39	288	41	155	.265	9	30	.300	102	11	59	0	91	2.3

DETROIT PISTONS

	G	Min.	FGM	FGA	Pct.	FTM	FTA	Pct.	Reb.	Ast.	PF	Dq.	Pts.	Avg.
Terry Dischinger	80	2698	568	1153	.493	320	424	.755	479	198	253	5	1456	18.2
Dave DeBusschere	79	2769	508	1196	.425	306	437	.700	874	253	242	5	1322	16.7
Eddie Miles	76	2074	439	994	.442	166	223	.744	258	157	201	1	1044	13.7
Ray Scott	66	2167	402	1092	.368	220	314	.701	634	239	209	5	1024	15.5
Reggie Harding	78	2699	405	987	.410	128	209	.612	906	179	258	5	938	12.0
Rod Thorn	74	1770	320	750	.427	176	243	.724	266	161	122	0	816	11.0
Joe Caldwell	66	1543	290	776	.374	129	210	.614	441	118	171	3	709	10.7
Don Kojis	65	836	180	416	.433	62	98	.633	243	63	115	1	422	6.5
Donnis Butcher	71	1157	143	353	.405	126	204	.618	200	122	183	4	412	5.8
Jackie Moreland	54	732	103	296	.348	66	104	.635	183	69	151	4	272	5.0
Hub Reed	62	753	84	221	.380	40	58	.690	206	38	136	2	208	3.4
Willie Jones	12	101	21	52	.404	2	6	.333	10	7	13	0	44	3.7
Bob Duffy	4	26	4	11	.364	6	7	.857	4	5	4	0	14	3.5

LOS ANGELES LAKERS

	G	Min.	FGM	FGA	Pct.	FTM	FTA	Pct.	Reb.	Ast.	PF	Dq.	Pts.	Avg.
Jerry West	74	3066	822	1655	.497	648	789	.821	447	364	221	2	2292	31.0
Elgin Baylor	74	3056	763	1903	.401	483	610	.792	950	280	235	0	2009	27.1
Rudy LaRusso	77	2588	381	827	.461	321	415	.773	725	198	258	3	1083	14.1
Dick Barnett	74	2026	375	908	.413	270	338	.799	200	159	209	1	1020	13.8
LeRoy Ellis	80	2026	311	700	.444	198	284	.697	652	49	196	1	820	10.3
Jim King	77	1671	184	469	.392	118	151	.781	214	178	193	2	486	6.3
Gene Wiley	80	2002	175	376	.465	56	111	.505	690	105	235	11	406	5.1
Darrall Imhoff	76	1521	145	311	.466	88	154	.571	500	87	238	7	378	5.0
Walt Hazzard	66	919	117	306	.382	46	71	.648	141	140	132	0	280	4.2
Don Nelson	39	238	36	85	.424	20	26	.769	73	24	40	1	92	2.4
Cotton Nash*	25	167	14	57	.246	25	32	.781	35	10	30	0	53	2.1
Bill McGill†	8	37	7	20	.350	1	1	1.000	12	3	6	0	15	1.9
Bill McGill‡	24	133	21	65	.323	13	17	.765	36	9	32	1	55	2.3
Jerry Grote	11	33	6	11	.545	2	2	1.000	4	4	5	0	14	1.3

NEW YORK KNICKERBOCKERS

	G	Min.	FGM	FGA	Pct.	FTM	FTA	Pct.	Reb.	Ast.	PF	Dq.	Pts.	Avg.
Willis Reed	80	3042	629	1457	.432	302	407	.742	1175	133	339	14	1560	19.5
Jim Barnes	75	2586	454	1070	.424	251	379	.662	729	93	312	8	1159	15.5
Bob Boozer	80	2139	424	963	.440	288	375	.768	604	108	183	0	1136	14.2
Howie Komives	80	2376	381	1020	.374	212	254	.835	195	265	246	2	974	12.2
Johnny Green	78	1720	346	737	.469	165	301	.548	545	129	194	3	857	11.0
Johnny Egan	74	1664	258	529	.488	162	199	.814	143	252	139	0	678	9.2
Tom Gola	77	1727	204	455	.448	133	180	.739	319	220	269	8	541	7.0
Dave Budd	62	1188	196	407	.482	121	170	.712	310	62	147	1	513	8.3
Emmette Bryant	77	1332	145	436	.333	87	133	.654	167	167	212	3	377	4.9
Len Chappell	43	655	145	367	.395	68	100	.680	140	15	73	0	358	8.3
Art Heyman	55	663	114	267	.427	88	132	.667	99	79	96	0	316	5.7
Barry Kramer†	19	231	27	86	.314	30	40	.750	41	15	31	1	84	4.4
Barry Kramer‡	52	507	63	186	.339	60	84	.714	100	41	67	1	186	3.6
Tom Hoover	24	153	13	32	.406	8	14	.571	58	12	37	0	34	1.4
John Rudometkin*	1	22	3	8	.375	0	0	...	7	0	5	0	6	6.0

PHILADELPHIA 76ERS

	G	Min.	FGM	FGA	Pct.	FTM	FTA	Pct.	Reb.	Ast.	PF	Dq.	Pts.	Avg.
Hal Greer	70	2600	539	1245	.433	335	413	.811	355	313	254	7	1413	20.2
Lucious Jackson	76	2590	419	1013	.414	288	404	.713	980	93	251	4	1126	14.8
Wilt Chamberlain†	35	1558	427	808	.528	200	380	.526	780	133	70	0	1054	30.1
Wilt Chamberlain‡	73	3301	1063	2083	.510	408	880	.464	1673	250	146	0	2534	34.7
Chet Walker	79	2187	377	936	.403	288	388	.742	528	132	200	2	1042	13.2
Dave Gambee	80	1993	356	864	.412	299	368	.813	468	113	277	7	1011	12.6
Larry Costello	64	1967	309	695	.445	243	277	.877	169	275	242	10	861	13.5
Red Kerr	80	1810	264	714	.370	126	181	.696	551	197	132	1	654	8.2
Paul Neumann*	40	1100	213	434	.491	148	184	.804	102	139	119	1	574	14.4

	G	Min.	FGM	FGA	Pct.	FTM	FTA	Pct.	Reb.	Ast.	PF	Dq.	Pts.	Avg.
Al Bianchi	60	1116	175	486	.360	54	76	.711	95	140	178	10	404	6.7
Ben Warley	64	900	94	253	.372	124	176	.705	277	53	170	6	312	4.9
Connie Dierking*	38	729	121	311	.389	54	83	.651	239	42	101	3	296	7.8
Larry Jones	23	359	47	153	.307	37	52	.712	57	40	46	2	131	5.7
Steve Courtin	24	317	42	103	.408	17	21	.810	22	22	44	0	101	4.2
Jerry Greenspan	5	49	8	13	.615	8	8	1.000	11	0	12	0	24	4.8

ST. LOUIS HAWKS

	G	Min.	FGM	FGA	Pct.	FTM	FTA	Pct.	Reb.	Ast.	PF	Dq.	Pts.	Avg.
Zelmo Beaty	80	2916	505	1047	.482	341	477	.715	966	111	328	11	1351	16.9
Lenny Wilkens	78	2854	434	1048	.414	416	558	.746	365	431	283	7	1284	16.5
Bob Pettit	50	1754	396	923	.429	332	405	.820	621	128	167	0	1124	22.5
Cliff Hagan	77	1739	393	901	.436	214	268	.799	276	136	182	0	1000	13.0
Bill Bridges	79	2362	362	938	.386	186	275	.676	853	187	276	3	910	11.5
Charles Vaughn	75	1965	344	811	.424	182	242	.752	173	157	192	2	870	11.6
Richie Guerin	57	1678	295	662	.446	231	301	.767	149	271	193	1	821	14.4
Mike Farmer	60	1272	167	408	.409	75	94	.798	258	88	123	0	409	6.8
Paul Silas	79	1243	140	375	.373	83	164	.506	576	48	161	1	363	4.6
John Barnhill	41	777	121	312	.388	45	70	.643	91	76	56	0	287	7.0
Jeff Mullins	44	492	87	209	.416	41	61	.672	102	44	60	0	215	4.9
Bill McGill*	16	96	14	45	.311	12	16	.750	24	6	26	1	40	2.5
Ed Burton	7	42	7	20	.350	4	7	.571	13	2	13	0	18	2.6
John Tresvant	4	35	4	11	.364	6	9	.667	18	6	9	0	14	3.5

SAN FRANCISCO WARRIORS

	G	Min.	FGM	FGA	Pct.	FTM	FTA	Pct.	Reb.	Ast.	PF	Dq.	Pts.	Avg.
Wilt Chamberlain*	38	1743	636	1275	.499	208	500	.416	893	117	76	0	1480	38.9
Nate Thurmond	77	3173	519	1240	.419	235	357	.658	1395	157	232	3	1273	16.5
Guy Rodgers	79	2699	465	1225	.380	223	325	.686	323	565	256	4	1153	14.6
Tom Meschery	79	2408	361	917	.394	278	370	.751	655	106	279	6	1000	12.7
Al Attles	73	1733	254	662	.384	171	274	.624	239	205	242	7	679	9.3
McCoy McLemore	78	1731	244	725	.337	157	220	.714	488	81	224	6	645	8.3
Gary Phillips	73	1541	198	553	.358	120	199	.603	189	148	184	3	516	7.1
Wayne Hightower*	48	1037	136	396	.343	133	173	.769	247	38	143	1	405	8.4
Paul Neumann†	36	934	152	338	.450	86	119	.723	96	94	99	2	390	10.8
Paul Neumann‡	76	2034	365	772	.473	234	303	.772	198	233	218	3	964	12.7
Bud Koper	54	631	106	241	.440	35	42	.833	61	43	59	1	247	4.6
Connie Dierking†	30	565	97	227	.427	46	85	.541	196	30	64	1	240	8.0
Connie Dierking‡	68	1294	218	538	.405	100	168	.595	435	72	165	4	536	7.9
John Rudometkin†	22	354	49	146	.336	34	50	.680	92	16	49	0	132	6.0
John Rudometkin‡	23	376	52	154	.338	34	50	.680	99	16	54	0	138	6.0
Barry Kramer*	33	276	36	100	.360	30	44	.682	59	26	36	0	102	3.1
George Lee	19	247	27	77	.351	38	52	.731	55	12	22	0	92	4.8
Cotton Nash†	20	190	33	88	.375	18	20	.900	48	9	27	0	84	4.2
Cotton Nash‡	45	357	47	145	.324	43	52	.827	83	19	57	0	137	3.0
Gary Hill*	9	88	10	35	.286	7	14	.500	15	6	10	0	27	3.0

* Finished season with another team. † Totals with this team only. ‡ Totals with all teams.

PLAYOFF RESULTS

EASTERN DIVISION

SEMIFINALS

Philadelphia 3, Cincinnati 1

Mar. 24—Wed.	Philadelphia 119 at Cincinnati	117
Mar. 26—Fri.	Cincinnati 121 at Philadelphia	120
Mar. 28—Sun.	Philadelphia 108 at Cincinnati	94
Mar. 31—Wed.	Cincinnati 112 at Philadelphia	119

FINALS

Boston 4, Philadelphia 3

Apr. 4—Sun.	Philadelphia 98 at Boston	108
Apr. 6—Tue.	Boston 103 at Philadelphia	109
Apr. 8—Thur.	Philadelphia 94 at Boston	112
Apr. 9—Fri.	Boston 131 at Philadelphia	*134
Apr. 11—Sun.	Philadelphia 108 at Boston	114
Apr. 13—Tue.	Boston 106 at Philadelphia	112
Apr. 15—Thur.	Philadelphia 109 at Boston	110

WESTERN DIVISION

SEMIFINALS

Baltimore 3, St. Louis 1

Mar. 24—Wed.	Baltimore 108 at St. Louis	105
Mar. 26—Fri.	Baltimore 105 at St. Louis	129
Mar. 27—Sat.	St. Louis 99 at Baltimore	131
Mar. 30—Tue.	St. Louis 103 at Baltimore	109

FINALS

Los Angeles 4, Baltimore 2

Apr. 3—Sat.	Baltimore 115 at Los Angeles	121
Apr. 5—Mon.	Baltimore 115 at Los Angeles	118
Apr. 7—Wed.	Los Angeles 115 at Baltimore	122
Apr. 9—Fri.	Los Angeles 112 at Baltimore	114
Apr. 11—Sun.	Baltimore 112 at Los Angeles	120
Apr. 13—Tue.	Los Angeles 117 at Baltimore	115

NBA FINALS

Boston 4, Los Angeles 1

Apr. 18—Sun.	Los Angeles 110 at Boston	142
Apr. 19—Mon.	Los Angeles 123 at Boston	129
Apr. 21—Wed.	Boston 105 at Los Angeles	126
Apr. 23—Fri.	Boston 112 at Los Angeles	99
Apr. 25—Sun.	Los Angeles 96 at Boston	129

*Denotes number of overtime periods.

1964-65

1963-64

1963-64 NBA CHAMPION BOSTON CELTICS
Front row (from left): Sam Jones, Frank Ramsey, K.C. Jones, head coach Red Auerbach, president Walter A. Brown, Bill Russell, John Havlicek. Back row (from left): Johnny McCarthy, Tom Sanders, Tom Heinsohn, Clyde Lovellette, Willie Naulls, Jim Loscutoff, Larry Siegfried, trainer Buddy LeRoux. Inset: vice president Lou Pieri.

FINAL STANDINGS

EASTERN DIVISION

	Bos.	Cin.	Phi.	N.Y.	S.F.	St.L.	L.A.	Balt.	Det.	W	L	Pct.	GB
Boston	..	5	10	10	5	7	6	9	7	59	21	.738	..
Cincinnati	7	..	9	11	5	4	4	8	7	55	25	.688	4
Philadelphia	2	3	..	8	4	3	4	5	5	34	46	.425	25
New York	2	1	4	..	1	4	2	3	5	22	58	.275	37

WESTERN DIVISION

	Bos.	Cin.	Phi.	N.Y.	S.F.	St.L.	L.A.	Balt.	Det.	W	L	Pct.	GB
San Francisco	3	4	4	8	..	6	7	7	9	48	32	.600	..
St. Louis	2	4	6	4	6	..	7	7	10	46	34	.575	2
Los Angeles	3	4	5	6	5	5	..	7	7	42	38	.525	6
Baltimore	1	2	5	7	3	3	3	..	7	31	49	.388	17
Detroit	1	2	3	4	3	2	5	3	..	23	57	.288	25

TEAM STATISTICS

	G	FGM	FGA	Pct.	FTM	FTA	Pct.	Reb.	Ast.	PF	Dq.	AVERAGE POINTS For	AVERAGE POINTS Agst.	AVERAGE POINTS Dif.
Boston	80	3619	8770	.413	1804	2489	.725	5736	1760	2125	19	113.0	105.1	+7.9
San Francisco	80	3407	7779	.438	1800	2821	.638	5499	1899	1978	33	107.7	102.6	+5.1
Cincinnati	80	3516	7761	.453	2146	2828	.759	5400	1916	2139	35	114.7	109.7	+5.0
St. Louis	80	3341	7776	.430	2115	2795	.757	4959	1901	2266	39	110.0	108.4	+1.6
Los Angeles	80	3272	7438	.440	2230	2910	.766	5025	1676	1997	26	109.7	108.7	+1.0
Baltimore	80	3456	7862	.440	2036	2958	.688	5460	1423	2073	45	111.9	113.6	-1.7
Philadelphia	80	3394	8116	.418	2184	2851	.766	5132	1643	2251	39	112.2	116.5	-4.3
New York	80	3512	7888	.445	1952	2852	.684	5067	1563	2222	33	112.2	119.6	-7.4
Detroit	80	3346	7943	.421	1928	2685	.718	5145	1633	2235	50	107.8	115.5	-7.7
Avgs.	80	3429	7926	.433	2022	2799	.722	5269	1713	2143	35.4	111.0	...	...

HOME/ROAD/NEUTRAL

	Home	Road	Neutral	Total		Home	Road	Neutral	Total
Baltimore	20-19	8-21	3-9	31-49	New York	10-25	8-27	4-6	22-58
Boston	26-4	21-17	12-0	59-21	Philadelphia	18-12	12-22	4-12	34-46
Cincinnati	26-7	18-18	11-0	55-25	St. Louis	27-12	17-19	2-3	46-34
Detroit	9-21	6-25	8-11	23-57	San Francisco	25-14	21-15	2-3	48-32
Los Angeles	24-12	15-21	3-5	42-38	Totals	185-126	126-185	49-49	360-360

POINTS

	G	FGM	FTM	Pts.	Avg.
Wilt Chamberlain, San Francisco	80	1204	540	2948	36.9
Oscar Robertson, Cincinnati	79	840	800	2480	31.4
Bob Pettit, St. Louis	80	791	608	2190	27.4
Walt Bellamy, Baltimore	80	811	537	2159	27.0
Jerry West, Los Angeles	72	740	584	2064	28.7
Elgin Baylor, Los Angeles	78	756	471	1983	25.4
Hal Greer, Philadelphia	80	715	435	1865	23.3
Bailey Howell, Detroit	77	598	470	1666	21.6
Terry Dischinger, Baltimore	80	604	454	1662	20.8
John Havlicek, Boston	80	640	315	1595	19.9
Sam Jones, Boston	76	612	249	1473	19.4
Dick Barnett, Los Angeles	78	541	351	1433	18.4
Cliff Hagan, St. Louis	77	572	269	1413	18.4
Ray Scott, Detroit	80	539	328	1406	17.6
Jerry Lucas, Cincinnati	79	545	310	1400	17.7
Wayne Embry, Cincinnati	80	556	271	1383	17.3
Gus Johnson, Baltimore	78	571	210	1352	17.3
Len Chappell, Philadelphia-N.Y.	79	531	288	1350	17.1
Red Kerr, Philadelphia	80	536	268	1340	16.8
Chet Walker, Philadelphia	76	492	330	1314	17.3

FIELD GOALS

(minimum 210 made)

	FGM	FGA	Pct.
Jerry Lucas, Cincinnati	545	1035	.527
Wilt Chamberlain, San Francisco	1204	2298	.524
Walt Bellamy, Baltimore	811	1582	.513
Terry Dischinger, Baltimore	604	1217	.496
Bill McGill, Baltimore-New York	456	937	.487
Jerry West, Los Angeles	740	1529	.484
Oscar Robertson, Cincinnati	840	1740	.483
Bailey Howell, Detroit	598	1267	.472
John Green, New York	482	1026	.470
Bob Pettit, St. Louis	791	1708	.463

FREE THROWS

(minimum 210 made)

	FTM	FTA	Pct.
Oscar Robertson, Cincinnati	800	938	.853
Jerry West, Los Angeles	584	702	.832
Hal Greer, Philadelphia	435	525	.829
Tom Heinsohn, Boston	283	342	.827
Richie Guerin, New York-St. Louis	347	424	.818
Cliff Hagan, St. Louis	269	331	.813
Bailey Howell, Detroit	470	581	.809
Elgin Baylor, Los Angeles	471	586	.804
Wayne Hightower, San Francisco	260	329	.790
Paul Neumann, Philadelphia	210	266	.789

ASSISTS

	G	No.	Avg.
Oscar Robertson, Cincinnati	79	868	11.0
Guy Rodgers, San Francisco	79	556	7.0
K.C. Jones, Boston	80	407	5.1
Jerry West, Los Angeles	72	403	5.6
Wilt Chamberlain, San Francisco	80	403	5.0
Richie Guerin, New York-St. Louis	80	375	4.7
Hal Greer, Philadelphia	80	374	4.7
Bill Russell, Boston	78	370	4.7
Lenny Wilkens, St. Louis	78	359	4.6
John Egan, Detroit-New York	66	358	5.4

REBOUNDS

	G	No.	Avg.
Bill Russell, Boston	78	1930	24.7
Wilt Chamberlain, San Francisco	80	1787	22.3
Jerry Lucas, Cincinnati	79	1375	17.4
Walt Bellamy, Baltimore	80	1361	17.0
Bob Pettit, St. Louis	80	1224	15.3
Ray Scott, Detroit	80	1078	13.5
Gus Johnson, Baltimore	78	1064	13.6
Red Kerr, Philadelphia	80	1017	12.7
Elgin Baylor, Los Angeles	78	936	12.0
Wayne Embry, Cincinnati	80	925	11.6

INDIVIDUAL STATISTICS, TEAM BY TEAM

BALTIMORE BULLETS

	G	Min.	FGM	FGA	Pct.	FTM	FTA	Pct.	Reb.	Ast.	PF	Dq.	Pts.	Avg.
Walt Bellamy	80	3394	811	1582	.513	537	825	.651	1361	126	300	7	2159	27.0
Terry Dischinger	80	2816	604	1217	.496	454	585	.776	667	157	321	10	1662	20.8
Gus Johnson	78	2847	571	1329	.430	210	319	.658	1064	169	321	11	1352	17.3
Rod Thorn	75	2594	411	1015	.405	258	353	.731	360	281	187	3	1080	14.4
Sihugo Green	75	2064	287	691	.415	198	290	.683	282	215	224	5	772	10.3
Kevin Loughery*	66	1459	236	631	.374	126	177	.712	138	182	175	2	598	9.1
Don Kojis	78	1148	203	484	.419	82	146	.562	309	57	123	0	488	6.3
Charles Hardnett	66	617	107	260	.412	84	125	.672	251	27	114	1	298	4.5
Barney Cable	71	1125	116	290	.400	28	42	.667	301	47	166	3	260	3.7
Gene Shue	47	963	81	276	.293	36	61	.590	94	150	98	2	198	4.2
Paul Hogue**	15	147	12	30	.400	2	7	.286	31	6	35	1	26	1.7
Larry Comley	12	89	8	37	.216	9	16	.563	19	12	11	0	25	2.1
Mel Peterson	2	3	1	1	1.000	0	0	...	1	0	2	0	2	1.0
Roger Strickland	1	4	1	3	.333	0	0	...	0	0	1	0	2	2.0

*Loughery—Played 1 Detroit, 65 Baltimore.
**Hogue—Played 6 New York, 9 Baltimore.

BOSTON CELTICS

	G	Min.	FGM	FGA	Pct.	FTM	FTA	Pct.	Reb.	Ast.	PF	Dq.	Pts.	Avg.
John Havlicek	80	2587	640	1535	.417	315	422	.746	428	238	227	1	1595	19.9
Sam Jones	76	2381	612	1359	.450	249	318	.783	349	202	192	1	1473	19.4
Tom Heinsohn	76	2040	487	1223	.398	283	342	.827	460	183	268	3	1257	16.5
Bill Russell	78	3482	466	1077	.433	236	429	.550	1930	370	190	0	1168	15.0
Tom Sanders	80	2370	349	836	.417	213	280	.761	667	102	277	6	911	11.4
Willie Naulls	78	1409	321	769	.417	125	157	.796	356	64	208	0	767	9.8
K.C. Jones	80	2424	283	722	.392	88	168	.524	372	407	253	0	654	8.2
Frank Ramsey	75	1227	226	604	.374	196	233	.841	223	81	245	7	648	8.6
Clyde Lovellette	45	437	128	305	.420	45	57	.789	126	24	100	1	301	6.7
Jim Loscutoff	53	451	56	182	.308	18	31	.581	131	25	90	1	130	2.5

1963-64

	G	Min.	FGM	FGA	Pct.	FTM	FTA	Pct.	Reb.	Ast.	PF	Dq.	SCORING Pts.	Avg.
Larry Siegfried................	31	261	35	110	.318	31	39	.795	51	40	33	0	101	3.3
Johnny McCarthy..............	28	206	16	48	.333	5	13	.385	35	24	42	0	37	1.3

CINCINNATI ROYALS

	G	Min.	FGM	FGA	Pct.	FTM	FTA	Pct.	Reb.	Ast.	PF	Dq.	SCORING Pts.	Avg.
Oscar Robertson	79	3559	840	1740	.483	800	938	.853	783	868	280	3	2480	31.4
Jerry Lucas	79	3273	545	1035	.527	310	398	.779	1375	204	300	6	1400	17.7
Wayne Embry	80	2915	556	1213	.458	271	417	.650	925	113	325	7	1383	17.3
Jack Twyman..................	68	1996	447	993	.450	189	228	.829	364	137	267	7	1083	15.9
Tom Hawkins	73	1770	256	580	.441	113	188	.601	435	74	198	4	625	8.6
Adrian Smith	66	1524	234	576	.406	154	197	.782	147	145	164	1	622	9.4
Arlen Bockhorn	70	1670	242	587	.412	96	126	.762	205	173	227	4	580	8.3
Larry Staverman*	60	674	98	212	.462	69	90	.767	176	32	118	3	265	4.4
Bud Olsen	49	513	85	210	.405	32	57	.561	149	29	78	0	202	4.1
Jay Arnette	48	501	71	196	.362	42	54	.778	54	71	105	2	184	3.8
Tom Thacker	48	457	53	181	.293	26	53	.491	115	51	51	0	132	2.8

*Staverman—Played 6 Baltimore, 20 Detroit, 34 Cincinnati.

DETROIT PISTONS

	G	Min.	FGM	FGA	Pct.	FTM	FTA	Pct.	Reb.	Ast.	PF	Dq.	SCORING Pts.	Avg.
Bailey Howell.................	77	2700	598	1267	.472	470	581	.809	776	205	290	9	1666	21.6
Ray Scott	80	2964	539	1307	.412	328	456	.719	1078	244	296	7	1406	17.6
Don Ohl	71	2366	500	1224	.408	225	331	.680	180	225	219	3	1225	17.3
Bob Ferry	74	1522	298	670	.445	186	279	.667	428	94	174	2	782	10.6
Jackie Moreland..............	78	1780	272	639	.426	164	210	.781	405	121	268	9	708	9.1
Willie Jones.................	77	1539	265	680	.390	100	141	.709	253	172	211	5	630	8.2
Donnis Butcher*	78	1971	202	507	.398	159	256	.621	329	244	249	4	563	7.2
Reggie Harding	39	1158	184	460	.400	61	98	.622	410	52	119	1	429	11.0
Eddie Miles	60	811	131	371	.353	62	87	.713	95	58	92	0	324	5.4
Darrall Imhoff	58	871	104	251	.414	69	114	.605	283	56	167	5	277	4.8
Bob Duffy** ....../.......	48	662	94	229	.410	44	65	.677	61	79	48	0	232	4.8
Dave DeBusschere............	15	304	52	133	.391	25	43	.581	105	23	32	1	129	8.6

*Butcher—Played 26 New York, 52 Detroit. **Duffy—Played 2 St. Louis, 4 New York, 42 Detroit.

LOS ANGELES LAKERS

	G	Min.	FGM	FGA	Pct.	FTM	FTA	Pct.	Reb.	Ast.	PF	Dq.	SCORING Pts.	Avg.
Jerry West...................	72	2906	740	1529	.484	584	702	.832	433	403	200	2	2064	28.7
Elgin Baylor.................	78	3164	756	1778	.425	471	586	.804	936	347	235	1	1983	25.4
Dick Barnett.................	78	2620	541	1197	.452	351	454	.773	250	238	233	3	1433	18.4
Rudy LaRusso................	79	2746	337	776	.434	298	397	.751	800	190	268	5	972	12.3
LeRoy Ellis	78	1459	200	473	.423	112	170	.659	498	41	192	3	512	6.6
Don Nelson	80	1406	135	323	.418	149	201	.741	323	76	181	1	419	5.2
Frank Selvy	73	1286	160	423	.378	78	122	.639	139	149	115	1	398	5.5
Gene Wiley	78	1510	146	273	.535	45	75	.600	510	44	225	4	337	4.3
Jim Krebs	68	975	134	357	.375	65	85	.765	283	49	166	6	333	4.9
Jim King	60	762	84	198	.424	66	101	.653	113	110	99	0	234	3.9
Hub Reed	46	386	33	91	.363	10	15	.667	107	23	73	0	76	1.7
Mel Gibson.................	8	53	6	20	.300	1	2	.500	4	6	10	0	13	1.6

NEW YORK KNICKERBOCKERS

	G	Min.	FGM	FGA	Pct.	FTM	FTA	Pct.	Reb.	Ast.	PF	Dq.	SCORING Pts.	Avg.
Len Chappell*	79	2505	531	1185	.448	288	403	.715	771	83	214	1	1350	17.1
Bob Boozer**	81	2379	468	1096	.427	272	376	.723	596	96	231	1	1208	14.9
Johnny Green	80	2134	482	1026	.470	195	392	.497	799	157	246	4	1159	14.5
Art Heyman	75	2236	432	1003	.431	289	422	.685	298	256	229	2	1153	15.4
Bill McGill***	74	1784	456	937	.487	204	282	.723	414	121	217	7	1116	15.1
Johnny Egan****	66	2325	334	758	.441	193	243	.794	191	358	181	3	861	13.0
Tom Gola...................	74	2156	258	602	.429	154	212	.726	469	257	278	7	670	9.1
Al Butler	76	1379	260	616	.422	138	187	.738	168	157	167	3	658	8.7
John Rudometkin	52	696	154	326	.472	87	116	.750	164	26	86	0	395	7.6
Dave Budd..................	73	1031	128	297	.431	84	115	.730	276	57	130	1	340	4.7
Tom Hoover.................	59	988	102	247	.413	81	132	.614	331	36	185	4	285	4.8
Gene Conley	46	551	74	189	.392	44	65	.677	156	21	124	2	192	4.2
Jerry Harkness	5	59	13	30	.433	3	8	.375	6	6	4	0	29	5.8

*Chappell—Played 1 Philadelphia, 78 New York. **Boozer—Played 32 Cincinnati, 49 New York. ***McGill—Played 6 Baltimore, 68 New York.
****Egan—Played 24 Detroit, 42 New York.

PHILADELPHIA 76ERS

	G	Min.	FGM	FGA	Pct.	FTM	FTA	Pct.	Reb.	Ast.	PF	Dq.	SCORING Pts.	Avg.
Hal Greer...................	80	3157	715	1611	.444	435	525	.829	484	374	291	6	1865	23.3
Red Kerr	80	2938	536	1250	.429	268	357	.751	1017	275	187	2	1340	16.8
Chet Walker.................	76	2775	492	1118	.440	330	464	.711	784	124	232	3	1314	17.3
Paul Neumann...............	74	1973	324	732	.443	210	266	.789	246	291	211	1	858	11.6

	G	Min.	FGM	FGA	Pct.	FTM	FTA	Pct.	Reb.	Ast.	PF	Dq.	Pts.	Avg.
Ben Warley	79	1740	215	494	.435	220	305	.721	619	71	274	5	650	8.2
Al Bianchi	78	1437	257	684	.376	109	141	.773	147	149	248	6	623	8.0
Lee Shaffer	41	1013	217	587	.370	102	133	.767	205	36	116	1	536	13.1
Larry Costello	45	1137	191	408	.468	147	170	.865	105	167	150	3	529	11.8
Connie Dierking	76	1286	191	514	.372	114	169	.675	422	50	221	3	496	6.5
Dave Gambee	41	927	149	378	.394	151	185	.816	256	35	161	6	449	11.0
Dolph Schayes	24	350	44	143	.308	46	57	.807	110	48	76	3	134	5.6
Jerry Greenspan	20	280	32	90	.356	34	50	.680	72	11	54	0	98	4.9
Hubie White	23	196	31	105	.295	17	28	.607	42	12	28	0	79	3.4

ST. LOUIS HAWKS

	G	Min.	FGM	FGA	Pct.	FTM	FTA	Pct.	Reb.	Ast.	PF	Dq.	Pts.	Avg.
Bob Pettit	80	3296	791	1708	.463	608	771	.789	1224	259	300	3	2190	27.4
Cliff Hagan	77	2279	572	1280	.447	269	331	.813	377	193	273	4	1413	18.4
Richie Guerin*	80	2366	351	846	.415	347	424	.818	256	375	276	4	1049	13.1
Lenny Wilkens	78	2526	334	808	.413	270	365	.740	335	359	287	7	938	12.0
Zelmo Beaty	59	1922	287	647	.444	200	270	.741	633	79	262	11	774	13.1
Bill Bridges	80	1949	268	675	.397	146	224	.652	680	181	269	6	682	8.5
Charles Vaughn	68	1340	238	538	.442	107	148	.723	126	129	166	0	583	8.6
John Barnhill	74	1367	208	505	.412	70	115	.609	157	145	107	0	486	6.6
Mike Farmer	76	1361	178	438	.406	68	83	.819	225	109	140	0	424	5.6
Gene Tormohlen	51	640	94	250	.376	22	46	.478	216	50	128	3	210	4.1
Bob Nordmann**	19	259	27	66	.409	9	19	.474	65	5	51	1	63	3.3
Gerry Ward	24	139	16	53	.302	11	17	.647	21	21	26	0	43	1.8
Ken Rohloff	2	7	0	1	.000	0	0	...	0	1	4	0	0	0.0

*Guerin—Played 2 New York, 78 St. Louis.
**Nordmann—Played 7 New York, 12 St. Louis.

SAN FRANCISCO WARRIORS

	G	Min.	FGM	FGA	Pct.	FTM	FTA	Pct.	Reb.	Ast.	PF	Dq.	Pts.	Avg.
Wilt Chamberlain	80	3689	1204	2298	.524	540	1016	.531	1787	403	182	0	2948	36.9
Tom Meschery	80	2422	436	951	.458	207	295	.702	612	149	288	6	1079	13.5
Wayne Hightower	79	2536	393	1022	.385	260	329	.790	566	133	269	7	1046	13.2
Guy Rodgers	79	2695	337	923	.365	198	280	.707	328	556	245	4	872	11.0
Al Attles	70	1883	289	640	.452	185	275	.673	236	197	249	4	763	10.9
Gary Phillips	66	2010	256	691	.370	146	218	.670	248	203	245	8	658	10.0
Nate Thurmond	76	1066	210	554	.395	95	173	.549	790	86	184	2	533	7.0
Gary Hill	67	1015	146	384	.380	51	77	.662	114	103	165	2	343	5.1
George Lee	54	522	64	169	.379	47	71	.662	97	25	67	0	175	3.2
Kenny Sears	51	519	53	120	.442	64	79	.810	94	42	71	0	170	3.3
John Windsor	11	68	10	27	.370	7	8	.875	26	2	13	0	27	2.5

1963-64

PLAYOFF RESULTS

EASTERN DIVISION

SEMIFINALS

Cincinnati 3, Philadelphia 2

Mar. 22—Sun.	Philadelphia 102 at Cincinnati	127
Mar. 24—Tue.	Cincinnati 114 at Philadelphia	122
Mar. 25—Wed.	Philadelphia 89 at Cincinnati	101
Mar. 28—Sat.	Cincinnati 120 at Philadelphia	129
Mar. 29—Sun.	Philadelphia 124 at Cincinnati	130

FINALS

Boston 4, Cincinnati 1

Mar. 31—Tue.	Cincinnati 87 at Boston	103
Apr. 2—Thur.	Cincinnati 90 at Boston	101
Apr. 5—Sun.	Boston 102 at Cincinnati	92
Apr. 7—Tue.	Boston 93 at Cincinnati	102
Apr. 9—Thur.	Cincinnati 95 at Boston	109

WESTERN DIVISION

SEMIFINALS

St. Louis 3, Los Angeles 2

Mar. 21—Sat.	Los Angeles 104 at St. Louis	115
Mar. 22—Sun.	Los Angeles 90 at St. Louis	106
Mar. 25—Wed.	St. Louis 105 at Los Angeles	107
Mar. 28—Sat.	St. Louis 88 at Los Angeles	97
Mar. 30—Mon.	Los Angeles 108 at St. Louis	121

FINALS

San Francisco 4, St. Louis 3

Apr. 1—Wed.	St. Louis 116 at San Francisco	111
Apr. 3—Fri.	St. Louis 105 at San Francisco	120
Apr. 5—Sun.	San Francisco 109 at St. Louis	113
Apr. 8—Wed.	San Francisco 111 at St. Louis	109
Apr. 10—Fri.	St. Louis 97 at San Francisco	121
Apr. 12—Sun.	San Francisco 95 at St. Louis	123
Apr. 16—Thur.	St. Louis 95 at San Francisco	105

NBA FINALS

Boston 4, San Francisco 1

Apr. 18—Sat.	San Francisco 96 at Boston	108
Apr. 20—Mon.	San Francisco 101 at Boston	124
Apr. 22—Wed.	Boston 91 at San Francisco	115
Apr. 24—Fri.	Boston 98 at San Francisco	95
Apr. 26—Sun.	San Francisco 99 at Boston	105

1962-63

1962-63 NBA CHAMPION BOSTON CELTICS
Front row (from left): K.C. Jones, Bill Russell, president Walter A. Brown, head coach Red Auerbach, treasurer Lou Pieri, captain Bob Cousy, Sam Jones. Back row (from left): Frank Ramsey, Gene Guarilia, Tom Sanders, Tom Heinsohn, Clyde Lovellette, John Havlicek, Jim Loscutoff, Dan Swartz, trainer Buddy LeRoux.

FINAL STANDINGS

EASTERN DIVISION

	Bos.	Syr.	Cin.	N.Y.	L.A.	St.L.	Det.	S.F.	Chi.	W	L	Pct.	GB
Boston	..	6	9	10	4	5	8	8	8	58	22	.725	..
Syracuse	6	..	5	10	4	4	6	5	8	48	32	.600	10
Cincinnati	3	7	..	10	3	3	4	6	6	42	38	.525	16
New York	2	2	2	..	3	3	1	2	6	21	59	.263	37

WESTERN DIVISION

	Bos.	Syr.	Cin.	N.Y.	L.A.	St.L.	Det.	S.F.	Chi.	W	L	Pct.	GB
Los Angeles	5	4	6	5	..	7	11	8	7	53	27	.663	..
St. Louis	3	5	5	6	5	..	8	9	7	48	32	.600	5
Detroit	0	3	4	8	1	4	..	7	7	34	46	.425	19
San Francisco	1	3	3	6	4	3	5	..	6	31	49	.388	22
Chicago	2	2	4	4	3	3	3	4	..	25	55	.313	28

TEAM STATISTICS

	G	FGM	FGA	Pct.	FTM	FTA	Pct.	Reb.	Ast.	PF	Dq.	AVERAGE POINTS For	AVERAGE POINTS Agst.	AVERAGE POINTS Dif.
Boston	80	3746	8779	.427	2012	2777	.725	5818	1960	2090	30	118.8	111.6	+7.2
Syracuse	80	3690	8290	.445	2350	3005	.782	5516	1742	2277	33	121.6	117.8	+3.8
Los Angeles	80	3506	7948	.441	2230	2931	.761	5282	1739	1775	18	115.5	112.4	+3.1
St. Louis	80	3355	7780	.431	2056	2820	.729	5096	1902	2077	35	109.6	107.8	+1.8
Cincinnati	80	3672	7998	.459	2183	2923	.747	5561	1931	2203	39	119.0	117.8	+1.2
San Francisco	80	3805	8449	.450	1870	2797	.669	5359	1906	1882	45	118.5	120.6	-2.1
Detroit	80	3534	8188	.432	2044	2852	.717	5315	1731	2181	40	113.9	117.6	-3.7
Chicago	80	3371	7448	.453	2053	2944	.697	5145	1773	2065	33	109.9	113.9	-4.0
New York	80	3433	8007	.429	1971	2778	.710	4952	1658	2144	49	110.5	117.7	-7.2
Avgs.	80	3568	8099	.441	2085	2870	.726	5338	1816	2077	35.8	115.3	...	...

HOME/ROAD/NEUTRAL

	Home	Road	Neutral	Total		Home	Road	Neutral	Total
Boston	25-5	21-16	12-1	58-22	New York	12-22	5-28	4-9	21-59
Chicago	17-17	3-23	5-15	25-55	St. Louis	30-7	13-18	5-7	48-32
Cincinnati	23-10	15-19	4-9	42-38	San Francisco	13-20	11-25	7-4	31-49
Detroit	14-16	8-19	12-11	34-46	Syracuse	23-5	13-19	12-8	48-32
Los Angeles	27-7	20-17	6-3	53-27	Totals	184-109	109-184	67-67	360-360

POINTS

	G	FGM	FTM	Pts.	Avg.
Wilt Chamberlain, San Francisco	.80	1463	660	3586	44.8
Elgin Baylor, Los Angeles	.80	1029	661	2719	34.0
Oscar Robertson, Cincinnati	.80	825	614	2264	28.3
Bob Pettit, St. Louis	.79	778	685	2241	28.4
Walt Bellamy, Chicago	.80	840	553	2233	27.9
Bailey Howell, Detroit	.79	637	519	1793	22.7
Richie Guerin, New York	.79	596	509	1701	21.5
Jack Twyman, Cincinnati	.80	641	304	1586	19.8
Hal Greer, Syracuse	.80	600	362	1562	19.5
Don Ohl, Detroit	.80	636	275	1547	19.3
Sam Jones, Boston	.76	621	257	1499	19.7
Jerry West, Los Angeles	.55	559	371	1489	27.1
Lee Shaffer, Syracuse	.80	597	294	1488	18.6
Terry Dischinger, Chicago	.57	525	402	1452	25.5
John Green, New York	.80	582	280	1444	18.1
Tom Heinsohn, Boston	.76	550	340	1440	18.9
Dick Barnett, Los Angeles	.80	547	343	1437	18.0
Wayne Embry, Cincinnati	.76	534	343	1411	18.6
Bill Russell, Boston	.78	511	287	1309	16.8
Red Kerr, Syracuse	.80	507	241	1255	15.7

FIELD GOALS

(minimum 210 made)

	FGM	FGA	Pct.
Wilt Chamberlain, San Francisco	1463	2770	.528
Walt Bellamy, Chicago	.840	1595	.527
Oscar Robertson, Cincinnati	.825	1593	.518
Bailey Howell, Detroit	.637	1235	.516
Terry Dischinger, Chicago	.525	1026	.512
Dave Budd, New York	.294	596	.493
Jack Twyman, Cincinnati	.641	1335	.480
Al Attles, San Francisco	.301	630	.478
Sam Jones, Boston	.621	1305	.476
Red Kerr, Syracuse	.507	1069	.474

FREE THROWS

(minimum 210 made)

	FTM	FTA	Pct.
Larry Costello, Syracuse	.288	327	.881
Richie Guerin, New York	.509	600	.848
Elgin Baylor, Los Angeles	.661	790	.837
Tom Heinsohn, Boston	.340	407	.835
Hal Greer, Syracuse	.362	434	.834
Frank Ramsey, Boston	.271	332	.816
Dick Barnett, Los Angeles	.343	421	.815
Jack Twyman, Cincinnati	.304	375	.811
Adrian Smith, Cincinnati	.223	275	.811
Oscar Robertson, Cincinnati	.614	758	.810

ASSISTS

	G	No.	Avg.
Guy Rodgers, San Francisco	.79	825	10.4
Oscar Robertson, Cincinnati	.80	758	9.5
Bob Cousy, Boston	.76	515	6.8
Sihugo Green, Chicago	.73	422	5.8
Elgin Baylor, Los Angeles	.80	386	4.8
Lenny Wilkens, St. Louis	.75	381	5.1
Bill Russell, Boston	.78	348	4.5
Richie Guerin, New York	.79	348	4.4
Larry Costello, Syracuse	.78	334	4.3
John Barnhill, St. Louis	.77	322	4.2

REBOUNDS

	G	No.	Avg.
Wilt Chamberlain, San Francisco	.80	1946	24.3
Bill Russell, Boston	.78	1843	23.6
Walt Bellamy, Chicago	.80	1309	16.4
Bob Pettit, St. Louis	.79	1191	15.1
Elgin Baylor, Los Angeles	.80	1146	14.3
Red Kerr, Syracuse	.80	1039	13.0
John Green, New York	.80	964	12.1
Wayne Embry, Cincinnati	.76	936	12.3
Bailey Howell, Detroit	.79	910	11.5
Bob Boozer, Cincinnati	.79	878	11.1

1962-63

BOSTON CELTICS

SCORING

	G	Min.	FGM	FGA	Pct.	FTM	FTA	Pct.	Reb.	Ast.	PF	Dq.	Pts.	Avg.
Sam Jones	76	2323	621	1305	.476	257	324	.793	396	241	162	1	1499	19.7
Tom Heinsohn	76	2004	550	1300	.423	340	407	.835	569	95	270	4	1440	18.9
Bill Russell	78	3500	511	1182	.432	287	517	.555	1843	348	189	1	1309	16.8
John Havlicek	80	2200	483	1085	.445	174	239	.728	534	179	189	2	1140	14.3
Bob Cousy	76	1975	392	988	.397	219	298	.735	193	515	175	0	1003	13.2
Tom Sanders	80	2148	339	744	.456	186	252	.738	576	95	262	5	864	10.8
Frank Ramsey	77	1541	284	743	.382	271	332	.816	288	95	259	13	839	10.9
K.C. Jones	79	1945	230	591	.389	112	177	.633	263	317	221	3	572	7.2
Clyde Lovellette	61	568	161	376	.428	73	98	.745	177	95	137	0	395	6.5
Jim Loscutoff	63	607	94	251	.375	22	42	.524	157	25	126	1	210	3.3
Dan Swartz	39	335	57	150	.380	61	72	.847	88	21	92	0	175	4.5
Gene Guarilia	11	83	11	38	.289	4	11	.364	14	2	5	0	26	2.4

CHICAGO ZEPHYRS

SCORING

	G	Min.	FGM	FGA	Pct.	FTM	FTA	Pct.	Reb.	Ast.	PF	Dq.	Pts.	Avg.
Walt Bellamy	80	3306	840	1595	.527	553	821	.674	1309	233	283	7	2233	27.9
Terry Dischinger	57	2294	525	1026	.512	402	522	.770	458	175	188	2	1452	25.5
Sihugo Green	73	2648	322	783	.411	209	306	.683	335	422	274	5	853	11.7
Charles Hardnett	78	1657	301	683	.441	225	349	.645	602	74	225	4	827	10.6
Johnny Cox	73	1685	239	568	.421	95	135	.704	280	142	149	4	573	7.8
Bill McGill	60	590	181	353	.513	80	119	.672	161	38	118	1	442	7.4
Don Nelson	62	1071	129	293	.440	161	221	.729	279	72	136	3	419	6.8
Barney Cable*	61	1200	173	380	.455	62	96	.646	242	82	136	0	408	6.7
Larry Staverman	33	602	94	194	.485	49	62	.790	158	43	94	3	237	7.2
Mel Nowell	39	589	92	237	.388	48	66	.727	67	84	86	0	232	5.9
Bob Leonard	32	879	84	245	.343	59	85	.694	68	143	84	1	227	7.1
Maurice King	37	954	94	241	.390	28	34	.824	102	142	87	0	216	5.8
Nick Mantis**	32	684	94	244	.385	27	49	.551	85	83	94	0	215	6.7
Al Ferrari	18	138	12	37	.324	14	17	.824	12	14	21	0	38	2.1
Jeff Slade	3	20	2	5	.400	0	1	.000	7	0	3	0	4	1.3
Ralph Wells	3	48	1	7	.143	0	7	.000	6	7	6	0	2	0.7

*Cable—Played 42 St. Louis, 19 Chicago. **Mantis—Played 9 St. Louis, 23 Chicago.

CINCINNATI ROYALS

	G	Min.	FGM	FGA	Pct.	FTM	FTA	Pct.	Reb.	Ast.	PF	Dq.	Pts.	Avg.
Oscar Robertson	80	3521	825	1593	.518	614	758	.810	835	758	293	1	2264	28.3
Jack Twyman	80	2623	641	1335	.480	304	375	.811	598	214	286	7	1586	19.8
Wayne Embry	76	2511	534	1165	.458	343	514	.667	936	177	286	7	1411	18.6
Bob Boozer	79	2488	449	992	.453	252	353	.714	878	102	299	8	1150	14.6
Arlen Bockhorn	80	2612	375	954	.393	183	242	.756	322	261	260	6	933	11.7
Tom Hawkins	79	1721	299	635	.471	147	241	.610	543	100	197	2	745	9.4
Adrian Smith	79	1522	241	544	.443	223	275	.811	174	141	157	1	705	8.9
Hub Reed	80	1299	199	427	.466	74	98	.755	398	83	261	7	472	5.9
Dave Piontek	48	457	60	158	.380	10	16	.625	96	26	67	0	130	2.7
Bud Olsen	52	373	43	133	.323	27	39	.692	105	42	78	0	113	2.2
Dan Tieman	29	176	15	57	.263	4	10	.400	22	27	18	0	34	1.2
Joe Buckhalter	2	12	0	5	.000	2	2	1.000	3	0	1	0	2	1.0

DETROIT PISTONS

	G	Min.	FGM	FGA	Pct.	FTM	FTA	Pct.	Reb.	Ast.	PF	Dq.	Pts.	Avg.
Bailey Howell	79	2971	637	1235	.516	519	650	.798	910	232	300	9	1793	22.7
Don Ohl	80	2961	636	1450	.439	275	380	.724	239	325	234	3	1547	19.3
Ray Scott	76	2538	460	1110	.414	308	457	.674	772	191	263	9	1228	16.2
Bob Ferry	79	2479	426	984	.433	220	339	.649	537	170	246	1	1072	13.6
Dave DeBusschere	80	2352	406	944	.430	206	287	.718	694	207	247	2	1018	12.7
Willie Jones	79	1470	305	730	.418	118	164	.720	233	188	207	4	728	9.2
Jackie Moreland	78	1516	271	622	.436	145	214	.678	449	114	226	5	687	8.8
Kevin Loughery	57	845	146	397	.368	71	100	.710	109	104	135	1	363	6.4
Johnny Egan	46	752	110	296	.372	53	69	.768	59	114	70	0	273	5.9
Walter Dukes	62	913	83	255	.325	101	137	.737	360	55	183	5	267	4.3
Darrall Imhoff	45	458	48	153	.314	24	50	.480	155	28	66	1	120	2.7
Danny Doyle	4	25	6	12	.500	4	5	.800	8	3	4	0	16	4.0

LOS ANGELES LAKERS

	G	Min.	FGM	FGA	Pct.	FTM	FTA	Pct.	Reb.	Ast.	PF	Dq.	Pts.	Avg.
Elgin Baylor	80	3370	1029	2273	.453	661	790	.837	1146	386	226	1	2719	34.0
Jerry West	55	2163	559	1213	.461	371	477	.778	384	307	150	1	1489	27.1
Dick Barnett	80	2544	547	1162	.471	343	421	.815	242	224	189	3	1437	18.0
Rudy LaRusso	75	2505	321	761	.422	282	393	.718	747	187	255	5	924	12.3
Frank Selvy	80	2369	317	747	.424	192	269	.714	289	281	149	0	826	10.3
Jim Krebs	79	1913	272	627	.434	115	154	.747	502	87	256	2	659	8.3
LeRoy Ellis	80	1628	222	530	.419	133	202	.658	518	46	194	1	577	7.2
Rod Hundley	65	785	88	262	.336	84	119	.706	106	151	81	0	260	4.0
Gene Wiley	75	1488	109	236	.462	23	68	.338	504	40	180	4	241	3.2
Ron Horn	28	289	27	82	.329	20	29	.690	71	10	46	0	74	2.6
Howie Jolliff	28	293	15	55	.273	6	9	.667	62	20	49	1	36	1.3

NEW YORK KNICKERBOCKERS

	G	Min.	FGM	FGA	Pct.	FTM	FTA	Pct.	Reb.	Ast.	PF	Dq.	Pts.	Avg.
Richie Guerin	79	2712	596	1380	.432	509	600	.848	331	348	228	2	1701	21.5
Johnny Green	80	2553	582	1261	.462	280	439	.638	964	152	243	5	1444	18.1
Gene Shue	78	2288	354	894	.396	208	302	.689	191	259	171	0	916	11.7
Tom Gola*	73	2670	363	791	.459	170	219	.776	517	298	295	9	896	12.3
Dave Budd	78	1725	294	596	.493	151	202	.748	395	87	204	3	739	9.5
Al Butler	74	1488	297	676	.439	144	187	.770	170	156	145	3	738	10.0
Gene Conley	70	1544	254	651	.390	122	186	.656	469	70	263	10	630	9.0
Donnis Butcher	68	1193	172	424	.406	131	194	.675	180	138	164	1	475	7.0
Paul Hogue	50	1340	152	419	.363	79	174	.454	430	42	220	12	383	7.7
Bob Nordmann**	53	1000	156	319	.489	59	122	.484	316	47	156	6	371	7.0
John Rudometkin	56	572	108	307	.352	73	95	.768	149	30	58	0	289	5.2
Tom Stith	25	209	37	110	.336	3	10	.300	39	18	23	0	77	3.1
Jack Foley***	11	83	20	51	.392	13	15	.867	16	5	8	0	53	4.8
Cleveland Buckner	6	27	5	10	.500	2	4	.500	4	5	6	0	12	2.0

*Gola—Played 21 San Francisco, 52 New York.
**Nordmann—Played 27 St. Louis, 26 New York.
***Foley—Played 5 Boston, 6 New York.

ST. LOUIS HAWKS

	G	Min.	FGM	FGA	Pct.	FTM	FTA	Pct.	Reb.	Ast.	PF	Dq.	Pts.	Avg.
Bob Pettit	79	3090	778	1746	.446	685	885	.774	1191	245	282	8	2241	28.4
Cliff Hagan	79	1716	491	1055	.465	244	305	.800	341	193	211	2	1226	15.5
John Barnhill	77	2692	360	838	.430	181	255	.710	359	322	168	0	901	11.7
Lenny Wilkens	75	2569	333	834	.399	222	319	.696	403	381	256	6	888	11.8
Woody Sauldsberry*	77	2034	366	966	.379	107	163	.656	447	78	241	4	839	10.9
Zelmo Beaty	80	1918	297	677	.439	220	307	.717	665	85	312	12	814	10.2
Charles Vaughn	77	1845	295	708	.417	188	261	.720	258	252	201	3	778	10.1
Mike Farmer	80	1724	239	562	.425	117	139	.842	369	143	155	0	595	7.4
Phil Jordon	73	1420	211	527	.400	56	101	.554	319	103	172	3	478	6.5
Bill Bridges	27	374	66	160	.413	32	51	.627	144	23	58	0	164	6.1

1962-63

	G	Min.	FGM	FGA	Pct.	FTM	FTA	Pct.	Reb.	Ast.	PF	Dq.	Pts.	Avg.
Bob Duffy	42	435	66	174	.379	22	39	.564	39	83	42	0	154	3.7
Gene Tormohlen	7	47	5	10	.500	2	10	.200	15	5	11	0	12	1.7

*Sauldsberry—Played 54 Chicago, 23 St. Louis.

SAN FRANCISCO WARRIORS

	G	Min.	FGM	FGA	Pct.	FTM	FTA	Pct.	Reb.	Ast.	PF	Dq.	SCORING Pts.	Avg.
Wilt Chamberlain	80	3806	1463	2770	.528	660	1113	.593	1946	275	136	0	3586	44.8
Guy Rodgers	79	3249	445	1150	.387	208	286	.727	394	825	296	7	1098	13.9
Tom Meschery	64	2245	397	935	.425	228	313	.728	624	104	249	11	1022	16.0
Willie Naulls*	70	1901	370	887	.417	166	207	.802	515	102	205	3	906	12.9
Al Attles	71	1876	301	630	.478	133	206	.646	205	184	253	7	735	10.4
Gary Phillips	75	1801	256	643	.398	97	152	.638	225	137	185	7	609	8.1
Wayne Hightower	66	1387	192	543	.354	105	157	.669	354	51	181	5	489	7.4
Kenny Sears**	77	1141	161	304	.530	131	168	.780	206	95	128	0	453	5.9
George Lee	64	1192	149	394	.378	152	193	.788	217	64	113	0	450	7.0
Howie Montgomery	20	364	65	153	.425	14	23	.609	69	21	35	1	144	7.2
Hubie White	29	271	40	111	.360	12	18	.667	35	28	47	0	92	3.2
Fred LaCour	16	171	28	73	.384	9	16	.563	24	19	27	0	65	4.1
Ted Luckenbill	20	201	26	68	.382	9	20	.450	56	8	34	0	61	3.1
Dave Fedor	7	27	3	10	.300	0	1	.000	6	1	4	0	6	0.9
Dave Gunther	1	5	1	2	.500	0	0	. . .	3	3	1	0	2	2.0

*Naulls—Played 23 New York, 47 San Francisco.
**Sears—Played 23 New York, 54 San Francisco.

SYRACUSE NATIONALS

	G	Min.	FGM	FGA	Pct.	FTM	FTA	Pct.	Reb.	Ast.	PF	Dq.	SCORING Pts.	Avg.
Hal Greer	80	2631	600	1293	.464	362	434	.834	457	275	286	4	1562	19.5
Lee Shaffer	80	2392	597	1393	.429	294	375	.784	524	97	249	5	1488	18.6
Red Kerr	80	2561	507	1069	.474	241	320	.753	1039	214	208	3	1255	15.7
Chet Walker	78	1992	352	751	.469	253	362	.699	561	83	220	3	957	12.3
Larry Costello	78	2066	285	660	.432	288	327	.881	237	334	263	4	858	11.0
Len Chappell	80	1241	281	604	.465	148	238	.622	461	56	171	1	710	8.9
Dave Gambee	60	1234	255	537	.438	199	238	.836	289	48	190	2	669	11.2
Paul Neumann	80	1581	237	503	.471	181	222	.815	200	227	221	5	655	8.2
Dolph Schayes	66	1438	223	575	.388	181	206	.879	375	175	177	2	627	9.5
Al Bianchi	61	1159	202	476	.424	120	164	.732	134	170	165	2	524	8.6
Joe Roberts	33	466	73	196	.372	35	51	.686	155	16	66	1	181	5.5
Bon Warley	26	206	50	111	.450	25	35	.714	86	4	42	1	125	4.8
Porter Meriwether	31	268	48	122	.393	23	33	.697	29	43	19	0	119	3.8

PLAYOFF RESULTS

EASTERN DIVISION

SEMIFINALS

Cincinnati 3, Syracuse 2
Mar. 19—Tue.	Cincinnati 120 at Syracuse	123
Mar. 21—Thur.	Syracuse 115 at Cincinnati	133
Mar. 23—Sat.	Cincinnati 117 at Syracuse	121
Mar. 24—Sun.	Syracuse 118 at Cincinnati	125
Mar. 26—Tue.	Cincinnati 131 at Syracuse	*127

FINALS

Boston 4, Cincinnati 3
Mar. 28—Thur.	Cincinnati 135 at Boston	132
Mar. 29—Fri.	Boston 125 at Cincinnati	102
Mar. 31—Sun.	Cincinnati 121 at Boston	116
Apr. 3—Wed.	Boston 128 at Cincinnati	110
Apr. 6—Sat.	Cincinnati 120 at Boston	125
Apr. 7—Sun.	Boston 99 at Cincinnati	109
Apr. 10—Wed.	Cincinnati 131 at Boston	142

WESTERN DIVISION

SEMIFINALS

St. Louis 3, Detroit 1
Mar. 20—Wed.	Detroit 99 at St. Louis	118
Mar. 22—Fri.	Detroit 108 at St. Louis	122
Mar. 24—Sun.	St. Louis 103 at Detroit	107
Mar. 26—Tue.	St. Louis 104 at Detroit	100

FINALS

Los Angeles 4, St. Louis 3
Mar. 31—Sun.	St. Louis 104 at Los Angeles	112
Apr. 2—Tue.	St. Louis 99 at Los Angeles	101
Apr. 4—Thur.	Los Angeles 112 at St. Louis	125
Apr. 6—Sat.	Los Angeles 114 at St. Louis	124
Apr. 7—Sun.	St. Louis 100 at Los Angeles	123
Apr. 9—Tue.	Los Angeles 113 at St. Louis	121
Apr. 11—Thur.	St. Louis 100 at Los Angeles	115

NBA FINALS

Boston 4, Los Angeles 2
Apr. 14—Sun.	Los Angeles 114 at Boston	117
Apr. 16—Tue.	Los Angeles 106 at Boston	113
Apr. 17—Wed.	Boston 99 at Los Angeles	119
Apr. 19—Fri.	Boston 108 at Los Angeles	105
Apr. 21—Sun.	Los Angeles 126 at Boston	119
Apr. 24—Wed.	Boston 112 at Los Angeles	109

*Denotes number of overtime periods.

1962-63

1961-62

1961-62 NBA CHAMPION BOSTON CELTICS
Front row (from left): K.C. Jones, Gary Phillips, president Walter A. Brown, head coach Red Auerbach, treasurer Lou Pieri, captain Bob Cousy, Sam Jones. Back row (from left): Frank Ramsey, Tom Sanders, Tom Heinsohn, Bill Russell, Gene Guarilia, Jim Loscutoff, Carl Braun, trainer Buddy LeRoux.

FINAL STANDINGS

EASTERN DIVISION

	Bos.	Phi.	Syr.	N.Y.	L.A.	Cin.	Det.	St.L.	Chi.	W	L	Pct.	GB
Boston	..	8	10	8	6	7	5	7	9	60	20	.750	..
Philadelphia	4	..	6	8	3	5	7	6	10	49	31	.613	11
Syracuse	2	6	..	9	2	4	5	4	9	41	39	.513	19
New York	4	4	3	..	2	4	4	4	4	29	51	.363	31

WESTERN DIVISION

	Bos.	Phi.	Syr.	N.Y.	L.A.	Cin.	Det.	St.L.	Chi.	W	L	Pct.	GB
Los Angeles	3	6	6	6	..	7	8	10	8	54	26	.675	..
Cincinnati	1	3	5	5	5	..	6	9	9	43	37	.538	11
Detroit	3	1	4	5	4	6	..	7	7	37	43	.463	17
St. Louis	2	3	4	4	2	3	5	..	6	29	51	.363	25
Chicago	1	0	1	6	2	1	3	4	..	18	62	.225	36

TEAM STATISTICS

	G	FGM	FGA	Pct.	FTM	FTA	Pct.	Reb.	Ast.	PF	Dq.	For	Agst.	Dif.
Boston	80	3855	9109	.423	1977	2715	.728	6080	2049	1909	28	121.1	111.9	+9.2
Philadelphia	80	3917	8929	.439	2201	3207	.686	5939	2073	2013	71	125.4	122.7	+2.7
Syracuse	80	3706	8875	.418	2246	2880	.780	5764	1791	2344	53	120.7	118.4	+2.3
Cincinnati	80	3806	8414	.452	2233	2969	.752	5665	2154	2081	31	123.1	121.3	+1.8
Los Angeles	80	3552	8315	.427	2378	3240	.734	5600	1878	2057	39	118.5	120.0	-1.5
Detroit	80	3472	8366	.415	2290	3142	.729	5823	1723	2040	46	115.4	117.1	-1.7
St. Louis	80	3641	8461	.430	2226	2939	.757	5557	1996	2166	51	118.9	122.1	-3.2
New York	80	3638	8696	.418	1911	2693	.710	5440	1765	2056	39	114.8	119.7	-4.9
Chicago	80	3461	8405	.412	1952	2901	.673	5547	1802	1954	30	110.9	119.4	-8.5
Avgs.	80	3672	8619	.426	2157	2965	.727	5713	1915	2069	43.1	118.8	...	...

The "AVERAGE POINTS" heading spans the For, Agst., and Dif. columns.

HOME/ROAD/NEUTRAL

	Home	Road	Neutral	Total		Home	Road	Neutral	Total
Boston	23-5	26-12	11-3	60-20	New York	19-14	2-23	8-14	29-51
Chicago	9-19	3-20	6-23	18-62	Philadelphia	18-11	18-19	13-1	49-31
Cincinnati	18-13	14-16	11-8	43-37	St. Louis	19-16	7-27	3-8	29-51
Detroit	16-14	8-17	13-12	37-43	Syracuse	18-10	11-19	12-10	41-39
Los Angeles	26-5	18-13	10-8	54-26	Totals	166-107	107-166	87-87	360-360

POINTS

	G	FGM	FTM	Pts.	Avg.
Wilt Chamberlain, Philadelphia	.80	1597	835	4029	50.4
Walt Bellamy, Chicago	.79	973	549	2495	31.6
Oscar Robertson, Cincinnati	.79	866	700	2432	30.8
Bob Pettit, St. Louis	.78	867	695	2429	31.1
Jerry West, Los Angeles	.75	799	712	2310	30.8
Richie Guerin, New York	.78	839	625	2303	29.5
Willie Naulls, New York	.75	747	383	1877	25.0
Elgin Baylor, Los Angeles	.48	680	476	1836	38.3
Jack Twyman, Cincinnati	.80	739	353	1831	22.9
Cliff Hagan, St. Louis	.77	701	362	1764	22.9
Tom Heinsohn, Boston	.79	692	358	1742	22.1
Paul Arizin, Philadelphia	.78	611	484	1706	21.9
Hal Greer, Syracuse	.71	644	331	1619	22.8
Bailey Howell, Detroit	.79	553	470	1576	19.9
Gene Shue, Detroit	.80	580	362	1522	19.0
Wayne Embry, Cincinnati	.75	564	356	1484	19.8
Bill Russell, Boston	.76	575	286	1436	18.9
Sam Jones, Boston	.78	596	243	1435	18.4
Rudy LaRusso, Los Angeles	.80	516	342	1374	17.2
Dave Gambee, Syracuse	.80	477	384	1338	16.7

FIELD GOALS

(minimum 200 made)

	FGM	FGA	Pct.
Walt Bellamy, Chicago	.973	1875	.519
Wilt Chamberlain, Philadelphia	.1597	3159	.506
Jack Twyman, Cincinnati	.739	1542	.479
Oscar Robertson, Cincinnati	.866	1810	.478
Al Attles, Philadelphia	.343	724	.474
Clyde Lovellette, St. Louis	.341	724	.471
Larry Foust, St. Louis	.204	433	.471
Cliff Hagan, St. Louis	.701	1490	.470
Wayne Embry, Cincinnati	.564	1210	.466
Rudy LaRusso, Los Angeles	.516	1108	.466

FREE THROWS

(minimum 200 made)

	FTM	FTA	Pct.
Dolph Schayes, Syracuse	.286	319	.897
Willie Naulls, New York	.383	455	.842
Larry Costello, Syracuse	.247	295	.837
Cliff Hagan, St. Louis	.362	439	.825
Frank Ramsey, Boston	.334	405	.825
Tom Meschery, Philadelphia	.216	262	.824
Richie Guerin, New York	.625	762	.820
Tom Heinsohn, Boston	.358	437	.819
Hal Greer, Syracuse	.331	404	.819
Sam Jones, Boston	.243	297	.818

ASSISTS

	G	No.	Avg.
Oscar Robertson, Cincinnati	.79	899	11.4
Guy Rodgers, Philadelphia	.80	643	8.0
Bob Cousy, Boston	.75	584	7.8
Richie Guerin, New York	.78	539	6.9
Gene Shue, Detroit	.80	465	5.8
Jerry West, Los Angeles	.75	402	5.4
Frank Selvy, Los Angeles	.79	381	4.8
Bob Leonard, Chicago	.70	378	5.4
Cliff Hagan, St. Louis	.77	370	4.8
Arlen Bockhorn, Cincinnati	.80	366	4.6

REBOUNDS

	G	No.	Avg.
Wilt Chamberlain, Philadelphia	.80	2052	25.7
Bill Russell, Boston	.76	1790	23.6
Walt Bellamy, Chicago	.79	1500	19.0
Bob Pettit, St. Louis	.78	1459	18.7
Red Kerr, Syracuse	.80	1176	14.7
John Green, New York	.80	1066	13.3
Bailey Howell, Detroit	.79	996	12.6
Oscar Robertson, Cincinnati	.79	985	12.5
Wayne Embry, Cincinnati	.75	977	13.0
Elgin Baylor, Los Angeles	.48	892	18.6

BOSTON CELTICS

	G	Min.	FGM	FGA	Pct.	FTM	FTA	Pct.	Reb.	Ast.	PF	Dq.	SCORING Pts.	Avg.
Tom Heinsohn	79	2383	692	1613	.429	358	437	.819	747	165	280	2	1742	22.1
Bill Russell	76	3433	575	1258	.457	286	481	.595	1790	341	207	3	1436	18.9
Sam Jones	78	2388	596	1284	.464	243	297	.818	458	232	149	0	1435	18.4
Frank Ramsey	79	1913	436	1019	.428	334	405	.825	387	109	245	10	1206	15.3
Bob Cousy	75	2114	462	1181	.391	251	333	.754	261	584	135	0	1175	15.7
Tom Sanders	80	2325	350	804	.435	197	263	.749	762	74	279	9	897	11.2
K.C. Jones	80	2054	294	724	.406	147	232	.634	298	343	206	1	735	9.2
Jim Loscutoff	79	1146	188	519	.362	45	84	.536	329	51	185	3	421	5.3
Gary Phillips	67	713	110	310	.355	50	86	.581	107	64	109	0	270	4.0
Carl Braun	48	414	78	207	.377	20	27	.741	50	71	49	0	176	3.7
Gene Guarilia	45	367	61	161	.379	41	64	.641	124	11	56	0	163	3.6

CHICAGO PACKERS

	G	Min.	FGM	FGA	Pct.	FTM	FTA	Pct.	Reb.	Ast.	PF	Dq.	SCORING Pts.	Avg.
Walt Bellamy	79	3344	973	1875	.519	549	853	.644	1500	210	281	6	2495	31.6
Bob Leonard	70	2464	423	1128	.375	279	371	.752	199	378	186	0	1125	16.1
Andy Johnson	71	2193	365	814	.448	284	452	.628	351	228	247	5	1014	14.3
Sihugo Green*	71	2388	341	905	.377	218	311	.701	399	318	226	3	900	12.7
Ralph Davis	77	1992	364	881	.413	71	103	.689	162	247	187	1	799	10.4
Woody Sauldsberry**	63	1765	298	869	.343	79	123	.642	536	90	179	5	675	10.7
Charlie Tyra	78	1606	193	534	.361	133	214	.621	610	86	210	7	519	6.7
Horace Walker	65	1331	149	439	.339	140	193	.725	466	69	194	2	438	6.7
Dave Piontek	45	614	83	225	.369	39	59	.661	155	31	89	1	205	4.6
Jack Turner	42	567	84	221	.380	32	42	.762	85	44	51	0	200	4.8
Howie Carl	31	382	67	201	.333	36	51	.706	39	57	41	1	170	5.5
George Bon Salle	3	9	2	8	.250	0	0	...	2	0	0	0	4	1.3

*Green—Played 14 St. Louis, 57 Chicago.
**Sauldsberry—Played 14 St. Louis, 49 Chicago.

1961-62

CINCINNATI ROYALS

	G	Min.	FGM	FGA	Pct.	FTM	FTA	Pct.	Reb.	Ast.	PF	Dq.	SCORING Pts.	Avg.
Oscar Robertson	79	3503	866	1810	.478	700	872	.803	985	899	258	1	2432	30.8
Jack Twyman	80	2991	739	1542	.479	353	435	.811	638	215	323	5	1831	22.9
Wayne Embry	75	2623	564	1210	.466	356	516	.690	977	182	286	6	1484	19.8
Arlen Bockhorn	80	3062	531	1234	.430	198	251	.789	376	366	280	5	1260	15.8
Bob Boozer	79	2488	410	936	.438	263	372	.707	804	130	275	3	1083	13.7
Adrian Smith	80	1462	202	499	.405	172	222	.775	151	167	101	0	576	7.2
Hub Reed	80	1446	203	460	.441	60	82	.732	440	53	267	9	466	5.8
Joe Buckhalter	63	728	153	334	.458	67	108	.620	262	43	123	1	373	5.9
Bob Nordmann	58	344	51	126	.405	29	57	.509	128	18	81	1	131	2.3
Bob Wiesenhahn	60	326	51	161	.317	17	30	.567	112	23	50	0	119	2.0
Dave Zeller	61	278	36	102	.353	18	24	.750	27	58	37	0	90	1.5

DETROIT PISTONS

	G	Min.	FGM	FGA	Pct.	FTM	FTA	Pct.	Reb.	Ast.	PF	Dq.	SCORING Pts.	Avg.
Bailey Howell	79	2857	553	1193	.464	470	612	.768	996	186	317	10	1576	19.9
Gene Shue	80	3143	580	1422	.408	362	447	.810	372	465	192	1	1522	19.0
Don Ohl	77	2526	555	1250	.444	201	280	.718	267	244	173	2	1311	17.0
Bob Ferry	80	1918	411	939	.438	286	422	.678	503	145	199	2	1108	13.9
Ray Scott	75	2087	370	956	.387	255	388	.657	865	132	232	6	995	13.3
Walter Dukes	77	1896	256	647	.396	208	291	.715	803	125	327	20	720	9.4
George Lee	75	1351	179	500	.358	213	280	.761	349	64	128	1	571	7.6
Jackie Moreland	74	1219	205	487	.421	139	186	.747	427	76	179	2	549	7.4
Willie Jones	69	1006	177	475	.373	64	101	.634	177	115	137	1	418	6.1
Johnny Egan	58	696	128	301	.425	64	84	.762	86	102	64	0	320	5.5
Chuck Noble	26	361	32	113	.283	8	15	.533	43	63	55	1	72	2.8

LOS ANGELES LAKERS

	G	Min.	FGM	FGA	Pct.	FTM	FTA	Pct.	Reb.	Ast.	PF	Dq.	SCORING Pts.	Avg.
Jerry West	75	3087	799	1795	.445	712	926	.769	591	402	173	4	2310	30.8
Elgin Baylor	48	2129	680	1588	.428	476	631	.754	892	222	155	1	1836	38.3
Rudy LaRusso	80	2754	516	1108	.466	342	448	.763	828	179	255	5	1374	17.2
Frank Selvy	79	2806	433	1032	.420	298	404	.738	412	381	232	0	1164	14.7
Jim Krebs	78	2012	312	701	.445	156	208	.750	616	110	290	9	780	10.0
Tom Hawkins	79	1903	289	704	.411	143	222	.644	514	95	244	7	721	9.1
Ray Felix	80	1478	171	398	.430	90	130	.692	473	55	266	6	432	5.4
Rod Hundley	78	1492	173	509	.340	83	127	.654	199	290	129	1	429	5.5
Howie Jolliff	64	1094	104	253	.411	41	78	.526	383	76	175	4	249	3.9
Bob McNeill*	50	441	56	136	.412	26	34	.765	56	89	56	0	138	2.8
Wayne Yates	37	263	31	105	.295	10	22	.455	94	16	72	1	72	1.9
Bobby Smith	3	7	0	1	.000	0	0	...	0	0	1	0	0	0.0

*McNeill—Played 21 Philadelphia, 29 Los Angeles.

NEW YORK KNICKERBOCKERS

	G	Min.	FGM	FGA	Pct.	FTM	FTA	Pct.	Reb.	Ast.	PF	Dq.	SCORING Pts.	Avg.
Richie Guerin	78	3348	839	1897	.442	625	762	.820	501	539	299	3	2303	29.5
Willie Naulls	75	2978	747	1798	.415	383	455	.842	867	192	260	6	1877	25.0
Johnny Green	80	2789	507	1164	.436	261	434	.601	1066	191	265	4	1275	15.9
Phil Jordon	76	2195	403	1028	.392	96	168	.571	482	156	258	7	902	11.9
Al Butler*	59	2016	349	754	.463	129	182	.709	337	205	156	0	827	14.0
Dave Budd	79	1370	188	431	.436	138	231	.597	345	86	162	4	514	6.5
Darrall Imhoff	76	1481	186	482	.386	80	139	.576	470	82	230	10	452	5.9
Cleveland Buckner	62	696	158	367	.431	83	133	.624	236	39	114	1	399	6.4
Whitey Martin	66	1018	95	292	.325	37	55	.673	158	115	158	4	227	3.4
Sam Stith	32	440	59	162	.364	23	38	.605	51	60	55	0	141	4.4
Donnis Butcher	47	479	48	155	.310	42	69	.609	79	51	63	0	138	2.9
George Blaney	36	363	54	142	.380	9	17	.529	36	45	34	0	117	3.3
Bill Smith	9	83	8	33	.242	7	8	.875	16	7	6	0	23	2.6
Ed Burton	8	28	7	14	.500	1	4	.250	5	1	3	0	15	1.9
Doug Kistler	5	13	3	6	.500	2	4	.500	1	0	2	0	8	1.6

*Butler—Played 5 Boston, 54 New York.

PHILADELPHIA WARRIORS

	G	Min.	FGM	FGA	Pct.	FTM	FTA	Pct.	Reb.	Ast.	PF	Dq.	SCORING Pts.	Avg.
Wilt Chamberlain	80	3882	1597	3159	.506	835	1363	.613	2052	192	123	0	4029	50.4
Paul Arizin	78	2785	611	1490	.410	484	601	.805	527	201	307	18	1706	21.9
Tom Meschery	80	2509	375	929	.404	216	262	.824	729	145	330	15	966	12.1
Al Attles	75	2468	343	724	.474	158	267	.592	355	333	279	8	844	11.3
Tom Gola	60	2462	322	765	.421	176	230	.765	587	295	267	16	820	13.7
Guy Rodgers	80	2650	267	749	.356	121	182	.665	348	643	312	12	655	8.2
Ed Conlin	70	963	128	371	.345	66	89	.742	155	85	118	1	322	4.6
York Larese*	59	703	122	327	.373	58	72	.806	77	94	104	0	302	5.1
Ted Luckenbill	67	396	43	120	.358	49	76	.645	110	27	67	0	135	2.0

1961-62

	G	Min.	FGM	FGA	Pct.	FTM	FTA	Pct.	Reb.	Ast.	PF	Dq.	Pts.	Avg.
Joe Ruklick	46	302	48	147	.327	12	26	.462	87	14	56	1	108	2.3
Frank Radovich	37	175	37	93	.398	13	26	.500	51	4	27	0	87	2.4

*Larese—Played 8 Chicago, 51 Philadelphia.

ST. LOUIS HAWKS

	G	Min.	FGM	FGA	Pct.	FTM	FTA	Pct.	Reb.	Ast.	PF	Dq.	Pts.	Avg.
Bob Pettit	78	3282	867	1928	.450	695	901	.771	1459	289	296	4	2429	31.1
Cliff Hagan	77	2786	701	1490	.470	362	439	.825	633	370	282	8	1764	22.9
Clyde Lovellette	40	1192	341	724	.471	155	187	.829	350	68	136	4	837	20.9
Barney Cable*	67	1861	305	749	.407	118	181	.652	563	115	211	4	728	10.9
Shellie McMillon**	62	1225	265	591	.448	108	182	.593	368	59	202	10	638	10.3
Al Ferrari	79	2046	208	582	.357	175	219	.799	213	313	278	9	591	7.5
Fred LaCour	73	1507	230	536	.429	106	130	.815	272	166	168	3	566	7.8
Larry Foust	57	1153	204	433	.471	145	178	.815	328	78	186	3	553	9.7
Bob Sims***	65	1345	193	491	.393	123	216	.569	183	154	187	4	509	7.8
Lenny Wilkens	20	870	140	364	.385	84	110	.764	131	116	63	0	364	18.2
Vern Hatton****	40	898	112	331	.338	98	125	.784	102	99	63	0	322	8.1
Cleo Hill	58	1050	107	309	.346	106	137	.774	178	114	98	1	320	5.5
Archie Dees*****	21	288	51	115	.443	35	46	.761	77	16	33	0	137	6.5
Stacey Arceneaux	7	110	22	56	.393	6	13	.462	32	4	10	0	50	7.1
Johnny McCarthy	15	333	18	73	.247	12	27	.444	56	70	50	1	48	3.2
Jimmy Darrow	5	34	3	15	.200	6	7	.857	7	6	9	0	12	2.4
Ron Horn	3	25	1	12	.083	1	2	.500	6	1	4	0	3	1.0
Dick Eichhorst	1	10	1	2	.500	0	0	...	1	3	1	0	2	2.0

*Cable—Played 15 Chicago, 52 St. Louis. **McMillon—Played 14 Detroit, 48 St. Louis. ***Sims—Played 19 Los Angeles, 46 St. Louis.
****Hatton—Played 15 Chicago, 25 St. Louis. *****Dees—Played 13 Chicago, 8 St. Louis.

SYRACUSE NATIONALS

	G	Min.	FGM	FGA	Pct.	FTM	FTA	Pct.	Reb.	Ast.	PF	Dq.	Pts.	Avg.
Hal Greer	71	2705	644	1442	.447	331	404	.819	524	313	252	2	1619	22.8
Dave Gambee	80	2301	477	1126	.424	384	470	.817	631	114	275	10	1338	16.7
Rod Korr	80	2768	641	1220	.443	222	302	.735	1176	243	272	7	1304	16.3
Lee Shaffer	75	2083	514	1180	.436	239	310	.771	511	99	266	6	1267	16.9
Larry Costello	63	1854	310	726	.427	247	295	.837	245	359	220	5	867	13.8
Al Bianchi	80	1925	336	847	.397	154	221	.697	281	263	232	5	826	10.3
Dolph Schayes	56	1480	268	751	.357	286	319	.897	439	120	167	4	822	14.7
Joe Roberts	80	1642	243	619	.393	129	194	.665	538	50	230	4	615	7.7
Paul Neumann	77	1265	172	401	.429	133	172	.773	194	176	203	3	477	6.2
Swede Halbrook	64	908	152	422	.360	96	151	.636	399	33	179	7	400	6.3
Joe Graboski*	38	468	77	221	.348	39	65	.600	154	28	62	0	193	5.1
Chuck Osborne	4	21	1	8	.125	3	4	.750	9	1	3	0	5	1.3

*Graboski—Played 3 St. Louis, 12 Chicago, 23 Syracuse.

PLAYOFF RESULTS

EASTERN DIVISION

SEMIFINALS

Philadelphia 3, Syracuse 2
Mar. 16—Fri.   Syracuse 103 at Philadelphia 110
Mar. 18—Sun.   Philadelphia 97 at Syracuse 82
Mar. 19—Mon.   Syracuse 101 at Philadelphia 100
Mar. 20—Tue.   Philadelphia 99 at Syracuse 106
Mar. 22—Thur. Syracuse 104 at Philadelphia 121

FINALS

Boston 4, Philadelphia 3
Mar. 24—Sat.   Philadelphia 89 at Boston 117
Mar. 27—Tue.   Boston 106 at Philadelphia 113
Mar. 28—Wed.   Philadelphia 114 at Boston 129
Mar. 31—Sat.   Boston 106 at Philadelphia 110
Apr. 1—Sun.   Philadelphia 104 at Boston 119
Apr. 3—Tue.   Boston 99 at Philadelphia 109
Apr. 5—Thur.   Philadelphia 107 at Boston 109

WESTERN DIVISION

SEMIFINALS

Detroit 3, Cincinnati 1
Mar. 16—Fri.   Cincinnati 122 at Detroit 123
Mar. 17—Sat.   Detroit 107 at Cincinnati 129
Mar. 18—Sun.   Cincinnati 107 at Detroit 118
Mar. 20—Tue.   Detroit 112 at Cincinnati 111

FINALS

Los Angeles 4, Detroit 2
Mar. 24—Sat.   Detroit 108 at Los Angeles 132
Mar. 25—Sun.   Detroit 112 at Los Angeles 127
Mar. 27—Tue.   Los Angeles 111 at Detroit 106
Mar. 29—Thur. Los Angeles 117 at Detroit 118
Mar. 31—Sat.   Detroit 132 at Los Angeles 125
Apr. 3—Tue.   Los Angeles 123 at Detroit 117

NBA FINALS

Boston 4, Los Angeles 3
Apr. 7—Sat.   Los Angeles 108 at Boston 122
Apr. 8—Sun.   Los Angeles 129 at Boston 122
Apr. 10—Tue.   Boston 115 at Los Angeles 117
Apr. 11—Wed.   Boston 115 at Los Angeles 103
Apr. 14—Sat.   Los Angeles 126 at Boston 121
Apr. 16—Mon.   Boston 119 at Los Angeles 105
Apr. 18—Wed.   Los Angeles 107 at Boston *110

*Denotes number of overtime periods.

1960-61

1960-61 NBA CHAMPION BOSTON CELTICS

Front row (from left): K.C. Jones, Bob Cousy, head coach Red Auerbach, president Walter A. Brown, Bill Sharman, Frank Ramsey. Back row (from left): trainer Buddy LeRoux, Tom Sanders, Tom Heinsohn, Gene Conley, Bill Russell, Gene Guarilia, Jim Loscutoff, Sam Jones. Inset: treasurer Lou Pieri.

FINAL STANDINGS

EASTERN DIVISION

	Bos.	Phi.	Syr.	N.Y.	St.L.	L.A.	Det.	Cin.	W	L	Pct.	GB
Boston	..	8	10	10	6	8	8	7	57	22	.722	..
Philadelphia 5		..	6	11	3	8	5	8	46	33	.582	11
Syracuse 3		7	..	8	4	4	6	8	38	41	.481	19
New York 3		2	5	..	1	3	5	2	21	58	.266	36

WESTERN DIVISION

	Bos.	Phi.	Syr.	N.Y.	St.L.	L.A.	Det.	Cin.	W	L	Pct.	GB
St. Louis 4		7	6	9	..	8	10	7	51	28	.646	..
Los Angeles 2		2	6	7	5	..	9	5	36	43	.456	15
Detroit 2		5	4	5	3	4	..	11	34	45	.430	17
Cincinnati 3		2	4	8	6	8	2	..	33	46	.418	18

TEAM STATISTICS

	G	FGM	FGA	Pct.	FTM	FTA	Pct.	Reb.	Ast.	PF	Dq.	AVERAGE POINTS For	AVERAGE POINTS Agst.	AVERAGE POINTS Dif.
Boston 79		3697	9295	.398	2062	2804	.735	6131	1872	2032	46	119.7	114.1	+5.6
St. Louis 79		3618	8795	.411	2147	2921	.735	5994	2136	2135	36	118.8	115.2	+3.6
Syracuse 79		3654	8746	.418	2278	2948	.773	5726	1786	2280	43	121.3	119.2	+2.1
Philadelphia 79		3768	8883	.424	2022	3108	.651	5938	1959	1936	38	121.0	120.1	+0.9
Los Angeles 79		3401	8430	.403	2204	2999	.735	5816	1728	2043	32	114.0	114.1	-0.1
Detroit 79		3481	8357	.417	2408	3240	.743	5813	1866	2157	47	118.6	120.1	-1.5
Cincinnati 79		3626	8281	.438	2060	2761	.746	5581	2107	2159	40	117.9	121.3	-3.4
New York 79		3422	8347	.410	2135	2838	.752	5315	1822	2223	37	113.7	120.1	-6.4
Avgs 79		3583	8642	.415	2165	2952	.733	5789	1910	2121	39.9	118.1	. . .	. . .

HOME/ROAD/NEUTRAL

	Home	Road	Neutral	Total		Home	Road	Neutral	Total
Boston	21-7	24-11	12-4	57-22	Philadelphia	23-6	12-21	11-6	46-33
Cincinnati	18-13	8-19	7-14	33-46	St. Louis	29-5	15-20	7-3	51-28
Detroit	20-11	3-19	11-15	34-45	Syracuse	19-9	8-21	11-11	38-41
Los Angeles	16-12	8-20	12-11	36-43	Totals	156-85	85-156	75-75	316-316
New York	10-22	7-25	4-11	21-58					

INDIVIDUAL LEADERS

POINTS

	G	FGM	FTM	Pts.	Avg.
Wilt Chamberlain, Philadelphia	79	1251	531	3033	38.4
Elgin Baylor, Los Angeles	73	931	676	2538	34.8
Oscar Robertson, Cincinnati	71	756	653	2165	30.5
Bob Pettit, St. Louis	76	769	582	2120	27.9
Jack Twyman, Cincinnati	79	796	405	1997	25.3
Dolph Schayes, Syracuse	79	594	680	1868	23.6
Willie Naulls, New York	79	737	372	1846	23.4
Paul Arizin, Philadelphia	79	650	532	1832	23.2
Bailey Howell, Detroit	77	607	601	1815	23.6
Gene Shue, Detroit	78	650	465	1765	22.6
Richie Guerin, New York	79	612	496	1720	21.8
Cliff Hagan, St. Louis	77	661	383	1705	22.1
Tom Heinsohn, Boston	74	627	325	1579	21.3
Hal Greer, Syracuse	79	623	305	1551	19.6
Clyde Lovellette, St. Louis	67	599	273	1471	22.0
Jerry West, Los Angeles	79	529	331	1389	17.6
Bob Cousy, Boston	76	513	352	1378	18.1
Bill Russell, Boston	78	532	258	1322	16.9
Dick Barnett, Syracuse	78	540	240	1320	16.9
Frank Ramsey, Boston	79	448	295	1191	15.1

FIELD GOALS

(minimum 200 made)

	FGM	FGA	Pct.
Wilt Chamberlain, Philadelphia	1251	2457	.509
Jack Twyman, Cincinnati	796	1632	.488
Larry Costello, Syracuse	407	844	.482
Oscar Robertson, Cincinnati	756	1600	.473
Bailey Howell, Detroit	607	1293	.469
Barney Cable, Syracuse	266	574	.463
Clyde Lovellette, St. Louis	599	1321	.453
Dick Barnett, Syracuse	540	1194	.452
Hal Greer, Syracuse	623	1381	.451
Wayne Embry, Cincinnati	458	1015	.451

FREE THROWS

(minimum 200 made)

	FTM	FTA	Pct.
Bill Sharman, Boston	210	228	.921
Dolph Schayes, Syracuse	680	783	.868
Gene Shue, Detroit	465	543	.856
Paul Arizin, Philadelphia	532	639	.833
Frank Ramsey, Boston	295	354	.833
Clyde Lovellette, St. Louis	273	329	.830
Dave Gambee, Syracuse	291	352	.827
Ken Sears, New York	268	325	.825
Oscar Robertson, Cincinnati	653	794	.822
Cliff Hagan, St. Louis	383	467	.820

ASSISTS

	G	No.	Avg.
Oscar Robertson, Cincinnati	71	690	9.7
Guy Rodgers, Philadelphia	78	677	8.7
Bob Cousy, Boston	76	587	7.7
Gene Shue, Detroit	78	530	6.8
Richie Guerin, New York	79	503	6.4
Johnny McCarthy, St. Louis	79	430	5.4
Larry Costello, Syracuse	75	413	5.5
Cliff Hagan, St. Louis	77	381	5.0
Elgin Baylor, Los Angeles	73	371	5.1
Rod Hundley, Los Angeles	79	350	4.4

REBOUNDS

	G	No.	Avg.
Wilt Chamberlain, Philadelphia	79	2149	27.2
Bill Russell, Boston	78	1868	23.9
Bob Pettit, St. Louis	76	1540	20.3
Elgin Baylor, Los Angeles	73	1447	19.8
Bailey Howell, Detroit	77	1111	14.4
Willie Naulls, New York	79	1055	13.4
Walter Dukes, Detroit	73	1028	14.1
Dolph Schayes, Syracuse	79	960	12.2
Red Kerr, Syracuse	79	951	12.0
Wayne Embry, Cincinnati	79	864	10.9

1960-61

INDIVIDUAL STATISTICS, TEAM BY TEAM

BOSTON CELTICS

	G	Min.	FGM	FGA	Pct.	FTM	FTA	Pct.	Reb.	Ast.	PF	Dq.	SCORING Pts.	SCORING Avg.
Tom Heinsohn	74	2256	627	1566	.400	325	424	.767	732	141	260	7	1579	21.3
Bob Cousy	76	2468	513	1382	.371	352	452	.779	331	587	196	0	1378	18.1
Bill Russell	78	3458	532	1250	.426	258	469	.550	1868	268	155	0	1322	16.9
Frank Ramsey	79	2019	448	1100	.407	295	354	.833	431	146	284	14	1191	15.1
Sam Jones	78	2028	480	1069	.449	211	268	.787	421	217	148	1	1171	15.0
Bill Sharman	61	1538	383	908	.422	210	228	.921	223	146	127	0	976	16.0
K.C. Jones	78	1605	203	601	.338	186	280	.664	279	253	190	3	592	7.6
Gene Conley	75	1242	183	495	.370	106	153	.693	550	40	275	15	472	6.3
Tom Sanders	68	1084	148	352	.420	67	100	.670	385	44	131	1	363	5.3
Jim Loscutoff	76	1153	144	478	.301	49	76	.645	291	25	238	5	337	4.4
Gene Guarilia	25	209	38	94	.404	3	10	.300	71	5	28	0	79	3.2

CINCINNATI ROYALS

	G	Min.	FGM	FGA	Pct.	FTM	FTA	Pct.	Reb.	Ast.	PF	Dq.	SCORING Pts.	SCORING Avg.
Oscar Robertson	71	3032	756	1600	.473	653	794	.822	716	690	219	3	2165	30.5
Jack Twyman	79	2920	796	1632	.488	405	554	.731	672	225	279	5	1997	25.3
Wayne Embry	79	2233	458	1015	.451	221	331	.668	864	127	286	7	1137	14.4
Arlen Bockhorn	79	2669	420	1059	.397	152	208	.731	434	338	282	9	992	12.6
Bob Boozer	79	1573	250	603	.415	166	247	.672	488	109	193	1	666	8.4
Mike Farmer*	59	1301	180	461	.390	69	94	.734	380	81	130	1	429	7.3
Hub Reed	75	1216	156	364	.429	85	122	.697	367	69	199	7	397	5.3
Ralph Davis	73	1210	181	451	.401	34	52	.654	86	177	127	1	396	5.4
Larry Staverman	66	944	111	249	.446	79	93	.849	287	86	164	4	301	4.6
Win Wilfong	62	717	106	305	.348	72	89	.809	147	87	119	1	284	4.6

*Farmer—Played 2 New York, 57 Cincinnati.

Oscar Robertson (far left) averaged 30.5 points for the Cincinnati Royals in 1960-61 en route to winning Rookie of the Year honors. In the same season Wilt Chamberlain (left) became the first NBA player to score 3,000 points.

DETROIT PISTONS

	G	Min.	FGM	FGA	Pct.	FTM	FTA	Pct.	Reb.	Ast.	PF	Dq.	SCORING Pts.	Avg.
Bailey Howell	77	2952	607	1293	.469	601	798	.753	1111	196	297	10	1815	23.6
Gene Shue	78	3361	650	1545	.421	465	543	.856	334	530	207	1	1765	22.6
Don Ohl	79	2172	427	1085	.394	200	278	.719	256	265	224	3	1054	13.3
George Lee	74	1735	310	776	.399	276	394	.701	490	89	158	1	896	12.1
Bob Ferry	79	1657	350	776	.451	189	255	.741	500	129	205	1	889	11.3
Walter Dukes	73	2044	286	706	.405	281	400	.703	1028	139	313	16	853	11.7
Shellie McMillon	78	1636	322	752	.428	140	201	.697	487	98	238	6	784	10.1
Chuck Noble	75	1655	196	566	.346	82	115	.713	180	287	195	4	474	6.3
Jackie Moreland	64	1003	191	477	.400	86	132	.652	315	52	174	3	468	7.3
Willie Jones	35	452	78	216	.361	40	63	.635	94	63	90	2	196	5.6
Archie Dees	28	308	53	135	.393	39	47	.830	94	17	50	0	145	5.2

LOS ANGELES LAKERS

	G	Min.	FGM	FGA	Pct.	FTM	FTA	Pct.	Reb.	Ast.	PF	Dq.	SCORING Pts.	Avg.
Elgin Baylor	73	3133	931	2166	.430	676	863	.783	1447	371	279	3	2538	34.8
Jerry West	79	2797	529	1264	.419	331	497	.666	611	333	213	1	1389	17.6
Rudy LaRusso	79	2593	416	992	.419	323	409	.790	781	135	280	8	1155	14.6
Rod Hundley	79	2179	323	921	.351	223	296	.753	289	350	144	0	869	11.0
Frank Selvy	77	2153	311	767	.405	210	279	.753	299	246	219	3	832	10.8
Tom Hawkins	78	1846	310	719	.431	140	235	.596	479	88	209	2	760	9.7
Jim Krebs	75	1655	271	692	.392	75	93	.806	456	68	223	2	617	8.2
Ray Felix	78	1510	189	508	.372	135	193	.699	539	37	302	12	513	6.6
Bob Leonard	55	600	61	207	.295	71	100	.710	70	81	70	0	193	3.5
Howie Jolliff	46	352	46	141	.326	11	23	.478	141	16	53	0	103	2.2
Ron Johnson*	14	92	13	43	.302	11	17	.647	29	2	10	0	37	2.6
Gary Alcorn	20	174	12	40	.300	7	8	.875	50	2	47	1	31	1.6

*Johnson—Played 6 Detroit, 8 Los Angeles.

NEW YORK KNICKERBOCKERS

	G	Min.	FGM	FGA	Pct.	FTM	FTA	Pct.	Reb.	Ast.	PF	Dq.	SCORING Pts.	Avg.
Willie Naulls	79	2976	737	1723	.428	372	456	.816	1055	191	268	5	1846	23.4
Richie Guerin	79	3023	612	1545	.396	496	626	.792	628	503	310	3	1720	21.8
Dick Garmaker	71	2238	415	943	.440	275	358	.768	277	220	240	2	1105	15.6
Phil Jordon*	79	2064	360	932	.386	208	297	.700	674	181	273	3	928	11.7
Johnny Green	78	1784	326	758	.430	145	278	.522	838	97	194	3	797	10.2
Kenny Sears	52	1396	241	568	.424	268	325	.825	293	102	165	6	750	14.4
Charlie Tyra	59	1404	199	549	.362	120	173	.694	394	82	164	7	518	8.8
Bob McNeill	75	1387	166	427	.389	105	126	.833	123	238	148	2	437	5.8
Dave Budd	61	1075	156	361	.432	87	134	.649	297	45	171	2	399	6.5
Jim Palmer	55	688	125	310	.403	44	65	.677	179	30	128	0	294	5.3
Darrall Imhoff	62	994	122	310	.394	49	96	.510	296	51	143	2	293	4.7
Phil Rollins**	61	816	109	293	.372	58	88	.659	97	123	121	1	276	4.5
Carl Braun	15	218	37	79	.468	11	14	.786	31	48	29	0	85	5.7
Jack George	16	268	31	93	.333	20	30	.667	32	39	37	0	82	5.1
Whitey Bell	5	45	7	18	.389	1	3	.333	7	1	7	0	15	3.0

*Jordon—Played 48 Cincinnati, 31 New York.

**Rollins—Played 7 St. Louis, 14 Cincinnati, 40 New York.

PHILADELPHIA WARRIORS

	G	Min.	FGM	FGA	Pct.	FTM	FTA	Pct.	Reb.	Ast.	PF	Dq.	SCORING Pts.	Avg.
Wilt Chamberlain	79	3773	1251	2457	.509	531	1054	.504	2149	148	130	0	3033	38.4
Paul Arizin	79	2935	650	1529	.425	532	639	.833	681	188	335	11	1832	23.2
Tom Gola	74	2712	420	940	.447	210	281	.747	692	292	321	13	1050	14.2
Guy Rodgers	78	2905	397	1029	.386	206	300	.687	509	677	262	3	1000	12.8
Andy Johnson	79	2000	299	834	.359	157	275	.571	345	205	249	3	755	9.6
Al Attles	77	1544	222	543	.409	97	162	.599	214	174	235	5	541	7.0
Ed Conlin	77	1294	216	599	.361	104	139	.748	262	123	153	1	536	7.0
Joe Graboski	68	1011	169	507	.333	127	183	.694	262	74	148	2	465	6.8
Vern Hatton	54	610	97	304	.319	46	56	.821	92	59	59	0	240	4.4
Joe Ruklick	29	223	43	120	.358	8	13	.615	62	10	38	0	94	3.2
Bill Kennedy	7	52	4	21	.190	4	6	.667	8	9	6	0	12	1.7

ST. LOUIS HAWKS

	G	Min.	FGM	FGA	Pct.	FTM	FTA	Pct.	Reb.	Ast.	PF	Dq.	SCORING Pts.	Avg.
Bob Pettit	76	3027	769	1720	.447	582	804	.724	1540	262	217	1	2120	27.9
Cliff Hagan	77	2701	661	1490	.444	383	467	.820	715	381	286	9	1705	22.1
Clyde Lovellette	67	2111	599	1321	.453	273	329	.830	677	172	248	4	1471	22.0
Lenny Wilkens	75	1898	333	783	.425	214	300	.713	335	212	215	5	880	11.7
Sihugo Green	76	1968	263	718	.366	174	247	.704	380	258	234	2	700	9.2
Johnny McCarthy	79	2519	266	746	.357	122	226	.540	325	430	272	8	654	8.3
Larry Foust	68	1208	194	489	.397	164	208	.788	389	77	185	0	552	8.1
Woody Sauldsberry	69	1491	230	768	.299	56	100	.560	491	74	197	3	516	7.5
Al Ferrari	63	1031	117	328	.357	95	116	.819	115	143	157	4	329	5.2
Fred LaCour	55	722	123	295	.417	63	84	.750	178	84	73	0	309	5.6
Dave Piontek	29	254	47	96	.490	16	31	.516	68	19	31	0	110	3.8

SYRACUSE NATIONALS

	G	Min.	FGM	FGA	Pct.	FTM	FTA	Pct.	Reb.	Ast.	PF	Dq.	SCORING Pts.	Avg.
Dolph Schayes	79	3007	594	1595	.372	680	783	.868	960	296	296	9	1868	23.6
Hal Greer	79	2763	623	1381	.451	305	394	.774	455	302	242	0	1551	19.6
Dick Barnett	78	2070	540	1194	.452	240	337	.712	283	210	189	0	1320	16.9
Dave Gambee	79	2090	397	947	.419	291	352	.827	581	101	276	6	1085	13.7
Larry Costello	75	2167	407	844	.482	270	338	.799	292	413	286	9	1084	14.5
Red Kerr	79	2676	419	1056	.397	218	299	.729	951	199	230	4	1056	13.4
Barney Cable	75	1642	266	574	.463	73	108	.676	469	85	246	1	605	8.1
Swede Halbrook	79	1131	155	463	.335	76	140	.543	550	31	262	9	386	4.9
Joe Roberts	68	800	130	351	.370	62	104	.596	243	43	125	0	322	4.7
Al Bianchi	52	667	118	342	.345	60	87	.690	105	93	137	5	296	5.7
Ernie Beck*	10	82	10	29	.345	6	7	.857	23	15	10	0	26	2.6
Cal Ramsey	2	27	2	11	.182	2	4	.500	7	3	7	0	6	3.0

*Beck—Played 7 St. Louis, 3 Syracuse.

PLAYOFF RESULTS

EASTERN DIVISION

SEMIFINALS

Syracuse 3, Philadelphia 0

Mar. 14—Tue.	Syracuse 115 at Philadelphia	107
Mar. 16—Thur.	Philadelphia 114 at Syracuse	115
Mar. 18—Sat.	Syracuse 106 at Philadelphia	103

FINALS

Boston 4, Syracuse 1

Mar. 19—Sun.	Syracuse 115 at Boston	128
Mar. 21—Tue.	Boston 98 at Syracuse	115
Mar. 23—Thur.	Boston 110 at Syracuse	133
Mar. 25—Sat.	Boston 120 at Syracuse	107
Mar. 26—Sun.	Syracuse 101 at Boston	123

WESTERN DIVISION

SEMIFINALS

Los Angeles 3, Detroit 2

Mar. 14—Tue.	Detroit 102 at Los Angeles	120
Mar. 15—Wed.	Detroit 118 at Los Angeles	120
Mar. 17—Fri.	Los Angeles 113 at Detroit	124
Mar. 18—Sat.	Los Angeles 114 at Detroit	123
Mar. 19—Sun.	Detroit 120 at Los Angeles	137

FINALS

St. Louis 4, Los Angeles 3

Mar. 21—Tue.	Los Angeles 122 at St. Louis	118
Mar. 22—Wed.	Los Angeles 106 at St. Louis	121
Mar. 24—Fri.	St. Louis 112 at Los Angeles	118
Mar. 25—Sat.	St. Louis 118 at Los Angeles	117
Mar. 27—Mon.	Los Angeles 121 at St. Louis	112
Mar. 29—Wed.	St. Louis 114 at Los Angeles	*113
Apr. 1—Sat.	Los Angeles 103 at St. Louis	105

NBA FINALS

Boston 4, St. Louis 1

Apr. 2—Sun.	St. Louis 95 at Boston	129
Apr. 5—Wed.	St. Louis 108 at Boston	116
Apr. 8—Sat.	Boston 120 at St. Louis	124
Apr. 9—Sun.	Boston 119 at St. Louis	104
Apr. 11—Tue.	St. Louis 112 at Boston	121

*Denotes number of overtime periods.

1960-61

1959-60

1959-60 NBA CHAMPION BOSTON CELTICS
Front row (from left): Frank Ramsey, Bob Cousy, head coach Red Auerbach, president Walter Brown, treasurer Lou Pieri, K.C. Jones, Bill Sharman. Back row (from left): Gene Guarilia, Tom Heinsohn, John Richter, Bill Russell, Gene Conley, Jim Loscutoff, Sam Jones, trainer Buddy LeRoux.

FINAL STANDINGS

EASTERN DIVISION

	Bos.	Phi.	Syr.	N.Y.	St.L.	Det.	Minn.	Cin.	W	L	Pct.	GB
Boston	..	8	8	12	6	9	8	8	59	16	.787	..
Philadelphia	5	..	8	9	4	7	7	9	49	26	.653	10
Syracuse	5	5	..	11	4	5	8	7	45	30	.600	14
New York	1	4	2	..	3	5	5	7	27	48	.360	32

WESTERN DIVISION

St. Louis.	3	5	5	6	..	8	10	9	46	29	.613	..
Detroit	0	2	4	4	5	..	7	8	30	45	.400	16
Minneapolis	1	2	1	4	3	6	..	8	25	50	.333	21
Cincinnati	1	0	2	2	4	5	5	..	19	56	.253	27

TEAM STATISTICS

	G	FGM	FGA	Pct.	FTM	FTA	Pct.	Reb.	Ast.	PF	Dq.	AVERAGE POINTS For	AVERAGE POINTS Agst.	AVERAGE POINTS Dif.
Boston	75	3744	8971	.417	1849	2519	.734	6014	1849	1856	42	124.5	116.2	+8.3
St. Louis	75	3179	7580	.419	2148	2885	.745	5343	1881	1995	40	113.4	110.7	+2.7
Syracuse	75	3406	8232	.414	2105	2662	.791	5406	1676	1939	39	118.9	116.4	+2.5
Philadelphia	75	3549	8678	.409	1797	2686	.669	5916	1796	1715	21	118.6	116.4	+2.2
New York.	75	3429	8153	.421	1942	2539	.765	5251	1667	1940	32	117.3	119.6	-2.3
Detroit	75	3146	7920	.397	2075	2847	.729	5491	1472	1983	49	111.6	115.0	-3.4
Minneapolis	75	3040	7884	.386	1965	2691	.730	5432	1444	1813	37	107.3	111.4	-4.1
Cincinnati	75	3210	7786	.412	1913	2672	.716	5251	1747	2097	38	111.1	117.4	-6.3
Avgs..	75	3338	8151	.410	1974	2688	.734	5513	1692	1917	37.3	115.3	. . .	. . .

HOME/ROAD/NEUTRAL

	Home	Road	Neutral	Total		Home	Road	Neutral	Total
Boston	25-2	23-9	11-5	59-16	Philadelphia	22-6	12-19	15-1	49-26
Cincinnati	9-22	2-20	8-14	19-56	St. Louis	28-5	12-20	6-4	46-29
Detroit	17-14	6-21	7-10	30-45	Syracuse	26-4	11-19	8-7	45-30
Minneapolis	9-13	9-22	7-15	25-50	Totals	149-84	84-149	67-67	300-300
New York	13-18	9-19	5-11	27-48					

POINTS

	G	FGM	FTM	Pts.	Avg.
Wilt Chamberlain, Philadelphia	.72	1065	577	2707	37.6
Jack Twyman, Cincinnati	.75	870	598	2338	31.2
Elgin Baylor, Minneapolis	.70	755	564	2074	29.6
Bob Pettit, St. Louis	.72	669	544	1882	26.1
Cliff Hagan, St. Louis	.75	719	421	1859	24.8
Gene Shue, Detroit	.75	620	472	1712	22.8
Dolph Schayes, Syracuse	.75	578	533	1689	22.5
Tom Heinsohn, Boston	.75	673	283	1629	21.7
Richie Guerin, New York	.74	579	457	1615	21.8
Paul Arizin, Philadelphia	.72	593	420	1606	22.3
George Yardley, Syracuse	.73	546	381	1473	20.2
Bob Cousy, Boston	.75	568	319	1455	19.4
Clyde Lovellette, St. Louis	.68	550	316	1416	20.8
Willie Naulls, New York	.65	551	286	1388	21.4
Bill Sharman, Boston	.71	559	252	1370	19.3
Bill Russell, Boston	.74	555	240	1350	18.2
Bailey Howell, Detroit	.75	510	312	1332	17.8
Kenny Sears, New York	.64	412	363	1187	18.5
Tom Gola, Philadelphia	.75	426	270	1122	15.0
Frank Ramsey, Boston	.73	422	273	1117	15.3

FIELD GOALS

(minimum 190 made)

	FGM	FGA	Pct.
Ken Sears, New York	.412	863	.477
Hal Greer, Syracuse	.388	815	.476
Clyde Lovellette, St. Louis	.550	1174	.468
Bill Russell, Boston	.555	1189	.467
Cliff Hagan, St. Louis	.719	1549	.464
Wilt Chamberlain, Philadelphia	.1065	2311	.461
Bill Sharman, Boston	.559	1225	.456
Bailey Howell, Detroit	.510	1119	.456
Sam Jones, Boston	.355	782	.454
George Yardley, Syracuse	.546	1205	.453

FREE THROWS

(minimum 185 made)

	FTM	FTA	Pct.
Dolph Schayes, Syracuse	.533	597	.893
Gene Shue, Detroit	.472	541	.872
Ken Sears, New York	.363	418	.868
Bill Sharman, Boston	.252	291	.866
Larry Costello, Syracuse	.249	289	.862
Willie Naulls, New York	.286	342	.836
Clyde Lovellette, St. Louis	.316	385	.821
George Yardley, Syracuse	.381	467	.816
Cliff Hagan, St. Louis	.421	524	.803
Paul Arizin, Philadelphia	.420	526	.798

ASSISTS

	G	No.	Avg.
Bob Cousy, Boston	.75	715	9.5
Guy Rodgers, Philadelphia	.68	482	7.1
Richie Guerin, New York	.74	468	6.3
Larry Costello, Syracuse	.71	449	6.3
Tom Gola, Philadelphia	.75	409	5.5
Dick McGuire, Detroit	.68	358	5.3
Rod Hundley, Minneapolis	.73	338	4.6
Slater Martin, St. Louis	.64	330	5.2
Jack McCarthy, St. Louis	.75	328	4.4
Cliff Hagan, St. Louis	.75	299	4.0

REBOUNDS

	G	No.	Avg.
Wilt Chamberlain, Philadelphia	.72	1941	27.0
Bill Russell, Boston	.74	1778	24.0
Bob Pettit, St. Louis	72	1221	17.0
Elgin Baylor, Minneapolis	.70	1150	16.4
Dolph Schayes, Syracuse	.75	959	12.8
Willie Naulls, New York	.65	921	14.2
Red Kerr, Syracuse	.75	913	12.2
Walter Dukes, Detroit	.66	883	13.4
Ken Sears, New York	.64	876	13.7
Cliff Hagan, St. Louis	.75	803	10.7

1959-60

INDIVIDUAL STATISTICS, TEAM BY TEAM

BOSTON CELTICS

	G	Min.	FGM	FGA	Pct.	FTM	FTA	Pct.	Reb.	Ast.	PF	Dq.	SCORING Pts.	Avg.
Tom Heinsohn	75	2420	673	1590	.423	283	386	.733	794	171	275	8	1629	21.7
Bob Cousy	75	2588	568	1481	.384	319	403	.792	352	715	146	2	1455	19.4
Bill Sharman	71	1916	559	1225	.456	252	291	.866	262	144	154	2	1370	19.3
Bill Russell	74	3146	555	1189	.467	240	392	.612	1778	277	210	0	1350	18.2
Frank Ramsey	73	2009	422	1062	.397	273	347	.787	506	137	251	10	1117	15.3
Sam Jones	74	1512	355	782	.454	168	220	.764	375	125	101	1	878	11.9
Gene Conley	71	1330	201	539	.373	76	114	.667	590	32	270	10	478	6.7
K.C. Jones	74	1274	169	414	.408	128	170	.753	199	189	109	1	466	6.3
John Richter	66	808	113	332	.340	59	117	.504	312	27	158	1	285	4.3
Jim Loscutoff	28	536	66	205	.322	22	36	.611	108	12	108	6	154	5.5
Gene Guarilia	48	423	58	154	.377	29	41	.707	85	18	57	1	145	3.0
Maurice King	1	19	5	8	.625	0	1	.000	4	2	3	0	10	10.0

CINCINNATI ROYALS

	G	Min.	FGM	FGA	Pct.	FTM	FTA	Pct.	Reb.	Ast.	PF	Dq.	SCORING Pts.	Avg.
Jack Twyman	75	3023	870	2063	.422	598	762	.785	664	260	275	10	2338	31.2
Phil Jordon	75	2066	381	970	.393	242	338	.716	624	207	227	7	1004	13.4
Arlen Bockhorn	75	2103	323	812	.398	145	194	.747	382	256	249	8	791	10.5
Wayne Embry	73	1594	303	690	.439	167	325	.514	692	83	226	1	773	10.6
Win Wilfong	72	1992	283	764	.370	161	207	.778	352	265	229	1	727	10.1
Hub Reed*	71	1820	270	601	.449	134	184	.728	614	69	230	6	674	9.5
Med Park	74	1849	226	582	.388	189	260	.727	301	214	180	2	641	8.7
Phil Rollins	72	1235	158	386	.409	77	127	.606	180	233	150	1	393	5.5
Dave Gambee**	61	656	117	291	.402	69	106	.651	229	38	83	1	303	5.0
Larry Staverman	49	479	70	149	.470	47	64	.734	180	36	98	0	187	3.8
Wayne Stevens	8	49	3	19	.158	7	10	.700	16	4	4	0	13	1.6

*Reed—Played 2 St. Louis, 69 Cincinnati.
**Gambee—Played 42 St. Louis, 19 Cincinnati.

DETROIT PISTONS

	G	Min.	FGM	FGA	Pct.	FTM	FTA	Pct.	Reb.	Ast.	PF	Dq.	Pts.	Avg.
Gene Shue	75	3338	620	1501	.413	472	541	.872	409	295	146	2	1712	22.8
Bailey Howell	75	2346	510	1119	.456	312	422	.739	790	63	282	13	1332	17.8
Walter Dukes	66	2140	314	871	.361	376	508	.740	883	80	310	20	1004	15.2
Ed Conlin	70	1636	300	831	.361	181	238	.761	346	126	158	2	781	11.2
Archie Dees	73	1244	271	617	.439	165	204	.809	397	43	188	3	707	9.7
Shellie McMillon	75	1416	267	627	.426	132	199	.663	431	49	198	3	666	8.9
Chuck Noble	58	1621	276	774	.357	101	138	.732	201	265	172	2	653	11.3
Earl Lloyd	68	1610	237	665	.356	128	160	.800	322	89	226	1	602	8.9
Dick McGuire	68	1466	179	402	.445	124	201	.617	264	358	112	0	482	7.1
Gary Alcorn	58	670	91	312	.292	48	84	.571	279	22	123	4	230	4.0
Billy Kenville	25	365	47	131	.359	33	41	.805	71	46	31	0	127	5.1
Tony Windis	9	193	16	60	.267	4	6	.667	47	32	20	0	36	4.0

MINNEAPOLIS LAKERS

	G	Min.	FGM	FGA	Pct.	FTM	FTA	Pct.	Reb.	Ast.	PF	Dq.	Pts.	Avg.
Elgin Baylor	70	2873	755	1781	.424	564	770	.732	1150	243	234	2	2074	29.6
Rudy LaRusso	71	2092	355	913	.389	265	357	.742	679	83	222	8	975	13.7
Rod Hundley	73	2279	365	1019	.358	203	273	.744	390	338	194	0	933	12.8
Bob Leonard	73	2074	231	717	.322	136	193	.705	245	252	171	3	598	8.2
Jim Krebs	75	1269	237	605	.392	98	136	.721	327	38	210	2	572	7.6
Frank Selvy*	62	1308	205	521	.393	153	208	.736	175	111	101	1	563	9.1
Tom Hawkins	69	1467	220	579	.380	106	164	.646	428	54	188	3	546	7.9
Ray Felix**	47	883	136	355	.383	70	112	.625	338	23	177	5	342	7.3
Boo Ellis	46	671	64	185	.346	51	76	.671	236	27	64	2	179	3.9
Ed Fleming	27	413	59	141	.418	53	69	.768	87	38	46	0	171	6.3
Charlie Share***	41	651	59	151	.391	53	80	.663	221	62	142	9	171	4.2
Ron Sobie****	16	234	37	108	.343	31	37	.838	48	21	32	0	105	6.6
Steve Hamilton	15	247	29	77	.377	18	23	.783	58	7	39	1	76	5.1
Bobby Smith	10	130	13	54	.241	11	16	.688	33	14	10	0	37	3.7
Nick Mantis	10	71	10	39	.256	1	2	.500	6	9	8	0	21	2.1

*Selvy—Played 19 Syracuse, 43 Minneapolis.
**Felix—Played 16 New York, 31 Minneapolis.
***Share—Played 38 St. Louis, 3 Minneapolis.
****Sobie—Played 15 New York, 1 Minneapolis.

NEW YORK KNICKERBOCKERS

	G	Min.	FGM	FGA	Pct.	FTM	FTA	Pct.	Reb.	Ast.	PF	Dq.	Pts.	Avg.
Richie Guerin	74	2420	579	1379	.420	457	591	.773	505	468	242	3	1615	21.8
Willie Naulls	65	2250	551	1286	.428	286	342	.836	921	138	214	4	1388	21.4
Kenny Sears	64	2099	412	863	.477	363	418	.868	876	127	191	2	1187	18.5
Charlie Tyra	74	2033	406	952	.426	133	189	.704	598	80	258	8	945	12.8
Dick Garmaker*	70	1932	323	815	.396	203	263	.772	313	206	186	4	849	12.1
Carl Braun	54	1514	285	659	.432	129	154	.838	168	270	127	2	699	12.9
Jack George	69	1604	250	650	.385	155	202	.767	197	240	148	1	655	9.5
Jim Palmer**	74	1482	246	574	.429	119	174	.684	389	70	224	6	611	8.3
Mike Farmer	67	1536	212	568	.373	70	83	.843	385	57	130	1	494	7.4
Johnny Green	69	1232	209	468	.447	63	155	.406	539	52	195	3	481	7.0
Whitey Bell	31	449	70	185	.378	28	43	.651	87	55	59	0	168	5.4
Bob Anderegg	33	373	55	143	.385	23	42	.548	69	29	32	0	133	4.0
Cal Ramsey***	11	195	39	96	.406	19	33	.576	66	9	25	1	97	8.8
Brendan McCann	4	29	1	10	.100	3	3	1.000	4	10	2	0	5	1.3

*Garmaker—Played 44 Minneapolis, 26 New York.
**Palmer—Played 20 Cincinnati, 54 New York.
***Ramsey—Played 4 St. Louis, 7 New York.

PHILADELPHIA WARRIORS

	G	Min.	FGM	FGA	Pct.	FTM	FTA	Pct.	Reb.	Ast.	PF	Dq.	Pts.	Avg.
Wilt Chamberlain	72	3338	1065	2311	.461	577	991	.582	1941	168	150	0	2707	37.6
Paul Arizin	72	2618	593	1400	.424	420	526	.798	621	165	263	6	1606	22.3
Tom Gola	75	2870	426	983	.433	270	340	.794	779	409	311	9	1122	15.0
Guy Rodgers	68	2483	338	870	.389	111	181	.613	391	482	196	3	787	11.6
Woody Sauldsberry	71	1848	325	974	.334	55	103	.534	447	112	203	2	705	9.9
Andy Johnson	75	1421	245	648	.378	125	208	.601	282	152	196	5	615	8.2
Joe Graboski	73	1269	217	583	.372	131	174	.753	358	111	147	1	565	7.7
Vern Hatton	67	1049	127	356	.357	53	87	.609	159	82	61	0	307	4.6
Ernie Beck	66	809	114	294	.388	27	32	.844	127	72	90	0	255	3.9
Joe Ruklick	39	384	85	214	.397	26	36	.722	137	24	70	0	196	5.0
Guy Sparrow	11	80	14	45	.311	2	8	.250	23	6	20	0	30	2.7

ST. LOUIS HAWKS

	G	Min.	FGM	FGA	Pct.	FTM	FTA	Pct.	Reb.	Ast.	PF	Dq.	SCORING Pts.	Avg.
Bob Pettit	72	2896	669	1526	.438	544	722	.753	1221	257	204	0	1882	26.1
Cliff Hagan	75	2798	719	1549	.464	421	524	.803	803	299	270	4	1859	24.8
Clyde Lovellette	68	1953	550	1174	.468	316	385	.821	721	127	248	6	1416	20.8
Larry Foust*	72	1964	312	766	.407	253	320	.791	621	96	241	7	877	12.2
Dave Piontek**	77	1833	292	728	.401	129	202	.639	461	118	211	5	713	9.3
Johnny McCarthy	75	2383	240	730	.329	149	226	.659	301	328	233	3	629	8.4
Al Ferrari	71	1567	216	523	.413	176	225	.782	162	188	205	7	608	8.6
Sihugo Green	70	1354	159	427	.372	111	175	.634	257	133	150	3	429	6.1
Slater Martin	64	1756	142	383	.371	113	155	.729	187	330	174	2	397	6.2
Bob Ferry	62	875	144	338	.426	76	119	.639	233	40	132	2	364	5.9
Jack McMahon	25	334	33	93	.355	16	29	.552	24	49	42	1	82	3.3

*Foust—Played 47 Minneapolis, 25 St. Louis.
**Piontek—Played 52 Cincinnati, 25 St. Louis.

SYRACUSE NATIONALS

	G	Min.	FGM	FGA	Pct.	FTM	FTA	Pct.	Reb.	Ast.	PF	Dq.	SCORING Pts.	Avg.
Dolph Schayes	75	2741	578	1440	.401	533	597	.893	959	256	263	10	1689	22.5
George Yardley	73	2402	546	1205	.453	381	467	.816	579	122	227	3	1473	20.2
Red Kerr	75	2372	436	1111	.392	233	310	.752	913	167	207	4	1105	14.7
Larry Costello	71	2469	372	822	.453	249	289	.862	388	449	234	4	993	14.0
Hal Greer	70	1979	388	815	.476	148	189	.783	303	188	208	4	924	13.2
Dick Barnett	57	1235	289	701	.412	128	180	.711	155	160	98	0	706	12.4
Bob Hopkins	75	1616	257	660	.389	136	174	.782	465	55	193	4	650	8.7
Al Bianchi	69	1256	211	576	.366	109	155	.703	179	169	231	5	531	7.7
Connie Dierking	71	1119	192	526	.365	108	188	.574	456	54	168	4	492	6.9
Barney Cable*	57	715	109	290	.376	44	67	.657	225	39	93	1	262	4.6
Togo Palazzi	7	70	13	41	.317	4	8	.500	14	3	7	0	30	4.3
Jim Ray	4	21	1	6	.167	0	0	...	0	2	3	0	2	0.5
Paul Seymour	4	7	0	4	.000	0	0	...	1	0	1	0	0	0.0

*Cable—Played 7 Detroit, 50 Syracuse.

PLAYOFF RESULTS

EASTERN DIVISION

SEMIFINALS

Philadelphia 2, Syracuse 1
Mar. 11—Fri.   Syracuse 92 at Philadelphia 115
Mar. 13—Sun.   Philadelphia 119 at Syracuse 125
Mar. 14—Mon.   Syracuse 112 at Philadelphia 132

FINALS

Boston 4, Philadelphia 2
Mar. 16—Wed.   Philadelphia 105 at Boston 111
Mar. 18—Fri.   Boston 110 at Philadelphia 115
Mar. 19—Sat.   Philadelphia 90 at Boston 120
Mar. 20—Sun.   Boston 112 at Philadelphia 104
Mar. 22—Tue.   Philadelphia 128 at Boston 107
Mar. 24—Thur. Boston 119 at Philadelphia 117

WESTERN DIVISION

SEMIFINALS

Minneapolis 2, Detroit 0
Mar. 12—Sat.   Minneapolis 113 at Detroit 112
Mar. 13—Sun.   Detroit 99 at Minneapolis 114

FINALS

St. Louis 4, Minneapolis 3
Mar. 16—Wed.   Minneapolis 99 at St. Louis 112
Mar. 17—Thur. Minneapolis 120 at St. Louis 113
Mar. 19—Sat.   St. Louis 93 at Minneapolis 89
Mar. 20—Sun.   St. Louis 101 at Minneapolis 103
Mar. 22—Tue.   Minneapolis 117 at St. Louis *110
Mar. 24—Thur. St. Louis 117 at Minneapolis 96
Mar. 26—Sat.   Minneapolis 86 at St. Louis 97

NBA FINALS

Boston 4, St. Louis 3
Mar. 27—Sun.   St. Louis 122 at Boston 140
Mar. 29—Tue.   St. Louis 113 at Boston 103
Apr. 2—Sat.   Boston 102 at St. Louis 86
Apr. 3—Sun.   Boston 96 at St. Louis 106
Apr. 5—Tue.   St. Louis 102 at Boston 127
Apr. 7—Thur.   Boston 102 at St. Louis 105
Apr. 9—Sat.   St. Louis 103 at Boston 122

*Denotes number of overtime periods.

1958-59

1958-59 NBA CHAMPION BOSTON CELTICS

Front row (from left): Gene Conley, Bob Cousy, head coach Red Auerbach, president Walter A. Brown, Bill Sharman, Bill Russell. Back row: trainer Buddy LeRoux, K.C. Jones, Lou Tsioropoulos, Tom Heinsohn, Bennie Swain, Jim Loscutoff, Sam Jones, Frank Ramsey. Inset: treasurer Lou Pieri.

FINAL STANDINGS

EASTERN DIVISION

	Bos.	N.Y.	Syr.	Phi.	St.L.	Minn.	Det.	Cin.	W	L	Pct.	GB
Boston	..	7	7	9	4	9	8	8	52	20	.722	..
New York 5	5	..	9	5	4	5	6	6	40	32	.556	12
Syracuse 5	5	3	..	8	2	4	7	6	35	37	.486	17
Philadelphia 3	3	7	4	..	4	3	4	7	32	40	.444	20

WESTERN DIVISION

	Bos.	N.Y.	Syr.	Phi.	St.L.	Minn.	Det.	Cin.	W	L	Pct.	GB
St. Louis. 5	5	5	7	5	..	8	8	11	49	23	.681	..
Minneapolis 0	0	4	5	6	4	..	8	6	33	39	.458	16
Detroit 1	1	3	2	5	4	4	..	9	28	44	.389	21
Cincinnati 1	1	3	3	2	1	6	3	..	19	53	.264	30

TEAM STATISTICS

	G	FGM	FGA	Pct.	FTM	FTA	Pct.	Reb.	Ast.	PF	Dq.	For	Agst.	Dif.
												AVERAGE POINTS		
Boston 72	72	3208	8116	.395	1963	2563	.766	5601	1568	1769	46	116.4	109.9	+6.5
Syracuse 72	72	3050	7490	.407	2046	2642	.774	4900	1340	1961	44	113.1	109.1	+4.0
St. Louis 72	72	2879	7015	.410	2072	2757	.752	5045	1567	1937	35	108.8	105.1	+3.7
New York. 72	72	2863	7170	.399	2217	2802	.791	4091	1383	1899	34	110.3	110.1	+0.2
Minneapolis. 72	72	2779	7084	.392	2071	2718	.762	5149	1373	1874	27	106.0	107.3	-1.3
Detroit. 72	72	2811	7305	.385	1943	2627	.740	4860	1317	1881	58	105.1	106.6	-1.5
Philadelphia 72	72	2826	7423	.381	1783	2425	.735	4910	1375	1776	36	103.3	106.3	-3.0
Cincinnati 72	72	2854	7340	.389	1713	2375	.721	4887	1369	1855	36	103.1	112.0	-8.9
Avgs. 72	72	2909	7368	.395	1976	2614	.756	4930	1412	1869	39.5	108.3	. . .	. . .

HOME/ROAD/NEUTRAL

	Home	Road	Neutral	Total		Home	Road	Neutral	Total
Boston 26-4	26-4	13-15	13-1	52-20	Philadelphia 17-9	17-9	7-24	8-7	32-40
Cincinnati 9-19	9-19	2-25	8-9	19-53	St. Louis 28-3	28-3	14-15	7-5	49-23
Detroit 13-17	13-17	8-20	7-7	28-44	Syracuse 19-12	19-12	12-17	4-8	35-37
Minneapolis 15-7	15-7	9-17	9-15	33-39	Totals 148-80	148-80	80-148	60-60	288-288
New York 21-9	21-9	15-15	4-8	40-32					

POINTS

	G	FGM	FTM	Pts.	Avg.
Bob Pettit, St. Louis	72	719	667	2105	29.2
Jack Twyman, Cincinnati	72	710	437	1857	25.8
Paul Arizin, Philadelphia	70	632	587	1851	26.4
Elgin Baylor, Minneapolis	70	605	532	1742	24.9
Cliff Hagan, St. Louis	72	646	415	1707	23.7
Dolph Schayes, Syracuse	72	504	526	1534	21.3
Ken Sears, New York	71	491	506	1488	21.0
Bill Sharman, Boston	72	562	342	1466	20.4
Bob Cousy, Boston	65	484	329	1297	20.0
Richie Guerin, New York	71	443	405	1291	18.2
Red Kerr, Syracuse	72	502	281	1285	17.8
Gene Shue, Detroit	72	464	338	1266	17.6
Tom Heinsohn, Boston	66	465	312	1242	18.8
George Yardley, Det.-Syracuse	61	446	317	1209	19.8
Bill Russell, Boston	70	456	256	1168	16.7
Woody Sauldsberry, Phil.	72	501	110	1112	15.4
Larry Costello, Syracuse	70	414	280	1108	15.8
Frank Ramsey, Boston	72	383	341	1107	15.4
Willie Naulls, New York	68	405	258	1068	15.7
Joe Graboski, Philadelphia	72	394	270	1058	14.7

FIELD GOALS

(minimum 230 made)

	FGM	FGA	Pct.
Ken Sears, New York	.491	1002	.490
Bill Russell, Boston	.456	997	.457
Cliff Hagan, St. Louis	.646	1417	.456
Clyde Lovellette, St. Louis	.402	885	.454
Hal Greer, Syracuse	.308	679	.454
Red Kerr, Syracuse	.502	1139	.441
Bob Pettit, St. Louis	.719	1640	.438
Larry Costello, Syracuse	.414	948	.437
Sam Jones, Boston	.305	703	.434
Paul Arizin, Philadelphia	.632	1466	.431

FREE THROWS

(minimum 190 made)

	FTM	FTA	Pct.
Bill Sharman, Boston	.342	367	.932
Dolph Schayes, Syracuse	.526	609	.864
Ken Sears, New York	.506	588	.861
Bob Cousy, Boston	.329	385	.855
Willie Naulls, New York	.258	311	.830
Clyde Lovellette, St. Louis	.205	250	.820
Paul Arizin, Philadelphia	.587	722	.813
Vern Mikkelsen, Minneapolis	.286	355	.806
Gene Shue, Detroit	.338	421	.803
Richie Guerin, New York	.405	505	.802
Larry Costello, Syracuse	.280	349	.802

ASSISTS

	G	No.	Avg.
Bob Cousy, Boston	65	557	8.6
Dick McGuire, Detroit	71	443	6.2
Larry Costello, Syracuse	70	379	5.4
Richie Guerin, New York	71	364	5.1
Carl Braun, New York	72	349	4.9
Slater Martin, St. Louis	71	336	4.7
Jack McMahon, St. Louis	72	298	4.1
Elgin Baylor, Minneapolis	70	287	4.1
Tom Gola, Philadelphia	64	269	4.2
Guy Rodgers, Philadelphia	45	261	5.8

REBOUNDS

	G	No.	Avg.
Bill Russell, Boston	70	1612	23.0
Bob Pettit, St. Louis	72	1182	16.4
Elgin Baylor, Minneapolis	70	1050	15.0
Red Kerr, Syracuse	72	1008	14.0
Dolph Schayes, Syracuse	72	962	13.4
Walter Dukes, Detroit	72	958	13.3
Woody Sauldsberry, Philadelphia	72	826	11.5
Cliff Hagan, St. Louis	72	783	10.9
Joe Graboski, Philadelphia	72	751	10.4
Willie Naulls, New York	68	723	10.6

1958-59

INDIVIDUAL STATISTICS, TEAM BY TEAM

BOSTON CELTICS

	G	Min.	FGM	FGA	Pct.	FTM	FTA	Pct.	Reb.	Ast.	PF	Dq.	SCORING Pts.	Avg.
Bill Sharman	72	2382	562	1377	.408	342	367	.932	292	179	173	1	1466	20.4
Bob Cousy	65	2403	484	1260	.384	329	385	.855	359	557	135	0	1297	20.0
Tom Heinsohn	66	2089	465	1192	.390	312	391	.798	638	164	271	11	1242	18.8
Bill Russell	70	2979	456	997	.457	256	428	.598	1612	222	161	3	1168	16.7
Frank Ramsey	72	2013	383	1013	.378	341	436	.782	491	147	266	11	1107	15.4
Sam Jones	71	1466	305	703	.434	151	196	.770	428	101	102	0	761	10.7
Jim Loscutoff	66	1680	242	686	.353	62	84	.738	460	60	285	15	546	8.3
Bennie Swain	58	708	99	244	.406	67	110	.609	262	29	127	3	265	4.6
Gene Conley	50	663	86	262	.328	37	64	.578	276	19	117	2	209	4.2
K.C. Jones	49	609	65	192	.339	41	68	.603	127	70	58	0	171	3.5
Lou Tsioropoulos	35	488	60	190	.316	25	33	.758	110	20	74	0	145	4.1

CINCINNATI ROYALS

	G	Min.	FGM	FGA	Pct.	FTM	FTA	Pct.	Reb.	Ast.	PF	Dq.	SCORING Pts.	Avg.
Jack Twyman	72	2713	710	1691	.420	437	558	.783	653	209	277	6	1857	25.8
Dave Piontek	72	1974	305	813	.375	156	227	.687	385	124	162	3	766	10.6
Wayne Embry	66	1590	272	702	.387	206	314	.656	597	96	232	9	750	11.4
Arlen Bockhorn	71	2251	294	771	.381	138	196	.704	460	206	215	6	726	10.2
Jim Palmer	67	1624	256	633	.404	178	246	.724	472	65	211	7	690	10.3
Johnny McCarthy	47	1827	245	657	.373	116	174	.667	227	225	158	4	606	12.9
Archie Dees	68	1252	200	562	.356	159	204	.779	339	56	114	0	559	8.2
Med Park*	62	1126	145	361	.402	115	150	.767	188	108	93	0	405	6.5
Jack Parr	66	1037	109	307	.355	44	73	.603	278	51	138	1	262	4.0
Larry Staverman	57	681	101	215	.470	45	59	.763	218	54	103	0	247	4.3
Phil Rollins**	44	691	83	231	.359	63	90	.700	118	102	49	0	229	5.2
Tom Marshall	18	272	23	79	.291	18	29	.621	52	27	22	0	64	3.6

*Park—Played 29 St. Louis, 33 Cincinnati.
**Rollins—Played 23 Philadelphia, 21 Cincinnati.

DETROIT PISTONS

	G	Min.	FGM	FGA	Pct.	FTM	FTA	Pct.	Reb.	Ast.	PF	Dq.	SCORING Pts.	Avg.
Gene Shue	72	2745	464	1197	.388	338	421	.803	335	231	129	1	1266	17.6
Phil Jordon	72	2058	399	967	.413	231	303	.762	594	83	193	1	1029	14.3
Walter Dukes	72	2338	318	904	.352	297	452	.657	958	64	332	22	933	13.0
Ed Conlin*	72	1955	329	891	.369	197	274	.719	394	132	188	6	855	11.9
Dick McGuire	71	2063	232	543	.427	191	258	.740	285	443	147	1	655	9.2
Earl Lloyd	72	1796	234	670	.349	137	182	.753	500	90	291	15	605	8.4
Joe Holup	68	1502	209	580	.360	152	200	.760	352	73	239	12	570	8.4
Dick Farley	70	1280	177	448	.395	137	186	.737	195	124	130	2	491	7.0
Chuck Noble	65	939	189	560	.338	83	113	.735	115	114	126	0	461	7.1
Shellie McMillon	48	700	127	289	.439	55	104	.529	285	26	110	2	309	6.4
Barney Cable	31	271	43	126	.341	23	29	.793	88	12	30	0	109	3.5

*Conlin—Played 57 Syracuse, 15 Detroit.

MINNEAPOLIS LAKERS

	G	Min.	FGM	FGA	Pct.	FTM	FTA	Pct.	Reb.	Ast.	PF	Dq.	SCORING Pts.	Avg.
Elgin Baylor	70	2855	605	1482	.408	532	685	.777	1050	287	270	4	1742	24.9
Vern Mikkelsen	72	2139	353	904	.390	286	355	.806	570	159	246	8	992	13.8
Dick Garmaker	72	2493	350	885	.395	284	368	.772	325	211	226	3	984	13.7
Larry Foust	72	1933	301	771	.390	280	366	.765	627	91	233	5	882	12.3
Rod Hundley	71	1664	259	719	.360	164	218	.752	250	205	139	0	682	9.6
Jim Krebs	72	1578	271	679	.399	92	123	.748	491	50	212	4	634	8.8
Bob Leonard	58	1598	206	552	.373	120	160	.750	178	186	119	0	532	9.2
Ed Fleming	71	1132	192	419	.458	137	190	.721	281	89	148	1	521	7.3
Boo Ellis	72	1202	163	379	.430	102	144	.708	380	59	137	0	428	5.9
Steve Hamilton	67	847	109	294	.371	74	109	.679	220	36	144	2	292	4.4

NEW YORK KNICKERBOCKERS

	G	Min.	FGM	FGA	Pct.	FTM	FTA	Pct.	Reb.	Ast.	PF	Dq.	SCORING Pts.	Avg.
Kenny Sears	71	2498	491	1002	.490	506	588	.861	658	136	237	6	1488	21.0
Richie Guerin	71	2558	443	1046	.424	405	505	.802	518	364	255	1	1291	18.2
Willie Naulls	68	2061	405	1072	.378	258	311	.830	723	102	233	8	1068	15.7
Carl Braun	72	1959	287	684	.420	180	218	.826	251	349	178	3	754	10.5
Ray Felix	72	1588	260	700	.371	229	321	.713	569	49	275	9	749	10.4
Frank Selvy	68	1448	233	605	.385	201	262	.767	248	96	113	1	667	9.8
Jack George*	71	1881	233	674	.346	153	203	.754	293	221	149	0	619	8.7
Charlie Tyra	69	1586	240	606	.396	129	190	.679	485	33	180	2	609	8.8
Mike Farmer	72	1545	176	498	.353	83	99	.838	315	66	152	1	435	6.0
Ron Sobie	50	857	144	400	.360	112	133	.842	154	78	84	0	400	8.0
Pete Brennan	16	136	13	43	.302	14	25	.560	31	6	15	0	40	2.5
Jerry Bird	11	45	12	32	.375	1	1	1.000	12	4	7	0	25	2.3
Brendan McCann	1	7	0	3	.000	0	0	...	1	1	1	0	0	0.0

*George—Played 46 Philadelphia, 25 New York.

The Philadelphia Warriors'
Paul Arizin finished third in
the NBA with 1,851 points in
1958-59.

PHILADELPHIA WARRIORS

	G	Min.	FGM	FGA	Pct.	FTM	FTA	Pct.	Reb.	Ast.	PF	Dq.	SCORING Pts.	Avg.
Paul Arizin	70	2799	632	1466	.431	587	722	.813	637	119	264	7	1851	26.4
Woody Sauldsberry	72	2743	501	1380	.363	110	176	.625	826	71	276	12	1112	15.4
Joe Graboski	72	2482	394	1116	.353	270	360	.750	751	148	249	5	1058	14.7
Tom Gola	64	2333	310	773	.401	281	357	.787	710	269	243	7	901	14.1
Guy Rodgers	45	1565	211	535	.394	61	112	.545	281	261	132	1	483	10.7
Andy Johnson	67	1158	174	466	.373	115	191	.602	212	90	176	4	463	6.9
Vern Hatton*	64	1109	149	418	.356	77	105	.733	178	70	111	0	375	5.9
Ernie Beck	70	1017	163	418	.390	43	65	.662	176	89	124	0	369	5.3
Guy Sparrow**	67	842	129	406	.318	78	138	.565	244	67	158	3	336	5.0
Neil Johnston	28	393	54	164	.329	69	88	.784	139	21	50	0	177	6.3
Lennie Rosenbluth	29	205	43	145	.297	21	29	.724	54	6	20	0	107	3.7

*Hatton—Played 24 Cincinnati, 40 Philadelphia.
**Sparrow—Played 44 New York, 23 Philadelphia.

ST. LOUIS HAWKS

	G	Min.	FGM	FGA	Pct.	FTM	FTA	Pct.	Reb.	Ast.	PF	Dq.	SCORING Pts.	Avg.
Bob Pettit	72	2873	719	1640	.438	667	879	.759	1182	221	200	3	2105	29.2
Cliff Hagan	72	2702	646	1417	.456	415	536	.774	783	245	275	10	1707	23.7
Clyde Lovellette	70	1599	402	885	.454	205	250	.820	605	91	216	1	1009	14.4
Slater Martin	71	2504	245	706	.347	197	254	.776	253	336	230	8	687	9.7
Jack McMahon	72	2235	248	692	.358	96	156	.615	164	298	221	2	592	8.2
Charlie Share	72	1713	147	381	.386	139	184	.755	657	103	261	6	433	6.0
Al Ferrari	72	1189	134	385	.348	145	199	.729	142	122	155	1	413	5.7
Sihugo Green*	46	1109	146	415	.352	104	160	.650	252	113	127	1	396	8.6
Hub Reed	65	950	136	317	.429	53	71	.746	317	32	171	2	325	5.0
Win Wilfong	63	741	99	285	.347	62	82	.756	121	50	102	0	260	4.1
Ed Macauley	14	196	22	75	.293	21	35	.600	40	13	20	1	65	4.6
Dave Gambee	2	7	1	1	1.000	0	0	...	2	0	2	0	2	1.0

*Green—Played 20 Cincinnati, 26 St. Louis.

SYRACUSE NATIONALS

	G	Min.	FGM	FGA	Pct.	FTM	FTA	Pct.	Reb.	Ast.	PF	Dq.	SCORING Pts.	Avg.
Dolph Schayes	72	2645	504	1304	.387	526	609	.864	962	178	280	9	1534	21.3
Red Kerr	72	2671	502	1139	.441	281	367	.766	1008	142	183	1	1285	17.8
George Yardley*	61	1839	446	1042	.428	317	407	.779	431	65	159	2	1209	19.8
Larry Costello	70	2750	414	948	.437	280	349	.802	365	379	263	7	1108	15.8
Hal Greer	68	1625	308	679	.454	137	176	.778	196	101	189	1	753	11.1
Al Bianchi	72	1779	285	756	.377	149	206	.723	199	159	260	8	719	10.0
Bob Hopkins	67	1518	246	611	.403	176	234	.752	436	67	181	5	668	10.0
Togo Palazzi	71	1053	240	612	.392	115	158	.728	266	67	174	5	595	8.4
Connie Dierking	64	726	105	260	.404	83	140	.593	233	34	148	2	293	4.6
George Dempsey**	57	694	92	215	.428	81	106	.764	160	68	95	0	265	4.6
Paul Seymour	21	266	32	98	.327	26	29	.897	39	36	25	0	90	4.3
Tom Kearns	1	7	1	1	1.000	0	0	...	0	0	1	0	2	2.0

*Yardley—Played 46 Detroit, 15 Syracuse.
**Dempsey—Played 23 Philadelphia, 34 Syracuse.

PLAYOFF RESULTS

EASTERN DIVISION

SEMIFINALS
Syracuse 2, New York 0
| Mar. 13—Fri. | Syracuse 129 at New York | 123 |
| Mar. 15—Sun. | New York 115 at Syracuse | 131 |

FINALS
Boston 4, Syracuse 3
Mar. 18—Wed.	Syracuse 109 at Boston	131
Mar. 21—Sat.	Boston 118 at Syracuse	120
Mar. 22—Sun.	Syracuse 111 at Boston	133
Mar. 25—Wed.	Boston 107 at Syracuse	119
Mar. 28—Sat.	Syracuse 108 at Boston	129
Mar. 29—Sun.	Boston 121 at Syracuse	133
Apr. 1—Wed.	Syracuse 125 at Boston	130

WESTERN DIVISION

SEMIFINALS
Minneapolis 2, Detroit 1
Mar. 14—Sat.	Detroit 89 at Minneapolis	92
Mar. 15—Sun.	Minneapolis 103 at Detroit	117
Mar. 18—Wed.	Detroit 102 at Minneapolis	129

FINALS
Minneapolis 4, St. Louis 2
Mar. 21—Sat.	Minneapolis 90 at St. Louis	124
Mar. 22—Sun.	St. Louis 98 at Minneapolis	106
Mar. 24—Tue.	Minneapolis 97 at St. Louis	127
Mar. 26—Thur.	St. Louis 98 at Minneapolis	108
Mar. 28—Sat.	Minneapolis 98 at St. Louis	*97
Mar. 29—Sun.	St. Louis 104 at Minneapolis	106

NBA FINALS

Boston 4, Minneapolis 0
Apr. 4—Sat.	Minneapolis 115 at Boston	118
Apr. 5—Sun.	Minneapolis 108 at Boston	128
Apr. 7—Tue.	Boston 123, Minneapolis (at St. Paul)	110
Apr. 9—Thur.	Boston 118 at Minneapolis	113

*Denotes number of overtime periods.

1958-59

1957-58

1957-58 NBA CHAMPION ST. LOUIS HAWKS
Front row (from left): head coach Alex Hannum, Cliff Hagan, Jack Coleman, captain Charlie Share, Bob Pettit, Walt Davis, Ed Macauley. Back row (from left): ballboy Max Shapiro, Slater Martin, Win Wilfong, Jack McMahon, Med Park, Frank Selvy, trainer Bernie Ebert.

FINAL STANDINGS

EASTERN DIVISION

	Bos.	Syr.	Phi.	N.Y.	St.L.	Det.	Cin.	Minn.	W	L	Pct.	GB
Boston	..	7	6	7	5	8	7	9	49	23	.681	..
Syracuse 5		..	9	7	4	4	5	7	41	31	.569	8
Philadelphia 6		3	..	8	7	4	3	6	37	35	.514	12
New York 5		5	4	..	3	5	5	8	35	37	.486	14

WESTERN DIVISION

St. Louis 4		5	2	6	..	6	9	9	41	31	.569	..
Detroit 1		5	5	4	6	..	6	6	33	39	.458	8*
Cincinnati 2		4	6	4	3	6	..	8	33	39	.458	8*
Minneapolis 0		2	3	1	3	6	4	..	19	53	.264	22

*Detroit and Cincinnati tied for second place. Detroit won coin flip for home-court advantage in playoffs.

TEAM STATISTICS

	G	FGM	FGA	Pct.	FTM	FTA	Pct.	Reb.	Ast.	PF	Dq.	AVERAGE POINTS For	AVERAGE POINTS Agst.	AVERAGE POINTS Dif.
Boston 72	72	3006	7759	.387	1904	2585	.737	5402	1508	1723	34	109.9	104.4	+5.5
Syracuse 72	72	2823	7336	.385	2075	2617	.793	4895	1298	1820	28	107.2	105.1	+2.1
New York 72	72	2884	7307	.395	2300	3056	.753	5385	1359	1865	41	112.1	110.8	+1.3
St. Louis 72	72	2779	7162	.388	2180	3047	.715	5445	1541	1875	40	107.5	106.2	+1.3
Cincinnati 72	72	2817	7339	.384	1688	2372	.712	4959	1578	1835	30	101.7	100.6	+1.1
Philadelphia 72	72	2765	7276	.380	1977	2596	.762	4836	1441	1763	31	104.3	104.4	-0.1
Detroit 72	72	2746	7295	.376	2093	2774	.755	5168	1264	1807	32	105.3	107.7	-2.4
Minneapolis 72	72	2660	7192	.370	2246	3007	.747	5189	1322	1982	60	105.1	111.5	-6.4
Avgs. 72	72	2810	7333	.383	2058	2757	.746	5160	1414	1834	37.0	106.6	. . .	. . .

HOME/ROAD/NEUTRAL

	Home	Road	Neutral	Total		Home	Road	Neutral	Total
Boston	25-4	17-13	7-6	49-23	Philadelphia	16-12	12-19	9-4	37-35
Cincinnati	17-12	10-19	6-8	33-39	St. Louis	23-8	9-19	9-4	41-31
Detroit	14-14	13-18	6-7	33-39	Syracuse	26-5	9-21	6-5	41-31
Minneapolis	13-17	4-22	2-14	19-53	Totals	150-85	85-150	53-53	288-288
New York	16-13	11-19	8-5	35-37					

INDIVIDUAL LEADERS

POINTS

	G	FGM	FTM	Pts.	Avg.
George Yardley, Detroit	.72	673	655	2001	27.8
Dolph Schayes, Syracuse	.72	581	629	1791	24.9
Bob Pettit, St. Louis	.70	581	557	1719	24.6
Clyde Lovellette, Cincinnati	.71	679	301	1659	23.4
Paul Arizin, Philadelphia	.68	483	440	1406	20.7
Bill Sharman, Boston	.63	550	302	1402	22.3
Cliff Hagan, St. Louis	.70	503	385	1391	19.9
Neil Johnston, Philadelphia	.71	473	442	1388	19.5
Ken Sears, New York	.72	445	452	1342	18.6
Vern Mikkelsen, Minneapolis	.72	439	370	1248	17.3
Jack Twyman, Cincinnati	.72	465	307	1237	17.2
Tom Heinsohn, Boston	.69	468	294	1230	17.8
Willie Naulls, New York	.68	472	284	1228	18.1
Larry Foust, Minneapolis	.72	391	428	1210	16.8
Carl Braun, New York	.71	426	321	1173	16.5
Bob Cousy, Boston	.65	445	277	1167	18.0
Bill Russell, Boston	.69	456	230	1142	16.6
Frank Ramsey, Boston	.69	377	383	1137	16.5
Dick Garmaker, Minneapolis	.68	390	314	1094	16.1
John Kerr, Syracuse	.72	407	280	1094	15.2

FIELD GOALS

(minimum 230 made)

	FGM	FGA	Pct.
Jack Twyman, Cincinnati	.465	1028	.452
Cliff Hagan, St. Louis	.503	1135	.443
Bill Russell, Boston	.456	1032	.442
Ray Felix, New York	.304	688	.442
Clyde Lovellette, Cincinnati	.679	1540	.441
Ken Sears, New York	.445	1014	.439
Neil Johnston, Philadelphia	.473	1102	.429
Ed Macauley, St. Louis	.376	879	.428
Larry Costello, Syracuse	.378	888	.426
Bill Sharman, Boston	.550	1297	.424

FREE THROWS

(minimum 190 made)

	FTM	FTA	Pct.
Dolph Schayes, Syracuse	.629	696	.904
Bill Sharman, Boston	.302	338	.893
Bob Cousy, Boston	.277	326	.850
Carl Braun, New York	.321	378	.849
Dick Schnittker, Minneapolis	.201	237	.848
Larry Costello, Syracuse	.320	378	.847
Gene Shue, Detroit	.276	327	.844
Willie Naulls, New York	.284	344	.826
Ken Sears, New York	.452	550	.822
Ron Sobie, New York	.196	239	.820

ASSISTS

	G	No.	Avg.
Bob Cousy, Boston	.65	463	7.1
Dick McGuire, Detroit	.69	454	6.6
Maurice Stokes, Cincinnati	.63	403	6.4
Carl Braun, New York	.71	393	5.5
George King, Cincinnati	.63	337	5.4
Jack McMahon, St. Louis	.72	333	4.6
Tom Gola, Philadelphia	.59	327	5.5
Richie Guerin, New York	.63	317	5.0
Larry Costello, Syracuse	.72	317	4.4
Jack George, Philadelphia	.72	234	3.3

REBOUNDS

	G	No.	Avg.
Bill Russell, Boston	.69	1564	22.7
Bob Pettit, St. Louis	.70	1216	17.4
Maurice Stokes, Cincinnati	.63	1142	18.1
Dolph Schayes, Syracuse	.72	1022	14.2
John Kerr, Syracuse	.72	963	13.4
Walter Dukes, Detroit	.72	954	13.3
Larry Foust, Minneapolis	.72	876	12.2
Clyde Lovellette, Cincinnati	.71	862	12.1
Vern Mikkelsen, Minneapolis	.72	805	11.2
Willie Naulls, New York	.68	799	11.8

1957-58

INDIVIDUAL STATISTICS, TEAM BY TEAM

BOSTON CELTICS

	G	Min.	FGM	FGA	Pct.	FTM	FTA	Pct.	Reb.	Ast.	PF	Dq.	SCORING Pts.	SCORING Avg.
Bill Sharman	63	2214	550	1297	.424	302	338	.893	295	167	156	3	1402	22.3
Tom Heinsohn	69	2206	468	1226	.382	294	394	.746	705	125	274	6	1230	17.8
Bob Cousy	65	2222	445	1262	.353	277	326	.850	322	463	136	1	1167	18.0
Bill Russell	69	2640	456	1032	.442	230	443	.519	1564	202	181	2	1142	16.6
Frank Ramsey	69	2047	377	900	.419	383	472	.811	504	167	245	8	1137	16.5
Lou Tsioropoulos	70	1819	198	624	.317	142	207	.686	434	112	242	8	538	7.7
Jack Nichols	69	1224	170	484	.351	59	80	.738	302	63	123	1	399	5.8
Arnold Risen	63	1119	134	397	.338	114	267	.427	360	59	195	5	382	6.1
Sam Jones	56	594	100	233	.429	60	84	.714	160	37	42	0	260	4.6
Andy Phillip	70	1164	97	273	.355	42	71	.592	158	121	121	0	236	3.4
Jim Loscutoff	5	56	11	31	.355	1	3	.333	20	1	8	0	23	4.6

CINCINNATI ROYALS

	G	Min.	FGM	FGA	Pct.	FTM	FTA	Pct.	Reb.	Ast.	PF	Dq.	SCORING Pts.	SCORING Avg.
Clyde Lovellette	71	2589	679	1540	.441	301	405	.743	862	134	236	3	1659	23.4
Jack Twyman	72	2178	465	1028	.452	307	396	.775	464	110	224	3	1237	17.2
Maurice Stokes	63	2460	414	1181	.351	238	333	.715	1142	403	226	9	1066	16.9
Jim Paxson	67	1795	225	639	.352	209	285	.733	350	139	183	2	659	9.8
George King	63	2272	235	645	.364	140	227	.617	306	337	124	0	610	9.7
Dick Ricketts	72	1620	215	664	.324	132	196	.673	410	114	277	8	562	7.8
Richie Regan	72	1648	202	569	.355	120	172	.698	175	185	174	0	524	7.3
Dave Piontek	71	1032	150	397	.378	95	151	.629	254	52	134	2	395	5.6
Don Meineke	67	792	125	361	.356	77	119	.647	226	38	155	3	327	4.9
Tom Marshall*	38	518	52	166	.313	48	63	.762	101	19	43		152	4.0
Dick Duckett	34	424	54	158	.342	24	27	.889	56	47	60	0	132	3.9
Jerry Paulson	6	68	8	23	.348	4	6	.667	10	4	5	0	20	3.3

*Marshall—Played 9 Detroit, 29 Cincinnati.

DETROIT PISTONS

	G	Min.	FGM	FGA	Pct.	FTM	FTA	Pct.	Reb.	Ast.	PF	Dq.	Pts.	Avg.
George Yardley	72	2843	673	1624	.414	655	808	.811	768	97	226	3	2001	27.8
Harry Gallatin	72	1990	340	898	.379	392	498	.787	749	86	217	5	1072	14.9
Gene Shue	63	2333	353	919	.384	276	327	.844	333	172	150	1	982	15.6
Walter Dukes	72	2184	278	796	.349	247	366	.675	954	52	311	17	803	11.2
Dick McGuire	69	2311	203	544	.373	150	255	.588	291	454	178	0	556	8.1
Nat Clifton	68	1435	217	597	.363	91	146	.623	403	76	202	3	525	7.7
Chuck Noble	61	1363	199	601	.331	56	77	.727	140	153	166	0	454	7.4
Phil Jordon*	58	898	193	467	.413	64	93	.688	301	37	108	1	450	7.8
Billy Kenville	35	649	106	280	.379	46	75	.613	102	66	68	0	258	7.4
Joe Holup**	53	740	91	278	.327	71	94	.755	221	36	99	2	253	4.8
Bob Houbregs	17	302	49	137	.358	30	43	.698	65	19	36	0	128	7.5
Bill Thieben	27	243	42	154	.273	16	27	.593	65	7	44	0	100	3.7
Dick Atha	18	160	17	47	.362	10	12	.833	24	19	24	0	44	2.4
William Ebben	8	50	6	28	.214	3	4	.750	8	4	5	0	15	1.9
Doug Bolstorff	3	21	2	5	.400	0	0	...	0	0	1	0	4	1.3

*Jordon—Played 12 New York, 46 Detroit.
**Holup—Played 16 Syracuse, 37 Detroit.

MINNEAPOLIS LAKERS

	G	Min.	FGM	FGA	Pct.	FTM	FTA	Pct.	Reb.	Ast.	PF	Dq.	Pts.	Avg.
Vern Mikkelsen	72	2390	439	1070	.410	370	471	.786	805	166	299	20	1248	17.3
Larry Foust	72	2200	391	982	.398	428	566	.756	876	108	299	11	1210	16.8
Dick Garmaker	68	2216	390	988	.395	314	411	.764	365	183	190	2	1094	16.1
Bob Leonard	66	2074	266	794	.335	205	268	.765	237	218	145	0	737	11.2
Ed Fleming	72	1686	226	655	.345	181	255	.710	492	139	222	5	633	8.8
Jim Krebs	68	1259	199	527	.378	135	176	.767	502	27	182	4	533	7.8
Walter Devlin	70	1248	170	489	.348	133	172	.773	132	167	104	1	473	6.8
Dick Schnittker	50	979	128	357	.359	201	237	.848	211	71	126	5	457	9.1
Rod Hundley	65	1154	174	548	.318	104	162	.642	186	121	99	0	452	7.0
Bo Erias	18	401	59	170	.347	30	47	.638	83	26	52	1	148	8.2
Frank Selvy*	38	426	44	167	.263	47	77	.610	88	35	44	0	135	3.6
McCoy Ingram	24	267	27	103	.262	13	28	.464	116	20	44	1	67	2.8
Bob Burrow	14	171	22	70	.314	11	33	.333	64	6	15	0	55	3.9
George Brown	1	6	0	2	.000	1	2	.500	1	0	1	0	1	1.0

*Selvy—Played 26 St. Louis, 12 Minneapolis.

NEW YORK KNICKERBOCKERS

	G	Min.	FGM	FGA	Pct.	FTM	FTA	Pct.	Reb.	Ast.	PF	Dq.	Pts.	Avg.
Kenny Sears	72	2685	445	1014	.439	452	550	.822	785	126	251	7	1342	18.6
Willie Naulls	68	2369	472	1189	.397	284	344	.826	799	97	220	4	1228	18.1
Carl Braun	71	2475	426	1018	.418	321	378	.849	330	393	183	2	1173	16.5
Richie Guerin	63	2368	344	973	.354	353	511	.691	489	317	202	3	1041	16.5
Ray Felix	72	1709	304	688	.442	271	389	.697	747	52	283	12	879	12.2
Guy Sparrow	72	1661	318	838	.379	165	257	.642	461	69	232	6	801	11.1
Ron Sobie	55	1399	217	539	.403	196	239	.820	263	125	147	3	630	11.5
Charlie Tyra	68	1182	175	490	.357	150	224	.670	480	34	175	3	500	7.4
Art Spoelstra*	67	1305	161	419	.384	127	187	.679	332	57	225	11	449	6.7
Larry Friend	44	569	74	226	.327	27	41	.659	106	47	54	0	175	4.0
Mel Hutchins	18	384	51	131	.389	24	43	.558	86	34	31	0	126	7.0
Brendan McCann	36	295	22	100	.220	25	37	.676	45	54	34	0	69	1.9
Ron Shavlik	1	2	0	1	.000	0	0	...	1	0	0	0	0	0.0

*Spoelstra—Played 50 Minneapolis, 17 New York.

PHILADELPHIA WARRIORS

	G	Min.	FGM	FGA	Pct.	FTM	FTA	Pct.	Reb.	Ast.	PF	Dq.	Pts.	Avg.
Paul Arizin	68	2377	483	1229	.393	440	544	.809	503	135	235	7	1406	20.7
Neil Johnston	71	2408	473	1102	.429	442	540	.819	790	166	233	4	1388	19.5
Woody Sauldsberry	71	2377	389	1082	.360	134	218	.615	729	58	245	3	912	12.8
Joe Graboski	72	2077	341	1017	.335	227	303	.749	570	125	249	3	909	12.6
Tom Gola	59	2126	295	711	.415	223	299	.746	639	327	225	11	813	13.8
Ernie Beck	71	1974	272	683	.398	170	203	.837	307	190	173	2	714	10.1
Jack George	72	1910	232	627	.370	178	242	.736	288	234	140	1	642	8.9
George Dempsey	67	1048	112	311	.360	70	105	.667	214	128	113	0	294	4.4
Lennie Rosenbluth	53	373	91	265	.343	53	84	.631	91	23	39	0	235	4.4
Pat Dunn	28	206	28	90	.311	14	17	.824	31	28	20	0	70	2.5
Jim Walsh	10	72	5	27	.185	10	17	.588	15	8	9	0	20	2.0
Ray Radziszewski	1	6	0	3	.000	0	0	...	2	1	1	0	0	0.0

ST. LOUIS HAWKS

	G	Min.	FGM	FGA	Pct.	FTM	FTA	Pct.	Reb.	Ast.	PF	Dq.	Pts.	Avg.
Bob Pettit	70	2528	581	1418	.410	557	744	.749	1216	157	222	6	1719	24.6
Cliff Hagan	70	2190	503	1135	.443	385	501	.768	707	175	267	9	1391	19.9

	G	Min.	FGM	FGA	Pct.	FTM	FTA	Pct.	Reb.	Ast.	PF	Dq.	SCORING Pts.	Avg.
Ed Macauley	72	1908	376	879	.428	267	369	.724	478	143	156	2	1019	14.2
Slater Martin	60	2098	258	768	.336	206	276	.746	228	218	187	0	722	12.0
Charlie Share	72	1824	216	545	.396	190	293	.648	749	130	279	15	622	8.6
Jack McMahon	72	2239	216	719	.300	134	221	.606	195	333	184	2	566	7.9
Win Wilfong	71	1360	196	543	.361	163	238	.685	290	163	199	3	555	7.8
Jack Coleman	72	1506	231	590	.392	84	131	.641	485	117	169	3	546	7.6
Med Park	71	1103	133	363	.366	118	162	.728	184	76	106	0	384	5.4
Walt Davis*	61	663	85	244	.348	61	82	.744	174	29	143	0	231	3.8
Dwight Morrison	13	79	9	26	.346	3	4	.750	26	0	12	0	21	1.6
Worthy Patterson	4	13	3	8	.375	1	2	.500	2	2	3	0	7	1.8

*Davis—Played 35 Philadelphia, 26 St. Louis.

SYRACUSE NATIONALS

	G	Min.	FGM	FGA	Pct.	FTM	FTA	Pct.	Reb.	Ast.	PF	Dq.	SCORING Pts.	Avg.
Dolph Schayes	72	2918	581	1458	.398	629	696	.904	1022	224	244	6	1791	24.9
Red Kerr	72	2384	407	1020	.399	280	422	.664	963	88	197	4	1094	15.2
Larry Costello	72	2746	378	888	.426	320	378	.847	378	317	246	3	1076	14.9
Ed Conlin	60	1871	343	877	.391	215	270	.796	436	133	168	2	901	15.0
Togo Palazzi	67	1001	228	579	.394	123	171	.719	243	42	125	0	579	8.6
Al Bianchi	69	1421	215	625	.344	140	205	.683	221	114	188	4	570	8.3
Bob Hopkins	69	1224	221	554	.399	123	161	.764	392	45	162	5	565	8.2
Bob Harrison	72	1799	210	604	.348	97	122	.795	166	169	200	1	517	7.2
Earl Lloyd	61	1045	119	359	.331	79	106	.745	287	60	179	3	317	5.2
Paul Seymour	64	763	107	315	.340	53	63	.841	107	93	88	0	267	4.2

PLAYOFF RESULTS

EASTERN DIVISION

SEMIFINALS

Philadelphia 2, Syracuse 1

Mar. 15—Sat.	Philadelphia 82 at Syracuse	.86
Mar. 16—Sun.	Syracuse 93 at Philadelphia	.95
Mar. 18—Tue.	Philadelphia 101 at Syracuse	.88

FINALS

Boston 4, Philadelphia 1

Mar. 19—Wed.	Philadelphia 98 at Boston	.107
Mar. 22—Sat.	Boston 109 at Philadelphia	.87
Mar. 23—Sun.	Philadelphia 92 at Boston	.106
Mar. 26—Wed.	Boston 97 at Philadelphia	.111
Mar. 27—Thur.	Philadelphia 88 at Boston	.93

NBA FINALS

St. Louis 4, Boston 2

Mar. 29—Sat.	St. Louis 104 at Boston	.102
Mar. 30—Sun.	St. Louis 112 at Boston	.136
Apr. 2—Wed.	Boston 108 at St. Louis	.111
Apr. 5—Sat.	Boston 109 at St. Louis	.98
Apr. 9—Wed.	St. Louis 102 at Boston	.100
Apr. 12—Sat.	Boston 109 at St. Louis	.110

WESTERN DIVISION

SEMIFINALS

Detroit 2, Cincinnati 0

Mar. 15—Sat.	Cincinnati 93 at Detroit	.100
Mar. 16—Sun.	Detroit 124 at Cincinnati	.104

FINALS

St. Louis 4, Detroit 1

Mar. 19—Wed.	Detroit 111 at St. Louis	.114
Mar. 22—Sat.	St. Louis 99 at Detroit	.96
Mar. 23—Sun.	Detroit 109 at St. Louis	.89
Mar. 25—Tue.	St. Louis 145 at Detroit	.101
Mar. 27—Thur.	Detroit 96 at St. Louis	.120

Bob Pettit averaged 24.6 points in 1957-58 and led the St. Louis Hawks to their only NBA title.

1956-57

1956-57 NBA CHAMPION BOSTON CELTICS
Front row (from left): Lou Tsioropoulos, Andy Phillip, Frank Ramsey, head coach Red Auerbach, captain Bob Cousy, Bill Sharman, Jim Loscutoff. Back row (from left): president Walter A. Brown, Dick Hemric, Jack Nichols, Bill Russell, Arnold Risen, Tom Heinsohn, trainer Harvey Cohn, treasurer Lou Pieri.

FINAL STANDINGS

EASTERN DIVISION

	Bos.	Syr.	Phi.	N.Y.	St.L.	Minn.	Ft.W.	Roch.	W	L	Pct.	GB
Boston	..	5	8	7	7	5	6	6	44	28	.611	..
Syracuse	7	..	7	6	4	5	4	5	38	34	.528	6
Philadelphia	4	5	..	8	7	4	5	4	37	35	.514	7
New York	5	6	4	..	6	6	4	5	36	36	.500	8

WESTERN DIVISION

	Bos.	Syr.	Phi.	N.Y.	St.L.	Minn.	Ft.W.	Roch.	W	L	Pct.	GB
Fort Wayne	3	5	4	5	4	7	..	6	34	38	.472	..
Minneapolis	4	4	5	3	4	..	5	9	34	38	.472	..
St. Louis	2	5	2	3	..	8	8	6	34	38	.472	..
Rochester	3	4	5	4	6	3	6	..	31	41	.431	3

TEAM STATISTICS

	G	FGM	FGA	Pct.	FTM	FTA	Pct.	Reb.	Ast.	PF	Dq.	AVERAGE POINTS For	AVERAGE POINTS Agst.	AVERAGE POINTS Dif.
Boston	72	2808	7326	.383	1983	2644	.750	4963	1464	1851	38	105.5	100.2	+5.3
Philadelphia	72	2584	6533	.396	2062	2658	.776	4305	1467	1732	36	100.4	98.8	+1.6
New York	72	2569	6645	.387	2117	2844	.744	4723	1312	1824	20	100.8	100.9	-0.1
St. Louis	72	2557	6669	.383	1977	2710	.730	4566	1454	1848	36	98.5	98.6	-0.1
Minneapolis	72	2584	6965	.371	2195	2899	.757	4581	1195	1887	49	102.3	103.1	-0.8
Syracuse	72	2550	6915	.369	2075	2613	.794	4350	1282	1809	34	99.7	101.1	-1.4
Rochester	72	2515	6807	.369	1698	2402	.707	4171	1298	1866	38	93.4	95.6	-2.2
Fort Wayne	72	2532	6612	.383	1874	2510	.747	4289	1398	1643	17	96.4	98.7	-2.3
Avgs.	72	2587	6809	.380	1998	2660	.751	4494	1359	1808	33.5	99.6	...	...

HOME/ROAD/NEUTRAL

	Home	Road	Neutral	Total		Home	Road	Neutral	Total
Boston	27-4	12-19	5-5	44-28	Rochester	19-12	9-22	3-7	31-41
Fort Wayne	23-8	7-24	4-6	34-38	St. Louis	18-13	11-20	5-5	34-38
Minneapolis	18-13	9-22	7-3	34-38	Syracuse	22-9	12-19	4-6	38-34
New York	18-10	9-20	9-6	36-36	Totals	172-76	76-172	40-40	288-288
Philadelphia	26-5	5-26	6-4	37-35					

INDIVIDUAL LEADERS

POINTS

	G	FGM	FTM	Pts.	Avg.
Paul Arizin, Philadelphia	71	613	591	1817	25.6
Bob Pettit, St. Louis	71	613	529	1755	24.7
Dolph Schayes, Syracuse	72	496	625	1617	22.5
Neil Johnston, Philadelphia	69	520	535	1575	22.8
George Yardley, Fort Wayne	72	522	503	1547	21.5
Clyde Lovellette, Minneapolis	69	574	286	1434	20.8
Bill Sharman, Boston	67	516	381	1413	21.1
Bob Cousy, Boston	64	478	363	1319	20.6
Ed Macauley, St. Louis	72	414	359	1187	16.5
Dick Garmaker, Minneapolis	72	406	365	1177	16.3
Jack Twyman, Rochester	72	449	276	1174	16.3
Tom Heinsohn, Boston	72	446	271	1163	16.2
Maurice Stokes, Rochester	72	434	256	1124	15.6
Harry Gallatin, New York	72	332	415	1079	15.0
Ken Sears, New York	72	343	383	1069	14.8
Joe Graboski, Philadelphia	72	390	252	1032	14.3
Carl Braun, New York	72	378	245	1001	13.9
Vern Mikkelsen, Minneapolis	72	322	342	986	13.7
Ed Conlin, Syracuse	71	335	283	953	13.4
Red Kerr, Syracuse	72	333	225	891	12.4

FIELD GOALS

(minimum 230 made)

	FGM	FGA	Pct.
Neil Johnston, Philadelphia	520	1163	.447
Jack Twyman, Rochester	449	1023	.439
Charlie Share, St. Louis	235	535	.439
Bob Houbregs, Fort Wayne	253	585	.432
Bill Russell, Boston	277	649	.427
Clyde Lovellette, Minneapolis	574	1348	.426
Paul Arizin, Philadelphia	613	1451	.422
Ed Macauley, St. Louis	414	987	.419
Ken Sears, New York	343	821	.418
Ray Felix, New York	295	709	.416

FREE THROWS

(minimum 190 made)

	FTM	FTA	Pct.
Bill Sharman, Boston	381	421	.905
Dolph Schayes, Syracuse	625	691	.904
Dick Garmaker, Minneapolis	365	435	.839
Paul Arizin, Philadelphia	591	713	.829
Neil Johnston, Philadelphia	535	648	.826
Bob Cousy, Boston	363	442	.821
Carl Braun, New York	245	303	.809
Vern Mikkelsen, Minneapolis	342	424	.807
Joseph Holup, Syracuse	204	253	.806
Harry Gallatin, New York	415	519	.800

ASSISTS

	G	No.	Avg.
Bob Cousy, Boston	64	478	7.5
Jack McMahon, St. Louis	72	367	5.1
Maurice Stokes, Rochester	72	331	4.6
Jack George, Philadelphia	67	307	4.6
Slater Martin, New York-St. Louis	66	269	4.1
Carl Braun, New York	72	256	3.6
Gene Shue, Fort Wayne	72	238	3.3
Bill Sharman, Boston	67	236	3.5
Larry Costello, Philadelphia	72	236	3.3
Dolph Schayes, Syracuse	72	229	3.2

REBOUNDS

	G	No.	Avg.
Maurice Stokes, Rochester	72	1256	17.4
Bob Pettit, St. Louis	71	1037	14.6
Dolph Schayes, Syracuse	72	1008	14.0
Bill Russell, Boston	48	943	19.6
Clyde Lovellette, Minneapolis	69	932	13.5
Neil Johnston, Philadelphia	69	855	12.4
Red Kerr, Syracuse	72	807	11.2
Walter Dukes, Minneapolis	71	794	11.2
George Yardley, Fort Wayne	72	755	10.5
Jim Loscutoff, Boston	70	730	10.4

1956-57

INDIVIDUAL STATISTICS, TEAM BY TEAM

BOSTON CELTICS

	G	Min.	FGM	FGA	Pct.	FTM	FTA	Pct.	Reb.	Ast.	PF	Dq.	Pts.	Avg.
Bill Sharman	67	2403	516	1241	.416	381	421	.905	286	236	188	1	1413	21.1
Bob Cousy	64	2364	478	1264	.378	363	442	.821	309	478	134	0	1319	20.6
Tom Heinsohn	72	2150	446	1123	.397	271	343	.790	705	117	304	12	1163	16.2
Jim Loscutoff	70	2220	306	888	.345	132	187	.706	730	89	244	5	744	10.6
Bill Russell	48	1695	277	649	.427	152	309	.492	943	88	143	2	706	14.7
Jack Nichols	61	1372	195	537	.363	108	136	.794	374	85	185	4	498	8.2
Frank Ramsey	35	807	137	349	.393	144	182	.791	178	67	113	3	418	11.9
Dick Hemric	67	1055	109	317	.344	146	210	.695	304	42	98	0	364	5.4
Arnold Risen	43	935	119	307	.388	106	156	.679	286	53	163	4	344	8.0
Andy Phillip	67	1476	105	277	.379	88	137	.642	181	168	121	1	298	4.4
Lou Tsioropoulos	52	670	79	256	.309	69	89	.775	207	33	135	6	227	4.4

FORT WAYNE PISTONS

	G	Min.	FGM	FGA	Pct.	FTM	FTA	Pct.	Reb.	Ast.	PF	Dq.	Pts.	Avg.
George Yardley	72	2691	522	1273	.410	503	639	.787	755	147	231	2	1547	21.5
Mel Hutchins	72	2647	369	953	.387	152	206	.738	571	210	182	0	890	12.4
Gene Shue	72	2470	273	710	.385	241	316	.763	421	238	137	0	787	10.9
Larry Foust	61	1533	243	617	.394	273	380	.718	555	71	221	7	759	12.4
Bob Houbregs	60	1592	253	585	.432	167	234	.714	401	113	118	2	673	11.2
Billy Kenville	71	1701	204	608	.336	174	218	.798	324	172	169	3	582	8.2
Walter Devlin	71	1242	190	502	.378	97	143	.678	146	141	114	0	477	6.7
Chuck Noble	54	1260	200	556	.360	76	102	.745	135	180	161	2	476	8.8
Red Rocha	72	1154	136	390	.349	109	144	.757	272	81	162	1	381	5.3
Bill Thieben	58	633	90	256	.352	57	87	.655	207	17	78	0	237	4.1
Dick Rosenthal	18	188	21	79	.266	9	17	.529	52	17	22	0	51	2.8

MINNEAPOLIS LAKERS

	G	Min.	FGM	FGA	Pct.	FTM	FTA	Pct.	Reb.	Ast.	PF	Dq.	SCORING Pts.	Avg.
Clyde Lovellette	69	2492	574	1348	.426	286	399	.717	932	139	251	4	1434	20.8
Dick Garmaker	72	2406	406	1015	.400	365	435	.839	336	190	199	1	1177	16.3
Vern Mikkelsen	72	2198	322	854	.377	342	424	.807	630	121	312	18	986	13.7
Bob Leonard	72	1943	303	867	.349	186	241	.772	220	169	140	0	792	11.0
Walter Dukes	71	1866	228	626	.364	264	383	.689	794	54	273	10	720	10.1
Charles Mencel	72	1848	243	688	.353	179	240	.746	237	201	95	0	665	9.2
Ed Kalafat	65	1617	178	507	.351	197	298	.661	425	105	243	9	553	8.5
Jim Paxson	71	1274	138	485	.285	170	236	.720	266	86	163	3	446	6.3
Dick Schnittker	70	997	113	351	.322	160	193	.829	185	52	144	3	386	5.5
Whitey Skoog	23	656	78	220	.355	44	47	.936	72	76	65	1	200	8.7
Bob Williams	4	20	1	4	.250	2	3	.667	5	0	2	0	4	1.0

NEW YORK KNICKERBOCKERS

	G	Min.	FGM	FGA	Pct.	FTM	FTA	Pct.	Reb.	Ast.	PF	Dq.	SCORING Pts.	Avg.
Harry Gallatin	72	1943	332	817	.406	415	519	.800	725	85	202	1	1079	15.0
Kenny Sears	72	2516	343	821	.418	383	485	.790	614	101	226	2	1069	14.8
Carl Braun	72	2345	378	993	.381	245	303	.809	259	256	195	1	1001	13.9
Ray Felix	72	1622	295	709	.416	277	371	.747	587	36	284	8	867	12.0
Nat Clifton	71	2231	308	818	.377	146	217	.673	557	164	243	5	762	10.7
Willie Naulls*	71	1778	293	820	.357	132	195	.677	617	84	186	1	718	10.1
Richie Guerin	72	1793	257	699	.368	181	292	.620	334	182	186	3	695	9.7
Ron Sobie	71	1378	166	442	.376	152	199	.764	326	129	158	0	484	6.8
Dick McGuire	72	1191	140	366	.383	105	163	.644	146	222	103	0	385	5.3
Jim Baechtold	45	462	75	197	.381	66	88	.750	80	33	39	0	216	4.8
Phil Jordon	9	91	18	49	.367	8	12	.667	34	2	15	0	44	4.9
Ron Shavlik	7	7	4	22	.182	2	5	.400	22	0	12	0	10	1.4
Gary Bergen	6	6	3	11	.273	2	2	1.000	8	1	4	0	8	1.3

*Naulls—Played with St. Louis, New York.

PHILADELPHIA WARRIORS

	G	Min.	FGM	FGA	Pct.	FTM	FTA	Pct.	Reb.	Ast.	PF	Dq.	SCORING Pts.	Avg.
Paul Arizin	71	2767	613	1451	.422	591	713	.829	561	150	274	13	1817	25.6
Neil Johnston	69	2531	520	1163	.447	535	648	.826	855	203	231	2	1575	22.8
Joe Graboski	72	2501	390	1118	.349	252	322	.783	614	140	244	5	1032	14.3
Jack George	67	2229	253	750	.337	200	293	.683	318	307	165	3	706	10.5
Larry Costello	72	2111	186	497	.374	175	222	.788	323	236	182	2	547	7.6
Ernie Beck	72	1743	195	508	.384	111	157	.707	312	190	155	1	501	7.0
Walt Davis	65	1250	178	437	.407	74	106	.698	306	52	235	9	430	6.6
George Dempsey	71	1147	134	302	.444	55	102	.539	251	136	107	0	323	4.5
Lew Hitch*	68	1133	111	296	.375	63	88	.716	253	40	103	0	285	4.2
Jackie Moore	57	400	43	106	.406	37	46	.804	116	21	75	1	123	2.2
Bob Armstrong	19	110	11	37	.297	6	12	.500	39	3	13	0	28	1.5
Hal Lear	3	14	2	6	.333	0	0	…	1	1	3	0	4	1.3

*Hitch—Played with Minneapolis, Philadelphia.

ROCHESTER ROYALS

	G	Min.	FGM	FGA	Pct.	FTM	FTA	Pct.	Reb.	Ast.	PF	Dq.	SCORING Pts.	Avg.
Jack Twyman	72	2338	449	1023	.439	276	363	.760	354	123	251	4	1174	16.3
Maurice Stokes	72	2761	434	1249	.347	256	385	.665	1256	331	287	12	1124	15.6
Dick Ricketts	72	2114	299	869	.344	206	297	.694	437	127	307	12	804	11.2
Richie Regan	71	2100	257	780	.329	182	235	.774	205	222	179	1	696	9.8
Dave Piontek	71	1759	257	637	.403	122	183	.667	351	108	141	1	636	9.0
Art Spoelstra	69	1176	217	559	.388	88	120	.733	220	56	168	5	522	7.6
Johnny McCarthy	72	1560	173	460	.376	130	193	.674	201	107	130	0	476	6.6
Bob Burrow	67	1028	137	364	.376	130	211	.616	293	41	165	2	404	6.0
Ed Fleming	51	927	109	364	.299	139	191	.728	183	81	94	0	357	7.0
Tom Marshall	40	460	56	163	.344	47	58	.810	83	31	33	0	159	4.0
Sihugo Green	13	423	50	143	.350	49	69	.710	37	67	36	1	149	11.5
Bobby Wanzer	21	159	23	49	.469	36	46	.783	25	9	20	0	82	3.9

ST. LOUIS HAWKS

	G	Min.	FGM	FGA	Pct.	FTM	FTA	Pct.	Reb.	Ast.	PF	Dq.	SCORING Pts.	Avg.
Bob Pettit	71	2491	613	1477	.415	529	684	.773	1037	133	181	1	1755	24.7
Ed Macauley	72	2582	414	987	.419	359	479	.749	440	202	206	2	1187	16.5
Jack Coleman	72	2145	316	775	.408	123	161	.764	645	159	235	7	755	10.5
Charlie Share	72	1673	235	535	.439	269	393	.684	642	79	269	15	739	10.3
Slater Martin*	66	2401	244	736	.332	230	291	.790	288	269	193	1	718	10.9
Jack McMahon	72	2344	239	725	.330	142	225	.631	222	367	213	2	620	8.6
Cliff Hagan	67	971	134	371	.361	100	145	.690	247	86	165	3	368	5.5
Med Park	66	1130	118	324	.364	108	146	.740	200	94	137	2	344	5.2
Irv Bemoras	62	983	124	385	.322	70	103	.680	127	46	76	0	318	5.1
Alex Hannum**	59	642	77	223	.345	37	56	.661	158	28	135	2	191	3.2

	G	Min.	FGM	FGA	Pct.	FTM	FTA	Pct.	Reb.	Ast.	PF	Dq.	SCORING Pts.	Avg.
Marion Spears***	11	118	12	38	.316	19	22	.864	15	7	24	0	43	3.9
Norm Stewart..................	5	37	4	15	.267	2	6	.333	5	2	9	0	10	2.0
John Barber	5	5	2	8	.250	3	6	.500	6	0	4	0	7	1.4

*Martin—Played with New York, St. Louis.
**Hannum—Played with Fort Wayne, St. Louis.
***Spears—Played with Fort Wayne, St. Louis.

SYRACUSE NATIONALS

	G	Min.	FGM	FGA	Pct.	FTM	FTA	Pct.	Reb.	Ast.	PF	Dq.	SCORING Pts.	Avg.
Dolph Schayes................	72	2851	496	1308	.379	625	691	.904	1008	229	219	5	1617	22.5
Ed Conlin....................	71	2250	335	896	.374	283	368	.769	430	205	170	0	953	13.4
Red Kerr	72	2191	333	827	.403	225	313	.719	807	90	190	3	891	12.4
Earl Lloyd	72	1965	256	687	.373	134	179	.749	435	114	282	10	646	9.0
Bob Harrison.................	66	1810	243	629	.386	93	130	.715	156	161	220	5	579	8.8
Al Bianchi	68	1577	199	567	.351	165	239	.690	227	106	198	5	563	8.3
Togo Palazzi*................	63	1013	210	571	.368	136	175	.777	262	49	117	1	556	8.8
Joe Holup	71	1284	160	487	.329	204	253	.806	279	84	177	5	524	7.4
Paul Seymour	65	1235	143	442	.324	101	123	.821	130	193	91	0	387	6.0
Bob Hopkins	62	764	130	343	.379	94	126	.746	233	22	106	0	354	5.7
Larry Hennessy	21	373	56	175	.320	23	32	.719	45	27	28	0	135	6.4
Bob Schafer.................	11	167	19	66	.288	11	13	.846	11	15	16	0	49	4.5
Jim Tucker	9	110	17	44	.386	0	1	.000	20	2	26	0	34	3.8
Don Savage	5	55	6	19	.316	6	7	.857	7	2	7	0	18	3.6
Jim Ray	4	43	2	11	.182	3	5	.600	5	3	4	0	7	1.8
Forest Able.................	1	1	0	2	.000	0	0	...	1	1	1	0	0	0.0

*Palazzi—Played with Boston, Syracuse.

PLAYOFF RESULTS

EASTERN DIVISION

SEMIFINALS
Syracuse 2, Philadelphia 0
Mar. 16—Sat. Syracuse 103 at Philadelphia 96
Mar. 18—Mon. Philadelphia 80 at Syracuse 91

FINALS
Boston 3, Syracuse 0
Mar. 21—Thur. Syracuse 90 at Boston 108
Mar. 23—Sat. Boston 120 at Syracuse 105
Mar. 24—Sun. Syracuse 80 at Boston 83

WESTERN DIVISION

TIEBREAKERS
Mar. 14—Thur. Fort Wayne 103 at St. Louis 115
Mar. 16—Sat. Minneapolis 111 at St. Louis................114

SEMIFINALS
Minneapolis 2, Fort Wayne 0
Mar. 17—Sun. Fort Wayne 127 at Minneapolis 131
Mar. 19—Tue. Minneapolis 110 at Fort Wayne 108

FINALS
St. Louis 3, Minneapolis 0
Mar. 21—Thur. Minneapolis 109 at St. Louis................118
Mar. 24—Sun. Minneapolis 104 at St. Louis 106
Mar. 25—Mon. St. Louis 143 at Minneapolis **135

NBA FINALS
Boston 4, St. Louis 3
Mar. 30—Sat. St. Louis 125 at Boston **123
Mar. 31—Sun. St. Louis 99 at Boston 119
Apr. 6—Sat. Boston 98 at St. Louis 100
Apr. 7—Sun. Boston 123 at St. Louis 118
Apr. 9—Tue. St. Louis 109 at Boston 124
Apr. 11—Thur. Boston 94 at St. Louis 96
Apr. 13—Sat. St. Louis 123 at Boston **125

*Denotes number of overtime periods.

1956-57

1955-56

1955-56 NBA CHAMPION PHILADELPHIA WARRIORS
Front row (from left): head coach George Senesky, Larry Hennessy, Paul Arizin, Jack George, George Dempsey, president Eddie Gottlieb. Back row (from left): Ernie Beck, Neil Johnston, Joe Graboski, Walt Davis, Tom Gola, Jackie Moore.

FINAL STANDINGS

EASTERN DIVISION

	Phi.	Bos.	N.Y.	Syr.	Ft.W.	Minn.	St.L.	Roch.	W	L	Pct.	GB
Philadelphia	..	7	6	9	5	6	6	6	45	27	.625	..
Boston 5		..	5	8	4	7	5	5	39	33	.542	6
Syracuse 3		4	8	..	5	5	6	4	35	37	.486	10
New York 6		7	..	4	4	4	4	6	35	37	.486	10

WESTERN DIVISION

	Phi.	Bos.	N.Y.	Syr.	Ft.W.	Minn.	St.L.	Roch.	W	L	Pct.	GB
Fort Wayne 4		5	5	4	..	5	7	7	37	35	.514	..
St. Louis. 3		4	5	3	5	7	..	6	33	39	.458	4
Minneapolis 3		2	5	4	7	..	5	7	33	39	.458	4
Rochester. 3		4	3	5	5	5	6	..	31	41	.431	6

TEAM STATISTICS

	G	FGM	FGA	Pct.	FTM	FTA	Pct.	Reb.	Ast.	PF	Dq.	AVERAGE POINTS For	AVERAGE POINTS Agst.	AVERAGE POINTS Dif.
Philadelphia. 72		2641	6437	.410	2142	2829	.757	4362	1886	1872	45	103.1	98.8	+4.3
Boston 72		2745	6913	.397	2142	2785	.769	4583	1834	1874	44	106.0	105.3	+0.7
Fort Wayne 72		2396	6174	.388	2002	2729	.734	3974	1752	1789	20	94.4	93.7	+0.7
Syracuse 72		2466	6661	.370	2044	2703	.756	4060	1710	1783	32	96.9	96.9	0.0
New York. 72		2508	6395	.392	2196	2913	.754	4562	1610	1923	43	100.2	100.6	-0.4
Minneapolis. 72		2541	6543	.388	2066	2627	.786	4133	1689	1978	43	99.3	100.2	-0.9
St. Louis 72		2506	6628	.378	1941	2761	.703	4493	1748	1971	42	96.6	98.0	-1.4
Rochester 72		2551	6890	.370	1798	2567	.700	4449	1747	1990	46	95.8	98.7	-2.9
Avgs. 72		2544	6580	.387	2041	2739	.745	4327	1747	1898	39.4	99.0	. . .	. . .

HOME/ROAD/NEUTRAL

	Home	Road	Neutral	Total		Home	Road	Neutral	Total
Boston	20-7	12-15	7-11	39-33	Rochester.	15-14	7-21	9-6	31-41
Fort Wayne.	19-8	10-17	8-10	37-35	St. Louis.	16-10	10-17	7-12	33-39
Minneapolis	13-12	6-21	14-6	33-39	Syracuse	23-8	9-19	3-10	35-37
New York	14-14	15-14	6-9	35-37	Totals	141-80	80-141	67-67	288-288
Philadelphia	21-7	11-17	13-3	45-27					

POINTS

	G	FGM	FTM	Pts.	Avg.
Bob Pettit, St. Louis	72	646	557	1849	25.7
Paul Arizin, Philadelphia	72	617	507	1741	24.2
Neil Johnston, Philadelphia	70	499	549	1547	22.1
Clyde Lovellette, Minneapolis	71	594	338	1526	21.5
Dolph Schayes, Syracuse	72	465	542	1472	20.4
Bill Sharman, Boston	72	538	358	1434	19.9
Bob Cousy, Boston	72	440	476	1356	18.8
Ed Macauley, Boston	71	420	400	1240	17.5
George Yardley, Fort Wayne	71	434	365	1233	17.4
Larry Foust, Fort Wayne	72	367	432	1166	16.2
Maurice Stokes, Rochester	67	403	319	1125	16.8
Carl Braun, New York	72	396	320	1112	15.4
Jack Twyman, Rochester	72	417	204	1038	14.4
Joe Graboski, Philadelphia	72	397	240	1034	14.4
Harry Gallatin, New York	72	322	358	1002	13.9
Jack George, Philadelphia	72	352	296	1000	13.9
Charles Share, St. Louis	72	315	346	976	13.6
Vern Mikkelsen, Minneapolis	72	317	328	962	13.4
Red Kerr, Syracuse	72	377	207	961	13.3
Jack Coleman, Roch.-St. Louis	75	390	177	957	12.8

FIELD GOALS

(minimum 230 made)

	FGM	FGA	Pct.
Neil Johnston, Philadelphia	499	1092	.457
Paul Arizin, Philadelphia	617	1378	.448
Larry Foust, Fort Wayne	367	821	.447
Bill Sharman, Boston	538	1229	.438
Ken Sears, New York	319	728	.438
Clyde Lovellette, Minneapolis	594	1370	.434
Charles Share, St. Louis	315	733	.430
Bob Houbregs, Fort Wayne	247	575	.430
Bob Pettit, St. Louis	646	1507	.429
Mel Hutchins, Fort Wayne	325	764	.425

FREE THROWS

(minimum 190 made)

	FTM	FTA	Pct.
Bill Sharman, Boston	358	413	.867
Dolph Schayes, Syracuse	542	632	.858
Dick Schnittker, Minneapolis	304	355	.856
Bob Cousy, Boston	476	564	.844
Carl Braun, New York	320	382	.838
Slater Martin, Minneapolis	329	395	.833
Paul Arizin, Philadelphia	507	626	.810
Vern Mikkelsen, Minneapolis	328	408	.804
Neil Johnston, Philadelphia	549	685	.801
Jim Baechtold, New York	233	291	.801

ASSISTS

	G	No.	Avg.
Bob Cousy, Boston	72	642	8.9
Jack George, Philadelphia	72	457	6.4
Slater Martin, Minneapolis	72	445	6.2
Andy Phillip, Fort Wayne	70	410	5.9
George King, Syracuse	72	410	5.7
Tom Gola, Philadelphia	68	404	5.9
Dick McGuire, New York	62	362	5.8
Bill Sharman, Boston	72	339	4.7
Maurice Stokes, Rochester	67	328	4.9
Carl Braun, New York	72	298	4.1

REBOUNDS

	G	No.	Avg.
Bob Pettit, St. Louis	72	1164	16.2
Maurice Stokes, Rochester	67	1094	16.3
Clyde Lovellette, Minneapolis	71	992	14.0
Dolph Schayes, Syracuse	72	891	12.4
Neil Johnston, Philadelphia	70	872	12.5
Charles Share, St. Louis	72	774	10.8
Harry Gallatin, New York	72	740	10.3
Jack Coleman, Rochester-St. Louis	75	688	9.2
George Yardley, Fort Wayne	71	686	9.7
Larry Foust, Fort Wayne	72	648	9.0

BOSTON CELTICS

	G	Min.	FGM	FGA	Pct.	FTM	FTA	Pct.	Reb.	Ast.	PF	Dq.	SCORING Pts.	SCORING Avg.
Bill Sharman	72	2698	538	1229	.438	358	413	.867	259	339	197	1	1434	19.9
Bob Cousy	72	2767	440	1223	.360	476	564	.844	492	642	206	2	1356	18.8
Ed Macauley	71	2354	420	995	.422	400	504	.794	422	211	158	2	1240	17.5
Jack Nichols	60	1964	330	799	.413	200	253	.791	625	160	228	7	860	14.3
Jim Loscutoff	71	1582	226	628	.360	139	207	.671	622	65	213	4	591	8.3
Arnold Risen	68	1597	189	493	.383	170	240	.708	553	88	300	17	548	8.1
Ernie Barrett	72	1451	207	533	.388	93	118	.788	243	174	184	4	507	7.0
Dick Hemric	71	1329	161	400	.403	177	273	.648	399	60	142	2	499	7.0
Togo Palazzi	63	703	145	373	.389	85	124	.685	182	42	87	0	375	6.0
Dwight Morrison	71	910	89	240	.371	44	89	.494	345	53	159	5	222	3.1

FORT WAYNE PISTONS

	G	Min.	FGM	FGA	Pct.	FTM	FTA	Pct.	Reb.	Ast.	PF	Dq.	SCORING Pts.	SCORING Avg.
George Yardley	71	2353	434	1067	.407	365	492	.742	686	159	212	2	1233	17.4
Larry Foust	72	2024	367	821	.447	432	555	.778	648	127	263	7	1166	16.2
Mel Hutchins	66	2240	325	764	.425	142	221	.643	496	180	166	1	792	12.0
Bob Houbregs	70	1535	247	575	.430	283	383	.739	414	159	147	0	777	11.1
Chuck Noble	72	2013	270	767	.352	146	195	.749	261	282	253	3	686	9.5
Walter Devlin	69	1535	200	541	.370	146	192	.760	171	138	119	0	546	7.9
Marion Spears	72	1378	166	468	.355	159	201	.791	231	121	191	2	491	6.8
Andy Phillip	70	2078	148	405	.365	112	199	.563	257	410	155	2	408	5.8
Charles Cooper*	67	1144	101	308	.328	100	133	.752	239	89	140	0	302	4.5
Frank Brian	37	680	78	263	.297	72	88	.818	88	74	62	0	228	6.2
Jesse Arnelle	31	409	52	164	.317	43	69	.623	170	18	60	0	147	4.7
Max Zaslofsky	9	182	29	81	.358	30	35	.857	16	16	18	1	88	9.8
Jim Holstein**	27	352	24	89	.270	24	37	.649	76	38	51	1	72	2.7
Don Bielke	7	38	5	9	.556	4	7	.571	9	1	9	0	14	2.0

*Cooper—Played with St. Louis, Fort Wayne.
**Holstein—Played with Minneapolis, Fort Wayne.

1955-56

While George Mikan (left) was winding down a stellar career, Dolph Schayes was emerging as a marquee name.

MINNEAPOLIS LAKERS

	G	Min.	FGM	FGA	Pct.	FTM	FTA	Pct.	Reb.	Ast.	PF	Dq.	Pts.	Avg.
Clyde Lovellette	71	2518	594	1370	.434	338	469	.721	992	164	245	5	1526	21.5
Vern Mikkelsen	72	2100	317	821	.386	328	408	.804	608	173	319	17	962	13.4
Slater Martin	72	2838	309	863	.358	329	395	.833	260	445	202	2	947	13.2
Whitey Skoog	72	2311	340	854	.398	155	193	.803	291	255	232	5	835	11.6
Dick Schnittker	72	1930	254	647	.393	304	355	.856	296	142	253	4	812	11.3
Ed Kalafat	72	1639	194	540	.359	186	252	.738	440	130	236	2	574	8.0
George Mikan	37	765	148	375	.395	94	122	.770	308	53	153	6	390	10.5
Dick Garmaker	68	870	138	373	.370	112	139	.806	132	104	127	0	388	5.7
Charles Mencel	69	973	120	375	.320	78	96	.813	110	132	74	1	318	4.6
Lew Hitch	69	1129	94	235	.400	100	132	.758	283	77	85	0	288	4.2
Bob Williams	20	173	21	46	.457	24	45	.533	54	7	36	1	66	3.3
Johnny Horan*	19	93	12	42	.286	10	11	.909	10	2	21	0	34	1.8
Ron Feireisel	10	59	8	28	.286	14	16	.875	6	6	9	0	30	3.0

*Horan—Played with Fort Wayne, Minneapolis.

NEW YORK KNICKERBOCKERS

	G	Min.	FGM	FGA	Pct.	FTM	FTA	Pct.	Reb.	Ast.	PF	Dq.	Pts.	Avg.
Carl Braun	72	2316	396	1064	.372	320	382	.838	259	298	215	3	1112	15.4
Harry Gallatin	72	2378	322	834	.386	358	455	.787	740	168	220	6	1002	13.9
Kenny Sears	70	2069	319	728	.438	258	324	.796	616	114	201	4	896	12.8
Ray Felix	72	1702	277	668	.415	331	469	.706	623	47	293	13	885	12.3
Jim Baechtold	70	1738	268	695	.386	233	291	.801	220	163	156	2	769	11.0
Gene Shue	72	1750	240	625	.384	181	237	.764	212	179	111	0	661	9.2
Nat Clifton	64	1537	213	541	.394	135	191	.707	386	151	189	4	561	8.8
Walter Dukes	60	1290	149	370	.403	167	236	.708	443	39	211	11	465	7.8
Dick McGuire	62	1685	152	438	.347	121	193	.627	220	362	146	0	425	6.9
Bob Peterson	58	779	121	303	.399	68	104	.654	223	44	123	0	310	5.3
Dick Atha	25	288	36	88	.409	21	27	.778	42	32	39	0	93	3.7
Ernie Vandeweghe	5	77	10	31	.323	2	2	1.000	13	12	15	0	22	4.4
Bob Santini	4	23	5	10	.500	1	2	.500	3	1	4	0	11	2.8

PHILADELPHIA WARRIORS

	G	Min.	FGM	FGA	Pct.	FTM	FTA	Pct.	Reb.	Ast.	PF	Dq.	Pts.	Avg.
Paul Arizin	72	2724	617	1378	.448	507	626	.810	530	189	282	11	1741	24.2
Neil Johnston	70	2594	499	1092	.457	549	685	.801	872	225	251	8	1547	22.1
Joe Graboski	72	2375	397	1075	.369	240	340	.706	642	190	272	5	1034	14.4
Jack George	72	2840	352	940	.374	296	391	.757	313	457	202	1	1000	13.9
Tom Gola	68	2346	244	592	.412	244	333	.733	616	404	272	11	732	10.8
Ernie Beck	67	1007	136	351	.387	76	106	.717	196	79	86	0	348	5.2
George Dempsey	72	1444	126	265	.475	88	139	.633	264	205	146	7	340	4.7
Walt Davis	70	1097	123	333	.369	77	112	.688	276	56	230	7	323	4.6
Larry Hennessy	53	444	85	247	.344	26	32	.813	49	46	37	0	196	3.7
Jackie Moore	54	402	50	129	.388	32	53	.604	117	26	80	1	132	2.4

ROCHESTER ROYALS

	G	Min.	FGM	FGA	Pct.	FTM	FTA	Pct.	Reb.	Ast.	PF	Dq.	Pts.	Avg.
Maurice Stokes	67	2323	403	1137	.354	319	447	.714	1094	328	276	11	1125	16.8
Jack Twyman.................	72	2186	417	987	.422	204	298	.685	466	171	239	4	1038	14.4
Ed Fleming	71	2028	306	824	.371	277	372	.745	489	197	178	1	889	12.5
Bobby Wanzer	72	1980	245	651	.376	259	360	.719	272	225	151	0	749	10.4
Art Spoelstra	72	1640	226	576	.392	163	238	.685	436	95	248	11	615	8.5
Dick Ricketts*	68	1943	235	752	.313	138	195	.708	490	206	287	14	608	8.9
Richie Regan	72	1746	240	681	.352	85	133	.639	174	222	179	4	565	7.8
Don Meineke...............	69	1248	154	414	.372	181	232	.780	316	102	191	4	489	7.1
Connie Simmons.............	68	903	144	428	.336	78	129	.605	235	82	142	2	366	5.4
Chris Harris**	41	420	37	149	.248	27	45	.600	44	44	43	0	101	2.5
James Davis.................	3	16	0	6	.000	2	2	1.000	4	1	2	0	2	0.7

*Ricketts—Played with St. Louis, Rochester.
**Harris—Played with St. Louis, Rochester.

ST. LOUIS HAWKS

	G	Min.	FGM	FGA	Pct.	FTM	FTA	Pct.	Reb.	Ast.	PF	Dq.	Pts.	Avg.
Bob Pettit	72	2794	646	1507	.429	557	757	.736	1164	189	202	1	1849	25.7
Charlie Share................	72	1975	315	733	.430	346	498	.695	774	131	318	13	976	13.6
Jack Coleman*	75	2738	390	946	.412	177	249	.711	688	294	242	2	957	12.8
Jack Stephens...............	72	2219	248	643	.386	247	357	.692	377	207	144	6	743	10.3
Bob Harrison	72	2219	260	725	.359	97	146	.664	195	277	246	6	617	8.6
Al Ferrari..................	68	1611	191	534	.358	164	236	.695	186	163	192	3	546	8.0
Jack McMahon**	70	1713	202	615	.328	110	185	.595	180	222	170	1	514	7.3
Alex Hannum	71	1480	146	453	.322	93	154	.604	344	157	271	10	385	5.4
Bob Schafer***	54	578	81	270	.300	62	81	.765	71	53	75	0	224	4.1
Frank Selvy	17	444	67	183	.366	53	71	.746	54	35	38	1	187	11.0
Med Park...................	40	424	53	152	.349	44	70	.629	94	40	64	0	150	3.8

*Coleman—Played with Rochester, St. Louis.
**McMahon—Played with Rochester, St. Louis.
***Schafer—Played with Philadelphia, St. Louis.

SYRACUSE NATIONALS

	G	Min.	FGM	FGA	Pct.	FTM	FTA	Pct.	Reb.	Ast.	PF	Dq.	Pts.	Avg.
Dolph Schayes................	72	2517	465	1202	.387	542	632	.858	891	200	251	9	1472	20.4
Red Kerr...................	72	2114	377	935	.403	207	316	.655	607	84	168	3	961	13.3
George King	72	2343	284	763	.372	176	275	.640	250	410	150	2	744	10.3
Red Rocha.................	72	1883	250	692	.361	220	281	.783	416	131	244	6	720	10.0
Paul Seymour	57	1826	227	670	.339	188	233	.807	152	276	130	1	642	11.3
Earl Lloyd..................	72	1837	213	636	.335	186	241	.772	492	116	267	6	612	8.5
Ed Conlin..................	66	1423	211	574	.368	121	178	.680	326	145	121	1	543	8.2
Billy Kenville	72	1278	170	448	.379	195	257	.759	215	159	132	0	535	7.4
Dick Farley.................	72	1429	168	451	.373	143	207	.691	165	151	154	2	479	6.7
Jim Tucker.................	70	895	101	290	.348	66	83	.795	232	38	166	2	268	3.8

PLAYOFF RESULTS

EASTERN DIVISION

THIRD-PLACE GAME
Mar. 15—Thur. New York 77 at Syracuse 82

SEMIFINALS
Syracuse 2, Boston 1
Mar. 17—Sat. Syracuse 93 at Boston 110
Mar. 19—Mon. Boston 98 at Syracuse 101
Mar. 21—Wed. Syracuse 102 at Boston 97

FINALS
Philadelphia 3, Syracuse 2
Mar. 23—Fri. Syracuse 87 at Philadelphia 109
Mar. 25—Sun. Philadelphia 118 at Syracuse 122
Mar. 27—Tue. Syracuse 96 at Philadelphia 119
Mar. 28—Wed. Philadelphia 104 at Syracuse 108
Mar. 29—Thur. Syracuse 104 at Philadelphia 109

WESTERN DIVISION

SECOND-PLACE GAME
Mar. 16—Fri. Minneapolis 103 at St. Louis 97

SEMIFINALS
St. Louis 2, Minneapolis 1
Mar. 17—Sat. Minneapolis 115 at St. Louis 116
Mar. 19—Mon. St. Louis 75 at Minneapolis 133
Mar. 21—Wed. St. Louis 116 at Minneapolis 115

FINALS
Fort Wayne 3, St. Louis 2
Mar. 22—Thur. St. Louis 86 at Fort Wayne 85
Mar. 24—Sat. Fort Wayne 74 at St. Louis 84
Mar. 25—Sun. St. Louis 84 at Fort Wayne 107
Mar. 27—Tue. Fort Wayne 93 at St. Louis 84
Mar. 29—Thur. St. Louis 97 at Fort Wayne 102

NBA FINALS

Philadelphia 4, Fort Wayne 1
Mar. 31—Sat. Fort Wayne 94 at Philadelphia 98
Apr. 1—Sun. Philadelphia 83 at Fort Wayne 84
Apr. 3—Tue. Fort Wayne 96 at Philadelphia 100
Apr. 5—Thur. Philadelphia 107 at Fort Wayne 105
Apr. 7—Sat. Fort Wayne 88 at Philadelphia 99

1955-56

1954-55

1954-55 NBA CHAMPION SYRACUSE NATIONALS
Front row (from left): Dick Farley, Billy Kenville. Center row (from left): Earl Lloyd, captain Paul Seymour, head coach Al Cervi, George King, Jim Tucker. Back row (from left): president Daniel Biasone, Wally Osterkorn, business manager Bob Sexton, Dolph Schayes, Red Kerr, Billy Gabor, Red Rocha, trainer Art Van Auken.

FINAL STANDINGS

EASTERN DIVISION

	Syr.	N.Y.	Bos.	Phi.	Ft.W.	Minn.	Roch.	Mil.	W	L	Pct.	GB
Syracuse	..	8	6	7	7	3	7	5	43	29	.597	..
New York	4	..	6	5	7	5	5	6	38	34	.528	5
Boston	6	6	..	7	4	3	4	6	36	36	.500	7
Philadelphia	5	7	5	..	3	3	5	5	33	39	.458	10

WESTERN DIVISION

	Syr.	N.Y.	Bos.	Phi.	Ft.W.	Minn.	Roch.	Mil.	W	L	Pct.	GB
Fort Wayne	2	2	5	6	..	9	8	11	43	29	.597	..
Minneapolis	6	4	6	6	3	..	8	7	40	32	.556	3
Rochester	2	4	5	4	4	4	..	6	29	43	.403	14
Milwaukee	4	3	3	4	1	5	6	..	26	46	.361	17

TEAM STATISTICS

	G	FGM	FGA	Pct.	FTM	FTA	Pct.	Reb.	Ast.	PF	Dq.	For	Agst.	Dif.
												AVERAGE POINTS		
Fort Wayne	72	2333	5980	.390	1986	2710	.733	3826	1737	1753	26	92.4	90.0	+2.4
Syracuse	72	2360	6343	.372	1837	2450	.750	3933	1778	1658	20	91.1	89.7	+1.4
Minneapolis	72	2506	6465	.388	1873	2517	.744	3865	1468	1935	56	95.6	94.5	+1.1
New York	72	2392	6149	.389	1887	2593	.728	4379	1744	1587	23	92.7	92.6	+0.1
Boston	72	2604	6533	.399	2097	2704	.776	4203	1905	1859	48	101.4	101.5	-0.1
Philadelphia......	72	2392	6234	.384	1928	2625	.734	4238	1744	1716	29	93.2	93.5	-0.3
Rochester	72	2399	6020	.399	1737	2420	.718	3904	1695	1865	26	90.8	92.4	-1.6
Milwaukee.......	72	2187	6041	.362	1917	2672	.717	3854	1544	1904	59	87.4	90.4	-3.0
Avgs...........	72	2397	6221	.385	1908	2586	.738	4025	1702	1785	35.9	93.1	...	...

HOME/ROAD/NEUTRAL

	Home	Road	Neutral	Total		Home	Road	Neutral	Total
Boston	20-5	5-22	11-9	36-36	Philadelphia 16-5		4-19	13-15	33-39
Fort Wayne	20-6	9-14	14-9	43-29	Rochester............. 17-11		4-19	8-13	29-43
Milwaukee	6-11	9-16	11-19	26-46	Syracuse 25-7		10-16	8-6	43-29
Minneapolis	18-6	10-14	12-12	40-32	Totals 139-59		59-139	90-90	288-288
New York	17-9	8-18	13-7	38-34					

INDIVIDUAL LEADERS

POINTS

	G	FGM	FTM	Pts.	Avg.
Neil Johnston, Philadelphia	.72	521	589	1631	22.7
Paul Arizin, Philadelphia	.72	529	454	1512	21.0
Bob Cousy, Boston	.71	522	460	1504	21.2
Bob Pettit, Milwaukee	.72	520	426	1466	20.4
Frank Selvy, Balt.-Milwaukee	.71	452	444	1348	19.0
Dolph Schayes, Syracuse	.72	422	489	1333	18.5
Vern Mikkelsen, Minneapolis	.71	440	447	1327	18.7
Clyde Lovellette, Minneapolis	.70	519	273	1311	18.7
Bill Sharman, Boston	.68	453	347	1253	18.4
Ed Macauley, Boston	.71	403	442	1248	17.6
Larry Foust, Fort Wayne	.70	398	393	1189	17.0
Carl Braun, New York	.71	400	274	1074	15.1
Harry Gallatin, New York	.72	330	393	1053	14.6
Paul Seymour, Syracuse	.72	375	300	1050	14.6
Ray Felix, New York	.72	364	310	1038	14.4
George Yardley, Fort Wayne	.60	363	310	1036	17.3
Jim Baechtold, New York	.72	362	279	1003	13.9
Slater Martin, Minneapolis	.72	350	276	976	13.6
Joe Graboski, Philadelphia	.70	373	208	954	13.6
Nat Clifton, New York	.72	360	224	944	13.1

FIELD GOALS

(minimum 210 made)

	FGM	FGA	Pct.
Larry Foust, Fort Wayne	.398	818	.487
Jack Coleman, Rochester	.400	866	.462
Neil Johnston, Philadelphia	.521	1184	.440
Ray Felix, New York	.364	832	.438
Clyde Lovellette, Minneapolis	.519	1192	.435
Bill Sharman, Boston	.453	1062	.427
Ed Macauley, Boston	.403	951	.424
Vern Mikkelsen, Minneapolis	.440	1043	.422
Red Kerr, Syracuse	.301	718	.419
George Yardley, Fort Wayne	.363	869	.418

FREE THROWS

(minimum 180 made)

	FTM	FTA	Pct.
Bill Sharman, Boston	.347	387	.897
Frank Brian, Fort Wayne	.217	255	.851
Dolph Schayes, Syracuse	.489	587	.833
Dick Schnittker, Minneapolis	.298	362	.823
Jim Baechtold, New York	.279	339	.823
Harry Gallatin, New York	.393	483	.814
Odie Spears, Rochester	.220	271	.812
Paul Seymour, Syracuse	.300	370	.811
Bob Cousy, Boston	.460	570	.807
Carl Braun, New York	.274	342	.801

ASSISTS

	G	No.	Avg.
Bob Cousy, Boston	.71	557	7.9
Dick McGuire, New York	.71	542	7.6
Andy Phillip, Fort Wayne	.64	491	7.7
Paul Seymour, Syracuse	.72	483	6.7
Slater Martin, Minneapolis	.72	427	5.9
Jack George, Philadelphia	.68	359	5.3
Bob Davies, Rochester	.72	355	4.9
George King, Syracuse	.67	331	4.9
Bill Sharman, Boston	.68	280	4.1
Ed Macauley, Boston	.71	275	3.9

REBOUNDS

	G	No.	Avg.
Neil Johnston, Philadelphia	.72	1085	15.1
Harry Gallatin, New York	.72	995	13.8
Bob Pettit, Milwaukee	.72	994	13.8
Dolph Schayes, Syracuse	.72	887	12.3
Ray Felix, New York	.72	818	11.4
Clyde Lovellette, Minneapolis	.70	802	11.5
Jack Coleman, Rochester	.72	729	10.1
Vern Mikkelsen, Minneapolis	.72	722	10.0
Arnie Risen, Rochester	.69	703	10.2
Larry Foust, Fort Wayne	.70	700	10.0

1954-55

INDIVIDUAL STATISTICS, TEAM BY TEAM

BALTIMORE BULLETS

	G	Min.	FGM	FGA	Pct.	FTM	FTA	Pct.	Reb.	Ast.	PF	Dq.	Pts.	Avg.
Rollen Hans	13	178	30	67	.448	13	25	.520	16	26	20	0	73	5.6
Jim Neal	13	194	12	59	.203	15	22	.682	47	9	27	0	39	3.0
Al McGuire	10	98	9	32	.281	5	7	.714	25	8	15	0	23	2.3
Dan King	12	103	7	22	.318	5	10	.500	9	3	5	0	19	1.6

Team disbanded November 27; players assigned to other clubs.

BOSTON CELTICS

	G	Min.	FGM	FGA	Pct.	FTM	FTA	Pct.	Reb.	Ast.	PF	Dq.	Pts.	Avg.
Bob Cousy	71	2747	522	1316	.397	460	570	.807	424	557	165	1	1504	21.2
Bill Sharman	68	2453	453	1062	.427	347	387	.897	302	280	212	2	1253	18.4
Ed Macauley	71	2706	403	951	.424	442	558	.792	600	275	171	0	1248	17.6
Don Barksdale	72	1790	267	699	.382	220	338	.651	545	129	225	7	754	10.5
Frank Ramsey	64	1754	236	592	.399	243	322	.755	402	185	250	11	715	11.2
Jack Nichols	64	1910	249	656	.380	138	177	.780	533	144	238	10	636	9.9
Bob Brannum	71	1623	176	465	.378	90	127	.709	492	127	232	6	442	6.2
Dwight Morrison	71	1227	120	284	.423	72	115	.626	451	82	222	10	312	4.4
Togo Palazzi	53	504	101	253	.399	45	60	.750	146	30	60	1	247	4.7
Freddie Scolari	59	619	76	249	.305	39	49	.796	77	93	76	0	191	3.2
Skippy Whitaker	3	15	1	6	.167	0	0	...	1	1	4	0	2	0.7

FORT WAYNE PISTONS

	G	Min.	FGM	FGA	Pct.	FTM	FTA	Pct.	Reb.	Ast.	PF	Dq.	Pts.	Avg.
Larry Foust	70	2264	398	818	.487	393	513	.766	700	118	264	9	1189	17.0
George Yardley	60	2150	363	869	.418	310	416	.745	594	126	205	7	1036	17.3
Mel Hutchins	72	2860	341	903	.378	182	257	.708	665	247	232	0	864	12.0
Max Zaslofsky	70	1862	269	821	.328	247	352	.702	191	203	130	0	785	11.2
Frank Brian	71	1381	237	623	.380	217	255	.851	127	142	133	0	691	9.7
Andy Phillip	64	2332	202	545	.371	213	308	.692	290	491	166	1	617	9.6

	G	Min.	FGM	FGA	Pct.	FTM	FTA	Pct.	Reb.	Ast.	PF	Dq.	Pts.	Avg.
Dick Rosenthal	67	1406	197	523	.377	130	181	.718	300	153	179	2	524	7.8
Bob Houbregs*	64	1326	148	386	.383	129	182	.709	297	86	180	5	425	6.6
Don Meineke	68	1026	136	366	.372	119	170	.700	246	64	153	1	391	5.8
Paul Walther	68	820	56	161	.348	54	88	.614	155	131	115	1	166	2.4
Al Roges**	17	201	23	61	.377	15	24	.625	24	19	20	0	61	3.6
Jim Fritsche	16	151	16	48	.333	13	16	.813	32	4	28	0	45	2.8

*Houbregs—Played with Baltimore, Boston, Fort Wayne.
**Roges—Played with Baltimore, Fort Wayne.

MILWAUKEE HAWKS

	G	Min.	FGM	FGA	Pct.	FTM	FTA	Pct.	Reb.	Ast.	PF	Dq.	Pts.	Avg.
Bob Pettit	72	2659	520	1279	.407	426	567	.751	994	229	258	5	1466	20.4
Frank Selvy*	71	2668	452	1195	.378	444	610	.728	394	245	230	3	1348	19.0
Charlie Share	69	1685	235	577	.407	351	492	.713	684	84	273	17	821	11.9
Bob Harrison	72	2300	299	875	.342	126	185	.681	226	252	291	14	724	10.1
Charles Cooper	70	1749	193	569	.339	187	249	.751	385	151	210	8	573	8.2
Bill Calhoun	69	2109	144	480	.300	166	236	.703	290	235	181	4	454	6.6
Alex Hannum	53	1088	126	358	.352	61	107	.570	245	105	206	9	313	5.9
Frank Saul	65	1139	96	303	.317	95	123	.772	134	104	126	0	287	4.4
Bobby Watson	63	702	72	223	.323	31	45	.689	87	79	67	0	175	2.8
Ken McBride	12	249	48	147	.327	21	29	.724	31	14	31	0	117	9.8
George Ratkovicz	9	102	3	19	.158	10	23	.435	17	13	15	0	16	1.8
Phil Martin	7	47	5	19	.263	2	2	1.000	10	6	7	0	12	1.7
Fred Diute	7	72	2	21	.095	7	12	.583	13	4	12	0	11	1.6
Ronnie McGilvray	6	57	2	12	.167	4	7	.571	9	11	5	0	8	1.3
Carl McNulty	1	14	1	6	.167	0	0	...	0	0	1	0	2	2.0

*Selvy—Played with Baltimore, Milwaukee.

MINNEAPOLIS LAKERS

	G	Min.	FGM	FGA	Pct.	FTM	FTA	Pct.	Reb.	Ast.	PF	Dq.	Pts.	Avg.
Vern Mikkelsen	71	2559	440	1043	.422	447	598	.747	722	145	319	14	1327	18.7
Clyde Lovellette	70	2361	519	1192	.435	273	398	.686	802	100	262	6	1311	18.7
Slater Martin	72	2784	350	919	.381	276	359	.769	260	427	221	7	976	13.6
Whitey Skoog	72	2365	330	836	.395	125	155	.806	303	251	265	10	785	10.9
Dick Schnittker	72	1798	226	583	.388	298	362	.823	349	114	231	7	750	10.4
Jim Pollard	63	1960	265	749	.354	151	186	.812	458	160	147	3	681	10.8
Lew Hitch*	74	1774	167	417	.400	115	169	.680	438	125	110	0	449	6.1
Ed Kalafat	72	1102	118	375	.315	111	168	.661	317	75	205	9	347	4.8
Jim Holstein	62	980	107	330	.324	67	94	.713	206	58	107	0	281	4.5
Don Sunderlage	45	404	33	133	.248	48	73	.658	56	37	57	0	114	2.5
Robert Carney	19	244	24	64	.375	21	40	.525	45	16	36	0	69	3.6

*Hitch—Played with Milwaukee, Minneapolis.

NEW YORK KNICKERBOCKERS

	G	Min.	FGM	FGA	Pct.	FTM	FTA	Pct.	Reb.	Ast.	PF	Dq.	Pts.	Avg.
Carl Braun	71	2479	400	1032	.388	274	342	.801	295	274	208	3	1074	15.1
Harry Gallatin	72	2548	330	859	.384	393	483	.814	995	176	206	5	1053	14.6
Ray Felix	72	2024	364	832	.438	310	498	.622	818	67	286	11	1038	14.4
Jim Baechtold	72	2536	362	898	.403	279	339	.823	307	218	202	0	1003	13.9
Nat Clifton	72	2390	360	932	.386	224	328	.683	612	198	221	2	944	13.1
Dick McGuire	71	2310	226	581	.389	195	303	.644	322	542	143	0	647	9.1
Jack Turner	65	922	111	308	.360	60	76	.789	154	77	76	0	282	4.3
Gene Shue*	62	947	100	289	.346	59	78	.756	154	89	64	0	259	4.2
Bob Peterson	37	503	62	169	.367	30	45	.667	154	31	80	2	154	4.2
Bert Cook	37	424	42	133	.316	34	50	.680	72	33	39	0	118	3.2
Fred Christ	6	48	5	18	.278	10	11	.909	8	7	3	0	20	3.3
Chuck Grigsby	7	45	7	19	.368	2	8	.250	11	7	9	0	16	2.3
Bob Knight	2	29	3	7	.429	1	1	1.000	1	8	6	0	7	3.5
Herman Hedderick	5	23	2	9	.222	0	1	.000	4	2	3	0	4	0.8
Don Anielak	1	10	0	4	.000	3	4	.750	2	0	0	0	3	3.0

*Shue—Played with Philadelphia, New York.

PHILADELPHIA WARRIORS

	G	Min.	FGM	FGA	Pct.	FTM	FTA	Pct.	Reb.	Ast.	PF	Dq.	Pts.	Avg.
Neil Johnston	72	2917	521	1184	.440	589	769	.766	1085	215	255	4	1631	22.7
Paul Arizin	72	2953	529	1325	.399	454	585	.776	675	210	270	5	1512	21.0
Joe Graboski	70	2515	373	1096	.340	208	303	.686	636	182	259	8	954	13.6
Jack George	68	2480	291	756	.385	192	291	.660	302	359	191	2	774	11.4
Ken Murray*	66	1590	187	535	.350	98	120	.817	179	224	126	1	472	7.2
Robert Zawoluk	67	1117	138	375	.368	155	199	.779	256	87	147	3	431	6.4
George Dempsey	48	1387	127	360	.353	98	141	.695	236	174	141	1	352	7.3
Danny Finn	43	820	77	265	.291	53	86	.616	157	155	114	3	207	4.8
Paul Hoffman**	38	670	65	216	.301	64	93	.688	124	94	93	0	194	5.1
Walt Davis	61	766	70	182	.385	35	48	.729	206	36	100	0	175	2.9

1954-55

	G	Min.	FGM	FGA	Pct.	FTM	FTA	Pct.	Reb.	Ast.	PF	Dq.	SCORING Pts.	Avg.
Larry Costello	19	463	46	139	.331	26	32	.813	49	78	37	0	118	6.2
Jackie Moore	23	376	44	115	.383	22	47	.468	105	20	62	2	110	4.8
Tom Brennan	11	52	5	11	.455	0	0	...	5	2	5	0	10	0.9
Mike Kearns	6	25	0	5	.000	1	4	.250	3	5	1	0	1	0.2

*Murray—Played with Baltimore, Philadelphia.
**Hoffman—Played with Baltimore, New York.

ROCHESTER ROYALS

	G	Min.	FGM	FGA	Pct.	FTM	FTA	Pct.	Reb.	Ast.	PF	Dq.	SCORING Pts.	Avg.
Bobby Wanzer	72	2376	324	820	.395	294	374	.786	374	247	163	2	942	13.1
Jack Coleman	72	2482	400	866	.462	124	183	.678	729	232	201	1	924	12.8
Bob Davies	72	1870	326	785	.415	220	293	.751	205	355	220	2	872	12.1
Arnie Risen	69	1970	259	699	.371	279	375	.744	703	112	253	10	797	11.6
Marion Spears	71	1888	226	585	.386	220	271	.812	299	148	252	6	672	9.5
Jack McMahon	72	1807	251	721	.348	143	225	.636	211	246	179	1	645	9.0
Tom Marshall	72	1337	223	505	.442	131	194	.675	256	111	99	0	577	8.0
Art Spoelstra	70	1127	159	399	.398	108	156	.692	285	58	170	2	426	6.1
Don Henriksen*	70	1664	139	406	.342	137	195	.703	484	111	190	2	415	5.9
Cal Christensen	71	1204	114	305	.374	124	206	.602	388	104	174	2	352	5.0
Boris Nachamkin	6	59	6	20	.300	8	13	.615	19	3	6	0	20	3.3

*Henriksen—Played with Baltimore, Rochester.

SYRACUSE NATIONALS

	G	Min.	FGM	FGA	Pct.	FTM	FTA	Pct.	Reb.	Ast.	PF	Dq.	SCORING Pts.	Avg.
Dolph Schayes	72	2526	422	1103	.383	489	587	.833	887	213	247	6	1333	18.5
Paul Seymour	72	2950	375	1036	.362	300	370	.811	300	483	167	0	1050	14.6
Red Rocha	72	2473	295	801	.368	222	284	.782	489	178	242	5	812	11.3
Red Kerr	72	1529	301	718	.419	152	223	.682	474	80	165	2	754	10.5
Earl Lloyd	72	2212	286	784	.365	159	212	.750	553	151	283	4	731	10.2
George King	67	2015	228	605	.377	140	229	.611	227	331	148	0	596	8.9
Billy Kenville	70	1380	172	482	.357	154	201	.766	247	150	132	1	498	7.1
Dick Farley	69	1113	136	353	.385	136	201	.677	167	111	145	1	408	5.9
Connie Simmons*	36	862	137	384	.357	72	114	.632	220	61	109	2	346	9.6
Jim Tucker	20	287	39	116	.336	27	38	.711	97	12	50	0	105	5.3
Wally Osterkorn	19	286	20	97	.206	16	32	.500	70	17	32	0	56	2.9
Billy Gabor	3	47	7	22	.318	3	5	.600	5	11	6	0	17	5.7

*Simmons—Played with Baltimore, Syracuse.

PLAYOFF RESULTS

EASTERN DIVISION

SEMIFINALS

Boston 2, New York 1
Mar. 15—Tue.   New York 101 at Boston 122
Mar. 16—Wed. Boston 95 at New York 102
Mar. 19—Sat.   Boston 116 at New York 109

FINALS

Syracuse 3, Boston 1
Mar. 22—Tue.   Boston 100 at Syracuse 110
Mar. 24—Thur. Boston 110 at Syracuse 116
Mar. 26—Sat.   Syracuse 97 at Boston *100
Mar. 27—Sun.   Syracuse 110 at Boston 94

WESTERN DIVISION

SEMIFINALS

Minneapolis 2, Rochester 1
Mar. 16—Wed. Rochester 78, Minneapolis (at St. Paul) 82
Mar. 18—Fri.   Minneapolis 92 at Rochester 94
Mar. 19—Sat.   Rochester 110, Minneapolis (at St. Paul) 119

FINALS

Fort Wayne 3, Minneapolis 1
Mar. 20—Sun.   Minneapolis 79, Fort Wayne (at Elkhart, Ind.) 96
Mar. 22—Tue.   Minneapolis 97, Fort Wayne (at Indianapolis) ...*98
Mar. 23—Wed. Fort Wayne 91 at Minneapolis *99
Mar. 27—Sun.   Fort Wayne 105 at Minneapolis 96

NBA FINALS

Syracuse 4, Fort Wayne 3
Mar. 31—Thur.   Fort Wayne 82 at Syracuse 86
Apr. 2—Sat.   Fort Wayne 84 at Syracuse 87
Apr. 3—Sun.   Syracuse 89, Fort Wayne (at Indianapolis) 96
Apr. 5—Tue.   Syracuse 102, Fort Wayne (at Indianapolis) 109
Apr. 7—Thur.   Syracuse 71, Fort Wayne (at Indianapolis) 74
Apr. 9—Sat.   Fort Wayne 104 at Syracuse 109
Apr. 10—Sun.   Fort Wayne 91 at Syracuse 92

*Denotes number of overtime periods.

1954-55

1953-54

1953-54 NBA CHAMPION MINNEAPOLIS LAKERS
From left: Slater Martin, Frank Saul, Jim Holstein, Jim Pollard, Clyde Lovellette, George Mikan, Vern Mikkelsen, Dick Schnittker, Whitey Skoog, head coach John Kundla.

FINAL STANDINGS

EASTERN DIVISION

	N.Y.	Bos.	Syr.	Phi.	Balt.	Minn.	Roch.	Ft.W.	Mil.	W	L	Pct.	GB
New York	..	5	5	7	7	3	7	5	5	44	28	.611	..
Boston	5	..	5	6	9	3	4	4	6	42	30	.583	2
Syracuse	5	5	..	4	7	3	5	6	7	42	30	.583	2
Philadelphia	3	4	6	..	6	2	1	2	5	29	43	.403	15
Baltimore	3	1	3	4	..	2	1	0	2	16	56	.222	28

WESTERN DIVISION

	N.Y.	Bos.	Syr.	Phi.	Balt.	Minn.	Roch.	Ft.W.	Mil.	W	L	Pct.	GB
Minneapolis	5	5	5	6	6	..	6	5	8	46	26	.639	..
Rochester	1	4	3	7	7	5	..	8	9	44	28	.611	2
Fort Wayne	3	4	2	6	8	5	3	..	9	40	32	.556	6
Milwaukee	3	2	1	3	6	3	1	2	..	21	51	.292	25

TEAM STATISTICS

	G	FGM	FGA	Pct.	FTM	FTA	Pct.	Reb.	Ast.	PF	Dq.	AVERAGE POINTS For	AVERAGE POINTS Agst.	AVERAGE POINTS Dif.
Syracuse	72	2054	5579	.368	1905	2650	.719	3652	1541	1852	28	83.5	78.6	+4.9
Minneapolis	72	2184	5803	.376	1512	2067	.731	3752	1323	1918	31	81.7	78.3	+3.4
Rochester	72	2010	5451	.369	1722	2518	.684	3494	1454	1904	44	79.8	77.3	+2.5
Boston	72	2232	5580	.400	1851	2550	.726	3867	1773	1969	46	87.7	85.4	+2.3
Fort Wayne	72	1952	5187	.376	1689	2315	.730	3785	1474	1669	27	77.7	76.1	+1.6
New York	72	1934	5177	.374	1820	2525	.721	3830	1469	1832	23	79.0	79.1	-0.1
Philadelphia	72	2023	5431	.372	1586	2272	.698	3589	1468	1741	42	78.2	80.4	-2.2
Milwaukee	72	1757	5087	.345	1524	2202	.692	3202	1298	1771	45	70.0	75.3	-5.3
Baltimore	72	2036	5539	.368	1566	2312	.677	3816	1385	1777	24	78.3	85.1	-6.8
Avgs	72	2020	5426	.372	1686	2379	.709	3665	1465	1826	34.4	79.5	...	...

HOME/ROAD/NEUTRAL

	Home	Road	Neutral	Total		Home	Road	Neutral	Total
Baltimore	12-20	0-20	4-16	16-56	New York	18-8	15-13	11-7	44-28
Boston	16-6	11-19	15-5	42-30	Philadelphia	10-9	6-16	13-18	29-43
Fort Wayne	19-8	11-17	10-7	40-32	Rochester	18-10	12-15	14-3	44-28
Milwaukee	10-14	6-17	5-20	21-51	Syracuse	27-5	10-19	5-6	42-30
Minneapolis	21-4	13-15	12-7	46-26	Totals	151-84	84-151	89-89	324-324

POINTS

	G	FGM	FTM	Pts.	Avg.
Neil Johnston, Philadelphia	72	591	577	1759	24.4
Bob Cousy, Boston	72	486	411	1383	19.2
Ed Macauley, Boston	71	462	420	1344	18.9
George Mikan, Minneapolis	72	441	424	1306	18.1
Ray Felix, Baltimore	72	410	449	1269	17.6
Dolph Schayes, Syracuse	72	370	488	1228	17.1
Bill Sharman, Boston	72	412	331	1155	16.0
Larry Foust, Fort Wayne	72	376	338	1090	15.1
Carl Braun, New York	72	354	354	1062	14.8
Bobby Wanzer, Rochester	72	322	314	958	13.3
Harry Gallatin, New York	72	258	433	949	13.2
Arnie Risen, Rochester	72	321	307	949	13.2
Joe Graboski, Philadelphia	71	354	236	944	13.3
Paul Seymour, Syracuse	71	316	299	931	13.1
Bob Davies, Rochester	72	288	311	887	12.3
Jim Pollard, Minneapolis	71	326	179	831	11.7
George King, Syracuse	72	280	257	817	11.3
Max Zaslofsky, Balt.-Milw.-Ft.W.	65	278	255	811	12.5
Vern Mikkelsen, Minneapolis	72	288	221	797	11.1
Don Sunderlage, Milwaukee	68	254	252	760	11.2

FIELD GOALS

(minimum 210 made)

	FGM	FGA	Pct.
Ed Macauley, Boston	462	950	.486
Bill Sharman, Boston	412	915	.450
Neil Johnston, Philadelphia	591	1317	.449
Clyde Lovellette, Minneapolis	237	560	.423
Ray Felix, Baltimore	410	983	.417
Larry Foust, Fort Wayne	376	919	.409
Eddie Miller, Baltimore	244	600	.407
Jack Coleman, Rochester	289	714	.405
Harry Gallatin, New York	258	639	.404
Mel Hutchins, Fort Wayne	295	736	.401

FREE THROWS

(minimum 180 made)

	FTM	FTA	Pct.
Bill Sharman, Boston	331	392	.844
Dolph Schayes, Syracuse	488	590	.827
Carl Braun, New York	354	429	.825
Paul Seymour, Syracuse	299	368	.813
Bob Zawoluk, Philadelphia	186	230	.809
Bob Cousy, Boston	411	522	.787
Harry Gallatin, New York	433	552	.784
George Mikan, Minneapolis	424	546	.777
Odie Spears, Rochester	183	238	.769
Ed Macauley, Boston	420	554	.758

ASSISTS

	G	No.	Avg.
Bob Cousy, Boston	72	518	7.2
Andy Phillip, Fort Wayne	71	449	6.3
Paul Seymour, Syracuse	71	364	5.1
Dick McGuire, New York	68	354	5.2
Bob Davies, Rochester	72	323	4.5
Jack George, Philadelphia	71	312	4.4
Paul Hoffman, Baltimore	72	285	4.0
George King, Syracuse	72	272	3.8
Ed Macauley, Boston	71	271	3.8
Daniel Finn, Philadelphia	68	265	3.9

REBOUNDS

	G	No.	Avg.
Harry Gallatin, New York	72	1098	15.3
George Mikan, Minneapolis	72	1028	14.3
Larry Foust, Fort Wayne	72	967	13.4
Ray Felix, Baltimore	72	958	13.3
Dolph Schayes, Syracuse	72	870	12.1
Neil Johnston, Philadelphia	72	797	11.1
Arnie Risen, Rochester	72	728	10.1
Mel Hutchins, Fort Wayne	72	695	9.7
Lew Hitch, Milwaukee	72	691	9.6
Joe Graboski, Philadelphia	71	670	9.4

1953-54

BALTIMORE BULLETS

	G	Min.	FGM	FGA	Pct.	FTM	FTA	Pct.	Reb.	Ast.	PF	Dq.	Pts.	Avg.
Ray Felix	72	2672	410	983	.417	449	704	.638	958	82	253	5	1269	17.6
Paul Hoffman	72	2505	253	761	.332	217	303	.716	486	285	271	10	723	10.0
Eddie Miller	72	1657	244	600	.407	231	317	.729	537	95	194	0	719	10.0
Bob Houbregs*	70	1970	209	562	.372	190	266	.714	375	123	209	2	608	8.7
Al Roges	67	1937	220	614	.358	130	179	.726	213	160	177	1	570	8.5
Rollen Hans	67	1556	191	515	.371	101	180	.561	160	181	172	1	483	7.2
Jim Fritsche**	68	1221	116	379	.306	49	68	.721	217	73	103	0	281	4.1
Joe Smyth	40	495	48	138	.348	35	65	.538	98	49	53	0	131	3.3
Jimmy Luisi	31	367	31	95	.326	27	41	.659	25	35	45	0	89	2.9
Hal Uplinger	23	268	33	94	.351	20	22	.909	31	26	42	0	86	3.7
Mark Workman	14	151	25	60	.417	6	10	.600	37	7	31	0	56	4.0
Bill Bolger	20	202	24	59	.407	8	13	.615	36	11	27	0	56	2.8
Connie Rea	20	154	9	43	.209	5	16	.313	31	16	13	0	23	1.2
Don Asmonga	7	46	2	15	.133	1	1	1.000	1	5	12	1	5	0.7
Paul Nolen	1	2	0	1	.000	0	0	...	1	0	1	0	0	0.0
Francis Mahoney	2	11	0	2	.000	0	0	...	2	1	0	0	0	0.0

*Houbregs—Played with Milwaukee, Baltimore.
**Fritsche—Played with Minneapolis, Baltimore.

BOSTON CELTICS

	G	Min.	FGM	FGA	Pct.	FTM	FTA	Pct.	Reb.	Ast.	PF	Dq.	Pts.	Avg.
Bob Cousy	72	2857	486	1262	.385	411	522	.787	394	518	201	3	1383	19.2
Ed Macauley	71	2792	462	950	.486	420	554	.758	571	271	168	1	1344	18.9
Bill Sharman	72	2467	412	915	.450	331	392	.844	255	229	211	4	1155	16.0
Don Barksdale	63	1358	156	415	.376	149	225	.662	345	117	213	4	461	7.3
Jack Nichols*	75	1607	163	528	.309	113	152	.743	363	104	187	2	439	5.9
Bob Harris	71	1898	156	409	.381	108	172	.628	517	94	224	8	420	5.9
Bob Brannum	71	1729	140	453	.309	129	206	.626	509	144	280	10	409	5.8
Bob Donham	68	1451	141	315	.448	118	213	.554	267	186	235	11	400	5.9

	G	Min.	FGM	FGA	Pct.	FTM	FTA	Pct.	Reb.	Ast.	PF	Dq.	SCORING Pts.	Avg.
Charles Cooper	70	1101	78	261	.299	78	116	.672	304	74	150	1	234	3.3
Ernie Barrett	59	641	60	191	.314	14	25	.560	100	55	116	2	134	2.3
Ed Mikan	9	71	8	24	.333	5	9	.556	20	3	15	0	21	2.3

*Nichols—Played with Milwaukee, Boston.

FORT WAYNE PISTONS

	G	Min.	FGM	FGA	Pct.	FTM	FTA	Pct.	Reb.	Ast.	PF	Dq.	SCORING Pts.	Avg.
Larry Foust	72	2693	376	919	.409	338	475	.712	967	161	258	4	1090	15.1
Max Zaslofsky*	65	1881	278	756	.368	255	357	.714	160	154	142	1	811	12.5
Andy Phillip	71	2705	255	680	.375	241	330	.730	265	449	204	4	751	10.6
Mel Hutchins	72	2934	295	736	.401	151	223	.677	695	210	229	4	741	10.3
George Yardley	63	1489	209	492	.425	146	205	.712	407	99	166	3	564	9.0
Freddie Scolari	64	1589	159	491	.324	144	180	.800	139	131	155	1	462	7.2
Leo Barnhorst**	72	2064	199	588	.338	63	88	.716	297	226	203	4	461	6.4
Don Meineke	71	1466	135	393	.344	136	169	.805	372	81	214	6	406	5.7
Frank Brian	64	973	132	352	.375	137	182	.753	79	92	100	2	401	6.3
Jack Molinas	29	993	108	278	.388	134	176	.761	209	47	74	2	350	12.1
Ken Murray	49	528	53	195	.272	43	60	.717	65	56	60	0	149	3.0
Emilio Sinicola	9	53	4	16	.250	3	6	.500	1	3	8	0	11	1.2

*Zaslofsky—Played with Baltimore, Milwaukee, Fort Wayne.
**Barnhorst—Played with Baltimore, Fort Wayne.

MILWAUKEE HAWKS

	G	Min.	FGM	FGA	Pct.	FTM	FTA	Pct.	Reb.	Ast.	PF	Dq.	SCORING Pts.	Avg.
Don Sunderlage	68	2232	254	748	.340	252	337	.748	225	187	263	8	760	11.2
Bill Calhoun	72	2370	190	545	.349	214	292	.733	274	189	151	3	594	8.3
Lew Hitch	72	2452	221	603	.367	133	208	.639	691	141	176	3	575	8.0
George Ratkovicz	69	2170	197	501	.393	176	273	.645	523	154	255	11	570	8.3
Charlie Share*	68	1576	188	493	.381	188	275	.684	555	80	210	8	564	8.3
Irv Bemoras	69	1496	185	505	.366	139	208	.668	214	79	152	2	509	7.4
Bill Tosheff	71	1825	168	578	.291	156	210	.743	163	196	207	3	492	6.9
Bob Harrison**	64	1443	144	449	.321	94	158	.595	130	139	218	9	382	6.0
Red Holzman	51	649	74	224	.330	48	73	.658	46	75	73	1	196	3.8
Dick Surhoff	32	358	43	129	.333	47	62	.758	69	23	53	0	133	4.2
Don Lofgran	21	380	35	112	.313	32	49	.653	64	26	34	0	102	4.9
Gene Dyker	11	91	6	26	.231	4	8	.500	16	5	21	0	16	1.5
Bob Peterson***	8	60	3	10	.300	9	11	.818	12	3	15	1	15	1.9
Isaac Walthour	4	30	1	6	.167	0	0	...	1	2	6	0	2	0.5

*Share—Played with Fort Wayne, Milwaukee.
**Harrison—Played with Minneapolis, Milwaukee.
***Peterson—Played with Baltimore, Milwaukee.

MINNEAPOLIS LAKERS

	G	Min.	FGM	FGA	Pct.	FTM	FTA	Pct.	Reb.	Ast.	PF	Dq.	SCORING Pts.	Avg.
George Mikan	72	2362	441	1160	.380	424	546	.777	1028	174	268	4	1306	18.1
Jim Pollard	71	2483	326	882	.370	179	230	.778	500	214	161	0	831	11.7
Vern Mikkelsen	72	2247	288	771	.374	221	298	.742	615	119	264	7	797	11.1
Slater Martin	69	2472	254	654	.388	176	243	.724	166	253	198	3	684	9.9
Clyde Lovellette	72	1255	237	560	.423	114	164	.695	419	51	210	2	588	8.2
Whitey Skoog	71	1877	212	530	.400	72	97	.742	224	179	234	5	496	7.0
Frank Saul	71	1805	162	467	.347	128	170	.753	159	139	149	3	452	6.4
Dick Schnittker	71	1040	122	307	.397	86	132	.652	178	59	178	3	330	4.6
Jim Holstein	70	1155	88	288	.306	64	112	.571	204	79	140	0	240	3.4

NEW YORK KNICKERBOCKERS

	G	Min.	FGM	FGA	Pct.	FTM	FTA	Pct.	Reb.	Ast.	PF	Dq.	SCORING Pts.	Avg.
Carl Braun	72	2373	354	884	.400	354	429	.825	246	209	259	6	1062	14.8
Harry Gallatin	72	2690	258	639	.404	433	552	.784	1098	153	208	2	949	13.2
Connie Simmons	72	2006	255	713	.358	210	305	.689	484	128	234	1	720	10.0
Nat Clifton	72	2179	257	699	.368	174	277	.628	528	176	215	0	688	9.6
Dick McGuire	68	2343	201	493	.408	220	345	.638	310	354	190	3	622	9.1
Fred Schaus	67	1515	161	415	.388	153	195	.785	267	109	176	3	475	7.1
Jim Baechtold	70	1627	170	465	.366	134	177	.757	183	117	195	5	474	6.8
Vince Boryla	52	1522	175	525	.333	70	81	.864	130	77	128	0	420	8.1
Al McGuire	64	849	58	177	.328	58	133	.436	121	103	144	2	174	2.7
Ernie Vandeweghe	15	271	37	103	.359	25	31	.806	20	29	38	1	99	6.6
Buddy Ackerman	28	220	14	63	.222	15	28	.536	15	23	43	0	43	1.5
Ed Smith	11	104	11	45	.244	6	10	.600	26	9	15	0	28	2.5

1953-54

PHILADELPHIA WARRIORS

	G	Min.	FGM	FGA	Pct.	FTM	FTA	Pct.	Reb.	Ast.	PF	Dq.	SCORING Pts.	Avg.
Neil Johnston	72	3296	591	1317	.449	577	772	.747	797	203	259	7	1759	24.4
Joe Graboski	71	2759	354	1000	.354	236	350	.674	670	163	223	4	944	13.3
Jack George	71	2648	259	736	.352	157	266	.590	386	312	210	4	675	9.5
Robert Zawoluk	71	1795	203	540	.376	186	230	.809	330	99	220	6	592	8.3
Danny Finn	68	1562	170	495	.343	126	196	.643	216	265	215	7	466	6.9
Paul Walther	64	2067	138	392	.352	145	206	.704	257	220	199	5	421	6.6
Walt Davis	68	1568	167	455	.367	65	101	.644	435	58	207	9	399	5.9
Joe Fulks	61	501	61	229	.266	28	49	.571	101	28	90	0	150	2.5
Ernie Beck	15	422	39	142	.275	34	43	.791	50	34	29	0	112	7.5
George Senesky	58	771	41	119	.345	29	53	.547	66	84	79	0	111	1.9
Jim Phelan	4	33	0	6	.000	3	6	.500	5	2	9	0	3	0.8
Norm Grekin	1	1	0	0	...	0	0	...	0	0	1	0	0	0.0

ROCHESTER ROYALS

	G	Min.	FGM	FGA	Pct.	FTM	FTA	Pct.	Reb.	Ast.	PF	Dq.	SCORING Pts.	Avg.
Bobby Wanzer	72	2538	322	835	.386	314	428	.734	392	254	171	2	958	13.3
Arnie Risen	72	2385	321	872	.368	307	430	.714	728	120	284	9	949	13.2
Bob Davies	72	2137	288	777	.371	311	433	.718	194	323	224	4	887	12.3
Jack McMahon	71	1891	250	691	.362	211	303	.696	211	238	221	6	711	10.0
Jack Coleman	71	2377	289	714	.405	108	181	.597	589	158	201	3	686	9.7
Marion Spears	72	1633	184	505	.364	183	238	.769	310	109	211	5	551	7.7
Alex Hannum	72	1707	175	503	.348	102	164	.622	350	105	279	11	452	6.3
Cal Christensen	70	1654	137	395	.347	138	261	.529	395	107	196	1	412	5.9
Norm Swanson	63	611	31	137	.226	38	64	.594	110	33	91	3	100	1.6
Frank Reddout	7	18	5	6	.833	3	4	.750	9	0	6	0	13	1.9

SYRACUSE NATIONALS

	G	Min.	FGM	FGA	Pct.	FTM	FTA	Pct.	Reb.	Ast.	PF	Dq.	SCORING Pts.	Avg.
Dolph Schayes	72	2655	370	973	.380	488	590	.827	870	214	232	4	1228	17.1
Paul Seymour	71	2727	316	838	.377	299	368	.813	291	364	187	2	931	13.1
George King	72	2370	280	744	.376	257	410	.627	268	272	179	2	817	11.3
Earl Lloyd	72	2206	249	666	.374	156	209	.746	529	115	303	12	654	9.1
Wally Osterkorn	70	2164	203	586	.346	209	361	.579	487	151	209	1	615	8.8
Billy Gabor	61	1211	204	551	.370	139	194	.716	96	162	183	4	547	9.0
Billy Kenville	72	1405	149	388	.384	136	182	.747	247	122	138	0	434	6.0
Bob Lavoy*	68	1277	135	356	.379	94	129	.729	317	78	215	2	364	5.4
Jim Neal	67	899	117	369	.317	78	132	.591	257	24	139	0	312	4.7
Al Masino**	27	181	26	62	.419	30	49	.612	28	22	44	0	82	3.0
Bato Govedarica	23	258	25	79	.316	25	37	.676	18	24	44	1	75	3.3
Dick Knostman	5	47	3	10	.300	7	11	.636	17	6	9	0	13	2.6
Ed Earle	2	12	1	2	.500	2	4	.500	2	0	0	0	4	2.0
Mike Novak	5	24	0	7	.000	1	2	.500	2	2	9	0	1	0.2

*Lavoy—Played with Milwaukee, Syracuse.
**Masino—Played with Rochester, Syracuse.

PLAYOFF RESULTS

EASTERN DIVISION

ROUND ROBIN
Mar. 16—Tue.	Boston 93 at New York	.71
Mar. 17—Wed.	Syracuse 96 at Boston	*95
Mar. 18—Thur.	New York 68 at Syracuse	.75
Mar. 20—Sat.	New York 78 at Boston	.79
Mar. 21—Sun.	Syracuse 103 at New York	.99
Mar. 22—Mon.	Boston 85 at Syracuse	.98

FINALS
Syracuse 2, Boston 0
Mar. 25—Thur.	Boston 94 at Syracuse	.109
Mar. 27—Sat.	Syracuse 83 at Boston	.76

WESTERN DIVISION

ROUND ROBIN
Mar. 16—Tue.	Fort Wayne 75 at Rochester	.82
Mar. 17—Wed.	Rochester 88 at Minneapolis	.109
Mar. 18—Thur.	Minneapolis 90 at Fort Wayne	.85
Mar. 20—Sat.	Fort Wayne 73 at Minneapolis	.78
Mar. 21—Sun.	Rochester 89 at Fort Wayne	.71
Mar. 23—Tue.	Minneapolis at Rochester (canceled)	

FINALS
Minneapolis 2, Rochester 1
Mar. 24—Wed.	Rochester 76 at Minneapolis	.89
Mar. 27—Sat.	Minneapolis 73 at Rochester	.74
Mar. 28—Sun.	Rochester 72 at Minneapolis	.82

NBA FINALS
Minneapolis 4, Syracuse 3
Mar. 31—Wed.	Syracuse 68 at Minneapolis	.79
Apr. 3—Sat.	Syracuse 62 at Minneapolis	.60
Apr. 4—Sun.	Minneapolis 81 at Syracuse	.67
Apr. 8—Thur.	Minneapolis 69 at Syracuse	.80
Apr. 10—Sat.	Minneapolis 84 at Syracuse	.73
Apr. 11—Sun.	Syracuse 65 at Minneapolis	.63
Apr. 12—Mon.	Syracuse 80 at Minneapolis	.87

*Denotes number of overtime periods.

1953-54

1952-53 NBA CHAMPION MINNEAPOLIS LAKERS
From left: head coach John Kundla, Slater Martin, Frank Saul, Jim Holstein, Vern Mikkelsen, Lew Hitch, George Mikan, Jim Pollard, Bob Harrison, Whitey Skoog, assistant coach Dave McMillan.

FINAL STANDINGS

EASTERN DIVISION

	N.Y.	Syr.	Bos.	Balt.	Phi.	Minn.	Roch.	Ft.W.	Ind.	Mil.	W	L	Pct.	GB
New York...........	..	6	4	10	10	2	3	2	5	5	47	23	.671	..
Syracuse...........	4	..	6	8	8	4	4	5	5	3	47	24	.662	.5
Boston	6	5	..	8	9	1	4	4	4	5	46	25	.648	1.5
Baltimore..........	0	2	2	..	6	1	0	0	2	3	16	54	.229	31
Philadelphia.......	0	2	1	4	..	0	2	0	1	2	12	57	.174	34.5

WESTERN DIVISION

	N.Y.	Syr.	Bos.	Balt.	Phi.	Minn.	Roch.	Ft.W.	Ind.	Mil.	W	L	Pct.	GB
Minneapolis.........	4	2	5	5	6	..	4	9	6	7	48	22	.686	..
Rochester	3	2	2	6	4	6	..	7	7	7	44	26	.629	4
Fort Wayne	4	1	2	6	5	1	3	..	7	7	36	33	.522	11.5
Indianapolis.......	1	1	2	4	5	4	3	3	..	5	28	43	.394	20.5
Milwaukee..........	1	3	1	3	4	3	3	3	6	..	27	44	.380	21.5

TEAM STATISTICS

	G	FGM	FGA	Pct.	FTM	FTA	Pct.	Reb.	Ast.	PF	Dq.	For	Agst.	Dif.
Minneapolis......	70	2166	5559	.390	1611	2221	.725	3406	1351	1917	58	85.3	79.2	+6.1
New York........	70	2059	5339	.386	1867	2652	.704	4007	1575	2053	68	85.5	80.3	+5.2
Syracuse........	71	1942	5329	.364	2197	2950	.745	3472	1459	2132	49	85.6	81.3	+4.3
Rochester	70	2019	5432	.372	2005	2747	.730	3625	1520	2210	107	86.3	83.5	+2.8
Boston	71	2177	5555	.392	1904	2617	.728	3865	1666	1911	56	88.1	85.8	+2.3
Fort Wayne	69	1876	5230	.359	1839	2491	.738	3548	1438	2119	93	81.0	81.1	-0.1
Indianapolis.....	71	1829	5204	.351	1637	2277	.719	3326	1281	1765	60	74.6	77.4	-2.8
Milwaukee.......	71	1873	5320	.352	1643	2400	.685	3429	1427	2120	93	75.9	78.8	-2.9
Baltimore........	70	2083	5615	.371	1745	2542	.686	3727	1514	2141	93	84.4	90.1	-5.7
Philadelphia......	69	1987	5546	.358	1560	2298	.679	3763	1513	1860	70	80.2	88.9	-8.7
Avgs..........	70.2	2001	5413	.370	1801	2520	.715	3617	1474	2023	75.1	82.7	...	...

The "AVERAGE POINTS" header spans the For, Agst., and Dif. columns.

HOME/ROAD/NEUTRAL

	Home	Road	Neutral	Total		Home	Road	Neutral	Total
Baltimore	11-20	1-19	4-15	16-54	New York.............	21-4	15-14	11-5	47-23
Boston...............	21-3	11-18	14-4	46-25	Philadelphia	4-13	1-28	7-16	12-57
Fort Wayne...........	25-9	8-19	3-5	36-33	Rochester.............	24-8	13-16	7-2	44-26
Indianapolis.........	19-14	4-23	5-6	28-43	Syracuse	32-2	10-19	5-3	47-24
Milwaukee	14-8	4-24	9-12	27-44	Totals	195-83	83-195	73-73	351-351
Minneapolis	24-2	16-15	8-5	48-22					

POINTS

	G	FGM	FTM	Pts.	Avg.
Neil Johnston, Philadelphia	.70	504	556	1564	22.3
George Mikan, Minneapolis	.70	500	442	1442	20.6
Bob Cousy, Boston	.71	464	479	1407	19.8
Ed Macauley, Boston	.69	451	500	1402	20.3
Dolph Schayes, Syracuse	.71	375	512	1262	17.8
Bill Sharman, Boston	.71	403	341	1147	16.2
Jack Nichols, Milwaukee	.69	425	240	1090	15.8
Vern Mikkelsen, Minneapolis	.70	378	291	1047	15.0
Bob Davies, Rochester	.66	339	351	1029	15.6
Bobby Wanzer, Rochester	.70	318	384	1020	14.6
Carl Braun, New York	.70	323	331	977	14.0
Leo Barnhorst, Indianapolis	.71	402	163	967	13.6
Larry Foust, Fort Wayne	.67	311	336	958	14.3
Paul Seymour, Syracuse	.67	306	340	952	14.2
Don Barksdale, Baltimore	.65	321	257	899	13.8
Joe Graboski, Indianapolis	.69	272	350	894	13.0
Arnie Risen, Rochester	.68	295	294	884	13.0
Harry Gallatin, New York	.70	282	301	865	12.4
Jim Pollard, Minneapolis	.66	333	193	859	13.0
Joe Fulks, Philadelphia	.70	332	168	832	11.9

FIELD GOALS

(minimum 210 made)

	FGM	FGA	Pct.
Neil Johnston, Philadelphia	.504	1114	.4524
Ed Macauley, Boston	.451	997	.4523
Harry Gallatin, New York	.282	635	.444
Bill Sharman, Boston	.403	925	.436
Vern Mikkelsen, Minneapolis	.378	868	.435
Ernie Vandeweghe, New York	.272	625	.435
Jack Coleman, Rochester	.314	748	.420
Slater Martin, Minneapolis	.260	634	.410
George King, Syracuse	.255	635	.402
Bob Lavoy, Indianapolis	.225	560	.402

FREE THROWS

(minimum 180 made)

	FTM	FTA	Pct.
Bill Sharman, Boston	.341	401	.850
Fred Scolari, Fort Wayne	.276	327	.844
Dolph Schayes, Syracuse	.512	619	.827
Carl Braun, New York	.331	401	.825
Fred Schaus, Fort Wayne	.243	296	.821
Odie Spears, Rochester	.199	243	.819
Paul Seymour, Syracuse	.340	416	.817
Bob Cousy, Boston	.479	587	.816
Bobby Wanzer, Rochester	.384	473	.812
Bill Tosheff, Indianapolis	.253	314	.806

ASSISTS

	G	No.	Avg.
Bob Cousy, Boston	.71	547	7.7
Andy Phillip, Philadelphia-Fort Wayne	.70	397	5.7
George King, Syracuse	.71	364	5.1
Dick McGuire, New York	.61	296	4.9
Paul Seymour, Syracuse	.67	294	4.4
Bob Davies, Rochester	.66	280	4.2
Ed Macauley, Boston	.69	280	4.1
Leo Barnhorst, Indianapolis	.71	277	3.9
George Senesky, Philadelphia	.69	264	3.8
Bobby Wanzer, Rochester	.70	252	3.6

REBOUNDS

	G	No.	Avg.
George Mikan, Minneapolis	.70	1007	14.4
Neil Johnston, Philadelphia	.70	976	13.9
Dolph Schayes, Syracuse	.71	920	13.0
Harry Gallatin, New York	.70	916	13.1
Mel Hutchins, Milwaukee	.71	793	11.2
Jack Coleman, Rochester	.70	774	11.1
Larry Foust, Fort Wayne	.67	769	11.5
Nat Clifton, New York	.70	761	10.9
Arnie Risen, Rochester	.68	745	11.0
Joe Graboski, Indianapolis	.69	687	10.0

BALTIMORE BULLETS

													SCORING	
	G	Min.	FGM	FGA	Pct.	FTM	FTA	Pct.	Reb.	Ast.	PF	Dq.	Pts.	Avg.
Don Barksdale	65	2298	321	829	.387	257	401	.641	597	166	273	13	899	13.8
Eddie Miller	70	2018	273	781	.350	187	287	.652	669	115	250	12	733	10.5
Paul Hoffman	69	1955	240	656	.366	224	342	.655	317	237	282	13	704	10.2
Jim Baechtold	64	1893	242	621	.390	177	240	.738	219	154	203	8	661	10.3
Don Henriksen	68	2263	199	475	.419	176	281	.626	506	129	242	12	574	8.4
Ray Lumpp*	55	1422	188	506	.372	153	206	.743	141	168	178	5	529	9.6
Jack Kerris	69	1424	93	256	.363	88	140	.629	295	156	165	7	274	4.0
Ralph O'Brien	55	758	96	286	.336	78	92	.848	70	56	74	0	270	4.9
Kevin O'Shea	46	643	71	189	.376	48	81	.593	76	87	82	1	190	4.1
George Kaftan	23	380	45	142	.317	44	67	.657	75	31	59	2	134	5.8
Dick Bunt	26	271	29	107	.271	33	48	.688	28	17	40	0	91	3.5
Robert Priddy	16	149	14	38	.368	8	14	.571	36	7	36	3	36	2.3
George McLeod	10	85	2	16	.125	8	15	.533	21	4	16	0	12	1.2
Blaine Denning	1	9	2	5	.400	1	1	1.000	4	0	3	0	5	5.0

*Lumpp—Played with New York, Baltimore.

BOSTON CELTICS

													SCORING	
	G	Min.	FGM	FGA	Pct.	FTM	FTA	Pct.	Reb.	Ast.	PF	Dq.	Pts.	Avg.
Bob Cousy	71	2945	464	1320	.352	479	587	.816	449	547	227	4	1407	19.8
Ed Macauley	69	2902	451	997	.452	500	667	.750	629	280	188	0	1402	20.3
Bill Sharman	71	2333	403	925	.436	341	401	.850	288	191	240	7	1147	16.2
Bob Harris	70	1971	192	459	.418	133	226	.588	485	95	238	6	517	7.4
Bob Brannum	71	1900	188	541	.348	110	185	.595	537	147	287	17	486	6.8
Charles Cooper	70	1994	157	466	.337	144	190	.758	439	112	258	11	458	6.5
Bob Donham	71	1435	169	353	.479	113	240	.471	239	153	213	8	451	6.4
John Mahnken	69	771	76	252	.302	38	56	.679	182	75	110	1	190	2.8
Kenny Rollins	43	426	38	115	.330	22	27	.815	45	46	63	1	98	2.3
Gene Conley	39	461	35	108	.324	18	31	.581	171	19	74	1	88	2.3
Francis Mahoney	6	34	4	10	.400	4	5	.800	7	1	7	0	12	2.0

FORT WAYNE PISTONS

	G	Min.	FGM	FGA	Pct.	FTM	FTA	Pct.	Reb.	Ast.	PF	Dq.	SCORING Pts.	Avg.
Larry Foust	67	2303	311	865	.360	336	465	.723	769	151	267	16	958	14.3
Freddie Scolari	62	2123	277	809	.342	276	327	.844	209	233	212	4	830	13.4
Frank Brian	68	1910	245	699	.351	236	297	.795	133	142	205	8	726	10.7
Don Meineke	68	2250	240	630	.381	245	313	.783	466	148	334	26	725	10.7
Fred Schaus	69	2541	240	719	.334	243	296	.821	413	245	261	11	723	10.5
Andy Phillip*	70	2690	250	629	.397	222	301	.738	364	397	229	9	722	10.3
Thomas Eddleman	69	1571	241	687	.351	133	237	.561	236	104	220	5	615	8.9
Don Boven	67	1373	153	427	.358	145	209	.694	217	79	227	13	451	6.7
Charlie Share	67	1044	91	254	.358	172	234	.735	373	74	213	13	354	5.3
Dick Groat	26	663	100	272	.368	109	138	.790	86	69	90	7	309	11.9
Jake Fendley	45	380	32	80	.400	40	60	.667	46	36	82	3	104	2.3
Ray Corley	8	65	3	24	.125	5	6	.833	5	5	18	0	11	1.4
Boag Johnson	3	30	3	9	.333	2	3	.667	1	5	6	0	8	2.7
Jack Kiley	6	27	2	10	.200	2	2	1.000	2	3	7	0	6	1.0

*Phillip—Played with Philadelphia, Fort Wayne.

INDIANAPOLIS OLYMPIANS

	G	Min.	FGM	FGA	Pct.	FTM	FTA	Pct.	Reb.	Ast.	PF	Dq.	SCORING Pts.	Avg.
Leo Barnhorst	71	2871	402	1034	.389	163	259	.629	483	277	245	8	967	13.6
Joe Graboski	69	2769	272	799	.340	350	513	.682	687	156	303	18	894	13.0
Bill Tosheff	67	2459	253	783	.323	253	314	.806	229	243	243	5	759	11.3
Paul Walther	67	2468	227	645	.352	264	354	.746	284	205	260	7	718	10.7
Bob Lavoy	70	2327	225	560	.402	168	242	.694	528	130	274	18	618	8.8
Mel Payton	66	1424	173	485	.357	120	161	.745	313	81	118	0	466	7.1
Gene Rhodes	65	1162	109	342	.319	119	169	.704	98	91	78	2	337	5.2
Ed Mikan*	62	927	78	292	.267	79	98	.806	237	39	124	0	235	3.8
Robert Zawoluk	41	622	55	150	.367	77	116	.664	146	31	83	1	187	4.6
Don Hanrahan	18	121	11	32	.344	11	15	.733	30	11	24	1	33	1.8
Kleggie Hermsen	10	62	4	31	.129	3	5	.600	19	4	18	0	11	1.1
Robert Naber	4	11	0	4	.000	1	2	.500	5	1	6	0	1	0.3

*Mikan—Played with Philadelphia, Indianapolis.

MILWAUKEE HAWKS

	G	Min.	FGM	FGA	Pct.	FTM	FTA	Pct.	Reb.	Ast.	PF	Dq.	SCORING Pts.	Avg.
Jack Nichols	69	2626	425	1170	.363	240	339	.708	533	196	237	9	1090	15.8
Mel Hutchins	71	2891	319	842	.379	193	295	.654	793	227	214	5	831	11.7
George Ratkovicz	71	2235	208	619	.336	262	373	.702	522	217	287	16	678	9.5
Bill Calhoun	62	2148	180	534	.337	211	292	.723	277	156	136	4	571	9.2
Stan Miasek	65	1584	178	488	.365	156	248	.629	360	122	229	13	512	7.9
Johnny Payak	68	1470	128	373	.343	180	248	.726	114	140	194	7	436	6.4
Dave Minor	59	1610	154	420	.367	98	132	.742	252	128	211	11	406	6.9
Al Masino	71	1773	134	400	.335	128	204	.627	177	160	252	12	396	5.6
Dillard Crocker	61	776	100	284	.352	130	189	.688	104	63	199	11	330	5.4
Don Otten	24	384	34	87	.391	64	91	.703	89	21	68	4	132	5.5
Jim Brasco	20	248	25	94	.266	27	34	.794	24	21	30	2	77	3.9
Bucky McConnell	14	297	27	71	.380	14	29	.483	34	41	39	0	68	4.9
John O'Boyle	5	97	8	26	.308	5	7	.714	10	5	20	1	21	4.2
George Feigenbaum	5	79	4	22	.182	8	15	.533	7	9	14	1	16	3.2
Mike O'Neil	4	50	4	17	.235	4	4	1.000	9	3	10	1	12	3.0
Pete Darcey	12	90	3	18	.167	5	9	.556	10	2	29	2	11	0.9
Andrew Levane	7	68	3	24	.125	2	3	.667	9	9	15	0	8	1.1

MINNEAPOLIS LAKERS

	G	Min.	FGM	FGA	Pct.	FTM	FTA	Pct.	Reb.	Ast.	PF	Dq.	SCORING Pts.	Avg.
George Mikan	70	2651	500	1252	.399	442	567	.780	1007	201	290	12	1442	20.6
Vern Mikkelsen	70	2465	378	868	.435	291	387	.752	654	148	289	14	1047	15.0
Jim Pollard	66	2403	333	933	.357	193	251	.769	452	231	194	3	859	13.0
Slater Martin	70	2556	260	634	.410	224	287	.780	186	250	246	4	744	10.6
Frank Saul	70	1796	187	471	.397	142	200	.710	141	110	174	3	516	7.4
Bob Harrison	70	1643	195	518	.376	107	165	.648	153	160	264	16	497	7.1
Jim Holstein	66	989	98	274	.358	70	105	.667	173	74	128	1	266	4.0
Lew Hitch	70	1027	89	255	.349	83	136	.610	275	66	122	2	261	3.7
Whitey Skoog	68	996	102	264	.386	46	61	.754	121	82	137	2	250	3.7
Howie Schultz	40	474	24	90	.267	43	62	.694	80	29	73	1	91	2.3

NEW YORK KNICKERBOCKERS

	G	Min.	FGM	FGA	Pct.	FTM	FTA	Pct.	Reb.	Ast.	PF	Dq.	SCORING Pts.	Avg.
Carl Braun	70	2316	323	807	.400	331	401	.825	233	243	287	14	977	14.0
Harry Gallatin	70	2333	282	635	.444	301	430	.700	916	126	224	6	865	12.4
Nat Clifton	70	2496	272	794	.343	200	343	.583	761	231	274	6	744	10.6
Ernie Vandeweghe	61	1745	272	625	.435	187	244	.766	342	144	242	11	731	12.0
Connie Simmons	65	1707	240	637	.377	249	340	.732	458	127	252	9	729	11.2
Vince Boryla	66	2200	254	686	.370	165	201	.821	233	166	226	8	673	10.2
Dick McGuire	61	1783	142	373	.381	153	269	.569	280	296	172	3	437	7.2
Al McGuire	58	1231	112	287	.390	128	201	.637	167	145	206	8	352	6.1
Max Zaslofsky	29	722	123	320	.384	98	142	.690	75	55	81	1	344	11.9

1952-53

	G	Min.	FGM	FGA	Pct.	FTM	FTA	Pct.	Reb.	Ast.	PF	Dq.	Pts.	Avg.
													SCORING	
Dick Surhoff 26	26	187	13	61	.213	19	30	.633	25	9	36	1	45	1.7
Sherwin Raiken 6	6	63	3	21	.143	3	8	.375	8	6	10	0	9	1.5

PHILADELPHIA WARRIORS

	G	Min.	FGM	FGA	Pct.	FTM	FTA	Pct.	Reb.	Ast.	PF	Dq.	Pts.	Avg.
													SCORING	
Neil Johnston 70	70	3166	504	1114	.452	556	794	.700	976	197	248	6	1564	22.3
Joe Fulks. 70	70	2085	332	960	.346	168	231	.727	387	138	319	20	832	11.9
Don Lofgran 64	64	1788	173	525	.330	126	173	.728	339	106	178	6	472	7.4
George Senesky. 69	69	2336	160	485	.330	93	146	.637	254	264	166	1	413	6.0
Danny Finn 31	31	1015	135	409	.330	99	182	.544	175	146	124	9	369	11.9
Nelson Bobb 55	55	1286	119	318	.374	105	162	.648	157	192	161	7	343	6.2
Mark Workman 65	65	1030	130	408	.319	70	113	.619	193	37	166	5	330	5.1
Jerry Fleishman 33	33	882	100	303	.330	96	140	.686	152	108	118	7	296	9.0
Ralph Polson* 49	49	810	65	179	.363	61	96	.635	211	24	102	5	191	3.9
Bill Mlkvy. 31	31	608	75	246	.305	31	48	.646	101	62	54	1	181	5.8
Frank Kudelka 36	36	567	59	193	.306	44	68	.647	88	70	109	2	162	4.5
Jim Mooney** 18	18	529	54	148	.365	27	40	.675	70	35	50	1	135	7.5
Claude Overton 15	15	182	19	75	.253	20	30	.667	25	15	25	0	58	3.9
Moe Radovich 4	4	33	5	13	.385	4	4	1.000	1	8	5	0	14	3.5
Jack McCloskey 1	1	16	3	9	.333	0	0	. . .	3	1	2	0	6	6.0

*Polson—Played with New York, Philadelphia. **Mooney—Played with Baltimore, Philadelphia.

ROCHESTER ROYALS

	G	Min.	FGM	FGA	Pct.	FTM	FTA	Pct.	Reb.	Ast.	PF	Dq.	Pts.	Avg.
													SCORING	
Bob Davies 66	66	2216	339	880	.385	351	466	.753	195	280	261	7	1029	15.6
Bobby Wanzer 70	70	2577	318	866	.367	384	473	.812	351	252	206	7	1020	14.6
Arnie Risen 68	68	2288	295	802	.368	294	429	.685	745	135	274	10	884	13.0
Jack Coleman 70	70	2625	314	748	.420	135	208	.649	774	231	245	12	763	10.9
Marion Spears 62	62	1414	198	494	.401	199	243	.819	251	113	227	15	595	9.6
Arnie Johnson 70	70	1984	140	369	.379	303	405	.748	419	153	282	14	583	8.3
Jack McMahon 70	70	1665	176	534	.330	155	236	.657	183	186	253	16	507	7.2
Alex Hannum 68	68	1288	129	360	.358	88	133	.662	279	81	258	18	346	5.1
Cal Christensen 59	59	777	72	230	.313	68	114	.596	199	54	148	6	212	3.6
Red Holzman 46	46	392	38	149	.255	27	38	.711	40	35	56	2	103	2.2

SYRACUSE NATIONALS

	G	Min.	FGM	FGA	Pct.	FTM	FTA	Pct.	Reb.	Ast.	PF	Dq.	Pts.	Avg.
													SCORING	
Dolph Schayes. 71	71	2668	375	1022	.367	512	619	.827	920	227	271	9	1262	17.8
Paul Seymour 67	67	2684	306	798	.383	340	416	.817	246	294	210	3	952	14.2
George King 71	71	2519	255	635	.402	284	442	.643	281	364	244	2	794	11.2
Red Rocha. 69	69	2454	268	690	.388	234	310	.755	510	137	257	5	770	11.2
Billy Gabor 69	69	1337	215	614	.350	217	284	.764	104	134	262	11	647	9.4
Earl Lloyd 64	64	1806	156	453	.344	160	231	.693	444	64	241	6	472	7.4
Noble Jorgensen 70	70	1355	145	436	.333	146	199	.734	236	76	247	7	436	6.2
Wally Osterkorn 49	49	1016	85	262	.324	106	168	.631	217	61	129	2	276	5.6
Bob Lochmueller 62	62	802	79	245	.322	74	122	.607	162	47	143	1	232	3.7
Al Cervi. 38	38	301	31	71	.437	81	100	.810	22	28	90	2	143	3.8
James Brasco 10	10	111	11	48	.229	11	14	.786	15	12	18	1	33	3.3

1952-53

PLAYOFF RESULTS

EASTERN DIVISION

SEMIFINALS

New York 2, Baltimore 0
Mar. 17—Tue.   Baltimore 62 at New York .80
Mar. 20—Fri.   New York 90 at Baltimore 81

Boston 2, Syracuse 0
Mar. 19—Thur.   Boston 87 at Syracuse 81
Mar. 21—Sat.   Syracuse 105 at Boston ****111

FINALS

New York 3, Boston 1
Mar. 25—Wed.   Boston 91 at New York 95
Mar. 26—Thur.   New York 70 at Boston .86
Mar. 28—Sat.   Boston 82 at New York 101
Mar. 29—Sun.   New York 82 at Boston .75

WESTERN DIVISION

SEMIFINALS

Fort Wayne 2, Rochester 1
Mar. 20—Fri.   Fort Wayne 84 at Rochester 77
Mar. 22—Sun.   Rochester 83 at Fort Wayne 71
Mar. 24—Tue.   Fort Wayne 67 at Rochester 65

Minneapolis 2, Indianapolis 0
Mar. 22—Sun.   Indianapolis 69 at Minneapolis 85
Mar. 23—Mon.   Minneapolis 81 at Indianapolis 79

FINALS

Minneapolis 3, Fort Wayne 2
Mar. 26—Thur.   Fort Wayne 73 at Minneapolis 83
Mar. 28—Sat.   Fort Wayne 75 at Minneapolis 82
Mar. 30—Mon.   Minneapolis 95 at Fort Wayne 98
Apr. 1—Wed.   Minneapolis 82 at Fort Wayne 85
Apr. 2—Thur.   Fort Wayne 58 at Minneapolis 74

NBA FINALS

Minneapolis 4, New York 1
Apr. 4—Sat.   New York 96 at Minneapolis 88
Apr. 5—Sun.   New York 71 at Minneapolis 73
Apr. 7—Tue.   Minneapolis 90 at New York 75
Apr. 8—Wed.   Minneapolis 71 at New York 69
Apr. 10—Fri.   Minneapolis 91 at New York 84
*Denotes number of overtime periods.

1951-52

1951-52 NBA CHAMPION MINNEAPOLIS LAKERS
From left: Slater Martin, Joe Hutton, Frank Saul, Bob Harrison, Jim Pollard, Howie Schultz, Vern Mikkelsen, Lew Hitch, George Mikan. Not pictured: head coach John Kundla, Whitey Skoog.

FINAL STANDINGS

EASTERN DIVISION

	Syr.	Bos.	N.Y.	Phi.	Balt.	Roch.	Minn.	Ind.	Ft.W.	Mil.	W	L	Pct.	GB
Syracuse...........	..	5	4	6	6	2	5	2	6	4	40	26	.606	..
Boston	4	..	4	6	8	3	3	3	3	5	39	27	.591	1
New York..........	5	5	..	6	7	2	2	3	3	4	37	29	.561	3
Philadelphia........	3	3	3	..	5	2	4	4	4	5	33	33	.500	7
Baltimore..........	3	1	2	4	..	2	0	2	2	4	20	46	.303	20

WESTERN DIVISION

	Syr.	Bos.	N.Y.	Phi.	Balt.	Roch.	Minn.	Ind.	Ft.W.	Mil.	W	L	Pct.	GB
Rochester	4	3	4	4	4	..	2	6	6	8	41	25	.621	..
Minneapolis........	1	3	4	2	6	7	..	5	4	8	40	26	.606	1
Indianapolis.......	4	3	3	2	4	3	4	..	4	7	34	32	.515	7
Fort Wayne	0	3	3	2	4	3	5	5	..	4	29	37	.439	12
Milwaukee.........	2	1	2	1	2	1	1	2	5	..	17	49	.258	24

TEAM STATISTICS

	G	FGM	FGA	Pct.	FTM	FTA	Pct.	Reb.	Ast.	PF	Dq.	AVERAGE POINTS For	AVERAGE POINTS Agst.	AVERAGE POINTS Dif.
Minneapolis......	66	2106	5733	.367	1436	1921	.748	3543	1389	1763	60	85.6	79.5	+6.1
Syracuse........	66	1894	5207	.364	1933	2589	.747	3603	1373	1970	49	86.7	82.2	+4.5
Boston	66	2131	5510	.387	1765	2406	.734	3750	1606	1734	47	91.3	87.3	+4.0
Rochester	66	2014	5172	.389	1661	2150	.773	3373	1590	1804	62	86.2	82.9	+3.3
New York.......	66	2022	5282	.383	1565	2185	.716	3834	1567	1770	16	85.0	84.2	+0.8
Indianapolis.....	66	2026	5513	.367	1422	1965	.724	3288	1290	1586	37	82.9	82.8	+0.1
Philadelphia......	66	2039	5367	.380	1634	2143	.762	3647	1593	1806	57	86.5	87.8	-1.3
Fort Wayne	66	1771	5013	.353	1609	2194	.733	3619	1403	1751	70	78.0	80.1	-2.1
Baltimore........	66	1882	5495	.342	1614	2211	.730	3780	1417	1719	55	81.5	89.0	-7.5
Milwaukee.......	66	1674	5055	.331	1485	2177	.682	3540	1229	1848	68	73.2	81.2	-8.0
Avgs..........	66	1956	5335	.367	1612	2194	.735	3598	1446	1775	52.1	83.7	...	...

HOME/ROAD/NEUTRAL

	Home	Road	Neutral	Total		Home	Road	Neutral	Total
Baltimore	17-15	2-22	1-9	20-46	New York	21-4	12-22	4-3	37-29
Boston	22-7	10-19	7-1	39-27	Philadelphia	24-7	6-25	3-1	33-33
Fort Wayne	22-11	6-24	1-2	29-37	Rochester	28-5	12-18	1-2	41-25
Indianapolis	25-6	4-24	5-2	34-32	Syracuse	26-7	12-18	2-1	40-26
Milwaukee	7-13	3-22	7-14	17-49	Totals	213-80	80-213	37-37	330-330
Minneapolis	21-5	13-19	6-2	40-26					

INDIVIDUAL LEADERS

POINTS

	G	FGM	FTM	Pts.	Avg.
Paul Arizin, Philadelphia	66	548	578	1674	25.4
George Mikan, Minneapolis	64	545	433	1523	23.8
Bob Cousy, Boston	66	512	409	1433	21.7
Ed Macauley, Boston	66	384	496	1264	19.2
Bob Davies, Rochester	65	379	294	1052	16.2
Frank Brian, Fort Wayne	66	342	367	1051	15.9
Larry Foust, Fort Wayne	66	390	267	1047	15.9
Bobby Wanzer, Rochester	66	328	377	1033	15.7
Arnie Risen, Rochester	66	365	302	1032	15.6
Vern Mikkelsen, Minneapolis	66	363	283	1009	15.3
Jim Pollard, Minneapolis	65	411	183	1005	15.5
Fred Scolari, Baltimore	64	290	353	933	14.6
Max Zaslofsky, New York	66	322	287	931	14.1
Joe Fulks, Philadelphia	61	336	250	922	15.1
Joe Graboski, Philadelphia	66	320	264	904	13.7
Fred Schaus, Fort Wayne	62	281	310	872	14.1
Dolph Schayes, Syracuse	63	263	342	868	13.8
Red Rocha, Syracuse	66	300	254	854	12.9
Leo Barnhorst, Indianapolis	66	349	122	820	12.4
Andy Phillip, Philadelphia	66	279	232	790	12.0

FIELD GOALS
(minimum 210 made)

	FGM	FGA	Pct.
Paul Arizin, Philadelphia	548	1222	.448
Harry Gallatin, New York	233	527	.442
Ed Macauley, Boston	384	888	.432
Bobby Wanzer, Rochester	328	772	.425
Vern Mikkelsen, Minneapolis	363	866	.419
Jack Coleman, Rochester	308	742	.415
George King, Syracuse	235	579	.406
Red Rocha, Syracuse	300	749	.401
Paul Walther, Indianapolis	220	549	.401
Bob Lavoy, Indianapolis	240	604	.397

FREE THROWS
(minimum 180 made)

	FTM	FTA	Pct.
Bobby Wanzer, Rochester	377	417	.904
Al Cervi, Syracuse	219	248	.883
Bill Sharman, Boston	183	213	.859
Frank Brian, Fort Wayne	367	433	.848
Fred Scolari, Baltimore	353	423	.835
Fred Schaus, Fort Wayne	310	372	.833
Joe Fulks, Philadelphia	250	303	.825
Bill Tosheff, Indianapolis	182	221	.824
Paul Arizin, Philadelphia	578	707	.818
Bob Cousy, Boston	409	506	.808

ASSISTS

	G	No.	Avg.
Andy Phillip, Philadelphia	66	539	8.2
Bob Cousy, Boston	66	441	6.7
Bob Davies, Rochester	65	390	6.0
Dick McGuire, New York	64	388	6.1
Fred Scolari, Baltimore	64	303	4.7
George Senesky, Philadelphia	57	280	4.9
Bobby Wanzer, Rochester	66	262	4.0
Leo Barnhorst, Indianapolis	66	255	3.9
Slater Martin, Minneapolis	66	249	3.8
Fred Schaus, Fort Wayne	62	247	4.0

REBOUNDS

	G	No.	Avg.
Larry Foust, Fort Wayne	66	880	13.3
Mel Hutchins, Milwaukee	66	880	13.3
George Mikan, Minneapolis	64	866	13.5
Arnie Risen, Rochester	66	841	12.7
Dolph Schayes, Syracuse	63	773	12.3
Paul Arizin, Philadelphia	66	745	11.3
Nat Clifton, New York	62	731	11.8
Jack Coleman, Rochester	66	692	10.5
Vern Mikkelsen, Minneapolis	66	681	10.3
Harry Gallatin, New York	66	661	10.0

1951-52

INDIVIDUAL STATISTICS, TEAM BY TEAM

BALTIMORE BULLETS

	G	Min.	FGM	FGA	Pct.	FTM	FTA	Pct.	Reb.	Ast.	PF	Dq.	Pts.	Avg.
Freddie Scolari	64	2242	290	867	.334	353	423	.835	214	303	213	6	933	14.6
Don Barksdale	62	2014	272	804	.338	237	343	.691	601	137	230	13	781	12.6
Stan Miasek	66	2174	258	707	.365	263	372	.707	639	140	257	12	779	11.8
Frank Kudelka	65	1583	204	614	.332	198	258	.767	275	183	220	11	606	9.3
Dave Minor	57	1558	185	522	.354	101	132	.765	275	160	161	2	471	8.3
Kevin O'Shea*	65	1725	153	466	.328	144	210	.686	201	171	175	7	450	6.9
Bill Calhoun	55	1594	129	409	.315	125	183	.683	252	117	84	0	383	7.0
Brady Walker	35	699	89	217	.410	26	34	.765	195	40	38	0	204	5.8
Joe McNamee**	58	695	68	222	.306	30	50	.600	137	40	108	4	166	2.9
Jim Slaughter	28	525	53	165	.321	41	68	.603	148	25	81	0	147	5.3

*O'Shea—Played with Milwaukee, Baltimore.
**McNamee—Played with Rochester, Baltimore.

BOSTON CELTICS

	G	Min.	FGM	FGA	Pct.	FTM	FTA	Pct.	Reb.	Ast.	PF	Dq.	Pts.	Avg.
Bob Cousy	66	2681	512	1388	.369	409	506	.808	421	441	190	5	1433	21.7
Ed Macauley	66	2631	384	888	.432	496	621	.799	529	232	174	0	1264	19.2
Bill Sharman	63	1389	244	628	.389	183	213	.859	221	151	181	3	671	10.7
Bob Donham	66	1980	201	413	.487	149	293	.509	330	228	223	9	551	8.3
Charles Cooper	66	1976	197	545	.361	149	201	.741	502	134	219	8	543	8.2
Bob Harris	66	1899	190	463	.410	134	209	.641	531	120	194	5	514	7.8
Bob Brannum	66	1324	149	404	.369	107	171	.626	406	76	235	9	405	6.1
Horace McKinney	63	1083	136	418	.325	65	80	.813	175	111	148	4	337	5.3
John Mahnken	60	581	78	227	.344	26	43	.605	132	63	91	2	182	3.0
Dick Dickey	45	440	40	136	.294	47	69	.681	81	50	79	2	127	2.8

FORT WAYNE PISTONS

	G	Min.	FGM	FGA	Pct.	FTM	FTA	Pct.	Reb.	Ast.	PF	Dq.	Pts.	Avg.
Frank Brian	66	2672	342	972	.352	367	433	.848	232	233	220	6	1051	15.9
Larry Foust	66	2615	390	989	.394	267	394	.678	880	200	245	10	1047	15.9
Fred Schaus	62	2581	281	778	.361	310	372	.833	434	247	221	7	872	14.1

	G	Min.	FGM	FGA	Pct.	FTM	FTA	Pct.	Reb.	Ast.	PF	Dq.	Pts.	Avg.
Thomas Eddleman*	65	1893	269	809	.333	202	329	.614	267	134	249	9	740	11.4
Jack Kerris	66	2148	186	480	.388	217	325	.668	514	212	265	16	589	8.9
Boag Johnson	66	2265	211	592	.356	101	140	.721	222	210	243	6	523	7.9
Bill Closs	57	1120	120	389	.308	107	157	.682	204	76	125	2	347	6.1
Charlie Share	63	882	76	236	.322	96	155	.619	331	66	141	9	248	3.9
Jake Fendley	58	651	54	170	.318	75	95	.789	80	58	118	3	183	3.2
Jack Kiley	47	477	44	193	.228	30	54	.556	49	62	54	2	118	2.5
Emilio Sinicola	3	15	1	4	.250	0	2	.000	1	0	2	0	2	0.7

*Eddleman—Played with Milwaukee, Fort Wayne.

INDIANAPOLIS OLYMPIANS

	G	Min.	FGM	FGA	Pct.	FTM	FTA	Pct.	Reb.	Ast.	PF	Dq.	Pts.	Avg.
Joe Graboski	66	2439	320	827	.387	264	396	.667	655	130	254	10	904	13.7
Leo Barnhorst	66	2344	349	897	.389	122	187	.652	430	255	196	3	820	12.4
Paul Walther	55	1903	220	549	.401	231	308	.750	246	137	171	6	671	12.2
Bob Lavoy	63	1829	240	604	.397	168	223	.753	479	107	210	5	648	10.3
Bill Tosheff	65	2055	213	651	.327	182	221	.824	216	222	204	7	608	9.4
Ralph O'Brien	64	1577	228	613	.372	122	149	.819	122	124	115	0	578	9.0
Don Lofgran	63	1254	149	417	.357	156	219	.712	257	48	147	3	454	7.2
Wallace Jones	58	1320	164	524	.313	102	136	.750	283	150	137	3	430	7.4
Joe Holland	55	737	93	265	.351	40	69	.580	166	47	90	0	226	4.1
Cliff Barker	44	494	48	161	.298	30	51	.588	81	70	56	0	126	2.9

MILWAUKEE HAWKS

	G	Min.	FGM	FGA	Pct.	FTM	FTA	Pct.	Reb.	Ast.	PF	Dq.	Pts.	Avg.
Don Otten*	64	1789	222	636	.349	323	418	.773	435	123	218	11	767	12.0
Dick Mehen	65	2294	293	824	.356	117	167	.701	282	171	209	10	703	10.8
Don Boven	66	1982	200	668	.299	256	350	.731	336	177	271	18	656	9.9
Mel Hutchins	66	2618	231	633	.365	145	225	.644	880	190	192	5	607	9.2
Dillard Crocker**	38	783	98	279	.351	97	145	.669	111	57	132	7	293	7.7
Don Rehfeldt***	39	788	99	285	.347	63	80	.788	243	50	102	2	261	6.7
Bob Wilson	63	1308	79	264	.299	78	135	.578	210	108	172	8	236	3.7
James Owens****	29	626	83	252	.329	64	114	.561	102	64	92	5	230	7.9
Walt Kirk	11	396	28	101	.277	55	78	.705	44	28	47	3	111	10.1
Art Burris*****	41	514	42	156	.269	26	39	.667	99	27	49	3	110	2.7
Cal Christensen	24	374	29	96	.302	30	57	.526	82	34	47	2	88	3.7
Nate DeLong	17	132	20	142	.141	24	35	.686	31	14	47	3	64	3.8
Gene Vance	7	118	7	26	.269	9	14	.643	15	9	18	0	23	3.3
Charlie Black	13	117	6	31	.194	5	12	.417	31	9	31	2	17	1.3
Elmer Behnke	4	55	6	22	.273	4	7	.571	17	4	13	1	16	4.0
John McConathy	11	106	4	29	.138	6	14	.429	20	8	7	0	14	1.3
John Rennicke	6	54	4	18	.222	3	9	.333	9	1	7	0	11	1.8
Jerry Fowler	6	41	4	13	.308	1	4	.250	10	2	9	0	9	1.5

*Otten—Played with Fort Wayne, Milwaukee. **Crocker—Played with Indianapolis, Milwaukee. ***Rehfeldt—Played with Baltimore, Milwaukee. ****Owens—Played with Baltimore, Milwaukee. *****Burris—Played with Fort Wayne, Milwaukee.

MINNEAPOLIS LAKERS

	G	Min.	FGM	FGA	Pct.	FTM	FTA	Pct.	Reb.	Ast.	PF	Dq.	Pts.	Avg.
George Mikan	64	2572	545	1414	.385	433	555	.780	866	194	286	14	1523	23.8
Vern Mikkelsen	66	2345	363	866	.419	283	372	.761	681	180	282	16	1009	15.3
Jim Pollard	65	2545	411	1155	.356	183	260	.704	593	234	199	4	1005	15.5
Slater Martin	66	2480	237	632	.375	142	190	.747	228	249	226	9	616	9.3
Frank Saul*	64	1479	157	436	.360	119	153	.778	165	147	120	3	433	6.8
Bob Harrison	65	1712	156	487	.320	89	124	.718	160	188	203	9	401	6.2
Howie Schultz	66	1301	89	315	.283	90	119	.756	246	102	197	13	268	4.1
Whitey Skoog	35	988	102	296	.345	30	38	.789	122	60	94	4	234	6.7
Lew Hitch	61	849	77	215	.358	63	94	.670	243	50	89	3	217	3.6
Joe Hutton	60	723	53	158	.335	49	70	.700	85	62	110	1	155	2.6
John Pilch	9	41	1	10	.100	3	6	.500	9	2	10	0	5	0.6

*Saul—Played with Baltimore, Minneapolis.

NEW YORK KNICKERBOCKERS

	G	Min.	FGM	FGA	Pct.	FTM	FTA	Pct.	Reb.	Ast.	PF	Dq.	Pts.	Avg.
Max Zaslofsky	66	2113	322	958	.336	287	380	.755	194	156	183	5	931	14.1
Harry Gallatin	66	1931	233	527	.442	275	341	.806	661	115	223	5	741	11.2
Nat Clifton	62	2101	244	729	.335	170	256	.664	731	209	227	8	658	10.6
Connie Simmons	66	1558	227	600	.378	175	254	.689	471	121	214	8	629	9.5
Dick McGuire	64	2018	204	474	.430	183	290	.631	332	388	181	4	591	9.2
Ernie Vandeweghe	57	1507	200	457	.438	124	160	.775	264	164	188	3	524	9.2
Vince Boryla	42	1440	202	522	.387	96	115	.835	219	90	121	2	500	11.9
Ray Lumpp	62	1317	184	476	.387	90	119	.756	125	123	165	4	458	7.4
George Kaftan	52	955	115	307	.375	92	134	.687	196	88	107	0	322	6.2
Al McGuire	59	788	72	167	.431	64	122	.525	121	107	136	8	208	3.5
Herb Scherer	12	167	19	65	.292	9	14	.643	26	6	25	0	47	3.9

PHILADELPHIA WARRIORS

	G	Min.	FGM	FGA	Pct.	FTM	FTA	Pct.	Reb.	Ast.	PF	Dq.	SCORING Pts.	Avg.
Paul Arizin	66	2939	548	1222	.448	578	707	.818	745	170	250	5	1674	25.4
Joe Fulks	61	1904	336	1078	.312	250	303	.825	368	123	255	13	922	15.1
Andy Phillip	66	2933	279	762	.366	232	308	.753	434	539	218	6	790	12.0
Ed Mikan	66	1781	202	571	.354	116	148	.784	492	87	252	7	520	7.9
George Senesky	57	1925	164	454	.361	146	194	.753	232	280	123	0	474	8.3
Neil Johnston	64	993	141	299	.472	100	151	.662	342	39	154	5	382	6.0
Nelson Bobb	62	1192	110	306	.359	99	167	.593	147	168	182	9	319	5.1
Walt Budko	63	1126	97	240	.404	60	89	.674	232	91	196	10	254	4.0
Vern Gardner	27	507	72	194	.371	15	23	.652	112	37	60	2	159	5.9
Mel Payton	45	471	54	140	.386	21	28	.750	83	45	68	2	129	2.9
Stan Brown	15	141	22	63	.349	10	18	.556	17	9	32	0	54	3.6
Ed Dahler	14	112	14	38	.368	7	7	1.000	22	5	16	0	35	2.5

ROCHESTER ROYALS

	G	Min.	FGM	FGA	Pct.	FTM	FTA	Pct.	Reb.	Ast.	PF	Dq.	SCORING Pts.	Avg.
Bob Davies	65	2394	379	990	.383	294	379	.776	189	390	269	10	1052	16.2
Bobby Wanzer	66	2498	328	772	.425	377	417	.904	333	262	201	5	1033	15.7
Arnie Risen	66	2396	365	926	.394	302	431	.701	841	150	258	3	1032	15.6
Jack Coleman	66	2606	308	742	.415	120	169	.710	692	208	218	7	736	11.2
Arnie Johnson	66	2158	178	411	.433	301	387	.778	404	182	259	9	657	10.0
Marion Spears	66	1673	225	570	.395	116	152	.763	303	163	225	8	566	8.6
Alex Hannum*	66	1508	170	462	.368	98	137	.715	336	133	271	16	438	6.6
Red Holzman	65	1065	104	372	.280	61	85	.718	106	115	95	1	269	4.1
Sam Ranzino	39	234	30	90	.333	26	37	.703	39	25	63	2	86	2.2
Ray Ragelis	51	337	25	96	.260	18	29	.621	76	31	62	1	68	1.3
Paul Noel	8	32	2	9	.222	2	3	.667	4	3	6	0	6	0.8

*Hannum—Played with Baltimore, Rochester.

SYRACUSE NATIONALS

	G	Min.	FGM	FGA	Pct.	FTM	FTA	Pct.	Reb.	Ast.	PF	Dq.	SCORING Pts.	Avg.
Dolph Schayes	63	2004	263	740	.355	342	424	.807	773	182	213	5	868	13.8
Red Rocha	66	2543	300	749	.401	254	330	.770	549	128	249	4	854	12.9
George King	66	1889	235	579	.406	188	264	.712	274	244	199	6	658	10.0
Paul Seymour	66	2209	206	615	.335	186	245	.759	225	220	165	4	598	9.1
Noble Jorgensen	66	1318	190	460	.413	149	187	.797	288	63	190	2	529	8.0
George Ratkovicz	66	1356	165	473	.349	163	242	.674	328	90	235	8	493	7.5
Wally Osterkorn	66	1721	145	413	.351	199	335	.594	444	117	226	8	489	7.4
Billy Gabor	57	1085	173	538	.322	142	183	.776	93	86	188	5	488	8.6
Al Cervi	55	850	99	280	.354	219	248	.883	87	148	176	7	417	7.6
Gerry Calabrese	58	937	109	317	.344	73	103	.709	84	83	107	0	291	5.0

PLAYOFF RESULTS

EASTERN DIVISION

SEMIFINALS

Syracuse 2, Philadelphia 1
Mar. 20—Thur.	Philadelphia 83 at Syracuse	102
Mar. 22—Sat.	Syracuse 95 at Philadelphia	100
Mar. 23—Sun.	Philadelphia 73 at Syracuse	84

New York 2, Boston 1
Mar. 19—Wed.	New York 94 at Boston	105
Mar. 23—Sun.	Boston 97 at New York	101
Mar. 26—Wed.	New York 88 at Boston	**87

FINALS

New York 3, Syracuse 1
Apr. 2—Wed.	New York 87 at Syracuse	85
Apr. 3—Thur.	New York 92 at Syracuse	102
Apr. 4—Fri.	Syracuse 92 at New York	99
Apr. 8—Tue.	Syracuse 93 at New York	100

WESTERN DIVISION

SEMIFINALS

Minneapolis 2, Indianapolis 0
| Mar. 23—Sun. | Indianapolis 70 at Minneapolis | 78 |
| Mar. 25—Tue. | Minneapolis 94 at Indianapolis | 87 |

Rochester 2, Fort Wayne 0
| Mar. 18—Tue. | Fort Wayne 78 at Rochester | 95 |
| Mar. 20—Thur. | Rochester 92 at Fort Wayne | 86 |

FINALS

Minneapolis 3, Rochester 1
Mar. 29—Sat.	Minneapolis 78 at Rochester	88
Mar. 30—Sun.	Minneapolis 83 at Rochester	78
Apr. 5—Sat.	Rochester 67 at Minneapolis	77
Apr. 6—Sun.	Rochester 80 at Minneapolis	82

NBA FINALS

Minneapolis 4, New York 3
Apr. 12—Sat.	New York 79, Minneapolis (at St. Paul)	*83
Apr. 13—Sun.	New York 80, Minneapolis (at St. Paul)	72
Apr. 16—Wed.	Minneapolis 82 at New York	77
Apr. 18—Fri.	Minneapolis 89 at New York	*90
Apr. 20—Sun.	New York 89, Minneapolis (at St. Paul)	102
Apr. 23—Wed.	Minneapolis 68 at New York	76
Apr. 25—Fri.	New York 65 at Minneapolis	82

*Denotes number of overtime periods.

1951-52

1950-51

1950-51 NBA CHAMPION ROCHESTER ROYALS
Front row (from left): Bob Davies, Bobby Wanzer, Red Holzman, Paul Noel, Frank Saul. Back row (from left): Bill Calhoun, Joe McNamee, Arnie Risen, Jack Coleman, Arnie Johnson. Inset: head coach Les Harrison.

FINAL STANDINGS

EASTERN DIVISION

	Phi.	Bos.	N.Y.	Syr.	Balt.	Was.	Minn.	Roch.	Ft.W.	Ind.	Tri-C	W	L	Pct.	GB
Philadelphia		4	3	6	6	3	2	4	3	5	4	40	26	.606	..
Boston 4		..	4	3	6	4	3	2	5	4	4	39	30	.565	2.5
New York 5	4		..	5	5	2	3	3	4	1	4	36	30	.545	4
Syracuse 2	5	5		..	5	2	2	2	3	3	3	32	34	.485	8
Baltimore 3	3	2	3		..	1	2	1	4	2	3	24	42	.364	16
Washington 0	3	1	0	2		..	0	0	1	2	1	10	25	.286	*

WESTERN DIVISION

	Phi.	Bos.	N.Y.	Syr.	Balt.	Was.	Minn.	Roch.	Ft.W.	Ind.	Tri-C	W	L	Pct.	GB
Minneapolis 4	3	3	4	4	2		..	4	3	7	10	44	24	.647	..
Rochester 2	4	3	4	5	5	4		..	5	4	5	41	27	.603	3
Fort Wayne 3	1	2	3	2	3	5	3		..	5	5	32	36	.471	12
Indianapolis 1	1	5	3	4	2	3	5	3		..	4	31	37	.456	13
Tri-Cities 2	2	2	3	3	1	0	3	5	4		..	25	43	.368	19

*Washington team was disbanded January 9; players assigned to other teams.

TEAM STATISTICS

	G	FGM	FGA	Pct.	FTM	FTA	Pct.	Reb.	Ast.	PF	Dq.	AVERAGE POINTS For	AVERAGE POINTS Agst.	AVERAGE POINTS Dif.
Minneapolis 68		2084	5590	.373	1464	1989	.736	3409	1408	1801	49	82.8	77.4	+5.4
Philadelphia 66		1985	5665	.350	1664	2181	.763	3586	1432	1710	61	85.4	81.6	+3.8
Rochester 68		2032	5377	.378	1692	2248	.753	3015	1368	1534	35	84.6	81.7	+2.9
Syracuse 66		1884	5365	.351	1912	2634	.726	3259	1493	1995	64	86.1	85.5	+0.6
New York 66		2037	5380	.379	1592	2231	.714	3421	1551	1810	47	85.8	85.4	+0.4
Boston 69		2065	5607	.368	1751	2415	.725	3499	1579	1881	52	85.2	85.5	-0.3
Fort Wayne 68		2002	5927	.338	1718	2387	.720	3725	1142	1961	79	84.1	86.0	-1.9
Baltimore 66		1955	5542	.353	1504	2020	.745	3044	1345	1736	53	82.0	84.3	-2.3
Indianapolis 68		2096	5779	.363	1363	1902	.717	2779	1455	1569	35	81.7	84.0	-2.3
Tri-Cities 68		1988	6041	.329	1754	2425	.723	3715	1476	2092	79	84.3	88.0	-3.7
Washington* 35		967	2893	.334	910	1244	.732	1567	584	1050	26	81.3	86.0	-4.7
Avgs. 64.4		1918	5379	.357	1575	2152	.732	3184	1348	1740	52.7	84.0	. . .	. . .

*Disbanded January 9.

HOME/ROAD/NEUTRAL

	Home	Road	Neutral	Total		Home	Road	Neutral	Total
Baltimore	21-11	3-25	0-6	24-42	Philadelphia	29-3	10-22	1-1	40-26
Boston	26-6	9-22	4-2	39-30	Rochester	29-5	12-22	0-0	41-27
Fort Wayne	27-7	5-27	0-2	32-36	Syracuse	24-9	8-25	0-0	32-34
Indianapolis	19-12	10-24	2-1	31-37	Tri-Cities	22-13	2-28	1-2	25-43
Minneapolis	29-3	12-21	3-0	44-24	Washington	6-11	4-13	0-1	10-25
New York	22-5	10-25	4-0	36-30	Totals	254-85	85-254	15-15	354-354

INDIVIDUAL LEADERS

POINTS

	G	FGM	FTM	Pts.	Avg.
George Mikan, Minneapolis	.68	678	576	1932	28.4
Alex Groza, Indianapolis	.66	492	445	1429	21.7
Ed Macauley, Boston	.68	459	466	1384	20.4
Joe Fulks, Philadelphia	.66	429	378	1236	18.7
Frank Brian, Tri-Cities	.68	363	418	1144	16.8
Paul Arizin, Philadelphia	.65	352	417	1121	17.2
Dolph Schayes, Syracuse	.66	332	457	1121	17.0
Ralph Beard, Indianapolis	.66	409	293	1111	16.8
Bob Cousy, Boston	.69	401	276	1078	15.6
Arnie Risen, Rochester	.66	377	323	1077	16.3
Dwight Eddleman, Tri-Cities	.68	398	244	1040	15.3
Fred Schaus, Fort Wayne	.68	312	404	1028	15.1
Vince Boryla, New York	.66	352	278	982	14.9
Bob Davies, Rochester	.63	326	303	955	15.2
Larry Foust, Fort Wayne	.68	327	261	915	13.5
Vern Mikkelsen, Minneapolis	.64	359	186	904	14.1
Fred Scolari, Wash.-Syracuse	.66	302	279	883	13.4
Ken Murray, Balt.-Fort Wayne	.66	301	248	850	12.9
George Ratkovicz, Syracuse	.66	264	321	849	12.9
Harry Gallatin, New York	.66	293	259	845	12.8

FIELD GOALS

(minimum 200 made)

	FGM	FGA	Pct.
Alex Groza, Indianapolis	.492	1046	.470
Ed Macauley, Boston	.459	985	.466
George Mikan, Minneapolis	.678	1584	.428
Jack Coleman, Rochester	.315	749	.421
Harry Gallatin, New York	.293	705	.416
George Ratkovicz, Syracuse	.264	636	.415
Paul Arizin, Philadelphia	.352	864	.407
Vince Boryla, New York	.352	867	.406
Vern Mikkelsen, Minneapolis	.359	893	.402
Bobby Wanzer, Rochester	.252	628	.401

FREE THROWS

(minimum 170 made)

	FTM	FTA	Pct.
Joe Fulks, Philadelphia	.378	442	.855
Bobby Wanzer, Rochester	.232	273	.850
Belus Smawley, Syracuse-Baltimore	.227	267	.850
Fred Scolari, Washington-Syracuse	.279	331	.843
Vince Boryla, New York	.278	332	.837
Fred Schaus, Fort Wayne	.404	484	.835
Sonny Hertzberg, Boston	.223	270	.826
Frank Brian, Tri-Cities	.418	508	.823
Al Cervi, Syracuse	.194	237	.819
Red Rocha, Baltimore	.242	299	.809

ASSISTS

	G	No.	Avg.
Andy Phillip, Philadelphia	.66	414	6.3
Dick McGuire, New York	.64	400	6.3
George Senesky, Philadelphia	.65	342	5.3
Bob Cousy, Boston	.69	341	4.9
Ralph Beard, Indianapolis	.66	318	4.8
Bob Davies, Rochester	.63	287	4.6
Frank Brian, Tri-Cities	.68	266	3.9
Fred Scolari, Washington-Syracuse	.66	255	3.9
Ed Macauley, Boston	.68	252	3.7
Dolph Schayes, Syracuse	.66	251	3.8

REBOUNDS

	G	No.	Avg.
Dolph Schayes, Syracuse	.66	1080	16.4
George Mikan, Minneapolis	.68	958	14.1
Harry Gallatin, New York	.66	800	12.1
Arnie Risen, Rochester	.66	795	12.0
Alex Groza, Indianapolis	.66	709	10.7
Larry Foust, Fort Wayne	.68	681	10.0
Vern Mikkelsen, Minneapolis	.64	655	10.2
Paul Arizin, Philadelphia	.65	640	9.8
Ed Macauley, Boston	.68	616	9.1
Jack Coleman, Rochester	.67	584	8.7

1950-51

INDIVIDUAL STATISTICS, TEAM BY TEAM

BALTIMORE BULLETS

	G	FGM	FGA	Pct.	FTM	FTA	Pct.	Reb.	Ast.	PF	Dq.	SCORING Pts.	Avg.
Red Rocha	64	297	843	.352	242	299	.809	511	147	242	9	836	13.1
Belus Smawley*	60	252	663	.380	227	267	.850	178	161	145	4	731	12.2
Charles Halbert**	68	164	449	.365	172	248	.694	539	158	216	7	500	7.4
Walt Budko	64	165	464	.356	166	223	.744	452	135	203	7	496	7.8
Kenny Sailors***	60	181	533	.340	131	180	.728	120	150	196	8	493	8.2
Don Rehfeldt	59	164	426	.385	103	139	.741	251	68	146	4	431	7.3
Brady Walker****	66	164	416	.394	72	103	.699	354	111	82	2	400	6.1
Paul Hoffman	41	127	399	.318	105	156	.673	202	111	135	2	359	8.8
Gene James*****	48	79	235	.336	44	71	.620	141	70	118	2	202	4.2
William Hassett	30	45	156	.288	40	60	.667	34	46	68	1	130	4.3
Norm Mager	22	32	126	.254	37	48	.771	44	22	56	3	101	4.6
Joe Dolhon	11	15	50	.300	9	13	.692	15	15	28	0	39	3.5
Ray Ellefson	3	0	4	.000	4	4	1.000	8	0	6	0	4	1.3

*Smawley—Played with Syracuse, Baltimore.
**Halbert—Played with Washington, Baltimore.
***Sailors—Played with Boston, Baltimore.
****Walker—Played with Boston, Baltimore.
*****James—Played with New York, Baltimore.

BOSTON CELTICS

	G	FGM	FGA	Pct.	FTM	FTA	Pct.	Reb.	Ast.	PF	Dq.	Pts.	Avg.
Ed Macauley	68	459	985	.466	466	614	.759	616	252	205	4	1384	20.4
Bob Cousy	69	401	1138	.352	276	365	.756	474	341	185	2	1078	15.6
Sidney Hertzberg	65	206	651	.316	223	270	.826	260	244	156	4	635	9.8
Charles Cooper	66	207	601	.344	201	267	.753	562	174	219	7	615	9.3
Kleggie Hermsen*	71	189	644	.293	155	237	.654	448	92	261	8	533	7.5
Frank Kudelka**	62	179	518	.346	83	119	.697	158	105	211	8	441	7.1
Bob Donham	68	151	298	.507	114	229	.498	235	139	179	3	416	6.1
Ed Leede	57	119	370	.322	140	189	.741	118	95	144	3	378	6.6
Bob Harris***	56	98	295	.332	86	127	.677	291	64	157	4	282	5.0
Horace McKinney****	44	102	327	.312	58	81	.716	198	85	136	6	262	6.0
Ed Stanczak	17	11	48	.229	35	43	.814	34	6	6	0	57	3.4
Andy Duncan	14	7	40	.175	15	22	.682	30	8	27	0	29	2.1

*Hermsen—Played with Tri-Cities, Boston.
**Kudelka—Played with Washington, Boston.
***Harris—Played with Fort Wayne, Boston.
****McKinney—Played with Washington, Boston.

FORT WAYNE PISTONS

	G	FGM	FGA	Pct.	FTM	FTA	Pct.	Reb.	Ast.	PF	Dq.	Pts.	Avg.
Fred Schaus	68	312	918	.340	404	484	.835	495	184	240	11	1028	15.1
Larry Foust	68	327	944	.346	261	296	.882	681	90	247	6	915	13.5
Ken Murray*	66	301	887	.339	248	332	.747	355	202	164	7	850	12.9
Jack Kerris	68	255	689	.370	201	295	.681	477	181	253	12	711	10.5
Boag Johnson	68	235	737	.319	114	162	.704	275	183	247	11	584	8.6
Don Otten**	67	162	479	.338	246	308	.799	404	62	255	15	570	8.5
Johnny Oldham	68	199	597	.333	171	292	.586	242	127	242	15	569	8.4
Dick Mehen***	66	192	532	.361	90	123	.732	223	188	149	4	474	7.2
Duane Klueh	61	157	458	.343	135	184	.734	183	82	143	5	449	7.4
Paul Armstrong	38	72	232	.310	58	90	.644	89	77	97	2	202	5.3
Jim Riffey	35	65	185	.351	20	26	.769	61	16	54	0	150	4.3
Art Burris	33	28	113	.248	21	36	.583	106	27	51	0	77	2.3

*Murray—Played with Baltimore, Fort Wayne.
**Otten—Played with Washington, Baltimore, Fort Wayne.
***Mehen—Played with Baltimore, Boston, Fort Wayne.

INDIANAPOLIS OLYMPIANS

	G	FGM	FGA	Pct.	FTM	FTA	Pct.	Reb.	Ast.	PF	Dq.	Pts.	Avg.
Alex Groza	66	492	1046	.470	445	566	.786	709	156	237	8	1429	21.7
Ralph Beard	66	409	1110	.368	293	378	.775	251	318	96	0	1111	16.8
Paul Walther	63	213	634	.336	145	209	.694	226	225	201	8	571	9.1
Leo Barnhorst	68	232	671	.346	82	119	.689	296	218	197	1	546	8.0
Bob Lavoy	63	221	619	.357	84	133	.632	310	76	190	2	526	8.3
Joe Holland	67	196	594	.330	78	137	.569	344	150	228	8	470	7.0
John Mahnken*	58	111	351	.316	45	70	.643	219	77	164	6	267	4.6
Wallace Jones	22	93	237	.392	61	77	.792	125	85	74	4	247	11.2
Don Lofgran**	61	79	270	.293	79	127	.622	157	36	132	4	237	3.9
Mal McMullan	51	78	277	.282	48	82	.585	128	33	109	2	204	4.0
Cliff Barker	56	51	202	.252	50	77	.649	100	115	98	0	152	2.7
Bruce Hale	26	40	135	.296	14	23	.609	49	42	30	0	94	3.6
Charles Mrazcvich	23	24	73	.329	28	46	.609	33	12	48	1	76	3.3
Carl Shaeffer	10	6	22	.273	3	3	1.000	10	6	15	0	15	1.5
Leon Blevins	3	1	4	.250	0	1	.000	2	1	3	0	2	0.7

*Mahnken—Played with Boston, Indianapolis.
**Lofgran—Played with Syracuse, Indianapolis.

MINNEAPOLIS LAKERS

	G	FGM	FGA	Pct.	FTM	FTA	Pct.	Reb.	Ast.	PF	Dq.	Pts.	Avg.
George Mikan	68	678	1584	.428	576	717	.803	958	208	308	14	1932	28.4
Vern Mikkelsen	64	359	893	.402	186	275	.676	655	181	260	13	904	14.1
Jim Pollard	54	256	728	.352	117	156	.750	484	184	157	4	629	11.6
Slater Martin	68	227	627	.362	121	177	.684	246	235	199	3	575	8.5
Bob Harrison	68	150	432	.347	101	128	.789	172	195	218	5	401	5.9
Arnie Ferrin	68	119	373	.319	114	164	.695	271	107	220	8	352	5.2
Kevin O'Shea	63	87	267	.326	97	134	.724	125	100	99	1	271	4.3
Tony Jaros	63	88	287	.307	65	103	.631	131	72	131	0	241	3.8
Bud Grant	61	53	184	.288	52	83	.627	115	71	106	0	158	2.6
Joe Hutton	60	59	180	.328	29	43	.674	102	53	89	1	147	2.5

NEW YORK KNICKERBOCKERS

	G	FGM	FGA	Pct.	FTM	FTA	Pct.	Reb.	Ast.	PF	Dq.	Pts.	Avg.
Vince Boryla	66	352	867	.406	278	332	.837	249	182	244	6	982	14.9
Harry Gallatin	66	293	705	.416	259	354	.732	800	180	244	4	845	12.8

1950-51

	G	FGM	FGA	Pct.	FTM	FTA	Pct.	Reb.	Ast.	PF	Dq.	Pts.	Avg.
Max Zaslofsky	66	302	853	.354	231	298	.775	228	136	150	3	835	12.7
Connie Simmons	66	229	613	.374	146	208	.702	426	117	222	8	604	9.2
Nat Clifton	65	211	656	.322	140	263	.532	491	162	269	13	562	8.6
Dick McGuire	64	179	482	.371	179	276	.649	334	400	154	2	537	8.4
Ray Lumpp	64	153	379	.404	124	160	.775	125	115	160	2	430	6.7
Ernie Vandeweghe	44	135	336	.402	68	97	.701	195	121	144	6	338	7.7
George Kaftan	61	111	286	.388	78	125	.624	153	74	102	1	300	4.9
Goebel Ritter	34	100	297	.337	49	71	.690	65	37	52	1	249	7.3
Tony Lavelli	30	32	93	.344	35	41	.854	59	23	56	1	99	3.3

PHILADELPHIA WARRIORS

	G	FGM	FGA	Pct.	FTM	FTA	Pct.	Reb.	Ast.	PF	Dq.	Pts.	Avg.
Joe Fulks	66	429	1358	.316	378	442	.855	523	117	247	8	1236	18.7
Paul Arizin	65	352	864	.407	417	526	.793	640	138	284	18	1121	17.2
Andy Phillip	66	275	690	.399	190	253	.751	446	414	221	8	740	11.2
George Senesky	65	249	703	.354	181	238	.761	326	342	144	1	679	10.4
Bill Closs	65	202	631	.320	166	223	.744	401	110	156	4	570	8.8
Ed Mikan*	61	193	556	.347	137	189	.725	344	63	194	6	523	8.6
Vern Gardner	61	129	383	.337	69	97	.711	237	89	149	6	327	5.4
Ron Livingstone	63	104	353	.295	76	109	.697	297	76	220	10	284	4.5
Nelson Bobb	53	52	158	.329	44	79	.557	101	82	83	1	148	2.8
Leo Mogus	57	43	122	.352	53	86	.616	102	32	60	0	139	2.4
Ike Borsavage	24	26	74	.351	12	18	.667	24	4	34	1	64	2.7
Easy Parham	7	3	7	.429	4	9	.444	12	3	5	0	10	1.4

*Mikan—Played with Rochester, Washington, Philadelphia.

ROCHESTER ROYALS

	G	FGM	FGA	Pct.	FTM	FTA	Pct.	Reb.	Ast.	PF	Dq.	Pts.	Avg.
Arnie Risen	66	377	940	.401	323	440	.734	795	158	278	9	1077	16.3
Bob Davies	63	326	877	.372	303	381	.795	197	287	208	7	955	15.2
Jack Coleman	67	315	749	.421	134	172	.779	584	197	193	4	764	11.4
Bobby Wanzer	68	252	628	.401	232	273	.850	232	181	129	0	736	10.8
Arnie Johnson	68	185	403	.459	269	371	.725	449	175	290	11	639	9.4
Bill Calhoun	66	175	506	.346	161	228	.706	199	99	87	1	511	7.7
Red Holzman	68	183	561	.326	130	179	.726	152	147	94	0	496	7.3
Frank Saul	65	105	310	.339	72	105	.686	84	68	85	0	282	4.3
Paul Noel	52	49	174	.282	32	45	.711	81	34	61	1	130	2.5
Joe McNamee	60	48	107	.287	27	42	.643	101	18	88	2	123	2.1

SYRACUSE NATIONALS

	G	FGM	FGA	Pct.	FTM	FTA	Pct.	Reb.	Ast.	PF	Dq.	Pts.	Avg.
Dolph Schayes	66	332	930	.357	457	608	.752	1080	251	271	9	1121	17.0
Freddie Scolari*	66	302	923	.327	279	331	.843	218	255	183	1	883	13.4
George Ratkovicz	66	264	636	.415	321	439	.731	547	193	256	11	849	12.9
Billy Gabor	61	255	745	.342	179	242	.740	150	125	213	7	689	11.3
Noble Jorgensen**	63	223	600	.372	182	265	.687	338	91	237	8	628	10.0
Alex Hannum	63	182	494	.368	107	197	.543	301	119	271	16	471	7.5
Al Cervi	53	132	346	.382	194	237	.819	152	208	180	9	458	8.6
Johnny Macknowski	58	131	435	.301	122	170	.718	110	69	134	3	384	6.6
Paul Seymour	51	125	385	.325	117	159	.736	194	187	138	1	367	7.2
Gerry Calabrese	46	70	197	.355	61	88	.693	65	65	80	0	201	4.4
Leroy Chollet	14	6	51	.118	12	19	.632	15	12	29	0	24	1.7

*Scolari—Played with Washington, Syracuse.
**Jorgensen—Played with Tri-Cities, Syracuse.

TRI-CITIES BLACKHAWKS

	G	FGM	FGA	Pct.	FTM	FTA	Pct.	Reb.	Ast.	PF	Dq.	Pts.	Avg.
Frank Brian	68	363	1127	.322	418	508	.823	244	266	215	4	1144	16.8
Thomas Eddleman	68	398	1120	.355	244	349	.699	410	170	231	5	1040	15.3
Marko Todorovich	66	221	715	.309	211	301	.701	455	179	197	5	653	9.9
Cal Christensen	67	134	445	.301	175	245	.714	523	161	266	19	443	6.6
Warren Perkins	66	135	428	.315	126	195	.646	319	143	232	13	396	6.0
Edward Peterson*	53	130	384	.339	99	150	.660	288	66	188	9	359	6.8
Harry Boykoff**	48	126	336	.375	74	100	.740	220	60	197	12	326	6.8
Robert Carpenter***	56	109	355	.307	105	128	.820	229	79	115	2	323	5.8
Johnny Logan	29	81	257	.315	62	83	.747	134	127	66	2	224	7.7
Thomas Byrnes****	48	83	275	.302	55	84	.655	72	69	86	0	221	4.6
Gene Vance	28	44	110	.400	43	61	.705	88	53	91	0	131	4.7
Ray Corley	18	29	85	.341	16	29	.552	43	38	26	0	74	4.1
Herb Scherer	20	24	84	.286	20	35	.571	50	17	56	1	68	3.4
John Hargis*****	14	25	66	.379	17	24	.708	30	9	26	0	67	4.8
Ed Gayda	14	18	42	.429	18	23	.783	38	13	32	0	54	3.9
Jack Nichols	5	18	48	.375	10	13	.769	52	14	18	0	46	9.2

1950-51

	G	FGM	FGA	Pct.	FTM	FTA	Pct.	Reb.	Ast.	PF	Dq.	SCORING Pts.	Avg.
Ed Beach****** 12	8	38	.211	6	9	.667	25	3	14	0	22	1.8
Hank DeZonie................5	6	25	.240	5	7	.714	18	9	6	0	17	3.4

*Peterson—Played with Syracuse, Tri-Cities.
**Boykoff—Played with Boston, Tri-Cities.
***Carpenter—Played with Fort Wayne, Tri-Cities.
****Byrnes—Played with Baltimore, Washington, Tri-Cities.
*****Hargis—Played with Fort Wayne, Tri-Cities.
******Beach—Played with Minneapolis, Tri-Cities.

WASHINGTON CAPITOLS

	G	FGM	FGA	Pct.	FTM	FTA	Pct.	Reb.	Ast.	PF	Dq.	SCORING Pts.	Avg.
Bill Sharman 31	141	361	.391	96	108	.889	96	39	86	3	378	12.2
Dick Schnittker 29	85	219	.388	123	139	.885	153	42	76	0	293	10.1
Ariel Maughan................35	78	250	.312	101	120	.842	141	48	91	2	257	7.3
Alan Sawyer 33	87	215	.405	43	54	.796	125	25	75	1	217	6.6
Ed Bartels 17	24	97	.247	24	46	.522	84	12	54	0	72	4.2
Dick O'Keefe 17	21	102	.206	25	39	.641	37	25	48	0	67	3.9
Chuck Gilmur 16	17	61	.279	17	32	.531	75	17	57	3	51	3.2
Earl Lloyd...................7	16	35	.457	11	13	.846	47	11	26	0	43	6.1
Don Carlson.................9	17	46	.370	8	16	.500	15	19	23	0	42	4.7
Thomas O'Keefe 6	10	28	.357	3	4	.750	7	10	5	0	23	3.8
Johnny Norlander.............9	6	19	.316	9	14	.643	9	5	14	0	21	2.3

(Washington team disbanded January 9; players assigned to other clubs.)

PLAYOFF RESULTS

EASTERN DIVISION

SEMIFINALS

New York 2, Boston 0
Mar. 20—Tue. New York 83 at Boston 69
Mar. 22—Thur. Boston 78 at New York 92

Syracuse 2, Philadelphia 0
Mar. 20—Tue. Syracuse 91 at Philadelphia *89
Mar. 22—Thur. Philadelphia 78 at Syracuse 90

FINALS

New York 3, Syracuse 2
Mar. 28—Wed. Syracuse 92 at New York 103
Mar. 29—Thur. New York 80 at Syracuse 102
Mar. 31—Sat. Syracuse 75 at New York 97
Apr. 1—Sun. New York 83 at Syracuse 90
Apr. 4—Wed. Syracuse 81 at New York 83

WESTERN DIVISION

SEMIFINALS

Rochester 2, Fort Wayne 1
Mar. 20—Tue. Fort Wayne 81 at Rochester 110
Mar. 22—Thur. Rochester 78 at Fort Wayne 83
Mar. 24—Sat. Fort Wayne 78 at Rochester 97

Minneapolis 2, Indianapolis 1
Mar. 21—Wed. Indianapolis 81 at Minneapolis 95
Mar. 23—Fri. Minneapolis 88 at Indianapolis 108
Mar. 25—Sun. Indianapolis 80 at Minneapolis 85

FINALS

Rochester 3, Minneapolis 1
Mar. 29—Thur. Rochester 73 at Minneapolis 76
Mar. 31—Sat. Rochester 70 at Minneapolis 66
Apr. 1—Sun. Minneapolis 70 at Rochester 83
Apr. 3—Tue. Minneapolis 75 at Rochester 80

NBA FINALS

Rochester 4, New York 3
Apr. 7—Sat. New York 65 at Rochester 92
Apr. 8—Sun. New York 84 at Rochester 99
Apr. 11—Wed. Rochester 78 at New York 71
Apr. 13—Fri. Rochester 73 at New York 79
Apr. 15—Sun. New York 92 at Rochester 89
Apr. 18—Wed. Rochester 73 at New York 80
Apr. 21—Sat. New York 75 at Rochester 79

*Denotes number of overtime periods.

1949-50

1949-50 NBA CHAMPION MINNEAPOLIS LAKERS
From left: Slater Martin, Billy Hassett, Don Carlson, Herm Schaefer, Bob Harrison, Tony Jaros, head coach John Kundla, Bud Grant, Arnie Ferrin, Jim Pollard, Vern Mikkelsen, George Mikan.

FINAL STANDINGS

CENTRAL DIVISION

	Syr.	N.Y.	Was.	Phi.	Balt.	Bos.	Minn.	Roch.	Ft.W.	Chi.	St.L.	Ind.	And.	Tri-C	Sheb.	Wat.	Den.	W	L	Pct.	GB
Rochester	1	5	6	5	3	6	3	..	3	4	5	1	2	2	1	2	2	51	17	.750	..
Minneapolis . . .	1	5	6	4	5	5	..	3	4	4	5	1	1	2	1	2	2	51	17	.750	..
Chicago	0	2	3	4	5	6	2	2	2	..	5	1	1	1	2	2	2	40	28	.588	11
Fort Wayne . . .	0	4	2	4	3	4	2	3	..	4	5	1	1	2	2	1	2	40	28	.588	11
St. Louis	1	2	0	4	3	4	1	1	1	1	..	1	0	2	2	1	2	26	42	.382	25

EASTERN DIVISION

	Syr.	N.Y.	Was.	Phi.	Balt.	Bos.	Minn.	Roch.	Ft.W.	Chi.	St.L.	Ind.	And.	Tri-C	Sheb.	Wat.	Den.	W	L	Pct.	GB
Syracuse		2	1	2	2	2	1	1	2	2	1	7	4	6	6	6	6	51	13	.797	..
New York	0	..	5	5	5	5	1	1	2	4	4	1	1	1	1	2	2	40	28	.588	13
Washington . . .	0	1	..	4	3	3	2	1	2	2	2	0	1	1	2	2	2	32	36	.471	21
Philadelphia . . .	1	1	2	..	4	3	0	0	4	3	6	1	1	1	0	1	2	26	42	.382	27
Baltimore	0	1	2	3	..	2	1	3	3	1	3	1	1	0	2	1	1	25	43	.368	28
Boston	0	1	3	3	4	..	1	0	2	0	2	1	2	0	1	1	1	22	46	.324	31

WESTERN DIVISION

	Syr.	N.Y.	Was.	Phi.	Balt.	Bos.	Minn.	Roch.	Ft.W.	Chi.	St.L.	Ind.	And.	Tri-C	Sheb.	Wat.	Den.	W	L	Pct.	GB
Indianapolis . . .	2	1	1	2	1	1	1	1	1	1	1	..	5	4	5	5	7	39	25	.609	..
Anderson	3	1	1	1	1	0	1	0	1	1	2	2	..	7	5	7	4	37	27	.578	2
Tri-Cities	1	1	1	1	2	2	0	0	0	1	0	3	2	..	4	4	7	29	35	.453	10
Sheboygan . . .	1	1	2	0	0	1	1	1	0	0	0	2	2	3	..	4	4	22	40	.355	16
Waterloo	1	0	1	0	1	1	0	0	1	0	1	2	0	3	3	..	5	19	43	.306	19
Denver	1	0	0	0	1	1	0	0	0	0	0	0	3	0	3	2	..	11	51	.177	27

TEAM STATISTICS

	G	FGM	FGA	Pct.	FTM	FTA	Pct.	Ast.	PF	AVERAGE POINTS		
										For	Agst.	Dif.
Minneapolis	68	2139	5832	.367	1439	1943	.741	1406	1672	84.1	75.7	+8.4
Syracuse	64	1869	5276	.354	1691	2396	.706	1473	1833	84.8	76.7	+8.1
Rochester.	68	1956	5247	.373	1690	2319	.729	1383	1585	82.4	74.6	+7.8
Anderson	64	1943	6254	.311	1703	2343	.727	1240	1806	87.3	83.6	+3.7
Indianapolis	64	1982	5283	.375	1529	2145	.713	1342	1676	85.8	82.1	+3.7
New York	68	1889	5351	.353	1710	2404	.711	1308	1718	80.7	78.6	+2.1
Chicago	68	2003	5892	.340	1346	1934	.696	1366	1977	78.7	77.1	+1.6
Fort Wayne.	68	1878	5901	.318	1634	2331	.701	1364	2065	79.3	77.9	+1.4
Tri-Cities.	64	1818	5515	.330	1677	2308	.727	1330	2057	83.0	83.6	-0.6

	G	FGM	FGA	Pct.	FTM	FTA	Pct.	Ast.	PF	For	Agst.	Dif.
										average points		
Washington	68	1813	5493	.330	1575	2111	.746	1057	1837	76.5	77.4	-0.9
Boston	68	1945	5756	.338	1530	2163	.707	1473	1644	79.7	82.2	-2.5
St. Louis	68	1741	5086	.342	1528	2149	.711	1285	1596	73.7	76.5	-2.8
Philadelphia	68	1779	5711	.312	1425	2037	.700	1142	1768	73.3	76.4	-3.1
Sheboygan	62	1727	5022	.344	1654	2338	.707	1279	1766	82.4	87.8	-5.4
Waterloo	62	1746	4904	.356	1429	2002	.714	1324	1780	79.4	84.9	-5.5
Baltimore	68	1712	5516	.310	1549	2123	.730	1189	1792	73.1	78.7	-5.6
Denver	62	1731	5182	.334	1355	1999	.678	1044	1692	77.7	89.1	-11.4
Avgs.	66.0	1863	5484	.340	1557	2179	.715	1294	1780	80.0	...	...

HOME/ROAD/NEUTRAL

	Home	Road	Neutral	Total		Home	Road	Neutral	Total
Anderson	23-9	11-18	3-0	37-27	Philadelphia	15-15	8-23	3-4	26-42
Baltimore	16-15	8-25	1-3	25-43	Rochester	33-1	17-16	1-0	51-17
Boston	12-14	5-28	5-4	22-46	Sheboygan	17-14	5-22	0-4	22-40
Chicago	18-6	14-21	8-1	40-28	St. Louis	17-14	7-26	2-2	26-42
Denver	9-15	1-26	1-10	11-51	Syracuse	31-1	15-12	5-0	51-13
Fort Wayne	28-6	12-22	0-0	40-28	Tri-Cities	22-13	4-20	3-2	29-35
Indianapolis	23-5	13-18	3-2	39-25	Washington	21-13	10-20	1-3	32-36
Minneapolis	30-1	18-16	3-0	51-17	Waterloo	17-15	1-22	1-6	19-43
New York	19-10	18-16	3-2	40-28	Totals	351-167	167-351	43-43	561-561

INDIVIDUAL LEADERS

POINTS

	G	FGM	FTM	Pts.	Avg.
George Mikan, Minneapolis	68	649	567	1865	27.4
Alex Groza, Indianapolis	64	521	454	1496	23.4
Frank Brian, Anderson	64	368	402	1138	17.8
Max Zaslofsky, Chicago	68	397	321	1115	16.4
Ed Macauley, St. Louis	67	351	379	1081	16.1
Dolph Schayes, Syracuse	64	348	376	1072	16.8
Carl Braun, New York	67	373	285	1031	15.4
Ken Sailors, Denver	57	329	329	987	17.3
Jim Pollard, Minneapolis	66	394	185	973	14.7
Fred Schaus, Fort Wayne	68	351	270	972	14.3
Joe Fulks, Philadelphia	68	336	293	965	14.2
Ralph Beard, Indianapolis	60	340	215	895	14.9
Bob Davies, Rochester	64	317	261	895	14.0
Dick Mehen, Waterloo	62	347	198	892	14.4
Jack Nichols, Wash.-Tri-Cities	67	310	259	879	13.1
Ed Sadowski, Phil.-Baltimore	69	299	274	872	12.6
Paul Hoffman, Baltimore	60	312	242	866	14.4
Fred Scolari, Washington	66	312	236	860	13.0
Vern Gardner, Philadelphia	63	313	227	853	13.5
Belus Smawley, St. Louis	61	287	260	834	13.7

FIELD GOALS
(minimum 200 made)

	FGM	FGA	Pct.
Alex Groza, Indianapolis	.521	1090	.478
Dick Mehen, Waterloo	.347	826	.420
Bob Wanzer, Rochester	.254	614	.414
Harry Boykoff, Waterloo	.288	698	.413
George Mikan, Minneapolis	.649	1595	.407
Red Rocha, St. Louis	.275	679	.405

	FGM	FGA	Pct.
John Hargis, Anderson	.223	550	.405
Vern Mikkelsen, Minneapolis	.288	722	.399
Ed Macauley, St. Louis	.351	882	.398
Jack Toomay, Denver	.204	514	.397

FREE THROWS
(minimum 170 made)

	FTM	FTA	Pct.
Max Zaslofsky, Chicago	.321	381	.843
Chick Reiser, Washington	.212	254	.835
Al Cervi, Syracuse	.287	346	.829
Belus Smawley, St. Louis	.260	314	.828
Francis Curran, Rochester	.199	241	.826
Frank Brian, Anderson	.402	488	.824
Fred Scolari, Washington	.236	287	.822
Fred Schaus, Fort Wayne	.270	330	.818
Leo Kubiak, Waterloo	.192	236	.814
Bob Wanzer, Rochester	.283	351	.806

ASSISTS

	G	No.	Avg.
Dick McGuire, New York	68	386	5.7
Andy Phillip, Chicago	65	377	5.8
Bob Davies, Rochester	64	294	4.6
Al Cervi, Syracuse	56	264	4.7
George Senesky, Philadelphia	68	264	3.9
Dolph Schayes, Syracuse	64	259	4.1
Jim Pollard, Minneapolis	66	252	3.8
Jim Seminoff, Boston	65	249	3.8
Carl Braun, New York	67	247	3.7
John Logan, St. Louis	62	240	3.9

INDIVIDUAL STATISTICS, TEAM BY TEAM

ANDERSON PACKERS

	G	FGM	FGA	Pct.	FTM	FTA	Pct.	Ast.	PF	Pts.	Avg.
										SCORING	
Frank Brian	64	368	1156	.318	402	488	.824	189	192	1138	17.8
Bill Closs	64	283	898	.315	186	259	.718	160	190	752	11.8
John Hargis	60	223	550	.405	197	277	.711	102	170	643	10.7
Milo Komenich	64	244	861	.283	146	250	.584	124	246	634	9.9
Ed Stanczak	57	159	456	.349	203	270	.752	67	166	521	9.1
Ralph Johnson*	35	133	426	.312	71	83	.855	104	112	337	9.6
Frank Gates	64	113	402	.281	61	98	.622	91	147	287	4.5
Howie Schultz*	35	83	316	.263	117	160	.731	88	125	283	8.1
Charlie Black†	29	101	378	.267	77	112	.688	88	133	279	9.6
Charlie Black‡	65	226	813	.278	209	321	.651	163	273	661	10.2
Rollie Seltz	34	93	309	.301	80	104	.769	64	72	266	7.8
Richie Niemiera†	29	51	143	.357	48	66	.727	55	35	150	5.2
Richie Niemiera‡	60	110	350	.314	104	139	.748	116	77	324	5.4
Walt Kirk*	26	31	125	.248	57	83	.687	43	63	119	4.6
Jim Owens†	35	44	151	.291	28	42	.667	41	87	116	3.3

	G	FGM	FGA	Pct.	FTM	FTA	Pct.	Ast.	PF	Pts.	Avg.
Jim Owens‡	61	86	288	.299	68	101	.673	73	152	240	3.9
Jake Carter†	11	10	30	.333	18	27	.667	8	32	38	3.5
Jake Carter‡	24	23	75	.307	36	53	.679	24	59	82	3.4
Jack Smiley*	12	6	50	.120	12	24	.500	14	35	24	2.0
Murray Mitchell	2	1	3	.333	0	0	...	2	1	2	1.0

BALTIMORE BULLETS

	G	FGM	FGA	Pct.	FTM	FTA	Pct.	Ast.	PF	Pts.	Avg.
Paul Hoffman	60	312	914	.341	242	364	.665	161	234	866	14.4
Ed Sadowski†	52	252	769	.328	222	298	.745	97	181	726	14.0
Ed Sadowski‡	69	299	922	.324	274	373	.735	136	244	872	12.6
Blackie Towery	68	222	678	.327	153	202	.757	142	244	597	8.8
Walt Budko	66	198	652	.304	199	263	.757	146	259	595	9.0
Joe Dolhon	64	143	458	.312	157	214	.734	155	193	443	6.9
Tommy Byrnes	53	120	397	.302	87	124	.702	88	76	327	6.2
Whitey Von Nieda	59	120	336	.357	73	115	.635	143	127	313	5.3
Johnny Ezersky*	38	107	351	.305	92	132	.697	64	100	306	8.1
Les Pugh	56	68	273	.249	115	136	.846	16	118	251	4.5
Buddy Jeannette	37	42	148	.284	109	133	.820	93	82	193	5.2
Marv Schatzman	34	43	174	.247	29	50	.580	38	49	115	3.4
Andy O'Donnell	25	38	108	.352	14	18	.778	17	32	90	3.6
Ron Livingstone*	16	25	102	.245	35	46	.761	24	54	85	5.3
Fred Lewis*	18	25	110	.227	13	19	.684	18	23	63	3.5
George Feigenbaum	12	14	57	.246	8	18	.444	10	15	36	3.0
Howie Janotta	9	9	30	.300	13	16	.813	4	10	31	3.4
Bob Tough*	8	11	39	.282	5	6	.833	2	15	27	3.4
Paul Cloyd*	3	1	8	.125	3	3	1.000	1	4	5	1.7
Mike McCarron*	3	1	5	.200	2	3	.667	1	5	4	1.3
John Mandic†	3	1	10	.100	2	2	1.000	1	7	4	1.3
John Mandic‡	25	22	75	.293	22	32	.688	8	54	66	2.6
Paul Gordon	4	0	6	.000	3	5	.600	3	3	3	0.8
Dick Triptow	4	0	5	.000	2	2	1.000	1	5	2	0.5
Leo Knorek	1	0	2	.000	0	0	...	0	4	0	0.0

BOSTON CELTICS

	G	FGM	FGA	Pct.	FTM	FTA	Pct.	Ast.	PF	Pts.	Avg.
Sonny Hertzberg	68	275	865	.318	143	191	.749	200	153	693	10.2
Bob Kinney	60	233	621	.375	201	320	.628	100	251	667	11.1
Howie Shannon	67	222	646	.344	143	182	.786	174	148	587	8.8
Ed Leede	64	174	507	.343	223	316	.706	130	167	571	8.9
George Kaftan	55	199	535	.372	136	208	.654	145	92	534	9.7
Brady Walker	68	218	583	.374	72	114	.632	109	100	508	7.5
Tony Lavelli	56	162	436	.372	168	197	.853	40	107	492	8.8
Bob Doll	47	120	347	.346	75	114	.658	108	117	315	6.7
Jim Seminoff	65	85	283	.300	142	188	.755	249	154	312	4.8
Gene Englund*	24	55	148	.372	86	106	.811	17	97	196	8.2
Dermie O'Connell*	37	72	275	.262	33	58	.569	64	62	177	4.8
John Mahnken†	24	44	168	.262	23	36	.639	42	74	111	4.6
John Mahnken‡	62	132	495	.267	77	115	.670	100	231	341	5.5
George Nostrand*	18	36	120	.333	36	59	.610	17	46	108	6.0
Johnny Ezersky†	16	36	136	.265	35	51	.686	22	39	107	6.7
Johnny Ezersky‡	54	143	487	.294	127	183	.694	86	139	413	7.6
Joe Mullaney	37	9	70	.129	12	15	.800	52	30	30	0.8
Ward Gibson*	2	3	4	.750	1	4	.250	1	3	7	3.5
Art Spector	7	2	12	.167	1	4	.250	3	4	5	0.7

CHICAGO STAGS

	G	FGM	FGA	Pct.	FTM	FTA	Pct.	Ast.	PF	Pts.	Avg.
Max Zaslofsky	68	397	1132	.351	321	381	.843	155	185	1115	16.4
Andy Phillip	65	284	814	.349	190	270	.704	377	210	758	11.7
Odie Spears*	68	277	775	.357	158	230	.687	159	250	712	10.5
Kleggie Hermsen	67	196	615	.319	153	247	.619	98	267	545	8.1
Stan Miasek	68	176	462	.381	146	221	.661	75	264	498	7.3
Leo Barnhorst	67	174	499	.349	90	129	.698	140	192	438	6.5
Frank Kudelka	65	172	528	.326	89	140	.636	132	198	433	6.7
Kenny Rollins	66	144	421	.342	66	89	.742	131	129	354	5.4
Joe Graboski	57	75	247	.304	53	89	.596	37	95	203	3.6
Ed Mikan*	21	31	127	.244	45	58	.776	14	48	107	5.1
George Nostrand†	36	37	125	.297	18	35	.514	11	71	92	2.6
George Nostrand‡	55	78	255	.306	56	99	.566	29	118	212	3.9
Joe Bradley	46	36	134	.269	15	38	.395	36	51	87	1.9
Bob Hahn	10	4	13	.308	2	7	.286	1	17	10	1.0

1949-50

DENVER NUGGETS

	G	FGM	FGA	Pct.	FTM	FTA	Pct.	Ast.	PF	Pts.	Avg.
Kenny Sailors	57	329	944	.349	329	456	.721	229	242	987	17.3
Bob Brown	62	276	764	.361	172	252	.683	101	269	724	11.7
Dillard Crocker	53	245	740	.331	233	317	.735	85	223	723	13.6
Jack Toomay	62	204	514	.397	186	264	.705	94	213	594	9.6
Floyd Volker†	37	146	474	.308	64	111	.577	105	137	356	9.6
Floyd Volker‡	54	163	527	.309	71	129	.550	112	169	397	7.4
Duane Klueh*	33	110	302	.364	111	153	.725	63	73	331	10.0
Jack Cotton	54	97	332	.292	82	161	.509	65	184	276	5.1
Jimmy Darden	26	78	243	.321	55	80	.688	67	67	211	8.1
Robert Royer	42	78	231	.338	41	58	.707	85	72	197	4.7
Al Guokas*	41	86	271	.317	25	47	.532	85	116	197	4.8
Ed Bartels*	13	21	82	.256	17	31	.548	20	27	59	4.5
Bill Herman	13	25	65	.385	6	11	.545	15	13	56	4.3
Jim Browne	31	17	48	.354	13	27	.481	8	16	47	1.5
Jake Carter*	13	13	45	.289	18	26	.692	16	27	44	3.4
Earl Dodd	9	6	27	.222	3	5	.600	6	13	15	1.7

FORT WAYNE PISTONS

	G	FGM	FGA	Pct.	FTM	FTA	Pct.	Ast.	PF	Pts.	Avg.
Fred Schaus	68	351	996	.352	270	330	.818	176	232	972	14.3
Robert Carpenter	66	212	617	.344	190	256	.742	92	168	614	9.3
Bob Harris	62	168	465	.361	140	223	.628	129	190	476	7.7
Curly Armstrong	63	144	516	.279	170	241	.705	170	217	458	7.3
Jack Kerris†	64	149	455	.327	159	248	.641	110	162	457	7.1
Jack Kerris‡	68	157	481	.326	169	260	.650	119	175	483	7.1
Leo Klier	66	157	516	.304	141	190	.742	121	177	455	6.9
Charlie Black*	36	125	435	.287	132	209	.632	75	140	382	10.6
Johnny Oldham	59	127	426	.298	103	145	.710	99	192	357	6.1
Howie Schultz†	32	96	355	.270	79	122	.648	81	119	271	8.5
Howie Schultz‡	67	179	771	.232	196	282	.695	169	244	554	8.3
Ralph Johnson†	32	110	353	.312	33	46	.717	67	95	253	7.9
Ralph Johnson‡	67	243	779	.312	104	129	.806	171	207	590	8.8
Bill Henry*	44	65	209	.311	84	125	.672	39	99	214	4.9
Richie Niemiera*	31	59	207	.285	56	73	.767	61	42	174	5.6
Duane Klueh†	19	49	112	.438	46	69	.667	28	38	144	7.6
Duane Klueh‡	52	159	414	.384	157	222	.707	91	111	475	9.1
Clint Wager	63	57	203	.281	29	47	.617	90	175	143	2.3
Jerry Nagel	14	6	28	.214	1	4	.250	18	11	13	0.9
John Mahnken*	2	3	8	.375	1	3	.333	2	8	7	3.5

INDIANAPOLIS OLYMPIANS

	G	FGM	FGA	Pct.	FTM	FTA	Pct.	Ast.	PF	Pts.	Avg.
Alex Groza	64	521	1090	.478	454	623	.729	162	221	1496	23.4
Ralph Beard	60	340	936	.363	215	282	.762	233	132	895	14.9
Wallace Jones	60	264	706	.374	223	297	.751	194	241	751	12.5
Bruce Hale	64	217	614	.353	223	285	.782	226	143	657	10.3
Joe Holland	64	145	453	.320	98	142	.690	130	220	388	6.1
Mal McMullan	58	123	380	.324	77	141	.546	87	212	323	5.6
Cliff Barker	49	102	274	.372	75	106	.708	109	99	279	5.7
Lefty Walther†	31	82	210	.390	52	88	.591	46	84	216	7.0
Lefty Walther‡	53	114	290	.393	63	109	.578	56	123	291	5.5
Marshall Hawkins	39	55	195	.282	42	61	.689	51	87	152	3.9
Carl Shaeffer	43	59	160	.369	32	57	.561	40	103	150	3.5
Bob Evans	47	56	200	.280	30	44	.682	55	99	142	3.0
Floyd Volker*	17	17	53	.321	7	18	.389	7	32	41	2.4
Jack Parkinson	4	1	12	.083	1	1	1.000	2	3	3	0.8

MINNEAPOLIS LAKERS

	G	FGM	FGA	Pct.	FTM	FTA	Pct.	Ast.	PF	Pts.	Avg.
George Mikan	68	649	1595	.407	567	728	.779	197	297	1865	27.4
Jim Pollard	66	394	1140	.346	185	242	.764	252	143	973	14.7
Vern Mikkelsen	68	288	722	.399	215	286	.752	123	222	791	11.6
Arnie Ferrin	63	132	396	.333	76	109	.697	95	147	340	5.4
Herm Schaefer	65	122	314	.389	86	101	.851	203	104	330	5.1
Bob Harrison	66	125	348	.359	50	74	.676	131	175	300	4.5
Slater Martin	67	106	302	.351	59	93	.634	148	162	271	4.0
Don Carlson	57	99	290	.341	69	95	.726	76	126	267	4.7
Tony Jaros	61	84	289	.291	72	96	.750	60	106	240	3.9
Billy Hassett†	42	38	145	.262	35	67	.522	69	82	111	2.6
Billy Hassett‡	60	84	302	.278	104	161	.646	137	136	272	4.5
Bud Grant	35	42	115	.365	7	17	.412	19	36	91	2.6
Lefty Walther*	22	32	80	.400	11	21	.524	10	39	75	3.4
Gene Stump*	23	27	95	.284	7	14	.500	23	32	61	2.7
Normie Glick	1	1	1	1.000	0	0	...	1	2	2	2.0

NEW YORK KNICKERBOCKERS

	G	FGM	FGA	Pct.	FTM	FTA	Pct.	Ast.	PF	SCORING Pts.	Avg.
Carl Braun	67	373	1024	.364	285	374	.762	247	188	1031	15.4
Harry Gallatin	68	263	664	.396	277	366	.757	56	215	803	11.8
Connie Simmons	60	241	729	.331	198	299	.662	102	203	680	11.3
Vince Boryla	59	204	600	.340	204	267	.764	95	203	612	10.4
Dick McGuire	68	190	563	.337	204	313	.652	386	160	584	8.6
Ernie Vandeweghe	42	164	390	.421	93	140	.664	78	126	421	10.0
Goebel Ritter	62	100	297	.337	125	176	.710	51	101	325	5.2
Ray Lumpp	58	91	283	.322	86	108	.796	90	117	268	4.6
Harry Donovan	45	90	275	.327	73	106	.689	38	107	253	5.6
Paul Noel	65	98	291	.337	53	87	.609	67	132	249	3.8
Butch van Breda Kolff	56	55	167	.329	96	134	.716	78	111	206	3.7
Gene James	29	19	64	.297	14	31	.452	20	53	52	1.8
Ed Bartels†	2	1	4	.250	2	3	.667	0	2	4	2.0
Ed Bartels‡	15	22	86	.256	19	33	.576	20	29	63	4.2

PHILADELPHIA WARRIORS

	G	FGM	FGA	Pct.	FTM	FTA	Pct.	Ast.	PF	SCORING Pts.	Avg.
Joe Fulks	68	336	1209	.278	293	421	.696	56	240	965	14.2
Vern Gardner	63	313	916	.342	227	296	.767	119	236	853	13.5
George Senesky	68	227	709	.320	157	223	.704	264	164	611	9.0
Leo Mogus	64	172	434	.396	218	300	.727	99	169	562	8.8
Francis Crossin	64	185	574	.322	79	101	.782	148	139	449	7.0
Ron Livingstone†	38	138	477	.289	87	131	.664	117	206	363	9.6
Ron Livingstone‡	54	163	579	.282	122	177	.689	141	260	448	8.3
Jerry Fleishman	65	102	353	.289	93	151	.616	118	129	297	4.6
Jake Bornheimer	60	88	305	.289	78	117	.667	40	111	254	4.2
Nelson Bobb	57	80	248	.323	82	131	.626	46	97	242	4.2
Ed Sadowski*	17	47	153	.307	52	75	.693	39	63	146	8.6
Mike Novak†	55	36	138	.261	24	46	.522	57	129	96	1.7
Mike Novak‡	60	37	149	.248	25	47	.532	61	139	99	1.7
Fred Lewis†	16	21	74	.284	12	13	.923	7	17	54	3.4
Fred Lewis‡	34	46	184	.250	25	32	.781	25	40	117	3.4
Johnny Payak*	17	12	32	.375	13	21	.619	8	18	37	2.2
Charlie Parsley	9	8	31	.258	6	7	.857	8	7	22	2.4
Al Guokas†	16	7	28	.250	3	3	1.000	10	27	17	1.1
Al Guokas‡	57	93	299	.311	28	50	.560	95	143	214	3.8
Jim Nolan	5	4	21	.190	0	0	. . .	4	14	8	1.6
Jerry Rullo	4	3	9	.333	1	1	1.000	2	2	7	1.8

ROCHESTER ROYALS

	G	FGM	FGA	Pct.	FTM	FTA	Pct.	Ast.	PF	SCORING Pts.	Avg.
Bob Davies	64	317	887	.357	261	347	.752	294	187	895	14.0
Bobby Wanzer	67	254	614	.414	283	351	.806	214	102	791	11.8
Arnie Risen	62	206	598	.344	213	321	.664	92	228	625	10.1
Jack Coleman	68	250	663	.377	90	121	.744	153	223	590	8.7
Bill Calhoun	62	207	549	.377	146	203	.719	115	100	560	9.0
Red Holzman	68	206	625	.330	144	210	.686	200	67	556	8.2
Arnie Johnson	68	149	376	.396	200	294	.680	141	260	498	7.3
Fran Curran	66	98	235	.417	199	241	.826	71	113	395	6.0
Andy Duncan	67	125	289	.433	60	108	.556	42	160	310	4.6
Pep Saul	49	74	183	.404	34	47	.723	28	33	182	3.7
Ed Mikan†	44	58	194	.299	47	62	.758	28	95	163	3.7
Ed Mikan‡	65	89	321	.277	92	120	.767	42	143	270	4.2
Price Brookfield	7	11	23	.478	12	13	.923	1	7	34	4.9
Mike Novak*	5	1	11	.091	1	1	1.000	4	10	3	0.6

ST. LOUIS BOMBERS

	G	FGM	FGA	Pct.	FTM	FTA	Pct.	Ast.	PF	SCORING Pts.	Avg.
Ed Macauley	67	351	882	.398	379	528	.718	200	221	1081	16.1
Belus Smawley	61	287	832	.345	260	314	.828	215	160	834	13.7
Red Rocha	65	275	679	.405	220	313	.703	155	257	770	11.8
Johnny Logan	62	251	759	.331	253	323	.783	240	206	755	12.2
Ariel Maughan	68	160	574	.279	157	205	.766	101	174	477	7.0
Easy Parham	66	137	421	.325	88	178	.494	132	158	362	5.5
Bill Roberts	67	77	222	.347	28	39	.718	24	90	182	2.7
Don Putnam	57	51	200	.255	33	52	.635	90	116	135	2.4
Mac Otten†	47	39	121	.322	25	59	.424	25	92	103	2.2
Mac Otten‡	59	51	155	.329	40	81	.494	36	119	142	2.4
Mike Todorovich*	14	31	116	.267	35	56	.625	19	47	97	6.9
Dermie O'Connell†	24	39	150	.260	14	31	.452	27	29	92	3.8
Dermie O'Connell‡	61	111	425	.261	47	89	.528	91	91	269	4.4
D.C. Willcutt	37	24	73	.329	29	42	.690	49	27	77	2.1
Johnny Orr*	21	17	47	.362	6	7	.857	6	19	40	1.9
Mike McCarron†	5	2	10	.200	1	2	.500	2	0	5	1.0
Mike McCarron‡	8	3	15	.200	3	5	.600	3	5	9	1.1

1949-50

SHEBOYGAN REDSKINS

	G	FGM	FGA	Pct.	FTM	FTA	Pct.	Ast.	PF	Pts.	Avg.
Max Morris	62	252	694	.363	277	415	.667	194	172	781	12.6
Bob Brannum	59	234	718	.326	245	355	.690	205	279	713	12.1
Noble Jorgensen	54	218	618	.353	268	350	.766	90	201	704	13.0
Jack Burmaster	61	237	711	.333	124	182	.681	179	237	598	9.8
Bobby Cook	51	222	620	.358	143	181	.790	158	114	587	11.5
Milt Schoon	62	150	366	.410	196	300	.653	84	190	496	8.0
George Sobek	60	95	251	.378	156	205	.761	95	158	346	5.8
Walt Lautenbach	55	100	332	.301	38	55	.691	73	122	238	4.3
Jack Phelan†	40	63	199	.317	39	66	.591	41	103	165	4.1
Jack Phelan‡	55	87	268	.325	52	90	.578	57	51	226	4.1
Dick Schulz†	29	38	122	.311	49	61	.803	48	67	125	4.3
Dick Schulz‡	50	63	212	.297	83	110	.755	66	106	209	4.2
Matt Mazza	26	33	110	.300	32	45	.711	27	34	98	3.8
Stan Patrick†	19	37	107	.346	19	39	.487	33	33	93	4.9
Stan Patrick‡	53	116	294	.395	89	147	.605	74	76	321	6.1
Danny Wagner	11	19	54	.352	31	35	.886	18	22	69	6.3
Glen Selbo	13	10	51	.196	22	29	.759	23	15	42	3.2
John Chaney†	10	15	49	.306	12	17	.706	5	10	42	4.2
John Chaney‡	16	25	86	.291	20	29	.690	20	23	70	4.4
Robert Wood	6	3	14	.214	1	1	1.000	1	6	7	1.2
Don Grate	2	1	6	.167	2	2	1.000	3	3	4	2.0

SYRACUSE NATIONALS

	G	FGM	FGA	Pct.	FTM	FTA	Pct.	Ast.	PF	Pts.	Avg.
Dolph Schayes	64	348	903	.385	376	486	.774	259	225	1072	16.8
Billy Gabor	56	226	671	.337	157	228	.689	108	198	609	10.9
Al Cervi	56	143	431	.332	287	346	.829	264	223	573	10.2
George Ratkovicz	62	162	439	.369	211	348	.606	124	201	535	8.6
Alex Hannum	64	177	488	.363	128	186	.688	129	264	482	7.5
Paul Seymour	62	175	524	.334	126	176	.716	189	157	476	7.7
Edward Peterson	62	167	390	.428	111	185	.600	33	198	445	7.2
Johnny Macknowski	59	154	463	.333	131	178	.736	65	128	439	7.4
Fuzzy Levane	60	139	418	.333	54	85	.635	156	106	332	5.5
Ray Corley	60	117	370	.316	75	122	.615	109	81	309	5.2
Leroy Chollet	49	61	179	.341	35	56	.625	37	52	157	3.2

TRI-CITIES BLACKHAWKS

	G	FGM	FGA	Pct.	FTM	FTA	Pct.	Ast.	PF	Pts.	Avg.
Dike Eddleman	64	332	906	.366	162	260	.623	142	254	826	12.9
Mike Todorovich†	51	232	736	.315	231	314	.736	188	183	695	13.6
Mike Todorovich‡	65	263	852	.309	266	370	.719	207	230	792	12.2
Don Otten*	46	165	451	.366	226	315	.717	73	180	556	12.1
Murray Wier	56	157	480	.327	115	166	.693	107	141	429	7.7
Red Perkins	60	128	422	.303	115	195	.590	114	260	371	6.2
Don Ray	61	130	403	.323	104	149	.698	60	147	364	6.0
Gene Vance	35	110	325	.338	86	120	.717	121	145	306	8.7
Dee Gibson	44	77	245	.314	127	177	.718	126	113	281	6.4
Jack Nichols†	18	82	219	.374	72	90	.800	61	61	236	13.1
Jack Nichols‡	67	310	848	.366	259	344	.753	142	179	879	13.1
Walt Kirk†	32	66	236	.280	98	33	2.970	60	92	230	7.2
Walt Kirk‡	58	97	361	.269	155	216	.718	103	155	349	6.0
John Mahnken*	36	85	319	.266	53	76	.697	64	149	223	6.2
Gene Englund†	22	49	126	.388	66	86	.767	24	70	164	7.5
Gene Englund‡	46	104	274	.380	152	192	.792	41	167	360	7.8
Billy Hassett*	18	46	157	.293	69	94	.734	68	54	161	8.9
Jim Owens*	26	42	137	.307	40	59	.678	32	65	124	4.8
Bill Henry†	19	24	69	.348	34	51	.667	9	23	82	4.3
Bill Henry‡	63	89	278	.320	118	176	.670	48	122	296	4.7
Dick Schulz*	8	13	45	.289	15	21	.714	8	12	41	5.1
Mac Otten*	12	12	34	.353	15	22	.682	11	27	39	3.3
John Chaney*	6	10	37	.270	8	12	.667	15	13	28	4.7
Jack Kerris*	4	8	26	.308	10	12	.833	8	13	26	6.5
George Nostrand*	1	5	10	.500	2	5	.400	1	1	12	2.4
Gene Berce	3	5	16	.313	0	5	.000	0	6	10	3.3

WASHINGTON CAPITOLS

	G	FGM	FGA	Pct.	FTM	FTA	Pct.	Ast.	PF	Pts.	Avg.
Freddie Scolari	66	312	910	.343	236	287	.822	175	181	860	13.0
Jack Nichols*	49	228	629	.362	187	254	.736	81	118	643	13.1
Chick Reiser	67	197	646	.305	212	254	.835	174	223	606	9.0
Horace McKinney	53	187	631	.296	118	152	.776	88	185	492	9.3
Bob Feerick	60	172	500	.344	139	174	.799	127	140	483	8.1
Dick O'Keefe	68	162	529	.306	150	203	.739	74	217	474	7.0
Chuck Gilmur	68	127	379	.335	164	241	.680	108	275	418	6.1
Chuck Halbert	68	108	284	.380	112	175	.640	89	136	328	4.8
Don Otten†	18	77	197	.391	115	148	.777	18	66	269	14.9

	G	FGM	FGA	Pct.	FTM	FTA	Pct.	Ast.	PF	Pts.	Avg.
										SCORING	
Don Otten‡	64	242	648	.373	341	463	.737	91	246	825	12.9
Johnny Norlander	40	99	293	.338	53	85	.624	33	71	251	6.3
Leo Katkaveck	54	101	330	.306	34	56	.607	68	102	236	4.4
John Mandic*	22	21	65	.323	20	30	.667	7	47	62	2.8
Dick Schulz*	13	12	45	.267	19	28	.679	10	27	43	3.3
Hooks Dillon	22	10	55	.182	16	22	.727	5	19	36	1.6

WATERLOO HAWKS

	G	FGM	FGA	Pct.	FTM	FTA	Pct.	Ast.	PF	Pts.	Avg.
										SCORING	
Dick Mehen	62	347	826	.420	198	281	.705	191	203	892	14.4
Harry Boykoff	61	288	698	.413	203	262	.775	149	229	779	12.8
Leo Kubiak	62	259	794	.326	192	236	.814	201	250	710	11.5
Don Boven	62	208	558	.373	240	349	.688	137	255	656	10.6
Wayne See	61	113	303	.373	94	135	.696	143	147	320	5.2
Jack Smiley†	47	92	314	.293	124	177	.701	147	158	308	6.6
Jack Smiley‡	59	98	364	.269	136	201	.677	161	193	332	5.6
Johnny Payak†	35	86	299	.288	108	152	.711	78	95	280	8.0
Johnny Payak‡	52	98	331	.296	121	173	.699	86	113	317	6.1
Stan Patrick*	34	79	187	.422	70	108	.648	41	43	228	6.7
Ward Gibson†	30	64	191	.335	41	60	.683	36	103	169	5.6
Ward Gibson‡	32	67	195	.344	42	64	.656	37	106	176	5.5
Charley Shipp	23	35	137	.255	37	51	.725	46	46	107	4.7
Gene Stump†	26	36	118	.305	30	40	.750	21	27	102	3.9
Gene Stump‡	49	63	213	.296	37	54	.685	44	59	163	3.3
Bob Tough†	21	32	114	.281	32	34	.941	36	25	96	4.6
Bob Tough‡	29	43	153	.281	37	40	.925	38	40	123	4.2
Jack Phelan*	15	24	69	.348	13	24	.542	16	48	61	4.1
Johnny Orr†	13	23	71	.324	6	7	.857	14	15	52	4.0
Johnny Orr‡	34	40	118	.339	12	14	.857	20	34	92	2.7
Moe Ollrich	14	17	72	.236	10	14	.714	24	34	44	3.1
Al Miksis	8	5	21	.238	17	21	.810	4	22	27	3.4
Dale Hamilton	14	8	33	.242	9	19	.474	17	30	25	1.8
Elmer Galner	15	9	35	.257	6	8	.750	7	28	24	1.6
John Pritchard	7	9	29	.310	4	11	.364	8	14	22	3.1
Ken Menke	6	6	17	.353	3	8	.375	7	7	15	2.5
Paul Cloyd†	4	6	18	.333	2	5	.400	1	1	14	3.5
Paul Cloyd‡	7	7	26	.269	5	8	.625	2	5	19	2.7

* Finished season with another team.   † Totals with this team only.   ‡ Totals with all teams.

PLAYOFF RESULTS

EASTERN DIVISION

SEMIFINALS
Syracuse 2, Philadelphia 0
Mar. 22—Wed.   Philadelphia 76 at Syracuse 93
Mar. 23—Thur.   Syracuse 59 at Philadelphia 53

New York 2, Washington 0
Mar. 21—Tue.   New York 90 at Washington 87
Mar. 22—Wed.   Washington 83 at New York 103

FINALS
Syracuse 2, New York 1
Mar. 26—Sun.   New York 83 at Syracuse *91
Mar. 30—Thur.   Syracuse 76 at New York 80
Apr. 2—Sun.   New York 80 at Syracuse 91

CENTRAL DIVISION

FIRST-PLACE GAME
Mar. 21—Tue.   Minneapolis 78 at Rochester 76

THIRD-PLACE GAME
Mar. 20—Mon.   Chicago 69 at Fort Wayne 86

SEMIFINALS
Minneapolis 2, Chicago 0
Mar. 22—Wed.   Chicago 75 at Minneapolis 85
Mar. 25—Sat.   Minneapolis 75 at Chicago 67

Fort Wayne 2, Rochester 0
Mar. 23—Thur.   Fort Wayne 90 at Rochester 84
Mar. 25—Sat.   Rochester 78 at Fort Wayne *79

FINALS
Minneapolis 2, Fort Wayne 0
Mar. 27—Mon.   Fort Wayne 79 at Minneapolis 93
Mar. 28—Tue.   Minneapolis 89 at Fort Wayne 82

WESTERN DIVISION

SEMIFINALS
Indianapolis 2, Sheboygan 1
Mar. 21—Tue.   Sheboygan 85 at Indianapolis 86
Mar. 23—Thur.   Indianapolis 85 at Sheboygan 95
Mar. 25—Sat.   Sheboygan 84 at Indianapolis 91

Anderson 2, Tri-Cities 1
Mar. 21—Tue.   Tri-Cities 77 at Anderson 89
Mar. 23—Thur.   Anderson 75 at Tri-Cities 76
Mar. 24—Fri.   Tri-Cities 71 at Anderson 94

FINALS
Anderson 2, Indianapolis 1
Mar. 28—Tue.   Anderson 74 at Indianapolis 77
Mar. 30—Thur.   Indianapolis 67 at Anderson 84
Apr. 1—Sat.   Anderson 67 at Indianapolis 65

NBA SEMIFINALS
Minneapolis 2, Anderson 0
Apr. 5—Wed.   Anderson 50 at Minneapolis 75
Apr. 6—Thur.   Minneapolis 90 at Anderson 71

NBA FINALS
Minneapolis 4, Syracuse 2
Apr. 8—Sat.   Minneapolis 68 at Syracuse 66
Apr. 9—Sun.   Minneapolis 85 at Syracuse 91
Apr. 14—Fri.   Syracuse 77, Minneapolis (at St. Paul) 91
Apr. 16—Sun.   Syracuse 69, Minneapolis (at St. Paul) 77
Apr. 20—Thur.   Minneapolis 76 at Syracuse 83
Apr. 23—Sun.   Syracuse 95 at Minneapolis 110

*Denotes number of overtime periods.

1948-49

1948-49 NBA CHAMPION MINNEAPOLIS LAKERS
From left: Donnie Forman, Herm Schaefer, Don Carlson, Don Smith, Tony Jaros, Johnny Jorgensen, Earl Gardner, Arnie Ferrin, Jack Dwan, Jim Pollard, George Mikan. Not pictured: head coach John Kundla.

FINAL STANDINGS

EASTERN DIVISION

	Was.	N.Y.	Balt.	Phi.	Bos.	Prov.	Roch.	Minn.	Chi.	St.L.	Ft.W.	Ind.	W	L	Pct.	GB
Washington	..	3	3	4	5	6	3	3	2	3	3	3	38	22	.633	..
New York	3	..	4	2	3	5	1	1	2	3	4	4	32	28	.533	6
Baltimore	3	2	..	4	4	2	1	1	1	2	4	5	29	31	.483	9
Philadelphia	2	4	2	..	3	6	0	1	3	3	0	4	28	32	.467	10
Boston	1	3	2	3	..	3	1	2	0	3	4	3	25	35	.417	13
Providence	0	1	4	0	3	..	2	0	0	0	1	1	12	48	.200	26

WESTERN DIVISION

	Was.	N.Y.	Balt.	Phi.	Bos.	Prov.	Roch.	Minn.	Chi.	St.L.	Ft.W.	Ind.	W	L	Pct.	GB
Rochester	2	4	4	5	4	3	..	2	4	6	6	5	45	15	.750	..
Minneapolis	2	4	4	4	3	5	4	..	4	4	4	6	44	16	.733	1
Chicago	3	3	4	2	5	5	2	2	..	3	4	5	38	22	.633	7
St. Louis	2	2	3	2	2	5	0	2	3	..	5	3	29	31	.483	16
Fort Wayne	2	1	1	5	1	4	0	2	2	1	..	3	22	38	.367	23
Indianapolis	2	1	0	1	2	4	1	0	1	3	3	..	18	42	.300	27

TEAM STATISTICS

	G	FGM	FGA	Pct.	FTM	FTA	Pct.	Ast.	PF	AVERAGE POINTS For	AVERAGE POINTS Agst.	AVERAGE POINTS Dif.
Minneapolis	60	1885	5146	.366	1272	1759	.723	1134	1386	84.0	76.7	+7.3
Rochester	60	1811	4869	.372	1420	2060	.689	1259	1539	84.0	77.4	+6.6
Chicago	60	1905	5750	.331	1228	1775	.692	1220	1731	84.0	80.0	+4.0
Washington	60	1751	5472	.320	1408	1914	.736	972	1710	81.8	79.4	+2.4
New York	60	1688	5237	.322	1376	1959	.702	1017	1559	79.2	77.7	+1.5
Baltimore	60	1736	5162	.336	1545	2053	.753	1000	1730	83.6	82.2	+1.4
Philadelphia	60	1831	5695	.322	1360	1897	.717	1043	1459	83.7	83.4	+0.3
Boston	60	1706	5483	.311	1181	1856	.636	1135	1382	76.6	79.5	-2.9
Fort Wayne	60	1536	5370	.286	1385	1979	.700	1082	1722	74.3	77.5	-3.2
St. Louis	60	1659	4858	.341	1229	1770	.694	1269	1480	75.8	79.4	-3.6
Indianapolis	60	1621	5367	.302	1240	1798	.690	1225	1393	74.7	79.4	-4.7
Providence	60	1750	5427	.322	1207	1742	.693	1026	1349	78.5	87.1	-8.6
Avgs.	60	1740	5320	.327	1321	1880	.703	1115	1537	80.0	...	...

HOME/ROAD/NEUTRAL

	Home	Road	Neutral	Total		Home	Road	Neutral	Total
Baltimore	17-12	11-17	1-2	29-31	New York	17-12	13-16	2-0	32-28
Boston	17-12	7-20	1-3	25-35	Philadelphia	19-10	9-21	0-1	28-32
Chicago	16-8	18-14	4-0	38-22	Providence	7-23	5-23	0-2	12-48
Fort Wayne	15-14	5-23	2-1	22-38	Rochester	24-5	20-10	1-0	45-15
Indianapolis	14-15	4-22	0-5	18-42	St. Louis	17-12	10-18	2-1	29-31
Minneapolis	26-3	16-13	2-0	44-16	Washington	22-7	15-14	1-1	38-22
					Totals	212-132	132-212	16-16	360-360

POINTS

	G	FGM	FTM	Pts.	Avg.
George Mikan, Minneapolis	...60	583	532	1698	28.3
Joe Fulks, Philadelphia	60	529	502	1560	26.0
Max Zaslofsky, Chicago	58	425	347	1197	20.6
Arnie Risen, Rochester	60	345	305	995	16.6
Ed Sadowski, Philadelphia	60	340	240	920	15.3
Belus Smawley, St. Louis	59	352	210	914	15.5
Bob Davies, Rochester	60	317	270	904	15.1
Ken Sailors, Providence	57	309	281	899	15.8
Carl Braun, New York	57	299	212	810	14.2
John Logan, St. Louis	57	282	239	803	14.1
Jim Pollard, Minneapolis	...53	314	156	784	14.8
Connie Simmons, Baltimore	...60	299	181	779	13.0
Ray Lumpp, Indianapolis-N.Y.	..61	279	219	777	12.7
Bob Feerick, Washington	58	248	256	752	13.0
Howie Shannon, Providence	..55	292	152	736	13.4
Horace McKinney, Washington	.57	263	197	723	12.7
Andy Phillip, Chicago	60	285	148	718	12.0
John Palmer, New York	58	240	234	714	12.3
Kleggie Hermsen, Washington	.60	248	212	708	11.8
Walter Budko, Baltimore	60	224	244	692	11.5

FIELD GOALS
(minimum 200 made)

	FGM	FGA	Pct.
Arnie Risen, Rochester	.345	816	.423
George Mikan, Minneapolis	.583	1403	.416
Ed Sadowski, Philadelphia	.340	839	.405
Jim Pollard, Minneapolis	.314	792	.396
Red Rocha, St. Louis	.223	574	.389
Bobby Wanzer, Rochester	.202	533	.379

	FGM	FGA	Pct.
Connie Simmons, Baltimore	.299	794	.377
Herm Schaefer, Minneapolis	.214	572	.374
Belus Smawley, St. Louis	.352	946	.372
Bob Davies, Rochester	.317	871	.364
Howie Shannon, Providence	.292	802	.364

FREE THROWS
(minimum 150 made)

	FTM	FTA	Pct.
Bob Feerick, Washington	.256	298	.859
Max Zaslofsky, Chicago	.347	413	.840
Bobby Wanzer, Rochester	.209	254	.823
Herm Schaefer, Minneapolis	.174	213	.817
Howie Shannon, Providence	.152	189	.804
Hal Tidrick, Indianapolis-Baltimore	.164	205	.800
John Logan, St. Louis	.239	302	.791
Walter Budko, Baltimore	.244	309	.790
John Pelkington, Fort Wayne-Baltimore	.211	267	.790
Joe Fulks, Philadelphia	.502	638	.787

ASSISTS

	G	No.	Avg.
Bob Davies, Rochester	.60	321	5.4
Andy Phillip, Chicago	.60	319	5.3
John Logan, St. Louis	.57	276	4.8
Ernie Calverley, Providence	.59	251	4.3
George Senesky, Philadelphia	.60	233	3.9
Jim Seminoff, Boston	.58	229	4.0
George Mikan, Minneapolis	.60	218	3.6
Ken Sailors, Providence	.57	209	3.7
Bob Feerick, Washington	.58	188	3.2
Bobby Wanzer, Rochester	.60	186	3.1

INDIVIDUAL STATISTICS, TEAM BY TEAM

BALTIMORE BULLETS

	G	FGM	FGA	Pct.	FTM	FTA	Pct.	Ast.	PF	Pts.	Avg.
Connie Simmons	60	299	794	.377	181	265	.683	116	215	779	13.0
Walt Budko	60	224	644	.348	244	309	.790	99	201	692	11.5
Chick Reiser	57	219	653	.335	188	257	.732	132	202	626	11.0
Fred Lewis†	53	241	719	.335	121	157	.771	88	142	603	11.4
Fred Lewis‡	61	272	834	.326	138	181	.762	107	167	682	11.2
Hal Tidrick†	53	182	549	.332	150	187	.802	90	173	514	9.7
Hal Tidrick‡	61	194	616	.315	164	205	.800	101	191	552	9.0
Jake Pelkington†	40	160	365	.438	153	192	.797	99	162	473	11.8
Jake Pelkington‡	54	193	469	.412	211	267	.790	131	216	597	11.1
Stan Stutz	59	121	431	.281	131	159	.824	82	149	373	6.3
Buddy Jeannette	56	73	199	.367	167	213	.784	124	157	313	5.6
Sid Tannenbaum†	14	50	162	.309	34	43	.791	54	21	134	9.6
Sid Tannenbaum‡	46	146	501	.291	99	120	.825	125	74	391	8.5
Irv Torgoff*	29	45	178	.253	43	56	.768	32	77	133	4.6
Johnny Ezersky†	27	44	149	.295	39	55	.709	27	36	127	4.7
Johnny Ezersky‡	56	128	407	.314	109	160	.681	67	98	365	6.5
Jack Toomay†	23	23	63	.365	27	41	.659	11	49	75	3.3
Jack Toomay‡	36	32	84	.381	36	53	.679	12	65	100	2.8
John Mahnken*	7	21	80	.263	11	18	.611	9	32	53	7.6
Leo Mogus*	13	10	50	.200	25	36	.694	3	29	45	3.5
Dan Kraus	13	5	35	.143	11	24	.458	7	24	21	1.6
Howie Rader	13	7	45	.156	3	10	.300	14	25	17	1.3
Doug Holcomb	3	3	12	.250	9	14	.643	5	5	15	5.0
Herb Krautblatt	10	4	18	.222	5	11	.455	4	14	13	1.3
Don Martin†	7	2	9	.222	1	2	.500	4	14	5	0.7
Don Martin‡	44	52	170	.306	30	47	.638	25	115	134	3.0
Darrell Brown	3	2	6	.333	0	2	.000	0	3	4	1.3
Ray Ramsey	2	0	1	.000	2	2	1.000	0	0	2	1.0

BOSTON CELTICS

	G	FGM	FGA	Pct.	FTM	FTA	Pct.	Ast.	PF	Pts.	Avg.
Eddie Ehlers	59	182	583	.312	150	225	.667	133	119	514	8.7
Gene Stump	56	193	580	.333	92	129	.713	56	102	478	8.5
Jim Seminoff	58	153	487	.314	151	219	.689	229	195	457	7.9
Bob Doll	47	145	438	.331	80	117	.684	117	118	370	7.9
Mel Riebe*	33	146	501	.291	70	116	.603	95	97	362	11.0
Art Spector	59	130	434	.300	64	116	.552	77	111	324	5.5
Chuck Halbert*	33	99	338	.293	112	188	.596	61	97	310	9.4
George Kaftan	21	116	315	.368	72	115	.626	61	28	304	14.5
George Nostrand†	27	91	267	.341	83	135	.615	38	74	265	9.8
George Nostrand‡	60	212	651	.326	165	284	.581	94	164	589	9.8
Bob Kinney†	21	75	224	.335	54	91	.593	26	89	204	9.7
Bob Kinney‡	58	161	495	.325	136	234	.581	77	224	458	7.9
Dermie O'Connell	21	87	315	.276	30	56	.536	65	40	204	9.7
Tom Kelly	27	73	218	.335	45	73	.616	38	73	191	7.1
Johnny Ezersky*	18	68	185	.368	49	80	.613	29	49	185	10.3

	G	FGM	FGA	Pct.	FTM	FTA	Pct.	Ast.	PF	Pts.	Avg.
Johnny Bach	34	34	119	.286	51	75	.680	25	24	119	3.5
Bill Roberts*	26	36	109	.330	9	19	.474	13	34	81	3.1
Stan Noszka	30	30	123	.244	15	30	.500	25	56	75	2.5
Phil Farman†	21	21	78	.269	30	38	.789	18	36	72	3.4
Phil Farman‡	48	50	163	.307	55	81	.679	36	86	155	3.2
Dutch Garfinkel	9	12	70	.171	10	14	.714	17	19	34	3.8
Hank Beenders	8	6	28	.214	7	9	.778	3	9	19	2.4
John Hazen	6	6	17	.353	6	7	.857	3	10	18	3.0
Earl Shannon†	5	2	11	.182	1	4	.250	4	2	5	1.0
Earl Shannon‡	32	34	127	.268	39	58	.672	44	33	107	3.3
Al Lucas	2	1	3	.333	0	0	...	2	0	2	1.0

CHICAGO STAGS

	G	FGM	FGA	Pct.	FTM	FTA	Pct.	Ast.	PF	Pts.	Avg.
Max Zaslofsky	58	425	1216	.350	347	413	.840	149	156	1197	20.6
Andy Phillip	60	285	818	.348	148	219	.676	319	205	718	12.0
Ed Mikan	60	229	729	.314	136	183	.743	62	191	594	9.9
Gene Vance	56	222	657	.338	131	181	.724	167	217	575	10.3
Odie Spears	57	200	631	.317	131	197	.665	97	200	531	9.3
Stan Miasek	58	169	488	.346	113	216	.523	57	208	451	7.8
Kenny Rollins	59	144	520	.277	77	104	.740	167	150	365	6.2
Chuck Gilmur	56	110	281	.391	66	121	.545	125	194	286	5.1
Joe Graboski	45	54	157	.344	17	49	.347	18	86	125	2.8
Mike Bloom†	21	22	89	.247	27	34	.794	17	31	71	3.4
Mike Bloom‡	45	35	181	.193	56	74	.757	32	53	126	2.8
Edwin Kachan*	33	22	100	.220	21	34	.618	25	57	65	2.0
Carl Meinhold*	15	16	36	.444	9	13	.692	9	12	41	2.7
Bill Miller*	14	5	23	.217	4	9	.444	8	17	14	1.0
Jim Browne	4	1	2	.500	1	2	.500	0	4	3	0.8
Bill Roberts*	2	1	3	.333	0	0	...	0	2	2	1.0
Jack Eskridge	3	0	0	...	0	0	...	0	1	0	0.0

FORT WAYNE PISTONS

	G	FGM	FGA	Pct.	FTM	FTA	Pct.	Ast.	PF	Pts.	Avg.
Bob Tough	53	183	661	.277	100	138	.725	99	101	466	8.8
Jack Smiley	59	141	571	.247	112	164	.683	138	202	394	6.7
Curly Armstrong	52	131	428	.306	118	169	.698	105	152	380	7.3
Richie Niemiera	55	115	331	.347	132	165	.800	96	115	362	6.6
John Mahnken†	37	136	514	.265	79	119	.664	82	143	351	9.5
John Mahnken‡	57	215	830	.259	104	167	.623	125	215	534	9.4
Leo Klier	47	125	492	.254	97	137	.708	56	124	347	7.4
Dick Triptow	55	116	417	.278	102	141	.723	96	107	334	6.1
Bruce Hale†	34	109	348	.313	102	136	.750	87	72	320	9.4
Bruce Hale‡	52	187	585	.320	172	228	.754	156	112	546	10.5
Bill Henry	32	96	300	.320	125	203	.616	55	110	317	9.9
Bob Kinney*	37	86	271	.317	82	143	.573	51	135	254	6.9
Ralph Hamilton*	10	16	66	.242	10	13	.769	3	10	42	4.2
Ward Williams	53	61	257	.237	93	124	.750	82	158	215	4.1
Leo Mogus*	20	59	176	.335	55	74	.743	27	66	173	8.7
Blackie Towery*	22	56	216	.259	52	73	.712	35	79	164	7.5
Charlie Black†	17	46	145	.317	38	62	.613	25	64	130	7.6
Charlie Black‡	58	203	691	.294	161	291	.553	140	247	567	9.8
Jake Pelkington*	14	33	104	.317	58	75	.773	32	54	124	8.9
Walt Kirk*	14	22	61	.361	25	33	.758	12	24	69	4.9
Roy Pugh*	4	4	8	.500	1	4	.250	1	3	9	2.3
Dillard Crocker	2	1	4	.250	4	6	.667	0	3	6	3.0

INDIANAPOLIS JETS

	G	FGM	FGA	Pct.	FTM	FTA	Pct.	Ast.	PF	Pts.	Avg.
Ray Lumpp*	37	162	489	.331	129	171	.754	124	99	453	12.2
Price Brookfield	54	176	638	.276	90	125	.720	136	145	442	8.2
Blackie Towery†	38	147	555	.265	143	190	.753	136	164	437	11.5
Blackie Towery‡	60	203	771	.263	195	263	.741	171	243	601	10.0
Charlie Black*	41	157	546	.288	123	229	.537	115	183	437	10.7
Walt Kirk†	35	118	345	.342	142	198	.717	106	103	378	10.8
Walt Kirk‡	49	140	406	.345	167	231	.723	118	127	447	9.1
Leo Mogus†	19	103	283	.364	97	133	.729	74	75	303	15.9
Leo Mogus‡	52	172	509	.338	177	243	.728	104	170	521	10.0
John Mandic	56	97	302	.321	75	115	.652	80	151	269	4.8
Fritz Nagy	50	94	271	.347	65	97	.670	68	84	253	5.1
Ralph Hamilton†	38	98	381	.257	51	78	.654	80	57	247	6.5
Ralph Hamilton‡	48	114	447	.255	61	91	.670	83	67	289	6.0
Lionel Malamed*	35	85	259	.328	58	69	.841	55	44	228	6.5
Bruce Hale*	18	78	237	.329	70	92	.761	69	40	226	12.6
Tommy Byrnes†	22	83	255	.325	46	68	.676	48	31	212	9.6
Tommy Byrnes‡	57	160	525	.305	92	149	.617	102	84	412	7.2
Andy Kostecka	21	46	110	.418	43	70	.614	14	48	135	6.4
John Mahnken*	13	58	236	.246	14	30	.467	34	40	130	10.0
George Glamack	11	30	121	.248	42	55	.764	19	28	102	9.3
Fred Lewis*	8	31	115	.270	17	24	.708	19	25	79	9.9
Jack Eskridge	20	25	69	.362	14	20	.700	14	24	64	3.2
Hal Tidrick*	8	12	67	.179	14	18	.778	11	18	38	4.8
Marty Passaglia	10	14	57	.246	3	4	.750	17	17	31	3.1
Dick Wehr	9	5	21	.238	2	6	.333	3	12	12	1.3
Roy Pugh*	6	1	7	.143	1	5	.200	2	2	3	0.5
Jim Spruill	1	1	3	.333	0	0	...	0	3	2	2.0
James Springer	2	0	0	...	1	1	1.000	0	0	1	0.5
Paul Napolitano	1	0	0	...	0	0	...	0	0	0	0.0
Jack Maddox	1	0	0	...	0	0	...	1	0	0	0.0

MINNEAPOLIS LAKERS

	G	FGM	FGA	Pct.	FTM	FTA	Pct.	Ast.	PF	SCORING Pts.	Avg.
George Mikan	60	583	1403	.416	532	689	.772	218	260	1698	28.3
Jim Pollard	53	314	792	.396	156	227	.687	142	144	784	14.8
Herm Schaefer	58	214	572	.374	174	213	.817	185	121	602	10.4
Don Carlson	55	211	632	.334	86	130	.662	170	180	508	9.2
Arnie Ferrin	47	130	378	.344	85	128	.664	76	142	345	7.3
Tony Jaros	59	132	385	.343	79	110	.718	58	114	343	5.8
Jack Dwan	60	121	380	.318	34	69	.493	129	157	276	4.6
Donnie Forman	44	68	231	.294	43	67	.642	74	94	179	4.1
Johnny Jorgensen	48	41	114	.360	24	33	.727	33	68	106	2.2
Earl Gardner	50	38	101	.376	13	28	.464	19	50	89	1.8
Mike Bloom*	24	13	92	.141	29	40	.725	15	22	55	2.3
Edwin Kachan†	19	16	42	.381	15	22	.682	12	24	47	2.5
Edwin Kachan‡	52	38	142	.268	36	56	.643	37	81	112	2.2
Donald Smith	8	2	13	.154	2	3	.667	2	6	6	0.8
Jack Tingle	2	1	6	.167	0	0	...	1	2	2	1.0
Ray Ellefson	3	1	5	.200	0	0	...	0	2	2	0.7

NEW YORK KNICKERBOCKERS

	G	FGM	FGA	Pct.	FTM	FTA	Pct.	Ast.	PF	SCORING Pts.	Avg.
Carl Braun	57	299	906	.330	212	279	.760	173	144	810	14.2
Bud Palmer	58	240	685	.350	234	307	.762	108	206	714	12.3
Lee Knorek	60	156	457	.341	131	183	.716	135	258	443	7.4
Harry Gallatin	52	157	479	.328	120	169	.710	63	127	434	8.3
Butch van Breda Kolff	59	127	401	.317	161	240	.671	143	148	415	7.0
Goebel Ritter	55	123	353	.348	91	146	.623	57	71	337	6.1
Ray Lumpp†	24	117	311	.376	90	112	.804	34	74	324	13.5
Ray Lumpp‡	61	279	800	.349	219	283	.774	158	173	777	12.7
Irv Rothenberg	53	101	367	.275	112	174	.644	68	174	314	5.9
Sid Tannenbaum*	32	96	339	.283	65	77	.844	71	53	257	8.0
Tommy Byrnes*	35	77	270	.285	46	81	.568	54	53	200	5.7
Paul Noel	47	70	277	.253	37	60	.617	33	84	177	3.8
Mel McGaha	51	62	195	.318	52	88	.591	51	104	176	3.5
Joe Colone	15	35	113	.310	13	19	.684	9	25	83	5.5
Gene James	11	18	48	.375	6	12	.500	5	20	42	3.8
Ray Kuka	8	10	36	.278	5	9	.556	11	16	25	3.1
Dick Shrider	4	0	0	...	1	3	.333	2	2	1	0.3

PHILADELPHIA WARRIORS

	G	FGM	FGA	Pct.	FTM	FTA	Pct.	Ast.	PF	SCORING Pts.	Avg.
Joe Fulks	60	529	1689	.313	502	638	.787	74	262	1560	26.0
Ed Sadowski	60	340	839	.405	240	350	.686	160	273	920	15.3
Angelo Musi	58	194	618	.314	90	119	.756	81	108	478	8.2
Gale Bishop	56	170	523	.325	127	195	.651	92	137	467	8.3
George Senesky	60	138	516	.267	111	152	.730	233	133	387	6.5
Jerry Fleishman	59	123	424	.290	77	118	.653	120	137	323	5.5
Howie Dallmar	38	105	342	.307	83	116	.716	116	104	293	7.7
Francis Crossin	44	74	212	.349	26	42	.619	55	53	174	4.0
Jerry Rullo	39	53	183	.290	31	45	.689	48	71	137	3.5
Jake Bornheimer	15	34	109	.312	20	29	.690	13	47	88	5.9
Phil Farbman*	27	29	85	.341	25	43	.581	18	50	83	3.1
Elmo Morgenthaler	20	15	39	.385	12	18	.667	7	18	42	2.1
Irv Torgoff†	13	14	48	.292	7	8	.875	12	33	35	2.7
Irv Torgoff‡	42	59	226	.261	50	64	.781	44	110	168	4.0
Roy Pugh†	13	8	36	.222	4	10	.400	6	12	20	1.5
Roy Pugh‡	23	13	51	.255	6	19	.316	9	17	32	1.4
Robert O'Brien*	16	5	32	.156	5	14	.357	8	21	15	0.9

PROVIDENCE STEAMROLLERS

	G	FGM	FGA	Pct.	FTM	FTA	Pct.	Ast.	PF	SCORING Pts.	Avg.
Kenny Sailors	57	309	906	.341	281	367	.766	209	239	899	15.8
Howie Shannon	55	292	802	.364	152	189	.804	125	154	736	13.4
Ernie Calverley	59	218	696	.313	121	160	.756	251	183	557	9.4
Brady Walker	59	202	556	.363	87	155	.561	68	100	491	8.3
Les Pugh	60	168	556	.302	125	167	.749	59	168	461	7.7
George Nostrand*	33	121	384	.315	82	149	.550	56	90	324	9.8
Chuck Halbert†	27	103	309	.333	102	157	.650	52	78	308	11.4
Chuck Halbert‡	60	202	647	.312	214	345	.620	113	175	618	10.3
Carl Meinhold†	35	85	270	.315	52	83	.627	38	48	222	6.3
Carl Meinhold‡	50	101	306	.330	61	96	.635	47	60	263	5.3
Bob Brown	20	37	111	.333	34	47	.723	14	67	108	5.4
Otto Schnellbacher*	23	34	118	.288	34	54	.630	19	48	102	4.4
Earl Shannon*	27	32	116	.276	38	54	.704	40	31	102	3.8
Buddy O'Grady†	17	33	117	.282	15	25	.600	25	21	81	4.8
Buddy O'Grady‡	47	85	293	.290	49	71	.690	68	57	219	4.7
Bob Hubbard	34	25	135	.185	22	34	.647	18	39	72	2.1
Mel Riebe†	10	26	88	.295	9	17	.529	9	13	61	6.1
Mel Riebe‡	43	172	589	.292	79	133	.594	104	110	423	9.8
Johnny Ezersky*	11	16	73	.219	21	25	.840	11	13	53	4.8
Giff Roux†	26	18	74	.243	14	27	.519	9	18	50	1.9
Giff Roux‡	45	29	118	.246	29	44	.659	20	30	87	1.9
Andy Tonkovich	17	19	71	.268	6	9	.667	10	12	44	2.6
Lee Robbins	16	9	25	.360	11	17	.647	12	24	29	1.8
Fred Paine	3	3	19	.158	1	5	.200	1	3	7	2.3
Ben Scharnus	1	0	1	.000	0	1	.000	0	0	0	0.0

1948-49

ROCHESTER ROYALS

	G	FGM	FGA	Pct.	FTM	FTA	Pct.	Ast.	PF	Pts.	Avg.
										SCORING	
Arnie Risen	60	345	816	.423	305	462	.660	100	216	995	16.6
Bob Davies	60	317	871	.364	270	348	.776	321	197	904	15.1
Bobby Wanzer	60	202	533	.379	209	254	.823	186	132	613	10.2
Red Holzman	60	225	691	.326	96	157	.611	149	93	546	9.1
Arnie Johnson	60	156	375	.416	199	284	.701	80	247	511	8.5
Andy Duncan	55	162	391	.414	83	135	.615	51	179	407	7.4
Bill Calhoun	56	146	408	.358	75	131	.573	125	97	367	6.6
Mike Novak	60	124	363	.342	72	124	.581	112	188	320	5.3
Fran Curran	57	61	168	.363	85	126	.675	78	118	207	3.6
Fuzzy Levane	36	55	193	.285	13	21	.619	39	37	123	3.4
Lionel Malamed†	9	12	31	.387	6	8	.750	6	9	30	3.3
Lionel Malamed‡	44	97	290	.334	64	77	.831	61	53	258	5.9
Bob Fitzgerald	18	6	29	.207	7	10	.700	12	26	19	1.1

ST. LOUIS BOMBERS

	G	FGM	FGA	Pct.	FTM	FTA	Pct.	Ast.	PF	Pts.	Avg.
										SCORING	
Belus Smawley	59	352	946	.372	210	281	.747	183	145	914	15.5
Johnny Logan	57	282	816	.346	239	302	.791	276	191	803	14.1
Red Rocha	58	223	574	.389	162	211	.768	157	251	608	10.5
Ariel Maughan	55	206	650	.317	184	285	.646	99	134	596	10.8
Easy Parham	60	124	404	.307	96	172	.558	151	134	344	5.7
Don Putnam	59	98	330	.297	52	97	.536	140	132	248	4.2
Otto Schnellbacher†	20	59	162	.364	55	79	.696	45	61	173	8.7
Otto Schnellbacher‡	43	93	280	.332	89	133	.669	64	109	275	6.4
Coulby Gunther	32	57	181	.315	45	71	.634	33	64	159	5.0
Grady Lewis	34	53	137	.387	42	70	.600	37	104	148	4.4
Bill Roberts†	22	52	155	.335	35	44	.795	28	77	139	6.3
Bill Roberts‡	50	89	267	.333	44	63	.698	41	113	222	4.4
Buddy O'Grady*	30	52	176	.295	34	46	.739	43	36	138	4.6
Don Martin*	37	50	161	.311	29	45	.644	21	101	129	3.5
D.C. Willcutt	22	18	51	.353	15	18	.833	31	9	51	2.3
Bill Miller†	14	16	49	.327	7	11	.636	12	15	39	2.8
Bill Miller‡	28	21	72	.292	11	20	.550	20	32	53	1.9
Giff Roux*	19	11	44	.250	15	17	.882	11	12	37	1.9
Robert O'Brien†	8	5	18	.278	7	18	.389	1	11	17	2.1
Robert O'Brien‡	24	10	50	.200	12	32	.375	9	32	32	1.3
Lonnie Eggleston	2	1	4	.250	2	3	.667	1	3	4	2.0

WASHINGTON CAPITOLS

	G	FGM	FGA	Pct.	FTM	FTA	Pct.	Ast.	PF	Pts.	Avg.
										SCORING	
Bob Feerick	58	248	708	.350	256	298	.859	188	171	752	13.0
Horace McKinney	57	263	801	.328	197	279	.706	114	216	723	12.7
Kleggie Hermsen	60	248	794	.312	212	311	.682	99	257	708	11.8
Freddie Scolari	48	196	633	.310	146	183	.798	100	150	538	11.2
Johnny Norlander	60	164	454	.361	116	171	.678	86	124	444	7.4
Sonny Hertzberg	60	154	541	.285	134	164	.817	114	140	442	7.4
Jack Nichols	34	153	392	.390	92	126	.730	56	118	398	11.7
Matt Zunic	56	98	323	.303	77	109	.706	50	182	273	4.9
Leo Katkaveck	53	84	253	.332	53	71	.746	68	110	221	4.2
Dick Schulz	50	65	278	.234	65	91	.714	53	107	195	3.9
Dick O'Keefe	50	70	274	.255	51	99	.515	43	119	191	3.8
Jack Toomay*	13	8	21	.381	9	12	.750	1	16	25	1.9

* Finished season with another team. † Totals with this team only. ‡ Totals with all teams.

PLAYOFF RESULTS

EASTERN DIVISION

SEMIFINALS

Washington 2, Philadelphia 0
Mar. 23—Wed.   Washington 92 at Philadelphia 70
Mar. 24—Thur.   Philadelphia 78 at Washington 80

New York 2, Baltimore 1
Mar. 23—Wed.   New York 81 at Baltimore 82
Mar. 24—Thur.   Baltimore 82 at New York 84
Mar. 26—Sat.   Baltimore 99 at New York *103

FINALS

Washington 2, New York 1
Mar. 29—Tue.   New York 71 at Washington 77
Mar. 31—Thur.   Washington 84 at New York *86
Apr. 2—Sat.   New York 76 at Washington 84

WESTERN DIVISION

SEMIFINALS

Rochester 2, St. Louis 0
Mar. 22—Tue.   St. Louis 64 at Rochester 93
Mar. 23—Wed.   Rochester 66 at St. Louis 64

Minneapolis 2, Chicago 0
Mar. 23—Wed.   Chicago 77 at Minneapolis 84
Mar. 24—Thur.   Minneapolis 101 at Chicago 85

FINALS

Minneapolis 2, Rochester 0
Mar. 27—Sun.   Minneapolis 80 at Rochester 79
Mar. 29—Tue.   Rochester 55, Minneapolis (at St. Paul) 67

NBA FINALS

Minneapolis 4, Washington 2
Apr. 4—Mon.   Washington 84 at Minneapolis 88
Apr. 6—Wed.   Washington 62 at Minneapolis 76
Apr. 8—Fri.   Minneapolis 94 at Washington 74
Apr. 9—Sat.   Minneapolis 71 at Washington 83
Apr. 11—Mon.   Minneapolis 66 at Washington 74
Apr. 13—Wed.   Washington 56, Minneapolis (at St. Paul) 77
*Denotes number of overtime periods.

1947-48

1947-48 NBA CHAMPION BALTIMORE BULLETS
From left: Connie Simmons, Kleggie Hermsen, Grady Lewis, Carl Meinhold, Paul Hoffman, Dick Schulz, Herm Fuetsch, Chick Reiser, Red Klotz, player/coach Buddy Jeanette.

FINAL STANDINGS

EASTERN DIVISION

	Phi.	N.Y.	Bos.	Prov.	St.L.	Balt.	Chi.	Was.	W	L	Pct.	GB
Philadelphia	..	4	4	8	3	4	2	2	27	21	.563	..
New York 4		..	7	7	4	1	0	3	26	22	.542	1
Boston 4		1	..	6	2	1	3	3	20	28	.417	7
Providence 0		1	2	..	0	0	2	1	6	42	.125	21

WESTERN DIVISION

	Phi.	N.Y.	Bos.	Prov.	St.L.	Balt.	Chi.	Was.	W	L	Pct.	GB
St. Louis. 3		2	4	6	..	5	5	4	29	19	.604	..
Baltimore 2		5	5	6	3	..	5	2	28	20	.583	1
Washington 4		3	3	5	4	6	3	..	28	20	.583	1
Chicago 4		6	3	4	3	3	..	5	28	20	.583	1

TEAM STATISTICS

	G	FGM	FGA	Pct.	FTM	FTA	Pct.	Ast.	PF	AVERAGE POINTS For	Agst.	Dif.
Baltimore 48		1288	4283	.301	994	1443	.689	320	1080	74.4	70.5	+3.9
New York 48		1355	4724	.287	868	1291	.672	376	1076	74.5	71.4	+3.1
Chicago 48		1390	4683	.297	860	1305	.659	432	1138	75.8	73.2	+2.6
Washington 48		1336	4785	.279	865	1203	.719	305	1084	73.7	71.1	+2.6
St. Louis. 48		1297	4551	.285	838	1244	.674	218	1050	71.5	69.5	+2.0
Philadelphia 48		1279	4875	.262	963	1349	.714	335	934	73.4	72.1	+1.3
Boston 48		1241	4323	.287	821	1246	.659	364	1065	68.8	72.7	-3.9
Providence 48		1268	4630	.274	782	1275	.613	347	1105	69.1	80.1	-11.0
Avgs. 48		1307	4607	.284	874	1295	.675	337	1067	72.6	. . .	. . .

HOME/ROAD

	Home	Road	Total		Home	Road	Total
Baltimore	17-7	11-13	28-20	Philadelphia	14-10	13-11	27-21
Boston	11-13	9-15	20-28	Providence	3-21	3-21	6-42
Chicago	14-10	14-10	28-20	St. Louis	17-7	12-12	29-19
New York	12-12	14-10	26-22	Washington	19-5	9-15	28-20
				Totals	107-85	85-107	192-192

INDIVIDUAL LEADERS

POINTS

	G	FGM	FTM	Pts.	Avg.
Max Zaslofsky, Chicago	48	373	261	1007	21.0
Joe Fulks, Philadelphia	43	326	297	949	22.1
Ed Sadowski, Boston	47	308	294	910	19.4
Bob Feerick, Washington	48	293	189	775	16.1
Stan Miasek, Chicago	48	263	190	716	14.9
Carl Braun, New York	47	276	119	671	14.3
John Logan, St. Louis	48	221	202	644	13.4
John Palmer, New York	48	224	174	622	13.0
Red Rocha, St. Louis	48	232	147	611	12.7

	G	FGM	FTM	Pts.	Avg.
Fred Scolari, Washington	47	229	131	589	12.5
Howie Dallmar, Philadelphia	48	215	157	587	12.2
Kleggie Hermsen, Baltimore	48	212	151	575	12.0
Ernie Calverley, Providence	47	226	107	559	11.9
Chick Reiser, Baltimore	47	202	137	541	11.5
Belus Smawley, St. Louis	48	212	111	535	11.1
Ken Sailors, Chicago-Phil.-Prov.	44	207	110	524	11.9
George Nostrand, Providence	45	196	129	521	11.6
Mike Bloom, Baltimore-Boston	48	174	160	508	10.6
Dick Holub, New York	48	195	114	504	10.5
Buddy Jeannette, Baltimore	46	150	191	491	10.7

FIELD GOALS
(minimum 200 made)

	FGM	FGA	Pct.
Bob Feerick, Washington	293	861	.340
Max Zaslofsky, Chicago	373	1156	.323
Ed Sadowski, Boston	308	953	.323
Carl Braun, New York	276	854	.323
Chick Reiser, Baltimore	202	628	.322
John Palmer, New York	224	710	.315
Red Rocha, St. Louis	232	740	.314
Mel Riebe, Boston	202	653	.309
Belus Smawley, St. Louis	212	688	.308
Stan Miasek, Chicago	263	867	.303

FREE THROWS
(minimum 125 made)

	FTM	FTA	Pct.
Bob Feerick, Washington	189	240	.788
Max Zaslofsky, Chicago	261	333	.784
Joe Fulks, Philadelphia	297	390	.762

	FTM	FTA	Pct.
Buddy Jeannette, Baltimore	191	252	.758
John Palmer, New York	174	234	.744
Howie Dallmar, Philadelphia	157	211	.744
John Logan, St. Louis	202	272	.743
John Norlander, Washington	135	182	.742
Chick Reiser, Baltimore	137	185	.741
Fred Scolari, Washington	131	179	.732

ASSISTS

	G	No.	Avg.
Howie Dallmar, Philadelphia	48	120	2.5
Ernie Calverley, Providence	47	119	2.5
Jim Seminoff, Chicago	48	89	1.9
Chuck Gilmur, Chicago	48	77	1.6
Andy Philip, Chicago	32	74	2.3
Ed Sadowski, Boston	47	74	1.6
Buddy Jeannette, Baltimore	46	70	1.5
John Logan, St. Louis	48	62	1.3
Carl Braun, New York	47	61	1.3
Saul Mariaschin, Boston	43	60	1.4

INDIVIDUAL STATISTICS, TEAM BY TEAM

BALTIMORE BULLETS

	G	FGM	FGA	Pct.	FTM	FTA	Pct.	Ast.	PF	SCORING Pts.	Avg.
Kleggie Hermsen	48	212	765	.277	151	227	.665	48	154	575	12.0
Chick Reiser	47	202	628	.322	137	185	.741	40	175	541	11.5
Buddy Jeannette	46	150	430	.349	191	252	.758	70	147	491	10.7
Paul Hoffman	37	142	408	.348	104	157	.662	23	123	388	10.5
Dick Schulz	48	133	469	.284	117	160	.731	28	116	383	8.0
Mike Bloom*	34	128	471	.272	123	172	.715	24	79	379	11.1
Carl Meinhold	48	108	356	.303	37	60	.617	16	64	253	5.3
Connie Simmons†	13	54	179	.302	30	54	.556	7	40	138	10.6
Connie Simmons‡	45	162	545	.297	62	108	.574	24	122	386	8.6
Grady Lewis†	21	55	187	.294	39	63	.619	28	66	149	7.1
Grady Lewis‡	45	114	425	.268	87	135	.644	41	151	315	7.0
Herm Fuetsch	42	42	140	.300	25	40	.625	17	39	109	2.6
Paul Seymour	22	27	101	.267	22	37	.595	6	34	76	3.5
Irv Rothenberg*	14	25	86	.291	11	23	.478	2	24	61	4.4
Red Klotz	11	7	31	.226	1	3	.333	7	3	15	1.4
Johnny Jorgensen†	2	2	7	.286	1	1	1.000	0	1	5	2.5
Johnny Jorgensen‡	3	4	9	.444	1	1	1.000	0	2	9	3.0
Elmer Gainer	5	1	9	.111	3	6	.500	3	8	5	1.0
Brooms Abramovic†	5	0	11	.000	2	3	.667	1	5	2	0.4

1947-48

	G	FGM	FGA	Pct.	FTM	FTA	Pct.	Ast.	PF	Pts.	Avg.
Brooms Abramovic‡	9	1	21	.048	4	7	.571	2	10	6	0.7
Jerry Rullo	2	0	4	.000	0	0	. . .	0	1	0	0.0
Chet McNabb	2	0	1	.000	0	0	. . .	0	1	0	0.0

BOSTON CELTICS

	G	FGM	FGA	Pct.	FTM	FTA	Pct.	Ast.	PF	Pts.	Avg.
Ed Sadowski	47	308	953	.323	294	422	.697	74	182	910	19.4
Mel Riebe.	48	202	653	.309	85	137	.620	41	137	489	10.2
Saul Mariaschin	43	125	463	.270	83	117	.709	60	121	333	7.7
Eddie Ehlers.	40	104	417	.249	78	144	.542	44	92	286	7.2
Dutch Garfinkel	43	114	380	.300	35	46	.761	59	78	263	6.1
Connie Simmons*	32	108	366	.295	32	54	.593	17	82	248	7.8
Art Spector	48	67	243	.276	60	92	.652	17	106	194	4.0
Gene Stump.	43	59	247	.239	24	38	.632	18	66	142	3.3
Mike Bloom†	14	46	169	.272	37	57	.649	14	37	129	9.2
Mike Bloom‡	48	174	640	.272	160	229	.699	38	116	508	10.6
Stan Noszka.	22	27	97	.278	24	35	.686	4	52	78	3.5
George Munroe	21	27	91	.297	17	26	.654	3	20	71	3.4
Cecil Hankins	25	23	116	.198	24	35	.686	8	28	70	2.8
Jack Hewson	24	22	89	.247	21	30	.700	1	9	65	2.7
Chuck Connors	4	5	13	.385	2	3	.667	1	5	12	3.0
Charlie Hoefer	7	3	19	.158	4	8	.500	3	17	10	1.4
John Janisch*	3	1	7	.143	1	2	.500	0	3	3	1.0

CHICAGO STAGS

	G	FGM	FGA	Pct.	FTM	FTA	Pct.	Ast.	PF	Pts.	Avg.
Max Zaslofsky	48	373	1156	.323	261	333	.784	29	125	1007	21.0
Stan Miasek.	48	263	867	.303	190	310	.613	31	192	716	14.9
Chuck Gilmur.	48	181	597	.303	97	148	.655	77	231	459	9.6
Gene Vance	48	163	617	.264	76	126	.603	49	193	402	8.4
Andy Phillip	32	143	425	.336	60	103	.583	74	75	346	10.8
Jim Seminoff	48	113	381	.297	73	105	.695	89	105	299	6.2
Paul Huston	46	51	215	.237	62	89	.697	27	82	164	3.6
Mickey Rottner.	44	53	184	.288	11	34	.324	46	49	117	2.7
Ben Schadler	37	23	116	.198	10	13	.769	6	40	56	1.5
Chuck Halbert*	6	12	55	.218	7	20	.350	2	14	31	5.2
Jack Toomay*	19	9	47	.191	11	20	.550	2	22	29	1.5
Gene Rock	11	4	18	.222	2	4	.500	0	8	10	0.9
Johnny Jorgensen*	1	2	2	1.000	0	0	. . .	0	1	4	4.0
Kenny Sailors*	1	0	3	.000	0	0	. . .	0	1	0	0.0

NEW YORK KNICKERBOCKERS

	G	FGM	FGA	Pct.	FTM	FTA	Pct.	Ast.	PF	Pts.	Avg.
Carl Braun	47	276	854	.323	119	183	.650	61	102	671	14.3
Bud Palmer	48	224	710	.315	174	234	.744	45	149	622	13.0
Dick Holub.	48	195	662	.295	114	180	.633	37	159	504	10.5
Stan Stutz	47	109	501	.218	113	135	.837	57	121	331	7.0
Tommy Byrnes.	47	117	410	.285	65	103	.631	17	56	299	6.4
Lee Knorek.	48	99	369	.268	61	120	.508	50	171	259	5.4
Sid Tannenbaum.	24	90	360	.250	62	74	.838	37	33	242	10.1
Ray Kuka	44	89	273	.326	50	84	.595	27	117	228	5.2
Butch van Breda Kolff.	44	53	192	.276	74	120	.617	29	81	180	4.1
Leo Gottlieb	27	59	288	.205	13	21	.619	12	36	131	4.9
Paul Noel	29	40	138	.290	19	30	.633	3	41	99	3.4
Wat Misaka.	3	3	13	.231	1	3	.333	0	7	7	2.3
Sonny Hertzberg*	4	1	14	.071	3	4	.750	1	3	5	1.3

1947-48

PHILADELPHIA WARRIORS

	G	FGM	FGA	Pct.	FTM	FTA	Pct.	Ast.	PF	Pts.	Avg.
Joe Fulks	43	326	1258	.259	297	390	.762	26	162	949	22.1
Howie Dallmar	48	215	781	.275	157	211	.744	120	141	587	12.2
Chuck Halbert†	40	144	550	.262	133	200	.665	30	112	421	10.5
Chuck Halbert‡	46	156	605	.258	140	220	.636	32	126	452	9.8
George Senesky	47	158	570	.277	98	147	.667	52	90	414	8.8
Jerry Fleishman	46	119	501	.238	95	138	.688	43	122	333	7.2
Angelo Musi	43	134	485	.276	51	73	.699	10	56	319	7.4
Ralph Kaplowitz	48	71	292	.243	47	60	.783	19	100	189	3.9
Francis Crossin	39	29	121	.240	13	23	.565	20	28	71	1.8
Hank Beenders†	24	23	69	.333	14	24	.583	7	31	60	2.5
Hank Beenders‡	45	76	269	.283	51	82	.622	13	99	203	4.5
Art Hillhouse	11	14	71	.197	30	37	.811	3	30	58	5.3
Stan Brown	19	19	71	.268	12	19	.632	1	16	50	2.6
Robert O'Brien	22	17	81	.210	15	26	.577	1	40	49	2.2
Jack Rocker	9	8	22	.364	1	1	1.000	3	2	17	1.9
Kenny Sailors*	2	2	3	.667	0	0	...	0	4	4	2.0

PROVIDENCE STEAMROLLERS

	G	FGM	FGA	Pct.	FTM	FTA	Pct.	Ast.	PF	Pts.	Avg.
Ernie Calverley	47	226	835	.271	107	161	.665	119	168	559	11.9
George Nostrand	45	196	660	.297	129	239	.540	30	148	521	11.6
Kenny Sailors†	41	205	683	.300	110	159	.692	59	157	520	12.7
Kenny Sailors‡	44	207	689	.300	110	159	.692	59	162	524	11.9
Earl Shannon	45	123	469	.262	116	183	.634	49	106	362	8.0
Johnny Ezersky	25	95	376	.253	63	104	.606	16	62	253	10.1
Lee Robbins	31	72	260	.277	51	93	.548	7	93	195	6.3
Jack Toomay†	14	52	144	.361	49	71	.690	5	49	153	10.9
Jack Toomay‡	33	61	191	.319	60	91	.659	7	71	182	5.5
Bob Hubbard	28	58	199	.291	36	52	.692	11	34	152	5.4
Hank Beenders*	21	53	200	.265	37	58	.638	6	68	143	6.8
Dino Martin	32	46	193	.238	9	20	.450	14	17	101	3.2
Pop Goodwin	24	36	155	.232	19	27	.704	7	36	91	3.8
Mel Thurston	14	32	113	.283	14	28	.500	4	42	78	5.6
George Mearns	24	23	115	.200	15	31	.484	10	65	61	2.5
Ariel Maughan*	14	22	91	.242	11	16	.688	2	36	55	3.9
John Janisch†	7	13	43	.302	8	14	.571	2	2	34	4.9
John Janisch‡	10	14	50	.280	9	16	.563	2	5	37	3.7
Ray Wertis	7	13	72	.181	6	14	.429	6	13	32	4.6
Jerry Kelly	3	3	10	.300	0	1	.000	0	3	6	2.0
Bill Downey	3	0	2	.000	0	0	...	0	0	0	0.0
Nat Hickey	1	0	3	.000	0	0	...	0	1	0	0.0
Wyndol Gray*	1	0	1	.000	0	1	.000	0	0	0	0.0
Dick Fitzgerald	1	0	3	.000	0	0	...	0	1	0	0.0

ST. LOUIS BOMBERS

	G	FGM	FGA	Pct.	FTM	FTA	Pct.	Ast.	PF	Pts.	Avg.
Johnny Logan	48	221	734	.301	202	272	.743	62	141	644	13.4
Red Rocha	48	232	740	.314	147	213	.690	39	209	611	12.7
Belus Smawley	48	212	688	.308	111	150	.740	18	88	535	11.1
Bob Doll	42	174	658	.264	98	148	.662	26	107	446	10.6
Don Putnam	42	105	399	.263	57	84	.679	25	95	267	6.4
Irv Rothenberg†	24	63	218	.289	60	106	.566	4	69	186	7.8
Irv Rothenberg‡	49	103	364	.283	87	150	.580	7	115	293	6.0
Giff Roux	46	68	258	.264	40	68	.588	12	60	176	3.8
Buddy O'Grady	44	67	257	.261	36	54	.667	9	61	170	3.9
Grady Lewis*	24	59	238	.248	48	72	.667	13	85	166	6.9
Ariel Maughan†	28	54	165	.327	21	37	.568	4	53	129	4.6

1947-48

	G	FGM	FGA	Pct.	FTM	FTA	Pct.	Ast.	PF	SCORING Pts.	Avg.
Ariel Maughan‡	42	76	256	.297	32	53	.604	6	89	184	4.4
Don Martin.	39	35	150	.233	15	33	.455	2	61	85	2.2
Wyndol Gray†	11	6	36	.167	1	3	.333	3	16	13	1.2
Wyndol Gray‡	12	6	37	.162	1	4	.250	3	16	13	1.1
Brooms Abramovic*	4	1	10	.100	2	4	.500	1	5	4	1.0

WASHINGTON CAPITOLS

	G	FGM	FGA	Pct.	FTM	FTA	Pct.	Ast.	PF	SCORING Pts.	Avg.
Bob Feerick	48	293	861	.340	189	240	.788	56	139	775	16.1
Freddie Scolari	47	229	780	.294	131	179	.732	58	153	589	12.5
Horace McKinney	43	182	680	.268	121	188	.644	36	176	485	11.3
Johnny Norlander.	48	167	543	.308	135	182	.742	44	102	469	9.8
Irv Torgoff	47	111	541	.205	117	144	.813	32	153	339	7.2
John Mahnken	48	131	526	.249	54	88	.614	31	151	316	6.6
Sonny Hertzberg†	37	109	400	.273	55	69	.797	22	58	273	7.4
Sonny Hertzberg‡	41	110	414	.266	58	73	.795	23	6	278	6.8
Dick O'Keefe.	37	63	257	.245	30	59	.508	18	85	156	4.2
Jack Tingle.	37	36	137	.263	17	33	.515	7	45	89	2.4
Irv Rothenberg*	11	15	60	.250	16	21	.762	1	22	46	4.2

* Finished season with another team. † Totals with this team only. ‡ Totals with all teams.

PLAYOFF RESULTS

WESTERN DIVISION TIEBREAKERS

Mar. 23—Tue. Washington 70 at Chicago 74
Mar. 25—Thur. Baltimore 75 at Chicago .72

QUARTERFINALS

Baltimore 2, New York 1
Mar. 27—Sat. New York 81 at Baltimore 85
Mar. 28—Sun. Baltimore 69 at New York 79
Apr. 1—Thur. New York 77 at Baltimore 84

Chicago 2, Boston 1
Mar. 28—Sun. Chicago 79 at Boston 72
Mar. 31—Wed. Chicago 77 at Boston 81
Apr. 2—Fri. Chicago 81 at Boston 74

SEMIFINALS

Philadelphia 4, St. Louis 3
Mar. 23—Tue. Philadelphia 58 at St. Louis 60
Mar. 25—Thur. Philadelphia 65 at St. Louis 64
Mar. 27—Sat. St. Louis 56 at Philadelphia 84
Mar. 30—Tue. St. Louis 56 at Philadelphia 51
Apr. 1—Thur. Philadelphia 62 at St. Louis 69
Apr. 3—Sat. St. Louis 61 at Philadelphia 84
Apr. 6—Tue. Philadelphia 85 at St. Louis 46

Baltimore 2, Chicago 0
Apr. 7—Wed. Baltimore 73 at Chicago .67
Apr. 8—Thur. Chicago 72 at Baltimore .89

NBA FINALS

Baltimore 4, Philadelphia 2
Apr. 10—Sat. Baltimore 60 at Philadelphia 71
Apr. 13—Tue. Baltimore 66 at Philadelphia 63
Apr. 15—Thur. Philadelphia 70 at Baltimore 72
Apr. 17—Sat. Philadelphia 75 at Baltimore 78
Apr. 20—Tue. Baltimore 82 at Philadelphia 91
Apr. 21—Wed. Philadelphia 73 at Baltimore 88

1947-48

1946-47

1946-47 NBA CHAMPION PHILADELPHIA WARRIORS
Front row (from left): Jerry Rullo, Angelo Musi, general manager Peter A. Tyrell, Petey Rosenberg, Jerry Fleishman. Back row (from left): assistant coach Cy Kaselman, George Senesky, Ralph Kaplowitz, Howie Dallmar, Art Hillhouse, Joe Fulks, Matt Guokas, head coach Ed Gottlieb.

FINAL STANDINGS
EASTERN DIVISION

	Was.	Phi.	N.Y.	Prov.	Tor.	Bos.	Chi.	St.L.	Cle.	Det.	Pit.	W	L	Pct.	GB
Washington		5	4	6	5	5	5	4	5	5	5	49	11	.817	..
Philadelphia	1	..	4	4	5	5	1	3	3	4	5	35	25	.583	14
New York	2	2	..	4	3	2	3	4	2	5	6	33	27	.550	16
Providence	0	2	2	..	3	5	3	2	4	4	3	28	32	.467	21
Boston	1	1	4	1	4	..	0	1	2	3	5	22	38	.367	27
Toronto..........	1	1	3	3	..	2	2	4	0	3	3	22	38	.367	27

WESTERN DIVISION

	Was.	Phi.	N.Y.	Prov.	Tor.	Bos.	Chi.	St.L.	Cle.	Det.	Pit.	W	L	Pct.	GB
Chicago	1	5	3	3	4	6	..	3	5	3	6	39	22	.639	..
St. Louis........	2	3	2	4	2	5	4	..	5	6	5	38	23	.623	1
Cleveland	1	3	4	2	6	4	1	1	..	4	4	30	30	.500	8.5
Detroit	1	2	1	2	3	3	3	0	2	..	3	20	40	.333	18.5
Pittsburgh.......	1	1	0	3	3	1	0	1	2	3	..	15	45	.250	23.5

TEAM STATISTICS

	G	FGM	FGA	Pct.	FTM	FTA	Pct.	Ast.	PF	For	Agst.	Dif.
Washington	60	1723	5794	.297	982	1391	.706	378	1144	73.8	63.9	+9.9
Chicago	61	1879	6309	.298	939	1550	.606	436	1473	77.0	73.3	+3.7
Philadelphia	60	1510	5384	.280	1098	1596	.688	343	1082	68.6	65.2	+3.4
St. Louis.........	61	1601	5877	.272	862	1400	.616	292	1234	66.6	64.1	+2.5
New York	60	1465	5255	.279	951	1438	.661	457	1218	64.7	64.0	+0.7
Cleveland	60	1674	5699	.294	903	1428	.632	494	1246	70.9	71.8	-0.9
Providence	60	1629	5582	.292	1092	1666	.655	481	1215	72.5	74.2	-1.7
Detroit	60	1437	5843	.246	923	1494	.618	482	1351	63.3	65.3	-2.0
Toronto..........	60	1515	5672	.267	966	1552	.622	463	1271	66.6	71.0	-4.4
Boston	60	1397	5133	.272	811	1375	.590	470	1202	60.1	65.0	-4.9
Pittsburgh	60	1345	4961	.271	984	1507	.653	272	1360	61.2	67.6	-6.4
Avgs.	60.2	1561	5592	.279	956	1491	.641	415	1254	67.7	...	...

(AVERAGE POINTS: For, Agst., Dif.)

HOME/ROAD

	Home	Road	Total		Home	Road	Total
Boston.	14-16	8-22	22-38	Pittsburgh	11-19	4-26	15-45
Chicago.	22-9	17-13	39-22	Providence.	19-11	9-21	28-32
Cleveland.	17-13	13-17	30-30	St. Louis.	22-8	16-15	38-23
Detroit.	12-18	8-22	20-40	Toronto.	15-15	7-23	22-38
New York.	18-12	15-15	33-27	Washington.	29-1	20-10	49-11
Philadelphia.	23-7	12-18	35-25	Totals.	202-129	129-202	331-331

POINTS

	G	FGM	FTM	Pts.	Avg.
Joe Fulks, Philadelphia	.60	475	439	1389	23.2
Bob Feerick, Washington	.55	364	198	926	16.8
Stan Miasek, Detroit	.60	331	233	895	14.9
Ed Sadowski, Toronto-Cleveland	.53	329	219	877	16.5
Max Zaslofsky, Chicago	.61	336	205	877	14.4
Ernie Calverley, Providence	.59	323	199	845	14.3
Charles Halbert, Chicago	.61	280	213	773	12.7
John Logan, St. Louis	.61	290	190	770	12.6
Leo Mogus, Cleveland-Toronto	.58	259	235	753	13.0
Coulby Gunther, Pittsburgh	.52	254	226	734	14.1
Don Martin, Providence	.60	311	111	733	12.2
Fred Scolari, Washington	.58	291	146	728	12.6
Henry Beenders, Providence	.58	266	181	713	12.3
John Janisch, Detroit	.60	283	131	697	11.6
Horace McKinney, Washington	.58	275	145	695	12.0
Earl Shannon, Providence	.57	245	197	687	12.1
Mel Riebe, Cleveland	.55	276	111	663	12.1
Mike McCarron, Toronto	.60	236	177	649	10.8
Frankie Baumholtz, Cleveland	.45	255	121	631	14.0
Don Carlson, Chicago	.59	272	86	630	10.7

FIELD GOALS
(minimum 200 made)

	FGM	FGA	Pct.
Bob Feerick, Washington	.364	908	.401
Ed Sadowski, Toronto-Cleveland	.329	891	.369
Earl Shannon, Providence	.245	722	.339
Coulby Gunther, Pittsburgh	.254	756	.336
Max Zaslofsky, Chicago	.336	1020	.329
Don Carlson, Chicago	.272	845	.322

Connie Simmons, Boston	.246	768	.320
John Norlander, Washington	.223	698	.319
Ken Sailors, Cleveland	.229	741	.309
Mel Riebe, Cleveland	.276	898	.307

FREE THROWS
(minimum 125 made)

	FTM	FTA	Pct.
Fred Scolari, Washington	.146	180	.811
Tony Kappen, Pittsburgh-Boston	.128	161	.795
Stan Stutz, New York	.133	170	.782
Bob Feerick, Washington	.198	260	.762
John Logan, St. Louis	.190	254	.748
Max Zaslofsky, Chicago	.205	278	.737
Joe Fulks, Philadelphia	.439	601	.730
Leo Mogus, Cleveland-Toronto	.235	325	.723
George Mearns, Providence	.126	175	.720
Tony Jaros, Chicago	.128	181	.707

ASSISTS

	G	No.	Avg.
Ernie Calverley, Providence	.59	202	3.4
Ken Sailors, Cleveland	.58	134	2.3
Ossie Schectman, New York	.54	109	2.0
Howie Dallmar, Philadelphia	.60	104	1.7
Marv Rottner, Chicago	.56	93	1.7
Stan Miasek, Detroit	.60	93	1.6
Earl Shannon, Providence	.57	84	1.5
Leo Mogus, Cleveland-Toronto	.58	84	1.5
John Logan, St. Louis	.61	78	1.3
Bob Feerick, Washington	.55	69	1.3
Horace McKinney, Washington	.58	69	1.2

INDIVIDUAL STATISTICS, TEAM BY TEAM

BOSTON CELTICS

	G	FGM	FGA	Pct.	FTM	FTA	Pct.	Ast.	PF	Pts.	Avg.
Connie Simmons	60	246	768	.320	128	189	.677	62	130	620	10.3
Al Brightman	58	223	870	.256	121	193	.627	60	115	567	9.8
Wyndol Gray	55	139	476	.292	72	124	.581	47	105	350	6.4
Art Spector	55	123	460	.267	83	150	.553	46	130	329	6.0
Johnny Simmons	60	120	429	.280	78	127	.614	29	78	318	5.3
Jerry Kelly	43	91	313	.291	74	111	.667	21	128	256	6.0
Chuck Connors	49	94	380	.247	39	84	.464	40	129	227	4.6
Charlie Hoefer†	35	76	316	.241	59	93	.634	24	81	211	6.0
Charlie Hoefer‡	58	130	514	.253	91	139	.655	33	142	351	6.1
Dutch Garfinkel	40	81	304	.266	17	28	.607	58	62	179	4.5
Harold Kottman	53	59	188	.314	47	101	.465	17	58	165	3.1
Red Wallace*	24	55	224	.246	21	48	.438	20	42	131	5.5
Bill Fenley	33	31	138	.225	23	45	.511	16	59	85	2.6
Tony Kappen†	18	25	91	.275	24	38	.632	6	24	74	4.1
Tony Kappen‡	59	128	537	.238	128	161	.795	28	78	384	6.5
Virgil Vaughn	17	15	78	.192	15	28	.536	10	18	45	2.6
Mel Hirsch	13	9	45	.200	1	2	.500	10	18	19	1.5
Moe Becker*	6	5	22	.227	3	4	.750	1	15	13	2.2
Robert Duffy†	6	2	7	.286	4	4	1.000	0	4	8	1.3
Robert Duffy‡	17	7	32	.219	5	7	.714	0	17	19	1.1
Hal Crisler	4	2	6	.333	2	2	1.000	0	6	6	1.5
Dick Murphy†	7	1	17	.059	0	4	.000	3	6	2	0.3
Dick Murphy‡	31	15	75	.200	4	9	.444	8	15	34	1.1
Don Eliason	1	0	1	.000	0	0	. . .	0	1	0	0.0

CHICAGO STAGS

	G	FGM	FGA	Pct.	FTM	FTA	Pct.	Ast.	PF	Pts.	Avg.
Max Zaslofsky	61	336	1020	.329	205	278	.737	40	121	877	14.4
Chuck Halbert	61	280	915	.306	213	356	.598	46	161	773	12.7
Don Carlson	59	272	845	.322	86	159	.541	59	182	630	10.7
Tony Jaros	59	177	613	.289	128	181	.707	28	156	482	8.2
Jim Seminoff	60	184	586	.314	71	130	.546	63	155	439	7.3

1946-47

	G	FGM	FGA	Pct.	FTM	FTA	Pct.	Ast.	PF	Pts.	Avg.
Mickey Rottner	56	190	655	.290	43	79	.544	93	109	423	7.6
Doyle Parrack	58	110	413	.266	52	80	.650	20	77	272	4.7
Chet Carlisle	51	100	373	.268	56	92	.609	17	136	256	5.0
Wilbert Kautz	50	107	420	.255	39	73	.534	37	114	253	5.1
Chuck Gilmur	51	76	253	.300	26	66	.394	21	139	178	3.5
Bill Davis	47	35	146	.240	14	41	.341	11	92	84	1.8
Buck Sydnor	15	5	26	.192	5	10	.500	0	6	15	1.0
Robert Duffy*	11	5	25	.200	1	3	.333	0	13	11	1.0
Garland O'Shields	9	2	11	.182	0	2	.000	1	8	4	0.4
Robert Rensberger	3	0	7	.000	0	0	...	0	4	0	0.0
Norm Baker	4	0	1	.000	0	0	...	0	0	0	0.0

CLEVELAND REBELS

	G	FGM	FGA	Pct.	FTM	FTA	Pct.	Ast.	PF	Pts.	Avg.
Ed Sadowski†	43	256	682	.375	174	262	.664	30	152	686	16.0
Ed Sadowski‡	53	329	891	.369	219	328	.668	46	194	877	16.5
Mel Riebe	55	276	898	.307	111	173	.642	67	169	663	12.1
Frankie Baumholtz	45	255	856	.298	121	156	.776	54	93	631	14.0
Kenny Sailors	58	229	741	.309	119	200	.595	134	177	577	9.9
George Nostrand†	48	146	520	.281	74	149	.497	21	123	366	7.6
George Nostrand‡	61	192	656	.293	98	210	.467	31	145	482	7.9
Bob Faught	51	141	478	.295	61	106	.575	33	97	343	6.7
Nick Shaback	53	102	385	.265	38	53	.717	29	75	242	4.6
Leo Mogus*	17	73	226	.323	63	88	.716	28	50	209	12.3
Ray Wertis†	43	41	195	.210	33	54	.611	21	53	115	2.7
Ray Wertis‡	61	79	366	.216	56	91	.615	39	82	214	3.5
Dick Schulz*	16	43	176	.244	20	31	.645	17	29	106	6.6
Ben Scharnus	51	33	165	.200	37	59	.627	19	83	103	2.0
Irv Rothenberg	29	36	167	.216	30	54	.556	15	62	102	3.5
Hank Lefkowitz	24	22	114	.193	7	13	.538	4	35	51	2.1
Kleggie Hermsen*	11	18	67	.269	7	15	.467	10	32	43	3.9
Ned Endress	16	3	25	.120	8	15	.533	4	13	14	0.9
Leon Brown	5	0	3	.000	0	0	...	0	2	0	0.0
Pete Lalich	7	0	1	.000	0	0	...	0	1	0	0.0
Ken Corley	3	0	0	...	0	0	...	0	0	0	0.0

DETROIT FALCONS

	G	FGM	FGA	Pct.	FTM	FTA	Pct.	Ast.	PF	Pts.	Avg.
Stan Miasek	60	331	1154	.287	233	385	.605	93	208	895	14.9
John Janisch	60	283	983	.288	131	198	.662	49	132	697	11.6
Ariel Maughan	59	224	929	.241	84	114	.737	57	180	532	9.0
Robert Dille	57	111	563	.197	74	111	.667	40	92	296	5.2
Tom King	58	97	410	.237	101	160	.631	32	102	295	5.1
Grady Lewis	60	106	520	.204	75	138	.543	54	166	287	4.8
Harold Brown	54	95	383	.248	74	117	.632	39	122	264	4.9
Milt Schoon	41	43	199	.216	34	80	.425	12	75	120	2.9
Art Stolkey	23	36	164	.220	30	44	.682	38	72	102	4.4
George Pearcy	37	31	130	.238	32	44	.727	13	68	94	2.5
Henry Pearcy	29	24	108	.222	25	34	.735	7	20	73	2.5
Chet Aubuchon	30	23	91	.253	19	35	.543	20	46	65	2.2
Moe Becker†	20	19	107	.178	3	10	.300	15	33	41	2.1
Moe Becker‡	43	70	358	.196	22	44	.500	30	98	162	3.8
Howie McCarty	19	10	82	.122	1	10	.100	2	22	21	1.1
Harold Johnson	27	4	20	.200	7	14	.500	11	13	15	0.6

NEW YORK KNICKERBOCKERS

	G	FGM	FGA	Pct.	FTM	FTA	Pct.	Ast.	PF	Pts.	Avg.
Sonny Hertzberg	59	201	695	.289	113	149	.758	37	109	515	8.7
Stan Stutz	60	172	641	.268	133	170	.782	49	127	477	8.0
Tommy Byrnes	60	175	583	.300	103	160	.644	35	90	453	7.6
Ossie Schectman	54	162	588	.276	111	179	.620	109	115	435	8.1
Bud Palmer	42	160	521	.307	81	121	.669	34	110	401	9.5
Leo Gottlieb	57	149	494	.302	36	55	.655	24	71	334	5.9
Robert Cluggish	54	93	356	.261	52	91	.571	22	113	238	4.4
Ralph Kaplowitz*	27	71	274	.259	52	71	.732	25	57	194	7.2
Lee Knorek	22	62	219	.283	47	72	.653	21	64	171	7.8

1946-47

	G	FGM	FGA	Pct.	FTM	FTA	Pct.	Ast.	PF	Pts.	Avg.
Nat Militzok*	36	52	214	.238	40	73	.548	28	91	144	4.0
Hank Rosenstein*	31	38	145	.262	57	95	.600	19	71	133	4.3
Frido Frey	23	28	97	.289	32	56	.571	14	37	88	3.8
Bob Fitzgerald†	29	23	121	.190	36	60	.600	9	67	82	2.8
Bob Fitzgerald‡	60	70	362	.193	81	130	.623	35	153	221	3.7
Bob Mullens*	26	27	104	.260	22	34	.647	18	32	76	2.9
Aud Brindley	12	14	49	.286	6	7	.857	1	16	34	2.8
Dick Murphy*	24	14	58	.241	4	5	.800	5	9	32	1.3
Butch van Breda Kolff	16	7	34	.206	11	17	.647	6	10	25	1.6
Moe Murphy*	9	8	25	.320	8	12	.667	0	3	24	2.7
Jake Weber*	11	7	24	.292	6	8	.750	1	20	20	1.8
Frank Mangiapane	6	2	13	.154	1	3	.333	0	6	5	0.8

PHILADELPHIA WARRIORS

	G	FGM	FGA	Pct.	FTM	FTA	Pct.	Ast.	PF	Pts.	Avg.
Joe Fulks	60	475	1557	.305	439	601	.730	25	199	1389	23.2
Angelo Musi	60	230	818	.281	102	123	.829	26	120	562	9.4
Howie Dallmar	60	199	710	.280	130	203	.640	104	141	528	8.8
George Senesky	58	142	531	.267	82	124	.661	34	83	366	6.3
Art Hillhouse	60	120	412	.291	120	166	.723	41	139	360	6.0
Jerry Fleishman	59	97	372	.261	69	127	.543	40	101	263	4.5
Ralph Kaplowitz†	30	75	258	.291	59	80	.738	13	65	209	7.0
Ralph Kaplowitz‡	57	146	523	.279	111	151	.735	38	122	403	7.1
Petey Rosenberg	51	60	287	.209	30	49	.612	27	64	150	2.9
Jerry Rullo	50	52	174	.299	23	47	.489	20	61	127	2.5
Matt Guokas	47	28	104	.269	26	47	.553	9	70	82	1.7
Fred Sheffield	22	29	146	.199	16	26	.615	4	34	74	3.4
Moe Murphy†	11	3	15	.200	2	3	.667	0	5	8	0.7
Moe Murphy‡	20	11	40	.275	10	15	.667	0	8	32	1.6

PITTSBURGH IRONMEN

	G	FGM	FGA	Pct.	FTM	FTA	Pct.	Ast.	PF	Pts.	Avg.
Coulby Gunther	52	254	756	.336	226	351	.644	32	117	734	14.1
Brooms Abramovic	47	202	834	.242	123	178	.691	35	161	527	11.2
Stan Noszka	58	199	693	.287	109	157	.694	39	163	507	8.7
Hank Zeller	48	120	382	.314	122	177	.689	31	177	362	7.5
Tony Kappen*	41	103	446	.231	104	123	.846	22	61	310	7.6
Ed Melvin	57	99	376	.263	83	127	.654	37	150	281	4.9
Press Maravich	51	102	375	.272	30	58	.517	6	102	234	4.6
Mike Bytzura	60	87	356	.244	36	72	.500	31	108	210	3.5
John Mills	47	55	187	.294	71	129	.550	9	94	181	3.9
Moe Becker*	17	46	229	.201	16	30	.533	14	50	108	6.4
Noble Jorgensen	15	25	112	.223	16	25	.640	4	40	66	4.4
Joe Fabel	30	25	96	.260	13	26	.500	2	64	63	2.1
Roger Jorgensen	28	14	54	.259	13	19	.684	1	36	41	1.5
Walt Miller	12	7	21	.333	9	18	.500	6	16	23	1.9
Nat Frankel	6	4	27	.148	8	12	.667	3	6	16	2.7
Red Mihalik	7	3	9	.333	0	0	. . .	0	10	6	0.9
Gorham Getchell	16	0	8	.000	5	5	1.000	0	5	5	0.3

PROVIDENCE STEAMROLLERS

	G	FGM	FGA	Pct.	FTM	FTA	Pct.	Ast.	PF	Pts.	Avg.
Ernie Calverley	59	323	1102	.293	199	283	.703	202	191	845	14.3
Dino Martin	60	311	1022	.304	111	168	.661	59	98	733	12.2
Hank Beenders†	58	266	1016	.262	181	257	.704	37	196	713	12.3
Earl Shannon	57	245	722	.339	197	348	.566	84	169	687	12.1
George Mearns	57	128	478	.268	126	175	.720	35	137	382	6.7
Pop Goodwin	55	98	348	.282	60	75	.800	15	94	256	4.7
Hank Rosenstein†	29	81	245	.331	87	130	.669	17	101	249	8.6
Hank Rosenstein‡	60	119	390	.305	144	225	.640	36	172	382	6.4
Jake Weber†	39	52	178	.292	49	71	.690	3	91	153	3.9
Jake Weber‡	50	59	202	.292	55	79	.696	4	111	173	3.5
George Pastushok	39	48	183	.262	25	46	.543	15	42	121	3.1
Bob Shea	43	37	153	.242	19	33	.576	6	42	93	2.2
Woodie Grimshaw	21	20	56	.357	21	44	.477	1	25	61	2.9
Tom Callahan	13	6	29	.207	5	12	.417	4	9	17	1.3
Elmo Morgenthaler	11	4	13	.308	7	12	.583	3	3	15	1.4
Red Dehnert	10	6	15	.400	2	6	.333	0	8	14	1.4

SCORING

1946-47

	G	FGM	FGA	Pct.	FTM	FTA	Pct.	Ast.	PF	Pts.	Avg.
Armand Cure	12	4	15	.267	2	3	.667	0	5	10	0.8
Lou Spicer	4	0	7	.000	1	2	.500	0	3	1	0.3
Ken Keller†	3	0	0	...	0	1	.000	0	1	0	0.0
Ken Keller‡	28	10	30	.333	2	5	.400	1	15	22	0.8

ST. LOUIS BOMBERS

SCORING

	G	FGM	FGA	Pct.	FTM	FTA	Pct.	Ast.	PF	Pts.	Avg.
Johnny Logan	61	290	1043	.278	190	254	.748	78	136	770	12.6
Bob Doll	60	194	768	.253	134	206	.650	22	167	522	8.7
George Munroe	59	164	623	.263	86	133	.647	17	91	414	7.0
Don Putnam	58	156	635	.246	68	105	.648	30	106	380	6.6
Giff Roux	60	142	478	.297	70	160	.438	17	95	354	5.9
Cecil Hankins	55	117	391	.299	90	150	.600	14	49	324	5.9
John Barr	58	124	438	.283	47	79	.595	54	164	295	5.1
Aubrey Davis	59	107	381	.281	73	115	.635	14	136	287	4.9
Belus Smawley	22	113	352	.321	36	47	.766	10	37	262	11.9
Don Martin	54	89	304	.293	13	31	.419	9	75	191	3.5
Herk Baltimore	58	53	263	.202	32	69	.464	16	98	138	2.4
Deb Smith	48	32	119	.269	9	21	.429	6	47	73	1.5
Fred Jacobs	18	19	69	.275	12	25	.480	5	25	50	2.8
Ralph Siewert*	7	1	13	.077	2	5	.400	0	8	4	0.6

TORONTO HUSKIES

SCORING

	G	FGM	FGA	Pct.	FTM	FTA	Pct.	Ast.	PF	Pts.	Avg.
Mike McCarron	60	236	838	.282	177	288	.615	59	184	649	10.8
Leo Mogus†	41	186	653	.285	172	237	.726	56	126	544	13.3
Leo Mogus‡	58	259	879	.295	235	325	.723	84	176	753	13.0
Red Wallace†	37	170	585	.291	85	148	.574	30	125	425	11.5
Red Wallace‡	61	225	809	.278	106	196	.541	58	167	556	9.1
Dick Fitzgerald	60	118	495	.238	41	60	.683	40	89	277	4.6
Kleggie Hermsen†	21	95	327	.291	64	97	.660	15	54	254	12.1
Kleggie Hermsen‡	32	113	394	.287	71	112	.634	25	86	297	9.3
Dick Schulz†	41	87	372	.234	74	107	.692	39	94	248	6.0
Dick Schulz‡	57	130	548	.237	94	138	.681	56	123	354	6.2
Roy Hurley	46	100	447	.224	39	64	.609	34	85	239	5.2
Bob Mullens†	28	98	341	.287	42	68	.618	36	62	238	8.5
Bob Mullens‡	54	125	445	.281	64	102	.627	54	94	314	5.8
Ed Sadowski*	10	73	209	.349	45	66	.682	8	42	191	19.1
Harry Miller	53	58	260	.223	36	82	.439	42	119	152	2.9
Charlie Hoefer*	23	54	198	.273	32	46	.696	9	61	140	6.1
Frank Fucarino	28	53	198	.268	34	60	.567	7	38	140	5.0
Bob Fitzgerald*	31	47	241	.195	45	70	.643	26		139	4.5
George Nostrand*	13	46	136	.338	24	61	.393	10	22	116	8.9
Nat Militzok†	21	38	129	.295	24	39	.615	14	29	100	4.8
Nat Militzok‡	57	90	343	.262	64	112	.571	42	120	244	4.3
Ray Wertis*	18	38	171	.222	23	37	.622	18	29	99	5.5
Ralph Siewert†	14	5	31	.161	6	10	.600	4	10	16	1.1
Ralph Siewert‡	21	6	44	.136	8	15	.533	4	18	20	1.0
Edward Kasid	8	6	21	.286	0	6	.000	6	8	12	1.5
Gino Sovran	6	5	15	.333	1	2	.500	1	5	11	1.8
Hank Biasatti	6	2	5	.400	2	4	.500	0	3	6	1.0

WASHINGTON CAPITOLS

SCORING

	G	FGM	FGA	Pct.	FTM	FTA	Pct.	Ast.	PF	Pts.	Avg.
Bob Feerick	55	364	908	.401	198	260	.762	69	142	926	16.8
Freddie Scolari	58	291	989	.294	146	180	.811	58	159	728	12.6
Horace McKinney	58	275	987	.279	145	210	.690	69	162	695	12.0
Johnny Norlander	60	223	698	.319	180	276	.652	50	122	626	10.4
John Mahnken	60	223	876	.255	111	163	.681	60	181	557	9.3
Irv Torgoff	58	187	684	.273	116	159	.730	30	173	490	8.4
Buddy O'Grady	55	55	231	.238	38	53	.717	20	60	148	2.7
Marty Passaglia	43	51	221	.231	18	32	.563	9	44	120	2.8
Bob Gantt	23	29	89	.326	13	28	.464	5	45	71	3.1
Albert Negratti	11	13	69	.188	5	8	.625	5	20	31	2.8
Ken Keller*	25	10	30	.333	2	4	.500	1	14	22	0.9
Gene Gillette	14	1	11	.091	6	9	.667	2	13	8	0.6
Al Lujack	5	1	8	.125	2	5	.400	0	6	4	0.8
Ben Goldfaden	2	0	2	.000	2	4	.500	0	3	2	1.0

* Finished season with another team.   † Totals with this team only.   ‡ Totals with all teams.

1946-47

QUARTERFINALS

Philadelphia 2, St. Louis 1
Apr. 2—Wed.	St. Louis 68 at Philadelphia	73
Apr. 5—Sat.	Philadelphia 51 at St. Louis	73
Apr. 6—Sun.	Philadelphia 75 at St. Louis	59

New York 2, Cleveland 1
Apr. 2—Wed.	New York 51 at Cleveland	77
Apr. 5—Sat.	Cleveland 74 at New York	86
Apr. 9—Wed.	Cleveland 71 at New York	93

SEMIFINALS

Chicago 4, Washington 2
Apr. 2—Wed.	Chicago 81 at Washington	65
Apr. 3—Thur.	Chicago 69 at Washington	53
Apr. 8—Tue.	Washington 55 at Chicago	67
Apr. 10—Thur.	Chicago 69 at Washington	76
Apr. 12—Sat.	Washington 67 at Chicago	55
Apr. 13—Sun.	Washington 61 at Chicago	66

Philadelphia 2, New York 0
Apr. 12—Sat.	New York 70 at Philadelphia	82
Apr. 14—Mon.	Philadelphia 72 at New York	53

NBA FINALS

Philadelphia 4, Chicago 1
Apr. 16—Wed.	Chicago 71 at Philadelphia	84
Apr. 17—Thur.	Chicago 74 at Philadelphia	85
Apr. 19—Sat.	Philadelphia 75 at Chicago	72
Apr. 20—Sun.	Philadelphia 73 at Chicago	74
Apr. 22—Tue.	Chicago 80 at Philadelphia	83

1946-47

INDEX